# The Oxford Handbook of Cognitive Psychology

OXFORD LIBRARY OF PSYCHOLOGY

*Editor in Chief* PETER E. NATHAN

# The Oxford Handbook of Cognitive Psychology

*Edited by*
Daniel Reisberg

OXFORD
UNIVERSITY PRESS

# OXFORD
## UNIVERSITY PRESS

Oxford University Press is a department of the University of Oxford.
It furthers the University's objective of excellence in research, scholarship,
and education by publishing worldwide.

Oxford    New York
Auckland    Cape Town    Dar es Salaam    Hong Kong    Karachi
Kuala Lumpur    Madrid    Melbourne    Mexico City    Nairobi
New Delhi    Shanghai    Taipei    Toronto

With offices in
Argentina    Austria    Brazil    Chile    Czech Republic    France    Greece
Guatemala    Hungary    Italy    Japan    Poland    Portugal    Singapore
South Korea    Switzerland    Thailand    Turkey    Ukraine    Vietnam

Published in the United States of America by
Oxford University Press
198 Madison Avenue, New York, NY 10016

Library of Congress Cataloging-in-Publication Data
The Oxford handbook of cognitive psychology / edited by Daniel Reisberg.
    p. cm.
ISBN 978–0–19–537674–6 (hardcover); 978-0-19-936419-0 (paperback)
1. Cognitive psychology.    I. Reisberg, Daniel.
BF201.O94 2013
153—dc23
2012028873

# SHORT CONTENTS

# OXFORD LIBRARY OF PSYCHOLOGY

The *Oxford Library of Psychology*, a landmark series of handbooks, is published by Oxford University Press, one of the world's oldest and most highly respected publishers, with a tradition of publishing significant books in psychology. The ambitious goal of the *Oxford Library of Psychology* is nothing less than to span a vibrant, wide-ranging field and, in so doing, to fill a clear market need.

Encompassing a comprehensive set of handbooks, organized hierarchically, the *Library* incorporates volumes at different levels, each designed to meet a distinct need. At one level are a set of handbooks designed broadly to survey the major subfields of psychology; at another are numerous handbooks that cover important current focal research and scholarly areas of psychology in depth and detail. Planned as a reflection of the dynamism of psychology, the *Library* will grow and expand as psychology itself develops, thereby highlighting significant new research that will impact on the field. Adding to its accessibility and ease of use, the *Library* will be published in print and, later on, electronically.

The *Library* surveys psychology's principal subfields with a set of handbooks that capture the current status and future prospects of those major subdisciplines. This initial set includes handbooks of social and personality psychology, clinical psychology, counseling psychology, school psychology, educational psychology, industrial and organizational psychology, cognitive psychology, cognitive neuroscience, methods and measurements, history, neuropsychology, personality assessment, developmental psychology, and more. Each handbook undertakes to review one of psychology's major subdisciplines with breadth, comprehensiveness, and exemplary scholarship. In addition to these broadly conceived volumes, the *Library* also includes a large number of handbooks designed to explore in depth more specialized areas of scholarship and research, such as stress, health and coping, anxiety and related disorders, cognitive development, or child and adolescent assessment. In contrast to the broad coverage of the subfield handbooks, each of these latter volumes focuses on an especially productive, more highly focused line of scholarship and research. Whether at the broadest or most specific level, however, all of the *Library* handbooks offer synthetic coverage that reviews and evaluates the relevant past and present research and anticipates research in the future. Each handbook in the *Library* includes introductory and concluding chapters written by its editor to provide a roadmap to the handbook's table of contents and to offer informed anticipations of significant future developments in that field.

An undertaking of this scope calls for handbook editors and chapter authors who are established scholars in the areas about which they write. Many of the nation's and world's most productive and best-respected psychologists have agreed to edit *Library* handbooks or write authoritative chapters in their areas of expertise.

For whom has the *Oxford Library of Psychology* been written? Because of its breadth, depth, and accessibility, the *Library* serves a diverse audience, including graduate students in psychology and their faculty mentors, scholars, researchers, and practitioners in psychology and related fields. All will find in the *Library* the information they seek on the subfield or focal area of psychology in which they work or are interested.

Befitting its commitment to accessibility, each handbook includes a comprehensive index, as well as extensive references to help guide research. And because the *Library* was designed from its inception as an online as well as a print resource, its structure and contents will be readily and rationally searchable online. Furthermore, once the *Library* is released online, the handbooks will be regularly and thoroughly updated.

In summary, the *Oxford Library of Psychology* will grow organically to provide a thoroughly informed perspective on the field of psychology, one that reflects both psychology's dynamism and its increasing interdisciplinarity. Once published electronically, the *Library* is also destined to become a uniquely valuable interactive tool, with extended search and browsing capabilities. As you begin to consult this handbook, we sincerely hope you will share our enthusiasm for the more than 500-year tradition of Oxford University Press for excellence, innovation, and quality, as exemplified by the *Oxford Library of Psychology*.

Peter E. Nathan
Editor-in-Chief
*Oxford Library of Psychology*

# ABOUT THE EDITOR

**Daniel Reisberg**

Daniel Reisberg is Professor of Psychology at Reed College, in Portland, Oregon. He has published extensively, with a focus on how people remember the emotional events of their lives, and also on the nature of mental imagery. In addition to his scholarly writing, he is the author of several successful textbooks, including *Cognition: Exploring the Science of the Mind,* published by W.W. Norton and now in its fifth edition. Reisberg has also been increasingly involved with the application of cognitive psychology to issues within the criminal justice system, and he has provided training sessions for police officers, attorneys, and judges, and sometimes appears in court as an expert witness, with the focus generally on how crime witnesses (or victims, or perpetrators) remember and report on a criminal event. Between projects, Reisberg is a devoted wilderness canoe paddler, and escapes when he can to the far north.

# CONTRIBUTORS

**Lisa Feldman Barrett**
Department of Psychology
Northeastern University
Massachusetts General Hospital
Boston, MA

**Isabelle M. Bauer**
Centre for Addiction and Mental Health
Toronto, Ontario, Canada

**Roy F. Baumeister**
Department of Psychology
Florida State University
Tallahassee, FL

**Mark Beeman**
Department of Psychology
Northwestern University
Evanston, IL

**Martha Ann Bell**
Department of Psychology
Virginia Polytechnic Institute and State
University
Blacksburg, VA

**Miri Besken**
Department of Psychology
University of North Carolina, Chapel Hill
Chapel Hill, NC

**Derek Bickerton**
University of Hawaii at Manoa
Honolulu, HI

**Matthew Tyler Boden**
Center for Health Care Evaluation
VA Palo Alto Health Care System
Menlo Park, CA

**Galen V. Bodenhausen**
Department of Psychology
Northwestern University
Evanston, IL

**Julie M. Bugg**
Department of Psychology
Washington University in St. Louis
St. Louis, MO

**Andrew C. Butler**
Department of Psychology and Neuroscience
Duke University
Durham, NC

**Laura A. Carlson**
Department of Psychology
University of Notre Dame
Notre Dame, IN

**Kyle R. Cave**
Department of Psychology
University of Massachusetts
Amherst, MA

**Caitlin Cole**
Institute of Child Development
The University of Minnesota
Minneapolis, MN

**Mary L. Courage**
Department of Psychology
Memorial University
St. John's, Newfoundland, Canada

**Rodica Ioana Damian**
Department of Psychology
University of California, Davis
Davis, CA

**Bhaktee Dongaonkar**
Department of Psychology
The University of Arizona
Tucson, AZ

**John Dunlosky**
Department of Psychology
Kent State University
Kent, OH

**Gilles O. Einstein**
Department of Psychology
Furman University
Greenville, SC

**K. Anders Ericsson**
Department of Psychology
Florida State University
Tallahassee, FL

**Jonathan St B. T. Evans**
School of Psychology
University of Plymouth
Plymouth, UK

**Jessica I. Fleck**
Department of Psychology
The Richard Stockton College of New Jersey
Galloway, NJ

**Carol Forsyth**
Institute for Intelligent Systems
Department of Psychology
University of Memphis
Memphis, TN

**Steven L. Franconeri**
Department of Psychology
Northwestern University
Evanston, IL

**David A. Gallo**
Department of Psychology
The University of Chicago
Chicago, IL

**Bertram Gawronski**
Social Cognition Lab
University of Western Ontario
London, Ontario, Canada

**Maria Gendron**
Department of Psychology
Boston College
Chestnut Hill, MA

**Dedre Gentner**
Department of Psychology
Northwestern University
Evanston, IL

**Morton Ann Gernsbacher**
Department of Psychology
University of Wisconsin Madison
Madison, WI

**Michael J. Gill**
Department of Psychology
Lehigh University
Bethlehem, PA

**Lila Gleitman**
Department of Psychology
University of Pennsylvania
Philadelphia, PA

**Arthur C. Graesser**
Department of Psychology
Psychology Department
University of Memphis
Memphis, TN

**James J. Gross**
Department of Psychology
Stanford University
Stanford, CA

**York Hagmayer**
Department of Psychology
University of Göttingen
Göttingen, Germany

**Brett K. Hayes**
School of Psychology
University of New South Wales
Sydney, Australia

**Evan Heit**
School of Social Sciences, Humanities, and Arts
University of California, Merced
Merced, CA

**John M. Henderson**
Department of Psychology
University of South Carolina
Columbia, SC

**Siobhan M. Hoscheidt**
Center for Cognitive Neuroscience
Department of Psychology and Neuroscience
Duke University
Durham, NC

**John E. Hummel**
Department of Psychology
University of Illinois
Urbana-Champaign, IL

**Jeffrey R. Huntsinger**
Department of Psychology
Loyola University Chicago
Chicago, IL

**Kathy E. Johnson**
Indiana University-Purdue University Indianapolis
Indianapolis, IN

**Philip N. Johnson-Laird**
Department of Psychology
New York University
New York, NY

**Michael Jones**
Department of Psychology and Brain Sciences
Indiana University
Bloomington, IN

**Michael P. Kaschak**
Department of Psychology
Florida State University
Tallahassee, FL

**James C. Kaufman**
Learning Research Institute
California State University, San Bernardino
San Bernardino, CA

**Scott Barry Kaufman**
New York University
New York, NY

**John F. Kihlstrom**
Department of Psychology
University of California, Berkeley
Berkeley, CA

**Ruth Kimchi**
Department of Psychology and Institute of
Information Processing and Decision Making
University of Haifa
Haifa, Israel

**Melissa Koenig**
Institute of Child Development
The University of Minnesota
Minneapolis, MN

**John Kounios**
Department of Psychology
Drexel University
Philadelphia, PA

**Maria Kozhevnikov**
Martinos Center
Massachusetts General Hospital
Harvard Medical School
Charlestown, MA
National University of Singapore
Singapore

**Cara Laney**
Forensic Psychology
University of Leicester
Leicester, UK

**Jason P. Leboe-McGowan**
Department of Psychology
University of Manitoba
Winnipeg, Manitoba, Canada

**Robert H. Logie**
Human Cognitive Neuroscience
Centre for Cognitive Ageing and Cognitive
Epidemiology
University of Edinburgh
Edinburgh, Scotland, UK

**James S. Magnuson**
Department of Psychology
University of Connecticut Haskins Laboratories
Groton, CT

**Arthur B. Markman**
Department of Psychology
University of Texas
Austin, TX

**Elizabeth J. Marsh**
Department and Psychology and Neuroscience
Duke University
Durham, NC

**Sven L. Mattys**
Department of Psychology
University of York
York, UK

**Richard E. Mayer**
Department of Psychology
University of California
Santa Barbara, CA

**Mark A. McDaniel**
Department of Psychology
Washington University in St. Louis
St. Louis, MO

**Ken McRae**
Department of Psychology
Social Science Centre
University of Western Ontario
London, Ontario, Canada

**Nathaniel G. Meadow**
Department of Psychology
Northwestern University
Evanston, IL

**Batja Mesquita**
Department of Psychology
University of Leuven
Leuven, Belgium

**Daniel Mirman**
Moss Rehabilitation Research Institute
Philadelphia, PA

**Yuri Miyamoto**
Department of Psychology
University of Wisconsin-Madison
Madison, WI

**Agnes Moors**
Department of Psychology
Ghent University
Ghent, Belgium

**Katherine C. Morasch**
Department of Psychology
Virginia Polytechnic Institute and State University
Blacksburg, VA

**Gordon B. Moskowitz**
Department of Psychology
Lehigh University
Bethlehem, PA

**Neil W. Mulligan**
Department of Psychology
University of North Carolina
Chapel Hill, NC

**Emily Myers**
Department of Communication Sciences
Department of Psychology
University of Connecticut Haskins Laboratories
Groton, CT

**Lynn Nadel**
Department of Psychology
The University of Arizona
Tucson, AZ

**Ben R. Newell**
School of Psychology
University of New South Wales
Sydney, Australia

**Anna Papafragou**
Department of Psychology
University of Delaware
Newark, DE

**Jessica Payne**
Department of Psychology
Notre Dame University
Notre Dame, IN

**Diane Pecher**
Psychology Department
Erasmus University
Rotterdam, The Netherlands

**Mary A. Peterson**
Department of Psychology and Cognitive Science
Program
University of Arizona
Tucson, AZ

**Jonathan A. Plucker**
Neag School of Education
University of Connecticut
Storrs, CT

**Alexander Pollatsek**
Department of Psychology
University of Massachusetts, Amherst
Amherst, MA

**Danielle Posthuma**
Sections Functional Genomics and Medical
Genomics
Center for Neurogenomics and Cognitive
Research (CNCR)
Neuroscience Campus Amsterdam (NCA)
Department of Clinical Genetics
VU University medical center (VUmc)
Amsterdam, The Netherlands
Department of Child & Adolescent Psychiatry
Sophia Children's Hospital
Rotterdam, The Netherlands

**Vinaya Raj**
Virginia Polytechnic Institute and State University
Blacksburg, VA

**Keith Rayner**
Department of Psychology
University of California, San Diego
La Jolla, CA

**Jonathan R. Rein**
Department of Psychology
University of Texas
Austin, TX

**Daniel Reisberg**
Department of Psychology
Reed College
Portland, OR

**Ronald A. Rensink**
Departments of Psychology and Computer
Science
University of British Columbia
Vancouver, British Columbia, Canada

**Greg D. Reynolds**
Department of Psychology
University of Tennessee, Knoxville
Knoxville, TN

**Gillian Rhodes**
ARC Centre of Excellence in Cognition and its
Disorders
School of Psychology
University of Western Australia
Crawley, Australia

**John E. Richards**
Department of Psychology
University of South Carolina
Columbia, SC

**Thais S. Rizzi**
Section Functional Genomics
Center for Neurogenomics and Cognitive Research
(CNCR)
Neuroscience Campus Amsterdam (NCA)
VU University Amsterdam
Amsterdam, The Netherlands

**David A. Rosenbaum**
Department of Psychology
Pennsylvania State University
University Park, PA

**Dana Samson**
Institut de recherche en sciences psychologiques
Université catholique de Louvain
Louvain-la-Neuve, Belgium

**Simone Schnall**
Department of Social and Developmental Psychology
University of Cambridge
Cambridge, UK

**Holger Schultheis**
Department of Computer Science
University of Bremen
Bremen, Germany

**Barry Schwartz**
Department of Psychology
Swarthmore College
Swarthmore, PA

**Linsey A. Smith**
Department of Psychology
Northwestern University
Evanston, IL

**David R. Shanks**
Division of Psychology and Language Sciences
University College London
London, UK

**Dean Keith Simonton**
Department of Psychology
University of California, Davis
Davis, CA

**Roseanna Sommers**
Department of Psychology
Swarthmore College
Swarthmore, PA

**Maarten Speekenbrink**
Division of Psychology and Language Sciences
University College London
London, UK

**Keith W. Thiede**
Department of Education
Boise State University
Boise, ID

**Tyler J. Towne**
Department of Psychology
Florida State University
Tallahassee, FL

**Barbara Tversky**
Department of Psychology
Stanford University
Stanford, CA

**David H. Uttal**
Department of Psychology
Northwestern University
Evanston, IL

**Paul Verhaeghen**
School of Psychology
Georgia Institute of Technology
Atlanta, GA

**Michael R. Waldmann**
Department of Psychology
University of Göttingen
Göttingen, Germany

**Mark E. Wheeler**
Department of Psychology
Learning Research & Development Center
University of Pittsburgh
Pittsburgh, PA

**Bruce W. A. Whittlesea**
Simon Fraser University
Department of Psychology
Burnaby, British Columbia, Canada

**Brooke Wilken**
Department of Psychology
University of Wisconsin-Madison
Madison, WI

**Andy J. Wills**
School of Psychology
Plymouth University
Plymouth, UK

**Liane Young**
Department of Psychology
Boston College
Chestnut Hill, MA

**Jeffrey M. Zacks**
Department of Psychology
Washington University
St. Louis, MO

# CONTENTS

# Introduction to the Handbook

Daniel Reisberg

**Abstract**

This brief opening chapter outlines and celebrates the enormous progress cognitive psychology has made in the last 50 years. It discusses some of the principles that guided the selection of topics for this handbook and then provides a brief road map for the handbook's overall organization.

**Key Words:** introduction, cognitive psychology, history

For many years, I playfully began my undergraduate Cognition course by telling students: "The field of Cognitive Psychology began when I was born." I would give the class a moment to gasp at this stunning bit of narcissism, and then I would deliver the clarification: "Let's be clear, though, that there's no cause and effect here; I'm just trying to let you know how long this field's been around."

Of course, this opening gambit worked more effectively—and led to the point I was after—when I was young. Then I could use the joke to convey that the field of Cognition was also youthful, and I could celebrate how much the field had achieved in just a few decades. But I am no longer a young man, and (far more interesting) the field of Cognition has reached an age that no longer counts as youthful. Indeed, Donald Broadbent's *Perception and Communication* and Jerry Bruner's *A Study in Thinking* were both published more than 50 years ago (in 1958 and 1956, respectively). George Miller's "magic number" paper is of comparable vintage (published in 1956). Dick Neisser's remarkable textbook (*Cognitive Psychology*)—a book that drew many of us into the field—was published in 1967.

The decades have been fabulously fruitful for us. If we consider only our "internal products," we could point to the proliferation of specialized

journals, or—perhaps better—the frequent contributions of cognitive psychologists to journals that reach everyone in our field (e.g., *Psychological Review* and *Psychological Science*) or journals that reach other scientists (e.g., *Nature* and *Science*). Alternatively, we can consider our "exports," including the many applications of our field (to questions in the justice system, questions about education, question about business decision making, and more). We can also consider a different type of export: books that carry our work out of the journals and into the minds of a broader audience (e.g., Ariely, 2010; Chabris & Simons, 2011; Gilbert, 2007; Kahneman, 2011; Lederer, 2010; Nisbett, 2009; Pinker, 2009; Schwartz, 2005). Or, as one last measure, we can look to the future and ask how psychology is training its students: Courses in cognition are available in almost every department, and there is a proliferation of textbooks (Amazon.com offers more than a dozen) for instructors to choose from.

By any of these measures, it is clear that cognitive psychologists are generating a lot of new ideas and a lot of new information, and it is also clear that many have found considerable value in this information. We can, in short, be proud of what our 50-plus years of effort have produced.

I offer these entry comments not just as a "feel-good" message for my colleagues but also as a partial explanation for why this handbook has come to be. As cognitive psychology has matured, we have developed research tools and theoretical frameworks that have allowed us to explore a broad array of topics. In the same vein, the *depth* of our understanding, as well as the methodological and theoretical sophistication, has also grown in wonderful ways. We can, of course, celebrate these increases in breadth and depth, but there is also a price to be paid: We have all been forced to specialize more and more, to keep up with our "corner" of cognition. With that, it has become increasingly difficult to maintain the status of cognitive generalist. Thus, researchers in autobiographical memory can drift out of touch with research on semantic memory; researchers focused on working memory (and so sometimes concerned with executive function) might have difficulty keeping up with research on judgment (often concerned with executive function).

These are common problems in any burgeoning field, and handbooks like this one are a key part of the repair—allowing researchers in one corner of the field to instruct researchers in other domains. Indeed, independent of my role as editor, let me say *as a reader* that I happily express my gratitude to the authors of this handbook's many chapters: I learned a great deal from them, and I'm certainly appreciative of coverage in the chapters that is broader in its view and more cohesive than, say, a journal article; more advanced than one would find in a textbook; and less intermittent than, say, an *Annual Review* article. In these (and other) ways, handbooks like this one serve an essential role—for aspiring generalists who might choose to read the book cover to cover, and for the many of us who are simply curious to know what is going on in other cognition laboratories working on other problems.

What is in the handbook? In designing the volume, I did what I could to cover all of cognitive psychology. I hasten to say, though, that I did not achieve this lofty goal because of space limitations, author availability, and my own errors in overlooking this or that important topic; of course, I regret all of these shortcomings.

It is also far from clear what it would *mean* for a handbook to cover "all of cognitive psychology." The problem, obviously, is that the boundaries of our field are difficult to locate. Even if we could neatly identify certain research topics as "cognitive," it is plain that we can gain insight into these topics by drawing on research in allied fields. Hence, the separation between cognitive psychology and social psychology can, for some research questions, seem arbitrary; likewise the separation between cognitive and developmental psychology. In the same vein, the study of language and the study of emotion are both powerful scientific endeavors, important in their own right. But these domains are surely intertwined with the topics traditionally regarded as "cognitive," and so it seems foolish to hold language or emotion to the side when we study cognition.

Guided by these sentiments, I have aimed for coverage in this handbook that errs on the side of inclusion. To be sure, the volume's coverage of social or developmental topics and its coverage of language and emotion are (at best) selective and therefore incomplete. My hope, though, is that the book covers at least some of the major points of connection between cognitive psychology and these other intellectual domains.

I should also note that, in choosing authors, I have done what I could to include many influential, persuasive, well-established figures in our field. But I have also done what I could to include younger colleagues—largely because, in obvious ways, they are our field's future, and so, by keeping track of their work and their views, we gain an understanding of our field's forward trajectory.

I have also aimed, in this book, for a mix of didactic, largely neutral, "tutorial" chapters and also chapters that plainly and powerfully represent a particular research team's point of view. After all, cognitive psychology includes a mix of well-established consensus claims and more contentious arguments, and I wanted both in the book. To be sure, a handbook seemed not the place to emphasize the latter, but I did want the book to reflect the vitality of the field, and that vitality is most easily seen in the claims that are still being energetically and productively debated.

One last point about the book's coverage is complicated, because it hinges on the relationship between cognitive psychology and cognitive *neuroscience*. As it turns out, Oxford University Press is publishing two separate handbooks—this one, focused on cognitive psychology, and a separate volume covering cognitive neuroscience. Is this sensible? On the one hand, cognitive neuroscience is itself a sophisticated discipline with its own methods, its own theoretical framework, and its own questions. This sophistication will inevitably increase in the coming years, as neuroscientists build on new data, new ideas, and new technology. For these reasons, cognitive neuroscience must be understood as an independent field and will surely become more independent, more autonomous in times to come. Hence, it makes sense that we should give the field the respect (and page count) it deserves, and so keep the topics separate, each in its own volume.

With this, many cognitive psychologists believe that our field risks overstating the value of neuroscience. To be sure, insights from neuroscience are enormously important, and data from neuroscience can help us resolve long-standing debates. Even so, psychology's increasing emphasis on neuroscience, some might suggest, can lead us to lose track of lessons learned, perhaps decades earlier, from behavioral results. Related, some have complained that the understandable excitement about neuroscience can sometimes draw attention away from questions and problems that are best explored through other means. On these grounds, too, we should separate the volumes, so that cognitive psychology itself gets the respect (and page count) it needs.

There is, however, also an argument in the opposite direction—for *integrating* the two fields and (perhaps) the two OUP handbooks: Cognitive neuroscience inevitably and necessarily builds on an understanding of how cognitive processes function, and so in that way depends on cognitive psychology. Likewise, cognitive psychologists must pay close attention to the results provided by cognitive neuroscience, results that can provide tests of our claims, and sometimes constrain our claims, and often enrich our claims. In this fashion, there is a mutual dependence between these two fields, and this dependence is likely to *grow* in the coming years: Each discipline will learn more, and so have more to export to the other. Each discipline will therefore have more and more reason to keep track of what is going on in the other.

For all of these reasons, we handicap ourselves by separating psychology and the relevant neuroscience. Indeed, I have already suggested that the point of a handbook is to allow investigators in one domain to learn about (useful, interesting) insights in other domains. Hence, the last thing we would want to do is leave an important source of these insights out of the present volume.

The resolution of this quandary is perhaps inevitable: On one side, there are compelling reasons to separate the handbook of cognitive psychology and the handbook of cognitive neuroscience, just as Oxford has. On the other side, there is a clear need to link the volumes. The best we can do, therefore, is to keep the books separate but hope colleagues will read both. In addition, for some topics, the exchange between cognition psychology and cognitive neuroscience is actively under way. For other topics, the exchange is an exciting prospect but not yet in view. It cannot be surprising, therefore, that some chapters in the present volume include coverage of neuroscience topics; others do not. How this mix will play out over the next decade is, I think, a topic for psychologists to ponder, as we try to anticipate the forward trajectory of our field.

Overall, the handbook is divided into 13 sections. I hope this ordering is helpful, although other sequences could easily be defended. Even with this point acknowledged, I hope the ordering aids the reader in navigating through these 1076 pages.

Part 1 tackles a set of issues pertinent to how we *gain information about the visual world.* Peterson and Kimchi (Chapter 2) discuss the issue of how we organize the information provided to us by vision, and then Hummel (Chapter 3) turns to the problem of how we recognize the objects we have now organized. Rhodes (Chapter 4) tackles a more specialized form of recognition: the recognition of faces. Then Henderson (Chapter 5) turns to an issue crucial for all aspects of perception: how we move our eyes. In the section's last chapter, Tversky and Zacks (Chapter 6) broaden the questions, by asking how we perceive complex real-world events.

Part 2 is concerned with a cluster of topics linking *attention and awareness.* Rensink (Chapter 7) links this part to the concerns of Part 1, discussing the interplay between perception and attention. Then, in Chapter 8, Cave turns to a key issue for visual attention: how we manage to focus our attention on discrete regions of space. In Chapter 9, Logie tackles directly an issue that comes up in many chapters: what we can learn from cases of brain damage, and, in particular, disorders of attention. In Chapter 10, however, Franconeri turns a critical eye on a notion that plays a large role in many theories of attention: the notion of visual resources. Then, in Chapter 11, Moors considers a set of claims in which (traditionally) resources have played a large role, namely, the idea of automaticity. Finally, in Chapter 12, Kihlstrom casts a wide net, confronting issues that are pertinent to this section and to many others, when he examines the broad notion of unconscious processes.

Part 3 focuses on *memory.* In Chapter 13, Gallo and Wheeler summarize what is known about episodic memory; in Chapter 14, McRae and Jones discuss semantic memory; in Chapter 15, Mulligan and Besken describe implicit memory. Then, in Chapter 16, Laney explores a domain with profound pragmatic applications as well as theoretical interest—the nature and sources of memory errors. In Chapter 17, however, Leboe and Whittlesea offer an alternative view of all these memory issues, challenging us with their SCAPE framework. Then the next three chapters turn to key but (for some readers) less familiar aspects of memory: In Chapter 18, Bugg, McDaniel, and Einstein explore the key issue of prospective memory, that is, the challenge of remembering, in the future, to carry out present intentions. Dunlosky and Thiede (Chapter 19) discuss the topic of metamemory—the sense that each of us has of our own memory and the functions that this self-monitoring has. Finally, Chapter 20, by Marsh and Butler, picks up a set of questions that again have both pragmatic implications and theoretical power: the functioning of memory in educational settings.

Part 4 is concerned with the nature of *knowledge and mental representation*. Markman and Rein (in Chapter 21) explore mental concepts. Johnson's coverage (Chapter 22) is the first of several chapters that explore how our claims (and, specifically, claims about concepts) need to be tuned when we consider people with differing levels of expertise or people living in different cultures. Wills (Chapter 23) discusses a different—but deeply important—approach to concepts: the development of formal models to express and test our theories of categorization. In Chapter 24, Pecher then argues for an alternative approach to mental categories, one that is grounded in sensory-motor processes. Then, related, Reisberg (Chapter 25) summarizes what is known about mental representations of a different sort: visual mental images.

Part 5 turns to some of the points of contact between cognitive psychology and the broad study of *language*. In Chapter 26, Mattys describes the state of the art in speech perception; Chapter 27, by Magnuson, Mirman, and Myers, then builds on this base in exploring the broad issue of spoken word recognition. Chapter 28, by Rayner and Pollatsek, is also concerned with language—but via the visual modality—and explores basic processes in reading. (And I would urge readers to explore the parallels between the coverage in these three chapters, on language-related perception, and the coverage in Part 1, concerned with other aspects of perception.) Chapters 29, by Gernsbacher and Kaschak, and 30, by Graesser and Forsyth, are linked, both exploring how people perceive and understand larger units of language; Chapter 29 emphasizes text comprehension; Chapter 30 explores discourse comprehension. Then Koenig and Cole (Chapter 31) turn to the issue of how children launch the process of word learning; Gleitman and Papafragou (Chapter 32) summarize the state of the art on the interplay between language and thought. (These two chapters are rich with implications for, and can also be enriched by, themes in Part 2 and Part 4, addressing the *nature of mental representation*.) The final chapter in this section, by Bickerton (Chapter 33) introduces a perspective that can often guide cognitive research and theorizing, examining the likely evolution of language.

For many years, theorists have assumed that cognitive and *emotional factors* were separable and often in tension with each other. In recent years, however, we have seen many reasons to challenge this perspective, and Part 6 samples some of the scholarship in this domain. Gendron, Mesquita, and Barrett (Chapter 34) consider how we perceive emotion (and so this chapter can be read in conjunction with the materials in Part 1). Hoschedit, Dongaonkar, Payne, and Nadel (Chapter 35) discuss the interplay between emotion, stress, and memory (and this chapter should probably be read in conjunction with materials in Part 3). Huntsinger and Schnall (Chapter 36) then survey emotion–cognition interactions more broadly, laying out the argument for why we must not separate these domains. Boden and Gross (Chapter 37) then work through an intriguing issue in this arena: the tie between emotion regulation and belief change.

Parts 7, 8, and 9 span a range of topics concerned with what is sometimes called "higher order cognition" but is more plainly called "thinking." Part 7 begins with chapters on *judgment and reasoning*: Newell (Chapter 38) surveys judgment under uncertainty, Hayes and Heit (Chapter 39) tackle the related issue of induction, and Evans (Chapter 40) explores the problem of reasoning. The next two chapters describe specific routes toward judgment and reasoning: Johnson-Laird (Chapter 41) describes the role of mental models, and Gentner and Smith (Chapter 42) focus on the role of analogies and analogical learning. Then the last two chapters in Part 7 turn to the issue of choice, with Speekenbrink and Shanks (Chapter 43) describing how people make decisions and Schwartz and Sommers (Chapter 44) surveying the broad problem of affective forecasting and its relation to well-being.

Part 8 narrows the focus somewhat and considers three more *specialized types of reasoning*: Schultheis and Carlson (Chapter 45) consider spatial reasoning, Waldmann and Hagmayer (Chapter 46) turn to reasoning about causal relationships, and then Young (Chapter 47) considers how people think about moral issues.

Part 9's chapters turn to a problem that has a considerable amount of folklore associated with it: the domain of *problem solving and creativity*. Mayer (Chapter 48) describes what is known about problem solving. Fleck, Beeman, and Kounios (Chapter 49) turn to the achievement called "insight." Simonton and Damian (Chapter 50) describe research on creativity.

For many years, Cognitive Psychology emphasized principles that described all humans; consideration of individual differences was consigned to a separate endeavor termed *psychometrics*. This trend has shifted in the last years, and so Part 10 contains a trio of chapters on *how we differ*. Kaufman, Kaufman, and Plucker (Chapter 51) describe current theorizing about intelligence. Rizzi and Posthuma (Chapter 52) then help the reader grasp the likely genetic roots of differences in intelligence. Kozhevnikov (Chapter 53) turns to the differences, from one person to the next, in cognitive style.

Cognitive Psychology has also traditionally emphasized "input processes" and then mentation about the things we have perceived. But what about the "output" side of things, and action? Some of the earlier chapters have already suggested that this "input/output" distinction may be unwise (e.g., Chapter 24). Part 11, however, tackles directly this broad issue and includes three chapters on *practice and skilled performance*. Rosenbaum (Chapter 54) describes the planning and implementation of physical action. Uttal and Meadow (Chapter 55) consider the impact of practice. Then Ericsson and Towne (Chapter 56) explore the sometimes extraordinary level of performance achieved by experts.

Finally, the last two parts of the book draw on domains often considered separate from Cognitive Psychology, but unmistakably these fields are our allies, with prospect for information exchange in both directions. Part 12 turns to the *social and cultural context*. Bauer and Baumeister (Chapter 57) discuss self-knowledge, Moskowitz and Gill (Chapter 58) consider person perception, and Samson (Chapter 59) considers the cognition we have about others, knowledge typically termed "theory of mind." In Chapter 60, Bodenhausen and Gawronski discuss the topic of attitude change. Finally, Miyamoto and Wilken (Chapter 61) describe the crucial importance of cultural differences in cognition.

The handbook's final part, Part 13, then briefly delves into developmental issues. In Chapter 62, Morasch, Raj, and Bell explore the development of cognitive control. In Chapter 63, Reynolds, Courage, and Richards discuss the development of attention. Finally, Verhaeghen (Chapter 64) considers the other end of the life span and discusses cognitive aging.

Then, in the handbook's ultimate chapter, I as editor take on the daunting but enjoyable task of offering some general remarks, trying to say a few words about our field overall and also reflecting on the pleasure I have found in putting this handbook together.

## References

Ariely, D. (2010). *Predictably irrational, revised and expanded edition: The hidden forces that shape our decisions*. New York: Harper.

Chabris, C., & Simons, D. (2011). *The invisible gorilla: How our intuitions deceive us*. New York: Broadway.

Gilbert, D. (2007). *Stumbling on happiness*. New York: Vintage.

Kahneman, D. (2011). *Thinking, fast and slow*. New York: Farrar, Straus, & Giroux.

Lederer, J. (2010). *How we decide*. New York: Mariner Books.

Nisbett, R. (2009). *Intelligence and how to get it*. New York: Norton.

Pinker, S. (2009). *How the mind works*. New York: Norton.

Schwartz, B. (2005). *The paradox of choice: Why more is less*. New York: Harper Perennial.

# PART 1

# Gaining Information About the Visual World

# Perceptual Organization in Vision

Mary A. Peterson *and* Ruth Kimchi

**Abstract**

Perceptual organization encompasses grouping and segregating processes; grouping processes assemble visual elements into perceptual wholes, and segregating processes parse visual input into separate objects. In this chapter, we review behavioral evidence regarding both image-based (objective) and perceiver-based (subjective) factors that operate to produce grouping and segregation. We consider both how these factors combine and compete and when in the course of processing they operate. The research reviewed in this chapter shows that the traditional view of perceptual organization as an early process that provides the substrate on which high-level perceptual processes operate is oversimplified. Recent research makes a case that perceptual organization is neither a stage of processing nor a monolithic entity. Instead, perceptual organization results from interactions among multiple cues and processes at many levels; it is a form of selection, in that only one of many interpretations that could be fit to a display is perceived.

**Key Words:** grouping, segregation, figure-ground perception, objective factors, subjective factors, Gestalt, past experience, cue integration, selection, direct measures, indirect measures

People readily perceive and act upon objects, but perceptual processes must operate to organize the input into these coherent units. *Perceptual organization* processes can be subclassified as *grouping* and *segregating* processes. *Grouping* refers to the processes by which visual elements are "put together" into perceptual wholes. *Segregating* refers to the processes by which these wholes are parsed into separate objects. In particular, the visual system must determine which borders in the visual field are likely to be bounding edges of objects or surfaces and which are pattern borders, shadow edges, or formed by the junction of two planar surfaces. Those deemed to be bounding edges are perceived to separate entities, with one of these entities shaped, or configured, by the border (this is the near object, or *figure*), while the other is not (and thus is perceived as a surface that constitutes the local background, or *ground*, to the figure).

In the late 19th century, the prevailing theory of perception was Structuralism. Proponents of this position attributed perceptual organization to past experience, proposing that those parts of the visual field that had been grouped or segmented in past experience were grouped and segmented in current experience as well. An explanation based totally on past experience will not work, however, as the Gestalt psychologists pointed out early in the 20th century. Among other considerations, they demonstrated that segregation and grouping *can* occur without input from memory or past experience, and they argued that segregation and grouping *must* operate before memory and conceptual content are accessed. Note, however, the potential slip here, because demonstrations that perceptual organization *can* occur without input from past experience do not entail that it *always* occurs without input from experience (Peterson, 1999).

In this chapter, we take an interactive processing approach to perceptual organization, arguing that high-level and low-level representations and processes interact to produce perceptual organization. On this view, perceptual organization is neither a stage of processing nor a monolithic entity; instead it is a confluence of multiple cues and processes (Behrmann & Kimchi, 2003; Kimchi, 2003; Peterson, 1994b, 2003b). Furthermore, we consider perceptual organization to be a form of selection, in that only one of many interpretations that could be fit to a display is perceived. We review both image-based (objective) and perceiver-based (subjective) factors that operate to produce *grouping* and *segregation*; we also review behavioral evidence regarding how these factors combine and compete. We will show that behavioral research is beginning to shed light on foundational perceptual organization process. We note that computational and neuropsychological approaches have also been applied to this issue but are beyond the scope of this chapter.

## Segregation

Segregating the visual field into separate objects is a multidetermined and complex process involving myriad cues. Julesz (1971) demonstrated, using random-dot stereograms, that the depth cue of binocular disparity alone can produce the perception of both depth and simple shape, and, since then, the influence of shape properties has often been overlooked. Some took Julesz's demonstrations to imply that cues that had been shown to influence figure assignment in two-dimensional displays are irrelevant in the three-dimensional world (e.g., Marr, 1982). But this conclusion is based on a reasoning error similar to that made by the Gestalt psychologists: The demonstration that binocular disparity alone *can* produce perceptual organization does not imply that other cues cannot operate singly as well; nor does it imply that other cues are irrelevant when binocular disparity is available (see Bertamini, Martinovic, & Wueger, 2008; Burge, Peterson, & Palmer, 2005; Burge et al., 2010; Peterson, 2003a; Peterson & Gibson, 1993).

In this chapter, we focus our review on properties other than depth cues that affect the likelihood that a border shared by two adjacent regions will be perceived as the bounding edge of a "figure" (a shaped entity) on one side with an unshaped region (the "ground") on the other side. All borders in the visual field are ambiguous, in that shapes that might

be seen on opposite sides are detected yet only one is perceived (e.g., Peterson & Enns, 2005; Peterson & Lampignano, 2003; Peterson & Skow, 2008). Hence, perceiving a figure on one side but not the other entails selection.

### *Image-Based Segregation Factors*

"Image-based factors" refer to segregation factors that can be defined on the image. The Gestalt psychologists introduced a number of these factors and held that they were independent of the viewer's experience (i.e., "autochthonous"), although there is no evidence for this point. Additional image-based segregation factors have been identified recently.

#### CLASSIC GESTALT IMAGE-BASED SEGREGATION FACTORS

The Gestalt psychologists showed that the figure was more likely to be perceived on the side of a border that is *convex* rather than concave, where the convex side is that side from which the border has a positive sign of curvature. For instance, Kanizsa and Gerbino (1976) showed that with displays like Figure 2.1A and 2.1B, in which multiple convex and concave regions alternate, convexity is an effective cue: 90% of their observers reported perceiving the convex regions as figures. Strictly speaking, the "convex" and "concave" regions in Figure 2.1 are not entirely convex or concave, but Stevens and Brooks (1988; Hoffman

(A)

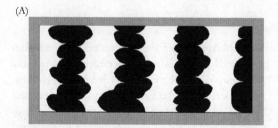

(B)

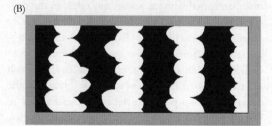

**Figure 2.1** (*A* and *B*) Displays with equal-area black and white regions. Regions with convex parts alternate with regions with concave parts. For simplicity these regions are called "convex" and "concave" regions; this nomenclature dates to the Gestalt psychologists. The convex regions are black in (*A*), white in (*B*).

& Singh, 1997) showed that convexity *can* operate locally; that is, when only small portions of the borders near part boundaries (minima of curvature) are convex. For brevity in what follows, therefore, we will use the terms "convex" and "concave" regions to refer to regions with convex and concave parts.

Most perception psychologists inferred that the effectiveness of convexity as a figural cue measured by Kanisza and Gerbino (1976) generalized to all types of displays. Some investigators, in fact, concluded that convexity alone could account for much of image-based segregation, and many computational models use convexity alone to account for figure assignment (e.g., Jehee, Lamme, & Roelfsema, 2007; Kogo, Strecha, Van Gool, & Wagemans, 2010).

However, Peterson and Salvagio (2008) showed that, in briefly exposed displays (100 ms, unmasked), the effectiveness of convexity as a figural cue decreases systematically as the number of alternating convex and concave regions decreases from eight to two (see Figs. 2.2A and 2.2B). In two-region displays, where one concave and one convex region lie on opposite sides of a central border, the likelihood of perceiving the figure on the convex side of the central border was 58%, which is significantly but not substantially greater than chance, and nowhere near the likelihood of perceiving the figure on the convex side of the central border in eight region displays (89%). Furthermore, Peterson and Salvagio observed these effects of region number only when the concave regions alternating with the convex regions were homogeneously colored, not when they were heterogeneously colored (Figs. 2.2C and 2.2D). Thus, much remains to be learned about how the image-based cue of convexity operates. What is certain is that it alone cannot account for figure assignment under many conditions. Peterson and Salvagio's results also indicate that local decisions regarding individual borders are influenced by global display-wide analyses (cf. Kim & Feldman, 2009).

Other image-based shape properties identified as figural cues by the Gestalt psychologists include *symmetry*, *small area*, and *closure* (Rubin, 1915/1958; for review, see Hochberg, 1971; Peterson, 2001; Pomerantz & Kubovy, 1986). But these image-based properties can also be attributes of grounds, as shown in Figure 2.3. Therefore, these cues must be operating probabilistically rather than deterministically. Furthermore, recent research shows that, like convexity, neither symmetry (Machilsen, Pauwels, & Wagemans, 2009; Mojica & Peterson, 2012; Salvagio, Mojica, & Peterson, 2008) nor small area (Salvagio et al., 2008) is a strong figural cue in displays with only two contiguous regions. This finding is again consistent with the idea that segregation is determined by ensembles of shape properties and by scene-wide information, rather than by individual, localized properties.

### NEW IMAGE-BASED SHAPE PROPERTIES

Hulleman and Humphreys (2004) introduced a new figural cue of *top/bottom polarity*, whereby regions with a wide base and a narrow top are more likely to be seen as figures than those with a narrow base and a wide top. An example is shown in Figure 2.4A. This cue, along with many of the others, may reflect a general feature of our environment: On the assumption that objects are more stable when they are wider at the base than at the top, objects with this property are probably more common in our environment than objects that are narrower at the base than at the top.

Vecera, Vogel, and Woodman (2002) systematically explored the cue of *lower region* that had been discussed but not investigated by Ehrenstein (1930; cf. Koffka, 1935; Metzger, 1953). Vecera et al. showed that, ceteris paribus, a horizontal border is more likely to be perceived as shaping the region below rather than above it (see Fig. 2.4B).

Other image-based figural cues have been introduced over the years, including *part salience* (Hoffman & Singh, 1997), whereby regions with protruding parts are more likely to be perceived as figures; *spatial frequency* (Klymenko & Weisstein, 1986), whereby regions filled with high spatial frequency gratings are more likely to be perceived as figures than regions filled with low spatial frequency gratings; *extremal edges* (Palmer & Ghose, 2008), whereby regions with shading gradients indicating a horizon of self-occlusion on a smoothly curved convex surface are more likely than abutting regons to be perceived as figures, as well as some dynamic cues (Barenholtz & Feldman, 2006). A figural property recently introduced by Palmer and Brooks (2008) integrates grouping and segregation (see section on "The Relationship Between Grouping and Segregation" for further explication).

In summary, even when depth cues are not considered, multiple image-based properties influence figure assignment, so it is clear that multiple sources of information are used to solve the critically important task of scene segregation.

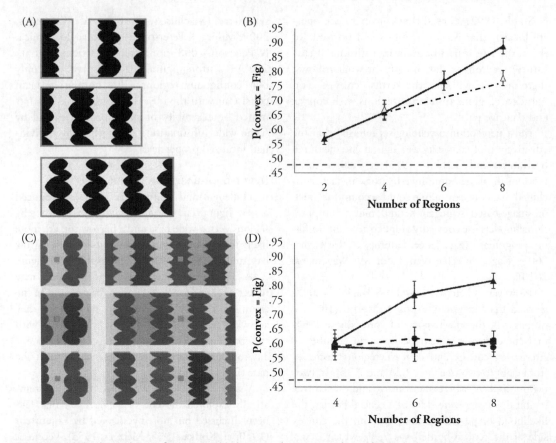

**Figure 2.2** (*A*) Displays with two-, four-, six-, and eight-region alternating equal-area black and white convex and concave regions. The convex regions are black in these displays, but they were white on half the trials in the experiments. Observers fixated the central border and reported whether the black or the white regions appeared to be figures. (Adapted from Peterson and Salvagio, 2008, *Journal of Vision*, Figure 2.) (*B*) The probability that observers perceived the convex regions as figures as a function of region number. (Region number was a between-subjects factor.) Solid black line: results obtained when all the convex regions had the same shape (as did all the concave regions); dashed black line: results obtained when each of the display regions had a different shape. The dashed red line indicates chance performance. (Adapted from Peterson and Salvagio, 2008, *Journal of Vision*, Figure 3.) (*C*) Sample four- and eight-region displays used to test whether homogeneity of color of the convex and/or the concave regions was necessary for the region number effects shown in (*B*). Top: both convex and concave regions are heterogeneously (HET) colored; no two regions of the same type are the same color (although all regions of one type are the same luminance; luminance was balanced across region type). Middle: Sample displays with homogeneously (HOM) colored convex regions and HET colored concave regions. Bottom: Sample HOM colored concave/HET colored convex displays. Note that the brightness values may not reproduce well here. Because displays were multicolored, direct report regarding the color of the figures was not possible. Accordingly on each trial a red response probe was placed on the region to the right or to the left of fixation. Observers reported whether the probe appeared to lie on or off the region they saw as figure. (Originally published as Peterson and Salvagio, 2008, *Journal of Vision*, Figure 4.) (*D*) The probability that convex regions were perceived as figure [P(convex = fig)] in multicolored displays as a function of region number. Dashed black line and disks: HET colored convex/HET colored concave displays. Solid black line and squares: HOM colored convex/HET colored concave displays; solid black line and triangles: HOM colored concave/HET colored convex displays. The dashed red line indicates chance performance. (Originally published as Peterson and Salvagio, 2008, *Journal of Vision*, Figure 5.) (*See* color insert.)

## Subjective Factors

A variety of subjective factors, including past experience (learning), attention, perceptual set, and the observers' fixation location, affect segregation.

**FAMILIAR CONFIGURATION: A LEARNED GEO-
METRIC SHAPE PROPERTY**

Until the early 1990s the Gestalt view that past experience could not affect figure assignment dominated (see also Fodor, 1984; Pylyshyn, 1999). But, since then, carefully controlled tests have shown that past experience in the form of familiar configuration serves as a segregation cue (e.g., Peterson, Harvey, & Weidenbacher, 1991; Peterson & Gibson 1994a, b). For instance, Peterson and Gibson (1994b; Gibson & Peterson, 1994) used vertically elongated rectangular displays divided in half by a central border. The displays were designed so that no

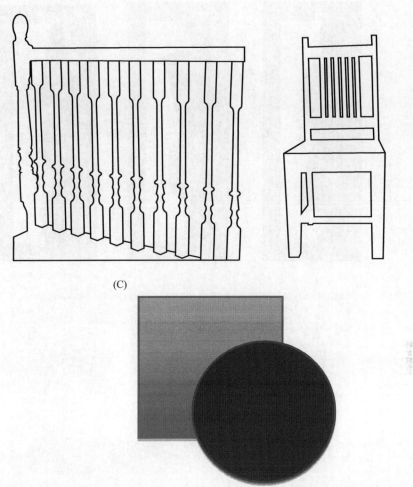

**Figure 2.3** (*A*) Bannisters: Both the turned wooden pieces (the figures) and the spaces between them are symmetric. (*B*) Chair: the small-area spaces between the slats on the back of the chair are not figures, nor are the enclosed horizontal spaces within the borders of the chair. (*C*) Both the light gray and dark gray regions are closed, yet only one is perceived as the figure at their shared border. (*See* color insert.)

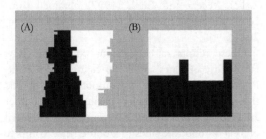

**Figure 2.4** (*A*) A display illustrating the figural cue of top/bottom polarity introduced by Hulleman and Humphreys (2004). The region on the left has a wide base and a narrow top. The region on the right has a narrow base and a wide top. Hulleman and Humphreys showed that regions like those on the left are more likely than regions like those on the right to be perceived as figures. (*B*) A display illustrating the figural cue of lower region introduced by Vecera et al. (2002).

known shape properties relevant to segregation distinguished the two halves of the display, yet the central border suggested a familiar, nameable, object on one side but not the other (see Fig. 2.5A). Observers were more likely to perceive the figure on the side of the border where the familiar configuration lay when the display was presented with the familiar object in its typical upright orientation rather than in an inverted orientation (see Fig. 2.5B; for review, see Peterson, 1994). Orientation dependency was critical for attributing these effects to past experience rather than to geometric properties of the display, because past experience effects plausibly should depend on typical orientation, whereas effects due to the geometric properties of the parts alone (e.g., part saliency) should not (also see Gibson & Peterson, 1994; Peterson et al., 1991). Furthermore, when

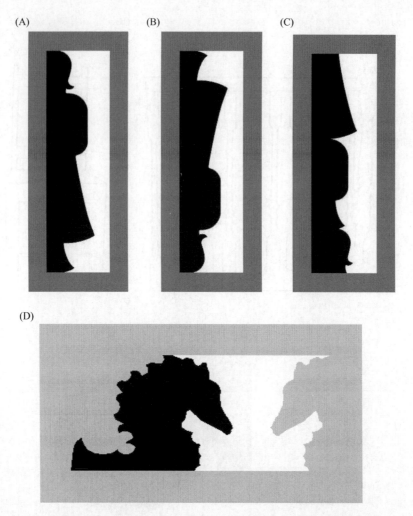

(A)     (B)     (C)

(D)

**Figure 2.5** (*A* and *B*) Sample bipartite displays in which two equal-area regions share a central border. The region on the left in black in these sample displays portrays a portion of a meaningful, familiar object, a woman. The woman is portrayed in an upright orientation in (*A*) and in an inverted orientation in (*B*). (*C*) The parts of the upright woman (delimited by successive minima of curvature along the central border) have been spatially rearranged. (*D*) A sample of a display used by Peterson and Gibson (1994) with an asymmetric region portraying a familiar configuration (a seahorse) in black on the left and a symmetric meaningless/novel region in white on the right.

familiar parts were spatially rearranged to form a novel configuration as in Fig. 2.5C, no effects of past experience were observed. This pattern of results led Peterson et al. to conclude that familiar configurations—and not familiar parts—were the origin of the past experience effects.

In their original experiments testing effects of familiarity on segregation, Peterson and colleagues used portions of well-known familiar objects (e.g., women, seahorses, coffee pots, table lamps). Later, they found that a single experience with a novel shape was sufficient for it to exert an influence on figure assignment the next time the border of that shape was encountered (Gibson & Peterson, 1994; Peterson & Enns, 2005; Peterson & Lampignano, 2003; also Treisman & DeSchepper, 1996; Peterson,

2012). Vecera and Farah (1997) obtained similar results with alphabetic letters (see also Navon, 2011).

These results raise questions concerning how familiarity operates prior to figure assignment. Peterson and Skow (2008) proposed that objects that might be perceived on opposite sides of a border are identified in a first pass of processing; potential objects on opposite sides of a border then compete for figural status (cf. Desimone & Duncan, 1995), and the most likely percept is seen.

### FIXATION LOCATION, ATTENTION, AND PERCEPTUAL SET

Subjective factors such as the location of observers' eyes or attention affect segregation as well.

Observers are more likely to perceive a given region as figure when they are fixating it than when they are fixating a contiguous region (Peterson & Gibson, 1994b). Effects of spatial attention, independent of fixation location, have been demonstrated as well. Baylis and Driver (1995) showed that the voluntary allocation of attention to one of two contiguous regions boosts the likelihood of seeing that region as figure. Later, Vecera, Flevaris, and Filapek (2004) demonstrated that involuntary attention, too, can influence figure-ground assignment. Additional evidence for attention effects came from tests of unilaterally brain-damaged participants. Such participants often allocate attention to the ipsilesional side of objects, regardless of where the objects are located in space (e.g., Behrmann & Tipper, 1994; Driver & Halligan, 1991; Gainotti, Messerle, & Tissot, 1972). In bipartite displays, each region constitutes a potential object, of which only one is selected for perception (see Figs. 2.5A-C). Unilaterally brain-damaged patients are more likely to perceive figures lying on the contralesional side of the central borders of bipartite displays (Driver, Baylis, & Rafal, 1992; Marshall & Halligan, 1994; Mattingly, Price, & Driver, 1996; Peterson, Gerhardstein, Mennemeier, & Rapscak, 1998), consistent with their attention having been allocated ipsilesionally within the two bipartite display regions. These results indicate that the potential objects on opposite sides of a border can serve as substrates for attention, consistent with Peterson and Skow's (2008) view that objects that might be perceived on opposite sides of a border are identified in a fast pass of processing, followed by a competition between them for figural status.

The perceiver's *perceptual set* (or intention) to perceive the figure on one side of a border (manipulated via instructions) also exerts an influence on segregation, even when fixation location is held constant (Peterson & Gibson, 1994b; Peterson et al., 1991). Intention effects are larger for upright than inverted familiar configurations, suggesting that intention operates at least in part via representations of familiar objects (see also Strüber & Stadler, 1999).

### Interactions Between Cues

There have been a few investigations exploring how different figural cues interact. Peterson and Gibson (1994b) found that effects of fixation were independent of those of past experience (i.e., the effects of fixation did not vary with the familiarity/meaningfulness of the shape depicted by a region). Fixation effects were also similar in size regardless of whether viewers had a perceptual set to try to perceive a region as figure.

Kanisza and Gerbino (1976) placed symmetry in competition with convexity, and they found that effects of convexity were undiminished by the competition. These results led some investigators to conclude that symmetry is a weak figural cue (e.g., Pomerantz & Kubovy, 1986). Inasmuch as Kanisza and Gerbino used multiregion displays, however, their results were likely context dependent (see discussion of region number effects in section on "Classic Gestalt Image-Based Segregation Factors"). Investigations of how convexity and symmetry compete in displays with fewer regions have yet to be conducted.

Peterson and Gibson (1994a) used brief masked exposures of two-region displays to examine how symmetry and familiar configuration interact. In their displays, a region that sketched a familiar meaningful configuration shared a central border with a region that portrayed a novel, meaningless configuration[1]; the two regions were equated for area and convexity. A sample of a display, with one symmetric but novel region and one asymmetric region portraying a familiar configuration (a seahorse) is shown in Figure 2.5D (color and left/right location were counterbalanced). When these displays were viewed in an inverted orientation, the symmetric regions were perceived as figure on approximately 62% of trials (averaged over all exposure durations) and the asymmetric region was perceived as figure on 38% of trials, documenting the effect of symmetry once again. When these displays were upright, however, and effects of familiar configuration were expected, the effect of symmetry was diminished: now symmetric regions were perceived as figure on only 52% of the trials, and the asymmetric familiar configuration was perceived as figure on 48% of the trials (again, averaged over variations in exposure duration). Thus, when symmetry and familiarity were in conflict, each cue determined the figure on approximately half the trials. These results suggest familiar configuration is not a dominant figural cue; instead it is one among many shape properties relevant to figure assignment (Peterson, 1994a,b).

On a competition view, the familiar configuration should be perceived as figure more often when the region on the opposite side of the central border is asymmetric. In fact, the familiar configuration was perceived as figure on 61% of trials when both regions were asymmetric and on 84% of trials when it was symmetric and the novel meaningless configuration on the opposite side of the border was asymmetric. (For more on this competition, see Peterson & Skow, 2008; Peterson & Kim, 2001; for computational models of the competition, see Keinker, Hinton, & Sejnowski, 1986; Vecera & O'Reilly, 1998, 2000).

### Figure-Ground Early or Late?

To accommodate the effects of familiarity on figure assignment, Palmer (1999) suggested that figure assignment occurs later in processing than had been proposed by the Gestalt psychologists. But this proposal seems inconsistent with the effects of exposure duration. Peterson and Gibson (1994a) exposed displays like Figure 2.5D for 14 ms, 28 ms, 57 ms, or 100 ms and followed them immediately with a mask. Effects of both familiar configuration and symmetry were evident when displays were viewed for 28 ms; effects of neither were evident in 14-ms exposures. Thus, at least via this index, figure assignment seems to occur early in processing for two region displays. Moreover, familiar configuration seems to operate as early in processing as symmetry. Other figural cues have not been tested at such short durations, either alone, in conflict, or in combination. Effects of convexity are evident in 100 ms masked exposures; shorter exposure durations were not tested. Effects of region number (i.e., context) on convexity (see section on "Classic Gestalt Image-Based Segregation Factors") are not evident in a 100-ms masked exposure; they require as long as 200 ms to emerge (Salvagio & Peterson, 2010; 2012). Thus, the processing time required for figure assignment is variable rather than fixed.

Another way to interpret the early versus late distinction is in terms of level of processing. In their interactive processing model, Vecera and O'Reilly (2000) place figure-ground perception lower than object representations in the hierarchy of visual processes. Effects of familiar configuration are therefore viewed as top-down effects on computation. Here, the Gestalt view that figure-ground perception precedes access to object memories is maintained in architectural terms, although not in temporal terms (since processing is interactive). Peterson and colleagues (Barense et al., 2012) have argued, though, that there is no single processing level at which figure assignment occurs; instead, competitions producing figure-ground perception occur at multiple levels of the visual system.

A third way to classify a process as early or late is to ask whether it can occur *preattentively*, that is, under conditions of distributed attention, before attention has been focused on a location in the input

array. Although "preattentive" implies a temporal ordering, one can also interpret "pre"-attentive as "a"-attentive, that is, as occurring without attention directed to the task at hand. Kimchi and Peterson (2008) showed that by this definition, too, figure-ground perception can occur early (see section on "Methods of Assessing Segregation: Direct Versus Indirect" for further explication).

## Grouping

Like segregation, grouping is a highly complex process, influenced by a variety of image-based factors as well as by past experience and attention. Researchers have investigated how multiple grouping cues combine, and they also have examined the time course of grouping and when grouping occurs in the functional hierarchy of visual processes.

### Image-Based Grouping Factors

#### CLASSICAL GESTALT IMAGE-BASED GROUPING FACTORS

Gestalt psychologists, most notably Max Wertheimer (1923/1938), proposed a set of grouping principles rooted in image properties. These classic factors include proximity, similarity, common fate, good continuation, and closure; they are presented in all textbooks on perception. The principle of *proximity*, perhaps the most fundamental grouping principle, states that closer elements tend to be grouped together (Fig. 2.6B). The *similarity* principle states that the most similar elements (in attributes such as color, orientation, or shape) tend to be grouped together (Fig. 2.6C-E). According to the *common fate* principle, elements tend to be grouped together if they move together (Fig. 2.6F). The principle of *good continuation* states that elements that form a smooth continuation are grouped together (Fig. 2.6G), and the principle of *closure* states that elements that form a closed figure tend to be grouped together (Fig. 2.6H).

#### NEW IMAGE-BASED GROUPING FACTORS

In recent years new grouping principles have been added. The principle of *common region* (Palmer, 1992) states that elements that are located within the same closed region of space tend to be grouped together (Fig. 2.6I). The principle of *element connectedness* (Palmer & Rock, 1994) states that elements that are connected tend to be grouped together (Fig. 2.6J). The principle of *synchrony* (Lee & Blake, 1999; Palmer & Levitin, 1998) suggests that visual events that change at the same time tend to group. Synchrony is related to the principle of

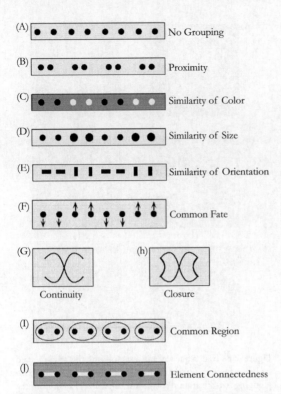

(A) ●　●　●　●　●　●　●　●　No Grouping

(B) ●●　　●●　　●●　　●●　Proximity

(C) ●　●　○　○　●　●　○　○　Similarity of Color

(D) ●　●　⬤　●　●　●　●　●　Similarity of Size

(E) ━ ━ │ │ ━ ━ │ │　Similarity of Orientation

(F) Common Fate

(G) Continuity　　(h) Closure

(I) Common Region

(J) Element Connectedness

**Figure 2.6** Classical and new image-based grouping factors. (Adapted from Palmer, Brooks, & Nelson, 2003.)

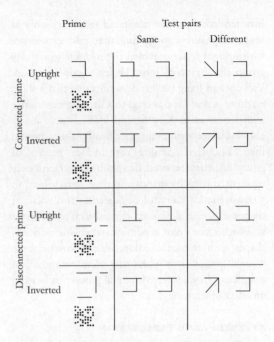

**Figure 2.7** Examples of the stimuli used by Kimchi and Hadad (2002) to show the influence of past experience on grouping. The primes and test figures were Hebrew letters. Disconnected letters were formed by introducing either small or large gaps at the interior concave discontinuities of the upright letter. The illustration depicts the letter "Bet" in the connected and the large gap conditions. The random array of dots served as a neutral prime, providing a baseline for each test pair. Connected letter prime facilitated "same" responses to the test pairs at brief exposures, regardless of orientation (upright or inverted), but when the primes were disconnected, only upright-letter primes facilitated judgments at brief exposures. (Adapted from Kimchi & Hadad, 2002.)

common fate, except that the simultaneous changes do not have to involve motion or to be "common" in any sense—for example, some elements can get brighter and others can get dimmer, as long as the change occurs at the same time (Palmer, 1999).

Palmer and Rock (1994) argued for an even more basic organization principle, the principle of *uniform connectedness* (UC), which precedes all forms of grouping (and parsing). According to this principle, a connected region of uniform visual property (such as luminance and color) is perceived initially as a single perceptual unit. Classical grouping principles operate only after uniformly connected units are designated as figures rather than background. However, the foundational status of UC has been challenged and several studies showed that other properties, such as collinearity and colsurer, were at least as important, if not more so, in intial organization (Kimchi, 1998, 2000; Peterson, 1994b).

### Subjective Factors
#### PAST EXPERIENCE

At the end of his seminal article on grouping, Wertheimer (1923/1938) listed "past experience" or "habit" as a *potential* grouping principle that, although championed by some had not been shown

to be an independent cue. However, he made it clear that he considered habit to be dominated by other principles and secondary to them in that it probably operated only after they had produced an initial organization.

Recent studies demonstrate that past experience can influence grouping (Kimchi & Hadad, 2002; Vickery & Jiang, 2009; Zemel, Behrmann, Mozer, & Bavelier, 2002). For example, Kimchi and Hadad (2002) asked subjects to judge whether two intact letters were the same or different. The target letters were preceded by a briefly presented letter prime (Fig. 2.7) and the exposure duration of the letter prime varied (40–690 ms). They found that a connected letter prime similar to the target letters sped up "same" judgments both when the prime and targets were upright and when they were inverted. However, when the prime letters were constructed of disconnected segments, only upright-letter primes facilitated judgments at brief exposures, whereas inverted-letter primes facilitated responses only at longer exposures, suggesting that past experience with upright letters enabled the subjects to quickly group the segments into the letter configuration. Vickery and Jiang (2009) demonstrated that a short learning period (as opposed to a lifelong experience with letters as in Kimchi and Hadad's study) can also influence grouping; specifically, they showed that associative learning can induce perceptual grouping. They exposed their subjects to explicitly segmented pairs of shapes and then tested them in a transfer task that required detecting two adjacent shapes of the same color. The subjects were faster at locating the color repetition when the adjacent shapes with the same color came from the same trained groups than when they were composed of two shapes from different trained groups, indicating an effect of learning.

## ATTENTION AND EXPECTATION

Subjective factors such as attention and the observer's knowledge or expectation can also influence perceptual grouping. For example, Freeman, Sagi, and Driver (2001) provided evidence that attention can affect basic grouping. They used displays that included a central target Gabor patch with low-contrast surrounded by two pairs of high-contrast Gabor flankers (Fig. 2.8) and measured contrast thresholds for detecting the central target. One flanker pair was collinear with the target, while the other was orthogonal. Flankers collinear with the target improved target detection—but only when the flankers were attended to as part of a simultaneous task (Fig. 2.8, left panel). The same flankers, when unattended (Fig. 2.8, right panel), did not interact with the target, as if they were not physically present in the display.

Beck and Palmer (2002) examined whether an observer's knowledge can influence grouping. They presented observers with a row of alternating circles and squares except for a single adjacent pair in which the same shape is repeated. The observers were asked to determine whether the repeated pair consisted of circles or squares. Observers were faster to find the target shapes when grouping factors (e.g., proximity, similarity, common region, connectedness) biased the pair to occur within a perceptual group. The probability of the within-group trials varied (25%, 50%, or 75%) and observers were informed about these probabilities prior to each condition. The grouping effect increased as the probability of the within-group trials increased. The influence of the probability was stronger for the grouping factors of

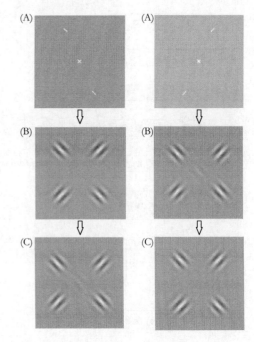

**Figure 2.8** Trial sequence and examples of the stimuli used by Freeman et al. (2001) to show the influence of attention on grouping. (*A*) Fixation display with bar markers indicating the relevant flanker pair and the direction of offset for the Vernier task. (*B* and *C*) Two successive stimulus intervals, each composed of two pairs of flanking Gabor patches, with a central target present only in one interval. One flanker pair was always collinear with the target, while the other was orthogonal. Each flanking pair had a Vernier offset. The observer made two responses, indicating first the interval in which the relevant flankers were offset in the prespecified direction, and then the interval in which the central target was present. The illustration depicts two examples. Left panel: the pre-specified Vernier offset's direction for the relevant flanker pair is in the first interval (*B*); the central target is present in the second interval (*C*); the attended flanker pair (for the Vernier task) is collinear with the target. Right panel: the prespecified Vernier offset's direction for the relevant flanker pair is in the second interval (*C*); the central target is present in the first interval (*B*); the attended flanker pair (for the Vernier task) is orthogonal to the target. The collinear flanker pair facilitated the central target detection only when attended for the Vernier task. (Adapted from Freeman, Sagi, & Driver, 2001.)

common region and connectedness than for proximity and color similarity.

## *Integrating Multiple Grouping Principles*

The grouping principles, as formulated by the Gestalt psychologists, hold only when everything else is equal, that is, when they are the only rule that applies and no other grouping factors are present. Perceptual organization, however, is clearly determined by the simultaneous operation of several grouping principles (e.g., Koffka, 1935). Recent developments of a quantitative approach to perceptual grouping address the issue of integration of multiple grouping factors, and studies have investigated the rules governing the combination of different principles (e.g., Claessens & Wagemans, 2005, 2008; Elder & Goldberg, 2002; Kimchi, 2000; Kubovy & van den Berg, 2008).

Kubovy and van den Berg (2008), using dot lattices, examined what happens when grouping by proximity and grouping by similarity in luminance are combined. Their strategy was to first measure grouping by proximity and then examine the relation between it and grouping by luminance similarity. Their results showed that the strength of the combined effect of these two grouping principles is equal to the sum of their separate effects. A reanalysis of Quinlan and Wilton's (1998) data by Kubovy and van den Berg showed that grouping by proximity and grouping by color similarity also combine additively. Additivity was also found for the combined effect of proximity and collinearity (Claessens & Wagemans, 2005, 2008).

Elder and Goldberg (2002; Elder, 2002) examined the principles of proximity, good continuation, and luminance similarity as they relate to contour grouping in natural images. They found that, statistically, in these real-world images, these grouping principles are approximately independent. They also found that these principles differ in their importance for contour grouping—the most powerful one is the principle of proximity. The question of whether the independence observed for these principles is true for other combinations of grouping principles awaits further research.

Ben Av and Sagi (1995) examined the interactions between grouping by proximity and grouping by similarity. They presented arrays with two principles in conflict followed by a mask and varied the array-mask interval. Grouping by proximity was perceived faster than grouping by similarity in luminance or in shape. Han (2004) examined the interaction between grouping by proximity and grouping by shape similarity in an event-related brain potential study and found both behavioral and ERP evidence for early dominance of proximity over shape similarity.

Other results suggest that collinearity can facilitate rapid grouping when proximity is relatively weak (Hadad & Kimchi, 2008; Kimchi, 2000). Interestingly, the ability to utilize collinearity to facilitate grouping of spatially distant lines into a global shape was observed in older children and adults, but not in 5-year olds (Hadad & Kimchi, 2006).

Recently, Shibata, Kawachi, and Gyoba (2010) examined the combined effects of grouping by proximity, closure, and orientation similarity, utilizing the phenomenon of motion-induced blindness (MIB), wherein salient visual stimuli alternately disappear from awareness and reappear when they are superimposed on a moving distractor pattern (Bonneh, Cooperman, & Sagi, 2001). Participants had to report whether the targets—a solid square embedded in an outline square—disappeared independently or simultaneously (Fig. 2.9A). The proportion of simultaneous versus independent disappearance was used as a measure of grouping. The combination of proximity and contour closure was examined by varying the relative separation between the inner and outer squares and the degree of closure of the outer square (Fig. 2.9B), and the combination of proximity and orientation similarity was examined by varying the relative separation and orientation difference between the two squares (Fig. 2.9C). The results showed that high proximity produced simultaneous disappearance, regardless of closure and orientation similarity. Closure produced simultaneous disappearance when the separation between the targets increased, and when the separation increased even further, the effect of orientation similarity was observed.

Thus, the findings to date regarding the integration of multiple grouping principles suggest that the different grouping principles are independent, their combined grouping effect is additive, and strong proximity appears to be the most powerful grouping cue.

### Is Grouping an Early or a Late Process?

Traditional theories of perception assumed that perceptual grouping operates at an early preattentive stage, in a bottom-up fashion, in order to create the units for which attention can be allocated for further, more elaborated processing (e.g., Kahneman & Henik, 1981; Marr, 1982; Neisser, 1967). This view implies that grouping occurs before other perceptual processes, in particular before perceptual constancies are achieved (Palmer, Brooks, & Nelson, 2003). Rock, Palmer, and colleagues, however, have argued that grouping does not occur early, but instead operates on a representation available only after depth perception, lightness constancy, and perceptual completion have been achieved.

For example, Rock and Brosgole (1964) presented observers with a two-dimensional array of luminous beads in a dark room either in the frontal

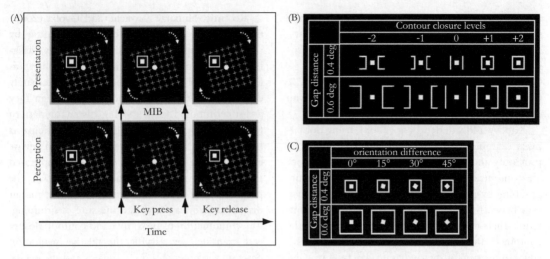

**Figure 2.9** Examples of the stimuli used by Shibata et al. (2010) to study the combined effects of grouping by proximity, closure, and orientation similarity. (*A*) Schematic representation of the MIB stimulus and the corresponding percept. The observers fixated on the center of the screen while attending to the inner and outer squares in the upper left quadrant. The background crosses rotated clockwise or counterclockwise at 180º/sec. The observers were required to press a key as soon as one of the targets (or both) disappeared and hold it down until the target(s) reappeared. The illustration depicts perceptual disappearance of both targets. (*B*) Examples of visual targets used to study the combined effect of proximity and contour closure. Proximity was manipulated by the gap distance between the inner and outer squares; for each gap distance, contour closure was manipulated by the length and direction (outward or inward) of the horizontal contour of the outer square. (*C*) Examples of the visual targets used to study the combined effect of proximity and orientation similarity. For each gap distance, the inner square was rotated. High proximity produced simultaneous disappearance, regardless of closure and orientation similarity. The closure cue produced simultaneous disappearance when the separation between the targets increased, as did the orientation similarity cue when the separation increased even further. (Adapted from Shibata, Kawachi, & Gyoba, 2010.)

plane or slanted in depth. The beads were closer together vertically than horizontally, so that when viewed in the frontal plane, they were always perceived as organized into columns. When the array was slanted in depth, however, the beads were retinally closer together in the horizontal direction, but observers who viewed it binocularly still reported seeing them grouped into columns. These results argue that grouping occurs after binocular depth perception.

Rock, Nijhawan, Palmer, and Tudor (1992) examined whether grouping by achromatic similarity operates on preconstancy retinal luminance or on postconstancy perceived lightness. They presented displays containing five columns of squares in which the central column was covered by a strip of translucent plastic (Fig. 2.10A) and asked observers to report whether the central column grouped with those to the left or right. The central squares were identical in reflectance to those on the left, but when seen behind the translucent strip their retinal luminance was identical to the squares on the right. The results showed that the central squares were grouped with the reflectance-matched squares on the left rather than with the luminance-matched ones on the right. Similar results were obtained when the central column was seen under shadow. These

results were not due to simple luminance ratio of the squares to their background, because when the central squares were seen as in front of an opaque strip of paper (Fig. 2.10B), they were grouped with the reflectance-matched ones on the right rather than the luminance ratio–matched ones on the left. Thus, these results support the hypothesis that grouping occurs on a postconstancy representation. Using a similar method, Palmer demonstrated that perceptual grouping operates after amodal completion (Palmer, Neff, & Beck, 1996) and modal completion (Palmer & Nelson, 2000) have been achieved.

Although these findings provide evidence for the view that grouping is a functionally late process that operates after constancy has been achieved, other findings showed that grouping by color similarity was based on retinal color at short exposure durations and on surface color at long exposure durations (Schulz & Sanocki, 2003), and that grouping can influence shape and lightness constancy (see Palmer et al., 2003). In light of these findings, Palmer at al. (2003) suggested that some form of grouping occurs both functionally early and functionally late in processing.

As noted earlier, the early versus late distinction can also be interpreted in temporal terms. Several

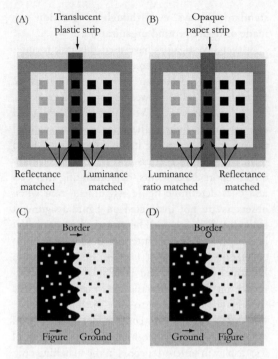

(A) Translucent plastic strip    (B) Opaque paper strip

Reflectance matched    Luminance matched    Luminance ratio matched    Reflectance matched

(C) Border →    (D) Border ○

Figure → Ground ○    Ground → Figure ○

**Figure 2.10** (*A* and *B*) The stimuli used by Rock et al. (1992) to show that grouping is influenced by lightness constancy. (*A*) When the central column of squares is seen behind a translucent strip of plastic, it groups with the reflectance-matched elements on the left rather than the luminance-matched ones on the right. (*B*) When the central column is seen as in front of an opaque strip of paper, they are grouped with the reflectance-matched ones on the right rather than the luminance ratio–matched ones on the left. (Reproduced from Palmer, Brooks, & Nelson, 2003.) (*C* and *D*) Stimulus displays used by Palmer and Brooks (2008) to show that grouping affects figure-ground perception. The stimuli are composed of two adjacent regions, one moving (indicated by the arrow at the bottom) and one stationary (indicated by a circle at the bottom). (*C*) When the border moves (indicated by the arrow at the top) in the same direction as the moving region—the border groups with the moving region by common fate—the moving region is seen as figural. (*D*) When the border does not move (indicated by the circle at the top)—the border groups with the stationary region—the stationary region is seen as figural. (Adapted from Palmer & Brooks, 2008.)

investigators examined the time course of grouping (e.g., Ben Av & Sagi, 1995; Han, Ding, & Song, 2002; Kimchi, 1998, 2000; Kurylo, 1997; Razpurker-Apfeld & Kimchi, 2007). For example, Razpurker-Apfeld and Kimchi (2007) found that grouping into columns or rows by common lightness was evident with a 40-ms exposure duration, whereas grouping by common lightness into a shape (e.g., square or a cross) was evident only at a much longer exposure. Furthermore, the time required for grouping depends on the grouping cue. Using relatively complex displays, Kuyrlo (1997) found that grouping by proximity required a mean of 87.6

ms for processing to be completed, whereas grouping by alignment required a mean of 118.8 ms. Ben Av and Sagi (1995; see section on "Integrating Multiple Grouping Principles") found that grouping by proximity was evident when the stimulus was available for just 60 ms, whereas grouping by similarity (in luminance or shape) was evident only when the stimulus was available for 160 ms. When cues are combined (e.g., proximity and collinearity) in relatively simple stimuli, grouping appears to emerge at shorter exposures (e.g., Hadad & Kimchi, 2008; Kimchi, 2000; see section on "Integrating Multiple Grouping Principles"). Thus, grouping is time dependent, and some forms of grouping are accomplished earlier than others.

## The Relationship Between Grouping and Segregation

Recall that segregation entails determining whether borders are bounding edges of objects, and if so where the object lies with respect to the border. Palmer and Brooks (2008) showed that grouping affects segregation via an "edge-region grouping" principle: When the border groups with one of its attached regions based on the classical grouping principle of similarity (in motion, blur, color, orientation, position, or synchronous flicker), the grouped side appears figural. For example, if the border between two regions moves together with the texture on one side and the texture on the other side is stationary (Fig. 2.10C), the border groups with the moving region by common fate, and the grouped region is perceived as figural; if the border is stationary (Fig. 2.10D), it groups with the stationary region, and the stationary region appears figural.

These results provide further evidence supporting the hypothesis that perceptual grouping occurs at different levels of visual processing (Palmer et al., 2003; see section "Is Grouping an Early or a Late Process?").

## Methods

We turn now to the methods that have been used to investigate segregation and grouping. The use of new methods has contributed to a rapid growth of knowledge regarding perceptual organization in recent years.

### Methods of Assessing Segregation: Direct Versus Indirect

Much of the evidence regarding segregation factors was gained from experiments in which perceivers reported directly about the regions they perceived as shaped entities at critical borders. Indirect methods of assessing segregation have been employed as well. In this section, we discuss a number of indirect indices that have been developed, and the relative merits of direct and indirect methods.

Driver and Baylis (1996) introduced a visual short-term memory (VSTM) task as an indirect measure of segregation. Their participants viewed "study" displays in which a stepped edge divided a large rectangle into two regions, one smaller than the other (its width was 33% of that of the larger region), and higher in contrast against the overall screen backdrop (a depth cue identified by O'Shea, Blackburn, & Ono, 1994). Driver and Baylis asked their subjects to remember the shape of the stepped border in the standard display because their task was to decide which of two test shapes shown after a short delay had the same stepped border. (A sample trial is shown in Fig. 2.11.) Driver and Baylis observed that test trial performance was faster and more accurate when the border was repeated as a boundary of a figure on the same side as the small high-contrast region in the study display (see Fig. 2.11B) rather than the opposite (ground) side (see Fig. 2.11C). Because (a) responses are expected to be faster if test shapes are similar to previously seen shapes, and (b) the shape of the figure is perceived but not that of the ground, Driver and Baylis concluded that figure assignment based on small area and high contrast had occurred automatically in the

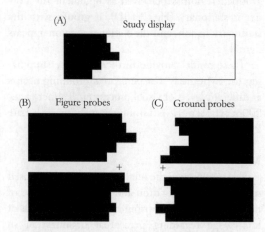

(A) Study display

(B) Figure probes    (C) Ground probes

**Figure 2.11** Sample trial in Driver and Baylis (1996). (*A*) Study display. (*B*) Figure probes with the boundary from the study display repeated as a boundary for a shape on the same side. (*C*) Ground probes with the boundary from the study display repeated as a boundary for a shape on the opposite side. (Originally published in Peterson and Enns, 2005, *Perception & Psychophysics*, Figure 2.)

standard displays, even though no mention was made of figure-ground organization.

Other investigators have used this task to infer which regions were perceived as figures in displays where top-bottom polarity (Hulleman & Humphreys, 2004), lower region (Vecera et al., 2002), and attention (Vecera et al., 2004) cued one region as figure. These investigators verified the inferences regarding figure assignment derived from the indirect measures in complementary direct-report experiments, demonstrating that certain cues determine figure assignment even when observers are not instructed on figure assignment beforehand. It should be noted, however, that inasmuch as volitional attentional allocation influences figure assignment (see section on "Fixation Location, Attention, and Perceptual Set"), performance on the VSTM task can be affected by the strategy observers adopt to solve the matching task. For instance, observers could adopt a strategy of attending to the smaller, higher contrast region of the display in order to succeed in the matching task. Consequently, the VSTM task might not index the operation of shape properties alone.

Hulleman and Humphreys (2004) introduced another indirect measure of segregation that cleverly combines a visual search task with a segregation task. Their subjects viewed single displays composed of multiple alternating black and white wide and narrow base regions like those in Figure 2.12A. They were instructed to search for a symmetric region that was present in only half the displays; no mention was made of figure-ground perception. Subjects detected symmetric targets faster and more accurately when they had a wide base and a narrow top rather than a narrow base and a wide top, as expected on the basis of the top/bottom polarity cue. The assumption underlying this measure is that observers will search for the target among the figures first before they search among the regions initially perceived as grounds.

Most recently, Kim and Feldman (2009) introduced a method that opens up exciting possibilities because it can be used to probe figure assignment along segments of a continuous border. They added a local perturbation to an otherwise smooth contour and set that perturbation in motion such that it would be perceived as a rigid part deforming at a concavity from one side and as a nonrigid part deforming at a convexity from the other side. Rather than asking subjects to report which side appeared to be figure, Kim and Feldman asked them to report which side of the boundary appeared to be moving.

Based on direct reports of participants in a previous study conducted by Barenholz and Feldman (2006), Kim and Feldman assumed that the side that appeared to move was perceived as the figure.

Kim and Feldman used this dynamic indirect measure to investigate whether the figure was perceived on the same side along a continuous border, and they found that figure assignment can reverse along a continuous border, replicating previous research (Peterson, 2003b; see Figs. 2.12B and 2.12C) and demonstrations (Hochberg, 1971; see Fig. 2.12D) that had used direct reports. Kim and Feldman's dynamic indirect probe measure is valuable both because it does not require instruction regarding figure-ground perception and because it is a useful probe of local figure-ground perception.

Indirect reports and direct reports are both useful indices of figure assignment. Direct reports can provide evidence regarding the probability that the shape property under investigation determines figural status; this is an important piece of information that most indirect measures cannot provide. Among

the indirect measures, only Kim and Feldman's (2008) dynamic indirect probe can assess the probability of a cue's effectiveness. On the other hand, inasmuch as perception is a private experience and subjects report what they perceive, those reports cannot be scored as correct or incorrect. Indirect reports can be scored as correct or incorrect, and response times for correct responses can provide a quantitative measure.

Indirect tasks can also be used to investigate the conditions under which figure-ground perception occurs. For instance, Kimchi and Peterson (2008) tested whether the presence of a change in the figure-ground organization of a task-irrelevant backdrop display affected participants' performance on a change detection task adapted from Russell and Driver (2005); see Figure 2.13. They observed congruency effects such that "same" judgments were faster and more accurate when the backdrop's figure-ground organization remained the same across successive exposures, whereas "different" judgments were faster and more accurate when figure-ground organization changed when the matrices differed. These effects were obtained even though, when probed with surprise questions, participants could report neither the figure-ground status of the region on which the matrix appeared nor any change in that status. Thus, the results clearly demonstrate that figure-ground segregation *can* occur without focal attention ("preattentively," in functional terms).

In addition to direct and indirect indices, implicit measures can be used to probe shape properties that are not reportable because they are properties of the regions ultimately perceived as grounds rather than as figures. Peterson and colleagues (Peterson & Enns, 2005; Peterson & Lampignano, 2003; Peterson & Skow, 2008) have shown via implicit measures that familiar configurations are accessed even when they do not win the competition for figural status. These results are consistent with the hypothesis mentioned earlier—that objects that might be perceived on opposite sides of a border are accessed in a fast pass of processing prior to figure assignment, they compete, and the loser is inhibited, accounting in part for the fact that grounds are shapeless near the borders they share with figures.

### Methods of Assessing Grouping: Direct and Indirect

The Gestalt psychologists used phenomenological demonstrations to investigate perceptual grouping, generating qualitative observations. Current

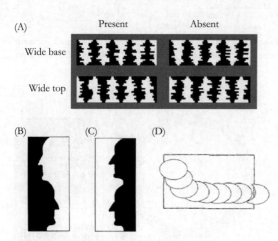

**Figure 2.12** (*A*) Sample displays used in a visual search task by Hulleman and Humphreys (2004). A symmetric region was either present or absent. When present, the symmetric region could have either a wide base or a wide top. (*B* and *C*) Sample displays discussed by Peterson (2003b). (*B*) A profile of a face is suggested in white on the top of the display and in black on the bottom of the display. Observers perceived the figure on the right in the top portion of this display and on the left in the bottom portion of this display, indicating that the figural cue of familiarity/meaningfulness can operate locally. Such "cross-over" interpretations were less likely in a display like (*C*), where a face profile is suggested in black in both the top and bottom portions of the display. (*D*) A display used by Hochberg (1971) to show that figure and ground assignments are local. Observers perceive multiple oval disks occluding one another. For all but the leftmost and rightmost regions, each region is perceived as figure along one portion of its boundary and as ground along another portion.

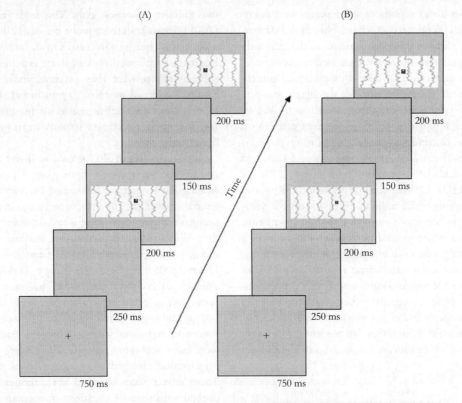

**Figure 2.13** Sequence of events in two trial types in Kimchi and Peterson (2008). (*A*) Same target (matrix is unchanged), different backdrop (target is on figure in first frame and on ground in second frame). (*B*) Different target (matrix changes), same backdrop (target is on figure in both frames).

work has used more rigorous, quantitative methods with more complex stimuli, allowing the measurement of the strength of a single grouping factor or the combined effect of multiple factors.

### DIRECT METHODS

Two popular methods that evaluate grouping directly are the multistable lattice paradigm and the contour detection paradigm. The multistable lattice paradigm uses stimuli in which two or more candidate organizations are simultaneously available and measures the probability with which observers report perceiving each possible organization (e.g., Ben Av & Sagi, 1995; Kubovy & Wagemans, 1995). A prime example of the use of the multistable lattice paradigm is the extensive and elegant work by Kubovy and his colleagues on quantifying the grouping principle of proximity (Kubovy, Holcombe, & Wagemans, 1998; Kubovy & van den Berg, 2008; Kubovy & Wagemans, 1995). They briefly presented multistable dot lattices in which the distances between dots were parametrically varied (see Fig. 2.14A and 2.14B) and asked observers to indicate which organization they perceived.

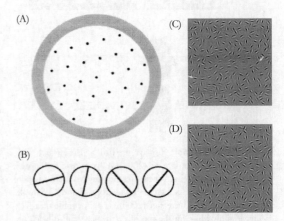

**Figure 2.14** (*A* and *B*) Examples of the stimuli used by Kubovy and Wagemans (1995) to measure proximity. (*A*) An example of stimulus display—a multistable dot lattice that can be grouped into stripes of different orientations. (*B*) A response screen—observers indicate the orientation of the dot lattice they saw by choosing the corresponding response alternative. (Adapted from Kubovy & Wagemans, 1995.) (*C* and *D*) Examples of the stimuli used in the contour detection paradigm (Field et al., 1993). (*C*) A contour (marked by white arrows) is embedded in similar background Gabor elements randomly oriented. (*D*) An otherwise similar display to the one in (*A*), except that all elements are randomly oriented. (Reproduced from Hess & Field, 1999.)

Their data were fit well by an exponential model: Grouping follows a decaying exponential function of the relative distance between dots. Other studies, however, suggested that the proximity cue follows a power law (e.g., Claessens & Wagemans, 2008; Elder & Goldberg, 2002). Further research is required to reconcile these differences. (For some of the rich results obtained with other uses of the multistable lattice paradigm, see Ben Av & Sagi, 1995; Claessens & Wagemans, 2005, 2008; Gepshtein & Kubovy, 2000, 2005; Kubovy & van den Berg, 2008; Palmer et al., 2003; Rock & Brosgole, 1964).

The contour detection paradigm is used mainly to study contour integration: Observers are required to detect a single contour in a background noise and the accuracy with which such detections are made is measured (e.g., Field, Hayes, & Hess, 1993; Kovacs & Julesz, 1993). In a typical experiment, observers are presented with arrays of randomly oriented Gabor elements in which a subset of the elements are locally coaligned—forming a virtual contour (see Fig. 2.14C), and an otherwise identical array where all of the elements are randomly oriented (Fig. 2.14D). Observers are asked in a two-alternative forced-choice procedure to indicate which of the stimuli contains the contour. To distinguish the contour from the background, the contour elements must be grouped, and the results show that contour detection is best for straight contours and becomes worse as the curvature of the contour increases (e.g., Field et al., 1993; Geisler, Perry, Super, & Gallogly, 2001; Hess & Dakin, 1997), and it is best when the orientations of the individual elements are aligned

with the contour (Field et al., 1993). Experiments also show that smooth contours are more detectable then jagged ones (e.g., Pettet, 1999), and contour integration can occur even when elements alternate between the two eyes (e.g., Kovacs, Papathomas, Yang, & Feher, 1996), and when the polarity of contour elements alternates (Field, Hayes, & Hess, 2000; see Hess & Field, 1999; Hess, Hayes, & Field, 2003, for reviews).

## INDIRECT METHODS

Several methods assess grouping indirectly. Some of these methods are adaptations of well-established psychophysical paradigms, such as visual search and primed matching. Elder and Zucker (1993, 1994, 1998) used visual search to measure perceptual *closure* and its utility in shape processing. Participants searched for a concave target among a variable number of convex distractors (Figs. 2.15A and 2.15B). The basic stimuli were composed of unconnected line segments, which were the same for the concave and convex stimuli, but bending inward for the concave stimuli and outward for the convex ones. Therefore, the discrimination between target and distractors required grouping of the contour segments into coherent shapes. Search efficiency, indicated by the slope of the best-fitting linear function relating response time to display size, was high (i.e., shallow slope) for closed stimuli (Fig. 2.15B), whereas search for the open stimuli (Fig. 2.15A) was inefficient (i.e., steep slope). When degree of closure of both target and distractors was manipulated (Fig. 2.15C), search speed decreased with

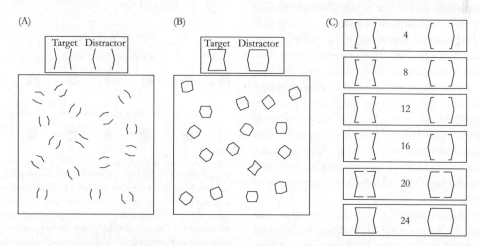

**Figure 2.15** Examples of the stimuli used by Elder and Zucker (1993) to measure perceptual closure. (*A* and *B*) Examples of search displays for the open (*A*) and the closed (*B*) outline shapes. The target and distractor for each example are indicated. The examples illustrate display size of 16. (*C*) Stimuli with different degrees of closure, created from the original open stimuli by adding pixels (the number of which is indicated in the middle) to form inward corners. (Adapted from Elder & Zucker, 1993.)

increased degree of closure. Based on their results, Elder and Zucker (1994) proposed the notion of a closure continuum (see also, Gillam, 1975; Peterson & Lampignano, 2003) and developed a measure of closure based on a sum of squares of contour gaps; this measure emphasizes large gaps relative to small ones (for a total gap size). However, Kimchi (2000; Hadad & Kimchi, 2006, 2008) demonstrated that grouping by closure also depends on the distribution of the gaps along the contours. Apparently, large gaps hinder rapid grouping when gaps occur at point of change in contour direction but not when gaps occur at straight, collinear contour segments.

Kimchi and colleagues (e.g., Hadad & Kimchi, 2008; Kimchi, 1998, 2000; Razpurker-Apfeld & Kimchi, 2007) adapted the primed-matching paradigm (Beller, 1971) to examine the microgenesis of grouping. In this paradigm observers are presented with a prime followed immediately by a pair of test figures to be matched for identity. Responses to "same" test pairs are faster when the figures in the pairs are similar to the prime than when they are dissimilar to it. Varying the exposure duration of the prime allows the researcher to probe changes in the representation over time—in this case, tracing the time course of grouping. For example, Kimchi (1998) examined the time course of grouping multiple elements that varied in number and relative size. The primes were elements (e.g., circles) grouped into a global configuration (e.g., global diamonds). The "same"-response test pairs were either similar to the elements of the prime (and dissimilar to the global configuration) or similar to the prime's global configuration (and dissimilar to the elements) (Fig. 2.16). The results showed priming of the global configuration of many-element stimuli at brief exposures, but priming of the local elements only at longer exposures. The converse pattern was observed for the few-element stimuli; here the relatively large elements were primed at brief exposures and the global configuration was primed at longer exposures. These results suggest rapid grouping of many small elements into configuration with elements individuation occurring later in time, whereas few, relatively large elements are individuated rapidly and their grouping into a configuration is time consuming.

The primed-matching paradigm was also used to study the time course of grouping by lightness similarity (Razpurker-Apfeld & Kimchi, 2007). Their primes were dot matrices grouped by lightness similarity into columns/rows or into a shape (square/cross or triangle/arrow). The results showed

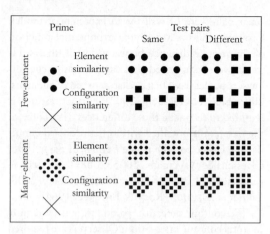

**Figure 2.16** Examples of the priming stimuli and the "same"-response and "different"-response test pairs for the few-element and many-element stimuli used by Kimchi (1998) to study the time course of grouping multiple elements into a global configuration. The "same"-response test pairs were similar to the prime either in elements (element-similarity test pair) or in configuration (configuration-similarity test pair). The X served as a neutral prime, providing a baseline for each of the test-pair type. The prime was presented for various durations (40–690 ms). The global configuration of the many-element patterns was primed at brief exposures, whereas the local elements were primed at longer exposures. In contrast, the few, relatively large elements were primed at brief exposures, whereas the global configuration was primed at longer exposures. (Adapted from Kimchi, 1998.)

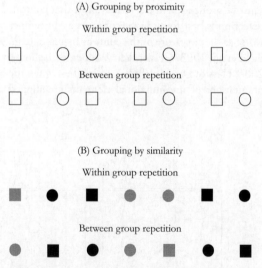

**Figure 2.17** An example of the repetition discrimination task (RTD) devised by Palmer and Beck (2007). Squares and circles alternated in a row except for a single adjacent pair of repeated shapes. Because of grouping, the adjacent repeated shapes could occur within a perceptual group or across perceptual groups (between groups). The example depicts proximity grouping (A) and color similarity grouping (B). The task was to find the repetition of shape and identify it as circles or squares. Repetition discrimination was faster when the adjacent repeated shapes were located within groups than between groups. (Adapted from Palmer & Beck, 2007.)

priming of the columns/rows under short prime durations, whereas priming of the square/cross (or triangle/arrow) was observed only under longer prime durations, indicating that grouping by lightness similarity into columns/rows was accomplished faster than grouping by lightness similarity into a shape. These results suggest that even when guided by the same principle, groupings can vary in their time course. This paradigm was also used to study the interaction between grouping by proximity, collinearity, and closure (Kimchi, 2000; Hadad & Kimchi, 2008; see section on "Integrating Multiple Grouping Principles"), and the influence of past experience on grouping (Kimchi & Hadad, 2002; see section on "Past Experience").

Another method to assess grouping indirectly is the repetition discrimination task (RDT), introduced by Palmer and Beck (2007). Participants have to identify repeated items in an otherwise alternating row of items. The items are grouped pair-wise by a certain grouping factor. The repeated items can occur within a group or between groups (see Fig. 2.17). The difference in response time between the within-group and the between-group trials is taken as a measure of the grouping effect of the

manipulated factor. Palmer and Beck found that, for grouping by proximity, color similarity, common region, and element connectedness, response times were faster in the within-group conditions (also see Beck & Palmer, 2002; Vickery & Jiang, 2009).

Several investigators used indirect tasks to examine whether grouping can be accomplished without focal attention (e.g., Kimchi & Razpurker-Apfeld, 2004; Moore & Egeth, 1997; Russell & Driver, 2005). For example, Kimchi and Razpurker-Apfeld (2004) used Russell and Driver's (2005) indirect task (see section on "Figure-Ground Early or Late?") to investigate grouping under inattention. On each trial, two successive displays were briefly presented, each comprising a central target matrix surrounded by elements (Fig. 2.18). The task was to judge whether the targets were the same or different. The organization of the background elements stayed the same or changed, independently of the targets. In two critical conditions, the background elements were organized by color similarity into columns and rows (Fig. 2.18A), and into square and cross (Fig. 2.18B). Changes in the background grouping of columns/rows produced congruency effects on the matrix-change judgments, even though participants

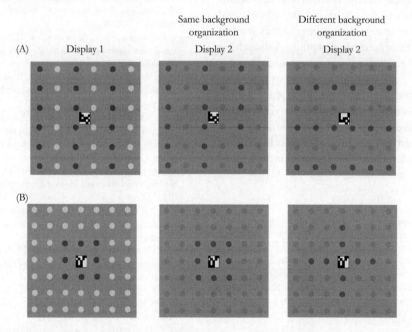

**Figure 2.18** Examples of the stimulus displays used by Kimchi and Razpurker-Apfeld (2004) to examine whether grouping can be accomplished without focal attention. Two successive displays were presented on each trial. The central target matrix in Displays 1 and 2 was either the same or different. The surrounding colored elements were grouped into (*A*) columns/rows by color similarity and (*B*) a square/cross by color similarity. The background organization either stayed the same across Displays 1 and 2 or changed, independently of whether the target matrix changed or remained the same. The colors of the background elements always changed between Displays 1 and 2. All colors were equiluminant in the experiment. Changes in the background grouping produced congruency effects on the matrix-change judgments for the grouping of columns/rows by color similarity (*A*), but not for the grouping of square/cross by color similarity (*B*). (Adapted from Kimchi & Razpurker-Apfeld, 2004.) (*See* color insert.)

reported no or little awareness of the background grouping. No effect of the background was observed for grouping of shape, however. Apparently, some forms of grouping can take place without focal attention (see also Moore & Egeth, 1997; Russell & Driver, 2005; Shomstein, Kimchi, Hammer, & Behrmann, 2010), whereas other groupings cannot, suggesting a continuum of attentional demands as a function of the processes involved in the grouping (for a review, see Kimchi, 2009).

## Conclusion

This chapter had reviewed behavioral evidence indicating that multiple factors act and interact to produce perceptual organization. It is clear that perceptual organization is influenced by multiple image-based factors: the classic factors introduced by the Gestalt psychologists and more recently identified factors, past experience, and various forms of attention and perceptual set. Although perceptual organization is a fundamental process, the research reviewed in this chapter has shown that the traditional view of perceptual organization as an early process that serves to provide the substrate on which high-level perceptual processes operate is highly simplified. Recent research and new methods have begun to shed light on how objective and subjective, low-level and high-level factors interact to produce the objects of perception. Although we have covered research on segregation and grouping separately, we consider them part of an integrated system of processes that accomplish the daunting task of imposing organization on the visual input. The recent research opens up the exciting prospect of elucidating this foundational process by unraveling the complex interactions among organizational cues in time and in space.

## Notes

1. Pilot studies showed that no shape is completely meaningless; that is some observers usually state that any shape resembles something familiar. Accordingly, we defined regions as meaningless/unfamiliar in shape if < 25% of pilot subjects agreed on a single interpretation for that region. We defined regions as meaningful/familiar in shape if > 75% of pilot observers agreed on a single interpretation for that region.

## References

Barenholtz, E., & Feldman, J. (2006). Determination of visual figure and ground in dynamically deforming shapes. *Cognition, 101*, 530–544.

Barense, M. G., Ngo, J., Hung, L., & Peterson, M. A. (2012). Interactions of memory and perception in amnesia: The figure-ground perspective. *Cerebral Cortex, 22*(11), 2680–2691.

Baylis, G. C., & Driver, J. (1995). One-sided edge assignment in vision: 1. Figure-ground segmentation and attention to objects. *Current Directions in Psychological Science, 4*, 140–146.

Beck, D. M., & Palmer, S. E. (2002). Top-down influences on perceptual grouping. *Journal of Experimental Psychology: Human Perception and Performance, 28*(5), 1071–1084.

Behrmann, M., & Kimchi, R. (2003). What does visual agnosia tell us about perceptual organization and its relationship to object perception? *Journal of Experimental Psychology: Human Perception and Performance, 29*(1), 19–42.

Behrmann, M., & Tipper, S. P. (1994). Object-based visual attention: Evidence from unilateral visual neglect. In C. Umilta & M. Moscovich (Eds.), *Attention and performance XIV: Conscious and non-conscious processing and cognitive functions* (pp. 351–375). Cambridge, MA: MIT Press.

Beller, H. K. (1971). Priming: Effects of advance information on matching. *Journal of Experimental Psychology, 87*, 176–182.

Ben Av, M. B., & Sagi, D. (1995). Perceptual grouping by similarity and proximity: Experimental results can be predicted by intensity autocorrelations. *Vision Research, 35*(6), 853–866.

Bertamini, M., Martinovic, J., & Wuerger, S. M. (2008). Integration of ordinal and metric cues in depth processing. *Journal of Vision, 8*, 1–12.

Bonneh, Y. S., Cooperman, A., & Sagi, D. (2001). Motion-induced blindness in normal observers. *Nature, 411*(6839), 798–801.

Burge, J., Fowlkes, C. C., & Banks, M. S. (2010). Natural scene statistics predict how the figure-ground cue of convexity affects human depth perception. *Journal of Neuroscience, 30*(21), 7269–7280.

Burge, J., Peterson, M. A., & Palmer, S. E. (2005). Ordinal configural cues combine with metric disparity in depth perception. *Journal of Vision, 5*(6), 534–542.

Claessens, P. M., & Wagemans, J. (2005). Perceptual grouping in Gabor lattices: Proximity and alignment. *Perception & Psychophysics, 67*(8), 1446–1459.

Claessens, P. M., & Wagemans, J. (2008). A Bayesian framework for cue integration in multistable grouping: Proximity, collinearity, and orientation priors in zigzag lattices. *Journal of Vision, 8*(7), 1–23.

Desimone, R., & Duncan, J. (1995). Neural mechanisms of selective visual attention. *Annual Review of Neuroscience, 18*, 193–222.

Driver, J., & Baylis, G.C. (1996). Figure-ground segmentation and edge assignment in short-term visual matching. *Cognitive Psychology, 31*, 248–306.

Driver, J., Baylis, G. C., & Rafal, R. D. (1992). Preserved figure-ground segregation and symmetry perception in visual neglect. *Nature, 360*, 73–75.

Ehrenstein, W. (1930). Untersuchungen u¨ber Figur-Grund Fragen [Investigations of more figure–ground questions]. *Zeitschrift fu¨r Psychologie, 117*, 339–412.

Elder, J. H. (2002). *Ecological statistics of contour grouping Proceedings of the 2nd International Workshop on Biologically Motivated Computer Vision*, Tubingen, Germany, in Lecture Notes in Computer Science, vol. 2525, H. H. Bulthoff et al., eds, Springer-Verlag, Berlin, 230–238.

Elder, J. H., & Goldberg, R. M. (2002). Ecological statistics of Gestalt laws for the perceptual organization of contours. *Journal of Vision, 2*(4), 324–353.

Elder, J. H., & Zucker, S. W. (1993). The effect of contour closure on the rapid discrimination of two-dimensional shapes. *Vision Research, 33*, 981–991.

Elder, J. H., & Zucker, S. W. (1994). A measure of closure. *Vision Research, 34*, 3361–3369.

Elder, J. H., & Zucker, S. W. (1998). Evidence for boundary-specific grouping. *Vision Research, 38*(1), 143–152.

Field, D. J., Hayes, A., & Hess, R. F. (1993). Contour integration by the human visual system: Evidence for a local "association field." *Vision Research, 33*(2), 173–193.

Field, D. J., Hayes, A., & Hess, R. F. (2000). The roles of polarity and symmetry in the perceptual grouping of contour fragments. *Spatial Vision, 13*(1), 51–66.

Fodor, J. (1984). *The Modularity of Mind.* Cambridge, MA: The MIT Press.

Freeman, E., Sagi, D., & Driver, J. (2001). Lateral interactions between targets and flankers in low-level vision depend on attention to the flankers. *Nature Neuroscience, 4,* 1032–1036.

Freeman, E., Sagi, D., & Driver, J. (2004). Configuration-specific attentional modulation of flanker-target lateral interactions. *Perception, 33*(2), 181–194.

Gainotti, G., Messerle, P., & Tissot, R. (1972). Quantitative analysis of unilateral spatial neglect in relation to laterally of cerebral lesions. *Journal of Neurology, Neurosurgery, and Psychiatry, 38,* 545–550.

Geisler, W. S., Perry, J. S., Super, B. J., & Gallogly, D. P. (2001). Edge co-occurrence in natural images predicts contour grouping performance. *Vision Research, 41*(6), 711–724.

Gepshtein, S., & Kubovy, M. (2000). The emergence of visual objects in space-time. *Proceedings of the National Academy of Sciences USA, 97*(14), 8186–8191.

Gepshtein, S., & Kubovy, M. (2005). Stability and change in perception: Spatial organization in temporal context. *Experimental Brain Research, 160*(4), 487–495.

Gibson, B. S., & Peterson, M. A. (1994). Does orientation-independent object recognition precede orientation-dependent recognition? Evidence from a cueing paradigm. *Journal of Experimental Psychology: Human Perception and Performance, 20,* 299–316.

Gillam, B. (1975). New Evidence for Closure in Perception. *Perception & Psychophysics,* 17(5), 521–524.

Hadad, B. S., & Kimchi, R. (2006). Developmental trends in utilizing perceptual closure for grouping of shape: Effects of spatial proximity and collinearity. *Perception & Psychophysics, 68*(8), 1264–1273.

Hadad, B. S., & Kimchi, R. (2008). Time course of grouping of shape by perceptual closure: Effects of spatial proximity and collinearity. *Perception & Psychophysics, 70*(5), 818–827.

Han, S. (2004). Interactions between proximity and similarity grouping: An event-related brain potential study in humans. *Neuroscience Letters, 367*(1), 40–43.

Han, S., Ding, Y., & Song, Y. (2002). Neural mechanisms of perceptual grouping in humans as revealed by high density event related potentials. *Neuroscience Letters, 319*(1), 29–32.

Han, S., Humphreys, G. W., & Chen, L. (1999). Uniform connectedness and classical Gestalt principles of perceptual grouping. *Perception & Psychophysics, 61*(4), 661–674.

Hess, R. F., & Dakin, S. C. (1997). Absence of contour linking in peripheral vision. *Nature, 390*(6660), 602–604.

Hess, R. F., & Field, D. J. (1999). Integration of contours: New insights. *Trends in Cognitive Sciences, 3*(12), 480–486.

Hess, R. F., Hayes, A., & Field, D. J. (2003). Contour integration and cortical processing. *Journal of Physiology (Paris), 97*(2–3), 105–119.

Hochberg, J. (1971). *Perception (2nd ed.).* Englewood Cliffs, NJ: Prentice Hall.

Hoffman, D. D., & Singh, M. (1997). Salience of visual parts. *Cognition, 63,* 29–78.

Hulleman, J., & Humphreys, G. W. (2004). A new cue to figure–ground coding: Top–bottom polarity. *Vision Research, 44*(24), 2779–2791.

Jehee, J. F. M., Lamme, V. A. F., & Roelfsema, P. R. (2007). Boundary assignment in a recurrent network architecture. *Vision Research, 47,* 1153–1165.

Julesz, B. (1971). *Cyclopean vision.* Chicago: University of Chicago Press.

Kahneman, D., & Henik, A. (1981). Perceptual organization and attention. In M. Kubovy & J. R. Pomerantz (Eds.), *Perceptual organization* (pp. 181–211). Hillsdale, NJ: Erlbaum.

Kanizsa, G., & Gerbino, W. (1976). Convexity and symmetry in figure-ground organization. In M. Henle (Ed.), *Vision and artifact* (pp. 25–32). New York: Springer.

Kim, S-H., & Feldman, J. (2009). Globally inconsistent figure/ground relations induced by a negative part. *Journal of Vision, 9*(10), 1–13.

Kimchi, R. (1998). Uniform connectedness and grouping in the perceptual organization of hierarchical patterns. *Journal of Experimental Psychology: Human Perception and Performance, 24*(4), 1105–1118.

Kimchi, R. (2000). The perceptual organization of visual objects: A microgenetic analysis. *Vision Research, 40*(10–12), 1333–1347.

Kimchi, R. (2003). Visual perceptual organization: A microgenetic analysis. In R. Kimchi, M. Behrmann, & C. R. Olson (Eds.), *Perceptual organization in vision: Behavioral and neural perspectives* (pp. 117–154). Mahwah, NJ: Erlbaum.

Kimchi, R. (2009). Perceptual organization and visual attention. *Progress in Brain Research, 176,* 15–33.

Kimchi, R., & Hadad, B. S. (2002). Influence of past experience on perceptual grouping. *Psychological Science, 13*(1), 41–47.

Kimchi, R., & Peterson, M. A. (2008). Figure-ground segmentation can occur without attention. *Psychological Science, 19*(7), 660–668.

Kimchi, R., & Razpurker-Apfeld, I. (2004). Perceptual grouping and attention: Not all groupings are equal. *Psychonomic Bulletin & Review, 11*(4), 687–696.

Klymenko, V., & Weisstein, N. (1986). Spatial frequency difference can determine figure-ground organization. *Journal of Experimental Psychology: Human Perception and Performance, 12,* 324–330.

Koffka, K. (1935). *Principles of Gestalt psychology.* New York: Harcourt, Brace.

Kogo, N., Strecha, C., Van Gool, L., & Wagemans, J. (2010). Surface construction by a 2-D differentiation-integration process: a neurocomputational model for perceived border ownership, depth, and lightness in Kanizsa figures. *Psychological Review, 117*(2), 406–439.

Kovacs, I., & Julesz, B. (1993). A closed curve is much more than an incomplete one: Effect of closure in figure-ground segmentation. *Proceedings of the National Academy of Sciences USA, 92,* 7495–7497.

Kovacs, I., Papathomas, T. V., Yang, M., & Feher, A. (1996). When the brain changes its mind: Interocular grouping during binocular rivalry. *Proceedings of the National Academy of Sciences USA, 93*(26), 15508–15511.

Kubovy, M., Holcombe, A. O., & Wagemans, J. (1998). On the lawfulness of grouping by proximity. *Cognitive Psychology, 35*(1), 71–98.

Kubovy, M., & van den Berg, M. (2008). The whole is equal to the sum of its parts: A probabilistic model of grouping by proximity and similarity in regular patterns. *Psychological Review, 115*(1), 131–154.

Kubovy, M., & Wagemans, J. (1995). Grouping by proximity and multistability in dot lattices: A quantitative gestalt theory. *Psychological Science, 6*(4), 225–234.

Kurylo, D. D. (1997). Time course of perceptual grouping. *Perception & Psychophysics, 59*(1), 142–147.

Lee, S. H., & Blake, R. (1999). Visual form created solely from temporal structure. *Science, 284*(5417), 1165–1168.

Machilsen, B., Pauwels, M., & Wagemans, J. (2009). The role of vertical mirror symmetry in visual shape detection. *Journal of Vision, 9*(12), 1–11.

Marr, D. (1982). *Vision.* San Francisco: W. H. Freeman.

Marshall, J. C. & Halligan, P. W. (1994). The ying and yang of visuospatial neglect: A case study. *Neuropsychologia, 32,* 1037–1057.

Mattingly, J. B., Price, M. C., & Driver, J. (1996). *Figure-ground segmentation and visual neglect. Cognitive Neuroscience Society 1996 annual meeting abstract program.* Cambridge, MA: MIT Press.

Metzger, W. (1953). *Gesetze des Sehens [Laws of seeing].* Frankfurt, Germany: Waldemar Kramer.

Mojica, A. J., & Peterson, M. A. (2012). *Symmetry context effects? Comparable to convexity context effects when accidental views are eliminated.* Manuscript under review.

Moore, C., & Egeth, H. (1997). Perception without attention: Evidence of grouping under conditions of inattention. *Journal of Experimental Psychology: Human Perception and Performance, 23*(2), 339–352.

Navon, D. (2011). The effect of recognizability on figure-ground processing: Does it affect parsing or only figure selection? *Quarterly Journal of Experimental Psychology, 64*(3), 608–624,

Neisser, U. (1967). *Cognitive psychology.* New York: Appleton Century Crofts.

O'Shea, R. P., Blackburn, S. G., & Ono, H. (1994). Contrast as a depth cue. *Vision Research, 34,* 1595–1604.

Palmer, S. E. (1992). Common region: A new principle of perceptual grouping. *Cognitive Psychology, 24,* 436–447.

Palmer, S. E. (1999). *Vision science: From photons to phenomenology.* Cambridge, MA: MIT Press.

Palmer, S. E., & Beck, D. M. (2007). The repetition discrimination task: An objective method for studying perceptual grouping. *Perception & Psychophysics, 69*(1), 68–78.

Palmer, S. E., & Brooks, J. L. (2008). Edge-region grouping in figure-ground organization and depth perception. *Journal of Experimental Psychology: Human Perception and Performance, 34*(6), 1353–1371.

Palmer, S. E., Brooks, J. L., & Nelson, R. (2003). When does grouping happen? *Acta Psychologica, 114,* 311–330.

Palmer S. E., & Ghose, T. (2008). Extremal edges: A powerful cue to depth perception and figure-ground organization. *Psychological Science, 19*(1), 77–84.

Palmer, S. E., & Levitin, D. J. (1998). *Synchrony: A new principle of perceptual grouping.* Paper presented at the 39th Annual Meeting of the Psychonomic Society, Dallas, TX, November 19–22.

Palmer, S. E., Neff, J., & Beck, D. (1996). Late influences on perceptual grouping: Amodal completion. *Psychonomic Bulletin and Review, 3*(1), 75–80.

Palmer, S. E., & Nelson, R. (2000). Late influence on perceptual grouping: Illusory figures. *Perception & Psychophysics, 62,* 1321–1331.

Palmer, S. E., & Rock, I. (1994). Rethinking perceptual organization: The role of uniform connectedness. *Psychonomic Bulletin and Review, 1*(1), 29–55

Peterson, M. A. (1994a). Object recognition processes can and do operate before figure-ground organization. *Current Directions in Psychological Science, 3,* 105–111.

Peterson, M. A. (1994b). The proper placement of uniform connectedness. *Psychonomic Bulletin and Review, 1,* 509–514.

Peterson, M. A. (1999). Organization, segregation, and recognition. *Intellectica, 28,* 37–51.

Peterson, M. A. (2001). Object perception. In E. B. Goldstein (Ed.), *Blackwell handbook of perception* (pp. 168–203). Oxford, England: Blackwell.

Peterson, M. A. (2003a). On figures, grounds, and varieties of amodal surface completion. In R. Kimchi, M. Behrmann, & C. Olson (Eds.), *Perceptual organization in vision: Behavioral and neural perspectives* (pp. 87–116). Mahwah, NJ: Erlbaum.

Peterson, M. A. (2003b). Overlapping partial configurations in object memory: An alternative solution to classic problems in perception and recognition. In M. A. Peterson & G. Rhodes (Eds.), *Perception of faces, objects, and scenes: Analytic and holistic processes* (pp. 269–294). New York: Oxford University Press.

Peterson, M. A. (2012). Plasticity, competition, and task effects in object perception. In J. M. Wolfe & L. Robertson. *From perception to consciousness: Searching with Anne Treisman* (pp. 253–262).

Peterson, M. A., & Enns, J. T. (2005). The edge complex: Implicit perceptual memory for cross-edge competition leading to figure assignment. *Perception & Psychophysics, 14,* 727–740.

Peterson, M. A., & Gibson, B. S. (1993). Shape recognition contributions to figure-ground organization in three-dimensional displays. *Cognitive Psychology, 25,* 383–429.

Peterson, M. A., & Gibson, B. S. (1994a). Must figure-ground organization precede object recognition? An assumption in peril. *Psychological Science, 5,* 253–259.

Peterson, M. A., & Gibson, B. S. (1994b). Object recognition contributions to figure-ground organization: Operations on outlines and subjective contours. *Perception & Psychophysics, 56,* 551–564.

Peterson, M. A., Gerhardstein, P. C., Mennemeier, M., & Rapcsak, S. Z. (1998). Object-centered attentional biases and object recognition contributions to scene segmentation in left- and right-hemisphere-damaged patients. *Psychobiology, 26,* 557–570.

Peterson, M. A., Harvey, E. H., & Weidenbacher, H. L. (1991). Shape recognition inputs to figure-ground organization: Which route counts? *Journal of Experimental Psychology: Human Perception and Performance, 17,* 1075–1089.

Peterson, M. A., & Kim, J. H. (2001). On what is bound in figures and grounds. *Visual Cognition, 8,* 329–348.

Peterson, M. A., & Lampignano, D. L. (2003). Implicit memory for novel figure-ground displays includes a history of border competition. *Journal of Experimental Psychology: Human Perception and Performance, 29,* 808–822.

Peterson, M. A., & Salvagio, E. (2008). Inhibitory competition in figure-ground perception: Context and convexity. *Journal of Vision*, *8*(16), 1–13.

Peterson, M. A., & Skow, E. (2008). Suppression of shape properties on the ground side of an edge: Evidence for a competitive model of figure assignment. *Journal of Experimental Psychology: Human Perception and Performance*, *34*(2), 251–267.

Pettet, M. W. (1999). Shape and contour detection. *Vision Research*, *39*(3), 551–557.

Pomerantz, J. R., & Kubovy, M. (1986). Theoretical approaches to perceptual organization: Simplicity and likelihood principles. In K. R. Boff, L. Kaufman, & J. P. Thomas (Eds.), *Handbook of perception and human performance: Vol. 2. Cognitive processes and performance* (pp. 1–46). NY: John Wiley and Sons.

Pylyshyn, Z. (1999). Is vision continuous with cognition? The case for cognitive impenetrability of visual perception. *Behavioral and Brain Sciences*, *22*, 341–365.

Quinlan, P. T., & Wilton, R. N. (1998). Grouping by proximity or similarity? Competition between the Gestalt principles in vision. *Perception*, *27*(4), 417–430.

Razpurker-Apfeld, I., & Kimchi, R. (2007). The time course of perceptual grouping: The role of segregation and shape formation. *Perception & Psychophysics*, *69*(5), 732–743.

Rock, I., & Brosgole, L. (1964). Grouping based on phenomenal proximity. *Journal of Experimental Psychology*, *67*, 531–538.

Rock, I., Nijhawan, R., Plamer, S. E., & Tudor, L. (1992). Grouping based on phenomenal similarity of achromatic color. *Perception*, *21*, 779–789.

Rubin, E. (1958). Figure and ground. In D. C. Beardslee & M. Wertheimer (Eds.), *Readings in perception* (pp. 194–203). Princeton, NJ: Van Nostrand. (Original work published 1915).

Russell, C., & Driver, J. (2005). New indirect measures of "inattentive" visual grouping in a change-detection task. *Perception & Psychophysics*, *67*(4), 606–623.

Salvagio, E., Mojica, A. J., & Peterson, M. A. (2008). Context effects in figure-ground perception: The role of biased competition, suppression and long-range connections. *Journal of Vision*, *8*(6), 1007, 1007a,

Salvagio, E., & Peterson, M. A. (2010). Temporal dynamics in convexity context effects. *Journal of Vision*, *10*(7), 1214. doi:10.1167/10.7.1214

Salvagio, E., & Peterson, M. A. (2012). Revealing the temporal dynamics of competitive interactions in figure-ground perception. *Journal of Vision*, *12*(9), 887. doi:10.1167/12.9.887

Schulz, M. F., & Sanocki, T. (2003). Time course of perceptual grouping by color. *Psychological Science*, *14*(1), 26–30.

Shibata, M., Kawachi, Y., & Gyoba, J. (2010). Combined effects of perceptual grouping cues on object representation: Evidence from motion-induced blindness. *Attention Perception & Psychophysics*, *72*(2), 387–397.

Shomstein, S., Kimchi, R., Hammer, M., & Behrmann, M. (2010). Perceptual grouping operates independently of attentional selection: Evidence from hemispatial neglect. *Attention Perception & Psychophysics*, *72*(3), 607–618.

Stevens, K. A., & Brookes, A. (1988). The concave cusp as a determiner of figure-ground. *Perception*, *17*, 35–42.

Strüber, D., & Stadler, M. (1999). Dfferences in top-down infuences on the reversal rate of different categories of reversible figures. *Perception*, *28*, 1185–1196.

Treisman, A., & DeSchepper, B. (1996). Object tokens, attention, and visual memory. In T. Inui & J. McClelland (Eds.), *Attention and performance, XVI: Information integration in perception and communication* (pp. 15–46). Cambridge, MA: MIT Press.

Vecera, S. P., & Farah, M. J. (1997). Is visual image segmentation a bottom-up or an interactive process? *Perception & Psychophysics*, *59*, 1280–1296.

Vecera, S. P., Flevaris, A. V., & Filapek, J. C. (2004). Exogenous spatial attention influences figure-ground assignment. *Psychological Science*, *15*, 20–26.

Vecera, S. P., & O'Reilly, R. C. (1998). Figure–ground organization and object recognition processes: An interactive account. *Journal of Experimental Psychology: Human Perception and Performance*, *24*, 441–462.

Vecera, S. P., & O'Reilly, R. C. (2000). Graded effects in hierarchical figure–ground organization: A reply to Peterson (1999). *Journal of Experimental Psychology: Human Perception and Performance*, *26*, 1221–1231.

Vecera, S. P., Vogel, E. K., & Woodman, G. F. (2002). Lower-region: A new cue for figure-ground assignment. *Journal of Experimental Psychology: General*, *131*, 194–205.

Vickery, T. J., & Jiang, Y. V. (2009). Associative grouping: Perceptual grouping of shapes by association. *Attention Perception & Psychophysics*, *71*(4), 896–909.

Wertheimer, M. (1923/1938). Laws of organization in perceptual forms. In W. D. Ellis (Ed.), *A source book of Gestalt psychology* (pp. 71–94). London, England: Routledge & Kegan Paul. (Original work published 1923.)

Zemel, R. S., Behrmann, M., Mozer, M. C., & Bavelier, D. (2002). Experience-dependent perceptual grouping and object-based attention. *Journal of Experimental Psychology: Human Perception and Performance*, *28*(1), 202–217.

# Object Recognition

John E. Hummel

### Abstract

The dominant approaches to theorizing about and modeling human object recognition are the *view-based* approach, which holds that we mentally represent objects in terms of the (typically two-dimensional [2D]) coordinates of their visible 2D features, and the *structural description* approach, which holds that we represent objects in terms of the (typically categorical) spatial relations among their (typically volumetric) parts. This chapter reviews the history and nature of these (and other) models of object recognition, as well as some of the empirical evidence for and against each of them. I will argue that neither account is adequate to explain the full range of empirical data on human object recognition and conclude by suggesting that the visual system uses an intelligent combination of structure- and view-based approaches.

**Key Words:** object recognition, view-based model, structural description, visual attention, viewpoint invariance

Object recognition is a fundamental process that serves as a gateway from vision to cognitive processes such as categorization, language, and reasoning. The visual representations that allow us to recognize objects do more than merely tell us what we are looking at. They also serve as a basis for visual reasoning and inference: We may recognize a hammer, not only as an object called "hammer" and an object for pounding nails into wood but also as an object of about the right weight to balance a beam of a certain length on a fulcrum, an object with which to prop open a door, or an object to tie to the end of a rope for the purposes of throwing it over a high branch in the service of making a swing.

One of the most remarkable properties of the human capacity for object recognition is our ability to recognize objects from a variety of viewpoints despite the fact that different viewpoints can project radically different—even nonoverlapping—images to the retina. And given the retinotopic mapping of early cortical visual processing (e.g., in V1, V2, and to a lesser extent, V4), nonoverlapping retinal images give rise to nonoverlapping cortical representations, even moderately "late" in the ventral processing stream (i.e., the visual pathway responsible for our ability to know what we are looking at, as opposed to knowing how to interact with it motorically; see, e.g., Goodale, Milner, Jakobson, & Carey, 1991). But despite the varying retinal and cortical representations resulting from different object views, we somehow manage to recognize all these different images as arising from the same object—an accomplishment that, on its face, is so remarkable that it largely dominated the study of object recognition for three decades or more (see Palmer, 1999, for a review). However, as important and impressive as this capacity is, it is just one aspect of our remarkable capacity for visual object recognition.

The process of recognizing an object is a process of matching a representation of a viewed object to a representation stored in long-term memory (LTM). These stored and matched representations consist largely (albeit not exclusively; Rossion & Pourtois, 2004) of information about an object's shape (Biederman & Ju, 1988; Mapelli & Behrmann, 1997; Op de Beeck, Beatse, Wagemans, Sunaert, & Van Hecke, 2000). Accordingly, the study of object recognition consists largely (although not exclusively) of the study of the mental representation of object shape, and the vast majority of theories of object recognition are, effectively, theories of the mental representation of shape.

This chapter is organized as follows. In aid of understanding the major theories of object recognition, I will begin by reviewing the formal properties of representations of shape. I will next describe the major theories of human shape perception and object recognition. The majority of the chapter will be spent reviewing the empirical literature on object recognition with an eye toward the implications of these findings for the two dominant theories of object recognition—the view-based account and the structural description account. I will argue that neither account is adequate to explain the full range of empirical data on human object recognition and conclude by suggesting that the visual system uses an intelligent combination of structure- and view-based approaches.

## Representations of Object Shape

A representation of shape is defined by four properties (Hummel, 1994; Palmer, 1978). The first is a set of primitive elements. These may be as simple as individual pixels (e.g., as found in some ideal observer models of object recognition; Liu, Knill, & Kersten, 1995), as complex as volumetric parts (e.g., Marr & Nishihara, 1978), or assertions about the categorical properties of object parts (e.g., Biederman, 1987; Hummel, 2001; Hummel & Biederman, 1992), or more commonly, features of intermediate complexity, such as image edges and vertices (e.g., Lowe, 1987; Poggio & Edelman, 1990) or collections of edges and vertices (e.g., Fukushima & Miyake, 1982; Riesenhuber & Poggio, 1999).

The second defining property of a representation of shape is a reference frame within which the arrangement of an object's features or parts is specified. These may be object centered (e.g., Marr & Nishihara, 1978), viewer centered (e.g., Hummel & Biederman, 1992; Poggio & Edelman, 1990; Riesenhuber & Poggio, 2002; Ullman & Basri, 1991), or a mixture of the two

(e.g., Hummel, 2001; Hummel & Stankiewicz, 1996a; Lowe, 1987; Ullman, 1989).

Mixtures of object- and viewer-centered reference frames come in two varieties. Three-dimensional (3D)-based models, such as those proposed by Lowe (1987) and Ullman (1989), hold that we mentally represent objects as detailed 3D models, which we match to 2D object images by a kind of "back projection" akin to the manner in which a 3D model is mapped to a specific object view in computer graphics.[1] The viewed 2D object image is then matched point by point against the 2D view produced by the back projection. These models represent a mixture of object- and viewer-centered reference frames in the sense that the stored 3D model is fully object centered, but the 2D back-projected view is matched to the object image in a viewer-centered reference frame.

The other way to mix reference frames is to specify some dimensions in viewer-centered terms and others in object-centered terms. This kind of mixture is possible because a reference frame is defined by three properties, any of which can be either viewer or object centered (or, for that matter, environment centered, although this latter approach is never used): The *origin* is the point relative to which the reference frame is defined (in the viewer-centered case, the origin is defined relative to the viewer, and in the object-centered case, it is defined relative to the object). A *scale* maps distances on the object or in the image to distances in the reference frame. And an *orientation* maps directions (in the image or on the object) to directions in the reference frame. A common way to mix object- and viewer-centered components is to define the origin and scale of the reference frame relative to the object but define the orientation relative to the viewer (Hummel, 2001; Hummel & Stankiewicz, 1996a; Olshausen, Anderson, & Van Essen, 1993).

The third dimension of the representation of shape is a vocabulary of relations specifying the arrangement of the primitives within the reference frame. The most straightforward approach is simply to specify the locations of primitives in terms of their coordinates, that is, their numerical relations to the origin of the reference frame. This approach characterizes "view-" or "appearance-based" models (Edelman & Intrator, 2003; Poggio & Edelman, 1990; Olshausen et al., 1993; Riesenhuber & Poggio, 2002; Ullman & Basri, 1991) as well as 3D model-matching models (Lowe, 1987; Ullman, 1989). Alternatively, more complex primitives (such as convex object parts

[Biederman, 1987; Marr & Nishihara, 1978] or surfaces [Leek, Reppa, & Arguin, 1995]) may be represented in terms of their relations, not to the origin of the reference frame, but to one another. Made explicit in this way, interpart relations may be represented metrically or categorically (e.g., "above" vs. "below" and "larger" vs. "smaller"; Biederman, 1987; Hummel & Biederman, 1992) or both (e.g., Hummel, 2001; Hummel & Stankiewicz, 1996a, 1998). In general, representing interpart relations explicitly provides tremendous representational flexibility, both in the vocabulary of relations that can be represented, and in the manner in which those relations can be specified.

The final dimension of a representation of shape, closely related to the issue of coordinates versus relations, is the distinction between *holistic* versus *analytic* representations. An analytic representation is one in which the components of the representation are made explicit and expressed relative to one another and/or to the representation as a whole. In the case of shape perception, a structural description specifying an object's shape in terms of the spatial relations among its component parts would be an analytic representation. Other examples of analytic representations include propositions (e.g., *loves* (John, Mary)) and sentences (e.g., "John loves Mary"). In all three cases, the component parts (e.g., the object parts, in the case of the structural description, or the relation *loves* and the actors John and Mary in the proposition and sentence) are represented explicitly in terms of their relations to one another (e.g., a structural description might express which object parts are connected to one another, which are larger than others, etc.; the proposition and sentence both express that John is the lover and Mary the beloved). In turn, representing these components explicitly implies representing them independently of one another. The independence of John with Mary and *loves* is what makes it possible for us to understand what *loves* (John, Mary) has in common with *hates* (John, Mary) or *loves* (John, Susan), and how they differ (Hummel & Biederman, 1992; Hummel & Holyoak, 1997, 2003).

A holistic representation is simply the opposite: It is one in which the components of the representation are not represented independently of one another or of their place in the representation as a whole. Quintessential examples of holistic representations in human vision include face perception (see Rhodes & Peterson, 2003) and color perception. Face perception is holistic in the sense that we match faces "all of a piece" to representations stored in memory, with little or no explicit knowledge of a face's details. As a result, we are generally capable of saying who looks like whom, but barring obvious categorical features such as scars or facial hair, we are generally at a loss to say why. Similarly, color perception tends to be quite holistic as evidenced by the fact that we have difficulty categorizing colors in terms of their underlying physical dimensions of hue, saturation, and brightness. Any color is some combination of these dimensions, but because we perceive them holistically we are at a loss to respond to them individually. (Contrast this situation with the case of "John loves Mary" or the case of a structural description specifying something like "cone on top of brick": Although we cannot easily say how one shade of red differs from another, we can easily say how "cone on top of brick" differs from "cylinder on top of brick.")

There is no necessary logical linkage between relations versus coordinates on the one hand and analytic versus holistic representations on the other. In principle, it is possible to imagine either analytic or holistic representations of either relations or coordinates. But as a matter of psychological fact, relational representations are analytic (i.e., when one thinks about relations, one is thinking explicitly; see, e.g., Holyoak & Thagard, 1995; Hummel & Holyoak, 1997; Stankiewicz, Hummel, & Cooper, 1998; Thoma, Hummel, & Davidoff, 2004), whereas coordinate-based representations lend themselves naturally to holistic coding (e.g., as in the case of face perception, for which there is evidence of coordinate-based coding of a face's features; Cooper & Wojan, 2000). As such, the issue of explicit relations versus coordinate-based coding in shape perception is de facto bound up with the issue of analytic versus holistic representations of shape: Structural description models, which propose that we represent the relations among an object's parts explicitly, therefore propose that the representation of shape is analytic, whereas view-based models, which represent objects in terms of their features coordinates, are naturally much more holistic. (At the same time, it is possible to reason explicitly, i.e., analytically, about coordinates, as when we solve problems in analytic geometry.)

## Models of Object Recognition

Any model of object recognition is a collection of commitments to the four dimensions of shape representation summarized earlier. Although in principle the dimensions are independent of one another, in practice commitments to particular values on them tend to cluster.

One group of models, collectively referred to as *view* or *appearance based*, are based on simple primitives such as vertices (Edelman & Intrator, 2001; Olshausen et al., 1993; Poggio & Edelman, 1990; Ullman & Basri, 1991) or collections of contour elements (Riesenhuber & Poggio, 1999), represented in terms of their numerical coordinates in a viewer-centered reference frame (or at least partly viewer-centered; many view-based models assume that images are normalized for translation and scale prior to recognition). In some of these models (e.g., Edelman & Intrator, 2003; Poggio & Edelman, 1990; Ullman & Basri, 1991), the representation of object shape is taken to be the vector of the 2D retinal coordinates of the vertices present in an object view; that is, the primitives themselves are not part of the representation at all except inasmuch as they determine which coordinates get into the vector. In these models, the primitives are simple local image elements (lines and/or vertices), the reference frame is viewer centered, the relations are numerical coordinates, and the representation is holistic.

As noted previously, a related group of models, *3D model-matching* models (e.g., Lowe, 1987; Ullman, 1989), assumes that objects are represented in LTM as 3D models but are matched to object images by back-projecting the models onto the image. These models assume an object-centered reference frame for the 3D model and a viewer-centered reference frame for the 2D matching process. Like the view-based models, matching in these models is based on local image features specified in terms of their retinotopic coordinates.

A third group of models assert that objects are represented as *structural descriptions* (e.g., Biederman, 1987; Clowes, 1967; Dickenson, Pentland, & Rosenfeld, 1992; Hummel & Biederman, 1992; Marr & Nishihara, 1978; Sutherland, 1968), which specify an object's volumetric parts in terms of their relations to one another. In these models, the primitives are volumetric parts or part attributes (i.e., generalized cylinders [Dickenson et al., 1992; Marr & Nishihara, 1978] or geons, which are classes of generalized cylinders that can be discriminated from one another based on nonaccidental properties of image edges [Biederman, 1987; Hummel, 2001; Hummel & Biederman, 1992; Hummel & Stankiewicz, 1996a]), the reference frame may either be object centered (Marr & Nishihara, 1978), viewer centered (Biederman, 1987; Hummel & Biederman, 1992), or mixed (Hummel, 2001;

Hummel & Stankiewicz, 1996a), the relations between an object's parts are represented explicitly, and the resulting representations are analytic. For example, a coffee mug might be represented as a curved cylinder (the handle) end-connected to the side of a straight vertical cylinder (the body of the mug).

Still a fourth class of models assumes a combination of the view- and structural-description-based approaches (Hummel, 2001; Hummel & Stankiewicz, 1996a). These models assume that the visual system generates part-based structural descriptions of attended objects and simultaneously generates view-like holistic representations (which are nonetheless invariant with translation and scale) of unattended objects.

## Evaluating View- and Structure-Based Models of Object Recognition

The view- and structural description-based approaches are the dominant approaches to modeling/theorizing about human object recognition and have motivated the majority of the theory-driven empirical research. Accordingly, I shall structure my review of the empirical literature around an evaluation of these two general theoretical approaches.

The structural description approach to object recognition was first proposed by Clowes (1967) and Sutherland (1968) and it was first proposed as a solution to the problem of view-invariant object recognition by Marr (1982; Marr & Nishihara, 1978). (Indeed, the roots of the structural description account, with its emphasis on relations rather than metric coordinates, date back at least as far as the Gestaltists; e.g., Köhler, 1940; Wertheimer, 1924/1950.) It was first popularized as a serious theory of human object recognition by Biederman (1987), who proposed that people recognize objects as collections of *geons*—classes of volumetric primitives that can be distinguished from one another based on nonaccidental 2D properties of image edges—in particular categorical relations to one another. The impact of Biederman's work was that it showed how the information necessary for view-invariant object recognition could be recovered from the information available in an object's 2D image. Hummel and Biederman (1992) later showed how the fundamental operations proposed by Biederman (1987) could be accomplished in a neural computing architecture, and demonstrated that the resulting model successfully simulated the strengths and limitations of the human ability to recognize objects despite variations in viewpoint.

The view- and structure-based approaches to object recognition grew from very different starting points. With Marr and Nishihara's (1978) work, the structural description approach started with an analysis of how view-invariant recognition could be accomplished, in the abstract, at Marr's (1982) computational theory-level of analysis. Biederman (1987) provided a psychologically plausible algorithmic account of this general approach, and Hummel and Biederman (1992) demonstrated how the resulting algorithm could be realized in neural hardware. Central to (especially more recent) structural description accounts is the assumption that objects are represented in terms of their parts' spatial relations to one another.

The view-based approach was arguably inspired much more from the opposite end: From the very beginning (e.g., Poggio & Edelman, 1990), the goal was to understand how neural networks could accomplish pattern recognition, and neural plausibility remains a primary motivation behind much view-based modeling (see, e.g., Riesenhuber & Poggio, 1999, 2002; Edelman & Intrator, 2003). Fundamental insights came from Poggio and Girosi (1990), who showed that a Gaussian radial basis function, which is easy to instantiate in a neural computing architecture, is in some senses an optimal classifier, and from Ullman and Basri (1991), who showed that, provided some basic assumptions could be satisfied (e.g., that all features of an object be visible in all possible views of that object), an object could be recognized in any 3D view as a linear combination of stored 2D views of the object. In other words, view-invariant recognition of 3D objects could be accomplished by simple vector operations (which are easy to implement in neural networks) on stored 2D views without having to store, compute, or even estimate any of the object's 3D properties. Central to all these modeling efforts is the assumption that objects are represented as vectors of features and/or feature coordinates.[2]

## The Effects of Viewpoint on Object Recognition

Throughout most of the 1990s and into the early 2000s, an often acrimonious debate raged—both in the literature and at scientific meetings—between the proponents of view-based models of object recognition and the proponents of structural description models. This debate centered on the question of just how view specific versus view invariant the representation of object shape really is. The proponents of structural description models argued (and

marshaled evidence demonstrating) that the visual representation of shape is largely invariant with (i.e., unaffected by changes in) the location of an object's image in the visual field (Biederman & Cooper, 1991a), the size of the image (up to the limits of visual acuity; Biederman & Cooper, 1992), left-right reflection (Biederman & Cooper, 1991a), and rotation in depth up to parts occlusion (Biederman & Bar, 1999, 2000; Biederman & Gerhardstein, 1993, 1995; Biederman & Subramaniam, 1997; Hayworth & Biederman, 2006; Kayaert, Biederman, Op De Beeck, & Vogels, 2005; Kayaert, Biederman & Vogels, 2003; Vogels, Biederman, Bar, & Lorincz, 2001).

By contrast, the proponents of view-based models of object recognition argued (and marshaled evidence demonstrating) that object recognition is largely sensitive to rotation in the picture plane (Tarr & Pinker, 1989; 1990) and rotation in depth (Edelman & Bülthoff, 1991; Logothetis, Pauls, Bülthoff, & Poggio, 1994; Poggio & Edelman, 1990; Tarr & Bülthoff, 1995; Tarr, Bülthoff, Zabinski, & Blanz, 1997).

It turns out that the question of whether object recognition looks view invariant or view sensitive hinges largely on the stimuli and tasks used to ask the question (Biederman & Subramaniam, 1997; Liu, Knill, & Kersten, 1995). With objects that can be easily segmented into distinct volumetric parts in distinct spatial relations, the visual representation of shape (as measured, for example, by visual priming) appears quite view invariant, up to parts occlusion: One view of a volumetric object will visually prime a different view of the same object just as much as it primes itself, so long as all the same parts are visible in both views (Biederman & Gerhardstein, 1993). It is this kind of stimulus that Biederman and colleagues used in the majority of their studies demonstrating view invariance. But with stimuli that are not easy to segment into distinct parts in distinct relations (e.g., the kind of object that would result from bending a paperclip in several places at various angles) the representation of shape is quite sensitive to the orientation from which the object is viewed. It is this kind of stimulus that Bülthoff, Tarr, and colleagues used in the majority of their studies demonstrating view sensitivity.[3]

The debate over the view dependence versus view invariance of object recognition was fueled largely by the fact that view-based models (as suggested by the name) *tend to be* more view sensitive than structural description models, whose early development (Biederman, 1987; Marr & Nishihara, 1978) was motivated largely by the question of how the visual system achieves view-invariant object recognition, and which therefore tends to predict substantial view invariance in the visual representation of object shape. The question of view dependence versus view invariance therefore *seemed to be* the deciding factor between these two classes of models.

But it is not (Hummel, 1994, 2000, 2003a; Hummel & Stankiewicz, 1996b, 1998). Models in either class can be modified to act more or less view invariant as demanded by the data. That is, neither are view-based models fundamentally view sensitive nor are structural description models fundamentally view invariant. For example, the view-based model of Ullman and Basri (1991) stores only 2D representations of individual object views in memory, but it predicts *complete* view invariance in object recognition provided enough such views are stored (where "enough" can be a surprisingly small number). 3D model-matching models, which are very much like view-based models in how they match object images to models in memory, also predict complete invariance in object recognition. And it is perfectly possible to render a structural description model more view sensitive simply by including, in an object's description, information about the angle in which it is viewed (see Hummel, 2001; Stankiewicz, 2002). As such, all the fighting about the view sensitivity versus view invariance of object recognition that dominated the 1990s and early 2000s turned out to be much ado about not very much.

Although view sensitivity is not the (or even a) fundamental difference between the view- and structure-based approaches to object recognition, there are four differences between these competing accounts that do turn out to be fundamental: (1) They differ in their commitment to strictly 2D information versus more 3D inferences about the representation of object shape. (2) They differ in their approach to representing the configuration of an object's features or parts, with view-based models strongly committed to representing an object's features in terms of their numerical coordinates (see Hummel, 2000, for an explanation of why; in brief, it is because feature vectors are mathematically well behaved, whereas categorical relations are not) and structural description theories committed to representing an object's features or parts in terms of their (typically categorical) spatial relations to one another. (3) View-based models are committed to a holistic coding of object shape, in which all an object's features are represented as coordinates in

the same, unitary feature vector, whereas structural descriptions are part-based analytic representations, which represent an object's part attributes independently of one another and of their interrelations (see Hummel, 2001, 2003b). And (4) because of (3), structural description models predict that the representation of an object's shape will differ qualitatively depending on whether it is attended or ignored; view-based models predict no qualitative effects of visual attention on the representation of object shape. On all four of these fundamental commitments, the view-based approach runs into difficulty as an account of human shape perception and object recognition. And on the fourth, so does the structural description approach.

## The Role of 2D and 3D Representations of Shape in Object Recognition

Liu, Knill, and Kersten (1995) did a groundbreaking study demonstrating that no model based strictly on 2D representations of object shape can provide an adequate account of human shape perception. They trained human observers to classify two kinds of objects: "bent paperclip"-like objects of the kind that have been used to demonstrate view sensitivity in object recognition and novel volumetric objects of the kind that have been used to demonstrate view invariance. They also trained two ideal observers (i.e., mathematical models that perform a task as well as it is logically possible to perform it with the information they are given) to classify the same objects. One of these ideal observers was a 2D ideal: an ideal observer that, like a view-based model, stored only 2D object views in memory and matched them against 2D images for classification. Being an ideal observer, this model performed as well as it is logically possible to perform the object classification task using only stored 2D views. The other ideal observer was a 3D ideal. It made inferences about an object's 3D shape based on the information in a 2D view of the object and used these inferences as the basis for classifying the viewed images. Since ideal observers are ideal, human observers rarely perform as well they do, with efficiency (i.e., human accuracy divided by ideal accuracy) typically well below 0.5. The only way a human can outperform an ideal observer is by having access to information to which the ideal does not.

With the bent paperclip objects, Liu et al. (1995) found that the 2D ideal observer outperformed the human observers (i.e., with human efficiency less than 1.0), a pattern consistent with the humans storing and matching 2D views of these objects.

However, with the volumetric objects, the human observers *outperformed* the 2D ideal, indicating that the human observers were using information about 3D shape to which the 2D ideal did not have access. (Unsurprisingly, the humans still underperformed the 3D ideal even with the volumetric objects.) The human observers' ability to outperform the 2D ideal with volumetric objects is very strong evidence that people do not recognize volumetric objects simply by storing and matching 2D views of those objects.

## The Role of Spatial Relations in Shape Perception and Object Recognition

Another fundamental difference between the view- and structure-based approaches (a difference that also happens to characterize the difference between nonhuman and human primates; see Penn, Holyoak, & Povenelli, 2008) concerns whether relations are represented explicitly. Structural descriptions (and humans) represent relations (e.g., relative size, relative location, relative orientation, etc.) explicitly; view-based models (and, apparently, nonhuman primates) do not. Along with language, the human ability to reason explicitly about relations is arguably the basis of virtually everything uniquely human, including art, science, mathematics, and engineering (see Holyoak & Thagard, 1995; Hummel & Holyoak, 1997, 2003).

That we can perceive the spatial relations among an object's parts is undeniable and is evidenced, for example, by our ability to name them and to use them as the basis for making analogies between objects (see Hummel, 2000). And although the perception of spatial relations—and the role of explicit relations in object recognition—have received comparatively little empirical attention, what evidence there is suggests that, as predicted by the structural description approach, explicit representations of an object's interpart spatial relations play an important role in the representation and encoding of object shape.

Hummel and Stankiewicz (1996b) directly tested categorical spatial relations against coordinate-based representations using a variety of object identification tasks (including basic recognition, same/different judgments, and similarity judgments). Specifically, we trained human subjects to recognize a collection of stick-arrangement objects like those used by Tarr and Pinker (1989, 1990) in their demonstrations of the sensitivity of object recognition to orientation in the picture plane. We deliberately chose these objects because they do not have distinguishable parts in distinguishable relations (all their "parts" are simply straight lines of various lengths connected at right angles); that is, we designed the objects to be similar to the kinds of objects typically used to demonstrate view-based effects in studies of object recognition.

After training, we tested our subjects for their ability to distinguish the trained objects from two kinds of distractors (see Fig. 3.1). One kind of distractor (*coordinate* distractors) was designed to maximize a distractor's similarity to a trained object in terms of the literal coordinates of its critical features (the line endpoints) while changing one categorical relation present in the trained object (e.g., one line might be moved so that it went from being *centered above* the line to which it was connected to being *centered below* the line to which it was connected, a change that affected exactly two sets of coordinates, namely, those of the endpoints of the moved line). The other kind of distractor (*categorical* distractors) were designed to distort more coordinates (four rather than two) but leave the categorical (e.g., *above/below*) relations between the parts intact.

To the extent that people represent the trained objects in terms of the coordinates of their critical points, they should find the coordinate distractors more confusable with the trained targets than the categorical distractors. But to the extent that they represent the trained targets in terms of the categorical relations among their parts, they should find the categorical distractors more confusable with the corresponding trained targets than the coordinate distractors. The results were not subtle. Across a variety of tasks, our subjects found the categorical distractors much more confusable with the corresponding targets than the coordinate distractors.

Cooper and Wojan (2000) conducted a similar study with faces as stimuli. Their interest was in

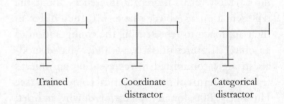

| Trained | Coordinate distractor | Categorical distractor |

**Figure 3.1** Illustration of the kind of stimuli used by Hummel and Stankiewicz (1996b). For each trained stimulus (Trained) there were two distractors, one designed to match the trained stimulus in terms of its literal feature coordinates but mismatch in one categorical spatial relation (Coordinate Distractor) and one designed to mismatch the trained stimulus in twice as many stimulus coordinates but to match the trained stimulus in terms of the categorical relations among its parts (Categorical Distractor).

whether face identification (as in "Who's face is this?") is based on a coordinate-based representation, whereas basic-level face recognition (as in "Is this a face or not?") is based on an explicit representation of the categorical relations among the face's parts. Their logic was similar to that of Hummel and Stankiewicz (1996b): They showed subjects either undistorted images of the faces of famous people, distortions in which one eye was moved up from its normal location on the face (changing its categorical spatial relation to the other eye but disrupting the coordinates of only one eye), or distortions in which both eyes had been moved up from their normal locations (preserving the categorical spatial relation between the eyes, but distorting twice as many feature coordinates as in the one-eye-moved case). To the extent that people use a coordinate-based representation, the two-eyes-moved images should be harder to recognize than the one-eye-moved images; but to the extent that they use a representation based on the categorical relations between the features of a face, the one-eye-moved images should be harder to recognize. Given a face identification task ("who is this?"), Cooper and Wojan found that subjects had more difficulty with the two-eyes-moved than the one-eye-moved stimuli, suggesting that face identification is based on a holistic, coordinate-based representation of the stimulus face (consistent with the vast literature on face identification; see, e.g., Rhodes & Peterson, 2003). But given a face recognition task ("is this a face or not?"), the one-eye-moved stimuli were harder to classify than the two-eyes-moved stimuli, consistent with a representation based on explicit categorical relations between the faces' parts.

Turning to object category learning, Saiki and Hummel (1996) showed that object categories defined by conjunctions of parts in specific spatial relations are much easier to learn than categories defined by conjunctions of parts in specific colors or colors in specific relations, even when the learnability of categories defined by colors, parts and relations, individually, is equated. In other words, the human object category learning system is biased to learn objects consisting of parts in specific spatial relations. In related research, Saiki and Hummel (1998) showed that people perceive the spatial relations among connected objects parts differently than the relations among nonconnected parts (e.g., among other things, people are more sensitive to part-relation bindings for connected than nonconnected parts).

In summary, the comparatively few data there are on the representation of spatial relations for object recognition suggest that people do explicitly represent the spatial relations among an object's parts in the service of object recognition and object category learning.

## Independence of Part Attributes in the Representation of Shape

One of the most basic predictions of Biederman's (1987) theory of object recognition is that people will activate a representation of an object's convex parts on the way to recognizing the object. In a now classic collection of experiments, Biederman and Cooper (1991b) used a visual priming paradigm to directly test this prediction. In Experiment 1, Biederman and Cooper formed complementary images of objects by starting with line drawings and removing half the contours and vertices from each of an object's parts. The removed contours and vertices were then used to make a second line drawing of the same object. The two line drawings were complements of one another in the sense that, although they depicted all the same volumetric parts, they had no local features (contours and vertices) in common. Biederman and Cooper showed that one member of an image-complement pair would visually prime the other member of the pair just as much as it primed itself: From the perspective of the visual priming, there was no difference between the two images, even though they had no local features in common.

In Experiment 2, Biederman and Cooper (1991b) formed complementary images by removing half the volumetric parts from one image in order to form the other. As with the complementary images from Experiment 1, together the two complements formed a complete line drawing of the object. But in Experiment 2, in contrast to Experiment 1, the two images depicted none of the same parts. This time, Biederman and Cooper found that complementary images did not visually prime one another at all. Taken together, the results of Experiments 1 and 2 show that two line drawings of the same object will visually prime one another if and only if they depict the same volumetric parts— a pattern that constitutes strong evidence for some kind of parts-based representation of shape being activated in the service of object recognition. Based on Biederman and Cooper's data, it is impossible to know whether the observed priming resides in a representation of volumetric parts, per se, versus whether it resides in a representation of the surfaces composing those volumes (Leek, Reppa, & Arguin, 2005). But regardless, it is clear that the priming resides in a representation of parts (surfaces or volumes) substantially more abstract than simple local image features.

Part of representing the relations among an object's parts explicitly is representing them independently of the parts so related (Arguin & Saumier, 2005; Hummel, 1994, 2000, 2001; Hummel & Biederman, 1992; Hummel & Holyoak, 1997, 2003). A corollary of this principle is that the visual system is well advised to represent high-level shape attributes, such as the attributes describing the shape of a geon, independently as well. In Hummel and Biederman's (1992) structural description model, JIM, as well as in JIM's successors, JIM2 (Hummel & Stankiewicz, 1996a) and JIM3 (Hummel, 2001), this independence takes the form of separate units representing the various shape attributes of an object part (e.g., one set of neuron-like units represents whether a geon's cross section is straight or curved, a separate set represents whether its major axis is straight or curved, and still other units represent its other shape attributes, its location in the visual field, etc.) and the relations between parts (e.g., separate units represent relations such as *above*, *below*, *larger*, *smaller*, etc.). This independence makes it possible to appreciate what different geons have in common and how they differ. Representing a cone-shaped part simply as the atom "cone" and a cylinder simply as "cylinder" fails to specify what cones have in common with cylinders. But representing a cone as "curved cross-section, straight major axis, nonparallel sides" and a cylinder as "curved cross section, straight major axis, parallel sides" makes explicit how a cone is similar to a cylinder and how they differ.

Behaviorally, independence predicts that part shape attributes ought to be perceptually separable from one another and from the relations in which a part is engaged. Using Garner's (1974) criteria, Saiki and Hummel (1998, Experiment 3) showed that object parts are perceived independently of their spatial relations, and using a visual search paradigm, Arguin and Saumier (2005) also found evidence for independent coding of object parts and their spatial relations. Using a noise-masking paradigm, Stankiewicz (2002) showed that part attributes such as aspect ratio and axis curvature are represented independently of one another. Stankiewicz also showed that part shape is perceptually independent of viewpoint. As predicted by the structure-based account, these findings indicate that part attributes

and their relations are represented explicitly and independently of one another. These findings are inconsistent with the view-based account's prediction that all aspects of object shape should be perceptually integral with (i.e., nonseparable from) one another and with the viewpoint in which the object is depicted.

Neurally, the independence implied by the structure-based account predicts that there ought to be neurons in visual cortex that respond to individual attributes of geons, independently of the geon's other attributes. Kayaert, Biederman, and Vogels (2005) report evidence for just such neurons in macaque inferotemporal cortex (specifically, in area TE). The same researchers also found that these neurons are more sensitive to changes in a geon's nonaccidental properties (e.g., a change from a straight to a curved major axis) than to otherwise equivalent (e.g., in terms of their impact on early visual representations in V1) metric changes in a geon's shape (e.g., in the degree of curvature of the major axis). Similar findings of independence were reported by Tanaka (1993) and Baker, Behrmann, and Olson (2002) using different stimulus materials.

## The Role of Attention in Shape Perception and Object Recognition

Representing visual properties independently of one another (i.e., analytically, rather than holistically) offers numerous advantages from a computational perspective (Hummel & Biederman, 1992), but it comes with a cost: If part attributes and relations are represented independently, then visual attention is necessary to ensure that they are bound together correctly (Hummel & Stankiewicz, 1996a; see also Treisman & Gelade, 1980; Treisman & Schmidt, 1982). It is here that the structure-based account runs into difficulty. This account correctly predicts that attention ought to be necessary to generate a structural description of object shape (Stankiewicz & Hummel, 2002; Stankiewicz, Hummel, & Cooper, 1998; Thoma et al., 2004; Thoma, Davidoff, & Hummel, 2007). However, it incorrectly predicts that, without the ability to generate a structural description, recognition of unattended objects should fail.

Evidence for the recognition of unattended objects comes in the form of both negative (Tipper, 1985; Treisman & DeSchepper, 1996) and positive (Stankiewicz et al., 1998; Stankiewicz & Hummel, 2002; Thoma et al., 2004, 2007) priming for unattended shapes. (Negative priming is an increase in response times and/or error rates to recognize previously seen items; positive priming [typically called simply "priming"] is a decrease in response times and/or error rates to recognize previously seen items. Whether priming for ignored objects is negative or positive depends on the difficulty of the selection task, with difficult selection [e.g., naming the green object in a display depicting a green line drawing of one object overlaid on a red line drawing of another] leading to negative priming and easy selection [e.g., naming one of two spatially separated line drawings] leading to positive priming; see Stankiewicz et al., 1998). Importantly, priming for ignored objects is not localized in low-level retinotopic features (e.g., as represented in V1). Tipper (1985) showed that negative priming for ignored objects extends all the way to the level of meaning, and Stankiewicz and Hummel (2002) showed that, in contrast to the visual features represented in V1 and V2, positive priming for unattended objects in invariant with translation and scale.

The view-based approach correctly predicts priming for unattended objects (since views are holistic, they do not depend on attention for binding; see Hummel & Stankiewicz, 1996a) but incorrectly predicts that the representation of an unattended shape should be the same as the representation of an attended shape. That is, whereas the structure-based account predicts too great a role for attention in object recognition (i.e., that recognition will fail completely in the absence of attention), the view-based account predicts too little.

Stankiewicz, Thoma, and their colleagues have shown that the visual representation of an attended object differs qualitatively from that of an unattended object. Whereas visual priming for both attended and unattended object images is invariant with translation across the visual field and changes in scale (Stankiewicz & Hummel, 2002), attended images visually prime their left-right reflections whereas ignored images do not (Stankiewicz et al., 1998). Similarly, visual priming for attended images is robust to configural distortions (as when an image is cut with a vertical line down the center and the left half is moved to the right and the right half to the left), whereas priming for ignored images is not (Thoma et al., 2004). Attended images also prime their inverted (i.e., upside-down) counterparts, whereas ignored images do not (Thoma et al., 2007).

The findings of Stankiewicz, Thoma, and colleagues can be accommodated neither by the structural account nor by the view-based account. Indeed, they were predicted (and the experiments themselves motivated) by a hybrid model (Hummel & Stankiewicz's, 1996, JIM2 and Hummel's, 2001, refinement, JIM3), whose development was a response to the strikingly complementary strengths and limitations of the structure- and view-based accounts. Hummel and Stankiewicz were motivated to develop JIM2 by the observation that structure-based models account for a large number of findings in the literature on object recognition and shape perception (as reviewed earlier), while at the same time being inconsistent with the automaticity and speed of object recognition. (Although not summarized earlier, object recognition is not only too automatic to be consistent with the structure-based approach, it is also too fast: At least for overlearned stimuli, object-sensitive neurons in macaque inferotemporal cortex will respond to their preferred stimulus in a feed-forward fashion [Tovee, Rolls, Treves, & Bellis, 1993]—processing that is much too fast to depend on the dynamic binding necessary to generate a structural description [Hummel & Stankiewicz, 1996a].)

The resulting model is a hybrid that generates geon-and-relation-based structural descriptions of attended object images but which uses a holistic "surface map" (akin to a view-based representation in the sense that features are represented at each of several locations in a reference frame, but at much lower spatial resolution than a view-based model and with more complex primitives than simple image features) to recognize familiar objects in familiar views rapidly and without the need for visual attention (see Hummel, 2001, for the most recent version of the model). In general, the model predicts that visual priming for attended images will reflect the properties of both the structured representation of shape and the holistic representation (both of which become active in response to an attended image), whereas priming for ignored images will reflect the properties of the holistic surface map only.

More specifically, the model makes a complex set of predictions about the effects of attention and images changes on visual priming in an object recognition task (predictions that, at the time of its first publication in 1996, were untested). As reviewed earlier, the model predicts that (a) priming for both attended and ignored images will be invariant with translation across the visual field and changes in scale (confirmed by Stankiewicz & Hummel, 2002); (b) attended images, but not ignored images, will visually prime their left-right reflections (confirmed by Stankiewicz et al., 1998); (c) attended images will prime configural distortions of themselves, but ignored images will not (confirmed by Thoma et al., 2004); and (d) attended images will prime inverted versions of themselves but ignored images will not (confirmed by Thoma et al., 2007).

## Summary and Conclusions

Human beings have large brains, and roughly half of the human brain (or a bit more) is involved in one way or another in processing visual information. Given this, it is perhaps unsurprising that we are extremely good at visually recognizing objects. When we attend to an object, we can visually segment it into its parts, perceive the attributes of those parts independently of one another and independently of the parts' relations to one another, and perceive and reason about the relations among the parts. Armed with these relational representations, we can recognize familiar objects in novel viewpoints and recognize novel instances of known object classes. We can also reason about the attributes of an object, its parts and the relations among them, in the service of making judgments about whether the object would make, say, an appropriate doorstop, a useful weapon, or a charming element in a modern sculpture to serve as a gift to our spouse on the occasion of our anniversary. All these abilities rely upon and reflect our capacity to represent objects relationally. Our relational representations of objects serve as a perceptual gateway to our ability to reason relationally about the world, which, in turn, sets us apart from all other primate species (and quite probably *all* other species).

At the same time, if all we had were these relational representations, object recognition would be attention demanding, labor intensive, calorie consuming, and frustratingly slow, as we would have to attend to every object in our environment in order to recognize it. So we appear to have evolved a shortcut (or, in all likelihood, the "shortcut" evolved before the relational ability, so it is probably more accurate to say that we simply did not evolve away our shortcut): Familiar objects in familiar views can be recognized rapidly and automatically, freeing up our attentional resources to focus on more interesting matters.

Together, the automatic holistic route to recognition and the effortful relational one give us the best of both worlds: We can be as fast and automatic as a view-based model most of the time, and as smart as a structural description when we need to be.

## Notes

1. Given a specification of an object's coordinates in 3D space (e.g., the coordinates of various features on its external surfaces) and given a specification of the angle and distance from which the object is viewed, the mathematics governing the projection of points on the object's visible surfaces to points in the resulting image of the object—that is, the mathematics of projective geometry—are well constrained and have been well understood for a long time. It is these mathematics that allow Pixar to create its movie magic.

2. At this point, students of cognitive psychology may be scratching their heads and wondering, "Hey, isn't this *view-based* approach just the same thing as *template matching*, which I read about in my intro to cog psych textbook and which is obviously wrong as an account of human object recognition?" The answer is, "Well, yes and no." Template matching, the whipping-boy presented and dismissed in intro texts, is most often presented as matching, pixel by pixel, a viewed image of an object to a literal image stored in the head. Inasmuch as view-based models match feature coordinates rather than individual pixels, the answer is, No, they are not the same (an object's image contains fewer "features" than pixels). However, in all other respects they are very much the same, in the sense of directly matching the exact 2D shape of an object's image to a set of precise 2D coordinates stored in memory. And in this sense, the view-based approach was basically falsified before Ullman and Basri (1991) or Poggio and Edelman (1990) published their first papers advocating the approach. At the time I, too, scratched my head and asked, "Hey, don't we already know what's wrong with this approach?" (see Hummel & Biederman, 1992; Hummel, 1994, 2000; Hummel & Stankiewicz, 1996b). But for whatever reason, the proponents of view-based models never bothered to cite the Gestaltists and others who had so long before demonstrated the fundamental inadequacy of their approach.

3. In response to this situation, it is natural to ask, "So: Who's right? Which kind of stimulus is 'better'?" By way of answering this question, it is worth noting that the use of bent paperclip-like stimuli was motivated by the fact that the view-based model of Ullman and Basri (1991) only works if all of an object's features are visible in all views. If one part of an object can occlude another part of that object (e.g., in the way that you cannot

see the backs of most objects when you are looking at their fronts), then the mathematics that form the foundation of the Ullman and Basri model become undefined (i.e., the system breaks, resulting in a runtime error if you happen to be running the model on a computer). Bent paperclips have the desirable property that all their features (i.e., the places where they bend) are visible in (virtually) all possible views. In other words, bent paperclips were chosen as stimuli because they are the only kind of stimulus most view-based models of the time were capable of recognizing. They are a "good" choice of experimental materials to the extent that they are representative of other objects in our visual world. Rather than passing judgment myself, I invite the reader to list as many objects as he or she can that, like bent paperclips, have all their features visible in all views.

## References

Arguin, M., & Saumier, D. (2005). Independent processing of parts and of their spatial organisation in complex visual objects. *Psychological Science, 15*, 629–633.

Baker, C., Behrmann, M., & Olson, C. (2002). Influence of visual discrimination training on the representation of parts and wholes in monkey inferotemporal cortex. *Nature Neuroscience, 5*, 1210–1216.

Biederman, I. (1987). Recognition-by-components: A theory of human image understanding. *Psychological Review, 94*(2), 115–147.

Biederman, I., & Bar, M. (1999). One-shot viewpoint invariance in matching novel objects. *Vision Research, 39*, 2885–2899.

Biederman, I., & Bar, M. (2000). Views on views: Response to Hayward & Tarr (2000). *Vision Research, 40*, 3901–3905.

Biederman, I., & Cooper, E. E. (1991a). Evidence for complete translational and reflectional invariance in visual object priming. *Perception, 20*, 585–593.

Biederman, I., & Cooper, E. E. (1991b). Priming contour deleted images: Evidence for intermediate representations in visual object recognition. *Cognitive Psychology, 23*, 393–419.

Biederman, I., & Cooper, E. E. (1992). Size invariance in visual object priming. *Journal of Experimental Psychology: Human Perception and Performance, 18*, 121–133.

Biederman, I., & Gerhardstein, P. C. (1993). Recognizing depth-rotated objects: Evidence and conditions for 3D viewpoint invariance. *Journal of Experimental Psychology: Human Perception and Performance, 19*, 1162–1182.

Biederman, I., & Gerhardstein, P. C. (1995). Viewpoint-dependent mechanisms in visual object recognition: A reply to Tarr & Bülthoff (1995). *Journal of Experimental Psychology: Human Perception and Performance, 21*, 1506–1514.

Biederman, I., & Ju, G. (1988). Surface versus edge-based determinants of visual recognition. *Cognitive Psychology, 20*, 38–64.

Biederman, I., & Subramaniam, S. (1997). Predicting the shape similarity of objects without distinguishing viewpoint invariant properties (VIPs) or parts. *Investigative Ophthalmology and Visual Science, 38*, 998.

Clowes, M. B. (1967). Perception, picture processing and computers. In N. L. Collins & D. Michie (Eds.), *Machine intelligence* (Vol. 1, pp. 181–197). Edinburgh, Scotland: Oliver & Boyd.

Cooper, E. E., & Wojan, T. J. (2000). Differences in the coding of spatial relations in face identification and basic-level object recognition. *Journal of Experimental Psychology: Learning, Memory, and Cognition, 26*, 470–488.

Dickinson, S. J., Pentland, A. P., & Rosenfeld, A. (1992). 3-D shape recovery using distributed aspect matching. *IEEE Transactions on Pattern Analysis and Machine Intelligence, 14*, 174–198.

Edelman, S., & Bülthoff, H. H. (1991). Orientation invariance in the recognition of familiar and novel views of 3-D objects. Unpublished manuscript, Weizmann Institute.

Edelman, S., & Intrator, N. (2003). Towards structural systematicity in distributed, statically bound visual representations. *Cognitive Science, 27*, 73–109.

Garner, W. R. (1974). *The processing of information and structure.* Hillsdale, NJ: Erlbaum.

Goodale, M. A., Milner, D. A., Jakobson, L. S., & Carey, D. P. (1991). A neurological dissociation between perceiving objects and grasping them. *Nature, 349*, 154–156.

Hayworth, K., & Biederman, I. (2006). Neural evidence for intermediate representations in object recognition, *Vision Research, 46*, 4024–4031.

Holyoak, K. J., & Thagard, P. (1995). *Mental leaps: Analogy in creative thought.* Cambridge, MA: MIT Press.

Hummel, J. E. (1994). Reference frames and relations in computational models of object recognition. *Current Directions in Psychological Science, 3*, 111–116.

Hummel, J. E. (2000). Where view-based theories break down: The role of structure in shape perception and object recognition. In E. Dietrich & A. Markman (Eds.), *Cognitive dynamics: Conceptual change in humans and machines* (pp. 157–185). Mahwah, NJ: Erlbaum.

Hummel, J. E. (2001). Complementary solutions to the binding problem in vision: Implications for shape perception and object recognition. *Visual Cognition, 8*, 489–517.

Hummel, J. E. (2003a). Effective systematicity in, effective systematicity out: A reply to Edelman & Intrator (2003). *Cognitive Science, 27*, 327–329.

Hummel, J. E. (2003b). The complementary properties of holistic and analytic representations of object shape. In G. Rhodes & M. Peterson (Eds.), *Perception of faces, objects, and scenes: Analytic and holistic processes* (pp. 212–234). Westport, CT: Greenwood.

Hummel, J. E., & Biederman, I. (1992). Dynamic binding in a neural network for shape recognition. *Psychological Review, 99*, 480–517.

Hummel, J. E., & Holyoak, K. J. (1997). Distributed representations of structure: A theory of analogical access and mapping. *Psychological Review, 104*, 427–466.

Hummel, J. E., & Holyoak, K. J. (2003). A symbolic-connectionist theory of relational inference and generalization. *Psychological Review, 110*, 220–264.

Hummel, J. E., & Stankiewicz, B. J. (1996a). An architecture for rapid, hierarchical structural description. In T. Inui & J. McClelland (Eds.), *Attention and performance XVI: Information integration in perception and communication* (pp. 93–121). Cambridge, MA: MIT Press.

Hummel, J. E., & Stankiewicz, B. J. (1996b). Categorical relations in shape perception. *Spatial Vision, 10*, 201–236.

Hummel, J. E., & Stankiewicz, B. J. (1998). Two roles for attention in shape perception: A structural description model of visual scrutiny. *Visual Cognition, 5,* 49–79.

Kayaert, G., Biederman, I., Op De Beeck, H., & Vogels, R. (2005). Tuning for shape dimensions in macaque inferior temporal cortex. *European Journal of Neuroscience, 22,* 212–224.

Kayaert, G., Biederman, I., & Vogels, R. (2003). Shape tuning in macaque inferior temporal cortex. *Journal of Neuroscience, 23,* 3016–3027.

Kayaert, G., Biederman, I., & Vogels, R. (2005). Representation of regular and irregular shapes in macaque inferotemporal cortex. *Cerebral Cortex, 15,* 1308–1321.

Kobatake, E., & Tanaka, K. (1994). Neuronal selection to complex object features in the ventral visual pathway of the macaque visual cortex. *Journal of Neuroscience, 71,* 856–867.

Köhler, W. (1940). *Dynamics in psychology.* New York: Liveright.

Leek, E. C., Reppa, I., & Arguin, M. (2005). The structure of 3D object shape representations: Evidence from whole-part matching. *Journal of Experimental Psychology: Human Perception and Performance, 31,* 668–684.

Liu, Z., Knill, D. C., & Kersten, D. (1995). Object classification for human and ideal observers. *Vision Research, 35,* 549–568.

Logothetis, N. K., Pauls, J., Bülthoff, H. H., & Poggio, T. (1994). View-dependent object representation by monkeys. *Current Biology, 4,* 401–414.

Lowe, D. G. (1987). The viewpoint consistency constraint. *International Journal of Computer Vision, 1,* 57–72.

Mapelli, D., & Behrmann, M. (1997). The role of color in object recognition: Evidence from visual agnosia. *NeuroCase, 3,* 237–247.

Marr, D. (1982). *Vision.* San Francisco: Freeman.

Marr, D., & Nishihara, H. K. (1978). Representation and recognition of three dimensional shapes. *Proceedings of the Royal Society of London, Series B, 200,* 269–294.

Olshausen, B. A., Anderson, C. H., & Van Essen, D. C. (1993). A neurobiological model of visual attention and invariant pattern recognition based on dynamic routing of information. *Journal of Neuroscience, 13,* 4700–4719.

Op de Beeck, H., Beatse, E., Wagemans, J., Sunaert, S., & Van Hecke P. (2000). The representation of shape in the context of visual object categorization tasks. *Neuroimage, 12,* 28–40.

Palmer, S. E. (1978). Fundamental aspects of cognitive representation. In E. Rosch & B. B. Lloyd (Eds.), *Cognition and categorization* (pp. 259–303). Hillsdale, NJ: Erlbaum.

Palmer, S. E. (1999). *Vision science: Photons to phenomenology.* Cambridge, MA: MIT Press.

Penn, D. C., Holyoak, K. J., & Povinelli, D. J. (2008). Darwin's mistake: Explaining the discontinuity between human and non-human minds. *Behavioral and Brain Sciences, 31,* 109–178.

Poggio, T., & Edelman, S. (1990). A neural network that learns to recognize three-dimensional objects. *Nature, 343,* 263–266.

Poggio, T., & Girosi, F. (1990). Regularization algorithms that are equivalent to multilayer networks. *Science, 277,* 978–982.

Rhodes, G., & Peterson, M. (2003). *Perception of faces, objects, and scenes: Analytic and holistic processe.* Westport, CT: Greenwood.

Riesenhuber, M., & Poggio, T. (1999). Hierarchical models of object recognition in cortex. *Nature Neuroscience, 11,* 1019–1025.

Rossion, B., & Pourtois, G. (2004). Revisiting Snodgrass and Vanderwart's object pictorial set: The role of surface detail in basic-level object recognition. *Perception, 33,* 217–236.

Saiki, J., & Hummel, J. E. (1996). Attribute conjunctions and the part configuration advantage in object category learning. *Journal of Experimental Psychology: Learning, Memory, and Cognition, 22,* 1002–1019.

Saiki, J. & Hummel, J. E. (1998). Connectedness and the integration of parts with relations in shape perception. *Journal of Experimental Psychology: Human Perception and Performance, 24,* 227–251.

Stankiewicz, B. J. (2002). Empirical evidence for independent dimensions in the visual representation of three-dimensional shape. *Journal of Experimental Psychology: Human Perception and Performance, 28*(4), 913–932.

Stankiewicz, B. J., & Hummel, J. E. (2002). The role of attention in scale- and translation-invariant object recognition. *Visual Cognition, 9,* 719–739.

Stankiewicz, B. J., Hummel, J. E., & Cooper, E. E. (1998). The role of attention in priming for left-right reflections of object images: Evidence for a dual representation of object shape. *Journal of Experimental Psychology: Human Perception and Performance, 24,* 732–744.

Sutherland, N. S. (1968). Outlines of a theory of visual pattern recognition in animals and man. *Proceedings of the Royal Society of London, Series B, 171,* 95–103.

Tanaka, K. (1993). Neuronal mechanisms of object recognition. *Science, 262,* 685–688.

Tarr, M. J., & Bülthoff, H. H. (1995). Is human object recognition better described by geon structural descriptions or by multiple views? Comment on Biederman and Gerhardstein (1993). *Journal of Experimental Psychology: Human Perception and Performance, 21,* 1494–1505.

Tarr, M. J., Bülthoff, H. H., Zabinski, M., & Blanz, V. (1997). To what extent do unique parts influence recognition across viewpoint? *Psychological Science, 8,* 282–289.

Tarr, M. J. & Pinker, S. (1989). Mental rotation and orientation dependence in shape recognition. *Cognitive Psychology, 21,* 233–283.

Tarr, M. J., & Pinker, S. (1990). When does human object recognition use a viewer-centered reference frame? *Psychological Science, 1*(4), 253–256.

Tarr, M. J., Williams, P., Hayward, W. G., & Gauthier, I. (1998). Three-dimensional object recognition is viewpoint dependent. *Nature Neuroscience, 1,* 275–277.

Thoma, V., Davidoff, J., & Hummel, J. E. (2007). Priming of plane-rotated objects depends on attention and view familiarity. *Visual Cognition, 15,* 179–210.

Thoma, V., Hummel, J. E., & Davidoff, J. (2004). Evidence for holistic representations of ignored images and analytic representations of attended images. *Journal of Experimental Psychology: Human Perception and Performance, 30,* 257–267.

Tipper, S. P. (1985). The negative priming effect: Inhibitory effects of ignored primes. *Quarterly Journal of Experimental Psychology, 37A,* 571–590.

Tovee, M. J., Rolls, E. T., Treves, A., & Bellis, R. P. (1993). Information encoding and the responses of individual neurons in the primate temporal visual cortex. *Journal of Neurophysiology, 70,* 640–654.

Treisman, A., & DeSchepper, B. (1996). Object tokens, attention, and visual memory. In T. Inui & J. McClelland (Eds.), *Attention and performance XVI: Information integration in perception and communication* (pp. 15–46). Cambridge, MA: MIT Press.

Treisman, A., & Gelade, G. (1980). A feature integration theory of attention. *Cognitive Psychology, 12*, 97–136.

Treisman, A. M., & Schmidt, H. (1982). Illusory conjunctions in the perception of objects. *Cognitive Psychology, 14*, 107–141.

Ullman, S. (1989). Aligning pictorial descriptions: An approach to object recognition. *Cognition, 32*, 193–254.

Ullman, S., & Basri, R. (1991). Recognition by linear combination of models. *IEEE Transactions on Pattern Analysis and Machine Intelligence, 13*, 992–1006.

Vogels, R., Biederman, I., Bar, M., & Lorincz, A. (2001). Inferior temporal neurons show greater sensitivity to non-accidental than metric differences. *Journal of Cognitive Neuroscience, 134*, 444–453.

Wertheimer, M. (1924/1950). Gestalt theory. In W. D. Ellis (Ed.), *A sourcebook of Gestalt psychology* (pp. 1–11). New York: The Humanities Press.

# Face Recognition

Gillian Rhodes

**Abstract**

People have an impressive ability to discriminate and recognize thousands of faces despite their similarity as visual patterns. In this chapter I ask how this is possible, focusing on how faces are mentally represented and whether specialized mechanisms contribute. I consider why unfamiliar faces can be surprisingly difficult to recognize, and why unfamiliar other-race faces can be even more difficult to recognize. I examine the mounting evidence for individual differences in face recognition ability and how these might help us understand face expertise. I ask why newborns have a visual bias for faces, how this bias interacts with early experience, whether there are sensitive periods for acquiring face expertise, and why face recognition performance does not reach adult levels until adolescence. I briefly consider the neural basis of face recognition, although readers are directed elsewhere for a comprehensive treatment of neural mechanisms. Finally, I offer some suggestions for future research directions.

**Key Words:** face recognition, face perception, holistic coding, configural coding, norm-based coding, other-race effect, development of face expertise

As a cognitive psychologist, I have always been struck by how good we are at discriminating and recognizing faces considering their similarity as visual patterns. All faces share a common first-order configuration of features, with a horizontal pair of eyes located above a nose, above a mouth, all inside an oval head outline (from a two-dimensional perspective, or on the front of the head, from a three-dimensional perspective). To make matters worse, the same face also projects numerous different retinal images, due to internal facial movements and changes in viewing perspective and illumination. Despite all this, we can discriminate many thousands of faces and can readily recognize or identify familiar faces, sometimes even after many years absence (Bahrick, Bahrick, & Wittlinger, 1975). I am impressed. Those who study eyewitness memory, however, are often less impressed, because people certainly make mistakes, particularly with unfamiliar faces (Burton & Jenkins, 2011).

There has been enormous growth in face recognition research over the last 40 years, and face recognition is now a major topic in cognitive psychology and cognitive neuroscience (Calder, Rhodes, Johnston, & Haxby, 2011). Why has face recognition generated so much interest? One reason is that person identification, which is central to human social interaction, is generally done using the face. Another is surely intellectual curiosity about how face recognition is possible given the difficult computational problems that must be solved. Another is the intriguing possibility, suggested by selective impairments in face recognition following brain damage (Farah, 1996), that we have specialized computational and neural mechanisms for face processing. Another is the possibility that some of these mechanisms may be innate, suggested by a visual bias for faces in newborns (Johnson & Morton, 1991).

In addition, cognitive and neural models of face processing (Bruce & Young, 1986; Haxby, Hoffman, & Gobbini, 2000) have helped organize knowledge (for example, by suggesting some separation of mechanisms for processing different aspects of faces, such as identity and expression) and generate research questions. Furthermore, advances in cognitive neuroscience methods (see *The Oxford Handbook of Cognitive Neuroscience*) and computer-graphic methods for manipulating realistic face images (for a review, see Vetter & Walker, 2011) have provided powerful new tools for addressing those questions. Controversies have also stimulated research: Are there specialized cognitive and neural mechanisms for face recognition, perhaps with innate origins, or are these mechanisms also used in other domains of perceptual expertise? Is the early interest of neonates in faces best understood in terms of specialized, innate face processing mechanisms or more general properties of the visual system? Does face recognition improve during childhood, because of maturation in face-selective coding mechanisms or in more general cognitive abilities, such as attention or executive functions? Are we poorer at recognizing other-race than own-race faces because of reduced perceptual expertise with such faces or reduced social motivation to individuate outgroup faces?

In this chapter, we will see how the evidence stacks up on some of these issues. In the first section, I ask how faces are represented, whether specialized coding mechanisms are used, and how the coding and recognition of familiar and unfamiliar faces might differ. In the second section, I review the well-known other-race effect (ORE), where other-race faces are recognized more poorly than own-race faces, and ask what factors contribute to it. This topic is interesting, not only for its applied significance but also because it can help us understand the nature of face expertise. In the third section, I examine individual differences in face recognition ability. Although not a traditional focus of cognitive psychology, individual differences may help reveal the basis of face expertise. In the fourth section, I consider the development of face recognition, which begins with a visual bias for faces at birth and follows a protracted course of development until adult levels are reached in adolescence. Finally, I outline current ideas about the neural basis of face recognition, although a comprehensive review of neural mechanisms is beyond the scope of this chapter (for reviews, see Calder et al., 2011).

## Representing Faces

To recognize a face, we must mentally represent those aspects of the face that distinguish it from other faces. Understanding how we do this is therefore fundamental to understanding face recognition, broadly construed to encompass discrimination and recognition of unfamiliar faces and identification of familiar faces. In this section, I will consider how faces are mentally represented. First, I will consider evidence that faces are coded holistically and ask whether this form of coding is specialized for faces. Second, I will consider evidence that faces are coded in relation to a norm or prototype that represents the central tendency (typical characteristics) of our visual diet of faces.

### *Holistic Coding*

Unlike many other visual objects, faces can seldom be recognized from diagnostic parts or the first-order arrangement of their parts. Instead, successful recognition entails sensitivity to more subtle second-order spatial relations. These are variations in the fixed first-order face configuration, such as spatial relations between internal features or between those features and the face outline (in two dimensions) or the rest of the head (in three dimensions) (Diamond & Carey, 1986). More generally, face recognition seems to entail integration of information across the face (for reviews, see Farah, Wilson, Drain, & Tanaka, 1998; Maurer, Le Grand, & Mondloch, 2002; McKone, Kanwisher, & Duchaine, 2007; McKone & Robbins, 2011; Peterson & Rhodes, 2003). Face representations have been characterized as "undifferentiated wholes" (e.g., Farah et al., 1998), which result from "glueing the features together into a gestalt" (Maurer et al., 2002, p. 255) with "simultaneous integration of the multiple features of a face into a single perceptual representation" (Rossion, 2008, p. 275).

A variety of terms have been used to characterize the kind of coding that seems to be important for face recognition: "holistic," "configural," "(second-order) relational," "coarse," and "global." Although these may differ in their precise meanings and/or operational definitions (for reviews, see Farah et al., 1998; Peterson & Rhodes, 2003), they share a focus on the overall structure of the face, in contrast with the coding of more local, feature-based information (variously referred to as "local," "piecemeal," "part-based," "componential," "fine-grained," or "analytic"). Unfortunately, not everyone uses the same terminology. For example, "configural" processing has been used variously as

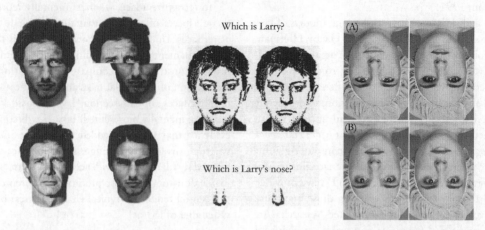

A. Composite effect    B. Wholes advantage    C. Inversion effect

Which is Larry?

Which is Larry's nose?

**Figure 4.1** (*A*) Composites effect: Pairing the top half of one face with the bottom half of another makes it harder to recognize the top face (top left), relative to a misaligned condition (top right) (Young et al., 1987). The faces used to make the composites are shown below. (*B*) Wholes-advantage: After seeing Larry, it is easier to recognize Larry's nose in the context of the whole face than in isolation (Tanaka & Farah, 1993). (*C*) Inversion effect: Inversion disrupts face perception, particularly sensitivity to spatial relations (row B faces differ in eye spacing). Sensitivity to feature appearance (row A faces have different eyes) is often less affected (but not always—for a review, see McKone & Yovel, 2009). Turning the faces up the right way makes it easier to see both differences, but especially the spacing difference. (Fig. 4.1C was adapted by permission from Macmillan Publishers Ltd: *Nature*. Le Grand, Mondloch, Maurer & Brent, copyright 2001.)

an umbrella term encompassing coding of first-order relations, second-order relations, and holistic processing (e.g., Maurer et al., 2002), an umbrella term encompassing holistic integration and coding of second-order relations (e.g., McKone, 2008), and a specific term referring to coding of second-order relations (e.g., Leder & Carbon, 2006; Rhodes, 1988; Rhodes, Hayward, & Winkler, 2006). Others have used the term "holistic" to encompass holistic integration across the face, including difficulty selectively attending to parts, and coding of second-order relations (McKone & Robbins, 2011; McKone, Kanwishwer, & Duchaine, 2007; Rossion, 2008; Tanaka & Gordon, 2011). I will follow that usage here.

Evidence that faces are coded holistically comes from three sources: the composite effect, the wholes-advantage, and the disproportionate inversion effect for faces (Fig. 4.1). The face composite effect was first demonstrated by Young and colleagues (1987). They mixed and matched top and bottom halves of different faces and found that participants were slower to identify the top halves in these composite faces than in misaligned noncomposites (which violate the first-order face configuration) (Fig. 4.1A). These results suggest that faces are perceived holistically, making identification of parts difficult. This composite effect is extremely robust, and variants of the task are now widely used

to assess holistic coding (despite some controversy over the best design—see Gauthier & Bukach, 2007; McKone & Robbins, 2007).

The part-whole effect provides additional evidence for holistic coding of faces (Tanaka & Farah, 1993). After studying a set of faces, participants find it harder to identify parts (eyes, nose, or mouth) presented in isolation ("Which is Larry's nose?") than in the context of the whole face ("Which is Larry?"—only the nose differed in the two test faces) (Fig. 4.1B). There is no such wholes advantage for scrambled study faces. Like the composite effect, the wholes-advantage is robust and variants of the parts-wholes task are widely used to measure holistic processing of faces.

A third, and less direct, line of evidence for holistic coding of faces comes from inversion effects (Fig. 4.1C). Yin (1969) observed that recognition of faces (photographs or drawings) was more disrupted by inversion in the picture plane (turning the images upside-down) than recognition of several other kinds of mono-oriented objects (photographs of houses, silhouettes of airplanes, and stick figures of men in motion). He attributed the *disproportionate* inversion effect to a "special factor related only to faces" and suggested that this might be related to the ability to "get a general impression of the whole picture" (p. 145), which participants reported being unable to do for inverted faces. Yin's (1969) hugely influential paper (cited over 700 times at last count) has stood the test of time, with two recent reviews concluding that loss of holistic processing explains the disproportionate effect of inversion on face recognition (McKone & Yovel, 2009; Rossion, 2008). This conclusion rests on several lines of evidence: (1) both the composite effect and wholes-advantage, described earlier, are lost with inversion, (2) inversion effects are large for second-order relational changes, and (3) inversion effects are large for feature-shape changes so long as the features are seen in the context of the face (for a review, see McKone & Yovel, 2009).

The idea that upright and inverted faces are coded in a qualitatively differently way has not gone unchallenged, with some studies reporting little difference in the processing of upright and inverted faces (Riesenhuber, Jarudi, Gilad, & Sinha, 2004; Sekuler, Gaspar, Gold, & Bennett, 2004). However, in some cases the tasks used seem unlikely to engage face processing mechanisms. For example, a few faces, obscured by visual noise and with local diagnostic features, may be presented thousands of times (Sekuler et al., 2004). Such stimuli may not engage face processing mechanisms, just as a word repeated endlessly no longer engages word-processing mechanisms (for a detailed critique, see Rossion, 2008).

So the evidence strongly suggests that faces are coded holistically and perhaps without explicit representation of isolated features. However, we should not take this conclusion to mean that features are not important for face recognition. Clearly they are. Altering internal features can have dramatic effects on appearance (e.g., Searcy & Bartlett, 1996; Thompson, 1980; Talati, Rhodes, & Jeffery, 2010) and adding features like facial hair and glasses is a classic form of disguise, at least for unfamiliar faces. The appearance of internal features, particularly the eyes, is important for recognition (Gilad, Meng, & Sinha, 2009; for a review see Bruce, 1988) and changing these features can alter the perceived identity of a face (Rotshtein, Geng, Driver, & Dolan, 2007). Furthermore, several lines of evidence indicate that features are integrated into holistic representations of faces. First, changing features within the context of the face can produce large inversion decrements (McKone & Yovel, 2009; Rossion, 2008). Second, old/new recognition of features is disrupted if spatial relations in some irrelevant part of the face are altered (Tanaka & Sengco, 1997). Third, discrimination of spacing and feature changes is correlated for upright, but not inverted, faces (Yovel & Kanwisher, 2008). These findings strongly suggest that features are integrated into holistic representations of upright faces and take us beyond the classic distinction between features and spatial relations between features that has driven so much research about what makes faces special (e.g., Peterson & Rhodes, 2003).

So we can conclude that (upright) faces are coded holistically. But does such coding actually help us recognize faces? Several lines of evidence suggest that it might. First, composite and part-whole effects are greatly reduced or absent for inverted faces, which are poorly recognized (see earlier). Second, both of these effects, and also inversion effects, are often reduced for other-race faces, which are recognized more poorly than own-race faces (Hancock & Rhodes, 2008; Hayward, Rhodes, & Schwaninger, 2008; Michel, Caldara, & Rossion, 2006; Michel, Corneille, & Rossion, 2007; Michel, Rossion, Han, Chung, & Caldara, 2006; Rhodes et al., 2006; Rhodes, Tan et al., 1989; Rhodes, Evangelista et al., 2009; Tanaka, Keifer, & Bukach, 2004; but see also Mondloch et al., 2010). Third, holistic coding is reduced in individuals with acquired prosopagnosia, who have difficulty recognizing faces following focal brain damage (e.g., Barton, Press, Keenan, & O'Connor, 2002; Barton, Zhao, & Keenan, 2003). It is also reduced in some (but not all) individuals with developmental prosopagnosia (Le Grand et al., 2006), and spacing discrimination training can improve face their identification (De Gutis, Bentin, Robertson, & D'Esposito, 2007). Fourth, holistic processing is strongest for face sizes corresponding to viewing distances that are functionally relevant for identification during approach in the environment (McKone, 2009). Taken together, these results suggest that holistic processing may help us recognize faces.

At an individual differences level the results are less clear. Although there are substantial individual differences in both face recognition ability and holistic processing of faces (Wilmer et al., 2010; Zhu et al., 2010), evidence that these are correlated is mixed. On the positive side, greater use of feature spacing information to discriminate faces is associated with better recognition performance (Rotshtein et al., 2007), "super-recognizers" who excel at face recognition have larger face inversion effects than controls (Russell, Duchaine, & Nakayama, 2009) and cross-race differences in holistic coding sometimes correlate with the size of the other-race effect in recognition (Hancock & Rhodes, 2008, but see Michel, Caldera, & Rossion, 2006; Michel,

Rossion et al., 2006). Degree of holistic coding measured using the either the composite effect or the part-whole effect is also correlated with face recognition performance (Richler, Cheung & Gauthier, 2011; Wang, et al., 2012). On the negative side, two other studies failed to find any correlation between face identification performance and degree of holistic coding, measured either by the composite effect (Konar, Bennett, & Sekuler, 2010) or by sensitivity to spacing of facial features (Mondloch & Desjarlais, 2010). However, in both cases identification was tested using matching tasks with little or no memory demands and in one case (Konar et al., 2010) hair cues were available.

There has been considerable controversy over whether holistic coding is a hallmark of face processing or of perceptual expertise more generally (e.g., Gauthier & Tarr, 2002; Gauthier, Williams, Tarr, & Tanaka, 1998; McKone et al., 2007). Early support for the "expertise hypothesis" came from evidence that inversion decrements for recognizing profile views of individual dogs were as large as those for recognizing faces, but only when participants were experts with the particular breeds used (Diamond & Carey, 1986, but see Robbins & McKone, 2007 for a recent failure to replicate). Early theorists were also struck by the large and ubiquitous effects of inversion on form perception generally, rather than any specificity for faces (Rock, 1973). Certainly, inverted handwriting, printed words, and maps all seemed difficult to read. Although more formal testing with such stimuli is needed to remove any doubt, it seems unlikely that large inversion effects are unique to faces. Nor is the wholes-advantage restricted to faces (e.g., Gauthier & Tarr, 1997, 2002; Tanaka & Farah, 2003).

In contrast, the classic composite effect (poorer identification or matching of top halves in aligned than misaligned composites with a different bottom half) may be restricted to (upright) faces (McKone & Robbins, 2011; Robbins & McKone, 2007). A possibly related congruency effect, of better performance when relevant and irrelevant halves both suggest the same response, has been reported for non-face objects (Richler, Bukach, & Gauthier, 2009; Wong, Palmeri, & Gauthier, 2009). However, it is not clear that such an effect reflects holistic *perception*.

Nor do these effects appear to be hallmarks of expert processing generally. Although these effects are sometimes found for classes of objects with which participants have expertise, they do not seem to be consistently associated with expertise, even when individuation is required. Expertise does not guarantee inversion effects as large as those seen for faces, and inversion effects do not consistently increase with expertise (for a detailed review, see McKone & Robbins, 2011). The wholes advantage is not restricted to objects of expertise (e.g., Gauthier & Tarr, 1997, 2002) and does not increase consistently with expertise (see McKone & Robbins, 2011). Composite effects are rare for objects of expertise (see McKone & Robbins, 2011) and can be larger for novices than experts in the case of Chinese character recognition (Hsiao & Cottrell, 2009). It seems, therefore, that holistic coding is not a hallmark of expert coding generally.

In summary, the evidence suggests that faces are coded holistically. Such coding may help us recognize faces, although more research is needed to determine whether individual differences in face recognition ability are related to individual variation in holistic coding of faces. In addition, holistic processing appears to be a hallmark of face processing rather than expert processing more generally. That said, however, holistic processing is certainly not unique to faces, a finding that should come as no surprise given the ubiquity of spatial context effects in vision (Schwartz, Hsu, & Dayan, 2007). These context effects can be seen in the many visual illusions where perception of one part of an array is influenced by other parts (e.g., tilt illusion, Muller-Lyer illusion).

### Norm-Based Coding of Faces

Holistic coding may be important for face expertise, but to recognize a face we need to know how that face differs from other faces. In this section, we consider how this distinctive information is coded. An elegant solution, proposed by many theorists, is to code faces relative to a perceptual norm or prototype that represents the central tendency of the faces we experience (Diamond & Carey, 1986; Goldstein & Chance, 1980; Hebb, 1949; Hochberg, 1978; Leopold, O'Toole, Vetter, & Blanz, 2001; Rhodes, 1996; Rhodes, Brennan, & Carey, 1987; Valentine, 1991). This form of coding, called norm-based coding, may allow the visual system to see past the shared structure common to all faces, to focus on what is distinctive about each face. In this section, I will consider the evidence for norm-based coding of faces.

In this context it is useful to think of faces as points or vectors in a multidimensional face space, whose dimensions correspond to whatever information is used to represent and recognize faces (Valentine, 1991) (Fig. 4.2). An average face lies at the center, and distance in the space corresponds to perceptual

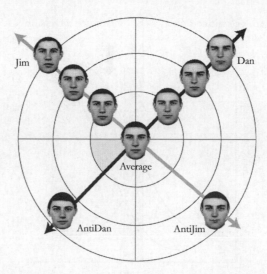

**Figure 4.2** A simple two-dimensional face-space with two faces, Dan and Jim, and an Average face, created by morphing 20 male, Caucasian faces, at the center. For each face we can construct a corresponding anti-face (antiDan and antiJim, also shown), with opposite properties, by morphing the original face toward the Average and beyond. Reduced identity strength versions (anticaricatures) of Dan and Jim, created by morphing those identities toward the Average, are also shown. Identity aftereffects occur when exposure to a face biases subsequent perception toward a face with opposite properties. For example, after viewing antiDan for a few seconds, we are biased (briefly) to see Dan. This identity aftereffect is measured as the reduction in identity strength needed to successfully identify a face (e.g., Dan) after viewing its opposite (antiDan).

dissimilarity, with similar faces lying closer together than less similar faces. Distinctiveness, or identity strength, generally increases with distance from the average, so that caricatures, which exaggerate distinctive information, lie further from the average than the original faces, and anticaricatures, which reduce that information, lie closer to the average.

Several lines of evidence suggest that the average face plays a functional role in coding faces. First, people seem to spontaneously abstract averages or prototypes from sets of seen faces (Bruce, Doyle, Dench, & Burton, 1991; Cabeza, Bruce, Kato, & Oda, 1999; De Haan, Johnson, Maurer, & Perrett, 2001; Inn, Walden, & Solso, 1993; MacLin & Webster, 2001; Reed, 1972; Rhodes, Jeffery, Clifford, & Leopold, 2003; Rhodes et al., 2004; Solso & McCarthy, 1981a,b; Strauss, 1979; Walton & Bower, 1993; Webster & MacLin, 1999). Second, distance from the average matters for recognition, with distinctive faces recognized better than typical faces (Valentine, 1991) and caricatures sometimes recognized better than the original faces (Benson & Perrett, 1994; Byatt & Rhodes, 2004; Lee, Byatt, & Rhodes, 2000; Rhodes, 1996; Rhodes et al., 1987).

Although suggestive, these findings could potentially be accommodated in exemplar-only recognition models in which performance depends only on proximity to stored exemplars (cf., Nosofsky

& Johansen, 2000). More compelling evidence for norm-based coding comes from face identity aftereffects, in which experience-induced changes to the average or norm affect our perception of faces (Anderson & Wilson, 2005; Leopold et al., 2001; Leopold, Rhodes, Müller, & Jeffery, 2005; Rhodes & Jeffery, 2006; Rhodes, Jeffery, Clifford, & Leopold, 2007; Rhodes & Leopold, 2011; Tsao & Freiwald, 2006). After viewing a face for a few seconds, we are biased to see the "opposite" identity, that is, a face with opposite properties (see Fig. 4.2) (Leopold et al., 2001, 2005; Rhodes & Jeffery, 2006; Rhodes et al., 2007). These aftereffects cannot be explained simply by adaptation to low-level image features, because they survive changes in the size and retinal position between adapt and test faces (see Rhodes & Leopold, 2011, for a review), and they are larger for upright than inverted faces (Rhodes, Evangelista, & Jeffery, 2009). Rather, viewing a face seems to temporarily shift some higher level representation of the average (norm) toward that face, so that low identity strength versions of Dan become more distinctive and look more like Dan. The selectivity of the bias for the identity that lies opposite the adapting face in face-space strongly suggests that identity is coded relative to the average face.

A simple model of norm-based coding has been proposed, with pairs of neural populations that are tuned to above-average (e.g., large eyes) and

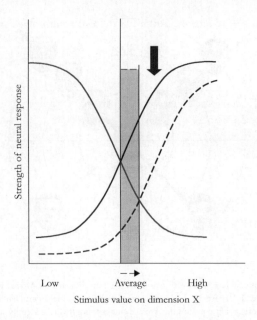

**Figure 4.3** A simple norm-based coding model in which each face dimension is coded by a pair of neural populations, one responding to below-average and the other to above-average values. Average values are coded implicitly, by equal (and low) activation of the two populations. Following adaptation to a face with a particular dimension value (large arrow), the relative contribution of the population that responds most strongly to that stimulus is diminished. As a result, the balance point (perceived average) shifts toward (small arrow, shaded area) the adapting value, biasing perception away from the adapting value.

below-average (e.g., small eyes) values, respectively, on each dimension (e.g., eye size) of face-space (Rhodes et al., 2005; Rhodes & Jeffery, 2006; Robbins & McKone, 2007; Susilo, McKone, & Edwards, 2010; Tsao & Freiwald, 2006) (Fig. 4.3). Such a model is computationally efficient because it focuses responses on distinctive information, which is what matters for recognition. It is neurally efficient because typical (common) faces produce lower responses than more distinctive faces (see low response to average face in Fig. 4.3), and it is consistent with neural responses to faces in humans (Loffler, Yourganov, Wilkinson, & Wilson, 2005) and monkeys (Leopold, Bondar, & Giese, 2006). Note that the model does not require any explicit representation of the norm, which is represented in the tuning functions of the neural populations, and signaled by equal (and low) activation in the two members of each pair (for details see Rhodes & Leopold, 2011). Therefore, it is not vulnerable to parsimony criticisms, which have been levelled at prototype models of concept representation (e.g., Nosofsky & Johansen, 2000).

We may also have different visual norms for different classes of faces, such as male and female faces, and faces of different races, because these can be selectively updated by experience. After viewing faces whose internal features have been

"expanded" from the center of the face (as if seen through a fish-eye lens), slightly expanded faces appear normal, whereas after viewing "contracted" faces, slightly contracted faces appear normal (e.g., Rhodes, Jeffery, Watson, Clifford, & Nakayama, 2003). If, however, one sees "expanded" male faces along with "contracted" female faces, or "expanded" Caucasian faces along with "contracted" Chinese faces, the most normal-looking configuration shifts in opposite directions for each class of faces (Bestelmeyer et al., 2008; Jaquet & Rhodes, 2008; Jaquet, Rhodes, & Hayward, 2007, 2008; Little, De Bruine, & Jones, 2005). If there was only a single underlying face norm, then it would be "pulled" in opposite directions by adapting to opposite distortions, resulting in no net aftereffect. Therefore, opposite aftereffects suggest that we maintain distinct norms for different kinds of faces. More generally, they suggest that faces of different races and sexes may form dissociable visual, as well as semantic, categories (for a review, see Rhodes & Jaquet, 2011).

Unlike holistic coding, norm-based coding is widely used in perception, where it may help us discriminate subtle differences in brightness, contrast, color, motion direction, shape, and other simple stimulus attributes (Bartlett, 2007; MacLeod & von der Twer, 2003; Mather, 1980; Regan &

Hamstra, 1992; Sutherland, 1961; Suzuki, 2005; Webster, 2003; Webster & Leonard, 2008). But does norm-based coding help us discriminate and recognize faces? Although the evidence is limited, there is support for a functional role from two sources. First, identity aftereffects are reduced in children with autism spectrum disorders (ASDs) (Pellicano, Jeffery, Burr, & Rhodes, 2007), who can have difficulty discriminating and recognizing faces (Behrmann et al., 2006; Behrmann, Thomas, & Humphreys, 2006; Blair, Frith, Smith, Abell, & Cipolotti, 2002; Boucher & Lewis, 1992; Dawson, Webb, & McPartland, 2005; Klin et al., 1999; Webb, Faja, & Dawson, 2011). Second, in typical adults a few minutes of adaptation to the average face of a particular race can facilitate identification of faces from that race relative to faces from an unadapted race (Rhodes, Watson, Jeffery, & Clifford, 2010). Nevertheless, the functional utility of norm-based coding, and of face adaptation more generally, remains poorly understood and is an important topic for future research.

### Faces in Three Dimensions

Much of the work described herein has approached face recognition as a problem of two-dimensional pattern recognition. However, three-dimensional information is clearly important for recognition (Hill & Bruce, 1993; 1996; O'Toole, Vetter, & Blanz, 1999). As with many other objects, shading provides cues to the three-dimensional shape of faces, which is useful information for recognition. The perception of shape from shading assumes (unconsciously) a single, overhead, light source (Ramachandran, 1988). This assumption contributes to two powerful face illusions. In the hollow-face illusion (Gregory, 1973), it makes a concave face mask illuminated from below appear convex (Hill & Bruce, 1993). It also contributes to the Thatcher illusion, where flipping the eyes and mouth upside-down in a face results in a grotesque appearance (Thompson, 1980). These locally bottom-lit features are now assumed to be top-lit, like the rest of the face, so they appear concave instead of convex, resulting in a sunken, ghoulish appearance (Talati et al., 2010).

Three-dimensional shape information provided by local contrast relations in the normal, upright eye region also appears to be important for face identification. It is well known that reversing the contrast relations in a face, as in a photographic negative, makes recognition difficult (Galper, 1970). However, restoring the correct contrast relations in the eye region alone greatly improves recognition (Gilad et al., 2009).

We can recognize faces from various views, including front-on and three-quarter views, although profiles are typically harder. Some have suggested that three-quarter views, which display information that is also visible in front and profile views (thus allowing good generalization across views), may be optimal for recognition (Baddeley & Woodhead, 1983). Findings vary and depend on numerous procedural factors (for recent reviews, see McKone, 2008; Van der Linde & Watson, 2010). Nevertheless, a recent comprehensive examination of viewpoint effects found that front views were best when study and test views matched, but that 30° views (the closest to a three-quarter view in their study) were best when study and test views differed, consistent with the idea that such views support good generalization (Van der Linde & Watson, 2010).

A central question in face perception (and object recognition more generally) is how we are able to recognize faces from different views, and more specifically whether this ability relies on view-specific or view-invariant representations. Studies examining transfer of face aftereffects across views have proved useful in addressing this question. These aftereffects are reduced when a change of view is introduced between adaptation and test faces, suggesting some view specificity (Benton, Jennings, & Chatting, 2006; Jeffery, Rhodes, & Busey, 2006; Jiang, Blanz, & O'Toole, 2006). However, they are not completely eliminated by a change of view, indicating some view invariance. Taken together, these results suggest that face representations contain both view-specific and view-invariant information.

As noted earlier, profiles are more difficult to recognize than front and three-quarter views. No doubt, limited experience with profiles contributes to this difficulty. Interestingly, however, there appears to be no reduction of holistic coding for profile views. Neither the composite effect nor the inversion effect is reduced for profile (or three-quarter) views (McKone, 2008). Moreover, profile recognition remains poor when normal holistic processing is disrupted (by misalignment in the composites task, inversion, or scrambling), suggesting that the difficulty lies in poor coding of unfamiliar parts or reduced availability of part information due to occlusion (McKone, 2008).

### Familiar Versus Unfamiliar Faces

Cognitive psychologists have generally emphasized our expertise in recognizing faces, which seems impressive given their similarity as visual patterns. However, we are far from perfect at recognizing unfamiliar faces, unless identical images are used (for a review, see Burton & Jenkins, 2011). For example, when shown high-quality photographs of faces and asked which of these people they had seen previously in poor-quality video sequences (showing people entering a building), participants did poorly unless they already knew these individuals (Burton, Wilson, Cowan, & Bruce, 1999). It can even be difficult to match one image of an unfamiliar person directly to another unless the images are identical (Bruce et al., 1999), and matching live unfamiliar people to their photographs is surprisingly difficult (Kemp, Towell, & Pike, 1997).

Recognition of unfamiliar faces is readily disrupted by superficial changes in expression, viewpoint, and lighting, which have little impact on recognition of familiar faces (e.g., Bruce, 1982; Bruce et al., 1999). In contrast with familiar faces, which are identified better from internal than external features, unfamiliar faces are identified equally well from internal and external features (Ellis, Shepherd, & Davies, 1979). Moreover, matching of familiar and unfamiliar faces is uncorrelated (despite good correlations between upright and inverted unfamiliar faces), suggesting qualitative differences in processing (Megreya & Burton, 2006). There appears to be greater reliance on two-dimensional, image-based, and pictorial cues for unfamiliar face recognition, presumably because it is difficult to abstract three-dimensional structure and identity-specific texture/color information about the facial surface from a single image that also contains effects of extrinsic factors like illumination and viewpoint (e.g., Hancock et al., 2000). As a face becomes more familiar and is seen under a variety of conditions, its representation should become more robust to changes in viewing conditions (Tong & Nakayama, 1999). Consistent with this proposal, information about three-dimensional facial structure in representations increases with familiarity (Jiang, Blanz, & O'Toole, 2007, 2009). An average representation may also be abstracted from multiple exposures, increasing the robustness of recognition to changes in viewing conditions (Burton & Jenkins, 2011).

Despite our rapid and apparently effortless encoding of faces, some attentional resources are required (for a review, see Palermo & Rhodes, 2007). Familiar faces, however, seem to require fewer attentional resources than unfamiliar faces. Famous faces survive the attentional blink (see Chapter 7) more readily than unfamiliar faces (Jackson & Raymond, 2006).

Extremely familiar faces, such as one's own face, are more easily detected in face arrays than unfamiliar faces (Tong & Nakayama, 1999). Working memory capacity is also larger for familiar than unfamiliar faces, suggesting more efficient coding (Jackson & Raymond, 2008). Therefore, converging evidence from a variety of paradigms suggests that familiarity reduces the attentional demand of face coding.

Jackson and Raymond (2008) suggested that stronger "within-item integration" of familiar faces might account for the greater capacity of working memory to deal with familiar faces. Thus, perhaps familiar faces are coded more holistically than unfamiliar faces. Consistent with this idea, Young et al. (1987) reported a slightly larger composite effect for familiar than unfamiliar faces, although no formal comparison was made. Moreover, both holistic coding and recognition of other-race faces can be increased to own-race levels by making the faces familiar, suggesting that familiarity at the level of a class of faces increases holistic coding (McKone, Kanwisher, & Duchaine, 2007). Note, however, that this does not always appear to be the case, because profile and front views seem to be coded equally holistically, although profile views are much less familiar (McKone, 2008). It remains to be seen whether individually familiar faces are coded more holistically than unfamiliar ones, and whether this contributes to the greater robustness and recognizability of familiar faces.

### The Other-Race Effect

I will use the term "race" to refer to a visually distinct social group with a common ethnicity. Poorer recognition of other-race than own-race faces is a robust effect that has been observed in field studies, simulated line-ups, and laboratory settings (for reviews and meta-analyses, see Hugenberg, Young, Bernstein & Sacco, 2010; Meissner & Brigham, 2001; Rossion & Michel, 2011; Sporer, 2001). The other-race effect (ORE) is not due simply to greater physical similarity of faces for some race than others, because it occurs for people from many races and full crossover interactions between race of participant and race of face are sometimes found (for reviews, see Brigham, Bennett, Meissner, & Mitchell, 2006; Meissner & Brigham, 2001). So what underlies the effect?

Many have proposed that the ORE is associated with reduced experience or contact with other-race faces (for a review, see Brigham et al., 2006). Consistent with this hypothesis, the ORE is sometimes reduced in populations with greater other-race experience (for reviews, see Brigham et al., 2006; Sporer, 2001). However, a large meta-analysis found that self-reported contact explained only 2% of variance in the size of the ORE (Meissner & Brigham, 2001). This small contribution could indicate a limited role for contact, although it might also reflect the intrinsically low reliability of OREs (Herzmann, Danther, Schact, Sommer, & Wilhelm, 2008; Meissner, Brigham, & Butz, 2005), which are difference scores with well-known psychometric problems (Edwards, 2001), and/or failure to assess quality, rather than simply quantity, of contact. Certainly, more recent evidence strongly implicates differential experience in the ORE. Importantly, the ORE emerges in infancy as a response to differential experience with own-race and other-race faces (Bar-Haim, Ziv, Lamy, & Hodes, 2006; Kelly et al., 2007). It can be reversed following cross-race adoption during childhood (Sangrigoli, Pallier, Argenti, Ventureyra, & de Schonen, 2005) and can be eliminated, at least temporarily in adults, by training on other-race faces (for a review, see McKone, Brewer, MacPherson, Rhodes, & Hayward, 2007). Finally, some studies have found links between the size of the ORE and a self-report measure of contact that assesses quality as well as quantity of other-race experience (Hancock & Rhodes, 2008; Rhodes, Ewing et al., 2009). So contact matters. However, this tells us little about the computational mechanisms involved in the ORE. Next we consider what those mechanisms might be.

## Perceptual Expertise

Several lines of evidence suggest that we have reduced perceptual expertise with other-race faces. People show reduced perceptual sensitivity to differences between other-race faces (Byatt & Rhodes, 2004; Mondloch et al., 2010; Rhodes et al., 2006; Walker & Hewstone, 2006; Walker & Tanaka, 2003) and reduced activation of neural face coding mechanisms by other-race faces (Golby, Gabrieli, Chiao, & Eberhardt, 2001). Several studies using Caucasian and Asian participants have also found less holistic coding of other-race faces (Michel, Caldera, & Rossion, 2006; Michel, Rossion et al., 2006; Rhodes et al., 1989; Tanaka, Kiefer, & Bukach, 2004). However, this difference is not always found and may be more robust for Caucasian than Asian individuals (for a recent discussion, see Mondloch et al., 2010).

These differences could reflect reduced perceptual learning opportunities for other-race faces, so that face-coding dimensions are better suited for

representing variation in own-race than other-race faces. As a result, mental representations of other-race faces would be less differentiated, and more difficult to remember, than own-race faces. Consistent with this proposal, Caucasian and Chinese participants discriminate and remember component and configural (spacing) information more poorly in other-race faces (Hayward et al., 2008; Mondloch et al., 2010). Similarly, reduced holistic coding of other-race faces, measured by the inversion decrement, significantly predicts cross-race recognition differences in Caucasian and Chinese participants (Hancock & Rhodes, 2008; but see Michel, Rossion et al., 2006). Furthermore, training White participants to attend to the lower part of faces, which contains useful information for discriminating Black faces, can eliminate their ORE for Black faces (Hills & Lewis, 2006). This result suggests that faces are spontaneously coded using dimensions that are better suited for recognizing own- than other-race faces. However, not all the evidence is readily explained in terms of differential perceptual expertise, as we will see in the next section.

## Socio-Cognitive Factors

People often display negative attitudes or prejudice to members of other races (e.g., Fazio, Jackson, Dunton, & Williams, 1995), which early theorists suggested might impair recognition of other-race faces (e.g., Brigham & Barkowitz, 1978; Caroo, 1987). However, there is little evidence that either explicit or implicit negative attitudes contribute to OREs (Ferguson, Rhodes, Lee, & Sriram, 2001; Meissner & Brigham, 2001). More recently, the opposite direction of causality has been proposed, whereby difficulty discriminating other-race faces might cause the negative attitudes (Lebrecht, Pierce, Tarr, & Tanaka, 2009). Consistent with this view, after Caucasian participants had received 5 days of individuation training on African American faces, they showed a significant correlation between the reduction in ORE and improvement of implicit attitudes to other-race faces. However, caution is needed in interpreting these results, because sample size was small (N = 10) and descriptive statistics were not presented. Moreover, one would also expect the size of ORE to correlate with attitudes, prior to training, but this correlation was not reported.

Other socio-cognitive factors, such as reduced motivation to individuate members of social outgroups and/or a tendency to treat outgroup members categorically have also been proposed to contribute to OREs (for reviews, see Bernstein, Young, &

Hugenberg, 2007; Hugenberg, Miller, & Claypool, 2007; Hugenberg et al., 2010; Levin, 1996, 2000; Shriver, Young, Hugenberg, Bernstein, & Lanter, 2008; Sporer, 2001). Such factors certainly affect face recognition, with ORE-like effects found for own-race faces that are categorized as belonging to a social outgroup (Bernstein et al., 2007; Shriver et al., 2008), and so might plausibly contribute to the ORE. If they do, then memory for other-race faces should improve when they are categorized as ingroup members, and it will be interesting to see whether this is the case.

Recognition of other-race faces can be improved by informing participants of the ORE and asking them to try to avoid it (Hugenberg et al., 2007; but see Tanaka & Pierce, 2009). Hugenberg et al. showed White US participants Black and White faces and instructed them to "pay close attention to what differentiates one particular face from another face of the same race, particularly when that faces is not of the same race as you" and to "pay close attention to the faces, especially when they are of a different race than you in order to try to avoid this Cross Race Effect" (p. 337; Hugenberg et al., 2007). These instructions reduced the ORE, indicating untapped capacity to individuate and remember other-race faces, consistent with reduced motivation to spontaneously individuate other-race faces. The participants in this study had considerable experience with, and opportunity to develop perceptual expertise for, other-race faces. It remains to be determined whether motivational instructions can also improve other-race recognition when other-race experience is more limited.

The effectiveness of motivational instructions in reducing the ORE might also indicate that other-race faces engage attentional resources less effectively than own-race faces, resources that are required for holistic coding (Palermo & Rhodes, 2002). There have, however, been reports that White US participants show attentional biases toward Black faces, which is not consistent with the idea that reduced attention to other-race faces contributes to OREs (Richeson & Trawalter, 2008; Trawalter, Todd, Baird, & Richeson, 2008). Nonetheless, these attentional effects are weak, easily eliminated by small changes in stimuli (no effect for averted gaze or happy expressions), may be restricted to extremely short exposure durations, and confined to participants with high external motivation to respond without prejudice, all of which suggest that they be unrelated to OREs in face recognition. More research is needed to clarify the role of attention in OREs.

An influential socio-cognitive hypothesis is that people spontaneously code race-specifying features at the expense of individuating information in other-race faces (Levin, 1996, 2000). Consistent with this hypothesis, Levin reported that White participants were faster to classify other-race (Black) than own-race faces by race (Levin, 1996), and that White participants who showed an ORE were faster to detect Black faces among White faces than vice versa (Levin, 1996, 2000). The search asymmetry suggested that race-specifying information functions as a visual feature, because feature-present targets are detected more quickly than feature-absent targets (Treisman & Gormican, 1988). However, neither race effect appears to be robust (for a review, see Rhodes, Locke, Ewing, & Evangelista, 2009).

Caution is also needed in interpreting other evidence presented as linking race categorization to the ORE. Adding race-stereotypic hairstyles to schematic ambiguous-race (Black-Hispanic) faces or presenting ambiguous-race (Black-White) morphed faces with White or Black "siblings" can generate ORE-like effects (MacLin & Malpass, 2001; Shutts & Kinzler, 2007). However, neither memory effect can be clearly attributed to race categorization, which was either not measured (Shutts & Kinzler, 2007) or was assessed using very different stimuli than used in the memory test (MacLin & Malpass, 2001). Furthermore, although perceptual adaptation to faces of one race strongly biases the perceived race of ambiguous-race morphs away from that race (e.g., making them look more Asian after adapting to Caucasian faces), it has no effect on memory or discrimination (Rhodes, Lie, Ewing, Evangelista, & Tanaka, 2010). There is also evidence that labelling ambiguous-race morphs as other-race faces reduces holistic coding (Michel et al., 2007). Given that holistic coding requires attention (Palermo & Rhodes, 2002), this effect may indicate reduced attention to other-race faces. Overall, the evidence that race categorization per se explains, or contributes to, the ORE seems weak.

In conclusion, although the ORE is a robust phenomenon, its cognitive basis remains hotly debated. Some favor a perceptual expertise account, pointing to early emergence of the ORE during infancy, reduced perceptual sensitivity to physical differences in other-race faces, and reduced holistic coding of other race faces (for a review, see Rossion & Michel, 2011). Others favor a socio-cognitive account, pointing to effects of instructions and race categorization (e.g., Hugenberg et al., 2007, 2010; Levin, 1996). Although these are often presented as competing accounts (e.g., Hugenberg et al., 2007; Levin, 1996; Rossion & Michel, 2011), both kinds of factors could contribute to the ORE. Although OREs have been reported for a wide range of races, a more systematic examination of the mechanisms underlying OREs in different groups would be useful. It remains to be seen, for example, whether socio-cognitive effects, which are well established for White US participants (typically viewing White and Black faces), generalize to other populations. Given that the ORE generalizes to other populations, so too must socio-cognitive effects if they are to help explain the ORE. For those interested in reducing OREs, there is encouraging evidence that individuation training can improve recognition of other-race faces (e.g., Lebrecht et al., 2009; Tanaka & Pierce, 2009; Tanaka & Pierce, 2009).

## Individual Differences

Face recognition is widely regarded as a prime example of perceptual expertise. However, it is becoming increasingly clear that we are not all equally good at it. Some individuals are so good they are characterized as "super-recognizers" (Russell et al., 2009), whereas others are so bad they are characterized as developmental prosopagnosics (for reviews, see Behrmann & Avidan, 2005; Behrmann, Avidan, & Nishimura, 2011; Duchaine, 2011). Interestingly, developmental prosopagnosia has a prevalence rate of around 2.5%, suggesting that it is not uncommon (Kennerknecht et al., 2006). Unlike acquired prosopagnosia, which results from damage to face-coding areas caused by stroke or other trauma, it is not associated with any obvious brain damage. Despite some behavioral heterogeneity, there appears to be a core deficit in deriving structural visual representations of faces (Duchaine & Nakayama, 2006a). The precise nature of the underlying computational problems, and their specificity for faces, are the subject of ongoing investigation (for a review, see Duchaine, 2011).

Russell and colleagues (2009) have proposed that developmental prosopagnosics and super-recognizers lie at opposite ends of a continuum of face recognition ability. If this is correct, then we might expect to see continuous variation in the underlying computational mechanisms, such as holistic coding, that is associated with variation in face recognition ability. First, we note that many developmental prosopagnosics have unimpaired holistic coding (Le Grand, et al., 2006). Nevertheless, recent studies have shown that individual differences in face recognition performance are associated with individual differences in holistic coding, as assessed by composite effects (Richler et al., 2011; Wang et al., 2012), part-whole effects (Wang et al., 2012) and inversion effects (Russell et al., 2009). There is also evidence for individual differences in face adaptation, measured using figural face aftereffects, that appear to be linked with differences in face recognition performance (Dennett, McKone, Edwards & Susilo, 2012). These studies provide good evidence for continuous variation in face-coding mechanisms that can be linked to performance.

Variation in face recognition ability seems to be at least partly genetically based. Developmental prosopagnosia can run in families (Behrmann & Avidan, 2005; de Haan, 1999; Duchaine & Nakayama, 2006a; Grueter et al., 2007; Kennerknecht et al., 2006; McConachie, 1976) and one study of 38 developmental prosopagnosics from 7 families identified a simple pattern of inheritance consistent with a single dominant autosomal gene (Grueter et al., 2007). If the face recognition deficit in developmental prosopagnosia represents the end of a continuous distribution of variation, as has been suggested, then it may be possible for large population-based studies to map variation in performance onto genetic variation. A recent twin study found a near-ceiling correlation (given the internal reliability of the CFMT test) between face recognition performance of monozygotic twins, which was significantly reduced for dizygotic twins, indicating a clear genetic basis for face recognition ability (Wilmer et al., 2009).

## Development

Newborn infants detect and visually orient to face-like patterns in preference to other complex patterns, such as scrambled or inverted faces (Goren, Sarty, & Wu, 1975; Johnson, Dziurawiec, Ellis, & Morton, 1991; for a review, see Johnson, 2005). These results suggest some innate bias toward faces (Johnson, 2011; Johnson & Morton, 1991). Some argue that this behavior reflects a more general visual bias, for example, for stimuli with more elements in the upper than the lower half (Cassia, Turati, & Simion, 2004). It is difficult, however, to determine whether the face bias results from the more general bias or whether the general bias results from the resemblance of other stimuli to faces. At a functional level, it difficult to see what biologically significant stimuli other than faces would drive the evolution of an innate bias. Irrespective of its source, this early bias for faces supports rapid learning, so that within days of birth infants prefer their mother's face to a stranger's (Bushnell, Sai, & Mullin, 1989; Pascalis, de Schonen, Morton, Deruelle, & Fabre-Grent, 1995). The bias also supports early visual preferences for faces with direct overaverted gaze (Farroni, Csibra, Simion, & Johnson, 2002; Farroni, Menon, & Johnson, 2006) and for attractive over unattractive faces (Slater, Quinn, Hayes, & Brown, 2000). Interestingly, both preferences are lost when faces are inverted, confirming early sensitivity to the first-order face configuration (eyes above nose above mouth). Although these preferences are present within days of birth, it is not yet known whether they are present at birth, or whether they emerge rapidly with experience of faces.

During the first year of life, face processing mechanisms are "tuned" by exposure to faces. This tuning causes "perceptual narrowing," analogous to the loss of early sensitivity to phonemic differences that are absent from the infant's language environment. In the case of faces, 6-month-olds can discriminate familiar from unfamiliar monkey faces as well as they can for human faces, but by 9 months they can no longer discriminate monkey faces (Pascalis, de Haan, & Nelson, 2002; Pascalis et al., 2005). A similar reduction of sensitivity occurs for faces from unfamiliar races (Kelly et al., 2007). In both cases exposure to other-species or other-race faces prevents the loss, so long as the faces must be individuated. Mere exposure or categorization (e.g., labeling faces as "monkey") is not sufficient (Scott & Monesson, 2009), highlighting the importance of quality rather than simply quantity of experience, as seen earlier in the other-race effect.

Exposure to faces in infancy also appears to be critical for the normal development of holistic face-coding mechanisms. Adults whose early exposure was disrupted by congenital cataracts show reduced sensitivity to feature spacing and reduced composite effects, despite removal of the cataracts by 6 months of age (Le Grand, Mondloch, Maurer, & Brent, 2001, 2004). Interestingly, it is early input to the right hemisphere that appears to be crucial, consistent with widespread evidence that the right hemisphere plays a critical role in face recognition (Le Grand, Mondloch, Maurer, & Brent, 2003). These results suggest that there may be an early sensitive period during which exposure to faces is essential for normal development, similar to that seen in other primates (Sugita, 2008).

Despite an early visual bias for faces and rapid perceptual learning about faces, face recognition performance continues to improve throughout childhood, and it does not reach adult levels until adolescence (Bruce et al., 2000; Carey, 1992; Carey, Diamond, & Woods, 1980; Chung & Thompson, 1995; Mondloch, Geldart, Maurer, & Le Grand, 2003; Mondloch, Le Grand, & Maurer, 2002). There has been much debate about whether this improvement reflects development of face-selective coding mechanisms or more general cognitive mechanisms (e.g., memory, executive function, attention). A recent review found little behavioral evidence for either qualitative or quantitative development of holistic face-coding during childhood (Crookes & McKone, 2009). Norm-based coding of faces also appears to be adult-like in young children (Jeffery et al., 2010; Nishimura, Maurer, Jeffery, Pellicano, & Rhodes, 2008; Pimperton, Pellicano, Jeffery, & Rhodes, 2009). Sensitivity to spacing changes, however, continues to improve throughout childhood and may be related to improvement in recognition (Mondloch et al., 2002, 2003). Imaging studies have also linked improved face recognition during childhood with expansion of face-selective cortex, suggesting a face-selective component to improved performance (Golari et al., 2007).

## A Neural Network for Face Recognition

A network of face-selective regions has been identified in human occipito-temporal cortex, using functional magnetic resonance imaging to identify voxels that respond more strongly to faces than other objects (Haxby et al., 2000) (Fig. 4.4). The face network consists of an occipital face area (OFA) in inferior occipital cortex, a fusiform face area (FFA) in the middle fusiform gyrus, and an area in the superior temporal sulcus (STS). The OFA may code an initial perceptual representation of the face, which is projected in parallel to the FFA and STS for further processing (Fairhall & Ishai, 2007; Haxby et al., 2000; Pitcher, Walsh, & Duchaine, 2011). The STS codes changeable aspects, such as gaze direction and emotional expression (Andrews & Ewbank, 2004; Calder & Young, 2005; Haxby, Hoffman, & Gobbini, 2002; Hoffman & Haxby, 2000), and the FFA codes invariant aspects of faces related to identity (Gauthier et al., 2000; George et al., 1999; Grill-Spector, Knouf, & Kanwisher, 2004; Haxby et al., 2000; Kanwisher & Yovel, 2006; Mazard, Schiltz, & Rossion, 2006; Rotshtein, Henson, Treves, Driver, & Dolan, 2005; Winston, Henson, Fine-Goulden, & Dolan, 2004), although it may also be sensitive to expression (for a review, see Calder, 2011).

Several studies have implicated the FFA in holistic coding of faces (Kanwisher & Yovel, 2006). It is

Traditionally, face recognition research has started from the assumption that we are all face experts. However, it is becoming clear that there are substantial individual differences in face recognition ability and face processing mechanisms. What is the source of this variation and can we exploit it to study the cognitive and neural bases of face recognition?

Why does face recognition improve during development? Is it because of maturation of face-selective coding mechanisms, or more general cognitive mechanisms, or both? Many studies have examined face processing in infants and school-age children, but little is known about development in the preschool years. Nor are the mechanisms that underlie perceptual narrowing of face discrimination during the first year of life well understood. Does this narrowing result from more precise tuning of coding dimensions to variation in a familiar population of faces, more categorical coding of faces from an unfamiliar population, or some combination of these?

The question of whether faces are special has stimulated a lot of research on face recognition. The bottom line seems to be that faces are special among visual stimuli in their social and evolutionary significance, in our innate visual bias for them, and in our rapid early learning about them. Holistic coding may also be special for faces in that it is not a hallmark of perceptual expertise generally, although it is not necessarily unique to faces. A methodological challenge for the future will be to determine whether the various indices of holistic coding all tap the same underlying process or whether they might map onto distinctions that matter for our understanding of face recognition.

## Glossary

**Face identity aftereffect**—a perceptual aftereffect in which viewing a face biases perception toward the opposite identity (a face with opposite values on the dimensions in face-space).

**Face-space**—a theoretical multidimensional space whose dimensions correspond to whatever information is used to discriminate and recognize faces. Typical faces lie closer to the center of the face than distinctive faces, and distance in the space corresponds to perceived dissimilarity.

**Features**—usually refer to local, internal components of a face, such as eyes, nose, and mouth, but they can also refer to more global, external features, such as hair and face outline.

**Fusiform face area (FFA)**—a face-selective region in the middle fusiform gyrus that responds more strongly to faces than other objects. Part of a larger network of face-selective regions.

**Holistic coding**—integration of information across the face, possibly with little explicit decomposition into component parts.

**Norm-based coding**—use of an average face as a perceptual norm for coding facial appearance. This form of coding allows the visual system to ignore information that is shared by many faces, and therefore useless for recognition, and focus on distinctive information.

**Other-race effect (ORE)**—poorer recognition of other-race than own-race faces. Sometimes called the cross-race effect.

**Prosopagnosia**—a selective impairment in face recognition, with relatively intact recognition of most other objects. May result from brain injury, in acquired prosopagnosia, or be present throughout life with no apparent brain injury, in developmental prosopagnosia (sometimes called congenital prosopagnosia).

**Second-order spatial relations**—spatial variations within the fixed first-order configuration (eyes above nose above mouth) that is shared by all faces. Second-order relations are sometimes experimentally manipulated by varying feature spacing.

## Acknowledgments

This work was supported by the ARC Centre of Excellence in Cognition and its Disorders (CE110001021) and an ARC Professorial Fellowship to Rhodes (DP0877379). I thank Linda Jeffery for helpful comments on an earlier draft of the chapter and Elinor McKone for helpful discussions about face recognition.

## References

Anderson, N. D., & Wilson, H. R. (2005). The nature of synthetic face adaptation. *Vision Research, 45*, 1815–1828.

Andrews, T. J., & Ewbank, M. P. (2004). Distinct representations for facial identity and changeable aspects of faces in the human temporal lobe. *Neuroimage, 23*, 905–913.

Baddeley, A., & Woodhead, M. (1983). Improving face recognition ability. In S. M. A. Lloyd-Bostock & B. R. Clifford (Eds.), *Evaluating eyewitness testimony* (pp. 125–136). Chichester, England: Wiley.

Bahrick, H. P., Bahrick, O. O., & Wittlinger, R. P. (1975). Fifty years of memory for names and faces: A cross-sectional approach. *Journal of Experimental Psychology: General, 104*, 54–75.

Bar-Haim, Y., Ziv, T., Lamy, D., & Hodes, R. M. (2006). Nature and nurture in own-race face processing. *Psychological Science, 17*, 159–163.

Bartlett, M. S. (2007). Information maximization in face processing. *Neurocomputing, 70*, 2204–2217.

Barton, J. J., Press, D. Z., Keenan, J. P., & O'Connor, M. (2002). Lesions of the fusiform face area impair perception of facial configuration in prosopagnosia. *Neurology, 58,* 71–78.

Barton, J. J. S., Zhao, J., & Keenan, J. P. (2003). Perception of global facial geometry in the inversion effect and prosopagnosia. *Neuropsychologia, 41,* 1703–1711.

Behrmann, M., & Avidan, G. (2005). Congenital prosopagnosia: Face-blind from birth. *Trends in Cognitive Sciences, 9,* 180–187.

Behrmann, M., Avidan, G., Leonard, G. L., Kimchi, R., Luna, B., Humphreys, K., & Minshew, N. (2006). Configural processing in autism and its relationship to face processing. *Neuropsychologia, 44,* 110–129.

Behrmann, M., Avidan, G., & Nishimura, M. (2011). Impairments in face perception. In A. J. Calder, G. Rhodes, M. H. Johnston, & J. V. Haxby (Eds.), *The Oxford handbook of face perception* (pp. 799–820). Oxford, England: Oxford University Press.

Behrmann, M., Thomas, C., & Humphreys, K. (2006). Seeing it differently: Visual processing in autism. *Trends in Cognitive Sciences, 10,* 258–264.

Benson, P. J., & Perrett, D. I. (1994). Visual processing of facial distinctiveness. *Perception, 23,* 75–93.

Benton, C. P., Jennings, S. J., & Chatting, D. J. (2006). Viewpoint dependence in adaptation to facial identity. *Vision Research, 46,* 3313–3325.

Bernstein, M. J., Young, S. G., & Hugenberg, K. (2007). The cross-category effect: Mere social categorization is sufficient to elicit an own-group bias in face recognition. *Psychological Science, 18,* 706–712.

Bestelmeyer, P. E. G., Jones, B. C., DeBruine, L. M., Little, A. C., Perrett, D. I., Schneider, A.,…Conway, C. A. (2008). Sex-contingent face aftereffects depend on perceptual category rather than structural coding. *Cognition, 107,* 353–365.

Blair, R. J. R., Frith, U., Smith, N., Abell, F., & Cipolotti, L. (2002). Fractionation of visual memory: Agency detection and its impairment in autism. *Neuropsychologia, 40,* 108–118.

Boucher, J., & Lewis, V. (1992). Unfamiliar face recognition in relatively able children with autism. *Journal of Child Psychology and Psychiatry, 33,* 843–859.

Bouvier, S. E., & Engel, S. A. (2006). Behavioral deficits and cortical damage loci in cerebral achromatopsia. *Cerebral Cortex, 16,* 183–191.

Brigham, J. C., & Barkowitz, P. (1978). Do "They all look alike?" The effect of race, sex, experience, and attitudes on the ability to recognise faces. *Journal of Applied Social Psychology, 8,* 306–318.

Brigham, J. C., Bennett, L. B., Meissner, C. A., & Mitchell, T. L. (2006). The influence of race on eyewitness memory. In R. C. L. Lindsay, D. Ross, J. Read, & M. Toglia (Eds.), *Handbook of eyewitness psychology: Memory for people* (pp. 257–281). Mahwah, NJ: Erlbaum.

Bruce, V. (1982). Changing faces: Visual and non-visual coding processes in face recognition. *British Journal of Psychology, 73,* 105–116.

Bruce, V. (1988). *Recognising faces.* Hove & London: Erlbaum.

Bruce, V., Campbell, R. N., Docherty-Sneddon G., Import, A., Langton, S., McAuley, S., & Wright, R. (2000). Testing face processing skills in children. *British Journal of Developmental Psychology, 18,* 319–333.

Bruce, V., Doyle, T., Dench, N., & Burton, M. (1991). Remembering facial configurations. *Cognition, 38,* 109–144.

Bruce, V., Henderson, Z., Greenwood, K., Hancock, P., Burton, A. M. & Miller, P. (1999). Verification of face identities from images captured on video. *Journal of Experimental Psychology: Applied, 5,* 339–360.

Bruce, V., & Young, A. W. (1986). Understanding face recognition. *British Journal of Psychology, 77,* 305–327.

Burton, A. M., & Jenkins, R. (2011). Unfamiliar face perception. In A. J. Calder, G. Rhodes, M. H. Johnston, & J. V. Haxby (Eds.), *The Oxford handbook of face perception* (pp. 287–306). Oxford, England: Oxford University Press.

Burton, A. M., Wilson, S., Cowan, M., & Bruce, V. (1999). Face recognition in poor quality video: Evidence from security surveillance. *Psychological Science, 10,* 243–248.

Bushnell, I. W. R., Sai, F. & Mullin, J. T. (1989). Neonatal recognition of the mother's face. *British Journal of Developmental Psychology, 7,* 3–15.

Byatt, G., & Rhodes, G. (2004). Identification of own-race and other-race faces: Implications for the representation of race in face-space. *Psychonomic Bulletin and Review, 11*(40), 735–741.

Cabeza, R., Bruce, V., Kato, T., & Oda, M. (1999). The prototype effect in face recognition: Extension and limits. *Memory and Cognition, 27,* 139–151.

Calder, A. J. (2011). Does facial identity and facial expression recognition involve separate visual routes? In A. J. Calder, G. Rhodes, M. H. Johnson & J. V. Haxby, (Eds.), *The Oxford handbook of face perception* (pp. 427–448). Oxford, England: Oxford University Press.

Calder, A. J., Rhodes, G., Johnson, M. H., & Haxby, J. V. (Eds.). (2011). *The Oxford handbook of face perception.* Oxford, England: Oxford University Press.

Calder, A. J., & Young, A. W. (2005). Understanding the recognition of facial identity and facial expression. *Nature Reviews Neuroscience, 6,* 641–651.

Carey, S. (1992). Becoming a face expert. *Philosophical Transactions of the Royal Society of London, Series B, 335,* 95–103.

Carey, S., Diamond, R., & Woods, B. (1980). Development of face recognition–a maturational component? *Developmental Psychology, 16,* 257–269.

Caroo, A. W. (1987). Recognition of faces as a function of race, attitudes and reported cross-racial friendships. *Perceptual and Motor Skills, 64,* 319–325.

Cassia, V. M., Turati, C., & Simion, F. (2004). Can a nonspecific bias toward top-heavy patterns explain newborns' face preference? *Psychological Science, 15,* 379–383.

Chung, M. S., & Thompson, D. M. (1995). Development of face recognition. *British Journal of Psychology, 86,* 55–87.

Corentin, J., & Rossion, B. (2006). The speed of individual face categorization. *Psychological Science, 16,* 485–492.

Crookes, K., & McKone, E. (2009). Early maturity of face recognition: No childhood development of holistic processing, novel face encoding or face-space. *Cognition, 111,* 219–247.

Dawson, G., Webb, S. J., & McPartland, J. (2005). Understanding the nature of face processing impairment in autism: Insights from behavioral and electrophysiological studies. *Developmental Neuropsychology, 27,* 403–424.

De Gutis, J. M., Bentin, S., Robertson, L. C., & D'Esposito, M. (2007). Functional plasticity in ventral temporal cortex following cognitive rehabilitation of a congenital prosopagnosic. *Journal of Cognitive Neuroscience, 19*(11), 1790–1802.

De Haan, M. (1999). A familial factor in the development of face recognition deficits. *Journal of Clinical and Experimental Neuropsychology, 21,* 312–315.

De Haan, M., Johnson, M. H., Maurer, D., & Perrett, D. I. (2001). Recognition of individual faces and average face prototypes by 1- and 3-month-old infants. *Cognitive Development, 16,* 659–678.

Dennett, H. W., McKone, E., Edwards, M., & Susilo, T. (2012). Face aftereffect predict individual differences in face recognition ability. *Psychological Science, 23,* 1279–1287.

Diamond, R., & Carey, S. (1986). Why faces are and are not special: An effect of expertise. *Journal of Experimental Psychology: General, 115,* 107–117.

Duchaine, B. C. (2011). Developmental prosopagnosia: Cognitive, neural, and developmental investigations. In A. J. Calder, G. Rhodes, M. H. Johnston, & J. V. Haxby (Eds.), *The Oxford handbook of face perception* (pp. 821–838). Oxford, England: Oxford University Press.

Duchaine, B. C., & Nakayama, K. (2006a). Developmental prosopagnosia: A window to content-specific face processing. *Current Opinion in Neurobiology, 16,* 166–173.

Duchaine, B. C., & Nakayama, K. (2006b). The Cambridge face memory test: Results for neurologically intact individuals and an investigation of its validity using inverted face stimuli and prosopagnosic participants. *Neuropsychologia, 44,* 576–585.

Edwards, J. R. (2001). Ten difference score myths. *Organizational Research Methods, 4,* 265–287.

Eimer, M. (2011). The face-sensitive N170 component of the event-related brain potential. In A. J. Calder, G. Rhodes, M. H. Johnson, & J. V. Haxby (Eds.), *The Oxford handbook of face perception* (pp. 329–344). Oxford: Oxford University Press.

Ellis, H. D., Shepherd, J. W., & Davies, G. M. (1979). Identification of familiar and unfamiliar faces from internal and external features: Some implications for theories of face recognition. *Perception, 8,* 431–439.

Fairhall, S. L., & Ishai, A. (2007). Effective connectivity within the distributed cortical network for face perception. *Cerebral Cortex, 17,* 2400–2406.

Farah, M. J. (1996). Is face recognition special? Evidence from neuropsychology. *Behavioural Brain Research, 76,* 181–189.

Farah, M. J., Wilson, K. D., Drain, M., & Tanaka, J. N. (1998). What is "special" about face perception? *Psychological Review, 105,* 482–498.

Farroni, T., Csibra, G., Simion, F., & Johnson, M. H. (2002). Eye contact detection in humans from birth. *Proceedings of the National Academy of Sciences USA, 99,* 9602–9605.

Farroni, T., Menon, E., & Johnson, M. H. (2006). Factors influencing newborns' preferences for faces with eye contact. *Journal of Experimental Child Psychology, 95,* 298–308.

Fazio, R. H., Jackson, J. R., Dunton, B. C., & Williams, C. J. (1995). Variability in automatic activation as an unobtrusive measure of racial attitudes: A bona fide pipeline? *Journal of Personality and Social Psychology, 69,* 1013–1027.

Ferguson, D. P., Rhodes, G., Lee, K., & Sriram, N. (2001). "They all look alike to me": Prejudice and cross-race face recognition. *British Journal of Psychology, 92,* 567–577.

Galper, R. E. (1970). Recognition of faces in photographic negative. *Psychonomic Science, 19,* 207–208.

Gauthier, I., & Bukach, C. (2007). Should we reject the expertise hypothesis? *Cognition, 103,* 322–330.

Gauthier, I., & Nelson, C. (2001). The development of face expertise. *Current Opinion in Neurobiology, 11,* 219–224.

Gauthier, I., & Tarr, M. J. (1997). Becoming a "greeble" expert: Exploring mechanisms for face recognition. *Vision Research, 37,* 1673–1682.

Gauthier, I., & Tarr, M. J. (2002). Unravelling mechanisms for expert object recognition: Bridging brain activity and behavior. *Journal of Experimental Psychology: Human Perception and Performance, 28,* 431–446.

Gauthier, I., Tarr, M. J., Moylan, J., Skudlarski, P., Gore, J. C., & Anderson, A. W. (2000). The fusiform face area is part of a network that processes faces at the individual level. *Journal of Cognitive Neuroscience, 12,* 495–504.

Gauthier, I., Williams, P., Tarr. M. J., & Tanaka, J. (1998). Training "greeble" experts: A framework for studying expert object recognition processes. *Vision Research, 38,* 2401–2428.

George, N., Dolan, R. J., Fink, G. R., Baylis, G. C., Russell, C., & Driver, J. (1999). Contrast polarity and face recognition in the human fusiform gyrus. *Nature Neuroscience, 2,* 574–580.

Gilad, S., Meng, M., & Sinha, P. (2009). Role of ordinal contrast relationships in face encoding. *Proceedings of the National Academy of Sciences USA, 106,* 5353–5358.

Gilchrest, A., & McKone, E. (2003). Early maturity of face processing in children: Local and relational distinctiveness effects in 7-year-olds. *Visual Cognition, 10,* 769–793.

Golari, G., Ghahremani, D. G., Whitfield-Gabrieli, S., Reiss, A., Eberhardt, J. L., Gabrieli, J. D., & Grill-Spector, K. (2007). Differential development of high-level visual cortex correlates with category-specific recognition memory. *Nature Neuroscience, 10,* 512–522.

Golby, A. J., Gabrieli, J. D., Chiao, J. Y., & Eberhardt, J. L. (2001). Differential responses in the fusiform region to same-race and other-race faces. *Nature Neuroscience, 4,* 845–850.

Goldstein, A. G., & Chance, J. E. (1980). Memory for faces and schema theory. *Journal of Psychology, 105,* 47–59.

Goren, C. C., Sarty, M., & Wu, P. Y. K. (1975). Visual following and pattern discrimination of face-like stimuli by newborn infants. *Pediatrics, 56,* 544–549.

Gregory, R. L. (1973). The confounded eye. In R. L. Gregory & E. H. Gombrich (Eds.), *Illusion in nature and art* (pp. 49–96). London: Duckworth.

Grill-Spector, K., Knouf, N., & Kanwisher, N. (2004). The fusiform face area subserves face perception, not generic within-category identification. *Nature Neuroscience, 7,* 555–562.

Grueter, M., Grueter, T., Bell, V., Horst, J., Laskowski, W., Sperling, K., Halligan, P. W., Ellis, H. D., & Kennerknecht, I. (2007). Hereditary prosopagnosia: The first case series. *Cortex, 43,* 734–749.

Hancock, K., & Rhodes, G. (2008). Contact, inversion and the other-race effect in face recognition. *British Journal of Psychology, 99,* 45–56.

Hancock, P. J. B., Bruce, V., & Burton, A. M. (2000). Recognition of unfamiliar faces. *Trends in Cognitive Science, 4*(9), 330–337.

Harris, A., & Aguirre, G. K. (2008). The representation of parts and wholes in face-selective cortex. *Journal of Cognitive Neuroscience, 20*(5), 863–878.

Haxby, J. V., Hoffman, E. A., & Gobbini, M. I. (2000). The distributed human neural system for face perception. *Trends in Cognitive Sciences, 4,* 223–233.

Haxby, J. V., Hoffman, E. A., & Gobbini, M. I. (2002). Human neural systems for face recognition and social communication. *Biological Psychiatry, 51,* 59–67.

Hayward, W. G., Rhodes, G., & Schwaninger, A. (2008). An own-race advantage for components as well as configurations in face recognition. *Cognition, 106,* 1017–1027.

Hebb, D. O. (1949). *The organisation of behaviour.* New York: Wiley.

Herzmann, G., Danther, V., Schacht, A., Sommer, W., & Wilhelm, O. (2008). Toward a comprehensive test battery for face cognition: Assessment of the tasks. *Behavior Research Methods, 40,* 840–857.

Hill, H., & Bruce, V. (1993). Independent effects of lighting, orientation, and stereopsis on the hollow-face illusion. *Perception, 22*(8), 887–897.

Hill, H., & Bruce, V. (1996). Effects of lighting on the perception of facial surfaces. *Journal of Experimental Psychology: Human Perception and Performance, 22,* 986–1004.

Hills, P. J., & Lewis, M. B. (2006). Reducing the own-race bias in face recognition by shifting attention. *Quarterly Journal of Experimental Psychology, 59,* 996–1002.

Hochberg, J. E. (1978). *Perception* (2nd ed.). Englewood Cliffs, NJ: Prentice-Hall.

Hoffman, E. A., & Haxby, J. V. (2000). Distinct representations of eye gaze and identity in the distributed human neural system for face perception. *Nature Neuroscience, 3,* 80–84.

Hsiao, J. H., & Cottrell, G. W. (2009). Not all visual expertise is holistic, but it may be leftist. *Psychological Science, 20,* 455–463.

Hugenberg, K., Miller, J., & Claypool, H. M. (2007). Categorization and individuation in the cross-race recognition deficit: Towards a solution to an insidious problem. *Journal of Experimental Social Psychology, 43,* 334–340.

Hugenberg, K., Young, S. G., Bernstein, M.J., & Sacco, D. (2010). The categorization-individuation model: An integrative account of the other-race recognition deficit. *Psychological Review, 117,* 1168–1187.

Inn, D., Walden, K. J., & Solso, R. L. (1993). Facial prototype formation in children. *Bulletin of the Psychonomic Society, 31,* 197–200.

Jackson, M. C., & Raymond, J. E. (2006). The role of attention and familiarity in face identification. *Perception and Psychophysics, 68,* 543–557.

Jackson, M. C., & Raymond, J. E. (2008). Familiarity enhances visual working memory for faces. *Journal of Experimental Psychology: Human Perception and Performance, 34,* 556–568.

Jaquet, E., & Rhodes, G. (2008). Face aftereffects indicate dissociable, but not distinct, coding of male and female faces. *Journal of Experimental Psychology: Human Perception and Performance, 34,* 101–112.

Jaquet, E., Rhodes, G., & Hayward, W. G. (2007). Opposite aftereffects for Chinese and Caucasian faces are selective for social category information and not just physical face differences. *Quarterly Journal of Experimental Psychology, 60,* 1457–1467.

Jaquet, E., Rhodes, G., & Hayward, W. G. (2008). Race-contingent aftereffects suggest distinct perceptual norms for different race faces. *Visual Cognition, 16,* 734–753.

Jeffery, L., McKone, E., Haynes, R., Firth, E., Pellicano, E., & Rhodes, G. (2010). Four-to-six-year-old children use norm-based coding in face-space. *Journal of Vision, 10*(5), 18.

Jeffery, L., Rhodes, G., & Busey, T. (2006). View-specific norms code face shape. *Psychological Science, 17,* 501–505.

Jiang, F., Blanz, V., & O'Toole, A. J. (2006). Probing the visual representation of faces with adaptation: A view from the other side of the mean. *Psychological Science, 17,* 493–500.

Jiang, F., Blanz, V., & O'Toole, A. J. (2007). The role of familiarity in three-dimensional view-transferability of face identity adaptation. *Vision Research, 47,* 525–531.

Jiang, F., Blanz, F., & O'Toole, A. J. (2009). Three-dimensional information in face representations revealed by identity aftereffects. *Psychological Science, 20,* 318–325.

Johnson, M. H. (2005). *Developmental cognitive neuroscience: An introduction* (2nd ed.). Oxford: Blackwell.

Johnson, M. H. (2011). Face perception: A developmental perspective. In A. J. Calder, G. Rhodes, M. H. Johnson, & J. V. Haxby (Eds.), *The Oxford handbook of face perception* (pp. 3–14). Oxford, England: Oxford University Press.

Johnson, M. H., Dziurawiec, S., Ellis, H., & Morton, J. (1991). Newborns' preferential tracking of face-like stimuli and its subsequent decline. *Cognition, 40,* 1–19.

Johnson, M., & Morton, J. (1991). *Biology and cognitive development. The case of face recognition.* Oxford, England and Cambridge, MA: Blackwell.

Kanwisher, N., McDermott, J., & Chun, M. M. (1997). The fusiform face area: A module in human extrastriate cortex specialized for face perception. *Journal of Neuroscience, 17,* 4302–4311.

Kanwisher, N., & Yovel, G. (2006). The fusiform face area: A cortical region specialized for the perception of faces. *Philosophical Transactions of the Royal Society of London, Series B, 361,* 2109–2128.

Kelly, D. J., Quinn, P. C., Slater, A. M., Lee, K., Ge, L., & Pascalis, O. (2007). The other-race effect develops during infancy. *Psychological Science, 18,* 1084–1089.

Kemp, R., Towell, N., & Pike, G. (1997). When seeing should not be believing: Photographs, credit cards and fraud. *Applied Cognitive Psychology, 11,* 211–222.

Kennerknecht, I., Grueter, T., Welling, B., Wentzek, S., Horst, J., Edwards, S., & Grueter, M. (2006). First report of prevalence of non-syndromic hereditary prosopagnosia (HPA). *American Journal of Medical Genetics Part A, 140A,* 1617–1622.

Klin, A., Sparrow, S. S., de Bildt, A., Cichetti, D. V., Cohen, D. J., & Volkmar, F. R. (1999). A normed study of face recognition in autism and related disorders. *Journal of Autism and Developmental Disorders, 29,* 499–508.

Konar, Y., Bennett, P. J., & Sekuler, A. B. (2010). Holistic processing is not correlated with face-identification accuracy. *Psychological Science, 21,* 38–43.

Le Grand, R., Cooper, P. A., Mondloch, C. J., Lewis, T. L., Sagiv, N., de Gelder, B., & Maurer, D. (2006). What aspects of face processing are impaired in developmental prosopagnosia? *Brain and Cognition, 61,* 139–158.

Le Grand, R., Mondloch, C. J., Maurer, D., & Brent, H. P. (2001). Early visual experience and face processing. *Nature, 410,* 890.

Le Grand, R., Mondloch, C. J., Maurer, D., & Brent, H. P. (2003). Expert face processing requires visual input to the right hemisphere during infancy. *Nature Neuroscience, 6*(10), 1108–1112.

Le Grand, R., Mondloch, C. J., Maurer, D., & Brent, H. P. (2004). Impairment in holistic face processing following early visual deprivation. *Psychological Science, 15,* 762–768.

Lebrecht, S., Pierce, L. J., Tarr, M. J., & Tanaka, J. W. (2009). Perceptual other-race training reduces implicit racial bias. *PLoS ONE, 4*(1), e4215.

Leder, H., & Carbon, C-C. (2006). Face-specific configural processing of relational information. *British Journal of Psychology*, *97*, 19–29.

Lee, K., Byatt, G., & Rhodes, G. (2000). Caricature effects, distinctiveness and identification: Testing the face-space framework. *Psychological Science*, *11*, 379–385.

Leopold, D. A., Bondar, I., & Giese, M. A. (2006). Norm-based face encoding by single neurons in the monkey inferotemporal cortex. *Nature*, *442*, 572–575.

Leopold, D. A., O'Toole, A. J., Vetter, T., & Blanz, V. (2001). Prototype-referenced shape encoding revealed by high-level aftereffects. *Nature Neuroscience*, *4*, 89–94.

Leopold, D. A., Rhodes, G., Müller, K-M & Jeffery, L. (2005). The dynamics of visual adaptation to faces. *Proceedings of the Royal Society of London, Series B*, *272*, 897–904.

Levin, D. T. (1996). Classifying faces by race: The structure of face categories. *Journal of Experimental Psychology: Learning, Memory, and Cognition*, *22*, 1364–1382.

Levin, D. T. (2000). Race as a visual feature: Using visual search and perceptual discrimination tasks to understand face categories and the cross-race recognition deficit. *Journal of Experimental Psychology: General*, *129*, 559–574.

Little, A. C., DeBruine, L. M., & Jones, B. C. (2005). Sex-contingent face aftereffects suggest distinct neural populations code male and female faces. *Proceedings of the Royal Society of London, Series B*, *272*, 2283–2287.

Loffler, G., Yourganov, G., Wilkinson, F., & Wilson, H. (2005). fMRI evidence for the neural representation of faces. *Nature Neuroscience*, *8*, 1386–1391.

MacLeod, D. I. A., & von der Twer, T. (2003). The pleistochrome: Optimal opponent codes for natural colours. In R. Mausfeld & D. Heyer (Eds.), *Color perception: Mind and the physical world* (pp. 155–184). Oxford, England: Oxford University Press.

MacLin, O. H., & Malpass, R. S. (2001). Race categorization of faces: The ambiguous race face effect. *Psychology, Public Policy and Law*, *7*(1), 98–118.

MacLin, O. H., & Webster, M. A. (2001). Influence of adaptation on the perception of distortions in natural images. *Journal of Electronic Imaging*, *10*, 100–109.

Mather, G. (1980). The movement aftereffect and a distribution-shift model for coding the direction of visual movement. *Perception*, *9*, 379–392.

Maurer, D., Le Grand, R., & Mondloch, C. J. (2002). The many faces of configural processing. *Trends in Cognitive Sciences*, *6*(6), 255–260.

Maurer, D., O'Craven, K. M., Le Grand, R., Modloch, C. J., Springer, M. V., Lewis, T. L., & Grady, C. L. (2007). Neural correlates of processing facial identity based on features versus their spacing. *Neuropsychologia*, *45*, 1438–1451.

Mazard, A., Schiltz, C., & Rossion, B. (2006). Recovery from adaptation to facial identity is larger for upright than inverted faces in the human occipito-temporal cortex. *Neuropsychologia*, *44*, 912–922.

McConachie, H. R. (1976). Developmental prosopagnosia: A single case report. *Cortex*, *12*, 76–82.

McKone, E. (2008). Configural processing and face viewpoint. *Journal of Experimental Psychology: Human Perception and Performance*, *34*(2), 310–327.

McKone, E. (2009). Holistic processing for faces operates over a wide range of sizes but is strongest at identification rather than conversational distances. *Vision Research*, *49*, 268–283.

McKone, E., Brewer, J. L., MacPherson, S., Rhodes, G., & Hayward, W. G. (2007). Familiar other-race faces show normal holistic processing and are robust to perceptual stress. *Perception*, *36*, 224–248.

McKone, E., Kanwisher, N., & Duchaine, B. C. (2007). Can generic expertise explain special processing for faces? *Trends in Cognitive Sciences*, *11*, 8–15.

McKone, E., & Robbins, R. (2007). The evidence rejects the expertise hypothesis: Reply to Gauthier & Bukach. *Cognition*, *103*(2), 331–336.

McKone, E., & Robbins, R. (2011). Are faces special? In A. J. Calder, G. Rhodes, M. H. Johnston & J. V. Haxby (Eds.), *The Oxford handbook of face perception* (pp. 149–176). Oxford, England: Oxford University Press.

McKone, E., & Yovel, G. (2009). Why does picture-plane inversion sometimes dissociate perception of features and spacing in faces, and sometimes not? Towards a new theory of holistic processing. *Psychonomic Bulletin and Review*, *16*(5), 778–797.

Megreya, A. M., & Burton, A. M. (2006). Unfamiliar faces are not faces: Evidence from a matching task. *Memory and Cognition*, *34*, 865–876.

Meissner, C. A., & Brigham, J. C. (2001). Thiry years of investigating the own-race bias memory for faces: A meta-analytic review. *Psychology, Public Policy and Law*, *7*(1), 3–35.

Meissner, C. A., Brigham, J. C., & Butz, D. A. (2005). Memory for own- and other-race faces: A dual-process approach. *Applied Cognitive Psychology*, *19*, 545–567.

Michel, C., Caldara, R., & Rossion, B. (2006). Same-race faces are perceived more holistically than other-race faces. *Visual Cognition*, *14*, 55–73.

Michel, C., Corneille, O., & Rossion, B. (2007). Race-categorization modulates holistic face encoding. *Cognitive Science*, *31*, 911–924.

Michel, C., Rossion, B., Han, J., Chung, C. H., & Caldara, R. (2006). Holistic processing is finely tuned for faces of one's own race. *Psychological Science*, *17*, 608–615.

Mondloch, C. J., & Desjarlais, M. (2010). The function and specificity of sensitivity to cues to facial identity: An individual differences approach. *Perception*, *39*, 819–829.

Mondloch, C. J., Elms, N., Maurer, D., Rhodes, G., Hayward, W. H., Tanaka, J. W., & Zhou, G. (2010). Processes underlying the cross-race effect: An investigation of holistic, featural and relational processing of own- versus other-race faces. *Perception*, *39*(8), 1065–1085.

Mondloch, C. J., Geldart, S., Maurer, D., & Le Grand, R. (2003). Developmental changes in face processing skills. *Journal of Experimental Child Psychology*, *86*, 67–84.

Mondloch, C. J., Le Grand, R., & Maurer, D. (2002). Configural face processing develops more slowly than featural face processing. *Perception*, *31*, 553–566.

Nishimura, M., Maurer, D., Jeffery, L., Pellicano, E., & Rhodes, G. (2008). Fitting the child's mind to the world: Adaptive norm-based coding of facial identity in 8-year-olds. *Developmental Science*, *11*, 620–627.

Nosofsky, R. M., & Johansen, M. K. (2000). Exemplar-based accounts of "multiple-system" phenomena in perceptual categorization. *Psychonomic Bulletin and Reivew*, *7*, 375–402.

O'Toole, A. J., Vetter, T., & Blanz, V. (1999). Two-dimensional reflectance and three-dimensional shape contributions to recognition of faces across viewpoint. *Vision Research*, *39*, 3145–3155.

Palermo, R., & Rhodes, G. (2002). The influence of divided attention on holistic face perception. *Cognition*, *82*, 225–257.

Palermo, R., & Rhodes, G. (2007). Are you always on my mind? A review of how face perception and attention interact. *Neuropsychologia, 45*, 75–92.

Pascalis, O., de Haan, M., & Nelson, C. A. (2002). Is face processing species-specified during the first year of life? *Science, 296*(5571), 1321–1323.

Pascalis, O., de Schonen, S., Morton, J., Deruell, C., & Fabre-Grenet, M. (1995). Mother's face recognition by neonates: A replication and an extension. *Infant Behavior and Development, 18*, 79–85.

Pascalis, O., Scott, L. S., Kelly, D. J., Shannon, R. W., Nicholson, E., Coleman, M., & Nelson, C. A. (2005). Plasticity of face processing in infancy. *Proceedings of the National Academy of Sciences USA, 102*, 5297–5300.

Pellicano, E., Jeffery, L., Burr, D., & Rhodes, G. (2007). Abnormal adaptive face-coding mechanisms in children with autism spectrum disorder. *Current Biology, 17*, 1508–1512.

Pellicano, E., Rhodes, G., & Peters, M. (2006). Are preschoolers sensitive to configural information in faces? *Developmental Science, 9*, 270–277.

Peterson, M. P., & Rhodes, G. (Eds.). (2003). *Perception of faces, objects and scenes: Analytic and holistic processing.* Cambridge, MA: Oxford University Press.

Pimperton, H., Pellicano, E., Jeffery, L., & Rhodes, G. (2009). The role of higher-level adaptive coding mechanisms in the development of face recognition. *Journal of Experimental Child Psychology, 104*, 229–238.

Pitcher, D., Walsh, V., & Duchaine, B. (2011). Transcranial magnetic stimulation studies of face processing. In A. J. Calder, G. Rhodes, M. H. Johnson, & J. V. Haxby (Eds.), *The Oxford handbook of face perception* (pp. 367–386). Oxford, England: Oxford University Press.

Pitcher, D., Walsh, V., Yovel, G., & Duchaine, B. (2007). TMS evidence for the involvement of the right occipital face area in early face processing. *Current Biology, 17*, 1568–1573.

Ramachandran, V. S. (1988). Perception of shape from shading. *Nature, 331*(6152), 163–166.

Reed, S. K. (1972). Pattern recognition and categorization. *Cognitive Psychology, 3*, 382–407.

Regan, D., & Hamstra, S. J. (1992). Shape discrimination and the judgment of perfect symmetry: Dissociation of shape from size. *Vision Research, 32*, 1845–1864.

Rhodes, G. (1988). Looking at faces: First-order and second-order features as determinants of facial appearance. *Perception, 17*, 43–63.

Rhodes, G. (1996). *Superportraits: Caricatures and recognition.* Hove, England: The Psychology Press.

Rhodes, G., Brennan, S., & Carey, S. (1987). Identification and ratings of caricatures: Implications for mental representations of faces. *Cognitive Psychology, 19*, 473–497.

Rhodes, G., Evangelista, E., & Jeffery, L. (2009). Orientation-sensitivity of face identity aftereffects. *Vision Research, 49*, 2379–2385.

Rhodes, G., Ewing, L., Hayward, W. G., Maurer, D., Mondloch, C. J., & Tanaka, J. W. (2009). Contact and other-race effects in configural and component processing of faces. *British Journal of Psychology, 100*, 717–728.

Rhodes, G., Hayward, W. G., & Winkler, C. (2006). Expert face coding: Configural and component coding of own-race and other-race faces. *Psychonomic Bulletin and Review, 13*, 499–505.

Rhodes, G., & Jaquet, E. (2011). Aftereffects reveal that adaptive face-coding mechanisms are selective for race and sex. In R. A. Adams, Jr., N. Ambady, K. Nakayama, & S. Shimojo (Eds.), *Social vision* (pp. 347–362). New York: Oxford University Press: New York.

Rhodes, G., & Jeffery, L. (2006). Adaptive norm-based coding of facial identity. *Vision Research, 46*, 2977–2987.

Rhodes, G., Jeffery, L., Clifford, C. W. G., & Leopold, D. A. (2007). The timecourse of higher-level face aftereffects. *Vision Research, 47*, 2291–2296.

Rhodes, G., Jeffery, L., Watson, T. L., Clifford, C. W. G., & Nakayama, K. (2003). Fitting the mind to the world: Face adaptation and attractiveness aftereffects. *Psychological Science, 14*, 558–566.

Rhodes, G., Jeffery, L., Watson, T., Jaquet, E., Winkler, C., & Clifford, C. W. G. (2004). Orientation-contingent face aftereffects and implications for face coding mechanisms. *Current Biology, 14*, 2119–2123.

Rhodes, G., & Leopold, D. L. (2011). Adaptive norm-based coding of face identity. In A. J. Calder, G. Rhodes, M. H. Johnson, & J. V. Haxby (Eds.), *The Oxford handbook of face perception* (pp. 263–286). Oxford, England: Oxford University Press.

Rhodes, G., Lie, H. C., Ewing, L. A., Evangelista, E., & Tanaka, J. W. (2010). Does perceived race affect discrimination and recognition of ambiguous-race faces? A test of the socio-cognitive hypothesis. *Journal of Experimental Psychology: Learning, Memory and Cognition, 36*, 217–223.

Rhodes, G., Locke, V., Ewing, L., & Evangelista, E. (2009). Race coding and the other-race effect in face recognition. *Perception, 38*, 232–241.

Rhodes, G., Michie, P. T., Hughes, M. E., & Byatt, G. (2009). FFA and OFA show sensitivity to spatial relations in faces. *European Journal of Neuroscience, 30*, 721–733.

Rhodes, G., Robbins, R., Jaquet, E., McKone, E., Jeffery, L., & Clifford, C. W. G. (2005). Adaptation and face perception: How aftereffects implicate norm-based coding of faces. In C. W. G. Clifford & G. Rhodes (Eds.), *Fitting the mind to the world: Adaptation and aftereffects in high-level vision* (pp. 213–240). Oxford, England: Oxford University Press.

Rhodes, G., Tan, S., Brake, S., & Taylor, K. (1989). Expertise and configural coding in face recognition. *British Journal of Psychology, 80*, 313–331.

Rhodes, G., Watson, T., Jeffery, L., & Clifford, C. W. G. (2010). Perceptual adaptation helps us identify faces. *Vision Research, 50*, 963–968.

Richeson, J. A., & Trawalter, S. (2008). The threat of appearing prejudiced and race-based attentional biases. *Psychological Science, 19*, 98–102.

Richler, J. J., Bukach, C., & Gauthier, I. (2009). Context influences holistic processing of nonface objects in the composite task. *Attention, Perception and Performance, 71*, 530–540.

Richler, J. J., Cheung, O. S., & Gauthier, I. (2011). Holistic processing predicts face recognition. *Psychological Science, 22*(4), 464–471.

Riesenhuber, M., Jarudi, I., Gilad, S., & Sinha, P. (2004). Face processing in humans is compatible with a simple, shape-based model of vision. *Proceedings of the Royal Society of London, Series B, 271*(Suppl.), S448–S450.

Robbins, R., & McKone, E. (2007). No face-like processing for objects-of-expertise in three behavioural tasks. *Cognition, 103*(1), 34–79.

Rock, I. (1973). *Orientation and form.* New York: Academic Press.

Rossion, B. (2008). Picture-plane inversion leads to qualitative changes of face perception. *Acta Psychologica (Amsterdam)*, *128*, 274–289.

Rossion, B., Caldara, R., Seghier, M., Schuller, A-M., Lazeyras, F., & Mayer, E. (2003). A network of occipito-temporal face-sensitive areas besides the right middle fusiform gyrus is necessary for normal face processing. *Brain*, *126*, 2381–2395.

Rossion, B., Dricot, L., Devolder, A., Bodart, J-M., Crommelinck, M., de Gelder, B., & Zoontjes, R. (2000). Hemispheric asymmetries for whole-based and part-based face processing in the human fusiform gyrus. *Journal of Cognitive Neuroscience*, *12*(5), 793–802.

Rossion, B., & Michel, C. (2011). An experience-based holistic account of the other-race face effect. In A. J. Calder, G. Rhodes, M. H. Johnson, & J. V. Haxby (Eds.), *The Oxford handbook of face perception* (pp. 215–244). Oxford, England: Oxford University Press.

Rotshtein, P., Geng, J. J., Driver, J. & Dolan, R. J. (2007). Role of features and second-order spatial relations in face discrimination, face recognition, and individual face skills: Behavioral and functional magnetic resonance imaging data. *Journal of Cognitive Neuroscience*, *19*, 1435–1452.

Rotshtein, P., Henson, R. N., Treves, A., Driver, J., & Dolan, R. J. (2005). Morphing Marilyn into Maggie dissociates physical and identity face representations in the brain. *Nature Neuroscience*, *8*(1), 107–113.

Russell, R., Duchaine, B., & Nakayama, K. (2009). Super-recognizers: People with extraordinary face recognition ability. *Psychonomic Bulletin and Review*, *16*, 252–257.

Sangrigoli, S., Pallier, C., Argenti, A. M., Ventureyra, V. A. G., & de Schonen, S. (2005). Reversibility of the other-race effect in face recognition during childhood. *Psychological Science*, *16*, 440–444.

Schiltz, C., & Rossion, B. (2006). Faces are represented holistically in the human occipito-temporal cortex. *Neuroimage*, *32*, 1385–1394.

Schwartz, O., Hsu, A., & Dayan, P. (2007). Space and time in visual context. *Nature Reviews: Neuroscience*, *8*, 522–535.

Scott, L. S., & Monesson, A. (2009). The origin of biases in face perception. *Psychological Science*, *20*, 676–680.

Searcy, J. H., & Bartlett, J. C. (1996). Inversion and processing of component and spatial-relational information of faces. *Journal of Experimental Psychology: Human Perception and Performance*, *22*, 904–915.

Sekuler, A. B., Gaspar, C. M., Gold, J. M., & Bennett, P. J. (2004). Inversion leads to quantitative, not qualitative, changes in face processing. *Current Biology*, *14*, 391–396.

Shriver, E. R., Young, S. G., Hugenberg, K., Bernstein, M. J., & Lanter, J. (2008). Class, race, and the face: Social context modulates the cross-race effect in face recognition. *Personality and Social Psychology Bulletin*, *34*, 260–274.

Shutts, K., & Kinzler, K. D. (2007). An ambiguous-race illusion in children's face memory. *Psychological Science*, *18*, 763–767.

Slater, A., Quinn, P. C., Hayes, R., & Brown, E. (2000). The role of facial orientation in newborn infants' preference for attractive faces. *Developmental Science*, *3*, 181–185.

Solso, R. L., & McCarthy, J. E. (1981a). Prototype formation of faces: A case of pseudomemory. *British Journal of Psychology*, *72*, 499–503.

Solso, R. L., & McCarthy, J. E. (1981b). Prototype formation: Central tendency models vs. attribute frequency model. *Bulletin of the Psychonomic Society*, *17*, 10–11.

Sporer, S. L. (2001). The cross-race effect: Beyond recognition of faces in the laboratory. *Psychology, Public Policy and Law*, *7*(1), 170–200.

Steeves, J. K., Culham, J. C., Duchaine, B. C., Pratesi, C. C., Valyear, K. F., Schindler, I.,…Goodale, M. A. (2006). The fusiform face area is not sufficient for face recognition: Evidence from a patient with dense prosopagnosia and no occipital face area. *Neuropsychologia*, *44*, 594–609.

Strauss, M. S. (1979). Abstraction of prototype information by adults and 10-month-old infants. *Journal of Experimental Psychology: Human Learning and Memory*, *5*, 618–632.

Sugita, Y. (2008). Face perception in monkeys reared with no exposure to faces. *Proceedings of the National Academy of Sciences USA*, *105*, 394–398.

Susilo, T., McKone, E., & Edwards, M. (2010). What shape are the neural response functions underlying opponent coding in face space? A psychophysical investigation. *Vision Research*, *50*, 300–314.

Sutherland, N. S. (1961). Figural aftereffects and apparent size. *Quarterly Journal of Experimental Psychology*, *13*, 222–228.

Suzuki, S. (2005). High-level pattern coding revealed by brief shape aftereffects. In C. W. G. Clifford & G. Rhodes (Eds.), *Fitting the mind to the world: Adaptation and aftereffects in high-level vision* (pp. 135–172). Oxford, England: Oxford University Press.

Talati, Z., Rhodes, G., & Jeffery, L. (2010). Now you see it, now you don't: Shedding light on the Thatcher illusion. *Psychological Science*, *21*(2), 219–221.

Tanaka, J. W., & Farah, M. J. (1993). Parts and wholes in face recognition. *Quarterly Journal of Experimental Psychology*, *46A*, 225–245.

Tanaka, J. W., & Farah, M. J. (2003). The holistic representation of faces. In M. P. Peterson & G. Rhodes (Eds.), *Perception of faces, objects and scenes: Analytic and holistic processing* (pp. 53–74). Cambridge, MA: Oxford University Press.

Tanaka, J. W., & Gordon, I. (2011). Features, configuration and holistic face processing. In A. J. Calder, G. Rhodes, M. H. Johnston, & J. V. Haxby (Eds.), *The Oxford handbook of face perception* (pp. 177–194). Oxford, England: Oxford University Press.

Tanaka, J. W., Kiefer, M., & Bukach, C. (2004). A holistic account of the own-race effect in face recognition: Evidence from a cross-cultural study. *Cognition*, *93*, B1–B9.

Tanaka, J. W., & Pierce, L. J. (2009). The neural plasticity of other-race face recognition. *Journal of Cognitive and Behavioral Neuroscience*, *9*(1), 122–131.

Tanaka, J. W., & Sengco, J. A. (1997). Features and their configuration in face recognition. *Memory and Cognition*, *25*(5), 583–592.

Thompson, P. (1980). Margaret Thatcher: A new illusion. *Perception*, *9*, 483–484.

Tong, F., & Nakayama, K. (1999). Robust representations for faces: Evidence from visual search. *Journal of Experimental Psychology: Human Perception and Performance*, *25*, 1016–1035.

Trawalter, S., Todd, A. R., Baird, A. A., & Richeson, J. A. (2008). Attending to threat: Race-based patterns of selective attention. *Journal of Experimental Social Psychology*, *44*, 1322–1327.

Treisman, A., & Gormican, S. (1988). Feature analysis in early vision: Evidence from search asymmetries. *Psychological Review*, *95*, 15–48.

Tsao, D. Y., & Freiwald, W. A. (2006). What's so special about the average face? *Trends in Cognitive Sciences, 10*, 391–393.

Valentine, T. (1991). A unified account of the effects of distinctiveness, inversion and race on face recognition. *Quarterly Journal of Experimental Psychology, 43A*, 161–204.

Van der Linde, I., & Watson, T. (2010). A combinatorial study of pose effects in unfamiliar face recognition. *Vision Research, 50*, 522–533.

Wang, R., Li, J., Fang, H., Tian, M., & Liu, J. (2012). Individual differences in holistic processing predict face recognition ability. *Psychological Science, 23*, 169–177.

Walker, P. M., & Hewstone, M. (2006). A perceptual discrimination investigation of the Own-Race Effect and intergroup experience. *Applied Cognitive Psychology, 20*, 461–475.

Walker, P. M., & Tanaka, J. W. (2003). An encoding advantage for own-race versus other-race faces. *Perception, 32*, 1117–1125.

Walton, G. E., & Bower, T. G. R. (1993). Newborns form "prototypes" in less than 1 minute. *Psychological Science, 4*, 203–205.

Webb, S. J., Faja, S., & Dawson, G. (2011). Face processing in autism. In A. J. Calder, G. Rhodes, M. H. Johnson, & J. V. Haxby (Eds.), *The Oxford handbook of face perception* (pp. 839–856). Oxford, England: Oxford University Press.

Webster, M. A. (2003). Light adaptation, contrast adaptation, and human vision. In R. Mausfeld & D. Heyer (Eds.), *Colour perception: Mind and the physical world* (pp. 67–110). Oxford: Oxford University Press.

Webster, M. A., & Leonard, D. (2008). Adaptation and perceptual norms in color vision. *Journal of the Optical Society of America, A, 25*, 2817–2825.

Webster, M. A., & MacLin, O. H. (1999). Figural aftereffects in the perception of faces. *Psychonomic Bulletin and Review, 6*(4), 647–653.

Webster, M. A., Werner, J. S., & Field, D. J. (2005). Adaptation and the phenomenology of perception. In C. Clifford & G. Rhodes (Eds.), *Fitting the mind to the world: Adaptation and aftereffects in high-level vision* (pp. 241–277). Oxford, England: Oxford University Press.

Wilmer, J. B., Germine, L., Chabris, C. F., Chatterjee, G., Williams, M., Loken, E.,...Duchaine, B. C. (2010). Human face recognition ability is specific and highly heritable. *Proceedings of the National Academy of Sciences USA, 107*, 5238–5241.

Wilmer, J. B., Germine, L., Williams, M. A., Nakayama, K., Chabris, C. F., & Duchaine, B. C. (2009). Genetic and environmental contributions to memory for faces: A twin study [Abstract]. *Journal of Vision, 9*(8), 509.

Winston, J. S., Henson, R. N. A., Fine-Goulden, M. R., & Dolan, R. J. (2004). fMRI-adaptation reveals dissociable neural representations of identity and expression in face perception. *Journal of Neurophysiology, 92*, 1830–1839.

Wong, A. C-N., Palmeri, T. J., & Gauthier, I. (2009). Conditions for facelike expertise with objects. *Psychological Science, 20*, 1108–1117.

Yin, R. K. (1969). Looking at upside-down faces. *Journal of Experimental Psychology, 81*, 141–145.

Young, A. W., Hellawell, D., & Hay, D. C. (1987). Configurational information in face perception. *Perception, 16*, 747–759.

Yovel, G., & Kanwisher, N. (2004). Face perception: Domain-specific, not process-specific. *Neuron, 44*, 889–898.

Yovel, G., & Kanwisher, N. (2005). The neural basis of the behavioral face-inversion effect. *Current Biology, 15*, 2256–2262.

Yovel, G., & Kanwisher, N. (2008). The representations of spacing and part-based information are associated for upright faces but dissociated for objects: Evidence from individual differences. *Psychonomic Bulletin and Review, 15*, 933–939.

Zhu, Q., Song, Y., Hu, S., Li, X., Tian, M., Zhen, Z.,...Liu, J. (2010). Heritability of the specific cognitive ability of face perception. *Current Biology, 20*, 137–142.

## Further Reading

Adams, R. B. Jr., Ambady, N., Nakayama, K., & Shimojo, S. (2011). *The science of social vision*. New York: Oxford University Press.

Calder, A. J., Rhodes, G., Johnson, M. H. & Haxby, J. V., (Eds.). (2011). *The Oxford handbook of face perception*. Oxford, England: Oxford University Press.

Maurer, D., Le Grand, R., & Mondloch, C. J. (2002). The many faces of configural processing. *Trends in Cognitive Sciences, 6*, 255–260.

McKone, E., Kanwisher, N., & Duchaine, B. C. (2006). Can generic expertise explain special processing for faces? *Trends in Cognitive Sciences, 11*, 8–15.

Peterson, M. P., & Rhodes, G. (Eds.). (2003). *Perception of faces, objects and scenes: Analytic and holistic processing*. Cambridge, MA: Oxford University Press.

# Eye Movements

John M. Henderson

**Abstract**

The active control of eye movements plays an important functional role in all visual and visuo-cognitive tasks. Eye movements ensure that visual input is available to the cognitive system as it is needed in the service of ongoing processing requirements. Eye movements are also an observable, behavioral manifestation of the allocation of attention, and the measurement of eye movements provides an unobtrusive, noninvasive, and sensitive window into the operation of the cognitive system as it unfolds in real time.

**Key Words:** eye movements, overt attention, perception, attention, scene perception, reading, face perception

The visual world contains an enormous amount of information, but human perception and cognition are capacity limited: Only a small percentage of the available information can be processed at any given moment. Efficient visual cognition therefore requires properly selecting the information that is most relevant given the current needs of the system. The primary way in which this selection takes place is via eye movements. Close or direct fixation of a region of a scene or other visual stimulus is typically necessary to perceive its visual details, to unambiguously determine its identity and meaning, and to encode that information into memory. What we see and understand about the world is in a very real sense determined by where we look.

In a classic demonstration of the relationship between eye movements and cognition, Yarbus (1967) presented a viewer with *Unexpected Visitor*, a painting by Ilya Repin depicting the homecoming of a soldier from war. The viewer was asked to look at the picture for a variety of purposes, and his eye movements changed systematically depending on the viewing task. For example, as can be seen in

Figure 5.1, when the viewer was asked to determine the ages of the people in the painting, he concentrated his fixations on their faces, but when he was asked to determine the material circumstances of the family in the painting, he directed his eye movements more generally over the objects in the scene.

Yarbus (1967) demonstrated that cognitive requirements can influence eye movements. The flip side is also true: Eye movements can influence cognitive activity. In a nice illustration of this point, Nelson and Loftus (1980) asked viewers to study line drawings of real-world scenes in preparation for a memory test. Eye movements were recorded during viewing. In the memory test, participants were asked to discriminate between objects that had originally appeared in the scenes and visually similar foils that differed in just a critical detail. Memory performance was highly related to the proximity of the closest fixation to the critical detail during memory encoding, with very good memory performance when the nearest fixation fell on the critical detail but near-chance performance when the closest fixation was 1.8 degrees or more away.

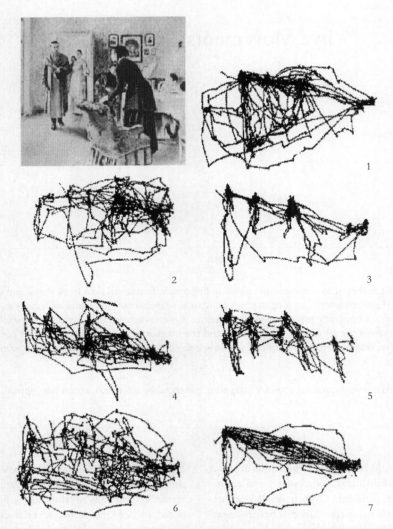

**Figure 5.1** Eye movements as a function of task while examining *Unexpected Visitors* by Ilya Rupin. (Reprinted from Yarbus, 1967.)

Another interesting example of the relationship between eye movements and visual cognition is observed in *change blindness*. In change blindness, viewers can be completely unaware of striking changes that take place right in front of their eyes (Levin & Simons, 1997). Hollingworth and Henderson (2002) directly manipulated whether a changing object in a scene was fixated. When viewers looked at a changing object before and after it changed, their ability to detect and report the change was dramatically improved compared to when they did not fixate the changing object. Consistent with Nelson and Loftus (1980), encoding information about the target object was highly related to fixating that object.

The reader can get a sense of the relationship between fixation and cognition by looking at Figure 5.2 depicting a famous Where's Waldo scene.

Choose any spot in the scene and try to understand other vignettes without making an eye movement. It is almost impossible to understand the individual vignettes in the picture without looking directly at each one of them, which is one of the reasons that this search is so difficult. The relationship between looking and seeing is highly counterintuitive for most people, and it is an important reason that we experience change blindness (Levin, Momen, Drivdahl, & Simons, 2000). Although we are not typically aware of the severe limitations in perception and cognition related to fixation, they are very strong.

### Gaze Control and Active Vision

Given the importance of where we look for perception and cognition, a critical issue in understanding

**Figure 5.2** An example from *Where's Waldo* of how important fixation is for perception and cognition. For example, look at the bumper cars in the right upper side of the scene. Think about the vignette. Did you notice that directly next to the vignette is a giant teddy bear? Or that there is a purveyor of cotton candy to the left? You probably did not notice any of these things until you moved your eyes directly to them, even though they are all directly in front of you.

eye movements concerns the representations and processes that govern where (and for how long) the eyes are directed within a complex image. We can define *gaze control* as the process of directing the eyes through a visual stimulus in real time in the service of ongoing perceptual, cognitive, and behavioral activity. Gaze control is an important topic for at least four reasons (Henderson & Hollingworth, 1999a). First, human vision is a dynamic process in which the viewer actively seeks out specific visual input as required given the current task and goals. Virtually all animals with developed visual systems actively control their direction of gaze using eye, head, and/or body movements (Land, 1999). Active vision via eye movements ensures that high-quality visual information is available when it is needed to support ongoing cognitive and behavioral activity, and it also can simplify a large variety of otherwise difficult computational problems (Ballard, Hayhoe, Pook, & Rao, 1997; Churchland, Ramachandran, & Sejnowski, 1994). A complete theory of visual cognition therefore requires understanding how ongoing visual and cognitive processes control the direction of the eyes. Second, because attention plays a central role in cognition, and because eye

movements provide a straightforward behavioral measure of the allocation of attention in a scene, eye movements serve as a window into the operation of the attentional system. Third, as already noted, where we look has important consequences for how we process the visual scene before us.

Finally, from a methodological standpoint, eye movements provide an unobtrusive, sensitive, real-time behavioral measure of visual and cognitive processing. This fact has been exploited to a significant degree in the study of reading (Rayner, 1998, 2009), and it is coming to play a similarly important role in many other areas of cognition, including scene understanding (Henderson, 2003), visual search (Zelinsky, 2008), memory (Henderson, 2008; Hollingworth, 2008), real-world behavioral tasks (Land & Hayhoe, 2001), spoken language comprehension and production (Henderson & Ferreira, 2004; Trueswell & Tanenhaus, 2004), and problem solving.

## Eye Movement Basics

Visual quality falls off rapidly and continuously from the center of gaze (the *fovea*) into a low-resolution visual surround, and all types of eye movements help to keep the fovea directed to a particular point or feature in space. This chapter will focus on saccadic eye movements because they have been the topic of the vast majority of research in cognitive psychology. Other types of eye movements include microsaccades, which help keep the image from fading on the retina due to fatigue; optokinetic nystagmus, which keeps fixation stable within a moving pattern; vergence movements, which direct the two eyes to a common point in depth; and smooth pursuit, which supports visual tracking over object or viewer motion. (For a general overview of eye movements in human vision, see Carpenter, 1988.) All types of eye movements operate when viewing the world, but it is less clear that they are directly reflective of ongoing cognitive processing than saccadic eye movements. However, there has been increasing interest in the hypothesis that both vergence movements (Kirby, Webster, Blythe, & Liversedge, 2008; Nuthmann & Kliegl, 2009) and microsaccades (Engbert & Kliegl, 2003) may provide additional insight into cognitive processes.

Saccadic eye movements are composed of two temporal epochs. During *fixations*, gaze position is held relatively still, and during *saccades*, the eyes move rapidly from one fixation location to another (Fig. 5.3). Saccadic eye movements are very fast (700 to 900 deg/sec; Carpenter, 1988), and due to a combination of visual masking and central suppression, visual uptake of pattern information is essentially shut down during the saccade, a phenomenon known as saccadic suppression (Matin, 1974; Thiele, Henning, Kubischik, & Hoffmann, 2002; Volkmann, 1961, 1986). There is evidence that some cognitive processes, particularly those associated with spatial cognition, are also suppressed during saccades (Irwin, 2004). Saccadic suppression implies that useful pattern information is acquired from complex visual stimuli only during fixations. The quality of the visual information available during a fixation falls off rapidly and continuously from the center of gaze due to the optical properties of the cornea and lens and the neuro-anatomical structure of the retina and visual cortex.

The highest quality visual information is acquired from the foveal region of a viewed scene, a spatial area subtending roughly 2 degrees of visual angle at and immediately surrounding the fixation point. The fovea is centered at the optical axis of the eye and has a high density of cones with minimal spatial summation. Although the cones require a relatively high level of luminance to operate, they support the perception of color and fine detail. Furthermore, a disproportionately large amount of primary visual cortex is devoted to the fovea, providing the neural machinery needed for initial visual computation that can take advantage of the high-resolution input from the fovea.

Saccadic eye movements are ubiquitous: On average the eyes move to a new fixation position about three times every second. Assuming 3 saccades per

**Figure 5.3** Scan pattern on a picture of a scene. The white circles represent fixations, the numbers represent the durations of those fixations, and the gray lines represent saccadic eye movements. The viewing task was to search for people in the picture. (From Henderson, 2003.)

second (180 per minute) and 16 waking hours per day, the average viewer makes about 172,800 saccades per day. In comparison, at an average of 60 heartbeats per minute, the eyes move about three times as frequently as the heart contracts.

### Saccades

Saccade amplitudes vary from an average of about 2 degrees in reading to about 4 degrees in picture viewing (Henderson & Hollingworth, 1998; Rayner, 1998). Larger average amplitudes are observed when eye movements are recorded during interaction with the world itself (Pelz & Canosa, 2001). To a good approximation, the duration of a saccade is a linear function of its amplitude, captured by the equation $D = 2.2A + 21$, where $D$ is the duration in milliseconds and $A$ is the amplitude in degrees (Carpenter, 1988). For example, the duration of a 2-degree saccade typical of reading would be about 25 ms, and of a 4-degree saccade typical of picture viewing would be about 30 ms. Saccade durations are roughly an order of magnitude shorter than the durations of fixations. With the notable exception of changes in saccadic trajectories as a function of attention and inhibition (Van der Stigchel, Meeter, & Theeuwes, 2006), saccades are typically not of direct interest in cognitive psychology except as the mechanism by which the point of fixation is moved from one location to another.

### Fixations

During fixations, the eyes are relatively still, though drifts and small corrective movements (microsaccades) are observed. Individual fixations average around a quarter to a third of a second in duration (Henderson & Hollingworth, 1998; Rayner, 1998, 2009), but there is a good deal of variability in these durations across viewing task, stimulus type, and individual (Henderson, 2003; Henderson & Hollingworth, 1998; Land & Hayhoe, 2001; Rayner, 1998). For example, fixation durations tend to average about 225 ms in reading and about 300 ms in picture viewing. These mean differences reflect differences in the underlying fixation duration frequency distributions, as shown in Figure 5.4. The mode of the fixation duration distribution in reading tends to be shifted to shorter durations, and there is less variability in the distribution compared to scene viewing (see also Henderson & Hollingworth, 1998). Fixation durations also vary as a function of task within a given stimulus type. For example, fixation durations are longer in picture viewing during memorization than during

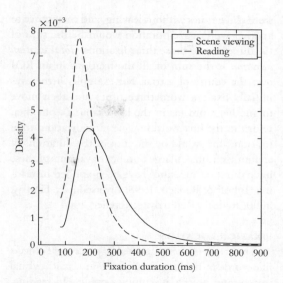

**Figure 5.4** Fixation duration distributions from scene viewing and reading. Data for the two tasks were collected using the same laboratory equipment and the same analysis procedures.

search (Henderson & Hollingworth, 1998; Võ & Henderson, 2009).

#### AGGREGATE FIXATION TIME

Aggregate fixation duration (sometimes called *dwell time*) is often used as a reflection of underlying cognitive processing. For example, the finding that fixation time on a word is longer if that word has a lower frequency in the language suggests that lexical frequency is an important psycholinguistic variable (see Chapter 28, this volume) and more generally that the cognitive system is highly sensitive to the relative frequency of environmental stimuli. Basic measures reported across a variety of tasks such as reading, search, and picture viewing include first fixation duration, gaze duration, and total fixation duration. These measures roughly rank from most to least fine-grained and are often thought to reflect influences from earlier to later stages of cognitive processing taking place within that fixation. *First fixation duration* is the elapsed time of the fixation resulting from the initial movement of the eyes into a region of interest (ROI) regardless of how many other fixations are made in that ROI. For example, in reading, first fixation duration in a word ROI is the duration of the very first fixation on that word, even if the word is immediately refixated. *Gaze durations* are the elapsed time of all fixations from the initial movement of the eyes entering an ROI until the first movement of the eyes exiting that ROI. For example, if the eyes move to a word, fixate that word three times without leaving, and then move to another word, gaze duration would be the sum of the durations of those three fixations. *Total fixation duration* is the sum of all the fixations in an ROI over the course of a trial. For example, if the eyes initially fixate a word three times and then move to another word (as in the last example), but then return to the first word for one more fixation, total fixation time would be the sum of the durations of all four fixations. A large number of variants of these basic duration measures have been applied in reading (Inhoff & Radach, 1998; Liversedge & Findlay, 2000; Radach, Kennedy, & Rayner, 2004).

## FIXATION LOCATION

The eyes tend to be directed to perceptual objects like words in reading, array items in classical visual search, and objects in complex scenes. In reading, the preferred viewing location (PVL) for fixation tends to be near the center (or just to the left of center) of a word (McConkie, Kerr, Reddix, & Zola, 1988; Rayner, 1979). A similar strong bias to fixate near the center of an object is observed for pictures of real-world objects in simple arrays (Henderson, 1993) and for objects in complex scenes (Nuthmann & Henderson, 2010).

In reading, the eyes tend to move in a generally stereotypical pattern, for example, left to right in English, though regressive (backward) eye movements occur about 20% of the time. Most words are fixated at least once, with short and predictable words sometimes skipped (Rayner, 2009). In difficult classical visual search, the eyes typically visit each item in an array, with regressive movements to previously visited items also observed as in reading (Williams, Henderson, & Zacks, 2005). When viewing pictures of real-world scenes, viewers tend to look at semantically important and cognitively relevant scene areas. Interestingly, the eyes also tend to cycle through the same scene regions rather than visiting new regions over time (Henderson & Hollingworth, 1998). This tendency can be seen in Figure 5.1 from the Yarbus (1967) study of picture viewing.

Fixation density represents the number of fixations in an ROI and when compared against fixations in other ROIs can be converted to the probability that a particular ROI will be fixated. As with fixation duration, a number of measures of fixation density can be generated. The *probability of region entry* measures the likelihood that an ROI is fixated at all. Empty or background regions of a search array or scene picture are often not fixated.

The *number of region entries* represents the number of times the eyes move to an ROI from outside of that ROI, and it reflects the tendency for the eyes to return to an ROI. *Gaze fixation count* represents the number of fixations in an ROI when it is entered, and it is related to gaze duration in that the durations of these fixations are summed for the latter measure. Similarly, *total fixation count* represents the number of total fixations in an ROI summed over all entries and is related to the total fixation duration measure.

Although density measures are often correlated, differences among them can be an important source of information about cognitive processing. For example, viewers may be unlikely to look at a particular ROI (low probability of entry), but given that they do look, they may fixate that ROI multiple times before exiting (high gaze fixation count), may return to the region multiple times (high number of entries), and may fixate multiple times on each entry (high total fixation count). This type of pattern can be found, for example, when a previously present object is deleted from a scene (Ryan, Althoff, Whitlow, & Cohen, 2000). In change blindness experiments, the ROI previously containing a deleted object may not typically be fixated. However, when the eyes do happen to land in the now-empty ROI, it tends then to receive many more fixations because, once fixated, the absence of the object is noted and the discrepancy leads to additional looks (Hollingworth & Henderson, 2002).

## Individual Differences

Individuals tend to be consistent in their average saccade amplitudes and average fixation durations from one viewing task or stimulus type to another (Andrews & Coppola, 1999; Castelhano & Henderson, 2008; Rayner, Li, Williams, Cave, & Well, 2007). Andrews and Coppola (1999) observed that fixation durations and saccade amplitudes covaried within individuals across reading and visual search tasks but not from those tasks to scene perception. Castelhano and Henderson (2008) reported that both fixation durations and saccade amplitudes tended to be stable within an individual across different types of scene images and faces. For example, people who averaged shorter fixation durations in scene viewing also tended to have shorter fixation durations during face viewing. The same correlations held for saccade amplitudes. Rayner et al. (2007) observed a strong relationship of mean fixation duration between scene and face viewing, consistent with Castelhano and Henderson, and a weak relationship between scene viewing and search, consistent with Andrews and Coppola. Interestingly, Castelhano and Henderson found no relationship between average fixation duration and average saccade amplitude: Although a person with short average fixation durations in one type of image also tended to have short average fixation durations in another type of image, this person might make either shorter or longer amplitude saccades. The consistency in eye movement parameters within individuals is striking and suggests that eye movements may provide a reliable psychometric measure. Exactly what underlying cognitive and neural processes these differences reflect has yet to be determined.

## Eye Movements in Cognitive Domains

Eye movements are important for and are used to study a wide variety of topics in cognition. Two important issues for understanding eye movements across these domains in cognition are *where* the eyes tend to be directed and *how long* they typically remain there in each area of investigation.

### Reading

A major motivation for the development of eye-tracking methods historically has been the study of skilled reading. Eyetracking has proved to be one of the richest and most important sources of information about the perceptual, cognitive, and linguistic processes that take place during reading. The literature on eye movements in reading is vast, and justice cannot be done to it in the space provided here. The interested reader is directed to the comprehensive review by Rayner (2009), the succinct overviews by Rayner and Liversedge (2004) and Starr and Rayner (2001), and Chapter 28 in this volume.

During reading, the eyes move across the page at a rate of about four fixations per second. Most words in a text are fixated, and many words receive more than one fixation. Shorter, higher frequency, and more highly constrained words tend to be skipped more often than longer, lower frequency, and less constrained words. The majority of saccades carry the eyes forward (rightward in English) through the text, though backward or regressive eye movements are not uncommon. The eyes also move right to left during return sweeps, taking them from the end of one line to the beginning of the next. Average fixation durations are about 225 ms, and average forward saccade amplitudes are about 8 character spaces or two degrees for normal text at a typical reading distance, with considerable variability for both measures. The durations of individual fixations on a word as well as cumulative durations are related to the perceptual and cognitive processes associated with that word. For example, the first fixation duration on a word is affected by lexical factors (e.g., word length and word frequency), syntactic factors (e.g., syntactic complexity), and discourse factors (e.g., anaphor resolution).

An important methodological development in the study of reading was the *eye-contingent display change technique* (McConkie & Rayner, 1975; Rayner, 1975). In this technique an eyetracker and display device are interfaced with a computer, and the text displayed on the monitor is changed contingent on characteristics of a reader's eye position or movement. This technique provides a powerful method for investigating central issues in vision and attention related to eye movements. For example, the perceptual span is defined as the distance beyond fixation from which useful information can be acquired during fixation. Initial investigations of the perceptual span involved the tachistoscope, which was developed for this use. However, estimates of the perceptual span in reading that were derived from the tachistoscope were misleading (Rayner, 1975, 1998). To circumvent the problems associated with brief stimulus presentations, George McConkie and Keith Rayner developed the *moving window paradigm* (McConkie & Rayner, 1975), a version of the eye-contingent display change technique in which the text surrounding fixation is displayed normally but the text at some distance from fixation is degraded. Because the display is updated based on the signal from the eyetracker, the region of text within the window moves with the eyes, providing clear text wherever the reader looks and degraded text elsewhere. By manipulating the size of the window of clear text and the nature of the degradation outside the window, the investigator can infer the size of the perceptual span in reading for various sorts of features such as letter identities, letter features, and word spaces (see Rayner, 2009). The inverse of the moving window, a moving mask at fixation that creates an artificial scotoma or blind spot, has also been used to study basic visual processes in reading. These studies demonstrate the critical importance of foveal vision in normal reading, with near-complete loss of reading comprehension when text is not available at the fovea (Rayner & Bertera, 1979; Rayner, Inhoff, Morrison, Slowiaczek, & Bertera, 1981).

## Scene Viewing

It has been known at least since the classic study by Buswell (1935) that the spatial distribution of fixations is not random in pictures of real-world scenes. Despite the elementary nature of his eye-tracker, Buswell discovered many of the basic facts about eye movements in picture viewing. For example, he was the first to report that viewers tend to cluster fixations on informative picture regions, and he was also able to estimate accurately the mean fixation durations and saccade amplitudes as well as the degree of variability within and across viewers, and within and across images, for these measures. Based on his observations, Buswell concluded that there is an important relationship between eye movements and visual attention. Perhaps better known even than Buswell, Yarbus (1967) also reported that eye movements over pictures are highly systematic and concluded that they are influenced by the viewer's task and goals. Indeed, many of the classic illustrations of eye movement patterns over pictures found in current textbooks (such as Fig. 5.1) are taken from the study reported by Yarbus. Both Buswell and Yarbus concluded from their observations that informative scene regions are more likely to receive fixations than less informative regions. This conclusion was based on what we might call a "natural history" approach, in the sense that the work involved interpreting observations rather than conducting controlled experiments. Even so, when the main aspects of the Yarbus study were reproduced with modern eyetracking equipment and more viewers, the primary results were replicated (DeAngelus & Pelz, 2009). There is now a wealth of evidence that viewers look at scene regions that are cognitively informative, both in pictures and in the world.

In scene viewing, an important issue concerns whether the eyes are "pulled" to a particular location by the visual features present at that location, or "pushed" to a particular location by cognitive factors related to active knowledge structures (Henderson, 2003, 2007). Intuitively, a dense, bright, or colorful region could attract the eyes in a bottom-up manner. Similarly, the eyes could move to particular locations simply on the basis of oculomotor tendencies, such as biases to move to the centers of words in reading (Rayner, 1979) or horizontally and in the same direction in pictures (Smith & Henderson, 2009; Tatler & Vincent, 2009). On the other hand, a viewer would likely want to look at a scene region that is relevant given current tasks and goals regardless of whether those regions are bright and colorful or otherwise visually conspicuous, and regardless of whether they are close to the current fixation location (Henderson, 2007; Henderson, Malcolm, & Schandl, 2009).

The dominance of cognitive factors on eye movements in scene viewing is easily illustrated by considering where you would look if you want to know the time. You would not look at the brightest or the most colorful thing in your visual field, but rather at an object in a location likely to provide the time (perhaps your wrist, or a clock on the wall). Fixation sites are far less strongly tied to visual saliency when meaningful scenes are viewed during active tasks (Land & Hayhoe, 2001). Completely nonsalient objects are quickly fixated when they are task relevant (Henderson et al., 2009). Even the initial saccades in a scene tend to move the eyes toward the likely location of a search target, regardless of whether the target is present, because a rapid understanding of the general meaning of a scene and its spatial layout provide important constraints on where a particular object is likely to be found (Castelhano & Henderson, 2007). These issues are taken up again in the section on "Cognition and Gaze Control."

## Visual Search

Although the topic of visual search is often introduced in terms of everyday behaviors like searching for car keys, it has traditionally been studied in the context of arrays of simple stimuli such as letters or geometric shapes. Similarly, many of the studies of eye movements in search have focused on traditional search arrays. More recently, eye movements have been used as a method to study visual search in real-world images, moving the investigation of search closer to the natural activity that inspires it. For example, recently eye movements have been used to investigate how quickly viewers can find specific target objects in photographs of complex real-world scenes (Henderson et al., 2009; Malcolm & Henderson, 2009, 2010; Rayner, Smith, Malcolm, & Henderson, 2009). Taking this one step further, Gajewski et al. (2005) studied search in the real environment using a portable eyetracker. These investigators had viewers search for coffee cups in an office and showed that the eyes are also intelligently controlled when scanning the world.

Eye movements also provide a method for dividing the underlying cognitive processes involved in search into observable behavioral epochs mapping onto sub-processes that otherwise are difficult to disentangle (Castelhano, Pollatsek, & Cave, 2008;

Malcolm & Henderson, 2009, 2010). For example, Malcolm and Henderson (2009) used eye movements to divide visual search into an initial preparation epoch, a scanning epoch, and a target verification epoch, and further were able to separate the spatial distribution of attention and distracter rejection during scanning. Their results showed that the visual specificity of the search target that viewers held in mind while searching affected the selection of potential target locations for attention as well as the time needed to reject distracters and verify the target once it was found.

### Face Viewing

In his early study, Yarbus (1967) studied viewers' eye movement patterns on a number of pictures of faces. The viewing pattern on the profile bust of Queen Nefertiti suggested that a large percentage of viewing time was spent on the outside bounding contours of the face. A second example from Yarbus showed eye movements on a picture of a face viewed from straight on. In this example eye movements were more concentrated on the internal features of the face, though fixations on the outer contours of the face were observed here as well. An often overlooked aspect of the Yarbus study is that these demonstrations were typically based on a single participant viewing a single image for a very long period of time. There is now considerable evidence that for static face images, eye movements tend to be directed predominantly to internal facial features during both face learning and face recognition (Groner, Walder, & Groner, 1984; Henderson, Williams, & Falk, 2005; Walker-Smith, Gale, & Findlay, 1977). For example, Henderson, Falk, and colleagues (2001) reported that close to 60% of fixation time was spent on the eyes in a face recognition task, and that about 90% of fixation time was spent on the eyes, nose, and mouth. These eye movements appear to play a functional role: Henderson, Williams, and Falk (2005) demonstrated that face recognition was greatly impaired when participants were restrained from making eye movements during face learning compared to a condition in which they were free to move their eyes, holding viewing time constant.

Like scene viewing, eye movements during face viewing have primarily been investigated using static pictures. In a study investigating eye movements during viewing of dynamic faces, viewers were more likely to fixate the centers of a face than the main features (Bindemann, Scheepers, & Burton, 2009). Võ, Smith, Mital, and Henderson (in press) found that fixations on the center of faces increased when those faces were moving. It may be that the observed tendency to heavily concentrate fixations on the eyes of a face is specific to static face pictures.

### The Real World

One of the most important limitations in the use of eyetracking in the past involves expanding the methodology to less constrained and more natural situations in which a viewer is free to move within and interact with the natural environment. Investigators have begun to study perception in the real environment using portable free-movement eyetrackers (Land & Hayhoe, 2001; Land, Mennie, & Rusted, 1999). This innovative use of eyetracking involves lightweight head-mounted optics and portable electronics that allow the viewer to move naturally and freely without being tethered to any stationary equipment. Though research using these devices is still relatively new, it has become apparent that there are important differences in eye movements for pictures of the environment and the environment itself. For example, frequency distributions of fixation durations and saccade amplitudes appear to differ depending on whether a viewer is examining a scene depiction or the real environment, with average saccade amplitudes significantly greater for the environment (Land & Hayhoe, 2001). Free-movement eyetracking allows investigators to study the nature of the eye movements that are made in the service of everyday tasks like driving (Land & Horwood, 1995) and tea and sandwich making (Hayhoe, Shrivastava, Mruczek, & Pelz, 2003; Land et al., 1999).

Recent eyetracking technologies have allowed mobile free-movement eyetracking. A limitation of these trackers, though, is that they tend to be less accurate than their stationary counterparts. Furthermore, the data that are collected from them are much more difficult to analyze because they require that video data be hand-scored. Although significant progress has been made in these areas, in many ways the use of free-movement eyetracking is in its infancy and will continue to progress as new methods for automated data analysis are developed. Furthermore, a limitation of studies using free-viewing eyetrackers in the world is that experimental control of the visual stimulus becomes very difficult. Therefore, continuing progress in the study of eye movements in perception and cognition is likely to involve converging evidence from both free-movement eyetrackers and highly accurate stationary eyetrackers.

## Spoken Language Comprehension and Production

A powerful tool for investigating language processing is to monitor the eye movements that people make as they listen to speech while simultaneously looking at a visual world containing relevant objects (Tanenhaus, Spivey-Knowlton, Eberhard, & Sedivy, 1995; for reviews see Ferreira & Tanenhaus, 2007; Henderson & Ferreira, 2004; Trueswell & Tanenhaus, 2004). Studies using this *visual world paradigm* have demonstrated that the interpretations listeners derive from language are often used to guide the eyes almost immediately to relevant objects that are present in the visual field. Moreover, listeners are highly likely to fixate a visual object within about a 1-second window following the onset of a related spoken word, even when nothing about the task seems to demand that the word and the object be linked. These results suggest that language can provide a strong source of top-down control over how attention and the eyes are directed through a visual scene. Similar results are observed in language production, where a tight temporal link is observed between a speaker's eye movements and utterance generation, with objects about to be spoken typically fixated just prior to (within 1 second of) mention (Griffin & Bock, 2000). Because of the apparent tight link between eye movements to visual entities and ongoing linguistic processing, the visual world paradigm has become a staple for investigating cognitive processes related to language comprehension and production. Eyetracking provides a powerful technique for investigating theoretical issues in language production and comprehension, and for understanding the interaction between language and vision.

## Memory

It is clear that people encode and retain a great deal of information about the objects that they fixate (Henderson, 2008; Hollingworth, 2008). Studies of change blindness have shown that change detection is facilitated when the eyes spontaneously return to the changed region compared to when they do not (Henderson & Hollingworth, 1999b; Hollingworth & Henderson, 2002). This latter effect has also been found when the eyes are directed to the changed region via an attentional cue (Hollingworth, 2006). Johansson et al. (2006) asked participants to view scenes while listening to a verbal description. When participants later described the scene from memory, their eye movements were found to be similar to the pattern executed during scene encoding. This tendency persisted even in complete darkness. Laeng and Teodorescu (2002) found that scan patterns made by participants when they imagined a stimulus they had previously viewed were similar to those executed during stimulus encoding. They also observed that similarity in eye movement patterns from encoding to imagery predicted memory accuracy, indicating that the eye movements made during the imagery task were functional. Thus, there is considerable evidence in the literature that attending to and looking at a location facilitates memory retrieval of information which had occupied that location.

## Social Attention

Where another person is looking is known to be a powerful source of social information. Humans are exquisitely sensitive to another person's direction of gaze (von Grünau & Anston, 1995). The human eye appears to have evolved so that the dark pupil and white sclera provide maximal information about gaze direction in others. The direction that another person is looking elicits a reflexive response in our own gaze in simple visual displays, an effect that is observed regardless of the relationship of the perceived gaze to the task at hand, and even when it is detrimental to performance (Driver et al., 1999; Friesen & Kingstone, 2003; Friesen, Ristic, & Kingstone, 2004; Langton & Bruce, 2000; Ricciardelli, Bricolo, Aglioti, & Chelazzi, 2002).

The gaze direction of another person provides a potentially important source of information concerning what is interesting and informative in a complex scene. Castelhano, Wieth, and Henderson (2008) conducted an eyetracking study in which participants watched a slideshow depicting an unfolding vignette. The slideshow portrayed the story of a janitor (the actor) cleaning a university office. Viewers' eye movements were strongly influenced by the gaze direction of the actor. The object that was the focus of the actor's gaze (the focused object) was fixated on a larger percentage of trials than any other scene region, including the actor's face. Furthermore, given that the focused object was fixated, it was fixated sooner, more often, and for a longer duration than any other scene region. The results provided the first demonstration that an observer's eye movements are influenced by the direction of gaze of an actor in an image of a real-world scene, and they clearly showed that what one person is looking at has a strong influence on what an observer will look at.

## Cognition and Gaze Control

What drives eye movements through a visual stimulus? A good deal of the literature on the relationship between cognition and eye movements has focused on this question, with answers ranging from random or stochastic processes, to simple oculomotor biases, to visual properties of the stimulus, to ongoing perceptual and cognitive processing. The answer to this question is of critical importance if eye movements are to be taken as relevant to the study of cognition. The tension especially between random, oculomotor, and stimulus-driven control on the one hand, and knowledge-driven control on the other, has historically been central in the study of eye movements in reading, and it continues to play out in the literature today. For example, the theoretical disagreement between the two most prominent models of eye movements in reading hinges partially on the emphasis placed on oculomotor and stimulus factors (the SWIFT model of Engbert, Nuthmann, Richtere, & Kliegl, 2005, versus linguistic and cognitive factors in the EZ Reader model of Reichle, Pollatsek, Fisher, & Rayner, 1998).

Similarly, much of the research on gaze control in scene perception has focused on the role of the visual stimulus in determining fixation placement (Itti & Koch, 2000, 2001; Koch & Ullman, 1985; Parkhurst, Law, & Niebur, 2002). This emphasis on stimulus control is motivated in part by research in attention suggesting that image differences perceptually "pop out" and capture attention (Treisman & Gelade, 1980; Wolfe, Cave, & Franzel, 1989). Because oculomotor biases and image properties are more tractable and easier to model than cognitive knowledge structures, initial attempts to generate computational models and quantitative predictions of human eye movements in scenes have tended to focus on them. And given the correlation between image features and interesting places to look (Elazary & Itti, 2008; Henderson, 2003; Henderson, Brockmole, Castelhano, & Mack, 2007), this approach makes sense from an engineering perspective where the goal may be to develop artificial vision systems that are able to actively orient sensors to potentially important input. However, from the perspective of understanding the causal mechanisms that drive human gaze control, it is clear that a theory based purely on oculomotor and image characteristics approach is severely limited (Henderson, 2007; Henderson et

al., 2007, 2009). Of course, this is not to say that the visual stimulus plays no role in human gaze control; there must be some internal map over which saccades are planned, and this map derives to a large degree from the visual input. In addition, relevant knowledge structures are activated in part based on the incoming visual information. Importantly, though, it is clear that selecting fixation locations is primarily a function of cognitive systems engaged in interpretation of the scene and task considerations, not by inherent differences in the image properties themselves. This is an important insight in the context of eye movements and cognition.

## Converging Methods and Future Directions
### Computational Modeling

An important growing area in the study of eye movements involves the use of computational modeling, particularly in the study of eye movements in reading, visual search, and complex scene perception. In each case, the aim has been to account for the spatial and temporal characteristics of eye movements and their relationship to perceptual and cognitive factors. In reading, current computational models are focused on predicting the basic statistics of eye movement control such as the means and frequencies of fixation durations and saccade amplitudes (Engbert et al., 2005; Reichle et al., 1998). In these models, specification of the relationship between covert attention and eye movements, and the degree to which lexical processing is serial versus parallel, are central issues of critical concern.

In scene perception, recent computational models have been inspired by known response properties of neurons in visual cortex, and the primary focus has been to determine where and in what order fixations will be placed in a scene (Itti & Koch, 2000; Kanan, Tong, Zhang, & Cottrell, 2009; Torralba, Oliva, Castelhano, & Henderson, 2006; Zelinsky, 2008), whereas issues of fixation durations have tended to be ignored (Henderson, 2003). An important step in redressing this imbalance is the appearance of a computational model accounting for fixation durations in scene viewing (Nuthmann et al., 2010, 2012).

It is understandable that models of scene viewing have been designed largely to explain fixation locations. In reading, selection of the next fixation location is relatively straightforward (typically, the next word) and variability in fixation duration is potentially more diagnostic of ongoing cognitive processing. In scene viewing, on the other hand, selection of the next fixation location is more complex, with two (for pictures) or three (for the world) dimensions to account for. By contrast, fixation durations during scene viewing can appear to be of secondary importance. A focus for future eye movement modeling will be to capture a more complete set of eye movement characteristics across multiple viewing situations and tasks. A convergence of modeling approaches across domains that accounts for both the where and when decisions is likely to provide a fruitful arena for generating and testing new theory.

## Neuroimaging

A final area ripe for significant progress is the integration of sophisticated eyetracking with methods of functional neuroimaging. For example, many magnetic resonance imaging (MRI) scanners used for functional MRI (fMRI) research have eyetrackers installed in them, but these eyetrackers have tended to be used to determine whether the subject is maintaining fixation, or at best to determine whether a saccade has been executed in a specific direction at a specific time, as for example in the anti-saccade task (Hallett, 1978). While these uses are important, they barely scratch the surface of the utility of the method for determining where and when perceptual, attentional, and cognitive processes have been deployed over a given complex visual stimulus. The combined integration of sophisticated eyetracking to measure the locus of eye fixations over time with methods for examining neural activity related to specific fixations (or saccades), in fMRI as well as other neuroimaging techniques such as event-related potentials (ERP) and magnetoencephalography (MEG), would seem to offer tremendous opportunity for advancing our knowledge of mind and brain.

## Conclusion

The active control of eye fixation plays an important functional role in all perceptual and cognitive tasks. Active vision ensures that visual input is available to the cognitive system as it is needed. The measurement of eye movements provides an unobtrusive, noninvasive, sensitive, behavioral window into the operation of the cognitive system as it unfolds in real time.

## References

Andrews, T. J., & Coppola, D. M. (1999). Idiosyncratic characteristics of saccadic eye movements when viewing different visual environments. *Vision Research, 39*(17), 2947–2953.

Ballard, D. H., Hayhoe, M. M., Pook, P. K., & Rao, R. P. N. (1997). Deictic codes for the embodiment of cognition. *Behavioral and Brain Sciences, 20*(4), 723–742.

Bindemann, M., Scheepers, C., & Burton, A. M. (2009). Viewpoint and center of gravity affect eye movements to human faces. *Journal of Vision, 9*(2), 1–16.

Buswell, G. T. (1935). *How people look at pictures: A study of the psychology of perception in art.* Chicago: University of Chicago Press.

Carpenter, R. H. S. (1988). *Movements of the eyes* (2nd ed.). London: Pion.

Castelhano, M. S., & Henderson, J. M. (2007). Initial scene representations facilitate eye movement guidance in visual search. *Journal of Experimental Psychology: Human Perception and Performance, 33*(4), 753–763.

Castelhano, M. S., & Henderson, J. M. (2008). Stable individual differences across images in human saccadic eye movements. *Canadian Journal of Experimental Psychology, 62,* 1–14.

Castelhano, M. S., Pollatsek, A., & Cave, K. (2008). Typicality aids search for an unspecified target, but only in identification and not in attentional guidance. *Psychonomic Bulletin and Review, 14*(4), 795–801.

Castelhano, M. S., Wieth, M. S., & Henderson, J. M. (2008). I see what you see: Eye movements in real-world scenes are affected by perceived direction of gaze. *Attention in cognitive systems.* Berlin: Springer.

Churchland, P. S., Ramachandran, V. S., & Sejnowski, T. J. (1994). A critique of pure vision. In C. Koch and J. L. Davis (Ed.), *Large-scale neuronal theories of the brain* (pp. 343). Cambridge, MA: MIT Press.

DeAngelus, M., & Pelz, J. B. (2009). Top-down control of eye movements: Yarbus revisited. *Visual Cognition, 17*(6), 790–811.

Driver, J., Davis, G., Kidd, P., Maxwell, E., Ricciardelli, P., & Baron-Cohen, S. (1999). Gaze perception triggers reflexive visuospatial orienting. *Visual Cognition, 6,* 509–541.

Elazary, L., & Itti, L. (2008). Interesting objects are visually salient. *Journal of Vision, 8*(3), 3 1–15.

Engbert, R., & Kliegl, R. (2003). Microsaccades uncover the orientation of covert attention. *Vision Research, 43,* 1035–1045.

Engbert, R., Nuthmann, A., Richter, E. M., & Kliegl, R. (2005). SWIFT: A dynamical model of saccade generation during reading. *Psychological Review, 112*(4), 777–813.

Ferreira, F., & Tanenhaus, M. K. (2007). Introduction to the special issue on language-vision interactions. *Journal of Memory and Language, 57,* 455–459.

Friesen, C. K., & Kingstone, A. (2003). Abrupt onsets and gaze direction cues trigger independent reflexive attentional effects. *Cognition, 87*(1), B1–B10.

Friesen, C. K., Ristic, J., & Kingstone, A. (2004). Attentional effects of counterpredictive gaze and arrow cues. *Journal of Experimental Psychology: Human Perception and Performance, 30*(2), 319–329.

Gajewski, D. A., Pearson, A. M., Mack, M. L., Bartlett, F. N., & Henderson, J. M. (2005). Human gaze control in real world search. *Attention and Performance in Computational Vision, 3368,* 83–99.

Griffin, Z. M., & Bock, K. (2000). What the eyes say about speaking. *Psychological Science, 11,* 274–279.

Groner, R., Walder, F., & Groner, M. (1984). Looking at faces: Local and global aspects of scanpaths. In F. Johnson & A. G. Gale (Eds.), *Theoretical and applied aspects of eye movement research* (pp. 523–533). Amsterdam, The Netherlands: Elsevier.

Hallett, P. E. (1978). Primary and secondary saccades to goals defined by instructions. *Vision Research, 18*, 1279–1296.

Hayhoe, M. M., Shrivastava, A., Mruczek, R., & Pelz, J. B. (2003). Visual memory and motor planning in a natural task. *Journal of Vision, 3*(1), 49–63.

Henderson, J. M. (1993). Eye-movement control during visual object processing—effects of initial fixation position and semantic constraint. *Canadian Journal of Experimental Psychology: Revue Canadienne De Psychologie Experimentale, 47*(1), 79–98.

Henderson, J. M. (2003). Human gaze control during real-world scene perception. *Trends in Cognitive Sciences, 7*(11), 498–504.

Henderson, J. M. (2007). Regarding scenes. *Current Directions in Psychological Science, 16*(4), 219–222.

Henderson, J. M. (2008). Eye movements and visual memory. In S. J. Luck & A. Hollingworth (Eds.), *Visual memory* (pp. 87–121). Oxford, England: Oxford University Press.

Henderson, J. M., Brockmole, J. R., Castelhano, M. S., & Mack, M. (2007). Visual saliency does not account for eye movements during visual search in real-world scenes. In R. v. Gompel, M. Fischer, W. Murray, & R. Hill (Eds.), *Eye movements: A window on mind and brain* (pp. 537–562). Oxford, England: Elsevier.

Henderson, J. M., Falk, R. J., Minut, S., Dyer, F. C., & Mahadevan, S. (2001). Gaze control for face learning and recognition in humans and machines. In T. Shipley & P. Kellman (Eds.), *From fragments to objects: Segmentation processes in vision* (pp. 463–481). New York: Elsevier.

Henderson, J. M., & Ferreira, F. (2004). *The interface of language, vision, and action: Eye movements and the visual world*. New York: Psychology Press.

Henderson, J. M., & Hollingworth, A. (1998). Eye movements during scene viewing: An overview. In G. Underwood (Ed.), *Eye guidance while reading and while watching dynamic scenes* (pp. 269–293). Oxford, England: Elsevier.

Henderson, J. M., & Hollingworth, A. (1999a). High-level scene perception. *Annual Review of Psychology, 50*, 243–271.

Henderson, J. M., & Hollingworth, A. (1999b). The role of fixation position in detecting scene changes across saccades. *Psychological Science, 10*(5), 438–443.

Henderson, J. M., Malcolm, G. L., & Schandl, C. (2009). Searching the the dark: Cognitive relevance drives attention in real-worls scenes. *Psychonomic Bulletin Review, 16*(5), 850–856.

Henderson, J. M., Williams, C. C., & Falk, R. J. (2005). Eye movements are functional during face learning. *Memory and Cognition, 33*(1), 98–106.

Hollingworth, A. (2006). Scene and position specificity in visual memory for objects. *Journal of Experimental Psychology: Learning, Memory and Cognition, 32*(1), 58–69.

Hollingworth, A. (2008). Visual memory for natural scenes. In S. J. Luck & A. Hollingworth (Eds.), *Visual memory* (pp. 123–162). New York: Oxford University Press.

Hollingworth, A., & Henderson, J. M. (2002). Accurate visual memory for previously attended objects in natural scenes. *Journal of Experimental Psychology: Human Perception and Performance, 28*(1), 113–136.

Inhoff, A. W., & Radach, R. (1998). Definition and computation of oculomotor measures in the study of cognitive processes. In G. Underwood (Ed.), *Eye guidance in reading and scene perception (pp. 29–53)*. Oxford, England: Elsevier.

Irwin, D. E. (2004). Fixation location and fixation duration as indices of cognitive processing. In J. M. Henderson & F. Ferreira (Eds.), *The interface of language, vision, and action: Eye movements and the visual world (pp. 105–133)*. New York: Psychology Press.

Itti, L., & Koch, C. (2000). A saliency-based search mechanism for overt and covert shifts of visual attention. *Vision Research, 40*(10–12), 1489–1506.

Itti, L., & Koch, C. (2001). Computational modelling of visual attention. *Nature Reviews Neuroscience, 2*(3), 194–203.

Johansson, R., Holsanova, J., & Holmqvist, K. (2006). Pictures and spoken descriptions elicit similar eye movements during mental imagery, both in light and in complete darkness. *Cognitive Science, 30*(6), 1053–1079.

Kanan, C., Tong, M. H., Zhang, L., & Cottrell, G. W. (2009). SUN: Top-down saliency using natural statistics. *Visual Cognition, 17*(6&7), 979–1003.

Kirby, J. A., Webster, L. A. D., Blythe, H. I., & Liversedge, S. P. (2008). Binocular coordination during reading and non-reading tasks. *Psychological Bulletin, 134*(5), 742–763.

Koch, C., & Ullman, S. (1985). Shifts in selective visual-attention—towards the underlying neural circuitry. *Human Neurobiology, 4*(4), 219–227.

Laeng, B., & Teodorescu, D. S. (2002). Eye scanpaths during visual imagery reenact those of perception of the same visual scene. *Cognitive Science, 26*(2), 207–231.

Land, M. F. (1999). Motion and vision: Why animals move their eyes. *Journal of Comparative Physiology: Neuroethology Sensory Neural and Behavioral Physiology, 185*(4), 341–352.

Land, M. F., & Hayhoe, M. (2001). In what ways do eye movements contribute to everyday activities? *Vision Research, 41*(25–26), 3559–3565.

Land, M. F., & Horwood, J. (1995). Which parts of the road guide steering. *Nature, 377*(6547), 339–340.

Land, M. F., Mennie, N., & Rusted, J. (1999). The roles of vision and eye movements in the control of activities of daily living. *Perception, 28*(11), 1311–1328.

Langton, S. R., & Bruce, V. (2000). You must see the point: Automatic processing of cues to the direction of social attention. *Journal of Experimental Psychology: Human Perception and Performance, 26*(2), 747–757.

Levin, D. T., Momen, N., Drivdahl, S. B., & Simons, D. J. (2000). Change blindness blindness: The metacognitive error of overestimating change-detection ability. *Visual Cognition, 7*(1–3), 397–412.

Levin, D. T., & Simons, D. J. (1997). Failure to detect changes to attended objects in motion pictures. *Psychonomic Bulletin & Review, 4*, 501–506.

Liversedge, S. P., & Findlay, J. M. (2000). Saccadic eye movements and cognition. *Trends in Cognitive Sciences, 4*(1), 6–14.

Malcolm, G. L., & Henderson, J. M. (2009). The effects of target template specificity on visual search in real-world scenes: Evidence from eye movements. *Journal of Vision, 9*(11):8.1–13.

Malcolm, G. L., & Henderson, J. M. (2010). Combining top-down processes to guide eye movements during real-world scene search. *Journal of Vision, 10*(2):4.1–11.

Matin, E. (1974). Saccadic suppression—review and an analysis. *Psychological Bulletin, 81*(12), 899–917.

McConkie, G. W., Kerr, P. W., Reddix, M. D., & Zola, D. (1988). Eye movement control during reading: I. The location of initial eye fixations on words. *Vision Research, 28,* 245–253.

McConkie, G. W., & Rayner, K. (1975). The span of the effective stimulus during a fixation in reading. *Perception and Psychophysics, 17,* 578–586.

Nelson, W. W., & Loftus, G. R. (1980). The functional visual-field during picture viewing. *Journal of Experimental Psychology: Human Learning and Memory, 6*(4), 391–399.

Nuthmann, A., & Kliegl, R. (2009). An examination of binocular reading fixations based on sentence corpus data. *Journal of Vision, 9*(5):31.1–28.

Nuthmann, A., Smith, T. J., Engbert, R., & Henderson, J. M. (2010). CRISP: A computational model of fixation durations in scene viewing. *Psychological Review, 117,* 382–405.

Nuthmann, A., & Henderson, J. M. (2012). Using CRISP to model global characteristics of fixation durations in scene viewing and reading with a common mechanism. *Visual Cognition, 20,* 457–494.

Parkhurst, D., Law, K., & Niebur, E. (2002). Modeling the role of salience in the allocation of overt visual attention. *Vision Research, 42*(1), 107–123.

Pelz, J. B., & Canosa, R. (2001). Oculomotor behavior and perceptual strategies in complex tasks. *Vision Research, 41*(25–26), 3587–3596.

Radach, R., Kennedy, A., & Rayner, K. (2004). Eye movements and information processing during reading—preface. *European Journal of Cognitive Psychology, 16*(1–2), 1–2.

Rayner, K. (1975). The perceptual span and peripheral cues in reading. *Cognitive Psychology, 7,* 65–81.

Rayner, K. (1979). Eye guidance in reading: Fixation locations within words. *Perception, 8,* 21–30.

Rayner, K. (1998). Eye movements in reading and information processing: 20 years of research. *Psychological Bulletin, 124*(3), 372–422.

Rayner, K. (2009). The Thirty Fifth Sir Frederick Bartlett Lecture: Eye movements and attention during reading, scene perception, and visual search. *Quarterly Journal of Experimental Psychology, 62,* 1457–1506.

Rayner, K., & Bertera, J. H. (1979). Reading without a fovea. *Science, 206,* 468–489.

Rayner, K., Inhoff, A. W., Morrison, R. E., Slowiaczek, M. L., & Bertera, J. H. (1981). Masking of foveal and parafoveal vision during fixations in reading. *Journal of Experimental Psychology: Human Perception and Performance, 7,* 167–179.

Rayner, K., Li, X., Williams, C. C., Cave, K. R., & Well, A. D. (2007). Eye movements during information processing tasks: Individual differences and cultural effects. *Vision Research, 47*(21), 2714–2726.

Rayner, K., & Liversedge, S. P. (2004). Visual and linguistic processing during eye fixations in reading. In J. M. Henderson & F. Ferreira (Eds.), *The interface of language, vision, and action: Eye movements and the visual world (pp. 59–104).* New York: Psychology Press.

Rayner, K., Smith, T. J., Malcolm, G. L., & Henderson, J. M. (2009). Eye movements and visual encoding during scene perception. *Psychological Science, 20*(1), 6–10.

Reichle, E. D., Pollatsek, A., Fisher, D. L., & Rayner, K. (1998). Toward a model of eye movement control in reading. *Psychological Review, 105*(1), 125–157.

Ricciardelli, P., Bricolo, E., Aglioti, S. M., & Chelazzi, L. (2002). My eyes want to look where your eyes are looking: Exploring the tendency to imitate another individual's gaze. *Neuroreport, 13*(17), 2259–2264.

Ryan, J. D., Althoff, R. R., Whitlow, S., & Cohen, N. J. (2000). Amnesia is a deficit in relational memory. *Psychological Science, 11*(6), 454–461.

Smith, T. J., & Henderson, J. M. (2009). Facilitation of return during scene viewing. *Visual Cognition, 17,* 1083–1108.

Starr, M. S., & Rayner, K. (2001). Eye movements during reading: Some current controversies. *Trends in Cognitive Sciences, 5,* 156–163.

Tanenhaus, M. K., Spivey-Knowlton, M. J., Eberhard, K. M., & Sedivy, J. C. (1995). Integration of visual and linguistic information in spoken language comprehension. *Science, 268*(5217), 1632–1634.

Tatler, B. W., & Vincent, B. T. (2009). The prominence of behavioural biases in eye guidance. *Visual Cognition, 17*(6–7), 1029–1054.

Thiele, A., Henning, P., Kubischik, M., & Hoffmann, K. P. (2002). Neural mechanisms of saccadic suppression. *Science, 295*(5564), 2460–2462.

Torralba, A., Oliva, A., Castelhano, M. S., & Henderson, J. M. (2006). Contextual guidance of eye movements and attention in real-world scenes: The role of global features in object search. *Psychological Review, 113*(4), 766–786.

Treisman, A. M., & Gelade, G. (1980). Feature-integration theory of attention. *Cognitive Psychology, 12*(1), 97–136.

Trueswell, J. C., & Tanenhaus, M. K. (Eds.). (2004). *Approaches to studying world-situated language use: Bridging the language-as-product and language-as-action traditions.* Cambridge, MA: MIT Press.

Van derStigchel, S., Meeter, M., & Theeuwes, J. (2006). Eye movement trajectories and what they tell us. *Neuroscience and Biobehavioral Reviews, 30,* 666–679.

Võ, M. L.-H., & Henderson, J. M. (2009). Does gravity matter? Effects of semantic and syntactic inconsistencies on the allocation of attention during scene perception. *Journal of Vision, 9*(3):24.1–15.

Võ, M. L.-H., Smith, T. J., Mital, P. K., & Henderson, J. M. (in press). Do the eyes really have it? Dynamic allocation of attention when viewing moving faces. Journal of Vision.

Volkmann, F. C. (1961). Vision during voluntary saccadic eye-movements. *American Psychologist, 16*(7), 415–415.

Volkmann, F. C. (1986). Human visual suppression. *Vision Research, 26*(9), 1401–1416.

von Grünau, M., & Anston, C. (1995). The detection of gaze direction: A stare-in-the-crowd effect. *Perception, 24*(11), 1297–1313.

Walker-Smith, G. J., Gale, A. G., & Findlay, J. M. (1977). Eye-movement strategies involved in face perception. *Perception, 6*(3), 313–326.

Williams, C. C., Henderson, J. M., & Zacks, R. T. (2005). Incidental visual memory for targets and distractors in visual search. *Perception and Psychophysics, 67*(5), 816–827.

Wolfe, J. M., Cave, K. R., & Franzel, S. L. (1989). Guided search—an alternative to the feature integration model for visual-search. *Journal of Experimental Psychology: Human Perception and Performance, 15*(3), 419–433.

Yarbus, A. L. (1967). *Eye movements and vision.* New York: Plenum Press.

Zelinsky, G. J. (2008). A theory of eye movements during target acquisition. *Psychological Review, 115*(4), 787–835.

# Event Perception

Barbara Tversky *and* Jeffrey M. Zacks

**Abstract**

Every waking moment, we are confronted with a continuous changing multimodal stream of information. To make sense of that information stream and to act effectively in the world, we need to reduce it to useful chunks. One important kind of chunk is an event, an integrated unit of space and time that has a beginning, middle, and end: having breakfast, attending class, seeing a movie. Events themselves are segmented into parts: buying a ticket, finding a seat, viewing the movie. A variety of cognitive and perceptual features converge at event boundaries; they are instants of relatively greater change in action, they are moments when goals and subgoals are accomplished, they are times when predictability breaks down. Event units are convenient packets for perception, comprehension, inference, prediction, imitation, learning, and planning.

**Key Words:** event, segmentation, breakpoint, action

Think, for a moment, about making a first acquaintance with life, like an infant, confronted with a rich and ever-changing stream of color, form, sound, smell, and touch. How do we make sense of what James called this blooming, buzzing confusion? We cope with this onslaught of sensation by reducing it, by packaging it into categories—people, objects, settings—categories with recognizable shapes that persist over time and space and allow inference and prediction. People provide food and make us laugh; cups are for drinking, beds for sleeping. Other categories, such as eating a meal, playing a game, going for a walk, are formed from time as well as space. We call these categories events, and they are the topic of this chapter. Events can be ordinary, like going to a restaurant or visiting a doctor, or extraordinary, like graduating from college or winning a prize. Events can be momentary, like the signing of a treaty, or extended, like a glacial age. Events may be public or private; they may be in the natural world or in the social world. Events may be

unique, the creation of the moon or a fifth birthday, or repeated, the cycles of the moon or making a birthday cake. What is critical is that events transpire in time and space, and like objects, events have parts, beginning, middles, and ends. How do we carve events and their parts from the rich and complex information stream impinging on our senses? And what is the significance of doing so?

## Early Research

Events are constructs of the mind, but this does not mean that they are figments of the imagination. On the contrary, the boundaries of events correspond with identifiable physical changes. Some of the earliest work on events beautifully demonstrated the stimulus regularities that allow us to carve events at their joints. That work ran a continuum from precisely controlled minimalist laboratory studies on the one hand and nonintrusive observations of people in the wild on the other. Both the laboratory research and the research in the wild have focused on the ordinary events that constitute our days and that can be brought into the laboratory: having a meal, going to work, doing the dishes, short interactions with others.

Michotte's (1963) studies were simple, elegant, systematic laboratory studies. Along with the Gestalt psychologists such as Koffka and Duncker, Michotte believed that causality could be perceived directly from events, notably from spatial and temporal coincidence. To study this, he showed viewers simple, highly controlled motion events and asked them to describe their impressions while viewing them. Imagine a sparse scene containing a single stationary blue spot on a surface. Now imagine a red spot approaching and contacting the blue spot. If the blue spot immediately starts to move, people perceive a single event, launching. The perception is that the red spot caused the blue spot to move. If, however, the red spot stops, and only later the blue spot begins to move, people perceive two separate events, and there is no perception of causality between the movements of the two spots. Michotte and his followers went on to explore the physical concomitants of perception of causality for and from variants of this situation.

This paradigm and its results highlight several key features of events. Events involve actions—actions on objects, like launching, or actions by objects, like rolling and stopping. They culminate in accomplishments or achievements, like launching or stopping. Events, then, are not the same as activities. Hitting a ball is an event but hitting is not. We think this generalizes to more complex events. Eating a meal is an event but eating is not. Events have a beginning, the start of the action that will lead to the accomplishment; a middle, the steps in the continuation of the action; and an end, the culmination and outcome of the sequence of actions.

Barker and Wright's (1951; 1954) studies anchor the other end of the continuum from minimal laboratory experiments to observations of complex human behavior in the wild. These researchers observed the everyday behaviors of ordinary people in a typical American city in the 1950s, coding those naturally occurring behaviors into "episodes," essentially events: "Behavior episodes are analogous to physical objects which can be seen with the naked eye. They are the common 'things' of behavior; they correspond to the stones, chairs, and buildings of the physical world" (1955, p. 6). Here are some behavior episodes: a group of boys moving a crate across a pit, a girl exchanging remarks with her mother, a boy going home from school. From the vast data they collected, they identified six characteristics that characterized the boundaries of behavior episodes (1954, p. 235):

1. A change in the sphere of the behavior between verbal, social, and intellectual
2. A change in the predominant part of the body
3. A change in the physical direction of the behavior
4. A change in the object of the behavior
5. A change in the behavior setting
6. A change in the tempo of the activity

Several more features of events are evident from this research and analysis. Events have boundaries, their beginnings and ends. The boundaries are marked by large, observable physical changes, in the setting or in the actors. Next, events bear analogies to objects, a point elaborated by others (Casati & Varzi, 1996; Tversky, Zacks, & Hard, 2008; Zacks & Tversky, 2001). Like objects, events are reified. Many are even referred to by nouns rather than verbs, such as conversation, contest, game, or birthday party. Like objects, events have parts, and their parts have parts. Where the parts of objects have a spatial configuration, the parts of events have a temporal configuration. Singing "Happy Birthday" comes after the candles are blown out, eating the cake comes after that, and only after that can the presents be opened.

The sorts of events studied by Michotte on one hand and Barker and Wright on the other differ in many respects, but perhaps the most salient is that Michotte's events were purely mechanical but Barker and Wright's were controlled by people. Simple billiard-ball interactions share some critical features with complex real-world events: They involve actions, they entail causality, they culminate in accomplishments or achievements, and they have beginnings, middles, and ends. However, even when abstracted into paths of motion, animate motion differs from inanimate, and when viewed as abstract paths, animate motion is interpreted differently from inanimate, even by infants (Gelman, Durgin, & Kaufman, 1995). There is also an essential causal difference: Both kinds of event are causal sequences, but the events involving people involve intentions. Like Michotte's minimalist studies, the path-breaking work of Heider and Simmel (1944) presented motion events of geometric figures, but their behavior was socially rather than physically determined.

Imagine a large triangle inside a box with a door. Two small figures, a smaller triangle and a circle, approach, bouncing. The large triangle exits the box, and comes near them. From here on, it is painstaking to describe the actions without interpreting them. The large triangle threatens the smaller figures, and the small triangle taunts the large one. As the large one attempts to bully back the small one, the circle sneaks into the house. The large triangle notices, goes back into the house, and begins to threaten the circle. The small triangle figures out how to enter as well and engages the large one, allowing the circle, and then the small triangle itself to escape. The large triangle attempts to catch them and fails, and then, in anger, goes back into his house and begins to break it apart. Note that the entire event can be reliably segmented into smaller units (Hard, Tversky, & Lang, 2006). Note also the wording of the description: not "move up," "move back and forth," "enter." Instead: "notice," "threaten," "taunt," "escape," and "anger," words that imply complex social intentions. Indeed, this is the sort of description that participants eventually gave of the films. Thus, simple actions on the part of these faceless, armless, legless, oddly shaped figures can be interpreted—in context—as highly articulated intentional social behaviors. Perceiving those intentions and interpretations is often not immediate; it can take several viewings (Hard, Tversky, & Lang, 2006). Importantly, however, the intentions can ultimately be perceived directly from the abstract movements of the abstract figures, using the physical context.

The review of these three seminal projects has revealed the essential characteristics of the kinds of events that will be considered here. Importantly, they are coherent chunks carved from the stream of ongoing behavior. They have beginnings, middles, and ends. They culminate in accomplishments or achievements. The endings are typically accompanied by large physical changes. Events can be segmented into parts. The parts have a temporal organization. Events entail causation, and human events entail intentions. As shall be seen, events, event segments, event causes, and event intentions have bases in the physical world, bottom-up determinants, as well as top-down interpretations and determinants.

## Sorting Events Into Kinds

New areas, like new things, are usually first explored by putting them into piles and by taking them apart; that is, categorizing them and segmenting them. The goal is to construct knowledge hierarchies around kinds and parts, taxonomies and partonomies (Miller & Johnson-Laird, 1976; Tversky, 1990). Research on objects preceded that on events and other kinds and has served as a paradigm (e. g., Rosch, 1978). Common objects can be sorted into kinds such as animals, vegetables, fruit, and furniture; these in turn have their own kinds such as dog, tomato, apple, and table. Continuing, there are kinds of dogs and tomatoes and apples and tables. That middle level of abstraction, the level of dog and tomato, turns out to have a special status in perception, action, and language. It is the most abstract level recognized by its contour, it has relatively more distinguishing properties, it is the most abstract level eliciting a common set of behaviors, it is the most frequently used label, it is the first level to enter the lexicon of a language or a child, and more. For these reasons, this level has been termed the basic level. In addition to kinds, dogs and peas and apples and tables have associated parts. Dogs have a head, body, and legs. Dogs' heads have ears, eyes, and a nose.

This approach, to study kinds and parts, is natural for the study of events. There has been some research on kinds of events (Morris & Murphy, 1995; Rifkin, 1985). That work suggests that there is a basic level for events parallel to a basic level for objects (e.g., Rosch, 1978), a level privileged in relative richness of associated perceptual and behavioral properties as well as in communication. For events, the level is that of breakfast rather than meal or going out for pancakes, the level of football rather than the level of sport or touch football, the level of movie rather than the level of entertainment or horror movie. Contemplating these examples reveals how much more multifaceted events are than objects, if only because events involve not only objects but much more: place, time, and actors, all interacting. Breakfast (in N. America) typically takes place indoors in the morning around a table in a kitchen or dining room with one or a small number of people usually living in the same house; it involves preparing and eating food like cereal, eggs, toast, and coffee. Football takes place outdoors on a special field with a small number of players appropriately dressed and divided into teams, throwing a special ball according to rules, observed by a large number of barely related fans of both teams. With so many interconnected elements, how is it possible to segment events into parts?

## Segmenting Events Into Parts
### The Segmentation Paradigm

Despite the richness, diversity, and multimodal nature of events, ongoing events can be reliably segmented into parts. Newtson and his collaborators (1973; Newtson & Engquist, 1976; Newtson, Engquist, & Bois, 1977) developed a straightforward technique for studying event segmentation: Participants watched films of some more or less organized human activities, such as arranging things in a room or operating a slide projector. They pressed a key whenever they thought that one behavioral unit had ended and another begun. Newtson termed the points at which people pressed the button "breakpoints." Others have used the term "event boundaries," which we will use here. Remarkably, there was good agreement both within and across observers on the locations of the event boundaries. That is, observers can consistently and reliably segment ongoing events into parts. Event boundaries form the junctures of coherent event parts in the continuous stream of behavior, much as changes in visual contours form the junctures of object parts.

Subsequent research using the same paradigm has shown that event categories form partonomies, that is, they are hierarchically organized into parts and parts of parts (e. g., Newtson, 1973; Hard et al., 2006; Zacks, Tversky, & Iyer, 2001) much as objects are organized into parts and parts of parts. Bodies consist of heads and trunks and arms and legs; arms consist of upper arms, lower arms, and hands, and so on. For events, when observers are asked to segment an event sequence twice, once at the coarsest level that makes sense and once at the finest level that makes sense (counterbalanced, of course), the fine units are contained in the larger ones, that is, finer units are parts of larger units. Making a bed consists of putting on the bottom sheet, putting on the top sheet, putting on the blanket, stuffing the pillows into pillow cases, and so on. Each of those coarse units in turn contains a set of finer units, so putting on the bottom sheet consists of spreading out the sheet, tucking in the corners, smoothing the sheet.

That events form hierarchical organizations of parts is substantiated by top-down conceptual studies as well. Bower, Black, and Turner (1979) asked people to list the actions that comprise common familiar events like going to a restaurant or visiting a doctor. There was impressive agreement in the listings. Actions frequently listed for going to a restaurant included the following: be seated, look at menu, order meal, eat food, pay bill. The actions that were less frequently listed were often included in the more frequent actions: "looking at menu" included "discuss menu," and "pay bill" included "leave tip."

Are events naturally and spontaneously segmented as they are observed or only when the task requires it? This seemingly unanswerable question can be addressed by observing the active brain during passive viewing of event sequences. Participants first viewed films of action sequences passively; on a second viewing, they segmented the films into event units, while undergoing functional magnetic resonance imaging (fMRI; Zacks, Braver, et al., 2001). Just prior to marked segment boundaries, the activity in several brain areas began to increase, peaking at segment boundaries, under both passive viewing and active segmentation, suggesting implicit segmentation of ongoing events.

### Boundaries

Some insight into what makes boundaries especially significant in the stream of behavior comes from observers' play-by-play descriptions of ongoing events. In one study, observers segmented films of people making beds, doing the dishes, fertilizing a plant, or assembling a saxophone (Zacks, Tversky, & Iyer, 2001). They segmented twice, once at the coarsest level that made sense and once at the finest level that made sense, in counterbalanced order. Half the observers were asked to describe what happened in each unit as they segmented. The vast majority of descriptions were of actions on objects: "he watered the plant," "she inserted the mouthpiece." The few remaining descriptions were self-actions: "she entered" or "he exited." For this kind of everyday event, analysis of the language of the descriptions showed that at the coarse level, segments were differentiated by different objects. For example, for making the bed, successive segments entailed actions on the bottom sheet, the top sheet, and the blanket. By contrast, the descriptions at the fine level were differentiated by different actions on the same object. For the fine level of making the bed, one observer described: "unfolding sheet," "laying it down," "putting on the top end of the sheet," "putting on the bottom," and "straightening it out." Other research corroborates that for everyday events, the highest level of event segmentation corresponds to objects or object parts. In people's spontaneous production of visual or verbal instructions to assemble an object, each new step corresponded to a new part (Tversky et al., 2007). Of course, in both natural and laboratory situations, the level of segmentation can vary;

for example, for unfamiliar situations, people tend to spontaneously segment events at a finer level (Vallacher & Wegner, 1997).

The ongoing descriptions of events as they unfold illustrate two other significant aspects of event units and boundaries of event units. Event boundaries correspond to completions of goals and subgoals. As noted, most segments are described as actions on objects, at different levels of analysis. As such, they describe local accomplishments or achievements, the causal outcomes of intentions, the completions of goals. In addition, describing while segmenting led to tighter hierarchical organization, suggesting that attending to accomplishments of goals brings top-down knowledge-based information in the service of segmentation (Zacks, Tversky, & Iyer, 2001). Altogether, many different features of events, bottom-up and top-down, converge at their boundaries. We turn to some of those now.

### Action Change

The continuous stream of behavior is segmented by the mind into events and event parts much as the continuous stream of speech is segmented into sentences and words and the continuous visual stream is segmented into objects and their parts. Objects are readily recognized by their canonical contours (e. g., Palmer, Rosch, & Chase, 1981). Good parts of objects are bounded by inflection points in their object contours (Hoffman & Richards, 1984)—think of how the leg of a bear or a chair joins its larger whole. Might there be a temporal analog for events of contour discontinuity for objects? Several projects investigating a range of different human action sequences suggest that event boundaries correspond to large changes in level of activity in the behavioral stream. In one study, the number of joints moving in an actor was found to be greater at boundaries than at other moments of the action sequence (Newtson et al., 1977). Other studies have shown that event boundaries coincided with moments of great physical change (Zacks, 2004) or with turns in paths of human motion (Shipley & Mcguire, 2008). Several studies have found that the number of different kinds of actions, such as change in speed or direction of actors (Hard et al., 2006) or movements of actors' hands as they performed various tasks (Zacks, Kumar, Abrams, & Mehta, 2009), was greater at event boundaries.

One project has investigated the joint time courses of action change and segmentation directly (Hard, Recchia, & Tversky, 2011). Participants viewed slide shows taken at 1 sec intervals from action sequences such as having breakfast or cleaning up a room. They were free to look at each slide as long as they liked, a measure termed "dwell time." Dwell time can be regarded as an index of attention to new information: the more new information to process, the longer viewers will look. After looking at the slide show of the action sequence, participants segmented the complete videos of the action sequences at coarse and fine levels. Together, these procedures reveal the temporal relationship between dwell time and event boundaries. Viewers looked longer at slides depicting boundaries than at nonboundary slides, and longer at coarse boundary slides than at fine boundary slides. Notably, dwell time began to increase several slides prior to boundaries, echoing findings for brain activation (Zacks, Braver, et al., 2001); dwell time dropped off quickly after boundaries. In short, viewers look at slides depicting boundary moments longer than at between-boundary slides, suggesting that there is more new information to process at these junctures.

That event boundaries are especially informative moments in the action stream was substantiated using an objective measure of moment-to-moment change in information. The slides were preprocessed to find edges and to filter out changes in lighting, color, and the like. Then the pixel-to-pixel difference or change was computed for each successive pair of slides, providing a continuous measure of degree of change. Because the only changes were the actor's actions on objects, the change measure is also a good index of the action contour. The next step was to compare the joint time courses of change, event boundaries, and dwell time. Importantly, the change measure was locally maximal at boundaries, and, like dwell time, greater for coarse than fine boundaries. Intriguingly, dwell (looking) time began to rise several slides before the change index, suggesting that qualitative aspects of the action sequence are signaling an impending boundary. Thus, both dwell time and action changes are maximal at boundaries. Participants look longer at boundaries presumably because these are moments of greatest change in action, hence more informative. Although the pixel-to-pixel change measure is an index of informativeness of the action contour, it is not equivalent to it. One can imagine situations where there would be great change, change that would draw attention, but the change would not be informative to the ongoing action sequence. Thus, although the temporal contours of dwell time and change maxima are in good correspondence with event boundaries, they are separable.

Event boundaries, to mix metaphors, are natural joints in the stream of behavior. A number of research efforts have converged to show that boundaries are especially significant moments in the behavior stream. The dwell-time research has shown that event boundaries correspond to moments of relatively large change in the degree of action in the stream of behavior, that is, they carry relatively greater amounts of new information. Because these points are especially informative, they attract comparably greater attention.

One general implication of these findings is that low-level, easily perceived information in the behavior stream can be and is used to segment the action sequence into chunks that are informative packets of information. Event boundaries correspond to the completion of one goal or intentional act and the initiation of a new goal or intentional act. As an actor is in the process of attaining one goal, such as soaping a dish or smoothing a sheet, each new movement is an incremental change from the previous movement. Shifting to a new goal, such as rinsing a dish or tucking in a corner, entails larger changes: finishing the earlier actions and initiating entirely different actions. Event boundaries mark transitions, and as such are likely to contain elements of both completion of one goal and initiation of another. Because goal completions coincide with substantial increases in the action contour, changes in low-level action and the consequent attention recruited to it can bootstrap inferring high-level information about intentions and goals. Research on novel abstract action sequences showed this process in action (Hard et al., 2006). Novice and experienced viewers segmented the action sequences identically though their interpretations of the actions differed dramatically. Novice viewers interpreted the novel sequences in terms of movements, whereas experienced viewers interpreted the action sequences in terms of intentions and goals.

If low-level action changes correspond to changes in goals and other conceptual features of activity, then such conceptual features should be associated with event segmentation. There is good evidence for this. In one study, participants watched one hour of a commercial film and segmented it by pausing a videotape player and noting the time code (Magliano, Miller, & Zwaan, 2001). Changes in space, time, and causality were all associated with the identification of event boundaries. Zacks, Speer, and Reynolds (2009) observed similar effects and extended them to changes in characters, objects, and goals. fMRI studies show that about half of the brain's response at event boundaries can be accounted for by activity associated with such changes (Speer, Reynolds & Zacks, 2007; Zacks, Speer, Swallow, & Maley, 2010).

### Statistical Dependencies of Units

Degree of change in action is not the only low-level information available to perceivers. Research has also investigated the perception of statistical dependencies among action units. The basic idea rests on the fact that there is a temporal organization to events, that certain units are more likely to be grouped and to be reliably ordered, and that the mind is likely to be sensitive to such statistical dependencies. The sequential dependencies are often causally constrained so that learning them can be used to bootstrap causal reasoning. The key must be inserted into the lock before the lock can be turned, the lock must be turned before the door can be opened, and the door must be opened before the room can be entered.

Research in other domains has shown that adults and even infants readily perceive statistical dependencies in temporal events. In particular, extensive work has demonstrated sensitivity to statistical dependencies among phonemes as early as infancy (e.g., Saffran, Aslin, & Newport, 1996). Most likely, detecting the statistical dependencies among event units depends on prior segmentation of events into units, but it is conceivable that the processes occur in tandem and augment one another.

What about the statistical dependencies among the action units of events? Evidence suggesting that people perceive statistical dependencies among event units comes from research in which dependencies of cartoon clips were varied (Avrahami & Kareev, 1994). They proposed the "cut hypothesis: A sub-sequence of stimuli is cut out of a sequence to become a cognitive unity if it has been experienced many times in different contexts (p. 245)." Although they found evidence supporting the cut hypothesis, both the events and the units were contrived, not representative of common coherent action sequences. Using somewhat more naturalistic materials, Swallow and Zacks (2008) found that observers could learn a repeated sequence of arm movements embedded in a longer series and use it to guide attention. Interestingly, observers could use this information without being explicitly aware of it. Other recent research has carefully explored viewers' sensitivity to statistical dependencies for novel sequences of familiar action units, finding support for such sensitivities (Baldwin, Andersson, Saffran,

& Meyer, 2008). The action units were a variety of differentiable actions such as poking, drinking, and stacking on objects such as bottles. Viewers could readily detect sequential dependencies among discrete action units and use the dependencies to form larger event categories. The implication is that these statistically dependent sequences create unitized events without any need to segment.

The role of statistical dependencies in the perception of events differs in a fundamental way from the role of statistical dependencies in the perception of language. Languages use a small closed set of phonemes, in the range of 20–50, to create tens of thousands of words. Most words use several phonemes from this limited set, and few, if any, words use phonemes not in the set. Furthermore, some sequences of phonemes are allowable, and others are not. Thus, statistical dependencies of phonemes are useful to differentiate and identify many words. By contrast, the number of action units is open and uncountable, so that even related action sequences, like preparing a meal and setting the table or washing the car and changing a tire, are unlikely to use the same units. Although there are statistical dependencies among the action units for most events, the statistical relations among units are not necessary for distinguishing among events. The event units themselves are likely to differ between different events and may be sufficient to distinguish and identify them. Changing the order of the units of setting the table or washing the car does not create different events. Rather, changing the order of units is likely to create an impossible event. For events, the statistical dependencies seem to serve another purpose. Learning the statistical relations among event units, that is, their temporal order, seems to be crucial for understanding the underlying causal relations of the events.

Like segmenting events by local maxima of change in the action stream, assessing the statistical dependencies among event units does not require understanding or interpretation of the events but can facilitate event understanding. The fact that large physical changes occur at boundaries and that boundaries mark completions of goals should encourage inferences about intentions and goals. Learning the statistical dependencies among action units, notably their temporal order, can provide the basis for inferring or learning the causal contingencies that enable completions of goals.

Is there a relationship between local maxima of change in action contours and statistical dependence among action units? Studies combining variations in statistical dependencies and dwell time suggest that there is (Hard, Baldwin, Meyer, & Sage, in preparation). Participants watched slide shows of novel action sequences with triples of actions that always occurred in the same order. Some viewers had seen the videos from which the slide shows were constructed; others had not. Those who had seen the videos and presumably learned the statistical dependencies looked longer at the first slide of the action triplet, that is, the first action of the triplet, and progressively less at the successive slides. This was not the case for viewers who had never seen the action sequence and who had not yet learned the statistical dependencies among the action units.

This research is consistent with the view that dwell time, an index of attention, responds to new information. On the first viewing, as in the Hard et al. (2011) studies, everything was new, so slides that were relatively different from the preceding slide, boundary slides, contained relatively more new information than slides that are more similar to their preceding slides. As the sequences were learned, even large physical changes could present little new information because they became predictable. Now, new information was more likely to result from the beginning of a new statistically constrained action sequence (see also Avrahami & Kareev, 1994). Over the course of learning, the beginning of a highly constrained set of actions may become unitized into a single functional unit. Unitization marks a transition to expertise; one mark of expertise is more abstract interpretations (e. g., Hard et al., 2006; Vallacher & Wegner, 1987).

### Prediction

Why do people perceive event boundaries when change is greatest and when activity is least predictable? One answer to these questions is given by Event Segmentation Theory (EST; Kurby & Zacks, 2007; Reynolds, Zacks, & Braver, 2007; Zacks, Speer, Swallow, Braver, & Reynolds, 2007). EST starts from the assumption that a major function of perception is to allow organisms to anticipate the near future and respond proactively. EST proposes that perceptual predictions are guided by short-term memory representations called *event models*. An event model is a structured representation of an event that captures features such as the characters, their goals, the location, and the objects involved. For example, an event model for tooth-brushing might include information about the water cup and toothbrush and their locations, the goal of cleaning teeth, and the person doing the brushing. For event models to be useful, they need to be stable in the face of moment-to-moment fluctuations in sensory input—the cup needs to remain in the model even if it is temporarily occluded. However, event models also need to be updated from time to time, else they will lead to errors: Once the tooth-brushing is over, a new model is needed, else the perceiver will make erroneous predictions that the activity will repeat or go on as before. Thus, there is a trade-off between stability and rigidity that must be resolved without any external signal telling the system when to update. EST proposes that the perceptual system monitors prediction error and updates event models when a transient increase in prediction error occurs. In the toothbrushing example, when the tooth-brushing is done, the brusher might reach into the medicine cabinet for some hair gel, and this unpredicted action would produce a prediction error. At this point the event model would be updated and a new representation would be formed.

EST proposes that, other things being equal, event boundaries tend to happen at changes because changes are generally less predictable than stasis. However, statistical dependencies in experience can alter the prediction error landscape: Large changes can become perfectly predictable if they are encountered repeatedly. We can even imagine that in some situations the absence of a change would be unpredicted. Imagine you have watched a daughter brush her teeth every evening and she consistently brushes for 45 s. If one evening 55 s had gone by and she is still brushing, this might produce a prediction error and therefore event model updating.

This account is consistent with the research reviewed earlier, showing that event boundaries tend to happen at large changes in physical or conceptual features. Further studies provide direct support for association between prediction error and event segmentation. Zacks, Kurby, Eisenberg, and Haroutunian (2011) presented observers with movies of everyday activities such as washing a car or putting up a tent. From time to time they stopped the movie and asked participants to make a prediction about what would happen in 5 s by selecting a picture. The movies had previously been segmented, and the stopping points were placed either 2.5 s before an event boundary or in the middle of an event. Predicting across an event boundary was harder than predicting during the middle of an event, and participants were less confident about their predictions. fMRI recordings showed that regions in the midbrain and the basal ganglia associated with prediction difficulty were selectively activated when attempting to predict—particularly when predicting across an event boundary. These data support the proposal of EST that event boundaries correspond to points at which observers make errors in predicting the near future.

As we have seen, events are naturally segmented into units whose boundaries are referred to as breakpoints. Breakpoints are distinguished by large increases in action and decreases in predictability. The segments are often composed of statistically dependent subunits. Breakpoints are not just the confluence of bottom-up information. Earlier we saw that breakpoints are also points where goals and subgoals are completed. As such, they link the perceptual concomitants of event boundaries and the conceptual meanings of event boundaries, providing support for inferences from one to the other.

## Action-Object Couplets

These varying perspectives on event segmentation converge on a prototypical event unit, an *action-object couplet* or a *turning point* in human action: opening a bottle, filling a glass, closing a door, cleaning a window, zipping a jacket, crossing a street, turning a corner. At turning points, there are relatively large changes in the stream of action, more information to process, and decreased predictability of action. At turning points, goals are accomplished. Turning points divide the action stream into units that can be assembled into statistically dependent sequential chains that accomplish larger goals.

Action-object couplets come in two varieties: transitive, that is, actions on objects, or intransitive, that is, self-actions. In the descriptions of action sequences like making a bed and doing the dishes, actions on objects accounted for the vast majority, 96%. Self-actions, like entering and exiting, were far fewer (Zacks, Tversky, & Iyer, 2001). The common transitive action sequences investigated in these and similar studies are what have been termed *events by hands*. Intransitive action units are more likely to be *events by feet*, whole-body movements that are used to take someone from place to place in an environment (cf. Tversky, Zacks, & Lee, 2004). Whereas events by hands are movements with respect to small hand-held objects, events by feet are movements with respect to large features in the world, corners, intersections, walls, and other landmarks. Whereas events by hands typically lead to changes in the objects by the actor, events by feet lead to changes in location of the actor. Of course, events by feet constitute a large, if unquantified, percent of human behavior. Perhaps the paradigmatic case of an event by feet is a route through an environment, a sequence of actions, usually turns, at landmarks (e.g., Denis, 1997; Tversky & Lee, 1998). Intransitive actions, then, should also be regarded as action-object couplets because the actions are with respect to and constrained by environmental objects, even if the actions do not involve manipulation of the objects.

## Recognizing Events Using Brain and Body

As noted earlier, the mind segments ongoing action even under passive viewing (Zacks, Braver, et al., 2001). Studies of event comprehension and action recognition have provided important information about how those segments are used in cognition and action control. Some of the most compelling data come from neurophysiology. The brain invests significant resources to recovering the identity of actions from signals arising in vision, hearing, and touch. For example, neuroimaging studies reveal multiple brain areas that are selectively activated by animate visual motion compared to motion that is not related to goal-directed action (Castelli, Happé, Frith, & Frith, 2000; Martin & Weissberg, 2003). Some of these regions contain individual neurons that respond selectively when one observes a particular goal-directed action. Much of the initial evidence came from electrical recordings of cortical cells in monkeys. In the premotor cortex of the frontal lobes, parietal cortex, and in the superior temporal sulcus, cells were found that responded when a monkey observed a particular goal-directed action—say, picking up a peanut. Some of these responses are highly specific—responding to picking up the peanut but not to putting it down or to picking up an apple (Perrett & Jellema, 2002). Importantly, for many of these cells the shape of the movement is not sufficient to evoke a response; the object of the action has to be present as well and the object appropriately contacted, either explicitly or implicitly. Action-selective cells appear to represent action units somewhat abstractly. Cells in the superior temporal sulcus have been found that continue to respond to a goal-directed action even when the action is hidden from view because the actor moves behind an obstacle (Perrett & Jellema, 2002). For certain familiar actions, the sound of the appropriate action alone is sufficient to trigger them, without any visual stimulation (Rizzolatti, 2005; Rizzolatti et al., 2001). These and similar results suggest that the perceptual input alone is not sufficient for understanding a perceived action, that

structures involved in the motor planning needed to perform the action must also be activated. Perhaps the most evocative evidence that the relevant representations overlap for perception and action comes from research on mirror neurons (e. g., Rizzolatti, 2005; Rizzolatti, Fogassi, & Gallese, 2001). Mirror neurons are a subset of the action-selective neurons that respond to the same actions whether they are performed or observed.

Further evidence for action-specific brain responses has come from studies of neural adaptation. Neurons in most brain areas adapt over time. For example, if a cell in early visual cortex that is selective for vertical bars in the upper left visual quadrant is presented with one of these, it will initially respond strongly but with repeated exposure, its response diminishes. In parts of the frontal and parietal lobes, researchers have observed brain responses that adapt when associated actions are repeated even if the low-level visual properties of the presentations vary (Dinstein, Hasson, Rubin, & Heeger, 2007; Hamilton & Grafton, 2009).

Studies of action observation in humans support a tight relationship between perception and action. The mirror system in humans is a network that includes the body as well as the brain. Perception of actions not only stimulates motor areas of the brain but also stimulates the appropriate muscles (e.g., Aziz-Zadeh, Maeda, Zaidel, Mazziotta, & Iacoboni, 2002; Buccino, Riggio, Melli, Binkofski, Gallese, & Rizzolatti, 2005; Fadiga, Craighero, Buccino, & Rizzolatti, 2002). In one project, ballet and capoeira dancers watched videos of ballet and capoeira dancing while in a brain scanner. Dancers showed greater activation for the dances they had been trained to perform in motor mirror neuron areas than for the dances that were less unfamiliar (Calvo-Merino, Glaser, Grezes, Passingham, & Haggard, 2005). Thus, the network of brain and presumably body regions that subserve event perception is enriched by experience.

In humans, perceptual and motor representations can be accessed from symbolic information alone, from language or music scores, for example. In one study, participants were faster to push or pull a lever when reading sentences that described a congruent action; for example, pulling a lever toward the body was faster when it signified liking than when it signified dislike (Glenberg & Kaschak, 2002). In neuroimaging studies, reading about actions performed with specific parts of the body activated brain areas associated with those body parts (Hauk, Johnsrude, & Pulvermüller,

2004), and reading about interacting with new objects activated regions associated with grasping (Speer, Reynolds, Swallow, & Zacks, 2009).

There is also evidence for the converse relation: that movements of the body affect thinking (e. g., Fischer & Zwaan, 2008; Hommel & Muesseler, 2006; Klatzky, Pellegrino, & McCloskey, 1989; Segal, Black, & Tversky, 2010). For example, holding the hand in an appropriate grip allows faster recognition of objects (Klatzky et al., 1989) and discrete gestures facilitate arithmetic performance and continuous ones facilitate number line estimation (Segal et al., 2010).

To sum up, action-object couplets are represented by tuned networks that incorporate specific perceptual and action areas of the brain as well as specific musculature of the body. The brain/body network that encompasses perception and action and that is tuned to specific actions serves as a distributed abstract representation of action units, accessible by many routes. It is tuned to specific actions, say of hands or feet or mouth. It can be accessed not just by vision but also by audition, by the imagination, and by purely symbolic stimuli. It can be augmented by experience, by expertise. The prototypic event unit is a Goldilocks-sized chunk, not too big and not too little, but just right. Putting on the bottom sheet, shooting a free-throw, hosing the car, putting on a shirt. And in other domains, finishing a sentence or a bar of music. These short, bounded units fit neatly into working memory. They are just the right size for attending and perceiving. Just the right size for comprehending. Just the right size for inferring intentions. Just the right size for predicting. Just the right size for imitating. Just the right size for learning. Just the right size for planning. Neat little packages that subserve myriad tasks: perception, comprehension, inferences, prediction, imitation, learning, and planning.

## Conclusion

Making sense of events, small and large, private and public, natural and social, is fundamental to understanding the world and to functioning in it. Segmenting events into action-object couplets is the crucial step in understanding. Event segments encapsulate an object and an action with respect to it, an intention and an accomplishment. Perceiving and understanding action-object couplets are mediated by the mirror neuron system, which links perception and imagination with action. The perception of action entails motor activation, allowing perceivers

to "feel" the action and its consequences. Sensing the actions contributes to imitating and learning the actions. Sensing the actions also allows realizing the intentions governing the actions, what observers would be intending if they were acting similarly. Understanding ongoing action in turn facilitates predicting what will happen next. It allows planning one's own behavior in response.

The world is never still. It presents an ever-changing barrage of information to eyes, ears, and body. Coping with the onslaught of information and acting in ways that fulfill our needs and accomplish our goals, perception and action, depend on the same trick of the brain and the body, to carve events from the endless stream of action.

## Acknowledgments

BT is indebted to the following grants: National Science Foundation HHC 0905417, IIS-0725223, IIS-0855995, and REC 0440103, the Stanford Regional Visualization and Analysis Center, and Office of Naval Research NOOO14-PP-1-O649, N000140110717, and N000140210534. JZ's research has been supported by the James S. McDonnell Foundation, National Science Foundation BCS-0236651, National Institute of Mental Health RO1-MH70674, and National Institute of Aging R01-AG031150.

## References

Avrahami, J., & Kareev, Y. (1994). The emergence of events. Cognition, 53, 239–261.

Aziz-Zadeh, L., Maeda, F., Zaidel, E., Mazziotta, J., & Iacoboni, M. (2002). Lateralization in motor facilitation during action observation: A TMS study. Experimental Brain Research, 144, 127–131.

Baldwin, D., Andersson, A., Saffran, J., & Meyer, M. (2008). Segmenting dynamic human action via statistical structure. Cognition, 106(3), 1382–1407.

Barker, R. G., & Wright, H. F. (1951). One boy's day: A specimen record of behavior. New York: Harper & Brothers.

Barker, R. G., & Wright, H. F. (1954). Midwest and its children: The psychological ecology of an American town. Evanston, IL: Row, Peterson and Company.

Bower, G. H., Black, J. B., & Turner, T. J. (1979). Scripts in memory for text. Cognitive Psychology, 11, 177–220.

Buccino, G., Riggio, L., Melli, G., Binkofski, F., Gallese, V., & Rizzolatti G. (2005). Listening to action-related sentences modulates the activity of the motor system: A combined TMS and behavioral study. Cognitive Brain Research, 24, 355–363.

Calvo-Merino, B., Glaser, D. E., Grezes, J., Passingham, R. E., & Haggard, P. (2005). Action observation and acquired motor skills: An fMRI study with expert dancers. Cerebral Cortex, 15, 1243–1249.

Casati, R., & Varzi, A. C. (1996). Events. Aldershot, England and Brookfield, VT: Dartmouth.

Castelli, F., Happe, F., Frith, U. & Frith, C. (2000). Movement and mind: A functional imaging study of perception and interpretation of complex intentional movement patterns. NeuroImage, 12, 314–325.

Denis, M. (1997). The description of routes: A cognitive approach to the production of spatial discourse. Current Psychology of Cognition, 16, 409–458.

Dickman, H. R. (1963). The perception of behavioral units. In R. G. Barker (Ed.), *The stream of behavior* (pp. 23–41). New York: Appleton-Century-Crofts.

Dinstein, I., Hasson, U., Rubin, N., & Heeger, D. J. (2007). Brain areas selective for both observed and executed movements. Journal of Neurophysiology, 98, 1415–1427.

Fadiga, L., Craighero, L., Buccino, G., & Rizzolatti, G. (2002). Speech listening specifically modulates the excitability of tongue muscles: A TMS study. European Journal of Neuroscience, 15, 399–402.

Fischer, M. H., & Zwaan, R. W. (2008). Embodied language: A review of the role of the motor system in language comprehension. Quarterly Journal of Experimental Psychology, 61, 825–850.

Gelman, R., Durgin, F., & Kaufman, L. (1995). Distinguishing between animates and inanimates: Not by motion alone. In D. Sperber, D. Premack, & A. J. Premack (Eds.), *Causal cognition: A multidisciplinary debate* (pp. 150–184). Oxford, England: Oxford University Press.

Glenberg, A. M., & Kaschak, M. P. (2002). Grounding language in action. Psychonomic Bulletin and Review, 9, 558–565.

Hamilton, A. F., & Grafton, S. T. (2009). Repetition suppression for performed hand gestures revealed by fMRI. Human Brain Mapping, 30, 2898–2906.

Hard, B. M., Recchia, G., & Tversky, B. (2011). The shape of events. Journal of Experimental Psychology: General, 140(4), 586–604.

Hard, B. M., Tversky, B., & Lang, D. S. (2006). Making sense of abstract events: Building event schemas. Memory and Cognition, 34, 1221–1235.

Hauk, O., Johnsrude, I., & Pulvermuller, F. (2004). Somatotopic representation of action words in human motor and premotor cortex. Neuron, 41, 301–307.

Heider, F., & Simmel, M. (1944). An experimental study of apparent behavior. American Journal of Psychology, 57, 243–259.

Hoffman, D. D., & Richards, W. A. (1984). Parts of recognition. Cognition, 18, 65–96.

Hommel, B., & Muesseler, J. (2006). Action-feature integration blinds to feature- overlapping perceptual events: Evidence from manual and vocal actions. Quarterly Journal of Experimental Psychology, 59, 509–523.

Klatzky, R. L., Pellegrino, J. W., & McCloskey, B. P. (1989). Can you squeeze a tomato? The role of motor representations in semantic sensibility judgments. Journal of Memory and Language, 28, 56–77.

Kurby, C. A., & Zacks, J. M. (2007). Segmentation in the perception and memory of events. Trends in Cognitive Science, 12, 72–79.

Magliano, J. P., Miller, J., & Zwaan, R. A. (2001). Indexing space and time in film understanding. Applied Cognitive Psychology, 15, 533–545.

Martin, A., & Weisberg, J. (2003). Neural foundations for understanding social and mechanical concepts. Cognitive Neuropsychology, 20, 575–587.

Mennie, N., Hayhoe, M., & Sullivan, B. (2007). Look-ahead fixations: Anticipatory eye movements in natural tasks. Experimental Brain Research, 179, 427–442.

Michotte, A. (1963). *The perception of causality.* New York: Basic Books. Translated from the French by T. R. and E. Miles.

Morris, M. W., & Murphy, G. L. (1990). Converging operations on a basic level in event taxonomies. Memory and Cognition, 18, 407–418.

Newtson, D. (1973). Attribution and the unit of perception of ongoing behavior. Journal of Personality and Social Psychology, 28, 28–38.

Newtson, D., & Engquist, G. (1976). The perceptual organization of ongoing behavior. Journal of Experimental Social Psychology, 12, 436–450.

Newtson, D., Engquist, G., & Bois, J. (1977). The objective basis of behavior units. Journal of Personality and Social Psychology, 35, 847–862.

Palmer, S., Rosch, E., & Chase, P. (1981). Canonical perspective and the perception of objects. In J. B. Long & A. D. Baddeley (Eds.), *Attention and performance, IX* (pp. 135–151). Hillsdale, NJ: Erlbaum.

Perrett, D. I., & Jellema, T . (2002). Coding of visible and hidden actions. In W. Prinz & B. Hommel (Eds.), *Common mechanisms in perception and action, attention and performance* (Vol. 19, pp. 356–380).

Reynolds, J. R., Zacks, J. M., & Braver, T. S. (2007). A computational model of event segmentation from perceptual prediction. Cognitive Science, 31, 613–643.

Rifkin, A. (1985). Evidence for a basic level in event taxonomies. Memory and Cognition, 13, 538–556.

Rizzolatti, G., Fadiga, L., Gallese, V., & Fogassi, L. (1996). Premotor cortex and the recognition of motor actions. Cognitive Brain Research, 3, 131–141.

Rosch, E. (1978). Principles of categorization. In E. Rosch & B. B. Lloyd (Eds.), *Cognition and categorization* (pp. 27–48). Hillsdale, NJ: Erlbaum.

Saffran, J., Aslin, R., & Newport, E. (1996). Statistical learning by 8-month-old infants. Science, 274, 1926–1928.

Segal, A., Black, J., & Tversky, B. (November, 2010). Embodied interaction: Congruent gestures promote performance in math. Paper presented at the Annual Meeting of the Psychonomic Society, St. Louis, MO.

Shipley, T. F., & Maguire, M. (2008). Geometric information for event segmentation. In T. F. Shipley & J. M. Zacks (Eds.), *Understanding events: From perception to action* (pp. 415–435). New York: Oxford University Press.

Speer, N. K., Reynolds, J. R., Swallow, K. M., & Zacks, J. M. (2009). Reading stories activates neural representations of perceptual and motor experiences. Psychological Science, 20, 989–999.

Speer, N. K., Reynolds, J. R., & Zacks, J. M. (2007). Human brain activity time-locked to narrative event boundaries. Psychological Science, 18, 449–455.

Swallow, K. M., & Zacks, J. M. (2008). Sequences learned without awareness can orient attention during the perception of human activity. Psychonomic Bulletin and Review, 15, 116–122.

Tversky, B. (1990). Where partonomies and taxonomies meet. In S. L. Tsohatzidis (Ed.), *Meanings and prototypes: Studies on linguistic categorization* (pp. 334–344). London: Routledge.

Tversky, B., Agrawala, M., Heiser, J., Lee, P. U., Hanrahan, P., Phan, D., Stolte, C., & Daniel, M -P. (2007). Cognitive design principles for generating visualizations. In G. Allen

(Ed.), *Applied spatial cognition: From research to cognitive technology* (pp. 53–73). Mahwah, NJ: Erlbaum.

Tversky, B., & Lee, P. U. (1998). How space structures language. In C. Freksa, C. Habel, & K. F. Wender (Eds.), *Spatial cognition: An interdisciplinary approach to representation and processing of spatial knowledge* (pp. 157–175). Berlin: Springer-Verlag.

Tversky, B., Zacks, J. M., & Hard, B. A. (2008). The structure of experience. In T. Shipley & J. Zacks (Eds.), *Understanding events: How humans see, represent, and act on events* (pp. 436–464). New York: Oxford University Press.

Tversky, B., Zacks, J. M., & Lee, P. (2004). Events by hand and feet. Spatial Cognition and Computation, 4, 5–14.

Vallacher, R. R., & Wegner, D. M. (1987). What do people think they're doing? Action identification and human behavior. Psychological Review, 94, 3–15.

Zacks, J. M. (2004). Using movement and intentions to understand simple events. Cognitive Science, 28, 979–1008.

Zacks, J. M., Braver, T. S., Sheridan, M. A., Donaldson, D. I., Snyder, A. Z., Ollinger, J. M.,...Raichle, M. E. (2001). Human brain activity time-locked to perceptual event boundaries. Nature Neuroscience, 4, 651–655.

Zacks, J. M., Kumar, S., Abrams, R. A., & Mehta, R. (2009). Using movements and intentions to understand human activity. Cognition, 112, 201–216.

Zacks, J. M., Kurby, C. A., Eisenberg, M. L., & Haroutunian, N. (2011). Prediction error associated with the perceptual segmentation of naturalistic events. Journal of Cognitive Neuroscience, 23(12), 4057–4066.

Zacks, J. M., Speer, N. K., & Reynolds, J. R. (2009). Segmentation in reading and film comprehension. Journal of Experimental Psychology: General, 138, 307–327.

Zacks, J. M., Speer, N. K., Swallow, K. M., Braver, T. S., & Reynolds, J. R. (2007). Event perception: A mind/brain perspective. Psychological Bulletin, 133, 272–293.

Zacks, J. M., Speer, N. K., Swallow, K. M., & Maley, C. J. (2010). The brain's cutting-room floor: Segmentation of narrative cinema. Frontiers in Human Neuroscience, 4, 1–15.

Zacks, J. M., & Tversky, B. (2001). Event structure in perception and conception. Psychological Bulletin, 127, 3–21.

Zacks, J., Tversky, B., & Iyer, G. (2001). Perceiving, remembering, and communicating structure in events. Journal of Experimental Psychology: General, 130, 29–58.

# PART 2

# Attention and Awareness

# Perception and Attention

Ronald A. Rensink

## Abstract

The relation between perception and attention is discussed, via a taxonomy of attention centered around function. Five kinds are distinguished. The first is sampling, involving the pickup of information by the eye. The second is filtering (or gating), the control of information considered relevant. The third is binding, involving the formation of more integrated structure over space. Fourth is holding, which creates the coherent structure necessary to perceive continuity over time. Fifth is indexing, which enables individuation of selected items. The function of each is discussed, along with several associated behavioral effects and perceptual deficits, the mechanisms believed to carry it out, and possible relation to conscious visual experience. Discussion is also given of the implicit processing carried out both prior to and independent of any kind of attention, in the complete absence of conscious visual experience.

**Key Words:** attention, awareness, binding, change blindness, consciousness, implicit perception, inattentional blindness, selection, taxonomy, tracking

Our visual experience of the world is one of diverse objects and events, each with particular colors, shapes, and motions. This experience is so coherent, so immediate, and so effortless that it seems to result from a single system that lets us experience everything in our field of view. But however appealing, this belief is mistaken: There are severe limits on what can be visually experienced.

For example, in a display for air-traffic control it is important to track all moving items. For a single item, this can be done without problem. Three or four can also be tracked, although some degree of effort may be needed. As the number is increased further, accurate tracking becomes more and more difficult—and eventually, impossible. Performance is evidently affected by a factor within the observer that enables certain kinds of perception to occur, but is limited in some way. This factor is generally referred to as *attention*.

At various times, attention has been associated with clarity of perception, intensity of perception, consciousness, selection, or the allocation of a limited "resource" enabling various operations (see Hatfield, 1998). During the past several decades, considerable progress has been achieved by focusing on the idea of selection (Broadbent, 1982). In particular, attention can be productively viewed as *contingently selective processing*. This can be embodied in various ways by various processes—there need not be a single quantity identified with all forms of attention, or a single site where it operates (Allport, 1993; Tsotsos, 2011). Although "paying attention" is often considered to be a unitary operation, it may simply refer to *the control of one or more selective processes*, ideally in a coordinated way. While this view has some cost in terms of conceptual simplicity, it can help make sense of a large set of phenomena.

This chapter surveys several of the major issues in our understanding of attention and how it relates to perception. It focuses on vision, since many—if not all—considerations are similar for all sensory modalities, and the level of understanding achieved in this domain is currently the most advanced. Although many of the issues discussed here also apply to higher level cognitive processes, coverage of those is best done separately.

## Kinds of Attention

A great deal of work has been carried out on attention over the years, with a wide variety of approaches used on a wide variety of issues (see, e.g., Parasuraman, 1998; Pashler, 1999; Wright, 1998). Partly because of such heterogeneity, studies of attention have tended to form "silos" that focus on a particular type of experimental approach or proposed mechanism. To provide a more comprehensive view, this discussion includes all of these issues, but it is organized around the possible *functions* that attention might have.

In the view taken here, "attention" is more an adjective than a noun: an attentional process is one that is *contingently selective*, controlled on the basis of global considerations (e.g., selection of a particular item to track, based on perceived importance). Any limited-capacity process is necessarily selective, in that it cannot handle everything; if coupled with appropriate control, it becomes ipso facto attentional. In the case of a limited-resource process, attention is sometimes considered a kind of "fuel" (see Hirst & Kalmar, 1987; Wickens, 1980). However, this does not really help with understanding—it is essentially just a different term for the same problem (Allport, 1989). It may instead be better to discuss processing resources in terms of more concrete measures such as time or processor connections, which if limited can create a need for selectivity, or may constrain a process, but which are not themselves a form of selection or control.

Given all this, it is evident that many kinds of selectivity are possible, each corresponding to a particular kind—or at least, aspect—of attention. These are organized here into a taxonomy describing several of the main kinds possible, as well as the relationships among them. This *function-centered taxonomy* characterizes each kind of attention primarily in terms of its (selective) function. This is followed by the perceptual effects associated with it, the mechanisms that carry it out, and the ways that it enters into our conscious experience of the world.

This taxonomy is incomplete in many ways, and parts of it are provisional. But it encompasses much of what is believed about attention, and provides a natural way to organize a wide variety of results obtained in a wide variety of ways.

## Attentional Sampling
### Function

The first step of visual perception is the pickup of information by the eye. This is carried out by the selective sampling of incoming light, via a retina with most of its information pickup in the central few degrees of visual angle (see e.g., Barlow, 1981). To compensate for the relatively poor pickup elsewhere, the eye is continually repositioned via brief jumps, or *saccades*. Augmented by head and body movements, these enable access to any part of the incoming light (see, e.g., Henderson & Hollingworth, 1998). A somewhat analogous situation exists in the third dimension (depth), with high-resolution pickup only for the depths that are in focus, a restriction compensated for by continually changing the focus of the lens. When controlled on the basis of global considerations, such *attentional sampling* can enable the right information to be obtained from the environment at the right time, thereby minimizing the computational resources needed for many tasks. In essence, processing over space is traded for processing over time (see Niebur & Koch, 1998). (Also see Chapter 5.)

Attentional sampling—sometimes referred to as *overt attention*—is not the only kind of attention possible. Others also exist, occasionally referred to collectively *as covert attention*. Overt and covert systems are at least partly separate: They need not—and often do not—act on the same information at the same time. For example, although covert spatial attention must go to a location before the eye can saccade there (Deubel & Schneider, 1996), it is not necessary to make—or even intend to make—a saccade to generate a covert shift (Juan, Shorter-Jacobi, & Schall, 2004). Indeed, much of the correlation between these two kinds of attention may arise simply because they tend to respond to the same informative parts of the visual input (Tsotos, 2011, ch. 1).

### Perceptual Effects

The limitations of sampling are generally compensated for by appropriate movements of the eye. But they can become evident when such movements are prevented, such as by having the observer fixate a location or view the stimulus during a brief flash. Results show that acuity and color perception are best in the central few degrees (or *foveal* area) and fall off rapidly with increasing eccentricity in the outer parts (or *periphery*); in contrast, motion perception is poor in the fovea but better in the periphery (e.g., Barlow & Mollon, 1982).

Most kinds of eye movement are rapid, and are made several times a second. The particular sequence (or *scan path*) used for viewing an image depends not only on its physical properties but also on the knowledge and interests of the viewer and his or her understanding of the task (Hayhoe & Ballard, 2005; Noton & Stark, 1971).

### Mechanism

Many of the systems underlying sampling are fairly well understood. Incoming light is transformed into neural signals by two interleaved arrays of photoreceptors: *cones* (for high levels of illumination) and *rods* (for low levels). Cones are located mostly in the fovea, rods in the periphery. Because cones alone distinguish color, this property is perceived only in the central few degrees of visual angle (see, e.g., Barlow & Mollon, 1982). Meanwhile, an array of *ganglion cells* takes the photoreceptor signals and—after several stages of processing—transmits the results to the brain via the optic nerve. Each ganglion cell receives input from the receptors in a particular area of the retina (its *receptive field*); the size of this increases with eccentricity (see e.g., Kaplan, 1991). Acuity is therefore best in the fovea, where receptive fields are small. Meanwhile, accurate measurement of motion requires the collection of information over a large area, and so motion perception is best in the periphery.

The eye itself is moved via three pairs of muscles, coordinated such that one member of each pair contracts while the other relaxes. These are controlled via several areas in the brain, such as the superior colliculus and the frontal eye fields (see, e.g., Crowne, 1983). And these in turn are under the control of areas involving higher level functions (see, e.g., Carpenter, 1988). (Also see Chapter 5)

### Relation to Consciousness

Because information pickup is required for visual perception, attentional sampling is necessary for any conscious (*explicit*) as well as nonconscious (*implicit*) process. But although our visual experience is quite compelling, it does not directly correspond to what is picked up by the retina. For example, the limited range of color and motion sampling is never noticed: We experience the same resolution and color information throughout. Likewise, although saccades are usually made several times each second (often over several degrees of visual angle), our impression is that of a single, stable image. The mechanisms that create such uniformity and stability are largely unknown (Bridgeman, van der Heijden, & Velichkovsky, 1994; O'Regan & Noe, 2001). But their involvement means that although attentional sampling may be necessary for visual experience, it cannot be sufficient.

The involvement of these mechanisms also explains why even though sampling may be necessary for visual experience at a global level, this necessity does not always apply locally. For example, the retina contains an area where the outputs of the ganglion cells exit, rendering it unable to pick up information. But although this *blind spot* may cover as much as 5–7 degrees of angle, it does not enter into our visual experience: Even when the eye is fixated, it appears "filled in," so the gap is not noticed (Ramachandran, 1992). Similar effects occur for blind spots created by small lesions elsewhere in the visual system, as well as by stimulus manipulations (Ramachandran & Gregory, 1991).

### Attentional Filtering
#### Function

Although a vast amount of information is generally picked up at any moment, most is irrelevant for any particular task. And irrelevant information can be harmful. For example, detection is affected by the noise—or more precisely, the *signal-to-noise ratio*—in the input (e.g., Palmer, Ames, & Lindsey, 1993). Since irrelevant information contains no signal but may contain noise, it can only hurt performance. Likewise, because recognition of a pattern is affected by context (e.g., Oliva & Torralba, 2007), irrelevant background can only interfere. And if not disregarded in some way, irrelevant information can place a load on some processors, causing them to slow down (Tsotsos, 1990). Thus, if perception is to be efficient, it must select the relevant, and only the relevant.

Such *filtering* is in some ways an internal form of sampling. But because it is controlled via changes in neural connections rather than physical forces on the eye, filtering can act more quickly. It can also be more flexible, selecting information from particular regions of space, and with particular ranges of properties (such as color or orientation). This need not be all-or-nothing—a filter can be graded, with inputs weighted as a function of particular values.

Two complementary approaches to filtering are possible: selection *for* and selection *against*. Selection *for* relevant information results in the contents being *expressed*. One way of doing so is *gating*—transmitting information at a particular location, or of a particular color, say. In addition, contents can be *enhanced*, having an effect—or at least, priority—above baseline levels. In a similar way, selection *against* irrelevant information results in the selected contents being *suppressed*. When applied to the control of process or behavior, the two approaches are often referred to, respectively, as *facilitation* and *inhibition* (Posner & Snyder, 1975). Both are largely equivalent, although practical considerations may favor one over the other.

Another issue—especially important in the case of space—is the extent of gating. When selection is *diffuse* (input from a large area), considerable information is simultaneously accessible, which can enable several kinds of process to be sped up. However, more noise may be introduced, creating greater risk of error. Conversely, when selection is *focused* (input from only a small area), processing is potentially less error-prone but slower. These are sometimes referred to, respectively, as *diffuse attention* and *focused attention*. There is consequently a trade-off between speed and accuracy depending on the size selected, with the most effective choice depending upon details of the task and environment (see Giordano, McElree, & Carrasco, 2009).

### Perceptual Effects

As in the case of sampling, most observers are unaware of the limitations imposed by filtering. But under the right conditions, they can lead to measurable effects. Although not all of these necessarily involve the same neural systems, they are similar in several ways.

#### CUEING EFFECTS

Observers can detect a target item more quickly and accurately if presented with advance information about its location. This *cueing* occurs even when eye movements are prevented, indicating that it is due to attentional (or covert) *orienting*, the adjustment of internal filters to task demands. These filters block information from irrelevant locations or properties, improving performance by reducing noise.

A transient form of enhancement begins within 50 ms of cue onset and peaks 50–100 ms later. It appears to be due to a *spotlight of attention* that expresses whatever is within the "beam" (Posner, Snyder, & Davidson, 1980) and suppresses whatever is just outside (Steinman, Steinman, & Lehmkuhle, 1995; Tsotsos, 2011). The size of this is about 1 degree at fixation, and it increases with eccentricity (Sagi & Julesz, 1986). It falls off gradually, rather than having a sharp edge (Laberge & Brown, 1989). Its location can be shifted extremely rapidly, at a rate of c. 10 ms/degree (Tsal, 1983) or faster (see Egeth & Yantis, 1997); intermediate locations do not appear to be affected (see Cave & Bichot, 1999). Only one spotlight usually exists at a time (Jonides, 1983), although under some conditions it may be split among several locations (Bichot, Cave, & Pashler, 1999; Kramer & Hahn, 1995; but see Wright & Ward, 2008, ch. 3).

Cueing is also possible for properties such as color and orientation (Humphreys, 1981; Maunsell & Treue, 2006; Rossi & Paradiso, 1995), as well as spatial frequency (Davis, Kramer, & Graham, 1983). It can also affect purely subjective aspects of perception, such as apparent contrast (Anton-Erxleben, Abrams, & Carrasco, 2010; Carrasco, Ling, & Read, 2004).

In general, cueing involves simple properties such as orientation or location. But there is also an influence of larger scale "preattentive" structures—or *segments*—in the background,[1] these apparently formed on the basis of luminance or texture boundaries at early levels of processing, before attentional filtering can act (e.g., Driver, Davis, Russell, Turrato, & Freeman, 2001; Lamme, 1995). For example, cueing is facilitated if cue and target are both in a region interpreted as the surface of the same segment (Egly, Driver, & Rafal, 1994), but not if this region is interpreted as a hole (Albrecht, List, & Robertson, 2008). Consistent with this, cueing appears to operate over perceived rather than retinal space (Robertson & Kim, 1999).

#### SEARCH ASYMMETRY

In *visual search*, observers must detect as quickly as possible the presence of a *target* item among a set of *distractors*—for example, a vertical line among a set of obliques. For many kinds of search, the time needed is proportional to the number of items in the display. This has been explained via a spotlight of attention that accesses information from each item in turn, at a rate of 30–50 ms per item (see Wolfe, Klempen, & Dahlen, 2000; but see Thornton & Gilden, 2007). Search slows with increasing eccentricity (Carrasco, Evert, Chang, & Katz, 1995), possibly due to the sparser representation of peripheral areas in the cortex (Carrasco & Frieder, 1997).

When the target and distractors differ only by the amount of a simple property (e.g., length or luminance), an interesting *asymmetry* emerges: Search is faster for a longer item among short ones, say, than the other way around. This has been explained by a pooling of the signals in the spotlight. When a target has more of a property, it creates a higher signal. Since accuracy is determined by the ratio of signal to noise, a larger spotlight—which collects more noise—can be used while keeping accuracy the same. Since a larger spotlight requires fewer shifts to cover an area, the result is faster search (Treisman & Gormican, 1988).

Although the properties involved in search may be simple (e.g., length or orientation), they are not directly obtained from simple structures such as line segments. Instead, they appear to be measurements of complex structures—*proto-objects*—of limited extent, formed at early levels prior to attentional filtering (Rensink, 2000a; Rensink & Enns, 1995). Search speed is also affected by background segmentation, being faster for items on the same surface (He & Nakayama, 1995).

### INTERFERENCE EFFECTS

Performance in brief displays can be degraded by nearby items, or flankers (Eriksen & Eriksen, 1974). This *flanker effect* is believed to be caused by a pooling of the information in the spotlight, with signals from the flankers being mixed in with those from the target. Such effects point to a spotlight with a minimum area of 1 degree of angle in the fovea (Eriksen & Eriksen, 1974). It can "zoom out" to a larger area if needed, changing size within 100 ms (Eriksen & St. James, 1986), and automatically becomes smaller when task difficulty or load is increased (Lavie, 1995). Only one such spotlight is believed to operate at a time (Eriksen & Yeh, 1985).

A related effect is *crowding*, where items in the periphery that are easy to recognize when alone become less so when other items are placed nearby; subjectively, their components become "scrambled." The size of the affected area increases with eccentricity (Bouma, 1970); it can be reduced somewhat if target location is cued (Yeshurun & Rashal, 2010). While part of crowding may be due to poor information pickup in the periphery, much of it appears due to the loss of positional information about the components; indeed, crowding may be much the same as the flanker effect (Strasburger, 2005).

As in the case of cueing and search, interference is influenced by structural factors. For example, it is greater for items grouped by common motion (Driver & Baylis, 1989) or on the same background segment (Kramer & Jacobson, 1991). And the expression of a face can be still perceived even when crowding destroys conscious awareness of the detailed configuration that conveys this (Fischer & Whitney, 2011).

### INATTENTIONAL BLINDNESS

Consider an observer carrying out a demanding primary task, such as determining which of two similar lines is longest. If an unexpected irrelevant item is shown at the same time, it will often not be seen, especially if less than 1 degree in size. This *inattentional blindness (IB)* has been explained by a failure to "attend" the irrelevant item—that is, a failure to transmit the information from its location (Mack & Rock, 1998). This can last for several seconds, provided that the irrelevant stimulus remains unexpected (Most et al., 2001; Simons & Chabris, 1999). Otherwise, IB virtually disappears, possibly because the filter(s) involved can be reconfigured quickly. IB appears to involve the suppression of items with visual properties similar to those that are ignored (Most et al., 2001).

An important issue is whether the failure to report an irrelevant item results from a failure to *perceive* it or to *remember* that it appeared (Wolfe, 1999). If the primary task is sufficiently demanding, a degree of IB can be induced for repeated stimuli (Cartwright-Finch & Lavie, 2007; Rensink, 2005). Assuming that advance knowledge about the appearance of an item (obtained via the repetition) can prepare the viewer to place a record of it into durable memory at the moment it appears, this indicates that IB is a failure of perception.

### INTEROCULAR SUPPRESSION

In *binocular rivalry (BR)*, two stimuli are simultaneously presented to an observer, one to each eye. But instead of the observer experiencing a combination of the two stimuli, the percept alternates, with only one stimulus experienced at any time (Blake, 2001). This occurs both for simple stimuli and complex events (Neisser & Becklen, 1975), and it likely results from the suppression of information on the basis of eye of origin.

A related effect is *continuous flash suppression (CFS)*, where a set of random images flashed into one eye at a rate of about 10 Hz completely suppresses the experience of an image shown to the other (Tsuchiya & Koch, 2005). This effect can be sustained for several minutes. The degree of suppression is more severe than that found in BR, although some of the same neural systems may be involved (Tsuchiya, Koch, Gilroy, & Blake, 2006). The afterimage of a suppressed stimulus is weakened, consistent with a suppression of information even to mechanisms not directly involved with conscious perception (Kaunitz, Fracasso, & Melcher, 2011; Tsuchiya & Koch, 2005).

## NEGLECT (HEMINEGLECT; UNILATERAL NEGLECT)

Damage to the right posterior parietal cortex can result in *neglect*—the absence of visual experience in some part of space (Bartolomeo & Chokron, 2002; Bisiach, 1993). Two variants can be distinguished. In *egocentric* neglect, the absence is of one side—usually the left—of viewer-centered space (Posner, Walker, Friedrich, & Rafal, 1984); in *allocentric* neglect, absence is of one side—usually the left—of each item in the entire visual field (Driver & Halligan, 1991). A related condition is *extinction*, where an item vanishes when a competing item appears on the opposite side of the visual field. These deficits appear to result from a failure to attentionally gate—that is, transmit—information from the appropriate area (or structure), causing either an outright failure to access the information it contains or at least a slowdown in the speed of processing (Posner et al., 1984). These deficits can be influenced by the structure of unseen objects, as well as by background segmentation (Rafal, 1994).

### Mechanism

The effects described earlier appear to involve a mechanism with a characteristic mode of operation: It acts within a very brief time (c. 50 ms), involves simple variables (such as spatial location, orientation, and color), and for spatial variables operates like a reconfigurable spotlight. It is modulated by a retinotopic (i.e., eye-centered) organization, with performance deteriorating as eccentricity increases, likely due to the sparser representation of peripheral areas in the cortex. The filtering common to all of these is sometimes referred to as *spatial attention* or *space-based attention* (see Cave & Bichot, 1999). The information transmitted does not seem to keep track of its precise position in the visual field; when it is pooled, confusions often arise.

Although the variables that control filtering are simple, the structures it operates upon are not, having at least some degree of organization (also see Duncan, 1984; Egeth & Yantis, 1997). Background structures—*segments*—appear to facilitate information

access (also see Franconeri, Bemis, & Alvarez, 2009; Kimchi, 2009). Filtering, in turn, can influence these, possibly via feedback connections (Driver et al., 2001). Likewise, although the variables transmitted (such as length) are simple, they are derived from relatively complex proto-objects in which various properties have already been bound together to some extent, presumably at low levels (Rensink, 2000a; Rensink & Enns, 1995). Also see Perceptual Organization in Vision (Chapter 2).

Models of these mechanisms include those of Posner et al. (1980) and Treisman and Gelade (1980). Neural implementation may involve the dynamic restriction of receptive fields of neurons in visual cortex (Desimone & Duncan, 1995; Moran & Desimone, 1985). Control has been modeled by a system with three components: disengagement, shifting, and reengagement (Posner et al., 1984). A more general framework for filtering is that of Nakayama (1990). Detailed computational models include those of Cave (1999), Niebur and Koch (1998), and Tsostos (2011). (Also see Chapter 8.)

### Relation to Consciousness

Much of consciousness appears to involve the consolidation of information over a global scale (Baars, 2005; Cohen & Dennett, 2011). This potentially connects to attention in at least two ways. First, conscious experience might be involved in transmitting the *output* of an attentional process elsewhere. Second, given that an attentional process can be responsive to global considerations, experience may enter into the control of its *operation*—for example, the override of automatic settings (Libet, 1985). As such, there may well be an association between conscious experience and at least some aspects of attentional filtering.

#### CONSCIOUS PERCEPTION

Attentional filtering—or at least, gating—appears necessary for conscious visual experience. In binocular rivalry, for example, observers simply fail to experience anything from the unmonitored eye (see Rensink, 2009). A similar failure occurs in inattentional blindness when the irrelevant stimulus is less than a few degrees (Mack & Rock, 1998), and in neglect, where gating has presumably failed entirely (Posner et al., 1984).

An even deeper relation may exist. When given a primary task of identifying a pattern at the center of a brief display, observers can still detect simple *features* elsewhere, such as localized colors or orientations (Braun & Sagi, 1990). They can also rapidly determine the meaning—or *gist*—of an image (Li, VanRullen, Koch, & Perona, 2002; Oliva & Torralba, 2006) and summary statistics such as average size of items (Ariely, 2001; Chong & Treisman, 2003). Here, gating may occur over a relatively large expanse, possibly in a sequential way (VanRullen, Reddy, & Koch, 2004). As the primary task becomes more demanding, gist perception begins to fail (Cohen, Alvarez, & Nakayama, 2011). If this is due to reduced gating (Lavie, 1995), it would suggest that gating—but possibly no other kind of attention—is necessary for any process concerned with the fragmentary aspects of an image.

The perception of these fragmentary aspects appears to correlate with a distinct kind of subjective experience. When an irrelevant IB stimulus is sufficiently large and the primary task not too demanding, observers often report a "fragmented" experience, being able to see "something" but not being able to say what it is (Neisser & Becklen, 1975). Such a base-level—or *ambient*—experience may be similar to the *background consciousness* of briefly presented displays (Iwasaki, 1993), where contents are fleeting, fragmentary, and seem to contain more than can be reported. It may also be related to the *phenomenal-* or *P-consciousness* taken to describe raw experience (Block, 1995; also see Lamme, 2003).

### NONCONSCIOUS PERCEPTION

Visual processing in the complete absence of visual experience—and presumably, spatial gating—is evident in many situations. During binocular rivalry, for example, faces and familiar stimuli in the unmonitored eye are not experienced, but they can enter conscious awareness more quickly (Jiang, Costello, & He, 2007). And during inattentional blindness, an unseen item can cause *priming*—speeding up the identification of a related item that is presented soon afterward (Mack & Rock, 1998). It can even draw attention to itself (Mack & Rock, 1998; but see Harris & Pashler, 2004).

Such effects are likely related to those found in *subliminal perception*, where observers generally fail to consciously experience a target that is presented extremely briefly (c. 20 ms), presumably because attentional processes are not given sufficient time to operate. But although not consciously experienced, stimuli presented under these conditions can still cause priming; interestingly, this occurs only when the time of their appearance is predictable, indicating the involvement of (possibly automatic) temporal gating (Naccache, Blandin, & Dehaene, 2002).

More generally, effects such as these suggest the existence of what might be called "*dark structure*"—structure that never can be part of visual experience, yet still affects perception. Whether the structures that influence filtering are also dark, or just the initial stages of structures that are later experienced, is an open question.

## Attentional Binding
### Function

At some point, the pieces of information obtained in the initial stages of vision must be *integrated*. This already occurs to an extent at early stages of processing, for example, the creation of background segments and proto-objects (see section on "Mechanism"). But to better capture the structure of the world, a more sophisticated structure is needed, one in which *all* the properties relevant at a moment in time are appropriately linked and are connected to a particular position in space.

One aspect of this is the linking of properties at the same location. This can occur at early levels of visual processing, with some neurons responding to particular combinations of simple properties (see e.g., Sincich & Horton, 2005); it also shows up at higher levels (e.g., van Dam & Hommel, 2010). But other aspects also exist, which may involve greater distances, greater precision, greater numbers of properties—and therefore, greater challenges (see Tsotsos, 2011, ch. 6). And all of these may require that structures be created—or at least modified—on the basis of global considerations. In other words, integration may require *attentional binding*.

Attentional binding is often associated with attentional filtering. Indeed, the two are sometimes considered to be much the same, with binding referred to as "focused attention." But binding involves rather different functions. For example, if a line segment cannot be assigned to a particular group on the basis of purely local factors, its assignment must be based on more global considerations. Similar concerns exist for other aspects of structure, for example, high-resolution estimates of orientation. More generally, the determination of integrated structure requires solving the *binding problem*: how to correctly link all relevant components (Robertson, 2003; Treisman, 1999). As such, binding is considered here to be a separate attentional process.

### Perceptual Effects

The limitations of attentional binding show up in various ways. As in the case of filtering, not all

## CONJUNCTION SEARCH

Experiments on visual search (see section on "Neglect", although I'll leave that up to you) show that the time needed to detect a unique combination (or *conjunction*) of simple features is proportional to the number of items present. This is believed to be due to a spotlight of attention that binds the features at each location, at a rate of 30–50 ms per item (Treisman & Gelade, 1980; Wolfe, 1998; but see Eckstein, 1998). Search is slower at greater eccentricity, perhaps due to sparser representation in the corresponding cortical areas (Carrasco et al., 1995; Carrasco & Frieder, 1997). Comparable rates are found when spatial form needs to be resolved (Duncan & Humphreys, 1989; Kleiss & Lane, 1986).

Not all combinations need attentional binding. Relatively fast search is possible for some scene properties and groups (Rensink & Enns, 1995, 1998), suggesting that it can access proto-objects that already contain a considerable degree of binding (but see VanRullen et al., 2004). In addition, some kinds of conjunction search can be sped up if the target is known ahead of time and the items are relatively far apart. Such *guided search* may occur because items with one of the target properties are picked out via filtering, resulting in a simpler task involving the remainder (Treisman & Sato, 1990; Wolfe, 1994). If the selection of one property in a structure can result in the immediate selection of the others, a possible explanation is that some degree of binding is in place prior to attentional processing.

## ILLUSORY CONJUNCTIONS

When nearby items with different properties are displayed briefly (e.g., 200 ms), viewers often report seeing the properties combined incorrectly (Prinzmetal, 1995; Treisman & Schmidt, 1982). These *illusory conjunctions* have been explained in terms of a process that requires 100–200 ms to link the features within the spotlight of attention and determine a definite position for each. If insufficient time is given, positional information remains poorly established, creating the possibility of erroneous bindings (Cohen & Ivry, 1989).

In foveal vision, illusory conjunctions occur primarily when items are within 1 degree of each other (Cohen & Ivry, 1989). In peripheral vision, they can occur for larger separations and slower speeds (Prinzmetal, Henderson, & Ivry, 1995), possibly because crowding (see section on "Neglect", although I'll leave that up to you) increases the difficulty of access to individual features (also see Pelli, Cavanagh, Desimone, Tjan, & Treisman, 2007). Illusory conjunctions occur more frequently within perceptual groups (Prinzmetal, 1995), showing the influence of background structures (such as segments) that contain a degree of organization. They are unlikely if the binding would create a semantic association not in the original items—for example, there is little illusory conjunction of circle plus black if the result would be a tire not present originally (Treisman, 1986).

## REPETITION BLINDNESS

If an observer looks for a target item in a stream of briefly presented stimuli (100–200 ms each), a repeated target is much less likely to be seen than a different item at the same position in the sequence. Such *repetition blindness (RB)* is thought to occur because the second item is perceived as an instance of a category (or *type*) encountered recently, which prevents triggering the formation of a new integrated structure (Kanwisher, 1987).

The type involved in RB is somewhat abstract, being invariant to size, orientation, and viewpoint (Kanwisher, Yin, & Wojciulik, 1999). This suggests it can be determined within about 100 ms, which in turn suggests that the process involved draws upon structures that already have some degree of binding. Only those items that are filtered in (e.g., those with a particular color or orientation) appear to be relevant for determining what constitutes a repetition (Kanwisher, Driver, & Machado, 1995).

## INTEGRATIVE AGNOSIA (APPERCEPTIVE AGNOSIA; VISUAL SPACE AGNOSIA)

Damage to the inferior temporal lobe sometimes results in *integrative agnosia*, an inability to perceive overall shape or configuration, with perception being only of simple features, such as color or texture (Farah, 2004; Riddoch & Humphreys, 1987). This is likely caused—at least in part—by a disabling of attentional binding. The ability to determine which items belong together appears to be unaffected, consistent with the idea that several aspects of (nonattentional) binding are carried out prior to attentional binding (Behrmann & Kimchi, 2003).

## *Mechanism*

The effects described earlier involve bound structures that enable processes such as recognition of complex shapes and characters. Most indicate a mechanism with a time constant of about 150 ms—shorter than the 300 ms typical of a fixation, but longer than the 50 ms characteristic of filtering. The 50 ms value encountered in conjunction search may reflect a mechanism based on filtering (Treisman & Gelade, 1980), but it could also simply reflect the time needed to gate an item into a pipeline that operates on several items concurrently, with each processed for several hundred milliseconds (Wolfe et al., 2000).

The mechanism involved appears to operate upon segments and proto-objects that already have a degree of binding, much—if not exactly—the same as the structures operated upon by filtering. Indeed, *feature integration theory* (Treisman & Gelade, 1980) posits that filtering is the basis of a good part of attentional binding. For example, when searching for a conjunction of different kinds of properties, or *dimensions* (e.g., a red T among red As and blue Ts), it proposes that the spotlight of attention restricts gating to a small location, resulting in the simultaneous detection of all features there.

But for many tasks, attentional filtering and attentional binding appear to be carried out by different mechanisms (Bravo & Nakayama, 1992; Briand & Klein, 1986; Maddox, Ashby, & Waldron, 2002; VanRullen et al., 2004); these may involve, respectively, the *transient* and *sustained* forms of attention that are sometimes distinguished (Nakayama & Mackeben, 1989). In addition, the resolving of fine detail appears to involve still another mechanism, one that combines information from filters operating within a single dimension (Laberge, 1998).

The neural systems that implement (attentional) binding are largely unknown (Robertson, 2003). One possibility is the synchrony in firings of neurons that belong to the same group (Singer, 1999). Another—not necessarily exclusive—account is based on the dynamic, selective routing of information from various areas of cortex (Olshausen, Anderson, & Van Essen, 1993), likely involving feedback connections between several levels of processing (Di Lollo, Enns, & Rensink, 2000; Lamme, 2003; Tsotsos, 2011, ch. 7).

### Relation to Consciousness

Just as conscious experience is associated with some aspects of attentional filtering, it may also be associated with some aspects of attentional binding. And as in the case of filtering, this could be in terms of both output and operation.

#### CONSCIOUS PERCEPTION

Attentional binding appears necessary to experience structure containing integrated properties,

spatial extension, and a well-defined position. This kind (or perhaps level) of *assembled experience* comprises ambient experience (providing basic sensory properties) along with a degree of additional (bound) structure; it may be related to the *access-* or *A-consciousness* involved with verbal reports (Block, 1995; also see Lamme, 2003). If attentional binding is diverted to some task, irrelevant visual stimuli can still be experienced, but only in ambient form, either the fragmentary features themselves (Braun & Sagi, 1990) or properties based directly upon them, such as scene gist (Li et al., 2002; VanRullen et al., 2004). Consistent with this, ambient experience alone appears to be encountered in integrative agnosia, likely due to the loss of attentional binding.

There is some possibility that attentional binding is involved in creating the "figure" in figure-ground organization (Vecera, Flavaris, & Filapek, 2004), while other kinds of attention—such as those involved in change detection—are not (Kimchi & Peterson, 2008). Given that "figure" is generally experienced in an assembled way (and "ground" in an ambient one), it may be that attentional binding is associated at least to some extent with assembled experience.

#### NONCONSCIOUS PERCEPTION

In integrative agnosia, the overall configuration of an object is not experienced in an assembled way (i.e., as a bound structure) but is still available for motor tasks such as grasping (Goodale & Milner, 1992). This suggests that integrated structure is still captured in other processing streams, possibly as dark structure that is never experienced consciously. Indeed, even when background organization is not seen in an assembled way, it can still affect the perception of stimuli that are (Driver et al., 2001; Moore & Egeth, 1997). Such phenomena are consistent with the proposal that attentional binding is involved in the control of processes that have already captured a considerable degree of structure.

### Attentional Holding
### Function

Although binding is important for various tasks, it is not always enough. For example, when a physical object changes, it is helpful to see it as a single *visual object* that endures over time, rather than a sequence of unrelated structures. Such *continuity* likely plays a central role in the perception of physical objects and events. However, establishing this additional level of structure is a complex process, in that both permanence (persistence of identity) and change (transformation of properties) must be handled simultaneously (Kahneman, Treisman, & Gibbs, 1992).Also see Object Recognition (Chapter 3).

Such continuity can be achieved via the idea of *coherent* representation. Here, properties are linked not only across space but also across time, so as to refer to a single persisting object (Rensink, 2000a). As in the case of binding (and to some degree, filtering), this process may take time. Indeed, owing to the greater complexity of coherent structure, such *attentional holding* may require considerably more in the way of various computational resources.

## Perceptual Effects

Similar to the situation for other kinds of attention, the limitations of attentional holding show up in various ways, with several common characteristics.

### OBJECT-SPECIFIC PREVIEW BENEFIT

When several items in a display are presented briefly (250 ms), a letter or digit located inside one of them can be identified more quickly the next time it appears, provided it remains inside the original item. This *object-specific preview benefit* lasts for over 600 ms and can survive considerable displacements of item location (Kahneman et al., 1992) and even the addition of a border that does not overlap existing components (Gao & Scholl, 2010).

This effect weakens as the number of items increases from 2 to 4, suggesting that some aspects of the process involved are extremely limited, possibly to one item at a time. The formation of the representations underlying this effect is believed to be largely complete by about 250 ms (Kahneman et al., 1992).

### CHANGE DETECTION/CHANGE BLINDNESS

If a change is made while the accompanying motion signals are swamped (e.g., by an image flicker or eye movement), it can be quite difficult to notice, even when large and continually repeated (Rensink, O'Regan, & Clark, 1997; Simons & Levin, 1997). This *change blindness* is believed to reflect a failure to attentionally hold the item at the moment of change (Rensink et al., 1997; Rensink, 2000a). Although reminiscent of inattentional blindness (see section on "Neglect", although I'll leave that up to you), the two are not the same; for example, change blindness can still occur when the observer is aware that a change could happen,

suggesting that the underlying processes are less flexible, or at least, slower (see Rensink, 2009).

When detecting the presence of change, up to 3–5 items can be monitored at a time (Luck & Vogel, 1997; Pashler, 1988; Rensink, 2000b). Relatively little information about each is stored (Alvarez & Cavanagh, 2004), and not all structural levels are represented (Austen & Enns, 2000). Filtering is able to control the properties considered relevant (Rensink, 2000b). When detecting an *absence* or *conjunction* of changing properties, only one item can be compared at a time, at a rate of about 300 ms per item. Thus suggests that information from the monitored items is not maintained in a set of independent representations but is collected into a single *nexus* (see Rensink, 2002).

### THIRD-ORDER MOTION

Three different kinds of motion are often distinguished. *First-order* motion is supported by differences in luminance and results from the operation of low-level detectors (Cavanagh & Mather, 1989; but see Petersik & Rice, 2006). *Second-order* is encountered for patterns with no luminance differences (e.g., textures or isoluminant colors); it appears to be based at least in part on the displacement of low-level structures (Seiffert & Cavanagh, 1998). Finally, *third-order* motion involves the tracking of movement patterns via higher level operations. It acts on extended spatial structures (e.g., a group of lines), and it can survive changes in their underlying properties (Lu & Sperling, 2001).

The perception of third-order motion is believed to require at least one kind of attention (Cavanagh, 1992). This differs from the kind that enables character recognition (presumably binding), although it may draw upon it. The mechanism involved has a time constant of about 300 ms; only one movement pattern can be seen at a time (Ho, 1998).

### ATTENTIONAL BLINK

If two prespecified targets in a stream of briefly presented stimuli appear at slightly different times, an observer will often see the first target but not the second. This phenomenon is called the *attentional blink (AB)*; it is thought to result from a failure to attentionally hold the second target, possibly because the representation of the first is not yet complete (Raymond, Shapiro, & Arnell, 1992). The mechanisms underlying this effect are selective. They differ from those that underlie repetition blindness but may involve coherent representation of some kind (Chun, 1997). The meaning of a word not consciously experienced during the blink can be implicitly perceived (Luck, Vogel, & Shapiro, 1996).

The separation needed for AB is 250–300 ms, a value known as the *attentional dwell time* (Duncan, Ward, & Shapiro, 1994; Theeuwes, Godijn, & Pratt, 2004). Only one such representation appears to be created at a time.

## SIMULTANAGNOSIA

*Simultanagnosia* is an inability to recognize more than one object at a time, resulting from damage to the brain (Coslett & Saffran, 1991). Two variants are known. The first, *dorsal* simultanagnosia, results from bilateral damage to the junction between the parietal and occipital lobes. It involves a failure to see more than one object or part of an object, with the rest of the input simply not experienced (Farah, 2004). The meaning of unseen items, however, can still have an effect (Jackson, Shepherd, Mueller, Husain, & Jackson, 2006). The second variant, *ventral* simultanagnosia, is caused by damage to the left inferior temporo-occipital region. It also involves a failure to recognize more than one object, but allows perception—including counting—of several simple shapes simultaneously (Farah, 2004). Both variants are believed to stem from an impairment of attentional processing (Coslett & Saffran, 1991; Duncan et al., 2003), likely including the engagement or disengagement of attentional hold, and—for dorsal simultanagnosia—attentional gating as well.

## *Mechanism*

The effects described earlier involve a mechanism—or set of mechanisms—with many of the following characteristics: relatively slow (c. 300 ms) access to only a few structures and a small amount of information from each, ability to filter inputs via simple properties, and only one overall structure in play at a time. Such a mechanism could represent at most only a few aspects of a physical object at any time. But if the relevant quantities could be created when requested, the result would be a *virtual representation* of the object, with any relevant aspect represented whenever needed (Ballard, Hayhoe, Pook, & Rao, 1997; Rensink, 2000a).

One model of this is the *object file*, a temporary representation of (bound) properties intended to capture the continuity of an object as it transforms or changes position (Kahneman et al., 1992). Containing only a handful of features and a single level of hierarchical structure, it forms a highly compact description of the object (including the spatial relations among its parts). Only a few object files are assumed to exist simultaneously, with only one updated at a time.

A proposal similar in many ways is the *coherence field*, in which information is "held" in reverberating circuits implemented via feedforward and feedback connections between selected proto-objects and a higher level nexus, with only a few properties in play at any moment (Rensink, 2000a). The selected proto-objects become part of a coherent visual object; when the circuit is broken, the object-level structure simply dissipates, without any accumulation of information in coherent form (also see Wolfe et al., 2000). Some information can be retained—although no longer in coherent form—for a small number of items (perhaps 10 or so), possibly as a memory to help guide subsequent allocation (Hollingworth & Henderson, 2002; Rensink, 2000a).

A more detailed quantitative model that handles many of the issues involved with the representation of coherent (and bound) structure is the *Visual Theory of Attention* (Bundesen, 1990). This incorporates several aspects of attentional processing in a unified way and provides a good fit to a considerable body of experimental data (e.g., Duncan et al., 2003).

In all these proposals a critical role is played by visual short-term memory (vSTM), which provides continuity over durations greater than a few hundred milliseconds. Although the contents of vSTM play an important role in coherent representation, the two are not necessarily the same, at least conceptually; the contents of vSTM, for example, can be maintained for several seconds after visual input disappears, whereas coherence collapses within a few hundred milliseconds afterward (Rensink, 2000a). Bindings between different dimensions appear to be maintained in vSTM (Gajewski & Brockmole, 2006; but see Wheeler & Treisman, 2002), whereas the status of these in coherent representation (where they are held only over short durations) is unknown. And while more sophisticated structures, such as movement patterns—or *sprites*—may be accessed by vSTM to enable the recognition and anticipation of complex movements (Cavanagh, Labianca, & Thornton, 2001), it is likewise unclear whether these are also part of a coherent representation. More generally, the heavy involvement—if not outright embedding—of vSTM in long-term memory (Cowan, 2001) might enable access to considerable knowledge about possible movements and other transformations, which could *guide* the creation of coherent representation.

But such knowledge need not be contained in the representation itself.

### Relation to Consciousness

As in the case of other kinds of attention, conscious experience is likely involved with at least some aspects of attentional holding, in regard to both output and control of operation. Indeed, the likelihood of such involvement is highest for this kind of attention. Given that coherence is expensive in terms of computational resources, it is extremely important to guide its usage effectively, both when transmitting it to the appropriate processes and deciding when to create it in the first place. The more global the basis of this guidance, the better.

#### CONSCIOUS PERCEPTION

Attentional holding appears necessary for a kind (or possibly level) of *coherent experience*, which includes not only ambient (and perhaps assembled) experience but also the impression of a persisting substrate. This may be similar to the *object consciousness* proposed on the basis of verbal reports of structure, which is believed to involve vSTM (Iwasaki, 1993). In the absence of attentional hold, coherence does not exist; experience is of a succession of static structures, somewhat akin to perception under stroboscopic conditions.

Whether attentional hold is also sufficient to perceive a coherent object depends on what is meant by "object." If this refers to a physical object, hold is clearly insufficient: Relatively little information is maintained in coherent form, and so most properties are not experienced in a coherent way. But if the term refers to a visual object—that is, the contents of a coherent representation—it may be both necessary *and* sufficient (Rensink, 2002).

Two types of change can be distinguished on the basis of subjective impression (Rensink, 2002). *Dynamic* change is experienced as the transformation of a structure that is *continually present* throughout the process. In contrast, *completed* change is experienced as an event that has simply *happened* at some time in the past. These appear to involve different time constants. Dynamic change cannot survive an interstimulus interval much beyond 300 ms, while completed change is far more robust; it also appears to be the only type experienced for changes made during eye movements (Rensink, 2002; also see Hollingworth, 2008). It may be that dynamic change involves coherent representation, and completed change, the contents of vSTM alone.

#### NONCONSCIOUS PERCEPTION

Although attentional hold may be necessary for the visual experience of change, implicit detection of change may still occur without it (Fernandez-Duque & Thornton, 2000; Laloyaux, Destrebecqz, & Cleeremans, 2006). The existence of this is controversial (Mitroff, Simons, & Franconeri, 2002). But if it does exist, it may reflect the operation of low-level feedback circuits that provide a degree of continuity over brief temporal gaps (cf. Di Lollo et al., 2000).

Another interesting phenomenon is the report of some observers of "sensing" or "feeling" a change without an accompanying visual experience. This may be a form of nonvisual—but still conscious—awareness involving mechanisms that differ to some extent from those underlying visual experience (Rensink, 2004). Such an account is controversial (Simons, Navarez, & Boot, 2005), but additional support for it has been found (Busch, Fründ, & Herrmann, 2010; Galpin, Underwood, & Chapman, 2008).

## Attentional Indexing
### Function

It is sometimes important to individuate a physical object—to see it not just as *an* object (coherent or otherwise) but as a *particular* object. This is especially so when more than one object must be dealt with, for example, determining spatial relations such as "between," assessing the configuration of a group, or ensuring that items in an image are processed in an optimal—or at least, effective—sequence (Pylyshyn, 2003; Ullman, 1984).

Although this might be done via multiple coherent representations, it is difficult to create more than one such representation at any time (see section on "Mechanism"). But fortunately, simultaneous coherence is rarely needed. Many operations involve only a few items, with each needing only to be distinguished in some way, such as by location. Consequently, an item only needs to contain enough information to be considered distinct at some point, and then kept track of as it moves about. If such *indexing* is successful, the item can be immediately accessed whenever needed.

### Perceptual Effects

Although indexing can be useful, it also has limitations. As in the case of other kinds of attention, these need not all involve the same neural systems. But they nevertheless appear to exhibit a degree of similarity.

## MULTIPLE-OBJECT TRACKING

In *multiple-object tracking (MOT)*, a set of identical items is displayed, a subset marked (e.g., briefly flashed), and the marked items tracked for several seconds as all items move around (Pylyshyn & Storm, 1988; Scholl, 2009). Accuracy is often good up to about 4 tracked items, this limit varying between 1 and 8, depending on task demands (Alvarez & Franconeri, 2007). Accuracy also depends on eccentricity. It is limited by a resolution coarser than that due to purely sensory limitations, possibly reflecting the involvement of attentional gating (Intriligator & Cavanagh, 2001). Indeed, tracking may help with the control of gating (Bettencourt & Somers, 2009). But it does not improve change detection (Bahrami, 2003), suggesting that it cannot help control holding.

Although tracked items are often considered independent, they can be perceived as the corners of a virtual polygon that deforms over time (Yantis, 1992). Tracking is not extrapolated when an item becomes occluded (Franconeri, Pylyshyn, & Scholl, 2006), and it does not appear to facilitate binding of the properties of the tracked item or their encoding into vSTM (Bahrami, 2003; Scholl, 2009). Meanwhile, it is possible to track the center of a simple extended structure (Scholl, Pylyshyn, & Feldman, 2001), but not the intersection perceived to result from two moving structures (Anstis, 1990). This suggests that tracking is of structures rather than simple features, but that these structures are not highly integrated, perhaps being preattentive segments or proto-objects. Tracking is based on perceived rather than retinotopic space (Liu et al., 2005).

## PRIORITIZATION OF SEARCH

A target item in visual search (see section on "Neglect", although I'll leave that up to you) is more rapidly detected if in a set of items whose locations are shown ahead of time. This *prioritization of search* is believed to reflect the existence of a set of preferred locations (Yantis & Jones, 1991; but see Watson & Humphreys, 1997), each corresponding to an indexed item.

Up to four locations can be prioritized this way; the effect does not seem to be affected by the distance between them (Burkell & Pylyshyn, 1997; Yantis & Jones, 1991). Considerably more can be prioritized under some conditions, but this may simply reflect a group that is perceived as a single indexed item (Belopolsky, Theeuwes, & Kramer, 2005).

## INHIBITION OF RETURN

When an item is attentionally gated, more time is needed to respond to it for a short while afterward (Posner & Cohen, 1984). This *inhibition of return (IOR)* takes at least 200–300 ms to develop (depending somewhat on task demands), and it can last several seconds. It appears only after the application of attentional operations involving space (Klein, 2000). It is believed to mark particular items or locations, so as to prevent attentional processes from returning too soon to a previously visited input (see Klein, 2000).

At least four locations (items) can be inhibited simultaneously; distance of separation does not appear to matter (Snyder & Kingstone, 2001; Wright & Richard, 1996). IOR acts in an object-centered rather than a retinotopic frame (Tipper, Driver, & Weaver, 1991).

## SUBITIZING

*Subitizing* is the rapid, effortless, and accurate counting of a small number of items. Up to four can be enumerated this way, at a rate of about 50 ms per item; beyond this, a slower process is needed (Trick & Pylyshyn, 1994; but see Piazza, Mechelli, Butterworth, & Price, 2002). Individuation is clearly involved, so as to ensure that the subitizing is of distinct elements.

Arbitrary combinations of features cannot be subitized, although localized groups can (Trick & Enns, 1997), suggesting that the process acts on structures (e.g., proto-objects) formed prior to attentional binding (Pylyshyn, 2003; Scholl, 2009). There appears to be no effect of spatial separation, but performance is slower for items on the same segment (or bound structure), indicating that these items are not considered separate, at least initially (Davis & Holmes, 2005).

## *Mechanism*

Each of the effects described earlier appears to involve a mechanism that can index about four items. Position is referenced not to an arbitrary point in retinotopic space, but to a structure—a segment, proto-object, or frame—created at early levels of processing. Selectivity can be allocated on the basis of global considerations, showing that this process is attentional (also see Scholl, 2009). But it operates rapidly and appears to be concerned with facilitating the control of other processes, perhaps explaining why it has not always been considered a form of attention (cf. Pylyshyn, 2003).

Coherent representations do not appear to be automatically indexed (van Dam & Hommel, 2010), suggesting that indexing may be carried out by mechanisms largely separate from those used for holding (also see Bahrami, 2003; Scholl, 2009). One proposed mechanism is the *fingers of instantiation (FINST)* model, which posits that 4–6 items can be simultaneously tracked (Pylyshyn, 2003; Pylyshyn & Storm, 1988). A variant is the *flexibly allocated index (FLEX)* model, in which 1–8 items can be tracked, with a minimal separation between them (Alvarez & Franconeri, 2007). The memory involved in indexing may be related to a spatial short-term memory concerned exclusively with location (e.g., Darling, Della Sala, & Logie, 2007; Xu & Chun, 2006).

### Relation to Consciousness

At the subjective level, indexing requires effort, consistent with it being a form of attention (see Scholl, 2009). It also appears to involve—at least during tracking—an experience of continuity, one similar to that experienced during holding, where objects maintain coherence over both time and space.

Whether indexing is also associated with a distinct kind of perceptual experience (corresponding to individuation, say) is an open issue. Given that it largely acts by facilitating the control of other attentional processes, the kinds of experience associated with indexing may not extend beyond those associated with other kinds of attention. More precisely, although indexing may enable more effective control of attentional processing, its effects may be exhibited mostly—if not entirely—via the facilitation of mechanisms found elsewhere; no new kinds of output or operational control may be involved. As such, no new kinds of conscious experience would be expected. The definitive resolution of this issue will likely require additional work in which the effects of indexing can be separated out from those of the processes it facilitates.

### Conclusion

Although the relation between perception and attention is complex, it is possible to clarify—and potentially, simplify—several of the issues involved. For visual perception, a *function-centered taxonomy* can distinguish at least five kinds of attention, each having a distinct function and characteristic mode of operation. Many of the behavioral effects associated with attention (including perceptual deficits) can be identified with one of these. In addition, at least three kinds of visual experience can be distinguished, involving increasingly sophisticated levels of represented structure, and each associated with a particular kind of attention. The results of many studies also indicate that processes of considerable sophistication occur both prior to and independent of any kind of attention, in the complete absence of conscious visual experience.

### Future Directions

1. *What exactly is an attentional kind?* The taxonomy used here centers around function, with each function appearing to be associated with a distinct set of effects and mechanisms.[2] But how real is this? Does each kind of attention correspond to an aspect or stage of a unitary process, or to something more? To answer this would include determining whether all effects believed to reflect the same kind of attention actually involve the same mechanism; this in turn would require careful measurement of things such as timing parameters and variables involved. It would also include determining the extent to which each mechanism is also used for other functions (e.g., a mechanism for filtering that is also used for binding). Some of these issues could be investigated via approaches such as the *attention operating characteristic (AOC)*, which shows the degree to which the same mechanism (or "resource") is used in two concurrent tasks (Sperling & Dosher, 1986).

2. *What kinds of attention exist?* Over the years, various processes have been lumped together under the name of "attention" (Allport, 1993; Chun, Golumb, & Turk-Browne, 2011; Tsotsos, 2011). It is important to determine what these are in a rigorous way. The approach used here might be extended to other kinds of contingently selective process, for example, assignment of semantic associations or control of motor actions. Additional kinds of attention might also be found via the splitting of existing categories—for example, binding separated into the linking of features and the formation of extended configurations across space. Progress here would include developing more rigorous criteria for determining what counts as a distinct kind of attentional process, as well as a more careful examination of effects currently considered to involve the same kind of attention.

3. *How do the various kinds of attention relate to each other?* This is essentially the generalization of the question of how eye movements relate to covert kinds of attention. A key step is to determine which

attentional processes depend on which. Although there could in principle be interactions among several processes simultaneously, much could likely be done simply by investigating pairs of interactions. If there is some dependence between particular processes, it becomes important to determine how closely their operation is aligned, both in space (operands selected) and in time (kinds of delays).

4. *What are the characteristics of the processes operating prior to attention?* The kinds of attention discussed here all appear to operate on the same preattentive structures: extended segments, localized proto-objects, and possibly frames of some kind. It is important to get a better understanding of these. Do they form a common substrate for all attentional processes? Are they distinct or different aspects of the same thing? To what extent can they be overridden—or at least, set—by attentional control allocated ahead of time? These questions can be investigated via modifications of the techniques outlined here.

5. *How do the different kinds of visual experience relate to the different kinds of attention?* Interest in how attention relates to conscious awareness spans centuries. Most proposals (e.g., Koch & Tsuchiya, 2007; Lamme, 2003) assume only one kind of attention and one kind of visual experience. However, given the distinctions that appear to be emerging, this issue needs to be recast into a more articulated form: Relationships may only exist between some kinds of attention and some kinds of experience. Given the number of possible combinations and the number of issues to consider in each, establishing such relationships will take considerable work. But once determined, they will likely give us important new insights into the nature of both attention and consciousness.

## Acknowledgments

This chapter is dedicated to the memory of Jon Driver.

Correspondence may be addressed to R.A. Rensink, Department of Psychology, University of British Columbia, 2136 West Mall, Vancouver BC V6T 1Z4, Canada. E-mail: rensink@psych.ubc.ca or rensink@cs.ubc.ca.

## Notes

1. These have often been referred to as "objects." But this word is overworked, having been used to refer to virtually any level of structure. Following Driver et al. (2001), simple large-scale background structures at early levels are referred to here as "segments"; following Rensink and Enns (1995), more complex localized structures are referred to as "proto-objects." "Object" (as in "visual object") is reserved for the highest level of visual structure, viz., a coherent representation in which all components refer—over both space and time—to a single underlying substrate, ideally capturing the structure of a physical object in the world.

2. The function-centered categorization developed here echoes to a large extent the approach advocated by Marr (1982) and Dennett (1994). This begins by analyzing the process in terms of its function, followed by analysis of the mechanisms/representations that carry it out, followed by analysis of the underlying neural implementation. Given the focus of this chapter, only the first two are discussed in the framework here.

## References

Albrecht, A.R., List, A., & Robertson, L.C. (2008). Attentional selection and the represention of holes and objects. *Journal of Vision, 8,* 8.1–10.

Allport, A. (1989). Visual attention. In M. I. Posner (Ed.), *Foundations of cognitive science* (pp. 631–682). Cambridge, MA: MIT Press.

Allport, A. (1993). Attention and control: Have we been asking the wrong questions? A critical review of twenty-five years. In D. E. Meyer & S. Kornblum (Eds.), *Attention and performance XIV: Synergies in experimental psychology, artificial intelligence, and cognitive neuroscience* (pp. 183–218). Cambridge, MA: MIT Press.

Alvarez, G. A., & Cavanagh, P. (2004). The capacity of visual short-term memory is set both by visual information load and by number of objects. *Psychological Science, 15,* 106–111.

Alvarez, G. A., & Franconeri, S. (2007). How many objects can you track? Evidence for a resource-limited attentive tracking mechanism. *Journal of Vision, 7,* 14.1–10.

Anstis, S. (1990). Imperceptible intersections: The chopstick illusion. In A. Blake & T. Troscianko (Eds.), *AI and the eye* (pp. 105–117). London: John Wiley.

Anton-Erxleben, K., Abrams, J., & Carrasco, M. (2010). Evaluating comparative and equality judgments in contrast perception: Attention alters appearance. *Journal of Vision, 10,* 6.1–22.

Ariely, D. (2001). Seeing sets: Representation by statistical properties. *Psychological Science, 12,* 157–162.

Austen, E., & Enns, J. T. (2000). Change detection: Paying attention to detail. *Psyche, 6*(11). Retrieved from cogprints.org/1055/3/psyche-6–11-austen.pdf

Baars, B. J. (2005). Global workspace theory of consciousness: Toward a cognitive neuroscience of human experience. *Progress in Brain Research, 150,* 45–53.

Bahrami, B. (2003) Object property encoding and change blindness in multiple object tracking. *Visual Cognition, 10,* 949–963.

Ballard, D. H., Hayhoe, M. M., Pook, P. K., & Rao, R. P. N. (1997). Deictic codes for the embodiment of cognition. *Behavioral and Brain Sciences, 20,* 723–767.

Barlow, H. B. (1981). Critical limiting factors in the design of the eye and visual cortex. *Proceedings of the Royal Society of London, Series B, 212*, 1–34.

Barlow, H. B., & Mollon, J. D. (Eds.). (1982). *The senses*. Cambridge, England: Cambridge University Press.

Bartolomeo, P., & Chokron, S. (2002). Orienting of attention in left unilateral neglect. *Neuroscience and Biobehavioral Reviews, 26*, 217–234.

Behrmann, M., & Kimchi, R. (2003). What does visual agnosia tell us about perceptual organization and its relationship to object perception? *Journal of Experimental Psychology: Human Perception and Performance, 29*, 19–42.

Belopolsky, A.V., Theeuwes, J., & Kramer, A. (2005). Prioritization by transients in visual search. *Psychonomic Bulletin and Review, 12*, 93–99.

Bettencourt, K. C., & Somers, D. C. (2009). Effects of target enhancement and distractor suppression on multiple object tracking capacity. *Journal of Vision, 9*, 9.1–11.

Bichot, N. P., Cave, K. R., & Pashler, H. (1999). Visual selection mediated by location: Feature-based selection of noncontiguous locations. *Perception and Psychophysics, 61*, 403–423.

Bisiach, E. (1993). Mental representation in unilateral neglect and related disorders: The twentieth Bartlett Memorial Lecture. *Quarterly Journal of Experimental Psychology, 46*, 435–561.

Blake, R. (2001). A primer on binocular rivalry, including current controversies. *Brain and Mind, 2*, 5–38.

Block, N. (1995). On a confusion about a function of consciousness. *Behavioral and Brain Science, 18*, 227–247.

Bouma, H. (1970). Interaction effects in parafoveal letter recognition. *Nature, 226*, 177–178.

Braun, J., & Sagi, D. (1990). Vision outside the focus of attention. *Perception and Psychophysics, 48*, 45–58.

Bravo, M. J., & Nakayama, K. (1992). The role of attention in different visual-search tasks. *Perception and Psychophysics, 51*, 465–472.

Briand, K. A., & Klein, R. M. (1986). Is Posner's "beam" the same as Treisman's "glue"? On the relation between visual orienting and feature integration theory. *Journal of Experimental Psychology: Human Perception and Performance, 13*, 228–241.

Bridgeman, B., van derHeijden, A. H. C., & Velichkovsky, B. M. (1994). A theory of visual stability across saccadic eye movements. *Behavioral and Brain Sciences, 17*, 247–292.

Broadbent, D. E. (1982). Task combination and selective intake of information. *Acta Psychologica, 50*, 253–290.

Bundesen, C. (1990). A theory of visual attention. *Psychological Review, 97*, 523–547.

Burkell, J. A., & Pylyshyn, Z. W. (1997). Searching through subsets: A test of the visual indexing hypothesis. *Spatial Vision, 11*, 225–258.

Busch, N. A., Fründ, I., & Herrmann, C. S. (2010). Electrophysiological evidence for different types of change detection and change blindness. *Journal of Cognitive Neuroscience, 22*, 1852–1869.

Carpenter, R. H. S. (1988). *Movements of the eyes* (2nd ed., text rev.). London: Pion.

Carrasco, M., Evert, D. L., Change, I., & Katz, S. M. (1995). The eccentricity effect: Target eccentricity affects performance on conjunction searches. *Perception and Psychophysics, 57*, 1241–1261.

Carrasco, M., & Frieder, K. S. (1997). Cortical magnification neutralized the eccentricity effect in visual search. *Vision Research, 37*, 63–82.

Carrasco, M., Ling, S., & Read, S. (2004). Attention alters appearance. *Nature Neuroscience, 7*, 308–313.

Cartwright-Finch, U., & Lavie, N. (2007). The role of perceptual load in inattentional blindness. *Cognition, 102*, 321–340.

Cavanagh, P. (1992). Attention-based motion perception. *Science, 257*, 1563–1565.

Cavanagh, P., Labianca, A. T., & Thornton, I. M. (2001). Attention-based visual routines: Sprites. *Cognition, 80*, 47–60.

Cavanagh, P., & Mather, G. (1989). Motion: The long and short of it. *Spatial Vision, 4*, 103–129.

Cave, K. R. (1999). The feature-gate model of visual selection. *Psychological Research, 62*, 182–194.

Cave, K. R., & Bichot, N. P. (1999). Visuospatial attention: Beyond a spotlight model. *Psychonomic Bulletin and Review, 6*, 204–223.

Chong, S. C., & Treisman, A. (2003). Representation of statistical properties. *Vision Research, 43*, 393–404.

Chun, M. M. (1997). Types and tokens in visual processing: A double dissociation between the attentional blink and repetition blindness. *Journal of Experimental Psychology: Human Perception and Performance, 23*, 738–755.

Chun, M. M., Golomb, J. D., & Turk-Browne, N. B. (2011). A taxonomy of external and internal attention. *Annual Review of Psychology, 62*, 73–101.

Cohen, M. A., Alvarez, G. A, & Nakayama, K. (2011). Natural-scene perception requires attention. *Psychological Science, 22*, 1165–1172.

Cohen, M. A., & Dennett, D. C. (2011). Consciousness cannot be separated from function. *Trends in Cognitive Sciences, 15*, 358–364.

Cohen, A., & Ivry, R. (1989). Illusory conjunctions inside and outside the focus of attention. *Journal of Experimental Psychology: Human Perception and Performance, 15*, 650–663.

Coslett, H. B., & Saffran, E. (1991). Simultanagnosia: To see but not two see. *Brain, 114*, 1523–1545.

Cowan, N. (2001). The magical number 4 in short-term memory: A reconsideration of mental storage capacity. *Behavioral and Brain Sciences, 24*, 87–18.

Crowne, D. P. (1983). The frontal eye field and attention. *Psychological Bulletin, 93*, 232–260.

Darling, S., Della Sala, S., & Logie, R. H. (2007). Behavioural evidence for separating components within visuo-spatial working memory. *Cognitive Processing, 8*, 175–181.

Davis, G., & Holmes, A. (2005). What is enumerated by subitization mechanisms? *Perception and Psychophysics, 67*, 1229–1241.

Davis, E. T., Kramer, P., & Graham, N. (1983). Uncertainty about spatial frequency, spatial position, or contrast of visual patterns. *Perception and Psychophysics, 33*, 20–28.

Dennett, D. C. (1994). Cognitive science as reverse engineering: Several meanings of "top-down" and "bottom-up." In D. Prawitz , B. Skyrms , & D. Westerståhl (Eds.), *Logic, methodology,and philosophy of science IX* (pp. 679–689). Amsterdam, The Netherlands: Elsevier.

Desimone, R., & Duncan, J. (1995). Neural mechanisms of selective visual attention. *Annual Review of Neuroscience, 18*, 193–222.

Deubel, H., & Schneider, W. X. (1996). Saccade target selection and object recognition: Evidence for a common attentional mechanism. *Vision Research, 36*, 1827–1837.

Di Lollo, V., Enns, J. T., & Rensink, R. A. (2000). Competition for consciousness among visual events: The psychophysics of reentrant visual processes. *Journal of Experimental Psychology: General, 129,* 481–507.

Driver, J., & Baylis, G. C. (1989). Movement and visual attention: The spotlight metaphor breaks down. *Journal of Experimental Psychology: Human Perception and Performance, 15,* 448–456.

Driver, J., Davis, G., Russell, C., Turrato, M., & Freeman, E. (2001). Segmentation, attention and phenomenal visual objects. *Cognition, 80,* 61–95.

Driver, J., & Halligan, P. W. (1991). Can visual neglect operate in object-centred coordinates? An affirmative single-case study. *Cognitive Neuropsychology, 8,* 475–496.

Duncan, J. (1984). Selective attention and the organization of visual information. *Journal of Experimental Psychology: General, 113,* 501–517.

Duncan, J., Bundesen, C., Olson, A., Humphreys, G., Ward, R., Kyllingsbæk, S.,…Chavda, S. (2003). Attentional functions in dorsal and ventral simultanagnosia. *Cognitive Neuropsychology, 20,* 675–701.

Duncan, J., & Humphreys, G. W. (1989). Visual search and stimulus similarity. *Psychological Review, 96,* 433–458.

Duncan, J., Ward, R., & Shapiro, K. (1994). Direct measurement of attentional dwell time in human vision. *Nature, 369,* 313–315.

Eckstein, M. P. (1998). The lower visual search efficiency for conjunctions is due to noise and not serial attentional processing. *Psychological Science, 9,* 111–118.

Egeth, H. E., & Yantis, S. (1997). Visual attention: Control, representation, and time course. *Annual Review of Psychology, 48,* 269–297.

Egly, R., Driver, J., & Rafal, R. D. (1994). Shifting visual attention between objects and locations: Evidence from normal and parietal lesion subjects. *Journal of Experimental Psychology: General, 123,* 161–177.

Eriksen, B. A., & Eriksen, C. W. (1974). Effects of noise letters upon the identification of a target letter in a non-search task. *Perception and Psychophysics, 16,* 143–149.

Eriksen, C. W., & St. James, J. D. (1986). Visual attention within and around the field of focal attention: A zoom lens model. *Perception and Psychophysics, 40,* 225–240.

Eriksen, C. W., & Yeh, Y -Y. (1985). Allocation of attention in the visual field. *Journal of Experimental Psychology: Human Perception and Performance, 11,* 583–597.

Farah, M. J. (2004). *Visual agnosia* (2nd ed.). Cambridge, MA: MIT Press.

Fernandez-Duque, D., & Thornton, I. M. (2000). Change detection without awareness: Do explicit reports underestimate the representation of change in the visual system? *Visual Cognition, 7,* 323–344.

Fischer, J., & Whitney, D. (2011). Object-level visual information gets through the bottleneck of crowding. *Journal of Neurophysiology, 106,* 1389–1398.

Franconeri, S. L., Bemis, D. K., & Alvarez, G. A. (2009). Number estimation relies on a set of segmented objects. *Cognition, 113,* 1–13.

Franconeri, S. L., Pylyshyn, Z. W., & Scholl, B. J. (2006). Spatiotemporal cues for tracking multiple objects through occlusion. *Visual Cognition, 14,* 100–103.

Gajewski, D. A., & Brockmole, J. R. (2006). Feature bindings endure without attention: Evidence from an explicit recall task. *Psychonomic Bulletin and Review, 13,* 581–587.

Galpin, A., Underwood, G., & Chapman, P. (2008). Sensing without seeing in comparative visual search. *Consciousness and Cognition, 17,* 672–687.

Gao, T., & Scholl, B. J. (2010). Are objects required for object-files? Roles of segmentation and spatiotemporal continuity in computing object persistence. *Visual Cognition, 18,* 82–109.

Giordano, A. M., Mc Elree, B., & Carrasco, M. (2009). On the automaticity and flexibility of covert attention: A speed-accuracy trade-off analysis. *Journal of Vision, 9,* 30. 1–10.

Goodale, M. A., & Milner, A. D. (1992). Separate visual pathways for perception and action. *Trends in Neurosciences, 15,* 20–22.

Harris, C. R., & Pashler, H. (2004). Attention and the processing of emotional words and names: Not so special after all. *Psychological Science, 15,* 171–178.

Hatfield, G. (1998). Attention in early scientific psychology. In R. D. Wright (Ed.), *Visual attention* (pp. 3–25). Oxford, England: Oxford University Press.

Hayhoe, M. M., & Ballard, D. H. (2005). Eye movements in natural behavior. *Trends in Cognitive Sciences, 9,* 188–194.

He, Z. J., & Nakayama, K. (1995). Visual attention to surfaces in 3-D space. *Proceedings of the National Academy of Sciences USA, 92,* 11155–11159.

Henderson, J. M., & Hollingworth, A. (1998). Eye movements during scene viewing: An overview. Eye guidance in reading and scene perception. In G. Underwood (Ed.), *Eye guidance in reading and scene perception* (pp. 269–293). Oxford, England: Elsevier.

Hirst, W., & Kalmar, D. (1987). Characterizing attentional resources. *Journal of Experimental Psychology: General, 116,* 68–81.

Ho, C. E. (1998). Letter recognition reveals pathways of second-order and third-order motion. *Proceedings of the National Academy of Sciences USA, 95,* 400–404.

Hollingworth, A. (2008). Visual memory for natural scenes. In S. J. Luck & A. Hollingworth (Eds.), *Visual memory* (pp. 123–162). New York: Oxford University Press.

Hollingworth, A., & Henderson, J. M. (2002). Accurate visual memory for previously attended objects in natural scenes. *Journal of Experimental Psychology: Human Perception and Performance, 28,* 113–136.

Humphreys, G. W. (1981). Flexibility of attention between stimulus dimensions. *Perception and Psychophysics, 30,* 291–302.

Intriligator, J., & Cavanagh, P. (2001) The spatial resolution of visual attention. *Cognitive Psychology, 43,* 171–216.

Iwasaki, S. (1993). Spatial attention and two modes of consciousness. *Cognition, 49,* 211–233.

Jackson, G. M., Shepherd, T., Mueller, S. C., Husain, M., & Jackson, S. R. (2006) Dorsal simultanagnosia: An impairment of visual processing or visual awareness? *Cortex, 42,* 740–749.

Jiang, Y., Costello, P., & He, S. (2007). Processing of invisible stimuli: Advantage of upright faces and recognizable words in overcoming interocular suppression. *Psychological Science, 18,* 349–355.

Jonides, J. (1983). Further toward a model of the mind's eye's movement. *Bulletin of the Psychonomic Society, 21,* 247–250.

Juan, C-H., Shorter-Jacobi, S. M., & Schall, J. (2004). Dissociation of spatial attention and saccade preparation. *Proceedings of the National Academy of Sciences USA, 101,* 15541–15544.

Kahneman, D., Treisman, A., & Gibbs, B. J. (1992). The reviewing of object files: Object-specific integration of information. *Cognitive Psychology, 24,* 175–219.

Kanwisher, N., Driver, J., & Machado, L. (1995). Spatial repetition blindness is modulated by selective attention to color or shape. *Cognitive Psychology, 29*, 303–337.

Kanwisher, N., Yin, C., & Wojciulik, E. (1999). Repetition blindness for pictures: Evidence for the rapid computation of abstract visual descriptions. In V. Coltheart (Ed.), *Fleeting memories: Cognition of brief visual stimuli* (pp. 119–150). Cambridge, MA: MIT Press.

Kanwisher, N. G. (1987). Repetition blindness: Type recognition without token individuation. *Cognition, 27*, 117–143.

Kaplan, E. (1991). The receptive field structure of retinal ganglion cells in cat and monkey. In. A. G. Leventhal (Ed.), *Vision and visual dysfunction* (pp. 10–40). Boston: CRC Press.

Kaunitz, L., Fracasso, A., & Melcher, D. (2011). Unseen complex motion is modulated by attention and generates a visible aftereffect. *Journal of Vision, 11*, 10.1–9.

Kimchi, R. (2009). Perceptual organization and visual attention. *Progress in Brain Research, 176*, 15–33.

Kimchi, R., & Peterson, M. A. (2008). Figure-ground segmentation can occur without attention. *Psychological Science, 19*, 660–668.

Klein, R. M. (2000). Inhibition of return. *Trends in Cognitive Sciences, 4*, 138–147.

Kleiss, J. A., & Lane, D. M. (1986). Locus and persistence of capacity limitations in visual information processing. *Journal of Experimental Psychology: Human Perception and Performance, 12*, 200–210.

Koch, C., & Tsuchiya, N. (2007). Attention and consciousness: Two distinct brain processes. *Trends in Cognitive Sciences, 11*, 16–22.

Kramer, A. F., & Hahn, S. (1995). Splitting the beam: Distribution of attention over noncontiguous regions of the visual field. *Psychological Science, 6*, 381–386.

Kramer, A. F., & Jacobson, A. (1991). Perceptual organization and focused attention: The role of objects and proximity in visual processing. *Perception and Psychophysics, 50*, 267–284.

LaBerge, D. (1998). Attentional emphasis in visual orienting and resolving. In R. D. Wright (Ed.), *Visual attention* (pp. 417–454). Oxford, England: Oxford University Press.

LaBerge, D., & Brown, V. (1989). Theory of attentional operations in shape identification. *Psychological Review, 96*, 101–124.

Laloyaux, C., Destrebecqz, A., & Cleeremans, A. (2006). Implicit change identification: A replication of Fernandez-Duque and Thornton (2003). *Journal of Experimental Psychology: Human Perception and Performance, 32*, 1366–1379.

Lamme, V. A. F. (1995). The neurophysiology of figure-ground segregation in primary visual cortex. *Journal of Neuroscience, 15*, 1605–1615.

Lamme, V. A. F. (2003). Why visual attention and awareness are different. *Trends in Cognitive Sciences, 7*, 12–18.

Lavie, N. (1995). Perceptual load as a necessary condition for selective attention. *Journal of Experimental Psychology: Human Perception and Performance, 21*, 451–468.

Li, F. F., VanRullen, R., Koch, C., & Perona, P. (2002). Rapid natural scene categorization in the near absence of attention. *Proceedings of the National Academy of Sciences USA, 99*, 9596–9601.

Libet, B. (1985). Unconscious cerebral initiative and the role of conscious will in voluntary action. *Behavioral and Brain Sciences, 8*, 529–66.

Liu, G., Austen, E. L., Booth, K. S., Fisher, B. D., Argue, R., Rempel, M. I., & Enns, J. T. (2005). Multiple-object tracking is based on scene, not retinal, coordinates. *Journal of Experimental Psychology: Human Perception and Performance, 31*, 235–247.

Lu, Z -L., & Sperling, G. (2001). Three-systems theory of human visual motion perception: Review and update. *Journal of the Optical Society of America A, 18*, 2331–2370.

Luck, S. J., & Vogel, E. K. (1997). The capacity of visual working memory for features and conjunctions. *Nature, 390*, 279–281.

Luck, S. J., Vogel, E. K., & Shapiro, K. L. (1996). Word meanings can be accessed but not reported during the attentional blink. *Nature, 383*, 616–618.

Mack, A., & Rock, I. (1998). *Inattentional blindness.* Cambridge, MA: MIT Press.

Maddox, W. T., Ashby, F. G., & Waldron, E. M. (2002). Multiple attention systems in perceptual categorization. *Memory and Cognition, 30*, 325–329.

Marr, D. (1982). *Vision: A computational investigation into the human representation and processing of visual information* (pp. 8–38). San Francisco: W.H. Freeman.

Maunsell, J. H. R., & Treue, S. (2006). Feature-based attention in visual cortex. *Trends in Neurosciences, 29*, 317–322.

Mitroff, S. R., Simons, D. J., & Franconeri, S. L. (2002). The siren song of implicit change detection. *Journal of Experimental Psychology: Human Perception and Performance, 28*, 798–815.

Moore, C. M., & Egeth, H. (1997). Perception without attention: Evidence of grouping under conditions of inattention. *Journal of Experimental Psychology: Human Perception and Performance, 23*, 339–352.

Moran, J., & Desimone, R. (1985). Selective attention gates visual processing in the extrastriate cortex. *Science, 229*, 782–784.

Most, S. B., Simons, D. J., Scholl, B. J., Jimenez, R., Clifford, E., & Chabris, C. F. (2001). How not to be seen: The contribution of similarity and selective ignoring to sustained inattentional blindness. *Psychological Science, 12*, 9–17.

Naccache, L., Blandin, E., & Dehaene, S. (2002). Unconscious masked priming depends on temporal attention. *Psychological Science, 13*, 416–424.

Nakayama, K. (1990). The iconic bottleneck and the tenuous link between early visual processing and perception. In C. Blakemore (Ed.), *Vision: Coding and efficiency* (pp. 411–422). New York: Cambridge University Press.

Nakayama, K., & MacKeben, M. (1989) Sustained and transient components of focal visual attention. *Vision Research, 29*, 1631–1647.

Neisser, U., & Becklen, R. (1975). Selective looking: Attending to visually significant events. *Cognitive Psychology, 7*, 480–494.

Niebur, E., & Koch, C. (1998). Computational architectures for attention. In R. Parasuraman (Ed.), *The attentive brain* (pp. 163–186). Cambridge, MA: MIT Press.

Noton, D., & Stark, L. (1971). Eye movements and visual perception. *Scientific American, 224*(6), 34–43.

Oliva, A., & Torralba, A. (2006). Building the gist of a scene: The role of global image features in recognition. *Progress in Brain Research, 155*, 23–36.

Oliva, A., & Torralba, A. (2007). The role of context in object recognition. *Trends in Cognitive Sciences, 11*, 520–527.

Olshausen, B. A., Anderson, C. H., & Van Essen, D. C. (1993). A neurobiological model of visual attention and invariant pattern recognition based on dynamic routing of information. *Journal of Neuroscience, 13*, 4700–4719.

O'Regan, J. K., & Noë, A. (2001.) A sensorimotor account of vision and visual consciousness. *Behavioral and Brain Sciences, 24*, 939–973.

Palmer, J., Ames, C. T., & Lindsey, D. T. (1993). Measuring the effect of attention on simple visual search. *Journal of Experimental Psychology: Human Perception and Performance, 19*, 108–130.

Parasuraman, R. (Ed.). (1998). *The attentive brain*. Cambridge, MA: MIT Press.

Pashler, H. E. (1988). Familiarity and visual change detection. *Perception and Psychophysics, 44*, 369–378.

Pashler, H. E. (1999). *The psychology of attention*. Cambridge, MA: MIT Press.

Pelli, D. G., Cavanagh, P., Desimone, R., Tjan, B., & Treisman, A. (2007). Crowding: Including illusory conjunctions, surround suppression, and attention. *Journal of Vision, 7*, 1.

Petersik, T. J., & Rice, C. M. (2006). The evolution of explanations of a perceptual phenomenon: A case history using the Ternus effect. *Perception, 35*, 807–821.

Piazza, M., Mechelli A., Butterworth, B., & Price, C. J. (2002). Are subitizing and counting implemented as separate or functionally overlapping processes? *NeuroImage, 15*, 435–446.

Posner, M. I., & Cohen, Y. (1984). Components of visual orienting. In H. Bouma & D. Bouwhuis (Eds.), *Attention and performance X* (pp. 531–556). Hillsdale, NJ: Erlbaum.

Posner, M. I., & Snyder, C. R. R. (1975). Attention and cognitive control. In R. L. Solso (Ed.), *Information processing and cognition* (pp. 55–85). Hillsdale, NJ: Erlbaum.

Posner, M. I., Snyder, C. R. R., & Davidson, B. J. (1980). Attention and the detection of signals. *Journal of Experimental Psychology: General, 109*, 160–174.

Posner, M. I., Walker, J. A., Friedrich, F. J., & Rafal, R. D. (1984). Effects of parietal injury on covert orienting of attention. *Journal of Neuroscience, 4*, 1863–1874.

Prinzmetal, W. (1995). Visual feature integration in a world of objects. *Current Directions in Psychological Science, 4*, 90–94.

Prinzmetal, W., Henderson, D., & Ivry, R. (1995). Loosening the constraints on illusory conjunctions: The role of exposure duration and attention. *Journal of Experimental Psychology: Human Perception and Performance, 21*, 1362–1375.

Pylyshyn, Z. W. (2003). *Seeing and visualizing: It's not what you think*. Cambridge MA: MIT Press.

Pylyshyn, Z. W., & Storm, R. W. (1988). Tracking multiple independent targets: Evidence for a parallel tracking mechanism. *Spatial Vision, 3*, 179–197.

Rafal, R. (1994). Neglect. *Current Opinion in Neurobiology, 4*, 231–236.

Ramachandran, V. S. (1992). Filling in gaps in perception: I. *Current Directions in Psychological Science, 1*, 199–205.

Ramachandran, V. S., & Gregory, R. L. (1991). Perceptual filling in of artificially induced scotomas in human vision. *Nature, 350*, 699–702.

Raymond, J. E., Shapiro, K. L., & Arnell, K. M. (1992). Temporary suppression of visual processing in an RSVP task: An attentional blink? *Journal of Experimental Psychology: Human Perception and Performance, 18*, 849–860.

Rensink, R. A. (2000a). The dynamic representation of scenes. *Visual Cognition, 7*, 17–42.

Rensink, R. A. (2000b). Visual search for change: A probe into the nature of attentional processing. *Visual Cognition, 7*, 345–376

Rensink, R. A. (2002). Change detection. *Annual Review of Psychology, 53*, 245–277.

Rensink, R. A. (2004). Visual sensing without seeing. *Psychological Science, 15*, 27–32.

Rensink, R. A. (2005). Robust inattentional blindness. *Journal of Vision, 5*, 790a.

Rensink, R. A. (2009). Attention: Change blindness and inattentional blindness. In W. Banks (Ed.), *Encyclopedia of consciousness* (Vol. 1, pp. 47–59). New York: Elsevier.

Rensink, R. A., & Enns, J. T. (1995). Preemption effects in visual search: Evidence for low-level grouping. *Psychological Review, 102*, 101–130.

Rensink, R. A., & Enns, J. T. (1998). Early completion of occluded objects. *Vision Research, 38*, 2489–2505.

Rensink, R. A., O' Regan, J. K., & Clark, J. J. (1997). To see or not to see: The need for attention to perceive changes in scenes. *Psychological Science, 8*, 368–373.

Riddoch, M. J., & Humphreys, G. W. (1987). A case of integrative visual agnosia. *Brain, 110*, 1431–1462.

Robertson, L. C. (2003). Binding, spatial attention and perceptual awareness. *Nature Reviews Neuroscience, 4*, 93–102.

Robertson, L. C., & Kim, M -S. (1999). Effects of perceived space on spatial attention. *Psychological Science, 10*, 76–79.

Rossi, A. F., & Paradiso, M. (1995). Feature-specific effects of selective visual attention. *Vision Research, 35*, 621–634.

Sagi, D., & Julesz, B. (1986). Enhanced detection in the aperture of focal attention during simple discrimination tasks. *Nature, 321*, 693–695.

Scholl, B. J. (2009). What have we learned about attention from multiple-object tracking (and vice versa)? In D. Dedrick & L. Trick (Eds.), *Computation, cognition, and Pylyshyn* (pp. 49–77). Cambridge, MA: MIT Press.

Scholl, B. J., Pylyshyn, Z. W., & Feldman, J. (2001). What is a visual object? Evidence from target merging in multiple-object tracking. *Cognition, 80*(1/2), 159–177.

Seiffert, A. E., & Cavanagh, P. (1998). Position displacement, not velocity, is the cue to motion detection of second-order stimuli. *Vision Research, 38*, 3569–3582.

Simons, D. J., & Chabris, C. F. (1999). Gorillas in our midst: Sustained inattentional blindness for dynamic events. *Perception, 28*, 1059–1074.

Simons, D. J., & Levin, D. T. (1997). Change blindness. *Trends in Cognitive Sciences, 1*, 261–267.

Simons, D. J., Nevarez, G., & Boot, W. R. (2005). Visual sensing is seeing: Why "mindsight," in hindsight, is blind. *Psychological Science, 16*, 520–524.

Sincich, J. C., & Horton, J. C. (2005). The circuitry of V1 and V2: Integration of color, form, and motion. *Annual Review of Neuroscience, 28*, 303–326.

Singer, W. (1999). Neuronal synchrony: A versatile code for the definition of relations? *Neuron, 24*, 49–65.

Snyder, J. J., & Kingstone, A. (2000). Inhibition of return and visual search: How many separate loci are inhibited? *Perception and Psychophysics, 62*, 452–458.

Sperling, G., & Dosher, B. A. (1986). Strategy and optimization in human information processing. In K. R. Boff , L. Kaufman, & J. P. Thomas (Eds.), *Handbook of perception and human performance* (Vol. 1, pp. 1–65). New York: Wiley.

Strasburger, H. (2005). Unfocussed spatial attention underlies the crowding effect in indirect form vision. *Journal of Vision, 5*, 1024–1037.

Steinman, B. A., Steinman, S. B., & Lehmkuhle, S. (1995). Visual attention mechanisms show a center—surround organization. *Vision Research, 35*, 1859–1869.

Theeuwes, J., Godijn, R., & Pratt, J. (2004). A new estimation of the duration of attentional dwell time. *Psychonomic Bulletin and Review, 11*, 60–64.

Thornton, T. L., & Gilden, D. L. (2007). Parallel and serial processes in visual search. *Psychological Review, 114*, 71–103.

Tipper, S. P., Driver, J., & Weaver, B. (1991). Object-centred inhibition of return of visual attention. *Quarterly Journal of Experimental Psychology A: Human Experimental Psychology, 43*, 289–298.

Treisman, A. (1986). Features and objects in visual processing. *Scientific American, 255*(Nov), 114B–125B.

Treisman, A. (1999). Solutions to the binding problem: Progress through controversy and convergence. *Neuron, 24*, 105–110.

Treisman, A. M., & Gelade, G. (1980). A feature-integration theory of attention. *Cognitive Psychology, 12*, 97–136.

Treisman, A., & Gormican, S. (1988). Feature analysis in early vision: Evidence from search asymmetries. *Psychological Review, 95*, 15–48.

Treisman, A., & Sato, S. (1990). Conjunction search revisited. *Journal of Experimental Psychology: Human Perception and Performance, 16*, 459–478.

Treisman, A., & Schmidt, H. (1982). Illusory conjunctions in the perception of objects. *Cognitive Psychology, 14*, 107–141.

Trick, L. M., & Enns, J. T. (1997). Clusters precede shapes in perceptual organization. *Psychological Science, 8*, 124–129.

Trick, L. M., & Pylyshyn, Z. W. (1994). Why are small and large numbers enumerated differently? A limited-capacity preattentive stage in vision. *Psychological Review, 101*, 80–102.

Tsal, Y. (1983). Movement of attention across the visual field. *Journal of Experimental Psychology: Human Perception and Performance, 9*, 523–530.

Tsotsos, J. K. (1990). Analyzing vision at the complexity level. *Behavioral and Brain Sciences, 13*, 423–469.

Tsotsos, J. K. (2011). *A computational perspective on visual attention.* Cambridge, MA: MIT Press.

Tsuchiya, N., & Koch, C. (2005). Continuous flash suppression reduces negative afterimages. *Nature Neuroscience, 8*, 1096–1101.

Tsuchiya, N., Koch, C., Gilroy, L. A., & Blake, R. (2006) Depth of interocular suppression associated with continuous flash suppression, flash suppression, and binocular rivalry *Journal of Vision, 6*, 1068–1078.

Ullman, S. (1984). Visual routines. *Cognition, 18*, 97–159.

van Dam, W. O., & Hommel, B. (2010). How object-specific are object files? Evidence for integration by location. *Journal of Experimental Psychology: Human Perception and Performance, 36*, 1184–1192.

VanRullen, R., Reddy, L., & Koch, C. (2004). Visual search and dual tasks reveal two distinct attentional resources. *Journal of Cognitive Neuroscience, 16*, 4–14.

Vecera, S. P., Flevaris, A. V., & Filapek, J. C. (2004). Exogenous spatial attention influences figure-ground assignment. *Psychological Science, 15*, 20–26.

Watson, D. G., & Humphreys, G. W. (1997). Visual marking: Prioritizing selection for new objects by top-down attentional inhibition of old objects. *Psychological Review, 104*, 90–122.

Wheeler, M. E., & Treisman, A. M. (2002). Binding in short-term visual memory. *Journal of Experimental Psychology: General, 131*, 48–64.

Wickens, C. D. (1980). The structure of attentional resources. In R. Nickerson (Ed.), *Attention and performance VIII* (pp. 239–257). Hillsdale, NJ: Erlbaum.

Wolfe, J. M. (1994). Guided search 2.0: A revised model of visual search. *Psychonomic Bulletin and Review, 1*, 202–238.

Wolfe, J. M. (1998). What can 1 million trials tell us about visual search? *Psychological Science, 9*, 33–39.

Wolfe, J. M. (1999). Inattentional amnesia. In V. Coltheart (Ed.), *Fleeting memories: Cognition of brief visual stimuli* (pp. 71–94). Cambridge, MA: MIT Press.

Wolfe, J. M., Klempen, N., & Dahlen, K. (2000). Postattentive vision. *Journal of Experimental Psychology: Human Perception and Performance, 26*, 693–716.

Wright, R. D. (Ed.). (1998). *Visual attention.* Oxford, England: Oxford University Press.

Wright, R. D., & Richard, C. M. (1996). Inhibition-of-return at multiple locations in visual space. *Canadian Journal of Experimental Psychology, 50*, 324–327.

Wright, R. D., & Ward, L. M. (2008). *Orienting of attention.* Oxford, England: Oxford University Press.

Xu, Y., & Chun, M. M. (2006). Dissociable neural mechanisms supporting visual short-term memory for objects. *Nature, 440*, 91–95.

Yantis, S. (1992). Multielement visual tracking: Attention and perceptual organization. *Cognitive Psychology, 24*, 295–340.

Yantis, S., & Jones, E. (1991). Mechanisms of attentional selection: Temporally modulated priority tags. *Perception and Psychophysics, 50*, 166–178.

Yeshurun, Y., & Rashal, E. (2010). Precueing attention to the target location diminishes crowding and reduces the critical distance. *Journal of Vision, 10*, 16.1–12.

Further Reading

Coltheart, V. (Ed.). (1999). *Fleeting memories: Cognition of brief visual stimuli.* Cambridge, MA: MIT Press

Itti, L., Rees, G., & Tsotsos, J. (2005). *The neurobiology of attention.* Burlington, MA: Academic.

Jensen, M. S., Yao, R., Street, W. N., & Simons, D. J. (2011). Change blindness and inattentional blindness. *Wiley Interdisciplinary Reviews: Cognitive Science, 2*, 529–546.

Koch, C. (2004). *The quest for consciousness: A neurobiological approach.* Englewood, CO: Roberts & Co.

Mack, A., & Rock, I. (1998). *Inattentional blindness.* Cambridge, MA: MIT Press.

Parasuraman, R. (Ed.). (1998). *The attentive brain.* Cambridge, MA: MIT Press.

Pashler, H. E. (1999). *The psychology of attention.* Cambridge, MA: MIT Press.

Rensink, R. A. (2002). Change detection. *Annual Review of Psychology, 53*, 245–277.

Scholl, B. J. (2009). What have we learned about attention from multiple-object tracking (and vice versa)? In D. Dedrick & L. Trick (Eds.), *Computation, cognition, and Pylyshyn* (pp. 49–77). Cambridge, MA: MIT Press.

Wright, R. D. (Ed.). (1998). *Visual attention.* Oxford, England: Oxford University Press.

# Spatial Attention

Kyle R. Cave

**Abstract**

Location plays a fundamental role in visual attention. Experiments using spatial cuing, spatial probes, flanker interference, and other methods show that visual information is often selected by its location. This spatial attention can take the form of a gradient, with facilitation that weakens with distance from the center. Although attention is easily allocated to a cued location, it can also be driven effectively by features such as motion, color, and orientation, and this feature-driven selection is accomplished at least in part by selecting locations with those features. Attention is flexible and often seems to be allocated to objects, as demonstrated in experiments with overlapping objects. Attention to one part of an object can increase attention to other parts of the same object, even though the object organization is irrelevant to the task. More experiments, including neuroscience studies, are necessary to determine the relationships between location-based, feature-based, and object-based attention.

**Key Words:** location, selection, cuing, flanker, feature, object, split, gradient

"Spatial attention" refers to selection that is based on location. In most circumstances, a perceptual system cannot fully process all the incoming information, and therefore some aspect of processing is limited to just information from a specific location or region. One aspect of spatial selection is very obvious in vision: At any given moment, the two eyes are fixated at a particular location in space, allowing the visual information from that location to be processed by the retinal fovea, which provides higher spatial resolution than any other part of the retina. Multiple times each second, the eyes will move to a new location, so that over a relatively brief time the powerful processing resources of the retina will be applied to many different locations in the environment. Thus, eye movements are one example of a limited resource (spatial acuity) and a selection mechanism for choosing how to allocate this resource to different locations. Because eye movements are

easily observed, this selection is often described as "overt attention."

Eye movements, however, are just the beginning of the story of spatial attention in vision. There are other limits on visual processing, and other types of visual selection to compensate for them. Von Helmholtz (1924) demonstrated "covert" visual attention that selected a specific region of the visual field without moving the eyes (see Van der Heijden, 1992). In a dark room, he fixated his eyes at the center of a large piece of paper on the wall covered with many different letters. He then generated an electric spark that illuminated the room. The flash was too brief for an eye movement, but Helmholtz found that he could attend to and perceive a small set of letters from one area. Before the next flash, he could shift his covert attention to a different location, and once they were illuminated, he could perceive those letters, even though his eyes had not moved.

## Visual System Limitations

Helmholtz's experiment demonstrates a basic limitation in visual processing, along with a method for coping with the limitation. Helmholtz was unable to identify all the letters in the visual field within the short time interval of the light flash, but he could direct his visual processing resources to a particular location, in order to process the letters there. The limitation in visual capacity is not surprising given the basic structure of the visual system. The initial neural processing stages, from the retina to the lateral geniculate nucleus of the thalamus and on to the occipital regions such as V1 and V2, are organized as large spatial maps in which the neurons have relatively small receptive fields. In other words, each neuron represents information from a small region of space, and the huge collection of neurons working simultaneously together represent the entire visual field. These structures feed into the "What" pathway that identifies visual objects, and in the upper levels of this pathway, the receptive fields become larger and larger. At these levels, each neuron can represent complex shape properties, but because of its large receptive field, it can be driven by multiple objects at different locations. Because information from different objects converges together in the What pathway, there can be much confusion about which properties belong to which object. This confusion can lead to "binding errors" in which features from different objects are incorrectly combined together to form an illusory conjunction. Binding errors can be prevented by a selection mechanism that only allows information from a single location or object to activate these neurons at any given time. Because of the potential for binding errors, the recognition system is effectively a limited-capacity processing resource, and the selection mechanism decides how to allocate this resource.

The early stages of visual processing appear to involve relatively simple neural operations that are performed in parallel across the visual field, while the later stages require more complex operations that can only be applied to a limited part of the input. Because the retina and other early structures are organized as spatial maps, it is perhaps not surprising that location seems to serve as a basis for selection. A huge number of experiments conducted over many years support the idea that visual attention works spatially, by selecting the information from a specific location in the visual field.

## Spatial Cuing Experiments

One key piece of evidence that visual attention selects from a spatially organized representation comes from spatial cuing experiments, which have demonstrated that a response to a visual stimulus is faster and/or more accurate when its location is known in advance. In these experiments, the test or probe stimulus to be reported is often preceded by a cue stimulus that indicates a particular location where the probe is likely to appear (Eriksen & Hoffman, 1974; Posner, Nissen, & Ogden, 1978; Posner, Snyder, & Davidson, 1980). After the cue, the eyes remain fixed in these experiments, which is confirmed in some cases either by tracking eye position or by limiting the display time between cue and probe stimulus. Thus, the facilitation at the cued location is due to covert attention and not to the higher spatial resolution at the fovea.

The cuing can be done in a couple of different ways, and the different results suggest two different attentional control mechanisms. The more straightforward approach is to position the cue at or very near the location where the upcoming probe can be expected. Attention is simply allocated to the location with the cue and is there waiting when the probe stimulus appears. This method is called exogenous or peripheral cuing, because the cue is usually located somewhere away from the center of gaze. The alternative is for the cue to be a symbol that appears at the fixated location. This method is known as endogenous or central cuing. Attention is generally allocated more slowly under endogenous cuing than under exogenous cuing, because of the extra step of interpreting the cue in order to determine the location to be attended. Exogenous cues also trigger an attention shift more automatically and are more difficult to ignore than endogenous cues. When a salient cue stimulus appears at a location, it is difficult not to attend to that location, even when it is known that the probe is no more likely to appear at the cued location than anywhere else.

A spatial cue can speed responses in a simple detection task in which no discrimination is necessary and in which few distracting stimuli are present. These strong attention effects from these simple tasks indicate that spatial attention may be playing some role other than the filtering out of interfering distractors, as suggested earlier. One alternative explanation is that spatial cues do not actually influence the effectiveness of visual processing, but only lower the threshold for responding, allowing faster responses but also more errors. However, Downing (1988) measured sensitivity using $d'$ (Macmillan & Creelman, 2005) in a collection of detection and discrimination tasks to show that foreknowledge of the stimulus location actually improved perceptual sensitivity, rather than simply lowering a response threshold.

## Spatial Probe Experiments

In the spatial cuing paradigm, a simple cue causes attention to be allocated to a particular location, and the effects of attention are measured on the perception of a probe stimulus. Probe stimuli can also be used to measure how spatial attention is allocated in the course of other visual tasks. Hoffman and Nelson (1981) combined two different tasks: searching for target letters in an array of rapidly changing letters, and monitoring for a small U-shaped stimulus (the probe) to appear. When subjects were correct in their response for the letter task, they were more likely to also correctly report the orientation of the U-shaped stimulus if it was near the target letter. On the other hand, when their letter response was incorrect, their report of the U-shaped orientation was more likely to be correct if it was not near the target letter. Attention allocated for the letter task also benefited the processing of the U-shaped stimulus when it was at a nearby location. Hoffman, Nelson, and Houck (1983) demonstrated that attention allocated in the detection of a flickering dot could enhance the identification of a nearby probe letter.

These two studies demonstrate the generality of spatial attention: When it is allocated for one task, it can benefit very different stimuli used in a very different task. They also address concerns that location only plays an important role in cuing tasks because the instructions emphasize location. In Hoffman et al.'s experiments, location was not part of the instructions, and yet the attention to the probe stimulus was still determined by its location relative to the stimulus from the other task. Finally, these experiments demonstrate how spatial probes can be used to measure attentional allocation during other visual tasks.

Kim and Cave (1995) combined a visual search task with two different types of spatial probes. In both sets of experiments, a small array of colored shapes was presented so briefly that there was not enough time to execute an eye movement before they disappeared. The search task was to find a red square among a set of red circles, green squares, and green circles. In one set of experiments, the search array was followed on some trials by a small dot at a location formerly occupied by one of the colored shapes. The response time to the dot indicated the degree to which that location had been attended. In the other set of experiments, the search array was followed by an array of small letters, with one letter at each of the locations formerly occupied by a shape. Subjects identified as many letters as possible, and the letters they reported indicated which locations had been attended. Thus, both methods served as a measure of spatial attention, because the probes differed from the search stimuli in color, shape, and most other properties, and shared only location. The fact that probe responses were affected by attention indicated that attention selected the location occupied by one of the search items, and ended up also selecting the probe that appeared at that location. A similar pattern emerged from both types of probe: Attention was strongest at the location of the red square target, and it was somewhat weaker at locations that had the target color (red) or the target shape (square) but not both. Attention was weakest at the locations of the green circles. Attention was apparently allocated to each location according to the target features present there.

Probe experiments like these are complicated by the fact that subjects must perform the primary and probe tasks together. The goal is to measure how spatial attention is allocated in the performance of a visual search or some other primary task. The measure of attention comes from the probe task. The executive control necessary for the probe task may interfere with the primary task, and the need to report the probe may alter the allocation of attention from what it would normally be for the primary task. Event-related potential (ERP) measures allow for the measurement of spatial attention without a probe response, allowing subjects to focus on performing just the primary task.

## Event-Related Potential Experiments

Many ERP attention experiments have used a procedure similar to the dot-probe experiments described earlier. While the subject is engaged in the primary task, a dot probe appears at some location in the display. The probe generates a wave of neural activity that can be measured with electroencephalographic (EEG) electrodes on the scalp. The changes in electrical potential over time can be plotted in a graph. When the changes are plotted relative to the time of the probe appearance, the resulting waveform is an ERP. The size of the changes in electrical potential over time is shaped by attention. When a probe appears at an attended location, the potential from electrodes at certain scalp locations will be more positive in some time windows and more negative in other time windows than they would without attention to the probed location (Luck, Woodman, & Vogel, 2000; Mangun & Hillyard, 1995). ERP thus provides another method for measuring how attention augments the signals from stimuli at selected locations in the visual field, without requiring that a probe task be combined with the primary task.

## Spotlight Metaphor

The results from these different experimental methods converge on the idea that visual information is selected according to its location. Posner, Snyder, and Davidson (1980) illustrated this idea by comparing visual attention to a spotlight. The attentional spotlight is directed at a single location, and anything that falls within its beam is selected, while everything in the dark regions outside is excluded. Thus, when the beam is directed to a specific location in the course of a visual search, a spatial probe that appears at the same location will be selected and facilitated. The spotlight metaphor has had an enormous effect on theorizing about visual attention, and it has suggested to many that because visual attention shares the spatial aspect with a spotlight, it must share other properties as well, such as its shape and manner of motion. Some of those assumptions have been substantiated, while others have not (Cave & Bichot, 1999).

## Attentional Gradient

In addition to demonstrating the spatial nature of visual selection, the spatial cuing, spatial probe, and ERP methods all provide ways for the pattern of attentional facilitation to be mapped across space. Some, but not all, attentional tasks produce a gradient pattern, in which attentional facilitation is strongest in the center and declines gradually with distance from the center. In other words, the spotlight of attention can often have a very fuzzy edge.

Some of the earliest evidence for an attentional gradient came from experiments by Eriksen and colleagues. Eriksen and Eriksen's (1974) subjects simply reported a target letter that appeared in the center of the display, accompanied by flanking distractor letters. Each target letter belonged to one of two categories, and subjects responded by pressing one of two buttons. Even though the location of the target was known in advance and it occurred in the fovea, the distracting flankers had a subtle but measurable effect on the responses. When the flankers were associated with the same response as the target, responses were faster, and when the flankers were associated with the other response, they were slower.

The results demonstrate a partial failure in spatial attention. The spatial nature of the selection in this task was demonstrated by moving the flankers more than 1 degree of visual angle away from the target, which eliminated the flanker interference. Attention that was allocated to the target location spilled out into the neighboring regions, where it allowed distractors to partially activate responses.

This spilling over of spatial attention was made more evident in cuing studies by Downing (1988; Downing & Pinker, 1985), which were similar to Posner's cuing experiments except that the target could appear at any of 10 or 12 locations, each marked by a box. When one location was cued as being the most likely location of an upcoming target stimulus, the attentional facilitation for that stimulus was strongest at the cued location, of course, but there was weaker but still measurable facilitation at nearby locations, falling off gradually with the distance between cued location and target location. The gradient findings suggest that spatial attention may not be all that precise; although attention is allocated for one stimulus at one location in the visual field, its effects sometimes spill over to neighboring regions.

This distance effect, in which response time rises with distance between cue and probe stimuli, has been interpreted in different ways. Once a location is cued, attention might be allocated in a gradient pattern, with strong facilitation in the center and weaker facilitation at the edges, and this pattern might stay in place as the probe stimulus appears and is processed. This account assumes that attention can speed processing along, but that a stimulus can still be identified and responded to even if it is at a location with little or no attentional facilitation. Under an alternative account, attention might be focused narrowly and precisely at the cued location, and then moved to the probe location once it appears. In this account, no stimulus can trigger a response until it is attended, making it necessary for attention to move to the location of a stimulus before response. This attentional movement would explain the distance effect in response times, but only if it takes more time to move attention longer distances.

However, there have been a number of arguments against the idea that movement time is proportional to distance (see Cave & Bichot, 1999, for a review). On top of that, LaBerge and Brown (1989) tested these two accounts against one another with a complex probe experiment. The primary stimulus was a target letter in the center of the display with distractors on both sides. It was quickly followed by a probe letter that appeared somewhere along the line of locations previously occupied by the target and distractors and was also accompanied by flanking distractors. Response time increased with the distance between the target and the probe, which could be explained with either a stationary attentional gradient allocated around the target location, or a small attentional spotlight sliding across from the target to the probe location. However, the distance effect was stronger when the probe was very similar to its flanking distractors. LaBerge and Brown argued that similarity should not affect the speed of a sliding spotlight, and so they concluded that there must be a stationary gradient of attention. There is an additional reason to favor the fixed gradient account over the moving spotlight account: Similar gradient patterns are found with ERP attention measurements (Mangun & Hillyard, 1988).

Surprisingly, not all experiments have produced a gradient pattern. Hughes and Zimba (1985, 1987) used a cuing paradigm similar to Downing and Pinker's but with a sparser stimulus array that had no boxes marking the possible stimulus location. They found uniformly fast responses whenever the cue and the target stimulus were both in the same hemifield, and slower responses when they were in different hemifields. The squares apparently have an important effect on attention in this task, because when Zimba and Hughes (1987) added squares to mark their potential target locations, they found a gradient pattern similar to Downing and Pinker's. Attention can thus take the form of a broad gradient in some circumstances, especially when there are items in the display that may produce a low level of interference. In emptier displays, attention seems to spread even further, constrained only by hemifield boundaries.

The cuing experiments by Downing (1988) mentioned earlier provide additional evidence that the size of the gradient can be adjusted to fit the circumstances. Using a signal detection approach (Macmillan & Creelman, 2005), she measured the falloff in sensitivity with distance from the cued location. Sensitivity fell off more quickly and thus produced a tighter, steeper gradient, when the stimulus items were closer together. Importantly, the shape of the gradient changed with the task, with luminance detection and brightness discrimination producing a broader gradient than orientation and form discrimination.

The flexibility in attentional allocation depending on the task suggests that spatial attention can be more narrowly focused when there is more potential for interference between different objects in a stimulus array. In Downing's experiments, this focusing occurred when there were more items present, when the items were closer together, or the discrimination was more demanding. For all these experiments, having a narrower focus of spatial attention facilitated task performance. In Kim and Cave's search task, in which each target was accompanied by multiple distractors sharing some features with it, there seemed to be little spread of attention from one object to the next, suggesting that spatial attention can be reasonably precise when it needs to be. Cave and Zimmerman (1997) found a similar pattern with a letter search task: All of the distractors were inhibited relative to the target location. Interestingly, although spatial attention was focused in a fairly narrow fashion in this task, it exerted a stronger effect when the distractor letters were more confusable with the target letter, demonstrating again that spatial attention varies according to the demands of the task.

Taken together, these results suggest that in tasks with higher distractor interference, the selected region can be smaller and the strength of the facilitation within this region can increase. Spatial attention is apparently serving to limit distractor interference, but it does not inhibit distractor processing any more than is necessary given the current task. This idea is generally consistent with the assumptions underlying perceptual load theory (Lavie, Hirst, de Fockert, & Viding, 2004), which postulates that more perceptually demanding tasks will require attention to be narrowly focused on a target object, while less demanding tasks will allow some attention to spill over onto distractor objects (but see Benoni & Tsal, 2010).

## Attentional Zoom

If spatial attention is as flexible as suggested here, then there needs to be an ability not only to direct attention to a specific location but also to adjust it to select a region of a certain size. Controlling the size of the selected region could also be advantageous in selecting stimuli of various sizes, or when the region within which a stimulus is expected to appear can vary in size over time. Eriksen and St. James (1986) compared attention to a zoom lens with the ability to select smaller or larger regions according to the situation.

LaBerge (1983) provided evidence for adjustments in attentional size using a probe paradigm similar to that from LaBerge and Brown described earlier. There were two conditions, which were tested in separate blocks. In the wide attention condition, the primary stimulus was a five-letter word, and in the narrow attention condition, it was a single letter with two distractor characters on either side. On some trials, the primary stimulus was replaced by a probe stimulus consisting of a single character at one of the five locations normally occupied by one of the characters in the primary stimulus. When the probe response times for the five different positions were compared against one another, they showed that attention was sharply focused in the narrow condition, producing fast response times for probes in the center location and slower response times for those at other locations. In the wide condition, however, attention was more evenly spread across the five conditions, producing more similar response times. Subjects were able to adjust their "attentional zoom" setting according to their expectations for the upcoming task.

The size adjustments demonstrated by LaBerge may or may not be related to a different type of size adjustment demonstrated by Larsen and Bundesen (1978) and by Cave and Kosslyn (1989). In these experiments, a single stimulus appeared by itself on each trial. Many of these stimuli were the same size as the preceding stimulus, so that subjects knew what size to expect. Some stimuli, however, appeared at a different size, and on these trials, the response time was proportional to the change in size from the previous stimulus to the current stimulus. Subjects appeared to prepare themselves to process a stimulus of a cued size, just as subjects in the standard spatial cuing experiments set themselves to process a stimulus at a cued location. In both the size and location experiments, the response time was proportional to the difference between the expected and actual stimulus properties. When these subjects prepare for a particular size, they may be selecting a region of that size, as suggested by LaBerge's (1983) experiment. On the other hand, the adjustment may not be linked to a particular location but may simply cause recognition mechanisms to expect a stimulus at a certain scale.

## Split Attention

In many circumstances, there are two or more important visual objects that are visible simultaneously. Given the ability to zoom attention in and out, it ought to be possible to select an area that is large enough to select all of the target objects. If there are distractor objects in between the target objects, however, then they would be selected as well, which would interfere with processing of the targets. A number of studies have tested whether two different locations can be selected simultaneously without selecting the regions in between. This has been a very difficult question to answer, because most of the experimental results that are predicted by split attention could also be produced by a single area of attention that moves quickly from one location to another, or that occupies one target location on some trials and another location on other trials.

There is only an advantage to splitting attention if there is also processing capacity to identify the two selected objects simultaneously. There is not a clear experimental demonstration of multiple objects being recognized simultaneously, but there is evidence for a generally high degree of visual processing capacity. Some experiments have demonstrated that the analysis of complex scenes is very fast, while others have demonstrated the effects of visual context on recognition of a target object, and still others have measured attention in the execution of tasks that require coordinating movements involving multiple objects (see Cave, Bush, & Taylor, 2010, for a review).

Doubts arose early on about the idea of split attention as a result of a cuing experiment by Posner, Snyder, and Davidson (1980). When they cued a secondary location along with a primary location, the secondary cue had no effect unless it was adjacent to the primary cue location. Posner et al. interpreted this pattern as evidence that the secondary location could only be selected by expanding the spotlight of attention, rather than by splitting it. However, a number of studies since then using methods other than simple spatial cuing have suggested that attention can be split, especially in circumstances in which the two targets will not interfere much with one another and share some feature such as color that sets them apart from distractors. Jans, Peters, and De Weerd (2010) have reviewed these studies in some detail, and they concluded that none of them definitively demonstrate split attention, although some argue that their criteria are overly stringent (Cave, Bush, & Taylor, 2010).

## Distractor Inhibition

Another way to select multiple target locations is to inhibit only the locations containing distractors, leaving the target locations and blank locations uninhibited. Because of the importance attached to the spotlight metaphor, most studies have been interpreted in terms of processing facilitation occurring at target locations, and this sort of attentional spotlight seems to be the most straightforward explanation for experiments such as Downing's (1988) showing a gradient of attention. However, in some circumstances the results could be explained by inhibition of distractor locations rather than facilitation of target locations, and Cepeda, Cave, Bichot, and Kim (1998) used spatial probes to show that in a search for a red digit among three green distractor digits, inhibition was focused specifically on the green locations. Thus, the attentional system apparently has the option of targeting inhibition specifically on distractor locations when that approach is beneficial.

The inhibition seen in this experiment may be related to negative priming, in which a stimulus that has been a distractor on one trial produces a weaker response on a later trial (Neill, 1977; Reisberg, Baron, & Kemler, 1980; Tipper, 2001). Negative priming can be associated with specific objects or stimuli, but it can also be very general in that it applies to objects independently of their location. Its underlying mechanisms are a topic of debate, making it difficult to know whether those mechanisms are responsible for the spatial inhibition that is driven by color in Cepeda et al.'s study.

Inhibition of distractor locations has been demonstrated a number of times for distractors that are positioned very close to a target object (e.g., Hopf et al., 2006; Mounts, 2000). This pattern is interesting not only because it demonstrates that attentional selection can work partly through inhibition but also because it suggests that distractors near a target interfere more with the target's processing than distractors farther away. This interference probably arises because the nearby distractors will fall within the receptive fields of many of the visual neurons that will be responding to the target. Inhibiting those distractors will therefore allow those neurons to represent the properties of the target more accurately, rather than the properties of the distractors. The pattern of facilitation at the target location surrounded by a ring of inhibition to block nearby distractors is very similar to the center-surround patterns that trigger neural responses most effectively at many levels within the visual system, starting with the retinal ganglion cells.

## Multiple Object Tracking

One task that seems to require split attention is the Multiple Object Tracking (MOT) task. At the beginning of a trial, a set of identical shapes are shown at random locations across the display. A subset of these shapes is then temporarily marked to indicate that they are targets, while the remaining shapes are distractors to be ignored. The marks disappear, and all the objects move across the display, each moving independently of the others. The targets must be tracked throughout this motion, and at the end of the trial, a test determines whether subjects can distinguish between targets and distractors. Typically four objects can be tracked with relatively few errors.

Are there four different spotlights of attention, each tracking a different target as it moves around the display? An experiment by Pylyshyn, Haladjian, King, and Reilly (2008) suggests a different explanation. They combined the MOT task with spatial attention probes similar to those used by Cepeda et al. and found evidence for inhibition that was targeted just at the locations with distractors. Interestingly, when the distractors were not moving or were in a different depth plane from the targets, they were not inhibited. Apparently those distractors were easily excluded by other means, and the distractor inhibition was only used for those distractors that were more easily confused with the targets. Pylyshyn et al. thus provide another piece of evidence that simultaneous attention to multiple objects can be accomplished by distractor inhibition.

## Visual Search

As is clear from the descriptions earlier, visual attention research benefits from being able to draw on a variety of different types of experiments. One of the most heavily used methods is visual search, in which a target object appears at an unknown location surrounded by many distractor objects. In many experiments, the task is simply to report whether a target is present in the array, although in some experiments, a target defined by one property (e.g., color) will be present on every trial, and once it is found, another of its properties (such as its shape) must be reported.

There are two aspects to attentional control in most visual search tasks. Usually, the eyes are allowed to move from location to location during the search. This overt attention is by definition spatial, since the goal is to choose the best location for the next fixation. Eyetracking measurements can reveal which locations in the search array are chosen, and thus indirectly indicate which visual properties are guiding overt attention. For instance, color is especially effective at guiding eye movements, and properties such as orientation and shape can also be used effectively (Williams & Reingold, 2001). The effectiveness of a particular feature in guiding overt attention will depend on the discriminability of the target feature relative to the corresponding distractor features. It is much easier to direct the eyes to a red target among green distractors than a red target among orange distractors.

The other aspect of attentional control in search is harder to measure. Given the evidence described earlier for covert attention shifts, it seems likely that covert attention will shift from one item to another during a single fixation. A number of theories, including Feature Integration Theory (Treisman & Gelade, 1980) have assumed that this covert attention is also selecting by location, although the spatial basis of covert attention is harder to demonstrate than it is for overt attention. The data produced by most visual search experiments are response times and error rates for finding the target, and although these data are useful for gauging the attentional limits on visual processing, they do not indicate whether selection is based on location or something else. One relevant piece of evidence for spatial section in search comes from Kim and Cave's (1995) spatial probe experiments with a search task in which eye movements are prohibited. Even though the targets are defined by a combination of shape and color, the responses to the spatial probes indicate that the covert selection is ultimately based on location.

If the assumption is correct that covert attention in visual search is selecting by location, there are other questions that arise about how much is selected at any given moment. Many theories (e.g., Treisman & Gelade, 1980) suggest that in difficult searches, one item is selected at a time, with attention moving serially from item to item until the target is found. This claim is supported by the fact that response times in many difficult searches increase linearly with the number of items in the display. However, the linear increase in response times is also consistent with a system that selects a small group of items and processes them simultaneously, and then moves serially from one clump to the next (Pashler, 1987). Given the evidence discussed earlier that "attentional zoom" can be adjusted to select either a small or a large region at any one time, it seems likely that easier searches might be conducted with a rather wide attentional zoom setting, which selects a large clump of items and processes them together, so that a large display can be processed with just a few attentional shifts. More difficult searches might require a more focused attentional zoom setting, so that fewer items are processed in each step, and more attentional shifts are necessary (see Nakayama & Joseph, 1998).

The flexibility in attentional control makes it difficult to know exactly how spatial attention is used in visual search, and the uncertainty gets worse as we consider this question further. Townsend (1990) has suggested that the fact that response times increase with the number of items in a search display does not necessarily indicate that the search is serial, with attention shifting from location to location. Instead, this pattern might reflect a process that is completely parallel but limited in capacity, so that a fixed amount of processing resources is distributed across all the objects in the search array. All of the items are processed simultaneously, but the processing speed for all the items is slower for large displays than for small displays, because a smaller proportion of the resources is applied to each item. Thus, there are a number of theoretical options for explaining visual search and the role of covert spatial selection in it, all making similar predictions. We know that visual attention must be flexible enough to deal with many different processing challenges, and that flexibility makes it very difficult to pin down.

## Selecting From Three-Dimensional Surfaces

By definition, spatial attention is selecting locations, but that definition does not specify what type of location-based representation the information is selected from. One straightforward assumption is that selection occurs within a two-dimensional representation early in the visual system, in which basic features such as color and orientation have been identified, but which has not been processed much beyond that. However, some experiments suggest that visual attention can be guided by information about depth. Nakayama and Silverman (1986) showed that search can be limited to one depth plane, ignoring distractors in other depth planes, just as it can be limited to one side of the display, ignoring distractors on the other side. This result suggests that search occurs within a three-dimensional (3D) rather than a two-dimensional representation. He and Nakayama (1992) extended this result. Their subjects searched for a patch of a specific color among other color patches, all organized into three different depth planes. When the three depth planes were all oriented vertically with respect to the viewer, and the color patches were also vertical so that they lay flat within the planes, search was easy. There was only one patch with the target color within the target depth plane, and subjects were able to limit search to that depth plane and easily find the uniquely colored target. However, when the color patches were all tilted so that they "stuck out" from their depth planes, search could no longer be limited to a single plane, and responses were much slower. The surprising result came when the depth planes were all tilted so that they were no longer vertical. With tilted depth planes, search was still efficient as long as the color patches were aligned with their depth planes, even though that meant that the color patches were now tilted with respect to the viewer. If the color patches were vertical and not aligned with the depth planes, search was difficult. Thus, visual search seems to be operating within a representation of a 3D surface.

Additional evidence for the use of depth information in search comes from Enns and Rensink (1990), who constructed a target pattern of three different four-sided polygons, each with a different level of shading. When this pattern was presented among distractors that were a different arrangement of the three component shapes, search was very difficult. However, when the three components of the target and distractor shapes were rearranged so that they looked like shaded 3D cubes, search became very easy. Once again, the results suggest that a 3D representation is constructed before search begins.

Marr (1982) theorized that visual processing could be broken down into three stages, and that the intermediate stage was devoted to reconstructing the third dimension. He described the representation produced by this stage as a "2½-D sketch." The "sketch" indicated that it was still a spatially oriented depiction of the scene represented from a specific viewpoint. The "2½-D" indicated that it was midway between the 2D representation from early vision and a full 3D model. The experiments in 3D search suggest that visual search may be conducted within a representation like a 2½-D sketch, which is organized spatially but includes information about the depth at each point.

## Attention Based on Locations or on Features?

The Kim and Cave (1995) study mentioned earlier indicates that when searching for a target defined by shape and color, attention is ultimately allocated to the locations containing the target features. There is plenty of additional evidence that when the task is to select a specific feature such as color, the feature selection is accomplished indirectly by selecting a location (Lamy & Tsal, 2000; Shih & Sperling, 1996; Tsal & Lavie, 1993). Harms and Bundesen (1983) found that when attention is focused on a target object, it spreads to a nearby distractor with the same color, providing another example of

selection driven by color, but Kim and Cave (2001) used spatial probes to show that it is ultimately location based. All of these studies are consistent with an attentional mechanism that facilitates processing at any location that has a specified target feature. As long as the facilitation applies to all stimuli at the selected location, including items that do not have the target feature, then this would be considered to be indirect feature selection that is mediated by location selection.

Even though location selection contributes to feature selection in many circumstances, there still might be a separate mechanism for pure feature-based selection. In other words, within the visual system there might be a representation organized by color (or some other feature) that is separate from the representations organized by location, and that color-indexed representation might be used to select information directly according to color, without selecting other items at the same locations. Finding experimental evidence for this direct feature selection, however, has been difficult. For instance, Vierck and Miller (2006) tried to make location irrelevant to a search task by presenting a series of letters one after the other in the center of the screen. This rapid serial visual presentation (RSVP) procedure effectively turns a spatial search into a temporal search, requiring subjects to monitor the stimulus stream over time until the target appears. Their letters appeared in different colors, and when subjects knew the target color in advance, their detection performance improved. This may be an example of direct color selection, but if we consider a location selection mechanism like the one suggested earlier in which the amount of facilitation at each location is controlled by the color at that location, then these results could also be explained by location selection. When a nontarget color appears in the target location, it is less facilitated than when the target color appears.

Although there are questions about the behavioral evidence for direct feature selection, neuroscience studies have provided more convincing evidence. Brain imaging has shown that while subjects are attending to a stimulus with a particular target feature (color or direction of motion) at one location, another stimulus at an unattended location can produce an enhanced neural response if it shares the target feature (Saenz, Buracas & Boynton, 2002; Treue & Martinez-Trujillo, 1999), and Zhang and Luck (2009) have used ERPs to demonstrate that under the right conditions, color selection can shape perceptual processing at a very early stage.

Thus, at some stages of visual processing, there does appear to be selection directly by features, although it seems to be used less often and have fewer measurable effects than selection by location.

## Attention to Objects

The evidence reviewed so far paints a picture of a spatial attention mechanism that selects locations and that can be guided by the presence of features such as color and orientation, augmented by a mechanism or mechanisms for selecting directly by those features without calling on spatial selection. There is another extensive body of evidence that reveals a different aspect of visual attention. In some tasks, spatial selection cannot easily separate a target from distractors, yet performance is sometimes very good, as was demonstrated early on by Neisser and Becklen (1975). They superimposed two different video clips. Their subjects could attend effectively to one clip while ignoring the other, even though both occupied the same general region in the display. In fact, as demonstrated more recently by Simons and Chabris (1999), the inhibition of the unattended information is so effective that very salient and surprising stimuli can be missed. Duncan (1984) kicked off the more controlled exploration of attention to a small target object with a superimposed distractor by asking subjects to report two properties from two simple geometric shapes. Performance was better when both properties were from the same shape, leading Duncan to conclude that attention could be allocated to one shape or the other, even though they occupied approximately the same location. When the two properties were from two different shapes, attention apparently had to shift from one object to the other, resulting in lower accuracy. Duncan's results could be explained by a very precise selection of location that could select only the contours of the target object while avoiding those of the distractor, but if spatial attention is as imprecise as suggested by Eriksen and Eriksen's (1974) flanker task and by Downing's (1988) demonstration of attentional gradients, then something else must underlie selection in Duncan's task. He suggested that in this task, attention was allocated to an object rather than a location.

Object-based attention has been studied with a variety of experimental procedures very different from Duncan's superimposed object paradigm (for reviews, see Chen, 2012; Scholl, 2001). The most popular was introduced by Egly, Driver, and Rafal (1994). The study was originally designed to explore attentional deficits in parietal patients, but their method has now been employed in many studies not involving brain damage. The method is an extension of the basic Posner cuing paradigm, in which two squares are presented, one on either side of fixation, and one of the squares is cued by making its contour brighter for a brief interval. A stimulus that appears in the cued square generates a faster response than a stimulus in the uncued square. This result was interpreted as evidence for location-based attention, but it could also be explained as the result of attention allocated to the cued object. To distinguish between these two possibilities, Egly, Driver, and Rafal extended the two boxes to make them long rectangles, both oriented in the same direction and one on each side of fixation. In their task, an entire rectangle was not cued; instead, the cue appeared only at the end of one of the rectangles. Thus, one of four locations could be cued (either end of either rectangle), and the probe stimulus could also appear at any of those four locations. As might be expected, responses to the probe were fastest when it appeared at the cued location. The key comparison in this experiment was between response times for probes at two other locations, both of which were equidistant from the cued location. One was on the same rectangle as the cue, but at the opposite end, and the other was at one end of the uncued rectangle. Responses to both of these locations were slower than responses to the cued location, but responses to the cued-object location were nonetheless faster than those to the uncued-object location. Because these two locations were equidistant from the cue, the difference could not be attributed to an attentional gradient. Instead, attention seemed to be stronger at all locations in the cued object than to locations in the uncued object. Attention seemed to spread to some extent to the entire object. The task in this experiment was to detect the probe regardless of which object it appeared in, and favoring locations in one object over locations in the other would not improve overall performance. Therefore, the result suggests that the attentional spread might occur automatically, regardless of the goals or the task. Avrahami (1999) demonstrated that these effects of stimulus organization did not require closed shapes.

Egly, Driver, and Rafal's object-based effect is very robust in the sense that it is easy to replicate, but it can be reduced or eliminated by manipulating a number of different factors. One important factor is attentional zoom. Goldsmith and Yeari (2003) demonstrated that the object boundaries only affect responses when attention is spread broadly across the display rather than narrowly focused. In Egly, Driver, and Rafal's original experiment, the cue was an exogenous cue, so subjects probably began each trial with attention distributed in order to detect the cue. The object effect disappeared in a study by Maquistan (1997) using endogenous cues, and Goldsmith and Yeari attributed this to the narrower attentional focus that Maquistan's subjects would have adopted to select the cue in the center of the display.

The role of attentional zoom is probably related to a finding by Shomstein and Yantis (2002) using measures of distractor interference within a cross-shaped configuration rather than the two parallel rectangles used by Egly, Driver, and Rafal. In their experiment, the object effect only arose when subjects did not know at the beginning of the trial where the target stimulus would appear. In experiments in which the target always appeared in the center of the display, the object effect disappeared. They concluded that the object effect required positional uncertainty, and they went on to claim that the effects were not the result of attention spreading to fill the boundaries of an object but instead the result of a process of prioritizing locations for a visual search. When the target location was not known in advance, a search was necessary to find it, and locations within the same object as the cue were given higher priority so that they would be more likely to be attended before locations outside the object.

Positional uncertainty does seem to be a relevant factor in the activation of object-based attention, perhaps because attention may be spread more broadly when the target location is unknown. However, it cannot be the only factor controlling object-based attention, because other studies have demonstrated object-based attention under positional certainty, including the Harms and Bundesen's (1983) study mentioned earlier, and another by Kramer and Jacobsen (1991). Chen and Cave (2006) used a stimulus in which the objects were in a cross configuration similar to that of Shomstein and Yantis. The object effect disappeared if the trials with the cross stimuli were mixed in with trials in which only one part of the complete configuration appeared. Because object-based attention can arise even with positional certainty, it does not seem to be simply a product of priority in visual search.

Lamy and Egeth (2002) proposed a different explanation of object-based attention. They concluded that object-based attention only arises after attention has shifted from one location to another. Their subjects compared two shapes that could appear either in the same rectangle or in different rectangles. The object effect only arose when one shape appeared after the other, allowing time for attention to select the first object and then shift to the second. Drummond and Shomstein (2010) argued that it was the positional uncertainty about the target locations in Lamy and Egeth's task rather than the attentional shift that triggered object-based attention.

Another factor that affects the object effect is the amount of time necessary to observe the stimulus. In a number of experiments (e.g., Avrahami, 1999; Chen & Cave, 2008; Law & Abrams, 2002; Shomstein & Behrmann, 2008), object effects become weaker or disappear if the stimulus is only available for a short time. These results suggest that organizing the scene into objects is not an obligatory step in the allocation of attention. Attention can be allocated spatially without the object representations playing a role. If more time is available, the object organization of the scene can be analyzed and used to shape attention.

A final factor that can affect object-based attention is the interpretation that the viewer imposes on the scene, as can be seen with stimuli that can be interpreted as either one object or multiple objects. Chen (1998) replaced Egly, Driver, and Rafal's two rectangles with a configuration made up of two V-shaped polygons joined at their points to form an X. When the configuration was described to subjects as two V's, the object effect was present, but when it was described as a single X, they disappeared. As mentioned earlier, Chen and Cave (2006) used a cross-shaped configuration. In this study, one group of subjects were encouraged to interpret the configuration as separate shapes by exposing them to trials in which only part of the configuration was present. On the trials with the complete configuration, those subjects showed an object effect, even though another group of subjects showed no object effect with the same stimuli. Perhaps the object effect can be avoided by treating the entire configuration as a single object.

Object-based attention does not arise in all tasks, but it does arise in many tasks in which the object organization is irrelevant. Its presence is affected by several factors, but there does not appear to be a single factor that triggers it in all circumstances. Attention is not automatically shaped by object boundaries in every task, and object-based attention can appear even when a search is not necessary. Although there has been much disagreement about what underlies object-based attention, and even disagreement about the terminology to use, there does seem to be a general understanding now emerging that object-based attention is a very flexible mechanism that will be activated under some conditions and not others (see Drummond & Shomstein, 2010). More research is necessary to determine exactly what those conditions are, and why object-based attention is activated in some cases when it does not seem to contribute to the task.

In the end, the problem of explaining the control of object-based attention is turning out to be similar to the problem of explaining exactly how attention is allocated during visual searches. As with search, there is more flexibility in the control of object-based attention than was first appreciated, and that flexibility makes it difficult to arrive at a single unambiguous account of its operation.

## The Relationship Between Spatial Attention and Object-Based Attention

If object-based attention is invoked in some circumstances, while location-based attention is left to work by itself in others, then what is the relationship between the two? They could be separate systems, operating at different levels of processing. As described earlier, the ventral or "What" visual pathway can be seen as a progression from spatially organized representations to representations organized by complex shape properties and ultimately to object representations. There could be selection mechanisms working throughout this hierarchy, with selection being more location based at the lower levels and more object based at the higher levels. At the highest level, object-based selection would be working among object representations that are coded independently of location, selecting some objects and/or inhibiting others.

Alternatively, there might be a single, more unified system. This system is ultimately spatial, selecting by location, but in many cases when there is enough time for building object representations, those representations can affect which locations are selected. Vecera and Farah (1994) referred to this location-mediated object selection as the "grouped array hypothesis." In this account, selection is more of an interaction between spatial representations and object representations, and it probably requires some communication back and forth between different processing systems. This need for interaction between upper and lower levels arises in aspects of visual processing other than just the control of attention, and it has led to recurrent theories of visual processing (Di Lollo, Enns, & Rensink, 2000; Hochstein & Ahissar, 2002). When a stimulus first

appears, there might be an initial wave of neural activity starting at the retina and working its way up through the LGN, V1, and the "What" pathway until high-level object representations are activated. Those object representations could then trigger another wave of activity back down the hierarchy to shape the allocation of attention at the lower, spatially organized levels.

## Spatial Attention in Nonvisual Modalities

Spatial location is a fundamental property in visual processing, but it is also an important factor in audition and touch. Although the majority of recent research in attention has been in the visual domain, audition was the modality of choice for much of the foundational attentional research of the 1960s, and the results showed that attention for auditory stimuli can clearly be allocated to a specific location. Selection by location is also possible for touch stimuli. Furthermore, in many circumstances there are links between these different modalities, so that attention to the location of a stimulus in one modality can affect the processing of stimuli in the other modalities (Reisberg, Scheiber, & Potemken, 1981; Spence & Driver, 2004). One important question for future research is how information about location is shared across the different modalities to control attention. The ability to select multimodal information from a single location is probably related to the ability to attend to an object, and the two issues should be considered together.

## Conclusion

Attention is necessary in vision to allocate higher level resources effectively and prevent interference between objects. An important aspect of visual attention is the selection of information from specific locations, and this spatial selection is apparently done within a three-dimensional mental representation. Spatial selection interacts with the presence of visual features, such as color and orientation, and also with boundaries and clusters that define objects and groups.

## Future Directions

1. Are there separate mechanisms to select locations, features, and objects, or is there a single location-based mechanism that is driven by the presence of features and by object boundaries?

2. When can spatial attention be split across multiple locations simultaneously? What are the costs and benefits of splitting attention?

3. When attention is set to select information at a specific size or scale, is it selecting a specific region of that size, or does this scale selection work independently of location?

4. In visual search, how large a region is selected at any given moment? How does the size of the selected region vary with the relationship between target and distractors?

## Acknowledgments

Thanks to Zhe Chen, Hayward Godwin, Michael J. Stroud, and Gemma Towers for comments and suggestions.

## References

Avrahami, J. (1999). Objects of attention, objects of perception. *Perception and Psychophysics, 61*, 1604–1612.

Benoni, H., & Tsal, Y. (2010). Where have we gone wrong? Perceptual load does not affect selective attention. *Vision Research, 50*, 1292–1298.

Cave, K. R., & Bichot, N. P. (1999). Visuo-spatial attention: Beyond a spotlight model. *Psychonomic Bulletin and Review, 6*, 204–223.

Cave, K. R., Bush, W. S., & Taylor, T. G. G. (2010). Split attention as part of a flexible attentional system for complex scenes: Comment on Jans, Peters, and De Weerd (2010). *Psychological Review, 117*, 685–696.

Cave, K. R., & Kosslyn, S. M. (1989). Varieties of size-specific visual selection. *Journal of Experimental Psychology: General, 118*, 148–164.

Cave, K. R., & Zimmerman, J. M. (1997). Flexibility in spatial attention before and after practice. *Psychological Science, 8*, 399–403.

Cepeda, N. J., Cave, K. R., Bichot, N. P., & Kim, M-S . (1998). Spatial selection via feature-driven inhibition of distractor locations. *Perception and Psychophysics, 60*, 727–746.

Chen, Z. (1998). Switching attention within and between objects: The role of subjective organization. *Canadian Journal of Experimental Psychology, 52*, 7–16.

Chen, Z. (2012). Object-based attention: A tutorial review. *Attention, Perception, and Psychophysics, 74*, 784–802.

Chen, Z., & Cave, K. R. (2006). Reinstating object-based attention under positional certainty: The importance of subjective parsing. *Perception and Psychophysics, 68*, 992–1003.

Chen, Z., & Cave, K. R. (2008). Object-based attention with endogenous cuing and positional certainty. *Perception and Psychophysics, 70*, 1435–1443.

Di Lollo, V., Enns, J., & Rensink, R. (2000). *Journal of Experimental Psychology: General, 129*, 481–507.

Downing, C. J. (1988). Expectancy and visual-spatial attention: Effects on perceptual quality. *Journal of Experimental Psychology: Human Perception and Performance, 14*, 188–202.

Downing, C. J., & Pinker, S. (1985). The spatial structure of visual attention. In M. I. Posner & O. S. M. Marin (Eds.), *Attention and performance XI: Mechanisms of attention.* Hillsdale, NJ: Erlbaum.

Drummond, L., & Shomstein, S. (2010). Object-based attention: Shifting or uncertainty? *Attention, Perception, and Psychophysics, 72, 1743–1755.*

Duncan, J. (1984). Selective attention and the organization of visual information. *Journal of Experimental Psychology: General, 113*, 501–517.

Egly, R., Driver, J., & Rafal, R. (1994). Shifting visual attention between objects and locations: Evidence from normal and parietal lesion subjects. *Journal of Experimental Psychology: General, 123*, 161–177.

Enns, J. T., & Rensink, R. A. (1990). Influence of scene-based properties on visual search. *Science, 247*, 721–723.

Eriksen, B. A., & Eriksen, C. W. (1974). Effects of noise letters upon the identification of a target letter in a nonsearch task. *Perception and Psychophysics, 16*, 143–149.

Eriksen, C. W., & Hoffman, J. E. (1974). Selective attention: Noise suppression or signal enhancement? *Bulletin of the Psychonomic Society, 4*, 587–589.

Eriksen, C. W., & St. James, J. D. (1986). Visual attention within and around the field of focal attention: A zoom lens model. *Perception and Psychophysics, 40*, 225–240.

Goldsmith, M., & Yeari, M. (2003). Modulation of object-based attention by spatial focus under endogenous and exogenous orienting. *Journal of Experimental Psychology: Human Perception and Performance, 29*, 897–918.

Harms, L., & Bundesen, C. (1983). Color segregation and selective attention in a nonsearch task. *Perception and Psychophysics, 33*, 11–19.

He, J. J., & Nakayama, K. (1992). Surfaces vs features in visual search. *Nature, 359*, 231–233.

Hochstein, S., & Ahissar, M. (2002). View from the top: Hierarchies and reverse hierarchies in the visual system. *Neuron, 36*, 791–804.

Hoffman, J. E., & Nelson, B. (1981). Spatial selectivity in visual search. *Perception and Psychophysics, 30*, 283–290.

Hoffman, J. E., Nelson, B., & Houck, M. R. (1983). The role of attentional resources in automatic detection. *Cognitive Psychology, 51*, 379–410.

Hopf, J. M., Boehler, C. N., Luck, S. J., Tsotsos, J. K., Heinze, H. J., & Schoenfeld, M. A. (2006). Direct neurophysiological evidence for spatial suppression surrounding the focus of attention in vision. *Proceedings of the National Acadamy of Sciences USA, 13*(4), 1053–1058.

Hughes, H. C., & Zimba, L. D. (1985). Spatial maps of directed visual attention. *Journal of Experimental Psychology: Human Perception and Performance, 11*, 409–430.

Hughes, H. C., & Zimba, L. D. (1987). Natural boundaries for the spatial spread of directed visual attention. *Neuropsychologia, 25*, 5–18.

Jans, B., Peters, J. C., & De Weerd, P. (2010). Visual spatial attention to multiple locations at once: The jury is still out. *Psychological Review, 117*, 637–684.

Kim, M-S., & Cave, K. R. (1995). Spatial attention in visual search for features and feature conjunctions. *Psychological Science, 6*, 376–380.

Kim, M-S., & Cave, K. R. (2001). Perceptual grouping via spatial selection in a focused-attention task. *Vision Research, 41*, 611–624.

Kramer, A. F., & Jacobson, A. (1991). Perceptual organization and focused attention: The role of objects and proximity in visual processing. *Perception and Psychophysics, 50*, 267–284.

LaBerge, D. (1983). Spatial extent of attention to letters and words. *Journal of Experimental Psychology: Human Perception and Performance, 9*, 371–379.

LaBerge, D., & Brown, V. (1989). Theory of attentional operations in shape identification. *Psychological Review, 96*, 101–124.

Lamy, D., & Egeth, H. (2002). Object-based selection: The role of attentional shifts. *Perception and Psychophysics, 64*(1), 52–66.

Lamy, D., & Tsal, Y. (2000). Object features, object locations, and object files: Which does selective attention activate and when? *Journal of Experimental Psychology: Human Perception and Performance, 26,* 1387–1400.

Larsen, A., & Bundesen, C. (1978). Size scaling in visual pattern recognition. *Journal of Experimental Psychology: Human Perception and Performance, 4,* 1–20.

Lavie, N., Hirst, A., de Fockert, J. W., & Viding, E. (2004). Load theory of selective attention and cognitive control. *Journal of Experimental Psychology: General, 133,* 339–354.

Law, M. B., & Abrams, R. A. (2002). Object-based selection within and beyond the focus of spatial attention. *Perception and Psychophysics, 64,* 1017–1027.

Luck, S. J., Woodman, G. F., & Vogel, E. K. (2000). Event-related potential studies of attention. *Trends in Cognitive Sciences, 4,* 432–440.

Macmillan, N. A., & Creelman, C. D. (2005). *Detection theory: A user's guide.* Mahwah, NJ: Erlbaum.

Mangun, G. R., & Hillyard, S.A. (1988). Spatial gradients of visual attention: Behavioral and electrophysiological evidence. *Electroencephalography and Clinical Neurophysiology, 70,* 417–428.

Mangun, G. R., & Hillyard, S.A. (1995). Mechanisms and models of selective attention. In M. D. Rugg & M. G. H. Coles (Eds.), *Electrophysiology of mind: Event-related brain potentials and cognition* (pp. 41–85). Oxford, England: Oxford University Press.

Maquistan, A. D. (1997). Object-based allocation of visual attention in response to exogenous, but not endogenous, spatial precues. *Psychonomic Bulletin and Review, 4,* 512–515.

Marr, D. (1982). *Vision.* San Francisco: W.H. Freeman.

Mounts, J. R. W. (2000). Evidence for suppressive mechanisms in attentional selection: Feature singletons produce inhibitory surrounds. *Perception and Psychophysics, 62,* 969–983.

Nakayama, K., & Joseph, J. S. (1998). Attention, pattern recognition and popout in visual search. In R. Parasuraman (Ed.), *The attentive brain* (pp. 279–298). Cambridge, MA: MIT Press.

Nakayama, K., & Silverman, G. H. (1986). Serial and parallel processing of visual feature conjunctions. *Nature, 320,* 264–265.

Neill, W. T. (1977). Inhibition and facilitation processes in selective attention. *Journal of Experimental Psychology: Human Perception and Performance, 3,* 444–450.

Neisser, U., & Becklen, R. (1975). Selective looking: Attending to visually specified events. *Cognitive Psychology, 7,* 480–494.

Pashler, H. (1987). Detecting conjunctions of color and form: Reassessing the serial search hypothesis. *Perception and Psychophysics, 41,* 191–201.

Posner, M. I., Nissen, M. J., & Ogden, W. C. (1978). Attended and unattended processing modes: The role of set for spatial location. In H. J. Pick & I. J. Saltzman (Eds.), *Modes of perception* (pp. 137—157). Hillsdale, NJ: Erlbaum.

Posner, M. I., Snyder, C. R. R., & Davidson, B. J. (1980). Attention and the detection of signals. *Journal of Experimental Psychology: General, 109,* 160–174.

Pylyshyn, Z. W., Haladjian, H. H., King, C. E., & Reilly, J. E. (2008). Selective nontarget inhibition in multiple object tracking. *Visual Cognition, 16,* 1011–1021.

Reisberg, D., Baron, J., & Kemler, D. G. (1980). Overcoming Stroop interference: The effects of practice and distractor potency. *Journal of Experimental Psychology: Human Perception and Performance, 6,* 140–150.

Reisberg, D., Scheiber, R., & Potemken, L. (1981). Eye position and the control of auditory attention. *Journal of Experimental Psychology: Human Perception and Performance, 7,* 318–323.

Saenz, M., Buracas, G. T., & Boynton, G. M. (2002). Global effects of feature-based attention in human visual cortex. *Nature Neuroscience, 5,* 631–632.

Scholl, B. (2001). Objects and attention: The state of the art. Cognition, 80, 1–46.

Shih, S-I., & Sperling, G. (1996). Is there feature-based attentional selection in visual search? *Journal of Experimental Psychology: Human Perception and Performance, 22,* 758–779.

Shomstein, S., & Behrmann, M. (2008). Object-based attention: Strength of object representation and attentional guidance. *Perception and Psychophysics, 70,* 132–144.

Shomstein, S., & Yantis, S. (2002). Object-based attention: Sensory modulation or priority setting? *Perception and Psychophysics, 64,* 41–51.

Simons, D. J., & Chabris, C. F. (1999). Gorillas in our midst: Sustained inattentional blindness for dynamic events. *Perception, 28,* 1059–1074.

Spence, C., & Driver, J. (Eds.). (2004). *Crossmodal space and crossmodal attention.* Oxford, England: Oxford University Press.

Tipper, S. P. (2001). Does negative priming reflect inhibitory mechanisms? A review and integration of conflicting views. *Quarterly Journal of Experimental Psychology, 54A,* 321–343.

Townsend, J. (1990). Serial versus parallel processing: Sometimes they look like Tweedledum and Tweedledee but they can (and should) be distinguished. *Psychological Science, 1,* 46–54.

Treisman, A., & Gelade, T. (1980). A feature integration theory of attention. *Cognitive Psychology, 12,* 97–136.

Treue, S., & Martinez-Trujillo, J. C. (1999). Feature-based attention influences motion processing gain in macaque visual cortex. *Nature, 399,* 575–579.

Tsal, Y., & Lavie, N. (1993). Location dominance in attending to color and shape. *Journal of Experimental Psychology: Human Perception and Performance, 19,* 131–139.

Van der Heijden, A.H.C. (1992). *Selective attention in vision.* London: Routledge.

Vecera, S., & Farah. M. (1994). Does visual attention select objects or locations? *Journal of Experimental Psychology: General, 123,* 146–160.

Vierck, E., & Miller, J. (2006). Effects of task factors on selection by color in the rapid serial visual presentation (RSVP) task. *Perception and Psychophysics, 68,* 1324–1337.

Von Helmholtz, H. (1924). *Treatise on physiological optics.* Rochester, NY: Optical Society of America.

Williams, D. E., & Reingold, E. M. (2001). Preattentive guidance of eye movements during triple conjunction search tasks: The effects of feature discriminability and saccadic amplitude. *Psychonomic Bulletin and Review, 8,* 476–488.

Zhang, W., & Luck, S. J. (2009). Feature-based attention modulates feed-forward visual processing. *Nature Neuroscience, 12,* 24–25.

Zimba, L. D., & Hughes, H. C. (1987). Distractor-target interactions during directed visual attention. *Spatial Vision, 2,* 117–149.

# Disorders of Attention

Robert H. Logie

**Abstract**

Attention covers a wide range of different concepts, variously referred to as spatial attention, divided attention, sustained attention, focused attention, visual attention, covert mental attention, inhibition of attention, and many others. There are likewise diverse disorders of attention resulting from different forms of brain damage. This chapter discusses forms of unilateral spatial neglect following unilateral brain damage as disorders of spatial attention and of visuospatial working memory, specific disorders of divided and sustained attention associated with Alzheimer's disease, and failures of inhibition and focused attention associated with focal brain damage in the prefrontal cortex. Behavioral and neuroanatomical evidence is considered along with accounts of the cognitive impairments observed and implications of this evidence for theories of healthy cognition.

**Key Words:** visuospatial working memory, unilateral spatial neglect, representational neglect, Alzheimer's disease, frontal lobe damage, brain damage

Attention conjures up a range of concepts in the lay public and in scientists alike. In everyday use, attention generally refers to the idea that humans have some kind of limited cognitive resource, and attention involves concentrating at least some of that resource on a specific task or a narrowly defined topic, or on a single source of information. However, this concept of attention can apply to quite complex tasks such as "paying attention while driving," or it can be rather narrow such as attending to the ticking of a clock or to a particularly attractive face to the exclusion of anything else around you. Attention can also apply to mental objects and events such as how to answer a difficult question in a job interview, the memory of a favorite landscape, or remembering to carry out each of a set of errands in the shopping mall.

Theories of attention in healthy adults are covered elsewhere in this volume (see Part 2). Disorders of cognition are generally better understood in the context of theories of cognition, and attention is no exception. Moreover, there are numerous instances in which testing theories of cognition when studying brain-damaged individuals has led to refinement of those theories. So studying the damaged brain can help us understand aspects of the healthy brain as well as understand the nature of the cognitive impairments associated with the damage. In this chapter, I will cover disorders of spatial attention, commonly associated with relatively focal right hemisphere lesions. I will also cover disorders of divided attention linked with degenerative brain diseases such as the dementias, and that are associated with more diffuse damage. Finally, there will be some discussion of disorders of sustained attention and of failures of inhibition that are often associated with damage to areas in the prefrontal cortex.

## Disorders of Spatial Attention
### *Unilateral Spatial Neglect*

Unilateral spatial neglect refers to an apparent lack of awareness of the side of space opposite to the brain hemisphere that is damaged. Moreover, patients seem to be unaware that they have this disorder, even when it is pointed out to them. It is not uncommon following a stroke or a brain injury. Two months post onset, 48% of right brain-damaged (left neglect) and 15% of left brain-damaged (right neglect) patients show neglect (Halligan, Marshall, & Wade, 1989; see also Vallar & Perani, 1986). Neglect of the left side is not only more frequent than right neglect (e.g., Kinsbourne, 1987), it is also more severe and tends to last longer (e.g., Stone et al., 1991). However, there is an ongoing debate as to its interpretation, largely because there are several different types of neglect but also because there are no clear links between the precise site of the lesion and the form of neglect that is observed. Indeed, neglect might arise from disruption of networks within each hemisphere of the brain, rather than from damage to any one particular site. In the discussion that follows I will describe the different forms of the disorder and the contrasting views as to their interpretation.

### PERCEPTUAL NEGLECT

The most widely studied forms of neglect involve a tendency to ignore one-half of extrapersonal space, most commonly on the left, following a lesion in the right parietal lobe (e.g., Paterson & Zangwill, 1944; for reviews, see Robertson & Halligan, 1999). These neglect types are linked with problems of perceiving the external world and so are referred to as perceptual neglect (Albert, 1973; Poppelreuter, 1917/1991). Thus, when asked to cross out items on a sheet in front of them, to copy a picture, or to indicate the center point of a line, patients with perceptual neglect will cross out items mainly on the right, reproduce only the right half of the picture, or will bisect a line well to the right of the true center (e.g., Schenkenberg, Bradford, & Ajax, 1980). When asked to describe their immediate environment, they will describe only the right half of the scene in front of them, and, in some cases, will eat from only the right half of their plate or fail to comb their hair or shave on their left side. For some patients, they show what is called "neglect dyslexia" in which they fail to read the left half of individual words (e.g., Miceli & Capasso, 2001). Others show the phenomenon of "allochiria" in which an item that actually appears on the left is reported by

the patients as having been presented on the right (e.g., Lepore, Conson, Ferrigno, Grossi, & Trojano, 2004). These deficits do not arise from failure of the visual sensory system such as poor vision or hearing loss, nor from a general intellectual impairment. The problem appears to arise from a failure of visual attention to areas of space.

There are multiple forms of perceptual neglect, for example, some patients show "personal" neglect, ignoring one side of their body, while others show "extrapersonal" neglect showing that they are not aware of the left side of space (e.g., Beschin & Robertson, 1997). Even within extrapersonal neglect, there are cases of neglect of the immediate environment (near space) but not of more distant aspects of the current scene (far space) (e.g., Calvanio, Petrone, & Levine, 1987; Halligan & Marshall, 1991). These diverse patterns among patients considered under the general umbrella of unilateral spatial neglect led Halligan and Marshall (1992) to question whether this classification of the disorder was "a meaningless entity." As we will see, this challenge contains an important kernel of truth, because there is diversity among the types of neglect, as well as a diversity of accounts for each type. Whether this renders the broader classification "meaningless," however, remains moot.

Although there are several different forms of neglect, one common interpretation is that they reflect an inability to attend to the neglected side of space or an inability to move attention away from the right (e.g., De Renzi, Gentilini, Faglioni, & Barbieri, 1989; Posner, Walker, Friedrich, & Rafal, 1984). In terms of underlying brain organization, Kinsbourne (1987) has suggested the hypothesis that the preponderance of left neglect following a right hemisphere lesion arises because the right hemisphere represents both the left and right sides of space, but the left hemisphere represents only the right side of space. Therefore, when the left hemisphere is damaged, the intact right hemisphere can continue to represent both right and left hemispace. When the right hemisphere is damaged, the left hemisphere can only deal with the right side of space, leaving the left side of space without representation in the brain. However, this hypothesis does not deal adequately with the observation that some patients do show right neglect following left hemisphere damage and an intact right hemisphere. A more recent view from Bartolomeo, Thiebaut de Schotten, and Doricchi (2007) has argued that left neglect is not so much linked with damage to specific brain areas within the right hemisphere, but more that damage in those areas disrupts a network of brain white matter that is used for communication between the prefrontal cortex and the parietal areas in the right hemisphere. It is often the latter that are damaged in neglect.

Some theoretical developments have focused on findings that aspects of neglect can be overcome on a temporary basis by providing external cues. So, for example, a number of studies have shown that line bisection in neglect patients tends to be much more accurate for very long lines than it is for short lines (e.g., Bisiach, Pizzamiglio, Nico, & Antonucci, 1994). Rossetti et al. (1998) showed that when neglect patients were asked to wear rightward displacing prismatic goggles, then they showed a dramatic reduction in a range of neglect symptoms. Although the benefit is clear, the explanation is much less so. One view is that perceptual neglect is a disorder of spatial attention, but it is uncertain whether this is an overemphasis on attention to the nonneglected side or an inability to direct attention to the neglected side. In either case, prism adaptation has been thought to help the patient initiate control of spatial attention to the neglected side (for a discussion see Nijboera, McIntosh, Nysc, Dijkermana, & Milner, 2008). An alternative account is that the prisms help the patient to orient more effectively toward external cues in the environment. For example, a series of studies by Robertson and colleagues (e.g., Robertson, Mattingley, Rorden, & Driver, 1998) has shown that presenting an "alerting" signal such as a tone can result in neglect patients noticing events on the neglected side that follow the tone. They have argued that the alerting stimulus activates remaining healthy cells in the damaged right hemisphere that support spatial attention, and that these cells do not operate effectively without the external cue.

As a contrast to these findings that an external cue might alleviate symptoms of neglect, in "extinction," the presence of a second stimulus is the source of the problem. In these cases, the patient can readily detect a single stimulus in his or her right or left visual field. However, if two stimuli are presented, one in each hemifield, then one of the stimuli appears to be ignored or is "extinguished" by the presence of the second stimulus (e.g., Humphreys, Riddoch, Nys, & Heinke, 2002; Valler, Rusconi, Bignamini, Geminiani, & Perani, 1994). Extinction can appear with other senses, such as hearing, touch and smell (e.g., Bender, 1952) and analogous methods are used to diagnose extinction in those other modalities. It is related to neglect in that the disorder appears to be

a failure to attend to a stimulus in a particular area of space. However, extinction tends to appear only with brief presentations of the two stimuli, such as the clinician holding up a finger in the left or right visual field or in both fields of the patient. Unlike neglect, extinction shows no preferential association with the right hemisphere, and it may follow damage to either side of the brain, affecting the side of space opposite to the damage. Its causes are not entirely clear, but like neglect, extinction appears to reflect the outcome of a spatially biased competition for attention.

Another line of study has explored whether some of the problems in neglect arise from an inability to keep track of scanning of visual scenes. Specifically, patients cannot remember which areas of a scene they have scanned and which they have not. Recordings of eye movements have shown that neglect patients tend to refixate the same items in an array that they have fixated before. When they are given an array of objects on a computer screen and asked to cancel as many items as they can within the array, they tend to cancel the same items on the right side repeatedly (Husain, Mannan, Hodgson, Wojciulik, & Driver, 2001). This has been interpreted as a failure of visuospatial working memory to retain and update a representation of what has and what has not been searched in an array. Husain et al. (2001) suggest further that impaired spatial working memory is the basis for pathological visual search observed in several patients with neglect, and they propose a possible link between visual spatial attention and visuospatial working memory (Logie, 1995). Some supportive evidence for this comes from studies of healthy adults showing that when people are asked to follow a moving target on screen, this disrupts their ability to remember spatial arrays (Pearson & Sahraie, 2003; Postle, Idzikowski, Della Sala, Logie, & Baddeley, 2006). This is then consistent with there being a link between visual attention and spatial working memory in the healthy brain, and with the idea that this link is damaged in at least some forms of neglect. However, it is not clear whether the Husain et al. (2001) finding is linked primarily with perceptual neglect, or if their patients had both perceptual and representational neglect (see later discussion), with the latter being at the core of the problem with visuospatial working memory.

## REPRESENTATIONAL NEGLECT

The debate continues with regard to explanations for perceptual neglect, but the issue is not made any simpler by observations of what has been referred to as representational neglect. The best known report is of two neglect patients living in Milan, Italy. Bisiach and Luzzatti (1978) asked these patients to try to imagine that they were standing in the main cathedral square in Milan (Piazza del Duomo), an area that they knew well. When asked to imagine that they were at one end of the square, facing the cathedral, they mentioned a range of buildings that are on the right side of the square, but they mentioned very few buildings from their imagined left. However, this was not because they had forgotten these details. They were next asked to try to imagine themselves at the other end of the square, with their back to the cathedral. This time, they reported buildings now on their imagined right that they had previously failed to mention, and they failed to report buildings now on their imagined left that they had mentioned before. So the problem was with the left side of their mental image or spatial mental representation of the square, regardless of their imagined viewpoint. The patients showed the same lateralized impairments of mental images when asked to describe a room in their home, so the effect seems to generalize to any familiar setting.

In the Bisiach and Luzzatti (1978) cases, the patients showed evidence of perceptual neglect for the left side of physical space as well as neglect of the left side of imagined space. However, there are multiple reports of patients who show only perceptual forms of neglect but have no difficulty describing familiar scenes from memory (e.g., Coslett, 1997). There are also reports of patients who show

a pure form of representational neglect (Beschin, Cocchini, Della Sala, & Logie, 1997; Guariglia, Padovani, Pantano, & Pizzamiglio, 1993). These patients show no symptoms of perceptual neglect in that they readily notice objects that are in view regardless of whether they are on the left or on the right, and they show no impairments in item cancellation tasks or line bisection. However, when asked to describe a familiar scene from memory, they fail to report details from the left side of their imagined perspective. Figure 9.1 shows an attempt by patient NL (Beschin et al., 1997) to draw a familiar country scene from memory. What is clear is that he drew considerable detail on the right of the picture and drew almost no details on the left. When questioned about this, he could see in the drawing that there were few details on the left, but he responded that there were very few details in that part of the real scene. His friends and family confirmed that there were indeed as many details on the left as on the right of this area of countryside, which he had visited many times. So he could see the lack of detail in his own drawing, showing no perceptual neglect, but he could not generate the required details from his memory for the scene. Cases like this point to the suggestion that perceptual neglect and representational neglect do not reflect variations of the same disorder, and the fact that both kinds of patient have been observed suggests it is not simply that, for example, more severely affected patients have both forms but less severely affected patients only have the most common, perceptual form.

**Figure 9.1** Example drawing of a familiar country scene by patient NL (Beschin et al., 1997), who suffered from pure representational neglect.

Pure representational neglect patients are much less commonly described. This could be in part because tests for representational neglect are rarely used in clinical assessment of stroke patients. However, such patients do appear to be less common even when neuropsychologists are specifically looking for them. In a group study of 17 right hemisphere–damaged patients, Denis, Beschin, Logie, and Della Sala (2002) found one patient with pure representational neglect, eight patients with both representational and perceptual neglect, and two patients with only perceptual neglect. Six of the patients had no neglect, showing that neglect is not inevitable following right hemisphere damage.

Moreover, there was no relationship between the precise site or the extent of brain damage and the type of neglect, consistent with the idea that different forms of neglect might arise from disruption to communication between brain areas rather than damage to any one specific area.

The Denis et al. (2002) study demonstrated another phenomenon that seriously undermined any suggestion that representational neglect somehow arises from some aspect of neglect in perception or visual attention. Denis and colleagues tested their patients on novel arrays of objects. Four objects were presented in a simple square layout as illustrated in Figure 9.2A. In the perception condition,

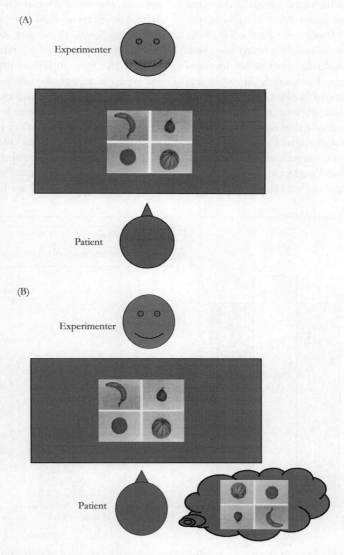

**Figure 9.2** Cartoon illustration of the layout for testing perceptual and representational neglect with patients reporting the layout as viewed (*A*) or from the perspective of the experimenter (*B*).

participants simply had to report what they saw while the objects were still in view, naming each object and its location in the array. In a memory condition, the array was removed after viewing and the participant was asked to recall from memory each of the objects and their location. In a third condition, the array was not shown to the participant, but instead they heard the layout of objects described by the experimenter. They then had to recall from memory each object and its location. Results showed that in the perception condition, the patients with both perceptual and representational neglect tended to report either zero or only one item from the left of this very simple array, but they could report both objects on the right. In the memory condition, the pattern of results was the same, except that overall performance was a bit lower. Most intriguing, the patients also reported fewer items on the left of the array that they did not see but only heard described. The patients had completely intact verbal immediate memory, so it seemed as though they were trying to remember the verbally described arrays using a damaged visuospatial working memory system, despite the fact that they could have remembered the items quite successfully by using their intact verbal memory. This points very clearly to the suggestion that representational neglect arises for different reasons than perceptual neglect. Moreover, because

representational and perceptual neglect are separate impairments (Coslett, 1997), this suggests that the visual attention system that supports perception of the world in the healthy brain is not the same as the system that supports our visual mental representations (Logie, 2003, 2011; Logie & van der Meulen, 2009). If they were the same, then damage to one should automatically result in damage to the other, and clearly this is not the case.

Can representational neglect be interpreted as an impairment in some form of covert or mental attention to parts of our mental representation? Logie, Beschin, Della Sala. and Denis (2005; Della Sala, Logie, Beschin, & Denis, 2004) addressed this question with two representational neglect patients who were given the same range of experimental conditions used by Denis et al. (2002). But in addition, there were conditions in which each patient was asked to report the location of each of the four objects as they would appear to the experimenter on the other side of the table (see Fig. 9.2B). Results from this experiment are shown in Figure 9.3. First, note that the neglect is clear in both patients when asked to recall the objects in their original locations (plain bars). However, when they were asked to imagine from the opposite perspective (i.e., mentally rotate their visual representation—shaded bars in Figure 9.3), there

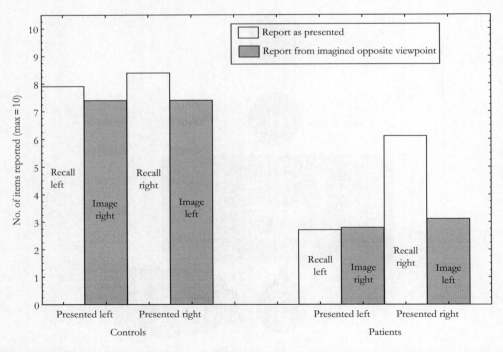

**Figure 9.3** Results from Della Sala et al. (2004) for a group of controls and two representational neglect patients reporting the layout of four objects as viewed or after rotation through 180 degrees.

is no further loss of items presented on the left but now recalled from the imagined right. However, for items presented on the right and recalled from the imagined left (the neglect side), performance drops to the level it would have been if the items had been presented on the left in the first place. Logie et al. (2005) interpreted these results to suggest that the patients could pay "mental attention" to material on both sides of the representation, and they could also control mental attention in order to carry out the mental rotation required. However, they performed poorly on the basis of whether the item that they were recalling was on the left of their mental representation. This pointed to an impairment in the representation system in visuospatial working memory, not to the control of mental attention. A possible analogy is that the left half of the "mental screen" was damaged, and that an intact covert attention system was dealing with a mental image that was impoverished on one side. Consistent with this interpretation, Baddeley and Lieberman (1980) speculated that representational neglect might reflect a deficit in the visuospatial system within working memory, a suggestion that was also raised by Bisiach (1993).

A further case illustrates that perceptual and representational neglect are really rather distinct. Beschin, Basso, and Della Sala (2000) reported the case of a very unfortunate patient who suffered strokes in both hemispheres. This patient showed both perceptual and representational neglect, but what was intriguing about this case was that he showed the two forms of neglect in different hemifields. Figure 9.4 shows attempts by the patient to draw a picture of a house shown at the top of the figure. The middle of the figure shows the patient's attempt to copy the picture of the house when it was still in view, and it is clear that he was copying only the left half of the picture (a right perceptual neglect). The bottom drawing is the attempt by the patient to reproduce the house from memory, and it is clear that he was recalling only the details from the right half of the house (a left representational neglect). The fact that his copying was intact shows that the absence of the left half of the house when drawing from memory was not due to a failure to attend to the left half of the drawing when it was in view. Finding the two forms of neglect independently for different hemifields in the same patient offers rather strong evidence that they reflect very different disorders. This reinforces the view that visual attention and perception rely on different neuronal pathways in the healthy brain than

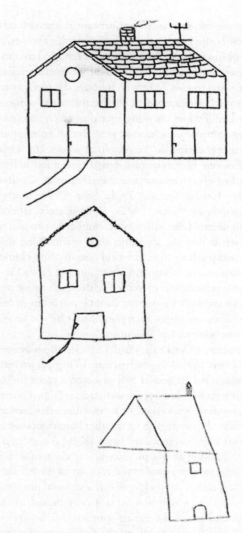

**Figure 9.4** Drawing from copying (*middle*) or from memory (*lower*) of a picture of a house by a patient suffering from right perceptual neglect and from left representational neglect (Reproduced from Beschin et al., 2000, with permission.)

visuospatial working memory and covert attention to mental processes.

## IMPLICIT PROCESSING IN NEGLECT

A final observation regarding neglect comes from a range of studies that demonstrate some form of implicit processing of material in the neglected field, at least in some patients. The most famous of these cases was reported by Marshall and Halligan (1988), in which a patient was shown a picture of two houses, one above the other. One of the houses looked perfectly symmetrical and normal, while the other house was depicted with flames issuing from a window on the left of the picture.

The patient was asked to indicate if she detected whether the two houses were the same, or were different in any way. She consistently reported that the houses were identical. However, when the patient was asked to choose in which house she would prefer to live, she tended to choose the house without the flames while claiming that this was a complete guess. Similar conclusions were drawn from studies using chimeric pictures that show the right half of one object/animal joined to the left half of another object/animal (e.g., Buxbaum & Coslett, 1994; Cantagallo and Della Sala, 1998; Young, Hellawell, & Welch, 1992). Some neglect patients demonstrated that they were implicitly processing the left half of the stimulus while maintaining that the two pictures were identical despite their chimeric nature. For example, Cantagallo and Della Sala's (1998) patient was presented with the drawing of a trombone with a rifle butt coming out from its left side. Spontaneously, he reported that he was seeing a "trombone which *fired* notes."

Recently, Della Sala, van der Meulen, Bestelmeyer, and Logie (2010) showed pictures to neglect patients in which the neglected half depicted a scene linked to either a well-known proverb such as "Don't put all your eggs in one basket" or to an unfamiliar proverb translated into English from other languages such as "Don't buy a cat in a bag" (see Figs. 9.5A and 9.5B). After looking at the picture, it was clear that each patient was not aware of the content of the left side. The experimenter then read out a series of proverbs, only one of which was semantically linked to the neglected half of the picture (printed in italic in Figs. 9.5A and 9.5B). Although the patients maintained that they were guessing, they successfully performed above chance in selecting the correct proverb, but only when proverbs were familiar. When proverbs were unfamiliar (such as the translated Dutch proverbs in Fig. 9.5B), performance was at chance. In that same study, a group of healthy participants was asked to carry out the same task, except that the target area of each picture was presented very rapidly, and below the perceptual threshold for each participant to be able to detect what had been presented. They showed the same pattern as the patients in that they could successfully select the correct proverb from a group of familiar proverbs, but they could not do so when the proverbs were unfamiliar.

These studies of implicit processing suggest that although neglect patients are not able to attend to the left half of their visual field, information from the neglected field is being processed at a level below conscious awareness. The flames of the burning

Still waters run deep
Blood is thicker than water
***Don't put all your eggs in one basket***
Walking on egg shells

**Figure 9.5A** Example of a picture used by Della Sala et al. (2010), with a target feature on the left of the picture to be matched with a *familiar* proverb from among those shown. The correct proverb is shown here in bold italics, but it was not highlighted in any way in the actual experiment.

Rowing goes well beneath an open sail
***Don't buy a cat in a bag***
Always keep an eye on the sail
First watch the cat out of the tree

**Figure 9.5B** Example of a picture used by Della Sala et al. (2010) with target feature on the left of the picture to be matched with an *unfamiliar* proverb. The correct proverb is shown here in bold italics, but it was not highlighted in any way in the actual experiment.

house in the Marshall and Halligan (1988) study appear to activate stored knowledge in the patient about the undesirability of a house on fire. The selection of the proverbs in the Della Sala et al. (2010) study suggests that the activation from the neglected field is sufficient to support quite complex semantic processing. That is, even when attention is impaired, this does not mean that the "unattended" material is not processed by the brain, possibly even at the semantic level. Other studies of neglect patients have shown that they can avoid obstacles when reaching or moving, even when those obstacles are in the neglected field and the patient would fail to report those objects if asked to describe what he or she can see (e.g., McIntosh et al., 2004).

Finally, the finding that there are patients with perceptual neglect but not representational neglect suggests that a disorder of visual attention will not necessarily imply that there is a disorder of covert attention to mental events within working memory. Conversely, the finding that there are patients with representational neglect who do not have perceptual neglect suggests that the representational neglect is not the direct result of a disorder of visual attention, and it does not appear to be a disorder of covert attention. Perceptual and representational neglect often occur together in stroke patients, but they do appear to reflect a combination of two different disorders that have rather different characteristics. Although lesion sites in neglect patients tend to be in the right fronto-parietal areas of the brain, as I have noted earlier in this chapter, whether there are specific areas of the brain linked with one or other form of the disorder is not clear. For example, in the Denis et al. (2004) study, there was no relationship between the locus or extent of the lesion in each patient and whether they showed perceptual or representational neglect or no neglect at all. A plausible hypothesis then is that it is the way in which the lesion affects connectivity (Bartolomeo et al., 2007) between the frontal and parietal lobes that leads to the form of cognitive impairment rather than the specific area of brain that is damaged by the lesion.

## Disorders of Divided Attention

While the disorder in neglect, at least in perceptual neglect, appears to be linked with impairments of attention to locations in space, the attentional disorder in people with Alzheimer-type dementia appears to be a problem of dividing attention. Alzheimer-type dementia is linked with a brain disease that gradually spreads through the brain. It most commonly (but not always) starts in the temporal lobes, and as the disease progresses, it affects other brain areas, notably the prefrontal cortex. The precise link between the areas of brain affected by the disease and the cognitive impairments from which these patients suffer is not entirely clear. Nevertheless, the cognitive impairments in such patients have been studied quite extensively, and episodic memory failure is a common early symptom of the disease, linked with the temporal lobe damage. However, impairments of episodic memory are also found in healthy older people and in people with other disorders such as chronic depression. So a major criterion for diagnosing Alzheimer's disease is that the person is shown to have impairments in episodic memory and in at least one other cognitive function, and that these cognitive functions get poorer over time, indicating that the disease is progressing. One particular "other" cognitive function that appears to be impaired in people with this disease is control of attention (e.g., Baddeley, Logie, Bressi, Della Sala, & Spinnler, 1986; Perry & Hodges, 1999), and specifically, the ability to divide attention in order to carry out two tasks at the same time, or dual tasking.

### DIVIDED ATTENTION IN DEMENTIA

Dual tasking in healthy adults tends to be studied broadly in three ways. One of these investigates when two tasks compete for a common processing stage, such as dealing with two simultaneous inputs or having two competing responses (for reviews, see Levy, Pashler, & Boer, 2006; Pashler & Johnston, 1998). A second approach focuses on the ability to switch back and forth between two tasks that have to be performed in a limited time period (e.g., Allport & Wylie, 2000; Monsell, 2003). However, the dual-task problem that is specific to Alzheimer's disease arises from experimental paradigms that explicitly avoid perceptual or response bottlenecks. Instead, the two tasks are chosen so that they can be performed largely in parallel by healthy adults (Cochini, Logie, Della Sala, & MacPherson, 2002; Logie, Cocchini, Della Sala, & Baddeley, 2004).

The first study to address divided attention in Alzheimer's disease was reported by Baddeley et al. (1986). A group of patients who had already been diagnosed as having the disease using formal clinical criteria were compared with a group of older healthy people matched on age with the patient group, and with a third group of younger healthy people. One difficulty with comparing different groups on their ability to divide attention between two tasks is that the groups might differ in their ability to do each

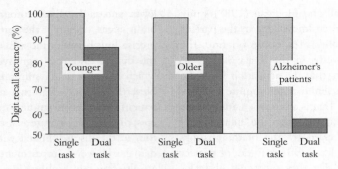

**Figure 9.6** Digit recall alone and with concurrent tracking for younger and older people and for people with mild Alzheimer's disease. (Based on data from Baddeley et al., 1986.)

task on its own. So, for example, Alzheimer's patients have an episodic memory deficit, and so their digit span will be lower than it is for healthy people of the same age. Older healthy people, in turn, might have a lower digit span than younger healthy people. So, if the experiment compares the groups on how well they can recall digits while they are doing something else at the same time, then the patient group will perform more poorly simply because they had trouble when even doing the single task. The dual-task impairment could then be explained as an episodic memory impairment. To get around this problem, Baddeley et al. (1986) adjusted the demand of each of their two tasks according to the ability of each participant. Each individual in each group was first assessed for his or her immediate serial order verbal memory with aural presentation of sequences of digits that the participant was asked to recall orally in the same order. The length of the sequence on each trial was gradually increased until the individual could no longer recall the sequence correctly, and this was taken as the individual digit span, or a measure of the individual maximum capacity for retaining a verbal ordered sequence. The second task involved asking participants to use a light-sensitive stylus to follow a moving single target around a computer screen. The computer recorded when the participant was on or off the target, and the speed of the target was gradually increased until people could no longer reliably keep the stylus on the target. This maximum speed for reliable tracking was taken as tracking span, or the maximum capacity for perceptual-motor tracking for each individual. This technique of titrating or adjusting demand for each person meant that everyone in all three groups was then performing at close to 100% of his or her own maximum ability on each task. That is, the initial, single task performance levels were the same across the three groups. So, when participants were asked

both to recall digit sequences and to track the moving target at the same time, any differences between the groups in dual-task performance have to be specific to dual task, and not due to differences in initial baseline levels of performance. The results of this study for digit recall are shown in Figure 9.6.

It is clear from Figure 9.6 that all three groups were indeed performing at their own maximum level when asked to perform digit recall on its own. However, when asked to listen to and recall digit sequences and at the same time to follow a moving target at their own individual maximum speed, then the healthy young and older adults showed about the same drop in performance of around 15%–20%, but the Alzheimer group show a very dramatic drop of around 45% compared with their own single task performance. A very similar result was found for the tracking performance in single and dual task. As noted earlier, this difference for the patient group cannot be attributed to initial differences in single-task performance between the groups, and so it appeared that the patients had a specific problem in carrying out two tasks at the same time. In a follow-up study, Baddeley, Bressi, Della Sala, Logie, and Spinnler (1991) tested the patients on three occasions, 6 months apart. The specific difficulty with doing two tasks at once became progressively larger as the disease progressed, again linking this dual-task impairment with the disease.

One possible criticism of the dual-task studies described earlier is that doing two tasks at the same time could be seen as simply more difficult or more cognitively demanding than doing one task at a time. This criticism arises from suggestions that cognition slows down in older people (e.g., Salthouse, 1993), and so it might be slowed down even further in people with progressive brain disease. A more cognitively demanding task will be more affected in people with progressive cognitive slowing as might

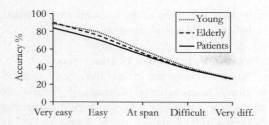

**Figure 9.7** Tracking accuracy as speed of target is gradually reduced or increased relative to the measured tracking speed (span) for each individual in a group of Alzheimer patients, age-matched healthy controls, and younger healthy controls. (Data reproduced from Logie et al., 2004.)

be the case with Alzheimer patients. To address this criticism, Logie et al. (2004) used a variation of the procedure used in the earlier Baddeley et al. (1986) studies. Again, the individual spans for each participant were assessed for digit recall and for tracking. However, Logie et al. (2004) next asked participants in each group to perform the digit recall on its own while the length of the sequence that they had to recall was reduced or increased. They then asked participants to perform the tracking as a single task as the speed of the target was increased or decreased. Results for the tracking task are shown in Figure 9.7, and very similar for digit recall. When the target moved more quickly or the length of the digit sequence increased, performance gradually became poorer, and when the target moved more slowly or the digit sequence was shorter, performance improved, but as is clear from Figure 9.7, the effect of changing demand in a single task was exactly the same for the patient group as it was for the other two groups. In a second experiment, the three groups were asked to perform the two tasks both set at a very easy level according to their own ability. Here, the patients had a problem in performing two easy tasks, while neither of the healthy groups showed a difference between single- and dual-task performance. Therefore, the patients showed a problem in carrying out two tasks at the same time, even when the tasks were extremely easy for them, and the effect of increasing demand had exactly the same effect on the patients as it did on the healthy participants. So it is the ability to perform two tasks at the same time that is a problem for the patients, and it is not an effect of overall demand on their damaged cognitive system.

The specific impairment of dual-task ability in Alzheimer patients has now been shown in a range of other studies (e.g., Baddeley, Baddeley, Bucks, & Wilcock, 2001; Della Sala, Cocchini, Logie, & MacPherson, 2010; MacPherson, Della Sala, Logie, & Wilcock, 2007; Ramsden, Kinsella, Ong, & Storey, 2008; Sebastian, Menor, & Elosua, 2006). Indeed, Baddeley et al. (2001) contrasted tests of focal and sustained attention, inhibition, and divided attention, or dual task. Focal attention, measured with simple and choice response time tests was shown to be broadly intact in patients with Alzheimer's disease, in contrast to the clear impairment of divided attention when dual tasking.

### INHIBITION AND DEMENTIA

The patients in the Baddeley et al. (2001) study also appeared to have difficulty inhibiting irrelevant visual stimuli. In their comprehensive review of cognitive deficits in Alzheimer's disease, Perry and Hodges (1999) identified inhibition as being a particular difficulty for such patients. In a later review, Amieva, Phillips, Della Sala, and Henry (2004) noted that some studies had shown dementia-related impairments in tasks requiring control of inhibition, such as the Stroop task in which participants are asked to inhibit their natural tendency to read a color word (e.g., RED) but instead to say aloud the color of the ink in which the word is printed (e.g., for the word "RED" printed in green ink, the correct response is "green"). However, they also noted a range of studies showing little or no impairment in tasks involving automatic inhibition of responses such as the tendency not to look back at a location that has been fixated a very short time before, known as inhibition of return. In summary, it appears that focal attention and automatic inhibition are intact in Alzheimer's disease, but controlled inhibition and divided attention are not. Amieva et al. (2004) concluded that some forms of attention can be damaged while others remain intact, indicating in turn that there are different forms of attention in the healthy brain that can be differentially impaired by brain damage. This conclusion is further reinforced by the observation from earlier sections of this chapter that spatial attention is specifically impaired in neglect patients, in contrast with the impairment of divided attention and controlled inhibition in Alzheimer patients. Attention is not a single entity or concept.

A recent set of studies has examined the phenomenon of "closing-in behavior" in dementia patients (e.g., Ambron, McIntosh, Allaria, & Della Sala, 2009; Lee, Chin, Kang, Kim, Park, & Na, 2004). Here, Alzheimer patients are asked to copy a simple drawing on a sheet of paper, but they have a tendency to produce their drawing very close to, or even on top of, the item that they are copying. This has been interpreted either as their attention being attracted toward the existing drawing on the page (or a failure to inhibit this tendency) or as a limitation of their visuospatial working memory that might be needed to keep parts of the target item in mind while they look at and produce their own drawing or to switch their gaze between their drawing and their target. Although the phenomenon has been known in clinical settings for a long time (Mayer Gross, 1935), there are relatively few systematic empirical studies and theoretical accounts for the phenomenon at an early stage. However, as Ambron et al. (2009) note, it does appear to be linked with a combination of failures of attention and of visuospatial working memory.

## Disorders of Sustained Attention

A further form of attention that has been studied in Alzheimer patients is vigilance or sustained attention. Here, the participant is asked to carry out a repetitive task over an extended period and has to detect the presence of an infrequently occurring event. The capacity to maintain attention over long intervals in order to detect infrequent signals assumed considerable practical importance during military conflicts in the mid 20th century, with the development of sonar and radar as submarine and aircraft detection devices. Performance in the radar/sonar operators tended to show a steady decrement over time, a finding that led to a considerable amount of research and contrasting interpretations as to its cause (see Broadbent, 1958, for a review). Parasuraman (1979, 1984) suggested that the decrement in sustained attention occurred in those conditions where participants had to hold information in memory for comparison with the signal that they were trying to detect, but it typically did not occur when participants had to make a simple perceptual judgement without any memory load. Parasuraman (1979) asked healthy participants to discriminate successive or simultaneous tones of different volume or light flashes of different intensity presented over periods of 45 minutes. Only the successive discrimination tasks resulted in progressive deterioration of performance. This led Parasuraman to argue that when vigilance tasks make ongoing demands on memory, this constitutes additional cognitive effort. A successive discrimination task involves retaining information in memory and so involves cognitive effort. Therefore, performance may begin to degrade earlier for a vigilance task with an ongoing memory load than it would in a task where the

target and the comparison stimulus are presented together (simultaneous discrimination).

### SUSTAINED ATTENTION IN DEMENTIA

Sustained attention deficits have been reported in clinical assessments of patients with Alzheimer's disease (e.g., Della Sala & Logie, 1993; Parasuraman & Haxby, 1993; Spinnler, 1991). Alexander (1973) reported that dementia patients showed poorer overall detection of letter targets in a string of letters than did age-matched controls, but neither group showed a further drop in detection performance over time. A similar lack of difference in sustained attention performance between dementia patients and age-matched controls was reported by Nebes and Brady (1993) and by Brazzelli, Cocchini, Della Sala, and Spinnler (1994). Parasuraman and Haxby (1993) concluded from the results available at that time that Alzheimer patients show no decrement in vigilance if the task involves perceptual discrimination, and the differential impairments in the patients is found only when there is some additional task demand.

As discussed in the section on divided attention, there are problems with interpreting an observed impairment as resulting from high task demand or difficulty. This interpretation immediately leads to the question of what is the source of the difficulty. It could be that there is too much information, or this information is too complex, or it is being presented at too fast a rate for the capacity of the cognitive system, whether that cognitive system is damaged or healthy. However, in the case of vigilance tasks, the whole point is that the task and the information are very simple and the information to which the participant has to respond is presented at a rather slow rate. Another possible source of difficulty could be that the information is degraded because of visual interference with the signal or noise in an auditory channel, or because the participant has poor vision or hearing. However, none of these problems were present in the experiments studying vigilance in dementia patients.

Baddeley, Cocchini, Della Sala, Logie, and Spinnler (1999) noted that there is no a priori reason why the Parasuraman (1979) perceptual discrimination between two tones or flashes presented at the same time should involve a lower task demand than a discrimination in which a second item presented on its own is compared to a previously presented item that is held in memory. If the second condition leads to a vigilance decrement while the first does not, then this indicates a specific additional cognitive cost of storing information in short-term memory.

Baddeley et al. (1999) followed an analogous procedure to that used in the dual-task experiments (Baddeley et al., 1986; Logie et al., 2004) to equate initial performance levels across conditions and between groups of dementia patients and of older controls. They used a discrimination task in which two lines were shown on the screen and participants were asked to decide whether the lines were the same length. The discrimination threshold was measured for each participant—that is, the smallest difference in line lengths at which each participant could detect that the lengths were different. This ensured that the discrimination task itself was set at the same level of difficulty for all of the participants. In the perceptual task, both lines were presented simultaneously. In the memory condition, the second line was presented on its own and its length was to be compared with the first line of the pair held in memory. Results showed that the healthy older group showed a progressive drop over time, reaching a peak of around 10% reduction in performance after 30 minutes of the memory-based task, but showed no drop over that same period in the perceptual task. The Alzheimer patients also showed a progressive drop in the memory condition but reached a 24% reduction over just 15 minutes of performing the task. They also showed a drop of around 7% in the perceptual task over the same period. Given that the initial levels of performance were equated by adjusting task demands for each individual, this suggests that there is a specific impairment in sustained attention in Alzheimer patients, and this impairment is particularly evident when they have to carry a memory load while performing the vigilance task.

## SUSTAINED ATTENTION AND FRONTAL LOBE DAMAGE

Damage to the prefrontal cortical areas of the brain are often associated with disorders of what are referred to as executive functions (e.g., Rabbitt, 1997), including inhibition, task switching, and focusing attention. The discussion so far in this chapter has considered possible links between damage to the frontal lobes with the progression of Alzheimer's disease, and impairments in divided and sustained attention. Patients with focal damage to the frontal lobes as a result of a stroke, or from neurosurgery, or from a serious head injury also appear to show impairments of attention. The most common clinical reports are that they exhibit "perseveration" in

which there is a tendency to repeat the same action, confabulation in which they tend to generate reports of events that could not possibly have occurred, and a lack of inhibition such as "utilization behavior" in which they find it impossible to avoid picking up or handling objects placed in front of them. They might also have a tendency to say things that are insulting or rude because they cannot prevent themselves from doing so. Such patients have been shown to be unable to perform a range of planning tasks, and have a particular problem in multitasking, for example, planning and carrying out a set of errands in a shopping mall (Shallice & Burgess, 1991).

Although the impairments mentioned earlier are observed following frontal lobe damage, no one patient tends to exhibit all of these difficulties, and this has led to the suggestion mentioned earlier when discussing the impact of Alzheimer's disease, that there are different kinds of attention that can be differentially impaired depending on the location and extent of the brain damage. For example, Simons, Marieke, Schölvinck, Gilbert, Frith, and Burgess (2006) demonstrated that an area at the very front of the frontal lobes, Brodmann area 10, appears to be involved in biasing attention to external events or to internal, mental events. They have suggested that this area plays a crucial role in prospective memory tasks which require participants to be aware of external or exogenous cues, or to mental or endogenous cues that act as reminders to perform particular actions. If the bias is to exogenous cues but the relevant current cue is endogenous, then this will result in a prospective memory failure.

One attentional impairment that does appear to be common to patients with frontal lobe damage is what has been referred to as "goal neglect" (e.g., Duncan, Elmslie, Williams, Johnson, & Freer, 1996). Here, the patient appears to ignore an instruction or particular aspect of a task when he or she has to perform it, even if the patient knows what the action is. So, for example, a patient might be asked to hold up his or her hand when a light comes on, and fail to do so. Yet he or she can say that when the light comes on he or she should hold up his or her hand. This neglect of current goals could be one reason why frontal lobe patients are poor at multitasking; they might know what the tasks are that they have to perform, but they neglect to perform them. Duncan and colleagues suggest that the action that is neglected loses out in a competition between a variety of mental activities or physical actions that the patient is asked to perform. As the set of goals or tasks becomes more complex, some of these are given priority reflected in a bias toward performing the higher priority tasks at the expense of others. Duncan has extended this idea to suggest that goal neglect might be characteristic of healthy individuals and linked to general mental capacity or general intelligence "g." Attending to multiple tasks or swapping attention between tasks is then more efficient for people who have greater mental capacity, who in turn will be less prone to show goal neglect. Given that prefrontal areas are thought to be important in supporting the planning of goals and switching attention between tasks, as well as switching attention between the external world and the mental world (Simons et al., 2006), then damage to these areas will be associated with an inability to deal with increasing task complexity, and hence goal neglect (Duncan et al., 2008).

## Conclusions

This discussion of disorders of attention should make clear that it would be more appropriate to refer to disorders of different kinds of attention. Impairments of spatial attention in unilateral spatial perceptual neglect appear to be rather different from impairments associated with representational neglect, and both differ from the impairments of divided attention or of inhibition in Alzheimer's disease. These, in turn, only partially overlap with the lack of inhibition and goal neglect in patients suffering from frontal lobe damage. It is equally clear that there are striking differences between failures of attention to the outside world and failures of attention to the mental world in addition to a failure to switch attention between them and the operation of online cognition within the mental workspace (Logie, 2011; Logie & van der Meulen, 2009). There are other disorders of attention linked with, for example, healthy ageing (e.g., Naveh-Benjamin, Moscovitch, & Roediger, 2001), or syndromes such as attention-deficit disorders in children (e.g., Brown, 2005), or everyday lapses of attention leading to human errors in healthy adults (e.g., Reason, 1990), and discussion of each of these topics would require several chapters of this book.

Given the plethora of attentional disorders, is there some coherent theory or framework that might encompass all or most of these disorders, or are we really forced to come up with separate explanations for each of them? The human brain is certainly complex and it can break down in complex ways. It also has sufficient plasticity to compensate for some forms of damage, and when we observe a particular pattern of impairment in a brain-damaged individual, it is not always clear whether we are observing the result of the damage or the result of using some alternative cognitive system that relies on remaining intact brain networks to perform the same task. Duncan's ideas of goal neglect coupled with biased competition between brain networks offers one possible general framework for attentional disorders. These ideas are also consistent with the long-standing view of the brain activity comprising differential levels of activation of different neuroanatomical networks, with the highest level of activation being given the highest priority (Selfridge, 1959; Selfridge & Neisser, 1960), the difference now being that this differential activity can be demonstrated rather than assumed (see review in Duncan, 2006). However, this cannot be the whole story given that the brain can process information in parallel, while focused and/or sustained attention might be elsewhere, and inhibitory processes can operate largely automatically. What has been discovered thus far appears to suggest that understanding both intact forms of attention and how they break down will require a combination of theories of controlled and automatic attention and theories of temporary storage and manipulation of material in the mental workspace of working memory.

## References

Albert, M. L. (1973). A simple test of visual neglect. *Neurology*, 23, 658–664.

Alexander, D. A. (1973). Attention dysfunction in senile dementia. *Psychological Report*, 32, 229–230.

Allport, A., & Wylie, G. (2000). Task-switching stimulus-response bindings and negative priming. In S. Monsell & J. S. Driver (Eds.), *Control of cognitive processes: Attention and performance XVIII* (pp. 35–70). Cambridge, MA: MIT Press.

Ambron, E., McIntosh, R. D., Allaria, F., & Della Sala, S. (2009). A large scale retrospective study of closing-in behaviour in Alzheimer's disease. *Journal of the International Neuropsychological Society*, 15, 787–792.

Amieva, H., Phillips, L. H., Della Sala, S., & Henry, J. D. (2004). Inhibitory functioning in Alzheimer's disease. *Brain*, 127, 949–964.

Baddeley, A.D. (2007). Working memory, thought and action. Oxford, UK: Oxford University Press.

Baddeley, A. D., Baddeley, H. A., Bucks, R. S., & Wilcock, G. K. (2001). Attentional control in Alzheimer's disease. *Brain*, 124, 1492–1508.

Baddeley, A. D., Bressi, S., Della Sala, S., Logie, R. H., & Spinnler, H. (1991). The decline of working memory in Alzheimer's disease: A longitudinal study. *Brain*, 114, 2521–2542.

Baddeley, A. D., Cocchini, G., Della Sala, S., Logie, R. H., & Spinnler, H. (1999). Working memory and vigilance: Evidence from normal aging and Alzheimer's disease. *Brain and Cognition*, 41, 87–108.

Baddeley, A. D., & Lieberman, K. (1980). Spatial working memory. In R. S. Nickerson (Ed.), *Attention and performance VIII* (pp. 521–539). Hillsdale, NJ: Erlbaum.

Baddeley, A., Logie, R., Bressi, S., Della Sala, S., & Spinnler, H. (1986). Senile dementia and working memory. *Quarterly Journal of Experimental Psychology, 38A*, 603–618.

Bartolomeo, P., Thiebaut de Schotten, M. T., & Doricchi, F. (2007). Left unilateral neglect as a disconnection syndrome. *Cerebral Cortex, 17*, 2479–2490.

Bender, M. B. (1952). *Disorders of perception.* Springfield, IL: Charles C Thomas.

Beschin, N., Basso, A., & Della Sala, S. (2000). Perceiving left and imagining right: Dissociation in neglect. *Cortex, 36*, 401–414.

Beschin, N., Cocchini, G., Della Sala, S., & Logie, R. H. (1997). What the eyes perceive, the brain ignores: A case of pure unilateral representational neglect. *Cortex, 33*, 3–26.

Beschin, N., & Robertson, I. (1997). Personal versus extrapersonal: A group study of their dissociation using a reliable clinical test. *Cortex, 33*, 3–26.

Bisiach, E. (1993). Mental representation in unilateral neglect and related disorders. *Quarterly Journal of Experimental Psychology, 46*, 435–461.

Bisiach, E., & Luzzatti, C. (1978). Unilateral neglect of representational space. *Cortex, 14*, 129–133.

Bisiach, E., Pizzamiglio, L., Nico, D., & Antonucci, G. (1996). Beyond unilateral neglect. *Brain, 119*, 851–857.

Brazzelli, M., Cocchini, G., Della Sala, S., & Spinnler, H. 1994. Alzheimer patients show a sensitivity decrement over time on a tonic alertness task. *Journal of Clinical and Experimental Neuropsycholgy, 16*, 851–860.

Broadbent, D. E. (1958). *Perception and communication.* London: Pergamon.

Brown, T. E. (2005). *Attention deficit disorder: The unfocused mind in children and adults.* New Haven, CT: Yale University Press.

Buxbaum, L. J., & Coslett, H. B. (1994). Neglect of chimeric figures—2 halves are better than a whole. *Neuropsychologia, 32*, 275–288.

Calvanio, R., Petrone, P. N., & Levine, D. N. (1987). Left visuo-spatial neglect is both environment-centred and body-centred. *Neurology, 37*, 1179–1181.

Cantagallo, A., & Della Sala, S. (1998). Preserved insight in an artist with extrapersonal spatial neglect. *Cortex, 34*, 163–189.

Cocchini, G., Logie, R. H., Della Sala, S., & MacPherson, S. E. (2002). Concurrent performance of two memory tasks: Evidence for domain specific working memory systems. *Memory and Cognition, 30*, 1086–1095.

Coslett, B. (1997). Neglect in vision and visual imagery: A double dissociation. *Brain, 120*, 1163–1171.

Della Sala, S., Cocchini, G., Logie, R. H., & MacPherson, S. E. (2010). Dual task during encoding, maintenance and retrieval in Alzheimer disease and healthy ageing. *Journal of Alzheimer's Disease, 19*, 503–515.

Della Sala, S., & Logie, R. H. (1993). When working memory does not work: The role of working memory in neuropsychology. In F. Boller & H. Spinnler (Eds.), *Handbook of neuropsychology* (pp. 1–62). Amsterdam, The Netherlands: Elsevier Science Publishers B.V.

Della Sala, S., Logie, R. H., Beschin, N., & Denis, M. (2004). Preserved visuo-spatial transformations in representational neglect. *Neuropsychologia, 42*, 1358–1364.

Della Sala, S., van der Meulen, M., Bestelmeyer, P., & Logie, R. H. (2010). Evidence for a workspace model of working memory from semantic implicit processing in neglect. *Journal of Neuropsychology, 4(Pt. 2), 147–166.*

De Renzi, E., Gentilini, M., Faglioni, P., & Barbieri, C. (1989). Attentional shift towards the rightmost stimuli in patients with left visual neglect. *Cortex, 25*, 231–237.

Denis, M., Beschin, N., Logie, R. H., & Della Sala, S. (2002). Visual perception and verbal descriptions as sources for generating mental representations: Evidence from representational neglect. *Cognitive Neuropsychology, 19*(2), 97–112.

Duncan, J. (2006). Brain mechanisms of attention. *Quarterly Journal of Experimental Psychology, 59*, 2–27.

Duncan, J., Elmslie, H., Williams, P., Johnson, R., & Freer, C. (1996). Intelligence and the frontal lobe: The organization of goal-diected behavior. *Cognitive Psychology, 30*, 257–303.

Duncan, J., Parr, A., Woolgar, A., Thomson, R., Bright, P., Cox, S.,... Nimmo-Smith, I. (2008). Goal neglect and Spearman's g: Competing parts of a complex task. *Journal of Experimental Psychology: General, 137*, 131–148.

Guariglia, C., Padovani, A., Pantano, P., & Pizzamiglio, L. (1993). Unilateral neglect restricted to visual imagery. *Nature, 364*, 235–237.

Halligan, P. W., & Marshall, J. C. (1991). Left neglect for near but not far space in man. *Nature, 350*, 498–500.

Halligan, P. W., & Marshall, J. C. (1992). Left visuo-spatial neglect: A meaningless entity? *Cortex, 28*, 525–535.

Halligan, P. W., Marshall, J. C., & Wade, D. T. (1989). Visuo-spatial neglect: Underlying factors and test sensitivity. *The Lancet, 2*, 980–910.

Humphreys, G. W., Riddoch, M. J., Nys, G., & Heinke, D. (2002). Transient binding by time: Neuropsychological evidence from anti-extinction. *Cognitive Neuropsychology, 19*, 361–380.

Husain, M., Mannan, S., Hodgson, T., Wojciulik, E., & Driver, J. (2001). Impaired spatial working memory across saccades contributes to abnormal search in parietal neglect. *Brain, 124*, 941–952.

Kinsbourne, M. (1987). Mechanisms of unilateral neglect. In M. Jeannerod (Ed.), *Neurophysiological and neuropsychological aspects of spatial neglect* (pp. 69–85). North Holland, The Netherlands: Elsevier.

Lee, B. H., Chin, J., Kang, S. J., Kim, E. J., Park, K. C., & Na, D. L. (2004). Mechanism of the closing-in phenomenon in a figure copying task in Alzheimer's disease patients. *Neurocase, 10*, 393–397.

Lepore, M., Conson, M., Ferrigno, A., Grossi, D., & Trojano, L. (2004). Spatial transpositions across tasks and response modalities: Exploring representational allochiria. *Neurocase, 10*, 386–392.

Levy, J., Pashler, H, & Boer, E (2006). Central interference in driving: Is there any stopping the psychological refractory period? *Psychological Science, 17*(3), 228–235

Logie, R. H. (1995). *Visuo-spatial working memory.* Hove, England: Erlbaum.

Logie, R. H. (2003). Spatial and visual working memory: A mental workspace. In D. Irwin & B. Ross (Eds.), *Cognitive vision: The psychology of learning and motivation* (Vol. 42, pp. 37–78). New York: Elsevier Science.

Logie, R. H. (2011). The functional organisation and the capacity limits of working memory. *Current Directions in Psychological Science, 20*(4), 240–245.

Logie, R. H., Beschin, N., Della Sala, S., & Denis, M. (2005). Dissociating mental transformations and visuo-spatial storage in working memory. Evidence from representational neglect. *Memory, 13*, 430–434.

Logie, R. H., Cocchini, G., Della Sala, S., & Baddeley, A. D. (2004). Is there a specific executive capacity for dual task co-ordination? Evidence from Alzheimer's Disease. *Neuropsychology, 18*, 504–513.

Logie, R. H., & van der Meulen, M. (2009). Fragmenting and integrating visuo-spatial working memory. In J. R. Brockmole (Ed.), *Representing the visual world in memory* (pp. 1–32). Hove, England: Psychology Press.

MacPherson, S. E., Della Sala, S., Logie, R. H., & Willcock, G. K. (2007). Specific AD impairment in concurrent performance of two memory tasks. *Cortex, 43*, 858–865.

Marshall, J. C., & Halligan, P. W. (1988). Blindsight and insight in visuo-spatial neglect. *Nature, 336*, 766–767.

Mayer Gross, W. (1935). Some observations on apraxia. *Proceedings of the Royal Society of Medicine, 28*, 63–72.

McIntosh, R. D., McClements, K. I., Schindler, I., Cassidy, T. P., Birchall, D., & Milner, A. D. (2004). Avoidance of obstacles in the absence of visual awareness. *Proceedings of the Royal Society of London B, 271*, 15–20.

Miceli, G., & Capasso, R. (2001). Word-centred neglect dyslexia: Evidence from a new case. *Neurocase, 7*, 221–237.

Monsell, S. (2003). Task switching. *Trends in Cognitive Sciences, 7*, 134–140.

Naveh-Benjamin, M., Moscovitch, M., & Roediger, H. L. (2001). *Human memory and cognitive aging.* Hove, England. Psychology Press.

Nebes, R. D., & Brady, C. B. 1993. Phasic and tonic alertness in Alzheimer's disease. *Cortex, 29*, 77–90.

Nijboera, T. C. W., Mc Intosh, R. D., Nysc, G. M. S., Dijkermana, H. C., & Milner, A. D. (2008). Prism adaptation improves voluntary but not automatic orienting in neglect. *Neuroreport, 19*, 293–298.

Parasuraman, R. (1979). Memory load and event rate control sensitivity decrements in sustained attention. *Science, 205*, 924–927.

Parasuraman, R. (1984). Sustained attention in detection and discrimination. In R. Parasuraman & D. R. Davies (Eds.), *Varieties of attention* (pp. 243–271). New York: Academic Press.

Parasuraman, R., & Haxby, J. (1993). Attention and brain function in Alzheimer's disease: A review. *Neuropsychology, 7*, 242–272.

Pashler, H., & Johnston, J. C. (1998). Attentional limitations in dual-task performance. In H. Pashler (Ed.), *Attention* (pp. 155–189). East Essex, England: Psychology Press.

Paterson, A., & Zangwill, O. L. (1944). Disorders of visual space perception associated with lesions of the right cerebral hemisphere. *Brain, 67*, 331–358.

Pearson, D. G., & Sahraie, A. (2003). Oculomotor control and the maintenance of spatially and temporally distributed events in visuo-spatial working memory. *Quarterly Journal of Experimental Psychology, 56A*, 1089–1111.

Perry, R. J., & Hodges, J. R. (1999). Attention and executive deficits in Alzheimer's disease: A critical review. *Brain, 122*, 383–404.

Poppelreuter, W. (1991). *Disturbances of lower and higher visual capacities caused by occipital damage with special reference to the psychopathological, pedagogical, industrial, and social implications (J. Zihl, Trans.).* Oxford, England: Oxford University Press. (Original work published 1917).

Posner, M. I., Walker, J. A., Friedrich, F. J., & Rafal, R. D. (1984). Effects of parietal injury on covert orienting of attention. *Journal of Neuroscience, 4*, 1863–1874.

Postle, B., Idzikowski, C., Della Sala, S., Logie. R. H., & Baddeley, A. D. (2006). The selective disruption of spatial working memory by eye movements. *Quarterly Journal of Experimental Psychology, 59*, 100–120.

Rabbitt, P. M. A. (Ed.). (1997). *Methodology of frontal and executive function.* Hove, England: Psychology Press.

Ramsden, C. M., Kinsella, G. J., Ong, B., & Storey, E. (2008). Performance of everyday actions in mild Alzheimer's disease. *Neuropsychology, 22*, 17–26.

Reason, J. (1990). *Human error.* Cambridge, England: Cambridge University Press.

Robertson, I. H., & Halligan, P. W. (1999). *Spatial neglect: A clinical handbook for diagnosis and treatment.* Hove, England: Psychology Press.

Robertson, I. H., Mattingley, J. B., Rorden, C., & Driver, J. (1998). Phasic alerting of neglect patients overcomes their spatial deficit in visual awareness. *Nature, 395*, 169–172.

Rossetti, Y., Rode, G., Pisella, L., Farnè, A., Li, L., Boisson, D., & Perenin, M.T. (1998). Prism adaptation to a rightward optical deviation rehabilitates left hemispatial neglect. *Nature, 395*, 166–169.

Salthouse, T. A. (1993). Speed mediation of adult age differences in cognition. *Developmental Psychology, 29*, 722–738.

Schenkenberg, T., Bradford, D. C., & Ajax, E. T. (1980). Line bisection and unilateral visual neglect in patients with neurological impairment. *Neurology, 30*, 509–517.

Sebastian, M. V., Menor, J., & Elosua, M. R. (2006). Attentional dysfunction of the central executive in AD: Evidence from dual task. *Cortex, 42*, 1015–1020.

Selfridge, O. (1959). Pandemonium: A paradigm for learning. In *Symposium on the mechanization of thought processes.* London: HM Stationery Office.

Selfridge, O., & Neisser, U. (1960). Pattern recognition by machine. *Scientific American, 203*, 60–68.

Shallice, T., & Burgess, P. W. (1991). Deficits in strategy application following frontal lobe damage in man. *Brain, 114*, 727–741.

Simons, J. S., Schölvinck, M. L., Gilbert, S. J., Frith, C. D., & Burgess, P. W. (2006). Differential components of prospective memory? Evidence from fMRI. *Neuropsychologia, 44*, 1388–1397.

Spinnler, H. 1991. The role of attention disorders in the cognitive deficits of dementia. In F. Boller & J. Grafman (Eds.), *Handbook of neuropsychology* (pp.79–122). Amsterdam, The Netherlands: Elsevier Science.

Stone, S. P., Wilson, B., Wroot, A., Halligan, P. W., Lange, L. S., Marshall, J. C., & Greenwood, R. J. (1991). The assessment of visuo-spatial neglect after acute stroke. *Journal of Neurology, Neurosurgery and Psychiatry, 54*, 345–350.

Vallar. G., & Perani, D. (1986). The anatomy of unilateral neglect after right hemisphere stroke lesions: A clinical/CT-correlation study in man. *Neuropsychologia, 24*, 609–622.

Vallar, G., Rusconi, M. L., Bignamini, L., Geminiani, G., & Perani, D. (1994). Anatomical correlates of visual and tactile extinction in humans: A clinical CT scan study. *Journal of Neurology, Neurosurgery and Psychiatry, 57*, 464–470.

Young, A. W., Hellawell, D. J., & Welch, J. (1992). Neglect and visual recognition. *Brain, 115*, 51–71.

# The Nature and Status of Visual Resources

Steven L. Franconeri

### Abstract

Across many types of tasks, our ability to process multiple objects or locations at once is limited by a finite processing resource. This chapter describes 15 classic examples of such resources limits. The chapter then reviews evidence suggesting that this resource primarily reflects competition for representation, across two types of representation. First, limits on the identification of objects may reflect competition within networks that represent object identity (the ventral visual stream). Second, limits on the selection of multiple locations may reflect competition between selected locations within representations of visual space (the dorsal visual stream). This definition of visual resources provides a parsimonious explanation for many effects in the visual cognition literature, and it makes concrete predictions about manipulations that should affect performance across a wide variety of visual tasks.

**Key Words:** visual attention, selection, resources, competition, crowding, surround inhibition, object tracking, visual search, subitizing

The goal of research in visual cognition is to explain how our visual system takes a stream of information from tens of millions of constantly changing visual "pixels" and produces a coherent visual experience that can lead to useful action in the world. This is a daunting problem, because it is difficult to comprehend the huge space of possible ways that the visual system might achieve this result. One way to reduce the scope of any problem is to break it into smaller pieces, in this case by reducing the visual system to more constrained systems. These subsystems might process certain kinds of stimuli, such as color, texture, or motion. Or they might perform a certain type of processing, such as edge detection, which is any process that seeks contrast among different colors, textures, or motion directions.

Among the constrained problems studied by vision researchers, *visual attention* is an odd class because it might be defined as "processing that fails when you give it too much to do at once." These failures, illustrated in Figure 10.1, seem to show that as people are asked to deal with a larger number of objects, there is a limited pool of visual "resources" that becomes depleted, leading to slower response time or lower accuracy. The chapter argues for a common root of these limited resources: competition for representation, either within a representational space of object identity (the ventral visual system), or a representational space that stores currently selected locations (a dorsal map of visual space).

The second section reviews the many examples of processing limitations depicted in Figure 10.1. The third section isolates the examples that reflect visual resource limitations (as opposed to, e.g., limits on higher level decision processes). The fourth section reviews evidence that visual processing can be limited by competition for representation, and the fifth and sixth sections argue that this resource can

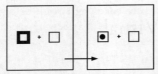

**Cueing benifits:** a location is cued with a flash or arrow, responses are faster or more accurate to probe at that location.

**Pop-out vs. slow visual search:** finding the bright object at left is immediate, finding the backward C at right takes time.

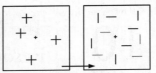

**Selecting multiple locations:** finding the grey vertical at right takes time, but we can select a limited number of hint locations

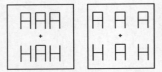

**Flanker interference:** deciding if center letter is A or H is slower when flankers are incompatible (bottom). greater spacing helps.

**Global interference:** deciding if smaller letter is A or H is slower when large letter is incompatible. smaller effect in opposite direction.

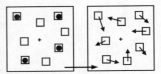

**Tracking multiple objects:** we can track a few cued moving objects at fast speeds, and up to 8 at slower speeds.

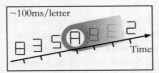

**Attentional blink:** while reporting letters in a rapidly changing number stream, processing 'blinks' after a target: 'A' is defined 'E' is missed.

**Crowding:** when fixating, letters at left are clear. letter at right seem to have floating or interchanging identities

**Fast vs. slow enumeration:** we can instantly count up to 4 objects. for more objects, counting is very slow (though we can quickly estimate).

**Averaging:** we can quickly judge average size in right display. remaining fixated on right display, note average orientation on left.

**Illustory conjunctions:** forcing attention to spread widely with number judgement, percept of shape features can miscombine.

**Slow tracking:** keeping your eyes fixed, is the dot at left inside or outside the shape? at right, are the two dots on the same line?

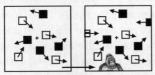

**Inattentional blindness:** count wall bounces of white objects. people miss appearance of new black objects, red objects, gorillas.

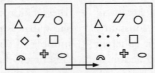

**Object substitution:** an array of shapes is briefly flashed, we can't report a shape masked by dots, unless its position is pre-cued.

**Spatial relationship perception:** is surprisingly slow. find the two pairs in each dispaly with unique relationship.

Ventral competition for identification

Dorsal competition for selection

**Figure 10.1** Fifteen examples of visual tasks that have been taken to reflect limits on visual resources. Examples on the left are argued to reflect competition for representation in the ventral visual stream and, on the right, the dorsal visual stream. (The "crowding" example is adapted from Pelli, Palomares, & Majaj, 2004.)

explain performance limits in ventral object identification (left side of Fig. 10.1) and dorsal object selection (right side of Fig. 10.1). The final section offers a broader picture of how these limits might affect everyday perception.

## Fifteen Examples of Visual Resource Limits

Figure 10.1 lists examples of tasks that reveal limitations in our ability to process visual information. All of them show that when we ask too much of our visual system, response times lengthen or accuracy falls. Some of these limitations may be illusory, but all have historically served as examples.

### Limits on Identification of Objects

*Cueing* effects can occur when observers are asked to make a fast response when a probe dot appears or to identify a letter that appears. There are two (or more) potential locations for this probe, and performance is faster or more accurate if the target's location is cued beforehand, relative to when another location is cued (Posner, 1980). The cue seems to allow faster processing when an observer focuses on a single location.

Limits on *visual search* can occur when observers are asked to find a target object in a field of distractor objects (Wolfe, 2007). For some versions of the task, response times are fast no matter how many distractor objects are added to the display. This might include searches for a bright object among dark objects, searches for a red object among green objects, or searches for a moving object among static objects. But for other versions of the task, response times increase as more distractors are added. These include searches for a target letter among other letters, or a search for a conjunction of two features (e.g., a gray vertical bar) among distractors that each carry one of the target's features (e.g., gray horizontal bars and black vertical bars, see the "Multiple location selection" example lower in the figure). For these searches, we appear to be limited in the number of objects that we can process at once.

*Flanker interference* effects occur when known target objects are flanked by nearby objects that carry an incompatible response. If an observer's task is to determine whether a center letter is an A or an H, and the center letter is an A, responses are slower when the flankers are H's than when the flankers are also A's. Moving the letters farther away, or making them less featurally similar (e.g., different colors), reduces this interference effect. Something about the addition of these incompatible letters limits the observer's ability to respond quickly (see Chajut, Schupak, & Algom, 2009; Mordkoff, 1996). In another type of interference effect labeled *global interference*, the identity of a larger object can interfere with recognition of smaller objects that comprise it. In the figure example, observers are asked to detect whether the small letters are A's or H's. Similar to the flanker effect, incompatible global letters slow processing of local letters (Navon, 1977).

*Attentional blink* effects seem like an effort by the visual system to prevent flanker interference effects across time instead of space. When asked to identify two letters in a rapidly changing stream of digits (about 100ms/character), we can identify the first letter, but we are reduced in our ability to identify the second one. The typical conclusion is that in order to isolate the first digit, the object identification system must briefly "blink" in order to shut out interfering input from the subsequent "flanking" characters (Chun & Potter, 1995; Raymond, Shapiro, & Arnell, 1992).

The presence of too many object identities can even limit performance when observers are given ample time to inspect a display. In *crowding* effects, objects placed too close together in the visual periphery become difficult or impossible to identify. In Figure 10.1, fixate at the center cross and notice that the objects at the right have strangely jumbled identities. You can tell that the objects are roughly A's and H's, but the identities seem to float among the four letters (this example was adapted from Pelli, Palomares, & Majaj, 2004). This limit is not due to poor visual acuity in the periphery; when the object identities are homogeneous as on the left side, the letters are easy to distinguish. Instead, the important limiting factor is the number of distinct letter types that must be identified.

Interestingly, in the crowding example information about the letters is not lost, but instead the identities seem to become mixed together. Findings from tasks that examine visual *averaging* effects show that even if there is a limit to how well the information can be organized, the information can still be used to produce a summary of the otherwise jumbled features. In the averaging example, fixate your eyes on the cross in the right box and try to determine the orientation of the center patch in the left box. Even if you cannot tell the orientation of an individual patch, you may be able to judge the average orientation of the group as a whole (a slight counterclockwise tilt). Results from a similar task suggest that this average orientation is available from a crowded group, even if the identity of the center patch alone cannot be recovered independently (Parkes, Lund, Angelucci, Solomon, & Morgan, 2001). Other results suggest that a similar average representation is available even when objects are not crowded. If observers broadly select the group of circles at right, they are able to determine the average size of a set of circles (Ariely, 2001; Chong & Treisman, 2005; but see Myczek & Simons 2009 for evidence that this ability might instead be due to sampling of one or more circles). Later in the chapter this ability to extract average representations from crowded objects will prove to be an interesting qualification to the limits implied by crowding.

The jumble of features created by crowding may have the same roots as a phenomenon called the *illusory conjunction* effect. Even when a display is not crowded, if observers are convinced to broadly select multiple objects (in the case in the figure, by requiring a response related to the numbers at each edge of the display), and the display is briefly flashed, the colors of the center shapes can become jumbled. A display containing a red triangle, green circle, and blue diamond might be misreported as containing a red triangle, blue circle, and green diamond (Treisman & Schmidt, 1982).

In the examples listed so far, limitations on visual processing appear to slow down responses, impair accuracy, or jumble the features of objects. But these limits can cause even more striking effects, where objects are never seen at all. In the phenomenon of *inattentional blindness*, engaging an observer in a demanding task, such as identifying line lengths in a quickly flashed display (Mack & Rock, 1998), counting the bounces of a set of moving shapes (Most, Scholl, Clifford, & Simons, 2005), or counting the bounces of a ball by a team of basketball players (Neisser & Becklen, 1975; Simons & Chabris, 1999), can cause observers to miss salient events right in front of their eyes. These events include novel shapes or colors (Mack & Rock, 1998; Most et al., 2005), a change in an ongoing action (Neisser & Becklen, 1975), or even a gorilla walking across the scene (Simons & Chabris, 1999). But if an observer is allowed to watch displays without focusing resources on the secondary task, they easily see the salient events (see Most et al., 2005, for review).

*Object substitution masking* effects rely on an even more direct manipulation that prevents an object from reaching awareness. If a set of objects is briefly displayed but then one is quickly replaced by a set of dots, the replaced object usually cannot be identified, even though the dots do not directly overlap the object's location (Enns & Di Lollo, 1997). However, if the observer is told where the object will appear before the trial so that he or she can focus on only one location, the observer easily sees the object.

### Limits on Object Selection

Another set of tasks, shown on the right side of Figure 10.1, reveals limits on how we select objects and their locations over time, even when object identification is no longer necessary. Some reveal a limit on *multiple location selection*. In a typical task, observers complete a difficult visual search but are first precued to a set of potential target locations. The target will always appear at one of these locations, so it is beneficial to select them. Performance suggests that at least five (Burkell & Pylyshyn, 1997) and up to eight (Franconeri, Alvarez, & Enns, 2007) locations can be selected simultaneously, but no more. *Multiple object tracking* adds a second requirement. A set of objects are precued, and observers are asked to select them, but now the objects also move (Pylyshyn & Storm, 1988). This task is similar to the street magician's game of placing a valuable object under one of several quickly moving cups. With carefully constructed displays, observers can simultaneously track up to eight moving objects in this task (Alvarez & Franconeri, 2007).

In another limitation, there are strong effects of the number of objects when we are required to *enumerate* objects. There is little cost in response time when producing fast counts of sets of four or fewer objects, but when more than four objects are present, the number is not immediately available. Instead, response times suggest that for larger collections we need to count each object one at a time or settle for a rough estimate of the number (for review, see Dehaene & Changeux, 1993; Gallistel & Gelman, 1992). This limit of about four has been linked to the number of objects that we can simultaneously attend at once (see Trick & Pylyshyn, 1994, for review).

Another example reveals limits on selecting the location of an entire complex shape at once, which instead seems to require *tracing* an imaginary movement through the shape over time. Keeping your eyes fixed, determine whether the center dot is located inside or outside of the shape (Jolicoeur, Ullman, & Mackay, 1986; McCormick & Jolicoeur, 1991, 1994; Ullman, 1984; for similar examples). You may feel as though you trace a position through the maze (or "spread attention" through the maze; Houtkamp, Sprekreijse, & Roelfsma, 2003) and then see whether the dot can exit the shape. The feeling is similar for the second task, where you must decide whether the two dots are on the same or different lines. Making these decisions takes more time for longer or more complex lines.

Determining the relative *spatial relationships* among even objects is a highly resource-demanding process. When asked to find a pair of objects in a given configuration in a visual search display, adding additional pairs to the display slows response times significantly (Logan, 1994, 1995). A review of visual search results shows spatial relationship searches to be among the more robustly difficult (Wolfe, 1998). Spatial relationship judgments are even time consuming with very small numbers of objects in a display—when deciding the relationship between two letters, adding just one additional letter can slow performance (Carlson & Logan, 2001).

## Why Is Processing Limited?

All of the tasks mentioned so far reveal that visual processing becomes slower or less accurate when observers are asked to process too much information or too many objects. Why? A typical answer is that the visual system has only a finite *capacity* for processing, and as limited processing *resources* are spread more thinly with increased task *load*, speed and accuracy must be sacrificed (e.g., Broadbent, 1958; Kahneman, 1973; Norman & Bobrow, 1975). Words like capacity, resources, and load identify phenomena that demand explanation (but see Navon, 1984, for a critique of the concept of "processing resources").

The challenge is to isolate a more concrete and useful picture of the limiting factor. Here is a good test of any possible definition: Given an omnipotent set of tools to change the mind and brain, could you predict what you would alter within the visual system to increase the capacity or resource, or reduce the limits or load? When speaking only of processing "resources," it's not clear what the answer should be. The next section discusses a more concrete proposal that can provide an answer to this question.

Before attempting to identify these roots in the examples mentioned earlier, it is important to acknowledge that many of the examples in Figure 10.1 may not reflect resource limitations after all (see Luck & Vecera, 2002, for additional discussion). First, just because a task feels difficult, takes time to complete, or is not performed with high accuracy, does not mean that more "resources" would necessarily help. Indeed, resource-limited processing can be contrasted with *data-limited* processing, where performance is capped by properties like the quality of incoming information (Norman & Bobrow, 1975). When processing is data limited, lowering the "task load," for example, asking observers to process fewer objects at once, does not help. As an example, imagine showing the observer a brief display of five letters that have been degraded with visual noise, and asking them to repeat the letters verbally. If recall averaged four letters (80% accuracy), it would be tempting to conclude that performance

reflected limited processing resources. But it is also likely that performance was data limited, by a letter that happened to be degraded in such a way that made it impossible to discern (say, a barely visible bottom section of a B made it confusable with a P). The critical test would be to manipulate the number of letters processed at once. If performance is data limited, then the overall score should not depend on the number of letters, but instead on the average performance combined across performance for each letter by itself. That is, it should depend solely on how many of those tricky B's are in the display. In contrast, resource-limited processing predicts that processing more letters at once, per se, should lower performance.

One important data limitation is the position of the eyes. Because visual resolution is best at the fovea, dropping off rapidly in the periphery, the position of the fovea represents a critical potential data limit. For example, in a visual search task, adding more objects slows responses. But adding more objects also increases the amount of space needed for objects in a display, usually pushing the objects farther from fixation. Thus, less accurate or slower processing of larger sets of objects might be due to lower quality of information for those objects, and performance for even one solitary object might also be lower at these more distant locations. The need to move the eyes in a task can even create set size effects that mimic a resource limit (Maioli, Beaglio, Siri, Sosta, & Cappa, 2001).

Another factor that can mimic a resource limit, but could be considered a data limit, is called decision noise. Consider the increase of response times with more distractors in visual search tasks, which is typically taken to reflect processing limitations. But these costs might occur even if every object in the display were identified simultaneously and independently. Because there is always noise in the visual system, there is always a chance that any one object will be recognized incorrectly (e.g., a distractor being mistaken as a target). Adding more objects to a display would therefore multiply the chances of at least one distractor being mistaken for the target, because there is a greater chance of at least one distractor having a sufficiently noisy representation (Duncan, 1980; Palmer, 1994).

One way to distinguish these decision limits from other resource limits is by presenting search objects independently over time instead of simultaneously. Decision limitations predict the same increasing difficulty with more distractors, because the same maximally noisy distractor representation should be present within N distractors presented either independently or simultaneously (Duncan, 1980; see Pashler, 1998 for discussion). Resource limitations predict that independent presentation will eliminate the costs from additional objects, resulting in ceiling performance. This manipulation has shown that in many visual search tasks the additional distractor costs claimed to reflect resource limits could actually be better explained by decision noise (Huang & Pashler, 2005; Palmer, 1994, 1995). Note that the mechanisms for reducing the effects of decision noise, reducing the number of total objects inspected, or allowing more time to accumulate more information about each object could be considered resource limited. But it seems more appropriate to think of the visual system making mistakes on occasion, and when asking for a greater number of objects in a shorter amount of time, the odds of at least one troublesome mistake grow, even though processing of any individual object is no less thorough.

There are also strategic factors that can create illusory performance limitations. For example, in cueing tasks, detection or discrimination performance is better for cued locations, suggesting that processing was faster or more accurate when a limited resource could be selectively applied to the cued location. But cueing effects have also been explained by a set of strategy changes, such as altering the criterion for responding to information at cued locations, which are usually more likely to contain the target, or more heavily weighting information from cued locations. Some have even concluded that no cueing data exist that demonstrate resource limits outside of these strategic biases (Shiu & Pashler, 1994; Pashler, 1998; but see Luck & Thomas, 1999).

Finally, it should be noted that the limits described here are not the only limiting factors within visual cognition. First, there are limits not just in online perception but in short-term memory for object identities and locations. Storing visual information is limited by memory storage capacity, which appears to be limited to about four objects in many cases (Luck & Vogel, 1997; Zhang & Luck, 2008; but see Hollingworth, 2006). This might also constitute competition for representation, though in a different medium (e.g., feature space) than the examples listed in Figure 10.1. There may also be a limit to the process that compares information in memory to the information in the present view (Mitroff, Simons, & Levin, 2004). Even when memory limits are removed from change detection

tasks by presenting both displays simultaneously, finding changes is slow and difficult, suggesting that the comparison process is highly limited (Scott-Brown, Baker, & Orbach, 2001). There are limits at processing levels beyond vision, such as response selection (for review, see Pashler, 1998) that may limit abilities to complete tasks involving multiple objects, even when the actual processing of those objects does not require visual "resources."

What does this list of potentially illusory resource limitations mean for the examples in Figure 10.1? It is controversial whether cueing reflects resource limitations at all. Many search tasks also seem suspect, though there is general agreement that many types of visual search are resource limited (Huang & Pashler, 2005; Palmer, 1994; Wolfe et al., 2008). But all of the other limits found using the tasks listed in Figure 10.1 seem fairly immune from these critiques. So for the remaining examples, when observers are asked to process too much information at once, what is the resource that causes responses to slow, accuracy to drop, or awareness to fail? A general principle that seems to fit many examples is competition for representation within the visual system.

## Competition for Representation

The first case of competition is for object recognition. Object recognition is handled primarily by the ventral stream of the visual system. This stream starts in primary visual cortex (V1), where networks filter incoming information by relatively simple properties like orientation or contrast polarity. Processing moves to subsequent areas that process more complex features (e.g., V4). The stream ends in inferior temporal (IT) cortex, where more sophisticated features such as shape are processed (see Grill-Spector & Malach, 2004 for review). In addition to increasing complexity of processing, moving farther along the ventral stream also greatly increases the area of the visual world that any cell responds to. In V1 this "receptive field" is less than 1 degree wide, but it grows to occupy large portions of the visual field by IT cortex, even whole visual hemifields (Desimone & Ungerleider, 1989).

Imagine placing an object in front of an observer, say the letter A. The small receptive fields of neurons in V1 might represent the presence of edges and their orientations, and the larger fields midstream might represent more complex junctions of edges, while the largest fields of IT cortex might represent the letters as wholes, or close to it (there is evidence for specialized areas for letter and word processing, but for the moment we can assume IT cortex). At each stage neurons encode a specific set of features, and the more clearly they signal that those features are present (and not others), the more confidence the system contains about which letter is present. If additional features that are not associated with the letter A are present, that signal will be exposed to increased noise (Tsotsos, 1990).

For example, imagine adding an H to the display as well (as in the crowding example in Fig. 10.1). In V1, the small receptive fields would separately encode the features of each object, and there would initially be no competition among them. But as the features of both objects travel up the ventral stream, at some point features from both objects will enter the same larger receptive field. If the neuron responded highly to horizontal symmetry or the presence of line intersections, then the signal from the A would remain high. But if the neuron responded to vertical symmetry or letter identity, the signal available that an A was present would be decreased due to the competition between the dueling properties. This competition would continue at higher areas of the ventral stream, which in turn feed back to lower areas in an attempt to clarify the conflict toward a winner.

In summary, if a neuron prefers a certain stimulus, and a nonpreferred object is added to its receptive field, that neuron's responses are altered toward the response it would give for the nonpreferred object (Luck, Chelazzi, Hillyard, & Desimone, 1997; Moran & Desimone, 1985; Reynolds & Desimone, 2003). While these neural recordings are only typically possible in monkeys, a similar effect can also be seen in humans using functional magnetic resonance imaging (fMRI). When shown pictures of objects close together on a display, observers showed lower activation in mid and late ventral stream areas (V4, IT cortex) when the pictures were shown simultaneously relative to being shown sequentially (Kastner, DeWeerd, Desimone, & Ungerleider, 1998). This result is consistent with the idea that in the simultaneous condition the pictures compete with each other, lowering the overall activation. The effects were smaller when the pictures were moved farther from each other, which should decrease the likelihood that they would fall within the same receptive fields. The effects were also smaller in earlier visual areas (V1), where receptive fields should be too small to allow competition between the pictures.

In this case of competition we assumed that adding more objects added noise, such that information would be lost. But in many other cases adding more objects or features might add activation that does not strongly spatially overlap across the receptive fields of neurons or across the types of features that those neurons respond to (Fujita, Tanaka, Ito, & Cheng, 1992; Komatsu & Ideura, 1993; Treisman & Gelade, 1980). If so, then all or most of the information could still be represented. But it could create a related case of competition for representation, by producing a "binding" problem. If the features of many objects are encoded simultaneously, and multiple objects are present within the same receptive fields, it may not be clear which features should be associated with each object (Luck, Girelli, McDermott, & Ford, 1997; Reynolds & Desimone, 2003; Treisman, 1996).

For example, some visual search data suggest that if a target is designated as an object that contains a set of features (e.g., a gray vertical line) that are also present individually in distractors (e.g., gray horizontals and black verticals), the task is relatively difficult, even though search for any feature alone is easy and immediate (Treisman & Gelade, 1980). The difficulty of these "conjunction searches" may be due to the ambiguity that would arise in determining whether all features were present on any one object (but see McLeod, Driver, & Crisp, 1988; VanRullen, 2009; and Wolfe, 1994, for evidence that many feature combinations that seem like they should produce binding errors can still lead to efficient search). Another case of this binding problem might be seen in the illusory conjunction effect depicted in Figure 10.1. The brief presentation of the display leads to too many features of too many objects being encoded at once, causing confusion about which features belong to which objects. In summary, this type of competition is not for representation alone, but for a type of representation that allows the features of any one object to remain tied together.

How does the visual system resolve these types of competition for representation? One strategy appears to be to reduce competition by suppression of representations of irrelevant information, or heightening representations of relevant information, allowing it to "win" the competition and inhibit competing possible conclusions. Biasing the competition in this way can help the relevant information to outweigh or exclude irrelevant information, and increase the signal from relevant objects (Desimone & Duncan, 1985; Moran & Desimone, 1985; Luck, Girelli, McDermott, & Ford, 1997; Reynolds & Desimone, 1999; Serences & Yantis,

2006). It would be impossible to isolate every bit of relevant information, but the visual system has several tools available that allow selection of types of incoming information that should be *correlated* with the relevant stimuli.

One tool is the selection of areas of the visual field that contain features relevant to the current task, such as certain colors, luminances, spatial frequencies, types or directions of motion, or orientations (see Wolfe & Horowitz, 2004 for a sample list). For example, making a certain color disambiguate relevant information within a display containing harmful irrelevant information can bias activity in the ventral stream toward objects with that color, according to direct neural recordings (Chelazzi et al., 1998), as well as behavioral (Saenz, Buracas, & Boynton, 2003) and electrophysiological (Anderson, Hillyard, & Muller, 2008) studies using human observers. Another tool is the selection of single locations or objects (Mozer & Vecera, 2005; Scholl, 2001) or multiple locations or objects (Awh & Pashler, 2001; Franconeri et al., 2007). Selection can be based either on top-down factors like the observer's current goals (Folk, Remington, & Johnston, 1992) or default bottom-up factors like stimulus salience (Franconeri, Simons, & Junge, 2004; Itti & Koch, 2001).

Selection can bias competition in powerful ways. One set of studies isolated neurons in V4 that produced different responses for preferred and nonpreferred stimuli. As mentioned earlier, when the preferred stimulus was in the neuron's receptive field, adding the nonpreferred stimulus decreased responses. But giving the monkey an incentive to select the location of the preferred stimulus virtually eliminated this decrease (Reynolds, Chelazzi, & Desimone, 1999). Likewise, selecting the nonpreferred stimulus drove the neuron to respond as if it were the only object in the field as well. A set of similar studies additionally showed that when the nonpreferred stimulus was placed outside of the receptive field of the recorded V4 neuron, selection effects were minimal (Luck, Chelazzi et al., 1997; Moran & Desimone, 1985), suggesting that there are few effects of selection when there is no competition to resolve. As another example of the role of selection in resolving competition, in the Kastner et al. (1998) study discussed earlier, simultaneous presentation of pictures caused competition that lowered overall responses in late ventral stream areas. But asking observers to attend to the location of the pictures reduced the suppressive effect of the other pictures.

Later sections of this chapter argue that competition for representation can cause most or all of the effects depicted in Figure 10.1. We start by dividing the types of limits according to a neurophysiologically inspired division between the ventral visual stream (discussed earlier), which is proposed to focus on object identity processing, and the dorsal visual stream, which is proposed to focus on processing of spatial and action-related properties (Ettlinger, 1990; Goodale & Milner, 1992; Mishkin & Ungerleider, 1982), though many argue that this division is not always clear (Cardoso-Leite & Gorea, 2010; Franz, Gegenfurtner, Bulthoff, & Fahle, 2000). The following section applies competition for representation within the ventral stream to the examples on the left side of Figure 10.1, and the section on "Competition for Representation of Selection Locations in the Dorsal Stream" applies competition for representation in the dorsal stream to the examples on the right side of Figure 10.1.

## Competition for Representation of Object Identity in the Ventral Stream

For cueing, it is not clear that the competition account could explain the advantage for the cued location, because there is no competing information from other stimuli that would need to be suppressed. However, as discussed in the section on "Why Is Processing Limited?" there is debate over whether cueing effects can be classified as reflecting resource limitations in the first place.

For visual search, there should be competition for representation among targets and distractors, especially when their features are more similar (Duncan & Humphreys, 1989). This should be especially true when objects are placed close together, which should make competition more likely (Motter & Simoni, 2007). Indeed, for conjunction searches where competition should be expected to be high due to binding errors, spacing objects further apart improves performance (Cohen & Ivry, 1991). This competition could be resolved by selecting single objects or handfuls of objects at once, either by their locations or features (see Wolfe, 1994 for review).

Flanker interference and global interference could be described as failures of selection to prevent competition. For the flanker effect, the amount of interference can be reduced by moving the flankers farther from the target, a manipulation that should enhance an observer's ability to select only the target for representation. Note that it is also possible that both target and flankers are processed completely and independently through the ventral stream, and only at the stage of response selection is there competition for control of action (Deutsch & Deutsch, 1963). However, it is difficult for this response selection account to explain effects of spacing between the letters. Global interference could also be due to a failure of selection, due to a default bias toward selecting larger objects or lower spatial frequencies (Navon, 1977; but see Rijpkema, van Aalderen, Schwarzbach, & Verstraten, 2007, for important limitations).

The attentional blink has also been explained in terms of selection that filters incoming information in order to reduce competition among them (DiLollo, Kawahara, Ghorashi, & Enns, 2005; Olivers, van der Stigchel, & Hulleman, 2007).[1] In the example in Figure 10.1, observers should have a selection "setting" for letters. As soon as the first letter ("A") appears, its identity begins to be processed by selecting that letter's location. But as the next character (a digit) appears, it is processed to some degree, which causes the selection "setting" to involuntarily switch over to a setting for "digits," causing the subsequent letter ("E") to be inhibited, and not reported. At first glance, this story sounds a bit post hoc, but it has impressive supporting data. Within the series of the first letter, intervening digit, and second letter, if the intervening digit is changed to a letter, the "blink effect" disappears and the observer can report *all three* letters with the same level of accuracy, consistent with the idea that the digit had reset the observer's selection settings. In contrast, a "resource" version of the blink account would predict that changing the intervening digit to a letter should have made the task more difficult.

For crowding, if objects are placed too closely to one another, such that their representations do not overlap at early ventral areas (allowing processing of basic features), but do compete at late ventral areas (creating ambiguity about which objects are present), the competition account could predict that the local features of objects would be accessible, but the exact identities and their bindings would be ambiguous (Pelli et al., 2004). Adding salient features that allow selection of one object reduces this crowding effect (Chakravarthi & Cavanagh, 2007). Straddling two crowded objects across the visual hemifield boundary also reduces crowding, presumably because high-level receptive fields are usually restricted to a single hemifield, preventing multiple objects from falling into the same receptive field (Chakravarthi & Cavanagh, 2009; Liu, Jiang, Sun, & He, 2009; Torralbo & Beck, 2008).

Having basic features represented at lower levels of the ventral stream, even without proper binding of features to specific objects at higher levels, may still provide some information about a set of crowded objects. The ability to average orientation and size in Figure 10.1 ("Averaging" panel) may reflect an ability to still combine these jumbled features in a useful way. When objects cannot be isolated within a receptive field, this coarser and more global representation may be the only one available (Choo & Franconeri, 2010; Parkes et al., 2001; see Balas, Nakano, & Rosenholtz, 2009 for a related idea). But when isolation of objects is possible, as in the size averaging example in Figure 10.1, broad selection of the space around an entire collection may also make this global representation available in the same way, by activating the features (e.g., size) of all circles at once (Chong & Treisman, 2005).

A similar global jumble may occur for illusory conjunctions. Because the task requires identification of two numbers flanking the shapes, the scope of selection is necessarily broad, encompassing all of the shapes. Simultaneous encoding of all features of all shapes would lead to precise and noncompetitive representations of their features at early stages of the ventral stream, but the broader receptive fields at higher areas would create ambiguity about the relative bindings of the features to each object (Reynolds & Desimone, 1999). Consistent with this idea, moving the objects closer together, which should make them more likely to fall in the same receptive fields, makes reports of illusory conjunctions more frequent (Cohen & Ivry, 1989; Sohn, Liederman, & Reisnity, 1996). Deficits in selection appear to make this illusion occur even outside of briefly flashed displays. For patients with damage to parietal areas known to participate in the control of visual selection, severe damage has led one patient to a state of enduring experiences of illusory conjunctions in everyday life (Robertson, Treisman, Friedman-Hill, & Grabowecky, 1997).

Inattentional blindness seems to be due more to the power of selection than competition per se. In one classic demonstration, observers were asked to count the basketball passes among a team in white shirts, who were interleaved with a team in black shirts, and subsequently missed a gorilla walking through the game (Simons & Chabris, 1999; see Most et al., 2005, for systematic variations using simpler displays). This result is consistent with selection of locations containing white in order to isolate the bounces made only by that team, leading to amplification of anything white in the display,

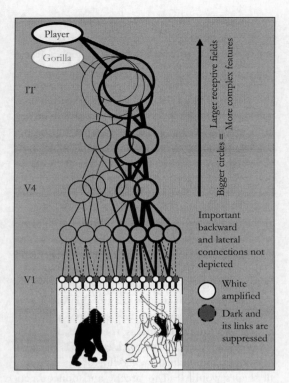

**Figure 10.2** An example of how competition for representation could explain missing a gorilla walking through a complex scene. See text for explanation.

Labels in figure: Player, Gorilla, IT, V4, V1. "Bigger circles = Larger receptive fields = More complex features". "Important backward and lateral connections not depicted". "White amplified". "Dark and its links are suppressed".

relative to suppression of anything black in the display, including the gorilla. Figure 10.2 depicts this process in a cartoon model of the ventral visual system (for clarity, many aspects of the diagram are abstracted, including the scale of receptive fields, the network creating the feature selection, the processing level of competition reduction, and a lack of lateral and backward connections). Two initial sets of feature detectors encode visual information for white and black areas (or contrast polarities) of the scene, and the observer's top-down goal leads to suppression of information from the black detectors (note that the layout of the example scene would allow equally good selection by location, but in the Simons & Chabris 1999 example the gorilla's walking path was interleaved among with the players). This suppression leads the information from the white detectors to win the competition for representation within progressively larger receptive fields. This lack of representation of the gorilla, at least at the highest levels that lead to an explicit memory (Wolfe, 1999), means that the observer fails to notice the gorilla at all.

Object substitution masking is an important example, because it suggests that competition need

not occur for different objects across space, but can also occur for two objects over time. Object substitution appears to occur when a first wave of visual information containing the target object is overwritten by a second wave containing the mask (see Enns, 2004 for review), such that the mask dots compete for representation with the original objects (and usually win) within a similar set of receptive fields. This competition can be biased toward the original object by cueing the location of the object that will be masked, allowing the selection mechanism to protect the original representation.

## Competition for Representation of Selection Locations in the Dorsal Stream

Because these limits on the *right* side of Figure 10.1 do not involve object identification (at least for the aspect of the task that is limited), these limits should not reflect competition for representation within the ventral stream. Instead, they may reflect a similar type of competition in the dorsal stream (Franconeri et al., 2007). Specifically, areas within this stream, notably the lateral intraparietal area (Gottlieb, 2007; Serences & Yantis, 2007) or inferior intraparietal sulcus (Todd & Marois, 2004; Xu & Chun, 2009), may represent currently selected locations in the visual field (Pylyshyn, 1989, 1994). When locations are selected in a complex display, there is a minimum size of a given selection region (Intrilligator & Cavanagh, 2001). That is, in a computer's display, you cannot choose to select a single pixel. Instead, the selection region size (which becomes larger in the periphery) is at minimum roughly one-third the distance of the selected location from fixation (Intrilligator & Cavanagh, 2001). Figure 10.3 depicts sample selection regions for the visual quadrant in panel one (not draw to exact scale), assuming fixation at the center of the figure. In a task requiring selection of multiple relevant "target" locations interleaved with distractor locations, moving locations closer together would cause these selection regions to begin to involuntarily include distractor locations (Franconeri et al., 2007).

To make mattes worse, selection regions are also known to have suppressive surrounds (Bachall & Kowler, 1999; Hopf et al., 2006; Tsotsos, Culhane, Wai, Davis, & Nuflo, 1995), possibly to maximize the amplification of selected information relative to nearby information that might create the most competition within the same receptive fields. As selection regions become closer, these suppressive surrounds would begin to overlap the selection

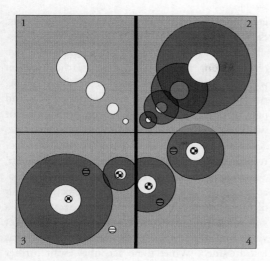

**Figure 10.3** Illustration of how competition for representation might explain a limit on the number of locations that can be selected, or the number of objects that can be tracked. See text for explanation.

regions (Franconeri, Jonathan, & Scimeca, 2010; Franconeri, Lin, Pylyshyn, Fisher, & Enns, 2008; Shim, Alvarez, & Jiang, 2008). The second panel of Figure 10.3 simulates this effect. Both of these effects would be worse in the periphery, where selection regions and their associated suppressive surrounds would be larger. The third panel of Figure 10.3 shows how two target locations (checkered circles) could be selected while excluding two distractor locations (striped circles). The fourth panel illustrates how inhibitory surrounds might not cross the vertical visual hemifield boundary, and it might only partially cross the horizontal boundary (Bachall & Kowler, 1999; Cave & Zimmerman, 1997), potentially explaining better performance in some tasks when objects are separated by these boundaries (Alvarez & Cavanagh, 2005; Carlson, Alvarez, & Cavanagh, 2007; Downing & Pinker, 1985). The presence of these boundaries might explain why performance on multiple location selection and multiple-object tracking tasks is limited to about eight objects—it is plausible that within each of the four quadrants, up to two locations or objects can be reliably selected without creating levels of competition that would lead to the loss of an object.

If the limiting factor is competition for representation within a spatial map, we can make a prediction—spacing the objects farther apart should decrease competition and improve performance. Indeed, although both were initially thought to be limited to 4–5 locations or objects (Burkell & Pylyshyn, 1997; Pylyshyn & Storm, 1988), more

recent work shows that these limits can be raised, by keeping the locations or objects as far apart as possible. Moving the objects closer can reduce either limit to 1–2, and moving them farther apart can increase the limit to 8–9 (Alvarez & Franconeri, 2007; Franconeri, Alvarez, & Enns, 2008).

So the limit on selecting multiple locations of moving objects can also be considered competition for representation, this time competing for representation of selection regions with minimum sizes, within the limits of the visual field. But one other effect seems to be inconsistent with this spatially modulated competition as the sole resource in these tasks. When performing a multiple-object tracking task, it is possible to track eight objects, but only when they move very slowly (Alvarez & Franconeri, 2007). When they move faster, performance drops unless the tracking load is reduced, and there are fast speeds at which only one object can be tracked. At first glance it is difficult to explain this limit with competition, because the same number of objects is present in the visual field for slow and fast speeds. There may be another unspecified resource that is drained when objects move faster, requiring a lower number of tracked targets to maintain the same levels of accuracy. But two recent studies suggest that competition over space can explain the speed effects as well. As objects move faster, they cover more distance during a trial (which typically lasts about 5–8 seconds). More distance covered means more opportunity to come too close to other objects, creating competitive interactions that can lead to lower performance. Lowering the number of tracked targets can offset this problem, by lowering the number of these interactions in the first place. This account correctly predicts that increasing the speed of the moving objects does not change performance,[2] as long as it is done in way that does not change the number of object interactions (Franconeri et al., 2008, 2010). These results allow competition for representation to explain the limits in multiple-object tracking tasks.

For rapid counting, the limit on how many objects can be quickly counted (about 4–5) might be similar to the limit on multiple-object selection. The "magic number" might be four instead of eight, because of higher requirements for a precise selection region for the counting process relative to the selection or tracking processes. The requirements of the counting task may require especially clear and noncompetitive selection regions for each object, resulting in a maximum of one object per quadrant. However, there are other plausible explanations for this fast-counting effect. These explanations include a data-limited cap on our ability to estimate number from correlates of number, such as bumps on a primitive segmentation map, spatial frequency, or display density (Franconeri, Bemis, & Alvarez, 2009; Durgin, 1995). The precision limit of this ability may be enough to tell four from five, but not five from six (Gallistel & Gelman, 1992). Or we might be able to recognize number within small collections according to the stereotypical shapes that they create (1 object is a dot, 2 a line, 3 a triangle, 4 a square or diamond). Larger numbers do not signal prototypical shapes and therefore would not produce efficient performance (Logan & Zbrodoff, 2003; Mandler & Shebo, 1982; Palmeri, 1997; Peterson & Simon, 2000). Because the competition account makes clear predictions about object spacing, there is an experiment that should dissociate these predictions. The competition account predicts that moving the collection of objects into the periphery, or simply one side of the visual field, should increase competition and therefore decrease counting accuracy for small collections.

For tracing, the competition account would state that when a shape becomes sufficiently complex, it is not possible to select multiple areas of that shape with sufficient precision (due to the competition) to differentiate that shape from another interleaved shape. Simplifying the shape, or moving the shape across more of the visual field in ways that decrease competition (e.g., especially across the visual hemifields), should boost performance. Otherwise, there is a salient impression that the task is completed by moving a single mental "spotlight" (which does not incur competition) along the shape or line, and waiting to see where it ends up (Cavanagh, 2004; Jolicoeur et al., 1986; McCormick & Jolicoeur, 1991, 1994; Ullman, 1984; see Houtkamp et al., 2003 for a different explanation).

The last example in Figure 10.1 is spatial relationship perception. This example is tentatively included as a "dorsal" limit, because there is little work exploring the mechanism that allows us to judge the relative locations of a pair of objects. But one strong possibility is that, like in the example of tracing, the position of the locus of selection itself is critical in coding interobject structure. The window of selection might form the "reference frame" for a relationship judgment (Logan, 1995), such that the "left" object is not really on the left of the other object, but on the left of the selection window encompassing both objects (Biederman, Lescroart, & Hayworth, 2007). This conclusion is not possible unless the selection window spans the two objects being judged, and therefore the selection window itself is a limited visual processing resource. Attempting to place a second window on a second pair of objects would lead to competition about which object is in which window and on which side. A second possibility is that the window of selection only covers one object at a time (Franconeri, Scimeca, Roth, Helseth, & Kahn, 2012). Instead, as selection moves from object to object, the path of the selection window over time is recorded as a vector, allowing the conclusion that the last object viewed is, for example, on the right of whatever was last attended. While these accounts await further empirical investigation, both rely on selection itself as a limited resource.

## Conclusions

Competition for representation appears to be a fundamental resource limit for the visual system. It is worth taking a moment to see whether this concept succeeds in unpacking visual "resources" into more concrete terms. Is "competition" just a rephrasing of words like "resource" or "capacity"? Have we merely passed the explanatory buck to the neural level? Competition does explain performance limits across a diverse set of tasks, and more important, it makes surprising and validated predictions about factors that should influence competition, such as object spacing. A generic resource account would have difficulty explaining why identification or multiple location selection improves when densely spaced displays are given more elbow room.

One test for a good account of visual resources mentioned at the start of the chapter is whether one would know what to change about the visual system to increase the resource. For the competition account, it would be more neurons and tighter receptive fields, especially at high-level areas in the ventral stream that typically have the largest fields. So why not do this? Major qualitative changes to a cognitive system (e.g., the advent of recursive processing) might take ages to evolve, but it would seem simple to make quantitative changes by adding more neurons or tightening receptive field sizes. It is possible that this option is limited by physical resource limits like oxygen, glucose, or space in the skull. Too many neurons or connections might be needed to make these changes at the highest level networks in the ventral stream, which are responsible for representing many different types and combinations of features (Luck & Vecera, 2002). Another likely possibility is that large receptive fields in high-level ventral areas serve an important purpose, reflecting an architecture designed to recognize objects regardless of their size or position on the retina (Lueschow, Miller, & Desimone, 1994). This design should allow the ventral stream to reuse learned patterns across widely varied conditions. Finally, it is possible that increases in visual resources (e.g., tightening receptive field sizes) might not result in processing improvements, because of other limitations on how the visual system's output is used by broader cognitive systems. More detailed information might make it harder to see the forest through trees when learning, notice patterns or correlations, or generate a fast action in response to the world.

Finally, the resource limits of our visual system may cause lower performance in tasks built for psychology labs, but in the natural world several other mechanisms may help us avoid reaching these limits. Even if information is lost through competition, we may still have summary information about the gist or category of a scene (Oliva & Torralba, 2005), the texture or features of objects (Ariely, 2001), or the layout of objects in an environment (Franconeri et al., 2009). When resource limits do become salient, we can guide selection toward information most relevant to our goals (Wolfe & Horowitz, 2004), and selection can be automatically captured by information that is likely to require urgent action (Franconeri & Simons, 2003; Yantis & Hillstron, 1994). Together, such mechanisms may support our perception of an outside world where visual information is fully processed and readily available, without a feeling that we expend resources for the vast majority of everyday visual tasks.

## Acknowledgments

I thank the following people for their helpful comments on this chapter: George Alvarez, Heeyoung Choo, Michael Gleicher, Brian Levinthal, Daniel Reisberg, and Jeremy Wolfe.

## Notes

1. This explanation is only part of the larger picture of the resource limitations that underlie the attentional blink effect, which is likely due to a larger set of processing bottlenecks at various stages, including object selection, identification, and memory (see Dux & Marois, 2009, for review).

2. More precisely, increased speed *could* impair performance, just not in a resource-limited way that is relevant for the present argument (e.g., the objects might become blurry). See Franconeri, Jonathan, and Scimeca (2010) for discussion.

## References

Alvarez, G. A., & Cavanagh, P. (2005). Independent resources for attentional tracking in the left and right visual hemifields. *Psychological Science, 16*(8), 637–643.

Alvarez, G. A., & Franconeri, S. L. (2007). How many objects can you track? Evidence for a resource-limited tracking mechanism. *Journal of Vision, 7*(13), 1–10.

Ariely, D. (2001). Seeing sets: Representation by statistical properties. *Psychological Science, 12*(2), 157–162.

Awh, E., & Pashler, H. (2000). Evidence for split attentional foci. *Journal of Experimental Psychology: Human Perception and Performance, 26*, 834–846.

Bachall, D. O., & Kowler, E. (1999). Attentional interference at small spatial separations. *Vision Research, 39*, 71–86.

Balas, B., Nakano, L., & Rosenholtz, R. (2009). A summary-statistic representation in peripheral vision explains visual crowding. *Journal of Vision, 9*(12), 13.1–18.

Biederman, I., Lescroart, M., & Hayworth, K. (2007). Sensitivity to object-centered relations in LOC [Abstract]. *Journal of Vision, 7*(9), 1030.

Broadbent, D. (1958). *Perception and communication.* London: Pergamon Press.

Burkell, J. A., & Pylyshyn, Z. W. (1997). Searching through subsets: A test of the visual indexing hypothesis. *Spatial Vision, 11*, 225–258.

Cardoso-Leite, P., & Gorea, A. (2010). On the perceptual/motor dissociation: A review of concepts, theory, experimental paradigms and data interpretations. *Seeing and Perceiving, 23*(2), 89–151.

Carlson, T. A., Alvarez, G. A., & Cavanagh, P. C. (2007). Quadrantic deficit reveals anatomical constraints on selection. *Proceedings of the National Academy of Sciences USA, 104*(33), 13496–13500.

Carlson, L. A., &Logan, G. D. (2001). Using spatial terms to select an object. *Memory and Cognition, 29*, 883–892.

Cavanagh, P. (2004). Attention routines and the architecture of selection. In M. Posner (Ed.), *Cognitive neuroscience of attention (pp. 13–28).* New York: Guilford Press.

Cave, K. R., & Zimmerman, J. M. (1997). Flexibility in spatial attention before and after practice. *Psychological Science, 8*, 399–403.

Chajut, E., Schupak, A., & Algom, D. (2009). Are spatial and dimensional attention separate? Evidence from Posner, Stroop, and Eriksen tasks. *Memory and Cognition, 37*(6), 924–934.

Chakravarthi, R., & Cavanagh, P. (2007). Temporal properties of the polarity advantage effect in crowding. *Journal of Vision, 7*(2),11.1–13

Chakravarthi, R., & Cavanagh, C. (2009). Bilateral field advantage in visual crowding. *Vision Research, 49*, 1638–1646.

Chelazzi, L., Duncan, J., Miller, E. K., & Desimone, R. (1998). Responses of neurons in inferior temporal cortex during memory-guided visual search. *Journal of Neurophysiology, 80*, 2918–2940.

Chong S. C., & Treisman, A. (2005). Attentional spread in the statistical processing of visual displays. *Perception and Psychophysics, 67*(1), 1–13.

Choo, H. Y., & Franconeri, S. L. (2010). Visual size averaging of objects unavailable to conscious awareness. *Attention, Perception, and Psychophysics, 72*(1), 86–99.

Chun, M. M., & Potter, M. C. (1995). A two-stage model for multiple target detection in rapid serial visual presentation.

*Journal of Experimental Psychology: Human Perception and Performance, 21*, 109–127.

Cohen, A., & Ivry, R. (1989). Illusory conjunctions inside and outside the focus of attention. *Journal of Experimental Psychology: Human Perception and Performance, 15*, 650–663.

Cohen, A., & Ivry, R. (1991). Density effects in conjunction search: Evidence for a coarse location mechanism of feature integration. *Journal of Experimental Psychology: Human Perception and Performance, 17*, 891–901.

Dehaene, S., & Changeux, J.-P. (2007). Development of elementary numerical abilities: A neuronal model. *Journal of Cognitive Neuroscience, 5*, 390–407.

Desimone, R., & Duncan, J. (1995). Neural mechanisms of selective visual attention. *Annual Review of Neuroscience, 18*, 193–222.

Deutsch, J., & Deutsch, D. (1963). Attention: Some theoretical considerations. *Psychological Review, 70*, 80–90.

Di Lollo, V., Kawahara, J., Ghorashi, S. M., & Enns, J. T. (2005). The attentional blink: Resource limitation or temporary loss of control? *Psychological Research, 69*, 191–200.

Downing, C. J., & Pinker, S. (1985). The spatial structure of visual attention. In M. Posner & O. Martin (Eds.), *Attention and performance XI* (pp. 171–187). Hillsdale, NJ: Erlbaum.

Duncan, J. (1980). The demonstration of capacity limitation. *Cognitive Psychology, 12*, 75–96.

Duncan, J., & Humphreys, G. W . (1989). Visual search and stimulus similarity. *Psychological Review, 96*, 433–58

Durgin, F. H. (1995). Texture density adaptation and the perceived numerosity and density of texture. *Journal of Experimental Psychology: Human Perception and Performance, 21*, 149–169.

Dux, P. E., & Marois, R. (2009). The attentional blink: A review of data and theory. *Attention, Perception and Psychophysics, 71*, 1683–1700.

Enns, J. T. (2004). Object substitution and its relation to other forms of visual masking. *Vision Research, 44*, 1321–1331.

Enns, J. T., & Di Lollo, V. (1997). Object substitution: A new form of visual masking in unattended visual locations. *Psychological Science, 8*(2), 135–139.

Ettlinger, G. (1990). "Object vision" and "spatial vision": The neuropsychological evidence for the distinction. *Cortex, 26*(3), 319–41.

Folk, C. L., Remington, R. W., & Johnston, J. C. (1992). Involuntary covert orienting is contingent on attentional control settings. *Journal of Experimental Psychology: Human Perception and Performance, 18*, 1030–1044.

Franconeri, S. L., Alvarez, G. A., & Enns, J. T. (2007). How many locations can you select? *Journal of Experimental Psychology: Human Perception and Performance, 33*(5), 1003–1012.

Franconeri, S. L., Bemis, D. K., & Alvarez, G. A. (2009). Number estimation relies on a set of segmented objects. *Cognition, 113*, 1–13.

Franconeri, S. L., Jonathan, S., & Scimeca, J. M. (2010). Tracking multiple objects is limited only by object spacing, not speed, time, or capacity. *Psychological Science, 21*(7), 920–925.

Franconeri, S. L., Lin, J., Pylyshyn, Z. W., Fisher, B., & Enns, J. T. (2008). Multiple object tracking is limited by crowding, but not speed. *Psychonomic Bulletin and Review, 15*(4), 802–808.

Franconeri, S. L., Scimeca, J. M., Roth, J. C., Helseth, S. A., & Kahn, L. (2011). Flexible visual processing of spatial relationships. *Cognition, 122*, 210–227.

Franconeri, S. L., & Simons, D. J. (2003). Moving and looming stimuli capture attention. *Perception and Psychophysics, 65*(7), 999–1010.

Franconeri, S. L., Simons, D. J., & Junge, J. A. (2004). Searching for stimulus-driven shifts of attention. *Psychonomic Bulletin and Review, 11*(5), 876–881.

Franz, V. H., Gegenfurtner, K. R., Bülthoff, H. H., & Fahle, M. (2000). Grasping visual illusions: No evidence for a dissociation between perception and action. *Psychological Science, 11*(1): 20–25.

Fujita, I., Tanaka, K., Ito, M., & Cheng, K. (1992). Columns for visual features of objects in monkey inferotemporal cortex. *Nature, 360*, 343–346.

Gallistel, C. R., & Gelman, R. (1992). Preverbal and verbal counting and computation. *Cognition, 44*, 43–74.

Goodale, M. A., & Milner, A. D. (1992). Separate visual pathways for perception and action. *Trends in Neuroscience, 15*(1), 20–25.

Gottlieb, J. (2007). From thought to action: The parietal cortex as a bridge between perception, action, and cognition. *Neuron, 53*, 9–16

Grill-Spector, K., & Malach, R. (2004). The human visual cortex. *Annual Reviews Neuroscience, 27*, 649–677.

Hollingworth, A. (2006). Visual memory for natural scenes: Evidence from change detection and visual search. *Visual Cognition, 14*, 781–807.

Hopf, J. M., Boehler, C. N., Luck, S. J., Tsotsos, J. K., Heinze, H. J., & Schoenfeld, A. M. (2006). Direct neurophysiological evidence for spatial suppression surrounding the focus of attention in vision. *Proceedings of the National Academy of Sciences USA, 103*, 1053–1058.

Houtkamp, R., Sprekreijse, H., & Roelfsma, P. R. (2003). A gradual spread of attention during mental curve tracing. *Perception and Psychophysics, 65*, 1136–1144.

Huang, L., & Pashler, H. (2005). Attention capacity and task difficulty in visual search. *Cognition, 94*, B101–B111.

Intriligator, J., & Cavanagh, P. (2001). The spatial resolution of visual attention. *Cognitive Psychology, 43*, 171–216.

Itti, L., &Koch, C. (2001). Computational modeling of visual attention. *Nature Reviews Neuroscience, 2*(3), 194–203.

Jolicoeur, P., Ullman, S., & Mackay, M. (1986). Curve tracing: A possible basic operation in the perception of spatial relations. *Memory and Cognition, 14*, 129–140.

Kahneman, D. (1973). *Attention and effort.* Englewood Cliffs, NJ: Prentice-Hall.

Kastner, S., DeWeerd, P., Desimone, R., & Ungerleider, L. G. (1998). Mechanisms of directed attention in the human extrastriate cortex as revealed by functional MRI. *Science, 282*, 108–111.

Komatsu, H., & Ideura, Y. (1993). Relationship between color, shape, and pattern selectivities in the inferior cortex of the monkey. *Journal of Neurophysiology, 70*, 677–694.

Liu, T., Jiang, Y., Sun, X., &He, S. (2009). Reduction of the crowding effect in spatially adjacent but cortically remote visual stimuli. *Current Biology, 19*(2), 127–132.

Logan, G. D. (1994). Spatial attention and the apprehension of spatial relations. *Journal of Experimental Psychology: Human Perception and Performance, 20*(5), 1015–1036.

Logan, G. D. (1995). Linguistic and conceptual control of visual spatial attention. *Cognitive Psychology, 28*(2), 103–174.

Logan, G. D., & Zbrodoff, N. J. (2003). Subitizing and similarity: Toward a pattern-matching theory of enumeration. *Psychonomic Bulletin and Review, 10*, 676–682.

Luck, S. J., Chelazzi, L., Hillyard, S. A., &Desimone, R. (1997). Neural mechanisms of spatial selective attention in areas V1, V2, and V4 of macaque visual cortex. *Journal of Neurophysiology, 77*, 24–42.

Luck, S. J.Girelli, M., Mc Dermot, M. T., & Ford, M. A. (1997). Bridging the gap betwen monkey neurophysiology and human perception: An ambiguity resolution theory of visual selective attention. *Cognitive Psychology, 33*, 64–87.

Luck, S. J., &Thomas S. J. (1999). What variety of attention is automatically captured by peripheral cues? *Perception and Psychophysics, 61*, 1424–1435.

Luck, S. J., &Vecera, S. P. (2002). Attention. In H. Pashler (Series Ed.) & S. Yantis (Volume Ed.), *Stevens' handbook of experimental psychology, Vol.1. Sensation and perception* (3rd ed., pp. 235–286). New York: Wiley.

Luck, S. J., & Vogel, E. K. (1997). The capacity of visual working memory for features and conjunctions. *Nature, 390*, 279–281.

Lueschow, A., Miller, E. K., & Desimone, R. (1994). Inferior temporal mechanisms for invariant object recognition. *Cerebral Cortex, 5*, 523–531.

Mack, A, & Rock, I. (1998). *Inattentional blindness.* Cambridge, MA: MIT Press.

Maioli, C., Benaglio, I., Siri, S., Sosta, K., & Cappa, S. (2001). The integration of parallel and serial processing mechanisms in visual search: Evidence from eye movement recording. *European Journal of Neuroscience, 13*, 364–372.

Mandler, G., & Shebo, B. J. (1982). Subitizing: An analysis of its component processes. *Journal of Experimental Psychology: General, 111*, 1–22.

McCormick, P. A., & Jolicoeur, P. (1991). Predicting the shape of distance functions in curve tracing: Evidence for a zoom lens operator. *Memory and Cognition, 19*, 469–486.

McCormick, P. A., & Jolicoeur, P. (1994). Manipulating the shape of distance effects in visual curve tracing: Further evidence for the zoom lens model. *Canadian Journal of Experimental Psychology, 48*, 1–24.

McLeod, P., Driver, J., & Crisp, J. (1988). Visual search for a conjunction of movement and form is parallel. *Nature, 332*,154–155.

Mishkin, M., & Ungerleider, L. G . (1982). Contribution of striate inputs to the visuospatial functions of parieto-preoccipital cortex in monkeys. *Behavioral and Brain Research, 6*(1), 57–77.

Mitroff, S. R., Simons, D. J., & Levin, D. T. (2004). Nothing compares two views: Change blindness can occur despite preserved access to the changed information. *Perception and Psychophysics, 66*, 1268–1281.

Moran, J., & Desimone, R. (1985). Selective attention gates visual processing in the extrastriate cortex. *Science, 229*, 782–784.

Mordkoff, J. T. (1996). Selective attention and internal constraints: There is more to the flanker effect than biased contingencies. In A. Kramer, M. G. H. Coles, & G. Logan (Eds.), *Converging operations in the study of visual selective attention* (pp. 483–502). Washington, DC: American Psycholgical Association Press.

Most, S. B., Scholl, B. J., Clifford, E., & Simons, D. J. (2005). What you see is what you set: Sustained inattentional blindness and the capture of awareness. *Psychological Review, 112*, 217–242.

Motter, B. C., & Simoni, D. A. (2007). The roles of cortical image separation and size in active visual search performance. *Journal of Vision, 7*(2), 6.1–15.

Mozer, M. C., & Vecera, S. P. (2005). Object- and space-based attention. In L. Itti, G. Rees, & J. Tsotsos (Eds.), *Neurobiology of attention* (pp. 130–134). New York: Elsevier.

Myczek, K., & Simons, D. J. (2008). Better than average: Alternatives to statistical summary representations for rapid judgments of average size. *Perception and Psychophysics, 70*(7), 772–788.

Navon, D. (1977). Forest before trees: The precedence of global features in visual perception. *Cognitive Psychology, 9*, 353–383.

Navon, D. (1984). Resources—A theoretical soup stone? *Psychological Review, 91*(2), 216–234.

Neisser, U., & Becklen, R. (1975). Selective looking: Attending to visually specified events. *Cognitive Psychology, 7*, 480–494.

Norman, D. A., & Bobrow, D. G. (1975). On data-limited and resource limited processes. *Cognitive Psychology, 7*, 44–64.

Oliva, A., &Torralba, A. (2006). Building the gist of a scene: The role of global image features in recognition. *Progress in Brain Research, 155*, 23–36

Olivers, N. L., van der Stigchel, S., & Hulleman, J. (2007). Spreading the sparing: Against a limited-capacity account of the attentional blink. *Psychological Research, 71*, 126–139

Palmer, J. (1994). Set-size effect in visual search: The effect of attention is independent of the stimulus for simpler tasks. *Vision Research, 34*, 1703–1721.

Palmer, J. (1995). Attention in visual search: Distinguishing four causes of set-size effects. *Current Directions in Psychological Science, 4*, 118–123.

Palmeri, T. J. (1997). Exemplar similarity and the development of automaticity. *Journal of Experimental Psychology: Learning, Memory, and Cognition, 23*, 324–354.

Parkes, L., Lund, J., Angelucci, A., Solomon, J. A., & Morgan, M. (2001). Compulsory averaging of crowded orientation signals in human vision. *Nature Neuroscience, 4*(7), 739–744.

Pashler, H. (1998). *The psychology of attention.* Cambridge, MA: MIT Press.

Pelli, D. G., Palomares, M., & Majaj, N. J. (2004). Crowding is unlike ordinary masking: Distinguishing feature integration from detection. *Journal of Vision, 4*(12), 1136–1169.

Peterson, S. A., & Simon, T. J. (2000). Computational evidence for the subitizing phenomenon as an emergent property of the human cognitive architecture. *Cognitive Science, 24*(1), 93–122.

Posner, M. I. (1980). Orienting of attention. *Quarterly Journal of Experimental Psychology, 32*, 3–25.

Pylyshyn, Z. (1989). A role of location indexes in spatial perception: A sketch of the FINST spatial index model. *Cognition, 32*, 65–97.

Pylyshyn, Z. (1994). Some primitive mechanisms of spatial attention. *Cognition, 50*, 363–384.

Pylyshyn, Z. W., & Storm, R. W. (1988). Tracking multiple independent targets: Evidence for a parallel tracking mechanism. *Spatial Vision, 3*, 1–19.

Raymond, J. E., Shapiro, K. L., & Arnell, K. M. (1992). Temporary suppression of visual processing in an RSVP task: An attentional blink? *Journal of Experimental Psychology: Human Perception and Performance, 18*(3), 849–860.

Reynolds, J. H., Chelazzi, L., & Desimone, R. (1999). Competitive mechanisms subserve attention in macaque areas V2 and V4. *Journal of Neuroscience, 19*, 1736–1753.

Reynolds, J. H., &Desimone, R. (1999). The role of neural mechanisms of attention in solving the binding problem. *Neuron, 24*, 19–29.

Reynolds, J. H., &Desimone, R. (2003). Interacting roles of attention and visual salience in V4. *Neuron, 37*(5), 853–863.

Rijpkema, M., van Aalderen, S., Schwarzbach, J., & Verstraten, F. A. J. (2007). Beyond the forest and the trees: Local and global interference in hierarchical visual stimuli containing three levels. *Perception, 36*(8), 1115–1122.

Robertson, L., Treisman, A., Friedman-Hill, S., & Grabowecky, M. F. (1997). The interaction of spatial and object pathways: Evidence from Balint's syndrome. *Journal of Cognitive Neuroscience, 9,* 295–317.

Saenz, M., Buracas, G. T., & Boynton, G. M . (2003). Global feature-based attention for motion and color. *Vision Research, 43,* 629–637.

Scott-Brown, K., Baker, M. J., & Orbach, H. (2000). Comparison blindness. *Visual Cognition, 7,* 253–267.

Scholl, B. J. (2001). Objects and attention: The state of the art. *Cognition, 80*(1/2), 1–46.

Serences, J. T., &Yantis, S. (2006). Selective visual attention and perceptual coherence. *Trends in Cognitive Sciences, 10,* 38–45.

Serences, J. T., &Yantis, S. (2007). Representation of attentional priority in human occipital, parietal, and frontal cortex. *Cerebral Cortex, 17,* 284–293.

Shim, W. M., Alvarez, G. A., & Jiang, Y. V. (2008). Spatial separation between targets constrains maintenance of attention on multiple objects. *Psychonomic Bulletin and Review, 15*(2), 390–397.

Shiu, L-P., & Pashler, H. (1994). Negligible effect of spatial precuing in identification of single digits.*Journal of Experimental Psychology: Human Perception and Performance, 20,* 1037–1054.

Simons, D. J., & Chabris, C. F. (1999). Gorillas in our midst: Sustained inattentional blindness for dynamic events. *Perception, 28,* 1059–1074.

Sohn, Y-S., Liederman, J., & Reinitz, M. T. (1996). Division of inputs between hemispheres eliminates illusory conjunctions. *Neuropsychologia, 34,* 1057–1068.

Todd, J., & Marois, R. (2004). Capacity limit of visual sort-term memory in human posterior parietal cortex. *Nature, 428*(15), 751–754.

Torralbo, A., &Beck, D. M. (2008). Perceptual-load-Induced selection as a result of local competitive interactions in visual cortex. *Psychological Science, 19*(10), 1045–1050.

Treisman, A. (1996). The binding problem. *Current Opinion in Neurobiology, 6,* 171–178.

Treisman, A. M., & Gelade, G. (1980). A feature-integration theory of attention. *Cognitive Psychology, 12,* 97–136.

Treisman, A., & Schmidt, H. (1982). Illusory conjunctions in the perception of objects. *Cognitive Psychology, 14,* 107–141.

Trick, L. M., & Pylyshyn, Z. W. (1994). Why are small and large numbers enumerated differently? A limited capacity preattentive stage in vision. *Psychological Review, 101,* 1–23.

Tsotsos, J. K. (1990). Analyzing vision at the complexity level. *Behavioral and Brain Sciences, 13,* 423–469.

Tsotsos, J. K., Culhane, S. W., Wai, Y. L., Davis, N., & Nuflo, F. (1995). Modeling visual attention via selective tuning. *Artificial Intelligence, 78,* 507–547.

Ullman, S. (1984). Visual routines. *Cognition, 18*(1–3), 97–159.

VanRullen, R. (2009). Binding hardwired vs. on-demand feature conjunctions. *Visual Cognition, 17*(1–2), 103–119.

Wolfe, J. M. (1994). Guided search 2.0: A revised model of visual search. *Psychonomic Bulletin and Review, 1*(2), 202–238.

Wolfe, J. M. (1998). What can 1,000,000 trials tell us about visual search? *Psychological Science, 9*(1), 33–39.

Wolfe, J. M. (1999). Inattentional amnesia. In V. Coltheart (Ed.), *Fleeting memories: Cognition of brief visual stimuli* (pp. 71–94). Cambridge, MA: MIT Press.

Wolfe, J. M. (2007). Guided search 4.0: Current progress with a model of visual search. In W. Gray (Ed.), *Integrated models of cognitive systems* (pp. 99–119). New York: Oxford University Press.

Wolfe, J., Alvarez, G., Rosenholtz, R., Oliva, A., Torralba, A., Kuzmova, Y., & Sherman, A. M. (2008). Search for arbitrary objects in natural scenes is remarkably efficient. *Journal of Vision, 8*(6), 1103–1103.

Wolfe, J. M., & Horowitz, T. S. (2004). What attributes guide the deployment of visual attention and how do they do it? *Nature Reviews Neuroscience, 5,* 1–7.

Xu, Y., &Chun, M. M. (2009). Selecting and perceiving multiple visual objects. *Trends in Cognitive Sciences, 13,* 167–174

Yantis, S., & Hillstrom, A. P. (1994). Stimulus-driven attentional capture: Evidence from equiluminant visual objects. *Journal of Experimental Psychology: Human Perception and Performance, 20,* 95–107.

Zhang, W., & Luck, S. J. (2008). Discrete fixed-resolution representations in visual working memory. *Nature, 453,* 233–235.

# Automaticity

Agnes Moors

## Abstract

This chapter discusses two classes of views of automaticity: mechanism-based views and feature-based views. For each view it is considered what the implications are for the diagnosis of a process or behavior as automatic. The class of feature-based views is discussed in further detail. First, definitions of features are listed. Then, it is proposed that features provide information about operating conditions. This broadens the scope toward examining operating conditions that are not included in the automaticity concept. Finally, various feature-based views are examined that differ with regard to the amount of coherence that they assume among features.

**Key Words:** automatic, uncontrolled, unintentional, goal independent, unconscious, efficient, fast, purely stimulus driven

The concept of automaticity is important across nearly all subareas of psychology. Pertinent questions are as follows: What is automaticity? What is automatization? How can one diagnose whether a process or behavior is automatic? I discuss two classes of views of automaticity and automatization: mechanism-based views and feature-based views. The class of feature-based views is discussed in further detail. First, I present definitions of features, in which the central ingredients of these features (goals, attention, consciousness, and duration) are specified. Then, I submit the proposal that features provide information about operating conditions. This broadens the scope toward examining operating conditions with ingredients that are not included in the automaticity concept (e.g., stimulus intensity). Finally, I examine various feature-based views that differ with regard to the amount of coherence that they assume among features or operating conditions. I advocate a decompositional view that argues for the separate investigation of automaticity features. Research about ingredients (goals, attention, consciousness, duration, stimulus intensity)

has revealed that the relations among these ingredients are complex. This complexity, however, does not seem to have infused many researchers' usage of automaticity. The present chapter tries to connect the dots. Ideally, recent (and future) insights in the relations between ingredients of automaticity features should inform researchers' usage of the term *automaticity*.

Before embarking on a discussion of views of automaticity, I wish to specify that the term *automatic* can be a predicate of processes or behavior. It may be good to keep in mind that processes can be described at different levels of analysis. Marr (1982), for example, distinguished between three levels of analysis. The first, functional level articulates the functional relation between input and output (i.e., what the process does). The second, algorithmic level specifies the mechanisms involved in transforming input into output as well as the format of the representations (i.e., codes) on which the mechanisms operate. Examples of mechanisms are the activation of associations, rule-based computation, and information integration (Hélie, Waldschmidt,

& Ashby, 2010). Examples of codes are propositional, conceptual, and perceptual codes. The third, implementational level is concerned with the physical implementation of processes in the brain. Processes described at higher levels of analysis can be explained by processes described at lower levels of analysis. This type of explanation has been called a vertical or synchronic explanation, and it has been contrasted with a horizontal, diachronic, or causal explanation (Crisp & Warfield, 2001).

### Views and Diagnosis of Automaticity

Views of automaticity can be divided into two classes: mechanism-based views and feature-based views. Mechanism-based views define automaticity in terms of a particular mechanism. Feature-based views define automaticity as an umbrella term for a number of features such as uncontrolled, unconscious, efficient, and fast. I discuss one mechanism-based view and several feature-based views. I discuss the implications of each view for the diagnosis of a process or behavior as automatic and highlight their strengths and weaknesses.

#### Mechanism-Based View

According to a mechanism-based view, a process or behavior described at the functional level of analysis is automatic when it can be explained by one particular mechanism at the algorithmic level. The best-known example of a mechanism-based view is that of Logan (1988). He proposed to define automaticity in terms of the mechanism of direct memory retrieval (i.e., associative mechanism). A process described at the functional level is automatic when it can be explained by direct memory retrieval at the algorithmic level. Logan defined automatization or the development toward automaticity as the transition from a computation of a complex procedure (i.e., rule-based mechanism) toward direct memory retrieval (i.e., associative mechanism). To solve arithmetic problems of the type "5+3+2=?," participants initially engage in a complex procedure that consists of two steps. In a first step, they retrieve the sum of 5 and 3, which leads to the intermediate outcome 8. In a next step, they retrieve the sum of 8 and 2, which leads to the final outcome 10. Once an association is formed between the set of digits and their sum, participants are able to directly produce the sum by activating this association.

The mechanism-based view proposes to diagnose a process as automatic when the underlying mechanism is an associative mechanism. It is notoriously difficult to determine whether a (high-level) process is based on an associative or a rule-based mechanism (cf. Hahn & Chater, 1998; Moors, in press; Moors & De Houwer, 2006b). The criterion for diagnosing a (high-level) process as automatic or nonautomatic is therefore difficult to apply.

Logan's (1988) view is incompatible with the view espoused by Anderson (1992) and Rosenbloom and Newell (1986) that automatization can be defined as the strengthening of procedures (i.e., a rule-based mechanism). These authors do not portray automatization as a shift from one type of mechanism to another, but rather as a change in the same underlying mechanism, the strengthening of procedures. Processes have the same underlying mechanism in the nonautomatic stage as in the automatic stage, but in the latter stage, the mechanism is executed faster and more efficiently. Hence, automatic and nonautomatic processes and behavior only differ with regard to the features (fast, efficient) they possess. In other words, these authors advocate a feature-based view of automaticity. Logan's view is also incompatible with a reconciling approach (e.g., Tzelgov, Henik, Sneg, & Baruch, 1996; Tzelgov, Yehene, Kotler, & Alon, 2000) in which it is argued that both mechanisms of procedure strengthening and a shift toward direct memory retrieval are equivalent mechanisms underlying automatization. Advocates of the reconciling view also define automaticity in terms of features.

In sum, Logan (1988) proposed a mechanism-based view in which automaticity is defined in terms of the underlying mechanism of direct memory retrieval. Partisans of the procedure-strengthening view and the reconciling view of automatization found this proposal to be unsatisfactory because it cannot integrate findings supporting the automatic nature of other mechanisms than direct memory retrieval (Carlson & Lundy, 1992; Hélie et al., 2010; Kramer, Strayer, & Buckley, 1990; Moors, De Houwer, & Eelen, 2004; Schneider & Fisk, 1984; Smith & Lerner, 1986; Tzelgov et al., 2000; Van Opstal, Moors, Fias, & Verguts, 2008). Of course, according to the mechanism-based view, these findings do not count as evidence for automaticity. The main reason to reject the mechanism-based view is precisely that it excludes certain (low-level) processes from the realm of automatic processes on an a priori basis. The question of which mechanisms can underlie automatic processes and behavior should be open to empirical study. It should not be answered a priori that only one mechanism can be automatic. The alternative option is to define automaticity in terms of features. I now turn to a discussion of feature-based views.

## Feature-Based Views

This section starts with definitions of the most current features of automaticity (for an extended justification of these definitions, see Moors & De Houwer, 2006a, 2007). The field is marked by the absence of explicit definitions of automaticity features and the inconsistent use of implicit definitions of these features. The definitions that I present are stipulative in nature, yet their choice is guided by three principles. I chose definitions (a) that are in line with dominant philosophical writings, (b) that remain close to natural language, and (c) that have minimal mutual overlap.

### DEFINITIONS OF FEATURES

I define the following features of (non)automaticity: (un)controlled, (un)intentional, (non) autonomous, goal (in)dependent, (un)conscious, (non)efficient, fast(slow), and (not) purely stimulus driven. For each of the features, I identify the (central) ingredients. I also specify what the features can be a predicate of. Features can be predicates of processes described at high (functional) or low (algorithmic) levels of analysis. All features can be predicates of entire processes, and some features can be predicates of parts of processes. Examples of parts are inputs and outputs of processes, at least when processes are defined at a high level of analysis as relations between an input and an output. I start with the features (un)controlled, (un)intentional, (non) autonomous, and goal (in)dependent. The central ingredient of these features is a goal (or the absence of a goal). I therefore call them goal-related features.

### (Un)controlled

A process is controlled when a person has a goal[1] about the process and this goal causes the desired effect (the state represented in the goal). This definition has three ingredients: a goal about a process, an effect, and a causal relation between goal and effect. Processing goals can be of the promoting type (i.e., the goal to engage in the process) or of the counteracting type (e.g., the goals to alter, stop, or avoid the process). In the case of a promoting goal, the desired effect is the actual occurrence of a process. In the case of a counteracting goal, the desired effect is a change, the interruption, or the prevention of a process.

A process is uncontrolled when one or more ingredients (the effect, the goal, or the causal relation) are missing. A process is uncontrolled when a person has a goal about the process, but the desired effect is absent. A process is also uncontrolled when the goal about the process is absent but an effect is present (i.e., the process occurs, changes, is interrupted, is prevented). For example, a process is uncontrolled when it is prevented despite the fact that the person did not have the goal to prevent it. Something else caused the prevention. Finally, a process is uncontrolled when both the goal and the desired effect are present, but the effect was not caused by the goal. For example, a person can have the goal to interrupt a process and the process is indeed interrupted. Yet the goal did not cause the interruption; something else did.

It is good to bear in mind that the terms *controlled* and *uncontrolled* are not synonymous with the terms *controllable* and *uncontrollable*. The former terms refer to an actual state of affairs; the latter terms refer to a possibility. A process is controlled (here and now) when a goal is active and causes the desired effect. A process is uncontrolled (here and now) when at least one of the three ingredients (goal, effect, causal relation between goal and effect) is missing. A process is controllable when there is at least one occasion on which activation of the goal causes the desired effect. A process is uncontrollable when there is no occasion whatsoever on which activation of the goal causes the desired effect. A process that is currently uncontrolled may be controlled on other occasions, and hence be controllable.

### (Un)intentional

A process is intentional when a person has the goal to engage in the process and this goal causes the occurrence of the process. It may be noted that intentional is identical to controlled in the promoting sense. Thus, intentional processes are a subset of controlled processes. Likewise, unintentional processes are a subset of uncontrolled processes. A process is unintentional when the process is present but the goal to engage in the process is absent. A process is also unintentional when both the process and the goal to engage in the process are present but the causal relation between them is absent.

It is good to keep in mind that a process can be intentional under one description but unintentional under another (e.g., Searle, 1983). For example, a person can evaluate a job candidate in an intentional manner but, while doing so, activate stereotypes about the person in an unintentional manner. The same process is intentional under the description of evaluating a person but unintentional under the description of activating stereotypes.

## (Non)autonomous

A process is autonomous when it is uncontrolled in both the promoting and the counteracting sense. A process is autonomous when it is not caused by the goal to engage in it and when it is not counteracted by a goal to counteract it. Autonomous processes are a subset of uncontrolled processes. They are at the intersection of processes that are uncontrolled in the promoting sense (i.e., unintentional) and those that are controlled in the counteracting sense. A process can be partially autonomous. For example, a process can be controlled in the promoting sense but uncontrolled in the counteracting sense.

## Goal (In)dependent

A process is goal dependent when a person has a goal (any goal) and this goal causes the occurrence of the process. The goal may be either the proximal goal to engage in the process or a remote goal that is not about the process. In the first case, the process is goal dependent and intentional; in the second case, the process is just goal dependent. Intentional processes are a subset of goal-dependent processes because intentions are a subset of goals; they are goals to engage in an act or a process. To illustrate these notions, the act of moving one's arm toward one's head may be caused by the proximal goal to move the arm toward the head (in this case the act is intentional) or directly by the goal to scratch the head (in this case the process is unintentional but goal dependent). Another scenario is that the remote goal causes the proximal goal, and that the latter, in turn, causes the process. The goal to scratch the head may cause activation of the goal to move the arm toward the head and this, in turn, may cause the arm to move toward the head. A process is goal independent when it is not caused by a (proximal or remote) goal.

Intentional processes are a subset of both goal-dependent processes and controlled ones; they are at the intersection of both. In the case of goal-dependent processes, the goal can be about the process (e.g., the proximal goal to engage in the process, in which case the process is intentional) or not about the process (a remote goal). In the case of controlled processes, the goal is always about the process. The goal can be of the promoting type (i.e., the goal to engage in the process, in which case the process is intentional) or of the counteracting type (e.g., the goals to change, interrupt, or prevent the process).

In the case of goal-dependent processes, the effect consists in the occurrence of the process. In the case of controlled processes, the effect can be manifold: the occurrence, a change, the interruption, or the prevention of the process.

## (Un)conscious

Many theorists have distinguished two aspects or ingredients of consciousness: an aboutness aspect and a phenomenal aspect. The aboutness aspect refers to the fact that consciousness is about something, that it has content; the phenomenal aspect refers to subjective feeling or qualia. The aboutness aspect is said to depend on attention, whereas the phenomenal aspect is said to escape attention. Block (1995) even argued that there are two types of consciousness based on these two aspects: access consciousness (or A-consciousness) and phenomenal consciousness (or P-consciousness). The feature unconscious refers to the absence of consciousness. The terms *conscious* and *unconscious* can be used as predicates of several things. They can refer to (a) the stimulus input of the process, (b) the output of the process, and (c) the process itself (i.e., the relation between input and output when the process is defined on a functional level of analysis). Processes that operate on conscious input can be unconscious themselves. Examples are the processes involved in reading and driving a car. Therefore, it is recommended to always specify the predicates of the terms *conscious* and *unconscious*.

## (Non)efficient

A process is efficient when it consumes little or no attentional capacity. The central ingredient of the feature efficient is attention. Attention has two aspects: a quantity and a direction.[2] Efficiency is only related to the quantity aspect. A process is efficient when it operates with very little or without this quantity. It is nonefficient when it consumes a substantial amount of this quantity.

Processes that depend on the direction of attention do not necessarily use a large amount of attention. For example, affective priming effects have been shown to disappear when attention was not directed at the primes (Musch & Klauer, 2001). This suggests that evaluation of the primes depends on the direction of attention. It is possible, however, that this evaluation process used only a small amount of attention and therefore still counts as efficient.

Like consciousness, attention may be directed at (a) the stimulus input of a process, (b) the output of a process, or (c) the process itself. It is also useful to distinguish (a) attention to a stimulus (i.e., stimulus-based attention) from (b) attention to a stimulus feature (feature-based attention), (c) attention to the spatial location in which the stimulus is presented (i.e., spatial or space-based attention), and (d) attention to the time window in which the stimulus is presented (i.e., temporal attention). Attention may have various objects, but the term *efficient* can only be used as a predicate of a process or behavior. In cases in which various processes may be at work, it is important to specify the process that one considers to be efficient.

### Fast (Slow)

The central ingredient of the feature fast is duration. A fast process is one with a short duration; a slow process is one with a long duration. The duration of a process should not be conflated with the duration of the stimulus input on which the process operates. A slow process may operate on a briefly presented stimulus, and a fast process may operate on a stimulus that is presented for a long time. The term *fast* can only be used as a predicate of a process.

### Purely Stimulus Driven

A process is purely stimulus driven when the only condition necessary for its occurrence is the presence of the stimulus. Purely stimulus-driven processes may require some background conditions (such as being awake and that the light is on in the case of visual stimuli) in addition to the stimulus input, but they do not require the presence of goals, consciousness, and attention. Thus, purely stimulus-driven processes are at the intersection of goal-independent processes, unconscious processes, and efficient processes. They are a subset of each of these sets of processes.

### FEATURES PROVIDE INFORMATION ABOUT OPERATING CONDITIONS

Automaticity features are not fixed features of processes. A process can be unintentional on some occasions but intentional on others, or it can be intentional at first but unintentional after practice. This has led to the proposal to view and redefine features of (non)automaticity in terms of operating conditions (Bargh, 1992). The features discussed earlier can be reformulated as follows. A process is uncontrolled in the promoting sense (intentional) when it occurs in the absence of a (causally efficacious) promoting goal (i.e., goal to engage in the process). A process is uncontrolled in the counteracting sense when it occurs despite the presence of a counteracting goal or in the absence of a (causally efficacious) counteracting goal. A process is autonomous when it occurs in the absence of a (causally efficacious) promoting goal and despite the presence of a counteracting goal or the absence of a (causally efficacious) counteracting goal. A process is goal independent when it occurs in the absence of any (causally efficacious) goal. A process is unconscious when it occurs in the absence of consciousness of the process. A process is efficient when it occurs in the absence of a large amount of attentional capacity. A process is fast when it occurs in the absence of a large amount of time. A process is purely stimulus driven when it occurs in the absence of goals, attention, and consciousness.

### EXTENDING THE SET OF OPERATING CONDITIONS

I suggest that the range of possible conditions that influence the occurrence (or nonoccurrence) of processes—and that are therefore worthy of study—can be extended beyond those that are related to (non)automaticity features (cf. Moors, Spruyt, & De Houwer, 2010). One example of a condition that is not included in most lists of automaticity features is salience, the quality of a stimulus (or stimulus feature) to stand out relative to other stimuli (or stimulus features; Itti, 2007). Salience is a property of a stimulus, but a stimulus is always salient for a person. Salience corresponds to the subjective intensity of a stimulus relative to other stimuli. The subjective intensity of a stimulus must be delineated from the objective intensity of a stimulus. Objective stimulus intensity corresponds to luminance in the visual domain, to amount of decibels in the auditory domain, and to amount of pressure in the tactile domain. Salience of a stimulus can be influenced by various factors such as the objective intensity, clarity, size, duration, and frequency of a stimulus, as well as by goals, expectations, attention, and recency (whether a representation of the stimulus was recently activated). Another condition that is not related to one of the automaticity features is the direction of attention. Some processes only occur when attention is directed to the stimulus or to the location of the stimulus (cf. Musch & Klauer, 2001). The list of possible conditions can, in principle, be extended to include any concrete or abstract aspect of an experimental procedure (e.g., specific instructions, stimulus set, context).

Operating conditions can be split into two groups: internal and external ones. Most of the conditions discussed here are internal. They refer to internal ingredients such as goals, consciousness, and attention. Some conditions are external. They refer to external ingredients such as duration, frequency, and intensity of stimuli.

It may be noted that in the case of internal operating conditions, there is often reference to a process (e.g., the goal to engage in or counteract a process, consciousness of a process, attention directed at a process). It is most likely that the processes that are referred to in these conditions are described at a high but not at a low level of analysis. For example, a person can become aware that she is engaged in the high-level process of evaluation, but probably not that she is engaged in the low-level process of activating associations. Likewise, a person can have the goal to engage in the high-level process of evaluation but probably not the goal to engage in the low-level process of activating associations.

### RELATIONS AMONG FEATURES OR OPERATING CONDITIONS

Various feature-based views of automaticity differ with regard to the amount of coherence they assume among features. Features have been grouped into two modes (dual-mode view) or three modes (triple-mode view), or they have been considered as entirely separable (essence view; decompositional view).

#### Dual-Mode View

The dual-mode view proposes that there are two modes of processing and behavior: the automatic mode and the nonautomatic mode. This view assumes a perfect coherence among the features of each mode. Assumptions of coherence stem from assumptions of conceptual overlap and logical relations among the ingredients of (non)automaticity features (see Moors, 2009, for a discussion of other sources of the dual-mode view). For example, the coherence among the features conscious and controlled stems from the idea that consciousness is an ingredient of control (i.e., conceptual overlap; e.g., Prinz, 2004) or that consciousness is a necessary condition for control (e.g., Uleman, 1989). For another example, the coherence among the features efficient and unconscious stems from the idea that consciousness and attention are identical or that attention is necessary and sufficient for consciousness (e.g., De Brigard & Prinz, 2010; Prinz, 2010, in press).

Because of the coherence among the features of each mode, processes in the automatic mode possess all automatic features, and those in the nonautomatic mode possess all nonautomatic features. The dual-mode view is therefore also called an all-or-none view.

The implications of the dual-mode view for the diagnosis of processes or behavior as automatic are the following: A process can be diagnosed as automatic when it has been demonstrated that it possesses one feature of automaticity. The remaining features of automaticity can then be inferred. In other words, evidence for the presence of one feature of one mode can be generalized to the remaining features of that mode. Proponents of the dual-mode view think of (non)automaticity features as fixed features of processes. In their view, (non)automaticity features do not refer to conditions that are sometimes present and sometimes not. In addition, they do not usually consider the influence of factors that are not included in the automaticity concept (such as salience).

It has become clear, however, that the dual-mode view is untenable. Studies have demonstrated that many processes possess a combination of automaticity and nonautomaticity features. For example, studies have demonstrated that the processes underlying the affective priming effect can be unintentional (e.g., Bargh, Chaiken, Raymond, & Hymes, 1996) and unconscious (e.g., Klauer, Eder, Greenwald, & Abrams, 2007), but that they can also be controlled in the counteracting sense (Teige-Mocigemba & Klauer, 2008). Lachter, Foster, and Ruthruff (2008) have shown that the processes underlying the word repetition priming effect can be unintentional and unconscious but nevertheless depend on (the direction and quantity of) attention. The processes underlying the color word Stroop effect have been shown to be unintentional and difficult to counteract. Yet studies showing a dilution of the Stroop effect when the to-be-named colors are spatially separated from the color words (e.g., Kahneman & Chajczyk, 1983; Lachter, Ruthruff, Lien, & McCann, 2008) suggest that these processes are influenced by (the direction and quantity of) attention. This and other evidence led researchers (e.g., Bargh, 1989; Shiffrin, 1988) to abandon the dual-mode view.

#### Triple-Mode View

One alternative to the dual-mode view is the triple-mode view. Several authors have separated nonautomatic processes from two types of automatic processes. Carver and Scheier (1999, 2002) distinguished between bottom-up automatic processes and top-down automatic processes. These two types of automatic processes come about at different stages in the evolution of a process during practice. In the initial stages of practice, there are bottom-up processes that are triggered by mere stimulus input. These processes are so weak that they remain inaccessible to consciousness and they cannot be controlled (i.e., bottom-up automatic stage). In intermediate stages of practice, processes become so strong that they become consciously accessible. As a result, they can be controlled (i.e., nonautomatic stage). In later stages of practice, processes become so strong and well trained that control is no longer required and they fall out of consciousness again (i.e., top-down automatic stage). Top-down automatic processes are usually unconscious, but they are not inaccessible to consciousness. They can become conscious when attention is directed to them. Several attention researchers made a similar distinction between preattentive automatic processes and learned ones (e.g., Treisman, Vieira, & Hayes, 1992). Preattentive automatic processes are those involved in the early stages of the processing sequence (e.g., sensory analysis). Learned automatic processes are those that become independent of attentional capacity as a result of practice. It may be noted that bottom-up automatic processes may not overlap entirely with preattentive ones. Not all unlearned automatic processes may be situated in the early stages of the processing sequence.

The triple-mode view faces the same problems as the dual-mode view. It is based on assumptions of coherence among features. For example, a strong coherence is assumed between the features conscious and controlled. It is assumed that a process can be controlled when it is conscious, and that a process falls out of consciousness when control is no longer required.

The implications of the triple-mode view for the diagnosis of processes or behavior as automatic are practically the same as those of the dual-mode view. Even though there are two types of automatic processes, both types include all automatic features and these cohere perfectly. Thus, a process can be diagnosed as automatic when it is demonstrated that it possesses one feature of automaticity (the other features can then be inferred).

## Essence View

The lack of coherence among automaticity features has led some authors to choose one necessary feature (i.e., an essence) that a process should have to belong to the set of automatic processes. The remaining features of automaticity are considered optional. For example, Bargh (1992) proposed to call a process automatic when it runs to completion without the need for conscious guidance, regardless of how it was initially caused (by a goal or not). Such processes can be called a special type of partially autonomous processes. The start of the process can be caused or not caused by a promoting goal. The completion of the process is not caused by a conscious goal (but it can still be caused by an unconscious goal, I presume).

To diagnose a process as automatic according to an essence view, one should investigate whether the process possesses the essential feature. The problem is that the choice of such a feature is always an arbitrary matter.

## Decompositional View

Another view that does not assume a priori coherence among the features of each mode is the decompositional view. According to this view, processes can, in principle, possess any random combination of automatic and nonautomatic features. It is up to empirical research to determine which features cohere in reality. The decompositional view rests on the assumption that most features of automaticity can be separated on conceptual and logical grounds.

Most features can be conceptually separated. They can be defined in such a way that they do not share ingredients. In the definitions of (non)automaticity features presented earlier, the goal-related features (un)controlled, (un)intentional, (non)autonomous, and goal (in)dependent do not overlap with (un)conscious, (non)efficient, and fast (slow) because they do not make reference to consciousness, attention, or duration. The features (un)conscious, efficient, and fast can also be conceptually separated from each other because they do not share ingredients (aboutness aspect, phenomenal aspect, attentional capacity, and duration). The definitions presented earlier do entail conceptual overlap among several goal-related features, as well as among purely stimulus driven and several other features. (Un)intentional processes are at the intersection of (un)controlled processes and goal-(in)dependent ones. Autonomous processes are at the intersection of processes that are uncontrolled in the promoting sense and ones that are uncontrolled in the counteracting sense. Purely stimulus-driven processes are at the intersection of goal-independent processes, unconscious ones, and efficient ones. On

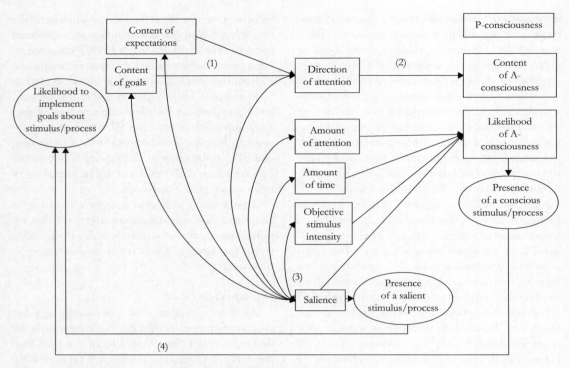

**Figure 11.1** Possible relations among the ingredients figuring in operating conditions

the other hand, processes that are (un)controlled in the promoting sense (i.e., [un]intentional) do not overlap with ones that are (un)controlled in the counteracting sense because they are based on different types of goals (promoting vs. counteracting).

Most features can also be logically separated. This does not mean that there are no relations among features. Ingredients of features do influence each other. The decompositional view, however, starts from the working hypothesis that these relations are not one-to-one relations. No ingredient is considered a necessary and/or sufficient condition for another ingredient. Figure 11.1 shows possible relations among the ingredients of (non)automaticity features and other operating conditions. As the figure shows, all ingredients are multidetermined. I discuss five sets of relations:

(1) Goals influence attention. The presence of a goal increases the likelihood that attention will be allocated to something. The content of the goal influences the direction (and hence object) of attention (e.g., Allport, 1989; Yantis, 2000). It seems reasonable to assume that this also holds for processing goals. The goal to engage in a process may steer attention to a suitable stimulus input. For example, the goal to evaluate a job candidate may steer attention to the candidate. The goal to

counteract a process may steer attention to the process itself. For example, the goal to counteract the process of stereotyping may call attention to this process. However, attention is not exclusively influenced by goals. Other possible factors are expectations, salience, and mismatches with goals (i.e., significance), mismatches with expectations (i.e., unexpectedness), and mismatches with memory representations (i.e., novelty) (e.g., Gati & Ben-Shakar, 1990; Mack & Rock, 1998; Öhman, 1992; Yantis, 2000).

(2) Attention influences consciousness. Relying on the distinction between the direction and the amount of attention, one can distinguish between two types of influences. First, the direction of attention influences the content of consciousness (e.g., Posner, 1994; Shiffrin & Schneider, 1977): Attention to a stimulus (or process) renders the stimulus (or process) conscious and not another one. Second, the amount of attention spent on something determines the likelihood that it will become conscious (or the amount of consciousness, for gradual views of consciousness). Empirical support for both types of influence comes from effects known as inattentional blindness (an unexpected stimulus with a long duration and high objective intensity fails to reach consciousness when

attention is directed to another stimulus, e.g., Mack & Rock, 1998), change blindness (i.e., a change in a visual pattern does not become conscious when attention is not focused on the changing part, e.g., Rensink, O'Regan, & Clark, 1997), the attentional blink (i.e., a stimulus fails to reach consciousness when attention is consumed by another stimulus that is presented around 200 ms earlier; Raymond, Shapiro, & Arnell, 1992), and load-induced blindness (i.e., the threshold for consciousness of a stimulus increases when attentional capacity is consumed by a secondary task; Macdonald & Lavie, 2008). The former two effects (inattentional blindness and change blindness) seem to be more supportive of the first type of influence (that the direction of attention influences the content of consciousness), whereas the latter two (attentional blink and load-induced blindness) seem more supportive of the second type of influence (that the amount of attention spent influences the likelihood or amount of consciousness).

Everybody agrees that attention influences consciousness, yet there is strong disagreement about whether attention is necessary and/or sufficient for consciousness. Some theorists hold that attention is *necessary* for consciousness (e.g., Kouider & Dehaene, 2007; De Brigard & Prinz, 2010), whereas others deny this (e.g., Koch & Tsuchiya, 2007; van Boxtel, Tsuchiya, & Koch, 2010). Still others argue that attention is necessary for some but not all aspects or types of consciousness. For example, Block (1995) distinguishes between access consciousness, which is dependent of attention, and phenomenal consciousness, which is not dependent of attention. In addition to these two first-order types of consciousness, there is a second-order type of consciousness, which is typically thought to be dependent of attention as well.

To demonstrate that attention is *necessary* for consciousness, one should demonstrate that in all instances in which attention is absent, consciousness is absent as well. To demonstrate that attention is *not necessary* for consciousness, one should find one instance in which consciousness is present but attention is absent. Investigating all instances in which attention is absent is not a realistic purpose. Common empirical practice consists of demonstrating one or a few instances in which attention and consciousness are both absent. These results are generalized to other instances. Examples of instances in which attention and consciousness are both absent are phenomena such as inattentional blindness, change blindness, attentional blink, and load blindness. Critics have questioned whether consciousness is really absent in these studies. For example, van Boxtel et al. (2010) review studies in which it is shown that participants in inattentional blindness studies are still conscious of the gist of the unattended stimuli. These studies count as evidence that attention is not necessary for consciousness. In turn, this (and other) evidence has been criticized on the grounds that attention is not really absent in these studies (e.g., Prinz, 2010a).

Some theorists hold that attention is *sufficient* for consciousness. More precisely, these theorists hold that attention to X is sufficient for consciousness of X. Attention to a location (i.e., space-based attention) is sufficient for becoming conscious of that location; attention to a feature (i.e., feature-based attention) is sufficient for becoming conscious of that feature; and attention to a stimulus (i.e., stimulus-based attention) is sufficient for becoming conscious of that stimulus. They do not make the claim that attention to a location is sufficient for becoming conscious of the stimulus presented in that location (De Brigard & Prinz, 2010; Mole, 2008).

To demonstrate that attention is *sufficient* for consciousness requires demonstrating that in all instances in which attention is present, consciousness is present as well. Investigating all instances in which attention is present is not a realistic purpose. Common empirical practice consists of demonstrating instances in which both attention and consciousness are present. These findings are generalized to other instances or it is provisionally maintained that attention is sufficient for consciousness until someone comes up with evidence to the contrary. To demonstrate that attention is *not sufficient* for consciousness, one should demonstrate that attention is present when consciousness is absent. Evidence for this position is adduced by (a) subliminal priming studies showing that attention influences the likelihood of unconscious processing (Lachter et al., 2004; Naccache, Blandin, & Dehaene, 2002), and (b) attentional bias studies showing that unconscious stimuli influence the direction of attention (Jiang, Costello, Fang, Huang, & He, 2006). Critics have argued that the data do not convincingly demonstrate that attention was directed to the stimulus (stimulus-based attention) instead of to the location of the stimulus (space-based attention) (Prinz, 2010b). Recent studies have demonstrated that feature-based attention is possible in the absence of consciousness of the stimulus, but whether stimulus-based attention is possible in the absence of consciousness of the stimulus remains a matter of debate (e.g., Tapia, Breitmeyer, & Broyles, 2011; Tapia, Breitmeyer, & Shooner, 2010).

Another way of demonstrating that attention is not sufficient for consciousness is to show that there are other factors besides attention that are necessary for consciousness. Factors that have been mentioned as necessary conditions for consciousness are stimulus intensity (Kouider & Dehaene, 2007) and stimulus duration (Prinz, 2010a). It seems that even defenders of the position that stimulus-based attention is sufficient for consciousness think that stimulus intensity and stimulus duration are necessary conditions. If they indeed agree that these other conditions are necessary, how can they maintain that attention is sufficient for consciousness? One proposal offered by these authors is that intensity and duration act as conditions for attention. Only when intensity and duration are high enough can attention do its work. And once attention does its work, consciousness is a fact (cf. Prinz, 2010a). Another proposal, however, is that the influence of attention, strength, and duration are additive (cf. Moors & De Houwer, 2007). Subliminal priming studies and threshold studies suggest that a lack of stimulus duration may be compensated by a high stimulus intensity and/or a high amount of attention directed to the stimulus. Likewise, a lack of stimulus intensity (e.g., when the stimulus is degraded) may be compensated by long presentation duration and/or a high amount of attention directed to the stimulus. Determining the precise nature of the relation between the ingredients attention, intensity, and duration remains a topic for future research. In the meanwhile, I think it is best to consider them as independent ingredients. This increases the likelihood that they are taken into account. Against the background of the ongoing debate between proponents and opponents of the claims that attention is necessary and/or sufficient for consciousness, I propose to define these ingredients in a nonoverlapping way and to investigate their presence or absence separately.

(3) The salience or subjective intensity of a stimulus is influenced by factors such as goals, expectations, the direction and amount of attention, and the objective stimulus intensity. These factors may also be additive.

(4) The presence of a salient and/or conscious stimulus (or process) influences the likelihood that a conscious goal of the promoting (or of the counteracting) kind will be implemented (cf. Shallice, 1988). For example, implementation of the goal to evaluate a job candidate is more likely when a job candidate is consciously available. Implementation of the goal to counteract the activation of stereotypes is more likely when the person is aware that this process is taking place. This being said, a conscious and/or salient stimulus input may not be necessary for the implementation of goals. The implementation of (conscious or unconscious) goals may suffice with an unconscious and/or nonsalient stimulus (or process) (e.g., Wolbers et al., 2006).

I wish to note that the set of interrelations among the ingredients sketched earlier is not exhaustive. Moreover, some relations have been empirically established, whereas others are theoretical possibilities that have not (or not sufficiently) been tested. Still other relations have been empirically investigated, but the interpretation of the results is subject to intense debate. Participants in these debates often use different definitions and models of attention and consciousness.

The arguments that motivate the choice for a decompositional view could also be taken as arguments to abandon the concept of automaticity altogether. This would indeed be an option. However, the decompositional view is also compatible with a gradual view of automaticity, which conceives of automaticity as a gradual concept (Moors & De Houwer, 2006a, 2007; Shiffrin, 1988). The notion *gradual* applies to two things. First, processes can be automatic with regard to more or fewer features. The more features of automaticity a process has, the more automatic it is. Second, each of the automaticity features discussed can themselves be considered as gradual. A process can be more or less controlled, more or less conscious, more or less efficient, and more or less fast.

The implication of this view for the diagnosis of automaticity is the following. One cannot simply diagnose a process as automatic or nonautomatic. One can examine whether certain features of automaticity are present or absent, or the degree to which they are present. This allows one to diagnose a process as more or less automatic. The assumption that features are conceptually and logically separable has the implication that each feature has to be investigated separately. The presence of one feature cannot be inferred from the presence of another feature.

## Conclusion

The present chapter discussed one mechanism-based view and four feature-based views of automaticity. The feature-based views differ with regard to the amount of coherence that they assume among features of automaticity. The dual-mode view proposes to organize processes into an automatic and a nonautomatic mode and assumes that there is perfect coherence among the features of each mode. The triple-mode view proposes to organize processes into three modes: a bottom-up automatic mode, a top-down automatic mode, and a nonautomatic mode. The essence view proposes to elect one feature as the necessary feature and to consider all the other features as optional ones. Like the decompositional approach, this view argues that there is no (a priori) coherence among features of automaticity. All features can be conceptually and logically separated and processes can, in principle, possess any random combination of features.

For each of the views discussed, it was examined what the implications are for the diagnosis of a process or behavior as automatic. The mechanism-based view recommends diagnosing a (functional-level) process as automatic when it is based on an associative mechanism (on the algorithmic level). The dual-mode view and the triple-mode view recommend diagnosing a process as automatic when there is evidence for the presence of one automaticity feature. From this, it can be inferred that the remaining automaticity features are present as well. The essence view recommends investigating the presence of the feature that is deemed essential. According to the gradual, decompositional view defended in this chapter, a process or behavior cannot be diagnosed as either automatic or nonautomatic. It can be diagnosed as more or less automatic based on the number of features that are present and the degree to which they are present. Instead of making absolute claims about automaticity, investigators can make relative claims about the automaticity of a process relative to other processes or relative to other occasions or stages of practice.

I elaborated the feature-based view with the proposal to reformulate features in terms of operating conditions. This opens the door for extending the set of conditions with ones that are not related to automaticity features. If the set of conditions is extended in this way, I suggest talking about processes that occur under optimal versus suboptimal conditions instead of about processes that are nonautomatic versus automatic. Suboptimal conditions include the absence of a promoting goal, the presence of a counteracting goal, the absence of a remote goal, the absence of a conscious stimulus input, the absence of a large amount of attentional capacity, the absence of attention being focused on the stimulus input, the absence of a large amount of time, and the absence of an objectively or subjectively intense stimulus input. Optimal conditions include the opposites of these conditions.

## Future Directions

Future research aimed at diagnosing the automaticity of processes or behavior may benefit from the following recommendations:

(1)  A first recommendation from the decompositional view is to investigate features of automaticity one by one. When calling some process automatic, one should specify which feature of automaticity one has in mind. One should also specify whether the feature under consideration can be applied to entire processes or to parts of them (inputs, outputs).

(2)  My proposal to reformulate features in terms of operating conditions and to extend the set of operating conditions beyond those strictly related to automaticity features leads to a second recommendation. I recommend studing a series of conditions for the occurrence of a process, including ones that are not strictly related to automaticity features such as the direction of attention and objective or subjective stimulus intensity.

(3)  The decompositional view recognizes that there are relations among the central ingredients that figure in the definitions of features or operating conditions. For example, research shows that goals do influence attention and that attention does influence consciousness. As argued earlier, however, there may not be one-to-one relations among these concepts. Attention can be influenced by other factors than goals, such as stimulus intensity. Likewise, consciousness can be influenced by other factors than attention, such as stimulus intensity and stimulus duration. The additional point that conditions may be interdependent has the implication that it is ultimately not very informative to have knowledge about a single operating condition. It is best to progressively investigate and map out the larger set of interdependent conditions at stake.

In conclusion, when calling a process automatic, one should specify the features of automaticity (or operating conditions) one has in mind, or even better, accompany them with empirical arguments. In addition, one should attempt to uncover the interrelations among the features (or operating conditions).

## Acknowledgments

Preparation of this chapter was supported by Methusalem grant BOF09/01M00209 of Ghent University.

## Notes

1. The term *goal* has two meanings. A first meaning is apparent in the phrase "a person/process is *directed toward* a goal." Here, goal means a desired state in the future. One way in which a person can be directed toward a future state is by forming a representation of it. This leads to a second meaning of the term *goal*, which is apparent in the phrase "a person/process is driven or *caused by* a goal." Here, goal means a representation of a state, which, when activated, may act as a cause.

2. Some authors have used these two aspects of attention (direction and quantity) as the basis for two types of attention (input attention and central attention) that have separate functions, and separate temporal and anatomical loci (cf. Johnston, McCann, & Remington, 1995). I prefer treating them as aspects that are not entirely separable. When attention is directed somewhere, there is always *some* amount of attention that is being spent.

## References

Allport, A. (1989). Visual attention. In M. I. Posner (Ed.), *Foundation of cognitive science* (pp. 631–682). Cambridge, MA: MIT Press.

Anderson, J. R. (1992). Automaticity and the ACT* theory. American Journal of Psychology, 105, 165–180.

Bargh, J. A. (1989). Conditional automaticity: Varieties of automatic influence in social perception and cognition. In J. S. Uleman & J. A. Bargh (Eds.), *Unintended thought* (pp. 3–51). New York: Guilford Press.

Bargh, J. A. (1992). The ecology of automaticity. Toward establishing the conditions needed to produce automatic processing effects. American Journal of Psychology, 105, 181–199.

Bargh, J. A., Chaiken, S., Raymond, P., & Hymes, C. (1996). The automatic evaluation effect: Unconditional automatic activation with a pronunciation task. Journal of Experimental Social Psychology, 32, 104–128.

Block, N. (1995). On a confusion about a function of consciousness. Behavioral and Brain Sciences, 18, 227–287.

Carlson, R. A., & Lundy, D. H. (1992). Consistency and restructuring in cognitive procedural sequences. Journal of Experimental Psychology: Learning, Memory, and Cognition, 18, 127–141.

Carver, C. S., & Scheier, M. F. (1999). Themes and issues in the self-regulation of behaviour. In R. S. Wyer (Ed.), *Advances in social cognition* (Vol.12, pp. 1–105). Mahwah, NJ: Erlbaum.

Carver, C. S., & Scheier, M. F. (2002). Control processes and self-organization as complementary principles underlying behaviour. Personality and Social Psychology Review, 6, 304–315.

Crisp, T. M., & Warfield, T. A. (2001). Kim's master argument. Noûs, 35, 304–316.

De Brigard, F., & Prinz, J. (2010). Attention and consciousness. In L. Nadel (Ed.), *Wiley interdisciplinary reviews: Cognitive science* (Vol. 1, pp. 51–59). Hoboken, NJ: Wiley.

Gati, I., & Ben-Shakar, G. (1990). Novelty and significance in orientation and habituation: A feature-matching approach. Journal of Experimental Psychology: General, 119, 251–263.

Hahn, U., & Chater, N. (1998). Similarity and rules: Distinct? Exhaustive? Empirically distinguishable? Cognition, 65, 197–230.

Hélie, S., Waldschmidt, J. G., & Ashby, F. G. (2010). Automaticity in rule-based and information-integration categorization. Attention, Perception, and Psychophysics, 72, 1013–1031.

Itti, L. (2007) Visual salience. Scholarpedia, 2(9), 3327.

Jiang, Y., Costello, P., Fang, F., Huang, M., & He, S. (2006). Gender and sexual orientation dependent attentional effect of invisible images. Proceedings of the National Academy of Sciences USA, 103, 17048–17052.

Johnston, J. C., McCann, R. S., & Remington, R. W. (1995). Chronometric evidence for two types of attention. Psychological Science, 6, 365–369.

Kahneman, D., & Chajczyk, D. (1983). Test of the automaticity of reading: Dilution of Stroop effects by color-irrelevant stimuli. Journal of Experimental Psychology: Human Perception and Performance, 9, 497–509.

Klauer, K. C., Eder, A. B., Greenwald, A. G., & Abrams, R. L. (2007). Priming of semantic classifications by novel subliminal prime words. Consciousness and Cognition, 16, 63–83.

Koch, C., & Tsuchiya, N. (2007). Attention and consciousness: Two distinct brain processes. Trends in Cognitive Science, 11, 16–22

Kouider, S., & Dehaene, S. (2007). Levels of processing during non-conscious perception: A critical review of visual masking. Philosophical Transactions of the Royal Society B, Biological Sciences, 362, 857–875.

Kramer, A. F., Strayer, D. L., & Buckley, J. (1990). Development and transfer of automatic processing. Journal of Experimental Psychology: Human Perception and Performance, 16, 505–522.

Lachter, J., Forster, K. I., & Ruthruff, E . (2004). Forty-five years after Broadbent (1958): Still no identification without attention. Psychological Review, 111, 880–913.

Lachter, J., Ruthruff, E., Lien, M-C., & McCann, R. S. (2008). Is attention needed for object identification? Evidence from the Stroop paradigm. Psychonomic Bulletin and Review, 15, 1110–1116.

Logan, G. D. (1988). Toward an instance theory of automatization. Psychological Review, 95, 492–527.

Macdonald, J. S., & Lavie, N. (2008). Load induced blindness. Journal of Experimental Psychology: Human Perception and Performance, 34, 1078–1091.

Mack, A., & Rock, I. (1998). *Inattentional blindness*. Cambridge, MA: MIT Press.

Marr, D. (Ed.). (1982). *Vision: A computational investigation into the human representation and processing of visual information.* New York: Freeman.

Mole, C. (2008). Attention in the absence of consciousness? Trends in Cognitive Sciences, 12, 44.

Moors, A. (2009). Automaticity. In T. Bayne, A. Cleeremans, & P. Wilken (Eds.), *Oxford companion to consciousness* (pp. 91–95). Oxford, England: Oxford University Press.

Moors, A. (in press). Examining the mapping problem in dual process models. In J. W. Sherman, B. Gawronski, & Y. Trope (Eds.), *Dual processes in social psychology*. NY: Guilford.

Moors, A., & De Houwer, J. (2006a). Automaticity: A theoretical and conceptual analysis. Psychological Bulletin, 132, 297–326.

Moors, A., & De Houwer, J. (2006b). Problems with dividing the realm of cognitive processes. Psychological Inquiry, 17, 199–204.

Moors, A., & De Houwer, J. (2007). What is Automaticity: An analysis of its component features and their interrelations. In J. A. Bargh (Ed.), *Social psychology and the unconscious: The automaticity of higher mental processes* (pp. 11–50). New York: Psychology Press.

Moors, A., De Houwer, J., & Eelen, P. (2004). Automatic stimulus-goal comparisons: Support from motivational affective priming studies. Cognition and Emotion, 18, 29–54.

Moors, A., Spruyt, A., & De Houwer, J. (2010). In search of a measure that qualifies as implicit: Recommentations based on a decompositional view of automaticity. In B. Gawronski & K. B. Payne (Eds.), *Handbook of implicit social cognition: Measurement, theory, and application* (pp. 19–37). New York: Guilford Press.

Musch, J., & Klauer, K. C. (2001). Locational uncertainty moderates affective congruency effects in the evaluation decision task. Cognition and Emotion, 15, 167–188.

Naccache, L., Blandin, E., & Dehaene, S. (2002). Unconscious masked priming depends on temporal attention. Psychological Science, 13, 416–424.

Öhman, A. (1992). Orienting and attention: Preferred preattentive processing of potentially phobic stimuli. In B. A. Campbell, H. Hayne, & R. Richardson (Eds.), *Attention and information processing in infants and adults* (pp. 263–295). Hillsdale, NJ: Erlbaum.

Posner, M. I. (1994). Attention: The mechanism of consciousness. Proceedings of the National Academy of Science USA, 91, 7398–7403.

Prinz, J. (2004). *Gut reactions: A perceptual theory of emotion*, Oxford, England: Oxford University Press.

Prinz, J. (2010). When is perception conscious? In B. Nanay (Ed.), *Perceiving the world: New essays on perception* (pp. 310–332). Oxford, England: Oxford University Press.

Prinz, J. (in press). Is attention necessary and sufficient for consciousness. In C. Mole, D. Smithies, & W. Wu (Eds.), *Attention: Philosophical and psychological essays*. Oxford, England: Oxford University Press.

Raymond, J. E., Shapiro, K. L., & Arnell, K. M. (1992). Temporary suppression of visual processing in an RSVP task: An attentional blink? Journal of Experimental Psychology: Human Perception and Performance, 18, 849–860.

Rensink, R. A., O'Regan, J. K., & Clark, J. J . (1997). To see or not to see: The need for attention to perceive changes in scenes. Psychological Science, 8, 368–373.

Rosenbloom, P. S., & Newell, A. (1986). The chunking of goal hierarchies: A generalized model of practice. In R. S. Michaliski, J. G. Carbonell, & T. M. Mitchell (Eds.), *Machine learning: An artificial intelligence approach* (Vol. 2, pp. 247–288). Los Altos, CA: Morgan Kaufmann.

Schneider, W., & Fisk, A. D. (1984). Automatic category search and its transfer. Journal of Experimental Psychology: Learning, Memory, and Cognition, 10, 1–15

Searle, J. R. (1983). *Intentionality: An essay in the philosophy of mind*. Cambridge, England: Cambridge University Press.

Shallice, T. (1988). Information-processing models of consciousness: Possibilities and problems. In A. J. Marcel & E. Bisiach (Eds.), *Consciousness in contemporary science* (pp. 305–333). Oxford, England: Oxford University Press.

Shiffrin, R. M. (1988). Attention. In R. C. Atkinson, R. J. Hernstein, G. Lindzey, & R. D. Luce (Eds.), *Stevens' handbook of experimental psychology* (Vol. 2, pp. 739–811). New York: Wiley.

Shiffrin, R. M., & Schneider, W. (1977). Controlled and automatic human information processing: II. Perceptual learning, automatic attending and a general theory. Psychological Review, 84, 127–190.

Smith, E. R., & Lerner, M. (1986). Development of automatism of social judgements. Journal of Personality and Social Psychology, 50, 246–259.

Tapia, E., Breitmeyer, B. G., & Broyles, E. C. (2011) Properties of spatial attention in conscious and nonconscious visual information processing. Consciousness and Cognition, 20, 426–431.

Tapia, E., Breitmeyer, B. G., & Shooner, C. R. (2010). Role of task-1050 directed attention in nonconscious and conscious response priming by form and color. Journal of Experimental Psychology: Human Perception and Performance, 36, 74–87.

Teige-Mocigemba, S., & Klauer, K. C. (2008). "Automatic" evaluation? Strategic effects on affective priming. Journal of Experimental Social Psychology, 44, 1414–1417.

Treisman, A., Vieira, A., & Hayes, A. (1992). Automaticity and preattentive processing. American Journal of Psychology, 105, 341–362.

Tzelgov, J., Henik, A., Sneg, R., & Baruch, B. (1996). Unintentional word reading via the phonological route: The Stroop effect with cross-script homophones. Journal of Experimental Psychology: Learning, Memory, and Cognition, 22, 336–349.

Tzelgov, J., Yehene, V., Kotler, L., & Alon, A. (2000). Automatic comparisons of artificial digits never compared: Learning linear ordering relations. Journal of Experimental Psychology: Learning, Memory, and Cognition, 26, 103–120.

Uleman, J. S. (1989). A framework for thinking intentionally about unintended thoughts. In J. S. Uleman & J. A. Bargh (Eds.), *Unintended thought* (pp. 425–449). New York: Guilford Press.

van Boxtel J. J., Tsuchiya, N., & Koch, C. (2010). Consciousness and attention: On sufficiency and necessity. Frontiers in Psychology, 1, 217.

Van Opstal, F., Moors, A., Fias, W., & Verguts, T. (2008). Offline and online automatic number comparison. Psychological Research, 72, 347–352.

Wolbers, T., Schoell, E. D., Verleger, R., Kraft, S., McNamara, A., Joskowski, P., & Buchel, C. (2006). Changes in connectivity profiles as a mechanism for strategic control over interfering subliminal information. Cerebral Cortex, 16, 857–864.

Yantis, S. (2000). Goal-directed and stimulus-driven determinants of attentional control. In S. Monsell & J. Driver (Eds.), Attention and performance (Vol. 18, pp. 73–103). Cambridge, MA: MIT Press.

# Unconscious Processes

John F. Kihlstrom

**Abstract**

Unconscious processes manifest themselves in two quite different ways. First, some processes are unconscious in the strict sense that they are executed automatically, in response to certain stimulus conditions. At least in principle automatic processes are unavailable to conscious introspection and are independent of conscious control. Second, some mental contents—percepts, memories, and the like—are unconscious in the sense that they are inaccessible to phenomenal awareness but nonetheless affect the person's ongoing experience, thought, and action. Solid evidence for this aspect of unconscious mental life is provided by dissociations between explicit (conscious) and implicit (unconscious) memory and perception. There is also mounting evidence for implicit learning and implicit thought, dissociated from their conscious counterparts, as well as explicit-implicit dissociations in the domains of emotion and motivation. The explicit-implicit distinction provides a vehicle for identifying some of the neural correlates of consciousness.

**Key Words:** automaticity, attentional blindness, implicit emotion, implicit learning, implicit memory, implicit motivation, implicit perception, implicit thought, inattentional blindness, priming

The unconscious mind was ostensibly discovered by Freud—though as Ellenberger (1970) makes clear, the idea had been expressed much earlier by Leibniz, Kant, and Helmholtz, among many others. After the dark age of functional behaviorism, the cognitive revolution in psychology promoted a resurgence of interest in both conscious and unconscious mental life (Kihlstrom, 1987, 1994). The new view of the unconscious, however, owes little to Freud.

## Consciousness, the Unconscious, and the Mental

Let me first make the terms of the discussion clear: We are talking about unconscious *mental* life. There are many physical and biological processes that, in some sense, proceed unconsciously: the expansion of the universe, the orbiting of planets around the sun, evolution by natural selection, photosynthesis,

and the machinations of DNA. The biochemistry of brain activity, which in humans at least gives rise to consciousness, itself goes on unconsciously. Considerations such as this led some Romantic philosophers, such as Edward von Hartmann, to declare that the unconscious pervades the universe. But as Searle (1992) has argued, the term *unconscious* only makes sense when applied to mental activity, as a contrast to *consciousness*. There is little point in talking about something being *unconscious* if that same thing cannot also be conscious. This leads us to ask what the hallmark of mental life is.

Here we turn to another philosopher, Franz Brentano, who in fact taught Freud and happily included him in his "school." Brentano argued (1874/1973) that *intentionality is the mark of the mental*: All mental states are intentional in nature, and only mental states are intentional. Put another way, mental states are representational: They are always *about* something. We do not think, or feel, or desire in the abstract; rather we think, feel, or desire *something*. The nature of intentional states was further explicated by Bertrand Russell (1912, and elsewhere) in terms of *propositional attitudes*, which state a cognitive relation between a person and some proposition P. These attitudes come in various forms: namely, knowing, feeling, and wanting—Kant's trilogy of mind (Hilgard, 1980)—or, more generically, *believing*. When I presented a version of this article at a conference at the University of Vienna, I *knew* that Vienna is the capital of Austria; I *believed* that it is a beautiful city; I *felt* honored to have been invited to speak there; and I *wanted* to make a good impression. All of these were conscious mental states. All of them were about something. And all of them represented my cognitive attitude toward that event.

Put in the standard language of cognitive psychology, mental representations take the form of percepts, memories, thoughts, images, and the like. In an experiment, subjects *perceive* words that are presented on a computer screen; they *remember* words that appeared on a list; they *learn* a new fact about the world; or they *think* about some problem they encounter in their environment. Usually, these representations are accessible to consciousness, in that the subjects are aware of what is on their minds. The question for us is whether these same representations can exist outside the scope of phenomenal awareness and nonetheless influence our ongoing experience, thought, and action.

## Automaticity and Unconscious Processing

It is important to frame the question in this way because in contemporary psychology the most popular construal of unconscious mental life is in terms of *automaticity* (e.g., Hassin, Uleman, & Bargh, 2005; see also Chapter 11, "Automaticity"). According to this view, some mental processes occur outside the scope of conscious awareness and control. These processes are inevitably evoked by the appearance of certain stimuli, are incorrigibly executed once set in motion, consume few or no cognitive resources, and do not interfere with conscious mental activities. Automatic processes, as exemplified by the Stroop color-word effect (MacLeod, 1991), are unconscious in the strict sense that they are not available to phenomenal awareness under any circumstances and can be known only by inference. The distinction between automatic and controlled processes is not without its problems (Moors & DeHouwer, 2006), but it has become widely accepted within

psychology, and lately a rather large industry has developed around its application in social psychology (Kihlstrom, 2008).

The notion of unconscious, automatic processing has its roots in Helmholtz's (1866/1968) idea that unconscious inferences are critical for conscious perception. For Helmholtz, the retinal image was insufficient to support visual perception, requiring the perceiver, in Bruner's (1973) words, to go "beyond the information given" by the proximal stimulus to make assumptions and inferences about the form, location, and movement of the distal stimulus. We are not consciously aware of making these inferences, but they are simply necessary for conscious perception to occur. Helmholtz's arguments were, of course, strenuously denied by Gibson's (1979) idea that we perceive the world directly, without any need for inferences, conscious or unconscious.

This article is not the place to settle that debate (see Chapter 7, "Perception and Attention"), and for present purposes let us simply stipulate that Helmholtz was onto something. But the fact that some mental processes can occur unconsciously says nothing about whether the mental representations on which they operate, and which they in turn generate, can be unconscious. Certainly automatic processes can act on what Freud would have called *preconscious* representations, before focal attention (cathexis) is directed to them. But the representations that they generate are generally thought to be consciously accessible. I may not know how unconscious inferences automatically generate the moon illusion (Kaufman & Rock, 1962; Rock & Kaufman, 1962), but I am certainly aware of the moon when I look at it, and I am aware that the moon looks larger on the horizon than it does at zenith. So the question remains: Can we have mental representations—percepts, memories, thoughts, bits of knowledge—which are themselves unconscious, yet influence our experience, thought, and action nonetheless? Can we see the moon without consciously being aware of it?

## The Cognitive Unconscious

Evidence for unconscious mental *contents*, which influence experience, thought, and action outside of phenomenal awareness, comes mostly from the cognitive domain of perception and memory. It is possible that unconscious percepts and memories are subject only to unconscious, automatic processing: It seems unlikely that we could engage in conscious, deliberate, controlled processing of mental contents of which we were unaware. But, in principle, it seems appropriate to discuss unconscious cognitive contents separately from the unconscious processes that might operate on (and generate) them (e.g., Nisbett & Wilson, 1977).

Granted, the process-content distinction is not always easy to make (e.g., White, 1980). It is clear enough in the classical multistage information-processing models of cognition, which distinguished between information-storage structures (which, after all, held informational content), and the control processes, which passed informational content from structure to structure, transforming it along the way (e.g., Atkinson & Shiffrin, 1968). And it is also clear enough in "symbolic" cognitive architectures based on a distinction between procedural and declarative knowledge (Anderson, 1983). But even in "connectionist" architectures (e.g., Rumelhart & McClelland, 1986), "content" can be identified with the layers of a neural network, network, and "process" with the weights of the connections between the nodes that comprise these layers, and which get from the input layer to the output layer. The input layer may or may not be represented in consciousness (think of Leibnitz's *petites perceptions*), but once a connectionist network settles into a relaxed state, the stable state of the output layer—whether it represents the past tense of a verb or the perspective of a Necker cube—is presumably available to conscious awareness.

The process-content distinction is blurred somewhat by the existence of "intermediate" products of information processing. Connectionist architectures, for example, interpose one or more "hidden" layers between the input and output layers, and the characterization of them as "hidden" might suggest that they are phenomenally unconscious. But that is not the meaning of "unconscious" intended in this chapter. The question to be addressed is whether we can sensibly ask whether the percepts, memories, and thoughts that would be represented by the output layer, normally in consciousness, can be inaccessible to phenomenal awareness yet nonetheless influence the person's ongoing experience, thought, and action.

## Implicit Memory

The study of implicit memory represents a milestone in our understanding of unconscious mental life. We now know that amnesic patients can show priming effects, in which the presentation of a prime affects processing of a target presented later, even though they cannot consciously remember the prime. Priming effects exemplify what Schacter

(1987) has labeled *implicit memory*—the influence of a past event on subsequent experience, thought, or action, in the absence of conscious recollection of that event (see also Chapter 15, "Implicit Memory").

An early demonstration of the dissociation between explicit and implicit memory in the amnesic syndrome was supplied by Warrington and Weiskrantz (1970). Their patients showed profound deficits in recalling or recognizing a previously studied list of words but normal levels of priming when completing word fragments or word stems. Graf and his colleagues confirmed spared priming in amnesia with stem completion when compared with an explicit memory task in which the same stems were used as cues for explicit recall (Graf, Squire, & Mandler, 1984). The best comparisons of explicit and implicit memory follow their model, equating explicit and implicit memory for the informational value of the cues supplied in the tests.

A great deal of subsequent research has shown that explicit (conscious) and implicit (unconscious) memory can be dissociated in a wide range of conditions, including the amnesic syndrome associated with damage to the medial temporal lobes or diencephalon, the anterograde and retrograde amnesias associated with electroconvulsive therapy for depression, the anterograde amnesias produced by both general anesthesia administered to surgical patients and conscious sedation in outpatient surgery, dementia, including Alzheimer's disease, normal aging, posthypnotic amnesia, and the functional amnesias associated with dissociative disorders such as fugue and multiple personality. Explicit and implicit memory can also be dissociated in normal, neurologically intact, nonamnesic subjects under conditions where explicit memory is impaired by shallow encoding or long retention intervals.

Although the dissociation of explicit and implicit memory is well established, controversy persists concerning the nature of implicit memory itself. One very popular view holds that explicit and implicit memory are the product of separate memory systems in the brain. A variant on this view, which goes back at least as far as the work of Ewald Hering (of color vision fame) and Samuel Butler (author of *Erewhon*), holds that there are not multiple memory systems as such, but rather that there are multiple cognitive systems for perception, conceptual processing, and the like, which each have an ability to learn. A competing view assumes that there is only a single memory system, but that explicit and implicit memory are dissociated when one task (typically, the implicit test) depends on "perceptually driven" processing, and the other (typically the explicit test) depends on "conceptually driven" processing. Another view, also assuming only a single memory system, is that implicit memory requires only the activation or preexisting knowledge stored in memory, while explicit memory requires, in addition, the elaboration and integration of activated knowledge structures. Yet another is that implicit memory is the product of automatic processing, while explicit memory is the product of controlled processing.

A major difficulty preventing resolution of this theoretical debate is that almost all research on implicit memory has involved repetition priming, and very little has involved semantic priming. Repetition priming, almost by definition, can be mediated by a perceptual representation system or by perceptually driven processing. Evidence that explicit memory extends to semantic processing would appear to contradict either approach. But so long as research on implicit memory is dominated by a single paradigm, repetition priming, theorists will not have to contend with this issue. The fact is that implicit memory does extend to semantic processing, and theories need to take this fact into account.

There is more at stake in this debate than understanding the nature of implicit memory: There is also the issue of the scope of unconscious mental life. According to Brentano's doctrine of intentionality, unconscious mental life—like *conscious* mental life—has to be *about* something. An image-like perception-based representation, produced by perceptually driven processing and perhaps stored in a perceptual representation system, is "about" physical structure—what the stimulus sounds or looks like. It is "about" something, but it is not "about" very much. Repetition priming can tell us a lot about perceptual processing and about how perceptual structure is represented in memory. But an unconscious memory that is limited to perception-based representations of past events is simply not very interesting (one thinks of the Jerry Leiber-Mike Stoller song, "Is That All There Is?"). Ever since Freud (for better or worse), when people have talked about unconscious memory, they have been talking about memory that has *meaning* attached to it. Therefore, the important question for future research on implicit memory is to determine whether unconscious memories can represent—can "be about"—the meaning, significance, and implications of events, as well as their physical structure.

## Implicit Perception

Just as implicit memory refers to the influence of past events that cannot be consciously remembered, so *implicit perception* refers to the influence of events in the current stimulus environment that cannot be consciously perceived (Kihlstrom, Barnhardt, & Tataryn, 1992). Explicit and implicit perception are dissociated in so-called subliminal perception, where priming effects occur even though the prime is presented at an intensity, or for a duration, that is below the threshold for conscious perception; or when the prime has been masked by another stimulus. Subliminal perception has been controversial almost since the first report of it in 1884 (Dixon, 1971, 1981). The alternative label of "implicit" perception avoids methodological controversies over the details of threshold-setting procedures and focuses the controversy on whether the stimulus is consciously perceptible (Cheesman & Merikle, 1984; Greenwald, Draine, & Abrams, 1996).

Dissociations between explicit and implicit perception can also be observed in other conditions, including blindsight associated with lesions to the striate cortex (Weiskrantz, 1986), visual neglect resulting from damage to the temporo-parietal area of the brain, prosopagnosia, hypnotic blindness and deafness, and the "hysterical" blindness and deafness observed in cases of conversion disorder (see Chapter 9, "Disorders of Attention"). In these cases, the stimuli in question are in no sense "subliminal," although they are not represented in conscious awareness. This is also the case in experiments on "preattentive" or "preconscious" processing employing such paradigms as parafoveal vision and dichotic listening, inattentional blindness (Mack & Rock, 1998), and various forms of attentional blindness (e.g., repetition blindness, the attentional blink, and change blindness). In these cases, too, the stimulus is in no sense subliminal, which is all the more reason to prefer *implicit perception* as the more appropriate umbrella term.

Subliminal perception effects are sometimes classified as instances of implicit memory, on the ground that the presentation of the prime occurs before the presentation of the target. But in subliminal perception, the stimulus-onset asynchrony is extremely brief, less than a second, with no intervening distraction, so that the prime is presented in what William James called "the specious present." More important, in implicit memory the subject is aware of the prime when it is presented but subsequently forgets it; in implicit perception the subject is never aware of the prime at all. On these grounds, priming by stimuli presented during general anesthesia is probably better counted as an instance of implicit perception.

The distinction between repetition and semantic priming, introduced in the discussion of implicit memory, is pertinent to implicit perception as well. The task of perception is not merely to form an internal mental representation of the physical structure of the stimulus—its form, location, and activity. As Bruner argued persuasively, every act of perception is an act of categorization. If so, then perception is not complete until the distal stimulus has been identified and categorized. Accordingly, at least since the work of Marcel (1983a, 1983b), the ultimate test of implicit perception has been semantic priming—evidence that the stimulus has been processed for meaning.

Evidence for semantic priming in implicit perception has sometimes been taken as justification for exaggerated claims for unconscious influence in advertising and psychotherapy (e.g., Packard, 1957) or magazine promotions of "subliminal" self-help tapes. In fact, the same research that indicates that implicit perception extends to semantic processing also indicates that semantic processing outside of awareness is analytically limited. For example, while the single word *doctor* may prime processing of the semantically related word *nurse*, it turns out to be difficult to process the meaning of even a two-word phrase presented outside of conscious awareness (Greenwald, 1992). Sleep learning does not appear to be possible, except to the extent that the subject stays awake (Simon & Emmons, 1955); and information processing during general anesthesia appears to be limited to repetition, but not semantic, priming (Kihlstrom & Cork, 2007). There is no good evidence for the efficacy of "subliminal" self-help tapes—nor, in some cases, any evidence that there is even any message on them, subliminal or otherwise (Moore, 2008).

Of course, statements about the analytic scope of implicit perception may have to take account of the processing demands of the experimental task. It stands to reason that unconscious percepts are ordinarily subject to automatic, but not controlled, processing. It would seem hard to consciously control the processing of a target of which one is not consciously aware. Presumably, many "perceptually driven" analyses of the physical features of a stimulus—enough to support repetition priming—are carried out automatically. The results of Marcel's experiments, and others like them, suggest that simple "conceptually driven" analyses—enough to

support semantic priming of the "doctor-nurse" type—are also carried out automatically. But more complex semantic analyses, of the sort required to understand phrases and whole sentences, may require conscious, controlled processes that simply cannot be applied to percepts of which the subject is not consciously aware. For that matter, there may well be complex perceptual analyses that also require conscious, controlled processing, and that are necessarily denied to unconscious percepts.

On the other hand, it is important to remember that most automatic processes are not innate but have become automatized through extensive practice—think of Ericsson's "10,000-hour" principle. It is entirely possible that even very complex semantic (or perceptual) analyses can be automatized if they are highly practiced. In a provocative experiment by Spelke, Hirst, and Neisser (1976), subjects were given extensive practice in taking dictation while simultaneously reading prose. Eventually, the subjects were able to do this successfully, taking accurate dictation and reading at normal speed with a high degree of comprehension—but they had little or no conscious recollection of the words that they had transcribed. At this stage, presumably, the dictated words were not subject to the kind of elaborate, semantic processing required to remember and categorize words. On later trials, however, they were able to recall the words, and to identify phonological and categorical relations within the dictated lists—even writing the category to which the words belonged as opposed to the words themselves. These investigators interpreted their results as indicating that attention is a skill that, with practice, can be deployed in several directions at once. But they also raise the possibility that the scope of implicit perception can include even extensive semantic processing—provided that the processing task has first been automatized through extensive practice.

### Implicit Learning

Apparently, subjects can also learn unconsciously, in the sense that new knowledge acquired through experience can affect their ongoing behavior, even though the subjects are not aware of what they have learned. So, for example, Reber (1993) has shown that subjects can pick up on the "grammar" by which meaningless strings of letters have been arranged, permitting them to discriminate between grammatical and ungrammatical letter strings, even though they cannot articulate the grammar itself. Similar *implicit learning* effects have been observed in a number of different paradigms, including categorization, the detection of covariation, sequence learning, and the control of complex systems (see Chapter 39, "Induction").

Again, implicit learning effects are sometimes classified as instances of implicit memory, but there is a difference. Implicit memory is an unconscious expression of episodic memory: Subjects do not consciously remember some past event. But implicit learning covers semantic and procedural knowledge. Source amnesia, where subjects are aware of what they know but cannot remember where they have learned it, is a better example of implicit memory. By contrast, subjects in implicit learning remember their learning experiences quite well—they just are not consciously aware of what they have learned from them. For example, Reber's subjects remember studying a list of letter strings but appear unaware of the grammatical rules that they abstracted from that experience. Accordingly, I prefer to reserve the term "implicit memory" for unconscious episodic memory—memory for events embedded in a specific spatiotemporal context.

In contrast to implicit memory and implicit perception, implicit learning has not yet been established to the satisfaction of all interested parties (e.g., Shanks & St.John, 1994). Partly this is because, again in contrast to memory and perception, it is not easy to equate the informational value of the cues provided for the explicit and implicit tests. In the case of memory, for example, subjects can be asked to complete the stem *ash___* with an item from the study list (explicit memory), or with the first word that comes to mind (implicit memory). But in the case of artificial-grammar learning, for example, the typical implicit task asks subjects to make a grammaticality judgment, while the typical explicit task requires them to specify the grammar itself, in whole or in part. These instructions entail quite different cues. Moreover, it may be that subjects lack complete awareness of the grammar but have enough that they can make discriminations at levels above chance. These are not easy methodological problems to solve.

There is also a nontrivial question of just what is learned in implicit learning. Returning to the artificial-grammar paradigm, the implication of most theorizing is that subjects unconsciously acquire something like a Markov-process grammar, a piece of procedural knowledge, which guides their grammaticality judgments. An alternative view is that they acquire something like a prototype of a grammatical string—which would be a piece of declarative knowledge. Or, given that the usual cover task in

these experiments is to memorize the letter strings, they may base their grammaticality judgments on comparisons with exemplars remembered from the study phase. The format of the knowledge acquired in implicit learning experiments bears on the critical question of whether the learning is truly implicit. If subjects abstracted a prototype instead of inducing a rule but are subsequently asked to specify the rule, they may appear to be unaware of what they have learned, even though they are completely aware of the prototype—about which they have not been asked.

### Implicit Thought

An emerging area of research interest is *implicit thought*—where subjects are influenced by ideas that are not, themselves, properly construed as percepts or memories (Dorfman, Shames, & Kihlstrom, 1996; Kihlstrom, Shames, & Dorfman, 1996). For example, Bowers and his colleagues (Bowers, Regehr, Balthazard, & Parker, 1990) showed that subjects could discriminate between problems that are soluble and those that are not, even though they had not actually arrived at the solutions in question. Along the same lines, Shames (1994) found that the unconscious solution nevertheless primed subjects' performance on a lexical-decision task. Similar effects have been observed in both neurological patients and intact subjects making risky choices (who may make the correct choice even though they do not consciously feel the anxiety that comes with the appreciation of risk) and also in studies of insight learning. Children who are learning to solve arithmetic problems show signs of shifting to a more efficient cognitive strategy before they are aware of having done so (Siegler, 2000). In each case, the source of the unconscious influence on task performance is neither a percept (i.e., a mental representation of some event in the current stimulus environment) nor a memory (i.e., a representation of some event in the past). Instead, it is something internally generated by the subject, albeit outside of conscious awareness: Call it a thought.

Bowers speculated that such "intimations" are related to the intuition phase of creative problem-solving, as described by Wallas (1921) and others (see Chapter 50, "Creativity"). In this view, the unconscious solution gathers strength during the incubation phase and emerges fully into consciousness as an insight (see Chapter 49, "Insight"). The subject feels that something is just over the horizon—an experience common among artists and mathematicians alike. The "heuristics and biases" program in research on judgment and decision making (see Chapter 38, "Judgment Under Uncetainty") has led some theorists to cast doubt on the utility of intuitions such as these (e.g., Metcalfe, 1986). And, more recently, "gut feelings" have been implicated in irrational (or, at least *non*rational), emotion-based theories of moral reasoning (e.g., Haidt, 2001). But the work of Bowers and others on implicit thought suggests that intuitions can have a purely cognitive basis. While it is certainly possible to construct situations where intuitions can lead us astray (e.g., Jacoby, Kelley, Brown, & Jasechko, 1989), it is also possible that, in the course of everyday living, intuitions can be rational guides to appropriate choice.

## The Emotional and Motivational Unconscious

In addition to this evidence for the cognitive unconscious (Kihlstrom, 1987), there are also hints of unconscious emotion and motivation.

### The Conative Unconscious

David McClelland and his colleagues, for example, claimed that procedures such as the Thematic Apperception Test assessed subjects' unconscious motives, while personality questionnaires such as Jackson's Personality Research Form assessed conscious motives (McClelland, Koestner, & Weinberger, 1989). Viewed from this perspective, the frequently lamented lack of substantial correlation between "projective" and "objective" assessments of motive dispositions suggests a dissociation between explicit and implicit motivation (Schultheiss, 2008; Schultheiss & Pang, 2007). In implicit motivation, the subject's experience, thought, and action are affected by a motive (or goal), in the absence of conscious awareness of that motive.

The very notion of unconscious motivation threatens to send us into Freudian territory (Shevrin, 1992), but most contemporary research on unconscious motivation shies away from the primitive sexual and aggressive instincts of classical psychodynamic theory and focuses on more benign, if not mundane, needs for achievement, power, intimacy, and the like. There is good evidence that explicit and implicit motives are elicited by different kinds of stimuli and predict performance on different types of tasks. Taken with the low correlations between "objective" and "projective" motive measures, such findings support the proposition that explicit and implicit motives are, indeed, dissociable.

The definition of implicit motivation parallels those offered in the domain of implicit cognition (memory, perception, learning, and thinking), but it has not been easy to clinch the case for unconscious motives. As with implicit learning, there are big differences in how explicit and implicit motives are assessed—big enough, frankly, to raise the question of whether the two types of tests are actually assessing the same motives; or whether the typically low correlation between them indicates that they differ in terms of accessibility to conscious awareness or is simply a reflection of method variance (Campbell & Fiske, 1959). The cases for implicit memory and implicit perception are strengthened by the fact that they are dissociable, even though the same cues are used to test for both conscious and unconscious expressions; the case for implicit learning is weakened by the absence of such closely matched tests. The same problem adheres to implicit motivation.

### The Affective Unconscious

On the affective side of the ledger, Peter Lang cogently argued that, in principle, every emotional state consists of three components: the subjective feeling, the physiological correlate, and the behavioral response (Lang, 1968). If so, then—at least in principle—we can identify explicit emotion with the subjective feeling state, and *implicit emotion* with the behavioral and physiological components. Where physiological or behavioral components of emotion occur in the absence of a feeling state we can rightly speak of a dissociation between explicit and implicit emotion (Kihlstrom, Mulvaney, Tobias, & Tobis, 2000). Some clinical psychologists refer to such a situation as a state of *desynchrony* (e.g., Rachman & Hodgson, 1974); but desynchronies can take multiple forms, and here we are interested only in dissociations between subjective feeling states and overt or covert behavioral manifestations of emotion.

The success in documenting implicit cognition, especially in the domains of perception and memory, makes the idea of implicit emotion plausible—even if, again, we are treading close to Freudian territory. But, as with implicit motivation, not much by way of compelling evidence has accrued so far. In the most interesting study to date, Winkielman and his colleagues found that masked presentation of happy or angry faces affected subjects' judgments in a consumer-testing situation (Winkielman, Berridge, & Wilbarger, 2005). The effect can be explained as follows: Perception of the emotional faces induced corresponding emotional states in the subjects, and these emotional states in turn affected their judgments. Because the faces were not consciously perceived, this outcome would count at the very least as an example of implicit perception. But because the subjects did not report any changes in emotional state either, it counts as an example of implicit emotion as well. The subjects' choice behavior was influenced not just by a percept but also an affective state, of which they were unaware.

Lately, Greenwald, Banaji, and their colleagues have introduced the Implicit Association Test, a reaction-time measure intended to reveal prejudices and other attitudes that subjects are not aware of harboring (e.g., Greenwald et al., 2002). As in the case of implicit motivation, the principal evidence that the IAT taps unconscious emotion is the relatively low correlation between attitudes as assessed by the IAT and corresponding attitudes measured by traditional methods, such as a rating scale. The point is controversial, as the IAT is infected by a number of potentially confounding variables (e.g., Arkes & Tetlock, 2004; for a reply, see Banaji, Nosek, & Greenwald, 2004). Moreover, the correlations in question are not, actually, all that low. Nosek (2007) reported a mean correlation of .48 between IAT and explicit "attitude thermometer" measures of the same attitude. However, it should be noted that this value is relatively high by the standards of multimethod personality research (e.g., Mischel, 1968). Even accepting the characterization of IAT correlations as "low," it is not yet clear that the IAT taps attitudes that are truly unconscious, as opposed to providing an unobtrusive measurement (Webb, Campbell, Schwartz, & Sechrest, 1966) of consciously accessible attitudes that the subject merely refuses to disclose to the investigator.

## Reflections and Implications

Although the findings cited here give sufficient reason for taking unconscious mental life seriously, it has to be said that the evidence in each of these domains is not equally strong. Implicit perception and implicit memory have now been established to the satisfaction of all but a few critics (and it is possible that no amount of evidence would convince these naysayers anyway). Implicit learning has been explored in the laboratory for more than 40 years, but still the dissociation between explicit and implicit learning has not been established with the rigor that characterizes research in the domains of perception and memory. Implicit thought is on somewhat softer ground, if only because there have been so few relevant studies. This holds true for implicit motives as well as implicit emotions.

There is also the matter of the comparative power of unconscious processing. Recently, in both the scientific literature and the popular press, authors have touted the power of unconscious learning and thought—that unconscious learning and automatic processing allow us to solve more complex problems, more efficiently, than is possible consciously (Gladwell, 2005; Wilson, 2002). In some sense, these claims revive Romantic notions of the power of *The Unconscious* that were popular in the 19th century (Hartmann, 1868/1931). But it has to be said that these claims are not well founded in scientific evidence—if for no other reason than that there are relatively few methodologically adequate comparisons of conscious and unconscious processing. There is every reason to think that unconscious perception is analytically limited, for example. The existence of schools and universities, and other cultural institutions for the deliberate transmission of knowledge from one person, and one generation, to another are ample evidence of the power and importance of conscious, deliberate thinking, and conscious, deliberate learning.

More to the point, the debate over automaticity testifies to the odd situation that consciousness still makes psychologists uncomfortable—what Flanagan (1992) calls *conscious shyness*. Partly as a holdover from the dark days of behaviorism, and partly as a reflection of the functionalist stance that is so popular in the philosophy of mind, psychologists and other cognitive scientists are often reluctant to take consciousness seriously, or even utter the word. Still, we must take care that our acceptance of unconscious mental life does not tilt unnecessarily into a stance of conscious inessentialism or epiphenomenalism. Unconscious states and processes can influence ongoing experience, thought, and action; but that fact does not warrant relegating conscious mental life to the dustbin of "folk psychology."

Beyond mere acceptance that the psychological unconscious is a viable concept after all, the phenomena I have described here may offer a new approach to one of the central problems in psychology, cognitive science, and neuroscience—what we might call the mysterious leap from the body to the mind: What are the neural substrates of conscious awareness? Studies of the physiology of sleep and dreams (e.g., Hobson, Pace-Schott, & Stickgold, 2000), and of general anesthesia (e.g., Hameroff & Penrose, 1996), will help us to understand the neural substrates of *being conscious* as opposed to unconscious. And studies of automatic and controlled processes (e.g., Schneider & Chein, 2003) will help us to understand the neural substrates of *acting consciously* as opposed to unconsciously.

Another piece of the puzzle will come from studies comparing the neural correlates of explicit and implicit perception, memory, thought, and the like (e.g., Schacter & Badgaiyan, 2001). The explicit-implicit distinction offers a natural control group for neuroscientifc research: what are the differences, in terms of neural activity, between the conscious and the unconscious influence of percepts and memories? In this way, we may get new insights into precisely what makes conscious percepts, and conscious memories, conscious. Among these insights may be that the neural correlates of consciousness are going to be as variable as consciousness itself. Conscious recollection has its seat in the hippocampus and the rest of the medial temporal lobe memory system, for example, but conscious (visual) perception has its seat in the striate cortex. Where the neural correlates of consciousness lie may depend precisely on what people are conscious of—what their conscious mental states are *about*. And, for that matter, the same point may be taken with regard to automaticity: the neural distinction between automatic and controlled processes may depend on precisely what has been automatized.

Setting neuroscience aside, the explicit-implicit distinction also gives us some insight into the *psychological* distinction between conscious and unconscious mental life. Returning to Brentano's and Russell's discussion of intentionality, note that each of their examples of a mental state invokes the self and delineates a kind of ownership between the person and what is going through his or her mind (see Chapter 57, "Self-Knowledge"). In linguistic terms, conscious mental states always include some reference to the self as the agent or patient of some action, or the stimulus or experiencer of some state.

Consider the sorts of tasks in which we demonstrate the dissociation between explicit and implicit memory. First, the subject studies a list of words, including the word *paragon*. On an explicit memory task, the subject is asked what he or she remembers and replies, in effect, "I remember" such-and-such an event from the past—with the emphasis on the first person: "*I* remember studying *this item*." But when a subject is asked to complete a word-stem or a fragment, or to identify a word, or to determine whether a letter string is a word, self-reference is missing, or is there in a very different way: "That fragment can be completed with *paragon*," instead of the more familiar response *parachute*, or *parallel*.

Whatever is going on in the brain during conscious perception and memory, what is going through the mind is a connection between some mental representation of some object or event, and a mental representation of the self. This link appears to be missing in instances of unconscious processing (Kihlstrom, 1997).

## Not a Tumbling-Ground for Whimsies

More than 200 years ago, Immanuel Kant asked whether the notion of unconscious mental states made any sense, and concluded that it does. But only 100 years ago, William James, writing in the *Principles*, warned that the unconscious was "the sovereign means for believing what one likes in psychology, and of turning what might become a science into a tumbling-ground for whimsies." It is all too easy for us, as psychologists, especially psychologists still living in the shadow of Freud, to tell people what they *unconsciously* believe, or feel, or want—how could they possibly contradict us? Studies of automatic and controlled processes, and of explicit and implicit perception, memory, and the like, offer a solution to James's warning, because they offer strict criteria for identifying unconscious mental processes and unconscious mental states—and for tying inferences about subjects' unconscious mental lives to objective evidence of their behavior in the controlled environmental circumstances of the laboratory. The result is that we can now talk about the unconscious in a scientifically respectable way, discover its scope and limitations, and seek to identify the neural correlates of consciousness—all of which represent a great advance in the science of mental life.

## References

Anderson, J. R. (1983). *The architecture of cognition*. Mahwah, NJ: Erlbaum.

Arkes, H. R., & Tetlock, P. E. (2004). Attributions of implicit prejudice, or "Would Jesse Jackson 'fail' the Implicit Association Test?" [with commentary and reply from authors]. *Psychological Inquiry, 15*, 257–321.

Atkinson, R. C., &Shiffrin, R. M. (1968). Human memory: A proposed system and its control processes. In K. W. Spence & J. T. Spence (Eds.), *The psychology of learning and motivation* (Vol. 2, pp. 89–105). New York: Academic Press.

Banaji, M. R., Nosek, B. A., & Greenwald, A. G. (2004). No place for nostalgia in science: A response to Arkes and Tetlock. *Psychological Inquiry, 15*, 279–289.

Bowers, K. S., Regehr, G., Balthazard, C., & Parker, K. (1990). Intuition in the context of discovery. *Cognitive Psychology, 22*, 72–110.

Brentano, F. (1874/1973) *Psychology from an empirical standpoint*, London: Routledge and Kegan Paul.Bruner, J. S. (1973). *Beyond the information given: Studies in the psychology of knowing*. New York: Norton.

Campbell, D. T., & Fiske, D. W. (1959). Convergent and discriminant validation by the multitrait-multimethod matrix. *Psychological Bulletin, 56*, 82–105.

Cheesman, J., & Merikle, P. M. (1984). Priming with and without awareness. *Perception and Psychophysics, 36*, 387–395.

Dixon, N. F. (1971). *Subliminal perception: The nature of a controversy.* London: McGraw-Hill.

Dixon, N. F. (1981). *Preconscious processing.* Chichester, England: Wiley.

Dorfman, J., Shames, V. A., & Kihlstrom, J. F. (1996). Intuition, incubation, and insight: Implicit cognition in problem solving. In G. Underwood (Ed.), *Implicit cognition* (pp. 257–296). Oxford, England: Oxford University Press.

Ellenberger, H. F. (1970). *The discovery of the unconscious: The history and evolution of dynamic psychiatry.* New York: Basic Books.

Flanagan, O. (1992). *Consciousness reconsidered.* Cambridge, MA: MIT Press.

Gibson, J. J. (1979). *The ecological approach to visual perception.* Boston: Houghton Mifflin.

Gladwell, M. (2005). *Blink: The power of thinking without thinking.* Boston: Little, Brown.

Graf, P., Squire, L. R., & Mandler, G. (1984). The information that amnesic patients do not forget. *Journal of Experimental Psychology: Learning, Memory, and Cognition, 10*, 164–178.

Greenwald, A. G. (1992). New look 3: Unconscious cognition reclaimed. *American Psychologist, 47*, 766–779.

Greenwald, A. G., Banaji, M. R., Rudman, L. A., Farnham, S. D., Nosek, B. A., & Mellott, D. S. (2002). A unified theory of implicit attitudes, stereotypes, self-esteem, and self-concept. *Psychological Review, 109*(1), 3–25.

Greenwald, A. G., Draine, S. C., & Abrams, R. L. (1996). Three cognitive markers of unconscious semantic activation. *Science, 273*, 1699–1702.

Haidt, J. (2001). The emotional dog and its rational tail: A social intuitionist approach to moral judgment. *Psychological Review, 108*(4), 814–834.

Hameroff, S. R., & Penrose, R. (1996). Conscious events as orchestrated spacetime selections. *Journal of Consciousness Studies, 3*(1), 36–53.

Hartmann, E. v. (1931). *Philosophy of the unconscious: Speculative results according to the inductive method of physical science.* London: Routledge and Kegan Paul. (Original work published in 1868).

Hassin, R. R., Uleman, J. S., & Bargh, J. A. (Eds.). (2005). *The new unconscious.* New York: Oxford University Press.

Hilgard, E. R. (1980). The trilogy of mind: Cognition, affection, and conation. *Journal for the History of the Behavioral Sciences, 16*, 107–117.

Helmholtz, H. v. (1866/1968). Concerning the perceptions in general. In R.M. Warren & R.P. Warren (Eds.), *Helmholtz on perception* (pp. 171–203). New York: Wiley.

Hobson, J. A., Pace-Schott, E., & Stickgold, R. (2000). Dreaming and the brain: Towards a cognitive neuroscience of conscious states. *Behavioral and Brain Sciences, 23*(6), 793–842.

Jacoby, L. L., Kelley, C., Brown, J., & Jasechko, J. (1989). Becoming famous overnight: Limits on the ability to avoid unconscious influences of the past. *Journal of Personality and Social Psychology, 56*, 326–338.

Kaufman, L., & Rock, I. (1962). The moon illusion: I. *Science, 136*, 953–961.

Kihlstrom, J. F. (1987). The cognitive unconscious. *Science, 237*(4821), 1445–1452.

Kihlstrom, J. F. (1994). The rediscovery of the unconscious. In H. Morowitz & J. L. Singer (Eds.), *The mind, the brain, and complex adaptive systems* (pp. 123–143). Reading, MA: Addison-Wesley.

Kihlstrom, J. F. (1997). Consciousness and me-ness. In J. D. Cohen & J. W. Schooler (Eds.), *Scientific approaches to consciousness* (pp. 451–468). Mahwah, NJ: Erlbaum.

Kihlstrom, J. F. (2008). The automaticity juggernaut. In J. Baer, J. C. Kaufman, & R. F. Baumeister (Eds.), *Psychology and free will* (pp. 155–180). New York: Oxford University Press.

Kihlstrom, J. F., Barnhardt, T. M., & Tataryn, D. J. (1992). Implicit perception. In R. F. Bornstein & T. S. Pittman (Eds.), *Perception without awareness: Cognitive, clinical, and social perspectives* (pp. 17–54). New York: Guilford Press.

Kihlstrom, J. F., & Cork, R. C. (2007). Anesthesia. In M. Velmans & S. Schneider (Eds.), *Blackwell companion to consciousness* (pp. 628–639). Oxford, England: Blackwell.

Kihlstrom, J. F., Mulvaney, S., Tobias, B. A., & Tobis, I. P. (2000). The emotional unconscious. In E. Eich, J. F. Kihlstrom, G. H. Bower, J. P. Forgas, & P. M. Niedenthal (Eds.), *Cognition and emotion* (pp. 30–86). New York: Oxford University Press.

Kihlstrom, J. F., Shames, V. A., & Dorfman, J. (1996). Intimations of memory and thought. In L. M. Reder (Ed.), *Implicit memory and metacognition* (pp. 1–23). Mahwah, NJ: Erlbaum.

Lang, P. J. (1968). Fear reduction and fear behavior: Problems in treating a construct. In J. M. Schlein (Ed.), *Research in psychotherapy* (Vol. 3, pp. 90–103). Washington, DC: American Psychological Association.

Mack, A., & Rock, I. (1998). *Inattentional blindness.* Cambridge, MA: MIT Press.

MacLeod, C. M. (1991). Half a century of research on the Stroop effect: An integrative review. *Psychological Bulletin, 109*(2), 163–203.

Marcel, A. J. (1983a). Conscious and unconscious perception: An approach to the relations between phenomenal experience and perceptual processes. *Cognitive Psychology, 15*, 238–300.

Marcel, A. J. (1983b). Conscious and unconscious perception: Experiments on visual masking and word recognition. *Cognitive Psychology, 15*, 197–237.

McClelland, D. C., Koestner, R., & Weinberger, J. (1989). How do self-attributed and implicit motives differ? *Psychological Review, 96*, 690–702.

Metcalfe, J. (1986). Premonitions of insight predict impending error. *Journal of Experimental Psychology: Learning, Memory, and Cognition, 12*, 623–634.

Mischel, W. (1968). *Personality and assessment.* New York: Wiley.

Moore, T. E. (2008). Subliminal perception: Facts and fallacies. In S. O. Lilienfeld, J. Ruscio, & S. J. Lynn (Eds.), *Navigating the mindfield: A user's guide to distinguishing science from pseudoscience in mental health* (pp. 589–601). Amherst, NY: Prometheus.

Moors, A., & DeHouwer, J. (2006). Automaticity: A theoretical and conceptual analysis. *Psychological Bulletin, 132*(2), 297–326.

Nisbett, R. E., & Wilson, T. D. (1977). Telling more than we can know: Verbal reports on mental processes. *Psychological Review, 84*(3), 231–259.

Nosek, B. A. (2007). Implicit-explicit relations. *Current Directions in Psychological Science, 16*(2), 65–69.

Packard, V. (1957). *The hidden persuaders.* New York: McKay.

Rachman, S., & Hodgson, R. E. (1974). Synchrony and desynchrony in measures of fear. *Behaviour Research and Therapy*, *12*, 311–318.

Reber, A. S. (1993). *Implicit learning and tacit knowledge: An essay on the cognitive unconscious*. Oxford, England: Oxford University Press.

Rock, I., & Kaufman, L. (1962). The moon illusion: II. *Science*, *136*, 1023–1031.

Rumelhart, D. E., & McClelland, J. L. (Eds.). (1986). *Parallel distributed processing: Explorations in the microstructure of cognition. Vol. 1: Foundations*. Cambridge, MA: MIT Press.

Russell, B. (1912). *The problems of philosophy*. New York; Holt.

Schacter, D. L. (1987). Implicit memory: History and current status. *Journal of Experimental Psychology: Learning, Memory, and Cognition*, *13*, 501–518.

Schacter, D. L., & Badgaiyan, R. D. (2001). Neuroimaging of priming: New perspectives on implicit and explicit memory. *Current Directions in Psychological Science*, *10*(1), 1–4.

Schneider, W., & Chein, J. M. (2003). Controlled and automatic processing: Behavior, theory, and biological mechanisms. *Cognitive Science*, *27*, 525–559.

Schultheiss, O. C. (2008). Implicit motives. In O. P. John, R. W. Robins, & L. A. Pervin (Eds.), *Handbook of personality: Theory and research* (3rd ed., pp. 603–633). New York: Guilford Press.

Schultheiss, O. C., & Pang, J. S. (2007). Measuring implicit motives. In R. W. Robins, R. C. Fraley, & R. Krueger (Eds.), *Handbook of research methods in personality psychology* (pp. 322–344). New York: Guilford Press.

Searle, J. R. (1992). *The rediscovery of the mind*. Cambridge, MA: MIT Press.

Shames, V. A. (1994). *Is there such a thing as implicit problem-solving?* Unpublished Ph.D. dissertation, University of Arizona, Tuscon.

Shanks, D. R., & St.John, M. F. (1994). Characteristics of dissociable human learning systems. *Behavioral and Brain Sciences*, *17*, 367–395.

Shevrin, H. (1992). The Freudian unconscious and the cognitive unconscious: Identical or fraternal twins? In J. W. Barron, M. N. Eagle, & D. L. Wolitzky (Eds.), *Interface of psychoanalysis and psychology* (pp. 313–326). Washington, DC: American Psychological Association.

Siegler, R. S. (2000). Unconscious insights. *Current Directions in Psychological Science*, *9*(3), 79–83.

Simon, C. W., & Emmons, W. H. (1955). Learning during sleep? *Psychological Bulletin*, *52*, 328–342.

Spelke, E., Hirst, W., & Neisser, U. (1976). Skills of divided attention. *Cognition*, *4*, 215–230.

Wallas, G. (1921). *The art of thought*. New York: Harcourt Brace.

Warrington, E. K., & Weiskrantz, L. (1970). Amnesia: Consolidation or retrieval? *Nature*, *228*, 628–630.

Webb, E. J., Campbell, D. T., Schwartz, R. D., & Sechrest, L. (1966). *Unobtrusive measures: Nonreactive research in the social sciences*. Chicago: Rand McNally.

Weiskrantz, L. (1986). *Blindsight: A case study and implications*. Oxford, England: Oxford University Press.

White, P. (1980). Limitations on verbal reports of internal events: A refutation of Nisbett and Wilson and of Bem. *Psychological Review*, *87*(1), 305–312.

Wilson, T. D. (2002). *Strangers to ourselves: Discovering the adaptive unconscious*. Cambridge, MA: Belknap Press of Harvard University Press.

Winkielman, P., Berridge, K. C., & Wilbarger, J. L. (2005). Unconscious affective reactions to masked happy versus angry faces influence consumption behavior and judgments of value. *Personality and Social Psychology Bulletin*, *31*, 121–135.

# PART 3

# Memory

# Episodic Memory

David A. Gallo *and* Mark E. Wheeler

## Abstract

This chapter provides a brief overview of episodic memory, or the ability to consciously recall events from one's personal past. The historical context of this concept is sketched, as well as its relationship to other kinds of memory. Defining characteristics are then outlined, including its role in consciousness and sense of self, the dynamics of encoding and retrieval, and the phenomena of amnesia, forgetting, and false memories. Recollection is described as being cue dependent, and it is argued that this principle can explain three major encoding factors that influence episodic retrieval (distinctiveness, depth, and organization). Finally, the major neural substrates are summarized, as well as the effects of development and aging. The chapter concludes with some far-reaching questions for future research.

**Key Words:** aging, amnesia, consciousness, development, event, encoding, false memory, recall, recollection, retrieval

Episodic memory refers to an organism's capacity to consciously retrieve previously experienced events. It is a form of mental time travel synonymous with "recollection," and it is commonly implied by the terms "remembering," "recalling," "reminding," and "reminiscing." In humans, episodic memory makes one's thoughts and experiences available over time, thereby enriching the sense of a continuous self and its relationships with the rest of the universe. The primary function of episodic memory is to provide useful information about the past that can guide decisions and behaviors in the present. It also can be involved when imagining new events and planning for the future.

## Historical Context

Episodic memory was popularized as a scientific concept by Endel Tulving, an influential cognitive psychologist who helped shape the direction of modern human memory research. The concept was originally introduced by Tulving (1972) and revised in subsequent works as the research literature rapidly expanded (Tulving, 1983, 1993, 2002b). By emphasizing the subjective experience of recollecting the past, Tulving's conceptualization of episodic memory closely follows the folk psychology or colloquial use of the term "memory." This also is the conceptualization of memory that William James offered in his great work *Principles of Psychology* (1890) and in other writings (Wheeler, Stuss, & Tulving, 1997).

Although the term "episodic memory" is relatively recent, the ability to consciously reexperience prior sensations and perceptions has been the target of scholarly consideration since ancient times (see Burnham, 1888, for a historical review). Plato and Aristotle likened this kind of memory to impressions made in wax, Saint Augustine made analogies to a storehouse of sensations, and philosophical empiricists such as John Locke and John Stuart Mill emphasized how associations bring prior perceptions back to mind. The susceptibility of this type of memory to brain damage was documented in the early clinical literature, as in the 19th-century works of Ribot and Korsakoff, and the early writings of Freud popularized the controversial idea that this type of memory could be impaired by psychogenic factors. Of course, many literary and artistic references to this type of memory also can be found throughout history, with Proust's autobiographical work often cited as an example because of its extensive and explicit reliance on memory of his past.

Despite these historical precursors, the study of episodic memory as a distinct type of learning and memory was not widely adopted by early experimental psychologists (see Bower, 2000, for an overview). In the first empirical studies of memory, Hermann Ebbinghaus (1885/1964) measured the degree of relearning that was required to recall previously memorized material. Although Ebbinghaus's method of rote recall likely evoked some of the same cognitive processes involved in episodic memory, he was more interested in the associative regularities of learning than in the subjective experience of recollection. Similarly, the verbal learning tradition that dominated mainstream North American research on memory in the early 20th century focused more on the principles of associative learning than on conscious experience. This trend was heavily influenced by the prevailing behaviorist paradigm in psychological science, which avoided consideration of mental states in theory and research. Studies that were concerned with conscious recollection can be found in early experimental psychology, with the paired-associates learning technique first developed by Mary Calkins (1894) and the prose recall studies of Sir Fredrick Bartlett (1932) being two prominent examples, but these approaches were overshadowed by those of the verbal learning tradition.

More systematic and widespread research on episodic memory awaited the rise of cognitive psychology in the mid 20th century. This paradigm shift introduced information processing concepts into psychological theories, concepts that were inspired by the mind-computer analogy and applied research on human–machine interactions. Experimental psychologists began to focus on mental transformations of information, such as the encoding, storage, and retrieval of information in memory (Melton, 1963), as well as the nature of internal representations and images that are characteristic of episodic memory. The cognitive approach also was shaped by neuroscience, starting with neurological case studies and nonhuman animal learning studies, and resurging in the late 20th century with advances in neuroimaging technology. By linking different mental processes to different structures and activity patterns in the brain, the idea of functionally distinct memory systems gained popularity. The term "episodic memory" is widely used today within cognitive psychology and cognitive neuroscience, and much research still is devoted toward understanding the basic cognitive and neural processes of episodic memory and its relationship to other kinds of memory.

## Relationship to Other Kinds of Memory

Tulving (1972) differentiated episodic memory from semantic memory, which refers to general knowledge that is detached from personally experienced events (e.g., vocabulary, mathematical laws, historical facts, etc.; Chapter 14, "Semantic Memory"). In this sense episodic memory is a more specific concept, referring only to the subjective experience of retrieving the past events of one's life, whereas the concept of semantic memory is used to refer to many other kinds of knowledge that are acquired through experience. According to Tulving (1985), the retrieval of these different kinds of memories is accompanied with a different subjective experience. Whereas episodic memory is associated with a sense of "remembering," semantic memory is associated with a sense of "knowing." It also has been suggested that visual mental imagery is more heavily associated with episodic than semantic memory, further underscoring the importance of subjective experience to episodic recollection (Brewer & Pani, 1996).

Episodic memory closely interacts with semantic memory, and both forms of memory share similarities that differentiate them from other forms of learning and memory. Both have been described as declarative, meaning that the retrieved information can be verbally described or asserted, in contrast to nondeclarative forms of memory (Squire, 1987). Forms of memory that have been described as nondeclarative include procedural skills (e.g., reading), motor skills (e.g., writing), and associative conditioning or habits (e.g., drinking coffee while reading or writing). These various types of memory serve different psychological functions, and they often are categorized into different memory systems based on functional and neuroanatomical characteristics (see Squire, 2004, for a brief historical review). Episodic and semantic memory also have been described as explicit, meaning that the retrieved information is consciously accessible, as opposed to implicit forms of memory that nonconsciously influence thoughts and behaviors (Schacter,

1987; see also Chapter 15, "Implicit Memory"). Of course, not all memory phenomena neatly fit into these dichotomies. For example, semantic knowledge can operate nonconsciously, as when the ability to perceive a word is briefly facilitated by recent exposure to related concepts (semantic priming) or when language production is automatically guided by the rules of grammar.

Episodic memory is different from working memory or short-term memory.[1] A defining feature of episodic memory is that the retrieved information is mentally reexperienced after some retention interval, or a period of time in which conscious attention was directed toward other experiences. In contrast, working memory involves the continuous activation or conscious rehearsal of information within the scope of attention, usually in the pursuit of a concurrent goal or task. Working memory can be considered a declarative or explicit form of memory, and by some theories working memory involves episodic-like components (Baddeley, 2000). In fact, the rehearsal of information in working memory can increase subsequent episodic recollection of that information. Nevertheless, working memory differs from episodic memory because of its transient nature and its limited storage capacity. The storage of episodic memories can span years, and episodic memory has no known capacity limits.

The concept of autobiographical memory also is closely related to episodic memory. Broadly defined, autobiographical memory refers to knowledge about one's self, and as such all episodic memory is necessarily a subset of autobiographical memory. However, autobiographical memory also can refer to general knowledge about oneself that is not necessarily accompanied by conscious recollection of past events (e.g., knowing when you were born, where you work, etc.). Thus, autobiographical memory is a combination of episodic memory and semantic memory. As illustrated by Conway (2005), autobiographical memory may be organized in a hierarchical fashion, with semantic knowledge about general lifetime periods near the top, and event-specific episodic memories near the bottom. Autobiographical memory research usually involves episodic memories of events that occurred in natural settings (e.g., early childhood memories, important milestones in one's life, etc.). A somewhat separate research tradition involves episodic memories created in the laboratory, including experimentally presented word lists, pictures, and stories, as well as more complex events such as movies, self-performed actions, and staged performances.

## Seven Defining Criteria

The concept of episodic memory can be characterized by seven criteria that differentiate this kind of memory from other kinds. Additional criteria might be proposed, such as those based on neural substrates or functional properties, but the following criteria are central elements to the concept as it has been used in mainstream cognitive psychology.

### It Involves Consciousness

Episodic memories are consciously experienced at retrieval, or replayed in the mind's eye, such that someone with verbal abilities could communicate aspects of the earlier experience to others. In this sense, episodic memory is a type of declarative or explicit memory that requires conscious awareness. The subjective experience of episodic memories also supports one's personal sense of a self that exists in time. The capacity to think about the self in this way has been dubbed "autonoetic" consciousness and differentiated from "noetic" consciousness, or the ability to think about other kinds of knowledge (Wheeler et al., 1997).

Episodic memory also contributes to our sense of conscious awareness, as illustrated by the case study of Clive Wearing, an individual who suffered a profound loss of episodic memory owing to viral encephalitis (Wearing, 2005). Many aspects of Wearing's learning and intelligence remained functional following his illness. For instance, he was able to engage informal conversation, to make coffee, and to read and play musical compositions on the piano. He also was able to recognize loved ones and to recall general autobiographical information (i.e., that he was married, had children, and was a musician). However, he was unable to consciously recollect many specific events that had occurred before the onset of his illness (retrograde amnesia) and almost none of the events occurring after the illness (anterograde amnesia). A poignant example is that he often greeted his wife with great joy each time he met her—as if he had not seen her for years—even though she might have left the room only for a brief moment. His amnesia was so dense that he would write the time in his diary, declaring that he had just gained consciousness, only to cross out this time a few minutes later and replace it with the newer time and a new declaration that he had just gained consciousness. Wearing's illness forced him to live in a perpetual state of the present, destroying his sense of autonoetic awareness.

Because episodic memory is so closely linked to conscious awareness, it is unknown whether nonhuman animals have episodic memory. Episodic memory is defined by the subjective experience of remembering, and it is difficult (if not impossible) to definitively determine whether nonhuman animals have such experiences (e.g., they cannot communicate these experiences using language). However, Clayton and colleagues have shown episodic-like memory in food-caching birds, in the sense that they have memory for the location of different types of foodstuffs, as well as when the food was earlier stored in that location (Clayton & Dickinson, 1998). Episodic-like behaviors also have been found in rats, including the forming of associations and learning temporal order, and these behaviors depend on a brain structure called the hippocampus (Eichenbaum & Fortin, 2005). Eichenbaum and colleagues' findings are particularly interesting because human episodic memory also is hippocampally dependent (as discussed later). Although these studies do not address the issue of consciousness, they indicate that several characteristics of human episodic memory are found in nonhuman animals.

### It Involves the Past

Episodic memories are understood by the rememberer to have happened at some time in his or her past, even though the exact time is not always known. This sense of retrieving something from the past usually is a relatively automatic aspect of episodic memory, although contextual information can help place the event in a specific temporal context. The belief that one is retrieving events from the past may partly originate from an automatic or nonconscious inference, based on the relative ease or fluency with which the information comes to mind (Jacoby, Kelley, & Dywan, 1989; see also Chapter 17, "Through the SCAPE Looking Glass"). It also may originate from the first-person perspective of the visual images that often characterize episodic memories (e.g., Nigro & Nisser, 1983), which would suggest that the information was personally encountered previously.

In addition to thinking about the past, it has been argued that episodic memory plays a critical role in future-oriented thinking and planning. When imagining the future, people can draw from past experiences to predict what may happen and also to mentally simulate plausible ways that future events may unfold. Evidence for this relationship comes from amnesic patients (such as Clive Wearing), who seem less likely to engage in elaborate future-oriented thought than people with intact episodic memory, as well as neuroimaging studies that have

revealed similarities in neural activity between episodic remembering and future simulation (Schacter, Addis, & Buckner, 2007). Of course, future-oriented thought also may involve general knowledge about the world and imagination-based processes that are independent from episodic remembering. The exact role of episodic memory for future-oriented thinking is an active research area.

### It Involves Events

Episodic memories are about episodes or events that were personally experienced by the individual. This means that the retrieved information is understood as having occurred at a specific point in space and time, within the context of surrounding events. The term "event" is flexible and has been used to describe a wide variety of occurrences, ranging from the relatively simple and trivial (e.g., hearing a word in a recently presented experimental list) to the relatively complex and consequential (e.g., spilling a punchbowl on the bride at a wedding). The term "context" also is flexible and generally refers to associated details that are peripheral to central elements of the event, such as the location of the event.

The content and organization of recollected events can be influenced by numerous factors. In addition to basic associative factors (e.g., spatial, temporal, etc.), these factors include a deeper comprehension of the objects and actions depicted in the events (e.g., inferences and causal relationships, see Brewer, 1977; Radvansky, Copeland, & Zwaan, 2005) as well as their personal or autobiographical significance (e.g., Conway, 2009). It has been argued that ongoing experiences are processed as meaningful units and segmented into corresponding events during their initial perception (Zacks & Swallow, 2007; see also Chapter 6, "Event Perception"). For example, setting up a tent involves a series of readily identifiable stages, including unpacking the gear, sorting and laying out the items, and assembling the pieces in the proper order. Alternatively, ongoing experiences might not be mentally segmented into events but instead may be initially perceived as a continuous flow of information about the world, analogous to James's (1890) stream of consciousness. Along these lines it has been argued that the types of information that are initially encoded into memory are primarily a by-product of the perceptual and conceptual processes that are engaged at the time (Craik & Lockhart, 1972). As such, the extent that information is organized into meaningful events may flexibly depend on information processing goals.

## Encoding Is Rapid and Often Automatic

Episodic memories can be rapidly acquired based on a single learning episode, without subsequent rehearsal. Such rapid acquisition is a functional necessity, given that each unique event in one's life occurs only once and is immediately replaced by subsequent events. In contrast, other types of learning and memory require multiple exposures to information in order for it to be subsequently used or retrieved. Many procedural skills such as how to read or do math require repeated and effortful practice to acquire, as does learning how to ride a bike or drive a car. Learning how to understand a foreign language as an adult is another example, as it requires extensive experience with the language in order to fluently perceive individual words, inflections, and the like. The acquisition of this kind of knowledge requires numerous exposures so that the learner can extract nonrandom patterns and regularities in the data. As argued by Sherry and Schacter (1987), the ability to gradually learn information over repeated encounters represents a fundamentally different kind of memory than episodic memory, one that has independently evolved to serve qualitatively different psychological functions.

In addition to being rapid, the encoding of episodic memories can be relatively automatic. People remember many events of their lives, even though they do not consciously attempt or intend to memorize the information at the time. This observation again suggests that the contents of episodic memories are primarily a by-product of other information processing demands (Craik & Lockhart, 1972). People can engage in special encoding strategies or mnemonics to enhance their ability to remember information, but as described next, these strategies typically involve mental transformations of what is encoded as opposed to the initiation of a different kind of encoding process itself. Despite the relatively automatic nature of encoding, the concept is not necessarily synonymous with attention or perception. The encoding of episodic memories may require specialized neural mechanisms that are not needed for perception or attention (see Tulving, 2002a, and the later section on "Neural Substrates").

A classic experiment by Hyde and Jenkins (1969) demonstrates the dependence of episodic retrieval on the type of processes engaged at encoding, as opposed to the intention to memorize. Healthy adults studied a list of words under different encoding tasks. In one condition they were told to focus on the surface form of each word (i.e.,

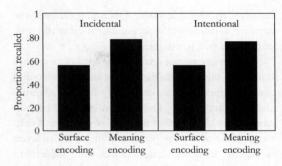

**Figure 13.1** Results selected from Hyde and Jenkins (1969, Experiment 3). The intention to memorize words at study did not affect recall, but the encoding task did. Not shown is a group that was given intentional instructions without an encoding task. This group recalled as many words as the meaningful conditions (75%), suggesting that meaning is the default method for processing words.

decide whether it contained the letter "e"), whereas in the other condition they focused on the meaning of each word (i.e., decide whether it is pleasant). Importantly, some subjects were told that their memory would subsequently be tested (intentional encoding), whereas others were not told that their memory would be tested (incidental encoding). Figure 13.1 illustrates two key results. First, the encoding task had a very large effect on subsequent recall, suggesting that attention to the meaning of the words led to more distinctive memories than attention to the surface form (this effect is discussed more later). Second, instructing subjects to intentionally memorize the words had no effect on subsequent recall, indicating that the type of processing engaged at encoding was more critical than the intention to learn. Attempts to encode information influence subsequent retrieval primarily by guiding attention to specific features of the stimuli.

## A Retrieval Process Is Required

Theories of learning and memory frequently distinguish between (a) the initial encoding, acquisition, or formation of a trace in the nervous system; (b) the subsequent storage or retention of this trace over time; and (c) the final retrieval or utilization of this trace. Importantly, an episodic memory only can be identified after it has been retrieved in the form of a conscious recollection (at least with current technologies). In a sense this is a circular point, because the very definition of episodic memory involves a description of the retrieval experience. It is an important point, though, because it highlights the possibility that the same encoding experience can influence subsequent cognition or behavior in multiple ways, depending on how the encoded information is accessed or used at the time of retrieval (see Roediger, 2000).

The importance of retrieval for episodic memory is illustrated by the distinction between implicit and explicit memory tests. In a study by Graf, Squire, and Mandler (1984), amnesic patients and healthy control subjects studied a list of words. On a subsequent test they were presented with a list of word stems (the first three letters of a word). Subjects in the explicit test condition were asked to complete the stems with the appropriate studied word. As expected, the amnesic subjects were less likely to consciously recollect the appropriate words on this test compared to the healthy subjects. Subjects in the implicit test condition were asked to complete the stems with the first word that came to mind, but they were not given explicit instructions to use memory. Even though this test did not require recollection of the studied words, studied words were more likely to be generated than nonstudied words on this test, due to the temporary activation or implicit priming of the word representation. Importantly, amnesics and controls showed the same degree of priming on this test, despite the fact that the encoding and storage conditions were equivalent to those in the explicit group. Amnesia only impaired memory when the retrieval conditions required episodic recollection.

The Graf et al. (1984) study also highlights some of the difficulties in disentangling the influence of encoding, storage, and retrieval processes on episodic memory performance. Although the amnesic patients were impaired in their ability to recollect the studied words, this deficit might have been caused by an inability to encode or store information in a way that is required for subsequent recollection, as opposed to an intrinsic retrieval deficit. Amnesic patients often can recall at least some autobiographical events that occurred prior to their brain injury, suggesting that their memory deficits may primarily be in the encoding or storage of new information (Alvarez & Squire, 1994). In fact, amnesics tend to exhibit temporally graded retrograde amnesia, so that memory for events occurring just prior to their brain injury is impaired more than memories from the more distant past. This observation suggests that experiences require a period of consolidation for some time after they are perceived in order to form lasting memory representations (but see Winocur & Moscovitch, 2011). Results from pharmacological studies, in which amnesia-inducing drugs are administered at different stages of a memory task,

also suggest that recently encoded information undergoes consolidation (Polster, 1993; Wixted, 2004).

## Retrieval Depends on Associated Cues

Episodic memories are retrieved when an appropriate cue is processed. Cues can be internally generated, as when we try to remember an event by thinking of associated details, or they can originate from external sources, as when some percept spontaneously triggers the recollection of an associated event. According to the encoding specificity principle, a cue will be effective at triggering a memory to the extent that information contained in the cue overlaps with stored information, which in turn depends on the originally encoded event (Tulving & Thompson, 1973). For example, Tulving and Pearlstone (1966) had subjects study several lists of categorized words (e.g., engineer, lawyer, etc.), along with their corresponding category label (e.g., professions). They found that subjects were more likely to recall the studied words if subjects were re-presented with the specific category labels as retrieval cues, as opposed to a condition where they were only given a very general retrieval cue (e.g., "recall all the items that you just studied"). This finding confirms the intuition that information that is available (i.e., stored in memory) is not always accessible (i.e., able to be retrieved) but depends on whether the appropriate cues are presented.

The encoding specificity principle has been used to explain context-dependent and state-dependent memory phenomena, or the finding that episodic retrieval can be enhanced when the person is in the same physical context (e.g., a room) or the same mental state (e.g., mood) at both encoding and retrieval. In a well-known example, Godden and Baddeley (1975) found that scuba divers who had initially studied a list of words underwater recalled more of the words when they were tested underwater compared to land, whereas if they had encoded the words on land they recalled them better on land (see Fig. 13.2). In cases like this it is believed that reinstating the encoding context at retrieval provides additional cues that trigger the episodic memories. More generally, these ideas are related to the principle of transfer appropriate processing, which states that the level of transfer in any learning or memory task will depend on the extent that similar processes are engaged at encoding and retrieval (Morris, Bransford, & Franks, 1977).

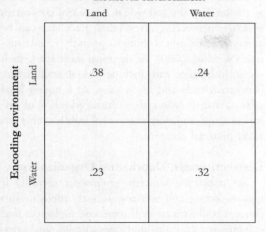

**Figure 13.2** Results selected from Godden and Baddeley (1975, Experiment 1). The proportion of correctly recalled studied words was greatest when the test environment matched the encoding environment.

## It Is Fallible and Reconstructive

Episodic memory is not a perfect record of the past, and research indicates that it is prone to error, distortion, and reconstruction. One common error is forgetting, or the failure to retrieve previously memorable events. An obvious cause of forgetting is amnesia caused by brain damage. Other causes of forgetting are a natural consequence of normal brain function. One cause of forgetting is interference, or the idea that similar memories can compete at the time of retrieval, reducing the likelihood that one or the other will be retrieved. The inability to remember where one parked his or her car is a well-known example, whereby previous parking locations get confused with the most recent location. Because the different instances of parking locations are relatively similar or nondistinctive, the same general retrieval cue ("Where did I park?") becomes ineffective at triggering the target memory. Many instances of forgetting in episodic memory are caused by a failure to have an appropriate retrieval cue (Tulving, 1974).

Unlike interference effects, which imply a memory error or difficulty, some types of forgetting actually may be advantageous. The directed forgetting phenomenon provides some evidence for this idea. In directed forgetting tasks, deliberate attempts to forget recently learned material can reduce the subsequent likelihood of remembering this material, and also can reduce the potentially interfering effects of this material on memory for

other information (Bjork, 1970). These effects may owe to several causes, such as the selective rehearsal of to-be-remembered information or the active process of inhibiting the memory traces associated with unwanted material (see Anderson, Bjork, & Bjork, 1994, for additional discussion of inhibition). More generally, Anderson and Schooler (1991) argued that the relative levels of activation of information in memory can be adaptive, enhancing the availability of memories that are likely to be relevant to one's current and future goals, while reducing the availability of other memories.

The idea that memories can be temporarily inhibited is central to the concept of repression, which was popularized by the work of Freud. Repression theories indicate that memories of traumatic or negative events can be rendered into an unconscious or temporarily forgotten state, in order to protect the psychological well-being of the individual. Although this concept has been used in some clinical settings, it is a controversial concept, and many have questioned the evidence provided in support of the existence of repression (Alpert et al., 1998; McNally & Geraerts, 2009). In fact, many researchers argue that emotionally intense events often have the opposite effect of being repressed, in the sense that they are difficult to forget. For example, people often report "flashbulb memories," or vivid and lasting recollections of having first learned about a unique and emotionally significant event, although researchers contend that these memories are not special and can be prone to reconstruction and error just like other memories (Neisser & Harsch, 1992). Similar issues have been raised regarding the concept of "flashbacks," or the intrusive images that have been associated with posttraumatic stress disorder (see Rubin, Berntsen, & Bohni, 2008).

Another common error is false memory, or the recollection of events or details of events that never actually occurred (Chapter 16, "The Sources of Memory Errors"). False memories have been considered throughout history, especially because they have significant implications outside the laboratory (e.g., understanding the accuracy of eyewitness testimony, or memories retrieved in clinical settings). However, they have been intensively researched only in the past few decades (Roediger, 1996; Schacter, 1995). One common cause of false memory is the confusion of details across previously experienced events or thoughts, or a breakdown in the associative processes that bind together the details of an event. These failures can cause people to falsely remember the source of information (e.g., who said what, where something happened, or whether something was actually perceived or imagined). According to the source-monitoring framework, episodic memory is not perfect and so individuals must rely on expectations and other kinds of decision processes in order to accurately reconstruct the past (Johnson, Hashtroudi, & Lindsay, 1993). Many false memories are caused by a failure to monitor retrieval.

As was the case with forgetting, advantageous or adaptive processes may cause some types of false memories. For example, Roediger and McDermott (1995) found that studying lists of associated words (bed, rest, awake, tired, etc.) often caused healthy adults to falsely remember associated words that were not actually presented (e.g., sleep, see Fig. 13.3). Much like a perceptual illusion, this memory illusion is very difficult to consciously avoid, potentially because it reflects associative processes that are usually beneficial to memory and thus are relatively automatic (for a review, see Gallo, 2006). The brain is unable to encode and remember all of the information it is presented, and so it often distills incoming information into the basic gist or meaningfulness of the material. This information is later used to reconstruct past events at the time of retrieval. This strategy is cognitively efficient, but it also enhances susceptibility to false memories of related material.

Reconstructive processes are well documented in memory research. Individuals sometimes falsely remember events that were only inferred from actual events. Individuals also distort memories to make them more consistent with their personal schemas or biases. In addition to these factors, which operate at the level of the individual, the social context in which remembering often takes place also can be a major factor contributing to memory reconstruction (Weldon, 2000). At the most basic level, such social influences can include casual reminiscing between friends and loved ones. At a higher level of social organization, the cultural adoption of historical scripts or interpretations of public events can affect personal memory.

## Distinctiveness, Depth, and Organization

An important concept in episodic memory is that encoding and retrieval factors interact. This concept is illustrated by three encoding factors that enhance retrieval: distinctiveness, depth, and organization. Although there are numerous theoretical explanations for how these factors affect memory, one way to explain them is to focus on the way that events are initially encoded, as well as the resulting consequences for the ability of cues to trigger these events at retrieval, as described next.

It is well established that distinctive events are more likely to be recalled than nondistinctive events, although the concept of distinctiveness has several connotations (Hunt, 2006). One useful definition is that distinctive events have more differentiated memory representations, or fewer overlapping features stored across memory traces, than nondistinctive events. According to this definition, distinctive events are dissimilar from other events along some dimension. As a result, distinctive events are more likely to be associated with unique retrieval cues, and hence more likely to be triggered when the corresponding cues are presented at retrieval. This explanation gains support from the cue-overload phenomenon, or the finding that the recall of an event in response to a retrieval cue decreases if other events are associated to the same retrieval cue (Watkins & Watkins, 1975). In essence, similar or nondistinctive events compete for the same retrieval cues, making any one of them less likely to be recalled due to interference.

A factor related to distinctiveness is the level or depth of processing at encoding. When an event is initially processed, it triggers related information stored in memory, as the person makes sense of the event and incorporates it with existing knowledge. This information becomes associated with the event at encoding, making it more distinctive and increasing the likelihood that a cue will trigger some aspect of the elaborated event at retrieval. Craik and Tulving (1975) argued that this sort of principle explained

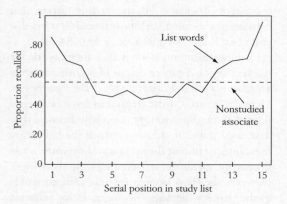

**Figure 13.3** Results selected from Roediger and McDermott (1995, Experiment 1). Recall of studied words demonstrated a typical serial position curve, with greater recall of words presented at the beginning of the list (primacy effect) and the end of the list (recency effect). False recall of the nonstudied associate (dashed line) occurred as frequently as true recall of words from the middle serial positions.

why words processed for meaning at encoding were better remembered than those processed for surface features, as in the aforementioned Hyde and Jenkins (1969) experiment. Because meaning primarily differentiates words, this type of processing increases the number of uniquely encoded or distinctive features for each word compared to the processing of surface features. Of course, for information other than words, the type of encoding processing that will maximize the number of uniquely encoded features might not be semantic meaningfulness, but instead will depend upon the types of preexisting knowledge (or expertise) that the individual can use to elaborate upon the particular type of information. For example, remembering faces usually requires considerable attention to the perceptual processing of surface features (e.g., the spacing between the eyes, thickness of the lips, etc.) and their holistic integration.

The degree of organization at encoding also can enhance episodic retrieval. Some organizational schemes allow one to associate information to preexisting knowledge, so that this knowledge can later be used to generate cues for subsequent retrieval (e.g., Bower, Clark, Lesgold, & Winzenz, 1969). This principle underlies many of the mnemonics that can be used to efficiently store information, such as those that were known to the Ancient Greeks (e.g., the method of loci, in which objects are associated with a spatial location, see Worthen & Hunt, 2011). By associating new information to the mnemonic scheme, the individual can later use this mnemonic scheme as a cue to trigger the original information. Even without explicit mnemonics, people tend to subjectively organize material in an effort to make meaningful associations that can facilitate recall (Tulving, 1962). The finding that similarity sometimes can enhance memory, in contrast to distinctiveness effects, also might be explained by such organizational factors (Hunt & McDaniel, 1993). Similarities can help to subjectively organize studied events by relating them to each other, so that the retrieval of one event can cue the retrieval of the other.

## Neural Substrates

Converging evidence from brain damage and cognitive (or functional) neuroimaging studies has elucidated many of the neural underpinnings of episodic memory. As illustrated in Figure 13.4 and described later, episodic memory is subserved by several distinct anatomical structures in the brain. This schematic is an oversimplification, and the exact contribution of specific brain structures to

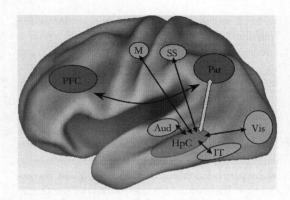

**Figure 13.4** Brain regions commonly involved in episodic memory retrieval. Regions are displayed on a cortical representation of the left hemisphere based on the PALs-B12 atlas (Van Essen, 2005). Aud, auditory cortex; HpC, hippocampus and adjacent areas; IT, inferotemporal cortex; M, motor cortex; Par, parietal cortex; PFC, prefrontal cortex; SS, somatosensory cortex; Vis, visual cortex.

episodic memory is still an area of active research. Nevertheless, several regions have been attributed specific roles in the encoding, storage, and retrieval of episodic memories.

Regions of the medial temporal lobes (MTL), primarily the hippocampus and surrounding structures, are involved in associative or relational processes. These structures are thought to bind different types of information or details of experience into a single trace at the time of encoding and also to mediate the reconstruction of the event when presented with a cue at retrieval. Evidence for the role of MTL structures in episodic memory comes from studies of amnesic patients with damage to these regions, who show profound episodic memory amnesia but relatively spared intellectual processes in other domains (Cohen & Eichenbaum, 1993), and also from many recent functional magnetic resonance imaging (fMRI) studies indicating that the hippocampus is activated during both the encoding and the retrieval of associations in memory (e.g., Davachi & Wagner, 2002; Giovanello, Schnyer, & Verfaellie, 2009). Neurons in the hippocampus are known to support long-term potentiation, or the formation of lasting connections between neurons, potentially providing a mechanism through which the hippocampus might form lasting associations. However, there is some debate as to whether the hippocampus is always required during recollection, or whether some memories can become consolidated into a more lasting form over time such that they no longer require the hippocampus to be retrieved (McClelland, McNaughton, & O'Reilly, 1995; Moscovitch et al., 2005).

MTL regions other than the hippocampus also contribute to episodic memory. The amygdala is known to be involved in emotional processing, and neuroimaging studies have shown that activity in the amygdala is related to both encoding and retrieval of emotionally arousing information in episodic memory (Cahill & McGaugh, 1998; Kensinger, 2007; see also Chapter 35, "Emotion, Stress and Memory"). It also has been argued that the other regions adjacent to the hippocampus, such as the perirhinal cortex, are involved in the subjective experience of familiarity. Familiarity is a feeling that a stimulus had earlier been encountered without a specific episodic recollection (Eichenbaum, Yonelinas, & Ranganath, 2007). The psychological relationship between recollection and familiarity is currently debated by memory researchers, and so too is the specific role of the hippocampus and surrounding structures in these different types of subjective experience (see Squire, Wixted, & Clark, 2007).

The actual information or contents of episodic memories are not necessarily coded by MTL regions, but rather, are probably represented in specialized neocortical areas. For example, an fMRI study by Wheeler, Petersen, and Buckner (2000) found that the recollection of visual memories (pictures) activated regions in visual cortex, whereas the recollection of auditory memories (sounds) activated regions of auditory cortex. Similar principles apply to other sensory or motor-specific information (Nyberg et al., 2001). Just as mental imagery tends to activate relatively high-level (or downstream) subsets of the sensory areas that are involved in actual perception (Ishai, Ungerleider, & Haxby, 2000; O'Craven & Kanwisher, 2000), memory-related activity tends to activate only a subset of the sensory areas that are involved in perception (Wheeler & Buckner, 2003). This targeted characteristic of retrieval may help individuals differentiate memories (or mental images) from actual perception, which involves bottom-up activity in sensory areas. In contrast, the representation of more abstract semantic or conceptual information has been linked to the lateral temporal lobes, primarily because patients with damage in these areas have problems comprehending categories (Hodges, Patterson, Oxbury, & Funnell, 1992).

Regions within the prefrontal cortex (PFC) are involved in the coordination or control of information processing across a variety of cognitive domains, including episodic memory. For example, the conscious rehearsal of information within working memory is heavily dependent on PFC regions (Smith & Jonides, 1997), and as discussed, the repeated rehearsal of information can enhance subsequent episodic memory retrieval. Neuroimaging studies also have demonstrated that different regions within the PFC subserve qualitatively different types of information processing (e.g., different areas within left inferior frontal gyrus are involved in semantic versus phonological processing of words; see McDermott, Petersen, Watson, & Ojemann, 2003), and that the level of activity in some of these regions during the encoding of words is positively related to subsequent episodic memory retrieval (Wagner et al., 1998). Thus, in addition to the active maintenance or rehearsal of information, specific regions of the PFC may help to encode different kinds of information.

PFC regions also play a large role in the reconstructive processes that occur during episodic memory retrieval. Lesions within PFC have long been known to cause episodic memory problems, such as difficulties recollecting the source of information, and in some instances, the confabulation (or fabrication) of details about events that never actually occurred (Burgess & Shallice, 1996; Moscovitch & Melo, 1997). Many neuroimaging studies in healthy adults further implicate PFC regions in the metacognitive monitoring or decision processes that are used to edit the accuracy of memory (Mitchell & Johnson, 2009). For example, an fMRI study by Gallo, McDonough, and Scimeca (2010) found that different patterns of activity in dorsolateral PFC were associated with the use of different types of retrieval monitoring. One type of monitoring involved the use of retrieval expectations to maximize memory accuracy and avoid false recollection (diagnostic monitoring), whereas the other involved the recollection of corroborating information to avoid false recollection (disqualifying monitoring).

Neuroimaging studies also have demonstrated that regions within the lateral inferior parietal cortex are active during episodic memory retrieval. Given that these regions are involved in visuospatial attentional processes, it has been proposed that they may support attention toward recollected information (Cabeza, Ciaramelli, Olson, & Moscovitch, 2008). Alternatively, activity of these regions during retrieval may be involved in coordinated processing along with PFC and MTL regions, as might be required if maintaining an episodic buffer in working memory (Vilberg & Rugg, 2008) or accumulating evidence about a memory decision over time (Donaldson, Wheeler, & Petersen, 2010).

## Development and Aging

The ability to retrieve episodic memories significantly changes across the life span. Perhaps the most striking aspect of childhood memory is infantile amnesia, or the inability of adults to recall episodic memories from early childhood (e.g., prior to 3 years of age). Most adults have little or no memory of their early childhood (see Rubin, 2000). The source of infantile amnesia is puzzling because children younger than 4 years can clearly recall events from the past, and at times do so in exquisite detail. For example, Myers, Clifton, and Clarkson (1987) found that children at the age of 3 years expressed memories for laboratory events that transpired 2 years earlier, indicating that fundamental episodic memory abilities are established and operational in early childhood. Thus, although some of the neocortical structures that are involved in episodic memory are known to mature in late childhood and adolescence, such as the prefrontal cortex (Fuster, 2002), infantile amnesia does not seem to be caused by the failure of these systems to support episodic memory in early childhood.

The cause of infantile amnesia remains an open question, but there are several noteworthy possibilities (Rovee-Collier & Hayne, 2000). One is that the acquisition of language abilities motivates a shift from sensory-based to language-based knowledge representations. According to the encoding specificity principle, it should be difficult to access experiences using language-based retrieval cues if they were originally encoded in a sensory format. In the same vein, temporal awareness can provide a rich source of organization in episodic memory, but a sense of time is undeveloped in young children. Without the temporal context, memories may be difficult to retrieve. Yet another possibility is based on the maturation of a sense of self and identity (Howe & Courage, 1993). Changes like these would make it difficult to think about one's self in the same way as in childhood, making it difficult if not impossible to find effective retrieval cues for the memories of that time period.

Another aspect of episodic memory that has been extensively investigated in children is their propensity for false memory. Children can be more susceptible than adults to a variety of false memories, including those based on imagination, suggestion, and other sources (e.g., Ceci & Bruck, 1993). These effects may be due to the relatively late maturation of the prefrontal cortex (Chapter 62, "The Development of Cognitive Control"). For example, children can be more likely than adults to confuse the source of episodic memories (Lindsay, Johnson, & Kwon, 1991), and source memory abilities in children have been linked to individual differences in prefrontal function (Rybash & Colilla, 1994). Research also indicates that children are less effective than adults in using retrieval monitoring processes to edit the accuracy of episodic memory (see Brainerd & Reyna, 2002; Ghetti, 2008), processes that are known to involve the prefrontal cortex (as reviewed earlier). Note, though, that developmental differences in false memories are not always obtained, and in some situations children may be less prone to false memories than adults (see Loftus & Davies, 1984). For example, in situations where children do not comprehend the gist of studied materials as effectively as adults, they can be less prone to gist-based false memory errors (e.g., Brainerd, Reyna, & Forrest, 2002).

At the other end of the age spectrum, it is well established that advanced aging can impair episodic memory on laboratory tasks (Chapter 64, "Cognitive Aging"). Older adults particularly have memory difficulty in situations that require resource-demanding or self-initiated processes (e.g., Craik & Anderson, 1999), such as strategic rehearsal at encoding or self-cuing at retrieval. Older adults perform well when automatic forms of memory are sufficient, such as when an item can be recognized based only on a feeling of familiarity, but can show deficits when the recollection of specific information is required (Jacoby, 1999). These recollection deficits usually involve the retrieval of the source of information or specific associations, as when trying to remember the name of a recently learned face (e.g., Naveh-Benjamin et al., 2009; Schacter, Koutstaal, Johnson, Gross, & Angell, 1997). Older adults also are more prone to false memories in laboratory tasks than are younger adults (Pierce, Simons, & Schacter, 2004). At least some of these aging effects can be attributed to reduced attention to details at encoding and retrieval, but even when encouraged to focus on details these age differences persist (Koutstaal, Schacter, Galluccio, & Stofer, 1999).

Reductions in memory performance in healthy aging are associated with both structural and functional changes in the brain. Normal aging is particularly associated with reduced neuronal density and other changes in the prefrontal cortex, although there is some evidence that MTL regions also may be disproportionately sensitive to advanced aging (e.g., Raz, Rodrigue, Kennedy, & Acker, 2007; Tisserand & Jolles, 2003). Source memory abilities in older adults have been linked to individual differences in prefrontal functions (e.g., Glisky, Polster, & Routhieaux, 1995), and neuroimaging studies indicate that older adults are less likely to activate MTL regions and other regions during episodic memory tasks (Grady, 2008). Interestingly, older adults sometimes recruit more prefrontal regions than younger adults during attempts to retrieve episodic memories, potentially reflecting compensatory processes (Cabeza, Anderson, Locantore, & McIntosh, 2002). A better understanding of these and other age-related changes in neural activity is an active area of cognitive aging research.

The effects of normal aging on cognition exhibit considerable variability across individuals, both in terms of neural changes and also in terms of actual abilities. Many elderly individuals show no declines in episodic memory performance. For instance, Butler et al. (2004) showed that older adults with reduced frontal function were more prone to false memories, but those with intact frontal functioning performed as well as college undergraduates. These individual differences may be due to biological predispositions as well as environmental or lifestyle factors that serve protective functions. A growing initiative in cognitive neuroscience is devoted toward strategies and interventions that may improve episodic memory in aging (Lustig, Shah, Seidler, & Reuter-Lorenz, 2009).

It is important to note that the types of memory difficulties found in normal aging differ from those in Alzheimer's disease. Whereas episodic memory declines in normal aging are primarily attributed to changes in the frontal lobes, those seen even in the earliest stages of Alzheimer's disease are due to more profound changes in MTL regions (e.g., Buckner, 2004). Alzheimer's disease is a progressive neurodegenerative condition characterized by increased density of plaques and neurofibrillary tangles, with early neuron loss primarily occurring in MTL regions such as the entorhinal cortex and the hippocampus (Hedden & Gabrieli, 2004). Consistent with this neurological profile, the early stages of the disease are characterized by a sharp decline in episodic memory abilities compared to age-matched controls, as measured in laboratory tasks and in memory for naturalistic events (e.g., Balota et al., 1999; Budson et al., 2007). These changes lead to episodic memory amnesia that increases in severity as the disease progresses, in addition to the eventual loss of many other cognitive functions. Alzheimer's disease ultimately distorts one's sense

of self (Morgabi, Brown & Morris, 2009), making it one of the most devastating disorders of episodic memory.

Unlike Alzheimer's disease, not all types of episodic memories are affected by normal aging. Age-related declines in self-initiated processing can have significant implications, such as failure to remember to take one's medication at the appropriate time (e.g., prospective memory; see Einstein, Richardson, Guynn, Cunfer, & McDaniel, 1995; see also Chapter 18, "Event-Based Prospective Memory"). However, whereas older adults have difficulties remembering relatively similar events, their memory can be quite good for other types of naturalistic information, such as the prices of groceries (Castel, 2005). Aging also is less likely to impair memory for more distinctive events. Figure 13.5 presents results from Gallo, Cotel, Moore, and Schacter (2007) that illustrate this point. In this study, older adults were severely impaired in recollecting nondistinctive information (i.e., whether a test word was studied in a red font), but they performed as well as undergraduates when tested for more distinctive information (i.e., whether a test word was studied with a unique colored picture).

One final factor to consider is that laboratory studies of aging typically do not capture all of the personally relevant variables that affect episodic memory in more naturalistic contexts, such as one's goals and motivations (Hess, 2005). Compared to the relatively simple events used in the laboratory, aging may be less likely to affect memory for the major life events that people cherish. For instance,

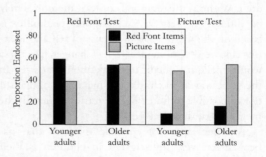

**Figure 13.5** Results selected from Gallo et al. (2007). Participants studied red words and colored pictures, and recollection later was tested for these items using black words as retrieval cues. On the red word test, subjects had to endorse items that were studied in red font (rejecting the others), whereas on the picture test they had to endorse items that were studied with a picture. Even though the same items were tested in each condition, age impaired the ability to discriminate test items on red font test but not on the picture test.

older adults retrieve a disproportionate number of autobiographical events from their late adolescence and young adulthood, a phenomenon known as the "reminiscence bump" (Berntsen & Rubin, 2002). Older adults also tend to recall more positive than negative memories, suggesting that some age-related changes in memory are driven by motivational factors (Carstensen, Mikels, & Mather, 2006). From this perspective, some age-related changes in memory are adaptive, allowing individuals to focus on positive aspects of their lives in order to promote social and emotional health.

## Summary and Future Directions

Episodic memory is one of the most salient aspects of conscious experience, and its complexities have been contemplated since ancient times in philosophy and literature. Within the relatively recent history of experimental psychology, significant empirical advances have been made toward understanding the cognitive principles that guide successful remembering, forgetting, and distortion in episodic memory. Further advances have been made by studying brain damage and nonhuman animals, and by the use of neuroimaging techniques. This relatively new cognitive neuroscience approach has begun to integrate psychological theories with principles of neural organization and function, leading to a more complete understanding of episodic memory.

This final section proposes four broad sets of questions about episodic memory that have far-reaching implications. These questions have yet to be fully answered, and many will require cross-disciplinary efforts to address. Nevertheless, recent findings suggest that answers to at least some of these questions may be within the reach of memory researchers in the very near future.

1. What is the exact sequence of neural events giving rise to the process of episodic recollection? How will the study of this neural time course constrain psychological concepts such as "mental representations," "retrieval cues," "memory traces," and the "associations" that are formed between them? Is synchronized and distributed neural activity required for the conscious experience of recollection?

2. How does memory consolidation work, and what is the role of sleep and dreaming? Does the retrieval of episodic memories temporarily render them susceptible to reconsolidation? How might psychoactive drugs affect the reinterpretation and reconsolidation of memories, and what are

the clinical, ethical, and legal implications for tampering with episodic memories?

3. Why did episodic memory evolve? What functions did it serve in humankind's prehistoric ancestors (e.g., tracking geographical locations and resources, navigating complex social environments and communication systems, mental simulation of future plans and goals, etc.)? Did the episodic-like memory of other species evolve for similar reasons, and how can comparative studies inform the way that different memory systems are conceptualized in the human brain?

4. Are there reliable individual differences in episodic memory distortion? If laboratory measures were devised to assess these propensities, how should they be used in applied situations such as eyewitness testimony? Would it be wise to take drugs that could enhance episodic memory accuracy, or might there be negative consequences of an unnaturally precise episodic memory?

## Acknowledgments

We are grateful to Endel Tulving for thoughtful comments on an earlier draft.

## Note

1. This use of the term "short-term memory" should not be confused with more colloquial usage, which tends to refer to memories of recently experienced events (e.g., daily events). Although this colloquial notion of short-term memory still is used in some clinical and neuroscience areas, many modern cognitive psychologists use the term "episodic memory" to refer to the conscious reexperiencing of past events from memory, irrespective of the retention interval. They restrict the term "short-term memory" for the transient activation of information in working memory. Short-term memory also is different from transient perceptual after-effects that may exist within sensory systems, such as iconic memory (in vision) and echoic memory (in audition).

## References

Alpert, J. L., Brown, L. S., Ceci, S. J., Courtois, C. A., Loftus, E. F., & Ornstein, P. A. (1998). Final report of the American Psychological Association working group on investigation of memories of childhood abuse. Psychology, Public Policy, and Law, 4, 931–1078.

Alvarez, P., & Squire, L. R. (1994). Memory consolidation and the medial temporal lobe: A simple network model. Proceedings of the National Academy of Sciences USA, 91, 7041–7045.

Anderson, M. C., Bjork, R. A., & Bjork, E. L. (1994). Remembering can cause forgetting: Retrieval dynamics in long-term memory. Journal of Experimental Psychology: Learning, Memory, and Cognition, 20, 1063–1087.

Anderson, J. R., & Schooler, L. J. (1991). Reflections of the environment in memory. Psychological Science, 2, 396–408.

Baddeley, A. (2000). The episodic buffer: A new component of working memory? Trends in Cognitive Sciences, 4, 417–423.

Balota, D. A., Cortese, M. J., Duchek, J. M., Adams, D., Roediger, H. L., III, McDermott, K. B., & Yerys, B. E. (1999). Veridical and false memories in healthy older adults and in dementia of the Alzheimer's type. Cognitive Neuropsychology, 16, 361–384.

Bartlett, F. C. (1932). *Remembering: A study in experimental and social psychology*. Cambridge, England: Cambridge University Press.

Berntsen, D., & Rubin, D. C. (2002). Emotionally charged autobiographical memories across the life span: The recall of happy, sad, traumatic, and involuntary memories. Psychology and Aging, 17, 636–652.

Bjork, R. A. (1970). Positive forgetting: The noninterference of items intentionally forgotten. Journal of Verbal Learning and Verbal Behavior, 9, 255–268.

Bower, G. H. (2000). A brief history of memory research. In E. Tulving & F. I. M. Craik (Eds.), *Oxford handbook of memory* (pp. 3–32). Oxford, England: Oxford University Press.

Bower, G. H., Clark, M. C., Lesgold, A. M., & Winzenz, D. (1969). Hierarchical retrieval schemes in recall of categorized word lists. Journal of Verbal Learning and Verbal Behavior, 8, 323–343.

Brainerd, C. J., & Reyna, V. F. (2002). Recollection rejection: How children edit their false memories. Developmental Psychology, 38, 156–172.

Brainerd, C. J., Reyna, V. F., & Forrest, T. J. (2002). Are young children susceptible to the false-memory illusion? Child Development, 73, 1363–1377.

Brewer, W. F. (1977). Memory for the pragmatic implications of sentences. Memory and Cognition, 5, 673–678.

Brewer, W. F., & Pani, J. R. (1996). Reports of mental imagery in retrieval from long-term memory. Consciousness and Cognition, 5, 265–287.

Buckner, R. L. (2004). Memory and executive function in aging and AD: Multiple factors that cause decline and reserve factors that compensate. Neuron, 44, 195–208.

Budson, A. E., Simons, J. S., Waring, J. D., Sullivan, A. L., Hussoin, T., & Schacter, D. L. (2007). Memory for the September 11, 2001, terrorist attacks one year later in patients with Alzheimer's disease, patients with mild cognitive impairment, and healthy older adults. Cortex, 43, 875–888.

Burgess, P. W., & Shallice, T. (1996). Confabulation and the control of recollection. Memory, 4, 359–411.

Burnham, W. H. (1888). Memory, historically and experimentally considered. I: An historical sketch of the older conceptions of memory. American Journal of Psychology, 2, 39–90.

Butler, K. M., Mc Daniel, M. A., Dornburg, C. C., Price, A. L., & Roediger, H. L. (2004). Age differences in veridical and false recall are not inevitable: The role of frontal lobe function. Psychonomic Bulletin and Review, 11, 921–925.

Cabeza, R., Anderson, N. D., Locantore, J. K., & McIntosh, A. R. (2002). Aging gracefully: Compensatory brain activity in high-performing older adults. Neuroimage, 17, 1394–1402.

Cabeza, R., Ciaramelli, E., Olson, I. R., & Moscovitch, M. (2008). The parietal cortex and episodic memory: An attentional account. Nature Reviews Neuroscience, 9, 613–625.

Cahill, L., & Mc Gaugh, J. L. (1998). Mechanisms of emotional arousal and lasting declarative memory. Trends in Neurosciences, 21, 294–299.

Calkins, M. W. (1894). Association: I. Psychological Review, 1, 476–483.

Carstensen, L. L., Mikels, J. A., & Mather, M. (2006). Aging and the intersection of cognition, motivation, and emotion. In J. Birren & K. W. Schaie (Eds.), *Handbook of the psychology of aging* (pp. 343–362). San Diego, CA: Psychology Press.

Castel, A. D. (2005). Memory for grocery prices in younger and older adults: The role of schematic support. Psychology and Aging, 20, 718–721.

Ceci, S. J., & Bruck, M. (1993). Suggestibility of the child witness: A historical review and synthesis. Psychological Bulletin, 113, 403–439.

Clayton, N. S., & Dickinson, A. D. (1998). Episodic-like memory during cache recovery by scrub jays. Nature, 395, 272–278.

Cohen, N. J., & Eichenbaum, H. (1993). *Memory, amnesia, and the hippocampal system*. Cambridge, MA: MIT Press.

Conway, M. A. (2005). Memory and the self. Journal of Memory and Langauge, 53, 594–628.

Conway, M. A. (2009). Episodic memories. Neuropsychologia, 47, 2305–2313.

Craik, F. I. M., & Anderson, N. D. (1999). Applying cognitive research to problems of cognitive aging. In D. Gopher & A. Koriat (Eds.), *Attention and performance XVII: Cognitive regulation of performance*, (Vol. 17, pp. 583–615). Cambridge, MA: MIT Press.

Craik, F. I. M., & Lockhart, R. S. (1972). Levels of processing: A framework for memory research. Journal of Verbal Learning and Verbal Behavior, 11, 671–684.

Craik, F. I. M., & Tulving, E. (1975). Depth of processing and the retention of words in episodic memory. Journal of Experimental Psychology: General, 104, 268–294.

Davachi, L., & Wagner, A. D. (2002.). Hippocampal contributions to episodic encoding: Insights from relational and item-based learning. Journal of Neurophysiology, 88, 982–990.

Donaldson, D. I., Wheeler, M. E., & Petersen, S. E. (2010). Remember the source: Dissociating frontal and parietal contributions to episodic memory. Journal of Cognitive Neuroscience, 22, 377–391.

Ebbinghaus, H. (1964). *Memory: A contribution to experimental psychology* (H. A. Ruger & C. E. Bussenius, Trans.). New York: Dover. (Original work published in 1885).

Eichenbaum, E., &Fortin, N. J. (2005). Bridging the gap between brain and behavior: Cognitive and neural mechanisms of episodic memory. Journal of the Experimental Analysis of Behavior, 84, 619–629.

Eichenbaum, H., Yonelinas, A. P., & Ranganath, C. (2007). The medial temporal lobe and recognition memory. Annual Review of Neuroscience, 30, 123–152.

Einstein, G. O., Richardson, S. L., Guynn, M. J., Cunfer, A. R., & Mc Daniel, M. A. (1995). Aging and prospective memory: Examining the influences of self-initiated retrieval-processes. Journal of Experimental Psychology: Learning, Memory and Cognition, 21, 996–1007.

Fuster, J. M. (2002). Frontal lobe and cognitive development. Journal of Neurocytology, 31, 373–385.

Gallo, D. A. (2006). *Associative illusions of memory*. New York: Psychology Press.

Gallo, D. A., Cotel, S. C., Moore, C. D., & Schacter, D. L. (2007). Aging can spare recollection-based retrieval monitoring: The importance of event distinctiveness. Psychology and Aging, 22, 209–213.

Gallo, D. A., Mc Donough, I. M., & Scimeca, J. (2010). Dissociating source memory decisions in prefrontal cortex: fMRI of diagnostic and disqualifying monitoring. Journal of Cognitive Neuroscience, 22, 955–969.

Ghetti, S. (2008). Rejection of false events in childhood: A metamemory account. Current Directions in Psychological Science, 17, 16–20.

Giovanello, K. S., Schnyer, D. M., & Verfaellie, M. (2009). Distinct hippocampal regions make unique contributions to relational memory. Hippocampus, 19, 111–117.

Glisky, E. L., Polster, M. R., & Routhieaux, B. C. (1995). Double dissociation between item and source memory. Psychology and Aging, 9, 229–235.

Godden, D. R., & Baddeley, A. D. (1975). Context-dependent memory in two natural environments: On land and underwater. British Journal of Psychology, 66, 325–331.

Grady, C. L. (2008). Cognitive neursocience of aging. Annals of the NY Academy of Sciences, 1124, 127–144.

Graf, P., Squire, L. R., & Mandler, G. (1984). The information that amnesic patients do not forget. Journal of Experimental Psychology: Learning, Memory, and Cognition, 10, 164–178.

Hedden, T., & Gabrieli, D. (2004). Insights into the ageing mind: A view from cognitive neuroscience. Nature Reviews Neuroscience, 5, 87–97.

Hess, T. M. (2005). Memory and aging in context. Psychological Bulletin, 131, 383–406.

Hodges, J. R., Patterson, K., Oxbury, S., & Funnell, E. (1992). Semantic dementia: Progressive fluent aphasia with temporal lobe atrophy. Brain, 115, 1783–1806.

Howe, M. L., & Courage, M. L. (1993). On resolving the enigma of infantile amnesia. Psychological Bulletin, 113, 305–326.

Hunt, R. R. (2006). The concept of distinctiveness in memory research. In R. R. Hunt & J. B. Worthen (Eds.), *Distinctiveness and memory* (pp. 3–26). New York: Oxford University Press.

Hunt, R. R., & Mc Daniel, M. A. (1993). The enigma of organization and distinctiveness. Journal of Memory and Language, 32, 421–445.

Hyde, T. S., & Jenkins, J. J. (1969). Differential effects of incidental tasks on the organization of recall of a list of highly associated words. Journal of Experimental Psychology, 82, 472–481.

Ishai, A., Ungerleider, L. G., & Haxby, J. V. (2000). Distributed neural systems for the generation of visual images. Neuron, 28, 979–990.

Jacoby, L. L. (1999). Ironic effects of repetition: Measuring age-related differences in memory. Journal of Experimental Psychology: Learning, Memory, and Cognition, 25, 3–22.

Jacoby, L. L., Kelley, C. M., & Dywan, J. (1989). Memory attributions. In H. L. Roediger & F. I. M. Craik (Eds.), *Varieties of memory and consciousness: Essays in honour of Endel Tulving* (pp. 391–422). Hillsdale, NJ: Erlbaum.

James, W. (1890). *Principles of psychology*. New York: Dover.

Johnson, M. K., Hashtroudi, S., & Lindsay, D. S. (1993). Source monitoring. Psychological Bulletin, 114, 3–28.

Kensinger, E. A. (2007). Negative emotion enhances memory accuracy: Behavioral and neuroimaging evidence. Current Directions in Psychological Science, 16, 213–218.

Koutstaal, W., Schacter, D. L., Galluccio, L., & Stofer, K. A. (1999). Reducing gist-based false recognition in older adults: Encoding and retrieval manipulations. Psychology and Aging, 14, 220–237.

Lindsay, D. S., Johnson, M. K., & Kwon, P. (1991). Developmental changes in memory source monitoring. Journal of Experimental Child Psychology, 52, 297–318.

Loftus, E. F., & Davies, G. M. (1984). Distortions in the memory of children. Journal of Social Issues, 40, 51–67.

Lustig, C., Shah, P., Seidler, R., & Reuter-Lorenz, P. A. (2009). Aging, training, and the brain: A review and future directions. Neuropsychology Review, 19, 504–522.

McClelland, J. L., McNaughton, B. L., & O'Reilly, R. C. (1995). Why are there complementary learning systems in the hippocampus and neocortex: Insights from the successes and failures of connectionist models of learning and memory. Psychological Review, 102, 419–457.

McDermott, K. B., Petersen, S. E., Watson, J. M., & Ojemann, J. G. (2003). A procedure for identifying regions preferentially activated by attention to semantic and phonological relations using functional magnetic resonance imaging. Neuropsychologia, 41, 293–303.

McNally, R. D., & Geraerts, E. (2009). A new solution to the recovered memory debate. Perspectives on Psychological Science, 4, 126–134.

Melton, A. W. (1963). Implications of short-term memory for a general theory of memory. Journal of Verbal Learning and Verbal Behavior, 2, 1–21.

Mitchell, K. J., & Johnson, M. K. (2009). Source monitoring 15 years later: What have we learned from fMRI about the neural mechanisms of source memory? Psychological Bulletin, 135, 638–677.

Morgabi, D. C., Brown, R. G., & Morris, R. G. (2009). Anosognosia in Alzheimer's disease: The petrified self. Consciousness and Cognition, 18, 989–1003.

Morris, C. D., Bransford, J. P., & Franks, J. J. (1977). Levels of processing versus transfer appropriate processing. Journal of Verbal Learning and Verbal Behavior, 16, 519–533.

Moscovitch, M., & Melo, B. (1997). Strategic retrieval and the frontal lobes: Evidence from confabulation and amnesia. Neuropsychologia, 35, 1017–1034.

Moscovitch, M., Rosenbaum, R. S., Gilboa, A., Addis, D. R., Westmacott, R., Grady, C., . . . Nadel, L . (2005). Functional neuroanatomy of remote episodic, semantic and spatial memory: A unified account based on multiple trace theory. Journal of Anatomy, 207(1), 35–66.

Myers, N. A., Clifton, R. K., & Clarkson, M. G. (1987). When they were very young: Almost-threes remember two years ago. Infant Behavior and Development, 10, 123–132.

Naveh-Benjamin, M., Shing, Y. L., Kilb, A., Werkle-Bergner, M., Lindenberger, U., & Li, S. (2009). Adult age differences in memory for name-face associations: The effects of intentional and incidental learning. Memory, 17, 220–232.

Neisser, U., & Harsch, N. (1992). Phantom flashbulbs: False recollections of hearing the news about Challenger. In E. Winograd & U. Neisser (Eds.), *Affect and accuracy in recall* (pp. 9–31). New York: Cambridge University Press.

Nigro, G., & Neisser, U. (1983). Point of view in personal memories. Cognitive Psychology, 15, 467–482.

Nyberg, L., Petersson, K. M., Nilsson, L. G., Sandblom, J., Åberg, C., & Ingvar, M. (2001). Reactivation of motor brain areas during explicit memory for actions. NeuroImage, 14, 521–528.

O'Craven, K. M., & Kanwisher, N. (2000). Mental imagery of faces and places activates corresponding stimulus-specific brain regions. Journal of Cognitive Neuroscience, 12, 1013–1023.

Pierce, B. H., Simons, J. S., & Schacter, D. L. (2004). Aging and the seven sins of memory. Advances in Cell Aging and Gerontology, 15, 1–40.

Polster, M. R. (1993). Drug-induced amnesia: Implications for cognitive neuropsychological investigations of memory. Psychological Bulletin, 114, 477–493.

Radvansky, G. A., Copeland, D. E., & Zwaan, R. A. (2005). A novel study: Investigating the structure of narrative and autobiographcial memories. Memory, 13, 796–814.

Raz, N., Rodrigue, K. M., Kennedy, K. M., & Acker, J. D. (2007). Vascular health and longitudinal changes in brain and cognition in middle-aged and older adults. Neuropsychology, 21, 149–157.

Roediger, H. L. (1996). Memory illusions. Journal of Memory and Language, 35, 76–100.

Roediger, H. L. (2000). Why retrieval is the key process in understanding human memory. In E. Tulving (Ed.), Memory, consciousness, and the brain: The Tallinn conference (pp. 52–73). Philadelphia, PA: Psychology Press.

Roediger, H. L., III, & Mc Dermott, K. B. (1995). Creating false memories: Remembering words not presented in lists. Journal of Experimental Psychology: Learning, Memory, and Cognition, 21, 803–814.

Rovee-Collier, C., & Hayne, H. (2000). Memory in infancy and early childhood. In E. Tulving & F. I. M. Craik (Eds.), Oxford handbook of memory. New York: Oxford University Press.

Rubin, D. C. (2000). The distribution of early childhood memories. Memory, 8, 265–269.

Rubin, D. C., Berntsen, D., & Bohni, M. K. (2008). A memory-based model of posttraumatic stress disorder: Evaluating basic assumptions underlying the PTSD diagnosis. Psychological Review, 115, 985–1011.

Rybash, J. M., & Colilla, J. L. (1994). Source memory deficits and frontal lobe functioning in children. Developmental Neuropsychology, 10, 67–73.

Schacter, D. L. (1987). Implicit memory: History and current status. Journal of Experimental Psychology: Learning, Memory, and Cognition, 13, 501–518.

Schacter, D. L. (1995). Memory distortion: History and current status. In D. L. Schacter, J. T. Coyle, G. D. Fischbach, M. M. Mesulam, & L. E. Sullivan (Eds.), Memory distortions: How minds, brains, and societies reconstruct the past (pp. 1–43). Cambridge, MA: Harvard University Press.

Schacter, D. L., Addis, D. R., & Buckner, R. L. (2007). Remembering the past to imagine the future: The prospective brain, Nature Reviews Neuroscience, 8, 657–661.

Schacter, D. L., Koutstaal, W., Johnson, M. K., Gross, M. S., & Angell, K. E. (1997). False recollection induced by photographs: A comparison of older and younger adults. Psychology and Aging, 12, 203–215.

Sherry, D. F., & Schacter, D. L. (1987). The evolution of multiple memory systems. Psychological Review, 94, 439–454.

Smith, E. E., & Jonides, J. (1997). Working memory: A view from neuroimaging. Cognitive Psychology, 33, 5–42.

Squire, L. R. (1987). Memory and brain. New York: Oxford University Press.

Squire, L. R. (2004). Memory systems of the brain: A brief history and current perspective. Neurobiology of Learning and Memory, 82, 171–177.

Squire, L. R., Wixted, J. T., & Clark, R. E. (2007). Recognition memory and the medial temporal lobe: A new perspective. Nature Reviews Neuroscience, 8, 872–883.

Tisserand, D. J., & Jolles, J. (2003). On the involvement of prefrontal networks in cognitive ageing. Cortex, 39, 1107–1128.

Tulving, E. (1962). Subjective organization in free recall of "unrelated" words. Psychological Review, 69, 344–354.

Tulving, E. (1972). Episodic and semantic memory. In E. Tulving & W. Donaldson (Eds.), Organization of memory (pp. 381–402). New York: Academic Press.

Tulving, E. (1974). Cue-dependent forgetting. American Scientist, 62, 74–82.

Tulving, E. (1983). Elements of episodic memory. Oxford, England: Clarendon Press.

Tulving, E. (1985). Memory and consciousness. Canadian Psychology, 26, 1–12.

Tulving, E. (1993). What is episodic memory? Current Directions in Psychological Science, 2, 67–70.

Tulving, E. (2002a). Does memory encoding exist? In M. Naveh-Benjamin, M. Moscovitch, & H. L. Roediger (Eds.), Perspectives on human memory and cognitive aging: Essays in honour of Fergus Craik (pp.6–27). New York: Psychology Press.

Tulving, E. (2002b). Episodic memory: From mind to brain. Annual Review of Psychology, 53, 1–25.

Tulving, E., & Pearlstone, Z. (1966). Availability versus accessibility of information in memory for words. Journal of Verbal Learning and Verbal Behavior, 5, 381–391.

Tulving, E., & Thompson, D. M. (1973). Encoding specificity and retrieval processes in episodic memory. Psychological Review, 80, 352–373.

Van Essen, D. C . (2005). A population-average, landmark- and surface-based (PALS) atlas of human cerebral cortex. Neuroimage, 28, 635–662.

Vilberg, K. L., & Rugg, M. D. (2008). Memory retrieval and the parietal cortex: A review of evidence from a dual-process perspective. Neuropsychologia, 46, 1787–1799.

Wagner, A. D., Schacter, D. L., Rotte, M., Koutstaal, W., Maril, A., Dale, A. M.,…Buckner, R. L. (1998). Building memories: Remembering and forgetting of verbal experiences as predicted by brain activity. Science, 281, 1188–1191.

Watkins, O. C., & Watkins, M. J. (1975). Buildup of proactive inhibition as a cue-overload effect. Journal of Experimental Psychology: Human Leanring and Memory, 1, 442–452.

Wearing, D. (2005, January 12). The man who keeps falling in love with his wife. The Telegraph. Retrieved January 2, 2010, from http://www.telegraph.co.uk/health/3313452/The-man-who-keeps-falling-in-love-with-his-wife.html

Weldon, M. S. (2000). Remembering as a social process. In D. L. Medin (Ed.), The psychology of learning and memory (Vol. 40, pp. 67–120). San Diego, CA: Academic press.

Wheeler, M. E., & Buckner, R. L. (2003). Functional dissociation among components of remembering: Control, perceived oldness, and content. Journal of Neuroscience, 23, 3869–3880.

Wheeler, M. E., Petersen, S. E., & Buckner, R. L. (2000). Memory's echo: Vivid remembering reactivates sensory-specific cortex. Proceedings of the National Academy of Sciences USA, 97, 11125–11129.

Wheeler, M. A., Stuss, D. T., & Tulving, E. (1997). Toward a theory of episodic memory: The frontal lobes and autonoetic consciousness. Psychological Bulletin, 121, 331–354.

Winocur, G., & Moscovitch, M. (2011). Memory transformation and systems consolidation. *Journal of the International Neuropsychological Society*, 17, 766–780.

Wixted, J. T. (2004). The psychology and neuroscience of forgetting. Annual Review of Psychology, 55, 235–269.

Worthen, J. B., & Hunt, R. R. (2011). *Mnemonology: Mnemonics for the 21st century*. New York: Psychology Press.

Zacks, J. M., & Swallow, K. M. (2007). Event segmentation. Current Directions in Psychological Science, 16, 80–84.

# Semantic Memory

Ken McRae *and* Michael Jones

**Abstract**

Concepts and word meaning are fundamental to nearly all aspects of human cognition. People use this knowledge daily to recognize entities and objects in their environment, generate expectancies for upcoming events, and interpret language. In this chapter, we review contemporary research in semantic memory. Our discussion is restricted to the meaning of individual words, focusing on recent experimental results and theoretical trends. Over the past number of years, semantic memory research has blossomed for a number of reasons, and our goal is to provide the reader with a feel for the exciting research and theoretical approaches that have resulted. The chapter deals primarily with the following topics: implications of grounded cognition for semantic memory, neural organization of concepts, the importance of people's knowledge of everyday events for semantic memory, distinctions among semantic and associative relations, research on abstract concepts, connectionist models of semantic computations, and distributional models of semantic representations.

**Key Words:** semantic memory models, grounded cognition, neural organization, semantic relations

Concepts and meaning are fundamental components of nearly all aspects of human cognition. We use this knowledge every day to recognize entities and objects in our environment, anticipate how they will behave and interact with each other, use them to perform functions, to generate expectancies for situations, and to interpret language. This general knowledge of meaning falls within the realm of *semantic memory*. For many years, semantic memory was viewed as an amodal, modular memory store for factual information about concepts, distinct from episodic memory (our memory for specific instances of personal experience). However, researchers now interpret semantic memory more broadly to refer to general world knowledge, entangled in experience, and dependent on culture. Furthermore, there is now considerable evidence suggesting that semantic memory is grounded in the sensory modalities, is distributed across brain regions, and depends on

episodic memories at least in terms of learning, with the possibility that there is no definite line between episodic and semantic memory. In this chapter, we review contemporary research in semantic memory. We limit our discussion to lexical semantics (the meaning of individual words), with particular focus on recent findings and trends, formal computational models, neural organization, and future directions.

## Classic View of Semantic Memory

Tulving (1972) viewed memory as a system of independent modules. Long-term memory was subdivided into declarative (facts) and procedural (skills) components. Declarative memory was further divided into semantic memory and episodic memory, with a clear distinction between them. Tulving characterized semantic memory as amodal. In an amodal view, when one thinks of an apple, the information retrieved from semantic memory is independent of the sensory modalities used to perceive an apple. Although semantic memory contains factual information about an apple's color and taste, this information is dissociated from the sensory systems used to actually see or taste.

Early neuropsychological evidence supported Tulving's (1972) view. For example, amnesic patients showed dissociations between episodic and semantic memory tasks (Squire, 1988); their impairment seemed to have little effect on semantic memory despite profound episodic deficiencies, bolstering the modularity claim. Research on "schema abstraction" tasks found that the decay of episodic and semantic memory followed different profiles (Posner & Keele, 1968). Although memory for episodes is stronger than for category prototypes immediately after training, episodic memory decays much faster than semantic memory (or at least, instances decay faster than do abstract prototypes).

Tulving's (1972) characterization of semantic memory as an amodal, modular system separate from episodic and procedural memory provided a useful foundation to study and understand human semantic representations. In retrospect, however, it may have actually stifled research in semantics by imposing a rigid framework that is unlikely to be correct. Recent research with improved experimental, computational, and neuroimaging techniques clearly contradicts the classic view. Semantic memory is now viewed more broadly as a part of an integrated memory system, grounded in the sensory, perceptual, and motor systems, and is distributed across key brain regions.

## Grounding Semantic Memory

Tulving's classic view of semantic memory as an amodal symbolic store has been challenged by contemporary research. There is a growing body of behavioral and neuroimaging research demonstrating that when humans access word meaning, they automatically activate sensorimotor information used to perceive and act on the real-world objects and relations to which a word refers. In theories of *grounded cognition*, the meaning of a word is grounded in the sensorimotor systems (Barsalou, 1999; see Pecher & Zwann, 2005, for a review). Hence, when one thinks of an apple, knowledge regarding motoric grasping, chewing, sights, sounds, and tastes used to encode episodic experiences of an apple are reinstated via sensorimotor simulation. Thus, a grounded simulation refers to context-specific reactivations that incorporate the important aspects of episodic experience into a current representation. In this sense,

simulations are guided and only partial (Barsalou, 2008). This approach challenges amodal views and makes a clear link between episodic experience and semantic memory.

A wealth of recent behavioral evidence supports the grounded simulation approach to semantics. For example, response latencies for images and feature names are faster when they have visual properties congruent with context (Solomon & Barsalou, 2001; Zwann, Stanfield, & Yaxley, 2002). Similarly, having participants perform particular motions (e.g., grasping) facilitates the comprehension of sentences describing actions involving these motions (Klatzky, Pellegrino, McCloskey, & Doherty, 1989), and prime-target pairs sharing motor-manipulation features (e.g., *typewriter-piano*) are responded to more quickly than pairs that do not (Myun, Blumstein, & Sedivy, 2006). Zwaan and Madden (2005) review numerous studies suggesting that the mental representations activated during comprehension also include information about object features, temporal and spatial perspective, and spatial iconicity. Barsalou (2008) and Pecher, Boot, and Van Dantzig (2011) contain surveys of the recent literature attesting to the importance of situation models, simulation (perceptual, motor, and affective), and gesture in language comprehension and abstract concepts.

## Semantic Organization in the Brain

Semantic memory research was for many years dominated by cognitive psychologists who generally were not concerned with neural organization. In cognitive neuropsychology, there is a history of studies investigating patients with semantic deficits (Warrington & Shallice, 1984). However, for a number of years, this line of research was divorced from semantic memory research using normal adult participants. With the advent of neuroimaging techniques, functional magnetic resonance imaging (fMRI) in particular, research on the neural organization of semantic memory blossomed.

Researchers have long known that brain regions responsible for perception tend to be specialized for specific sensory modalities. Given that perception is distributed across specialized neural regions, one possibility is that conceptual representations are organized in a similar fashion. For the past 40 years, Paivio (1971) has advocated a form of modality-specific representations in his dual-coding theory. Furthermore, studies of patients with category-specific semantic deficits have been used as a basis for arguing for multimodal representations for the past 25 years or so.

In early work, Warrington and McCarthy (1987) put forward their sensory/functional theory to account for patterns of category-specific impairments of knowledge in patients with focal brain damage. The basic assumption is that living things depend primarily on visual knowledge, whereas although visual knowledge is also important for nonliving things, knowledge of an object's function is primary. Building on Allport (1985), recent research has used analyses of large-scale feature production norms to extend the sensory-functional theory to other senses and types of knowledge, and move beyond the binary living-nonliving distinction (Cree & McRae, 2003). There do remain some accounts of category-specific semantic deficits that are amodal (Caramazza & Shelton, 1998; Tyler & Moss, 2001), but even these researchers have begun to find support for theories in which knowledge is tied to modality-specific brain areas (Mahon & Caramazza, 2003; Raposo, Moss, Stamatakis, & Tyler, 2009).

The behavioral and neuropsychological evidence in favor of grounded semantics is corroborated by recent neuroimaging studies supporting a distributed multimodal system. A few researchers have used evoked response potentials to investigate this issue (Sitnikova, West, Kuperberg, & Holcomb, 2006), but the vast majority of studies have used fMRI. For example, Goldberg, Perfetti, and Schneider (2006) tied together previously reported neuroimaging evidence supporting modally bound tactile, color, auditory, and gustatory representations. They found that sensory brain areas for each modality are recruited during a feature verification task using linguistic stimuli (e.g., *banana-yellow*). The same pattern emerges in single-word processing. Hauk, Johnsrude, and Pulvermüller (2004) showed that reading action words correlates with activation in somatotopically corresponding areas of the motor cortex (*lick* activates tongue regions, while *kick* activates foot regions), indicating that word meaning is modally distributed across brain regions. Furthermore, within brain regions that encode modality-specific, possibly feature-based representations, some studies suggest a category-based organization (Chao, Haxby, & Martin, 1999). Finally, some studies have shown that semantic representations are located just anterior to primary perceptual or motor areas, whereas others have found evidence for activation of primary areas (see Thompson-Schill, 2003). In summary, there is a large amount of converging evidence supporting a distributed multimodal semantic system (for thorough reviews, see

Binder, Desai, Graves, & Conant, 2009; Martin, 2007).

Perhaps one of the most important remaining issues concerns the fact that people's concepts are not experienced as a jumble of features, disjointed across space and time, but instead are experienced as coherent unified wholes. Multimodal feature-based theories therefore need to include a solution to the binding problem, specifying how representational elements are integrated into conceptual wholes, both within and between modalities. One solution involves temporal synchrony of neuronal firing rates (von der Malsburg, 1999). Semantic representations may be integrated by coincidental firing rates of distributed neural populations. However, the most frequently invoked solution is based on the idea of a convergence zone, which can be considered as a set of processing units that encode coincidental activity among multiple input units (Damasio, 1989). In connectionist models, a convergence zone may be thought of as a hidden layer (Rogers et al., 2004). Because they encode time-locked activation patterns, an important property of convergence zones is that they transform their input, rather than just repeat signals. In this way, successive convergence zones build more complex or abstract representations. Current theories of multimodal semantic representations incorporate either single convergence zones, as in Patterson, Nestor, and Rogers' (2007) anterior temporal lobe hub theory, or a hierarchy of convergence zones encoding information over successively more complex configurations of modalities (Simmons & Barsalou, 2003). At the moment, it is unclear which of these hypotheses is correct.

In summary, recent research supports the idea that semantic representations are grounded across modality-specific brain regions. Researchers are working toward fleshing out details of precisely what these regions encode, the degree to which subregions are specific to types of concepts, and how semantic representations are experienced as unified wholes. Furthermore, the vast majority of research has been conducted on concrete concepts, so research on other concepts, such as verbs or abstract concepts, will play a key role over the next few years.

## Event-Based Semantic Representations

Another way in which the semantic-episodic distinction has been blurred in recent years concerns research on event-based knowledge in semantic memory. People's knowledge of common everyday events includes actions that are part of those events, and common primary participants or components, such as agents (the people doing the action), patients (the people or objects upon which the action is performed), instruments involved in actions, and locations at which various events take part. Furthermore, people have knowledge of temporal aspects of events. This generalized event knowledge is learned through our experience with everyday events, watching television and movies, and reading and hearing about what people have done, what they are doing, and what they are going to do.

Language provides many cues into event knowledge. For example, verbs like *travel* or *cook* denote events and actions, some nouns like *breakfast* refer to events, and other nouns refer to entities or objects that typically play a role in specific situations, such as *waitress, customer, fork,* or *cafeteria*. A number of studies have shown that such event knowledge is computed rapidly from single words. These experiments have tended to use a priming paradigm with a short stimulus onset asynchrony (SOA, the time between the onset of the prime and the onset of the target), which is viewed as providing a window into the organization of semantic memory.

Moss, Ostrin, Tyler, and Marslen-Wilson (1995) showed priming effects based on instrument relations (such as *broom-floor*) and what they called script relations, in which the primes were a mixture of locations and events (*hospital-doctor* and *war-army*). Subsequent studies have shown that verbs prime their typical agents (*arresting-cop*), patients (*serving-customer*), and instruments (*stirred-spoon*), but not locations (*skated-arena*; Ferretti, McRae, & Hatherell, 2001). Furthermore, typical agents, patients, instruments, and locations prime verbs (McRae, Hare, Elman, & Ferretti, 2005). In addition, Hare, Jones, Thomson, Kelly, and McRae (2009) showed that event nouns prime the types of people and things commonly found at those events (*sale-shopper, breakfast-eggs*), location nouns prime entities and objects typically found at those locations (*stable-horse, sandbox-shovel*), and instrument nouns prime the types of things on which they typically are used (*key-door*) but not the people who typically use them (*hose-gardener*, although priming was found in the other direction). Hare et al. used a corpus-based model, BEAGLE (Jones, Kintsch, & Mewhort, 2006), to simulate their results.

Chwilla and Kolk (2005) showed that people can integrate words rapidly to construct situations, thus producing priming. They presented two words simultaneously that were unrelated except when considered in the context of some broader event

(*director bribe*) and demonstrated priming of a third word (*dismissal*) related to the situation. Chwilla and Kolk's results depend on conceptually integrating both primes with the target, thus speaking to rapid activation of knowledge of situations. In addition, Khalkhali, Wammes, and McRae (2012) found that relatedness decision latencies were shorter when three events were presented in the order corresponding to their usual real-world sequence (*marinate-grill-chew*) than when the order of the first two events was reversed (*grill-marinate-chew*), suggesting that such temporal information is encoded in semantic memory.

An interesting consequence of these studies is that they move toward a stronger tie between semantic memory and sentence comprehension. For example, a number of the studies used thematic roles of verbs as the basis for testing relations, thus making direct contact with a key construct in sentence processing research. Along this same line, Jones and Love (2007) provide a point of contact between sentence processing and how people learn lexical concepts. Participants studied sentences such as *The polar bear chases the seal* and *The German shepherd chases the cat*. In a test phase, similarity ratings increased for entities and objects participating in common relational systems. The increase was largest for objects playing the same role within a relation (e.g., the chaser) but also was present for those playing different roles in the same relation (e.g., the chaser or the chasee role in the chase relation), and this happened regardless of whether they participated in the same sentence/event.

In summary, recent studies have investigated people's episodic-based knowledge of common generalized events. These studies show that semantic memory is organized so that this knowledge is computed and used rapidly, and they demonstrate direct links between episodic and semantic memory.

## Semantic and Associative Relations
There are long-standing issues in semantic memory research regarding associative versus semantic relations. Association has a long history in psychology and philosophy, and normative word association has often been used to explain performance in semantic memory experiments (Nelson, McEvoy, & Dennis, 2000; Roediger, Watson, McDermott, & Gallo, 2001). Bower (2000) defined associations as "sensations that are experienced contiguously in time and/or space. The memory that sensory quality or event A was experienced together with, or immediately preceding, sensory quality or event

B is recorded in the memory bank as an association from idea *a* to idea *b*" (p. 3). In 1965, Deese stated that "almost all the basic propositions of current association theory derive from the sequential nature of events in human experience" (p. 1). More recently, Moss et al. (1995) claimed that associations between words are "built up through repeated co-occurrence of the two word forms" (p. 864). In general, the consensus seems to be that contiguity is key to forming a link between two concepts.

In contrast, association in cognitive psychology almost invariably is defined in terms of its operationalization. In a word association task, a participant hears or reads a stimulus word and produces the first word that comes to mind (Nelson, McEvoy, & Schreiber, 1998). Thus, two words are associated if one is produced as a response to the other. There exist significant discrepancies between the definition of association and its operationalization. Association is learning based, whereas word association is production based. Association is based on sensory information, whereas word association is linguistically based. Association is based on contiguity, whereas word associations are virtually always meaningful.

The construct of semantic relatedness was for a long time limited to exemplars from the same category, or featurally similar concepts (as in *cow-horse*; Frenck-Mestre & Bueno, 1999; Lupker, 1984). Recently, however, researchers have investigated a much wider array of relations. The event-based relations discussed in the section "Event-Based Semantic Representations" are examples. In addition, researchers have been studying what are often called thematic relations (see Estes, Golonka, & Jones, 2011, for a recent review). These include, for example, *cow-milk*, where a cow produces milk, or *wind-erosion*, where wind causes erosion.

A thorny issue concerns delineating between the influences of semantic and associative relatedness. Lucas (2000) concluded from a meta-analysis of priming experiments that "pure" semantic priming (in the absence of word association) exists, whereas there is no evidence for association-based priming in the absence of semantic relatedness. In contrast, Hutchison (2003) reviewed individual studies and concluded that both semantic and associative relatedness produce priming. One possibility is that it may not be fruitful to distinguish between associative and semantic relations because word associations are best understood in terms of semantic relations (Anisfeld & Knapp, 1968; Brainerd, Yang, Reyna, Howe, & Mills, 2008). In some views, the word association task unambiguously taps associative connections between words/concepts in people's semantic memory. In contrast, word association can be considered an open-ended task on which performance is driven almost exclusively by types of semantic relations. Researchers who have classified word associates according to their semantic relations have shown that almost all stimulus-response pairs, with the exception of rhymes, have clear semantic relations (Guida & Lenci, 2007). Furthermore, Brainerd et al. found that a number of semantic variables correlate with word association strength.

This is likely the primary reason why it has been so difficult to distinguish empirically between associative and semantic relations. In studies of associative priming, the items are a mixture of semantic relations, such as *hammer-nail* or *engine-car*. McNamara (2005) stated the issue clearly: "Having devoted a fair amount of time perusing free-association norms, I challenge anyone to find two highly associated words that are not semantically related in some plausible way. Under this view, the distinction between purely semantically and associatively related words is an artificial categorization of an underlying continuum" (p. 86). Furthermore, in studies of pure semantic relatedness priming, items that appear in word association norms are excluded. However, it does not appear to make sense to argue that items in these studies are not associated in the general sense. For example, Hare et al. (2009) analyzed subsets of stimuli not associated according to word association norms, showing priming in the absence of association. This logic appears at first glance to be valid because concepts such as *sale* and *shopper* are not associated according to Nelson et al.'s (1998) norms. However, shoppers are found at sales, and the entire point of a sale is to attract shoppers. So these concepts definitely are associated in the general sense, even though forward and backward association statistics indicate that they are not.

The line between association and semantics has now been questioned in a number of areas of research. McRae, Khalkhali, and Hare (2012) discuss this issue with respect to research using the Deese-Roediger-McDermott false memory paradigm, picture-word facilitation and interference, the development of associative learning through adolescence, and semantic priming. Although association is a critical aspect of learning, one possibility is that virtually all retained associations are meaningful and thus can be understood in terms of semantic relations. On the other hand, given long-standing views on the primacy of association-based links in memory (as indexed by normative word association), this debate is likely to continue.

## Abstract Concepts

The structure and content of abstract concepts such as *lucky*, *advise*, and *boredom* have been studied to a much lesser extent than concrete concepts and thus are not nearly as well understood. In general, there is little consensus regarding how abstract concepts are represented and computed. The lack of obvious physical referents in the world for abstract concepts makes theorizing, model building, and experimentation quite difficult but also an important and intriguing issue. We use the phrase "obvious physical referents" in the previous sentence because many abstract concepts are at least partly experienced by the senses or have internal states that correspond to them. For example, we have all experienced boredom, we have internal thoughts and emotions that are tied to the meaning of *boredom*, and we can visually recognize boredom in other people.

The most influential theory has been Paivio's (1971, 2007) dual-coding theory, in which the processing of lexical concepts involves the activation of functionally independent but interconnected verbal and nonverbal representational systems. The verbal system consists of associatively interconnected linguistically based units, whereas the nonverbal system consists of spatially organized representations of objects and events that can be experienced as mental images. Activation spreads within and between systems. Concrete concepts are represented in both systems, whereas abstract concepts are represented in the verbal system only. Dual-coding theory has been used to explain differences between concrete and abstract words in memory tasks, lexical decision, electroencephalography (EEG), and fMRI experiments.

Dual-coding theory is contrasted frequently with context-availability theory, in which the major difference between abstract and concrete concepts is that abstract words and sentences are more difficult to comprehend because it is challenging to access relevant world knowledge contextual information when comprehending abstract materials (Schwanenflugel & Shoben, 1983). At present, however, dual-coding theory has received much more support.

The vast majority of experiments on abstract concepts compare performance on concrete versus abstract words, either in isolation or in sentence contexts. A consistent finding is that memory is better for concrete concepts (Paivio, 2007). A number of studies have also found shorter lexical decision latencies to concrete than to abstract words in isolation (Schwanenflugel & Shoben, 1983), and a larger N400 to concrete words (Kounios & Holcomb, 1994). Some patients have been reported with better performance on concrete concepts (Coltheart, Patterson, & Marshall, 1980). However, a frustrating aspect of this research is that, although the memory results are stable, some studies show shorter lexical decision latencies to abstract words (Kousta, Vigliocco, Del Campo, Vinson, & Andrews, 2011), and some patients perform better on abstract concepts (Breedin, Saffran, & Coslett, 1994). In addition, there is no compelling explanation for the N400 results. Finally, the fMRI literature on concrete versus abstract concepts has produced highly variable results (Grossman et al., 2002; Kiehl et al., 1999; Wise et al., 2000).

There are at least two reasons for the inconsistency in results. First, some differences may be task related because the manner in which people process words influences the form of concrete-abstract differences. Second, there may be important differences among item sets across studies. Typically, researchers select concrete and abstract words using concreteness and/or imageability ratings. However, the categories of concrete and abstract concepts are large, and selecting small subsets from these large classes has presumably led to inconsistent results. To deal with this issue, researchers have begun to classify abstract words on further dimensions, such as emotional valence (Kousta et al., 2011).

More recent theories of the structure and content of abstract concepts have emerged. In Barsalou's (1999) perceptual simulation theory, abstract and concrete concepts can be simulated from prior experience. One issue involves the type of simulations that might be key to abstract concepts that do not, at least at first glance, have sensory-motor correspondences. Barsalou and Weimer-Hastings (2005) focused on situations as the key to abstract concepts. Concepts such as *lucky*, *advise*, and *boredom* are tied both to situations in which people have learned the meaning of those concepts, and to internally generated cognitive and emotional states. At present, however, little research has been conducted to flesh out these ideas.

One other prominent theory of abstract concepts is conceptual metaphor or image schema theory (Lakoff, 1987). In this view, abstract concepts are mapped to sensory-motor grounded image schemas. For example, studies suggest that the abstract concept of time is grounded in our knowledge of space (Casasanto & Boroditsky, 2008). At the moment, however, the notion of a conceptual metaphor or image schema is inconsistent among theorists (Pecher et al., 2011).

A promising avenue for studying abstract concepts comes from corpus-based distributional models. One advantage of corpus-based models is that they provide representations for all types of words using the same computational mechanisms. As described in the section "Integrating Perceptual Information Into Distributional Models," these models can also be combined with other approaches to form hybrids.

In summary, understanding the organization and content of abstract concepts is a major challenge for all current theories of semantic memory. Addressing the relevant issues will require a deeper appreciation of the similarities and differences among types of abstract concepts; how abstract concepts depend differentially on sensory, motor, and internally generated cognitive and emotional information; and the manner which they are tied to situations or contexts in which they are important.

## Computational Models of Semantic Memory

There is a fuzzy boundary in the literature between models of semantic processing and semantic representation. We define the former to be models of how learned semantic structure is used in tasks, and the latter to be models that specify a mechanism by which semantic memory is formed from experience. We first review models of semantic processing, and then models of learning semantic structure from experience (primarily corpus-based models). However, we acknowledge that this distinction between the two "levels" of models is an oversimplification: How we learn new semantic information depends on the current contents of semantic memory, and semantic structure and process influence each other when explaining behavioral data (Johns & Jones, 2010).

### Models of Semantic Processing

Connectionist networks have been used to provide insight into how word meaning is represented and computed, and to simulate numerous empirical semantic memory phenomena. In these models, concepts are typically represented as distributed patterns of activity across sets of representational units that often represent features (<has four legs>), but not necessarily nameable ones. Units are organized into layers and are linked by weighted connections.

These connections control processing, and their weights are established using a learning algorithm.

The impact of connectionist models has been at least four-fold. First, due to distributed representations, they naturally encode concept similarity in terms of shared units, and thus simulate similarity-based phenomena (Cree, NcNorgan, & McRae, 1999; Masson, 1995; Plaut & Booth, 2000). Second, because they learn statistical regularities between and within patterns, they have led researchers to focus on the distributional statistics underlying semantic representations and computations (McRae, de Sa, & Seidenberg, 1997; Tyler & Moss, 2001). Third, because many connectionist models settle into representations over time (e.g., attractor networks), they can be used to simulate response latencies and provide insight into the temporal dynamics of computing word meaning (Masson, 1995). Fourth, one can train a model and then damage it in various ways, thus simulating brain-damaged patients (Hinton & Shallice, 1991; Plaut & Shallice, 1993; Rogers et al., 2004). Finally, all of these properties of connectionist models are interrelated.

Semantic processing unfolds over time. When we read or hear a word, components of meaning become active at different rates over the first several hundred milliseconds. Attractor networks, in which units update their states continuously based on both their prior states and input from other units, are well suited to simulate this process. Because priming has played such a large role in semantic memory research, a number of researchers have simulated it. Given that similar concepts have overlapping distributed representations, connectionist networks have been successful at simulating priming between featurally similar concepts such as *eagle* and *hawk*, providing insight into factors such as correlations among semantic features and the degree of similarity between concepts (Cree et al., 1999; McRae et al., 1997). Furthermore, researchers have simulated contiguity-based (associative) priming and individual differences in priming (Masson, 1995; Plaut & Booth, 2000).

One way in which distributional statistics underlying semantic representations have been studied is the feature verification task, in which participants judge whether a feature such as <has an engine> is reasonably true of a concept such as *van*. These studies and accompanying simulations have highlighted the role of correlational structure. That is, some features tend to occur with others across basic-level concepts, such as <has feathers> and <has

a beak>, and there is a continuum of feature correlational strength. Studies such as McRae et al. (1997) and Randall, Moss, Rodd, Greer, and Tyler (2004) show that connectionist models predict influences of feature correlations that are observed in human data. Furthermore, the degree to which features are distinctive (the inverse of the number of concepts in which a feature occurs) plays a privileged role in semantic computations in both people and connectionist simulations (Cree et al., 2006; Randall et al., 2004). Distributional statistics such as these are bases for theories such as the conceptual structure account (Tyler & Moss, 2001), and they are also strongly implicated in understanding data from category-specific deficits and semantic dementia patients (Rogers et al., 2004; Tyler & Moss, 2001). Finally, they may form the basis for understanding how superordinate categories such as *clothing* and *fruit* are learned and computed (O'Connor, Cree, & McRae, 2009).

Much of the research on simulating neurally impaired adults has drawn on work by Hinton and Shallice (1993) and Plaut and Shallice (1993). A nice example is Rogers and colleagues' work in which they provide detailed accounts of the performance of semantic dementia patients (Rogers et al., 2004; Rogers & McClelland, 2004). Rogers et al. damaged a trained attractor network, and then simulated patient performance in a number of tasks. For example, they showed that loss of knowledge followed a specific-to-general trajectory because of the nature in which regularities across visual and verbal patterns are captured by their model's hidden units. Features that were shared and correlated across numerous concepts tended to be represented in larger and more neighboring regions of semantic space than were highly distinctive features. Thus, distinctive features were more likely to be influenced by damage, so the model showed a tendency to lose its ability to discriminate among similar concepts early in the course of semantic dementia.

Finally, Rogers and McClelland (2004) present a large set of arguments and simulations in which, among other things, they provide connectionist accounts of several phenomena that have been highlighted in knowledge-based theories of concepts. The issues are too complex and numerous to do them justice in a short paragraph, but their book is highly recommended.

## Models of Semantic Representation

Classic models of semantic structure assumed that meaning was represented either as a hierarchical network of interconnected nodes (Collins & Quillian, 1969) or as arrays of binary features (Smith, Shoben, & Rips, 1974). A major limitation of both of these early models is that neither specifies how its representations are learned. Instead, their representations must be hand coded by the theorist or collected from adult participants.

More recent *distributional models* specify cognitive mechanisms for constructing semantic representations from statistical experience with text corpora. In general, these models are all based on the *distributional hypothesis* (Harris, 1970): Words that appear in similar linguistic contexts are likely to have related meanings. For example, *apple* may frequently co-occur with *seed, worm,* and *core*. As a result, the model can infer that these words are related. In addition, the model can induce that *apple* is similar to *peach* even if the two never directly co-occur, because they occur around the same types of words. In contrast, *apple* and *staple* rarely appear in the same or similar contexts.

There are a large number of distributional models (for reviews, see Bullinaria & Levy 2007; Riordan & Jones, 2011). To simplify our discussion, we classify them into three families based on their learning mechanism: (1) latent inference models, (2) passive co-occurrence models, and (3) retrieval-based models. For an in-depth review of new advances in distributional modeling, we refer readers to the recent pair of special issues of *Topics in Cognitive Science* (2011).

### LATENT INFERENCE MODELS

This family of models reverse-engineers the cognitive variables responsible for how words co-occur across linguistic contexts. The process is similar to other types of latent inference in psychology. For example, personality psychologists commonly administer structured questionnaires, constructing items to tap hypothetical psychological constructs. Singular value decomposition (SVD) is applied to the pattern of responses over questionnaire items to infer the latent psychological variables responsible for the cross-item response patterns. Latent inference models of semantic memory work in an analogous way, but they apply this decomposition to the pattern of word co-occurrences over documents in a corpus.

The best-known latent inference model is *Latent Semantic Analysis* (LSA; Landauer & Dumais, 1997). LSA begins with a word-by-document frequency matrix from a text corpus. Each word is weighted relative to its entropy over documents;

"promiscuous" words appearing in many contexts are dampened more than are "monogamous" words that appear more faithfully in particular contexts. Finally, the matrix is factored using SVD, and only the components with the largest eigenvalues are retained (typically 300–400). These are the latent semantic components that best explain how words co-occur over documents, similar to the way that the psychological constructs of introversion and extroversion might explain response patterns over hundreds of questionnaire items. With this reduced representation, each word in the corpus is represented as a pattern over latent variables. In the reduced space, indirect relationships emerge— even though two words may never have directly co-occurred in a document (e.g., two synonyms), they can have similar patterns.

Landauer and Dumais (1997) suggested that the human brain performs some data reduction operation similar to SVD on contextual experience to construct semantic representations. However, they were careful not to claim that what the brain does is *exactly* SVD on a perfectly remembered item-by-episode representation of experience. Regardless of whether LSA is a plausible model of human semantic representation (for criticisms, see Glenberg & Robertson, 2000; Perfetti, 1998), it has been remarkably successful at accounting for data ranging from human performance on synonymy tests (Landauer & Dumais, 1997) to metaphor comprehension (Kintsch, 2000). LSA set the stage for future distributional models to better study the specific mechanisms that might produce a reduced semantic space. In addition, the model made a clear formal link between semantic memory structure and episodic experience.

More recently, Griffiths, Steyvers, and Tenenbaum's (2007) *Topic* model extended LSA in a Bayesian framework, specifying a generative mechanism by which latent semantic variables could produce the pattern of word co-occurrences across documents. The Topic model operates on the same initial data representation as LSA—it assumes that we experience words over discrete episodic contexts (operationalized as documents in a corpus). However, it specifies a cognitive inference process based on probabilistic reasoning to discover word meaning. To novice users of semantic models, the computational machinery of the Topic model can be daunting. However, the theoretical underpinning of the model is simple and elegant, and it is based on the same idea posited for how children infer unseen causes for observable events. Consider

an analogy: Given a set of co-occurring symptoms, a dermatologist must infer the unseen disease or diseases that led to the observed symptoms. Over many instances of the same co-occurring symptoms, she can infer the likelihood that they result from a common cause. The topic model works in an analogous manner, but on a much larger scale of inference and with mixtures of causal variables. Given that certain words tend to co-occur in contexts and this pattern is consistent over many contexts, the model infers the likely latent "topics" that are responsible for the co-occurrence patterns, where the document is a probabilistic mixture of topics. A word's meaning is a probability distribution over possible topics, where a topic is a probability distribution over words (just as a disease would be a probability distribution over symptoms, and a symptom is a probability distribution over possible diseases that produced it).

This results in two key distinctions from LSA. First, the Topic model is generative in that it defines a process by which documents could be constructed from mixtures of mental variables. Second, a word's representation is a probability distribution rather than a point in semantic space. This allows the Topic model to represent multiple meanings of ambiguous words, whereas in LSA, ambiguity is collapsed to a single point. The Topic model is able to account for free association data, sense disambiguation, word-prediction, and discourse effects that are problematic for LSA (Griffiths et al., 2007).

## PASSIVE CO-OCCURRENCE MODELS

Passive co-occurrence models posit simple Hebbian type accumulation mechanisms that give rise to sophisticated semantic representations. Hence, these models tend not to need a full word-by-document matrix but gradually develop semantic structure by simple co-occurrence "counting" as a text corpus is continuously experienced.

The first passive co-occurrence model was the *hyperspace analogue to language* model (HAL; Lund & Burgess, 1996). HAL slides an *n*-word window across a text corpus, and counts the co-occurrence frequency of words within the window (where frequency is inversely proportional to distance between words in the window). A word's semantic representation is a vector of distance-weighted co-occurrence values to all other words in the corpus. Hence, a word is defined relative to other words in HAL. Comparing the vectors for two words yields their semantic similarity, producing both direct and indirect semantic relations as in LSA. HAL has accounted for a range of semantic priming phenomena (Lund & Burgess, 1996). Modern variants of HAL have improved the model to produce better fits to human data (Rohde, Gonnerman, & Plaut, 2005), and a HAL-like model was used by Mitchell et al. (2008) to predict fMRI activation patterns associated with the meanings of concrete nouns.

A second type of passive co-occurrence model uses the accumulation of random vectors as a mechanism for semantic abstraction (Jones et al., 2006; Kanerva, 2009). For example, in the BEAGLE model (Jones & Mewhort, 2007) words are initially represented by random patterns of arbitrary dimensionality. Hence, before any episodic experience, the representation for *apple* is no more similar to *peach* than it is to *staple*. As text is experienced, each word's memory pattern is updated as the sum of the random initial patterns representing the words with which it co-occurs. Thus, *apple*, *peach*, and *core* move closer to one another in semantic space as text is experienced, while *staple* moves away (but closer to *paper*, *pencil*, etc.). Random accumulation can be considered as semantic abstraction from the coincidental co-occurrence of (initially random) brain states representing the words in the episodic context. Because of the arbitrary nature of the features, BEAGLE can simultaneously learn about the positional information of words in the context similar to HAL-type models (Jones & Mewhort, 2007 use convolution to encode order information). Hence, a word's representation becomes a pattern of arbitrary "features" that reflects its history of co-occurrence with, and position relative to, other words in contexts. BEAGLE simulates a number of phenomena, including semantic priming, typicality, and semantic constraints in sentence completions.

**RETRIEVAL-BASED MODELS**

Rather than assuming that humans store semantic representations, retrieval-based models construct meaning as part of episodic memory retrieval. Retrieval-based models are similar to exemplar-based theories of categorization (Nosofsky, 1986) and multiple-trace theories of global memory (Hintzman, 1986). Just as Hintzman's Minerva 2 model demonstrated that schema abstraction can be simulated by a model containing only episodic traces, Kwantes' (2005) constructed semantics model demonstrates that semantic phenomena are possible without requiring a semantic memory. In this model, memory *is* the episodic word-by-context matrix. When a word is read or heard, its semantic representation is constructed as an average of other words in memory, weighted by their contextual similarity to the target. Although semantic abstraction differs radically from LSA, similar representations are produced. Dennis (2005) has used a similar approach, accounting for an impressive array of semantic phenomena.

## Integrating Perceptual Information Into Distributional Models

Distributional models have been criticized as psychologically implausible because they learn from only linguistic information and do not contain information about sensorimotor perception contrary to grounded cognition (for a review, see de Vega, Glenberg, & Graesser, 2008). Hence, representations in distributional models are not a replacement for feature norms. Feature-based representations contain a great deal of sensorimotor features of words that cannot be learned from purely linguistic input, and both types of information are core to human semantic representation (Louwerse, 2007). Riordan and Jones (2011) recently compared a variety of feature-based and distributional models on semantic clustering tasks. Their results demonstrated that whereas there is information about word meaning redundantly coded in both feature norms and linguistic data, each has its own unique variance and the two information sources serve as complementary cues to meaning.

Research using recurrent networks trained on child-directed speech corpora has found that pre-training a network with features related to children's sensorimotor experience produced significantly better word learning when subsequently trained on linguistic data (Howell, Jankowicz, & Becker, 2005). Durda, Buchanan, and Caron (2009) trained a feedforward network to associate LSA-type semantic vectors with their corresponding activation of features from McRae et al.'s (2005) norms. Given the semantic representation for *dog*, the model attempts to activate the output feature <has fur> and inhibit the output feature for <made of metal>. After training, the network was able to infer the correct pattern of perceptual features for words that were not used in training because of their linguistic similarity to words that were used in training.

A recent flurry of models using the Bayesian Topic model framework has also explored parallel learning of linguistic and featural information (Andrews, Vigliocco, & Vinson, 2009; Baroni, Murphy, Barba, & Poesio, 2010; Steyvers, 2009). Given a word-by-document representation of a text corpus and a word-by-feature representation of feature production norms, the models learn a word's meaning by simultaneously considering inference across documents and features. This enables learning from joint distributional information: If the model learns from the feature norms that *sparrows* have beaks, and from linguistic experience that *sparrows* and *mockingbirds* are distributionally similar, it infers that *mockingbirds* also have beaks, despite having no feature vector for *mockingbird*. Integration of linguistic and sensorimotor information allows the model to better fit human semantic data than a model trained with only one source (Andrews et al., 2009). This information integration is not unique to Bayesian models, but it can also be accomplished within passive co-occurrence models (Jones & Recchia, 2010; Vigliocco, Vinson, Lewis, & Garrett, 2004) and retrieval-based models (Johns & Jones, 2012).

## Summary

Over the past 25 years or so, semantic memory research has blossomed for a number of reasons, all of which are equally important. The generation of intriguing patient data and theories of the organization of semantic memory that resulted from them, and the acceptance of this patient research into what some might call mainstream cognitive psychology, was an important step. Furthermore, connectionist models of semantic processing enabled implementations of meaning-based computations, generating new ideas, experiments, and simulations. The advent of neuroimaging methods allowed researchers to study semantic processing in the brain, to integrate neurally based theories with those resulting from implemented models as well as normal adult and patient data, and to generate novel theories of semantic representation and processing. In addition, theories of grounded cognition added excitement and paved the way for a large number of novel experiments designed to test them. Finally, corpus-based models of meaning have provided new ways to think about semantic representations, and a plethora of new ideas for designing experiments, and techniques for simulating human performance. The present high level of enthusiasm surrounding the study of semantic memory should continue as researchers refine, compare, and integrate theories, and test predictions that result from those theoretical endeavors. We hope that we have communicated some of this excitement to the reader.

## Acknowledgments

This work was supported by Natural Sciences and Engineering Council grant OGP0155704 and National Institutes of Health grant HD053136 to Ken McRae and by National Science Foundation grant BCS-1056744 to Michael Jones.

## References

Allport, D. A. (1985). Distributed memory, modular subsystems and dysphasia. In S. K. Newman & R. Epstein (Eds.), *Current perspectives in dysphasia* (pp. 207–244). Edinburgh, Scotland: Churchill Livingstone.

Andrews, M., Vigliocco, G., & Vinson, D. P. (2009). Integrating experiential and distributional data to learn semantic representations. Psychological Review, 116, 463–498.

Anisfeld, M., & Knapp, M. (1968). Association, synonymity, and directionality in false recognition. Journal of Experimental Psychology, 77, 171–179.

Baroni, M., Murphy, B., Barbu, E., & Poesio, M. (2010). Strudel: A corpus-based semantic model based on properties and types. Cognitive Science, 34, 222–254.

Barsalou, L. W. (1999). Perceptual symbol systems. Behavioral Brain Science, 22, 577–660.

Barsalou, L. W. (2008). Grounding symbolic operations in the brain's modal systems. In G. R. Sermin & E. R. Smith (Eds.), *Embodied grounding: Social, cognitive, affective, and neuroscientific approaches* (pp. 9–42). New York: Cambridge University Press.

Barsalou, L. W., & Wiemer-Hastings, K. (2005). Situating abstract concepts. In D. Pecher & R. A. Zwaan (Eds.), *Grounding cognition: The role of perception and action in memory, language, and thinking* (pp. 129–163). Cambridge, England: Cambridge University Press.

Binder, J. R., Desai, R. H., Graves, W. W., & Conant, L. L. (2009). Where is the semantic system? A review of 120 functional neuroimaging studies. Cerebral Cortex, 19, 2767–2796.

Bower, G. H. (2000). A brief history of memory research. In E. Tulving & F. I. M. Craik (Eds.), *The Oxford handbook of memory* (pp. 3–32). New York: Oxford University Press.

Brainerd, C. J., Yang, Y., Reyna, V. F., Howe, M. L., & Mills, B. A. (2008). Semantic processing in "associative" false memory. Psychonomic Bulletin and Review, 15, 1035–1053.

Breedin, S. D., Saffran, E. M., & Coslett, H. B. (1994). Reversal of the concreteness effect in a patient with semantic dementia. Cognitive Neuropsychology, *11*, 617–660.

Bullinaria, J. A., & Levy, J.P. (2007). Extracting semantic representations from word co-occurrence statistics: A computational study. Behavior Research Methods, 39, 510–526.

Caramazza, A., & Shelton, J.R. (1998). Domain specific knowledge systems in the brain: The animate-inanimate distinction. Journal of Cognitive Neuroscience, 10, 1–34.

Casasanto, D., & Boroditsky, L. (2008). Time in the mind: Using space to think about time. Cognition, 106, 579–593.

Chao, L. L., Haxby, J. V., & Martin, A. (1999). Attribute-based neural substrates in temporal cortex for perceiving and knowing about objects. Nature Neuroscience, 2, 913–919.

Chwilla, D. J., & Kolk, H. H. J. (2005). Accessing world knowledge: Evidence from N400 and reaction time priming. Cognitive Brain Research, 25, 589–606.

Collins, A. M., & Quillian, M. R. (1969). Retrieval time from semantic memory. Journal of Verbal Learning and Verbal Behavior, 8, 240–247.

Coltheart, M., Patterson, K., & Marshall, J. (1980). *Deep dyslexia*. London: Routledge.

Cree, G. S., McNorgan, C., & McRae, K. (2006). Distinctive features hold a privileged status in the computation of word meaning: Implications for theories of semantic memory. Journal of Experimental Psychology: Learning, Memory, and Cognition, 32, 643–658.

Cree, G. S., & McRae, K. (2003). Analyzing the factors underlying the structure and computation of the meaning of chipmunk, cherry, chisel, cheese, and cello (and many other such concrete nouns). Journal of Experimental Psychology: General, 132, 163–201.

Cree, G. S., McRae, K., & McNorgan, C. (1999). An attractor model of lexical conceptual processing: Simulating semantic priming. Cognitive Science, 23, 371–414.

Damasio, A. R. (1989). The brain binds entitites and events by multiregional activation from convergence zones. Neural Computation, 1, 123–132.

Deese, J. (1965). The structure of associations in language and thought. Baltimore: Johns Hopkins Press.

Dennis, S. (2005). A memory-based theory of verbal cognition. Cognitive Science, 29, 145–193.

De Vega, M., Glenberg, A. M., & Graesser, A. C. (2008). Symbols and embodiment: debates on meaning and cognition. Oxford, England: Oxford University Press.

Durda, K., Buchanan, L., & Caron, R. (2009). Grounding co-occurrence: Identifying features in a lexical co-occurrence model of semantic memory. Behavior Research Methods, 41, 1210–1223.

Estes, Z., Golonka, S., & Jones, L. L. (2011). Thematic thinking: The apprehension and consequences of thematic relations. In B. Ross (Ed.), The psychology of learning and motivation (Vol. 54, pp. 249–278). Burlington, VT: Academic Press.

Ferretti, T. R., McRae, K., & Hatherell, A. (2001). Integrating verbs, situation schemas, and thematic role concepts. Journal of Memory and Language, 44, 516–547.

Frenck-Mestre, C., & Bueno, S. (1999). Semantic features and semantic categories: Differences in the rapid activation of the lexicon. Brain and Language, 68, 199–204.

Glenberg, A., & Robertson, D. (2000). Symbol grounding and meaning: A comparison of high-dimensional and embodied theories of meaning. Journal of Memory and Language, 43, 379–401.

Goldberg, R. F., Perfetti, C. A., & Schneider, W. (2006). Perceptual knowledge retrieval activates sensory brain regions. Journal of Neuroscience, 26, 4917–4921.

Griffiths, T. L., Steyvers, M., & Tenenbaum, J. B. (2007). Topics in semantic representation. Psychological Review, 114, 211–244.

Grossman, M., Koenig, P., De Vita, C., Glosser, G., Alsop, D., Detre, J., & Gee, J. (2002). The neural basis for category-specific knowledge: An fMRI study. Neuroimage, 15, 936–948.

Guida, A., & Lenci, A. (2007). Semantic properties of word associations to Italian verbs. Italian Journal of Linguistics, 19, 293–326.

Hare, M., Jones, M. N., Thomson, C., Kelly, S., & Mc Rae, K. (2009). Activating event knowledge. Cognition, 111, 151–167.

Harris, Z. S. (1970). Distributional structure. In Z. S. Harris (Ed.), Papers in structural and transformational linguistics. Formal linguistics series, Volume 1 (pp. 775–794). Dordrecht, The Netherlands: Reidel.

Hauk, O., Johnsrude, I., & Pulvermüller, F. (2004). Somatotopic representation of action words in human motor and premotor cortex. Neuron, 41, 301–307.

Hinton, G. E., & Shallice, T. (1991). Lesioning an attractor network: Investigations of acquired dyslexia. Psychological Review, 98, 74–95.

Hintzman, D. L. (1986). "Schema abstraction" in a multiple-trace memory model. Psychological Review, 93, 411–428.

Howell, S., Jankowicz, D., & Becker, S. (2005). A model of grounded language acquisition: Sensorimotor features improve lexical and grammatical learning. Journal of Memory and Language, 53, 258–276.

Hutchison, K. A. (2003). Is semantic priming due to association strength or feature overlap? A microanalytic review. Psychonomic Bulletin abd Review, 10, 785–813.

Johns, B. T., & Jones, M. N. (2010). Evaluating the random representation assumption of lexical semantics in cognitive models. Psychonomic Bulletin and Review, 17, 662–672.

Johns, B. T., & Jones, M. N. (2012). Perceptual inference from global lexical similarity. Topics in Cognitive Science, 4, 103–120.

Jones, M., & Love, B. C. (2007). Beyond common features: The role of roles in determining similarity. Cognitive Psychology, 55, 196–231.

Jones, M. N., Kintsch, W., & Mewhort, D. J. K. (2006). High-dimensional semantic space accounts of priming. Journal of Memory and Language, 55, 534–552.

Jones, M. N., & Mewhort, D. J. K. (2007). Representing word meaning and order information in a composite holographic lexicon. Psychological Review, 114, 1–37.

Jones, M. N., & Recchia, G. L. (2010). You can't wear a coat rack: A binding framework to avoid illusory feature migrations in perceptually grounded semantic models. In Proceedings of the 32nd Annual Meeting of the Cognitive Science Society (pp. 877–882). Austin, TX: Cognitive Science Society.

Kanerva, P. (2009). Hyperdimensional computing: An introduction to computing in distributed representations with high-dimensional random vectors. Cognitive Computation, 1, 139–159.

Khalkhali, S., Wammes, J., & McRae, K. (2012). Integrating words denoting typical sequences of events. Canadian Journal of Experimental Psychology, 66, 106–114.

Kiehl, K. A., Liddle, P. F., Smith, A. M., Mendrek, A., Forster, B. B., & Hare, R. D. (1999). Neural pathways involved in the processing of concrete and abstract words. Human Brain Mapping, 7, 225–233.

Kintsch, W. (2000). Metaphor comprehension: A computational theory. Psychonomic Bulletin and Review, 7, 257–266.

Klatzky, R. L., Pellegrino, J. W., Mc Closkey, B. P., & Doherty, S. (1989). Can you squeeze a tomato? The role of motor representations in semantic sensibility judgments. Journal of Memory and Language, 28, 56–77.

Kounios, J., & Holcomb, P. J. (1994). Concreteness effects in semantic processing: ERP evidence supporting dual-coding theory. Journal of Experimental Psychology: Learning, Memory, and Cognition, 20, 804–823.

Kousta, S., Vigliocco, G., Del Campo, E., Vinson, D. P., & Andrews, M. (2011). The representation of abstract words: Why emotion matters. Journal of Experimental Psychology: General, 140, 14–34.

Kwantes, P. J. (2005). Using context to build semantics. Psychonomic Bulletin and Review, 12, 703–710.

Lakoff, G. (1987). Women, fire, and dangerous things. Chicago: Chicago University Press.

Landauer, T. K., & Dumais, S. (1997). A solution to Plato's problem: The latent semantic analysis theory of the acquisition, induction, and representation of knowledge. Psychological Review, 104, 211–240.

Louwerse, M. M. (2007). Symbolic or embodied representations: A case for symbol interdependency. In T. K. Landauer , D. S. Macnamara , S. Dennis, & W. Kintsch (Eds.), *Handbook of latent semantic analysis* (pp. 107–120). Mahwah, NJ: Erlbaum.

Lucas, M. (2000). Semantic priming without association: A meta-analytic review. Psychonomic Bulletin and Review, 7, 618–630.

Lund, K., & Burgess, C. (1996). Producing high-dimensional semantic spaces from lexical co-occurrence. Behavioral Research Methods, Instrumentation, and Computers, 28, 203–208.

Lupker, S. J. (1984). Semantic priming without association: A second look. Journal of Verbal Learning and Verbal Behavior, 23, 709–733.

Mahon, B. Z., & Caramazza, A. (2003). Constraining questions about the organization and representation of conceptual knowledge. Cognitive Neuropsychology, 20, 433–450.

Martin, A. (2007). The representation of object concepts in the brain. Annual Review of Psychology, 58, 25–45.

Masson, M. E. J. (1995). A distributed memory model of semantic priming. Journal of Experimental Psychology: Learning, Memory, and Cognition, 21, 3–23.

McNamara, T. (2005). *Semantic priming*. New York: Psychology Press.

McRae, K., Cree, G. S., Seidenberg, M. S., & McNorgan, C. (2005). Semantic feature production norms for a large set of living and nonliving things. Behavior Research Methods, 37, 547–559.

McRae, K., de Sa, V., & Seidenberg, M. S. (1997). On the nature and scope of featural representations of word meaning. Journal of Experimental Psychology: General, 126, 99–130.

McRae, K., Hare, M., Elman, J. L., & Ferretti, T. R. (2005). A basis for generating expectancies for verbs from nouns. Memory and Cognition, 33, 1174–1184.

McRae, K., Khalkhali, S., & Hare, M. (2012). Semantic and associative relations: Examining a tenuous dichotomy. In V. F. Reyna, S. Chapman, M. Dougherty, & J. Confrey (Eds.), *The adolescent brain: Learning, reasoning, and decision making* (pp. 39–66). Washington, DC: APA.

Mitchell, T. M., Shinkanerva, S. V., Carlson, A., Chang, K., Malave, V. L., Mason, R. A., & Just, M. A. (2008). Predicting human brain activity associated with the meanings of nouns. Scienced 1191–1195.

Moss, H. E., Ostrin, R. K., Tyler, L. K., & Marslen-Wilson, W. D. (1995). Accessing different types of lexical semantic information: Evidence from priming. Journal of Experimental Psychology: Learning, Memory, and Cognition, 21, 863–883.

Myun, J., Blumstein, S. E., & Sedivy, J. C. (2006). Playing on the typewriter, typing on the piano: Manipulation knowledge of objects. Cognition, 98, 223–243.

Nelson, D. L., Mc Evoy, C. L., & Dennis, S. (2000). What is free association and what does it measure? Memory and Cognition, 28, 887–899.

Nelson, D. L., McEvoy, C. L., & Schreiber, T. A. (1998). The University of South Florida word association, rhyme, and word fragment norms. Retrieved August 1, 2012, from http://web.usf.edu/FreeAssociation/

Nosofsky, R. M. (1986). Attention, similarity, and the identification-categorization relationship. Journal of Experimental Psychology: General, 115, 39–57.

O'Connor, C. M., Cree, G. S., & McRae, K. (2009). Conceptual hierarchies in a flat attractor network: Dynamics of learning and computations. Cognitive Science, 33, 665–708.

Paivio, A. U. (1971). *Imagery and verbal processes*. New York: Holt, Rinehart, and Winston.

Paivio, A. U. (2007). *Mind and its evolution: A dual coding theoretical approach*. Mahwah, NJ: Erlbaum.

Patterson, K., Nestor, P. J., & Rogers, T. T. (2007). Where do you know what you know? The representation of semantic knowledge in the human brain. Nature Reviews Neuroscience, 8, 976–987.

Pecher, D., Boot, I., & Van Dantzig, S. (2011). Abstract concepts: Sensory-motor grounding, conceptual metaphors, and beyond. In B. Ross (Ed.), *The psychology of learning and motivation* (Vol. 54, pp. 217–248). Burlington, VT: Academic Press.

Pecher, D., & Zwaan, R. A. (2005). *Grounding cognition: The role of perception and action in memory, language, and thinking*. Cambridge, England: Cambridge University Press.

Perfetti, C. (1998). The limits of co-occurrence: Tools and theories in language research. Discourse Processes, 25, 363–377.

Plaut, D. C., & Booth, J. R. (2000). Individual and developmental differences in semantic priming: Empirical and computational support for a single-mechanism account of lexical processing. Psychological Review, 107, 786–823.

Plaut, D. C., & Shallice, T. (1993). Deep dyslexia: A case study of connectionist neuropsychology. Cognitive Neuropsychology, 10, 377–500.

Posner, M. I., & Keele, S. W. (1968). On the genesis of abstract ideas. Journal of Experimental Psychlogy, 77, 353–363.

Randall, B., Moss, H. E., Rodd, J., Greer, M., & Tyler, L. K. (2004). Distinctiveness and correlation in conceptual structure: Behavioral and computational studies. Journal of Experimental Psychology: Language, Memory, and Cognition, 30, 393–406.

Raposo, A., Moss, H. E., Stamatakis, E. A., & Tyler, L. K. (2009). Modulation of the motor and premotor cortices by actions, action words, and action sentences. Neuropsychologia, 47, 388–396.

Riordan, B., & Jones, M. N. (2011). Redundancy in linguistic and perceptual experience: Comparing distributional and feature-based models of semantic representation. Topics in Cognitive Science, 3, 303–345.

Roediger, H. L., III, Watson, J. M., McDermott, K. B., & Gallo, D. A. (2001). Factors that determine false recall: A multiple regression analysis. Psychonomic Bulletin and Review, 8, 385–407.

Rogers, T. T., Lambon Ralph, M. A, Garrard, P., Bozeat, S., McClelland, J. L., Hodges, J. R., & Patterson, K. (2004). The structure and deterioration of semantic memory: A neuropsychological and computational investigation. Psychological Review, 111, 205–235.

Rogers, T. T., & McClelland, J. L. (2004). *Semantic cognition: A parallel distributed processing approach*. Cambridge, MA: MIT Press.

Rohde, D. L. T., Gonnerman, L., & Plaut, D. C. (2005). An improved model of semantic similarity based on lexical co-occurrence. Unpublished manuscript.

Schwanenflugel, P. J, & Shoben, E. J. (1983). Differential context effects in the comprehension of abstract and concrete verbal materials. Journal of Experimental Psychology: Learning, Memory, and Cognition, 9, 82–102.

Simmons, K. W., & Barsalou, L. (2003). The similarity-in-topography principle: Reconciling theories of conceptual deficits. Cognitive Neuropsychology, 20, 451–486.

Sitnikova T., West, W. C., Kuperberg, G. R., & Holcomb, P. J. (2006). The neural organization of semantic memory: Electrophysiological activity suggests feature-based segregation. Biological Psychology, 71, 326–340.

Smith, E. E., Shoben, E. J., & Rips, L. J. (1974). Structure and process in semantic memory: A featural model for semantic decisions. Psychological Review, 81, 214–241.

Solomon, K. O., & Barsalou, L. W. (2001). Representing properties locally. Cognitive Psychology, 43, 129–169.

Squire, L. R. (1988). Episodic memory, semantic memory, and amnesia. Hippocampus, 8, 205–211.

Steyvers, M. (2009). Combining feature norms and text data with topic models. Acta Psychologica, 133, 234–243.

Thompson-Schill, S. (2003). Neuroimaging studies of semantic memory: Inferring how from where. Neuropsychologia, 41, 280–292.

Tulving, E. (1972). Episodic and semantic memory. In E. Tulving & W. Donaldson (Eds.), Organization of memory (pp. 381–403). New York: Academic Press.

Tyler, L. K., & Moss, H. E. (2001). Towards a distributed account of conceptual knowledge. Trends in Cognitive Sciences, 5, 244–252.

Vigliocco, G., Vinson, D. P., Lewis, W., & Garrett, M. (2004). Representing the meanings of object and action words: The featural and unitary semantic space hypothesis. Cognitive Psychology, 48(4), 422–488.

von der Malsburg, C. (1999). The what and why of binding: The modeler's perspective. Neuron, 24, 95–104.

Warrington, E. K., & McCarthy, R. A. (1987). Categories of knowledge. Further fractionation and an attempted integration. Brain, 110, 1273–1296.

Warrington, E. K., & Shallice, T. (1984). Category specific semantic impairments. Brain, 107, 829–854.

Wise, R. J. S., Howard, D., Mummery, C. J., Fletcher, P., Leff, A., Buchel, C., & Scott, S. K. (2000). Noun imageability and the temporal lobes. Neuropsychologia, 38, 985–994.

Zwaan, R. A., & Madden, C. J. (2005). Embodied sentence comprehension. In D. Pecher & R. A. Zwaan (Eds.), Grounding cognition: The role of perception and action in memory, language, and thinking (pp. 224–245). Cambridge, England: Cambridge University Press.

Zwann, R. A., Stanfield, R. A., & Yaxley, R. H. (2002). Language comprehenders mentally represent the shape of objects. Psychological Science, 13, 168–171.

# Implicit Memory

Neil W. Mulligan *and* Miri Besken

**Abstract**

Although memory is typically defined in terms of conscious, intentional recollection of the past (explicit memory), it is clear that memory can also be expressed through unconscious changes in behavior (implicit memory). Modern research on memory has uncovered numerous differences between these forms of memory. For example, patients with anterograde amnesia exhibit dramatic impairments in explicit memory but often show little impairment on tests of implicit memory. Likewise, variations in the conditions of learning can produce very different effects on implicit and explicit tests. Finally, research on the neural underpinnings of memory indicates that these forms of memory are mediated by different parts of the brain.

**Key Words:** memory, implicit memory, explicit memory, amnesia

> Memory…is the knowledge of a former state of mind after it has already once dropped from consciousness; or rather *it is the knowledge of an event*, or fact, of which meantime we have not been thinking, *with the additional consciousness that we have thought or experienced it before.* [italics in original] (James, 1890, p. 648)
>
> …vanished mental states give proof of their continued existence even if they themselves do not return to consciousness. (Ebbinghaus, 1885/1964, p. 2)

The quote from William James meshes with our everyday use of the term "memory" as the ability to consciously and intentionally recollect past events, to mentally review an event and to know that it is a *re*experience. But a moment's reflection (and Ebbinghaus's quote) implies that not all influences of the past are accompanied by conscious recollection. For example, when we execute a well-learned motor skill, such as playing the piano or swinging a golf club, we typically do not recollect specific instances of practice nor individual lessons, although we are clearly influenced by these past events as we carry out the skill.

Researchers have long supposed that memory for the past can influence present behavior without conscious recollection. Ebbinghaus (1885/1964) had just this issue in mind when he developed his famous savings measure. Ebbinghaus argued that only strong memory traces reach the threshold of conscious awareness, whereas other traces are too weak to produce recollection, although they still might influence ongoing behavior. The savings measure (which requires the relearning of previously learned information) was developed to measure all aspects of memory, strong traces as well as weak. Likewise, Korsakoff (cited in Schacter, 1987) concluded that memory for the past can sometimes evince itself without conscious awareness. Korsakoff studied amnesic patients who showed little conscious recollection of recent events but demonstrated classical conditioning. Korsakoff attributed this preserved learning to the formation of weak memory traces that, although not reaching the threshold for consciousness, could still influence the course of thought and behavioral responses. Thus, early notions of unconscious memory placed it on a continuum with conscious recollection, the primary difference being the quantitative strength of memory traces. As we shall see, this contrasts with the modern view of qualitative differences between different forms of memory.

Korsakoff's notion of preserved learning in amnesia is thrown into vivid relief by an observation of the Swiss neurologist Edouard Claparede in a case report of a patient with anterograde amnesia (Claparede, 1911/1951), a disorder in which a patient can recall little about new events occurring after the onset of brain injury. Despite the apparent lack of memory for the past, Claparede suspected that his patient had residual memory abilities that did not produce conscious recollection. Claparede tested this possibility by hiding a pin in his hand and giving the patient a painful pinprick upon shaking hands. The next time Claparede met the patient, she refused to take his hand but could not provide a reason for the refusal. Claparede pressed the patient for an explanation; she finally explained her reluctance by saying that people sometimes hide pins in their hands as a type of practical joke. Clearly the patient formed some type of memory of the original event, but this memory was not recollected as a personal experience.

## Implicit Memory in the Modern Era

Modern research supports the distinction between conscious and unconscious influences of memory, embodied in the distinction between *explicit* and *implicit* memory. Explicit memory refers to conscious, intentional recollection of the past, whereas implicit memory refers to changes in behavior attributable to specific past events but unaccompanied by conscious or intentional recollection. Much of the modern interest in this distinction stems from

research on patients with anterograde amnesia, the form of amnesia exhibited by Claparede's patient. The traditional definition of anterograde amnesia is an inability to remember new experiences along with preserved perceptual and intellectual abilities. However, research beginning in the 1970s demonstrated a remarkable range of preserved learning abilities in patients with amnesia, reminiscent of Claparede's demonstration.

A classic, early demonstration was provided by Warrington and Weiskrantz (1970), who compared the memory abilities of a group of patients with anterograde amnesia and a group of matched control subjects. Both groups were presented with a list of words for a later memory test. Two of the tests required the participants to think back and try to remember materials from the study phase of the experiment. That is, these were tests of explicit remembering. The first was free recall, in which participants simply try to recall as many of the study words as possible; the other was a test of recognition, in which studied words are mixed with new words, and the participant tries to determine which words were presented earlier in the experiment. The other test conditions did not require explicit memory. In these tests, participants were presented with fragmented or partial words (e.g., MET___), some of which corresponded to words from the study list (e.g., METAL) and some did not. For this test, participants are not required to recall or consciously remember any of the studied information; they are merely asked to try to complete each fragment with a word. On the recall and recognition tests, the amnesics remembered fewer of the words than the control subjects, thus exhibiting the defining symptom of their disorder. However, on the word completion tests, the amnesics were more likely to complete partial words with previously studied words, and this enhancement occurred to the same degree as in the control group. Thus, when the memory test did not require intentional or conscious recollection, the amnesic subjects showed the same level of retention as the normal control subjects, despite dramatically deficient conscious recollection.

The foregoing experiment illustrates a standard approach for studying explicit and implicit memory. The standard memory experiment begins with a study phase, in which the participant is presented with some type of controlled experience, such as a series of words or pictures presented on a computer screen. Some time later, a memory test is given to assess how much of the studied information is retained. The memory test is either an explicit test, in which the subject is asked to think back and try to retrieve information about the study episode, or an implicit test, in which the subject is asked to perform a task that is nominally unrelated to the study episode. The operative difference between these two types of test is the task instructions. Examples of explicit memory tests include free recall, in which the participant is simply asked to report as much as possible about prior events, cued recall, in which the participant is presented with cues to aid in recall (e.g., category names after seeing a study list composed of examples from different categories), and recognition memory tests, in which the subject is asked to discriminate between previously experienced information and new information. Examples of implicit memory tests include word-stem completion (WSC) and word-fragment completion (WFC). In these tasks, the subject is presented with a series of word stems (e.g., ora___) or fragments (e.g., "_ r _ n g _") and asked to complete each with the first appropriate word that comes to mind (e.g., "orange"). Unbeknownst to the subject, some of the stems and fragments correspond to studied words and others correspond to new words that were not presented during the study phase. The proportion of completions is typically greater for the studied words than the new words. This difference can occur even in the absence of intention to retrieve the studied materials, and in the absence of awareness that the implicit task relates to the earlier portion of the experiment. Other implicit tests use conceptual as opposed to fragmentary perceptual cues. For example, on the category-production task, participants are presented with the names of categories (e.g., FRUIT) and are asked to generate examples from each. This task is presented as a general knowledge or semantic fluency test, but, of course, some of the categories correspond to words on the study list and others do not. Subjects are more likely to produce studied examples than counterbalanced, nonstudied examples. In general, the increased accuracy, ease, or speed of processing for studied versus nonstudied materials is referred to as *repetition priming*, and it serves as the measure of implicit memory. Although priming is the most common measure of implicit memory, some researchers have also used sequence learning, skill acquisition, or classical conditioning to investigate unconscious forms of memory.

## Dissociations Between Implicit and Explicit Memory

The principles that govern implicit and explicit memory differ in a number of ways as reflected by *dissociations* between implicit and explicit memory tests. The term *dissociation* refers to a data pattern in which a variable produces different effects on an implicit and an explicit memory test. Dissociations help delineate the differences between these forms of memory and constitute the data for which theories of implicit memory must account.

### Population Dissociations

The findings of Warrington and Weiskrantz reviewed earlier constitute a particularly surprising dissociation in which the variable of neurological population (amnesic vs. control) dissociated performance on implicit and explicit memory tests. Subsequent research demonstrated that this dissociation was quite general, holding over a range of materials and measures of implicit memory. First, the memory cues as well as type of memory test varied over the implicit and explicit tests used by Warrington and Weiskrantz.[1] An early order of business was to determine whether Warrington and Weiskrantz's results were driven by the types of memory cues rather than the distinction between explicit and implicit memory. Graf et al. (1984) examined this question by testing amnesic and control subjects with implicit and explicit tests that were matched on types of cues. Specifically, both groups were presented with a study list of words and later tested. The implicit test was WSC used by Warrington and Weiskrantz. The explicit test was word-stem cued recall, in which the very same word-stem cues were coupled with explicit instructions to use the word stems to try to remember words from the list. The amnesics were quite impaired on the explicit test but showed normal levels of priming on the implicit test, demonstrating that the critical factor in the dissociation was not the memory cues but rather whether the memory test required intentional, conscious recollection.

Many of the early implicit tests require the completion or identification of fragmented perceptual cues, as in the WSC and WFC tasks. It was natural to wonder whether preserved learning in amnesia extended to more meaningful material. Graf et al. (1985) presented amnesics and control subjects with a list of words containing examples from various categories. Subsequently, memory was tested with one of two tests, either the explicit test of category-cued recall or the implicit test of category production. The amnesics exhibited poor memory on the explicit, cued-recall test (as is typical) but produced normal amounts of priming on the implicit test. Thus, preserved implicit memory in amnesia encompasses memory retrieval guided by meaningful cues, as well as retrieval guided by degraded perceptual cues.

A final example of preserved implicit memory in amnesics focuses on skill learning. In a classic study on this topic, Cohen and Squire (1980) taught amnesics and normal control subjects a new perceptual skill, reading mirror-reversed text. Amnesics acquired this skill at the same rate as the control subjects and retained the skill over a period of 3 months. Furthermore, both the amnesics and the control subjects were quicker at reading repeated text than new text, a form of repetition priming embedded in the skill-learning task. Strikingly, amnesics exhibited very little explicit memory for specific passages of text on a recognition memory test, whereas the control subjects could recognize substantial numbers of these passages. Consistent with the repetition priming studies, this form of skill learning was intact in a population with greatly compromised recollective ability. Such dissociations between implicit and explicit memory for amnesic patients has been documented many times since these early studies, although as discussed later, emerging research places important limits on the generality of preserved implicit memory in amnesia (Keane & Verfaellie, 2006).

Similar dissociations have been reported across the life span. Many studies comparing younger and older adults reveal different patterns for their explicit and implicit memory, with older adults performing worse on explicit memory tasks even though their implicit memory performance is not statistically different than younger adults (e.g. Fay, Isingrini, & Clarys, 2005). There has been some debate about the absolute preservation of implicit memory in old age. In an earlier meta-analytical study, LaVoie and Light (1994) found that the confidence interval of the effect size for adult age differences in repetition priming did not include 0; therefore, they concluded that priming decreases with age, but less so than performance on explicit tests of recall and recognition. Alternatively, Fleischman and Gabrieli (1998) found that 85% of the studies that compared healthy older adults to young adults found age to be an invariant factor in priming, and argued that implicit memory is preserved. However, neither of these two reviews took into account explicit contamination, the possibility that participants may use explicit memory retrieval to aid performance on a nominally implicit test. Because younger adults are better in using their explicit memory, this may give them an unfair advantage in producing critical

responses on priming tests, which in turn would produce the appearance of an age effect in implicit memory. In a study designed to eliminate the effects of explicit contamination, Mitchell and Bruss (2003) compared young and old adults on five implicit measures (WFC, picture-fragment completion, category-exemplar production, WSC, and picture naming) and one explicit memory measure (category-cued recall). The results indicated that priming was equivalent for old and young adults when test-aware participants were excluded; in contrast, younger adults outperformed older adults in the cued recall test. Mitchell and Bruss concluded that priming is preserved throughout adulthood in spite of decreased explicit memory. In a recent review, Fleischman (2007) also argued that priming is preserved in healthy aging, and that appearances to the contrary are due to studies that do not adequately screen out older adults with incipient forms of dementia.

Developmental studies also reveal dissociations between explicit and implicit measures. Many studies that have compared the priming for children (from ages 3 to 14) to young adults have found that children perform similarly to adults on implicit memory tasks, such as picture-fragment completion, even though young adults outperform children in explicit tests (e.g., Drummey & Newcombe, 1995; Graf, 1990). Research with conceptual implicit tests, on the other hand, provides some evidence that implicit memory may increase with age. Murphy, McKone, and Slee (2003) investigated explicit and implicit memory with perceptual and conceptual tests across four age groups ranging from kindergarten to young adults. These authors found developmental changes in conceptual priming but not on the perceptual tasks. Murphy et al. (2003) concluded that the developmental trend for conceptual implicit memory was guided by the development of the underlying knowledge structures about categories.

A number of other population dissociations have been reported. For example, patients with depression commonly report difficulties in memory and concentration. In formal tests, such patients often exhibit deficient memory on explicit tests compared to healthy control subjects. However, a number of studies indicate that depressed patients exhibit similar amounts of repetition priming on implicit tests (Barry, Naus, & Lynn, 2004). Likewise, patients with schizophrenia exhibit memory deficits in explicit remembering (as compared to healthy control subjects) but still produce intact implicit memory (Kazes et al., 1999). In both of these cases, a population with deficient explicit memory produces normal or near-normal implicit memory.

## Functional Dissociations

Additional evidence for the separability of different forms of memory comes from experimental variables that dissociate performance on explicit and implicit memory tests. An example of such a functional dissociation is the effect of study modality. If some study words are presented visually and some are presented aurally, later explicit memory for the words is typically unaffected. However, when memory is tested with the implicit tests of WSC and WFC, study modality has a large impact; visually presented study words lead to more priming than the aurally presented words. Much of the initial research in implicit memory used visual materials during both study and test phase. However, some studies have assessed priming in the auditory modality as well, producing results that are largely consistent with implicit memory as measured visually. Auditory tests are designed to be analogs of visual implicit tests. For example, in the auditory perceptual identification test, participants are presented with spoken words presented with white noise, and they try to identify the word. In auditory WFC and auditory WSC tests, part of the spoken word is replaced with silence, and participants try to complete the item with the first word that comes to mind. Studies using these tests indicate that the words studied during the encoding phase lead to better identification or completion than unstudied items, confirming that auditory testing produces significant priming just like in the visual modality. Moreover, auditory priming exhibits similar patterns of results as visual priming. For example, auditory implicit tests exhibited greater priming for study words presented in the same modality, just as visual implicit tests do (e.g., Loveman, van Hooff & Gale, 2002). Other similarities are noted later. One potential difference is that auditory priming may be more consistent across early ages than is visual priming, a difference that may reflect developmental differences between perceiving speech and perceiving visual language (Carlesimo, Vicari, Albertoni, Turriziani, & Caltagirone, 2000).

Varying the perceptual features of the stimulus often has a greater impact on implicit than explicit memory. Conversely, varying the amount of semantic processing during the study episode typically has a marked effect on explicit memory but less effect on such implicit memory tests as WSC and perceptual identification. In the classical levels of processing manipulation, participants are asked to perform two encoding tasks, in which they are either encouraged to process items in a "shallow" or a "deep" manner (Craik & Lockhart, 1972). Shallow processing refers to the analysis of perceptual characteristics of a stimulus, such as counting the number of vowels or syllables of a word, or identifying the type-case. Deep processing entails evaluation about the meaning of the stimulus, required by tasks such as the categorizing the item or rating its pleasantness. The superiority of deep processing over shallow processing is well documented in explicit memory, and this manipulation has also been used widely in implicit memory studies. In an experiment by Graf and Mandler (1984), participants were asked to perform deep processing tasks (rating of concreteness or pleasantness) or shallow processing tasks (counting letters, finding common vowels) at study. At test, participants were given either the explicit tests of free recall, recognition or cued recall, or the implicit test of WSC. They found that the deep encoding produced better memory than shallow encoding on the explicit memory tasks, but not on the implicit memory test. Similarly, Schacter and Church (1992) found that the levels-of-processing manipulation did not affect auditory priming, even though deeper encoding enhanced explicit recall.

Although this dissociation is well documented, deep processing tasks often produce a numerical advantage in priming (even if not significant) over nonsemantic tasks. In a meta-analysis, Brown and Mitchell (1994) examined 33 levels-of-processing studies with 166 results, which revealed the semantic (deep) tasks were superior to nonsemantic (shallow) tasks in 79% of the studies using implicit memory measures, as compared to 97% of the studies using explicit memory tasks. However, many of these earlier studies may not have adequately handled the issue of explicit contamination. Other researchers have argued that when stringent criteria are applied to rule out explicit contamination, then levels-of-processing effects on perceptually based priming tasks are minimized (e.g., Mace, 2003).

All of the preceding dissociations may be regarded as single dissociations, in which a variable (e.g., neurological population, study modality, levels of processing) impacts one memory test (be it explicit or implicit) but not the other. Crossover dissociations are instances in which a variable produces opposite effects on implicit and explicit tests. Such dissociations are important because they provide stronger evidence of qualitative differences between the two measures of memory (a point to which we return later). An example of such a dissociation is produced by the generation manipulation, as originally demonstrated by Jacoby (1983). In this experiment, participants read some of the words in isolation (e.g., xxx-COLD), read some others along with their antonyms (e.g., hot-COLD), and generated the rest of the words from their antonyms (e.g., hot-????). At test, participants either took the explicit test of recognition or the implicit test of perceptual identification (which involves the identification of briefly presented words). The results create a crossover dissociation: The participants who took the recognition test had the best memory for generated words, followed by words read in context, which in turn was better than the words read in isolation. On the implicit test, the results were reversed, with the greatest priming for the words read in isolation, intermediate priming for the words read in context, and the least priming for generated words. This crossover dissociation has been replicated with many other perceptual tasks, such as WFC and WSC, and it has been replicated in the auditory modality with auditory versions of perceptual identification and WSC (Dew & Mulligan, 2008; although see Mulligan & Dew, 2009, for a review of some limitations on this dissociation).

### *Pharmacological Dissociations*

Another set of dissociations between implicit and explicit memory are produced by the amnestic effects of a class of drugs called benzodiazepines (which includes triazolam, diazepam, and midazolam). These drugs are used to treat anxiety and to induce anesthesia. At low dosages (too low to induce sleep or stupor), these drugs produce a powerful but temporary form of anterograde amnesia, despite the fact that the patient exhibits normal language and cognitive abilities. Information encountered while under the effects of the drug is very poorly remembered. As the effects of the drug wear off, so do the amnestic effects. Research motivated by findings with organic amnesia demonstrates that these drugs predominantly impact explicit forms of memory. The typical study entails two groups of participants, one receiving a low dose of a benzodiazepine and a second receiving a placebo. After an absorption period that allows time for the drug to take effect, participants are presented with the study phase of the experiment. Some time later (an interval sufficient to allow the effects of the drug to wash out), a memory test is administered. The group given benzodiazepine produces very poor explicit memory for the study materials on tests such as free recall (thus evincing amnesia for information encountered while under the effects of the drug). However, if memory is measured with an implicit test, such as WSC or WFC, then the drug and placebo group produce equivalent levels of priming. Thus, pharmacological amnesia produces the same type of dissociation as produced by organic amnesia: It affects conscious recollection but appears to have little effect on unconscious influences of memory (see Curran, 2000 for a review).

### *Neuroimaging Dissociations*

Neuroimaging research, using positron emission tomography (PET) and functional magnetic resonance imaging (fMRI), provides convergent evidence for differences between explicit and implicit forms of memory. In a typical neuroimaging analysis, participants are presented with study materials in the initial phase of the experiment, and then given a memory test during which the brain scan occurs. In some conditions, the memory test is an explicit test such as recall or recognition, and in other conditions, an implicit test is given. Thus, brain activity is measured during memory retrieval, allowing researchers to examine differences in brain function during implicit or explicit memory retrieval.

Several such differences in brain activity have been found. Explicit memory retrieval typically produces an increase in neural activity in prefrontal cortex (especially in the right hemisphere) and in the medial temporal lobe and hippocampus. The activity in the frontal lobe appears to reflect a mental set in which the individual is oriented toward the past and intentionally tries to retrieve information. Activity in medial-temporal areas reflects the recollective experience itself, when the memory is successfully retrieved. These patterns of activation are typically missing when participants engage in implicit retrieval, providing an initial difference in neural activity between explicit and implicit tests. Furthermore, priming on implicit tests is associated with decreased activity in various brain areas. Specifically, researchers compare brain activity on trials in which a studied word may be produced (an old trial) with trials on which a study word is not a potential response (new trials). This comparison allows the researcher to isolate the unique influence of implicit memory as opposed to the ongoing demands of the task that are common to both old and new trials (e.g., the common processes necessary to complete a fragmented word regardless of its old-new status). The old condition typically produces less neural activity than the new condition in regions of the brain that contribute to the ongoing task. This phenomenon is called repetition suppression and reflects a reduction in processing demands when a stimulus is processed a second time (Horner & Henson, 2008). The brain regions involved depend on the nature of the implicit test. For perceptual tests such as WSC or WFC, the decreased processing is found in visual areas of the brain (in occipital lobe). On conceptual implicit tests, the pattern of repetition suppression is found in inferior frontal lobe and mid-temporal lobe. In general, these results imply that the same neural substrates responsible for the initial (perceptual or conceptual) processing are reengaged at the time of test and exhibit the effects of the initial processing by their subsequent reduced activity. In sum, the difference in brain regions engaged by implicit and explicit memory tests argues for qualitative differences between the forms of memory invoked by these tasks.

## The Methodological Challenge of Explicit Contamination

An important challenge in research on implicit memory, alluded to earlier, is the possibility of explicit contamination. Specifically, it is possible that a participant could "catch on" to the nature of the experiment and intentionally retrieve information from the study phase during the nominally implicit test. This possibility may be unlikely in studies with amnesic patients for whom explicit memory is minimal, but it is a much more pointed concern when implicit memory is studied in healthy young adults. Researchers have developed a number of techniques to try to mitigate this potential problem, a detailed discussion of which is beyond the scope of the present chapter. We merely mention some common techniques and point the reader to MacLeod (2008) for a thorough review of this issue.

Roediger and McDermott (1993) recommend a number of design features to minimize the possibility and utility of explicit retrieval on implicit tests: (1) study (and test) instructions are incidental; (2) the test instructions emphasize providing the first response that comes to mind; (3) multiple filler tasks intervene between the study and test portion of the experiment; (4) the set of study items is relatively large; (5) the proportion of old items on the tests is below 50%; and (6) the tests begin with filler items not from the study portion of the experiment. A second technique is the use of a posttest questionnaire, designed to assess whether the participant was aware of the nature of the implicit test and whether the participant engaged in explicit retrieval (see Barnhardt & Geraci, 2008, for evidence on the validity of this technique). Another common approach is the retrieval-intentionality criterion (Schacter, Bowers, & Booker, 1989), which compares performance on matched implicit and explicit tests. If a variable can be found that dissociates the two tests, the logic goes, then the implicit test must not have been meaningfully contaminated by explicit memory. Otherwise the two tests would demonstrate a similar effect of the variable. Finally, Jacoby (1991) has developed a process-dissociation procedure that attempts to measure implicit and explicit contributions to performance within a single memory test. This is done by comparing two conditions, one in which the implicit and explicit influences work together to increase test performance, and another in which the two influences are placed in opposition. Jacoby developed an algebraic model to compare performance in these two conditions, and to derive measures of conscious and unconscious memory influences.

## Breadth of Implicit Memory Phenomena

To experimentally analyze implicit memory, researchers often make use of repetition priming tasks. However, implicit memory is not limited to simplified tasks requiring identification or classification of individual words. Rather, implicit memory has been found to influence a wide variety of cognitive and affective processes. Kunst-Wilson and Zajonc (1980) provide a classic demonstration in which participants were presented with abstract geometric figures for very brief exposures (1 ms), a duration designed to eliminate conscious perception of the figures. A later test of explicit recognition indicated that participants could not distinguish figures presented earlier from those not presented. However, when asked to rate the figures for aesthetic appearance, participants preferred old figures over new. This "mere exposure" effect has also been demonstrated in populations with deficits in explicit memory. For example, Johnson, Kim, and Risse (1985) presented amnesic and control participants with previously unfamiliar melodies. Later, both groups received a preference test, in which they rated how much they liked both old and new melodies. Both the amnesics and the controls demonstrated the same increase in preference for old melodies. On an explicit recognition test, however, the amnesics had very poor memory for the old versus new melodies. This same pattern of results is found when Alzheimer patients are compared to age-matched control participants (Willems, Adam, & Van der Linden, 2002).

The false-fame effect is another interesting demonstration of implicit memory. Participants are initially presented with a set of famous and nonfamous names. Later, in a separate phase of the experiment, the participants are asked to indicate which names on a list are famous. Participants give higher fame ratings to the nonfamous names presented earlier than new nonfamous names (Jacoby, Woloshyn, & Kelley, 1989). Jacoby and colleagues have argued that the old nonfamous names are processed with greater fluency, and this fluency is misattributed to the fame of the name rather than its prior presentation. Such fluency misattributions can occur in a number of other ways. For example, when participants hear sentences masked in white noise, the noise appears quieter when masking previously presented sentences than new sentences, even though the white noise is actually equally loud in both cases (Jacoby, Allens, Collins, & Larwill, 1988). Likewise, the repetition of a statement increases the likelihood that the statement will be regarded as true later on, even when the statement was initially labeled as false (Begg, Anas, & Farinacci, 1992). This memory illusion appears to be driven by increased fluency in the absence of conscious recollection of the source of the statement. In all of these cases, memory-based fluency is misattributed to some other characteristic of the stimulus. Finally, the dual-process model (Yonelinas, 2002) argues that implicit memory contributes to performance on nominally explicit tests. According to this view, fluency is one basis for recognizing that a stimulus or an event has occurred earlier. In contrast to the prior examples, in which fluency is misattributed to some other source (fame, truth, current perceptual conditions), the dual-process view claims that when one is oriented toward the past, fluency can be correctly interpreted as evidence for re-presentation.

## Theoretical Frameworks

Several theoretical frameworks have evolved to account for dissociations between implicit and explicit memory. These accounts have been further complicated as dissociations among different measures of implicit memory have joined the dissociations between implicit and explicit memory. Extant theoretical accounts generally have greater success accounting for some types of dissociations

than others, but all shed light on varying aspects of implicit memory.

### Implicit Memory as Weak Trace or Residual Activation

Two early accounts of implicit memory that have largely been discarded are the "weak trace" view and the activation view. Mentioned earlier was Korsakoff's view that amnesics were capable of creating only weak memory traces, too weak to reach the threshold for conscious awareness but nevertheless capable of producing effects on behavior (similar to Ebbinghuas's view). This view, which argues that implicit and explicit memory differ only in degree, has largely been discounted in the modern era given evidence for qualitative differences between implicit and explicit measures of memory. For example, cross-over dissociations, in which a variable (such as the generation manipulation) produces opposite effects on implicit and explicit measures of memory is generally taken as evidence for a qualitative difference in the forms of memory underlying the two tests. Likewise, neuroimaging dissociations imply qualitative dissimilarity at the basis of neural substrate.

Another early view attributed implicit memory phenomena to the temporary activation of preexisting knowledge representations. According to this view, processing a stimulus activates representations in long-term memory, leaving the representations in a temporarily heightened state of activation for some time thereafter. This residual activation increases the subsequent accessibility of those representations, enhancing the speed or accuracy of processing for items that had been recently perceived compared to those that had not. Although the activation account was consistent with initial evidence, several lines of evidence against this view have accrued. First, this view assumes that residual activation is short lived, returning to baseline within a period of minutes or hours. However, it has been found that repetition priming can persist over periods of days, weeks, or even months. Such longevity is inconsistent with standard notions of activation. Second, the activation view predicts that only those stimuli that are familiar and well integrated (i.e., stimuli with preexisting representations) should exhibit priming. In contradiction, priming effects have been obtained for novel stimuli, such as nonsense words and line-drawings of nonsense objects. Third, the perceptual specificity of many priming phenomena (e.g., effects of study modality) appears incompatible with an activation view that attributes priming to abstract, amodal representations of words and concepts.

## Multiple Memory Systems

Modern analysis indicate that human memory is not a unitary ability but rather a set of functionally and neural distinct systems. One familiar distinction is that between working memory and long-term memory, which is supported by a host of behavioral, neuropsychological, and brain-imaging data. Likewise, the dissociations between implicit and explicit memory has been taken as evidence for multiple, distinct long-term memory systems. For example, the common finding that amnesics perform poorly on explicit tests but typically exhibit intact implicit memory is interpreted as indicating that the brain areas damaged in amnesia (typically the hippocampus and/or medial temporal lobe) are critical to the formation of memories that later produce conscious recollection. In contrast, the system(s) that underlies unconscious influences of memory must reside elsewhere in the brain.

Initial versions of this view were dichotomous, proposing two systems (e.g., declarative vs. procedural, episodic vs. semantic) to account for explicit and implicit memory, respectively. However, subsequent research indicated that different forms of implicit memory were mutually dissociable. Consequently, current versions of this theory propose four memory systems (Schacter et al., 2000; see also Squire, Clark, & Bayley, 2004). Episodic memory refers to memory for specific episodes that are tied to a particular place and time. According to the multiple memory systems (MMS) view, episodic memory underlies our ability to recollect the past. Semantic memory stores general knowledge about the world, including facts, conceptual information, and vocabulary. Episodic and semantic memory are sometimes jointly referred to as declarative memory, referring to knowledge that can be verbalized (knowing that). The perceptual representation system (PRS) stores and processes information about the form and structure of words and objects. Finally, procedural memory represents knowledge of cognitive and motor skills (knowing how). In the MMS view, only one of the systems is thought to produce explicit memory (i.e., the episodic system), whereas the other three systems give rise to various forms of implicit memory, allowing the theory to accommodate dissociates among implicit memory measures as well as dissociations between implicit and explicit memory.

Most of the population and pharmacological dissociations fit naturally with the MMS view. For example, anterograde amnesia produces deficits on explicit memory, implying disruption to the episodic memory system, but typically not on verbal implicit memory tests (such as WSC and WFC) or on tests of skill learning, implying that the other systems are not disrupted. Thus, dissociations of implicit and explicit memory tests are interpreted as reflecting the operation of distinct memory systems. The MMS view obtains strong support from reports of double dissociations, in which two different patient groups (with damage to different parts of the brain) exhibit complementary dissociative patterns on implicit and explicit memory tests. For example, amnesic patients (with damage to medial-temporal regions of the brain) have disrupted memory on explicit tests but not on implicit tests, as noted. The opposite dissociation occurs in patients with occipital-lobe lesions, who exhibit preserved explicit memory coupled with deficits in implicit memory for visual-perceptual information (Gabrieli, Fleishman, Keane, Reminger, & Morrell, 1995). This provides strong support for the view that brain systems mediating performance on these two types of tests differ. Similar dissociative patterns support distinctions among the other proposed memory systems (Schacter, Wagner, & Buckner, 2000; Squire et al., 2004)

## Transfer-Appropriate Processing

Another important theoretical perspective on implicit memory is the transfer-appropriate processing (TAP) framework (Jacoby, 1983; Roediger & McDermott, 1993). The framework was initially developed as an alternative to the MMS view and attempted to account for functional dissociations in terms of different processes operating within a single memory system. Although the bulk of the research argues against a single-system account of all of the data, the TAP view highlights several important issues and draws a number of theoretical contrasts of continuing importance. The TAP view draws on earlier research indicating that memory performance is a function of the overlap in encoding and retrieval processes. Applied to implicit memory phenomena, the TAP framework distinguishes between conceptual processing (involved in the analysis of meaning) and perceptual processing (involved in the analysis of perceptual or surface-level features of a stimulus). Many of the commonly used implicit tests require identification of degraded or ambiguous perceptual stimuli, such as word fragments, briefly presented words, or fragmented pictures. Under the TAP view, such tests are considered perceptually driven. Consequently, encoding conditions that require greater perceptual processing should transfer well to these tests. Alternatively, according to the TAP view, explicit memory instructions generally encourage the reengagement of conceptual memory processes, leading to greater transfer for conceptual encoding conditions.

As an example of the TAP account of a functional dissociation, consider the results of Jacoby (1983) discussed earlier. Identifying a word without context requires perceptual processing of the word (of course) but does not mandate much conceptual processing. In contrast, generating a word from an antonym requires conceptual processing but provides little opportunity for visual or perceptual analysis. Reading a word in context presumably occupies a middle ground in which both perceptual and conceptual processing occur. According to the TAP view, perceptual encoding conditions should transfer well to implicit memory tests focusing on perceptual retrieval, whereas conceptual encoding conditions should transfer well to explicit tests, consistent with the observed results.

Although many implicit tests are perceptual in nature, and many explicit tests conceptual, this is not a necessary correspondence. With the appropriate choice of memory cues and response requirements, one can develop implicit memory tests that reengage conceptual processes as well as explicit memory tests that reengage perceptual processes. For example, the category production task, in which participants generate examples from provided category cues, is an example of a conceptual implicit test. The TAP framework predicts that dissociations are likely to occur between two implicit tests if one is perceptual and the other conceptual, and a number of such dissociations have been reported. For example, study modality affects perceptual implicit tests such as WSC and WFC (as noted earlier) but not the conceptual implicit test of category production. Alternatively, levels-of-processing and divided attention have minimal impact on perceptual tasks such as WFC and perceptual identification but produce substantial effects on conceptual priming tasks. Finally, the read/generate manipulation likewise dissociates perceptual and conceptual priming tasks; reading produces more perceptual priming than the generate condition, but generating produces more conceptual priming than does reading.

The TAP framework has had substantial success in accounting for functional dissociations between explicit and implicit tests, and among implicit tests of different types (i.e., perceptual and conceptual). Thus, the perceptual-conceptual processing dimension is an important element in accounting for implicit memory phenomena. However, it is unlikely to provide a complete explanation because the view does not readily account for some of the population and pharmacological dissociations so important to the multiple systems view. In particular, it has generally been found that explicit tests, whether relying on conceptual or perceptual retrieval cues, are affected by anterograde amnesia and amnestic drug treatments like the benzodiazepines. In addition, both organic amnesia and drug (benzodiazepines)-induced amnesia produce normal levels of priming on conceptual as well as perceptual implicit tests. That is, in these cases, perceptual and conceptual tests produce similar rather than different outcomes. However, the perceptual-conceptual distinction may prove useful for other population dissociations. In particular, children have preserved perceptual priming, but current results imply that their conceptual priming continues to develop relative to young adults (Murphy et al., 2003). Likewise, although schizophrenic patients demonstrate preserved priming on perceptual implicit tests, conceptual priming appears to be reduced compared to normal control subjects (Ruiz, Soler, Fuentes, & Tomás, 2007). These results indicate that even in the domain of population dissociations, the TAP account may have applicability.

## Emerging Issues in Implicit Memory Research

The traditional finding with respect to amnesia is that explicit memory is impaired but that implicit forms of memory are preserved. This characterization has been challenged in recent research using implicit tests that measure the formation of new associations. Such associative priming tasks reveal memory deficits in anterograde amnesia (Keane & Verfaellie, 2006). Likewise, benzodiazepine-induced amnesia demonstrates a similar pattern, with performance on nonassociative implicit tests preserved but associative priming impaired (Chun, 2005). These and related findings have spurred some researchers to argue that implicit and explicit memory may not be as different as traditionally supposed by the MMS view. Rather, differences between explicit memory and the traditional (nonassociative) implicit tests may hinge not on conscious awareness but instead on their differential reliance on the formation of new associations (e.g., Reder, Park, & Kieffaber, 2009). This is certain to be a topic of great research interest in the next few years.

## Note

1. It should be noted that Warrington and Weiskrantz did not use the terms *implicit memory* and *explicit memory*, and thus they did not focus on the strict comparability of memory tests so categorized by later researchers.

## References

Barnhardt, T. M., & Geraci, L. (2008). Are awareness questionnaires valid? Investigating the use of posttest questionnaires for assessing awareness in implicit memory tests. Memory and Cognition, 36, 53–64.

Barry, E. S., Naus, M. J., & Lynn P. R. (2004). Depression and implicit memory: Understanding mood congruent memory bias. Cognitive Therapy and Research, 28, 387–414.

Begg, I. A., Anas, A., & Farinacci, S. (1992). Dissociation of processes in belief: Source recollection, statement familiarity and the illusion of truth. Journal of Experimental Psychology: General, 121, 446–458.

Brown, A. S., & Mitchell, D. B. (1994). A reevaluation of semantic versus nonsemantic processing in implicit memory. Memory and Cognition, 22, 533–541.

Carlesimo, G. A., Vicari, S., Albertoni, A., Turriziani, P., & Caltagirone, C. (2000). developmental dissociation between visual and auditory repetition priming: The role of lexicon inputs. Cortex, 36, 181–193.

Chun, M. M. (2005). Drug-induced amnesia impairs implicit relational memory. Trends in Cognitive Sciences, 9, 355–357.

Claparede, E. (1951). Recognition and "me-ness." In D. Rapaport (Ed.), *Organization and pathology of thought* (pp. 58–75). New York: Columbia University Press. (Original work published in 1911).

Cohen, N. J., & Squire, L. R. (1980). Preserved learning and retention of pattern-analyzing skill in amnesia: Dissociation of knowing how and knowing that. Science, 210, 207–210.

Craik, F. I. M., & Lockhart, R. S. (1972). Levels of processing: A framework for memory research. Journal of Verbal Learning and Verbal Behavior, 11, 671–684.

Curran, H. V. (2000). Psychopharmacological perspectives on memory. In E. Tulving & F. I. M. Craik (Eds.), *The Oxford handbook on memory* (pp. 539–554). New York: Oxford University Press.

Dew, I. T. Z., & Mulligan, N. W. (2008). The effects of generation on auditory implicit memory. Memory and Cognition, 36, 1157–1167.

Drummey, A. B., & Newcombe, N. (1995). Remembering versus knowing the past: Children's explicit and implicit memory for pictures. Journal of Experimental Child Psychology, 59, 549–565.

Ebbinghaus, H. (1964). *Memory: A contribution to experimental psychology*. New York: Dover. (Original work published in 1885).

Fay, S., Isingrini, M., & Clarys, D. (2005). Effects of depth-of-processing and ageing on word-stem and word-fragment implicit memory tasks: Test of the lexical-processing hypothesis. European Journal of Cognitive Psychology, 17, 785–802.

Fleischman, D. A. (2007). Repetition priming in aging and Alzheimer's disease: An integrative review and future directions. Cortex, 43, 889–897.

Fleischman, D. A., & Gabrieli, J. D. E. (1998). Repetition priming in normal aging and Alzheimer's disease: A review of findings and theories. Psychology and Aging, 13, 88–119.

Gabrieli, J. D. E., Fleishman, D. A., Keane, M. M., Reminger, S. L., & Morrell, F. (1995). Double dissociation between memory systems underlying explicit and implicit memory in the human brain. Psychological Science, 6, 76–82.

Graf, P. (1990). Life-span changes in implicit and explicit memory. Bulletin of the Psychonomic Society, 28, 353–358.

Graf, P., & Mandler, G. (1984). Activation makes words more accessible, but not necessarily more retrievable. Journal of Verbal Learning and Verbal Behavior, 23, 553–568.

Graf, P., Shimamura, A., & Squire, L. (1985). Priming across modalities and priming across category levels: Extending the domain of preserved functions in amnesia. Journal of Experimental Psychology: Learning, Memory and Cognition, 11, 386–396.

Graf, P., Squire, L. R., & Mandler, G. (1984). The information that amnesic patients do not forget. Journal of Experimental Psychology: Learning, Memory, and Cognition, 10, 164–178.

Horner, A. J., & Henson, R. N. (2008). Priming, response learning and repetition suppression. Neuropsychologia, 46, 1979–1991.

Jacoby, L. L. (1983). Remembering the data: Analyzing interactive processes in reading. Journal of Verbal Learning and Verbal Behavior, 22, 485–508.

Jacoby, L. L. (1991). A process dissociation framework: Separating automatic from intentional uses of memory. Journal of Memory and Language, 30, 513–541.

Jacoby, L. L., Allan, L. G., Collins, J. C., & Larwill, L. K. (1988). Memory influences subjective experience: Noise judgments. Journal of Experimental Psychology: Learning, Memory, and Cognition, 14, 240–247.

Jacoby, L. L., Woloshyn, V., & Kelley, C. (1989). Becoming famous without being recognized: Unconscious influences of memory produced by divided attention. Journal of Experimental Psychology: General, 118, 115–125.

James, W. (1890). *The principles of psychology*. London: MacMillan.

Johnson, M. K., Kim, J. K., & Risse, G. (1985). Do alcoholic Korsakoff's syndrome patients acquire affective reactions? Journal of Experimental Psychology: Learning, Memory, and Cognition, 11, 22–36.

Kazes, M., Berthet, L., Danion, J., Amado, I., Willard, D., Robert, P., & Poirier, M. F. (1999). Impairment of consciously controlled use of memory in schizophrenia. Neuropsychology, 13, 54–61.

Keane, M. M., & Verfaellie, M. (2006). Amnesia II: Cognitive issues. In M. J. Farah & T. E. Feinberg (Eds.), *Patient-based approaches to cognitive neuroscience (2nd ed.,* pp. 303–314). Cambridge, MA: MIT Press.

Kunst-Wilson, W. R., & Zajonc, R. B. (1980). Affective discrimination of stimuli that cannot be recognized. Science, 207, 557–558.

La Voie, D., & Light, L. L. (1994). Adult age differences in repetition priming: A meta-analysis. Psychology and Aging, 9, 539–533.

Loveman, E., van Hooff, J. C., & Gale, A. (2002). A systematic investigation of same and cross modality priming using written and spoken responses. Memory, 10, 267–276.

Mace, J. H. (2003). Study-test awareness can enhance priming on an implicit memory task: Evidence from a word completion task. *American Journal of Psychology, 166*, 257–279.

MacLeod, C. M. (2008). Implicit memory tests: Techniques for reducing conscious intrusion. In R. A. Bjork (Ed.), *Handbook of metamemory and memory* (pp. 245–263). New York: Psychology Press.

Mitchell, D. B., & Bruss, P. J. (2003). Age differences in implicit memory: Conceptual, perceptual, or methodological? *Psychology and Aging, 18*, 897–822.

Mulligan, N. W., & Dew, I. T. Z. (2009). Generation and perceptual implicit memory: Different generation tasks produce different effects on priming. *Journal of Experimental Psychology: Learning, Memory, and Cognition, 35*, 1522–1538.

Murphy, K., McKone, E., & Slee, J. (2003). Dissociations between implicit and explicit memory in children: The role of strategic processing and the knowledge base. *Journal of Experimental Child Psychology, 84*, 124–165.

Reder, L. M., Park, H., & Kieffaber, P. D. (2009). Memory systems do not divide on consciousness: Reinterpreting memory in terms of activation and binding. *Psychological Bulletin, 135*, 23–49.

Roediger, H. L., & Mc Dermott, K. B. (1993). Implicit memory in normal human subjects. In F. Boller & J. Grafman (Eds.), *Handbook of neuropsychology* (Vol. 8, pp. 63–131). Amsterdam, The Netherlands: Elsevier.

Ruiz, J. C., Soler, M. J., Fuentes, I., & Tomás, P. (2007). Intellectual functioning and memory deficits in schizophrenia. *Comprehensive Psychiatry, 48*, 276–282.

Schacter, D. L. (1987). Implicit memory: History and current status. *Journal of Experimental Psychology: Learning, Memory and Cognition, 13*, 501–518.

Schacter, D. L., Bowers, J., & Booker, J. (1989). Intention, awareness, and implicit memory: The retrieval intentionality criterion. In S. Lewandowsky, J. C. Dunn, & K. Kirsner (Eds.), *Implicit memory: Theoretical issues* (pp. 47–65). Hillsdale, NJ: Erlbaum.

Schacter, D. L., & Church, B. A. (1992). Auditory priming: Implicit and explicit memory for words and voices. *Journal of Experimental Psychology: Learning, Memory, and Cognition, 18*, 915–930.

Schacter, D. L., Wagner, A. D., & Buckner, R. L. (2000). Memory systems of 1999. In E. Tulving & F. I. M. Craik (Eds.), *The Oxford handbook on memory*. New York: Oxford University Press.

Squire, L. R., Clark, R. E., & Bayley, P. J. (2004). Medial temporal lobe function and memory. In M. Gazzaniga (Ed.), *The cognitive neurosciences III* (pp. 691–708). Cambridge, MA: MIT Press.

Warrington, E. K., & Weiskrantz, L. (1970). Amnesic syndrome: Consolidation or retrieval. *Nature, 217*, 972–974.

Weiskrantz, L., & Warrington, E. K. (1970). Verbal learning and retention by amnesic patients using partial information. *Psychonomic Science, 20*, 210–211

Willems, S., Adam, S., & Van, D. L. (2002). Normal mere exposure effect with impaired recognition in Alzheimer's disease. *Cortex, 38*, 77–86.

Yonelinas, A. P. (2002). The nature of recollection and familiarity: A review of 30 years of research. *Journal of Memory and Language, 46*, 441–517.

# The Sources of Memory Errors

Cara Laney

**Abstract**

This chapter discusses some of the various types of errors that are the by-products of highly efficient and practical human memory systems. The errors vary in size, commonness, and potential for impact. Errors may be of omission (forgetting details and whole events that did happen), commission (remembering details and whole events that did not actually happen), or a combination of the two. Errors can happen at any stage from initial perception to final memory retrieval. Critically, some errors are so compelling for the rememberer that they cannot be "undone" once they have occurred.

**Key Words:** encoding failure, retrieval failure, schemata, stress, misinformation, false memory

Several of the chapters in this book are a testament to the complexities of human memory, as well as to its power to hold tremendous amounts of information for impressive periods of time. This chapter will discuss some of the downsides of this complexity and capacity—that is, the errors that can result. In particular, underlying commonalities in apparently different errors will be noted and discussed.

Memory errors include both errors of omission and of commission. Errors of omission that will be discussed here include failures to initially encode information and failures to correctly retrieve it later. Errors of commission to be discussed include the adoption of incorrect details into existing memories and the creation of completely new, wholly false, memories.

Memory errors are part of daily living. Some of these errors are small and correctable, like temporarily forgetting a particular word or name. Errors that are not corrected may go completely unnoticed. Other errors are substantial and can have huge impacts on people's lives, even including convictions

for crimes committed by someone else. Part of the reason that these latter memory errors can have such consequences is that they can be extremely compelling for those who have them (and those who hear about them). Some of the factors that can make false memories so compelling will be discussed later in this chapter.

Contrary to common intuition, forgetting is a very important part of remembering. As William James (1890) put it, "If we remembered everything, we should on most occasions be as ill off as if we remembered nothing" (p. 68). If this seems strange, consider briefly what would happen if every memory of parking your car was as vivid as every other memory of parking your car, and then try to consider how you might go about finding your way home.

Instead of remembering with equal strength everything that has ever happened to us, and everything we have ever learned, we have a necessarily incomplete record of the past, plus a set of resources to help us organize and make sense of these incomplete records. These resources include schemata, biases of various kinds, abilities to prioritize, assumptions, and reconstructive capabilities. These resources are mostly highly functional and make practical memory possible. But they also backfire in predictable ways and thus create predictable and testable patterns of errors (see also Schacter, 2001, for a further discussion of the adaptiveness of memory errors).

Because memory is a series of processes—broadly encoding, storage, and retrieval—there are a variety of opportunities for errors. In order for a memory to be successfully formed, saved, and accessed when needed, a number of things have to go right. Notably, the information or event has to be perceived (and thus to be readily perceptible), attended to, stored (and perhaps rehearsed) until needed, found again when required, and brought back into awareness. Each of these steps introduces error potential, and although these errors work somewhat differently from one another, they also share a variety of often telling commonalities.

As we will see later, errors in human memory are particularly likely in the presence of several factors. Memory errors are more likely when contradictory evidence is lacking (often because it was not recorded or has since been lost), when erroneous information fits in with our understanding of the world and expectations about it, when we are motivated to believe the erroneous information, and when the erroneous information comes from reliable sources. This is not to say that all of these factors must be present for a memory error to occur, but rather that the presence of more factors makes errors (and more substantial errors) more likely.

## Incomplete Records

At any given moment in time, there are thousands if not millions of bits of information in one's immediate surroundings that one might attend to. Even in the relatively calm and banal environment of an academic office, for example, there are normally sights (computers, books, lights, pens, papers, knick-knacks), sounds (computer fans and keystrokes, vents, office neighbors), and smells (dust, caffeinated beverages) that one might notice. Taking in all of this sensory information continually in a meaningful way is simply not possible. And even attempting to do so would mean that we had little time for anything else. So we do not constantly attend to all of this input. Instead, we pay attention to what matters in the moment. But because only parts of the available information are attended to, there is a necessarily incomplete record available

later. Schacter (1999, 2001) calls this the memory "sin" of absent-mindedness.

More precisely, sensory memory holds a huge amount of rich information but only for very short periods of time (see Cowan, 2008). From here, information that is attended to is processed by working memory and is thus more likely to end up in longer term store (Mulligan, 2008; Schacter, 2001), while information that is not attended to may well be lost forever (see Cowan, 2008). The particular role of attention in perceptual processes has been a major source of debate in perception research for decades (e.g., Mack & Rock, 1998; Rensink, 2002).

There are a variety of factors that affect the extent to which we pay attention to information, and whether this information is subsequently stored in memory. The first such factor is the simple availability of attention. Dividing attention between multiple tasks limits the amount of information that can be held on to for the long term (e.g., Craik, Govoni, Naveh-Benjamin, & Anderson, 1996). (This is something that frequent multitaskers might want to keep in mind.)

For example, Fernandes, Craik, Bialystok, and Kreuger (2007) gave subjects lists of words to learn and then repeat. Each list of 20 words was presented aurally and all the words in each list were from a single category (e.g., animals, tools). For some word lists, subjects were asked to make judgments about other, visually presented words (e.g., Is the object this word represents smaller or larger than a computer mouse?) at the same time as they listened to the word lists—that is, they were asked to encode the word lists under divided attention. Relative to conditions in which they were able to give the word lists their full attention, subjects were able to remember fewer words that they had learned in this divided attention condition. Divided attention has also been shown to influence retrieval, though not as strongly (Baddeley, Lewis, Eldridge, & Thomas, 1984).

In cases where sufficient attention is available, how that attention is utilized can make a substantial difference. Craik and Lockhart (1972) demonstrated that attending to shallow dimensions of stimuli, for example, whether to-be-remembered words are in *CAPITAL LETTERS* or *lowercase letters*, leads to relatively poor memory for those stimuli later. By contrast, deeper processing of the same information, for example by semantically categorizing words, leads to better memory. This helps to explain why meaningful events are typically more memorable than nonmeaningful events—they are processed more deeply (e.g., Elias & Perfetti, 1973). Deep processing of information apparently leads to better memory because it facilitates the making of connections between new and old information (see Reisberg, 2010).

Further evidence that attention can influence what is originally encoded comes from recent research on the memory implications of change blindness and inattention blindness (see Laney & Loftus, 2010). A person is change blind when he or she fails to notice a significant change in the visual environment. For example, Levin, Simons, Angelone, and Chabris (2002) brought undergraduate volunteers into a lab for an experiment. An experimenter briefly explained the study to each participant from behind a counter, and then ducked below the counter on the pretence of picking up a stack of study materials. During this very brief interlude, the experimenter changed places with another individual, who had been hiding behind the counter out of view of the subject. This second individual popped up with the study materials and continued the conversation with the subject, as if nothing unusual had happened. Fifteen of the 20 subjects in the study failed to notice the change of experimenters, even though they were in the middle of a face-to-face conversation when the change occurred.

Inattention blindness is a similar phenomenon, whereby a person fails to notice an event entirely. The classic experimental demonstration of this involves a woman in a gorilla suit who subjects fail to notice in a video—even though she walks right into the middle of the scene and waves—because they are attending to people dressed in white and intentionally ignoring people dressed in black (Simons & Chabris, 1999).

It is also worth noting that there is a related line of research showing that people are particularly bad at predicting the errors that have been demonstrated in change blindness and inattention blindness research. This "change blindness blindness" work shows that people fail to predict that they would be change blind in scenarios where change blindness is, in fact, quite likely (Beck, Levin, & Angelone, 2007).

The memory implications of change blindness and inattention blindness are perhaps obvious, for the reasons already discussed. That is, if one failed to notice something when it happened, it is hardly surprising that he or she fails to remember it later. And yet the potential implications of this very particular kind of memory failure are impressive. Recent research has shown that change blindness can lead people to falsely identify perpetrators of crime (Davies & Hine, 2007; Nelson, Laney, Bowman Fowler, Knowles, & Loftus, 2011).

For example, Nelson et al. (2011) showed subjects a video depicting a student stealing money from another student. After the thief takes the money and tucks it into a book, she is seen leaving the room and walking down the hall. For half of subjects, the thief is then switched for another actor as she walks around a corner. Subjects in the change conditions were quite unlikely to notice this change of actors (just 4.5% noticed), but it certainly did affect their later memory for the video. The subjects who experienced the change of actors were as likely to identify the innocent actor (35%) as the actual thief (36%) in a subsequent lineup. By comparison, just 9% of subjects in the no-change conditions identified the innocent actor and 64% correctly identified the thief.

## Biased Encoding

Because it is not possible (or desirable) to remember every detail about the world around us, we are left in a position where we are forced to make assumptions and inferences about that world. These assumptions save time and energy—think how inconvenient it would be if you could not make and rely upon assumptions about how, for example, cars work. When getting into a strange car you will likely need to adjust the seat and note whether there is a clutch, but you can safely assume that there will be a steering wheel, a gas pedal, and a review mirror (to say nothing of four wheels and an engine). But these assumptions also come at a cost. Because we tend not to notice aspects of events that fit with our expectations, we tend not to fully remember these details later (though we may think we do). Likewise, aspects of events that do *not* fit with our expectations, unless they earn special attention at the time of encoding, are unlikely to be remembered later. Note that biased encoding can lead to errors both of omission and of commission. Unnoticed details are not remembered accurately, while assumptions take over and fill in some details, and not necessarily correctly.

In an interesting demonstration of the importance of both attention and expectations, Friedman (1979) recorded subjects' eye movements as they carefully studied complex line drawings. The time that subjects spent looking at each detail of the drawings was determined by the appropriateness of each detail to the scene. So subjects spent approximately twice as long looking at details that did *not* fit in a scene (like a steamer trunk in an office scene) relative to those that did (like a chair). These attentional biases then led to biased memories. Details were changed between successive viewings of the pictures. Sometimes plausible details (like a sheep in a farm scene) were changed for other plausible details (like a goat). These changes tended not to be noticed or remembered. But other changes were less plausible (like a cow being replaced by a hippopotamus), and these were almost always noticed and remembered.

### Schemata

Researchers at least as far back as Bartlett (1932; see also Alba & Hasher, 1983) have noted that our knowledge and beliefs about the world influence what and how we perceive and thus remember. Many parts of human life are predictable, based on past experience. Our memory systems take advantage of this predictability, by forming and utilizing schemata. Schemata are memory templates, describing the typical elements of the events (and places, information, etc.) that we repeatedly experience. Because our lives are full of redundancies, this prior knowledge is, in fact, quite helpful in predicting what will happen in the future. Because I have been in hotel rooms before, I know to expect a bed, a bathroom, a Gideon's Bible, and probably a TV, and also not to expect an ice cream maker. This is because my hotel room schema tells me that the former are common and the latter is highly unlikely. Because of a hotel room schema, the average adult upon entering a hotel room will toss his or her suitcase on the bed without first stopping to comment on the presence of a bed or bathroom or TV. By contrast, a small child who does not yet have a hotel room schema (because of lack of experience across multiple hotel rooms) may well be excited about any of these things.

Brewer and Treyens (1981) tested this type of schematic knowledge experimentally. They asked each of 86 undergraduate subjects to wait in a graduate student office on the pretence of the experimenter needing to check whether the study was ready to run. After a delay of 35 seconds, the experimenter returned, escorted the subject to a different room, and informed the subject that the true purpose of the study was to test subjects' memory for the first room. Subjects' memories were guided by what might be called their academic office schemata. For example, although they were highly likely to remember schema-relevant items like a desk and

shelves, they were unlikely to remember items that were neither salient in themselves nor relevant to the office schema, like a picnic basket. But they were also likely to *falsely* remember seeing items that were highly relevant to the schema, like books, even when they had not actually been present in the room. Schemata amount to very convenient memory shortcuts, and our memory systems tend to rely on them. This reliance can lead to incomplete memories, because we do not notice and thus do not encode elements of our world that fit in with our schemata. For more on this problem, see the section on "Memory Reconstruction." Reliance on schemata can also lead to the blurring of similar and recurring events in our memories, and it can lead us to forget to perform repeated tasks, like taking medications (Schacter, 1999).

### Motivation to Remember

People who are motivated to remember something at the time the memory is encoded sometimes show better memory than those who are less motivated (Loftus & Wickens, 1970). Loftus and Wickens gave subjects a paired-associates memory test, where different words were rewarded to differing degrees at test. Subjects were more likely to remember high-value words than low-value words, especially when they were told the values of the words as they were learning them, rather than after the fact. This differential impact of motivation at encoding versus retrieval has been supported by other work (e.g., Naveh-Benjamin, Craik, Gavrilescu, & Anderson, 2000). This result is apparently counterintuitive, however, as outside judges assume that all motivation to remember is equivalent, no matter the timing (Kassam, Gilbert, Swencionis, & Wilson, 2009).

### Stress

Emotionality of to-be-remembered events is another key factor considered in other chapters in this book. To avoid redundancy, just one type of emotional response will be considered, briefly, here: stress. Unlike emotional arousal and even trauma, which normally improve the accuracy and fluency of memory (Conway et al., 1994; McNally, 2003; Peace & Porter, 2004; Shobe & Kihlstrom, 1997), stress has been shown to have a generally negative effect on memory (e.g., Morgan et al., 2004; see Reisberg & Heuer, 2007, for a review). Morgan et al. (2004) found that soldiers in an extreme wilderness and mock captivity training camp who experienced 40 minutes of extremely stressful interrogation were subsequently less able to identify their inter-rogators than other soldiers who experienced less stressful interrogation (see also Lieberman et al., 2005; Southwick, Morgan, Nicolauou, & Charney, 1997). That is, these highly stressed subjects had poor memories for the details of the interrogation that they had experienced, even though their inter-rogators had been demanding direct eye contact.

Even comparatively mild acute stressors like being asked to give a short speech can have a nega-tive effect on memory, as can drugs that work to mimic these stressors (Payne, Nadel, Britton, & Jacobs, 2004). In a meta-analysis of studies of stress and memory, Deffenbacher, Bornstein, Penrod, and McGorty (2004) found that stress was a reliable impediment to accurate memory.

Stress, unlike other types of emotionality, seems to produce a defensive response that leads people to focus their attention on something, anything, apart from the source of the stress (Reisberg & Heuer, 2007). In this sense, it is like other sources of mem-ory error discussed earlier. Stress alters attention and thus what is encoded and subsequently available for retrieval.

## Effort and Goals During Retrieval

Memory retrieval is not a simple event—some-thing that simply happens because we want to remember X—but rather a set of processes that are used in different ways depending on our particular goals. This is evident in the fact that sometimes it is worth searching hard in memory to try to recall exactly what happened and how, whereas at other times a vague notion of some element of the past suffices (see, e.g., Dalgleish et al., 2007; Davis & Friedman, 2007). In the former cases, relative to the latter cases, searching through memory can take time and effort (see Hockley, 2008). In addi-tion to tradeoffs between completeness and speed, there are tradeoffs between completeness and accu-racy. Specifically, in cases where we are only willing to accept details that we are sure are accurate, our memories are likely to be incomplete.

Retrieval cues are the specific reminders that link us back to specific memories (see Rajaram & Barber, 2008). These can come from the content of questions or from images, words, feelings, noises, or smells in the environment. One memory can also form a powerful retrieval cue for another memory. Some memories are easier to retrieve when one can match the circumstances in which the memory was encoded, a phenomenon called context-dependent memory (Eich, 1980). This explains why going back

to one's childhood hometown or school as an adult can bring up memories that one has not thought of for many years.

## Retrieval Failure

Memory retrieval happens smoothly and effort-lessly most of the time, yet we are often painfully aware of the occasional breakdowns in this process, called retrieval failures. Nearly every time we speak or write or recall a personal anecdote, we do so flu-ently. Yet failures to recall a specific word or event can sometimes seem to be constantly occurring. (Whenever I tell someone that I study memory, I am immediately regaled with tales of this type of memory failure.)

One highly familiar type of retrieval failure is a so-called tip-of-the-tongue (TOT) state, where one experiences a failure to recall a word (often a name) but has a strong subjective feeling of it being stored in memory but just out of reach (see Brown, 1991; Shafto, Burke, Stamatakis, Tam, & Tyler, 2007). The phenomenon seems to be universal, but it is particularly common in older adults and bilinguals. Because less frequently used words are more likely to lead to TOT states, research suggests that TOTs are likely caused by a breakdown of communication between semantic and phonological processes in the brain. That is, we know what we want to say, but we cannot quite remember how to go about saying it.

There is also evidence that the act of working to retrieve a particular piece of information can inhibit retrieval of other, closely related pieces of informa-tion (Anderson, Bjork, & Bjork, 1994; MacLeod, Saunders, & Chalmers, 2010). So-called retrieval-induced forgetting is normally demonstrated in studies where subjects learn lists of semantically related words, then are given practice at retrieving some (but not all) words from some (but not all) categories. Later, subjects are asked to recall the full lists of words. Typical results show improved mem-ory for rehearsed words but also, less intuitively, poorer memory for unrehearsed words from cat-egories where some words were rehearsed, relative to words from categories that were not rehearsed at all. Other research has shown similar effects with more complex materials (e.g., Koutstaal, Schachter, Johnson, & Galluccio, 1999; Shaw, Bjork, & Handal, 1995).

## Memory Reconstruction

Memory is not just accessed from storage; it is in many situations reconstructed at the point of retrieval (Barlett, 1932; see Davis & Loftus, 2007).

That is, bits of the original event are combined with information learned before or since, as well as current thoughts and feelings, to produce a new, conglomerated memory. Note that at this stage we have moved from primarily discussing errors of omission to primarily discussing errors of commission.

## Source Monitoring

Sometimes we remember information but fail to remember, or incorrectly remember, the source of this information. Daniel Schacter (1999, 2001) calls this the memory sin of "misattribution." The source monitoring framework (Johnson, Hastroudi, & Lindsay, 1993; Lindsay, 2008; Mitchell & Johnson, 2009) explains that although we often lack specific information about the source of a particular memory (because memories do not come with attached tags labeling them as real or imagined events, for example, or with other specific source information), we can and do make assumptions about the source of a memory based on certain qualitative and quantitative characteristics of that memory. So a remembered dream feels subjectively different than a remembered experience, and some information (e.g., a personal anecdote from one's childhood) is more likely to have come from some sources (one's mother) than others (the nightly news). These subjective characteristics and knowledge-based assumptions work well enough for accurate source monitoring most of the time, but, as with other memory systems, there are opportunities for error.

## Misinformation

The fact that information from multiple sources (including misidentified sources) can be blended to form reconstructed memories leads to the so-called misinformation effect (see Davis & Loftus, 2007). Misinformation is incorrect information that can be blended in with memory after the fact. The misinformation can be incorporated quickly after the original event, or much later, but the key is that this alteration of memory may occur without the knowledge of the rememberer, such that he or she may be entirely sure about a memory that is, in fact, quite compromised.

In typical studies of the misinformation effect, mock witnesses watch an event, often a crime, usually presented via slides or video (e.g., Loftus, Miller, & Burns, 1978). Later they are given extra information that is relevant to the event, often in the form of misleading questions or written summaries. Critically, this extra information is misinformation, and this misinformation leads to memory errors. (There is some debate in the field regarding whether the misinformation completely alters subjects' memories for the original event, or, for example, creates a separate alternate version of the memory that leads to confusion; see Ayers & Reder, 1998; Brainerd & Reyna, 2005.)

In an early demonstration of the power of leading questions to cause memory errors, Loftus (1975) showed subjects a film of a car accident and then later asked a series of questions about the crash. The critical question varied between groups. One group was asked, "Did you see a broken headlight?" while another group was asked, "Did you see the broken headlight?" The latter group was significantly more likely to answer in the affirmative, even though the two questions varied by only a single (and phonetically similar) word. The reason for that is that the second question is essentially informing the witness that there was a broken headlight, and asking whether he or she managed to notice it. The first question does not carry any presumption about the existence of a broken headlight. The similarity of the two questions means that there need not be any malice (or forensic context) for leading questions to distort memories—a simple slip of the tongue or mishearing of the question could suffice.

Recent research has sought to quantify the misinformation effect in new ways. Okado and Stark (2005) showed subjects events and then gave them misinformation about those events, while they were in a functional magnetic resonance imaging (fMRI) machine. Subjects were then given memory tests outside of the fMRI. The levels of activation in certain structures of the brain (notably the medial temporal lobe and prefrontal cortex) were different depending on whether subjects went on to report correct or erroneous information at test. That is, differences in brain activation during encoding predicted correct versus incorrect memory later.

The misinformation effect also happens outside of the laboratory (see Loftus & Castelle, 2000) and for memories that have nothing to do with crime (e.g., Wilson & French, 2008).

### SOCIAL INFLUENCES

In the last few years, one particular type of misinformation has come to the foreground: social misinformation. Research has shown that misinformation from co-witnesses to events has particular power with subjects. Although the effects of co-witness comments on memory have been studied for decades (e.g., Loftus, 1979; Loftus & Greene, 1980), there has been a recent explosion in this research area (e.g, French, Sutherland, & Garry, 2006; Gabbert, Memon, & Allan, 2003; Gabbert, Memon, Allan, & Wright, 2004; Hope, Ost, Gabbert, Healey, & Lenton, 2008; Takarangi, Parker, & Garry, 2006; Wright, Mathews, & Skagerberg, 2005).

Witnesses often assume that other witnesses have seen and heard the same events in the same way as themselves, and thus trust these other witnesses' memories as much as their own—especially where their own memory is incomplete. As such, conversations between co-witnesses (which do happen outside of the laboratory; see Paterson & Kemp, 2006) can be detrimental to the truth, by leading people to "remember" far more than they actually encoded.

A new technique for studying social misinformation has recently been fruitful. Called the "manipulation of overlapping rivalrous images by polarizing filters" (MORI) paradigm (Garry, French, Kinzett, & Mori, 2008; Mori, 2003), it allows for two subjects to sit in front of a single screen to watch a video. The two subjects assume (quite reasonably) that they are seeing the same images, but because each subject is wearing a different type of polarized glasses, they are in fact watching different videos (projected onto the same screen, much like for 3D movies). Because the two subjects believe they have seen exactly the same event, they are particularly likely to allow their co-witness's memories of the video to affect their own.

There is also new evidence that what witnesses say to other witnesses can also bias their own memories for the witnessed events (Kopietz, Echterhoff, Niemeier, Hellman, & Memon, 2009). That is, not only does hearing about other people's memories lead to bias but so does telling other people about one's own. Specifically, Kopietz et al. had subjects tell a fellow student about a bar brawl they had seen on video. Subjects were told either that their audience liked or disliked one of the characters involved in the fight. Subjects adjusted their telling of the story based on this information (though only if their audience was assumed to be sufficiently like themselves) and subsequently showed biased memory for the original video, in the direction of their own retelling.

## False Memory

The reconstructive nature of memory can have some extreme consequences. Sometimes memory is not merely distorted by suggestion but created out of whole cloth by suggestion. False memories can be created in laboratories using a variety of techniques (see Loftus & Bernstein, 2005), and they can also be a by-product of everyday memory reconstruction (e.g., Clancy, 2005; Sheen, Kemp, & Rubin, 2001; Taylor, 1965)—perhaps particularly in the context of techniques used by some therapists (see Loftus 1993, 2004; Loftus & Ketcham, 1994).

Suggestive techniques that have been used to produce false memories range from word list memorization tasks (e.g., Read, 1996; Roediger & McDermott, 1996) to computer-generated false feedback (e.g., Bernstein, Laney, Morris, & Loftus, 2005; Laney & Loftus, 2008) to intensive interviews and mock dream interpretation methods (Loftus & Pickrell, 1995; Mazzoni, Lombardo, Malvagia, & Loftus, 1999) to digitally altered images and hypnosis (e.g., Scoboria, Mazzoni, Kirsch, & Milling, 2002; Wade, Garry, Read, & Lindsay, 2002). But the reasons that the memory system falls for these tactics are not really different than the reasons for other types of errors already discussed. That is, these suggestions are believable (and thus lead to false memories) because one or more factors apply: They fill a void in our existing memories (i.e., we do not specifically remember the opposite to be true), they fit in with our expectations and are thus plausible, they link in with our existing knowledge, they come from reliable (and even authoritative) sources, and/or people are somehow motivated to believe them. (Note that, as with other types of errors, these factors need not all apply, but more and stronger factors can lead to more and larger errors.)

For example, Laney and Loftus (2008) used a false feedback manipulation to give undergraduate subjects false memories for three different emotional childhood events: being hospitalized overnight, catching their parents having sex, and witnessing a violent fight between their parents. In the false feedback procedure, subjects are asked to fill out a set of questionnaires on a particular topic—in this case emotional childhood events. They are then told (falsely) that their data will be entered into a special computer program that will provide specific feedback for them. This special computer program thus serves as the reliable and authoritative source of information in these studies. After a delay, subjects are given their "feedback" (which is, in fact, not specific at all but is the false memory manipulation) and then asked to fill out more questionnaires. Subjects frequently become more confident that they had experienced a particular event that had been suggested by the false feedback. They may also produce very specific detailed memory descriptions that conform to the feedback suggestions.

In this study, some 21% of manipulated subjects ended up forming false memories for one of the three false events (this ranged from 15% for the parent fight item to 38% for the hospitalized item). In other studies using the false feedback procedure with less controversial items, this proportion has ranged as high as 53% (Laney, Morris, Bernstein, Wakefield, & Loftus, 2008).

Because the suggested events in the Laney and Loftus (2008) study were at least a decade in the past for subjects, many did not have specific memories to contradict them. For some (but not all) subjects, suggestions that they had been hospitalized or even witnessed parental violence were plausible because they fit in with their general understanding of their own childhoods, even when they did not remember these events happening to them (cf. Lampinen, Meier, Arnal, & Leding, 2005). For other subjects, these events were less plausible or fit less well with their other memories, and were thus more likely to be rejected. (For further discussion of plausibility in the formation of false memories, see Hart & Schooler, 2006; Mazzoni, Loftus, & Kirsch, 2001.) These subjects were probably not particularly motivated to believe any of the three false events in this study, but this merely suggests that there is scope for even more people to believe (and believe more strongly) in contexts where they are motivated to believe (see Sharman & Calacouris, 2010).

Once established, false memories can be extremely compelling for those who have them (see Loftus & Bernstein, 2005). This leads to great difficulties in telling established false memories apart from true memories. This is particularly problematic in court cases where one party claims to remember a horrible event (like child sexual abuse), while another party claims that no such event occurred. Researchers have identified numerous possible characteristics on which true and false memories might theoretically be distinguished—from quantity of detail and confidence to consequentiality and emotional content—but as yet no definitive factor has been found that categorically discriminates between true and false memories. That is, false memories, like true memories, can be confidently held, detailed, long lasting, consequential, and even emotional, such that none of these characteristics can be used to guarantee a particular memory's truth (Laney & Loftus, 2008; Laney, Bowman Fowler, Nelson, Bernstein, & Loftus, 2008, Laney, Morris et al., 2008; Loftus & Bernstein, 2005). As such, when memory errors are at their most extreme, they can also be very difficult to correct.

## Conclusion

Because memory is not a static storehouse of information, but rather a set of keenly adapted dynamic processes, it is infinitely more efficient for our everyday needs. This efficiency has a downside, though, in the form of proneness to various types of errors, including errors of omission and of commission. These errors show broad commonalities, in that they tend to result from the combination of incomplete original information and inferences (based on experience or assumptions), plus perhaps confusion about the sources of different bits of information.

## References

Alba, J. W., & Hasher, L. (1983). Is memory schematic? *Psychological Bulletin, 93*, 203–231.

Anderson, M. C., Bjork, R. A., & Bjork, E. L. (1994). Remembering can cause forgetting: Retrieval dynamics in long-term memory. *Journal of Experimental Psychology: Learning, Memory, and Cognition, 20*, 1063–1087.

Ayers, M. S., & Reder, L. M. (1998). A theoretical review of the misinformation effect: Predictions from an activation-based memory model. *Psychonomic Bulletin and Review, 5*, 1–21.

Baddeley, A. D., Lewis, V., Eldridge, M., & Thompson, N. (1984). Attention and retrieval from long-term memory. *Journal of Experimental Psychology: General, 113*, 518–540.

Bartlett, F. C. (1932). *Remembering*. Cambridge, England: Cambridge University Press.

Beck, M. R., Levin, D. T., & Angelone, B. (2007). Change blindness blindness: Believes about the roles of intention and scene complexity in change detection. *Consciousness and Cognition, 16*, 31–51.

Bernstein, D. M., Laney, C., Morris, E. K., & Loftus, E. F. (2005). False memories about food can lead to food avoidance. *Social Cognition, 23*, 11–34.

Brainerd, C. J., & Reyna, V. F. (2005). *The science of false memory*. New York: Oxford University Press.

Brewer, W. F., & Treyens, J. C. (1981). Role of schemata in memory for places. *Cognitive Psychology, 13*, 207–230.

Brown, A. S. (1991). A review of tip of the tongue experience. *Psychological Bulletin, 109*, 79–91.

Clancy, S. A. (2005). *Abducted: How people come to believe they were kidnapped by aliens*. Cambridge, MA: Harvard University Press.

Conway, M. A., Anderson, S., Larsen, S., Donnelly, C., Mc Daniel, M., McClelland, A. G. R., ... Logie, R. H. (1994). The formation of flashbulb memories. *Memory and Cognition, 22*, 326–343.

Cowan, N. (2008). Sensory memory. In H. L. Roediger, III & J. H. Byrne (Eds.), *Learning and memory: A comprehensive reference* (Vol. 2, pp. 23–32). London: Academic Press.

Craik, F. I. M., Govoni, R., Naveh-Benjamin, M., & Anderson, N. D. (1996). The effects of divided attention on encoding and retrieval processes in human memory. *Journal of Experimental Psychology: General, 125*, 159–180.

Craik, F. I. M., & Lockhart, R. S. (1972). Levels of processing: A framework for memory research. *Journal of Verbal Learning and Verbal Behavior, 11*, 671–684.

Dalgleish, T., Williams, J. M. G., Golden, A. J., Perkins, N., Barrett, L. F., Barnard, P. J., ... Watkins, E. (2007). Reduced specificity of autobiographical memory and depression: The role of executive control. *Journal of Experimental Psychology: General*, *136*, 23–42.

Davies, G., & Hine, S. (2007). Change blindness and eyewitness testimony. *Journal of Psychology: Interdisciplinary and Applied*, *14*, 423–434.

Davis, D., & Friedman, R. D. (2007). Memory for conversation: The orphan child of witness memory researchers. In M. P. Toglia, J. D. Read, D. F. Ross, & R. C. L. Lindsay (Eds.) *The handbook of eyewitness psychology. Volume 1: Memory for events* (pp. 3–52). Mahwah, NJ: Erlbaum.

Davis, D., & Loftus, E. F. (2007) Internal and external sources of misinformation in adult witness memory. In M. P. Toglia, J. D. Read, D. F. Ross, & R. C. L. Lindsay (Eds.), *The handbook of eyewitness psychology. Volume 1: Memory for events* (pp. 195–237). Mahwah, NJ: Erlbaum.

Deffenbacher, K. A., Bornstein, B. H., Penrod, S. D., & McGorty, E. K. (2004). A meta-analytic review of the effects of high stress on eyewitness memory. *Law and Human Behavior*, *28*, 687–706.

Eich, J. E. (1980). The cue-dependent nature of state dependent retrieval. *Memory and Cognition*, *8*, 157–173.

Elias, C. S., & Perfetti, C. A. (1973). Encoding task and recognition memory: The importance of semantic encoding. *Journal of Experimental Psychology*, *99*, 151–156.

Fernandes, M. A., Craik, F., Bialystok, E., & Kreuger, S. (2007). Effects of bilingualism, aging, and semantic relatedness on memory under divided attention. *Canadian Journal of Experimental Psychology*, *61*, 128–141.

French, L., Sutherland, R., & Garry, M. (2006). Discussion affects memory for true and false childhood events. *Applied Cognitive Psychology*, *20*, 671–680.

Friedman, A. (1979). Framing pictures: The role of knowledge in automatized encoding and memory for gist. *Journal of Experimental Psychology: General*, *130*, 316–355.

Gabbert, F., Memon, A., & Allan, K. (2003). Memory conformity: Can eyewitnesses influence each other's memories for an event? *Applied Cognitive Psychology*, *17*, 533–543.

Gabbert, F., Memon, A., Allan, K., & Wright, D. B. (2004). Say it to my face: Examining the effects of socially encountered misinformation. *Legal and Criminological Psychology*, *9*, 215–227.

Garry, M., French, L., Kinzett, T., & Mori, K. (2008). Eyewitness memory following discussions: Using the MORI technique with a Western sample. *Applied Cognitive Psychology*, *22*, 431–439.

Hart, R. E., & Schooler, J. W. (2006). Increasing belief in the experience of an invasive procedure that never happened: The role of plausibility and schematicity. *Applied Cognitive Psychology*, *20*, 661–669.

Hockley, W. E. (2008). Memory search: A matter of time. In H. L. Roediger, III & J. H. Byrne (Eds.), *Learning and memory: A comprehensive reference* (Vol. *2*, pp. 417–444). London: Academic Press.

Hope, L., Ost, J., Gabbert, F., Healey, S., & Lenton, E. (2008). "With a little help from my friends...": The role of co-witness relationship in susceptibility to misinformation. *Acta Psychologica*, *12*, 76–484.

James, W. (1890). *The principles of psychology* (Vol. 1). New York: Holt.

Johnson, M. K., Hashtroudi, S., & Lindsay, D. S., (1993). Source monitoring. *Psychological Bulletin*, *114*, 3–28.

Kassam, K. S., Gilbert, D. T., Swencionis, J. K., & Wilson, T. D. (2009). Misconceptions of memory: The Scooter Libby effect. *Psychological Science*, *20*, 551–552.

Kopietz, R., Echterhoff, G., Niemeier, S., Hellmann, J. H., & Memon, A. (2009). Audience-congruent biases in eyewitness memory and judgment: Influence of a co-witness' liking for a suspect. *Social Psychology*, *40*, 133–144.

Koutstall, W., Schacter, D. L., Johnson, M. K., &. Galluccio, L. (1999). Facilitation and impairment of event memory produced by photograph review. *Memory and Cognition*, *27*, 478–493.

Lampinen, J. M., Meier, C. R., Arnal, J. D., & Leding, J. K. (2005). Compelling untruths: Content borrowing and vivid false memories. *Journal of Experimental Psychology: Learning, Memory, and Cognition*, *31*, 954–963.

Laney, C., Bowman Fowler, N., Nelson, K. J., Bernstein, D. B., & Loftus, E. F. (2008). The persistence of false beliefs. *Acta Psychologica*, *129*, 190–197.

Laney, C., & Loftus, E. F. (2008). Emotional content of true and false memories. *Memory*, *16*, 500–516.

Laney, C., & Loftus, E. F. (2010). Change blindness and eyewitness testimony. In G. M. Davies & D. B. Wright (Eds.), *Current issues in applied memory research* (pp. 142–159). Hove, England: Psychology Press.

Laney, C., Morris, E. K., Bernstein, D. M., Wakefield, B. M., & Loftus, E. F. (2008). Asparagus, a love story: Healthier eating could be just a false memory away. *Experimental Psychology*, *55*, 291–300.

Levin, D. T., Simons, D. J., Angelone, B. L., & Chabris, C. F. (2002). Memory for centrally attended changing objects in an incidental real-world change detection paradigm. *British Journal of Psychology*, *93*, 289–302.

Lieberman, H. R., Bathalon, G. P., Falco, C. M., Kramer, F. M., Morgan, C. A., III, & Niro, P. (2005). Severe decrements in cognition function and mood induced by sleep loss, heat, dehydration, and undernutrition during simulated combat. *Biological Psychiatry*, *57*, 422–429.

Lindsay, D. S. (2008). Source monitoring. In H. L. Roediger, III & J. H. Byrne, *Learning and memory: A comprehensive reference* (Vol. *2*, pp. 325–347). London: Academic Press.

Loftus, E. F. (1975). Leading questions and the eyewitness report. *Cognitive Psychology*, *7*, 560–574.

Loftus, E. F. (1979). *Eyewitness testimony*. Cambridge, MA: Harvard University Press.

Loftus, E. F. (1993). The reality of repressed memories. *American Psychologist*, *48*, 518–537.

Loftus, E. F. (2004). Dispatch from the (un)civil memory wars. *Lancet*, *364*, 20–21.

Loftus, E. F., & Bernstein, D. M. (2005). Rich false memories. In A. F. Healy (Ed.), *Experimental cognitive psychology and its applications* (pp. 101–113). Washington, DC: American Psychological Association Press.

Loftus, E. F., & Castelle, G. (2000). Crashing memories in legal cases. In P. J. VanKoppen & N. H. M. Roos (Eds.), *Rationality, information and progress in law and psychology* (pp. 115–127). Maastricht, The Netherlands: Maastricht University Press.

Loftus, E. F., & Greene, E. (1980). Warning: Even memory for faces can be contagious. *Law and Human Behavior*, *4*, 323–334.

Loftus, E. F., & Ketcham, K. (1994). *The myth of repressed memory*. New York: St. Martin's Press.

Loftus, E. F., Miller, D. G., & Burns, H. J. (1978). Semantic integration of verbal information into a visual memory. *Journal of Experimental Psychology: Human Learning and Memory, 4*, 19–31.

Loftus, E. F., & Pickrell, J. E. (1995). The formation of false memories. *Psychiatric Annals, 25*, 720–725.

Loftus, G. R., & Wickens, T. D. (1970). Effect of incentive on storage and retrieval processes. *Journal of Experimental Psychology: General, 85*, 141–147.

Mack, A., & Rock, I. (1998). *Inattentional blindness*. Cambridge, MA: MIT Press.

MacLeod, M. D., Saunders, J., & Chalmers, L. (2010). Retrieval-induced forgetting: The unintended consequences of unintended forgetting. In G. M. Davies & D. B. Wright (Eds.), *Current issues in applied memory research* (pp. 50–71). Hove, England: Psychology Press.

Mazzoni, G. A. L., Loftus, E. F., & Kirsch, I. (2001). Changing beliefs about implausible autobiographical events: A little plausibility goes a long way. *Journal of Experimental Psychology: Applied, 7*, 51–59.

Mazzoni, G. A. L., Lombardo, P., Malvagia, S., & Loftus, E. F. (1999). Dream interpretation and false beliefs. *Professional Psychology: Research and Practice, 30*, 45–50.

McNally, R. J. (2003). *Remembering trauma*. Cambridge, MA: Harvard University Press.

Mitchell, K. J., & Johnson, M. K. (2009). Source monitoring 15 years later: What have we learned from fMRI about the neural mechanisms of source monitoring? *Psychological Bulletin, 135*, 638–677.

Morgan, C. A., Hazlett, G., Doran, A., Garrett, S., Hoyt, G., Thomas, P., ... Southwich, S. M. (2004). Accuracy of eyewitness memory for persons encountered during exposure to highly intense stress. *International Journal of Law and Psychiatry, 27*, 265–279.

Mori, K. (2003). Surreptitiously projecting different movies to two subsets of viewers. *Behavior Research Methods, Instruments, and Computers, 35*, 599–604.

Mulligan, N. W. (2008). Attention and memory. In H. L. Roediger, III & J. H. Byrne (Eds.), *Learning and memory: A comprehensive reference* (Vol. 2, pp. 7–22). London: Academic Press.

Naveh-Benjamin, M., Craik, F. I. M., Gavrilescu, D., & Anderson, N. D. (2000). Asymmetry between encoding and retrieval processes: Evidence from divided attention and a calibration analysis. *Memory and Cognition, 28*, 965–976.

Nelson, K. J., Laney, C., Bowman Fowler, K., Knowles, E. D., & Loftus, E. F. (2011). Change blindness can cause mistaken eyewitness identification. *Legal and Criminological Psychology, 16, 62–74*.

Okado, Y., & Stark, C. E. L. (2005). Neural activity during encoding predicts false memories created by misinformation. *Learning and Memory, 12*, 3–11.

Paterson, H. M., & Kemp, R. I. (2006). Co-witnesses talk: A survey of eyewitness discussion. *Psychology, Crime and Law, 12*, 181–191.

Payne, J. D., Nadel, L., Britton, W. B., & Jacobs, W. J. (2004). The biopsychology of trauma and memory. In D. Reisberg & P. Hertel (Eds.), *Memory and emotion. Series in affective science* (pp. 76–128). New York: Oxford University Press.

Peace, K. A., & Porter, S. (2004). A longitudinal investigation of the reliability of memory for trauma and other emotional experiences. *Applied Cognitive Psychology, 18*, 1143–1159.

Rajaram, S., & Barber, S. J. (2008). Retrieval processes in memory. In H. L. Roediger, III & J. H. Byrne (Eds.), *Learning and memory: A comprehensive reference* (Vol. 2, pp. 261–283). London: Academic Press.

Read, J. D. (1996). From a passing thought to a false memory in 2 minutes: Confusing real and illusory events. *Psychonomic Bulletin and Review, 3*, 105–111.

Rensink, R. A. (2002). Change detection. *Annual Review of Psychology, 53*, 245–277.

Reisberg, D. (2010). *Cognition: Exploring the science of the mind* (4th ed.). New York: W. W. Norton.

Reisberg, D., & Heuer, F. (2007). The influence of emotion on memory in forensic settings. In M. P. Toglia , J. D. Read, D. F. Ross , & R. C. L. Lindsay (Eds.) *The handbook of eyewitness psychology. Volume 1: Memory for events* (pp. 81–116). London: Erlbaum.

Roediger, H. L., III & McDermott, K. B. (1996). Creating false memories: Remembering words not presented in lists. *Journal of Experimental Psychology: Learning, Memory and Cognition, 21*, 803–814.

Schacter, D. L. (1999). The seven sins of memory: Insights from psychology and cognitive neuroscience. *American Psychologist, 54*, 182–203.

Schacter, D. L. (2001). *The seven sins of memory: How the mind forgets and remembers*. New York: Houghton Mifflin.

Scoboria, A., Mazzoni, G. A. L., Kirsch, I., & Milling, L. S. (2002). Immediate and persisting effects of misleading questions and hypnosis on memory reports. *Journal of Experimental Psychology: Applied, 8*, 26–32.

Shafto, M. A., Burke, D. M., Stamatakis, E. A., Tam, P. P., & Tyler, L. K. (2007). On the tip-of-the-tongue: Neural correlates of increased word-finding failures in normal aging. *Journal of Cognitive Neuroscience, 19*, 2060–2070.

Sharman, S. J., & Calacouris, S. (2010). Do people's motives influence their susceptibility to imagination inflation? *Experimental Psychology, 57*, 77–82.

Shaw, J. S., Bjork, R. A., & Handal, A. (1995). Retrieval-induced forgetting in an eyewitness memory paradigm. *Psychonomic Bulletin and Review, 2*, 249–253.

Sheen, M., Kemp, S., & Rubin, D. (2001). Twins dispute memory ownership: A new false memory phenomenon. *Memory and Cognition, 29*, 779–788.

Shobe, K. K., & Kihlstrom, J. F. (1997). Is traumatic memory special? *Current Directions in Psychological Science, 6*, 70–74.

Simons, D. J., & Chabris, C. F. (1999). Gorillas in our midst: Sustained inattentional blindness for dynamic events. *Perception, 28*, 1059–1074.

Southwick, S. M., Morgan, C. A., Nicolaou, A. L., & Charney, D. S. (1997). Consistency of memory for combat-related traumatic events in veterans of Operation Desert Storm. *American Journal of Psychiatry, 154*, 173–177.

Takarangi, M. K. T., Parker, S., & Garry, M. (2006). Modernizing the misinformation effect: The development of a new stimulus set. *Applied Cognitive Psychology, 20*, 583–590.

Taylor, F. K. (1965). Cryptomnesia and plagiarism. *British Journal of Psychiatry, 4*, 1111–1118.

Wade, K. A., Garry, M., Read, J. D., & Lindsay, S. A. (2002). A picture is worth a thousand lies. *Psychonomic Bulletin and Review, 9*, 597–603.

Wilson, K., & French, C. C. (2008). Misinformation effects for psychic readings and belief in the paranormal. *Imagination, Cognition and Personality, 28*, 155–171.

Wright, D. B., Mathews, S. A., & Skagerberg, E. M. (2005). Social recognition memory: The effect of other people's responses for previously seen and unseen items. *Journal of Experimental Psychology: Applied, 11*, 200–209.

## Further Reading

Baddely, A. D. (1990). *Human memory: Theory and practice.* Needham Heights, MA: Allyn & Bacon.

Craik, F. I. M., & Lockhart, R. S. (1972). Levels of processing: A framework for memory research. *Journal of Verbal Learning and Verbal Behavior, 11*, 671–684.

Loftus, E. F. (1993). The reality of repressed memories. *American Psychologist, 48*, 518–537.

Schacter, D. L. (2001). The seven sins of memory: Insights from psychology and cognitive neuroscience. *American Psychologist, 54*, 182–203.

# 17

# Through the SCAPE Looking Glass— Sources of Performance and Sources of Attribution

Jason P. Leboe-McGowan *and* Bruce W. A. Whittlesea

**Abstract**

In the present chapter, we provide a summary of the major features of the Selective Construction and Preservation of Experience (SCAPE) framework of memory (Whittlesea, 1997) and describe how that framework differs from many other conventional approaches to memory. We also provide a review of the past 15 years of research inspired by the SCAPE framework, organizing the discussion into the two primary functions of mind identified by that framework: the production function and the evaluation function. Under the *production* function, we focus on the value of applying the SCAPE framework to explain immediate priming phenomena. Under the *evaluation* function, we identify the common processes underlying feelings of familiarity, recollective experiences, and other subjective judgments that people make in the context of nonremembering tasks. The broad goal of this discussion is to orient the reader to the impressive similarity in principles that guide mental functioning across a wide range of tasks and contexts.

**Key Words:** memory, immediate priming, transfer-appropriate processing, familiarity, recall, attribution

Approximately 15 years ago, the second author of the current chapter outlined a unique approach to mind and memory (Whittlesea, 1997), which he called the SCAPE (Selective Construction and Preservation of Experience) framework. This framework was unique in that it flatly contradicted many of the most broadly accepted views about memory. As of now, it remains in direct conflict with most conventional approaches to memory. Thus, this chapter offers a timely opportunity to present a case for the utility of the SCAPE framework over its competitors, with a particular emphasis on recent empirical developments in cognitive psychology. It also offers us an opportunity to describe the critical refinements to the framework that have occurred over the past dozen years or so.

## The Nature of Memory Under the SCAPE Framework

Perhaps the most controversial premise of the SCAPE framework is that memory has only one function: the preservation of specific experiences. This idea that memory contains prior processing episodes was borrowed from others (Brooks, 1978; Craik & Lockhart, 1972; Jacoby, 1983; Kolers & Roediger, 1984) and so is not an especially novel or contentious feature of the framework on its own. What makes the SCAPE framework provocative is the contention that memory contains *only* representations of the cognitive operations that one engages in during specific events. Without denying that memory generates these *episodic representations*, most other contemporary approaches ascribe substantially more sophisticated capacities to memory. Typically, cognitive scientists have also attributed to memory the inherent function of generating summary representations across multiple experiences. The implication is that memory automatically preserves both the details of specific experiences *and* also computes the common properties associated with classes of specific experiences. In consequence, one can remember details about the specific experience of having visited the dentist and also can make statements about what typically occurs during visits to the dentist. This distinction between *remembering* an event and *knowing* what is common across multiple events of the same type is taken as fundamental in many modern conceptualizations of memory's structure and function. This distinction lies at the root of multiple systems approaches to memory, such as the semantic/episodic (Schacter, 1987; Tulving, 1985), types/tokens (Anderson, 1996; Kanwisher, 1987), and the declarative/nondeclarative frameworks (Squire & Zola-Morgan, 1991; Zola-Morgan & Squire, 1993). These approaches to memory are incompatible with SCAPE. Under the SCAPE framework, the same episodic representations guide all instances of thought and behavior. Any form of knowledge that emerges from multiple episodes preserved in memory derives through making contact with those episodes, in parallel. Such knowledge does not require a separate form of representation in memory that contains abstract information about types of events. The SCAPE framework presumes that representations of specific experiences form the basic unit of knowledge and consist of three components: the *stimulus* that is the focus of current processing, the *task* or purpose for which one is engaging that stimulus, and the *context* within which processing of that stimulus occurs. These combined features of a past or current episode form what Whittlesea (1997) referred to as a stimulus complex.

## Production Versus Evaluation

It is seductive to form distinctions between types of cognitive process and, in turn, to treat those distinctions as qualitatively different psychological functions. The distinction between using memory to recall specific prior experiences (*remembering*) and using memory to express general knowledge associated with many prior experiences (*knowing*) provides one example. Another, related example is the distinction between conscious and unconscious influences of memory. One can report the capital of Australia in response to a trivia question and consciously remember when they learned that fact. Alternatively, one might generate the correct answer without any remembrance of the source of that knowledge. Such distinctions are plentiful in cognitive psychology (see also serial versus parallel processing; automatic versus controlled processing; recollection versus familiarity; algorithmic processing versus instance retrieval; short-term memory versus long-term memory). Under the SCAPE framework, primary emphasis is on the contrast between *production* and *evaluation* as the most essential and qualitatively distinct functions of mind.

When engaging the *production* function, one generates some reaction to present circumstances by making contact with similar episodes preserved in memory. That reaction can be purely mental, reflecting some comprehension of the present (e.g., Here comes the bus!). Alternatively, the reaction might include an overt motor response, such as catching a flying ball. In either case, an act of production is defined by the current stimulus complex (encountering a stimulus for some purpose in some context) as the primary object of current processing. By contrast, when engaging the *evaluation* function, the object of processing is processing itself. It involves a reflection on the nature and quality of the act of production just performed. Within the SCAPE framework, the evaluation function of mind is the origin of all feeling states and subjective judgments. A more detailed description of the evaluation function will be provided later in this chapter. Briefly, however, affective states emerge depending on an evaluation as to whether an act of production unfolded in a way that is consistent with one's expectations as to how that production should have unfolded based on similar prior experiences. That affective state then motivates one's efforts to identify the source of the expectancy violation. In such cases, the evaluation function leads the individual to arrive at some attitude as to the significance of the current production. The attitude that emerges can relate to any number of a multitude of possible levels of analysis. For example, evaluation of one's processing of some stimulus, such as a person's face, might stimulate an inference about that stimulus directly, leading one to experience that person as more or less attractive or that her hairstyle does or does not suit her. In another context, such an evaluation might terminate in a judgment about whether one has encountered that person before. In still other circumstances, that type of evaluation might guide one's attitude regarding the other person's likely value as an employee.

## Production in Remembering and Nonremembering Tasks

Under the SCAPE framework, a person is in a state of remembering whenever she is convinced that her current processing is under the control of a specific event from her past. Furthermore, we conceive of *memory* as controlling the remembering process, but the two words should not be used interchangeably. Memory perpetually controls current processing, but remembering only occurs when one develops an attitude that her processing is being guided by a prior experience. We prefer this definition of remembering because it is neutral regarding the accuracy of the rememberer's interpretation of her current processing. A person might incorrectly think that some detail that she remembers about a past event actually originated from that experience, as in studies of the misinformation effect (Lindsay & Johnson, 1989; Loftus, Miller, & Burns, 1978; Loftus & Palmer, 1974; McCloskey & Zaragoza, 1985). It is also possible for a person to remember an entire event as having actually occurred either because she was misled (Hyman & Pentland, 1996; Lindsay, Hagen, Read, Wade, & Garry, 2004; Loftus & Pickrell, 1995) or because she mistook a previously imagined event for a real experience (Johnson, 1988). Separate from the range of errors that can occur, we consider it sensible to treat people's distorted or even entirely false conceptions of their past as valid instances of remembering. Moreover, a person may bring to mind details about a prior event, but simply bringing to mind those details does not necessarily constitute an act of remembering. A person might describe a trip to the zoo as part of a creative writing exercise that overlaps perfectly with an event that occurred in her life. Failing to experience that creative storytelling as originating from an actual experience disqualifies the description of those events as a legitimate case of remembering. This approach highlights the subjective nature of remembering in a way that is analogous to most cognitive scientists' view of perception. Experiencing a perceptual illusion reveals the subjective nature of perception, yet they are as much instances of perception as any other. Likewise, a false recollection is no less an instance of remembering than one that is perfectly accurate.

Inherent in the previous discussion about how *remembering* ought to be defined is that there are clear differences between a remembering experience and an influence of memory that is not accompanied by the conviction that current processing is under the control of a previous experience. This difference has dominated theoretical approaches to memory for most of the past three decades, through the development of separate-systems approaches by Tulving (2002), Squire (1992), and others (Gabrieli, 1998; Graf & Schacter, 1985; McClelland, McNaughton, & O'Reilly, 1995; Nadel & Moscovitch, 1997). Under these approaches, separate systems control conscious remembering and the use of knowledge preserved in memory to perform nonremembering tasks, such as those that require motor skills (e.g., riding a bicycle or using a fork) or object categorization (e.g., being able to identify bicycles and forks). Although other ways of subdividing memory often accompany these approaches, the most common and agreed-upon basis for separate memory systems is the distinction between using memory for remembering (also known as explicit memory) versus influences of memory that occur in the absence of conscious remembering (also known as implicit memory). These separate-systems approaches draw much of their support from observations that different brain structures underlie remembering and the use of memory to perform nonremembering tasks. Supporters of the separate-systems perspective also point to demonstrations that different factors contribute to success in performing remembering and nonremembering tasks. For example, the time interval between a study phase and a subsequent memory test dramatically impairs successful recognition of studied items (an explicit memory test), but it does not impact success in completing word fragments with studied items (an implicit memory test; Tulving, Schacter, & Stark, 1982). That is, it seems as though remembering processes follow different rules than other influences of memory.

For proponents of the separate-systems approach, the most critical difference between the use of memory for remembering and the use of memory to perform nonremembering tasks is that remembering relies on representations of specific experiences, whereas using memory for other purposes typically relies on knowledge that is not tied to any specific past event. A logical inference, then, is that the system for remembering contains representations for specific experiences, whereas the system for performing nonremembering tasks contains abstract representations that preserve only the properties that are common across types of events and do not contain features that are idiosyncratic to particular experiences. Such representations include constructs, such as prototypes, logogens, schemas, and the like, which we made reference to earlier.

Contrary to these approaches, a major premise of the SCAPE framework is that a single memory system controls the use of memory for remembering and nonremembering purposes. Biologically, that memory system is equivalent to the brain operating as a unit, despite the divisions of labor that can be observed when investigating separate brain areas within that system. Different uses of memory will naturally arise from different brain structures, but the remembering/nonremembering distinction is only one example of a staggering number of specializations that may be identified by studying the brain as a collection of distinct structures. Few would deny that remembering relies on different brain areas than visual perception, that visual perception relies on different brain areas than speech comprehension, and that comprehension of a psychology journal article involves different patterns of brain activity than comprehension of an article in *People* magazine. Where the SCAPE framework diverges from other contemporary approaches to cognitive processing is in the premise that *none* of the differences in patterns of brain activity that can be observed are informative as to the most basic principles of mind. Instead, these differences are seen as a natural outcome of the broad diversity of circumstances that people find themselves in. Processing differs across tasks, stimuli, and contexts; therefore, differences in patterns of brain activity are expected but are not useful for revealing the common mental functions that underlie disparate forms of mental and behavioral experience. Similarly, observations that the factors which improve success in remembering are often different from those that improve success in the performance of nonremembering tasks do not necessitate carving up memory into separate subsystems. Different factors may determine success in remembering and nonremembering tasks because their *requirements* for success often differ, in the same way that the neurological requirements of different mental activities differ. Indeed, when remembering and nonremembering tasks require similar types of processing, it is common to observe similarities in the factors that promote successful performance (MacLeod & Masson, 2000; Roediger & Blaxton, 1987; Roediger, Weldon, & Challis, 1989; Vriezen, Moscovitch, & Bellos, 1995).

To a great extent, the SCAPE framework developed out of a profound skepticism regarding the popular view that memory is necessarily comprised of multiple subsystems. Particularly objectionable was the assumption that memory possesses the capacity to abstract the common properties across similar experiences and to represent those properties in a separate form (and a separate system) from the system that represents specific experiences. In his original description of the framework, Whittlesea (1997) made reference to several studies which revealed that particular experiences control performance on nonremembering tasks, such as categorization and perceptual identification tasks, just as they determine performance on remembering tasks (Brooks, 1978; Medin & Schaffer, 1978; Nosofsky, 1984; Whittlesea, 1987; Whittlesea & Brooks, 1988; Whittlesea, Brooks, & Westcott, 1994; Whittlesea & Cantwell, 1987; Whittlesea & Dorken, 1993; Whittlesea & Wright, 1997; Wright & Whittlesea, 1998). Other research has since further confirmed that specific events control performance of these nonremembering tasks across a range of conditions (Barsalou, 2008; Jamieson & Mewhort, 2009; Johnstone & Shanks, 2001; Smith & Medin, 2002). To avoid redundancy with these earlier writings, in the current chapter we will illustrate the central role of particular experiences in guiding current performance of nonremembering tasks in the context of *immediate priming*.

## Traditional Approaches to Immediate Priming

In immediate priming experiments, researchers expose participants to a series of trials, usually consisting of two critical stimulus events: a prime followed by a probe. Collections of trials, which may be presented as a block or randomly intermixed, are designed to contrast the effect of some association between the prime and the probe on generation of a response to the probe. For instance, on some trials the prime and probe might be matching colored rectangles, whereas on other trials the prime and probe might be rectangles that differ in color. The task might then be to identify the probe's color by making a voice response or a button-press. The mean response times and proportion of accurate responses to the probe would then be separately computed for trials corresponding to each of the color-same and color-different conditions. *Priming* occurs when performance differs in responding to the probe (participants are faster, slower, less accurate, or more accurate) when a similarity exists between the prime and probe than when the prime and probe differ on the critical dimension. Many studies have investigated priming effects on nonremembering tasks across relatively long time intervals, ranging from several minutes (Jacoby & Witherspoon, 1982) to a week (Tulving et al., 1982) to a year (Kolers, 1976;

for a review of these relatively long-term priming effects, see Roediger, 2003). In contrast, immediate priming procedures measure these effects across intervals that are rarely longer than a few seconds. We will focus on this subcategory of priming effects in the current chapter because it is within this domain that cognitive psychologists are most convinced as to the role of abstract representations.

Immediate priming effects provide a measure of the influence of a very recent event on current performance of a task. The most common interpretation of these effects is that exposure to a prime event activates or inhibits abstract representations that exist for the purpose of signaling the perceiver about the appearance of particular stimulus features (Forster & Davis, 1984; Houghton & Tipper, 1994; Monsell, 1985; Morton, 1969, 1979; Paap, Newsome, & Noel, 1984). For example, the phenomenon of repetition priming, in which participants are able to identify a stimulus more quickly after a recent exposure (Forbach, Stanners, & Hochhaus, 1974; Kirsner & Smith, 1974; Scarborough, Cortese, & Scarborough, 1977; Scarborough, Gerard, & Cortese, 1979), is frequently interpreted as occurring because the previous encounter with the stimulus raised the activation of its lexical representation above resting level and closer to the threshold level necessary to invoke an identification response (Monsell, 1985; Morton, 1969). Similarly, participants often exhibit faster responding to a stimulus that is meaningfully related to one recently encountered (Meyer & Schvaneveldt, 1971). This phenomenon of semantic priming (for reviews, see Hutchison, 2003; Neely, 1991) was explained as resulting from activation spreading from the representation of the prime stimulus to semantically related representations (Collins & Loftus, 1975).

Immediate priming effects can also generate costs to performance in responding to a probe. Perhaps most notably, many studies have investigated impaired responding to a repeated stimulus to which participants withheld a response during the prime event, a phenomenon commonly referred to as *negative priming*. In a typical negative priming study, participants attend and respond selectively to one of two dimensions of a prime display, such as when identifying color (and withholding a word identification response) in the Stroop (1935) color-word task. Performance costs then arise when the relevant dimension for responding to the probe matches the irrelevant dimension in the prime display (Tipper, 1985; Tipper & Cranston, 1985; see Tipper, 2001, for a review). One explanation for this result is that ignoring and/or withholding a response to a stimulus dimension during the prime event results in inhibition of its mental representation, causing slowed responses to that dimension when it later becomes central to the probe task (Neill, 1977; Tipper, 1985). Thus, from this Activation/Inhibition (A/I) perspective, priming effects measure the change in activation state of abstract mental representations resulting from processing that occurs at the time of the prime event.

## A SCAPE-Inspired Approach to Immediate Priming

From the SCAPE perspective, the effect of a prior event (the prime episode) on current performance (the probe task) ought to obey the same principles in the immediate priming context as it does in all other contexts in which a specific episode in memory gains control of current processing. In particular, the principles that control priming effects should be precisely the same as those that determine success in remembering. Boiled down to the essence, success in remembering an event accurately depends on two primary factors: (1) the degree of overlap between present conditions and those present at the time of encoding (the transfer-appropriate processing principle; Morris, Bransford, & Franks, 1977) and (2) the elaborateness of encoding (Craik & Lockhart, 1972; Lockhart & Craik, 1990). Within the SCAPE framework, the only compatible approach to explaining the phenomena of positive and/or negative priming would involve the application of these two principles.

### Priming Effects as Transfer Affects

Regarding the first principle identified earlier, many immediate priming effects follow easily from the principle of transfer-appropriate processing (TAP), which simply asserts that a previous experience will facilitate current performance of a task to the extent that it involved processing that is appropriate for performing that task. Likewise a previous experience will impair performance of a current task to the extent that it involved processing that is inappropriate for performing that task. When applied to a nonremembering task, the influence of a memory representation on current processing depends on feature overlap between that prior event and present conditions; the overlap serves as a cue for making contact with the relevant episode preserved in memory. It is the extent of overlap that determines whether the memory episode contributes a benefit or a cost to current performance of a task. Relative to an episode that differs completely from present conditions, an episode that overlaps on some dimensions, but not others, will tend to impair performance. In contrast, when compared against an episode that differs completely from present conditions, a high overlap between present conditions and a prior episode (i.e., a match on most or all dimensions) will tend to benefit performance. This nonmonotonic association between the similarity between a current and prior event and the effect of that prior event on current performance has been investigated previously by a number of priming researchers (Hommel, 1998; Hommel, Musseler, Aschersleben, & Prinz, 2002; Leboe, Leboe, & Milliken, 2010; Leboe & Milliken, 2004; Leboe, Whittlesea, & Milliken, 2005; Milliken, Joordens, Merikle, & Seiffert, 1998; Neill & Mathis, 1998; Rothermund, Wentura, & de Houwer, 2005; Wood & Milliken, 1998).

Evaluating whether a SCAPE or an A/I approach is more effective at explaining immediate priming effects presents a major challenge because either approach can accommodate a wide range of these effects. In particular, both of these approaches are well equipped to explain repetition effects that are based on a stimulus dimension that is relevant to the probe task. To illustrate, Bowers, Vigliocco, and Haan (1998, Experiment 5) measured priming effects for homophones, manipulating the phonological requirements of the probe task. On each of a series of trials, all participants were presented with a masked, lowercase prime word for 50 ms, followed by an uppercase probe word that was either the same as the prime (*read* followed by *READ*), a homophone of the prime (*sale* followed by *SAIL*), and a word that was unrelated to the prime (*read* followed by *SAIL*). For one group of participants the task was speeded naming and, for the other group, it was a word/nonword lexical decision task. The critical result was that the presentation of a homophone prime facilitated naming performance much more than it facilitated lexical decision performance. That is, the phonological overlap between the prime and probe facilitated a task that requires phonological processing (naming) more than it facilitated a task that is less reliant on phonological processing (lexical decision). The A/I framework can explain this type of result because it is founded on the premise that processing some stimulus feature leads to temporary activation of a corresponding mental code. In turn, this activation facilitates processing of that feature in a subsequent display. Of course, such effects can also be explained by the emphasis on the TAP principle

inherent to the SCAPE account. In the study conducted by Bowers et al. (1998), the phonology of the prime stimulus made available resources appropriate for meeting a subsequent demand for phonological processing when the probe task was word naming. These resources were less useful for aiding participants in performing the lexical decision task. Leboe et al. (2005) referred to this type of immediate priming as *task-relevant transfer*.

Other immediate priming effects may be more readily explained by a SCAPE than by an A/I approach. For example, matches on some dimension irrelevant to the probe task that modulate the effect of task-relevant transfer have provided a compelling argument for the role of the TAP principle in explaining longer term examples of priming. In particular, some authors have reported higher repetition benefits on identification of briefly presented words and letters (Ratcliff & McKoon, 1988) and categorization of artificial grammar stimuli (Brooks, 1987; Whittlesea & Dorken, 1993) when some contextual overlap (an overlap in a stimulus feature that is not the object of processing during either the prime and probe events) exists between study and test conditions. Leboe et al. (2005) referred to this source of influence on priming as *task-irrelevant transfer*.

When the dimension is truly unrelated to the probe task, this contribution to priming effects is not easy to accommodate by the A/I framework. Naturally, that framework does not rule out that immediate priming effects may depend on stimulus dimensions that differ somewhat from the target dimension of the probe task. Activation of one stimulus dimension could influence responding to a probe display through its effect on activation of some associated stimulus dimension. To illustrate, Cheesman and Merikle (1986) observed speeded responses to a colored rectangle following masked presentation of a congruent color word. Even though word processing is not precisely the same as color processing, explanation of this result by the A/I framework merely requires the assumption that representations responsible for color and color word identification can interact. In this way, semantic-level activation of a color word might speed later color responses by increasing activation of mental representations responsible for detecting the presence of color.

Our use of the phrase "task-irrelevant transfer" applies only to instances in which priming is heightened by repetition of a stimulus dimension that is entirely uncorrelated with the probe task. This form of immediate priming challenges the A/I framework because there is no mechanism by which activation of a feature code during the prime event can contribute to performance when it bears no association to the focal dimension of the probe task. The A/I framework requires an established associative link between stimulus dimensions before this type of interactive activation can occur. In contrast, under the TAP principle, it is associations generated within particular episodes that control the impact of that event on subsequent performance. Thus, a match between the prime and probe on a task-irrelevant dimension should contribute to performance of a probe task. This match between the prime and probe serves as a contextual cue for reinstatement of processes that occurred during the prime event. Depending on the processes retrieved by this contextual cue, the contribution to performance may be positive, negative, or neutral. If the processes recruited are appropriate for performing the current task, then the contextual overlap will benefit performance (a case of *task-irrelevant positive transfer*), whereas recruitment of processes inappropriate for performing the current task will introduce a cost to performance (a case of *task-irrelevant negative transfer*).

In studies of immediate priming, there have been many demonstrations of task-irrelevant positive and negative transfer effects. Observations of heightened negative priming effects when the prime and probe events match on some task-irrelevant contextual dimension (Fox & DeFockert, 1998; Neill & Mathis, 1998; Neill, Valdes, Terry, & Gorfein, 1992) represent examples of this form of immediate priming. To illustrate, Stolz and Neely (2001) presented participants with a five-item letter string on each of a series of trials. The first, third, and fifth *distractor* letters are identical. Participants were instructed to ignore those distractor letters and judge whether the second and fourth *target* letters were the *same* or *different* by making a button-press. Thus, presentation of the string *XAXAX* would prompt a *same* response, whereas presentation of the string *RLRSR* would prompt a *different* response. As with priming experiments more generally, trials of negative priming experiments consist of pairs of events with the critical conditions of the experiment defined by the association between items in a first *prime* display and those presented in a second *probe* display. In the Stolz and Neely study, on *primed trials*, the distractor letters present in the prime display matched the target letters in the following probe display, whereas on *unprimed*

*trials*, there was no overlap between letters in the prime display and the letters presented during the probe display. In this type of procedure, the negative priming effect occurs when participants make slower and/or less accurate responses on *primed trials* than on *unprimed trials*. A SCAPE-consistent, episodic explanation for such effects assumes that impairment on *primed trials* occurs because accessing a memory representation for the prime event contributes a source of interference when responding to the probe event. After treating a letter as a distractor when responding to the prime event, accessing a memory representation for that event at the time of the probe event will conflict with the requirement to treat that same letter as a target for generating a same/different response. In turn, this conflict slows response times and reduces response accuracy. Stolz and Neely (2001, Experiment 2) manipulated the brightness of distractors and targets, such that the intensity of prime distractor letters (bright vs. dim) would either match or differ from the intensity of probe target letters. Bright prime distractors did not generate significant negative priming effects, presumably because proper ignoring did not occur for brightly presented prime distractors. However, a significant negative priming effect did occur when dim prime distractor letters appeared as dim target letters in the following probe display, whereas significant negative priming was not observed when dim prime distractor letters appeared as bright probe target letters. Because stimulus intensity was not a relevant dimension for completing the same-different task in response to either the prime or probe display, this influence on the occurrence of negative priming represents an instance of task-irrelevant negative transfer. The common interpretation of priming effects that depend on the presence of overlap on some irrelevant feature is that the overlap enhances access to a memory representation for the prime episode during the probe event. Enhanced access to the prime event results in greater interference from having previously ignored the probe target when it was assigned the role of distractor in the preceding prime display (see Mayr & Buchner, 2007, for a review of the evidence for an episodic origin of negative priming effects).

### Transfer Effects and Task-Switching Costs

Most often, discussion of the relative merits of the A/I and SCAPE frameworks for priming effects has centered on results from studies that use a single-task procedure; that is, a procedure in which participants perform the same task for all trials encountered in the experiment. With the single-task procedure, arguments that favor the TAP framework over the A/I framework rest heavily on task-irrelevant transfer (i.e., contextual similarity) effects. Leboe et al. (2005) argued that the task-switching procedure provides an additional means of evaluating the utility of the TAP principle over A/I accounts. In particular, when a task switch is required between prime and probe displays, a match in some property of the prime and probe stimuli often impairs performance. We refer to this influence on immediate priming as "repetition-modulated switch costs." Central to this type of immediate priming influence is the combination of feature similarity between prime and probe *and* a difference between the prime and probe tasks. As a result, such effects are distinct from the task-relevant and task-irrelevant transfer effects described earlier. Repetition-modulated switch costs may result from dimensions that are either central to or irrelevant for performing either the prime or probe tasks.

This class of immediate priming effects is expected by a TAP approach because slowed performance should occur when features of the probe display cue reinstatement of irrelevant processes engaged when responding to the prime task. In contrast, by an A/I account, such an effect would require that impaired performance originates from an inhibitory influence at the time of the prime event. This explanation only has merit if there is reason to suspect that the repeated feature was suppressed in the process of responding to the prime task.

Leboe et al. (2005) sought evidence for task-irrelevant transfer and repetition-modulated switch costs. In two experiments, participants either performed a lexical decision task (judging whether the item presented was a word or nonword) or a color identification task in response to prime and probe displays. Across trials, they manipulated the association between prime and probe words and nonwords on the dimensions of color, orthography, and lexical status. Several instances of task-irrelevant transfer emerged. In Experiment 1, when participants made a lexical decision in response to both prime and probe, the irrelevant dimension of color match speeded responses to the probe. By the A/I framework, accounting for this result might rely on the idea that exposure to a color during the prime event heightened the activation of mental codes corresponding to that feature, facilitating subsequent performance on the lexical decision task. Leboe et al. argued that this explanation is implausible given that stimulus color ought to be irrelevant for

activating the mental codes necessary for arriving at a lexical decision. Instead, they proposed that a match in color provided a contextual cue that facilitated contact with the prime episode preserved in memory. The appropriateness of the lexical decision task engaged in during the prime event then facilitated performance of the lexical decision required by the probe task. Similarly, in Experiment 2, when the prime and probe task both required a color identification response, participants were faster at identifying the color of probes when the prime and probe were similar in orthographic structure. In this case as well, explaining this result by the A/I approach requires a preexisting link between representations that code for stimulus orthography and those that code for stimulus color. Leboe et al. carefully chose their stimulus set to avoid the presence of this type of preexisting association and paired each stimulus equally often with each color during the experimental session. In contrast, according to the TAP principle, performance on an irrelevant task might benefit from color match or a match in orthographic structure by serving as a contextual cue to appropriate processes engaged in during the prime event.

Leboe et al. also observed repetition-modulated switch costs that could not be explained by inhibition of the repeated feature at the time of the prime display. In both Experiments 1 and 2, color repetition produced especially poor performance in identifying probe color after participants judged the lexical status of the prime. This result could be seen as an outcome of suppressing prime color while performing the lexical decision task. As discussed earlier, the construct of inhibition has been applied to explain a host of previous such demonstrations of "negative priming," in which participants are slower at responding to a stimulus dimension that was ignored in a preceding display (see Fox, 1995; May, Kane, & Hasher, 1995; Tipper, 2001, for reviews). Leboe et al. rejected this interpretation, in part, because of their observation of the same effect based on overlap in orthographic structure in Experiment 2. When the prime task was lexical decision and the probe task was color identification, orthographic similarity between the prime and probe also increased the cost of switching tasks. This finding is significant because it reveals a repetition-modulated switch cost based on the stimulus dimension that participants relied upon to complete the prime task. Participants must first perceive stimulus orthography before judging its lexical status. Therefore, not attending to a property of the prime stimulus was not necessary for repetition of that property to increase the cost of switching to an alternative task. The A/I framework is not well equipped to explain how ignoring (or inhibiting) one stimulus dimension and attending to (or activating) another one could produce the same outcome for task switching.

## Priming Effects as a Function of Elaborateness of Encoding

The quality of initial encoding has long been understood as promoting success in later remembering, beginning with the levels of processing framework developed by Craik and Lockhart (1972; Moscovitch & Craik, 1976; see Lockhart, 2002, for a review). A straightforward prediction derived from the SCAPE account is that the same encoding factors that promote success in remembering should also increase the impact of a specific prior experience on subsequent performance of a nonremembering task. To illustrate, Wong and Leboe (2009) investigated the role of elaborateness of encoding in generating switch-cost asymmetries with the goal of distinguishing between an A/I approach to task-switching costs and an approach that is more compatible with the SCAPE framework.

The A/I framework that has dominated explanations of priming generally has also been vigorously applied to the task-switching literature. Specifically, costs associated with switching from one task to another might occur via inhibition of abstract task-set representations during a prime event that then impairs performance of that task during a subsequent probe event. Inhibition of a task set would tend to be applied when performance of that task is currently irrelevant, such as when one is occupied by the need to perform some other task. In a number of studies of task switching (Goschke, 2000; Meuter & Allport, 1999; Wylie & Allport, 2000), participants experience a greater cost when switching from a difficult task to one that is relatively easy than when they are required to make the reverse task switch (but see Monsell, Yeung, & Azuma, 2000 and Yeung & Monsell, 2003, for some exceptions). This observation is typically referred to as a "switch-cost asymmetry." The Stroop (1935) color-word task has provided one frequent basis for demonstrating a switch-cost asymmetry. Studies using incongruent Stroop stimuli consistently reveal that participants are more readily able to name words than to name the color of words (see MacLeod, 1991, for a review). The consequence of this difference in the ease of word naming versus color identification is that switching from the color identification to the word-naming task often results in higher switching costs than the requirement to switch from word naming to color identification (Allport et al., 1994; Wylie & Allport, 2000). From an A/I perspective, participants might have difficulty suppressing the more familiar task of word reading during the prime event. As a result, considerable inhibition of that task might be necessary to allow people to respond on the basis of color. In contrast, processing of color is a less dominant task and interferes less with performing the task of word reading. Consequently, reading a word in the prime display might involve less inhibition of the alternative task of color naming. Greater costs of switching to word reading than to color naming would then simply reflect differences in the amount of task-set inhibition that occurred when responding to the preceding task.

A SCAPE-inspired approach would explain this switch cost asymmetry with reference to the elaborateness of processing that occurred during the prime event. Whether the probe task is color or word identification, having performed a different task in response to the prime provides an opportunity for making contact with inappropriate processes that could provide a source of interference. Still, the amount of actual interference observed depends on whether those inappropriate processes are made available through the accessibility of the prime episode. If the prime task requires a color identification response, the relative difficulty of that task will generate a more elaborate representation for that event in memory. If so, at the time of the probe there would be a greater likelihood that the prime episode will influence performance of the probe task when the prime task is color identification than when it is word identification. As a consequence, on switch trials, inappropriate processes engaged during the prime event would be more readily accessed to interfere with word naming than when the subsequent task is color identification.

To test this episodic memory explanation of task-switch asymmetries, Wong and Leboe (2009, Experiment 1) had participants generate a button-press response to the appearance of animal names (TIGER, ELEPHANT, WHALE). On each trial participants were required to perform the same task in response to successive animal names or to switch from one task to another. Across four groups of participants, the procedure was designed to measure the cost of switching from one relatively easy perceptual task (word font size vs. word font color) to another relatively difficult, meaning-based task (animal size—big/small vs. animal habitat—land/

water) and vice versa. The outcome was that the cost of switching was greater when participants were required to switch from a conceptual task to a perceptual task than when they were required to make the reverse task switch. This result replicated the often-observed switch-cost asymmetry described earlier. In a second experiment, Wong and Leboe (2009, Experiment 2) measured the cost of switching between the two easier tasks for one group of participants and between the two difficult tasks for another group of participants. Thus, across the two experiments, they were able to determine whether the cost of switching depends on the difficulty of the task *performed* at the time of the prime event *or* the difficulty of the task *not performed* at the time of the prime event. The outcome was that the difficulty of the task not performed during the prime event (i.e., the to-be-inhibited task set) had no significant influence on the magnitude of switching costs. Instead, it was the difficulty of the task performed during the prime event that mattered, with larger switch costs occurring when participants switched from conceptual prime tasks than when they switched from perceptual prime tasks. Wong and Leboe offered this evidence as favoring an account of switch-cost asymmetries that highlights the role of elaborate processing at the time of the prime event in magnifying switch costs. More elaborate processing results in greater accessibility of a memory representation for the prime episode in memory, therefore generating more interference when participants are required to switch to an alternative task.

The accessibility of the prime episode due to the quality of encoding has been implicated as heightening priming effects in a number of other context as well, including in studies of negative priming (Leboe, Mondor, & Leboe, 2006; Mondor, Leboe, & Leboe, 2005), repetition priming (Bodner & Masson, 1997, 2001), and semantic priming (Becker, Moscovitch, Behrmann, & Joordens, 1997; Joordens & Becker, 1997). An especially compelling demonstration was provided by Hughes and Whittlesea (2003) in the context of semantic priming. Semantic priming is the observation of faster responding to a stimulus following the earlier presentation of a meaningfully related stimulus (e.g., faster responses to *DOCTOR* following presentation of *NURSE*). Most demonstrations of semantic priming last for no more than 2 seconds (Neely, 1991) and frequently do not survive the insertion of even one intervening event (Masson, 1995). As noted earlier, the earliest and still dominant accounts of semantic priming make reference to spreading

activation within an interconnected network of abstract semantic representations (Anderson, 1976, 1983; Collins & Loftus, 1975; Collins & Quillian, 1969). By this view, presentation of a word spreads activation to associated concepts in the network, facilitating access to the meaning of probe words that follow meaningfully related primes. Semantic priming effects ought to be short lived and fragile based on a spreading activation account.

In contrast, adopting a SCAPE approach would lead one to expect that the short-lived nature of semantic priming effects reflects the traditional procedure for investigating those effects, rather than reflecting a fundamental feature of the underlying cause of those effects. In particular, the prime episode generated in conventional studies of semantic priming is quite sparse and should not be expected to impact performance across delays longer than a few moments and should not be expected to survive intervening events. Often, presentation of the prime in semantic priming studies requires only a simple identification response or no response at all. Indeed, primes are frequently masked in semantic priming studies such that participants may not even be aware of the identity of the prime word (Cheesman & Merikle, 1986; Marcel, 1983; Merikle & Reingold, 1990; Merikle, Smilek, & Eastwood, 2001). Thus, short and fragile semantic priming effects may merely be an outcome of providing participants with an extremely weak episodic representation for the prime word. Hughes and Whittlesea (2003) proposed that the creation of more elaborate memory representations for primes should result in longer term semantic priming effects that are able to survive the insertion of multiple intervening events.

In multiple experiments, Hughes and Whittlesea (2003) confirmed their suspicions that more elaborately processed prime words should yield more robust semantic priming effects, particularly when the processes engaged in during the relevant prime event were maximally appropriate for generating a response to semantically related probes. Rather than the conventionally sparse processing of primes that occurs in most semantic priming experiments, participants performed categorical judgments in response to a list of prime words presented in a study phase and a list of probe words in a test phase, some of which were related to prime words and some of which were not. Each prime (e.g., *EAGLE*) was presented along with two category labels (e.g., *BIRD* and *GRASS*), one to which the item belonged and one to which it clearly did not belong. Participants were required to select the correct category as quickly as possible. On the subsequent probe trial, the probe (e.g., *HAWK*) was presented with the same two categories. On other trials, other primes and probes were shown with different category labels (the prime *COBRA–PYTHON* with *SNAKE* and *MACHINE*). The critical result was that significant semantic priming effects occurred in a procedure for which the average delay between the relevant prime and probe events was around 20 minutes and was separated by approximately 90 intervening trials. Based on their findings, Hughes and Whittlesea proposed that semantic priming effects are a consequence of accessing an episodic memory representation for the prime event during efforts to generate a response to the probe. Because the cognitive operations necessary for responding to a probe are similar to those engaged by the earlier processing of a meaningfully related word, the memory episode for the prime event facilitates completion of the probe task.

In this section, we reviewed evidence that principles that are known to be critical to performance of remembering tasks (transfer-appropriate processing and elaborateness of encoding) are also central to understanding immediate priming effects. The goal was to illustrate how the *production* function of memory operates by the same principles, regardless as to whether the current task requires conscious access to a specific prior experience. In the section that follows, we will describe what we have learned about the *evaluation* function of memory and the rules that govern its operation in the context of remembering and nonremembering tasks.

## Evaluation as the Root of Subjective Judgments in Remembering and Nonremembering Tasks
### Remembering and the SCAPE Framework

The SCAPE approach to remembering is rooted in the constructivist traditions of Bartlett (1932) and Elizabeth Loftus (Loftus, 1993, 1996; Loftus & Palmer, 1974; Loftus et al., 1978), the reality/source monitoring framework developed by Marcia Johnson and her colleagues (Johnson, Hashtroudi, & Lindsay, 1993; Johnson & Raye, 1981; Lindsay & Johnson, 1989), and the fluency attribution framework developed by Larry Jacoby and his colleagues (Jacoby & Dallas, 1981; Jacoby, Kelley, & Dywan, 1989; Jacoby & Whitehouse, 1989). The major premise is that remembering is most certainly not "mental time travel," as some theorists have described it (Tulving, 2002)—at least, not in any literal sense. Remembering never allows a person to directly relive a prior experience, and any

correspondence between a remembering experience and an actual prior event is incidental. Such accuracy occurs because of the appropriateness of present cues and the uniqueness of the original event. Accuracy is not a definitive property of remembering experiences. Instead, remembering involves the current production of some mental experience or physical action with a subjective evaluation that current processing originates from a specific prior experience. Since the raw materials of a remembering experience are *constructed* in the present, deviations between what a person remembers and what actually occurred are a natural consequence of the remembering process. Furthermore, under the SCAPE framework, the term *retrieval* is objectionable because there is nothing compatible between the process implied by that term and the conception of remembering as an error-prone construction.

### Forms of Evaluation and the Subjective Experience of Remembering

Since proposing the SCAPE framework in 1997, Whittlesea and his colleagues have made substantial progress in the development of categories of evaluative response that can lead to the subjective experience of remembering (or not remembering). These evaluations stem from a person's assessment of the quality and content of her current thoughts and actions (i.e., memory fulfilling its production function) and her *expectations* as to how that production ought to have occurred, given how her thoughts and actions have unfolded during similar events that occurred in the past. The term *expectations* can be misleading in this context, because it is not meant to refer to conscious a priori predictions about what ought to occur. Instead, *expectation* in this context refers to the degree of similarity between past and current events that are of the same type. Such expectations are merely a description of the contents of a person's memory and how those contents relate to present conditions.

In that sense, these *expectations* should be thought of as a *latent readiness* to make an easy accommodation for certain event details and not others.

When present circumstances confirm one's expectations, the result is one of two forms of evaluation. One possible outcome is a sense of *coherence*, which occurs whenever events unfold in a more or less unsurprising way, but one had no clearly defined expectation as to what should occur. Subjectively, one experiences this evaluation as comprehension and goodness. It is the feeling of things going smoothly. It is a feeling commonly generated when having a conversation with a longtime friend. The interaction is fluid and comfortable, just as one ought to expect, even though one might not have any definite expectation as to the content of the conversation. Another potential outcome is a sense of *integrality*, which occurs whenever one confirms clearly defined expectations about what should occur in some context. For example, in a grocery store one might look for the milk display in the same general area that the cheese is located. Knowing where the cheese is might lead to the specific expectation that the milk must be nearby. *Integrality* is the feeling one might experience by confirming that "Yes(!), the milk is indeed quite close to the cheese." The sense of "Aha, just as I expected!" is the signature of experiencing integrality.

When present circumstances violate one's expectations, two forms of evaluation are also possible. When one's expectations are violated, but the source of that violation is not readily identifiable, the evaluation will generate a feeling of *discrepancy*. The outcome is a sense that something is not quite right, which generates a tension or feeling of unease. It is the feeling one might have when arriving home prepared to unlock the front door and finding the front door already unlocked. Thus, *discrepancy* is the feeling generated by an unsolved mystery. When there is violation of an expectation about what should occur in some context, and the source of that violation is obvious, the evaluation that results is *incongruity*. The outcome is a sense that things are just wrong because the components of an experience are simply not compatible with one another. It is the kind of feeling one might have when encountering another receiving praise for incompetent job performance. It is the experience that occurs upon learning that a police officer has committed a crime. The emotional response that accompanies *incongruity* can be strong, but unlike experiences of *discrepancy* there is no mystery as to the origin of that response.

### The Discrepancy Attribution Hypothesis

Over the past few years, Whittlesea and colleagues have explored the role of each of these categories of evaluation in guiding remembering judgments. In the earliest investigations, the focus was on investigating the role of *discrepancy* in generating feelings of familiarity. The dominant explanation as to the cause of feelings of familiarity was first proposed by Mandler (1980), who suggested that the subjective experience of familiarity originated from intraitem integration or the efficiency with which one integrated the features of a stimulus

into a coherent whole. Mandler proposed that prior exposure to a stimulus generates a memory representation that facilitates integration of the features of that stimulus during a subsequent exposure and the perceiver consciously experiences this fast perceptual integration as a feeling of familiarity. This proposal was a sensible one because prior exposure to a stimulus does tend to facilitate subsequent perception of that stimulus—the phenomenon of repetition priming (Bowers, 2000; Jacoby, 1983; Logan, 1990; Tenpenny, 1995). Feelings of familiarity might be a subjective state that accompanies repetition priming effects.

Later, however, Jacoby and colleagues (Jacoby & Dallas, 1981; Jacoby et al., 1989; Jacoby & Whitehouse, 1989) elaborated upon Mandler's idea, developing a *fluency attribution hypothesis* as to the origin of feelings of familiarity. By their view, the feeling of familiarity may or may not derive from a memory representation for having encountered a stimulus previously. Across a number of studies, they demonstrated that any source of fluent stimulus perception could generate feelings of familiarity in the perceiver, whether that fluent perception originated from a prior encounter with a stimulus or some aspect of the present situation.

The best support for the fluency attribution hypothesis came from recognition studies showing that enhancing the perceptual fluency of recognition test items increased the likelihood that participants would judge those items as *old*, even when they were not actually presented in the preceding study phase (Jacoby & Whitehouse, 1989; Whittlesea, 1993; Whittlesea, Jacoby, & Girard, 1990). In other words, enhancing the perceptual fluency of *new* items presented during a recognition test, causes participants to experience an illusion of familiarity.

More recently, Whittlesea and Williams (1998) noted that strong feelings of familiarity tend to occur when the fluency of processing a stimulus exceeds what one ought to expect given the context in which that item occurs. For example, a mere acquaintance will generate a strong (and even irritating) feeling of familiarity in contexts for which one expects only to encounter strangers (e.g., when one encounters her dentist at the mall). In contrast, upon encountering a person in the context within which she typically appears, extremely fluent processing of that person's features often does not generate strong feelings of familiarity (e.g., when one encounters one's spouse in the kitchen). These observations led to a *discrepancy attribution hypothesis* that feelings of familiarity occur when current processing unfolds in a surprising way and one unconsciously attributes the source of that surprise to a prior stimulus exposure. By this view, previous observations that fluency attributions lie at the root of feelings of familiarity were not actually caused by experiencing *absolute fluency of processing* but originated from the surprise reaction generated by experiencing *relative fluency of processing*—stimulus processing that is more fluent than one ought to expect under present circumstances.

In the context of the recognition task, Whittlesea and colleagues vigorously studied the role of discrepancy attributions in generating feelings of familiarity (Whittlesea & Leboe, 2003; Whittlesea & Williams, 1998, 2000, 2001a, 2001b). In one critical example, Whittlesea and Williams (1998) presented participants with a mixture of words (*station, daisy, table*), orthographically regular nonwords (*hension, bardle, brender*), and orthographically irregular nonwords (*stofwus, lictpub, gertpris*) in a study phase. In a subsequent test phase, participants were presented with old and new words, regular nonwords, and irregular nonwords and their task was to identify which items appeared in the study phase (by making an *old* judgment) and which items were not shown previously (by making a *new* judgment). Other experiments measured the fluency of processing for each of these item types, as indexed by pronunciation latencies and lexical decision performance (Whittlesea & Williams, 1998, 2000). These measures revealed that real words were processed most fluently, regular nonwords were processed with intermediate fluency, and irregular nonwords were processed with the lowest degree of fluency. Thus, based solely on the absolute fluency of processing for these items, one can generate a straightforward prediction as to the likelihood that participants should incorrectly judge novel items as *old* (also known as *false alarms*). If feelings of familiarity are a direct consequence of the absolute fluency of stimulus processing, then the highest proportion of false alarms should be observed for real words, followed by regular nonwords, followed by irregular nonwords. Contrary to this prediction, Whittlesea and Williams have consistently observed that the proportion of false alarms for regular nonwords are between 2–3 times higher than the proportion of false alarms for real words and are between 3–4 times higher than the proportion of false alarms for irregular nonwords.

This *Hension effect* contradicts a straightforward application of the fluency attribution hypothesis as an explanation as to what causes feelings of familiarity. Instead, Whittlesea and Williams (1998, 2000,

2001a) suggested that regular nonwords generate a surprise reaction because they are extremely word-like, yet they lack meaning. They proposed that the surprise reaction generated by regular nonwords frequently generates a feeling of familiarity because, in the context of a recognition test, participants unconsciously attribute the source of this reaction to prior exposure to those items in the preceding study phase. Whittlesea and Williams reasoned that, if this assertion is correct, then orienting participants away from the surprising wordiness of regular nonword should reduce the capacity of those items to generate false alarms. They confirmed this idea in a number of experiments, but we will only provide a couple of key examples.

In the first example, Whittlesea and Williams (2000, Experiment 4) presented only regular nonwords in a study phase and then presented a mixture of *old* and *new* regular nonwords in a later recognition test. Half of these *old* and *new* items appeared alone and the other half appeared flanked by one nonword that rhymed and another nonword that did not rhyme with the recognition target. For example, the nonword *pingle* might be flanked by the nonwords *bingle* and *pinget* on either side. For recognition targets flanked by nonwords, participants were asked to indicate which of the two flankers rhymed prior to making their recognition judgment. The outcome was that both hits and false alarms for regular nonwords were significantly lower when participants' recognition judgment followed the rhyming judgment. Whittlesea and Williams argued that the discrepancy participants normally experienced from regular nonwords was reduced by their requirement to make a rhyme judgment because, instead of those items seeming surprisingly word-like for nonwords, those items seemed word-like *and* useful for making rhyme judgments in response to similar looking nonwords. Reducing the discrepancy normally generated by the regular nonwords also reduced the likelihood of claiming those items as old.

In a second example, Whittlesea and colleagues applied a sentence-stem paradigm to evaluate their discrepancy attribution hypothesis for the high false alarms generated by regular nonwords in their previous studies. In a study phase, Whittlesea and Williams (2001a, Experiment 1) presented participants with a mixture of real words and regular nonwords. During the later recognition test, both *old* and *new* words and nonwords were then presented at the end of sentence stems. Words either sensibly completed these sentence stems (e.g., The old priest gave the nuns his *BLESSING*) or not (e.g., The train came roaring out of the *PENCIL*). Obviously, regular nonwords never sensibly completed any sentence stems (e.g., The stormy seas tossed the *HENSION*). Despite the consistent observation of high false alarm rates for regular nonwords in previous studies, the proportion of false alarms in this experiment were highest for words that sensibly completed the sentence stem that they appeared in (.21) than words that did not (.10) and regular nonwords (.08). When presented alone, regular nonwords produce a state of discrepancy (and illusions of familiarity) because their lack of meaning conflicts with their word-like structure. At the end of a sentence stem, however, they just seem meaningless. In that context, they do not generate a state of discrepancy (or feelings of familiarity). Rather, they generate a state of incongruity; the components of the event violate expectations, but the source of that violation is clear and requires no reference to prior stimulus exposure.

In addition to its application in investigations of the Hension effect, the sentence-stem paradigm also provided an additional context for exploring the role of discrepancy in producing feelings of familiarity. Whittlesea (1993) first employed a sentence-stem paradigm to investigate whether illusions of familiarity would emerge as a direct consequence of absolute processing fluency. In these studies, Whittlesea observed a high rate of false alarms for novel words presented at the end of *predictive* sentence stems compared to those presented at the end of *nonpredictive* sentence stems. For predictive stems, the terminal word that sensibly completed the sentence was one of only a relatively small set of words (e.g., The stormy seas tossed the *BOAT*). In contrast, nonpredictive stems could be sensibly completed by a considerably larger set of words (e.g., She saved up her money and bought a *BOAT*). The original explanation for the high rate of false alarms generated by predictive sentence stems was that the sentence stem enhanced the fluency of processing the terminal word, which participants then unconsciously attributed to prior exposure, causing them to consciously experience an illusion of familiarity.

Later research disconfirmed this simple explanation, revealing that heightened false alarms for words presented at the end of predictive sentences only occurred when a brief pause separated participants' reading of the sentence stem and presentation of the terminal word. Presenting words at the end of predictive sentences did not lead to illusions of familiarity when the sentence stem and terminal word were presented simultaneously (Whittlesea & Williams, 2001b, Experiment 1). Whittlesea and Williams identified this source of feelings of familiarity as another instance of discrepancy attribution. A pause following the presentation of a predictive sentence stem produces tension as to what will follow and a relatively narrow set of expectations as to what type of word should complete the sentence. When a word that fits is ultimately presented, the goodness-of-fit between the terminal word and the sentence stem exceeds the participants' expectations (e.g., "Oh, yes, that's the one!"). In turn, the state of discrepancy generated by presentation of the terminal word gets attributed to prior exposure to that word in the study phase.

When the terminal word and sentence stem are presented simultaneously, participants do not have time to generate expectations about what the terminal word will be. It already completes the sentence, so it is experienced as merely fitting, rather than as fitting better than expected. Nonpredictive sentences also do not produce a state of discrepancy (or illusions of familiarity) because their meaning provides little constraint on the participants' expectations as to what the terminal word will be. If the effect of the pause is to cause participants to experience discrepancy when the terminal word appears, simultaneous presentation of the terminal word with the sentence stem or presentation of a word at the end of a nonpredictive sentence stem causes participants to experience a state of mere coherence. The sentence makes sense, but not in any way that exceeds expectations.

To summarize, Whittlesea and Williams suggested that fluency is not directly responsible for feelings of familiarity. Instead, it is tension arising from an experience of *discrepancy* that compels an attribution as to its source. People may resolve this discrepancy to their satisfaction by attributing it to the most salient source available. When their current task requires making recognition judgments, prior stimulus exposure is the most obvious cause of the discrepancy. This unconscious attribution then results in the conscious experience of familiarity.

### Coherence, Incongruity, and Integrality in the Context of Recognition Judgments

Although most investigations of the four states of evaluation described earlier have focused on discrepancy, some progress has been made in determining the role that the other three states have in guiding remembering judgments. As mentioned earlier, the state of coherence does not compel strong feelings of remembering because processing does not unfold particularly better or worse than one ought to expect, given the present context. One of the assumptions of the SCAPE account is that people need to be somehow impressed by the quality of their own processing (whether that processing goes well or badly) for that processing to guide judgments about the past.

The state of incongruity is compelling enough to guide remembering judgments, because it emerges through an obvious violation of one's expectations. Nevertheless, since the source of the violation is known, the state of incongruity cannot generate strong feelings that current processing is under the control of prior experience. Instead, incongruity tends to produce strong feelings of wrongness that have a suppressant effect on feelings of remembering. For example, Whittlesea and Williams (2001b, Experiment 3) presented participants with a series of words in a study phase. In a later test phase, they presented *old* and *new* words at the end of sentence stems, generating three categories of sentence stem/terminal word combinations. On every trial, a brief pause separated presentation of the sentence stem and the terminal word. In the *simple violation condition*, terminal words incorrectly completed common phrases (Let them eat...*PIE*). In the *clang violation condition*, the terminal words incorrectly completed common phrases *and* rhymed with the word that normally completes the phrase (Row, row, row, your...*GOAT*). Finally, in the *no violation condition*, the terminal words correctly completed common phrases (Raindrops keep falling on my...*HEAD*). In both the *simple violation* and *clang violation* conditions, the terminal word is unexpected, but it is easy to realize the source of that expectancy violation. The outcome was that false alarms were 13% higher for words in the *no violation condition* (.34) than in the *simple* (.21) and *clang violation* (.21) *conditions*. Unlike the state of discrepancy, this result illustrates that the state of incongruity tends to *reduce* the likelihood of attributing current processing to a prior experience.

The state of integrality is also compelling enough to guide remembering judgments. This state emerges when one experiences confirmation of a relatively well-defined set of expectations. This is a satisfying state to be in because it occurs when one's previously acquired knowledge allows for quite specific predictions about what should happen in the future. In the context of remembering, it is when one feels as though one has successfully solved the challenge of reconstructing the details of some prior

event through reasoning (e.g., Yes, I knew that my keys would be in the second most typical place that I always put them!).

Whittlesea (2002, Experiment 2; see also Whittlesea, 2004) had participants study a list of words that were each presented at the end of predictive and nonpredictive sentence stems. During the later test phase, old and new words were presented at the end of the same sentence stems that had appeared in the study phase. For example, if the predictive sentence, *After the accident he was covered in GLASS*, was presented at study, the same sentence stem/terminal word combination would also appear at test if *GLASS* was selected to be an old word. If *GLASS* was not selected to be an old word, the predictive sentence might be, *After the accident he was covered in BLOOD*. Similarly, if the nonpredictive sentence, *On the corner of the table there was a bit of TOAST*, was presented at study, the same sentence stem/terminal word combination would also appear at test if *TOAST* was selected to be an old word. If *TOAST* was not selected to be an old word, the nonpredictive sentence might be, *On the corner of the table there was a bit of INK*. The presence of a pause between presentation of the sentence stem and the terminal word was also manipulated independent of the old/new word and predictive/nonpredictive sentence stem factors. The outcome was that false alarms were heightened for words appearing at the end of predictive sentences, regardless as to whether a pause separated presentation of the sentence stem and the terminal word. The observation that the presence of a pause had no effect on the observation of this illusion of remembering rules out a role for the state of discrepancy that generated illusions of familiarity in previous studies using the sentence-stem paradigm. Instead, the remembering errors that occurred in this study originate from the state of integrality generated by preservation of the general theme of the predictive sentence-stem/terminal word combinations presented at study and the general theme of predictive sentence stems/novel terminal word combinations presented at test.

As Bartlett (1932) originally noted, and others have since observed (Bransford & Franks, 1971; Bransford & Johnson, 1972), people find it easier to recall the gist of an experience than the specific details. The result is that people tend to be susceptible to remembering errors when presented with the task of deciding whether some event occurred that is consistent with the theme of the original event yet deviates somewhat from the precise details of that experience. In the context of the present discussion, studying the sentence, *After the accident he was covered in GLASS*, would leave participants readily able to remember the theme of the statement (accident/injury) but less able to remember the specific details. Thus, in order to decide that the terminal word appeared in the earlier study phase, participants would require that the theme derived from the study phase be more or less duplicated during the test phase. This is achieved by replacement of the terminal word *GLASS* with *BLOOD*. *After the accident he was covered in BLOOD* preserves the injury theme, although it is not precisely the same as the original statement. Note that, for the most part, preservation of the theme of the study sentence is only possible for predictive sentences. For nonpredictive sentences (*On the corner of the table there was a bit of TOAST*), the terminal word plays a larger role in defining the theme of the sentence. If participants demand a statement that stays true to the theme of what they encountered at study, changing the terminal word will not satisfy them. The statement, *On the corner of the table there was a bit of INK*, represents quite a different set of thematic circumstances than the statement, *On the corner of the table there was a bit of TOAST*. In the case of nonpredictive sentences, then, replacement of the terminal word generates a state of incongruity in reference to the information that can be brought to mind from the study phase, rather than a state of integrality. This state of incongruity decreases the likelihood of judging new words presented at the end of nonpredictive sentences as old, whereas the state of integrality increases the likelihood of judging new words presented at the end of predictive sentences as old.

### Evaluation, Familiarity, and Recollection

Under the SCAPE framework, the four states generated by the evaluation function of memory partly represent an effort to classify the phenomenological conditions under which people arrive at decisions about their past. They also represent the basic experiential categories that generate all other affective states and that govern all other subjective judgments. Even so, comprehensive investigations as to the role of *discrepancy, incongruity, coherence*, and *integrality* outside of the domain of remembering have yet to be undertaken. Despite this present imbalance, however, the SCAPE approach does not give any remembering process a special status. In this section, we will describe implications of the SCAPE framework for the popular distinction that

is typically drawn between two categories of remembering: *familiarity* and *recollection*. In the subsequent and final section, we will summarize evidence revealing that an essential similarity exists between the processes that underlie remembering judgments and those that control judgments in nonremembering tasks.

Although the processes that generate remembering experiences often operate at an unconscious level, such experiences always involve some form of reasoning that allows people to make a best guess as to what happened in their past. Remembering is a subjective state that is the combined outcome of these reasoning processes (the evaluation function of mind) and information about the past that is brought to mind by cues available in the present context (the production function of mind). That is, under the SCAPE framework, all instances of remembering are constructive and inferential. Remembering never involves passive reception of the details associated with a prior experience, even though that is the process implied by the commonly used phrase "memory retrieval." This view is contrary to prevailing dual-process approaches to recognition performance. According to these theories (Jacoby, 1991; Jacoby & Dallas, 1981; Mandler, 1980; Tulving, 1985), people have two bases for identifying a stimulus as previously encountered. *Old* judgments can arise from either a feeling of *familiarity* for the stimulus or from successful *recollection* of the context surrounding a prior exposure to that stimulus (see Yonelinas, 2002, for a review). This dual-process approach has tended to orient researchers toward differences between the processes of familiarity and recollection. For example, feelings of familiarity are commonly seen as originating from a heuristic *fluency attribution* or *discrepancy attribution* process that is prone to error (Jacoby & Dallas, 1981; Jacoby & Whitehouse, 1989; Whittlesea, 1993; Whittlesea & Williams, 1998, 2000). In contrast, recollection is often seen as the more dominant and accurate basis for making recognition judgments. Indeed, rather than generated by a faulty heuristic attribution process, recollective experiences are seen as arising from a successful search of memory and a direct retrieval of details about the past into consciousness.

Unlike recognition judgments guided by a vague sense of familiarity for the stimulus, recollection often does permit conscious access to details about the context in which that stimulus was encountered. The result is that recognition judgments based on recollection are often more valid and less prone to

SOURCES

error than recognition judgments based solely on familiarity. Development of the process-dissociation procedure (Jacoby, 1991) further highlighted this typically dominant role of the recollection process in supporting accurate recognition judgments. That framework placed emphasis on the corrective function of recollection; participants may use their recall of contextual details to avoid claiming a recognition test item as *old*, even when that item generates a strong feeling familiarity. Recollection provides a useful basis for rejecting a stimulus as having appeared in some context (e.g., "She wasn't at the party") by providing knowledge about the presence of the stimulus in some other context (e.g., "I remember seeing her at the mall").

Even so, the role of recollection in promoting accurate recognition judgments can be overstated. It is possible for the information provided by the recollection process to be insufficient for determining whether some stimulus was encountered in one or another context (Gruppuso, Lindsay, & Kelley, 1997). It is also possible for people to use the familiarity they experience when presented with a stimulus as a basis for inferring the context in which that item occurred (Diana, Yonelinas, & Rangarath, 2008; Dodson & Johnson, 1996). Evidence also reveals that false recollections do occur and can be a source of error in the recognition task (Brainerd & Reyna, 2005; Brainerd, Wright, & Reyna, 2001; Higham & Vokey, 2004), and that experiencing a recollection as a true reflection of the past depends on the application of heuristics that are prone to error (Kurilla & Westerman, 2008, 2011; Leboe & Whittlesea, 2002; Lindsay & Kelley, 1996; Whittlesea & Leboe, 2000, 2003). Supported by these studies, the inferential basis of recollection serves to blur the clear distinction that is often presumed to exist between the processes of recollection and familiarity. Nevertheless, the more typical conception of remembering as strictly dichotomous (familiarity is a heuristic, error-prone basis for making recognition judgments; recollection is direct retrieval of the details surrounding an experience with a stimulus) has discouraged research into the inferential origins of recollective experiences, at least in the context of the recognition task. Investigations into how accurate recollections form the basis of inferences about past events are also extremely rare (but see Dodson & Schacter, 2002; Kleider & Goldinger, 2006, for exceptions).

To illustrate the role of recollection in generating remembering errors, Ansons and Leboe (2011) tested whether people would use detailed recollections when making judgments about the past, even when the content of those recollections was nondiagnostic of the remembering task they were asked to perform. Under those conditions, participants used their recollection of interactive images generated in an *initial encoding phase* to infer either the presence or absence of items in a separate *recency phase*, depending on whether the type of processing engaged in during the *recency phase* was consistent with the recollection of interactive images at test. Ansons and Leboe described this bias as reflecting a metacognitive understanding of the principle of transfer-appropriate processing, an understanding that current processing represents a compelling instance of remembering to the extent that it matches the type of processing engaged in during some prior event. In the context of a recognition test, they suggested that participants will rely on a *resemblance of processing* heuristic when using detailed recollections to make decisions about the context in which some stimulus occurred. This heuristic is related to the resemblance heuristic that was first identified by Whittlesea and Leboe (2000), but with an emphasis on the primacy of processing resemblance over other dimensions of resemblance between study items and recognition test items (e.g., structural similarities between stimuli presented during the study and test phases of a recognition experiment).

Further highlighting the fundamental similarity between familiarity and recollection as categories of remembering, Westerman, Lloyd, and Miller (2002) provided evidence that a similar inferential process can determine whether people will rely on feelings of familiarity to make *old* judgments. Ansons and Leboe also observed that application of a *resemblance of processing* heuristic occurred mainly when test items were less likely to promote recollection of interactive images, whereas participants abandoned reliance on this heuristic when a high proportion of test items were capable of promoting such recollections. Inspired by the SCAPE framework, Ansons and Leboe's study was designed to reveal the fundamentally inferential and constructive nature of recollection and recollection-based remembering judgments. It is precisely these same processes that control people's use of familiarity when making remembering judgments.

### The Evaluation Function of Mind Also Controls Nonremembering Judgments

Whittlesea and Leboe (2000) listed a set of three heuristics already known to guide remembering judgments in the context of recognition experiments. We identified these bases for making recognition judgments as heuristics because, although they often result in accurate decisions, they are also prone to error. First, participants can decide that a stimulus was presented during an earlier study phase based on the ease of processing that stimulus; that is, they could rely on a *fluency heuristic*. Second, participants might make an *old* judgment when the features of a recognition test item match the typical features present during the set of items that they encountered at study—a *resemblance heuristic*. Third, participants might identify a test item as *old* if presentation of that item at test cues the recollection of details associated with a prior encounter with that stimulus during the study phase—a *generation heuristic*.

In a series of experiments, Whittlesea and Leboe demonstrated that these same three heuristics can also guide participants' classification judgments in an artificial grammar paradigm. This type of paradigm involves presentation of a series of items in a study phase that all conform to the same rule or set of rules. Following the study phase, participants are presented with new items, some of which conform to the same rule(s) used to construct the study items and some of which do not. Their task is to discriminate between rule-following and rule-violating items despite expressing no conscious knowledge of the rule(s) used to construct the items presented at study. The typical finding in experiments that apply this basic procedure is that participants can somewhat discriminate rule-following from rule-violating test items, even though they are unable to express any conscious awareness that they learned anything useful during the study phase (Dienes, Broadbent, & Berry, 1991; Knowlton & Squire, 1996; Reber, 1989; Whittlesea & Dorken, 1993). This phenomenon is commonly referred to as *implicit learning* and the dominant view is that acquiring unconscious knowledge of the rules used to construct an artificial grammar relies on a system of memory that operates independent of the memory system that promotes conscious remembering of specific previous experiences.

As a challenge to this separate-systems account of implicit learning, Whittlesea and Leboe developed a set of six-letter nonwords that all conformed to the same simple rule; the fourth letter must always be either a *b* or a *d*. For example, *barden* followed the rule, whereas *wintep* did not. As in previous investigations of implicit learning using the artificial grammar paradigm, most of the experiments required

participants to study rule-following nonwords in the study phase and then to discriminate rule-following from rule-violating nonwords during a subsequent test phase. No participant ever expressed conscious awareness of the rule used to define *legal* nonwords. The critical experiments in the series were designed to isolate participants' reliance on the fluency, resemblance, or generation heuristics when classifying test items as *legal*. The study obtained evidence that, independent of the actual legality of test items, participants will make *legal* classification judgments based on the ease of processing items (the *fluency heuristic*), based on their similarity to the set of items presented during the study phase (the *resemblance heuristic*) and based on the nature of recollections cued by the presentation of test items (the *generation heuristic*). Naturally, if this type of classification judgment can be based on precisely the same type of heuristics that also guide recognition judgments, one might reasonably question the validity of treating recognition and classification judgments as controlled by separate underlying memory systems.

Indeed, there is considerable evidence that the same heuristic basis that people rely on to make remembering judgments also controls a range of other subjective judgments. A number of researchers have observed this similarity in a specific sense (see Oppenheimer, 2008, for a review), observing that the ease of processing a stimulus contributes to judgments of stimulus beauty or pleasantness (Reber, Schwarz, & Winkielman, 2004; Whittlesea, 1993; Whittlesea & Price, 2001), stimulus duration (Masson & Caldwell, 1998; Whittlesea, 1993; Witherspoon & Allan, 1985), stimulus clarity (Jacoby, Allan, Collins, & Larwill, 1988; Kleider & Goldinger, 2004; Whittlesea, et al., 1990), and judgments about the likelihood of recalling an item on a future memory test (Rhodes & Castel, 2008; Tiede, Derksen, & Leboe, 2009). Beyond fluency-based heuristics, researchers have begun to identify people's reliance on other heuristics when making judgments about the basic perceptual features of stimuli. For example, Launa Leboe and colleagues have recently demonstrated that participants will apply a *change heuristic* when judging both the duration and intensity of simple auditory stimuli, identifying sounds that contain a frequency change as both longer in temporal duration and louder in intensity than sounds that maintain a static frequency (Leboe & Mondor, 2008, 2010). Under the SCAPE framework, remembering is fundamentally the outcome of a reasoning process based on whatever evidence is presently available, although much of the processing that underlies that reasoning is presumed to be unconscious. Moreover, remembering is also an active construction, rather than an active reception of information about prior experience. It is becoming increasingly clear that a comprehensive understanding as to how people make even the simplest perceptual judgments must proceed from the realization that, like remembering, instances of perception are also constructed through heuristic reasoning processes.

## Summary Comments

In the current chapter, we have reviewed some of the research that has been inspired by the SCAPE framework, since its inception just over a decade ago. Central to the SCAPE framework is the idea that mind serves two main functions: production and evaluation. Regarding the *production* function, the studies described herein primarily focused on investigating the applicability of well-known remembering principles to nonremembering contexts, such as in the domains of immediate priming and task switching. Research on the *evaluation* function has been aimed at identifying the basic categories of subjective experience and revealing a role for constructive and inferential processes in guiding people's performance of both remembering and nonremembering tasks.

Cognitive scientists have sought to identify fundamental boundaries of mind and memory based on a number of promising dimensions. As described earlier, the distinction between (1) knowledge derived from specific experiences and (2) abstracted knowledge based on the combined influence of multiple experiences of the same type represents one of the more popular demarcation lines within cognitive psychology. In other models, a core assumption is that the mind operates differently on memory representations that occurred a longer amount of time ago than those that occurred only a few moments ago (Atkinson & Shiffrin, 1968). Another approach highlights the importance of distinguishing between conscious and unconscious influences on current thought and behavior. This distinction forms a critical foundation for separate-systems accounts of memory (Squire, 1992; Tulving, 1985), and it is one of the primary bases for distinguishing between processes of familiarity and recollection (Jacoby, 1991; Jacoby, Toth, & Yonelinas, 1993). Similarly, other theorists have suggested that it is the amount of resources consumed by performing different tasks that represents a core division of mind. Specifically, completing some tasks requires *automatic processes*,

in that they occur unconsciously and consume little or no mental resources, whereas completing other tasks require consciously *controlled processes* that are resource demanding (Posner & Snyder, 1975; Schneider & Shiffrin, 1977). Over the past 50 to 60 years, these distinctions have dominated theoretical approaches to human cognitive processing.

A little over a decade ago, Whittlesea (1997) developed the SCAPE framework in explicit opposition to these earlier approaches to human mind and memory. He suggested that by highlighting distinctions between explicit and implicit or long- and short-term memory, automatic and controlled processing, abstract and specific forms of knowledge, and so on, these approaches are useful for clarifying important differences in the requirements of tasks and in phenomenological experience. Nevertheless, such distinctions do not represent the essential categories of mind or memory. Instead, the essential categories of mental function are *production* and *evaluation*. It is in the operation of those two basic mental functions that the same principles should be applicable across a staggering range of stimuli, tasks, and contexts.

## References

Anderson, J. R. (1976). *Language, memory, and thought*. Oxford, England: Erlbaum.

Anderson, J. R. (1983). A spreading activation theory of memory. *Journal of Verbal Learning and Verbal Behavior*, 22(3), 261–295.

Anderson, J. R. (1996). *The architecture of cognition*. Mahwah, NJ: Erlbaum.

Ansons, T. L., & Leboe, J. P. (2011). The constructive nature of recollection. In P. Higham & J. P. Leboe (Eds.), *Constructions of remembering and metacognition: Essays in honour of Bruce Whittlesea*. Houndmills, England: Palgrave-MacMillan.

Atkinson, R. C., & Shiffrin, R. M. (1968). Human memory: A proposed system and its control processes. In K. W. Spence & J. T. Spence (Eds.), *The psychology of learning and motivation: Advances in research and theory* (Vol. 2, pp. 89–195). New York: Academic Press.

Barsalou, L. W. (2008). Cognitive and neural contributions to understanding the conceptual system. *Current Directions in Psychological Science*, 17(2), 91–95.

Bartlett, F. C. (1932). *Remembering: A study in experimental and social psychology*. Cambridge, England: Cambridge University Press.

Becker, S., Moscovitch, M., Behrmann, M., & Joordens, S. (1997). Long-term semantic priming: A computational account and empirical evidence. *Journal of Experimental Psychology: Learning, Memory, and Cognition*, 23(5), 1059–1082.

Bodner, G. E., & Masson, M. E. J. (1997). Masked repetition priming of words and nonwords: Evidence for a nonlexical basis for priming. *Journal of Memory and Language*, 37(2), 268–293.

Bodner, G. E., & Masson, M. E. J. (2001). Prime validity affects masked repetition priming: Evidence for an episodic resource account of priming. *Journal of Memory and Language*, 45(4), 616–647.

Bowers, J. S. (2000). In defense of abstractionist theories of repetition priming and word identification. *Psychonomic Bulletin and Review*, 7(1), 83–99.

Bowers, J. S., Vigliocco, G., & Haan, R. (1998). Orthographic, phonological, and articulatory contributions to masked letter and word priming. *Journal of Experimental Psychology: Human Perception and Performance*, 24(6), 1705–1719.

Brainerd, C. J., & Reyna, V. F. (2005). *The science of false memory*. New York: Oxford University Press.

Brainerd, C. J., Wright, R., & Reyna, V. F. (2001). Conjoint recognition and phantom recollection. *Journal of Experimental Psychology: Learning, Memory, and Cognition*, 27, 307–327.

Bransford, J. D., & Franks, J. J. (1971). The abstraction of linguistic ideas. *Cognitive Psychology*, 2(4), 331–350.

Bransford, J. D., & Johnson, M. K. (1972). Contextual prerequisites for understanding: Some investigations of comprehension and recall1. *Journal of Verbal Learning and Verbal Behavior*, 11(6), 717–726.

Brooks, L. R. (1978). Non-analytic concept formation and memory for instances. In E. Rosch & B. Lloyd (Eds.), *Cognition and categorization* (pp. 169–211). Hillsdale, NJ: Erlbaum.

Brooks, L. R. (1987). Decentralized control of categorization: The role of prior processing episodes. In U. Neisser (Ed.), *Concepts and conceptual development: Ecological and intellectual factors in categorization* (pp. 141–174). New York: Cambridge University Press.

Cheesman, J., & Merikle, P. M. (1986). Distinguishing conscious from unconscious perceptual processes. *Canadian Journal of Psychology/Revue canadienne de psychologie*, 40(4), 343–367.

Collins, A. M., & Loftus, E. F. (1975). A spreading-activation theory of semantic processing. *Psychological Review*, 82(6), 407–428.

Collins, A. M., & Quillian, M. R. (1969). Retrieval time from semantic memory. *Journal of Verbal Learning and Verbal Behavior*, 8(2), 240–247.

Craik, F. I. M., & Lockhart, R. S. (1972). Levels of processing: A framework for memory research. *Journal of Verbal Learning and Verbal Behavior*, 11(6), 671–684.

Diana, R. A., Yonelinas, A. P., & Ranganath, C. (2008). The effects of unitization on familiarity-based source memory: Testing a behavioral prediction derived from neuroimaging data. *Journal of Experimental Psychology: Learning Memory and Cognition*, 34(4), 730–740.

Dienes, Z., Broadbent, D. E., & Berry, D. (1991). Implicit and explicit knowledge bases in artificial grammar learning. *Journal of Experimental Psychology: Learning, Memory, and Cognition*, 17(5), 875–887.

Dodson, C. S., & Johnson, M. K. (1996). Some problems with the process-dissociation approach to memory. *Journal of Experimental Psychology: General*, 125(2), 181–194.

Dodson, C. S., & Schacter, D. L. (2002). When false recognition meets metacognition: The distinctiveness heuristic. *Journal of Memory and Language*, 46(4), 782–803.

Forbach, G. B., Stanners, R. F., & Hochhaus, L. (1974). Repetition and practice effects in a lexical decision task. *Memory and Cognition*, 2(2), 337–339.

Forster, K. I., & Davis, C. (1984). Repetition priming and frequency attenuation in lexical access. *Journal of Experimental Psychology: Learning, Memory, and Cognition*, 10(4), 680–698.

Fox, E. (1995). Negative priming from ignored distractors in visual selection: A review. *Psychonomic Bulletin and Review*, 2(2), 145–173.

Fox, E., & de Fockert, J. W. (1998). Negative priming depends on prime–probe similarity: Evidence for episodic retrieval. *Psychonomic Bulletin and Review*, 5(1), 107–113.

Gabrieli, J. D. E. (1998). Cognitive neuroscience of human memory. *Annual Review of Psychology*, 49, 87–115.

Goschke, T. (2000). Intentional reconfiguration and involuntary persistence in task set switching. In S. Monsell & J. Driver (Eds.), *Control of cognitive processes* (pp. 320–355). Cambridge, MA: MIT Press.

Graf, P., & Schacter, D. L. (1985). Implicit and explicit memory for new associations in normal and amnesic subjects. *Journal of Experimental Psychology: Learning, Memory, and Cognition*, 11(2), 501–518.

Gruppuso, V., Lindsay, D. S., & Kelley, C. M. (1997). The process-dissociation procedure and similarity: Defining and estimating recollection and familiarity in recognition memory. *Journal of Experimental Psychology: Learning, Memory, and Cognition*, 23(2), 259–278.

Higham, P. A., & Vokey, J. R. (2004). Illusory recollection and dual-process models of recognition memory. *The Quarterly Journal of Experimental Psychology Section A*, 57(4), 714–744.

Hommel, B. (1998). Event files: Evidence for automatic integration of stimulus-response episodes. *Visual Cognition*, 5(1), 183–216.

Hommel, B., Müsseler, J., Aschersleben, G., & Prinz, W. (2002). The theory of event coding (TEC): A framework for perception and action planning. *Behavioral and Brain Sciences*, 24(05), 849–878.

Houghton, G., & Tipper, S. P. (1994). A model of inhibitory mechanisms in selective attention. Inhibitory processes in attention, memory, and language. In D. Dagenbach & T. H. Carr (Eds.), *Inhibitory processes in attention, memory, and language* (pp. 53–112). San Diego, CA: Academic Press.

Hughes, A. D., & Whittlesea, B. W. A. (2003). Long-term semantic transfer: An overlapping-operations account. *Memory and Cognition*, 31, 401–411.

Hutchison, K. A. (2003). Is semantic priming due to association strength or feature overlap? A microanalytic review. *Psychonomic Bulletin and Review*, 10, 785–813.

Hyman, J. I. E., & Pentland, J. (1996). The role of mental imagery in the creation of false childhood cemories. *Journal of Memory and Language*, 35(2), 101–117.

Jacoby, L. L. (1983). Remembering the data: Analyzing interactive processes in reading. *Journal of Verbal Learning and Verbal Behavior*, 22(5), 485–508.

Jacoby, L. L. (1991). A process dissociation framework: Separating automatic from intentional uses of memory. *Journal of Memory and Language*, 30(5), 513–541.

Jacoby, L. L., Allan, L. G., Collins, J. C., & Larwill, L. K. (1988). Memory influences subjective experience: Noise judgments. *Journal of Experimental Psychology: Learning, Memory, and Cognition*, 14(2), 240–247.

Jacoby, L. L., & Dallas, M. (1981). On the relationship between autobiographical memory and perceptual learning. *Journal of Experimental Psychology: General*, 110(3), 306–340.

Jacoby, L. L., Kelley, C. M., & Dywan, J. (1989). Memory attributions. In H. L. Roediger & F. I. M. Craik (Eds.), *Varieties of memory and consciousness: Essays in honour of Endel Tulving* (pp. 391–422). Hillsdale, NJ: Erlbaum.

Jacoby, L. L., Toth, J. P., & Yonelinas, A. P. (1993). Separating conscious and unconscious influences of memory: Measuring recollection. *Journal of Experimental Psychology: General*, 122, 139–154.

Jacoby, L. L., & Whitehouse, K. (1989). An illusion of memory: False recognition influenced by unconscious perception. *Journal of Experimental Psychology: General*, 118(2), 126–135.

Jacoby, L. L., & Witherspoon, D. (1982). Remembering without awareness. *Canadian Journal of Psychology*, 36(2), 300–324.

Jamieson, R. K., & Mewhort, D. J. K. (2009). Applying an exemplar model to the artificial-grammar task: Inferring grammaticality from similarity. *Quarterly Journal of Experimental Psychology*, 62, 550–575.

Johnson, M. K. (1988). Reality monitoring: An experimental phenomenological approach. *Journal of Experimental Psychology: General*, 117(4), 390–394.

Johnson, M. K., Hashtroudi, S., & Lindsay, D. S. (1993). Source monitoring. *Psychological Bulletin*, 114, 3–28.

Johnson, M. K., & Raye, C. L. (1981). Reality monitoring. *Psychological Review*, 88, 67–85.

Johnstone, T., & Shanks, D. R. (2001). Abstractionist and processing accounts of implicit learning. *Cognitive Psychology*, 42, 61–112.

Joordens, S., & Becker, S. (1997). The long and short of semantic priming effects in lexical decision. *Journal of Experimental Psychology: Learning, Memory, and Cognition*, 23(5), 1083–1105.

Kanwisher, N. G. (1987). Repetition blindness: Type recognition without token individuation. *Cognition*, 27(2), 117–143.

Kirsner, K., & Smith, M. C. (1974). Modality effects in word identification. *Memory and Cognition*, 2(4), 637–640.

Kleider, H. M., & Goldinger, S. D. (2004). Illusions of face memory: Clarity breeds familiarity. *Journal of Memory and Language*, 50(2), 196–211.

Kleider, H. M., & Goldinger, S. D. (2006). The generation and resemblance heuristics in face recognition: Cooperation and competition. *Journal of Experimental Psychology: Learning, Memory, and Cognition*, 32(2), 259–276.

Knowlton, B. J., & Squire, L. R. (1996). Artificial grammar learning depends on implicit acquisition of both abstract and exemplar-specific information. *Journal of Experimental Psychology: Learning, Memory, and Cognition*, 22(1), 169–181.

Kolers, P. A. (1976). Pattern-analyzing memory. *Science*, 191(4233), 1280–1281.

Kolers, P. A., & Roediger III, H. L. (1984). Procedures of mind. *Journal of Verbal Learning and Verbal Behavior*, 23(4), 425–449.

Kurilla, B. P., & Westerman, D. L. (2008). Processing fluency affects subjective claims of recollection. *Memory and Cognition*, 36(1), 82–92.

Kurilla, B. P., & Westerman, D. L. (2011). Inferential processes in subjective reports of recollection. In P. Higham & J. P. Leboe (Eds.). *Constructions of remembering and metacognition: Essays in honour of Bruce Whittlesea*. Houndmills, England: Palgrave-MacMillan.

Leboe, L. C., & Mondor, T. A. (2008). The role of a change heuristic in judgments of sound duration. *Psychonomic Bulletin and Review*, 15(6), 1122–1127.

Leboe, L. C., & Mondor, T. A. (2010). The role of a change heuristic in judgments of sound intensity. *Experimental Psychology, 57, 398–404.*

Leboe, J. P., Leboe, L. C., & Milliken, B. (2010). Constraints on the observation of partial match costs: Implications for transfer appropriate processing approaches to immediate priming. *Journal of Experimental Psychology: Human Perception and Performance, 36, 634–648.*

Leboe, J. P., & Milliken, B. (2004). Single-prime negative priming in the shape-matching task: Implications for the role of perceptual segmentation processes. *Visual Cognition*, 11(5), 603–630.

Leboe, J. P., Mondor, T. A., & Leboe, L. C. (2006). Feature mismatch effects in auditory negative priming: Interference as dependent on salient aspects of prior episodes. *Perception and Psychophysics*, 68(6), 897–910.

Leboe, J. P., & Whittlesea, B. W. A. (2002). The inferential basis of familiarity and recall: Evidence for a common underlying process. *Journal of Memory and Language*, 46(4), 804–829.

Leboe, J. P., Whittlesea, B. W. A., & Milliken, B. (2005). Selective and nonselective transfer: Positive and negative priming in a multiple-task environment. *Journal of Experimental Psychology: Learning, Memory, and Cognition*, 31(5), 1001–1029.

Lindsay, D. S., Hagen, L., Read, J. D., Wade, K. A., & Garry, M. (2004). True photographs and false memories. *Psychological Science*, 15(3), 149–154.

Lindsay, D. S., & Johnson, M. K. (1989). The eyewitness suggestibility effect and memory for source. *Memory and Cognition*, 17(3), 349–358.

Lindsay, D. S., & Kelley, C. M. (1996). Creating illusions of familiarity in a cued recall remember/know paradigm. *Journal of Memory and Language*, 35, 197–211.

Lockhart, R. S. (2002). Levels of processing, transfer-appropriate processing, and the concept of robust encoding. *Memory*, 10(5), 397–403.

Lockhart, R. S., & Craik, F. I. M. (1990). Levels of processing: A retrospective commentary on a framework for memory research. *Canadian Journal of Psychology*, 44(1), 87–112.

Loftus, E. F. (1993). The reality of repressed memories. *American Psychologist*, 48(5), 518–537.

Loftus, E. F. (1996). *Eyewitness testimony*. Cambridge, MA: Harvard University Press.

Loftus, E. F., Miller, D. G., & Burns, H. J. (1978). Semantic integration of verbal information into a visual memory. *Journal of Experimental Psychology: Human Learning and Memory*, 4(1), 19–31.

Loftus, E. F., & Palmer, J. C. (1974). Reconstruction of automobile destruction: An example of the interaction between language and memory. *Journal of Verbal Learning and Verbal Behavior*, 13(5), 585–589.

Loftus, E. F., & Pickrell, J. E. (1995). The formation of false memories. *Psychiatric Annals*, 25(12), 720–725.

Logan, G. D. (1990). Repetition priming and automaticity: Common underlying mechanisms? *Cognitive Psychology*, 22(1), 1–35.

MacLeod, C. M. (1991). Half a century of research on the Stroop effect: An integrative review. *Psychological Bulletin*, 109(2), 163–203.

MacLeod, C. M., & Masson, M. E. J. (2000). Repetition priming in speeded word reading: Contributions of perceptual and conceptual processing episodes. *Journal of Memory and Language*, 42(2), 208–228.

Mandler, G. (1980). Recognizing: The judgment of previous occurrence. *Psychological Review*, 87(3), 252–271.

Marcel, A. J. (1983). Conscious and unconscious perception: Experiments on visual masking and word recognition. *Cognitive Psychology*, 15(2), 197–237.

Masson, M. E. J. (1995). A distributed memory model of semantic priming. *Journal of Experimental Psychology: Learning, Memory, and Cognition*, 21(1), 3–23.

Masson, M. E. J., & Caldwell, J. I. (1998). Conceptually driven encoding episodes create perceptual misattributions. *Acta Psychologica*, 98(2–3), 183–210.

May, C. P., Kane, M. J., & Hasher, L. (1995). Determinants of negative priming. *Psychological Bulletin*, 118(1), 35–54.

Mayr, S., & Buchner, A. (2007). Negative priming as a memory phenomenon: A review of 20 years of negative priming research. *Zeitschrift für Psychologie/Journal of Psychology*, 215(1), 35–51.

McClelland, J. L., Mc Naughton, B. L., & O'Reilly, R. C. (1995). Why there are complementary learning systems in the hippocampus and neocortex: Insights from the successes and failures of connectionist models of learning and memory. *Psychological Review*, 102(3), 419–457.

McCloskey, M., & Zaragoza, M. (1985). Misleading postevent information and memory for events: Arguments and evidence against memory impairment hypotheses. *Journal of Experimental Psychology: General*, 114(1), 1–16.

Medin, D. L., & Schaffer, M. M. (1978). Context theory of classification learning. *Psychological Review*, 85(3), 207–238.

Merikle, P. M., & Reingold, E. M. (1990). Recognition and lexical decision without detection: Unconscious perception? *Journal of Experimental Psychology: Human Perception and Performance*, 16(3), 574–583.

Merikle, P. M., Smilek, D., & Eastwood, J. D. (2001). Perception without awareness: Perspectives from cognitive psychology. *Cognition*, 79(1–2), 115–134.

Meuter, R. F. I., & Allport, A. (1999). Bilingual language switching in naming: Asymmetrical costs of language selection. *Journal of Memory and Language*, 40(1), 25–40.

Meyer, D. E., & Schvaneveldt, R. W. (1971). Facilitation in recognizing pairs of words: Evidence of a dependence between retrieval operations. *Journal of Experimental Psychology*, 90(2), 227–234.

Milliken, B., Joordens, S., Merikle, P. M., & Seiffert, A. E. (1998). Selective attention: A reevaluation of the implications of negative priming. *Psychological Review*, 105(2), 203–229.

Mondor, T. A., Leboe, J. P., & Leboe, L. C. (2005). The role of selection in generating auditory negative priming. *Psychonomic Bulletin and Review*, 12(2), 289–294.

Monsell, S. (1985). Repetition and the lexicon. In A. W. Ellis (Ed.), *Progress in the psychology of language* (Vol. 2, pp. 147–195). London: Erlbaum.

Monsell, S., Yeung, N., & Azuma, R. (2000). Reconfiguration of task-set: Is it easier to switch to the weaker task? *Psychological Research*, 63, 250–264.

Morris, C. D., Bransford, J. D., & Franks, J. J. (1977). Levels of processing versus transfer appropriate processing. *Journal of Verbal Learning and Verbal Behavior*, 16(5), 519–533.

Morton, J. (1969). Interaction of information in word recognition. *Psychological Review*, 76(2), 165–178.

Morton, J. (1979). Facilitation in word recognition: Experiments causing change in the logogen models. In P. A. Kolers , M. E. Wrolstad, & H. Bouma (Eds.), *Processing of visible language* (Vol. 1, pp. 259–268). New York: Plenum.

Moscovitch, M., & Craik, F. I. M. (1976). Depth of processing, retrieval cues, and uniqueness of encoding as factors in recall. *Journal of Verbal Learning and Verbal Behavior*, 15(4), 447–458.

Nadel, L., & Moscovitch, M. (1997). Memory consolidation, retrograde amnesia and the hippocampal complex. *Current Opinion in Neurobiology*, 7(2), 217–227.

Neely, J. H. (1991). Semantic priming effects in visual word recognition: A selective review of current findings and theories. In D. Besner & G. W. Humphreys (Eds.), *Basic processes in reading: Visual word recognition* (pp. 264–336). Hillsdale, NJ: Erlbaum.

Neely, J. H. (1997). Semantic priming and retrieval from lexical memory: Roles of inhibitionless spreading activation and limited-capacity attention. *Journal of Experimental Psychology: General*, 106(3), 226–254.

Neill, W. T. (1977). Inhibitory and facilitatory processes in selective attention. *Journal of Experimental Psychology: Human Perception and Performance*, 3(3), 444–450.

Neill, W. T., & Mathis, K. M. (1998). Transfer-inappropriate processing: Negative priming and related phenomena. In D. L. Medin (Ed.), *The psychology of learning and motivation: Advances in research and theory* (Vol. 38, pp. 1–44). San Diego, CA: Academic Press.

Neill, W. T., Valdes, L. A., Terry, K. M., & Gorfein, D. S. (1992). Persistence of negative priming: II. Evidence for episodic trace retrieval. *Journal of Experimental Psychology: Learning, Memory, and Cognition*, 18(5), 993–1000.

Nosofsky, R. M. (1984). Choice, similarity, and the context theory of classification. *Journal of Experimental Psychology: Learning, Memory, and Cognition*, 10(1), 104–114.

Oppenheimer, D. M. (2008). The secret life of fluency. *Trends in Cognitive Sciences*, 12(6), 237–241.

Paap, K. R., Newsome, S. L., & Noel, R. W. (1984). Word shape's in poor shape for the race to the lexicon. *Journal of Experimental Psychology: Human Perception and Performance*, 10, 413–428.

Posner, M. I., & Snyder, C. R. R. (1975). Facilitation and inhibition in the processing of signals. In P. M. A. Rabbitt & S. Dornic (Eds.), *Attention and performance V* (pp. 669–682). New York: Academic Press.

Ratcliff, R., & McKoon, G. (1988). A retrieval theory of priming in memory. *Psychological Review*, 95(3), 385–408.

Reber, A. S. (1989). Implicit learning and tacit knowledge. *Journal of Experimental Psychology: General*, 118(3), 219–235.

Reber, R., Schwarz, N., & Winkielman, P. (2004). Processing fluency and aesthetic pleasure: Is beauty in the perceiver's processing experience? *Personality and Social Psychology Review*, 8(4), 364–382.

Rhodes, M. G., & Castel, A. D. (2008). Memory predictions are influenced by perceptual information: Evidence for metacognitive illusions. *Journal of Experimental Psychology: General*, 137(4), 615–625.

Roediger, H. L., III. (2003). Reconsidering implicit memory. In J. S. Bowers & C. J. Marsolek (Eds.), *Rethinking implicit memory* (pp. 3–18). New York: Oxford University Press.

Roediger, H. L., III., & Blaxton, T. A. (1987). Retrieval modes produce dissociations in memory for surface information. In D. S. Gorfein & R. R. Hoffman (Eds.), *Memory and learning* (pp. 349–379). Hillsdale, NJ: Erlbaum.

Roediger, H. L., III., Weldon, M. S., & Challis, B. H. (1989). Explaining dissociations between implicit and explicit measures of retention: A processing account. In H. L. Roediger III & F. I. M. Craik (Eds.), *Varieties of memory and consciousness: Essays in honour of Endel Tulving* (pp. 3–41). Hillsdale, NJ: Erlbaum.

Rothermund, K., Wentura, D., & De Houwer, J. (2005). Retrieval of incidental stimulus-response associations as a source of negative priming. *Journal of Experimental Psychology: Learning, Memory, and Cognition*, 31(3), 482–495.

Scarborough, D. L., Cortese, C., & Scarborough, H. S. (1977). Frequency and repetition effects in lexical memory. *Journal of Experimental Psychology: Human Perception and Performance*, 3(1), 1–17.

Scarborough, D. L., Gerard, L., & Cortese, C. (1979). Accessing lexical memory: The transfer of word repetition effects across task and modality. *Memory and Cognition*, 7(1), 3–12.

Schacter, D. L. (1987). Implicit memory: History and current status. *Journal of Experimental Psychology: Learning, Memory, and Cognition*, 13(3), 501–518.

Schneider, W., & Shiffrin, R. M. (1977). Controlled and automatic human information processing: I. Detection, search, and attention. *Psychological Review*, 84, 1–66.

Smith, E. E., & Medin, D. L. (2002). The exemplar view. In D. Levitin (Ed.), *Foundations of cognitive psychology: Core readings* (pp. 277–292). Cambridge, MA: The MIT Press.

Squire, L., & Zola-Morgan, S. (1991). The medial temporal lobe memory system. *Science*, 253(5026), 1380–1386.

Squire, L. R. (1992). Declarative and nondeclarative memory: Multiple brain systems supporting learning and memory. *Journal of Cognitive Neuroscience*, 4(3), 232–243.

Stolz, J. A., & Neely, J. H. (2001). Taking a bright view of negative priming in the light of dim stimuli: Further evidence for memory confusion during episodic retrieval. *Canadian Journal of Experimental Psychology*, 55, 219–230.

Stroop, J. R. (1935). The basis of Ligon's theory. *American Journal of Psychology*, 47, 499–504.

Tenpenny, P. L. (1995). Abstractionist versus episodic theories of repetition priming and word identification. *Psychonomic Bulletin and Review*, 2(3), 339–363.

Tiede, H. L., Derksen, C., & Leboe, J. P. (2009). An investigation of increases in metamemory confidence across multiple study trials. *Memory*, 17(3), 288–300.

Tipper, S. P. (1985). The negative priming effect: Inhibitory priming by ignored objects. *Quarterly Journal of Experimental Psychology Section A: Human Experimental Psychology*, 37(4), 571–590.

Tipper, S. P. (2001). Does negative priming reflect inhibitory mechanisms? A review and integration of conflicting views. *Quarterly Journal of Experimental Psychology Section A: Human Experimental Psychology*, 54(2), 321–343.

Tipper, S. P., & Cranston, M. (1985). Selective attention and priming: Inhibitory and facilitatory effects of ignored primes. *Quarterly Journal of Experimental Psychology Section A: Human Experimental Psychology*, 37(4), 591–611.

Tulving, E. (1985). Memory and consciousness. *Canadian Psychology-Psychologie Canadienne*, 26(1), 1–12.

Tulving, E. (2002). Episodic memory: From mind to brain. *Annual Review of Psychology*, 53, 1–25.

Tulving, E., Schacter, D. L., & Stark, H. A. (1982). Priming effects in word-fragment completion are independent of recognition memory. *Journal of Experimental Psychology: Learning, Memory, and Cognition*, 8(4), 336–342.

Vriezen, E. R., Moscovitch, M., & Bellos, S. A. (1995). Priming effects in semantic classification tasks. *Journal of Experimental Psychology: Learning, Memory, and Cognition*, 21(4), 933–946.

Westerman, D. L., Lloyd, M. E., & Miller, J. K. (2002). The attribution of perceptual fluency in recognition memory: The role of expectation. *Journal of Memory and Language*, 47(4), 607–617.

Whittlesea, B. W. A. (1987). Preservation of specific experiences in the representation of general knowledge. *Journal of Experimental Psychology: Learning, Memory, and Cognition*, 13(1), 3–17.

Whittlesea, B. W. A. (1993). Illusions of familiarity. *Journal of Experimental Psychology: Learning, Memory, and Cognition*, 19(6), 1235–1253.

Whittlesea, B. W. A. (1997). Production, evaluation and preservation of experiences: Constructive processing in remembering and performance tasks. *The psychology of learning and motivation: Advances in research and theory*, 37, 211–264.

Whittlesea, B. W. A. (2002). Two routes to remembering (and another to remembering not). *Journal of Experimental Psychology: General*, 131(3), 325–348.

Whittlesea, B. W. A. (2004). The perception of integrality: Remembering through the validation of expectation. *Journal of Experimental Psychology: Learning, Memory, and Cognition*, 30(4), 891–908.

Whittlesea, B. W. A., & Brooks, L. R. (1988). Critical influence of particular experiences in the perception of letters, words, and phrases. *Memory and Cognition*, 16(5), 387–399.

Whittlesea, B. W. A., Brooks, L. R., & Westcott, C. (1994). After the learning is over: Factors controlling the selective application of general and particular knowledge. *Journal of Experimental Psychology: Learning, Memory, and Cognition*, 20(2), 259–274.

Whittlesea, B. W. A., & Cantwell, A. L. (1987). Enduring influence of the purpose of experiences: Encoding-retrieval interactions in word and pseudoword perception. *Memory and Cognition*, 15(6), 465–472.

Whittlesea, B. W. A., & Dorken, M. D. (1993). Incidentally, things in general are particularly determined: An episodic-processing account of implicit learning. *Journal of Experimental Psychology: General*, 122(2), 227–248.

Whittlesea, B. W. A., Jacoby, L. L., & Girard, K. (1990). Illusions of immediate memory: Evidence of an attributional basis for feelings of familiarity and perceptual quality. *Journal of Memory and Language*, 29(6), 716–732.

Whittlesea, B. W. A., & Leboe, J. P. (2000). The heuristic basis of remembering and classification: Fluency, generation, and resemblance. *Journal of Experimental Psychology: General*, 129(1), 84–106.

Whittlesea, B. W. A., & Leboe, J. P. (2003). Two fluency heuristics (and how to tell them apart). *Journal of Memory and Language*, 49(1), 62–79.

Whittlesea, B. W. A., & Price, J. R. (2001). Implicit/explicit memory versus analytic/nonanalytic processing: Rethinking the mere exposure effect. *Memory and Cognition*, 29(2), 234–246.

Whittlesea, B. W. A., & Williams, L. D. (1998). Why do strangers feel familiar, but friends don't? A discrepancy-attribution account of feelings of familiarity. *Acta Psychologica*, 98(2–3), 141–165.

Whittlesea, B. W. A., & Williams, L. D. (2000). The source of feelings of familiarity: The discrepancy-attribution hypothesis. *Journal of Experimental Psychology: Learning, Memory, and Cognition*, 26(3), 547–565.

Whittlesea, B. W. A., & Williams, L. D. (2001a). The discrepancy-attribution hypothesis: I. The heuristic basis of feelings and familiarity. *Journal of Experimental Psychology: Learning, Memory, and Cognition*, 27(1), 3–13.

Whittlesea, B. W. A., & Williams, L. D. (2001b). The discrepancy-attribution hypothesis: II. Expectation, uncertainty, surprise, and feelings of familiarity. *Journal of Experimental Psychology: Learning, Memory, and Cognition*, 27(1), 14–33.

Whittlesea, B. W. A., & Wright, R. L. (1997). Implicit (and explicit) learning: Acting adaptively without knowing the consequences. *Journal of Experimental Psychology: Learning, Memory, and Cognition*, 23(1), 181–200.

Witherspoon, D., & Allan, L. G. (1985). The effect of a prior presentation on temporal judgments in a perceptual identification task. *Memory and Cognition*, 13(2), 101–111.

Wong, J., & Leboe, J. P. (2009). Distinguishing between inhibitory and episodic processing accounts of switch-cost asymmetries. *Canadian Journal of Experimental Psychology*, 63(1), 8–23.

Wood, T. J., & Milliken, B. (1998). Negative priming without ignoring. *Psychonomic Bulletin and Review*, 5(3), 470–475.

Wright, R. L., & Whittlesea, B. W. A. (1998). Implicit learning of complex structures: Active adaptation and selective processing in acquisition and application. *Memory and Cognition*, 26(2), 402–420.

Wylie, G., & Allport, A. (2000). Task switching and the measurement of "switch costs." *Psychological Research*, 63(3), 212–233.

Yeung, N., & Monsell, S. (2003). Switching between tasks of unequal familiarity: The role of stimulus-attribute and response-set selection. *Journal of Experimental Psychology: Human Perception and Performance*, 29(2), 455–469.

Yonelinas, A. P. (2002). The nature of recollection and familiarity: A review of 30 years of research. *Journal of Memory and Language*, 46(3), 441–517.

Zola-Morgan, S., & Squire, L. R. (1993). Neuroanatomy of memory. *Annual Review of Neuroscience*, 16, 547–563.

# Event-Based Prospective Remembering: An Integration of Prospective Memory and Cognitive Control Theories

Julie M. Bugg, Mark A. McDaniel, *and* Gilles O. Einstein

**Abstract**

Event-based prospective memory refers to remembering to perform an intended action in response to an anticipated event at some point in the future. In this chapter, we describe the primary components that support prospective memory. These components include encoding, storage, and retrieval. For encoding, we consider one effective strategy, implementation intentions, and the mechanism(s) by which such intentions improve prospective remembering. For storage, we review research that examines whether individuals have privileged access to intention-related information during a retention interval, and the role of retrievals in fostering retention. For retrieval, we discuss theorizing regarding the role of monitoring and spontaneous processes in prospective memory. Throughout, we highlight several features that differentiate prospective and retrospective remembering. In a final section we emphasize one such feature, the need to coordinate ongoing activities with retrieval. To gain traction on such coordination, we propose an integration of cognitive control and prospective memory theories.

**Key Words:** prospective memory, implementation intentions, intention superiority, monitoring, spontaneous retrieval, cognitive control

Event-based prospective memory (PM) refers to remembering to perform an intended action in response to an anticipated event at some point in the future. PM challenges are ubiquitous in our everyday lives and include remembering to turn off your cell phone when you attend a lecture and remembering to stop at the local coffee shop on your way to work in the morning. Although the consequences of PM failures for such tasks may be relatively mild (e.g., you may feel embarrassed or suffer caffeine withdrawal), some PM failures have devastating consequences. Consider, for example, an airline pilot who must remember to set the airplane's wing flaps after an unanticipated holding pattern (see Nowinski, Holbrook, & Dismukes, 2003) or a surgeon who must remember to check a patient's body for surgical instruments prior to closing the incision (see Fig. 18.1; Dembitzer & Lai, 2003).

For these types of PM challenges, and many others, failure to perform the intended action may be life threatening.

Consequently, it is important to understand the critical components that underlie both successful and unsuccessful prospective remembering. Three primary components have been emphasized in research studies over the past few decades. One component process is *encoding*. Taking the example from earlier, imagine that you awoke one morning to discover that you were out of coffee beans. Knowing you could not possibly make it through the day without caffeine, you formulate an intention (e.g., I will buy a cup of coffee at Café Espresso di Cincotta on my drive in to work). You long for a cup of coffee while showering and eating breakfast, and these additional reminders may serve to bolster the encoding of the intention. Upon hitting

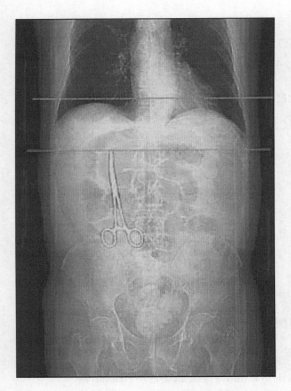

**Figure 18.1** Scan of a 16-cm clamp left in the abdominal area of a patient. (Reprinted with permission from Dembitzer, A., & Lai, E. J. (2003). Retained surgical instrument. New England Journal of Medicine, 348, 228.)

the highway you begin to think about the numerous items (i.e., additional PM intentions) on your to-do list (e.g., meet with a student, grade an exam, work on a manuscript). You reach your exit 30 minutes later and proceed toward the university. Thus, there is some delay between the formulation of the intention (i.e., encoding) and the occurrence of the event (passing the Café) that signals that the window of opportunity has arrived for execution of the intention. We refer to the processes that support maintenance of the intention over the course of this delay as reflecting a *storage* component. You now catch sight of Café Espresso di Cincotta, the intention of buying a cup of coffee pops into mind, and you head for the finish line. It is the occurrence of this final component, *retrieval*, which serves to complete a PM task.

As may be obvious from this example, there appears to be parallels between prospective remembering and the often-researched retrospective remembering. For purposes of organizing and describing the component processes that support prospective remembering, we have adopted the

same framework that has frequently been used to organize and describe retrospective memory (RM) processes. Briefly, this framework recognizes that some information is *encoded* and following a delay during which it is *stored*, the information is subsequently *retrieved*. Although these surface similarities exist, deeper consideration of the primary components reveals a number of features that differentiate prospective and retrospective remembering (e.g., see McDaniel & Einstein, 2007). In this chapter, we will highlight the unique challenges and properties associated with PM tasks during encoding, storage, and especially retrieval.

Another aim of this chapter is to relate general theories of cognitive control to prospective remembering and, by so doing, extend current theoretical understanding of PM. This perspective further highlights a primary difference between prospective and retrospective remembering (i.e., the need to coordinate performance of ongoing activities with the recognition of a PM signal [i.e., target event] and retrieval of an intention), and additionally, it provides new directions for investigating the control processes that support the fulfillment of PM intentions.

## Laboratory-Based Prospective Memory Tasks

Before considering the primary components involved in prospective remembering, it is useful to first briefly describe the typical laboratory paradigm used to investigate PM. In a typical laboratory paradigm (see Fig. 18.2), a participant is given an instruction to perform an ongoing activity (e.g., a lexical decision task in which she must judge whether a string of letters is a word or nonword) and an instruction to remember to perform an intention (i.e., the phase during which encoding occurs). For example, the participant may be asked to press the "Q" key if she encounters a target event such as the word "tornado" or the syllable "tor." Instructions often encourage participants to prioritize performance on the ongoing task and to characterize the PM task as secondary. The participant is then busily engaged in the ongoing activity. The storage demand is reflected by the fact that many (e.g., 100) trials of the lexical decision task can occur prior to the appearance of the first target event. Retrieval is measured by whether the participant remembers to retrieve the intention and press the Q key when the target occurs. In total there are often just a few targets (e.g., four)

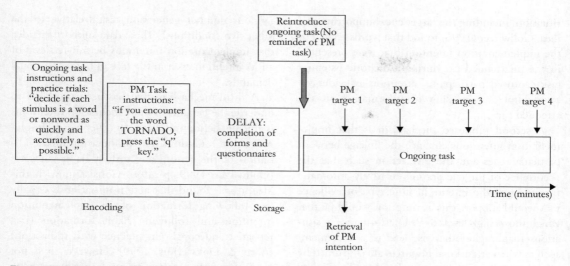

**Figure 18.2** Primary components of a typical laboratory prospective memory (PM) paradigm.

among hundreds of lexical-decision trials. Spacing the targets in this manner is intended to simulate real-world remembering where PM target events may occur infrequently in the context of engaging ongoing activities. Participants are also typically questioned at the end of the experiment to help identify the source of any memory failures. Specifically, they are tested for their memory of the PM target and action to determine whether any forgetting was the result of a PM failure or a retrospective memory failure associated with forgetting the task demands.

## Contributions of Encoding, Storage, and Retrieval Components

### Encoding

A characteristic of PM challenges is that they often involve a priori knowledge of the cues that will be available to activate retrieval. Thus, for PM it is often possible to systematically formulate a strategy or plan during encoding that will maximize the likelihood of retrieval upon the onset of the expected cue. Perhaps the most clear-cut and well-researched example of use of such an encoding strategy in PM tasks is implementation intentions (Gollwitzer, 1999). Implementation intentions refer to "If Situation x, then Response y" statements. For example, "When I see the Café Espresso di Cincotta sign on my way to work, I will stop to buy a coffee." Note that the triggering situation is specifically indicated (and in good detail) in this statement relative to a general goal statement such as "I will buy a cup of coffee." The implementation

intention entails a more contextualized cue-action plan in that it includes components such as where and when the intention will be carried out, and in some cases involves visualization of oneself performing the intended action upon onset of the cue (Chasteen, Park, & Schwarz, 2001; McFarland & Glisky, 2012).

Several studies have revealed that the additional effort applied at encoding to formulate an implementation intention is well rewarded, and the strategy appears applicable for a variety of PM challenges. For instance, Sheeran and Orbell (1999) found a 35% reduction in the rate with which participants forgot to take at least one vitamin C pill over a 3-week period for a group that formed an implementation intention relative to a group that formed a more general goal statement. Similarly, implementation intentions have been shown to effectively increase the proportion of individuals who engage in exercise in the week following formulation of the intention (Milne, Orbell, & Sheeran, 2002). About 29% of individuals who formed general goal statements and 39% of individuals who received motivational material engaged in exercise, whereas a whopping 91% of those who formed an implementation intention, in addition to being given motivational material, exercised.

A key theoretical question concerns why this particular type of encoding has such pronounced benefits. It appears several potential mechanisms may converge to benefit PM (Gollwitzer, 1999). One is that implementation intentions enhance the accessibility/activation of the anticipated PM situation, including the target cue. Supporting this idea, Gollwitzer (1996) found that words related to the implementation intention that were presented in the unattended ear during a dichotic listening task captured participants' attention as evidenced by disrupted processing of information in the attended ear.

A second proposed mechanism is that implementation intentions enhance the linkage between particular cues and the PM action such that the occurrence of the cue permits relatively automatic triggering of the intention. One type of evidence that would support this assumption would be that which shows high levels of PM performance in situations that might otherwise lead to a decrement, such as when attentional resources are consumed by other tasks. Providing support for this view, Cohen and Gollwitzer (2008) found that the formation of an implementation intention, relative to standard prospective memory instructions, bolstered PM performance. In addition, only the implementation intention condition was associated with an absence of cost to ongoing task performance. (As will be discussed in the *Retrieval* section, cost refers to the degree to which the presence of a PM intention interferes with ongoing task performance.)

Additional support for this view stems from a study in which attentional resources were further challenged by asking participants to sometimes perform a demanding secondary task (random number generation) in addition to the ongoing activity and the PM task (McDaniel, Howard, & Butler, 2008; Exp. 2). PM performance was evaluated for a standard instructional group, an imagery encoding group, and an implementation intentions group that read, imagined, and stated their intention of performing the action in response to the appropriate cue. PM performance was higher for participants in the implementation intention condition relative to either the standard instructional or imagery encoding conditions. The key finding was that for the implementation intentions condition, PM performance was not degraded by the presence of a high attentional load; by contrast, in the two conditions in which implementation intentions were not formulated, PM declined under high attentional load (but see, McDaniel & Scullin, 2010). Equally important, intact PM performance for the implementation intention group under conditions of high attentional load could not be explained by differential resource allocation policies (e.g., neglecting the ongoing task, or showing greater cost on the ongoing task) or reduced effort toward the secondary,

random number generation task (relative to the other two conditions). These data support the idea that implementation intentions permit retrieval of a PM intention even in the face of high attentional demands.

A third mechanism that has been proposed to underlie the benefits of implementation intentions is efficient action initiation. In other words, implementation intentions may produce automatic initiation of the action, an "instant habit" of sorts (Gollwitzer, 1999, p. 499). Consistent with this idea, it was found that action initiation is equally fast following formation of an implementation intention and following habit formation (i.e., repeated and consistent practice with the action) (Aarts & Dijksterjuis, 1999). However, it is not clear that this mechanism underlies benefits to PM performance. Recently, McDaniel and Scullin (2010; Exp. 3) found that repeated practice performing the intended action in response to the target cue led to significantly better performance than implementation intentions in a subsequent PM test phase with high attentional load (a finding that could not be accounted for by differential resource allocation policies). If implementation intentions promoted PM through automatic initiation, then performance in the implementation-intention condition should have been comparable to the performance observed in the repeated practice condition (a condition that presumably created reflexive response initiation). Thus, these findings do not support the view that implementation intentions produce completely automatic prospective remembering.

Implementation intentions did, however, produce equivalent PM performance to that obtained in a generation-encoding condition, a condition that was expected to strengthen the association between the cue and intended action (McDaniel & Scullin, 2010, Exp. 2). Taken in concert, the current evidence is consistent with the conclusion that implementation intentions bolster linkages between cues and intentions. These linkages may stimulate retrieval of the intention upon presentation of the cue, but they need not produce automatized responding (i.e., automatic initiation of the action). We now consider storage characteristics of PM intentions.

## Storage
### HEIGHTENED ACTIVATION
An unresolved issue in the PM literature is whether prospective memories are stored with heightened

activation relative to retrospective memories. In the preceding section we referred to changes in the activation level of intention-related information as a function of forming implementation intentions. The implication is that a by-product of effective encoding strategies may be a boost in the activation level of a PM intention. Even without these strategies, however, some researchers have suggested that intended actions are stored in a privileged state relative to other items in memory. One can imagine, for instance, a continuum of baseline activation levels with PM intentions falling toward the high end of the continuum such that less "triggering" may be needed (e.g., via a target event or cue) to bring the intention to mind (cf. Yaniv & Meyer, 1987). This idea has been empirically tested by comparing how quickly memory judgments are generated for PM intentions relative to other memory contents when similarly cued.

A series of experiments by Goschke and Kuhl (1993) provided initial support for what they called the *intention superiority effect*. In their paradigm, participants studied two scripts. Each script was composed of a short list of actions (e.g., sort the file cards, stack the articles) that was affiliated with a particular event (e.g., clearing a desk). Following study of both scripts, one was designated the prospective script and the other the neutral script. Participants were told that a recognition test would be given on both scripts, and that they would be asked to later execute the actions from the prospective but not the neutral script. Designating scripts as prospective or neutral following study ensured that any differences in the activation level of actions from each script were not attributable to differential encoding strategies. The recognition test, consisting of actions from the prospective and neutral scripts, as well as distracter actions, was administered next. Consistent with the idea that intention-related actions are stored at a higher baseline level of activation, and thus more accessible when cued, recognition judgments were faster for the prospective as compared to the neutral actions (for a similar finding using lexical-decision judgments, see Marsh, Hicks, & Bink, 1998).

Using variations of the aforementioned paradigm, Goschke and Kuhl (1993) ruled out alternative explanations of the intention superiority effect. In one variant, for example, participants were told that they would have to recall both scripts at the end of the experiment, and a distracter activity was inserted immediately after the prospective script was identified to prevent additional rehearsal. Speeded recognition of the prospective, to-be-executed

actions was still found relative to the neutral actions, suggesting that the effect cannot be accounted for by differential strategies that were developed following designation of a script as prospective or neutral.

In another experiment, Goschke and Kuhl (1993) included a second group that was given identical instructions as in the original experiment except that the prospective script was now termed the observe script. This group was told that they would later be asked to determine whether an experimenter performed all actions from the observe script. Critically, then, participants in both the prospective and observe groups expected to use information from these scripts at a later point in the experiment. Thus, comparing the accessibility of actions from the prospective and observe scripts permits one to evaluate whether the activation level of prospective actions is higher (i.e., facilitated) than other information that is as relevant to an upcoming decision (i.e., the nonneutral observe actions). Further supporting the notion of intention superiority, recognition judgments were faster for the prospective relative to the observe actions (see Fig. 18.3). As for the neutral items, recognition judgments were slower in the presence of prospective as compared to observe actions (see Fig. 18.3). This suggests that the greater accessibility of prospective intentions likely reflects a combination of heightened activation of intention-related actions as well as suppression of actions that are not relevant to the intention.

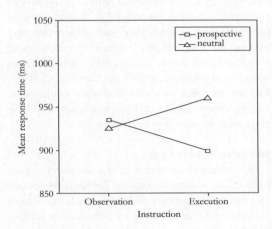

**Figure 18.3** Mean recognition latencies for prospective and neutral items in the observation and execution conditions. (Reprinted with permission from Goschke, T., & Kuhl, J. (1993). Representation of intentions: Persisting activation in memory. *Journal of Experimental Psychology: Learning, Memory and Cognition, 19*(5), 1211–1226.)

Whereas the work of Goschke and Kuhl (1993) is compelling, it is not without limitations. For present purposes, perhaps the most critical limitation is that this work differs in an important way from the large majority of PM research. That is, participants are never asked to self-initiate performance of the prospective script in response to a particular event or cue that signals retrieval of the intention-related actions. We are left to assume that a higher state of prospective intention-related activation would lead to better PM performance, which is reasonable, but an assumption nonetheless. Countering this concern somewhat, the work of Freeman and Ellis (2003) showed that the general level of activation of to-be-enacted information and the advantage for to-be-enacted items was still found when participants had to self-initiate retrieval (i.e., they did not expect to be cued by the experimenter).

A second limitation is that the possibility remains that the intention superiority effect reflects differential activation of motor information during encoding (i.e., an *action superiority* interpretation), and not privileged storage of information that is intended for later enactment. In support of this view, Freeman and Ellis (2003) found that recognition judgments were speeded for to-be-enacted (intended) actions (analogous to Goschke & Kuhl's, 1993, prospective condition) relative to neutral items, but the advantage for to-be-enacted actions disappeared when motor processing was prevented by an interference task that followed encoding. A verbal interference task did not disrupt the advantage. This combined pattern is contrary to the notion of privileged access to intention-related information. It appears then that participants may prepare for a prospective intention by developing a motor-based action schema that then facilitates access to the intention (but see Goschke & Kuhl, Exp. 4). In other words, at least some of the time, storage-related effects in PM paradigms may have their roots in encoding operations.

### RETENTION INTERVAL

Regardless of the locus of the intention superiority effect, a critical question for both theoretical and practical purposes is how long the enhanced activation of intention-related information persists. This is a more specified version of the general question concerning the retention principles that underlie PM. In Goschke and Kuhl's (1993) work, the heightened activation persisted for at least 15 minutes. Similarly, in other work, it has been shown that PM performance does not decline with increasing retention intervals from 15 to 30 minutes (Einstein, Holland, McDaniel, & Guynn, 1992) or 4 to 20 minutes (Guynn, McDaniel, & Einstein, 1998). Note that the retention interval in these studies was defined as the time between the formation of the intention and the occurrence of the target cue. Retention interval might also be thought of as the time between the formation of the intention and the beginning of the ongoing activity during which a PM target cue is expected. When so defined, there is evidence that PM performance may actually increase as the retention interval increases. Hicks, Marsh, and Russell (2000) used filled retention intervals wherein participants performed a series of distracter tasks that were either 2.5 min or 15 min in length. In two experiments, PM performance was 17% and 21% better for the long- as compared to short-retention interval. One conclusion that can be drawn on the basis of this work is that, at least for retention intervals of these durations, PM does not appear to adhere to the same retention principles as RM, where classically a negatively accelerating logarithmic forgetting curve is observed as a function of the retention interval.

A possible reason for why PM performance may improve with a longer retention interval is that participants may have more opportunities to retrieve the intention (either spontaneously or intentionally). It is plausible, for instance, that retrievals of a PM intention during a retention interval help to maintain its heightened state of activation, and facilitate subsequent retrieval of the intention. Indeed, Kvavilashvili (1987) found that thoughts about the intention during the ongoing activity positively correlated with PM performance, and Kvavilashvili and Fisher (2007) found that throughout the retention interval (6 days in their experiments) people reported that chance encounters with cues related to the intention stimulated retrievals of the intention (e.g., seeing someone on a phone triggered recollection of the intention to telephone the experimenter at an appointed day and time). This dynamic likely pervades PM in everyday contexts. For instance, for the intention to get coffee, one is likely to experience both internal cues (feeling tired) and external cues (smelling the aroma of coffee when walking by someone's office) that would trigger retrieval of that intention.

In laboratory experiments, instructing participants to use breaks that were inserted during an ongoing activity to retrieve the intention significantly enhanced PM performance relative to an instruction to relax during breaks (Finstad, Bink,

McDaniel, & Einstein, 2006, Exp. 1). The nature of the retrieval also seems to be important. Guynn et al. (1998) incorporated a retrieval prompt 1 minute prior to the appearance of a PM target cue. Relative to a control group that was not prompted, retrieving the complete intention (target + action) improved PM performance by an astounding 51%. Critically, however, it appears that not all retrievals are created equal. A significantly smaller benefit was observed for a retrieval prompt that cued only the action, and no benefit occurred as a result of a retrieval prompt that focused on the target cues alone (e.g., subjects were instructed "remember the three words that you studied at the beginning of the experiment," referring to the three target cues). Thus far the data indicate that the best kind of retrieval cue or reminder is one that includes thinking about the target and action together.

Further specification of the factors that yield a positive association between retrieval of intentions and PM performance will be both theoretically and practically fruitful. In this vein, Kvavilashvili (1987) found that thoughts about the intention (i.e., retrievals) during the retention interval were more frequent when the ongoing task was less absorbing and when the instructions emphasized that remembering to fulfill the PM intention was very important, with a higher frequency of thoughts associated with better PM. Additional factors that might be explored include the length of the retention interval and whether the interval includes sleep (e.g., Scullin & McDaniel, 2010).

Other relevant factors likely include the number of ongoing tasks as well as the number of currently activated intentions. Real-world PM is often characterized by having several concurrent intentions that are differentially prioritized, and that must be coordinated with constantly changing goals and activities. The fact that humans can continue to successfully perform PM tasks under these situations is impressive. This likely reflects, at least in part, the use of external reminders (Meacham & Leiman, 1982) and our ability to quite naturally deactivate performed intentions, which might otherwise produce interference. Supporting the latter possibility, Marsh, Hicks, and Bink (1998; cf. Scullin, Einstein, & McDaniel, 2009) showed that the intention superiority effect disappears once the prospective actions are performed (but see Scullin & Bugg, 2012; Scullin, Bugg, & McDaniel, 2012; Walser, Fischer, & Goschke, 2012, for evidence of the failure to deactivate previously relevant intentions).

## Retrieval

Although there are clearly many interesting research questions regarding encoding and storage processes in PM, the majority of research in PM has addressed the retrieval properties of PM (for a detailed overview, see McDaniel & Einstein, 2007). Perhaps the most striking difference between RM and PM is retrieval. Unlike an RM task, where participants are directed to initiate a search of memory (e.g., in the laboratory, "Please recall the word that was associated with the cue PRANCE in the previous list," or in everyday life, "How do you get to Barberry Street?"), prospective remembering involves retrieval in the absence of a direct instruction to engage in a retrieval search. For example, after forming the intention to pick up bread at the store, there is no one present to prompt you to search your memory for what you are supposed to do when you pass the store. In other words, RM involves the adoption of a retrieval mode (but see Berntsen, 2009, for spontaneous RM in the absence of a retrieval mode), but PM does not (see Guynn, 2003, for an alternative view of PM). How, then, is retrieval of PM intentions accomplished? Research to date suggests two primary types of processes that support retrieval, attentional monitoring and spontaneous retrieval. We will describe each of these in turn.

### MONITORING

Attentional monitoring entails resource-consuming processes that are engaged to support prospective remembering (Smith, 2003; Smith & Bayen, 2004). These "preparatory" attentional processes monitor events to determine whether the target event is present and, if so, the intended action can be initiated. According to Smith's preparatory attention and memory (PAM) model, attentional monitoring processes combine with memory processes that discriminate target events from nontarget events and recollect the intended action upon encountering the target event. In the context of a laboratory experiment, the idea would be that while performing an ongoing lexical decision task, the participant is actively checking each letter string (e.g., BRUB, THORN, FALLOT, TORCH) to determine whether it is the target (e.g., TORCH). This determination is made through a recognition check. Thus, in the preceding example, in turn, BRUB, then THORN, then FALLOT, then TORCH would be compared with the target in memory (i.e., TORCH), and once there is a match the participant will start to initiate the action.

Within this view, forgetting occurs because of a failure to maintain the preparatory attention process (i.e., a failure to initiate the recognition check) or because of a recognition failure (i.e., forgetting that TORCH is the target item). A primary signature of the preparatory monitoring process is cost, which refers to the decrement in ongoing task performance that is associated with the presence of a PM intention. Cost is typically calculated by comparing average reaction time (and/or accuracy) on the ongoing task in a control block that does not include the PM intention with average reaction time on the ongoing task in an experimental block where the PM intention is present.

The PAM theory makes several predictions. One is that PM performance should suffer with increases in the attentional demands associated with the ongoing task, as this would leave fewer resources for monitoring. Supporting this prediction, it has been shown that the addition of a secondary task to the ongoing task often interferes with PM performance (McDaniel, Robinson-Riegler, & Einstein, 1998; Park, Hertzog, Kidder, Morrell, & Mayhorn, 1997), particularly when the secondary task engages resources that overlap with those that are presumed to support monitoring (Marsh & Hicks, 1998).

A second prediction is that cost, the primary signature of monitoring, should always accompany successful PM performance. Smith (2003) was the first to evaluate cost by focusing solely on the non-target trials of the ongoing task, rather than focusing on or including PM target trials. This is important because the interpretation of slowing for target trials is ambiguous, as these trials are expected to be slowed in an experimental block with a PM intention regardless of whether a participant is monitoring (Marsh, Hicks, & Watson, 2002). In contrast, according to Smith, slowing on nontarget trials decisively implicates the presence of monitoring, or in other words the deployment of attention toward checking for the PM target. Indeed, studies using a range of ongoing tasks (e.g., lexical decision, category judgment, color matching) have shown that the experimental block is often accompanied by significant cost relative to a control block (Einstein et al., 2005; Guynn, 2003; Marsh, Hicks, Cook, Hansen, & Pallos, 2003; Smith, 2003; Smith & Bayen, 2004). Moreover, on average, participants who perform better on the PM task show greater cost than those who perform more poorly on the PM task (Smith, 2003). Though such an effect has not consistently been reported, it is important

because it suggests a functional relationship between monitoring and PM performance.

The aforementioned findings support the role of monitoring in facilitating retrieval of an intention in laboratory PM paradigms. However, one might question the degree to which a resource-consuming process would be utilized to support everyday PM challenges. Everyday PM challenges often involve retention intervals that are rather lengthy relative to those used in the laboratory and often filled with various tasks for which performance is at a premium. For example, would you actively monitor for a coffee shop as soon as you begin your commute to work? Would you continuously sacrifice the ongoing task (driving safely) to free up resources for monitoring? There is some laboratory-based evidence to suggest that the answer to these questions is "no."

Marsh, Hicks, and Cook (2006) gave participants a PM task (remembering to press a particular key if they encountered an animal word) and told participants in advance that the animal words would appear in Phase 3. The ongoing, lexical-decision task was given in Phase 1 and Phase 3, with Phase 2 consisting of questionnaires. This unique design permitted Marsh and his colleagues to evaluate cost for the context in which the target event was expected (i.e., Phase 3) as well as the context in which the target event was not expected (i.e., Phase 1). Here, continuous monitoring was not observed. Instead, the presence of cost, and by implication monitoring, was limited to Phase 3. This suggests that we tend to associate intentions with particular contexts and restrict monitoring to these contexts. Returning to the coffee shop example, then, the implication is that one might monitor at particular locations (e.g., a strip mall) where it seems likely that a coffee shop would be present, rather than continuously checking visible signs for the phrase "Coffee Shop." The idea that monitoring is contextually driven as opposed to continuous, thus, provides a reasonable account of how humans manage to remember everyday PM intentions.

## MULTIPLE PROCESSES: SPONTANEOUS RETRIEVAL PROCESSES

The other major theoretical perspective that attempts to explain PM retrieval is the multiprocess theory proposed by McDaniel and Einstein (2000; see also McDaniel & Einstein, 2007). According to this theory, people can use spontaneous retrieval processes in addition to monitoring processes in order to accomplish PM retrieval. By spontaneous retrieval, they mean that the occurrence of a target event (or a related event) triggers retrieval under conditions in which no resources are devoted to monitoring the environment for the target event. McDaniel and Einstein (2007) have identified two spontaneous retrieval mechanisms. The *reflexive associative process* assumes that after forming an association between the target event and the intended action (and storing it in long-term memory), later processing of the target event will cause the intended action to be delivered to awareness.

The *discrepancy plus search process* follows from Whittlesea and Williams's (2001) view that people are sensitive to the discrepancy between the actual quality of processing of an event and the expected quality of processing. As applied to PM, the idea is that upon encountering a target event (at retrieval), a person experiences it with more or less fluency than is expected in that context and this discrepancy stimulates a search of memory to identify the source of the discrepancy (i.e., that the target event is a cue for an intended action). As described at the outset of this paragraph, neither of these processes requires monitoring or *preparatory* attentional processes in order to accomplish retrieval of an intention.

The multiprocess framework assumes that people prefer to rely on these spontaneous retrieval processes to support prospective remembering (cf. Bargh & Chartrand, 1999). In line with this assumption, participants often indicate that intentions simply "pop into mind" (Einstein & McDaniel, 1990), and participants report that they rarely (<5% of the time) think about the PM intention while performing the ongoing task (Reese & Cherry, 2002). It is important to note that the multiprocess theory also assumes that the process that the person relies on in a given situation (as well as the effectiveness of that process) depends on a number of factors, including the nature of the PM task, the nature and demands of the ongoing task, and individual differences. For example, research thus far has shown that participants are more likely to rely on spontaneous retrieval processes with one target event (Cohen & Gollwitzer, 2008), when the importance of the ongoing task is emphasized (and the importance of the PM task is deemphasized; Einstein et al., 2005; Kliegel, Martin, McDaniel, & Einstein, 2004) and when focal cues are used. As illustrated in Table 18.1, focal cues are those whose processing overlaps with the processing participants engage in as they perform the ongoing task, whereas nonfocal cues are those that require processing that does not overlap with that which is engaged during the ongoing task (see McDaniel & Einstein, 2007, for

further elaboration of the distinction between focal and nonfocal cues).

Perhaps the most direct evidence in support of spontaneous retrieval processes in PM stems from experiments in which participants perform the PM task at high levels but with no evidence of cost (see Einstein & McDaniel, 2010). One critical experiment that provides this evidence was conducted by Einstein et al. (2005, Exp. 2; see also Scullin, McDaniel, & Einstein, 2010) in which a category judgment task was used as the ongoing task (i.e., decide whether the lowercase word presented on screen [e.g., tiger] was a member of the category written in capital letters [e.g., ANIMAL]) and a word (e.g., tortoise) served as the cue. Under these conditions, PM performance was very high (93%), and importantly significant slowing (cost) was not observed. This supports the idea that a spontaneous retrieval process, rather than monitoring, may underlie successful PM performance on some tasks. A key factor that was believed to stimulate such retrieval and bias participants away from monitoring in Experiment 2 is that the task entailed focal processing.

Additional evidence in support of spontaneous retrieval processes was obtained in a subsequent experiment by Einstein et al. (2005, Exp. 5). A lexical decision task was interleaved between the PM instructions and the ongoing image-rating task. Participants were told to press a particular key whenever they encountered the target word in the image-rating task. Furthermore, they were told to ignore the PM task during the lexical-decision task, which would occur following some trials of the image-rating task. The key manipulation was the inclusion of two types of words in the lexical decision task. One type was the target words that participants were instructed to respond to during image-rating. The second type was words that were presented in the initial, brief phase of the image-rating task prior to the beginning of the lexical decision task.

The predictions were as follows. Responding was expected to be slowed for the PM target words but speeded for the words for which an imagery rating was provided (due to priming) relative to matched neutral items in the lexical decision phase. These predictions were confirmed. For present purposes, the critical finding was slowed processing of the target words. This finding implicates spontaneous retrieval of the PM intention because the slowing occurred for targets that were presented in a context in which the intention was not relevant. A reader

**Table 18.1** Representative Examples of Task Conditions, Some of Which Have Been Used in Published Research, That We Assume Reflect Nonfocal and Focal Processing

| Processing | Ongoing Task | Prospective Memory Task |
|---|---|---|
| Nonfocal | Words were presented in the center of a computer monitor and participants had to learn them for recall tests that occurred at unpredictable times. | Respond when you see a particular background pattern (background pattern changes every 3 seconds). |
| Focal | Participants had to keep track of the number of occurrences of each background screen pattern. | Respond when you see a particular background pattern (background pattern is changed every 3 seconds). |
| Nonfocal | Lexical decision task | Respond to items from the "animal" category. |
| Focal | Lexical decision task | Respond to the word "cat." |
| Nonfocal | Pairs of words were presented, and participants decided whether the word on the left was a member of the category on the right. | Respond to the syllable "tor." |
| Focal | Pairs of words were presented, and participants decided whether the word on the left was a member of the category on the right. | Respond to the word "tortoise." |
| Nonfocal | Pictures of famous faces were presented, and the task was to name the face. | Respond when you see a face with eyeglasses. |
| Focal | Pictures of famous faces were presented, and the task was to name the face. | Respond when you see a face with the first name of "John." |

*Source*: From Einstein, G. O., & McDaniel, M. A. (2005). Prospective memory: Multiple retrieval processes. *Current Directions in Psychological Science, 14,* 286–290.

might rightfully suggest that participants were perhaps monitoring during the lexical decision task even though instructions clearly noted that PM targets would not occur within this context. This seemed unlikely given the finding of context-specific monitoring (Marsh et al., 2006), which we reviewed earlier. Nonetheless, Einstein et al. evaluated this possibility and found no evidence of monitoring. The data, therefore, suggest that stimuli can elicit intention-related thoughts rather spontaneously, a process that may facilitate retrieval.

Recall that in a previous section we presented evidence that increasing the attentional demands of the ongoing task interfered with PM performance, and this was taken as evidence for the monitoring theory. However, the divided attention results are not as decisively in the favor of the monitoring theory as originally thought (Smith, 2003). First, dividing attention may interfere with spontaneous retrieval itself. For instance, dividing attention may compromise full processing of the target event, which in turn interferes with retrieval of the associated action (cf. Moscovitch, 1994). Dividing attention may also

prevent a retrieved intention from reaching awareness (see Einstein & McDaniel, 2008).

Secondly, dividing attention may interfere with postretrieval processes (e.g., interrupting the ongoing task, holding the retrieved intention in mind, and coordinating the ongoing task and PM responses) that are necessary for ensuring that the PM intention is executed subsequent to retrieval (Einstein, Smith, McDaniel, & Shaw, 1997; McDaniel et al., 1998). These postretrieval processes have received relatively little attention in theories of PM. In the following section, we explore the fruitfulness of incorporating cognitive control theories into a comprehensive view of PM, a view that would embrace consideration of the postretrieval control processes necessary for PM execution.

## Contributions of Control Processes

The view that PM retrieval is accomplished through multiple processes dovetails nicely with a range of dual-process theories in the cognitive literature (e.g., dual-process models of RM; Jacoby, 1991). The multiprocess theory also shares some striking similarities with the recently proposed dual mechanisms of control (DMC) account that provides a general theoretical framework for contextual influences on cognitive control (Braver, Gray, & Burgess, 2007). That very similar theories have emerged from a consideration of the cognitive processes that support performance in very different paradigms speaks to the ubiquity and fruitfulness of dual-process approaches.

The DMC account proposes two types of cognitive control, proactive and reactive, which have been examined primarily in classic cognitive control paradigms such as the Stroop, task-switching, and the AX Continuous Performance task (AX-CPT). According to Braver et al. (2007), *proactive control* involves preparatory establishment and sustained activation of goal-relevant attentional settings. These settings bias attention toward the processing of task-relevant information and prevent or minimize interference from goal-irrelevant information. In the AX-CPT, for example, participants are instructed to make a target response to an X probe when it follows a particular cue (an A stimulus) and a nontarget response otherwise. The AX trial type occurs frequently (e.g., 70% of trials) relative to all other trial types (e.g., 30% of trials are AY, BX, and BY). As such, processing of the A cue leads participants to expect an X probe, which permits them to prepare the target response in advance of the occurrence of the probe. Intact proactive control, thus, facilitates performance on AX trial types.

*Reactive control*, in contrast, is engaged as needed after the occurrence of a stimulus or target event. Reactive control is believed to be triggered by the occurrence of interference from goal-irrelevant information or other processing conflicts. In the AX-CPT, the BX trial type assesses reactive control. On these trial types, the occurrence of an X probe is unexpected (i.e., its occurrence is not predicted by the presentation of the B cue). Its occurrence triggers a tendency to produce the target response (because this is the correct response for most X probes due to the presence of a disproportionate number of AX trials), and participants must engage control to inhibit this prepotent response and make the nontarget response. Following the engagement of reactive control, the attentional settings decay quickly such that it is considered a relatively transient mode of processing. In the following sections, we discuss the similarities between the multiprocess theory of PM and the DMC account, then consider how applying a dual cognitive control perspective to PM might identify new directions for PM research.

## Similarities Between the Multiprocess Theory of Prospective Memory and the Dual Mechanisms of Control Account

A key similarity between the multiprocess theory of PM and the DMC account pertains to the nature of the two processes that support PM, on the one hand, and performance on traditional cognitive control tasks, on the other hand. For both accounts, one process involves preparation (e.g., activation of a task set, biasing of attention toward goal-relevant information, adoption of a strategy for monitoring the environment for particular cues) prior to the imperative stimulus or event. For the multiprocess theory of PM, this process is attentional monitoring, and for the DMC account, this process is proactive control. Mechanistically speaking, both attentional monitoring and proactive control can be thought of as top-down influences on behavior. For both accounts, the second process they describe is more reflexive, as it is triggered by bottom-up influences such as the onset of imperative stimuli, cues, or events. For the multiprocess theory, this process is spontaneous retrieval, and for the DMC account, this process is reactive control.

In addition to specifying two distinct, but mechanistically similar processes, the multiprocess theory and DMC account are also similar in recognizing that contextual factors play an important role in modulating reliance on one versus the other process. Whereas both accounts have posited that the preferred mode for humans is to rely on the relatively more reflexive process (cf. Bargh & Chartrand, 1999), both also acknowledge factors that justify the use of a preparatory process. This reflects that there are trade-offs associated with each type of process. For example, in the AX-CPT, implementing proactive control in response to the occurrence of an A cue benefits performance on the AX trial type, but it can hinder performance on the AY trial type because processing of the A cue leads to an invalid expectancy. Next we highlight two contextual factors that have been addressed by both accounts, albeit using different terminology.

One such factor is the metabolic and/or capacity costs associated with use of proactive control and monitoring processes. As noted by Braver and colleagues (2007), such costs may not be justifiable when there are very long retention intervals (e.g., between a cue and probe in the AX-CPT; between a PM instruction and target event in PM paradigms) or when contextual cues do not reliably predict the occurrence of particular stimuli or events (Braver et al., 2007). When such factors are apparent, one would expect reliance on reactive control or spontaneous retrieval. This expectation finds support in the existing PM literature. For instance, Einstein and McDaniel (1996) have shown that performance of delayed intentions reflects use of episodic retrieval processes that are activated in response to the presentation of the target event. Recent work by Loft, Kearney, and Remington (2008) has shown that cost, the signature of preparatory monitoring processes, is significantly lower in contexts where participants have been told to expect PM cues, but they do not occur for up to 640 trials. One interpretation is that participants have begun to shift away from a proactive mode at this point, possibly because use of such an effortful process is not reinforced. In contrast, frequent presentation of PM targets is related to increased costs, thereby reflecting greater use of proactive processes such as monitoring (Cohen & Gollwitzer, 2008), and in tasks where reliable contextual cues predict the presence of PM targets, evidence of monitoring (i.e., proactive control) is robust (see Marsh et al., 2006).

Another contextual factor is the quality of cue, stimulus, or target event processing. Reactive control and spontaneous retrieval depend heavily upon cues, stimuli, and/or target events to trigger retrieval of attentional settings and facilitate prospective remembering. Thus, cues that are not salient, are difficult to detect perceptually (e.g., a coffee shop that is not right along the side of the road), or are not focally processed may not effectively trigger these reflexive processes. Such cues include those that have been considered to be nonfocal in prior PM studies, (e.g., a particular syllable is the PM target event, e.g., "tor," and participants are engaged in a lexical decision task) and the evidence to date suggests use of proactive monitoring processes to support PM performance for such cues (Einstein et al., 2005).

In contrast, when cues are salient, are easy to detect perceptually, or are focally processed, reliance on spontaneous retrieval is expected to produce high levels of PM performance in most situations. Indeed, for such cues, including those that have been considered focal in prior studies (e.g., a particular word is the PM target event [e.g., PARROT] and participants are engaged in a lexical-decision task), PM performance is high without significant cost (prior to the target cues), supporting the notion that a spontaneous retrieval process supported PM (Einstein et al., 2005).

## New Directions for Prospective Memory Research Based on Considerations of the Dual Mechanisms of Control Account

One issue that remains to be fully explored is the extent to which reactive control processes, per se, are involved in PM tasks that are supported by spontaneous retrieval processes. Even when retrieval appears to be stimulated by a spontaneous as opposed to a preparatory monitoring process, it seems reasonable to assume that cognitive control mechanisms must be involved in facilitating task coordination and task switching (i.e., switching away from the ongoing task to performance of the PM intention). These mechanisms most likely involve reactive control. Indeed, as noted earlier, one factor that is believed to trigger reactive control is the occurrence of response conflict or interference, and spontaneous retrieval of an intention may produce response conflict. That is, the target event or cue elicits both the ongoing task response (e.g., if the ongoing task is lexical decision, responding "yes" it is a word) and the PM response (e.g., pressing the escape key on the keyboard). The implication of this view is that PM may always involve some cognitive control. In cases where retrieval of a PM intention is stimulated by spontaneous retrieval, the use of cognitive control may be reactive and follow retrieval. In cases where retrieval is stimulated by monitoring, the use of cognitive control is proactive in that it precedes and may also coincide with retrieval.

The assumption that PM involves reactive control processes leads to several interesting directions for future PM research. For instance, earlier we described the use of divided attention manipulations in studies aimed at investigating the role of monitoring versus spontaneous retrieval. The assumption has generally been that divided attention would interfere with performance on PM tasks that are supported by monitoring. However, on the view that performance on PM tasks that are supported by spontaneous retrieval also requires control, of the reactive type, then one might anticipate performance decrements as a result of dividing attention. For example, a cue could trigger the retrieval of an intended action into working memory, but divided attention conditions could interfere with selecting and executing the action while it is still accessible (Einstein, McDaniel, Williford, Pagan, & Dismukes, 2003; Einstein et al., 1997; Guynn et al., 2001).

Another direction for future research on PM that is stimulated by consideration of the DMC account is to examine the neural activation patterns that characterize spontaneous retrieval and preparatory monitoring processes. According to Braver et al., (2007), activation patterns differ for reactive control and proactive control. Because reactive control is often triggered by processing conflicts, activation of the anterior cingulate cortex is expected, as is activation of medial temporal areas, which may facilitate retrieval or reactivation of control settings. While an overlapping region, the lateral prefrontal cortex, characterizes both proactive and reactive control, reactive control is reflected by transient activation in this region, while proactive control is reflected by sustained activation in this region (see De Pisapia & Braver, 2006). The activation patterns that characterize preparatory attentional monitoring processes do in fact overlap with those associated with proactive control (Burgess, Scott, & Frith, 2003; Reynolds, West, & Braver, 2009). However, no studies to date have examined the activation patterns for PM tasks that entail contextual factors that bias participants toward use of spontaneous retrieval mechanisms (e.g., focal processing, emphasis on ongoing task performance) (but see Gordon, Shelton, Bugg, McDaniel, & Head (2011) for evidence that the volume of medial temporal regions including hippocampus correlates with PM performance on a focal task presumed to be supported by spontaneous retrieval). Thus, it is not yet clear whether these patterns overlap with those associated with reactive control. Similar patterns would provide converging evidence for the role of reactive control processes in PM tasks that are stimulated by spontaneous retrieval.

### Everyday Prospective Memory: Multiple Goals, Multiple Processes

Finally, we return to the topic of everyday PM challenges. Unlike in most laboratory studies, PM challenges in everyday life are just one of many simultaneously activated goals. Thus, it is not unusual for individuals to be faced with the *shielding-monitoring dilemma* (e.g., Goschke, 2000; Goschke & Dreisbach, 2008). The dilemma is that while it may be beneficial to tightly shield one's current goal from interference (e.g., environmental distraction, internalized interruptions), doing so may prevent one from monitoring the environment, including aspects that would be considered irrelevant to one's current goal, for imperative events or cues. This dilemma speaks directly to the trade-offs that are associated with proactive control processes in the context of ever-changing

environments and goals. Let us illustrate with an example.

Imagine that you have been invited to give a talk in an unfamiliar city. You are staying at a downtown hotel and have been invited to a dinner party at the home of a faculty member. You have a rental car at your disposal, but before leaving the hotel you decide to pick up a few bottles of wine as a gift to the hostess and consult the concierge for the location of a wine shop. The concierge indicates that there is a wine shop "somewhere" on Purchase Ave., a street that the directions indicate you will be driving on for 3 miles. Traffic is hectic and you are focused on driving, somewhat defensively, and not getting lost. In this situation, your primary goal is to drive safely and to follow the directions accurately. To achieve this goal, a proactive, sustained approach may be quite useful whereby you filter out the many bits of irrelevant environmental information (e.g., signs, lights, people along the sidewalks) that you encounter. Indeed, it is easy to see how proactive control would benefit driving-related goals but may come at a cost to other, simultaneously activated goals such as purchasing wine. This secondary goal, after all, requires the detection of a cue (e.g., a sign advertising a wine shop) whose location is uncertain, and which you may inadvertently filter.

Recently, Bugg, McDaniel, Scullin, and Braver (2011) explored the potential costs to PM that may be associated with the use of proactive control during performance of an ongoing task. The ongoing task they used was a Stroop color-word task where participants were asked to name the ink color of congruent (e.g., BLUE written in blue ink), incongruent (e.g., BLUE written in red ink), and neutral (e.g., WINDOW written in green ink) stimuli. Participants were instructed that their primary task was to name the ink colors as quickly and accurately as possible. They were also told that the researchers had a secondary interest in their ability to remember to press a key on a response box whenever they encountered the word "HORSE." Neutral stimuli (which included HORSE) occurred infrequently (15% of trials).

The primary manipulation pertained to the remaining 85% of the trials. In the mostly congruent condition, 70% of these trials were congruent and 15% were incongruent. In the mostly incongruent condition, 70% of these trials were incongruent and 15% were congruent. In the latter condition, then, interference was frequent. Based on a rich literature on proportion congruence effects in Stroop paradigms (see e.g., Lindsay & Jacoby, 1994; Logan &

Zbrodoff, 1979), we predicted that the proportion congruency manipulation would bias participants in the mostly incongruent condition to adopt a proactive control mode when performing the Stroop task. By this view, participants would be expected to engage a sustained process for blocking out the irrelevant, distracting words. In contrast, in the mostly congruent condition, word reading would largely be permitted, and reactive control activated as needed to block out word reading on the occasional incongruent trial.

The key predictions were as follows. The adoption of a proactive control mode was expected to enhance performance on the Stroop task such that Stroop interference, the reaction time slowing on incongruent relative to congruent trials, would be attenuated in the mostly incongruent as compared to the mostly congruent condition (e.g., Lindsay & Jacoby, 1994). However, it was expected that this benefit would come at the cost of lower PM performance. That is, use of a sustained process for proactively blocking out the irrelevant words was expected to decrease the likelihood that the word HORSE would be detected and the PM response performed. The results were precisely as anticipated. There was significantly less Stroop interference in the mostly incongruent as compared to the mostly congruent condition, consistent with the idea that proactive control processes were operating to filter words in the mostly incongruent condition. The use of proactive control, however, came at the cost of missing PM cues. PM performance was significantly higher in the mostly congruent condition ($M = .96$), where word reading was permitted, compared to the mostly incongruent condition ($M = .85$). These contrasting interference and PM patterns demonstrate, respectively, the benefits and drawbacks of goal shielding in the context of a multigoal environment.

## Conclusion

The overarching framework presented throughout our chapter suggests that PM performance depends on an interrelation among encoding components, storage components, and components in the retrieval environment. The retrieval components seem especially dynamic, as they can depend on preparatory monitoring (proactive control processes), spontaneous retrieval, or both; furthermore, reactive control processes may support these components to ensure PM execution. We suggest that a complete specification of these components is needed in order to achieve a full understanding of everyday PM challenges.

## Acknowledgments

We dedicate this chapter to the late Rich Marsh, who died at the prime of his career. A gifted teacher, mentor, and scholar, he played a pivotal role in developing the field of PM.

## References

Aarts, H., & Dijksterjuis, A. (1999). How often did I do it? Experienced ease of retrieval and frequency estimates of past behavior. *Acta Psychologica, 103*, 77–99.

Bargh, J. A., & Chartrand, T. L. (1999). The unbearable automaticity of being. *American Psychologist, 54*, 462–479.

Braver, T. S., Gray, J. R., & Burgess, G. C. (2007). Explaining the many varieties of working memory variation: Dual mechanisms of cognitive control. In A. R. A. Conway , C. Jarrold , M. J. Kane , A. Miyake, & J. N. Towse (Eds.), *Variation in working memory* (pp. 76–106). New York, NY: Oxford University Press.

Bugg, J. M., McDaniel, M. A., Scullin, M. K., & Braver, T. S. (2011). Revealing list-level control in the Stroop task by uncovering its benefits and a cost. *Journal of Experimental Psychology: Human Perception and Performance, 37*, 1595–1606.

Burgess, P. W., Scott, S. K., & Frith, C. D. (2003). The role of the rostral frontal cortex (area 10) in prospective memory: A lateral versus medial dissociation. *Neuropsychologia, 41*, 906–918.

Berntsen, D. (2009). *Involuntary autobiographical memories: An introduction to the unbidden past*. New York: Cambridge University Press.

Chasteen, A. L., Park, D. C., & Schwarz, N. (2001). Implementation intentions and facilitation of prospective memory. *Psychological Science, 12*, 457–461.

Cohen, A. L., & Gollwitzer, P. M. (2008). The cost of remembering to remember: Cognitive load and implementation intentions influence ongoing task performance. In M. Kliegl, M. A. McDaniel, & G. O. Einstein (Eds.), *Prospective memory: Cognitive, neuroscience, developmental, and applied perspectives*. Mahwah, NJ: Erlbaum.

Dembitzer, A., & Lai, E. J. (2003). Retained surgical instrument. *New England Journal of Medicine, 348*, 228.

De Pisapia, N., & Braver, T. S. (2006). A model of dual control mechanisms through anterior cingulated and prefrontal cortex interactions. *Neurocomputing, 69*, 1322–1326.

Einstein, G. O., Holland, L. J., McDaniel, M. A., & Guynn, M. J. (1992). Age-related deficits n prospective memory: The influence of task complexity. *Psychology and Aging, 7*, 471–478.

Einstein, G. O., & McDaniel, M. A. (2005). Prospective memory: Multiple retrieval processes. *Current Directions in Psychological Science, 14*, 286–290.

Einstein, G. O., & McDaniel, M. A. (1990). Normal aging and prospective memory. *Journal of Experimental Psychology: Learning, Memory, and Cognition, 16*, 717–726.

Einstein, G. O., & McDaniel, M. A. (1996). Retrieval processes in prospective memory: Theoretical approaches and some new empirical findings. In M. Brandimone, G. Einstein, & M. McDaniel (Eds.), *Prospective memory: Theory and applications* (pp. 115–142). Hillsdale, NJ: Erlbaum.

Einstein, G. O., & McDaniel, M. A. (2008). Prospective memory and metamemory: The skilled use of basic attentional and memory processes. In A. S. Benjamin & B. Ross (Eds.), *The Psychology of Learning and Motivation* (Vol. 48, pp. 145–173). San Diego, CA: Elsevier.

Einstein, G. O., & McDaniel, M. A. (2010) Prospective memory and what costs do not reveal about retrieval processes: A commentary on Smith, Hunt, McVay, and McConnell (2007). *Journal of Experimental Psychology: Learning, Memory, and Cognition, 36*, 1082–1088.

Einstein, G. O., Mc Daniel, M. A., Thomas, R., Mayfield, S., Shank, H., Morisette, N., & Breneiser, J. (2005). Multiple processes in prospective memory retrieval: Factors determining monitoring versus spontaneous retrieval. *Journal of Experimental Psychology: General, 134*(3), 327–342.

Einstein, G. O., McDaniel, M. A., Williford, C. L., Pagan, J. L., & Dismukes, R. K. (2003). Forgetting of intentions in demanding situations is rapid. *Journal of Experimental Psychology: Applied, 9*, 147–162.

Einstein, G. O., Smith, R. E., Mc Daniel, M. A., & Shaw, P. (1997). Aging and prospective memory: The influence of increased task demands at encoding and retrieval. *Psychology and Aging, 12*, 479–488.

Finstad, K., Bink, M., McDaniel, M. A., & Einstein, G. O. (2006). Breaks and task switches in prospective memory. *Applied Cognitive Psychology, 20*, 705–712.

Freeman, J. E., & Ellis, J. (2003). The representation of delayed intentions: A prospective subject-performed task? *Journal of Experimental Psychology: Learning, Memory, and Cognition, 29*, 976–992.

Gollwitzer, P. M. (1996). The volitional benefits of planning. In P. M. Gollwitzer & J. A. Bargh (Eds.), *The psychology of action: Linking cognition and motivation to behavior* (pp. 287–312). New York: Guilford Press.

Gollwitzer, P. M. (1999). Implementation intentions: Strong effects of simple plans. *American Psychologist, 54*, 493–503.

Gordon, B. A., Shelton, J. T., Bugg, J. M., McDaniel, M. A., & Head, D. (2011). Structural correlates of prospective memory. *Neuropsychologia, 49*, 3795–3800.

Goschke, T. (2000). Intentional reconfiguration and involuntary persistence in task-set switching. In S. Monsell & J. Driver (Eds.), *Attention and performance XVIII: Control of cognitive processes* (pp. 331–355). Cambridge, MA: MIT Press.

Goschke, T., & Dreisbach, G. (2008). Conflict-triggered goal shielding: Response conflicts attenuate background monitoring for prospective memory cues. *Psychological Science, 19*(1), 25–32.

Goschke, T., & Kuhl, J. (1993). Representation of intentions: Persistent activation in memory. *Journal of Experimental Psychology: Learning, Memory, and Cognition, 19*, 1211–1226.

Guynn, M. J. (2003). A two-process model of strategic monitoring in event-based prospective memory: Activation/retrieval mode and checking. *International Journal of Psychology, 38*, 245–256.

Guynn, M. J., McDaniel, M. A., & Einstein, G. O. (1998). Prospective memory: When reminders fail. *Memory and Cognition, 26*, 287–298.

Hicks, J. L., Marsh, R. L., & Russell, E. J. (2000). The properties of retention intervals and their affect on retaining prospective memories. *Journal of Experimental Psychology: Learning, Memory, and Cognition, 26*, 1160–1169.

Jacoby, L. L. (1991). A process dissociation framework: Separating automatic from intentional uses of memory. *Journal of Memory and Language, 30*, 3, 513–541.

Kliegel, M., Martin, M., McDaniel, M. A., & Einstein, G. O. (2004). Importance effects in event-based prospective memory tasks. *Memory, 12*, 553–561.

Kvavilashvili, L. (1987). Remembering intention as a distinct form of memory. *British Journal of Psychology, 78*, 507–518.

Kvavilashvili, L., & Fisher, L. (2007). Is time-based prospective remembering mediated by self-initiated rehearsals? Effects of incidental cues, ongoing activity, age, and motivation. *Journal of Experimental Psychology: General, 136*, 112–132.

Lindsay, D. S., & Jacoby, L. L. (1994). Stroop process dissociations: The relationship between facilitation and interference. *Journal of Experimental Psychology: Human Perception and Performance, 20*, 219–234.

Logan, G. D., & Zbrodoff, N. J. (1979). When it helps to be misled: Facilitative effects of increasing the frequency of conflicting stimuli in a Stroop—like task. *Memory and Cognition, 7*, 166–174.

Loft, S., Kearney, R., & Remington, R. (2008). Is task interference in event-based prospective memory dependent on cue presentation? *Memory and Cognition, 36*, 139–148.

Marsh, R. L., & Hicks, J. L. (1998). Event-based prospective memory and executive control of working memory. *Journal of Experimental Psychology: Learning, Memory, and Cognition, 24*, 336–349.

Marsh, R. L., Hicks, J. L., & Bink, M. L. (1998). Activation of completed, uncompleted, and partially completed intentions. *Journal of Experimental Psychology: Learning, Memory, and Cognition, 24*, 350–361.

Marsh, R. L., Hicks, J. L., & Cook, G. I. (2006). Task interference from prospective memories covaries with contextual associations of fulfilling them. *Memory and Cognition, 34*, 1037–1045.

Marsh, R. L., Hicks, J. L., Cook, G. I., Hansen, J. S., & Pallos, A. L. (2003). Interference to ongoing activities covaries with the characteristics of an event-based intention. *Journal of Experimental Psychology: Learning, Memory, and Cognition, 29*, 861–870.

Marsh, R. L., Hicks, J. L., & Watson, V. (2002). The dynamics of intention retrieval and coordination of action in event-based prospective memory. *Journal of Experimental Psychology: Learning, Memory, and Cognition, 28*, 652–659.

McDaniel, M. A., & Einstein, G. O. (2000). Strategic and automatic processes in prospective memory retrieval: A multiprocess framework. *Applied Cognitive Psychology, 14*, S127–S144.

McDaniel, M. A., & Einstein, G. O. (2007). *Prospective memory: An overview and synthesis of an emerging field.* Thousand Oaks, CA: Sage.

McDaniel, M. A., Guynn, M. J., Einstein, G. O., & Breneiser, J. E. (2004). Cue focused and automatic-associative processes in prospective memory. *Journal of Experimental Psychology: Learning, Memory, and Cognition, 30*, 605–614.

McDaniel, M. A., Howard, D. C., & Butler, K. (2008). Implementation intentions facilitate prospective memory under high attention demands. *Memory and Cognition, 36*, 716–724.

McDaniel, M. A., Robinson-Riegler, B., & Einstein, G. O. (1998). Prospective remembering: Perceptually driven or conceptually driven processes? *Memory and Cognition, 26*, 121–134.

McDaniel, M. A., & Scullin, M. K. (2010). Implementation intention encoding does not automatize prospective memory responding. *Memory and Cognition, 38*, 221–232.

McFarland, C., & Glisky, E. (2012). Implementation intentions and imagery: Individual and combined effects on prospective memory among young adults. *Memory & Cognition, 40*, 62–69.

Meacham, J. A., & Leiman, B. (1982). Remembering to perform future actions. In U. Neisser (Ed.), *Memory observed: Remembering in natural contexts* (pp. 327–336). San Francisco: Freeman.

Milne, S., Orbell, S., & Sheeran, P. (2002). Combining motivational and volitional interventions to promote exercise participation: Protection motivation theory and implementation intentions. *British Journal of Health Psychology, 7*, 163–184.

Moscovitch, M. (1994). Memory and working with memory: Evaluation of a component process model and comparisons with other models. In D. L. Schacter & E. Tulving (Eds.), *Memory systems* (pp. 269–310). Cambridge, MA: MIT Press.

Nowinski, J. L., Holbrook, J. B., & Dismukes, R. K. (2003). Human memory and cockpit operations: An ASRS study. In *Proceedings of the 12th International Symposium on Aviation Psychology* (pp. 888–893). Dayton, OH: The Wright State University. Retrieved October 20, 2006, from http://humanfactors.arc.nasa.gov/ihs/flightcognition/Publications/NowinskiI_etal_ISAP03.pdf

Park, D. C., Hertzog, C., Kidder, D. P., Morrell, R. W., & Mayhorn, C. B. (1997). Effect of age on event-based and time-based prospective memory. *Psychology and Aging, 12*, 314–327.

Reese, C. M., & Cherry, K. E. (2002). The effects of age, ability, and memory monitoring on prospective memory task performance. *Aging, Neuropsychology, and Cognition, 9*, 98–113.

Reynolds, J. R., West, R., & Braver, T. (2009). Distinct neural circuits support transient and sustained processes in prospective memory and working memory. *Cerebral Cortex, 19*, 1208–1221.

Scullin, M. K., & Bugg, J. M. (2012). Failing to forget: Prospective memory commission errors can result from spontaneous retrieval and impaired executive control. *Journal of Experimental Psychology: Learning, Memory, and Cognition.* doi: 10.1037/a0029198.

Scullin, M. K., Bugg, J. M., & McDaniel, M. A. (2012). Whoops, I did it again: Commission errors in prospective memory. *Psychology and Aging, 27*, 46–53.

Scullin, M. K., Einstein, G. O., & Mc Daniel, M. A. (2009). Evidence for spontaneous retrieval of suspended but not finished prospective memories. *Memory and Cognition, 37*, 425–433.

Scullin, M. K., & Mc Daniel, M. A. (2010). Remembering to execute a goal: Sleep on it! *Psychological Science, 21(7)*, 1028–1035.

Scullin, M. K., McDaniel, M. A., & Einstein, G. O. (2010). Control of monitoring in prospective memory: Evidence for spontaneous retrieval processes. *Journal of Experimental Psychology: Learning, Memory, and Cognition, 36*, 196–203.

Sheeran, P., & Orbell, S. (1999). Implementation intentions and repeated behavior: Augmenting the predictive validity of the theory of planned behavior. *European Journal of Social Psychology, 29*, 349–369.

Smith, R. E. (2003). The cost of remembering to remember in event-based prospective memory: Investigating the capacity demands of delayed intention performance. *Journal of Experimental Psychology: Learning, Memory, and Cognition, 29*, 347–361.

Smith, R. E., & Bayen, U. J. (2004). A multinomial model of event-based prospective memory. *Journal of Experimental Psychology: Learning, Memory, and Cognition, 30*, 756–777.

Walser, M., Fischer, R., & Goschke, T. (2012). The failure of deactivating intentions: Aftereffects of completed intentions in the repeated prospective memory cueparadigm. *Journal of Experimental Psychology: Learning, Memory, and Cognition. 38*, 1030–1044.

Whittlesea, B. W. A., & Williams, L. D. (2001). The discrepancy-attribution hypothesis: II. Expectation, uncertainty, surprise, and feelings of familiarity. *Journal of Experimental Psychology: Learning, Memory, and Cognition, 27*, 14–33.

Yaniv, I. & Meyer, D. E. (1987). Activation and metacognition of inaccessible store information: Potential bases for incubation effects in problem solving. *Journal of Experimental Psychology: Learning, Memory, and Cognition, 13*, 187–205.

# Metamemory

John Dunlosky *and* Keith W. Thiede

**Abstract**

Metamemory refers to people's beliefs about their memory and to how people monitor and control their learning and retrieval. In this chapter, we describe monitoring and control processes involved in learning and retrieval, how these processes have been measured, and key outcomes relevant to human metamemory. Based on these outcomes, general conclusions include the following: (a) people's judgments of their memory are based on a variety of cues; hence (b) judgment accuracy arises from the diagnosticity of the cues, so that above-chance accuracy of any metamemory judgment only arises when the available cues are predictive (or diagnostic) of criterion performance; and finally, (c) people use their memory judgments to guide their study and retrieval. Thus, people's memory monitoring plays a pivotal role in the effectiveness of their self-regulated learning and retrieval, so a major aim of metamemory research is to discover techniques that yield high levels of judgment accuracy and optimal regulation.

**Key Words:** metamemory, self-regulated learning, memory monitoring, control, judgments of learning, feeling of knowing, confidence judgments, metacognition

*Metamemory* refers to people's thoughts about their memory and how memory operates. Although the term *metamemory* may seem esoteric to some, people rely on their metamemory as they perform many activities. When heading to a grocery store, one person may believe that he can remember all 10 items that need to be purchased, whereas another person with the same items to purchase may believe that her memory will fail and hence decides to take a list along. An eyewitness may point the finger at the accused, and do so with extreme confidence that the accused had committed the crime; however, such high confidence can be illusory, such as when confidence is inadvertently based on a memory of seeing the accused in a lineup instead of actually witnessing the accused commit the crime (for real-life examples, see Loftus & Ketcham, 1991).

Unfortunately, jurors believe the testimony of a highly confident eyewitness, regardless of whether his or her confidence is well placed. On a lighter note, when playing games (such as Trivial Pursuit), players may withhold answers when they believe that those answers are wrong, yet they will try to persuade their team to respond with an answer when their confidence in it is high. And when failing to generate answers to some questions, an emotionally charged tip-of-the-tongue state may arise when they believe the sought-after answer is available in memory. Being a student can put an even higher premium on the effective use of metamemory, because to learn efficiently, students must be able to accurately judge how well key concepts have been learned and make appropriate decisions about which concepts require further study.

This short list illustrates several metamemory processes that can occur while people are learning new materials or are attempting to retrieve old ones. Moreover, they illustrate the multifaceted nature of metamemory, which includes knowledge (and beliefs) about memory, monitoring of memory, and control of memory. *Metamemory knowledge* refers to declarative knowledge or beliefs that an individual holds about how memory operates and whether those beliefs are accurate. In the earlier example, the individual who decided to write down the grocery list may know from experience that memory tends to fail after four or five items from a grocery list need to be remembered. The individual who went without a list may believe that he has a very good memory—that is, he has high memory self-efficacy—and hence will be able to recall even lengthier lists without having difficulties.

*Memory monitoring* refers to assessing progress during learning or the current state of a previously studied item. For example, when studying for an upcoming test, students may attempt to monitor and evaluate their ongoing progress while studying. Their monitoring of memory yields a confidence judgment about whether they will remember the key concepts on the upcoming exam. Finally, *memory control* involves regulating any aspect of learning or retrieval. For the control of learning, one example of a control process includes deciding to spend more time studying materials that one believes have not been well learned. For retrieval, accusing a defendant of committing a crime is a prime example, because the eyewitness allegedly must be highly confident in his or her memory of the crime to potentially condemn the defendant.

Based on these examples, it may be evident why so many people have become interested in metamemory: Faulty metamemory can lead to poor memory and low achievement, whereas accurate metamemory can enhance memory and achievement. For instance, if students inaccurately assess that they are ready for an upcoming test, then they may prematurely stop studying. In this case, poor monitoring leads to a nonoptimal control decision, which in turn would lead to less-than-expected performance on the examination. To expand on this example, consider two students who are studying for an upcoming test in a class of introductory psychology. Both students are trying to learn the core concepts relevant to memory, such as what is short-term memory, long-term memory, and encoding specificity. Both students

judge that they will be able to remember about 90% of the concepts, which they believe is fine for the test, so they stop studying to join each other for a late-night movie. Whereas Julie actually will retain 90% of the concepts (her judgments were accurate), Mike was highly overconfident and will remember only 50%. In this case, Mike was overconfident and hence he stopped studying before he met his desired learning goal; unfortunately, Mike will not perform well on the test, and he may even tell the teacher, "But I thought I knew all these concepts. Why did I earn such a poor grade on the exam?"

Although the importance of accurate metamemory may be intuitive, research in this area did not begin in earnest until about 1970 when John Flavell coined the term "metamemory." In the 1970s, the term "meta" began to appear in articles and in conference papers, and groundbreaking research was also conducted by John Flavell, Ellen Markman, and Ann Brown, among others. Perhaps most important for solidifying a specialized field of metamemory was Flavell's (1979) *American Psychologist* article, called "Metacognition and Cognitive Monitoring: A New Area of Cognitive-Developmental Inquiry." This article has been highly influential because it is here where Flavell defines core concepts for the field, such as metacognitive knowledge and metacognitive experiences (which are most closely aligned with metamemory knowledge and memory monitoring, as described earlier). As important, he developed numerous testable hypotheses about how the development of metamemory in childhood would in turn influence the developmental progress of core cognitive processes.

John Flavell and his colleagues—most notably, Henry Wellman—first captured our attention with persuasive arguments about the importance of metamemory, but it was Joseph Hart who provided the first method to assess metamemory in an objective manner. One can best understand Hart's breakthrough within the context of the introspection method that was used in the infancy of psychological research. In the early 1900s, a researcher interested in associations may ask a (trained) participant to introspect about the psychological processes that produce a free association. For instance, what is the first word that comes to mind when you read "guitar"? Perhaps you think "Stratocaster," but if you were an introspectionist, you would also need to describe the cognitive processes that preceded the thought "Stratocaster." Doing so may seem difficult, but participants in these studies (at times the experimenters themselves) were highly practiced. A downfall of this method was that the introspective reports were viewed as a window into the mind; that is, the reports were assumed by some to be accurate and complete. This view is most evident in R. S. Woodworth's (1921) definition of introspection as the "observation by an individual of his own conscious action... Notice that it is a form of observation, and not speculation or reasoning from past experience. It is a direct observation of fact" (p. 10). This definition emphasizes introspection as a metacognitive act, because introspection involves directly observing a mental action. Unfortunately, even in 1901, it was evident that introspective methods would fall well short of direct observation of mental actions involved in a response (for a historical review, see Humphrey, 1951).

Six decades later, Joseph Hart introduced a method to systematically explore distortions in people's introspections about their memory. In particular, participants were asked general-information questions. When they did not answer a question, they were simply asked to predict whether they could choose the correct answer on a multiple-choice recognition test. These predictions—which are called *feeling-of-knowing* (FOK) judgments—are introspective reports, but in contrast to earlier introspection research, Hart (1965) did not assume that they were valid. Instead, he evaluated their accuracy against objective performance by administering recognition tests. By doing so, people's judgments could be validated against their performance: When they were in a tip-of-the-tongue state and were sure they knew the correct answer even when they could not retrieve it, would they then recognize the correct answer? Hart (1965, 1966) found that people's FOK judgments showed above-chance accuracy. That is, their judgments were higher for correctly recognized answers than for ones that were not recognized.

Hart's methods focused on the monitoring of retrieval, as measured by FOK judgments. The method is invaluable because it has allowed researchers to systematically explore the biases in people's FOK judgments, which we consider in some detail later. As important, his methods can be readily applied to evaluate how people monitor all aspects of learning—from study through retrieval. And extensions of his methods have been used to explore people's control of study and retrieval. In the remainder of this chapter, we first provide a bird's eye view of the kinds of monitoring and control processes investigated in the field. We then discuss current theory pertaining to two widely investigated metamemory judgments relevant to study and retrieval: judgments of learning (JOLs) and FOK judgments, respectively.

In 1990, Nelson and Narens unified the field of metamemory by organizing the various monitoring and control processes into a single framework. An expanded version of this framework is presented in Figure 19.1, which illustrates measures of memory monitoring and memory control that correspond to each phase of learning. For instance, during study ("acquisition" in Fig. 19.1), one may monitor memory for to-be-learned items, which is measured by having people judge how well an item has been learned. This JOL may also influence the control of study, such as by informing people's decisions about when to terminate study of a given item. The measures depicting memory monitoring are presented in the top portion of Figure 19.1, and the measures depicting memory control are presented in the bottom portion. Definitions of each measure are in Table 19.1.

Modern research on metamemory largely focuses on answering just a few questions about monitoring and control. Concerning memory monitoring, one primary question is, How do people monitor various phases of learning? Answers to this question are obtained by investigating how people make the various monitoring judgments. For instance, JOLs are investigated to understand how people monitor their learning, whereas confidence judgments and FOK judgments are investigated to understand how people monitor their retrieval. The accuracy of these judgments is often of central interest, and taking the lead from Hart (1965), accuracy is measured by comparing a given judgment to its corresponding criterion measure. JOLs (which are predictions of future performance) are compared to future performance, FOK judgments for predicting future recognition of currently unrecallable information are compared to future recognition performance, and confidence judgments are compared to performance on the criterion test being judged. These and other judgments often demonstrate a positive correlation with criterion performance. For instance, Souchay, Moulin, Clarys, Taconnat, and Isingrini (2007) had older (*M* age = 72 years) and younger (*M* age = 27) adults attempt to answer general-information questions and then make an FOK judgment for any question they did not answer. After this judgment phase, the

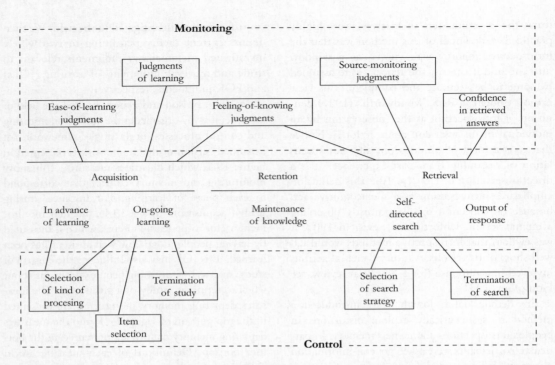

**Figure 19.1** Overview of metamemory monitoring and control components that occur throughout study (acquisition), retention, and retrieval. (Adapted from Nelson & Narens, 1990, to include judgments that were absent from their original framework.)

**Table 19.1** Names and Common Definitions of Metacognitive Judgments and Control Processes

| Name | Definition |
|---|---|
| *Metacognitive judgments* | |
| Ease-of-learning (EOL) judgments | Judgments of how easy to-be-studied items will be to learn. |
| Judgments of learning (JOLs) | Judgments of the likelihood of remembering recently studied items on an upcoming test |
| Feeling-of-knowing (FOK) judgments | Judgments of the likelihood of recognizing currently unrecallable answers on an upcoming test |
| Source-monitoring judgments | Judgments made during a criterion test pertaining to the source of a particular memory |
| Confidence in retrieved answers | Judgments of the likelihood that a response on a test is correct. Often referred to as retrospective confidence (RC) judgments |
| *Control processes* | |
| Selection of kind of processing | Selection of strategies to employ when attempting to commit an item to memory |
| Item selection | Decision about whether to study an item on an upcoming trial |
| Termination of study | Decision to stop studying an item currently being studied |
| Selection of search strategy | Selecting a particular strategy in order to produce a correct response during a test |
| Termination of search | Decisions to terminate searching for a response |

*Source*: From Dunlosky, J., Serra, M., & Baker, J. M. C. (2007). Metamemory applied. In F. Durso et al. (2nd ed.) *Handbook of applied cognition*. New York: Wiley.

participants completed a recognition test for each of the unrecalled questions. Means across intraindividual correlations between FOK judgments and recognition performance were .35 for younger adults and .46 for older adults, indicating that people of all ages can accurately predict future recognition performance for currently unrecallable information (for extended primers on metamemory measurement and analyses, see Dunlosky & Bjork, 2008; Dunlosky & Metcalfe, 2009).

Concerning memory control, a primary question is, How do people use monitoring to control their memory? To address this question, researchers often examine the relationship between a measure of monitoring and a measure of control. For instance, to examine control of study, JOLs made during an initial study trial may be compared to subsequent self-paced study time (Mazzoni, Cornoldi, & Marchitelli, 1990). JOLs are often negatively related to later self-paced study time—that is, learners tend to spend more time studying information that has been less well learned (lower JOLs) than better learned (higher JOLs). As we discuss later, explaining this negative relationship between JOLs and self-paced study times—and exceptions to it—has become a principal focus of current theories of self-paced study.

## Theory and Data of Basic Monitoring and Control Processes

The literature on metamemory includes basic research on metamemory knowledge, monitoring, and control; analyses of changes in metamemory that occur throughout the life span; and the neuroscience and neuropsychology of monitoring and control processes (Dunlosky & Metcalfe, 2009). Given the size of this literature, our overview here must be limited in scope, so we have decided to focus largely on two questions: How do people make metamemory judgments during study and retrieval? And how do people control their study and retrieval? To answer them, we could rely on the literature of almost any of the measures presented in Figure 19.1. Presently, however, we consider only JOLs and FOK judgments, because the literature in both cases is extensive and offers some basic principles that apply to all metamemory judgments. A more thorough introduction to the literature on each of the monitoring and control functions in Figure 19.1 is provided by Dunlosky and Metcalfe (2009) and Dunlosky, Serra, and Baker (2007).

## Monitoring of Study and Retrieval

### HOW DO PEOPLE MAKE JUDGMENTS OF LEARNING AND FEELING-OF-KNOWING JUDGMENTS?

Some of the earliest theoretical work on the bases of FOK judgments explored the degree to which they directly measure memory. According to this *direct-access view*, people's judgments reflect the underlying strength of an item in memory (cf. trace-access mechanisms in Nelson, Gerler, & Narens, 1984). So, if you made a JOL after you had just studied "dog—spoon," your judgment would directly tap how well the association between "dog" and "spoon" was stored in memory. Such direct access echoes the early introspectionists' belief that self-evaluations arise from a "direct observation of fact," and perhaps not surprisingly, predictions from the direct-access view have been disconfirmed with regard to JOLs and FOK judgments.

Let's just consider a disconfirmation of this view from the JOL literature, which will also serve to introduce cue-based accounts for metamemory judgments. Benjamin, Bjork, and Schwartz (1998) had participants answer general-knowledge questions that were moderate to easy in difficulty level, so participants could generate an answer to most questions. Immediately after they generated an answer, participants made a JOL concerning the likelihood that they would recall the answer on a test of free recall; for this test, they were given a blank sheet of paper and had to recall only the previously retrieved answers (without the question cues). JOLs were related to the fluency of initial retrieval—the faster they could generate an answer to a general-knowledge question, the more likely they judged that they would be able to freely recall it on the criterion test. By contrast, the opposite was true for the criterion test; that is, the faster the answer was retrieved during the initial phase, the less likely they were to recall it during the free-recall criterion test. Thus, people's JOLs did not directly access how well each target answer was stored in memory. Instead, JOLs tracked retrieval fluency: As they retrieved answers more quickly during the initial test, they judged the answer would be easier to remember, even though this assessment did not reflect actual storage strength (as assessed by free recall on the criterion test).

This outcome, among many others, suggests that people use processing fluency as a cue to make JOLs. In fact, people tend to use fluency for almost all metamemory judgments when processing fluency differs across to-be-judged items (Alter

& Oppenheimer, 2009). This conclusion not only pertains to retrieval fluency (as in Benjamin et al., 1998) but other forms of processing fluency as well. Another example involves fluency of generating encoding strategies. In one study (Hertzog, Dunlosky, Robinson, & Kidder, 2003), college students studied word pairs and were asked to generate an interactive image to associate both words. During study, participants pressed the space bar once they had generated an image. The time from an item's presentation and this key press was a measure of the fluency of image generation. Across three experiments, encoding fluency was negatively related to JOLs; that is, the more fluently participants generated an image (faster latency), the higher people's judgment that they would correctly recall the item. Even subtle aspects of the stimulus environment can influence encoding fluency and JOLs. For instance, Rhodes and Castel (2009) manipulated the fluency of perceptually processing items. Participants listened to items that were presented at different volumes and made a JOL after each item was presented. JOLs were higher for items presented loudly than those presented quietly, presumably because the former were more fluently processed. Thus, both encoding fluency and retrieval fluency influence people's JOLs.

People also use fluency when making FOK judgments. The potential influence of this cue is most evident in Koriat's (1997) accessibility hypothesis. According to this hypothesis, when people make an FOK judgment for an unrecalled item, it is based on the information that they had accessed while searching for an answer. So, if you are asked, "What city is the capital of Washington State?" you may fail to come up with an answer, but in trying to retrieve one from memory, you may remember "emerald," that it begins with an "s," and that it is in the far northwest portion of the state. For another question, "Who wrote *Moll Flanders*?" you do not respond but think the author's name begins with a "D." A prediction from this hypothesis is that the more information you access—and the more fluently you access it—prior to making an FOK judgment, the higher your FOK is expected to be. So you may judge that you will absolutely recognize the capital of Washington State but will unlikely recognize the name of the author who wrote *Moll Flanders*.

Importantly, Koriat (1993) proposed that the quality of what is accessed is irrelevant—even if a lot of incorrect information is fluently accessed, then a high FOK will result. In the present example, note that all the accessed information about Washington's

capital pointed toward Seattle (the "Emerald City"), when in fact, the correct answer is Olympia. By contrast, "D" is the first letter of the author's first and last names (Daniel Defoe). Nevertheless, according to the accessibility hypothesis, the sheer amount retrieved and the fluency of retrieval are most influential, so FOK judgments are expected to be greater for the question about Washington's capital, even though the partial information retrieved about it was incorrect. In a series of creative studies, Koriat (1993) demonstrated the powerful influence of accessibility on FOK judgments. In one experiment, participants studied tetragrams—four-letter strings that were nonwords, such as RFSC and FKRD. A tetragram was briefly presented for study, which was followed by a short retention interval and a retrieval attempt. After the retrieval attempt, an FOK judgment was made for that tetragram, and then after all tetragrams were studied and judged, a recognition test was administered so that FOK accuracy could be measured. Most relevant for now, people's FOK judgments were related to how many letters were recalled prior to making the judgment, even when those letters were not in the studied tetragram. Put differently, FOK judgments were based on how much information was accessed, regardless of whether the information recalled was correct.

We have focused almost exclusively on people's use of fluency as a basis for their judgments. More generally, however, people appear to base their judgments on many cues that appear to distinguish between items in a manner that may be relevant to criterion performance. For instance, another cue that is available when people make FOK judgments is the familiarity of the cue used to prompt the retrieval attempt. The cue for "What city is the capital of Washington State?" is the question itself. For a variety of reasons (e.g., perhaps you recently read an article about Washington State), you may find the cue itself familiar and hence judge that you are likely to recognize the correct answer. Research has established that FOK judgments are influenced by cue familiarity in this manner (Metcalfe, Schwartz, & Joaquim, 1993; Miner & Reder, 1994).

Given that metamemory judgments can be based on multiple cues, researchers are beginning to explore how various cues are integrated into a judgment. For FOK judgments, Koriat and Levy-Sadot (2001) proposed that cue familiarity has the first influence. If your familiarity with a cue is low, then you would spend little, if any, time attempting to retrieve the correct answer and your FOK would be low. However, if you are familiar with the cue, then you would search for an answer, and any information you accessed during this search would in turn influence your FOK judgment. That is, accessibility is expected to have a greater influence on FOK judgments when cue familiarity is high than when it is low. For instance, if you were asked, "Who is the mayor of Ravenna, Ohio?" you would likely have no familiarity with this particular cue and quickly respond with the lowest FOK judgment without even attempting to search for the answer (cf. Kolers & Palef, 1976). However, if you were asked, "Who was the second president of the United States?" if you had familiarity with the presidents of the United States, then you would likely search for the correct answer. While searching, any information that you accessed along the way would then influence your subsequent FOK judgments. Across three experiments, Koriat and Levy-Sadot (2001) provided evidence consistent with this interactive hypothesis. Moreover, Benjamin (2005) demonstrated how cue familiary and target accessibility both influence people's JOLs, but the time course for their influence differs. When JOLs are made under time pressure, cue familiarity has an influence. Without time pressure, people have more time to attempt retrieval, and hence this cue has a larger influence on people's JOLs.

To conclude this section, we will return to our initial question, How do people make JOLs and FOK judgments? Processing fluency and cue familiarity have a joint influence on these judgments, but they also can be influenced by any number of cues that are available when the judgments are made. For instance, in some experiments on JOLs, participants study paired associates consisting of either unrelated (dog—spoon) or related (king—crown) words. JOLs are much higher for related than unrelated items (e.g., Carroll, Nelson, & Kirwan, 1997). In some cases, people's JOLs are influenced by the serial position of items on a list, with higher judgments being made for items in the first positions (the primacy items) than for those in the middle of the list (Castel, 2008; Dunlosky & Matvey, 2001).

Given the number of cues that do influence JOLs, it is perhaps surprising that some relatively obvious ones have a rather minimal (or inconsistent) influence. For instance, when studying paired associates, people can use numerous strategies, such as interactive imagery (for "dog—spoon," imaging a dog paddling in a large spoon filled with milk) or repetition (repeating "dog—spoon" together during study). The strategies differ in their effectiveness, with final recall performance typically being

much higher after interactive imagery than rote repetition. When people judge items studied under these two different strategies, however, their JOLs typically do not differ for items that were studied using imagery rather than repetition (Rabinowitz, Ackerman, Craik, & Hinchley, 1982; Shaughnessy, 1981). Likewise, other studies have demonstrated that people's JOLs can be insensitive to retention interval and to the number of learning trials (e.g., Carroll et al., 1997; Koriat, Bjork, Sheffer, & Bar, 2004; Kornell & Bjork, 2008, respectively), which often have a substantial influence on criterion recall performance.

Why are some cues influential (e.g., fluency), whereas other cues (e.g., encoding strategy or number of learning trials) are not? One answer is based on the assumption that all judgments are inferential. That is, people use various cues to infer the likelihood of correctly performing on the criterion test. What makes one cue more potent than another can partly be ascertained from Koriat and colleagues' (Koriat, Nussinson, Bless, & Shaked, 2008) inference-based account that emphasizes a distinction between whether the source of an inference is experience based (EB) or information based (IB). IB (or theory-based) judgments rely on people's declarative knowledge and beliefs about how a particular cue influences memory. For instance, as noted earlier, JOLs do not distinguish between items that are studied by imagery versus rote repetition, and this null effect presumably arises because most people do not know that imagery is a more effective strategy. Once people are given experience using both strategies, however, they obtain declarative knowledge that "imagery is better," and in subsequent trials, JOLs (and other metmamemory judgments) are higher after imagery than repetition (Hertzog, Price, & Dunlosky, 2008).

EB judgments involve two processing stages: "first a process that gives rise to a sheer subjective feeling and second a process that uses that feeling as a basis for memory predictions" (Koriat et al., 2008, p. 118). The idea here is that various cues trigger feelings, which in turn boost metamemory judgments. According to Koriat et al. (2008), EB judgments for JOLs rely on the ease with which items are encoded or retrieved during learning, and EB judgments for FOKs rely on the fluency of accessing partial information when searching for a target answer. Put differently, differences in the fluency of processing presumably give rise to different feelings that then influence people's metamemory judgments.

This taxonomy does provide some insight into why various cues influence—or do not influence—people's metamemory judgments. For instance, if a participant does not believe a particular cue will influence memory (IB) and if the cue does not give rise to a metacognitive experience (EB), then it should not influence the judgments. This situation presumably holds for different encoding strategies that most participants would not have experience using in a novel associative task, such as imagery and repetition. Another possibility is that a cue which produces a strong metacognitive experience (e.g., processing fluency) could override the influence of other IB cues. Thus, when people study "archer—tree" and then make a JOL for it, they may be captured by the ease of developing an image for the word pair (and hence make a high JOL), and altogether ignore the fact that the word pair is slated to be tested weeks after study (and hence should probably receive a low JOL). In this way, even obvious IB cues (e.g., retention interval) may not influence JOLs when other strong EB cues are available in the environment. This taxonomy is useful for explaining the influence of various cues on metamemory judgments, and it has intuitive appeal. Even so, the taxonomy is not entirely orthogonal, because people apparently have theories about fluency cues; that is, learners believe that fluently processed information is easier to remember. So this EB cue (fluency) may actually have its influence on metamemory judgments vis-à-vis IB processing (as in Matvey, Dunlosky, & Guttentag, 2001).

## WHEN WILL METAMEMORY JUDGMENTS BE ACCURATE?

Hart's groundbreaking research demonstrated that the accuracy of people's FOK judgments was above chance, and the seminal work on JOLs by Arbuckle and Cuddy (1969) also revealed that they had above-chance accuracy. Why? One straightforward answer is offered by cue-based accounts of metamemory judgments, which are themselves founded on Egon Brunswik's lens model of perceptual judgments (Brunswik, 1956). These accounts highlight the importance of the three relationships among a cue, judgment, and criterion performance—which are illustrated in Figure 19.2. The relationship between cue and judgment is referred to as *cue utilization*, which represents the degree to which a cue influences (or is related to) the judgment. As described earlier, cue utilization for processing fluency is usually high for metamemory judgment. A second relationship occurs between

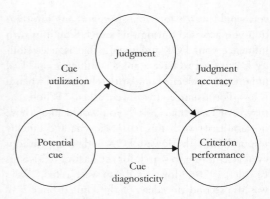

**Figure 19.2** Relationships among cues, judgments, and recall that emphasize the central role of cue utilization and diagnosticity in determining judgment accuracy.

judgment and criterion performance, which represents *judgment accuracy*. Finally, the relationship between cue and performance is referred to as *cue diagnosticity* and represents the degree to which a particular cue predicts criterion test performance (cf. ecological validity, Brunswik, 1956).

According to the cue-based accounts, judgment accuracy is a function of cue utilization and cue diagnosticity, and hence, above-chance accuracy occurs whenever (a) a cue influences (or is related to) a judgment and (b) the cue itself accurately predicts—or rather, is diagnostic of—criterion performance. Above-chance accuracy is not ensured, because even when a cue is used to make a judgment, the cue itself may have nil diagnosticity or even negative diagnosticity. In the latter case, the judgments would show below-chance accuracy, with higher confidence in performance (e.g., higher JOLs) being indicative of *lower* criterion performance. In fact, the most impressive support for such inference-based accounts of accuracy comes from studies in which the accuracy of people's judgments was zero or negative.

One excellent example comes from Benjamin et al. (1998), which was described earlier. Recall that participants used initial fluency of retrieving answers to general-information questions as a cue to make JOLs for predicting subsequent free recall of the answers. In this case, the cue of retrieval fluency was *negatively* related to cued recall: The more quickly they retrieved answers to general-information questions (the cue), the less likely they would later recall the answers on the criterion test. Such negative cue diagnosticity in turn led to inaccurate JOLs. The general point here is that when people use a cue, its diagnosticity will in part drive judgment accuracy.

Thus, for Benjamin et al. (1998), if retrieval fluency on the first test had been predictive of performance on the second (criterion) test, then JOL accuracy should be above chance. This prediction has received empirical support. In particular, when the first test is a cued recall test (as in Benjamin et al., 1998) but the second criterion test is *also* cued recall, then (a) JOLs are still based on the fluency of retrieval on the first test, but (b) now this cue of retrieval fluency is predictive of final recall performance. As the cue is diagnostic of criterion performance, JOL accuracy is relatively high (Serra & Dunlosky, 2005).

This example also suggests one way that the accuracy of JOLs and FOK judgments can be improved or fine-tuned to match levels of performance. Namely, to assess memory well, one must evaluate it in contexts that yield diagnostic cues. For instance, when studying paired associates (e.g., dog—spoon), two kinds of JOLs can be made. An *immediate* JOL occurs immediately after an item is studied. So one would study "dog—spoon," and then ask, "Will I later recall spoon when shown 'dog' on the test?" Immediate JOLs are not highly accurate because the cues available for the JOL (e.g., processing fluency) usually are not highly predictive of criterion performance. By contrast, a *delayed* JOL occurs after other items have been studied, so when the prompt for JOL is presented (i.e., "dog—?"), one must try to recall the response from memory (i.e., "spoon"). For paired associates, the outcome of this delayed retrieval attempt is highly diagnostic of future memory performance, so delayed JOLs are highly accurate (Nelson & Dunlosky, 1991).

Another avenue to improve judgment accuracy is to provide people with experience about the diagnosticity of various cues. For instance, as noted earlier, people's JOLs do not differ for paired associates studied by imagery more than for those studied by rote repetition, even though this cue (strategy used) is highly diagnostic of performance. That is, criterion recall performance is much higher after imagery than repetition. When people are given experience using these strategies during an initial study-test trial and then make JOLs on a second study-test trial in which imagery and repetition are used, people's JOLs begin to favor imagery items (Hertzog et al., 2008). Thus, even if people's JOLs and FOK judgments are not initially accurate, they can be tuned to better reflect memory performance (for further discussion of a variety of tactics to improve judgment accuracy, see Dunlosky & Metcalfe, 2009).

## THE BASES AND ACCURACY OF OTHER METAMEMORY JUDGMENTS

Although we have focused exclusively on JOLs and FOK judgments, the ideas described earlier pertain to any of the judgments listed in the top half of Figure 19.1. Each of the judgments is presumably inferential in nature in that people infer the likelihood of criterion performance based on available cues. Even so, they are not always empirically correlated because they also differ in other ways. Concerning their intercorrelations, Nelson and Leonesio (1988) had participants make multiple judgments during a multiphase experiment—including ease-of-learning (EOL) judgments, JOLs, and FOK judgments. Within individual participants, the judgments were not highly correlated: +.19 between EOL judgments and JOLs, +.12 between EOL judgments and FOKs, and +.17 between JOLs and FOK judgments. One explanation for these small intercorrelations follows from cue-based accounts of metamemory judgments, because the cues available can differ as people judge different aspects of memory. As the cues differ, the relationship between the judgments will diverge; however, when the same cues are available for different judgments, the judgments will show a stronger relationship.

These points can be illustrated with a simple experiment. Participants study 40 paired associates; 20 pairs consist of related words (king—crown) and 20 consist of unrelated words (turtle—bean). Before studying any pairs, participants are shown each pair and asked to make this ease-of-learning (EOL) judgment: How difficult will this item be to learn (0 = difficult to 100 = easy)? Then, each pair is presented individually for 6 seconds, and a JOL is made (0 = 0% likelihood of recall to 100 = 100% likelihood). Finally, a cued recall test is administered across all pairs, and for those in which a correct response could not be recalled, participants made a FOK judgment for a subsequent recognition test. Notice that some cues are similar but others differ across the judgments. For EOL judgments and JOLs, the relatedness of pairs is available as a cue and it has a major influence: Both judgments are higher for related than unrelated pairs. In this case, the judgments are highly correlated (e.g., +.71 and +.65 in two different conditions; Dunlosky & Matvey, 2001). By contrast, note that pair relatedness is not available when people make FOK judgments, because these judgments are made when people cannot retrieve the response to a pair. Thus, the cue of pair relatedness would not be available for FOK judgments, and hence other cues would be used to infer the likelihood that the correct answers will be recognized. This context more closely matches the method used by Nelson and Leonesio (1988), which yielded low correlations.

Given the usefulness of a cue-based account for understanding metamemory judgments, a general agenda for research has been to identify (a) the cues that are available when any particular judgment is made, (b) the degree to which people use a given cue when making a judgment, (c) the diagnosticity of the available cues, and, of course, (d) the degree to which the available cues support above-chance accuracy. Any particular research study typically only explores a subset of these issues, but the entire enterprise has consistently led to converging conclusions about all the metamemory judgments listed in Table 19.1. In particular, when monitoring our memories, we do not possess the skill to *directly* assess how well a memory has been stored or how accurately it can be retrieved, and hence the accuracy of people's metamemory judgments is not ensured. Instead, judgment accuracy depends on the available cues, the degree to which those cues are used in constructing a metamemory judgment, and the diagnosticity of the cues for predicting criterion performance.

## Control of Memory

A major focus of metamemory research concerns how people control their study and retrieval processes. In the next two sections, we review the extensive literature on these control processes. The main issues that we address here are whether and how monitoring is used to make control decisions.

### HOW DO LEARNERS CONTROL THEIR STUDY?

To begin answering this question, we describe a standard method used to investigate the control of study. Participants are asked to learn a list of word pairs, and during an initial trial, each pair (e.g., cat—boat) is presented at a fixed rate (e.g., 2 seconds an item). Participants then make a JOL for each item. Afterward, they have another chance to study each pair. During this self-paced study trial, participants may be shown all the pairs in an array (such as in a textbook page of foreign language translation equivalents), and then they select pairs that they want to restudy. Alternatively, each pair may be presented individually, and participants study each pair as long as they want. A key question is, Do people use their monitoring (as measured by JOLs) to make decisions about which items to select for restudy or to decide how long to study each item?

The modal (and nearly universal) finding from the earliest studies using this method was a negative relationship between JOLs and subsequent study time (either item selection or self-paced study). That is, as people rated items as more difficult to remember (lower JOLs), they spent more time studying (for reviews, see Son & Kornell, 2008; Son & Metcalfe, 2000). This relationship suggests that people do use monitoring to control their study time. Nevertheless, it is correlational, and hence some other variable may be responsible for why JOLs are related to the allocation of study time. To evaluate whether JOLs are causally related to allocation, Metcalfe and Finn (2008) used a variant of the aforementioned method. On an initial study trial, participants either studied pairs (cat—boat) once or three times; a cued recall test then occurred (e.g., cat—?), and of course, recall was greater for pairs presented thrice than once. Next, a second study trial occurred in which items initially presented once were now presented three times, whereas items initially presented three times were presented only once. After each pair was studied (either once or thrice), participants made a JOL for the pair and then made a decision about whether to restudy the pair.

On this judgment-selection trial, memory performance for the two sets of items was statistically equivalent, because all items were studied four times, either being studied once during the first trial and three times during the second, or vice versa. Thus, when people made decisions about which items to restudy, on average, memory across all items was the same. However, people's JOLs were different for the two sets of items: On the second trial, people made higher JOLs for items that were *initially* studied three times on the first trial than for those studied only once. Note that JOLs made on the second study trial are inaccurate here: People believe they will remember items studied more time on the first trial, when in fact, all items were studied the same number of times when JOLs were made, so recall did not differ for them. Thus, if people's JOLs drive study-time allocation, then they should more often select to restudy those items studied once on the first trial, because people believe those items have been less well learned. Across three experiments, Metcalfe and Finn (2008) demonstrated that people use their JOLs to control their allocation of study time (see also, Hines, Touron, & Hertzog, 2009).

Now that we have established that people do use their monitoring of learning to guide study, an intriguing issue becomes how it is used in allocating study time. According to the discrepancy-reduction model, people set a goal for learning items, and then continue studying each one until the goal is met. That is, learners continue studying an item until the discrepancy between current learning and the goal is completely reduced. As it takes longer to reduce this discrepancy for more difficult-to-learn items than easier ones, people use more time studying the more difficult items. In this manner, the discrepancy-reduction model predicts the modal outcome in which people spend more time studying items given lower than higher JOLs (Son & Metcalfe, 2000, 2005).

Although discrepancy reduction may underlie some study behaviors (Benjamin & Bird, 2006), people's allocation of study time is more flexible. We do more than (perhaps mindlessly) continue studying items until they all meet the same preset goal. In some situations, learners use monitoring to prioritize the *easiest* items for study and do not even study the more difficult items (Son & Metcalfe, 2000; Thiede & Dunlosky, 1999), and in other situations, they abandon memory monitoring in deciding how to allocate study time across items (Ariel, Dunlosky, & Bailey, 2009). Let's consider the former case first. The modal outcome (i.e., more study to items judged as most difficult) has typically been found when participants are encouraged to learn all the items on a list. To learn them all (i.e., meet a mastery goal), more time would likely need to be spent studying the more difficult items. In some situations, however, learners do not have mastery goals: Perhaps they have little time to study and cannot master all the items, or perhaps they do not desire to master the list (e.g., students who only need to pass a final exam to obtain their desired grade). If learners are trying to efficiently meet their goals, in both cases, they should focus on the easiest items, because using extra effort on the more difficult ones would be a waste of time. Consistent with such possibilities, when study time is limited (e.g., 15 seconds to study 30 items) and when people set low performance goals (e.g., learn only 6 of 30 items), they spend the most time studying a subset of the easiest-to-learn items (Dunlosky & Thiede, 2004; Son & Metcalfe, 2000).

Note that in these cases, people are using monitoring of learning to decide which items should be selected and prioritized for study. Beyond monitoring, people also tend to focus their restudy on items that they expect will provide the most reward. For instance, college students more often select to study (a) items that are more likely (than less likely) to appear on the criterion test and (b) items that will be worth more points (or reward) if correctly recalled on the criterion test (Ariel et al., 2009; Thiede & Dunlosky, 1999). In both cases, college students prioritize the more highly valued items for study, regardless of whether they are difficult or easy to learn.

Thus, students often appear to attempt to maximize their performance in the most efficient manner, which is a central premise of the *agenda-based regulation* (ABR) framework of study-time allocation (Ariel et al., 2009; Dunlosky, Ariel, & Thiede, 2011). According to the ABR framework, people construct and execute agenda—or simple plans—for allocating study time to meet these dual criteria: meeting current task goals and doing so efficiently. Although this framework highlights the importance of agendas, factors other than agenda construction and execution are expected to influence how (and how well) learners allocate their study time. For instance, individual differences in working-memory abilities can limit the quality of agenda use that leads to the dysregulation of study time (Dunlosky & Thiede, 2004). Bottom-up processes that are triggered by prepotent responses to the stimulus environment also can influence study time (Rhodes & Castel, 2009).

The ABR framework is an example of just one of several theories of people's allocation of study time (see also, Koriat, Ma'ayan, & Nussinson, 2006; Metcalfe, 2009; Winne & Hadwin, 1998). These theories differ with respect to their explanatory scope and are not mutually exclusive. For instance, Metcalfe's (2009) *region-of-proximal-learning* framework emphasizes how students in some cases prioritize the easiest of the unlearned items for study, because focusing on those items presumably would increase the likelihood that students would efficiently obtain their learning goals (Kornell & Metcalfe, 2006). In the context of the ABR framework, prioritizing items within this region of proximal learning constitutes just one of many agendas that people can use to allocate their time across items. Given that research on self-regulated learning is largely in its infancy, new evidence will likely help to shape these recent theories as we move toward a general theory of study-time allocation that can both describe how people control their study as well as prescribe how they should control study to efficiently meet their goals.

## CONTROL OF OTHER FACETS OF LEARNING

Researchers have just begun exploring how students control other facets of learning, such as making decisions to mass or space their study (Son, 2004; Toppino, Cohen, Davis, & Moors, 2009) or whether they elect to test themselves during study (Karpicke, 2009; Kornell & Bjork, 2007). Deciding how (or whether) to use these study strategies is important, because they can boost performance if used properly. For instance, memory performance is often better when study of each item is spaced throughout a study session than when it is massed together; fortunately, when given the choice, students often decide to space their study (Pyc & Dunlosky, 2010). Memory performance also benefits from testing; in fact, testing oneself on previously studied items typically is better for memory than is restudying the same items again (Roediger & Karpicke, 2006). Unfortunately, college students tend to underuse testing as a study strategy (Kornell & Bjork, 2007). Understanding why students appropriately use some effective strategies and underuse others is becoming an important goal for metamemory research, partly because it has obvious implications for improving student scholarship.

## HOW DO PEOPLE CONTROL THEIR RETRIEVAL?

A great way to begin answering this question involves asking another one: Which country won the World Cup in 2006? If you are a soccer fan, you would be familiar with the World Cup. Thus, if you cannot recall the answer, you may spend quite a bit of time trying to retrieve it. If your first thought was, "What is the World Cup?" you may not even search for an answer. Understanding how people control their retrieval has been central to metamemory research on retrieval processes. Just like research on the control of study, much of the research on the control of retrieval has sought to understand how people use their monitoring to control the time. As implied by the earlier example, FOK judgments as well as confidence in retrieved answers may play a role in people's decisions about how long to search for a response ("termination of search") and whether to output a response that had been retrieved.

Concerning termination of search, Singer and Tiede (2008) investigated whether FOK judgments are related to search times for general-knowledge questions that lead to "don't know" responses. That is, when people ultimately cannot retrieve answers to questions, do their feelings of knowing drive them to use more or less time while searching? To answer this question, some participants were used to develop FOK norms for a set of general-knowledge questions. These participants attempted to answer each question and then rated their confidence in recognizing the correct answer (1 = sure I would not recognize it to 9 = sure I would recognize it). An average FOK for each item was computed, and such norms across participants were positively correlated with individual FOK judgments from single individuals. Thus, using them allowed Singer and Tiede (2007) to estimate the FOK judgments of a second group of participants who were instructed to merely retrieve the answers. The prediction was that the normative FOKs would be positively correlated with retrieval latencies (i.e., the time taken to retrieve an answer before giving up) when participants could not retrieve an answer. Consistent with this prediction, the correlation between FOKs and retrieval latencies for unrecalled answers was +.50.

This outcome is intuitive: When we really feel we know an answer, we typically spend more time trying to pull it from memory. Even when we do retrieve an answer to a question, however, it does not mean we will share it with others. In fact, withholding incorrect responses is often just as important as responding correctly, such as when a witness is admonished to "tell the truth, and nothing but the truth." Koriat and Goldsmith (1996) proposed an influential model of memory retrieval that explained why (and when) people would either volunteer a response or withhold it (see also Higham & Arnold, 2007). Importantly, this model illustrates how accurate monitoring is critical for the quality of people's decision to output a response. Their model is presented in Figure 19.3. After being asked a question ("Input Question" in Fig. 19.3), people attempt to retrieve candidate answers from memory. For the question "Which country won the World Cup in 2006?" you may have retrieved United States, Brazil, and Italy. As answers are retrieved, you would evaluate their quality, such as by judging your confidence in the retrieved answer from "0" (meaning there is no way it is correct) to "1.0" (meaning you are sure it is correct). Perhaps you feel that there is only a .10 probability that United States is correct, a .70 chance that Brazil is correct, and a .40 chance that Italy is correct. In the model, these are the assessed probabilities ($Pa$). If you did not retrieve any other candidates, you would choose the best one (in this case, Brazil), but even now, you would not necessarily respond with "Brazil." Instead, you would compare your assessed probability ($Pa = .70$) with a response criterion ($Prc$). This criterion can be influenced by a variety of factors,

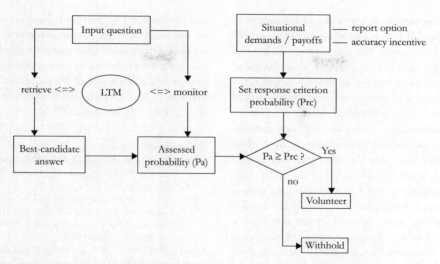

**Figure 19.3** Model of self-regulated retrieval that explains whether someone will report an answer that is retrieved when asked a given input question. See text for details. (From Koriat & Goldsmith, 1996.)

such as the current set of payoffs for responses. For instance, you may be taking a test over sports trivia where the reward for a correct response is high and where the penalty for an incorrect response is small. In this case, your response criterion would likely be low. By contrast, if you are on the witness stand and were told not to report any incorrect evidence, you may set a very high response criterion. Let's assume that you set a $Prc$ at .40, and hence you would volunteer the response "Brazil," because your assessed probability exceeds your response criterion; that is, $Pa$ (.70) > $Prc$ (.40).

Based on this example, it should be clear why monitoring accuracy is critical for the quality (and quantity) of what responses people will volunteer. Concerning accuracy, if your assessed probabilities do not reflect the actual probabilities of being correct (i.e., poor judgment accuracy), then incorrect answers could be volunteered. This mistake is illustrated in the earlier example: Italy is the correct answer, so the assessed probabilities were not accurate. Thus, your overconfidence in Brazil's team led you to respond incorrectly. If instead, Italy had a much higher $Pa$ (e.g., close to 1.0), then the enhanced judgment accuracy would have led to the correct response.

To evaluate this implication of the model, Koriat and Goldsmith (1996) used the following method. Participants were forced to answer general-knowledge questions so that the experimenters would know what each participant's best candidate answer was for every question; for each answer, participants provided a confidence judgment, which was used as

a measure of $Pa$. Next, the participants answered the questions again, but this time, they could withhold answers—that is, they were not forced to respond. As important, two different sets of questions were used. Some were considered standard questions and supported high levels of judgment accuracy and some were deceptive and led to inaccurate judgments. The latter consisted of questions that people often answer incorrectly with high confidence; for instance, "What is the capital of Australia?" is often confidently answered with "Syndey" when the correct answer is "Canberra." During the first round of questions, performance was greater for the standard questions (28%) than for the deceptive ones (12%). This outcome is not surprising, given that it merely demonstrates that the deceptive questions are in fact deceptive. The more important outcomes concern performance for the free-report phase. If participants use their confidence judgments to make decisions about which answers to withhold, their performance should increase for standard questions but may not change for deceptive ones. As expected, the percentage of accurate recall for the free-report phase was 75% for the standard questions, but it was only 21% for the deceptive questions. According to the model, people had difficulties with the deceptive questions because they would have failed to withhold incorrect responses that were inadvertently held with high confidence.

How long one persists in trying to retrieve an item and whether one elects to respond are not the only facets of retrieval that are under people's control. Others include (a) whether to even attempt to retrieve an answer or to use some other means to obtain one and (b) decisions about the grain size of information to report. For the former, Reder and Ritter (1992) investigated factors that influence people's decision to retrieve an answer to a difficult math problem or to compute it. People attempted retrieval when they believed problems were familiar (even when they were actually not familiar with them) and elected to compute answers when familiarity was low. For the latter, the instruction to "speak the truth and nothing but the truth" may influence the grain size of reports; in this case, people will tend to give more general reports that are more likely to be true and withhold details that have a higher chance of not being accurate (cf. Goldsmith, Koriat, & Weinberg-Eliezer, 2002). According to Ackerman and Goldsmith (2008), people control the grain size of their reports (either by providing more precise or more coarse answers) in order to be both informative and confident in their responses. Although we have much to learn about how people control their retrieval and whether such control can be optimal (for discussions of optimality, see Higham, 2007), one conclusion is certain: People do use their monitoring to make decisions about how long to search for answers and whether to volunteer responses. Thus, as with the control of study, accurate monitoring is essential for effective self-regulation.

## Conclusion

In the present chapter, we provided an introduction to many of the common measures, methods, and issues that drive research on metamemory. Some major conclusions included that people's monitoring judgments can be accurate, but only when the cues that are used to construct the judgments are diagnostic of criterion performance. As cue diagnosticity increases, then the upper limit on judgment accuracy also increases. Regardless of judgment accuracy, monitoring is also used in the service of controlling memory, whether it be in deciding which items to prioritize for study or when to volunteer (or withhold) a response during retrieval. Our overview, however, did not cover the entire field, which has sought to answer many intriguing questions about metamemory. How does metamemory develop in childhood and does it decline as we age? Do animals have metamemory—do they know when they know and when they do not? How do individual differences in metamemory influence educational outcomes? What are the neurological underpinnings of metamemory, and what kinds of brain insult

and psychological disorders lead to disruptions of metamemory? For those interested in further exploring metamemory, answers to these and other questions are available in a variety of more extensive sources (e.g., Dunlosky & Metcalfe, 2009; Hacker, Dunlosky, & Graesser, 2009; Higham & Leboe, 2011; Terrace & Metcalfe, 2005).

## References

Alter, A. L., & Oppenheimer, D. M. (2009). Uniting the tribes of fluency to form a metacognitive nation. *Personality and Social Psychology Review, 13,* 219–235.

Ackerman, R., & Goldsmith, M. (2008). Control over grain size in memory reporting: With and without satisficing knowledge. *Journal of Experimental Psychology: Learning, Memory, and Cognition, 34,* 1224–1245.

Arbuckle, T. Y., & Cuddy, L. L. (1969). Discrimination of item strength at time of presentation. *Journal of Experimental Psychology, 81,* 126–131.

Ariel, R., Dunlosky, J., & Bailey, H. (2009). Agenda-based regulation of study-time allocation: When agendas override item-based monitoring. *Journal of Experimental Psychology: General, 138,* 432–447.

Benjamin, A. S. (2005). Response speeding mediates the contributions of cue familiarity and target retrievability to metamnemonic judgments. *Psychonomic Bulletin and Review, 12,* 874–879.

Benjamin, A. S., & Bird, R. D. (2006). Metacognitive control of the spacing of study repetitions. *Journal of Memory and Language, 55,* 126–137.

Benjamin, A. S., Bjork, R. A., & Schwartz, B. L. (1998). The mismeasure of memory: When retrieval fluency is misleading as a metamnemonic index. *Journal of Experimental Psychology: General, 127,* 55–68.

Brunswik, E. (1956). *Perception and representative design of psychological experiments.* Berkeley: University of California Press.

Carroll, M., Nelson, T. O., & Kirwan, A. (1997). Tradeoff of semantic relatedness and degree of overlearning: Differential effects on metamemory and on long-term retention. *Acta Psychologica, 95,* 239–253.

Castel, A. D. (2008). Metacognition and learning about primacy and recency effects in free recall: The utilization of intrinsic and extrinsic cues when making judgments of learning. *Memory and Cognition, 36,* 429–437.

Dunlosky, J., Ariel, R., & Thiede, K. W. (2011). Agenda-based regulation of study-time allocation. In P. Higham & J. P. Leboe (Eds.), *Constructions of remembering and metacognition* (pp. 182–200). Hampshire, England: Palgrave Macmillan.

Dunlosky, J., & Bjork, R. A. (Eds.). (2008). *A handbook of metamemory and memory.* New York: Psychology Press.

Dunlosky, J., & Matvey, G. (2001). Empirical analysis of the intrinsic-extrinsic distinction of judgments of learning (JOLs): Effects of relatedness and serial position on JOLs. *Journal of Experimental Psychology: Learning, Memory, and Cognition, 27,* 1180–1191.

Dunlosky, J., & Metcalfe, J. (2009). *Metacognition.* Los Angeles: Sage.

Dunlosky, J., Serra, M. J., & Baker, J. M. C. (2007). Metamemory. In F. T. Durso, Nickerson, R. S., Dumais, S. T., Lewandowsky, S., & Perfect, T. J. (Eds.), *Handbook* of applied cognition (2nd ed., pp. 137–160). Hoboken, NJ: Wiley.

Dunlosky, J., & Thiede, K. W. (2004). Causes and constraints of the shift-to-easier-materials effect in the control of study. *Memory and Cognition, 32*, 779–788.

Flavell, J. H. (1979). Metacognition and cognitive monitoring: A new area of cognitive-developmental inquiry. *American Psychologist, 34*, 906–911.

Goldsmith, M., Koriat, A., & Weinberg-Eliezer, A. (2002). Strategic regulation of grain size memory reporting. *Journal of Experimental Psychology: General, 131*, 73–95.

Hacker, D. J., Dunlosky, J., & Graesser, A. C. (Eds.). (2009). *Handbook of metacognition and self-regulated learning.* Mahwah, NJ: Erlbaum.

Hart, J. T. (1965). Memory and the feeling-of-knowing experience. *Journal of Educational Psychology, 56*, 208–216.

Hart, J. T. (1966). Methodological note on feeling-of-knowing experiments. *Journal of Educational Psychology, 57*, 347–349.

Hertzog, C., Dunlosky, J., Robinson, A. E., & Kidder, D. P. (2003). Encoding fluency is a cue used for judgments about learning. *Journal of Experimental Psychology: Learning, Memory, and Cognition, 29*, 22–34.

Hertzog, C., Price, J., & Dunlosky, J. (2008). How is knowledge generated about memory encoding strategy effectiveness? *Learning and Individual Differences, 18*, 430–445.

Higham, P. A. & Leboe, J. P. (Ed.). (2011). *Constructions of remembering and metacognition.* Hampshire, England: Palgrave Macmillan.

Higham, P. A. (2007). No Special K! A signal detection framework for the strategic regulation of memory accuracy. *Journal of Experimental Psychology: General, 136*, 1–22.

Higham, P. A., & Arnold, M. M. (2007). How many questions should I answer? Using bias profiles to estimate optimal bias and maximum score on formula-scored tests. *European Journal of Cognitive Psychology, 19*, 718–742.

Hines, J. C., Touron, D. R., & Hertzog, C. (2009). Metacognitive influences on study time allocation in an associative recognition task: An analysis of adult age differences. *Psychology and Aging, 24*, 462–475.

Humphrey, G. (1951). *Thinking: an introduction to its experimental psychology.* New York: Wiley.

Karpicke, J. D. (2009). Metacognitive control and strategy selection: Deciding to practice retrieval during learning. *Journal of Experimental Psychology: General, 138*, 469–486.

Kolers, P. A., & Palef, S. R. (1976). Knowing not. *Memory and Cognition, 4*, 553–558.

Koriat, A. (1993). How do we know that we know? The accessibility model of the feeling of knowing. *Psychological Review, 100*, 609–639.

Koriat, A. (1997). Monitoring one's own knowledge during study: A cue-utilization approach to judgments of learning. *Journal of Experimental Psychology: General, 126*, 349–370.

Koriat, A., Bjork, R. A., Sheffer, L., & Bar, S. K. (2004). Predicting one's own forgetting: The role of experience-based and theory-based processes. *Journal of Experimental Psychology: General, 133*, 643–656

Koriat, A., & Goldsmith, M. (1996). Monitoring and control processes in the strategic regulation of memory accuracy. *Psychological Review, 103*, 490–517.

Koriat, A., & Levy-Sadot, R. (2001). The combined contributions of the cue-familiarity and accessibility heuristics to feelings of knowing. *Journal of Experimental Psychology: Learning, Memory, and Cognition, 27*, 34–53.

Koriat, A., Ma'ayan, H., & Nussinson, R. (2006). The intricate relationships between monitoring and control in metacognition: Lessons for the cause-and-effect relation between subjective experience and behavior. *Journal of Experimental Psychology: General, 135*, 36–69.

Koriat, A., Nussinson, R., Bless, H., & Shaked, N. (2008). Information-based and experience-based metacognitive judgments: Evidence from subjective confidence. In J. Dunlosky & R. A. Bjork (Eds.), *Handbook of metamemory and memory* (pp. 117–135). New York: Psychology Press.

Kornell, N., & Bjork, R. A. (2007). The promise and perils of self regulated study. *Psychonomic Bulletin and Review, 14*, 219–224.

Kornell, N., & Bjork, R. A. (2008). Optimizing self-regulated study: The benefits-and costs-of dropping flashcards. *Memory, 16*, 125–136.

Kornell, N., & Metcalfe, J. (2006). Study efficacy and the region of proximal learning framework. *Journal of Experimental Psychology: Learning, Memory, and Cognition, 32*, 609–622.

Loftus, E., & Ketchum, K. (1991). *Witness for the defense: The accused, the eyewitness, and the expert who puts memory on trial.* New York: St. Martin's Press.

Matvey, G., Dunlosky, J., & Guttentag, R. (2001). Fluency of retrieval at study affects judgments of learning (JOLs): An anlaytic or nonanalytic basis for JOLs? *Memory and Cognition, 29*, 222–232.

Mazzoni, G., Cornoldi, C., & Marchitelli, G. (1990). Do memorability ratings affect study-time allocation? *Memory and Cognition, 18*, 196–204.

Metcalfe, J. (2002). Is study time allocated selectively to a region of proximal learning? *Journal of Experimental Psychology: General, 131*, 349–363.

Metcalfe, J. (2009). Metacognitive judgments and control of study. *Current Directions in Psychological Science, 18*, 159–163.

Metcalfe, J., & Finn, B. (2008). Evidence that judgments of learning are causally related to study choice. *Psychonomic Bulletin and Review, 15*, 174–179.

Metcalfe, J., Schwartz, B. L., & Joaquim, S. G. (1993). The cue-familiarity heuristic in metacognition. *Journal of Experimental Psychology: Learning, Memory, and Cognition, 19*, 851–861.

Miner, A. C., & Reder, L. M. (1994). A new look at feeling of knowing: Its metacognitive role in regulating question answering. In J. Metcalfe & A. Shimamura (Eds.), *Metacognition: Knowing about knowing* (pp. 47–70). Cambridge, MA: MIT Press.

Nelson, T. O., & Dunlosky, J. (1991). When people's judgments of learning (JOLs) are extremely accurate at predicting subsequent recall: The "delayed-JOL effect." *Psychological Science, 2*, 267–270.

Nelson, T. O., & Narens, L. (1990). Metamemory: A theoretical framework and new findings. In G. H. Bower (Ed.), *The psychology of learning and motivation* (Vol. 26, pp. 125–141). New York: Academic Press.

Nelson, T. O., Gerler, D., & Narens, L. (1984). Accuracy of feeling of knowing judgments for predicting perceptual identification and relearning. *Journal of Experimental Psychology: General, 113*, 282–300.

Nelson, T. O., & Leonesio, R. J. (1988). Allocation of self-paced study time and the "labor-in-vain effect." *Journal of*

*Experimental Psychology: Learning, Memory, and Cognition, 14,* 676–686.

Pyc, M. A. & Dunlosky, J. (2010). Toward an understanding of students' allocation of study time: Why do they decide to mass or space their practice? *Memory and Cognition, 38,* 431–440.

Rabinowitz, J. C., Ackerman, B. P., Craik, F. I. M., & Hinchley, J. L. (1982). Aging and metamemory: The roles of relatedness and imagery. *Journal of Gerontology, 37,* 688–695.

Reder, L. M., & Ritter, F. E. (1992). What determines initial feeling of knowing? Familiarity with question terms, not with the answer. *Journal of Experimental Psychology: Learning, Memory, and Cognition, 18,* 435–451.

Rhodes, M. G., & Castel, A. D. (2009). Metacognitive illusions for auditory information: Effects on monitoring and control. *Psychonomic Bulletin and Review, 16,* 550–554.

Roediger, H. L., III, & Karpicke, J. D. (2006). The power of testing memory: Basic research and implications for educational practice. *Perspectives on Psychological Science, 1,* 181–210.

Serra, M. J., & Dunlosky, J. (2005). Does retrieval fluency contribute to the underconfidence-with-practice effect? *Journal of Experimental Psychology: Learning, Memory, and Cognition, 31,* 1258–1266.

Shaughnessy, J. J. (1981). Memory monitoring accuracy and modification of rehearsal strategies. *Journal of Verbal Learning and Verbal Behavior, 20,* 216–230.

Singer, M., & Tiede, H. L. (2008). Feeling of knowing and duration of unsuccessful memory search. *Memory and Cognition, 36,* 588–597.

Son, L. K. (2004). Spacing one's study: Evidence for a metacognitive control strategy. *Journal of Experimental Psychology: Learning, Memory, and Cognition, 30,* 601–604.

Son, L. K., & Kornell, N. (2008). Research on the allocation of study time: Key studies from 1890 to the present (and beyond). In J. Dunlosky & R. A. Bjork (Eds.), *Handbook of metamemory and memory* (pp. 333–351). New York: Psychology Press.

Son, L., & Metcalfe, J. (2005). Judgments of learning: Evidence for a two-stage process. *Memory and Cognition, 33,* 1116–1129.

Son, L. K., & Metcalfe, J. (2000). Metacognitive and control strategies in study-time allocation. *Journal of Experimental Psychology: Learning, Memory, and Cognition, 26,* 204–221.

Souchay, C., Moulin, C. J. A., Clarys, D., Taconnat, L., & Isingrini, M. (2007). Diminished episodic memory awareness in older adults: Evidence from feeling-of-knowing and recollection. *Consciousness and Cognition, 16,* 769–784.

Terrace, H. S., & Metcalfe, J. (Eds.). (2005). *The missing link in cognition: Origins of self-reflective consciousness.* New York: Oxford University Press.

Thiede, K. W., & Dunlosky, J. (1999). Toward a general model of self-regulated study: An analysis of selection of items for study and self-paced study time. *Journal of Experimental Psychology: Learning, Memory, and Cognition, 25,* 1024–1037.

Toppino, T. C., Cohen, M. S., Davis, M. L., & Moors, A. C. (2009). Metacognitive control over the distribution of practice: When is spacing preferred? *Journal of Experimental Psychology: Learning, Memory, and Cognition, 5,* 1352–1358.

Winne, P. H., & Hadwin, A. F. (1998). Studying as self-regulated learning. In D. Hacker, J. Dunlosky, & A. C. Graesser (Eds.), *Metacognition in educational theory and practice* (pp. 277–304). Hillsdale, NJ: Erlbaum.

Woodworth, R. S. (1921). *Psychology: A study of mental life.* New York: Henry Holt.

# Memory in Educational Settings

Elizabeth J. Marsh *and* Andrew C. Butler

**Abstract**

We describe three theoretical principles from cognitive science that have implications for educational practice: introducing desirable difficulties during learning, processing information to extract meaning, and the importance of a match between the processing that occurs during initial learning and the processing required by the criterial task. We use these principles to evaluate the effectiveness of three strategies typically used to guide the initial learning of material (advance organizers, underlining and highlighting, and note taking) and three strategies for poststudy processing (retrieval practice, feedback processing, and spacing of practice). Finally, we consider the issues of long-term retention, transfer, and the relativity of memory phenomena, all of which often constrain the applicability of basic research to educational settings.

**Key Words:** memory, education, learning, long-term retention, transfer-appropriate processing, desirable difficulties, levels of processing

Cognitive psychologists and educators share a common goal: Both want to understand how to promote long-term learning and memory. Both are interested in the answers to questions like "How should people study material in order to remember it after time has passed?" and "What causes people to forget material they once knew?" However, cognitive psychologists tend to answer these questions using convenience samples (i.e., college undergraduates), relatively short delays between study and test, laboratory experiments, and simple stimuli such as word lists. But the educator is interested in specific student populations, very long-term memory, applications in the classroom, and complex educational materials such as lectures and textbooks. These differences in approaches have limited conversation between cognitive psychologists and educators, which is unfortunate as there is great potential for both groups to benefit from interacting. This chapter reflects a recent interest in the field to shrink this divide and summarizes a growing body of work aimed at connecting basic cognitive research to educational situations.

We begin this chapter with some guiding theoretical principles and then turn to specific applications. We are interested in general cognitive principles that can be applied to education, regardless of the subject matter or particular classroom. To this end, we will describe some basic research from cognitive psychology that is important for understanding the theory, and we will consider the implications for educational practice. We will then discuss some specific strategies (including ones implemented during the initial learning of material as well as some implemented after material has been studied) and provide an example of how such strategies can be combined to optimize learning. Next we will explore some issues with applying these guiding principles and learning strategies in educational settings. Finally, we will close by considering the relativity of memory and pointing out some future directions for research.

## Guiding Theoretical Principles
### Introducing "Desirable Difficulties" During Learning

In education, techniques that speed up the process of learning are commonplace—from language-learning programs like Rosetta Stone (a commercial product) to speed reading strategies like skimming. The logic behind such techniques seems reasonable: Why would one want to spend a longer period of time mastering material when it is possible to learn it faster? The problem with this idea is the implicit assumption that the level of performance attained during learning will be maintained over the long run. However, this assumption is false—learning material to some criterion does not guarantee that it will be remembered in the future. Performance during learning is a poor predictor of future performance because it reflects the momentary accessibility of knowledge (i.e., retrieval strength) rather than how well it has been stored in memory (i.e., storage strength) (see Bjork & Bjork, 1992).

To understand the distinction between retrieval strength and storage strength, try answering the following question: What did you eat for dinner last night? You probably retrieved the answer very quickly and easily because retrieval strength is high for that particular memory (since it is very recent and you have not eaten any other dinners in the interim). However, a month from now you would be unlikely to remember what you ate last night because retrieval strength dissipates over time. Instead, remembering your dinner a month from now would depend upon the storage strength of the memory of that particular dinner. Storage strength increases when a memory is retrieved or the event is reexperienced. If last night's dinner is like most dinners, the memory will not accumulate much storage strength because you are unlikely to think about it or tell someone else about it (i.e., retrieve or reexperience it). Returning to education, if knowledge is to be retained over long periods of time, then the goal of learning must be to increase storage strength, not momentary accessibility. A student being able to quickly retrieve an answer at one time does not guarantee long-term learning.

Based on the distinction between retrieval strength and storage strength, R. A. Bjork and colleagues developed the concept of "desirable difficulties" in learning (Bjork, 1994a, 1994b; Christina & Bjork, 1991; Schmidt & Bjork, 1992). The main idea is that introducing difficulties during learning

will result in superior long-term retention because the greatest gains in storage strength occur when retrieval strength is low. For example, consider the practice of using flash cards to study vocabulary words. If you study a word and then try to remember it immediately, then the gain in storage strength will be relatively low because it is so easy to retrieve the word right away (retrieval strength is high). However, if you wait 5 minutes before attempting to retrieve the word (when retrieval strength will be lower), then the gain in storage strength will be larger. The implication for educational practice is that instead of arranging the conditions of learning to be easier and faster for the learner, educators should introduce difficulties into the learning process in order to promote long-term retention of knowledge.

In short, the theory of desirable difficulties encourages us to think about introducing conditions that will slow the learner down, and make learning a bit harder—with benefits for long-term learning. As will be developed later in the chapter, however, this theory is not to be interpreted as "make learning impossible"—the learner must be able to overcome the difficulty for it to be a desirable one.

### Processing Information to Extract Meaning

A second relevant theoretical idea involves how people simultaneously process information on many different levels. At the most basic level, incoming information is processed by the nervous system in order to organize and understand sensory input. At higher levels, the information is processed with respect to existing knowledge in order to extract meaning. According to the levels-of-processing framework (Craik & Lockhart, 1972; Craik & Tulving, 1975), much of this processing occurs automatically, but attention can be directed toward any given level. Critically, directing attention at a lower or "shallow" level of processing (e.g., focusing on the orthography of words while reading) disrupts higher or "deeper" levels of processing (e.g., determining what those words mean). As a result, the type of processing in which one consciously engages determines what information will be encoded into memory and retained. The type of processing is more important than the intent to learn (e.g., Craik & Tulving, 1975); the implication is that a student who deliberately prepares for a test but who does not engage in deep processing will not do as well as the student who processes the material deeply, even if the latter student is not deliberately trying to learn the material.

For the purposes of the present chapter, we are more concerned with types of processing in which meaning is extracted from information, since most educational tasks emphasize meaning over perceptual information. With that in mind, it is important to point out that there are many different ways in which information can be processed at this "deeper" level (e.g., Packman & Battig, 1978). One helpful distinction involves *item-specific processing* versus *relational processing* (Hunt & Einstein, 1981). Item-specific processing involves encoding the various characteristics or properties of a particular piece of information. For example, judging the pleasantness of a word, filling in missing letters in a text, and creating a mental image of each step in a science experiment all focus the learner on a single to-be-remembered item.

In contrast, relational processing refers to the encoding of similarities and differences across pieces of information. For example, sorting words into categories, ordering sentences to create a coherent text, and explaining why each subsequent step in a science experiment follows the preceding step all involve comparing to-be-remembered events to each other. In short, both item-specific and relational processing can involve meaning extraction, but they direct the learner to different aspects of the to-be-remembered events.

To summarize, it is key to consider what type of processing different learning strategies encourage. For most educational tasks, students will benefit from strategies that encourage them to extract the meaning of to-be-remembered information. However, as will be described in the next section, it is also important to think about what type of processing will be required later on to succeed on the criterial task.

### Importance of Match Between Processing at Encoding and Retrieval

Although processing information at "deeper" levels involving meaning extraction generally results in superior memory performance (e.g., Craik & Lockhart, 1972; Craik & Tulving, 1975), the way in which information is processed is not the sole determinate of what will be remembered. Rather, memory performance is the joint product of the way in which the memory was encoded (i.e., the memory trace that is stored) and the way in which it is retrieved (i.e., the cues provided) (e.g., Tulving & Pearlstone, 1966; Tulving & Osler, 1968). This idea is codified in the theory of transfer-appropriate processing, which states that memory performance

will be enhanced to the extent that the processes engaged during initial learning match the processes required for the criterial task (Morris, Bransford, & Franks, 1977; for a review see Roediger, Weldon, & Challis, 1989). Thus, "goodness" of encoding is important for establishing the potential for good memory performance, but the match between processing at encoding and retrieval is critical to realizing that potential (e.g., Fisher & Craik, 1977; Moscovitch & Craik, 1976).

To illustrate the concept of transfer-appropriate processing, consider an experiment by McDaniel and colleagues (McDaniel, Hines, Waddill, & Einstein, 1994, Experiment 1). Subjects read a text that described baseball and performed one of three tasks: generating words in the text by inserting deleted letters (an item-specific processing condition), ordering scrambled sentences to form a coherent text (a relational processing condition), or simply reading the text (a control condition). Later, subjects took a short-answer test that probed item-specific information (e.g., the name of the baseball stadium) and relational information (e.g., the sequence of events during a major play in the game). Having inserted letters or ordered the sentences led to better performance on both types of final questions, relative to simply reading the text (see Fig. 20.1). However, more importantly, subjects who had inserted missing letters performed the best on the item-specific questions, whereas subjects who had ordered sentences performed the best on the relational questions. Memory performance on the final test was enhanced when there was a match between processing at encoding and retrieval.

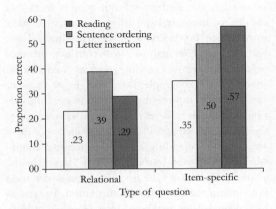

**Figure 20.1** Proportion correct on the final test as a function of encoding task (reading, sentence ordering, letter insertion) and question type (relational vs. item-specific). (Data from McDaniel, Hines, Waddill, & Einstein, 1994, Experiment 1.)

In short, there is not always a single right answer about which study strategy will be best. Rather, as reflected in ideas about transfer-appropriate processing, the ideal study strategy depends upon what the student will need to do later.

## Summary

We have presented three general cognitive principles that are critical for determining memory performance in educational settings: introducing desirable difficulties during learning, engaging in processes that emphasize meaning extraction, and matching learning processes to the processes needed to excel on the final criterial task (i.e., transfer-appropriate processing). We turn now to applying these theoretical ideas to specific educational activities.

## Learning Strategies for Studying Material

Much research has focused on strategies for learning material, and to review all possible strategies is beyond the scope of this chapter. Instead, we focus on a few common strategies and apply the guiding theoretical principles described earlier to help us understand how each strategy can be used to optimize learning. We chose one strategy (advance organizers) that is typically implemented by the instructor or in course materials (e.g., textbooks) and two strategies (highlighting/underlining and note taking) that are normally under student control.

### Receiving Advance Organizers

It is important that the student approach the learning situation with the information he or she needs to appropriately process the to-be-remembered information. Without the relevant background knowledge, the student will not be able to extract the desired meaning from a text or lecture (in other words, deep processing will be impossible). Thus, the first study strategy we will consider, advance organizers, involves giving readers information (normally in paragraph form) that helps them to orient to and understand the important information in a to-be-read text, as well as connect it to their prior knowledge. Critically, advance organizers are aimed at providing a larger conceptual framework for the to-be-learned material; they help the reader to understand the upcoming material but do not contain the exact same information. For example, in one of the earliest studies (Ausubel, 1960), students in the experimental group read an advance organizer explaining the relationship between metals and alloys before reading the target passage on

the metallurgy of steel. In contrast, students in the control group also read a paragraph before reading the critical passage on steel, but they read about the history of steel-making methods (which would not help them understand the science of steel). Both groups read their introductory passages 48 hours before reading the target passage on steel; 3 days after that, they answered a series of multiple-choice questions about the steel passage. Subjects in the experimental group, who received the advance organizer, outperformed subjects in the control group (Ms of 46% and 39% correct, respectively).

Numerous studies have replicated this benefit of advance organizers (see Corkill, 1992, and Mayer, 1979, for reviews). Advance organizers can help the student to be more efficient; for example, students who read an advance organizer did not need to listen to a lecture on 35 mm cameras more than once to reach the same level of learning as observed in control subjects who repeatedly listened to it (Bromage & Mayer, 1986; see also Mayer, 1983). However, advance organizers are not always helpful, and understanding when they do versus do not help the reader is informative about how they work. Advance organizers work by providing a framework or schema for integrating the incoming information—thus, if the framework is already activated, advance organizers will not provide any additional benefit. Consequently, advance organizers help students learn disorganized material but not organized material (Mayer, 1978). Advance organizers are also less effective when students are likely already familiar with their content. For example, Ausubel and Fitzgerald (1961) examined the usefulness of an advance organizer comparing Christianity and Buddhism, prior to reading a text about Buddhism. The advance organizer was helpful, but only for subjects who scored low on a test about Christianity. Students who knew a lot about Christianity presumably did not need that schema activated prior to passage reading. Overall, advance organizer studies often use math or science materials, as students are unlikely to be familiar with the overarching conceptual frameworks for such topics (Mayer, 1979).

Advance organizers work primarily by improving the encoding of the to-be-learned material. Standard manipulations known to increase encoding have their expected effects when applied to advance organizers. The benefits of advance organizers increase following deep processing (by requiring students to paraphrase the organizer; Dinnel & Glover, 1985) and with spacing (reading the organizer ahead of time is better than reading it immediately before the critical text; Glover, Bullock, & Dietzer, 1990). Because advance organizers are typically aimed at overarching conceptual frameworks, they help students to process the target relationally (according to the relevant schema) as opposed to focusing on individual details (item-specific processing). Consequently, advance organizers promote transfer of knowledge. For example, Mayer (1975, 1976) examined how advance organizers affected the ability to apply new knowledge about a computer language called FORTRAN. In these studies, the advance organizer explained how a computer works using concrete analogies, such as comparing a computer's output to a telephone note pad. Subjects in both the advance organizer and control groups learned computer commands such as READ, WRITE, GO TO, and IF, but only the advance organizer subjects had learned an overarching model of the computer before encountering the specific programming commands. When asked to recall what they had learned, subjects who had received an advance organizer were more likely to recall conceptual information and to make appropriate inferences (Mayer, 1976). Subjects who had received advance organizers were also better able to write and interpret programming statements than were control subjects (Mayer, 1975).

While typically treated as an encoding phenomenon, advance organizers can also influence retrieval. Although the benefits of advance organizers depend upon reading them before encoding the target text (readers do not benefit from reading an organizer after encoding; Mayer & Bromage, 1980), rereading the organizer before a *delayed* test can also help performance (Corkill, Glover, Bruning, & Krug, 1988). Rereading the organizer right before test likely reactivates the original encoding context, increasing the overlap between encoding and retrieval, as well as providing a spaced rehearsal of the crucial conceptual information.

In short, advance organizers can be connected to the theoretical ideas laid out earlier in this chapter. Most obviously, they encourage deep processing of unfamiliar material by giving students the knowledge they need to process the material meaningfully. Advance organizers are less useful when read immediately before the target text; it is a desirable difficulty to insert a delay between these two phases and require readers to retrieve the information from the advance organizers from long-term memory. Finally, advance organizers work by helping the learner to link to-be-remembered information to a larger conceptual framework, meaning the benefits are most visible on tests that tap relational information.

## Highlighting and Underlining

Students often face a large amount of information and need to figure out how to best allocate their study time. As described in the last section, the teacher can help students to appropriately direct their attention with tools such as advance organizers. However, students need to be able to identify important concepts on their own, and one common technique is to highlight or underline information that needs to be remembered. The one study we found that directly compared highlighting and underlining found no difference between these conceptually similar strategies (Fowler & Barker, 1974), so we will discuss these techniques together.

Highlighting and underlining have potential as learning strategies, because it has been demonstrated that students are more likely to remember text that appears in a distinctive format. For example, students who read *Scientific American* articles with five statements underlined were more likely to later correctly answer questions about those statements than were students who read the same texts without any underlining (Cashen & Leicht, 1970). In such cases, underlining or highlighting presumably captures the reader's attention, increasing encoding of the distinctive text. Several studies support the idea that readers benefit from attentional cues in texts that include underlining, highlighting, capitalization, and other ways of making text distinctive (e.g., Lorch, Lorch, & Klusewitz, 1995).

However, a second step is involved when the student uses highlighting or underlining as a study strategy: He or she must decide which text to mark. No benefit has been observed in several studies that allowed students to underline as much or as little of texts as desired (e.g., Idstein & Jenkins, 1972; Stordahl & Christensen, 1956). Two issues may drive such results. First, even if marking text does not lead to an overall boost in recall, it may promote memory for the parts of the text that were highlighted—the issue is that this benefit is potentially at the expense of other nonhighlighted text (e.g., Fowler & Barker, 1974). The literature is unclear about the effects of marking part of a text on other nearby but unmarked sentences, and whether it should hurt or help memory for the unmarked sentences (e.g., Cashen & Leicht, 1970). Second, students often highlight too much of a text, and people are less likely to remember marked text if it is more prevalent (Lorch et al., 1995). In addition to reducing the distinctiveness of the marked text, over-highlighting and over-underlining may reduce deep processing. That is, it may take more cognitive effort to figure out which one or two points in a paragraph are most important, and thus selective highlighting may be better than highlighting the bulk of a text. Some data to support this idea comes from Fowler and Barker (1974), who examined the relationship between the amount of *Scientific American* texts that were highlighted and performance on later multiple-choice items. Students who highlighted more text performed worse on the later test ($r = -.287$), although the small sample size ($n = 19$ in the relevant condition) meant the result was not significant. Supporting the idea that less highlighting might be better, Rickards and August (1975) found that students asked to underline just one sentence per paragraph later recalled more of a science text than did a no-underlining control group.

In short, highlighting (or underlining) as typically implemented is not a strong study strategy, even though it is a popular one. One issue is that overuse of this technique may reduce deep processing. A better strategy is to select just one sentence to highlight per paragraph, as this likely increases both deep processing and relational processing as sentences are compared to one another. In addition, highlighting in this way represents a desirable difficulty because of the effort required to identify the key sentence in a given paragraph.

## Note Taking

Note taking is also a common strategy that students report using when listening to lectures or while reading texts (e.g., Palmatier & Bennett, 1974). Note taking may affect memory through two different routes: one involving initial learning (encoding) and the other involving storage. Our focus will be on encoding; that is, how does note taking change the way the to-be-remembered information is processed, with consequences for later memory? However, this focus is not meant to minimize the importance of reviewing notes after encoding; an important consequence of note taking is that it yields external storage of the to-be-remembered material, which can then be used for poststudy review (see Kiewra, 1983, for an overview of the review function of note taking, and see the next section of this chapter for discussion of other poststudy activities).

Overall, research supports the common belief that taking notes promotes memory, with the benefits of note taking observed both in the classroom (e.g., Crawford, 1925a) and the lab (e.g., Crawford, 1925b), and with both text (e.g., Bretzing & Kulhavy, 1981) and lecture materials (e.g., Di Vesta & Gray, 1972). Some of the earliest evidence comes

from Crawford (1925a), who examined the relationship between students' notes and performance on quizzes in seven college classes. Across studies, there was a median correlation of .50 between the number of correct points in a student's notes and his or her quiz score. In contrast, there was no relationship between the number of vague points noted and later quiz performance. This early study highlights two themes in the note-taking literature: first, the quantity of notes matters (with more complete notes generally yielding greater memorial benefits) and, second, the quality of the notes matters (with precise notes being better than vague ones).

Consistent with these two themes, instructor-provided support that improves the quality of notes benefits memory. For example, Moore (1968) held up red/green cards to cue students on whether to write down lecture points or not; students liked this technique and it improved later performance relative to a control group that took notes without cues. Similarly, students can benefit from receiving partial notes or handouts from the instructor to guide note taking (e.g., Austin, Lee, Thibeault, Carr, & Bailey, 2002). On the other hand, if the educational situation will not permit the student to take complete and/or quality notes, the student will not benefit from note taking. In fact, note taking may even hurt performance in such situations because students must pay attention to both the lecture and note taking, and dividing attention during encoding impairs memory (e.g., Craik, Govoni, Naveh-Benjamin, & Anderson, 1996). The student listening to a fast-paced lecture does not have the resources to take good notes and thus may be worse off if she tries to take notes while listening (e.g., Peters, 1972).

Understanding *why* note taking benefits memory requires an analysis of the processing involved. Two findings suggest that note taking may help students to extract the "big picture" of a text or lecture. The first piece of support comes from detailed analyses of the content of notes and later recall of the target material, to see whether listeners recalled all lecture propositions equally (Einstein, Morris, & Smith, 1985). In this study, an independent group of subjects rated the importance of 126 propositions in a lecture on the history of individual differences, and these ratings were used to classify the importance of what note takers recorded and recalled. Critically, note takers remembered more important propositions than did subjects who only listened to the lecture. It was *not* that note takers recalled more of everything. Instead, note takers only recalled more of the most important propositions, a finding Einstein et al. (1985) argued was consistent with organizational processing because determining importance requires comparisons across to-be-remembered items.

Even more critically, note taking promotes transfer (e.g., Peper & Mayer, 1986). For example, in one experiment (Peper & Mayer, 1978, Experiment 2) subjects learned about the chi-square statistic, either via a video lecture or via text. A later test consisted of both near- and far-transfer questions; near-transfer questions were straight-forward applications of the formula, whereas far-transfer questions went beyond the material covered in the experiment (e.g., requiring the subject to say the situation did not allow the use of the chi-square statistic). Note takers and control subjects performed similarly on the near-transfer problems, but note takers outperformed the controls on the far-transfer problems. This benefit of note taking occurred regardless of whether students heard the lecture or read the text, but it was particularly salient for low-ability subjects who had not scored as well on the SAT math test (see Fig. 20.2).

Although note taking yields memorial benefits, the type of notes naturally taken may not be the most powerful mnemonic possible. One issue involves how much note taking involves going beyond the to-be-remembered information (versus simply copying; see Marsh & Sink, 2010), including paraphrasing the to-be-remembered information and connecting it to stored knowledge. Returning to the

levels of processing framework, the key issue is the depth of processing note taking naturally affords. We have just reviewed evidence that note taking encourages relational processing that affords transfer. Nevertheless, additional benefit may come from techniques that encourage the reader or listener to process the material even more deeply. For example, King (1992) trained students to summarize material, specifically how to identify and encapsulate the main idea. This group of students was compared to another group who took notes naturally, and who later had a chance to review those notes. Students who summarized the lecture performed better on both immediate and delayed comprehension tests than students who took notes (see Bretzing & Kulhavy, 1979, for similar results). Similarly, the note-taking group did not do as well as a group of students trained to ask themselves (and answer) questions about the material. Students might benefit from incorporating some of these deep processing techniques into their notes; in other words, training might help students to take notes that include more of the generative processing thought to be key for transfer (e.g., Peper & Mayer, 1978).

In summary, the literature on note taking is consistent with the theoretical ideas laid out at the beginning of this chapter. Note taking promotes transfer, suggesting that it does involve deep processing of the to-be-remembered material. However, it is important that the situation not be one that makes note taking too hard; the difficulty must be desirable and not impossible to overcome.

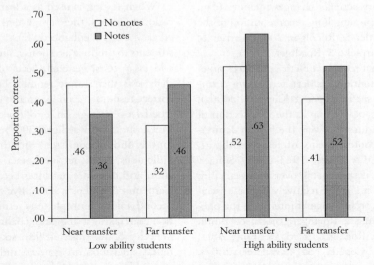

**Figure 20.2** Proportion correct on the final test as a function of note taking (notes vs. no notes), question type (near transfer vs. far transfer), and student ability (high vs. low). (Data from Peper & Mayer, 1978, Experiment 2.)

## Learning Strategies for Poststudy

After the initial processing of material is complete, there are many ways in which that information can be further processed (such as reviewing one's notes, as already discussed). One of the most popular strategies involves repeatedly reading the material (e.g., Karpicke, Butler, & Roediger, 2009; see too Kornell & Bjork, 2007). As the reader can likely surmise from the concept of desirable difficulties, this strategy tends to be relatively ineffective (see Callender & McDaniel, 2009). However, there are many strategies for reprocessing information that produce substantial mnemonic benefits. We will describe three such strategies: engaging in retrieval practice, processing feedback to correct errors, and spacing out practice over time.

### Retrieval Practice

In most educational settings, testing is used as an assessment tool. As such, it serves two purposes: (1) evaluating student learning (i.e., summative assessment) and (2) providing feedback to guide future learning activities (i.e., formative assessment). Much has been written about each of these purposes (for an excellent review, see Black & Wiliam, 1998), and thus we will focus on a less appreciated reason for testing: the use of tests as a learning tool. In both educational and psychological theories of learning, testing is often assumed to be a neutral event, much like measuring someone's weight. Just as stepping on a scale does not change how much someone weighs, testing is assumed to measure the contents of memory but leave them unchanged. However, memory research has shown that retrieving information from memory actually changes memory (e.g., Bjork, 1975), improving long-term retention of the material (e.g. Butler & Roediger, 2007; Carrier & Pashler, 1992; Karpicke & Roediger, 2008).

The finding that retrieval practice produces superior long-term retention has been termed *the testing effect* (for review, see Roediger & Karpicke, 2006a). Memory researchers working at the intersection of psychology and education were the first to demonstrate the mnemonic benefits of testing (Abbott, 1909; Gates, 1917; Jones, 1923–1924; Spitzer, 1939). However, despite being over 100 years old, the testing effect remained relatively underappreciated until a recent resurgence of interest in the phenomenon (see Marsh, Roediger, Bjork, & Bjork, 2007; McDaniel, Roediger, & McDermott, 2007; Pashler, Rohrer, Cepeda, & Carpenter, 2007). Importantly, retrieval practice improves retention even in the absence of feedback or additional study

opportunities (e.g., Glover, 1989). In addition, the benefits of retrieval practice cannot be explained by reexposure to the material, because students remember more after retrieval practice than if they restudy the original material for an equivalent amount of time (Roediger & Karpicke, 2006b).

Retrieval practice (i.e., testing) represents a strategy for reprocessing material that yields significant memorial benefits in educational settings (e.g., Carpenter, Pashler, & Cepeda, 2009; McDaniel, Agarwal, Huelser, McDermott, & Roediger, in press; McDaniel, Anderson, Derbish, & Morrisette, 2007; Metcalfe, Kornell, & Son, 2007; for review, see Bangert-Drowns, Kulik, & Kulik, 1991). For example, Larsen, Butler, and Roediger (2009) investigated whether retrieval practice enhances long-term retention of medical information that was taught during a weekly didactic conference for residents on a neurology rotation. A group of pediatric and emergency medicine residents participated in an interactive teaching session that covered two topics: (1) status epilepticus and (2) myasthenia gravis (two types of neurological disorders). For one of the topics, the residents took a series of three short-answer tests on the material with each test spaced about 2 weeks apart. For the other topic, the residents studied a review sheet at the same intervals. After 6 months, a final test was given for both topics. Performance on the final test showed that repeated testing on the material led to much better retention relative to repeated studying—and the difference in performance between the two groups was almost one standard deviation (effect size = .91).

When testing is used as a learning tool in educational settings, there are several ways in which its efficacy can be enhanced. First, tests that require students to produce a response, such as short-answer and essay tests, generally lead to better retention than tests that simply require the selection of the correct response, such as multiple-choice tests and true/false tests (e.g., Butler & Roediger, 2007; Kang, McDermott, & Roediger, 2007). One explanation for this finding, consistent with the idea of desirable difficulties, is that retrieval practice requires greater effort and therefore produces better retention (e.g., Carpenter & DeLosh, 2006; Pyc & Rawson, 2009). Second, taking multiple tests results in better retention than taking a single test (Bahrick & Hall, 2005; Wheeler & Roediger, 1992), so it is beneficial to repeat questions on quizzes and give cumulative exams. Third, successful retrieval is the key to learning from tests, so providing feedback after the test is essential, especially if test-takers do not retrieve many correct responses (e.g., Kang et al., 2007).

To summarize, retrieval practice represents an effective method for promoting long-term retention. This strategy constitutes a desirable difficulty because testing requires the learner to effortfully retrieve information from memory (particularly when a response must be produced by the learner) and may initially slow learning relative to comparable tasks like repeated study. Retrieval practice also provides the learner with an opportunity to reprocess the material in a way that results in the extraction of additional meaning (i.e., above and beyond that gleaned from initial study). We now turn to describing when and how to give feedback.

### Processing Feedback to Correct Errors

Providing feedback after an attempt to retrieve information from memory is critical, because it helps to correct memory errors (e.g., Pashler, Cepeda, Wixted, & Rohrer, 2005) and maintain correct responses (e.g., Butler, Karpicke, & Roediger, 2008; Fazio, Huelser, Johnson, & Marsh, 2010). An extensive literature exists to support the efficacy of feedback in both controlled laboratory experiments and applied studies in educational settings (for reviews, see Bangert-Drowns, Kulik, Kulik, & Morgan, 1991; Butler & Winne, 1995; Hattie & Timperley, 2007; Kulhavy & Stock, 1989). Researchers have identified a variety of factors that determine the effectiveness of feedback, such as the nature of the to-be-learned material, the amount of prior learning before retrieval is attempted, and the retention interval between feedback and the subsequent use of that knowledge (e.g., retrieval on a final test). However, given the limited space we can devote to this topic, we will focus on two of the more important factors: the content of the feedback message and the timing of feedback.

Perhaps the most important aspect of feedback is the nature of the information provided. At the minimum, the feedback message needs to inform the learner whether one's response is correct or incorrect. However, there are many different ways of elaborating the feedback message beyond this basic form (for a taxonomy of feedback messages, see Kulhavy & Stock, 1989), and numerous studies have explored the efficacy of including additional information in the message. The most consistent result is that providing learners with the correct answer in the feedback message produces better subsequent performance than simply indicating whether an answer is correct or incorrect (e.g., Pashler et al., 2005; for a

meta-analysis, see Bangert-Drowns, Kulik, Kulik, & Morgan, 1991). This finding makes sense because informing the learner that a given response is incorrect will not help the learner to correct the error if the learner does not have any recourse to learn the correct answer.

There is little consensus as to whether feedback should contain additional information beyond the correct answer. Some studies have found that elaborating the basic feedback message has a positive effect on learning; for example, learning can be improved by providing students with the original study materials so that they can self-grade their tests (Andre & Thieman, 1988) or requiring them to generate the feedback by rearranging letters to form the correct answer (Lhyle & Kulhavy, 1987). However, many other elaborations have shown no effect or, occasionally, a negative effect on learning (see Kulhavy & Stock, 1989). One reason for these disparate findings may be the way in which learning is assessed on the final test. For example, studies on explanation feedback (i.e., providing an explanation of why the learner's response is correct or incorrect) often find no benefit relative to correct answer feedback (e.g., Kulhavy, White, Topp, Chan, & Adams, 1985; McDaniel & Fisher, 1991). However, these studies generally assess learning with verbatim repetitions of the same questions, so that the learner merely has to memorize the correct responses rather than understand the concepts. Explanation feedback may be more effective for promoting transfer to situations in which learners must apply their knowledge in a new context (Butler, Godbole, & Marsh, 2010).

Another key factor involves the timing of the feedback message. Studies have produced contradictory results on feedback timing. Some studies have found it is better to give feedback immediately, while others have found it is better to give it after a delay (for a meta-analysis, see Kulik & Kulik, 1988). The literature on this topic is complicated by differences in how "immediate" and "delayed" feedback are defined across studies, serious methodological flaws (e.g., confounding the timing of feedback with the type of feedback; Angell, 1949), and the deeply entrenched notion that feedback must be given immediately to be effective (e.g., Skinner, 1954). Although some reviewers have concluded that feedback should be given as soon as possible to be effective (e.g., Mory, 2004; Kulik & Kulik, 1988), the weight of evidence seems to suggest that delayed feedback produces superior retention. In fact, many studies have shown that even short delays produce better retention, such as waiting until the end of the test rather than giving feedback after each question (e.g., Butler & Roediger, 2008). Of course, the key assumption in comparing the effectiveness of immediate and delayed feedback is that feedback is processed in the same way regardless of its timing (see Butler, Karpicke, & Roediger, 2007). For example, if students are motivated to study all the feedback when it is given immediately, but only study some of it if it is given a week later, then immediate feedback may be more effective.

In summary, processing feedback helps to correct errors and maintain correct responses. Consistent with the notion of processing material to extract meaning, feedback messages that are elaborated beyond the basic form of verification (i.e., correct/incorrect) may promote deeper learning and therefore produce superior transfer to new tasks. All things being equal, delayed feedback seems to be more effective than immediate feedback. Delaying feedback represents a desirable difficulty because it generally takes more effort to reinstate the initial learning context when processing feedback after a delay. However, it is important to note that if full processing of the delayed feedback cannot be guaranteed, then giving immediate feedback is probably the better choice.

### Spacing Out Practice Over Time

Students often put off studying until the last possible moment (oftentimes the night before an exam). Procrastination is a behavior that is manifested at all levels of education (even teachers wait until the night before to compose a test). In the literature, this pattern of behavior has been termed the "procrastination scallop" (Michael, 1991). Study behavior remains relatively infrequent over time, but then it increases rapidly as an exam or some other reason to learn the material approaches. For instance, Mawhinney and colleagues (Mawhinney, Bostow, Laws, Blumenfeld, & Hopkins, 1971) conducted a classroom experiment in which they tested students either every day or every 3 weeks. When students were tested daily, they studied for 60 to 80 minutes every day. In contrast, students who were tested every 3 weeks studied about 20 minutes a day at first and then increased the amount of time that they studied until they reached 120 minutes a day right before the test (i.e., the classic procrastination scallop pattern).

Why is procrastination so common in educational settings? One likely factor is that cramming, which results from procrastination, is a very effective strategy in the short term. When students cram or "mass" practice, they probably do fairly well on an immediate test, leading to the illusion that they know the material. However, as we discussed in the section on "Introducing 'Desirable Difficulties' During Learning," performance on an immediate test is not a good predictor of long-term retention. As any student will readily attest, most of the information that is learned from cramming is quickly forgotten. Thus, cramming may be useful under some circumstances, but it is not an effective way of producing knowledge that will be retained over long periods of time.

Many studies have shown that spacing or distributing practice over time produces better long-term retention of material than massing practice (i.e., cramming), a finding called *the spacing effect* (e.g., Glenberg, 1976; Melton, 1970). Ebbinghaus (1885/1967) described the spacing effect in his pioneering investigation of human memory, making this finding one of the oldest in the literature. After over a century of investigation, the spacing effect has been shown to be extremely robust and easy to replicate (for a review, see Cepeda, Pashler, Vul, Wixted, & Rohrer, 2006; Dempster, 1989). Based on the ubiquity of the spacing effect, the Institute of Education Sciences recommended spacing as a strategy to promote retention in a practice guide entitled *Organizing Instruction and Study to Improve Student Learning* (Pashler, Bain, et al., 2007; see recommended readings).

Although many studies of the spacing effect have used lists of words and other simple information, the finding has also been demonstrated with more complex sets of material. For example, Kornell and Bjork (2008; Experiments 1a and 1b) investigated whether spacing would lead to better inductive learning of the styles of different painters in a pair of experiments. They had subjects study six paintings by 10 different artists in either a massed fashion (all the paintings from a given artist were presented consecutively) or spaced out in time (the paintings from each artist were interleaved with paintings from other artists). [1] Spacing was manipulated within subjects in Experiment 1a and between subjects in Experiment 1b. After each presentation block, subjects took a test in which they saw new paintings by the same artists, and they had to indicate which artists had painted them. Figure 20.3 shows the results of the test that was given after the first block (i.e., before subjects received any feedback). As the results clearly show, subjects in both experiments were better able to correctly identify the artist

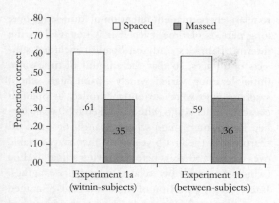

**Figure 20.3** Proportion of artists selected correctly on the multiple-choice test given after the first block of trials as a function of learning condition (spacing vs. massing) for Experiments 1a (left side) and 1b (right side). (Data from Kornell & Bjork, 2008, Experiments 1a and 1b.)

when they had studied the paintings under spaced conditions rather than massed conditions.

Is there an optimal interval for spacing practice? Studies have shown benefits of distributing practice over intervals that range from a few seconds (see Underwood, 1961) to many years (e.g. Bahrick, Bahrick, Bahrick, & Bahrick, 1993), so there is not just one optimal interval. Rather, it seems that the optimal interval depends on how long the knowledge needs to be retained after the last practice (i.e., the retention interval). Cepeda and colleagues (2006; see also Cepeda, Vul, Rohrer, Wixted, & Pashler, 2008) performed a meta-analysis that included 317 experiments from 184 articles on the spacing effect. They found that the optimal spacing interval is approximately 10%–20% of the retention interval. Thus, if the goal is to retain the material for 5 days, then practice should be spaced over intervals between 12 and 24 hours. However, if the desired retention interval is 10 years, then the optimal interval between practices is about 1 to 2 years.

Overall, spacing out practice over time is a powerful method for promoting long-term retention. Reprocessing material after a delay may lead to the extraction of different information (and different meaning, increasing deep processing), which can facilitate transfer in certain situations (e.g., Kornell & Bjork, 2008). Spacing constitutes a desirable difficulty in that it may initially slow learning as people have a harder time remembering previously learned material after a delay (and probably forget some of it); however, these initial difficulties will pay dividends over the long run because spacing will produce better retention relative to massing practice. In

terms of identifying the spacing schedule that will optimize retention, the ratio described earlier may sound complicated; however, it can be simplified by stating that spacing over greater intervals generally leads to retention over longer periods of time.

## Combining Techniques

Successful students are unlikely to limit themselves to a single technique, so future research should assess how to combine the kinds of techniques reviewed here. We alluded earlier to one combination known to benefit memory: reviewing notes (a poststudy strategy) taken during a lecture (a study strategy). A second example involves the 3R technique, a self-controlled method of learning that McDaniel, Howard, and Einstein (2009) created by shortening an older technique (Robinson, 1941). The 3R technique involves reading the text, reciting aloud all the information that can be remembered without looking at the text, and then rereading the text (i.e., read-recite-review—hence the 3R name). The 3R technique incorporates two of the poststudy learning strategies discussed earlier: retrieval practice (the recite part of the technique) and processing feedback (obtained when the text is reviewed).

In one experiment, McDaniel et al. (2009, Experiment 2) compared the 3R technique with two other common techniques: rereading and note taking (the latter of which we reviewed earlier as an effective strategy). Subjects read engineering texts while using one of the three techniques (3R, rereading, or note taking). Learning was assessed via a series of tests given either immediately or after a 1-week delay. A free-recall test measured memory for the entire text, a multiple-choice test measured retention of facts from the text, and a short answer test required inferences to be made based on information from the text. Subjects who used the 3R technique recalled more of the texts than subjects who either reread the texts or took notes, and this result held both immediately and a week later. Using the 3R technique also increased performance on both fact-based, multiple-choice questions and inference-based, short-answer questions, relative to rereading. The 3R technique and note taking led to similar performance on the multiple-choice and short-answer tests, but the 3R technique required less time during the initial study phase (meaning it was a more efficient way to learn the material).

The 3R technique is probably effective because it requires significant effort on the part of the learner—recalling a text is much harder to do than simply rereading it, and actively reviewing a text to obtain feedback is more difficult than passively receiving feedback. Furthermore, additional meaning is extracted when the student practices retrieval and then reviews each text for feedback. That is, when students reread the text *after* having attempted retrieval, the processing will change, leading to the encoding of new information as well as reencoding learned information in new ways.

In short, strategies that combine techniques have the potential to be even more effective than a single approach. However, more is not always better; a complex strategy that combines ineffective techniques may not be helpful and may even hurt the learner. The guiding principles can be used to evaluate the components of more complex strategies to yield predictions about whether techniques will help the learner.

## Applying the Guiding Principles and Learning Strategies in Educational Settings

Now that we have described several guiding principles and learning strategies, it is important to think about their application in the classroom. We note that most of the strategies reviewed here have been studied in some form in the classroom (e.g., Crawford, 1925a; Larsen et al., 2009). However, when thinking about the transition between the laboratory and the classroom, two obstacles must be considered: Experimenters often use short delays and simple materials, whereas educators are interested in long-term learning and mastery of more complex materials. In this section, we will highlight the advances that have been made toward solving each of these problems.

### *Long-Term Learning*

First, consider the issue of long-term learning. Cognitive psychologists often think they are using long delays when they examine memory over days or even weeks (in fact, delays as short as 20 minutes are often labeled "long-term memory"). Even in the majority of studies cited in this chapter, many of which explicitly claim to have educational applications, learning is often assessed after a few days. However, the goal of education is learning that will be retained for years. This is difficult to study in the laboratory, for obvious reasons. However, Harry Bahrick brilliantly tackled this challenge using naturalistic studies; for example, he examined people's memory for Spanish vocabulary and grammar learned during high school (Bahrick, 1984). As will be described, these studies have yielded a unique finding: the concept of a *permastore*, which refers

to relatively permanent retention of knowledge over long periods of time, even if it is not used in the interim. Bahrick's study on Spanish included subjects of all ages, so that the amount of time since initial learning varied widely—from high school students who were currently enrolled in Spanish classes to older adults who had taken it 50 years earlier. Retention of high school Spanish dropped off sharply over the first 5 years, but then stayed stable over the next 30 years before showing a final decline (which was probably related to cognitive aging). Interestingly, a portion of the knowledge remained accessible up to 50 years later, even though it had not been used since high school, leading Bahrick to propose the concept of the permastore.

Of interest is how the types of learning strategies reviewed in this chapter may contribute to the type of long-term learning studied by Bahrick and emphasized by educators. Many studies have shown that knowledge acquired in the classroom is retained over long periods of time (e.g., Conway, Cohen, & Stanhope, 1991; Landauer & Ainsle, 1975; Semb, Ellis, & Araujo, 1993; for review, see Semb & Ellis, 1994), and our focus is on the techniques that promote this long-term retention. While noting that many of these studies are naturalistic in their design (i.e., no independent variables, no random assignment to groups, many uncontrolled variables, etc.), and thus the conclusions drawn from them must be interpreted with some caution, it is important that many of these studies yield results that converge with the results of careful laboratory studies. For example, Bahrick and colleagues provided evidence that spaced poststudy sessions promote long-term memory for foreign language vocabulary (Bahrick et al., 1993). Similarly, taking a test on material helps students to remember the information a year later (e.g., Landauer & Ainslie, 1975; see also Semb & Ellis, 1994).

Intriguingly, some of the strategies reviewed here may also be useful for recovering knowledge, long after it has been forgotten. That is, just because students learned something at one point in time does not mean they will be able to retrieve it in the future. Bahrick referred to this type of knowledge as *marginal knowledge*: information that was stored but cannot currently be retrieved (this distinction is very similar to Tulving's distinction between *availability* and *accessibility* of information in memory; see Tulving & Pearlstone, 1966). In one study, the power of feedback to reactivate marginal knowledge was examined, using general-knowledge materials (Berger, Hall, & Bahrick, 1999). Subjects received

5 seconds of answer feedback after they failed to correctly answer each of a series of short-answer questions (e.g., they saw "Einstein" if they failed to correctly answer the question, "What is the last name of the person who proposed the theory of relativity?"). Critically, half of the items referenced real facts (like the Einstein fact just shown) and half were yoked controls that referenced fictional entities (e.g., "What is the last name of the person who proposed the theory of maladaptivity?" Answer: Alfred). The fictional items were important as a control for new learning; the feedback could only activate pre-existing marginal knowledge for real items and not for fictional items. After various retention intervals of up to 9 days, subjects were asked the critical questions again. Feedback boosted performance on the real items, even after 9 days, whereas performance on the fictional items quickly dropped to zero after a delay, since there was no marginal knowledge to activate for these items.

In short, strategies like retrieval practice, spacing, and feedback have the potential to enhance learning over the long run, as desired by educators. One of the major challenges for future research is to further connect the learning strategies reviewed in this chapter to the types of retention intervals important in education.

### Learning Beyond Facts

Experimentalists have a tendency to simplify the materials used, in order to control for as many potentially confounding factors as possible. This is not possible in actual classrooms, nor is it desirable. Rather, in the classroom, educators have many different goals for their students, and these goals vary as a function of the level of education, the type of course, and the time frame given for learning, among many other factors. One way of categorizing these goals is through Bloom's (1956) taxonomy of educational objectives, which conceptualizes learning as a hierarchy in which the various levels must be mastered in sequential order. The cognitive domain is comprised of six levels (from lowest to highest): knowledge (e.g., learning facts, concepts, etc.), comprehension (e.g., understanding the relationship between ideas), application (e.g., using knowledge to solve new problems), analysis (e.g., finding evidence to support a hypothesis), synthesis (e.g., combining different accounts of an event to understand what occurred), and evaluation (e.g., assessing the validity of an idea according to certain criteria). Although Bloom's taxonomy has been criticized over the years (e.g., Moore, 1982), it has proven to be a valuable tool for both researchers and educators. In fact, its massive influence on the fields of education and educational psychology recently led to a major effort to update the taxonomy so that it could continue to be used (Anderson et al., 2001).

Cognitive psychologists often claim to be using educationally relevant materials when they are using general-knowledge facts (e.g., Lima is the capital of Peru) or simple texts. However, such learning is classified as Level 1 in Bloom's taxonomy, reflecting the learning of simple facts and concepts. To the extent that research on learning strategies will be translated to the classroom, it must move beyond the learning of facts and concepts to higher levels of knowledge (e.g., evaluation). Throughout this chapter we have highlighted instances where learning strategies afford transfer; for example, as described earlier, receiving advance organizers promoted interpretation of new programming statements, note taking improved performance on conceptual questions about the chi-square statistic, and reading explanation feedback enhanced transfer of knowledge about complex concepts such as diffusion.

Recent work suggests that retrieval practice may also facilitate transfer. In one study, Butler (2010, Experiment 2) had subjects study a set of prose passages, each of which contained several critical concepts (e.g., how bats use echolocation to navigate and find prey in the dark). A concept was defined as information that had to be extracted from multiple sentences. After reading each passage, the subjects either repeatedly restudied the entire passage, repeatedly restudied isolated sentences from the passage that contained the critical concepts, or repeatedly answered test questions about the critical concepts and received feedback on their answers (e.g., Some bats use echolocation to navigate the environment and locate prey. How does echolocation help bats to determine the distance and size of objects?). The feedback provided after each test question was essentially the same information as that presented in the condition in which subjects restudied the isolated sentences from the passage.

After a 1-week delay, students took a transfer test that consisted of questions that required the application of the critical concepts from the passages (e.g., "An insect is moving toward a bat. Using the process of echolocation, how does the bat determine that the insect is moving toward it [i.e., rather than away from it]?"). When subjects were repeatedly tested on the concepts, they performed significantly better on the transfer test relative to when they repeatedly studied the passages or repeatedly studied the isolated sentences. The comparison between repeated testing and repeated study of the isolated sentences is particularly important, because these two conditions were well matched in terms of exposure to the material and total time spent learning. In fact, the only real difference between these conditions was that the subjects attempted to retrieve the critical concepts in one condition and not in the other.

The finding that testing promoted transfer of knowledge is an important one (see also Johnson & Mayer, 2009; Rohrer, Taylor, & Sholar, 2010). However, encouraging as these results are, the tasks involved were still quite simple ones, and they did not require the use of knowledge as proposed in the highest levels in Bloom's taxonomy. Future research should continue to investigate transfer and should tackle goals such as evaluation and synthesis.

## The Relativity of Memory

A recurring theme in the last section involved concerns that basic research may not generalize to actual educational situations; we discussed whether the learning strategies reviewed in this chapter are likely to boost memory over long delays, with more complex materials, and for more sophisticated learning goals involving transfer of knowledge. In effect, such questions emphasize the importance of considering memory in particular contexts (e.g., McKeachie, 1974; see Roediger, 2008). This emphasis on the relativity of memory differs from the emphasis of the first half-century of cognitive research, when memory researchers focused on discovering general laws that governed how we remember and forget (e.g., Jost, 1897; Ribot, 1881; Thorndike, 1911). The switch to emphasizing the relativity of memory means that when questions like "Does X lead to better memory?" are posed, the answer is almost always "Well, it depends. . . ."

To better understand why memory effects tend to be relative, it is helpful to consider the classes of variables that can influence memory performance in any given circumstance. Figure 20.4 presents a tetrahedral model of memory that was created by James Jenkins (1979). In the model, each vertex of the tetrahedron represents a class of variables: the learning or encoding tasks, the to-be-learned materials, the characteristics of the learner, and the criterial tasks that assess memory (see Roediger, 2008 for a possible fifth vertex). Cognitive psychologists often carefully control for these different factors by specifying how the learner should process to-be-remembered information (e.g., by judging its

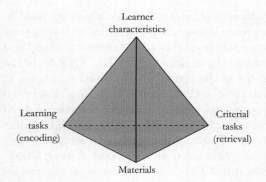

**Figure 20.4** The tetrahedral model of memory experiments. (Adapted from Jenkins, 1979.)

pleasantness) and using words for materials, college students for learners, and standard tests such as recall to measure retrieval. In contrast, educators are often at the other extreme, arguing for interventions aimed at specific populations in specific contexts, as opposed to a "one-size-fits-all" approach. The best approach likely falls in the middle, with the goal being as general of advice as possible, while considering how the advice to an educator might change depending on factors such as learner characteristics or test type.

We have already discussed how the interaction of encoding and retrieval tasks can have a profound effect on memory performance. In passing we also mentioned some of the different types of materials that researchers have used, as well as some individual differences. However, we did not have the opportunity to review research on how certain types of materials naturally afford specific types of processing (e.g., the narrative structure of fairytales invites relational processing). Research has shown that learning is better when the processing induced by the materials is complementary to the processing that is induced by the learning task (see McDaniel & Einstein, 1989, 2005). For example, performing a relational processing task (e.g., sorting mixed-up sentences into the correct order) on a fairytale would not be an effective way of learning because the processing induced by the task is redundant with the processing induced by the materials. In contrast, performing such a relational processing task on an expository text (which does not naturally induce relational processing) would be effective, because it would be complementary to the processing naturally afforded by the text.

Likewise, characteristics of the learner will impact whether the processing induced by a particular task enhances memory. If the learner has difficulty with a particular type of processing or tends to naturally engage in a certain type of processing, then giving that learner a task that induces that same type of processing will be detrimental and redundant, respectively. For example, readers who score poorly on the Nelson-Denny Reading Test (Brown, Nelson, & Denny, 1973) do not benefit from processing a text using a letter-insertion task like the one described earlier (e.g., McDaniel, Hines, & Guynn, 2002). The Nelson-Denny Reading Test is a measure of reading ability that reflects, among other things, people's proficiency at decoding words. If people have trouble decoding words, then performing a task that requires generating words from fragments will not be helpful because it places additional stress on word decoding.

The relativity of memory means that desirable difficulties must be considered within the context of the other three vertices of Jenkins's model (for discussion, see McDaniel & Butler, 2010). The desirability of any difficulty will be determined by three factors. First, the particular type of processing in the learning task must match the type of processing in the retrieval task (e.g., deWinstanley, Bjork, & Bjork, 1996). Second, the type of processing invited by the materials must be complementary to that induced by the learning task (e.g., McDaniel & Einstein, 1989). Third, and finally, the abilities of the learner must allow the difficulty induced by the learning task to be overcome (e.g., McDaniel et al., 2002).

## Conclusions and Future Directions

In this chapter, we described three cognitive theories that can guide educational practice: desirable difficulties (and how it can be a good thing to make learning harder), meaning extraction (and how it is important that learning tasks encourage the student to process the material at "deeper" levels), and transfer-appropriate processing (and how the strategy should make the learner attend to whatever it is he or she will need to succeed on the final criterial task). We used these three theories to evaluate the effectiveness of strategies that guide the initial learning of material (advance organizers, underlining/highlighting, and note taking) as well as strategies that guide poststudy processing (retrieval practice, feedback, and spacing). We could have sampled additional strategies, such as the use of adjunct questions during reading (a strategy involving retrieval practice), summarization exercises (which can be completed during learning or poststudy,

encouraging meaning extraction), and the use of imagery (which is often involved in mnemonics created during study), to name just a few. The application of the theories is not limited to the examples we chose, and future research will continue to connect the theories to additional encoding and poststudy strategies.

When applying cognitive psychology to education, it is critical to think about long-term retention and transfer of knowledge (two important directions for future research). The results of experiments are more likely to generalize to the classroom if researchers keep Jenkins's tetrahedral model in mind, by thinking about how results might change for different students, materials, strategies, and criterial tasks. Earlier in this chapter we alluded to the practice guide published by the Institute of Education Sciences (Pashler, Bain, et al., 2007; see suggested readings); this guide made recommendations for the classroom based on basic cognitive science research. One key criterion for inclusion in the guide was that a principle had to have been shown in both the classroom and the laboratory. Successful translation of cognitive research will likely require explicit classroom demonstrations, as educators are unlikely to be convinced by assumptions of generality. Moving into the classroom may also benefit cognitive psychologists because effects that persist in the classroom are likely to be robust (see Rubin, 1989) and careful observation of the classroom may reveal interesting new phenomena to study. By increasing the collaboration and communication between cognitive psychologists and educators, we will enhance our understanding of how to optimize learning to promote long-term retention and transfer of knowledge.

## Acknowledgments

The writing of this chapter was supported by a collaborative activity award from the James S. McDonnell Foundation. The opinions expressed are those of the authors and do not represent the views of the James S. McDonnell Foundation. We thank Anna Goswick for her assistance with research and editing.

## Note

1. The careful reader may have noticed that the example just described involves spacing during *initial learning*, as opposed to spacing of *poststudy* activities. To be clear, spacing is important for both behaviors, and we could have included it in either section of the chapter.

# References

Abbott, E. E. (1909). On the analysis of the factors of recall in the learning process. *Psychological Monographs, 11*, 159–177.

Anderson, L. W., Krathwohl, D. R., Airasian, P. W., Cruikshank, K. A., Mayer, R. E., Pintrich, P. R., ... Wittrock, M. C. (Eds.). (2001). *A taxonomy for learning, teaching, and assessing: A revision of Bloom's taxonomy of educational objectives.* New York: Longman.

Andre, T., & Thieman, A. (1988). Level of adjunct question, type of feedback, and learning concepts by reading. *Contemporary Educational Psychology, 13*, 296–307.

Angell, G. W. (1949). The effect of immediate knowledge of quiz results on final examination scores in freshman chemistry. *Journal of Educational Research, 42*, 391–394.

Austin, J. L., Lee, M. G., Thibeault, M. D., Carr, J. E., & Bailey, J. S. (2002). Effects of guided notes on university students' responding and recall of information. *Journal of Behavioral Education, 11*, 243–254.

Ausubel, D. P. (1960). The use of advance organizers in the learning and retention of meaningful verbal material. *Journal of Educational Psychology, 51*, 267–272.

Ausubel, D. P., & Fitzgerald, D. (1961). The role of discriminability in meaningful verbal learning and retention. *Journal of Educational Psychology, 52*, 266–274.

Bahrick, H. P. (1984). Semantic memory content in permastore: 50 years of memory for Spanish learned in school. *Journal of Experimental Psychology: General, 113*, 1–29.

Bahrick, H. P., Bahrick, L. E., Bahrick, A. S., & Bahrick, P. E. (1993). Maintenance of foreign language vocabulary and the spacing effect. *Psychological Science, 4*, 316–321.

Bahrick, H. P., & Hall, L. K. (2005). The importance of retrieval failures to long-term retention: A metacognitive explanation of the spacing effect. *Journal of Memory and Language, 52*, 566–577.

Bangert-Drowns, R. L., Kulik, J. A., & Kulik, C. C. (1991). Effects of frequent classroom testing. *Journal of Educational Research, 85*, 89–99.

Bangert-Drowns, R. L., Kulik, C. C., Kulik, J. A., & Morgan, M. (1991). The instructional effect of feedback in test-like events. *Review of Educational Research, 61*, 213–238.

Berger, S. A., Hall, L. K., & Bahrick, H. P. (1999). Stabilizing access to marginal and submarginal knowledge. *Journal of Experimental Psychology: Applied, 5*, 438–447.

Bjork, R. A. (1975). Retrieval as a memory modifier. In R. Solso (Ed.), *Information processing and cognition: The Loyola Symposium* (pp. 123–144). Hillsdale, NJ: Erlbaum.

Bjork, R. A. (1994a). Memory and metamemory considerations in the training of human beings. In J. Metcalfe & A. Shimamura (Eds.), *Metacognition: Knowing about knowing* (pp. 185–205). Cambridge, MA: MIT Press.

Bjork, R. A. (1994b). Institutional impediments to effective training. In D. Druckman & R. A. Bjork (Eds.), *Learning, remembering, believing: Enhancing human performance* (pp. 295–306). Washington, DC: National Academy Press.

Bjork, R. A., & Bjork, E. L. (1992). A new theory of disuse and an old theory of stimulus fluctuation. In A. Healy, S. Kosslyn, & R. Shiffrin (Eds.), *From learning processes to cognitive processes: Essays in honor of William K. Estes* (Vol. 2, pp. 35–67). Hillsdale, NJ: Erlbaum.

Black, P., & Wiliam, D. (1998). Assessment and classroom learning. *Assessment in Education: Principles, Policy, and Practice, 5*, 7–74.

Bloom, B. S. (1956). *Taxonomy of educational objectives: The classification of educational goals.* Essex, England: Harlow.

Bretzing, B. H., & Kulhavy, R. W. (1979). Notetaking and depth of processing. *Contemporary Educational Psychology, 4*, 145–153.

Bretzing, B. H., & Kulhavy, R. W. (1981). Note-taking and passage style. *Journal of Educational Psychology, 73*, 242–250.

Bromage, B. K., & Mayer, R. E. (1986). Quantitative and qualitative effects of repetition from learning from technical text. *Journal of Educational Psychology, 78*, 271–278.

Brown, J. I., Nelson, M. J. B., & Denny, E. C. (1973). *The Nelson-Denny reading test.* Boston, MA: Houghton Mifflin.

Butler, A. C. (2010). Repeated testing produces superior transfer of learning relative to repeated studying. *Journal of Experimental Psychology: Learning, Memory, and Cognition, 36, 1118–1133.*

Butler, A. C., Godbole, N., & Marsh, E. J. (in press). Explanation feedback is better than correct answer feedback for promoting transfer of learning. *Journal of Educational Psychology.*

Butler, A. C., Karpicke, J. D., & Roediger, H. L., III. (2007). The effect of type and timing of feedback on learning from multiple-choice tests. *Journal of Experimental Psychology: Applied, 13*, 273–281.

Butler, A. C., Karpicke, J. D., & Roediger, H. L., III. (2008). Correcting a meta-cognitive error: Feedback enhances retention of low confidence correct responses. *Journal of Experimental Psychology: Learning, Memory, and Cognition, 34*, 918–928.

Butler, A. C., & Roediger, H. L., III. (2007). Testing improves long-term retention in a simulated classroom setting. *European Journal of Cognitive Psychology, 19*, 514–527.

Butler, A. C., & Roediger, H. L., III. (2008). Feedback enhances the positive effects and reduces the negative effects of multiple-choice testing. *Memory and Cognition, 36*, 604–616.

Butler, D. L., & Winne, P. H. (1995). Feedback and self-regulated learning: A theoretical synthesis. *Review of Educational Research, 65*, 245–281.

Callender, A. A., & McDaniel, M. A. (2009). The limited benefits of rereading educational texts. *Contemporary Educational Psychology, 34*, 30–41.

Carpenter, S. K., & DeLosh, E. L. (2006). Impoverished cue support enhances subsequent retention: Support for the elaborative retrieval explanation of the testing effect. *Memory and Cognition, 34*, 268–276.

Carpenter, S. K., Pashler, H., & Cepeda, N. J. (2009). Using tests to enhance 8th grade students' retention of U. S. history facts. *Applied Cognitive Psychology, 23*, 760–771.

Carrier, M., & Pashler, H. (1992). The influence of retrieval on retention. *Memory and Cognition, 20*, 632–642.

Cashen, V. M., & Leicht, K. L. (1970). Role of the isolation effect in a formal educational setting. *Journal of Educational Psychology, 61*, 484–486.

Cepeda, N. J., Pashler, H., Vul, E., Wixted, J. T., & Rohrer, D. (2006). Distributed practice in verbal recall tasks: A review and quantitative synthesis. *Psychological Bulletin, 132*, 354–380.

Cepeda, N. J., Vul, E., Rohrer, D., Wixted, J. T., & Pashler, H. (2008). Spacing effect in learning: A temporal ridgeline of optimal retention. *Psychological Science, 19*, 1095–1102.

Christina, R. W., & Bjork, R. A. (1991). Optimizing long-term retention and transfer. In D. Druckman & R. A. Bjork

(Eds.), *In the mind's eye: Enhancing human performance* (pp. 23–56). Washington, DC: National Academy Press.

Conway, M. A., Cohen, G., & Stanhope, N. (1991). On the very long-term retention of knowledge acquired through formal education: Twelve years of cognitive psychology. *Journal of Experimental Psychology: General, 120*, 395–409.

Corkill, A. J. (1992). Advance organizers: Facilitators of recall. *Educational Psychology Review, 4*, 33–67.

Corkill, A. J., Glover, J. A., Bruning, R. H., & Krug, D. (1988). Advance organizers: Retrieval context hypothesis. *Journal of Educational Psychology, 80*, 304–311.

Craik, F. I. M., Govoni, R., Naveh-Benjamin, M., & Anderson, N. D. (1996). The effects of divided attention on encoding and retrieval processes in human memory. *Journal of Experimental Psychology: General, 125*, 159–180.

Craik, F. I., & Lockhart, R. S. (1972). Levels of processing: A framework for memory research. *Journal of Verbal Learning and Verbal Behavior, 11*, 671–684.

Craik, F. I. M., & Tulving, E. (1975). Depth of processing and the retention of words in episodic memory. *Journal of Experimental Psychology: General, 104*, 268–294.

Crawford, C. C. (1925a). The correlation between college lecture notes and quiz papers. *Journal of Educational Research, 12*, 282–291.

Crawford, C. C. (1925b). Some experimental studies of the results of college note-taking. *Journal of Educational Research, 12*, 379–386.

Dempster, F. N. (1989). Spacing effects and their implications for theory and practice. *Educational Psychology Review, 1*, 309–330.

deWinstanley, P. A., Bjork, E. L., & Bjork, R. A. (1996). Generation effects and the lack thereof: The role of transfer-appropriate processing. *Memory, 4*, 31–48.

Dinnel, D., & Glover, J. A. (1985). Advance organizers: Encoding manipulations. *Journal of Educational Psychology, 77*, 514–521.

Di Vesta, F. J., & Gray, G. S. (1972). Listening and note taking. *Journal of Educational Psychology, 63*, 8–14.

Ebbinghaus, H. (1967). *Memory: A contribution to experimental psychology* (H. A. Ruger & C. E. Bussenius, Trans.). New York: Dover. (Original work published 1885).

Einstein, G. O., Morris, J., & Smith, S. (1985). Note-taking, individual differences, and memory for lecture information. *Journal of Educational Psychology, 77*, 522–532.

Fazio, L. K., Huelser, B. J., Johnson, A., & Marsh, E. J. (2010). Receiving right/wrong feedback: Consequences for learning. *Memory, 18*, 335–350.

Fisher, R. P., & Craik, F. I. M. (1977). Interaction between encoding and retrieval operations in cued recall. *Journal of Experimental Psychology: Human Learning and Memory, 3*, 701–711.

Fowler, R. L., & Barker, A. S. (1974). Effectiveness of highlighting for retention of text material. *Journal of Applied Psychology, 59*, 358–364.

Gates, A. I. (1917). Recitation as a factor in memorizing. *Archives of Psychology, 6*(40), 1–104.

Glenberg, A. M. (1976). Monotonic and nonmonotonic lag effects in paired-associate and recognition memory paradigms. *Journal of Verbal Learning and Verbal Behavior, 15*, 1–16.

Glover, J. A. (1989). The "testing" phenomenon: Not gone but nearly forgotten. *Journal of Educational Psychology, 81*, 392–399.

Glover, J. A., Bullock, R. G., & Dietzer, M. L. (1990). Advance organizers: Delay hypotheses. *Journal of Educational Psychology, 82*, 291–297.

Hattie, J., & Timperley, H. (2007). The power of feedback. *Review of Educational Research, 77*, 81–112.

Hunt, R. R., & Einstein, G. O. (1981). Relational and item-specific information in memory. *Journal of Verbal Learning and Verbal Behavior, 20*, 497–514.

Idstein, P., & Jenkins, J. R. (1972). Underlining versus repetitive reading. *Journal of Educational Research, 65*, 321–323.

Jenkins, J. J. (1979). Four points to remember: A tetrahedral model of memory experiments. In L. S. Cermak & F. I. M. Craik (Eds.), *Levels of processing in human memory* (pp. 429–446). Hillsdale, NJ: Erlbaum.

Johnson, C. I., & Mayer, R. E. (2009). A testing effect with multimedia learning. *Journal of Educational Psychology, 101*, 621–629.

Jones, H. E. (1923–1924). The effects of examination on the performance of learning. *Archives of Psychology, 10*, 1–70.

Jost, A. (1897). Die Assoziationsfestigkeit in ihrer Abhängigkeit von der Verteilung der Wiederholungen [The strength of associations in their dependence on the distribution of repetitions]. *Zeitschrift fur Psychologie und Physiologie der Sinnesorgane, 16*, 436–472.

Kang, S. H. K., McDermott, K. B. & Roediger, H. L., III. (2007). Test format and corrective feedback modulate the effect of testing on memory retention. *European Journal of Cognitive Psychology, 19*, 528–558.

Karpicke, J. D., Butler, A. C., & Roediger, H. L., III. (2009). Metacognitive strategies in student learning: Do students practice retrieval when they study on their own? *Memory, 17*, 471–479.

Karpicke, J. D., & Roediger, H. L., III. (2008). The critical importance of retrieval for learning. *Science, 15*, 966–968.

Kiewra, K. A. (1983). The process of review: A levels of processing approach. *Contemporary Educational Psychology, 8*, 366–374.

King, A. (1992). Comparison of self-questioning, summarizing, and notetaking-review as strategies for learning from lectures. *American Educational Research Journal, 29*, 303–323.

Kornell, N., & Bjork, R. A. (2007). The promise and perils of self-regulated study. *Psychonomic Bulletin and Review, 14*, 219–224.

Kornell, N., & Bjork, R. A. (2008). Learning concepts and categories: Is spacing the "enemy of induction"? *Psychological Science, 19*, 585–592

Kulhavy, R. W., & Stock, W. A. (1989). Feedback in written instruction: The place of response certitude. *Educational Psychology Review, 1*, 279–308.

Kulhavy, R. W., White, M. T., Topp, B. W., Chan, A. L., & Adams, J. (1985). Feedback complexity and corrective efficiency. *Contemporary Educational Pscyhology, 10*, 285–291.

Kulik, J. A., & Kulik, C. C. (1988). Timing of feedback and verbal learning. *Review of Educational Research, 58*, 79–97.

Landauer, T. K., & Ainslie, K. I. (1975). Exams and use as preservatives of course-acquired knowledge. *Journal of Educational Research, 69*, 99–104.

Larsen, D. P., Butler, A. C., & Roediger, H. L., III. (2009). Repeated testing improves long-term retention relative to repeated study: A randomized, controlled trial. *Medical Education, 43*, 1174–1181.

Lhyle, K. G., & Kulhavy, R. W. (1987). Feedback processing and error correction. *Journal of Educational Psychology, 79,* 320–322.

Lorch, R. F., Lorch, E. P., & Klusewitz, M. A. (1995). Effects of typographical cues on reading and recall of text. *Contemporary Educational Psychology, 20,* 51–64.

Marsh, E. J., Roediger, H. L., III, Bjork, R. A., & Bjork, E. L. (2007). The memorial consequences of multiple-choice testing. *Psychonomic Bulletin and Review, 14,* 194–199.

Marsh, E. J., & Sink, H. E. (2010). Access to handouts of presentation slides during lecture: Consequences for learning. *Applied Cognitive Psychology, 24,* 691–706.

Mawhinney, V. T., Bostow, D. E., Laws, D. R., Blumenfeld, G. J., & Hopkins, B. L. (1971). A comparison of students studying-behavior produced by daily, weekly, and three-week testing schedules. *Journal of Applied Behavior Analysis, 4,* 257–264.

Mayer, R. E. (1975). Different problem-solving competencies established in learning computer programming with and without meaningful models. *Journal of Educational Psychology, 67,* 725–734.

Mayer, R. E. (1976). Some conditions of meaningful learning for computer programming: Advance organizers and subject control of frame order. *Journal of Educational Psychology, 68,* 143–150.

Mayer, R. E. (March 27–3l, 1978). *Can advance organizers counter the effects of text organization?* Paper presented at the Annual meeting of the American Educational Research Association, Toronto, Canada.

Mayer, R. E. (1979). Twenty years of research on advance organizers: Assimilation theory is still the best predictor of results. *Instructional Science, 8,* 133–167.

Mayer, R. E. (1983). Can you repeat that: Qualitative effects of repetition and advance organizers on learning from science prose. *Journal of Educational Psychology, 75,* 40–49.

Mayer, R. E., & Bromage, B. K. (1980). Different recall protocols for technical texts due to advance organizers. *Journal of Educational Psychology, 72,* 209–225.

McDaniel, M. A., Agarwal, P. K., Huelser, B. J., McDermott, K. B., & Roediger, H. L., III. (2011). Test-enhanced learning in a middle school science classroom: The effects of quiz frequency and placement. *Journal of Educational Psychology, 103,* 399–414.

McDaniel, M. A., Anderson, J. L., Derbish, M. H., & Morrisette, N. (2007). Testing the testing effect in the classroom. *European Journal of Cognitive Psychology, 19,* 494–513.

McDaniel, M. A., & Butler, A. C. (2010). A contextual framework for understanding when difficulties are desirable. In A. S. Benjamin (Ed.), *Successful remembering and successful forgetting: Essays in honor of Robert A. Bjork* (pp. 175–199). New York: Psychology Press.

McDaniel, M. A., & Einstein, G. O. (1989). Material appropriate processing: A contextualist approach to reading and studying strategies. *Educational Psychology Review, 1,* 113–145.

McDaniel, M. A., & Einstein, G. O. (2005). Material appropriate difficulty: A framework for determining when difficulty is desirable for improving learning. In A. F. Healy (Ed.), *Experimental cognitive psychology and its applications* (pp. 73–85). Washington, DC: American Psychological Association.

McDaniel, M. A., & Fisher, R. P. (1991). Tests and test feedback as learning sources. *Contemporary Educational Psychology, 16,* 192–201.

McDaniel, M. A., Hines, R. J., & Guynn, M. J. (2002). When text difficulty benefits less-skilled readers. *Journal of Memory and Language, 46,* 544–561.

McDaniel, M. A., Hines, R. J., Waddill, P. J., & Einstein, G. O. (1994). What makes folk tales unique: Content familiarity, causal structure, scripts, or superstructures? *Journal of Experimental Psychology: Learning, Memory, and Cognition, 20,* 169–184.

McDaniel, M. A., Howard, D. C., & Einstein, G. O. (2009). The read-recite-review study strategy: Effective and portable. *Psychological Science, 20,* 516–522.

McDaniel, M. A., Roediger, H. L., III, & McDermott, K. B. (2007). Generalizing test-enhanced learning from the laboratory to the classroom. *Psychonomic Bulletin and Review, 14,* 200–206.

McKeachie, W. J. (1974). Instructional psychology. *Annual Review of Psychology, 25,* 161–193.

Melton, A. W. (1970). The situation with respect to the spacing of repetitions and memory. *Journal of Verbal Learning and Verbal Behavior, 9,* 596–606.

Metcalfe, J., Kornell, N., & Son, L. K. (2007). A cognitive-science based program to enhance study efficacy in a high and low-risk setting. *European Journal of Cognitive Psychology, 19,* 743–768.

Michael, J. (1991). A behavioral perspective on college teaching. *Behavior Analyst, 14,* 229–239.

Moore, D. S. (1982). Reconsidering Bloom's taxonomy of educational objectives, cognitive domain. *Educational Theory, 32,* 29–34.

Moore, J. C. (1968). Cueing for selective note-taking. *Journal of Experimental Education, 36,* 69–72.

Morris, C. D., Bransford, J. D., & Franks, J. J. (1977). Levels of processing versus transfer-appropriate processing. *Journal of Verbal Learning and Verbal Behavior, 16,* 519–533.

Mory, E. H. (2004). Feedback research review. In D. Jonassen (Ed.), *Handbook of research on educational communications and technology* (pp. 745–783). Mahwah, NJ: Erlbaum.

Moscovitch, M., & Craik, F. I. M. (1976). Depth of processing, retrieval cues, and uniqueness of encoding as factors in recall. *Journal of Verbal Learning and Verbal Behavior, 15,* 447–458.

Packman, J. L., & Battig, W. F. (1978). Effects of different kinds of semantic processing on memory for words. *Memory and Cognition, 6,* 502–508.

Palmatier, R. A., & Bennett, J. M. (1974). Notetaking habits of college students. *Journal of Reading, 18,* 215–218.

Pashler, H., Bain, P., Bottge, B., Graesser, A., Koedinger, K., McDaniel, M., & Metcalfe, J. (2007). *Organizing instruction and study to improve student learning: A practice guide (NCER 2007–2004).* Washington, DC: National Center for Education Research, Institute of Education Sciences, U.S. Department of Education.

Pashler, H., Cepeda, N. J., Wixted, J. T., & Rohrer, D. (2005). When does feedback facilitate learning of words? *Journal of Experimental Psychology: Learning, Memory, and Cognition, 31,* 3–8.

Pashler, H., Rohrer, D., Cepeda, N. J., & Carpenter, S. K. (2007). Enhancing learning and retarding forgetting: Choices and consequences. *Psychonomic Bulletin and Review, 14,* 187–193.

Peper, R. J., & Mayer, R. E. (1978). Note taking as a generative activity. *Journal of Educational Psychology, 70,* 514–522.

Peper, R. J., & Mayer, R. E. (1986). Generative effects of note-taking during science lectures. *Journal of Educational Psychology, 78*, 34–38.

Peters, D. L. (1972). Effects of note taking and rate of presentation on short-term objective test performance. *Journal of Educational Psychology, 63*, 276–280.

Pyc, M. A., & Rawson, K. A. (2009). Testing the retrieval effort hypothesis: Does greater difficulty correctly recalling information lead to higher levels of memory? *Journal of Memory and Language, 60*, 437–447.

Ribot, T. (1881). *Les maladies de la memoire [Diseases of memory].* Paris: Germer Bailliere.

Rickards, J. P., & August, G. J. (1975). Generative underlining strategies in prose recall. *Journal of Educational Psychology, 67*, 800–805.

Robinson, F. P. (1941). *Effective study.* New York: Harper and Brothers.

Roediger, H. L., III. (2008). Relativity of remembering: Why the laws of memory vanished. *Annual Review of Psychology, 59*, 225–254.

Roediger, H. L., III, & Karpicke, J. D. (2006a). The power of testing memory: Basic research and implications for educational practice. *Perspectives on Psychological Science, 1*, 181–210.

Roediger, H. L., III, & Karpicke, J. D. (2006b). Test-enhanced learning: Taking memory tests improves long-term retention. *Psychological Science, 17*, 249–255.

Roediger, H. L., III, Weldon, M. S., & Challis, B. H. (1989). Explaining dissociations between implicit and explicit measures of retention: A processing account. In H. L. Roediger, III, & F. I. M. Craik (Eds.), *Varieties of memory and consciousness: Essays in honor of Endel Tulving* (pp. 3–41). Hillsdale, NJ: Erlbaum.

Rohrer, D., Taylor, K., & Sholar, B. (2010). Tests enhance the transfer of learning. *Journal of Experimental Psychology: Learning, Memory, and Cognition, 36*, 233–239.

Rubin, D. C. (1989). Issues of regularity and control: Confessions of a regularity freak. In L. W. Poon , D. C. Rubin, and B. A. Wilson (Eds.), *Everyday cognition in adulthood and late life.* Cambridge, England: Cambridge University Press.

Schmidt, R. A., & Bjork, R. A. (1992). New conceptualizations of practice: Common principles in three paradigms suggest new concepts for training. *Psychological Science, 3*, 207–217.

Semb, G. B., & Ellis, J. A. (1994). Knowledge taught in school: What is remembered? *Review of Educational Research, 64*, 253–286.

Semb, G. B., Ellis, J. A., & Araujo, J. (1993). Long-term memory for knowledge learned in school. *Journal of Educational Psychology, 85*, 305–316.

Skinner, B. F. (1954). The science of learning and the art of teaching. *Harvard Educational Review, 24*, 86–97.

Spitzer, H. F. (1939). Studies in retention. *Journal of Educational Psychology, 30*, 641–656.

Stordahl, K. E., & Christensen, C. M. (1956). The effect of study techniques on comprehension and recall. *Journal of Educational Research, 49*, 561–570.

Thorndike, E. (1911). *Animal intelligence: Experimental studies.* Oxford, England: Macmillan.

Tulving, E., & Pearlstone, Z. (1966). Availability versus accessibility of information in memory for words. *Journal of Verbal Learning and Verbal Behavior, 5*, 381–391.

Tulving, E., & Osler, S. (1968). Effectiveness of retrieval cues in memory for words. *Journal of Experimental Psychology, 77*, 593–601.

Underwood, B. J. (1961). Ten years of massed practice on distributed practice. *Psychological Review, 68*, 229–247.

Wheeler, M. A., & Roediger, H. L., III. (1992). Disparate effects of repeated testing: Reconciling Ballard's (1913) and Bartlett's (1932) results. *Psychological Science, 3*, 240–245.

## Further Reading

McDaniel, M., & Einstein, G. O. (2005). Material appropriate difficulty: A framework for determining when difficulty is desirable for improving learning. In A. F. Healy (Ed.), *Experimental cognitive psychology and its applications* (pp. 73–86). Washington, DC: APA.

Pashler, H., Bain, P. M., Bottge, B. A., Graesser, A., Koedinger, K., McDaniel, M., & Metcalfe, J. (2007). *Organizing instruction and study to improve student learning (NCER 2007–2004).* Washington, DC: National Center for Education Research, Institute of Education Sciences, U.S. Department of Education.

Roediger, H. L., III, & Karpicke, J. D. (2006). The power of testing memory: Basic research and implications for educational practice. *Perspectives on Psychological Science, 1*, 181–210.

Willingham, D. T. (2009). *Why don't students like school? A cognitive scientist answers questions about how the mind works and what it means for the classroom.* San Francisco: Jossey-Bass.

# PART 4

# Knowledge and Mental Representation

# The Nature of Mental Concepts

Arthur B. Markman *and* Jonathan R. Rein

**Abstract**

Concepts are crucial for understanding the world. This chapter aims to lay a foundation for other discussions of categories in this book. We begin by exploring the interplay between concepts and memory. Then, we discuss types of categories and distinguish among proposals about the way categories are represented. In particular, we examine differences among feature-based, thematic, and relational categories. Next, the chapter focuses on the functions that categories play within cognition, such as classification, inference, and communication. This discussion ends with an examination of the interplay of category use and category learning.

**Key Words:** categories, concepts, prototypes, features, relations, inference, communication, classification, implicit memory, explicit memory

Categories are collections of items in the world that we choose to treat as equivalent for some purpose. Our ability to create categories of things is central to our capacity to make use of past experience to help us understand new situations. We use our category knowledge to make predictions about new events and to communicate with others about those events. Category information is also central to our ability to make effective decisions.

The psychology literature often makes a distinction between categories and concepts. When these terms are used differently, a *category* refers to a collection of items that are treated as equivalent. A *concept* is the mental representation of that category. In practice, it is hard to make this distinction clearly, and though we think this distinction is potentially useful, we will use these terms interchangeably in this chapter.

The aim of this chapter is to provide key background information for understanding the structure of our categories. The chapter begins by discussing the relationship between category knowledge

and memory systems. The mental representations of our categories are part of memory, and thus it is crucial to understand how memory influences categorization.

Next, we examine the main types of categories that people have. Traditionally, research in psychology and the philosophy of mind has assumed that categories are best described by collections of features that are (typically) true of category members. However, more recent research has demonstrated that categories can be organized around many properties of items beyond just the features that describe them.

Finally, we explore the functions that categories play within the cognitive system. There are two reasons to want to examine the uses of categories. First, to really understand theories of categorization within psychology, it is crucial to know what roles categories play within the cognitive system broadly. Second, the information people acquire about category members is strongly influenced by the tasks they perform while the categories are being learned.

Thus, the use of categories affects what is learned about them.

## Categories and Memory Systems

Research on memory has made clear that there are many different systems of memory that are anatomically distinct in the brain and store different kinds of information for different purposes (Cohen & Eichenbaum, 1993; Tulving, 1983). Within the categorization literature, the broad distinction between explicit and implicit memory has had the most impact. Explicit memory involves systems that enable people to consciously recollect stored information and reason about aspects of categories. This is the kind of memory you use when you recall the color of your first car or when you assert that all cars have engines. In contrast, implicit memory systems enable habitual stimulus-response associations, independent of conscious awareness and perceptual learning. This is the kind of memory that you use when you drive your car along a familiar route or recognize the sound of a car approaching behind you.

The influence of these memory systems on categorization has been studied most extensively in experiments on perceptual classification (e.g., F. G. Ashby, Alfonso-Reese, Turken, & Waldron, 1998). Perceptual classification involves learning to classify items into one of a small number of categories based on their visual properties. In the typical experiment, people are shown simple stimuli such as lines that vary in their length and orientation on a computer screen. They respond by pressing a button to signify which of a set of categories this stimulus belongs to. They are given feedback about their response and are then shown another stimulus. This process continues until people can reliably distinguish among members of the categories. Although these experiments usually involve very simple stimuli, they are analogous to more perceptually rich classifications, like male versus female or cat versus dog.

The explicit memory system seeks rules that can be stated verbally that will correctly classify the items. For example, if a person's task is to classify lines that vary in length and orientation into one of two categories, then the individual might explicitly try the rule that steep lines are in one category and shallow lines are in the other. This system can learn quite quickly. Furthermore, if someone decides that a particular rule is not sufficiently successful at classifying the stimuli, the participant can change the rule that he or she is using, leading to abrupt changes in performance.

The implicit system learns associations between stimuli and responses. This system tends to learn quite slowly. Thus, it takes many trials before this system can control responding in a classification task. Some research has found that amnesics, who cannot learn new information explicitly, may still acquire information from perceptual classification tasks (Knowlton, Squire, & Gluck, 1994). Furthermore, this system is quite inflexible in its behavior. So, in a classification learning task, this implicit system will learn the relationship between the perceptual stimuli and the classification responses. However, this system cannot perform flexibly. If the perceptual information about these categories must be used for any other purpose than for classifying the items, then the information acquired by this implicit system will not support correct responding. The implicit system will also fail to classify correctly if the nature of the response changes, because this disrupts the stimulus-response habits that the system learns.

The evidence suggests that these memory systems compete (Ashby, Ennis, & Spiering, 2007; Ashby & Maddox, 2005; Poldrack, 2002). Thus, factors that allow the explicit learning system to succeed at learning will tend to decrease engagement of the implicit system. When the explicit learning system is not successful at learning a set of categories, then the implicit system will be engaged more fully. Over time, if there is a consistent mapping between stimuli and classification responses, then the implicit system will come to govern responding in perceptual classification tasks.

Obviously, other chapters in this volume are focused on memory systems. However, to understand category learning, it is important to remember that our categories are represented as concepts in memory. Thus, what we know about memory is deeply relevant to our understanding of the way that concepts are formed. We now turn to a discussion of the kinds of categories that people form.

## Kinds of Categories

In this section, we describe different ways that categories can be formed and represented. We start with a discussion of feature-based categories, which are the typical way that theories of categorization have assumed categories are structured. Then, we turn to other types of categories that people may form. For example, people have categories that describe events. They also have thematic categories that link together elements that commonly appear together. They have categories that link together items that are related to a common goal. Finally,

**Table 21.1** Summary of Category Types

| Category Type | Representation | Example |
|---|---|---|
| Feature based | Collection of characteristic features | Birds: sparrow, eagle, penguin |
| Goal derived | Organized around some kind of goal | Picnic food; method of payment |
| Relational | Describes the relationship among some set of items | Competitions: war, chess match, beauty contest |
| Role governed | Objects that fill a particular role in a relational structure | Barriers: roadblock, cell membrane, glass ceiling |
| Thematic | Entities that characteristically co-occur in an event | Kitchen items: chef, stove, fruit |

they have categories that group objects that play a common role in an event. For reference, the main types of categories discussed in this chapter are summarized in Table 21.1.

## Feature-Based Categories

Traditionally, categories were thought to be represented by the properties that described the category members. We call categories of this type *feature-based categories*. There are many different ways that feature-based categories can be constructed, but what they all have in common is that their representations focus on properties that are common to members of the category. There are many different ways that feature-based categories can be represented, however.

For example, Smith and Medin (1981) describe the classical view of categories. On this view, category membership is determined by a rule that proposes the *necessary* and *sufficient* features for category membership. The necessary features are those that an item must have to be a member of a category. The sufficient features are those that, as a collection, are sufficient to determine that an item really is a member of that category. This is the kind of category description that is found in dictionaries. A straightforward example is the category *bachelor*. Unmarried and male appear to be the two features that jointly define membership in this category.

Unfortunately, the classical view of categories does not seem to be a good description of people's categories. Analyses of the categories people form have not been able to find a set of necessary and sufficient features for most of people's categories. For example, Wittgenstein (1968) famously analyzed the category *game* and could not find any necessary and sufficient features that made something a game. For now, consider the category *bird*. There are many

features that birds commonly have (such as wings, feathers, beaks, flying, and singing). None of these features individually guarantees that something is a bird. However, there are many examples of things that are birds but do not have these typical properties (such as penguins and emus that do not fly). Even the apparently simple *bachelor* category cannot be described with a rule based on features. For instance, the Pope is an unmarried male, but classifying him as a bachelor seems incorrect.

Other proposals for feature-based categories take a similarity-based view of categorization (Smith & Medin, 1981). On the *similarity-based* view, category representations contain some set of properties that are often or characteristically true of category members, but not necessarily true of all category members. A new example is classified as a member of a category to the degree that it is similar to the category representation.

For example, the *prototype* view of categories assumes that people form an average category member based on the various members of categories experienced in the past (Posner & Keele, 1970; Rosch & Mervis, 1975). Then, a new example is classified as a member of a category if it is sufficiently similar to the prototype of the category. Research on categorization has led to a number of findings consistent with this prototype view. For example, when people learn new categories, the prototype is the best recognized item, even if the prototype itself was never seen during learning (e.g., Posner & Keele, 1970). In addition, when people judge items as examples of categories, their ratings of example goodness go up as an item gets more similar to the category prototype (Rosch, 1975; Rosch & Mervis, 1975).

An alternative feature-based approach to categories comes from exemplar models (Medin & Schaffer, 1978; Nosofsky, 1987). Exemplar models assume that people store every single category member that they experience. Each category member is stored as the set of that item's unique combination of features along with the label of the category to which the exemplar belongs. New items are classified by determining the similarity of that item to all previously experienced exemplars and selecting category membership based on those exemplars most similar to the new item. Somewhat counterintuitively, exemplar models account for many of the findings first taken as evidence in favor of prototypes. For example, because many experienced exemplars are likely to be close to the category prototype, the prototype will be classified easily, even if it has never been seen before. Furthermore, items close to the prototype will be seen as better exemplars of a category than those exemplars far from the prototype.

As you may have noticed, a crucial part of this discussion revolves around the concept of *similarity*. That is, in order to decide whether a concept is part of a particular category, it is important to have some method for calculating the similarity among items. Once items and categories have been represented, it is straightforward to match up their features and have similarity increase with the number of shared features and decrease with the number of nonshared (or distinctive) features (Tversky, 1977).

However, in order for this process to work, there has to be some process that determines the features that are used to represent category members. After all, it is logically possible to create features that would make any pair seem infinitely similar (Goodman, 1972). For example, both eggs and chickens weigh less than 10 pounds, and they weigh less than 11 pounds, and they weigh less than 12 pounds, and so on. If all of these features were used to represent eggs and chickens, they might be seen to be extremely similar. Somehow, psychological representations and similarity processes are able to focus only on those properties that are relevant to the current situation (Medin, Goldstone, & Gentner, 1993; Sperber & Wilson, 1986). A full discussion of the ways that this focus on relevance is achieved is beyond the scope of this chapter, but the issue is worth raising nonetheless.

There are many other computational models of categorization. Some employ various mixtures of rules, prototypes, and exemplars, while others contain hybrid representations that lie between these levels of abstraction. Despite their many differences, virtually all existing categorization models assume that categories are feature based.

## Thematic and Goal-Derived Categories

For many years, research on categorization focused almost exclusively on feature-based categories. Gradually, however, there was a recognition that some categories do not seem to be well described by particular features. One class of categories that generated considerable interest was those that are organized around people's goals.

Barsalou (1983, 1985) pointed out that there are many categories that are goal derived. For example, categories like exercise equipment or diet foods are organized around goals that people are trying to satisfy. There is little featural similarity between a barbell, a treadmill, and an exercise mat. However, all of them can be used to help a person satisfy his or her goal of exercising, and so there is coherence to this set of items as a category.

One interesting difference between goal-derived and feature-based categories is that people judge the goodness of examples of goal-derived categories based on their similarity to the ideal member of the category rather than to the prototype of the category. For example, the ideal piece of exercise equipment is one that supports strength and cardiovascular fitness. So an elliptical trainer is a good member of the category. An exercise mat is a common piece of exercise equipment, but it is not close to the ideal, and so it is not as good a member of the category.

Another interesting observation about goal-derived categories is that people are good at deriving them on the fly when they are needed. For example, Barsalou asked people to name members of the new goal-derived category, *things to take out of the house in the event of a fire*. Even though the participants in the study had never thought about this category explicitly before, they had no trouble listing examples that belonged in the category. In addition, just like goal-derived categories that people have stored in memory, the goodness of these ad hoc goal-derived categories was based on the similarity of the item to the ideal member of the category. For example, the ideal member of the category *things to take out of the house in the event of a fire* is something that is valuable, easily carried, and irreplaceable.

A second type of category that is related to goal-derived categories is thematic categories such as *tableware* (Lin & Murphy, 2001; Murphy & Ross, 1999). Thematic categories group all of the items that you would expect to see in a particular setting. For example, tableware consists of all of the things you would place on a table in order to set the table (including plates, utensils, glasses, and serving pieces). Thematic categories differ from goal-derived categories, because the members need not satisfy a particular goal. They only need to appear together in common settings. Thematic categories are quite a powerful mechanism for grouping items, because they allow people to predict the other items that are likely to be present in a particular context (Lin & Murphy, 2001). Indeed, children seem to be much more sensitive to thematic relationships among items than to other kinds of categorization relationships (e.g., Markman & Hutchinson, 1984).

### Relational and Role-Governed Categories

Two other types of categories are related to people's ability to represent relationships among things in the world (Markman, 1999). There are a few kinds of these *relational* categories that people use frequently (Gentner & Kurtz, 2005). A simple kind of relational category just names a particular relationship between individuals. For example, the concept *rivalry* names the relationship between two entities such that they are in competition. The rest of the entities' characteristics are not important for whether they can appropriately be called rivals. Competitions in sport, business, and evolution can all be described as rivalries despite the vast differences in features.

To illustrate relational categories, we draw a simple diagram in Figure 21.1. In this figure, the relation *hunting* depicts a relationship between something doing the hunting and something being hunted. We can name this relational category with the noun *hunting*. Any pair of items that are engaged in a hunting relationship can be described as being part of this relational category.

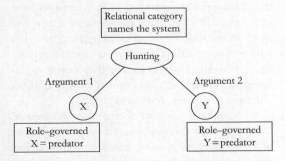

**Figure 21.1** A sample relational structure that can be used to define relational and role-governed categories. The relation hunting (X, Y) names an entire relation, while the terms *predator* and *prey* name the roles within that relational system.

A more complex kind of relational category is an event category (Rifkin, 1985; Rips & Conrad, 1989). Event categories name interactions among people and objects such as *shopping trips*, *visits*, *football games*, and *dates*. These categories represent the relationships among the various actors in a situation and the objects that typically appear in them. For example, a football game includes players from each of two teams, fans watching the game, referees, and objects such as the ball and goalposts. An event can be identified both by the presence of particular objects as well as by the relationships that hold among people and objects in them. Like goal-derived categories, the goodness of an event category is typically related to its similarity to the ideal event. For example, the ideal *date* involves a pleasant activity undertaken between two people who are romantically interested in each other. A date that was missing some of these ideal properties (e.g., the activity was not that much fun, a third person tagged along, or the people did not really like each other that much) would be a worse example of a date than one that had all of these properties.

As shown in Figure 21.1, an important aspect of these relational categories is that they point outward to other concepts in order to bind them together. When people describe these relational categories, then, they tend to list properties that relate the category to other categories. For example, when people talk about a *football game*, they talk about teams, equipment, and fans, each of which exists outside of the football game itself. Features that refer to properties outside of the category are called *extrinsic features*, and they are contrasted with *intrinsic features*, which name features that are part of the item itself (Barr & Caplan, 1987; Caplan & Barr, 1989). All categories will have both intrinsic and extrinsic features to some degree, but people will generally list more extrinsic properties for relational categories than for feature-based categories.

Event categories are also deeply related to the verbs people have in language (Gentner, 1981). Verbs bind together the elements of a sentence. Thus, they point outward to other words and create a relational structure. For example, consider the simple sentence, John gave a book to Mary.

In this sentence, the verb *gave* relates the three objects in the sentence (John, Mary, and the book) in the relationship in which the book transfers possession from John to Mary (Gentner, 1975).

Another important type of category is related to relational categories. These categories, called *role-governed categories*, name the roles that people and objects can play in events and verbs (Ferretti, McRae, & Hatherell, 2001; Markman & Stilwell, 2001). For example, the relational category *hunting* shown in Figure 21.1 has two associated role-governed categories. The item doing the hunting is a *predator* or *hunter*. The item being hunted is the *prey*. What makes an item a member of a role-governed category is that it fills that role within the relational category, regardless of the other properties that it might have.

There are a few ways that people learn role-governed categories. As children, we tend to acquire role-governed categories by first treating them as feature-based categories and gradually transitioning to understanding the role they play within a relational system. For example, Keil (1989) found that children first assume that members of role-governed categories share a set of properties in common, and only gradually come to understand that their role in the relational system defines the category. For example, young children assume that a *robber* is someone who is mean, and has a mask and a gun, while older children realize that anyone who takes something that does not belong to them qualifies as a robber, even if they do not have characteristics that are typical of a robber.

Role-governed categories are also learned along with verbs. Ferretti, McRae, and Hatherell (2001) demonstrated that verbs like *arrest* are strongly associated with the categories that can fill roles within the verb, like *cop*. Other studies suggest that when people learn a new verb, they can easily learn role-governed categories that relate to it. For example, upon hearing the novel verb, "John whiskied himself stupid last night," people can quickly learn the category of the *whiskier*, meaning the person who gets drunk on whisky (Goldwater & Markman, 2010)

Finally, role-governed categories also have many of the characteristics of relational categories. For example, as with relational categories, the features that people list for role-governed categories are primarily extrinsic features rather than intrinsic features (Goldwater & Markman, 2010). In addition, the goodness of an example as a member of a role-governed category is related to the closeness of that example to the ideal member of the category (Goldwater & Markman, 2010).

In summary, many categories can be described by characteristic features. However, people also have a number of categories in which relations play a crucial role. It is important to bear in mind that people's ability to use categories involving relations relies crucially on their capacity to represent relations and the elements that they relate (like the simple structure shown in Fig. 21.1). Some of those categories (such as those that name events) are represented by a set of relationships among a set of other objects. These relational categories also bear a similarity to the categories named by verbs. Finally, people have role-governed categories that name the objects that play particular roles within a broader relational system.

## Category Uses

A primary reason why so much research has focused on people's ability to form categories is that categories are central to many of our cognitive abilities. Obviously, our categories help us to classify things into groups. These groups would not be that useful, though, unless there were other functions that categories could serve. Among the important ones are inference, communication, and preference formation.

In this section, we discuss these functions of categories and also examine how these uses of categories affect what is learned about the category (Markman & Ross, 2003). In general, people are cognitive misers, and so they will focus on the information that is most useful for whatever cognitive task they are pursuing. Thus, the information that people acquire about categories is strongly influenced by what they are doing when they learn those categories.

Obviously, classification is a central part of our ability to categorize. Much of our discussion of categorization so far has been focused on aspects of classification. Of interest in this section is that classification often influences what people learn about category members. For example, if people are learning to classify items from different categories at the same time, then they tend to focus on the properties that distinguish the members of the categories from each other. In contrast, if people learn a new category in isolation from other categories, then they tend to focus on the features most commonly associated with the category so that they can recognize category members at a later time (Goldstone, 1996; Goldstone, Steyvers, & Rogosky, 2003).

A second key function of categories is inference. Inference is the ability to predict unknown features of a new category member based on knowledge of the category. For example, if you see a small furry animal on the street and you classify it as a dog, then you can predict a number of other properties about it, such as that it may bark or that it likes to chew on bones. Some theorists have suggested that the ability to predict properties of new examples based on the way they are classified is the most important function of people's categories (Anderson, 1990).

To predict unknown properties of a new example, people must focus on the relationship between the category label and the features of the category. They must also focus on causal and statistical relationships among the features. This information allows people to succeed at predicting the value of an unknown feature. Thus, when people make predictions about features of new examples, it tends to reinforce their knowledge of the relationship between the category label and the properties most typical of category members (Yamauchi & Markman, 1998, 2000).

In addition to making inferences about individual items based on category knowledge, we can also reason in the opposite direction, making inferences about the entire category based on individual instances. For instance, if you learn that a single robin has sesamoid bones, you can reasonably infer that all robins and even all birds have sesamoid bones, even if you do not know what sesamoid bones are. Much like classification behavior, exemplars' similarity to other category members strongly influences these inferences (Osherson, Smith, Wilkie, Lopez, & Shafir, 1990).

A third function of categories is communication (Brown, 1958). One reason why people form categories and then give those categories labels is so that they can refer to those items later when speaking to others. When people communicate about items, they learn how to use labels from the people around them in the process of talking to them (Garrod & Doherty, 1994). The set of items that a particular label is used to describe ultimately ends up serving as a category (Markman & Makin, 1998).

The influence of communication on category acquisition helps to answer a long-standing puzzle in categorization research. It has long been known that people's categories are reasonably coherent across people. That is, if you ask different people about their intuitions about categories, you get similar answers from different people. Research on this question has tended to focus on one of two possibilities (Malt, 1995). One possibility is that categories are coherent, because there really are coherent categories out there in the world. A second possibility is that categories are coherent, because there are aspects of our cognitive system that place constraints on the categories that people form.

A third possibility, however, is that people form categories in part in the process of learning to communicate with others. On this view, categories are shared across individuals, because we must use category labels in the same ways during discourse. For example, if two people are talking, and one mistakenly refers to an object using a particular label that the other does not think refers to that object, then they will not communicate effectively. They will repair this error in the conversation by trying to figure out what each other meant (Clark, 1996). Ultimately, repeated conversations will allow them to use their labels in a coordinated fashion. And because each of them speaks to many other people, their entire social network ultimately ends up having labels that are used in reasonably similar ways. Thus, there are important social forces that help to create category structures that are coherent across people.

Another example of the interplay between categorization and communication is the use of metaphor. When someone says, "My job is a jail," he or she is making an analogy between the two, using familiar properties of jails to describe their job. Some researchers have argued that such metaphors are actually classification statements; that "my job is a jail" means "my job is a member of the category of jail-like things" (Glucksberg & Keysar, 1990). It is likely that people have to learn what this means at first by comparing the two domains (e.g., comparing jobs to jails). Over time, however, these can become conventionalized category labels. For example, after repeated use as a metaphor, "goldmine" now functions as a role-governed category describing not just sources of a particular mineral but any source of substantial gain (Bowdle & Gentner, 2005).

One final use of categories that we discuss in this section is preference construction. One reason that we need to know about the things in our world is because we need to know whether they are things we like, and therefore hope to acquire, or things we dislike, and therefore hope to avoid. Thus, knowing that an object is a member of a particular category helps us to determine whether we like it.

There are two general strategies that people use to determine their preferences for items: attribute-based processing and alternative-based processing (Payne, Bettman, & Johnson, 1993). In attribute-based processing, people compare different items to each other to determine which one has the best properties. This strategy is particularly effective for people just learning a domain, because they do not yet know how to evaluate the various features (Hsee, 1996). For example, someone who does not know anything about computers might not know whether a computer with 2 Gb of RAM is good or bad. However, if it is compared to a second computer with 4 Gb or RAM, then it is clear that the first computer is worse than the second. Attribute-based processing tends to focus people on the differences among a set of options, and thus people will learn the distinctive features of the options when they learn them through attribute-based processing (Houston, Sherman, & Baker, 1989).

In alternative-based processing, people process each option individually, focusing on creating an overall evaluation of that option. It is called "alternative-based" processing because each of the alternatives is considered separately rather than in comparison. Alternative-based processing is more characteristic of evaluations done by experts than of evaluations done by novices (Klein, 2000). Alternative-based processing is also done when people learn about the first new product in a general class (Zhang & Markman, 1998). For example, when people encountered an mp3 player for the first time, they had no other product to compare it to, and so they had to learn all of the central properties of this first example. Thereafter, this example became the initial basis for the category of mp3 players. Because alternative-based processing is done without regard to the other options to which it might be compared, learning about new options through alternative-based processing will lead people to learn about all of the important features of an option, regardless of whether they will turn out to be commonalities or differences when compared to other options.

As this section makes clear, people perform a variety of tasks with their categories. Thus, the information that they acquire about their categories must be sufficient to serve these functions. At the same time, the information that they use when performing these functions becomes a more central part of the concepts that people have represented. Thus, there is an interplay between the use of categories and what is learned about them.

## Summary

Categorization is a core cognitive ability. It allows people to draw information from memory about past experience and to apply that past experience to new situations. In this chapter, we reviewed three core aspects of categorization that are fundamental for understanding the more detailed aspects described by other chapters in this volume. First, we reviewed how categorization abilities are intertwined with memory systems. Category information is stored in memory, and so it is important to understand how general memory systems influence what is learned about categories.

Next, we reviewed a variety of types of categories that people form. These category types are summarized in Table 21.1. It is important to keep these category types in mind, because much research on categorization has focused on feature-based categories. As Table 21.1 makes clear, though, there are a number of important kinds of categories that people form and use.

Finally, we discussed some core uses of category knowledge. To place the importance of category knowledge in perspective, it is crucial to understand the variety of ways that people take their knowledge of categories and apply it to common tasks. In this chapter, we reviewed research on inference, communication, and decision making to demonstrate the ways that people can bring their knowledge and experience to bear on new situations.

## References

Anderson, J. R. (1990). *The adaptive character of thought.* Hillsdale, NJ: Erlbaum.

Ashby, F. G., Alfonso-Reese, L. A., Turken, A. U., & Waldron, E. M. (1998). A neuropsychological theory of multiple systems in category learning. *Psychological Review, 105*(3), 442–481.

Ashby, F. G., Ennis, J. M., & Spiering, B. J. (2007). A neurobiological theory of automaticity in perceptual categorization. *Psychological Review, 114*(3), 632–656.

Ashby, F. G., & Maddox, W. T. (2005). Human category learning. *Annual Review of Psychology, 56,* 149–178.

Barr, R. A., & Caplan, L. J. (1987). Category representations and their implications for category structure. *Memory and Cognition, 15*(5), 397–418.

Barsalou, L. W. (1983). Ad hoc categories. *Memory and Cognition, 11,* 211–227.

Barsalou, L. W. (1985). Ideals, central tendency and frequency of instantiation as determinants of graded structure in categories. *Journal of Experimental Psychology: Learning, Memory and Cognition, 11*(4), 629–654.

Bowdle, B. F., & Gentner, D. (2005). The career of metaphor. *Psychological Review, 112*(1), 193–216.

Brown, R. (1958). How shall a thing be called? *Psychological Review, 65*(1), 14–21.

Caplan, L. J., & Barr, R. A. (1989). On the relationship between category intensions and extensions in children. *Journal of Experimental Child Psychology, 47,* 413–429.

Clark, H. H. (1996). *Using language.* New York: Cambridge University Press.

Cohen, N. J., & Eichenbaum, H. (1993). *Memory, amnesia, and the hippocampal system.* Cambridge, MA: MIT Press.

Ferretti, T. R., Mc Rae, K., & Hatherell, A. (2001). Integrating verbs, situation schemas, and thematic role concepts. *Journal of Memory and Language, 44,* 516–547.

Garrod, S., & Doherty, G. (1994). Conversation, co-ordination and convention: An empirical investigation of how groups establish linguistic conventions. *Cognition, 53,* 181–215.

Gentner, D. (1975). Evidence for the psychological reality of semantic components: The verbs of possession. In D. A. Norman & D. E. Rumelhart (Eds.), *Explorations in cognition* (pp. 211–246). San Francisco: W.H. Freeman.

Gentner, D. (1981). Some interesting differences between nouns and verbs. *Cognition and Brain Theory, 4*(2), 161–178.

Gentner, D., & Kurtz, K. J. (2005). Relational categories. In W. K. Ahn, R. L. Goldstone, B. C. Love, A. B. Markman, & P. Wolff (Eds.), *Categorization inside and outside the laboratory: Essays in honor of Douglas L. Medin* (pp. 151–175). Washington, DC: American Psychological Association.

Glucksberg, S., & Keysar, B. (1990). Understanding metaphorical comparisons: Beyond similarity. *Psychological Review, 97*(1), 3–18.

Goldstone, R. L. (1996). Isolated and interrelated concepts. *Memory and Cognition, 24*(5), 608–628.

Goldstone, R. L., Steyvers, M., & Rogosky, B. J. (2003). Conceptual interrelatedness and caricatures. *Memory and Cognition, 31*(2), 169–180.

Goldwater, M. B., & Markman, A. B. (2010). The empirical case for role-governed categories. *Cognition.* ePub ahead of print.

Goodman, N. (1972). *Problems and prospects.* Indianapolis, IN: Bobbs-Merrill.

Houston, D. A., Sherman, S. J., & Baker, S. M. (1989). The influence of unique features and direction of comparison on preferences. *Journal of Experimental Social Psychology, 25*, 121–141.

Hsee, C. K. (1996). The evaluability hypothesis: An explanation for preference reversals between joint and separate evaluations of alternatives. *Organizational Behavior and Human Decision Processes, 67*(3), 247–257.

Keil, F. C. (1989). *Concepts, kinds and cognitive development.* Cambridge, MA: MIT Press.

Klein, G. (2000). *Sources of power.* Cambridge, MA: MIT Press.

Knowlton, B. J., Squire, L. R., & Gluck, M. A. (1994). Probabilistic classification learning in amnesia. *Learning and Memory, 1*, 106–120.

Lin, E. L., & Murphy, G. L. (2001). Thematic relations in adults' concepts. *Journal of Experimental Psychology: General, 130*(1), 3–28.

Malt, B. C. (1995). Category coherence in cross-cultural perspective. *Cognitive Psychology, 29*, 85–148.

Markman, A. B. (1999). *Knowledge representation.* Mahwah, NJ: Erlbaum.

Markman, A. B., & Makin, V. S. (1998). Referential communication and category acquisition. *Journal of Experimental Psychology: General, 127*(4), 331–354.

Markman, A. B., & Ross, B. H. (2003). Category use and category learning. *Psychological Bulletin, 129*(4), 592–613.

Markman, A. B., & Stilwell, C. H. (2001). Role-governed categories. *Journal of Experimental and Theoretical Artificial Intelligence, 13*(4), 329–358.

Markman, E. M., & Hutchinson, J. E. (1984). Children's sensitivity to constraints on word meaning: Taxonomic vs. thematic relations. *Cognitive Psychology, 16*(1), 1–27.

Medin, D. L., Goldstone, R. L., & Gentner, D. (1993). Respects for similarity. *Psychological Review, 100*(2), 254–278.

Medin, D. L., & Schaffer, M. M. (1978). Context theory of classification. *Psychological Review, 85*(3), 207–238.

Murphy, G. L., & Ross, B. H. (1999). Induction with cross-classified categories. *Memory and Cognition, 27*(6), 1024–1041.

Nosofsky, R. M. (1987). Attention and learning processes in the identification and categorization of integral stimuli. *Journal of Experimental Psychology: Learning, Memory and Cognition, 13*(1), 87–108.

Osherson, D. N., Smith, E. E., Wilkie, O., Lopez, A., & Shafir, E. (1990). Category based induction. *Psychological Review, 97*(2), 185–200.

Payne, J. W., Bettman, J. R., & Johnson, E. J. (1993). *The adaptive decision maker.* New York: Cambridge University Press.

Poldrack, R. A. (2002). Neural systems for perceptual skill learning. *Behavioral and Cognitive Neuroscience Reviews, 1*(1), 76–83.

Posner, M. I., & Keele, S. W. (1970). Retention of abstract ideas. *Journal of Experimental Psychology, 83*, 304–308.

Rifkin, A. (1985). Evidence for a basic level in event taxonomies. *Memory and Cognition, 13*(6), 538–556.

Rips, L. J., & Conrad, F. G. (1989). Folk psychology of mental activities. *Psychological Review, 96*(2), 187–207.

Rosch, E. (1975). Cognitive reference points. *Cognitive Psychology, 7*, 532–547.

Rosch, E., & Mervis, C. B. (1975). Family resemblances: Studies in the internal structure of categories. *Cognitive Psychology, 7*, 573–605.

Smith, E. E., & Medin, D. L. (1981). *Categories and concepts.* Cambridge, MA: Harvard University Press.

Sperber, D., & Wilson, D. (1986). *Relevance.* Cambridge, MA: Blackwell.

Tulving, E. (1983). *Elements of episodic memory.* New York: Oxford University Press.

Tversky, A. (1977). Features of similarity. *Psychological Review, 84*(4), 327–352.

Wittgenstein, L. (1968). *Philosophical investigations* (G. E. M. Anscombe, Trans.). New York: MacMillan.

Yamauchi, T., & Markman, A. B. (1998). Category learning by inference and classification. *Journal of Memory and Language, 39*(1), 124–148.

Yamauchi, T., & Markman, A. B. (2000). Inference using categories. *Journal of Experimental Psychology: Learning, Memory, and Cognition, 26*(3), 776–795.

Zhang, S., & Markman, A. B. (1998). Overcoming the early entrant advantage: The role of alignable and nonalignable differences. *Journal of Marketing Research, 35*, 413–426.

# Culture, Expertise, and Mental Categories

Kathy E. Johnson

**Abstract**

Humans' capacity for representing categories is inherently flexible and capable of adapting to varying levels of experience with the world. Two factors that influence these levels of experience are *culture* (reflecting learned networks of knowledge shared by people who live in close proximity and interact with each other often) and *expertise* (heightened domain-specific knowledge typically motivated by interest). The chapter reviews a wide range of cognitive consequences for categorization that arise when individuals are highly familiar with objects to be categorized. An integrated approach is adopted, considering both research from cognitive science and cognitive anthropology on object categorization, as well as the perceptual expertise literature that focuses primarily on visual perception. Key directions for future research are delineated.

**Key Words:** culture, expertise, concepts, perceptual expertise, categorization

The study of mental categories has provided a fertile ground for psychologists, linguists, and anthropologists to consider the effects that both culture and the domains of expertise that cultures support can have on those conceptual representations. Cultures shape the typical patterns of experience and everyday behaviors of individuals residing within them, and thus they impact mental categories corresponding to domains of objects, actions, and events. Though the capacity for forming mental categories is universal (and shared by a number of other animal species), the specific categories that humans acquire and use depend heavily on those habits of mind that are aligned with one's culture, as well as the pockets of expertise that emerge as a function of the interests and experiences manifest by the individuals that reside (and develop) within them.

For the sake of clarity, *mental categories* are construed as synonymous with *concepts*—they are mental representations of kinds that can be viewed, touched, smelled, tasted, heard, imagined, and responded to similarly in everyday life. Mental categories provide the conceptual foundation for acts of categorization—the rendering of discriminably different things as equivalent in some sense. Categorization in turn supports identification, labeling, and higher order cognitive activities that depend on mental categories, such as reasoning and analogical problem solving. Although mental categories could correspond to any "like kinds" that are concrete or abstract, stable or dynamic, and perceived through any sensory modality, the present chapter will focus primarily on mental categories pertaining to *objects in the world*, as these are the concepts that have most frequently been studied by cognitive scientists and cognitive anthropologists with interest in culture and expertise.

Mental categories are bound by similarity relations and most critically share theoretical coherence (Carey, 1985; Medin, Lynch, & Solomon, 2000; Murphy, 2002; Murphy & Medin, 1985). They are embedded within explanatory frameworks that are domain specific and that can vary as a function of both culture and expertise (Medin, Ross, Atran, Burnett, & Blok, 2002). They also are lexicalized—humans use individual nouns or noun phrases to refer to them, and such labels can be applied with varying levels of precision. Generally, people who possess more enriched knowledge about mental categories tend to acquire and use labels that are highly specific (e.g., chipping sparrow, Chevy Volt), while novices use labels that are less precise (e.g., bird, car). Though individuals who know little about a domain may indeed possess some specific "subordinate-level" category names, the representations supporting those names may be fairly sparse. For example, citified adults may know that elm and beech are kinds of trees yet be utterly unable to use those labels to actually identify types of leaves or trees. Not only do experts use labels that are highly specific to identify objects accurately, such labels are accessed as rapidly as the more general "default" labels (i.e., "tree") typically favored by novices (Johnson & Mervis, 1997; Tanaka & Taylor, 1991).

In this review, *culture* is defined as *learned networks of shared knowledge* that include routine ways of thinking, feeling, and interacting with others, as well as beliefs about aspects of the world (Barth, 2002; Hong, 2009). Though culture often covaries with racial, ethnic, or national groups, the present definition more clearly stipulates that the effects of culture on mental categories are rooted in the activation of shared knowledge, rather than the behaviors, language, or ideas expressed by the people that make up cultural groups. Cognitive psychologists typically have acknowledged that culture contributes to individual differences in thinking, but until relatively recently, the experimental methods (and statistical analyses) most frequently used to examine mental categories have tended to focus on the most typical behaviors exhibited under controlled conditions—treating variability as a nuisance that should be controlled (Markman, Grimm, & Kim, 2009). In contrast, anthropologists tend to exploit this variability through detailed and more qualitatively oriented analyses of how people engage with categories of objects in the natural world.

*Expertise* typically is defined by relatively high levels of domain-specific knowledge (Chi, Glaser, & Farr, 1988; Glaser, 1987; Gobbo & Chi, 1986; Johnson, Scott, & Mervis, 2004) or outstanding levels of skilled performance that depend on at least 10 years of deliberate practice to accrue (Ericsson & Smith, 1991; Ericsson, Krampe, & Tesch-Römer, 1993). Some domains of expertise are relatively ubiquitous among individuals from the same community, usually because such knowledge is transmitted formally through school (e.g., reading, long division) or because such knowledge is fundamental to everyday routines within one's community (e.g., manioc cultivation among the Aguaruna Jivaro; Boster, 1986). More frequently, expertise is considered to be a basis for individual differences in cognitive processing that varies among individuals that share the same culture. Domain-specific knowledge accrual is fueled either by interests that are idiosyncratic and intrinsically motivated (Renninger, 1992) or by training that is delivered only to specific subgroups (Biederman & Shiffrar, 1987).

Regardless of the motivational origins, the consequence of expertise on mental categories is isomorphic to that of culture. Expertise and culture contribute to predictable changes in the rate at which mental categories are acquired, the levels of specificity or "scope" of such categories, and the ways that such categories are used in communication, reasoning, and other forms of higher order cognitive processing. The present chapter is divided into five general sections. In the first section, the nature of mental categories is considered together with aspects of perception, representation, and categorization that adapt to varying levels of experience. In the second, cross-cultural variability in mental categories is reviewed. Third, literature drawn from the study of experts is reviewed, followed by a section dedicated to analyses of perceptual expertise. Finally, future directions for research are considered.

## The Adaptiveness of Mental Categories

The capacity to form categories is essential for nearly all aspects of what we consider to be thought—encoding and retaining information, reasoning by analogy, deducing and inferring, and simply identifying what things are. Although many nonhuman animals are able to form equivalence classes based on perceptual information (Lazareva & Wasserman, 2010; Zentall, Wasserman, Thompson, & Ratterman, 2008), only humans learn mental categories that can be ordered hierarchically to facilitate labeling at multiple levels of abstraction (all recliners are chairs and all chairs are furniture, which are artifacts—kinds of objects) and exploited to construct new knowledge through inductive and deductive reasoning. Humans' capacity for representing aspects of the world is inherently flexible and adaptive. Yet analyses of this flexibility have typically focused either on the perceptual bases for this flexibility or on the conceptual bases (and consequences) of this flexibility in reasoning, communicating with others, and problem solving. The current review intentionally integrates these approaches, emphasizing the bidirectional relation between perception and mental categories (Goldstone, 2010; Goldstone & Barsalou, 1998; Goldstone, Gerganov, Landy, & Roberts, 2008; Smith & Heise, 1992). Experts—by virtue of culture or intrinsic motivation—use perception to cultivate their vast networks of conceptual knowledge, which in turn tune and further sharpen perception.

In categorization, a wide array of perceptual inputs (percepts) are reduced to a smaller array of equivalence classes (categories), for which memory representations (mental categories or concepts) support language, thinking, and other behaviors (Schyns, 1997). Properties associated with categories also may be lexicalized, and category labels used in conjunction with such properties help people to infer how broadly such properties can be generalized (e.g., hearing that "mammals have spleens inside" would lead to more pervasive generalizations than hearing that "black and white ruffed lemurs have spleens inside"). Sloutsky (2010) maintains that lexicalized properties that must be inferred because they refer to nonvisible features are "conceptual" properties, and lexicalized mental categories that include such properties are *concepts*.

In her seminal theory of perceptual learning, Eleanor Gibson (1969, 1991) was among the first to maintain that with learning and practice, organisms increase their ability to extract information from the environment. This process of perceptual learning is inherently self-regulating—the types of interactions that people have with objects in the environment are inextricably linked to the ways that those objects are perceived. Very frequent interactions typically culminate in the discovery of distinctive features and structures in the world that originally were undifferentiated. Experts on various domains of food, drink, disease, artifacts, and biological domains of the natural world come to be able to selectively attend to increasingly subtle features that distinguish among kinds. In many cases, these features are discovered independently through repeated exposure or interactions with objects. For example, in the world of poultry farming, the ability to distinguish the gender of newly hatched chicks is a tricky business. Yet skill in this specialized discrimination improves with repeated exposure to a distinctive cloacal region of chicks, particularly when it is emphasized during training (Biederman & Shiffrar, 1987). Adding language to this process can have an accelerating effect. Words can indeed facilitate perceptual learning by drawing attention to previously unnoticed features that help to differentiate among kinds (Gibson, 1969). When a child hears an adult label two previously undifferentiated dinosaurs, "parasaurolophus" and "lambeosaurus," she infers that the labels signify distinct subcategories and could (particularly if motivated by an intrinsic interest in dinosaurs) initiate a search for the perceptual characteristics that distinguish these kinds.

Traditional models of memory have maintained that perceptual processes provide feature information that is critical to "downstream" aspects of information processing, including the acquisition of conceptual representations and their use during thinking. In contrast, Goldstone and Barsalou (1998) maintain that a common representational system underlies both conception and perception, and that concepts depend on perceptual representations and processes—both during concept acquisition and as concepts are used. Perceptual processes are fairly conservative in their potential for adaptation as a result of experience—perceptual learning requires high levels of repetition or practice in order to give rise to neurological changes that affect subsequent perceptual processing—and these neurological modifications take time. Yet this flexibility is well worth it from the standpoint of humans' capacity to respond quickly to familiar stimuli at minimal "cost" in terms of the deployment of online attentional resources. Such changes have been examined primarily by cognitive neuroscientists interested in the mechanisms supporting perceptual expertise. As will be reviewed in the third and fourth sections of this chapter, perceptual tuning of attention may culminate in unique patterns of neuronal activation when domain-specific stimuli are presented. It also can impact the speed with which identification takes place at the individual or specific levels, and the bases for similarity grouping within the domain. In sum, the flexibility inherent in mental categories' capacity to adapt to experience, whether as a function of participation in activities that culminate in shared cultural knowledge or because of individuals' acquisition of expertise, is grounded in both changes to perception and alterations in the relative salience of conceptual properties. The consequences of these changes on human behavior are reviewed in the next two sections.

## Culture and Mental Categories

Culture comprises the broad and relatively stable distribution of mental categories across members of the same population (Atran, Medin, & Ross, 2005). Cultural anthropologists typically emphasize the emergence of mental categories through human social interactions that give rise to learning through informal conversations, folklore, and everyday behaviors. Ross and Tidwell (2010) argue that while cognitive scientists focusing on expertise tend to highlight people's relative *levels* of knowledge, anthropologists examining cultural variations in mental categories tend to emphasize the *kinds* of knowledge acquired, and the alignment of those kinds with cultural frameworks that translate into patterns of reasoning and generalizations based on mental categories. Cognitive anthropological analyses of categorization frequently have emphasized biological domains of plants and animals (folk biology), as these provide a relatively constant set of stimuli to evaluate against a backdrop of potential variations in categorization behaviors fueled by culture. Such domains also have a scientific standard—taxonomic relations grounded in the study of biological systematics—that informants' categories can be compared against (Boster, Berlin, & O'Neill, 1986; Johnson, Mervis, & Boster, 1992; Malt, 1995).

## Names for Things

Names for things reflect conventions concerning how entities should be divided into categories. Across individuals with different cultural backgrounds, different entities within the world may be lexicalized. Among cultures that possess nominals referring to the same real-world kinds, differences may exist in terms of the level of specificity routinely used to identify or name those kinds. Cognitive psychologists and cognitive anthropologists have long grappled with the issue of why members of different cultures use some groupings but not others. Some variation appears due to functional utility of the categories themselves. For example, Diamond (1966) reported that the Fore people of the New Guinea Highlands use very specific labels to differentiate among kinds of birds, which are frequently hunted.[1] On the other hand, the Fore refer to all butterflies with a single label, as butterflies are less significant than birds to everyday life in this region. Other variations in how things in the world are grouped stem from culturally shared belief systems that may be reinforced through folktales or rituals. For example, Bulmer (1967) reported that the cassowary (a

large, flightless bird) was not classified as a bird by the Karam of Papua New Guinea because it was believed to possess a mythical relationship to humans. Theorists tend to differ in terms of whether they emphasize that mental categories reflect structural information that is readily evident in the world versus emphasizing that human categorizers impose structure through a constructive process of category formation (for an excellent review of these alternatives, see Malt, 1995). Regardless, it is clear from the cognitive anthropological literature that culture exudes significant effects on how mental categories are structured and used—a perspective that is frequently masked in reviews of categorization that are based on studies based on the behaviors of college undergraduates typically recruited in Western postindustrial societies.

Anthropologists frequently have considered patterns of nomenclature to be accurate reflections of the underlying categories of objects into which members of cultures divide their worlds. The linguistic structure of names for things also may be used to determine the level of inclusiveness of the categories to which those names refer. Berlin, Breedlove, and Raven (1973, p. 216) argue that "nomenclature is often a near perfect guide to folk taxonomic structure. Furthermore, when nomenclature fails to mirror accurately the taxonomic structure of a particular biological class, it can usually be shown that the class in question is undergoing semantic change."

Morphological similarity generally has been found to be a more important basis for classifying and naming kinds than function (Berlin, 1972, 1992; Berlin et al., 1973). Berlin has emphasized that folk conceptualizations of plants and animals are strikingly similar across different regions of the world, which must reflect that human beings possess an unconscious appreciation of the biological structure present in the environment. When informants are asked to sort objects in terms of similarity, decisions based on perceptible characteristics (things with the same shape or configurations of parts) typically trump decisions based on functional or utilitarian properties (things that one hunts, things that are used during religious rituals). Considerable agreement exists between local informants and biologists regarding groupings of familiar populations of plants and animals. However, this agreement breaks down when species that are less familiar are included (Hull, 1992). The highest levels of agreement occur for large vertebrate animals, followed by plants that are conspicuously plentiful. In contrast, there is very little agreement between folk and scientists for most invertebrates and inconspicuous plants.

In studying biological taxa, ethnobiologists generally consider there to be multiple, nested ranks of categories at which plants and animals can be conceptualized and often named (Berlin, 1972, 1978; Berlin, Breedlove, & Raven, 1973, 1974). At the broadest level, or *unique beginner*, plants are differentiated from animals, although Berlin points out that many languages have no translatable labels for these domains. The unique beginner is considered a covert category because although it may be unmarked by a specific label, other words (e.g., fur, stem) are semantically aligned with a specific domain, providing evidence that such domains are differentiated. Other ranks include the *life form* (bird, mammal, tree), *folk generic* (dog, pine), *folk specific* (sparrow, terrier, white pine), and *folk varietal* (e.g., chipping sparrow, Yorkshire terrier, Eastern white pine). The "folk generic" level has been argued to embody the core of any folk taxonomy (Atran, 2002). It is the most fundamental level at which an object may be categorized, and it is roughly comparable to what psychologists have referred to as the *basic* level (Rosch, Mervis, Gray, Johnson, & Boyes-Braem, 1976). It is the level at which the smallest conceptually relevant groupings of biological taxa are referred to by members sharing the same culture (Berlin, 1972). At the generic level, the discontinuities between biological categories are readily perceived. Names that refer to generic-level categories are usually simple lexemes and are the most commonly used terms within communities of informants and hence are the first terms typically encountered by ethnobiological researchers. Berlin reported that 61% of Tzeltal folk generic category labels mapped directly to scientific species, suggesting that there was a close correspondence between scientific taxonomy and folk mental categories within communities for which plants are highly salient (Berlin, 1992).

## Classification

Naming conventions implicitly reflect groupings that are recognized by language users. On the other hand, more systematic analyses of relations among mental categories that are conceptually related can be derived through sorting behavior—frequently elicited through requests to sort like kinds into piles. A task frequently used to shed light on such relations is the *successive sorting task*. Informants are presented with cards depicting kinds of animals, plants, or humanmade objects. Cards may

be labeled or not, depending on the literacy skills of the informants; labels are generally preferable given that they are less prone to bias through perceptual characteristics depicted in drawings or photographs (e.g., color patterns). Informants are then typically asked to sort cards according to how they "go together by nature" (Lopez, Atran, Coley, & Medin, 1997) or "go together as companions...of the same natural lineage" (Atran, 1999). After the initial set of piles has been created, informants are invited to combine piles again according to how they might go together in nature (with the aim of deriving superordinate-level groupings). Finally, the initial set of piles is restored and the informant is invited to subdivide those piles until he or she no longer wishes to do so (to yield subordinate-level groupings).

Hierarchical relations among mental categories are inferred through people's patterns of sorting behavior. Each individual's taxonomy can be inferred by translating groupings during the free pile, successive pile, and successive subpile phase into a taxonomic tree; the "taxonomic distance" between any two entities is inferred from where in the sorting sequence the items were first grouped together. The "distance matrix" for each informant can then be compared against those of other informants from the same culture, as well as with actual scientific taxonomic distances using the Cultural Consensus Model (CCM; Romney, Weller, & Bachelder, 1986; Romney, Bachelder & Weller, 1987). The CCM is a statistical approach based on principal components factor analysis that uses patterns of agreement among individuals to infer each person's relative level of cultural competence. The CCM also can be used to determine whether there is a single consensus across different subgroups, or whether individuals within groups agree with each other to a greater extent than would be predicted by the overall pattern of agreement.

As is the case for naming data, analyses of pile sort data generated by members of the same culture tend to be highly correlated and also converge moderately well with scientific taxonomy (Bailenson, Shum, Atran, Medin, & Coley, 2002; Boster, 1986; Lopez et al., 1997). Yet systematic differences among subgroups of individuals help to illuminate the ways that expertise and culturally shared systems independently affect mental categories of biological kinds. As an illustrative example, Bailenson et al. used a "triangulation strategy" (Medin et al., 2002) to disentangle the sources of variation among cultural groups. The primary comparison focused on

Itza' Maya and US undergraduate novices' categorization of North and Central American passerines (birds of the order *Passeriformes*, which are sometimes referred to as "perching birds" or "songbirds"). A third group (US bird experts) is then introduced that resembles one group in certain ways (US experts and Itza' Maya share extensive knowledge with species of passerines) and the second group in other ways (US experts and US novices share the same culture). Bailenson et al. found that the pile sorting behavior of US experts was more similar to that of Itza' (and to corresponding scientific taxonomy) than to that of US novices. Expertise (whether supported by cultural relevance or intrinsic motivation to engage in birding) seems to support people's ability to abstract important (and often perceptually subtle) relationships among biological categories that novices fail to detect (see also Johnson & Mervis, 1998). While continuities across cultures in the ways that flora and fauna are named and grouped into categories suggests that there is a universal categorization scheme that is sensitive to structural information present in nature and detected by the human perceptual system (Berlin, 1992), the perceptual system can be further "tuned" through engagement with domain-specific categories. As will be pointed out in the next section, this general scheme may be overridden in some cases by goal-related knowledge that is aligned with particular types of expertise.

## Patterns of Reasoning

In contrast to relatively stable patterns of agreement derived from analyses of names used to refer to categories and the sorting of instances into groups, cultural variations seem particularly pronounced in inductive reasoning contexts. Induction fuels the construction of categorical knowledge by supporting the generalization of properties across kinds. When one learns about a property of a particular instance (X has a spleen; Y is susceptible to a particular kind of disease), children and adults tend to generalize such properties to other instances. In general, the probability of a particular inductive inference is predicted by the relevant relations that are believed to exist among classes of entities. This is where cultures wield their impact—of the many possible relationships that could be construed to exist among kinds, cultures select those that are most salient for guiding inductive inferences (Coley, Shafto, Stepanova, & Baraff, 2005).

Traditional accounts of category-based induction emphasize the importance of global similarity (or shared features) for guiding induction (e.g., Similarity Coverage Model; Osherson et al., 1990). Inductive arguments are considered strong to the extent that premise categories are more similar to the conclusion category. For example, generalization of a property known to be shared by oak trees and maple trees to an elm tree is more likely than generalization of that same property to a blue spruce. Similarly when premise categories are more typical (e.g., sparrow/bird), arguments are considered stronger than when they are less typical (e.g., ostrich/bird). Yet other dimensions may be important to individuals from different cultures. Lopez et al. (1997) studied the inductions of industrialized Americans and traditional Itza'-Mayan informants in relation to instances of mammals and palms. While both groups used their taxonomic knowledge to make similarity-based and typicality-based inductive inferences, cultural variations also emerged. Americans used their knowledge to make diversity-based inductions (the more diverse the premise categories, the stronger the argument) while Itza' made ecologically based inductions. For example, one informant preferred the argument COCONUT, ROYAL PALM/PALM over the more diverse premises, COCONUT, BASKET WHIST/ PALM, explaining that because both the coconut and the royal palm were tall and tree-like, disease would be more able to spread to all other palms. Itza' frequently considered arguments to be stronger when premise categories shared the same habitat, regardless of how similar or dissimilar the premise categories were.

Similar patterns have been reported by Ross, Medin, Coley, and Atran (2003) for Menominee, rural, and urban children. While urban children displayed traditional patterns of property projections (based on similarity to humans), older rural children and Menominee children of all ages were found to base inductions on ecological relations among plants and animals. For example, Menominee children frequently generalized from bees to bears on the basis of justifications such as bees stinging bears, or bears' affinity for honey. Similar justifications were produced by older rural majority culture children, but never by urban children.

## Expertise Fueled by Interest

Regardless of one's culture, people have the capacity to delve deeply into fields that spark curiosity or even passion. Interest is a source of intrinsic motivation that fuels learning and that culminates in the construction of mental categories that are considerably richer than those of nonexperts. Renninger (1990) characterized *individual interests* as ongoing and deepening relations between individuals and nonhuman objects or activity domains that are personally meaningful and that result in knowledge acquisition. Experts naturally spend a great deal of time observing or interacting with category exemplars, and over time they become able to identify instances with a high degree of specificity and accuracy (Johnson & Mervis, 1997; Palmer, Jones, Hennesy, Unze, & Pick, 1989; Tanaka & Taylor, 1991). As described later, experts can classify and reason about objects in ways that novices do not (e.g., Medin, Lynch, & Coley, 1997) and have advantages in terms of both the amount of conceptual information stored in semantic memory and the manner in which this information is organized (Chi et al., 1988; Gobbo & Chi, 1986). Furthermore different kinds of expertise can be associated with different kinds of interactions with object categories, and these inter-expert variations may subsequently lead to variations in conceptual structure (Medin et al., 1997). For example, birders pride themselves on the diversity of specimens that can be successfully identified, and rarely do such experts constrain their interest to a single specific subcategory. In contrast, dog breeders tend to develop expertise on specific kinds of dogs, which culminates in different patterns of knowledge effects from those described for bird experts (Diamond & Carey, 1986; Tanaka & Taylor, 1991).

### Names for Things

Although taxonomies may vary in the number of levels of inclusiveness they contain, there is always a *basic* level somewhere near the middle (Neisser, 1987). In contrast to anthropologists, psychologists generally have considered only three major levels of categorization in their research. The *superordinate* is the most inclusive level (e.g., vehicle, animal) and the *subordinate* is the least inclusive level (e.g., sedan, Chihuahua). The basic level (e.g., car, dog) is most informative in terms of category members sharing a large quantity of information. It is cognitively privileged, in that processing advantages are evident across a range of tasks, including object naming, identification based on shape, attribute listing, and verification of category labels as correct or incorrect (Rosch et al., 1976). For practical purposes, the cognitive anthropologists' "folk generic" level and the psychologists' basic level refer to the same level of inclusiveness.

The effect of knowledge on mental categories was initially introduced by Rosch et al. (1976) through an anecdote involving a former airplane mechanic. Whereas *airplane* appeared to be a basic level kind for other participants, the airplane mechanic's mental categories appeared different. He was able to list far more attributes for various kinds of airplanes, and his motor programs for subordinates of the airplane category were geared specifically toward the attributes of the engines of those kinds of airplanes. Rosch et al. (1976) suggested that "categories such as airplanes can have differing sets of correlational structures, depending upon the degree of knowledge of the perceiver" (p. 430).

Experts can detect differences among object categories that nonexperts fail to differentiate, as features that differentiate among coordinate categories increase in salience through the perceptual tuning that arises through repeated exposure (Johnson & Mervis, 1998; Proctor & Dutta, 1995). Experts acquire a wealth of knowledge pertaining to subordinate (e.g., sparrow) and even sub-subordinate (e.g., chipping sparrow) level kinds (Johnson & Mervis, 1997; Tanaka & Taylor, 1991). Within some domains of expertise, subordinate and sub-subordinate levels may eventually function as basic, in that they come to acquire the same cognitive processing advantages with regard to naming and speed of identification. Dougherty (1978) points out that discrepancies between the findings of Berlin et al. (1973) and Rosch et al. (1976) with respect to the naming of plants could well be attributed to the effects of knowledge: California residents simply know less about the attributes that are indicative of subordinate-level plant categories than Tzeltal informants. Californians tend to name and to group objects at a more general level (*tree*) rather than at the more specific levels preferred by the Tzeltal.

In a study of the cognitive processes involved in the identification of gulls, Hunn (1975) evoked perceptual processes as the chief difference between novice and expert birders. From a series of interviews with six experts conducted in part during field identifications, Hunn concluded that different identification routines were used by novices and experts on gulls. Novices typically employed a "generic" identification procedure in which the perceptual features of gulls were processed at a glance as a whole or "gestalt." Experts, however, used a "specific" identification procedure that involved attention to features that were less salient and less easily visible, but that enabled them to rapidly identify species of gulls. Hunn's findings are in keeping with the premise that expertise involves a shift in the level of categorization that functions as basic. He notes:

> We have seen that as birdwatchers gain experience they gradually "push" the level of generic identification downwards so that more terminal taxa are recognizable as generics. Those whose livelihood depends on their ability to recognize natural "species" push the level of generic identification down to where most terminal taxa are immediately and automatically recognized. The few taxa which resist this process, or taxa which differ in but a single feature from each other, are the most likely candidates for specific names. (p. 63)

A hallmark of expertise effects on labeling, particularly in young children, is that "the rich get richer" as knowledge accrues. Because experts know more names for things to begin with, they can more readily encode related information and more easily assimilate new instances into existing mental categories. In a microgenetic analysis of very young children's acquisition of expertise on shorebirds, Johnson and Mervis (1994) found that possessing relevant background knowledge pertaining to birds (and, separately, possessing higher levels of verbal ability) had a facilitative effect on the acquisition of domain-specific knowledge related to shorebirds. Knowing more names for things, particularly at the subordinate level, provides a rich foundation for reasoning, generalization, and analogical problem solving.

## Classification

In a commentary on how expertise affects categories, Honeck, Firment, and Case (1987) argued that experts and novices differ principally in the abstractness of their categories. While novices are bound to perceptible or literal features, experts are freed to go beyond this information and base their categories on more abstract features. Experts may recognize more potential bases for similarity relations among kinds as a result of their enriched conceptual knowledge of properties, functions, and themes related to familiar objects. In a representative study, Boster and Johnson (1989) contrasted expert fisherman with novices in a task that involved unconstrained similarity judgments generated in reference to labeled line drawings of fish. Experts were recreational sport fisherman recruited from the southeast United States, and novices were undergraduate students. After arranging the 43 target fish species into piles according to "which they believed were similar to one another," participants were asked to describe their reasons for forming the groups that they did. Data were aggregated across informants, and similarity judgments were compared to actual morphological similarity, estimated by calculating taxonomic distances (Boster et al., 1986) between pairs of species that reflected the number of nodes that one must ascend along the scientific taxonomic tree in order to reach a node that includes both species in the pair. Because closely related species are highly morphologically similar, this measure serves as a useful proxy of similarities in form across species.

Boster et al. reported that novices' judgments of similarity were highly aligned with scientific taxonomy (this contrasts somewhat with the pattern of results reported by Bailenson et al., 2002, for novices' classification of passerine birds). This pattern presumably emerged because novices' mental categories were relatively impoverished and thus they relied heavily on visible, morphological characteristics depicted in the line drawings. The piles of experts and novices differed most significantly when morphological criteria for sorting conflicted directly with functional criteria for sorting. Experts routinely grouped species that were similar in terms of their behavior. Finally experts exhibited far more variability in their groupings of fish than novices did, presumably because different experts used functional versus morphological information to different degrees than did novices, who are largely ignorant of functional characteristics.

## Determination of Typicality

It has been well established that everyday mental categories possess a graded structure (Mervis & Rosch, 1981; Rosch, 1978). Some exemplars of categories are recognized to be more typical or representative than others, and these "prototypes" tend to share higher proportions of features in common with each other. Even infants under a year of age are capable of acquiring an internal graded representation based on exposure to varied instances from within the same category (Quinn, 1987; Younger, 1990). If experts' awareness of features indicative of particular specific categories is heightened, typicality gradients associated with more specific categories may come to resemble novice gradients for more general categories. For example, novices might have difficulty distinguishing different Chihuahuas from each other and they may be hopelessly unable to recognize a prototypical Chihuahua. Expert judges of Chihuahuas, on the other hand, distinguish them readily and can evaluate instances against idealized prototypes by focusing on relatively subtle attributes such as ear shape and position, the arch of a tail, and the balance of features in proportion to the dog's size.

Determinations of typicality are informed by multiple sources of information (Barsalou, 1985; Hampton, 1998; Malt & Smith, 1982), including the goals and ideals associated with utilitarian categories described in the previous section (Lynch, Coley, & Medin, 2000). Johnson (2001) set out to contrast these patterns of influence in a study of predictors of typicality ratings for US novices, intermediate experts, and advanced experts. Both North American and Australian passerine exemplars were included to disentangle effects of instantiation frequency (the frequency with which instances are represented in the environment; Barsalou, 1985, 1987), subjective impressions of familiarity, and central tendency on determinations of typicality. Among experts, the degree to which a passerine was judged to be a good example was predicted by the extent to which it was considered familiar. While instantiation frequency and subjective impressions of familiarity were correlated, instantiation frequency did not contribute unique variance above and beyond the effects of subjective familiarity. Central tendency was significantly correlated with typicality only when categories were moderately heterogeneous and when knowledge was relatively low.

## Patterns of Reasoning and the Influence of Goals and Ideals

People use different cognitive strategies to reason about mental categories for which they possess expertise in contrast to those for which they do not. Murphy (2010, p. 25) maintains that a mental category can "serve as a nexus for reasoning and learning." The concepts that we possess and the theoretical frameworks within which they are embedded provide a platform for subsequent learning and for everyday reasoning.

Expertise is particularly prone to influence the contexts in which experts interact with objects, which affect subsequent decisions about intradomain relations, "best examples," and patterns of reasoning. Dougherty and Keller (1982) were among the first to apply the notion of goal-directed theories to domains of expertise. They maintained that for goal-oriented domains, knowledge is organized in response to particular tasks, rather than taxonomically. For the domain of blacksmithing, such traditional classification tasks as asking, "Which two go together?" in reference to a group of three tools, or sorting tools into natural groups made no sense to skilled blacksmiths. Rather, blacksmiths organized their solutions to categorization requests around particular tasks that are relevant to doing the work of a blacksmith. Dougherty and Keller propose that such domains be considered "taskonomies," which are characterized by *flexibility* in categorization.

This theme is echoed in more recent work by Medin and colleagues. In a seminal contrast of three types of tree experts—scientists, landscaper workers, and parks maintenance personnel—Medin et al. (1997) reported some similarities across groups in terms of the classification of a subset of trees, and the fact that genus-level categories were privileged for induction. However, clear differences emerged in terms of the structure of individuals' taxonomies and their explanations concerning how they formed their groupings. Parks maintenance workers relied on morphological characteristics of trees, yielding taxonomies that were broad but shallow. Parks maintenance staff formed many initial groupings of trees (justified on the basis of both morphological and utilitarian features), but these groupings were not extensively subdivided into smaller categories or collapsed into higher order groupings. Utilitarian categories were aligned with their work (e.g., weed trees). Scientists' taxonomies were deep and broad, aligning well with classical scientific taxonomy. Finally, landscapers' taxonomies were narrow, yet deep—and only weakly correlated with scientific relations. Landscapers preferred utilitarian categories relevant to the field of landscaping (e.g., ornamental trees, street trees) and initially formed relatively few groups. However, these were subdivided into many lower order groupings based on a wide variety of functional bases (e.g., large native-specimen trees). As was the case for the effects of culture, people's patterns of classification diverge most sharply from formal scientific relations when alternative bases for categorization are present that align with the unique ways that different types of experts engage with objects.

### Perceptual Expertise

Most of the literature reviewed thus far on culture and expertise has addressed the issue of perception from the standpoint that universality in patterns of categorization and reasoning must be attributable to "natural" structure available in the world. Relatively few connections have been made with the field of perceptual expertise, which has been dominated by considerations of the neural mechanisms that support visual object perception. While cognitive psychologists and anthropologists request that participants or informants label, sort, rate, generalize properties, and even sometimes justify or explain their responses, researchers studying perceptual expertise focus almost exclusively on the visual perception processes evidenced by experts (either "natural" experts recruited based on their possession of high levels of knowledge or "cultivated" experts who are created following extensive practice with visual stimuli). Many examinations of perceptual expertise have been theoretically motivated by the issue of modularity and questions concerning whether the mechanisms underlying face recognition are domain specific or extendable to other domains (Bukach, Gauthier, & Tarr, 2006). The key questions are grounded in which neural mechanisms support perceptual "tuning" (Gauthier, Tarr, & Bub, 2010). Training studies also permit investigations of the nature of cortical plasticity in the mature adult brain.

As mentioned at the outset of this chapter, perceptual learning involves discrimination of low-level perceptible properties (that can be seen, heard, touched, tasted, or smelled) as a function of everyday, repeated exposure (Ahissar, & Hochstein, 1997; Gibson, 1969). The process of perceptual learning is initiated relatively soon after exposure, generally occurs outside the realm of conscious awareness, and does not typically support much transfer of learning to novel stimuli. For example, children learn to visually discriminate letters of the alphabet as they encounter words in books, on signs, and in various media. Some letters are discriminated relatively early because of their distinctiveness (x, o), whereas others take longer because they share more features in common with other letters (Gibson, 1969). However, improvements in letter differentiation as a function of perceptual learning do not transfer to other symbols, such as Chinese characters.

The term "perceptual expertise" is typically used to refer to the extreme consequences of domain-specific perceptual learning. Perceptual expertise reflects heightened capacity for perceptual discrimination and generally depends on the accumulation of real-world experience through practice that can extend across a decade or more (Diamond & Carey, 1986)—or on massed practice that is supported through intense training. The rudiments of perceptual expertise are present in infancy. Quinn and Tanaka (2007) demonstrated that by 6 to 7 months, infants can be induced to form subordinate-level category representations (e.g., beagle) after engaging in a subordinate formation task involving an initial subordinate-level category that was drawn from the same basic-level category (e.g., St. Bernard) but not from a different basic-level category (e.g., Siamese cat). Although this is an important start, the "downward shift" in the basic level that is the hallmark of perceptual expertise depends on far higher concentrations of exposure—and repeated engagement in the identification of objects at the subordinate level appears critically important (Scott, Tanaka, Sheinberg, & Curran, 2008).

It has long been recognized that humans are uniquely equipped to recognize faces holistically. Neuroimaging data have identified the fusiform face area (FFA) within the fusiform gyrus on the underside of the temporal lobe as the region that responds specifically to faces, and the region that is typically damaged in patients with prosopagnosia (Kanwisher, McDermott, & Chun, 1997). Bornstein (1963) initially reported on a case of a patient with prosopagnosia who had been an avid birdwatcher—yet who became unable to identify either birds or faces. In an elegant series of studies, Gauthier and colleagues demonstrated that acquired expertise on artificial objects (Greebles) configured similarly to faces resulted in higher levels of activation to the FFA (Gauthier & Tarr, 1997; Gauthier, Tarr, Anderson, Skudlarski, & Gore, 1999), and that similar patterns of activation were evident when experts on birds or cars engaged in a matching task involving stimuli from the domain of expertise (Gauthier, Skudlarski, Gore, & Anderson, 2000). Furthermore, experts are able to "bootstrap" new category learning onto previously learned categories, as exemplified by Greeble experts learning the names of newly encountered Greebles in fewer trials than novices. Clearly the perceptual aspects of some forms of expertise manifested by individuals across and within cultures have neurophysiological origins in the FFA region.

Perceptual expertise has been shown to generalize, or transfer to new contexts. At the behavioral level, Johnson and Mervis (1998) reported that advanced experts on passerine birds or tropical fish were more apt to solve triads involving unfamiliar exemplars from the contrasting domain on the basis of subtle perceptual features that were correlated with taxonomic membership. A similar study involving both children and adults matched on levels of dinosaur expertise revealed that adults who were highly knowledgeable about dinosaurs—but not children—demonstrated similarly accurate patterns of category extensions with both dinosaurs and with unfamiliar examples of shorebirds, suggesting that knowledge transfer was mediated by age-related strategies (Johnson & Eilers, 1998). This generalizeability appears to be limited to "near transfer" effects involving stimuli from related domains that possess similar structure (as opposed to "far transfer" effects that would extend even to the categorization of stimuli from different domains such as cars or tools). Similarly, Tanaka, Curran, and Sheinberg (2005) trained participants to classify wading birds and owls at either the basic or the subordinate levels and found that subordinate-level categorization (but not categorization at more general levels) improved participants' discrimination of trained instances. Furthermore, this training effect generalized to improve discrimination of novel species from the same domain (i.e., participants who learned to categorize green herons, limpkins, and American bitterns at the subordinate level were better able to discriminate among novel species of wading birds). Tanaka et al. suggest that subordinate-level training prompted a perceptual strategy that could be deployed with novel category instances.

At the neural level, electrophysiological studies have linked perceptual expertise to the magnitude of early negative event-related potential (ERP) components known as the N170 and the N250. Tanaka and colleagues initially demonstrated that the N170 was larger when experts categorized objects from the domain of expertise (either dogs or birds), and that the effect was similar in timing and in scalp distribution to that reported for face perception (Curran, Tanaka, & Weiskopf, 2002; Tanaka & Curran, 2001). Scott, Tanaka, Sheinberg, and Curran (2006) replicated the near transfer effects reported by Tanaka et al. (2005) in an ERP study, reporting that both the N170 and the N250 components were correlated with the development of perceptual expertise. While the N170 appeared specific to the encoding of shape information, the N250 appeared specific to the processing of more detailed perceptual features required for subordinate-level categorization. More recently, Scott, Tanaka, Sheinberg, and Curran (2008) extended these findings in a training study involving cars (rather than the typical natural kind domains that dominate the perceptual expertise literature). In examining the ERPs and classification accuracy of participants trained to classify cars at either the basic or subordinate level, Scott et al. found that the N250 was enhanced only in relation to subordinate-level training. Furthermore,

expert-like categorization (and changes in the N250 response) persisted for at least a week following training. Long-term learning mechanisms reflected by enhanced N250 responses appear to be a hallmark of perceptual expertise in adults.

## Summary

The world is replete with objects, events, people, and qualities that can be discriminated. Yet people avoid becoming "slaves to the particular" through their capacity for categorization (Bruner, Goodnow, & Austin, 1956). Mental categories contain a history of the perceiver's experiences in the world and enable people to identify and to make inferences about instances that they have never before encountered. Both culture and expertise foster systematic variations in the structure and function of mental categories, and both exert their effects through shaping individuals' theories, goals, and ideals related to particular domains, as well as through an accretion of perceptual experiences that incrementally build over time to fundamentally change perception and to create systematic deviations in the way that mental categories are used during classification, identification, and reasoning.

## Future Directions

Examination of interactions among culture, expertise, and categorization across the past several decades has yielded a rich literature informed by both interdisciplinary and multidisciplinary research engaged in by anthropologists, cognitive psychologists, and cognitive neuroscientists. There is recognition among most cognitive scientists that the majority of research published on categorization, more generally, is based heavily on data gathered from a very small minority group—college undergraduates (though this is not always conveyed in textbooks). Cross-cultural psychology has evolved from simple comparisons of task performance across individuals from different geographic regions to more sophisticated analyses of how interactions among people from the same community lead to networks of shared understanding that give rise to predictable patterns of behavior. Yet there are still many intriguing sets of questions to address.

1. *What are the social and cognitive mechanisms of cultural transmission of knowledge?* Cognitive neuroscience has begun to clarify the neural mechanisms that support perceptual expertise, but little study has been directed toward the social channels and cognitive mechanisms that support

the cultural transfer of knowledge. Children must acquire "habits of mind" through interactions with parents, siblings, peers, and teachers that support knowledge construction. While bases for categorization are readily abstracted through engagement with objects and learning names for things, cultural variations in the degree to which ecological relations are emphasized in reasoning contexts suggest that goal orientations and "utilitarian categories" are socially learned and have a significant impact on categorization. Little is known concerning how such information is passed on to children, and whether similar social channels support the acculturation of adults moving to different regions of the world—or the education of apprentices and protégés acquiring expertise in formal or informal learning environments. Once understood, such findings have potential for translation to educational interventions that can increase the efficiency of learning across a range of contexts.

2. *Expanding the focus to neglected types of categories and neglected populations.* A wealth of knowledge has been gleaned through systematic investigations of how individuals from around the world acquire and use mental categories that correspond to objects, and the vast majority of this work has been directed at a very specific subset of objects: those corresponding to biological kinds that comprise the natural world. Yet clearly such kinds represent just a slim proportion of those object categories that humans acquire; we know very little about representations of artifacts and cultural tools such as money (Lotto, Rubaltelli, Rumiati, & Savadori, 2006) or of representations corresponding to other sensory modalities (e.g., wine expertise; Solomon, 1997; learning to read Braille or to identify songbirds by ear) or dynamic categories pertaining to events that are aligned with expertise on domains as diverse as athletics, poetry, and surgery.

Although cultural anthropology has helped to diversify the pool of participants whose category representations are sampled and analyzed, comparative studies of development in diverse populations of children within the same culture are needed (Coley, 2000). In the United States, the field of conceptual development has been derived almost exclusively from studies involving middle- to upper-class children from communities adjacent to research universities, whose parents provide consent to participate in cognitive developmental research. Very little is known concerning the types of expertise acquired by children from families that are socioeconomically vulnerable, and how such knowledge is constructed through interactions with family members, peers, and teachers.

3. *Reuniting perception with concepts throughout the continuum of expertise.* Though compelling arguments have been made for the more explicit integration of conception and perception (e.g., Goldstone, 2010; Goldstone & Barsalou, 1998; Smith & Heise, 1992), the literatures on perceptual expertise and the cognitive consequences of possessing enriched domain-specific knowledge (whether acquired via culture or through individual interests) have remained quite separate. It is critical that we begin to integrate findings on perceptual aspects of expertise with those that are more conceptual. Similarly, we must examine the gap between infancy and the preschool period in terms of children's acquisition of subordinate-level categories. While infants can acquire subordinate categories by 6 or 7 months (Quinn & Tanaka, 2007), young children typically do not learn subordinate category labels until after age 3 years (Johnson, Scott, & Mervis, 1997), preferring instead to name (and to group) objects at the basic level. Furthermore, the extensions of children's subordinate categories may differ from those of adults. Mervis (1984, 1987) points out that differences between the categories of children and adults, and between the categories of novices and experts, are to be expected. Although the principles that lead to the acquisition of mental categories are expected to be universal, categories formed on the basis of these principles may vary as a function of the particular attributes to which groups of individuals attend.

The degree to which perception and conception are influenced by expertise (and ultimately integrated) might also vary as a function of the domain that the individual is interested in. While many experts on object domains cultivate knowledge reflecting a breadth of domain-specific categories, other types of experts may spend inordinate amounts of time interacting with instances that are highly similar. Individuals who raise (or judge) specific breeds of dogs can immediately recognize candidates for "best of breed" among golden retrievers based on dynamic properties such as the animal's gait, and subtle perceptual properties such as head shape and hock joint angulation. Variations in these experiences may yield different types of experts who represent different sets of features (and theories pertaining to feature correlations) for the same domain-specific categories.

4. *Delineating processes that support the acquisition and use of expert knowledge at varying levels of proficiency and across developmental time.* For reasons both theoretical and pragmatic, researchers examining variations in mental categories as a function of either shared cultural knowledge or idiosyncratically acquired expertise typically recruit participants representing extreme points along the continuum of knowledge. Anthropologists contrast groups of informants representing cultures that diverge along a number of salient dimensions, and cognitive psychologists contrast experts with individuals who possess very low levels of knowledge (and presumably little interest) in the domain in question (e.g., Boster & Johnson, 1989; Chi, Glaser, & Rees,1982; Chi, Hutchinson, & Robin, 1989). Some have used within-subject designs that contrast experts' performance across familiar and less familiar domains (Johnson & Mervis, 1997, 1998; Tanaka & Curran, 2001; Tanaka & Taylor, 1991). Yet to truly understand mechanisms that support changes in mental categories throughout the continuum of knowledge acquisition, one must focus as well on intermediate levels of knowledge—and ultimately conduct careful microgenetic analyses focused on the process of knowledge construction.

Attempting to understand interactions among culture, expertise, and mental categories is challenging, even when limiting analyses to adult informants. However, applying a developmental framework to such analyses provides unique opportunities for examining an array of intriguing questions concerning the extent to which content knowledge, framework theories, and maturation of basic processes (e.g., executive function) affect the process of expertise acquisition and potentially limit aspects of expert performance. Some children develop relatively narrow interests that culminate in expertise (Alexander, Johnson, & Leibham, 2008; DeLoache, Simcock, & Macari, 2007; Johnson, Alexander, Spencer, Leibham, & Neitzel, 2004). One can begin to disentangle effects of maturation, knowledge acquisition, and shared culture by comparing groups of children and adults with similar levels of domain-specific knowledge who reside in communities that share different types of cultural knowledge (e.g., Coley, 2000; Ross et al., 2003). When children and adults with comparable levels of

domain-specific knowledge and experience are contrasted (e.g., Chi, 1978; Johnson & Eilers, 1998; Johnson, Scott, & Mervis, 2004), the role of knowledge acquisition in shaping developmental changes over time becomes more apparent. Future studies should involve adults to determine the developmental "end state" related to cultural and expertise effects on mental categories. Yet studies of children are critical for elucidating whether there are variations in the underlying mechanisms supporting brain plasticity associated with acquiring expertise at varying points in the life span.

## Note

1. While it is generally the case that culturally significant categories tend to be referred to with highly specific nouns, it should be noted that one frequently cited example of this phenomenon is based on spotty scholarship. Martin (1986) provided compelling evidence that the myriad "words for snow" reportedly used by the Inuit people is largely unfounded. Reports have been distorted by misinterpretations of the data and perpetuated through careless scholarship.

## References

Ahissar, M., & Hochstein, S. (1997). Task difficulty and the specificity of perceptual learning. *Nature, 387,* 401–406

Alexander, J. M., Johnson, K. E., & Leibham, M. E. (2008). The development of conceptual interests in young children. *Cognitive Development, 23,* 324–334.

Atran, S. (1999). Itzaj Maya folkbiological taxonomy: Cognitive universals and cultural particulars. In D. L. Medin & S. Atran (Eds.), *Folkbiology* (pp. 119–203). Cambridge, MA: MIT Press.

Atran, S. (2002). Modular and cultural factors in biological understanding: an experimental approach to the cognitive basis of science. In P. Carruthers , S. P. Stich, & M. Siegal (Eds.), *The cognitive basis of science* (pp. 41–72). Cambridge, England: Cambridge University Press.

Atran, S., Medin, D., & Ross, N. (2005). The cultural mind: Environmental decision making and cultural modeling within and across populations. *Psychological Review, 112*(4), 744–776.

Bailenson, J. N., Shum, M. S., Atran, S., Medin, D. L., & Coley, J. D. (2002). A bird's eye view: Biological categorization and reasoning within and across cultures. *Cognition, 84,* 1–53.

Barsalou, L.W. (1985). Ideals, central tendency, and frequency of instantiation as determinants of graded structure in categories. *Journal of Experimental Psychology: Learning, Memory, and Cognition, 11,* 629–654.

Barsalou, L.W. (1987). The instability of graded structure: Implications for the nature of concepts. In U. Neisser (Ed.), *Concepts and conceptual development: Ecological and intellectual factors in categorization* (pp. 101–140). Cambridge, England: Cambridge University Press.

Barth, F. (2002). An anthropology of knowledge. *Current Anthropology, 43,* 1–18.

Berlin, B. (1972). Speculations on the growth of ethnobotanical nomenclature. *Language in Society, 1,* 51–86.

Berlin, B. (1978). Ethnobiological classification. In E. Rosch & B. B. Lloyd (Eds.), *Cognition and categorization* (pp. 9–26). Hillsdale, NJ: Erlbaum.

Berlin, B. (1992). *Ethnobiological classification: Principles of categorization of plants and animals in traditional societies.* Princeton, NJ: Princeton University Press.

Berlin, B., Breedlove, D. E., & Raven, P. H. (1973). General principles of classification and nomenclature in folk biology. *American Anthropologist, 75,* 214–242.

Berlin, B., Breedlove, D. E., & Raven, P. H. (1974). *Principles of plant classification: An introduction to the botanical ethnography of a Mayan-speaking community of highland Chiapis.* New York: Academic Press.

Biederman, I., & Shiffrar, M. M. (1987). Sexing day-old chicks: A case study and expert systems analysis of a difficult perceptual learning task. *Journal of Experimental Psychology: Learning, Memory, and Cognition, 13,* 640–645.

Bornstein, B. (1963). Prosopagnosia. In L. Halpern (Ed.), *Problems in dynamic neurology* (pp. 283–318). Jerusalem: Hadassah Medical School.

Boster, J. S. (1986). Exchange of varieties and information between Aguaruna manioc cultivators. *American Anthropologist, 88,* 428–436.

Boster, J. S., Berlin, B., & O' Neill, J. (1986). The correspondence of Jivaroan to scientific ornithology. *American Anthropologist, 88,* 569–583.

Boster, J. S., & Johnson, J. C. (1989). Form or function: A comparison of expert and novice judgments of similarity among fish. *American Anthropologist, 91,* 866–889.

Bruner, J. S., Goodnow, J. J., & Austin, G. A. (1956). *A study of thinking.* New Brunswick, NJ: Wiley.

Bukach, C. M., Gauthier, I., & Tarr, M. J. (2006). Beyond faces and modularity: The power of an expertise framework. *Trends in Cognitive Sciences, 10,* 159–166.

Bulmer, R. N. H. (1967). Why is the cassowary not a bird? A problem of zoological taxonomy among the Karam of the New Guinea highlands. *Man, 2,* 1–25.

Carey, S. (1985). *Conceptual change in childhood.* Cambridge, MA: MIT Press.

Chi, M. T. H. (1978). Knowledge structure and memory development. In R. Siegler (Ed.), *Children's thinking: What develops?* (pp. 73–96). Hillsdale, NJ: Erlbaum.

Chi, M. T. H., Glaser, R., & Farr, M. J. (1988). *The nature of expertise.* Hillsdale, NJ: Erlbaum.

Chi, M. T. H., Glaser, R., & Rees, E. (1982). Expertise in problem solving. In R. Sternberg (Ed.), *Advances in the psychology of human intelligence* (Vol. 1, pp. 7–75). Hillsdale, NJ: Erlbaum.

Chi, M. T. H., Hutchinson, J. E., & Robin, A. F. (1989). How inferences about novel domain-related concepts can be constrained by structured knowledge. *Merrill-Palmer Quarterly, 35,* 27–62.

Coley, J. D. (2000). On the importance of comparative research: The case of folkbiology. *Child Development, 71,* 82–90.

Coley, J. D., Shafto, P., Stephanova, O., & Baraff, E. (2005). Knowledge and category-based induction. In W. Ahn , R. L. Goldson , B. C. Love, A. B. Markman (Eds.), *Categorization inside andoutside the laboratory: Essays in honor of Douglas L. Medin. APA Decade of behavior series* (pp. 69–85). Washington, DC: American Psychological Association.

Curran, T., Tanaka, J. W., & Weiskopf, D. (2002). An electrophysiological comparison of visual categorization and recognition memory. *Cognitive, Affective, and Behavioral Neuroscience, 2,* 1–18.

DeLoache, J. S., Simcock, G., & Macari, S. (2007). Planes, trains, automobiles—and tea sets: Extremely intense interests in very young children. *Developmental Psychology, 43,* 1579–1586.

Diamond, J. (1966). Zoological classification system of a primitive people. *Science, 151,* 1102–1104.

Diamond, R., & Carey, S. (1986). Why faces are and are not special: An effect of expertise. *Journal of Experimental Psychology: General, 115,* 107–117.

Dougherty, J. W. D. (1978). Salience and relativity in classification. American Ethnologist, 5, 66–80.

Dougherty, J. W. D., & Keller, C. M. (1982). Taskonomy: A practical approach to knowledge structures. *American Ethnologist, 9,* 763–774.

Ericsson, K. A., & Smith, J. (1991). Prospects and limits of the empirical study of expertise: An introduction. In K. A. Ericsson & J. Smith (Eds.), *Toward a general theory of expertise: Prospects and limits* (pp. 1–38). New York: Cambridge University Press.

Ericsson, K. A., Krampe, R. T., & Tesch-Römer, C. (1993). The role of deliberate practice in the acquisition of expert performance. *Psychological Review, 100*(3), 363–406.

Gauthier, I., Skudlarski, P., Gore, J. C., & Anderson, A. W. (2000). Expertise for cars and birds recruits brain areas involved in face recognition. *Nature Neuroscience, 3*(2), 191–197.

Gauthier, I., & Tarr, M. J. (1997). Becoming a "greeble" expert: Exploring mechanisms for face recognition. *Vision Research, 37,* 1673–1682.

Gauthier, I., Tarr, M. J., & Bub, D. (2010). *Perceptual expertise: Bridging brain and behavior.* New York: Oxford University Press.

Gauthier, I., Tarr, M. J., Anderson, A. W., Skudlarski, P., & Gore, J. C. (1999). Activation of the middle fusiform "face area" increases with expertise recognizing novel objects. *Nature Neuroscience, 2*(6), 568–573.

Gibson, E. J. (1969). *Principles of perceptual learning and development.* Englewood Cliffs, NJ: Prentice Hall.

Gibson, E. J. (1991). *An odyssey in learning and perception.* Cambridge, MA: MIT Press.

Glaser, R. (1987). Thoughts on expertise. In C. Schooler & K. W. Schaie (Eds.), *Cognitive functioning and social structure over the life course* (pp. 81–94). Norwood, NJ: Ablex.

Gobbo, C., & Chi, M. (1986). How knowledge is structured and used by expert and novice children. *Cognitive Development, 1,* 221–237.

Goldstone, R. L. (2010). Forward. In I. Gauthier , M. J. Tarr, & D. Bubb (Eds.), *Perceptual expertise: Bridging brain and behavior* (pp. v-x). Oxford, England: Oxford University Press.

Goldstone, R. L., & Barsalou, L. W. (1998). Reuniting perception and conception. *Cognition, 65,* 231–262.

Goldstone, R. L., Gerganov, A., Landy, D., & Roberts, M. E. (2008). Learning to see and conceive. In L. Tommasi , M. Peterson, & L. Nadel (Eds.), *The new cognitive sciences* (pp. 163–188). Cambridge, MA: MIT Press.

Hampton, J. (1998). Similarity-based categorization and fuzziness of natural categories. In S. A. Sloman & L. J. Rips

(Eds.), *Similarity and symbols in human thinking* (pp. 51–79). Cambridge, MA: MIT Press.

Honeck, R. P., Firment, M., & Case, T. J. S. (1987). Expertise and categorization. *Journal of the Psychonomic Society, 25,* 431–434.

Hong, Y. (2009). A dynamic constructivist approach to culture: Moving from describing culture to explaining culture. In R. S. Wyer , C. Chiu, & Y. Hong (Eds.), *Understanding culture: Theory, research, and application* (pp. 3–23). New York: Psychology Press.

Hull, D. (1992). Biological species: An inductivist's nightmare. In M. Douglas & D. Hull (Eds.), *How classification works: Nelson Goodman among the social sciences* (pp. 42–68). Edinburgh, Scotland: Edinburgh University Press.

Hunn, E. (1975). *Cognitive processes in folk ornithology: The identification of gulls. Working Paper No. 42: Language Behavior Research Laboratory,* University of California, Berkeley.

Johnson, K. E. (2001). Determinants of typicality throughout the continuum of expertise. *Memory and Cognition, 29,* 1036–1050.

Johnson, K. E., Alexander, J. M., Spencer, S., Leibham, M. E., & Neitzel, C. (2004). Factors associated with the early emergence of intense interests within conceptual domains. *Cognitive Development, 19,* 325–343.

Johnson, K. E., & Eilers, A. T. (1998). Effects of knowledge and development on the extension and evolution of subordinate categories. *Cognitive Development, 13,* 515–545.

Johnson, K. E., & Mervis, C. B. (1994) Microgenetic analysis of first steps in the acquisition of expertise on shorebirds. *Developmental Psychology, 30,* 418–435.

Johnson, K. E., & Mervis, C. B. (1997). Effects of varying levels of expertise on the basic level of categorization. *Journal of Experimental Psychology: General, 126,* 248–277.

Johnson, K. E., & Mervis, C. B. (1998). Impact of intuitive theories on feature recruitment throughout the continuum of expertise. *Memory and Cognition, 26,* 382–401.

Johnson, K. E., Mervis, C. B., & Boster, J. S. (1992). Developmental changes in the structure of the mammal domain. *Developmental Psychology, 28,* 74–83.

Johnson, K. E., Scott, P. D., & Mervis, C. B. (1997). The development of children's understanding of basic-subordinate inclusion relations. *Developmental Psychology, 33,* 745–763.

Johnson, K. E., Scott, P., & Mervis, C. B. (2004). What are theories for? Concept use throughout the continuum of expertise. *Journal of Experimental Child Psychology, 87,* 171–200.

Kanwisher, N., Mc Dermott, J., & Chun, M. M. (1997). The fusiform face area: A module in human extrastriate cortex specialized for face perception. *Journal of Neuroscience, 17,* 4302–4311.

Lazareva, O. F., & Wasserman, E. A. (2010). Category learning and concept learning in birds. In D. Mareschal , P. C. Quinn, & S. E. G. Lee (Eds.), *The making of human concepts* (pp. 151–172). New York: Oxford University Press.

Lopez, A., Atran, S., Coley, J. D., & Medin, D. L. (1997). The tree of life: Universal and cultural features of folkbiological taxonomies and inductions. *Cognitive Psychology, 32,* 251–295.

Lotto, L., Rubaltelli, E., Rumiati, R., & Savadori, L. (2006). Mental representation of money in experts and nonexperts after the introduction of the Euro. *European Psychologist, 11,* 277–288.

Lynch, J. E., Coley, J. D., & Medin, D. L. (2000). Tall is typical: Central tendency, ideal dimensions, and graded structure among tree experts and novices. *Memory and Cognition, 28,* 41–50.

Malt, B. C. (1995). Category coherence in cross-cultural perspective. *Cognitive Psychology, 29,* 85–148.

Malt, B. C., & Smith, E. E. (1982). The role of familiarity in determining typicality. *Memory and Cognition, 10,* 69–75.

Markman, A. B., Grimm, L. R., & Kim, K. (2009). Culture as a vehicle for studying individual differences. In R. S. Wyer , C. Chiu, & Y. Hong (Eds.), *Understanding culture: Theory, research, and application* (pp. 93–106). New York: Psychology Press.

Martin, L. (1986). Eskimo words for snow: A case study in the genesis and decay of an anthropological example. *American Anthropologist, 88,* 418–423.

Medin, D. L., Lynch, E. B., & Coley, J. D. (1997). Categorization and reasoning among tree experts: Do all roads lead to Rome? *Cognitive Psychology, 32,* 49–96.

Medin, D. L., Lynch, E. B., & Solomon, K. E. (2000). Are there kinds of concepts? *Annual Review of Psychology, 51,* 121–147.

Medin, D. L., Ross, N., Atran, S., Burnett, R., & Blok, S. (2002). Categorization and reasoning in relation to culture and expertise. *Psychology of Learning and Motivation, 41,* 1–41.

Mervis, C. B. (1984). Early lexical development: The contributions of mother and child. In C. Sophian (Ed.), *Origins of cognitive skills* (pp. 339–370). Hillsdale, NJ: Erlbaum.

Mervis, C. B. (1987). Child-basic object categories and early lexical development. In U. Neisser (Ed.), *Concepts and conceptual development: Ecological and intellectual factors in categorization* (pp. 201–233). New York: Cambridge University Press.

Mervis, C. B., & Rosch, E. (1981). Categorization of natural objects. *Annual Review of Psychology, 32,* 89–115.

Murphy, G. L. (2002). *The big book of concepts.* Cambridge, MA: MIT Press.

Murphy, G. L. (2010). What are categories and concepts? In D. Mareschal, P. C. Quinn, & S. E. G. Lea (Eds.), *The making of human concepts* (pp. 11–28). New York: Oxford University Press.

Murphy, G. L., & Medin, D. L. (1985). The role of theories in conceptual coherence, *Psychological Review, 92,* 289–316.

Neisser, U. (1987). From direct perception to conceptual structure. In U. Neisser (Ed.), *Concepts and conceptual development: Ecological and intellectual factors in categorization* (pp. 11–24). New York: Cambridge University Press.

Osherson, D. N., Smith, E. E., Wilkie, O., Lopez, A., & Shafir, E. (1990). Category-based induction. Psychological Review, 97, 185–200.

Palmer, C. F., Jones, R. K., Hennesy, B. L., Unze, M. G., & Pick, A. D. (1989). How is a trumpet known? The "basic object level" concept and perception of musical instruments. American Journal of Psychology, 102, 17–37.

Proctor, R. W., & Dutta, A. (1995). Sill acquisition and human performance. Thousand Oaks, CA: Sage.

Quinn, P. C. (1987). The categorical representation of visual pattern information by young infants. *Cognition, 27,* 145–179.

Quinn, P. C., & Tanaka, J. W. (2007). Early development of perceptual expertise: Within-basic-level categorization experience facilitates the formation of subordinate-level category representations in 6- to 7-month-old infants. *Memory and Cognition, 36,* 1422–1431.

Renninger, K. A. (1990). Children's play interests, representation, and activity. In R. Fivush & J. Hudson (Eds.), *Knowing and remembering in young children* (Vol. III, pp. 127–165). New York: Cambridge University Press.

Renninger, K. A. (1992). Individual interest and development: Implications for theory and practice. In K. Renninger, S. Hidi, & A. Krapp (Eds.), *The role of interest in learning and development* (pp. 361–395). Hillsdale, NJ: Erlbaum.

Romney, A. K., Bachelder, W. H., & Weller, S. C. (1987). Recent applications of cultural consensus theory. American Behavioral Sciences, 31, 129–141.

Romney, A. K., Weller, S. A., & Batchelder, W. H. (1986). Culture as consensus: A theory of culture and informant accuracy. American Anthropologist, 88, 313–338.

Rosch, E. (1978). Principles of categorization. In E. Rosch & B. B. Lloyd (Eds.), *Cognition and categorization* (pp. 27–48). Hillsdale, NJ: Erlbaum

Rosch, E., Mervis, C. B., Gray, W. D., Johnson, D., & Boyes-Braem, P. (1976). Basic objects in natural categories. *Cognitive Psychology, 8*, 382–439.

Ross, N., Medin, D., Coley, J. D., & Atran, S. (2003). Cultural and experiential differences in the development of folkbiological induction. *Cognitive Development, 18*, 25–47.

Ross, N., & Tidwell, M. (2010). Concepts and culture. In D. Mareschal , P. C. Quinn, & S. E. G. Lee (Eds). *The making of human concepts* (pp. 131–148). New York: Oxford University Press.

Schyns, P. G. (1997). Categories and percepts: A bi-directional framework for categorization. *Trends in Cognitive Sciences, 1*(5), 183–189.

Scott, L. S., Tanaka, J. W., Sheinberg, D. L., & Curran, T. (2006). A reevaluation of the electrophysiological correlates of expert object processing. *Journal of Cognitive Neuroscience, 18*, 1453–1465.

Scott, L. S., Tanaka, J. W., Sheinberg, D. L., & Curran, T. (2008). The role of category learning in the acquisition and retention of perceptual expertise: A behavioral and neurophysiological study. *Brain Research, 1210*, 204–215.

Sloutsky, V. (2010). From perceptual categories to concepts: What develops? *Cognitive Science, 34*, 1244–1286.

Smith, E. E., & Medin, D. L. (1981). *Categories and concepts*. Cambridge, MA: Harvard University Press.

Smith, L. B., & Heise, D. (1992). Perceptual similarity and conceptual structure. In B. Burns (Ed.), *Percepts, concepts, and categories: Representation and processing of information. Advances in psychology* (pp. 233–272). Mahwah, NJ: Elsevier.

Solomon, G. E. A. (1997). Conceptual change and wine expertise. *Journal of the Learning Sciences, 6*, 41–60.

Tanaka, J. W. & Curran, T. (2001). A neural basis for expert object recognition. *Psychological Science, 12*, 43–47.

Tanaka, J. W., Curran, T., & Sheinberg, D. L. (2005). The training and transfer of real-world perceptual expertise. *Psychological Science, 16*, 145–151.

Tanaka, J. W., & Taylor, M. (1991). Object categories and expertise: Is the basic level in the eye of the beholder? *Cognitive Psychology, 23*, 457–482.

Younger, B. A. (1990). Infants' detection of correlations among feature categories. *Child Development, 61*, 614–620.

Zentall, T. R., Wasserman, E. A., Lazareva, O. F., Thompson, R. K. R., & Ratterman, M. J. (2008). Concept learning in animals. *Comparative Cognition and Behavior Reviews, 3*, 13–45.

## Further Reading

Gauthier, I., Tarr, M. J., & Bub, D. (2010). *Perceptual expertise: Bridging brain and behavior*. New York: Oxford University Press.

Johnson, K., & Mervis, C. (1997). Effects of varying levels of expertise on the basic level of categorization. *Journal of Experimental Psychology: General, 126*, 248–277.

Malt, B. C. (1995). Category coherence in cross-cultural perspective. *Cognitive Psychology, 29*, 85–148.

Medin, D. L., & Atran, S. (1999). *Folkbiology*. Cambridge, MA: MIT Press.

Medin, D. L., Lynch, E., Coley, J. D., & Atran, S. (1997). Categorization and reasoning among tree experts: Do all roads lead to Rome? *Cognitive Psychology, 32*, 49–96.

Medin, D. L., Ross, N., Atran, S., Burnett, R., & Blok, S. (2002). Categorization and reasoning in relation to culture and expertise. In *The psychology of learning and motivation* (Vol. *41*, pp. 1–41). New York: Academic Press.

Tanaka, J. W., & Taylor, M. (1991). Object categories and expertise: Is the basic level in the eye of the beholder? *Cognitive Psychology, 23*, 457–482.

# CHAPTER
# 23

# Models of Categorization

Andy J. Wills

**Abstract**

This chapter reviews some of the main ways in which theories of categorization have been expressed in formal, mathematical terms. The focus of the models discussed is the categorization of abstract visual forms by adults in situations where prior knowledge is unlikely to contribute much to performance. Each of the main components of categorization models is discussed: input representations, attentional processes, intermediate representations (e.g., prototypes, exemplars), evidential mechanisms (e.g., similarity, rules), and decision mechanisms (e.g., the choice axiom; Luce, 1959). Models discussed include the Generalized Context Model (Nosofsky, 1986), ALCOVE (Kruschke, 1992), prototype models (e.g., Smith & Minda, 1998), clustering models (e.g., SUSTAIN; Love, Medin & Gureckis, 2004), and multiprocess models (e.g., COVIS; Ashby, Alfonso-Reese, Turken, & Waldron, 1998).

**Key Words:** categorization, models, formal, mathematical, connectionist, exemplar, prototype, GCM, ALCOVE, COVIS, SUSTAIN

Previous chapters in this volume outlined some of the phenomena and descriptive theories in the study of mental categories. The purpose of the current chapter is to describe some of the main ways in which theories of categorization have been expressed in formal, mathematical terms. Formal description of theories is important to the development of cognitive psychology as a science—it encourages theorists to be explicit in their assumptions and to describe their theories in a way that permits independent objective verification of the theory's predictions. Formal description also, in principle, permits the possibility of unambiguous rejection of a theory.

The theories described in this chapter focus on adults categorizing abstract visual forms in situations where prior knowledge of real-world categories is unlikely to contribute much to performance. The level of experimental control this permits is often assumed to assist the development of formal theory. Of course, the study of categorization is much broader than the study of the classification

of abstract forms, and this is reflected in the other chapters of Part IV.

Another way in which this chapter is narrower than the field it describes is that only models that might be loosely described as process models are discussed. Process models, at varying levels of abstraction, attempt to characterize the representations and information processing assumed to underlie categorization behavior. This tends to be done without much consideration of what adaptive purpose categorization might serve. A complementary approach is functional modeling, which considers the purposes categorization might serve, and then seeks to describe ways in which an optimal system (i.e., one with infinite time and resources) might best serve those purposes (Anderson, 1991; Pothos & Chater, 2002).

In this chapter, I discuss the components of formal process models of categorization. I do this in the order that information is assumed to pass through these components (at least in the first instance—models differ in the extent to which they assume

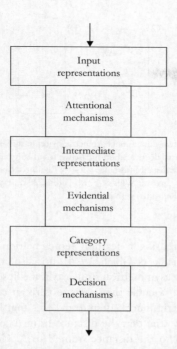

**Figure 23.1** Components of a model of categorization. Reprinted from "On the Adequacy of Current Empirical Evaluations of Formal Models of Categorization" by A. J. Wills & E. M. Pothos, 2012, Psychological Bulletin, 138, 104. Copyright 2012 by the American Psychological Association. Reprinted with permission.

information flows in both directions). This flow of information is represented schematically in Figure 23.1. Categorization is seldom modeled from a retinal starting point—most modelers assume some form of higher level input representation of the presented stimulus. The information from this input representation is sometimes modulated by attentional mechanisms, usually with attention directed to maximize categorization accuracy. The attentionally modulated information from the input representations is sometimes assumed to activate one or more intermediate representations, which are defined in the coordinates of the input representation system. Among the types of intermediate representations assumed are exemplars, prototypes, clusters, and distributed representations.

Information from the intermediate representations is assumed to activate one or more category representations. The process by which a category representation or representations are activated is described, for the purposes of this chapter, as an evidential mechanism. Examples of evidential mechanisms include associative links, decision bounds, and rules.

Sometimes an evidential mechanism will activate more than one category representation. In the laboratory, and in everyday life, there is often a requirement to produce a categorical response (i.e., "it's a dog," rather than "it's quite similar to a dog, a bit similar to a cat, and not very similar at all to a bagel"). Therefore, there is a need for a decision mechanism that is able to turn graded information into a categorical response. This categorical decision ultimately results in an observable action, although the stages of information processing beyond the categorical decision are seldom considered by models of categorization.

This introductory section comprised a brief overview of the representations and processes generally assumed in models of categorization. In the sections that follow, some of the main approaches to modeling each of these components are discussed.

## Input Representations

All formal models inevitably make assumptions about the nature of the information that is available to them at input. In the case of models of categorization, those assumptions generally take one of two forms: geometric models and featural models.

Featural (also known as elemental or microfeatural) models assume that any presented stimulus, even an apparently simple one such as a monochromatic light, is represented by a number of features. Two stimuli are similar to the extent that they have common features and the extent to which they do not have distinctive features. Some of the assumptions often found in a featural approach are that any given stimulus activates a relatively small subset of the features within the representational system (sparse coding; e.g., Granger, Ambros-Ingerson, & Lynch, 1989), that the subset of features activated by a given stimulus varies somewhat from one presentation to the next (stimulus sampling; Estes, 1950), and that features can have graded levels of activity (rather than simply being either "on" or "off"). Featural accounts have a long history (e.g., Estes, 1950), and they are also at the heart of some recent (Harris, 2006; McLaren & Mackintosh, 2000, 2002) and some very famous (McClelland & Rumelhart, 1985; Tversky, 1977) formal models.

Geometric models have a similarly impressive pedigree (Ashby & Gott, 1988; Nosofsky, 1986; Shepard, 1958) and, in recent times, have been more common in the modeling of adult categorization data than have featural models. This is in large part due to the success of two geometric models: the Generalized Context Model (Nosofsky, 1986) and General Recognition Theory (Ashby & Gott, 1988). Geometric models assume that any presented

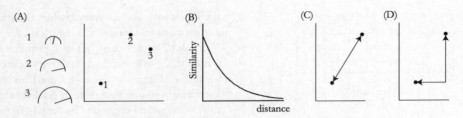

**Figure 23.2** (*A*) Representing the similarity structure of stimuli 1, 2, and 3 in a two-dimensional geometric space; in this example the dimensions of this space are readily interpretable as size and angle. (*B*) An exponential decay relationship between similarity and distance in psychological space. (*C*) Euclidean distance (distance$^2$ = x$^2$ + y$^2$). (*D*) City-block distance (distance = x + y). Reprinted from "On the Adequacy of Current Empirical Evaluations of Formal Models of Categorization" by A. J. Wills & E. M. Pothos, 2012, *Psychological Bulletin*, 138, 105. Copyright 2012 by the American Psychological Association. Reprinted with permission.

stimulus can be represented as a point (or a distribution; Ashby & Gott, 1988) in a psychological similarity space. Two stimuli are similar to the extent that they are close to each other in this space. Figure 23.2A illustrates this. The Generalized Context Model (GCM) assumes that similarity is an exponential decay function of distance (see Fig. 23.2B; Shepard, 1958). Sometimes, a Gaussian function is used instead (Nosofsky, 1991; this approximates trial-to-trial variability in the perception of highly confusable stimuli in models that represent individual stimuli as points in space, rather than as distributions; Ennis, 1988).

Although in common usage "distance" implies Euclidean distance (Fig. 23.2C), other interpretations are possible, for example, "city-block" distance (Fig. 23.2D). The GCM typically employs Euclidean distance where stimulus dimensions are integral (e.g., hard to selectively attend, such as hue and saturation; Garner, 1978) and city-block distance where stimuli are separable (the antonym of integral).

There are well-known statistical methods for deriving a geometric representation of a stimulus set from data such as similarity ratings, or the extent to which two stimuli are confused in an identification task. The statistical method, known as multidimensional scaling (e.g., Kruskal, 1964), is akin to deriving the relative position of towns from the distances between them. To the extent that multidimensional scaling produces a good approximation to the psychological similarity data in a low-dimensional space (and it often does; Shepard, 1987), geometric models can provide an elegant and readily comprehensible representation of the information available to the categorization process.

The representational power of both geometric and featural systems is greater than might initially be apparent. For example, it is possible to approximate continuous dimensions with an arbitrary degree of

precision using a featural representation (Restle, 1959; Shanks & Gluck, 1994). It is also possible to represent asymmetrical similarity (an ellipse is more similar to a circle than a circle is to an ellipse) in a geometric model, despite the fact that it is self-evidently true that the distance from A to B must be equal to the distance from B to A. Geometric models can account for asymmetric similarity by assuming stimulus-specific biases (a circle is more easily brought to mind than an ellipse). In fact, a geometry-plus-bias model is mathematically equivalent to certain featural models (Holman, 1979).

## Mechanisms of Attention

Some models of categorization assume that the information provided by the input representations can be modulated by attentional processes, and that the function of this attentional modulation is to increase categorization accuracy. Attentional modulation is sometimes assumed to operate at the level of the dimensions of a geometric input representation (Nosofsky, 1986; see also Sutherland & Mackintosh, 1971) and sometimes assumed to operate in a more stimulus-specific or feature-specific manner (Kruschke, 2001; Mackintosh, 1975). At the level of dimensions, attentional modulation can be conceptualized as the stretching and compressing of a geometric input representation along one or more of its dimensions. Figures 23.3A and 23.3B illustrate this form of attentional modulation; note that the effect of the modulation is that the within-category similarities are increased and the between-category similarities are decreased. This will make it easier for the model to correctly categorize the presented stimuli, and it is this kind of process that underlies the success of certain models in capturing the relative difficulty people have in acquiring different category structures (Nosofsky, Gluck, Palmeri, McKinley, & Glauthier, 1994). For

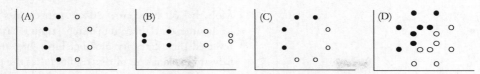

**Figure 23.3** (*A*) Geometric representation of two categories, each of four stimuli (category membership denoted by type of dot). (*B*) Stretching along the x-axis and compression along the y-axis, thereby increasing within-category similarity and decreasing between-category similarity. (*C*) A category structure for which selective attention to the x-axis would be less helpful than in Figure 23.3A. (*D*) Overall expansion of psychological similarity space. Reprinted from "On the Adequacy of Current Empirical Evaluations of Formal Models of Categorization" by A. J. Wills & E. M. Pothos, 2012, *Psychological Bulletin*, 138, 105. Copyright 2012 by the American Psychological Association. Reprinted with permission.

example, the category structure in Figure 23.3C is harder for people to learn than the structure in Figure 23.3A (Kruschke, 1993), and one appealing explanation for this is that selective attention to one dimension facilitates the learning of the latter, but not the former, problem.

Similar processes of attentional modulation can also be applied to models with featural input representations. In these kinds of models (e.g., Mackintosh, 1975; Kruschke, 2001), attention to a feature is assumed to increase to the extent that it is a better predictor of the category label than other features that are simultaneously present. Symmetrically, attention to a feature is assumed to decrease if it is a worse predictor of the category label than other present features. The consequence of this attentional allocation will be to increase categorization accuracy, and the existence of such a process in humans is supported by behavioral (Le Pelley & McLaren, 2003; Lochmann & Wills, 2003), eye-tracking (Kruschke, Kappenman, & Hetrick, 2005), and electrophysiological (Wills, Lavric, Croft, & Hodgson, 2007) data. Eye-tracking data are also consistent with dimensional allocation of attention (Rehder & Hoffman, 2005).

In addition to these processes of selective attention, some models assume that overall differentiation of the input representation is possible—typically as a result of extended exposure to the stimuli. Within geometric input representations, this can be conceptualized as an overall expansion of psychological similarity space (Fig. 23.3D; Nosofsky, 1986). With featural input representations, differentiation can be represented by a reduction in the activity levels of features that stimuli have in common (McLaren & Mackintosh, 2000, 2002). One notable aspect of a featural account of stimulus differentiation is that it predicts when exposure to stimuli will aid the subsequent categorization of those stimuli, and when exposure will impair subsequent classification (Wills & McLaren, 1998: Wills, Suret, & McLaren, 2004). Another phenomenon that is naturally

conceptualized within a featural representation is that of unitization. There is evidence that, with extended experience, the components of multiattribute stimuli become "psychologically fused" into a more unitary representation (Goldstone, 2000). The formation of associations between featural input representations is one way to conceptualize the process of unitization (McLaren & Mackintosh, 2000, 2002).

## Intermediate Representations

Some models of categorization assume the presence of intermediate representations that mediate between the (sometimes attentionally modulated) input representation and the evidential process. Intermediate representations are generally expressed in the same mode of representations as the input representation. In other words, if a geometric input representation is assumed, then the intermediate representations are also expressed in that geometric space. If the input representation is featural, then so is the intermediate representation. For illustrative convenience, this section will describe most intermediate representations geometrically, but they can also be expressed in featural terms.

The assumed nature of the intermediate representations varies greatly between different accounts of categorization. In this section, I will outline some of the types of intermediate representation that have been assumed.

### Cluster Representations

Cluster representations (e.g., Anderson, 1991; Love et al., 2004; Vanpaemel & Storms, 2008) are activated by a region of the input representation. Clusters are usually constrained to represent coherent regions of the input representation, and they are generally assumed to be some form of average of the stimuli that activate the cluster representation. For example, Figure 23.4 shows one possible way in which the 16 stimuli shown might result in four cluster representations (marked "C"). Note

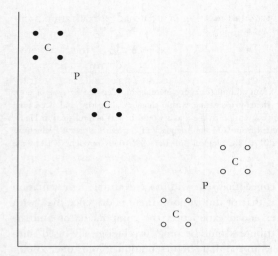

**Figure 23.4** Geometric representation of two categories, each of eight items; category membership denoted by type of circle. C, cluster; P, prototype.

that, as shown in this example, there is no necessity for a cluster representation to correspond exactly with any of the stimuli the participant has experienced.

Prototype representations (e.g., Reed, 1972; Smith & Minda, 1998) and exemplar representations (Medin & Schaffer, 1978; Generalized Context Model, Nosofsky, 1986) are special types of cluster representation. In prototype-based representation, each category label is assumed to result in exactly one cluster representation (marked "P" in Fig. 23.4). In exemplar-based representation each experimenter-defined stimulus is assumed to correspond to exactly one cluster (the 16 circles in Fig. 23.4). Some of the better-known debates in categorization research have centered on the question of whether exemplar-based or prototype-based representation is the better basis for models of categorization. One possible answer (Love et al., 2004) is that cluster size is a function of the stimuli participants are presented with and the level of experience participants have with those stimuli (Smith & Minda, 1998).

Other evidence that clusters less specific than exemplars are formed includes the effect of partially reversing a category structure. For example, train participants on 16 A stimuli and 16 B stimuli. Now train a partial reversal of those category assignments—for example, 6 As are now labeled B, and 6 Bs are now labeled A—and do not present the remaining 20 stimuli during this partial reversal. Under some circumstances (e.g., Wills, Noury,

Moberly, & Newport, 2006) participants seem to assume that these remaining stimuli have also reversed their category membership. One straightforward explanation of this result is that the partial reversal leads participants to reverse the mapping between representations of the categories and representations of their labels. For this explanation to work, the representations have to be less specific than exemplar representations. One possible solution to this problem for exemplar-based models is to assume another, categorical, representation layer in addition to an exemplar representation layer (Kruschke, 1996).

### Distributed Hidden-Layer Representations

Some of the best known models of certain cognitive processes assume that distributed representations mediate between input and output representations (for example, Seidenberg & McClelland's, 1989, account of word naming). Distributed hidden-layer representations are most naturally conceived in featural terms, although geometric interpretations are also possible. Each input representation produces a set of activities across the features of the distributed hidden-layer representation. This pattern of hidden-layer activities arises through the, initially random, connections from the input representation. The hidden-layer representations are assumed to develop over time by a process of error attribution and reduction, typically via the back-propagation algorithm (Rumelhart, Hinton, & Williams, 1986; Werbos, 1974).

Distributed hidden-layer representations are relatively rare in models of categorization, but they have been used with some success in models that attempt to characterize the effects of hippocampal damage on the ability to categorize (Gluck & Myers, 1997).

### Evidential Mechanisms

Most models of categorization convert the information from the intermediate representations (or input representations) into a set of evidence magnitudes, generating one evidence magnitude for each category under consideration. So, for example, a particular pattern of activity in the intermediate representations might give the evidence magnitudes of 0.87 and 0.42 for categories A and B, respectively. It is these numbers that eventually give rise to a decision about the category membership of the presented item, via a categorical decision process. In the next three sections, some of the more common ways of calculating evidence terms are discussed.

## Summed Similarity

Probably the most common form of evidence magnitude is a summed similarity (e.g., Nosofsky, 1986; Smith & Minda, 1998). When a stimulus X is presented, the evidence that it belongs to category Y is assumed to be the sum of the similarity of stimulus X to all relevant intermediate representations associated with category Y. For example, if the intermediate representation is exemplar based, then the evidence magnitude for category Y is the sum of the similarities of stimulus X to all stored exemplars known to belong to category Y. Similarity is calculated in the manner described in the "Input Representations" section of this chapter. For example, in a geometric exemplar model, similarity is related to distance in a psychological space by an exponential or Gaussian decay function (see Fig. 23.2). In featural model, similarity is an increasing function of the number of features shared, and a decreasing function of the number of features that are different. Stewart and Brown (2005) have recently proposed a geometric exemplar-based model that employs both similarity to category Y exemplars, and dissimilarity to members of other categories, in the calculation of the evidence term for category Y.

## Decision Bounds

Decision bounds are most naturally conceptualized as working directly on a geometric input representation. The input representation is often expressed in terms of physical measurements of the stimuli (e.g., size), rather than a psychological space derived from similarity or confusability data. A decision bound is a line through that space that separates one category from another (see Fig. 23.5A). Sometimes that line is assumed to be straight (Ashby & Gott, 1988); sometimes it is assumed to be quadratic (Ashby & Maddox, 1992). In some applications of a decision-bound evidential process, the decision bound is assumed to be placed optimally (Ashby & Gott, 1988); in other words, its form and location is such that categorization accuracy is maximized.

The position of the presented stimulus relative to that line determines its category membership. As should be apparent, there are certain category structures that cannot be captured by a single linear or quadratic decision bound. An example is given in Figure 23.5B; a potential solution is to assume that more than one decision bound is used.

Note that, unlike a summed similarity mechanism, on any given presentation of a stimulus the evidence magnitudes for all categories except one are zero, and for the remaining category the evidence is maximal. In Figure 23.5A, the presentation of any stimulus in category 1 results in maximal evidence magnitude for category 1 and zero evidence magnitude for category 2. However, decision-bound models typically assume perceptual noise (Ashby & Gott, 1988), so a given stimulus will not always be represented in exactly the same location in the input representation. Some decision-bound models also assume decisional noise—in other words, that the decision bound varies somewhat from decision to decision.

One striking aspect of a decision-bound evidential mechanism is that it is distance from the decision boundary, rather than distance from the known examples of a category, that determines categorization accuracy. This is illustrated in Figure 23.5C, where the novel stimuli marked "2" are predicted to be classified at least as accurately as the novel stimuli marked "1," and more accurately if one assumes substantial perceptual and decisional noise. Hence, a decision-bound evidence mechanism can be said to extrapolate from the known members of category. Extrapolation is observed in categorization experiments, and at least some extrapolation phenomena seem difficult to explain without positing a decision-bound evidence mechanism (Denton, Kruschke, & Erickson, 2008).

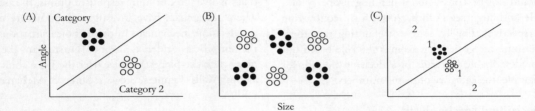

**Figure 23.5** (*A*) Geometric representation of two categories, and a linear decision bound separating them; category membership denoted by type of circle. (*B*) A category structure that cannot be represented by a single linear or quadratic decision bound. (*C*) In a decision-bound account, novel stimuli marked "2" will be responded to at least as accurately as novel stimuli marked "1."

## Verbalizable Rules

The idea that people make decisions on the basis of "rules" is a pervasive concept in psychology and in everyday life, but what does it mean to say performance is "rule-based"? Decision-bound theories seem in some ways to be quite rule-like, for example, in their ability to predict extrapolation. On the other hand, some would argue (Ashby et al., 1998) that the decision bound in Figure 23.5A is unlikely to represent a rule, because it is not easily verbalizable. A verbal representation of this decision bound would have to be of the form "It's category 1 if it's more obtuse than it is large, and category 2 if it's less obtuse than it is large." Among the problems with formulating and applying a rule of this type is that the things being compared have different units. In other words, what does it mean to say something is more obtuse than it is large? In contrast, the rule "category A is composed of small obtuse items" is readily formulated verbally and can be applied without having to compare things measured in different units.

Hence, what some theorists mean when they talk of a categorization model being rule based is a decision bound that can be readily expressed in verbal terms. Limiting the concept of "rules" to things that are verbalizable is not an idea that is universally accepted in psychology, but it does currently have currency in the modeling of categorization. This view of rules as verbalizable naturally leads to the assumption that easy-to-verbalize rules (e.g., "Category A is blue") are more likely to be employed than hard-to-verbalize rules (e.g., "Category A is small and blue, or large and red"). This assumption is instantiated in some rule-based models of categorization such as RULEX (Nosofsky, Palmeri, & McKinley, 1994) and COVIS (Ashby et al., 1998). The extent to which participants spontaneously prefer simple rules over complex rules depends on the time available for a decision (e.g., Milton, Longmore, & Wills, 2008), with greater preference for complex rules where time permits. Hence, while rules are sometimes simple, simplicity should not be considered a defining property of a rule (although see Pothos, 2005, for a contrasting perspective). Finally, it is worth noting that there are some categories that seem to be rule based but not describable in terms of a decision bound, for example, the category of prime numbers.

## Decisional Mechanisms

In some models, the evidential mechanisms themselves result in a categorical decision (e.g., certain decision-bound models; see earlier). However, in most models, the output of the evidential mechanism is a set of non-zero evidence magnitude terms. For example, the evidence terms for a presented item being a cat, a dog, or a bagel might be 0.83, 0.41, and 0.05, respectively. In many situations, a decision is required—should I call this thing a cat, a dog, or a bagel?

The seemingly obvious answer to this question is that I should call it a cat, because that is the category for which the evidence is greatest. This strategy of "pick the biggest" is not, however, what the vast majority of models of categorization do. Instead, they engage in a form of probability matching. Applying the simplest form of probability matching to the earlier example, the probability of the model responding "cat" would be $0.83/(0.83 + 0.41 + 0.05) = 0.64$. So despite "cat" being the most likely answer, that answer is only produced on 64% of occasions. This decision mechanism is generally known as the Luce choice rule (Luce, 1959).

Although it is well known that organisms probability match (e.g., Herrnstein, 1961), it is generally accepted that the level of probability matching seen in studies of categorization is much lower than a simple application of the Luce choice axiom would predict (Ashby & Gott, 1988; McKinley & Nosofsky, 1995). One solution to this problem is to transform the evidence terms (v) in some way— for example, by using $v^k$ or $e^{kv}$. Increasing the value of k reduces the level of probability matching predicted by the model—large values of k approximate a "pick the biggest" strategy. Applying $v^{10}$ to our earlier example, the probability of responding "cat" exceeds 0.999.

The fact that the Luce choice axiom can approximate the behavior of a pick-the-biggest strategy does not imply that the two formulations are equivalent. In fact, Yellott (1977) demonstrated mathematically that noisy pick-the-biggest (in other words, picking the biggest under conditions where the evidence terms for a given item vary) is not equivalent to the Luce choice axiom in virtually all situations that involve three or more response options. In cases where researchers have investigated the nature of the decision mechanism in three-choice situations, the empirical evidence favors Thurstonian (i.e., noisy pick-the-biggest) choice over the Luce choice axiom (Wills, Reimers, Stewart, Suret, & McLaren, 2000).

## Multiprocess Models

Over the last decade, it has become increasingly common to propose that there are multiple categorization processes at work. For example, ATRIUM (Erickson & Kruschke, 1998) assumes the presence of both a decision-bound process and an exemplar-based process. Each of these processes provides a set of evidence terms for the possible category responses, and hence part of the decision process involves the integration of this information. In ATRIUM, this process involves keeping track of the past success of each process in providing the correct answer for the stimulus presented. The COVIS model (Ashby et al., 1998) also assumes a rule-like and exemplar-like process, although the details are different.

## The Time Course of Categorization

To summarize what has been said so far, models of categorization assume the passing of information from attentionally modulated input representations, through intermediate representations, to evidential and decisional processes. A categorical decision is the result. In this context, the time course of categorization can be considered in two ways. First, one can consider the time course within a single decision—how is information accumulated over the time course from stimulus presentation to decision, and what additional phenomena can be captured by modeling this accumulation of information? Second, one can consider the time course across multiple decisions—what are the mechanisms that allow the system's ability to categorize to improve with experience? These two questions are considered in the following sections.

### Single-Decision Time Course

There are two main ways information is assumed to accumulate over the course of a single decision: at the level of input representations, and at the level of categorical decisions. At the level of input representations, models such as the Extended Generalized Context Model (Lamberts, 1995) assume that the dimensions of the input representation become available at different intervals after the presentation of the stimulus, with the average interval being a function of both the perceptual salience of that dimension and its usefulness in determining category membership of the item. Evidence in support of this form of information accumulation includes the fact that time pressure can systematically change the category into which a stimulus is placed. For example, under time pressure the stimulus might be systematically considered to be in category A, while in the absence of time pressure, it was systematically considered to be in category B. Such

"cross-over" effects (Lamberts & Freeman, 1999) can be explained by assuming that, under time pressure, not all of the dimensions of the stimulus representation are available to later components of the categorization process (Lamberts, 1995; Milton et al., 2008).

Some models, such as the Exemplar-based Random Walk model (Nosofsky & Palmeri, 1997), the EGCM-RT model (Lamberts, 2000), and the winner-take-all model (Wills & McLaren, 1997), also assume that information accumulates over time at the level of categorical decisions. Making this assumption allows these models to predict the time taken to make a decision, in addition to the more standard prediction of the probability with which a particular category will be chosen.

### Multiple-Decision Time Course

The discussion of the components of categorization models in this chapter assumed the presence of a lot of information. Models are assumed to have information about which dimensions and/or features to attend to in order to maximize accuracy. They are assumed to have information about how the structure of the stimuli can best be represented within the model's chosen intermediate representations (e.g., prototypes). Models are also assumed to know which intermediate representations correspond to which category labels and/or which decision bound to use to maximize categorization accuracy. How is this information acquired?

Perhaps surprisingly, many models of categorization have no specific mechanisms by which they can acquire the information they are assumed to have; those that do mainly rely on the concept of reduction of prediction error through, for example, changing the structure of associative connections

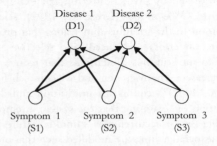

**Figure 23.6** A simple associative learning model of a disease prediction task. Units representing symptoms have connections of variable strength to units representing disease. Representational units are shown as circles; associative connections are shown as arrows. The thickness of the arrows denotes the relative strength of the connections in this example.

between representations (Gluck & Bower, 1988; Rescorla & Wagner, 1972; Widrow & Hoff, 1960).

This principle is illustrated in the very simple featural model shown in Figure 23.6. The model is too simplistic to be a convincing account of categorization, but it serves to illustrate the principle of the reduction of prediction error. In an experiment where participants have to predict which fictitious disease a patient has on the basis of his symptoms (e.g., Gluck & Bower, 1988), it is presumably the case that participants will not start the experiment with the information required to solve it. This state of affairs is illustrated in Figure 23.6 by assuming a series of associations of arbitrary strength between the input and category representations. Now assume that the participant sees a patient with symptoms 1 and 2. On the basis of the connections shown in Figure 23.6, there is more evidence (within this initially arbitrary knowledge) that the patient has disease 1 than that he has disease 2. Assuming a take-the-best decision mechanism, the model predicts that the patient has disease 1 but is told that the patient actually has disease 2. The model has therefore made a prediction error. To reduce the likelihood of a future error, the model increases the strength of the connection between symptom 1 and disease 2 (S1-D2), increases S2-D2, decreases S1-D1, and decreases S2-D1. In this particular instantiation of prediction-error-driven learning, connections from absent symptoms (symptom 3) do not change. The process just described is approximately that undertaken by the Widrow-Hoff rule (1960), and it is closely related to the Rescorla-Wagner theory (1972) and the LMS rule (Gluck & Bower, 1988).

The acquisition of other information within the categorization process is also commonly assumed to be driven by prediction error. For example, in the ALCOVE model (Kruschke, 1992), selective attention to the stimulus dimensions that produce prediction errors is reduced, and selective attention to the stimulus dimensions that reduce error is increased. The McLaren and Mackintosh model (2000, 2002) accounts for unitization and differentiation by assuming that the system attempts to predict the co-occurrence of stimulus features, and that associative links are modified such that prediction errors are reduced. The SUSTAIN model (Love et al., 2004) assumes that a new cluster representation is formed when the existing clusters fail to predict the category membership of the presented stimulus

### Role of Feedback

The concept of prediction error, discussed earlier, could be taken to imply that category learning is only possible where some external agent (e.g., a teacher) or the environment provides specific information about the category membership of presented stimuli. This is not the case; category learning can and does occur in the absence of feedback (e.g., Homa & Cultice, 1984; Wills & McLaren, 1998). Relatively few models of categorization can account for this phenomenon. Those that can—such as Adaptive Resonance Theory (Grossberg, 1976), the Rumelhart and Zipser model (1986), and SUSTAIN (Love et al., 2004)—do so by assuming that the categorical decision produced by the model is correct, and adjusting associative strengths and other parameters in the same way as if "correct" feedback had been received. Where the stimuli presented to the model are well structured (as in, for example, Fig. 23.5A), such models are able to produce categorical representations that capture much of that structure.

## Conclusions and Future Directions

Over the last 35 years, there has been a great deal of progress in the modeling of categorization. Since Hull's work (Hull, 1920) and, perhaps more famously, the work of Bruner and colleagues (Bruner, Goodnow, & Austin, 1956), the field had been steadily accumulating empirical phenomena, but it was not until the early 1970s (e.g., Reed, 1972) that theories of these phenomena started routinely taking mathematical form. The late 1970s to the mid-1990s saw the introduction and development of a number of still highly influential single-process models, such as the Generalized Context Model (Nosofsky, 1986) and General Recognition Theory (Ashby & Gott, 1988). Toward the end of the 1990s, there was increasing recognition that categorization may involve more than one competing process, and the development of multiprocess theories such as COVIS (Ashby et al., 1998) and ATRIUM (Erickson & Kruschke, 1998), and also the idea that intermediate representations may develop and change in specificity over time (e.g., Smith & Minda, 1998). COVIS is also notable in that it is a theory of categorization specified in both formal mathematical terms and related to the assumed underlying neuroscience (another example of this combined approach is the Gluck-Myers model; e.g., Gluck & Myers, 1997).

The first decade of the 21st century saw a rapidly increasing data set on the neuroscience of categorization and the development of existing theories to account for these data (e.g., Ashby, Ennis & Spiering, 2007). It also saw attempts to expand the range of behavioral phenomena to be modeled to include, for example, classification in the absence of feedback, classification and feature inference (e.g., Love et al., 2004), and the effects of background knowledge (e.g., Rehder & Murphy, 2003). The broadening of data to both more behavioral phenomena and to neuroscientific data is very welcome, as both sets of information should serve to constrain and reduce the number of formal models that remain plausible accounts of the known phenomena.

In conclusion, formal modeling of psychological phenomena is a complex and time-consuming task. What indicates that it is a worthwhile enterprise? Probably the single biggest advantage of formal modeling over more informal forms of theorizing is that the ability of a formal theory to encompass an empirical phenomenon is unambiguously determinable. This can sometimes lead to surprising conclusions. For example, asymmetry in similarity relations (an ellipse is more similar to a circle than a circle is to an ellipse) seems, informally, to be incompatible with the idea that similarity relations can be represented in a geometric space. Yet categorization models employing a geometric space can unambiguously be demonstrated to be able to capture certain asymmetric similarity relations (Nosofsky, 1991). Another example is that some philosophers have argued the concept of similarity is ill defined because any two objects have an arbitrary number of things in common (e.g., An ostrich and an aircraft carrier? Both weigh more than one gram, neither can fly, both can be found on the Earth, both can carry people, etc.). This is known as Goodman's paradox (Goodman, 1972). Models of categorization may help us work through Goodman's paradox by specifying, for example, the ways in which attention to features is directed through experience.

The unambiguous specification of theory that formal modeling brings should also, in principle, confer two further advantages. First, it should be possible to compare different theories in an unambiguous manner and come to a consensual conclusion about which theory encompasses more of the known empirical phenomena. Second, the formal specification of theories of psychological processes should bring with it the possibility of re-creating those processes in artificial systems (automated cognition). However, the potential of both these aspects currently remains largely unfulfilled in the formal

modeling of categorization. The relative adequacy of different models of categorization is seldom systematically compared, and never across a broad range of empirical phenomena. Perhaps as a result of this, the field continues to have a large range of competing formal theories with no consensus over their relative adequacy. The lack of such consensus may in part explain the relative lack of successes in the application of formal categorization theory to the development of automated cognition. The resolution of these issues is the single biggest challenge that the formal modeling of categorization must address in the coming years.

## References

Anderson, J. R. (1991). The adaptive nature of human categorization. *Psychological Review, 98*(3), 409–429.

Ashby, F. G., Alfonso-Reese, L. A., Turken, A. U., & Waldron, E. M. (1998). A neuropsychological theory of multiple systems in category learning. *Psychological Review, 105*(3), 442–481.

Ashby, F. G., Ennis, J. M., & Spiering, B. J . (2007). A neurobiological theory of automaticity in perceptual categorization. *Psychological Review, 114*, 632–656.

Ashby, F. G., & Gott, R. E. (1988). Decision rules in the perception and categorization of multidimensional stimuli. *Journal of Experimental Psychology: Learning, Memory, and Cognition, 14*(1), 33–53.

Ashby, F. G., & Maddox, W. T. (1992). Complex decision rules in categorization: Contrasting novice and experienced performance. *Journal of Experimental Psychology: Human Perception and Performance, 18*, 50–71.

Bruner, J. S., Goodnow, J. J., & Austin, G. A. (1956). *A study of thinking*. New York: Wiley.

Denton, S. E., Kruschke, J. K., & Erickson, M. A. (2008). Rule-based extrapolation: A continuing challenge for exemplar models. *Psychonomic Bulletin and Review, 15*(4), 780–786.

Ennis, D.M. (1988). Confusable and discriminable stimuli: Comment on Nosofsky (1986) and Shepard (1986). *Journal of Experimental Psychology: General, 117*, 408–411.

Erickson, M. A., & Kruschke, J. K. (1998). Rules and exemplars in category learning. *Journal Of Experimental Psychology: General, 127*(2), 107–140.

Estes, W. K. (1950). Toward a statistical theory of learning. *Psychological Review, 57*, 94–107.

Garner, W. R. (1978). Aspects of a stimulus: Features, dimensions and configurations. In E. Rosch & B. B. Lloyd (Eds.), *Cognition and categorization (pp. 99–133)*. Hillsdale, NJ: Erlbaum.

Gluck, M. A., & Bower, G. H. (1988). Evaluating an adaptive network model of human learning. *Journal of Memory and Language, 27*, 166–195.

Gluck, M. A., & Myers, C. E. (1997). Psychobiological models of hippocampal function in learning and memory. *Annual Review of Psychology, 48*, 481–514.

Goldstone, R. L. (2000). Unitization during category learning. *Journal of Experimental Psychology: Human Perception and Performance, 26*(1), 86–112.

Goodman, N. (1972). Seven strictures on similarity. In N. Goodman (Ed.), *Problems and projects (pp. 437–447)*. New York: Bobbs-Merrill.

Granger, R., Ambros-Ingerson, J., & Lynch, G. (1989). Derivation of encoding characteristics of layer II cerebral cortex. *Journal of Cognitive Neuroscience, 1,* 61–87.

Grossberg, S. (1976). Adaptive pattern classification and universal recoding: Part I. Parallel development and coding of neural feature detectors. *Biological Cybernetics, 23,* 121–134.

Harris, J. A. (2006). Elemental representations of stimuli in associative learning. *Psychological Review, 113,* 584–605.

Herrnstein, R. J. (1961). Relative and absolute strength of response as a function of frequency of reinforcement. *Journal of the Experimental Analysis of Behavior, 4,* 267–272.

Holman, E. W. (1979). Monotonic models for asymmetric proximities. *Journal of Mathematical Psychology, 20,* 1–15.

Homa, D., & Cultice, J. C. (1984). Role of feedback, category size, and stimulus distortion on the acquisition and utilization of ill-defined categories. *Journal of Experimental Psychology: Learning, Memory and Cognition, 10*(1), 83–94.

Hull, C. L. (1920). Quantitative aspects of the evolution of concepts: An experimental study. *Psychological Monographs, 28*(1), No. 123.

Kruschke, J. K. (1992). ALCOVE: An exemplar-based connectionist model of category learning. *Psychological Review, 99,* 22–44.

Kruschke, J. K. (1993). Human category learning: Implications for backpropagation models. *Connection Science, 5*(1), 3–36.

Kruschke, J. K. (1996). Dimensional relevance shifts in category learning. *Connection Science, 8*(2), 225–247.

Kruschke, J. K. (2001). Toward a unified model of attention in associative learning. *Journal of Mathematical Psychology, 45,* 812–863.

Kruschke, J. K., Kappenman, E. S., & Hetrick, W. P. (2005). Eye gaze and individual differences consistent with learned attention in associative blocking and highlighting. *Journal of Experimental Psychology-Learning Memory and Cognition, 31*(5), 830–845.

Kruskal, J. (1964). Multidimensional scaling by optimizing goodness-of-fit to a nonmetric hypothesis. *Psychometrika, 29,* 1–28.

Lamberts, K. (1995). Categorization under time pressure. *Journal of Experimental Psychology: General, 124*(2), 161–180.

Lamberts, K. (2000). Information-accumulation theory of speeded categorization. *Psychological Review, 107*(2), 227–260.

Lamberts, K., & Freeman, R. P. J. (1999). Building object representations from parts: Tests of a stochastic sampling model. *Journal of Experimental Psychology: Human Perception and Performance, 25*(4), 904–926.

Le Pelley, M. E., & McLaren, I. P. L. (2003). Learned associability and associative change in human causal learning. *Quarterly Journal of Experimental Psychology, 56B,* 68–79.

Lochmann, T., & Wills, A.J. (2003). Predictive history in an allergy prediction task. In F. Schmalhofer, R. M. Young, & G. Katz (Eds.), *Proceedings of EuroCogSci 03: The European Cognitive Science Conference (pp. 217–222).* Mahwah, NJ: Erlbaum.

Love, B. C., Medin, D. L., & Gureckis, T. M. (2004). SUSTAIN: A network model of category learning. *Psychological Review, 111*(2), 309–332.

Luce, R. D. (1959). *Individual choice behavior.* New York: Wiley.

Mackintosh, N. J. (1975). A theory of attention: Variations in the associability of stimuli with reinforcement. *Psychological Review, 82,* 276–298.

McClelland, J. L., & Rumelhart, D. E. (1985). Distributed memory and the representation of general and specific information. *Journal of Experimental Psychology: General, 114*(2), 159–188.

McKinley, S. C., & Nosofsky, R. M. (1995). Investigations of exemplar and decision-bound models in large-size, ill-defined category structures. *Journal of Experimental Psychology: Human Perception and Performance, 21,* 128–148.

McLaren, I. P. L., & Mackintosh, N. J. (2000). An elemental model of associative learning: I. Latent inhibition and perceptual learning. *Animal Learning and Behavior, 28,* 211–246.

McLaren, I. P. L., & Mackintosh, N. J. (2002). Associative learning and elemental representation: II. Generalization and discrimination. *Animal Learning and Behavior, 30,* 177–200.

Medin, D. L., & Schaffer, M. M. (1978). Context theory of classification learning. *Psychological Review, 85*(3), 207–238.

Milton, F., Longmore, C. A., & Wills, A. J. (2008). Processes of overall similarity sorting in free classification. *Journal of Experimental Psychology: Human Perception and Performance, 34*(3), 676–692.

Nosofsky, R. M. (1986). Attention, similarity and the identification-categorization relationship. *Journal of Experimental Psychology: General, 115*(1), 39–57.

Nosofsky, R. M. (1991). Stimulus bias, asymmetric similarity, and classification. *Cognitive Psychology, 23,* 94–140.

Nosofsky, R. M., Gluck, M. A., Palmeri, T. J., McKinley, S. C., & Glauthier, P. (1994). Comparing models of rule-based classification learning: A replication and extension of Shepard, Hovland, and Jenkins (1961). *Memory and Cognition, 22*(3), 352–369.

Nosofsky, R. M., & Palmeri, T. J. (1997). An exemplar-based random walk model of speeded classification. *Psychological Review, 104*(2), 266–300.

Nosofsky, R. M., Palmeri, T. J., & McKinley, S. C. (1994). Rule-plus-exception model of classification learning. *Psychological Review, 101*(1), 53–79.

Pothos, E. M. (2005). The rules versus similarity distinction. *Behavioral and Brain Sciences, 28,* 1–49.

Pothos, E. M., & Chater, N. (2002). A simplicity principle in unsupervised human categorization. *Cognitive Science, 26,* 303–343.

Reed, S. K. (1972). Pattern recognition and categorization. *Cognitive Psychology, 3,* 382–407.

Rehder, B., & Hoffman, A.B. (2005). Eyetracking and selective attention in category learning. *Cognitive Psychology, 51,* 1–41.

Rehder, B., & Murphy, G. L. (2003). A knowledge-resonance (KRES) model of category learning. *Psychonomic Bulletin and Review, 10,* 759–784.

Rescorla, R. A., & Wagner, A. R. (1972). A theory of Pavlovian conditioning: Variations in the effectiveness of reinforcement and nonreinforcement. In A. H. Black & W. F. Prokasy (Eds.), *Classical conditioning II: Current research* (pp. 64–99). New York: Appleton-Century-Crofts.

Restle, F. (1959). A metric and an ordering on sets. *Psychometrika, 24*(3), 207–220.

Rumelhart, D. E., Hinton, G. E., & Williams, R. J. (1986). Learning internal representations by error propagation. In D. E. Rumelhart & J. L. McClelland (Eds.), *Parallel distributed processing: Explorations in the microstructure of cognition (Vol. 1, pp. 318–362).* Cambridge, MA: MIT Press.

Rumelhart, D. E., & Zipser, D. (1986). Feature discovery by competitive learning. In D. E. Rumelhart & J. L. McClelland

(Eds.), *Parallel distributed processing: Explorations in the microstructure of cognition (Vol. 1, pp. 151–193)*. Cambridge, MA: MIT Press.

Seidenberg, M. S., & McClelland, J. L. (1989). A distributed developmental model of word recognition and naming. *Psychological Review, 96*, 523–568.

Shanks, D. R., & Gluck, M. A. (1994). Tests of an adaptive network model for the identification and categorization of continuous-dimension stimuli. *Connection Science, 6*(1), 59–89.

Shepard, R. (1987). Towards a universal law of generalization for psychological science. *Science, 237*, 1317–1323.

Shepard, R. N. (1958). Stimulus and response generalization: Tests of a model relating generalization to distance in psychological space. *Journal of Experimental Psychology, 55*, 509–523.

Smith, J. D., & Minda, J. P. (1998). Prototypes in the mist: The early epochs of category learning. *Journal of Experimental Psychology: Learning, Memory, and Cognition, 24*, 1411–1436.

Stewart, N., & Brown, G. D. A. (2005). Similarity and dissimilarity as evidence in perceptual categorization. *Journal of Mathematical Psychology, 49*, 403–409.

Sutherland, N. S., & Mackintosh, N. J. (1971). *Mechanisms of animal discrimination learning*. New York: Academic Press.

Tversky, A. (1977). Features of similarity. *Psychological Review, 84*(4), 327–352.

Vanpaemel, W., & Storms, G. (2008). In search of abstraction: The varying abstraction model of categorization. *Psychonomic Bulletin and Review, 15*(4), 732–749.

Werbos, P. J. (1974). *Beyond regression: New tools for prediction and analysis in the behavioral sciences*. Unpublished Ph.D. dissertation, Harvard University, Boston.

Widrow, B., & Hoff, M. E. (1960). *Adaptive switching circuits*. Paper presented at the IRE WESCON Convention, Los Angeles, CA. August 23–26.

Wills, A. J., Lavric, A., Croft, G. S., & Hodgson, T. L. (2007). Predictive learning, prediction errors, and attention: Evidence from event-related potentials and eye tracking. *Journal of Cognitive Neuroscience, 19*(5), 843–854.

Wills, A. J., & McLaren, I. P. L. (1997). Generalization in human category learning: A connectionist explanation of differences in gradient after discriminative and non-discriminative training. *Quarterly Journal of Experimental Psychology, 50A*(3), 607–630.

Wills, A. J., & McLaren, I. P. L. (1998). Perceptual learning and free classification. *Quarterly Journal of Experimental Psychology, 51B*(3), 235–270.

Wills, A. J., Noury, M., Moberly, N. J., & Newport, M. (2006). Formation of category representations. *Memory and Cognition, 34*(1), 17–27.

Wills, A. J., Reimers, S., Stewart, N., Suret, M., & McLaren, I. P. L. (2000). Tests of the ratio rule in categorization. *Quarterly Journal of Experimental Psychology, 53A*(4), 983–1011.

Wills, A. J., Suret, M., & McLaren, I. P. L. (2004). The role of category structure in determining the effects of stimulus preexposure on categorization accuracy. *Quarterly Journal of Experimental Psychology, 57B*(1), 79–88.

Yellott, J. I., Jr. (1977). The relationship between Luce's choice axiom, Thurstone's theory of comparative judgment, and the double exponential distribution. *Journal of Mathematical Psychology, 15*, 109–144.

## Further Reading

Kruschke, J. K. (2008). Models of categorization. In: R. Sun (Ed.), *The Cambridge Handbook of Computational Psychology*, pp. 267–301. New York: Cambridge University Press.

Pothos, E.M. & Wills, A.J. (2011). *Formal approaches in categorization*. Cambridge University Press.

Wills, A. J. (2009). Prediction errors and attention in the presence and absence of feedback. *Current Directions in Psychological Science, 18*(2), 95–100.

Wills, A. J., & Pothos, E. M. (2012). On the adequacy of current empirical evaluations of formal models of categorization. *Psychological Bulletin, 138*, 102–125.

# The Perceptual Representation of Mental Categories

Diane Pecher

**Abstract**

Many studies have shown that mental categories share processing mechanisms with perception and action. According to a strong view of grounded cognition, these sensory-motor mechanisms are sufficient for mental representations, while more moderate views might say that other, more abstract mechanisms also play a role. Several lines of research support the idea that mental categories are grounded in sensory-motor processes. Behavioral studies show interactions between cognition and perception or action, suggesting that they share mechanisms. Neuroscientific studies have collected evidence that sensory-motor brain areas are involved in cognition. Several connectionist models show how sensory-motor experiences can be combined and result in categorical representations. These findings suggest a highly flexible and interactive system in which the strict distinction between sensory-motor processing and other types of processing may no longer be relevant.

**Key Words:** grounded cognition, concepts, sensory-motor simulation

Many categories in the world have perceptual qualities that allow us to recognize and interact with them. We recognize apples by their shape and color, and when we eat an apple we recognize the feel in our hand, the texture of skin and flesh when we bite, and the taste and smell of the fruit. But what about the categories in our minds? Do they also have perceptual qualities, and if they do, to what extent do we use these perceptual qualities to categorize, make inferences and predictions, and, in short, to think? This chapter discusses some recent theories that have proposed that the mental representation of categories shares processing mechanisms with perception and action.

## Perceptual Theories of Concepts

The starting point for this chapter is the assumption that most of our mental categories are relevant to us because they allow us to perceive our environment and perform actions (Glenberg, 1997). The most influential theory on the role of perception

for mental categories is Barsalou's (1999) Perceptual Symbols theory. Perceptual symbols are the neural states that underlie perception and action. The perceptual symbols that represent categories are learned through recurrent experiences of perceiving and interacting with exemplars. These experiences are captured by modality-specific sensory-motor systems and integrated via hierarchical association areas (Barsalou, 2008; Barsalou, Simmons, Barbey, & Wilson, 2003). At the perceptual level are the modality-specific activations that represent the states of sensory-motor systems. At this level, association areas connect the neuronal patterns that resulted from a specific experience in order to capture such states. Higher level cross-modal association areas then integrate these modality-specific patterns into multimodal experiences. These association networks represent categorical knowledge that can be recruited for cognitive processing. Mental representation of a category is achieved by simulators that reactivate aspects of experience in a top-down fashion from higher level association areas back to the modality-specific sensory-motor systems.

Such mechanism might be achieved by connectionist networks, in which simple processing units are highly interconnected. In such connectionist networks, experiences or categories are represented by activation patterns across the units. Learning takes place by adjustments of the strength of connections between units. Through repeated activation of a pattern the connections between units that are activated simultaneously become stronger and the whole pattern becomes an attractor. An attractor is a stable state of the network in which energy is low. An important characteristic of such attractors is that when the pattern is only partially activated, the network can complete the pattern by a process of iterative spreading activation. Because strength of the connection between units determines how much they activate (or inhibit) each other, and units that were part of the same pattern have strong connections, the previously learned pattern is recovered in a number of updating cycles in which the activation level of each unit is adjusted according to the activation levels of the other units and the strength of the connections between the units (e.g., Masson, 1995; McRae, Cree, Westmacott, & de Sa, 1999; McRae, de Sa, & Seidenberg, 1997; Plaut, 2002; Pulvermüller, 1999). A simulator might work the same way by completing patterns of activation in sensory-motor systems in order to represent experiential knowledge.

Several other theories have also proposed that concepts are grounded in sensory-motor processing (Glenberg, 1997; Prinz, 2002; Pulvermüller, 1999). It is important to note that the actual representation is achieved by the sensory-motor systems and not by the higher level association areas, and that this aspect of the theory is essentially different from a symbolic account of cognition, which would assume that abstract representations suffice for categories. A middle position was proposed by Mahon and Caramazza (2008), who argue that sensory-motor systems enrich representations, but that categories are at least partially abstract. Before looking at specific models I will first review the studies that have contributed to the idea that sensory-motor simulations and mental categories are strongly associated.

Researchers should always be hesitant to claim that particular results provide conclusive *evidence* for a theory. As various authors (e.g., Dove, 2009; Mahon & Caramazza, 2008) have noted, showing sensory-motor effects does not necessarily entail that all representations consist purely of sensory-motor

simulations. Rather, sensory-motor simulations may be only part of a representation, or even a mere by-product of representation. Providing conclusive evidence might be extremely difficult, similar to the difficulties associated with distinguishing exemplar and prototype models of categorization. In exemplar models, each experience with a category is stored, and abstractions are computed at the time of retrieval by combining a whole set of exemplars (Hintzman, 1986; Nosofsky, 1988). In contrast, prototype models assume that category abstractions (prototypes) are stored in memory. These models make almost identical predictions because it is impossible to distinguish between stored and computed abstractions (Barsalou, 1990; Murphy, 2002). For the sake of parsimony one might therefore favor the exemplar model approach. A similar situation exists for the distinction between fully grounded and partially grounded theories of cognition. Thus, one should be careful to interpret evidence for sensory-motor simulations as support for the fully grounded view. On the other hand, in the absence of decisive evidence, a fully grounded view might be more parsimonious and therefore preferable.

## Evidence for Perceptual Simulation
### Representation and Perception of Categories Interact

Grounded theories argue that sensory-motor simulations underlie representations of categories. In this view, a category, for example, apple, is represented by simulation of an experience with an apple, such as seeing a round, red object, which can be grasped by one hand and feels firm, is sweet, tart, and juicy when bitten, and so on. Because the simulation is supported by sensory-motor systems, there should be interactions between representational processes and perceptual processes. An important line of evidence comes from studies that show effects of mental representation on processing of visual stimuli. The idea is that representation of a category and perception of a category used (partly) overlapping perceptual features, which are then processed more easily when they are activated by two sources. For example, in a series of studies Zwaan and colleagues (Stanfield & Zwaan, 2001; Zwaan, Madden, Yaxley, & Aveyard, 2004; Zwaan, Stanfield, & Yaxley, 2002) showed that sentences in which an object's orientation, shape, or motion was implied (e.g., *He hammered the nail into the floor* vs. *He hammered the nail into the wall*) affected the speed of picture processing in which the relevant dimension either matched or mismatched the sentence (e.g., a picture of a nail oriented horizontally or vertically). Connell (2007) showed similar effects for color. Thus, processing is affected by the overlap in perceptual features between representation and perception.

The effect of such overlap might be due to task-induced strategies. When linguistic stimuli and perceptual stimuli are alternated and the task involves comparison of two consecutive stimuli, participants may be induced to consciously generate images of the objects described by the sentences. Therefore, the effects may reflect strategic rather than automatic activation of perceptual information. To circumvent this problem, Pecher, van Dantzig, Zwaan, and Zeelenberg (2009) presented all sentences blocked, and after a delay, all pictures were presented. Thus, during sentence processing participants did not know yet that they would see pictures of the objects that were mentioned in the sentences. Recognition performance was still better for matching than mismatching pictures even 45 minutes after reading the sentences. Thus, implied orientation and shape are not only represented during online language processing but also affect representations at longer delays. Both short- and long-term effects indicate that the mental representations of categories not only contain perceptual features but also that the particular features that are represented (e.g., orientation) are context dependent.

### Representation Has Perceptual Qualities

The representation of categories by sensory-motor systems implies that these representations retain perceptual qualities. Several studies have shown that the representation of categories itself is influenced by variables that are perceptual in nature, even if the stimuli themselves are words and do not contain any perceptual information of their referents. Solomon and Barsalou (2001) asked participants to verify, for example, whether *a horse has mane*. Earlier in the experiment the same property had been presented with a different category. The critical manipulation was whether the property has a similar perceptual form on the context trial (e.g., *pony-mane*) or a different perceptual form (e.g., *lion-mane*). They showed that performance was better if the context and target property had a similar form than if they did not. Priming for shape similarity (e.g., *banjo-tennis racket*) has also been observed in tasks that require less semantic processing such as word naming and lexical decision (Pecher, Zeelenberg, & Raaijmakers, 1998), although the effect tends to be quite fragile in such tasks. Thus, overlap in

perceptual features facilitates processing. This effect of shape similarity indicates that participants have visual representations of categories.

Other studies have shown effects of visual perspective. Solomon and Barsalou (2004) showed that verification times for object-property word pairs were affected by perceptual variables such as the relative size and location of the property on the object. Wu and Barsalou (2009) asked participants to generate properties for objects that were presented in isolation (*watermelon*) or with a modifier that changed which properties would be visible if the object were actually present (*half watermelon*). Visible properties were more likely to be generated than occluded properties. For example, the property *seeds* was generated more often for *half watermelon* than for *watermelon* without modifier. Borghi, Glenberg, and Kaschak (2004) presented sentences that invoked a particular perspective (*You are driving a car* vs. *You are washing a car*) and subsequently asked participants to verify properties. Performance in the property verification task was affected by whether the property was visible from the particular perspective invoked by the sentence (e.g., *tires, steering wheel*).

Of course, categories are not only represented visually. Action and other sensory modalities also contribute to representation. Pecher, Zeelenberg, and Barsalou (2003) demonstrated that, just as in perceptual tasks (Spence, Nicholls, & Driver, 2001), switching between sensory modalities in conceptual judgments incurred a processing cost. Category names were presented with a property name from a specific modality in a property verification task. Responses were faster and more accurate if a target trial (e.g., *apple-red*) was preceded by a context trial from the same modality (e.g., *diamond-sparkling*) than if it was preceded by a context trial from a different modality (e.g., *airplane-noisy*). The explanation for this effect is that when participants perform the property verification task, they simulate experiencing an exemplar from the category in such a way that they can observe whether the exemplar has the property. In that way, they focus their attention on the relevant modality. A switching cost occurs because when the next pair is presented, attention is still focused on the modality that was relevant for the previous trial. The modality-switch effect has been replicated (Marques, 2006) and extended to switching between affective and perceptual representations (Vermeulen, Niedenthal, & Luminet, 2007). In addition to the modality-switch effect, Marques showed that performance was not affected by switching between superordinate categories. He presented animals and artifacts with modality-specific features. Whereas performance was affected by switching modalities (e.g., *mirror-reflect*, *telephone-ring*), there was no effect of superordinate switching (e.g., *donkey-heehaw*, *telephone-ring*). These results strongly suggest that categories are represented by perceptual modalities rather than by hierarchical domains.

Finally, there is an important role of action for representing categories. Since the main function of categories is to support our interactions with the environment, action should be central to representations. That this is very likely the case is demonstrated by the interaction between representation and action. When interacting with objects, the first action is often to touch the object. Therefore, grasping and pushing actions might be strongly activated. Having the hand in the appropriate shape to grasp a particular object facilitates subsequent processing of the object name (Klatzky, Pellegrino, McKloskey, & Doherty, 1989). In Klatzky et al.'s study, participants learned to make specific hand shapes such as a pinch in response to icons. These icons were then presented as primes, followed by target sentences (e.g., *Insert a coin*) to which participants made sensibility judgments. Performance was affected positively when the primed hand shape matched the shape that would be needed to interact with the object in the sentence. The reverse was shown by Masson, Bub, and Warren (2008; see also Van Elk, van Schie, & Bekkering, 2008), who found that processing of object and action names primed subsequent actions for which the matching hand shape was needed. Similar findings have shown facilitation due to a match between the direction of a movement implied by a sentence and the actual movement needed to make a response, the action-compatibility effect (Borghi et al., 2004; Glenberg & Kaschak, 2002;

Scorolli, Borghi, & Glenberg, 2009; Taylor, Lev-Ari, & Zwaan, 2008). Glenberg and Kaschak showed that when participants made sensibility judgments to sentences describing actions toward the body (e.g., *Open the drawer*), they were faster if the response required them to move their hand toward themselves than if it required them to move their hand away from their body. The opposite was found when the sentence described an action away from the body (e.g., *Close the drawer*). These and similar findings strongly suggest that the motor system is involved in representing categories.

## Sensory-Motor Systems Are Directly Involved in Representation

The studies discussed so far investigated the role of sensory-motor systems for categories in paradigms in which the perceptual and conceptual information was meaningfully related. For example, in Klatzky et al.'s (1989) experiments, the grasp that was primed was related to the grasp that would be needed for the object mentioned in the sentence. In Stanfield and Zwaan's (2001) experiment, the object in the picture was the same as the object in the sentence. It could be argued that these results show that sensory-motor information plays a role, but the locus of the effect might still be at some higher, more abstract semantic level rather than at the level of the sensory-motor systems. Therefore, we need to look at studies that have used paradigms in which a perceptual task and a conceptual task without a meaningful relation were used. McCloskey, Klatzky, and Pellegrino (1992) showed that concurrent motor planning of an unrelated action interfered with the hand shape priming effect on sentence processing. Investigating the role of perception, Van Dantzig, Pecher, Zeelenberg, and Barsalou (2008) adjusted the modality-switch paradigm. Rather than conceptual trials, they used a perceptual task (detection of meaningless visual, auditory, and tactile stimuli) as the context for conceptual property verification trials. They observed a modality-switch effect between the perceptual and conceptual trials. In particular, they observed a cost when the modality of the perceptual trial was different from that of the feature in the conceptual trial, paralleling the findings in the conceptual-only studies (Marques, 2006; Pecher et al., 2003). In contrast, Vermeulen, Corneille, and Niedenthal (2008) found that a concurrent perceptual memory load (meaningless visual shapes or auditory signals) interfered more with conceptual property verification trials if the property was from the same than from a different modality. Other studies have also shown that concurrent perceptual processing can interfere rather than facilitate conceptual processing. For example, Kaschak and colleagues (Kaschak et al., 2005, Kaschak, Zwaan, Aveyard, & Yaxley, 2006) showed that perceiving visual or auditory stimuli that depicted motion in a particular direction interfered with concurrent sentence comprehension if the sentence described an object moving in the same rather than different direction.

These studies suggest that whether overlap in perceptual and conceptual processing facilitates or harms performance depends on whether the tasks are performed at the same time or alternating. When the tasks are performed at the same time, they compete for resources, so greater overlap increases competition. When they alternate, there is no competition, and overlap may cause priming, for example, by focusing attention on the relevant modality. This picture is complicated, however, by studies that showed interference in an alternating paradigm. When participants processed linguistic stimuli in which a verb (e.g., *climb*; Richardson, Spivey, Barsalou, & McRae, 2003) or noun (e.g., *hat*; Estes, Verges, & Barsalou, 2008; Pecher, Van Dantzig, Boot, Zanolie, & Huber, 2010) pointed to a particular spatial location (e.g., *up* or *down*), their identification of a subsequently presented visual target (e.g., X or O) was harmed if the location of the visual target matched the implied location of the verb or noun. A possible explanation for these different findings is that in the studies by Richardson et al. and Estes et al. the perceptual representation of the conceptual stimulus was much richer than the simple perceptual stimuli used by Van Dantzig et al. The richer representation may have caused interference and may explain the differences in results.

### Flexibility of Representations

An important issue is whether category representations should be considered in isolation or in context. In daily life, people seldom encounter categories in isolation. We never interact with just an apple in some empty space. Categories are usually embedded in a context; for example, we have an apple with our lunch in the cafeteria, or we pick an apple from a crate at the supermarket. Several studies have shown that context affects which features of categories are activated. In the previous sections I already discussed some studies that showed such an effect. For example, the studies on modality switching (Pecher et al., 2003) suggest that the activation of features from certain modalities is determined by the modality of a previous trial. Zwaan and colleagues showed that linguistic context affects the visual features of categories (e.g., whether a bird is represented with its wings stretched or folded). Another interesting finding is that goals (e.g., such as defined by the experimental task) affect which sensory-motor features are used for performance. Bub, Masson, and Bukach (2003; see also Bub, Masson, & Cree, 2008) showed that action-related information is activated only when the task required participants to perform those actions (e.g., grasp). Iachini, Borghi, and Senese (2008) showed that when participants made similarity judgments, shape

was the most relevant feature, but when they sorted objects into categories, type of grip was the most relevant feature. Thus, various types of contexts affect categorical representations in different ways.

Further evidence for the flexibility of representations is provided by studies that show effects of prior context. Pecher et al. (1998) found priming for words that referred to objects with similar shapes (e.g., *banjo-tennis racket*), even though such information was irrelevant for the current task (lexical decision and word naming) as long as shape information had been activated in an earlier task. They argued that activation of the visual features in the prior task had made those features still more available later in the experiment (Barsalou, 1993), possibly due to altered representations (Goldstone, Lippa, & Shiffrin, 2001). Also using only words as stimuli, Pecher, Zeelenberg, and Barsalou (2004) extended these findings to other modalities in a property verification task. Even though initial processing was on word stimuli, further studies showed that the perceptual features that were made more available affected picture recognition (Pecher et al., 2009; Pecher, Zanolie, & Zeelenberg, 2007). For example, Pecher et al. (2007) presented object names (e.g., *chocolate*) with visual (e.g., *brown*) or nonvisual (e.g., *sweet*) property names in a property verification task. Later in the experiment, recognition of object pictures (e.g., a black-and-white drawing of a chocolate bar) was better for objects that had been presented with visual properties than with nonvisual properties, even though the particular visual property itself was not present in the picture. These findings suggest that during property verification participants simulated a visual representation of the object in order to verify the property. During this simulation, not only the relevant feature was activated but also other visual features such as shape. During the later recognition test the previously activated features were still more available. If the property was nonvisual, the simulation included no or fewer visual features. This flexibility of representations along modalities suggests that category representations are organized by sensory-motor modalities and that features can be strengthened selectively.

### Perceptual Simulation in the Brain
#### Activation of Sensory-Motor Systems

The similarity between sensory-motor processing and category representation implies that they are supported by the same brain structures. Several studies have used functional neuroimaging techniques to identify activity in the brain while participants process categories. Chao and Martin (1999) presented colored and grayscale pictures and asked participants to passively view the pictures, name the objects, or name the color of objects. By contrasting passive viewing of colored and grayscale pictures, the areas involved in perception of color could be identified. By contrasting object naming and color naming for grayscale pictures, the areas involved in retrieving color knowledge could be identified. Retrieving color knowledge was associated with a wide network of activity. Of particular interest were occipital areas that were activated during color knowledge retrieval; these areas were adjacent rather than overlapping with color perception. In contrast, Simmons et al. (2007) found overlap in left fusiform gyrus between an active color perception task and color name retrieval for objects. They argued that it is important to compare brain activation for perception and representation within subjects and in both domains use tasks that require active processing.

Brain regions associated with processing of other modalities have also been shown to be more activated during processing of categories. Simmons, Martin, and Barsalou (2005) showed that while participants performed a memory task with pictures of foods there was increased activation of circuits associated with taste and reward processing. While Simmons et al. used pictures of foods, Goldberg, Perfetti, and Schneider (2006) showed that even when words were presented brain regions associated with visual, auditory, gustatory, and tactile processing were activated. They asked participants to verify properties from these modalities for objects, and they showed increased activations in the corresponding regions. Hauk, Johnsrude, and Pulvermüller (2004) obtained evidence that the activation of motor and premotor areas was organized somatotopically, such that words referring to actions with specific body parts (e.g., kick) were associated with activations in the corresponding region (e.g., the leg area). The involvement of different sensory-motor systems suggests that categories are supported by a widely distributed network of activation (Barsalou, 2008; Cree & McRae, 2003; Martin, 2007).

## Domain-Specific Deficits

This view of categories as distributed patterns of activation may seem to be in contradiction with reports of patients who have category-specific deficits. A number of cases have been reported in the literature of patients with temporal lobe damage who show selective loss of knowledge for items from specific categories (Caramazza & Shelton, 1998; Warrington & Shallice, 1984). In the majority of cases these patients have lost knowledge of living things compared to nonliving things, although the opposite has also been reported. This double dissociation has led Caramazza and Shelton to argue for specialized mechanisms for living and nonliving things. They argued that conceptual knowledge is organized categorically in the brain. Such a categorical division would have evolved from evolutionary pressure to act with fast flight or feeding responses to certain animals and plants. As these specialized structures are selectively impaired, category-specific knowledge loss results.

Farah and McClelland (1991; see also Humphreys & Forde, 2001) demonstrated, however, that category-specific deficits can emerge from an architecture that has no separate structures for different categories. In their model, illustrated in Figure 24.1, categorical knowledge was distributed over patterns of units that represent functional and sensory features. These units were fully interconnected and activation was updated in parallel. They assumed that the proportions of sensory and functional features differed between living and nonliving things. Living things (e.g., *zebra*) are distinguished primarily by sensory features, whereas nonliving things (e.g., *hammer*) are distinguished primarily by functional features. For example, knowledge of most animals consists of what they look like and what sounds they make. Knowledge of tools, on the other hand, consists more of what they are used for. Farah and McClelland implemented this distinction in their model. They demonstrated that when the visual units were damaged, the model was impaired more for living than nonliving things, and when

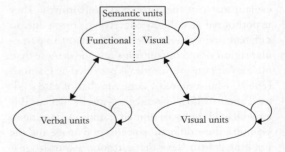

**Figure 24.1** Farah and McClelland's (1991) model. The model has 24 verbal units, 24 picture units, 60 visual semantic units, and 20 functional semantic units. In the basic model, 20 living things were represented with 16.1 visual units and 2.1 functional units on average; 20 nonliving things were represented with 9.4 visual units and 6.7 functional units on average.

the functional units were damaged, the model was impaired more for nonliving than living things.

The distinction in impairments is not just between living and nonliving, however, because some categories (animals, fruits, vegetables, human-made foods, gems, and musical instruments) can be impaired separately or with the opposite domain (Cree & McRae, 2003). Cree and McRae (see also McRae & Cree, 2002) used feature production norms (McRae et al., 1997; McRae, Cree, Seidenberg, & McNorgan, 2005) to investigate the actual distribution of features from different knowledge types. The norms were collected by asking participants to list features for a total of 541 concepts from about 35 categories. For example, for the concept *pumpkin*, participants would produce properties such as *is round, is orange, has seeds, grows on vines, is eaten in pies*, and so on. Cree and McRae used the Wu and Barsalou (2009) knowledge type taxonomy to classify these responses into classes that correspond to sensory modalities, emotion, function, and more abstract features such as taxonomic knowledge. They showed that the pattern of impairments found in patients was best explained by a combination of differences in distribution over knowledge types between categories, differences in the number of distinguishing features, and concept familiarity. The most important finding was that categories differed greatly in the distribution of features over different modalities. For example, fruits and vegetables had a much higher number of color and taste features than creatures and nonliving things, and a much lower number of visual motion features than creatures. On the other hand, fruits and vegetables are similar to nonliving things because they are high on functional features and low on visual motion features. The distribution of features over knowledge types for different categories allowed Cree and McRae to explain many of the patterns of impairment. They hypothesized that knowledge types correspond to different brain regions, and that damage to a particular region would impair some categories more than others. Support for this idea is provided by Gainotti (2000), who reviewed a large number of case studies. Patients who show category-specific deficits differ widely in the locus of their lesions. According to Gainotti, these different patterns of damage and the resulting deficits show that categorical knowledge is supported by a network of brain areas that represent sensory-motor information.

In addition, Cree and McRae also showed that categories with more distinguishing features are less susceptible to damage than categories with fewer distinguishing features. Distinguishing features allow discrimination between concepts. For example, *has a trunk* distinguishes *elephants* from other animals, whereas *has ears* does not distinguish animals from each other. If features are lost, categories with fewer distinguishing features are more likely to be damaged than categories with more distinguishing features because the information that allows discrimination from other categories is no longer available. This finding also shows that a distributed explanation is more likely than a domain-specific explanation.

The models discussed so far assumed that categories are represented by patterns of activation in different brain regions that correspond to sensory modalities. A slightly different approach was taken by Plaut (2002). He also developed a distributed connectionist model of semantic knowledge, illustrated in Figure 24.2. In addition to different sets of units that represented visual, tactile, action, and phonological information, a set of hidden units formed the semantic knowledge representations. The architecture was such that the set of hidden units formed a sort of hub between the specialized units. The specialized units were connected only to other units within the same set and to the hidden semantic units. In this way the semantic units mediated between different modalities.

The model was trained to perform in two ways. First, it was trained to generate a name when given visual or tactile object input. Second, it was trained

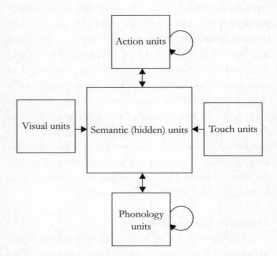

**Figure 24.2** Plaut's (2002) model. The visual and touch units are input units, and each has 20 units. The action and phonology units are output units and also have 20 units each. There are 225 semantic units. The model represented 100 concepts, 20 exemplars each from five categories.

to generate both the name and an action when given visual or tactile input. The result of training was that the semantic units showed both categorical and modality-specific organization. Representations generated within the same modality had higher similarity than representations generated cross-modally. However, cross-modal representations of the same object were also highly similar. In fact, activation levels in the semantic units were not affected by modality, but the connection weights between semantic units and specialized units showed topographic organization. Semantic units near the specialized units had larger weights on input connections from that modality.

Other models also have hidden units that act as a hub. Using verbal descriptions of objects and visual features present in people's drawings of the same objects as input, Rogers et al. (2004) trained a connectionist model to represent objects in a layer of hidden "semantic" units. Their model is illustrated in Figure 24.3. Damage to these semantic units resulted in similar deficits as those observed in patients with semantic dementia, including failures to retrieve or use visual or verbal information. The deficits of the model across a wide variety of tasks could be explained by the similarity structure in the semantic units. As object representations were more similar, damage to the connection weights in the model caused them to drift, resulting in increasing difficulty to distinguish between similar representations. Thus, although the objects' similarities were expressed in the verbal or visual descriptions, the semantic units were sensitive to these similarities as well. However, Rogers et al. argued that the stability of the model's semantic representation still relied on the connectivity between the hidden units and the perceptual and verbal input units. Damage to the connections between visual and semantic units

could cause deficits in a variety of tasks, including tasks in which no visual information is involved.

An important question is to what extent such hidden units truly represent semantic knowledge or whether they only mediate between different kinds of knowledge of objects. Rogers et al. (2004) stated that their model captures the similarities between objects across domains in an abstract form. However, their semantic units do not explicitly encode information but should be viewed as links between visual and verbal representations. As such, they should be considered semantic in the function they perform and not in their content. Given an input pattern at one of the sets of input units (visual, verbal, or name), the model settled into a stable state that included patterns at the other input units. As an example, one of the tasks that the model was made to perform was naming from visual input. To simulate presenting a picture, a pattern of activation was presented at the visual input units. Because there were no direct connections between visual and name units, updating had to happen via the hidden semantic units. Once the name units were in a stable state, the object name was produced. Thus, the semantic units encoded neither visual nor verbal information but allowed updating of the name units by mediating between visual and verbal units. Thus, the semantic units form a convergence zone (Damasio, Grabowski, Tranel, Hichwa, & Damasio, 1996) or a semantic hub (Patterson, Nestor, & Rogers, 2007; see also Kellenbach, Brett, & Patterson, 2001).

Another type of model does not assume a separation between different types of input modalities but rather has one single layer of semantic units. McRae et al. (1997) used feature production norms to train their model, which consisted of a layer of word-form units and a layer of semantic units, as illustrated in Figure 24.4. This model was able to explain various results from speeded semantic tasks with healthy subjects. An important finding was that variability in the degree of feature intercorrelations can explain differences between categories. Artifacts have fewer intercorrelated features than natural kinds. McRae et al. showed that priming effects for artifacts were predicted better by overlap in individual features, whereas priming effects for natural kinds were predicted better by overlap in intercorrelated features. Devlin, Gonnerman, Andersen, and Seidenberg (1998; see also Tyler, Moss, Durrant-Peatfield, & Levy, 2000) showed that a model in which such differences in intercorrelated features was preserved could account for the double dissociation observed

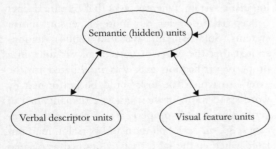

**Figure 24.3** Rogers et al.'s (2004) model. The verbal descriptor units consisted of 40 name units, 64 perceptual units, 32 functional units, and 16 encyclopedic units. In addition, there were 64 visual feature units and 64 semantic units. Inputs were verbal features from production norms and descriptions of drawings for 62 objects.

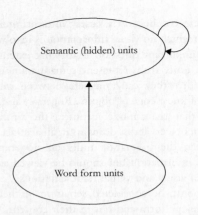

**Figure 24.4** McRae et al.'s (1997) model. The model had 379 word-form units and 646 semantic units and represented 84 words. The representations were based on feature production norms.

in Alzheimer's patients. At low levels of damage, categories that had lots of intercorrelated features were less susceptible to nonfocal damage (as is typically found with Alzheimer's patients), because the strong intercorrelations allowed pattern completion even for weaker features. However, as damage got more severe, entire sets of intercorrelated features were lost, resulting in impairment of entire superordinate categories. Devlin et al.'s simulations showed that the pattern of deficits paralleled those found for patients. When only small proportions of semantic connections were damaged, there was, on average, a small artifact deficit. With more damage, however, there was a larger deficit of natural kinds. The simulations also showed large variability in patterns, consistent with the variability found between patients.

The distributed nature of these models seems to be at odds with functional magnetic resonace imaging (fMRI) data that show specialized areas for certain categories of objects such as faces and houses (Haxby et al., 2001). This may be due to the sort of subtraction techniques often used with fMRI research. In typical studies, participants process two types of stimuli (e.g., faces vs. tools), and the areas that show significantly more BOLD activation for one category than the other are appointed the role of specialized processor of that category. Such techniques ignore the role of areas that are involved in more than one category because these get subtracted out.

Although most fMRI research thus focuses on finding localized areas for categories, it is possible to investigate the kind of distributed representations as are assumed by the models described earlier. Haxby et al. (2001) used an analysis technique that was aimed at distributed patterns of activation across large parts of the cortex. They presented pictures of different exemplars from seven categories and examined the patterns of voxel activation in the ventral temporal cortex. For each category, correlations between different runs of the same category were higher than correlations between runs of different categories. More important, even if the voxels that responded maximally to that particular category were removed, the remaining pattern was still more similar to other same category patterns than to different category patterns. Thus, these data indicate that categories are represented by a distributed pattern of activation rather than specialized areas.

## The Role of Language
### Language Binds Experiences

Building on earlier proposals (Glaser, 1992; Pavio, 1986), Simmons, Hamann, Harenski, Hu, and Barsalou (2008; see also Louwerse & Jeuniaux, 2008) argued that conceptual processing is a mixture of superficial linguistic processing and deeper, sensory-motor simulations. Using fMRI, Simmons et al. showed that a conceptual task (property generation) shared patterns of brain activation with both word association and situation generation. Moreover, they argued that the activation associated with linguistic processing peaked earlier than the activations associated with sensory-motor simulations. They proposed that conceptual processing is supported by two parallel streams of activation. The faster stream is based on the linguistic system and reflects associations between words. The slower stream is based on sensory-motor systems and reflects situated simulations of concepts. Differences in task requirements cause differences in recruitment of these two streams. Tasks that can be performed at a superficial level rely mostly on the linguistic system, whereas tasks that require deeper conceptual processing rely more on sensory-motor systems. Solomon and Barsalou (2004) demonstrated that the effect of perceptual variables in a property verification task was modulated by the extent to which the task could be performed by word association. In their task, participants had to verify whether the property was a part of the concept (e.g., *cat-ear*). Solomon and Barsalou manipulated whether the false trials contained associated concept-property pairs (e.g., *owl-tree*). When only the true trials were associated, participants could use superficial processing based on word associations. When both true and false trials were associated, however, participants had to use deeper processing, and in that case perceptual variables affected their performance.

Although some people may think of linguistic processing and simulation as two separate routes, it is much more likely that these types of processing interact and share processing mechanisms. A possible mechanism for the interaction between linguistic processing and simulation is the idea of a convergence zone (Damasio et al., 1996) or semantic hub (Patterson et al., 2007). Linguistic information and sensory-motor information from different modalities are represented in modality-specific systems, and they are linked through central areas whose function is to link information from these different modalities together. With such a mechanism, object identities are formed and linked to names. For example, the word *apple* will be linked to a shape representation on one occasion, while on another occasion the word *apple* will be linked to a taste representation. Models such as those developed by Plaut (2002) and Rogers et al. (2004) show that the resulting representations in semantic hubs (the hidden layers in their models) are organized according to semantic similarity. It is important to note that these representations do not contain any meaning. The hub does not represent the color or taste of an apple; it only allows this information to be activated in the specialized sensory areas when, for example, the word *apple* is presented. However, because the hub has a semantic organization, activation of a pattern in the hub could lead to activation of related words without the need to activate the word's meaning. Therefore, it is possible that for superficial processing the links between the language area and the hub are sufficient.

The role of language might be to connect different sensory-motor experiences to the same category. In this way, category identities may develop even when experiences do not share features. For example, the experience of drinking apple juice and the experience of picking up an apple in a shop have little in common. By using the same category name (*apple*) for both experiences, they become connected and form rich representations.

Andrews, Vigliocco, and Vinson (2009) argue that both types of input are important. In their model, sensory-motor information and language information are treated as a single combined data set. They used feature production norms as a proxy for sensory-motor experiences, and word co-occurrences as linguistic input. The word co-occurrence data were based on an approach similar to LSA (Landauer & Dumais, 1997). In LSA, text is used as input, and the model computes how often words occur in particular texts. Based on a large corpus of texts, words are represented as vectors of co-occurrence frequencies in the texts. Landauer and Dumais showed that words that occur in similar sets of texts have similar vectors and can be viewed as nearby points in a multidimensional co-occurrence space. Distances in this space tend to be highly correlated to semantic similarity. Andrews et al. argued that a probabilistic model that was trained using the linguistic and sensory-motor data concurrently was a better predictor of human performance than models based on either source of data alone or based on using the two sources independently.

Thus, instead of language and sensory-motor representations as being separate, parallel processes, they are part of the same network. Language binds different sensory-motor experiences to form coherent categories. During language processing, meaning is represented by activation of a pattern across sensory-motor systems. However, in tasks in which performance can be based on word associations, activation of other words via the semantic hub might be sufficient. The advantage of such shortcuts is that the system does not need to wait for full activation of representations in the sensory-motor system. To represent meaning fully, however, these representations are necessary.

### Abstract Concepts

An interesting aspect of the Andrews et al. (2009) model is that it can infer features for concepts for which no sensory-motor input was available. This might provide a solution to the problem of how abstract categories are represented (Barsalou, 1999; Barsalou & Wiemer-Hastings, 2005; Dove, 2009; Prinz, 2002). Since abstract categories (e.g., *democracy*, *respect*) have no perceptual features, explaining how they can be grounded in sensory-motor representations provides a challenge. Andrews et al. attempted to solve this problem by attributing features from words that have similar word co-occurrence vectors. However, from the examples that they provided, it is not immediately obvious that the resulting features are perceptual. For example, the features that are produced (by the model) for the abstract word *obsession* are *women, scream, crave, desire, relieve, love, discomfort, burn, explode,* and *attack*. Rather than describing perceptual experiences, some of these words are abstract themselves, and of those that do describe perceivable features, some seem only indirect aspects of the experience of *obsession* (e.g., *burn, explode, attack*). The question is, of course, what sensory-motor experiences would represent such concepts.

Several other ideas for how abstract concepts might be grounded have been proposed (e.g., Barsalou, 1999, Barsalou & Wiemer-Hastings, 2005; Prinz, 2002). At present, the most popular theory is that people use metaphors and image schemata to ground abstract concepts in bodily experiences. For example, people may understand the process of solving a problem in terms of travelling from a starting point (the problem situation) to a destination (the solution) along a path (the method that is used to solve the problem), as is illustrated by expressions such as *to get sidetracked* or *to have something get in one's way* (Gibbs, 1994, 2005; Lakoff, 1987; Lakoff & Johnson, 1980; but see Barsalou & Wiemer-Hastings, 2005; Murphy, 1996). Thus, the concrete situation of travelling along a path is used as a metaphor for an abstract situation such as solving a problem. Because the metaphor refers to a concrete physical experience, embodied theories can explain how the abstract concept is grounded in the perceptual and motor systems.

Whereas most of the evidence given in support of this theory comes from cognitive linguistics, recent studies have provided some evidence that image schemata are activated by abstract concepts (Boot & Pecher, 2010, 2011; Boroditsky & Ramscar, 2002; Richardson et al., 2003; Spivey, Richardson, & Gonzalez-Marquez, 2005; Zanolie, Van Dantzig, Boot, Wijnen, Schubert, Giessner, & Pecher, 2012; see Pecher, Boot, & Van Dantzig, 2011, for an extended discussion). The question is to what extent these results are proof of grounded representations. Although image schemata refer to basic bodily experiences, they do so in quite an abstract way. For example, several concepts might be represented with the verticality image schema, such as *power, valence, status,* and so on. However, the concept of *power* must be much richer than just the verticality image schema. Image schemata may represent some features of abstract concepts, but the full representation needs additional features.

A second proposal for grounding abstract concepts is by simulations of introspective experiences (Barsalou, 1999; Barsalou & Wiemer-Hastings, 2005). For example, introspective experiences may be associated with being hungry, feeling happy, or having a goal. People can perceive their internal states and can simulate internal states to represent concepts. Introspection could be considered another sensory modality. Just as for sensory modalities, people can switch attention from introspection to other modalities such as visual perception (Oosterwijk et al., 2009). Barsalou and Wiemer-Hastings found a greater focus on introspective properties for abstract than for concrete concepts. The idea of introspection needs further investigation, however. While it may be more or less clear how people perceive that they are hungry or aroused, it is less obvious how people know that they have goals or beliefs, or that they are trying to retrieve something from memory, without postulating a homunculus. Possibly, introspective experiences can be part of a representation as grounded features, but they do not provide the full meaning of a concept.

A third proposal is that abstract concepts are represented by concrete situations (Barsalou & Wiemer-Hastings, 2005). Likely, a collection of concrete situations that share the abstract concept combine to form a rich representation. This proposal has similarities to exemplar models of categorization (Hintzman, 1986; Nosofsky, 1988). In exemplar models, each encounter with an exemplar is stored. Abstraction across exemplars is achieved when a cue activates several different exemplars. These are then combined as a response to the cue (e.g., as a combined similarity measure or as a summary representation) in order to be used for processing. Representation by concrete situations allows these representations to be grounded in sensory-motor simulations. For example, the concept *democracy* may be represented by *a meeting of parliament, a succession of speeches, votes on proposals during meetings, election campaigns, a voter deciding on her vote, going into a booth with a ballot, availability of multiple views in the media,* and so on. Barsalou and Wiemer-Hastings found that situations were important aspects for all types of concepts, constituting about half of all produced properties, but even more for abstract than concrete concepts. Thus, this idea has great promise. So far, however, it is still in its early stages of development.

## General Discussion
### Is Sensory-Motor Simulation Necessary?

In this chapter I have set out to describe the role of sensory-motor simulations for mental categories. The evidence from behavioral studies, brain imaging, patient studies, and models of category representation are consistent with the idea that sensory-motor systems support representation by a simulation mechanism. An important question, however, is whether these sensory-motor simulations are necessary for representation. Theories of grounded cognition propose that they are, because the core assumption of such theories is that a simulation and a concept are the same thing. For example, Glenberg (1997) proposes that concepts are potential action patterns. Thus, in this view, there are no amodal symbols that represent a concept. Mahon and Caramazza (2008), on the other hand, have argued that much of the evidence is also consistent with a system in which representation is initially separate from sensory-motor systems, and in which activation cascades to those systems only *after* a category has been represented by amodal symbols, or in which activation spreads in parallel to amodal and sensory-motor systems, but the sensory-motor activation is not fundamental to the category representation. Thus, studies that show activation of sensory-motor systems in the brain while participants perform a representational task (e.g., read language) do not necessarily show that such activation supports representation. The activation of sensory-motor systems might merely be a side effect of representing categories. The same explanation might be applied to behavioral studies that show activation of sensory-motor information during representation.

It is more difficult (but perhaps not impossible) for such a coactivation account to explain data that show an effect of perceptual variables that precede representation. For example, studies show deficits in performance when sensory-motor systems are damaged or occupied by other tasks. Although some models have shown that domain-specific deficits are predicted by models that assume a single semantic system (Devlin et al., 1998; McRae et al., 1997), more detailed studies showed that deficits are most likely due to damage to processing areas for specific sensory-motor information (Cree & McRae, 2003; Gainotti, 2000). Healthy participants also showed deteriorated performance in a verbal property verification task when the property was from the same modality as a concurrently performed perceptual task (Vermeulen et al., 2008). The fact that representation is more difficult when the specific sensory system has fewer resources strongly suggests that these systems perform an essential role. Using a slightly different paradigm, Van Dantzig et al. (2008) showed facilitation for verbal property verification if a previous perceptual stimulus was from the same modality. Again, this is hard to reconcile with an explanation that assumes mere coactivation of sensory information. Although it remains possible that some aspects of representation are more symbolic, at least an important part has to be supported by sensory-motor systems in order to explain these findings.

## Is Simulation Task-Induced Imagery?

An important question is to what extent the evidence presented so far reflects automatic representation. In laboratory experiments participants may develop strategies in order to cope with a task. In cases where sensory-motor variables affect conceptual processing, one may wonder whether conscious imagery rather than automatic representational processing can explain such effects. Thus, much of the work on the role of sensory-motor systems for category representations may suggest that representation is a form of imagery. As with categories, there is evidence that mental imagery shares modality-specific mechanisms at behavioral (Rouw, Kosslyn, & Hamel, 1997) and neurological levels (Borst & Kosslyn, 2008). On the other hand, important differences exist between imagery and categorical representations (Barsalou, 1999, 2009). First, there is a difference in conscious control. Imagery tasks require effortful processes such as rotating or reorganizing mental images, whereas the representation of a category may take place without conscious awareness or control. Second, imagery ability varies widely between individuals (Blajenkova, Kozhevnikov, & Motes, 2006; Burton & Fogarty, 2003; Kosslyn, Brunn, Cave, & Wallach, 1984), whereas representing conceptual knowledge is performed easily by anyone with normal cognitive abilities. Several studies have shown that perceptual effects in representation do not vary with imagery ability or preference (Pecher, Van Dantzig, & Schifferstein, 2009; Stanfield & Zwaan, 2001), suggesting that the involvement of sensory-motor systems for representation is automatic.

## Conclusion

Mental categories are (at least for a part) supported by sensory-motor simulations. There is a wealth of evidence showing that mental categories retain the sensory-motor qualities of their physical counterparts, such as modality-specific features. These simulations are highly flexible, and just as in sensory-motor interactions, they can focus on specific modalities, change according to context, take perspective into account, and so on. Although simulations are temporary processes that represent categories during online processing, they can have longer lasting impacts. Several studies have shown that when concepts are repeated, later representations are affected by earlier ones as if they had been interacted with physically. Several findings of interactions between representation and perception and the activation of similar brain areas for representation and perception all point to the conclusion that they are supported by the same processing mechanisms.

## Future Directions

Although the aforementioned conclusion is supported by a lot of research, there are some important remaining questions. First of all, as was already discussed earlier, more research is needed to show how fundamental the role of sensory-motor mechanisms is for representations. Are simulations essential for representation, do they support representation only partly, or are they merely by-products of otherwise symbolic operations? As some connectionist frameworks show, representations might be widely distributed, which complicates the question of what is essential and what is a by-product. In such models, all kinds of information interact and support each other. Thus, even if there are more abstract, symbolic aspects to representation, they might still be affected by manipulations that tap into sensory-motor processes. Therefore, the distinction between grounded and nongrounded theories may turn out to be artificial.

A second, very important question is how sensory-motor simulations can represent abstract concepts. Research supporting the grounded cognition framework so far has mainly found evidence for representations of concrete things such as *apples* and *eagles*. It can be argued, however, that most of our representations and other cognitive operations concern abstract things such as *democracy* or *regret*. Several mechanisms have been proposed, and of these, the conceptual metaphor theory has received most attention. It is unlikely, however, that this theory can fully explain abstract concepts, because these concepts are much richer than simple image schemata. Other ideas are still in too early stages to allow evaluation. It is crucial that this question gets resolved, because a theory that can deal only with concrete concepts is too limited.

A more methodological challenge is how we can measure what people's sensory-motor experiences are. Most researchers have used their own (informed) intuitions when manipulating sensory-motor features of representations. Some have been more thorough and collected norms (e.g., McRae et al., 2005). Still, often the kinds of features that are used are those that can be described by words. One may wonder whether words can accurately describe sensory-motor experiences. Take, for example, colors. The color red may be used for various things (hair, wine, earth, fire truck) that are all red but in very different ways. For other modalities it is often even harder to accurately describe sensory experiences. For example, there are hardly any words that describe smells except for names of other things that have that smell, hence the interesting vocabulary of wine tasters. Even if there are words to describe an experience, one may wonder whether this is the right grain size for perceptual symbols.

Finally, as some research has shown, concepts are affected by context. As things in the world are not experienced in isolation, it seems likely that concepts are also not represented in isolation. The framework I have discussed in this chapter views representations as simulations of experiences. It seems likely, therefore, that such a framework is especially suited to take context into account.

## References

Andrews, M., Vigliocco, G., & Vinson, D. (2009). Integrating experiential and distributional data to learn semantic representations. *Psychological Review, 116*, 463–498.

Barsalou, L. W. (1990). On the indistinguishability of exemplar memory and abstraction in category representation. In T. K. Srull & R. S. Wyer (Eds.), *Advances in social cognition, volume III: Content and process specificity in the effects of prior experiences* (pp. 61–88). Hillsdale, NJ: Lawrence Erlbaum Associates.

Barsalou, L. W. (1993). Flexibility, structure, and linguistic vagary in concepts: Manifestations of a compositional system of perceptual symbols. In A. F. Collins , S. E. Gathercole , M. A. Conway , & P. E. Morris (Eds.), *Theories of memory* (pp. 29–101). Hove, England: Erlbaum.

Barsalou, L. W. (1999). Perceptual symbol systems. *Behavioral and Brain Sciences, 22*, 577–660.

Barsalou, L. W. (2008). Grounding symbolic operations in the brain's modal systems. In G. R. Semin & E. R. Smith (Eds.), *Embodied grounding: Social, cognitive, affective, and neuroscientific approaches* (pp. 9–42). New York: Cambridge University Press.

Barsalou, L. W. (2009). Simulation, situated conceptualization, and prediction. *Philosophical Transactions of the Royal Society B, 364*, 1281–1289.

Barsalou, L. W., Simmons, W. K., Barbey, A. K., & Wilson, C. D. (2003). Grounding conceptual knowledge in modality-specific systems. *Trends in Cognitive Sciences, 7*, 84–91.

Barsalou, L. W., & Wiemer-Hastings, K. (2005). Situating abstract concepts. In D. Pecher & R. A. Zwaan (Eds.), *Grounding cognition: The role of perception and action in memory, language, and thinking* (pp. 129–163). Cambridge, England: Cambridge University Press.

Blajenkova, O., Kozhevnikov, M., & Motes, M. A. (2006). Object-spatial imagery: A new self-report imagery questionnaire. *Applied Cognitive Psychology, 20*, 239–263.

Boot, I., & Pecher, D. (2010). Similarity is closeness: Metaphorical mapping in a perceptual task. *Quarterly Journal of Experimental Psychology, 63*, 942–954.

Boot, I., &Pecher, D. (2011). Representation of categories: Metaphorical use of the container schema. *Experimental Psychology, 58, 162–170.*

Borghi, A. M., Glenberg, A. M., & Kaschak, M. P. (2004). Putting words in perspective. *Memory and Cognition*, *32*, 863–873.

Boroditsky, L., & Ramscar, M. (2002). The roles of body and mind in abstract thought. *Psychological Science*, *13*, 185–189.

Borst, G., & Kosslyn, S. M. (2008). Visual mental imagery and visual perception: Structural equivalence revealed by scanning processes. *Memory and Cognition*, *36*, 849–862.

Bub, D. N., Masson, M. E. J., & Bukach, C. M. (2003). Gesturing and naming: The use of functional knowledge in object identification. *Psychological Science*, *14*, 467–472.

Bub, D. N., Masson, M. E. J., & Cree, G. S. (2008). Evocation of functional and volumetric gestural knowledge by objects and words. *Cognition*, *106*, 27–58.

Burton, L. J., & Fogarty, G. J. (2003). The factor structure of visual imagery and spatial abilities. *Intelligence*, *31*, 289–318.

Caramazza, A., & Shelton, J. R. (1998). Domain-specific knowledge systems in the brain: The animate-inanimate distinction. *Journal of Cognitive Neuroscience*, *10*, 1–34.

Chao, L. L., & Martin, A. (1999). Cortical regions associated with perceiving, naming, and knowing about colors. *Journal of Cognitive Neuroscience*, *11*, 25–35.

Connell, L. (2007). Representing object colour in language comprehension. *Cognition*, *102*, 476–485.

Cree, G. S., & Mc Rae, K. (2003). Analyzing the factors underlying the structure and computation of the meaning of chipmunk, cherry, chisel, cheese, and cello (and many other such concrete nouns). *Journal of Experimental Psychology: General*, *132*, 163–201.

Damasio, H., Grabowski, T. J., Tranel, D., Hichwa, R. D., & Damasio, A. R. (1996). A neural basis for lexical retrieval. *Nature*, *380*, 499–505.

Devlin, J. T., Gonnerman, L. M., Andersen, E. S., & Seidenberg, M. S. (1998). Category-specific semantic deficits in focal and widespread brain damage: A computational account. *Journal of Cognitive Neuroscience*, *10*, 77–94.

Dove, G. (2009). Beyond perceptual symbols: A call for representational pluralism. *Cognition*, *110*, 412–431.

Estes, Z., Verges, M., & Barsalou, L. W. (2008). Head up, foot down: Object words orient attention to the objects' typical location. *Psychological Science*, *19*, 93–97.

Farah, M. J., & Mc Clelland, J. L. (1991). A computational model of semantic memory impairment: Modality specificity and emergent category specificity. *Journal of Experimental Psychology: General*, *120*, 339–357.

Gainotti, G. (2000). What the locus of brain lesion tells us about the nature of the cognitive defect underlying category-specific disorders: A review. *Cortex*, *36*, 539–559.

Gibbs, R. W. J. (1994). *The poetics of mind: Figurative thought, language, and understanding*. New York: Cambridge University Press.

Gibbs, R. W. J. (2005). Embodiment in metaphorical imagination. In D. Pecher & R. A. Zwaan (Eds.), *Grounding cognition: The role of perception and action in memory, language, and thinking* (pp. 65–92). Cambridge, England: Cambridge University Press.

Glaser, W. R. (1992). Picture naming. *Cognition*, *42*, 61–105.

Glenberg, A. M. (1997). What memory is for. *Behavioral and Brain Sciences*, *20*, 1–55.

Glenberg, A. M., & Kaschak, M. P. (2002). Grounding language in action. *Psychonomic Bulletin and Review*, *9*, 558–565.

Goldberg, R. F., Perfetti, C. A., & Schneider, W. (2006). Perceptual knowledge retrieval activates sensory brain regions. *Journal of Neuroscience*, *26*, 4917–4921.

Goldstone, R. L., Lippa, Y., & Shiffrin, R. M. (2001). Altering object representations through category learning. *Cognition*, *78*, 27–43.

Hauk, O., Johnsrude, I., & Pulvermüller, F. (2004). Somatotopic representation of action words in human motor and premotor cortex. *Neuron*, *41*, 301–307.

Haxby, J. V., Gobbini, M. I., Furey, M. L., Ishai, A., Schouten, J. L., & Pietrini, P. (2001). Distributed and overlapping representations of faces and objects in ventral temporal cortex. *Science*, *293*, 2425–2430.

Hintzman, D. L. (1986). Schema abstraction in a multiple-trace memory model. *Psychological Review*, *93*, 411–428.

Humphreys, G. W., & Forde, E. M. E. (2001). Hierarchies, similarity, and interactivity in object recognition: "Category-specific" neuropsychological deficits. *Behavioral and Brain Sciences*, *24*, 453–509.

Iachini, T., Borghi, A. M., & Senese, V. P. (2008). Categorization and sensorimotor interaction with objects. *Brain and Cognition*, *67*, 31–43.

Kaschak, M. P., Madden, C. J., Therriault, D. J., Yaxley, R. H., Aveyard, M., Blanchard, A. A., & Zwaan, R. A. (2005). Perception of motion affects language processing. *Cognition*, *94*, B79–B89.

Kaschak, M. P., Zwaan, R. A., Aveyard, M., & Yaxley, R. H. (2006). Perception of auditory motion affects language processing. *Cognitive Science*, *30*, 733–744.

Kellenbach, M. L., Brett, M., & Patterson, K. (2001). Large, colorful, or noisy? Attribute- and modality-specific activations during retrieval of perceptual attribute knowledge. *Cognitive, Affective and Behavioral Neuroscience*, *1*, 207–221.

Klatzky, R. L., Pellegrino, J. W., Mc Closkey, B. P., & Doherty, S. (1989). Can you squeeze a tomato? The role of motor representations in semantic sensibility judgments. *Journal of Memory and Language*, *28*, 56–77.

Kosslyn, S. M., Brunn, J., Cave, K. R., & Wallach, R. W. (1984). Individual differences in mental imagery ability: A computational analysis. *Cognition*, *18*, 195–243.

Lakoff, G. (1987). *Women, fire, and dangerous things*. Chicago: Chicago University Press.

Lakoff, G., & Johnson, M. (1980). *Metaphors we live by*. Chicago: Chicago University Press.

Landauer, T. K., & Dumais, S. T. (1997). A solution to Plato's problem: The latent semantic analysis theory of acquisition, induction, and representation of knowledge. *Psychological Review*, *104*, 211–240.

Louwerse, M. M., & Jeuniaux, P. (2008). Language comprehension is both embodied and symbolic. In M. De Vega , A. M. Glenberg, & A. C. Graesser (Eds.), *Embodiment and meaning: A debate* (pp. 309–326). Oxford, England: Oxford University Press.

Mahon, B. Z., & Caramazza, A. (2008). A critical look at the embodied cognition hypothesis and a new proposal for grounding conceptual content. *Journal of Physiology (Paris)*, *102*, 59–70.

Marques, J. F. (2006). Specialization and semantic organization: Evidence for multiple semantics linked to sensory modalities. *Memory and Cognition*, *34*, 60–67.

Martin, A. (2007). The representation of object concepts in the brain. *Annual Review of Psychology*, *58*, 25–45.

Masson, M. E. J. (1995). A distributed memory model of semantic priming. *Journal of Experimental Psychology: Learning, Memory, and Cognition, 21,* 3–23.

Masson, M. E. J., Bub, D. N., & Warren, C. M. (2008). Kicking calculators: Contribution of embodied representations to sentence comprehension. *Journal of Memory and Language, 59,* 256–265.

Mc Closkey, B. P., Klatzky, R. L., & Pellegrino, J. W. (1992). Rubbing your stomach while tapping your fingers: Interference between motor planning and semantic judgments. *Journal of Experimental Psychology: Human Perception and Performance, 18,* 948–961.

McRae, K., & Cree, G. S. (2002). Factors underlying category-specific semantic deficits. In E. M. E. Forde & G. W. Humphreys (Eds.), *Category specificity in brain and mind* (pp. 211–249). Hove, England: Psychology Press.

McRae, K., Cree, G. S., Seidenberg, M. S., & McNorgan, C. (2005). Semantic feature production norms for a large set of living and nonliving things. *Behavior Research Methods, 37,* 547–559.

McRae, K., Cree, G. S., Westmacott, R., & De Sa, V. R. (1999). Further evidence for feature correlations in semantic memory. *Canadian Journal of Experimental Psychology, 53,* 360–373.

McRae, K., De Sa, V. R., & Seidenberg, M. S. (1997). On the nature and scope of featural representations of word meaning. *Journal of Experimental Psychology: General, 126,* 99–130.

Murphy, G. L. (1996). On metaphoric representation. *Cognition, 60,* 173–204.

Murphy, G. L. (2002). *The big book of concepts.* Cambridge: MIT Press.

Oosterwijk, S., Winkielman, P., Pecher, D., Zeelenberg, R., Rotteveel, M., & Fischer, A. H. (2012). Mental states inside out: Switching costs for emotional and nonemotional sentences that differ in internal and external focus. *Memory and Cognition, 40,* 93–100.

Nosofsky, R. M. (1988). Similarity, frequency, and category representations. *Journal of Experimental Psychology: Learning, Memory, and Cognition, 14,* 54–65.

Patterson, K., Nestor, P. J., & Rogers, T. T. (2007). Where do you know what you know? The representation of semantic knowledge in the human brain. *Nature Reviews: Neuroscience, 8,* 976–987.

Pavio, A. (1986). *Mental representations: A dual coding approach.* Oxford, England: Oxford University Press.

Pecher, D., Boot, I., & Van Dantzig, S. (2011). Abstract concepts: Sensory-motor grounding, metaphors, and beyond. In B. H. Ross (Ed.), *The psychology of learning and motivation* (pp. 217–248). Burlington: Academic Press.

Pecher, D., van Dantzig, S., Boot, I., Zanolie, K., & Huber, D. E. (2010). Congruency between word position and meaning is caused by task induced spatial attention. *Frontiers in Cognition, 1,* 30.

Pecher, D., v an Dantzig, S., & Schifferstein, H. N. J. (2009). Concepts are not represented by imagery. *Psychonomic Bulletin and Review, 16,* 914–919.

Pecher, D., van Dantzig, S., Zwaan, R. A., & Zeelenberg, R. (2009). Language comprehenders retain implied shape and orientation of objects. *Quarterly Journal of Experimental Psychology, 62,* 1108–1114.

Pecher, D., Zanolie, K., & Zeelenberg, R. (2007). Verifying visual properties in sentence verification facilitates picture recognition memory. *Experimental Psychology, 54,* 173–179.

Pecher, D., Zeelenberg, R., & Barsalou, L. W. (2003). Verifying different-modality properties for concepts produces switching costs. *Psychological Science, 14,* 119–124.

Pecher, D., Zeelenberg, R., & Barsalou, L. W. (2004). Sensorimotor simulations underlie conceptual representations: Modality-specific effects of prior activation. *Psychonomic Bulletin and Review, 11,* 164–167.

Pecher, D., Zeelenberg, R., & Raaijmakers, J. G. W. (1998). Does pizza prime coin? perceptual priming in lexical decision and pronunciation. *Journal of Memory and Language, 38,* 401–418.

Plaut, D. C. (2002). Graded modality specific specialisation in semantics: A computational account of optic aphasia. *Cognitive Neuropsychology, 19,* 603–639.

Prinz, J. J. (2002). *Furnishing the mind: Concepts and their perceptual basis.* Cambridge, MA: MIT Press.

Pulvermüller, F. (1999). Words in the brain's language. *Behavioral and Brain Sciences, 22,* 253–336.

Richardson, D. C., Spivey, M. J., Barsalou, L. W., & McRae, K. (2003). Spatial representations activated during real-time comprehension of verbs. *Cognitive Science, 27,* 767–780.

Rogers, T. T., Lambon Ralph, M. A., Garrard, P., Bozeat, S., McClelland, J. L., Hodges, J. R., & Patterson, K. (2004). Structure and deterioration of semantic memory: A neuropsychological and computational investigation. *Psychological Review, 111,* 205–235.

Rouw, R., Kosslyn, S. M., & Hamel, R. (1997). Detecting high-level and low-level properties in visual images and visual percepts. *Cognition, 63,* 209–226.

Scorolli, C., Borghi, A. M., & Glenberg, A. M. (2009). Language-induced motor activity in bi-manual object lifting. *Experimental Brain Research, 193,* 43–53.

Simmons, W. K., Hamann, S. B., Harenski, C. L., Hu, X. P., & Barsalou, L. W. (2008). fMRI evidence for word association and situated simulation in conceptual processing. *Journal of Physiology Paris, 102,* 106–119.

Simmons, W. K., Martin, A., & Barsalou, L. W. (2005). Pictures of appetizing foods activate gustatory cortices for taste and reward. *Cerebral Cortex, 15,* 1602–1608.

Simmons, W. K., Ramjee, V., Beauchamp, M. S., McRae, K., Martin, A., & Barsalou, L. W. (2007). A common neural substrate for perceiving and knowing about color. *Neuropsychologia, 45,* 2802–2810.

Solomon, K. O., & Barsalou, L. W. (2001). Representing properties locally. *Cognitive Psychology, 43,* 129–169.

Solomon, K. O., & Barsalou, L. W. (2004). Perceptual simulation in property verification. *Memory and Cognition, 32,* 244–259.

Spence, C., Nicholls, M. R., & Driver, J. (2001). The cost of expecting events in the wrong sensory modality. *Perception and Psychophysics, 63,* 330–336.

Spivey, M. J., Richardson, D. C., & Gonzalez- Marquez, M. (2005). On the perceptual-motor and image-schematic infrastructure of language. In D. Pecher & R. A. Zwaan (Eds.), *Grounding cognition: The role of perception and action in memory, language, and thinking* (pp. 246–281). Cambridge, England: Cambridge University Press.

Stanfield, R. A., & Zwaan, R. A. (2001). The effect of implied orientation derived from verbal context on picture recognition. *Psychological Science, 12,* 153–156.

Taylor, L. J., Lev-Ari, S., & Zwaan, R. A. (2008). Inferences about action engage action systems. *Brain and Language, 107,* 62–67.

Tyler, L. K., Moss, H. E., Durrant-Peatfield, M. R., & Levy, J. P. (2000). Conceptual structure and the structure of concepts: A distributed account of category-specific deficits. *Brain and Language, 75*, 195–231.

Van Dantzig, S., Pecher, D., Zeelenberg, R., & Barsalou, L. W. (2008). Perceptual processing affects conceptual processing. *Cognitive Science, 32*, 579–590.

Van Elk, M., Van Schie, H. T., & Bekkering, H. (2009). Action semantic knowledge about objects is supported by functional motor activation. *Journal of Experimental Psychology: Human Perception and Performance, 35*, 1118–1128.

Vermeulen, N., Corneille, O., & Niedenthal, P. M. (2008). Sensory load incurs conceptual processing costs. *Cognition, 109*, 287–294.

Vermeulen, N., Niedenthal, P. M., & Luminet, O. (2007). Switching between sensory and affective systems incurs processing costs. *Cognitive Science, 31*, 183–192.

Warrington, E. K., & Shallice, T. (1984). Category specific semantic impairments. *Brain, 107*, 829–853.

Wu, L., & Barsalou, L. W. (2009). Perceptual simulation in conceptual combination: Evidence from property generation. *Acta Psychologica, 132*, 173–189.

Zanolie, K., Van Dantzig, S., Boot, I., Wijnen, J., Schubert, T. W., Giessner, S. R., & Pecher, D. (2012). Mighty metaphors: Behavioral and ERP evidence that power shifts attention on a vertical dimension. *Brain and Cognition, 78*(1), 50–58.

Zwaan, R. A., Madden, C. J., Yaxley, R. H., & Aveyard, M. E. (2004). Moving words: Dynamic representations in language comprehension. *Cognitive Science, 28*, 611–619.

Zwaan, R. A., Stanfield, R. A., & Yaxley, R. H. (2002). Language comprehenders mentally represent the shape of objects. *Psychological Science, 13*, 168–171.

## Further Reading

Barsalou, L. W. (1999). Perceptual symbol systems. *Behavioral and Brain Sciences, 22*, 577–660.

Cree, G. S., & Mc Rae, K. (2003). Analyzing the factors underlying the structure and computation of the meaning of chipmunk, cherry, chisel, cheese, and cello (and many other such concrete nouns). *Journal of Experimental Psychology: General, 132*, 163–201.

Martin, A. (2007). The representation of object concepts in the brain. *Annual Review of Psychology, 58*, 25–45.

# Mental Images

Daniel Reisberg

**Abstract**

The experience of "mental pictures" viewed by the "mind's eye" is familiar for almost all of us, but what are these "mental pictures"? This chapter reviews evidence documenting the resemblance between mental pictures and actual visual stimuli – in their information content, the processes needed to inspect them, and in the neural circuitry that supports these processes. However, the chapter also examines points of contrast between mental pictures and ordinary pictures, arguing that mental pictures are indeed depictions (just as actual pictures are) but are organized in ways that actual pictures are not. In addition, several lines of evidence demand an often-neglected distinction between visual images and spatial images. This distinction is supported by neuroimaging and neuropsychology data, behavioral data, and studies of imagery abilities in people born blind. The same distinction may help untangle discussions of the conscious experience of imagery, and, in particular, discussions of "image vividness," a quality of visual, not spatial, imagery.

**Key Words:** blind; depiction, mind's eye, spatial imagery, visualization, visual imagery, vividness

There you are in the store, trying on a new shirt. Will it look good with the blue pants at home in your closet? To decide, you may try to visualize the blue of the pants, using your "mind's eye" to ask how they will look with the new top. Likewise, you might believe that Sam was at the seminar last week, but you are not certain. As a way of checking on your belief, you might form a "mental picture" of the seminar room—trying to visualize who was sitting where around the table. When you detect Sam's face in the group, you conclude that he was indeed present.

Examples like these illustrate the everyday use of visual images, but these examples—and the common-sense terms in which we have described them—also raise a number of concerns. There is, after all, no tiny eye somewhere deep in the brain, and so the phrase "mind's eye" cannot be taken literally. Likewise, mental "pictures" cannot be actual pictures; with no eye deep inside the brain, who or what would inspect such images?

Therefore, we plainly need to find an account of mental imagery that avoids these problematic notions.

In this chapter, we explore what is known about mental imagery, in particular, about visual imagery. We review the findings that make it clear visual images do function in important ways as if they were mental pictures, and that the processes of imaging do resemble actual seeing. We also present evidence that visual imagery relies heavily on brain areas ordinarily involved in visual *perception*, and thus point the way toward a conception of imagery that avoids the problematic notions of a "mind's eye" and "mental pictures."

However, the commonalities between imagery and perception need to be placed alongside key points of *contrast* between imagery and perception, and likewise, between visual images and actual out-in-the-world pictures. We review these contrasts, and this will lead us to the question of just how "visual" visual images truly are.

## The Resemblance Between Images and Pictures

### Chronometric Studies of Imagery

Introspectively, visual imagery seems for many people to resemble actual seeing. Imagers routinely report that their images resemble pictures, and that they "read" information off the image much as one reads information off of a picture. No wonder, then, that Shakespeare's Hamlet spoke of the "mind's eye," and, of course, this expression remains in common use 400 years after Shakespeare coined it.

Of course, we need to be wary of these introspectively based self-reports, but, even so, studies make it plain that (this time, at least) the self-reports capture some essential properties of mental imagery. More precisely, data strongly indicate that mental images are qualitatively distinct from other forms of mental representation, and, moreover, that mental images truly seem to *depict* the represented content (much as a picture would), whereas other forms of representation seem instead to *describe* the represented content.

As one point of evidence, mental images differ from other representations in the pattern of what information is easily available within the image (Kosslyn, 1976). Specifically, participants are very fast in "locating" within their image features that would be prominent in the corresponding picture—parts that are large, or parts that would be at the "front" of the represented form from common or canonical viewing angles. Participants are slower in "locating" within the image features that would be small or hidden from view in most depictions, even if these features have a strong semantic association to the represented target. Importantly, this pattern of information availability reverses if participants are asked to confirm the relevant features without use of a mental image. In this condition, responses are very quick for strongly associated features, and there is no relationship between response times and size or prominence.

Similarly, mental images seem to be represented from a determinate viewing angle and distance, much as a picture must be. (A descriptive representation, in contrast, can be entirely neutral with regard to viewing perspective.) This fact is evident in the data just described, since "visibility from a specific perspective" and "occlusion" both seem to play a role in those data: Response times are short when participants are asked about an imaged cat's head, for example, because the head is prominent *from a particular viewing angle*. Likewise, response times are long when participants are asked about

the cat's claws because these are *occluded from view* from a particular viewing angle. Thus, the data just described make no sense unless we assume a representation that somehow specifies viewing angle, and which somehow respects occlusion.

In addition, studies have directly examined the role of "viewing position" in mental imagery—asking participants to "zoom in" to scrutinize details or "zoom back" to examine large-scale features (Kosslyn, 1983). The data show clearly that the greater the imagined zoom required for a particular trial, the slower the response. Thus, we can meaningfully speak of the image *having a viewing perspective*, consistent with the broader claim that images depict the represented content rather than describing it.

The lawful relation between amount of "zoom" required and response time also indicates that the *transformation* of mental images respects the principles associated with depictions, rather than those associated with descriptions. Concretely, actual, out-in-the-world depictions are obviously displayed in two or three dimensions, so that we can measure the *distance* between two points or between two viewing perspectives. If we now add straightforward assumptions about movement across these distances, we are led to predictions about travel time within this depicted landscape. At the least, we might expect a positive monotonic relation between travel time and distance on the depiction. If we also assume a constant velocity, then this relation will also be *linear*.

If mental images act like depictions, then the same claims should be true of images, and, indeed, they are. The time needed to imagine "zooming" in on a scene is a positive function of the amount of zoom required. The time needed to imagine "scanning" across an image is a strikingly linear function of the "distance traveled" across the image (Denis & Kosslyn, 1999; Kosslyn, Ball, & Reiser, 1978). The time needed to imagine an image rotating into a new position is a positive function (and, in many studies, a linear function) of the degree of rotation required (Shepard & Cooper, 1982).

Finally, these results with imagined transformation also make it clear that images directly represent a set of important spatial relationships. Thus, there does seem to be a one-to-one correspondence, at a fairly fine grain, between the parts of the out-in-the-world scene that is being represented and the parts of the scene as represented in imagery. Likewise, points that are close to each other in the depicted scene seem to be functionally close in the image, and points that are aligned in the depicted scene seem to be functionally aligned in the imagined scene. These (and other) geometric relationships are reflected in the pattern of response times, and these relationships, in turn, make it clear that the image represents in a direct fashion the spatial layout of the represented scene, exactly as one would expect for a depiction of that scene.

## Images and the Brain

The results just catalogued make it all too easy to think of images as akin to actual pictures, projected on some viewing screen deep within the brain. However, as we have noted, this conception is problematic. There is no little eye inside the brain; there is no viewing screen. Why, therefore, do images behave as they do? The answer grows out of the fact that the neural substrate of mental imagery overlaps heavily with that of vision. This, in turn, has strong implications for the nature of imagery, and we return to those implications after a brief survey of the relevant neuroscience data.

Neuroimaging studies show that, when participants are visualizing, activity levels are high in various parts of the occipital cortex; this brain area is, of course, crucially involved in visual perception (Behrmann, 2000; Farah, 1988, 1989; Ishai & Sagi, 1995; Kosslyn, 1994; Miyashita, 1995; Thompson & Kosslyn, 2000). Moreover, the exact pattern of brain activation during imagery depends on the type of image being maintained. For high-resolution, detailed images, Areas V1 and V2 (which we know to be spatially organized) are particularly active, and, remarkably, the amount of brain tissue showing activation increases as participants imagine larger and larger objects (Behrmann, 2000; Kosslyn et al., 1993, 1999; Kosslyn, Thompson, Kim, & Alpert, 1995; Mellet et al., 2000). In a similar fashion, Area MT/MST, sensitive to motion in ordinary perception, is particularly activated when participants are asked to imagine movement patterns (Goebel, Khorram-Sefat, Muckli, Hacker, & Singer, 1998); brain areas that are especially active during the perception of faces are also highly activated when people are imagining faces (O'Craven & Kanwisher, 2000), and so on.

Further evidence comes from studies using *transcranial magnetic stimulation* to disrupt Area V1 (primary visual cortex) in an otherwise normal brain. Not surprisingly, this procedure causes problems in vision but also causes parallel problems in visual imagery, plainly indicating that Area V1 is crucial both for the processing of visual information and for the creation of visual images (Kosslyn et al., 1999).

Likewise, in many cases, patients who have suffered brain damage that disrupts their vision also suffer parallel deficits in their imagery—as we would expect if these two activities rely on overlapping neural areas. Thus, patients who (because of stroke) have lost the ability to perceive color often seem to lose the ability to imagine scenes in color; patients who lose the ability to perceive fine detail seem also to lose the ability to visualize fine detail, and so on. If (as a result of occipital damage) patients have a restriction on the *extent* of visual space, they are likely to have a corresponding limit on their visual imagery (DeRenzi & Spinnler, 1967; Farah, 1988, 1989; Farah, Soso, & Dasheiff, 1992; Kosslyn, 1994; Kosslyn & Thompson, 1999; we will, however, consider some contrasting evidence in a later section).

All of these results point the way toward a particular conception of visual imagery: In ordinary *perceiving*, one begins with a stimulus and derives from it an internal representation of that stimulus. This representation is, of course, far more than a mere "transcription" of the stimulus, because the representation is organized and interpreted in ways the stimulus is not (more on this point later). Nonetheless, this representation—the *percept*—does depict the external stimulus, that is, does show directly what (many aspects of) the stimulus looks like. However, the percept is not some sort of "mental picture." Instead, the percept is a representation instantiated in a neural substrate, with this representation containing a lot of the same information that a picture would. "Inspection" of this representation, therefore, does not require an "inner eye" with which to view a mental picture; instead, what is required is a set of processes (again, obviously instantiated in the neural substrate) that take this representation as their input.

Images may be thought of in roughly the same way, and, according to the evidence just reviewed, may be instantiated in the same neural substrate, and analyzed through roughly the same processes, as percepts. Images, therefore, just like percepts, depict, with no need for appeals to "mental pictures" or "inner eyes." And, because they are depictions, images can have all the properties described in the previous section, with no need for any "projection screen," deep within the brain, nor for any homunculus sitting and viewing this "screen."

Note also that these points illuminate some of the issues that were contentious during the "imagery debate" of the late 1970s and early 1980s. (For a sample of that debate, see the papers in Block, 1981.) The debate focused on whether imagery was encoded in the mind in some sort of *propositional* format (e.g., Pylyshyn, 1981) or in some sort of *analog* format. Those who defended the *analog* position argued that imagery was mentally represented in some sort of specialized "imagery medium" (Kosslyn, 1981), and that the properties of that medium governed imagery functioning in important ways. We can now, with the advantage of hindsight, see that this latter position captured an important truth: Imagery does seem to rely on a special medium: the topographically organized "maps" of the visual cortex, and it is likely that the properties of these maps (e.g., their degree of resolution, the relationship between resolution and position within the map, and, of course, the topographic organization itself) do shape mental imagery. In crucial ways, then, the "analog / special medium" side of the imagery debate was correct in its view of imagery. (We will, however, return to this issue later in this chapter and argue that the "propositional" side of the debate was also correct on some key points.)

### Sensory Effects in Imagery

If mental imagery relies on the mechanisms of perception, then we should expect mutual interference between imagery and perception, on the assumption that the mechanisms needed for each cannot be used for more than one task at a time. Closely related, we might expect that imagery will show many of the functional patterns observed in perception. Both of these predictions have been confirmed.

Segal and Fusella (1971, 1970) asked participants to detect faint signals, either dim visual stimuli or soft tones. Participants did this either while forming a visual image or while forming an auditory imagery and the results showed a selective interference pattern: Auditory imagery made it difficult to detect faint sounds; visual imagery made it difficult to detect faint visual signals (see also Craver-Lemley, Arterberry, & Reeves, 1997; Craver-Lemley & Reeves, 1987, 1992; Farah & Smith, 1983; Johnson, 1982; Logie, 1986; Matthews, 1983; once again, though, we note that there are some contrasting data, and we discuss these later).

In other studies, participants have been asked to image stimuli *related to* the one they are trying to perceive. In this case, imagery produces a priming effect, with perception facilitated if participants have just been visualizing the target form in the appropriate position (Farah, 1985; Heil, Rösler, & Hennighausen, 1993; Ishai & Sagi, 1997; also see McDermott & Roediger, 1994).

Other studies have documented various "sensory" effects in mental imagery. For example, participants in one study were shown two dots, then the dots were removed but participants were asked to imagine that they were still present. The participants then moved their eyes away from the imaged dots' position, and, as they looked further and further away, they had to judge whether they could still "see" that the dots were indeed separate. In this way, acuity was measured with imagined stimuli, and the data show impressive correspondence between performance with actually perceived dots and performance with imagined dots (Finke & Kosslyn, 1980). In both cases, acuity fell off abruptly if the dots were not in the center of vision, and the decline in acuity was virtually the same in perception and in imagery. Qualitatively and quantitatively, the imagery data match the perceptual data.

### Images Are Not Pictures
#### Neutral Depictions, Organized Depictions

We have now surveyed evidence documenting the fact that images depict the represented content, but we still need to ask *what sort of depiction* images provide. Consider the Necker cube (Fig. 25.1A). The drawing of this cube (the stimulus itself) is ambiguous: It is compatible with both the construal shown in Figure 25.1B and also the one in Figure 25.1C. Thus, the *drawing* is indeterminate with regard to interpretation, and, specifically, the drawing is neutral with regard to configuration in depth.

Our perception of the cube, in contrast, is not indeterminate; it is not neutral. Instead, we perceive the cube either as similar to Figure 25.1B or to Figure 25.1C. Our perception, in other words, goes beyond the information given by specifying a configuration in depth.

The same point can be made for an endless series of other stimuli. The actual pixel pattern in the classic vase/profiles figure (Fig. 25.1D) is not "vase-and-not-profiles," nor is it "profiles-and-not-vase." Instead, the figure itself is neutral with regard to interpretation, and so it affords either interpretation. Our perception, though, lacks this equipotentiality. The perception specifies that we are looking at the vase and not the profiles, *or* that we are looking at profiles and not the vase. This then turns out to have a variety of consequences: for how the dimensions of the figure are understood,

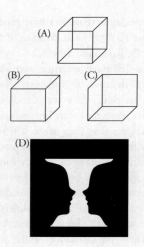

**Figure 25.1** The actual drawing of the Necker cube (shown in A) is a "neutral depiction," entirely compatible with a construal that involves an orientation like that shown (unambiguously) in B or like the one shown in C. Our *perception* of the Necker cube, in contrast, is an "organized depiction," specifying an orientation in space (and so specifying whether the cube-as-perceived is more similar to B or to C). Similarly, the vase/profiles figure itself (D) is a neutral depiction, compatible with more than one interpretation. Our perception of the figure, in contrast, provides an organized depiction—and thus shows either the vase or the profiles.

for how attention is deployed across the figure, and so on (Goldmeier, 1937/1972; Rock, 1983).

These points, simple as they are, remind us about some essential properties of *percepts*, our mental representations of the stimulus world around us. Percepts are depictions, and, in some regards, can be thought of (somewhat crudely) as akin to pictures. At the same time, percepts are different from pictures. A picture of the Necker cube is indeterminate regarding depth; the percept specifies depth. The picture of the vase/profiles is neutral regarding whether it is a vase or profiles, but the percept specifies one or the other.

Let us call the sort of depiction that is in a picture a *neutral depiction*, and the sort that is in a percept an *organized depiction*. In describing this contrast, terminology proposed by Peterson, Kihlstrom, Rose, and Glisky (1992) is useful: A percept exists within what Peterson et al. call a *perceptual reference frame* that specifies how the percept is to be understood. The reference frame does not specify the referent of the form (does not tell what the representation is a representation *of*) but does specify how the form is configured in depth, what the figure-ground relationships are, what its top and bottom are, and so on—a small set of perceptual specifications detailing how the form is organized, and governing subsequent processing of the form.

With this context, what sort of depictions are mental images—neutral depictions, like pictures, indeterminate with regard to the various specifications just mentioned? Or are they organized depictions, the way percepts are, existing within a perceptual reference frame? Evidence on this point comes from a series of studies by Chambers and Reisberg (1985, 1992; Reisberg & Chambers, 1991). They led participants to memorize some of the classic ambiguous figures, including the duck/rabbit. Participants were then asked to form a "mental picture" of the form and tried to reinterpret this imaged form, just as they had reinterpreted a series of training figures. The result was clear: Zero participants were able to discover the duck in a rabbit image, or the rabbit in a duck image. In sharp contrast, all of the participants were able, moments later, to draw a picture of the form they had been imaging and to reverse the figure in their own drawings.

Other laboratories have not been able to replicate the zero rate of image-based reversals (Brandimonte & Gerbino, 1993; Hyman, 1993; Kaufman & Helstrup, 1993; Peterson et al., 1992; for an account of this point, see Reisberg, 1994). Even so, these laboratories have replicated the finding that the reversal of mental images is difficult and quite rare, with 80% or 90% of the participants failing to reverse the image, even though reversal of the corresponding *picture* is extremely easy, with 100% of the participants succeeding in this reversal.

### Image-Based Discovery

The results just cited are just what we would expect if images are *organized depictions*—understood within a perceptual reference frame, and, as such, determinate with regard to the various appearance specifications mentioned earlier. One might say, therefore, that images (like percepts) are "already interpreted," and thus resistant to reinterpretation.

This claim, however, seems to pose a puzzle. It is clear that imagery can be a rich source of new ideas and inventions; images can remind us and instruct us. This is easily documented in the laboratory (e.g., Anderson & Helstrup, 1993; Finke, 1990; Finke, Pinker, & Farah, 1989; Pinker & Finke, 1980; Thompson, Kosslyn, Hoffman, & Kooij, 2008) but is also evident in the broader history of ideas, which is, after all, filled with instances in which great discoveries (discoveries that led to great works of art, or important new inventions, or scientific innovations) were all inspired by mental images of one sort or another (Miller, 1986; Shepard, 1988).

Against this backdrop, why did Chambers and Reisberg's participants fail to make a simple discovery in their image—failing, for example, to find the duck in a rabbit image? The reason is simple: Whenever one examines a mental image, seeking some new perspective or some new idea, one is, in essence, asking: *What does the depicted form resemble?* Furthermore, we know from much research in perception that the pattern of resemblance depends both on stimulus geometry *and* on the perceptual reference frame that is organizing that geometry (i.e., the specification of figure/ground, the assignment of orientation, and so on). It follows from this that discoveries will flow easily from an image *if* the discovery is compatible with both the depicted geometry and also the reference frame. In that case, the resemblance pattern will favor the image-based discovery. But if the discovery is incompatible with either the geometry or the reference frame, then the discovery will be much more difficult and much less frequent.

As an illustration, participants in one study were shown the shape shown in Figure 25.2. Participants memorized this "nonsense shape," just as they had the training figures, and then were asked to imagine the shape rotated 90 degrees clockwise. At this point, the participants were asked what familiar geographic form this figure resembled (Reisberg & Chambers, 1991).

It seems likely that participants encoded this form with a reference frame that identified the top-most edge in the drawing as being the form's top. When

**Figure 25.2** When research participants formed an image of this figure, the depiction was understood within a perceptual reference frame that identified the figure's "top." If this "top" happened to be the upper-most edge in the drawing (as it would naturally be), then participants routinely failed to recognize the shape of Texas in their own image—even if they imaged the form rotated ninety degrees clockwise.

they imagined the form rotated into a new position, they probably maintained this perceptual reference frame. As a result, their image depicted the proper geometry for Texas, but with the wrong reference frame, and, as a result, they should not recognize Texas in their image, and this is why, in fact, zero participants recognized Texas in their own image.

The key idea here is that participants in this procedure were imaging the Texas geometry with the wrong reference frame, one that identified the eastern edge of Texas as the form's top. As a result, their image (with this reference frame) did not resemble Texas, and it did not call the Texas shape to mind. If this is correct, then the result should change if participants are led to the "proper" reference frame, by means of suitable instruction. Thus, in a follow-up study, Reisberg and Chambers again had participants encode the shape shown in Figure 25.2, and then asked them (with the drawing removed from view) to form an image of the form. This time, participants were told directly to think of the form as having a "new top," and, specifically, to think of the left side as the top. With this instruction, performance was vastly improved, and now a third of the participants recognized Texas in the imaged form, in contrast to the zero success rate in the earlier procedure. (For similar data, also showing the effects of suitable hints, see Hyman, 1993; Peterson et al., 1992.)

Notice two key themes within this data pattern. First, it is important that participants *succeed* in image-based discovery in many contexts—they can, for example, recognize Texas in their image if the image is organized appropriately, and they can find the duck in a rabbit image if given a suitable hint. This is possible only because an image represents a form's geometry in a fashion that lets us judge what the imaged form *looks like*. This is presumably what images (in contrast to a purely descriptive mode of representation) are *for*—why we use them, why we evolved the capacity for imaging. More to the point, all of this reminds us once again that images *depict*.

At the same time, the fact that participants *fail* to recognize Texas (for example), when they understand the image in the wrong way, underscores the importance of the image's reference frame—a reference frame that somehow *describes* how the depiction is to be organized. When the frame is inappropriate, it can render image-based discoveries much less likely, and in some cases, it seems, rule them out altogether. (For other data on this point, and, more generally, for studies exploring the nature of image-based problem solving, see Anderson and

Helstrup, 1993; Verstijnen, Hennessey, Leeuwen, Hamel, & Goldschmidt, 1998; Verstijnen, Leeuwen, Goldschmidt, Hamel, & Hennessey, 1998.)

Thus, mental images have a "duplex" quality—containing both depictive information (which represents the geometry of the imaged form) and also descriptive information (which stipulates how that geometry is organized). With this base, we can revisit the "imagery debate" of the 1970s and 1980s. We noted earlier that the "analog / special medium" side of the debate was correct on some crucial points. It now appears, though, that the "propositional/descriptive" side of the debate was also right on some issues. As Pylyshyn (1981) argued, images are "cognitively penetrated" in ways that neutral depictions (such as pictures) are not; this point is obviously related to the argument we are offering here, that images are organized depictions, not neutral depictions, and that this seems to demand some degree of propositional encoding as part of the mental image. In short, then, images are neither pictures nor propositions, but a hybrid of both.

## Visual Images and Spatial Images
### Imagery and the Blind

So far, our discussion has emphasized the similarity between vision and mental imagery. There are many points of functional resemblance between these activities, and manipulations that influence one often seem to influence the other. Likewise, circumstances that cause *deficits* in one of these activities (transcranial magnetic stimulation or brain damage) typically cause deficits in the other.

Other data, however, point to important distinctions between vision and visual imagery. For example, consider the congenitally blind. With no history of vision, one might expect impairment in this population in tasks requiring imagery. The data are otherwise. In tests involving mental rotation or image scanning, these individuals yield data quite similar to those obtained with sighted research participants—with response times proportionate to the "distance" traveled. Likewise, people who are congenitally blind show a memory advantage for materials that are more readily "imaged"; they also benefit from specific instructions to use imagery as an aid to memory (Carpenter & Eisenberg, 1978; Jonides, Kahn, & Rozin, 1975; Kerr, 1983; Marmor & Zabeck, 1976; Paivio & Okovita, 1971; Vecchi, 1998; Zimler & Keenan, 1983).

Presumably, the congenitally blind have some means other than visual imagery for performing these imagery tasks, and it seems plausible that this other means involves *body* imagery or *motion* imagery. In other words, blind individuals might perform these tasks by imagining a series of movements. Alternatively, perhaps their imagery is not tied to any sensory modality but is part of their broader cognition about spatial layout. No matter how we answer these questions, though, the data from the blind suggest that many imagery tasks can be performed without relying on a representation that is in some way visual. This raises a new question: Do *sighted* participants have recourse to a nonvisual mode of spatial representation when performing imagery tasks? If so, what adjustment does this demand in our theorizing about the relationship between mental imagery and perception? We return to this issue after more of the data are in view.

### Do Visual Tasks Interfere With Imagery?

As we have noted, several lines of evidence speak to the functional and biological overlap between mental imagery and visual perception, and one line concerns the *mutual interference* between imagery and perception. In general, participants visualizing one target have difficulty in discerning some other simultaneous visual target. Other studies, however, yield a different result. Baddeley and Lieberman (1980) asked participants to imagine a 4 x 4 matrix. Within the matrix, a particular cell was designated the "starting square," and, from this anchor, participants were instructed in how to "fill" this imagined matrix: "In the starting square, place a '1'; in the next square to the right, put a '2'; in the next square up, put a '3,'" and so on. Then, after a short delay, the participants had to report back the contents of the matrix.

It seems likely that this task requires imagery, but imagery of what sort? In one condition, participants tried to remember these matrices while doing a visual interference task. As they were hearing the sentences, they were shown a series of lights, some bright and some dim, and had to press a key whenever they saw a bright stimulus. In a second condition, participants had to remember the matrices while doing a spatial interference task. They were required to move their hands in a particular pattern, but they were blindfolded so that they could not rely on vision in guiding their motions.

No interference was observed when participants were asked to memorize the matrices while doing the visual task. Interference was observed, though, when the matrix task was combined with the spatial task. Apparently, memorizing these matrices depends on some sort of spatial skill, and, correspondingly, the imagery relevant for this task seems to be spatial, not visual, in nature. (For related evidence, see Logie & Marchetti, 1991; Morris, 1987; Quinn, 1988; Quinn & Ralston, 1986; Smyth & Pendleton, 1989; for a closely related distinction among types of imagery, see Kosslyn & Thompson, 1999; for other data emphasizing the importance of a visual/spatial distinction, Hegarty, 2004; Klauer & Zhao, 2004.)

### Neuroscience Points of Contrast Between Imagery and Perception

Thus, in some cases, there is interference between imagery and vision; in other cases, this interference is not observed. Instead, the data show interference between imagery and (nonvisual) *spatial* tasks. One plausible interpretation of this pattern rests on the simple idea that there are different *types* of imagery. One type is indeed visual and so disrupted by simultaneous visual activity. The other type involves some sort of spatial representation and thus is available to the congenitally blind and is disrupted by simultaneous spatial activity.

This framework also helps with another complication in the overall data pattern. As already noted, there are many cases in which brain damage has led to parallel damage in imaging and perceiving; this is, of course, one of the arguments that these activities overlap in their neural substrates. However, there are also cases in which parallel deficits are not observed. For example, Goldenberg, Müllbacher, and Nowak (1995) describe a patient whose occipital lobe lesions have produced cortical blindness, but, despite this profound visual deficit, the patient does well on many mental imagery tasks (also see Chatterjee & Southwood, 1995). Similarly, a number of investigators have described patients who do well on imagery tasks despite severe visual agnosia (Bartolomeo et al., 1998; Behrman, Moscovitch, & Winocur, 1994; Behrmann, Winocur, & Moscovitch, 1992; Jankowiak, Kinsbourne, Shalev, & Bachman, 1992; Servos & Goodale, 1995). Other cases show the reverse pattern: impaired imagery performance despite intact perception (Farah, 1984).

Why do imagery and perception sometimes show parallel deficits, and sometimes not? The answer surely has several parts, but one part likely hinges on the distinction among types of imagery. Some imagery is surely *visual* and relies on brain structures ordinarily used in vision. Damage to these structures will therefore cause parallel deficits in vision and tasks relying on this type of imagery.

Other imagery is not visual; we have suggested that it may involve a representation based on *body movements*, perhaps representing how one would move to explore certain layouts or manipulate the layouts. In fact, and fully consistent with this latter proposal, some functional magnetic resonance imaging data link the task of mental rotation to motor areas in the brain (e.g., Goldenberg, 1999; Richter et al., 2000; also see Sirigu & Duhamel, 2001). Thus, this type of imagery does not rely on brain structures typically used for vision, and so it will be spared if these visual structures are damaged.

### Neuroscience Distinctions Between Visual and Spatial Imagery

Overall, then, it is clear that humans employ mental representations that depict the perceptual environment. In some cases, these representations seem truly visual—and so show interference with simultaneous vision and are disrupted by damage (permanent or temporary) to structures in the brain needed for vision. In other cases, though, our depictive representations are not visual (and so show neither of the traits just listed, and are also available to the congenitally blind).

In addition, if visual imagery is distinct from spatial imagery, then we would expect dissociations not just between perception and imagery but also between the *types* of imagery. Consider the case of L. H., who suffered a brain lesion as the result of an automobile accident (Farah, Hammond, Levine, & Calvanio, 1988). After his recovery, L. H. continued to have difficulties with a variety of visual tasks. In one test, L. H. performed poorly in reporting the colors of common objects (e.g., football—brown). In another test, the experimenter named an animal, and L. H. had to indicate whether the animal had a long tail or short, relative to its body size. L. H. got 13 of 20 items correct—only slightly above chance.

In contrast, L. H. does well in spatial tasks, including image scanning and mental rotation. Indeed, on the matrix task (described earlier), L. H. was correct on 18 or 20 items, virtually identical to the performance of control participants. Thus, L. H. does well on tasks requiring spatial manipulations or memory for spatial positions but poorly on tasks requiring judgments about visual appearance. This pattern fits well with the claim that visual imagery is indeed distinct from spatial imagery.

The distinction between visual and spatial imagery may also allow us to resolve an apparent discrepancy in the neuroimaging data. Some authors have reported that mental imagery tasks produce activation in primary visual cortex, Area 17; other authors, however, report the opposite finding, with imagery producing no activation in primary visual cortex (e.g., Mellet, Tzourio, Denis, & Mazoyer, 1995; Mellet et al., 1996). Kosslyn and Thompson (1999) note, however, that the latter studies have relied on imagery tasks that required judgments about spatial positions (e.g., a task requiring image scanning). Studies showing activation in Area 17 have relied on tasks that required a higher resolution depictive image. The suggestion, therefore, is that Area 17 is likely to be well activated during tasks that require visual imagery, but not tasks requiring spatial imagery. This, in turn, provides further warrant for including this distinction within our theorizing. (For further data, confirming via neuroimaging the distinction between types of imagery, see Thompson, Slotnick, Burrage, & Kosslyn, 2009.)

## Image Vividness
### The Trouble With Vividness

Many historical accounts point to Galton's investigations as the first research on mental imagery (Galton, 1883). Galton asked his participants to describe for him the nature of their mental images and found enormous variation in these descriptions. Many participants described images of photographic clarity, rich in detail, almost as if they were *seeing* the imaged scene rather than visualizing it. Others reported sketchy images or no images at all. They were certainly able to think about the scenes or objects Galton named for them, but in no sense were they "seeing" these scenes. Their self-reports rarely included mention of color, size, or viewing perspective; indeed, their reports were devoid of any visual qualities. In recounting Galton's data, William James (1890, p. 57) commented: "some people undoubtedly have no visual images at all worthy of the name."

Across the last century, though, researchers have often voiced skepticism about these imagery self-reports. As one concern (and despite James's endorsement), perhaps all of Galton's participants had the same imagery capacity, but some were cautious in how they described their imagery, whereas others were more extravagant. In this way, Galton's data might reveal differences in how people *talk* about their imagery, rather than differences in the imagery per se.

In addition, studies have sought empirical correlates of these imagery self-reports, with the expectation that people who claim to have vivid imagery should have a corresponding performance advantage on tasks that require imagery. Conversely, people who report sparse (or no) imagery should be unable to imagine rotated objects, use imagery mnemonics, and so on. However, tests of these suggestions have routinely yielded null findings. There is no difference, for example, between vivid imagers and sparse imagers in their speed or accuracy of mental rotation, how quickly they scan across their images, or how effective their images are in supporting memory. Indeed, people who insist they have *no* imagery do as well as everyone else on these tasks; individuals who boast of clear and detailed imagery show no corresponding processing advantage (e.g., Ernest, 1977; Katz, 1983; Kosslyn, Brunn, Cave, & Wallach, 1985; Marks, 1983; Reisberg, Culver, Heuer, & Fischman, 1986; Richardson, 1980).

### Image Vividness and the Visual/Spatial Distinction

One could read these results as an indication that self-reports of imagery vividness have no validity. Perhaps, despite Galton's observations, people all have the same imagery prowess. Or perhaps people differ in their imagery experience, but we have no means of measuring these differences.

There is, however, another possibility. Researchers have employed different instruments to measure image vividness (Richardson, 1999, provides a review), but some themes are prominent in virtually all of these instruments, including an explicit invitation to participants to *compare their imagery to actual vision*. For example, the instructions for Marks's (1977) Vividness of Visual Imagery Questionnaire (VVIQ) repeatedly invite participants to form a picture before their "mind's eye." Moreover, the response scale for the VVIQ offers, as one endpoint, a response indicating that the image is "perfectly clear and as vivid as *normal vision*" (italics added). And of the sixteen items that comprise the VVIQ, six items explicitly mention *color*, perhaps the clearest case of a property that is essentially visual, not spatial. (A seventh item on the test mentions a rainbow, and so invites participants again to think about the colors.)

It would seem, then, that introspective reports of image vividness are gauging the visual richness of mental imagery—or, more succinctly, are assessing visual imagery, not spatial. This is plausibly the reason why these self-reports are uncorrelated with performance in many imagery tasks. If a task relies on *spatial* imagery, the visual qualities provided by a "vivid image" are likely to be neither necessary nor helpful (cf. McKelvie, 1999.) This, in short, is why studies find no relationship between VVIQ scores and mental rotation, mental scanning, the use of imagery mnemonics and so on.

Using this logic, though, we should expect tests like the VVIQ to be predictive of performance on *visual* tasks, and several studies confirm this expectation. For example, the two-point acuity experiment (discussed earlier) requires little in the way of spatial judgments; instead, it requires someone to maintain a high-resolution image and to make exact judgments about what this depiction would *look like*. This therefore seems likely to be a task drawing on visual, not spatial, imagery, and, indeed, performance in this task is related to vividness self-report. People who describe their imagery as vivid yield data in close correspondence to the perceptual data; people with less vivid imagery do not show this close correspondence (Finke & Kosslyn, 1980).

Other studies show a lawful relationship between image vividness and *color memory* (e.g., Reisberg et al., 1986), consistent with the claim that judgments about color require a visual representation, rather than a spatial one. Likewise, vividness is predictive of memory for faces (Reisberg & Leak, 1987), another task that plausibly involves visual imagery. (For related findings, see Cui, Jeter, Yang, Montague, & Eagleman, 2006; Kozhevnikov, Kosslyn, & Shephard, 2005.)

Finally, at least some neuroscience evidence accords with these claims. Farah and Peronnet (1989) measured event-related potentials (ERPs) while their participants were generating mental images. They found that the occipital ERPs were consistently larger for participants who rated their images as particularly vivid. This is, of course, sensible on the view being developed here: Image vividness is an index of the quality of *visual* imagery; visual imagery, in turn, is likely to be instantiated in the visual cortex. It is appropriate, therefore, that vivid imagery is associated with increased activity levels in the occipital lobe (see also Goldenberg, Podreka, & Steiner, 1990; Marks, 1990).

### Vividness and Memory

There are, to be sure, many null findings associated with vividness measures, and at least some of these may be attributed to methodological concerns that are inevitable when trying to measure some aspect of conscious experience. Other null findings, though, may reflect a failure in previous studies to distinguish between visual and spatial tasks, and visual and spatial imagery. Once this distinction is made, the data pattern becomes more orderly than it initially appeared to be.

At the same time, we must not overstate our argument here. The data on imagery vividness are messy. There continue to be null findings in the literature, and even when systematic relationships are found, the direction of the relationship is sometimes positive, and sometimes *negative*. For example, both Reisberg et al. (1986) and Reisberg and Leak (1987) found that participants with vivid imagery were *less* accurate in their memory tasks. Likewise, McKelvie (1995) reviews many studies showing a positive relation between image vividness (measured by the VVIQ) and performance on cognitive tasks, with a mean correlation of .273. McKelvie reports, though, that the relationship between vividness and tasks involving memory was weaker (mean correlation = .137), plausibly because some studies (as already noted) report a negative relation between imagery and memory, and this obviously weakens the overall data pattern. (For contrasting cases, with *positive* relations between imagery vividness and memory accuracy, see Riske, Wallace, & Allen, 2000; Walczyk & Taylor, 2000.)

Thus, work clearly remains to be done before we can claim to understand the full nature of, and influences of, vivid imagery. Why are correlations sometimes not observed? Why is the influence sometimes positive, sometimes negative? On the latter point, one suggestion grows out of the research on *source monitoring*. This research highlights the fact that remembering is more than a matter of simply bringing the desired content into mind. In addition, one must become convinced that the "memory" is indeed a memory, and not just a passing fantasy or a thought merely associated with the retrieval cue. Similarly, if one decides that a remembered thought *is* a memory, one must still become convinced that it is a memory from the right source (and not, for example, a recollection of some event other than the target event). Only when these assessments have been made does one take the memory seriously and take action based on it.

Of course, the assessments just described will be more difficult if the false leads provided by memory are recalled (or imagined) in vivid and rich detail, especially sensory detail. In other words, vividly imagined fictions will be difficult to distinguish from accurate recollections, with the result that vivid imagery may sometimes be an obstacle to accurate memory. Consistent with this view, several studies have reported a link between vivid imagery (measured by the VVIQ) and vulnerability to certain types of memory error (e.g., Tomes & Katz, 1997; Wilkinson & Hyman, 1998; Winograd, Peluso, & Glover, 1998; for contrasting data, though, see Heaps & Nash, 1999).

These last points provide at least one way to think about the negative correlation sometimes observed between image vividness and memory accuracy. In addition, this linkage between imagery and source monitoring offers another lesson for us: It is all too easy to focus our discussion on tasks specifically designed to tap mental imagery, and correspondingly easy to think of the *function* of imagery as somehow defined by these tasks. However, the interaction between imagery and memory accuracy reminds us that imagery (vivid or otherwise) can influence us in a wide range of other settings (including problem solving, decision making, or inductive judgment), and the contribution of imagery to these other domains remains an issue in need of further scrutiny.

## Imagery in Other Modalities

Finally, we wish to close with a brief further point. Our exploration of mental imagery has drawn attention to the fact that there are (not surprisingly) different *types* of imagery, and our understanding of the available research is surely improved by a consideration of how these types of imagery are alike (functionally and biologically) and also how they differ. In the same spirit, it seems likely that our understanding of visual *or* spatial imagery will benefit from a consideration of how this imagery resembles, and how it differs from, imagery in other modalities—including auditory imagery, tactile imagery, kinesthetic imagery, and so on.

Some of the research needed for this consideration is already available. Halpern (1988, 1991), for example, has argued that auditory images are extended in time in the same way that visual images seem to be (functionally) extended in space; her research draws on the image-scanning task already used effectively in the study of visual imagery. Researchers have likewise shown that the neural mechanisms serving auditory imagery overlap with those of audition, again in parallel with the relevant research on visual imagery (e.g., Zatorre & Halpern, 1993; Zatorre, Halpern, Perry, Meyer, & Evans, 1996). Studies also indicate that auditory images are resistant to reinterpretation just as the visual image of, say, the duck-rabbit is (Reisberg, 1994; Reisberg, Smith, Baxter, & Sonenshine, 1989), and so on.

Our point here, however, is not to survey auditory imagery in detail. Instead, we mention these other findings simply to highlight the fact that many aspects of visual imagery will find parallels in other domains, while surely other aspects will not. Exploring these (possible) parallels seems certain to enrich our understanding of all modalities, and it is a prospect that imagery researchers should welcome.

## References

Anderson, R., & Helstrup, T. (1993). Visual discovery in mind and on paper. *Memory and Cognition, 21,* 283–293.

Baddeley, A. D., & Lieberman, K. (1980). Spatial working memory. In R. Nickerson (Ed.), *Attention and performance* (pp. 521–539). Hillsdale, NJ: Erlbaum.

Bartolomeo, P., Bachoud-Levi, A. C., De Gelder, B., Denes, G., Dalla Barba, G., Brugieres, P., & Degos, J. D. (1998). Multiple-domain dissociation between impaired visual perception and preserved mental imagery in a patient with bilateral extrastriate lesions. *Neuropsychologia, 36,* 239–249.

Behrmann, M. (2000). The mind's eye mapped onto the brain's matter. *Current Directions in Psychological Science, 9,* 50–54.

Behrman, M., Moscovitch, M., & Winocur, G. (1994). Intact visual imagery and impaired visual perception in a patient with visual agnosia. *Journal of Experimental Psychology: Human Perception and Performance, 20,* 1068–1087.

Behrmann, M., Winocur, G., & Moscovitch, M. (1992). Dissociation between mental imagery and object recognition in a brain-damaged patient. *Nature, 359*(6396), 636–637.

Block, N. (Ed.). (1981). *Imagery.* Cambridge, MA: MIT Press.

Brandimonte, M. A., & Gerbino, W. (1993). Mental image reversal and verbal recoding: When ducks become rabbits. *Memory and Cognition, 21,* 23–33.

Carpenter, P. A., & Eisenberg, P. (1978). Mental rotation and the frame of reference in blind and sighted individuals. *Perception and Psychophysics, 23,* 117–124.

Chambers, D., & Reisberg, D. (1985). Can mental images be ambiguous? *Journal of Experimental Psychology: Human Perception and Performance, 11,* 317–328.

Chambers, D., & Reisberg, D. (1992). What an image depicts depends on what an image means. *Cognitive Psychology, 24,* 145–174.

Chatterjee, A., & Southwood, M. H. (1995). Cortical blindness and visual imagery. *Neurology, 45,* 2189–2195.

Craver-Lemley, C., Arterberry, M. E., & Reeves, A. (1997). Effects of imagery on vernier acuity under conditions of induced depth. *Journal of Experimental Psychology: Human Perception and Performance, 23*(1), 3–13.

Craver-Lemley, C., & Reeves, A. (1987). Visual imagery selectively reduces vernier acuity. *Perception, 16*(5), 599–614.

Craver-Lemley, C., & Reeves, A. (1992). How visual imagery interferes with vision. *Psychological Review, 99,* 633–649.

Cui, X., Jeter, C., Yang, D., Montague, P. R., & Eagleman, D. M. (2006). Vividness of mental imagery: Individual variability can be measured objectively. *Vision Research, 47,* 474–478.

Denis, M., & Kosslyn, S. M. (1999). Scanning visual mental images: A window on the mind. *Cahiers de Psychologie Cognitive/Current Psychology of Cognition, 18,* 409–465.

DeRenzi, E., & Spinnler, H. (1967). Impaired performance on color tasks in patients with hemispheric lesions. *Cortex, 3,* 194–217.

Ernest, C. (1977). Imagery ability and cognition: A critical review. *Journal of Mental Imagery, 2,* 181–216.

Farah, M. (1984). The neurological basis of mental imagery. *Cognition, 18,* 245–272.

Farah, M. (1985). Psychophysical evidence for a shared representational medium for mental images and percepts. *Journal of Experimental Psychology: General, 114,* 91–103.

Farah, M. (1988). Is visual imagery really visual? Overlooked evidence from neuropsychology. *Psychological Review, 95,* 307–317.

Farah, M. (1989). Mechanisms of imagery-perception interaction. *Journal of Experimental Psychology: Human Perception and Performance, 15,* 203–211.

Farah, M., & Smith, A. (1983). Perceptual interference and facilitation with auditory imagery. *Perception and Psychophysics, 33,* 475–478.

Farah, M. J., Hammond, K. M., Levine, D. N., & Calvanio, R. (1988). Visual and spatial mental imagery: Dissociable systems of representation. *Cognitive Psychology, 20,* 439–462.

Farah, M. J., & Peronnet, F. (1989). Event-related potentials in the study of mental imagery. *Journal of Psychophysiology, 3,* 99–109.

Farah, M. J., Soso, M., & Dasheiff, R. (1992). Visual angle of the mind's eye before and after unilateral occipital lobectomy. *Journal of Experimental Psychology: Human Perception and Performance, 18,* 241–246.

Finke, R. (1990). *Creative imagery: Discoveries and inventions in visualization.* Hillsdale, NJ: Erlbaum.

Finke, R., & Kosslyn, S. (1980). Mental imagery acuity in the peripheral visual field. *Journal of Experimental Psychology: Human Perception and Performance, 6,* 126–139.

Finke, R., Pinker, S., & Farah, M. (1989). Reinterpreting visual patterns in mental imagery. *Cognitive Science, 13,* 51–78.

Galton, F. (1883). *Inquiries into human faculty.* London: Dent.

Goebel, R., Khorram-Sefat, D., Muckli, L., Hacker, H., & Singer, W. (1998). The constructive nature of vision: Direct evidence from functional magnetic resonance imaging studies of apparent motion and motion imagery. *European Journal of Neuroscience, 10*(5), 1563–1573.

Goldenberg, G. (1999). Mental scanning: A window on visual imagery? *Cahiers de Psychologie Cognitive, 18*(4), 522–526.

Goldenberg, G., Müllbacher, W., & Nowak, A. (1995). Imagery without perception—A case study of anosognosia for cortical blindness. *Neuropsychologia, 33,* 39–48.

Goldenberg, G., Podreka, I., & Steiner, M. (1990). The cerebral localization of visual imagery: Evidence from emission computerized tomography of cerebral blood flow. In P. J. Hampson & D. F. Marks (Eds.), *Imagery: Current developments. International library of psychology* (pp. 307–332). London: Routledge.

Goldmeier, E. (1937/1972). Similarities in visually perceived forms. *Psychological Issues, 8,* 1–136.

Halpern, A. (1988). Mental scanning in auditory imagery for songs. *Journal of Experimental Psychology: Learning, Memory and Cognition, 14,* 434–443.

Halpern, A. (1991). Musical aspects of auditory imagery. In D. Reisberg (Ed.), *Auditory imagery.* Hillsdale, NJ: Erlbaum.

Heaps, C., & Nash, M. (1999). Individual differences in imagination inflation. *Psychonomic Bulletin and Review, 6,* 313–318.

Hegarty, M. (2004). Mechanical reasoning by mental simulation. *Trends in Cognitive Sciences, 8,* 280–285.

Heil, M., Rösler, F., & Hennighausen, E. (1993). Imagery-perception interaction depends on the shape of the image: A reply to Farah. *Journal of Experimental Psychology: Human Perception and Performance, 19,* 1313–1319.

Hyman, I. (1993). Imagery, reconstructive memory, and discovery. In B. Roskos-Ewoldsen, M. Intons-Peterson, & R. Anderson (Eds.), *Imagery, creativity and discovery: A cognitive approach* (pp. 99–122). Amsterdam, The Netherlands: Elsevier.

Ishai, A., & Sagi, D. (1995). Common mechanisms of visual imagery and perception. *Science, 268,* 1772–1774.

Ishai, A., & Sagi, D. (1997). Visual imagery facilitates visual perception: Psychophysical evidence. *Journal of Cognitive Neuroscience, 9*(4), 476–489.

James, W. (1890). *The principles of psychology, Vol. II.* New York: Dover.

Jankowiak, J., Kinsbourne, M., Shalev, R. S., & Bachman, D. L. (1992). Preserved visual imagery and categorization in a case of associative visual agnosia. *Journal of Cognitive Neuroscience, 4,* 119–131.

Johnson, P. (1982). The functional equivalence of imagery and movement. *Quarterly Journal of Experimental Psychology, 34a,* 349–365.

Jonides, J., Kahn, R., & Rozin, P. (1975). Imagery instructions improve memory in blind subjects. *Bulletin of the Psychonomic Society, 5,* 424–426.

Katz, A. (1983). What does it mean to be a high imager? In J. Yuille (Ed.), *Imagery, memory and cognition* (pp. 39–63). Hillsdale, NJ: Erlbaum.

Kaufman, G., & Helstrup, T. (1993). Mental imagery: Fixed or multiple meanings? In B. Roskos-Ewoldsen, M. Intons-Peterson, & R. Anderson (Eds.), *Imagery, creativity and discovery: A cognitive approach* (pp. 123–150). Amsterdam, The Netherlands: Elsevier.

Kerr, N. H. (1983). The role of vision in "visual imagery" experiments: Evidence from the congenitally blind. *Journal of Experimental Psychology: General, 112,* 265–277.

Klauer, K. C., & Zhao, Z. (2004). Double dissociations in visual and spatial short-term memory. *Journal of Experimental Psychology: General, 133,* 355–381.

Kosslyn, S., Brunn, J., Cave, K., & Wallach, R. (1985). Individual differences in mental imagery ability: A computational analysis. *Cognition, 18,* 195–243.

Kosslyn, S. M. (1976). Can imagery be distinguished from other forms of internal representation? Evidence from studies of information retrieval times. *Memory and Cognition, 4,* 291–297.

Kosslyn, S. M. (1981). The medium and the message in mental imagery: A theory. *Psychological Review, 88,* 46–66.

Kosslyn, S. M. (1983). *Ghosts in the mind's machine.* New York: Norton.

Kosslyn, S. M. (1994). *Image and brain: The resolution of the imagery debate.* Cambridge, MA: MIT Press.

Kosslyn, S. M., Alpert, N. M., Thompson, L., Maljkovic, V., Weise, S., Chabris, C., Hamilton, S. E., & Buonanno, F. S. (1993). Visual mental imagery activates topographically organized visual cortex: PET investigations. *Journal of Cognitive Neuroscience, 5,* 263–287.

Kosslyn, S. M., Ball, T. M., & Reiser, B. J. (1978). Visual images preserve metric spatial information: Evidence from studies of image scanning. *Journal of Experimental Psychology: Human Perception and Performance, 4,* 1–20.

Kosslyn, S. M., Pascual-Leone, A., Felician, O., Camposano, S., Keenan, J. P., Thompson, W. L., ... Alpert, N. M. (1999).

The role of area 17 in visual imagery: Convergent evidence from PET and rTMS. *Science, 284,* 167–170.

Kosslyn, S. M., & Thompson, W. L. (1999). Shared mechanisms in visual imagery and visual perception: Insights from cognitive neuroscience. In M. S. Gazzaniga (Ed.), *The new cognitive neurosciences (pp. 975–985).* Cambridge, MA: MIT Press.

Kosslyn, S. M., Thompson, W. L., Kim, I. J., & Alpert, N. M. (1995). Topographical representations of mental images in primary visual cortex. *Nature, 378*(6556), 496–498.

Kozhevnikov, M., Kosslyn, S., & Shephard, J. (2005). Spatial versus object visualizers: A new characterization of visual cognitive style. *Memory and Cognition, 33,* 710–726.

Logie, R. (1986). Visuo-spatial processing in working memory. *Quarterly Journal of Experimental Psychology, 38A,* 229–247.

Logie, R. H., & Marchetti, C. (1991). Visuo-spatial working memory: Visual, spatial or central executive. In R. H. Logie & M. Denis (Eds.), *Mental images in human cognition* (pp. 105–115). Amsterdam, The Netherlands: Elsevier.

Marks, D. (1977). Imagery and consciousness: A theoretical review from an individual differences perspectives. *Journal of Mental Imagery, 2,* 275–290.

Marks, D. (1983). Mental imagery and consciousness: A theoretical review. In A. Sheikh (Ed.), *Imagery: Current theory, research and application.* New York: Wiley.

Marks, D. F. (1990). On the relationship between imagery, body, and mind. In P. J. Hampson & D. F. Marks (Eds.), *Imagery: Current developments. International library of psychology* (pp. 1–38). London: Routledge.

Marmor, G. S., & Zabeck, L. A. (1976). Mental rotation by the blind: Does mental rotation depend on visual imagery? *Journal of Experimental Psychology: Human Perception and Performance, 2,* 515–521.

Matthews, W. A. (1983). The effects of concurrent secondary tasks on the use of imagery in a free recall task. *Acta Psychologica, 53,* 231–241.

McDermott, K., & Roediger, H. (1994). Effects of imagery on perceptual implicit memory tests. *Journal of Experimental Psychology: Learning, Memory and Cognition, 20,* 1379–1390.

McKelvie, S. (1995). The VVIQ as a psychometric test of individual differences in visual imagery vividness: A critical quantitative review and plea for direction. *Journal of Mental Imagery, 19,* 1–106.

McKelvie, S. J. (1999). Metric properties of visual images: Only a partial window on the mind. *Cahiers de Psychologie Cognitive, 18*(4), 556–563.

Mellet, E., Tzourio, N., Crivello, F., Joliot, M., Denis, M., & Mazoyer, B. (1996). Functional anatomy of spatial mental imagery generated from verbal instructions. *Journal of Neuroscience, 16,* 6504–6512.

Mellet, E., Tzourio, N., Denis, M., & Mazoyer, B. (1995). A positron emission topography study of visual and mental spatial exploration. *Journal of Cognitive Neuroscience, 7,* 433–445.

Mellet, E., Tzourio-Mazoyer, N., Bricogne, S., Mazoyer, B., Kosslyn, S. M., & Denis, M. (2000). Functional anatomy of high-resolution visual mental imagery. *Journal of Cognitive Neuroscience, 12*(1), 98–109.

Miller, A. (1986). *Imagery in scientific thought.* Cambridge, MA: MIT Press.

Miyashita, Y. (1995). How the brain creates imagery: Projection to primary visual cortex. *Science, 268,* 1719–1720.

Morris, N. (1987). Exploring the visuo-spatial scratch pad. *Quarterly Journal of Experimental Psychology, 39A,* 409–430.

O'Craven, K., & Kanwisher, N. (2000). Mental imagery of faces and places activates corresponding stimulus-specific brain regions. *Journal of Cognitive Neuroscience, 12,* 1013–1023.

Paivio, A., & Okovita, H. W. (1971). Word imagery modalities and associative learning in blind and sighted subjects. *Journal of Verbal Learning and Verbal Behavior, 10,* 506–510.

Peterson, M., Kihlstrom, J., Rose, P., & Glisky, M. (1992). Mental images can be ambiguous: Reconstruals and reference-frame reversals. *Memory and Cognition, 20,* 107–123.

Pinker, S., & Finke, R. (1980). Emergent two-dimensional patterns in images in depth. *Journal of Experimental Psychology: Human Perception and Performance, 6,* 244–264.

Pylyshyn, Z. (1981). The imagery debate: Analogue media versus tacit knowledge. In N. Block (Ed.), *Imagery* (pp. 151–206). Cambridge, MA: MIT Press.

Quinn, G. (1988). Interference effects in the visuo-spatial sketch-pad. In M. Denis, J. Engelkamp, & J. T. E. Richardson (Eds.), *Cognitive and neuropsychological approaches to mental imagery* (pp. 181–189). Boston, MA: Martinus Nijhoff.

Quinn, J. G., & Ralston, G. E. (1986). Movement and attention in visual working memory. *Quarterly Journal of Experimental Psychology, 38A,* 689–703.

Reisberg, D. (1994). The non-ambiguity of mental images. In C. Cornold, R. Logie, M. Brandimonte, G. Kaufmann, & D. Reisberg (Eds.), *Images and pictures: On perception and mental representation* (pp. 119–171). New York: Oxford University Press.

Reisberg, D., & Chambers, D. (1991). Neither pictures nor propositions: What can we learn from a mental image? *Canadian Journal of Psychology, 45,* 288–302.

Reisberg, D., Culver, C., Heuer, F., & Fischman, D. (1986). Visual memory: When imagery vividness makes a difference. *Journal of Mental Imagery, 10,* 51–74.

Reisberg, D., & Leak, S. (1987). Visual imagery and memory for appearance: Does Clark Gable or George C. Scott have bushier eyebrows? *Canadian Journal of Psychology, 41,* 521–526.

Reisberg, D., Smith, J. D., Baxter, D. A., & Sonenshine, M. (1989). "Enacted" auditory images are ambiguous; "Pure" auditory images are not. *Quarterly Journal of Experimental Psychology, 41A,* 619–641.

Richardson, J. (1980). *Mental imagery and human memory.* New York: St. Martin's Press.

Richardson, J. T. E. (1999). *Imagery.* East Sussex, England: Psychology Press.

Richter, W., Somorjai, R., Summers, R., Jarmasz, M., Menon, R. S., Gati, J. S., ... Kim, S -G. (2000). Motor area activity during mental rotation studied by time-resolved single-trial fMRI. *Journal of Cognitive Neuroscience, 12*(2), 310–320.

Riske, M. L., Wallace, B., & Allen, P. A. (2000). Imaging ability and eyewitness accuracy. *Journal of Mental Imagery, 24*(1–2), 137–148.

Rock, I. (1983). *The logic of perception.* Cambridge, MA: MIT Press.

Segal, S., & Fusella, V. (1971). Effect of images in six sense modalities on detection of visual signal from noise. *Psychonomic Science, 24,* 55–56.

Segal, S. J., & Fusella, V. (1970). Influence of imaged pictures and sounds in detection of visual and auditory signals. *Journal of Experimental Psychology, 83,* 458–474.

Servos, P., & Goodale, M. A. (1995). Preserved visual imagery in visual form agnosia. *Neuropsychologia, 33*(11), 1383–1394.

Shepard, R. (1988). The imagination of the scientist. In K. Egan & D. Nadaner (Eds.), *Imagination and education* (pp. 153–185). New York: Teachers College Press.

Shepard, R. N., & Cooper, L. A. (1982). *Mental images and their transformations.* Cambridge, MA: MIT Press.

Sirigu, A., & Duhamel, J. R. (2001). Motor and visual imagery as two complementary but neurally dissociable mental processes. *Journal of Cognitive Neuroscience, 13,* 910–919.

Smyth, M. M., & Pendleton, L. R. (1989). Working memory for movements. *Quarterly Journal of Experimental Psychology, 41A,* 235–250.

Thompson, W. L., & Kosslyn, S. M. (2000). Neural systems activated during visual mental imagery: A review and meta-analyses. In J. Mazziotta & A. Toga (Eds.), *Brain mapping II: The applications.* New York: Academic Press.

Thompson, W. L., Kosslyn, S. M., Hoffman, M. S., & Kooij, K. v. D. (2008). Inspecting visual mental images: Can people "see" implicit properities as easily in imagery and perception? *Memory and Cognition, 36,* 1024–1032.

Thompson, W. L., Slotnick, S. D., Burrage, M. S., & Kosslyn, S. M. (2009). Two forms of spatial imagery: Neuroimaging evidence. *Psychological Science, 20,* 1245–1253.

Tomes, J. L., & Katz, A. N. (1997). Habitual susceptibility to misinformation and individual differences in eyewitness testimony. *Applied Cognitive Psychology, 11,* 233–252.

Vecchi, T. (1998). Visuo-spatial imagery in congenitally totally blind people. *Memory, 6*(1), 91–102.

Verstijnen, I. M., Hennessey, J. M., Leeuwen, C. v., Hamel, R., & Goldschmidt, G. (1998). Sketching and creative discovery. *Design Studies, 19,* 519–546.

Verstijnen, I. M., Leeuwen, C. v., Goldschmidt, G., Hamel, R., & Hennessey, J. M. (1998). Creative discovery in imagery and perception: Combining is relatively easy, restructuring takes a sketch. *Acta Psychologica, 99,* 177–200.

Walczyk, J. J., & Taylor, R. W. (2000). Reverse-spelling, the VVIQ and mental imagery. *Journal of Mental Imagery, 24*(1–2), 177–188.

Wilkinson, C., & Hyman, I. E., Jr. (1998). Individual differences related to two types of memory errors: Word lists may not generalize to autobiographical memory. *Applied Cognitive Psychology, 12*(Spec Issue), S29–S46.

Winograd, E., Peluso, J. P., & Glover, T. A. (1998). Individual differences in susceptibility to memory illusions. *Applied Cognitive Psychology, 12,* S5–S28.

Zatorre, R. J., & Halpern, A. R. (1993). Effect of unilateral temporal-lobe excision on perception and imagery of songs. *Neuropsychologia, 31*(3), 221–232.

Zatorre, R. J., Halpern, A. R., Perry, D. W., Meyer, E., & Evans, A. C. (1996). Hearing in the mind's ear: A PET investigation of musical imagery and perception. *Journal of Cognitive Neuroscience, 8*(1), 29–46.

Zimler, J., & Keenan, J. M. (1983). Imagery in the congenitally blind: How visual are visual images? *Journal of Experimental Psychology: Learning, Memory and Cognition, 9,* 269–282.

# PART 5

# Text and Language

# Speech Perception

Sven L. Mattys

**Abstract**

Speech perception is conventionally defined as the perceptual and cognitive processes leading to the discrimination, identification, and interpretation of speech sounds. However, to gain a broader understanding of the concept, such processes must be investigated relative to their interaction with long-term knowledge—lexical information in particular. This chapter starts with a review of some of the fundamental characteristics of the speech signal and by an evaluation of the constraints that these characteristics impose on modeling speech perception. Long-standing questions are then discussed in the context of classic and more recent theories. Recurrent themes include the following: (1) the involvement of articulatory knowledge in speech perception, (2) the existence of a speech-specific mode of auditory processing, (3) the multimodal nature of speech perception, (4) the relative contribution of bottom-up and top-down flows of information to sound categorization, (5) the impact of the auditory environment on speech perception in infancy, and (6) the flexibility of the speech system in the face of novel or atypical input.

**Key Words:** coarticulation, phonemes, categorical perception, lexical access, segmentation, bottom-up, top-down, perceptual learning

The complexity, variability, and fine temporal properties of the acoustic signal of speech have puzzled psycholinguists and speech engineers for decades. How can a signal seemingly devoid of regularity be decoded and recognized almost instantly, without any formal training, and despite being often experienced in suboptimal conditions? Without any real effort, we identify over a dozen speech sounds (phonemes) per second, recognize the words they constitute, almost immediately understand the message generated by the sentences they form, and often elaborate appropriate verbal and nonverbal responses before the utterance ends.

Unlike theories of letter perception and written-word recognition, theories of speech perception and spoken-word recognition have devoted a great deal of their investigation to a description of the signal itself, most of it carried out within the field of

phonetics. In particular, the fact that speech is conveyed in the auditory modality has dramatic implications for the perceptual and cognitive operations underpinning its recognition. Research in speech perception has focused on the constraining effects of three main properties of the auditory signal: sequentiality, variability, and continuity.

## Nature of the Speech Signal
### Sequentiality

One of the most obvious disadvantages of the auditory system compared to its visual counterpart is that the distribution of the auditory information is time bound, transient, and solely under the speaker's control. Moreover, the auditory signal conveys its acoustic content in a relatively serial fashion, one bit of information at a time. The extreme spreading of information over time in the speech domain

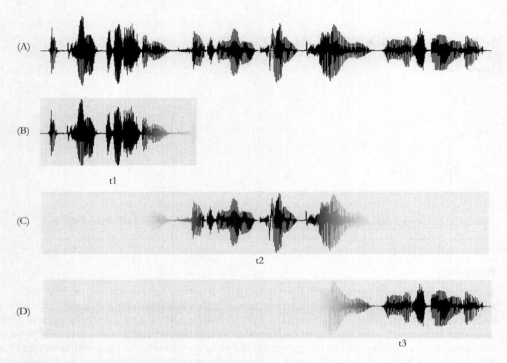

**Figure 26.1** Illustration of the sequential nature of speech processing. (*A*) Waveform of a complete sentence, that is, air pressure changes (Y axis) over time (X axis). (*B–D*) Illustration of a listener's progressive processing of the sentence at three successive points in time. The visible waveform represents the portion of signal that is available for processing at time t1 (*B*), t2 (*C*), and t3 (*D*).

has important consequences for the mechanisms involved in perceiving and interpreting the input.

In particular, given that relatively little information is conveyed per unit of time, the extraction of meaning can only be done within a window of time that far exceeds the amount of information that can be held in echoic memory (Huggins, 1975; Nooteboom, 1979). Likewise, given that there are no such things as "auditory saccades," in which listeners would be able to skip ahead of the signal or replay the words or sentences they just heard, speech perception and lexical-sentential integration must take place sequentially, in real time (Fig. 26.1).

For a large part, listeners are extremely good at keeping up with the rapid flow of speech sounds. Marslen-Wilson (1987) showed that many words in sentences are often recognized well before their offset, sometimes as early as 200 ms after their onset, the average duration of one or two syllables. Other words, however, can only be disentangled from competitors later on, especially when they are short and phonetically reduced, for example, "you are" pronounced as "you're" (Bard, Shillcock, & Altmann, 1988). Yet, in general, there is a consensus that speech perception and lexical access closely shadow the unfolding of the signal (e.g., the Cohort Model;

Marslen-Wilson, 1987), even though "right-to-left" effects can sometimes be observed as well (Dahan, 2010).

Given the inevitable sequentiality of speech perception and the limited amount of information that humans can hold in their auditory short-term memory, an obvious question is whether fast speech, which allows more information to be packed into the same amount of time, helps listeners handle the transient nature of speech and, specifically, whether it affects the mechanisms leading to speech recognition. A problem, however, is that fast speech tends to be less clearly articulated (hypoarticulated), and hence, less intelligible. Thus, any processing gain due to denser information packing might be offset by diminished intelligibility. However, this confound can be avoided experimentally. Indeed, speech rate can be accelerated with minimal loss of intrinsic intelligibility via computer-assisted signal compression (e.g., Foulke & Sticht, 1969; van Buuren, Festen, & Houtgast, 1999). Time compression experiments have led to mixed results. Dupoux and Mehler (1990), for instance, found no effect of speech rate on how phonemes are perceived in monosyllabic versus disyllabic words. They started from the observation that the initial consonant of a monosyllabic word is detected faster if the word is high frequency than if it is low frequency, whereas frequency has no effect in multisyllabic words. This difference can be attributed to the use of a lexical route with short words and of a phonemic route with longer words. That is, short words are mapped directly onto lexical representations, whereas longer words undergo a process of decomposition into phonemes first. Critically, Dupoux and Mehler reported that a frequency effect did not appear when the duration of the disyllabic words was compressed to that of the monosyllabic words, suggesting that whether listeners use a lexical or phonemic route to identify phonemes depends on structural factors (number of phonemes or syllables) rather than time. Thus, on this account, the transient nature of speech has only a limited effect on the mechanisms underlying speech recognition.

In contrast, others have found significant effects of speech rate on lexical access. For example, both Pitt and Samuel (1995) and Radeau, Morais, Mousty, and Bertelson (2000) observed that the uniqueness point of a word, that is, the sequential point at which it can be uniquely specified (e.g., "spag" for "spaghetti"), could be dramatically altered when speech rate was manipulated. However, most changes were observed at slower rates, not at faster rates. Thus, changes in speech rate can have effects on recognition mechanisms, but these are observed mainly with time expansion, not with time compression. In sum, although the studies by Dupoux and Mehler (1990), Pitt and Samuel (1995), and Radeau et al. (2000) highlight different effects of time manipulation on speech processing, they all agree that packing more information per unit of time by accelerating speech rate does not compensate for the transient nature of the speech signal and for memory limitations. This is probably due to intrinsic perceptual and mnemonic limitations on how fast information can be processed by the speech system—at *any* rate.

In general, the sequential nature of speech processing is a feature that many models have struggled to implement not only because it requires taking into account echoic and short-term memory mechanisms (Mattys, 1997) but also because the sequentiality problem is compounded by a lack of clear boundaries between phonemes and between words, as described later.

### Continuity

The inspection of a speech waveform does not reveal clear acoustic correlates of what the human ear perceives as phoneme and word boundaries. The lack of boundaries is due to coarticulation between phonemes (the blending of articulatory gestures between adjacent phonemes) within and across words. Even though the degree of coarticulation between phonemes is somewhat less pronounced across than within words (Fougeron & Keating, 1997), the lack of clear and reliable gaps between words, along with the sequential nature of speech delivery, makes speech continuity one of the most challenging obstacles for both psycholinguistic theory and automatic speech recognition applications. Yet the absence of phoneme and word boundary markers hardly seems to pose a problem for everyday listening, as the subjective experience of speech is not one of continuity but, rather, of discreteness—that is, a string of sounds making up a string of words.

A great deal of the segmentation problem can be solved, at least in theory, based on lexical knowledge and contextual information. Key notions, here, are lexical competition and segmentation by lexical subtraction. In this view, lexical candidates are activated in multiple locations in the speech signal—that is, multiple alignment—and they compete for a segmentation solution that does not leave any fragments lexically unaccounted for (e.g., "great wall" is favored over "gray twall," because "twall" in not an English word). Importantly, this knowledge-driven approach does not assign a specific computational status to segmentation, other than being the mere consequence of mechanisms associated with lexical competition (e.g., McClelland & Elman, 1986; Norris, 1994).

Another source of information for word segmentation draws upon broad prosodic and segmental regularities in the signal, which listeners use as heuristics for locating word boundaries. For example, languages whose words have a predominant rhythmic pattern (e.g., word-initial stress is predominant in English; word-final lengthening is predominant in French) provide a relatively straightforward—though probabilistic—segmentation strategy to their listeners (Cutler, 1994). The heuristic for English would go as follows: *every time a strong syllable is encountered, a boundary is posited before that syllable.* For French, it would be: *every time a lengthened syllable is encountered, a boundary is posited after that syllable.* Another documented heuristic is based on phonotactic probability, that is, the likelihood that specific phonemes follow each other in the words of a language (McQueen, 1998). Specifically, phonemes that are rarely found next to each other in words (e.g., very few English words contain the /fh/ diphone) would be probabilistically interpreted as having occurred across a word boundary (e.g., "tou*gh h*ero"). Finally, a wide array of acoustic-phonetic cues can also give away the position of a word boundary (Umeda & Coker, 1974). Indeed, phonemes tend to be realized differently depending on their position relative to a word or a syllable boundary. For example, in English, word-initial vowels are frequently glottalized (brief closure of the glottis, e.g., /e/ in "isle *e*nd," compared to no closure in "I l*e*nd"), word-initial stop consonants are often aspirated (burst of air accompanying the release of a consonant, e.g., /t/ in "gray *t*anker" compared to no aspiration in "grea*t* anchor").

It is important to note that, in everyday speech, lexically and sublexically driven segmentation cues usually coincide and reinforce each other. However, in suboptimal listening conditions (e.g., noise) or in rare cases where a conflict arises between those two sources of information, listeners have been shown to downplay sublexical discrepancies and give more heed to lexical plausibility (Mattys, White, & Melhorn, 2005; Fig. 26.2).

### Variability

Perhaps the most defining challenge for the field of speech perception is the enormous variability of

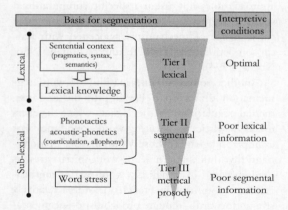

**Figure 26.2** Sketch of Mattys, White, and Melhorn's (2005) hierarchical approach to speech segmentation. The relative weights of speech segmentation cues are illustrated by the width of the gray triangle. In optimal listening conditions, the cues in Tier I dominate. When lexical access is compromised or ambiguous, the cues in Tier II take over. Cues from Tier III are recruited when both lexical and segmental cues are compromised (e.g., background of severe noise). (Reprinted from Mattys, S. L., White, L., & Melhorn, J. F [2005]. Integration of multiple speech segmentation cues: A hierarchical framework. *Journal of Experimental Psychology: General, 134,* 477–500 [Figure 7], by permission of the American Psychological Association.)

the signal relative to the stored representations onto which it must be matched. Variability can be found at the word level, where there are infinite ways a given word can be pronounced depending on accents, voice quality, speech rate, and so on, leading to a multitude of surface realizations for a unique target representation. But this many-to-one mapping problem is not different from the one encountered with written words in different handwritings or object recognition in general. In those cases, signal normalization can be effectively achieved by defining a set of core features unique to each word or object stored in memory and by reducing the mapping process to those features only.

The real issue with speech variability happens at a lower level, namely, phoneme categorization. Unlike letters whose realizations have at least some commonality from one instance to another, phonemes can vary widely in their acoustic manifestation—even within the same speaker. For example, as shown in Figure 26.3A, the realization of the phoneme /d/ has no immediately apparent acoustic commonality in /di/ and /du/ (Delattre, Liberman, & Cooper, 1955). This lack of acoustic invariance is the consequence of coarticulation: The articulation of /d/ in /di/ is partly determined by the articulatory preparation for /i/, and likewise for /d/ in /du/. The power of coarticulation is easily demonstrated by observing a speaker's mouth prior to saying /di/ compared to /du/. The mode of articulation of /i/ (unrounded) versus /u/ (rounded) is visible on the speaker's lips even before /d/ has been uttered. The resulting acoustics of /d/ preceding each vowel have therefore little in common.

The success of the search for acoustic cues, or invariants, capable of uniquely identifying phonemes or phonetic categories has been highly feature specific. For example, as illustrated in Figure 26.3A, the place of articulation of phonemes (i.e., the place in the vocal tract where the airstream is most constricted, which distinguishes, e.g., /b/, /d/, /g/) has been difficult to map onto specific acoustic cues. However, the difference between voiced and unvoiced stop consonants (/b/, /d/, /g/ vs. /p/, /t/, /k/) can be traced back fairly reliably to the duration between the release of the consonant and the moment when the vocal folds start vibrating, that is, the voice onset time (VOT; Liberman, Delattre, & Cooper, 1958). In English, the VOT of voiced stop consonants is typically around 0 ms (or at least shorter than 20 ms), whereas it is generally over 25 ms for voiceless consonants. Although this contrast has been shown to be somewhat influenced by

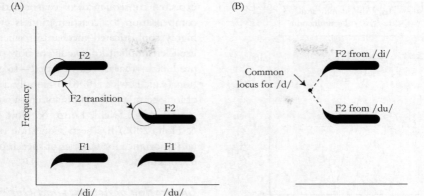

(A)                                                    (B)

**Figure 26.3** (*A*) Stylized spectrograms of /di/ and /du/. The dark bars, or formants, represent areas of peak energy on the frequency scale (Y axis), which correlate with zones of high resonance in the vocal tract. The curvy leads into the formants are formant transitions. They show coarticulation between the consonant and the following vowel. Note the dissimilarity between the second formant transitions in /di/ (rising) and /du/ (falling). However, as shown in (*B*), the extrapolation back in time of the two second formants' transitions point to a common frequency locus.

consonant type and vocalic context (e.g., Lisker & Abramson, 1970), VOT is a fairly robust cue for the voiced-voiceless distinction.

Vowels are subject to coarticulatory influences, too, but the spectral structure of their middle portion is usually relatively stable, and hence, a taxonomy of vowels based on their unique distribution of energy bands along the frequency spectrum, or formants, can be attempted. However, such distribution is influenced by speaking rate, with fast speech typically leading to the target frequency of the formants being missed or leading to an asymmetric shortening of stressed versus unstressed vowels (Lindblom, 1963; Port, 1977). In general, speech rate variation is particularly problematic for acoustic cues involving time. Even stable cues such as VOT can lose their discriminability power when speech rate is altered. For example, at fast speech rates, the VOT difference between voiced and voiceless stop consonants decreases, making the two types of phonemes more difficult to distinguish (Summerfield, 1981). The same problem has been noted for the difference between /b/ and /w/, with /b/ having rapid formant transitions into the vowel and /w/ less rapid ones. This difference is less pronounced at fast speech rates (Miller & Liberman, 1979).

Yet, except for those conditions in which subtle differences are manipulated in the laboratory, listeners are surprisingly good at compensating for the acoustic distortions introduced by coarticulation and changes in speech rate. Thus, input variability, phonetic-context effects, and the lack of invariance do not appear to pose a serious problem for everyday speech perception. As reviewed later, however,

theoretical accounts aiming to reconcile the complexity of the signal with the effortlessness of perception vary greatly.

## Basic Phenomena and Questions in Speech Perception

Following are some of the observations that have shaped theoretical thinking in speech perception over the past 60 years. Most of them concern, in one way or another, the extent to which speech perception is carried out by a part of the auditory system dedicated to speech and involving speech-specific mechanisms not recruited for nonspeech sounds.

### Categorical Perception

Categorical perception in a sensory phenomenon whereby a physically continuous dimension is perceived as discrete categories, with abrupt perceptual boundaries between categories and poor discrimination within categories (e.g., perception of the visible electromagnetic radiation spectrum as discrete colors). Early on, categorical perception was found to apply to phonemes—or at least some of them. For example, Liberman, Harris, Hoffman, and Griffith (1957) showed that synthesized syllables ranging from /ba/ to /da/ to /ga/ by gradually adjusting the transition between the consonant and the vowel's formants (i.e., the formant transitions) were perceived as falling into coarse /b/, /d/, and /g/ categories, with poor discrimination between syllables belonging to a perceptual category and high discrimination between syllables straddling a perceptual boundary (Fig. 26.4). Importantly, categorical perception was not observed for matched auditory

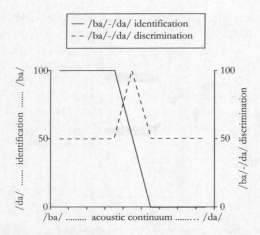

**Figure 26.4** Idealized identification pattern (solid line, left Y axis) and discrimination pattern (dashed line, right Y axis) for categorical perception. Illustration with a /ba/ to /da/ continuum. Identification shows a sharp perceptual boundary between categories. Discrimination is finer around the boundary than inside the categories.

stimuli devoid of phonemic significance (Liberman, Harris, Eimas, Lisker, & Bastian, 1961). Moreover, since categorical perception meant that easy-to-identify syllables (spectrum endpoints) were also easy syllables to pronounce, whereas less-easy-to-identify syllables (spectrum midpoints) were generally less easy to pronounce, categorical perception was seen as a highly adaptive property of the speech system, and hence, evidence for a dedicated speech mode of the auditory system. This claim was later weakened by reports of categorical perception for nonspeech sounds (e.g., Miller, Wier, Pastore, Kelly, & Dooling, 1976) and for speech sounds by non-human species (e.g., Kluender, Diehl, & Killeen, 1987; Kuhl, 1981).

### Effects of Phonetic Context

The effect of adjacent phonemes on the acoustic realization of a target phoneme (e.g., /d/ in /di/ vs. /du/) was mentioned earlier as a core element of the variability challenge. This challenge, that is, achieving perceptual constancy despite input variability, is perhaps most directly illustrated by the converse phenomenon, namely, the varying perception of a constant acoustic input as a function of its changing phonetic environment. Mann (1980) showed that the perception of a /da/-/ga/ continumm was shifted in the direction of reporting more /ga/ when it was preceded by /al/ and more /da/ when it was preceded by /ar/. Since these shifts are in the opposite direction of coarticulation between adjacent phonemes, listeners appear to compensate for the

expected consequences of coarticulation. Whether compensation for coarticulation is evidence for a highly sophisticated mechanism whereby listeners use their implicit knowledge of how phonemes are produced—that is, coarticulated—to guide perception (e.g., Fowler, 2006) or simply a consequence of long-term association between the signal and the percept (e.g., Diehl, Lotto, & Holt, 2004; Lotto & Holt, 2006) has been a question of fundamental importance for theories of speech perception, as discussed later.

### Integration of Acoustic and Optic Cues

The chief outcome of speech production is the emission of an acoustic signal. However, visual correlates, such as facial and lip movements, are often available to the listener as well. The effect of visual information on speech perception has been extensively studied, especially in the context of the benefit provided by visual cues for listeners with hearing impairments (e.g., Lachs, Pisoni, & Kirk, 2001) and for speech perception in noise (e.g., Sumby & Pollack, 1954). Visual-based enhancement is also observed for undegraded speech with a semantically complicated content or for foreign-accented speech (Reisberg, McLean, & Goldfield, 1987). In the laboratory, audiovisual integration is strikingly illustrated by the well-known McGurk effect. McGurk and McDonald (1976) showed that listeners presented with an acoustic /ba/ dubbed over a face saying /ga/ tended to report hearing /da/, a syllable whose place of articulation is intermediate between /ba/ and /ga/. The robustness and automaticity of the effect suggest that the acoustic and (visual) articulatory cues of speech are integrated at an early stage of processing. Whether early integration indicates that the primitives of speech perception are articulatory in nature or whether it simply highlights a learned association between acoustic and optic information has been a theoretically divisive debate (see Rosenblum, 2005, for a review).

### Lexical and Sentential Effects on Speech Perception

Although traditional approaches to speech perception often stop where word recognition begins (in the same way that approaches to word recognition often stop where sentence comprehension begins), speech perception has been profoundly influenced by the debate on how higher order knowledge affects the identification and categorization of phonemes and phonetic features. A key observation is that lexical knowledge and sentential context can aid phoneme identification, especially when the signal is ambiguous or degraded. For example, Warren and Obusek (1971) showed that a word can be heard as intact even when a component phoneme is missing and replaced with noise, for example, "legi*lature," where the asterisk denotes the replaced phoneme. In this case, lexical knowledge dictates what the listener should have heard rather than what was actually there, a phenomenon referred to as phoneme restoration. Likewise, Warren and Warren (1970) showed that a word whose initial phoneme is degraded, for example, "*eel," tends to be heard as "wheel" in "It was found that the *eel was on the axle" and as "peel" in "It was found that the *eel was on the orange." Thus, phoneme identification can be strongly influenced by lexical and sentential knowledge even when the disambiguating context appears later than the degraded phoneme.

But is this truly of interest for speech *perception*? In other words, could phoneme restoration (and other similar speech illusions) simply result from postperceptual, strategic biases? In this case, "*eel" would be interpreted as "wheel" simply because it makes pragmatic sense to do so in a particular sentential context, not because our perceptual system is genuinely tricked by high-level expectations. If so, contextual effects are of interest to speech-perception scientists only insofar as they suggest that speech perception happens in a system that is unpenetrable by higher order knowledge—an unfortunately convenient way of indirectly perpetuating the confinement of speech perception to the study of phoneme identification. The evidence for a postperceptual explanation is mixed. While Norris, McQueen, and Cutler (2000), Massaro (1989), and Oden and Massaro (1978), among others, found no evidence for online top-down feedback to the perceptual system and no logical reasons why such feedback should exist, Samuel (1981, 1997, 2001), Connine and Clifton (1987), and Magnuson, McMurray, Tanenhaus, and Aslin (2003), among others, have reported lexical effects on perception that challenge feedforward models—for example, evidence that lexical information truly alters low-level perceptual discrimination (Samuel, 1981). This debate has fostered extreme empirical ingenuity over the past decades but comparatively little change to theory. One exception, however, is that the debate has now spread to the *long-term* effects of higher order knowledge on speech perception. For example, while Norris, McQueen, and Cutler (2000) argue against online top-down feedback, the same group (2003) recognizes that perceptual

(re-)tuning can happen over time, in the context of repeated exposure and learning. Placing the feedforward/feedback debate in the time domain provides an opportunity to examine the speech system at the interface with cognition, and memory functions in particular. It also allows more applied considerations to be introduced, such as the role of perceptual recalibration for second-language learning and speech perception in difficult listening conditions (Samuel & Kraljic, 2009), as discussed later.

## Theories of Speech Perception (Narrowly and Broadly Construed)
### Motor and Articulatory-Gesture Theories

The Motor Theory of speech perception, reported in a series of articles in the early 1950s by Liberman, Delattre, Cooper, and other researchers from the Haskins Laboratories, was the first to offer a conceptual solution to the lack-of-invariance problem. As mentioned earlier, the main stumbling block for speech-perception theories was the observation that many phonemes cannot uniquely be identified by a set of stable and reliable acoustic cues. For example, the formant transitions of /d/, especially the second formant, differ as a function of the following vowel. However, Delattre et al. (1955) found commonality between different /d/s by extrapolating the formant transitions back in time to their convergence point, or *locus* (or *hub*; Potter, Kopp, & Green, 1947), as shown in Figure 26.3B. Thus, what is common to the formants of all /d/s is the frequency at their origin, that is, the frequency that would best reflect the position of the articulators prior to the release of the consonant. This led to one of the key arguments in support of the motor theory, namely that a one-to-one relationship between acoustics and phonemes can be established if the speech system includes a mechanism that allows the listener to work backward through the rules of production in order to identify the speaker's intended phonemes. In other words, the lack-of-invariance problem can be solved if it can be demonstrated that listeners perceive speech by identifying the speaker's intended speech gestures rather than (or in addition to) relying solely on the acoustic manifestation of such gestures. The McGurk effect, whereby auditory perception is dramatically altered by seeing the speaker's moving lips (articulatory gestures), was an important contributor to the view that the perceptual primitives of speech are gestural in nature.

In addition to claiming that the motor system is recruited for perceiving speech (and partly because of this claim), the Motor Theory also posits that speech perception takes place in a highly specialized and speech-specific module that is neurally isolated and is most likely a unique and innate human endowment (Liberman, 1996; Liberman & Mattingly, 1985). However, even among supporters of a motor basis for speech perception, agreeing upon an operational definition of intended speech gestures and providing empirical evidence for the contribution of such intended gestures to perception proved difficult. This led Fowler and her colleagues to propose that the objects of speech perception are not *intended* articulatory gestures but *real* gestures, that is, actual vocal tract movements that are inferable from the acoustic signal itself (e.g., Fowler, 1986, 1996). Thus, although Fowler's Direct Realism approach aligns with the Motor Theory in that it claims that perceiving speech is perceiving gestures, it asserts that the acoustic signal itself is rich enough in articulatory information to provide a stable (i.e., invariant) signal-to-phoneme mapping algorithm. In doing so, Direct Realism can do away with claims about specialized and/or innate structures for speech perception.

Although the popularity of the original tenets of the Motor Theory—and, to some extent,

associated gesture theories—has waned over the years, the theory has brought forward essential questions about the specificity of speech, the specialization of speech perception, and, more recently, the neuroanatomical substrate of a possible motor component of the speech apparatus (e.g., Gow & Segawa, 2009; Pulvermüller et al., 2006; Sussman, 1989; Whalen et al., 2006), a topic that regained interest following the discovery of mirror neurons in the premotor cortex (e.g., Rizzolatti & Craighero, 2004; but see Lotto, Hickok, & Holt, 2009). The debate has also shifted to a discussion of the extent to which the involvement of articulation during speech perception might in fact be under the listener's control and its manifestation partly task specific (Yuen, Davis, Brysbaert, & Rastle, 2010, Fig. 26.5; see comments by McGettigan, Agnew, & Scott, 2010; Rastle, Davis, & Brysbaert, 2010). The Motor Theory has also been extensively reviewed—and revisited—in an attempt to address problems highlighted by auditory-based models, as described later (e.g., Fowler, 2006, 2008; Galantucci, Fowler, & Turvey, 2006; Lotto & Holt, 2006; Massaro & Chen, 2008).

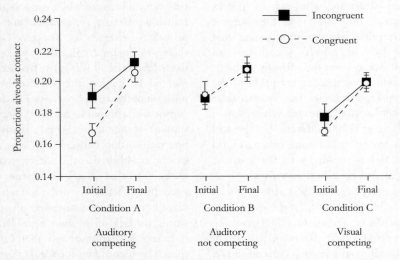

**Figure 26.5** Electropalatographic data showing the proportion of tongue contact on alveolar electrodes during the initial and final portions of /k/-initial (e.g., *kib*) or /s/-initial (e.g., *sib*) syllables (collapsed) while a congruent or incongruent distractor is presented (Yuen et al., 2010). The distractor was presented auditorily in conditions A and B and visually in condition C. With the target *kib* as an example, the congruent distractor in the A condition was *kib* and the incongruent distractor started with a phoneme involving a different place of articulation (e.g., *tib*). In condition B, the incongruent distractor started with a phoneme that differed from the target only by its voicing status, not by its place of articulation (e.g., *gib*). Condition C was the same as condition A, except that the distractor was presented visually. The results show "traces" of the incongruent distractors in target production when the distractor is in articulatory competition with the target, particularly in the early portion of the phoneme (condition A), but not when it involves the same place of articulation (condition B), or when it is presented visually (condition C). The results suggest a close relationship between speech perception and speech production. (Reprinted from Yuen, I., Davis, M. H., Brysbaert, M., Rastle, K. [2010]. Activation of articulatory information in speech perception. *Proceedings of the National Academy of Sciences USA, 107*, 592–597 [Figure 2], by permission of the National Academy of Sciences.)

## Auditory Theory(ies)

The role of articulatory gestures in perceiving speech and the special status of the speech-perception system progressively came under attack largely because of insufficient hard evidence and lack of computational parsimony. Recall that recourse to articulatory gestures was originally posited as a way to solve the lack-of-invariance problem and turn a many(acoustic traces)-to-one(phoneme) mapping problem into a one(gesture)-to-one(phoneme) mapping solution. However, the lack of invariance problem turned out to be less prevalent and, at the same time, more complicated than originally claimed. Indeed, as mentioned earlier, many phonemes were found to preserve distinctive features across contexts (e.g., Blumstein & Stevens, 1981; Stevens & Blumstein, 1981). At the same time, lack of invariance was found in domains for which a gestural explanation was only of limited use, for example, voice quality, loudness, and speech rate.

Perhaps most problematic for gesture-based accounts was the finding by Kluender, Diehl, and Killeen (1987) that phonemic categorization, which was viewed by such accounts as necessitating access to gestural primitives, could be observed in species lacking the anatomical prerequisites for articulatory knowledge and practice (Japanese quail; Fig. 26.6). This result was seen by many as undermining both the motor component of speech perception and its human-specific nature. Parsimony became the new driving force. As Kluender et al. put it, "A theory of human phonetic categorization may need to be no more (and no less) complex than that required to explain the behavior of these quail" (p. 1197). The gestural explanation for compensation for coarticulation effects (Mann, 1980) was challenged by a general auditory mechanism as well. In Mann's experiment, the perceptual shift on the /da/-/ga/ continumm induced by the preceding /al/ versus /ar/ context was explained by reference to articulatory gestures. However, Lotto and Kluender (1998) found a similar shift when the preceding context consisted of nonspeech sounds mimicking the spectral characteristics of the actual syllables (e.g., tone glides). Thus, the acoustic composition of the context, and in particular its spectral contrast with the following syllable, rather than an underlying reference to abstract articulatory gestures, was able to account for Mann's context effect (but see Fowler, Brown, & Mann's, 2000, subsequent multimodal challenge to the auditory account).

However, auditory theories have been criticized for lacking in theoretical content. Auditory accounts are indeed largely based on counterarguments (and counterevidence) to the motor and gestural theories, rather than resting on a clear set of falsifiable principles (Diehl et al., 2004). While it is clear that a great deal of phenomena previously believed to

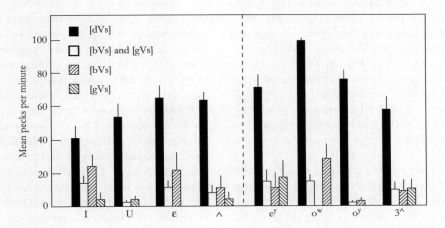

**Figure 26.6** Pecking rates at test for positive stimuli (/dVs/) and negative stimuli (all others) for one of the quail in Kluender et al.'s (1987) study in eight vowel contexts. The test session was preceded by a learning phase in which the quail learned to discriminate /dVs/ syllables (i.e., syllables starting with /d/ and ending with /s/, with a varying intervocalic vowel) from /bVs/ and /gVs/ syllables, with four different intervocalic vowels not used in the test phase. During learning, the quail was rewarded for pecking in response to /d/-initial syllables (positive trials) but not to /b/- and /g/-initial syllables (negative trials). The figure shows that, at test, the quail pecked substantially more to positive than negative syllables, even though these syllables contained entirely new vowels, that is, vowels leading to different formant transitions with the initial consonant than those experienced during the learning phase. (Reprinted from Kluender, K. R., Diehl, R. L., & Killeen, P. R. [1987]. Japanese Quail can form phonetic categories. *Science, 237*, 1195–1197 [Figure 1], by permission of the National Academy of Sciences.)

require a gestural account can be explained within an arguably simpler auditory framework, it remains to be seen whether auditory theories can provide a satisfactory explanation for the entire class of phenomena in which the many-to-one puzzle has been observed (e.g., Pardo & Remez, 2006).

### Top-Down Theories

This rubric and the following one (bottom-up theories) review theories of speech perception *broadly construed*. They are broadly construed in that they consider phonemic categorization, the scope of the *narrowly construed* theories, in the context of its interface with lexical knowledge. Although the traditional separation between narrowly and broadly construed theories originates from the respective historical goals of speech perception and spoken-word recognition research (Pisoni & Luce, 1987), an understanding of speech perception cannot be complete without an analysis of the impact of long-term knowledge on early sensory processes (see useful reviews in Goldinger, Pisoni, & Luce, 1996; Jusczyk & Luce, 2002).

The hallmark of top-down approaches to speech perception is that phonetic analysis and categorization can be influenced by knowledge stored in long-term memory, lexical knowledge in particular. As mentioned earlier, phoneme restoration studies (e.g., Warren & Obusek, 1971; Warren & Warren, 1970) showed that word knowledge could affect listeners' interpretation of what they heard, but they did not provide direct evidence that phonetic categorization per se (i.e., *perception*, as it was referred to in that literature) was modified by lexical expectations. However, Samuel (1981) demonstrated that auditory acuity was indeed altered when lexical information was available (e.g., "pr*gress" [from "progress"], with * indicating the portion on which auditory acuity was measured) compared to when it was not (e.g., "cr*gress" [from the nonword "crogress"]).

This kind of result (see also, e.g., Ganong, 1980; Marslen-Wilson & Tyler, 1980; and, more recently, Gow, Segawa, Ahlfors, & Lin, 2008) led to conceptualizing the speech system as being deeply interactive, with information flowing not only from bottom to top but also from top down. For example, the TRACE model (more specifically, TRACE II; McClelland & Elman, 1986) is an interactive-activation model made of a large number of units organized into three levels: features, phonemes, and words (Fig. 26.7A). The model includes bottom-up excitatory connections (from features to phonemes

and from phonemes to words), inhibitory lateral connections (within each level), and, critically, top-down excitatory connections (from words to phonemes and from phonemes to features). Thus, the activation levels of features, for example, voicing, nasality, and burst, are partly determined by the activation levels of phonemes, and these are partly determined by the activation levels of words. In essence, this architecture places speech perception within a system that allows a given sensory input to yield a different *perceptual experience* (as opposed to interpretive experience) when it occurs in a word versus a nonword or next to phoneme x versus phoneme y, and so on. TRACE has been shown to simulate a large range of perceptual and psycholinguistic phenomena, for example, categorical perception, cue trading relations, phonetic context effects, compensation for coarticulation, lexical effects on phoneme detection/categorization, segmentation of embedded words, and so on. All this takes place within an architecture that is neither domain nor species specific. Later instantiations of TRACE have been proposed by McClelland (1991) and Movellan and McClelland (2001), but all of them preserve the core interactive architecture described in the original model.

Like TRACE, Grossberg's Adaptive Resonance Theory (ART; e.g., Grossberg, 1986; Grossberg & Myers, 1999) suggests that perception emerges from a compromise, or stable state, between sensory information and stored lexical knowledge (Fig. 26.7B). ART includes *items* (akin to subphonemic features or feature clusters) and *list chunks* (combinations of items whose composition is the result of prior learning; e.g., phonemes, syllables, or words). In ART, a sensory input activates items that, in turn, activate list chunks. List chunks feed back to component items, and items back to list chunks again in a bottom-up/top-down cyclic manner that extends over time, ultimately creating stable resonance between a set of items and a list chunk. Both TRACE and ART posit that connections between levels are only excitatory and connections within levels are only inhibitory. In ART, in typical circumstances, attention is directed to large chunks (e.g., words), and hence the content of smaller chunks is generally less readily available. Small mismatches between large chunks and small chunks do not prevent resonance, but large mismatches do. In other words, unlike TRACE, ART does not allow the speech system to "hallucinate" information that is not already there (however, for circumstances in which it could, see Grossberg,

2000a). Large mismatches lead to the establishment of new chunks, and these gain resonance via subsequent exposure. In doing so, ART provides a solution to the stability-plasticity dilemma, that is, the unwanted erasure of prior learning by more recent learning (Grossberg, 1987), also referred to as *catastrophic interference* (e.g., McCloskey & Cohen, 1989).

Thus, like TRACE, ART posits that speech perception results from an online interaction between prelexical and lexical processes. However, ART is more deeply grounded in, and motivated by biologically plausible neural dynamics, where reciprocal connectivity and resonance states have been observed (e.g., Felleman & Van Essen, 1991). Likewise, ART replaces the hierarchical structure of TRACE with a more flexible one, in which tiers self-organize over time through competitive dynamics—as opposed to being predefined. Although sometimes accused of placing too few constraints on empirical expectations (Norris et al., 2000), the functional architecture of ART is thought to be more computationally economical than that of TRACE and more amenable to modeling both real-time and long-term temporal aspects of speech processing (Grossberg, Boardman, & Cohen, 1997).

### Bottom-Up Theories

Bottom-up theories describe effects of lexical and sentential knowledge on phoneme categorization as a consequence of postperceptual biases. In this conceptualization, reporting "progress" when presented with "pr*gress" simply reflects a strategic decision to do so and the functionality of a system that is geared toward meaningful communication—we generally hear words rather than nonwords. Here, phonetic analysis itself is incorruptible by lexical or sentential knowledge. It takes place within an autonomous module that receives no feedback from lexical and postlexical layers. In Cutler and Norris's (1979) Race model, phoneme identification is the result of a time race between a sublexical route and a lexical route activated in parallel in an entirely bottom-up fashion (Fig. 26.7C). In normal circumstances, the lexical route is faster, which means that a sensory input that has a match in the lexicon (e.g., "progress") is usually read out from that route. A nonlexical sensory input (e.g., "crogress") is read out from the prelexical route. In this model, "pr*gress" is reported as containing the phoneme /o/ because the lexical route receives enough evidence to activate the word "progress" and, being faster, this route determines the response. In contrast, "cr*gress" does

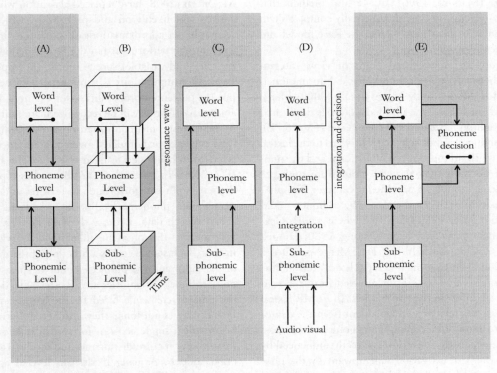

**Figure 26.7** Simplified architecture of (*A*) TRACE, (*B*) ART, (*C*) Race, (*D*) FLMP, and (*E*) Merge. Layers are labeled consistently across models for comparability. Excitatory connections are denoted by arrows. Inhibitory connections are denoted by closed black circles.

not lead to an acceptable match in the lexicon, and hence, readout is performed from the sublexical route, with the degraded phoneme being faithfully reported as degraded.

Massaro's Fuzzy Logical Model of Perception (FLMP; Massaro, 1987, 1996; Oden & Massaro, 1978) also exhibits a bottom-up architecture, in which various sources of sensory input—for example, auditory, visual—contribute to speech perception without any feedback from the lexical level (Fig. 26.7D). In FLMP, acoustic-phonetic features are activated multimodally and each feature accumulates a certain level of activation (on a continuous 0-to-1 scale), reflecting the degree of certainty that the feature has appeared in the signal. The profile of features' activation levels is then compared against a prototypical profile of activation for phonemes stored in memory. Phoneme identification occurs when the match between the actual and prototypical profiles reaches a level determined by goodness-of-fit algorithms. Critically, the match does not need to be perfect to lead to identification; thus, there is no need for lexical top-down feedback. Prelexical and lexical sources of information are then integrated into a conscious percept. Although the extent to which the integration stage can be considered a true instantiation of bottom-up processes is a matter for debate (Massaro, 1996), FLMP also predicts that auditory acuity of * is fundamentally comparable in "pr*gress" and "cr*gress"—like the Race model and unlike top-down theories.

From an architectural point of view, integration between sublexical and lexical information is handled differently by Norris et al.'s (2000) Merge model. In Merge, the phoneme layer is duplicated into an input layer and a decision layer (Fig. 26.7E). The phoneme input layer feeds forward to the lexical layer (with no top-down connections) and the phoneme decision layer receives input from both the phoneme input layer and the lexical layer. The phoneme decision layer is the place where phonemic and lexical inputs are integrated and where standard lexical phenomena arise (e.g., Ganong, 1980; Samuel, 1981). While both FLMP and Merge produce a decision by integrating unaltered lexical and sublexical information, the input received from the lexical level differs in the two models. In FLMP, lexical activation is relatively independent from the degree of activation of its component phonemes, whereas, in Merge, lexical activation is directly influenced by the pattern of activation sent upward by the phoneme input layer. While Merge has been criticized for exhibiting a contorted architecture (Gow, 2000;

Samuel, 2000), being ecologically improbable (e.g., Grossberg, 2000b; Montant, 2000; Stevens, 2000), and being simply a late instantiation of FLMP (Massaro, 2000; Oden, 2000), it has gathered the attention of both speech-perception and spoken-word-recognition scientists around a question that is as yet unanswered.

### Bayesian Theories

Despite important differences in functional architecture between top-down and bottom-up models, both classes of models agree that speech perception involves distinct levels of representations (e.g., features, phonemes, words), multiple lexical activation, lexical competition, integration (of some sort) between actual sensory input and lexical expectations, and corrective mechanisms (of some sort) to handle incompleteness or uncertainty in the input. A radically different class of models based on optimal Bayesian inference has recently emerged as an alternative to the ones mentioned earlier—recently in psycholinguistics at least. These models eschew the concept of lexical activation altogether, sometimes doing away with the bottom-up/top-down debate itself—or at a minimum blurring the boundaries between the two mechanisms. For instance, in their Shortlist B model, Norris and McQueen (2008) have replaced activation with the concepts of likelihood and probability, which are seen as better approximations of actual (i.e., imperfect) human performance in the face of actual (i.e., complex and variable) speech input. The appeal of Bayesian computations is substantial because output (or posterior) probabilities, for example, probability that a word will be recognized, are estimated by tabulating both confirmatory and disconfirmatory evidence accumulated over past instances, as opposed to being tied to fixed activation thresholds (Fig. 26.8). In particular, Shortlist B has replaced discrete input categories such as features and phonemes with phoneme likelihoods calculated from actual speech data. Because they are derived from real speech, the phoneme likelihoods vary from instance to instance and as a function of the quality of the input and the phonetic context. Thus, while noisier, these probabilities are a better reflection of the type of challenge faced by the speech system in everyday conditions. They also allow the model to provide a single account for speech phenomena that usually require distinct ad-hoc mechanisms in other models. A general criticism leveled against Bayesian models, however, concerns the legitimacy of their *priors*, that is, the set of assumptions used

$$P(word_i \mid evidence) = \frac{P(evidence \mid word_i) \times P(word_i)}{\sum\limits_{j=1}^{j=n} P(evidence \mid word_j) \times P(word_j)}$$

**Figure 26.8** Main Bayesian equation in Shortlist B (Norris & McQueen, 2008). *P(word_i|evidence)* is the conditional probability of a specific word (*word_i*) having been heard given the available (intact or degraded) input (*evidence*). *P(word_i)* represents the listener's prior belief, before any perceptual evidence has been accumulated, that *word_i* will be present in the input. *P(word_i)* can be approximated from lexical frequencies and contextual variables. The critical term of the equation is *P(evidence|word_i)*, which is the likelihood of the evidence given *word_i*, that is, the product of the probabilities of the sublexical units (e.g., phonemes) making up *word_i*. This term is important because it acknowledges and takes into account the variability of the input (noise, ambiguity, idiosyncratic realization, etc.) in the input-to-representation mapping process. The probability of *word_i* so calculated is then compared to that of all other words in the lexicon (*n*). Thus, Bayesian inference provides an index of word recognition that considers both lexical and sublexical factors as well as the complexity of a real and variable input.

to determine initial probabilities before any evidence has been gathered (e.g., how expected is a word or a phoneme a priori). Because priors can be difficult to establish, their arbitrariness or the modeler's own biases can have substantial effects on the model's outcome. Likewise, compared to the models reviewed earlier, models based on Bayesian inference often lead to less straightforward hypotheses, which makes their testability somewhat limited—even though their performance level in terms of replicating known patterns of data is usually high.

## Tailoring Speech Perception: Learning and Relearning
### Learning

The literature reviewed so far suggests that perceiving speech involves a set of highly sophisticated processing skills and structures. To what extent are these skills and structures in place at birth? Of particular interest in the context of early theories of speech perception is the way in which speech perception and speech production develop relative to each other and the degree to which perceptual capacities responsible for subtle phonetic discrimination (e.g., voicing distinction) are present in prelinguistic infants. Eimas, Siqueland, Jusczyk, and Vigorito (1971) showed that 1-month-old infants perceive a voicing-based /ba/-/pa/ continuum categorically, just as adults do. Similarly, like adults (Mattingly, Liberman, Syrdal, & Halwes, 1971), young infants show a dissociation between categorical perception with speech and continuous perception with matched nonspeech (Eimas, 1974). Infants also seem to start off with

an open-ended perceptual system, allowing them to discriminate a wide range of subtle phonetic contrasts—far more contrasts than they will be able to discriminate in adulthood (e.g., Aslin, Werker, & Morgan, 2002; Trehub, 1976). There is therefore strong evidence that fine speech-perception skills are in place early in life—at least well before the onset of speech production—and operational with minimal, if any, exposure to ambient speech. These findings have led to the idea that speech-specific mechanisms are part of the human biological endowment and have been taken as evidence for the innateness of language, or at least some of its perceptual aspects (Eimas et al., 1971). In that sense, an infant has very little to *learn* about speech perception. If anything, attuning to one's native language is rather a matter of losing sensitivity to (or *unlearning*) phonetic contrasts that have little communicative value for that particular language, for example, the /r/-/l/ distinction for Japanese listeners.

However, the idea that infants are born with a universal discrimination device operating according to a use-it-or-lose-it principle has not been unchallenged. For instance, on closer examination, discrimination capacities at the end of the first year appear far less acute and far less universal than expected (e.g., Lacerda & Sundberg, 2001). Likewise, discrimination of irrelevant contrasts does not wane as systematically and as fully as the theory would have it (e.g., Polka, Colantonio, & Sundara, 2001). For example, Bowers, Mattys, and Gage (2009) showed that language-specific phonemes learned in early childhood but never heard or produced subsequently, as would be the case for young children of temporarily expatriate parents, can be relearned relatively easily even decades later (Fig. 26.9A). Thus, discriminatory attrition is not as widespread and severe as previously believed, suggesting that the representations of phonemes from "forgotten" languages, that is, those we stop practicing early in life, may be more deeply engraved in our long-term memory than we think.

By and large, however, the literature on early speech perception indicates that infants possess fine language-oriented auditory skills from birth as well as impressive capacities to learn from the ambient auditory scene during the first year of life (Fig. 26.10). Auditory deprivation during that period (e.g., otitis media; delay prior to cochlear implantation) can have severe consequences on speech perception and later language development (e.g., Clarkson, Eimas, & Marean, 1989; Mody, Schwartz, Gravel, & Ruben, 1999), possibly due to a general decrease of attention to sounds (e.g., Houston, Pisoni, Kirk, Ying, & Miyamoto, 2003). However, even in such circumstances, partial sensory information is often available through the visual channel (facial and lip information), which might explain the relative resilience of basic speech perception skills to auditory deprivation. Indeed, Kuhl and Meltzoff (1982) showed that, as early as 4 months of age, infants show a preference for matched audiovisual inputs (e.g., audio /a/ with visual /a/) over mismatched inputs (e.g., audio /a/ with visual /i/). Even more striking, infants around that age seem to integrate discrepant audiovisual information following the typical McGurk pattern observed in adults (Rosenblum, Schmuckler, & Johnson, 1997). These results suggest that the multimodal (or amodal) nature of speech perception, a central tenet of Massaro's Fuzzy Logical Model of Perception (FLMP; cf. Massaro, 1987), is present early in life and operates without much prior experience with sound-gesture association. Although the *strength* of the McGurk effect is lower in infants than adults (e.g., Massaro, Thompson, Barron, & Laren, 1986; McGurk & MacDonald, 1976), early cross-modal integration is often taken as evidence for gestural theories of speech perception and as a challenge to auditory theories.

## Relearning

A question of growing interest concerns the flexibility of the speech-perception system when it is faced with an unstable or changing input. Can the perceptual categories learned during early infancy be undone or retuned to reflect a new environment? The issue of perceptual (re)learning is central to research on second-language (L2) perception and speech perception in degraded conditions. Evidence for a speech-perception-sensitive period during the first year of life (Trehub, 1976) suggests that attuning to new perceptual categories later on should be difficult and perhaps not as complete as it is for categories learned earlier. Late learning of L2 phonetic contrasts (e.g., /r/-/l/ distinction for Japanese L1 speakers) has indeed been shown to be slow, effortful, and imperfect (e.g., Logan, Lively, & Pisoni, 1991). However, even in those conditions, learning appears to transfer to tokens produced by new talkers (Logan et al., 1991) and, to some degree, to production (Bradlow, Pisoni, Akahane-Yamada, & Tohkura, 1997). Successful learning of L2 contrasts is not systematically observed, however. For example, Bowers et al. (2009) found no evidence that English L1 speakers could learn to discriminate Zulu contrasts (e.g., /b/-/ʘ/) or Hindi contrasts (e.g., /t/ vs. /ʈ/) even after 30 days of daily training (Fig. 26.9 B). Thus, although possible, perceptual learning of L2 contrasts is greatly constrained by the age of L2 exposure, the nature and duration of training, and the phonetic overlap between the L1 and L2 phonetic inventories (e.g., Best, 1994; Kuhl, 2000).

Perceptual learning of accented L1 and noncanonical speech follows the same general patterns as

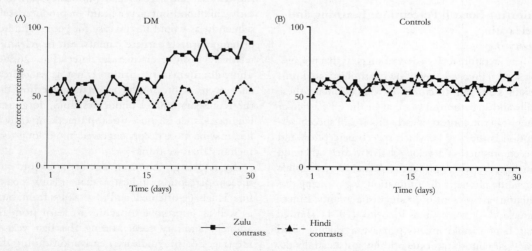

**Figure 26.9** (*A*) AX discrimination scores over 30 consecutive days (50% chance level; feedback provided) for Zulu contrasts (e.g., /b/-/ʘ/) and Hindi contrasts (e.g., /t/ vs. /ʈ/) by DM, a 20-year-old, male, native English speaker who was exposed to Zulu from 4 to 8 years of age but never heard Zulu subsequently. Note DM's improvement with the Zulu contrasts over the 30 days, in sharp contrast with his inability to learn the Hindi contrasts. (*B*) Performance on the same task by native English speakers with no prior exposure to Zulu or Hindi. (Adapted with permission from Bowers, J. S., Mattys, S. L., & Gage, S. H., [2009]. Preserved implicit knowledge of a forgotten childhood language. *Psychological Science, 20,* 1064–1069 [partial Figure 1].)

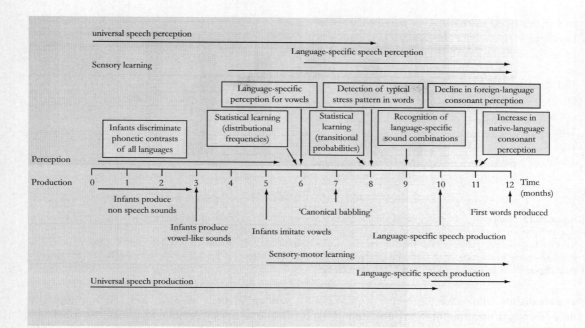

**Figure 26.10** Summary of key developmental landmarks for speech perception and speech production in the first year of life. (Reprinted from Kuhl, P. K. [2004]. Early language acquisition: Cracking the speech code. *Nature Reviews Neuroscience*, 5, 831–843 [Figure 1], by permission of the Nature Publishing Group.)

L2 learning, but it usually leads to faster and more complete retuning (e.g., Bradlow & Bent, 2008; Clarke & Garrett, 2004). A reason for this difference is that, while L2 contrast learning involves the formation of new perceptual categories, whose boundaries are sometimes in direct conflict with L1 categories, accented L1 learning "simply" involves retuning existing perceptual categories, often by broadening their mapping range. This latter feature makes perceptual learning of accented speech a special instance of the more general debate on the episodic versus abstract nature of phonemic and lexical representations. At issue, here, is whether phonemic and lexical representations consist of a collection of episodic instances in which surface details are preserved (voice, accent, speech rate) or, alternatively, single, abstract representations (i.e., one for each phoneme and one for each word). That at least some surface details of words are preserved in long-term memory is undeniable (e.g., Goldinger, 1998). The current debate focuses on (1) whether lexical representations include both indexical (e.g., voice quality) and allophonic (e.g., phonological variants) details (Luce, McLennan, & Charles-Luce, 2003); (2) whether such details are of a lexical nature (i.e., stored within the lexicon), rather than sublexical (i.e., stored at the subphonemic, phonemic, or syllabic level; McQueen, Cutler, & Norris, 2006);

(3) the online time course of episodic trace activation (e.g., Luce et al., 2003; McLennan, Luce, & Charles-Luce, 2005); (4) the mechanisms responsible for consolidating newly learned instances or new perceptual categories (e.g., Fenn, Nusbaum, & Margoliash, 2003); and (5) the possible generalization to other types of noncanonical speech, such as disordered speech (e.g., Lee, Whitehall, & Coccia, 2009; Mattys & Liss, 2008).

According to Samuel and Kraljic (2009), the aforementioned literature should be distinguished from a more recent strand of research that focuses on the specific variables affecting perceptual learning and the mechanisms linking such variables to perception. In particular, Norris, McQueen, and Cutler (2003) found that lexical information is a powerful source of perceptual recalibration. For example, Dutch listeners repeatedly exposed to a word containing a sound halfway between two existing phonemes (e.g., *witlo*\*, where \* is ambiguous between /f/ and /s/, with *witlof* a Dutch word—chicorey—and *witlos* a nonword) subsequently perceived a /f/-/s/ continuum as biased in the direction of the lexically induced percept (more /f/ than /s/ in the *witlo*\* case). Likewise, Bertelson, Vroomen, and de Gelder (2003) found that repeated exposure to McGurk audiovisual stimuli (e.g., audio /a\*a/ and visual /aba/ leading to the auditory perception of /

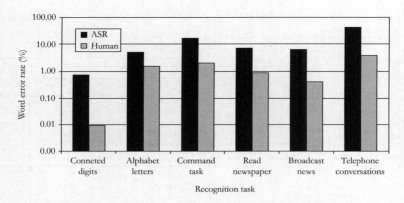

**Figure 26.11** Comparison of speech recognition error rate by machines (ASR) and humans. The logarithmic scale on the Y axis shows that ASR performance is approximately one order of magnitude behind human performance across various speech materials (ASR error rate for telephone conversation: 43%). The data were collated by Lippmann (1997). (Reprinted from Moore, R. K. [2007]. Spoken language processing by machine. In G. Gaskell [Ed.], *Oxford handbook of psycholinguistics* (pp. 723–738). Oxford, UK: Oxford University Press [Figure 44.6], by permission of Oxford University Press.)

aba/) biased the subsequent perception of an audio-only /aba/-/ada/ continuum in the direction of the visually induced percept. Although visually induced perceptual learning seems to be less long-lasting than its lexically induced counterpart (Vroomen, van Linden, Keetels, de Gelder, & Bertelson, 2004), the Norris et al. and Bertelson et al. studies demonstrate that even the mature perceptual system can show a certain degree of flexibility when it is faced with a changing auditory environment.

## Speech Recognition by Machines

This chapter was mainly concerned with human speech recognition (HSR), but technological advances in the past decades have allowed the topic of speech perception and recognition to become an economically profitable challenge for engineers and applied computer scientists. A complete review of Automatic Speech Recognition's (ASR) historical background, issues, and state of the art is beyond the scope of this chapter. However, a brief analysis of ASR in the context of the key topics in HSR reviewed earlier reveals interesting commonalities as well as divergences among the preoccupations and goals of the two fields.

Perhaps the most notable difference between HSR and ASR is their ultimate aim. Whereas HSR aims to provide a description of how the speech system works (processes, representations, functional architecture, biological plausibility), ASR aims to deliver speech transcriptions as error-free as possible, regardless of the biological and cognitive validity of the underlying algorithms. The success of ASR is typically measured by the percentage of words correctly identified from speech samples

varying in their acoustic and lexical complexity. While increasing computer capacity and speed have allowed ASR performance to improve substantially since the early systems of the 1970s (e.g., Jelinek, 1976; Klatt, 1977), ASR accuracy is still about an order of magnitude behind its HSR counterpart (Moore, 2007; see Fig. 26.11).

What is the cause of the enduring performance gap between ASR and HSR? Given that the basic constraints imposed by the signal (sequentiality, continuity, variability) are the same for humans and machines, it is tempting to conclude that the gap between ASR and HSR will not be bridged until the algorithms of the former resemble those of the latter. And currently, they do not. The architecture of most ASR systems is almost entirely data driven: Its structure is expressed in terms of a network of sequence probabilities calculated over large corpora of natural speech (and their supervised transcription). The ultimate goal of the corpora, or training data, is to provide a database of acoustic-phonetic information sufficiently large that an appropriate match can be found for any input sound sequence. The larger the corpora, the tighter the fit between the input and the acoustic model (e.g., triphones instantiated in hidden Markov models, HMM, cf. Rabiner & Juang, 1993), and the lower the ASR system's error rate (Lamel, Gauvain, & Adda, 2000). By that logic, hours of training corpora, not human-machine avatars, are the solution for increased accuracy, giving support to the controversial assertion that human models have so far hindered rather than promoted ASR progress (Jelinek, 1985). However, Moore and Cutler (2001) estimated that increasing corpus sizes from their current average capacity (1,000 hours or less, which is the equivalent of the average hearing time of a 2-year-old) to 10,000 hours (average hearing time of a 10-year-old) would only drop the ASR error rate to 12%.

Thus, a data-driven approach to speech recognition is constrained by more than just the size of the training data set. For example, the lexical and syntactic content of the training data often determines the application for which the ASR system is likely to perform best. Domain-specific systems (e.g., banking transactions by phone) generally reach high recognition accuracy levels even when they are fed continuous speech produced by various speakers, whereas domain-general systems (e.g., speech-recognition packages on personal computers) often have to compromise on the number of speakers they can recognize and/or training time in order to be effective (Everman et al., 2005). Therefore, one of the current stumbling blocks of ASR systems is language modeling (as opposed to acoustic modeling), that is, the extent to which the systems include higher order knowledge—syntax, semantics, pragmatics—from which inferences can be made to refine the mapping between the signal and the acoustic model. Existing ASR language models are fairly simple, drawing upon the distributional methods of acoustic models in that they simply provide the probability of all possible word sequences based on their occurrences in the training corpora. In that sense, an ASR system can predict that "necklace" is a possible completion of "The burglar stole the..." because of its relatively high transitional probability in the corpora, not because of the semantic knowledge that burglars tend to steal valuable items, and not because of the syntactic knowledge that a noun phrase typically follows a transitional verb. Likewise, ASR systems rarely include the kind of lexical feedback hypothesized in HSR models like TRACE (McClelland & Elman, 1986) and ART (Grossberg, 1986). Like Merge (Norris et al., 2000), ASR systems only allow lexical information and the language model to influence the relative weights of activated candidates, but not the fit between the signal and the acoustic model (Scharenborg Norris, ten Bosch, & McQueen, 2005).

While the remaining performance gap between ASR and HSR is widely recognized in the ASR literature, there seems to be no clear consensus on the direction to take in order to reduce it (Moore, 2007). Given today's ever-expanding computer power, increasing the size of training corpora is probably the easiest way of gaining a few percentage points in accuracy, at least in the short term. More radical solutions are also being envisaged, however. For example, attempts are being made to build more linguistically plausible acoustic models by using phonemes (as opposed to di/triphone HMMs) as basic segmentation units (Ostendorf, Digilakis, & Kimball, 1996; Russell, 1993) or by preserving and exploiting fine acoustic detail in the signal instead of treating it as noise (Carlson & Hawkins, 2007; Moore & Maier, 2007).

## Conclusion

The scientific study of speech perception started in the early 1950s under the impetus of research carried out at the Haskins Laboratories, following the development of the *Pattern Playback* device. This machine allowed Franklin S. Cooper and his colleagues to visualize speech in the form of a decomposable spectrogram and, reciprocally, to create artificial speech by *sounding out* the spectrogram. Contemporary speech perception research is both a continuation of its earlier preoccupations with the building blocks of speech perception and a departure from them. On the one hand, the quest for universal units of speech perception and attempts to crack the many-to-one mapping code are still going strong. Still alive, too, is the debate about the involvement of gestural knowledge in speech perception, reignited recently by neuroimaging techniques and the discovery of mirror neurons. On the decline are the ideas that speech is special with respect to audition and that infants are born with speech- and species-specific perceptual capacities. On the other hand, questions have necessarily spread beyond the sublexical level, following the assumption that decoding the sensory input must be investigated in the context of the entirety of the language system—or, at the very least, some of its phonologically related components. Indeed, lexical feedback, online or learning related, has been shown to modulate the perceptual experience of an otherwise unchanged input. Likewise, what used to be treated as speech surface details (e.g., indexical variations), and commonly filtered out for the sake of modeling simplicity, are now more fully acknowledged as being preserved during encoding, embedded in long-term representations, and used during retrieval. Speech-perception research in the coming decades is likely to expand its interest not only to the rest of the language system but also to domain-general cognitive functions such as attention and memory as well as practical applications (e.g., ASR) in the field of artificial intelligence. At the same time, researchers have become increasingly concerned with the external validity of their models. Attempts to enhance the ecological contribution of speech research are manifest in a sharp increase in studies using *natural* speech (conversational, accented, disordered) as the front end of their models.

# References

Aslin, R. N., Werker, J. F., & Morgan, J. L. (2002). Innate phonetic boundaries revisited. *Journal of the Acoustical Society of America, 112*, 1257–1260.

Bard, E. G., Shillcock, R. C., & Altmann, G. T. M. (1988). The recognition of words after their acoustic offsets in spontaneous speech: Effects of subsequent context. *Perception and Psychophysics, 44*, 395–408.

Bertelson, P., Vroomen, J., & de Gelder, B. (2003). Visual recalibration of auditory speech identification: A McGurk aftereffect. *Psychological Science, 14*, 592–597.

Best, C. T. (1994). The emergence of native-language phonological influences in infants: A perceptual assimilation model. In H. Nusbaum & J. Goodman (Eds.), *The transition from speech sounds to spoken words: The development of speech perception* (pp. 167–224). Cambridge, MA: MIT Press.

Blumstein, S. E., & Stevens, K. N. (1981). Phonetic features and acoustic invariance in speech. *Cognition, 10*, 25–32

Bowers, J. S., Mattys, S. L., & Gage, S. H. (2009). Preserved implicit knowledge of a forgotten childhood language. *Psychological Science, 20*, 1064–1069.

Bradlow, A. R., & Bent, T. (2008). Perceptual adaptation to non-native speech. *Cognition, 106*, 707–729.

Bradlow, A. R., Pisoni, D. B., Yamada, R. A., & Tohkura, Y. (1997). Training Japanese listeners to identify English /r/ and /l/: IV. Some effects of perceptual learning on speech production. *Journal of the Acoustical Society of America, 101*, 2299–2310.

Carlson, R., & Hawkins, S. (2007). When is fine phonetic detail a detail? In *Proceedings of the 16th ICPhS Meeting* (pp. 211–214). Saarbrücken, Germany.

Clarke, C. M., & Garrett, M. F. (2004). Rapid adaptation to foreign-accented English. *Journal of the Acoustical Society of America, 116*, 3647–3658.

Clarkson, R. L., Eimas, P. D., & Marean, G. C. (1989). Speech perception in children with histories of recurrent otitis media. *Journal of the Acoustical Society of America, 85*, 926–933.

Connine, C. M., & Clifton, C. (1987) Interactive use of lexical information in speech perception. *Journal of Experimental Psychology: Human Perception and Performance, 13*, 291–299.

Cutler, A. (1994). Segmentation problems, rhythmic solutions. *Lingua, 92*, 81–104

Cutler, A., & Norris, D. (1979). Monitoring sentence comprehension. In W. E. Cooper & E. C. T. Walker (Eds.), *Sentence processing: Psycholinguistic studies presented to Merrill Garrett* (pp. 113–134). Hillsdale, NJ: Erlbaum.

Dahan, D. (2010). The time course of interpretation in speech comprehension. *Current Directions in Psychological Science, 19*, 121–126.

Delattre, P. C., Liberman, A. M., & Cooper, F. S. (1955). Acoustic loci and transitional cues for consonants. *Journal of the Acoustical Society of America, 27*, 769–773.

Diehl, R. L., Lotto, A. J., & Holt, L. L. (2004). Speech perception. *Annual Review of Psychology, 55*, 149–179.

Dupoux, E., & Mehler, J. (1990). Monitoring the lexicon with normal and compressed speech: Frequency effects and the prelexical code. *Journal of Memory and Language, 29*, 316–335.

Eimas, P. D. (1974). Auditory and linguistic processing of cues for place of articulation by infants. *Perception and Psychophysics, 16*, 513–521.

Eimas, P. D., Siqueland, E. R., Jusczyk, P., & Vigorito, J. (1971). Speech perception in infants. *Science, 171*, 303–306.

Everman, G., Chan, H. Y., Gales, M. J. F, Jia, B., Mrva, D., & Woodland, P. C. (2005). Training LVCSR systems on thousands of hours of data. In *Proceedings of the IEEE ICASSP* (pp. 209–212).

Felleman, D., & Van Essen, D. (1991). Distributed hierarchical processing in primate cerebral cortex. *Cerebral Cortex, 1*, 1–47.

Fenn, K. M., Nusbaum, H. C., & Margoliash, D. (2003). Consolidation during sleep of perceptual learning of spoken language. *Nature, 425*, 614–616.

Fougeron, C., & Keating, P. A. (1997). Articulatory strengthening at edges of prosodic domains. *Journal of the Acoustical Society of America, 101*, 3728–3740.

Foulke, E., & Sticht, T. G. (1969). Review of research on the intelligibility and comprehension of accelerated speech. *Psychological Bulletin, 72*, 50–62.

Fowler, C. A. (1986). An event approach to the study of speech perception from a direct-realist perspective. *Journal of Phonetics, 14*, 3–28.

Fowler, C. A. (1996). Listeners do hear sounds not tongues. *Journal of the Acoustical Society of America, 99*, 1730–1741.

Fowler, C. A. (2006). Compensation for coarticulation reflects gesture perception, not spectral contrast. *Perception and Psychophysics, 68*, 161–177.

Fowler, C. A. (2008). The FLMP STMPed. *Psychonomic Bulletin and Review, 15*, 458–462

Fowler, C. A., Brown, J. M., & Mann, V. A. (2000). Contrast effects do not underlie effects of preceding liquids on stop-consonant identification by humans. *Journal of Experimental Psychology: Human Perception and Performance, 26*, 877–888.

Galantucci, B., Fowler, C. A., & Turvey, M. T. (2006). The motor theory of speech perception reviewed. *Psychonomic Bulletin and Review, 13*, 361–377.

Ganong, W. F. (1980). Phonetic categorization in auditory word perception. *Journal of Experimental Psychology: Human Perception and Performance, 6*, 110–125.

Goldinger, S. D. (1998). Echoes of echoes? An episodic theory of lexical access. *Psychological Review, 105*, 251–279.

Goldinger, S. D., Pisoni, D. B., & Luce, P. A. (1996). Speech perception and spoken word recognition: Research and theory. In N. J. Lass (Ed.), *Principles of experimental phonetics* (pp. 277–327). St. Louis, MO: Mosby.

Gow, D. W. (2000). One phonemic representation should suffice. *Behavioral and Brain Science, 23*, 331.

Gow, D. W., & Segawa, J. A. (2009). Articulatory mediation of speech perception: A causal analysis of multi-modal imaging data. *Cognition, 110*, 222–236.

Gow, D. W., Segawa, J. A., Ahlfors, S. P., & Lin, F. H. (2008). Lexical influences on speech perception: A Granger causality analysis of MEG and EEG source estimates. *Neuroimage, 43*, 614–23.

Grossberg, S. (1986). The adaptive self-organization of serial order in behavior: Speech, language, and motor control. In

E. C. Schwab & H. C. Nusbaum (Eds.), *Pattern recognition by humans and machines, Vol 1. Speech perception* (pp. 187–294). New York: Academic Press.

Grossberg, S. (1987). Competitive learning: From interactive activations to adaptive resonance. *Cognitive Science, 11*, 23–63

Grossberg, S. (2000a). How hallucinations may arise from brain mechanisms of learning, attention, and volition. *Journal of the International Neuropsychological Society, 6*, 579–588.

Grossberg, S. (2000b). Brain feedback and adaptive resonance in speech perception. *Behavioral and Brain Science, 23*, 332–333.

Grossberg, S., Boardman, I., & Cohen, M. A. (1997). Neural dynamics of variable-rate speech categorization. *Journal of Experimental Psychology: Human Perception and Performance, 23*, 481–503.

Grossberg, S., &Myers, C. (1999). The resonant dynamics of conscious speech: Interword integration and duration-dependent backward effects. *Psychological Review, 107*, 735–767.

Houston, D. M., Pisoni, D. B., Kirk, K. I., Ying, E. A., & Miyamoto, R. T. (2003). Speech perception skills of infants following cochlear implantation: A first report. *International Journal of Pediatric Otorhinolaryngology, 67*, 479–495.

Huggins, A.W. F. (1975). Temporally segmented speech and "echoic" storage. In A. Cohen & S. G. Nooteboom (Eds.), *Structure and process in speech perception* (pp. 209–225). New York: Springer-Verlag.

Jelinek, F. (1976). Continuous speech recognition by statistical methods. *Proceedings of the IEEE, 64*, 532–556.

Jelinek, F. (1985). *Every time I fire a linguist, the performance of my system goes up.* Public statement at the IEEE ASSPS Workshop on Frontiers of Speech Recognition, Tampa, Florida.

Jusczyk, P. W., & Luce, P. A. (2002). Speech perception and spoken word recognition: Past and present. *Ear and Hearing, 23*, 2–40.

Klatt, D. H. (1977). Review of the ARPA speech understanding project. *Journal of the Acoustical Society of America, 62*, 1345–1366.

Kluender, K. R., Diehl, R. L., & Killeen, P. R. (1987). Japanese quail can form phonetic categories. *Science, 237*, 1195–1197.

Kuhl, P. K. (1981). Discrimination of speech by non-human animals: Basic auditory sensitivities conductive to the perception of speech-sound categories. *Journal of the Acoustical Society of America, 95*, 340–349.

Kuhl, P. K. (2000). A new view of language acquisition. *Proceedings of the National Academy of Sciences USA, 97*, 11850–11857.

Kuhl, P. K. (2004). Early language acquisition: Cracking the speech code. *Nature Reviews Neuroscience, 5*, 831–843.

Kuhl, P. K., &Meltzoff, A. N. (1982). The bimodal development of speech in infancy. *Science, 218*, 1138–1141.

Lacerda, F., &Sundberg, U. (2001). Auditory and articulatory biases influence the initial stages of the language acquisition process. In F. Lacerda , C. von Hofsten, & M. Heimann (Eds.), *Emerging cognitive abilities in early infancy* (pp. 91–110). Mahwah, NJ: Erlbaum.

Lachs, L., Pisoni, D. B., & Kirk, K. I. (2001). Use of audio-visual information in speech perception by pre-lingually deaf children with cochlear implants: A first report. *Ear and Hearing, 22*, 236–251.

Lamel, L., Gauvain, J-L., & Adda, G. (2000). Lightly supervised acoustic model training. In *Proceeding of the ISCA Workshop on Automatic Speech Recognition* (pp. 150–154).

Lee, A., Whitehall, T. L., & Coccia, V. (2009). Effect of listener training on perceptual judgement of hypernasality. *Clinical Linguistics and Phonetics, 23*, 319–334.

Liberman, A. M. (1996). *Speech: A special code.* Cambridge, MA: MIT Press.

Liberman, A. M., Delattre, P. C., & Cooper, F. S. (1958). Some cues for the distinction between voiced and voiceless stops in initial position. *Language and Speech, 1*, 153–167.

Liberman, A. M., Harris, K. S., Eimas, P., Lisker, L., & Bastian, J. (1961). An effect of learning on speech perception: The discrimination of durations of silence with and without phonemic significance. *Language and Speech, 4*, 175–195.

Liberman, A. M., Harris, K. S., Hoffman, H. S., & Griffith, B. C. (1957). The discrimination of speech sounds within and across phoneme boundaries. *Journal of Experimental Psychology, 54*, 358–368.

Liberman, A. M., & Mattingly, I. G. (1985). The motor theory of speech perception revised. *Cognition, 21*, 1–36.

Lindblom, B. (1963). Spectrographic study of vowel reduction. *Journal of the Acoustical Society of America, 35*, 1773–1781.

Lippmann, R. (1997). Speech recognition by machines and humans. *Speech Communication, 22*, 1–16.

Lisker, L., & Abramson, A. S. (1970). The voicing dimensions: Some experiments in comparative phonetics. In *Proceedings of the Sixth International Congress of Phonetic Sciences* (pp. 563–567). Prague, Czechoslovakia: Academia.

Logan, J. S., Lively, S. E., & Pisoni, D. B. (1991). Training Japanese listeners to identify English /r/ and /l/: A first report. *Journal of the Acoustical Society of America, 89*, 874–886.

Lotto, A. J., Hickok, G. S., & Holt, L. L. (2009). Reflections on mirror neurons and speech perception. *Trends in Cognitive Science, 13*, 110–114.

Lotto, A. J., & Holt, L. L. (2006). Putting phonetic context effects into context: A commentary on Fowler (2006). *Perception and Psychophysics, 68*, 178–183.

Lotto, A. J., & Kluender, K. R. (1998). General contrast effects in speech perception: Effect of preceding liquid on stop consonant identification. *Perception and Psychophysics, 60*, 602–619.

Luce, P. A., Mc Lennan, C. T., & Charles-Luce, J. (2003). Abstractness and specificity in spoken word recognition: Indexical and allophonic variability in long-term repetition priming. In J. Bowers & C. Marsolek (Eds.), *Rethinking implicit memory* (pp. 197–214). New York: Oxford University Press.

Magnuson, J. S., McMurray, B., Tanenhaus, M. K., & Aslin, R. N. (2003). Lexical effects on compensation for coarticulation: The ghost of Christmas past. *Cognitive Science, 27*, 285–298.

Mann, V. A. (1980). Influence of preceding liquid on stop-consonant perception. *Perception and Psychophysics, 28*, 407–412.

Marslen-Wilson, W. D. (1987). Functional parallelism in spoken word recognition. *Cognition, 25*, 71–102.

Marslen-Wilson, W. D., &Tyler, L. K. (1980). The temporal structure of spoken language understanding. *Cognition, 8*, 1–71.

Massaro, D. W. (1987). *Speech perception by ear and eye: A paradigm for psychological inquiry.* Hillsdale, NJ: Erlbaum.

Massaro, D. W. (1989). Testing between the TRACE model and the Fuzzy Logical Model of speech perception. *Cognitive Psychology, 21*, 398–421.

Massaro, D. W. (1996). Integration of multiple sources of information in language processing. In T. Inui & J. L. McClelland (Eds.), *Attention and performance XVI: Information integration in perception and communication* (pp. 397–432). Cambridge, MA: MIT Press.

Massaro, D. W. (2000). The horse race to language understanding: FLMP was first out of the gate and has yet to be overtaken. *Behavioral and Brain Science, 23*, 338–339.

Massaro, D. W., &Chen, T. H. (2008). The motor theory of speech perception revisited. *Psychonomic Bulletin and Review, 15*, 453–457.

Massaro, D. W., Thompson, L. A., Barron, B., & Laren, E. (1986). Developmental changes in visual and auditory contributions to speech perception. *Journal of Experimental Child Psychology, 41*, 93–113.

Mattingly, I. G., Liberman, A. M., Syrdal A. K., & Halwes T. (1971). Discrimination in speech and nonspeech modes. *Cognitive Psychology, 2*, 131–157.

Mattys, S. L. (1997). The use of time during lexical processing and segmentation: A review. *Psychonomic Bulletin and Review, 4*, 310–329.

Mattys, S. L., &Liss, J. M. (2008). On building models of spoken-word recognition: When there is as much to learn from natural "oddities" as from artificial normality. *Perception and Psychophysics, 70*, 1235–1242.

Mattys, S. L., White, L., & Melhorn, J. F (2005). Integration of multiple speech segmentation cues: A hierarchical framework. *Journal of Experimental Psychology: General, 134*, 477–500.

McClelland, J. L. (1991). Stochastic interactive processes and the effect of context on perception. *Cognitive Psychology, 23*, 1–44.

McClelland, J. L., &Elman, J. L. (1986). The TRACE model of speech perception. *Cognitive Psychology, 18*, 1–86.

McCloskey, M., &Cohen, N. J. (1989). Catastrophic interference in connectionist networks: The sequential learning problem. *The Psychology of Learning and Motivation, 24*, 109–165.

McGettigan, C., Agnew, Z. K., & Scott, S. K. (2010). Are articulatory commands automatically and involuntarily activated during speech perception? *Proceedings of the National Academy of Sciences USA, 107*, E42.

McGurk, H., &MacDonald, J. W. (1976). Hearing lips and seeing voices. *Nature, 264*, 746–748.

McLennan, C. T., Luce, P. A., & Charles-Luce, J. (2005). Examining the time course of indexical specificity effects in spoken word recognition. *Journal of Experimental Psychology: Learning Memory and Cognition, 31*, 306–321.

McQueen, J. M. (1998). Segmentation of continuous speech using phonotactics. *Journal of Memory and Language, 39*, 21–46.

McQueen, J. M., Cutler, A., & Norris, D. (2006). Phonological abstraction in the mental lexicon. *Cognitive Science, 30*, 1113–1126.

Miller, J. D.Wier, C. C., Pastore, R., Kelly, W. J., & Dooling, R. J. (1976). Discrimination and labeling of noise-buzz sequences with varying noise lead times: An example of categorical perception. *Journal of the Acoustical Society of America, 60*, 410–417.

Miller, J. L., & Liberman, A. M. (1979). Some effects of later-occurring information on the perception of stop consonant and semivowel. *Perception and Psychophysics, 25*, 457–465.

Mody, M., Schwartz, R. G., Gravel, R. S., & Ruben, R. J. (1999). Speech perception and verbal memory in children with and without histories of otitis media. *Journal of Speech, Language and Hearing Research, 42*, 1069–1079.

Montant, M. (2000). Feedback: A general mechanism in the brain. *Behavioral and Brain Science, 23*, 340–341.

Moore, R. K. (2007). Spoken language processing by machine. In G. Gaskell (Ed.), *Oxford handbook of psycholinguistics* (pp. 723–738). Oxford, England: Oxford University Press.

Moore, R. K., &Cutler, A. (2001, July 11-13). *Constraints on theories of human vs. machine recognition of speech.* Paper presented at the SPRAAC Workshop on Human Speech Recognition as Pattern Classification, Max-Planck-Institute for Psycholinguistics, Nijmegen, The Netherlands.

Moore, R. K., &Maier, V. (2007). Preserving fine phonetic detail using episodic memory: Automatic speech recognition using MINERVA2. In *Proceedings of the 16th ICPhS Meeting (pp. 197–203).* Saarbrücken, Germany.

Movellan, J. R., &McClelland, J. L. (2001). The Morton-Massaro law of information integration: Implications for models of perception. *Psychological Review, 108*, 113–148.

Nooteboom, S. G. (1979). The time course of speech perception. In W. J. Barry & K. J. Kohler (Eds.), *"Time" in the production and perception of speech* (Arbeitsberichte 12). Kiel, Germany: Institut für Phonetik, University of Kiel.

Norris, D. (1994). Shortlist: A connectionist model of continuous speech recognition. *Cognition, 52*, 189–234.

Norris, D., & McQueen, J. M. (2008). Shortlist B: A Bayesian model of continuous speech recognition. *Psychological Review, 115*, 357–395.

Norris, D., McQueen. J. M., & Cutler, A. (2000). Merging information in speech recognition: Feedback is never necessary. *Behavioral and Brain Sciences, 23*, 299–370.

Norris, D., McQueen, J. M., & Cutler, A. (2003). Perceptual learning in speech. *Cognitive Psychology, 47*, 204–238.

Oden, G. C. (2000). Implausibility versus misinterpretation of the FLMP. *Behavioral and Brain Science, 23*, 344.

Oden, G. C., &Massaro, D. W. (1978). Integration of featural information in speech perception. *Psychological Review, 85*, 172–191.

Ostendorf, M., Digilakis, V., & Kimball, O. A. (1996). From HMMs to segment models: A unified view of stochastic modelling for speech recognition. *IEEE Transactions, Speech and Audio Processing, 4*, 360–378.

Pardo, J. S., & Remez, R. E. (2006). The perception of speech. In M. Traxler & M. A. Gernsbacher (Eds.), *Handbook of psycholinguistics (2nd ed.,* pp. 201–248). New York: Academic Press.

Pisoni, D. B., &Luce, P. A. (1987). Acoustic-phonetic representations in word recognition. *Cognition, 25*, 21–52.

Pitt, M. A., & Samuel, A. G. (1995). Lexical and sublexical feedback in auditory word recognition. *Cognitive Psychology, 29*, 149–188.

Polka, L., Colantonio, C., & Sundara, M. (2001). A cross-language comparison of /d/–/Δ/ perception: Evidence for a new developmental pattern. *Journal of the Acoustical Society of America, 109*, 2190–2201.

Port, R. F. (1977). *The influence of speaking tempo on the duration of stressed vowel and medial stop in English Trochee words.* Unpublished Ph.D. dissertation, Indiana University, Bloomington.

Potter, R. K., Kopp, G. A., & Green, H. C. (1947). *Visible speech.* New York: D. Van Nostrand.

Pulvermüller, F., Huss, M., Kherif, F., Moscoso Del Prado Martin, F., Hauk, O., & Shtyrof, Y. (2006). Motor cortex maps articulatory features of speech sounds. *Proceedings of the National Academy of Sciences USA, 103,* 7865–7870.

Rabiner, L., & Juang, B. H. (1993). Fundamentals of speech recognition. Englewood Cliffs, NJ: Prentice Hall.

Radeau, M., Morais, J., Mousty, P., & Bertelson, P. (2000). The effect of speaking rate on the role of the uniqueness point in spoken word recognition. *Journal of Memory and Language, 42,* 406–422.

Rastle, K., Davis, M. H., & Brysbaert, M., (2010). Response to McGettigan et al.: Task-based accounts are not sufficiently coherent to explain articulatory effects in speech perception. *Proceedings Proceedings of the National Academy of Sciences USA, 107,* E43.

Reisberg, D., Mc Lean, J., & Goldfield, A. (1987). Easy to hear but hard to understand: A lip-reading advantage with intact auditory stimuli. In R. Campbell & B. Dodd (Eds.), *Hearing by eye: The psychology of lip-reading* (pp. 97–114). Hillsdale, NJ: Erlbaum.

Rizzolatti, G., &Craighero, L. (2004). The mirror-neuron system. *Annual Review of Neuroscience, 27,* 169–192,

Rosenblum, L. D. (2005). Primacy of multimodal speech perception. In D. B. Pisoni & R. E. Remez (Eds.), *The handbook of speech perception* (pp. 51–78). Oxford, England: Blackwell.

Rosenblum, L. D., Schmuckler, M. A., & Johnson, J. A. (1997). The McGurk effect in infants. *Perception and Psychophysics, 59,* 347–357.

Russell, M. J. (1993). A segmental HMM for speech pattern modeling. In *Proceedings of the IEEE International Conference on Acoustics, Speech and Signal Processing* (pp. 640–643)

Samuel, A. G. (1981). Phonemic restoration: Insights from a new methodology. *Journal of Experimental Psychology: General, 110,* 474–494.

Samuel, A. G. (1997). Lexical activation produces potent phonemic percepts. *Cognitive Psychology, 32,* 97–127.

Samuel, A. G. (2000). Merge: Contorted architecture, distorted facts, and purported autonomy. *Behavioral and Brain Science, 23,* 345–346.

Samuel, A. G. (2001). Knowing a word affects the fundamental perception of the sounds within it. *Psychological Science, 12,* 348–351.

Samuel, A. G., &Kraljic, T. (2009). Perceptual learning for speech. *Attention, Perception, and Psychophysics, 71,* 1207–1218.

Scharenborg, O., Norris, D., ten Bosch, L., & Mc Queen, J. M. (2005). How should a speech recognizer work? *Cognitive Science, 29,* 867–918.

Stevens, K. N. (2000). Recognition of continuous speech requires top-down processing. *Behavioral and Brain Science, 23,* 348.

Stevens, K. N., &Blumstein, S. E. (1981). The search for invariant acoustic correlates of phonetic features. In P. Eimas & J. Miller (Eds.), *Perspectives on the study of speech* (pp. 1–38). Hillsdale, NJ: Erlbaum.

Sumby, W. H., &Pollack, I. (1954). Visual contribution to speech intelligibility in noise. *Journal of the Acoustical Society of America, 26,* 212–215.

Sussman, H. M. (1989). Neural coding of relational invariance in speech: Human language analogs to the barn owl. *Psychological Review, 96,* 631–642.

Summerfield, A. Q. (1981). Articulatory rate and perceptual constancy in phonetic perception. *Journal of Experimental Psychology: Human Perception and Performance, 7,* 1074–1095.

Trehub, S. E. (1976). The discrimination of foreign speech contrasts by infants and adults. *Child Development, 47,* 466–472.

Umeda, N., &Coker, C. H. (1974). Allophonic variation in American English. *Journal of Phonetics, 2,* 1–5.

van Buuren, R. A., Festen, J., & Houtgast, T . (1999). Compression and expansion of the temporal envelope: Evaluation of speech intelligibility and sound quality. *Journal of the Acoustical Society of America, 105,* 2903–2913.

Vroomen, J., Van Linden, B., Keetels, M., de Gelder, B., & Bertelson, P. (2004). Selective adaptation and recalibration of auditory speech by lipread information: Dissipation. *Speech Communication, 44,* 55–61.

Warren, R. M., & Obusek, C. J. (1971). Speech perception phonemic restorations. *Perception & Psychophysics, 9,* 358–362.

Warren, R. M., &Warren, R. P. (1970). Auditory illusions and confusions. *Scientific American, 223,* 30–36.

Whalen, D. H., Benson, R. R., Richardson, M., Swainson, B., Clark, V. P., Lai, S.,... Liberman, A. M. (2006). Differentiation of speech and nonspeech processing within primary auditory cortex. *Journal of the Acoustical Society of America, 119,* 575–581.

Yuen, I., Davis, M. H., Brysbaert, M., & Rastle, K. (2010). Activation of articulatory information in speech perception. *Proceedings of the National Academy of Sciences USA, 107,* 592–597.

# Spoken Word Recognition

James S. Magnuson, Daniel Mirman, *and* Emily Myers

## Abstract

Spoken word recognition is the study of how lexical representations are accessed from phonological patterns in the speech signal. That is, we conventionally make two simplifying assumptions: Because many fundamental problems in speech perception remain unsolved, we provisionally assume the input is a string of phonemes that are the output of speech perception processes, and that the output is a string of recognized words that are passed onto mechanisms supporting, for example, sentence processing. These kinds of assumptions allow psycholinguists to break language understanding into manageable research domains, and as we review, they have afforded great progress in understanding spoken word recognition. However, we also review a growing body of results that are incompatible with these assumptions: Spoken word recognition is constrained by subphonemic details and top-down influences from higher level processing. We argue that these findings are incompatible with current theoretical frameworks, and that a new theoretical paradigm is needed.

**Key Words:** lexical access, computational models, segmentation, embedded word problem, interaction, top-down influences

When we comprehend spoken language, we accomplish many amazing feats. We map the acoustics of speech onto phonological categories, despite a rapid signal,[1] with tremendous variation in talker characteristics, acoustic environment, speaking rate, and many other dimensions (see Chapter 26, this volume). We also build syntactic structures on the fly as we hear speech, allowing us to derive a talker's intended meaning, overcoming rampant syntactic and semantic ambiguity along the way (Trueswell & Tanenhaus, 1994). The study of word recognition focuses on processes that intervene, more or less, between phonological and syntactic processing: how do listeners map phonological forms onto words in memory, taking into account prior probabilities, linguistic and nonlinguistic context, including the phonetic, phonological, lexical, semantic, and syntactic structures that have been activated by the speech signal as it unfolds in time. As we

shall see, there may not be distinct processes or representations that are concerned purely with spoken word recognition.[2] Word recognition is influenced by (and in turn influences processing of) low-level acoustic and phonetic details of speech as well as semantic and syntactic processing; there is no sharp boundary between speech perception and word recognition, nor between word recognition and sentence processing.

Nonetheless, psycholinguistics is divided into intuitively identifiable levels of organization in human language processing—*speech perception, spoken word recognition, sentence processing,* and so on—providing a logical division of labor among psycholinguists. This way, rather than waiting until all fundamental problems at the level of speech perception are solved, researchers can make progress on the word level by making simplifying assumptions about the nature of the input and the goals of word-level processing (see Magnuson, 2008, for a detailed discussion). The nature of the input and the goals of processing are what David Marr (1982) called the *computational level* of theorizing about information processing systems. We need to articulate a computational-level theory before we can discuss what sorts of representations and mechanisms support human spoken word recognition.

## The Computational Problem

Marr (1982) described three levels of information processing theories: computational, algorithmic, and implementational. The idea is that when we are faced with some sort of information processing system—a thermostat, a calculator, a computer, or human language processing—and want to figure out through empirical investigation what the system does and how it works, we need to posit theories at multiple levels of analysis to guide our investigations. The most abstract level is the *computational* theory, which is an analysis of the goals or purpose of the system based on the mapping between the system's input and output—which defines the information processing the system does. For a basic calculator, the input might be numbers and symbols for mathematical operations, and the output would be the result the calculator displays.

At the *algorithmic* level, we develop a theory of the "software" that could achieve the computational mapping. For example, we might posit that for multiplication, the calculator performs a sequence of additions (given 4 x 3, it adds 4 + 4 + 4) or that it just looks up the result from a list of pairwise products coded in its memory. We might then propose an empirical test of these two theories by measuring how long the calculator takes to display its answer in cases where the two theories would require a similar number of operations versus cases where the serial addition theory would involve many more operations.

The third level is the *implementational* level, which in the case of our calculator would be the hardware level. Here, we examine the inner workings of the calculator—perhaps taking it apart, enumerating the components and their interconnections. In a modern calculator, this would be a circuit board. We take as given that the relevant implementational level for spoken word recognition is that of neural systems. Despite the advent in recent years of sophisticated neuroimaging techniques, understanding of the neural basis of language remains rather coarse (for recent reviews, see Blumstein & Myers, in press; Hickok & Poeppel, 2007; Ueno,

Saito, Rogers, & Lambon Ralph, 2011). While we argue at the end of the chapter that integration with cognitive neuroscience via lesion studies, neuroimaging, and genetics will be necessary for full understanding of human language processing, our focus will remain firmly on cognitive psychology in this review.

One of Marr's goals in identifying these three levels of information processing theory was to make clear that they can be addressed independently. Theories at different levels need not have contact with each other to make progress (although a computational level theory—the relevant input-output mapping and its purpose—is a prerequisite to an algorithmic theory and a crucial source of constraints in studying the implementational level), but they can be mutually constraining. For example, if we are comparing algorithmic theories of multiplication that posit serial addition vs. memory lookup (for single digits), we might search for circuits at the implementational level that perform addition when a multiplication operation is called for. Conversely, if we determine at the implementational level that the device has a memory limited to 1 kilobyte, we should not propose algorithmic theories that require megabytes of memory.

Now imagine we have a device that happens to be a calculator—but we do not know that, because the Arabic numerals and mathematical symbols have been replaced with arbitrary symbols. What should our first step be in figuring out what information processing this device does? We will have to observe what symbols are displayed as we input different key sequences. We should arrive at the same computational theory as we would with a "normal" calculator, but it will take a lot of work to document the input-output mappings and surmise the purpose of the information processing the device does. Enumerating all possible inputs and their results would not be feasible—depending on the limits of the calculator, these may be infinite or at least impractically many. If we have no clue that this device is a calculator, imagine how difficult it would be to jump to the algorithmic or implementational level before establishing a computational theory—that is, figuring out that the purpose of the device is calculation. And this is largely the position we find ourselves in when attempting to develop theories of cognition. So let's begin by deriving a computational theory of *spoken word recognition*: What are the inputs, the outputs, and the mapping between them?

The input is a trickier issue than one might think. It may seem obvious that for *spoken* word recognition, the input is speech. This turns out to be an impractical starting point, because of unsolved mysteries in speech perception. The central one is called the *lack of invariance problem*, and it refers to the fact that there is not a simple mapping between acoustic patterns and percepts (such as consonants and vowels, syllables, or words). Instead, there is a many-to-many mapping (e.g., Lisker, 1985). The acoustic patterns that map to a particular phoneme (consonant or vowel) vary depending on phonetic context (what phonemes precede and follow), acoustic environment (an open field vs. an echoey stairwell vs. a noisy party), talker characteristics (physical size, sex, dialect, idiolect, emotional state), speaking rate ... and this is a partial list! (See Chapter 26, this volume, for a review.) The result is that many acoustic patterns can map to the same percept. Compounding this problem is the fact that phonological categories overlap in acoustic space and an identical acoustic pattern can map onto multiple percepts depending on context. For instance, a given vowel can sound like the vowel in "bit" in the context of one talker, but like the vowel in "bet" in another talker's voice (Ladefoged & Broadbent, 1957; Peterson & Barney, 1952), and the same acoustic pattern can sound like "b" in the context of slow speech but "w" in fast speech (Miller & Liberman, 1979; for examples of how speech rate affects spoken word recognition, see Dilley & Pitt, 2010).

The acoustic variability in different phonetic contexts arises due to the fact that speech is *coarticulated*, meaning that the vocal tract gestures we use to produce successive speech sounds overlap. If we try to identify the time intervals where the vocal tract is making the motor movements for the phonemes /b/, /æ/, and /g/ in the word "bag," we find that the gestures for /æ/ extend over the entire production of the word, and even gestures for /b/ and /g/ overlap in time (for a review, see Fowler & Magnuson, 2012). Coarticulation contributes to the lack of invariance problem (the acoustics for a phoneme will change given the motoric constraints of producing adjacent phonemes with which it is coarticulated) but is also at the heart of the *segmentation* problem: There are few acoustic cues to where one phoneme ends and another begins because articulation and therefore acoustics are usually continuous. Discontinuities—actual breaks and pauses in the signal, which would seem like a logical acoustic cue to boundaries—are not reliable cues to phoneme boundaries. These discontinuities rarely occur "between" phonemes and are likely to happen "within" a phoneme, such as

the sudden reduction in sound when a constriction for a voiceless stop consonant like /p/ is made (the constriction gesture being the brief, air-stopping closure of the lips).

Rather than waiting until these mysteries are resolved, psycholinguists make simplifying assumptions that allow them to tackle higher levels of processing. Typically, psycholinguists allow themselves to assume that the input to word recognition will be a string of phonemes generated by a speech perception mechanism (and scientists studying sentence processing make a similar assumption and assume a string of words to be a plausible input to sentence processing—and so on, as one moves to higher levels of organization). This simplifying assumption allows us to get started, but as we shall see later in this chapter, it paradoxically makes some aspects of theories of spoken word recognition more complex than they need be.

For now, let's consider what this assumption buys us. If we consider the input to be a string of phonemes, the next step in deriving a computational-level theory of spoken word recognition is to ask what the output should be, in order to identify the *goal* of the information processing system we are studying. The ultimate goal is, of course, a full specification of the listener's understanding of the speaker's message, but the complexities of semantics and syntax render this, as with the input, too large a problem to take on simultaneously with word-level processing. We would also have to grapple with how words map onto syntactic and semantic structures of various sorts, how those result in appreciation of the speaker's intent (or not) in light of linguistic and nonlinguistic context, the listener's prior experiences, and so on. Rather than grappling with all of these details in one go, psycholinguists break the problem into manageable chunks. For spoken word recognition, we assume the intermediate goal of the system is to achieve a match to a *lexical representation* of a word in memory and feed it forward for higher levels of processing.

What should be the contents of lexical representations? Certainly, there will have to be a *phonological form*—a sequenced list of the phonemes that should occur (the most typical assumption) or some other acoustic form (e.g., episodic traces; Goldinger, 1998), or detailed phonetic or phonological form. While one possibility we have just listed is explicitly nonphonological (acoustic episodes), we will use "phonological form" to mean any coding scheme that maps the speech signal onto words in the lexicon. While phonological form will be the primary key for accessing lexical representations, what else should we assume lexical representations contain? We might minimally expect *lexical semantics* and *grammatical class*, although contemporary linguistic and psycholinguistic theories of grammar and sentence processing attribute even more syntactic and semantic knowledge to lexical representations (Altmann & Mirković, 2009; MacDonald, Pearlmutter, & Seidenberg, 1994; Pusteyevsky, 1995; Trueswell & Tanenhaus, 1994). Again, theories of spoken word recognition typically defer consideration of details beyond phonological form to higher levels, such as sentence processing. As with input representation, the risk of seemingly simplifying assumptions may make the problem of spoken word recognition paradoxically more difficult if they exclude contributions of semantic, syntactic, and pragmatic factors to resolving word-level ambiguities (e.g., Barr, 2008; Dahan & Tanenhaus, 2004; Magnuson, Tanenhaus, & Aslin, 2008).

So now we have a basic definition of the computational problem: The input is a string of speech sounds represented either abstractly (as symbolic representations) or episodically (as memory traces preserving surface details),[3] and the goal is access of a lexical representation, which includes at least parsing the phonemes onto phonological forms of words in memory, and may include accessing some degree of semantic, syntactic, and pragmatic knowledge (though these details tend to be beyond the scope of current theories of spoken word recognition). The next steps in determining how the system achieves this goal are characterizing the mappings between inputs and outputs through experimental observation, and then enumerating the computational challenges the system must overcome in achieving the mapping, and constraints on how it does so (How quickly are particular words processed? What kinds of errors do listeners make?). With a sufficiently large body of results of this sort in hand, one can begin to construct algorithmic ("software") level theories specifying cognitive mechanisms that could achieve the observed mapping. This sets the stage for competition among algorithmic theories, as theories generate experimentally testable predictions that go beyond the phenomena that have been observed so far, and the knowledge base and level of detail about the input-output mapping grows. Thus, as algorithmic theories are posited and tested, the computational theory—the mapping that any algorithmic theory must account for—becomes more detailed and refined.

We will use an even more abstract lens—Kuhn's (1962) three phases of scientific paradigms—to present our view of the literature and history of spoken word recognition: *preparadigm*, where basic facts are enumerated and preliminary, incomplete theories begin to point the way to a theoretical consensus; *normal science*, where theories drift toward consensus in response to an ever-growing corpus of empirical details, but eventually anomalous findings that cannot be accommodated by extant theories push the paradigm toward a crisis; and *revolutionary science*, where a new paradigm arises from insights that allow for a new theoretical perspective that accommodates the anomalies (a classic example from Kuhn is Gallileo's insight that friction can explain why terrestrial objects in motion stop without some force pushing them, rather than this being an intrinsic natural property of objects, which paved the way for a paradigm shift to Copernican cosmology). With this framework in mind, we will next present a selective and not purely chronological review of the spoken word recognition literature in three parts: the foundational, preparadigm consensus (the initial computational-level facts on which spoken word recognition researchers agree); the progression to an initial phase of normal science, where models and measures of the time course of processing pushed theory development; and finally, where we find ourselves today—(hopefully) late in a period of normal science, with a growing body of anomalous findings that cannot be easily fit into current theories. We will conclude the chapter with a discussion of what we view as the most pressing crises, and possible avenues to a revolution. These include grappling with the actual speech signal, integration of word-level processing with the context of language understanding, development throughout the life span, and neurobiological constraints on algorithmic theories.

## Basic Science Phase: Foundations of a Computational Theory of Spoken Word Recognition

To set the stage for our review of foundational empirical results, the basic facts on which all theories of spoken word recognition agree are summarized in Table 27.1.[4] These basic facts were discovered in the middle- to late-1900s as the essential technologies, methods, and theoretical framework emerged. These developments, namely the advent of chronometric (i.e., precise reaction time) experimental methods, digital speech analysis and manipulation methods, and the development of theories of

**Table 27.1** Basic, Agreed-Upon Facts About Spoken Word Recognition

| Spoken Word Recognition Is... | Details, Implications, Challenges, Etc. |
| --- | --- |
| Incremental | As a word is being heard, that is, as soon as even the initial sound is heard:<br>➢ Multiple words are activated in *parallel* in memory,<br>➢ With strength proportional to their *similarity* (both phonetic and semantic) to the input and *prior probability* (*frequency* of occurrence and, to a lesser degree, fit to lexical, sentential, or other *contextual constraints*); and<br>➢ Activated words *compete* for recognition |
| Sequential | ➢ *Coarticulation*: sound patterns corresponding to phonological categories such as consonants and vowels are constellations of temporally overlapping (but not necessarily coincident) buzzes, chirps, and frication that must be bound together to map onto phonological categories<br>➢ *Phoneme segmentation problem*: phonemes overlap in time and there are no invariant boundary cues[6]<br>➢ *Lexical segmentation problem*: there are no invariant cues to word boundaries<br>➢ *Embedding problem*: segmentation must not lead to "recognition" of embedded words (e.g., when hearing *window*, the system should recognize just that word, and not *win*, *wind*, *in*, or *dough*). This is potentially a very large problem; McQueen et al. (1995) estimate that 84% of English polysyllabic words contain at least one embedded word. |
| Interactive | Spoken word recognition *influences* performance on speech perception tasks and is *influenced by* semantic, syntactic, and pragmatic context. |

cognitive psychology, still form the core of spoken word recognition research.[5] Next, we will unpack this consensus, beginning by focusing on phonological form, introducing some of the "basic," "incomplete" theories of the preparadigm phase, and eventually turning to meaning and context.

First, we can intuit the necessity of spoken word recognition being sequential from the *segmentation problem*: Despite our subjective impression that words "pop out" from continuous speech, there are in fact no perfectly reliable cues to word boundaries (Aslin, Woodward, LaMendola, & Bever, 1996; Cole & Jakimik, 1980; Lehiste, 1970); indeed, as we have already reviewed briefly, there are no such things as phoneme boundaries (see Chapter 26, this volume). (To refute your subjective impression that there are breaks between words when listening to a language you know, try discerning word boundaries when listening to someone speak an unfamiliar language.) The absence of robust acoustic boundary cues makes it impossible, for example, for spoken word recognition to depend on a process that buffers the acoustic input until a boundary is detected, and then performs recognition on the entire word form in parallel.

Sequential processing can also be inferred from behavior. The first time-course method devised to study spoken word recognition was the *gating task*

(Grosjean, 1980). In gating, a small portion of the onset of a word—the first "gate"—is presented, and the subject is asked for the most likely completion. Then, the second gate—a slightly longer portion of the word, beginning from word onset—is presented, and the subject guesses at a completion. This continues with successively longer gates until the entire word is presented. Recognition is operationalized as the gate by which the correct word is always given. Even at the first gate, participants are able to offer completions. As more of the word is presented, the number of completions offered decreases, in a fashion consistent with the phonemes heard so far. Given /b/ as the first gate, participants provide completions that begin with /b/. If the second gate provides strong evidence that the second phoneme is /æ/, the completions narrow to words beginning with /bæ/. Gating reveals many additional details about word recognition. For example, word frequency is an important predictor of completion probability (e.g., given /bæ/, *bat* is a more likely response than *bass*). Gating results also suggest that words are often recognized before they have been fully heard; that is, high identification accuracy is often possible before the entire word is presented. This *recognition point* is highly correlated with the *uniqueness point*—the phoneme at which there is only one possible (uninflected) completion of a word, such as the /f/ sound in *elephant*. In some cases, though, the recognition point can even precede the uniqueness point (e.g., when one possible completion is much more probable due to word frequency). Thus, gating suggests that lexical activation is incremental (people are able to provide highly likely completions that are consistent with the gated input), that multiple words are activated (given the variety of completions offered), and that word onsets are crucial keys to accessing lexical items—subjects virtually never provide a completion that mismatches with the initial sounds in the gate (e.g., given /bæ/, subjects do not suggest *cat* as a completion).

So far we have support for (a) sequential/incremental/continuous processing beginning from word onset, (b) multiple activation, and (c) roles for similarity and prior probability (frequency). However, the gating task is rather unusual, and one could argue that it bears little similarity to word recognition "in the wild," and may be instead a guessing game subject to various strategies. Converging evidence, though, comes from tasks like *lexical decision* and *naming*. In a lexical decision task, you hear a spoken word (*ball*) or a spoken nonword (*balt*), and press a button to indicate whether what you heard was a word. In naming (sometimes called *shadowing* or *repetition*), you hear a word and repeat it as quickly as you can. In tasks like these, response latencies decline and/ or accuracy increases (especially when the speech signal is degraded or noise is added) with word frequency (e.g., Luce, 1986; Luce & Pisoni, 1998). These measures also provide evidence for activation of and competition among multiple words, as reaction times increase and/or accuracy declines with the number of words in the lexicon that are phonologically similar to a target word.

It is more challenging to detect the sequential nature of processing with tasks like lexical decision and naming. They provide a single, presumably postperceptual measure, and like gating, arguably have little connection to word recognition outside the laboratory. Furthermore, lexical decision has the potential to index something other than the actual recognition of a target word; for example, one might achieve high accuracy just from responding based on a sense of familiarity, or based on the summed activation of multiple words, before one has truly identified the word (Grainger & Jacobs, 1996; Rogers, Lambon Ralph, Hodges, & Patterson, 2004). The coordination of perception and production required by the naming task might direct attention to different details of the signal than a situation where there is no need to repeat a word as you hear it.

However, an extremely clever variant of lexical decision, the *cross-modal semantic priming* paradigm, provides converging evidence for other details from the gating task. The paradigm exploits the phenomenon of semantic priming (Meyer & Schvaneveldt, 1971), where hearing or seeing a related word appears to preactivate or prime semantically related words (e.g., you are faster to recognize *doctor* if it is preceded by *nurse* than if it is preceded by *sandwich*). In cross-modal priming, your task is to perform lexical decision on visually presented letter strings, which are interspersed with auditory stimuli (e.g., Marslen-Wilson & Zwitserlood, 1989). This allows experimenters to look for semantic or other effects between the spoken and written words. In fact, the paradigm might be better called "cross-modal, *phonologically mediated* semantic priming." Rather than looking for direct competition between the spoken prime and visual target, Marslen-Wilson and Zwitserlood (1989) predicted that if a spoken word (e.g., *castle*) activates a cohort of words with similar onsets (*candy, cabin,* etc.) to a significant degree, those words should spread detectable activation to semantic relatives (*sweet, log,* etc.). If instead word onsets are not crucial, other highly similar words should also be in the competition cohort (and so *castle* should activate *hassle*, which should prime *bother*). The former predictions were borne out: Priming was found for pairs like *castle-sweet*, but not pairs like *castle-bother* (even when word frequency and other factors were controlled). It is important to note that these results also imply that the set of activated words includes items that are semantically related to words that are phonologically consistent with the spoken input. However, the ramifications of this implication are mostly ignored by models of spoken word recognition—a point to which we will return at the end of this section and in the next section.

Marslen-Wilson and colleagues took the gating and priming results to rather transparently reflect the workings of human spoken word recognition and proposed the *Cohort Theory* of spoken word recognition (Marslen-Wilson & Tyler, 1980; Marslen-Wilson & Welsh, 1978); because their definition of the competition cohort was based on onset overlap, "cohort" has become a synonym for onset competitor.) One of their key insights was that the apparent complication of sequential input actually provides a basis for understanding not just isolated word recognition but also how the system might address the embedding and segmentation problems in isolated words and word sequences.

They proposed a mechanism that at utterance onset begins activating all words consistent with the input. Given the input /b/, all /b/-initial words receive modest activation. As the input continues to /bæ/, all /bæ/-initial words receive more activation, and all /b/-initial words that do not continue to /æ/ are removed from the activation cohort (or begin to be inhibited). This continues as more input comes in. If only a single word is uttered, the latest point at which the word will be recognized is after the final phoneme is heard. However, the word can be very strongly activated prior to word offset as the cohort decreases in size. In the extreme case that a single word remains in the cohort prior to word offset (e.g., /bænIst^r/-*banister*, which becomes unique at /s/), uniqueness point effects are predicted. The original version of the model was interactive. It allowed context to activate words so strongly they could be recognized significantly earlier than their uniqueness points. The model was revised (Marlen-Wilson, 1987, 1989) with strong bottom-up priority—making initial processing autonomous, to avoid the problem that words unexpected in a context can still be clearly recognized (e.g., the system should not recognize *nice* instead of *knife* given *he cut the bread with a nice switchblade*). In the next section, we will discuss how these difficulties with interaction can be avoided when one does not assume there is actually an instant of definitive recognition (the so-called "magical moment"; Balota, 1990), rather than flux in the relative activations of lexical representations.

In the case of a sequence of words, phoneme-by-phoneme winnowing of the cohort provides a potential solution to the segmentation problem (the absence of reliable bottom-up cues to word boundaries). For example, if the utterance so far is /bæn/ (*ban*), and the next sound is /I/ (*ih*, as in *banish* or *banister*), a word boundary cannot be posited. Even though *ban* is a word, longer words beginning with that string remain in the cohort (set of activated words). If instead the next sound is /v/, a word boundary must be posited, because there are no words that begin *banv*. In some cases, a boundary must be posited at an earlier position. For example, if the input has so far been /bænI/ (*bani-*) and the next sounds is /f/ (as in the word sequence *ban if*), a boundary must be posited before the /I/. This algorithm also provides an explanation for how the embedding problem might be handled. In the case of *banister*, *ban* is not recognized because longer words remain in the cohort when /bæn/ has been heard. Thus, segmentation and handling of embeddings emerge from a simple parsing mechanism

motivated by the need to handle sequential input and result in a very specific *similarity metric*, that is, the basis for including a word in the activation set. In the case of the Cohort Model, the similarity metric is roughly that two words will compete strongly if they overlap in the first one or two phonemes (Marslen-Wilson, 1987).

But this is where we encounter our first basis for debate about the basic empirical facts for form activation. We cited work by Luce and colleagues earlier in support of the basic fact that recognition facility (speed and accuracy) increases with word frequency and decreases with competitor set size (Goldinger, Luce, & Pisoni, 1989; Luce, 1986; Luce & Pisoni, 1998). While one obtains the same results manipulating the size of the onset cohort (e.g., Zhang, Randall, Stamtakis, Marslen-Wilson, & Tyler, 2011), Luce and colleagues tested a very different similarity metric. This metric, known as neighborhood density, was motivated by the observation that the Cohort Model must assume virtually noise-free input to work as we have just described it (otherwise, the cohort cannot be winnowed accurately), but in the real world, speech is often heard in noisy contexts. So they devised a more forgiving metric that assumes less input certainty and so greater confusability. Extending some previous notions of structure in the auditory lexicon (Greenberg & Jenkins, 1964; Landauer & Streeter, 1973), they proposed what is now called the "DAS" similarity metric: Two words are considered neighbors (and likely to activate each other) if they differ by no more than one phonemic deletion (D), addition (A), or substitution (S). As they predicted, the more neighbors a word has, the more slowly and/or inaccurately it is processed. This is consistent with the notion that neighbors are activated and compete for recognition, and further evidence for competition comes from the result that the neighborhood effects are amplified by neighbor frequency; if two words are matched in frequency and number of neighbors, but the mean frequency of one word's neighbors is higher, that word will be harder to process (Luce & Pisoni, 1998).

This leads to a very different conception of the competitor set compared to Cohort. The word *cat*, for example, has the deletion neighbor *at*, addition neighbors *scat* and *cast*, and substitution neighbors like *bat*, *cot*, and *can*. Many items that would be in the Cohort competitor set are excluded: monosyllables like *camp* and *cask*, and many longer words (*cabin, cabinet, cabbie, caddy, calcium, candy, catalog*, etc.). Thus, this metric conflicts with the Cohort metric by including words that mismatch at onset, and by excluding many words for which Marslen-Wilson and colleagues reported robust competition effects. Luce and Pisoni gloss over these seemingly problematic items by maintaining their focus on monosyllabic words, acknowledging that aspects of Cohort theory may need to be integrated into their similarity metric later to handle longer words.

Luce and colleagues also showed that the DAS rule can be improved by using a graded similarity metric. Instead of counting complete matches or mismatches, you calculate pairwise similarity between words phoneme-by-phoneme. Luce and colleagues have done this by using actual confusion probabilities measured when speech was presented in noise, but one could also use a metric based on similarity in phonetic features. While this approach provides a modicum of greater precision, Luce and colleagues have reported that the DAS rule works nearly as well, with one important exception: The graded similarity approach predicts inhibitory priming between words that are highly similar at every position but do not overlap in even a single phoneme, such as *veer* and *bull* (these examples differ from each other by a single phonetic feature at each phoneme; see Luce, Golding, Auer, & Vitevitch, 2000, for priming results supporting this prediction).

Luce and colleagues proposed a model based on their results: the *Neighborhood Activation Model* (NAM). NAM does not address the time course of processing—and so is mute on questions of incrementality—focusing instead on multiple, parallel activation and competition. NAM models an assumed final stage of spoken word recognition where acoustic-phonetic detectors have accumulated activation from bottom-up input, which they combine with lexical knowledge, such as word frequencies. Decision unit activations are assumed to be proportional to *frequency-weighted neighborhood probability*; here is our slightly streamlined version of the FWNP:

$$FWNP = \frac{f_t S_{tt}}{\sum f_w S_{wt}} \qquad (1)$$

Thus, the *FWNP* for target word $t$ is the ratio of $f_t s_{t_t}$, where $f_t$ is $t$'s log frequency, and $s_{tt}$ is $t$'s similarity to an utterance of $t$ (which is not necessarily 1.0, as one might confuse the /t/ of *bat* with /d/, for example), to the sum of the similarity to $t$ of every word, $w$, in the lexicon ($s_{wt}$), weighted by its log frequency ($f_w$). We can simplify further if we base similarity on

the DAS rule. Now a word is either a neighbor or it is not, because it either meets the 1-phoneme difference threshold or it does not. Since $s$ will be 1 for all neighbors and 0 for every other word, we drop it, leaving the ratio of $t$'s log frequency to the sum of all its neighbors' log frequencies (Equation 2, where $w$ has been replaced by $n$ in the denominator, as the summation is now over all neighbors, not all words). Because $t$ will be included in the denominator, since it is a neighbor of itself, we can think of this as representing the proportion of the frequency weight of its own neighborhood that a word contributes.

$$FWNP_{DAS} = \frac{f_t}{\sum f_n} \qquad (2)$$

This compact, elegant equation (essentially a simplified variant of the R. D. Luce [1959] choice rule) simultaneously represents the core theoretical stance of NAM and provides a crucial methodological tool—studies of spoken word recognition routinely use Equation 2 to control neighborhood (or at least control the raw neighbor counts). Thus, decision unit activations are assumed to be proportional to FWNP, and human behavior is predicted to be proportional to decision unit activations, such that the higher the FWNP for a word, the faster and/or more accurately it should be recognized. The FWNP has largely been tested in the aggregate, with factorial manipulations of FWNP or number of neighbors or with regressions examining how well the FWNP predicts recognition facility for a large number of words (Luce & Pisoni, 1998), as opposed to the typical approach in testing the Cohort model—assessing priming of specific words or enumerating gating completions for specific words. In regression analyses, FWNP accounts for approximately 15% of the variance beyond the 5% accounted for by word frequency alone. We will have more to say about these competing visions of the competitor set in the next section.

Now let's consider evidence for contextual constraints on spoken word recognition. The question is whether semantic, sentential, or other contextual information interacts directly with the bottom-up mapping of sublexical information to lexical representations, or if bottom-up lexical activation is initially *autonomous*—protected from context, which is integrated at a later stage. Frauenfelder and Tyler (1987) made a useful distinction between structural and nonstructural context. Nonstructural context is like word-to-word priming; it does not cross levels of hierarchical organization. If we assume that semantic and (phonological) form representations exist at the same lexical level, finding priming of the sort we have already described does not address the autonomy issue. Experiments by Tyler, Voice, and Moss (2000) showing that high imageability facilitates recognition of words with many cohort competitors suggests that form and meaning are indeed integral (we will discuss this more in the next section). Evidence of early impact of structural context (e.g., sentence or discourse details), however, would violate bottom-up autonomy. An example of structural context comes from a study by Tanenhaus, Leiman and Seidenberg (1979; see also similar work by Swinney, 1979). They used cross-modal semantic priming, but with auditory stimuli presented in sentence contexts. Their critical items were homophones that were presented in contexts that favored one meaning (*they all rose*) or the other (*he gave her a rose*). Their first question was whether priming would be found for associates of both senses (*stand, flower*). When they presented the probe item visually at homophone offset, they found statistically equivalent priming for associates of both meanings. If they waited 250 msec, there was selective priming for the context-appropriate meaning. Tanenhaus et al. interpreted this as consistent with a mechanism where autonomous, full access to all items matching the bottom-up input is quickly followed by a process integrating the bottom-up signal with sentential context. Shillcock and Bard (1993) used more constraining contexts that strongly predicted closed-class words (e.g., *would*) over open-class homophones (e.g., *wood*) and found selective priming as early as they could look for it (partway through the homophone). This study tends to be neglected in reviews of this literature, but we shall see later that this result has been replicated and extended using newer techniques.

Interaction in the opposite direction—from words to sublexical processing—has been of great interest in spoken word recognition. Examples where lexical knowledge affects sublexical performance include the word superiority effect (Rubin, Turvey, & Van Gelder, 1976), where phonemes can be detected more quickly in the context of a word than nonword, and phoneme restoration (Samuel, 1981, 1996; Warren, 1970), where a phoneme replaced with noise appears to be filled in in a context-appropriate fashion, even having perceptual effects like those of clear phonemes, such as selective adaptation (Samuel, 1997, 2001). While such effects are consistent with the idea that there is direct feedback from words to phonemes, lexical effects on

*performance* in phoneme tasks could also arise post-perceptually. We will discuss this possibility later; for now, the important thing to note is that theories of speech perception must provide some account of these top-down effects.

The issues we have reviewed have emerged as the primary questions theories of spoken word recognition address—that is, as the boundaries of spoken word recognition theories. In particular, research in the latter half of the 20th century established a framework that assumes that phonemic input activates multiple words in parallel as a function of similarity and prior probability, and activated words compete for recognition. In the next section, we discuss how research over the last couple of decades has filled in many details about these questions, but has also begun to strain at these borders.

## The Normal Science Phase: An Emerging Consensus

Here is where this review departs from chronology to discuss the *normal science* phase of contemporary research on spoken word recognition. "Normal science" is what Kuhn (1962) calls the "puzzle-solving" or filling-in period, as (and after) a consensus on a *paradigm* emerges. To mix Kuhn and Marr, this is the consensus on Marr's (1982) computational level theory and agreement on the sorts of experimental methods and measures that provide valid evidence (the most common experimental tasks, along with their advantages and disadvantages are summarized in Table 27.2). On our view, the best way to get a sense of the current paradigm is by walking through the details of the TRACE model of speech perception and spoken word recognition (McClelland & Elman, 1986). This is not to say that TRACE *is* the consensus. However, there is substantial agreement that the *functions* TRACE provides—for example, activation of representations at multiple levels (phonemes, words), inhibition providing the means for competition among activated representations—are needed, even if there is disagreement (and occasional fractious debate) about the best ways to "wire up" those functions (e.g., What is the best similarity metric for predicting what words will be coactive? Is lexical competition better modeled by lateral inhibition between words or bottom-up inhibition from phonemes to words? Should we allow feedback between levels of representation in language processing, or does information flow only in a bottom-up direction?). Most crucially, TRACE ushered in a new level of detail in predictions about not just recognition time but also

**Table 27.2** Common Paradigms for Studying Spoken Word Recognition

| Task | Advantages | Disadvantages |
|---|---|---|
| *Lexical decision*: Nonwords (e.g., "blat") are mixed with words, and participants press a button indicating YES for words and another indicating NO for nonwords (an alternative "go/no-go" version asks participant to press a button for words and withhold a response for nonwords, or vice versa) | • Fast<br>• Commonly used | • Correct responses do not require full word recognition, but just a relative sense of familiarity or partial activation of multiple words<br>• RT on critical word stimuli is sensitive to design of nonword filler items |
| *Naming (also called Shadowing or Repetition)*: Participants hear a word and repeat it as quickly as possible (alternative: participants report what word they heard by typing it into a computer keyboard). | • Direct measure of recognition: processing entire word form is required | • Slow: Participants need more time for each trial, so they can complete fewer trials<br>• Does not guarantee deep (e.g., semantic-level) processing<br>• Accuracy requires coding the responses, which can be time consuming and ambiguous (e.g., should mispronunciations/misspellings count as correct or incorrect responses?) |
| *Semantic judgments*: Participants indicate whether some semantic property (living thing vs. artifact, something you can touch, etc.) is true of the concept named by the spoken word | • Fast<br>• Requires access to lexical semantic knowledge | • Semantic variables may complicate results (e.g., edible plants such as "tomato" are somewhat ambiguous with regard to their status as living things—when it is on the plant it is living, when it is on the plate it is not) |
| *Word-to-picture matching*: Participants indicate which of several pictures matches a spoken word. | • Fast<br>• Requires semantic access<br>• Naturalistic (does not require meta-linguistic judgments)<br>• Can be combined with eye- or hand-tracking to measure the time course of spoken word recognition | • Limited to words that refer to pictureable objects or actions<br>• Reaching movements can make RTs noisy<br>• Sensitive to number of alternatives and their similarities |
| *Priming*: Using any of the above tasks, test processing of a word when the preceding word is related on some dimension compared to when it is unrelated. Variants:<br>• Phonological (BALD—BALLS, HAND—SAND)<br>• Phonetic (BULL—VEER)<br>• Semantic (DOCTOR—NURSE)<br>• Cross-modal: prime presented auditorily, target presented visually (or vice versa, depending on which modality the researcher wants to drive initial access to lexical memory) | • Fast<br>• Sensitive<br>• Can measure time course by manipulating the relative timing of the prime and target ("interstimulus interval") | • Priming can be positive (facilitatory—related prime causes better performance) or negative (inhibitory—related prime causes worse performance), and the literature is rife with conflicting positive and negative priming effects<br>• Phonological and semantic priming are susceptible to bias and strategy (e.g., sensitive to proportion of related-prime trials; see Luce et al., 2000, for the relative susceptibility of phonological vs. phonetic priming) |

the subphonemic time course of lexical activation and competition. In this section, we will begin with a description of TRACE and the motivation for its architecture and processing components. This sets the stage for debates about the specific mechanisms a model should employ, and the advent of experimental methods that provided time course measures comparable to the time course predictions of models like TRACE. Time course modeling and measures brought about a period of intense research aimed at filling in fine-grained details in the corpus of empirical knowledge (which continues today). In the section following this one, we will argue that current debates are really a matter of fine-tuning the consensus on how one might model the agreed-upon computational theory (that phonemic input activates multiple words in parallel as a function of similarity and prior probability, and activated words compete for recognition)—especially when compared with emerging crises of empirical facts that cannot be accommodated in current theory; a harbinger of a scientific revolution, according to Kuhn (1962).

## TRACE and the Time Course of Word Recognition

### THE TRACE MODEL OF SPEECH PERCEPTION AND SPOKEN WORD RECOGNITION

Let's walk through how the TRACE model implements the core theoretical consensus (along with some debatable details). TRACE (McClelland & Elman, 1986; McClelland, 1991) was inspired by the Cohort model, but the competition dynamics of the *interactive activation* framework (McClelland & Rumelhart, 1981) were substituted for bottom-up inhibition (inhibiting words that do not include a perceived phoneme) *and* for the notion of an explicit segmentation tracking device. Recall that in Cohort, the system tracks possible completion of words given the input so far; a word boundary is detected when the input so far corresponds to a word and the following segment cannot be added to it. In TRACE, competition and segmentation are emergent properties; there is no explicit tracking of word boundaries. Figure 27.1 shows how this works. On the left, we show a conceptual schematic of the interactive activation framework as it is implemented in TRACE. "Pseudo-spectral" inputs (shown in the center of the figure) activate feature detector nodes, which activate phonemes that contain them. Phonemes send activation forward to words that contain them. Words send feedback to phonemes that they contain. Competition comes from lateral inhibition within the phoneme and word levels. Inhibition among activated units usually leads one node at each level to dominate (achieve the highest activation) for some period of time. Activations wax and wane as a function of bottom-up input, lateral inhibition, and top-down feedback, as the set of strongly activated words changes gradually over time. When a sequence of words is presented, there is nothing inherent in the model that corresponds to a discrete, "magical moment" (Balota, 1990) of word recognition for each word; instead, as the input unfolds, the lexical nodes for the presented words briefly dominate the lexical level in series.[7] To make explicit comparisons with a specific task, such as lexical decision, one must construct a linking hypothesis between the behavior of the model and measures of human performance, such as reaction times (see Magnuson, Mirman, & Harris, 2012).

The actual architecture of TRACE is more complex than the conceptual schematic suggests. A problem that any *implemented* model of spoken word recognition must grapple with is temporal order. Many preceding theories side-stepped this problem; since they were not implemented, they simply stipulated that lexical representations would be sensitive to temporal order (the Cohort Model being a notable exception). Addressing this problem is crucial and very difficult, so it is instructive to walk through how TRACE handles it. If the network were really as simple as the conceptual schematic, it would have no way of telling /bæad/ from /dæb/ or even /æbd/; all three inputs would simultaneously activate all word nodes containing those three phonemes. What TRACE does is sketched in the rightmost panel of Figure 27.1. Rather than having a single node for the word *bad*, TRACE has many, each aligned with a different point in time. The same scheme applies at the phoneme level: There are /b/ nodes aligned at successive time slices. This provides the model with phonemic and lexical memory—the "trace" behind the model's name.

Consider the input in the center of Figure 27.1. The featural code corresponding to /b/ spreads from time 0 to time 11. There are /b/ nodes aligned with every time slice. So when the input is "heard" by the model, the input at slice 1 is fed to feature nodes aligned with slice 1, then the input at slice 2 is fed to aligned feature nodes, and so on. Feature nodes send activation forward to phoneme nodes aligned with them. Phoneme nodes in turn send activation forward to word nodes aligned with them. In Figure 27.1, connections between /b/ nodes at the right edge of the figure to a *bad* node are shown. Those

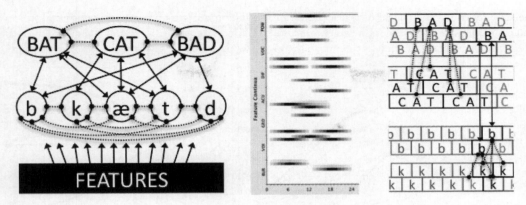

**Figure 27.1** The TRACE Model. (*Left*) Conceptual schematic showing feedforward connections from features to phonemes and phonemes to words, feedback from words to phonemes, and lateral inhibition (dashed "bulb" connectors) within phoneme and lexical levels. (*Middle*) TRACE input for the word "bat," showing how activations ramp up at different levels of different features for phonemes, and how phonemes overlap in time. (*Right*) More detailed schematic of the actual design of phoneme and lexical levels in TRACE. Each phoneme node is replicated at multiple time steps, allowing TRACE to "spatialize" time, such that independent nodes can detect the presence of the same or different phonemes at different points in time. The same scheme is used at the word level. Only the phoneme-word connections for one of the last "BAD" word nodes from /b/ are shown. Only the lateral inhibition connections from those /b/ nodes to the /k/ nodes they would inhibit are shown (nodes only inhibit nodes with which they overlap in time). Only the lexical lateral inhibition nodes between one highlighted BAD node and the CAT nodes with which it overlaps in time are shown.

/b/ nodes also have (mutually) inhibitory links with all other phoneme nodes *that overlap with them in time*. This last point is crucial, as it allows multiple phoneme nodes to become highly active; that is, a series of nodes that do not overlap in time can become highly activated since they do not inhibit each other. This allows the model to robustly represent temporal order, since each phoneme is associated not just with a featural code, but with that featural code linked to a particular point in time. For a word node to get robustly activated, the correct temporal series of phonemes must be activated. Just as this scheme allows a series of phonemes to become strongly activated, it also allows TRACE to "recognize" a series of words; nodes aligned with the points in time where the words occurred get activated and do not interfere with earlier and later words with which they do not overlap in time.

A common way for TRACE's behavior to be quantified is with a time course plot, as in Figure 27.2, where we use an example that illustrates how TRACE handles embedded word effects and differences it predicts in the time course of biases for short versus long words. On the left, the input is the word *artist*; on the right, it is *art*. We track activations of several words activated by this input. Note that there is an early short-word advantage apparent in both panels. We also see a late advantage for long words: Note how dramatically higher the activation for *artist* on the left becomes compared to that for *art* on the right. Finally, note as well that TRACE

is handling the embedded word problem—*artist* eventually wins the competition on the left despite the fact that the entire patterns corresponding to *are* and *art* have been encountered. The early short-word advantage and late long-word advantage are particularly interesting because Pitt and Samuel (2006) reported evidence for both.

Let's walk through how TRACE does this. The easiest piece of this to understand is the basis for the late advantage for long words: Long words simply accrue more bottom-up activation than short words—the more phonemes there are in a word, the more feedforward activation it will receive. There is a flip side to this advantage, though: Because word nodes receive inhibition from word nodes with which they overlap in time, longer words have more "inhibition sites" than shorter words (that is, they simply overlap temporally with more word nodes because they extend further in time), which puts them at a disadvantage compared to shorter words. Even the tiny bit of bottom-up activation that nodes send when they do not have strong similarity to the input can have a large effect.[8] In the case of embeddings, the fact that *artist* receives more bottom-up input allows it to eventually overcome the activations of embedded words because it can send them more inhibition than they can send to it.

The aspect of TRACE that is conceptually difficult is understanding where the activations in a time course plot come from. This is illustrated in the upper panels of Figure 27.3, which also illustrates

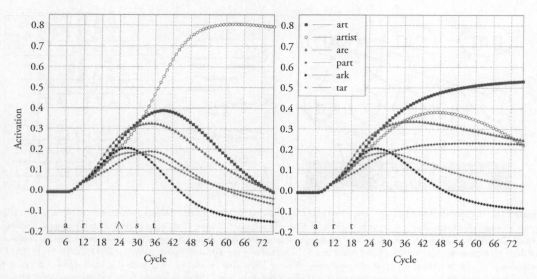

**Figure 27.2** Embedded word and word length effects in TRACE. TRACE phonemic inputs are shown in the lower left of each panel, aligned with the cycle at which they were presented. TRACE's handling of embedded words can be seen on the left, where *artist* wins out over even the fully embedded word, *art*. The early short-word bias can also be seen on the left, where the activations of *art* and *are* rise more quickly than that of *artist*. This can also be seen by comparing how quickly *artist* rises in the left panel (hitting activation of 0.3 at cycle 30) and how quickly *art* rises in the right panel (hitting 0.3 around cycle 27). The late advantage for long words can be seen in comparing the peak target activations on the left and right.

what word "segmentation" looks like in TRACE. The figure shows what happens as the series of words *boy pats dog* (/buipatsdag/) has been presented to the network. The "floating" phonemes, for example, have a specific "temporal alignment"—a slice of the model's memory "trace." As time goes by, phonemes (and words) at particular alignments become more or less active as a function of their current and earlier bottom-up support, top-down support (lexical feedback to phonemes), and inhibition from other nodes at the same level. You can also see that the network is successfully inhibiting the word, *pat*, which is embedded in *pats*, and the word *stack*, which is highly similar to the string of phonemes straddling the second word boundary, /sdag/. The bottom panel of Figure 27.3 shows the corresponding lexical time course plot, where the maximally active nodes for a set of words of interest are plotted.

**THE TIME COURSE OF COMPETITION**

The competition dynamics of TRACE also shed light on the competitor set disagreements between the Cohort and Neighborhood Activation models (reviewed earlier). Cohort predicts that words overlapping at onset will activate one another, even if they are of different length, and that activation of words mismatching at onset will be negligible, even if overall (global) similarity is high. NAM ignores

onsets and instead posits that global similarity is what matters, predicting that words will compete if they differ by no more than one phoneme. TRACE predicts something in between the two and offers a resolution to this debate. The left panel of Figure 27.4 shows simulations from Allopenna, Magnuson, and Tanenahus (1998), who examined what TRACE predicts for a target word, *beaker*; a cohort competitor, *beetle*; a rhyme, *speaker*; and an unrelated word, *carriage* (the figure actually averages over several item sets, and an analog to the carrier phrase, "click on the . . .," was presented prior to the target word; also, to conform to the way Allopenna et al. presented simulations, activations less than zero are plotted as zero). As the input unfolds, the target and cohort activate together since they are consistent with the bottom-up input, /bi/. Once the input begins to favor the target (once the /k/ is presented for *beaker*), the activation of cohort items begins to drop off both because of lesser bottom-up support but also because the target is able to inhibit them. Simultaneously, the input has become more similar to the rhyme (*speaker*), and it becomes much more activated than the unrelated comparison item. However, its peak activation remains substantially below that of cohort items—despite its overall greater similarity to the input (in the example set, the rhyme overlaps in four phonemes with the target, but the cohort only overlaps in two). This is

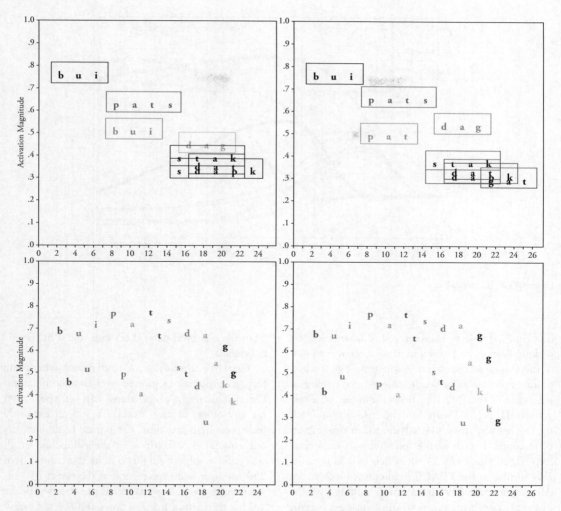

**Figure 27.3a** Activations over time in TRACE. (*Left*) Snapshots of phoneme (*middle*) and word (*top*) activations just as the /g/ in /buipatsdag/ ("boy pats dog"; note that we are transcribing with phonemes from TRACE's limited inventory rather than accurate English phonemic transcriptions) has been presented (cycle 72, corresponding to temporal alignment 24). (*Right*) Snapshots slightly later (cycle 78, alignment 26). Note the multiple /b/ activations at the left side of the phoneme plots. These show the activations of /b/ nodes aligned with different time slices. The word activations make clear that there is not a magical moment of word recognition in TRACE; rather, there is flux in the relative activation of word units aligned with different portions of the temporal memory "trace." Note, for example, how the DOG (/dag/) node emerges as the late time course "winner" over just the few time steps between the left and right graphs. The plots also illustrate that TRACE solves the lexical embedding problem (PATS wins over PAT). The bottom panel presents a conventional activation time-course plot. Here, each word is represented by the activation of one node—the node for that word that had the highest activation. Note, for example, that activation of *boy* persists, overlapping with high activation of the following words. This does not mean that the model is simulating "hearing" these simultaneously. In the top panel, we can see that the *boy* node we are tracking is aligned with temporal slice 2, which corresponds to processing cycle 6, while the maximally activated (and therefore tracked) node for *pats* aligns with temporal slice 8/processing cycle 24, and the tracked node for *dog* is at slice 16/cycle 48. This illustrates how TRACE maintains an active memory of what words have been presented over time; word activations tracked here are linked to specific instants in memory, such that the tracked activation for *boy* indicates not just that *boy* is active, but that it occurred at a specific time (position, really) in memory. Plots were generated using jTRACE (Strauss, Harris, & Magnuson, 2007).

because it is inhibited not just by the already-activated target but also by the cohort items. Thus, the "head start" that the onset overlap affords to cohort items turns into a significant activation advantage compared to rhymes. But how do these time course predictions correspond to human performance?

The other panels of Figure 27.4 illustrate how Allopenna et al. tested these predictions, using the then new "visual world paradigm" (Tanenhaus, Spivey-Knowlton, Eberhard, & Sedivy, 1995.)[9] Subjects saw displays like the one in the center panel (there were also filler trials where all items were

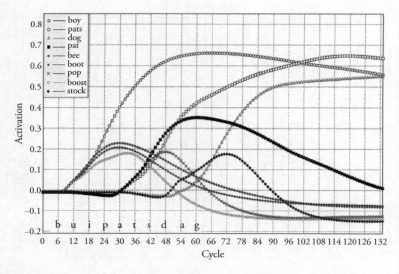

**Figure 27.3b** (*Continued*)

unrelated). Subjects heard a verbal instruction to pick up one of the items and place it relative to one of the shapes on the screen. Allopenna et al. tracked point of gaze using a head-mounted eye tracker as subjects did this. Starting from the onset of a target word, such as *beaker* in the instruction "pick up the beaker," they plotted the mean proportion of fixations to each of the four items at each time step (right panel, Fig. 27.4), which looked remarkably similar to the TRACE predictions (indeed, see Allopenna et al., 1998 for a simple linking hypothesis that transforms raw activations using a variant of the R. D. Luce [1959] choice rule into response probabilities that are virtually indistinguishable

from the observed data). Let's examine some essential details.

First, it's important to understand where the fixation proportions plotted over time come from. On a single trial, "proportions" can only be 1 or 0 for any object at any instant—a subject can only fixate one item at a time. On typical trials, subjects only made ~1.5 fixations in the Allopenna et al. study. So a subject might look at the cohort item 250 ms after word onset, and at the target 350 ms after word onset. For that trial, the data would be 1.0 for the central fixation cross and 0.0 for everything else from word onset to 250 ms, 1.0 for the cohort and 0.0 for everything else from 250–350

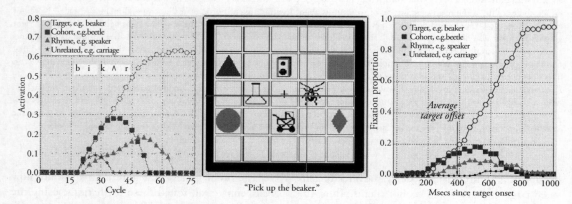

**Figure 27.4** (*Left*) Relative activation of cohort (onset) and rhyme competitors in TRACE. (Adapted from Allopenna et al., 1998.) (*Center*) Sample stimulus display and (spoken) instruction from Allopenna et al. (1998). (*Right*) Proportions of fixations over time to each item of interest. Proportions do not sum to 1.0 because fixations outside the four items of interest (e.g., to the central fixation cross) are not plotted.

ms, and 1.0 for the target and 0.0 for everything else from 350 ms until the end of the trial. Trials for each condition are averaged within participants, and then participant means are averaged to arrive at plots like the one in Figure 27.4. Then, the same sorts of statistical approaches that are used for other kinds of psychological data can be applied (e.g., ANOVA; but see Barr, 2008 and Mirman, Dixon, & Magnuson, 2008, for alternative approaches explicitly designed for assessing change over time). Second, when we look at the time course plots, we can see that changes in mean fixation proportions tended to lag behind phonetic details by about 200 ms. Given that it takes approximately 150 ms to plan and launch an eye movement to a point of light in a darkened room (Fischer, 1992; Matin, Shao, & Boff, 1993; Saslow, 1967) and that inter-saccade intervals are typically in the 200–300 ms range in similar tasks, such as visual search (Viviani, 1990), this lag was nearly as short as could theoretically be.[10] Third, proportions of eye movements over time map onto phonetic similarity over time: Target and cohort looks increased in the early time course, and as the bottom-up input favored the target, fixation proportions to the cohort diminished. This is consistent with results from the gating task. Simultaneously, however, the input had become more similar to the rhyme, and the rhyme fixation proportion eventually exceeded that for the unrelated baseline item. Recall that rhymes are never offered as completions in the gating task, nor are they predicted to compete in the Cohort Model. Why might rhyme effects emerge in this task?

One possibility is that presenting rhymes in the visual display primes them. Allopenna et al., though, pointed out that fixation proportions map onto phonetic similarity over time—rhymes are not fixated until there is phonetic overlap between them and the input. However, this does not rule out priming; it could be that picture priming boosts the resting level of the rhyme's lexical representation. Allopenna et al. also provided an empirical case for differences between tasks. In a second experiment, they combined the gating task with the visual world task. They presented gated auditory inputs with the same visual displays. Rhyme effects disappeared. Allopenna et al. (1998) argued that this demonstrated that the gating task emphasizes word onsets, leading to overactivation of onset competitors compared to what happens when fluent speech is presented. A later study explicitly tested effects of displaying competitor pictures empirically and with computational modeling (Dahan, Magnuson,

Tanenhaus, & Hogan, 2001), and the results suggested that displaying a competitor emphasizes competition effects slightly—but likely because the possibility of fixating the competitor when it is on the screen better *reveals* competition rather than amplifying it. Competition effects persisted when competitors were not displayed. Magnuson, Dixon, Tanenhaus, and Aslin (2007) found effects of frequency-weighted competitor counts (neighborhood and cohort densities, discussed later) even when no competitors were displayed at all.

Now with strong evidence that TRACE simulations of cohort and rhyme effects are largely borne out in time course measures with human subjects, let's return to the debate over the nature of the competitor set. Recall that many results support the Cohort Model (e.g., the absence of evidence for rhyme activation from cross-modal semantic priming), while others support NAM (the variance for recognition and naming data accounted for by the frequency-weighted neighborhood probability metric that includes many offset competitors). Think about what must happen for priming to be detected in the cross-modal semantic priming paradigm. A target like *beaker* must activate a competitor like *beetle* strongly enough that activation spreads to the competitor's semantic associates (like *insect*). If rhymes are activated later and less strongly than cohorts, less activation will spread to their semantic associates, making it difficult to detect priming. By combining the gating and visual world paradigm, Allopenna et al.'s (1998) second experiment suggests that the failure to find evidence of rhyme activation in gating may be an artifact of repeated presentation of onsets in gating, which boosts activation of onset competitors. Thus, it appears that including items that mismatch at onset in the competitor set, as in the NAM, is justified.

However, the NAM is clearly incorrect in excluding onset competitors that mismatch in multiple phonemes (e.g., it would exclude *beetle* from *beaker* neighborhood), and in treating neighbors as equivalent competitors no matter where (when) they differ from a target; clearly, onset competitors need to be weighted more heavily. A study by Magnuson et al. (2007) suggests that the temporal distribution of phonetic similarity has complex impacts on the time course of lexical activation and competition that may be difficult to formalize in a revised NAM metric. Magnuson et al. (2007) attempted to examine the relative contributions of cohort and neighbor definitions by factorially manipulating word frequency, frequency-weighted neighborhood probability, and frequency-weighted cohort probability. That is, they tested words that were high or low frequency, had low or high neighborhood probability, and low or high cohort probability. Neighborhood probability was estimated by the ratio of a word's log frequency to the summed log frequency of all its neighbors using the NAM 1-phoneme difference definition. Cohort probability was estimated the same way, with cohorts defined as words overlapping in at least the first two phonemes, with no limit on how many subsequent phonemes could differ. Magnuson et al. used the visual world paradigm, presenting target pictures among pictures of three phonologically and semantically unrelated items. They found clear effects of word frequency (high-frequency targets were fixated more quickly than low-frequency targets) and cohort density (low-cohort targets were fixated more quickly than high-cohort targets). The results for neighborhood were more complex. There was an unexpected *early* advantage for high-neighborhood density items, followed by the expected low-neighborhood advantage. This led Magnuson et al. to more carefully examine the makeup of their items' neighborhoods. Although the low- and high-neighborhood items were matched on cohort *density* (that is, the ratio of the target's frequency to the summed frequencies of its cohorts), it turned out that a larger proportion of low-neighborhood items' neighbors were also cohorts. This explained the early disadvantage for low-neighborhood items: Their neighborhoods were "front-loaded." If we consider phonetic overlap between targets and competitors phoneme-by-phoneme, the point of greatest phonetic overlap—and therefore greatest moment of competition—in the low neighborhoods was shifted toward word onset.

## THE TIME COURSE OF WORD FREQUENCY EFFECTS

Other experiments comparing the predictions of the TRACE model with time course estimates from the visual world paradigm have revealed that the time course predictions of TRACE are surprisingly robust and very much illustrate the "puzzle solving" of normal science. One example is the temporal locus of frequency effects. Word frequency (frequency of usage) has long been known to influence word recognition, with higher frequency associated with faster and/or more accurate recognition performance (e.g., Howes & Solomon, 1951; Luce & Pisoni, 1998; Marslen-Wilson, 1987). Some cross-modal priming studies suggested that frequency seemed to have an early, transient effect

(Marslen-Wilson, 1987; Zwitserlood, 1989). For example, in presenting the word *captain*, one can test for priming of semantic associates of *captain* and its lower frequency onset competitor, *captive*. Stronger priming is found for visually presented associates of higher frequency items (for this example, more priming is found for *ship* than *guard*), but only when the visual probe is presented as the word is being heard. McQueen (1991) also found larger frequency effects in fast responses in a phoneme decision task than in slow responses—again, suggesting frequency has an early influence. Connine, Titone, and Wang (1993) employed an ingenious method for assessing temporal locus from single-response method. They used the Fox Effect (Fox, 1984), in which participants identify the initial consonant of tokens drawn from a continuum between two words (e.g., *best-pest*). Fox found that if one endpoint has higher frequency, responses shift in its favor. Connine et al. used this method but manipulated whether a block of trials was biased toward high-frequency words, low-frequency words, or was balanced (mixed). In the low-frequency list, for example, ambiguous tokens from low-high frequency pairs (e.g., *pest-best*) were presented, as was the low-frequency endpoint (e.g., *pest*). The prediction was that if frequency were an integral part of the initial activation and perception of a word, this "extrinsic" frequency manipulation (that is, of the probability of low- or high-frequency words being heard) should not matter, and results should be similar whether items were blocked by frequency or mixed. However, they found that extrinsic frequency did matter—so much so that subjects exhibited a bias for low-frequency responses in low-frequency blocks. Their interpretation was that for subjects to be able to modulate attention to word frequency as a function of their extrinsic frequency manipulation, frequency must apply postperceptually, as a decision-stage bias.

Dahan, Magnuson, and Tanenhaus (2001) explored this issue further by testing three implementations of frequency in the TRACE model: (1) making the resting-level activations of words proportional to word frequency, so that a higher frequency word would have a permanent head start; (2) making phoneme-word connections proportional to word frequency (so that the connection from /b/ to *bed* would be stronger than the connection from /b/ to *bench*), consistent with the idea that experience should tune connection strengths; and (3) as a postperceptual effect, where frequency is suddenly applied late in the processing of a word. The resting-level implementation predicts a constant frequency advantage that diminishes as a word is heard and bottom-up input disambiguates between competitors. The postperceptual bias predicts exactly the same thing, except with no frequency effect at all until the "magical moment" where frequency is applied, at which point it becomes identical to the resting-level simulation. The connection strength simulation predicts a constant effect of frequency, but one that is "gated" by the bottom-up input. That is, the connection strength basis for the frequency effect is the multiplication of the bottom-up signal strength by the frequency-weighted connection. When input is weak, the frequency difference is small. As the input becomes stronger, the difference between low- and high-frequency word units becomes much more robust. Then, as with the other implementations, the frequency effect declines as the bottom-up input disambiguates between high- and low-frequency alternatives. When Dahan and colleagues tested these predictions using the visual world paradigm, they found that fixation proportions over time were best modeled by the connection strength implementation: A constant effect of frequency was apparent in the fixation proportions, but it was subtle near word onset, became robust in response to the ambiguous portion of a word (compatible with two alternatives differing in frequency, e.g., *be-* with the alternatives *bed* and *bench*), and then disappeared once the full word had been heard.

As we mentioned before, our focus on the TRACE model is just to illustrate functions that most current theories regard as necessary—which are the functions we have reviewed thus far. These are as follows: a degree of phonetic sensitivity in input representations (/p/ should be more similar to /b/ than to /s/ or /a/), a sublexical level of representation mediating the signal-lexical mapping, sensitivity to prior probability at the word level (frequency), the ability to segment a series of words without explicit word boundary markers, and the ability to handle embedded words (the latter two details are achieved through lateral inhibition at the word level, and through the reduplication of phoneme and word units over time). Next, let's consider details where there continues to be debate.

## Points of Disagreement
### LATERAL INHIBITION
First, not all models agree that lateral inhibition at the phoneme level is required. The Cohort Model approach favors bottom-up inhibition, for

example (Marslen-Wilson & Warren, 1994), and at least one study has argued that inhibition among phoneme units eliminates sensitivity to phonetic detail too quickly to account for behavioral recovery from "lexical garden-paths" (McMurray, Tanenhaus, & Aslin, 2009). Second, it is not clear that direct lateral inhibition between units is the best way to capture competitive dynamics. Gaskell and Marslen-Wilson (1997, 2002) proposed that "emergent inhibition" among overlapping distributed lexical-semantic representations provides a better account (we discuss this account in more detail later).

### WORD SEGMENTATION
Even models that agree that lateral inhibition is required at the word level do not buy into the TRACE strategy of reduplicating phoneme and word units to solve the segmentation problem. The Shortlist Model (Norris, 1994) rejects both unit reduplication and feedback. Instead, Shortlist proposes that as words are activated by their bottom-up fit to spoken input, "shortlists" of lateral inhibition networks are created where activated words compete for recognition. This does away with the need for reduplicated units with massive numbers of feedforward, feedback, and lateral inhibition connections (Hannagan, Magnuson, & Grainger, 2012, estimate that a TRACE implementation with a realistically sized lexicon of 20,000 words and a 2-second memory trace would require about 4 million nodes and 80 billion connections). However, Shortlist requires that there be an as-yet unimplemented mechanism that could wire up the needed networks continuously as speech is heard, as well as an as-yet-unimplemented "lookup" network for finding shortlists reduplicated at each phoneme in the input, making the actual savings in terms of numbers of units and connections somewhat unclear. One particularly intriguing aspect of Shortlist is the use of stress information and the *possible-word constraint* (pressure on the model to arrive at parses that result in only a series of words, without leaving residual phonemes that could not form a word according to the phonotactics of English; for example, if *apple* were recognized on hearing *fapple*, this would leave *f* as "residue" that could not form a word, and indeed, listeners have more trouble noticing they have heard *apple* in that case than on hearing an item like *vuffapple*, where parsing *apple* leaves a word-like remainder, *vuff*; Norris, McQueen, Cutler, & Butterfield, 1997).

## INTERACTIVITY

There is disagreement about the need for lexical-sublexical feedback, which aficionados of spoken word recognition will recognize as one of the most visible debates in the field. Such feedback is a common feature of interactive activation models, and it is posited to have two beneficial properties: (1) it provides an implicit implementation of probabilistic phonotactics, with common sequences of phonemes receiving boosted activation via resonance from the many words that contain them[11]; and (2) it makes the model robust against noise, whether external (literal noise in the case of speech) or internal. Note that feedback also crucially provides an explanation for top-down effects on speech perception, but these are side effects of a mechanism that make the model more robust.

Norris, McQueen, and Cutler (2000) marshaled a comprehensive theoretical and empirical case against the need for feedback in word recognition. They claimed that logically, feedback could not improve recognition beyond the best performance possible with well-tuned feedforward connections, and that feedback would override bottom-up input to cause hallucinations. They then went on to demonstrate that the majority of top-down effects could be simulated without feedback in a new extension of the Shortlist model that they dubbed *Merge*. In Merge, phonemes feed to lexical nodes, and there is no lexical-phonemic feedback. To simulate, for example, lexical effects on phoneme decisions, Merge posits a set of *postlexical* phoneme decision units that receive input directly from phoneme input nodes and directly from lexical nodes. This allows phonemic and lexical information to be merged—thus accounting for lexical effects on phoneme decisions—but postperceptually, and without contaminating phonemic processing nodes with top-down input (i.e., avoiding hallucinations).

The argument that feedback does not do anything useful in TRACE was based on simulations by Frauenfelder and Peeters (1998) that tested a set of 21 words selected for other simulations. When this analysis was extended to about 900 words, nearly 75% of words were recognized more quickly with feedback on than off (Magnuson, Strauss, & Harris, 2005). Furthermore, Magnuson et al. (2005) tested the performance of the model as noise was added (recall that a primary motivation for feedback is protecting the model against noise effects) and found that feedback substantially preserved accuracy.

The hallucination argument is surprising in light of Figure 7 of the original TRACE paper (McClelland & Elman, 1986), which clearly shows that lexical feedback *modulates* phonemic activation but does not overwhelm bottom-up input (and so, for an input like *shigarette*, lexical feedback would boost activation of /s/, but /ʃ/ would still be much more active than /s/). Mirman, McClelland, and Holt (2005) explored this issue more thoroughly, confirming that lexical feedback in TRACE could not overwhelm bottom-up input, but it could delay recognition of lexically inconsistent phonemes in some cases. Their behavioral experiments then confirmed that human listeners do indeed exhibit lexically induced delays in phoneme recognition in precisely the contexts predicted by TRACE. Furthermore, Mirman, Bolger, Khaitan, and McClelland (in press) demonstrated that it is trivially easy to balance feedforward and feedback gain to preclude hallucination, and they extended earlier arguments by Movellan and McClelland (2001) that interactive models such as TRACE implement optimal perceptual inference.

Most damaging for the Merge account, there appear to be "knock-on" or "indirect" effects of lexical activation on sublexical processing, which are only possible if lexical information is feeding back directly to sublexical levels during online processing. The first demonstration of such effects was lexically mediated compensation for coarticulation (Elman & McClelland, 1988; see also Magnuson, McMurray, Tanenhaus, & Aslin, 2003a; Samuel & Pitt, 2003), which has been disputed (McQueen, Jesse, & Norris, 2009[12]; Pitt & McQueen, 1998; see also the exchange between McQueen, 2003, and Magnuson, McMurray, Tanenhaus, & Aslin, 2003b). However, there are at least two other such indirect effects: lexically induced selective adaptation (Samuel, 1997, 2001) and lexically guided tuning of speech perception (Norris, McQueen, & Cutler, 2003; for a review see Samuel & Kraljic, 2009). The latter of these is particularly important because it is less controversial (both camps agree it requires feedback, but they debate when feedback happens; Norris et al. argue that the learning signal is somehow stored in memory and applied later—"feedback for learning" rather than the online feedback in TRACE) and has opened new avenues for investigating the representation of speech sounds and the interplay between lexical and sublexical representations (more on this later).

For more detailed discussion of interactivity in speech perception and other cognitive and perceptual domains, see McClelland, Mirman, and Holt (2006), the exchange between McQueen, Norris, and Cutler (2006) and Mirman, McCelland, and Holt (2006), Mirman (2008), and Mirman et al. (in press). While our position on this topic is likely clear, we think it is fair to say that the preponderance of evidence supports interactive processing as a central principle across cognitive and perceptual domains, including spoken word recognition and speech perception. Convincing all parties will likely take substantially more empirical and computational work.

## Moving Beyond the Limitations of the TRACE Model

It is essential that we keep TRACE's limitations in mind. TRACE achieves deep and broad coverage only of sound form recognition—not meaning—and it is a "hand-wired" model with fixed parameters set by the experimenter. Given that the goal of spoken word recognition is to support perception of a speaker's message, the absence of semantics and connections to sentence processing in TRACE and nearly all other models of spoken word recognition is a serious gap. And while an accurate model of average adult performance in word recognition is an invaluable tool, it can only be a waypoint in the quest to understand language comprehension, which eventually must include an account of development.

A handful of efforts have been made at addressing spoken word recognition in a developmental context with models of word learning using simple recurrent networks (Christiansen, Allen, & Seidenberg, 1998; Gaskell & Marslen-Wilson, 1997, 1999; Magnuson, Tanenhaus, Aslin, & Dahan, 2003). Each of these has modeled some important aspects of word learning and word recognition, but the Gaskell and Marslen-Wilson *Distributed Cohort Model* stands out for tackling form and meaning simultaneously. The Distributed Cohort Model simulates several aspects of spoken word recognition (largely consistent with the earlier Cohort Model) and leads to some new puzzles for models of spoken word recognition to grapple with that would have been difficult to intuit without a working model that simultaneously activates form and meaning. For example, in the midst of phonological competition (e.g., between *captain* and *captive* when just the /kæpt/ portion has been heard), semantic representations will be in a rather odd state: a blend of the semantic features of the items in the phonologically activated competitor set. This has the potential to interact with phonological competition and to provide insights into how context might influence form recognition.

This is an important consideration, as during the current normal science phase of spoken word recognition research, a handful of visual world paradigm studies on semantic competition and contextual constraints have appeared that are at odds with the older research we reviewed earlier—and with each other. First, consider evidence of semantic competition. At the coarsest level, visual world studies show that semantic competitors include words that are members of the same semantic category (e.g., *piano—trumpet*, Huettig & Altmann, 2005), semantic associates (e.g., *ham—eggs*, Yee & Sedivy, 2006), and concepts that frequently co-occur in situations or events (e.g., *balloon—clown*, Mirman & Graziano, 2011). Just as greater phonological similarity produces stronger phonological competition, greater semantic similarity produces more semantic competition (Mirman & Magnuson, 2009). Importantly, these competition effects are truly "semantic" in nature—simple lexical co-occurrence is not sufficient to cause the effect: When hearing *lettuce*, there is no evidence of activation of *iceberg*, even though the two words frequently co-occur (Yee, Overton, & Thompson-Schill, 2009). A concern with studying semantically related items in the visual world paradigm is that competition may be induced just by presenting pictures of related items. A follow-up study conducted by Yee and Sedivy (2006) addresses this possibility. Again, they found semantic competition effects that resembled (in terms of timing and magnitude) the phonological competition effects seen in Figure 27.4. For example, as subjects heard *lock*, they were significantly more likely to fixate a picture of a *key* than an unrelated item. In a second experiment, they tested whether this could be due just to picture priming by looking for phonologically mediated semantic activation. Instead of using *lock* as the target, they used *logs*. The logic was that as the participant hears *logs*, *lock* should be activated by phonological similarity, and then should spread activation to *key* via semantic associations. This is just what they found.[13]

Semantic competition can be driven by specific semantic features. For example, there is partial activation of objects that are similar in shape (e.g., *rope—snake*, Dahan & Tanenhaus, 2005; Yee, Huffstetler, & Thompson-Schill, 2011), motor actions (e.g., *piano—typewriter*, Lee, Middleton, Mirman, Kalenine, & Buxbaum, in press; Myung, Blumstein, & Sedivy, 2006), or function (e.g., *broom—sponge*, Kalenine, Mirman, Middeton, & Buxbaum, in press; Yee et al., 2011). In addition, there appears to be a time course to semantic feature activation: Kalenine et al. found that features shared by objects that are used together (e.g., *broom—dustpan*) are activated faster than general function features (e.g., *broom—sponge*), Lee et al. found that structural action features are activated faster than functional action features (i.e., "grasp" features faster than "use" features), and shape features may be activated faster than function features (Yee et al., 2011).

The fact that people look to items with only tangential connection to the bottom-up input presents us with yet another puzzle when we consider visual world studies looking at sentential and other constraints, which suggest that lexical competition can be flexibly restricted. Dahan and Tanenhaus (2004) used the visual world and found that sentential contexts in Dutch like "never before climbed a..." led to a strong and even anticipatory advantage for the Dutch word for *goat* (*bok*) compared to a phonological competitor (*bot*, Dutch for *bone*). A manipulation of the speech file favoring *bot* was able to modulate the result, demonstrating the online interplay between sentential constraints and details of the speech signal. Chambers, Tanenhaus, and Magnuson (2004) had subjects follow instructions to interact with real objects. When subjects were told to pick up an *egg* and there were two eggs available—one in the shell and a liquid one that had been cracked into a bowl—subjects looked at both and needed clarification to proceed. But if the instruction were to *pour the egg*, subjects did not even look at the unpourable egg still in the shell (similar results were found as a function of the affordances of implements; subjects holding a hook restricted attention to "hookable" objects when they were told to pick up some object!). Magnuson, Tanenhaus, and Aslin (2008) used an artificial lexicon paradigm to implement a stronger version of the Tanenhaus et al. (1979) and Shillcock and Bard (1993) experiments we reviewed earlier and found that strong form-class expectations based on the pragmatics of visual displays (whether bare noun reference would suffice, or whether an adjective was required for unambiguous reference) were able to wipe out cross-form class competition (phonologically similar nouns and adjectives did not compete with each other). Similarly, pragmatic expectations about which objects will be referred to by a speaker appear to influence lexical activation (Barr, 2008; Hanna, Tanenhaus, & Trueswell, 2003). The puzzle here is that on the one hand, the semantic competition effects suggest promiscuous, automatic spreading of activation over pathways sensitive to phonological

and semantic relatedness, but at the same time, strong sentential and pragmatic constraints seem able to prevent activation of individual items or even classes of items. At first blush, the semantic effects appear to be a case of facilitation, but the sentential/pragmatic constraint effects appear to be inhibition. It may be that both kinds of findings have to do with facilitation; sentential/pragmatic constraints may just boost activation of compatible items (see footnote 12). However, it is difficult to intuit how such mechanisms would operate without implementing them in a simulation model, and it appears that progress on this front will require implemented models.

Similar findings are emerging at the interface of words and sentences. There is growing evidence that words activate in an anticipatory fashion based on context and inferences about what will be heard from properties of animate and inanimate objects depicted in a visual scene (e.g., Altmann & Kamide, 1999; see Altmann & Mirkovic, 2009, for a review, and Kukona, Fang, Aicher, Chen, & Magnuson, 2011, for details about the time course of sentential and lexical-thematic constraints). As with the priming literature, understanding whether such mechanisms are driven primarily by facilitation or inhibition, and how lexical and sentential constraints interact, will require implemented models.

On our view, we are in the thick of the normal science phase of research on spoken word recognition. The field finds itself with a rough consensus about the data that need to be explained, the computational theory of the input-output mapping, and the essential functions the mechanisms of spoken word recognition must include. There is vastly more agreement than disagreement about these matters. However, a closer look at the data we have just reviewed reveals some discomfiting incongruencies between the empirical findings and our current models. First, no current model can accommodate *all* of the results we have just reviewed; TRACE (McClelland & Elman, 1986) simulates a surprisingly broad and deep array of form recognition phenomena at a fine-grained time scale, but it cannot address meaning. The Distributed Cohort Model (Gaskell & Marslen-Wilson, 1997, 1999) is a learning model that simulates a combination of form and meaning phenomena and reveals interesting problems that emerge when such representations interact. However, it is unknown whether that model can be extended to the range of phenomena TRACE simulates. Furthermore, there are some results that extant models cannot accommodate.

One simple example is priming, whether phonological, phonetic, or semantic. Priming seems like it should be easy to accommodate in cognitive psychological models of language processing; it is a basic, long-standing phenomenon that has motivated and constrained theories in many cognitive domains—how could priming be incompatible with current theories of spoken word recognition? All the same, most current theories of spoken word recognition cannot accommodate it (we will discuss the one counterexample, Goldinger [1998], later). Claims that priming effects can be modeled by connectionist models of spoken word recognition (Luce et al., 2000) typically boil down to the fact that simultaneous activations of prime, probe, and baseline items (e.g., *veer, bull, soft,* where *veer* primes *bull* due to high phonetic similarity at each phoneme) within the model show a pattern of some sort of connection (e.g., simply that the prime and probe are both active). What current simulation models are incapable of is showing priming like that of human listeners, where the prime has a postive or negative impact on *subsequent* processing of the probe. This may not seem like a crucial example, but it illustrates the fact that our theories and models may do an even worse job of accounting for empirical facts than we realize.

This leaves us with a consensus but without a unified model. Instead, we have separate microtheories of form and meaning, activation and priming, and so on, that nonetheless appear to be compatible with one another in broad strokes because each is consistent with general principles of cognitive psychology. On top of these gaps, though, there are more troubling anomalies looming—results that seem truly incompatible with current theories and that may require a new theoretical formulation.

## Waiting for the Revolution

The gaps we have just reviewed are minor in comparison to a growing set of results that are truly incommensurate with current theories. Kuhn (1962) argues that scientific revolutions, or paradigm shifts, are triggered by the accrual of so many anomalous results that a dominant paradigm cannot continue in the normal science mode of incorporating more and more fine-grained details into an existing theoretical framework. Normal science can withstand a number of anomalies; they can be ignored, treated as curiosities, or so nearly compatible with current theory that integration seems imminent. Eventually, though, so many anomalies accrue that a tipping point is reached. It would appear that we are nearing this point in spoken word recognition. In this section we present a selective review of the most pressing anomalies.

### Surface Details in the Speech Signal

We began this chapter with a discussion of the simplifying assumption that the input to spoken word recognition can be temporarily assumed to be a string of phonemes output by a speech perception mechanism. Such simplifying assumptions are common throughout science and allow progress at multiple levels of analysis, rather than a purely bottom-up approach that does not progress until all fundamental problems are cracked. However, temporary simplifying assumptions can take on the functional status of true theoretical assumptions and hide constraints—ironically becoming complicating assumptions (Magnuson, 2008). Let's consider how the phonemic input assumption has done just that.

A fundamental finding in speech perception is the categorical perception of many speech sounds (Liberman, Harris, Hoffman, & Griffith, 1957). There tends to be a sharp boundary between phonemic categories, such that a change in a critical dimension (e.g., voice onset time) is difficult to detect within a category, but change of the same magnitude that straddles the category boundary is obvious. However, it has been known for a long time that human speech perception *is* sensitive to within-category variation (e.g., Pisoni & Tash, 1974) and that that sensitivity can be observed in spoken word recognition (Andruski, Blumstein, & Burton, 1994; Marslen-Wilson & Warren, 1994). Studies using the visual world paradigm have demonstrated this sensitivity in great detail in speech perception (e.g., McMurray, Tanenhaus, & Aslin, 2002), as well as exquisite sensitivity to subcategorical (subphonemic) detail, such as coarticulatory cues (Dahan, Magnuson, Tanenhaus, & Hogan, 2001). These results should have led directly to the insight that the phonemic input assumption is just plain wrong, and that the computational theory of spoken word recognition cannot be compartmentalized away from speech perception—especially in light of well-known phonetic studies demonstrating, for example, that vowel durations differ systematically (albeit probabilistically) as a function of word length (e.g., Peterson & Lehiste, 1960). Salverda, Dahan, and McQueen (2003) finally made this connection explicit in a visual world study (see also Davis, Marslen-Wilson, & Gaskell, 2002, for related results using a priming paradigm).

They confirmed that, on average, vowel durations in longer words (e.g., *hamster*) were shorter (by only about 20 ms at an average speaking rate) than in shorter words (e.g., *ham*), and then demonstrated that listeners use subtle cues like these immediately to constrain spoken word recognition (e.g., the *ham-* of *hamster* leads to greater activation of *hammer*, which is compatible with cues to word length present already in /æ/, than the short word, *ham*). On the one hand, building in a correlation between word length and vowel duration would be fairly easy in a model like TRACE; on the other hand, such durations just scratch the surface of the complex prosodic patterns to which listeners are sensitive (see Salverda et al. for some of these). Consider the implications for the *embedding problem* if the initial segments in spoken words essentially tell the listener how long the word they are hearing will be; this substantially mitigates the embedding problem (i.e., if vowel duration is consistent with a two-syllable word, *ham* should be less active, reducing the magnitude of the embedding problem). Thus, simplifying assumptions about the nature of the input hid subphonemic constraints available in the speech signal.

This is just one example of surface details that spoken word recognition is sensitive to. Another is assimilation. In English, *place assimilation* can straddle word boundaries, with actual place of articulation shifting with the context of an adjacent segment. For example, the sequence *green boat* is often pronounced as a rhyme or near rhyme of *dream boat*, but this appears not to impede perception of the intended word. If there is truly full assimilation (e.g., Gaskell, 2003; Gaskell & Marslen-Wilson, 1998), this might be a problem situated at the level of spoken word recognition. However, evidence that characteristics of the intended segment shift only partially toward the assimilating place (e.g., Gow, 2001, 2002, 2003a, 2003b) suggest a degree of interaction between speech perception and spoken word recognition that cannot be trivially accommodated in current models, especially when the phonemic input assumption is in play.

Word segmentation is another place where the phonemic input assumption may be complicating rather than simplifying. Relatively easy to quantify surface details—such as stress patterns—are not difficult to integrate with current frameworks (Norris, McQueen, & Cutler, 1995). Mattys and colleagues (e.g., Mattys, White, & Melhorn, 2005) have been mapping out complex interactions between knowledge-based (lexical) and signal-based cues to segmentation, the relative weights of which vary with context. Again, aspects of these details could be built into a model like TRACE. But it does not seem plausible that the full number and complexity of constraints Mattys and colleagues have documented could be hand-coded into such models. In fact, attempting to do so would amount to replacing the phonemic input assumption with another simplifying assumption, albeit one that would be more complex and realistic. That is, building in such correlations with any simplified/abstract analog to the acoustics of real speech is still a matter of constructing a pretend signal, rather than grappling with actual speech. Without tackling the signal, we will not know what helpful constraints we have hidden with the abstractions of our simplifying assumptions.

A case where surface detail seems complicating rather than simplifying, though, is the great sensitivity listeners exhibit to surface details that do not seem to provide general constraints on the signal-word mapping reported by Goldinger (1998). Memory for and naming of a word heard earlier in a session (e.g., in an old-new recognition test) benefit from preservation of seemingly nonessential details such as talker identity. Goldinger (1998) proposed an episodic model of the lexicon, where the storage of unanalyzed memory traces provides the basis for word recognition. While several fundamental problems would have to be overcome for this to be a viable model of word recognition (see Magnuson & Nusbaum, 2007, and footnote 2), Goldinger's simulations with an episodic model (based on MINERVA2; Hintzman, 1986) provide a potential starting point for understanding priming and recognition within a single system.

Further need for some sort of flexible, active, and context-dependent episodic learning based on complex contingencies between talkers and surface details is illustrated by recent studies showing rapid, but conservative, learning. Norris, McQueen, and Cutler (2003) and Bertelson, Vroomen, and DeGelder (2003) reported rapid "perceptual recalibration" when ambiguous phonetic stimuli are accompanied by some kind of disambiguating context. Bertelson et al. used videos of the oral gestures of speakers to disambiguate segments halfway between /b/ and /d/. Norris et al. predicted that lexically disambiguated segments (Ganong, 1980) could lead to lexically guided learning. They used segments halfway between /f/ and /s/ that were lexically disambiguated as subjects did a lexical decision task (e.g., in English, the ambiguous token in the context of *distre-* would most likely be *distress*, but the same ambiguous segment would most likely be /f/ in the context of *himsel-*). In both studies, the contexts drove learning that changed performance on subsequent phonetic identification assessments. Thus, phonetic-to-phonemic mappings are not static but can change dynamically based on recent experience. Later studies showed that such learning is robust over time (25 minutes: Kraljic & Samuel, 2005; 12 hours: Eisner & McQueen, 2006) and re-exposure to canonical, unambiguous tokens (Kraljic & Samuel, 2005). Perhaps most remarkably, this learning appears to depend on history with a speaker *and* the absence of a causal explanation for perturbed speech production; Kraljic, Samuel, and Brennan (2008) found that learning is talker-specific and depends on the first utterances heard by a particular talker (early unambiguous tokens are not overridden by later, lexically disambiguated tokens) *and* that such learning is blocked if a causal, external factor would explain temporary deviance from canonical pronunciation (such as a pen in the talker's mouth).

One last related phenomenon we will touch on here is word learning in adults, which both highlights further the need to grapple with learning and the need to integrate the cognitive psychology of language with the cognitive neuroscience of language (and eventually the neurochemistry and genetics, etc.). Gaskell and Dumay (2003) pioneered a new learning paradigm where subjects are exposed to word-like patterns (e.g., *cathedruke*) as nonword foils in lexical decision over a period of 5 days. They found that eventually, these nonwords began to act as though they were becoming lexicalized, as indicated by increased competition evident when subjects processed similar real words (e.g., *cathedral*). Dumay and Gaskell (2007) explicitly tested whether the advent of lexical competition is dependent upon sleep-based consolidation. With a classic sleep + delay versus no-sleep + delay approach, they found that the emergence of competition does depend on consolidation. Leach and Samuel (2007) pointed out that this requires two different phases of learning, and possibly two different forms of learning: *lexical configuration* is a matter of learning to recognize a pattern, and this seems to emerge before *lexical engagement*, when that pattern begins to show evidence (via competition with existing lexical items) of integration with the lexicon. While in this chapter we have steadfastly stuck to our charge of reviewing the cognitive psychology of spoken word recognition, ambitious behavioral and neuroimaging work on consolidation in lexical learning by

Davis and Gaskell (2009) at the intersection of neuroscience and cognitive psychology illustrates that maintaining boundaries between these domains is becoming less tenable every day. We only have time to mention in passing the growing need for theories and models of spoken word recognition to respect computational constraints emerging from the cognitive neuroscience of language, and the fact that this represents another source of Kuhnian crisis for current theories.

## Revolutionary Frameworks?

In closing, we see three avenues as most promising for pushing the field beyond the tipping point and to new theoretical frameworks: (1) the need to grapple with the speech signal itself, (2) integration of the study of spoken word recognition with descriptively higher levels of language processing, (3) the need for theories and models to grapple with learning across the life span, including language development in childhood and rapid, flexible learning in adults, and (4) the need to respect neurobiological constraints on mechanisms for language processing. Two existing approaches might provide paths forward on some of these.

The first is the adaptive resonance framework of Grossberg and colleagues (e.g., Grossberg, Boardman, & Cohen, 1997; Grossberg, Govindarajan, Wyse, & Cohen, 2004; Grossberg & Myers, 2000), who have ignored the simplifying assumptions embraced elsewhere in the field and have stubbornly refused to abandon the speech signal or neurobiologically realistic learning models. A pessimistic view of this work would be that progress has been slight, leading thus far neither to anything like the breadth of the TRACE model nor to a plausible developmental model. As we have discussed, simplifying assumptions about the input signal can actually complicate the problem of spoken word recognition. Working with the signal is necessary both in terms of demonstrating that our models could actually work with the signal whose perception we intend to model, and in uncovering further constraints our simplifying assumptions have hidden. Similar benefits may also emerge from realistic neural modeling.

The second promising framework is a connectionist model that integrates the development of speech perception and speech production (Plaut & Kello, 1999), using acoustic and articulatory representations that are still abstractions but are tremendously more realistic than TRACE (McClelland & Elman, 1986), the next best simplified approach in current models, providing a waypoint perhaps between current approaches and adaptive resonance. The model learns to recognize words based on "adult" input and learns to control its articulatory apparatus by attempting to mimic the sound patterns in that input. More generally, it may be time for theories and models of spoken word recognition to move away from stipulated representations to emergent representations (McClelland, 2010; McClelland et al., 2010).

But, of course, a framework encompassing learning is even more important when we turn our attention to language development. As we suggested earlier, models of adult "endpoints" are invaluable tools for making progress on understanding spoken word recognition (even if endpoints are another example of a useful but misleading simplifying assumption, given the results for adult plasticity we have just reviewed), but full understanding of language processing will require developmental models. Plaut and Kello did not develop the model beyond this first report, but a framework of this sort may be just what is needed to push the field forward.

## Notes

1. Typical speaking rates range from approximately 12 phonemes per second (moderate) to 30 (fast) phonemes per second (Liberman, Cooper, Shankweiler, & Studdert-Kennedy, 1967). Even though 12 phonemes per second is already three to four times the rate at which sequences of arbitrary sounds can be perceived (Warren, Obusek, Farmer, & Warren, 1969), word recognition remains stable at unusually fast rates up to 50–60 phonemes per second.

2. Although the field continues to be known as "spoken word *recognition*," we will see that current theories largely eschew the notion of a "magical moment" (Balota, 1990) where the system enters a state of one word being recognized, embracing instead notions of change over time in relative activations of lexical representations in memory (e.g., McClelland & Elman, 1986) or Bayesian probability estimates that particular words have been or are being heard (e.g., Norris & McQueen, 2008). For better or worse, we will follow standard practice of using "spoken word recognition" as a catchall term to indicate processes intervening between speech perception and sentence processing.

3. Whether one must fully commit to abstract or episodic representations is a complex issue beyond the scope of this chapter. See Magnuson and Nusbaum (2007) for a discussion of the possibility that both support speech perception and word recognition.

4. Note that a more conventional way of reviewing spoken word recognition is to divide the problem is divided into three functions: access, selection, and integration (e.g., Dahan & Magnuson, 2006; Frauenfelder & Tyler, 1987; Marslen-Wilson, 1987). Access, or initial contact, is how the speech signal is mapped to phonological (or possibly other) representational forms that are the key to accessing lexical entries. The selection function identifies the lexical item with the best fit to the bottom-up input, possibly constrained by top-down context. The integration function must output a form that can be the basis for the syntactic and semantic processing. While we agree

these are necessary functions, we do not view them as necessarily independent, nor even distinct.

5. Or rather, many of the basic facts reemerged. Bagley (1900) reports the results of a research program that presaged much of the basic work at the intersection of speech perception and spoken word recognition of the 1970s and 1980s, including ingenious modifications ("mutilations") of wax drum recordings for manipulation of spoken words. In the interest of concision and utility, we will focus on recent work with modern techniques, even when Bagley's work presents an interesting precedent. Intrigued readers should see the comparison of Bagley's methods and results with those of 1970s and 1980s psycholinguists by Cole and Rudnick (1983).

6. We must mention two things here. First, these latter two problems (resolving phonological patterns and segmenting phonemes) are problems typically deferred to speech perception specialists, via the simplifying assumption that the input is a series of parsed phonemes, as reviewed earlier. Second, it is not a given that the speech signal must be parsed into phonemes before it can be mapped onto words, even though almost all theories of spoken word recognition assume there is some level of sublexical representation mediating the mapping from acoustics to words; for example, Klatt (1979) proposed a theory in which acoustic patterns (spectra) were mapped directly to words.

7. Note that this avoids the problems with interaction that led to the abandonment of top-down interaction in the Cohort Model (Marslen-Wilson, 1987, reviewed above). Even without interaction, the notion of the recognition point in the Cohort Model has serious problems. We have no trouble realizing we have *not* just heard a word when we hear *banisfer*, even though we hit the uniqueness point for *banister* at the /s/—pushing Cohort to predict recognition of *banister*. If we view this as a case where a word has reached a high degree of activation relative to other words, rather than reaching an all-or-none recognition state, we avoid this problem. High activation allows a listener to *expect* a word and to perform as though it has been recognized, but without absolute commitment to that word.

8. The interested reader can test this for herself using jTRACE (Strauss et al., 2007); even if you reduce the lexicon to a single pair, such as *artist* and *art*, there is still an early short-word advantage because each *artist* node receives more inhibition from overlapping *art* nodes, and the only way to eliminate the effect completely is to turn off lateral inhibition. A short-word advantage persists even if you reduce the lexicon to one long word and one unrelated short word (e.g., *artist* and *blue*) and compare the recognition time for the two words (again, you can eliminate the bias by turning off lateral inhibition).

9. An early version of this task was reported by Cooper (1974), but its potential was not appreciated at the time. Recently, a version was developed that tracks hand movements instead of eye movements and provides a different perspective on time course (Spivey, Grosjean, & Knoblish, 2005).

10. Note that 200 ms is the mean lag, which means that there are faster and slower initial fixations. See Altmann and Kamide (2007; also Altmann, 2011) for assessments of saccade latency distributions.

11. We are using the term *probabilistic phonotactics* here to capture the general idea that words can vary in just how word-like they sound, with more common sequences sounding more word-like. This term also has been given an operational definition in spoken word recognition research as well. Vitevitch and Luce (1999) define this as a sum of diphone probabilities within a word (so not exactly a probability). While this is strongly

correlated with neighborhood density, Vitevitch and Luce have demonstrated that in a task where attention is manipulated to a sublexical locus (by presenting many nonwords in a naming task, for example), phonotactic probability facilitates processing.

12. Indeed, McQueen et al. (2010) failed to replicate the findings of Magnuson et al. (2003a) using the original materials. Using better materials provided by Magnuson et al., McQueen et al. mostly found null effects, as well as one reliable effect in the same direction as Magnuson et al. and one in the opposite direction, which they argue depended on perceptual learning based on the types of items included in practice trials. While positive results still outnumber negative ones (see Magnuson et al., 2003b, for a scorecard), it is clear that this experimental paradigm is fragile, and that resolving this debate may require a different form of evidence.

13. There is a puzzle lurking here. After seeing or hearing one item and then responding to a semantically related item, we typically observe classical positive priming: lexical decision or naming responses to the second item are speeded relative to responses to that item when preceded by an unrelated item. But inhibitory priming is observed for phonological relatedness in such tasks (Luce et al., 2000). The puzzle emerges when we consider what happens in the visual world paradigm. The presence of phonologically related items results in apparent competition; fixations are diverted to the competitor, and target fixations are proportionally depressed. This is interpreted both as evidence for activation of the competitor and inhibition of the target. When a semantic associate is present, the same pattern is observed. However, this may be a case where the paradigm masks the true effect; if the semantic associate is activated, it will attract fixations by virtue of that activation, but it may not actively inhibit activation of the target. This might also suggest the caution is warranted in interpreting the phonological case as demonstrating both competitor activation and target inhibition. All the same, we shall follow the literature and refer to both phonological and semantic cases as instances of competition.

# References

Allopenna, P. D., Magnuson, J. S., & Tanenhaus, M. K. (1998). Tracking the time course of spoken word recognition using eye movements: Evidence for continuous mapping models. *Journal of Memory and Language*, 38, 419–439.

Altman, G. T. M. (2010). Language can mediate eye movement control within 100 milliseconds, regardless of whether there is anything to move the eyes to. *Acta Psychologica, 137*(2), 190–200.

Altmann, G. T. M., & Kamide, Y. (1999). Incremental interpretation at verbs: Restricting the domain of subsequent reference. *Cognition, 73*, 247–264.

Altmann, G. T. M., & Kamide, Y. (2007). The real-time mediation of visual attention by language and world knowledge: Linking anticipatory (and other) eye movements to linguistic processing. *Journal of Memory and Language, 57*, 502–518.

Altmann, G. T. M., & Mirković, J. (2009). Incrementality and prediction in human sentence processing. *Cognitive Science, 33*(4), 583–609.

Andruski, J. E., Blumstein, S. E., & Burton, M. (1994). The effect of subphonetic differences on lexical access. *Cognition, 52*, 163–187.

Aslin, R. N., Woodward, J., LaMendola, N., & Bever, T. G. (1996). Models of word segmentation in fluent maternal speech to infants. In J. L. Morgan & K. Demuth (Eds.),

*Signal to syntax: Bootstrapping from speech to grammar in early acquisition* (pp. 117–134). Mahwah, NJ: Erlbaum.

Balota, D. A. (1990). The role of meaning in word recogni- tion. In D. A Balota, G. B. Flores d'Arcais, & K. Rayner (Eds.), *Comprehension processes in reading* (pp. 9–32). Hillsdale, NJ: Erlbaum.

Barr, D. J. (2008). Pragmatic expectations and linguistic evidence: Listeners anticipate but do not integrate common ground. *Cognition, 109*(1), 18–40.

Bertelson, P., Vroomen, J., & DeGelder, B. (2003). Visual recalibration of auditory speech identification: A McGurk aftereffect. *Psychological Science, 14*(6), 592–597.

Blumstein, S. E. & Myers, E. (in press). Speech perception. In *Oxford handbook of cognitive neuroscience*.

Chambers, C. G., Tanenhaus, M. K., & Magnuson, J. S. (2004). Actions and affordances in syntactic ambiguity resolution. *Journal of Experimental Psychology: Learning, Memory, and Cognition, 30*, 687–696.

Christiansen, M. H., Allen, J., & Seidenberg, M. S. (1998). Learning to segment speech using multiple cues: A connectionist model. *Language and Cognitive Processes, 13*, 221–268.

Cole, R. A., & Jakimik, J. (1980). A model of speech perception. In R. A. Cole (Ed.), *Perception and production of fluent speech* (pp. 133–163). Hillsdale, NJ: Erlbaum.

Connine, C. M., Titone, D., & Wang, J. (1993). Auditory word recognition: Extrinsic and intrinsic effects of word frequency. *Journal of Experimental Psychology: Learning Memory and Cognition, 19*(1), 81–94.

Cooper, R. M. (1974). The control of eye fixation by the meaning of spoken language. A new methodology for the real time investigation of speech perception, memory, and language processing. *Cognitive Psychology, 6*, 84–107.

Dahan, D., Magnuson, J. S., & Tanenhaus, M. K. (2001). Time course of frequency effects in spoken-word recognition: Evidence from eye movements. *Cognitive Psychology, 42*, 317–367.

Dahan, D., Magnuson, J. S., Tanenhaus, M. K., & Hogan, E. M. (2001). Tracking the time course of subcategorical mismatches: Evidence for lexical competition. *Language and Cognitive Processes, 16*(5/6), 507–534.

Dahan, D., & Tanenhaus, M. K. (2004). Continuous mapping from sound to meaning in spoken-language comprehension: Immediate effects of verb-based thematic constraints. *Journal of Experimental Psychology: Learning, Memory, and Cognition, 30*, 498–513.

Dahan, D., & Tanenhaus, M. K. (2005). Looking at the rope when looking for the snake: Conceptually mediated eye movements during spoken-word recognition. *Psychonomic Bulletin & Review, 12*, 453–459.

Davis, M. H., Marslen-Wilson, W. D., & Gaskell. M. G. (2002). Leading up the lexical garden-path: Segmentation and ambiguity in spoken word recognition. *Journal of Experimental Psychology: Human Perception and Performance, 28*, 218–244.

Davis, M. H., & Gaskell, M. G. (2009). A complementary systems account of word learning: Neural and behavioural evidence. *Philosophical Transactions of the Royal Society B, 364*, 3773–3800.

Dilley, L. C., & Pitt, M. A. (2010). Altering context speech rate can cause words to appear or disappear. *Psychological Science, 21*(11), 1664–1670.

Dumay, N., & Gaskell, M. G. (2007). Sleep-associated changes in the mental representation of spoken words. *Psychological Science, 18*, 35–39.

Eisner, F., & McQueen, J. M. (2006). Perceptual learning in speech: Stability over time. *Journal of the Acoustical Society of America, 119*(4), 1950–1953.

Elman, J. L., & McClelland, J. L. (1988). Cognitive penetration of the mechanisms of perception: Compensation for coarticulation of lexically restored phonemes. *Journal of Memory and Language, 27,* 143–165.

Fischer, B. (1992). Saccadic reaction time: Implications for reading, dyslexia and visual cognition. In K. Rayner (Ed.), *Eye movements and visual cognition: Scene perception and reading* (pp. 31–45). New York: Springer-Verlag.

Fowler, C. A., & Magnuson, J. S. (2012). Speech perception. In M. Spivey, M. Joanisse, & K. McRae (Eds.), *The Cambridge handbook of psycholinguistics* (pp. 3–25). Cambridge: Cambridge University Press.

Fox, R. A. (1984). Effect of lexical status on phonetic categorization. *Journal of Experimental Psychology: Human Perception and Performance, 10,* 526–540.

Frauenfelder, U. H., & Peeters, G. (1998). Simulating the time course of spoken word recognition: An analysis of lexical competition in TRACE. In J. Grainger & A. M. Jacobs (Eds.), *Localist connectionist approaches to human cognition* (pp. 101–146). Mahwah, NJ: Erlbaum.

Frauenfelder, U. H., & Tyler, L. K. (1987). The process of spoken word recognition: An introduction. *Cognition, 25,* 1–20.

Ganong, W. F. (1980). Phonetic categorization in auditory word perception. *Journal of Experimental Psychology: Human Perception and Performance, 6,* 110–125.

Gaskell, M. G. (2003). Modelling regressive and progressive effects of assimilation in speech perception. *Journal of Phonetics, 31,* 447–463.

Gaskell, M. G., & Dumay, N. (2003). Lexical competition and the acquisition of novel words. *Cognition, 89,* 105–132.

Gaskell, M. G., & Marslen-Wilson, W. D. (1997). Integrating form and meaning: A distributed model of speech perception. *Language and Cognitive Processes, 12*(5), 613–656.

Gaskell, M. G., & Marslen-Wilson, W. D. (1998). Mechanisms of phonological inference in speech perception. *Journal of Experimental Psychology: Human Perception & Performance, 24,* 380–396.

Gaskell, M. G., & Marslen-Wilson, W. D. (1999). Ambiguity, competition, and blending in spoken word recognition. *Cognitive Science, 23,* 439–462.

Gaskell, M. G., & Marslen-Wilson, W. D. (2002). Representation and competition in the perception of spoken words. *Cognitive Psychology, 45*(2), 220–266.

Goldinger, S. D. (1998). Echoes of echoes? An episodic theory of lexical access. *Psychological Review, 105,* 251–279.

Goldinger, S. D., Luce, P. A., & Pisoni, D. B. (1989). Priming lexical neighbors of spoken words: Effects of competition and inhibition. *Journal of Memory and Language, 28,* 501–518.

Gow, D. W., Jr. (2001). Assimilation and anticipation in continuous spoken word recognition. *Journal of Memory and Language, 45,* 133–159.

Gow, D. W., Jr. (2002). Does English coronal place assimilation create lexical ambiguity? *Journal of Experimental Psychology: Human Perception and Performance, 28,* 163–179.

Gow, D. W., Jr. (2003a). Feature parsing: Feature cue mapping in spoken word recognition. *Perception and Psychophysics, 65,* 575–590.

Gow, D. W., Jr. (2003b). How representations help define computational problems: Commentary on Grossberg, Gaskell and Greenberg. *Journal of Phonetics, 31,* 487–493.

Grainger, J., & Jacobs, A. M. (1996). Orthographic processing visual word recognition: A multiple read-out model. *Psychological Review, 103,* 674–691.

Greenberg, J. H., & Jenkins, J. J. (1964). Studies in the psychological correlates of the sound system of American English. *Word, 20,* 157–177.

Grosjean, F. (1980). Spoken word recognition processes and the gating paradigm. *Perception and Psychophysics, 28,* 267–283.

Grossberg, S., Boardman, I., & Cohen, M. (1997). Neural dynamics of variable-rate speech categorization. *Journal of Experimental Psychology: Human Perception and Performance, 23*(2), 481–503.

Grossberg, S., Govindarajan, K. K., Wyse, L. L., & Cohen, M. A. (2004). ARTSTREAM: A neural network model of auditory scene analysis and source segregation. *Neural Networks, 17*(4), 511–536.

Grossberg, S., & Myers, C. W. (2000). The resonant dynamics of speech perception: Interword integration and duration-dependent backward effects. *Psychological Review, 107*(4), 735–767.

Hanna, J. E., Tanenhaus, M. K., & Trueswell, J. C. (2003). The effects of common ground and perspective on domains of referential interpretation. *Journal of Memory and Language, 49*(1), 43–61.

Hannagan, T., Magnuson, J., & Grainger, J. (2012). A time-invariant connectionist model of spoken word recognition. *Proceedings of the 34th Annual Conference of the Cognitive Science Society,* 1638–1643.

Hickok, G. S., & Poeppel, D. (2007). The cortical organization of speech processing. *Nature Reviews Neuroscience, 8,* 393–402.

Hintzman, D. L. (1986). "Schema abstraction" in a multiple-trace memory model. *Psychological Review, 93,* 411–428.

Howes, D. H., & Solomon, R. L. (1951). Visual duration threshold as a function of word-probability. *Journal of Experimental Psychology, 41,* 401–410.

Huettig, F., & Altmann, G. T. M. (2005). Word meaning and the control of eye fixation: Semantic competitor effects and the visual world paradigm. *Cognition, 96,* B23–B32.

Kalénine, S., Mirman, D., Middleton, E. L., & Buxbaum, L. J. (in press). Temporal dynamics of activation of thematic and functional action knowledge during auditory comprehension of artifact words. *Journal of Experimental Psychology: Learning, Memory, and Cognition.*

Klatt, D. H. (1979). Speech perception: A model of acoustic-phonetic analysis and lexical access. *Journal of Phonetics, 7*(3), 279–312.

Kraljic, T., & Samuel, A. G. (2005). Perceptual learning for speech: Is there a return to normal? *Cognitive Psychology, 51*(2), 141–178.

Kraljic, T., Samuel, A. G ,. & Brennan, S. E. (2008). First impressions and last resorts: How listeners adjust to speaker variability. *Psychological Science, 19,* 332–38

Kuhn, T. (1962). *The structure of scientific revolutions.* Chicago: University of Chicago Press.

Kukona, A., Fang, S., Aicher, K. A., Chen, H., & Magnuson, J. S. (2011). The time course of anticipatory constraint integration. *Cognition, 119,* 23–42.

Ladefoged, P., & Broadbent, D. E. (1957). Information conveyed by vowels. *Journal of the Acoustical Society of America, 29,* 98–104.

Landauer, T. K., & Streeter, L. A. (1973). Structural differences between common and rare words: Failure of equivalence assumptions for theories of word recognition. *Journal of Verbal Learning and Verbal Behavior, 12,* 119–131.

Leach, L., & Samuel, A. G. (2007). Lexical configuration and lexical engagement: When adults learn new words. *Cognitive Psychology, 55*, 306–353.

Lee, C-L., Middleton, E. L., Mirman, D., Kalénine, S., & Buxbaum, L. J. (in press). Incidental and context-responsive activation of structure- and function-based action features during object identification. *Journal of Experimental Psychology: Human Perception and Performance.*

Lehiste, I. (1970). *Suprasegmentals.* Cambridge, MA: MIT Press.

Liberman, A. M., Cooper, F. S., Shankweiler, D. P., & Studdert-Kennedy, M. (1967). Perception of the speech code. *Psychological Review, 74,* 431–461.

Liberman, A. M., Harris, K. S., Hoffman, H. S., & Griffith, B. C. (1957). The discrimination of speech sounds within and across phoneme boundaries. *Journal of Experimental Psychology, 54*(5), 358–368.

Lisker, L. (1985). The pursuit of invariance in speech signals. *Journal of the Acoustical Society of America, 77,* 1199–1202.

Luce, P. A. (1986). Neighborhoods of words in the mental lexicon. (Research on Speech Perception, Technical Report No. 6). Bloomington: Speech Research Laboratory, Department of Psychology, Indiana University.

Luce, P. A., Goldinger, S. D., Auer, E. T., Jr., & Vitevitch, M. S. (2000). Phonetic priming, neighborhood activation, and parsyn. *Perception and Psychophysics, 62,* 615–625.

Luce, P. A., & Pisoni, D. B. (1998). Recognizing spoken words: The neighborhood activation model. *Ear and Hearing, 19,* 1–36.

Luce, R. D. (1959). *Individual choice behavior.* Oxford, England: Wiley.

MacDonald, M. C., Pearlmutter, N. J., & Seidenberg, M. S. (1994). The lexical nature of syntactic ambiguity resolution. *Psychological Review, 101,* 676–703.

Magnuson, J. S. (2008). Nondeterminism, pleiotropy, and single word reading: Theoretical and practical concerns. In E. Grigorenko & A. Naples (Eds.), *Single word reading (pp. xx–xx).* Mahweh, NJ: Erlbaum.

Magnuson, J. S., Dixon, J., Tanenhaus, M. K., & Aslin, R. N. (2007). The dynamics of lexical competition during spoken word recognition. *Cognitive Science, 31,* 133–156.

Magnuson, J. S., McMurray, B., Tanenhaus, M. K., & Aslin, R. N. (2003a). Lexical effects on compensation for coarticulation: The ghost of Christmash past. *Cognitive Science, 27,* 285–298.

Magnuson, J. S., McMurray, B., Tanenhaus, M. K., & Aslin, R. N. (2003b). Lexical effects on compensation for coarticulation: A tale of two systems? *Cognitive Science, 27,* 801–805.

Magnuson, J. S., Mirman, D., & Harris, H. D. (2012). Computational models of spoken word recognition. In M. Spivey, M. Joanisse, & K. McRae (Eds.), *The Cambridge handbook of psycholinguistics* (pp. 76–103). Cambridge: Cambridge University Press.

Magnuson, J. S., & Nusbaum, H. C. (2007). Acoustic differences, listener expectations, and the perceptual accommodation of talker variability. *Journal of Experimental Psychology: Human Perception and Performance, 33,* 391–409.

Magnuson, J. S., Strauss, T., & Harris, H. D. (2005). Interaction in spoken word recognition models: Feedback helps. In *Proceedings of the Annual Meeting of the Cognitive Science Society* (pp. 1379–1384).

Magnuson, J. S., Tanenhaus, M. K., & Aslin, R. N. (2008). Immediate effects of form-class constraints on spoken word recognition. *Cognition, 108*(3), 866–873.

Magnuson, J. S., Tanenhaus, M. K., Aslin, R. N., & Dahan, D. (2003). The microstructure of spoken word recognition: Studies with artificial lexicons. *Journal of Experimental Psychology: General, 132*(2), 202–227.

Marr, D. (1982). *Vision.* San Francisco: W. H. Freeman.

Marslen-Wilson, W. (1987). Functional parallelism in spoken word-recognition. *Cognition, 25,* 71–102.

Marslen-Wilson, W. (Ed.). (1989). *Lexical representation and process.* Cambridge, MA: MIT Press.

Marslen-Wilson, W. D., & Tyler, L. K. (1980). The temporal structure of spoken language understanding. *Cognition, 8,* 1–71.

Marslen-Wilson, W., & Warren, P. (1994). Levels of perceptual representation and process in lexical access: Words phonemes and features. *Psychological Review, 101,* 653–675.

Marslen-Wilson, W., & Welsh, A. (1978). Processing interactions and lexical access during word recognition in continuous speech. *Cognitive Psychology, 10,* 29–63.

Marslen-Wilson, W. D., & Zwitserlood, P. (1989). Accessing spoken words: The importance of word onsets. *Journal of Experimental Psychology: Human Perception and Performance, 15*(3), 576–585.

Matin, E., Shao, K., & Boff, K. (1993). Saccadic overhead: Information processing time with and without saccades. *Perception and Psychophysics, 53,* 372–380.

Mattys, S. L., White, L., & Melhorn, J. F. (2005). Integration of multiple speech segmentation cues: A hierarchical framework. *Journal of Experimental Psychology: General, 134,* 477–500.

McClelland, J. L. (1991). Stochastic interactive processes and the effect of context on perception. *Cognitive Psychology, 23,* 1–44.

McClelland, J. L. (2010). Emergence in cognitive science. *Topics in Cognitive Science, 2*(4), 751–770.

McClelland, J. L., Botvinick, M. M., Noelle, D. C., Plaut, D. C., Rogers, T. T., Seidenberg, M. S., & Smith, L. B. (2010). Letting structure emerge: Connectionist and dynamical systems approaches to cognition. *Trends in Cognitive Sciences, 14*(8), 348–356.

McClelland, J. L., & Elman, J. L. (1986). The TRACE model of speech perception. *Cognitive Psychology, 18,* 1–86.

McClelland, J. L., Mirman, D., & Holt, L. L. (2006). Are there interactive processes in speech perception? *Trends in Cognitive Sciences, 10*(8), 363–369.

McClelland, J. L., & Rumelhart, D. E. (1981). An interactive activation model of context effects in letter perception: I An account of basic findings. *Psychological Review, 88*(5), 375–407.

McMurray, B., Tanenhaus, M. K., & Aslin, R. N. (2002). Gradient effects of within-category phonetic variation on lexical access. *Cognition, 86,* B33–B42.

McMurray, B., Tanenhaus, M. K., & Aslin, R. N. (2009). Within-category VOT affects recovery from "lexical" garden paths: Evidence against phoneme-level inhibition. *Journal of Memory and Language, 60*(1), 65–91.

McQueen, J. M. (1991). The influence of the lexicon on phonetic categorization: Stimulus quality in word-final ambiguity. *Journal of Experimental Psychology: Human Perception and Performance, 17,* 433–443.

McQueen, J. M. (2003). The ghost of Christmas future: Didn't Scrooge learn to be good? Commentary on Magnuson,

McMurray, Tanenhaus, and Aslin (2003). *Cognitive Science*, *27*(5), 795–799.

McQueen, J. M., Cutler, A., Briscoe, T., & Norris, D. (1995). Models of continuous speech recognition and the contents of the vocabulary. *Language and Cognitive Processes, 10*, 309–331.

McQueen, J. M., Jesse, A., & Norris, D. (2009). No lexical–prelexical feedback during speech perception or: Is it time to stop playing those Christmas tapes? *Journal of Memory and Language, 61*, 1–18.

McQueen, J. M., Norris, D., & Cutler, A. (2006). Are there really interactive processes in speech perception? *Trends in Cognitive Sciences, 10*(12), 533.

Meyer, D. E., & Schvaneveldt, R. W. (1971). Facilitation in recognizing pairs of words: Evidence of a dependence between retrieval operations. *Journal of Experimental Psychology, 90*, 227–234.

Miller, J. L., & Liberman, A. M. (1979). Some effects of later-occurring information on the perception of stop consonant and semivowel. *Perception and Psychophysics, 25*, 457–465.

Mirman, D. (2008). Mechanisms of semantic ambiguity resolution: Insights from speech perception. *Research on Language and Computation, 6*(3–4), 293–309.

Mirman, D., Bolger, D. J., Khaitan, P., & McClelland, J. L. (in press). Interactive activation and mutual constraint satisfaction in perception and cognition. *Cognitive Science*.

Mirman, D., Dixon, J. A., & Magnuson, J. S. (2008). Statistical and computational models of the visual world paradigm: Growth curves and individual differences. *Journal of Memory & Language, 59*(4), 475–494.

Mirman, D., & Graziano, K. M. (2011). Individual differences in the strength of taxonomic versus thematic relations. *Journal of Experimental Psychology: General*. doi:10.1037/a0026451

Mirman, D., & Magnuson, J. S. (2009). Dynamics of activation of semantically similar concepts during spoken word recognition. *Memory and Cognition, 37*(7), 1026–1039. doi:10.3758/MC.37.7.1026

Mirman, D., McClelland, J. L., & Holt, L. L. (2005). Computational and behavioral investigations of lexically induced delays in phoneme recognition. *Journal of Memory and Language, 52*(3), 424–443.

Mirman, D., McClelland, J. L., & Holt, L. L. (2006). Reply to McQueen et al.: Theoretical and empirical arguments support interactive processing. *Trends in Cognitive Sciences, 10*(12), 534.

Movellan, J. R., & McClelland, J. L. (2001). The Morton-Massaro law of information integration: Implications for models of perception. *Psychological Review, 108*(1), 113–148.

Myung, J., Blumstein, S. E., & Sedivy, J. C. (2006). Playing on the typewriter and typing on the piano: Manipulation knowledge of objects. *Cognition, 98*, 223–243.

Norris, D. (1994). Shortlist: A connectionist model of continuous speech recognition. *Cognition, 52*, 189–234.

Norris, D., & McQueen, J. M. (2008). Shortlist B: A Bayesian model of continuous speech recognition. *Psychological Review, 115*, 357–395.

Norris, D., McQueen, J. M., & Cutler, A. (1995). Competition and segmentation in spoken-word recognition. *Journal of Experimental Psychology: Learning, Memory, and Cognition, 21*(5), 1209–1228.

Norris, D., McQueen, J. M., & Cutler, A. (2000). Merging information in speech recognition: Feedback is never necessary. *Behavioral and Brain Sciences, 23*, 299–370.

Norris, D., McQueen, J. M., & Cutler, A. (2003). Perceptual learning in speech. *Cognitive Psychology, 47*, 204–238.

Norris, D., McQueen, J. M., Cutler, A., & Butterfield, S. (1997). The possible-word constraint in the segmentation of continuous speech. *Cognitive Psychology, 34*(3), 191–243.

Peterson, G. E., & Barney, H. L. (1952). Control methods used in a study of the vowels. Journal of the Acoustical Society of America, 24, 175–184.

Peterson, G., & Lehiste, I. (1960). Durations of syllabic nuclei in English. *Journal of the Acoustical Society of America, 32*, 693–703.

Pisoni, D., & Tash, J. (1974) Reaction times to comparisons with and across phonetic categories. *Perception and Psychophysics, 15*(2), 285–290

Pitt, M. A., & McQueen, J. M. (1998). Is compensation for coarticulation mediated by the lexicon? *Journal of Memory and Language, 39*, 347–370.

Pitt, M. A., & Samuel, A. G. (2006). Word length and lexical activation: Longer is better. *Journal of Experimental Psychology: Human Perception and Performance, 32*, 1120–1135.

Plaut, D. C., & Kello, C. T. (1999). The emergence of phonology from the interplay of speech comprehension and production: A distributed connectionist approach. In B. MacWhinney (Ed.), *The emergence of language* (pp. 381–415). Mahwah, NJ: Erlbaum.

Pustejovsky, J. (1995). *The generative lexicon*. Cambridge, MA: MIT Press.

Rogers, T. T., Lambon Ralph, M. A., Hodges, J. R., & Patterson, K. E. (2004). Natural selection: The impact of semantic impairment on lexical and object decision. *Cognitive Neuropsychology, 21*(2–4), 331–352.

Rubin, P., Turvey, M. T., & van Gelder, P. (1976). Initial phonemes are detected faster in spoken words than in spoken nonwords. *Perception and Psychophysics, 19*, 384–398.

Salverda, A. P., Dahan, D., & McQueen, J. M. (2003). The role of prosodic boundaries in the resolution of lexical embedding in speech comprehension. *Cognition, 90*, 51–89.

Samuel, A. G. (1981). Phonemic restoration: Insights from a new methodology. *Journal of Experimental Psychology: General, 110*, 474–494.

Samuel, A. G. (1996). Does lexical information influence the perceptual restoration of phonemes? *Journal of Experimental Psychology: General, 125*(1), 28–51.

Samuel, A. G. (1997). Lexical activation produces potent phonemic percepts. *Cognitive Psychology, 32*(2), 97–127.

Samuel, A. G. (2001). Knowing a word affects the fundamental perception of the sounds within it. *Psychological Science, 12*, 348–351.

Samuel, A. G., & Pitt, M. A. (2003). Lexical activation (and other factors) can mediate compensation for coarticulation. *Journal of Memory and Language, 48*(2), 416–434.

Saslow, M. G. (1967). Latency for saccadic eye movement. *Journal of the Optical Society of America, 57*, 1030–1033.

Shillcock, R. C., & Bard, E. G . (1993). Modularity and the processing of closed class words. In G. T. M. Altmann & R. C. Shillock (Eds.), *Cognitive models of speech processing. The Second Sperlonga Meeting* (pp. 163–185). Mahwah, NJ: Erlbaum.

Spivey, M., Grosjean, M., & Knoblich, G. (2005). Continuous attraction toward phonological competitors. *Proceedings of the National Academy of Sciences USA, 102*(29), 10393–10398.

Strauss, T., Harris, H. D., & Magnuson, J. S. (2007). jTRACE: A reimplementation and extension of the TRACE model of speech perception and spoken word recognition. *Behavior Research Methods, Instruments and Computers, 39*, 19–30.

Swinney, D. A. (1979). Lexical access during sentence comprehension: (Re)consideration of con- text effects. *Journal of Verbal Learning and Verbal Behavior, 18*, 645–659.

Tanenhaus, M. K., Leiman, J. M., & Seidenberg, M. S. (1979). Evidence for multiple stages in the processing of ambiguous words in syntactic contexts. *Journal of Verbal Learning and Verbal Behavior, 18*, 427–440.

Tanenhaus, M. K., Spivey-Knowlton, M. J., Eberhard, K. M., & Sedivy, J. C. (1995). Integration of visual and linguistic information in spoken language comprehension. *Science, 268*(5217), 632–634.

Trueswell, J. C., & Tanenhaus, M. K. (1994). Toward a lexicalist framework for constraint-based syntactic ambiguity resolution. In C. Clifton, L. Frazier, & K. Rayner (Eds.), *Perspectives in sentence processing* (pp. 155–179). Hillsdale, NJ: Erlbaum.

Tyler, L. K., Voice, J. K., & Moss, H. E. (2000). The interaction of meaning and sound in spoken word recognition. *Psychonomic Bulletin and Review, 7*, 320–326.

Ueno, T., Saito, S., Rogers, T. T., & Lambon Ralph, M. A. (2011). Lichtheim 2: Synthesizing aphasia and the neural basis of language in a neurocomputational model of the dual dorsal-ventral language pathways. *Neuron, 72*(2), 385–396.

Vitevitch, M. S., & Luce, P.A. (1999). Probabilistic phonotactics and neighborhood activation in spoken word recognition. *Journal of Memory and Language, 40*, 374–408.

Viviani, P. (1990). Eye movements in visual search: Cognitive, perceptual, and motor control aspects. In E. Kowler (Ed.), *Eye movements and their role in visual and cognitive processes. Reviews of oculomotor research (Vol. 4, pp. xx–xx)*. Amsterdam, The Netherlands: Elsevier.

Warren, R. M. (1970). Perceptual restoration of missing speech sounds. *Science, 167*, 392–93.

Warren, R. M., Obusek, C. J., Farmer, R. M., & Warren, R. P. (1969). Auditory sequence: Confusion of patterns other than speech and music. *Science, 196*, 586–587.

Yee, E., & Sedivy, J. (2006). Eye movements to pictures reveal transient semantic activation during spoken word recognition. *Journal of Experimental Psychology: Learning, Memory and Cognition, 32*(1), 1–14.

Yee, E., Huffstetler, S., & Thompson-Schill, S. L. (2011). Function follows form: Activation of shape and function features during object identification. *Journal of Experimental Psychology: General, 140*(3), 348–363.

Yee, E., Overton, E., & Thompson-Schill, S. L. (2009). Looking for meaning: Eye movements are sensitive to overlapping semantic features, not association. *Psychonomic Bulletin and Review, 16*(5), 869–874.

Zhuang, J., Randall, B., Stamatakis, E. A., Marslen-Wilson, W. D., & Tyler, L. K. (2011). The interaction of lexical semantics and cohort competition in spoken word recognition: An fMRI study. *Journal of Cognitive Neuroscience, 23*(12), 3778–3790.

Zwitserlood, P. (1989). The locus of the effects of sentential-semantic context in spoken-word processing. *Cognition, 32*, 25–64.

# Basic Processes in Reading

Keith Rayner *and* Alexander Pollatsek

**Abstract**

Two important basic processes in reading, eye movement control and word recognition, are discussed in this chapter. While other aspects of reading are very important, we view eye movement control and word recognition as essential basic processes in learning to read and in skilled reading. We first review research on the characteristics of eye movements during reading and also discuss the perceptual span (or area of effective vision) during an eye fixation, preview benefit, and the control of eye movements. We then review research on word recognition, discussing how letters and words are processed, the role of phonological coding in word processing, and the role of context in word recognition.

**Key Words:** reading, eye movements, word recognition

Skilled reading is a remarkable achievement of the human mind (Huey, 1908; Rayner & Pollatsek, 1989; Rayner, Pollatsek, Ashby, & Clifton, 2011). Whereas most children acquire spoken language without much difficulty and without formal instruction, reading can be quite difficult to acquire and generally involves formal instruction (Rayner, Foorman, Perfetti, Pesetsky, & Seidenberg, 2001, 2002). Yet, once the basics of reading are mastered, readers are able to efficiently process the written versions of their language.

Cognitive psychologists have long been interested in skilled reading. While the topic of learning to read generally falls within the purview of developmental and educational psychology, the issue of how the mind/brain processes written language has been an important topic of research for cognitive psychology. In this chapter, we address basic processes in reading and focus on two aspects of the overall skill: eye movement control and word recognition. We quite readily acknowledge that there are many other aspects to skilled reading besides eye movement control and word recognition (see Rayner & Pollatsek, 1989; Rayner, Pollatsek, Ashby, & Clifton, 2011, for discussion of other important components of reading). For example, a lot of research has examined sentence processing (i.e., syntactic parsing) and discourse processing, and both topics are important and worthy of discussion. However, we focus on eye movement control and word recognition since both are central to the ability to process written text. Quite simply, we cannot read and comprehend text if we cannot (1) control our eye movements efficiently so as to obtain maximal information from the text and (2) understand and recognize individual words in text. While it is possible to read without eye movements (so that either the head moves or the text moves), clearly most reading involves readers making eye movements. Likewise, it is quite obvious that reading cannot proceed efficiently if readers cannot recognize the individual words on a page of text. Indeed, recognizing the printed words is perhaps the most basic component of skilled reading. We begin the chapter by first addressing some basic issues related to eye movements during reading and then turn to issues related to word recognition.

## Eye Movements During Reading

When we read, our eyes do not simply glide across the page, even though that is how it feels to us. Rather, we make a series of very fast eye movements (called *saccades*) separated by periods of time when the eyes are relatively still (called *fixations*). Since vision is suppressed during a saccade (Matin, 1974; Wolverton & Zola, 1983), new information is only acquired during fixations, though cognitive processing does continue in most situations during the saccade (Irwin, 1998; Irwin & Carlson-Radvansky, 1996). Fixations typically last about 200–250 ms, though there is considerable variability as some fixations are under 100 ms and some are well over 500 ms (Rayner, 1998, 2009a). Reading is thus a bit like a slide show where information is acquired from brief snapshots of the text. Saccade latency, the time needed to encode the location of a target in the visual field and initiate an eye movement, is on the order of 175–200 ms (Becker & Jürgens, 1979; Rayner, Slowiaczek, Clifton, & Bertera, 1983). However, it varies quite a bit as a function of the exact nature of the situation and readers can probably make the decision to move their eyes in the dynamic task of reading faster than 175–200 ms. Saccade duration, the amount of time that is takes to actually move the eyes, is a function of the distance moved. A typical saccade in reading, about 2 degrees in visual angle, takes about 30 ms. However, it has been demonstrated that a more appropriate index of saccade length in reading is letter spaces, rather than visual angle (Morrison & Rayner, 1981). Thus, the average saccade is about 7–9 letter spaces, but again with considerable variability – with some saccades smaller than a single letter and some as long as 25 or more letter spaces.

Eye movements are necessary because of the anatomy of the retina. In reading, for example, the line of text that the reader is looking at can be divided into three regions: the foveal region (i.e., the 2 degrees in the center of vision), the parafoveal region (which extends from the foveal region to about 5 degrees on either side of fixation), and the peripheral region (which includes everything on a line beyond the parafoveal region). Because acuity is high in the center of vision and drops off precipitously beyond the fovea, we move our eyes so as to place the fovea on that word (or words) we wish to process next.

Regressions (saccades that move backward in the text) are the third important component of eye movements in reading and occur about 10%–15% of the time in skilled readers. They need to be distinguished, however, from return sweeps, which are right-to-left saccades from the end of one line to the beginning of the next. The long forward saccades of 25 or more letter spaces just mentioned tend to follow a regression since readers typically move forward in the text past the point from which they originally launched the regression. Most regressions tend to be to the immediately preceding word, though when comprehension is not going well or the text is particularly difficult, more long-range regressions occur to earlier words in the text. Regressions are not particularly well understood because it is difficult to control them experimentally.

Thus, the eyes do not relentlessly move forward in the text given that readers regress about 10% to 15% of the time. Another important fact is that every word in the text is not directly fixated. The first and last fixations on a line are typically 5–7 letter spaces from the end of the line. Thus, about 80% of the text typically falls between the extreme fixations. Overall, up to one-third of the words in a text are skipped. Usually the skipped words are short function words or words that are highly predictable from the preceding context. It is a mistake, however, to assume that if a word is not fixated that it is not processed. It is generally believed that skipped words are processed on the fixation prior to the skip (and perhaps to some extent after the skip as well).

Eye movements are influenced by text difficulty, reading skill, and characteristics of the writing system. Thus, as text gets more difficult, fixations get longer, saccades get shorter, and more regressions are made. Also, typographical variables such as font difficulty can influence eye movements; more difficult-to-encode fonts yield longer fixations, shorter saccades, and more regressions (Rayner, Reichle, Stroud, Williams, & Pollatsek, 2006; Slattery & Rayner, 2010). Beginning, dyslexic, and other less skilled readers have longer fixations, shorter saccades, and more regressions than skilled readers (see Rayner, 1998, 2009a). As far as a writing system is concerned, the one that is most different from English is Chinese, yet Chinese readers tend to have average fixation durations that are quite similar to readers of English, and their regression rate does not differ dramatically from English readers. Where they do differ is that their average saccade length is much shorter than that of readers of alphabetic writing systems (as measured in number of characters) as they typically move their eyes only 2–3 characters (which makes sense given that linguistic information in Chinese is more densely packed than in English). Likewise, readers of Hebrew (a language that is also more densely packed than English, largely because most vowels are deleted in the printed orthography) tend to have shorter saccades (about 5.5 letter spaces) than readers of English (Pollatsek, Bolozky, Well, & Rayner, 1981), though their fixation durations are comparable.

Three central issues with respect to eye movements during reading will now be discussed. They are as follows: (1) the perceptual span, (2) preview benefit, and (3) the control of eye movements.

### The Perceptual Span in Reading

How much information does a skilled reader process and use during each fixation? In other words, how large is the perceptual span, or region of effective vision, during an eye fixation in reading? We often have the impression that we can clearly see the entire line of text, even the entire page of text. However, this is an illusion as experiments utilizing a gaze-contingent, moving-window paradigm (McConkie & Rayner, 1975; Rayner & Bertera, 1979) have clearly demonstrated. In experiments using the moving-window paradigm, the rationale is to vary how much information is available to a reader and then determine how large the window of normal text has to be before readers read normally (see top panels of Fig. 28.1). Thus, within the window area, text is normally displayed; in contrast, outside of the window, the letters are replaced (with other letters or with X's or a homogenous masking pattern). The size of the window can be varied so that it is either very small or quite large. Wherever the reader looks, the window is available, but outside of the window the words/letters from the normal text are not available. This is possible because the eyes are tracked by a highly accurate eye tracking system (with very high spatial resolution) interfaced to a high-speed computer. Thus, the window moves in synchrony with the eyes and is in place when the reader's saccade ends.

Research using this paradigm has demonstrated that skilled readers of English and other alphabetic writing systems obtain useful information from an asymmetric region extending roughly 3–4 character spaces to the left of fixation to about 14–15 character spaces to the right of fixation (see Rayner, 1998, 2009a, for reviews). If readers have the fixated word and the word to the right of fixation available on a fixation (and all other letters are replaced with

```
our eyes don't simply glide across the page even though

xxxxeyes don't simpxxxxxxxxxxxxxxxxxxxxxxxxxxxxxxxxxxxxxx
       +
Xxxxxxxxxxxn't simply glidxxxxxxxxxxxxxxxxxxxxxxxxxxxxxxxx
          +

avn eyes don't simptj ptnbc ornazz fkc goyc cwcm fhcnpb
        +
avn cjcr ban't simply glidc ornazz fkc goyc cwcm fhcnpb
           +


Our eyesxxxxxxxxxxmply glide across the page even though
          +
our eyes don'txxxxxxxxxxlide across the page even though
          +
```

**Figure 28.1** Example of a moving window and a moving mask. The first line shows a normal line of text. The second and third lines show what two consecutive fixations would be like with a 15-letter window. The + indicates the location of the readers' fixation (though it would be on the line of text and our representation shows it below the line). In these examples, all letters and spaces outside of the window are replaced with x's. The fourth and fifth lines show what two consecutive fixations would be like with a 15-letter window, but with the spaces outside the window preserved and letters replaced with similar letters. The sixth and seventh lines show what two consecutive fixations would be like with a 9-letter mask.

visually similar letters), they are not aware that the words outside of the window are not normal, and their reading speed only decreases by about 10%. If two words to the right of fixation are available within the window, there is very little slowdown in reading (Rayner, Well, Pollatsek, & Bertera, 1982). That the asymmetry of the perceptual span is a function of attention is evident from the finding that the asymmetry is reversed for readers of Hebrew (Pollatsek, Bolozky, Well, & Rayner, 1981), which is printed from right to left; they obtain more information from the left than from the right of fixation. It is also clear that the span is not simply the result of acuity limitations as Miellet, O'Donnell, and Sereno (2009) demonstrated that the span to the right of fixation remained 14–15 letter spaces to the right of fixation when they used a parafoveal magnification technique in which letters on each fixation became increasingly larger further from fixation (to offset acuity limitations).

Readers do not utilize information from the words on the lines below the one they are currently fixating. However, if the task is visual search rather than reading, then information can be obtained below the currently fixated line (Pollatsek, Raney, LaGasse, & Rayner, 1993). Finally, in moving-mask experiments (Rayner & Bertera, 1979; Rayner, Inhoff, Morrison, Slowiaczek, & Bertera, 1981) in which a visual mask moves in synchrony with the eyes on each fixation (see bottom panel of Fig. 28.1), reading is very difficult if not impossible as central foveal vision is masked (and only letters in parafoveal vision are available for reading). In essence, the moving-mask paradigm creates an artificial foveal scotoma mimicking patients with brain damage that effectively eliminates their use of foveal vision.

Characteristics of the writing system influence the size of the perceptual span. Thus, for readers of Chinese (which is now typically read from left to right in mainland China), the perceptual span extends 1 character to the left of fixation to 2–3 characters to the right (Inhoff & Liu, 1998). And, as noted earlier, the perceptual span for Hebrew readers is asymmetric and larger to the left of fixation (Pollatsek et al., 1981). In addition, reading skill influences the size of the perceptual span since beginning readers (Häikiö, Bertram, Hyönä, & Niemi, 2009; Rayner, 1986) and dyslexic readers (Rayner, Murphy, Henderson, & Pollatsek, 1989) have smaller spans than more skilled readers. Presumably, difficulty encoding the fixated word leads to smaller spans for both beginning and dyslexic readers. Older readers read more slowly than younger college-age readers (Laubrock, Kliegl, & Engbert, 2006; Rayner, Reichle, Stroud, Williams & Pollatsek, 2006) and their perceptual span seems to be slightly smaller (and less asymmetric) than younger readers (Rayner, Castelhano, & Yang, 2009a). In addition, the amount of preview benefit they obtain from a word is somewhat attenuated, particularly in cases where refixations or regressions are made (Rayner, Castelhano, & Yang, 2009b).

Finally, reading speed is related to the size of the perceptual span as Rayner, Slattery, and Bélanger (2010) recently found that slower readers (reading about 200 wpm) have a smaller perceptual span than faster readers (reading about 330 wpm). Rayner et al. (2010) argued that slower readers, like dyslexic, beginning, and older readers have more difficulty encoding the fixated word. Interestingly, they also varied the font in their experiment using a standard fixed width font (which for technical reasons has been typically used in moving-window

experiments) and proportional width fonts and found that this manipulation did not have an effect on the size of the perceptual span. This too is consistent with the conclusion that the number of letters/words that can be processed is primarily influenced by attention.

## Preview Benefit in Reading

Research using another type of gaze-contingent display change paradigm—the boundary paradigm (Rayner, 1975)—has also revealed important information about what kind of information is obtained from parafoveal words and integrated across saccades. In the boundary paradigm, an invisible boundary is just to the left of a target word (see Fig. 28.2) and before the reader crosses the boundary, there is typically a preview that is different from the target word. When the eyes cross the boundary, the preview is replaced by the target word; because of saccadic suppression, readers are generally unaware of the identity of the preview and of the display change. Research using this paradigm has revealed that when readers have a valid preview of the word to the right of fixation (i.e., the actual target word), they spend less time fixating that word (following a saccade to it) than when they do not have a valid preview (i.e., as when another word or nonword or random string of letters initially occupied the target word location). The size of this *preview benefit* is typically on the order of 30–50 ms. Research using this technique and related techniques has revealed a number of interesting findings (see Rayner, 2009a, for a review).

This research has demonstrated that readers do not combine a literal representation of the visual information across saccades. This is clear from studies that employed words written in mixed case LiKe ThIs (McConkie & Zola, 1979; Rayner, McConkie, & Zola, 1980). These experiments demonstrate that, with a little bit of practice, people can read such text just about as well as normal text, especially if the tops and bottoms of all the lowercase

Our eyes don't simply happy across the page even though

+

Our eyes don't simply glide across the page even though

+

**Figure 28.2** Example of the boundary paradigm. The first line shows a line with the reader fixated on the word *simply*. When the reader's eyes cross an invisible boundary just after the "y" in *simply*, the display change occurs and the target word *glide* replaces the preview word *happy*.

letters are aligned with the tops and bottoms of the uppercase letters. Moreover, McConkie and Zola switched the case of all the letters on every fixation (e.g., "like" would switch back and forth between LiKe and lIkE) and found that this had no effect on reading speed or comprehension. These experiments not only demonstrate that what is preserved across fixations is an abstract (case-independent) form of letters. They also indicate that the visual form of the whole word is largely irrelevant for word identification and that the initial stage of word recognition involves the identification of the component abstract letters. Moreover, other experiments indicate that not all letters of words in the parafovea seem to be of equal importance (Inhoff, 1989; Johnson, Perea, & Rayner, 2007); beginning letters of the word to the right of the fixated word have the most influence on later processing, and its end letters are more important than middle letters (especially for shorter words).

We will document later that phonological codes, as well as abstract phonological codes, are integrated across saccades. However, somewhat surprisingly, semantic information is not (Hyönä & Häikiö, 2005; Rayner, Balota, & Pollatsek, 1985; White, Bertram, & Hyönä, 2008). That is, words that typically produce priming in a standard naming or lexical decision task (e.g., the prime word *tune* primes the target word *song*) do not yield priming when the prime word is in parafoveal vision[1] (with the target word presented as soon as the reader crosses the invisible boundary location). Although this result is sometimes considered puzzling, it is probably due to the fact that words in parafoveal vision are degraded sufficiently that readers cannot typically process their meaning. This is not to say that words in parafoveal vision cannot be identified, because they clearly can. When words are short or sufficiently constrained by context, as discussed later, readers skip them, and it is generally agreed that these words are identified on the fixation prior to the skip.

Just as there is no strong evidence that semantic information is integrated across saccades, there is also no evidence in English that morphological information from a parafoveal word facilitates processing when the word is later fixated (Inhoff, 1989; Juhasz, White, Liversedge, & Rayner, 2008; Kambe, 2004; Lima, 1987). Specifically, readers do not have shorter fixations on a word when the preview was a prefix than when it was a pseudo-prefix. On the other hand, readers of Hebrew apparently do integrate morphological information across saccades (Deutsch, Frost, Peleg, Pollatsek, & Rayner,

2003; Deutsch, Frost, Pollatsek, & Rayner, 2000, 2005), as morphological information is more central to processing Hebrew than English.

The amount of preview benefit readers obtain varies as a function of the difficulty of the fixated word. If the fixated word is difficult to process, readers get little or no preview benefit from the word to the right of fixation (Henderson & Ferreira, 1990; White, Rayner, & Liversedge, 2005). Conversely, if the fixated word is easy to process, readers get larger preview benefit from the word to the right of fixation (Balota, Pollatsek, & Rayner, 1985; Drieghe, Rayner, & Pollatsek, 2005). It has also been found that preview benefit is larger within words than across words (Hyönä, Bertram, & Pollatsek, 2004; Juhasz, Pollatsek, Hyönä, Drieghe, & Rayner, 2009; Pollatsek & Hyönä, 2005).

Another interesting issue concerns the spatial extent of preview benefit. Specifically, do readers obtain preview benefit from word $n + 2$ (the word two to the right of the currently fixated word)? While it is clear that readers generally obtain preview benefit from word $n + 1$, readers typically do not get preview benefit from word $n + 2$ (Angele, Slattery, Yang, Kliegl, & Rayner, 2008; Kliegl, Risse, & Laubrock, 2007; McDonald, 2005, 2006; Rayner, Juhasz, & Brown, 2007). It may be that when word $n + 1$ is a very short word (2–3 letters), readers obtain preview benefit from word $n + 2$. Also, preview benefit may be obtained from word $n + 2$ when readers target their next saccade to that word. However, when readers fixate word $n + 1$ and word $n + 2$ in sequence, they obtain preview benefit from word $n + 1$ but not word $n + 2$.

## PARAFOVEAL-ON-FOVEAL EFFECTS

Do characteristics of the word to the right of fixation influence the duration of the fixation on the currently fixated word? Such effects, when they occur, are called parafoveal-on-foveal effects (see Rayner, 2009a for review). Some research has found that orthographic properties of the word to the right of fixation can influence the duration of the current fixation, while other studies have found no such effects. Furthermore, some recent studies have suggested that the meaning of the word to the right of fixation can produce parafoveal-on-foveal effects, while other studies have shown inconsistent or no parafoveal-on-foveal effects due to word frequency. Other studies have likewise shown no evidence of lexical parafoveal-on-foveal effects (see Rayner, 2009a for a review and discussion of these studies).

Are parafoveal-on-foveal effects real or are there other reasons why such effects sometimes appear in the eye movement record? There are two possible (and reasonable) explanations for parafoveal-on-foveal effects that do not assume that such effects are real. First, some fixations in reading are mislocated because saccades are not perfectly accurate and do not land on the intended target (Nuthmann, Engbert, & Kliegl, 2005); thus, parafoveal-on-foveal effects may arise due to inaccurately targeted saccades (Drieghe, Rayner, & Pollatsek, 2008; Rayner, Warren, Juhasz, & Liversedge, 2004). That is, some saccades that are meant to land on a given target word fall short of the target and land on the end of the previous word. However, in this case, attention would still be allocated to the word that was intended to be the target of the saccade so that processing of the target word influences the fixation on the previous word. Second, the studies that have typically reported evidence of parafoveal-on-foveal effects have largely been based on analyses of large data sets across a corpus of data, whereas those that have found no evidence for lexical parafoveal-on-foveal effects are based on experimental studies that provide greater control over other variables (see Rayner, Pollatsek, Drieghe, Slattery, & Reichle, 2007).

At this point, there seems to be some converging agreement concerning the validity of ortho-graphic parafoveal-on-foveal effects. However, there is controversy concerning the validity of lexical parafoveal-on-foveal effects. Given the possibility of mislocalized fixations and the fact that most of the positive evidence for these effects is based on corpus-based analyses, it seems quite reasonable to view such effects with caution (Rayner, Pollatsek, et al., 2007; White, 2008).

## The Control of Eye Movements in Reading

What determines *when* and *where* to move the eyes? Across large segments of text, there is no cor-relation between how long the eyes remain fixated and how far they move (Rayner & McConkie, 1976). This has generally been taken to suggest that these two decisions are made somewhat inde-pendently and there is compelling evidence for this view. Specifically, Rayner and Pollatsek (1981) var-ied physical aspects of the text and found that prop-erties of an eye movement mirrored aspects of the display on the current fixation. In one experiment, we used the moving-window paradigm described earlier and varied the size of the window from fixation to fixation. We found that saccade length varied as a function of the immediately preceding window size. Thus, when the window was small, saccade size was shorter than when the window was large. In a second experiment, the text was delayed at the onset of a fixation by a mask (with the time of the delay varying randomly from fixation to fixation). Here we found that a large percentage of fixation durations varied according to the text delay. From this, we argued that most fixations in reading are under direct cognitive control, though there was also a subset of fixations that appeared to be preprogrammed (see also Morrison, 1984). Importantly, the manipulations affected saccade length and fixation duration independently, rein-forcing the view that the decisions about where to move and when to move are made somewhat independently.

In general, it appears from a considerable amount of research that the decision of where to move next is largely driven by low-level properties of the text while the decision of when to move the eyes is largely driven by lexical properties of the fixated word (Rayner, 1998). However, as we discuss later, lexical effects (specifically related to word predict-ability and word frequency) have some influence on where the eyes move (and considerable influence on how long they remain fixated).

### WHERE TO MOVE THE EYES

For English and other alphabetic languages, where to move the eyes next is strongly influenced by low-level cues provided by word length and space information. Thus, saccade length is influenced by the length of the fixated word and the word to the right of it. If the word to the right of fixation is either very long or very short, the next saccade will be lon-ger than when a medium size word is to the right of fixation. For example, if the 9 character spaces to the right of the fixated word consists of a single 9-letter word, the saccade will be longer than if it consists of two 4-letter words (with a space between). If there is a short word (2 to 4 letters to the right of fixation) to the right of fixation, the next saccade will tend to be longer than when the next word is 5 to 7 letters, largely because the short word tends to be skipped (Juhasz, White, et al., 2008).

It is also clear that the spaces between words (which demarcate how long words are) are used in targeting where the next saccade will land. When space information is removed, reading slows down considerably. Specifically, when spaces are removed or spaces are filled with irrelevant characters, read-ing slows down by as much as 30%–50% (Rayner,

Fischer, & Pollatsek, 1998). Moreover, even though spaces between words are not present in all writing systems, inserting spaces between words or morphemes[2] in writing systems that do not use them seems to generally help, even though these spaces are "illegal" in the writing system. For example, Kohsom and Gobet (1997) demonstrated that when space information was provided for readers of Thai (who are not used to reading with spaces between words), they read more effectively than normal. Also, work with three-lexeme compound words in German (where three words are often strung together as one word such as datasystemsanalyist) showed that inserting spaces between the three lexemes actually reduces overall reading time on the compounds (Inhoff, Radach, & Heller, 2000). In the experiment by Inhoff et al., the interword spaces were more beneficial than other manipulations that were used to mark lexeme boundaries (e.g., capitalizing the first letter of each lexeme). More recently, Bai, Yan, Liversedge, Zang, and Rayner (2008) inserted spaces between Chinese words or between Chinese characters (for a similar study with Japanese, see Sainio, Hyönä, Bingushi, & Bertram, 2007). (In Chinese, a character is a morpheme, and words typically are two characters.) Whereas inserting a space between every two characters interfered with reading, inserting spaces between words did not. Actually, it is quite surprising that the insertion of spaces between words was not interfering, given that the Chinese readers have a lifetime of experience reading without spaces. All of these pieces of evidence suggest that even when interword spaces are orthographically illegal, they are beneficial to reading.

**LANDING POSITION EFFECTS**

The spaces between words provide information about an upcoming word's length in parafoveal vision, leading to systematic tendencies with respect to where the eyes typically land. Rayner (1979) demonstrated that readers' eyes tend to land halfway between the middle of a word and the beginning of that word (the *preferred viewing location*). It is generally argued that readers attempt to target the center of words, but their saccades tend to fall short. When readers' eyes land at a nonoptimal position in a word, they are more likely to refixate that word. Experiments using the boundary change paradigm, which provided readers with an incorrect length preview of an upcoming word in the parafovea, have demonstrated that when readers send their eyes to what will turn out to be a nonoptimal position in

the parafoveal word, there will be an increase in reading time on the word once fixated (Inhoff, Radach, Eiter, & Juhasz, 2003; Juhasz, White, et al., 2008; White et al., 2005).

Where readers fixate in a word is not only determined by the intended landing site on the word but by where the saccade was launched from (McConkie, Kerr, Reddix, & Zola, 1988; Rayner, Sereno, & Raney, 1996). Although the average landing position in a word lies between the beginning and the middle of a word, this position varies as a function of the prior launch site. Thus, if the launch site for a saccade landing on a target word is far from that word (say 8 to 10 letter spaces), the landing position will be shifted to the left. Likewise, if the distance is small (2–3 letter spaces), the landing position is shifted to the right.

**SKIPPING EFFECTS**

As noted earlier, words are sometimes skipped during reading. Two factors have a big impact on skipping: word length and contextual constraint. First, the most important variable in skipping is word length (Rayner, 1998): Short words are much more likely to be skipped than long words. When two or three short words occur in succession, there is a good chance that two of them will be skipped. In addition, short words (like *the*) preceding a content word are often skipped (Drieghe, Pollatsek, Staub, & Rayner, 2008). In situations such as this, groups of words (e.g., three short words in succession and when an article precedes a content word) tend to be processed on a single fixation. Second, words that are highly constrained by the prior context are much more likely to be skipped than those that are not predictable (Ehrlich & Rayner, 1981; Rayner & Well, 1996). Chinese words that are predictable from prior context are also skipped more than those that are not (Rayner, Li, Juhasz, & Yan, 2005). Word frequency also has an effect on word skipping, but the effect is smaller than that of predictability (Rayner, Sereno, & Raney, 1996). While predictability influences whether a word is skipped, it does not influence where in the word the fixation lands (Rayner, Binder, Ashby, & Pollatsek, 2001; Vainio, Hyönä, & Pajunen, 2009). However, predictability does influence how long readers look at a word. Finally, Rayner, Slattery, Drieghe, and Liversedge (2011) recently demonstrated that while longer words were less likely to be skipped than short words, long predictable words (over 10–12 letters long) were skipped more than long unpredictable words.

## WHEN TO MOVE THE EYES

The ease or difficulty associated with processing the currently fixated word strongly influences when the eyes move (for reviews, see Liversedge & Findlay, 2000; Rayner, 1998, 2009a; Starr & Rayner, 2001). Thus, fixation time on a word is influenced by a host of lexical and linguistic variables such as word frequency, word predictability, number of meanings, age of acquisition, phonological properties of words, semantic relations between the fixated word and prior words, and word familiarity. The effects of word frequency (Yan, Tian, Bai, & Rayner, 2006) and word predictability (Rayner et al., 2005) on fixation times on words also hold for skilled readers of Chinese. It is also interesting to note that when viewers are presented passages of text and are asked to search for a target word in the text, the frequency effect disappears (Rayner & Fischer, 1996; Rayner & Raney, 1996). This is consistent with the view that what influences *when* to move the eyes during reading is different from visual search.

Perhaps the most compelling evidence that cognitive processing of the fixated word is driving the eyes through the text comes from experiments in which the fixated word either disappears or is masked after 50–60 ms (Ishida & Ikeda, 1989; Liversedge et al., 2004; Rayner et al., 1981; Rayner, Liversedge, White, 2006; Rayner, Liversedge, White, & Vergilino-Perez, 2003). Basically, these studies show that if readers are allowed to see the fixated word for 50–60 ms before it disappears, they read quite normally. This does not mean that words are completely processed in 50–60 ms, but rather that this amount of time is sufficient for the visual processing system to encode the word for further processing. Interestingly, if the word to the right of fixation also disappears or is masked, then reading is disrupted (Rayner, Liversedge, & White, 2006). This indicates both (a) that the word to the right of fixation is very important in reading and (b) that it is typically not attended at the beginning of a fixation so that when it disappears after 50–60 ms it is not preserved for further processing. More critically, when the fixated word disappears after 50–60 ms, how long the eyes remain in place is determined by the frequency of the word that disappeared: If it is a low-frequency word, the eyes remain in place longer (Rayner et al., 2003, Liversedge, & White, 2006). Thus, even though the word is no longer there, how long the eyes remain in place is determined by that word's frequency. This is very compelling evidence that the cognitive processing associated with a fixated word is the primary engine driving the eyes through the text.

It is thus clear that lexical variables have strong and immediate effects on how long readers look at a word. While other linguistic variables can have an influence on how soon readers move their eyes on in the text, it is generally the case that higher level linguistic variables have somewhat later effects, unless the variable more or less "smacks you in the eye." One clear example of an immediate effect on processing from a higher level linguistic variable is when readers fixate on the disambiguating word in a syntactic "garden path" sentence such as "While Mary was mending the sock fell off her lap." in which readers boggle when they get to "fell" because they parsed "the sock" as the object of "was mending." In such cases, when readers fixate the disambiguating word ("fell"), they make regressions back to earlier parts of the sentence (Frazier & Rayner, 1982). Readers also have longer fixations at the end of clauses and sentences, suggesting that they are taking time to "wrap up" processing of that unit before moving ahead (Rayner, Kambe, & Duffy, 2001). Also, when readers encounter an anomalous word, the effect is quite immediate, as they fixate on it longer (Rayner et al., 2004; Staub, Rayner, Pollatsek, Hyönä, & Majewski, 2007; Warren & McConnell, 2007); when a word indicates an implausible, but not truly anomalous event, there will be an effect registered in the eye movement record, but it is typically delayed a bit, showing up in later processing measures (Joseph, Liversedge, Blythe, White, Gathercole, & Rayner, 2008; Rayner et al., 2004). Thus, if readers encounter a sentence like "Jane used an axe to chop the carrots for dinner," the effect of the implausible nature of using an axe to chop carrots is registered in measures reflecting later processing activities, such as go-past time (the time from when a word is first encountered until the eyes move forward past that word in the text).

Interestingly, when sentences with an anomalous word (such as *carrot* in "Jane used a pump to inflate the large carrot.") are embedded in cartoon or fantasy-like contexts and compared with real-world contexts where inflating a carrot with a pump is anomalous (Warren, McConnell, & Rayner, 2008), the earliest measures of fixation time (first fixation duration and gaze duration) still yield longer fixations on the anomalous word than the control word (*carrot* in a sentence like "Jane used a knife to chop the large carrot."). However, go-past time revealed disruption only in the real-world context. These results suggest that contextual information did not eliminate the initial disruption but moderated it quickly thereafter. They also indicate that these fairly immediate effects are not merely due to the combination of a few weird words that do not normally occur together (such as "blow up" and "carrots") but to the reader's ongoing processing of the meaning of the text.

Finally, although we do not have space to discuss them in this chapter, the last 15 years has seen the development of a large number of computational models that can account for most of the details of eye movements that we have discussed earlier. The models differ on a number of key dimensions (see Rayner, 2009b; Reichle, Rayner, & Pollatsek, 2003, for overviews of the different models), but because they are quite explicit in their details they have generated a lot of recent research.

## Word Recognition

The topic of visual word recognition (usually studied with printed words as opposed to words written in script) has been a major area of research in cognitive psychology for the last 40 years. This is possibly because it touches on many basic topics in the field—most notably, object recognition, the relation between visual forms and meaning, and the relationship between spoken and written language. With respect to object recognition, although printed words are clearly unusual and "artificial" objects to study, they have the promise of shedding light on the general topic of object recognition because it is clearer what the components are (e.g., letters), whereas for most real-world objects, it is still far from clear what the features or parts are in the object recognition process.

Before going on, however, it must be acknowledged that the concept of "word" is not completely uncontroversial. In an alphabetic language like English, it may seem clear that a word is the sequence of letters between the spaces. However, the concept is really a bit fuzzier than that. In particular, in English, compound words are sometimes written without a space between the components (e.g., basketball) and sometimes written with a space (e.g., tennis ball). There really is not any principled reason for this difference, and in some languages, such as Finnish and German, all compound words (including ones with more than two constituents) are written without spaces.

The problem is deeper in other languages such as Chinese, where some researchers even question whether the concept of "word" is meaningful. That is, characters in Chinese are written without spaces between them within and between sentences. In addition, as noted earlier, characters in Chinese represent morphemes rather than words. Although there is evidence that the concept of "word" is meaningful in Chinese (although some Chinese words are one character, as we also noted earlier, the modal Chinese word is two characters), it is even less clear how to define it than in English, and it is not marked in the writing system. However, for the purposes of the present chapter, we will largely confine our discussion to alphabetic languages and, for the most part, talk about a word as "the sequence of letters between two spaces."

## Letters and Words—Parallel and Serial Processing Within and Between Words

As indicated earlier, one of the reasons that word identification has been of interest to cognitive psychologists is that it has the potential for helping our understanding of object recognition. This is because printed words have obvious visual components (letters) and thus the issue of how processing of parts relates to processing of the whole object seems more tractable than for other types of object recognition.[3] The earlier data we presented involving mixed-case words indicate that an overall word visual pattern (word shape) is, at best, a small part of the word identification process. But what is the process by which words are identified through their component letters? A major issue in cognitive psychology is whether components are processed in parallel (i.e., all at the same time) or serially (i.e., one at a time) and the answer (for short words, at least) is quite clear: The letters are processed in parallel. Perhaps the clearest demonstration of this is from a paradigm using isolated words (Reicher, 1969; Wheeler, 1970).

In this paradigm, the subject sees a target stimulus briefly followed by a *pattern mask*. (Many experiments have shown that such masks terminate low-level visual processing, but that whatever information has been extracted at that level remains in the processing system and can be processed further.) Simultaneous with the mask, a probe of two letters is presented (one above and one below one of the letters in the target stimulus) and the subject has to choose which of the two letters was in that location in the target stimulus (see Fig. 28.3). In these experiments, the time between the presentation of target stimulus and the pattern mask (the *stimulus onset asynchrony* or *SOA*) is held fixed at a value of something like 50–60 ms such that performance is above chance (50% correct) but well below perfect performance.

READ

O

#######

E

**Figure 28.3** Example of the word superiority effect paradigm. A target word (*read*) is presented followed by a mask and two letters. The subject must choose which letter was present. Notice that either letter (*o* or *e*) forms a word. Likewise, all of the letter positions can be replaced with two letters that make a word: READ and LEAD, READ and ROAD, READ and REND, and READ and REAL.

For our purposes, there are three conditions and two comparisons of interest. The first comparison is between when a single letter is presented and when four unrelated letters are presented. The data indicate that performance (percent correct identification of the probed letter) is the same when four letters are presented as when one is! This pretty clearly indicates that the four letters are processed in parallel, because a serial process that took any appreciable time would imply that performance should be worse when there were four letters to process. The second finding of interest was that, when the four letters formed a word, performance was even better than in either of the other two conditions. This implies that, not only are the letters in a word processed in parallel, but that there is some kind of mutual facilitation between the processing of the letters that is making performance even better. Note that this is not an artifact of guessing as, in all cases (not just the example in the figure), both of the probe letters presented would form a word given the other three letters. Moreover, later experiments (Baron, 1973) showed that there was also an advantage over single letters when the four-letter stimulus was a pseudoword (i.e., a pronounceable nonword) such as MARD.

These experiments pretty clearly show that, in the encoding of a word, units of at least four letters can be processed in parallel; furthermore, something about their "wordlikeness" aids in the encoding process. There are now a large number of models that can explain how this happens (e.g., McClelland & Rumelhart, 1981; Paap, Newsome, McDonald, & Schvaneveldt, 1982; Seidenberg & McClelland, 1989). They differ in their details, but the general idea in all of them is as follows. They all posit that there are letter detectors that operate in parallel. They all also posit that there is something like "word

knowledge" that is activated by these letter detectors but that also feeds back to the letter detectors. One difference in the models is that the word knowledge is stored specifically by word detectors in some of the models, whereas other models have what are generally called "hidden units" that are related to what words a person has seen in his or her lifetime but a hidden unit is not tied to a specific word. As the former models are easier to illustrate, we will briefly indicate how such a model could explain the aforementioned findings.

When a word is presented, it is assumed to excite the relevant letter detectors and word detectors. However, none of the units at either level is perfectly accurate (especially in conditions where the stimulus is presented briefly and masked). Thus, a *d* will not only excite the "d" detector, but it will also excite similar letters (such as *b*), but to a lesser extent. Similarly, the letters *dog* will not only excite the "dog" detector but will excite the "dot," "log," and "dig" detectors—but again to a lesser extent. These excited word detectors then feed back excitation to the letter detectors, and if the stimulus is a word, provide extra support for identifying the component letters. For example, if "dog" is presented, there would be quite a bit of excitation flowing back to support that the middle letter was an *o* and not a *c*. Moreover, these models do in fact predict that one would get about as much support from these word detectors even if the stimulus was a pseudoword like *mard* because words like *maid*, *yard*, and *mark* will help to support identification of the component letters. It may seem surprising that such models predict about as much facilitation in these tasks for pseudowords as words, but they do.

These experiments thus raise the question of what the limits are of how much can be processed in parallel and whether the limits are influenced by the spaces between words. As the prior section indicated, there are definite limits due to visual acuity: Letters that are further than about 14–15 characters from fixation cannot be processed even when the information closer to fixation is clearly irrelevant. Moreover, the prior section indicated that there are attentional constraints on what is being processed: Letters to the left of the fixated word are not processed, presumably because that word has already been identified and is now irrelevant and thus its letters are not attended to.

Currently, there is considerable controversy about how much is processed in parallel in reading, and we cannot review all the issues. Instead, we will discuss two experiments that we think shed light on the limitations of what can be processed in parallel in service of word identification. Juhasz, Pollatsek, Hyönä, Drieghe, and Rayner (2009) employed the boundary technique described earlier using compound words such as *basketball*. In this case, before the reader's eyes moved to the right of the initial morpheme *basket*, all but the initial letters of the rest of the word were replaced by nonsense letters (*basketbadk*). One interesting finding was that, as with the between-word boundary studies described earlier, readers were unaware of the incorrect letters. Moreover, the gaze duration on the initial morpheme was not affected by the presence of the unusual letters (i.e., it was the same regardless of whether *basketball* or *basketbadk* was presented). However, when readers' eyes landed on the second part of the word, their gaze duration on the second part was longer when the letters had been mutilated.

Drieghe, Pollatsek, Juhasz, and Rayner (2010) tested whether this was merely due to the length of the compound word or whether it was because compound words have two meaningful units. They compared the aforementioned preview effect for compound words to equally long words that were not compound words (e.g., *bathroom* vs. *fountain*). (In this example, the boundary was set between the fourth and fifth letters, and in one condition, all the letters after the sixth letter were changed to "nonsense letters.") They replicated the earlier study for the compound words but found considerable cost on the gaze duration on the first part of the control words. That is, in some sense, the mutilated letters affected initial processing when the word was a single meaningful unit but not when the word contained two meaningful units. This is not to say that there was no processing of the second part of the word, even when the word was a compound word; gaze durations on the whole word were lengthened considerably when there was a bad preview. (This is consistent with the boundary experiments described in the prior section where fixation time on a word is lengthened if an incorrect preview was present before it is fixated.) However, because this incorrect letter information has no effect in the case of the compound words until the second part is fixated, this indicates that, in some sense, the whole word was not processed as a unit in parallel.

How can this pattern of results be explained? One view that posits massive parallel processing in reading (Kliegl, Nuthmann, & Engbert, 2006) explains phenomena such as this by positing only a loose coupling of ongoing cognitive processing with the control of eye movements. However, we think that the data presented in the prior section indicate that this is not true; instead, there is quite tight coupling of cognitive processes and eye movements, even though there are some delayed effects of cognitive processing. We think a more serial view of how word information is processed is more consistent with the data (Reichle, Liversedge, Pollatsek, & Rayner, 2009). In this view, spatial attention is a key construct. That is, at any given time, the reader's spatial attention "window" is focused on processing a certain set of letters. For shorter words, this window of attention is almost certainly the entire word that is fixated.[4] Then, when the word is identified, covert attention shifts to the next word and some information from these letters is processed prior to the eyes actually moving to the next word. (This attentional shift obviously explains preview effects and can also explain word skipping.)

For longer words, such as the ones in the aforementioned studies, the process is undoubtedly more complex. It appears that the reader's initial focus of attention may only be on the beginning of the word but spreads out over the first few milliseconds of the fixation. However, if the initial part of the word is a unit such as a morpheme, the reader apparently does not initially attend to all the letters but assembles the initial letters as a unit and only then shifts attention to the rest of the word. Thus, the process for compound words may not be fundamentally different than for two separate words. The only difference may be that, for compound words, it takes a while to identify and isolate the first unit, whereas when there is a space between two words, the division is obvious.

To summarize, we think that in reading, the goal of the reader on each fixation is to identify a meaningful unit. Most of the time, this is the word being fixated, but some of the time, it is even a smaller unit. This unit is what is attended to on the first part of a fixation. When it is processed, attention shifts to the next unit in the text and processing begins on that before the eyes actually move to this new focus of attention. In some extreme cases, when the material in that next unit is very easy to identify because it is a very short word, predictable, and/or frequent in the language, it is actually fully identified and is skipped. Space limitations do not permit us to outline how this interplay between cognition and the eye movement system can occur, but there is a well-worked-out computational model in which all these phenomena (including skipping words and refixating words) can be explained.[5]

Before moving on to the next major topic—how the sounds of words influence the reading process—we need to finish this unit with a brief discussion of how the order of letters in a word is coded. In the early versions of the models we discussed earlier, such as the McClelland and Rumelhart model, it was tacitly assumed that the order of the letters was automatically encoded correctly. Although this may seem plausible for short words, it seems less so for words like *basketball*. That is, how would a system be able to code in a few milliseconds that *e* was the fifth rather than the fourth or sixth letter? One "solution" to this problem is to assert that letter order does not matter, and there are claims circulating on the Internet that people can read words in which the order of the letters is changed just as easily as normal text. Although it is true that people can usually tell what word was intended in such texts (assuming the scrambling is not too extreme), it is clear that the identification of words is quite a bit slower than with normal text (White et al., 2005).

There have been two attempts to explain how letter order is encoded well enough to be useful to the word processing system. The first relies on encoding the relative positions of neighboring letters (which seems plausible). One simple encoding scheme of this kind is bigrams. Thus, with bigrams, the order of the letters of *basket* would be captured by encoding the bigrams *ba*, *as*, *sk*, and so on. (Other subword units such as trigrams have also been proposed to help encode letter order.) The second type of model, in contrast, assumes that the system encodes the absolute position of all the letters, but that there is error involved in this coding (Gomez, Ratcliff, & Perea, 2008).

There is a phenomenon known as the transposed letter (TL) effect that supports the latter hypothesis. Different experimental paradigms have investigated the TL effect, but perhaps the easiest to explain is the masked priming paradigm (Forster & Davis, 1984). In this paradigm, a prime stimulus is presented briefly followed by a second target stimulus on top of the first stimulus that masks it so the viewer is unaware of the prime stimulus. There is also a pattern mask (often ######) that appears before the prime stimulus that helps in the masking process.[6] The typical task that is used in this paradigm is a *lexical decision task*, where the subject judges whether the target stimulus is a word. Our focus will be on those trials when the target stimulus was indeed a word.

The key comparison in these experiments is between the TL condition when the prime stimulus transposes two of the letters with a replacement letter (RL) condition where the same two letters of the target word are replaced by other letters (usually visually similar to the transposed letters). Thus, if *basket* was the target, a TL prime could be *bakset* and the RL prime could be *barlet*. The results of these experiments are quite consistent: Lexical decision times are faster when there is a TL prime than when there is an RL prime (Perea & Lupker, 2003; Schoonbaert & Grainger, 2004). (A similar result also occurs in the boundary paradigm, where either a TL or RL version of the stimulus is presented as a preview; Johnson et al., 2007.) Indeed, TL primes are sometimes almost as effective as when the prime is identical.

Perhaps you think that this result is not surprising and that virtually any model of word encoding could handle it. However, this is not the case as it is quite hard for a model of order encoding such as the bigram model to explain it. That is, if letters and their order are encoded as bigrams, then *basket* would have the following bigrams: [space]b, ba, as, sk, ke, et, t[space]. The prime *bakset* would have the bigrams [space]b, ba, ak, ks, se, et, t[space], and the prime *barlet* would have the bigrams [space] b, ba, ar, rl, le, et, t[space]. That is, there would be just as many bigram mismatches between the TL prime and the target word as between the RL prime and the target word. It is possible that one could try to fix this by positing that, for example, ks is more similar to sk than rl is. However, when one does this, then the feature of using the bigram to store the order of the letters gets lost. Moreover, there has been a satisfactory simulation of the TL data using a variant of the absolute coding of position with error model (Davis, 2010).

## Role of Phonological Coding in Word Processing

The role of phonological coding, or converting what is being read to a representation in the mind that is close to the sound of the spoken language, has been a contentious issue for decades, if not centuries. Certainly, in the popular culture, there is an often held belief that converting what is being read to a representation of speech is a bad habit that needs to be corrected if one is to read at a normal rate. This belief is certainly true if that conversion process is actually saying the words out loud in turn because normal silent reading (which is something like 300–350 words per minute for easy text) is much more rapid than spoken language. However, the real issue is not whether skilled readers either do or should read the text aloud, but instead, whether they form something like an acoustic image of the words (and text) in their minds while they are reading.

We think that the answer is clearly "yes"—that skilled readers do convert the printed language to sound when they read—and, furthermore, there is no reason to believe that it is not functional. First, by all evidence, the formation of such a phonological code is rapid and automatic and is not a hindrance to reading rapidly. Second, there is considerable evidence that short-term memory is quite dependent on a short-term rehearsal "buffer" in which acoustic codes play a major role (Baddeley & Hitch, 1974). In addition, of course, language for humans evolved as spoken language (with writing a relatively recent invention in terms of evolution); thus, it makes good sense that reading would be aided by bootstrapping on auditory language.

Plausible and functional arguments aside, we think the data solidly support the claim that skilled readers do automatically create a phonological representation of the words they are reading, and furthermore, that this process occurs early and is part of the process of accessing the meaning of a word. One of the more striking demonstrations of this comes from a paradigm developed by Van Orden (1987), which had subjects judge the meaning of a single word. More specifically, on each trial, he gave subjects a target category (e.g., TREE) and then had them judge whether the target word was a member of this category. The surprising finding was that when the target word was a homophone of a member of the category (e.g., BEACH), subjects took much longer to reject the word as not being in the category than a control word (e.g., BENCH) and made a considerable number of errors as well. Moreover, a similar, but slightly reduced, effect was found by Van Orden, Johnston, and Hale (1987) for pseudoword targets (e.g., judging that SUTE was not an article of clothing). Such a finding is hard to reconcile with a view that says that one goes directly from the printed word to the meaning, and only later (if at all) accesses the sound of the printed word. That is, in our example, BEACH should activate its "sandy seaside" meaning and thus the orthographic representation should not bias a person to respond that the word is a type of food. Moreover, even if BEACH later accesses the sound of the word, which then accesses the "beech tree" meaning, it is hard to see why people should falsely classify BEACH as a tree 30% of the time if they have earlier accessed the other meaning.

Thus, we think it is safe to say that there is little current controversy about whether skilled readers do access a phonological code while reading a word. However, there is still controversy about how early it does so in the reading process and how important sound coding is. To explain what is at issue, it will help if we define two terms: *addressed phonology* and *assembled phonology*. "Addressed phonology" refers to a process in which the visual stimulus goes to the reader's internal *lexicon* (mental dictionary) and then the sound is obtained there, roughly as one would find the correct pronunciation of a word in a real dictionary. In contrast, "assembled phonology" refers to a process in which the sound of the written stimulus is constructed from something like rules for converting print to sound or by analogies to words that are already in one's mental lexicon. (There are some theorists who maintain that there are not two distinct processes, but we think our exposition will be easier if we assume there are.)

Much of the early work on phonological coding in reading suggested that, although phonological coding was occurring in the identification of printed words, it was a relatively minor part of the process and perhaps mainly occurring for words that were low frequency in the language. (This is obviously quite a different picture from that presented in the semantic category judgment experiments described earlier.) These earlier experiments relied on the comparison of *regular* and *exception* words. This distinction assumes that there are rules governing how letter combinations should sound. For example, because virtually all monosyllabic words ending in *ave* have an "ay" vowel sound (e.g., gave, wave, pave, save, etc.), it is positive that there is a rule governing that the *a* in –*ave* is pronounced "ay"; thus, these rule-consistent words are called "regular" and a word in which the *a* is pronounced differently (*have*) is called an exception word.

The logic of these experiments is that if sound coding (especially assembled sound coding) is an important part of the word identification process, the time to identify an exception word should be slowed down because of the contradiction between its assembled sound code (which would be incorrect) and its actual pronunciation. The typical experiment examined the difference in response time to regular and irregular words that were matched on frequency in the language. These experiments usually employed isolated words, and identification time was assessed either with the lexical decision task (described earlier) or a naming task, in which the subject attempted to say the word aloud as rapidly as possible, consistent with good accuracy and the time is measured between when the word was presented and the beginning of the speech utterance. As indicated earlier, the findings from both paradigms confirmed that times were slower to the exception words, but that the difference in times was relatively small and largely absent for the higher frequency words.

These earlier findings, as indicated, suggested to some researchers that phonological coding was not very important, but the Van Orden experiments revived interest in the topic. There is still disagreement about the ultimate conclusion here, but we think that many researchers would agree that a major reason for the relatively small regularity effects in these naming and lexical decision experiments is that the irregular words were not all that irregular (almost always only off by one phoneme). Moreover, there is evidence from the eye movement literature that phonological coding occurs early in the word identification process and, as the Van Orden result suggests, decisively.

The first result that indicates this comes from the boundary paradigm discussed earlier (Pollatsek, Lesch, Morris, & Rayner, 1992). In this experiment, in the key condition, the wrong homophone (e.g., *beech*) was in the text until the reader crossed a boundary location and actually fixated the target word (e.g., *beach*). This condition was compared to a condition where a word that had the same number of matching letters was in the location before the target word was fixated (e.g., *bench*). The finding was that fixation time on the target word was shorter for the homophone preview than for the control preview. This implies that phonological coding relevant to identifying a word begins even before the word is fixated. Ashby and Rayner (2004) showed that this phonological representation extracted from the preview is more than the sounds of individual letters because it mattered whether the preview's syllable structure matched that of the target word. Their target words had either a two- or three-segment initial syllable (e.g., *magic* or *magnet*) and the preview contained either the exact first syllable of the target (e.g., *maxxx* as a preview for *magic* or magxx as a preview for magnet) or one letter more or fewer than the target's initial syllable (e.g., *magxx* as a preview for *magic*, *maxxxx* as a preview for *magnet*). They found that fixation time on the target word was shorter when the preview and target had matching initial syllables.

The above data, however, do not necessarily imply that this phonological coding in the preview is due to an assembly process; that is, the preview word may be fully identified before it is fixated. Indeed, the homophone preview benefit cannot be completely due to assembled phonology as it was observed in a character-naming experiment in Chinese as well (Pollatsek, Tan, & Rayner, 2000), where there is no assembled phonology. Later experiments in Chinese indicated, however, that phonological preview effects in reading are only reliable when the *radical* (a sub-character unit) in the preview character was also pronounced the same as the target character (Liu, Inhoff, Ye, & Wu, 2002; Tsai, Lee, Tzeng, Hung, & Yen, 2004).

Perhaps the most convincing demonstration of an early assembled phonological effect in word identification comes from an experiment using isolated words in the masked priming paradigm described earlier (Pollatsek, Perea, & Carreiras, 2005). This paradigm took advantage of a phenomenon in Spanish orthography that is similar to that in English: The sound of *c* is different when the vowel following it is *a*, *o*, and *u* than when it is *e* or *i*. (In Castillian Spanish, there is a "hard c" after *a*, *o*, and *u*, but a "th" sound after *e* or *i*.) To ensure that the effects from the primes were not due to accessing the prime as a word, nonword primes were employed. Thus, *conal* and *cinal* (nonwords) were primes for the target word *canal* (which is a word in Spanish with the same meaning as in English). Thus, if assembled phonology is occurring prior to the target word appearing, identification times (assessed in a lexical decision task) on *canal* should be faster when the prime is *conal* than when it is *cinal*.

The finding was that lexical decision times were shorter when the prime vowel signaled the appropriate pronunciation of *c* than when it did not, and that this occurred for both types of target words (i.e., those that had a "k" sound and those that had a "th" sound). To further ensure that the effect was not due to a visual difference (e.g., *o* may look more like *a* than *i*), there was a control condition with similar nonword preview pairs where the vowel does not affect the pronunciation of the initial consonant: Target words beginning with another consonant and a vowel (e.g., beginning with *pa*) had. Here, there was no difference between the priming conditions. Thus, the effect with the "c" target words was not due to either the sound or form of the preview vowel, but because the vowel causes people either to activate the "right" or the "wrong" sound for the initial *c*.

## Role of Prior Context on Word Identification

Earlier in this chapter, we presented data that indicated that the prior context dramatically influenced reading in that predictable words were skipped and implausible words often caused quite immediate regressions back to the prior text. One thing that should be firmly kept in mind about these results is that they indicate that the processing of the individual word is quite immediate—such that it can influence when a saccade occurs and where it occurs some time even before the word is fixated, or within something like a quarter of a second after it is fixated. There are many such context phenomena, but we thought that two particular examples were particularly important to mention with respect to how words are processed.

The first experiments (Duffy, Morris, & Rayner, 1988; Rayner & Duffy, 1987) deal with semantically ambiguous words, such as *bank*: words that happen to be both spelled and pronounced identically but have two completely unrelated meanings (as distinct from words like *garbage*, which have two related meanings—a literal and a more metaphorical meaning). The dual question that this research addressed is how readers deal with the ambiguity and how (and when) the prior context enters to disambiguate the two meanings. The basic design of the experiments is that: (a) they employed two types of ambiguous words—*balanced* (e.g., straw) where the two meanings have about equal frequency in the language and *biased* (e.g., port) where one of the meanings was much more frequent than the other and (b) they had passages in which the prior context was disambiguating or where the prior context was neutral with respect to which meaning was appropriate. In all the passages, when the prior context did not disambiguate the meaning, the subsequent context did. Moreover, the context always biased people to the less frequent meaning of the word (which was only slightly less frequent for the balanced words).

The basic findings were the following. First, fixation times on the target words (even first fixation durations) were affected by the prior context. However, the pattern was the opposite for the two types of words. For the balanced words, disambiguating prior context shortened fixation times on the target word, probably because it reduced the competition between the two meanings. In contrast, for the biased words, the prior context lengthened fixations on the target word, presumably because the context forced readers to get to the lower frequency

meaning of the word, whereas with neutral prior context, they encoded the higher frequency meaning. This interpretation is strengthened by the fact that there were many more regressions back to the target word when the prior context was neutral, indicating that readers had indeed encoded the word's meaning as inconsistent with the subsequent context (which supported the lower frequency meaning of the word).

To summarize, these results indicate that not only is a word encoded up to the level of knowing what its visual form is and what it sounds like, but, on a reasonable percent of fixations in reading, the meaning of the word has been encoded as well and the meaning extracted is affected by prior context. In one successful attempt to model these context effects, the prior context either strengthens or inhibits the strength of the various meanings of an ambiguous word (Reichle, Pollatsek, & Rayner, 2007).

An analogous experiment with heterophonic homographs (e.g., *bows*) indicated that phonological encoding was tightly connected to accessing the meaning of the word for these ambiguous words (Folk & Morris, 1995). These words were embedded in neutral sentence frames (i.e., where both meanings are consistent with the prior context) and compared to control words matched on frequency on length. The differences they obtained between these heterophonic homographs and the control words on fixation times on the target words were an order of magnitude greater than for homophones like *bank*: 40 ms on first fixation duration and 81 ms on gaze duration. Moreover, fixation times on the immediately following words were also lengthened considerably. These large effects indicate that the presence of two different phonological codes for the word is making the fact that there are two alternate meanings for the word more apparent and is delaying arriving at a decision for what the meaning of the word is.

## Summary and Conclusions

The study of reading, especially word recognition, is a major area of interest in cognitive psychology. In the last 40 years, great strides have been made in understanding much about how people read. As indicated earlier, a major impetus for this is that one can study people reading sentences and connected discourse in a controlled manner by measuring where readers fixate, how long the fixations are, and by manipulating aspects of the text from fixation to fixation. A major reason why this methodology works so well is that there is quite a tight linkage between where the eyes are (and how long fixations are) and what is being read. Although there have also been important discoveries about how people process syntax and discourse, space limitations necessitated that we focus on what has been learned about word identification.

We think the major findings of this research are the following. First, the area of the page from which skilled readers extract information is quite limited—on most fixations, this area is the fixated word and the following word (or two words if they are short) in the text. Second, most processing of a word is completed before the reader leaves the word; the time spent fixating the word is reflected by various indices of the time to identify a word such as its frequency, whether it is consistent with the prior text, and whether it has more than one meaning. Moreover, although these variables do have effects on subsequent fixations, they are fairly small. Third, getting to the sound of a word is an important part of word encoding, even in its early stages so that even skilled readers do not go directly from print to meaning. Finally, although there are differing opinions about how many words are processed at any given instant, we think that the hypothesis that readers are only lexically processing one word at a time is a tenable one and consistent with the data. This does not mean, however, that only one word is processed on a fixation; instead, the reader typically begins a fixation by processing the fixated word and then shifts attention to the following word in the later part of the fixation.

While significant strides have been made in understanding the cognitive processes involved in reading over the past 40 years, we are also optimistic that future research will provide an even finer grained description of the reading process. We would hope that such work will also further impact on the teaching of reading in children and those who experience difficulty in learning the task in the first place (Rayner et al., 2001, 2002).

## Acknowledgments

Preparation of this chapter was supported by grant HD26765 from the National Institute of Child Health and Human Development.

## Notes

1. Recent studies with Chinese readers have reported evidence for semantic preview benefit (Yan, Risse, Zhou, & Kliegl, 2012; Yang, Wang, Tong, & Rayner, 2012) as has a recent experiment with German readers (Hohenstein, Laubrock, & Kliegl, 2010). With Chinese, it is perhaps not surprising that semantic preview benefit would occur given the closer link between meaning and the orthography. It will be interesting to see if the German result replicates and/or extends to English.

2. We will discuss morphemes later in more detail, but for now think of "basket" and "ball" as morphemes of "basketball."

3. This is a slight oversimplification, as there are some languages (e.g., Arabic) that do not have a nonscript format. Thus, even in printed Arabic, letters are not visually separated.

4. It is even plausible that two common short words like "of the" can be processed in parallel. We should also point out that it is likely that attention is not always on the fixated word; there is evidence that there is error in targeting saccades so that the reader's fixation may sometimes be close to, but not on, the word attended to.

5. The account we are giving here explains the forward movement of the eyes through the text. One obviously needs another mechanism to explain regressions, such as in the "garden path" example given earlier; that is, some sort of mechanism that indicates a failure of comprehension and a signal to either pause or go back in the text to "repair the damage."

6. A standard feature of the paradigm worth commenting on is that the prime is in lowercase and the target is in uppercase to minimize the actual physical overlap of the prime and target.

## References

Angele, B., Slattery, T. J., Yang, J., Kliegl, R., & Rayner, K. (2008). Parafoveal processing in reading: Manipulating n + 1 and n + 2 previews simultaneously. *Visual Cognition, 16*, 697–707.

Ashby, J., & Rayner, K. (2004). Representing syllable information during silent reading: Evidence from eye movements. *Language and Cognitive Processes, 19*, 391–426.

Baddeley, A. D., & Hitch, G. (1974). Working memory. In G. Bower (Ed), *The psychology of learning and motivation* (Vol. 8). New York: Academic Press.

Bai, X, Yan, G., Liversedge, S. P., Zang, X., & Rayner, K. (2008). Reading spaced and unspaced Chinese text: Evidence from eye movements. *Journal of Experimental Psychology: Human Perception and Performance, 34*, 1277–1287.

Balota, D. A., Pollatsek, A., & Rayner, K. (1985). The interaction of contextual constraints and parafoveal visual information in reading. *Cognitive Psychology, 17*, 364–390.

Baron, J. (1973). Phonemic stage not necessary for reading. *Quarterly Journal of Experimental Psychology, 25*, 241–246.

Becker, W., & Jürgens, R. (1979). Analysis of the saccadic system by means of double step stimuli. *Vision Research, 19*, 967–983.

Davis, C. J. (2010). The spatial coding model of visual word identification. *Psychological Review, 117,* 713–758.

Deutsch, A., Frost, R., Peleg, S., Pollatsek, A., & Rayner, K. (2003). Early morphological effects in reading: Evidence from parafoveal preview benefit in Hebrew. *Psychonomic Bulletin & Review, 10,* 415–422.

Deutsch, A., Frost, R., Pollatsek, A., & Rayner, K. (2000). Early morphological effects in word recognition: Evidence from parafoveal preview benefit. *Language and Cognitive Processes, 15,* 487–506.

Deutsch, A., Frost, R., Pollatsek, A., & Rayner, K. (2005). Morphological parafoveal preview benefit effects in reading: Evidence from Hebrew. *Language and Cognitive Processes, 20,* 341–371.

Drieghe, D., Juhasz, B.J., Pollatsek, A., & Rayner, K. (2010). Parafoveal processing during reading is reduced across a morpheme boundary. *Cognition, 116,* 136–142.

Drieghe, D., Pollatsek, A., Staub, A., & Rayner, K. (2008). The word grouping hypothesis and eye movements in reading. *Journal of Experimental Psychology: Learning, Memory, and Cognition, 34,* 1552–1560.

Drieghe, D., Rayner, K., & Pollatsek, A. (2005). Eye movements and word skipping during reading revisited. *Journal of Experimental Psychology: Human Perception and Performance, 31,* 954–969.

Drieghe, D., Rayner, K., & Pollatsek, A. (2008). Mislocated fixations can account for parafoveal-on-foveal effects in eye movements during reading. *Quarterly Journal of Experimental Psychology, 61,* 1239–1249.

Duffy, S. A., Morris, R. K., & Rayner, K. (1988). Lexical ambiguity and fixation times in reading. *Journal of Memory and Language, 27,* 429–446.

Ehrlich, S. F., & Rayner, K. (1981). Contextual effects on word recognition and eye movements during reading. *Journal of Verbal Learning and Verbal Behavior, 20,* 641–655.

Folk, J. R., & Morris, R. K. (1995). Multiple lexical codes in reading: Evidence from eye movements, naming time, and oral reading. *Journal of Experimental Psychology: Learning, Memory, and Cognition, 21,* 1412–1429.

Forster, K. I., & Davis, C. (1984). Repetition priming and frequency attenuation in lexical access. *Journal of Experimental Psychology: Learning, Memory, and Cognition, 10,* 680–698.

Frazier, L., & Rayner, K. (1982). Making and correcting errors during sentence comprehension: Eye movements in the analysis of structurally ambiguous sentences. *Cognitive Psychology, 14,* 178–210.

Gomez, P., Ratcliff, R., & Perea, M. (2008). The overlap model: A model of letter position coding. *Psychological Review, 115,* 577–601.

Häikiö, T., Bertram, R., Hyönä, J., & Niemi, P. (2009). Development of the letter identity span in reading: Evidence from the eye movement moving window paradigm. *Journal of Experimental Child Psychology, 102,* 167–181.

Henderson, J. M., & Ferreira, F. (1990). Effects of foveal processing difficulty on the perceptual span in reading: Implications for attention and eye movement control. *Journal of Experimental Psychology: Learning, Memory, and Cognition, 16,* 417–429.

Hohenstein, S., Laubrock, J., & Kliegl, R. (2010). Semantic preview benefit in eye movements during reading: A parafoveal fast-priming study. *Journal of Experimental Psychology: Learning, Memory, and Cognition, 36,* 1150–1170.

Huey, E. B. (1908). *The psychology and pedagogy of reading.* New York: Macmillan.

Hyönä, J., Bertram, R., & Pollatsek, A. (2004). Are long compound words identified serially via their constituents? Evidence from an eye-movement-contingent display change study. *Memory & Cognition, 32,* 523–532.

Hyönä, J., & Häikiö, T. (2005). Is emotional content obtained from parafoveal words during reading? An eye movement analysis. *Scandinavian Journal of Psychology, 46,* 475–483.

Inhoff, A. W. (1989). Parafoveal processing of words and saccade computation during eye fixations in reading. *Journal of Experimental Psychology: Human Perception and Performance, 15,* 544–555.

Inhoff, A. W., & Liu, W. (1998). The perceptual span and oculomotor activity during the reading of Chinese sentences. *Journal of Experimental Psychology: Human Perception and Performance, 24,* 20–34.

Inhoff, A. W., Radach, R., Eiter, B. M., & Juhasz, B. (2003). Distinct subsystems for the parafoveal processing of spatial and linguistic information during eye fixations in reading. *Quarterly Journal of Experimental Psychology, 56A,* 803–828.

Inhoff, A. W., Radach, R., & Heller, D. (2000). Complex compounds in German: Interword spaces facilitate segmentation but hinder assignment of meaning. *Journal of Memory and Language, 42,* 23–50.

Irwin, D. E. (1998). Lexical processing during saccadic eye movements. *Cognitive Psychology, 36,* 1–27.

Irwin, D. E., & Carlson-Radvansky, L. A. (1996). Cognitive suppression during saccadic eye movements. *Psychological Science, 7,* 83–88.

Ishida, T., & Ikeda, M. (1989). Temporal properties of information extraction in reading studied by a text-mask replacement technique. *Journal of the Optical Society A: Optics and Image Science, 6,* 1624–1632.

Johnson, R. L., Perea, M., & Rayner, K. (2007). Transposed-letter effects in reading: Evidence from eye movements and parafoveal preview. *Journal of Experimental Psychology: Human Perception and Performance, 33,* 209–229.

Joseph, H. S. S. L., Liversedge, S. P., Blythe, H. I., White, S. J., Gathercole, S. E., & Rayner, K. (2008). Children's and adults' processing of implausibility during reading. *Quarterly Journal of Experimental Psychology, 61,* 708–723.

Juhasz, B. J., Pollatsek, A., Hyönä, J., Drieghe, D., & Rayner, K. (2009). Parafoveal processing within and between words. *Quarterly Journal of Experimental Psychology, 62,* 1356–1376.

Juhasz, B. J., White, S. J., Liversedge, S. P., & Rayner, K. (2008). Eye movements and the use of parafoveal word length information in reading. *Journal of Experimental Psychology: Human Perception and Performance, 34,* 1560–1579.

Kambe, G. (2004). Parafoveal processing of prefixed words during eye fixations in reading: Evidence against morphological influences on parafoveal preprocessing. *Perception & Psychophysics, 66,* 279–292.

Kliegl, R., Nuthmann, A., & Engbert, R. (2006). Tracking the mind during reading: The influence of past, present, and future words on fixation durations. *Journal of Experimental Psychology: General, 135,* 12–35.

Kliegl, R., Risse, S., & Laubrock, J. (2007). Preview benefit and parafoveal-on-foveal effects from word n + 2. *Journal of Experimental Psychology: Human Perception and Performance, 33,* 1250–1255.

Kohsom, C., & Gobet, F. (1997). Adding spaces to Thai and English: Effects on reading. *Proceedings of the Cognitive Science Society, 19*, 388–393.

Laubrock, J., Kliegl, R., & Engbert, R. (2006). SWIFT explorations of age differences in eye movements during reading. *Neuroscience and Biobehavioral Reviews, 30*, 872–884.

Lima, S. D. (1987). Morphological analysis in sentence reading. *Journal of Memory and Language, 26*, 84–99.

Liu, W., Inhoff, A. W., Ye, Y., & Wu, C. (2002). Use of parafoveally visible characters during the reading of Chinese sentences. *Journal of Experimental Psychology: Human Perception and Performance, 28*, 1213–1227.

Liversedge, S. P., & Findlay, J. M. (2000). Saccadic eye movements and cognition. *Trends in Cognitive Sciences, 4*, 6–14.

Liversedge, S. P., Rayner, K., White, S. J., Vergilino-Perez, D., Findlay, J. M., & Kentridge, R. W. (2004). Eye movements while reading disappearing text: Is there a gap effect in reading? *Vision Research, 44*, 1013–1024.

Matin, E. (1974). Saccadic suppression: A review and an analysis. *Psychological Bulletin, 81*, 899–917.

McClelland, J. L., & Rumelhart, D. E. (1981). An interactive activation model of context effects in letter perception: Part 1. An account of basic findings. *Psychological Review, 88*, 375–407.

McConkie, G. W., Kerr, P. W., Reddix, M. D., & Zola, D. (1988). Eye movement control during reading: I. The location of initial fixations in words. *Vision Research, 28*, 1107–1118.

McConkie, G. W., & Rayner, K. (1975). The span of the effective stimulus during a fixation in reading. *Perception & Psychophysics, 17*, 578–586.

McConkie, G. W., & Zola, D. (1979). Is visual information integrated across successive fixations in reading? *Perception & Psychophysics, 25*, 221–224.

McDonald, S. A. (2005). Parafoveal preview benefit in reading is not cumulative across multiple saccades. *Vision Research, 45*, 1829–1834.

McDonald, S. A. (2006). Parafoveal preview benefit in reading is only obtained from the saccade goal. *Vision Research, 46*, 4416–4424.

Miellet, S., O'Donnell, P. J., & Sereno, S. C. (2009). Parafoveal magnification: Visual acuity does not modulate the perceptual span in reading. *Psychological Science, 20*, 721–728.

Morrison, R. E. (1984). Manipulation of stimulus onset delay in reading: Evidence for parallel programming of saccades. *Journal of Experimental Psychology: Human Perception and Performance, 10*, 667–682.

Morrison, R. E., & Rayner, K. (1981). Saccade size in reading depends upon character spaces and not visual angle. *Perception and Psychophysics, 30*, 395–396.

Nuthmann, A., Engbert, R., & Kliegl, R. (2005). Mislocated fixations during reading and the inverted optimal viewing position effect. *Vision Research, 45*, 2201–2217.

Paap, K. R., Newsome, S. L., McDonald, J. E., & Schvaneveldt, R. W. (1982). An activation-verification model for letter and word recognition: The word superiority effect. *Psychological Review, 89*, 573–594.

Perea, M., & Lupker, S. J. (2003). Does jugde activate COURT? Trasposed-letter confusability effects in masked associate priming. *Memory & Cognition, 31*, 829–841.

Pollatsek, A., Bolozky, S., Well, A. D., & Rayner, K. (1981). Asymmetries in the perceptual span for Israeli readers. *Brain and Language, 14*, 174–180.

Pollatsek, A., & Hyönä, J. (2005). The role of semantic transparency in the processing of Finnish compound words. *Language and Cognitive Processes, 20*, 261–290.

Pollatsek, A., Lesch, M., Morris, R. K., & Rayner, K. (1992). Phonological codes are used in integrating information across saccades in word identification and reading. *Journal of Experimental Psychology: Human Perception and Performance, 18*, 148–162.

Pollatsek, A., Perea, M., & Carreiras, M. (2005). Does conal prime CANAL more than cinal? Masked phonological priming effects in Spanish with the lexical decision task. *Memory & Cognition, 33*, 557–565.

Pollatsek, A., Raney, G. E., LaGasse, L., & Rayner, K. (1993). The use of information below fixation in reading and in visual search. *Canadian Journal of Experimental Psychology, 47*, 179–200.

Pollatsek, A., Tan, L. H., & Rayner, K. (2000). The role of phonological codes in integrating information across saccadic eye movements in Chinese character identification. *Journal of Experimental Psychology: Human Perception and Performance, 26*, 607–633.

Rayner, K. (1975). Parafoveal identification during a fixation in reading. *Acta Psychologica, 39*, 272–282.

Rayner, K. (1979). Eye guidance in reading: Fixation locations in words. *Perception, 8*, 21–30.

Rayner, K. (1986). Eye movements and the perceptual span in beginning and skilled readers. *Journal of Experimental Child Psychology, 41*, 211–236.

Rayner, K. (1998). Eye movements in reading and information processing: 20 years of research. *Psychological Bulletin, 124*, 372–422.

Rayner, K. (2009a). The Thirty Fifth Sir Frederick Bartlett Lecture: Eye movements and attention in reading, scene perception and visual search. *The Quarterly Journal of Experimental Psychology, 62*, 1457–1506.

Rayner, K. (2009b). Eye movements in reading: Models and data. *Journal of Eye Movement Research, 2*(5), 1–10.

Rayner, K., Balota, D., &Pollatsek, A. (1985). Against parafoveal semantic processing during eye fixations during reading. *Canadian Journal of Psychology, 40*, 473–483.

Rayner, K., & Bertera, J. H. (1979). Reading without a fovea. *Science, 206*, 468–469.

Rayner, K., Binder, K. S., Ashby, J., & Pollatsek, A. (2001). Eye movement control in reading: Word predictability has little influence on initial landing positions in words. *Vision Research, 41*, 943–954.

Rayner, K., Castelhano, M. S., & Yang, J. (2009a). Eye movements when looking at unusual/weird scenes. Are there cultural differences? *Journal of Experimental Psychology: Learning, Memory, and Cognition, 35*, 254–259.

Rayner, K., Castelhano, M. S., & Yang, J. (2009b). Eye movements and the perceptual span in older and younger readers. *Psychology and Aging, 24*, 755–760.

Rayner, K., & Duffy, S. A. (1987). Eye movements and lexical ambiguity. In J. K. O'Regan & A. Levy-Schoen (Eds.), *Eye movements: From physiology to cognition*. Amsterdam: Elsevier.

Rayner, K., & Fischer, M. H. (1996). Mindless reading revisited: Eye movements during reading and scanning are different. *Perception & Psychophysics, 58*, 734–747.

Rayner, K., Fischer, M. H., & Pollatsek, A. (1998). Unspaced text interferes with both word identification and eye movement control. *Vision Research, 38*, 1129–1144.

Rayner, K., Foorman, B. F., Perfetti, C. A., Pesetsky, D., & Seidenberg, M. S. (2001). How psychological science informs the teaching of reading. *Psychological Science in the Public Interest, 2*, 31–74.

Rayner, K., Foorman, B. F., Perfetti, C. A., Pesetsky, D., & Seidenberg, M. S. (2002). How should reading be taught? *Scientific American, 286*(3), 84–91.

Rayner, K., Inhoff, A. W., Morrison, R. E., Slowiaczek, M. L., & Bertera, J. H. (1981). Masking of foveal and parafoveal vision during eye fixations in reading. *Journal of Experimental Psychology: Human Perception and Performance, 7*, 167–179.

Rayner, K., Juhasz, B. J., & Brown, S. J. (2007). Do readers obtain preview benefit from word n + 2? A test of serial attention shift versus distributed lexical processing models of eye movement control in reading. *Journal of Experimental Psychology: Human Perception and Performance, 33*, 230–245.

Rayner, K., Kambe, G., & Duffy, S.A. (2001). Clause wrap-up effects on eye movements during reading. *Quarterly Journal of Experimental Psychology, 53*, 1061–1080.

Rayner, K., Li, X., Juhasz, B. J., & Yan, G. (2005). The effect of word predictability on the eye movements of Chinese readers. *Psychonomic Bulletin & Review, 12*, 1089–1093.

Rayner, K., Liversedge, S. P., & White, S. J. (2006). Eye movements when reading disappearing text: The importance of the word to the right of fixation. *Vision Research, 46*, 310–323.

Rayner, K., Liversedge, S. P., White, S. J., & Vergilino-Perez, D. (2003). Reading disappearing text: Cognitive control of eye movements. *Psychological Science, 14*, 385–389.

Rayner, K., & McConkie, G. W. (1976). What guides a reader's eye movements? *Vision Research, 16*, 829–837.

Rayner, K., McConkie, G. W., & Zola, D. (1980). Integrating information across eye movements. *Cognitive Psychology, 12*, 206–226.

Rayner, K., Murphy, L., Henderson, J. M., & Pollatsek, A. (1989). Selective attentional dyslexia. *Cognitive Neuropsychology, 6*, 357–378.

Rayner, K., & Pollatsek, A. (1981). Eye movement control during reading: Evidence for direct control. *Quarterly Journal of Experimental Psychology, 33A*, 351–373.

Rayner, K., & Pollatsek, A. (1989). *The psychology of reading*. Englewood Cliffs, NJ: Prentice Hall.

Rayner, K., Pollatsek, A., Ashby, J., & Clifton, C. (2011). *The psychology of reading* (2nd ed.). New York: Psychology Press.

Rayner, K., Pollatsek, A., Drieghe, D., Slattery, T. J., & Reichle, E. D. (2007). Tracking the mind during reading via eye movements: Comments on Kliegl, Nuthmann, and Engbert (2006). *Journal of Experimental Psychology: General, 136*, 520–529.

Rayner, K., & Raney, G. E. (1996). Eye movement control in reading and visual search: Effects of word frequency. *Psychonomic Bulletin & Review, 3*, 245–248.

Rayner, K., Reichle, E. D., Stroud, M. J., Williams, C. C., & Pollatsek, A. (2006). The effect of word frequency, word predictability, and font difficulty on the eye movements of young and older readers. *Psychology and Aging, 21*, 448–465.

Rayner, K, Sereno, S. C., & Raney, G. E. (1996). Eye movement control in reading: A comparison of two types of models. *Journal of Experimental Psychology: Human Perception and Performance, 22*, 1188–1200.

Rayner, K., Slattery, T. J., & Bélanger, N. (2010). Eye movements, perceptual span, and reading speed. *Psychonomic Bulletin & Review,17*, 834–839.

Rayner, K., Slattery, T. J., Drieghe, D., & Liversedge, S. P. (2011). Eye movements and word skipping during reading: Effects of word length and predictability. *Journal of Experimental Psychology: Human Perception and Performance, 37*, 514–528.

Rayner, K., Slowiaczek, M. L., Clifton, C., & Bertera, J. H. (1983). Latency of sequential eye movements: Implications for reading. *Journal of Experimental Psychology: Human Perception and Performance, 9*, 912–922.

Rayner, K., Warren, T., Juhasz, B.J., & Liversedge, S.P. (2004). The effect of plausibility on eye movements in reading. *Journal of Experimental Psychology: Learning, Memory, and Cognition, 30*, 1290–1301.

Rayner, K., & Well, A. D. (1996). Effects of contextual constraint on eye movements in reading: A further examination. *Psychonomic Bulletin & Review, 3*, 504–509.

Rayner, K., Well, A. D., Pollatsek, A., & Bertera, J. H. (1982). The availability of useful information to the right of fixation in reading. *Perception & Psychophysics, 31*, 537–550.

Reicher, G. (1969). Perceptual recognition as a function of meaningfulness of stimulus material. *Journal of Experimental Psychology, 81*, 275–280.

Reichle, E., Liversedge, S., Pollatsek, A., &Rayner, K. (2009). Encoding multiple words simultaneously in reading is implausible. *Trends in Cognitive Science, 13*, 115–119.

Reichle, E. D., Pollatsek, A., & Rayner, K. (2007). Modeling the effects of lexical ambiguity on eye movements during reading. In R. van Gompel, M. H. Fischer, W. S. Murray, & R. L. Hill (Eds). *Eye movements: A window on mind and brain* (pp. 271–292). Amsterdam: Elsevier.

Reichle, E. D., Rayner, K., & Pollatsek, A. (2003). The E-Z Reader model of eye-movement control in reading: Comparisons to other models. *Behavioral and Brain Sciences, 26*, 445–476.

Sainio, M., Hyönä, J., Bingushi, K., & Bertram, R. (2007). The role of interword spacing in reading Japanese: An eye movement study. *Vision Research, 47*, 2575–2584.

Schoonbaert, S., & Grainger, J. (2004). Letter position coding in printed word perception: Effects of repeated and transposed letters. *Language and Cognitive Processes, 19*, 333–367.

Seidenberg, M. S., & McClelland, J. L. (1989). A distributed, developmental model of word recognition and naming. *Psychological Review, 96*, 523–568.

Slattery, T. J., & Rayner, K. (2010). The influence of text legibility on eye movements during reading. *Applied Cognitive Psychology, 24*, 1129–1148.

Starr, M. S., & Rayner, K. (2001). Eye movements during reading: Some current controversies. *Trends in Cognitive Sciences, 5*, 156–163.

Staub, A., Rayner, K., Pollatsek, A., Hyönä, J., & Majewski, H. (2007). The time course of plausibility effects on eye movements during reading: Evidence from noun–noun compounds. *Journal of Experimental Psychology: Learning, Memory, and Cognition, 33*, 1162–1169.

Tsai, J., Lee, C., Tzeng, O. J. L., Hung, D. L., & Yen, N. (2004). Use of phonological codes for Chinese characters: Evidence from processing of parafoveal preview when reading sentences. *Brain and Language, 91*, 235–244.

Vainio, S., Hyönä, J., & Pajunen, A. (2009). Lexical predictability exerts robust effects on fixation duration, but not on initial landing position during reading. *Experimental Psychology, 56*, 66–74.

Van Orden, G.C. (1987). A rows is a rose: Spelling, sound, and reading. *Memory and Cognition, 15*, 181–198.

Van Orden, G. C., Johnston, J. C., & Hale, B. L. (1987). Word identification in reading proceeds from spelling to sound to meaning. *Journal of Experimental Psychology: Learning, Memory, and Cognition, 14*, 371–386.

Warren, T., & McConnell, K. (2007). Investigating effects of selectional restriction violations and plausibility violation severity on eye-movements in reading. *Psychonomic Bulletin & Review, 14*, 770–775.

Warren, T., McConnell, K., & Rayner, K. (2008). Effects of context on eye movements when reading about possible and impossible events. *Journal of Experimental Psychology: Learning, Memory, and Cognition, 34*, 1001–1010.

Wheeler, D. (1970). Processes in word recognition. *Cognitive Psychology, 1*, 59–85.

White, S. J. (2008). Eye movement control during reading: Effects of word frequency and orthographic familiarity. *Journal of Experimental Psychology: Human Perception and Performance, 34*, 205–223.

White, S., Bertram, R., &Hyönä, J. (2008). Semantic processing of previews within compound words. *Journal of Experimental Psychology: Learning, Memory and Cognition, 34*, 988–993.

White, S. J., Rayner, K., & Liversedge, S. P. (2005). The influence of parafoveal word length and contextual constraint on fixation durations and word skipping in reading. *Psychonomic Bulletin and Review, 12*, 466–471.

Wolverton, G. S., & Zola, D. (1983). The temporal characteristics of visual information extraction during reading. In K. Rayner (Ed.), *Eye movements in reading: Perceptual and language processes* (pp. 301–313). New York: Academic Press.

Yan, G., Tian, H., Bai, X., & Rayner, K. (2006). The effect of word and character frequency on the eye movements of Chinese readers. *British Journal of Psychology, 97*, 259–268.

Yan, M., Risse, S., Zhou, X., & Kliegl, R. (2012). Preview fixation duration modulates identical and semantic preview benefit in Chinese reading. *Reading and Writing, 25*, 1093–1111.

Yang, J., Wang, S., Tong, X., & Rayner, K. (2012). Semantic and plausibility effects on preview benefit during eye fixations in Chinese reading. *Reading and Writing, 25*, 1031–1052.

# Text Comprehension

Morton Ann Gernsbacher *and* Michael P. Kaschak

**Abstract**

The study of text comprehension is the study of the cognitive processes involved as people process (and ultimately understand) the words, phrases, and sentences that make up larger bodies of language use (e.g., stories, magazine articles, novels, and so on). This chapter provides an introduction to several aspects of research on text comprehension: the methods commonly employed to study text comprehension, the major themes that have emerged over the past several decades of work in this field, and the theories that have been proposed to explain the comprehension process. In examining each of these aspects of the field, we highlight not only the state of the art in what is currently known about text comprehension but also the wide range of techniques and research questions that have come to characterize this area of psychological research.

**Key Words:** language comprehension, situation models, mental models, discourse

The use of language permeates our existence. We spend virtually all of our waking moments (and perhaps many of our sleeping moments) engaged in some kind of linguistic activity—writing e-mail, having conversations with friends, running through thoughts in our heads, and the like. A common factor across these situations is that language is almost always experienced in chunks larger than single words or single sentences. Thus, in most cases the comprehension of language requires not just understanding the meaning of the individual words or sentences, but the integration of the meaning of those words or sentences into a larger understanding of what is being talked or read about. The processes involved in comprehending these larger units of language (stories, newspaper articles, conversations, etc.) have been studied in some detail over the past several decades (see Graesser, Gernsbacher, & Goldman, 2003, for reviews). The present chapter provides an overview of research in this area, with a particular focus on reviewing the work that has examined comprehension of texts.

Text comprehension is a complex cognitive activity. To illustrate the complexity, consider what it takes to understand the following passage:

> Jane woke up in a panic on Thursday morning. Her rent check was due the next day, but there was no money in her bank account. When she walked into the kitchen, she remembered that she had not yet deposited the large refund check that she had gotten from the IRS. After getting dressed, she grabbed the check and drove to the bank.

At the most basic level, understanding this passage requires the reader to decode the orthographic symbols on the page, to recognize the words that the clumps of symbols form, and to recover the syntactic structure of the sentences. Beyond this, the reader must make sense of the whole text. The reader is told that Jane is in a panic, that her rent is due, and that she has no money. It seems clear that these statements are related (i.e., Jane is panicked because she cannot pay her rent), but the text does not state these relations explicitly; rather, readers must infer the relations based on their knowledge of the world. Jane's goal, namely to reduce her distress by finding a way to pay the rent, is also not explicitly stated in the text. The next sentence about her check from the IRS fits within the structure of this goal and therefore is easily incorporated into the ongoing situation. Finally, we are told that Jane drives to the bank as a way of meeting her goal. Note that if the final sentence had indicated that Jane drove to the beach, most readers would be confused, and their confusion would indicate a clash between their understanding of the situation conveyed by the text and their world knowledge: People who need to pay their rent do not usually take important checks to the beach.

This brief example highlights the major themes that have characterized research on text comprehension. Readers need to establish a representation to keep track of the events in the story, to be aware of the goals of the characters, and so on. Readers also need to draw on their knowledge of the world to draw inferences that fill the blanks of components of the situation not explicitly described. Finally, readers need to monitor the information that is presented in the text to make sure it is coherent with the representation that they have constructed based on the previous sentences. The main focus of this chapter will be to describe the cognitive mechanisms that underlie readers' ability to accomplish these tasks.

## Methods of Studying Text Comprehension

Text comprehension is a complex activity that involves cognitive operations on every level of linguistic representation. Accordingly, a broad range of research methodologies has been used to investigate the mechanisms involved in the comprehension process. In this section of the chapter, we discuss the methods that are most frequently used in the field.

### Verbal Protocols

When thinking about the question of how a text is understood, one might be interested in noting the kinds of overt strategies that readers employ to structure the comprehension task (Graesser, 2007). The collection of verbal protocols, or "think aloud" measures (see Ericsson & Simon, 1993), provides an efficient means of doing so. Research participants may be asked to provide a report of whatever they are thinking as they read a text, or they may be asked to respond to specific questions. For example, at a given point during a text, a reader may be asked why a character performed a particular action, what the reader thinks will happen next in the story, or how well the reader thinks she or he is understanding what she or he is reading. Although verbal reports may not accurately reflect the moment-by-moment processing that goes into the comprehension of a text, they do provide a valuable source of information about the ways that readers are approaching the comprehension task (e.g., what elements of the text they are paying attention to and which elements they are ignoring). Verbal reports can also be used in conjunction with other research methods (see Magliano & Graesser, 1991; Trabasso & Suh, 1993).

### Probe Response Measures

Although verbal protocols provide researchers with insight into the knowledge that readers are retrieving as they process a text, verbal protocols do not allow researchers to ascertain when this knowledge is retrieved during the real-time, moment-by-moment processing involved in comprehension. A widespread method for accomplishing that goal is the use of probe response tasks. In this method, research participants are asked to read a text. At various points in their reading, they are interrupted with a secondary task that requires them to respond to a single word. For example, participants may read a sentence such as (1).

(1) John walked down the street with a smile on his face.

After reading this sentence, the word *happy* may be presented visually or auditorily. The reader may be asked to decide whether *happy* is a word (i.e., a *lexical decision task*) or may be asked to simply say the word *happy* aloud (i.e., a *naming* task). The logic of these tasks is that if the reader has used the information presented in sentence (1) to infer that John is happy, then the response to the probe task should be faster when the probe word is *happy* (or, a related word, such as *joyful*) than when the probe word is *sad* (or a word completely unrelated to this inference, e.g., *table*).

### Reading Time Measures

Whereas probe response tasks have provided a valuable tool for studying the moment-by-moment retrieval of knowledge during text comprehension, they have the unfortunate feature of disrupting the normal reading process: To respond to the probe, participants need to stop reading and attend to a secondary task. Therefore, researchers have used other methods to assess the reading process under more normal processing conditions. Reading time methods range from those that are fairly coarse (e.g., measuring the time it takes readers to process a whole clause or sentence) to those that are more precise (e.g., measuring the reading time for each word as the sentence is read, either by asking the reader to push a button to move from one word to the next in a sentence, or by monitoring the position of the eyes as they move across the sentence). Reading time measures are typically used as an index of processing difficulty. Increases in reading time suggest an increase in processing difficulty, which itself can be caused by many factors (e.g., the need to generate an inference to maintain the coherence of the text).

### Brain Measures

Several methods of studying brain activity have been employed to study text comprehension. One such method involves measuring event related potentials (ERPs), which are changes in electrical activity in the brain that occur during text comprehension. For example, readers may be presented with a sentence such as (2).

(2) Jane wanted to deposit her paycheck, so she drove to the beach.

The word *beach* is anomalous in this context, and so it is expected that a change in brain activity should occur as participants read the word and notice the inconsistency. ERP methods provide very good temporal resolution in that the changes in brain activity are closely time-locked to particular events that occur while processing language. However, because ERPs are detected by electrodes placed on the scalp, ERPs are not very good for localizing the activity to a particular part of the brain. Other measures of brain activity are functional magnetic resonance imaging (fMRI) and positron emission tomography (PET). Both fMRI and PET use changes in blood flow in the brain to determine which brain regions are involved in a given cognitive task. These methods are useful for localizing changes in brain activity that occur during text comprehension, but they suffer from relatively poor temporal resolution due to the slow rate of onset and offset for changes in blood flow in the brain, which is unfortunate considering how rapidly a process like text comprehension occurs.

### Theoretical Issues in Text Comprehension

Our discussion of the processes involved in text comprehension will be centered on several theoretical issues that have received attention in the literature. The first issue concerns the kinds of representation that are constructed during text comprehension. Here we will consider the multiple ways that a text can be represented and the role that each of these representations can play in the comprehension process. The second issue concerns the medium that is used to construct representations of text content. The final issue we tackle concerns the processes involved in comprehending a text. Of concern here will be the moment-by-moment processes involved in text comprehension, particularly the ways that readers "fill in the blanks" so that they can understand what the text is trying to convey, even though the text itself may leave important information unsaid.

### Levels of Representation

Beginning with van Dijk and Kintsch (1983), approaches to text comprehension have broadly accepted the claim that readers construct three levels of representation during the comprehension process. The first of these is the *surface-level* representation, which is a verbatim representation of the wording used in the text. Generally speaking, the surface-level representation is short lived (e.g., Barclay, Bransford, Franks, McCarell, & Nitsch, 1974; Gernsbacher, 1985). Kintsch et al. (1990) asked participants to read texts, then gave them a recognition test to assess their memory for the different levels of text representation. Whereas memory for the surface form declined quickly (and was almost entirely lost over a period of a few days), memory for textbase and situation model representations remained somewhat accurate even several days after encountering the original texts. Nonetheless, there are cases in which memory for the surface form of the text is long-lasting. For example, Murphy and Shapiro (1994) demonstrated that memory for the surface form of a text can be high in cases where the text presents a joke or an insult (both being contexts in which remembering the surface form of the language would be of some import).

The second layer of representation is the *textbase*. The textbase is a propositional representation of the ideas explicitly stated in the text. As seen in the brief story presented at the beginning of this chapter, texts are rarely explicit about everything that is relevant to the comprehension of the situation that is being described. The textbase level of representation does not function to fill in all of these gaps, but it does begin to glue some of the elements presented in the text together. Consider sentence (3).

(3) The boy gave his mother a cupcake.

A verb such as *give* has a particular argument structure, or configuration of noun phrases, that fills different roles in the action of giving. The boy is referred to as the *agent* of the action (i.e., the "doer"), the mother is the *recipient* of the action (i.e., the "receiver"), and the cupcake is the *patient* of the action (i.e., the thing being acted on). The binding of elements in the text (boy, mother, and cupcake) to particular roles in the action *(agent, recipient, patient)* is accomplished in the textbase level of representation. It is worth noting that although the textbase is traditionally considered to be a level of representation in discourse processing, there are some who argue that this level of representation is unnecessary. For example, it has been proposed that individual lexical items may provide the comprehension system with "instructions" about how to produce the situation model, thus eliminating the need to have a textbase that connects the surface level and situation model levels of representation (e.g., Gernsbacher, 1990).

The third layer of representation constructed during text comprehension, and the one that has received the most attention, has been variously called the *mental model, discourse model,* or *situation model.* These terms have been used for very specific purposes in the literature, but for the present purposes we will treat them as equivalent and adopt the convention of referring to this level of representation as the situation model. The situation model is a representation of what the text is about. It is an amalgam of information that is contained in the textbase and information that has been retrieved from the comprehender's general store of world knowledge (Kintsch, 1988). It is here that information not explicitly mentioned in the text can be brought to bear in the service of understanding the events that are being described. The generation of the inferences necessary to make sense of the content of the text takes place during the construction of a situation model.

Zwaan et al. (1995; Zwaan & Radvansky, 1998) proposed that situation models are structured around five dimensions:

*Protagonist*: Who is involved in the events being described?

*Time*: At what time is the event taking place?

*Space*: What are the spatial relations between the characters, objects, and events being described?

*Causality*: Which events in the text are causally related to each other?

*Intentionality*: Is the incoming information relevant to the protagonist's goals and intentions?

Readers track information along these, and possibly other, dimensions as they process a text. Zwaan et al.'s (1995) account has two important implications. First, events that are interrelated among several dimensions will be more closely linked in memory than events that are interrelated among fewer dimensions. Second, the ease with which incoming information will be integrated into the existing situation model depends on the number of dimensions on which the incoming text content matches the immediately preceding content. Overall, the more overlap between the incoming content and the existing state of the situation model, the easier it will be to integrate the new information into the model.

A number of studies support Zwaan et al.'s (1995) general claim that readers monitor several dimensions during the comprehension of text. Space is the most explored of the dimensions. Some early views of situation models held that comprehenders constructed spatial representations of text content in a spatial medium that was analogous to the three-dimensional world in which we live (Glenberg, Kruley & Langston, 1994; Johnson-Laird, 1983). Rinck and Bower (1995; see also Morrow, Bower & Greenspan, 1989) found evidence for this claim in experiments in which participants were asked to read texts about the protagonists' movements around a building. They found that the reading time for sentences referring to objects in the building increased as a function of the number of rooms between the location of the object and the current location of the main character in the building. That is, the more "space" the participants needed to cover to get from their current location to the location of the object that was mentioned, the harder it was to process the sentence.

Early indications were that situation models contained analogical spatial representations; however, subsequent work put important qualifications on this claim. Langston, Kramer, and Glenberg (1998) report a series of studies in which they failed to find anything like analogical spatial representation. Moreover, Radvansky and Copeland (2000) used a combination of reading time measures and memory assessments to demonstrate that sentences describing functional spatial relationships between entities are read faster and remembered better than sentences describing nonfunctional relationships. Current thinking on the role of space in situation models has thus shifted somewhat from the initial positions that appeared in the literature. Specifically, it appears that readers do not routinely construct detailed spatial representations in their situation models unless (a) the text is explicitly spatial, or (b) there is some strategic reason to do so (see Langston et al., 1998, for a discussion). Furthermore, the spatial relationships that are constructed are rarely analogical.

Temporal representations in situation models have also been studied. Zwaan (1996) reports a seminal set of experiments that explored the processing of sentences that indicate a time shift in narratives, as in (4).

(4a) A moment later, the fireman....
(4b) A day later, the fireman...
(4c) A month later, the fireman...

Zwaan (1996) found that the processing speed of such sentences was related to the magnitude of the time shift that was indicated. The longer the time shift, the longer the processing time. This seems to indicate that comprehenders are sensitive to the magnitude of time shifts as they construct their situation models—longer time shifts represent larger breaks in the timeline of the narrative and therefore require more updating of the situation.

The other dimensions proposed by Zwaan et al. (1995) have received comparatively less attention in the literature (see Zwaan & Radvansky, 1998, for a review). Nonetheless, there is empirical support for the general notion that these dimensions of a situation are tracked during text comprehension. It is important to note that most studies of the dimensional approach to text processing examine the tracking of a single dimension; few studies have explored multiple dimensions at once (but see Therriault, Rinck, & Zwaan, 2006, for an example). Gaining an understanding of how comprehenders simultaneously track multiple dimensions during text comprehension will be an important topic for further research in this area.

### What Are Situation Models Made of?

The situation model is the level of representation that is taken to be synonymous with full comprehension of a text. It is here that comprehenders integrate information presented in the text with their general store of knowledge and use this integration to fashion an understanding of the situations that are described. While virtually all language comprehension researchers would agree that a situation model (or something like it) is essential for successful text comprehension, there has been somewhat less agreement about the nature of situation models themselves.

One prominent view of the representational medium of situation models has been to propose that the models are, like the textbase, propositional in nature (Kintsch, 1988, 1998). To illustrate this type of representation, consider again sentence (3): The boy gave his mother a cupcake. The nature of this action could be represented via the proposition (GIVE, AGENT:boy, PATIENT:cupcake, RECIPIENT:mother). This view holds that knowledge (generally speaking) is stored in propositional format, that propositions can be derived explicitly from the text when forming the textbase, and these propositions can be united with propositions from the reader's general knowledge base to form a situation model. Proposition-based accounts of situation models have achieved wide-ranging success in explaining empirical phenomena associated with situation models. As one example, the activation and inhibition of propositions, as instantiated in Kintsch's (1988) Construction-Integration model, has proven to be relatively successful in predicting what information will be available (and what information will not be available) at various points during the comprehension of a text, the kinds of inferences that readers will make as reading a text, and the kinds of performance that students will demonstrate as they comprehend and solve mathematical word problems (a task that inherently involves the comprehension of text).

An alternative view of situation models holds that the representational medium is not propositional, but rather analogical. The key distinction between these views is that whereas the propositional approach holds that the information presented in the text is converted into a propositional "language of thought," the analogical view holds that the information presented in the text is used to retrieve representations that are akin to perceptual and spatial representations of the sort that forms our mental imagery (putting aside the contentious debate about whether imagery comes from propositional representations). Johnson-Laird's (1983) approach to mental models is an early example of this perspective. A more recent exemplar of this view is the claim that language comprehension requires the construction of sensorimotor simulations of the events being described (e.g., Barsalou, 1999; Zwaan, 2004). That is, a sentence such as "The car approached you" would be understood by using the visual system to simulate what it would look like for a car to come toward you (Kaschak et al., 2005), and a sentence such as "The boy gave his mother a cupcake" would be understood by using the motor system to simulate the action of transferring something from one person to another (Glenberg & Kaschak, 2002; Zwaan & Taylor, 2006).

Both propositional and analogical representations have their proponents in the literature. Proponents of the propositional representation format point to the empirical successes of the formal models that have been constructed based on this sort of representation. As noted earlier, Kintsch's (1988) Construction-Integration theory has been employed to model a range of comprehension data in the text-reading literature and in educational settings. More broadly, there is a large body of literature showing that nonanalogical representations play a role in language processing. Examples of such representations include knowledge of abstract syntactic rules (e.g., Frazier & Clifton, 1996) and probabilistic knowledge concerning the patterns of use of individual words, sentence constructions, syllables, and the like (e.g., Landauer & Dumais, 1997; MacDonald, Pearlmutter, & Seidenberg, 1994; Roland, Dick, & Elman, 2007). This sort of information has been shown to play a role in language acquisition (e.g., Saffran, Aslin, & Newport, 1996), language comprehension (e.g., MacDonald et al., 1994; McRae, Spivey-Knowlton, & Tanenhaus, 1998), and language production (e.g., Chang, Dell, & Bock, 2006).

Proponents of analogical representations point to a growing body of evidence from behavioral studies (e.g., Glenberg & Kaschak, 2002; Meteyard, Bahrami, & Vigliocco, 2007; Zwaan & Taylor, 2006) and neuroimaging studies (e.g., Buccino et al., 2005; Glenberg et al., 2008; Hauk, Johnschrude, & Pulvermuller, 2004; Speer, Reynolds, Swallow, & Zacks, 2009) showing that the systems involved in perception and action planning are recruited during the comprehension of sentences describing both concrete and abstract situations. Behavioral studies have shown that the comprehension of sentences about action (e.g., "Open the drawer") facilitates the preparation and execution of congruent actions (e.g., pulling your arm toward your body; Glenberg & Kaschak, 2002; Zwaan & Taylor, 2006), and both that the comprehension of language about motion affects one's acuity in perceiving motion in a visual stimulus (e.g., Meteyard et al., 2007) and that the perception of visual motion affects the comprehension of sentences about motion (e.g., Kaschak et al., 2005). Consistent with these behavioral results, fMRI studies have shown that asking participants to process words about perception and action activates the neural regions that have been identified as being involved in the processing of perceptual or motor information. As one example, Hauk et al. (2004) demonstrated that the parts of the motor strip that have been identified as controlling the lips, fingers, and legs were activated when participants processed the words lick, pick, and kick, respectively.

Given that situation models are central to the process of comprehending language, a resolution of the question about the representational format of such models will be important to developing an understanding of what it means to understand. It is not our goal to resolve this issue here, but a few points can be made. First, most studies of language comprehension are not incisive on the matter of what kinds of representation underlie the comprehension process. With the exception of some recent studies of the interplay between language comprehension and systems of perception and action planning, task performance in studies of language comprehension are generally open to explanation from both a propositional and analogical perspective (witness the parallels between this debate and the analogical/propositional debate in the literature on mental imagery; e.g., Kosslyn, 1994). More studies need to assess the nitty-gritty of the representational formats that are used in text comprehension.

Second, it is possible that some types of abstract representational formats (e.g., some types of propositional representations) may turn out to be represented analogically. As one example of this, Lakoff and Nunez (2000) argue that abstract mathematical representations (such as mathematical sets) can be represented in terms of concrete, analogical representations (e.g., a set can be represented as a container). Third, although some have called for approaches that incorporate both abstract types of linguistic representation and analogical, experiential types of representation (e.g., Louwerse, 2008), it remains to be seen whether such hybrid approaches can produce a satisfactory theory of language comprehension.

## Processing a Text

At the beginning of this chapter, we walked through a brief example of what would be involved in comprehending a short text about a person who needed to pay her rent. It was clear that understanding even a short, relatively straightforward text involves a host of cognitive processes ranging from the detection and recognition of letters to the construction of inferences needed to fill in the gaps in the information presented explicitly in the text. In this section of the chapter, we discuss the major processes involved in comprehending a text.

## FIRST THINGS FIRST

Although the processing of all sentences in a text requires some degree of cognitive work, a number of studies have shown that the processing of initial sentences in a text requires more effort than the processing of subsequent sentences. Gernsbacher (1990) has described this phenomenon in terms of *laying a foundation* for subsequent comprehension to take place. Thus, processing the first sentences of a text involves the initial construction of a situation model, and this initial construction involves extra processing effort since the model needs to be started from scratch. Once the model is constructed, it becomes easier to add more information as the text proceeds. It should be noted that this phenomenon also holds for segments of a text where shifts of various sorts occur. For example, a comprehender may create a new submodel within a larger situation model of a text to represent an extensive flashback that is presented. The creation of this submodel requires additional processing work and thus results in slower comprehension of the first few sentences after the shift takes place.

## GATHERING RAW MATERIALS

The information presented explicitly in a text forms the basis of text comprehension. The words and phrases that are used provide the initial triggers for retrieving information from memory, and it is the combination of information retrieved directly based on the words and phrases used in the text and information that is already present in the reader's situation model that combine to form the interpretation of a given sentence.

We are describing the process of using lexical information to retrieve information from memory as a process of gathering raw materials for the construction of a situation model largely because this initial stage of processing is initially indiscriminate with respect to what is retrieved. Beginning with Swinney (1979), it has been shown that a wide range of information is activated when one initially processes a word. Consider sentence (5).

(5) The spy placed a bug on the table.

Swinney (1979) asked participants to listen to sentences such as (5). When the critical word (in this case, *bug*) was reached, participants were visually presented with a string of letters on a computer screen and participants had to decide whether it was a word. The words that were presented were either related to the different senses of the critical word (e.g., *spy* and *insect* are related to different meanings of *bug*) or were unrelated to the critical word (e.g., *sew*). Swinney (1979) found that when the test words were presented immediately after the critical word in the sentence, participants were fast to respond to the words related to the meaning of the critical word and comparatively slower to respond to the unrelated word. This suggests that comprehenders immediately access all relevant information when processing a word with multiple meanings. Nonetheless, it has also been shown that the contextually inappropriate meanings of the word are quickly dampened; activation of inappropriate meanings seems to decay within around 750 msec from the processing of the word (Gernsbacher & Faust, 1995).

Successful language comprehension requires the resolution of ambiguity. Ambiguity exists at every representational level of language (phonology, lexicon, syntax, etc.), and most theories of language comprehension employ some mechanism through which ambiguity (e.g., selecting the meaning of an ambiguous word such as *bug*) is handled. For example, Gernsbacher (1990) suggests that ambiguities in word meaning are resolved by higher level representations inhibiting the contextually inappropriate lexical representations of the word in question (e.g., inhibiting the *insect* meaning of *bug* in a context about espionage). The quick resolution of ambiguity is central to comprehension as a failure to resolve ambiguities (e.g., by not selecting a single meaning of *bug*) can lead to the development of an incorrect representation of the content of the text. Indeed, Gernsbacher and colleagues have shown that an important distinction between good and poor language comprehenders is the ability to inhibit contextually inappropriate meanings. Gernsbacher and Faust (1995) review several studies using methods similar to the one employed by Swinney (1979) in which it is shown that whereas all readers initially activate a wide range of information relevant to the interpretation of a word with multiple meanings (such as *bug*), good comprehenders inhibit contextually inappropriate information within a few hundred milliseconds, but poor comprehenders do not. Thus, all comprehenders successfully recruit information for potential inclusion in one's representation of the meaning of a sentence or text, but poor comprehenders struggle because they are unable to successfully inhibit the information that is not relevant to the comprehension of the ongoing text.

## ADDING TO THE STRUCTURE

Theories of text comprehension typically posit that information is added to a situation model on a clause-by-clause or sentence-by-sentence basis (e.g., Kintsch, 1988). Here, the information that is retrieved based on the explicit content of the text is integrated with both the existing structure of the situation model and additional knowledge that has been retrieved from memory. This process is referred to as *updating* the situation model. It is the updating of situation models that allows the comprehender to keep the content of a text together in a coherent representation.

The updating of situation models raises three issues. First, how does the reader know that a series of sentences is intended to be integrated into a single representation? There are several linguistic cues that signal the reader to interpret sentences as a discourse. Robertson et al. (2000) asked readers to process a series of sentences such as "The family rode together in a car." When the series of sentences began with the definite article *the*, readers tended to interpret the series of sentences as part of a connected discourse. On the other hand, when the same sentences were presented with the indefinite article *a*, readers tended to interpret the sentences as being unrelated to each other. The use of the article *the* implies that the entities being discussed are entities to which reference has already been made in the preceding sentences, and thus it cues the reader to treat the sentences as being related. Connectives such as *because, however, meanwhile*, and others play a similar role. For example, consider the sentences, "The grandparents prepared the food for their party. Meanwhile, the family was loading into their minivan." The focus of the two sentences is completely different, but the use of the connective *meanwhile* tells the reader that the two actions should be treated as part of the same event.

The second updating-related issue concerns the question of what information should be integrated into the situation model. Here, the linguistic distinction between *given* and *new* information (e.g., Haviland & Clark, 1974) is relevant. Given information is information that is already present in the situation model. New information is information that is being introduced in the current clause or sentence. The given information in the current sentence provides an anchor to the current state of the situation model, and it indicates which elements of the model will be updated. For example, mentioning the name of one character in a story will anchor the current sentence to the representation of that character in the situation model, and it will signal that the new information in the sentence can be added to the model to update the representations involving that character. Although much information is retrieved from memory during the processing of a clause, only that information that can be anchored to existing elements of the situation model will be easily integrated into the updated version of the model.

The final updating-related issue to be addressed here regards the means through which readers keep track of entities that are mentioned repeatedly in a text. When texts are written, they do not repeatedly use the same word to refer to a particular object or person. A character may be introduced as "Jane," and in the next sentence be referred to as "she," and later in the text be referred to as "the woman with the brown hair." To maintain order in his or her situation model, the reader must realize that "Jane," "she," and "the woman with the brown hair" all refer to the same person.

The most studied case of reference in discourse processing is the comprehension of *anaphoric* reference, or reference to a person or object that has previously been mentioned (as in the earlier example). One factor that influences the comprehension of anaphoric references is the nature of the information currently active in memory (and foregrounded in the mental model). If there is one female character currently in the foreground of the model (Jane), then pronouns such as "she" will be mapped onto Jane. If there is more than one female character in the foreground of the model, the pronoun will be mapped to the one whose representation is most active. In some cases, further knowledge is needed in order to determine the referent of an anaphor. When Jane is referred to as "the woman with brown hair," the reader needs to know that Jane has brown hair in order to easily understand the reference as intended.

The choice of reference for an entity in the text depends largely on the circumstances in which the entity is being mentioned. When a person or object is initially mentioned, it is usually marked with the article *a* or *an*, and the description provided is typically somewhat detailed. Subsequent references are less detailed and may be made by pronouns or other "shorthand" referring expressions. The more the entity has been mentioned in the text, the shorter the referring terms tend to be. These linguistic cues provide the reader with information as to whether a person or object that is being mentioned is one that has previously been mentioned in the text, or whether a new entity has been introduced to the situation.

## MAINTAINING COHERENCE

The preceding paragraphs have discussed several means through which readers integrate a series of sentences into a larger representation of the text. As seen in the examples that were provided, it is possible to create such larger representations by connecting information explicitly presented in the text to information that is already present in one's situation model. Such connections are made through processes of memory retrieval, where elements of the incoming language (e.g., a pronoun such as *she*, or a proper name such as *Jane*) serve as cues to retrieve information from the existing situation model (e.g., Myers & O'Brien, 1998). Thus, a pronoun such as *she* serves as a cue to retrieve the identity of a female person who is currently represented in the situation model. These memory-driven processes are no doubt an important component of text comprehension, but they are not sufficient to explain the entirety of how readers maintain a coherent representation of a text. To make sense of a text, readers often need to do additional processing work to figure out how the incoming sentence relates to the existing situation model. That is, they need to do processing work to maintain the coherence of the text as new information comes in.

Text comprehenders may strive to maintain coherence in their representation of a text in many ways. They might connect each incoming sentence to the most recently encountered sentences (as discussed earlier). In doing so, the reader is attempting to maintain *local coherence* (e.g., McKoon & Ratcliff, 1992) in his or her situation model. On the other hand, readers may attempt to maintain *global coherence* in their discourse model (e.g., Graesser, Singer, & Trabasso, 1994). That is, readers connect each incoming sentence to both the local content of the situation model and the global structure of the model (which includes information about the structure of the text, the overarching goals of the characters, and so on).

In general, readers attempt to maintain both local and global coherence when they construct mental models (e.g., O'Brien & Albrecht, 1992). Consider the short text presented at the beginning of this chapter. The narrative begins by presenting a goal for Jane (she needs to get money into her bank account). Several sentences later, the reader is told that Jane is going to the bank to deposit her check. As noted in our discussion of that example, if readers had been told that Jane is going to the beach with her check, they would no doubt find the sentence incongruous. Part of the reason that readers find that statement to be inconsistent with the rest of the text is that the behavior it describes is inconsistent with Jane's goals. That is, readers are keeping track of Jane's goals in order to maintain the global coherence of the text. In addition to tracking information needed to maintain global coherence, it is clear that readers attempt to maintain coherence from sentence to sentence (as seen in the previous section of this chapter; McKoon & Ratcliff, 1992). If readers fail to maintain global coherence in their discourse models, they may focus instead on maintaining local coherence. If a given text has too little local coherence, it will be viewed as altogether incoherent.

To achieve global and local coherence, the reader must often fill in details that are not explicitly presented in the text. That is, the reader must generate inferences about the events being described in order to maintain a coherent representation of the text. For example, when they encounter a pair of sentences such as "It was cold that morning. Joe slipped on the sidewalk," readers need to draw the inference that there may have been snow or ice on the sidewalk in order to integrate the two statements into a coherent discourse model. Although theories differ on the exact mechanisms through which inferences are generated, the general picture that emerges from the literature is that inference generation arises through the knowledge activation mechanisms that were discussed earlier in the context of "gathering raw materials" for the comprehension process. Comprehenders retrieve not just information relevant to the interpretation of individual words but also information associated with those meanings. For example, the *spy* meaning of *bug* implies not only espionage but also that the spy and the person being spied upon are enemies (or at least working for different government agencies). This knowledge forms the basis for inference generation, such that when we are told that one character in a story plants a bug in the hotel room of another character, we can use the knowledge retrieved to integrate the fact that the characters work for different governments into our situation model.

One of the major research questions about inference generation during text processing has centered on the issue of when inferences are generated and when they are not. According to the *minimalist* position (McKoon & Ratcliff, 1992), readers mostly attempt to maintain local coherence when they process a text. The only inferences that are routinely generated by readers are those that are required to maintain local coherence (such as the inference that there was ice on the sidewalk from the example in the previous paragraph). Readers are capable of drawing more global inferences from text, but these inferences are only drawn under certain circumstances (e.g., when the reader is attempting to process the text more deeply than usual). In contrast, the *promiscuous generation* position maintains that readers routinely generate a wide range of inferences from the text, including those that are not strictly necessary to ensure local coherence (Kintsch, 1988). These inferences include inferences about the goals of the characters, the emotional state of the characters, the cause-and-effect relationship between events in the text, the intent of the writer in conveying particular pieces of information, and so on.

A compromise between these extreme positions is the *constructivist* position (Graesser et al., 1994). The constructivist position holds that readers routinely draw inferences that meet their goals as comprehenders, inferences that maintain the coherence of the text, and inferences that explain why different events in the text are taking place. On this view, readers may appear to behave in accord with the minimalist position under certain conditions, and behave in accord with the promiscuous generation position in other conditions depending on the nature of the text and the goals they have in comprehending that text. For example, if the reader is attempting to skim the text in an effort to quickly glean information, he or she may draw few inferences (in keeping with the minimalist position). On the other hand, if individuals are reading a text for enjoyment (say, if they are reading a detective novel) or if they are trying to learn about a new field of study, they may read the text more carefully and draw a wider range of inferences (see Foertsch & Gernsbacher, 1994).

## STRATEGIC PROCESSING

We conclude our discussion of the theoretical issues surrounding text comprehension by saying a few words about the ways that reading strategies play a role in the comprehension process. We have already discussed some of this in the context of constructionist approaches to text comprehension, where the general idea is that readers can choose to read a text in great detail or can choose to skim over the text and skip over a lot of the detail. Indeed, it has been noted that readers typically adopt a minimalist approach to comprehension and construct text representations that are just "good enough" to allow comprehension to proceed (e.g., Foertsch & Gernsbacher, 1994; Ferreira, 2003). It is clear that the amount of effort that a reader puts into comprehending a text has a strong influence on the representations that are constructed.

Another way that strategic processing can affect text comprehension is through the expectations that readers bring to bear about the text based on genre information. Experienced readers know that newspaper stories, detective novels, science fiction stories, and romantic comedies have typical structures, and knowledge of these structures can affect the ways that readers glean information from the text and the kinds of situation models that are constructed (e.g., Graesser, Kassler, Kreuz, & McLain-Allen, 1998; Zwaan, 1994).

## Theories of Text Comprehension

In this section, we briefly introduce several theories that have been put forth to explain text comprehension.

### *Construction-Integration Model*

Kintsch's (1988) Construction-Integration (CI) model is one of the most successful models of text comprehension. Although the model is not universally endorsed, there is a fairly wide consensus that the CI model captures nearly all of the basic processes that are required for successful comprehension. The CI model proposes that text is comprehended in two iterative stages. During the Construction stage, the incoming textbase enters working memory and retrieves potentially relevant information from long-term memory. This stage of processing happens quickly and automatically. During the Integration stage, the comprehension system assimilates the new information with the previously existing model of the discourse. The Integration stage is comparatively slow and resource consuming, as the comprehension system pares down the information activated in the Construction stage and integrates only the information that is most relevant to the present situation into the model of the discourse. The CI model provides a framework through which to understand the processes involved as information is activated, inhibited, and integrated into a coherent situation model, and as such can be applied to many of the research findings discussed throughout this chapter.

### Structure Building Framework

The Structure Building Framework was outlined by Gernsbacher (1990). The theory proposes that discourse comprehension proceeds by building structured representations of the information presented in the textbase. The "structure" is based around the initial elements presented in the textbase. For example, if a narrative began, "Jane woke up on Thursday morning...," Jane would be the focus of the new structure. The process of initiating a structure is called *laying a foundation*. When new information is presented, it can either be *mapped* to the existing structure, or it can prompt the comprehension system to *shift* to a new structure. Finally, some information in the structure can be *enhanced* and made more available for further processing, whereas other information can be *suppressed* and made temporarily unavailable for further processing. The Structure Building Framework has been an influential account of the processes through which coherence is maintained in the ongoing comprehension of a situation model.

### The Memory-Based Approach to Discourse Processing

Myers and O'Brien (1998) describe the memory-based approach to discourse processing. Whereas the Construction-Integration model and the Structure Building Framework posit the operation of "active" processing mechanisms (in the sense that these mechanisms actively retrieve or inhibit information when building a representation of the discourse), the memory-based approach is built on passive mechanisms of memory retrieval. The memory-based approach is based on Hintzman's (1986) MINERVA and its resonance process of memory retrieval. On this view, incoming information resonates both with the existing model of the discourse and with information in long-term memory. Information from memory is used to interpret the incoming sentence to the extent that it resonates with the new information. The primary contribution of the memory-based approach has been to outline a passive memory retrieval mechanism that serves as a theoretical alternative to the more active "activation and inhibition" mechanisms that have played a large role in many extant theories of text comprehension (e.g., Gernsbacher, 1990; Kintsch, 1988).

### Event-Indexing Model

Zwaan et al.'s (1995) Event-Indexing model proposes that readers continually monitor the discourse model to maintain coherence on five dimensions: protagonist (who is involved in the events being described), time (when the events take place), space (where the characters, objects, and events are located), causality (why the events happen), and intentionality (what drives the protagonist, i.e., his goals and intentions). Shifts on any one of those dimensions—for example, if the text indicates a temporal delay between one event and the next—are typically associated with some processing cost as readers update their mental model. The largest processing costs tend to be associated with discontinuities on the time and protagonist dimensions. The Event-Indexing model has been influential in shaping research on how the dynamics involved in updating many aspects of a situation model at once affect the comprehension process.

### Conclusions

Text comprehension is a complex cognitive operation that requires several levels of linguistic processing and the integration of information presented in the text with knowledge from the reader's long-term memory. As discussed in this chapter, research conducted during the past decades has productively enumerated the processes involved in text comprehension, and several valuable theories have been developed. Nonetheless, there are many exciting frontiers of text comprehension research that are only beginning to be explored. For example, several researchers have begun to apply basic research on text comprehension to problems related to the remediation of reading difficulties (e.g., Rapp, van den Broek, McMaster, Kendeou, & Espin, 2007; see also chapters in McNamara, 2007). There is promise that research of the sort that has been reviewed in this chapter can contribute to the development of educational practices and interventions. As another example, there is growing interest in the question of whether the comprehension of texts reflects the same sort of processes that are involved in the comprehension of the events that occur in our lives. This research has suggested that similar principles can applied to the understanding of text processing and both event processing (e.g., Speer & Zacks, 2005) and the processing of episodes in films (e.g., Magliano, Miller, & Zwaan, 2001; Zacks, Speer, & Reynolds, 2009). Finally, the use of neuroimaging techniques such as fMRI to explore text comprehension promises to open new possibilities for exploring the processes and representations involved in the comprehension process (e.g., Robertson et al., 2000; Speer et al., 2009). Exploration of these new frontiers of research will no doubt deepen our understanding of text comprehension and ensure that the next decades of research in this area are as exciting and productive as the previous decades have been.

# References

Barsalou, L. W. (1999). Perceptual symbol systems. *Behavioral and Brain Sciences, 22*, 577–660.

Barclay, J. R., Bransford, J. D., Franks, J. J., McCarell, N. S., & Nitsch, K. (1974). Comprehension and semantic flexibility. *Journal of Verbal Learning and Verbal Behavior, 13*, 471–481.

Buccino, G., Riggio, L., Hellia, G., Binkofski, F., Gallese, V., & Rizzolatti, G. (2005). Listening to action-related sentences modulates the activity of the motor system: A combined TMS and behavioral study. *Cognitive Brain Research, 24*, 355–363.

Chang, F., Dell, G. S., & Bock, K. (2006). Becoming syntactic. *Psychological Review, 113*, 2, 234–272.

Ericsson, K. A., & Simon, H. A. (1993). *Protocol analysis: Verbal reports as data* (rev. ed.). Cambridge, MA: MIT Press.

Ferreira, F. (2003). The misinterpretation of noncanonical sentences. *Cognitive Psychology, 47*, 164–203.

Foertsch, J., & Gernsbacher, M. A. (1994). In search of complete comprehension: Getting "minimalists" to work. *Discourse Processes, 18*, 271–296.

Frazier, L., &Clifton, C., Jr. (1996). *Construal*. Cambridge, MA: MIT Press.

Gernsbacher, M. A. (1985). Surface information loss in comprehension. *Cognitive Psychology, 17*, 324–363.

Gernsbacher, M. A. (1990). *Language comprehension as structure building*. Hillsdale, NJ: Erlbaum.

Gernsbacher, M. A., & Faust, M. (1995). Skilled suppression. In F. N. Dempster & C. N. Brainerd (Eds.), *Interference and inhibition in cognition* (pp. 295–327). San Diego, CA: Academic Press.

Glenberg, A. M., & Kaschak, M. P. (2002). Grounding language in action. *Psychonomic Bulletin and Review, 9*, 558–565.

Glenberg, A. M., Kruley, P., & Langston, W. E. (1994). Analogical processes in comprehension: Simulation of a mental model. In M. A. Gernsbacher (Ed.), *Handbook of psycholinguistics*. San Diego, CA: Academic Press.

Glenberg, A. M., Sato, M., Cattaneo, L., Riggio, L., Palumbo, D., & Buccino, G. (2008). Processing abstract language modulates motor system activity. *Quarterly Journal of Experimental Psychology, 61*, 905–919.

Graesser, A. C. (2007). An introduction to strategic reading comprehension. In D. S. McNamara (Ed.), *Reading comprehension strategies: Theories, interventions, and technologies* (pp. 3–26). Mahwah, NJ: Erlbaum.

Graesser, A. C., Gernsbacher, M. A., & Goldman, S. R. (Eds.). (2003). *Handbook of discourse processes*. Mahwah, NJ Erlbaum.

Graesser, A. C., Kassler, M. A., Kreuz, R. J., & McLain-Allen, B. (1998). Verification of statements about story worlds that deviate from normal conceptions of time: What is true about Einstein's Dreams? *Cognitive Psychology, 35*, 246–301.

Graesser, A. C., Singer, M., & Trabasso, T. (1994). Constructing inferences during narrative text comprehension. *Psychological Review, 101*, 371–395.

Hauk, O., Johnschrude, I., &Pulvermuller, F. (2004) Somatotopic representation of action words in human motor and premotor cortex. *Neuron, 41*, 301–307.

Haviland, S. E., &Clark, H. H. (1974). What' new? Acquiring new information as a process in comprehension. *Journal of Verbal Learning and Verbal Behavior, 13*, 512–521.

Hintzman, D. L. (1986). "Schema-abstraction" in a multiple trace model. *Psychological Review, 93*, 411–428.

Johnson-Laird, P. N. (1983). *Mental models: Towards a cognitive science of language, inference, and consciousness*. Cambridge, MA: Harvard University Press.

Kaschak, M. P, Madden, C. J., Therriault, D. J., Yaxley, R. H., Aveyard, M., Blanchard, A. A., &Zwaan, R. A. (2005). Perception of motion affects language processing. *Cognition, 94*, B79–B89

Kintsch, W. (1988). The role of knowledge in discourse comprehension: A construction-integration model. *Psychological Review, 95*, 163–182.

Kintsch, W. (1998). *Comprehension: A paradigm for cognition*. New York: Cambridge University Press.

Kintsch, W., Welsch, D., Schmalhofer, F., & Zimny, S. (1990). Sentence memory: A theoretical analysis. *Journal of Memory and Language, 29*, 133–159.

Kosslyn S. M. (1994). *Image and brain: the resolution of the imagery debate*. Cambridge, MA: MIT Press.

Lakoff, G., & Nunez, R. (2000). *Where mathematics comes from: How the embodied mind brings mathematics into being*. New York: Basic Books.

Landauer, T. K., & Dumais, S. T. (1997). A solution to Plato's problem: The latent semantic analysis theory of acquisition, induction and representation of knowledge. *Psychological Review, 104*, 211–240.

Langston, W., Kramer, D. C., & Glenberg, A. M. (1998). The representation of space in mental models derived from text. *Memory and Cognition, 26*, 247–262.

Louwerse, M. M. (2008). Embodied relations are encoded in language. *Psychonomic Bulletin and Review, 15*, 838–844.

MacDonald, M. C., Pearlmutter, N. J., & Seidenberg, M. S. (1994). The lexical nature of syntactic ambiguity resolution. *Psychological Review, 101*, 676–703.

Magliano, J. P., & Graesser, A. C. (1991). A three-pronged method for studying inference generation in literary text. *Poetics, 20*, 193–232.

Magliano, J. P., Miller, J., & Zwaan, R. A. (2001). Indexing space and time in film understanding. *Applied Cognitive Psychology, 15*, 533–545.

McKoon, G., & Ratcliff, R. (1992). Inferences during reading. *Psychological Review, 99*, 440–466.

McNamara, D. S. (Ed.). (2007). *Reading comprehension strategies: Theories, interventions, and technologies*. Mahwah, NJ: Erlbaum.

McRae, K., Spivey-Knowlton, M. J., & Tanenhaus, M. K. (1998). Modeling the influence of thematic fit (and other constraints) in on-line sentence comprehension. *Journal of Memory and Language, 38*, 283–312.

Meteyard, L., Bahrami, B., &Vigliocco, G. (2007) Motion detection and motion words: Language affects low-level visual perception. *Psychological Science, 18*, 1007–1013.

Morrow, D. G., Bower, G. H., & Greenspan, S. L. (1989). Updating situation models during narrative comprehension. *Journal of Memory and Language, 28*, 293–312.

Murphy, G. L., & Shapiro, A. M. (1994). Forgetting of verbatim information in discourse. *Memory and Cognition, 22*, 85–94.

Myers, J. L., & O'Brien, E. J. (1998). Accessing the discourse representation during reading. *Discourse Processes, 26*, 131–157.

O'Brien, E. J., & Albrecht, J. E. (1992). Comprehension strategies in the development of a mental model. *Journal of Experimental Psychology: Learning, Memory, and Cognition, 18*, 777–784.

Radvansky, G. A., &Copeland, D. E. (2000). Functionality and spatial relations in situation models. *Memory and Cognition, 28*, 987–992.

Rapp, D. N., van den Broek, P., McMaster, K. L., Kendeou, P., & Espin, C. A. (2007). Higher-order comprehension processes in struggling readers: A perspective for research and intervention. *Scientific Studies of Reading, 11*, 289–312.

Rinck, M., & Bower, G. H. (1995). Anaphora resolution and the focus of attention in situation models. *Journal of Memory and Language, 34*, 110–131.

Robertson, D. A., Gernsbacher, M. A., Guidotti, S. J., Robertson, R. R. W., Irwin, W., Mock, B. J., & Campana, M. E. (2000). Functional neuroanatomy of the cognitive process of mapping during discourse comprehension. *Psychological Science, 11*, 255–260.

Roland, D., Dick, F., & Elman, J.L. (2007). Frequency of basic English grammatical structures: A corpus analysis. *Journal of Memory and Language, 57*, 348–379.

Saffran, J. R., Aslin, R. N., & Newport, E. L. (1996) Statistical learning by 8-month-old infants. *Science, 274*, 1926–1928.

Speer, N. K., Reynolds, J. R., Swallow, K. M., & Zacks, J. M. (2009). Reading stories activates neural representations of perceptual and motor experiences. *Psychological Science, 20*, 989–999.

Speer, N. K., & Zacks, J. M. (2005). Temporal changes as event boundaries: Processing and memory consequences of narrative time shifts. *Journal of Memory and Language, 53*, 125–140.

Swinney, D. (1979). Lexical access during sentence comprehension: (Re) consideration of context effects. *Journal of Verbal Learning and Verbal Behavior, 18*, 645–659

Therriault, D. J., Rinck, M., & Zwaan, R. A. (2006). Assessing the influence of dimensional focus during situation model construction. *Memory and Cognition, 34*, 78–89.

Trabasso, T., & Suh, S. (1993). Understanding text: Achieving explanatory coherence through on-line inferences and mental operations in working memory. *Discourse Processes, 16*, 3–34.

van Dijk, T. A., & Kintsch, W. (1983). *Strategies of discourse comprehension*. New York: Academic Press.

Zacks, J., Speer, N., & Reynolds, J. R. (2009). Segmentation in reading and film comprehension. *Journal of Experimental Psychology: General, 138*, 307–327.

Zwaan, R. A. (1994). Effect of genre expectations on text comprehension. *Journal of Experimental Psychology: Learning, Memory, and Cognition, 20*, 920–933

Zwaan, R. A. (1996). Processing narrative time shifts. *Journal of Experimental Psychology: Learning, Memory, and Cognition, 22*, 1196–1207.

Zwaan, R. A. (2004). The immersed experiencer: Toward an embodied theory of language comprehension. In B. H. Ross (Ed.), *The psychology of learning and motivation* (pp. 35–62). New York: Academic Press.

Zwaan, R. A., Langston, M. C., & Graesser, A. C. (1995). The construction of situation models in narrative comprehension: An event-indexing model. *Psychological Science, 6*, 292–297.

Zwaan, R. A., & Radvansky, G. A. (1998). Situation models in language comprehension and memory. *Psychological Bulletin, 123*, 162–185.

Zwaan, R. A., &Taylor, L. J. (2006). Seeing, acting, understanding: motor resonance in language comprehension. *Journal of Experimental Psychology: General, 135*, 1–11.

# Discourse Comprehension

Arthur C. Graesser *and* Carol M. Forsyth

**Abstract**

Discourse comprehension is viewed from a multilevel framework that includes the levels of words, syntax, textbase, situation model, rhetorical structure, genre, and pragmatic communication. Discourse researchers investigate the cognitive representation of these levels and the process of constructing them during comprehension. Comprehension frequently is successful at all levels, but sometimes there are communication misalignments, information gaps, ungrounded symbols, and other comprehension obstacles that increase processing time or that lead to comprehension breakdowns. Psychologists have developed a number of psychological models of discourse comprehension, such as the the construction-integration, constructionist, and indexical-embodiment models. Advances in corpus and computational linguistics have allowed interdisciplinary researchers to systematically analyze the words, syntax, semantics, cohesion, situation model, world knowledge, and global structure of texts with computers. These computer analyses help researchers discover new discourse patterns, test hypotheses more rigorously, assess potential confounding variables, and scale texts on difficulty.

**Key Words:** discourse processing, comprehension

## Discourse Comprehension

Our definition of discourse includes both oral conversation and printed text. The spoken utterances in oral conversation and the sentences in printed text are composed by the speaker/writer with the intention of communicating interesting and informative messages to the listener/reader. Therefore, naturalistic discourse is likely to be coherent, understandable to the community of discourse participants, and relevant to the situational goals. Sometimes discourse communication breaks down, however. Communication breakdowns occur when the writer and reader (or speaker and listener) are faced with substantial gulfs in language, prior knowledge, or discourse skills. Minor misalignments often grab the comprehender's attention, as in the case of a mispronounced word, a rare word in a text, an ungrammatical sentence, or a sentence that does not fit into the discourse flow. A model of discourse

comprehension should handle instances when there are communication breakdowns in addition to successful comprehension.

Psychological theories of comprehension have identified the representations, structures, strategies, and processes at multiple levels of discourse (Clark, 1996; Graesser & McNamara, 2011; Graesser, Millis, & Zwaan, 1997; Kintsch, 1998; Pickering & Garrod, 2004; Snow, 2002; Van Dijk & Kintsch, 1983). The taxonomy we adopt in this chapter is an expanded version of one presented by Graesser et al. (1997): *words, syntax*, the explicit *textbase*, the referential *situation model* (sometimes called the mental model), the discourse *genre and rhetorical structure* (the type of discourse and its composition), and the *pragmatic communication* level (between speaker and listener, or writer and reader). Words and syntax are self-explanatory and form what is sometimes called the surface code. The textbase contains explicit propositions in the text in a form that preserves the meaning but not the surface code of wording and syntax. The situation model is the referential content or microworld that the text is describing. This would include the people, objects, spatial setting, actions, events, processes, plans, thoughts and emotions of people, and other referential content. The text genre is the type of discourse, such as a news story, a folk tale, a persuasive editorial, or a science text that explains a causal mechanism. The argument can be made that there is a psychological foundation for differentiating these six levels, as will be clarified throughout this chapter. However, it would be a mistake to view them as crisp separable levels because there are systematic links between levels and occasionally it is debatable on where information components reside.

Table 30.1 elaborates on these six levels by identifying the codes, constituents, and content associated with each level. This chapter will not precisely define each level and the associated terminology, but the table does provide example components of each level. Table 30.1 depicts the levels of discourse as compositional components that are constructed as a *result* of comprehension. It is important not to lose sight of the fact that this *compositional* viewpoint is incomplete without considering the affiliated *knowledge* and *process* viewpoints. For any given compositional entity C, the person needs to have had the prerequisite knowledge about C through prior experiences and training. The person needs to be able to process C by identifying its occurrence in the discourse and by executing relevant cognitive processes, procedures, and strategies proficiently.

The remainder of this chapter has three sections. The first section discusses some of the mechanisms that operate when readers/listeners experience comprehension difficulties, breakdowns, or communication misalignments. Such comprehension challenges are informative because they predict measures of attention, reading time, memory, reasoning, behavior, and other manifestations of cognition. The second section reviews psychological models of discourse that attempt to explain comprehension processes and representations. The third section describes advances in corpus and computational linguistics that have computers automatically analyze texts on the various discourse levels: words,

**Table 30.1** Levels of Language and Discourse

| Level | Example Components of Level |
|---|---|
| 1. Words | Lexical meaning representation<br>Word composition (graphemes, phonemes, syllables, morphemes, lemmas)<br>Parts of speech (noun, verb, adjective, adverb, determiner, connective) |
| 2. Syntax | Syntax (noun-phrase, verb-phrase, prepositional phrase, clause)<br>Linguistic style |
| 3. Textbase | Semantic meaning<br>Explicit propositions or clauses<br>Referents linked to referring expressions<br>Bridging inferences that connect propositions, clauses, or words<br>Connectives that explicitly link clauses |
| 4. Situation model | Situation conveyed in the text<br>Agents, objects, and abstract entities<br>Dimensions of temporality, spatiality, causality, intentionality<br>Inferences that elaborate text and link to the reader's experiential knowledge<br>Given versus new information<br>Images and mental simulations of events |
| 5. Genre and rhetorical structure | Discourse category (narrative, persuasive, expository, descriptive)<br>Rhetorical composition (cause + effect, claim + evidence, problem + solution)<br>Epistemological status of propositions and clauses (claim, evidence, warrant)<br>Speech act categories (assertion, question, command, request, greeting, etc.)<br>Theme, moral, or point of discourse |
| 6. Pragmatic communication | Goals of author<br>Attitudes and beliefs (humor, sarcasm, eulogy, deprecation) |

syntax, semantics, cohesion, situation models, global structure, and world knowledge. These three sections are written from the lens of the multilevel discourse comprehension framework.

## Obstacles of Multilevel Comprehension

Comprehenders can face obstacles at any of the levels in Table 30.1. There can be deficits in the comprehender (e.g., lack of knowledge or skill) or the discourse (e.g., incoherent text, unintelligible speech). The severity of a comprehension obstacle can range from a minor irregularity that adds some cost in processing time to a complete breakdown in comprehension. At one end of the continuum is a misspelled word that adds a small amount of processing time to fill in its meaning. At the other end of the continuum is a student who gives up trying to understand a complex text on electronics. Attempts can be made to compensate for a comprehension obstacle at one (or more) of the six levels by recruiting information from other levels of discourse, from prior knowledge, from external sources (e.g., other people or technologies), or from strategies. Sometimes deeper levels of comprehension can compensate for deficits at the shallower levels. However, such compensation will obviously not work if information at the shallow levels needs to be successfully registered. Compensatory processing will also not be successful when the deeper levels have errors, misconceptions, or irrelevant content. The scenarios that follow illustrate some discourse obstacles and the resulting consequences and compensations with respect to the other levels of the multilevel framework.

**Scenario 1.** A student in a foreign language course has mastered the phonemes but very little of the vocabulary. The vocabulary deficit prevents him from understanding any of the conversations in class. The breakdown at discourse level 1 also blocks the deeper levels of 2–6 (see Table 30.1).

**Scenario 2.** An employee reads a health insurance document that has lengthy sentences with embedded clauses and numerous quantifiers (*all, many, rarely*) and Boolean operators (*and, or, not, if*). She understands nearly all of the words but has only a vague idea what the document explicitly states because of complex syntax, a dense textbase, and an ungrounded situation model (i.e., deficits at levels 2–4). However, she signs the contract because she understands its purpose and trusts the Human Resources Department of the employer. Levels 5 and 6 circumvent the need to understand levels 2–4 completely.

**Scenario 3.** A couple read the directions to assemble a new computer. They argue about how to hook up the cables on the dual monitors. They have no problem understanding the words and textbase in the directions (levels 1–3) and no problem understanding the genre and purpose of the document (levels 5 and 6), but they do have a deficit at the situation model level (level 4).

**Scenario 4.** A science student asks his roommate to proofread a term paper, but the roommate is a journalism major who knows little about science and complains that there is a problem with logical flow. The science major revises the text by adding connectives (e.g., *because, so, therefore, before*) and other words to improve the cohesion. The revised composition is deemed more comprehensible. In this case, improvements at levels 1 and 3 compensated for a deficit at level 4.

**Scenario 5.** Parents take their children to a new Disney movie that they discover has a few adult themes. The children notice the parents laughing at different points in the movie than they do. The children are making it successfully through discourse levels 1–4, but levels 5 and 6 are not intact.

**Scenario 6.** A jury receives instructions on a case, their decision options, and the legal ground rules of justice. However, the jury has trouble understanding the jargon, abstractions, and dense legal language, so they instead appeal to their intuitions on common-sense justice. In this case, the schema for common-sense justice at level 4 interferes with comprehension at levels 1–3.

These scenarios illustrate how deficiencies at one or more discourse levels can have substantial repercussions on the processing at other levels. Discourse researchers need to understand the processing mechanisms both *within* levels and *between* levels.

Metacognition is the knowledge that a person has about cognitive mechanisms—thinking about thinking (Hacker, Dunlosky, & Graesser, 2009). Research on metacomprehension has revealed that people may have deficits at one or more comprehension levels without being aware of it. For example, in research on *comprehension calibration* (Dunlosky & Lipko, 2007; Maki, 1998), ratings are collected from readers on how well they believe they have comprehended texts and these ratings are correlated with objective tests of text comprehension. The comprehension calibration correlations are alarmingly low ($r = .27$) even among college students. Readers often have an illusion of comprehension when they read text because they settle for shallow levels of analysis as a criterion for adequate comprehension (Baker, 1985; Daneman, Lennertz, & Hannon, 2006; Otero & Kintsch, 1992). Shallow readers believe they have adequately comprehended text if they can recognize the content words and can understand most of the sentences, when in fact they are missing the deeper knowledge and occasional contradictions or false claims. Deep comprehension requires inferences, linking ideas coherently, scrutinizing the validity of claims with a critical stance, and understanding the motives of authors (Kendeou & Van den Broek, 2007; Rapp, 2008; Rouet, 2006; Wiley et al., 2009). Deep comprehension may only be selectively achieved in everyday comprehension experiences. Many readers settle for shallow comprehension for discourse unless they have a high amount of background knowledge (O'Reilly & McNamara, 2007), the information is in the discourse focus (Sanford & Graesser, 2006; Sturt, Sanford, Steward, & Dawydiak, 2004; Ward & Sturt, 2007), the genre dictates careful scrutiny of information (Kendeou & van den Broek, 2007), or the information is highly relevant to the readers' goals (Kaakinen & Hyona, 2007; McCruddin & Schraw, 2007).

In studies conducted in our laboratory (Graesser et al., 2004; VanLehn et al., 2007), college students read textbooks on technical topics such as computer literacy and Newtonian physics. They subsequently completed a rigorous test on deep knowledge with multiple-choice questions similar to the Force Concept Inventory in physics (Hestenes, Wells, & Swackhamer, 1992). We were surprised to learn that the college students had zero learning gains from reading the textbook and that the posttest scores did not differ from a condition in which the students read nothing at all. In contrast, the learning gains were quite substantial when there was a learning environment that challenged their comprehension of the material and engaged in tutorial dialogue (through a computer system called AutoTutor). Results such as these strongly suggest that the reading strategies of literate adults are far from optimal when considering deep comprehension. Our college students did not achieve deep comprehension on texts about physics and computer literacy even when they had a nontrivial amount of world knowledge on these topics and sufficient reading strategies to land them in college.

Comprehension deficits also periodically occur in conversations. An important foundation for communication is forming a *common ground* (shared knowledge) among speech participants (Bard et al., 2007; Clark, 1996; Holler & Wilkin, 2009; Schober & Brennan, 2003). This requires making appropriate assumptions on what each other already knows ("old" or "given" knowledge in the common ground) and by performing acts of communication (verbal or nonverbal) about new information that is properly *coordinated* with what each other knows. People normally assume that knowledge is in the common ground if it (a) is physically co-present and salient (all parties in the communication can perceive it); (b) has been verbally expressed and understood in the discourse space, in front of the sender, recipients, and side audience; and/or (c) it is common knowledge for members of a group, culture, or target community. Communication breakdowns occur to the extent that one or more of these conditions are in jeopardy.

Regarding the coordination of acts of communication, there are discourse devices that facilitate successful communication. Clark (1996) has proposed four levels in the *joint action ladder*:

*Level A: Attention.* Is the intended recipient paying attention?
*Level B: Listening.* Is the recipient actively listening and identifying signals?
*Level C: Understanding.* Does the recipient understand the message of the sender?
*Level D: Action.* Does the recipient perform a verbal or physical action that reflects understanding?

Breakdowns occur when there is a misfire at any one of these levels. However, it can be difficult to know which level is problematic when there is no response from a recipient. Clark's *principle of upward causality* predicts that disruption at lower levels propagates to higher levels. Indeed, failure at the attention Level A accounts for many of the disruptions that occur in communication technologies, such as e-mail and instant messaging (Hancock & Dunham, 2001). Simply put, it is not clear whether the recipient is paying attention. The sender can ask questions to inquire about the status of the listener with respect to these four levels: "Are you there?" "Are you listening?" "Do you understand?" "Could you recap/summarize?" These discourse acts correspond to a second track discussion (Track 2, metacommunication) that specifically addresses communication problems.

One important signal of a recipient is *backchannel feedback*. Backchannel feedback ("uh huh," "okay," head nod) from the recipient acknowledges the sender's message (i.e., conversation tracks 1 and 2 are in check). In face-to-face conversations in English, backchannel feedback is typically provided by the recipient after every 10–15 syllables, on the average. The recipient who gives more backchannel feedback could possibly be viewed as annoying, whereas much less feedback makes the recipient appear distracted, skeptical, or unresponsive. In e-mail, backchannel feedback is an important courtesy after a sender's message, but some recipients do not extend this courtesy. Sometimes it is appropriate to withhold backchannel feedback, as in the case of a large teleconference on a telephone system that imposes transmission latencies after every party turn; when this occurs, the organizer needs to declare rules such as "Whenever I say something and then pause, please respond only if you disagree or have something new to say."

Degrees of comprehension are manifested in *conversation patterns* that span larger sequences of turns between conversational participants. The conversation patterns are quite different in different sociocultural settings. For example, consider different educational settings. In the context of classroom teaching, a common pattern is the IRE sequence (Sinclair & Coulthard, 1975) in which the instructor asks a question (Initiate), the student answers (Response), and the instructor gives feedback on the answer (Evaluate). In tutorial dialogue, there is a five-step tutoring frame in which the tutor asks a difficult question, the student answers, the tutor gives short feedback (positive, negative, or neutral), there is an optional extended multiturn elaboration of the answer, the tutor asks a comprehension-gauging question (e.g., "Do you understand?"), and the student designates his or her level of understanding (Graesser, D'Mello, & Person, 2009). In dialogues between a leader and follower that require referential grounding, there often are four-step sequences: Leader: "You lift the red bar." Follower: "The red bar?" Leader: "Yes, that red bar." Follower: "Okay, the red bar" (Clark & Wilkes-Gibbs, 1986). This four-step frame can be more economically expressed in face-to-face interaction by pointing gestures, directing a person's gaze, and other nonverbal channels (Bard et al., 2007; Hanna & Brennan, 2007; Holler & Wilkin, 2009; Van der Sluis & Krahmer, 2007).

Available psychological research supports a number of generalizations about the processing order, constraints, interaction, and compensatory mechanisms of the different levels of discourse comprehension. Some of these generalizations are briefly described next.

## Bottom-Up Dependencies of Meaning

In a strictly bottom-up model of reading, the ordering on depth is assumed to be levels $1 \rightarrow 2 \rightarrow 3 \rightarrow 4 \rightarrow 5 \rightarrow 6$ (see Table 30.1). Most researchers endorse an interactive model of reading rather than a strictly bottom-up model (Rayner & Pollatsek, 1994; Rumelhart, 1977; Taraban & McClelland, 1988; van den Broek, Rapp, & Kendeou, 2005). However, they also assume asymmetry in the constraints, such that the lower levels constrain the higher levels more than vice versa. The reading of words is robustly influenced by the bottom-up constraints of the letters and syllables (Gough, 1972; Rayner, 1998; Rayner & Pollatsek, 1994). The quality of a person's lexicon has a large impact on the proficiency and speed of interpreting sentences and generating inferences at levels 2 and higher (Perfetti, 2007; Stanovich, 1986). It is important for readers to establish an interpretation of the textbase before they can productively move on to the construction of the situation model and higher levels (O'Reilly & McNamara, 2007). A partial to full analysis of levels 1–4 is presumably needed to adequately construct the rhetorical structure.

There is some question about the extent to which top-down processes influence lower level processes. Top-down processing is known to influence the speed and construction of word meanings (Rayner & Pollatsek, 1994), but there is less certainty about top-down influences on the construction of the textbase and situation model. Bransford and Johnson (1972) conducted a series of studies with vague abstract texts that were very difficult to comprehend without the introduction of a title that identifies a higher order schema (such as washing clothes) that coherently organizes the text content. Zwaan (1994) reported that the encoding of the surface code, textbase, and situation model had different profiles when college students were told they were reading a newspaper article versus literature. As predicted, the literature instructions enhanced the surface code, whereas the newspaper instructions enhanced the situation model. These top-down influences of comprehending the textbase and situation model are provocative, but the effects are confined to texts that are extremely ambiguous or malleable in interpretation. The vast majority of texts are much more constrained.

## Novel Information Requires More Processing Effort Than Familiar and Automatized Components

Novelty of information is a foundational cognitive dimension that attracts attention, effort, and processing resources, and that predicts salience in memory (Tulving & Kroll, 1995). In spoken conversation, there are prosodic features that signal the occurrence of given information versus new information in the discourse space (Clark, 1996; Nygaard, Herold, & Namy, 2009; Riesco-Bernier & Romero-Trillo, 2008). Reading studies with eye tracking or self-paced reading times show that more processing time is allocated to rare words than high-frequency words (Just & Carpenter, 1987; Pollatsek, Slattery, & Juhasz, 2008; Rayner, 1998) and to new information expressed in the textbase and situation model than to old information already mentioned (Haberlandt & Graesser, 1985; Kaakinen & Hyona, 2007). Graesser and McNamara (2011) proposed that the highest density of novel information resides in lower frequency words, the textbase level, and the situation model (levels 1, 3, and 4). In contrast, most aspects of syntax, genre, and author characteristics (levels 2, 5, and 6) are frequently experienced and therefore overlearned and automatized; these levels are quickly processed or are invisible to the comprehender unless there are obstacles.

### Attention, Consciousness, and Effort Gravitate to Comprehension Obstacles

Obstacles at any level of analysis are likely to draw cognitive resources. Reading time studies have shown that extra processing time is allocated to pronouns that have unresolved or ambiguous referents (Gernsbacher, 1990; Rayner, 1998), to sentences that have breaks in textbase cohesion (Gernsbacher, 1990), to sentences that have coherence breaks in the situation model on the dimensions of temporality, spatiality, causality, and intentionality (Magliano & Radvansky, 2001; Zwaan, Magliano & Graesser, 1995; Zwaan & Radvansky, 1998), and to sentences that contradict ideas already established in the evolving situation model (Kendeou & van den Broek, 2007; O'Brien, Rizzella, Albrecht, & Halleran, 1998; Rapp, 2008). Attention drifts toward sources of cognitive disequilibrium, such as impasses, anomalies, discrepancies, and contradictions (Graesser, Lu, Olde, Cooper-Pye, & Whitten, 2005).

### Comprehension Obstacles May Be Repaired or Circumvented by World Knowledge, Information at Other Discourse Levels, or External Sources

The scenarios described earlier illustrate some compensatory mechanisms that repair or circumvent the comprehension obstacles. For example,

the syntax, textbase, and situation model deficits in scenario 2 are circumvented by the information in discourse levels 5 and 6; in this case the person has enough information about levels 5 and 6 to know that deep understanding of levels 2–4 is unnecessary. The gaps and misalignments in the situation model of scenario 3 are rectified by extended conversations between the couple and by active problem solving. Coherence gaps in the textbase and situation model of scenario 4 are rectified by augmenting the discourse at levels 1 and 2 with connectives and other cohesion markers. Inserting these connectives and markers is known to improve comprehension, particularly for readers with low subject matter knowledge or low reading comprehension skill (Britton & Gulgoz, 1991; McNamara & Kintsch, 1996; O'Reilly & McNamara, 2007).

The multilevel comprehension framework outlined in this section has provided a plausible sketch of the complexities of constructing meaning on different levels during discourse comprehension. There are multiple levels of meaning that mutually, but asymmetrically, constrain each other. The components at each level are successfully built if the text is naturalistic and the reader has prerequisite background knowledge and reading skills. However, there are periodic comprehension obstacles that range from minor misalignments and comprehension difficulties to complete communication breakdowns. The misfires are magnets of attention that sometimes trigger compensatory mechanisms that repair or circumvent the problems.

## Psychological Models of Discourse Comprehension

Discourse psychologists have developed several theoretical models of comprehension during the last two decades. It is beyond the scope of this chapter to cover all of these models, but we will contrast three models that are representative of particular classes of models. A construction-integration model (Kintsch, 1998) will represent a class of bottom-up models, which would also include the memory-based resonance model developed by Myers and O'Brien (Myers, O'Brien, Albrecht, & Mason, 1994; O'Brien et al., 1998). A constructionist model by Graesser, Singer, and Trabasso (1994) will represent a class of strategy-driven models, which would also include the structure-building framework (Gernsbacher, 1990) and the event-indexing model (Zwaan et al., 2005; Zwaan & Radvansky, 1998). An indexical model by Glenberg (Glenberg & Robertson, 1999) will represent a class of embodied cognition models

(Glenberg, 1997; de Vega, Glenberg, & Graesser, 2008). There are other models that that can be viewed as hybrids of these three classes, such as the landscape model (Van den Broek, Virtue, Everson, Tzeng, & Sung, 2002), the CAPS/Reader model (Just & Carpenter's, 1992), and the 3CAPS model (Goldman, Varma, & Cote, 1996).

### Construction-Integration Model

Kintsch's (1998) construction-integration (CI) model is currently regarded as the most comprehensive psychological model of comprehension. The model accommodates a large body of psychological data, including reading times, activation of concepts at different phases of comprehension, sentence recognition, text recall, and text summarization. Comprehension strategies exist, but they do not drive the comprehension engine. Instead, comprehension lies in (a) the bottom-up activation of knowledge in long-term memory from textual input (the *construction* phase) and (b) the integration of activated ideas in working memory (the *integration* phase). As each sentence or clause in a text is comprehended, there is a construction phase followed by an integration phase.

The construction phase for each sentence activates hundreds of *nodes*, which correspond to concepts, propositions, rules, and other forms of content. The nodes cover the various levels of representation in the multilevel comprehension framework (see Table 30.1). The model assumes that a connectionist network (Mayberry, Crocker, & Knoeferle, 2009; Taraban & McClelland, 1988) is iteratively created, modified, and updated during the course of comprehension. That is, as text is read, sentence by sentence (or clause by clause), a set of word concept nodes and proposition nodes are activated (constructed). Some nodes correspond to explicit constituents in the text, whereas others are activated inferentially. The activation of each node in the network fluctuates systematically during the course of comprehension as each sentence is read. When a sentence (or clause) S is read, the set of N activated nodes include (a) the explicit and inference nodes affiliated with S and (b) the nodes that are held over in working memory from the previous sentence S-1 by virtue of meeting some threshold of activation. There are N nodes that have varying degrees of activation while comprehending sentence S. These N nodes are fully connected to each other in a weight space. The set of weights in the resulting N by N *connectivity matrix* specifies the extent to which each node activates or inhibits the activation of each of the N nodes. The values of the weights in the connectivity matrix are theoretically motivated by the multiple levels of language and discourse. For example, if two proposition nodes (A and B) are closely related semantically, they would have a high positive weight, whereas if the two propositions contradict each other, they would have a high negative weight.

The integration phase modifies activation of the N nodes dynamically. At construction, the N nodes are activated to varying degrees, specified by an initial activation vector $(a_1, a_2, \ldots a_N)$. The connectivity matrix then operates on this initial node activation vector in multiple activation cycles until there is a settling of the node activations to a new final stable activation profile for the N nodes. At that point, integration of the nodes has been achieved. This is computed mathematically by the initial activation vector being multiplied by the same connectivity matrix in multiple iterations until the N output vectors of two successive interactions show extremely small differences (signifying a stable settling of the integration phase). Sentences that are more difficult to comprehend would presumably require more cycles to settle. The settling process history and/or final activation values of the N nodes are able to predict different types of experimental measures, such as reading times, word priming, recall, recognition, and summarization.

### Constructionist Model

Comprehension is more directed and strategic according to the constructionist theory proposed by Graesser, Singer, and Trabasso (1994). The distinctive strategies of this model are reflected in its three principal assumptions: reader goals, coherence, and the explanation. The *reader goal* assumption states that readers attend to content in the text that is relevant to the goals of the reader (McCrudden & Schraw, 2007). For example, adults read newspaper articles for the purpose of being updated about events and factual information, whereas novels are read for the purpose of being entertained. Newspapers are rarely read front to back, whereas novels often are completed even though they are much longer. The *coherence* assumption states that readers attempt to construct meaning representations that are coherent at both local and global levels. Therefore, coherence gaps in the text will stimulate the reader to actively think, generate inferences, and reinterpret the text in an effort to fill in, repair, or take note of the coherence gap. The *explanation* assumption states that good comprehenders tend to generate explanations of *why* events and actions in the text occur, *why* states exist, and *why* the author bothers expressing particular ideas. Why-questions encourage analysis of causal mechanisms, justifications of claims, and other deeper levels of the situation model. There are other assumptions of the constructionist theory that are shared by many other models, assumptions that address memory stores, levels of representation, world knowledge, activation of nodes, automaticity, and so on, but its signature assumptions address reader goals, coherence, and explanation. As in the case of the construction-integration model, the constructionist theory has accounted for data involving reading times, word priming, inference generation, recall of text information, and summarization.

The notion that coherence and explanation strategies are the hallmarks of good comprehension places constraints on comprehension. These strategies determine the selection of content that gets encoded, the inferences that are generated, and the time spent processing text constituents. For example, proficient readers are driven by why-questions more than how, when, where, and what-if, unless there are special goals to track the latter information. The explanations of the motives of characters and of the causes of unexpected events in a story are much more important than the spatial position of the characters in a setting, what the character looks like, and the procedures and style of how characters' actions are performed. Such details about space, perceptual attributes, and actions are important when they serve an explanatory function or they address specific reader goals. When readers are asked to monitor why-questions during comprehension, their processing and memory for the text is very similar to normal comprehension without such orienting questions; however, when asked to monitor how questions and what happens next questions, their processing and memory show signs of being disrupted (Magliano, Trabasso, & Graesser, 1999). The explanation assumption of the constructionist theory applies to expository text in addition to stories. Students comprehend expository text more deeply when they normally build or are experimentally prompted to generate self-explanations of the material (Chi, deLeeuw, Chiu, & LaVancher, 1994; McNamara, 2004; Millis et al., 2004).

### Indexical Hypothesis and Embodiment

Glenberg's *Indexical Hypothesis* (Glenberg & Robertson, 1999) adopts an embodied theory of language and discourse comprehension (Glenberg, 1997; Glenberg & Kaschak, 2004; Pecher & Zwaan, 2005). The central theoretical claim is that meaning is grounded in how we use our bodies as we perceive and act in the world. For example, comprehension of a story is predicted to improve after children have been able to perceive and manipulate the characters and objects in a story scenario. When adults read a manual on assembling a piece of equipment, their comprehension is expected to improve to the extent that they can enact the procedures or at least form visual images of the objects and actions. Readers who have the metacognitive strategy of grounding the entities and events mentioned in the text are expected to show comprehension advantages over those who do not bother taking such extra cognitive steps. It should be noted that the constructionist model would not encourage these strategies unless they served the strategies of building explanations, coherent representations, and representations that address particular reader goals. Similarly, the construction-integration model would not directly predict the importance of embodied representations.

A recent edited volume published some debates on the conceptual differences and the empirical evidence for embodied versus symbolic theories of comprehension (de Vega et al., 2008). A *strong* sense of embodiment exists in a representation that incorporates the constraints of an organism's body, its location in the world, its perspective in perceiving the world, and its perceptual-motor interactions with the world. A *weak* sense of embodiment exists when there are vestiges of perceptions, actions, and perspectives in the representation, but the components are less detailed or underspecified, yet to some extent systematic or recoverable. A representation is *not* embodied when the symbols have an arbitrary relationship with the various components of perceptual-motor interactions with the world. In contrast, a symbolic representation is a structured set of symbols, each of which stands for some aspect of a referential domain. What it stands for may or may not be embodied. An *amodal* symbolic representation is not grounded in any embodied representation. A *modal* symbolic representation is connected to perceptual-motor experience either indirectly through interpretive mechanisms or directly through sensory transduction and motoric actuators. Consequently, embodied and symbolic representations are not necessarily mutually exclusive.

There is growing support for the embodied framework, even though it has enjoyed only a decade of empirical testing (de Vega et al., 2008; Masson, Bub, & Warren, 2008; Pecher & Zwaan,

2005). However, as would be expected, there are some fundamental challenges for the embodiment framework in explaining discourse comprehension. The first challenge is that it is difficult to explain how embodied representations can be constructed at a normal reading rate of 150–400 words per minute. It takes approximately 300–1000 milliseconds to construct a new referent in a discourse space (i.e., in the mind's eye), several hundred milliseconds to move an entity from one location to another, a few hundred more milliseconds to have the mental camera zoom in on an entity within a crowded mental space, and so on (Kosslyn, 1980; Millis, King, & Kim, 2001). These considerations on timing and complexity raise some doubts that all referring expressions and clauses in the text have fully embodied representations during reading. It should be noted that this challenge about comprehension time also would apply to the constructionist theorists who claim that deep explanations are constructed during comprehension. It may be impossible to construct deep explanations at a reading rate of 150–400 words per minute, which would explain the results of the studies that were reported earlier that very little deep knowledge is acquired from reading textbooks.

The second challenge is that embodied representations appear to be constructed only under very restricted conditions. Graesser and Jackson (2008) have argued that the embodied framework is essentially correct under the following conditions: (1) when tasks and tests involve goals and representations that are directly aligned with action, (2) when the stimuli are simple (e.g., few actors and objects in the mind's eye), (3) when there is an existing visual-spatial grounding (e.g., an established spatial layout), and (4) when there is sufficient time and cognitive resources to carry out these processing operations. It is plausible that the small amount of content in the discourse focus is an excellent candidate for being a recipient of such cognitive activities. In contrast, disembodied symbolic representations are more explanatory when the relevant task goals do not encourage embodied processing, when the stimulus is complex, when there is minimal visual-spatial grounding, and when the reading rate is at the fast end of 150–400 words per minute. Much of the content that is presupposed and highly embedded will not be a good candidate for becoming a fully fleshed out embodied representation.

The aforementioned analysis addresses the relatively time-consuming integration phase of Kintsch's construction integration model (Kintsch, 1998) rather than the initial activation of representations. It is possible to have quick activations of many types of representations, both embodied and symbolic, during the initial activation of information associated with content words. Much of this automatic activation of representations end up dying away and never make it to the integration phase that establishes a more coherent representation of the meaning of the text.

## Computer Tools for Analyzing Language and Discourse at Multiple Levels

This is a unique point in history because there is widespread access to hundreds of computer tools that analyze specific texts and large text corpora. This increase in automated text analyses can be attributed to landmark advances in computational linguistics (Jurafsky & Martin, 2008), discourse processes (Graesser, Gernsbacher, & Goldman, 2003), statistical representations of world knowledge (Landauer, McNamara, Dennis, & Kintsch, 2007), and corpus analyses (Biber, Conrad, & Reppen, 1998). Thousands of texts can be quickly accessed and analyzed on thousands of measures in a short amount of time. Of course, many theoretical components of discourse cannot currently be automated. In such cases it is necessary to have human experts annotate the texts systematically. However, human annotation is an expensive and time-consuming alternative, so it is essential to offload much of the work to computers. Moreover, an objective analysis of discourse should not rely entirely on human intuitions for scoring and annotation.

This chapter will present recent work on automated text analysis through the lens of Coh-Metrix (Graesser & McNamara, 2011; Graesser, McNamara, Louwerse, & Cai, 2004; McNamara, Louwerse, & Graesser, in press; McNamara, Louwerse, McCarthy, & Graesser, 2010). Coh-Metrix is a computer facility that analyzes texts on most of the discourse levels in Table 30.1, namely levels 1 through 5. The original purpose of the Coh-Metrix project was to concentrate on the cohesion of the textbase and situation model because those levels needed a more precise specification. However, it quickly became apparent that there is a need to automatically measure language and discourse processing at all of the levels under the rubric of the multilevel comprehension framework. The theoretical vision behind Coh-Metrix was to use the tool to (a) assess the overall cohesion and language difficulty of discourse on multiple levels, (b) investigate the constraints of discourse within levels and between levels, and (c) test models of multilevel discourse comprehension. There were also some practical goals in our vision: (a) to enhance standard text difficulty measures by providing scores on various cohesion and language characteristics and (b) to determine the appropriateness of a text for a reader with a particular profile of cognitive characteristics.

Coh-Metrix is available in both a public version for free on the Web (http://cohmetrix.memphis.edu, version 2.0) and an internal version (versions 2.1 and 3.0). The public version has over 60 measures of language and discourse at levels 1–5 in Table 30.1, whereas the internal research version has nearly a thousand measures that are at various stages of testing. Coh-Metrix is used by simply entering a text, filling in identifier information about the text, and clicking on a button. After a few seconds, the system produces a long list of measures on the text. If the text is extremely lengthy, the text can be divided into textiles of 500–1000 words. There is a help system that defines the measures and that provides various forms of contextual support. Discussed next are measures associated with the various levels of the multilevel framework. Examples of these measures can be found in Table 30.2.

## Words

Coh-Metrix was designed to move beyond standard readability formulas that rely on word length and sentence length to difficulty. Widely adopted measures of text difficulty are the Flesch-Kincaid Grade Level (Klare, 1974–5), Degrees of Reading Power (DRP; Koslin, Zeno, & Koslin, 1987), and Lexile scores (Stenner, 1996). Formula 1 shows the Flesch-Kincaid Grade Level metric. *Words* refers to mean number of words per sentence and *syllables* refers to mean number of syllables per word.

$$\text{Grade Level} = .39 * \text{Words} + 11.8 * \text{Syllables} - 15.59 \tag{1}$$

The lengths of words and sentences no doubt have important repercussions on psychological processes, but we need Coh-Metrix to scale texts on more levels.

Many Coh-Metrix measures refer to characteristics of individual words. Much can be discovered from computer facilities that link words to psychological dimensions, as in the case of *WordNet* (Fellbaum, 1998) and *Linguistic Inquiry Word Count* (Pennebaker, Booth, & Francis, 2007). Coh-Metrix measures words on dozens of characteristics that were extracted from established psycholinguistic and corpus analyses, including WordNet

and many of the categories of LIWC. The MRC Psycholinguistic Database (Coltheart, 1981) is a collection of human ratings of several thousands of words along several psychological dimensions: meaningfulness, concreteness, imagability, age of acquisition, and familiarity. Coh-Metrix computes scores for word frequency, ambiguity, abstractness, and parts of speech, as is documented in the Coh-Metrix help system. There is a relative frequency per 1000 words for each particular category of words.

## Syntax

Coh-Metrix analyzes sentence syntax with the assistance of a syntactic parser developed by Charniak (2000). The parser assigns part-of-speech categories to words and syntactic tree structures to sentences. There are two notable measures of syntactic complexity that are predicted to place a high load on working memory. First, the *number of modifiers per noun phrase* is an index of the complexity of referencing expressions. "The very large angry dog" is a noun phrase with four modifiers of the head noun "dog." Second, the number of words before the main verb of the main clause is an index of syntactic complexity because it places a burden on the working memory of the comprehender (Graesser, Cai, Louwerse, & Daniel, 2006; Just & Carpenter, 1987, 1992). Sentences with preposed clauses and left-embedded syntax require comprehenders to keep many words in working memory before getting to the meaning of the main clause.

## Textbase

The *textbase* theoretically contains explicit propositions in the text, referential links between explicit propositions, and a small number of inferences that connect the explicit propositions (van Dijk & Kintsch, 1983). The propositions are in a stripped-down form that removes surface code features captured by determiners, quantifiers, tense, aspect, and auxiliary verbs. *Co-reference* is an important linguistic method of connecting propositions, clauses, and sentences in the textbase (Britton & Gulgoz, 1991; Halliday & Hasan, 1976; McNamara & Kintsch, 1996; van Dijk & Kintsch, 1983). Referential cohesion occurs when a noun, pronoun, or noun phrase refers to another constituent in the text. For example, in the sentence *When the intestines absorb the nutrients, the absorption is facilitated by some forms of bacteria*, the word *absorption* in the second clause refers to the event (or alternatively the verb *absorb*) in the first clause. There is a referential cohesion gap when the

**Table 30.2** Example Coh-Metrix Measures and Indices (Over 700 Available)

| Level or Class | Measure (Index) |
| --- | --- |
| Words | Frequency, concreteness, imagery, age of acquisition, part of speech, content words, pronouns, negations, connectives (different categories), logical operators, polysemy, hypernym/hyponym (reflects abstractness); these counts per 1000 words. |
| Syntax | Syntactic complexity (words per noun phrase, words before main verb of main clause). |
| Textbase cohesion | Cohesion of adjacent sentences as measured by overlapping nouns, pronouns, meaning stems (lemma, morpheme). Proportion of content words that overlap. Cohesion of all pairs of sentences in a paragraph. |
| Situation model cohesion | Cohesion of adjacent sentences with respect to causality, intentionality, temporality, spatiality, and latent semantic analysis (LSA). Cohesion among all sentences in paragraph and between paragraphs via LSA. Given versus new content. |
| Genre and rhetoric | Type of genre (narrative, science, other). Topic sentence-hood |
| Other | Flesch-Kincaid grade level, type token ration, syllables per word, words per sentence, sentences and paragraphs per 1000 words. |

words in a sentence or clause do not connect to other sentences in the text.

Coh-Metrix tracks five major types of lexical co-reference: *common noun overlap*, *pronoun overlap*, *argument overlap*, *stem overlap*, and *content word overlap*. Common noun overlap is the proportion of all sentence pairs that share one or more common nouns, whereas pronoun overlap is the proportion of sentence pairs that share one or more pronoun. Argument overlap is the proportion of all sentence pairs that share common nouns or pronouns (e.g., *table/table*, *he/he*, or *table/tables*). Stem overlap is the proportion of sentence pairs in which a noun (or pronoun) in one sentence has the same semantic morpheme (called a lemma) in common with any word in any grammatical category in the other sentence (e.g., the noun *photograph* and the verb *photographed*). The fifth co-reference index, content word overlap, is the proportion of content words that are the same between pairs of sentences. There are different variants of the five measures of co-reference. Some indices consider only pairs of *adjacent* sentences, whereas others consider *all possible pairs* of sentences in a paragraph.

Coh-Metrix treats pronouns carefully because pronouns are known to create problems in comprehension when readers have trouble linking the pronouns to referents. Coh-Metrix computes the incidence scores for personal pronouns (I, you, we) and the proportion of noun phrases that are filled with any pronoun (including it, these, that). *Anaphors* are pronouns that refer to previous nouns and constituents in the text. There are measures of anaphor overlap in Coh-Metrix that approximate binding the correct referent to a pronoun, but the pronoun resolution mechanism is not perfect. A pronoun is scored as having been filled with a referent corresponding to a previous constituent if there is any prior noun that agrees with the pronoun in number and gender and that satisfies some syntactic constraints (Lappin & Leass, 1994).

Connectives and discourse markers have the special function of linking clauses and sentences in the textbase (Halliday & Hasan, 1976; Louwerse, 2001; Sanders & Noordman, 2000). The categories of connectives in Coh-Metrix include additive (*also, moreover*), temporal (*and then, after, during*), causal (*because, so*), and logical operators (*therefore, if, and, or*). A higher relative frequency of these connectives increases cohesion in the textbase and also the situation model.

## Situation Model

Text comprehension researchers have investigated five dimensions of the situational model (Zwaan et al., 1995; Zwaan & Radvansky, 1998): causation, intentionality, time, space, and protagonists. A break in cohesion or coherence occurs when there is a discontinuity on one or more of these situation model dimensions. Such discontinuities are known to increase reading times and trigger the generation of elaborative inferences (Zwaan & Radvansky, 1998). Whenever such discontinuities occur, it is important to have connectives, transitional phrases, adverbs, or other signaling devices that convey to the readers that there is a discontinuity; we refer to these different forms of signaling as *particles*. Cohesion is facilitated by particles that clarify and stitch together the actions, goals, events, and states in the text.

Coh-Metrix analyzes the situation model dimension on causation, intentionality, space, and time, but not protagonists. For *causal and intentional cohesion*, Coh-Metrix computes the ratio of cohesion particles to the incidence of relevant referential content (i.e., main verbs that signal state changes, events, actions, and processes, as opposed to states). The ratio metric is essentially a conditionalized relative frequency of cohesion particles: Given the occurrence of relevant content (such as clauses with events or actions, but not states), Coh-Metrix computes the density of particles that stitch together the clauses. For example, the referential content for intentional information includes intentional actions performed by agents (*kill, help, give*, as in stories, scripts, and common procedures); in contrast, the intentional cohesion particles include infinitives and intentional connectives (*in order to, so that, by means of*).

Measuring *temporal cohesion* is important because of its ubiquitous presence in organizing language and discourse. Time is represented through inflected tense morphemes (e.g., *-ed, is, has*) in sentences of the English language. The temporal dimension also depicts unique internal event timeframes, such as an event that is complete (i.e., *telic*) or ongoing (i.e., *atelic*), by incorporating a diverse tense-aspect system. The occurrence of events at a point in time can be established by a large repertoire of adverbial cues, such as *before, after, then*. The temporal measures of Coh-Metrix compute a repetition score that tracks the consistency of tense (e.g., *past* and *present*) and aspect (*perfective* and *progressive*) across a passage of text. The repetition scores decrease as shifts in tense and aspect are encountered. A low score indicates that the representation of time in the text is disjointed, thus having a possible negative influence on the construction of a mental representation. When such temporal shifts occur, the readers would encounter difficulties without explicit particles that signal such shifts in time, such as the temporal adverbial (*later on*), temporal connective (*before*), or prepositional phrases with temporal nouns (*on the previous day*). A low particle-to-shift ratio is a symptom of problematic temporal cohesion.

In addition to the co-reference variables discussed earlier, Coh-Metrix assesses conceptual overlap between sentences by a statistical model of word meaning: Latent Semantic Analysis (LSA; Landauer et al., 2007). LSA is an important method of computing the conceptual similarity between words, sentences, paragraphs, or texts because it considers implicit knowledge. LSA is a mathematical, statistical technique for representing world knowledge, based on a large corpus of texts. The central intuition is that the meaning of a word is captured by the company of other words that surround it in naturalistic documents. Two words are similar in meaning to the extent that they share similar surrounding words. For example, the word *glass* will be highly associated with words of the same functional context, such as *cup, liquid*, and *pour*. LSA uses a statistical technique called singular value decomposition to condense a very large corpus of texts to 100–500 statistical dimensions (Landauer et al., 2007). The conceptual similarity between any two text excerpts (e.g., word, clause, sentence, text) is computed as the geometric cosine between the values and weighted dimensions of the two text excerpts. The value of the cosine typically varies from 0 to 1. LSA-based cohesion was measured in several ways in Coh-Metrix, such as LSA similarity between adjacent sentences, LSA similarity between all possible pairs of sentences in a paragraph, and LSA similarity between adjacent paragraphs. The statistical representation of words in LSA depends on the corpus of texts on which they are trained. Coh-Metrix has different corpus options, but the default is the TASA corpora of academic textbooks; this is a corpus of over 10 million words that cover a broad range of topics.

Coh-Metrix supplies a LSA-based measure of *given versus new information* in text. Each sentence has a measure of the amount of given (G) versus new (N) information and a proportion score is computed for newness [N/(N + G)]. A text with a low newness score is considered redundant.

## Genre and Rhetorical Composition

Coh-Metrix distinguishes texts in three genres that are typical of high-school reading exercises: *narrative*, *social studies*, and *science*. The indices are derived from discriminant analyses conducted to identify the language and discourse features that diagnostically predict the genre to which a text belongs (McCarthy, Myers, Briner, Graesser, & McNamara, 2009). A reader's comprehension of a text can be facilitated by correctly identifying the textual characteristics that signal its genre (Biber, 1988). Researchers in educational psychology have shown that training struggling readers to recognize genre and global text structures helps them improve comprehension (Meyer & Wijekumar, 2007; Williams, Stafford, Lower, Hall, & Pollini, 2009). As discussed earlier, students read texts very differently if they view it as a newspaper article versus literature (Zwaan, 1994).

Identification of topic sentences in paragraphs is also an important component of rhetorical composition, at least for informational texts. These sentences are claims or main points that are elaborated by other sentences in the paragraph. They ideally occur in the *paragraph initial* position, although that ideal does not hold up in naturalistic texts (Popken, 1991). Coh-Metrix provides a number of measures of topic sentencehood that are either intrinsic characteristics of sentences or relative measures that involve comparisons between sentences in a paragraph.

## Psychological Tests of Coh-Metrix

Coh-Metrix has been used in dozens of projects that investigate characteristics of discourse, comprehension, memory, and learning (Crossley, Louwerse, McCarthy, & McNamara, 2007; Graesser, Jeon, Yang, & Cai, 2007; McNamara et al., in press). These studies have validated the Coh-Metrix measures by comparing the computer output to language and discourse annotations by experts, to texts scaled on cohesion, to psychological data (e.g., ratings, reading times, memory, test performance), and to samples of texts that serve as gold standards. Coh-Metrix has uncovered differences among a wide range of discourse categories at level 5, such as differences between (a) spoken and written samples of English; (b) physics content in textbooks, texts prepared by researchers, and conversational discourse in tutorial dialogue; (c) articles written by different authors; (d) sections in typical science texts, such as *introductions*, *methods*, *results*, and *discussions*; and (e) texts that were *adopted* (or

authentic) versus *adapted* (or simplified) for second language learning.

Graesser and McNamara (2012) recently conducted a principal components analysis (PCA, a type of factor analysis) on a large corpus of texts to investigate what dimensions of language and discourse account for variations among texts. The analysis was performed on 37,520 texts in a corpus provided by TASA (Touchstone Applied Science Associates). This corpus represents the texts that a typical senior in high school would have encountered between kindergarten and 12th grade. The texts were scaled on Degrees of Reading Power, which can approximately be translated into grade level (McNamara et al., in press). The genres of texts were also classified by TASA researchers, with most being in language arts (narrative), science, and social studies/history, but others in various categories of informational texts (business, health, home economics, and industrial arts). Nearly 100 measures of Coh-Metrix were explored in various PCAs, but the final analysis had 53 measures.

The PCA uncovered eight dimensions that accounted for an impressive 67% of the variability among texts. The major five dimensions were as follows:

1. *Narrativity.* Narrative text tells a story, with characters, events, places, and things that are familiar to the reader. Narrative is closely affiliated with everyday oral conversation.

2. *Referential cohesion (textbase).* High cohesion texts contain explicit words and ideas that overlap across sentences and the text.

3. *Situation model cohesion.* Causal, intentional, and temporal connectives help the reader to form a more coherent and deeper understanding of the text.

4. *Syntactic simplicity.* Sentences with few words and simple, familiar syntactic structures are easier to understand. Complex sentences have structurally embedded syntax.

5. *Word concreteness.* Concrete words evoke mental images and are more meaningful to the reader than abstract words.

It is quite apparent that these dimensions are closely aligned with the first five levels of the multilevel framework summarized in Table 30.1.

The five dimensions also predict measures that reflect psychological mechanisms (Graesser & McNamara, 2012). Standardized z-scores were computed for the five dimensions on the 37,520 TASA texts and were correlated with DRP grade-level scores. The correlations were substantial and predictable for narrativity (–.69), syntactic simplicity (–.47), and word concreteness (–.23), but lower for referential cohesion (.03) and situation model cohesion (.11). Moreover, McNamara, Louwerse, McCarthy, and Graesser (2010) reported that Coh-Metrix scores on referential and situational cohesion significantly predicted comprehension measures and recall measures in 19 studies (conducted by other researchers) that experimentally manipulated cohesion. These studies support the claim that the five dimensions of Coh-Metrix have some modicum of psychological reality. The Coh-Metrix tool should help advance theory and empirical research in discourse comprehension on a number of fronts. First, researchers can scale their texts on multiple levels of comprehension in order to perform manipulation checks, assess the impact of potential extraneous variables, and explore how the different levels of meaning are interrelated. Discourse researchers are routinely haunted that some extraneous variable may be responsible for their claims about the impact of text on psychological processes; Coh-Metrix can be used to measure and assess the potential extraneous variables. Second, researchers can test theoretical claims that texts have particular properties by collecting Coh-Metrix measures on a large corpus of naturalistic texts that are selected with rigorous scientific sampling procedures. This is a landmark advance over research 20 years ago when researchers cherry picked a handful of texts to suit their purposes. Third, researchers can discover new discourse patterns by applying data-mining procedures to the hundreds of Coh-Metrix dimensions when applied to thousands of texts. We anticipate many new research breakthroughs on multilevel discourse comprehension with computation tools such as Coh-Metrix, particularly if it is used in interdisciplinary efforts with researchers in psychology, linguistics, education, language arts, communication, computer science, and many other areas of the cognitive sciences.

## Acknowledgments

This research was supported by the National Science Foundation (ALT-0834847, DRK12 0918409, BCS 0904909), the Institute of Education Sciences (R305G020018, R305H050169, R305B070349, R305A080589, R305A080594), and the US Department of Defense Counterintelligence Field Activity (H9C104–07–0014). Any opinions, findings, and conclusions or recommendations expressed in this material are those of the authors and do not necessarily reflect the views of the National Science Foundation, the Institute of Education Sciences, or the Department of Defense. Our gratitude goes to Zhiqiang Cai for his software development of Coh-Metrix, and to Nia Dowell, Jonna Kulikowich, Max Louwerse, Phil McCarthy, Danielle McNamara, and Jeremiah Sullins for their testing of Coh-Metrix on text samples.

## References

Baker, L. (1985). Differences in standards used by college students to evaluate their comprehension of expository prose. *Reading Research Quarterly, 20*, 298–313.

Bard, E. G., Anderson, A. H., Chen, Y., Nicholson, H. B. M., Harvard, C., & Dalzel-Job, S. (2007). Let's you do that: Sharing the cognitive burdens of dialogue. *Journal of Memory and Language, 57*, 616–641.

Biber, D. (1988). *Variation across speech and writing*. Cambridge, England: Cambridge University Press.

Biber, D., Conrad, S., & Reppen, R. (1998). *Corpus linguistics: Investigating language structure and use*. Cambridge, England: Cambridge University Press.

Bransford, J., & Johnson, M. K. (1972). Contextual prerequisites for understanding: Some investigations of comprehension and recall. *Journal of Verbal Learning and Verbal Behavior, 11*, 717–796.

Britton, B. K., & Gulgoz, S. (1991). Using Kintsch's computational model to improve instructional text: Effects of repairing inference calls on recall and cognitive structures. *Journal of Educational Psychology, 83*, 329–345.

Charniak, E. (2000). A maximum-entropy-inspired parser. In J. Wiebe (Ed.), *Proceedings of the First Conference on North American Chapter of the Association for Computational Linguistics* (pp. 132–139). San Francisco: Morgan Kaufmann.

Chi, M. T. H., de Leeuw, N., Chiu, M., & LaVancher, C. (1994). Eliciting self-explanation improves understanding. *Cognitive Science, 18*, 439–477.

Clark, H. H. (1996). *Using language*. Cambridge, England: Cambridge University Press.

Clark, H. H., & Wilkes-Gibbs, D. (1986). Referring as a collaborative process. *Cognition, 22*, 1–39.

Coltheart, M. (1981). The MRC Psycholinguistic Database. *Quarterly Journal of Experimental Psychology, 33A*, 497–505.

Crossley, S. A., Louwerse, M., McCarthy, P. M., & McNamara, D. S. (2007). A linguistic analysis of simplified and authentic texts. *Modern Language Journal, 91*, 15–30.

Daneman, M., Lennertz, T., & Hannon, B. (2007). Shallow semantic processing of text: Evidence from eye movements. *Language and Cognitive Processes, 22*, 83–105.

De Vega, M., Glenberg, A. M., & Graesser, A. C. (Eds.). (2008). *Symbols and embodiment: Debates on meaning and cognition*. Oxford, England: Oxford University Press.

Dunlosky, J., & Lipko, A. (2007). Metacomprehension: A brief history and how to improve its accuracy. *Current Directions in Psychological Science, 16*, 228–232.

Fellbaum, C. (Ed.). (1998). *WordNet: An electronic lexical database. [CD-ROM]*. Cambridge, MA: MIT Press.

Gernsbacher, M. A. (1990). *Language comprehension as structure building*. Hillsdale, NJ: Erlbaum.

Glenberg, A. M. (1997). What memory is for? *Behavior and Brain Sciences, 20,* 1–55.

Glenberg, A. M., & Kaschak, M. P. (2002). Grounding language in action. *Psychonomic Bulletin and Review, 9,* 558–565.

Glenberg, A. M., & Robertson, D. A. (1999). Indexical understanding of instructions. *Discourse Processes, 28,* 1–26.

Goldman, S. R., Varma, S., & Cote, N. (1996). Extending capacity-constrained construction integration: Toward "smarter" and flexible models of text comprehension. In B. K. Britton & A. C. Graesser (Eds.), *Models of understanding text* (pp. 73–114). Mahwah, NJ: Erlbaum.

Gough, P. B. (1972). One second of reading. In J. F. Kavanaugh & J. G. Mattingly (Eds.), *Language by ear and by eye* (pp. 331–358). Cambridge, MA: MIT Press.

Graesser, A. C., Cai, Z., Louwerse, M. M., & Daniel, F. (2006). Question Understanding Aid (QUAID): A web facility that tests question comprehensibility. *Public Opinion Quarterly, 70,* 3–22.

Graesser, A. C., D' Mello, S., & Person, N. K. (2009). Metaknowledge in tutoring. In D. Hacker, J. Dunlosky, & A. C. Graesser (Eds.), *Handbook of metacognition in education (pp. 361–382).* Mahwah, NJ: Taylor & Francis.

Graesser, A. C., Gernsbacher, M. A., & Goldman, S. (Eds.). (2003). *Handbook of discourse processes.* Mahwah, NJ: Erlbaum.

Graesser, A. C., & Jackson, G. T. (2008). Body and symbol in AutoTutor: Conversations that are responsive to the learners' cognitive and emotional states. In M. de Vega, A. Glenberg, & A. C. Graesser (Eds.), *Symbols and embodiment: Debates on meaning and cognition* (pp. 33–56). Oxford, England: Oxford University Press.

Graesser, A. C., Jeon, M., Yang, Y., & Cai, Z. (2007). Discourse cohesion in text and tutorial dialogue. *Information Design Journal, 15,* 199–213.

Graesser, A. C., Lu, S., Jackson, G. T., Mitchell, H., Ventura, M., Olney, A., & Louwerse, M. M. (2004). AutoTutor: A tutor with dialogue in natural language. *Behavioral Research Methods, Instruments, and Computers, 36,* 180–193.

Graesser, A. C., Lu, S., Olde, B. A., Cooper-Pye, E., & Whitten, S. (2005). Question asking and eye tracking during cognitive disequilibrium: Comprehending illustrated texts on devices when the devices break down. *Memory and Cognition, 33,* 1235–1247.

Graesser, A. C., & McNamara, D. S. (2011). Computational analyses of multilevel discourse comprehension. *Topics in Cognitive Science, 3,* 371–398.

Graesser, A. C., & McNamara, D. S. (2012). Reading instruction: Technology based supports for classroom instruction. In C. Dede & J. Richards (Eds.), *Digital teaching platforms: Customizing classroom learning for each student* (pp. 71–87). New York: Teacher's College Press.

Graesser, A. C., McNamara, D. S., Louwerse, M. M., & Cai, Z. (2004). Coh-Metrix: Analysis of text on cohesion and language. *Behavioral Research Methods, Instruments, and Computers, 36,* 193–202.

Graesser, A. C., Millis, K. K., & Zwaan, R. A. (1997). Discourse comprehension. *Annual Review of Psychology, 48,* 163–189.

Graesser, A. C., Singer, M., & Trabasso, T (1994). Constructing inferences during narrative text comprehension. *Psychological Review, 101,* 371–395.

Haberlandt, K. F., & Graesser, A. C. (1985). Component processes in text comprehension and some of their interactions. *Journal of Experimental Psychology: General, 114,* 357–374.

Hacker, D. J., Dunlosky, J., & Graesser, A. C. (Eds.). (2009). *Handbook of metacognition in education.* Mahwah, NJ: Erlbaum/Taylor & Francis.

Halliday, M. A. K., & Hasan, R. (1976). *Cohesion in English.* London: Longman.

Hancock, J., & Dunham. P. (2001). Language use in computer-mediated communication: The role of coordination devices. *Discourse Processes, 31,* 91–110.

Hanna, J. E., & Brennan, S. E. (2007). Speakers' eye gaze disambiguates referring expressions early during face-to face conversation. *Journal of Memory and Language, 57,* 596–615.

Hestenes, D., Wells, M., & Swackhamer, G. (1992). Force concept inventory. *The Physics Teacher, 30,* 141–158.

Holler, J., & Wilkin, K. (2009). Communicating common ground: How mutually shared knowledge influences speech and gesture in a narrative task. *Language and Cognitive Processes, 24,* 267–289.

Jurafsky, D., & Martin, J. (2008). *Speech and language processing.* Englewood Cliffs, NJ: Prentice Hall.

Just, M. A., & Carpenter, P. A. (1987). *The psychology of reading and language comprehension.* Boston: Allyn & Bacon.

Just, M. A., & Carpenter, P. A. (1992). A capacity theory of comprehension: Individual differences in working memory. *Psychological Review, 99,* 122–149.

Kaakinen, J. K., & Hyona, J. (2007). Perspective effects in repeated reading: An eye movement study. *Memory and Cognition, 35,* 1323–1336.

Kendeou, P., & van den Broek, P. (2007). The effects of prior knowledge in text structure on comprehension processes during reading scientific texts. *Memory and Cognition, 35,* 1567–1577.

Kintsch, W. (1998). *Comprehension: A paradigm for cognition.* Cambridge, England: Cambridge University Press.

Klare, G. R. (1974–1975). Assessing readability. *Reading Research Quarterly, 10,* 62–102.

Koslin, B. I., Zeno, S., & Koslin, S. (1987). *The DRP: An effective measure in reading.* New York: College Entrance Examination Board.

Kosslyn, S. M. (1980). *Image and mind.* Cambridge, MA: Harvard University Press.

Landauer, T., McNamara, D. S., Dennis, S., & Kintsch, W. (Eds.). (2007). *Handbook of latent semantic analysis.* Mahwah, NJ: Erlbaum.

Lappin, S., & Leass, H. J. (1994). An algorithm for pronominal coreference resolution. *Computational Linguistics, 20,* 535–561.

Louwerse, M. M. (2001). An analytic and cognitive parameterization of coherence relations. *Cognitive Linguistics, 12,* 291–315.

Magliano, J. P., & Radvansky, G. A. (2001). Goal coordination in narrative comprehension. *Psychonomic Bulletin and Review, 8,* 372–376.

Magliano, J., Trabasso, T., & Graesser, A. C. (1999). Strategic processing during comprehension. *Journal of Educational Psychology, 91,* 615–629.

Maki, R. H. (1998). Test predictions over text material. In D. J. Hacker, J. Dunlosky, & A. C. Graesser (Eds.), *Metacognition in educational theory and practice* (pp. 117–144). Mahwah, NJ: Erlbaum.

Masson, M. E. J., Bub, D. N., & Warren, C. M. (2008). Kicking calculators: Contribution of embodied representations to sentence comprehension. *Journal of Memory and Language, 59,* 256–265.

Mayberry, M., Crocker, M., & Knoeferle, P. (2009).Learning to attend: A connectionist model of situated language comprehension. *Cognitive Science, 33*, 449–496.

McCarthy, P. M., Myers, J. C., Briner, S. W., Graesser, A. C., & McNamara, D. S. (2009). Are three words all we need? A psychological and computational study of genre recognition. *Journal for Language Technology and Computational Linguistics, 1*, 23–57.

McCrudden, M. T., & Schraw, G. (2007). Relevance and goal-focusing in text processing. *Educational Psychology Review, 19*, 113–139.

McNamara, D. S. (2004). SERT: Self-explanation reading training. *Discourse Processes, 38*, 1–30.

McNamara, D. S., Graesser, A., & Louwerse, M. (in press). Sources of text difficulty: Across the ages and genres. In J. P. Sabatini & E. Albro (Eds.), *Assessing reading in the 21st century: Aligning and applying advances in the reading and measurement sciences.*

McNamara, D. S., & Kintsch, W. (1996). Learning from text: Effects of prior knowledge and text coherence. *Discourse Processes, 22*, 247–287.

McNamara, D. S., Louwerse, M. M., McCarthy, P. M., & Graesser, A. C. (2010). Coh-Metrix: Capturing linguistic features of cohesion. *Discourse Processes, 47*, 292–330.

Meyer, B. J. F., & Wijekumar, K. (2007). Web-based tutoring of the structure strategy: Theoretical background, design, and findings. In D. S. McNamara (Ed.), *Reading comprehension strategies: Theories, interventions, and technologies* (pp. 347–375). Mahwah, NJ: Erlbaum.

Millis, K. K., Kim, H. J., Todaro, S., Magliano, J., Wiemer-Hastings, K., & McNamara, D. S. (2004). Identifying reading strategies using latent semantic analysis: Comparing semantic benchmarks. *Behavior Research Methods, Instruments, and Computers, 36*, 213–221.

Millis, K. K., King, A., & Kim, J. (2001). Updating situation models from descriptive texts: A test of the situational operator model. *Discourse Processes, 30*, 201–236.

Myers, J. L., O'Brien, E. J., Albrecht, J. E., & Mason, R. A. (1994). Maintaining global coherence during reading. *Journal of Experimental Psychology: Learning, Memory, and Cognition, 20*, 876–886.

Nygaard, L. C., Herold, D. S., & Namy, L. L. (2009). The semantics of prosody: Acoustic and perceptual evidence of prosodic correlates to word meaning. *Cognitive Science, 33*,127–146.

O'Brien, E. J., Rizzella, M. L., Albrecht, J. E., & Halleran, J. G. (1998). Updating a situation model: A memory-based text processing view. *Journal of Experimental Psychology: Learning, Memory, and Cognition, 24*, 1200–1210.

O'Reilly, T., &McNamara, D. S. (2007). The impact of science knowledge, reading skill, and reading strategy knowledge on more traditional "high-stakes" measures of high school students' science achievement.*American Educational Research Journal, 44*,161–197.

Otero, J., & Kintsch, W. (1992). Failures to detect contradictions in text: What readers believe versus what the read. *Psychological Science, 3*, 229–235.

Pecher, D., &Zwaan, R.A. (2005). *Grounding cognition: The role of perception and action in memory, language, and thinking.* Cambridge, England: Cambridge University Press.

Pennebaker, J. W., Booth, R. J., & Francis, M. E. (2007). *Linguistic inquiry and word count.* Austin, TX: LIWC.net.

Perfetti, C. A. (2007). Reading ability: Lexical quality to comprehension. *Scientific Studies of Reading, 11*, 357–383.

Pickering, M., & Garrod, S. (2004). Toward a mechanistic psychology of dialogue. *Behavioral and Brain Sciences, 27*, 169–226.

Pollatsek, A., Slattery, T., & Juhasz, B. (2008). The processing of novel and lexicalised prefixed words in reading. *Language and Cognitive Processes, 23*, 1133–1158.

Popken, R. (1991). A study of topic sentence use in technical writing. *The Technical Writing Teacher, 18*, 49–58.

Rapp, D. N. (2008). How do readers handle incorrect information during reading? *Memory and Cognition, 36*, 688–701.

Rayner, K. (1998) Eye movements in reading and information processing: 20 years of research. *Psychological Bulletin, 124*, 372–422.

Rayner, K., & Pollatsek, A. (1994). *The psychology of reading.* Mahwah, NJ: Erlbaum.

Riesco-Bernier, S., & Romero-Trillo, J. (2008). The acoustics of "newness" and its pragmatic implications in classroom discourse. *Journal of Pragmatics, 40*, 1103–1116.

Rouet, J. (2006). *The skills of document use: From text comprehension to web-based learning.* Mahwah, NJ: Erlbaum.

Rumelhart, D. E. (1977). Toward an interactive model of reading In S. Dornie (Ed.), *Attention and performance* (pp. 573–603). Hillsdale, NJ: Erlbaum.

Sanders, T. J. M., & Noordman, L. G. M. (2000). The role of coherence relations and their linguistic markers in text processing. *Discourse Processes, 29*, 37–60.

Sanford, A. J., & Graesser, A. C. (2006). Introduction: Shallow processing and underspecification. *Discourse Processes, 42*, 99–108.

Schober, M. F., &Brennan, S. E. (2003). Processes of interactive spoken discourse. In A. C. Graesser, M. A. Gernsbacher, & S. Goldman (Eds.), *Handbook of discourse processes* (pp. 123–164). Mahwah, NJ: Erlbaum.

Sinclair, J. M., & Coulthard, R. M. (1975). *Towards an analysis of discourse: The English used by teachers and their pupils.* London: Oxford University Press.

Snow, C. (2002). *Reading for understanding: Toward an R&D program in reading comprehension.* Santa Monica, CA: RAND Corporation.

Stanovich, K. E. (1986). Matthew effects in reading: Some consequences of individual differences in the acquisition of literacy. *Reading Research Quarterly, 21*, 360–407.

Stenner, A. J. (1996). *Measuring reading comprehension with the Lexile framework.* Durham, NC: Metametrics, Inc.

Sturt, P., Sanford, A. J., Stewart, A. J., & Dawydiak, E. (2004). Linguistic focus and good-enough representations: An application of the change detection paradigm. *Psychonomic Bulletin and Review, 11*, 882–888.

Taraban, R., &McClelland, J. L. (1988). Constituent attachment and thematic role assignment in sentence processing: Influences of content-based expectations. *Journal of Memory and Language, 27*, 597–632.

Tulving, E., & Kroll, N. (1995). Novelty assessment in the brain: Long-term memory encoding. *Psychonomic Bulletin and Review, 2*, 387–390.

Van den Broek, P., Virtue, S., Everson, M. G., Tzeng, Y., & Sung, Y. (2002). Comprehension and memory of science texts: Inferential processes and the construction of a mental representation. In J. Otero, J. Leon, & A. C. Graesser (Eds.), *The psychology of science text comprehension* (pp. 131–154). Mahwah, NJ: Erlbaum.

Van den Broek, P., Rapp, D. N., & Kendeou, P. (2005). Integrating memory-based and constructionist processes in accounts of reading comprehension. *Discourse Processes*, *39*, 299–316.

Van der Sluis, L., & Krahmer, E. (2007). Generating multimodal references. *Discourse Processes*, *44*, 145–174.

van Dijk, T.A., & Kintsch, W. (1983). *Strategies of discourse comprehension*. New York: Academic Press.

VanLehn, K., Graesser, A. C., Jackson, G. T., Jordan, P., Olney, A., & Rose, C. P. (2007). When are tutorial dialogues more effective than reading? *Cognitive Science*, *31*, 3–62.

Ward, P., &Sturt, P. (2007). Linguistic focus and memory: An eye movement study. *Memory and Cognition*, *35*, 73–86.

Wiley, J., Goldman, S. R., Graesser, A. C., Sanchez, C. A., Ash, I. K., & Hemmerich, J. A. (2009). Source evaluation, comprehension, and learning in Internet science inquiry tasks. *American Educational Research Journal*, *46*, 1060–1106.

Williams, J. P., Stafford, K. B., Lauer, K. D., Hall, K. M., & Pollini, S. (2009). Embedding reading comprehension training in content-area instruction. *Journal of Educational Psychology*, *101*, 1–20.

Zwaan, R. A. (1994). Effect of genre expectations on text comprehension. *Journal of Experimental Psychology: Learning, Memory, Cognition*, *20*, 920–933.

Zwaan, R. A., Magliano, J. P., & Graesser, A. C. (1995). Dimensions of situation model construction in narrative comprehension. *Journal of Experimental Psychology: Learning, Memory, and Cognition*, *21*, 386–397.

Zwaan, R. A., & Radvansky, G. A. (1998). Situation models in language comprehension and memory. *Psychological Bulletin*, *123*, 162–185.

# Early Word Learning

Melissa Koenig *and* Caitlin Cole

**Abstract**

Words carry social information by reflecting the intentions and interests of individual speakers. In this chapter, we argue for the possibility that early developments in infants' social understanding may support word learning in the first year of life. We begin by first focusing on the literature that has isolated the earliest time points at which infants' segmentation and associative capacities have been found in laboratory environments. In the second half of this chapter, we discuss a diverse range of research in infant cognitive development to highlight the ways in which social information might aid even young infants' ability to acquire and interpret words. Infants younger than 12 months may not spontaneously or accurately track others' referential cues; however, existing research raises the important possibility that certain components of early word learning may be enhanced when intentions are made clear, available, and salient.

**Key Words:** word learning, infancy, early social cognition

In some sense, words are simple. As we typically think about them, words are arbitrary symbols used by people to communicate information. However, definitions that focus on how words function for adults can overlook the intricate, layered, and interacting processes involved in word acquisition. Some words point to referents in the world; others do not. Some words (i.e., concrete object labels) carry meanings that may be acquired intact after a number of exposures; many others are acquired and finessed over a much more extended mapping process (Carey, 2010; Swingley, 2010). Words are often learned in episodes of joint attention in the contexts of dyadic conversations; however, children learn words under many conditions of exposure (Akhtar, Jipson, & Callanan, 2001; Ochs & Schieffelin, 1984). Given the flexibility and power of our early word-learning capacities, our goal in this chapter is to focus on and integrate research in infancy in order to stress the overarching continuity of word-learning processes and to highlight the range of candidate processes, social and nonsocial, that support word learning.

Learning a word requires, among other things, mapping a phonological form to a referent. It is not enough to appreciate that people use words to communicate their ideas; one also needs to attend to the putative links between sounds and objects and store them in memory. However, it is also the case that words refer only because people use them to do so, and in this way, words consistently reflect the interests of the speakers who use them. From the outset, words stand in relation both to things external and internal to the speaker's mind. Given the ubiquity and the significance of words' relations to external objects and to speakers' internal concepts and interests, we consider the possibility that words reflect both of these component understandings in the first year of life.

As we review later, infants by at least 6 to 7 months of age have the segmentation and associative capacities required to get some degree of word learning off the ground. Indeed, by 6 months, many infants know a small number of word forms that they have linked to objects or events. It is not until the second year, however, that infants are said to actively and spontaneously track social cues indicative of others' intentions and use such cues to make inferences about word meaning (see Baldwin & Moses, 2001; Tomasello, 1999 for reviews). Thus, a common tenet in the early word-learning literature is that infants first understand an external, "goes with" relation between a word and a referent *before* they understand that words, as symbols, reflect the intentions of others (Golinkoff, Mervis, & Hirsh-Pasek, 1994; Werker, Cohen, Lloyd, Casasola, & Stager, 1998). The experimental methods used to reveal the earliest associations between words and objects largely dispose of human speakers and do so for good reasons—by eliminating potentially complex procedural distractions, researchers simplify the task and isolate the components that participate in early associations. However, by removing human speakers from word learning experiments that test our earliest capacity to form sound-object links, the task may indeed be made more difficult for infants, rather than less so. In what follows, we first focus on the literature that has isolated the earliest time points at which infants' segmentation and associative capacities can be found in laboratory environments. In the second half of this review, we discuss a diverse range of research in infancy to highlight the ways in which social information might aid even young infants' ability to acquire and interpret words.

## Words in Isolation

Learning a word depends on component skills such as the ability to segment the speech stream into appropriate word-level units and to retain the sound pattern of individual word forms. By 6 to 8 months of age, infants segment words from continuous streams of speech using lexical stress patterns (Echols, Crowhurst, & Childers, 1997; Jusczyk, Houston, & Newsome, 1999), familiarity (Bortfeld, Morgan, Golinkoff, & Rathbun, 2005; Jusczyk & Aslin, 1995), phonotactic cues (Jusczyk, Friederici, Wessels, Svenkerud, & Jusczyk, 1993; Mattys, Jusczyk, Luce, & Morgan, 1999), and transitional probabilities (Saffran, Aslin, & Newport, 1996). The strategies or cues infants rely on to segment words change with age; for example, Johnson and Jusczyk (2001) showed that when multiple cues were available, 8-month-olds weighed prosodic cues more

heavily than statistical cues, whereas 7-month-old infants relied on statistical rather than prosodic cues. Similarly, Thiessen and Saffran (2003) demonstrated that 6-month-old infants pay more attention to transitional probabilities than to stress when the two cues are pitted against one another. While the best evidence for segmentation is seen in infants aged 7 to 8 months, it is worth noting that Mandel, Jusczyk, and Pisoni (1995) found indirect evidence for segmentation among 4.5-month-old infants, who preferred to listen to their own name over foil words matched in syllable length and stress.

The earliest report of word comprehension comes from work by Tincoff and Jusczyk (1999), who found that 6-month-olds could appropriately pick out comprehended instances of "mommy" and "daddy." Infants looked longer to videotaped films of the appropriate parent when acoustically variable tokens of "mommy" and "daddy" were presented. Furthermore, infants who link familiar names to the appropriate individual can use such names, including their own, as a segmenting anchor that allows them to identify the word forms that follow them (Bortfeld et al., 2005; Mandel et al., 1995). Gradually, between 6 and 11 months this top-down strategy of familiar-words-as-anchors gets extended to familiar, well-pronounced count nouns (Swingley, 2005) and familiar function words (like *the, her, its*). Both English- and French-learning infants prefer listening to noun phrases that contain real determiners, like *the*, over noun phrases that contain made-up foils (Halle, Durand, & de Boysson-Bardies, 2008; Shi, Cutler, Werker, & Cruickshank, 2006). Thus, by at least 6 months of age, infants use familiar word forms to cut into the continuous speech stream and identify word forms.

When infants start by extracting an oft-used word form, like "Mommy," and associate it with an individual entity in the world, how accurately do they represent the phonological form? In one sense and perhaps for certain tasks, the word form is represented with remarkable accuracy. Research by Bortfeld et al (2005) showed that infants at 6 months recognized target words that followed "Mommy's" but failed to recognize those word forms that followed a similar-sounding but unfamiliar unit like "Tommy's" (see also Tincoff & Jusczyk, 1999). Similarly, at 11 months, the enhanced attention infants give to familiar over unfamiliar words simply does not hold if the familiar words are mispronounced (Swingley, 2005). In another sense, some early word forms may be *too precise* in that infants fail to ignore naturally occurring variations in speaker and intonation. For example, 7.5-month-olds do not show recognition of the same word when spoken by a man and then a woman nor when the same form is produced with neutral versus happy intonation (Houston & Jusczyk, 2000; Singh, Morgan & White, 2004). One implication of this specificity is that part of what might make word learning "slow" in the first year is the difficulty inherent in recognizing (and re-recognizing) varying tokens of "cup" as instances of the word "cup."

Indeed, there is further reason to think that infants might benefit when the "segmentation problem" and the "mapping problem" are separated in time. As discussed by Swingley (2005, 2007), children probably have identified many candidate word forms before they begin to learn what those words mean. Swingley (2007) reported that 18-month-old infants did better in a word-learning task when they were exposed to a set of novel words before information about meaning was provided. A similar result was reported by Estes, Evans, Alibali, and Saffran (2007), who first presented 17-month-olds with a statistical word segmentation task in which infants distinguished between "words" (syllables that occurred in sequence reliably) and "nonwords" (syllables that co-occurred less reliably). Interestingly, when the segmentation task was followed by a word-learning task that presented meaning information with both "words" and "nonwords," children were able to learn the meanings of the "words," not the "nonwords." Both of these studies demonstrate that exposure to word forms first facilitates the acquisition of word meaning later.

What about the first year of life? Evidence that young infants extract and retain information about the sound pattern of particular word forms over time can be seen in work by Jusczyk and Hohne (1997), who visited 8-month-olds in their homes 10 times over the course of 2 weeks and, at each visit, played 30-minute audio recordings of women reading a series of three stories. Two weeks after the tenth visit, infants were presented with lists of words in isolation, and they indeed gave selectively more attention to the familiar words from the stories over foils. Thus, word forms can be encoded and retained by 8-month-old infants for at least a 2-week period, forms that were previously repeated on average 13 times per visit in the context of stories. Further research by Jusczyk and Aslin (1995) showed that 7.5-month-olds preferred fluent passages of speech that contained words like "feet," "bike," and "cup," words that infants had heard previously in isolation, during a brief familiarization period. Given extant

experimental evidence mentioned earlier, it is likely that infants use some combination of stored forms, stress patterns, and statistical and prosodic cues to identify and recognize a sample of words (Cutler & Carter, 1987; Jusczyk et al., 1999; Saffran & Thiessen, 2003). Here, we wish to stress the possibility that *social cues* may have helped support such learning. In the study by Jusczyk and Hohne (1997), while infants heard the audio recordings of stories, an experimenter in the home turned the pages of a story book and quietly interacted with infants. Thus, the presence of natural, live, contingent, social interaction may have aided infants' long-term learning of new word forms. Whether social interaction itself, or the arousal, attention, and contingency that accompany social interaction, are crucial for learning remains an important question.

### Associating Words and Objects

At the same general point that infants are showcasing tools that help them extract new forms and identify recurrent word forms like "Mommy" (Tincoff & Jusczyk, 1999), experimental studies demonstrate infants' sensitivity to trained associations between objects and sounds. In research that stresses infants' detection of redundant information present in the environment, Gogate and Bahrick (2001) found that 7-month-old infants can learn the links between synchronously moving images and syllables and remember such links over a significant period of time. Infants were habituated to consistent pairings between two toys and two syllables (/a/ and /i/). Some infants experienced synchrony between the movement of a toy and the sound, whereas other infants experienced the same movements and syllables but no synchrony between them. Following habituation, infants' comprehension was tested with familiar trials that presented the same pairing as seen during habituation as well as "switched" pairings, which presented infants with a new, mismatched syllable-toy pairing. Infants looked longer on these "switch" trials but only when syllables and toy movement were synchronized. In a follow-up study, this pattern was replicated in infants who were habituated in the synchronous condition only. When infants were brought back to the laboratory 4 days later, they showed lasting retention of these associations by giving significantly more attention to the image that matched the sound they heard over the one that did not match.

Given that the aforementioned methodology used vocalic sounds, not words, and infants required synchrony between sound and object to detect violations of the association, most agree that this type of intermodal learning falls short of demonstrating true "word" learning in infancy. However, the brute associative capacity that is required to succeed in both intermodal perceptual paradigms and word-learning tasks should not be dismissed or taken for granted. Without the associative memories that infants and young children use to learn words, vocabulary growth would not even start. Further evidence that infants can make associations between words and associated objects comes from work by Werker, Cohen, Lloyd, Casasola, and Stager (1998). While seated on their parents' laps, infants were exposed to two word-object associations. Novel words (like "lif" and "neem") were delivered in isolation, using infant-directed prosody, and objects were depicted on a video monitor. After habituating infants to the co-occurrence between words and objects, their learning of associations was tested by presenting test trials that preserved the link ("same trials") and test trials that violated the link ("switch trials"). By 14 months of age, infants were able to learn both of the associations when the words are dissimilar in form (Stager & Werker, 1997). However, it is important to note that even 8-month-olds could form a single word-object association when the task was simplified (one word–one object pairing) (Stager & Werker, 1997; Werker et al., 1998).

One question that arises from evidence of this early ability to associate spoken words with visual information is how this ability relates to true word learning later in development. On the one hand, early integration of information from two modalities (e.g., vision and audition) may be necessarily and causally related to later word learning (Gogate, Walker-Andrews, & Bahrick, 2001). According to this view, learning links between sounds and objects in the first year of life is an early step in the development of word learning in the second year, with both being consequences of earlier integration of information from two sensory domains. In other words, word learning grows out of intermodal perceptual capacities in the first year. On the other hand, full word learning may not simply be a consequence of earlier bimodal perception; it may require additional conceptual developments (Werker & Patterson, 2001) and social developments (Baldwin, 1995; Tomasello, 1999). While the integration of sensory information from two domains may be necessary for word learning, it is not sufficient for learning the referential relation between words and what they stand for. To understand words as referential, some level of social understanding, in addition to bimodal mapping and associative memory, may be required.

## Count Nouns and Cross-Situational Learning

The impact of count nouns on categorization and concept formation can be seen very early in life. More specifically, from 9 months of age, object labels seem to constrain the search for meaning across situations. For example, in work by Balaban and Waxman (1997), 9-month-old infants were presented with a series of pairs of category members (e.g., birds) and either heard a count noun, "a bird," in the Word condition, or heard a tone in the Tone condition. At test, infants were presented with a new instance of the category (i.e., a new bird) along with an instance from a new category (e.g., a rabbit). If infants formed a category of birds prior to test, then they are expected to look longer at the rabbit. In contrast, if they formed no category, they should look indiscriminately at the two test items. Nine-month-old infants looked longer at the rabbit in the Word condition, but they showed no systematic looking pattern in the Tone condition. One inference drawn from this was that the presence of a count noun invited infants to look for commonalities across different objects (see also Fulkerson & Haaf, 2003). Another line of work suggests that count nouns support individuation such that the presence of two different words leads young infants to expect two distinct objects (Xu, 1997, 2002; Xu & Carey, 1996) and, furthermore, that objects with different shapes should have different labels (Diesendruck & Bloom, 2003; Landau, Smith, & Jones, 1998). Such findings underscore the ways in which infants' associative abilities are constrained by their expectations about how certain types of words (e.g., novel count nouns) relate to aspects of the world (e.g., objects of similar shape).

The putative links formed by way of infants' associative abilities become increasingly powerful over time and help infants learn word-object links that might not be obvious in any given instance. Recent work by Smith and Yu (2008) examined infants' associative learning across multiple situations. They showed that infants are able to gather evidence across situations in order to determine word-referent pairings. In this study, 12- and 14-month-olds viewed pairs of novel objects and heard labels for each object. Across 30 trials, the object pairings differed, but each object always occurred with the same label, and each correct word-object pairing occurred 10 times. For example, in one trial, infants might see novel objects A and B and hear the novel words "bosa" and "gasser." In a later trial, infants might see object A paired with object C and hear the novel words "manu" and "bosa." Then in a third trial, they might see objects B and C and hear "manu" and "gasser." Although the pairs of objects changed from trial to trial, an object was never presented without the correct label. Within a single trial, infants did not have sufficient evidence to determine the correct word-object pairing, but evidence for the correct pairings accumulated across trials. Following the training phase, infants were presented with target-distracter object pairs and heard a single label. Both 12- and 14-month-olds looked significantly longer toward target objects, suggesting that they used cross-situational evidence to discover the correct word-object pairings.

The authors propose that the learning mechanism involved in discovering the correct word-object pairings may benefit from the complexity of a word-learning situation. This is supported by previous evidence from adults (Yu & Smith, 2007). Adults viewed four novel objects at a time, hearing four novel words on each trial, with no indication of which word corresponded to each object. The number of words to be learned (9 or 18) and the number of repetitions of each word differed across conditions. At test, participants heard a single word and were asked to choose the corresponding object from among four objects they had seen during training. Results showed that the mean number of words learned was higher in the 18-word condition than in the 9-word condition. One explanation the authors suggest is that adults were aided by the fewer spurious correlations between the target word and the incorrect objects in the 18-word condition. Though there were more words to learn in the 18-word context, the context was less ambiguous because each word was less likely to occur with its nonreferents.

These findings suggest that infants and adults are able to learn word-object pairings after repeated exposures, even if a pairing is not obvious in any one exposure. One question that remains is how infants would perform in a task like that used in Yu and Smith (2007). If it is indeed the case that the learning mechanism used for cross-situational word-learning benefits from complexity, then infants should also perform better in more complex but less ambiguous situations than in less complex situations with fewer target words. A second open question concerns how words are treated in such experiments. Do infants treat a word as categorical in scope in such experiments or as a paired associate

for a single item? When infants (or adults) learn the putative links between words and objects, it is important to discern whether the learned association is between a word and a single item or a word and a category.

While Smith and Yu have shown that infants and adults can learn word-object pairings across contexts, the pairings occurred together 100% of the time. Although other objects were present, providing competition, the correct word-object pairing was always available in a given situation, which is not always the case in the natural environment. The real world is full of words that refer to absent or invisible referents, so that the objects visible in the environment do not necessarily correspond to the words being spoken. Vouloumanos and Werker (2009) examined 18-month-olds' learning of word-object pairs that differed in their degree of co-occurrence. Infants viewed 30 labeling events, during which three words and three objects co-occurred at different rates. One object appeared with the same word ten times, and the other two objects appeared eight times with one remaining word and twice with the other. Results suggest that infants tracked the frequency of occurrence of the word-object pairings. When presented at test with a word and a pair of objects, one of which had co-occurred with the word with high frequency (8 out of 10 trials) and the other which had never co-occurred with the word, infants looked longer at the high-frequency object. However, when each object had occurred with a given word (eight and two times, respectively), infants looked equally at each object, suggesting that they kept track of both high-probability and low-probability information across trials. Tracking words that occur with objects with low frequency may be important for learning words that do not refer to basic-level categories and thus may occur with a wide range of different objects.

To sum, infants who are 6 to 8 months old can learn word forms in isolation, and this learning can aid them in the discovery of additional forms. Furthermore, they associate sounds to significant individuals and to objects that move in synchrony together. By 9 months of age, infants hold expectations or assumptions regarding count nouns and their referents. A short time later, their associative abilities help them attend to cross-situational statistics between words and objects. Taken together, these findings demonstrate that infants can extract and retain word forms, most of which they do not produce. Given the evidence for early segmentation, lexical assumptions, and the later evidence for putative associative links, perhaps infants often extract a word form first, represent it with some degree of phonetic accuracy, and then gradually add meaning to the form as the situation allows over time.

## Words Presented in a Social Context

From birth, the language that infants hear is saturated with information relevant to meaning. Human infants grow up in a language-rich world filled with other people, including parents, siblings, other family members, friends, and strangers. Adult speakers in many cultures are known to exaggerate intonation in ways that signal their interests and intentions when talking to infants (Fernald, 1989). Adults also tend to utter words in isolation and talk about things available in the present situation (Brent & Siskind, 2001; Snow & Ferguson, 1977). Furthermore, infants' lives are typically structured by adults into predictable patterns of events or socially coordinated interactions, and this likely helps infants experience well-rehearsed words, phrases, and commonly encountered objects (Bates, Benigni, Bretherton, Camaioni, & Volterra, 1979; Bruner, 1990). Thus, we raise the possibility that any association-focused picture of early word learning in the first year of life may be distorted by the use of methods—like those discussed earlier—that restrict or prohibit the use of human speakers. The ability to learn from other humans is perhaps one of the most important adaptations of our species (Adolphs, 2003; Csibra & Gergely, 2006; Tomasello, 1999), making it reasonable to suggest that hearing language in a social context might result in a different kind of learning than hearing them in nonsocial contexts.

Research shows us that infants in the second year of life use social cues appropriately and effectively to guide their word learning. By 12 months of age, infants seek out social information prior to making inferences in a word-learning task, checking the gaze direction of a speaker who produces a novel label more often when two objects were present than when just one object is present (Baldwin, Bill, & Ontai, 1996; Vaish, Demir, & Baldwin, 2011). This suggests that already by the beginning of the second year, infants use social cues from a speaker to clarify an ambiguous reference. Tomasello and Haberl (2003) found that 12-month-old infants are able to keep track of what a person has and has not seen and to use this information to interpret her novel word use. Specifically, infants assumed that an adult's expressions of surprise and excitement must refer to an object that the adult had not previously seen. In another study, Woodward (2004) reported that 13-month-old infants accepted a novel word as the name for an object when the speaker had indicated the object with gaze and pointing. However, when the speaker's attention was directed elsewhere, they did not accept the new label, in spite of the strong contiguity that occurred between seeing the object and hearing the label. Furthermore, several studies have shown that infants as young as 12–14 months interpret new words (and emotional expressions) based on information about the speaker's attention and apparent intention (Campbell & Namy 2003; Moses, Baldwin, Rosicky, & Tidball, 2001; Tomasello, Strosberg, & Akhtar, 1996). By 19–20 months, social information appears to be necessary for infants to establish word-object associations, and when social information is absent, infants resist making the connection between a spoken word and an object (Baldwin & Moses, 2001; Baldwin, Markman, et al., 1996).

Although there is much evidence for social influences on word learning in the second year of life, we believe that there is reason to think that social information may be relevant for word learning at earlier time points. As we will discuss, the social information that younger infants, in the first year, attend to is likely not the same as what has been found with older children (Baldwin etc.). However, it is worth considering the type of social understanding that 6- to 8-month-olds might bring to the task of interpreting speech/words around them. Language learning begins and continues in the ubiquitous context of social others, making it reasonable to suspect that infant word-learning abilities are at their best in that context. Without a live human interlocutor, infants may not even interpret speech as signaling a communicative situation (Csibra, 2003). As we review in the next section, behavioral, cognitive, and brain research on infant social understanding in the first year of life (for a review, see Grossman & Johnson, 2007) informs our understanding of the types of social information that might be used by the very early word learner.

## Infants Use of Social Cues: Object Processing, Joint Attention, Phonetic Learning
### Object Processing

As mentioned earlier, 4.5-month-old infants respond preferentially to their own names over other names (Mandel et al., 1995). Furthermore, 6-month-olds, not 4.5-month-olds, prefer tokens of "baby" but not "mommy." This suggests that infants listen preferentially to words typically directed to themselves. In research by Parise, Friederici, and Striano (2010), 5-month-olds not only detected their own name but also used it to guide their subsequent attention to objects and events. Using event-related potential (ERP) methods, infants were first exposed to their own name or a stranger's name. After a brief time interval, they then saw a picture of a toy. As a result, infants' own name showed greater amplitude of the anterior positive shift component than the stranger's name, which suggests greater sensitivity to the sound of their own name as compared to a stranger's name. In addition, the ERP to objects preceded by the infants' own name showed a later peak in the negative central component than the ERP to objects preceded by a stranger's name. One possibility, highlighted by the authors, is that an object forecasted by the infant's own name was processed more slowly and required more neural resources than objects that were preceded by a stranger's name.

Similar evidence derives from research that manipulates eye gaze as an attentional cue in infancy. Research by Striano and colleagues demonstrates a developmental trajectory for infants' use of gaze direction in object processing. In a series of studies (Cleveland, Schug, & Striano, 2007; Cleveland & Striano, 2007; Striano, Chen, Cleveland, & Bradshaw, 2006), infants watched as an experimenter alternated gaze between the infant and an object (joint-attention condition) or alternated gaze between the ceiling and the object, never looking at the infant (object-only condition). Infants were then presented with the object they had already seen and a novel object, and their preference to look toward the novel object was measured. If the social cue in the joint-attention condition resulted in heightened attention toward the cued object, then infants should show a greater novelty preference in the joint-attention condition than in the object-only condition. The results of these studies showed that while 7- and 9-month-olds displayed a greater novelty preference in the joint-attention condition, 4- and 5-month-olds' novelty preferences did not vary as a function of condition, suggesting that infants' use of gaze direction as an attentional cue undergoes development from the first half to the second half of the first year. However, note that there is neural evidence to suggest that even by 4 months, infants perceive objects that an adult has gazed at as more familiar than objects the adult previously looked away from (Reid, Striano, Kaufman, & Johnson, 2004). Reid and colleagues (2004) presented 4-month-olds with a still photograph of an adult looking toward an object or an adult looking away from an object. Then, they viewed a photograph of the previously viewed object alone while an electroencephalogram (EEG) was recorded. The amplitude of slow-wave ERP was greater in response to objects that the adult had looked away from (uncued) than in response to objects that the adult had looked toward (cued), suggesting that the infants processed the pictures of uncued objects as more novel than the cued objects. Given the salience that cues like own name and eye gaze have for young infants in attentional contexts, it seems plausible that they come to be treated as conversational signals soon thereafter (Kampe, Frith, & Frith, 2003; Grossman, Parise, & Friederici, 2010).

Studies that isolate and distinguish socially relevant cues from nonsocial ones do indicate development in the first year of life, with social cues being used to different ends by younger versus older infants. Wu and Kirkham (2010) familiarized 8-month-old and 4-month-old infants to an array of four objects, one of which was highlighted either by a face gazing toward the object or by a flashing outline around the object. Eight-month-olds who received social cues to direct their attention to an object learned that object's identity and its spatial location, expecting a particular object to appear in the location it had appeared before. Eight-month-olds who received perceptual cues learned only the spatial location, expecting an object to appear in the same location that had been highlighted before, but not expecting the object to be the same as the previously highlighted object. Four-month-olds who received social cues also only learned the spatial location of the object. These findings suggest that, for 8-month-old infants, social cues may lead to deeper, more specific learning about objects than do perceptual cues. On the other hand, for 4-month-olds, social cues do not yet have this effect. Thus, the tendency to learn from a social cue develops during the first year, with experimental evidence pointing to fairly systematic use of eye gaze during the second half of the first year.

### Joint Attention

Joint attentional contexts provide natural world tests of infants' use of eye gaze. Episodes of joint attention are thought to promote language acquisition because these are the types of social interactions that would help infants identify the referents to which their parents or caregivers intend to refer

(Baldwin, 1995; Scaife & Bruner, 1975; Tomasello & Farrar, 1986). Indeed, mothers who more frequently engage in follow-in labeling have infants who show relatively larger vocabularies later (Akhtar, Dunham, & Dunham, 1991; Harris, Jones, Brookes, & Grant, 1986; Tomasello & Todd, 1983). Morales, Mundy, and Rojas (1998) investigated the age at which meaningful differences could be observed in infants' capacity to follow their mother's direction of gaze. Six-month-old infants and their mothers were videotaped during a 12-minute interaction. At two different time points, mothers turned and fixated a target that was 90 degrees to the right or left of the infant or 180 degrees behind the infant while saying the child's name three times to help support their attention. The authors found that first, a large number of 6-month-olds reliably matched their mother's direction of gaze when targets appeared to the left or right of the infants' visual field. Second, this ability was positively related to the size of the infants' productive vocabulary, as measured by parental report (MacArthur Communicative Development Inventory [MCDI] at 12, 18, and 24 months [rs = .47 to .51]). Thus, not only is there a capacity for tracking a speaker's direction of gaze at 6 months, this nascent ability is related to early language development. An interesting study would be one that used this same methodology to train actual word-object pairings, followed with a paired-preference assessment of infants' comprehension.

A comprehensive follow-up investigation by Morales et al. (2000) demonstrated the most significant gains in infants' responding to joint attention between 8 to 10 months and 10 to 12 months of age, with the further consolidation of skills occurring between 12 and 18 months. Again, the authors found that infants' success in responding to bids for joint attention was correlated with MCDI at 24 and 30 months. The authors discuss a discrepancy in the literature between those studies that demonstrate joint attentional skills at 6 months (Butterworth & Cochran, 1980; Butterworth & Jarrett, 1991; Morales et al., 1998, 1999; Scaife & Bruner, 1975) and those that do not find such evidence until 10 or 12 months (Corkum & Moore, 1998; Morissette, Ricard, & Gouin-Decarie, 1995). The ecological factors they suspect are relevant include (1) use of a familiar experimenter (four out of five studies finding competence at 6 months used parents in place of experimenters); (2) whether vocal information is used as well as visual information (the auditory channel may be especially potent in channeling infant attention); and (3) whether infants are aware of the targets before the bids for joint attention are made (8-month-olds who had not followed gaze did so after they were first made aware of the targets in the laboratory (Corkum & Moore, 1998). Evidence of sensitivity to joint attention has been found even earlier in the first year: Striano and colleagues (2007) found that 3-month-olds looked longer toward an experimenter when she alternated her gaze between the infant and an object than when she looked only at the object.

## Phonetic Learning

Finally, the importance that social interaction carries for language learning is seen vividly in work on foreign phonetic learning by Kuhl, Tsao, and Liu (2003), who examined the effects of a foreign-language exposure intervention on the decline in ability to discriminate nonnative phonemes in infancy. Nine-month-old English-learning infants participated in twelve 25-minute language-exposure sessions conducted over the course of 4 weeks. In one condition, four live Mandarin-speaking adults (one in each session) read storybooks to and played with sets of three infants. In another condition, infants heard an audio recording, or viewed an audio-visual video, of the same Mandarin speakers doing the same activities (reading the same storybooks and playing with the same toys). Finally, a control group of English-learning infants was exposed to live English-speaking adults reading storybooks and playing with toys.

After the fourth exposure session, infants returned to the lab and were tested on their discrimination of Mandarin phonemes using a head-turn conditioning procedure. Infants in the live Mandarin-exposure condition with the live speaker performed significantly better than infants in the English-exposure condition on the Mandarin phoneme discrimination task. In addition, infants in the live exposure condition outperformed infants in the audio and audio-visual conditions, suggesting that exposure to the Mandarin language was not enough to affect the decline of phonemic discrimination. Rather, social interaction with a native speaker seems to be required for the reversal of decline to occur. While both the live speaker and the recordings provided general social cues, such as infant-directed speech, only the live interaction provided infants with more specific referential information, such as a gaze toward an object. Only in the live language exposure did infants have the opportunity to participate in joint attention with the speaker. Such active participation in the language exposure sessions is likely to have contributed to infants' ability to attend to meaningful units in the stream of foreign speech.

Social influences on language learning are also apparent in work on speech production. Research by Goldstein, King, and West (2003) shows that the vocalizations of 8-month-old infants vary according to social cues from their mothers. Researchers observed infant-mother dyads interacting in a playroom and manipulated the mothers' responses to their infants' vocalizations. Mothers in the contingent response group were instructed to respond positively, by smiling and moving toward the infant, immediately after the infant produced a vocalization. Mothers in the yoked control group were instructed to respond noncontingently, with their responses timed according to responses from mothers in the contingent group. Infants who received contingent responses from their mothers not only produced more vocalizations across the response period, but the phonological quality of their responses showed more mature voicing, more syllable structure, and faster consonant-vowel transitions than infants in the control group. These results suggest that infants' vocal production in the first year of life is not simply a matter of imitation; rather, even nonvocal social responsiveness of others is related to the sophistication of infants' early vocalizations.

As mentioned earlier, using and understanding words involves appreciating their multifaceted nature as instances of symbols, conventions, category terms, grammatical unit, and intentional actions (Koenig & Woodward, 2007). Infants' symbolic understanding undergoes development between 13 and 18 months of age in that the youngest infants appear to learn nonverbal "names" for objects (e.g., gestures, icons, noises) just as readily as verbal labels (Campbell & Namy 2003; Namy & Waxman 1998; Woodward & Hoyne 1999). Starting at around 18–20 months, a narrowing expectation for specifically verbal forms emerges among hearing infants, grows increasingly stronger (Namy & Waxman, 1998; Woodward & Hoyne, 1999), and by 26 months interferes with children's ability to learn arbitrary gestures. The fact that the youngest infants accept nonword items as symbols raises the possibility that infants place an initial priority on how the symbol is used by an interlocutor. As long as a human speaker uses a symbol intentionally and meaningfully, infants may be prepared to assign meaning to the symbol.

More generally, early sociocognitive research demonstrates that infants respond differently to human and nonhuman sources. By 6 months, infants selectively attended longer to a human agent's reach when it was directed toward a new goal object than when it was extended to the same goal across a new path. This heightened attention to a new goal object did not emerge when infants saw an inanimate entity "reach" toward objects. Thus, infants interpreted reaches as goal directed only when the action was well formed and performed by human hands. Similarly, infants track and imitate the facial and hand gestures of humans, not inanimate objects (Legerstee, 1991; Meltzoff, 1995; Meltzoff & Moore, 1977). As communicators, infants produce gestures such as points, requests, and displays for other people (Bates, Camaioni, & Volterra, 1975; Brooks & Meltzoff, 2002; Carpenter, Nagell, Tomasello, Butterworth, & Moore, 1998), successfully track others' gaze across distances (Moll & Tomasello, 2004), and they monitor the success of their bids for attention (Tomasello & Haberl, 2003; for a review, see Tomasello, Carpenter, Call, Behne, & Moll, 2005). While many of these findings are demonstrated in nonverbal or nonlinguistic contexts, many researchers currently see these and other behaviors as reflections of the infants' intentional attributions toward others, attributions of mental states with content. More direct evidence for the significance of human speakers for infants' understanding of words can be seen in research by Koenig and Echols (2003). By 16 months, most infants have acquired the conventional labels for some objects and give priority to those forms by correcting adults when they offer inappropriate forms, such as calling a cup "a dog" or a duck "a chair" (Pea, 1982). In research by Koenig and Echols, one group of infants was presented with repeated instances of labels that accurately named a visual target (True Condition) and another group experienced labels that inaccurately named the same targets (False Condition). In one study, the labels, either true or false, were produced by a live human speaker who was seated near the infant and who directed her gaze at the visual targets. In another two studies, labels came from a visible audio speaker in the same location or from a live human person with her back to the objects. We measured infants' corrections as well as the visual attention they gave both to the labeling source and to the object being labeled. Infants were more likely to correct false labels in responses to a live human speaker looking at the objects (15/16 infants) than in the other conditions. They also looked longer at this speaker when she offered false labels than when she offered true ones. In contrast, they looked longer to the facing-backward human labeler when she produced true labels. First, infants appear to appreciate critically that human speakers, not inanimate sources, are typically truthful communicators. Furthermore, they also understand the way in which truthful labeling—or the capacity for truthful labeling—interacts with the perceptual experience of the speaker. The finding that by 16 months, infants carry unique expectations for human speakers under certain informational conditions indicates that they monitor what human speakers say in terms of what they have access to. It would be very informative to know whether infants who at the very beginning of lexical development would also be influenced by the nature of the labeling source (human vs. nonhuman) and her intentional cues, such as perceptual gaze.

## Conclusions

To sum, language is inherently social. Language input to children is infused with a rich set of social cues to meaning, and existing research suggests that infants are highly sensitive to many of these cues. For some theorists, children's word learning results, in part, from mechanisms that they use for understanding a whole range of human behaviors (Bloom, 2000). Indeed, by approximately 12 months of age, evidence suggests that infants actively monitor and use social cues relevant to meaning.

Our aim in this chapter has been to underline the word-relevant abilities possessed by infants in the first year of life. Infants younger than 12 months may not spontaneously or accurately track others' referential cues; however, existing research raises the important possibility that certain components of early word learning may be enhanced when intentions are made clear, available, and salient. Young infants' inability to actively track a particular social cue might not mean that sensitivity to that cue is unavailable or absent but rather that they are not well tuned to that cue when they compete with other cues. Addressing this issue will bring us closer to an account that recognizes the intricate links between our early social understanding, as it unfolds in the first year, and the other cognitive capacities that support early word learning.

## References

Adolphs, R. (2003). Cognitive neuroscience of human social behaviour. *Nature Reviews, 4*, 165–178.

Akhtar, N., Dunham, F., & Dunham, P. J. (1991). Directive interactions and early vocabulary development: the role of joint attentional focus. *Journal of Child Language, 18*, 41–49.

Akhtar, N., Jipson, J., & Callanan, M. A. (2001). Learning words through overhearing. *Child Development, 72*, 416–430.

Balaban, M. T., & Waxman, S. R. (1997). Do words facilitate object categorization in 9-month-old infants? *Journal of Experimental Child Psychology, 64*, 3–26.

Baldwin, D. A. (1995). Understanding the link between joint attention and language. In C. Moore & P. J. Dunham (Eds.). *Joint attention: Its origins and role in development* (pp. 131–158). Hillsdale, NJ: Erlbaum.

Baldwin, D. A., Bill, B., & Ontai, L. L. (1996). Infants' tendency to monitor others' gaze: Is it rooted in intentional understanding or a result of simple orienting? *Infant Behavior and Development, 19*, 270.

Baldwin, D. A., Markman, E. M., Bill, B., Desjardins, R. N., Irwin, J. M., & Tidball, G. (1996). Infants' reliance on a social criterion for establishing word-object relations. *Child Development, 67*, 3135–3153.

Baldwin, D. A., & Moses, L. J. (2001). Links between social understanding and early word learning: Challenges to current accounts. *Social Development, 10*, 309–329.

Bates, E., Benigni, L., Bretherton, I., Camaioni, L., & Volterra, V. (1979). *The emergence of symbols: Cognition and communication in infancy*. New York: Academic Press.

Bates, E., Camaioni, L., & Volterra, V. (1975). The acquisition of performatives prior to speech. *Merrill-Palmer Quarterly, 21*, 205–226.

Bloom, P. (2000). Language and thought: Does grammar makes us smart? *Current Biology, 10*, R516–R517.

Bortfeld, H., Morgan, J. L., Golinkoff, R. M., & Rathbun, K. (2005). Mommy and me: Familiar names help launch babies into speech-stream segmentation. *Psychological Science, 16*, 298–304.

Brent, M. R., & Siskind, J. M. (2001). The role of exposure to isolated words in early vocabulary development. *Cognition, 81*, B33–B44.

Brooks, R., & Meltzoff, A. N. (2002). The importance of eyes: How infants interpret adult looking behavior. *Developmental Psychology, 38*, 958–966.

Bruner, J. S. (1990). *Acts of meaning*. Cambridge, MA: Harvard University Press.

Butterworth, G., & Cochran, E. (1980). Towards a mechanism of joint visual attention in human infancy. *International Journal of Behavioral Development, 3*, 253–272.

Butterworth, G., & Jarrett, N. (1991). What minds have in common is space: Spatial mechanisms serving joint visual attention in infancy. *British Journal of Developmental Psychology, 9*, 55–72.

Campbell, A. L., & Namy, L. L. (2003). The role of social-referential context in verbal and nonverbal symbol learning. *Child Development, 74*, 549–563.

Carpenter, M., Nagell, K., Tomasello, M., Butterworth, G., & Moore, C. (1998). Social cognition, joint attention, and communicative competence from 9 to 15 months. *Monographs of the Society for Research in Child Development, 63*, 1–174.

Carey, S., (2010). Beyond fast mapping. *Language Learning and Development, 6*(3), 184–205.

Cleveland, A., Schug, M., & Striano, T. (2007). Joint attention and object learning in 5- and 7-month-old infants. *Infant and Child Development, 16*, 295–306.

Cleveland, A., & Striano, T. (2007). The effects of joint attention on object processing in 4- and 9-month-old infants. *Infant Behavior and Development, 30*, 499–504.

Corkum, V., & Moore, C. (1998). The origins of joint visual attention in infants. *Developmental Psychology, 34*, 28–38.

Csibra, G. (2003). Teleological and referential understanding of action in infancy. *Philosophical Transactions: Biological Sciences, 358,* 447–458.

Csibra, G., &Gergely, G. (2006). Social learning and social cogniton: The case for pedagogy. In Y. Munakata & M. H. Johnson (Eds.), *Processes of change in brain and cognitive development. Attention and Performance XXI* (pp. 249–274). Oxford, England: Oxford University Press.

Cutler, A., &Carter, D. M. (1987). The predominance of strong initial syllables in the English vocabulary. *Computer Speech and Language, 2,* 133–142.

Diesendruck, G., &Bloom, P. (2003). How specific is the shape bias? *Child Development, 74,* 168–178.

Echols, C. H., Crowhurst, M. J., & Childers, J. B. (1997). The perception of rhythmic units in speech by infants and adults. *Journal of Memory and Language, 36,* 202–225.

Estes, K. G., Evans, J. L., Alibali, M. W., & Saffran, J. R. (2007). Can infants map meaning to newly segmented words? Statistial segmentation and word learning. *Psychological Science, 53,* 1742–1756.

Fernald, A. (1989). Intonation and communicative intent in mothers' speech to infants. *Child Development, 60,* 1497–1510.

Fulkerson, A. L., &Haaf, R. A. (2003). The influence of labels, non-labeling sounds, and source of auditory input on 9- and 15-month-olds' object categorization. *Infancy, 4,* 349–369.

Gogate, L. J., &Bahrick, L. E. (2001). Intersensory redundancy and 7-month-olds infants' memory for arbitrary syllable-object relations. *Infancy, 2,* 219–232.

Gogate, L. J, Walker-Andrews, A. S., & Bahrick, L. E. (2001). The intersensory origins of word comprehension: An ecological-dynamic systems view. *Developmental Science, 4,* 1–18.

Goldstein, M. H., King, A. P., & West, M. J. (2003). Social interaction shapes babbling: Testing parallels between birdsong and speech. *Proceedings of the National Academy of Sciences USA, 100,* 8030–8035.

Golinkoff, R. M., Mervis, C. B., & Hirsh-Pasek, K. (1994). Early object labels: The case for a developmental lexical principles framework. *Journal of Child Language, 21,* 125–155.

Grossmann, T., &Johnson, M. H. (2007). The development of the social brain in human infancy. *European Journal of Neuroscience, 25,* 909–919.

Grossmann, T., Parise, E., & Friederici, A. D. (2010). Detection of communicative signals directed at the self in infant prefrontal cortex. *Frontiers in Human Neuroscience, 4,* 201.

Halle, P. A., Durand, C., & de Boysson-Bardies, B. (2008). Do 11-month-old French infants process articles? *Language and Speech, 51,* 23–44.

Harris, M., Jones, D., Brookes, S., & Grant, J. (1986). Relations between the non-verbal contex of maternal speech and rate of language development. *British Journal of Developmental Psychology, 4,* 261–268.

Houston, D. M., &Jusczyk, P. W. (2000). The role of talker-specific information in word segmentation by infants. *Journal of Experimental Psychology, 26,* 1570–1582.

Johnson, E. K., & Jusczyk, P. W. (2001). Word segmentation by 8-month-olds: When speech cues count more than statistics. *Journal of Memory and Language, 44,* 548–567.

Jusczyk, P. W., &Aslin R. N. (1995). Infants' detection of the sound patterns of words in fluent speech. *Cognitive Psychology, 29,* 1–23.

Jusczyk, P. W., Friederici, A. D., Wessels, J. M., Svenkerud, V. Y., & Jusczyk, A. M. (1993). Infants' sensitivity to the sound patterns of native language words. *Journal of Memory and Language, 32,* 402–420.

Jusczyk, P. W., &Hohne, E. A. (1997). Infants' memory for spoken words. *Science, 277,* 1984–1985.

Jusczyk, P. W., Houston, D. M., & Newsome, M. (1999). The beginnings of word segmentation in English-learning infants. *Cognitive Psychology, 39,* 159–207.

Kampe, K. K. W., Frith, C. D., & Frith, U. (2003). "Hey John": Signals conveying communicative intention toward the self activate brain regions associated with "mentalizing," regardless of modality. *Journal of Neuroscience, 23,* 5258–5263.

Koenig, M. A., &Echols, C. H. (2003). Understanding of false labeling events: The referential roles of words and the speakers who use them. *Cognition, 87,* 179–208.

Koenig, M. A., & Woodward, A. L. (2007). Word learning. In M. G. Gaskell (Ed.), *Oxford handbook of psycholinguistics* (pp. 617–626). New York: Oxford University Press.

Kuhl, P. K., Tsao, F., & Liu, H. (2003). Foreign-language experience in infancy: Effects of short-term exposure and social interaction on phonetic learning. *Proceedings of the National Academy of Sciences USA, 100,* 9096–9101.

Landau, B., Smith, L., & Jones, S. (1998). Object shape, object function, and object name. *Journal of Memory and Language, 38,* 1–27.

Legerstee, M. (1991). The role of person and object in eliciting early imitation. *Journal of Experimental Child Psychology, 51,* 423–433.

Mandel, D. R., Jusczyk, P. W., & Pisoni, D. B. (1995). Infants' recognition of the sound patterns of their own names. *Psychological Science, 6,* 314.

Mattys, S. L., Jusczyk, P. W., Luce, P. A., & Morgan, J. L. (1999). Phonotactic and prosodic effects on word segmentation in infants. *Cognitive Psychology, 38,* 465–494.

Meltzoff, A. N. (1995). Understanding the intentions of others: Re-enactment of intended acts by 18-month-old children. *Developmental Psychology, 31,* 838–850.

Meltzoff, A. N., &Moore, M. K. (1977). Imitation of facial and manual gestures by human neonates. *Science, 7,* 75–78.

Moll, H., &Tomasello, M. (2004). 12- and 18-month-old infants follow gaze to spaces behind barriers. *Developmental Science, 7,* F1–F9.

Morales, M., Mundy, P., Delgado, C. E. F., Yale, M., Messinger, D., Neal, R., & Schwartz, H. K. (2000). Responding to joint attention across the 6- through 24-month age period and early language acquisition. *Journal of Applied Developmental Psychology, 21,* 283–298.

Morales, M., Mundy, P., & Rojas, J. (1998). Following the direction of gaze and language development in 6-month-olds. *Infant Behavior and Development, 21,* 373–377.

Morissette, P., Ricard, M., & Gouin-Decarie, T. (1995). Joint visual attention and point in infancy: A longitudinal study of comprehension. *British Journal of Developmental Psychology, 13,* 163–175.

Moses, L. J., Baldwin, D. A., Rosicky, J. G., & Tidball, G. (2003). Evidence for referential understanding in the emotions domain at twelve and eighteen months. *Child Development, 72,* 718–735.

Namy, L. L., &Waxman S. R. (1998). Words and gestures: Infants' interpretations of different forms of symbolic reference. *Child Development, 69,* 295–308.

Ochs, E., & Schieffelin, B. (1984). Language acquisition and socialization: Three developmental stories and their implications. In R. Shweder & R. A. LeVine (Eds.), *Culture theory: Essays on mind, self, and emotion* (pp. 276–320). New York: Cambridge University.

Parise, E., Friederici, A. D., & Striano, T. (2010). "Did you call me?" 5-month-old infants own name guides their attention. *PLoS ONE, 5,* e14208.

Pea, R. D. (1982). Origins of verbal logic: spontaneous denials by two- and three-year-olds. *Journal of Child Language, 9,* 597–626.

Reid, V. M., Striano, T., Kaufman, J., & Johnson, M. H. (2004). Eye gaze cueing facilitates neural processing of objects in 4-month-old infants. *Cognitive Neuroscience and Neuropsychology, 15,* 2553–2555.

Saffran, J. R., Aslin, R. N., & Newport, E. L. (1996). Statistical learning by 8-month-old infants. *Science, 274,* 1926–1928.

Saffran, J. R., &Thiessen, E. D. (2003). Pattern induction by infant language learners. *Developmental Psychology, 39,* 484–494.

Scaife, M., &Bruner, J. S. (1975). The capacity for joint visual attention in the infant. *Nature, 253,* 265–266.

Shi, R., Cutler, A., Werker, J. F., & Cruickshank, M. (2006). Frequency and form as determinants of functor sensitivity in English-acquiring infants. *Journal of the Acoustical Society of America, 119,* EL61–EL67.

Smith, L., & Yu, C. (2008). Infants rapidly learn word-referent mappings via cross-situational statistics. *Cognition, 106,* 1558–1568.

Snow, C. E., & Ferguson, C. A. (1977). *Talking to children: language input and acquisition.* Cambridge, England: Cambridge University Press.

Stager, C. L., &Werker, J. F. (1997). Infants listen for more phonetic detail in speech perception than in word-learning tasks. *Nature, 388,* 381–382.

Striano, T., Chen, X., Cleveland, A., & Bradshaw, S. (2006). Joint attention social cues influence infant learning. *European Journal of Developmental Psychology, 3,* 289–299.

Striano, T., Stahl, D., Cleveland, A., & Hoehl, S. (2007). Sensitivity to triadic attention between 6 weeks and 3 months of age. *Infant Behavior and Development, 30,* 529–534.

Swingley, D. (2005). 11-month-olds knowledge of how familiar words sound. *Developmental Science, 8,* 432–443.

Swingley, D. (2007). Lexical exposure and word-form encoding in 1.5-year-olds. *Developmental Psychology, 43,* 454–464.

Swingley, D. (2010). Fast mapping and slow mapping in children's word learning. *Language Learning and Development, 6,* 179–183.

Thiessen, E. D., &Saffran, J. R. (2003). When cues collide: Use of stress and statistical cues to word boundaries by 7- to 9-month-old infants. *Developmental Psychology, 39,* 706–716.

Tincoff, R., &Jusczyk, P. W. (1999). Some beginnings of word comprehension in 6-month-olds. *Psychological Science, 10,* 172–175.

Tomasello, M. (1999). *The cultural origins of human cognition.* Cambridge, MA: Harvard University Press.

Tomasello, M., Carpenter, M., Call, J., Behne, T., & Moll, H. (2005). Understanding and sharing intentions: The origins of cultural cognition. *Behavioral and Brain Sciences, 28,* 675–691.

Tomasello, M., &Farrar, M. J. (1986). Joint attention and early language. *Child Development, 57,* 1454–1463.

Tomasello, M., &Haberl, K. (2003). Understanding attention: 12- and 18-month-olds know what is new for other persons. *Developmental Psychology, 39,* 906–912.

Tomasello, M., Strosberg, R., & Akhtar, N. (1996). Eighteen-month-old children learn words in non-ostensive contexts. *Journal of Child Language, 23,* 157–176.

Tomasello, M., &Todd, J. (1983). Joint attention and lexical acquisition style. *First Language, 4,* 197–211.

Vaish, A., Demir, O.E., & Baldwin, D. (2011). Thirteen- and 18-month-old infants recognize when they need referential information. *Social Development, 20,* 431–449.

Vouloumanos, A., &Werker, J. F. (2009). Infants' learning of novel words in a stochastic environment. *Developmental Psychology, 45,* 1611–1617.

Werker, J. F., Cohen, L. B., Lloyd, V. L., Casasola, M., & Stager, C. L. (1998). Acquisition of word-object associations by 14-month-old infants. *Developmental Psychology, 34,* 1289–1309.

Werker, J. F., &Patterson, M. L. (2001). Does perceptual learning really contribute to word learning? *Developmental Science, 4,* 26–28.

Woodward, A. L. (2004). Infants' use of action knowledge to get a grasp on words. In D. G. Hall & S. R. Waxman (Eds.), *Weaving a lexicon* (pp. 149–172). Cambridge, MA: MIT Press.

Woodward, A. L., &Hoyne, K. (1999). Infants' learning about words and sounds in relation to objects. *Child Development, 70,* 65–77.

Wu, R., &Kirkham, N. Z. (2010). No two cues are alike: Depth of learning during infancy is dependent on what orients attention. *Journal of Experimental Child Psychology, 107,* 118–136.

Xu, F. (1997). From Lot's wife to a pillar of salt: Evidence for physical object as a sortal concept. *Mind and Language, 12,* 365–392.

Xu, F. (2002). The role of language in acquiring object kind concepts in infancy. *Cognition, 85,* 223–250.

Xu, F., &Carey, S. (1996). Infants' metaphysics: The case of numerical identity. *Cognitive Psychology, 30,* 111–153.

Yu, C., &Smith, L. (2007). Rapid word learning under uncertainty via cross-situational statistics. *Psychological Science, 18,* 414–420.

# Relations Between Language and Thought

Lila Gleitman *and* Anna Papafragou

**Abstract**

In this chapter we consider the question of whether the language one speaks affects one's thinking. We discuss arguments showing that language cannot be taken to be the vehicle of thought. We then review evidence from several domains in which language has been proposed to reorganize conceptual representations, including color, objects and substances, space, motion, number, and spatial orientation. We conclude that linguistic representations have significant online processing effects in these and other cognitive and perceptual domains but do not alter conceptual representation.

**Key Words:** linguistic relativity, linguistic determinism, Whorf

Traditionally it has been assumed that language is a conduit for thought, a system for converting our preexisting ideas into a transmissible form (sounds, gestures, or written symbols) so that they can be passed into the minds of others equipped with the same language machinery. During the early and mid 20th century, however, several linguistic anthropologists, most notably Benjamin Whorf and Eric Sapir, proposed that language is not merely an interface but also plays a formative role in shaping thought itself. At its strongest, this view is that language "becomes" thought or becomes isomorphic to it. Here is this position as Whorf stated it:

> We are thus introduced to a new principle of relativity, which holds that all observers are not led by the same physical evidence to the same picture of the universe, unless their linguistic backgrounds are similar, or can in some way be calibrated. (Whorf, 1956, p. 214)

This linguistic-relativistic view entails that linguistic categories will be the "program and guide for an individual's mental activity" (Whorf, 1956, p. 212), including categorization, memory, reasoning,

and decision making. If this is right, then the study of different linguistic systems may throw light onto the diverse modes of thinking encouraged or imposed by such systems. The importance of this position cannot be overestimated: Language here becomes a vehicle for the growth of *new* concepts—those which were not theretofore in the mind, and perhaps could not have been there without the intercession of linguistic experience. At the limit it is a proposal for how new thoughts can arise in the mind as a result of experience with language rather than as a result of experience with the world of objects and events.

The possibility that language is a central vehicle for concept formation has captured the interest of many linguists, anthropologists, philosophers, and psychologists and led to a burgeoning experimental exploration that attempts to find the origins and substance of aspects of thought and culture in the categories and functions of language. Before turning to these specifics, however, we want to emphasize that most modern commentators fall somewhere between the extremes—either that language simply "is" or "is not" the crucial progenitor of higher order cognition. To our knowledge, none of those who are currently advancing linguistic-relativistic themes and explanations believe that infants enter into language acquisition in a state of complete conceptual nakedness, later redressed (perhaps we should say "dressed") by linguistic information. Rather, infants are believed to possess some "core knowledge" that enters into the first categorizations of objects, properties, and events in the world (e.g., Baillargeon, 1993; Carey, 1982, 2008; Gelman & Spelke, 1981; Gibson & Spelke, 1983; Kellman, 1996; Leslie & Keeble, 1987; Mandler, 1996; Prasada, Ferenz, & Haskell, 2002; Quinn, 2001; Spelke, Breinliger, Macomber, & Jacobson, 1992). The viable question is how richly specified this innate basis may be; how experience refines, enhances, and transforms the mind's original furnishings; and, finally, whether specific language knowledge may be one of these formative or transformative aspects of experience.

We will try to draw out aspects of these issues within several domains in which commentators and investigators are currently trying to disentangle cause and effect in the interaction of language and thought. But two kinds of general consideration, sketched in the next section, are worth keeping in mind as a framework for how far language can serve as a central causal force for cognitive growth and substance.

## Language Is Sketchy; Thought Is Rich

There are several reasons to believe that thought processes, while perhaps influenced by the forms of language, are not literally definable over representations that are isomorphic to linguistic representations. One is the pervasive ambiguity of words and sentences. *Bat*, *bank*, and *bug* all have multiple meanings in English and hence are associated with multiple concepts, but these concepts themselves are clearly distinct in thought, as shown inter alia by the fact that one may consciously construct a pun. Moreover, several linguistic expressions, including pronouns (*he, she*) and indexicals (*here, now*), crucially rely on context for their interpretation, while the thoughts they are used to express are usually more specific. Our words are often semantically general, that is, they fail to make distinctions that are nevertheless present in thought: *uncle* in English does not semantically specify whether the individual comes from the mother's or the father's side or whether he is a relative by blood or marriage, but usually the speaker who utters this word (*my uncle …*) possesses the relevant information. Indeed, lexical items typically take on different interpretations tuned to

the occasion of use (*He has a square face; The room is hot*) and depend on inference for their precise construal in different contexts. For example, the implied action is systematically different when we *open an envelope/a can/an umbrella/a book* or when an instance of that class of actions is performed to serve different purposes: *open the window to let in the evening breeze/the cat*. Moreover, there are cases where linguistic output does not even encode a complete thought/proposition (*Tomorrow, Maybe*). Finally, the presence of implicatures and other kinds of pragmatic inference ensures that—to steal a line from the Mad Hatter—while speakers generally mean what they say, they do not and could not say exactly what they mean.

From this and related evidence, it appears that linguistic representations underdetermine the conceptual contents they are used to convey: Language is *sketchy* compared to the richness of our thoughts (for related discussions, see Fisher & Gleitman, 2002; Papafragou, 2007). In light of the limitations of language, time, and sheer patience, language users make reference by whatever catch-as-catch-can methods they find handy, including the waitress who famously told another that "The ham sandwich wants his check" (Nunberg, 1978). In this context, *Table 8*, *the ham sandwich*, and *the man seated at Table 8* are communicatively equivalent. What chiefly matters to talkers and listeners is that successful reference be made, whatever the means at hand. If one tried to say all and exactly what one meant, conversation could not happen; speakers would be lost in thought. Instead, conversation involves a constant negotiation in which participants estimate and update each others' background knowledge as a basis for what needs to be said versus what is mutually known and inferable (e.g., Bloom, 2000; Clark, 1992; Grice, 1975; Sperber & Wilson, 1986).

In limiting cases, competent listeners ignore linguistically encoded meaning if it patently differs from (their estimate of) what the speaker intended, for instance, by smoothly and rapidly repairing slips of the tongue. Oxford undergraduates had the wit, if not the grace, to snicker when Reverend Spooner said, or is reputed to have said, "Work is the curse of the drinking classes." Often the misspeaking is not even consciously noticed but is repaired to fit the thought, evidence enough that the word and the thought are two different matters.[1] The same latitude for thought to range beyond established linguistic means holds for the speakers, too. Wherever the local linguistic devices and locutions seem insufficient or overly constraining, speakers invent or borrow words from another language, devise similes and metaphors, and sometimes make permanent additions and subtractions to the received tongue. It would be hard to understand how they do so if language were itself, and all at once, both the format and the vehicle of thought.

## How Language Influences Thought: A Processing Perspective

So far we have emphasized that language is a relatively impoverished and underspecified vehicle of expression which relies heavily on inferential processes outside the linguistic system for reconstructing the richness and specificity of thought. If correct, this seems to place rather stringent limitations on how language could serve as the original engine and sculptor of our conceptual life. Phrasal paraphrase, metaphor, and figurative language are heavily relied on to carry ideas that may not be conveniently lexicalized or grammaticized. Interpretive flexibility sufficient to overcome these mismatches is dramatically manifested by simultaneous translators at the United Nations who more or less adequately convey the speakers' thoughts using the words and structures of dozens of distinct languages, thus crossing not only differences in the linguistic idiom but enormous gulfs of culture and disagreements in belief and intention.

Despite the logical and empirical disclaimers just discussed, it is still reasonable to maintain that certain formal properties of language causally affect thought in more local, but still important, ways. In the remainder of this chapter we consider two currently debated versions of the view that properties of language influence aspects of perception, thinking, and reasoning. The first is that language exerts its effects more or less *directly and permanently*, by revising either the mental categories, shifting the boundaries between them, or changing their prominence ("salience"). The second is that particulars of a language exert *indirect and transient* effects imposed during the rapid-fire business of talking and understanding. The latter position, which we will explicate as we go along, comes closer than the former to unifying the present experimental literature, and, in essence, reunites the Whorf-inspired position with what we might call "ordinary psycholinguistics," the machinery of online comprehension.

### Use It or Lose It: When Language Reorganizes the Categories of Thought

We begin with the most famous and compelling instance of language properties reconstructing

perceptual categories: categorical perception of the phoneme (Kuhl, Williams, Lacerda, Stevens, & Lindblom, 1992; Liberman, 1970; Werker & Lalonde, 1988).

Children begin life with the capacity and inclination to discriminate among all of the acoustic-phonetic properties by which languages encode distinctions of meaning, a result famously documented by Peter Eimas (Eimas, Siqueland, Jusczyk, & Vigorito, 1971) using a dishabituation paradigm (for details and significant expansions of this basic result see, e.g., Jusczyk, 1985; Mehler & Nespor, 2004; Werker & DesJardins, 1995). These authors showed that an infant will work (e.g., turn its head or suck on a nipple) to hear a syllable such as *ba*. After some period of time, the infant habituates; that is, its sucking rate decreases to some base level. The high sucking rate can be reinstated if the syllable is switched to, say, *pa*, demonstrating that the infant detects the difference. These effects are heavily influenced by linguistic experience. Infants only a year or so of age—just when true language is making its appearance—have become insensitive to phonetic distinctions that are not phonemic (play no role at higher levels of linguistic organization) in the exposure language (Werker & Tees, 1984). While these experience-driven effects are not totally irreversible in cases of long-term second-language immersion (Werker & Lalonde, 1988), they are pervasive and dramatic (for discussion, see Best, McRoberts, & Sithole, 1988; Werker & Logan, 1985). Without special training or unusual talent, the adult speaker-listener can effectively produce and discriminate the phonetic categories required in the native tongue, and little more. These discriminations are categorical in the sense that sensitivity to within-category phonetic distinctions is poor and sensitivity at the phonemic boundaries is especially acute.

When considering these findings in the context of linguistic relativity, one might be tempted to write them off as a limited tweaking at the boundaries of acoustic distinctions built into the mammalian species, a not-so-startling sensitizing effect of language on perception (Aslin, 1981; Aslin & Pisoni, 1980). But a more radical language-particular restructuring occurs as these phonetic elements are organized into higher level phonological categories. For example, American English speech regularly lengthens vowels in syllables ending with a voiced consonant (compare *ride* and *write*) and neutralizes the t/d distinction in favor of a single dental flap in certain unstressed syllables. The effect is that (in most dialects) the consonant sounds in the middle of *rider* and *writer* are indistinguishable if removed from their surrounding phonetic context. Yet the English-speaking listener perceives a *d/t* difference in these words all the same, and—except when asked to reflect carefully—fails to notice the characteristic difference in vowel length that his or her own speech faithfully reflects. The complexity of this phonological reorganization is often understood as a reconciliation (interface) of the cross-cutting phonetic and morphological categories of a particular language. *Ride* ends with a *d* sound; *write* ends with a *t* sound; morphologically speaking, *rider* and *writer* are just *ride* and *write* with *er* added on; therefore, the phonetic entity between the syllables in these two words must be *d* in the first case and *t* in the second. Morphology trumps phonetics (Bloch & Trager, 1942; Chomsky, 1964; for extensions to alphabetic writing, Gleitman & Rozin, 1977).

## The Perception of Hue

The perception of hue seems at first inspection to provide a close analogy to the language-perception analysis just presented. Is it so, then, that learning the terminology of hue in a particular language will invade and recharacterize whatever is our "native" hue perception much as experience with particular phonological categories reforms our speech perception? After all, languages differ in their terms for color just as they do in their phonetic and phonemic inventories. Moreover, again there is a powerful tradition of psychophysical measurement in this area that allows for the creation of test materials that can be scaled and quantitatively compared, at least roughly, for differences in magnitudes, discriminability, and so on. Finally, the fact that humans can discriminate hundreds of thousands of hues, coupled with the fact that it is impossible to learn a word for each, makes this domain a likely repository of linguistic difference.

Accordingly, a very large descriptive and experimental literature has been directed toward the question of whether color memory, learning, and similarity are influenced by color category boundaries in the languages of the world. Significant evidence supports the view that color labeling is at least partly conditioned by universal properties of perception. Berlin and Kay (1969), in a cross-linguistic survey, showed that color vocabularies develop under strong universal constraints that are unlikely to be describable as effects of cultural diffusion (for recent discussion and amplifications, see especially

Regier, Kay, Gilbert, & Ivry, 2010). Nevertheless, there is considerable variance in the number of color terms encoded, so it can be asked whether these linguistic labeling practices affect perception. Heider and Oliver (1972) made a strong case that they do not. They reported that the Dugum Dani, a preliterate Papuan tribe of New Guinea with only two color labels (roughly, warm-dark and cool-light), remembered and categorized new hues that they were shown in much the same way as English speakers who differ from them both culturally and linguistically.

Intriguing further evidence of the independence of perception and labeling practices comes from red-green color-blind individuals (*deuteranopes*; Jameson & Hurvich, 1978). The perceptual similarity space of the hues for such individuals is systematically different from that of individuals with normal trichromatic vision. Yet a significant subpopulation of deuteranopes *names* hues, even of new things, consensually with normal-sighted individuals and consensually orders these hue *labels* for similarity as well. That is, these individuals do not order a set of color chips by similarity with the reds at one end, the greens at the other end, and the oranges somewhere in between (rather, by alternating chips that the normal trichromat sees as reddish and greenish; that is what it means to be color blind). Yet they do organize the color words with *red* semantically at one end, *green* at the other, and *orange* somewhere in between. In the words of Jameson and Hurvich:

> the language brain has learned denotative color language as best it can from the normal population of language users, exploiting whatever correlation it has available by way of a reduced, or impoverished, sensory system, whereas the visual brain behaves in accordance with the available sensory input, ignoring what its speaking counterpart has learned to say about what it sees. (1978, p. 154)

Contrasting findings had been reported earlier by Brown and Lenneberg (1954), who found that colors that have simple verbal labels are identified more quickly than complexly named ones in a visual search task (e.g., color chips called "blue" are, on average, found faster among a set of colors than chips called "purplish blue," etc.), suggesting that aspects of naming practices do influence recognition. In a series of recent studies in much the same spirit, Regier, Kay, Gilbert, and Ivry (2006; see also Regier, Kay, & Cook, 2005; Regier, Kay, & Khetarpal, 2009) have shown that reaction time in visual search is longer for stimuli with the same label (e.g., two shades both called "green" in English) than for stimuli with different labels (one a consensual "blue" and one a consensual "green"). Crucially, however, this was the finding only when the visual stimuli were delivered to the right visual field (RVF), that is, projecting to the left, language-dominant, hemisphere. Moreover, the RVF advantage for differently labeled colors disappeared in the presence of a task that interferes with verbal processing but not in the presence of a task of comparable difficulty that does not disrupt verbal processing (see also Kay & Kempton, 1984; Winawer, Witthoft, Frank, Wu, & Boroditsky, 2007). This response style is a well-known index of categorical perception, closely resembling the classical results for phoneme perception.

Looking at the literature in broadest terms, then, and as Regier et al. (2010) discuss in an important review, the results at first glance seem contradictory: On the one hand, perceptual representations of hue reveal cross-linguistic labeling commonalities and are independent of such terminological differences as exist within these bounds. On the other hand, there are clear effects of labeling practices, especially in speeded tasks, where within-linguistic category responses are slower and less accurate than cross-category responses. The generalization appears to be that when language is specifically mobilized as a task requirement (e.g., the participant is asked for a verbal label) or when linguistically implicated areas of the brain are selectively measured, the outcomes are sensitive to linguistic categories; otherwise, less so or not at all: Language tasks recruit linguistic categories and functions that do not come into play in nonlinguistic versions of very similar tasks.[2] *The effects of language on thought seem to consist mainly in short-term—though important and consequential—processing influences rather than long-term category reorganization.* As we next show, this generalization holds as well in a variety of further domains where linguistic effects on thinking have been explored.

### Objects and Substances

The problem of reference to *stuff* versus *objects* has attracted considerable attention because it starkly displays the indeterminacy in how language refers to the world (Chomsky, 1957; Quine, 1960). Whenever we indicate some physical object, we necessarily indicate some portion of a substance as well; the reverse is also true. Languages differ in their expression of this distinction. Some languages make a grammatical distinction that roughly distinguishes object from substance (Chierchia, 1998; Lucy & Gaskins, 2001). Count nouns in such languages denote individuated entities, for example, object kinds. These are marked in English with determiners like *a, the,* and *many* and are subject to counting and pluralization (*a horse, horses, two horses*). Mass nouns typically denote nonindividuated entities, for example, substance rather than object kinds. These are marked in English with a different set of determiners (*more toothpaste*), and they need an additional term that specifies quantity to be counted and pluralized (*a tube of toothpaste* rather than *a toothpaste*).

Soja, Carey, and Spelke (1991) asked whether children approach this aspect of language learning already equipped with the ontological distinction between things and substances, or whether they are led to make this distinction through learning count/mass syntax. Their subjects, English-speaking 2-year-olds, did not yet make these distinctions in their own speech. Soja et al. taught these children words in reference to various types of unfamiliar displays. Some were solid objects such as a T-shaped piece of wood, and others were nonsolid substances such as a pile of hand cream with sparkles in it. The children were shown such a sample, named with a term presented in a syntactically neutral frame that identified it neither as a count nor as a mass noun, for example, *This is my blicket* or *Do you see this blicket?* In extending these words to new displays, 2-year-olds honored the distinction between object and substance. When the sample was a hard-edged solid object, they extended the new word to all objects of the same shape, even when made of a different material. When the sample was a nonsolid substance, they extended the word to other-shaped puddles of that same substance but not to shape matches made of different materials. Soja et al. took this finding as evidence of a conceptual distinction between objects and stuff, independent of and prior to the morphosyntactic distinction made in English.

This interpretation was put to stronger tests by extending such classificatory tasks to languages that differ from English in these regards: Either these languages do not grammaticize the distinction, or they organize it in different ways (see Lucy, 1992; Lucy & Gaskins, 2001, for findings from Yucatec Mayan; Mazuka & Friedman, 2000; Imai & Gentner, 1997, for Japanese). Essentially, these languages' nouns all start life as mass terms, requiring a special grammatical marker (called *a classifier*) if their quantity is to be counted. One might claim, then, that substance is in some sense linguistically basic for Japanese, whereas objecthood is basic for English speakers because of the dominance of its count-noun morphology.[3] So if children are led to differentiate object and substance reference by the language forms themselves, the resulting abstract semantic distinction should differ cross-linguistically. To test this notion, Imai and Gentner replicated Soja et al.'s original tests with Japanese and English children and adults. Some of their findings appear to strengthen the evidence for a universal prelinguistic ontology that permits us to think both about individual objects and about portions of stuff, for both American and Japanese children (even 2-year-olds) extended names for complex hard-edged nonsense objects on the basis of shape rather than substance. Thus, the lack of separate grammatical marking did not put the Japanese children at a disadvantage in this regard.

But another aspect of the results hints at a role for language itself in categorization. For one thing, the Japanese children tended to extend names for mushy hand-cream displays according to their substance, while the American children were at chance for these items. There were also discernible language effects on word extension for certain very simple stimuli (e.g., a kidney-bean-shaped piece of colored wax) that seemed to fall at the ontological midline between object and substance. While the Japanese at ages 2 and 4 were at chance on these items, the English speakers showed a tendency to extend words for them by shape.

How are we to interpret these results? Several authors have concluded that ontological boundaries literally shift to where language makes its cuts; that the substance/object distinction works much like the categorical perception effects we noticed for phonemes (and perhaps colors; see also Gentner & Boroditsky, 2001). Lucy and Gaskins (2001) bolstered this interpretation with evidence that populations speaking different languages differ increasingly with increasing age. While their young Mayan speakers are much like their English-speaking peers, by age 9 years members of the two communities differ significantly in relevant classificatory and memorial tasks. The implication is that long-term use of a language influences ontology, with growing conformance of concept grouping to linguistic grouping. Of course, the claim is not for a rampant reorganization of thought, only for boundary shifting. Thus, for displays that clearly fall to one side or the other of the object/substance boundary, the speakers of all the tested languages sort the displays in the same ways.

The results just discussed may again be limited to the influence of linguistic categories on linguistic performances, as we have noted before for the cases of phoneme and hue perception. This time the ultimate culprit is the necessarily sketchy character of most utterances, given ordinary exigencies of time and attention. One does not say (or rarely says), "Would you please set the table that is made of wood, is 6 feet in length, and is now standing in the dining room under the chandelier?" One says instead just enough to allow reference making to go through in a particular situational context. "Just enough," however, itself varies from language to language owing to differences in the basic vocabulary. Interpretations from this perspective have been offered by many commentators. Bowerman (1996), Brown (1957), Landau, Dessalegn, and Goldberg (2009), Landau and Gleitman (1985), Slobin (1996, 2001), and Papafragou, Massey, and Gleitman (2006), among others, propose that native speakers not only learn and use the individual lexical items their language offers but also learn the *kinds* of meanings typically expressed by a particular grammatical category in their language, and they come to expect new members of that category to have similar meanings. Languages differ strikingly in their most common forms and locutions—preferred fashions of speaking, to use Whorf's phrase. These probabilistic patterns could bias the interpretation of *new words*. Such effects come about in experiments when subjects are offered language input (usually nonsense words) under conditions in which implicitly known form-to-meaning patterns in the language might hint at how the new word is to be interpreted.

Let us reconsider the Imai and Gentner (1997) object-substance effects in light of this hypothesis. As we saw, when the displays themselves were of nonaccidental-looking hard-edged objects, subjects in both language groups opted for the object interpretation. But when the world was uninformative (e.g., for softish waxy lima bean shapes), the listeners fell back upon linguistic cues if available. No relevant morphosyntactic clues exist in Japanese, and so Japanese subjects chose at random for these indeterminate stimuli. For the English-speaking subjects, the linguistic stimulus too was in a formal sense interpretively neutral: *This blicket* is a template that accepts both mass and count nouns (*this horse/toothpaste*). But here principle and probability part company. Recent experimentation leaves no doubt that child and adult listeners incrementally exploit probabilistic facts about word use to guide the comprehension process online (e.g., Gleitman, January, Nappa, & Trueswell, 2007; Snedeker, Thorpe, & Trueswell, 2001; Tanenhaus, 2007; Trueswell, Sekerina, Hill, & Logrip, 1999). In the present case, any English speaker equipped with even a rough subjective probability counter should take into account the great preponderance of count nouns to mass nouns in English and so conclude that a new word *blicket*, used to refer to some indeterminate display, is very probably a new count noun rather than a new mass noun. Count nouns, in turn, tend to denote individuals rather than stuff and so have shape predictivity (Landau, Smith, & Jones, 1998; Smith, 2001). On this interpretation, it is not that speaking English leads one to tip the scales toward object representations of newly seen referents for perceptually ambiguous items; only that hearing English leads one to tip the scales toward count-noun representation of newly heard nominals in linguistically ambiguous structural environments. Derivatively, then, count syntax hints at object representation of the newly observed referent. Because Japanese does not have a corresponding linguistic cue, subjects choose randomly between the object/substance options where world observation does not offer a solution. Such effects can be expected to increase with age as massive lexical-linguistic mental databases are built, consistent with the findings from Lucy and Gaskins (2001).[4]

Li, Dunham, and Carey (2009) recently tested the language-on-language interpretation conjectured by Fisher and Gleitman (2002) and Gleitman and Papafragou (2005), using an expanded set of object-like, substance-like, and neutral stimuli, in the Imai and Gentner (1997) paradigm. They replicated the prior finding in several comparisons of Mandarin and English speakers. However, they added a new task, one that, crucially, did not require the subjects to interpret the meaning of the noun stimuli. This manipulation completely wiped out the cross-linguistic effect. As so often, the implication is that it is the linguistic nature of the task that elicits linguistic categories and functions. Languages differ in their vocabulary and structural patterns, impacting the procedures by which forms resolve to their meanings. But in nonlinguistic tasks, individuals with different linguistic backgrounds are found to respond in terms of the same conceptual categories.

## Spatial Relationships

Choi and Bowerman (1991) studied the ways in which common motion verbs in Korean differ from their counterparts in English. First, Korean motion verbs often contain location or geometric information that is more typically specified by a spatial preposition in English. For example, to describe a scene in which a cassette tape is placed into its case, English speakers would say, "We put the tape *in the case.*" Korean speakers typically use the verb *kkita* to express the *put in* relation for this scene. Second, *kkita* does not have the same extension as English *put in*. Both *put in* and *kkita* describe an act of putting an object in a location; but *put in* is used for all cases of containment (fruit in a bowl, flowers in a vase), while *kkita* is used only in case the outcome is a tight fit between two matching shapes (tape in its case, one Lego piece on another, glove on hand). Notice that there is a cross-classification here: While English appears to collapse across tightnesses of fit, Korean makes this distinction but conflates across *putting in* versus *putting on*, which English regularly differentiates. Very young learners of these two languages have already worked out the language-specific classification of such motion relations and events in their language, as shown by both their usage and their comprehension (Choi & Bowerman, 1991).

Do such cross-linguistic differences have implications for spatial cognition? McDonough, Choi, and Mandler (2003) focused on spatial contrasts between relations of tight containment versus loose support (grammaticalized in English by the prepositions *in* and *on* and in Korean by the verbs *kkita* and *nohta*) and tight versus loose containment (both grammaticalized as *in* in English but separately as *kkita* and *nehta* in Korean). They showed that prelinguistic infants (9- to 14-month-olds) in both English- and Korean-speaking environments are sensitive to such contrasts, and so are Korean-speaking adults (see also Hespos & Spelke, 2004, who show that 5-month-olds are sensitive to this distinction). However, their English-speaking adult subjects showed sensitivity only to the tight containment versus loose support distinction, which is grammaticalized in English (*in* vs. *on*). The conclusion drawn from these results was that some spatial relations that are salient during the prelinguistic stage become less salient for adult speakers if their language does not systematically encode them: "Flexible infants become rigid adults."

This interpretation again resembles the language-on-language effects in other domains but in this case by no means as categorically as for the perception of phoneme contrasts. For one thing, the fact that English speakers learn and readily use verbs like *jam*, *pack*, and *wedge* weakens any claim that the lack of common terms seriously diminishes the availability of categorization in terms of tightness of fit. One possibility is that the observed language-specific effects with adults are due to verbal mediation: Unlike preverbal infants, adults may have turned the spatial classification task into a linguistic task. Therefore, it is useful to turn to studies that explicitly compare performance when subjects from each language group are instructed to classify objects or pictures by *name*, versus when they are instructed to classify the same objects by *similarity*.

In one such study, Li, Gleitman, Gleitman, and Landau (1997) showed Korean- and English-speaking subjects pictures of events such as putting a suitcase on a table (an example of *on* in English, and of "loose support" in Korean). For half the subjects from each language group (each tested fully in their own language), these training stimuli were labeled by a videotaped cartoon character who performed the events (*I am Miss Picky and I only like to put things on things. See?*), and for the other subjects the stimuli were described more vaguely (*… and I only like to do things like this. See?*). Later categorization of new instances followed language in the labeling condition: English speakers identified new pictures showing tight fits (e.g., a cap put on a pen) as well as the original loose-fitting ones as belonging to the category that Miss Picky likes, but Korean speakers generalized only to new instances of loose fits. These language-driven differences radically diminished in the similarity sorting condition, in which the word (*on* or *nohta*) was not invoked; in this case the categorization choices of the two language groups were essentially the same.

The "language-on-language" interpretation thus unifies the various laboratory effects in dealing with spatial relations, much as it does for hue perception, and for the object-substance distinction.

## Motion

Talmy (1985) described two styles of motion expression that are typical for different languages: Some languages, including English, usually use a verb plus a separate path expression to describe motion events. In such languages, manner of motion is encoded in the main verb (e.g., *walk*, *crawl*, *slide*, or *float*), while path information appears in nonverbal elements such as particles, adverbials, or prepositional phrases (e.g., *away*, *through the forest*,

*out of the room*). In Greek or Spanish, the dominant pattern instead is to include path information within the verb itself (e.g., Greek *bjeno* "exit" and *beno* "enter"); the manner of motion often goes unmentioned or appears in gerunds, prepositional phrases, or adverbials (*trehontas* "running"). These patterns are not absolute. Greek has motion verbs that express manner, and English has motion verbs that express path (*enter*, *exit*, *cross*). But several studies have shown that children and adults have learned these dominant patterns. Berman and Slobin (1994) showed that child and adult Spanish and English speakers vary in the terms that they most frequently use to describe the very same picture-book stories, with English speakers displaying greater frequency and diversity of manner of motion verbs. Papafragou, Massey, and Gleitman (2002) showed the same effects for the description of motion scenes by Greek- versus English-speaking children and, much more strongly, for Greek- versus English-speaking adults. Reasonably enough, the early hypothesis from Slobin and Berman was that the difference in language typologies of motion leads their speakers to different cognitive analyses of the scenes that they inspect. In the words of these authors, "children's attention is heavily channeled in the direction of those semantic distinctions that are grammatically marked in the language" (Berman & Slobin, 1994), a potential salience or prominence effect of the categories of language onto the categories of thought.

Later findings did not sustain so strong a hypothesis, however. Papafragou, Massey, and Gleitman (2002) tested their English- and Greek-speaking subjects on either *(a)* memory of path or manner details of motion scenes, or *(b)* categorization of motion events on the basis of path or manner similarities. Even though speakers of the two languages exhibited an asymmetry in encoding manner and path information in their verbal descriptions, they did not differ from each other in terms of classification or memory for path and manner.[5] Similar results have been obtained for Spanish versus English by Gennari, Sloman, Malt, and Fitch (2002). Corroborating evidence also comes from studies by Munnich, Landau, and Dosher (2001), who compared English, Japanese, and Korean speakers' naming of spatial locations and their spatial memory for the same set of locations. They found that, even in aspects where languages differed (e.g., encoding spatial contact or support), there was no corresponding difference in memory performance across language groups.

Relatedly, the same set of studies suggests that the mental representation of motion and location is independent of linguistic naming *even within a single language*. Papafragou et al. (2002) divided their English- and Greek-speaking subjects' verbal descriptions of motion according to whether they included a path or manner verb, regardless of native language. Though English speakers usually chose manner verbs, sometimes they produced path verbs; the Greek speakers varied too but with the preponderances reversed. It was found that verb choice did not predict memory for path/manner aspects of motion scenes, or choice of path/manner as a basis for categorizing motion scenes. In the memory task, subjects who had used a path verb to describe a scene were no more likely to detect later path changes in that scene than subjects who had used a manner verb (and vice versa for manner). In the classification task, subjects were not more likely to name two motion events they had earlier categorized as most similar by using the same verb. Naming and cognition, then, are distinct under these conditions: Even for speakers of a single language, the linguistic resources mobilized for labeling underrepresent the cognitive resources mobilized for cognitive processing (e.g., memorizing, classifying, reasoning, etc.; see also Papafragou & Selimis, 2010b, for further evidence). An obvious conclusion from these studies of motion representation is that the conceptual organization of space and motion is robustly independent of language-specific labeling practices; nevertheless, specific language usage influences listeners' interpretation of the speaker's intended meaning if the stimulus situation leaves such interpretation unresolved.[6]

Other recent studies have shown that motion event representation is independent of language even at the earliest moments of event apprehension. Papafragou, Hulbert, and Trueswell (2008) compared eye movements from Greek and English speakers as they viewed motion events while *(a)* preparing verbal descriptions or *(b)* memorizing the events. During the verbal description task, speakers' eyes rapidly focused on the event components typically encoded in their native language, generating significant cross-language differences even during the first second of motion onset. However, when freely inspecting ongoing events (memorization task), people allocated attention similarly regardless of the language they spoke. Differences between language groups arose only after the motion stopped, such that participants spontaneously studied those aspects of the scene that their language did not

routinely encode in verbs (e.g., English speakers were more likely to focus on the path and Greek speakers on the manner of the event). These findings indicate that attention allocation during event perception is not affected by the perceiver's native language; effects of language arise only when linguistic forms are recruited to achieve the task, such as when committing facts to memory. A separate study confirmed that the linguistic intrusions observed at late stages of event inspection in the memory task of Papafragou et al. (2008) disappear under conditions of linguistic interference (e.g., if people are asked to inspect events while repeating back strings of numbers) but persist under conditions of nonlinguistic interference (e.g., if people view events while tapping sounds they hear; Trueswell & Papafragou, 2010). Together, these studies suggest that cross-linguistic differences do not invade (nonlinguistic) event apprehension. Nevertheless, language (if available) can be recruited to help event encoding, particularly in tasks that involve heavy cognitive load.

### Spatial Frames of Reference

Certain linguistic communities (e.g., Tenejapan Mayans) customarily use an externally referenced ("absolute") spatial-coordinate system to refer to nearby directions and positions ("to the north"); others (e.g., Dutch speakers) typically use a viewer-perspective ("relative") system ("to the left"). Brown and Levinson (1993) and Pederson et al. (1998) claim that these linguistic practices affect spatial reasoning in language-specific ways. In one of their experiments, Tenejapan Mayan and Dutch subjects were presented with an array of objects (toy animals) on a tabletop; after a brief delay, subjects were taken to the opposite side of a new table (they were effectively rotated 180 degrees), handed the toys, and asked to reproduce the array "in the same way as before." The overwhelming majority of Tenejapan ("absolute") speakers rearranged the objects so that they were heading in the same cardinal direction after rotation, while Dutch ("relative") speakers massively preferred to rearrange the objects in terms of left-right directionality. This covariation of linguistic terminology and spatial reasoning seems to provide compelling evidence for linguistic influences on nonlinguistic cognition.[7]

However, as so often in this literature, it is quite hard to disentangle cause and effect. For instance, it is possible that that the Tenejapan and Dutch groups think about space differently because their languages pattern differently, but it is just as possible that the two linguistic-cultural groups developed different spatial-orientational vocabulary to reflect (rather than cause) differences in their spatial reasoning strategies. Li and Gleitman (2002) investigated this second position. They noted that absolute spatial terminology is widely used in many English-speaking communities whose environment is geographically constrained and includes large stable landmarks such as oceans and looming mountains. For instance, the absolute terms *uptown*, *downtown*, and *crosstown* (referring to north, south, and east-west) are widely used to describe and navigate in the space of Manhattan Island; Chicagoans regularly make absolute reference to the lake; and so on. It is quite possible, then, that the presence/absence of stable landmark information, rather than language spoken, influences the choice of absolute versus spatial-coordinate frameworks. After all, the influence of such landmark information on spatial reasoning has been demonstrated with nonlinguistic (rats; Restle, 1957) and prelinguistic (infants; Acredolo & Evans, 1980) creatures.

To examine this possibility, Li and Gleitman replicated Brown and Levinson's rotation task with English speakers, but they manipulated the presence/absence of landmark cues in the testing area. The result, just as for the rats and the infants, was that English-speaking adults respond absolutely in the presence of landmark information (after rotation, they set up the animals going in the same cardinal direction) and relatively when it is withheld (in this case, they set up the animals going in the same body-relative direction).

More recent findings suggest that the spatial reasoning findings from these investigators are again language-on-language effects, the result of differing understanding of the instruction to make an array "the same" after rotation. Subjects should interpret this blatantly ambiguous instruction egocentrically if common linguistic usage in the language is of left and right, as in English, but geocentrically if common linguistic usage is of east or west as in Tseltal. But what should happen if the situation is not ambiguous, that is, if by the nature of the task it requires either one of these solution types or the other? If the subjects' capacity to reason spatially has been permanently transformed by a lifetime of linguistic habit, there should be some cost—increased errorfulness or slowed responding, for instance—in a task that requires the style of reasoning that mismatches the linguistic encoding. Li, Abarbanell, Gleitman, and Papafragou (2011) experimented with such nonambiguous versions of the spatial rotation tasks, yielding the finding that all cross-linguistic differences

disappeared. Tseltal-speaking individuals solved these unambiguous rotation tasks at least as well (often better) when they required egocentric strategies as when they required geocentric strategies.

Flexibility in spatial reasoning when linguistic pragmatics does not enter into the task demands should come as little surprise. The ability to navigate in space is hardwired in the brain of moving creatures, including bees and ants; for all of these organisms, reliable orientation and navigation in space is crucial for survival (Gallistel, 1990); not surprisingly, neurobiological evidence from humans and other species indicates that the brain routinely uses a multiplicity of coordinate frameworks in coding for the position of objects in order to prepare for directed action (Gallistel, 2002). It would be pretty amazing if, among all the creatures that walk, fly, and crawl on the earth, only humans in virtue of acquiring a particular language lose the ability to use both absolute and relative spatial-coordinate frameworks flexibly.

### Number

Prelinguistic infants and nonhuman primates share an ability to represent both exact numerosities for very small sets (roughly up to three objects) and approximate numerosities for larger sets (Dehaene, 1997). Human adults possess a third system for representing number, which allows for the representation of exact numerosities for large sets, has (in principle) no upper bound on set size, and can support the comparison of numerosities of different sets as well as processes of addition and subtraction. Crucially, this system is *generative*, since it possesses a rule for creating successive integers (the successor function) and is thus characterized by discrete infinity.

How do young children become capable of using this uniquely human number system? One powerful answer is that the basic principles underlying the adult number system are innate; gaining access to these principles thus gives children a way of grasping the infinitely discrete nature of natural numbers, as manifested by their ability to use verbal counting (Gelman & Gallistel, 1978). Other researchers propose that children come to acquire the adult number system by conjoining properties of the two prelinguistic number systems via natural language. Specifically, they propose that grasping the *linguistic* properties of number words (e.g., their role in verbal counting, or their semantic relations to quantifiers such as *few*, *all*, *many*, *most*; see Spelke & Tsivkin, 2001a and Bloom, 1994; Carey, 2001, respectively) enables children to put together elements of the two previously available number systems in order to create a new, generative number faculty. In Bloom's (1994b, p. 186) words, "in the course of development, children 'bootstrap' a generative understanding of number out of the productive syntactic and morphological structures available in the counting system."

For instance, upon hearing the number words in a counting context, children realize that these words map onto both specific representations delivered by the exact-numerosities calculator and inexact representations delivered by the approximator device. By conjoining properties of these two systems, children gain insight into the properties of the adult conception of number (e.g., that each of the number words picks out an exact set of entities, that adding or subtracting exactly one object changes number, etc.). Ultimately, it is hypothesized that this process enables the child to compute exact numerosities even for large sets (such as *seven* or *twenty-three*)—an ability which was not afforded by either one of the prelinguistic calculation systems.

Spelke and Tsivkin (2001a, b) experimentally investigated the thesis that language contributes to exact large-number calculations. In their studies, bilinguals who were trained on arithmetic problems in a single language and later tested on them were faster on large-number arithmetic if tested in the training language; however, no such advantage of the training language appeared with estimation problems. The conclusion from this and related experiments was that the particular natural language is the vehicle of thought concerning large exact numbers but not about approximate numerosities. Such findings, as Spelke and her collaborators have emphasized, can be part of the explanation of the special "smartness" of humans. Higher animals, like humans, can reason to some degree about approximate numerosity, but not about exact numbers. Beyond this shared core knowledge, however, humans have language. If language is a required causal factor in exact number knowledge, this in principle could explain the gulf between creatures like us and creatures like them. In support of the dependence of the exact number system on natural language, recent findings have shown that members of the Pirahã community that lack number words and a counting system seem unable to compute exact large numerosities (Gordon, 2004).

How plausible is the view that the adult number faculty presupposes linguistic mediation? Recall that, on this view, children infer the generative structure of number from the generative structure of grammar when they hear others counting. However, counting systems vary cross-linguistically, and in a language like English, their recursive properties are not really obvious from the outset. Specifically, until number eleven, the English counting system presents no evidence of regularity, much less of generativity: A child hearing *one, two, three, four, five, six*, and up to *eleven* would have no reason to assume—based on properties of form—that the corresponding numbers are lawfully related (namely, that they successively increase by one). For larger numbers, the system is more regular, even though not fully recursive due to the presence of several idiosyncratic features (e.g., one can say *eighteen* or *nineteen* but not *tenteen* for twenty). In sum, it is not so clear how the "productive syntactic and morphological structures available in the counting system" will provide systematic examples of discrete infinity that can then be imported into number cognition.

Can properties of other natural language expressions bootstrap a generative understanding of number? Quantifiers have been proposed as a possible candidate (Carey, 2001). However, familiar quantifiers lack the hallmark properties of the number system: They are not strictly ordered with respect to one another and their generation is not governed by the successor function. In fact, several quantifiers presuppose the computation of cardinality of sets: for example, *neither* and *both* apply only to sets of two items (Barwise & Cooper, 1981; Keenan & Stavi, 1986). Moreover, quantifiers and numbers compose in quite different ways. For example, the expression *most men and women* cannot be interpreted to mean a large majority of the men and much less than half the women. In light of the semantic disparities between the quantifier and the integer systems, it is hard to see how one could bootstrap the semantics of the one from the other.

Experimental findings suggest, moreover, that young children understand certain semantic properties of number words well before they know those of quantifiers. One case involves the scalar interpretation of these terms. In one experiment, Papafragou and Musolino (2003) had 5-year-old children watch as three horses are shown jumping over a fence. The children would not accept *Two of the horses jumped over the fence* as an adequate description of that event (even though it is necessarily true that if three horses jumped, then certainly two did). But at the same age, they would accept *Some of the horses jumped over the fence* as an adequate description, even though it is again true that all of the horses jumped. In another experiment, Hurewitz, Papafragou, Gleitman, and

Gelman (2006) found that 3-year-olds understand certain semantic properties of number words such as *two* and *four* well before they know those of quantifiers such as *some* and *all*. It seems, then, that the linguistic systems of number and natural language quantification are developing rather independently. If anything, the children seem more advanced in knowledge of the meaning of number words than quantifiers, so it is hard to see how the semantics of the former lexical type is to be bootstrapped from the semantics of the latter.

How then are we to interpret the fact that linguistic number words seem to be crucially implicated in nonlinguistic number cognition (Gordon, 2004; Spelke & Tsivkin, 2001a, b)? One promising approach is to consider number words as a method for online encoding, storage, and manipulation of numerical information that complements, rather than altering or replacing, nonverbal representations. Evidence for this claim comes from recent studies that retested the Pirahã population in tasks used by Gordon (Frank, Everett, Fedorenko, & Gibson, 2008). Pirahã speakers were able to perform exact matches with large numbers of objects perfectly, but, as previously reported, they were inaccurate on matching tasks involving memory. Other studies showed that English-speaking participants behave similarly to the Pirahã population on large number tasks when verbal number representations are unavailable due to verbal interference (Frank, Fedorenko, & Gibson, 2008). Nicaraguan signers who have incomplete or nonexistent knowledge of the recursive count list show a similar pattern of impairments (Flaherty & Senghas, 2007). Together, these data are consistent with the hypothesis that verbal mechanisms are necessary for learning and remembering large exact quantities—an online mnemonic effect of language of a sort we have already discussed.

### Orientation

A final domain that we will discuss is spatial orientation. Cheng and Gallistel (1984) found that rats rely on geometric information to reorient themselves in a rectangular space, and they seem incapable of integrating geometrical with nongeometrical properties (e.g., color, smell, etc.) in searching for a hidden object. If they see food hidden at the corner of a long and a short wall, they will search equally at either of the two such walls of a rectangular space after disorientation; this is so even if these corners are distinguishable by one of the long walls being painted blue or having a special smell. Hermer and Spelke (1994, 1996) reported

a very similar difficulty in young children. Both animals and young children can navigate and reorient by the use of either geometric or nongeometric cues; it is integrating across the cue types that makes the trouble. These difficulties are overcome by older children and adults who are able, for instance, to go straight to the corner formed by a long wall to the left and a short blue wall to the right. Hermer and Spelke found that success in these tasks was significantly predicted by the spontaneous combination of spatial vocabulary and object properties such as color within a single phrase (e.g., *to the left of the blue wall*).[8] Later experiments (Hermer-Vasquez, Spelke, & Katsnelson, 1999) revealed that adults who were asked to shadow speech had more difficulty in these orientation tasks than adults who were asked to shadow a rhythm with their hands; however, verbal shadowing did not disrupt subjects' performance in tasks that required the use of nongeometric information only. The conclusion was that speech shadowing, unlike rhythm shadowing, by taking up linguistic resources, blocked the integration of geometrical and object properties that is required to solve complex orientation tasks. In short, success at the task seems to require encoding of the relevant terms in a specifically linguistic format.

In an influential review article, Carruthers (2002) suggests even more strongly that in number, space, and perhaps other domains, language is the medium of intermodular communication, a format in which representations from different domains can be combined in order to create novel concepts. However, on standard assumptions about modularity, modules are characterized as computational systems with their own proprietary vocabulary and combinatorial rules. Since language itself is a module in this sense, its computations and properties (e.g., generativity, compositionality) cannot be "transferred" to other modules, because they are defined over—and can only apply to—language-internal representations. One way out of this conundrum is to give up the assumption that language is—on the appropriate level—modular:

> Language may serve as a medium for this conjunction … because it is a domain-general, combinatorial system to which the representations delivered by the child's … [domain-specific] nonverbal systems can be mapped. (Spelke & Tsivkin, 2001b, p. 84)

And:

> Language is constitutively involved in (some kinds of) human thinking. Specifically, language is the

vehicle of non-modular, non-domain-specific, conceptual thinking which integrates the results of modular thinking. (Carruthers, 2002, p. 666)

On this view, the output of the linguistic system just IS Mentalese: There is no other level of representation in which the information *to the left of the blue wall* can be entertained. This picture of language is novel in many respects. In the first place, replacing Mentalese with a linguistic representation challenges existing theories of language production and comprehension. Traditionally, the production of sentences is assumed to begin by entertaining the corresponding thought, which then mobilizes the appropriate linguistic resources for its expression (e.g., Levelt, 1989). On some proposals, however,

We cannot accept that the production of a sentence "The toy is to the left of the blue wall" begins with a tokening of the thought THE TOY IS TO THE LEFT OF THE BLUE WALL (in Mentalese), since our hypothesis is that such a thought cannot be entertained independently of being framed in a natural language. (Carruthers, 2002, p. 668)

Inversely, language comprehension is classically taken to unpack linguistic representations into mental representations, which can then trigger further inferences. But in Carruthers' proposal, after hearing *The toy is to the left of the blue wall*, the interpretive device cannot decode the message into the corresponding thought, since there is no level of Mentalese independent of language in which the constituents are lawfully connected to each other. Interpretation can only dismantle the utterance and send its concepts back to the geometric and landmark modules to be processed. In this sense, understanding an utterance such as *The picture is to the right of the red wall* turns out to be a very different process than understanding superficially similar utterances such as *The picture is to the right of the wall* or *The picture is on the red wall* (which do not, on this account, require cross-domain integration).

Furthermore, if language is to serve as a domain for cross-module integration, then the lexical resources of each language become crucial for conceptual combination. For instance, lexical gaps in the language will block conceptual integration, since there would be no relevant words to be inserted into the linguistic string. As we have discussed at length, color terms vary across languages (Kay & Regier, 2002); more relevantly, not all languages have terms for *left* and *right* (Levinson, 1996). It follows that speakers of these languages should fail to combine

geometric and object properties in the same way as do English speakers in order to recover from disorientation. In other words, depending on the spatial vocabulary available in their language, disoriented adults may behave either like Spelke and Tsivkin's English-speaking population or like prelinguistic infants and rats. This prediction, although merely carrying the original proposal to its apparent logical conclusion, is quite radical: It allows a striking discontinuity among members of the human species, contingent not on the presence or absence of human language and its combinatorial powers (as the original experiments seem to suggest), or even on cultural and educational differences, but on vagaries of the lexicon in individual linguistic systems.

Despite its radical entailments, there is a sense in which Spelke's proposal to interpret concept configurations on the basis of the combinatorics of natural language can be construed as decidedly nativist. In fact, we so construe it. Spelke's proposal requires that humans be equipped with the ability to construct novel structured syntactic representations, insert lexical concepts at the terminal nodes of such representations (*left, blue*, etc.), and interpret the outcome on the basis of familiar rules of semantic composition (*to the left of the blue wall*). In other words, humans are granted principled knowledge of how phrasal meaning is determined by lexical units and the way they are composed into structured configurations. That is, what is granted is the ability to read the semantics off of phrase structure trees. Furthermore, the assumption is that this knowledge is not itself attained through learning but belongs to the in-built properties of the human language device.

But notice that granting humans the core ability to build and interpret phrase structures is granting them quite a lot. Exactly these presuppositions have been the hallmark of the nativist program in linguistics and language acquisition (Chomsky, 1957; Gleitman, 1990; Jackendoff, 1990; Pinker, 1984) and the target of vigorous dissent elsewhere (Goldberg, 1995; Tomasello, 2000). To the extent that Spelke and Tsivkin's arguments about language and cognition rely on the combinatorial and generative powers of language, they make deep commitments to abstract (and unlearnable) syntactic principles and their semantic reflexes. Notice in this regard that since these authors hold that *any* natural language will do as the source and vehicle for the required inferences, the principles at work here must be abstract enough to wash out the diverse surface-structural realizations of *to the left of the blue wall* in the languages of the world. An organism with such principles in place could—independently of particular experiences—generate and *systematically* comprehend novel linguistic strings with meanings predictable from the internal organization of those strings—and, for different but related reasons, *just as systematically* fail to understand other strings such as *to the left of the blue idea*. We would be among the very last to deny such a proposal in its general form. We agree that there are universal aspects of the syntax-semantics interface. Whether these derive from or augment the combinatorial powers of thought is the question at issue here.

Recent developmental studies from Dessalegn and Landau (2008) offer useful ways to understand the issue just raised (see also Landau et al., 2009). These investigators studied 4-year-olds' ability to keep track of two features of a visual array simultaneously: color and position. Classic work from Treisman and Schmidt (1982) has shown that such visual features are initially processed independently, so that under rapid presentation, a red "O" next to a green "L" might be reported as a green O even by adults. Young children are even more prone to such errors, often giving mirror-image responses to, for example, a square green on its left side and red on its right. Directions such as "Look very hard" or "Look! The red is touching the green" do not reduce the prevalence of such errors. But subjects told "Look! The red is on the right" improve dramatically. Landau and colleagues point out that this finding in itself is not very surprising—except that they show that these preschoolers did not have a stable grasp of the meanings of the terms *left* versus *right*, when tested for this separately. Yet their partial, possibly quite vague, sensitivity to these egocentric spatial terms was enough to influence perceptual performance "in the moment." Two properties of these findings further support the interpretation that applies to most of the results we have reported. First, the linguistic influence is highly transient—a matter of milliseconds. Second, the effect, presumably like those of Hermer and Spelke, is independent of *which* language is being tested. Rather, as Landau and colleagues put it, there is a momentary "enhancement" of cognitive processing in the presence of very specific linguistic labeling.

## Conclusions and Future Directions

We have just reviewed several topics within the burgeoning psychological and anthropological literature that are seen as revealing causal effects of language on thought, in senses indebted to Sapir and Whorf. We began discussion with the many difficulties involved in radical versions of the linguistic "determinism" position, including the fact that language seems to underspecify thought and to diverge from it as to the treatment of ambiguity, paraphrase, and deictic reference. Moreover, there is ample evidence that several forms of cognitive organization are independent of language: Infants who have no language are able to entertain relatively complex thoughts; for that matter, they can learn languages or even invent them when the need arises (Feldman, Goldin-Meadow, & Gleitman, 1978; Goldin-Meadow, 2003; Senghas, Coppola, Newport, & Suppala, 1997); many bilinguals as a matter of course "code-switch" between their known languages even within a single sentence (Joshi, 1985); aphasics sometimes exhibit impressive propositional thinking (Varley & Siegal, 2000); animals can form representations of space, artifacts, and perhaps even mental states without linguistic crutches (Gallistel, 1990; Hare, Call, & Tomasello, 2001). All these nonlinguistic instances of thinking and reasoning dispose of the extravagant idea that language just "is" thought.

However, throughout this chapter we have surveyed approximately half a century of investigation in many cognitive-perceptual domains that document systematic population differences in behavior, attributable to the particular language spoken. Consistent and widespread as these findings have been, there is little scientific consensus on their interpretation. Quite the contrary, recent positions range from those holding that specific words or language structures cause "radical restructuring of cognition" (e.g., Majid, Bowerman, Kita, Haun, & Levinson, 2004) to those that maintain—based on much the same kinds of findings—that there is a "remarkable independence of language and thought" (e.g., Heider & Oliver, 1972; Jameson & Hurvich, 1978). To approach these issues, it is instructive to reconsider the following three steps that have always characterized the relevant research program:

(1) *Identify a difference* between two languages, in sound, word, or structure.

(2) *Demonstrate a concordant cognitive or perceptual difference* between speakers of the languages identified in (1).

(3) *Conclude that, at least in some cases, (1) caused (2)* rather than the other way round.

Though there is sometimes interpretive difficulty at step (3)—recall Eskimos in the snow—the major problem is to disambiguate the source of the differences discovered at step (2). To do so, investigators either compare results when a linguistic response is or is not part of the task (e.g., Jameson & Hurvich, 1978; Li et al., 2009; Papafragou et al., 2008); or that do or do not interfere with simultaneous linguistic functioning (e.g., Frank et al., 2008; Kay & Kempton, 1984; Trueswell & Papafragou, 2010; Winawer et al., 2008); or where hemispheric effects, implicating or not implicating language areas in the brain, can be selectively measured (e.g., Regier et al., 2010). The cross-language differences are usually diminished or disappear under those conditions where language is selectively excluded. Traditionally, investigators have concluded from this pattern of results that language categories do not penetrate deeply into nonlinguistic thought, and therefore that the Sapir-Whorf-conjecture has been deflated or discredited altogether.

But surprisingly, recent commentary has sometimes stood this logic on its head. Interpretation of these same patterns has been to the effect that, when behavioral differences arise if and only if language *is* implicated in the task, this is evidence *supporting* the Sapir-Whorf thesis, that is, vindicating the view that language causally impacts and transforms thought. Here is L. Boroditsky (2010) in a recent commentary on the color-category literature:

> … disrupting people's ability to use language while they are making colour judgments eliminates the cross-linguistic differences. This demonstrates that language per se plays a causal role, meddling in basic perceptual decisions as they happen.

Thus, at first glance, investigators are in the quandary of fact-immune theorizing, in which no matter how the results of experimentation turn out, the hypothesis is confirmed. As Regier et al. (2010) put this in a recent review, such findings

> … act as a sort of Rorschach test. Those who "want" the Whorf hypothesis to be true can point to the fact that the manipulation clearly implicates language. At the same time, those who "want" the hypothesis to be false can point to how easy it is to eliminate effects of language on perception, and argue on that basis that Whorfian effects are superficial and transient. (p. 179)

In the present chapter, we have understood the literature in a third way, one that situates the findings in each of the domains reviewed squarely within the "ordinary" psycholinguistic literature, as "language-on-language" effects: Language-specific patterns of cognitive performance are a product of the online language processing that occurs during problem solving. These patterns are indeed transient in the sense that they do not change the nature of the domain itself yet are by no means superficial. In some cases they are outcomes of linguistic information handling, as these emerge online, in the course of understanding the verbal instructions in a cognitive task. For instance, because of the differential frequencies, and so on, of linguistic categories across languages, slightly different problems may be posed to the processing apparatus of speakers of different languages by what appear to be "identical" verbal instructions in an experiment (see discussion of Imai & Gentner's, 1997, results on object individuation). In other cases, linguistic information may be used online to recode nonlinguistic stimuli even if the task requires no use of language. This is particularly likely to happen in tasks with high cognitive load (Trueswell & Papafragou, 2010), because language is an efficient way to represent and store information. In neither case of linguistic intrusion does language reshape or replace other cognitive formats of representation, but it does offer a mode of information processing that is often preferentially invoked during cognitive activity (for related statements, see Fisher & Gleitman, 2002; Papafragou et al., 2002, 2008; Trueswell & Papafragou, 2010).

Other well-known findings about the role of language in cognition are consistent with this view. For example, a major series of developmental studies demonstrate that a new linguistic label "invites" the learner to attend to certain types of classification criteria over others or to promote them in prominence. Markman and Hutchinson (1984) found that if one shows a 2-year-old a new object and says, *See this one; find another one*, the child typically reaches for something that has a spatial or encyclopedic relation to the original object (e.g., finding a bone to go with the dog). But if one uses a new word (*See this fendle, find another fendle*), the child typically looks for something from the same category (e.g., finding another dog to go with the first dog). Balaban and Waxman (1997) showed that labeling can facilitate categorization in infants as young as 9 months (cf. Xu, 2002). Beyond categorization, labeling has been shown to guide infants' inductive inference (e.g., expectations about nonobvious properties of novel objects), even more so than perceptual similarity (Welder & Graham, 2001). Other recent experimentation shows that labeling may help children solve spatial tasks by pointing to specific systems of spatial relations (Loewenstein & Gentner, 2005). For learners, then, the presence of linguistic labels constrains criteria for categorization and serves to foreground a *codable* category out of all the possible categories a stimulus could be said to belong to (Prasada et al., 2002; and see Brown & Lenneberg, 1954, for an early statement to this effect). Here, as well, the presence of linguistic labels does not intervene in the sense of replacing or reshaping underlying (nonlinguistic) categories; rather, it offers an alternative, efficient system of encoding, organizing, and remembering experience.

## Acknowledgments

Preparation of this chapter has been supported in part by grant 4-R01-HD055498 from the National Institutes of Health (NICHD) to Anna Papafragou and John Trueswell and in part by grant 1-R01-HD37507 from the National Institutes of Health (NICHD) to Lila R. Gleitman and John Trueswell.

## Notes

1. In one experimental demonstration, subjects were asked: *When an airplane crashes, where should the survivors be buried?* They rarely noticed the meaning discrepancy in the question (Barton & Sanford, 1993).

2. These results are fairly recent, and a number of follow-up studies suggest that the picture that finally emerges may be more complicated than foreseen in Gilbert et al. For instance, Lindsey et al. (2010) report that some desaturated highly codable colors (notably, certain pinks) are not rapidly identified. Liu et al. (2009) do replicate the between-category advantage finding of Gilbert et al. but, critically, not the hemispheric advantage. If so, the suggestion is that labeling practice is penetrating to the level of nonlinguistic cognition. Roberson and colleagues adopt this very view (e.g., Roberson, 2005; Roberson, Davies, & Davidoff, 2000; Roberson, Davidoff, Davies, & Shapiro, 2005).

3. This argument is not easy. After all, one might argue that English is a classifier language much like Yucatec Mayan or Japanese, that is, that all its words start out as mass nouns and become countable entities only through adding the classifiers *the* and *a* (compare *brick* the substance to *a brick*, the object). However, detailed linguistic analysis suggests that there is a genuine typological difference here (see Slobin, 2001 and Chierchia, 1998; Krifka, 1995; Lucy & Gaskins, 2001, for discussion).

4. We should point out that this hint is itself at best a weak one, another reason why the observed interpretive difference for Japanese and English speakers, even at the perceptual midline, is also weak. Notoriously, English often violates the semantic generalization linking mass noun morphology with substancehood (compare, e.g., *footwear, silverware, furniture*).

5. Subsequent analysis of the linguistic data revealed that Greek speakers were more likely to include manner of motion in their verbal descriptions when manner was unexpected or noninferable, while English speakers included manner information regardless of inferability (Papafragou et al., 2006). This suggests that speakers may monitor harder-to-encode event components and choose to include them in their utterances when especially informative. This finding reinforces the conclusion that verbally encoded aspects of events vastly underdetermine the subtleties of event cognition. As Brown and Dell had shown earlier (1987), English actually shows the same tendency but more probabilistically.

6. In another demonstration of this language-on-language effect, Naigles and Terrazas (1998) asked subjects to describe and categorize videotaped scenes, for example, of a girl skipping toward a tree. They found that Spanish- and English-speaking adults differed in their preferred interpretations of new (nonsense) motion verbs in manner biasing (*She's kradding toward the tree* or *Ella está mecando hacia el árbol*) or path biasing (*She's kradding the tree* or *Ella está mecando el árbol*) sentence structures. The interpretations were heavily influenced by syntactic structure. But judgments also reflected the preponderance of verbs in each language—Spanish speakers gave more path interpretations, and English speakers gave more manner interpretations. Similar effects of language-specific lexical practices on presumed verb extension have been found for children (Papafragou & Selimis, 2010a).

7. It might seem perverse to hold (as Levinson and colleagues do) that it is "lacking 'left,'" rather than "having 'east,'" that explains the navigational skills of the Mayans, and the relative lack of such skills in speakers of most European languages. The reason, presumably, is that all languages have and widely use vocabulary for geocentric location and direction, so to point to one language's geocentric vocabulary would not account for the presumptive behavioral difference in navigational skill. Therefore, by hypothesis, it must be the mere presence of the alternate vocabulary (of

body-centered terms) that's doing the damage. Here L. Boroditsky (2010) makes this position explicit: "For example, unlike English, many languages do not use words like 'left' and 'right' and instead put everything in terms of cardinal directions, requiring their speakers to say things like 'there's an ant on your south-west leg.' As a result, speakers of such languages are remarkably good at staying oriented (even in unfamiliar places or inside buildings) and perform feats of navigation that seem superhuman to English speakers. In this case, just a few words in a language make a big difference in what cognitive abilities their speakers develop."

8. Further studies show that success in this task among young children is sensitive to the size of the room—in a large room, more 4-year-olds succeed in combining geometric and landmark information (Learmonth, Nadel, & Newcombe, 2002). Also, when adults are warned about the parameters of the task, they are able to fall back on alternative representational strategies (Ratliff & Newcombe, 2008). Moreover, it is claimed that other species (chickens, monkeys) can use both types of information when disoriented (Gouteux, Thinus-Blanc, & Vauclair, 2001; Vallortigara, Zanforlin, & Pasti, 1990).

## References

Acredolo, L., & Evans, D. (1980). Developmental changes in the effects of landmarks on infant spatial behavior. *Developmental Psychology, 16*, 312–318.

Aslin, R. N. (1981). Experiential influences and sensitive periods in perceptual development: A unified model. In R. N. Aslin, J. R. Alberts, & M. R. Petersen (Eds.), *Development of perception: Psychobiological perspectives* (Vol. 2, pp. 45–93). New York: Academic Press.

Aslin, R. N., & Pisoni, D. B. (1980). Some developmental processes in speech perception. In G. H. Yeni-Komshian, J. F. Kavanagh & C. A. Ferguson (Eds.), *Child Phonology: Volume 2, Perception* (pp. 67–96). New York: Academic Press.

Baillargeon, R. (1993). The object concept revisited: New directions in the investigation of infants' physical knowledge. In C. E. Granrud (Ed.), *Carnegie Mellon Symposia on Cognition, Vol. 23. Visual perception and cognition in infancy* (pp. 265–315). Hillsdale, NJ: Erlbaum.

Balaban, M. T., & Waxman, S. R. (1997). Do words facilitate object categorization in 9-month-old infants? *Journal of Experimental Child Psychology, 64*, 3–26.

Barton, S. B., & Sanford, A. J. (1993). A case study of anomaly detection: Shallow semantic processing and cohesion establishment. *Memory and Cognition, 21*, 477–487.

Barwise, J., & Cooper, R. (1981). Generalized quantifiers and natural language. *Linguistics and Philosophy, 4*, 159–219.

Berlin, B., & Kay, P. (1969). *Basic color terms: Their universality and evolution*. Berkeley: University of California Press.

Berman, R., & Slobin, D. (Eds.). (1994). *Relating events in narrative: A cross-linguistic developmental study*. Hillsdale, NJ: Erlbaum.

Best, C., McRoberts, G., & Sithole, N. (1988). The phonological basis of perceptual loss for nonnative contrasts: Maintenance of discrimination among Zulu clicks by English-speaking adults and infants. *Journal of Experimental Psychology: Human Perception and Performance, 14*, 345–360.

Bloch, B., & Trager, G. L. (1942) *Outline of linguistic analysis*. Baltimore: Waverly Press.

Bloom, P. (1994). Generativity within language and other cognitive domains. *Cognition, 51*, 177–189.

Bloom, P. (2000). *How children learn the meaning of words*. Cambridge, MA: MIT Press.

Boroditsky, L. (2001). Does language shape thought? Mandarin and English speakers' conception of time. *Cognitive Psychology, 43*, 1–22.

Boroditsky, L. (2010, December 13). "Pro," Debate on language and thought. *TheEconomist,* http://www.economist.com/debate/days/view/626/print/all [8.30.2012].

Bowerman, M. (1996). The origins of children's spatial semantic categories: Cognitive versus linguistic determinants. In J. Gumperz & S. C. Levinson (Eds.), *Rethinking linguistic relativity* (pp. 145–176). Cambridge, England: Cambridge University Press.

Brown, R. (1957). Linguistic determinism and the parts of speech. *Journal of Abnormal and Social Psychology, 55*, 1–5.

Brown, P., & Dell, G. S. (1987). Adapting production to comprehension: The explicit mention of instruments. *Cognitive Psychology, 19*, 441–472.

Brown, P., & Levinson, S. C. (1993). "Uphill" and "downhill" in Tzeltal. *Journal of Linguistic Anthropology, 3*, 46–74.

Brown, R., & Lenneberg, E. (1954). A study of language and cognition. *Journal of Abnormal and Social Psychology, 49*, 454–462.

Carey, S. (1982). The child as word learner. In M. Halle, J. Bresnan, & G. Miller (Eds.), *Linguistic theory and psychological reality* (pp. 264–293). Cambridge, MA: MIT Press.

Carey, S. (2001). Whorf versus continuity theorists: Bringing data to bear on the debate. In M. Bowerman & S. Levinson (Eds.), *Language acquisition and conceptual development* (pp. 185–214). Cambridge, England: Cambridge University Press.

Carey, S. (2008). Math schemata and the origins of number representations. *Behavioral and Brain Sciences, 31*(6), 645–646.

Carruthers, P. (2002). The cognitive functions of language. *Behavioral and Brain Sciences, 25*, 657–674.

Cheng, K., & Gallistel, C. R. (1984). Testing the geometric power of an animal's spatial representation. In H. Roitblat, T. G. Bever, & H. Terrace (Eds.), *Animal cognition* (pp. 409–423). Hillsdale, NJ: Erlbaum.

Chierchia, G. (1998). Reference to kinds across languages. *Natural Language Semantics, 6*, 339–405.

Choi, S., & Bowerman, M. (1991). Learning to express motion events in English and Korean: The influence of language-specific lexicalization patterns. *Cognition, 41*, 83–121.

Chomsky, N. (1957). *Syntactic structures*. The Hague, The Netherlands: Mouton.

Chomsky, N. (1964) *Current issues in linguistic theory*. The Hague, The Netherlands: Mouton.

Chomsky, N. (1975). *Reflections on language*. New York: Pantheon.

Clark, H. (1992). *Arenas of language use*. Chicago: University of Chicago Press.

Dehaene, S. (1997). *The number sense*. New York: Oxford University Press.

Dessalegn, B., & Landau, B. (2008). More than meets the eye: The role of language in binding visual properties. *Psychological Science, 19*,189–195.

Eimas, P., Siqueland, E., Jusczyk, P., & Vigorito, J. (1971). Speech perception in infants. *Science, 171*, 303–306.

Feldman, H., Goldin-Meadow, S., & Gleitman, L.R. (1978). Beyond Herodotus: The creation of language by linguistically deprived deaf children. In A. Lock (Ed.), *Action, gesture, and symbol: The emergence of language* (pp. 351–414). London: Academic Press.

Fisher, C., & Gleitman, L. R. (2002). Breaking the linguistic code: Current issues in early language learning. In H. F. Pashler (Series Ed.) & R. Gallistel (Vol. Ed.), *Steven's handbook of experimental psychology, Vol. 1. Learning and motivation (3rd ed.*, pp. 445–496). New York: Wiley.

Flaherty, M., & Senghas, A. (2007). *Numerosity and number signs in deaf Nicaraguan adults. In Proceedings of the 31st Annual Boston University Conference on Language Development.* Somerville, MA: Cascadilla Press.

Frank, M. C., Everett, D. L., Fedorenko, E., & Gibson, E., (2008). Number as a cognitive technology: Evidence from Pirahã language and cognition. *Cognition, 108*, 819–824.

Frank, M. C., Fedorenko, E., & Gibson, E. (2008). Language as a cognitive technology: English-speakers match like Pirahã when you don't let them count. In *Proceedings of the 30th Annual Meeting of the Cognitive Science Society.* Hillsdale, NJ: Erlbaum.

Gallistel, C. R. (1990). *The organization of learning*. Cambridge, MA: MIT Press.

Gallistel, C. R. (2002). Language and spatial frames of reference in mind and brain. *Trends in Cognitive Science, 6*, 321–322.

Gelman, R., & Gallistel, C. R. (1978). *The child's understanding of number*. Cambridge, MA: Harvard University Press.

Gelman, R., & Spelke, E. (1981). The development of thoughts about animate and inanimate objects: Implications for research on social cognition. In J. H. Flavell & L. Ross (Eds.), *Social cognitive development: Frontiers and possible futures* (pp. 43–66). Cambridge, England: Cambridge University Press.

Gennari, S., Sloman, S., Malt, B., & Fitch, W. (2002). Motion events in language and cognition. *Cognition, 83*, 49–79.

Gentner, D., & Boroditksy, L. (2001). Individuation, relativity and early word learning. In M. Bowerman & S. Levinson (Eds.), *Language acquisition and conceptual development* (pp. 215–256). Cambridge, England: Cambridge University Press.

Gibson, E. J., & Spelke, E. S. (1983). The development of perception. In P. Mussen (Series Ed.) & J. H. Flavell & E. Markman (Vol. Eds.), *Handbook of child psychology* (Vol. 3). New York: Wiley.

Gleitman, L. (1990). The structural sources of verb meaning. *Language Acquisition, 1*, 1–55.

Gleitman, L. R., January, D., Nappa, R., & Trueswell, J.T. (2007). On the give and take between event apprehension and sentence formulation. *Journal of Memory and Language, 57*(4), 544–569.

Gleitman, L. R., & Papafragou, A. (2005). Language and thought. In R. Morrison & K. Holyoak (Eds.), *Cambridge handbook of thinking and reasoning* (pp. 663–662). Cambridge, England: Cambridge University Press.

Gleitman, L., & Rozin, P. (1977). The structure and acquisition of reading I: Relations between orthographies and the structure of language. In A. Reber & D. Scarborough (Eds.), *Toward a psychology of reading* (pp. 447–493). Hillsdale, NJ: Erlbaum.

Goldberg, A. (1995). *Constructions: A construction grammar approach to argument structure*. Chicago: University of Chicago Press.

Goldin-Meadow, S. (2003). Thought before language: Do we think ergative? In D. Gentner & S. Goldin-Meadow (Eds.), *Language in mind: Advances in the study of language and thought* (pp. 493–522). Cambridge, MA: MIT Press.

Gordon, P. (2004). Numerical cognition without words: Evidence from Amazonia. *Science, 306*, 496–499.

Gouteux, S., Thinus-Blanc, C., & Vauclair, S. (2001). Rhesus monkeys use geometric and nongeometric information during a reorientation task. *Journal of Experimental Psychology: General, 130*, 505–519.

Grice, P. (1975). Logic and conversation. In P. Cole & J. Morgan (Eds.), *Syntax and Semantics, Vol. 3. Speech acts* (pp. 41–58). New York: Academic Press.

Hare, B., Call, J. & Tomasello, M. (2001). Do chimpanzees know what conspecifics know? *Animal Behaviour, 61*, 139–151.

Heider, E., & Oliver, D. C. (1972). The structure of color space in naming and memory for two languages. *Cognitive Psychology, 3*, 337–354.

Hermer, L., & Spelke, E. (1994). A geometric process for spatial representation in young children. *Nature, 370*, 57–59.

Hermer, L., & Spelke, E. (1996). Modularity and development: The case of spatial reorientation. *Cognition, 61*, 195–232.

Hermer-Vasquez, L., Spelke, E., & Katsnelson, A. (1999). Sources of flexibility in human cognition: Dual-task studies of space and language. *Cognitive Psychology, 39*, 3–36.

Hespos, S., & Spelke, E. (2004). Conceptual precursors to spatial language. *Nature, 430*, 453–456.

Hurewitz, F., Papafragou, A., Gleitman, L., & Gelman, R. (2006). Asymmetries in the acquisition of numbers and quantifiers. *Language Learning and Development, 2*, 77–96.

Imai, M., & Gentner, D. (1997). A crosslinguistic study of early word meaning: Universal ontology and linguistic influence. *Cognition, 62*, 169–200.

Jackendoff, R. (1990). *Semantic structures*. Cambridge, MA: MIT Press.

Jameson, D., & Hurvich, L.M. (1978). Dichromatic color language: "Reds" and "greens" do not look alike but their colors do. *Sensory Processes, 2*, 146–155.

Joshi, A. (1985). How much context-sensitivity is necessary for assigning structural descriptions: Tree adjoining grammars. In D. Dowty, L. Karttunen, & A. Zwicky (Eds.), *Natural language parsing* (pp. 206–250). Cambridge, England: Cambridge University Press.

Jusczyk, P. (1985). On characterizing the development of speech perception. In J. Mehler & R. Fox (Eds.), *Neonate cognition: Beyond the blooming buzzing confusion* (pp. 199–229). Hillsdale, NJ: Erlbaum.

Kay, P., & Kempton, W. (1984). What is the Sapir-Whorf hypothesis? *American Anthropologist, 86*, 65–79.

Kay, P., & Regier, T. (2002). Resolving the question of color naming universals. *Proceedings of the National Academy of Sciences USA, 100*(15), 9085–9089.

Kay, P. & Regier, T. (2007). Color naming universals: The case of Berinmo. *Cognition, 102*, 289–298.

Keenan, E., & Stavi, J. (1986). A semantic characterization of natural language determiners. *Linguistics and Philosophy*, 9, 253–326.

Kellman, P. (1996). The origins of object perception. In R. Gelman & T. Au (Eds.), *Perceptual and cognitive development* (pp. 3–48). San Diego, CA: Academic Press.

Krifka, M. (1995). Common nouns: A contrastive analysis of Chinese and English. In G. Carlson & F. J. Pelletier (Eds.), *The generic book* (pp. 398–411). Chicago & London: University of Chicago Press.

Kuhl, P., Williams, K., Lacerda, F., Stevens, K., & Lindblom, B. (1992). Linguistic experience alters phonetic perception in infants by six months of age. *Science*, 255, 606–608.

Landau, B., Dessalegn, B., & A. Goldberg (2009). Language and space: Momentary interactions. In P. Chilton & V. Evans (Eds.), *Language, cognition, and space: The state of the art and new directions. Advances in Cognitive Linguistics Series (pp. xx–xx)*. London: Equinox Publishing.

Landau, B., & Gleitman, L. (1985). *Language and experience: Evidence from the blind child*. Cambridge, MA: Harvard University Press.

Landau, B., Smith, L., & Jones, S. (1998). The importance of shape in early lexical learning. *Cognitive Development*, 3, 299–321.

Learmonth, A., Nadel, L., & Newcombe, N. (2002). Children's use of landmarks: Implications for modularity theory. *Psychological Science*, 13, 337–341.

Leslie, A., & Keeble, S. (1987). Do six-month-old infants perceive causality? *Cognition*, 25, 265–288.

Levelt, W. (1989). *Speaking: From intention to articulation*. Cambridge, MA: MIT Press.

Levinson, S. C. (1996). Frames of reference and Molyneux's question: Crosslinguistic evidence. In P. Bloom, M. Pederson, L. Nadel, & M. Garrett (Eds.), *Language and space* (pp. 109–169). Cambridge, MA: MIT Press.

Li, P., Abarbanell, L., Gleitman, L., & Papafragou, A. (2011). Spatial reasoning in Tenejapan Mayans. *Cognition*, 120, 33–53.

Li, P., Dunham, Y., & Carey, S. (2009). Of substance: The nature of language effects on entity construal. *Cognitive Psychology*, 58(4), 487–524.

Li, P., & Gleitman, L. (2002). Turning the tables: Spatial language and spatial cognition. *Cognition*, 83, 265–294.

Li, P., Gleitman, H., Gleitman, L., & Landau, B. (1997), Spatial language in Korean and English. *Proceedings from the 19th Annual Boston University Conference on Language Development*. Somerville: Cascadilla Press.

Liberman, A. M. (1970). The grammars of speech and language. *Cognitive Psychology*, 1, 301–323.

Lindsey, D. T., Brown, A. M., Reijnen, E., Rich, A. N., Kuzmova, Y. I., & Wolfe, J. M. (2010). Color channels, not color appearance or color categories, guide visual search for desaturated color targets. *Psychological Science*, 21, 1208–1214.

Liu, Q., Li, H., Campos, J. L., Wang, Q., Zhang, Y., Qiu, J., ... Sun, H-J., (2009). The N2pc component in ERP and the lateralization effect of language on colour perception. *Neuroscience Letters*, 454, 58–61.

Loewenstein, J., & Gentner, D. (2005). Relational language and the development of relational mapping. *Cognitive Psychology*, 50, 315–353.

Lucy, J. (1992). *Grammatical categories and cognition: A case study of the linguistic relativity hypothesis*. Cambridge, England: Cambridge University Press.

Lucy, J., & Gaskins, S. (2001). Grammatical categories and the development of classification preferences: A comparative approach. In M. Bowerman & S. Levinson (Eds.), *Language acquisition and conceptual development* (pp. 257–283). Cambridge, England: Cambridge University Press.

Majid, A., Bowerman, M., Kita, S., Haun, D. B., & Levinson, S. C. (2004). Can language restructure cognition? The case for space. *Trends in Cognitive Science*, 8(3), 108–114.

Mandler, J. (1996). Preverbal representation and language. In P. Bloom, M. Peterson, L. Nadel, & M. Garrett (Eds.), *Language and space* (pp. 365–384). Cambridge, MA: MIT Press.

Markman, E., & Hutchinson, J. (1984). Children's sensitivity to constraints on word meaning: Taxonomic versus thematic relations. *Cognitive Psychology*, 16, 1–27.

Mazuka, R., & Friedman, R. (2000). Linguistic relativity in Japanese and English: Is language the primary determinant in object classification? *Journal of East Asian Linguistics*, 9, 353–377.

McDonough, L., Choi, S., & Mandler, J. M. (2003). Understanding spatial relations: Flexible infants, lexical adults. *Cognitive Psychology*, 46, 229–259.

Mehler, J., & Nespor, M. (2004). Linguistic rhythm and the development of language. In A. Belletti & L. Rizzi (Eds.), *Structures and beyond: The cartography of syntactic structures (pp. 213–222)*. Oxford, England: Oxford University Press.

Munnich, E., Landau, B., & Dosher, B. A. (2001). Spatial language and spatial representation: a cross-linguistic comparison. *Cognition*, 81, 171–207.

Naigles, L., & Terrazas, P. (1998). Motion-verb generalizations in English and Spanish: Influences of language and syntax. *Psychological Science*, 9, 363–369.

Nunberg, G. (1978). *The pragmatics of reference*. Bloomington: Indiana University Linguistics Club.

Papafragou, A. (2007). Space and the language-cognition interface. In P. Carruthers, S. Laurence, & S. Stich (Eds.), *The innate mind: Foundations and the future* (pp. 272–292). Oxford, England: Oxford University Press.

Papafragou, A., Hulbert, J., & Trueswell, J. (2008). Does language guide event perception? Evidence from eye movements. *Cognition*, 108, 155–184.

Papafragou, A., & Musolino, J. (2003). Scalar implicatures: Experiments at the semantics-pragmatics interface. *Cognition*, 86, 153–182.

Papafragou, A., Massey, C., & Gleitman, L. (2002). Shake, rattle "n" roll: The representation of motion in language and cognition. *Cognition*, 84, 189–219.

Papafragou, A., Massey, C., & Gleitman, L. (2006). When English proposes what Greek presupposes: The cross-linguistic encoding of motion events. *Cognition*, 98, B75–B87.

Papafragou, A., & Selimis, S. (2010a). Lexical and structural biases in the acquisition of motion verbs. *Language Learning and Development*, 6, 87–115.

Papafragou, A., & Selimis, S. (2010b). Event categorisation and language: A cross-linguistic study of motion. *Language and Cognitive Processes*, 25, 224–260.

Pederson, E., Danziger, E., Wilkins, D., Levinson, S., Kita, S., & Senft, G. (1998). Semantic typology and spatial conceptualization. *Language*, 74, 557–589.

Pinker, S. (1984). *Language learnability and language development*. Cambridge, MA: Harvard University Press.

Prasada, S., Ferenz, K., & Haskell, T. (2002). Conceiving of entities as objects and stuff. *Cognition*, 83, 141–165.

Quine, W. V. O. (1960). *Word and object*. Cambridge, MA: MIT Press.

Quinn, P. (2001). Concepts are not just for objects: Categorization of spatial relational information by infants. In D. Rakison & L. Oakes (Eds.), *Early category and object development: Making sense of the blooming, buzzing confusion (pp. 50–76)*. Oxford, England: Oxford University Press.

Ratliff, K., & Newcombe, N. (2008). Is language necessary for human spatial reorientation? Reconsidering evidence from dual task paradigms. *Cognitive Psychology, 56*(2), 142–163.

Regier, T., Kay, P., & Cook, R. S. (2005). Focal colors are universal after all. *Proceedings of the National Academy of Sciences USA, 102*, 8386–8391.

Regier, T, Kay, P., Gilbert, A. L., & Ivry, R. B. (2010) Language and thought: Which side are you on anyway? In B. Malt & P. Wolff (Eds.), *Words and the mind: How words capture human experience* (pp. 165–182). Oxford, England: Oxford University Press.

Regier, T., Kay, P., & Khetarpal, N. (2009). Color naming and the shape of color space. *Language, 85*, 884–892.

Restle, F. (1957). Discrimination of cues in mazes: A resolution of the place-vs.-response question. *Psychological Review, 64*, 217–228.

Roberson, D. (2005). Color categories are culturally diverse in cognition as well as in language. *Cross-Cultural Research, 39*, 56–71.

Roberson, D., Davidoff, J., Davies, I., & Shapiro, L. (2005) Colour categories in Himba: Evidence for the cultural relativity hypothesis. *Cognitive Psychology, 50*, 378–411.

Roberson, D., Davies, I., & Davidoff, J. (2000). Color categories are not universal: Replications and new evidence from a stone-age culture. *Journal of Experimental Psychology: General, 129*, 369–398.

Senghas, A., Coppola, M., Newport, E., & Suppala, T. (1997). Argument structure in Nicaraguan Sign Language: The emergence of grammatical devices. In *Proceedings of the 21st Annual Boston University Conference on Language Development (pp. xx–xx)*. Somerville, MA: Cascadilla Press.

Slobin, D. (1996). From "thought and language" to "thinking for speaking." In J. Gumperz & S. C. Levinson (Eds.), *Rethinking linguistic relativity* (pp. 70–96). Cambridge, England: Cambridge University Press.

Slobin, D. (2001). Form-function relations: How do children find out what they are? In M. Bowerman & S. Levinson (Eds.), *Language acquisition and conceptual development* (pp. 406–449). Cambridge, England: Cambridge University Press.

Smith, L. (2001). How domain-general processes may create domain-specific biases. In M. Bowerman & S. C. Levinson (Eds.), *Language acquisition and conceptual development* (pp. 101–131). Cambridge, England: Cambridge University Press.

Snedeker, J., Thorpe, K., & Trueswell, J. (2001). On choosing the parse with the scene: The role of visual context and verb bias in ambiguity resolution. In *Proceedings of the 23rd Annual Conference of the Cognitive Science Society (pp. 964–969)*. Mahwah, NJ: Erlbaum.

Soja, N., Carey, S., & Spelke, E. (1991). Ontological categories guide young children's inductions of word meaning: Object terms and substance terms. *Cognition, 38*, 179–211.

Spelke, E., Breinliger, K., Macomber, J., & Jacobson, K. (1992). The origins of knowledge. *Psychological Review, 99*, 605–632.

Spelke, E., & Tsivkin, S. (2001a). Language and number: A bilingual training study. *Cognition, 78*, 45–88.

Spelke, E., & Tsivkin, S. (2001b). Initial knowledge and conceptual change: Space and number. In M. Bowerman & S. C. Levinson (Eds.), *Language acquisition and conceptual development* (pp. 70–100). Cambridge, England: Cambridge University Press.

Sperber, D., & Wilson, D. (1986). *Relevance: Communication and cognition*. Cambridge, MA: Harvard University Press.

Talmy, L. (1985). Lexicalization patterns: Semantic structure in lexical forms. In T. Shopen (Ed.), *Language typology and syntactic description* (pp. 57–149). New York: Cambridge University Press.

Tanenhaus, M. K. (2007). Spoken language comprehension: Insights from eye movements. In G. Gaskell (Ed.), *Oxford handbook of psycholinguistics* (pp. 309–326). Oxford, England: Oxford University Press.

Tomasello, M. (2000). Do young children have adult syntactic competence? *Cognition, 74*, 209–253.

Treisman, A., & Schmidt, H. (1982). Illusory conjunctions in the perception of objects. *Cognitive Psychology, 14*(1), 107–141.

Trueswell, J., & Papafragou, A. (2010). Perceiving and remembering events cross-linguistically: Evidence from dual-task paradigms. *Journal of Memory and Language, 63*, 64–82.

Trueswell, J. C., Sekerina, I., Hill, N. M., & Logrip, M. L. (1999). The kindergarten-path effect: Studying on-line sentence processing in young children. *Cognition, 73*, 89–134.

Vallortigara, G., Zanforlin, M., & Pasti, G. (1990). Geometric modules in animals' spatial representations: A test with chicks. *Journal of Comparative Psychology, 104*, 248–254.

Varley, R., & Siegal, M. (2000). Evidence for cognition without grammar from causal reasoning and "theory of mind" in an agrammatic aphasic patient. *Current Biology, 10*, 723–726.

Welder, A. N., & Graham, S. A. (2001). The influence of shape similarity and shared labels on infants' inductive inferences about nonobvious object properties. *Child Development, 72*, 1653–1673.

Werker, J. F., & Lalonde, C. E. (1988). Cross-language speech perception: Initial capabilities and developmental change. *Developmental Psychology, 24*(5), 672–683.

Werker, J., & Logan, J. (1985). Cross-language evidence for three factors in speech perception. *Perception and Psychophysics, 37*, 35–44.

Werker, J., & Tees, R. (1984). Cross-language speech perception: Evidence for perceptual reorganization during the first year of life. *Infant Behavior and Development, 7*, 49–63.

Werker, J. F., & Desjardins, R. N. (1995). Listening to speech in the first year of life: Experiential influences on phoneme perception. *Current Directions in Psychological Sciences, 4*(3), 76–81.

Whorf, B. L. (1956). Language, thought and reality. (J. Carroll, Ed.) . Cambridge, MA: MIT Press.

Winawer, J., Witthoft, N., Frank, M.C., Wu, L., & Boroditsky, L. (2007). Russian blues reveal effects of language on color discrimination. *Proceedings of the National Academy of Science USA, 104*(19), 7780–7785.

Xu, F. (2002). The role of language in acquiring object kind concepts. *Cognition, 85*, 223–250.

# The Evolution of Language

Derek Bickerton

**Abstract**

Language evolution remains contentious and to some extent speculative. While most writers agree that language depends to some extent on some degree of biological infrastructure, the extent and nature of the biological contribution is still controversial. One much-debated issue concerns whether (or to what extent) language shows continuity with other species' communication. Possible contributions from primate behaviors and capacities have received intense study, fostering neglect of nonprimate species that show some degree of language readiness; moreover, too little attention is paid to contrasting ecologies of great apes and human ancestors. While social intelligence constitutes the most popular selective pressure, specific proposals face formidable problems. Another controversial issue concerns the nature of the earliest stages of language. For later stages, estimates of the role of natural selection vary from 100% to 0. Yet despite continuing disagreements, knowledge in relevant sciences is accumulating fast enough for the issues to be resolved this century.

**Key Words:** language, evolution, biology, intelligence, communication, continuity, protolanguage, universals, selection

How is it that among all the countless species evolution has produced, only one species, our own, has language? This question has vexed human minds from time immemorial, but in the last century and a half it has become more focused. While some scholars continue to claim that language is a human invention created by a highly developed general intelligence, the evidence against this (see section on "Language and General Intelligence") seems overwhelming. A majority of investigators believe that language arose through the regular evolutionary processes that have produced every other distinctive trait among humans and non-humans alike; debate among these is limited to the precise means by which language came about (Bickerton & Szathmary, 2009). But this issue remains difficult to resolve. Since no other species has language, biology's most reliable approach, that of comparative studies, is of little use. Fossil and archaeological data can give only the slenderest and vaguest of suggestions, while our knowledge of neurology is still too immature to explain exactly what happens when the human brain creates a simple sentence. Only by gathering and collating facts and theories from a dozen disciplines can one produce even a speculative account of language evolution. However, there is a broad consensus that the problem is now potentially solvable, if only by the process of eliminating potential explanations until only a single theory is left standing. I hope in what follows to show something of the contentious nature of the field, as well as conveying a little of its persistent fascination.

## Language and General Intelligence

Some writers continue to express a belief that human ancestors developed a keen general (or specifically social) form of intelligence and that this alone somehow gave rise to language without any evolutionary process specific to language being required. In the view of Tomasello, for instance, language emerged "as one part of the much larger process of human culture" and was simply "a complex outcome of human cognitive and social processes taking place in evolutionary, historical and ontogenetic time" (2003, 109). Similar views are expressed in somewhat different form by Donald (1991), Fauconnier and Turner (2008), and others.

If language evolved, and thus forms part of the biological heritage of the species, it must be (in some sense) innate. It is a historical fact that controversy over the psychological status of language antedated the serious study of language evolution by at least a couple of decades. This leaves one to wonder how many of those who now deny language-specific evolution do so at least in part because their chips were already down in the "innateness" debate. Be that as it may, there are a number of factors that such writers usually ignore or dismiss. For instance, they do not deal with the claim that children can produce linguistic structures to which they were never exposed, either in the context of pidgin-to-creole development (Bickerton 1981, 1984) or in the development of new sign languages (Kegl, Senghas, & Coppola, 1999). They do not address problems involving the reference of empty categories (Lasnik & Uriagereka, 1988; that is to say, nouns that are not phonologically expressed, though their reference is quite unambiguous, for example, the "missing" subject and object in *Mary is not easy* SUBJ *to talk to* OBJ); since these categories have no sensorily perceptible content, rules that determine their reference cannot have been learned inductively, although every speaker of English knows that the subject refers to "anyone" and the object to "Mary." They do not explain how any kind of general-purpose intelligence could have evolved—what would select for a general ability, and why should such selection, if it happened, affect only one species? If advocates of intelligence models really grappled with such issues, one might have more confidence in their claims. As things are, the remainder of this chapter will concern itself solely with accounts that involve at some stage some kind of recognizable evolutionary process.

## The Continuity Issue and Communication

Since language is widely regarded as a form of communicative behavior, it has seemed only natural to many that language should have evolved out of animal communication. In other words, if we look at forms of communication among other species, we should be able to find precursors that evolution could have modified and shaped into at least some simpler version of human language. This is assumed in much recent work (Hurford, 2007; Johansson, 2005; Pollick & de Waal, 2007).

While it has often been observed (Bickerton, 1990; Chomsky, 1968) that language may be better regarded as primarily a formal system for the structuring of reality, rather than as a means of communication, it has been less frequently noted that nonhuman "communication" systems (NCSs) too may not have communication as their primary aim. Most NCS signals are simply hypertrophied versions, culled by natural selection, of behaviors primarily designed not to communicate information to the recipient but to confer fitness on the sender (Tinbergen, 1952). For instance, the placatory noises and postures produced by lower status social animals in confrontations with higher status conspecifics do not convey any information that benefits the latter; such signals exist only because they prolong the life (hence the procreative potential) of their sender. Contrast this with what happens in language. If I explain to someone that a certain type of footprint belongs to a dangerous predator, the fitness benefit to me, as sender of the message, is (apart from what I might gain from future reciprocity) zero. However, the receiver directly benefits in terms of potentially life-saving (hence procreation-extending) information. In short, NCSs primarily benefit the sender, while language primarily benefits the receiver.

Once we view so-called NCSs as vehicles for the enhancement of individual (sender) fitness rather than the transmission of information per se, their features, often puzzling when NCSs are seen as communication, begin to make more sense. For instance, one factor that militates against any "progressive" view of NCS-to-language development is the absence of any evolutionary development in the complexity or scope of NCSs. NCS signals, regardless of species, have only three domains of reference: mating, social interaction, and survival (Hauser, 1996). While NCSs of "higher" species may have more signals than those of "lower," this difference stems from a broader behavioral range rather than any specifically cognitive increment. Also there is considerable overlap between systems in different phyla (some fish and insects have more signals than some mammals) and the difference between NCSs with most and fewest signals falls into the lower double digits (Wilson, 1972).

## Continuity in Words?

With regard to more specific language precursors to language, cases of what is often described as "functional reference" are sometimes hailed as precursors of words. Typical examples are the predator warning calls of vervet monkeys (Cheney & Seyfarth, 1990), chickens (Evans et al., 1993), and many other species, which are taken as incipient "words" for the predator species involved. However, there is no evidence that, in the minds of vervets or chickens, such signals bear any kind of referential relationship to the predators concerned. If they do have reference, it is purely indexical, existing only if some member of the class of predator in question is present; if they are used mistakenly, or for purely deceptive purposes (Whiten & Byrne 1988), they do not refer at all. In contrast, words can (and mostly do) freely refer to entities that are currently absent. But "functionally referential" signals could, with at least as much plausibility, be interpreted as simply triggers for the appropriate evasive behaviors (climbing trees, if the predator is a leopard; hiding in bushes if it is an eagle). Moreover, it has been noted (Mithen, 2005) that such signals are conspicuously absent from the NCSs of our closest relatives, the great apes. In fact, apes lack such signals because they do not augment fitness in these species, due to the fact that predation on apes is relatively infrequent. Indeed, NCSs in general reflect the adaptive needs of particular species, rather than representing any kind of incremental development such as is found in the evolution of eyes, wings, and so on.

## Continuity in Structure?

On a different linguistic level, it has been suggested that some NCSs may contain precursors of syntax. Most signals of most species will not combine at all, not even into the two-unit structures that emerge in the speech of infants around the age of 20 months. However, recent research has turned up a handful of phenomena that have been claimed to show combinable signals. For instance, according to Zuberbuhler (2002, 2005), Campbell's monkeys sometimes preface warning calls with a "boom" vocalization, and this is interpreted by a sympatric species (Diana monkeys) who attend to and repeat Campbell's monkey calls as indicating that the danger is remote and can safely be ignored. This is a bizarre case, since it involves two species rather than one; more telling evidence comes from studies of putty-nosed monkeys (Arnold & Zuberbuhler, 2006). This species has two calls, a "pyow" call that warns of the presence of eagles, and a "hack" call

that signals the presence of leopards. However, a combination of two to three "pyow" calls followed by up to four "hack" calls led in many cases to subsequent movement of the group, and it has been interpreted as something along the lines of "Let's move on, folks."

Note, however, that (in contrast with concatenated words) the coupling of "pyow" and "hack" calls produces a meaning that has no connection with the meanings of the two calls in isolation. In contrast, what characterizes linguistic utterances of only two units is the fact that they stand in a subject-predicate relationship with one another, so that while one focuses on a particular topic, the other provides information about that topic (*dogs bark, John agreed, temperatures rose*). Moreover, it is surely significant that these behaviors, like "functional reference" calls, are found in species that are not closely related to ours, but not in those that are. As with "precursor words," these phenomena show no cumulative increase across species; hence, they can in no sense be regarded as steps on the road to syntax. Indeed, since animal signals are complete in themselves and modeled for use in specific situations, it would seem quite pointless to concatenate them.

Note that there are, of course, both cognitive and purely physiological *prerequisites for* (as opposed to *precursors of*) language. Before language can arise, brains presumably have to reach a certain (as yet undetermined) degree of complexity and sheer size. If language is to be vocal, certain minimal requirements in flexibility and control of vocal organs are mandatory, plus the ability to distinguish a wide range of sounds. Regardless of modality, cognitive capacities have to be sufficiently developed to distinguish between and assign to categories a wide range of entities in the objective world. But such specifications, though they may be necessary, can never be sufficient prerequisites even for the simplest imaginable language. Thus, the difference between NCSs and language is no mere matter of degree. The two have different functions and work in different ways; hence, the gap between them is not merely wider than, but different in kind from, what many researchers have so far assumed.

### The Continuity Issue and Descent

Evolution, Darwin said, is descent with variation. Consequently, it has seemed logical to seek the roots of language among our closest living relatives, the great apes, and especially among the closest: chimpanzees and bonobos. If the required connective links did not exist in the field of communication, then they must surely exist in other aspects of primate behavior.

Following a seminal essay by Humphrey (1976), attention focused on the social life of apes. This, as numerous ethological studies showed, had attained a high degree of complexity (de Waal, 1982; Goodall, 1986; Smuts, 1985). Consequently it seemed natural to suppose that developments in social intelligence were a major driving force behind, and/or the main selective pressure toward, the emergence of language in humans or their immediate ancestors. In particular, it was concluded that theory of mind—conceiving that others can have thoughts and intentions different from one's own—formed an essential prerequisite for even the simplest form of language, and from Premack and Woodruff (1978) on there has been an ongoing debate over whether (or to what extent) other primates have a theory of mind (see Heyes, 1998 for a summary).

Accordingly, the great apes have been taken as approximate but still valid models for recent human ancestors (those who immediately preceded or actually achieved the emergence of language). But genetic closeness does not guarantee behavioral closeness. The closest relatives of elephants are dugongs and manatees, but there is little behavioral similarity between them. The ecological niches that species inherit or create are as powerful determinants of behavior as genes and indeed strongly affect the ways in which genes are expressed (Odling-Smee, Laland, & Feldman, 2003). Consequently, before we can adopt contemporary apes as models for early hominids, we have to take into account that the ecological niches these inhabited were strikingly different from one another in several ways.

The fossil and archaeological records of human ancestry are notoriously vague and/or ambiguous at crucial stages of development, yet they suffice to show that the environments human ancestors exploited, and the means they used to exploit them, differed dramatically from those of contemporary apes. The habitat of great apes is tropical forest (with small numbers of chimpanzees living on its edges). The habitat of human ancestors was first mosaic woodland and later open savanna. These habitats and their increasing distance from ape habitats dictated very different patterns of behavior with respect to social life, foraging, and predation.

With regard to predation, human ancestors were exposed to a wide variety of predators that included eagles (Berger & Clarke 1995) and even giant weasels (Anderson, 2004) as well as many members of the Canidae, Felidae, and Hyaenidae families larger and more dangerous than their modern counterparts. For at least the first half of the period since the last common ancestor of humans and chimpanzees/bonobos, protohumans were considerably smaller than modern humans and lacked any artifacts usable in self-defense. Consequently they would have spent more time watching for and evading predators than modern apes, and thus less time on the intense social interaction found among those relatively predator-free species.

With regard to foraging, terrains inhabited by protohumans were more hostile than those inhabited by apes and were destined to become still more so as drying trends continued through the closing years of the Pliocene. While apes are (and presumably were) able to subsist almost entirely on fruit, nuts, and leaves, protohumans would have had to become omnivores, with a consequent diversification of foraging strategies. While apes have (and presumably had) relatively small day ranges, day ranges of protohumans must have exceeded these by several hundred percent. Time spent searching for food and returning to safe havens at night would also have reduced the time available for social interaction, Machiavellian strategizing, and the like.

In other words, both anti-predation strategies and foraging practices would have acted against any increase in the complexity of hominid social interaction and might in some ways have even reduced the types of interaction found among forest-dwelling apes. Moreover, those conditions would have limited the degree of competitiveness, which is one source for the complexity of apes' social life, and replaced it with patterns of cooperative behavior unknown among primates and rare, if they exist at all, outsiders of eusocial species.

The evolutionary origins of human cooperation have long been a puzzle for students of social behavior (Henrich & Henrich, 2006; Richerson, Boyd, & Henrich, 2003—notice that these and most similar studies are concerned with cooperative behavior in the abstract and do not even take into account the added layer of difficulty encountered when we compare human behavior to that of apes). Indeed, cooperation poses a problem for evolutionists just as acute as language does; one inevitably wonders how two such innovations could have occurred in the same species during what, in terms of evolution, is a relatively short time, and whether they might not be connected with one another in some way.

All of the foregoing considerations point to the conclusion that, in dealing with language evolution, the possible contribution of primatological studies can easily be overestimated. Reinforcing this conclusion is the fact that language-like systems can be taught to a variety of species, including some—dolphins (Herman, Kuczaj, & Holder, 1993), and even sea lions (Schusterman & Krieger, 1984) and African gray parrots (Pepperberg. 1987)—that are evolutionarily quite remote from humans. This suggests that a number of species may, in the sense of Szamado and Szathmary (2006), be "selection limited" rather than "variation limited"—that is to say, their genome contains material that might serve as the substrate for some kind of language, were they to undergo an appropriate kind of selective pressure. Consequently, those inquiring into the evolution of language should place at least as much emphasis on ecology and niche-construction processes (Odling-Smee, Laland, & Feldman, 2003) as they do on lines of descent.

## Selective Pressure

It is a tenet of Darwinian evolution that no substantive change in the form or behavior of organisms can become fixed in the genome unless it is favored by some kind of selective pressure. It follows therefore that language cannot have developed unless an appropriate pressure developed at some stage of human evolution. But here we are confronted by an *embarrass de richesse*: Over the course of time a large number of pressures have been proposed, none of which seems to have any decisive advantage over the others, and virtually all of which have to face substantial counterarguments. In the face of this situation, some have resorted to a belief in "multiple pressures," a formula that is untestable and that absolves its adopters from doing any serious work.

Proposed selective pressures in earlier work included communal hunting and the making of tools. Nowadays, few if any evolutionists support these suggestions (see introduction to Hurford, Studdert-Kennedy, & Knight, 1998). Communal hunting is carried out by a number of species without benefit of language, while tool-making (and even instruction in tool-making) has been found to be performed through observation and imitation, rather than verbally, by the preliterate hunters and gatherers, who, we assume (perhaps even correctly), form the best models for the behavior of our remote ancestors (Gibson & Ingold, 1993). Moreover, since these proposals were first made, it has been found that a number of other species use tools and hunt communally without benefit of language.

## Social Pressures

Since Humphrey (1976) suggested that the likeliest driving force behind increased cognition and language was intraspecific competition, the search for a selective pressure has focused on the "Machiavellian strategies" (attempts to deceive others to the deceiver's advantage) and high degree of social sophistication found among primates generally, and in particular among the great apes. The line of reasoning went as follows: When (presumably among australopithecines) social life grew more complex, intelligence increased to cope with these complexities, until either our ancestors became clever enough to invent language (Donald, 1991) or language spontaneously emerged to satisfy some social function. However, as was shown in the section on "The Continuity Issue and Descent," the nature of life for australopithecines and early *Homo* was not such as to encourage social complexities that might have required language for their solution (indeed, most complexities of human society are introduced by our possession of language, rather than serving to resolve such complexities).

Despite this fact, much work since 1990 has seen some kind of social pressure as being the main force driving the evolution of language. It has been proposed that language evolved for intergroup gossip as a substitute for grooming (Dunbar, 1993); as a consequence of theory-of-mind development (Kwistout, 2006; Worden, 1998); as a way of competing for female choice (Miller, 1997); or as a part of some ritual (Deacon, 1997; Knight, 1998). Some of these proposals, such as competition for female choice, run up against a problem that also confronts tool use and hunting theories; since similar pressures have operated on many other species, why is it that none of these species has even begun to develop language? But virtually all of them fail to deal with what one might call the problem of initial functionality.

This problem can be best understood if we examine in greater detail one of the more coherent (and more popular) selective pressure theories, that of Dunbar (1993, 1996). Dunbar's theory has the advantage of being based on an assumption that would, if correct, provide a pressure unique to human ancestors. Extrapolating from a strong correlation among primates between intelligence level and group size, Dunbar assumes that at some stage of human evolution, group size grew to such an extent that time required for the requisite amount of peer grooming became excessive and a substitute had to be found; this substitute had to be gossip, since only gossip about other group members would be interesting enough to fulfill the grooming function. Although there is no direct evidence of variation in human group size at different stages of evolution, let us grant Dunbar's assumption.

However, for any behavioral trait to become fixed, it must from its inception fulfill some function that results in increased fitness for those that possess the trait. To discharge any function whatsoever, language has to have at least a handful of meaningful signs; indeed, at its very beginning, it could not have had more than a handful of such signs. If that handful did not immediately confer some adaptive benefit, why would additional signs ever have developed? In the case of gossip, it would have to have been possible immediately to produce information that would be of interest to other group members. This presents Dunbar's proposal with at least three obstacles. First, there is no item of gossip of any possible interest that could be conveyed with only a handful of signs. Second, the signs would have to be concatenated in some way, which presupposes the existence of syntax, but there is wide agreement (even among those with opposing views on protolanguage; see later) that syntax could not have existed at this stage of development. Third, signs capable of dealing with social interactions are for the most part not susceptible to ostensive definition, and hence are extremely unlikely to have been the first signs to be produced.

While the foregoing obstacles apply particularly to the "grooming/gossip" theory, the problem of initial functionality applies generally. Nor is it the only problem that language-evolution theories must face. Other problems would have had to be overcome, including that of selfishness (i.e., why would an individual give away information, a valuable commodity, with no sure prospect of reward?) and that of "cheap tokens" (Zahavi, 1977; i.e., why would a species capable of deception trust things as easy to produce as words?)?

But perhaps the most fundamental error of selective-pressure hypotheses is their failure to consider how symbolic signs could have been born. Symbolism—a sign's capacity to refer to classes of entities in the absence of any physical representative of those classes—is not only the most fundamental property of language but something that is entirely absent from other species, as was well explained by Deacon (1997). The mere idea that objects in the real world can be identified by means of arbitrary symbols seems to be completely alien to nonhuman minds, yet at the same time is so taken for granted

by human minds that its acquisition by some ancestor of ours seems to require no special explanation and, in consequence, is almost universally ignored. Yet if this is the most neglected, it is also perhaps the most central feature in language evolution, without which no theory in this field can hope to be adequate.

### An Alternative Form of Pressure

The discrediting of tool-making and hunting hypotheses led a large majority of investigators to neglect environmental, as opposed to social, scenarios for the emergence of language. This abandonment was premature, for several reasons. Subsistence provides, for any species, a concern at least as vital to fitness as social relations; indeed, it forms the bedrock upon which all other behaviors rest. Moreover, the fact that primate inheritance and a focus on the social seemed to dovetail nicely with one another led investigators to neglect the crucial differences between ape and prehuman niches and ecologies detailed in the section on "The Continuity Issue and Descent"; hardly any work in the last two decades even attempts to integrate language into the overall process of human evolution, of which it forms a crucial and indispensible part. Also, the rejection of environmental factors renders nugatory any attempt to apply that keystone of biological research, the comparative method. As we have seen, comparison of communication is fruitless. But comparison of niches, subsistence methods and their consequences, ignoring degrees of genetic relatedness, is a potentially rewarding process, especially if we rephrase the question "How did language begin?" as "How did symbolic signs begin?"

A scenario designed to answer this question in terms of niche construction and consequent foraging patterns is elaborated in Bickerton (2009, 2010); the result is claimed to pass the tests of immediate functionality, selfishness, and cheap tokens discussed earlier.

### The Earliest Stages of Language

What was language like at its inception? A minority of scholars assumes that it emerged in something not unlike its present condition (see section on "Putative Universals"). However, most in the field hold that the first medium distinguishable from an NCS was strikingly different from human language as we know it today. In other words, there was some form of protolanguage (Bickerton, 1990) that preceded, and subsequently developed into, true language. It is widely assumed that such a protolanguage developed in some human ancestor and that true language is a relatively recent development, probably limited to modern humans. However, there has been considerable controversy over the precise nature of this protolanguage, the disputants falling into two clearly delineated camps.

## A Compositional Protolanguage

As originally proposed by Bickerton (1990), protolanguage would have been compositional from the beginning, consisting of a gradually increasing number of words that would have been linked together paratactically, like beads on a string, on a purely ad hoc basis, rather than through a set of regular syntactic processes like that which assembles words in true language. Several lines of argument appear to support such a hypothesis. Normal processes of evolution could hardly have produced anything with the complexity of modern language, so a more primitive antecedent seemed intrinsically plausible. Chomsky's (1980) distinction between conceptual and computational aspects of language (roughly, lexicon and syntax) was supported by evidence from early-stage pidgins (Bickerton, 1981) and early child language (Brown, 1970), suggesting that these two aspects are dissociable and that words can be strung together without any syntactic structure. Early-stage pidgins provide the strongest evidence, since these are spontaneously developed by adults who have a fully developed language faculty but insufficient exposure to any potential common language to master its syntax. The experience of speakers who have tried to acquire a first language after the critical period (such as Genie; Curtiss, 1977) and who have consequently been unable to acquire full syntax suggests that protolanguage is more robust than modern human language, and might therefore be phylogenetically older. Finally, apes under instruction (Savage-Rumbaugh, 1986; Terrace, Pettito, Sanders, & Bever, 1979) have been able to acquire lexical items; however, without further explicit instruction (beyond passive exposure) they can also string such items together to form elementary, unstructured propositions.

An oft-debated issue is whether protolanguage was signed or spoken. Since the notion of an original signed language (which had been around for centuries) was revived by Hewes (1973), it has been supported by a number of writers (Armstrong, Stokoe, & Wilcox, 1995; Corballis, 2002). However, there is no decisive evidence for either a spoken or a signed protolanguage, and a decision either way would do little or nothing to resolve the more crucial issues in language evolution, such as how symbolic signs evolved or how syntax evolved. Since today signed and spoken languages can be acquired with equal ease, we may suppose that language is modality neutral and may always have been so. Indeed, for all we know, the original protolanguage may well have employed a mixture of sounds and manual gestures.

A further issue involves whether we can reify protolanguage as an autonomous concept or whether it should be decomposed into a series of stages culminating in true language. This might seem merely the old argument of "lumpers" versus "splitters," but it turns to some extent on the validity of the developmental stages that are hypothesized. Jackendoff (2002) sees a total of nine distinct stages between an alingual condition and full language. Bickerton (1990, 2009) sees only two significant stages, a protolanguage whose constituents are linked by the operation "sequence" (beads on a string) and a language whose constituents are linked by the operation "merge" (Chomsky, 1995, a process that builds integrated, hierarchical structures). However, the most radical proposal is that protolanguage was not compositional but holophrastic.

## A Holophrastic Protolanguage

The notion of a holophrastic protolanguage was originally proposed by Wray (1998, 2000). A holophrastic protolanguage would consist of constituents that represented a rough equivalent of sentences rather than words; a unit like *tebima* might represent something like "Give that to her"—in other words, would be roughly equivalent to a sentence, rather than to a word—but could not be broken down into parts; there would originally be no segment of *tebima* that meant, in isolation, "give" or "this" or "her." However, once a stock of such holophrases had been assembled, chance similarities between segments would be noted and interpreted. For instance, if the same segment, say *ma*, should turn up in two or more holophrases that included references to a singular feminine third person with the thematic role of "Patient"—the recipient of some action—then it would be easy to interpret *ma* as an equivalent of "her." Holophrases would then continue to be analyzed until they finally disappeared into a series of discrete segments, compositionally linked. In other words, instead of words being linked to form sentences, eventually giving rise to modern syntax, sentences would appear as an emergent property of the dissolution of holophrases.

The holophrastic proposal naturally drew support from those who believed that there was a continuity in the communication of nonhumans and humans. After all, the sense of many signals in NCSs could be better conveyed by a sentence than by any single word: "I'm-higher-than-you-in-the-pecking-order," "Look-out-a-predator-is-appro aching," "I-want-to-mate-with-you." This apparent resemblance between holophrases and NCS signals seemed to promise a direct link between NCSs and language; the relevant NCSs simply had to multiply and come under volitional control, after which an automatic decomposition would complete the process. The notion of a holophrastic protolanguage also appealed to those computational linguists who sought to model language evolution; many of these had assumed initial forms some of which were holophrastic, and which, in the process of iterated learning, gradually decomposed into discrete compositional units (Briscoe, 2003).

However, any resemblance between holophrases and NCSs is only apparent. Although this is seldom if ever made explicit, the resemblance depends on two tacit assumptions. The first assumption is that for any given holophrase or NCS signal there is only one permissible paraphrase in human language. This has to be so; otherwise, there would be no agreement on the meaning of segments that might ultimately qualify as words. Utterances would be like the vervet eagle alarm, which could be interpreted as "Look out, here comes an eagle!" or "Danger from the air!" or "Quick, hide in the bushes" (would "come" and "eagle," or "danger" and "air," or "hide" and "bushes" fall out from analysis of such a signal?). The second assumption is that holophrastic speakers could already interpret an arbitrary sound or gesture as symbolizing an entity or action in the real world. There is not the slightest suggestion of any such capacity in any nonhuman species. Symbolism cannot just be taken for granted, as holophrastic advocates apparently assume; it had to evolve, just like anything else. And if, despite everything, symbolism had already been present when language began, why would human ancestors not have gone directly to a compositional language? Additional arguments against a holophrastic protolanguage are given in Tallerman (2008); for an overview of the entire debate, see Arbib and Bickerton (2008).

## Development to Full Language

However language began, and whatever form its first manifestations took, there is a broad consensus that its earliest stages fell considerably short of the richness and complexity found universally in language today. But the question of how language reached this level has been answered in a variety of ways. Disagreements involve the extent to which natural selection determined the ultimate structure of language, whether linguistic universals could have been incorporated into the genome, and even whether processes quite distinct from natural selection could have shaped the ultimate structure of language.

### The Role of Natural Selection

That language evolved in strict obedience to the laws of natural selection was first argued by Pinker and Bloom (1990; see also Pinker 1994, 2003); if the eye and other complex organs had evolved in accordance with those laws, then surely something as complex yet as fully functional as language must have a similar history. However plausible this analogy might seem, it runs into problems if, as Pinker and Bloom did, one assumes that specific rules, principles, and properties of language were individually selected for. How, for example, would features such as Subjacency or the Empty Category Principle enhance the fitness of those who possessed them as compared with the fitness of those who did not? (Jenkins, 2000; Lightfoot, 1991, 2000).

It could be argued that particular features were not selected for per se, but because in conjunction they formed a coherent and easily learnable system; any feature that contributed to such a system might have been chosen, regardless of its individual nature. Such a proposal, however, would lead away from an orthodox adaptationist view toward the position held by Deacon (1997), Christiansen and Kirby (2003), and others—that language adapts itself to accord with the properties of the human mind and so becomes easily learnable by children. Many, however, find this notion difficult to grasp. To some, it seems merely an inversion of the doctrine of innate universals, one version of which claims that the properties of the human mind determine the properties of language (Chomsky, 1968). To others, it seems an abuse of the term "adaptation," since it reifies an abstraction, language, and attributes to that reification adaptive capacities that in reality can belong only to living organisms.

### Putative Universals

Clearly allied to the notion of adaptation is the debate over whether linguistic universals can be instantiated in the genome. As noted earlier (see section on "Language and General Intelligence"), the issue of whether there can be innate universals of language preceded serious study of language evolution and thus inevitably colored the debate over whether universals were in fact evolvable. Deacon (1997) gave a negative answer to the latter question, mainly on the grounds that languages constituted a "moving target changing too rapidly for their properties to be assimilated through a "Baldwin effect" (Hinton & Nowlan, 1987) or any other means.

Under these circumstances, while language as a whole (and perhaps some of its supporting elements, such as a highly developed vocal tract) might have served as a target, more detailed features of language would have been invisible to natural selection. However, this position seems to depend on the rather curious view that languages are constantly changing all of their features. This is not so; different levels of language change at very different rates, with the deepest and most abstract level changing little if at all. Clearly we would expect only such relatively or absolutely unchanging properties to be incorporated in the genome—exactly the result that appears, from synchronic studies of a wide range of language, to be the case.

A somewhat different view of how universals might have been internalized is suggested in Bickerton (2009). Assuming that words predated any kind of formal linguistic structure, they would have presented the brain with just another type of information that required processing. Brains had faced similar tasks before, each time a new faculty (sight, smell, hearing, etc.) was added to the sensorium. Accordingly, similar processing methods of local and distributed storage and facilitated neural pathways for the merging of fragmentary information into structured wholes would have been deployed. In the present case, such a procedure might have taken considerable evolutionary time, since until the emergence of words, brains had had to deal only with information from outside the brain. In other words, linguistic universals (hence most of the post-protolanguage development of language) would stem neither from the development of a novel and dedicated organ (as assumed in Chomsky, 1968 and subsequent work) nor by Baldwinian assimilation of empirical linguistic phenomena (as proposed by Kirby, 1998, among others) but from autonomous reorganization of preexisting brain functions along lines suggested by Szathmary (2001). Viewed from this perspective, Chomsky's "knowledge of grammar" would be a case of "knowing how..." rather than "knowing that... ": a series of algorithms for the creation of sentences from lexical and semantic

material. But clearly, any such proposal is, at the moment, no more than a promissory note that needs to be cashed out in terms of linguistic and neurobiological research.

## Evolution Without Selection

To some linguists, the claim that language evolved through natural selection has always been dubious. According to Chomsky (1968), "It is perfectly safe to attribute this development to 'natural selection,' so long as we realize that there is no substance to this assertion, that it amounts to nothing more than a belief that there is some naturalistic explanation for these phenomena." One reason for this choice is Chomsky's belief that language is primarily a cognitive/computational device and only secondarily an instrument of communication.

Subsequently, Chomsky has subscribed (in Hauser, Chomsky, & Fitch, 2002) to the belief that the only purely linguistic component of language could be Merge, the recursive procedure that, according to the Minimalist Program (Chomsky, 1995), was basic to syntax. He was willing to concede that other components of language could have been derived by humans or nonhumans for nonlinguistic purposes through natural selection—even that recursive processes might have been originally developed by other species for some nonlinguistic function—but insisted that the Merge process first developed brain internally, being used for purposes of thought, and was only later "externalized" and employed for communicative purposes (Chomsky, 2010).

An interesting consequence of this line of thought is that, since all necessary components of language are assumed to have been present before its emergence, and since Merge was the only component then needed to complete the structure of language as we know it, language must have emerged fully fledged in its present condition, and even the notion of a protolanguage must be fallacious. "What would a *non-compositional* protolanguage be, once you strip *words as we know them* from their internal structure and their compositional valence?" (Piatelli-Palmerini, 2010, p. 161, emphasis added). Answers can be found in any early-stage pidgin or the speech of any child under about 2 years of age; such a protolanguage would not have to be "non-compositional," and "words as we know them" obviously bear no relation to "words as they were 2 million years ago."

But in any case Chomsky's proposals suffer from a crucial and potentially fatal problem. Chomsky assumes, correctly, that there are "critical differences between human conceptual systems and symbolic/representational systems of other animals" (Chomsky, 2010, p. 57), and that Merge can operate only the first of these. But this merely replaces one evolutionary question with another: Where did the human conceptual system come from? The most plausible answer seems to be that human cognition and human language developed in tandem, by a process of reciprocal coevolution that can only have taken place if language was "externalized" from the very beginning (for an admittedly brief sketch as to how this might have come about, see Bickerton, 2009, Ch. 10).

## Conclusion and Future Directions

As the foregoing suggests, the field of language evolution remains, a century and a half after the publication of *The Origin of Species*, a contentious one, still with areas where little can be said that is not at least partly speculative. But we can now claim that we know much better what it is that we do not know.

An ongoing problem has been uncertainty about exactly what has evolved. There is as yet no consensus among linguists as to the nature of language itself, and as Jackendoff 's (2010) title clearly states, "Your theory of language evolution depends on your theory of language." Unfortunately, with several contrasting theories of grammar still in the field, agreement cannot be expected any time soon.

It seems likely that any progress here will be triggered not by new findings or conjectures in linguistics itself but from a growing understanding of how the brain produces and understands sentences. After all, the best grammar should be the one that most faithfully mirrors the actual operations that the brain performs in the course of these tasks. But research summarized in Chapters 11 through 14 of Bickerton and Szathmary (2009) indicates that we are still some distance away from being able to construct, for example, a flowchart that would show, millisecond by millisecond, the sequence of brain regions activated when an experimental subject utters a novel sentence, with a similar chart for the neural activity of a recipient.

One reason why language evolution is "the hardest problem in science" (Christiansen & Kirby, 2003) is that, unlike almost any other problem, it is not amenable to experimental testing. It would be easy to design an experiment that would determine the extent to which the structure of language is biologically determined, and thus resolve a debate that has raged unchecked for more than half a century: Take a dozen or so children at birth, isolate them, supply them with a basic stock of individual words, but prevent them from ever hearing any combination of words in any language. A failure to acquire anything beyond those individual words (an unlikely finding) would prove that language structure is culturally learned; any other result would show the extent to which linguistic capacities do not depend on the internalization of any model but must be biologically based. Unfortunately, any such experiment would be almost universally regarded as inhumane.

There have, of course, been a number of "natural experiments"—situations where, through sheer historical accident, input to a particular generation of children has been reduced and/or deformed. Such situations include those that resulted in creole languages (Bickerton, 1981) or new sign languages, such as that which emerged in Nicaragua in the 1980s (Kegl et al., 1999). However, in creolization it is difficult to rule out input from preexisting languages, while Nicaraguan Sign Language, though arguably freer from such influences, awaits a comprehensive comparison between signed and spoken languages that would allow generalizations valid for both to be made.

Experiments can be, and indeed are, carried out by computer scientists in the form of computer simulations (see Bickerton & Szathmary, 2009, Ch. 18, for overviews of this highly productive field; see also Briscoe, 2003). However, doubts inherent in any form of study that attempts to replicate mechanically the behaviors of complex biological organisms have been augmented here by choice of initial conditions and modes of interaction between agents that seem, to many outside the field, overly artificial and unrealistic. Similar experiments involving robots (e.g. Steels, 2003) hold out much more promise, since robots have a degree of autonomy denied to computers and could at least in principle be presented with real-life problems, the solution of which might require some form of language-like behavior.

In addition, there are a couple of proposals relevant to language evolution that might be empirically testable. One involves the nature of the original protolanguage. Human subjects could be equipped with minimal vocabularies of either compositional or holophrastic units and could then interact with one another in a variety of simulated situations such as might have been encountered by human ancestral species, to test the communicative efficacy of different modes and vocabulary sets. A start in this direction has been made by Bowie (2008), and hopefully further studies will follow.

Another proposal involves the stimulus for the first step toward human language. Bickerton (2009) hypothesizes that it was recruitment for confrontational scavenging of megafauna, a procedure that necessarily involved transfer of factual information otherwise inaccessible to the receiver—in other words, displacement, one of the most basic properties of language. Work by Heinrich (1991) suggests that a similar recruitment strategy is actually employed by immature ravens. Whether prehumans developed such a strategy cannot, of course, be directly tested, but its overall feasibility, and the possibility that it could introduce displacement into an NCS, is currently in the process of being tested for ravens (Fitch, Hubert, & Bugnyar, 2010).

This brings us to the most central (and certainly the most easily remedied) weakness in current language evolution theory. The evolution of language forms part (arguably the most crucial part) of human evolution. Yet hardly any work on language evolution even attempts to integrate language into the broader process. Research in the field is still overwhelmingly "primate-centric," to use Pepperberg's (2005) term, despite much work on the substantial cognitive capacities of corvids and psittacids (with their potential to help define minimal prerequisites for a language-ready state), and despite the problematic status of ape models discussed earlier. While caution should clearly be exercised in making claims about the cognitive capacities of such species, further studies should clarify what it might mean to be "language-ready," making it potentially possible to determine at what stage human ancestors achieved this level. Moreover, though the fossil and archaeological records for ancestral human species are meager, they do exist, and they can potentially be useful for more than mere attempts to ascertain the date by which full language was established—about the only use to which they have so far been put (and still a pretty ambiguous one at that).

Given a refocusing on human ancestry, an increase in types of experiment, and significant advances in neurobiology and paleoanthropology, we can reasonably expect significant progress, if not a final resolution, by the bicentenary of Darwin's ground-breaking work.

# References

Anderson, K. I. (2004) Elbow-joint morphology as a guide to forearm function and foraging behaviour in mammalian carnivores. *Zoological Journal of the Linnean Society, 142*(1), 91–104.

Arbib, M. A., & Bickerton, D. (Eds.). (2008). Holophrasis versus compositionality in the emergence of protolanguage. [Special issue] *Interaction Studies 9*(1).

Armstrong, D. F., Stokoe, W. C., & Wilcox, S. E. (1995). *Gesture and the nature of language.* Cambridge, England: Cambridge University Press.

Arnold, K., & Zuberbuhler, K. (2006). Language evolution: Semantic combination in primate calls. *Nature, 441,* 303.

Berger, L., & Clarke, R. B. (1995). Eagle involvement in accumulation of the Taung child fauna. *Journal of Human Evolution, 29,* 275–299.

Bickerton, D. (1981). *Roots of language.* Ann Arbor, MI: Karoma Press.

Bickerton, D. (1984). The language hierogram hypothesis. *Behavioral and Brain Sciences, 7,* 173–221.

Bickerton, D. (1990). *Language and species.* Chicago: University of Chicago Press.

Bickerton, D. (2009). *Adam's tongue: How humans made language, how language made humans.* New York: Hill & Wang.

Bickerton, D. (2010). On two incompatible theories of language evolution. In R. K. Larsen, V. Depress, & H. Yamakido (Eds.), *The evolution of human language* (pp. 199–210). Cambridge, England: Cambridge University Press.

Bickerton, D., & Szathmary, E. (2009). *Biological foundations and origins of syntax.* Cambridge, MA: MIT Press.

Bowie, J. (2008). Proto-discourse and the emergence of compositionality. *Interaction Studies, 9*(1), 18–33.

Briscoe, T. (Ed.). (2003). *Linguistic evolution through language acquisition: Formal and computational models.* Cambridge, England: Cambridge University Press.

Brown, R. (1970). *A first language.* Cambridge, MA: Harvard University Press.

Cheney, D., & Seyfarth, R. (1990). *How monkeys see the world.* Chicago: Chicago University Press.

Chomsky, N. (1968). *Language and mind.* New York: Harcourt, Brace & World.

Chomsky, N. (1980). *Rules and representations.* New York: Columbia University Press.

Chomsky, N. (1995). *The minimalist program.* Cambridge, MA: MIT Press.

Chomsky, N. (2010). Some simple evo-devo theses: How true might they be for language? In R. K. Larsen, V. Depress, & H. Yamakido (Eds.), *The evolution of human language* (pp. 45–62). Cambridge, England: Cambridge University Press.

Christiansen, M. H., & Kirby, S. (Eds.). (2003). *Language evolution.* Oxford, England: Oxford University Press.

Corballis, M. C. (2002) *From hand to mouth: The origins of language.* Princeton, NJ: Princeton University Press.

Curtiss, S. (1977) *Genie: A psycholinguistic study of a modern-day "wild child."* New York: Academic Press.

Deacon, T. (1997). *The symbolic species.* New York: Norton.

De Waal, F. B. M. (1982). *Chimpanzee politics: Power and sex among apes.* London: Cape.

Donald, M. (1991). *Origins of the modern mind.* Cambridge, MA: Harvard University Press.

Dunbar, R. I. M. (1993). Co-evolution of neocortical size, group size and language in primates. *Behavioral and Brain Sciences, 16,* 681–735.

Dunbar, R. I. M. (1996). *Grooming, gossip and the evolution of language.* London: Faber & Faber.Evans, C. S., Evans, L., & Marler, P. (1993). On the meaning of alarm calls: functional reference in an avian vocal system. *Animal Behaviour, 46*(1), 23–38.

Fauconnier, G., & Turner, M . (2008). The origin of language as a product of the evolution of modern cognition. In B. Laks et al. (Eds.), *Origin and evolution of languages: Approaches, models, paradigms (pp.* 1–33). London: Equinox.

Fitch, W. T., Huber, L., & Bugnyar, T. (2010). Social cognition and the evolution of language: Constructing cognitive phylogenies. *Neutron, 65,* 795–814.

Gibson, K. R., & Ingold, T. (Eds.). (1993). *Tools, language and cognition in human evolution.* Cambridge, England: Cambridge University Press.

Goodall, J. (1986). *The chimpanzees of Gombe: Patterns of behavior.* Cambridge, MA: Harvard University Press.

Hauser, M. D. (1996). *The evolution of communication.* Cambridge, MA: MIT Press.

Hauser, M. D., Chomsky, N., & Fitch, W. T. (2002). The language Faculty: What is it, who has it, and how did it evolve? *Science, 298,* 1569–1579.

Heinrich, B. (1991). *Ravens in winter.* London: Vintage.

Henrich, J., & Henrich, N. (2006). Culture, evolution and the puzzle of human cooperation. *Cognitive Systems Research, 7,* 220–245.

Herman, L. M., Kuczaj, S A., & Holder, M. D. (1993). Responses to anomalous gestural sequences by a language-trained dolphin: Evidence for processing of semantic relations and syntactic information. *Journal of Experimental Psychology: General, 122*(2), 184–194.

Hewes, G. W. (1973). Primate communication and the gestural origins of language. *Current Anthropology, 14,* 5–24.

Heyes, C. M. (1998). Theory of mind in nonhuman primates. *Behavioral and Brain Sciences, 21,* 101–114.

Hinton, G. E., & Nowlan, S. J. (1987). How learning can guide evolution. *Complex Systems, 1,* 495–502.

Humphrey, N. K. (1976). The social function of intellect. In P. P. G. Bateson & R. A. Hinde (Eds.), *Growing points in ethology* (pp. 303–317). Cambridge, England: Cambridge University Press.

Hurford, J. (2007). *The origins of meaning.* Oxford, England: Oxford University Press.

Hurford, J. R., Studdert-Kennedy, M., & Knight, C. (Eds.). (1998). *Approaches to the evolution of language: Social and cognitive bases.* New York: Cambridge University Press.

Jackendoff, R. (2002). *Foundations of language: Brain, meaning, grammar, evolution.* New York: Basic Books.

Jenkins, L. (2000). *Biolinguistics: Exploring the biology of language.* Cambridge, England: Cambridge University Press.

Johannson, S. (2005). *Origins of language: Constraints on hypotheses.* Amsterdam, The Netherlands: Benjamins.

Kegl, J., Senghas, A., & Coppola, M. (1999). Creation through contact: Sign language emergence and sign language change in Nicaragua. In. M. DeGraff (Ed.), *Language creation and language change: Creolization, diachrony and development (pp.* 179–238). Cambridge, MA: MIT Press.

Kirby, S. (1998). Fitness and the selective adaptation of language. In J. R. Hurford M. Studdert-Kennedy, & C. Knight (Eds.), *Approaches to the evolution of language: Social and cognitive bases* (pp. 359–383).

Knight, C. (1998). Ritual/speech coevolution: a solution to the problem of deception. In J. R. Hurford, M. Studdert-Kennedy, & C. Knight (Eds.), *Approaches to the evolution of language: Social and cognitive bases* (pp. 148–168). Cambridge, England: Cambridge University Press.

Kwisthout, J. (2006). *Joint attention, language evolution, and development.* Unpublished Master's thesis, Radboud University, Nijmegen, The Netherlands.

Lasnik, H., & Uriagereka, J. (1988). *A course in GB syntax: Lectures on binding and empty categories.* Cambridge, MA: MIT Press.

Lightfoot, D. (1991). Subjacency and sex. *Language and Communication, 11,* 67–69.

Lightfoot, D. (2000). The spandrels of the linguistic genotype. In C. Knight, M. Studdert-Kennedy, & J. R. Hurford (Eds.), *The evolutionary emergence of language: Social function and the origins of linguistic form* (pp. 231–247). Cambridge, England: Cambridge University Press.

Miller, G. F. (1997). Mate choice: From sexual cues to cognitive adaptations. In G. Cardew (Ed.), *Characterizing human psychological adaptations, Ciba Foundation Symposium 208* (pp. 71–87). New York: Wiley.

Mithen, S. (2005). *The singing Neanderthals: The origin of language, music, body and mind.* London: Weidenfeld and Nicolson.

Odling-Smee, F. J., Laland, K. N., & Feldman, M. W. (2003). *Niche construction: The neglected process in evolution.* Princeton, NJ: Princeton University Press.

Pepperberg, I. M. (1987). Acquisition of the same/different concept by an African grey parrot. *Animal Behavior and Learning, 15,* 423–432.

Pepperberg, I. M. (2005). An avian perspective on language evolution. In M. Tallerma(Ed.), *Language origins: Perspectives on evolution* (pp. 239–262). Oxford, England: Oxford University Press.

Piatelli-Palmerini, M. (2010). What is language, that it may have evolved, and what is evolution, that it may apply to language. In R. K. Larsen, V. Deprez, & H. Yamakido (Eds.), *The evolution of human language* (pp. 148–162). Cambridge, England: Cambridge University Press.

Pinker, S. (1994). *The language instinct.* New York: Harper/Collins.

Pinker, S. (2003). Language as an adaptation to the cognitive niche. In M. H. Christiansen & S. Kirby (Eds.), *Language evolution* (pp. 16–37). Oxford, England: Oxford University Press.

Pinker, S., & Bloom, P. (1990). Natural language and natural selection. *Behavioral and Brain Sciences, 13,* 707–784.

Pollick, A. S., & de Waal, F. B. M. (2007). Ape gestures and language evolution. *Proceedings of the National Academy of Sciences USA, 104*(19), 8184–8189. Cambridge, England: Cambridge University Press.

Premack, D., & Woodruff, G. (1978). Does the chimpanzee have a theory of mind? *Behavioral and Brain Sciences, 1,* 515–526.

Richerson, P. J., Boyd, R. T., & Henrich, J. (2003). Cultural evolution of human co-operation. In P. Hammerstein (Ed.), *Genetic and cultural evolution of cooperation (pp. 357–388).* Cambridge, MA: MIT Press.

Savage-Rumbaugh, S. (1986). *Ape language: from conditioned response to symbol.* New York: Columbia University Press.

Schusterman, R. J., & Krieger, K. (1984). California sea lions are capable of semantic interpretation. *Psychological Record, 34,* 3–23.

Smuts, B. B. (1985). *Sex and friendship in baboons.* Piscataway, NJ: Transaction.

Steels, L. (2003). Evolving grounded communication for robots. *Trends in Cognitive Science, 7*(7), 308–312.

Szamado, S., & Szathmary, E . (2006). Selective scenarios for the emergence of natural language. *Trends in Ecology and Evolution, 21*(10), 555–561.

Szathmary, E. (2001). The origin of the human language faculty: The language amoeba hypothesis. In J. Trabant & S. Ward (Eds.), *New essays on the origin of language* (pp. 41–54). Berlin: Walter de Gruyter.

Tallerman, M. (2008). Holophrastic protolanguage: Planning, processing, storage and retrieval. *Interaction Studies, 9*(1), 84–99.

Terrace, H. S., Pettito, L. A., Sanders, R. J., & Bever, T. G. (1979). Can an ape create a sentence? *Science, 206*, 891–900.

Tinbergen, N. (1952) "Derived" activities: Their causation, biological significance, origin and emancipation during evolution. *Quarterly Review of Biology, 27*, 1–32.

Tomasello, M. (2003). On the different origins of symbols and grammar. In M. H. Christiansen & S. Kirby (Eds.), *Language evolution (pp.* 94–110). Oxford, England: Oxford University Press.

Whiten, A ., & Byrne, R. W . (1988). Tactical deception in primates. *Behavioral and Brain Sciences, 11*, 233–244.

Wilson, E. O. (1972) Animal communication. In W. S-Y. Wang (Ed.), *The emergence of language: Development and evolution* (pp. 3–15). New York: Freeman.

Worden, R. (1998) The evolution of language from social intelligence. In J. Hurford, M. Studdert-Kennedy, & C. Knight (Eds.), *Approaches to the evolution of language: Social and cognitive bases* (pp. 148–166).

Wray, A. (1998). Protolanguage as a holistic system for social interaction. *Language and Communication, 18*, 47–67.

Wray, A. (2000). Holistic utterances in protolanguage: The link from primates to humans. In C. Knight, M. Studdert-Kennedy, & J. R. Hurford (Eds.), *The evolutionary emergence of language: Social function and the origins of linguistic form* (pp. 285–302). Cambridge, England: Cambridge University Press.

Zahavi, A. (1977). The cost of honesty (further remarks on the handicap principle). *Journal of Theoretical Biology, 67*, 603–605.

Zuberbuhler, K. (2002). A syntactic rule in forest monkey communication. *Animal Behavior, 63*, 293–299.

Zuberbuhler, K. (2005). Linguistic prerequisites in the primate lineasge. In M. Tallerman (Ed.), *Language origins* (pp. 262–282). Oxford, England: Oxford University Press.

# PART 6

# The Role for Emotion

# Emotion Perception: Putting the Face in Context

Maria Gendron, Batja Mesquita, *and* Lisa Feldman Barrett

**Abstract**

Emotion perception research is dominated by the assumption that emotions are written on the face as particular arrangements of facial actions. This face-focused paradigm assumes that posed, static configurations of facial muscle movements provide sufficient cues to emotion, such that the study of context is secondary. As a result, it has been assumed that the mechanisms for perceiving posed, static facial actions reveal the mechanisms that support emotion perception outside of the laboratory setting. In this chapter, we review this face-focused paradigm in emotion perception and contrast it with experimental findings that place the face in context. Furthermore, we question whether a posed face is ever without context, even in a lab. We discuss how features of an experiment can serve (however unintentionally) as a context that influences performance in emotion perception tasks. Based on the literature reviewed, we conclude that the study of emotion perception is necessarily contextualized, such that context not only influences emotion perception, but it might be intrinsic to seeing an emotion in the first place.

**Key Words:** emotion, perception, facial expression, context

An iconic *fear* face looks startled—eyes wide, mouth agape, and eyebrows raised. An iconic *anger* face is scowling—brows furrowed, eyes glowering, and jaw tightened. An iconic *sad* face is frowning—lips pouting, brows pulled together. These posed, exaggerated faces dominate a research paradigm in the psychology of emotion perception. Simply exposing a perceiver to one of these faces is assumed to produce an automatic "recognition" that reflects some statistical regularity in the faces that populate the emotion category, and this automatic perception is taken as evidence that there is an evolutionarily preserved capability to "decode" facial actions for their psychological meaning. Several notable experiments (Ekman, 1972, 1973; Ekman & Freisen, 1971; Ekman, Sorensen, & Friesen, 1969; Izard, 1971) within this face-focused approach have captured the attention of textbook writers and have become part of the standard curriculum in psychology.

These experiments have also captured the imagination of other academic disciplines. The face-focused approach to emotion perception (where emotional information is written on the face) guides cognitive neuroscience studies of emotion perception (e.g., Breiter, Etcoff, Whalen, Kennedy, Rauch, Buckner, et al., 1996; Phillips et al., 1997; Sprengelmeyer, Rauch, Eysel, & Przuntek, 1998; for a discussion, see Watson, 2004). Research investigating social and emotional deficits in people with mental disorders, brain lesions, and neurodegenerative disease almost exclusively relies on the face-focused approach (e.g., Kohler, Walker, Martin, Healey, & Moberg, 2010). The face-focused approach also informs government spending on security training. For example, over 3,000 TSA employees have received security training to "read" emotion in the face, in the hopes of keeping citizens safe (Weinberger, 2010). Even the popular media is enamored with this paradigm, as evidenced by television shows such as "Lie to Me" and popular science writing such as Malcolm Gladwell's *The Naked Face* (2002).

The face-focused approach to emotion perception has several key features. First, this approach views the face as transmitting evolved signals that broadcast the internal state of a target person for perceivers to see (Keltner, Ekman, Gonzaga, & Beer, 2003). Data to support this view come in several varieties: (1) descriptions of facial behaviors that occur in emotion across cultures (e.g., Scherer & Wallbott, 1994); (2) cross-cultural production of facial behaviors during the experience of emotion (e.g., "negative" facial behaviors in Japanese and American students, Ekman, 1973; for review, see Matsumoto, Keltner, Shiota, Frank, & O'Sullivan, 2008, pp. 215–216); or (3) expressions produced by congenitally blind individuals as compared to sighted individuals (e.g., Matsumoto & Willingham, 2009). In this regard, "emotion perception" is redefined as "emotion recognition."

A second aspect of the face-focused approach is that emotion perception is an innate psychological process (e.g., Schyns, Petro, & Smith, 2009). Data used to support this point come from (1) studies on cross-cultural recognition of emotion (for reviews, see Ekman, 1998; Izard, 1977; but see Russell, 1994), (2) work on the "efficiency" or automaticity of perception (e.g., Schyns et al., 2009; Tracy & Robins, 2008), (3) work on the categorical perception of emotion (e.g., Etcoff & Magee, 1992), and (4) emotion perception in infants (e.g., Hoehl & Striano, 2008; for review, see Hoehl & Striano, 2010).

A third aspect of this view is that context (i.e., information aside from the face) is not necessary for successful emotion perception. For example, seeing emotion in another person is assumed to proceed "automatically, silently, and without the benefit of language" (Izard, 1994, p. 289). In some views, emotion perception is even resistant to contextual influences (e.g., Nakamura, Buck, & Kenny, 1990). Emotion perception is assumed to proceed in a feed-forward fashion, with more complex "cognitive" processing coming online relatively late and secondary to the perceptual processing of emotional faces (for a discussion, see Vuilleumier & Pourtois, 2007).

Because of these assumptions, the face-focused approach to studying emotion perception typically presents[1] perceivers with faces that are posing exaggerated facial actions that are devoid of a bodily, vocal, or situational context. Yet in everyday life, faces move in concert with bodies and vocalizations

in a way that is typically calibrated to the situation at hand. Even proponents have noted the oddity of the face-focused experimental paradigm (e.g., Ekman & O'Sullivan, 1988). Unfortunately, much of the literature has yet to take these ecological concerns to heart—researchers routinely present posed, static faces like those from Ekman and Freisen's (1976) set to examine how accurately perceivers can categorize these disembodied, posed faces.

In this chapter, we discuss recent empirical challenges to a face-focused approach to emotion perception. We focus on research that places the face into context, demonstrating that context dramatically shapes how faces portraying emotion are processed. We also explore the idea that the typical laboratory paradigm serves as its own form of context, one that is often unintended (and unrecognized) by the experimenter. We close the chapter by discussing the implications of context-based modulation for the future of emotion perception research. We suggest that context does more than modulate emotion perception; instead, it might serve as a necessary source of information in emotion perception.

## Putting the Face in Context

Early investigations of context effects in emotion perception were motivated by relatively low "accuracy" in experiments that relied exclusively on the face (Hunt, 1941; Landis 1934). Accuracy was (and still is) defined as seeing (1) what the target intended to portray (in posed facial actions), (2) what the stimulus developer intended (in directed facial actions often based on predetermined configurations that have been described in the literature, e.g., EMFACS; Ekman & Friesen, 1982), (3) the emotion associated with the stimulus "condition" in which a target's facial actions occurred (for spontaneous facial actions), or (4) the self-reported state of the target individual (again for spontaneous facial actions). Citing a number of experiments in which perceivers failed to agree on the emotion conveyed by faces, Hunt and Landis concluded that the face does not provide reliable information about emotion for the perceiver. This conclusion led researchers to explore what information, in addition to the face, is needed for perceptions of discrete emotions like anger, sadness, and fear. These experiments, published mainly between the 1920s and 1930s, examined whether contexts such as bodies, hands, vocalizations, and situational knowledge contributed to emotion perception over and above the facial actions that they were paired with. Although this research was criticized on methodological grounds

(Ekman, Freisen, & Ellsworth, 1972), more recent, well-designed research has emerged to again raise the question of whether context is an important determinant in emotion perception. As we will see in the coming pages, this more modern research makes it clear that a face does not speak for itself, at least where emotion[2] is concerned.

## Stimulus-Based Context

One of the most obvious sources of context in studies of emotion perception is the physical array in which a face is embedded, or what we refer to as "stimulus-based" context. Some stimulus-based context derives from the target person who produced the facial actions, such as bodily posture or movement, vocalizations, and even the target's sweat. Other forms of context characterize the broader "event" in which a face appears. Studies investigating stimulus-based forms of context have examined both influence of congruent (e.g., a startled face on a fearful body) and incongruent contexts (e.g., a pouting face following an anger situation), demonstrating both facilitation and interference effects.

### BODIES

In 1935, Kline and Johannesen demonstrated that perceivers are more accurate (i.e., to select the emotion category intended by the researcher) when a face portraying emotion was presented in a congruent bodily context (compared to when the face was presented alone). These data indicated that the body helps to increase interrater agreement about the feelings of a target over information derived from the face alone. In the last few years, there has been a spike of interest in the idea that body postures are a salient cue that perceivers use to understand others' emotional states (see de Gelder, 2009). For example, when posed faces and bodies portray the same emotion category, emotion perception in the face is facilitated; when body and face are incongruent, emotion perception in the face is impaired (Meeren, van Heijnsbergen, & de Gelder, 2005). Perception of a wide-eyed face on a body adopting an angry posture was less accurate than when that same face was placed on a body adopting a fearful posture. Strikingly, event-related potential (ERP) recordings reflect the incongruence between facial and bodily portrayals of emotion as soon as 115 ms after stimulus onset. And, remarkably, bodies also provide information about emotion for nonhuman perceivers: A computer classifier trained separately on faces and bodies portraying emotion demonstrated higher classification accuracy for the two

cues combined than with either one alone (Gunes & Piccardi, 2007). There are even times when bodies dominate over faces during emotion perception. A scowl (i.e., a portrayal of *anger*) is more likely to be perceived as disgusted when it is paired with a body posture involving a soiled object (Aviezer, Hassin, Ryan, et al., 2008, Study 1) and a face portraying disgust can even by perceived as displaying a positive emotion (i.e., pride) when paired with a muscled body whose arms are raised in triumph (Aviezer, Hassin, Ryan, et al., 2008, Study 2). Not all studies have found that bodies provide incremental information over faces during emotion perception, however (e.g., Rozin, Taylor, Ross, Bennett, & Hejnadi, 2005).

Hand gestures, too, can influence emotion perception in a face (Hietanen & Leppänen, 2008). Participants were more accurate to judge scowling faces as angry when paired with congruent hand gestures (a neutral sentence signed in Finnish Sign Language in an angry manner) and were least accurate to judge anger when scowls were paired with happy hand gestures (that same sentence signed in a happy manner). Perception of neutral faces was also biased toward "anger" when paired with angry hand gestures.

### VOCALIZATIONS

The voice constitutes a second type of stimulus-based context for perception of emotion in facial actions. The voice alone is an important conduit of affective tone, most effectively conveying arousal (Bachorowski, 1999; Pittam, Gallois, & Callan, 1990) and valence to a lesser extent (Bachorowski & Owren, 2008; Pereira, 2000). Importantly, vocal depictions shape emotion perception based on facial actions (e.g., de Gelder & Vroomen, 2000; Massaro & Egan, 1996; for a review, see de Gelder et al., 2006).[3] For example, perceivers judge ambiguous facial actions (i.e., a morph between a smiling "happy" face and a frowning "sad" face) in line with the affective value conveyed by vocalizations (i.e., prosody conveying sadness or happiness) even when they are told to judge the face alone (de Gelder & Vroomen, 2000). The effect of prosody on emotion perception in a face is most robust when the face is ambiguous (i.e., does not portray a single emotion in a caricatured manner; de Gelder & Vroomen, 2000), neutral (Massaro & Egan, 1996), or visually noisy (Collignon et al., 2008), although prosody also primes judgments of faces portraying congruent emotional content (Pell, 2005). Additional work is needed to clarify whether the effects of vocal prosody reflect affect congruence or a more specific discrete emotion congruence effect. Future work could use stimuli that are controlled for valence and arousal (e.g., fear and disgust in Phillips et al., 1998) to evaluate whether congruence or interference effects occur when vocal portrayals matched in affect, but not emotion, accompany facial actions.

Neuroimaging studies suggest that facial and vocal information are integrated in a variety of brain regions involved in perception. For example, facial and vocal portrayals of fear and disgust separately produced an increase in activation within the superior temporal gyrus, inferior posterior temporal gyrus, middle temporal gyrus, and medial frontal cortex (Phillips et al., 1998). Congruent combinations of negative facial and vocal cues produced an increase in activation in the left amygdala and right fusiform and several other structures in the distributed face-processing network (Dolan, Morris, & de Gelder, 2001). However, positive facial and vocal congruency produced increases in a distinct network of regions (i.e., left superior parietal lobule, the left medial parietal cortex, the left superior frontal gyrus, and the right anterior cingulate cortex). In another study, brain activity in some of these same regions—the medial prefrontal cortex (MPFC) and left superior temporal sulcus (STS) was linked to the category of emotion being perceived, regardless of the modality in which the cues occured (Peelen, Atkinson, & Vuilleumier, 2010). The amygdala, on the other hand, appears to be particularly important to the processing of combined facial and vocal cues. When startled faces portraying fear were accompanied by a sentence spoken in a fearful tone, perceivers judged the face as more negative than when that same face was presented alone, and these judgments were correlated with amygdala activation, which the authors interpret as evidence that the amygdala computes affective meaning based on multiple cues (Ethofer et al., 2007). It is also possible, however, that the faces were unfamiliar and ambiguous (i.e., not clearly indicative of one discrete emotion) to perceivers (Somerville & Whalen, 2006) and the vocal cues made their psychological meaning even more uncertain. Similar effects have been demonstrated in nonhuman primates, such that the same neurons in the central nucleus of the amygdala fired to the presentation of vocalizations and facial actions representing aggressive threat, scream, or coo (Kuraoka & Nakamura, 2007), which are thought to be homologous with expressions in humans (Parr & Waller, 2006).

Some work has investigated the time course of vocalization context effects, with discrepant results.

Research using magnetoencephalography (MEG) demonstrates that the integration of voices and faces portraying emotion occurs within 250 ms after stimulus onset in the superior temporal sulcus (Hagan et al., 2009).[4] Yet other data suggest that the time frame of prosody effects is much slower than 250 ms. In an implicit priming task where prosodic cues preceded faces, only vocalizations longer than 600 ms produced facilitation in judgments of a congruent emotional faces (Pell, 2005). It is unclear what this time constraint means, but one possibility is that despite early integration in the STS, behavioral facilitation will only occur with stimuli of sufficiently long duration, perhaps because conceptual knowledge based on vocalizations determines whether the emotion judgment will be affected. Alternatively, a longer presentation duration might only be important for instances when vocalizations and faces are not presented simultaneously. This would suggest that distinct mechanisms might be responsible for context effects based on simultaneous versus sequential presentation of cues.

## CHEMOSIGNALS

Even a target person's sweat can influence perception of emotion from the face (Zhou & Chen, 2009). For example, researchers collected sweat from target individuals while they viewed videos designed to induce fear or happiness. A second group of individuals then sniffed this sweat as they were completing an emotion perception task. Perceivers demonstrated better accuracy for the perception of startled "fear" faces when sniffing the "fearful" sweat compared to those sniffing the "happy" sweat. Interestingly, perceivers could not distinguish between the two types of sweat via self-report, suggesting this was not an explicit conceptual priming effect. This study did not investigate whether this facilitation might be driven by the quantity of sweat perceivers were exposed to (sweat was not measured, only collected on a gauze pad under the arms of participants). Furthermore, it is possible that sweat influences the perception of affect, rather than the perception of discrete emotion categories (given that happiness and fear differ in their basic affective quality).

## SITUATIONS

In the 1910s and 1920s, Lev Kuleshov performed filmmaking "experiments" that famously demonstrated how situational context influences the emotion perceived in another person's facial actions. He spliced the same neutral expression with different scenes that were emotional in nature, leading audiences to believe that the expression on the actor's face was changing. With no "signal" present in the face, perceivers still saw emotion when the context called for it. In fact, audiences raved about the superb acting in the film. More recently, the "Kuleshov effect" has proved to be somewhat more complex. When neutral faces were paired with common causes of emotion, such as missing a train, participants made judgments that reflected either the situation or the face, in equivalent amounts (Carrera-Levillain & Fernández-Dols, 1994). When the situation was more extreme, such as brake failure on a mountain pass, the "neutral" facial behaviors tended to dominate the judgment—perceivers overwhelmingly saw that face as neutral.

Other experiments investigating the influence of situational effects on emotion perception are as old as the first studies on the Kuleshov effect. For example, two different sets of perceivers judged spontaneous facial actions in infants that were either isolated from the context or paired with the eliciting situation (Sherman, 1927). Perceivers generated up to 25 different emotion labels for a given set of spontaneous facial actions in infants when they were presented in isolation. Agreement was higher for the perceivers who judged the facial actions in their eliciting circumstances (e.g., without context 15% of perceivers saw "fear," with context 65% did) (see also Munn, 1940). These experiments have been critiqued based on their methods (see Ekman et al., 1972), but more recent, better controlled, studies confirm that perceivers agree more on the emotion conveyed by a face when the facial actions are placed in a congruent context than when they are presented alone (Carroll & Russell 1996; Knudsen & Muzekari, 1983). Apparently, context can diminish the ambiguity (i.e., lack of interrater agreement about the emotional meaning) of posed facial actions, even when the actions depict highly caricatured expressions as in recent experiments.

A number of findings also point to a situational modulation of judgments when facial actions and the situation are "incongruent." For example, participants asked to make emotion judgments based on combinations of incongruent situational descriptions and facial actions made 55.7% of judgments consistent with the situation and 31.6% consistent with the facial behaviors (Goodenough & Tinker, 1931). These data suggest that the situation may be a stronger cue when it is inconsistent with information from a face. This general finding was replicated using bodily and situational

information conveyed by a visual scene (Munn, 1940), film clips (Goldberg, 1951), and video of the actual eliciting circumstances (Sherman, 1927). More recently, this finding has received further support (Fernandez-Dols, Sierra, & Ruiz-Belda, 1993; Fernandez-Dols, Wallbot & Sanchez, 1991, Study 2; Spignesi & Shor, 1981; Wallbott, 1988a, Study 2; Wallbott, 1988b). For example, portrayals of anger are more likely to be perceived as fearful when paired with the description of a dangerous situation (Carroll & Russell, 1996, Study 1). Yet other studies have failed to show that contextual information can override information in the face in driving emotion judgments (Fernandez-Dols et al., 1991, Study 1, 3; Nakamura et al., 1990; Wallbott, 1988a, Study 1; for a review see, Fernandez-Dols & Carroll, 1997).[5] Situational information tends to dominate perception of emotion in faces both when situations are common, everyday (Carrera-Levillain & Fernández-Dols, 1994) and even when situations are more ambiguous (i.e., contain less source clarity) than the exaggerated facial actions being perceived (Carroll & Russell, 1996, Study 3). This integration of situational context and facial actions also appears to develop over the lifespan, with children (ages 4–10) using situational over facial information for all emotions portrayals except surprise (Widen & Russell, 2010). Other data suggests that older children (third grade) are most accurate when both types of cues are present, and younger children (preschool) demonstrate advantages for stories (situational information) over faces portraying emotion (Reichenbach & Masters, 1983).

The use of situational context might be enhanced by the epistemic goal to perceive emotion as opposed to affect. For example, informationally irrelevant context is automatically encoded when perceivers were asked to judge the emotion in posed faces (i.e., "Is this person afraid or disgusted?") but not when they were asked to perceive affect (i.e., "Would you approach or avoid this person?"), suggesting that the structural configuration of faces carries information about the affective state of the target, but processing a face in context is necessary for perceiving emotion (Barrett & Kensinger, 2010). (This is consistent with earlier work showing that perceivers use basic affective dimensions like valence and arousal rather than discrete categories of emotion to understand posed facial behaviors in isolation; Russell & Bullock, 1986; Schlosberg, 1952.) Interestingly, perceivers' memory for the situational context was just as strong as memory for the focal face itself during emotion perception, suggesting that faces and contexts are processed configurally during emotion perception. (For related results, see Frühholz, Fehr, & Herrmann, 2009; Warner & Shields, 2009.)

The impact of situational context during emotion perception extends beyond explicit judgments of emotion to the gaze pattern used for faces. Perceivers' visual fixations on a face reflect the larger context (including the body) in which that face is embedded (Aviezer, Hassin, Ryan, et al., 2008) suggesting that the context changes which facial features are visually salient.

The neural responses that realize emotion perception are also shaped by situational context. Neural activity associated with a surprised face preceded by a negative sentence was greater in ventral regions of the amygdala, in comparison to when a surprise face was preceded by a positive sentence (Kim et al., 2004). Amygdala activity was also modulated by the congruence of a situational context and facial actions in a recent demonstration of the Kuleshov effect (Mobbs et al., 2006). A network of regions associated with processing the "emotionality" of a face (i.e., ACC, left STS, right STS, right amygdala, and the bilateral temporal pole) was more engaged when a face was presented following an "emotional" video compared to a "neutral" video. Incongruent context revealed specific activity in the ventromedial prefrontal cortex, whereas the combination of a fearful face and negative context revealed activity in the right amygdala, fusiform gyrus, and bilateral temporal pole and insula. It is believed that this network of regions works together to instantiate an emotion percept based on both facial actions and the context that accompanies them. Similarly, visual regions such as bilateral inferior occipital, bilateral fusiform, right inferior frontal gyrus, as well as left amygdala were engaged when participants were asked to match an emotional face to a context (Sommer, Döhnel, Meinhardt, & Hajak, 2008), suggesting that these regions play a role in integrating situational context and facial actions when the goal is to produce a coherent emotional percept. Amygdala activation was related to the goal to perceive emotion based on context and facial actions, because when these same stimuli were presented but were incidental to a color-matching task, amygdala activity did not differ from a control condition. Taken together, these findings suggest that when the epistemic goal is to perceive emotion, neural activity in regions involved in the perceptual processing of faces is shaped by the context in which faces are embedded. Since context modulates the same regions that are typically associated with the formation of an emotional percept to begin with, it can be argued that context is integral to the emotional percept itself, rather than a postperceptual decision process.

## OTHER FACES

Finally, other faces serve as another strong form of stimulus-based context in emotion perception, even when those other faces are irrelevant to the task at hand. For example, in an early study designed to examine "social context," perceivers were presented with a line drawing of two faces oriented toward one another (Cline, 1956). The faces depicted either a low-arousal negative emotion ("glum"), a high-arousal negative emotion ("frown"), or high-arousal positive emotion ("smile"). Participants assigned a different meaning to the face depending on the other face it was paired with. For example, participants perceived smiles as bolder when paired with the low-arousal "glum" expression than when paired with the high-arousal "frown" expression. In more recent experiments, perceivers judged faces as more intense when they followed with several faces of opposite valence (e.g., a frowning face following a smiling face) (Thayer, 1980). Similarly, perceived arousal level of anger and surprised facial portrayals can also be shifted based on the facial portrayal they follow (Russell & Fehr, 1987, Studies 5 & 6). Perception of a neutral face also shifted when it was presented concurrently with (Russell & Fehr, 1987, Studies 1 & 2) or following another face portraying emotion (Tanaka-Matsumi, Attivissimo, Nelson, & D'Urso, 1995). These effects occurred despite instructions for participants to judge the target face independently of the other stimuli. The size of the context effect produced by other faces appears to be culturally relative, however (Masuda, Ellsworth, Mesquita, Leu, & Veerdonk, 2008). Japanese perceivers' judgments of a target individual reflected the emotions conveyed by the other figures in a scene, but this was less true for Americans perceivers, who focused mainly on the target person.

The processing of surrounding nontarget faces is also evident in patterns of brain activity (Amtig, Miller, Chow, & Mitchell, 2009). Posterior regions of visual cortex are more engaged when all faces are consistent in affective content, whereas the amygdala response is selectively lessened for positive faces in the context of neutral or negative faces. Enhanced functional connectivity emerged between the amygdala and medial prefrontal cortex on trials where the target face was inconsistent in affective value with the nontarget faces, and this functional connectivity predicted longer reaction times. These data suggest that connectivity between the amygdala and medial prefrontal cortex reflects a process aimed at resolving competition between conflicting affective content (c.f. Lieberman et al., 2007). It is unclear based on these data whether this same connectivity would result from within valence competition, however.

## Perceiver-Based Context

Whereas stimulus-based forms of context are driven by something in the external surroundings, perceiver-based forms of context are driven by the internal state of the perceiver. In this section, we focus on how emotion perception in the face is influenced by the perceiver's immediate psychological state. Other forms of context that might be categorized as "perceiver based," such as those based on personality, culture, ethnicity, gender, or psychopathology, are beyond the scope of the present review.

### COGNITIVE LOAD

Emotion perception depends on the amount of executive attention that is available to a perceiver, and so attention becomes a relevant aspect of the perceiver-based context. Although researchers often believe that emotion perception is automatic (e.g., emotion recognition is above-chance under conditions of cognitive load; Tracy & Robins, 2008), there are often methodological circumstances that should constrain explanations for observed effects. For example, in the Tracy and Robbins study, perceivers were asked to judge the faces according to a single emotion word, which might have sufficiently constrained their perceptual choices (see later section on forced choice as an experimental context). Consistent with this interpretation, a recent study by Phillips, Channon, Tunstall, Hendenstrom, and Lyons (2008) found that placing participants under working memory load affected emotion perception judgments far less when the task was to choose between two labels (as opposed to four or six). Futhermore, perceivers under cognitive load still show performance decrements compared to when they are not placed under load (Phillips et al., 2008; Tomasik, Ruthruff, Allen, & Lien, 2009; Tracy & Robbins, 2008). For example, perceivers under cognitive load were less able to distinguish perceptually between scowling and smiling faces (Tomasik et al., 2009). This effect of load appears to be somewhat downstream in visual processing, however, given that early encoding of the visual input (indexed by early ERP components) remains intact when perceivers are placed under cognitive load at encoding (Holmes, Kragh Neilsen, Tipper, & Green, 2009).

### AFFECTIVE STATE

Several studies indicate that a perceiver's affective state shapes affect perception. Perceivers induced into an unpleasant affective state, compared to those feeling neutral, were more likely to see negative emotion in an ambiguous schematic (line drawing) face (Bouhuys, Bloem, & Groothuis, 1995). In a second study, perceivers in an unpleasant affective state were more likely to see "fear" in schematic faces that contained both positive and negative features. In contrast, perceivers in another study (Leppanen & Hietanen, 2003) who were induced to feel pleasant perceived happiness in low-intensity smiling faces more quickly than they perceived disgust in low-intensity disgust faces, although they had roughly equivalent reaction times to judge happiness and disgust in those faces following induction of unpleasant feelings. (Because this experiment did not include a neutral condition, it is unclear whether these were facilitation and interference effects.) The affective aspects of emotional experiences also shape affect perception, such that participants induced to feel the discrete state of disgust via audiotaped messages were more accurate at judging negatively valenced emotional faces generally (Schiffenbauer, 1974). These effects on emotion perception appear to be specific to momentary experiences of affect, however; retrospective ratings of emotion, as measured by the profile of mood states questionnaire, were unrelated to the perception of emotion (Harris & Synder, 1992).

The affective state of the perceiver not only influences the emotional content of what is perceived, but it also influences the dynamics of perception. Perceivers induced to feel an unpleasant affective state (i.e., sadness) perceived frowns, but not smiles, as lasting longer than they did, whereas the reverse finding was found for those induced to feel a pleasant (i.e., happy) state (Niedenthal, Halberstadt, Margolin, & Innes-Ker, 2000). Affective state also shapes how "believable" perceivers find portrayals of emotion. The experience of positive compared to negative affect leads perceivers to judge all facial portrayals (i.e., positive, negative, and neutral portrayals) as more believable (Forgas & East, 2008). Perceived *intensity* of emotional faces also appears to be influenced by the affective state of the perceiver. Participants in a pleasant affective state judged faces portraying positive, but not negative, emotion as more intense (Forgas & East, 2008). Taken together, these data indicate that the affective state of the perceiver is an important factor that contributes to emotion perception. Furthermore, changes in affective state might be a mechanism by which other context-based effects occur because odors, sounds, sights, and scenes all might shape ongoing perception by virtue of the fact that they have the potential to perturb a perceiver's affective state.

## EMBODIMENT

Embodiment refers to the various ways in which the body influences cognition. Embodiment is reflected, for example, in the idea that the brain systems used to represent the concept of an emotion (e.g., "anger") are also involved in seeing that emotion in another person and experiencing that emotion oneself (Niedenthal, Barsalou, Winkielman, Krauth-Gruber, & Ric, 2005). One implication of this work is that categorizing a face as "anger" versus "fear" might rely on the perceiver's ability to reenact the brain state that controls the relevant facial muscle movements associated with that emotion (cf. Niedenthal et al., 2005). Studies testing an embodiment hypothesis have a long history. As early as 1918, it was established that perceivers reported using facial mimicry as a strategy for emotion perception (Langfield, 1918b). Perceivers spontaneously mimic facial muscle movements in static portrayals of emotion (e.g., Dimberg, 1982, 1990) even when they are backwardly masked (Dimberg, Thunberg, & Elmehed, 2000). More recently, experimental studies have shown that facial mimicry is associated with perceptual accuracy (Wallbott, 1991), and with the ability to judge a smile as authentic versus faked (for review, see Niedenthal, Mermillod, Maringer, & Hess, 2010). Participants allowed to mimic facial behaviors saw the onset and offset of facial expressions sooner than participants who were unable to mimic because they were holding a pen in their mouth (Niedenthal, Brauer, Halberstadt, & Innes-Ker, 2001; see also Stel & van Knippenberg, 2008). Patients with "locked-in" syndrome, who have complete paralysis of voluntary (but not spontaneous) facial movements due to a brainstem lesion, have impaired accuracy for discrete emotion perception of negative faces (i.e., anger, fear, sadness) (Pistoia et al., 2010). Yet individuals with Mobius syndrome, who also have paralysis of facial muscles that results from the underdevelopment of the cranial nerves, do not show decrements in emotion perception (Rives Bogart & Matsumoto, 2010). These data suggest that central nervous system impairments

disrupt emotion perception, whereas more peripheral causes of muscle impairments might not. Similarly, a central representation of how a set of facial muscle movements feels may also be necessary to emotion perception; transcranial magnetic stimulation (TMS) applied to somatosensory cortex leads to decrements in emotion perception (Pitcher, Garrido, Walsh, & Duchaine, 2008; see also Adolphs, Damasio, Tranel, Cooper, & Damasio, 2000; Pourtois et al., 2004). Embodied representations may have particular utility for understanding static faces, however, given that an increase in motor cortex activity was not observed for perception of emotion in *dynamic* facial movements (Kilts, Egan, Gideon, Ely, & Hoffman, 2003).

## *Experimental Context*

Even with all the evidence that context routinely influences emotion perception, there are still experiments where faces are presented in isolation—no bodies or situational context—and emotion perception still proceeds. Some of the most well cited studies to make this point date from the early 1970s. This work demonstrated that even individuals from preliterate cultures have higher accuracy than would be expected by chance when perceiving emotion in static posed faces (e.g., Ekman & Friesen, 1971; Ekman et al., 1969, 1972; Izard, 1977). Yet these experiments, arguably some of the most visible and salient in all of psychology, contain certain contextual factors in the experimental setup that contributed to emotion perception in an important way.

### POSED FACIAL ACTIONS

Most studies in the face-focused paradigm (including our own) use faces that pose particular configurations of muscle movements to portray emotion instead of spontaneously elicited facial actions. Standard "facial expression" stimulus sets were created by either directing posers to move particular facial muscles according to a predetermined configuration (e.g., as prescribed by EMFACS) or by merely asking them to pose their faces to convey a particular emotion category. It is not clear how ecologically valid these particular configurations are with respect to actual spontaneous muscle movements during emotion experience (e.g., do people you know pout when they are sad or scowl when they are angry?). Facial electromyography, a direct measure of muscle activity, indicates that people do not always pout in sadness or scowl in anger; in fact, the electromyography data produce little differentiation beyond positive and negative affect (for a review, see Cacioppo, Berntson, Larsen, Poehlmann, & Ito, 2000). Photographs of posed facial actions thus introduce statistical regularities into emotion perception experiments that are not necessarily present in real life, and they have the potential to inflate emotion perception accuracy in the lab compared to what it would be in everyday life (if such perceptions were only based on a face). In fact, Landis (1924a, 1924b, 1929) observed that judgments of spontaneous expressions were at chance levels. More recent work is consistent with (although not as extreme as) these early findings (e.g., Yik, Meng, & Russell, 1998), even when the spontaneous facial actions were identified as emotional by "expert" coders (Naab & Russell, 2007). One argument, of course, is that target people are using display rules (see Ekman et al., 1969) to modify their spontaneous facial actions, making it harder to recognize expressions when they occur. To address this concern, it is instructive to compare emotion perception based on covertly acquired spontaneous facial actions (acquired in a social context that would not encourage the use of display rules) with actions that are posed. Accuracy rates are much lower for covert spontaneous facial actions, although they are still above chance levels (Hall, Gunnery, & Andrzejewski, 2011; Wagner, MacDonald, & Manstead, 1986; Zuckerman, Hall, DeFrank, & Rosenthal, 1976). Participants' accuracy to judge emotion drops even further when the target's facial behaviors occurred during conversation (Zuckerman et al., 1976; also see Motley & Camden, 1988).

In contrast to recognition advantages seen for posed facial actions, perceivers appear more willing to *attribute* emotional experience based on spontaneous expressions. Spontaneous facial actions are judged to convey emotions more clearly and reflect true feelings more than are posed facial actions (McLellan, Johnston, Dalrymple-Alford, & Porter, 2010). McLellan and colleagues also demonstrated that spontaneous facial actions serve as more effective affective primes than do posed actions. Even though posed facial actions do well in studies where the question is about the emotion displayed on the face, spontaneous facial actions appear to do well when the question is about the experience of the target individual (c.f. Aviezer, Hassin, Bentin, & Trope, 2008). The ability to explicitly distinguish between posed and spontaneous expressions (i.e., smiles) appears to be more developed in older adults, however (Murphy, Lehrfeld, & Isaacowitz, 2010; for review of aging and context in emotion perception, see Isaacowitz & Stanley, 2011). Future work should address whether judgments of "true feelings" and priming effects based on spontaneous stimuli are also enhanced with age.

## STATIC FACES

The face-focused approach to studying emotion perception relies on face stimuli that are not only *posed* but also faces that are unmoving or *static*. In these stimuli, facial muscle movements are frozen in time with no temporal dynamics. The static stimulus is often the "apex" of the supposed expression—the most intense and caricatured instance of facial actions. Thus, all "sad" faces are pouting; all "angry" faces are frowning; all "happy" faces are smiling, and so on. When combined with other method choices (e.g., forced choice among a small set of words, discussed in the next subsection), perceivers are able to see the intended emotion with high accuracy (between 60% and 80%; Keltner et al., 2003, p. 415), and many scientists have interpreted these findings as evidence that information in the face is sufficient for emotion perception (e.g., Matsumoto et al., 2008). But it is important to ask whether the high accuracy rates are, in part, a function of using static faces. Like posed material, static faces might create statistical regularities that do not normally exist in the facial actions that are produced in the real world. Dynamic facial actions contain facial movements that have their own psychological meaning. Furthermore, a static display extends the length of an expression's "apex" beyond its typical duration in dynamic face, although exposure durations that are meant to mimic brief facial muscle movements (called "micro expressions"; Ekman & Friesen, 1969) may not do so.

Unfortunately, it is difficult to assess the consequences of presenting static compared to dynamic facial actions because there are few studies that directly compare the two within the same experiment. One study, although limited in its methods, is suggestive. Perceptions of spontaneous smiles were compared based on whether the smiles were dynamic or static. Perceivers had higher accuracy for perceiving happiness in static smiles than dynamic smiles (Miles & Johnston, 2007). In contrast, when using artificially constructed (posed) faces, perceivers are more accurate in judging the emotions conveyed by dynamic facial actions than those depicted in static faces. This dynamic advantage holds true for judgments based on video footage of posed facial muscle movements (Ambadar, Schooler, & Cohn, 2005; Cunningham & Wallraven, 2009, Study

1), for synthetically created faces (Wehrle, Kaiser, Schmidt, & Scherer, 2000), and even for point light displays of motion created by facial muscle movements (Bassili, 1979). Developmental data, on the other hand, do not converge with these findings. Specifically, in preschoolers (3–5 years of age) there is no documented advantage for the perception of emotion from dynamic versus static expressions (Nelson & Russell, 2011), suggesting that use of dynamic cues may require learning that occurs over the lifespan.

In any case, the temporal dynamics of facial actions carry important information. When the speed of onset is manipulated either by changing the number of frames in a dynamic display (Kamachi et al., 2001) or the speed at which the individual frames are presented (Sato & Yoshikawa, 2004), some emotions are more easily perceived with slower onsets (e.g., sadness), whereas some (e.g., surprise) are more readily perceived with faster onsets. Importantly, this does not appear to be due to the duration of the "apex" (null findings for manipulating duration of static displays; Kamachi et al., 2001), but rather the dynamics of how the facial actions onset.

## EMOTION WORDS

Most experiments using a face-focused approach to emotion perception ask participants to match face stimuli to emotion words that are included as part of the experimental protocol. These words provide an important but hidden source of context that shapes emotion perception and increases accuracy (Barrett, Lindquist , &Gendron , 2007). A number of studies, dating back to the early years of psychology, provide evidence for the important influence of words in creating the high accuracy rates we are used to seeing in studies of emotion perception. Perceivers asked to judge emotion, but not provided with a list of emotion terms, had very low agreement on the meaning of a set of facial actions (Kanner, 1931). Providing perceivers with emotion words (vs. asking perceivers to free label) increases accuracy anywhere from 16% (Kline & Johannsen, 1935) to 26% (Izard, 1971), on average. Related, providing any label, even if it is not the correct one, can produce a false consensus in emotion perception. For example, participants presented with caricatured illustrations of emotional faces accompanied by incongruent labels tended to accept the labels as descriptors of the face more often if they previously had been unable to identify the emotion depicted on the face (Langfield, 1918a). More

recent studies confirm this finding (e.g., Russell, 1993; Widen, Christy, Hewett, & Russell, 2010; Widen & Russell, 2008). Similarly, when participants were presented with a list of choices that contained a number of foils, they had generally low accuracy (Buzby, 1924). One interpretation is that even posed, static, highly caricatured portrayals of emotion are somewhat ambiguous as to their psychological meaning, and emotion words can narrow the range of responses. Thus, any time a study reports high accuracy rates for emotion perception (in any cue), it is important to consider whether the experiment explicitly included emotion words that could influence perceivers' performance (cf. Russell, 1994).

A number of experiments have now demonstrated language effects in emotion perception when words are not directly introduced as choices in the experimental paradigm. Emotion words produce biases in perceptual memory for a face, such that memory is shifted toward words that were presented at encoding (Halberstadt & Niedenthal, 2001). Furthermore, a completely false perceptual memory (i.e., remembering a smile) can be created based on a context that primes a specific semantic category (e.g., wining a sporting event) (Fernández-Dols, Carrera, Barchard, & Gacitua, 2008). Words also support categorical perception of facial expressions (Fugate, Gouzoules, & Barrett, 2010). Perceivers learned chimpanzee expressions (e.g., a *hoot*) either with an arbitrary label or without. Only those perceivers who learned the expressions with labels showed the hallmark of categorical perception—an advantage at discriminating morphs that crossed the categorical boundary between two expressions.

Emotion perception can be impaired by reducing the accessibility of emotion words, even when such words are not necessary to perform the experimental task. When emotion word meaning is made less accessible by semantic satiation[6] (for a review, see Black, 2003), accuracy on a perceptual matching task drops to just above chance levels (even though emotion words are not necessary to say whether two faces match in their emotional content; Lindquist, Barrett, Bliss-Moreau, & Russell, 2006). Furthermore, when participants are placed under verbal load categorical perception for posed, caricatured faces is wiped out (such that perceptual advantages for distinguishing between stimuli from two different emotion categories is no longer observed) (Roberson, Damjanovic, & Pilling, 2007). Given these data, it is difficult to conclude that the structural features of expressions drive categorical perception all by themselves.

Words also provide an advantage to young children's emotion perception. Specifically, young children are more accurate at matching emotional faces in a sorting task when the box they are sorting into is marked by a word, compared to when it is marked with a perceptually similar face (Russell & Widen, 2002).[7] Furthermore, emotion perception accuracy increases in parallel with children's vocabulary for emotion words (for a review of this work, see Widen & Russell, 2008). For example, in Widen and Russell's work, children acquire the term "disgust" relatively late, at a mean age of 56 months (4.6 years) and only around this time do children distinguish between high arousal fear and disgust portrayals.

Finally, the neural representation of an emotional face is also shaped by emotion words. Providing perceivers with emotion words significantly reduced amygdala response to posed faces depicting emotion (Lieberman et al., 2007). This result is likely due to the reduced uncertainty produced by helping to resolve competing "perceptual hypotheses" that arose from a structural analysis of the face alone. Furthermore, when perceivers judged a structurally neutral face as emotional, this engaged a network of regions (e.g., right superior temporal sulcus, bilateral orbitofrontal cortex, right anterior insula) (Thieschler & Pessoa, 2007) that are typically thought of as the distributed network for emotional face perception (Haxby, Hoffman, & Gobbini, 2000). In addition, evidence from a neural adaptation paradigm suggests that the representation of emotional faces, within this same neural network, is driven by perceiver conceptualization (i.e., judgments of the emotion category) rather than by structural features of the face alone (Fox, Moon, Iaria, & Barton, 2009). Even when repeated stimuli are changed so drastically that they are "perceptually" drawn from a different category, and theoretically should release the brain from adaptation (i.e., neural responses should go back up because the perceptual aspects of the stimuli have changed), they fail to do so when perceivers judge that the emotion category has not changed. Plainly, the neural representation of an emotional face involves conceptual processing and is not determined by the stimulus features of a face alone. The role of language in emotion perception is also evident in a meta-analysis comparing brain activity during the perception and experience of emotion; the analysis consistently showed activation in language-related regions, including inferior frontal gyrus (IFG), extending from the pars opercularis (Broca's area, BA 44) through pars triangularis (BA 45) and pars orbitalis on the inferior frontal convexity (BA 47/12 l) (Wager et al., 2008).

Taken together, these studies indicate that emotion words (regardless of whether they are offered) constrain how people understand the psychological meaning of a face, even if that face is posing an intense, stereotyped set of muscle actions. Words provide a context that contributes to emotion perception and increases accuracy. In some ways, this is unsurprising, given how powerful words are in the economy of the mind (e.g., Mani & Plunkett, 2010).

### REPEATED MEASURES

A final form of context that is embedded in nearly all investigations of emotion perception is the use of a small set of faces presented repeatedly to the perceiver. This repetition allows (and perhaps encourages) perceivers to form ad hoc perceptual categories by extracting statistical regularities from these posed faces (e.g., all angry faces are scowling, all sad faces are pouting, all happy faces are smiling, and so on).[8] Indeed, attaching a label to an emotional face in an explicit emotion perception task may help overcome perceptual variation and support category formation as is seen for other types of stimuli (see Lupyan, Rakison, & McClelland, 2007). A careful look suggests that repeating faces over and over creates a strong form of experiment-based context in the face-focused approach to understanding emotion perception. For example, research investigating the impact of training on emotion perception indicates that participants demonstrate substantial accuracy increases (Guilford, 1929). These training effects are greater for more unfamiliar stimuli, such as faces portraying emotion posed by someone from another cultural group (Elfenbein, 2006).

## Conclusions

To understand how humans perceive emotion, we must focus our research efforts on more than just the face. People rarely pose their faces into predetermined configurations when in an emotional state, and even when they do, facial actions often are moving targets, embedded in other facial actions, as well as the body movements, smells, and vocalizations that occur during conversation and other cognitively taxing events. In addition, other factors appear crucial to perceivers' emotion perception, including knowledge of the situation and their own internal state. And in the context of laboratory experiments, it is clear that scientists do many things that serve to contextualize emotion perception, often in ways that are unlike what occurs in everyday life.

Nevertheless, it is reasonable to ask what the face alone can tell us about a person's emotional state. Unfortunately, the published literature does not really answer this question because the experiments themselves usually contain hidden forms of context that contribute to emotion perception accuracy. The handful of studies that have attempted to strip away experimental forms of context from the face, with more or less success, almost always show notable decreases in accuracy. Most of these experiments remove only one form of experimental context, leaving the others intact. It is important to remember that every experiment involves some context, even if it is unintended by the experimenter.

More broadly, the context in which emotion perception unfolds might help explain how perceivers can routinely, and with little effort, perceive when another person is angry or afraid, despite the fact that the objective measures of the face (e.g., electromyographic measurements) and voice (e.g., acoustical measures) fail to reveal diagnostic patterns for each emotion (Barrett, 2006a). Barrett (2006b) has termed this the "Emotion Paradox": Instrument-based measures of the face do not reveal muscle movements that distinguish discrete emotions (Cacioppo et al., 2000; Mauss & Rpbinson, 2009), yet perceivers can readily look at someone's face and judge how that person is feeling. One hypothesis to solve the emotion paradox is that perceivers initially extract affective information from a face (whether to approach or avoid it, for example) and the context activates more nuanced conceptual knowledge that allows for the construction of discrete emotion percept of anger, sadness, or fear (for a similar view, see Roberson, Damjanovic, & Kikutani, 2010). The various forms of context reviewed in this chapter might help to shape broadly "affective" actions into discrete emotional percepts. Consistent with this hypothesis, perceivers routinely encode and remember the context better when they are asked to judge the emotion in a face than to judge whether to approach or avoid it (Barrett & Kensinger, 2010). Furthermore, the more readily a situation points to a single emotion category, the stronger its impact on subsequent emotion perception from the face (Fernández-Dols et al., 1991). As such, it might be that the forms of "context" reviewed here are vital to emotion perception as a highly constructive process.

Whatever the mechanisms by which context shapes emotion perception, the findings reviewed here should prompt us to reconsider long-held assumptions about emotion perception. They also suggest that we should question the experimental paradigms that dominate research based on these long-held assumptions. The field of emotion perception seems firmly rooted in the idea that a static, posed face is a useful cue for us to model the perception of discrete emotional states such as anger and sadness. The present review, in contrast, suggests that the face may not be "figure" and the context merely "ground." After all, the epistemic goal in emotion perception in everyday life is not to determine what a *face* is displaying. The goal, instead, is to determine what the person is experiencing, based on whatever is most information relevant at the time. Thus, the processing of "context" is not a secondary consideration, but instead is routine when the goal is to understand the emotion that another person is experiencing (Barrett & Kensinger, 2010).

As perceivers, we are drawn to faces. Our attention rests on them. It is therefore no accident that scientists assume that faces must be the key source of information in emotion perception. To be sure, faces convey important psychological information, but they very likely do not provide sufficient information to a person's emotional state (especially if the person himself or herself is using the context to construct that state; Barrett, 2006a, 2009). Future research that addresses emotion perception as a contextualized phenomenon will help build our understanding of how people see emotions in other people, and how they use those perceptions to get along and get ahead in the world.

## Notes

1. The use of the forced-choice method has recently been extended to studies testing the sufficiency of nonverbal emotional vocalizations as cues to discrete emotion (Sauter, Eisner, Ekman, & Scott, 2009; Simon-Thomas et al., 2009) and has been used in studies examining whether posture/bodily movements convey discrete emotion to perceivers (e.g., Coulson, 2004; De Silva & Bianchi-Berthouze, 2004; Ekman, 1965; Ekman & Friesen, 1967; Pitterman & Nowicki, 2004; Schouwstra & Hoogstraten, 1995).

2. "Affect" versus "emotion" perception must be distinguished. This distinction rests on the judgment that perceivers are asked to make. When a perceiver is asked to judge the discrete emotion content of a face, for example, "Is this face angry?" the task is typically assumed to be an emotion perception. If, however, the perceiver is asked to make a judgment about how intense, positive/negative, aroused/unaroused a target person is, or whether to approach/avoid that target person, the task is categorized as affect perception. Nonetheless, it is often the case that effects are interpreted as emotion perception when they might, in

fact, be affect perception. For example, presenting a facial depiction of "anger" within a "happy" context is incongruent both in terms of discrete emotion categories and also in terms of valence. Likewise, facilitation due to pairing a a scowling face with an anger-inducing situational description might be due merely to the affective value of the context instead of the match on discrete emotion category (if the effect is defined by comparing perception of the face in the absence of context or in a neutral context). Similarly, studies that compare the perception of started "fear" faces to neutral faces, or "happy" faces to "sad" faces, might be studies of affect (valence) perception rather than studies of emotion perception per se. A similar point can be made for comparisons of "fear" faces to "sad" faces because they differ in affective arousal.

3. There are additional data to suggest that context effects extend in the other direction: Facial behaviors serve as a context to emotion perception based on vocal cues (e.g., de Gelder, Böcker, Tuomainen, Hensen, & Vroomen, 1999; de Gelder, Pourtois, & Weiskrantz, 2002; de Gelder & Vroomen, 2000; Pourtois, de Gelder, Vroomen, Rossion, & Crommelinck, 2000; Pourtois, Debatisse, Despland, & de Gelder, 2002; Vroomen, Driver, & de Gelder, 2001). Furthermore, the influence of facial behaviors on the perception of emotion in the voice is maintained under a dual task, suggesting this effect is not dependent on attentional resources (Vroomen et al., 2001).

4. There are some data to suggest that these two sources of information can be integrated even earlier. When facial behaviors serve as a context for vocal cues, integration appears to occur very rapidly. For example, a mismatch negativity at 178 ms was detected for prosody following an incongruent face portraying emotion (de Gelder et al., 1999). When facial and vocal stimuli were presented simultaneously and were congruent, an enhancement of the N1 was demonstrated at 110 ms after onset (Pourtois et al., 2000). One possibility is that the time course of integration depends on which cue, face or voice, is the "object" of perception.

5. Interestingly, the Nakamura et al. (1990) paper is typically cited as some of the best evidence that the face is a stronger cue to emotion than is the situational context because the researchers matched each in its source clarity (i.e., the extent to which perceivers thought the cue was associated with a single emotion). Yet this research strikingly only looked at contexts and situations that differed in valence (e.g., a "pleasant" face paired with an "unpleasant" slide) so that a much more limited interpretation is warranted: situations fail to override facial information that differs in valence (although other work shows that bodies with props can over-ride valence; Aviezer et al., 2008, Study 2).

6. In semantic satiation, on a given trial, participants repeat a word 30 times (as compared to the typical control condition where they repeat the word three times). The massive repetition of the word produces a temporary functional equivalent of semantic dementia (characterized by impairments in the semantic representation of words).

7. Recent data suggest that the face can still be a relatively effective cue to a discrete emotion label. When young children (ages 2–4, a younger sample than the 2002 sample demonstrating the label superiority effect) are asked to generate a label in response to a face or a description of a cause or consequence for emotion, for some categories, faces were a better cue to the emotion label (Widen & Russell, 2010). These data suggest that facial actions may be one of the first types of content that "populate" emotion categories, perhaps given their relatively concrete nature.

8. In real life, it is unclear whether people routinely scowl when they are angry, or pout when they are sad, and so it is unclear whether emotion categories are, in fact, perceptual categories (cf. Barrett, 2006a; see also Mauss & Robinson, 2009).

# References

Adolphs, R., Damasio, H., Tranel, D., Cooper, G., & Damasio, A. R. (2000). A role for somatosensory cortices in the visual recognition of emotion as revealed by 3-D lesion mapping. *Journal of Neuroscience, 20,* 2683–2690.

Ambadar, Z., Schooler, J. W., & Cohn, J. F. (2005). Deciphering the enigmatic face: The importance of facial dynamics in interpreting subtle facial expressions. *Psychological Science, 16,* 403–410.

Amtig, J. A., Miller, J. E., Chow, M., & Mitchell, D. G. V. (2009). Getting mixed messages: The impact of conflicting social signals on the brain's target emotional response. *Neuroimage, 47,* 1950–1959.

Aviezer, H., Hassin, R., Bentin, S., & Trope, Y. (2008). Putting facial expressions back in context. In N. Ambady & J. Skowroski (Eds.), *First impressions* (pp. 255–288). New York: Guilford Press.

Aviezer, H., Hassin, R. R., Ryan, J., Grady, C., Susskind, J., Anderson, A.,... Bentin, S. (2008). Angry, disgusted, or afraid? Studies on the malleability of emotion perception. *Psychological Science, 19,* 724–732.

Bachorowski, J. A. (1999). Vocal expression and perception of emotion. *Current Directions in Psychological Science, 8,* 53–57.

Bachorowski, J. A., & Owren, M. J. (2008). Vocal expressions of emotion. In M. Lewis, J. M. Haviland-Jones, & L. F. Barrett (Eds.), *The handbook of emotion (3rd ed.,* pp. 196–210). New York: Guilford Press.

Barrett, L. F. (2006a). Emotions as natural kinds? *Perspectives on Psychological Science, 1,* 28–58.

Barrett, L. F. (2006b). Valence as a basic building block of emotional life. *Journal of Research in Personality, 40,* 35–55.

Barrett, L. F. (2009). The future of psychology: Connecting mind to brain. *Perspectives in Psychological Science, 4,* 326–339.

Barrett, L. F., & Kensinger, E. A. (2010). Context is routinely encoded during emotion perception. *Psychological Science, 21,* 595–599.

Barrett, L. F., Lindquist, K., & Gendron, M. (2007). Language as a context for emotion perception. *Trends in Cognitive Sciences, 11,* 327–332.

Bassili, J. N. (1979). Emotion recognition: The role of facial movement and the relative importance of upper and lower areas of the face. *Journal of Personality and Social Psychology, 37,* 2049–2058.

Black, S. R. (2003). A review of semantic satiation. In S. P. Shohov (Ed.), *Advances in psychology research* (Vol. 26, pp. 95–106). Huntington, NY: Nova Science.

Bouhuys, A. L., Bloem, G. M., & Groothuis, T. G. (1995). Induction of depressed and elated mood by music influences the perception of facial emotional expressions in healthy subjects. *Journal of Affective Disorders, 33,* 215–226.

Breiter, H. C., Etcoff, N. L., Whalen, P. J., Kennedy, W. A., Rauch, S. L., Buckner, R. L.,... Rosen, B. R. (1996). Response and habituation of the human amygdala during visual processing of facial expression. *Neuron, 17,* 875–887.

Buzby, D. E. (1924). The interpretation of facial expression. *American Journal of Psychology, 35,* 602–604

Cacioppo, J. T., Berntson, G. G., Larsen, J. T., Poehlmann, K. M., & Ito, T. A. (2000). The psychophysiology of emotion. In M. Lewis & R. J. M. Haviland-Jones (Eds.), *The handbook of emotions (2nd ed.,* pp. 173–191). New York: Guilford Press.

Carrera-Levillain, P., & Fernandez-Dols, J. M. (1994). Neutral faces in context: Their emotional meaning and their function. *Journal of Nonverbal Behavior, 18,* 281–299.

Carroll, J. M., & Russell, J. A. (1996). Do facial expression signal specific emotions? Judging emotion from the face in context. *Journal of Personality and Social Psychology, 70,* 205–218.

Cline, M. G. (1956). The influence of social context on the perception of faces. *Journal of Personality, 25,* 142–158.

Collignon, O., Girard, S., Gosselin, F., Roy, S., Saint-Amour, D., Lassonde, M., & Lepore, F. (2008). Audio-visual integration of emotion expression. *Brain Research, 1242,* 126–135.

Coulson, M. (2004). Attributing emotion to static body postures: Recognition accuracy, confusions, and viewpoint dependence. *Journal of Nonverbal Behavior, 28,* 117–139.

Cunningham, D. W., & Wallraven, C. (2009). Dynamic information for the recognition of conversational expressions. *Journal of Vision, 9,* 1–17.

de Gelder, B. (2009). Why bodies? Twelve reasons for including bodily expressions in affective neuroscience. *Philosophical Transactions of the Royal Society B: Biological Sciences, 364,* 3475–3484.

de Gelder, B., & Vroomen, J. (2000). The perception of emotions by ear and by eye. *Cognition and Emotion, 14,* 289–311.

de Gelder, B., Böcker, K. B., Tuomainen, J., Hensen, M., & Vroomen, J. (1999). The combined perception of emotion from voice and face: Early interaction revealed by human electric brain responses. *Neuroscience Letters, 260,* 133–136.

de Gelder, B., Meeren, H. K. M., Righart, R., Van den Stock, J., van de Riet, W. A. C., & Tamietto, M. (2006). Beyond the face: Exploring rapid influences of context on face processing. *Progress in Brain Research, 155,* 37–48.

de Gelder, B., Pourtois, G., & Weiskrantz, L. (2002). Fear recognition in the voice is modulated by unconsciously recognized facial expressions but not by unconsciously recognized affective pictures. *Proceedings of the National Academy of Sciences USA, 99,* 4121–4126.

De Silva, R. R., & Bianchi-Berthouze, M. (2004). Modeling human affective postures: An information theoretic characterization of posture features. *Journal of Visualization and Computer Animation, 15,* 269–276.

Dimberg, U. (1982). Facial reactions to facial expressions. *Psychophysiology, 19,* 643–647.

Dimberg, U. (1990). Facial electromyography and emotional reactions. *Psychophysiology, 27,* 481–194.

Dimberg, U., Thunberg, M., & Elmehed, K. (2000). Unconscious facial reactions to emotional facial expressions. *Psychological Science, 11,* 86–89.

Dolan, R. J., Morris, J. S., & de Gelder, B. (2001). Crossmodal binding of fear in voice and face. *Proceedings of the National Academy of Sciences USA, 98,* 10006–10010.

Ekman, P. (1965). Differential communication of affect by head and body cues. *Journal of Personality and Social Psychology, 2,* 726–35.

Ekman, P. (1972). Universal and cultural differences in facial expressions of emotions. In J. K. Cole (Ed.), *Nebraska symposium on motivation, 1971* (pp. 207–283). Lincoln: University of Nebraska Press.

Ekman, P. (1973). Cross-cultural studies of facial expression. In P. Ekman (Ed.), *Darwin and facial expression: A century of research in review* (pp. 169–222). New York: Academic Press.

Ekman, P. (1998). Introduction to the third edition. In P. Ekman (Ed), *Third edition of Charles Darwin's the expression of the emotions in man and animals, with introduction, afterwords, and commentaries* (pp. xxi–xxxvi). London: HarperCollins.

Ekman, P., & Friesen, W. V. (1967). Head and body cues in the judgment of emotion: A reformulation. *Perceptual and Motor Skills, 24,* 711–24.

Ekman, P., & Friesen, W. V. (1969). Nonverbal leakage and clues to deception. *Psychiatry, 32,* 88–105.

Ekman, P., & Freisen, W. V. (1971). Constants across cultures in the face and emotion. *Journal of Personality and Social Psychology, 17,* 124–129.

Ekman, P., & Friesen, W. V. (1976). *Pictures of facial affect.* Palo Alto, CA: Consulting Psychologist Press.

Ekman, P., & Friesen, W. (1982). EMFACS. Unpublished manuscript. San Francisco, CA.

Ekman, P., Freisen, W. V., & Ellsworth, P. (1972). *Emotion in the human face.* New York: Pergamon Press.

Ekman, P., & O'Sullivan, M. (1988). The role of context in interpreting facial expression: comment on Russell and Fehr (1987). *Journal of Experimental Psychology General, 117,* 86–90.

Ekman, P., Sorenson, E. R., Friesen, W. V. (1969). Pan-cultural elements in facial displays of emotion. *Science, 164,* 86–88.

Elfenbein, H. A. (2006). Learning in emotion judgments: Training and the cross-cultural understanding of facial expressions. *Journal of Nonverbal Behavior, 30,* 21–36.

Etcoff, N. L., & Magee, J. J. (1992). Categorical perception of facial expressions. *Cognition, 44,* 227–240.

Ethofer, T., Anders, S., Erb, M., Droll, C., Royen, L., Saur, R.,... Wildgruber, D. (2006). Impact of voice on emotional judgment of faces: An event-related fMRI study. *Human Brain Mapping, 27,* 707–714.

Fernández-Dols, J. M., Carrera, P., Barchard, K. A., & Gacitua, M. (2008). False recognition of facial expressions of emotion: Causes and implications. *Emotion, 8,* 530–539.

Fernandez-Dols, J. M., & Carroll, J. M. (1997). Is the meaning perceived in facial expression independent of its context? In J. A. Russell & J. M. Fernandez-Dols (Eds.), *The psychology of facial expression: Studies in emotion and social interaction, 2nd series* (pp. 3–30). New York: Cambridge University Press.

Fernandez-Dols, J. M., Sierra, B., & Ruiz-Belda, M. A. (1993). On the clarity of expressive and contextual information in the recognition of emotions: A methodological critique. *European Journal of Social Psychology, 23,* 195–202.

Fernandez-Dols, J. M., Wallbott, H., & Sanchez, F. (1991). Emotion category accessibility and the decoding of emotion from facial expression and context. *Journal of Nonverbal Behavior, 15,* 107–123.

Forgas, J. P., & East, R. (2008). How real is that smile? Mood effects on accepting or rejecting the veracity of emotional facial expressions. *Journal of Nonverbal Behavior, 32,* 157–270.

Fox, C. J., Moon, S., Iaria, G., & Barton, J. J. (2009). The correlates of subjective perception of identity and expression in the face network: An fMRI adaptation study. *Neuroimage, 44,* 569–580.

Frühholz, S., Fehr, T., & Herrmann, M. (2009). Early and late temporo-spatial effects of contextual interference

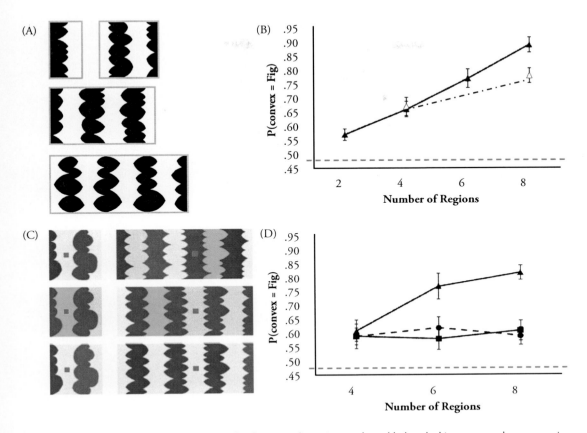

**Figure 2.2** (A) Displays with two-, four-, six-, and eight-region alternating equal-area black and white convex and concave regions. The convex regions are black in these displays, but they were white on half the trials in the experiments. Observers fixated the central border and reported whether the black or the white regions appeared to be figures. (Adapted from Peterson and Salvagio, 2008, *Journal of Vision,* Figure 2.) (B) The probability that observers perceived the convex regions as figures as a function of region number. (Region number was a between-subjects factor.) Solid black line: results obtained when all the convex regions had the same shape (as did all the concave regions); dashed black line: results obtained when each of the display regions had a different shape. The dashed red line indicates chance performance. (Adapted from Peterson and Salvagio, 2008, *Journal of Vision,* Figure 3.) (C) Sample four- and eight-region displays used to test whether homogeneity of color of the convex and/or the concave regions was necessary for the region number effects shown in (B). Top: both convex and concave regions are heterogeneously (HET) colored; no two regions of the same type are the same color (although all regions or one type are the same luminance; luminance was balanced across region type). Middle: Sample displays with homogeneously (HOM) colored convex regions and HET colored concave regions. Bottom: Sample HOM colored concave/ HET colored convex displays. Note that the brightness values may not reproduce well here. Because displays were multicolored, direct report regarding the color of the figures was not possible. Accoridngly, on each trial a red response probe was placed on the region to the right or to the left of fixation. Observers reported whether the probe appeared to lie on or off the region they saw as figure. (Originally published as Peterson and Salvagio, 2008, *Journal of Vision,* Figure 4.) (D) The probability that convex regions were perceived as figure [P(convex = fig)] in multicolored displays as a function of region number. Dashed black line and disks: HET colored convex/HET colored concave displays. Solid black line and squares: HOM colored convex/HET colored concave displays; solid black line and triangles: HOM colored concave/HET colored convex displays. The dashed red line indicates chance performance. (Originally published as Peterson and Salvagio, 2008, *Journal of Vision,* Figure 5.)

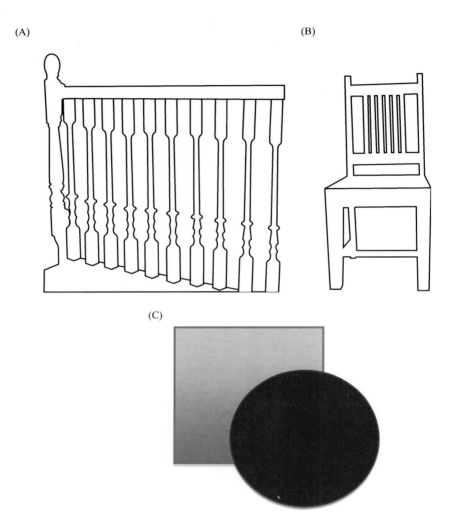

(A)                                                    (B)

(C)

**Figure 2.3** (A) Bannisters: Both the turned wooden pieces (the figures) and the spaces between them are symmetric. (B) Chair: the small-area spaces between the slats on the back of the chair are not figures, nor are the enclosed horizontal spaces within the borders of the chair. (C) Both the blue and purple regions are closed, yet only one is perceived as the figure at their shared border.

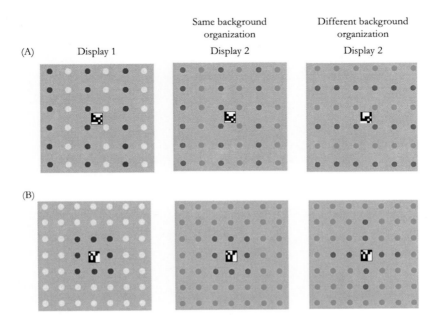

**Figure 2.18** Examples of the stimulus displays used by Kimchi and Razpurker-Apfeld (2004) to examine whether grouping can be accomplished without focal attention. Two successive displays were presented on each trial. The central target matrix in Displays 1 and 2 was either the same or different. The surrounding colored elements were grouped into (A) columns/rows by color similarity and (B) a square/cross by color similarity. The background organization either stayed the same across Displays 1 and 2 or changed, independently of whether the target matrix changed or remained the same. The colors of the background elements always changed between Displays 1 and 2. All colors were equiluminant in the experiment. Changes in the background grouping produced congruency effects on the matrix-change judgments for the grouping of columns/rows by color similarity (A), but not for the grouping of square/cross by color similarity (B). (Adapted from Kimchi & Razpurker-Apfeld, 2004.)

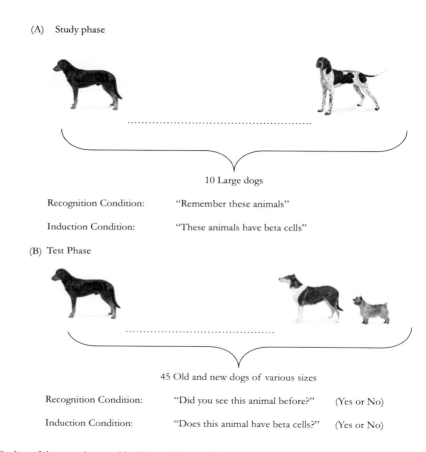

**(A)  Study phase**

10 Large dogs

Recognition Condition:     "Remember these animals"

Induction Condition:     "These animals have beta cells"

**(B)  Test Phase**

45 Old and new dogs of various sizes

Recognition Condition:     "Did you see this animal before?"     (Yes or No)

Induction Condition:     "Does this animal have beta cells?"     (Yes or No)

**Figure 39.1** Outline of the procedure used by Heit and Hayes (2008, 2011) to compare inductive reasoning and memory.

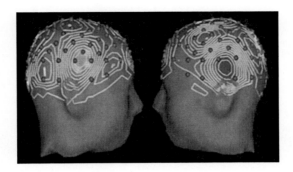

**Figure 49.5** Differences in neural activity immediately preceding insight and noninsight solutions. As noted in orange, greater activity was revealed through fMRI analysis for insight solutions than for noninsight solutions in the right superior temporal gyrus.

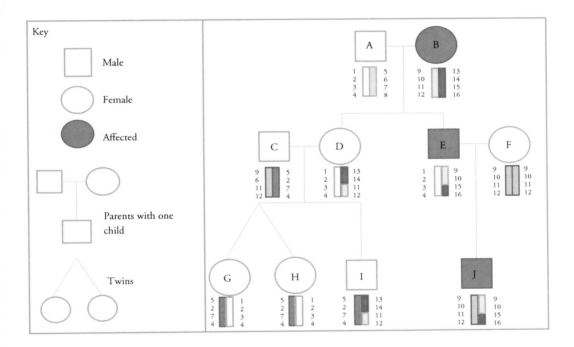

**Figure 52.1** Linkage, segregation and crossing over.

**Note:** This figure shows a pedigree with 10 individuals, identified with letters from A to J. Three individuals (B, E, and J) are affected with a certain disease. Each bar represents one chromosome, and each individual has 1 pair of a chromosome. The two founder individuals (A and B) have colored bars indicating that the white bar was inherited from the father of A, the blue bar from the mother of A, the yellow bar was inherited from the father of B and the red bar from the mother of B. On each chromosome, 4 markers are genotyped. Each pair of chromosomes contains the same markers in the same order, but the sequences are not identical. Numbers 1–16 represent the different alleles from each of the four markers. Each marker has 4 possible alleles. For example, the first marker has possible alleles coded 1, 5, 9, and 13, the second marker has alleles 2, 6, 10, and 14 etcetera. Individual C and F are not genetically related to the two founders and have grey chromosomes that have the same order of markers with the same possible alleles, but not necessarily with the same combination of alleles. Individuals D and E (children from parents A and B) have one chromosome (represented in white) that was inherited from the father. These individuals also have a chromosome inherited from the mother, however a genetic recombination took place and the children inherited a mixture of the two maternal grandparental chromosomes (combination of yellow and red), this phenomenon is known as crossover. If we follow the disease in the pedigree we notice that affected individuals always carry alleles 15 and 16 of the third and fourth marker. These alleles are flanking a region that segregates with the trait. We can conclude from the fictitious family pedigree that the red region (between 15 and 16) shared by all the affected individuals likely contains the gene or casual variant for the disease. We then say that this region is linked to the trait.

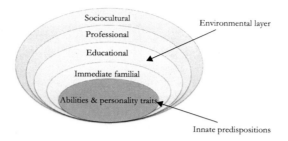

**Figure 53.2** Layers constituting individual differences in cognition.

(A)  American perceptual environment  (B)  Japanese perceptual environment

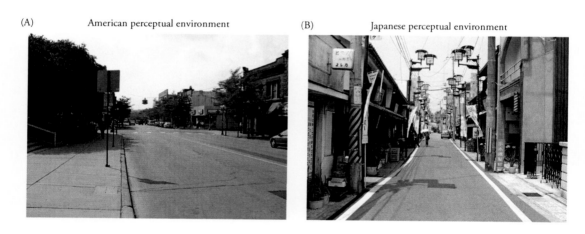

**Figure 61.2** Examples of an American perceptual environment and a Japanese perceptual environment (Miyamoto et al., 2006). Hotels, public elementary schools, and post offices in small, medium, and large cities in both Japan and the United States were randomly sampled, and photographs were taken at each sampled location.

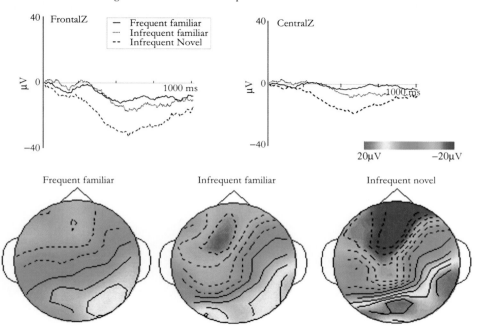

**Figure 63.3** The Nc component following frequent familiar, infrequent familiar, and infrequent novel stimulus presentations. The event-related potential waveforms are shown by stimulus type in the top panel at FrontalZ and CentralZ electrode locations (see Reynolds & Richards, 2005). The bottom panel shows the topographical scalp potential maps of the distribution of this component for the three stimulus types at the peak of Nc (approximately 500 ms following stimulus onset).

Cortical sources of the negative central ERP component

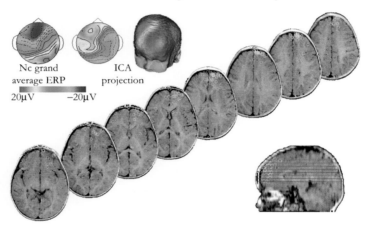

**Figure 63.4** The sequence of magnetic resonance imaging (MRI) slides shows the dipole locations (yellow circles) for an event-related potential (ERP) component known as the Negative central (Nc) (topographical scalp potential maps on upper left figures). The dipoles represent the best-fitting cortical sources of the Nc for individual participants obtained through cortical source analysis of high-density ERP data.

during perception of facial affect. *International Journal of Psychophysiology, 74,* 1–13.

Fugate, J. M. B., Gouzoules, H., & Barrett, L. F. (2010). Reading Chimpanzee faces: A test of the structural and conceptual hypotheses. *Emotion, 10,* 544–554.

Gendron, M., & Barrett, L. F. (2009). Reconstructing the past: A century of ideas about emotion in psychology. *Emotion Review, 1,* 1–24.

Gladwell, M. (2002, August 5). The naked face. *The New Yorker,* 38–49.

Goldberg, H. D. (1951). The role of "cutting" in the perception of the motion picture. *Journal of Applied Psychology, 35,* 70–71.

Goodenough, F. L., & Tinker, M. A. (1931). The relative potency of facial expression and verbal description of stimulus in the judgment of emotion. *Journal of Comparative Psychology, 12,* 365–370.

Guilford, J. P. (1929). An experiment in learning to read facial expressions. *Abnormal and Social Psychology, 24,* 191–202.

Gunes, H., & Piccardi, M. (2007). Bi-modal emotion recognition from expressive face and body gestures. *Journal of Network and Computer Applications, 30,* 1334–1345.

Hagan, C., Woods, W., Johnson, S., Calder, A. J., Green, G. G. R., & Young, A. W. (2009). MEG demonstrates a supra-additive response to facial and vocal emotion in right superior temporal sulcus. *Proceedings of the National Academy of Sciences USA, 106,* 20010–20015.

Halberstadt, J., & Niedenthal, P. M. (2001). Effects of emotion concepts on perceptual memory for emotional expressions. *Journal of Personality and Social Psychology, 81,* 587–598.

Hall, J. A., Gunnery, S. D., & Andrzejewski, S. A. (2011). Nonverbal emotion displays, communication modality, and the judgment of personality. *Journal of Research in Personality, 45,* 77–83.

Harris, L. J., & Snyder, P. J. (1992). Subjective mood state and the perception of emotion in chimeric faces. *Cortex, 28,* 471–481.

Hawk, S. T., van Kleef, G. A., Fischer, A. H., & van der Schalk, J. (2009). Worth a thousand words: Absolute and relative decoding of affect vocalizations. *Emotion, 9,* 293–305.

Haxby, J. V., Hoffman, E. A., & Gobbini, M. I. (2000). The distributed human neural system for face perception. *Trends in Cognitive Sciences, 4,* 223–233.

Hietanen, J. K., & Leppänen, J. M. (2008). Judgment of other people's facial expressions of emotions is influenced by their concurrent affective hand movements. *Scandinavian Journal of Psychology, 49,* 221–230.

Hoehl, S., & Striano, T. (2008). Neural processing of eye gaze and threat-related emotional facial expressions in infancy. *Child Development, 79,* 1752–1760.

Hoehl, S., & Striano, T. (2010). Discrete emotions in infancy: Perception without production? *Emotion Review, 2,* 132–133.

Holmes, A., Kragh Nielsen, M., Tipper, S., & Green, S. (2009). An electrophysiological investigation into the automaticity of emotional face processing in high versus low trait anxious individuals. *Cognitive, Affective and Behavioral Neuroscience, 9,* 323–334.

Hunt, W. A. (1941). Recent developments in the field of emotion. *Psychological Bulletin, 38,* 249–276.

Isaacowitz, D. M., & Stanley, J. T. (2011). Bringing an ecological perspective to the study of aging and recognition of emotional facial expressions: Past, current, and future methods. *Journal of Nonverbal Behavior, 35,* 261–278.

Izard, C. E. (1971). *The face of emotion.* New York: Appleton-Century-Crofts.

Izard, C. (1977). *Human emotions.* New York: Plenum.

Izard, C. E. (1994). Innate and universal facial expressions: Evidence from developmental and cross-cultural research. *Psychological Bulletin, 115,* 288–299.

Kamachi, M., Bruce, V., Mukaida, S., Gyoba, J., Yoshikawa S., & Akamatsu, S. (2001). Dynamic properties influence the perception of facial expressions. *Perception, 30,* 875–887.

Kanner, L. (1931). Judging emotion from facial expressions. *Psychological Monographs, 41,* 93.

Keltner, D., Ekman, P., Gonzaga, G. C., & Beer, J. (2003). Facial expression of emotion. In R. J. Davidson, K. R. Scherer, & H. H. Goldsmith (Eds.), *Handbook of affective sciences (pp. 415–131).* New York: Oxford University Press.

Kilts, C. D., Egan, G., Gideon, D. A., Ely, T. D., & Hoffman, J. M. (2003). Dissociable neural pathways are involved in the recognition of emotion in static and dynamic facial expressions. *Neuroimage, 18,* 156–168.

Kim, H., Somerville, L. H., Johnstone, T., Polis, S., Alexander, A. L, Shin, L. M., & Whalen, P. J. (2004). Contextual modulation of amygdala responsivity to surprised faces. *Journal of Cognitive Neuroscience, 16,* 1730–1745.

Kline, L. W., & Johannsen, D. E. (1935). Comparative role of the face and of the face-body-hands in identifying emotions. *Journal of Abnormal and Social Psychology, 2,* 415–426.

Knudsen, H. R., & Muzekari, L. H. (1983). The effects of verbal statements of context on facial expressions of emotion. *Journal of Nonverbal Behavior, 7,* 202–212.

Kohler, C. G., Walker, J. B., Martin, E. A., Healey, K. M., & Moberg, P. J. (2010). Facial emotion perception in schizophrenia: A meta-analytic review. *Schizophrenia Bulletin, 36,* 1009–1019.

Kuraoka, K., & Nakamura, K. (2007). Responses of single neurons in monkey amygdala to facial and vocal emotions. *Journal of Neurophysiology, 97,* 1379–1387.

Landis, C. (1924a). Studies of emotional reactions: I. A preliminary study of facial expression. *Journal of Experimental Psychology, 7,* 325–341.

Landis, C. (1924b). Studies of emotional reactions: II. General behavior and facial expression. *Journal of Comparative Psychology, 4,* 477–509.

Landis, C. (1929). The interpretation of facial expression in emotion. *Journal of General Psychology, 2,* 59–72.

Landis, C. (1934). Emotion: II. The expressions of emotion. In C. Murchison (Ed.), *A handbook of general experimental psychology* (pp. 312–351). Worcester, England: Clark University Press.

Langfeld, H. S. (1918a). Judgments of facial expression and suggestion. *Psychological Review, 25,* 488–494.

Langfield, H. S. (1918b). The judgment of emotions from facial expressions. *Journal of Abnormal Social Psychology, 13,* 172–184.

Leppänen, J. M., & Hietanen, J. K. (2003). Affect and face perception: Odors modulate the recognition advantage of happy faces. *Emotion, 3,* 315–326.

Lieberman, M. D., Eisenberger, N. I., Crockett, M. J., Tom, S. M., Pfeifer, J. H., & Way, B. M. (2007). Putting feelings into words: Affect labeling disrupts amygdala activity to affective stimuli. *Psychological Science, 18,* 421–428.

Lindquist, K. A., Barrett, L. F., Bliss-Moreau, E., & Russell, J. A. (2006). Language and the perception of emotion. *Emotion, 6*, 125–138.

Lupyan, G., Rakison, D. H., & Mcclelland, J. L. (2007). Language is not just for talking redundant labels facilitate learning of novel categories. *Psychological Science, 18*, 1077–1083.

Mani, N., & Plunkett, K. (2010). In the infant's mind's ear: Evidence for implicit naming in 18-month-olds. *Psychological Science, 21*, 908–913.

Massaro, D. W., & Egan, P. B. (1996). Perceiving affect from the voice and the face. *Psychonomic Bulletin and Review, 3*, 215–221.

Masuda, T., Ellsworth, P., Mesquita, B., Leu, J., & Veerdonk, E. (2008). Placing the face in context: Cultural differences in perceiving emotions from facial behavior. *Journal of Personality and Social Psychology, 94*, 365–381.

Matsumoto, D., Keltner, D., Shiota, M., Frank, M., & O'Sullivan, M. (2008). Facial expressions of emotions. In M. Lewis, J. Haviland, & L. Feldman-Barrett (Eds.), *Handbook of emotion* (pp. 211–234). New York: Guilford Press.

Matsumoto, D., & Willingham, B. (2009). Spontaneous facial expressions of emotion of congenitally and noncongenitally blind individuals. *Journal of Personality and Social Psychology, 96*, 1–10.

Mauss, I. B., & Robinson, M. D. (2009). Measures of emotion: A review. *Cognition and Emotion, 23*, 209–237.

McLellan, T., Johnston, L., Dalrymple-Alford, J., & Porter, R. (2010). Sensitivity to genuine versus posed emotion specified in facial displays. *Cognition and Emotion, 24, 1277–1292*.

Meeren, H. K. M., van Heijnsbergen, C., & de Gelder, B. (2005). Rapid perceptual integration of facial expression and emotional body language. *Proceedings of the National Academy of Sciences USA, 102*, 16518–16523.

Miles, L., & Johnston, L. (2007). Detecting happiness: Perceiver sensitivity to enjoyment and non-enjoyment smiles. *Journal of Nonverbal Behavior, 31*, 259–275.

Mobbs, D., Weiskopf, N., Lau, H. C., Featherstone, E., Dolan, R. J., & Frith, C. D. (2006). The Kuleshov effect: The influence of contextual framing on emotional attributions. *Social Cognitive and Affective Neuroscience, 1*, 95–106.

Motley, M. T., & Camden, C. T. (1988). Facial expression of emotion: A comparison of posed versus spontaneous expressions in an interpersonal-communication setting. *Western Journal of Speech Communication, 52*, 1–22.

Munn, N. L. (1940). The effect of knowledge of the situation upon judgment of emotion from facial expressions. *Journal of Abnormal and Social Psychology, 35*, 324–338.

Murphy, N. A, Lehrfeld, J. M., & Isaacowitz, D. M. (2010). Recognition of posed and spontaneous dynamic smiles in young and older adults. *Psychology and Aging, 25*, 811–821.

Naab, P. J., & Russell, J. A. (2007). Judgments of emotion from spontaneous facial expressions of New Guineans. *Emotion, 7*, 736–744.

Nakamura, M., Buck, R., & Kenny, D. A. (1990). Relative contribution of expressive behavior and contextual information to the judgment of the emotional state of another. *Journal of Personality and Social Psychology, 59*, 1032–1039.

Nelson, N. L., & Russell, J. A. (2011). Preschoolers' use of dynamic facial, bodily, and vocal cues to emotion. *Journal of Experimental Child Psychology, 110*, 52–61.

Niedenthal, P. M., Barsalou, L. W., Winkielman, P., Krauth-Gruber, S., & Ric, F. (2005). Embodiment in attitudes, social perception, and emotion. *Personality and Social Psychology Review, 9*, 184–211.

Niedenthal, P. M., Brauer, M., Halberstadt, J. B., & Innes-Ker, A. H. (2001). When did her smile drop? Facial mimcry and the influences of emotional state on the detection of change in emotional expression. *Cognition and Emotion, 15*, 853–864.

Niedenthal, P. M., Halberstadt, J. B., Margolin, J., & Innes-Ker, A. H. (2000). Emotional state and the detection of change in facial expression of emotion. *European Journal of Social Psychology, 30*, 211–222.

Niedenthal, P. M., Mermillod, M., Maringer, M., & Hess, U. (2010). The simulation of smiles (SIMS) model: Embodied simulation and the meaning of facial expression. *Behavioral and Brain Sciences, 33*, 417–33.

Parr, L. A., & Waller, B. M. (2006). Understanding chimpanzee facial expression: Insights into the evolution of communication. *Social Cognitive and Affective Neuroscience, 1*, 221–228.

Peelen, M. V., Atkinson, A. P., & Vuilleumier, P. (2010). Supramodal representations of perceived emotions in the human brain. *Journal of Neuroscience, 30*, 10127–10134.

Pell, M. C. (2005). Prosody-face interactions in emotional processing as revealed by the facial affect decision task. *Journal of Nonverbal Behavior, 29*, 193–215.

Pereira, C. (2000). Dimensions of emotional meaning in speech. In R. Cowie, E. Douglas-Cowie, & M. Schröder (Eds.), *Proceedings of the ISCA Workshop on Speech Emotion*. Belfast, Northern Ireland: Textflow.

Phillips, L. H., Channon, S., Tunstall, M., Hedenstrom, A., & Lyons, K. (2008). The role of working memory in decoding emotions. *Emotion, 8*, 184–191.

Phillips, M. L., Young, A. W., Scott, S. K., Calder, A. J., Andrew, C., Giampietro, V., . . . Gray, J. A. (1998). Neural responses to facial and vocal expressions of fear and disgust. *Proceedings of the Royal Society B, 265*, 1809–1817.

Phillips, M. L., Young, A. W., Senior, C., Brammer, M., Andrews, C., Calder, A. J., . . . David, A. S. (1997). A specific neural substrate for perceiving facial expressions of disgust. *Nature 389*, 495–498.

Pistoia, F., Conson, M., Trojano, L., Grossi, D., Ponari, M., Colonnese, C., . . . Sara, M. (2010). Impaired conscious recognition of negative facial expressions in patients with locked-in syndrome. *Journal of Neuroscience, 30*, 7838–7844.

Pitcher, D., Garrido, L., Walsh, V., & Duchaine, B. (2008). TMS disrupts the perception and embodiment of facial expressions. *Journal of Neuroscience, 28*, 8929–8933.

Pittam, J., Gallois, C., & Callan, V. (1990). The long-term spectrum and perceived emotion. *Speech Communication, 9*, 177–187.

Pitterman, H., & Nowicki, S., Jr. (2004). A test of the ability to identify emotion in human standing and sitting postures: The diagnostic analysis of nonverbal accuracy-2 posture test (DANVA2-POS). *Genetic, Social, and General Psychology Monographs, 130*, 146–162.

Pourtois, G., de Gelder, B., Vroomen, J., Rossion, B., & Crommelinck, M. (2000). The time-course of intermodal binding between seeing and hearing affective information. *Neuroreport, 11*, 1329–1333.

Pourtois, G., Debatisse, D., Despland, P. A., & de Gelder, B. (2002). Facial expressions modulate the time course of long latency auditory brain potentials. *Brain Research Cognitive Brain Research, 14*(1), 99–105.

Pourtois, G., Sander, D., Andres, M., Grandjean, D., Reveret, L., Olivier, E., & Vuilleumier, P. (2004). Dissociable roles of the human somatosensory and superior temporal cortices for processing social face signals. *European Journal of Neuroscience, 20*, 3507–3515.

Reichenbach, L., & Masters, J. C. (1983). Children's use of expressive and contextual cues in judgments of emotion. *Child Development, 54*, 993–1004.

Rives Bogart, K., & Matsumoto, D. (2010). Facial mimicry is not necessary to recognize emotion: Facial expression recognition by people with Moebius syndrome. *Social Neuroscience, 5*, 241–251.

Roberson, D., Damjanovic, L., Kikutani, M. (2010). Show and tell: The role of language in categorizing facial expression of emotion. *Emotion Review, 2, 255–260.*

Roberson, D., Damjanovic, L., & Pilling, M. (2007). Categorical perception of facial expressions: Evidence for a "Category Adjustment" model. *Memory and Cognition, 35*, 1814–1829.

Rozin, P., Taylor, C., Ross, L., Bennett, G., & Hejmadi, A. (2005). General and specific abilities to recognize negative emotions, especially disgust, as portrayed in the face and the body. *Cognition and Emotion, 19*, 397–412.

Russell, J. A. (1993). Forced-choice response format in the study of facial expression. *Motivation and Emotion, 17*, 41–51.

Russell, J. A. (1994). Is there universal recognition of emotion from facial expression? A review of the cross-cultural studies. *Psychological Bulletin, 115*, 102–141.

Russell, J. A., & Bullock, M. (1986). On the dimensions preschoolers use to interpret facial expressions of emotion. *Developmental Psychology, 22*, 97–102.

Russell, J. A., & Fehr, B. (1987). Relativity in the perception of emotion in facial expressions. *Journal of Experimental Psychology: General, 116*, 223–237.

Russell, J. A., & Widen, S. C. (2002). A label superiority effect in children's categorization of facial expressions. *Social Development, 11*, 30–52.

Sato, W., & Yoshikawa, S. (2004). The dynamic aspects of emotional facial expressions. *Cognition and Emotion, 18*, 701–710.

Sauter, D. A., Eisner, F., Ekman, P., & Scott, S. K. (2010). Cross-cultural recognition of basic emotions through non-verbal emotional vocalizations. *Proceedings of the National Academy of Sciences USA, 107(6), 2408–2412.*

Scherer, K. L., & Wallbot, H. B. (1994). Evidence for universality and cultural variation of differential emotion response patterning. *Journal of Personality and Social Psychology, 66*, 310–328.

Schiffenbauer, A. (1974). Effect of observer's emotional state on judgments of the emotional state of others. *Journal of Personality and Social Psychology, 30*, 31–35.

Schlosberg, H. (1952). The description of facial expressions in terms of two dimensions. *Journal of Experimental Psychology, 44*, 229–237.

Schouwstra, S. J., & Hoogstraten, J. (1995). Head position and spinal position as determinants of perceived emotional state. *Perceptual Motor Skills, 81*, 673–674.

Schyns, P. G., Petro, L. S., & Smith, M. L. (2009). Transmission of facial expressions of emotion co- evolved with their efficient decoding in the brain: Behavioral and brain evidence. *Plos One, 4*, 1–16.

Sherman, M. (1927). The differentiation of emotional responses in infants: II. The ability of observers to judge the emotional

characteristics of the crying of infants and of the voice of an adult. *Journal of Comparative Psychology, 7*, 335–351.

Simon-Thomas, E. R., Keltner, D. J., Sauter, D., Sinicropi-Yao, L., & Abramson, A. (2009). The voice conveys specific emotions: evidence from vocal burst displays. *Emotion, 9*, 838–846.

Somerville, L. H., & Whalen, P. J. (2006). Prior experience as a stimulus category confound: An example using facial expressions of emotion. *Social, Cognitive, and Affective Neuroscience, 1*, 271–274.

Sommer, M., Döhnel, K., Meinhardt, J., & Hajak, G. (2008). Decoding of affective facial expressions in the context of emotional situations. *Neuropsychologia, 46*, 2615–2621.

Spignesi, A., & Shor, R. (1981). The judgment of emotion from facial expressions, contexts and their combination. *Journal of General Psychology, 104*, 41–59.

Sprengelmeyer, R., Rausch, M., Eysel, U. T., & Przuntek, H. (1998). Neural structures associated with recognition of facial expressions of basic emotions. *Proceedings of the Royal Society of London B: Biological Sciences, 265*, 1927–1931.

Stel, M., & van Knippenberg, A. (2008). The role of facial mimicry in the recognition of affect. *Psychological Science, 19*, 984–985.

Tanaka-Matsumi, J., Attivissimo, D., Nelson S., & D'Urso, T. (1995). Context effects on the judgment of basic emotions in the face. *Motivation and Emotion, 19*, 139–155.

Thayer, S. (1980). The effect of expression sequence and expressor identity on judgments of the intensity of facial expression. *Journal of Nonverbal Behaivor, 5*, 71–79.

Thielscher, A., & Pessoa, L. (2007). Neural correlates of perceptual choice and decision making in fear-disgust discrimination. *Journal of Neuroscience, 27*, 2908–2917.

Tomasik, D., Ruthruff, E., Allen, P. A., & Lien, M. C. (2009). Non-automatic emotion perception in a dual-task situation. *Psychonomic Bulletin and Review, 16*, 282–288.

Tracy, J. L., & Robins, R. W. (2008). The automaticity of emotion recognition. *Emotion, 7*, 789–801.

Vuilleumier, P., & Pourtois, G. (2007). Distributed and interactive brain mechanisms during emotion face perception: Evidence from functional neuroimaging. *Neuropsychologia, 45*, 174–94.

Vroomen, J., Driver, J., & de Gelder, B. (2001). Is cross-modal integration of emotional expressions independent of attentional resources? *Cognitive, Affective and Behavioral Neuroscience, 1*, 382–387.

Wager, T. D., Barrett, L. F., Bliss-Moreau, E., Lindquist, K., Duncan, S., Kober, H.,... Mize, J. (2008). The neuroimaging of emotion. In M. Lewis, J. M. Haviland-Jones, & L.F. Barrett (Eds.), *The handbook of emotion* (3rd ed., pp. 249–271). New York: Guilford Press.

Wagner, H. L., MacDonald, C. J., & Manstead, A. S. R. (1986). Communication of individual emotions by spontaneous facial expressions. *Journal of Personality and Social Psychology, 50*, 737–743.

Wallbott, H. G. (1988a). Faces in context: The relative importance of facial expressions and context information in determining emotion attributions. In K. R. Scherer (Ed.), *Facets of emotion* (pp. 139–160). Hillsdale, NJ: Erlbaum.

Wallbott, H. G. (1988b). In and out of context: Influences of facial expression and context information on emotion attributions. *British Journal of Social Psychology, 27*, 357–369.

Wallbott, H. G. (1991). Recognition of emotion from facial expression via imitation? Some indirect evidence for an old theory. *British Journal of Social Psychology, 30*, 207–219.

Warner, L. R., & Shields, S. A. (2009). Judgments of others' emotional appropriateness are multidimensional. *Cognition and Emotion, 23,* 876–888.

Watson, J. C. (2004). From interpretation to identification: A history of facial images in the sciences of emotion. *History of the Human Sciences, 17,* 29–51.

Wehrle, T., Kaiser, S., Schmidt, S., & Scherer, K. R. (2000). Studying the dynamics of emotional expression using synthesized facial muscle movements. *Journal of Personality and Social Psychology, 78,* 105–119.

Weinberger, S. (2010). Airport security: Intent to deceive? *Nature, 465,* 412–415.

Widen, S. C., Christy, A. M., Hewett, K., & Russell, J. A. (2011). Do proposed facial expressions of contempt, shame, embarrassment, and compassion communicate the predicted emotion? *Cognition & Emotion, 25,* 898–906.

Widen, S. C., & Russell, J. A. (2008). Young children's understanding of other's emotions. In M. Lewis & J. M. Haviland-Jones (Eds.), *Handbook of emotions* (3rd ed., pp. 348–363). New York: Guilford Press.

Widen, S. C., & Russell, J. A. (2010). Differentiation in preschooler's categories of emotion. *Emotion, 10,* 651–61.

Widen, S. C., & Russell, J. A. (2010). Children's scripts for social emotions: Causes and consequences are more central than are facial expressions. *British Journal of Developmental Psychology, 28,* 565–581.

Yik, M. S. M., Meng, Z., & Russell, J. A. (1998). Adults' freely produced emotion labels for babies' spontaneous facial expressions. *Cognition and Emotion, 12,* 723–730.

Zhou, W., & Chen, D. (2009). Chemosignals of fear modulate fear recognition in ambiguous facial expressions. *Psychological Science, 20,* 177–183.

Zuckerman, M., Hall, J. A., DeFrank, R. S., & Rosenthal, R. (1976). Encoding and decoding of spontaneous and posed facial expressions. *Journal of Personality and Social Psychology, 34,* 966–977.

# Emotion, Stress, and Memory

Siobhan M. Hoscheidt, Bhaktee Dongaonkar, Jessica Payne, *and* Lynn Nadel

**Abstract**

Memory is influenced by emotion and stress in a variety of ways. Typically we remember emotional events better than neutral ones. This chapter considers how emotion and stress might influence memory at the biological level, and with due attention paid to the stage of the memory process we are considering. It turns out that there are important differences between mild to moderate emotion and severe stress. We discuss the biology of each of these in turn.

**Key Words:** memory, emotion, stress, hippocampus, amygdala, cortisol, PTSD, memory consolidation, encoding, retrieval

Emotional events are remembered from days to years, can be retrieved with little effort, and are usually reported in vivid detail (Denburg, Buchanan, Tranel, & Adolphs, 2003; Kensinger & Schacter, 2006; Mickley & Kensinger, 2009; Sharot, Martorella, Delgado, & Phelps, 2007; Talarico, Berntsen, & Rubin, 2009; Talarico, LaBar, & Rubin, 2004). By contrast, memories of nonemotional events are characteristically harder to retrieve and tend to be less detailed. Storage and efficient recollection of memories for emotional events can be highly adaptive, particularly in situations that are potentially harmful or threatening (Nairne, 2007). Memory for previously experienced negative events informs future behaviors so that negative situations may be successfully avoided or addressed (Koster, Crombez, Vershuere, Vanvolsem, & De Houwer, 2007). The finding that emotional information is better remembered than nonemotional information has been widely reported across numerous studies and for a variety of stimuli (e.g., word lists, scenes, and stories; Anderson, Yamaguchi, Grabski, & Lacka, 2006; Harris & Pashler, 2005; Kensinger, Garoff-Eaton, & Schacter, 2007b; Payne et al., 2006,

2007; Segal & Cahill, 2009; Touryan, Marian, & Shimamura, 2007). Research conducted over the past two decades has contributed a wealth of new knowledge to the field's understanding of how emotion affects memory, and it has demonstrated that effects vary as a function of the emotional experience (e.g., positive or negative arousal, fear, anger, happiness, etc.) and the phase of memory processing influenced by emotion (i.e., attention/encoding, consolidation, or retrieval). The current chapter reviews modulation of various memory processes by mild to severe negative emotion (i.e., stress) through key biologically defined mechanisms. At the outset we note two limitations on our review. First, we focus primarily on negative emotion, which connects readily to stress, the other focus of the chapter. Second, the processes we review are not the only relevant mechanisms through which emotions modulate memory. Functionally defined mechanisms also play an important role in modulation of memory processes by emotion. For example, emotional events are typically perceived as distinct and relevant to the self and thus are more likely to undergo postevent elaboration compared to nonemotional events. This may be, in part, why emotional events are typically remembered better than nonemotional events. A full review of functionally defined mechanisms is beyond the scope of this chapter; however, some of these mechanisms will be discussed briefly where relevant.

We start by discussing the effects of mild to moderate negative emotion on different memory phases, and then we discuss more severe negative emotion, or stress. This chapter aims to provide an integrated overview of (1) how mild to severe negative emotion modulates memory processes and (2) the underlying key biological mechanisms that contribute to the formation of well-preserved emotional memory.

## Modulation of Memory Processes by Moderate Emotion

Emotion can modulate memory by influencing any phase of processing—attention/encoding, working memory, consolidation, or retrieval. Studies have shown that the phase of processing influenced by emotion plays a significant role in how subsequent memory is affected, resulting in either memory enhancements or impairments (Liu, Graham, & Zorawski, 2008; Roozendaal, Barsegyan, & Lee, 2008; Talmi, Anderson, Riggs, Moscovitch, & Caplan, 2008; van Stegeren et al., 2005; Waring, Kensinger, Payne, & Schacter, 2010). In this section, we review the underlying mechanisms by which mild to moderate levels of negative emotion modulate (1) attention and encoding, (2) working memory, (3) consolidation, and (4) retrieval.

### Emotion-Based Modulation of Attention and Encoding

Emotional stimuli are often referred to as "attention magnets" because they readily attract attention and remain the focus of attention during encoding (Alpers, 2008; Calvo & Lang, 2005; Laney, Heuer, & Reisberg, 2003; Nummenmaa, Hyönä, & Calvo, 2006). Spontaneous preferential processing of negative emotional information in perceptual and attentional systems, an effect commonly referred to as attention narrowing, contributes to the overall effect of emotion on memory, allowing negative emotional information to have privileged access to working memory and beyond (see review by Mather, 2007). Eye-tracking and event-related potential (ERP) studies have provided evidence that automatic attentional shifts toward negatively arousing stimuli occur very early in emotion perception, within 100 ms to 300 ms after exposure to

a stimulus (Bradley, Hamby, Löw, & Lang, 2007; Huang & Luo, 2006; Schaefer, Pottage, & Rickart, 2011). These effects appear to be both automatic and uninfluenced by attentional load during the earliest stages of encoding (Luo et al., 2010). Fast and efficient perceptual processing of negative arousing materials can achieve two things, both of which are adaptive for survival: (1) elicit an autonomic response and (2) trigger the evaluation of an affective stimulus before an individual is consciously aware of perceiving it.

Autonomic activation elicits the release of hormones that automatically and rapidly modulate subcortical systems, causing pupil dilation (Sterpenich et al., 2006), and further biasing of perceptual and attentional systems toward processing aversive emotionally relevant information (Brosch, Pourtois, & Sander, 2010; Ohman, 2005; Talmi et al., 2008). The amygdala plays a critical role in this process, directing eye movements, via projections to low-level visual areas, to selectively attend to (Adolphs, 2004) and encode emotionally salient information (Compton, 2003; Kensinger & Corkin, 2004; Pessoa & Ungerleider, 2004). It is worth noting here that noradrenergic hormones also modulate encoding of aversive emotional materials by mediating neural processes in the amygdala. Several neuroimaging studies have demonstrated the important role of noradrenergic mediation of amygdala activity during encoding of aversive emotional material by administration of a beta blocker (i.e., propranolol) just prior to encoding. Overall, these studies demonstrate that beta blockade selectively disrupts normal activation patterns in the amygdala during acquisition, selectively decreasing activation in this region. Critically, in these studies, decreased amygdala activation during encoding predicted selective subsequent memory retrieval impairment for emotional materials (Strange & Dolan, 2004; van Stegeren et al., 2005). The integral role the amygdala plays in encoding emotional information has also been demonstrated in studies of patients with amygdala damage, who at times show minimal physiological arousal to negative material (Bernston, Bechara, Damasio, Tranel, & Cacioppo, 2007) and unbiased visual attention when encoding fearful faces or scenes with emotional and nonemotional components (Adolphs et al., 2005; Anderson & Phelps, 2001). An absence of emotion modulation of perceptual and attentional processes and impaired normal amygdala and noradrenergic function may be a few of the many reasons that memory for negative emotional information is typically not enhanced in amygdala patients, as it is in intact individuals.

Unlike negative emotional information, non-emotional information does not benefit from amygdala-driven modulation of perceptual and attention systems or arousal-evoked release of hormones (Kensinger & Corkin, 2004; Segal & Cahill, 2009). In fact, allocation of attention to favor negative emotional information diminishes resources, constraining attention that would be allocated across all aspects of an event otherwise. Viewing negative emotional stimuli dramatically narrows the functional field of view (FFOV), making it less probable that attention will be allocated to non-emotional or positive stimuli (Nobata, Hakoda, & Ninose, 2010). As a result, subsequent memory for nonemotional and positive information is typically poor, compared to memory for negative emotional information, particularly when presented within or in close proximity to a negative emotionally arousing stimulus or event (Kensinger et al., 2007b; Touryan et al., 2007).

Preferential remembering of negative emotional information at the expense of nonemotional information is often referred to as an emotion-induced memory trade-off (see Buchanan & Adolphs, 2002; Kensinger, 2009; Reisberg & Hertel, 2004 for reviews). For instance, if one sees a picture of a car accident on a street, one tends to have excellent memory for the car accident but poor memory for the street. In fact, memory for the street is often worse if one saw a car accident on the street than if one saw a nonemotional version of the scene, such as an intact car parked on the street. Such trade-offs can occur not only for nonemotional information presented in close spatial proximity to a negative emotional item but also for nonemotional information presented in temporal proximity to negative emotional information (Hurlemann et al., 2005). These findings suggest that memory trade-off effects may be tied to the strength of the emotional "attention magnet" in a scene.

Exceptions to this pattern of findings are seen when nonemotional and negative emotional information are integrated spatially (e.g., the font color or spatial location of an emotional word; Kensinger, Garoff-Eaton, & Schacter, 2007a), temporally or conceptually (Adolphs, Denburg, & Tranel, 2001; Schmidt, 2002), or are equally relevant to goal attainment (Compton, 2003; Gable & Harmon-Jones, 2008; Levine & Edelstein, 2009; Levine & Pizarro, 2004). In such cases, nonemotional information appears to be remembered as

well as negative emotional information (Adolphs et al., 2001). For example, studies have shown that encoding processes can be manipulated by altering instructions that direct participants to allocate their attention toward particular aspects of scenes. The logic behind these studies is that if focal effects arise due to attention focusing during encoding, it should be possible to alter the types of details that are remembered by manipulating how people process the information. Kensinger et al. (2005) demonstrated that when young adults intentionally encoded scenes with instructions to remember all aspects of the scenes, their ability to remember the nonemotional background (e.g., the street) was as good as their ability to remember the negative object (e.g., the car accident). Similar reductions of memory trade-off effects can occur if participants are asked to describe a scene so that an artist could reproduce it accurately. With this type of focused encoding task, most people are just as good at remembering the nonemotional background details of a negative scene than of an entirely nonemotional scene. Additionally, it has been shown that memory for thematically induced arousal, or arousal produced by empathy instead of a salient visual stimulus, enhances memory for an event overall with no memory-narrowing effects (Laney et al., 2003; Laney, Campbell, Heuer, & Reisberg, 2004). These data suggest that although perceptual processes may initially be automatically biased toward emotionally negative salient stimuli, controlled shifts in attention to intentionally encode nonemotional aspects of a negative emotional scene can alter later memory performance, reducing or eliminating emotion-induced memory trade-offs.

Successful encoding of negative emotional memories has been shown to critically depend on interactions between the hippocampus and amygdala (Dolcos, LaBar, & Cabeza, 2004; Richardson, Strange, & Dolan, 2004) and arousal-induced release of hormones. Neuroimaging studies highlight the important role of emotional arousal on activation in the hippocampus and amygdala during encoding of emotional stimuli. Some studies have suggested that an affective attentional network (amygdala, orbitofrontal cortex, ventral striatum, and anterior cingulate gyrus) focuses and guides encoding processes, ensuring that salient information is attended to and encoded in the hippocampus, often at the cost of nonemotional elements (Kensinger et al., 2007a) in the absence of intentional encoding instructions. Interestingly, implicitly driven emotion-induced memory trade-offs may vary depending on individual differences, particularly levels of anxiety, working memory capacity, and executive function abilities. A study recently conducted by Waring et al. (2010) demonstrated that individuals with greater anxiety, poor visuospatial working memory, and poor executive function show more prominent emotion-induced memory trade-offs than individuals without these traits. Aside from individual differences, Deffenbacher et al. (2004) suggests, in a meta-analytic review, that the type of arousal evoked is also critical in determining how emotion modulates attention. Deffenbacher makes a distinction between an arousal mode of attention, a mode that initiates orientation and allocation of attention to the most informative aspects of a particular stimulus, and an activation mode of attention control, by which attention is restricted to specific semantic or motivational content of a stimulus. In the former case one may be more likely to allocate attention across multiple features of a stimulus compared to the latter case where one's attention may be significantly restricted to a specific feature. While further research is needed to understand additional factors that may influence and modulate attentional resources and encoding of emotional scenes, emotion-induced memory trade-off has been demonstrated across many studies and is a robust effect. Preferential processing of negative emotional information in perceptual and attentional networks creates ideal conditions for emotional information to have privileged access to working memory.

## Emotion-Based Modulation of Working Memory

Working memory is a limited-capacity system that regulates and maintains information through conscious rehearsal or rumination (Baddeley, 2001). Only a handful of studies have examined the effects of emotion on working memory and findings remain mixed (Edelstein, 2006; Kensinger & Corkin, 2003). Some find that working memory capacity appears greater for emotional (both positive and negative) than nonemotional words (Edelstein, 2006), while others report that working memory performance does not differ for emotional and nonemotional information (Kensinger & Corkin, 2003). Mixed results may arise, in part, from task demand differences across studies. Working memory tasks incorporating instructions that require individuals to remember both nonemotional and emotional items typically result in no memory differences, while emotional items show enhancement if individuals are not provided with task instructions

(Kensinger & Corkin, 2003). High task demands appear to negatively impact working memory performance, most likely by straining its limited capacity, while emotional information is more likely to be maintained in working memory than nonemotional information in the absence of specific instructions to the contrary. Another possible functional mechanism for enhanced memory for emotional items in working memory may be the ease with which emotional items can be related to one another. This may facilitate chunking and thereby increase the capacity for emotional information in working memory.

Although it is known that rehearsal is the primary means by which information is maintained and processed in working memory, it has been shown that rehearsal alone does not account for emotional memory enhancement in working memory tasks. Studies have demonstrated that eliminating the opportunity for rehearsal by having participants perform a distracter task (e.g., math task) or an immediate recall test does not eliminate the memory advantage for negative emotional information in working memory (Harris & Pashler, 2005; Hulse, Allan, Memon, & Read, 2007). Similar to emotion modulation of perceptual and attentional systems, negative emotional memory advantages in working memory may reflect the influence of arousal-induced release of hormones (i.e., norepinephrine). Indeed, it has been shown that drugs that block arousal-induced hormone release selectively impair emotional memory in working memory tasks (Chamberlain, Müller, Blackwell, Robbins, & Sahakian, 2006). Given that emotional information is maintained in working memory, it can then be consolidated into long-term memory storage. Emotion has been shown to modulate consolidation processes as well.

## Emotion-Based Modulation of Consolidation

Memory consolidation involves a complex set of neurobiological processes that occur over time and that can be modulated by emotion (see McGaugh, 2000 for a review). Animal studies have provided evidence that arousal-induced activation of the noradrenergic system (i.e., norepinephrine) and activation of the amygdala, which promotes consolidation, drive the preferential consolidation of emotional memory (Ashby, Isen, & Turken, 1999; Cahill, Gorski, & Le, 2003; Canli, Zhao, Brewer, Gabrieli, & Cahill, 2000; Hurlemann et al., 2005; McGaugh, 2004). Although much of the research in this area has been conducted with animals, human research has also demonstrated that emotional memory is consolidated into long-term memory more efficiently than memory for nonemotional information, particularly under conditions of arousal-induced activation of the noradrenergic system. Research has shown that memory consolidation is facilitated by both pleasant and aversive postlearning arousal for positive and negative, but not nonemotional, stimuli (Liu et al., 2008; Nielson & Powless, 2007). Moreover, once encoded, emotional memories have been shown to be susceptible to strengthening by postlearning arousal from 30 minutes (Nielson & Powless, 2007) to 50 minutes and in some cases up to 2 hours (Pelletier, Likhtik, Filali, & Paré, 2005) after learning. Although some studies have focused on the effects of endogenous increases in arousal hormones, studies have shown that memory consolidation for negative materials is enhanced by exogenous increases in norepinephrine as well (Cahill & Alkire, 2003). Memory traces for negatively arousing events are additionally strengthened over time; enhancement effects are observed after brief delays from hours to days (Sharot & Phelps, 2004), and especially following postlearning nocturnal sleep (Payne & Kensinger, 2010, 2011; Payne, Swanberg, Stickgold, & Kensinger, 2008). An extended window of time for emotion to influence consolidation processes after initial acquisition, and preferential consolidation of emotional memory traces during sleep, serve important adaptive functions, ensuring that memory for emotionally salient negative events is well preserved. Aside from these biologically defined mechanisms, postevent elaboration and rumination of emotional events likely strengthens emotional memory traces over time.

### Emotion-Based Modulation of Retrieval

Clearly, research has shown that the more arousing an event is, the better it is remembered. Preferential processing of negative emotional information in perception/attention, working memory, consolidation, and long-term memory systems culminates in negative emotional information being more reliably and accurately retrieved than nonemotional information. Memories laden with great emotional intensity or of personal significance are remembered more accurately than memories that are emotionally neutral or are of little personal relevance (Buchanan, 2007; Reisberg & Hertel, 2004; Sharot et al., 2007).

Overall, there is less conclusive evidence regarding how emotion influences retrieval, when induced just prior to or during remembering. It has been suggested that retrieval of negative emotional information may be facilitated by reactivation of affective states similar to those experienced during encoding. In this sense, affective states act as internal retrieval cues that could aid in remembering past emotional experiences. Reactivation of affective states may additionally elicit activation in the amygdala, including release of noradrenergic hormones (Murchinson et al., 2004), which may aid in memory retrieval. Pharmacological studies support this notion, demonstrating that beta-adrenergic blockade during memory retrieval significantly diminishes the typical enhancement of memory for emotional materials (Kroes, Strange, & Dolan, 2010). Numerous studies have demonstrated that the amygdala is activated during retrieval of negative emotional information and that activation in this region corresponds to successful remembering of emotional, but not neutral, materials (Dolcos, LaBar, & Cabeza, 2005; Keightley, Anderson, Grady, & Chiew, 2011). Amygdala involvement in retrieval of emotional memories is critical and persists over time. Dolcos, LaBar, and Cabeza (2005) demonstrated that after a retention interval of a year, memory was greater overall for emotional versus neutral items, and that successful retrieval of emotional items elicited greater activation in the hippocampus and amygdala than did successful retrieval of neutral items. Furthermore, emotional items reported as being recollected, as opposed to being familiar, elicited greater activation in the amygdala and hippocampus. Thus, the hippocampus and amygdala not only play an integral role in retrieval of emotional information but also, as discussed earlier, show correlated activation during the encoding of emotional events.

In summary, moderate emotion facilitates processing of negative information in attention and perception (i.e., encoding), working memory, consolidation, and retrieval systems. As a result, subsequent memory for emotional materials is enhanced. By comparison, under conditions of moderate emotion, memory for emotionally neutral information is often impaired. Impairments are thought to result from a lack of attention allocated to nonemotional items, when in the presence of emotionally negative material during acquisition, a failure to engage norepinephrine and amygdala mechanisms that selectively promote the encoding and consolidation of emotional materials, and the fact that negative emotional information and events elicit more postevent elaboration and rumination than do nonemotional information and events.

## Modulation of Memory Processes by Intense Emotion

While the effects of intense emotion, or stress, on memory processes are similar to those just described for moderate emotion, memory impairments and enhancements are more pronounced. These potentiated effects are primarily driven by the release of cortisol, a stress hormone shown to modulate neural processing in several memory regions, including the hippocampus and amygdala. Cortisol effects on memory processes are mediated by two factors: (1) the degree to which an individual is emotionally aroused and (2) the phase of memory processing directly influenced by elevated cortisol levels (i.e., acquisition/encoding, consolidation, or retrieval).

### The Physiological Stress Response and Learning

The term *stress* is usually applied to situations that disrupt homeostasis, including situations where one faces emotional distress or is physically challenged. In response to stress, cortisol is released into the blood by the adrenal cortex, travels through the circulatory system, crosses the blood-brain barrier, and binds to mineralocorticoid receptors (MRs) and glucocorticoid receptors (GRs) in various brain regions. The frontal cortex, hippocampus, and amygdala have an abundance of these receptors; however, cortisol activation of MRs and GRs modulates processes quite differently in these regions. For the purpose of this discussion, we will focus on the effects of cortisol on the hippocampus and amygdala; however, it is important to note that stress has also been shown to modulate frontal lobe function (see Dedovic, D'Aguair, & Pruessner, 2005 for review; van Stegeren, Kindt, Roozendaal, Wolf, & Joëls, 2010). In the medial temporal lobes, a high level of circulating cortisol typically facilitates neural processes in the amygdala but impairs neural processes in the hippocampus.

Cortisol facilitates amygdala function by influencing both intracellular and extracellular neural processes. In the presence of high cortisol levels, amygdala neurons become more excitable, showing a positive shift in resting membrane potential and enhanced input resistance. Additionally, GABA-A receptors within this region show overall decreased amplitude of inhibitory postsynaptic potentials. Duvarci and Paré (2007) reported cortisol-driven shifts in amygdala neurons when varying amounts of cortisol were administered, in vitro, to basal lateral amygdala (BLA) slices. Larger dosages of cortisol resulted in greater facilitation of synaptic

plasticity. The functional implication of these effects seems clear: Learning and memory can be facilitated in the amygdala when stress levels are high.

Facilitation of amygdala plasticity is not solely dependent on cortisol activation of GRs and MRs. Much as the release of norepinephrine is necessary for enhanced emotional learning in the amygdala, the facilitating effects of cortisol on BLA plasticity are modulated by, and perhaps even dependent upon, arousal-induced noradrenergic activation within the BLA. Animal studies have provided support for this notion, demonstrating that blockade of beta-adrenoceptors in the BLA prevents the memory-enhancing effects of cortisol on amygdala function (McGaugh & Roozendaal, 2002; Roozendaal, Okuda, Van der Zee, & McGaugh, 2006b). These findings suggest that emotional arousal and stress must co-occur for subsequent memory of emotional materials to be enhanced. This is particularly true regarding stress modulation of encoding and consolidation processes, which will be discussed in the next section.

In contrast to what appears to be a positive linear relation between cortisol levels and amygdala function, cortisol effects on hippocampal learning are more complex and depend on the ratio of cortisol-bound MRs to GRs. There are important differences in affinity between these two receptor types: MRs have a much higher affinity for cortisol than GRs. Thus, at low and moderate levels of stress, binding of cortisol can be limited primarily to MRs, which facilitate hippocampal LTP processes (Joëls & de Kloet, 1990, 1991). When this occurs, hippocampal plasticity is at its maximum and performance on hippocampal-dependent tasks is optimal. However, when stress levels are sufficiently high, cortisol levels increase, MRs saturate, and GRs are activated. Activation of GRs facilitates long-term depression (LTD) in the hippocampus. As a result, hippocampal plasticity and hippocampal-dependent tasks can be impaired (Kim & Diamond, 2002). Given the dissociative effects of cortisol on hippocampal plasticity, the relationship between stress and performance on hippocampal-dependent tasks is traditionally described as an inverted U-shaped function (Yerkes & Dodson, 1908). Optimal behavioral performance occurs when cortisol levels are moderate (MRs are largely occupied but GR activation is minimal), and impaired behavioral performance occurs when cortisol levels are too low or too high (in the latter case, MRs are fully saturated and a large proportion of GRs are occupied).

## Severe Emotion Modulation of Encoding and Consolidation

Disentangling the effects of stress on encoding and consolidation has proved to be difficult. Traditionally the effects of stress on encoding are examined by inducing stress immediately prior to acquisition. Although these methods allow examination of the effects of stress on encoding processes, they also influence early consolidation processes, which are thought to begin immediately after encoding. By contrast, stress induction immediately after acquisition allows for the examination of the effects of stress on consolidation processes relatively independent of those on encoding. In this section we discuss the effects of stress on encoding and consolidation.

### INTENSE EMOTION AND THE MODULATION OF ENCODING

Behavioral studies have shown that stress induction, just prior to acquisition of emotional and nonemotional materials, can result in both enhanced and impaired declarative memory performance (Abercrombie, Kalin, Thurow, Rosenkranz, & Davidson, 2003). More specifically, enhanced emotional memory, but impaired memory for nonemotional information, has been observed (de Quervain, Aerni, Shelling, & Roozendaal, 2009; Payne et al., 2006, 2007). Dissociative effects of stress on memory for emotional versus nonemotional information is perhaps best understood in terms of the dissociative effects of cortisol on hippocampal versus amygdala function, discussed in the previous section. Neuroimaging studies have provided supporting evidence for impairing effects of cortisol on hippocampal function and enhancing effects of cortisol on amygdala function in humans during encoding, in that hippocampal activation decreases (Dedovic et al., 2009; Henckens, Hermans, Pu, Joëls, & Fernández, 2009; Pruessner et al., 2008), whereas amygdala activation increases (van Stegeren et al., 2010), under conditions of elevated stress. Furthermore, hippocampal activation and cortisol levels are negatively correlated; thus, as cortisol levels increase, activation in the hippocampus decreases (Pruessner et al., 2008).

Behavioral studies that have examined the effects of stress under conditions of arousal or nonarousal have demonstrated the critical role arousal plays in stress modulation of encoding processes. It appears that arousal and physiological stress must both occur for emotional memory enhancement effects to arise (Roozendaal et al., 2006a, 2006b; Segal & Cahill,

2009). Under conditions of stress and arousal, cortisol and norepinephrine appear to work within the BLA synergistically, facilitating amygdala learning during encoding. Payne et al. (2007) examined memory for arousing versus nonarousing episodes using identical visual stimuli. A slideshow depicting a car accident and subsequent injuries (cf., Cahill & McGaugh, 1995) was presented to all participants; the arousal group heard an emotionally arousing narrative while the nonarousal group heard a nonemotional narrative (i.e., participants are told that the injuries depicted are not real but rather part of a mock hospital drill). Results showed that memory for the events in the slideshow was enhanced in the stress-arousal group but impaired in the stress/nonarousal group. These results suggest that, when all things are held equal, arousal must be present for stress to enhance emotional memory, while stress alone can cause memory impairment for nonarousing materials.

Pharmacological studies have examined independent contributions of cortisol and norepinephrine on amygdala function, providing further evidence for the importance of co-occurring stress and arousal in the facilitation of emotional memory encoding. These studies have demonstrated that blockage of norepinephrine release or administration of a noradrenergic antagonist results in impaired long-term memory for emotionally arousing material (Maheu, Joober, Beaulieu, & Lupien, 2004; van Steregen et al., 2005, 2007). Results of neuroimaging studies support these findings, showing that the administration of a noradrenergic antagonist decreases amygdala activation, even under conditions of extreme stress (van Steregen et al., 2005, 2007). Together, these results support the notion that arousal plays an integral role in modulation of amygdala processes during encoding of emotionally salient information to produce emotional memory enhancement under high levels of stress.

Clearly, cortisol and norepinephrine interact in important ways to produce memory enhancement effects in the amygdala during encoding. However, research has also shown that enhanced BLA activation, during arousal, in turn mediates the effects of cortisol within areas of the hippocampus (McGaugh & Roozendaal, 2002; Nathan, Griffith, McReynolds, Hahn, & Roozendaal, 2004; Roozendaal, 2002; Strange & Dolan, 2004), allowing this region to successfully encode emotional information under stress (de Quervain et al., 2009; Lupien, Maheu, Tu, Fiocco, & Schramek, 2007; Richter-Levin, 2004; Roozendaal et al., 2008).

Although elevated cortisol levels can impair hippocampal plasticity, impaired hippocampal encoding under stress may be most likely in the absence of amygdala-driven noradrenegic modulation. In contrast, given the engagement of the amygdala, and the release of norepinephrine, the hippocampus can preferentially encode emotionally relevant information under conditions of stress (van Stegeren et al., 2010). In fact, at least one animal study has demonstrated that an intact hippocampus is necessary for the modulation of learning by stress, showing that hippocampal lesions prevented stress-induced enhancements as well as stress-induced impairments of learning after stress (Bangasser & Shors, 2007). Few human studies have investigated emotional memory in hippocampal-damaged individuals and findings remain mixed. One study, conducted by Buchanan, Tranel, and Adolphs (2005), demonstrated that unpleasant autobiographical memory reports of hippocampal patients were strikingly similar to those of brain-damaged and healthy controls. By contrast, patients with damage to the hippocampus and surrounding cortical regions (e.g., amygdala) reported fewer unpleasant memories overall. A critical component for interpreting these results is determining whether these structures were intact at the time the reported emotional events were encoded and the extent of damage to these regions. Provided what is known regarding the critical role of the amygdala and hippocampus in encoding and retrieving emotional memories, one might suspect that patients with partial hippocampal damage and an intact amygdala would be able to report a number of remote emotional memories while individuals with hippocampal and amygdala damage might produce fewer emotional memories overall. Additionally, research suggests that results may vary depending on whether the right or left medial temporal lobe region is damaged. Patients with right-sided anteromedial temporal lobe (i.e., anterior hippocampus and amygdala) damage demonstrate severely impaired recollection of unpleasant memories compared to right temporal lobectomy patients who perform similarly to intact individuals (Buchanan, Tranel, & Adolphs, 2006b).

## SEVERE EMOTION MODULATION OF CONSOLIDATION

Similar to the facilitating effects of stress administered prior to encoding, increased cortisol levels after encoding are positively correlated with enhanced memory for emotionally laden information in aroused individuals (Abercrombie et al., 2003; Buchanan & Lovallo, 2001; Cahill et al., 2003). Numerous studies have demonstrated that endogenous and exogenous increases in cortisol after training lead to enhanced memory consolidation of emotionally arousing materials (Kuhlmann & Wolf, 2006a; McGaugh & Roozendaal, 2002; Roozendaal, 2002). It is postulated that the emotional memory enhancement effect is the product of a "special" consolidation process involving interactions between cortisol and norepinephrine within the BLA and concomitant BLA modulation of hippocampal activity that promotes consolidation of emotional material (de Quervain et al., 2009; Lupien et al., 2007; Richardson et al., 2004; Richter-Levin, 2004; Roozendaal et al., 2008).

However, the effects of stress on consolidation processes remain unclear. Some studies have reported mixed results showing impaired emotional memory or enhanced nonemotional memory when cortisol levels are elevated after encoding. Buchanan, Tranel, and Adolphs (2006a) subjected participants to a cold pressor stress task 1 hour after learning negative and neutral words. This stress manipulation, which involves submerging one's arm in very cold water, reliably elevates cortisol in human participants. Stress responders showed impaired memory for moderately arousing negative words, while memory for highly arousing negative words and neutral words was unaffected. Mixed results may exist, in part, due to the phase of memory consolidation (i.e., early vs. late) modulated by cortisol. Neural mechanisms that underlie early consolidation processes, believed to begin immediately after encoding, may significantly differ from those involved in late consolidation processes. Thus, stress induced a few hours after encoding may produce very different memory effects than stress induced shortly after encoding, during the early phase of consolidation. It may be the case that once the optimal window of time during which cortisol can modulate consolidation processes has passed emotional memory enhancement is not observed. Additionally, the time between stress induction and memory testing is critical if one wishes to determine the effects of stress on consolidation processes independent of retrieval. In the study of Buchanan, Tranel, and Adolphs (2006a) memory was tested 10 minutes after the cold pressor; thus, cortisol levels were likely elevated during retrieval and, as we will discuss in the next section, stress has been shown to impair memory retrieval.

## Severe Emotion Modulation of Memory Retrieval

In contrast to the facilitatory effects of cortisol on encoding and consolidation of emotional materials, increased cortisol levels at retrieval typically result in memory impairments overall (de Quervain et al., 2009; Kuhlmann, Piel, & Wolf, 2005; Merz, Wolf, & Hennig, 2010; Tollenaar, Elzinga, Spinhove, & Everaerd, 2008b). Impairing effects of stress on retrieval are robust, generalizing across various types of stimuli with varying levels of valence and arousal (e.g., words; Domes, Heinrichs, Rimmele, Reichwald, & Hautzinger, 2004; Kuhlmann et al., 2005), word pair associations (Tollenaar et al., 2008a, 2008b), slideshows (Buchanan & Tranel, 2008), and socially relevant information (Merz et al., 2010). Studies examining the effects of exogenous increases in cortisol levels, through the oral administration of hydrocortisone, show that cortisol increases at the time of retrieval not only impair memory for experimental materials but also generally impair episodic memory performance (Tollenaar, Elzinga, Spinhove, & Everaerd, 2009a, 2009b). The driving factor of impaired retrieval under conditions of stress is thought to be disrupted hippocampal function via the binding of cortisol to both GRs and MRs. Neuroimaging studies examining the effects of stress on activation in regions involved in retrieval processes have provided evidence for this notion, demonstrating that activity in the hippocampus is significantly reduced when cortisol levels are high (Dedovic, Renwick, et al., 2005; Wang et al., 2005). Additionally, it has been shown that the degree of hippocampal deactivation significantly correlates with impaired declarative memory retrieval (Dedovic et al., 2009) as well as the cortisol stress response (Pruessner et al., 2008). Although impairing effects of stress on memory retrieval appear to be primarily driven by cortisol (Buchanan et al., 2006a), whether arousal-induced release of hormones modulates or even enables these cortisol effects on memory retrieval is still under debate. Some studies suggest that this might be the case, demonstrating that memory in nonarousing testing situations (Kuhlmann & Wolf, 2006b) and for nonarousing materials (Kuhlmann, Kirschbaum, & Wolf, 2005) is unaffected by exogenous cortisol administration prior to retrieval.

Although impaired memory retrieval may seem maladaptive, impaired memory retrieval under conditions of stress may serve an adaptive purpose. Hippocampal deactivation may prevent previously stored information from being retrieved at a time when it could interfere with the encoding and consolidation of salient new emotional information. Thus, stress-induced retrieval impairments might allow stressful experiences to be encoded rapidly and efficiently. Additionally, impaired retrieval may prevent remote memories for traumatic events from being updated through reconsolidation mechanisms during new stressful situations. This would guarantee that emotional memories remain distinct from one another (Roozendaal et al., 2008), an important feature for adaptive future behavior. Provided the stress is not chronic, such retrieval impairments are usually temporary, and memory performance is reinstated once the cortisol effects wear off (de Quervain, Aerni, & Roozendaal, 2007).

## Conclusions

All the effects we described herein reflect acute emotion or stress. While there is not a great deal known about the effects of chronic stress, it is worth briefly discussing what is known.

For obvious reasons, the effects of chronic stress have been studied mostly in animals. Elevating stress levels for long periods of time impairs hippocampal and prefrontal functions (de Kloet, Vreugdenhil, Oitzl, & Joëls, 1998; see Herbert et al., 2006, for review; Liston, Casey, & McEwen, 2009; McEwen, 1998, 2005), causing profound disruption of long-term potentiation and reduced density of dendritic spines in the hippocampus (Chen et al., 2010) that ultimately results in hippocampal volume loss. By contrast, chronic stress has been shown to enhance sensitivity of the amygdala (Vyas, Bernal, & Chattarji, 2003; Vyas, Mitra, Rao, & Chattarji, 2002), making this region more active overall. For example, heightened activity of the amygdala after traumatic stress has been shown to increase sensitivity to information related to the trauma (Bremner et al., 1999) and also to fear-inducing information (Shin et al., 2005). Deleterious effects on the hippocampus and enhanced sensitivity in the amygdala may be among the reasons some individuals develop pathological conditions such as depression and posttraumatic stress disorder (PTSD) in reaction to chronic stress. One mechanism at play in stress-related disorders might be a reduction of the inhibitory control the medial prefrontal cortex normally exerts over the amygdala, resulting in increased basal activity within this region (McEwen, 2005; Shekhar, Truitt, Rainnie, & Sajdyk, 2005). As a result, individuals may become more responsive to stressful situations and less able to moderate mood and anxiety levels.

Little is known about the relationship between stress hormones and depression, but what is known is that a correlation exists. Although the neural mechanisms underlying the relationship between chronic stress and depression remain unknown, it is plausible that depression and chronic stress are related in terms of decreased prefrontal and hippocampal function and increased amygdala activity. Long periods of depression have been shown to decrease volume in hippocampal and prefrontal cortex (MacQueen et al., 2003; Sheline, Gado, & Kraemer, 2003), while amygdala volume has been observed to increase, particularly after the first bout of depression (Frodl et al., 2003).

Finally, chronic stress suppresses long-term changes in the input pathways to and within subregions of the hippocampus that are implicated in long-term memory (Alkadhi, Srivareerat, & Tran, 2010; Pavlides, Nivon, & McEwen, 2002) as well as hippocampal neurogenesis, which may result in age-related memory deficits (Borcel et al., 2008). It is interesting to note, in this light, that acute prenatal stress can diminish the neurogenesis typically triggered by learning (Lemaire, Koehl, Le Moal, & Abrous, 2000), an effect that can be reversed by providing rich learning environments in early postnatal life (Yang et al., 2007).

Although there has been relatively little work in humans, chronic stress in animals does seem to have a number of negative effects on neural structures subject to modulation by stress hormones. While some of these effects are reversible, normal function is frequently impaired. Given that amygdala, hippocampus, and frontal cortex are prominent among the affected structures, learning and memory are not surprisingly compromised and disorders such as PTSD and depression develop in some individuals. Clearly, more research in humans is needed, although the difficulties involved in obtaining such information are clear.

The situation is much better understood with respect to acute stress. Our review, which focused on negative emotion, suggests that low to moderate levels of emotion enhance memory for emotional, relative to nonemotional, information. These effects are observed across all phases of memory and appear to be norepinephrine driven. By contrast, intense levels of emotion (i.e., stress) cause the release of the stress hormone cortisol which modulates the facilitating effects of norepinephrine, resulting in enhanced encoding of emotional versus nonemotional items, facilitated consolidation of emotional items and impaired memory retrieval, overall. These impairing and enhancing effects may be best understood in terms of how cortisol affects neuronal function in the hippocampus and amygdala, impairing learning in the former and facilitating learning it in the latter.

## References

Abercrombie, H. C., Kalin, N. H., Thurow, M. E., Rosenkranz, M. A., & Davidson, R. J. (2003). Cortisol variation in humans affects memory for emotionally laden and neutral information. *Behavioral Neuroscience*. *117*(3), 505–516.

Adolphs, R. (2004). Emotional vision. *Nature Neuroscience*, *7*(11), 1167–1168.

Adolphs, R., Denburg, N. L., & Tranel, D. (2001). The amygdala's role in long-term declarative memory for gist and detail. *Behavioral Neuroscience*, *115*(5), 983–992.

Adolphs R., Gosselin F., Buchanan T. W., Tranel D., Schyns P., & Damasio, A. R. (2005). A mechanism for impaired fear recognition after amygdala damage. *Nature*, *433*(7021), 68–72.

Alkadhi, K. A., Srivareerat, M., & Tran, T. T. (2010). Intensification of long-term memory deficit by chronic stress and prevention by nicotine in a rat model of Alzheimer's disease. *Molecular and Cellular Neuroscience*, *45*(3), 289–296.

Alpers, G. W. (2008). Eye-catching: Right hemisphere attentional bias for emotional pictures. *Laterality*, *13*(2), 158–178.

Anderson, A. K., & Phelps, E. A. (2001). Lesions of the human amygdala impair enhanced perception of emotionally salient events. *Nature*, *411*(6835), 305–309.

Anderson, A. K., Yamaguchi, Y., Grabski, W., & Lacka, D. (2006). Emotional memories are not all created equal: Evidence for selective memory enhancement. *Learning and Memory*, *13*(6), 711–718.

Ashby, F. G., Isen, A. M., & Turken, A. U. (1999). A neuropsychological theory of positive affect and its influence on cognition. *Psychological Review*, *106*(3), 529–550.

Baddeley, A. D. (2001). Is working memory still working? *American Psychologist*, *56*(11), 851–864.

Bangasser, D. A., & Shors, T. J. (2007). The hippocampus is necessary for enhancements and impairments of learning following stress. *Nature Neuroscience*, *10*(11), 1401–1403.

Berntson, G. G., Bechara, A., Damasio, H., Tranel, D., & Cacioppo, J. T. (2007). Amygdala contribution to selective dimensions of emotion. *Social Cognitive and Affective Neuroscience*, *2*(2), 123–129.

Borcel, E., Pérez-Alvarez, L., Herrero, A. I., Brionne, T., Varea, E., Berezin, V., ... Venero C. (2008). Chronic stress in adulthood followed by intermittent stress impairs spatial memory and the survival of newborn hippocampal cells in aging animals: Prevention by FGL, a peptide mimetic of neural cell adhesion molecule. *Behavioural Pharmacology*, *19*(1), 41–49.

Bradley, M. M., Hamby, S., Löw, A., & Lang, P. J. (2007). Brain potentials in perception: Picture complexity and emotional arousal. *Psychophysiology*, *44*(3), 364–373.

Bremner, J. D., Staib, L. H., Kaloupek, D., Southwick, S. M., Soufer, R., & Charney, D. S. (1999). Neural correlates of exposure to traumatic pictures and sound in Vietnam combat veterans with and without posttraumatic stress disorder: A positron emission tomography study. *Biological Psychiatry*, *45*(7), 806–816.

Brosch, T., Pourtois, G., & Sander, D. (2010). The perception and categorisation of emotional stimuli: A review. *Cognition and Emotion*, *24*(3), 377–400.

Buchanan, T. W. (2007). Retrieval of emotional memories. *Psychological Bulletin*, *133*(5), 761–779.

Buchanan, T. W., & Adolphs, R. (2002). The role of the human amygdala in emotional modulation of long-term declarative memory. In S. Moore & M. Oaksford (Eds.), *Emotional cognition: From brain to behavior* (pp. 9–34). Amsterdam, The Netherlands: Benjamins.

Buchanan, T. W., & Lovallo, W. R. (2001). Enhanced memory for emotional material following stress-level cortisol treatment in humans. *Psychoneuroendocrinology*, *26*(3), 307–317.

Buchanan, T. W., & Tranel, D. (2008). Stress and emotional memory retrieval: Effects of sex and cortisol response. *Neurobiology of Learning and Memory*, *89*(2), 134–141.

Buchanan, T. W., Tranel, D., & Adolphs, R. (2005). Emotional autobiographical memories in amnesic patients with medial temporal lobe damage. *Journal of Neuroscience*, *25*(12), 3151–3160.

Buchanan, T. W., Tranel, D., & Adolphs, R. (2006a). Impaired memory retrieval correlates with individual differences in cortisol response but not autonomic response. *Learning and Memory*, *13*(3), 382–387.

Buchanan, T. W., Tranel, D., & Adolphs, R. (2006b). Memories for emotional autobiographical events following unilateral damage to medial temporal lobe. *Brain*, *129*(1), 115–127.

Cahill, L., & Alkire, M. T. (2003). Epinephrine enhancement of human memory consolidation: Interaction with arousal at encoding. *Neurobiology of Learning and Memory*, *79*(2), 194–198.

Cahill, L., Gorski, L., & Le, K. (2003). Enhanced human memory consolidation with post-learning stress: Interaction with the degree of arousal at encoding. *Learning and Memory*, *10*(4), 270–274.

Cahill, L., & McGaugh, J. L. (1995). A novel demonstration of enhanced memory associated with emotional arousal. *Consciousness and Cognition*, *4*(4), 410–421.

Calvo, M. G., & Lang, P. J. (2005). Parafoveal semantic processing of emotional visual scenes. *Journal of Experimental Psychology: Human Perception and Performance*, *31*(3), 502–519.

Canli, T., Zhao, Z., Brewer, J., Gabrieli, J. D. E., & Cahill, L. (2000). Event-related activation in the human amygdala associates with later memory for individual emotional experience. *Journal of Neuroscience*, *20*(RC99), 1–5.

Chamberlain, S., Müller, U., Blackwell, A., Robbins, T., & Sahakian, B. (2006). Noradrenergic modulation of working memory and emotional memory in humans. *Psychopharmacology*, *188*(4), 397–407.

Chen, Y., Rex, C. S., Rice, C. J., Dube, C. M., Gall, C. M., Lynch, G., & Baram, T.Z. (2010). Correlated memory defects and hippocampal dendritic spine loss after acute stress involve corticotropin-releasing hormone signaling. *Proceedings- National Academy of Sciences USA*, *107*(29), 13123–13128.

Compton, R. J. (2003). The interface between emotion and attention: A review of evidence from psychology and neuroscience. *Behavioral and Cognitive Neuroscience Reviews*, *2*(2), 115–129.

de Kloet, E. R., Vreugdenhil, E., Oitzl, M. S., & Joëls, M. (1998). Brain corticosteroid receptor balance in health and disease. *Endocrine Reviews*, *19*(3), 269–301.

de Quervain, D. J., Aerni, A., & Roozendaal, B. (2007). Preventive effect of beta-adrenoceptor blockade on glucocorticoid-induced memory retrieval deficits. *American Journal of Psychiatry*, *164*(6), 967–969.

de Quervain, D. J., Aerni, A., Shelling, G., & Roozendaal, B. (2009). Glucocorticoids and the regulation of memory in health and disease. *Frontiers in Neuroendocrinology*, *30*(3), 358–370.

Dedovic, K., D'Aguiar, C., & Pruessner, J. C. (2005). What stress does to your brain: A review of neuroimaging studies. *Canadian Journal of Psychiatry*, *54*(1), 6–15.

Dedovic, K., Renwick, R., Mahani, N. K., Engert, V., Lupiën, S. J., & Pruessner, J. C. (2005). The Montreal imaging stress task: Using functional imaging to investigate the effects of perceiving and processing psychosocial stress in the human brain. *Journal of Psychiatry and Neuroscience*, *30*(5), 319–25.

Dedovic, K., Rexroth, M., Wolff, E., Duchesne, A., Scherling, C., Beaudry, T., ... Pruessner, J. C. (2009). Neural correlates of processing stressful information: An event-related fMRI study. *Brain Research*, *1293*, 49–60.

Deffenbacher, K. A., Bornstein, B. H., Penrod, S. D., & McGorty, E. K. (2004). A meta-analytic review of the effects of high stress on eyewitness memory. *Law and Human Behavior*, *28*(6), 687–706.

Denburg, N. L., Buchanan, T. W., Tranel, D., & Adolphs, R. (2003). Evidence for preserved emotional memory in normal older persons. *Emotion*, *3*(3), 239–253.

Dolcos, F., LaBar, K. S., & Cabeza, R. (2004). Interaction between the amygdala and the medial temporal lobe memory system predicts better memory for emotional events. *Neuron*, *42*(5), 855–863.

Dolcos, F., LaBar, K. S., & Cabeza, R. (2005). Remembering one year later: Role of the amygdala and the medial temporal lobe memory system in retrieving emotional memories. *Proceedings of the National Academy of Sciences USA*, *102*(7), 2626–2631.

Domes, G., Heinrichs, M., Rimmele, U., Reichwald, U., & Hautzinger, M. (2004). Acute stress impairs recognition for positive words-association with stress-induced cortisol secretion. *Stress*, *7*(3), 173–181.

Duvarci, S., & Paré, D. (2007). Glucocorticoids enhance the excitability of principal basolateral amygdala neurons. *Journal of Neuroscience*, *27*(16), 4482–4491.

Edelstein, R. S. (2006). Attachment and emotional memory: Investigating the source and extent of avoidant memory impairments. *Emotion*, *6*(2), 340–345.

Frodl, T., Meisenzahl, E. M., Zetzsche, T., Born, C., Jäger, M., Groll, C., ... Möller, H. (2003). Larger amygdala volumes in first depressive episode as compared to recurrent major depression and healthy control subjects. *Biological Psychiatry*, *53*(4), 338–344.

Gable, P. A., & Harmon-Jones, E. (2008). Approach-motivated positive affect reduces breadth of attention. *Psychological Science*, *19*(5), 476–482.

Harris, C. R., & Pashler, H. (2005). Enhanced memory for negatively emotionally charged pictures without selective rumination. *Emotion*, *5*(2), 191–199.

Henckens, M. J., Hermans, E. J., Pu, Z., Joëls, M., & Fernández, G. (2009). Stressed memories: How acute stress affects memory formation in humans. *Journal of Neuroscience*, *29*(32), 10111–10119.

Herbert, J., Goodyer, I. M., Grossman, A. B., Hastings, M. H., de Kloet, E. R., Lightman, S. L., ... Seckl, J. R.

(2006). Do corticosteroids damage the brain? *Journal of Neuroendocrinology, 18*(6), 393–411.

Huang, Y., & Luo, Y. (2006). Temporal course of emotional negativity bias: An ERP study. *Neuroscience Letters, 398*(1), 91–96.

Hulse, L. M., Allan, K., Memon, A., & Read, J. D. (2007). Emotional arousal and memory: A test of the poststimulus processing hypothesis. *American Journal of Psychology, 120*(1), 73–90.

Hurlemann, R., Hawellek, B., Matusch, A., Kolsch, H., Wollersen, H., Madea, B.,... Dolan, R. (2005). Noradrenergic modulation of emotion-induced forgetting and remembering. *Journal of Neuroscience, 25*(27), 6343–6349.

Joëls, M., & de Kloet, E. R. (1990). Mineralocorticoid receptor-mediated changes in membrane properties of rat CA1 pyramidal neurons in vitro. *Proceedings of the National Academy of Sciences USA, 87*(12), 4495–4498.

Joëls, M., & de Kloet, E. R. (1991). Effect of corticosteroid hormones on electrical activity in rat hippocampus. *Journal of Steroid Biochemistry and Molecular Biology, 40*(1–3), 83–86.

Keightley, M. L., Anderson, J., Grady, C., & Chiew, K. (2011). Neural correlates of recognition memory for emotional faces and scenes. *Cognitive and Affective Neuroscience, 6*(1), 24–37.

Kensinger, E. A. (2009). Remembering the details: Effects of emotion. *Emotion Review, 1*(2), 99–113.

Kensinger, E. A., & Corkin, S. (2003). Effect of negative emotional content on working memory and long-term memory. *Emotion, 3*(4), 378–393.

Kensinger, E. A., & Corkin, S. (2004). Two routes to emotional memory: Distinct neural processes for valence and arousal. *Proceedings of the National Academy of Sciences USA, 101*(9), 3310–3315.

Kensinger, E. A., Garoff-Eaton, R. J., & Schacter, D. L. (2007a). How negative emotion enhances the visual specificity of a memory. *Journal of Cognitive Neuroscience, 19*(11), 1872–1887.

Kensinger, E. A., Garoff-Eaton, R. J., & Schacter, D. L. (2007b). Effects of emotion on memory specificity: Memory trade-offs elicited by negative visually arousing stimuli. *Journal of Memory and Language, 56*(4), 575–591.

Kensinger, E. A., Piguet, O., Krendl, A. C., & Corkin, S. (2005). Memory for contextual details: Effects of emotion and aging. *Psychology and Aging, 20*(2), 241–250.

Kensinger, E. A., & Schacter, D. L. (2006). When the Red Sox shocked the Yankees: Comparing negative and positive memories. *Psychonomic Bulletin and Review, 13*(5), 757–763.

Kim, J. J., & Diamond, D. M. (2002). The stressed hippocampus, synaptic plasticity and lost memories. *Nature Reviews Neuroscience, 3*(6), 453–462.

Koster, E. H., Crombez, G., Verschuere, B., Vanvolsem, P., & De Houwer, J. (2007). A time-course analysis of attentional cueing by threatening scenes. *Experimental Psychology, 54*(2), 161–171.

Kroes, M. C., Strange, B. A., & Dolan, R. J. (2010). Beta-Adrenergic blockade during memory retrieval in humans evokes a sustained reduction of declarative emotional memory enhancement. *Journal of Neuroscience, 30*(11), 3959–3963.

Kuhlmann, S., Kirschbaum, C., & Wolf, O. T. (2005). Effects of oral cortisol treatment in healthy young women on memory retrieval of negative and neutral words. *Neurobiology of Learning and Memory, 83*(2), 158–162.

Kuhlmann, S., Piel, M., & Wolf, O. T. (2005). Impaired memory retrieval after psychosocial stress in healthy young men. *Journal of Neuroscience, 25*(11), 2977–2982.

Kuhlmann, S., & Wolf, O. T. (2006a). Arousal and cortisol interact in modulating memory consolidation in healthy young men. *Behavioral Neuroscience, 120*(1), 217–223.

Kuhlmann, S., & Wolf, O. T. (2006b). A non-arousing test situation abolishes the impairing effects of cortisol on delayed memory retrieval in healthy women. *Neuroscience Letters, 399*(3), 268–272.

Laney, C., Campbell, H. V., Heuer, F., & Reisberg, D. (2004). Memory for thematically arousing events. *Memory and Cognition, 32*(7), 1149–1159.

Laney, C., Heuer, F., & Reisberg, D. (2003). Thematically-induced arousal in naturally-occurring emotional memories. *Applied Cognitive Psychology, 17*, 995–1004.

Lemaire, V., Koehl, M., Le Moal, M., & Abrous, D. N. (2000). Prenatal stress produces learning deficits associated with an inhibition of neurogenesis in the hippocampus. *Proceedings of the National Academy of Sciences USA, 97*(20), 11032–11037.

Levine, L. J., & Edelstein, R. S. (2009). Emotion and memory narrowing: A review and goal-relevance approach. *Cognition and Emotion, 23*(5), 833–875.

Levine, L. J., & Pizarro, D. A. (2004). Emotion and memory research: A grumpy overview. *Social Cognition, 22*(5), 530–554.

Liston, C., Casey, B. J., & McEwen, B. S. (2009). Psychosocial stress reversibly disrupts prefrontal processing and attentional control. *Proceedings of the National Academy of Sciences USA, 106*(3), 912–917.

Liu, D. L., Graham, S., & Zorawski, M. (2008). Enhanced selective memory consolidation following post-learning pleasant and aversive arousal. *Neurobiology of Learning and Memory, 89*(1), 36–46.

Luo, Q., Holroyd, T., Majestic, C., Cheng, X., Schechter, J., & Blair, J. R. (2010). Emotional automaticity is a matter of timing. *Journal of Neuroscience, 30*(17), 5825–5829.

Lupien, S. J., Maheu, F., Tu, M., Fiocco, A., & Schramek, T. E. (2007). The effects of stress and stress hormones on human cognition: Implications for the field of brain and cognition. *Brain Cognition, 65*, 209–237.

MacQueen, G. M., Campbell, S., McEwen, B. S., Macdonald, K., Amano, S., Joffe, R. T.,... Young, L. T. (2003). Course of illness, hippocampal function, and hippocampal volume in major depression. *Proceedings of the National Academy of Sciences USA, 100*(3), 1387–1392.

Maheu, F. S., Joober, R., Beaulieu, S., & Lupien, S. J. (2004). Differential effects of adrenergic and corticosteroid hormonal systems on human short- and long-term declarative memory for emotionally arousing material. *Behavioral Neuroscience, 118*(2), 420–428.

Mather, M. (2007). Emotional arousal and memory binding: An object-based framework. *Perspectives on Psychological Science, 2*(1), 33–52.

McEwen, B. S. (1998). Protective and damaging effects of stress mediators. *New England Journal of Medicine, 338*(3), 171–179.

McEwen, B. S. (2005). Glucocorticoids, depression, and mood disorders: Structural remodeling in the brain. *Metabolism: Clinical and Experimental, 54*(5), 20–23.

McGaugh, J. L. (2000). Memory: A century of consolidation. *Science, 287*, 248–251.

McGaugh, J. L. (2004). The amygdala modulates the consolidation of memories of emotionally arousing experiences. *Annual Review of Neuroscience*, *27*, 1–28.

McGaugh, J. L., & Roozendaal, B. (2002). Role of adrenal stress hormones in forming lasting memories in the brain. *Current Opinion in Neurobiology*, *12*(2), 205–210.

Merz, C. J., Wolf, O. T., & Hennig, J. (2010). Stress impairs retrieval of socially relevant information. *Behavioral Neuroscience*, *124*(2), 288–293.

Mickley, K. R., & Kensinger, E. A. (2009). Phenomenological characteristics of emotional memories in younger and older adults. *Memory Memory*, *17*(5), 528–543.

Murchison, C. F., Zhang, X. Y., Zhang, W. P., Ouyang, M., Lee, A., & Thomas, S. A. (2004). A distinct role for norepinephrine in memory retrieval. *Cell*, *117*(1), 131–143.

Nairne, J. S. (2007). *The foundations of remembering: Essays in honor of Henry L. Roediger III*. New York: Psychology Press.

Nathan, S. V., Griffith, Q. K., McReynolds, J. R., Hahn, E. L., & Roozendaal, B. (2004). Basolateral amygdala interacts with other brain regions in regulating glucocorticoid effects on different memory functions. *Annals of the New York Academy of Sciences*, *1032*, 179–182.

Nielson, K. A., & Powless, M. (2007). Positive and negative sources of emotional arousal enhance long-term word-list retention when induced as long as 30 min after learning. *Neurobiology of Learning and Memory*, *88*(1), 40–47.

Nobata, T., Hakoda, Y., & Ninose, Y. (2010). The functional field of view becomes narrower while viewing negative emotional stimuli. *Cognition and Emotion*, *24*(5), 886–891.

Nummenmaa, L., Hyönä, J., & Calvo, M. G. (2006). Eye movement assessment of selective attentional capture by emotional pictures. *Emotion*, *6*(2), 257–268.

Ohman, A. (2005). The role of the amygdala in human fear: Automatic detection of threat. *Psychoneuroendocrinology*, *30*(10), 953–958.

Pavlides, C., Nivon, L. G., & McEwen, B. S. (2002). Effects of chronic stress on hippocampal long-term potentiation. *Hippocampus*, *12*(2), 245–257.

Payne, J., Jackson, E., Hoscheidt, S., Ryan, L., Jacobs, W. J., & Nadel, L. (2007). Stress administered prior to encoding impairs neutral but enhances emotional long-term episodic memories. *Learning and Memory*, *14*(12), 861–868.

Payne, J., Jackson, E., Ryan, L., Hoscheidt, S., Jacobs, J., & Nadel, L. (2006). The impact of stress on neutral and emotional aspects of episodic memory. *Memory*, *14*(1), 1–16.

Payne, J., & Kensinger, E. (2010). Sleep's role in the consolidation of emotional episodic memories. *Current Directions in Psychological Science*, *19*(5), 290–295.

Payne, J., & Kensinger, E. (2011). Sleep leads to qualitative changes in the emotional memory trace: Evidence from fMRI. *Journal of Cognitive Neuroscience*, 23(6), 1285–1297.

Payne, J., Swanberg, K., Stickgold, R., & Kensinger, E. A. (2008). Sleep preferentially enhances memory for emotional components of scenes. *Psychological Science*, *19*(8), 781–788.

Pelletier, J. G., Likhtik, E., Filali, M., & Paré, D. (2005). Lasting increases in basolateral amygdala activity after emotional arousal: Implications for facilitated consolidation of emotional memories. *Learning and Memory*, *12*(2), 96–102.

Pessoa, L., & Ungerleider, L. G. (2004). Section III—perception and attention—12 neuroimaging studies of attention and the processing of emotion-laden stimuli. *Progress in Brain Research*, *144*, 171–182.

Pruessner, J. C., Dedovic, K., Khalili-Mahani, N., Engert, V., Pruessner, M., Buss, C.,… Lupien, S. (2008). Deactivation of the limbic system during acute psychosocial stress: Evidence from positron emission tomography and functional magnetic resonance imaging studies. *Biological Psychiatry*, *63*(2), 234–240.

Reisberg, D., & Hertel, P. (2004). *Memory and emotion*. Oxford, England and New York: Oxford University Press.

Richardson, M. P., Strange, B. A., & Dolan, R. J. (2004). Encoding of emotional memories depends on amygdala and hippocampus and their interactions. *Nature Neuroscience*, *7*, 278–285.

Richter-Levin, G. (2004). The amygdala, the hippocampus, and emotional modulation of memory. *Neuroscientist*, *10*(1), 31–39.

Roozendaal, B. (2002). Stress and memory: Opposing effects of glucocorticoids on memory consolidation and memory retrieval. *Neurobiology of Learning and Memory*, *78*(3), 578–595.

Roozendaal, B., Barsegyan, A., & Lee, S. (2008). Adrenal stress hormones, amygdala activation, and memory for emotionally arousing experiences. *Progress in Brain Research*, *167*, 79–95.

Roozendaal, B., Okuda, S., de Quervain, D. J. F., & McGaugh, J. L. (2006a). Glucocorticoids interact with emotion-induced noradrenergic activation in influencing different memory functions. *Neuroscience*, *138*(3), 901–910.

Roozendaal, B., Okuda, S., Van der Zee, E. A., & McGaugh, J. L. (2006b). Glucocorticoid enhancement of memory requires arousal-induced noradrenergic activation in the basolateral amygdala. *Proceedings of the National Academy of Sciences USA*, *103*(17), 6741–6746.

Schaefer, A., Pottage, C. L., & Rickart, A. J. (2011). Electrophysiological correlates of remembering emotional pictures. *NeuroImage*, *54*(1), 714–724.

Schmidt, S. R. (2002). Outstanding memories: The positive and negative effects of nudes on memory. *Journal of Experimental Psychology: Learning, Memory, and Cognition*, *28*(2), 353–361.

Segal, S. K., & Cahill, L. (2009). Endogenous noradrenergic activation and memory for emotional material in men and women. *Psychoneuroendocrinology*, *34*(9), 1263–1271.

Sharot, T., Martorella, E. A., Delgado, M. R., & Phelps, E. A. (2007). How personal experience modulates the neural circuitry of memories of September 11. *Proceedings of the National Academy of Sciences USA*, *104*(1), 389–394.

Sharot, T., & Phelps, E. A. (2004). How arousal modulates memory: Disentangling the effects of attention and retention. *Cognitive, Affective, and Behavioral Neuroscience*, *4*(3), 294–306.

Shekhar, A., Truitt, W., Rainnie, D., & Sajdyk, T. (2005). Role of stress, corticotrophin releasing factor (CRF) and amygdala plasticity in chronic anxiety. *Stress*, *8*(4), 209–219.

Sheline, Y. I., Gado, M. H., & Kraemer, H. C. (2003). Untreated depression and hippocampal volume loss. *American Journal of Psychiatry*, *160*, 1516–1518.

Shin, L. M., Wright, C., Cannistraro, P., Wedig, M., McMullin, K., Martis, B.,… Rauch, S. (2005). A functional magnetic resonance imaging study of amygdala and medial prefrontal cortex responses to overtly presented fearful faces in posttraumatic stress disorder. *Archives of General Psychiatry*, *62*, 273–281.

Sterpenich, V., Argembeau, A.D., Desseilles, M., Balteau, E., Albouy, G., Vandewalle, G.,… Maquet, P. (2006). The locus ceruleus is involved in the successful retrieval of emotional memories in humans. *Journal of Neuroscience, 26*(28), 7416–7432.

Strange, B. A., & Dolan, R. J. (2004). Beta-adrenergic modulation of emotional memory-evoked human amygdala and hippocampal responses. *Proceedings of the National Academy of Sciences USA, 101*(31), 11454–11458.

Talarico, J. M., Berntsen, D., & Rubin, D. C. (2009). Positive emotions enhance recall of peripheral details. *Cognition and Emotion, 23*(2), 380–398.

Talarico, J. M., LaBar, K. S., & Rubin, D. C. (2004). Emotional intensity predicts autobiographical memory experience. *Memory and Cognition, 32*(7), 1118–1132.

Talmi, D., Anderson, A. K., Riggs, L., Moscovitch, M., & Caplan, J. B. (2008). Immediate memory consequences of the effect of emotion on attention to pictures. *Learning and Memory, 15*(3), 172–182.

Tollenaar, M. S., Elzinga, B. M., Spinhoven, P., & Everaerd, W. (2008a). Long-term outcomes of memory retrieval under stress. *Behavioral Neuroscience, 122*(3), 697–703.

Tollenaar, M. S., Elzinga, B. M., Spinhoven, P., & Everaerd, W. (2008b). The effects of cortisol increase on long-term memory retrieval during and after acute psychosocial stress. *Acta Psychologica, 127*(3), 542–552.

Tollenaar, M. S., Elzinga, B. M., Spinhoven, P., & Everaerd, W. (2009a). Autobiographical memory after acute stress in healthy young men. *Memory, 17*(3), 301–310.

Tollenaar, M. S., Elzinga, B. M., Spinhoven, P., & Everaerd, W. (2009b). Immediate and prolonged effects of cortisol, but not propranolol, on memory retrieval in healthy young men. *Neurobiology of Learning and Memory, 91*(1), 23–31.

Touryan, S. R., Marian, D. E., & Shimamura, A. P. (2007). Effect of negative emotional pictures on associative memory for peripheral information. *Memory, 15*(2), 154–166.

van Stegeren, A. H., Goekoop, R., Everaerd, W., Scheltens, P., Barkhof, F., Kuijer, J. P., & Rombouts, S. (2005). Noradrenaline mediates amygdala activation in men and women during encoding of emotional material. *NeuroImage, 24*(3), 898–909.

van Stegeren, A. H., Kindt, M., Roozendaal, B., Wolf, O. T., & Joëls, M. (2010). Interacting noradrenergic and corticosteroid systems shift human brain activation patterns during encoding. *Neurobiology of Learning and Memory, 93*(1), 56–65.

van Stegeren, A. H., Wolf, O. T., Everaerd, W., Scheltens, P., Barkhof, F., & Rombouts, S. (2007). Endogenous cortisol level interacts with noradrenergic activation in the human amygdala. *Neurobiology of Learning and Memory, 87*(1), 57–66.

Vyas, A., Bernal, S., & Chattarji, S. (2003). Effects of chronic stress on dendritic arborization in the central and extended amygdala. *Brain Research, 965*(1–2), 290–294.

Vyas, A., Mitra, R., Rao, B. S., & Chattarji, S. (2002). Chronic stress induced contrasting patterns of dendritic remodeling in hippocampal and amygdaloid neurons. *Journal of Neuroscience, 22*(15), 6810–6818.

Wang, J., Rao, H., Wetmore, G. S., Furlan, P. M., Korczykowski, M., Dinges, D. F., & Detre, J. (2005). Perfusion functional MRI reveals cerebral blood flow pattern under psychological stress. *Proceedings of the National Academy of Sciences USA, 102*(49), 17804–17809.

Waring, J. D., Kensinger, E. A., Payne, J. D., & Schacter, D. L. (2010). Impact of individual differences upon emotion-induced memory trade-offs. *Cognition and Emotion, 24*(1), 150–167.

Yang, J., Hou, C., Ma, N., Liu, J., Zhang, Y., Zhou, J., Xu, L., & Li, L. (2007). Enriched environment treatment restores impaired hippocampal synaptic plasticity and cognitive deficits induced by prenatal chronic stress. *Neurobiology of Learning and Memory, 87*(2), 257–263.

Yerkes, R. M., & Dodson, J. D. (1908). The relation of strength of stimulus to rapidity of habit formation. *Journal of Comparative Neurology and Psychology*, 459–482.

# Emotion–Cognition Interactions

Jeffrey R. Huntsinger *and* Simone Schnall

**Abstract**

Viewing affect and cognition as independent from one another has had a long history. Even if interaction between the two was entertained, affect was seen as contaminating cognition, leading to errant thinking and suboptimal decisions. A quite different perspective has emerged in recent years. From this view, rather than constituting distinct constructs or opposing forces, affect and cognition are intimately intertwined and the influence of affect is seen as functional rather than dysfunctional. This chapter reviews how affective states, such as moods and emotions, influence memory, perception, judgment, and cognitive processing style. Many of these influences can be understood by the idea that affect provides information. It is noted that many of the hallmark findings in cognitive psychology appear to have an affective trigger.

**Key Words:** emotion, mood, affective states, memory, perception, judgment, cognition

*Feeling without [thinking] is a washy draught indeed; but [thinking] untempered by feeling is too bitter and husky a morsel for human deglutition.*
　　　　　　　　　　—Charlotte Brontë (1847/2005, p. 190)

Does affect influence cognition? If one looks to classic philosophical and psychological treatments of emotion and cognition the answer is: Not much. According to these perspectives, affect and cognition are utterly independent and opposing influences on judgment and decision making (Aristotle, 1991; Plato, 1992). These ideas are echoed in contemporary affect-cognition models, in particular affect-primacy models, which argue for the independence of affect and cognition (Bargh, 1997; Zajonc, 1980). Even among perspectives that entertained the possibility that affect and cognition interact in meaningful ways, affect was believed to contaminate cognition and reason, leading to suboptimal decisions and behaviors (Kant, 1960).

In contrast to these views, a consensus has emerged across various subfields of psychology that affect and cognition are fundamentally intertwined (for reviews, see Martin & Clore, 2001). Research informing this view reveals that affect, in the form of moods and emotions, plays a critical role in regulating how people perceive, remember, and think about their physical and social worlds. Likewise, this research also shows that cognition is crucial to the generation, experience, and regulation of emotion. Indeed, some have gone so far as to argue that the distinction between affect and cognition may be more phenomenological than ontological (Duncan & Barrett, 2007; Pessoa, 2008).

Although we think it premature to cast aside the distinction between affect and cognition, our point here is that a wealth of empirical evidence shows that affect permeates cognition just as cognition permeates affect. As the epigraph that begins this chapter suggests, rather than having a dysfunctional role, affect plays a largely functional role in regulating cognition (Barrett & Salovey, 2002; Clore, 2005; Damasio, 1994; Frijda, 1986). When the ability to experience emotional reactions is impaired or absent, for example, the ability to make the most mundane through the most important decisions is impaired (Damasio, 1994). Delineating how emotion and cognition interact is, therefore, critical to understanding how people effectively navigate their social and physical worlds.

In what follows, we outline how affect informs judgments and regulates cognition. We begin by sketching historical developments to understanding how affect regulates cognition. We then review the different ways that affect has been shown to regulate cognition, including memory, perception, judgment, and decision making, and cognitive processing style. The affect-as-information approach serves to organize our discussion of how affect regulates cognition.

Before we continue, however, it is necessary to define some key terms. The first concerns what we mean by *affect*. According to Clore and Huntsinger (2007), affect is a representation of value (i.e., the goodness or badness of something) and can take several different forms, including neurological, physiological, experiential, cognitive, and behavioral. An affective state involves the co-occurrence of several of these reactions. *Emotions* represent affective states with an object and reflect an underlying appraisal. Although emotions can be classified according to valence, their influence on cognition depends on the appraisal pattern that accompanies their experience. In contrast, *moods* are diffuse affective states that lack specific objects and appraisals. We thus speak of affect as the category that comprises both emotion and mood.

## Models of Affect–Cognition Interactions

Classic understandings of affect–cognition interaction relied either on psychodynamic or conditioning principles. From the psychodynamic view, affect creeps into cognition unconsciously, leading people to see the world and others through affect-tinged lenses. Consistent with this idea, people experiencing a particular emotion such as anger or fear, for example, tend to perceive similar emotions in others (e.g., Feshbach & Singer, 1957). As with much psychodynamic theory, empirical examination of its ideas proved difficult, if not impossible. Early conditioning perspectives concentrated on the role of affect in shaping attitudes (e.g., Razran, 1954; Staats & Staats, 1958). For example, Razran's (1954) studies showed that the positive affect evoked by a free luncheon led to more positive evaluations of ethnic outgroups, political slogans, paintings, and a variety of other attitude objects.

As the cognitive revolution swept across psychology in the 1960s, the study of emotion and mood fell out of favor and so too did these approaches to affect and cognition. When the study of motivation and emotion regained a foothold in psychology in the late 1970s and early 1980s, there emerged two decidedly different ways of understanding affect–cognition interaction: spreading activation models and the affect-as-information approach. We first discuss the former because these were some of the earliest formulations of how affect influences cognition. Because evidence for such models is limited, our treatment is brief. We then describe the affect-as-information approach, which provides the theoretical framework for our discussion of affective influences on cognition throughout the chapter.

### Spreading Activation Models

Spreading activation models propose that affect influences what thoughts come to mind (Clark & Isen, 1982; Forgas, 1995; Isen, Shalker, Clark, & Karp, 1978). This work was motivated by Bower's (1981) associative network model of mood and memory, in which mood states are represented as specific nodes in memory that become activated, and subsequently this activation spreads to other material in memory. When a person is happy, for example, this activates happy memories and other positive mental content. When making evaluative judgments, memory-priming models propose that the positive or negative thoughts primed by positive and negative moods, respectively, bias judgment in a mood-congruent fashion.

Although early research revealed mood-congruent recall for both positive and negative moods (Bower, 1981), later research revealed that this effect was both weak and only occurred under certain conditions (for reviews, see Blaney, 1986; Matt, Vasquez, & Campbell, 1992; Wyer, Clore, & Isbell, 1999). Mood-congruent recall, for example, is more likely to emerge for positive moods than negative moods

(Singer & Salovey, 1988). Mood-*in*congruent recall among *both* happy and sad participants has also been observed (Parrott & Sabini, 1990). Furthermore, evidence of mood-congruent recall is most consistent when mood is induced prior to encoding (Bower, Gilligan, & Monteiro, 1981), suggesting that mood directs how people process the story rather than activating mood-congruent material from memory.

Although spreading activation models originally were designed to explain affective influences on judgment and memory, they were later expanded to describe how affect influences cognitive processing in general. According to some accounts, positive moods activate a greater amount and more diverse mental content than negative moods, which then reduces the ability of people in positive moods to deploy cognitive resources to meet task demands (e.g., Mackie & Worth, 1991). People in positive moods, therefore, engage in more heuristic and simplified processing than those in negative moods. According to other accounts, rather than constraining cognitive capacity, the more diverse mental content called to mind by positive moods actually allows for a more divergent and flexible style of cognitive processing (Isen, 1987).

Despite the intuitive appeal of spreading activation models, evidence supporting the idea that affect primes memories and other thoughts of similar valence is mixed at best. First, emotions do not appear to be stored in memory. Just as memory in general is reconstructive (Bartlett, 1932), memories of past emotions are reconstructed based on subsequent reinterpretations of past events (Levine, 1997). For example, participants' recollection of their emotional responses to a salient event changed if their current appraisal of the event had changed from the time the event had occurred (Levine, Prohaska, Burgess, Rice, & Laulhere, 2001).

In addition, mood and emotion manipulations unlikely to elicit much mental content—such as posing happy or sad facial expressions or listening to cheery or gloomy musical selections—lead to the same effects on cognition as more elaborate mood and emotion inductions. Finally, these models have difficulty explaining why individual differences in attention to feelings (Gasper & Clore, 2000) and bodily cues (Schnall, Haidt, Clore, & Jordan, 2008) moderate the influence of affect on judgment and processing. These results are more readily understandable via the affect-as-information approach, which we discuss next.

## Affect–Cognition Interactions: Affect as Information

As its name implies, the affect-as-information approach focuses on the information conveyed by affect. Although there are several different variations on this approach, each with a slightly different set of assumptions (for a collection, see Martin & Clore, 2001), they all share the basic idea that affect provides embodied information about the value of whatever happens to be in mind at the time (Clore & Huntsinger, 2007, 2009; Schwarz & Clore, 1983, 2007). Such an influence is direct, because the affective cue itself, rather than its association with other similarly valenced material, guides cognitive processes. The affect-as-information approach applies to affective cues from both moods and specific emotions. In the case of emotions, this approach proposes that different emotions convey different information about the ways in which objects are positive or negative so that emotions of similar valence can have different effects and their implications for cognition depend on their object.

The influence of affect on cognition is revealed across a wide variety of domains and comprises influences on memory, perception, judgment, and cognitive processing style. In what follows, using the affect-as-information approach as an explanatory framework, we review evidence of affective influences in these four domains. Although we discuss both mood and emotional influences on cognition, more research attention has been devoted to studying the former than the latter; thus, our review is necessarily tilted more toward mood than emotion.

### Memory

We first discuss the influence of mood on memory because in some sense the ground work was done in this domain, and then discuss how specific emotions convey information about importance, and thus enhance memory for words, stories, and events by directing encoding and consolidation.

The affect-as-information approach presumes that affect is not directly stored in memory (Wyer et al. 1999; see also Robinson & Clore, 2002). Thus, any observation of mood-congruent recall is not the result of affect per se, but rather the result of the cognitive content called to mind by the mood inductions used in prior research. For example, participants are explicitly asked to get into a happy or sad mood, watch films with explicit happy and sad themes, or are given success or failure feedback, all of which likely activated mood-relevant concepts. Indeed, mood inductions unlikely to explicitly activate mood-relevant concepts fail to produce mood-congruent recall (Rholes, Riskind, & Lane, 1987), which suggests that rather than being a general memory phenomenon, effects of mood-congruent recall depend on very specific experimental paradigms. Moreover, research (Storbeck & Robinson, 2004) directly comparing descriptive versus evaluative priming suggests that memory is primarily organized in terms of descriptive categories (i.e., animals, furniture) rather than in terms of networks of spreading activation based on valence (i.e., positive thoughts, negative thoughts).

Another early effort to uncover mood influences on memory examined what is called mood-dependent memory. This assumes better recall of material for which the mood at recall matches the mood at encoding. As with mood-congruent memory, later research failed to reliably demonstrate mood-dependent retrieval. Indeed, after repeated failures to replicate their earlier findings, Bower and Mayer (1985, p. 42) concluded that "mood-dependent retrieval is an evanescent will-o'-the-wisp, and not the robust outcome suggested by earlier reports."

Rather than influencing memory by activating valence-congruent memories and thoughts, recent research reveals that mood influences the styles of cognitive processing that people utilize during memory experiments. The tasks commonly used in memory research often evoke relational processing—relating incoming information to what is already known. According to the affect-as-information approach, when this is the case mood should shape performance on such tasks by signaling the value of this accessible or dominant processing style.

This idea is illustrated in research on false memory and intentional forgetting. In false memory experiments, people study lists of words (i.e., bed, pillow, rest, etc.), implying a related, but not presented, concept called a critical lure—in this case *sleep*. During a recall phase of the experiment, people often falsely "recall" the nonpresented critical lure (i.e., sleep). Such false memories are assumed to reflect relational or gist processing (Roediger, Balota, & Watson, 2001). Affect as information proposes that positive mood should promote, and negative mood should inhibit, such relational processing, leading to mood-related differences in false memory. Across several studies, Storbeck and Clore (2005) found precisely that individuals in happy and neutral moods displayed high numbers of false memories, whereas this tendency was significantly reduced among individuals in sad moods.

Retrieval-induced forgetting occurs when rehearsal of a subset of previously observed material inhibits memory for nonrehearsed material (MacLeod, 2002). As in production of false memory, retrieval-induced forgetting is thought to be promoted by relational processing and inhibited by item-specific processing. Consistent with the idea that affect regulates use of accessible processing styles, retrieval-induced forgetting is sustained in positive moods and is inhibited in negative moods (Bäuml & Kuhbandner, 2007).

Emotion, on the other hand, appears to enhance memory. The influence of emotion on memory can be understood via the idea that emotional arousal provides information about importance, which guides attention and selection of material that is encoded and consolidated into long-term memory (for a review, see Storbeck & Clore, 2008b). This effect of emotional arousal appears quite general, occurring for both emotional memories and for nonemotional declarative mental content (McGaugh, 2004). The influence of emotion on memory appears more pronounced for long-term than short-term memory.

### Perception

The possibility of affective influences on perception was first raised by New Look theorists (Bruner & Postman, 1947; Postman, Bruner, & McGinnies, 1948). Rather than treating perception as a process in which the mind constructs a veridical model of the world via a passive registration of sensory input, New Look theorists treated perception as a dynamic process in which internal cues from motivation and emotion and external cues from the environment combine to shape how people perceived their worlds. Despite promising early results, devastating methodological and theoretical critiques left much of the New Look approach in shambles.

Recent work, however, has revived research questions relating states of the perceiver with his or her current perceptions of the physical environment. Following Gibson's (1979) ecological approach, spatial perception is seen to be informed by a person's potential to carry out certain actions in a given environment (Proffitt, 2006). For instance, when a person is standing in front of a steep hill, that hill will appear steeper to her when she is wearing a heavy backpack, compared to when she is not (Bhalla & Proffitt, 1999). Factors such as age and aerobic fitness also influence hill slant perception, with elderly or nonfit individuals perceiving hills as steeper than young or fit individuals (Proffitt,

Bhalla, Gossweiler, & Midgett, 1995). Presumably, such factors constrain perception because they are relevant to actions: A hill would be more difficult to climb when wearing a backpack, or for an elderly or unfit person, and thus, looks steeper. This describes an *economy of action* (Proffitt, 2006), namely an individual's attempt to scale the world in terms of the actions that are afforded by her bodily capabilities.

Direct evidence for such an economy of action comes from the findings that when physiological energy is provided in the form of glucose, high levels of blood glucose make hills appear less steep than low levels of blood glucose (Schnall, Zadra, & Proffitt, 2010). In addition to physiological resources, psychosocial resources such as social support also influence hill slant perception (Schnall, Harber, Stefanucci, & Proffitt, 2008), as do participants' current affective states. Riener, Stefanucci, Proffitt, and Clore (2010) investigated the influence of mood on hill slant. Participants were induced to feel happy or sad by music in one study, and by recalling a happy or sad life event in the other study, and then completed slant estimates of a steep hill. In both studies, sad participants judged the hill as being steeper than those in the happy condition. In a related manner, the influence of fear on hill perception has been explored. In one study participants were asked to stand on a skateboard at the top of a hill, and their perception of hill slant was compared to participants who stood on a wooden box at the top of the hill (Stefanucci, Proffitt, Clore, & Parekh, 2008). Participants who felt afraid when standing on the skateboard gave higher slant estimates than participants standing on the wooden box. People's perception of height can also be changed by fear (Stefanucci & Proffitt, 2009). Participants stood either on a balcony and looked down to estimate the vertical distance to the ground, or they stood underneath the balcony and looked up to estimate the distance to the handrail. These vertical estimates generally lead to overestimation relative to equivalent horizontal distance. More important, this overestimation was greater when looking down compared to when looking up, and when looking down from a high balcony rather than low balcony, suggesting that the fear of falling when standing on a high balcony influences estimates of height. Fear of heights also is associated with more exaggerated height estimates (Teachman, Stefanucci, Clerkin, Cody, & Proffitt, 2008). In addition to stable individual differences regarding fear of height, fear arousal can also have an effect (Stefanucci & Storbeck, 2009).

Participants were first shown either arousing or non-arousing visual images. Subsequent height estimates from a balcony were greater for participants who had been exposed to arousing stimuli, presumably because the arousal from the images amplified the fear of falling associated with looking down from a high balcony.

### Evaluative Judgment

When making evaluative judgments, people often implicitly ask themselves, "How do I feel about it?" Current moods then inform people of the value of whatever happens to be the object of judgment (Schwarz & Clore, 1983) and are experienced as liking or disliking. The use of feelings as information in judgments occurs quickly and is often considered a more compelling basis for judgment than whatever thoughts about an object come to mind (Pham, Cohen, Pracejus, & Hughes, 2001). As a result, feelings-based judgments frequently produce more optimal decisions than more considered or sophisticated evaluative strategies (e.g., Wilson & Schooler, 1991).

Schwarz and Clore (1983) first demonstrated the informational influence of mood in studies examining life-satisfaction judgments. In a telephone survey people were called on either rainy or sunny spring days and asked how satisfied they were with their lives as a whole. The weather reliably influenced people's moods—people called on sunny days were happier than those called on dreary days. As part of an implicit misattribution process, these feelings were then drawn on by respondents when rating their levels of life satisfaction, leading them to report being more satisfied with life on a sunny than a rainy day. The influence of mood on judgments of life satisfaction, however, disappeared when participants were first asked about the weather. Asking about the weather did not change their feelings, but it did change what their feelings seemed to be about.

A parallel influence of mood can be seen in risk judgments. The experience of positive affect, as compared to negative affect, leads people to see less risk in their environment (Gasper & Clore, 1998). Similarly, Slovic and colleagues (Slovic, Finucane, Peters, & MacGregor, 2002) propose an "affect heuristic" in the context of risk perception. Furthermore, mood effects on risk judgments are stronger for people who pay attention to their feelings than those who do not (Gasper & Clore, 2000): Only people who attended to their feelings were influenced by the positive or negative mood they experienced when judging risk, presumably because they are more inclined to use the information conveyed by their current affective reactions than people who tend to ignore their feelings.

Although a similar influence of mood on judgment has been observed across a wide variety of domains, including judgments of consumer products, other people, the self-concept, and so forth (for a review, see Schwarz & Clore, 2007), mood-*in*congruent judgments also occur. In a clever series of experiments (Martin, Abend, Sedikides, & Green, 1997) positive and negative moods were induced prior to participants rating the success of stories designed to elicit happy or sad emotions. In this situation, rather than mood providing direct information about the object of judgment, people should consult their feelings to determine whether a story successfully elicited a specific emotion (i.e., happiness or sadness). Indeed, when participants' current feelings and a story's intended emotion matched (i.e., positive mood–happy story or negative mood–sad story), they judged the story positively, but when feelings and the story's emotion clashed, they judged it negatively.

In the case of emotions, specific appraisals direct judgment rather than affective valence per se. For example, anger and anxiety, clearly two negative emotions, have very different effects on judgments of risk because each involves a different pattern of appraisal, with different implications for risk judgments. Fear and anxiety involve displeasure about the prospect of an undesirable outcome and are accompanied by feelings of threat and uncertainty. As such, the experience of fear and anxiety is linked to increased judgments of risk (e.g., Gasper & Clore, 1998). In research on perceptions of terrorism and the second Iraq war, for example, fearful people perceived greater risk from terrorism (Lerner, Gonzalez, Small, & Fischhoff, 2003) and anxiety increased the perceived risk associated with the Iraq war as well as decreased support for the war (Huddy, Feldman, & Cassese, 2007). Fear and anxiety are also linked to a tendency to make risk-averse decisions, a more pessimistic outlook on future events (Lerner & Keltner, 2001), and preferences for consumer products that emphasize safety (Raghunathan, Pham, & Corfman, 2006).

Disgust involves dislike of the unappealing attributes of an object (Ortony, Clore, & Collins, 1988). The object of disgust can be anything from foul-tasting foods to offensive ideas (Rozin, Haidt, & McCauley, 2008). Thus, the experience of disgust decreases the perceived value of objects. An illustration is the endowment effect, which refers to people's tendency to set higher selling prices than buying prices on objects they own. Consistent with a decrease of perceived value of objects, feelings of disgust eliminate the endowment effect (Lerner, Small, & Lowenstein, 2003).

The influence of disgust on judgments has been most thoroughly mapped out in studies of morality, because people often report finding immoral acts physically disgusting. In fact, similar neutral structures appear to be involved in the experience of physical and moral disgust (Moll et al., 2005). Furthermore, the same facial muscle involved in the expression of physical disgust, namely the levator labii facial muscle, is contracted when participants are confronted with an unfair decision (Chapman, Kim, Susskind, & Anderson, 2009), and such facial activity predicts participants' moral judgments of transgressions violating assumptions of purity (Cannon, Schnall, & White, 2011).

Experimentally induced feelings of disgust can be misattributed to moral judgments such that, for example, the feeling of disgust derived from being exposed to a foul smell is incorrectly interpreted as being diagnostic about a moral transgression, thus leading the person to infer that a particular moral action is quite wrong (Schnall, Haidt, et al., 2008; Wheatley & Haidt, 2005). This effect can be eliminated or reversed by either priming participants with the concept of cleanliness, or allowing them to physically cleanse themselves after the experimental disgust induction, thus resulting in less severe moral judgments (Schnall, Benton, & Harvey, 2008). In addition to experimental manipulations of disgust and cleanliness, individual differences in people's predisposition to experience disgust are associated with moral attitudes. Jones and Fitness (2008) describe what they call moral hypervigilance in people high on disgust sensitivity (Haidt, McCauley, & Rozin, 1994), namely an increased propensitiy to see potential transgressions as morally wrong, and a desire to reduce one's own exposure to the moral transgressions of others. Furthermore, relative to people low in disgust sensitivity, those high in disgust sensitivity are more likely to be politically conservative (Inbar, Pizarro, & Bloom, 2009) and show a higher implicit bias against homosexual people (Inbar, Pizarro, Knobe, & Bloom, 2009).

Anger is a relatively complex emotion that has two key ingredients: being displeased at an undesirable outcome and disapproval of the blameworthy actions that caused them (Ortony et al., 1988). As such, anger has been shown to increase judgments of blame (Keltner, Ellsworth, & Edwards, 1993). Because anger is also associated with a feeling of one's position being correct (Clore & Huntsinger, 2009), it has been shown to increase support for actions associated with one's group. In the research discussed earlier on emotional reactions to terrorism, for example, anger after the September 11 attacks was associated with support for the Iraq war and the perception that it was less risky (Lerner et al., 2003). Similar to disgust, anger becomes relevant in the moral domain. However, in contrast to disgust, which does not seem to require reasoned justification, the experience of anger is often justified by presumed harm to other people, even when no harm is present (Gutierrez & Giner-Sorolla, 2007).

## Cognitive Processing Style

Explanations for the connection between mood and cognitive processing style have included the notion that positive mood reduces cognitive capacity (e.g., Mackie & Worth, 1991) or processing motivation (e.g., Schwarz, Bless, & Bohner, 1991), thus increasing reliance on heuristics and other cognitive shortcuts. Positive moods are hypothesized to activate more mental content than negative moods, thereby reducing the ability of people in positive moods to deploy cognitive resources to meet task demands. The motivational perspective holds that people in positive moods use little cognitive effort because they either see little reason to do so or because they want to preserve their positive mood. These perspectives have been challenged on a number of grounds (for a review, see Schwarz & Clore, 2007).

As both the cognitive capacity and motivation explanations became less influential, the idea emerged that positive and negative affect are linked to specific styles of cognitive processing. For example, positive affect has been associated with heuristic processing, a global focus, relational processing, enhanced creativity, and assimilation, to name but a few (see Martin & Clore, 2001). Such findings, and the theories that evolved with them, suggest a direct or dedicated link between affect and particular styles of cognitive processing.

Another (or perhaps additional) way of accounting for the link between affect and cognitive processing is that affect regulates cognitive processing by serving as evaluative feedback about currently accessible thoughts and response tendencies (Clore & Huntsinger, 2007; 2009). From this view, rather than directly instigating differences in cognitive processing, positive mood signals that accessible thoughts and response tendencies are valuable or valid, encouraging their use, whereas negative mood signals such thoughts and response tendencies are not valuable or invalid, discouraging their use. Thus, under this idea, links between affect and cognitive processing should be highly variable and should depend on what thoughts and response tendencies happen to be in mind at the moment.

### COGNITIVE PRIMING: SEMANTIC, AFFECTIVE, AND CATEGORY ACTIVATION

Various priming phenomena commonly observed in cognitive and social psychology should be more frequent among people in positive moods than those in negative moods because positive moods promote, and negative moods inhibit, the use of semantic, affective, and category associations. Indeed, people in positive moods are more likely than those in negative moods to exhibit semantic, evaluative, and categorical priming (Storbeck & Clore, 2008a), whereas sad moods eliminate priming. This effect is evident not only in the priming of words but also in the priming of social categories: Priming the category "elderly" can lead people to express more conservative attitudes and to walk more slowly (Dijksterhuis, Chartrand, & Aarts, 2007). If affect confers positive or negative value on activated cognitions, then people should be more likely to show such effects in happy moods than in sad moods. In several experiments (Ashton-James, Huntsinger, Clore, & Chartrand, unpublished data), for example, the category elderly or young was primed in several ways. The results showed that positive moods led to more conservative social attitudes and slower walking after the category "elderly" was primed compared to when the category "young" was primed. In contrast, negative moods led to more liberal attitudes and faster walking after exposure to elderly faces than young faces.

### HEURISTICS

A similar influence of mood on the use of accessible mental content and response tendencies can be seen in research on mood and judgmental heuristics. People often base frequency judgments on the ease with which examples of an event come to mind (Tversky & Kahneman, 1974). Similarly, when people make self-relevant judgments, the more easily instances of past behavior exemplifying a trait come to mind, the more likely it is a person will think the trait is self-descriptive (Schwarz Bless, Strack, Klumpp, Rittenauer-Schatka , & Simons 1991).

This is called the availability or ease-of-retrieval heuristic. People in positive moods are more likely than those in negative moods to rely on the ease or difficulty with which trait-relevant behaviors come to mind to determine whether they possess a given trait (Rüder & Bless, 2003; see also Isen & Means, 1983). A similar influence of mood on reliance on the availability heuristic can be seen with more chronic affective states, such as mild depression (Greifeneder & Bless, 2008).

People often evaluate a new product more positively if it is from an already established brand than from an unknown brand (Aaker, 1991). This brand heuristic is more evident among those in positive moods than those in negative moods (Barone, Miniard, & Romeo, 2000). Importantly, this effect depends on whether the brand is favorable or unfavorable (Greifeneder, Bless, & Kuschmann, 2007). As in past research, for favorable brands, positive moods led to more positive evaluations of the new product than negative moods. For unfavorable brands, by contrast, positive moods led to more negative evaluations than negative moods. Such findings would be difficult to explain via memory-priming models, but they can readily be accommodated by the affect-as-information approach.

## IMPLICIT-EXPLICIT ATTITUDE CORRESPONDENCE

Recent research on mood regulation of implicit-explicit attitude correspondence is also consistent with the idea that moods confer value on accessible cognitions, which then regulates their use. Implicit attitudes reflect automatically activated tendencies to respond in a positive or negative fashion toward an attitude object, whereas explicit attitudes reflect more controlled evaluative tendencies (Gawronski & Bodenhausen, 2006). In most circumstances people base their endorsed evaluative judgments on their automatic reactions (i.e., implicit attitudes), unless these reactions are considered an invalid basis for an evaluative judgment (Gawronski & Bodenhausen, 2006). In addition, positive moods validate, and negative moods invalidate, these automatic reactions, leading to differences in implicit-explicit attitude correspondence between the two types of mood (Huntsinger & Smith, 2009).

People reliably differ in whether they trust and rely on their intuitions. Differences in this tendency to trust or distrust one's intuitions, whether measured or manipulated, moderate correspondence between implicit and explicit attitudes—people who trust their intuitions, as compared to those who distrust

them, display greater implicit-explicit attitude correspondence (Jordan, Whitfield, & Zeigler-Hill, 2007). A recent set of studies (Huntsinger, 2011) explored the idea that, rather than directly influencing implicit-explicit attitude correspondence, mood would do so indirectly by signaling the value of momentarily primed tendencies to trust or distrust intuition. Supporting this reasoning, for both self and academic attitudes, when trust in intuition was primed, people in positive moods displayed greater implicit-explicit attitude correspondence than those in negative moods. When distrust in intuition was primed, however, the opposite pattern was found—people in positive moods now displayed lesser implicit-explicit attitude correspondence than those in negative moods.

## PERSUASION

Mood effects on the validation and use of accessible thoughts can be seen when examining responses to persuasive messages (Brinol, Petty, & Barden, 2007). Participants in this research first were exposed to persuasive appeals consisting of either strong arguments or weak arguments and then wrote down their thoughts, which tended to be positive for strong arguments and negative for weak arguments. Positive or negative moods were then induced and participants rated their agreement with the persuasive appeal. Positive mood validated thoughts about the messages so that participants were more persuaded by strong than by weak arguments. In contrast, negative mood invalidated such thoughts, reversing these effects.

This research may, at first glance, appear to contradict past research in which people in positive moods are found to be equally persuaded by strong and weak persuasive appeals, whereas those in negative moods are found to be more persuaded by strong than weak appeals (Schwarz et al., 1991). The key to resolving this discrepancy is to locate the object of mood in each of these types of studies. In past research on mood and persuasion, mood is induced prior to reading persuasive appeals, thus it signaled the value of accessible response tendencies, mood management strategies, and so forth, which then influenced persuasion. In the Brinol et al. (2007) studies, affect was induced after participants read the persuasive appeals; thus, it signaled the value of participants' thoughts about the message.

## TRANSFER OF LEARNING

A similar influence of mood on the use of accessible mental content and response tendencies can be found when investigating the influence of mood on transfer and learning on cognitive tasks (Brand, Reimer, & Opwis, 2007). Participants first learned to master the Tower of Hanoi problem and then experienced either a positive or negative mood induction. When trying to solve several tasks with similar or dissimilar surface features to the Tower of Hanoi problem, for both tasks with similar and dissimilar features, participants in positive moods, as compared to those in negative moods, relied on previously learned problem-solving strategies and algorithms, leading to superior performance on the second set of tasks.

## STEREOTYPES

People in positive moods are more likely than those in negative moods to use stereotypes. When judging a defendant's guilt, for example, people in positive moods rely more on stereotypes than those in negative and neutral moods (Bodenhausen, Kramer, & Süsser, 1994). Although most studies in this area simply examine downstream judgments, rather than disentangling the role of stereotype activation versus application, recent findings suggest that the effects of mood occur at the stereotype activation stage (Huntsinger, Sinclair, & Clore, 2009). Using Payne's (2001) weapon-identification task, people in positive moods displayed greater stereotypical bias than did those in negative moods. Process-dissociation analyses, used to decompose performance into separate estimates of automatic and controlled processing, revealed that mood influenced the use and, consequently, the activation of race-related stereotypes rather than influencing the extent of controlled, data-driven processing (i.e., stereotype application).

Although there might appear to be a direct connection between positive and negative moods and stereotyping, from the affect-as-information approach, this connection rests on the fact that, for most people and in most circumstances, stereotypes are highly accessible responses whenever people encounter or merely entertain thoughts about members of stereotyped groups (Bargh, 1997). Thus, positive moods simply encourage people to embrace, and negative moods encourage people to avoid, this highly accessible response. Consistent with this idea, the usual relation between mood and stereotyping can be reversed by varying the accessibility of stereotype-relevant thoughts and responses. In research directly exploring this idea (Huntsinger, Sinclair, Dunn, & Clore, 2010), mood was manipulated to be positive or negative and egalitarian

response tendencies were measured or manipulated, or counterstereotypical thoughts were made accessible. Stereotype activation was measured using a variety of reaction-time measures, including the implicit association task and the weapon-identification task. In the presence of accessible egalitarian response tendencies or counterstereotypic thoughts, people in positive moods exhibited less stereotype activation than those in negative moods—a reversal of the standard link between mood and stereotyping. By contrast, in the absence of such response tendencies and thoughts, people in positive moods displayed greater stereotype activation.

## GLOBAL-LOCAL FOCUS

People in positive moods tend to focus on the forest, whereas those in negative moods focus on the trees. For example, when judging the similarity between a series of geometric figures, people in positive moods tend to base their judgments on the global features of the stimuli more than people in negative moods (Fredrickson & Branigan, 2005; Gasper & Clore, 2002). Similar effects already occur for 6- to 7-year-old children completing the Embedded Figures Task, with sad children outperforming happy children because successful performance requires focusing on details while ignoring global information (Schnall, Jaswal, & Rowe, 2008). When recalling autobiographical events, people in positive moods, compared to those in negative moods, describe such events using more abstract, global representations (Beukeboom & Semin, 2005). However, drawing participants' attention to the true cause of their affective reactions eliminates mood-related differences in a global or local focus (Gasper, 2004a). Many explanations for this link suggest that positive and negative moods are uniquely dedicated to global and local orientations, respectively (for a review, see Schwarz & Clore, 2007).

Similar to the case of mood and stereotyping, however, the connection between mood and global-local focus appears to rest on the fact that a global focus is frequently a dominant or highly accessible orientation toward incoming information (Bruner, 1957; Kimchi, 1992). In past research, then, mood may have had its influence by signaling the value of this accessible response orientation, rather than by directly sparking a global or local focus. Consistent with this reasoning, recent research found no dedicated relationship between affect and perceptual focus when a global versus local focus was manipulated (Huntsinger, in press; Huntsinger, Clore, &

Bar-Anan, 2010). Instead, affect acted on whichever orientation was momentarily more accessible. When a global focus was more accessible, positive moods led to a greater global focus than negative moods, thus replicating past research. But when a local focus was made more accessible, then positive moods led to a greater local focus than negative moods.

## CREATIVITY

People in positive moods tend to display greater creativity and flexibility in their thinking than do those in negative moods (Isen, 1987). In general, positive emotions expand a person's thought-action repertoire and build social and intellectual resources (Fredrickson, 1998), and as a consequence, this can broaden attention (Fredrickson & Branigan, 2005). Effects on creativity are revealed in research employing a variety of different tasks, such as the remote associates task (RAT; Mednick, 1962), in which, for example, people are asked to write down uses for a brick, as well as the Tower of Hanoi problem, and categorization tasks. These findings are often taken to indicate that positive mood directly activates greater cognitive flexibility and a divergent thinking style (Isen, 1987). Although this certainly could be the case, consistent with the affect-as-information approach, the link between mood and creativity appears quite flexible and depends on what thoughts and responses happen to be in mind at the moment.

Altering whether a focus on similarities or differences is accessible, for instance, changes the relation between mood and creativity. When a focus on differences is accessible, people in positive moods display greater breadth of categorization than those in negative moods. However, when a focus on similarities is accessible, people in positive moods display less breadth of categorization than those in negative moods (Murray, Sujan, Hirt, & Sujan, 1990).

The influence of mood on creativity also depends on the framing of the task. When people are enjoyment focused, those in positive moods may persist longer on a creativity task than those in negative moods because positive mood signals the task is enjoyable, which may then lead to mood-related differences in creativity (Wyer et al., 1999). Consistent with this idea, when a task is framed in a way that stresses enjoyment, people in positive moods, as compared to those in negative moods, devote more time to the task, and thus come up with more creative responses (Martin, Ward, Achee, & Wyer, 1993). When performance is stressed, by contrast, people in positive moods devote less time to the task, and thus come up with less creative responses, than those in negative moods. One might speculate that many creativity tasks are probably among the more enjoyable tasks that participants in psychology experiments complete. This suggests that participants may spontaneously adopt an enjoyment focus when completing creativity tasks in laboratory experiments, which may underlie many of the mood-related differences in creativity found in past research (see also Wyer et al., 1999).

Another way that mood shapes creativity is by influencing whether people use currently accessible thoughts. For example, when contemplating uses for a brick, mood may signal the value of thoughts that come to mind (e.g., "A brick would make a useful doorstop"), influencing whether they are reported during the task. Because they view accessible thoughts as valid and valuable, people in positive moods should be more likely to report those thoughts than those in negative moods. This may then contribute to mood-related differences in divergent and creative thinking. Indeed, people in negative moods were less likely than those in positive moods to report thoughts that came to mind while completing a creativity task (Gasper, 2004b). This difference in reporting thoughts and thus creativity vanished, however, when participants in positive and negative moods were instructed to write down whatever thoughts came to mind while completing the task. Thus, rather than shaping what type of thoughts come to mind during a creativity task, as is often assumed (e.g., Isen, 1987), mood influences what people do with their thoughts.

## SPECIFIC EMOTIONS

As with evaluative judgments, research shows that the influence of specific emotions on cognitive processing depends on the pattern of appraisal associated with the emotion rather than its valence per se. The appraisal pattern associated with specific emotions, and thus their influence on cognitive processing, will be elaborated on later.

As discussed earlier, anger involves displeasure over undesirable outcomes and disapproval of the blameworthy action that caused them (Ortony et al., 1988). Although anger is a negative emotion, its influence on cognitive processing is similar to that of positive mood. Specifically, the experience of anger is accompanied by feelings of confidence in one's point of view (Clore & Huntsinger, 2009), which encourages reliance on accessible thoughts and response tendencies. This influence is nicely illustrated in studies of stereotyping and persuasion. Anger has been shown to increase reliance on stereotypes in jury decision-making contexts (Bodenhausen, Sheppard, & Kramer, 1994; Tiedens & Linton, 2001) and also to increase the display of implicit intergroup bias (DeSteno, Dasgupta, Bartlett, & Cajdric, 2004). In the persuasion domain, research demonstrates that anger increases reliance on heuristic cues when processing persuasive messages (Moons & Mackie, 2007; Tiedens & Linton, 2001).

Fear and anxiety are accompanied by feelings of threat and uncertainty (Ortony et al., 1988; Tiedens & Linton, 2001), which lead people to avoid relying on accessible mental content and routine response tendencies. Fearful people, for example, avoid relying on stereotypes when making judgments and, when processing persuasive message, they also avoid relying on heuristic cues (Tiedens & Linton, 2001).

## Conclusion

Affective reactions, in the form of emotions and moods, exert a far-reaching and largely functional influence on cognition (Clore, 2005; Damasio, 1994; Frijda, 1986). We discussed both classic and contemporary approaches to affective influences on cognition. These included psychodynamic perspectives, classical conditioning models, memory-priming models, and the affect-as-information approach. The latter perspective served as the theoretical framework for organizing our discussion of how affect influences four important cognitive domains: memory, perception, judgment, and cognitive processing. As this research reveals, many classic findings in cognitive psychology appear to have an affective trigger.

## Future Directions

1. What is the neurological basis for mood and emotional influences on cognition? It is imperative that a neurologically plausible model of affect–cognition interaction be developed in order to fully understand their interaction.

2. Cognitive feelings, such as fluency and certainty; bodily cues, such as head nodding and shaking; and so forth often have a similar influence on cognition as corresponding affective feelings. And some research reveals they may serve a similar information function as mood and emotion. Future research is necessary to establish whether these seemingly disparate internal cues can be unified under a single theoretical framework.

3. The information about value conveyed by affect can be represented at multiple levels, including neurological, physiological, experiential, cognitive, and behavioral. What are the consequences for cognition of coherence versus incoherence between these levels? Some research indicates that feelings of affective coherence versus incoherence produce epistemic advantages and disadvantages, respectively (Centerbar, Schnall, Clore, & Garvin, 2008). Does this influence extend beyond the epistemic realm? Does affective coherence serve an information function like mood and emotion?

## References

Aaker, D. A. (1991). *Managing brand equity: Capitalizing on the value of a brand name.* Free Press: New York.

Aristotle . (1991). *The art of rhetoric* (H. Lawson-Tancred, Trans.) . London: Penguin.

Bargh, J. A. (1997). The automaticity of everyday life. In R. S.Wyer, Jr . (Ed.), *The automaticity of everyday life: Advances in social cognition* (Vol. 10, pp. 1–61). Mahwah, NJ: Erlbaum.

Barone, M. J., Miniard, P. W., & Romeo, J. B. (2000). The influence of positive mood on brand extension evaluations. *Journal of Consumer Research, 26,* 386–400.

Barrett, L. F., & Salovey, P. (Eds.). (2002). *The wisdom in feeling: Processes underlying emotional intelligence.* New York: Guilford Press.

Bartlett, F. C. (1932). *Remembering: A study in experimental and social psychology.* Cambridge, England: Cambridge University Press.

Bäuml, K-H. & Kuhbandner, C. (2007). Remembering can cause forgetting—but not in negative moods. *Psychological Science, 18,* 111–115.

Beukeboom, C. J., & Semin, G. R., (2005). Mood and representations of behavior: The how and why. *Cognition and Emotion, 19,* 1242–1251.

Bhalla, M., & Proffitt, D. R. (1999). Visual-motor recalibration in geographical slant perception. *Journal of Experimental Psychology: Human Perception and Performance, 25,* 1076–1096.

Blaney, P. H. (1986). Affect and memory: A review. *Psychological Bulletin, 99,* 229–246.

Bodenhausen, G. V., Kramer, G., & Sü sser, K. (1994). Happiness and stereotypic thinking in social judgment. *Journal of Personality and Social Psychology, 66,* 621–632.

Bodenhausen, G. V., Sheppard, L., & Kramer, G. (1994). Negative affect and social perception: The differential impact of anger and sadness. *European Journal of Social Psychology, 24,* 45–62.

Bower, G. H. (1981). Emotional mood and memory. *American Psychologist, 36,* 129–148.

Bower, G. H., Gilligan, S. G., & Monteiro, K. P. (1981). Selectivity of learning caused by affective states. *Journal of Experimental Psychology: General, 110,* 451–473.

Bower, G. H., & Mayer, J. D. (1985). Failure to replicate mood-dependent retrieval. *Bulletin of the Psychonomic Society, 23,* 39–42.

Brand, S., Reimer, T., & Opwis, K. (2007). How do we learn in a negative mood? Effects of a negative mood on transfer and learning. *Learning and Instruction, 17,* 1–16.

Bruner, J. (1957). On perceptual readiness. *Psychological Review*, *64*, 123–152.

Bruner, J. S., & Postman, L. (1947). Tension and tension-release as organizing factors in perception. *Journal of Personality*, *15*, 300–308.

Cannon, P. R., Schnall, S., & White, M. (2011). Transgressions and expressions: Affective facial muscle activity predicts moral judgments. *Social Psychological and Personality Science*, *2*, 325–331.

Centerbar, D. B., Schnall, S., Clore, G. L., & Garvin, E. (2008). Affective incoherence: When affective concepts and embodied reactions clash. *Journal of Personality and Social Psychology*, *94*, 560–578.

Chapman, H. A., Kim, D. A., Susskind, J. M., & Anderson, A. K. (2009). In bad taste: Evidence for the oral origins of moral disgust. *Science*, *323*, 1222–1226.

Clark, M. S., & Isen, A. M. (1982). Toward understanding the relationship between feeling states and social behavior. In A. H. Hastrof & A. M. Isen (Eds.), *Cognitive social psychology* (pp. 73–108). New York: Elsevier.

Clore, G. L. (2005). For love or money: Some emotional foundations of rationality. *Chicago Kent Law Review*, *80*, 1151–1165.

Clore, G. L., & Huntsinger, J. R. (2007). How emotions inform judgment and regulate thought. *Trends in Cognitive Sciences*, *9*, 393–399.

Clore, G. L., & Huntsinger, J. R. (2009). How the object of affect guides its impact. *Emotion Review*, *1*, 39–54.

Damasio, A. (1994). *Descartes' error: Emotions, reason, and the human brain*. New York: Avon Books.

DeSteno, D., Dasgupta, N., Bartlett, M. Y., & Cajdric, A. (2004). Prejudice from thin air: The effect of emotion on automatic intergroup attitudes. *Psychological Science*, *15*, 319–325.

Dijksterhuis, A., Chartrand, T. L., & Aarts, H. (2007). Effects of priming and perception on social behavior and goal pursuit. In J. A. Bargh (Ed.), *Social psychology and the unconscious* (p. 51–132). Philadelphia: Psychology Press.

Duncan, S., & Barrett, L. F. (2007). Affect as a form of cognition: A neurobiological analysis. *Cognition and Emotion*, *21*, 1184–1211.

Feshbach, S., & Singer, R. D. (1957). The effects of fear arousal and suppression of fear upon social perception. *Journal of Abnormal and Social Psychology*, *55*, 283–288.

Forgas, J. P. (1995). Mood and judgment: The affect infusion model (AIM). *Psychological Bulletin*, *117*, 39–66.

Fredrickson, B. L. (1998). What good are positive emotions? *Review of General Psychology*, *2*, 300–319.

Fredrickson, B. L., & Branigan, C. (2005). Positive emotions broaden the scope of attention and thought-action repertoires. *Cognition and Emotion*, *19*, 313–332.

Frijda, N. H. (1986). *The emotions*. Cambridge, England: Cambridge University Press.

Gasper, K. (2004a). Do you see what I see? Affect and visual information processing. *Cognition and Emotion*, *18*, 405–421.

Gasper, K. (2004b). Permission to seek freely? The effect of happy and sad moods on generating old and new ideas. *Creativity Research Journal*, *16*, 215–229.

Gasper, K., & Clore, G. L. (1998). The persistent use of negative affect by anxious individuals to estimate risk. *Journal of Personality and Social Psychology*, *74*, 1350–1363.

Gasper, K., & Clore, G. L. (2000). Do you have to pay attention to your feelings to be influenced by them? *Personality and Social Psychology Bulletin*, *26*, 698–711.

Gasper, K., & Clore, G. L. (2002). Attending to the big picture: Mood and global vs. local processing of visual information. *Psychological Science*, *13*, 34–40.

Gawronski, B., & Bodenhausen, G. V. (2006). Associative and propositional processes in evaluation: An integrative review of implicit and explicit attitude change. *Psychological Bulletin*, *132*, 692–731.

Gibson, J. J. (1979). *The ecological approach to visual perception*. Boston: Houghton Mifflin.

Greifeneder, R., & Bless, H. (2008). Depression and reliance on ease-of-retrieval experiences. *European Journal of Social Psychology*, *38*, 213–230.

Greifeneder, R., Bless, H., & Kuschmann, T. (2007). Extending the brand image on new products: The facilitative effect of happy mood states. *Journal of Consumer Behavior*, *6*, 19–31

Gutierrez, R., & Giner-Sorolla, R. S. (2007) Anger, disgust, and presumption of harm as reactions to taboo-breaking behaviors. *Emotion*, *7*, 853–868.

Haidt, J., McCauley, C. R., & Rozin, P. (1994). A scale to measure disgust sensitivity. *Personality and Individual Differences*, *16*, 701–713.

Huddy, L., Feldman, S., & Cassese E. (2007). On the distinct political effects of anxiety and anger. In A. Crigler, M. MacKuen, G. E. Marcus, & W. R. Neuman (Eds), *The political dynamics of feeling and thinking*. Chicago: University of Chicago Press.

Huntsinger, J. R. (in press). Does positive affect broaden and negative affect narrow attentional scope? A new answer to an old question. *Journal of Experimental Psychology: General*.

Huntsinger, J. R. (2011). Mood and trust in intuition interactively orchestrate correspondence between implicit and explicit attitudes. *Personality and Social Psychology Bulletin*, *37*, 1245–1258.

Huntsinger, J. R., Clore, G. L., & Bar-Anan, Y. (2010). Mood and global-local focus: Priming a local focus reverses the link between mood and global-local processing. *Emotion*, *10*, 722–726.

Huntsinger, J. R., Sinclair, S., & Clore, G. L. (2009). Affective regulation of implicitly measured attitudes and stereotypes: Automatic and controlled processes. *Journal of Experimental Social Psychology*, *45*, 560–566.

Huntsinger, J. R., Sinclair, S., Dunn, E., & Clore, G. L. (2010). Affective regulation of automatic stereotype activation: It's the (accessible) thought that counts. *Personality and Social Psychology Bulletin*, *36*, 564–577.

Huntsinger, J. R., & Smith, C. T. (2009). First thought, best thought: Positive mood maintains and negative mood disrupts implicit-explicit attitude correspondence. *Personality and Social Psychology Bulletin*, *35*, 187–197.

Inbar, Y., Pizarro, D. A., & Bloom, P. (2009) Conservatives are more easily disgusted than liberals. *Cognition and Emotion*, *23*, 714–725.

Inbar, Y., Pizarro, D. A., Knobe, J., & Bloom, P. (2009) Disgust sensitivity predicts intuitive disapproval of gays. *Emotion*, *9*, 435–439.

Isen, A. (1987). Positive affect, cognitive processes, and social behavior. *Advances in Experimental Social Psychology*, *20*, 203–253.

Isen, A., & Means, B. (1983). The influence of positive affect on decision-making strategy. *Social Cognition*, *2*, 18–31.

Isen, A., Shalker, R., Clark, M., & Karp, L. (1978). Affect, accessibility of material in memory and behavior. A cognitive loop? *Journal of Personality and Social Psychology*, *36*, 1–12.

Jones, A., & Fitness, J. (2008). Moral hypervigilence: The influence of disgust sensitivity in the moral domain. *Emotion, 8*, 613–627.

Jordan, C. H., Whitfield, M., & Zeigler-Hill, V. (2007). Intuition and the correspondence between implicit and explicit self-esteem. *Journal of Personality and Social Psychology, 93*, 1067–1079.

Kant, I. (1960) *Observations on the feeling of the beautiful and the sublime* (J. T. Goldthwait, Trans.) . Berkeley: University of California Press.

Keltner, D., Ellsworth, P., & Edwards, K. (1993). Beyond simple pessimism: Effects of sadness and anger on social perception. *Journal of Personality and Social Psychology, 64*, 740–752.

Kimchi, R. (1992). Primacy of wholistic processing and global/local paradigms: A critical review. *Psychological Bulletin, 112*, 24–38.

Lerner, J. S., Gonzalez, R. M., Small, D. A., & Fischhoff, B. (2003). Effects of fear and anger on perceived risks of terrorism: A national field experiment. *Psychological Science, 14*, 144–150.

Lerner, J. S., & Keltner, D. (2001). Fear, anger, and risk. *Journal of Personality and Social Psychology, 81*, 146–159.

Lerner, J. S., Small, D. A., & Loewenstein, G. (2004). Heart strings and purse strings: Carry-over effects of emotions on economic decisions. *Psychological Science, 15*, 337–341.

Levine, L. J. (1997). Reconstructing memory for emotions. *Journal of Experimental Psychology: General, 126*, 165–177.

Levine, L. J., Prohaska, V., Burgess, S. L., Rice, J. A., & Laulhere, T. M. (2001). Remembering past emotions: The role of current appraisals. *Cognition and Emotion, 15*, 393–417.

Mackie, D. M., & Worth, L. T. (1991). Feeling good, but not thinking straight: The impact of positive mood on persuasion. In J. Forgas (Ed.), *Emotion and social judgment* (pp. 201–220). Oxford, England: Pergamon.

MacLeod, M. D. (2002). Retrieval-induced forgetting in eyewitness memory: Forgetting as a consequence of remembering. *Applied Cognitive Psychology, 16*, 135–149.

Martin, L. L., Abend, T., Sedikides, C., & Green, J. D. (1997). How would it feel if…? Mood as input to a role fulfillment evaluation process. *Journal of Personality and Social Psychology, 73*, 242–253.

Martin, L. L., & Clore, G. L. (Eds.). (2001). *Theories of mood and cognition: A user's guidebook*. Mahwah, NJ: Erlbaum.

Martin, L. L., Ward, D. W., Achee, J. W., & Wyer, R. S. (1993). Mood as input: People have to interpret the motivational implication of their moods. *Journal of Personality and Social Psychology, 64*, 317–326.

Matt, G., Vasquez, C., & Campbell, W. K. (1992). Mood-congruent recall of affectively toned stimuli: A meta-analytic review. *Clinical Psychology Review, 12*, 227–255.

McGaugh, J. (2004). The amygdala modulates the consolidation of memories of emotionally arousing experiences. *Annual Review of Neuroscience, 27*, 1–28.

Mednick, S. A. (1962). The associative basis of the creative process. *Psychological Review, 69*, 220–232.

Moll, J., de Oliveira-Souza, R., Moll, F. T., Ignácio, F. A., Bramati, I., Caperlli-Dáquer, E., & Eslinger, P. J. (2005). The moral affiliations of disgust: A functional MRI study. *Cognitive and Behavioral Neurobiology, 18*, 68–78.

Moons, W. G., & Mackie, D. M. (2007). Thinking straight while seeing red: The influence of anger on information processing. *Personality and Social Psychology Bulletin, 33*, 706–720.

Murray, N., Sujan, H., Hirt, E. R., & Sujan M. (1990). The influence of mood on categorization: A cognitive flexibility interpretation. *Journal of Personality and Social Psychology, 59*, 411–425.

Ortony, A., Clore, G. L., & Collins, A. (1988). *The cognitive structure of emotions*. New York: Cambridge University Press.

Parrott, G., & Sabini, J. (1990). Mood and memory under natural conditions: Evidence for mood incongruent recall. *Journal of Personality and Social Psychology, 59*, 321–336.

Payne, B. K. (2001). Prejudice and perception: The role of automatic and controlled processes in misperceiving a weapon. *Journal of Personality and Social Psychology, 81*, 181–192.1

Pessoa, L. (2008). On the relation between emotion and cognition. *Nature Reviews Neuroscience, 9*, 148–158.

Pham, M. T., Cohen, J. B., Pracejus, J. W., & Hughes, G. D. (2001). Affect monitoring and the primacy of feelings in judgment. *Journal of Consumer Research, 28*, 167–188.

Plato. (1992). *Republic* (G. M. A. Grube, Trans.). Indianapolis, IN: Hackett.

Postman, L., Bruner, J. S., & McGinnies, E., (1948). Personal values as selective factors in perception. *Journal of Abnormal and Social Psychology, 43*, 142–154.

Proffitt, D. R. (2006). Embodied perception and the economy of action. *Perspectives on Psychological Science, 1*, 110–122.

Proffitt, D. R., Bhalla, M., Gossweiler, R., & Midgett, J. (1995). Perceiving geographical slant. *Psychonomic Bulletin and Review, 2*, 409–428.

Raghunathan, R., Pham, M., & Corfman, K. P. (2006). Informational properties of anxiety and sadness, and displaced coping. *Journal of Consumer Research, 32*, 596–601.

Razran, G. H. S. (1954). The conditioned evocation of attitudes (cognitive conditioning?) *Journal of Experimental Psychololgy, 48*, 278–282.

Rholes, W. S., Riskind, J. H., & Lane, J. (1987). Emotional mood states and memory biases: The effects of cognitive priming and mood. *Journal of Personality and Social Psychology, 52*, 91–99.

Riener, C., Stefanucci, J., Proffitt, D., & Clore, G.L. (2010). Mood and the perception of spatial layout. *Cognition and Emotion, 25, 174–182*.

Robinson, M. D., & Clore, G. L. (2002). Beliefs, situations, and their interactions: Towards a model of emotion reporting. *Psychological Bulletin, 128*, 934–960.

Roediger, H. L., III, Balota, D., & Watson, J. (2001). Spreading activation and arousal of false memories. In H. L. Roediger, III, J. Nairne, I. Neath, & A. M. Surprenant (Eds.), *The nature of remembering: Essays in honor of Robert G. Crowder* (pp. 95–115). Washington, DC: American Psychological Association.

Rozin, P., Haidt, J., & McCauley, C. R. (2008). Disgust. In M. Lewis & J. M. Haviland (Eds.), *Handbook of emotions* (3rd ed., pp. 757–776). New York: Guilford Press.

Rüder, M., & Bless, H. (2003). Mood and the reliance on the ease of retrieval heuristic. *Journal of Personality and Social Psychology, 85*, 20–32.

Schnall, S., Benton, J., & Harvey, S. (2008). With a clean conscience: Cleanliness reduces the severity of moral judgments. *Psychological Science, 19*, 1219–1222

Schnall, S., Haidt, J., Clore, G. L., & Jordan, A. H. (2008). Disgust as embodied moral judgment. *Personality and Social Psychology Bulletin, 34*, 1096–1109.

Schnall, S., Harber, K. D., Stefanucci, J., & Proffitt, D. R. (2008). Social support and the perception of geographical slant. *Journal of Experimental Social Psychology, 44*, 1246–1255.

Schnall, S., Jaswal, V., & Rowe, C. (2008). A hidden cost of happiness in children. *Developmental Science, 11*, F25–F30.

Schnall, S., Zadra, J. R., & Proffitt, D. R. (2010). Direct evidence for the economy of action: Glucose and the perception of geographical slant. *Perception, 39*, 464–482.

Schwarz, N., Bless, H., & Bohner, G. (1991). Mood and persuasion: Affective states influence the processing of persuasive communications. *Advances in Experimental Social Psychology, 23*, 161–197.

Schwarz, N., Bless, H., Strack, F., Klumpp, G., Rittenauer-Schatka, H., & Simons, A. (1991). Ease of retrieval as information: another look at the availability heuristic, *Journal of Personality and Social Psychology, 61*, 195–202.

Schwarz, N., & Clore, G. L. (1983). Mood, misattribution, and judgments of well-being: Informative and directive functions of affective states. *Journal of Personality and Social Psychology, 45*, 513–523.

Schwarz, N., & Clore, G. L. (2007). Feelings and phenomenal experiences. In E. T. Higgins & A. Kruglanski (Eds.), *Social psychology: A handbook of basic principles* (Vol. 2, pp. 385–407). New York: Guilford Press.

Singer, J. A., & Salovey, P. (1988). Mood and memory: Evaluating the network theory of affect. *Clinical Psychology Review, 8*, 211–251.

Slovic, P., Finucane, M., Peters, E., & MacGregor, D. G. (2002). The affect heuristic. In T. Gilovich, D. Griffin, & D. Kahneman (Eds.), *The psychology of intuitive judgment heuristics and biases* (pp. 397–420). Cambridge, England: Cambridge University Press.

Staats, A. W., & Staats, C. K. (1958). Attitudes established by classical conditioning. *Journal of Abnormal and Social Psychology, 57*, 37–40.

Stefanucci, J. K., & Proffitt, D. R. (2009). The roles of altitude and fear in the perception of heights. *Journal of Experimental Psychology: Human Perception and Performance, 35*, 424–438.

Stefanucci, J. K., Proffitt, D. R., Clore, G. L., & Parekh, N. (2008). Skating down a steeper slope: Fear influences the perception of geographical slant. *Perception, 37*, 321–323.

Stefanucci, J. K., & Storbeck, J. (2009). Don't look down: Emotional arousal elevates height perception. *Journal of Experimental Psychology: General, 138*, 131–145.

Storbeck, J., & Clore, G. L. (2005). With sadness comes accuracy, with happiness, false memory: Mood and the false memory effect. *Psychological Science, 16*, 785–791.

Storbeck, J., & Clore, G. L. (2008a). Affective regulation of cognitive priming. *Emotion, 8*, 208–215.

Storbeck, J., & Clore, G. L. (2008b). Affective arousal as information: How affective arousal influences judgments, learning, and memory. *Social and Personality Psychology Compass, 2*, 1824–1843.

Storbeck, J., & Robinson, M. D. (2004). Preferences and inferences in encoding visual objects: A systematic comparison of semantic and affective priming. *Personality and Social Psychology Bulletin, 30*, 81–93.

Teachman, B. A., Stefanucci, J. K., Clerkin, E. M., Cody, M. W., & Proffitt, D. R. (2008). A new mode of fear expression: Perceptual bias in height fear. *Emotion, 8*, 296–301.

Tiedens, L. Z., & Linton, S. (2001). Judgment under emotional certainty and uncertainty: The effects of specific emotions and their associated certainty appraisals on cognitive processing. *Journal of Personality and Social Psychology, 81*, 973–988.

Tversky, A., & Kahneman, D. (1974). Judgment under uncertainty: Heuristics and biases. *Science, 185*, 1124–1131.

Wheatley, T., & Haidt, J. (2005). Hypnotic disgust makes moral judgments more severe. *Psychological Science, 18*, 780–784.

Wilson, T. D., & Schooler, J. W. (1991). Thinking too much: Introspection can reduce the quality of preferences and decisions. *Journal of Personality and Social Psychology, 60*, 181–192.

Wyer, R. S., Clore, G. L., & Isbell, L. (1999). Affect and information processing. *Advances in Experimental Social Psychology, 31*, 3–78.

Zajonc, R. B. (1980). Feeling and thinking: Preferences need no inferences. *American Psychologist, 35*, 151–175.

# An Emotion Regulation Perspective on Belief Change

Matthew Tyler Boden *and* James J. Gross

### Abstract

Theory and research have long supported the premise that the way a person thinks powerfully shapes what that person feels. Following, changing what a person is thinking alters his or her emotional responses, even if the situation itself remains objectively unchanged. This idea has played an important role in the development of the field of emotion regulation, which has considered how moment-by-moment changes in thinking influence the unfolding emotional response. In this chapter, we extend prior work by considering the possibility that longer-term cognitive changes or changes in beliefs can lead to changes in emotion, and that belief change may partly serve emotion regulation motives. The empirically supported framework we present may help to stimulate new theory and research on the bidirectional relations between emotion and belief, with further implications for understanding why people believe what they do and how to treat emotional disturbances that contribute to psychological disorders.

**Key Words:** belief, emotion, belief change, emotion change, affect

It is widely appreciated that "the same" situation can evoke very different emotional responses in different people. For example, some people living in India reacted with awe to a recent solar eclipse, the longest of this century. Others reacted with fear or even terror. According to appraisal perspectives on emotion, these emotional reactions were generated by differing beliefs, such as beliefs from Western science that an eclipse is a rare astronomical occurrence, or beliefs from Hindu mythology that an eclipse is caused by a dragon-demon swallowing the sun. These differing beliefs—and the emotions they generated—are consequential in that they can lead to quite different patterns of behavior. In this case, people interested in the eclipse took photographs because they wished to share their pleasure with others. People terrified by the eclipse engaged in rituals (e.g., chanting prayers, washing in the Ganges River) because they believed these actions would protect them from harm.

One particularly intriguing implication of the idea that the way a person thinks powerfully shapes what that person feels is that changing what a person is thinking should alter his or her emotional responses, even if the situation itself remains objectively unchanged. This idea has played an important role in the development of the field of emotion regulation, which—among other things—has considered how moment-by-moment changes in thinking influence the unfolding emotional response (e.g., Gross, 2007). In this chapter, we extend prior work by considering the possibility that longer term cognitive changes or changes in beliefs can lead to changes in emotion, and that belief change may partly serve emotion regulation motives.

## Emotions and Beliefs

Emotions and beliefs have typically been treated by psychologists as distinct mental phenomena. Hence, the persistent debates about whether one should follow one's mind or one's gut, or whether one should rely on intuition or logic when making important life decisions. However, consistent with philosophers who have described beliefs as being emotional states or having emotional aspects (Hume, 1739/1969; Price, 1954), a growing body of theory and research suggests that emotions and beliefs are mutually informative and constantly interacting (see Boden & Berenbaum, 2010, for a review). In the following sections, we say what we mean by *emotions* and *beliefs*, and then focus our discussion on the link from belief to emotion in those cases in which belief change is driven by emotion regulation motives.

### Emotions

Although the concept of emotion is notoriously difficult to define, many find it useful to consider three core features of a prototypical or commonly experienced emotion that together form the modal model of emotion (see Fig. 37.1): (a) emotion antecedents, (b) emotion responses, and (c) the link between emotion antecedents and responses.

Emotion antecedents are situations that are relevant to the present concerns of an individual. Concerns, which may be expressed as goals, traits, attitudes, beliefs, and sensitivities to particular stimuli, predispose individuals to emotionally respond to particular situations. According to appraisal theory, emotions are elicited and differentiated as an individual assesses the personal significance of a situation on a number of dimensions (Scherer, 1999). Appraisals represent these moment-by-moment evaluations of the personal significance of the situation in terms of dimensions such as pleasantness, novelty, and goal significance (Scherer, 1999). Appraisals are typically fast, and they often occur outside of awareness.

As emotion appraisals are made, they give rise to multifaceted, whole-body emotion responses, which involve loosely integrated changes in subjective experience, cognition (e.g., attention), behavior, and central and peripheral physiology (Mauss, Levenson, McCarter, Wilhelm, & Gross, 2005). Emotions are mentally represented as subjective

experience, or "feelings" (see Barrett, Ochsner, & Gross, 2007). They are often expressed as behavior via bodily responses involving motivation and motor systems (e.g., attacking a person who threatens you) that are supported by changes in central (e.g., neuroendocrine changes) and peripheral physiology (e.g., increased blood flow to the limbs). These physiological changes immediately precede and follow the behavioral response and support the motor system responses associated with emotions.

Emotion antecedents and responses are flexibly linked in a manner that allows for continual changes in emotional responses. In other words, emotional responses can be continually tailored to the specific requirements of a given situation as these requirements change due to changes in (a) the situation itself or (b) the meaning of the situation in terms of the goals of the individual. For example, I may become angry when the power at my apartment is shut off due to the negligence of my landlord, who forgot to pay the bill. This situation directly relates to my goal of cooking dinner while listening to music. However, my emotional responses may change when the situation changes (e.g., I call the landlord, who immediately pays the bill) or the meaning of the situation in terms of my goal changes (e.g., the landlord tells me she did not pay the bill because she was hospitalized for the past month). It is in part because of the flexibility of links between emotion antecedents and responses that emotional responses are so often adaptive, and when they are not, they may be regulated in various ways.

### Beliefs

Most psychological definitions of belief share two common features (e.g., Ajzen & Fishbein, 1975; Eagly & Chaiken, 1993). First, beliefs are about something; that is, they have content that is gained through subjective experience and is mentally represented. As one can potentially mentally represent any aspect of a subjective experience, beliefs can be about anything that one has subjectively experienced, from reading about the existence of Martians (e.g., "Martians do not exist"), to seeing a giraffe (e.g., "Giraffes are yellow with black spots"), to contemplating how one might die (e.g., "I will die by gunshot"), to attending a church service (e.g., "God loves all people equally"). We do not conceptualize belief content as do many philosophical definitions, as being propositions, statements, or premises that are held to be true or not by the holder of the belief (e.g., Schwitzgebel, 2006). In other words, we do not limit our conceptualization of belief content

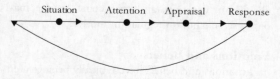

**Figure 37.1** The modal model of emotion with recursive feedback loop depicted (Gross & Thompson, 2007).

to the proposition that describes a particular phenomenon in the world. Instead, we think of belief content more broadly, as the phenomena itself, which are often encapsulated in a proposition that expresses the belief.

A second defining feature of beliefs is that to have a belief, one must be convinced that the content of the belief, or the belief object (e.g., "God"; "God interferes in the affairs of human beings"), exists or does not exist (e.g., "God" exists; "God interferes in the affairs of human beings" does not exist). We include conviction as both a defining feature of beliefs and a dimension of beliefs, as evidence has shown that belief conviction varies continuously over time and context for any given belief for any given individual (Appelbaum, Robbins, & Vasselinov, 2004; Inzlicht, McGregor, Hirsh, & Nash, 2009; Sharp et al., 1996; Strauss, 1969). In other words, without conviction regarding the existence of a belief object, one does not have a belief. Not being convinced one way or the other of the existence of a belief object (i.e., having conviction at a level of chance) is not to have a belief but to instead have an attribution, interpretation, hypothesis, or idea that may become more or less convincing through further subjective experience.

Beliefs arise as a result of our experiences. The generation of a belief includes both (a) the strengthening of conviction in the existence or nonexistence of a belief object from a level indicative of an attribution, interpretation, or hypothesis, to a level indicative of a belief; and (b) the consideration of a new belief object whose existence or nonexistence is immediately held with a level of conviction indicative of a belief (see Gilbert, 1991 for a related discussion). It thus follows that belief generation involves both the selecting of a belief object and the immediate or delayed strengthening in the conviction of a belief object.

## Relations Between Emotions and Beliefs

A growing body of theory and research has specified the bidirectional relations between emotion and belief (see Boden & Berenbaum, 2010 for a comprehensive discussion). People routinely react to their experiences, especially those that are difficult to understand, with both emotional arousal and beliefs, which mutually influence each other (e.g., see Wilson & Gilbert, 2008). The bidirectional relations between emotion and belief are driven both by a need to make sense of experience and by a need to regulate emotions in valued directions. The latter

need is especially salient in the link from belief to emotion, which we describe here.

Beliefs powerfully shape emotions via their influence on appraisal processes. Indeed, several influential appraisal theories have posited that beliefs are one of the most important influences on appraisal processes, and thereby determine when and what type of emotion will be elicited in response to environmental contingencies (Lazarus, 1991). Beliefs are sometimes proximal concerns that orient individuals to the personal salience of a particular situation and the meaning of events, as assessed through the appraisal process (Frijda & Mesquita, 2000). For example, among individuals with breast cancer who received surgery, higher levels of optimism were associated with lower levels of unpleasant emotions over the following months (Carver et al., 1993). In other words, beliefs (e.g., the belief that one would recover one's health) predisposed individuals to react to specific events with more positive appraisals, and these positive appraisals in turn led to lower levels of unpleasant emotions over time. It has also been proposed that different types of emotions result, in part, from different belief patterns that serve as the concerns that predispose one to experience emotions (Lazarus, 1991). For example, whereas the belief, "God loves all its children" may predispose the holder of the belief to experience sadness in response to the death of a child, the belief, "God does not exist" may predispose the holder to experience anger in response to a similar situation.

When individuals reflect upon any aspect of the emotion generation process (e.g., the cause of the emotion), they are using deliberate and conscious attribution processes to identify, understand, label, or articulate the less conscious and deliberate, and more reflexive appraisal process (Frijda, 1986). Attributions in part determine the intensity and type of emotion that will occur in response to future similar events (Weiner, 1974, 1985). Attributions can be more hypothesis-like, or open for further investigation and testing, or more fixed and belief-like. Any attribution that is thought to be true to an extent greater than a level of chance can be considered a belief, and therefore, the literature discussing the influence of attributions on emotions supports the hypothesis that beliefs influence emotion generation.

For example, Averill (see 1982, 1983 for a review) has conducted studies on anger in which he asked participants to describe situations in which they were made angry, and analyzed the results to determine the situational antecedents of the experience of anger. It was found that attributions of blame were causally associated with anger, such as when participants believed they were the subject of negative consequences resulting from an unjustified act or avoidable accidents. These results support the link from beliefs to emotion, as any of the attributions that were strongly held could be considered beliefs. Results showing that shame and guilt are, respectively, caused by attributions of failure (e.g., due to low ability) can be interpreted in the same way (Brown & Weiner, 1984; Covington & Omelich, 1984; Jagacinski & Nicholls, 1984).

It is important to note that beliefs influence emotions in a conceptually and temporally broad manner. During the typically long temporal duration with which they are held, beliefs have the potential to be concerns or influence concerns that contribute to many discrete emotions. In this manner, a single belief can influence many emotions across time. Further increasing the breadth of their influence on emotions, any specific belief can serve as or influence a concern that predisposes an individual to emotionally respond to a great number of situations. For example, the belief "Life has no inherent meaning" may predispose someone to react with despair and hopelessness when his daughter unexpectedly dies, when his country preemptively begins war with another, when his partner leaves him for another person, and so on. In this manner, all beliefs have the potential to influence the generation of many different types of emotional events over extended periods of time. We note that although all beliefs have the potential to influence emotions, only some beliefs will actually do so, and in a limited set of circumstances (see Boden & Berenbaum, 2010 for more details).

## Emotion and Belief Change

Whereas beliefs are generally stable and emotions in flux, both beliefs and emotions can and do change in a relatively short time frame (Appelbaum et al., 2004; Gilbert, 1991; Inzlicht et al., 2009; Sharp et al., 1996; Strauss, 1969). In the following sections, we consider the dynamics of changing emotions and beliefs, and argue that one reason that beliefs may change is because these changes produce desirable alterations in the emotions a person has.

### Emotion Change

Once they are generated, emotions are not stable, but continually change. Individual emotional episodes arise and then recede as the situations that give rise to them (and the related appraisals) change

over time. Over longer periods of time, repeated experiences with particular situations may lead emotional responses to increase (sensitization) or decrease (adaptation) (Wilson & Gilbert, 2008).

These changing emotions seem to play out beyond our control. However, emotions can be—and frequently are—intentionally altered. Emotion regulation may be defined as one type of emotion change in which an individual purposefully changes the latency, rise time, magnitude, duration, and offset of either pleasant or unpleasant emotional responses. Emotion regulation may involve increasing or maintaining an emotion response (i.e., up-regulating) or decreasing or avoiding an emotional response (i.e., down-regulating), depending on an individual's goals and ability to regulate emotions in valued directions. Emotion regulation processes may target one domain of emotional responding (e.g., facial expression), while others (e.g., cardiovascular responding) may be left untouched, and emotion regulation processes may be more or less conscious, and more or less automatic or controlled. The value of emotion regulation processes must be defined in terms of their relevance to the goals and aims of the individual engaging in them (see section "Relations Between Emotion Change and Belief Change"). Moreover, emotion regulation processes may be perceived by others as maladaptive while accomplishing a person's own goals or vice versa.

In the process model of emotion regulation, we have previously elucidated five families of emotion regulation processes, each of which is distinguished by the point during the emotion process at which they influence that process (e.g., Gross, 1998; Gross & Thompson, 2007). Each family consists of a set of related processes, all of which may be employed to influence emotions. As depicted in Figure 37.2, four families are considered antecedent focused in that they occur prior to when appraisals contribute to emotion response tendencies. These families include situation selection, situation modification, attentional deployment, and cognitive change. The fifth family, response modulation, occurs after the responses are generated.

*Situation selection* involves acting in ways that make it more or less likely that we will be in situations in which we experience particular emotions (e.g., to reduce fear associated with traveling in airplanes, one could avoid flying altogether and drive instead). Should the situation be unavoidable (i.e., one cannot adequately select the situation), one may try to *modify the situation* by changing some aspect of it to lessen or increase the emotional response

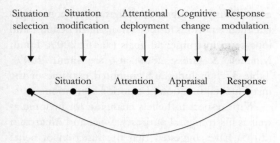

Figure 37.2 A process model of emotion regulation including the five families of emotion regulation strategies (Gross & Thompson, 2007).

once in the situation (e.g., one could take an anxiety-reducing drug [e.g., benzodiazepine] before she gets on the plane to reduce the chances she experiences anxiety). *Attentional deployment* refers to a set of strategies by which individuals direct their attention within a given situation to regulate their emotions (e.g., looking out the window of the airplane, looking at beautiful vacation locations depicted in a magazine). *Cognitive change* refers to altering one's appraisal (i.e., reappraisal) of the situation so as to change its emotional significance once the emotion response has begun. We conceptualize cognitive change broadly as (a) the manipulation of the significance and meaning of a situation or emotion through any change in the cognitive appraisal, or (b) reappraisal of the affective state itself, the eliciting situation, and/or the demands of the situation (Gross & Thompson, 2007; Larsen, 2000). For example, to reduce the fear one experiences during the plane flight, one may change the situational core meaning from "I am going to die in a plane crash" to "Planes are actually very safe, and I have a higher likelihood of dying in a car crash." *Response modulation* refers to directly influencing physiological, experiential, or behavioral responding after they have been initiated (e.g., one could drink a few Scotch's on the plane to reduce fear).

As we are especially interested in one type of cognitive change, belief change, we note that cognitive reappraisal is considered one of the more adaptive emotion regulation strategies. Reappraisal has been shown to successfully reduce negative emotions and related expressive and physiological behavior (e.g., Abelson, Liberzon, Young, & Khan, 2005; Dillon & LaBar, 2005; Gross, 1998). Studies have found that individuals who frequently use reappraisal tend to experience greater life satisfaction, more positive emotions, fewer negative emotions, and they tend to face stressful situations by remaining optimistic while they reinterpret what is stressful and take

active efforts to repair bad moods (Gross & John, 2003). Furthermore, it has been found that reappraisal does not impair memory for information that is presented while an individual is engaged in reappraisal strategies, as do strategies such as expressive suppression (e.g., Richards & Gross, 1999, 2000). This has adaptive consequences as an individual who remembers the causes, experience, and consequences of using reappraisal may be better able to successfully regulate emotions in future situations.

## Belief Change

Although many of the beliefs we hold tend to be stable throughout our lives, beliefs can and do change. Sometimes these changes in beliefs are the result of changes in the world around us. At other times, these changes in beliefs occur independently of changes in the world around us.

Belief change can be considered one type of cognitive change. Consistent with our definition of beliefs, belief change consists of changes in the conviction in a belief, content of a belief, and/or activation of/attending to a belief. Conviction in the existence or nonexistence of a belief object (e.g., God exists) can be increased, resulting in strengthening of the belief, or decreased, resulting in weakening of a given belief. When belief conviction decreases gradually or immediately (e.g., when strong contrary evidence is gained) to the level of chance (i.e., the belief object may or may not exist), the belief is rejected.

The content of a given belief can be expanded, which refers to the incorporation of new information into the belief structure, leading to increasingly complicated beliefs and networks in which they are embedded (e.g., Abelson, 1986). For example, one's belief that "It is always foggy in San Francisco" may be revised to "It is foggy in San Francisco primarily during the summer, the following two months of which are extremely sunny and warm" after living in San Francisco for a year. Belief content can also be revised when information is substituted into an existing belief object. For example, a child's belief that "Christopher Columbus discovered North America" may be revised to "North America was 'discovered' by people who lived there for thousands of years prior to Christopher Columbus's voyages."

Lastly, a belief can change from a deactivated state, in which it is not consciously attended to, to an activated state, in which it is consciously attended to for some period of time. For example, upon receiving a poor grade on a test, one's belief,

"I am a failure," which was initially deactivated and unconscious, may be activated and further attended to.

## Relations Between Emotion Change and Belief Change

Traditionally, theorists and researchers have considered the primary function of emotion regulation to be hedonic, and the primary function of belief change to be instrumental. In other words, emotions have been thought to be regulated primarily to increase/maintain positive affect and decrease/avoid negative affect, and beliefs have been thought to develop and change for the purpose of maintaining accurate mental representations of the world and oneself. We provide hypothetical examples of the instrumental function of belief change and the hedonic function of emotion regulation in Table 37.1. Indeed, philosophers, historians, and psychologists have all generally agreed that regulating emotions for hedonic purposes and changing beliefs for instrumental purposes are important motivations that shape human life. However, we propose that emotion regulation and belief change can serve *both* hedonic and instrumental functions.

With respect to emotions being regulated for instrumental purposes, recent empirical research has shown that emotions can facilitate achievement of instrumental goals, and that people are willing to forgo immediate hedonic gains to pursue instrumental, or long-term, goals (Mischel, Shoda, & Rodriquez, 1989). We use the term *goals* to refer to overall organizations of sets of activities that energize and motivate people in service of particular ends, and in doing so provide meaning to peoples' existences (see Miller & Read, 1987; Read & Miller, 1989; also see Cantor & Kihlstrom, 1987; Emmons, 1986). Therefore, as supported by

a small but growing body of literature, people regulate their emotions for both short-term hedonic and long-term instrumental goals (Tamir 2009; Tamir, Mitchell, & Gross, 2008; also see Tamir, 2009). Table 37.1 includes a highlighted example of the instrumental function of emotion regulation.

With respect to beliefs changing for hedonic as well as instrumental purposes, Wyer and Albarracin (2005) have suggested that the function of belief formation and change is: "to construct a representation of oneself and the world that permits one to cope effectively with life situations and, therefore, to lead a happy and successful life" (p. 306). This quote highlights that similar to emotions, beliefs sometimes have both instrumental functions (i.e., to construct a representation of oneself and the world that permits one to cope effectively with life situations) and hedonic functions (i.e., to lead a happy and successful life). In fact, we can classify the many motives that have been posited to drive belief formation and change as being representative of either the instrumental or hedonic functions. For example, the accurate reflecting and making sense of oneself, the world, and ongoing experience (e.g., Kruglanski, 1980) can be classified as instrumental functions. Hedonic functions include maintaining a positive self-image (Baumeister, 1997) and believing in a just world (Lerner, Miller, & Holmes, 1976). See Table 37.1 for a highlighted example of the hedonic function of belief change.

We think of the hedonic and instrumental functions of emotion regulation as continually integrated in service of the goals of the individual. In some instances, hedonic goals take priority, and in other instances, instrumental goals take priority. Often, there is a tension between hedonic and instrumental goals. For example, avoiding the experience of anxiety by drinking a few beers before

**Table 37.1** Examples of the Instrumental Function of Belief Change and the Hedonic Function of Emotion Regulation

|  | Hedonic Functions | Instrumental Functions |
|---|---|---|
| Emotion regulation | To reduce her anger, Sally consumes alcohol. | *To keep herself motivated to find a new job, Sally increases her anxiety by contemplating being unemployed.* |
| Belief change | *To calm herself, Sally activates and attends to the belief "God selected this as a trial of my faith."* | To increase her odds of keeping her next job, Sally revises the content of her belief "My communication skills are perfect" to "I need to improve my communication skills." |

*Note:* Traditional views propose that the primary function of emotion regulation is hedonic, and the primary function of belief change is instrumental. Our framework is derived from the premise that emotion regulation and belief change serve *both* hedonic and instrumental functions. Depicted in the cells are examples of how a hypothetical person who has been fired from her job could regulate emotions or change beliefs for both hedonic and instrumental purposes. Italicized examples represent the nondominant views that emotion regulation serves instrumental functions, and belief change serves hedonic functions.

an important exam may help to achieve a hedonic goal, but it will likely impede achievement of the instrumental goal of obtaining a passing grade in the class. Similarly, belief change is often motivated by an integration of hedonic and instrumental goals, with these goals sometimes being in tension. For example, after an individual fails a test his belief that "This professor is unfair in his distribution of grades" may become more convincing in service of a hedonic goal, and at the expense of instrumental goals, such as identifying and remediating academic weaknesses through the development of accurate beliefs regarding why he failed the test. As we discuss later (see section "Why Do People Believe What They Do?"), we hypothesize that an important part of mental health is clarifying why one believes (or acts) as one does, and then coordinating these beliefs (actions) in a way that increases real, long-term well-being, rather than short-term emotion regulatory goals.

## Emotion Regulation Through Belief Change

Although previous scholars have theorized that beliefs serve hedonic functions, these theories have not clearly and comprehensively discussed when and how beliefs regulate emotions. We propose that in accordance with theory and empirical evidence showing that beliefs influence emotion generation via their impact on the appraisal process, beliefs can be directly targeted to regulate emotions in valued directions. The successful fulfillment of this hedonic function of beliefs has important consequences for the emotional experience of the individual and on the beliefs he or she holds.

### Theory and Examples

According to our framework, belief change can serve an important emotion regulation function. More specifically, as depicted in Figure 37.3, our framework proposes three ways belief change can regulate emotions in valued directions: (1) through activation of and attending to beliefs, with no change in content or conviction (see Fig. 37.3A), (2) through increases or decreases in conviction of beliefs (see Fig. 37.3B), and (3) through revisions or expansion of the content of beliefs (see Fig. 37.3C). When referring to beliefs that can regulate emotions in these ways, we are referring to both beliefs directly related (as concerns or as attributions) to the emotion that is being regulated, and also to beliefs not directly related to the emotion-eliciting situation. Our framework proposes that beliefs can be

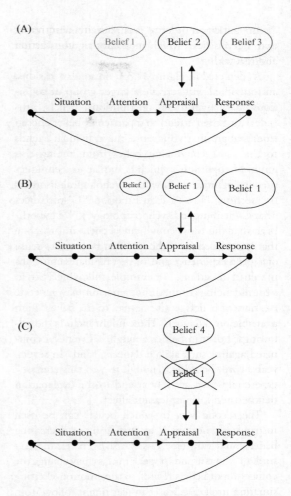

**Figure 37.3** A framework of emotion regulation through belief change. Our framework posits that there are at least three ways by which belief change can regulate emotions in valued directions. First, as depicted in (A), activation of and attending to beliefs (i.e., Belief 2 is activated and attended to while Beliefs 1 and 3 are not) with no change in content or conviction will regulate emotions in valued directions. Second, as depicted in (B), decreases or increases in conviction of beliefs (i.e., Belief 1) will regulate emotions in valued directions. Third, as depicted in (C), revision or expansion of the content of beliefs (i.e., Belief 4 is an expanded version of Belief 1) will regulate emotions in valued directions.

successfully targeted to both up-regulate and down-regulate both pleasant and unpleasant emotions.

The first way beliefs can be used to regulate emotions is by activating and attending to a belief. For example, a parent who learns that a child has been diagnosed with cancer may activate and attend to the belief "God is looking out for my child" in order to down-regulate the unpleasant emotions of fear and sadness. In a similar fashion, a professional surfer may activate and attend to her belief, "I am the best surfer in the entire world," prior to a competition in order to ensure excitement, rather than nervousness, which motivates rigorous action and risk taking.

As depicted in Figure 37.3A, on some occasions, an individual will activate a larger group of cognitions (e.g., hypotheses, attributions, beliefs, attitudes) and then attend to a particular belief chosen from that group. In this sense, the individual attends to the most convincing belief from among this group of cognitions, which is similar to techniques used in cognitive therapy for psychological disorders (see section "How to Treat Emotional Disturbances That Contribute to Psychopathology"). We hypothesize that the most convincing belief, and the one that is attended to, is the one that best makes sense of a given experience and/or best regulates emotions in valued directions. For example, following a loss in a breakdancing competition, a person may generate a variety of beliefs as alternatives to the belief "I am a terrible breakdancer." These might include the following: "I didn't practice enough," "I've never competed against such skilled dancers," and "In several years, I will be skilled enough to win this contest." One could then actively attend to the explanation that best reduces unpleasant affect.

The second way in which beliefs can be used to regulate emotions is by increasing or decreasing belief conviction (see Fig. 37.3B). For example, a student who is afraid to speak in class may change the conviction of beliefs related to the emotion-eliciting situation itself. Decreases in fear might follow from *increases* in conviction in beliefs about the situation itself (e.g., "I don't expect many people to come to class that day"), the situation's core meaning (e.g., "It does not matter what my classmates think of me"), and/or the student's capacity to manage the demands of the situation (e.g., "I am capable of giving the best speech this professor has ever heard"). Fear reduction might also result from *decreases* in conviction in beliefs about the situation, the situation's core meaning, and/or her capacity to manage the demands of the situation (e.g., "I am a terrible public speaker"). We posit that increases and decreases in conviction of beliefs unrelated to the situation (e.g., "I am going to have a fantastic weekend with my friends") will also have the effect of down-regulating fear or other unpleasant emotions, or it will up-regulate pleasant emotions.

The third way in which beliefs can be used to regulate emotions is by revising or expanding belief content, such as depicted in Figure 37.3C. Changes in belief content occur when new information is incorporated into an existing belief object or

substituted for existing information (e.g., resulting in expanded beliefs). For example, the fear experienced by a pregnant, reverent Hindu woman upon viewing a full solar eclipse may be down-regulated through revision of the belief "Being uncommon and unnatural, solar eclipses cause birth defects" to "Being uncommon and *natural*, solar eclipses do not cause birth defects." Similarly, upon reading about peoples' myriad reactions to the solar eclipse, an astronomer may contemplate her existing belief, "Religious ideology serves only to misinform and hurt people," and experience frustration. Through expansion of the belief to "Although religious ideology sometimes misinforms and hurts people, it also serves beneficial purposes," the astronomer may down-regulate her unpleasant affect.

At present, there is much more evidence supporting our framework's core premise that changes in belief conviction can regulate emotions than evidence supporting the emotion regulation effects of changes in activation of/attending to belief and changes in belief content. Here we briefly review evidence supporting the former core premise, while saving a discussion of the empirical status of the latter two premises for the "Applications and Future Directions" section.

### Supporting Empirical Evidence

Theory and research on cognitive consistency theory provides general support for our framework. Cognitive consistency theories propose that people are motivated to remediate discrepancies between conflicting cognitions and cognitions and behaviors (i.e., dissonance) to reduce resulting unpleasant affect (e.g., Festinger, 1957; Harmon-Jones & Mills, 1999). The presence of emotional arousal is necessary for the dissonance reduction, such as through belief change, to take place (Cooper, Zanna, & Taves, 1978). These results can be interpreted as showing that belief change is motivated by a desire to reduce unpleasant affect, and belief change fulfills a hedonic function.

There are several differences between our framework and cognitive consistency theories more generally. The primary difference is that our framework does not require discrepant cognitions and/ or behaviors to motivate belief change. Instead, according to our framework, belief change is motivated by the desire to regulate emotions in valued directions. Cognitive discrepancies are just one of many potential causes of emotional arousal that can give rise to the desire to regulate emotions. However, there are some similarities between our framework and cognitive consistency theory (e.g., emotional arousal motivates belief change) and dissonance reduction has been conceptualized as a mood regulation strategy (e.g., Jonas, Graupmann, & Frey, 2006). Therefore, many research findings regarding cognitive consistency theories support our own framework. For example, it has been found that discrepancies in beliefs and behaviors give rise to unpleasant affect, which in turn contributes to further belief change (e.g., Burris, Harmon-Jones, & Tarpley, 1997; Elliot & Devine, 1994; Harmon-Jones, 2000).

Two influential theories—Terror Management Theory (TMT) and System Justification Theory (SJT)—posit that changes in belief conviction can regulate emotions. TMT states that we have developed beliefs, values, rules, and sociocultural norms (i.e., world of meaning) partly to protect ourselves from potentially paralyzing thoughts of mortality and death (Solomon, Greenberg, & Pyszczynski, 1991). According to TMT, people engage in defense strategies to remove and protect themselves from thoughts of mortality by affirming one's symbolic or literal immortality. One type of defense is the worldview defense, which refers to increases in conviction and expansion of beliefs related to the world of meaning (Pyszczynski, Greenberg, & Solomon, 1999). According to SJT (Jost & Banaji, 1994; Jost & Hunyady, 2002), people are motivated to justify and rationalize the status quo, and systems supporting the status quo (e.g., conservative political ideological systems), to maintain and establish order, closure, certainty, and perceptions of a safe and reassuring environment in the face of threat. One way in which they do this is to endorse, accept, and strengthen beliefs that support the status quo. To frame TMT and SJT in emotion regulation terms: Increases in conviction in beliefs related to one's worldview or beliefs that support the status quo down-regulate unpleasant emotions in situations with salient threats.

Research on TMT has shown that following situations in which mortality is made salient beliefs related to the world of meaning are strengthened and expanded (see Sheldon, Greenberg, & Pyszczynski, 2004 for a review). For example, it has been found that following an experience through which mortality was made salient, among participants who initially had strong beliefs in an afterlife, beliefs in an afterlife were strengthened while anxiety remained stable (Osarchuk & Tatz, 1973). In a series of related studies, it was found that beliefs in supernatural existence (e.g., the existence of God)

and agency (e.g., efficacy of divine intervention) increased among those for whom mortality was made salient versus those for whom mortality was not made salient (Norenzayan & Hansen, 2006). We can interpret these results as evidence that increases in belief conviction can regulate emotions by preventing the generation or increase of fear that accompanies situations in which mortality is made salient.

Research on SJT also supports the idea that the change of beliefs favoring maintenance of the status quo results is associated with regulation of negative affect (Bonanno & Jost, 2006; Jost, Glaser, Kruglanski, & Sulloway, 2003; Landau et al., 2004; Wakslak, Jost, Tyler, & Chen, 2007). A meta-analysis including over 22,000 participants in 88 individual samples from 12 countries found that death anxiety and fear of threat and loss were positively associated with conservative political ideology, which includes beliefs favoring preservation of the status quo (liberal and radical ideology, on the other hand, tends to seek to reform of the status quo; Jost et al., 2003). Following a significant threat to the status quo and enhanced mortality salience in the form of the 9/11 attacks in the United States, individuals were more likely to endorse conservative, system-justifying beliefs (e.g., Bonanno & Jost, 2006; Landau et al., 2004). Presumably, in these instances, increases in system-justifying beliefs following threats to the status quo and one's mortality served to down-regulate unpleasant affect. At least one study directly tested this hypothesis, finding that the increases in conviction in system-justifying beliefs were causally associated with decreases in guilt and frustration (Wakslak et al., 2007).

## Applications and Future Directions

Although our framework is based solidly on well-articulated emotion theory (e.g., Lazarus, 1991), empirical support for core premises and specific hypotheses is needed, and in the following section we first consider the type of evidence that seems most pressing. Then, in the following sections, we argue that a firm understanding of how beliefs change and regulate emotions can be applied to further explain (a) why people hold the beliefs they do, and (b) how to treat emotional disturbances that contribute to psychopathology

### Testing Core Premises and Specific Hypotheses

As reviewed earlier, the core premise that increases and decreases in belief conviction can regulate emotions is well supported. Furthermore, this evidence supports the specific hypothesis that these changes in belief conviction down-regulate unpleasant emotions. However, more evidence is needed about whether changes in belief conviction can be used to up- and down-regulate pleasant emotions, and up-regulate unpleasant emotions. In addition, our framework's core premises that emotions can be regulated through changes in belief activation/attending and content are more speculative, as are the specific ways that emotions will be regulated in this regard.

In our view, the most important future tests of our framework will come from experimental studies, which enable researchers to induce and manipulate moods, measure and manipulate beliefs, and have participants actively regulate emotions through the use of belief change. An important first test will be to determine whether belief change successfully regulates emotions. For example, following a mood induction, participants could be cued or instructed to regulate their emotions through the recall or generation of beliefs, and changes in belief and in emotional experience could be measured. Longitudinal studies might also be used to measure changes in beliefs self-identified by participants as having important emotion regulation functions (e.g., belief in the existence of God). One could then investigate whether frequency of changes in activation/attending, content, and conviction covary with important life events (e.g., death of a relative; diagnosis of major illness) and long-term emotion experience.

Firm empirical grounding of our framework will provide the basis for further extensions of our framework. A particularly important extension would be to more directly test the premise that the relations between belief change and emotion regulation are bidirectional. Consistent with a cognitive and emotional constraint satisfaction framework of emotion regulation (Barrett et al., 2007; Westen & Blagov, 2007), affect-as-information theory (see Clore, 1992; Clore & Gasper, 2000)[1], and a framework of the bidirectional relations between belief and affect (Boden & Berenbaum, 2010), we hypothesize that changes in beliefs that regulate emotions in desired ways are likely to lead to the changed belief becoming more convincing. This will occur when (a) the successful regulation of emotions by the changed belief serves as evidence that the belief is true; and (b) the unsuccessful regulation of emotions by the changed belief serves as evidence that the belief is false.

For example, to reduce unpleasant affect following the power in my apartment being shut off due to lack of payment by my landlord, I may target the belief "My landlord has little respect for me" for change by generating a list of alternative beliefs. One of these beliefs (e.g., "The landlord could not pay the power bill due to unforeseen circumstances") may become increasingly convincing as reductions in unpleasant emotions that ensue serve as evidence that the belief is true. Should further change of the belief "The landlord could not pay the power bill due to unforeseen circumstance" not result in further decreases in unpleasant affect, the belief may be weakened or rejected.

We note that all beliefs are not equally amenable to change, and all emotions are not equally amenable to regulation through cognitive change strategies. Furthermore, people hold myriad beliefs, and it is likely that different beliefs are called upon to different extents and in different contexts to regulate emotions. Therefore, one might also investigate the conditions under which bidirectional relations between belief change and emotion regulation are strong and those under which they are weak or nonexistent. For example, religious/spiritual beliefs likely serve an emotion regulation function in many people and in many contexts. Alternatively, the belief that one must find his or her own meaning in this inherently meaningless world would likely serve an emotion regulation function only in an individual inclined to study and value existential philosophy. Furthermore, successful or unsuccessful regulation of emotion by these beliefs may only serve as evidence for their validity under conditions in which the source of emotions and the belief object is one in the same (see Boden & Berenbaum, 2010 for a comprehensive explication of the conditions under which affect and belief are bidirectionally related).

### Why Do People Believe What They Do?

Any given person has a large number of distinct beliefs and the potential to form an infinite number of new beliefs. Whereas many of the beliefs we hold are of little importance to us (e.g., "Pluto is not a planet"), others are much more important. For example, political and religious beliefs not only guide behavior (e.g., voting for presidential candidates, engaging in rituals), but they distinguish people and the sociocultural groups to which they belong (see Jost, 2006). Whereas some beliefs have a great deal of supporting evidence (e.g., "I will die sooner than I would like"), others do not (e.g., "My soul will exist after I die"). Furthermore, people hold beliefs that are maladaptive and distressing (e.g., "I am a worthless human being") and outright bizarre (e.g., "Jim Jones, orchestrator of the Jonestown Massacre, was the reincarnation of Jesus, Buddha, Mahatma Gandhi, and Vladimir Lenin").

This raises the questions of why we hold the beliefs we do, including those that are maladaptive, distressing, bizarre, and/or those that have little evidence to support them. As discussed previously, one reason people hold particular beliefs is because they successfully regulate emotions in valued directions, and in doing so, they are held with greater conviction.

We hypothesize that the emotion regulation function of beliefs may be especially important to understanding why people hold beliefs that play a prominent role in psychological disorders. Examples of these beliefs include an emaciated individual with anorexia nervosa believing she is fat, someone with panic disorder believing he is at risk of dying of a heart attack when he has a panic attack, and someone with body dysmorphic disorder believing she has a defect in appearance when most, if not all, people she encounters would agree that she does not. In short, we hypothesize that people with psychological disorders might hold these beliefs, even though they are distressing, maladaptive, or bizarre, because they help to regulate emotions. For example, the belief that one has a defect in appearance when, in fact, there exists no discernable defect may help to reduce unpleasant emotions associated with being rejected by others, the true cause of which lies elsewhere (e.g., the individual holding the belief is rude, obnoxious, or annoying). Although the belief seems to be increasing rather than decreasing unpleasant emotions, in fact, the unpleasant emotions that are evident are experienced at will to avoid unpleasant emotions of greater intensity or of a different type.

It is noteworthy that these beliefs are often held even when there is very little evidence to support them. Delusional beliefs are an example of often maladaptive, distressing, and bizarre beliefs that are in part defined as having less evidence or less convincing evidence to support their existence (Leeser & O'Donohue, 1999). The emotion regulation function of delusions is reflected in several prominent frameworks of delusion formation. These frameworks characterize the formation of delusions as an adaptive process that functions to protect the believer from the potential impact of unpleasant thoughts and emotions (e.g., Bentall, Corcoran, Howard, Blackwood, & Kinderman, 2001; Maher,

1974, 1988; Zigler & Glick, 1988). For example, Maher (1974, 1988) posits that delusional explanations for anomalous perceptual experiences are reinforced by a reduction in negative emotional arousal that accompanies the understanding of the anomalous experiences. In other words, although the delusional belief itself may be distressing (e.g., "The government is tracking me and trying to ruin my life"), the successful regulation of unpleasant emotional arousal that results from finding an explanation for experience contributes to the believability of the delusion. Furthermore, as may be the case with many delusional beliefs, the hedonic function is fulfilled at the cost of the instrumental function of accurately mentally representing one's experiences.

Future research is needed to gain a comprehensive understanding of how different functions, including regulating emotions, influence which beliefs people hold. In regard to delusional beliefs, studies including populations at risk for developing a psychotic disorder could longitudinally investigate whether delusion formation is associated with reductions in psychological distress, and thereby serves an emotion regulation function. Or emotionally arousing anomalous experiences could be induced in nonpsychotic participants to investigate whether delusion-like beliefs regulate emotions by reducing emotional distress. Of course, as not every delusional belief serves an emotion regulatory function, and not every belief that serves an emotion regulatory function is delusional, it will be important to investigate under what circumstances delusional beliefs form to regulate emotions. This holds true for other types of psychopathological beliefs that serve an emotion regulation function.

Finally, it would be useful to investigate when and how the different functions served by a given belief come into tension, and how this tension plays out in terms of mental health and illness. As previously stated, we hypothesize that part of mental health is sorting out why one believes (or acts) as one does, and then coordinating these beliefs (actions) in a way that increases real, long-term well-being, rather than short-term emotion regulatory goals. When and how this plays out in the context of mental health and well-being and mental illness has yet to be empirically addressed.

### How to Treat Emotional Disturbances That Contribute to Psychopathology

Emotional disturbances, including those involving difficulties with emotion regulation, are a sign or symptom of many psychological disorders. For example, over 75% of the diagnostic categories for psychiatric disorders in the *DSM-IV* (American Psychological Association, 2000) include problems with emotion or emotion regulation (Barlow, 2000; Kring & Werner, 2004). Specific examples of problematic emotion regulation include "quick angry reactions" in paranoid personality disorder, "elevated, expansive, irritable mood" in bipolar disorder, and "affective instability due to a marked reactivity of mood" in borderline personality disorder. As stated by Werner and Gross (2010, p. 1), "The pervasiveness of emotion dysregulation across these and other DSM disorders suggests that emotion regulatory difficulties lie at the heart of many types of psychopathology and may be a key to their treatment."

As we have discussed, beliefs can be purposefully targeted to regulate emotions for both hedonic and instrumental purposes. As applied in a therapeutic context, beliefs might be actively targeted for change to create greater success at regulating emotions in valued directions. Furthermore, success in this regard may be enhanced by first identifying and balancing the tension between hedonic and instrumental functions of both belief change and emotion regulation.

Changing maladaptive cognition (e.g., thoughts, beliefs) to decrease emotional disturbances, including disturbances in emotion regulation, is a primary focus of cognitive therapy (CT; Hollon & Beck, 1994). A central tenet of CT is that maladaptive cognitions contribute to emotional disturbances that are the core of many psychiatric disorders (Hollon & Beck, 1994). In other words, it is not situations themselves that generate emotional disturbances, such as excesses in fear or sadness, but instead one's interpretations of situations (Beck & Clark, 1997). Therefore, much of the work in CT is devoted to testing and correcting inaccurate, maladaptive cognitions. One technique used for such purposes is helping the client alter the meaning of particular "automatic" thoughts to seem less threatening, more within one's control, and less permanent (Heimberg, 2002). Another technique is to collect tangible evidence for and against mental representations, with the purpose of identifying and using the most accurate and adaptive mental representations.

Although rarely measured or tested in a valid and reliable manner in studies of CT, it is thought that maladaptive beliefs will change through the accumulation of evidence disputing maladaptive beliefs and/ or the evidence supporting more adaptive beliefs.

Several studies investigating factors that account for positive CT treatment outcomes (i.e., mechanisms of change) have found that reductions in maladaptive beliefs are causally associated with reductions in symptoms of psychiatric disorders that are characterized by emotional disturbances, such as major depressive disorder and generalized anxiety disorder (e.g., Kwon & Oei, 2003; Hofmann et al., 2007; see Garratt, Ingram, Rand, & Sawalani, 2007). For example, reductions in negative evaluative beliefs about oneself were causally associated with a reduction in depressive symptoms among individuals receiving CT (Kwon & Oei, 2003). These results suggest that belief change can be targeted to reduce symptoms of psychiatric disorders characterized by emotional disturbances.

Studies on emotional resistance/nonacceptance of one's current emotional experience (Hayes, Luoma, Bond, Masuda, & Lillis, 2006) suggest that belief change can be targeted not only to reduce symptoms of psychological disorders but to enhance emotion regulation in a clinical context. Beliefs about what emotions are valued and acceptable to experience and which are devalued and unacceptable greatly influence how emotions are experienced and regulated. Furthermore, people vary in the extent to which they view particular emotions as acceptable or not (e.g., European Americans value high-arousal positive affect [e.g., excitement] more than do Hong Kong Chinese; Tsai, Knutson, & Fung, 2006).

The belief that a particular emotional experience is unacceptable is associated with resistance to experiencing that emotion and an attempt to regulate emotions in such a way that that emotional experience is avoided or reduced, and psychopathology (Hayes et al., 2006; Turk, Heimberg, Luterek, Mennin, & Fresco, 2005; Tull, 2006). Resistance to emotional experiences leads to new emotional responses, or secondary emotional responses (i.e., dirty emotions; Greenberg & Safran, 1990; Hayes et al., 2006), whose eliciting situation is the initial emotional response. Theorists propose that initial emotional responses are not problematic, or indicative of psychological disturbance, but instead psychological suffering is exacerbated by patients' reappraisals and responses to their initial emotional reactions. In other words, beliefs about the unacceptability of emotions, and actions based upon these beliefs (e.g., unwillingness), are casually related to emotional disturbances and psychopathology. Therefore, changing these beliefs will directly influence emotional experience and the frequency and efficacy of use of particular emotion regulation strategies. For example, reducing conviction in the belief "It is unacceptable to experience anxiety in social situations because I will embarrass myself" will lead to less use of suppression to reduce anxiety and a greater experience and tolerance of anxiety. All of these changes may be extremely beneficial for someone with social phobia, who avoids social contact for fear of embarrassment.

Our framework can be of service in a clinical context by providing researchers with a basis by which to investigate how and when belief change contributes to enhanced emotion regulation and, through this, less psychopathology. Based on our framework, we posit that treatment studies of psychiatric disorders that include emotion dysregulation as a core disturbance would benefit from including comprehensive, valid, and reliable measures of beliefs (e.g., "core" maladaptive beliefs), in addition to measures of other cognitions targeted for change. Also important are measures of emotional experience that complement measures of broad psychiatric disorders. Researchers could then assess whether emotion regulation through belief change accounted for positive treatment outcomes. Researchers might also use our framework to guide measurement of the functions served by different beliefs characteristic of psychopathology, how well beliefs serve these functions, and the tension (if any) arising from a belief serving more than one function. This information could lead to a greater understanding of how the tension between and attempts to balance hedonic and instrumental functions of belief change and emotion regulation give rise to mental health and illness.

## Summary

In this chapter, we considered how belief change can regulate emotions. To set the stage for our perspective, we began by defining emotions and beliefs, and discussing theory and research supporting the link from beliefs to emotions. Next, we discussed emotion change and belief change, and the hedonic and instrumental functions of each. We then described our framework and reviewed supporting empirical evidence. Lastly, we articulated further research needed to support and expand our framework, and we applied our framework to understand why people believe what they do, and how to treat emotional disturbances that contribute to psychological disorders. We believe that this framework may help to stimulate new theory and research on the bidirectional relations between emotion and belief.

## Notes

1. Affect-as-information theory describes how emotions influence cognitive processing by serving as an informational basis, or heuristic, that people assess to varying degrees when making judgments and decisions. Building upon affect-as-information theory, Clore and Gasper (2000) argued that emotions influence beliefs by serving as evidence for or against particular beliefs and, by doing so, influence belief conviction. Clore and Gasper (2000) also hypothesized that emotions influence beliefs by guiding attention to belief-relevant information, which can either serve as evidence for or against a belief or serve as the belief object itself.

## References

Abelson, J. L., Liberzon, I., Young, E. A., & Khan, S. (2005). Cognitive modulation of the endocrine stress response to a pharmacological challenge in normal and panic disorder subjects. *Archives of General Psychiatry, 62*, 668–675.

Abelson, R. P. (1986). Beliefs are like possessions. *Journal for the Theory of Social Behaviour, 16*, 223–250.

Ajzen, I., & Fishbein, M. (1975). A Bayesian analysis of attribution processes. *Psychological Bulletin, 82*, 261–277.

American Psychiatric Association. (2000). *Diagnostic and statistical manual of mental disorders (4th ed., text rev.).* Washington, DC: Author.

Appelbaum, P. S., Robbins, P. C., & Vesselinov, R. (2004). Persistence and stability of delusions over time. *Comprehensive Psychiatry, 45*, 317–324.

Averill, J. R. (1982). *Anger and aggression: An essay on emotion.* New York: Springer-Verlag.

Averill, J. R. (1983). Studies on anger and aggression: Implications for theories of emotion. *American Psychologist, 11*, 1145–1160.

Barlow, D. H. (2000). Unraveling the mysteries of anxiety and its disorders from the perspective of emotion theory. *American Psychologist, 55*, 1247–1263.

Barrett, L. F., Ochsner, K. N., & Gross, J. J. (2007). On the automaticity of emotion. In J. Bargh (Ed.), *Social psychology and the unconscious: The automaticity of higher mental processes* (pp. 173–217). New York: Psychology Press.

Baumeister, R. F. (1997). Esteem threat, self-regulatory breakdown and emotional distress as factors in self-defeating behavior. *Review of General Psychology, 1*, 145–174.

Beck, A. T., & Clark, D. A. (1997). An information processing framework of anxiety: Automatic and strategic processes. *Behaviour Research and Therapy, 35*, 49–58.

Bentall, R., Corcoran, R., Howard, R., Blackwood, N., & Kinderman, P. (2001). Persecutory delusions: A review and theoretical integration. *Clinical Psychology Review, 21*, 1143–1192.

Boden, M. T., & Berenbaum, H. (2010). The bidirectional relations between affect and belief. *Review of General Psychology, 14*, 227–239.

Bonanno, G. A., & Jost, J. T. (2006). Conservative shift among high-exposure survivors of the September 11th terrorist attacks. *Basic and Applied Social Psychology, 28*, 311–323.

Brown, J., & Weiner, B. (1984). Affective consequences of ability versus effort ascriptions: Controversies, resolutions and quandaries. *Journal of Education Psychology, 76*, 146–158.

Burris, C. T., Harmon-Jones, E., & Tarpley, W. R. (1997). "By faith alone": Religious agitation and cognitive dissonance. *Basic and Applied Social Psychology, 19*, 17–31.

Cantor, N., & Kihlstrom, J. F. (1987). *Personality and social intelligence.* Englewood Cliffs, NJ: Prentice Hall.

Carver, C. S., Pozo, C., Harris, S. D., Noriega, V., Scheier, M. F., Robinson, D. S., ... Clark, K. C. (1993). How coping mediates the effect of optimism on distress: A study of women with early state breast cancer. *Journal of Personality and Social Psychology, 65,* 375–390.

Clore, G. L. (1992). Cognitive phenomenology: Feelings and the construction of judgment. In L. L. Martin & A. Tesser (Eds.), *The construction of social judgments* (pp. 133–163). Hillsdale, NJ: Erlbaum.

Clore, G. L., & Gasper, K. (2000). Feeling is believing: Some affective influences on belief. In N. H. Frijda, A. S. R. Manstead, & S. Bem (Eds.), *Emotions and belief: How feelings influence thoughts* (pp. 10–44). Cambridge, England: Cambridge University Press.

Cooper, J., Zanna, M. P., & Taves, P. A. (1978). Arousal as necessary condition for attitude change following induced compliance. *Journal of Personality and Social Psychology, 36,* 1101–1106.

Covington, M. V., & Omelich, C. L. (1984). Task oriented versus competitive learning structures: Motivational and performance consequences. *Journal of Education Psychology, 76,* 1038–1050.

Dillon, D. G., & La Bar, K. S. (2005). Startle modulation during conscious emotion regulation is arousal-dependent. *Behavioral Neuroscience, 119,* 1118–1124.

Eagly, A. H., & Chaiken, S. (1993). *The psychology of attitudes.* Orlando, FL: Harcourt Brace Jovanovich College Publishers.

Elliot, A. J., & Devine, P. G. (1994). On the motivational nature of cognitive-dissonance: Dissonance as psychological discomfort. *Journal of Personality and Social Psychology, 67,* 382–394.

Emmons, R. A. (1986). Personal strivings: An approach to personality and subjective well-being. *Journal of Personality and Social Psychology, 51,* 1058–1068.

Festinger, L. (1957). *A theory of cognitive dissonance.* Stanford, CA: Stanford University Press.

Frijda, N. H. (1986). *The emotions.* Cambridge, England: Cambridge University Press.

Frijda, N. H., & Mesquita, B. (2000). Beliefs through emotions. In N. H. Frijda, A. S. R. Manstead, & S. Bem (Eds.), *Emotions and beliefs: How feelings influence thoughts* (pp. 45–77). Cambridge, England: Cambridge University Press.

Garratt, G., Ingram, R. E., Rand, K. L., & Sawalani, G. (2007). Cognitive processes in cognitive therapy: Evaluation of the mechanisms of change in the treatment of depression. *Clinical Psychology: Science and Practice, 14,* 224–239.

Gilbert, D. T. (1991). How mental systems believe. *American Psychologist, 46,* 107–119.

Greenberg, L. S., & Safran, J. D. (1990). *Emotion in psychotherapy.* New York: Guilford Press.

Gross, J. J. (1998). Antecedent- and response-focused emotion regulation: Divergent consequences for experience, expression, and physiology. *Journal of Personality and Social Psychology, 74,* 224–237.

Gross, J. J. (Ed.). (2007). *Handbook of emotion regulation.* New York: Guildford Press.

Gross, J. J., & John, O. P. (2003). Individual differences in two emotion regulation processes: Implications for affect, relationships, and well-being. *Journal of Personality and Social Psychology, 85,* 348–362.

Gross, J. J., & Thompson, R. A. (2007). Emotion regulation: Conceptual foundations. In J. J. Gross (Ed.), *Handbook of emotion regulation* (pp. 3–26). New York: Guilford Press.

Harmon-Jones, E. (2000). Cognitive dissonance and experienced negative affect: Evidence that dissonance increases experienced negative affect even in the absence of aversive consequences. *Personality and Social Psychology Bulletin, 26,* 1490–1501.

Harmon-Jones, E., & Mills, J. (1999). *Cognitive dissonance: Progress on a pivotal theory in social psychology.* Washington, DC: American Psychological Association.

Hayes, S. C., Luoma, J. B., Bond, F. W., Masuda, A., & Lillis, J. (2006). Acceptance and commitment therapy: Framework, processes and outcomes. *Behaviour Research and Therapy, 44,* 1–25.

Heimberg, R. G. (2002). Cognitive-behavioral therapy for social anxiety disorder: Current status and future directions. *Biological Psychiatry, 51,* 101–108.

Hofmann, S. G., Maueret, A. E., Rosenfield, D., Suvak, M. K., Barlow, D. H., Gorman, J. M., ... Woods, S. W. (2007). Preliminary evidence for cognitive mediation during cognitive-behavioral therapy of panic disorder. *Journal of Consulting and Clinical Psychology, 75,* 374–379.

Hollon, S. D., & Beck, A. T. (1994). Cognitive and cognitive behavior therapies. In A. E. Bergin, & S. L. Garfield (Eds.), *Handbook of psychotherapy and behavior change* (pp. 428–466). New York: Wiley.

Hume, D. (1969). A treatise of human nature. (E. C. Mossner, Ed. ) Harmondsworth, England: Penguin. (Original work published in 1739).

Inzlicht, M., Mc Gregor, I., Hirsh, J. B., & K. Nash. (2009). Neural markers of religious conviction. *Psychological Science, 20,* 385–392.

Jagacinski, C. M., & Nicholls, J. G. (1984). Conceptions of ability and related affects in task involvement and ego involvement. *Journal of Educational Psychology, 76,* 909–919.

Jonas, E., Graupmann, V., & Frey, D. (2006). The influence of mood on the search for supporting versus conflicting information: Dissonance reduction as a means of mood regulation? *Personality and Social Psychology Bulletin, 32,* 3–15.

Jost, J. T. (2006). The end of the end of ideology. *American Psychologist, 61,* 651–670.

Jost, J. T., & Banaji, M. R. (1994). The role of stereotyping in system-justification and the production of false consciousness. *British Journal of Social Psychology, 33,* 1–27.

Jost, J. T., Glaser, J., Kruglanski, A. W., & Sulloway, F. J. (2003). Political conservatism as motivated social cognition. *Psychological Bulletin, 129,* 339–375.

Jost, J. T., & Hunyady, O. (2002). The psychology of system justification and the palliative function of ideology. *European Review of Social Psychology, 13,* 111–153.

Kring, A. M., & Werner, K. H. (2004). Emotion regulation and psychopathology. In P. Philippot & R. S. Feldman (Eds.), *The regulation of emotion* (pp. 359–385). Mahwah, NJ: Erlbaum.

Kruglanski, A. W. (1980). Lay epistemologic process and contents: Another look at attribution theory. *Psychological Review, 87,* 70–87.

Kwon, S. M., & Oei, T. P. S. (2003). Cognitive change processes in a group cognitive behavior therapy of depression. *Journal of Behavioral Therapy and Experimental Psychiatry, 3,* 73–85.

Landau, M. J., Solomon, S., Greenberg, J., Cohen, F., Pyszczynski, T., Arndt, J., ... Cook, A. (2004). Deliver us from evil: The effects of mortality salience and reminders of 9/11 on support for President George W. Bush. *Personality and Social Psychology Bulletin, 30,* 1136–1150.

Larsen, R. J. (2000). Toward a science of mood regulation. *Psychological Inquiry, 11,* 129–141.

Lazarus, R. S. (1991). *Emotion and adaptation.* New York: Oxford University Press.

Leeser, J., & O'Donohue, W. (1999). What is a delusion? Epistemological dimensions. *Journal of Abnormal Psychology, 108,* 687–694.

Lerner, M. J., Miller, D. T., & Holmes, J. G. (1976). Deserving and the emergence of forms of justice. In L. Berkowitz (Ed.), *Advances in experimental social psychology* (Vol. 9, pp. 133–162). New York: Academic Press.

Maher, B. A. (1974). Delusional thinking and perceptual disorder. *Journal of Individual Psychology, 30,* 98–113.

Maher, B. A. (1988). Anomalous experience and delusional thinking: The logic of explanations. In T. F. Oltmanns & B. A. Maher (Eds.), *Delusional beliefs. Wiley Series on Personality Processes* (pp. 15–33). New York: Wiley.

Mauss, I. B., Levenson, R. W., McCarter, L., Wilhelm, F. H., & Gross, J. J. (2005). The tie that binds? Coherence among emotion experience, behavior, and physiology. *Emotion, 5,* 175–190.

Mischel, W., Shoda, Y., & Rodriguez, M. L. (1989). Delay of gratification in children. *Science, 244,* 933–938.

Miller, L. C., & Read, S. J. (1987). Why am I telling you this? Self-disclosure in a goal-based framework of personality. In V. J. Derlega & J. Berg (Eds.), *Self-disclosure: Theory, research and therapy* (pp. 35–58). New York: Plenum Press.

Norenzayan, A., & Hansen, I. G. (2006). Belief in supernatural agents in the face of death. *Personality and Social Psychology Bulletin, 32,* 174–187.

Osarchuk, M., & Tatz, S. J. (1973). Effect of induced fear of death on belief in afterlife. *Journal of Personality and Social Psychology, 27,* 256–260.

Price, H. H. (1954). Belief and will. In *Proceedings of the Aristotelian Society* (Suppl. Vol. 28, pp. 1–26). Wiley-Blackwell publishing on behalf of the Aristotelian Society.

Pyszczynski, T., Greenberg, J., & Solomon, S. (1999). A dual-process framework of defense against conscious and unconscious death-related thoughts: An extension of terror management theory. *Psychological Review, 106,* 835–845.

Read, S. J., & Miller, L. C. (1989). Inter-personalism: Toward a goal-based theory of persons in relationships. In L. Pervin (Ed.), *Goal concepts in personality and social psychology* (pp. 413–472). Hillsdale, NJ: Erlbaum.

Richards, J. M., & Gross, J. J. (1999). Composure at any cost? The cognitive consequences of emotion suppression. *Personality and Social Psychology Bulletin, 25,* 1033–1044.

Richards, J. M., & Gross, J. J. (2000). Emotion regulation and memory: The cognitive costs of keeping one's cool. *Journal of Personality and Social Psychology, 79,* 410–424.

Scherer, K. R. (1999). Appraisal theories. In T. Dalgleish & M. Power (Eds.), *Handbook of cognition and emotion* (pp. 637–63). Chichester, England: Wiley.

Schwitzgebel, E. (2006). Belief. In E. Zalta (Ed.), *The Stanford encyclopedia of philosophy.* Retrieved August 10, 2010, from The Metaphysics Research Lab web site, http://plato.stanford.edu/entries/belief/

Sharp, H. M., Fear, C. F., Williams, M. G., Healy, D., Lowe, C. F., Yeadon, H., & Holden, R. (1996). Delusional phenom-

enology—dimensions of change. *Behavioural Research and Therapy, 34,* 123–142.

Sheldon, S., Greenberg, J. L., & Pyzszynki, T. A. (2004). Lethal consumption: Death-denying materialism. In T. Kasser & A. D. Kanner (Eds.), *Psychology of a consumer culture: The struggle for a good life in a materialistic world* (pp. 127–146). Washington, DC: American Psychological Association.

Solomon, S., Greenberg, J., & Pyszczynski, T. (1991). Terror management theory of self-esteem. In C. R. Snyder & R. D. Forsyth (Eds.), *Handbook of social and clinical psychology: The health perspective* (pp. 21–40). Elmsford, NY: Pergamon Press.

Strauss, J. S. (1969). Hallucinations and delusions as points on continua function: Rating scale evidence. *Archives of General Psychiatry, 21,* 581–586.

Tamir, M. (2009). What do people want to feel and why? Pleasure and utility in emotion regulation. *Current Directions in Psychological Science, 18,* 101–105.

Tamir, M. (2009). What do people want to feel and why? Pleasure and utility in emotion regulation. *Current Directions in Psychological Science, 18,* 101–105.

Tamir, M., Mitchell, C., & Gross, J. J. (2008). Hedonic and instrumental motives in anger regulation. *Psychological Science, 19,* 324–328.

Tsai, J. L., Knutson, B., & Fung, H. H. (2006). Cultural variation in affect valuation. *Journal of Personality and Social Psychology, 90,* 288–307.

Tull, M. T. (2006). Extending an anxiety sensitivity framework of uncued panic attack frequency and symptom severity: The role of emotion dysregulation. *Cognitive Therapy and Research, 30,* 177–184.

Turk, C. L., Heimberg, R. G., Luterek, J. A., Mennin, D. S., & Fresco, D. M. (2005). Emotion dysregulation in generalized anxiety disorder: A comparison with social anxiety disorder *Cognitive Therapy and Research, 29,* 89–106.

Wakslak, C., Jost, J. T., Tyler, T. R., & Chen, E. (2007). Moral outrage mediates the dampening effect of system justification on support for redistributive social policies. *Psychological Science, 18,* 267–274.

Weiner, B. (Ed.). (1974). *Achievement motivation and attribution theory.* Morristown, NJ: General Learning Press.

Weiner, B. (1985). "Spontaneous" causal thinking. *Psychological Bulletin, 97,* 74–84.

Werner, K., & Gross, J. J. (2010). Emotion regulation and psychopathology: A conceptual framework. In A. Kring & D. Sloan (Eds.), *Emotion regulation and psychopathology (pp. 13–37).* New York: Guilford Press.

Westen, D., & Blagov, P. S. (2007). A clinical-empirical framework of emotion regulation: From defense and motivated reasoning to emotional constraint satisfaction. In J. J. Gross (Ed.), *Handbook of emotion regulation* (pp. 373–392). New York: Guildford Press.

Wilson, T. D., & Gilbert, D. T. (2008). Explaining away: A framework of affective adaptation. *Perspectives on Psychological Science, 3,* 370–386.

Wyer, R. S., & Albarracin, D. (2005). The origins and structure of beliefs and goals. In D. Albarracin, B. T. Johnson, & M. P. Zanna (Eds.), *Handbook of attitudes* (pp. 273–322). Hillsdale, NJ: Erlbaum.

Zigler, E., & Glick, M. (1988). Is paranoid schizophrenia really camouflaged depression? *American Psychologist, 43,* 284–290.

# PART 7

# Judgment, Reasoning, and Choice

# Judgment Under Uncertainty

Ben R. Newell

**Abstract**

This chapter traces a path through over 50 years worth of research on judgment under uncertainty. The literature is viewed through the lens of two criteria for appraising judgment. The first, correspondence, emphasizes the empirical accuracy of judgment; the second, coherence, emphasizes internal consistency and rationality. Major findings from research traditions aligned with these criteria are reviewed (e.g., correspondence: fast and frugal heuristics; coherence: heuristics and biases), and a case is made for viewing the criteria as complementary rather than contrasting. The importance of considering the role of the environment and the mind in understanding judgment is emphasized, and the potential for integrating correspondence and coherence in a causal Bayesian framework is outlined briefly.

**Key Words:** judgment, uncertainty, coherence, correspondence, rationality, heuristics, biases, fast and frugal heuristics, lens model, dual systems, Bayes, causal models

> As we know, there are known knowns. There are things we know we know. We also know there are known unknowns. That is to say we know there are some things we do not know. But there are also unknown unknowns, the ones we don't know we don't know.
>
> —Donald Rumsfeld

Donald Rumsfeld's quote neatly illustrates the fact that uncertainty is a pervasive feature of our lives. Many decisions from the momentous to the mundane are based on our beliefs about the chances of future events. Should we go to war against a country? It depends on the chance that the war will be a "success." Should we take an umbrella when we leave for work in the morning? It depends on the chance of rain during the day. This chapter focuses on how people assess the probability of events, make judgments and predictions, and cope with living in an inherently uncertain world. The chapter

proceeds by first considering how we can evaluate the quality of judgment made under uncertainty and then traces a path through research programs that have aligned themselves with two different ways of appraising judgments: via coherence and correspondence.

## What Is Good Judgment?

How do we know if a judgment is good or bad? If we take the umbrella to work and it rains, then our judgment about the weather would be considered good. If it does not rain, then our judgment would be considered bad. Thus, in this situation the quality of our judgment is determined by whether what we predicted to happen did, in fact, occur. That is, whether our judgment *corresponded* with the eventual state of the world. Hammond (1996) contrasted *correspondence* with *coherence*—criteria that are concerned not with the accuracy of predicting events, but with the *rationality* of a judgment. Hammond describes the two approaches as follows:

> Correspondence theory focuses on the empirical accuracy of judgments, irrespective of whether the cognitive activity of the judge can be justified or even described.
> Coherence theorists... examine the question of whether an individual's judgment processes meet the test of rationality—internal consistency—irrespective of whether the judgment is empirically accurate.
> (Hammond, 1996, p. 106)

The emphasis on the empirical accuracy of judgments in correspondence theory has led researchers to focus on the ability of judges in many real-world environments to predict the outcome of uncertain events (e.g., the chance of a patient dying given a particular diagnosis). In contrast, coherence theorists have tended to focus on decontextualized problems, which lend themselves to being solved by normative rules, such as the laws of probability (e.g., predicting the outcomes of successive coin flips). Although these criteria are often presented as conflicting (Dunwoody, 2009; see also Gigerenzer, 1996; Kahneman & Tversky, 1996), it is perhaps more useful to see them as complementary. The different foci of the two approaches elucidate different aspects of judgment behavior that together can help place our understanding of human judgment into a general cognitive framework (see Newell, Lagnado, & Shanks, 2007). This chapter develops this view by exploring the synergies between the approaches and concludes by advocating a potential new path in which the criteria can be combined. The next section introduces the correspondence-based approach, which is primarily concerned with quantitative judgment (or prediction) under uncertainty.

## Correspondence-Based Approaches

Egon Brunswik's research on visual perception (e.g., Brunswik, 1956) is often credited as inspiring the correspondence approach to human judgment (Dunwoody, 2009). The main ideas in the Brunswikian approach are that an object in the environment (a "distal" stimulus) produces multiple cues through the stimulation of the perceiver's sense organs. These "proximal" cues are necessarily fallible (due to the probabilistic nature of the relation between the cues and the environment) and therefore only imperfectly indicate the true state of the external environment. Thus, perception is a constructive process, involving inferences drawn on the basis of incomplete and ambiguous sensory information. Hammond's (1955) important contribution was to demonstrate that the principles of perception proposed by Brunswik could be applied to the study of judgment.

Beginning with clinical judgment, Hammond and his colleagues demonstrated that Social Judgment Theory, as it became known, could be applied to a wide range of situations involving judgment. The main "tool" of the social judgment theorist is the Lens Model: a metaphor for thinking about how a "to-be-judged" criterion in the world (e.g., whether a patient is psychotic or neurotic) relates to the judgment made in the "mind" of the judge, that is, how well the judgment *corresponds* with the event in the world. The "lens" captures the notion that the judge views the world through an imperfect set (or lens) of cues.

Karelaia and Hogarth (2008) conducted a meta-analysis on over 240 different lens-model studies comprising both laboratory and field studies of judgment and drew three major conclusions: (1) that people are capable of achieving high levels of judgmental performance—as indicated by an average "achievement" correlation between the environmental criterion and the judgment of .56; (2) in studies where feedback was provided people learned best when the feedback instructed them about the characteristics of the task (e.g., how much "weight" a particular cue should be given in forming a judgment); and (3) that *models* of people's judgments tend to be more accurate than people's own judgments. The first conclusion is heartening, the second perhaps not overly surprising, but the third seems counterintuitive and a little worrying. Why should a model of people's judgments outperform their own judgments?

### Judgments Made by Humans and Models

Meehl (1954) demonstrated that judgments made by experts—usually clinicians—were often inferior in terms of accuracy to simple statistical models provided with the same information. Two classes of model can be identified—one in which information from the environment is fed into a statistical model, and one in which information derived from the judgments made by a person (typically an expert) is used.

To illustrate these techniques, consider the following example, adapted from Baron (2008). Imagine that you wanted to predict the performance in a final exam from students' performance on three pieces of assessment (A, B, and C) completed during the term. A statistical technique for prediction is to conduct a multiple linear regression—this simply finds a linear sum of the predictors (the assessment scores) in which the weight assigned to each assessment minimizes the error between the predicted and actual final exam performance. For example, the model might settle on ideal weights of .3 for assessment A and B, and .4 for assessment C. Provided the predictors have a linear relationship with the criterion, as we would expect to occur here, such a technique can work well.

The second technique is to give the same information to a judge (e.g., the professor teaching the course) and ask him or her to make a prediction about the final exam scores. The inputs would be the same—the assessment scores—but the weights and the rule for combining the inputs might be different. For example, the professor might believe that assessment B is a better indicator of final performance than assessment A. By analyzing the judgments the professor makes about several students, it is possible to develop a "model" of the judge that captures the way in which he or she weights the cues. Once we have this model we do not need the judge anymore but can simply "plug in" the assessment scores for other students and make predictions.

The superiority of these statistical techniques has been corroborated by hundreds of studies in diverse contexts (e.g., Dawes, Faust, & Meehl, 1989; Grove, Zald, Lebow, Snitz, & Nelson, 2000), leading some researchers to conclude, "Whenever possible, human judges should be replaced by simple linear models" (Hastie & Dawes, 2001, p. 63).

## The Advantages of Statistical Models

Dawes et al. (1989) list several factors that can contribute to the superior performance of statistical methods. Two key factors are, first, a statistical method will always arrive at the same judgment for a given set of data. Experts, on the other hand, are susceptible to the effects of fatigue, information presentation (framing), and recent experience. Second, experts are often exposed to a skewed sample of evidence, making it difficult to assess the actual relation between variables and a criterion of interest. This means that there is little opportunity to obtain the "task information" feedback that Karelaia and

Hogarth (2008) identified as being so important for improving judgment.

There are, however, times when a model will not prove superior; in particular, when the idiosyncratic knowledge of a judge is not captured by a linear model. Imagine, for example that the professor knew that a particular student had been sick during the term and had underperformed on her assessments. This information could be included by the professor to modify his prediction, but the model, with only the scores as input, would miss this subtlety. However, Karelaia and Hogarth (2008) conclude that, these subtleties notwithstanding, "the inconsistency that people exhibit in making judgments is sufficient for models of their judgments to be more accurate than they are themselves" (p. 420).

In summary, studies in the lens model tradition have emphasized that human quantitative judgment can show relatively good correspondence with the environment (e.g., the overall achievement correlation of .56; Karelaia & Hogarth, 2008) but that models, which are unaffected by the vagaries of human cognition, show better correspondence. Thus, human judges are not superfluous because they still serve an important role as the provider of information for the models of their judgment, but models should be used to weight and integrate this information (Baron, 2008). The next section considers how the vagaries of cognition impact on a different type of judgment under uncertainty: probability judgment.

## Coherence-Based Approaches

The coherence tradition investigates whether our judgments follow or *cohere* with normative theory. For example, when we check the weather in the morning, our judgment about the chance that it will rain and the chance that it will not must be complements of one another. If we believe that there is a 30% chance of rain, then to maintain a coherent set of beliefs, we must also believe that there is a 70% chance of no rain; believing otherwise would violate the laws of probability.

These laws were developed in the 17th century (Hacking, 1975) and can be thought of as a set of rules or axioms that should be followed to ensure sound judgment and reasoning (e.g., Ramsey, 1931). Failure to cohere to these laws leads to poor or defective judgments because, among other things, it allows unscrupulous individuals to take advantage of your incoherency. The best example of this vulnerability is the so-called Dutch book. This is a situation in which your probability judgments lead you to accept bets in which you are bound to lose no matter how the events you bet on turn out (see Newell et al., 2007, chapter 5 for a worked example).

Coherent beliefs by themselves, however, are not sufficient to ensure the truth of a judgment. We could be entirely coherent in judging the probability of the moon being made out of cheese as .8, provided we also judged the probability that it was not as .2. Thus, although coherence and correspondence are often cast as contrasting, they are, in fact, inescapably entwined. Dunwoody (2009) makes this point cogently: "If nature is necessarily lacking in self-contradictions, as the coherence theorists argue, then beliefs that correspond with nature should ultimately be coherent as well" (Dunwoody, 2009, p. 117). This idea accords with the thesis of this chapter that both criteria need to be considered in appraising judgment. Nonetheless, many studies have examined coherence in "isolation," as the next section illustrates.

### Bayes's Theorem and Conservatism

Put simply, Bayes's theorem is a method for working out what we do not know from what we do know. The theorem tells us how we should update our belief about an event or hypothesis in light of new evidence relevant to the hypothesis. Consider the following example taken from Edwards (1968):

> In front of you are two bags each containing 100 poker chips. You know that one bag has 70% red and 30% blue chips, and the other has 30% red and 70% blue. One bag is chosen at random (coin flip). Eight red and four blue chips are then drawn with replacement, in 12 consecutive drawings. What is the probability that the bag the chips are drawn from is the predominantly red bag?

To answer the question, you need to consider the prior odds of the bag being the predominantly red one (i.e., the strength of your belief before any chips had been drawn), and multiply this by the likelihood ratio of the data (the information provided by the sampled chips) to get the posterior odds (your revised belief). The prior odds are clearly .5 because the bag was chosen via a coin flip, but what are the correct posterior odds? Ward Edwards and colleagues (e.g., Edwards, 1968; Phillips & Edwards, 1966) gave problems like this to participants to see whether the difference between their prior and posterior odds was in accord with that prescribed by Bayes's theorem. In the example, appropriate belief revision leads to posterior odds of .97 for the

selected bag being the predominantly red one (see Sedlmeier, 1999 for a worked example if you find this answer difficult to fathom!). However, Edwards and colleagues found that the difference in probability estimates provided by participants was typically too small. People tended not to "extract from the data as much certainty as is theoretically implied by Bayes's Theorem" (Phillips & Edwards, 1966, p. 346)—an effect labeled *conservatism*.

Faced with this departure from the predictions of the theorem, Edwards's solution was to modify the theorem to account for the data rather than abandoning the model as an inappropriate benchmark. This approach was characteristic of much of the literature on human judgment at that time (e.g., Peterson & Beach, 1967; see also McKenzie, 2005). However, the view that normative models provided good approximations for psychological theories of judgment under uncertainty was about to be challenged.

### Judgment Heuristics (and Biases)

Writing in 1983, Ward Edwards lamented that his work on conservatism in probabilistic judgment had led to a "spate of studies that purport to show that men are incompetent intellectually" (p. 216). The comment was a reaction to the now seminal work of Tversky and Kahneman (1974), which focussed on the *heuristics* that people adopted in making judgments under uncertainty and the predictable *biases* that resulted from their use. This work led to a reversal of the optimistic way in which departures from the predictions of normative models had been interpreted. Now such failures of coherence were taken, by some at least, to paint the picture of man as a "cognitive cripple." Although this was not Tversky and Kahneman's intended message, as the following section illustrates, it is easy to see how one might be left with this pessimistic impression.

The heuristics and biases approach can best be explained via appeal to two related concepts: attribute substitution and natural assessment (Kahneman & Frederick, 2002). Attribute substitution refers to the idea that when people are asked to make a judgment about a specific *target attribute* (e.g., How probable is X?), they instead make a judgment about a *heuristic attribute* (e.g., How representative is X?), which they find easier to answer. This ease of answering often arises because the heuristic attributes relied upon are readily accessible via the "natural assessment" of properties such as size, distance, similarity, cognitive fluency, causal propensity, and affective valence. Kahneman and Frederick (2002;

see also Tversky & Kahneman, 1983) argue that because such properties are "routinely evaluated as part of perception and comprehension" (p. 55) they come more easily to mind than the often *inaccessible* target attributes. Hence, target attributes are *substituted* for heuristic attributes.

The evidence for attribute substitution and natural assessment comes in two main guises. The first is the simple demonstration that judgments of target attributes correlate very highly with judgments of the heuristic attributes with which they have been substituted. The second is that the failure to cohere with normative laws lead, in certain situations, to striking biases. There is an abundance of evidence documenting various heuristics and biases (see the volumes by Kahneman, Slovic, & Tversky, 1982 and Gilovich, Griffin, & Kahneman, 2002 for examples); one of the most famous demonstrations is the so-called Linda problem.

### The Linda Problem: Representativeness as a Heuristic Attribute

Tversky and Kahneman (1982) gave participants the following simple personality sketch:

> Linda is 31 years old, single, outspoken, and very bright. She majored in philosophy. As a student, she was deeply concerned with issues of discrimination and social justice, and also participated in anti-nuclear demonstrations.

They then asked separate groups of participants to rank a set of eight statements about Linda either by how *representative* they appeared to be or how *probable* they were. The correlation between the rankings was .99. Tversky and Kahneman took this as very powerful evidence that when people were asked a question about probability, they substituted this target attribute with a heuristic one about representativeness; that is, the degree to which one "object" (Linda in the personality sketch) resembles the "object" of the statement (e.g., Linda is a psychiatric social worker).

However, there was an additional "experimental flourish" (Kahneman & Frederick, 2002) that provided the dramatic demonstration of judgment via representative thinking. In another version of the problem (Tversky & Kahneman, 1983), participants were asked: Which of these two statements is more probable? (1) Linda is a bank teller; (2) Linda is a bank teller and active in the feminist movement. The overwhelming majority response was to rank (2) as more probable than (1). This is a clear violation of the conjunction rule of probability: A conjunction cannot be more probable than either of its conjuncts. All feminist bank tellers are, by definition, bank tellers so a person cannot be *more likely* to be a *feminist* bank teller than just a bank teller. Nonetheless, the description of Linda is highly representative of active feminists but not of bank tellers; thus, a judgment by representativeness leads to statement (2) receiving the higher ranking.

Representativeness-based explanations have also been applied to a related class of problems in which participants appear to neglect base-rate frequency information and rely on specific details of scenarios. In the well-known "lawyers and engineers" problem, participants were shown brief personality sketches of several individuals allegedly sampled at random from a group of 100 lawyers and engineers. They were then asked to assess for each one the likelihood that the person was an engineer rather than a lawyer. In one condition participants were told that the group comprised 70 lawyers and 30 engineers; in the other condition the composition was reversed. Bayes's rule dictates that the odds of any particular individual being an engineer are 5.44 times higher in the second condition than the first. In striking contradiction of the rule, participants' judgments in the two conditions were remarkably similar. Tversky and Kahneman (1974) argued that the judgments were made "by the degree to which this description was representative of the two stereotypes with little or no regard to the prior probabilities of the two categories" (p. 1125).

### Availability as a Heuristic Attribute

Although the heuristics and biases approach is typically associated with departures from coherence criteria, this focus is not exclusive (cf. Dunwoody, 2009). Availability, a pervasive heuristic attribute, has been invoked to explain errors of correspondence. Availability has been described both as a measure of the ease with which instances come to mind (Kahneman & Tversky, 1996) and the number of instances that come to mind (Tversky & Kahneman, 1973). Most of the time this heuristic will serve us well as a substitute for estimating frequencies or probabilities—typically more likely events come to mind more readily. However, at times the heuristic will produce errors, and it is these errors that have been the focus of research. Take, for example, a judgment of whether homicide or suicide is more likely in the US adult male population. The majority response is homicide, although in fact suicides are far more common (Lichenstein, Slovic, Fischoff, Layman, & Coombs, 1978). The explanation for this error is simply that instances of homicide come more readily to mind (are more available) than those of suicide (perhaps due to a bias in media coverage).

Note that the biased judgment of homicide arises because of the way in which information is presented to us from external sources (e.g., the media), but availability can also sometimes be a poor guide when we search through information in our memories. Consider this example: What is more probable: that a word starts with the letter *k* or has *k* as its third letter? Words with *k* as the third letter are in fact far more common, but people tend not to give this answer. Tversky and Kahneman (1973) argued that because we tend to organize words by their initial letters—and thus search our memories for them in this way—we tend to think that words starting with *k* occur more frequently.

## Affect as a Heuristic Attribute

The notion of an "affect heuristic" is strongly tied to availability. Indeed, the only difference between the two seems to be that the former is invoked in situations involving affectively loaded responses. Kahneman and Frederick (2002) point out that the affective valence of a stimulus is something that is often "naturally assessed" (we cannot avoid our affective reaction to many stimuli—disgust, desire, etc). Thus, affect is an obvious candidate for a heuristic attribute. According to Finucane, Peters, and Slovic (2003), the basic tenet of the affect heuristic is that "positive and negative affective feelings, attached to images, guide and direct judgments and decisions" (p. 341). In essence, the affect heuristic works via the generation of instances or images, which are "tagged" with particular feelings. These feelings or "affects" are then used as substitutes for whatever target attribute is being interrogated.

To test this idea, Finucane, Alhakami, Slovic, and Johnson (2000) presented participants with vignettes designed to manipulate affect by describing either the benefits or risks of nuclear power. They then collected perceived risk and benefit ratings. The general pattern in the results was that providing information about one attribute (e.g., risk) had a carryover effect on the attribute about which nothing had been learned directly (e.g., benefit). Finucane et al. interpreted this pattern in terms of people "consulting their overall affective evaluation of the item when judging its risk and benefit" (p. 13)—in other words, people relied on an affect heuristic to make risk/benefit judgments.

The notion that affect influences judgment is also supported by work examining the effect of different ways of presenting statistical information. Slovic, Monahan, and MacGregor (2000) demonstrated that clinicians provided with recidivism risks presented as frequencies (e.g., 20 out of 100) judged mental patients as posing higher risks than when the same information was presented as probabilities (e.g., 20%). The explanation was that only the frequency presentation generated a "terrifying image" of the recidivist in the mind of the clinician and that the affect associated with this imagery led to the more extreme judgments. In a similar vein, Newell, Mitchell, and Hayes (2008) demonstrated that participants were more willing to take part in positive activities (e.g., playing a lottery) but less willing to take part in negative activities (e.g., complex laser surgery) when frequencies were used to communicate the chances/risks involved than when probabilities were used.

## Anchoring and Adjustment

Anchoring—the tendency to insufficiently adjust from an initial value when estimating continuous variables (e.g., age, height, weight, price, etc.)—was introduced as one of the three major heuristics (alongside availability and representativeness) by Tversky and Kahneman (1974). However, Kahneman and Frederick (2002) note that anchoring does not fit within the attribute substitution framework. Rather, the heuristic works by increasing the plausibility of a particular value of the target attribute. The typical task involves providing a high (or low) anchor to separate groups of participants (e.g., Do you think Gandhi died before or after the age of 140 (9) years old?) and then asking for an estimate (e.g., How old was Gandhi when he died?). The highly robust finding is that those given the high anchor will estimate a higher value (67 years old, in this case) than those given a low anchor (50 years old) (Strack & Mussweiler 1997). Thus, although the initial value is irrelevant, it tends to be assimilated into the provided estimate.

## Critiques of the Heuristics and Biases Approach

The heuristics and biases program has been highly influential; however, some have argued that in recent years the influence, at least in psychology, has waned (McKenzie, 2005). This waning has been due in part to pointed critiques of the approach (e.g., Gigerenzer, 1996). The critique comprises two main arguments: (1) that by focussing mainly on coherence standards the approach ignores the role played by the environment or the context in which a judgment is made; and (2) that the explanations of phenomena via one-word labels such as availability, anchoring, and representativeness are vague, insufficient, and say nothing about the processes underlying judgment (see Kahneman, 2003; Kahneman & Tversky, 1996 for responses to this critique).

The accuracy of some of the heuristics proposed by Tversky and Kahneman can be compared to correspondence criteria (availability and anchoring). Thus, arguing that the tradition only uses the "narrow norms" (Gigerenzer, 1996) of coherence criteria is not strictly accurate (cf. Dunwoody, 2009). Nonetheless, responses in famous examples like the Linda problem can be reinterpreted as sensible rather than erroneous if one uses conversational or pragmatic norms rather than those derived from probability theory (Hilton, 1995). For example, Hertwig, Benz, and Krauss (2008) asked participants which of the following two statements is more probable:

[X] The percentage of adolescent smokers in Germany decreases at least 15% from current levels by September 1, 2003.

[X&Y] The tobacco tax in Germany is increased by 5 cents per cigarette and the percentage of adolescent smokers in Germany decreases at least 15% from current levels by September 1, 2003.

According to the conjunction rule, X cannot be more probable than X&Y and yet the majority of participants ranked the statements in that order. However, when subsequently asked to rank order four statements in order of how well each one described their understanding of X&Y, there was an overwhelming tendency to rank statements like "X and therefore Y" or "X and X is the cause for Y" higher than the simple conjunction "X and Y." Moreover, the minority of participants who did not commit the conjunction fallacy in the first judgment showed internal coherence by ranking "X and Y" as best describing their understanding in the second judgment. These results suggest that people adopt a causal understanding of the statements, in essence ranking the probability of X, given Y as more probable than X occurring alone. If so, then arguably their conjunction "error" is no longer incorrect. (See Moro, 2009 for extensive discussion of the reasons underlying the conjunction fallacy, including why "misunderstanding" cannot explain all instances of the fallacy.)

The "vagueness" argument can be illustrated by considering two related phenomena: the gambler's fallacy and the hot-hand (Gigerenzer & Brighton, 2009). The gambler's fallacy is the tendency for people to predict the opposite outcome after a run of the same outcome (e.g., predicting heads after a run of tails when flipping a fair coin); the hot-hand, in contrast, is the tendency to predict a run will continue (e.g., a player making a shot in basketball after a succession of baskets; Gilovich, Vallone, & Tversky, 1985). Ayton and Fischer (2004) pointed out that although these two behaviors are opposite—ending or continuing runs—they have both been explained via the label "representativeness." In both cases a faulty concept of randomness leads people to expect short sections of a sequence to be "representative" of their generating process. In the case of the coin, people believe (erroneously) that long runs should not occur, so the opposite outcome is predicted; for the player, the presence of long runs rules out a random process so a continuation is predicted (Gilovich et al., 1985). The "representativeness" explanation is therefore incomplete without specifying a priori which of the opposing prior expectations will result. More important, representativeness alone does not explain *why* people have the misconception that random sequences should exhibit local representativeness when in reality they do not (Ayton & Fischer, 2004).

Gigerenzer (1996) argued that for progress to be made in understanding judgment, the field needed to abandon coherence criteria, return to a focus on correspondence, and move away from vague labels of heuristics. The adaptive toolbox of fast and frugal heuristics borne from this approach is reviewed in the next section.

### Fast and Frugal Heuristics

At the heart of the fast and frugal approach lies the notion of *ecological rationality*. Ecological rationality is a type of correspondence criterion that emphasizes "the structure of environments, the structure of heuristics, and the match between them" (Gigerenzer, Todd, & ABC Research Group, 1999, p. 18). Thus, the concern is not so much with whether a heuristic is inherently accurate or biased, but rather why and when a heuristic will fail or succeed (Gigerenzer & Brighton, 2009). This focus on the "ecology," echoing the traditions of Brunswik's functionalism (1956) and Simon's bounded rationality (1955), brings context to the fore and overcomes the perceived "cognition in a vacuum" criticism of the heuristics and biases approach (McKenzie,

2005). The other central pillar of the approach is an emphasis on detailed models of the processes underlying each heuristic.

## Building Blocks and the Adaptive Toolbox

The fundamental building blocks of simple heuristics are rules for *searching* for information, *stopping* search, and *deciding*. Different types of search, stopping, and decision rules are combined into judgment heuristics for particular environments. The metaphor of the mind as an *adaptive toolbox* captures the notion that these heuristics are contained within a central resource from which tools are selected depending on the constraints of the environment and the goals of the decision maker. The emphasis is on using heuristics that do well, rapidly, and on the basis of a small amount of information. The following example serves to illustrate the approach.

Which US city has more inhabitants: San Diego or San Antonio? Goldstein and Gigerenzer (2002) posed this question to groups of students from the University of Chicago and the University of Munich. Sixty-two percent of University of Chicago students inferred correctly that San Diego was larger, but surprisingly, every single Munich university student answered correctly. Goldstein and Gigerenzer explained the result through the operation of the *recognition heuristic*, which states that when you are faced with two objects (e.g., cities) and you have heard of one but not the other, you should choose the former. Most of the Chicago students had heard of both cities so could not rely on this heuristic; in contrast, the ignorance of the Munich students (very few had heard of San Antonio) facilitated their judgment (a "less is more" effect; cf. Gigerenzer & Brighton, 2009). Thus, the recognition heuristic can be described in simple process rules: *Search* your memory for both objects; *stop search* if only one object is recognized; *choose* the recognized object.

If both objects are recognized, then a second heuristic from the toolbox is invoked: *take the best* (TTB). Here, search in memory (or the experimental environment) continues until a cue that discriminates between the two options is found. For example, you might recognize both San Diego and San Antonio but then recall that of the pair only San Diego has a world-famous zoo and infer that San Diego is larger. More formally, TTB states that cues are *searched* in descending order of their predictive validity of the criterion (in this case, city size), *stops* when a single discriminating cue is found, and *chooses* the object to which that cue "points."

The principle of ecological rationality emphasizes that these heuristics will only be successful in certain types of environments. The recognition heuristic will only work when the criterion of interest is correlated with recognition. Typically cities that are larger are more likely to be well known, but this is not always the case (cf. Oppenheimer, 2003). Likewise, TTB will be most successful in environments with sharply decreasing cue validities or weights—a so-called noncompensatory environment. In these environments, cues lower in validity, which are "ignored" by TTB, cannot outweigh the evidence provided by the "best" discriminating cue. In contrast, when cue weights are compensatory— all the pieces of information available have approximately equal validity—then TTB suffer because it will ignore important information (see Hogarth & Karelaia, 2005).

## Empirical Evidence for the Use of Fast and Frugal Heuristics

Like the heuristics and biases tradition that preceded it, the fast and frugal approach has inspired a wealth of studies. This research provides clear evidence that in certain environments simple strategies like TTB can be as effective and less resource intensive than more complex ones, such as multiple regression (e.g., Gigerenzer & Goldstein, 1996); that relying on simple name recognition can be very useful, for example, it performs just as well as the ATP rankings in predicting winners of Wimbledon tennis matches (e.g., Serwe & Frings, 2006); and that participants' behavior in experimental judgment tasks sometimes accords with the predictions of simple strategies (e.g., Bergert & Nosofsky, 2007; Bröder & Schiffer, 2003; Rieskamp & Otto, 2006) and at other times does not (Hilbig & Pohl, 2009; Newell, 2005; Newell & Fernandez, 2006; Newell & Shanks, 2003, 2004; Newell, Weston, & Shanks, 2003; Richter & Spath, 2006).

Perhaps most contentious is whether the fast and frugal approach provides a different class of explanation to that of the heuristics and biases tradition (e.g., Chater, Oaksford, Nakisa, & Redington, 2003; Dougherty, Thomas, & Franco-Watkins, 2008; Newell, 2005). There is no doubt that the renewed emphasis on the role of the environment, the attempt to understand the interface between the mind and the environment (cf. Fiedler & Juslin, 2006), and the exploration of how behavior is adaptive and adaptable represents important progress (e.g., McKenzie, 2005; see also Anderson, 1990; Oaksford & Chater, 1998). However, the extent to which behavior described in terms of the selection and implementation of heuristics from a toolbox is any more or less vague than behavior described in terms of natural assessment and attribute substitution remains debatable, as outlined in the next section.

## Critiques of Fast and Frugal Heuristics

The appeal of fast and frugal heuristics lies in their simplicity, precision, and testability. However, once we scratch beneath the surface of this appealing veneer, each of these qualities becomes somewhat tarnished. The simplicity of the heuristics belies a large amount of precomputation or prior learning/knowledge of the validities of particular cues in particular environments (Dougherty, Franco-Watkins, & Thomas, 2008; Juslin & Persson, 2002; Newell, 2005). Although a model like TTB can predict judgments as well as multiple regression (e.g. Gigerenzer & Goldstein, 1996), one of the principal reasons it does so is that TTB is provided with a validity-ordered hierarchy of all of the important cues for a given environment. Thus, the "simple" rules for search, stopping, and deciding are dependent on much more complex (and ill-specified or understood) mechanisms for determining cue hierarchies. Indeed, many researchers have acknowledged and demonstrated the difficulty that participants exhibit in learning the kind of cue-validity hierarchies necessary for implementing TTB (e.g., Bergert & Nosofsky, 2007; Rakow, Newell, Fayers, & Hersby, 2005).

One way of responding to this issue is to suggest that cue hierarchies might be constructed in ways other than individual learning. For example, Gigerenzer, Hoffrage, and Goldstein (2008) suggest that cues might be learned via evolution, or by social learning; the latter simply amounting to being told what cues are important for a given judgment (e.g., diagnosing acute heart disease). The problem with these alternatives is first that they somewhat beg the question (presumably the person telling us what cues to look at must have learned the importance at some point), but more worryingly they reduce the precision of the heuristics. If the "best" in TTB no longer only refers to cues with the highest ecological validity but can mean any subjective rank-ordering of cues—be it one provided by evolution, social learning, the idiosyncratic (and often erroneous) learning of an individual (Gigerenzer et al., 2008), or even the "environmental accessibility" of cues (Gigerenzer & Brighton, 2009, p. 129), then the precision of the heuristic is lost (cf.,

Dougherty, Thomas, et al., 2008; Newell, 2011; but see Katsikopoulos, Schooler, & Hertwig, 2010).

The testability of the approach can be critiqued on the grounds that the process by which different heuristics are selected for use in particular environments remains unspecified. Gigerenzer and Brighton (2009) suggest that selection occurs via a "mostly unconscious process" (p. 129) but go onto to describe three potential selection mechanisms: constraints of memory, constraints of the environment, and feedback on the performance of heuristics.

How does the state of memory at the time of judgment dictate heuristic choice? Gigerenzer and Brighton suggest that if you are asked to predict who of two players will win a tennis match at Wimbledon and you have heard of one but not the other, you "select" the recognition heuristic and predict that the recognized player will win. If you have heard of both but the name of one came to mind more quickly than the other, then you use the *fluency heuristic* (Schooler & Hertwig, 2005) and predict that the more fluently processed player will win. Finally, if you know both players and can recall some facts about each (e.g., their rankings, previous performance at Wimbledon), then memory "selects" TTB, and you choose the player pointed to by the most valid discriminating cue. The environmental constraints mesh with the memory ones to ensure that only heuristics that are ecologically rational are selected. The recognition heuristic is useful in predicting tennis tournament winners because the correlation between recognition and winners is strong and positive; if the correlation had been low (or even negative), then the environment/memory would have "selected" a different heuristic.

Such descriptions of how the selection of heuristics occurs make intuitive sense, but how different are they from the ideas of natural assessment and attribute substitution? One can describe fast and frugal heuristics according to the implementation of particular rules, but the underlying processes seem remarkably similar. When faced with a judgment about a target attribute (e.g., How likely is it that Andrew Murray will beat Roger Federer?), one *substitutes* it with information provided through natural assessments of recognition, fluency, or cue-based knowledge. Certainly these heuristic models can be implemented and tested in computer programs (e.g., Schooler & Hertwig, 2005), but this does not privilege them; other plausible and accurate models of human judgment that do not require recourse to the selection of discrete heuristics from an adaptive toolbox can also be represented as computational models (e.g., Chater et al. 2003; Dougherty, Gettys, & Ogden, 1999; Dougherty, Franco-Watkins, et al., 2008; Juslin & Persson, 2002; Lee & Cummins, 2004; Lee & Newell, 2011; Newell & Lee, 2011).

The third selection mechanism—feedback—has been emphasized in recent computational models of strategy selection. Rieskamp and colleagues (Rieskamp, 2008; Rieskamp & Otto, 2006) demonstrate how principles of reinforcement learning can explain how people learn to adopt (and adapt) strategies that search for and integrate more or fewer cues depending on the structure of the environment. Although, again, the adaptive toolbox model is not privileged in being able to explain such adaptation—(see Lee & Cummins, 2004; Newell, 2005; Newell & Lee, 2011; for an alternative framework based on evidence-accumulation models)—attempting to explain how people adapt judgment behavior is a useful advance on a problem that has plagued the literature for a long time (cf., Bröder & Newell, 2008; Payne, Bettman, & Johnson, 1993). The approach also emphasizes the key role for learning from feedback—something that was often absent in the heuristics and biases approach due to its focus on one-shot judgments (cf., Newell et al., 2007).

## Looking Inside, Outside, and Ahead

The fast and frugal approach has had a positive effect on the drive to "take the interface between mind and environment seriously" (Fiedler & Juslin, 2006, p. 9). This renewed emphasis on the ecology of judgment has brought the ideas of Brunswik (1956) and Simon (1955) back into vogue and also offers a way to reconcile the uneasy juxtaposition of the numerous studies that exhibit impressive judgment accuracy (e.g., Karelaia & Hogarth, 2008) and dramatic errors and biases (e.g., Tversky & Kahneman, 1974). By thinking carefully about how information presented to us in the world "outside" influences the representation of information "inside" our minds, a deeper understanding of the judgment process can be gained (e.g., Kahneman & Klein, 2009).

The *naïve* intuitive statistician approach (Fiedler, 2000; Fiedler & Juslin, 2006) focuses directly on this interface between mind and environment. The metaphor echoes the historical view (mentioned earlier) that statistical models provided good approximations for psychological theories of judgment (the *intuitive statistician* metaphor; Peterson & Beach, 1967). The novel insight is to argue that

when judgments go awry it is not because the internal cognitive mechanisms per se are at fault; rather, the judge is naïve with respect to the samples that provide the input for these mechanisms. These *biased samples* may be created via bias in the external environment (e.g., the heightened media coverage of homicide over suicide, Lichenstein et al., 1978), bias in memory representations (the letter "k" effect, Tversky & Kahneman, 1974), or even bias induced via the use of unrepresentative experimental materials (such as in the overconfidence phenomena in general knowledge; see Juslin, 1994).

The important point is that while previous explanations of these kinds of effects have appealed to cognitive algorithms that sometimes lead us astray ("availability"), the sampling explanation shifts the onus of explanation to the property of the sample. Thus, biased judgments are not due to faulty metacognition about ease of recall; the deficit in metacognition is in the inability to correct for the bias in the input. When more representative samples are used, such as using a large sample of letters rather than only the five consonants that *do* appear more often in the third than first position of words, "availability biases" like the "letter k" effect can be shown to disappear (Sedlmeier, Hertwig, & Gigerenzer, 1998).

### *Rethinking the Sample: Inside and Outside Views on Judgment*

The rhetoric of the naïve intuitive statistician approach implies that judgment should be improved by increasing awareness of the potential bias in external samples of information. This may be difficult to achieve. Fiedler (2000) gives the example of an expert estimating the causal impact of alcohol (of a certain concentration) on traffic accidents. Although the expert may be fully aware that the available samples are conditional on the criterion (i.e., the occurrence of an accident), taking this into account when quantifying an estimate—perhaps via Bayes's theorem—may not be possible because the base rate $p$(alcohol) and the false alarm rate $p$(alcohol/no accident) are unknown.

Although it may sometimes not be possible to find necessary information in the external environment, careful thought about the representation of information in our minds can help to overcome erroneous judgments. Consider a judgment about how long it will take you to write an essay (Buehler, Griffin, & Ross, 1994). You could consider the qualities of the particular essay (e.g., complexity of the topic, word limit, etc.) or you could consider the essay in the context of other similar ones that you have written and the time that they took. Kahneman and Lovallo (1993) label these two approaches as "inside" and "outside" views, respectively. Here, the inside and outside refer not to mind and environment, but rather to ways of constructing the representation of information in the mind. Kahneman and Lovallo argue that although an "outside view" is often nonintuitive, adopting one diminishes the types of "planning fallacies" that occur when the specifics of a single case are relied upon (Kahneman & Lovallo, 1993). In sampling terms, the outside view promotes the gathering of a set of instances, but with the caveat that the judge needs to be sensitive to how the instances are generated. A similar idea is found in the advice to "consider the opposite" (Larrick, 2004) when making judgments. Simply asking why an initial judgment might be wrong, or whether you should change some of your assumptions before committing to an answer, has been shown to be effective in overcoming anchoring biases in numerical estimation tasks (e.g., Mussweiler, Strack, & Pfeiffer, 2000) and improving estimates in general knowledge tasks (Herzog & Hertwig, 2009).

### Are There Two Systems Underlying Judgment?

This general notion that sometimes "more thinking" about a judgment can alleviate errors is sometimes discussed in terms of the competition between two distinct systems. The typical contrast is between a "System 1," depicted as intuitive or associative, and a "System 2," which is analytic, reflective, or rule-based (e.g., Evans, 2008; Kahneman, 2003; Kahneman & Frederick, 2002; Sloman, 1996; Stanovich & West, 2000). The basic idea is that initial, intuitive answers are proposed by System 1 (e.g., "Linda must be a *feminist* bank teller") but are simultaneously monitored by System 2 and, if necessary, (and circumstances permit) can be overridden (e.g., "She can't be because that violates a basic law of probability"). This characterisation leads to important questions about how such monitoring happens and what determines which system we "listen to" in giving our final response (i.e., What are the circumstances that permit endorsement, correction, or the overriding of System 1 by System 2?)

These are not trivial questions, and indeed a large literature has evolved attempting to identify when System 1 or 2 processes dominate (e.g., Evans, 2008; Kahneman, 2003). This literature highlights factors such as the time available or taken for a decision (e.g., DeNeys & Glumicic, 2008), the availability of cognitive resources (DeNeys, 2006), individual differences in intelligence (e.g., Stanovich & West, 2000), and the effect of instructions encouraging people to think "logically" (e.g., Bonner & Newell, 2010).

Despite the voluminous research and the obvious allure of the dual-system framework, there is debate about the explanatory role that such a framework plays. The advantages of describing processes and heuristics as under the operation of System 1 and System 2 are, some argue, outweighed by the disadvantages for theoretical progress. A key problem in the dual-system literature is the plethora of often vague and imprecise terms used to describe the characteristics of the systems, and a failure to specify the manner in which systems interact and/or exchange information. This has led, arguably, to an illusion of convergence whereby researchers appear to be describing similar models and frameworks that, in fact, differ in many crucial aspects (Evans, 2008). This tendency could impede progress on understanding the phenomena of interest through a (potentially misguided) desire to dichotomize (e.g., Bonner & Newell, 2010; Gigerenzer & Regier, 1996; Keren & Schul, 2009; Marewski, Gaissmaier, & Gigerenzer, 2010; see also Newell, Dunn, & Kalish, 2011, for a related discussion in category learning research).

Nevertheless, some argue that even imprecise frameworks such as those offered by dual-process protagonists are useful because of their potential to guide search for commonalities in processes, identify analogies across domains, and prevent overly narrow interpretations of phenomena (e.g., Kahneman, 2003, 2011). Time will tell whether such optimism is warranted; what is clear is that the development of dual-process accounts will be keenly watched and debated in the coming years.

### A Causal Framework: Integrating Coherence and Correspondence?

Whatever the eventual outcome of the dual-system debate, it is clear from the path followed in this chapter through traditions that have emphasized coherence and correspondence criteria that any successful approach will need to apply both to understand judgment. A novel approach that has the potential to achieve this integration is one which incorporates a role for causal knowledge.

Krynski and Tennenbaum (2007) suggest that deviations from normative standards, such as that exemplified by base rate neglect, can be explained via a mismatch between the statistics provided to participants and the intuitive causal models that participants construct when attempting to answer probability judgment problems. Krynski and Tennenbaum argue that when faced with a problem a participant engages in three steps of reasoning. First, causal domain knowledge is used to construct a causal model of the situation; second, the available statistical data (the probabilities presented in the problem) are used to set parameter values on the model, and finally judgments are made via Bayesian inference over the parameterized model. Krynski and Tennenbaum demonstrated that when inferences were made over intuitive causal models, base-rate neglect was reduced relative to problems in which the models were nonintuitive (e.g., a medical diagnosis task in which false-positive rates had to be included).

The approach taken by Krynski and Tennenbaum (2007) is consistent with a current popular view that emphasizes the potential of a causal Bayesian framework for understanding cognition (e.g., Chater & Oaksford, 2008). The approach provides a possible way to incorporate correspondence and coherence criteria into our explanations of judgment behavior. Coherence standards are readily accommodated via the prescription of an optimal standard—Bayes's rule—for inference. The departure from earlier research focusing on Bayes (e.g., Edwards, 1968) is the inclusion of causal mental models (Pearl, 2000) that specify and typically reduce the number of parameters over which the inference needs to be computed. Correspondence criteria are incorporated via the inclusion of causal knowledge in the models. As Krynski and Tennenbaum note, "causal Bayesian reasoning is often more ecologically adaptive, because it can leverage available causal knowledge to make appropriate judgments even when there is not sufficient statistical data available to make rational inferences under noncausal Bayesian norms" (p. 434). Thus, the causal Bayesian framework can combine coherence via Bayesian inference and correspondence via causal models (or priors) about the facts of the world to provide largely accurate judgments. The brief sketch provided here can only indicate the potential, but maybe the causal Bayesian framework can capitalize on the inseparability of coherence and correspondence and further elucidate how we make judgments under uncertainty.

## Conclusion

Psychological investigations of judgment under uncertainty have proved fertile ground over the past 50 years. This chapter viewed key findings from this rich tradition through the lens of correspondence and coherence criteria for appraising judgment. The research highlights the inseparability of the two criteria and the need to consider both in developing a fully fledged account of judgment. The research appears to be heading in an exciting and fruitful direction—a direction in which the properties of tasks and the constraints of the external environment are given their deserved prominence (e.g., Edwards, 1983; Fiedler & Juslin, 2006) and are combined with appropriate rational benchmarks for assessing judgment (e.g., Anderson, 1990; Chater & Oaksford, 2008; Juslin, Nilsson, & Winman, 2009; Krynski & Tennenbaum, 2007; McKenzie, 2005). With luck, and good judgment, continuing on this promising path will lead us to discover some of things we do not know about judgment under uncertainty (even if we do not yet know what we do not know).

## Future Directions

1. Why is some information more accessible and thus more readily relied upon during the judgment process? (See Shah & Oppenheimer, 2009, for recent work on this topic.)

2. Do we need to posit multiple discrete heuristics to explain judgment, or will a domain-general perspective prove more fruitful?

3. Can we develop a taxonomy of tasks to examine the interaction of task and individual variables and better relate coherence and correspondence criteria? (See Juslin, Nilsson, & Winman, 2009, for a fascinating exploration of how this might be achieved.)

4. What is the potential of the causal Bayesian framework for explaining judgment under uncertainty?

## Acknowledgements

Preparation of this chapter was supported by a Discovery Project grant (DP110100797) and a Future Fellowship (FT 110100151) from the Australian Research Council.

## References

Anderson, J. R. (1990). *The adaptive character of thought*. Hillsdale, NJ: Erlbaum.

Ayton, P., & Fischer, I. (2004). The hot hand fallacy and the gambler's fallacy: Two faces of subjective randomness? *Memory and Cognition, 32,* 1369–1378.

Baron, J. (2008). *Thinking and deciding (4th ed.).* New York: Cambridge University Press.

Bergert, F. B., & Nosofsky, R. M. (2007). A response-time approach to comparing generalized rational and take-the-best models of decision making. *Journal of Experimental Psychology: Learning, Memory, and Cognition, 33,* 107–129.

Bonner, C., & Newell, B. R. (2010). In conflict with ourselves? An investigation of heuristic and analytic processes in decision making. *Memory and Cognition, 38,* 186–196.

Bröder, A., & Newell, B. R. (2008). Challenging some common beliefs: Empirical work within the adaptive toolbox metaphor. *Judgment and Decision Making, 3i,* 25–214.

Bröder, A., & Schiffer, S. (2003). "Take-the-best" versus simultaneous feature matching: Probabilistic inferences from memory and the effects of representation format. *Journal of Experimental Psychology General, 132,* 277–293.

Brunswik, E. (1956). *Perception and the representative design of psychological experiments.* Berkeley: University of California Press.

Buehler, R., Griffin, D., & Ross, M. (1994). Exploring the "planning fallacy": Why people underestimate their task completion times. *Journal of Personality and Social Psychology, 67,* 366–381.

Chater, N., & Oaksford, M. (Eds.). (2008). *The probabilistic mind: Prospects for Bayesian cognitive science.* Oxford, England: Oxford University Press.

Chater, N., Oaksford, M., Nakisa, R., & Redington, M. (2003). Fast, frugal and rational: How rational norms explain behavior. *Organizational Behavior and Human Decision Processes, 90,* 63–80.

Dawes, R. M., Faust, D., & Meehl, P. E. (1989). Clinical versus actuarial judgment. *Science, 243,* 1668–1674.

De Neys, W. (2006). Dual processing in reasoning: Two systems but one reasoner. *Psychological Science, 17,* 428–433.

De Neys, W., & Glumicic, T. (2008). Conflict monitoring in dual process theories of thinking. *Cognition, 106,* 1248–1299.

Dougherty, M. R., Franco-Watkins, A. M., & Thomas, R. (2008). Psychological plausibility of the theory of probabilistic mental models and the fast and frugal heuristics. *Psychological Review, 115,* 199–211.

Dougherty, M. R. P., Gettys, C. F., & Ogden, E. E. (1999). Minerva-DM: A memory processes model for judgments of likelihood. *Psychological Review, 106,* 180–209.

Dougherty, M. R., Thomas, M. R., & Franco-Watkins, A. M. (2008). Postscript: Vague heuristics revisited. *Psychological Review, 115,* 211–213.

Dunwoody, P. T. (2009). Theories of truth as assessment criteria in judgment and decision making. *Judgment and Decision Making, 4,* 116–125.

Edwards, W. (1968). Conservatism in human information processing. In B. Kleinmuntz (Ed.), *Formal representation of human judgment* (pp. 17–52). New York: Wiley.

Edwards, W. (1983/2009). Human cognitive capabilities, representativeness, and ground rules for research. In J. W., & D. J. Wiess (Eds.), *A science of decision making: The legacy of Ward Edwards* (pp. 215–219). New York: Oxford University Press.

Evans, J. St. B. T. (2008). Dual-processing accounts of reasoning, judgement, and social cognition. *Annual Review of Psychology, 59,* 255–278.

Fiedler, K. (2000). Beware of samples! A cognitive-ecological sampling approach to judgment biases. *Psychological Review, 107,* 659–676.

Fiedler, K., & Juslin, P. (2006). Taking the interface between mind and environment seriously. In K. Fiedler & P. Juslin (Eds.). *Information sampling and adaptive cognition* (pp. 3–29). Cambridge, England: Cambridge University Press.

Finucane, M. L., Alhakami, A., Slovic, P., & Johnson, S. M. (2000). The affect heuristic in judgments of risks and benefits. *Journal of Behavioral Decision Making, 13,* 1–17.

Finucane, M. L., Peters, E., & Slovic, P. (2003). Judgment and decision making: The dance of affect and reason. In S. L. Schneider & J. Shanteau (Eds.), *Emerging perspectives on judgment and decision research* (pp. 327–364). Cambridge, England: Cambridge University Press.

Gigerenzer, G. (1996). On narrow norms and vague heuristics: A reply to Tversky and Kahneman. *Psychological Review, 103,* 592–596.

Gigerenzer, G., & Brighton, H. (2009). Homo heuristicus: Why biased minds make better inferences. *Topics in Cognitive Science, 1,* 107–143.

Gigerenzer, G., & Goldstein, D.G. (1996). Reasoning the fast and frugal way: Models of bounded rationality. *Psychological Review, 103,* 650–669.

Gigerenzer, G., Hoffrage, U., & Goldstein, D. G. (2008). Fast and frugal heuristics are plausible models of cognition: Replay to Dougherty, Franco-Watkins, and Thomas (2008). *Psychological Review, 115,* 230–237.

Gigerenzer, G., & Regier, T. (1996). How do we tell an association from a rule? Comment on Sloman (1996). *Psychological Bulletin, 11,* 23–26

Gigerenzer, G., Todd, P. M., & ABC Research Group. (1999). *Simple heuristics that make us smart.* New York: Oxford University Press.

Gilovich, T., Griffin, D., & Kahneman, D. (Eds.). (2002). *Heuristics and biases.* New York: Cambridge University Press.

Gilovich, T., Vallone, R., & Tversky, A. (1985). The hot hand in basketball: On the misperception of random sequences. *Cognitive Psychology, 17,* 295–314.

Goldstein, D. G., & Gigerenzer, G. (2002). Models of ecological rationality: The recognition heuristic. *Psychological Review, 109,* 75–90.

Grove, W., Zald, D., Lebow, B., Snitz, B., & Nelson, C. (2000). Clinical versus mechanical prediction: A meta-analysis. *Psychological Assessment, 12,* 19–30.

Hacking, I. (1975). *The emergence of probability: A philosophical study of early ideas about probability, induction and statistical inference.* Cambridge, England: Cambridge University Press.

Hammond, K. R. (1955). Probabilistic functioning and the clinical method. *Psychological Review, 62,* 255–262.

Hammond, K. R. (1996). *Human judgment and social policy. Irreducible uncertainty, inevitable error, unavoidable injustice.* New York: Oxford University Press.

Hastie, R., & Dawes, R. M. (2001). *Rational choice in an uncertain world.* Thousand Oaks, CA: Sage.

Hertwig R., Benz, B., & Krauss, S. (2008). The conjunction fallacy and the many meanings of "and." *Cognition, 108,* 740–753.

Herzog, S. M., & Hertwig, R. (2009). The wisdom of many in one mind: Improving individual judgments with dialectical bootstrapping. *Psychological Science, 20,* 231–237.

Hilbig, B. E., & Pohl, R. F. (2009). Ignorance-versus evidence-based decision making: A decision time analysis of the recognition heuristic. *Journal of Experimental Psychology: Learning, Memory, and Cognition, 35*, 1296–1305.

Hilton, D. J. (1995). The social context of reasoning: Conversational inference and rational judgment. *Psychological Bulletin, 118*, 248–271.

Hogarth, R. M., & Karelaia, N. (2005). Ignoring information in binary choice with continuous variables: When is less "more"? *Journal of Mathematical Psychology, 49*, 115–124.

Juslin, P. (1994). The overconfidence phenomenon as a consequence of informal experimenter-guided selection of almanac items. *Organizational Behavior and Human Decision Processes, 57*, 226–246.

Juslin, P., Nilsson, H., & Winman, A. (2009). Probability theory, not the very guide of life. *Psychological Review, 116*, 856–874.

Juslin, P., & Persson, M. (2002). PROBabilities from EXemplars (PROBEX): A "lazy" algorithm for probabilistic inference from generic knowledge. *Cognitive Science, 95*, 1–40.

Kahneman, D. (2003). A perspective on judgment and choice: Mapping bounded rationality. *American Psychologist, 58*, 697–720.

Kahneman, D. (2011). *Thinking fast and slow.* New York: Farrar, Strauss, & Giroux.

Kahneman, D., & Frederick, S. (2002). Representativeness revisited: Attribute substitution in intuitive judgment. In T. D. Gilovich, D. W. Griffin, & D. Kahneman (Eds.), *Heuristics and biases* (pp. 49–81). New York: Cambridge University Press.

Kahneman, D., & Klein, G. (2009). Conditions for intuitive expertise: A failure to disagree. *American Psychologist, 64*, 515–526.

Kahneman, D., & Lovallo, D. (1993). Timid choices and bold forecasts: A cognitive perspective on risk and risk taking. *Management Science, 39*, 17–31.

Kahneman, D., Slovic, P., & Tversky, A. (Eds.). (1982). *Judgment under uncertainty: Heuristics and biases.* Cambridge, England: Cambridge University Press.

Kahneman, D., & Tversky, A. (1996). On the reality of cognitive illusions. *Psychological Review, 103*, 582–591.

Karelaia, N., & Hogath, R. M. (2008). Determinants of linear judgment: A meta-analysis of lens model studies. *Psychological Bulletin, 134*, 404–426.

Katsikopoulos, K. V., Schooler, L. J., & Hertwig, R. (2010). The robust beauty of ordinary information. *Psychological Review, 117(4), 1259–1266.*

Keren, G., & Schul, Y. (2009). Two is not always better than one: A critical evaluation of two-system theories. *Perspectives on Psychological Science, 4*, 533–550.

Krynski, T. R., & Tennenbaum, J. B. (2007). The role of causality in judgment under uncertainty. *Journal of Experimental Psychology: General, 136*, 430–450.

Larrick, R. P. (2004). Debiasing. In D. J. Koehler & N. Harvey (Eds.), *The Blackwell handbook of judgment and decision making* (pp. 316–337). Malden, MA: Blackwell.

Lee, M. D., & Cummins, T. D. R. (2004). Evidence accumulation in decision making: Unifying "take the best" and "rational" models. *Psychonomic Bulletin and Review, 11*, 343–352.

Lee, M. D., & Newell, B. R. (2011). Using hierarchical Bayesian methods to examine the tools of decision making. *Judgment and Decision Making, 6*, 832–842.

Lichenstein, S., Slovic, P., Fischoff, B., Layman, M., & Coombs, B. (1978). Judged frequency of lethal events. *Journal of Experimental Psychology: Human Learning and Memory, 4*, 551–578.

Marewski, J., Gaissmaier, W., & Gigerenzer, G. (2010). We favor models of heuristics over loose lists and dichotomies. A reply to Evans & Over. *Cognitive Processing, 11*, 177–179.

McKenzie, C. R. M. (2005). Judgment and decision making. In K. Lamberts & R. Goldstone (Eds.), *Handbook of cognition* (pp. 321–338). Thousand Oaks, CA: Sage.

Meehl, P. E. (1954). *Clinical vs. statistical prediction.* Minneapolis: University of Minnesota Press.

Moro, R. (2009). On the nature of the conjunction fallacy. *Synthese, 171*, 1–24.

Mussweiler, T., Strack, F., & Pfeiffer, T. (2000). Overcoming the inevitable anchoring effect: Considering the opposite compensates for selective accessibility. *Personality and Social Psychology Bulletin, 26*, 1142–1150.

Newell, B. R. (2005). Re-visions of rationality? *Trends in Cognitive Science, 9*, 11–15.

Newell, B. R. (2011). Recognising the Recognition Heuristic for what it is (and what it's not). *Judgment and Decision Making, 6*, 409–412.

Newell, B. R., Dunn, J. C., & Kalish, M. (2011). Systems of category learning: Fact or fantasy? In B. H. Ross (Ed.), *The psychology of learning and motivation* (Vol. 54, pp. 167–215). Burlington: Academic Press.

Newell, B. R., & Fernandez, D. (2006). On the binary quality of recognition and the inconsequentially of further knowledge: Two critical tests of the recognition heuristic. *Journal of Behavioral Decision Making, 19*, 333–346.

Newell, B. R., Lagnado, D. A., & Shanks, D. R. (2007). *Straight choices: The psychology of decision making.* Hove, England: Psychology Press.

Newell, B. R., & Lee, M. D. (2011). The right tool for the job? Comparing an evidence accumulation and a naïve strategy selection model of decision making. *Journal of Behavioral Decision Making, 24*, 456–481.

Newell, B. R., Mitchell, C. J., & Hayes, B. K. (2008). Getting scarred and winning lotteries: Effects of exemplar cuing and statistical format on imagining low-probability events. *Journal of Behavioral Decision Making, 21*, 317–335.

Newell, B. R., & Shanks, D. R. (2003). Take-the-best or look at the rest? Factors influencing "one-reason" decision making. *Journal of Experimental Psychology: Learning, Memory and Cognition, 29*, 53–65.

Newell, B. R., & Shanks, D. R. (2004). On the role of recognition in decision making. *Journal of Experimental Psychology: Learning, Memory and Cognition, 30*, 923–935.

Newell, B. R., Weston, N. J., & Shanks, D. R. (2003). Empirical tests of a fast and frugal heuristic: Not everyone "takes-the-best." *Organizational Behavior and Human Decision Processes, 91*, 82–96.

Oaksford, M., & Chater, N. (1998). *Rationality in an uncertain world: Essays on the cognitive science of human reasoning.* Hove, England: Psychology Press.

Oppenheimer, D. M. (2003). Not so fast (and not so frugal!): Rethinking the recognition heuristic. *Cognition, 90*, B1–B9.

Payne, J. W., Bettman, J. R., & Johnson, E. J. (1993). *The adaptive decision maker.* New York: Cambridge University Press.

Pearl, J. (2000). *Causality: Models, reasoning, and inference.* Cambridge, England: Cambridge University Press.

Peterson, C. R., & Beach, L. R. (1967). Man as an intuitive statistician. *Psychological Bulletin, 68*, 29–46.

Phillips, L. D., & Edwards, W. (1966). Conservativism in a simple probability inference task. *Journal of Experimental Psychology, 72*, 346–354.

Rakow, T., Newell, B. R., Fayers, K., & Hersby, M. (2005). Evaluating three criteria for establishing cue-search hierarchies in inferential judgment. *Journal of Experimental Psychology: Learning, Memory and Cognition, 31*, 1088–1104.

Ramsey, F. P. (1931). *The foundations of mathematics and other logical essays.* London: Routledge and Kegan Paul.

Richter, T., & Späth, P. (2006). Recognition is used as one cue among others in judgment and decision making. *Journal of Experimental Psychology: Learning, Memory and Cognition, 32*, 150–162.

Rieskamp, J. (2008). The importance of learning when making inferences. *Judgment and Decision Making, 3*, 261–277.

Rieskamp, J., & Otto, P. (2006). SSL: A theory of how people learn to select strategies. *Journal of Experimental Psychology: General, 135*, 207–236.

Schooler, L. J., & Hertwig, R. (2005). How forgetting aids heuristic inference. *Psychological Review, 112*, 610–628.

Sedlmeier, P. (1999). *Improving statistical reasoning: Theoretical models and practical implications.* Mahwah, NJ: Erlbaum.

Sedlmeier, P., Hertwig, R., & Gigerenzer, G. (1998). Are judgments of the positional frequencies of letters systematically biased due to availability? *Journal of Experimental Psychology: Learning, Memory, and Cognition, 24*, 754–770.

Serwe, S., & Frings, C. (2006). Who will win Wimbledon? The recognition heuristic in predicting sports events. *Journal of Behavioral Decision Making, 19*, 321–332.

Shah, A. K., & Oppenheimer, D. (2009). The path of least resistance: Using easy-to-access information. *Current Directions in Psychological Science, 18*, 232–236.

Simon, H. A. (1955). A behavioral model of rational choice. *Quarterly Journal of Economics, 69*, 99–118.

Sloman, S. A. (1996). The empirical case for two systems of reasoning. *Psychological Bulletin, 119*, 3–22.

Slovic, P., Monahan, J., & MacGregor, D. M. (2000). Violence risk assessment and risk communication: The effects of using actual cases, providing instructions, and employing probability vs. frequency formats. *Law and Human Behavior, 24*, 271–296.

Stanovich, K. E., & West, R. F. (2000). Individual differences in reasoning: Implications for the rationality debate. *Behavioral and Brain Sciences, 23*, 645–726.

Strack, F., & Mussweiler, T. (1997). Explaining the enigmatic anchoring effect: Mechanisms of selective accessibility. *Journal of Personality and Social Psychology, 73*, 437–446.

Tversky, A., & Kahneman, D. (1973). Availability: A heuristic for judging frequency and probability. *Cognitive Psychology, 5*, 207–232.

Tversky, A., & Kahneman, D. (1974). Judgment under uncertainty: Heuristics and biases. *Science, 185*, 1124–1131.

Tversky, A., & Kahneman, D. (1982). Judgments of and by representativeness. In D. Kahneman, P. Slovic & A. Tversky (Eds.), *Judgment under uncertainty: Heuristics and biases* (pp. 84–98). Cambridge, England: Cambridge University Press.

Tversky, A., & Kahneman, D. (1983). Extensional versus intuitive reasoning: The conjunction fallacy in probability judgment. *Psychological Review, 90*, 293–315.

# Further Reading

Fiedler, K., & Juslin, P. (Eds.). (2006). *Information sampling and adaptive cognition.* Cambridge, England: Cambridge University Press.

Gigerenzer, G., Todd, P. M., & ABC Research Group. (1999). *Simple heuristics that make us smart.* New York: Oxford University Press.

Gilovich, T., Griffin, D., & Kahneman, D. (Eds.). (2002). *Heuristics and biases.* New York: Cambridge University Press.

Newell, B. R., Lagnado, D. A., & Shanks, D. R. (2007). *Straight choices: The psychology of decision making.* Hove, England: Psychology Press.

# Induction

Brett K. Hayes *and* Evan Heit

**Abstract**

This chapter examines recent empirical research and theoretical accounts of inductive reasoning. The first section focuses on property induction between categories. Key phenomena are described and major theoretical models of induction are compared. This section highlights the importance of induction in domains where people have rich background knowledge and research on inductive development in the evaluation of competing models. The next section considers the important but neglected issue of how people make inductive inferences about specific instances. The final sections examine three emerging areas of inductive research: induction when category membership is uncertain, the relationship between inductive and deductive reasoning, and the neural substrates of reasoning. We conclude that future progress in the field will come through the development of broader paradigms that examine induction across a wider range of stimulus domains and models that link induction to other kinds of reasoning and cognitive activities.

**Key Words:** induction, reasoning, categorization, concepts, knowledge, probability judgment, uncertainty

Inductive reasoning involves using past observations and knowledge to make predictions about novel cases. Inductive inferences are probabilistic. For example, if you are told that swans, ravens, and swallows all have "sesamoid bones," then you might be reasonably confident, but not absolutely certain, that this property is shared by other birds. Its probabilistic nature distinguishes induction from deductive reasoning, where the goal is to evaluate whether certain conclusions *necessarily* follow from the evidence given (see Chapters 40–41).

Much of the reasoning that people do in everyday life could be described as a form of induction. Predicting the next round of football results, deciding on the most suitable applicant for a job, or inferring whether your children will like a new brand of ice cream, all involve induction. Given its central role in human thought, it is important to understand the cognitive and neural processes that underlie

induction. Although the definition of induction is broad enough to encompass a range of psychological phenomena, including object recognition (Nosofsky, 1986), categorization (Anderson, 1991), and word learning (Xu & Tenenbaum, 2007), this chapter will focus primarily on research concerning property induction—how people generalize a novel property from a given category or exemplar known to have this property to other cases. In later sections, however, we will consider the links between property induction and other tasks like categorization and recognition memory (see also Kemp, Shafto, & Tenenbaum, 2012).

There have been quite a few previous reviews of property induction research (e.g., Feeney & Heit, 2007; Hayes, Heit, & Swendsen, 2010; Sloman & Lagnado, 2005). In this chapter we try to avoid going over the same ground by offering a novel way of organizing induction research and theory. In addition to examining property induction between categories (e.g., generalizing a novel property from dogs to horses, or from dogs to mammals), we will review relevant work on induction between individual instances (e.g., between Rex, our neighbor's dog; and other dogs). This distinction has generally been overlooked in previous reviews. However, we will show that it is critical because these two forms of induction often involve different kinds of perceptual and cognitive processes. Another factor that distinguishes this chapter from previous reviews is our inclusion of developmental as well as adult induction research. Some of the earliest systematic studies of inductive reasoning were carried out with young children (e.g., Carey, 1985). Such developmental data can inform and constrain the development of theoretical models of induction. Our final aim is to familiarize the reader with what we believe to be some of the most important new areas in research on property induction. These include inferences about exemplars whose category membership is uncertain, the relationship between inductive and deductive reasoning, and the neural processes that subserve reasoning.

## Property Induction Between Categories

Much of the work on this topic has been carried out using a paradigm introduced by Rips (1975) and refined by Osherson, Smith, Wilkie, and López (1990). The basic method involves presenting a novel property (e.g., "has sesamoid bones") shared by all (or most) members of a category or categories (e.g., "swans" and "ravens"). These categories serve as argument premises. The generalization of this property to other categories is then examined, often by asking people to evaluate the strength of a conclusion (e.g., "that all birds have sesamoid bones") given the premises. In early work the property being generalized was usually unfamiliar or "blank" so that the effect of taxonomic relations on induction could be studied independently of property knowledge. This work has uncovered a number of important principles that influence the relative strength of inductive arguments. Because these have been examined in some detail previously (e.g., Hayes et al., 2010; Heit, 2000), we will not attempt an exhaustive review but instead will concentrate on a number of key phenomena that are particularly important for developing process theories of induction (summarized in Table 39.1).

### Key Inductive Phenomena
#### PREMISE-CONCLUSION SIMILARITY AND PREMISE TYPICALITY

The most elementary forms of induction involve generalizing a novel property from a single premise category to a single conclusion. One robust finding

**Table 39.1** Examples of Some Key Inductive Phenomena Using a Blank Property

| Phenomena | Example of a Stronger Argument | Example of a Weaker Argument |
|---|---|---|
| Premise-conclusion similarity promotes induction | Orangutans *have property X*/ Gorillas *have property X* | Orangutans *have property X*/ Hippos *have property X* |
| Premise typicality promotes induction | Crows *have property X*/ Birds *have property X* | Ostriches *have property X*/ Birds *have property X* |
| Greater diversity and sample size (monotonicity) of positive premises promotes induction | *Diversity* <br> Africans + Americans *have property X*/ <br> All people *have property X* <br> *Monotonicity* <br> Africans + Americans + Europeans + Asians *have property X*/ All people have *property X* | *Diversity* <br> Canadians + Americans *have property X*/ <br> All people *have property X* <br> *Monotonicity* <br> Africans + Americans *have property X*/ All people *have property X* |
| Causal relations override similarity relations | *Causal violation of similarity* <br> Cheese *has property X*/ Mice *have property X* <br> *Causal nondiversity* <br> Fleas + Butterflies *have property X*/ Sparrows *have property X* <br> *Causal asymmetry* <br> Antelopes *have property X*/ Lions *have property X* | *Causal violation of similarity* <br> Monkeys have *property X*/ Mice *have property X* <br> *Causal nondiversity* <br> Fleas + Dogs *have property X*/ Sparrows *have property X* <br> *Causal asymmetry* <br> Lions *have property X*/ Antelopes *have property X* |

with these kinds of arguments is that the more similar the premise and conclusion categories, the stronger the inductive argument (Osherson et al., 1990; Rips, 1975; Sloman, 1993). This effect has been found across a wide range of category types and seems to be present in some form at a very early point in development (e.g., Welder & Graham, 2001).

Understanding the cognitive mechanisms that drive this effect is not quite as straightforward as it might seem because it presumes that we always know how people evaluate category similarity. There is good evidence, however, that the way people assess the similarity between categories can vary markedly across different judgment contexts (e.g., Medin, Goldstone, & Gentner, 1993), a point to which we will return shortly. Moreover, in developmental research there is an ongoing debate as to whether similarity effects in young children's induction reflect an overlap between the perceptual or conceptual/semantic features of premise and conclusion items (see Gelman & Waxman, 2007; Hayes, McKinnon, & Sweller, 2008; Sloutsky & Fisher, 2004, for contrasting views).

Another important finding is that premise instances that are seen as more typical or representative of a general category lead to stronger inductive projections than less typical premises (Osherson et al., 1990). Hence, a novel property that is true of bears is more likely to be generalized to other mammals than is a property that is true of bats. Again, this effect seems to be quite a general principle in human induction, affecting property inferences in both natural categories and more ad-hoc categories that are defined by a shared goal such as "game" or "friend" (Rein, Goldwater, & Markman, 2010). Like an understanding of the similarity principle, the effects of typicality on induction also emerge relatively early in childhood (López, Gelman, Gutheil, & Smith, 1992; Rhodes, Brickman, & Gelman, 2008).

Notably, little evidence for a corresponding effect of the typicality of the conclusion category has been found (Gelman & O'Reilly, 1988; Rips, 1975; but see Hampton & Cannon, 2004). Gelman and O'Reilly (1988), for example, showed that children and adults were equally likely to generalize a novel property of typical-looking chairs to typical (e.g., a bed) and atypical (e.g., a crib) kinds of furniture. Such findings suggest that when people learn new properties of a typical exemplar, they spontaneously infer these properties to other members of the conclusion category, regardless of exemplar typicality.

## PREMISE DIVERSITY AND MONOTONICITY

Adults' inductive inferences are sensitive to the diversity of premise categories. Properties shared by diverse or dissimilar categories that belong to the same superordinate (e.g., lions and goats) are more likely to be generalized than properties shared by similar categories (e.g., lions and leopards) (Feeney & Heit, 2011; Kim & Keil, 2003). In adults, inductive strength is also positively related to the number of premise categories known to share a property, an effect referred to as "premise monotonicity" (Osherson et al., 1990; for a recent review, see Heit & Rotello, 2012).

Premise diversity and montonicity effects are consistent with normative principles for probabilistic evidence, which hold that conclusions are stronger to the extent that they are based on a broader evidential base and on a greater number of observations (Nagel, 1939).[1] It is interesting, therefore, that an understanding of these principles seems to emerge relatively late in development. Although there are some exceptions (e.g., Heit & Hahn, 2001), most studies have found little evidence that children below the age of 8 years appreciate the value of diverse evidence for property induction (Lawson & Fisher, 2011; López et al., 1992; Rhodes, et al., 2008; Rhodes, Gelman, & Brickman, 2009). Recent work suggests that this may be because adults and children have different expectations about category homogeneity (Rhodes et al., 2008, 2009). Children view categories as more homogeneous than adults, expecting that most category members will share the same essential properties (Diesendruck & HaLevi, 2006; Gelman & Bloom, 2007). This could explain their failure to use premise diversity; if lions, goats, and leopards all belong to the same category (mammals) and young children assume that all category members have the same internal properties, premise diversity will have little effect on their inferences. Supporting this interpretation is the finding that explicitly instructing children about within-category variability promotes use of premise diversity in induction (Rhodes et al., 2009).

## CAUSAL RELATIONS OVERRIDE TAXONOMIC RELATIONS

The induction phenomena discussed so far are driven by taxonomic relationships between premise and conclusion categories. In many situations however, people use more complex relations between categories (e.g., thematic, script-based, ecological, causal) as a basis for generalizing properties (Medin, Coley, Storms, & Hayes, 2003; Rehder, 2009;

Sloman, 2005). Causal relations seem particularly important since they can override taxonomic similarity as a basis for induction. A good illustration comes from work by Rehder (2006). In one study participants first learned about members of an artificial category (e.g., Kehoe ants) made up of a number of discrete features. They were then taught a novel property of Kehoe ants (e.g., "has a venom that gives it a stinging bite") and asked whether this property generalizes to novel instances that had many features in common with the training category (high similarity) or few features in common (low similarity). Critically, on some trials participants were told that a particular feature of Kehoe ants was the cause of the novel property (e.g., the stinging sensation was caused by a high concentration of iron sulfate in the venom). When no causal explanation was given, people generalized the novel property based on similarity. When an explanation was given, people generalized on the presence or absence of the causal feature, regardless of overall similarity. Rehder (2006) also found that the presence of a causal explanation could override taxonomic effects like typicality and diversity.

Causal relations are also important for induction with natural categories. Medin et al. (2003) compared the strength of inductive arguments that used identical categories but varied whether the respective categories were presented as premises or conclusions (e.g., a novel property was generalized from antelopes to lions, or from lions to antelopes). When there was a plausible causal relation linking the premise to the conclusion (e.g., lions eat antelopes) property induction was more likely than in the reversed version, even though category similarity was identical in each case. The presence of a strong causal relation can also override standard taxonomic effects like premise-conclusion similarity, diversity, and monotonicity (see Table 39.1 for examples, but see Heit, Hahn, & Feeney, 2005 for a different account of causal nondiversity).

Children as young as 5 years of age use causal relations in induction (Hayes & Thompson, 2007; Hayes & Rehder, 2012; Opfer & Bulloch, 2007) and by 8 years children see causal relations as a better basis for generalizing properties than global similarity (Hayes & Thompson, 2007). There are some respects, however, in which young children's use of causal relations in inductive reasoning differs from that of older children and adults. For example, young children are precocious in their use of teleological causes (i.e., those based on an object function) in reasoning. Both adults and children use

such explanations for artifacts (Lombrozo & Carey, 2006), but children appear less selective in their application of teleology, believing that natural phenomena are subject to the same kinds of explanations. For example, while all age groups agreed that "pens are for writing," 4- to 5-year-olds also claimed that "mountains are for climbing" (Kelemen, 1999).

## Sources of Relational Knowledge in Induction

Given that adults and older children use a range of relations in induction, an important goal is to identify factors that lead people to rely on one kind of relation rather than another. At least three such factors have been identified so far. The first is experience with the categories and properties involved in induction (see Chapter 35). Experts with training and experience in biological domains are more likely to rely on causal /ecological relations when generalizing biological properties than are novices, who rely mainly on taxonomic similarity (Coley, 2012; Proffitt, Coley, & Medin, 2000; Shafto & Coley, 2003). The same pattern has been found in comparisons of biological induction by people from cultures with a close contact with the biological world like the Itza Maya of Central America or midwestern Native Americans, with urban undergraduates (Atran, Medin, & Ross, 2005; López, Atran, Coley, Medin, & Smith, 1997). Differences in experience and education may also go some way toward explaining certain developmental changes in induction. For example, children may become more selective in their teleological reasoning as they learn about the variety of causal mechanisms that operate in the natural and technological world. This is suggested by research showing that adults with limited education overgeneralize teleological explanations in much the same way as young children (Casler & Kelemen, 2008).

A second factor that can prompt the use of more complex relations in induction is the nature of the property being generalized. The use of familiar or "nonblank" properties in inductive arguments can have a profound effect on the way that people compare categories in induction. Heit and Rubinstein (1994), for example, found that anatomical properties (e.g., "has an ulnar artery") are more likely to be generalized from sparrows to hawks than from tigers to hawks but that for behavioral properties (e.g., "studies its food before attacking") the pattern reverses. Background knowledge about the property appeared to shift the dimensions used in assessing the similarity of premises and conclusions. In the case of anatomic properties, taxonomic similarity is relevant, but in the case of behavior, predation patterns are relevant (see Shafto, Coley, & Vitkin, 2007, for further examples of the selective generalization of different kinds of properties).

A third factor is the amount of time available to think about a given problem. Shafto, Coley, and Baldwin (2007) showed that when participants had more time to make inductive judgments, they selectively used ecological relations between animals for generalizing disease properties and taxonomic relations for generalizing structural properties like "has a gene." When the same inductive judgments were presented under a short response deadline, however, taxonomic relations were used for both kinds of properties (see Heit & Rotello, 2010, for a related finding, in which speeding up a judgment of deductive validity leads to a focus on taxonomic similarity).

These findings also speak to the important question of whether there is a "default" relation for property induction. A conclusive answer to this question requires more extensive examination of property effects across a range of conceptual domains. Based on existing work, however, it seems safe to suggest that taxonomic similarity is used as a default for generalizing novel properties with biological kinds (Shafto & Coley, 2003; Shafto et al., 2007), whereas information about object function is most frequently accessed in induction with artifacts (Bloom, 1996).

## Theoretical Models of Category-Based Induction

One consequence of the recent proliferation of induction research has been the development of a range of competing theoretical models of how people do category-based induction. In this section we will briefly review several of the most prominent models, examining their strengths and limitations and, wherever possible, pointing out where they converge on core principles.

### Similarity-Based Models

We use the term "similarity-based" to refer to models that were originally designed to explain induction phenomena that only involve taxonomic relations between premise and conclusion categories. Perhaps the best known is Osherson et al.'s (1990) *Similarity-Coverage* (Sim-Cov) model, which assumes that two processes drive the projection of novel properties between categories.

The *similarity* component computes the similarity between the premise and conclusion category with maximal premise-conclusion similarity being used when there is more than one premise. The *coverage* component involves computing the average maximum similarity of the premise categories to samples of the lowest level category, which includes both premises and conclusions. For example, in the argument bears/lions, coverage would involve first generating a superordinate that includes the premise and conclusion categories (e.g., mammals) and then computing the average similarity of the premises to instances from the superordinate.

The similarity component is sufficient to explain phenomena such as premise-conclusion similarity. Other phenomena, however, are driven by both components. Premise typicality, for example, arises because more typical premises (like bears) will have a higher average similarity to the more inclusive conclusion category (i.e., better coverage) than less typical premises (like bats). Diversity effects occur because more diverse premise sets like bears and bats provide better coverage of categories like mammal than do less diverse sets like bears and deer.

One strength of Sim-Cov is that it offers a relatively straightforward account of both adult induction and patterns of inductive development. The coverage component in the model involves more complex computations than the similarity component, particularly for arguments where one has to generate an inclusive conclusion. This suggests a developmental progression that begins with an understanding of arguments based only on the similarity component (e.g., premise-conclusion similarity) followed by arguments involving coverage with a more general conclusion supplied (e.g., bears, bats/mammals), followed by arguments where the inclusive conclusion has to be generated (e.g., bears, bats/lions). This predicted progression is close to what has been observed in many developmental studies (e.g., López et al., 1992).

An important limitation, however, is that the construct of "similarity" is underspecified, even though it is identified as a core component of the Sim-Cov model. Applications of the model (e.g., Osherson et al., 1990) operationalize similarity by obtaining global "similarity" ratings between various categories. But it not always clear what such ratings are measuring. They could reflect an assessment of the semantic relationships between categories, but it is also possible that the category labels activate memories for specific instances whose semantic and perceptual features might be compared.

Like Similarity-Coverage, Sloman's (1993) *Feature-based induction (FBI)* model emphasises the similarity of premise and conclusion categories as a basis for induction. However, it does so without the retrieval of superordinate categories. Instead, the model assumes that individual categories are encoded in terms of their typical features. Property generalization is proportional to the number of features shared by premises and conclusions, divided by a "magnitude" term, which represents the number of features in the conclusion category. A general prediction of the model is that generalization will increase as a function of similarity (defined in terms of feature overlap) between the premises and conclusions but will be reduced by the presence of "rich" conclusion categories that contain many features.

As well as providing a clear specification of how similarity between categories is computed, FBI makes novel predictions that lie outside the remit of Sim-Cov. For example, it predicts a boundary condition for the effects of premise diversity on induction. According to the model, increasing premise diversity will have little effect on inductive projection when the additional premise has few features in common with the conclusions. For example, even though the argument German shepards, blue whales have property X/Moles have property X involves highly diverse premises, and the premises and conclusions belong to the same superordinate of mammals, the model correctly predicts that participants will judge the argument as inductively weak.

A significant problem for FBI, however, is that it fails to give a complete account of the core phenomenon of premise typicality. Previous work on typicality effects has shown that this result obtains even when the respective similarities between the typical and atypical premises and the specific conclusion category are equated (Rips, 1975). But FBI incorrectly predicts that once premise-conclusion similarity is controlled for there should be no independent effect of typicality. Moreover, the model implies that the typicality of the conclusion category should also affect inductive strength, a prediction that has not generally been supported.

Of course, an even more serious problem for both Similarity-Coverage and FBI is that they fail to provide principled explanations of the effects of causal and property knowledge on induction. In part because it is a more flexible model, FBI fares slightly better in this respect. For example, reversals in patterns of inductive projection driven by different kinds of properties (e.g., Heit & Rubinstein, 1994) could be explained in FBI by assuming that

features shared by all premise categories would have the greatest weight in computing overlap with the conclusion category. It is not clear, however, how either Sim-Cov or FBI could explain the primacy of causal relations in induction when these are placed in conflict with similarity. More generally, some have argued that the construct of similarity, which is core to Similarity-Coverage and FBI, is not sufficiently constrained to explain induction (Medin et al., 1989; Sloman & Lagnado, 2005). The category members used in inductive arguments can be compared in an infinite number of ways (e.g., orangutans and gorillas are both apes, hairy, and intelligent, but they are also larger than caterpillars, have fewer than six legs, live on the planet Earth, and so on). Models like Sim-Cov and FBI ignore this complexity, assuming that a reasoner always knows which features of premise and conclusion categories are most relevant for a given prediction, and how features should be weighted and combined in similarity computations. Because of these limitations, recent interest has shifted to the broader and more flexible theoretical frameworks reviewed in the next sections.

### Relevance Theory

Relevance theory (Medin et al., 2003) is a broad theoretical framework that aims to account for the effects of causal and property knowledge on induction. A key contribution of relevance theory is that it provides some general principles for identifying the kinds of features that should be considered when evaluating the inductive strength of an argument. The core assumption is that this involves a comparison between the *most distinctive* features of premise and conclusion categories and, in the multiple-premise case, a comparison between different premises. The most distinctive relations activated during this process guide inductive projection. All things being equal, causal relations are generally assumed to be highly distinctive, and therefore more likely to influence property induction, than taxonomic or thematic relations. Nonblank properties can suggest the relevant dimensions for comparing premises and premises, so that the use of different kinds of more familiar properties (e.g., biological vs. behavioral) can prime different sorts of inductive projections.

A positive feature of relevance theory is that it applies the same general principles to explain the touchstone effects involving taxonomic similarity as well as the effects of causal knowledge. For example, a property of kangaroos and koalas is less likely to be generalized to project to "all mammals" than a property of kangaroos and polar bears, because the less diverse set activates a distinctive property ("native to Australia") that is not shared by most instances of the conclusion. The same mechanism, however, predicts that an even more diverse set like polar bears and penguins will be less inductively potent for the conclusion category of "animals" (because the premises share a distinctive habitat that is not shared by most other animals).

Although the breadth of relevance theory is appealing, a number of its assumptions need to be refined so that it can generate further testable assumptions. Most notably, the process by which the distinctiveness of the features of premise and conclusions is computed, and how this varies with different reasoning contexts, needs to be specified more clearly. Moreover, a number of the key process assumptions of the model (e.g., that comparisons between the distinctive relations of multiple premises precede comparison between premise-conclusion relations) have yet to be tested. Although much of this work is still to be carried out, there have been some recent positive developments. Most notably, some ideas similar to those in relevance theory have been implemented in a formal model (*SimProb*; Blok, Medin, & Osherson, 2007) and successfully applied to predict probability ratings for inductive arguments with nonblank features.

### Bayesian Models

Heit (1998, 2000) suggested that induction is best thought of as a form of Bayesian belief revision. His Bayesian model assumes that when generalizing a novel property (e.g., disease X) between familiar categories (e.g., from sparrows to crows), people will access their prior knowledge about the distribution of familiar properties. They will know, for example, that certain properties are true of all birds, including sparrows and crows, but that other properties are limited just to the premise or the conclusion. The question is which of these distributions the novel property most closely resembles. To solve the problem, the Bayesian model treats the premise or premises in an inductive argument as evidence, which is used to revise beliefs about the prior hypotheses, according to Bayes's theorem. Once these beliefs have been revised, the plausibility of the conclusion is estimated.

This model predicts most of the key results in Table 39.1. It can be extended to nonblank cases by assuming that different kinds of familiar properties cause the retrieval of different kinds of priors. So

when asked whether a biological property of hawks is more likely to generalize to sparrows or tigers, people will retrieve prior knowledge about the anatomical properties across these categories, whereas inductions about behavior will prime retrieval of familiar behavioral properties.

Like other early Bayesian models of induction (e.g., Tenenbaum & Griffiths, 2001), Heit's model is not precise about how prior probabilities are computed. One possibility is that they are proportional to the number of common and distinctive properties retrieved from memory for premise and conclusion categories. Heit also suggested that prior hypotheses could be influenced by placeholders for essential properties of categories that cannot be listed (cf., Medin & Ortony, 1989). It is not clear whether the model gives priority to causal relations over other properties.

Some of these issues have been addressed in more recent Bayesian accounts such as the structured statistical model of Kemp and Tenenbaum (2009). Like earlier models, this approach assumes that the problem of induction can be approached as one of making a statistical inference about the probability of a conclusion given the observed premises. Notably, the model assumes that the relevant priors used as inputs into Bayesian calculus are based on peoples' intuitive theories. These theories are instantiated as structural models of the relations between categories and prior beliefs about the distribution of features across categories. Different kinds of structured representations will be retrieved depending on the type of property being generalized. For example, when the induction involves taxonomic properties, the default structure is a hierarchical tree. For spatial or quantitative properties categories are represented according to their distance in dimensional space on known attributes relevant to the target property. When induction involves causal properties, then categories are represented in a directed graph (a Bayes net). Each structure leads to the activation of a different set of priors about the distribution of known features. So in the causal case, knowing that a mouse carries a particular disease may lead to retrieval of knowledge of relevant food-chain relations, activating many features of cats.

This model has been successfully applied to a range of induction data sets, which include many of the key findings in Table 39.1. The relative fit of models based on different structured representations depends on the kind of property being generalized. Bayesian predictions based on the taxonomic model of prior knowledge produce a good fit to generalization across a range of animal stimuli when genetic properties were used but a poor fit for disease properties. Predictions based on a causal structural model show the opposite trend, providing a close fit to disease properties that could be propagated via predator-prey relations but a poor fit to inferences about biological properties.

The structured statistical approach provides a clear mechanism for deriving prior probabilities from background knowledge, and it allows for the flexible application of different kinds of knowledge depending on the conceptual domain and nature of the property being generalized. Not surprisingly, there are still some effects of knowledge on induction that the model has difficulty with. Although it can deal with causal relationships that can be represented in a chain or web, it is not clear how the model would deal with cases of induction where premises and conclusion categories are seen as similar because they fulfil similar causal *roles* (e.g., hawks and tigers are similar because they both take the role of predator in their respective environments).

Perhaps the main weakness of the structured statistical model is a by-product of one of its strengths, namely its flexible application of different knowledge structures. The model says little about exactly how people ensure that they activate the correct structured representation for a given problem. When told that mice have a certain disease, it seems likely that people would consider a range of possible routes for property generalization (taxonomic, predator-prey relations, ecological relations, etc.), each of which is associated with a different structured representation for generating priors. Exactly how a particular representation is selected (and other representations discarded) remains to be specified.

### *Summary and Synthesis*

This review suggests that most induction models could be located on a continuum. At one end we have models like Sim-Cov and FBI that are relatively well specified in their processing assumptions and have been formally implemented, but which are relatively circumscribed in scope. These models give a good account of induction in the absence of detailed knowledge about the distinctive properties of premise and conclusion categories. At the other end we have approaches like relevance theory that have a broad scope but whose processing assumptions have yet to be fully specified or tested. An important development in the field, therefore, is the appearance of models like Structured Statistical Representations, which incorporate many of the

strengths of the alternate approaches; the model's core assumptions are specified precisely, but it has the scope to explain both elementary and more complex forms of induction.

It seems likely that the next decade will see the emergence of more precisely specified models that attempt to explain both similarity-based and causal induction. For example, Rogers and McClelland (2004) have proposed a connectionist model of property induction that includes generalization of causal properties. As such models proliferate we will need some principled ways of comparing them and ultimately deciding which provides the best account. First, we will need to examine whether, in fact, these models represent qualitatively different kinds of theoretical explanations. McClelland (1998), for example, has suggested that despite their many apparent differences, connectionist and Bayesian models of cognition may share some underlying assumptions and principles. Second, the trade-off between model complexity and success in fitting the data needs to be carefully evaluated. The Structured Statistical approach, for example, explains a far greater range of results than SimCov but does so at the cost of a considerable increase in complexity. Selection of the most appropriate model will need to be guided by inferential procedures that take account of differences in computational complexity and flexibility (Pitt, Myung, & Zhang, 2002). Third, future formal models will need to account not only for phenomena summarized in Table 39.1 but also for patterns of developmental continuity (e.g., Hayes et al., 2008) and discontinuity (e.g., Rhodes et al., 2008) in induction.

The most important principle for deciding on the best model of induction, however, is not whether the model accounts for known phenomena but whether the model can generate and explain novel (and preferably counterintuitive) patterns of data. In this respect, heuristic approaches like relevance theory have been especially successful. It remains to be seen whether the more recent formal induction models can also generate novel, testable predictions that lead to new discoveries about the way that people do property induction.

### Emerging Directions in Induction Research

This section examines a number of new trends in research on human induction. Some of these topics (e.g., induction with exemplars, induction with multiple categories) are of interest because they involve inductive phenomena that are very common in everyday life but have been overlooked in previous research. Other topics are of interest because they link induction to other cognitive domains like memory and deductive reasoning.

## Induction With Specific Exemplars

Much of the work discussed so far has been based on studies of property generalization between categories. Far less attention, however, has been devoted to how people generalize novel properties between specific exemplars.[2] One reason for the neglect of exemplar-based approaches in induction is that many current theories assume (at least implicitly) a prototype model of representation, where categories are represented by a summary of the most typical category features (see Markman & Ross, 2003 for a discussion of one such approach). This contrasts with the assumptions of many theories of category learning where the similarity between specific exemplars has been recognized as a critical factor in the way people assign objects to categories (e.g., Allen & Brooks, 1991; Nosofsky, 1986).

Understanding how people reason about specific exemplars is important for a number of reasons. First, reasoning about specific objects is ubiquitous in everyday life and may involve the consideration of factors that are not usually considered in category-based approaches. If asked to feed our neighbor's dog, Rex, our knowledge of the general properties of *dogs* can only take us so far when making predictions about Rex's behavior and preferences. To make these predictions, we may have to look at Rex's particular features. If Rex is large and barks a lot, we may infer that he is also aggressive toward strangers and should to be approached with caution. Alternately, if Rex is small, beautifully groomed, and has been entered in dog shows, we might predict that he will be a fussy eater. Note that in these cases property predictions are not just based on category-level knowledge. Instead, the predictions are based on knowledge about relationships between features rather than categories (e.g., large, barking dogs are often aggressive).

Is there any evidence that people reason this way? A recent study by Murphy and Ross (2010a) suggests they do. In one study participants were shown artificial categories containing cars that varied in color and in the nature of a "free" feature that came with each particular car (e.g., satellite radio, alloy wheels, heated seat). The categories represented cars produced by different manufacturers (e.g., Honda vs. Ford). The stimuli were designed so that in the crucial condition, one free feature was characteristic of each category overall (e.g., Fords most often had

satellite radio). Within the category, however, a different feature was strongly correlated with specific colors (e.g., yellow cars most often had alloy wheels). After hearing about these categories, people were presented with a novel car and told its color (e.g., "I have a new car that is yellow"). They were then asked to classify the instance and to predict what other feature it would have. Even though almost everyone assigned the test instance to the correct category, they did not use category-level information to make feature predictions. Instead, most people used the correlations between specific features as a basis for property induction. This result shows that when people have knowledge about some of the features of an object, they will often use feature-feature relations rather than feature-category relations as a basis for inductive prediction.

Another important reason for examining how people reason about specific instances is that it offers the prospect of linking the study of induction to other important areas of cognitive science. Much of the work in other key domains like memory, attention, and identification has focused on how people make judgments about individual objects rather than categories of objects. This has led to the development of sophisticated models that can explain a wide range of empirical phenomena (e.g., Malmberg, 2008). If the experimental paradigms used to study induction included inferences about individual objects, then we will be in a better position to examine the similarities and differences between the processes involved in induction and those involved in other tasks like object recognition.

To this end we have developed an experimental paradigm that makes induction and recognition memory tasks as comparable as possible (Hayes, Fritz, & Heit, 2012; Heit & Hayes, 2011). The basic approach is illustrated in Figure 39.1. People were presented with a common study set (e.g., pictures of several large dogs) and told that their task was either to learn about animals that shared a novel anatomical property (induction) or to memorize each item (recognition). All participants were subsequently presented with a test set that included study dogs and new dogs. Those in the induction condition were asked to respond "yes" if they thought a test animal had the target property, while those in the recognition condition responded "yes" if they thought they had seen the animal before. In general, those doing induction were more likely to respond "yes" to new test items than those doing recognition. However, the similarities between response

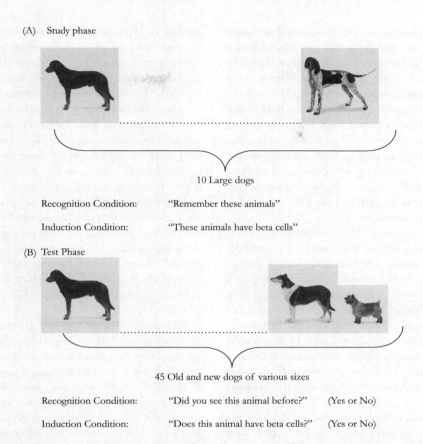

(A) Study phase

10 Large dogs

Recognition Condition:     "Remember these animals"

Induction Condition:       "These animals have beta cells"

(B) Test Phase

45 Old and new dogs of various sizes

Recognition Condition:     "Did you see this animal before?"     (Yes or No)

Induction Condition:       "Does this animal have beta cells?"    (Yes or No)

**Figure 39.1** Outline of the procedure used by Heit and Hayes (2011) to compare inductive reasoning and memory. (*See* color insert.)

patterns across the two tasks were equally striking. The correlation between the probability of making a "yes" response to the various test items under induction and recognition instructions was very high (0.84 or greater). Moreover, various task manipulations, such as increasing exposure to study items, increasing the length of the study list, and changing the perceptual context in which study and test items were seen, had similar effects on induction and recognition responses. Notably, a close relation between patterns of induction and recognition has also been found in 5–6-year-old children (Hayes et al., 2012).

These results suggest that induction and recognition share some component processes. One process likely to be shared is an assessment of the specific similarity between test items for which a judgment is required and previously experienced category exemplars. The notion that the total similarity between a test item and previously experienced instances affects judgments about new cases has long been a central feature of formal models of recognition (e.g., Dennis & Humphreys, 2001) and categorization

(Nosofsky, 1986). The value of incorporating this principle into models of induction is illustrated by the fact that a modification of Nosofsky's (1986) Generalized Context Model, which relies primarily on an assessment of the total similarity between old and new exemplars, produced an excellent fit to both the induction and recognition data in Heit and Hayes (2011).

There are two important implications of this work. First, it provides clear evidence for the overlap in underlying processes between induction and other well-studied cognitive phenomena. Second, it suggests that in order to deal with induction based on specific exemplars, future models of induction will have to build in mechanisms for comparing the similarity between instances as well as categories.

### Induction With Uncertain Categorization

Much of the research on induction reviewed so far has been concerned with making inferences about objects whose category membership is known with certainty. If you know an object is an apple, then you can be reasonably certain that it will taste sweet and have small seeds. If a persistent cough is known to be caused by bronchitis, one can predict that it will eventually subside. In many cases, however, we may have to make inductive predictions about instances whose category membership is ambiguous. Even though bronchitis may be a likely cause for the cough, other causes, such as early-stage lung cancer, are possible alternatives. Clearly our predictions about these cases (e.g., future symptoms and best course of treatment) will depend on whether we consider only the most likely category assignment or whether we factor in the properties of less likely category alternatives.

Bayesian theories like Anderson's (1991) Rational model predict that people will consider multiple categories when making feature predictions about objects whose category membership is uncertain. However, a considerable body of research with natural (Murphy & Ross, 1994, 2010b) and artificial categories (Ross & Murphy, 1996) suggests that people rarely do this; instead they usually ignore the uncertainty and make predictions based on the properties of the category to which an object is *most likely* to belong (referred to as the "primary category").

To illustrate, consider the artificial disease categories of Burlosis and Terragitis in Table 39.2. Each category contains eight "patients" with two characteristic symptoms. Imagine that a new test instance (e.g., a patient with a *headache*) is encountered and you are asked to predict another symptom that the patient is likely to have. Burlosis is the primary category because it contains more patients suffering from headaches. If only this category were considered, then the most likely symptom would be "rash" (as this is the most common symptom on dimension *d2* within Burlosis). Note, however, that some patients with Terragitis also have headaches. Hence, according to the Rational model, the properties of this secondary category should also be considered, leading to the prediction of "sore gums" (the most common symptom on *d2* across both categories). When people are presented with such problems, they readily acknowledge that the uncertainty regarding the category membership of the test instance. Nevertheless, most participants ignore this uncertainty, basing their predictions only on the features of the primary category (e.g., Hayes & Newell, 2009; Murphy & Ross, 1994, 2010b).

Exactly why people violate Bayesian prescriptions and make "single category" predictions is not yet clear. One possibility is that this reflects a general constraint on hypothetical reasoning, referred to by Evans (2007) as *the singularity principle*. According to this principle, when people reason hypothetically, they prefer to consider only one possible situation at a time. Hence, people will acknowledge uncertainty when deciding on category membership but focus only on the most likely scenario (i.e., the primary category) category when making a feature prediction.

**Table 39.2** Examples of Stimuli Used in Studies of Induction With Uncertain Categories

| | Burlosis | | | Terragitis | |
| Patient | Symptom Dimension 1 (d1) | Symptom Dimension 2 (d2) | Patient | Symptom Dimension 1 (d1) | Symptom Dimension 2 (d2) |
| --- | --- | --- | --- | --- | --- |
| B1 | Headache | Rash | T1 | Fever | Sore gums |
| B2 | Headache | Sore gums | T2 | Headache | Dizziness |
| B3 | Headache | Rash | T3 | Fever | Sore gums |
| B4 | Headache | Rash | T4 | Headache | Sore gums |
| B5 | Headache | Sore gums | T5 | Fever | Sore gums |
| B6 | Headache | Sore gums | T6 | Headache | Rash |
| B7 | Stomach pains | Rash | T7 | Headache | Dizziness |
| B8 | Headache | Runny nose | T8 | Fever | Sore gums |

*Induction test*: "Patient X is a new patient. This patient has a headache. What other symptom are they most likely to have?"
*Multiple category prediction* = "sore gums"; *Single category prediction* = "rash."
*Source*: Adapted from Hayes & Newell, 2009.

As with other cognitive heuristics (e.g., Kahneman & Tversky, 1973), however, there is evidence that people can overcome their tendency to make single-category predictions when the other category alternatives are seen as especially relevant or important for the prediction. Hayes and Newell (2009), for example, presented inductive problems like the one in Table 39.2 but told some participants that the less likely category (Terragitis in this example) was "serious and potentially fatal." This led to a marked increase in predictions based on information from both categories. Ross and Murphy (1996) found that when a less likely category alternative was seen as particularly relevant to the feature being predicted, then that category was considered when making feature predictions (e.g., when the feature was whether a stranger walking up a driveway would "pay attention to the sturdiness of the doors" and the category alternative was "burglar"). Hayes and Chen (2008) have also found that certain kinds of domain expertise can promote use of multiple categories for inductive predictions relevant to that domain.

Another important finding is that when people are faced with making inductive predictions about instances whose category membership is uncertain, they may abandon the use of categories altogether. Papadopoulos, Hayes, and Newell (2011) presented artificial categories with a statistical structure similar to the example in Table 39.2 except that across both categories certain features were highly correlated (e.g., headache was frequently paired with the symptom "difficulty swallowing"). The categories were designed so that feature predictions based on these conjunctions were distinguishable from those based on either single or multiple categories. When presented with a test patient with a headache, people overwhelmingly made inductive predictions based on feature conjunctions rather than using either of the category-based strategies (see Griffiths, Hayes, & Newell, 2012; Murphy & Ross, 2010a for similar findings). This again highlights that when making feature predictions about individual objects, people often rely on similarity to specific instances rather than category-level information.

It seems likely that we will see more research on inductive inference with uncertain categories in the coming years. One reason is that this work has the potential to strengthen the links between research on inductive reasoning and areas such as decision making and judgment under uncertainty (see Chapters 38 and 43). A second reason is that this work has some important implications for theories of induction. Induction with uncertain categories appears to involve factors that lie outside the scope of the Bayesian theories (e.g., Kemp & Tenenbaum, 2009) that have been successful in explaining other forms of category-based induction. Finally, this work is important is because it is closely linked to an even more fundamental problem in induction; how people make inferences about cross-classified objects. All objects are members of multiple categories. For example, *Hilary Clinton* is secretary of state, the wife of a former president, a Democrat, an American, and a woman. An important question that remains unresolved is how people coordinate information from these different categories when making feature predictions (but see Hayes, Kurniawan, & Newell, 2011; Murphy & Ross, 1999 for some possible answers).

### Relations Between Induction and Deduction

Inductive reasoning is not the only kind of reasoning. The traditional alternative to induction is deduction, which is linked to making valid inferences that are 100% certain given a set of premises and do not depend on background knowledge. Deduction appears very different from induction, which is probabilistic and knowledge rich. But where do you draw the line between induction and deduction, and how are they related? Heit (2007) distinguished between two approaches, the problem view and the process view. According to the problem view, induction and deduction refer to different kinds of reasoning problems. For example, deductive problems could be defined as those arguments that are valid according to the rules of a well-specified logic, and other arguments could be referred to as inductive problems. Alternately, deductive problems could be defined as those with 100% (or perhaps 99.9%) likely conclusions, inductively strong problems could be those with highly probable conclusions (perhaps 75%–99.9%), and other problems could be considered weak.

Unlike the problem view, the process view is concerned with psychological processes rather than the form of the problem. The question of interest is what processes underlie induction and deduction, and whether these are the same or different. Some researchers have suggested that induction and deduction depend on the same cognitive processes. This approach will be referred to as the one-process view. Several influential research programs embody the one-process view, by applying a common framework to both inductive and deductive problems. For example, Osherson et al. (1990) and Sloman

(1993) noted that their models of inductive reasoning could, without additional assumptions, account for some deductive reasoning phenomena. Similarly, Johnson-Laird (1994) explained how mental models theory, typically applied to problems of deduction, can also be applied to problems of induction.

In contrast, according to two-process accounts (Evans, 2007; Stanovich, 2009), both heuristic and analytic processes contribute to reasoning. Both induction and deduction could be influenced by these two processes, but in different ways. Induction judgments would be particularly influenced by quick heuristic processes that tap into associative information about similarity and background knowledge. In contrast, deduction judgments would be more heavily influenced by slower analytic processes that encompass more deliberative, and typically more accurate, reasoning. Two-process accounts have provided an explanatory framework for many results, but in general they have not been implemented computationally.

A recent line of work (Heit & Rotello, 2010; Heit, Rotello, & Hayes, 2012; Rotello & Heit, 2009) has directly pitted one- and two-process accounts against each other, by implementing the accounts as computational models and applying them to experimental data. The method, adapted from Rips (2001), is to take a set of arguments and have one group of subjects judge whether the arguments are deductively valid and another group judge whether they are inductively strong. If different variables affect deduction versus induction, then this can be seen as evidence for the two-process account. Indeed, Heit and Rotello found that logical validity itself has a greater effect on deduction judgments, whereas more superficial variables such as similarity and the length of an argument (the similarity and numerosity phenomena in Table 39.1) have a greater effect on induction judgments. Furthermore, forcing people to make very fast deduction judgments led these judgments to resemble induction judgments, suggesting that analytic processing had been impaired and heuristic processing had been emphasized. Heit and Rotello implemented a two-dimensional model of reasoning (see Fig. 39.2) that successfully accounted for these results by assuming that deduction and induction rely on differing proportions of two kinds of underlying information, which could be the outputs of analytic and heuristic processes. In comparison, a one-process model, simply assuming a single underlying process for evaluating argument strength, could not account for the results. It appears that by varying instructions as

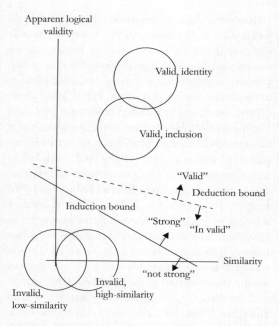

**Figure 39.2** Two-dimensional model of reasoning, showing arguments varying in apparent deductive correctness (y-axis) and similarity information (x-axis). The dotted line shows the decision boundary for judging whether an argument is deductively valid or invalid. The dashed line shows the decision boundary for judging whether an argument is inductively strong or weak. (Adapted from Heit & Rotello, 2010.)

well as speed of responding (see also Shafto et al., 2007), there will be a rich set of results that will be an important test bed for developing and testing models of reasoning.

### Neuroscience of Induction

Technological advances such as functional magnetic resonance imaging (fMRI) have spurred research on the neuroscience of reasoning, with the potential to address important theoretical questions in reasoning research. Researchers use fMRI to measure blood flow related to neural activity in the brain—sampling every few seconds from different positions and producing detailed, three-dimensional images of brain structure and activation (Henson, 2006). Although it seems plausible that induction takes place throughout the brain, given the probabilistic and context-dependent nature of induction, some research has aimed to localize some of the processes involved in induction (and deduction) in regard to particular brain regions. Henson (2006, p. 64) referred to this method as "forward inference," namely "the use of qualitatively different patterns of activity over the brain to distinguish between competing cognitive theories."

Several studies (Goel & Dolan, 2004; Goel, Gold, Kapur, & Houle, 1997; Osherson et al., 1998; Parsons & Osherson, 2001) have compared deductive and inductive reasoning tasks, in an attempt to compare one- and two-process accounts of reasoning. To the extent that qualitatively different patterns of brain activity are observed for deduction versus induction tasks, holding everything else equal between experimental conditions, by forward inference, two-process accounts will be supported over single-process alternatives. Indeed, these four studies found somewhat different patterns of brain activation for deduction versus induction. For example, three (Goel & Dolan, 2004; Goel et al., 1997; Osherson et al., 1998) found increased activation for induction, relative to deduction, in left frontal cortex, although in different regions at a finer level. Overall, these results help make the case for two-process accounts over one-process accounts, although there are still unanswered questions, such as why different brain regions are activated in different induction tasks. (See also Goel, 2009). More generally, as Henson (2006) notes, forward inferences are theory dependent: These are used to contrast the predictions of an opposing pair of theories, but it is always possible that neither theory is correct and that some third theory is the best explanation of the results (see Hayes et al., 2010, for further discussion of neuroscience studies of induction).

## Concluding Comments

Having reviewed some of the highlights from four decades of experimental and developmental research on induction, increasingly sophisticated models, and the newest work on the neuroscience of reasoning, we find ourselves enthusiastic about the progress that has been made. At the same time, we are aware of the limitations of induction research so far. Along with progress on incorporating rich domain knowledge into reasoning, we believe that models of induction need to become broader and more widely applied. One way that research on induction ought to become more ambitious is in terms of the induction task itself. Many of the experiments we have reviewed involved learning that a set of animals has a hidden property and inferring whether other animals have that property. Yet induction is much broader than that. For example, Heit and Nicholson (2010) have suggested that political reasoning is formally equivalent to some already-studied inductive tasks, and that models of induction might also be applied to reasoning by elected officials in terms of which legislation they will support, or decisions by voters

on which candidate to support. Thinking even more broadly, because induction is closely connected to other forms of reasoning, such as deduction (Heit & Rotello, 2010; Heit et al., 2012; Rotello & Heit, 2009), and other cognitive activities, such as categorization, memory, and decision making (Hayes & Newell, 2009; Heit & Hayes, 2005), we pose the question of whether in the future it will be sufficient to focus on induction alone. We suggest that the next generation of theoretical models should be more ambitious, spanning multiple reasoning tasks, such as induction and deduction together, or even multiple cognitive activities, such as induction, categorization, and memory.

## Notes

1. Some readers may be struck by the contrast between the relatively normative way that adults use sample size and information diversity in inductive reasoning and the range of biases that have been revealed in studies of adult probabilistic judgments (see Chapter 38 for a review). One reason for this discrepancy may be that, in contrast to the tasks often used in studies of judgment, the probability information in most induction tasks is relatively straightforward. Novel properties are usually attributed to *all* members of a premise category and interest is focused on factors that cause shifts in the probability that the property will generalize, rather than on whether probability estimates are normative. Some recent studies (e.g., Lawson & Kalish, 2009), however, have begun to examine feature induction involving more complex probabilistic relationships between features, premise and conclusion categories, and how inductive predictions are affected by a reasoners' sampling assumptions.

2. It could be argued that many studies of children's induction (e.g., Gelman & Markman, 1986) are exceptions to this generalization since much of this work has been devoted to examining how children generalize the novel properties of specific exemplars rather than categories.

## References

Allen, S. W., & Brooks, L. R. (1991). Specializing the operation of an explicit rule. *Journal of Experimental Psychology: General, 120,* 3–19.

Anderson, J. R. (1991). The adaptive nature of human categorization. *Psychological Review, 98,* 409–429.

Atran, S., Medin, D. L., &Ross, N. O. (2005). The cultural mind: Environmental decision making and cultural modelling within and across populations. *Psychological Review, 112,* 744–776.

Blok, S. V., Medin, D. L., &Osherson, D. N. (2007). Induction as conditional probability judgement. *Memory and Cognition*, *35*, 1353–1364.

Bloom, P. (1996). Intention, history, and artefact concepts. *Cognition*, *60*, 1–29.

Carey, S. (1985*). Conceptual change in childhood*. Cambridge, MA: Bradford Books.

Casler, K., &Kelemen, D. (2008). Developmental continuity in teleo-functional explanation: Reasoning about nature among Romanian Romani adults. *Journal of Cognition and Development*, *9*, 340–362.

Coley, J. D. (2012). Where the wild things are: Informal experience and ecological reasoning, Child Development, *83*, 992–1006.

Dennis, S., &Humphreys, M. S. (2001). A context noise model of episodic word recognition. *Psychological Review*, *108*, 452–477.

Diesendruck, G., & Ha Levi, H. (2006). The role of language, appearance, and culture in children's social category-based induction. *Child Development*, *77*, 539–553.

Evans, J. S. B. (2007). *Hypothetical thinking: Dual processes in reasoning and judgment*. Hove, England: Psychology Press.

Feeney, A., &Heit, E. (2007) *Inductive reasoning: Experimental, developmental and computational approaches*. New York: Cambridge University Press.

Feeney, A., & Heit, E. (2011). Properties of the diversity effect in category-based inductive reasoning, *17*, 156–181

Gelman, S. A., & Bloom, P. (2007). Developmental changes in the understanding of generics. *Cognition*, *105*, 166–183.

Gelman, S. A., &Markman, E. M. (1986). Categories and induction in young children. *Cognition*, *23*, 186–209.

Gelman, S. A., & O' Reilly, A. W. (1988). Children's inductive inferences within superordinate categories: The role of language and category structure. *Child Development*, *59*, 876–887.

Gelman, S. A., & Waxman, S. R. (2007). Looking beyond looks: Comments on Sloutsky, Kloos, and Fisher (2007). *Psychological Science*, *18*, 554–555.

Goel, V. (2009). Fractionating the system of deductive reasoning. In E. Kraft, B. Guylas, & E. Poppel (Eds.), *Neural correlates of thinking* (pp. 203–218). Berlin: Springer.

Goel, V., & Dolan, R. J. (2004). Differential involvement of left prefrontal cortex in inductive and deductive reasoning. *Cognition*, *93*, B109–B121.

Goel, V., Gold, B., Kapur, S., & Houle, S. (1997). The seats of reason: A localization study of deductive and inductive reasoning using PET (O15) blood flow technique. *NeuroReport*, *8*, 1305–1310.

Hampton, J. A., & Cannon, I. (2004).Category-based induction: An effect of conclusion typicality. *Memory and Cognition*, *32*, 235–243.

Hayes, B. K., &Chen, T. J. (2008). Clinical expertise and reasoning with uncertain categories. *Psychonomic Bulletin and Review*, *15*, 1002–1007.

Hayes, B. K., Heit, E., & Swendsen, H. (2010). Inductive reasoning. *Wiley Interdisciplinary Reviews: Cognitive Science*, *1*, 278–292.

Hayes, B. K., Fritz, K., & Heit, E. (2012). The relationship between memory and inductive reasoning: Does it develop? Develpmental Psychology, Online first, doi:10.1037/ a0028891

Hayes, B. K., McKinnon, R., & Sweller, N. (2008). The development of category-based induction: Re-thinking conclusions from the induction then recognition paradigm. *Developmental Psychology*, *44*, 1430–1444.

Hayes, B. K., &Newell, B. R. (2009). Induction with uncertain categories: When do people consider the category alternatives? *Memory and Cognition*, *37*, 730–743.

Hayes, B. K., &Thompson, S. P. (2007). Causal relation and feature similarity in children's inductive reasoning. *Journal of Experimental Psychology: General*, *136*, 470–484.

Hayes, B. K., & Rehder, B. (2012). The development of causal categorization. *Cognitive Science*, 1102–1128.

Hayes, B. K., Kurniawan, H., & Newell, B. R. (2011). Rich in vitamin C or just a convenient snack? Multiple-category reasoning with cross-classified foods. *Memory and Cognition*, *39*, 92–106.

Heit, E. (1998). A Bayesian analysis of some forms of inductive reasoning. In M. Oaksford & N. Chater (Eds.), *Rational models of cognition* (pp. 248–274). Oxford, England: Oxford University Press.

Heit, E. (2000). Properties of inductive reasoning. *Psychonomic Bulletin and Review*, *7*, 569–592.

Heit, E. (2007). What is induction and why study it? In A. Feeney & E. Heit (Eds.), *Inductive reasoning* (pp. 1–24). Cambridge, England: Cambridge University Press.

Heit, E., &Hahn, U. (2001). Diversity-based reasoning in children. *Cognitive Psychology*, *43*, 243–273.

Heit, E., Hahn, U., & Feeney, A. (2005). Defending diversity. In W. Ahn, R. L. Goldstone, B. C. Love, A. B. Markman, & P. Wolfe (Eds.), *Categorisation inside and outside the laboratory: Essays in honor of Douglas L. Medin* (pp. 87–99). Washington, DC: American Psychological Association.

Heit, E., &Hayes, B. K. (2005). Relations between categorization, induction, recognition and similarity. *Journal of Experimental Psychology: General*, *134*, 596–605.

Heit, E., & Hayes, B.K. (2011). Predicting reasoning from memory. *Journal of Experimental Psychology: General*, *140(1)*, 76–101.

Heit, E., & Nicholson (2010). The opposite of Republican: Polarization and political categorization. *Cognitive Science*, *34(8)*, 1503–1516.

Heit, E., & Rotello, C. (2010). Relations between inductive reasoning and deductive reasoning. *Journal of Experimental Psychology: Learning, Memory, and Cognition*, *36*, 805–812.

Heit, E., & Rotello, C. M. (2012). The pervasive effects of argument length on inductive reasoning. *Thinking & Reasoning* (Special issue on Reasoning and Argumentation), *18*, 244–277.

Heit, E., & Rubinstein, J. (1994). Similarity and property effects in inductive reasoning. *Journal of Experimental Psychology: Learning, Memory, and Cognition*, *20*, 411–422.

Heit, E., Rotello, C., & Hayes, B. K. (2012). Relations between memory and reasoning. In B. L. Ross (Ed.), *The Psychology of Learning and Motivation* (Vol. 57, pp. 57–102). San Diego, CA: Academic Press.

Henson, R. (2006). Forward inference using functional neuroimaging: Dissociations versus associations. *Trends in Cognitive Sciences*, *10*, 64–69.

Johnson-Laird, P. N. (1994). Mental models and probabilistic thinking. *Cognition*, *50*, 189–209.

Kahneman, D., &Tversky, A. (1973). On the psychology of prediction. *Psychological Review*, *80*, 237–251.

Kelemen, D. (1999). The scope of teleological thinking in preschool children. *Cognition*, *70*, 241–272.

Kemp, C., Shafto, P., & Tenenbaum, J. B. (2012). An integrated account of generalization across objects and features. *Cognitive Psychology, 64*, 35–73.

Kemp, C., & Tenenbaum, J. B. (2009). Structured statistical models of inductive reasoning. *Psychological Review, 116*, 20–58.

Kim, N. S., &Keil, F. C. (2003). From symptoms to causes: Diversity effects in diagnostic reasoning. *Memory and Cognition, 31*, 155–165.

Lawson, C. A., & Kalish, C. W. (2009). Sample selection and inductive generalization, *Memory and Cognition, 37*, 596–607.

Lawson, C. A., & Fisher, A. V. (2011). It's in the sample: The effects of sample size and sample diversity on the breadth of inductive generalization. *Journal of Experimental Child Psychology, 110*, 499–519.

Lombrozo, T., &Carey, S. (2006). Functional explanation and the function of explanation. *Cognition, 99*, 167–204.

López, A., Atran, S., Coley, J. D., Medin, D. L., & Smith, E. E. (1997). The tree of life: Universal and cultural features of folkbiological taxonomies and inductions. *Cognitive Psychology, 32*, 251–295.

López, A., Gelman, S. A., Gutheil, G., &Smith, E. E. (1992). The development of category-based induction. *Child Development, 63*, 1070–1090.

Malmberg, K. J. (2008). Recognition memory: A review of the critical findings and an integrated theory for relating them. *Cognitive Psychology, 57*, 335–384.

Markman, A. B., &Ross, B. H. (2003). Category use and category learning. *Psychological Bulletin, 129*, 592–613.

McClelland, J. L. (1998). Connectionist models and Bayesian inference. In M. Oaksford & N. Chater (Eds.), *Rational models of cognition* (pp. 21–53). Oxford, England: Oxford University Press.

Medin, D. L., Coley, J. D., Storms, G., & Hayes, B. K. (2003). A relevance theory of induction. *Psychonomic Bulletin and Review, 10*, 517–532.

Medin, D. L., Goldstone, R. L., & Gentner, D. (1993). Respects for similarity. *Psychological Review, 100*, 254–278.

Medin, D. L., &Ortony, A. (1989). Psychological essentialism. In S. Vosniadou & A. Ortony (Eds.), *Similarity and analogical reasoning* (pp. 179–195). New York: Cambridge University Press.

Murphy, G. L., &Ross, B. H. (1994). Predictions from uncertain categorizations. *Cognitive Psychology, 27*, 148–193.

Murphy, G. L., & Ross, B. H. (1999). Induction with cross-classified categories. *Memory and Cognition, 27*, 1024–1041.

Murphy, G. L., &Ross, B. H. (2010a). Category vs. object knowledge in category-based induction. *Journal of Memory and Language, 63*, 1–17.

Murphy, G. L., &Ross, B. H. (2010b). Uncertainty in category-based induction: When do people integrate across categories? *Journal of Experimental Psychology: Learning, Memory, and Cognition, 36*, 263–276.

Nagel, E. (1939). *Principles of the theory of probability*. Chicago: University of Chicago Press.

Nosofsky, R. M. (1986). Attention, similarity, and the identification-categorization relationship. *Journal of Experimental Psychology: General, 115*, 39–57.

Opfer, J. E., &Bulloch, M. J. (2007). Causal relations drive young children's induction, naming, and categorization. *Cognition, 105*, 206–217.

Osherson, D., Perani, D., Cappa, S., Schnur, T., Grassi. F., & Fazio, F. (1998). Distinct brain loci in deductive versus probabilistic reasoning. *Neuropsychologia, 36*, 369–376.

Osherson, D. N., Smith, E. E., Wilkie, O., &López, A. (1990). Category-based induction. *Psychological Review, 97*, 185–200.

Papadopoulos, C., Hayes, B. K., & Newell, B. (2011). Non-categorical approaches to feature prediction with uncertain categories. *Memory and Cognition, 39(2)*, 304–318.

Parsons, L. M., & Osherson, D. (2001). New evidence for distinct right and left brain systems for deductive versus probabilistic reasoning. *Cerebral Cortex, 11*, 954–965.

Pitt, M. A., Myung, I. J., &Zhang, S. (2002). Toward a method of selecting among computational models of cognition. *Psychological Review, 109*, 472–491.

Proffitt, J. B., Coley, J. D., & Medin, D. L. (2000). Expertise and category-based induction. *Journal of Experimental Psychology: Learning, Memory, and Cognition, 26*, 811–828.

Rehder, B. (2006). When similarity and causality compete in category-based property generalization. *Memory and Cognition, 34*, 3–16.

Rehder, B. (2009). Causal-based property generalization. *Cognitive Science, 33*, 301–343.

Rein, J. R., Goldwater, M. B., &Markman, A. B. (2010). What is typical about the typicality effect in category-based induction? *Memory and Cognition, 38*, 377–388

Rhodes, M., Brickman, D., & Gelman, S. A. (2008). Sample diversity and premise typicality in inductive reasoning: Evidence for developmental change. *Cognition, 108*, 543–556.

Rhodes, M., Gelman, S. A., & Brickman, D. (2009). Children's attention to sample composition in learning, teaching, and discovery. *Developmental Science, 13*, 421–429.

Rips, L. J. (1975). Inductive judgements about natural categories. *Journal of Verbal Learning and Verbal Behavior, 14*, 665–681.

Rips, L. J. (2001). Two kinds of reasoning. *Psychological Science, 12*, 129–134.

Rogers, T. T., &McClelland, J. L. (2004). *Semantic cognition: A parallel distributed processing approach*. Cambridge, MA: MIT Press.

Ross, B. H., &Murphy, G. L. (1996). Category-based predictions: Influence of uncertainty and feature associations. *Journal of Experimental Psychology: Learning, Memory, and Cognition, 22*, 736–753.

Rotello, C. M., & Heit, E. (2009). Modelling the effects of argument length and validity on inductive and deductive reasoning. *Journal of Experimental Psychology: Learning, Memory, and Cognition, 35*, 1317–1330.

Shafto, P., & Coley, J. D. (2003). Development of categorization and reasoning in the natural world: Novices to experts, naive similarity to ecological knowledge. *Journal of Experimental Psychology: Learning, Memory, and Cognition, 29*, 641–649.

Shafto, P., Coley, J. D., & Baldwin, D. (2007). Effects of time pressure on context-sensitive property induction. *Psychonomic Bulletin and Review, 14*, 890–894.

Shafto, P., Coley, J. D., & Vitkin, A. (2007). Availability in category-based induction. In A. Feeney & E. Heit (Eds.), *Inductive reasoning: Experimental, developmental, and computational approaches* (pp. 114–136). New York: Cambridge University Press

Sloman, S. (2005). *Causal models*. New York: Oxford University Press.

Sloman, S. A. (1993). Feature-based induction. *Cognitive Psychology, 25,* 231–280.

Sloman, S. A., & Lagnado, D. A. (2005). The problem of induction. In K. J. Holyoak & R. G. Morrison (Eds.), *The Cambridge handbook of thinking and reasoning* (pp. 95–116). New York: Cambridge University Press.

Sloutsky, V. M., & Fisher, A. V. (2004). Induction and categorization in young children: A similarity-based model. *Journal of Experimental Psychology: General, 133,* 166–188.

Tenenbaum, J. B., & Griffiths, T. L. (2001). Generalization, similarity and Bayesian inference. *Behavioral and Brain Sciences, 24,* 629–640.

Stanovich, K. E. (2009). *What intelligence tests miss: The psychology of rational thought*. New Haven, CT: Yale University Press.

Welder, A. N., &Graham, S. A. (2001). The influences of shape similarity and shared labels on infants' inductive inferences about nonobvious object properties. *Child Development, 72,* 1653–1673.

Xu, F., &Tenenbaum, J. B. (2007). Word learning as Bayesian inference. *Psychological Review, 114,* 245–272.

# Reasoning

Jonathan St B. T. Evans

## Abstract

This chapter covers the traditional study of deductive reasoning together with a change in the paradigm that has occurred in recent years. The traditional method involves asking logically untrained participants to assume the truth of premises and draw logically necessary conclusions. Contrary to initial expectations most people perform quite poorly on these tasks making many logical errors and exhibiting systematic biases. Moreover, reasoning turns out to be highly dependent on content and context. While this work produced a wealth of psychological findings and theories, authors have begun to change their methodological and theoretical approach in order to focus on how people reasoning with uncertain and personal beliefs. Many now consider Bayesiansim to be a more appropriate normative and computational model of reasoning than classical logic. Dual-process theories of reasoning have adapted to this paradigm shift and feature prominently in the current literature.

**Key Words:** deductive reasoning, new paradigm, Bayesianism, dual processes

The psychology of reasoning is usually taken to refer to the tradition of studying deduction. The standard paradigm for this field, which has been with us since the start of the 20th century, is based upon formal logic: Participants are tested for their ability, without formal training, to judge correctly the validity of arguments. There are, of course, other kinds of human inference to be studied, especially inductive and causal reasoning, which are the topics of Chapters 30 and 46 in this volume. Even the deductive reasoning tradition has, however, diversified in recent years to such an extent that many of the researchers in this field have moved away from the traditional paradigm. Many now think of reasoning as probabilistic or pragmatic and have adapted their methods of study as well as their theories to accommodate this change of perspective. Dual-process theories distinguishing fast, intuitive processes from slow, reflective ones have also become popular. The standard paradigm is still used, however, and often adopted when the intention is to engage participants in effortful and difficult reasoning.

The move away from the standard deduction paradigm means the distinction between this tradition and that of studying inductive reasoning appears no longer conceptually clear (but see Evans & Over, in press), at least conceptually. However, the literatures for these traditions remain largely separate, and so I will review work in both the traditional and new paradigms of the psychology of reasoning within this chapter. The simplest way to present this to the reader is to describe first the traditional paradigm, with its aims, methods, theories, and findings. I will then show how the paradigm has been shifting in the past 15 years or so and discuss changes in methods and theories as well as new findings that have emerged as a result.

## The Traditional Paradigm: Deductive Reasoning
### Aims

The psychology of deductive reasoning has a relatively long history with studies published well before World War II (Wilkins, 1928; Woodworth & Sells, 1935). Indeed, these early studies established one of the key methods still in use—syllogistic reasoning—as well as introducing the idea that logical errors are caused by cognitive biases. In more recent times the field has been active since the 1960s (see Wason & Johnson-Laird, 1972) and has gradually expanded up to the present day. In common with the study of decision making, and in contrast with most other fields of cognitive psychology, the study of reasoning has long been associated with an interest in normative rationality. Indeed, the principal aims of the standard paradigm were (a) to establish by experimental observation the extent to which people are competent in logical reasoning and (b) to describe theoretically how naïve participants are able to perform deductive reasoning. As much logical error was observed, an additional objective became (c) to describe the cognitive biases that interfere with the process of logical reasoning.

The qualification to (b) that theories should focus on naïve participants is of key importance. It is standard practice to avoid using participants with training in logic and few studies in the traditional paradigm provide instruction on key logical concepts. This reflects a long philosophical tradition in which it is proposed that logic is the foundation of rational thinking (Henle, 1962) as well as the once very influential claim of Jean Piaget that ordinary people develop sophisticated logical reasoning at the stage of formal operations (Inhelder & Piaget, 1958). Hence, the ability to reason logically should not depend upon any kind of training. The modern psychology of reasoning (from the 1960s onward) was thus founded upon both normative logicism (the belief that logic was the standard for rational thought) and the search for descriptive logicism (the belief that naïve participants reason using logic).

Highly influential in the development of the modern field was the British psychologist Peter Wason, who invented several ingenious tasks for studying reasoning and published extensively on the topic during the 1960s and 1970s. It was principally Wason who founded objective (c)—the study of cognitive biases in reasoning. As I have detailed elsewhere (Evans, 2002), Wason accepted normative logicism while strongly challenging the descriptive logicism of Piaget. In other words, he accepted that people should be logical in their reasoning, while declaring that they were frequently illogical. This suggests that people are irrational, as Wason indeed asserted. However, such arguments were strongly disputed by those convinced that people must be inherently rational and logical (Cohen, 1981; Henle, 1962). While the debate about rationality in reasoning has persisted to the present day, Wason's contribution in establishing evidence of cognitive biases is equally enduring.

## Methods

The principal method for studying deductive reasoning is to ask people to evaluate logical arguments. For example, a syllogism (a simple logical system devised by Aristotle) consists of the two premises and a conclusion, which link together three terms such as:

No A are B.
Some C are B.
Therefore, some A are not C. (1)

In many studies participants have been shown abstract syllogisms like these and asked to decide whether their conclusion necessarily follows from the premises. To my knowledge, however, the only study to have presented every possible syllogism for evaluation is that of Evans, Handley, Harper, and Johnson-Laird (1999). There are many possible syllogisms, as there are four types of statements used (all, no, some, some not) which can be presented in either premises or conclusion, as well as four different arrangements of the terms A, B, and C. The great majority of these are logically invalid, meaning that their conclusions do not necessarily follow. However, the predominant tendency is for participants to say that conclusions do, in fact, follow so that they endorse many fallacies (see Evans, Newstead, & Byrne, 1993). For example, argument 1 is a fallacy, but 63% of participants said that it necessarily followed from the premises in the study of Evans et al. (1999). Syllogistic arguments can also be presented with semantically rich content about which people have prior beliefs, for example:

No millionaires are hard workers.
Some rich people are hard workers.
Therefore, some millionaires are not rich people. (2)

Such content may have a dramatic effect on responding. Although argument 2 has the same logical form as 1, only 10% of participants endorsed its conclusion in the study of Evans, Barston, and Pollard (1983). With this particular content, the fallacy becomes transparent.

The syllogistic method can be varied by presenting only premises and asking participants to draw their own conclusions (e.g., Johnson-Laird & Bara, 1984); we can term this "the production method," as opposed to the standard evaluation method. It turns out that this change can substantially affect the patterns of reasoning observed (Morley, Evans, & Handley, 2004). Evaluation and production methods can also be applied to other types of logical argument, such as those involved in relational and propositional reasoning. A commonly used method to study deduction is that of conditional inference (see Table 40.1). As with syllogisms, these inferences can be presented using the evaluation or production method and with abstract or realistic materials. In the table, I illustrate the evaluation method with abstract materials in the examples. In the deduction paradigm, standard logic is applied so that two of these inferences (MP, MT) are deemed valid and two others (DA, AC) invalid. It is commonly observed that MP is endorsed more frequently than MT, and that both fallacies are often endorsed. As with syllogistic reasoning, therefore, logical accuracy is quite poor for naïve participants.

The other main method used to study deductive competence in this tradition is the Wason selection task (Wason, 1966), although this problem requires hypothesis testing as well as logical reasoning. In a typical abstract form, participants are told that a statement applies to four cards, each of which has a letter on one side and a number on the other side. The statement is as follows:

If a card has an A on one side, then it has a 3 on the other side.

The four cards are shown, but obviously with only the upper side visible as follows:

A  D  3  7

The instruction is then to decide which cards and only which cards need to be turned over in order to decide whether the statement is true or false. The logically correct answer is to choose the A and 7, although only 10%–20% of participants manage to do so, making this an exceptionally hard problem. Typical responses are to choose A and 3, or A alone. Finding a confirming combination on any given card (A and 3) will not prove the statement true of the whole set. Only a falsifying combination (A and not-3) would be decisive. The only two cards that could reveal such a combination are A and 7 (not a 3).

The selection task is also studied in another form, which is both deontic (concerned with rules and regulations) and realistic. An example is the drinking age rule (Griggs & Cox, 1983), an adapted version of which is the following:

You are a police officer watching people drinking in a bar, in order to check whether the following rule is being obeyed:

If a person is drinking beer, then that person must be over 18 years of age.

The following cards represent four drinkers and show on one side the beverage being drunk, and on the side the age:

Beer  Coke  20 years of age  16 years of age

By contrast with the abstract Wason task, this one is very easy to solve. Most people choose to investigate the beer drinker and the underage drinker, who are indeed the only ones who could be breaking the rule.

## Theories

There are many specific theories and models that have been proposed to explain performance on particular deductive reasoning tasks. In this section, I consider only theories framed at the level of the paradigm as a whole. During the 1970s and 1980s two major frameworks emerged to address aim (b):

**Table 40.1** The Four Basic Conditional Inferences, Together With Examples in Typical Abstract Form as Presented to Participants

| Modus Ponens | MP | If p, then q, p; therefore q |
| | | If the letter is A, then the number is 6 |
| | | The letter is A; therefore the number is 6 |
| Denial of the antecedent | DA | If p, then q; not-p therefore not-q |
| | | If the letter is P, then the number is 3 |
| | | The letter is not P; therefore the number is not 3 |
| Affirmation of the consequent | AC | If p, then q; q therefore p |
| | | If the letter is D, then the number is 1 |
| | | The number is 1; therefore the letter is D |
| Modus Tollens | MT | If p, then q; not-q; therefore not-p |
| | | If the letter is J, then the number is 8 |
| | | The number is not 8; therefore the letter is not J |

How can naïve participants engage in deductive reasoning? The first of these is known as the mental logic approach and primarily been applied to conditional reasoning and other forms of propositional inference (Braine & O'Brien, 1998; Rips, 1994). Some methods used by logicians, such as the truth table analysis to be found in standard logic textbooks, are most unlikely to be the basis for human reasoning. Hence, philosophers have suggested that people might have "natural" logics based upon sets of inference rules, an idea first introduced to psychologists by Braine (1978). The various theories of this type have in common the idea that some forms of deductive reasoning are quick, direct, and largely error free, while others are slow, indirect, and error prone. The former occurs where people have direct rules of inference stored in their minds, such as Modus Ponens, which is endorsed almost 100% of the time when presented using the standard method (Evans et al., 1993). The much greater difficulty of the valid Modus Tollens (MT) inference (endorsed about 60% of the time by university students) is attributed to the fact that there is no direct rule in the mental logic. Instead, they suggest that MT requires difficult and indirect reduction and absurdum reasoning. Consider the following:

If there is an A on the card, then there is a 4 on the card.
There is not a 4 on the card.
Therefore, there is not an A on the card.

According to mental logicians, people have no rule of inference in their minds corresponding to this. However, they can solve the problem by a thought experiment of the following kind. Imagine that there is an A on the card. What follows? There must be a 4. But there is not a 4. Hence, the supposition that there is an A must be false. So there cannot be an A on the card, or else we would have a contradiction. This more difficult reasoning is error prone, hence the lower endorsement rate of MT.

An important alternative to this account emerged when Johnson-Laird developed his mental model theory of deduction (Johnson-Laird, 1983; Chapter 41, this volume; Johnson-Laird & Byrne, 1991). Indeed this theory dominated the deduction paradigm up until the mid 1990s and the development of the new paradigm, and it is still influential today. In this account people represent premises and conclusion as mental models. These models are (primarily) semantic, meaning that they represent possible situations in the real world. Hence, they are also truth verifiable so that a particular mental model is either true or false

in the actual world (for a theory based on epistemic mental models, which represent beliefs about the world, see Evans, 2007). The basic mechanism for reasoning with mental models is the following:

1. Formulate a mental model of the premises.
2. Check whether the conclusion is true in the model (or generate a conclusion consistent with the model).
3. Test the putative conclusion by searching for counterexamples to it; that is, seek a mental model that is consistent with the premises but not the conclusion.

Put more simply, the theory proposed that deductive competence is founded not on a set of inferences rules but on a simple semantic principle: An inference is valid if there is no counterexample to it. The theory was originally applied to syllogistic reasoning (Johnson-Laird & Bara, 1984) and later to conditional reasoning (see Johnson-Laird & Byrne, 2002, for the most recent version), as well as a number of other deduction tasks. Unlike the mental logic theory, which had to add on a variety of explanations for logical errors and biases, the possibility for error was built in from the start in the mental models account. For example, it was assumed that reasoning would be limited by working memory capacity and that therefore reasoning with multiple mental models would be error prone. The theory also provided an alternative account of the MP/MT difference to that of the mental logic theory. It was assumed that a conditional, if p then q, was initially represented with only one explicit model: p & q. However, it was also implicit that there might be models consistent with not-p. In the case of MP, the minor premise p eliminates the implicit model, so q follows immediately. In the case of MT, the minor premise not-q leads to no conclusion unless the participant manages to "flesh out" the implicit mental model not-p & not-q. Reasoning with MT is hence more difficult.

In the 1980s, a major debate appeared between mental logic and mental model theorists with numerous claims and counterclaims published in the literature. As later commentators observed, however, the argument was entirely founded within the traditional, deduction paradigm (Evans & Over, 1996; Oaksford & Chater, 1995). Both sides agreed that deductive competence was the key to rational reasoning and that it was of paramount importance to understand the mechanisms by which people achieved it. However strong the disagreement, it was confined to the details of the method by which deductive reasoning was achieved. What this debate also obscured was the extent to which observed reasoning in these tasks was not logical at all: There was extensive evidence emerging that reasoning was both highly content dependent and subject to a whole range of cognitive biases.

Working in the tradition started by Peter Wason, I was more concerned to explain the biases observed in reasoning rather than its supposed logicality (aim (c)). I hence developed the heuristic-analytic (H-A) theory of reasoning. In its original form (Evans, 1989), the theory explained errors and biases as occurring at a heuristic stage that preceded an analytic stage of reasoning. Heuristic processing led to selective representations of problem content, both by selective attention to problem features and retrieval of relevant knowledge from memory. The idea was that biases would occur if logically relevant information was selected out or logically irrelevant information selected in at the heuristic stage. The mechanism of analytic reasoning was unspecified, although I was more sympathetic to the mental model than the mental logic theory. The H-A theory has recently been radically revised (Evans, 2006; 2007) and forms part of the new paradigm described below. A key difference is that cognitive biases are now attributed as much to analytic as heuristic processes. This is because people are inclined to accept the first possibility they consider without systematic consideration of alternatives. One inspiration for this is the observation that the search for the counterexamples stage specified in the mental model theory often fails to materialize (Evans et al., 1999).

The H-A theory falls within a broader category of dual-process theories and accounts that have been around in the psychology of reasoning since the 1970s (Wason & Evans, 1975). These arose originally within the standard paradigm as an attempt to distinguish between processes that underlie logical reasoning from those responsible for cognitive biases often portrayed a kind of conflict (e.g., Evans et al., 1983). I will, however, defer discussion of dual-process theory more generally to the later part of the chapter when we look at the shifting paradigm of more recent research.

Study of content-rich versions of the Wason selection task became very popular during the 1980s and 1990s, involving several authors who did not usually work within the deduction paradigm. As a result, a number of theories were introduced that emphasized domain-specific and content-based mechanisms, in contrast with the traditional emphasis on general-purpose reasoning systems. Cheng and Holyoak (1985) introduced the idea that deontic contexts activate pragmatic reasoning schemas that have been acquired for dealing with situations involving permission and obligation. More controversially, evolutionary psychologists argued that people have innate, modular reasoning systems that apply in particular contexts such as social exchange or hazard avoidance, and reported experiments on the selection task purporting to support these claims (Cosmides, 1989; Fiddick, Cosmides, & Tooby, 2000; Gigerenzer & Hug, 1992). An alternative view presented was that the domain-general pragmatic procedures produce domain-specific effects when applied to particular content (Sperber, Cara, & Girotto, 1995). All of these offered explanations of why some content-rich versions of the selection task are easy to solve but were mutually incompatible and led to several published exchanges between rival camps. However, the collective effect of such content-based theories was clearly a factor in undermining the traditions of the deduction paradigm.

## Findings

The three main tasks studied in the traditional paradigm—syllogistic reasoning, conditional inference, and the Wason selection task—have yielded a wealth of interesting and important findings about human reasoning. None of this is denied by critics of the deduction paradigm: It is simply that these findings seem themselves to undermine its basis. First, there is the finding that logical error rates are very high indeed on these tasks, even though the main participant population tested (university students) is above average in general intelligence. If people were designed to be logical reasoners, how can this be so? The difficulty is exacerbated by the fact that reasoning is shown on these tasks to be highly content and context dependent. But again, logical reasoning requires one to focus on the form of arguments, disregarding their content. These findings also undermined the normative justification for the deduction paradigm. If people, in fact, reason in a pragmatic and probabilistic manner, as the data suggest, then perhaps logic is not as important for real-world reasoning as first thought.

As there are far too many findings to discuss here, I have summarized some of the major ones in Table 40.2. I will, however, discuss some highlights, focusing mostly on the effect of problem content and context. Consider first the finding that realistic versions of the selection task are much easier to solve than the original abstract form. It was originally assumed that

**Table 40.2** Some Key Findings on Human Reasoning With the Deduction Paradigm

| Phenomenon | Description | Key References |
|---|---|---|
| Logical errors | Frequent endorsement of fallacies. Very poor performance on Wason's selection task (WST) and THOG problem | Evans et al. (1993); Manktelow (2012); Stanovich & West (2007), reviews |
| Figural bias in syllogistic reasoning | A preference for choosing conclusions that order terms in a similar manner to the premises | Johnson-Laird & Bara (1984) |
| Heuristic biases in syllogistic reasoning | The tendency to prefer conclusions to syllogisms that match the mood of the premises or to choose on the basis of information value | Woodworth & Sells (1935); Chater & Oaksford (1999) |
| Belief bias in syllogistic reasoning | Tendency to judge believable conclusions as valid and unbelievable conclusions as invalid | Evans et al. (1983); Klauer et al. (2000) |
| Matching bias on the selection task | Preference for cards that share lexical content with conditional statement | Evans (1998, review) |
| Content dependent reasoning on WST | General facilitation with deontic task | Griggs & Cox (1983); Evans & Over (2004, review) |
| Perspective shifts on WST | Cards chosen depend on role cued in scenario | Cosmides (1989); Gigerenzer & Hug (1992); Manktelow & Over (1991) |
| Negation biases in conditional inference | Double negation effects; matching bias when implicit negation is used | Evans & Handley (1999); Schroyens, Schaeken, & d'Ydewalle (2001) |
| Belief effects in conditional inference | Inferences depend upon believability of conditional statement and perceived links between p and q | Cummins et al. (1991); Thompson (1994); Stevenson & Over (1995) |
| Conditional suppression effect | Both valid and invalid conditional inferences may be withdrawn when extra premises are added | Byrne (1989); Byrne, Espino, & Santamaria (1999) |
| Cognitive correlates of reasoning | In general, deductive reasoning accuracy is correlated with intelligence and working memory capacity | Kyllonen & Crystal (1990); Stanovich (2011); Stanovich & West (2000b) |
| Neurological correlates of reasoning | Different brain areas are activated for belief-based materials; evidence for conflict detection and inhibition | Goel & Dolan (2003); Goel (2008, review); De Neys et al. (2008) |

this reflected improved logical reasoning (Wason & Johnson-Laird, 1972) as befits thinking within the traditional, logicist paradigm. In the light of the large amount of research that has taken place since on the selection task (see Evans & Over, 2004, for a recent review), this conclusion is impossible to sustain. Early doubts were raised by the observation that there was no transfer of performance from easy versions like the drinking age problem to subsequently performed abstract tasks (Cox & Griggs, 1982). If the former induces a logical insight, why should it then disappear? It soon became clear that pragmatic cues, based on prior experience, directed people's attention to the relevant cards (e.g., Evans, 1996). Some authors have even suggested that some versions of the deontic selection task require no reasoning at all for their solution (Sperber & Girotto, 2002). However, studies of individual differences show a moderate relation of cognitive ability to success on the deontic selection task, suggesting some kind of reasoning is required. In addition, only participants of very high IQ seem able to solve the abstract selection task (Newstead,

Handley, Harley, Wright, & Farelly, 2004; Stanovich & West, 1998).

The intense interest in the deontic (and content-rich) selection task between the mid-1980s and 1990s led to discovery of some interesting new phenomena. In particular, a number of different authors showed that manipulating scenarios which framed the decision in different ways had a marked effect on card choices. In particular, changing perspective of the person required to check compliance with the rule could result in an opposite pattern of card choices (Cosmides, 1989; Gigerenzer & Hug, 1992; Manktelow & Over, 1991; Politzer & Nguyen-Xuan, 1992). While results were similar, explanations were not. Perspective shifts were variously attributed to pragmatic mechanism, decision-theoretic choices, and innate Darwinian algorithms. To my knowledge, these arguments have never been satisfactorily resolved. However, findings like these certainly helped to undermine the traditional view that performance on reasoning tasks was based on the general logical form of the arguments presented.

There has also been a debate about whether most participants reason at all on the abstract version of the selection task, not including the 10% or so who manage to solve it. Evans and Over (2004) suggested that card choices were entirely caused by heuristics which prompted attention selectively to the cards usually chosen, a conclusion apparently supported by evidence that people attend only to the cards that they select (Ball, Lucas, Miles, & Gale, 2003; Evans, 1996). However, a recent reanalysis of these studies shows that while people attend selectively to cards which "match" the lexical content of the conditional statement, their subsequent decision to choose these cards is strongly affected by their logical status. Together with other evidence (Evans & Ball, 2010; Feeney & Handley, 2000; Handley, Feeney, & Harper, 2002; Lucas & Ball, 2005), it now seems clear that nonsolvers of the abstract selection task are indeed reasoning about hidden values on the cards. But this also leads us to another important conclusion: We cannot use the normative correctness of participants' responding as diagnostic evidence of their engagement in reasoning. The detachment of the definition of analytic reasoning from logical performance is an important aspect of the new paradigm, discussed later.

Content-rich versions of the selection task are usually used to demonstrate facilitation of performance. Given the very low base rate of correct choices on the abstract version, it is hard to see that they could do otherwise. However, the effect of content in another major paradigm, syllogistic

reasoning, appears to be quite the opposite—a major cause of bias in reasoning. The belief bias effect was first discovered by Wilkins (1928), but the modern history dates from the paper of Evans et al. (1983), who established the key phenomena with all relevant controls. The standard method involves presentation of four types of syllogism which differ in their validity as well as the believability of their conclusions: valid-believable, valid-unbelievable, invalid-believable, invalid-unbelievable. Despite clear instructions to reason logically, drawing only necessary conclusions, Evans et al. observed a large belief bias effect, with many more conclusions endorsed with believable than unbelievable conclusions. However, there was an equally large validity effect (valid conclusions preferred) and a belief by logic interaction: more belief bias on invalid arguments. These findings have been replicated many times since and interpreted within the mental model framework (Newstead, Pollard, Evans, & Allen, 1992; Oakhill, Johnson-Laird, & Garnham, 1989). Recently, the belief bias effect has been modeled in detail by Klauer, Musch, and Naumer (2000).

The role of content and context has also been studied within the conditional inference paradigm. In contrast with syllogistic reasoning, it is the belief in the major premises (the conditional statement) rather than the conclusion that seems to be the main factor. People are reluctant to draw inferences from conditional statements that they disbelieve, as many studies have shown. This conditional belief effect is, however, less marked when people are given strong deductive reasoning instructions than when simply asked to judge what follows (George, 1995; Stevenson & Over, 1995; see also Evans, Handley, Neilens, Bacon, & Over, 2010). This is one of many findings that led to a greater interest in dual-process accounts in the recent literature, as it seems that there may be an effortful form of reasoning that can be adopted which is more "logical" and less pragmatic in nature. Like belief bias, this conditional belief effect has been studied with some of the recently developed methodologies that I discuss in the second part of the chapter.

To summarize, research with the standard, deduction paradigm led to the discovery of many systematic logical errors and biases, both in abstract reasoning problems and those with semantically rich content. The use of this paradigm led to the labeling of any systematic deviation from the logically correct choice as a "bias," for example, matching bias and belief bias. However, during the 1990s authors became increasingly uncomfortable with the idea that participants must be poor reasoners, given the real-world intelligence of the human species (e.g. Evans & Over, 1996; Oaksford & Chater, 1994) and hence questioned the assumption that illogical means irrational. This was one of the foundations for the major paradigm shift that I now discuss.

## The Shifting Paradigm

Although some of my colleagues like to talk of the "new" paradigm in the psychology of reasoning, I think that is perhaps a little premature, at least in a strict Kuhnian sense. While there has been much movement away from both the theoretical and methodological constraints of the traditional deductive paradigm, there is as yet no really clear consensus on the alternative. In theoretical terms, there is now much interest in probabilistic and Bayesian models of reasoning, the role of pragmatics in human inference, and the case for dual-process and dual-system theories. The reason that it is difficult to call this a new paradigm is that there is also wide disagreement about the objectives to be followed. Nevertheless, I will follow the same structure as that adopted in the description of the traditional paradigm.

### Aims

Many contemporary reasoning researchers have dispensed with aims of the traditional deductive paradigm, which has received much criticism within the reasoning community (e.g., Evans, 2002; Oaksford & Chater, 1998). In particular, there is a lot less interest in whether people reason logically and a lot less belief that it matters. The major aims pursued in contemporary research seem to be the following: (a) to develop alternative normative systems for human reasoning than that of standard logic, and (b) to develop an accurate descriptive account of the actual processes that underlie human reasoning. In pursuit of (b), many have explored the dual-process approach. The reason that the paradigm is not yet integrated is that while the authors who are vigorously pursuing aim (a), such as Oaksford and Chater (2007), seem less interested in developing a descriptive account, those such as myself who are very interested in (b)—developing descriptive and dual-process accounts—do not necessarily see an important role for normative theory at all (Elqayam & Evans, 2011; Evans, 2007).

### Methods

Reasoning researchers no longer rely simply on asking people to assume premises and draw necessary conclusions from logical arguments, or on traditional variants such as the Wason selection task.

Where people are asked to draw inferences from premises, this may be done pragmatically, without the usual logical instructions and perhaps with an opportunity for people to rate the degree of believability of the conclusions, rather than its validity. Participants may be asked to judge the persuasiveness of arguments or simply to assess the believability of conditional statements and so on. In addition, a number of auxiliary methods have been developed in recent years to attempt to elucidate the nature of the underlying cognitive processes. In common with all other areas of cognitive psychology, neural imaging studies have been employed to trace the activity of different brain areas during reasoning. A number of methods have also been developed for the study of dual processes in reasoning, including instructional manipulations intended to induce more or less effortful reasoning, the use of speeded tasks and concurrent working memory loads to disrupt such reasoning, and the correlation of reasoning performance with individual differences in cognitive ability and cognitive style. I will illustrate the application of each of these methods by discussion of sample studies in due course.

### Theories

The 1990s was a period of major theoretical change in the psychology of reasoning. First, there was a revival of interest in dual-process theory, following the parallel publications of Evans and Over (1996) and Sloman (1996), and incorporation of dual-process theory into the major individual differences research program of Stanovich and West (Stanovich, 1999, 2011; Stanovich & West, 2000b). Such theories distinguish between two kinds of process: fast, automatic, and high capacity (type 1) and slow, effortful, and low capacity (type 2). Stronger forms of dual-process theory attribute these to two distinct cognitive systems that evolved separately (Epstein, 1994; Evans, 2010; Evans & Over, 1996; Reber, 1993; Stanovich, 1999), now usually known as System 1 and 2. Dual-process theories are not confined to the idea that there are two methods of reasoning, but they may also propose two forms of knowledge, two ways of deciding, and a basic distinction between explicit and implicit forms of social knowledge.

Within the standard paradigm, dual-process theories were originally developed to distinguish logical reasoning (type 2) from cognitive biases (type 1). (Attributing these to Systems 1 and 2, respectively, is popular but problematic; see Evans, 2008; Keren & Schul, 2009). This way of thinking has, however, radically changed. It is still considered that slow, effortful type 2 reasoning is generally necessary for solution of logical reasoning problems, but by no means sufficient. While some authors like to describe type 2 reasoning as "rule based," it is not some form of mental logic, as contemporary theories attribute a much wider role to System 2 than simply solving deduction problems. It is more common now to think of type 2 reasoning as that which requires central working memory resources (Evans, 2008), explaining its slow, sequential, limited capacity nature as well as the correlation with individual differences in cognitive ability. However, nothing in this definition implies that type 2 processes necessarily conform to logic or any other normative system. Type 2 processes can be the cause of biases (Evans, 2007; Stanovich, 2011), and type 1 processes can cue normatively correct answers, when the pragmatic cues align with the logical structure (e.g., Stanovich & West, 1998). Nor is it any longer deemed that type 1 processes are sensitive to context and prior belief, while type 2 processes are abstract. It now appears that both kinds of processing can be influenced by beliefs, albeit in a different way (Verschueren, Schaeken, & d'Ydewalle, 2005; Weidenfeld, Oberauer, & Hornig, 2005).

The 1990s also saw the emergence of the rational analysis program of Oaksford and Chater (1998). They attacked logicism and argued for alternative accounts of several reasoning tasks that recast participants' choices as rational. Examples include the proposal that card choices on the selection task are designed to maximize information about categories (Oaksford & Chater, 1994), the probability heuristics model of syllogistic reasoning (Chater & Oaksford, 1999), and the proposal that conditional inferences align with the conditional probability of the conclusion given the minor premise (Oaksford, Chater, & Larkin, 2000). Recently, these authors have integrated these various accounts within a general Bayesian framework (Oaksford & Chater, 2007). It is this program that primarily addresses objective (a) of the new paradigm, as they insist that it is important to replace logic with an alternative normative standard to logic.

My colleagues and I, by contrast, have primarily pursued the objective of finding an accurate description of human reasoning and one that integrates it more broadly with decision making. The new framework incorporates a form of dual-process theory and is known as hypothetical thinking theory or HTT (Evans, 2007; Evans, Over, & Handley, 2003). The general theory proposes that people conduct mental simulations to examine possibilities in both reasoning and decision making constrained by three principles: (1) singularity (only one possibility or mental model is considered at a time), (2) relevance (that which is most plausible or pragmatically cued by the context), and (3) satisficing (current model is accepted as the basis for inference or action unless there is good reason to give it up). The process model for HTT combines type 1 and 2 processes within a category of dual-process models described as "default-interventionist" (Evans, 2008). That is, rapid type 1 processes propose default intuitive responses that may or may not be intervened upon by type 2 processing (similar processing assumptions are made by Stanovich, 2011, and by Kahneman & Frederick, 2002).

A particular instantiation of HTT is the suppositional theory of conditionals (Evans & Over, 2004; Evans, Handley, & Over, 2003, 2005), which is strongly indicative of the paradigm shift in the psychology of reasoning. Whereas the mental logic and mental model accounts of conditional inference involve modified versions of the standard propositional calculus of logic, the suppositional theory is inspired by probability logic and the proposal of non-truth functional conditionals by philosophical logicians (Adams, 1998; Edgington, 1995). However, our purpose was to develop a psychologically plausible theory of ordinary conditionals, rather than to propose an alternative normative system. Inspired by philosophical discussions of the Ramsey test (Edgington, 1995), we suggested that ordinary conditionals are used by speakers to provoke mental simulations or thought experiments in the listener. The suppositional conditional is not the material conditional of standard logic and cannot be expressed by the disjunction "either not-p or q." Consider the following conditional:

If the US economy recovers, then Obama will be re-elected. (3)

If this were a material conditional, as in logic textbooks, then it would mean the same as

Either the US economy does not recover or Obama will be re-elected. (4)

Statement 4 is clearly true if the economy does not recover or if Obama is reelected. Surely, we would not say the same about 3! According to the suppositional theory of conditionals, deciding the truth of an ordinary conditional like 3 requires a mental simulation of a supposition. We have to imagine a world in which the US economy does recover and use our knowledge of economics and politics to decide the likelihood that Obama will be reelected. If that probability is high, we will find the conditional statement believable. If we think that there is no chance of the economy recovering in time, we would consider 3 to be irrelevant, rather than true.

## Findings

One of the new methods to have been applied to the psychology of reasoning in recent years is neural imaging by functional magnetic resonance imaging (fMRI) and other methods. Anyone hoping to find an organ in the brain that functions as a mental logic across the various tasks would be disappointed by the findings. In fact, a wide variety of brain regions have been shown to be active in different experiments on reasoning, with no common area consistently present across studies (Goel, 2008). However, several findings are broadly supportive of the dual-process theory. It appears that the brain detects conflict when type 1 and 2 processing would lead to different answers, signaled by activation of the anterior cingulate cortex. Only when the default response is overridden by reasoning, however, does a different region, in the right lateral prefrontal cortex, "light up" (De Neys, Vartanian, & Goel, 2008; Goel & Dolan, 2003; Tsujii & Watanabee, 2009). It should be noted, however, that research using these methods is in its infancy as compared with the extensive application of neuroscience methods in other fields of cognitive psychology.

In recent years, interest in the selection task has waned. The study of conditional inference has been the dominant method, with particular interest in the pragmatic factors that influence reasoning with and interpretation of statements with realistic content. There has been particular interest in causal conditionals, in which p represents a cause and q an effect, as well as in a range of "utility" conditionals (Bonnefon, 2009), which include those used as advice, inducement, and persuasion. In the case of causal conditionals, there is established work (Cummins, Lubart, Alksnis, & Rist, 1991; Thompson, 1994, 2000) showing that beliefs that participants hold about the relations between p and q strongly influence their tendency to endorse all four forms of conditional inference shown in Table 40.1, even if strict deductive reasoning instructions are employed. One way that this can happen, consistent with the mental model theory, is that people retrieve counterexamples from memory which may lead them, by explicit reasoning, to inhibit an

inference they might otherwise make. For example, the Modus Ponens inference might be resisted for a conditional such as "If the ignition key is turned, then the engine will start" because the participant recalls a case where she had a flat battery in her car (a type 2 process). On the other hand, the inference will probably be endorsed if the participant goes on associative strength or conditional probability (type 1) as engines do start most times that the key is turned. There is now evidence that beliefs can influence these inferences in each of these ways (Verschueren et al., 2005; Weidenfeld et al., 2005).

When people reason in the type 2 manner using counterexamples, it appears that the validity of the inference is relevant. A recent finding is that participants of higher working memory capacity are more able to retrieve counterexamples to all four kinds of conditional inference than those of lower capacity, but that they inhibit these when they would result in the withholding of a valid, rather than fallacious inference (De Neys, Schaeken, & d'Ydewalle, 2005a, 2005b). The reason is that higher ability participants make more effort to reason deductively in compliance with the instructions set (Newstead et al., 2004). However, the inhibition of beliefs in causal conditional reasoning by higher ability participants occurs only when they are given strict deductive rather than pragmatic reasoning instructions (Evans et al., 2010). This is consistent with contemporary dual-process theory (e.g., Stanovich, 2011). The ability to engage in effective reasoning in compliance with instructions requires both a sufficient level of cognitive ability and a disposition to reason in an analytic and effortful manner.

Recent studies of utility conditionals illustrate the diversification of methods within new paradigm studies of reasoning. Thompson, Evans, and Handley (2005) looked at conditional persuasions and dissuasions, also known as consequential conditionals. These are statements used in argumentation to persuade people of a point of view, rather than directly to cause an action. Such conditionals are often used by politicians, for example, "If the UK builds more nuclear power stations, then carbon emissions will be reduced." The assumption here is that reducing carbon emissions is a good thing, due to global warming fears, and that therefore building nuclear power stations is a good thing, too. Opponents of nuclear power would draw our attention to other, negative consequences, such as the problems of disposing of radioactive waste. Thompson et al. studied such statements using a wide variety of methods, not just conditional inference. Participants were, for example, quite easily able to infer the motives of the speaker, and to judge the inferences they intended the listener to draw, even when their own actual inferences were quite different. In studies such as these, conditionals are studied as illocutionary acts of communication, intended to influence the beliefs and actions of the listener. This is far removed from older studies that tested the people's ability to understand the logic of conditional statements, based on material implication.

A major class of utility conditionals is inducements (promises, threats) and advice (tips, warnings). One finding is that people draw more conditional inferences, of all four kinds (Table 40.1), with inducements than with advice statements (Newstead, Ellis, Evans, & Dennis, 1997). This was later shown to be due to the fact with the former, participants believe the speaker to be more in control of the consequence (Evans & Twyman-Musgrove, 1998). From the viewpoint of the suppositional conditional theory, this means that P(q|p) is higher. So this is another case where the degree of belief in a conditional statement influences the extent to which people draw inferences from it. If instead we ask people to rate the extent to which conditional advice is useful and likely to be heeded, or the extent to which conditional inducements will be effective, we find again that P(q|p) is a significant factor (Evans, Neilens, Handley, & Over, 2008). However, such judgements are also influenced by the costs and benefits associated with both actions and consequences. For example, advice is judged to be good when the cost of p is low, the benefit of q is high, and the likelihood that p leads to q is high.

In direct support of the suppositional and other probabilistic theories of conditionals, recent studies have shown that most people do indeed judge the probability of a conditional statement if p then q, on the basis of the conditional probability, P(q|p), whether the statements are abstract (Evans, Handley, & Over, 2003; Oberauer & Wilhelm, 2003) or realistic (Evans et al., 2010; Over, Hadjichristidis, Evans, Handley, & Sloman, 2007). However, the results are not quite straightforward. A sizeable minority instead assign the probability of the conditional statements as the conjunctive probability, P(p&q). It turns out that this is related to cognitive ability: Participants of higher IQ are more suppositional. They are both more likely to give P(q|p) as the probability of if p then q, and also to assign defective truth tables in which not-p cases are described as irrelevant (Evans, Handley, Neilens, & Over, 2007; Evans et al., 2010; Oberauer, Geiger, Fischer, & Weidenfeld, 2007). Barrouillet, Gauffroy, and Lecas (2008) have linked these findings with developmental trends, in which children are progressively more likely to interpret conditionals in terms of both conditional probability and defective truth tables as they grow older. This apparently conflicts with the account of the defective truth table given by Johnson-Laird and Byrne (2002). They suggest that people overlook the relevance of not-p cases as they fail to flesh out these implicit possibilities. But this should be more likely to occur in those with lower rather than higher working memory capacity. Recently, Johnson-Laird (2010) has offered an explanation of the conditional probability finding and other results in the suppositional conditional research programme within his own framework. The suppositional theory has also been critiqued on the basis of modeling conditional inference rates by Oberauer (2006).

While I have focused here on findings with conditional inference, it should be noted that the new paradigm has also freed reasoning researchers to work on any task which is informative about the cognitive processes that interest them. It is now common for reasoning researchers to make direct theoretical links with tasks on decision making and statistical inference, often studying these alongside traditional reasoning tasks (for examples, see De Neys & Glumicic, 2008; Evans, 2007; Stanovich & West, 2008b). Some have branched out into the study of informal reasoning and argumentation, which further blurs the distinction between this tradition and the study of inductive inference (Hahn & Oaksford, 2007; Stanovich & West, 2007, 2008a).

As has been mentioned several times, contemporary researchers quite commonly use measures of individual differences as either the main factor of interest or as an additional variable. Some researchers use SAT scores, some IQ tests and others measures of working memory capacity, but it makes little difference as all are highly correlated with one another (Colom, Rebollo, Palacios, Juan-Espinosa, & Kyllonen, 2004). The study of individual differences in cognitive ability and cognitive style was introduced by Stanovich and West (Stanovich, 1999; Stanovich & West, 2000a) during the 1990s initially with the conclusion that higher ability participants were more able to find normatively correct solutions to reasoning and decision problems. This perhaps led to the unfortunate conclusion that type 1 processes are responsible for biases and type 2 processes for abstract, normative reasoning. However, we know that both kinds of processing can causes biases (Evans, 2007), and it is now clear that higher cognitive ability fails to protect people from a range of cognitive biases (Stanovich & West, 2008a, 2008b). There are also some paradoxical findings as yet unexplained. For example, higher ability participants are better at Modus Ponens reasoning (considered rapid and automatic) and no better (or possibly worse) at solving Modus Tollens (a difficult and effortful inference) (Evans et al., 2007; Newstead et al., 2004). From the perspective of dual-process theory, this seems to be the wrong way around.

## Conclusions

While the psychology of reasoning has its roots in the study of deduction, it is quite clear that the paradigm has been shifting significantly away from interest in logical reasoning in the past 15 years or so. What we inherit from the study of deductive reasoning is substantial, if paradoxical: an understanding that human reasoning is *not*, in fact, well adapted to dealing with abstract, logical problems. Only participants of high cognitive ability fare at all well with these, and even they are still subject to a range of cognitive biases. Studies within the traditional paradigm showed that reasoning was highly dependent upon content and context (see Table 40.2). While such findings were originally interpreted as showing that people's efforts to reason deductively were subject to biasing influence of knowledge, that perspective has shifted with the paradigm. The new perspective is that people have reasoning systems designed to deal with the pragmatically rich and uncertain nature of the real world, rather than with logical abstractions. Thus, reasoning on the traditional tasks is more "rational" than was previously assumed. At the same time, there is little sense in confining the study of human reasoning to tasks that require people to disregard their beliefs and draw necessary conclusions from arbitrary premises.

While dual-process theories developed during the period of traditional study, their interpretation has been updated with the paradigm shift. Originally, type 1 processing was seen as contextually dependent and the cause of cognitive biases while type 2 processing was seen as abstract and logical, responsible for normative solutions. This is clearly wrong as both kinds of processing may be influenced by context, either may lead to biases, and either may also lead to normatively correct solutions. The only sensible basis for a dual-process theory now seems to be that type 1 processes are rapid and automatic leading to default judgements and inferences, while type 2 processes are slow and effortful, capable of intervening upon these default responses (Evans & Stanovich, in press). Most researchers implicitly or explicitly define type 2 processing by the involvement of working memory. From this assumption, the main methodologies for studying dual processes arise: Type 2 processes are expected selectively to correlate with individual differences in cognitive ability and selectively to be disrupted by concurrent working memory loads or speeded tasks. There is also current interest in dispositional and situational factors that might encourage type 2 processing, including cognitive style, instructional set, and feelings of confidence (Shynkarkuk & Thompson, 2006; Stanovich, 2011; Thompson, 2009; Thompson, Prowse Turner, & Pennycook, 2011).

While the shift away from the traditional deductive paradigm has liberated reasoning researchers in both their theories and their methods, it is not entirely clear what the new paradigm is that replaces it. While some authors think it is important to construct an alternative normative model to that of logic to define human reasoning as right or wrong, others see this as unnecessary or undesirable. The new methods, which involve studying reasoning in a pragmatic and probabilistic way, as well as making direct judgements of belief, probability, or argument strength clearly blur the boundaries with other distinct traditions, such as the study of inductive reasoning, argumentation, or persuasion. At the same time, things are not yet fully joined up, as cross-references to these alternative traditions are few and far between. However, explicit linkage with studies of statistical reasoning and decision making is now common and much to be welcomed.

## Future Directions

1. While the paradigm for the psychology of reasoning has clearly shifted away from logic and the traditional deduction paradigm, the rationality debate that engulfed the field in the 1980s is still to be resolved. Do we need an alternative normative framework for the psychology of reasoning, or should we simply focus on descriptive accounts?

2. The description of reasoning in the new paradigm appears to blur the distinction between induction and deduction. Should inheritors of the deductive tradition make more effort to integrate their work with paradigms (such as category-based induction, rule learning, and causal inference) traditionally studied in separate literature on inductive reasoning?

3. Dual-process theories that are conceptually similar to those in the psychology of reasoning have been investigated for many years

within social psychology, in largely separated literatures (see Evans, 2008). Such theories are also attracting interest from other cognitive scientists and philosophers of mind (see the recent collection of papers edited by Evans & Frankish, 2009). There is much work to be done in integrating these literatures and placing dual-process theory within a cognitive architecture for the mind as a whole.

4. Neural imaging and neuropsychological methods have been quite sparingly applied in the psychology of reasoning so far, compared with their extensive use in cognitive psychology generally. We can expect to see a large expansion in this enterprise in the near future.

5. Research within the past two decades has indicated that the ability to engage in effective analytic reasoning is related to cognitive ability, rational thinking dispositions, and a range of situational variables. The practical implications of these findings, for example, in education, are yet to be worked out in detail.

## Acknowledgments

I would like to thank Shira Elqayam for a detailed critical reading of an earlier draft of this chapter.

## References

Adams, E. (1998). *A primer of probability logic*. Stanford, CA: CLSI publications.

Ball, L. J., Lucas, E. J., Miles, J. N. V., & Gale, A. G. (2003). Inspection times and the selection task: What do eye-movements reveal about relevance effects? *Quarterly Journal of Experimental Psychology, 56A*, 1053–1077.

Barrouillet, P., Gauffroy, C., & Lecas, J. F. (2008). Mental models and the suppositional account of conditionals. *Psychological Review, 115*, 760–772.

Bonnefon, J. B. (2009). A theory of utility conditionals: Paralogical reasoning from decision-theoretic leakage. *Psychological Review, 118*, 888–907.

Braine, M. D. S. (1978). On the relation between the natural logic of reasoning and standard logic. *Psychological Review, 85*, 1–21.

Braine, M. D. S., & O'Brien, D. P. *(Eds.)*. (1998). *Mental logic*. Mahwah, NJ: Erlbaum.

Byrne, R. M. J. (1989). Suppressing valid inferences with conditionals. *Cognition, 31*, 61–83.

Byrne, R. M. J., Espino, O., & Santamaria, C. (1999). Counterexamples and the suppression of inferences. *Journal of Memory and Language, 40*, 347–373.

Chater, N., & Oaksford, M. (1999). The probability heuristics model of syllogistic reasoning. *Cognitive Psychology, 38*, 191–258.

Cheng, P. W., & Holyoak, K. J. (1985). Pragmatic reasoning schemas. *Cognitive Psychology, 17*, 391–416.

Cohen, L. J. (1981). Can human irrationality be experimentally demonstrated? *Behavioral and Brain Sciences, 4*, 317–370.

Colom, R., Rebollo, I., Palacios, A., Juan-Espinosa, M., & Kyllonen, P. C. (2004). Working memory is (almost) perfectly predicted by g. *Intelligence, 32*, 277–296.

Cosmides, L. (1989). The logic of social exchange: Has natural selection shaped how humans reason? *Cognition, 31*, 187–276.

Cox, J. R., & Griggs, R. A. (1982). The effects of experience on performance in Wason's selection task. *Memory and Cognition, 10*, 496–502.

Cummins, D. D., Lubart, T., Alksnis, O., & Rist, R. (1991). Conditional reasoning and causation. *Memory and Cognition, 19*, 274–282.

De Neys, W., & Glumicic, T. (2008). Conflict monitoring in dual process theories of thinking. *Cognition, 106*, 1248–1299.

De Neys, W., Schaeken, W., & d'Ydewalle, G. (2005a). Working memory and counterexample retrieval for causal conditionals. *Thinking and Reasoning, 11*, 123–150.

De Neys, W., Schaeken, W., & d'Ydewalle, G. (2005b). Working memory and everyday conditional reasoning: Retrieval and inhibition of stored counterexamples. *Thinking and Reasoning, 11*, 349–381.

De Neys, W., Vartanian, O., & Goel, V. (2008). Smarter than we think: When our brains detect that we are biased. *Psychological Science, 19*, 483–489.

Edgington, D. (1995). On conditionals. *Mind, 104*, 235–329.

Elqayam, S., & Evans, J. St. B. T. (2011). Subtracting 'ought from 'is': Descriptivism versus normativism in the study of human thinking. *Behavioral and Brain Sciences, 34,* 233–290.

Epstein, S. (1994). Integration of the cognitive and psychodynamic unconscious. *American Psychologist, 49*, 709–724.

Evans, J. St. B. T. (1989). *Bias in human reasoning: Causes and consequences*. Hove, UK: Erlbaum.

Evans, J. St. B. T. (1996). Deciding before you think: Relevance and reasoning in the selection task. *British Journal of Psychology, 87*, 223–240.

Evans, J. St. B. T. (1998). Matching bias in conditional reasoning: Do we understand it after 25 years? *Thinking and Reasoning, 4*, 45–82.

Evans, J. St. B. T. (2002). Logic and human reasoning: An assessment of the deduction paradigm. *Psychological Bulletin, 128*, 978–996.

Evans, J. St. B. T. (2006). The heuristic-analytic theory of reasoning: Extension and evaluation. *Psychonomic Bulletin and Review, 13*, 378–395.

Evans, J. St. B. T. (2007). *Hypothetical thinking: Dual processes in reasoning and judgement*. Hove, England: Psychology Press.

Evans, J. St. B. T. (2008). Dual-processing accounts of reasoning, judgment and social cognition. *Annual Review of Psychology, 59*, 255–278.

Evans, J. St. B. T. (2010). *Thinking twice: Two minds in one brain*. Oxford, England: Oxford University Press.

Evans, J. St. B. T., & Ball, L. J. (2010). Do people reason on the Wason selection task: A new look at the data of Ball et al. (2003). *Quarterly Journal of Experimental Psychology, 63*, 434–441.

Evans, J. St. B. T., Barston, J. L., & Pollard, P. (1983). On the conflict between logic and belief in syllogistic reasoning. *Memory and Cognition, 11*, 295–306.

Evans, J. St. B. T., & Frankish, K. *(Eds.)*. (2009). *In two minds: Dual processes and beyond*. Oxford, England: Oxford University Press.

Evans, J. St. B. T., Handley, S., Neilens, H., Bacon, A. M., & Over, D. E. (2010). The influence of cognitive ability and instructional set on causal conditional inference. *Quarterly Journal of Experimental Psychology, 63*, 892–909.

Evans, J. St. B. T., Handley, S., Neilens, H., & Over, D. E. (2007). Thinking about conditionals: A study of individual differences. *Memory and Cognition, 35*, 1772–1784.

Evans, J. St. B. T., Handley, S. J., Harper, C., & Johnson-Laird, P. N. (1999). Reasoning about necessity and possibility: A test of the mental model theory of deduction. *Journal of Experimental Psychology: Learning, Memory, and Cognition, 25*, 1495–1513.

Evans, J. St. B. T., Handley, S. J., & Over, D. E. (2003). Conditionals and conditional probability. *Journal of Experimental Psychology: Learning, Memory, and Cognition, 29*, 321–355.

Evans, J. St. B. T., Neilens, H., Handley, S., & Over, D. E. (2008). When can we say "if"? *Cognition, 108*, 100–116.

Evans, J. St. B. T., Newstead, S. E., & Byrne, R. M. J. (1993). *Human reasoning: The psychology of deduction.* Hove, England: Erlbaum.

Evans, J. St. B. T., & Over, D. E. (1996). *Rationality and reasoning.* Hove, England: Psychology Press.

Evans, J. St. B. T., & Over, D. E. (2004). *If.* Oxford, England: Oxford University Press.

Evans, J. St .B. T., & Over, D. E. (in press). Reasoning to and from belief: Deduction and induction are still distinct. *Thinking & Reasoning.*

Evans, J. St. B. T., Over, D. E., & Handley, S. J. (2003). A theory of hypothetical thinking. In D. Hardman & L. Maachi (Eds.), *Thinking: Psychological perspectives on reasoning, judgement and decision making* (pp. 3–22). Chichester, England: Wiley.

Evans, J. St. B. T., Over, D. E., & Handley, S. J. (2005). Supposition, extensionality and conditionals: A critique of Johnson-Laird & Byrne (2002). *Psychological Review, 112*, 1040–1052.

Evans, J. St. B. T., & Stanovich, K. E. (in press). Dual process theories of higher cognition: Advancing the debate. *Perspectives on psychological science.*

Evans, J. St. B. T., & Twyman-Musgrove, J. (1998). Conditional reasoning with inducements and advice. *Cognition, 69*, B11–B16.

Feeney, A., & Handley, S. J. (2000). The suppression of q card selections: Evidence for deductive inference in Wason's selection task. *Quarterly Journal of Experimental Psychology, 53A*, 1224–1243.

Fiddick, L., Cosmides, L., & Tooby, J. (2000). No interpretation without representation: The role of domain-specific representations and inferences in the Wason selection task. *Cognition, 77*, 1–79.

George, C. (1995). The endorsement of the premises: Assumption-based or belief-based reasoning. *British Journal of Psychology, 86*, 93–111.

Gigerenzer, G., & Hug, K. (1992). Domain-specific reasoning: Social contracts, cheating and perspective change. *Cognition, 43*, 127–171.

Goel, V. (2008). Anatomy of deductive reasoning. *Trends in Cognitive Sciences, 11*, 435–441.

Goel, V., & Dolan, R. J. (2003). Explaining modulation of reasoning by belief. *Cognition, 87*, B11–B22.

Griggs, R. A., & Cox, J. R. (1983). The effects of problem content and negation on Wason's selection task. *Quarterly Journal of Experimental Psychology, 35A*, 519–533.

Hahn, U., & Oaksford, M. (2007). The rationality of informal argumentation: A Bayesian approach to reasoning fallacies. *Psychological Review, 114*, 704–732.

Handley, S. J., Feeney, A., & Harper, C. (2002). Alternative antecedents, probabilities and the suppression of fallacies on Wason's selection task. *Quarterly Journal of Experimental Psychology, 55A*, 799–813.

Henle, M. (1962). On the relation between logic and thinking. *Psychological Review, 69*, 366–378.

Inhelder, B., & Piaget, J. (1958). *The growth of logical thinking.* New York: Basic Books.

Johnson-Laird, P. N. (1983). *Mental models.* Cambridge, England: Cambridge University Press.

Johnson-Laird, P. N. (2010). The truth about conditionals. In K. I. Manktelow, D. E. Over, & S. Elqayam (Eds.), *The science of reason: A Festschrift for Jonathan St B T Evans* (pp. 119–144). Hove, England: Psychology Press.

Johnson-Laird, P. N., & Bara, B. G. (1984). Syllogistic inference. *Cognition, 16*, 1–61.

Johnson-Laird, P. N., & Byrne, R. M. J. (1991). *Deduction.* Hove, England & London: Erlbaum.

Johnson-Laird, P. N., & Byrne, R. M. J. (2002). Conditionals: A theory of meaning, pragmatics and inference. *Psychological Review, 109*, 646–678.

Kahneman, D., & Frederick, S. (2002). Representativeness revisited: Attribute substitution in intuitive judgement. In T.Gilovich, D. Griffin, & D. Kahneman (Eds.), *Heuristics and biases: The psychology of intuitive judgment* (pp. 49–81). Cambridge: Cambridge University Press.

Keren, G., & Schul, Y. (2009). Two is not always better than one: A critical evaluation of two-system theories. *Perspectives on Psychological Science, 4*, 533–550.

Klauer, K. C., Musch, J., & Naumer, B. (2000). On belief bias in syllogistic reasoning. *Psychological Review, 107*, 852–884.

Kyllonen, P., & Christal, R. E. (1990). Reasoning ability is (little more than) working memory capacity!? *Intelligence, 14*, 389–433.

Lucas, E. J., & Ball, L. J. (2005). Think-aloud protocols and the selection task: Evidence for relevance effects and rationalisation processes. *Thinking and Reasoning, 11*, 35–66.

Manktelow, K. I. (1999). *Reasoning and thinking.* Hove, England: Psychology Press.

Manktelow, K. I. (2012). *Thinking and reasoning.* Hove, UK: Psychology Press.

Manktelow, K. I., & Over, D. E. (1991). Social roles and utilities in reasoning with deontic conditionals. *Cognition, 39*, 85–105.

Morley, N. J., Evans, J. St. B. T., & Handley, S. J. (2004). Belief bias and figural bias in syllogistic reasoning. *Quarterly Journal of Experimental Psychology, 57*, 666–692.

Newstead, S. E., Ellis, C., Evans, J. St. B. T., & Dennis, I. (1997). Conditional reasoning with realistic material. *Thinking and Reasoning, 3*, 49–76.

Newstead, S. E., Handley, S. J., Harley, C., Wright, H., & Farelly, D. (2004). Individual differences in deductive reasoning. *Quarterly Journal of Experimental Psychology, 57A*, 33–60.

Newstead, S. E., Pollard, P., Evans, J. St. B. T., & Allen, J. L. (1992). The source of belief bias effects in syllogistic reasoning. *Cognition, 45*, 257–284.

Oakhill, J., Johnson-Laird, P. N., & Garnham, A. (1989). Believability and syllogistic reasoning. *Cognition, 31*, 117–140.

Oaksford, M., & Chater, N. (1994). A rational analysis of the selection task as optimal data selection. *Psychological Review, 101*, 608–631.

Oaksford, M., & Chater, N. (1995). Theories of reasoning and the computational explanation of everyday inference. *Thinking and Reasoning, 1*, 121–152.

Oaksford, M., & Chater, N. (1998). *Rationality in an uncertain world*. Hove, England: Psychology Press.

Oaksford, M., & Chater, N. (2007). *Bayesian rationality*. Oxford, England: Oxford University Press.

Oaksford, M., Chater, N., & Larkin, J. (2000). Probabilities and polarity biases in conditional inference. *Journal of Experimental Psychology: Learning, Memory, and Cognition, 26*, 883–889.

Oberauer, K. (2006). Reasoning with conditionals: A test of the formal models of four theories. *Cognitive Psychology, 53*, 238–283.

Oberauer, K., Geiger, S. M., Fischer, K., & Weidenfeld, A. (2007). Two meanings of "If": Individual differences in the interpretation of conditionals. *Quarterly Journal of Experimental Psychology, 60*, 790–819.

Oberauer, K., & Wilhelm, O. (2003). The meaning(s) of conditionals: Conditional probabilities, mental models and personal utilities. *Journal of Experimental Psychology: Learning, Memory, and Cognition, 29*, 680–693.

Over, D. E., Hadjichristidis, C., Evans, J. St. B. T., Handley, S. J., & Sloman, S. A. (2007). The probability of causal conditionals. *Cognitive Psychology, 54*, 62–97.

Politzer, G., & Nguyen-Xuan, A. (1992). Reasoning about conditional promises and warnings: Darwinian algorithms, mental models, relevance judgements or pragmatic schemas? *Quarterly Journal of Experimental Psychology, 44*, 401–412.

Reber, A. S. (1993). *Implicit learning and tacit knowledge*. Oxford, England: Oxford University Press.

Rips, L. J. (1994). *The psychology of proof*. Cambridge, MA: MIT Press.

Schroyens, W., Schaeken, W., & d'Ydewalle, G. (2001). The processing of negations in conditional reasoning: A meta-analytic study in mental models and/or mental logic theory. *Thinking and Reasoning, 7*, 121–172.

Shynkarkuk, J. M., & Thompson, V. A. (2006). Confidence and accuracy in deductive reasoning. *Memory and Cognition, 34*, 619–632.

Sloman, S. A. (1996). The empirical case for two systems of reasoning. *Psychological Bulletin, 119*, 3–22.

Sperber, D., Cara, F., & Girotto, V. (1995). Relevance theory explains the selection task. *Cognition, 57*, 31–95.

Sperber, D., & Girotto, V. (2002). Use or misuse of the selection task? Rejoinder to Fiddick, Cosmides and Tooby. *Cognition, 85*, 277–290.

Stanovich, K. E. (1999). *Who is rational? Studies of individual differences in reasoning*. Mahwah, NJ: Elrbaum.

Stanovich, K. E. (2011). *Rationality and the reflective mind*. New York: Oxford University Press.

Stanovich, K. E., & West, R. F. (1998). Cognitive ability and variation in selection task performance. *Thinking and Reasoning, 4*, 193–230.

Stanovich, K. E., & West, R. F. (2000a). Advancing the rationality debate. *Behavioral and Brain Sciences, 23*, 701–726.

Stanovich, K. E., & West, R. F. (2000b). Individual differences in reasoning: Implications for the rationality debate. *Behavioral and Brain Sciences, 23*, 645–726.

Stanovich, K. E., & West, R. F. (2007). Natural myside bias is independent of cognitive ability. *Thinking and Reasoning, 13*, 225.

Stanovich, K. E., & West, R. F. (2008a). On the failure of cognitive ability to predict myside and one-sided thinking biases. *Thinking and Reasoning, 14*, 129–167.

Stanovich, K. E., & West, R. F. (2008b). On the relative independence of thinking biases and cognitive ability. *Journal of Personality and Social Psychology, 94*, 672–695.

Stevenson, R. J., & Over, D. E. (1995). Deduction from uncertain premises. *Quarterly Journal of Experimental Psychology, 48A*, 613–643.

Thompson, V. A. (1994). Interpretational factors in conditional reasoning. *Memory and Cognition, 22*, 742–758.

Thompson, V. A. (2000). The task-specific nature of domain-general reasoning. *Cognition, 76*, 209–268.

Thompson, V. A. (2009). Dual-process theories: A metacognitive perspective. In J. St. B. T. Evans & K. Frankish (Eds.), *In two minds: Dual processes and beyond* (pp. 171–196). Oxford, England: Oxford University Press.

Thompson, V. A., Evans, J. St. B. T., & Handley, S. J. (2005). Persuading and dissuading by conditional argument. *Journal of Memory and Language, 53*, 238–257.

Thompson, V. A., Prowse Turner, J. A., & Pennycook, G. (2011). Intuition, reason, and metacognition. *Cognitive Psychology, 63*, 107–140.

Tsujii, T., & Watanabee, S. (2009). Neural correlates of dual-task effect on belief-bias syllogistic reasoning: A near-infrared spectroscopty study. *Brain Research, 1287*, 118–125.

Verschueren, N., Schaeken, W., & d' Ydewalle, G. (2005). A dual-process specification of causal conditional reasoning. *Thinking and Reasoning, 11*, 239–278.

Wason, P. C. (1966). Reasoning. In B. M. Foss (Ed.), *New horizons in psychology I* (pp. 106–137). Harmandsworth, England: Penguin.

Wason, P. C., & Evans, J. St. B. T. (1975). Dual processes in reasoning? *Cognition, 3*, 141–154.

Wason, P. C., & Johnson-Laird, P. N. (1972). *Psychology of reasoning: Structure and content*. London: Batsford.

Weidenfeld, A., Oberauer, K., & Hornig, R. (2005). Causal and noncausal conditionals: An integrated model of interpretation and reasoning. *Quarterly Journal of Experimental Psychology, 58*, 1479–1513.

Wilkins, M. C. (1928). The effect of changed material on the ability to do formal syllogistic reasoning. *Archives of Psychology, 16*, No 102.

Woodworth, R. S., & Sells, S. B. (1935). An atmosphere effect in syllogistic reasoning. *Journal of Experimental Psychology, 18*, 451–460.

# The Mental Models Perspective

Philip N. Johnson-Laird

## Abstract

This chapter begins with mental models as the end product of vision, as a repository of knowledge, and as underlying visual imagery. It contrasts them with the alternative hypothesis that mental representations are syntactic expressions in a mental language. To resolve this controversy, it shows that the structure of models, which differs from that of syntactic representations, plays a major role in accounting for the comprehension and memory of discourse. It reports evidence corroborating another major principle of mental models—that they normally represent only what is true—for models of concepts and models of propositions. The chapter then describes how intuitions are based on a single mental model, whereas deductions call for the representation of alternative models, especially those representing counterexamples to putative conclusions. It reports the corroboration of these predictions. Next, it turns to inductive reasoning. It shows how models underlie common forms of induction in daily life, and it reports evidence corroborating the prediction that individuals prefer explanations that resolve inconsistencies over minimal amendments to the offending propositions. Finally, it concludes with an overview of the main principles governing mental models.

**Key Words:** concepts, deduction, explanation, induction, logic, mental models

The immediate precursor to the modern theory of mental models is a hypothesis due to the prescient psychologist and physiologist, Kenneth Craik (1943). What he wrote conveys the essence of the modern theory:

> If the organism carries a "small-scale model" of external reality and of its own possible actions within its head, it is able to try out various alternatives, conclude which is the best of them, react to future situations before they arise, utilize the knowledge of past events in dealing with the present and the future, and in every way to react in a much fuller, safer, and more competent manner to the emergencies which face it. (Craik, 1943, p. 61)

Before Craik, various philosophers and physicists had proposed analogous ideas. The great 19th-century American logician C. S. Peirce, for example, postulated that reasoning depends on diagrams that are models of propositions (Peirce, 1931–58, Vol. 4). Readers can find a fuller history of mental models elsewhere (Johnson-Laird, 2006), and so the aim of the present chapter is to describe the modern theory, which began to be formulated about 30 years ago, and which has had an impact on various aspects of cognitive psychology—from the study of perception to high-level reasoning.

This chapter begins with mental models as the end product of vision, as a repository of knowledge, and as underlying visual imagery. It contrasts them with the alternative hypothesis that mental representations are syntactic expressions in a mental language. To resolve this controversy, it shows that the structure of models, which differs from that of syntactic representations, plays a major role in accounting for the comprehension and memory of discourse. It reports evidence corroborating another major principle of mental models—that they normally represent only what is true—both for models of concepts and for models of propositions. The chapter then describes how intuitions are based on a single mental model, whereas deliberations call for the representation of alternative models, especially those representing counterexamples to putative conclusions. It reports the corroboration of these predictions. Next, it turns to inductive reasoning. It shows how models underlie common forms of induction in daily life, and it reports evidence corroborating the prediction that individuals prefer explanations that resolve inconsistencies over minimal amendments to the offending propositions. Finally, it concludes with an overview of the main principles distinguishing mental models from other sorts of putative mental representation.

## The Modern Theory of Mental Models

You may have the intuition that vision, hearing, and your other senses put you into direct contact with reality. In fact, you have no such contact. Consider, for example, the old riddle: If a tree falls down in the middle of a forest, miles from any sentient entity, does it make a sound? The answer is: no. It makes vibrations in the air, but sound itself depends on hearing. Similarly, objects in the world reflect light, but colors, textures, and shapes depend on a visual system. Vision, as Marr (1982) argued, is an unconscious inference, starting from the patterns of light falling on your retinas, and leading to a mental model that makes explicit the three-dimensional structure of the scene in front of you. To move around safely, you need a representation of the world that is independent from your viewpoint: You need to know what things are where in the world. You can recognize, say, that a street contains shops, pedestrians, and passing cars; and you can readily make your way to a distant landmark even if you have never been on that particular street before. Vision solves three problems to enable you to do so: It constructs a mental model that makes explicit three-dimensional shapes, it uses these shapes to identify objects, and it makes explicit the spatial relations among them.

How these tasks are carried out is not known with any certainty. Marr supposed that you have a catalog of the three-dimensional mental models of familiar objects, and that your visual system computes the shape of entities in the scene in terms of their major axes, for example, a furled umbrella is a long tapering cylinder. It compares this shape with the shapes in its catalog, which at their highest level capture the overall shape of objects but at lower levels flesh out the detailed shapes of the parts of objects. One possibility is that a visual cue about the shape of an object may trigger access to a model in the catalogue, which is then used to try to match the rest of the percept (cf. Biederman, 1995; Ullman, 1996; for alternative hypotheses).

The term "mental model" is often used in a promiscuous way to refer to any systematic representation of knowledge (Gentner & Stevens, 1983). Such a model of the world could have a three-dimensional structure (Hegarty, 1992; Metzler & Shepard, 1982), or it could consist of propositional representations, which are syntactically structured expressions in a mental language (Pylyshyn, 2003). This latter view dovetails with theories of reasoning in which formal rules of inference akin to those of logic are applied to representations of the logical form of propositions (e.g., Braine & O'Brien, 1998; Rips, 1994). In stark contrast, other psychologists have argued for theories that eschew abstract representations in favor of ones rooted in perception (Barsalou, 1999; Markman & Dietrich, 2000). Surprisingly, the resolution of this controversy comes, not from the study of perception or imagery, but from investigations of language and reasoning. They offer a more precise notion of mental models, and they provide evidence corroborating their psychological reality.

## Mental Models and Comprehension
### The Interpretation of Discourse

You construct models of the world from perception, but you can also construct them from descriptions of the world, which enable you to experience it by proxy. A good writer or storyteller has the power to initiate a process similar to the one that occurs when you perceive or imagine events. Indeed, experiments show that individuals rapidly forget the surface form of sentences, their underlying grammatical relations, and even the gist of individual sentences. And so when you understand discourse, you use the meaning of sentences and your general knowledge to construct mental models of the situations under description (e.g., Johnson-Laird, 1983; Van Dijk & Kintsch, 1983). But what distinguishes a mental model from, say, a propositional representation in a mental language?

The answer according to the present author is that a mental model has a structure corresponding to the structure of what it represents (Johnson-Laird, 1983). It is *iconic*. That is, its parts are interrelated in the same way that the parts of the entities that it represents are interrelated (see Peirce, 1931–1958, Vol. 4, paragraph 433 for this notion of iconicity). Models accordingly represent what things are where in a visual scene or in its verbal depiction, though in the latter case the model is compatible with an indefinite number of scenes. The model represents each referent with a single mental token, the properties of referents with properties of the tokens, and the relations among referents with relations among the tokens. This property of iconicity therefore distinguishes mental models from other sorts of representation, such as those in a mental language, which have a syntactic structure rather than an iconic one.

To illustrate the iconicity of a mental model, consider a simple spatial description (see Byrne & Johnson-Laird, 1989):

The talk button is on the left of the close-doors button. The open-doors button is on the right of the close-doors button.

Your interpretative system constructs a representation of the meaning of each sentence, and it can use this meaning to construct or to update a mental model of the spatial layout of the buttons. This model is depicted in the following diagram in which the left-to-right axis corresponds to that of the panel of buttons:

Talk    Close-doors    Open-doors

As the diagram illustrates, the model is iconic in that its layout corresponds to the layout of the three buttons, but a mental model represents actual buttons on an elevator, not just their verbal labels. You could use the model to infer that the talk button is to the left of the open-doors button. No alternative model of the description is a counterexample to this conclusion, and so it must be true given the truth of the description.

Experimental evidence shows that the number of mental models that individuals need to construct to make an inference predicts its difficulty, whereas the length of a logical proof based on propositional representations does not (e.g., Byrne & Johnson-Laird, 1989, Johnson-Laird & Byrne, 1991). Likewise, other evidence suggests that mental models underlie memory for descriptions (Bransford, Barclay, & Franks, 1972; Garnham, 1987). Mental models of a story can be dynamic and unfold in time (Johnson-Laird, 1983, Ch. 6), and Oatley and his colleagues have argued that fiction is a device for creating such simulations (e.g., Mar & Oatley, 2008). As a corollary, changes in location in a story should affect your ease of accessing the various individuals and entities in the story. For example, if the protagonist walks from one room to another carrying an object, then it is easier for you to access this object and the entities in the new room than those in the room the protagonist has just left. It takes you longer to respond to questions or to a probe word about them; and similar effects occur for stories (e.g., Glenberg, Mayer, & Lindem, 1987; Rinck & Bower, 1995), movies (e.g., Magliano, Miller, & Zwaan, 2001), and "virtual reality" (Radvansky & Copeland, 2006). Hence, you maintain a model of discourse similar to one that you construct from perceiving the events.

Spatial relations, such as those in the earlier description of the buttons in an elevator, are easy to envisage. You might therefore assume that mental models are nothing more than visual images. This assumption is wrong. Some descriptions are easy to visualize yet do not elicit spatial representations, for example, "The dog is dirtier than the cat." When individuals reason from such propositions, they are slower in comparison with their reasoning from propositions that do not elicit images (Knauff & Johnson-Laird, 2002). The reason may be that only descriptions eliciting imagery activate regions in visual cortex (Knauff, Fangmeier, Ruff, & Johnson-Laird, 2003). Some propositions, such as "Ann is cleverer than Beth," are plainly impossible to represent solely in a visual image. You can imagine, say, Ann as higher on a vertical scale than Beth, but nothing in such a representation makes explicit the meaning of *cleverer than*. Not all properties or relations are rooted in a sensory modality. Mental models can contain abstract elements, which, as Peirce realized, are symbolic rather than iconic.

The idea that discourse is represented in mental models of the situations under description is relatively uncontroversial (see, e.g., Gernsbacher, 1990; Kintsch, 1988). The major problem for the system that builds such models is to establish the appropriate referent for each expression. Speakers refer back to entities that they have already introduced in the discourse, and they can use different noun phrases, demonstratives, or pronouns to do so. The interpretative system uses many cues to co-reference—from the meaning of sentences to the grammatical roles of noun phrases (Almor, 1999; Stevenson, Nelson, & Stenning, 1995). The most comprehensive account within the framework of mental models is due to Garnham and his colleagues (e.g., Cowles & Garnham 2005; Garnham, 2001). It postulates that a critical factor is the number of potential antecedents for a referring expression, and so a noun phrase needs enough content to pinpoint its antecedent among them. But a noun phrase can also signal the future direction of the discourse and perhaps a shift in theme. No current theory, however, has led to a theory comprehensive enough to yield a computer program that copes with natural language.

A mental model captures what is common to the different ways in which a possibility can occur, and so the theory is an analog of "possible world" semantics (Kripke, 1963) and its more recent variants such as "situation semantics" (Barwise, 1987) and "discourse representation" theory (Kamp & Reyle, 1993). But representations according to these theories are always correct, whereas, as the next section shows, mental models have intrinsic shortcomings that lead individuals into error.

## The Principle of Truth

A central assumption of the model theory is known as the principle of *truth*. It postulates that mental models represent only what is true (Johnson-Laird & Savary, 1999). The principle is subtle, because it operates on two levels. Given an "exclusive" disjunction, such as:

Either the man pressed the open-doors button or else the woman pressed the close-doors button, but not both

a truth table lays out the truth or falsity of the disjunction for all four possible contingencies depending on the truth or falsity of its two constituent clauses. The disjunction is true when one clause is true and the other clause is false, and otherwise it is false. In contrast, the mental models of the proposition represent only the two contingencies that are possible given the truth of the proposition, which are laid out in this diagram on separate lines:

man pressed open-doors button
woman pressed close-doors button

For convenience, sentences stand in for mental models of actions in these diagrams. At the second level of the principle of truth, the models above do not represent explicitly that in the first possibility it is false that the woman pressed the close-doors button, and that in the second possibility it is false that the man pressed the open-doors button. The theory allows, however, that certain circumstances may lead individuals to flesh out their mental models into *fully explicit* models, which use negation to represent the status of each clause in each possibility:

man pressed open-doors button & woman did *not* press close-doors button
man did *not* press open-doors button & woman pressed close-doors button

The principle of truth reduces the load on working memory in comparison with a truth table, which represents all four possible contingencies. And the principle seems benign. Yet it can lead individuals into the illusion that they understand a description when, in fact, they have misunderstood it. A computer program implementing the principle led to the discovery of a variety of such illusions, and subsequent studies have corroborated their occurrence (Johnson-Laird, 2006). The problem arises when mental models of one proposition fail to take into account the concurrent falsity of another proposition, and so the mental models differ from the correct fully explicit models of the description.

A striking illusion of this sort occurs with the description:

Suppose only one of the following assertions is true:

1. You have the bread.
2. You have the soup or the salad, but not both.
Also, suppose you have the bread. What, if anything, follows? Could you have both the soup and the salad?

Most participants (78%) say, "no" (Khemlani & Johnson-Laird, 2009), and this answer is predicted by the mental models of the two initial assertions, which yield three alternative possibilities for what you can have:

bread
soup
salad

In contrast, the fully explicit models, which represent the status of each clause in the description in each model, are quite different. Given that you have the bread, then assertion 1 is true, and so assertion 2 is false. And there are two ways in which it can be false. One way is that you have neither the soup nor the salad, but the other way is that you have both of them. The fully explicit models of the description are accordingly:

bread & no soup & no salad
bread & soup & salad

where each model is a conjunction of entities. So, the correct answer to the question is: "Yes, given that I have the bread, I can also have both the soup and salad."

## MODELS OF CONCEPTS

An earlier part of the chapter described how models of entities can be part of the models of a visual scene. Similarly, models of concepts are components of the models of propositions, for example, your model of the concept of, say, "soup" is part of your model of the assertion, "You have the soup." You begin to acquire concepts in infancy and continue to do so, and to devise novel concepts, throughout your life (Medin, Lynch, & Solomon, 2000). One way to create new concepts is by combining existing ones using logical connectives, such as negation, conjunction, and disjunction. For example, the concept of a "ball" in baseball is defined as a pitch at which the batter does *not* swing *and* which does *not* pass through the strike zone. Systems based on these connectives, and those that can be defined in terms of them, are known as "Boolean" in honor of George Boole, the logician who first systematized their logic. But even informal concepts often depend on Boolean connectives, for example, the relation of ownership, as in *she owns it*, means in part that it is permissible for her to use it, *and* it is *not* permissible for others to prevent her from using it (Miller & Johnson-Laird, 1976, p. 560).

If thought depends on representations in a mental language, Boolean concepts should depend on them too, with expressions of the form, for example, *a and b, or not-a or not-b*. Likewise, the acquisition of a concept should call for individuals to find a minimal Boolean description of the instances of a concept (Feldman, 2000), or some sort of logical description of them (Nosofsky, Palmeri, & McKinley, 1994; Vigo, 2009). The resulting description could yield a decision tree that yields a correct classification of instances and noninstances of the concept (e.g., Bruner, Goodnow, & Austin, 1956; Hunt, 1962; Shepard, Hovland, & Jenkins, 1961). In contrast, the model theory postulates instead that a concept is represented in mental models of its possible instances, which are each a conjunction of properties and relations (Goodwin & Johnson-Laird, 2012). For example, the concept *tall and thin, or else short and fat* has these two mental models of its instances:

tall    thin
short  fat

Each model represents one sort of possible instance consisting of a conjunction of attributes, but here and henceforth, for simplicity, the sign for conjunction, "&", is omitted from these diagrams.

The simplest way to acquire a concept is to commit to memory each of its exemplars (see, e.g., Medin & Smith, 1984). The model theory, however, postulates that individuals detect those attributes that

are irrelevant given the values of other attributes, and they then eliminate the irrelevancies (Goodwin & Johnson-Laird, 2010). As an example, consider a concept that has these two instances:

tall thin muscular
tall thin not-muscular

Clearly, the attribute of *muscular or not* is irrelevant to the concept, which can be represented in a single model:

tall thin

The particular simplifications that humans discover are likely to depend on the order in which they encounter the instances of a concept, and on the relative saliency of their attributes. However, the overall number of models that result from the elimination of irrelevant attributes does not change as a result of these differences, and it provides a better predictor of the difficulty of acquiring concepts than either the number of decisions in a decision tree (Hunt, 1962) or the length of a minimal description of concepts (Feldman, 2000). So when individuals learn to categorize instances and noninstances of concepts, they do not seek a minimal description of the concept but instead seek to minimize the number of mental models required to represent its instances (Goodwin & Johnson-Laird, 2012). They eliminate any irrelevant property or relation. They also base their *descriptions* of a concept on mental models of its instances. That is, they describe disjunctions of instances, omitting irrelevant attributes.

If concepts are represented in models, then illusory concepts should exist, and recent studies have corroborated their existence (Goodwin & Johnson-Laird, 2010). Consider, for instance, this description of a set of objects based on their color and shape:

red if and only if square, or else red.

The description yields two mental models:

red    square
red

Hence, individuals think that the concept includes red squares. But the fully explicit models of the concept show that this concept is illusory:

not-red not-square (the first clause of the disjunction holds, but the second does not)

red not-square (the first clause does not hold, but the second does)

Readers may think that such concepts are highly artificial, and that errors are merely a consequence of this artificiality. A simple control inference, however, is just as artificial. It depends on changing the disjunction to an *inclusive* one, which allows that both its clauses could be true. In this case, the mental models yield the correct answer, and individuals tended to make it, too. Performance was also good on other control inferences based on exclusive disjunctions. The following description:

red and green, or else green.

should not elicit the illusory model:

red green

because individuals know that the objects under description cannot be both red and green. An experiment corroborated this prediction. Individuals were much less likely to succumb to illusions when the content of the descriptions blocked an illusory model, leaving only a correct model of the concept (Goodwin & Johnson-Laird, 2010, Experiment 3). Content had only a small effect on performance when it blocked an illusory model, but the participant still had to recover the correct models. And it had no effect whatsoever when it blocked one illusory model but not another. No other current theory, including recent probabilistic accounts (Kemp & Tenenbaum, 2008), predicts the occurrence of illusory concepts. Hence, their occurrence is a crucial corroboration of the model theory.

## Logical Reasoning
### Deduction and Logic

Reasoning is a systematic mental process that generates or evaluates implications among propositions. Implications are of two main sorts: deductive and inductive. Deduction is a central cognitive process and a major component of intelligence (Stanovich, 1999), and so tests of intelligence include problems of deductive reasoning. You know, for instance:

If one earns a salary, then one pays income tax.
President Obama earns a salary.

And so you can infer:

President Obama pays income tax.

This inference is *valid*, that is, if its premises are true, then its conclusion must be true, too. Logicians define a valid inference as one whose conclusion is true in every possibility in which all its premises are true (Jeffrey, 1981, p.1). In other words, there are no counterexamples to a valid deduction, that is, no possibilities in which the premises hold but the conclusion does not.

Psychologists studying reasoning once aimed to identify the particular logic that people have in their heads—an idea going back to the ancient doctrine that the laws of logic are the laws of thought. One difficulty was the vast number of different logics, including the indefinitely many "modal" logics for possibility and necessity. Nevertheless, theorists argued for a century that logic is a theory of human deductive competence; and Inhelder and Piaget (1958, p. 305) proposed that reasoning is nothing more than logic itself. Others have similarly argued that deductive performance depends on formal rules of inference (e.g., Braine & O'Brien, 1998; Rips, 1994). But several difficulties confront any psychological theory based on logic. Some are theoretical, such as the fact that in logic infinitely many conclusions—most of which are trivial—follow validly from any set of premises, whereas individuals often say, quite sensibly, that nothing follows from certain premises. Logic has nothing to say about which logical conclusions are sensible. What naïve individuals—those who have not mastered logic—tend to infer are conclusions that do not add disjunctive alternatives to those possibilities to which the premises refer, that simplify matters rather than include redundant propositions, and that make explicit what was only implicit in the premises (Johnson-Laird & Byrne, 1991, p. 22).

Another problem for theories based on logic is the difficulty of establishing the logical *form* of everyday propositions. In logic, deductions are expressed in sentences in a formal language with a grammar that makes logical form explicit, and they are proved using rules of inference sensitive only to these logical forms. But, in everyday life, implications hold, not between sentences, but between the propositions that sentences express in a particular context, or propositions that derive from perception, memory, or imagination. What proposition an everyday sentence expresses depends on its meaning, on what it refers to, and on knowledge. The one computer program implementing a psychological theory based on formal rules accordingly calls for users themselves to provide the logical form of the premises and conclusion (Rips, 1994). So what is an alternative basis for reasoning?

Craik postulated that models help us to navigate our way through life, but he did not consider their role in reasoning, which he took to depend on "verbal rules"—an idea on which he did not elaborate (Craik, 1943, p. 81). Models, however, are a way in which to make inferences. Reasoners construct models based on descriptions, on perception, and on knowledge. They formulate a conclusion that holds in the models and that was not overtly asserted in any single premise. A conclusion that holds in all the models is necessary given the premises (Johnson-Laird & Byrne, 1991). A conclusion that holds in most of the models is probable given the premises (Johnson-Laird, Legrenzi, Girotto, Legrenzi, & Caverni, 1999). And a conclusion that holds in at least one model is possible given the premises (Bell & Johnson-Laird, 1998). Models accordingly provide a unified theory of logical, modal, and probabilistic reasoning—at least the sort of probabilistic reasoning that depends on adding the probabilities of the different ways in which an event can occur. In fact, models have been successfully applied to most aspects of everyday deduction (for a review, see Johnson-Laird, 2006), but here the focus is on sentential reasoning, which depends on negation and connectives, such as "if," "or," and "and," that is, the same connectives that are used in describing Boolean concepts (see the earlier section).

## Intuitions and Deliberations: A Dual-Process Account

The modern theory of mental models from its inception differentiated between intuitions and deliberations (Johnson-Laird, 1983, Ch. 6). On the one hand, you make rapid, effortless, and unconscious inferences. For example, you read the following description:

> There was a fault in the signaling circuit. The crash led to the deaths of two people.

You infer that the crash killed them. The text makes no such assertion, and it could continue:

> They were arrested after the accident, convicted of deliberately causing the fault, and shot as saboteurs.

On the other hand, you make voluntary, effortful, and conscious inferences that take time. Psychologists have largely focused on these inferences at the expense of implicit inferences, which were discovered by computer scientists trying to write programs that "understand" natural language. The crucial difference between the two sorts of inference according to the model theory is that intuitive inferences depend on "a *single* mental model [based on] the discourse, its context, and background knowledge" (Johnson-Laird, 1983, p. 128). No attempt is made to search for alternative models unless evidence occurs to overrule the model. Hence, the process can be rapid and unconscious, but there is no guarantee that its results are valid. In contrast, deliberate reasoning depends on working memory and on carrying out recursive processes, including

a search for alternative models. Hence, the process is slow and you are aware of reasoning.

Many psychologists have proposed such "dual-process" accounts of reasoning (e.g., Johnson-Laird & Wason, 1976, p. 5–6; Kahneman & Frederick, 2002; Rader & Sloutsky, 2002; Schroyens, Schaeken, & Handley, 2003; Sloman, 1996; Stanovich, 1999). But Evans and his colleagues have perhaps explored the idea in more depth than other investigators (e.g., Evans, 2003; and Evans & Over, 1996; Wason & Evans; 1975). Not all theories specify how the two sorts of reasoning work together or what the processes are on which they rely. Such an algorithm, however, is built into those programs implementing the model theory (e.g., Johnson-Laird & Byrne, 1991, Ch. 9): the intuitive process constructs a single model of the premises, and the deliberative process searches recursively for alternative models.

A conditional assertion such as:

If one earns a salary, then one pays income tax usually refers to three possibilities:

| | |
|---|---|
| earns salary | pays income tax |
| doesn't earn salary | pays income tax |
| doesn't earn salary | doesn't pay income tax |

The Queen of England is an example of the second possibility. When you understand such a conditional, you normally construct only one explicit mental model that represents the most salient possibility—the first one in the list above, and another model with no explicit content to allow for the other possibilities. The further assertion, say, that Obama earns a salary, eliminates this implicit model, leaving only the explicit mental model, and it suffices for you to infer that Obama pays income tax. In the different case in which, say, Charles does *not* pay income tax, your mental models of the conditional yield no conclusion, and a common error is to think that nothing follows from such premises. When you deliberate, however, you can flesh out your mental models into fully explicit models representing all three possibilities above. Now, you can infer from the premise about Charles that he does not earn a salary (see Verschueren, Schaeken, & d'Ydewalle, 2005). Oberauer (2006) showed that this "dual-process" theory of mental models gives a better account of reasoning from conditional assertions than its rivals.

## Models and Sentential Reasoning

The theory of mental models yields five main predictions about sentential reasoning. First, more models mean more work; that is, the greater the number of models of possibilities that you need to think about, the harder an inference will be. Second, you can use counterexamples to overturn invalid inferences. Third, the principle of truth, which was described earlier, implies that you should make illusory inferences. Fourth, you can develop various strategies for reasoning, but, regardless of your strategy, the previous predictions should still hold. And, fifth, the meaning of clauses and general knowledge can modulate your interpretation of sentential connectives, such as "if" and "or," so that they no longer refer to three possibilities illustrated earlier. This section of the chapter examines each of these predictions in turn.

## MORE MODELS MEAN MORE WORK

The greater the number of models that individuals have to think about, the harder deductions should be, taking longer and being more prone to error. These errors should consist in drawing conclusions that overlook at least one model of a possibility consistent with the premises. A corroboration of this prediction concerns the difference in reasoning from an exclusive disjunction, for example:

> The man pressed a button or else the woman pressed a button, but not both.

and in reasoning from an inclusive disjunction, for example:

> The man pressed a button or the woman pressed a button, or both.

As we saw earlier, an exclusive disjunction refers to two possibilities, whereas an inclusive disjunction refers to three possibilities, because it allows that both of its clauses could be the case. Granted, say, the further premise:

> The man did not press a button

it is a valid inference from either sort of disjunction that:

> The woman pressed a button.

The model theory predicts that the inference from the exclusive disjunction (two possibilities) should be easier than the inference from the inclusive disjunction (three possibilities). The theories based on formal logic make the opposite prediction, because they have a rule for inclusive disjunction, but not for exclusive disjunction, and so the inference from it calls for a sequence of steps. Reasoning from verbal premises and from diagrams has corroborated the model theory's prediction (Bauer & Johnson-Laird, 1993; Johnson-Laird, Byrne, & Schaeken, 1992).

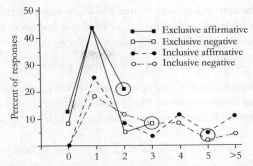

**Figure 41.1** The number of models of the premises underlying the participants' conclusions from four sorts of pairs of disjunctive premises (from Johnson-Laird et al., 1992). The circled items are the correct valid conclusions.

Likewise, reasoning from a conjunction, which refers to only one possibility, is easier than reasoning from a disjunction (García-Madruga, Moreno, Carriedo, Gutiérrez, & Johnson-Laird, 2001).

The erroneous conclusions that individuals draw tend to hold for only some of the possibilities to which the premises refer. Figure 41.1 presents the number of models of the premises that the participants' conclusions took into account in disjunctive reasoning (Johnson-Laird et al., 1992). The premises were pairs of either inclusive or exclusive disjunctions, and the second disjunction contained a clause that either affirmed or negated a clause in the first disjunction. The circled points in the figure correspond to the valid conclusions, which depend, respectively, on two, three, or five models. The participants drew just over 20% of valid conclusions for the two-model inferences, and less than 10% for the remaining inferences. And, as the figure shows, the modal errors were conclusions consistent with only one model, that is, the participants overlooked many possibilities to which the premises referred. Formal rule theories make no use of representations of possibilities, and so they cannot explain these results.

## COUNTEREXAMPLES OVERTURN INVALID INFERENCES

A counterexample to an inference is a possibility in which the premises hold, but the conclusion does not. There are two main sorts of invalid inference: one sort yields a conclusion that is consistent with the premises but that does not follow from them, for example:

> The fault is in the cable or the printer, or both.
> Therefore, the fault is in the cable and the printer.

The conclusion holds in one possibility to which the premise refers, but not in all of them, and so it is invalid, as the following counterexample shows:

fault in cable & not a fault in the printer.

The other sort of invalid inference yields a conclusion that is not even consistent with the premises—it is impossible given that they hold, for example:

The fault is in the cable or the printer, or both.

Therefore, the fault is not in the cable and not in the printer.

The best way in which to elicit counterexamples from naïve individuals is to ask them to evaluate given conclusions that are invalid but consistent with the premises. When the participants write justifications for their correct evaluations of such inferences, they tend to describe counterexamples (Johnson-Laird & Hasson, 2003). Studies of other sorts of reasoning have also shown that individuals use counterexamples spontaneously in drawing their own conclusions (e.g., Bucciarelli & Johnson-Laird, 1999). And, as brain imaging showed, only a search for counterexamples triggered activity in the region of the right frontal hemisphere known as the "frontal pole" (Kroger, Nystrom, Cohen, & Johnson-Laird, 2008). Psychological theories based on formal rules make no use of counterexamples, and so cannot account for these results.

## ILLUSORY SENTENTIAL INFERENCES

Readers are invited to solve the following problem:

Either Jane is kneeling by the fire and she is looking at the TV or otherwise Mark is standing by the window and he is peering into the garden.
Jane is kneeling by the fire.
Does it follow that she is looking at the TV?

Most people say, "yes" (Walsh & Johnson-Laird, 2004). The computer program implementing the model theory predicts that the premise yields two mental models:

Jane: kneeling by fire and looking at TV
Mark: standing by window and peering into garden

Hence, the theory predicts the affirmative answer. In fact, the answer is wrong. If the second conjunction is true, then the first conjunction is false, and one way in which it could be false is that Jane is kneeling by the fire but *not* looking

at TV. This example is a paradigm case of an illusory inference, and the present author should confess that he succumbed to it when Walsh and he were designing the materials for an experiment. A common criticism of such studies is that the materials are artificial, and so why should we care about their results? The principal answer is that reasoning is often about artificial contents both in logic and in daily life—the worldwide popularity of Sudoku puzzles is an excellent example (Lee, Goodwin, & Johnson-Laird, 2008). Their solution depends on pure deductive reasoning, but their contents are utterly artificial. In studies of illusory inferences, we can be sure that neither the contents nor the framing of problems causes such poor performance, because the participants are highly accurate in responding to the control problems.

Illusory inferences occur with all sorts of sentential connective, including "or" in both its inclusive and exclusive senses, and "if" and "if and only if" (e.g., Johnson-Laird & Savary, 1999). They also occur in various other domains of reasoning (e.g., Bucciarelli & Johnson-Laird, 2005; Goldvarg & Johnson-Laird; 2000; for a review, see Johnson-Laird, 2006). Many experts have fallen for them, and then proposed ingenious explanations for their errors, for example, the premises are so complex or artificial that they confuse people. But reasoners are highly confident in their conclusions, and, as I mentioned earlier, the control inferences, which participants get right, are equally complex and artificial. Other putative explanations concern the interpretation of conditionals. But the illusions occur with disjunctions too, and their interpretation is not controversial. Certain procedures do alleviate the illusions (e.g., Barrouillet & Lecas, 2000; Santamaria & Johnson-Laird, 2000; Yang & Johnson-Laird, 2000), but a perfect antidote for them has yet to be discovered.

## INDIVIDUAL STRATEGIES IN SENTENTIAL REASONING

Readers might suppose that individuals are equipped with a single deterministic strategy for deduction, which unwinds like an algorithm for long multiplication. One reason for this view is that many experiments are insensitive to the use of different strategies. Yet there are long-standing impediments to the notion of a single reasoning strategy. For example, the order of premises has robust effects on inferences—in a way that the model theory predicts (Girotto, Mazzocco, & Tasso, 1997). And when individuals carry out a series of sentential inferences, they develop different strategies for coping with them. This phenomenon is obvious when they think aloud and are permitted to use pencil and paper (Van der Henst, Yang, & Johnson-Laird, 2002). Consider, for instance, the following sort of inference about the contents of a box:

There is a red marble in the box if and only if there is a brown marble.
Either there is a brown marble or else there is a gray marble, but not both.
There is a gray marble if and only if there is a black marble.
Does it follow that: If there is not a red marble then there is a black marble?

The inference is easy, and the correct answer is "yes." Over the course of several problems of a similar sort, different individuals develop different strategies for reasoning about them.

Some people spontaneously develop a strategy based on suppositions. When they think aloud, they say, for instance:

Suppose there isn't a red marble. It follows from the first premise (above) that there isn't a brown one. It then follows from the second premise that there's a gray marble. The third premise then implies that there's a black one. So, yes, the conclusion does follow.

Each of these inferential steps can be carried out using models. The participants do not always use suppositions correctly. Given the conclusion in the previous example, participants sometimes made the supposition: suppose there's a black marble. They then inferred from the premises that there is not a red marble, and so they responded that the conditional followed from the premises. They made the correct response, but not for the right reason. The "then" clause of conditional can be true even when its "if" clause is false, and so the right way to proceed is to make a supposition of the "if" clause and to show that it leads to the truth of the "then" clause.

Another strategy is to make an inference from a pair of premises, and then to make another from its conclusion and the third premise. One strategy was totally unexpected, and no previous mention of it appears to be in either the psychological or logical literature. Reasoners transform each premise, where necessary, into a conditional, so that the result is a chain of conditionals leading from one clause in the conditional conclusion to its other clause, for example:

If there isn't a red marble then there isn't a brown marble.
If there isn't a brown marble then there is a gray marble.
If there is a gray marble then there is a black marble.
So, if there isn't a red marble then there is a black marble.

The strategy is correct provided that reasoners make the correct transformations into conditionals, and that they construct a chain leading from the "if" clause of the conclusion to its "then" clause. However, they sometimes worked incorrectly in the opposite direction. The model theory predicts that it should be easier to make inferences from conditionals than from disjunctions (see also Ormerod & Richardson, 2003), because conditionals have only one explicit mental model, whereas disjunctions have at least two explicit mental models. Hence, the construction of chains of conditionals should be much more likely than the construction of chains of disjunctions. Indeed, not a single participant ever transformed a conditional into a disjunction.

The most frequent strategy was to draw a single diagram that represented all the premises. For example, some participants drew a horizontal line across the middle of the page and wrote down the two possibilities to which the premises referred:

| red | brown |
| --- | --- |
| gray | black |

A tell-tale sign of this strategy is that individuals work through the premises in whatever order they are stated, even taking into account irrelevant premises. When individuals are taught to use this strategy in a systematic way, as Victoria Bell has shown in unpublished studies in the author's laboratory, their reasoning is both faster and more accurate.

Participants mix strategies, and switch from one to another. Sometimes a switch occurs in the middle of a problem; sometimes from one problem to another. There are no fixed sequences of steps that anyone invariably followed. But, regardless of strategy, as a further study showed, inferences that call for only one mental model are easier than those that call for two mental models, which in turn are easier than those that call for three mental models (Van der Henst et al., 2002). Reasoners also develop diverse strategies for reasoning about relations such as "taller than" (Goodwin & Johnson-Laird, 2005, 2006; Roberts, 2000), for reasoning from suppositions (Byrne & Handley, 1997), and for reasoning with quantifiers such as "all" and "some" (Bucciarelli & Johnson-Laird, 1999). All the strategies so far observed reflected a reliance on meaning, and they can be explained in terms of models. But individuals who know logic could make a strategic use of formal rules, and one study has detected signs of the development of formal intuitions (Galotti, Baron, & Sabini, 1986).

## MEANING, KNOWLEDGE, AND MODULATION

When human beings reason, they take their knowledge into account. As a result, they often go beyond the explicit information given to them. Suppose, for instance, that the following assertion is true:

Pat listened to a song, or she listened to some music.

From the further premise that Pat didn't listen to a song, you can infer that she listened to some music. In logic, the *form* of this inference is treated as valid, and psychological theories based on formal rules (e.g., Braine & O'Brien, 1998; Rips, 1994) include such a rule:

A or B.
Not A.
Therefore, B.

They also include a similar rule for cases in which the categorical premise is, *not-B*, and it yields the conclusion, *A*. But, suppose instead that Pat didn't listen to any music. Would you infer that she listened to a song? Obviously not. You know that songs are music, and so if Pat didn't listen to music, she didn't listen to a song. That's part of the meaning of the word "song." Your knowledge of the world can have a similar effect. Given the premises:

Pat listened to the Beatles' *Yellow Submarine* or she listened to some music.
Pat didn't listen to any music.

You are unlikely to infer that Pat listened to the Beatles' *Yellow Submarine*, because you know that it is a piece of music.

These two examples are instances of what is known as *modulation* (Johnson-Laird & Byrne, 2002). Meaning, reference, or general knowledge blocks the construction of an otherwise feasible model of an assertion. An inclusive disjunction, *A or B*, is normally interpreted as referring to three possibilities, which have these fully explicit models:

A not-B
not-A B
A B

But the disjunction, *Pat listened to a song or she listened to some music*, is modulated so that it refers to just two possibilities for Pat's listening:

song music
not-song music

Modulation blocks the third possibility in which Pat listened to a song but not to music.

Most investigations of modulation have concerned conditionals (e.g., Quelhas, Johnson-Laird, & Juhos, 2010). The model theory postulates that the core meaning of *If A then B* also corresponds to a logical interpretation that refers to three possibilities:

A B
not-A B
not-A not-B

But modulation can block any of these models, apart from the possibility of A and B when A may, or may not, occur, to yield various other interpretations (Johnson-Laird & Byrne, 2002). In addition, it can introduce spatial, temporal, or other relations between the situations referred to in the if-clause and the then-clause. (It can also introduce these relations into disjunctions.) These modulations, in turn, affect the inferences that individuals draw from conditionals. Here is an example from Quelhas et al. (2010):

If Lisa received the money, then she paid Frederico.
If she paid Frederico, then he bought a new laptop.
Lisa received the money.
Did Lisa receive the money before Frederico bought a new laptop?

Most participants responded, "yes," evidently inferring that the if-clauses in the two premises refer to events that preceded those referred to in the then-clauses. Here is a contrasting example:

If Tania gave Mauro a scooter, then he did well on the exams.
If he did well on the exams, then he studied a lot.
Tania gave Mauro a scooter.
Did Tania gave Mauro a scooter after he studied a lot?

Again, most participants responded, "yes," but now they evidently inferred that the if-clauses in the two premises referred to events that came after those referred to in the then-clauses. Many studies have shown that models are used to represent explicit spatial and temporal relations (e.g., Byrne & Johnson-Laird, 1989; Carreiras & Santamaria, 1997; Schaeken & Johnson-Laird, 2000; Schaeken, Johnson-Laird, & d'Ydewalle, 1996; Vandierendonck & De Vooght, 1996). But the studies discussed earlier show that individuals use their knowledge to infer temporal relations that are only implicit in the premises.

The potential for meaning, reference, and knowledge to modulate the interpretation of sentential connectives, such as "or" and "if," implies that the system for interpreting sentences must take these factors into account—even if, in the end, a sentence turns out to receive only a logical interpretation. It follows that the interpretative system for sentential connectives cannot work in the "truth functional" way of logic, which takes into account only the truth values of clauses (see, e.g., Jeffrey, 1981). The process of human interpretation is never purely logical: Modulation can add spatial and temporal relations between the events described in a sentence. Hence, sentences of a given grammatical form, such as conditionals or disjunctions, have an indefinite number of different interpretations (pace Evans & Over, 2004).

## Inductive Reasoning

Deduction comes with the guarantee that the conclusion of a valid inference must be true if its premises are true. Induction has no such guarantee. Many of the inferences that you make in daily life are inductive—you aim for truth but may miss the target even if your premises are true. For instance, when the starter doesn't turn over your car's engine, your immediate thought is that the battery is dead. You are likely to be right, but there is no guarantee. Likewise, when the car ferry, *Herald of Free Enterprise*, sailed from Zeebrugge on March 6, 1987, its master made the plausible induction that the bow doors had been closed. They had always been closed in the past, and there was no evidence to the contrary. But the doors had *not* been closed, the sea rushed in and the vessel capsized, and over a hundred people drowned. Induction is a risky business. A corollary is that it rules out possibilities over and above those that the premises rule out. It does so because it relies on knowledge, and knowledge is fallible.

Induction is a source of propositions about specific events, such as the closing of the bow doors, and a source of generalizations, such as that car ferries put out to sea with their bow doors closed.

And, most important, it is source of explanations. All inductions depend on knowledge and on various constraints, such as its availability (Tversky & Kahneman, 1973), the need for informative hypotheses consistent with the facts, and the similarity of one situation to others (see Johnson-Laird, 2006, Ch. 13). In logic, when a conclusion follows validly from premises, no subsequent information can invalidate it. As new premises are added to existing ones, increasing numbers of logical conclusions therefore follow. Logic is thus "monotonic." But, in daily life, you often withdraw conclusions in the light of subsequent information. Your inferences are "nonmonotonic." Sometimes, you withdraw a conclusion because it was based on an assumption that you made by default, for example, millionaires are right-wing. You encounter a politician who is a millionaire, and so you infer that she is right-wing. But then you learn that she's a Democrat, and so you withdraw your conclusion. The model theory allows for the withdrawal of the consequences of default assumptions. Indeed, this process is an integral part of reasoning based on models (Johnson-Laird & Byrne, 1991). On the one hand, the failure to find a model that serves as a counterexample to a conclusion implies that its inference is valid. On the other hand, the failure to find a model that is consistent with a conclusion—by overturning, say, an assumption made by default—implies that the conclusion is inconsistent with the premises.

### Reasoning to Consistency

Many inferences in daily life lead to conflicts with reality. Suppose you know, for example:

> If Ann has gone to get the car, then she will return in 5 minutes.
> Ann has gone to get the car.

You deduce that Ann will return in 5 minutes. In fact, Ann does not return, not even in 20 minutes. You are in a typical situation in which there is a conflict between the consequences of your beliefs and an incontrovertible fact. Something has to "give." At the very least, you have to withdraw your conclusion. You also have to modify your beliefs, but in what way? Should you cease to believe that Ann went to get the car, or that if she did she will return in 5 minutes, or both? Researchers in artificial intelligence have developed various systems of nonmonotonic reasoning to try to deal with such cases (see, e.g., Brewka, Dix, & Konolige, 1997), but psychologists have lagged behind in their investigations of the process. At its heart, there appears to be the creation of diagnostic explanations. You try to imagine a scenario that explains why Ann is not back in 5 minutes. Reasoning that leads in this way from inconsistency to consistency calls for the detection of an inconsistency, the creation of an explanation that accounts for its origins, and perhaps the revision of beliefs (Johnson-Laird, Girotto, & Legrenzi, 2004). But evidence strongly suggests that naïve individuals tend to seek explanations, which as a by-product lead to the revision of their beliefs. The rest of this section accordingly focuses on the discovery of inconsistencies and the creation of explanations that resolve them.

### The Discovery of Inconsistencies

A set of propositions is consistent if at least one possibility exists in which they are all true, and it is inconsistent if no such possibility exists. Hence, there is a close relation between consistency and deduction: An inference is valid if the negation of its conclusion is inconsistent with the premises. Inconsistency in a set of propositions implies that at least one proposition in the set is false, and so it is a serious matter in daily life. Sometimes individuals have a plausible model of the world, which turns out to be inconsistent with the facts of the matter, and as a result a disaster occurs, such as a collision at sea (Perrow, 1984, p. 230). The ability to detect inconsistencies is accordingly central to rationality.

You could use logic to detect an inconsistency in a set of propositions, but the method is psychologically implausible: You are supposed to select a proposition from the set and try to prove its negation from the remaining propositions. If you succeed, then the original set is inconsistent; otherwise, it is consistent. It follows that inconsistency should be easier to establish than consistency: With an inconsistency, you can stop as soon as you have proved the negated proposition, but with consistency you must go on searching until you have exhausted all possible proofs (or yourself). But, however you seek to assess consistency, the task is computationally intractable. The demands it places on time and memory increase at such a rate as the size of the set of propositions increases that the task soon defeats any feasible computational system. The question remains, however: Even with a small set of propositions, how do you assess their consistency?

The model theory provides this answer: Individuals evaluate the consistency of a set of propositions by searching for a model of a possibility in which all the propositions are true. If they find such a model, the propositions are consistent; otherwise,

they are inconsistent (Johnson-Laird, Legrenzi, Girotto, & Legrenzi, 2000). Hence, contrary to the logical account given earlier, consistency should be easier to establish than inconsistency, because you can stop as soon as you have found one possibility in which all the propositions hold, whereas with an inconsistency you have to examine the possibilities exhaustively in order to establish that not one exists in which all the propositions hold.

Experiments have supported the model theory. Consider, for instance, whether these propositions about what is on a table could all be true at the same time:

If there isn't an apple then there is a banana.
If there is a banana then there is a cherry.
There isn't an apple and there is a cherry.

You are likely to begin by considering an obvious possibility for the first proposition, which corresponds to its one explicit mental model (see earlier):

not-apple banana.

This possibility fits the second proposition, which adds a further fruit on top of the table:

not-apple banana cherry

The third proposition holds in this model, and so you infer that the set of propositions is consistent. In contrast, consider this description:

There is an apple or there is a banana.
There isn't a banana or there is a cherry.
There isn't an apple and there is a cherry.

You begin by considering the obvious possibility for the first proposition, corresponding to its first mental model:

apple

You update this model according to the second proposition:

apple not-banana

But this possibility is not consistent with the third proposition, and so you have to retrace your steps. At length, you discover a possibility in which all three propositions hold:

not-apple banana cherry

But this sort of problem in which your initial model leads you astray should be harder than the first sort of problem. An experiment in which the participants were over 500 of the best high school graduates in

Italy showed that the first sort of problem had a robust advantage in accuracy (of 15%) over the second sort of problem—even when conditionals and disjunctions were counterbalanced. Likewise, as the model theory predicts, the consistent problems were easier than the inconsistent problems.

The principle of truth is central to the model theory, because it predicts the occurrence of illusory inferences. Consider this description:

The tray is portable or else not both beautiful and heavy.
The tray is portable and not beautiful.

The first mental model of the tray according to the disjunction is:

portable

The tray lacks the property of being beautiful, and so individuals should judge that the second assertion is consistent with it. They would be wrong. If the tray is portable, the first clause of the disjunction is true and so its second clause is false, that is, the tray *is* both beautiful and heavy. This tray is not consistent with the second assertion in the description. But if it is false that the tray is portable, then the tray is also inconsistent with the second assertion. Hence, the two assertions are inconsistent. An experiment compared the illusory problems with similar control problems, and it corroborated the theory's predictions. The participants responded more accurately to the control problems (86% correct) than to the illusory problems (27% correct), and only 11 of 459 participants went against this trend (Legrenzi, Girotto, & Johnson-Laird, 2003). A further experiment conveyed the meaning of "or else" with an unambiguous statement of an exclusive disjunction: "Only one of the following assertions is true." Once again, the participants succumbed to illusions, but they responded correctly to control problems.

## The Creation of Explanations

Reasoning in daily life often calls for the generation of explanations, especially when you have detected an inconsistency among the propositions that you believe. For example, in the case of Ann's failure to return in 5 minutes when she went to get the car, you try to make explanatory inductions about what may have happened:

Perhaps the battery was dead and she couldn't get the car to start.
Perhaps she didn't remember where we were and got lost on the way.

You use your knowledge and any relevant evidence to generate possibilities. Human reasoners easily outperform any current computer program in envisaging putative explanations. Given two sentences selected at random from different stories, such as:

Celia made her way to a shop that sold TV sets.
She had recently had her ears pierced.

they readily offer explanations of what's going on, such as: Celia was getting reception in her ears and wanted the TV shop to investigate, or Celia had bought some new earrings and wanted to see how they looked on closed-circuit TV (Johnson-Laird, 2006, Ch. 14). This ability to create explanations underlies both science and superstition. The difference is that scientists test their explanations.

When you discover an inconsistency, you try to frame a causal explanation that accounts for its origin. The model theory postulates that the basic unit of explanations is a cause and its effect, in which the effect resolves the inconsistency. It makes possible the facts of the matter, and it repudiates at least one of your previous premises, which you then take to refer to a counterfactual possibility, that is, a situation that was once possible but that did not occur (see Byrne, 2002, 2005; Quelhas & Byrne, 2003). According to the model theory, the *meaning* of a causal relation between two states of affairs, a cause and its effect, refers to what is possible and what is impossible in their co-occurrences. The claim is controversial, but it has been corroborated experimentally (Goldvarg & Johnson-Laird, 2001). In daily life, the normal constraint is that an effect does not precede its cause in time (see, e.g., Tversky & Kahneman, 1982). Hence, the theory adopts this constraint. A computer program implements this account for simple inconsistencies, such as:

If the trigger is pulled then the pistol will fire.
The trigger is pulled.
But the pistol does not fire. Why not?

The program constructs mental models of the premises, detects the inconsistency with the facts, and uses its knowledge base of explicit models of causal relations to construct a causal chain that resolves the inconsistency, for example, a person emptied the pistol and so there were no bullets in the pistol (Johnson-Laird et al., 2004). When individuals were given 20 different inconsistencies, such as this example about the pistol, but from varied domains, they were usually able to create a causal explanation (Johnson-Laird et al., 2004). Most of these explanations repudiated the conditional. In two further experiments with the scenarios, the participants rated the statements of a cause and its effect as the most probable explanations, for example: A prudent person had unloaded the pistol and there were no bullets in the chamber. The cause alone was rated as less probable, but as more probable than the effect alone, which in turn was rated as more probable than an explanation that repudiated the categorical premise, for example, the trigger wasn't really pulled. The greater probability assigned to the conjunction of the cause and effect than to either of its clauses is an instance of the "conjunction" fallacy in which a conjunction is wrongly judged to be more probable than its constituents (Tversky & Kahneman, 1983). Recent studies have similarly shown that participants rate such explanations as more probable than simple denials of either the conditional premise or the categorical premise (Khemlani & Johnson-Laird, 2011).

In sum, reasoners can resolve inconsistencies. They use their knowledge to try to create a causal model that makes sense of the facts. Their reasoning may resolve the inconsistency or fail to yield any explanation whatsoever. One view of rational changes to beliefs is that they should incorporate the facts with minimal changes. As William James (1907, p. 59) wrote: "[The new fact] preserves the older stock of truths with a minimum of modification, stretching them just enough to make them admit the novelty." Such parsimony is sensible, and many cognitive scientists have advocated minimalism both for science and for daily life (e.g., Gärdenfors, 1992; Harman, 1986). Likewise, computer programs for artificial intelligence have modeled minimal changes (e.g., deKleer, 1986), and measures have been developed to calculate what counts as a minimal change (Elio & Pelletier, 1997; Harman, 1986). What the results reviewed in this section show is that naïve individuals are happy to sacrifice minimalism in the cause of an explanation (see also Walsh & Johnson-Laird, 2009).

## Conclusions

What is a mental model? The answer to this question conveys the main points of this chapter. A mental model is a representation of the world that is constructed from perception, memory, or imagination, and that underlies thinking. Three key properties distinguish a mental model from other proposed sorts of mental representation:

1. A mental model represents a possibility: It is a conjunction of entities, their properties, and interrelations. Strictly speaking, a mental model

of a situation captures what is common to the different ways in which it could occur. Hence, a description that makes explicit several alternative possibilities has models corresponding to each of them. As a result, you have greater difficulty in envisaging the description and in reasoning from it than from a description that yields only a single mental model. You infer that a conclusion that holds in all models is necessary given the description, one that holds in most models is probable, and one that holds in at least one model is possible. And you can refute a putative conclusion by discovering a model that is a counterexample to it.

2. A mental model is iconic insofar as it can be, which is to say that its structure corresponds to the structure of what it represents unlike, say, the syntactic structure of a sentence. Visual images are iconic, but mental models can also contain symbolic elements, such as negation (see Schroyens, Schaeken, & d'Ydewalle, 2001). And they can represent properties and relations that have meanings that cannot be visualized. As a corollary, models differ from propositional representations, which are syntactically structured representations in a mental language. The symbolic components of models also distinguish them from putative representations rooted in a sensory modality.

3. A mental model represents what is true as opposed to what is false. This principle of truth enables models to be much more parsimonious than, say, truth tables, which represent both what is true and what is false. As a result, models put much less of a load on the processing capacity of working memory. But sometimes you err as a result. In the case of those inferences for which falsity matters, you are likely to succumb to the illusion that a conclusion is valid when in fact it is not, and vice versa. Suppose, for instance, you know that either Pat called her mother on Monday or otherwise she went to see her mother on Tuesday or else on Wednesday but not both days. You are likely to think of these as three alternative possibilities. So, given, say, that she went to see her mother on Tuesday, you are likely to infer that she didn't go to see her on Wednesday. But suppose that Pat called her mother on Monday. The first clause of the principal exclusive disjunction is true, and so it is false that she went to see her mother either on Tuesday or Wednesday, but not both. And one way in which it could be false is that she went to see her mother on both days. Your inference isn't valid, even though it is compelling.

Finally, mental models have been proposed for domains remote from mainstream cognitive psychology. Bowlby (1988), for example, argued that models of caregivers play a crucial part in the development of children. Models also appear to underlie the reasoning of individuals suffering from psychological illnesses, and their reasoning—contrary to an assumption of cognitive therapy (e.g., Beck, 1976)—is superior to the reasoning of nonclinical controls, though only on topics relating to the patients' illnesses (Johnson-Laird, Mancini, & Gangemi, 2006). Models also predict an effect of personality on reasoning: Individuals who are open to experience tend to think of possibilities outside the premises and therefore they tend to make inductions, whereas those with the mirror-image traits tend to stick to the possibilities to which the premises refer and therefore they tend to make deductions (Fumero, Santamaría, & Johnson-Laird, 2010).

## Future Directions

1. How might mental models underlie the mental representation of stereotypes and prototypes?

2. Models appear to underlie "extensional" estimates of probability based on the different possible ways in which an event might occur, but what role, if any, do they play in "intensional" estimates based on intuitions about evidence?

3. How do children develop the ability to construct and to manipulate mental models?

## Acknowledgments

The theory of mental models has developed as a result of the work of many researchers, too numerous to list here, but readers should consult the references for the names of many of them. Much of the research reported in the chapter was made possible by grants from the National Science Foundation (BCS 0076287 and SES 0844851) to study strategies in reasoning, and deductive and probabilistic reasoning.

## References

Almor, A. (1999). Noun-phrase anaphora and focus: The informational load hypothesis. *Psychological Review, 106,* 748–765.

Barrouillet, P., & Lecas, J-F. (2000). Illusory inferences from a disjunction of conditionals: A new mental models account. *Cognition, 76,* 3–9.

Barsalou, L.W. (1999). Perceptual symbol systems. *Behavioral and Brain Sciences, 22,* 577–660.

Barwise, J. (1987). *The situation in logic.* Stanford, CA: CSLI.

Bauer, M. I., & Johnson-Laird, P. N. (1993). How diagrams can improve reasoning. *Psychological Science, 4,* 372–378

Beck, A. T. (1976). *Cognitive therapy and the emotional disorders.* New York: Meridian.

Bell, V., & Johnson-Laird, P. N. (1998). A model theory of modal reasoning. *Cognitive Science, 22,* 25–51.

Biederman, I. (1995). Visual object recognition. In S. M. Kosslyn & D. N. Osherson (Eds.), *An invitation to cognitive science, Vol. 2. Visual cognition* (2nd ed., pp. 121–165). Cambridge, MA: MIT Press.

Bowlby, J. (1988). *A secure base: Clinical applications of attachment theory.* London: Routledge.

Braine, M. D. S., & O'Brien, D. P. (Eds.). (1998). *Mental logic.* Mahwah, NJ: Erlbaum.

Bransford, J. D., Barclay, J. R., & Franks, J. J. (1972). Sentence memory: A constructive versus an interpretive approach. *Cognitive Psychology, 3,* 193–209.

Brewka, G., Dix, J., & Konolige, K. (1997). *Nonmonotonic reasoning: An overview.* Stanford, CA: CLSI, Stanford University.

Bruner, J. S., Goodnow, J. S., & Austin, G. G. (1956). *A study of thinking.* New York: Wiley.

Bucciarelli, M., & Johnson-Laird, P. N. (1999). Strategies in syllogistic reasoning. *Cognitive Science, 23,* 247–303.

Bucciarelli, M., & Johnson-Laird, P. N. (2005). Naïve deontics: A theory of meaning, representation, and reasoning. *Cognitive Psychology, 50,* 159–193.

Byrne, R. M. J. (2002). Mental models and counterfactual thoughts about what might have been. *Trends in Cognitive Sciences, 6,* 426–431

Byrne, R. M. J. (2005). *The rational imagination: How people create alternatives to reality.* Cambridge, MA: MIT Press.

Byrne, R. M. J., & Handley, S. J. (1997). Reasoning strategies for suppositional deductions. *Cognition, 62,* 1–49

Byrne, R. M. J., & Johnson-Laird, P. N. (1989). Spatial reasoning. *Journal of Memory and Language, 28,* 564–575.

Carreiras, M., &Santamaria, C. (1997). Reasoning about relations: Spatial and nonspatial problems. *Thinking and Reasoning, 3,* 191–208.

Cowles, W., & Garnham, A. (2005). Antecedent focus and conceptual distance effects in category noun-phrase anaphora. *Language and Cognitive Processes, 20,* 725–750.

Craik, K. (1943). *The nature of explanation.* Cambridge, England: Cambridge University Press.

de Kleer, J. (1986). An assumption-based TMS. *Artificial Intelligence, 28,* 127–162

Elio, R., & Pelletier, F. J. (1997). Belief change as prepositional update. *Cognitive Science, 21,* 419–460.

Evans, J.St. B. T. (2003). In two minds: Dual process accounts of reasoning. *Trends in Cognitive Sciences, 7,* 454–459.

Evans, J. St. B. T., & Over, D. E. (1996). *Rationality and reasoning.* Hove, England: Psychology Press.

Evans, J. St. B. T., & Over, D. E. (2004). *If.* Oxford, England: Oxford University Press.

Feldman, J. (2000). Minimization of Boolean complexity in human concept learning. *Nature, 407,* 630–633.

Fumero, A., Santamaría, C., & Johnson-Laird, P. N. (2010). Reasoning and autobiographical memory for personality. *Experimental Psychology, 57,* 215–220.

Galotti, K. M., Baron, J., & Sabini, J. P. (1986). Individual differences in syllogistic reasoning: Deduction rules or mental models? *Journal of Experimental Psychology: General, 115,* 16–25.

García-Madruga, J. A., Moreno, S., Carriedo, N., Gutiérrez, F., & Johnson-Laird, P. N. (2001). Are conjunctive inferences easier than disjunctive inferences? A comparison of rules and models. *Quarterly Journal of Experimental Psychology, 54A*, 613–632.

Gärdenfors, P. (1992). Belief revision: An introduction. In P. Gärdenfors (Ed.), *Belief revision* (pp. 1–20). Cambridge, England: Cambridge University Press.

Garnham, A. (1987). *Mental models as representations of discourse and text.* Chichester, England: Ellis Horwood.

Garnham, A. (2001). *Mental models and the interpretation of anaphora.* Hove, England: Psychology Press.

Gentner, D., & Stevens, A. L. (Eds.). (1983). *Mental models.* Hillsdale, NJ: Erlbaum.

Gernsbacher, M. A. (1990). *Language comprehension as structure building.* Hillsdale, NJ: Erlbaum.

Girotto, V., Mazzocco, A., & Tasso. A. (1997). The effect of premise order in conditional reasoning: a test of the mental model theory. *Cognition, 63*, 1–28.

Glenberg, A. M., Meyer, M., & Lindem, K. (1987). Mental models contribute to foregrounding during text comprehension. *Memory and Language, 26*, 69–83.

Goldvarg, Y., & Johnson-Laird, P. N. (2000). Illusions in modal reasoning. *Memory and Cognition, 28*, 282–294.

Goldvarg, Y., & Johnson-Laird, P. N. (2001). Naïve causality: A mental model theory of causal meaning and reasoning. *Cognitive Science, 25*, 565–610.

Goodwin, G., & Johnson-Laird, P. N. (2005). Reasoning about relations. *Psychological Review, 112*, 468–493.

Goodwin, G., & Johnson-Laird, P. N. (2006). Reasoning about the relations between relations. *Quarterly Journal of Experimental Psychology, 59*, 1047–1069.

Goodwin, G., & Johnson-Laird, P. N. (2010). Conceptual illusions. *Cognition, 114*, 253–265.

Goodwin, G. P., & Johnson-Laird, P. N. (2011). Mental models of Boolean concepts. *Cognitive Psychology, 63*, 34–59.

Harman, G. (1986). *Change in view: Principles of reasoning.* Cambridge, MA: MIT Press.

Hegarty, M. (1992). Mental animation: Inferring motion from static diagrams of mechanical systems. *Journal of Experimental Psychology: Learning, Memory, and Cognition, 18*, 1084–1102.

Hunt, E. B. (1962). *Concept learning: An information processing problem.* New York: Wiley.

Inhelder, B., & Piaget, J. (1958). *The growth of logical thinking from childhood to adolescence.* London: Routledge & Kegan Paul.

James, W. (1907). *Pragmatism—A new name for some old ways of thinking.* New York: Longmans, Green.

Jeffrey, R. (1981). *Formal logic: Its scope and limits* (2nd ed.). New York: McGraw-Hill.

Johnson-Laird, P. N. (1983). *Mental models.* Cambridge, MA: Harvard University Press.

Johnson-Laird, P. N. (2006). *How we reason.* Oxford, England: Oxford University Press.

Johnson-Laird, P. N., & Byrne, R. M. J. (1991). *Deduction.* Hillsdale, NJ: Erlbaum.

Johnson-Laird, P. N., & Byrne, R. M. J. (2002). Conditionals: A theory of meaning, pragmatics, and inference. *Psychological Review, 109*, 646–678.

Johnson-Laird, P. N., Byrne, R. M. J., & Schaeken, W. S. (1992). Propositional reasoning by model. *Psychological Review, 99*, 418–439.

Johnson-Laird, P. N., Girotto, V., & Legrenzi, P. (2004). Reasoning from inconsistency to consistency. *Psychological Review, 111*, 640–661.

Johnson-Laird, P. N., & Hasson, U. (2003). Counterexamples in sentential reasoning. *Memory and Cognition, 31*, 1105–1113.

Johnson-Laird, P. N., Legrenzi, P., Girotto, P., & Legrenzi, M. S. (2000). Illusions in reasoning about consistency. *Science, 288*, 531–532.

Johnson-Laird, P. N., Legrenzi, P., Girotto, V., Legrenzi, M., & Caverni, J-P. (1999). Naïve probability: A mental model theory of extensional reasoning. *Psychological Review, 106*, 62–88.

Johnson-Laird, P. N., Mancini, F., & Gangemi, A. (2006). A hyper emotion theory of psychological illnesses. *Psychological Review, 113*, 822–841.

Johnson-Laird, P. N., & Savary, F. (1999). Illusory inferences: A novel class of erroneous deductions. *Cognition, 71*, 191–229.

Johnson-Laird, P. N., & Wason, P. C. (Eds.). (1976). *Thinking: Readings in cognitive science.* Cambridge, England: Cambridge University Press.

Kahneman, D., & Frederick, S. (2002). Representativeness revisited: Attribute substitution in intuitive judgement. In T. Gilovich, D. Griffin, & D. Kahneman (Eds.), *Heuristics and biases: The psychology of intuitive judgement* (pp. 49–81.) Cambridge, England: Cambridge University Press.

Kamp, H., & Reyle, U. (1993). *From discourse to logic.* Dordrecht, The Netherlands: Kluwer.

Kemp, C., & Tenenbaum, J. B. (2008). The discovery of structural form. *Proceedings of the National Academy of Sciences USA, 105*, 10687–10692.

Khemlani, S., & Johnson-Laird, P. N. (2009). Disjunctive illusory inferences and how to eliminate them. *Memory and Cognition, 37*, 615–623.

Khemlani, S., & Johnson-Laird, P. N. (2011). The need to explain. *Quarterly Journal of Experimental Psychology, 64*, 276–288.

Kintsch, W. (1988). The role of knowledge in discourse comprehension: A construction-integration model. *Psychological Review, 95*, 163–182.

Knauff, M., Fangmeier, T., Ruff, C. C., &Johnson-Laird, P. N. (2003). Reasoning, models, and images: Behavioral measures and cortical activity. *Journal of Cognitive Neuroscience, 4*, 559–573.

Knauff, M., & Johnson-Laird, P. N. (2002). Imagery can impede inference. *Memory and Cognition, 30*, 363–371.

Kripke, S. (1963). Semantical considerations on modal logic. *Acta Philosophica Fennica, 16*, 83–94.

Kroger, J. K., Nystrom, L. E., Cohen, J. D., & Johnson-Laird, P. N. (2008). Distinct neural substrates for deductive and mathematical processing. *Brain Research, 1243*, 86–103.

Lee, N. Y. L., Goodwin, G. P., & Johnson-Laird, P. N. (2008). The psychological problem of Sudoku. *Thinking and Reasoning, 14*, 342–364.

Legrenzi, P., Girotto, V., & Johnson-Laird, P. N. (2003). Models of consistency. *Psychological Science, 14*, 131–137.

Magliano, J. P., Miller, J., & Zwaan, R. A. (2001). Indexing space and time in film understanding. *Applied Cognitive Psychology, 15*, 533–545.

Mar, R. A., & Oatley, K. (2008). The function of fiction is the abstraction and simulation of social experience. *Perspectives on Psychological Science, 3*, 173–192.

Markman, A. B., & Dietrich, E. (2000). Extending the classical view of representation. *Trends in Cognitive Science, 4*, 470–475.

Marr, D. (1982). *Vision: A computational investigation into the human representation and processing of visual information.* San Francisco: W. H. Freeman.

Medin, D. L., Lynch, E. B., & Solomon, K. O. (2000). Are there kinds of concepts? *Annual Review of Psychology, 51*, 121–147.

Medin, D. L., & Smith, E. E. (1984). Concepts and concept formation. *Annual Review of Psychology, 35*, 113–138.

Metzler, J., & Shepard, R. N. (1982). Transformational studies of the internal representations of three-dimensional objects. In R. N. Shepard & L. A. Cooper *Mental images and their transformations* (pp. 25–71.) Cambridge, MA: MIT Press.

Miller, G. A., & Johnson-Laird, P. N. (1976). *Language and perception.* Cambridge, MA: Harvard University Press.

Nosofsky, R. M., Palmeri, T. J., & Mc Kinley, S. C. (1994). Rule-plus-exception model of classification learning. *Psychological Review, 101*, 53–79.

Oberauer, K. (2006). Reasoning with conditionals: A test of formal models of four theories. *Cognitive Psychology, 53*, 238–283.

Ormerod, T. C., & Richardson, J. (2003). On the generation and evaluation of inferences from single premises. *Memory and Cognition, 31*, 467–478.

Peirce, C. S. (1931–1958). *Collected papers of Charles Sanders Peirce* (C. Hartshorne, P. Weiss, & A. Burks, Eds.). Cambridge, MA: Harvard University Press.

Perrow, C. (1984). *Normal accidents: Living with high-risk technologies.* New York: Basic Books.

Pylyshyn, Z. (2003). Return of the mental image: Are there really pictures in the head? *Trends in Cognitive Science, 7*, 113–118.

Quelhas, A. C., & Byrne, R. M. J. (2003). Reasoning with deontic and counterfactual conditionals. *Thinking and Reasoning, 9*, 43–66.

Quelhas, A. C., Johnson-Laird, P. N., & Juhos, C. (2010). The modulation of conditional assertions and its effects on reasoning. *Quarterly Journal of Experimental Psychology, 63*, 1716–1739.

Rader, A.W., & Sloutsky, V. M. (2002). Processing of logically valid and logically invalid conditional inferences in discourse comprehension. *Journal of Experimental Psychology: Learning, Memory, and Cognition, 28*, 59–68.

Radvansky, G. A., & Copeland, D. E. (2006). Walking through doorways causes forgetting: Situation models and experienced space. *Memory and Cognition, 34*, 1150–1156.

Rinck, M., & Bower, G. (1995). Anaphor resolution and the focus of attention in situation models. *Memory and Language, 34*, 110–131.

Rips, L. J. (1994). *The psychology of proof.* Cambridge, MA: MIT Press.

Roberts, M. J. (2000). Strategies in relational inference. *Thinking and Reasoning, 6*, 1–26.

Santamaría, C., & Johnson-Laird, P. N. (2000). An antidote to illusory inferences. *Thinking and Reasoning, 6*, 313–333.

Schaeken, W., & Johnson-Laird, P. N. (2000). Strategies in temporal reasoning. *Thinking and Reasoning, 6*, 193–219.

Schaeken, W. S., Johnson-Laird, P. N., & d' Ydewalle, G. (1996). Mental models and temporal reasoning. *Cognition, 60*, 205–234.

Schroyens, W., Schaeken, W., & Handley, S. (2003). In search of counter examples: Deductive rationality in human reasoning. *Quarterly Journal of Experimental Psychology, 56A*, 1129–1145.

Schroyens, W., Schaeken, W., & d'Ydewalle, G. (2001). The processing of negations in conditional reasoning: A meta-analytic case study in mental model and/or mental logic theory. *Thinking and Reasoning, 7*, 121–172.

Shepard, R. N., Hovland, C. I., & Jenkins, H. M. (1961). Learning and memorization of classifications. *Psychological Monographs: General and Applied, 75*, 1–42.

Sloman, S. A. (1996). The empirical case for two systems of reasoning. *Psychological Bulletin, 119*, 3–22.

Stanovich, K. E. (1999). *Who is rational? Studies of individual differences in reasoning.* Mahwah, NJ: Erlbaum.

Stevenson, R. J., Nelson, A. W. R., & Stenning, K. (1995). The role of parallelism in strategies of pronoun comprehension. *Language and Speech, 38*, 393–418.

Tversky, A., & Kahneman, D. (1973). Availability: A heuristic for judging frequency and probability. *Cognitive Psychology, 5*, 207–232.

Tversky, A., & Kahneman, D. (1982). Causal schemas in judgements under uncertainty. In D. Kahneman, P. Slovic, & A. Tversky (Eds.), *Judgement under uncertainty: Heuristics and biases.* (pp. 117–128). Cambridge, England: Cambridge University Press.

Tversky, A., & Kahneman, D. (1983). Extensional versus intuitive reasoning: The conjunction fallacy in probability judgment. *Psychological Review, 90*, 292–315.

Ullman, S. (1996). *High-level vision: Object recognition and visual cognition.* Cambridge, MA: MIT Press.

Van der Henst, J-B., Yang, Y., & Johnson-Laird, P. N. (2002). Strategies in sentential reasoning. *Cognitive Science, 26*, 425–468.

Vandierendonck, A., & De Vooght, G. (1996). Evidence for mental-model based reasoning: A comparison of reasoning with time and space concepts. *Thinking and Reasoning, 2*, 249–272.

Van Dijk, T. A., & Kintsch, W. (1983). *Strategies of discourse comprehension.* New York: Academic Press.

Verschueren, N., Schaeken, W., & d' Ydewalle, G. (2005). A dual-process specification of causal conditional reasoning. *Thinking and Reasoning, 11*, 278–293.

Vigo, R. (2009). Modal similarity. *Journal of Experimental and Theoretical Artificial Intelligence*, iFirst, 1–16.

Walsh, C., & Johnson-Laird, P. N. (2004). Co-reference and reasoning. *Memory and Cognition, 32*, 96–106.

Walsh, C. R., & Johnson-Laird, P. N. (2009). Changing your mind. *Memory and Cognition, 37*, 624–631.

Wason, P. C., & Evans, J. St. B. T. (1975). Dual processes in reasoning? *Cognition, 3*, 141–154.

Yang, Y., & Johnson-Laird, P. N. (2000). How to eliminate illusions in quantified reasoning. *Memory and Cognition, 28*, 1050–1059.

## Further Reading

Byrne, R. M. J. (2005). *The rational imagination: How people create alternatives to reality.* Cambridge, MA: MIT Press.

Johnson-Laird, P. N. (2006). *How we reason.* Oxford, England: Oxford University Press.

Khemlani, S., & Johnson-Laird, P. N. (2012). The processes of inference. *Argument and Computation*, 1–17, iFirst.

# Analogical Learning and Reasoning

Dedre Gentner *and* Linsey A. Smith

### Abstract

Analogy is a kind of similarity in which the same system of relations holds across different objects. Analogies thus capture parallels across different situations. When such a common structure is found, then what is known about one situation can be used to infer new information about the other. This chapter describes the processes involved in analogical reasoning, reviews foundational research and recent developments in the field, and proposes new avenues of investigation.

**Key Words:** analogy, mapping, inference, reasoning, relational structure, structural alignment, relational similarity, structure mapping, metaphor

Analogical ability—the ability to perceive like relational structure across different contexts—is a core mechanism of human cognition. The ability to perceive and use purely relational similarity is a major contributor—arguably *the* major contributor—to our species' remarkable mental powers (Gentner, 2003; Kurtz, Gentner, & Gunn, 1999; Penn, Holyoak, & Povinelli, 2008). Understanding the processes that underlie analogy is thus important in any account of "why we're so smart" (Gentner, 2003).

Analogy is ubiquitous in human cognition. People often understand a new situation by drawing an analogy to a familiar situation. This can be seen in words like "iron horse" for a locomotive or "horsepower" as applied to cars. Studies of problem solving show that students often try to solve problems by mapping solutions from known problems (e.g., Ross, 1987). Analogical processes are central in learning and transfer, as discussed later. In educational settings, a familiar, well-structured domain is often used to help students grasp a less-well-understood domain. Even without instruction, in everyday life people draw on experiential analogies to form mental models of phenomena in

the world. For example, it appears that people form an (erroneous) notion of "curvilinear momentum" by analogy with linear momentum (Kaiser & Profitt, 1985; McCloskey, 1983). Additionally, analogy is important in scientific discovery and creativity. Studies in the history of science show that analogy was a means of discovery for scientists like Faraday (Tweney, 1991), Maxwell (Nersessian, 1984), and Kepler (Gentner, 2002), as well as among contemporary scientists (Dunbar, 1995).

Analogical comparison is also used in social judgment. People often draw on experiences with familiar people or situations when asked to judge strangers (Andersen & Chen, 2002) or to evaluate new social experiences (Mussweiler & Rüter, 2003). Indeed, Mussweiler and Epstude (2009) found that people who were primed to use analogical comparison in social judgments were faster, but just as accurate, as those who did not use comparison—suggesting that social comparison is a natural processing strategy. Finally, analogy is used in persuasion and argumentation. For example, Jared Diamond (1995) offered the history of Easter Island as a cautionary analogy for the future of earth as a whole. Diamond argues that as the island, once rich in vegetation, became increasingly overpopulated, deforestation occurred. This caused the bird population to dwindle, and, without trees with which to build canoes, the islanders could no longer catch ocean fish. The result was famine, societal upheaval, and war, all of which put still more strain on the ecosystem. This analogy portrays the idea of the earth as an island, rich in resources but ultimately finite.

Thus, analogy is pervasive in human thought and speech. In this chapter, we begin by presenting an overview of analogical reasoning and its component processes. We then discuss each process in greater detail. We go on to review the role of analogy in learning and reasoning, including how analogy is used in everyday life and how it can go wrong. We discuss current research in analogy, including implicit uses of analogy and the neural basis of analogical processes.

## Defining Analogy

A good analogy both reveals common structure between two situations and suggests further inferences. That is, analogical mapping involves recognizing a common relational system between two situations and generating further inferences guided by these commonalities (Gentner, 1983; Gentner & Markman, 1997; Holyoak & Thagard, 1989; Hummel & Holyoak, 1997; Kokinov & French, 2003). The commonalities may include concrete property matches between the situations, but this is not necessary; what is crucial is *similarity in relational structure*.

In the most typical case of analogy, a familiar concrete domain (the *base* or *source*) serves as a model by which one can understand and draw new inferences about a less familiar or abstract domain (the *target*). We illustrate with an analogy used in geoscience education, which explains processes within the earth's mantle (the area between the core of the earth and the outer crust) by analogy with processes in a lava lamp (Tolley & Richmond, 2003):

> The bulb at the bottom of the lava lamp slowly begins to heat the solid lava on top of it. As its density is reduced by thermal expansion, the lava begins to rise. The lava continues to rise to the top of the lamp and away from its heat source; thus, it begins to cool and sinks back to the bottom of the lamp. As the lava begins to heat up again, the process starts anew.
> Likewise, the earth's outer core begins to heat the solid mantle above it. The mantle then begins to rise

toward the surface and away from the outer core; consequently, the mantle begins to cool.

In this analogy, the bulb corresponds to the core, the lava to the mantle, and the top of the lamp to the earth's crust. This analogy highlights a common relational structure: the process of thermal convection. This analogy also invites the (correct) inference that the mantle rises when heated because its density is reduced by thermal expansion. A process that cannot be seen becomes easier to grasp by virtue of the analogy with a concrete base domain. This example illustrates the potential value of analogy as a tool for education.

## Processes in Analogical Reasoning

As demonstrated in the earlier examples, analogies vary widely in their appearance, content, and usage. This raises an obvious question: Are all of these processed in the same way? Some theorists think not. For example, Lee and Holyoak (2008) argued that causal analogies are processed differently from other analogies. However, there is considerable evidence that the same kinds of analogical processes operate across many domains. The same basic set of phenomena has been found for perceptual analogies as for conceptual analogies, and for close similarity as for more distant analogies (Kokinov & French, 2003; Markman & Gentner, 1993b). Most theorists agree that all analogies share a basic set of processes:

- *Retrieval*: given some current topic that a person is thinking about, *analogical retrieval* occurs when a person is reminded of a prior relationally similar case.
- *Mapping*: given two cases that are simultaneously present (either physically or mentally), *mapping* involves a process of aligning the representations. This process of structural alignment often gives rise to new *inferences*, drawing a new abstraction and/or noticing a salient difference between the two cases, as amplified later.
- *Evaluation*: once the mapping has been achieved, *evaluation* involves judging the analogy, along with any inferences that have been generated.

We begin with mapping, the core process in analogical reasoning, reserving retrieval for later. While analogical reasoning invariably involves a mapping process, it does not always involve retrieval. For example, often both cases are presented to the reasoner, as in persuasive analogies like "Afghanistan is like Vietnam" or instructional analogies like "electric current is like waterflow."

## Mapping: Alignment and Inference Projection

Mapping is the core process of analogy, and it has been the central focus of much analogy research in both psychology and computer science (Gentner & Forbus, 2010). Theories of analogy have largely converged on a set of assumptions like those outlined in Gentner's (Gentner, 1983; Gentner & Markman, 1997) structure-mapping theory (see reviews by Gentner & Forbus, 2010; Kokinov & French, 2003). According to this theory, analogical mapping involves establishing a *structural alignment* between two representations based on finding the maximal set of commonalities between them.

The structural alignment process is heavily dependent on finding common relational structure. This means that the corresponding objects in the base and target need not resemble each other; what is important is that they hold like roles in the matching systems of relations. However, as discussed later, both object matches and relational matches enter into the process of alignment, so it is easier to establish an alignment if the corresponding objects do resemble one another. For example, it should be faster to match ■ ■ ■ with ▩ ▩ ▩ than with ● ● ●.

Nonetheless, people (especially adults) are highly likely to focus on relational commonalities even when there are conflicting object matches, as in the pair of scenes shown in Figure 42.1. The two scenes share a common relational system of a vehicle towing another conveyance. When asked to say what the VW in the left scene (Figure 42.1A) goes with in the right scene (Figure 42.1B), people often choose the other VW—an obvious object match. But if participants first compare the two scenes, they instead choose the boat, which plays the same role in the corresponding relational structure—both are being towed (Markman & Gentner, 1993b). Thus,

analogy provides a way to focus on relational commonalities independently of the objects in which those relations are embedded.

### STRUCTURAL ALIGNMENT

The alignment process is guided by a set of tacit constraints that lead to structural consistency. Structural consistency entails *one-to-one correspondence*, which requires that each element of a representation match (at most) one element of the other representation. For example, in the analogy above, the VW in the top scene cannot correspond to both the boat and the VW in the bottom scene. Structural consistency also involves *parallel connectivity*, which requires that if two predicates (i.e., relations) are put into correspondence, then their arguments must also be placed into correspondence. Returning to the lava lamp analogy, if the relation HEATS is matched between the two cases, then the elements that fill the corresponding roles in the two relations will also be placed into correspondence; that is, the bulb will be mapped to core (both are the things that HEAT), and the lava will be mapped to the mantle (both are being HEATED):

HEATS (bulb, lava) → HEATS (core, mantle)
Bulb → Core
Lava → Mantle

There is considerable evidence that people abide by structural consistency in mapping (e.g., Krawczyk, Holyoak, & Hummel, 2005; Markman, 1997; Markman & Gentner, 1993b; Spellman & Holyoak, 1992). For example, Spellman and Holyoak (1992) asked people to analogize Operation Desert Storm to World War II, with Saddam Hussein corresponding to Hitler. People who mapped George Bush to FDR went on to map the United States during Desert Storm to the United States during World War II. Those who mapped George Bush to Winston Churchill almost always mapped the United States during Desert Storm to Britain during World War II. Thus, people varied in

**Figure 42.1** Causal analogy (taken from Markman & Gentner, 1993b). The VW in the scene on the left (*A*) has both an object match (the VW) and a relational match (the boat) in the scene on the right (*B*). People who first compare the two scenes are likely to match the car with the boat, based on the structural alignment between the two scenes.

their preferred mapping but were structurally consistent within each mapping.

Analogical processing is also guided by an implicit preference for finding large connected systems of relations. This preference, termed the *systematicity principle*, can be stated more precisely as a bias to prefer interpretations in which the lower order matches (such as events) are connected by higher order constraining relations, such as causal relations (Clement & Gentner, 1991; Falkenhainer, Forbus, & Gentner, 1989). In other words, what people implicitly seek in an analogy is a common structure with a deeply connected system of relations. For example, the appeal of the lava lamp analogy stems from the sense that the same causal pattern of thermal convection applies in both cases.

## ANALOGICAL INFERENCE

Once two situations are aligned—that is, once correspondences have been established between them—further information can often be imported from base to target based on this alignment. This process of *analogical inference* is a crucial component of the mapping process. Two key points concerning analogical inference are (1) analogical inference is highly selective; we do not simply bring across everything known about the base; and (2) the inferences are *candidate inferences*; they are not guaranteed to be true. To begin with the first point, selectivity, a key issue for theories of analogy is capturing how potential inferences are constrained. Without such selection criteria, any fact known about the base could be posited about the target. Clearly, analogical reasoning would be useless if we had to spend time rejecting inferences such as the *earth's mantle comes in many attractive colors*, which could be derived from the lava lamp analogy. Thus, characterizing the constraints on analogical inference is essential to any account of analogy.

The structural consistency and systematicity preferences discussed earlier also guide inference projection. That is, candidate inferences are made in accord with the structural correspondences that were established during alignment. One way to think about inference generation is as a process of *structural pattern completion*: Once the base and target have been aligned and their common structure found (Fig. 42.2a), if there are additional assertions connected to that common structure in the base (and not yet present in the target), then this structure will be brought over as a candidate inference (Fig. 42.2b). Of course, these candidate inferences may not be correct; further evaluation is needed, as

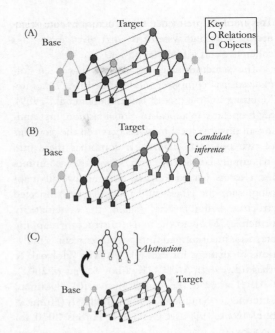

**Figure 42.2** Analogy as structure mapping. (*A*) Initial alignment of common relational structure. Relations are matched between domains, and their arguments are also matched. (*B*) Candidate inferences are generated by a process of structural pattern completion. (*C*) A possible outcome of structural alignment is abstraction of the common relational structure.

discussed later. Furthermore, not all analogies yield inferences; sometimes the point of an analogy is simply to convey a common abstraction (Fig. 42.2c).

Candidate inferences are derived by extending the common relational structure. This provides a natural filter on which inferences will be considered. For example, in the lava lamp analogy, suppose you make an initial alignment between *The bulb heats up the lava, and then the lava rises* with the fact that *The core heats up the mantle, and then the mantle rises*. If you then learn more about the causal connections in the lava lamp—for example, that *the lava rises because of its decreased density due to thermal expansion*—then you may carry this pattern over to the earth as a candidate inference: *Likewise, the mantle rises because of its decreased density due to thermal expansion*. This inference is warranted by its connection to the aligned relational structures between the two domains. The claim that inferences are guided by systematicity and structural consistency has empirical support. For example, people prefer to make inferences from structurally consistent mappings (Markman, 1997); and people are more likely to import an inference from base to target when that fact is causally connected to other matching facts (Clement & Gentner, 1991).

This implicit preference for structurally consistent, deeply matching systems is what gives analogy its coherence and inferential power.

The structure-mapping process has been formalized in a computer model called the Structure-Mapping Engine (SME; Falkenhainer et al., 1989). SME operates in a local-to-global fashion, first finding all possible local matches between the elements of two potential analogs. It combines these into structurally consistent clusters, and then combines the clusters (called kernels) into an overall mapping, with the largest and most deeply connected structure being favored (again, the systematicity principle). Many of the tenets of structure mapping are also incorporated into other current simulations of analogy, for example, ACME (Holyoak & Thagard, 1989), AMBR (Kokinov & Petrov, 2001), CAB (Larkey & Love, 2003), DORA (Doumas, Hummel, & Sandhofer, 2008), and LISA (Hummel & Holyoak, 1997; see Gentner & Forbus, 2010, for a review).

### Evaluation

After the structural alignment between two analogs has been found and the inferences projected, both the analogy and its inferences are evaluated. Evaluation of particular inferences contributes to the larger evaluation of the analogy. At least three factors enter into evaluating the inferences from an analogy. The first is the *factual correctness* of the inferences. If an analogy yields inferences that are clearly false, people will generally reject both the inferences and the analogy that gave rise to them (Smith & Gentner, 2010). Of course, in some cases one cannot immediately identify whether an inference is true, as when making new predictions about a scientific outcome by analogy with another domain. In these cases we must decide whether the prediction is sufficiently interesting to justify trying to test it. A related factor in evaluating inferences is *adaptability* (Keane, 1996): how easy it is to modify a fact from the base to fit the target. People accept inferences that are highly adaptable to the target more readily than those that are less adaptable (Keane, 1996). Novick and Holyoak (1991) have demonstrated the importance of adaptation in solving mathematics problems by analogy to stories. They showed that even when subjects knew the correspondences between two domains, they often had difficulty applying the solution plan in the base story (the mathematical procedure of finding the lowest common multiple) to a target problem.

A second factor that governs the evaluation of inferences is *goal relevance*. Inferences that are relevant to the current goals of the reasoner are more important in evaluation of the analogy than those that are not (e.g., Clement & Gentner, 1991; Holyoak, 1985). This constraint is especially pertinent in problem solving. People often map solutions from previously solved problems to current problems; in these cases, the key issue is whether the analogy yields inferences relevant to the goal of solving the current problem. For example, Spellman and Holyoak (1996) showed that when two possible mappings are available for a given analogy, people select the mapping whose inferences are most applicable to their goals.

A third factor in evaluation is the amount of new knowledge generated by the analogy (Forbus, Gentner, Everett, & Wu, 1997). If an analogy yields startling new inferences, this could potentially constitute a significant gain in knowledge. Even if somewhat risky, such an analogy is often desirable, especially when brainstorming about a new domain.

### Similarity Is Like Analogy

The framework developed for analogy extends to literal similarity (Gentner & Markman, 1997; Goldstone, Medin, & Gentner, 1991; Markman & Gentner, 1993a, 1993b; Medin, Goldstone, & Gentner, 1993). The distinction between analogy and literal similarity is that in analogy, only the relational structure is shared, whereas in literal similarity (or overall similarity), both relational structure and object properties are shared. In the lava lamp analogy, there is no physical resemblance between the earth and the lava lamp. Contrast this to a literal similarity match in which one lava lamp is compared to another: The lava lamps physically resemble one another, in addition to sharing a causal structure. The difference between analogy and similarity can be thought of within a similarity space defined by the degree of object-attribute similarity and the degree of relational similarity, as shown in Figure 42.3. When a comparison shares a high degree of relational similarity, but has very little attribute similarity, we consider it an analogy. As the amount of attribute similarity increases, the comparison becomes one of literal similarity. Thus, the distinction between literal similarity and pure analogy is a continuum, not a dichotomy: A pair of cases that shares relational structure can be purely analogical (*anger is like a teakettle*), literally similar (*this teakettle is like that teakettle*), or somewhere in between

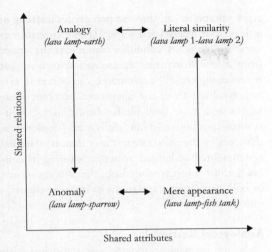

**Figure 42.3** Similarity space defined by the degree of relational similarity and object-attribute similarity (adapted from Gentner & Markman, 1997). These dimensions are continuous rather than categorical: A pair of cases can range from an overall similarity match to a purely relational (analogical) match (moving right to left along the top), and from an overall match to a purely surface match (moving top to bottom along the right).

(*a steam engine is like a teakettle*). These distinctions are not merely a matter of terminology; they are important psychologically. Overall similarity comparisons are far easier to notice and map than purely analogical comparisons, and they can serve as the entry point for children and other novice learners, as discussed later in this chapter.

## Analogical Learning

Analogy is an extremely powerful learning mechanism. One way in which analogy fosters knowledge acquisition is via *inference projection*—bringing across information from one analog to the other, as discussed earlier. While inference projection is perhaps the most obvious learning outcome of analogy (and also the most widely considered), analogy can augment knowledge in at least three other ways: schema abstraction (or generalization), difference detection (or contrast), and re-representation. We now discuss these in turn.

### Schema Abstraction (Generalization)

In structural alignment, relational similarities between two exemplars are highlighted, which can lead to the extraction of this relational structure. Extracting the common relational structure increases the likelihood that it will be used again later (Gick & Holyoak, 1983; Loewenstein, Thompson, & Gentner, 1999; Markman & Gentner, 1993b; Namy & Gentner, 2002). In the lava lamp analogy,

for example, one might extract the relational structure that describes thermal convection; this general schema can then be used to make sense of other convection systems, such as those that occur in the atmosphere.

Evidence that structural alignment promotes abstraction of relational schema comes from research in transfer of learning. Comparing two analogous scenarios (i.e., completing a structural alignment) dramatically increases the likelihood that a principle common to both exemplars will be transferred to a future item (relative to seeing just one exemplar, or even the same two items without encouragement to compare) (Catrambone & Holyoak, 1989; Gick & Holyoak, 1983). For example, Loewenstein et al. (1999) found that business school students who compared two negotiation scenarios were more than twice as likely to transfer the negotiation strategy to an analogous test negotiation as those who studied the same two scenarios separately. Additionally, when participants are asked to write the commonalities resulting from an analogical comparison, the quality of their relational schema predicts the degree of transfer to another example with the same structure (e.g., Gentner, Loewenstein, & Thompson, 2003; Gick & Holyoak, 1983; Loewenstein et al., 1999). Thus, through schema abstraction, analogy can promote the formation of new relational abstractions (Gentner & Kurtz, 2005) and abstract rules (Gentner & Medina, 1998); these generalizations can then be applied to new situations.

### Difference Detection (Contrast)

Structural alignment not only makes salient the relational commonalities between analogs, but it also leads naturally to the highlighting of *alignable differences* between analogs (Gentner & Markman, 1994; Markman & Gentner, 1993a). Alignable differences are differences that are connected to the common relational structure. Research has shown that alignable differences are highly salient. For example, when asked to state a difference between

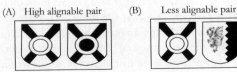

**Figure 42.4** In the pair on the left (*A*), which is easy to align, people readily notice an alignable difference (the color of the center circles). People are faster to name a difference for pairs like (*A*) than for less alignable pairs like the pair on the right (*B*) (Gentner & Sagi, 2006; Sagi, Gentner, & Lovett, 2012).

two figures like those in Figure 42.4, people are much faster to identify a difference for pair A than for pair B. Because pair A is easily aligned, the difference in the central circle pops out (Gentner & Sagi, 2006; Sagi, Gentner, & Lovett, 2012). Using conceptual pairs, Markman and Gentner (1993a) found a high correlation between the number of commonalities listed and the number of alignable differences listed. Furthermore, these alignable differences were related to the commonalities people generated. For instance, for the pair *car-motorcycle*, participants frequently listed *both have wheels* as a commonality and *cars have four wheels while motorcycles have two* as a difference. These results suggest that structural alignment influences which differences people notice. Alignable differences become highly apparent to the learner, thus making them available for learning by contrast.

### Re-Representation

Sometimes there is good reason to believe two nonidentical relations should match. This can happen, for example, if an instructor has provided an analogy between two seemingly disparate domains. In this case, the relations in the analogs may be re-represented to create a better match (e.g., Forbus et al., 1995; Kotovsky & Gentner, 1996; Yan, Forbus, & Gentner, 2003). Re-representation typically involves substituting a more abstract relation for the specific relations in the two analogs. For example, when people are given the following analogy, they typically arrive at the commonality "Each *got rid of* something they no longer wanted."

Walcorp divested itself of Acme Tires.
Likewise, Martha divorced George.

Re-representation can occur in perceptual as well as conceptual analogies (Hofstadter, 1995). Consider the perceptual analogy presented at the beginning of this chapter (Fig. 42.1). If you were to see either (A) or (B) by itself, you might well form a representation that was closely tied to the perceptual properties of the figure—for example, noting that (A) depicts *a car being towed* or that (B) shows *a boat hitched to a car*. However, once the figures are structurally aligned, these local descriptions are re-represented at a more abstract level: Both become seen as an instance of *a vehicle towing another conveyance*.

### Summary

The structural alignment process is geared toward finding a system of identical relations between two representations. This process potentiates learning in at least four interrelated ways: (1) inference projection: spontaneous candidate inferences are made from a well-structured representation to one that is less complete; (2) abstraction: the common system resulting from the alignment becomes more salient and more available for future use; (3) difference detection: alignable differences—differences that occupy the same role in the common relational system—are highlighted, fostering learning by contrast; and (4) re-representation: the altering of one or both analog representations to improve the relational match.

### Analogical Retrieval

So far, we have considered a scenario in which the two analogs are present (mentally and/or physically). However, analogies can also occur via spontaneous reminding: that is, while thinking about a topic, we may experience a reminding to some similar or analogous past experience. We now turn to the question of how this happens—what leads people to retrieve potential analogs from long-term memory? The news here is a bit on the gloomy side. People often fail to retrieve analogous cases, even ones that would be highly useful if retrieved. Gick and Holyoak (1980, 1983) were the first to show that people in a problem-solving situation often fail to be reminded of a prior analogous case that could help them solve the problem. This failure to access prior analogous cases is an example of "inert knowledge" (Whitehead, 1929)—knowledge that is not accessed when needed.

Much research has shown that similarity-based retrieval of prior cases is typically driven largely by surface similarities, such as similar objects and contexts, rather than by similarities in relational structure (Brooks, Norman, & Allen, 1991; Catrambone, 2002; Gentner, Rattermann, & Forbus, 1993; Holyoak & Koh, 1987; Reed, 1987; Ross, 1984, 1987). Strong surface similarity and content effects seem to dominate remindings and to limit the transfer of learning across domains. For example, Gentner, Rattermann, and Forbus (1993) gave participants a large set of stories to remember. Later, participants were given new stories that varied in their surface and relational similarity to the originals and were asked to write out any original stories they were reminded of. The remindings that resulted were strongly governed by surface commonalities, such as similar characters. In contrast, when asked to rate the similarity and inferential soundness of pairs of stories, the same participants

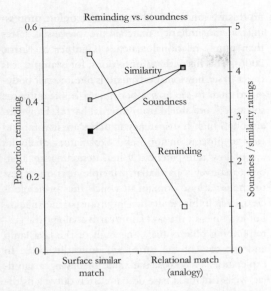

**Figure 42.5** Results from Gentner, Rattermann, and Forbus (1993), Experiment 2. Surface-similar matches produced more remindings, whereas relational matches were rated higher in soundness and in similarity.

relied primarily on higher order relational commonalities, such as matching causal structure. Participants even rated their own surface-similar remindings as poor matches. Figure 42.5 shows this striking dissociation between the kind of similarity that promotes memory retrieval and the kind of similarity that licenses mapping and inference. This pattern is also found in problem-solving tasks: Remindings of prior problems are strongly influenced by surface similarity, but success in solving the problem is best predicted by structural similarity (e.g., Ross, 1987).

Of course, it is important to bear in mind that in all of these studies, some people show genuine relational retrieval. It is not the case that relational remindings never occur; it is just that they are much rarer than remindings and overall similarity remindings (Forbus, Gentner, & Law, 1995). This may be partly because people often encode cases in a content-specific manner, so that later retrieval occurs only for highly surface-similar cases. In this case we would expect that experts, whose encodings presumably include more relational knowledge, will show better retrieval of structurally similar examples. Novick (1988) found this pattern when she compared people with varying degrees of mathematics expertise. Compared to novices, experts were more likely to retrieve structurally similar cases, rather than surface-similar ones; and when they did retrieve prior surface-similar cases, they were quicker to reject them.

## Development of Analogical Ability

When given an analogy, young children are highly influenced by object matches and are less able to attend to relational matches than are older participants (e.g., Gentner, 1988; Halford, 1993; Mix, 2008; Paik & Mix, 2006; Richland, Morrison, & Holyoak, 2006). This shift from a focus on objects to a focus on relations has been termed the *relational shift* (Gentner, 1988). Although there is widespread agreement that such a shift occurs, developmental researchers differ on why. One proposal is that the relational shift is driven primarily by gains in relational knowledge (Gentner & Rattermann, 1991). Another proposal is that the shift results from maturational increases in processing capacity (Halford, 1993); the idea is that making relational matches requires more processing capacity than making attribute matches. A third view explains the relational shift as stemming from a maturational increase in inhibitory control, which permits the child to suppress object matches in favor of relational matches (Richland et al., 2006; Thibaut, French, & Vezneva, 2010). These views are not mutually exclusive; it could well turn out that the best explanation for the relational shift will be some combination of these proposals.

Perhaps rather surprisingly, one way young children can come to perceive relational commonalities is through processing very close similarity comparisons (DeLoache, Kolstad, & Anderson, 1991; Kotovsky & Gentner, 1996; Loewenstein & Gentner, 2001)—a phenomenon described as *progressive alignment* (Gentner & Medina, 1998). Developmental research has shown (a) that young children can succeed with overall similarity matches well before they can succeed with purely relational matches and (b) that young learners can benefit from close literal similarity matches to gain the beginnings of relational insight. For example, in DeLoache's (1987) classic search task, children watched an experimenter hide a toy in a small model room and had to find another toy hidden "in the same place" in the full-sized room. Children under 3 years of age did very poorly at this task. Building on these results, Marzolf and DeLoache (1994) showed (a) if 2 ½-year-olds are given a similar-scale search task (so that model and room are highly similar) they perform very well (67% correct searches); and (b) when these children are brought back the next day and tested in the standard model-room task (small model and full-sized room), they are far more successful than age-mates who did not receive the highly similar pair first (35% correct).

This is related to the pattern discussed for adults, wherein comparing a pair of examples results in abstracting a relational schema, which can then be transferred to future examples. For adults, the initial comparison pair can be quite dissimilar—presumably because adults possess firm enough relational knowledge to allow them to align purely on the basis of relational similarity. But for young children, whose relational knowledge may be limited, close literal matches are important steppingstones, because they are very easy to align; the object matches support the relational alignment. This alignment results in a slight highlighting of the common relational structure, which then permits further alignments with more distant exemplars.

The finding that an easily aligned literal match can bootstrap young children to a more distant relational mapping via progressive alignment offers a route by which children's ordinary experiential learning can gradually lead them to the discovery of analogical matches (Gentner & Medina, 1998; Kotovsky & Gentner, 1986). Such overall similarity comparisons are far easier to notice and map than purely analogical comparisons, and they can serve as the entry point for children and other novice learners.

## Supports and Pitfalls

Analogy can be a valuable tool for learning and reasoning, but it can also be misleading. Several kinds of factors influence the outcome of an analogical mapping: first, factors internal to the mapping process itself, such as systematicity; second, characteristics of the reasoner, such as age and expertise; and, third, task factors such as processing load and time pressure, and context.

Among internal factors, *systematicity*—whether two analogs share a deeply connected relational structure—is crucial; people are more likely to make a relational alignment when they perceive a substantial relational match. Another factor internal to the mapping process is *transparency*: the degree to which the relationally corresponding objects in the two domains appear similar. A high-transparency analogy is one in which objects that share the same role are highly similar and noncorresponding objects are highly dissimilar. Such analogies are generally obvious and easy to align. For example, we noted earlier that *literal similarity* matches—which constitute the prototypical case of high-transparency matches—are more reliably retrieved from memory than are purely relational analogies. We also noted that young children are more likely to succeed in the alignment process when given a high-transparency (literal-similarity) match.

To this we can now add that even in online processing, literal-similarity matches are processed faster than purely relational matches (Gentner & Kurtz, 2006). This fits with our intuitions; for example, it is easier to see how one bodyguard is like another bodyguard than to see how a bodyguard is like antivirus software (both shield from external harm). However, although high-transparency matches are natural and easy to process, many useful explanatory analogies are of low transparency. When designing an analogy to convey a particular principle, it is often best to choose a base domain in which that principle is clear, even if this results in a low-transparency match. For example, in the lava lamp/earth analogy, the corresponding objects (e.g., the bulb of the lava lamp and the core of the earth) are quite dissimilar. In explanatory analogies, the value of having a familiar, well-structured base domain often outweighs the advantages of transparency.

Similarity between corresponding objects facilitates structural alignment, but similarity between noncorresponding objects impedes it. A *cross-mapped* comparison (Gentner & Toupin, 1986) is one in which similar (or identical) objects play different roles in the common relational structure. These extraneous matches can slow processing or even interfere with arriving at a relational match (Ross, 1987). Cross-mapped comparisons are very low in transparency; not only is the relationally correct object match not obvious, but also there is a competing object match.

Transparency and systematicity interact with each other and with characteristics of the reasoner, notably age and experience. For example, cross-mapped comparisons are particularly difficult for children and novices (Gentner & Rattermann, 1991; Gentner & Toupin, 1986; Richland et al., 2006), especially if the object matches are rich and distinctive (Gentner & Rattermann, 1991; Paik & Mix, 2006). But systematicity of relational structure can sometimes compensate for low transparency. For example, Gentner and Toupin (1986) gave children a simple story and asked them to re-enact the story with new characters. Both both 6- and 9-year-olds were sensitive to the transparency of the correspondences. Their mappings were highly accurate in the high-transparency condition (similar characters in corresponding roles), less accurate in the medium-transparency condition (dissimilar characters in corresponding roles), and least accurate in the cross-mapped condition (similar characters in different roles). In addition, older (but not younger) children benefited strongly from systematicity: When they were given a summary statement that provided a higher order plot structure, their mapping accuracy stayed high regardless of transparency. They were able to use the relational constraints provided by the higher order structure to maintain relational correspondences despite the tempting object matches. This finding is a microcosm of learning and development: the deeper and better-established our relational knowledge, the better we can maintain that structure in the face of competing local matches (Gentner & Toupin, 1986; Markman & Gentner, 1993b).

The third class of factors affecting analogical processing involves task conditions and their interaction with processing capacity. One generalization that emerges from several studies is that making relational matches requires more time and processing resources than making object attribute matches. For example, Goldstone and Medin (1994) found that when people are forced to terminate comparison processing early, they are strongly influenced by local attribute matches, even in cases where they would choose a relational match if given sufficient time. Waltz et al. (1999) asked people to state correspondences between two cross-mapped scenes taken from Markman and Gentner's (1993b) study (see Fig. 42.1) while carrying out a dual task designed to tax working memory and/or executive control—either generating random numbers or continually repeating the word *the*. Both dual tasks decreased the frequency with which participants identified relational correspondences and increased the frequency of choosing matching objects, suggesting that achieving a relational alignment requires more processing resources than does the process of matching objects.

One additional factor that influences whether an analogy will be useful involves the selection of the base domain. When we talk about analogical processing, it is usually with the assumption that an appropriate base domain has been selected. However, people sometimes choose inappropriate source analogs, which can lead to misguided inferences and faulty knowledge. For example, Kempton (1986) examined heating patterns used by households in winter and discovered that some households used a costly and ecologically wasteful strategy of constantly moving their thermostat setting from very high to very low and back. He concluded based on a series of interviews that this behavior stemmed from an incorrect model formed by analogy with other devices—namely, that the higher the thermostat setting, the more heat pours out, analogous to the way a faucet works. (In fact, most furnaces work at a constant rate; the thermostat simply determines when they turn off and on.) Because such incorrect mental models can be an impediment to science learning, some educators advise diagnosing and debugging these models in science classes (Collins, Stevens, & Goldin, 1979).

## Analogy in the Real World

Analogy researchers believe that analogy—and structural alignment more generally—is ubiquitous in human thinking. However, most of the research on analogy has been carried out in the experimental psychology laboratory, where people are explicitly provided with analogies and asked to respond in some way. Is real-world analogy guided by the same constraints seen in experimental studies? We now turn to research on analogy in naturalistic settings.

In a pioneering study of scientific reasoning, Dunbar (1993, 1995) studied the day-to-day processes of scientists in microbiology laboratories, Dunbar (1993, 1995) found that analogical thinking was a key component of all aspects of scientific reasoning, ranging from hypothesis generation to experimental design and data interpretation. Interestingly, Dunbar observed that many of the analogies scientists made were of high transparency, sharing not only causal structure but also many superficial features. For example, a scientist trying to determine the function of a gene in one organism (e.g., a gene in oysters) might draw an analogy to a gene in another organism (e.g., a similar gene in clams), whose function is well understood (Dunbar, 1997). These findings suggest that surface similarity aids in noticing potential comparisons, as many theories of analogy would predict. However, historical analyses reveal that scientists do sometimes use the kind of far-domain analogies that constitute a true leap in understanding (Holyoak & Thagard, 1997; Nersessian, 1984). These more dramatic analogies may be vehicles for large shifts in paradigm (Thagard, 1992).

We noted in the introduction that analogies are often used in argumentation and persuasion. In cases of disagreement, opponents often attack the analogy by pointing out critical differences. For example, after the BP oil spill in April of 2010, critics of the Obama administration offered an analogy exemplified by a *Washington Examiner* headline: "Gulf oil spill becoming Obama's Katrina: A timeline of presidential delay." The invited parallel is:

*The Bush administration's mismanagement exacerbated the results of Hurricane Katrina.*

*The Obama administration's mismanagement is exacerbating the results of the oil spill.*

Those who disagreed with this assessment denied the analogy's applicability. For example, a CNN correspondent stated that "unlike naturally occurring events such as Hurricane Katrina, the oil spill was something unforeseen and a never-before-happened moment." This move argues that the two situations are not causally analogous because Katrina was predictable from weather patterns, while the BP spill was unforeseen.

Analogy underlies much of humor. For example, Benjamin Franklin observed that "Genius without education is like silver in the mine." A more elaborate example comes from John Cassidy, writing in the *New Yorker* of November 29, 2010: "I came across an announcement that Citigroup, the parent company of Citibank, was to be honored ... for 'Advancing the Field of Asset Building in America.' This seemed akin to, say, saluting BP for services to the environment or praising Facebook for its commitment to privacy." Loewenstein and Heath (2009) surveyed jokes, children's stories, and advertisements from around the world and found that they often follow a *repetition-break plot structure*—essentially a progressive alignment structure. This structure is familiar to anyone who has heard a "rule of three" joke (e.g., "A doctor, a lawyer, and a psychologist walk into a bar ... ") or the story of the Three Little Pigs. Jokes and stories of this form begin with two highly similar episodes. Aligning these is essentially effortless, and this results in abstracting the common plot structure. The third episode is partly similar but contains a *break*—a sudden departure from this parallel plot structure. The humor or surprise comes from this break with expectations.

A further case of everyday analogy is the use of conceptual metaphors such as "their relationship has reached a crossroads" or "their marriage has been rather rocky" (Lakoff & Johnson, 1980). These are instances of the *A RELATIONSHIP IS A JOURNEY* metaphor, one of many widely used metaphoric systems. These kinds of metaphoric systems chiefly convey relational commonalities, and there is evidence that they are processed as conventionalized structure mappings (Bowdle & Gentner, 2005). Another everyday use of analogy occurs in the introduction of new technical concepts, such as (*computer*) *virus* (Gust, Kühnberger, & Schmid, 2006).

## Recent Avenues of Research in Analogy
### *Neuropsychology of Analogical Reasoning*

Recent studies have begun investigating the neural correlates of analogical processing (e.g., Green, Kraemer, Fugelsang, Gray, & Dunbar, 2010; Green, Fugelsang, Shamosh, Kraemer, & Dunbar, 2006; Krawczyk et al., 2008; Morrison et al., 2004; Wharton et al., 2000). Studies so far converge on areas within the left prefrontal cortex (l-PFC) as important in analogical reasoning. For example, Krawzyck et al. (2008) found that damage to the left prefrontal cortex was associated with poor performance on pictorial analogies of the form A:B::C:?. Several studies have implicated the left rostrolateral PFC in analogical mapping during semantic analogy problems (Green et al., 2006, 2010; Bunge, Wendelken, Badre, & Wagner, 2005; Krawczyk, McClelland, Donovan, Tillman, & Maguire, 2010). For example, Bunge, Helskog, and Wendelken (2009) showed that the rostrolateral prefrontal cortex was more heavily involved in a task that required relational comparison than in a task that required only featural processing. Of course, much remains to be discovered. For example, much of this work has involved four-term analogies of the form A:B::C:?. While these have the advantage of being tractable to investigate, they are fairly simple analogies. As neuroimaging techniques develop, we should be able to explore a greater range of depth and complexity in analogical materials and arrive at a more complete picture.

### *Analogical Reasoning Without Awareness*

Most experimental work tends to focus on the deliberate, conscious use of analogy; people retrieve or are given an analogy and are asked to interpret it and/or to derive new inferences. However, research in the past decade has demonstrated that not all analogical reasoning is deliberate. Blanchette and Dunbar (2002) first demonstrated the *analogical insertion effect*, in which analogical inferences are integrated unknowingly into mental representations of the target domain. They gave participants passages that explained a target issue (legalizing marijuana) by analogy with a familiar scenario (legalizing alcohol by repealing Prohibition). When asked to recognize assertions from the target passage, participants often misidentified analogical inferences as facts actually presented about the target; that is, they thought they had read statements about marijuana when what they had actually read were the analogous statements about alcohol. These findings show that analogical inference may occur without explicit awareness. But in these studies, the analogy was explicitly given to participants.

Day and Gentner (2007) took this phenomenon one step further. They asked whether analogical inference can occur without explicit awareness of the analogy itself. In their studies, people read a series of brief passages and then answered questions about them. Unbeknownst to the participants, each set of passages contained a later passage (the target) that was analogous to a prior passage. Participants' responses to the target passage revealed that they had aligned the target with the earlier passage and had mapped inferences from the prior passage to the target. Yet people reported that each passage had been understood on its own, without invoking other passages. Further studies of online reading time showed that these unaware analogical inferences were made during the processing of the target story.

These results show that information from a single analogous instance can spontaneously influence the way in which another situation is understood and remembered. Many questions remain. For example, in the Day and Gentner study the initial and final passages shared surface similarity as well as relational similarity. Would unaware inferences occur without this kind of strong overlap? Although there is much to discover, this line of research suggests that analogy may be the mechanism by which we apply existing knowledge to structure new situations.

## Conclusion

Analogy is at the core of higher order cognition (Gentner, Holyoak, & Kokinov, 2001; Hofstadter, 2001). Analogical processes underlie complex cognition, from scientific discovery to humor. The same basic processes of alignment and mapping also come into play in a vast range of human cognition, from perceptual similarity to categorization and decision-making.

Three decades of analogy research has led to great gains in our understanding of analogical processing. But there remain many open questions. We need a better understanding of how analogy plays out in everyday life and in how children and adults learn about the world. For example, how prevalent is the phenomenon of spontaneous, nonaware analogy? Could it account for the development of stereotypes? Another area that is largely open is that of the neural underpinnings of analogical processing. Aside from the left PFC areas noted earlier, are other areas of the brain involved, and do they differ for (for

example) spatial versus causal analogies? Finally, we are just beginning to explore analogical processing in other species (e.g., Haun & Call, 2009). Cross-species comparisons will help to delineate the cognitive components of analogical ability.

## References

Andersen, S. M., & Chen, S. (2002). The relational self: An interpersonal social-cognitive theory. *Psychological Review, 109*, 619–645.

Blanchette, I., & Dunbar, K. (2002). Representational change and analogy: How analogical inferences alter representations. *Journal of Experimental Psychology: Learning, Memory, and Cognition, 28*, 672–685.

Bowdle, B., & Gentner, D. (2005). The career of metaphor. *Psychological Review, 112*, 193–216.

Brooks, L. R., Norman, G. R., & Allen, S. W. (1991). Role of specific similarity in a medical diagnostic task. *Journal of Experimental Psychology: General, 120*(3), 278–287.

Bunge, S. A., Helskog, E. H., & Wendelken, C. (2009). Left, but not right, rostrolateral prefrontal cortex meets a stringent test of the relational integration hypothesis. *NeuroImage, 46*, 338–342.

Bunge, S. A., Wendelken, C., Badre, D., & Wagner, A. D. (2005). Analogical reasoning and prefrontal cortex: Evidence for separable retrieval and integration mechanisms. *Cerebral Cortex, 15*, 239–249.

Catrambone, R. (2002). The effects of surface and structural feature matches on the access of story analogs. *Journal of Experimental Psychology: Learning, Memory, and Cognition, 28*, 318–334.

Catrambone, R., & Holyoak, K. J. (1989). Overcoming contextual limitations on problem-solving transfer. *Journal of Experimental Psychology: Learning, Memory, and Cognition, 15*(6), 1147–1156.

Clement, C. A., & Gentner, D. (1991). Systematicity as a selection constraint in analogical mapping. *Cognitive Science, 15*, 89–132.

Collins, A. M., Stevens, A. L., & Goldin, S. (1979). Misconceptions in student's understanding. *International Journal of Man-Machine Studies, 11*, 145–156.

Day, S., &Gentner, D. (2007). Nonintentional analogical inference in text comprehension. *Memory and Cognition, 35*, 39–49.

DeLoache, J. S. (1987). Rapid change in the symbolic functioning of very young children. *Science, 238*, 1556–1557.

DeLoache, J. S., Kolstad, V., & Anderson, K. N. (1991). Physical similarity and young children's understanding of scale models. *Child Development, 62*, 11 1–126.

Diamond, J. (1995). Easter's end. *Discover, 9*, 62–69.

Doumas. L. A. A., Hummel, J. E., & Sandhofer, C. M. (2008). A theory of the discovery and predication of relational concepts.*Psychological Review, 115*, 1–43.

Dunbar, K. (1993). Concept discovery in a scientific domain. *Cognitive Science, 17*, 397–434

Dunbar, K. (1995). How scientists really reason: Scientific reasoning in real-world laboratories. In R. J. Sternberg & J. Davidson (Eds.). *Mechanisms of insight (pp. 365–395)*. Cambridge, MA: MIT Press.

Dunbar, K. (1997). How scientists think: Online creativity and conceptual change in science. In T. B. Ward, S. M. Smith, & S. Vaid (Eds.), *Conceptual structures and processes: Emergence, discovery and Change*. APA Press. Washington DC.

Falkenhainer, B., Forbus, K. D., & Gentner, D. (1989). The structure-mapping engine: Algorithm and examples. *Artificial Intelligence, 41*, 1–63.

Forbus, K. D., Gentner, D., Everett, J. O., & Wu, M. (1997). Towards a computational model of evaluating and using analogical inferences. In M. G. Shafto & P. Langley (Eds.), *Proceedings of the Nineteenth Annual Conference of the Cognitive Science Society* (pp. 229–234). Mahwah: Erlbaum.

Forbus, K. D., Gentner, D., & Law, K. (1995). MAC/FAC: A model of similarity-based retrieval. *Cognitive Science: A Multidisciplinary Journal, 19*(2), 141–205.

Gentner, D. (1983). Structure-mapping: A theoretical framework for analogy. *Cognitive Science, 7*, 155–170.

Gentner, D. (1988). Metaphor as structure mapping: The relational shift. *Child Development, 59*(1), 47–59.

Gentner, D. (2002). Analogy in scientific discovery: The case of Johannes Kepler. In L. Magnani & N. J. Nersessian (Eds.), *Model-based reasoning: Science, technology, values* (pp.21–39). New York: Kluwer Academic/Plenum Publisher.

Gentner, D. (2003). Why we're so smart. In D. Gentner & S. Goldin-Meadow (Eds.), *Language in mind: Advances in the study of language and thought* (pp. 195–235). Cambridge, MA: MIT Press.

Gentner, D., & Forbus, K. (2010). Computational models of analogy. *WIREs Cognitive Science.* doi: 10.1002/wcs.105

Gentner, D., Holyoak, K. J., & Kokinov, B. (Eds.). (2001). *The analogical mind: Perspectives from cognitive science.* Cambridge, MA: MIT Press.

Gentner, D., & Kurtz, K. (2005). Relational categories. In W. K. Ahn, R. L. Goldstone, B. C. Love, A. B. Markman, & P. W. Wolff (Eds.), *Categorization inside and outside the lab* (pp. 151–175). Washington, DC: American Psychological Association.

Gentner, D., & Kurtz, K. (2006). Relations, objects, and the composition of analogies. *Cognitive Science, 30*, 609–642.

Gentner, D., Loewenstein, J., & Thompson, L. (2003). Learning and transfer: A general role for analogical encoding. *Journal of Educational Psychology, 95*(2), 393–405.

Gentner, D., & Markman, A. B. (1994). Structural alignment in comparison: No difference without similarity. *Psychological Science, 5*(3), 152–158.

Gentner, D., & Markman, A. B. (1997). Structure mapping in analogy and similarity. *American Psychologist, 52*, 45–56.

Gentner, D., & Medina, J. (1998). Similarity and the development of rules. *Cognition, 65*(2), 263–297.

Gentner, D., & Rattermann, M. J. (1991). Language and the career of similarity. In S. A. Gelman & J. P. Brynes (Eds.), *Perspectives on thought and language: Interrelations in development* (pp. 225–277). London: Cambridge University Press.

Gentner, D., Rattermann, M. J., & Forbus, K. D. (1993). The roles of similarity in transfer: Separating retrievability from inferential soundness. *Cognitive Psychology, 25*, 524–575.

Gentner, D., & Sagi, E. (2006). Does "different" imply a difference? A comparison of two tasks. In R. Sun & N. Miyake (Eds.), *Proceedings of the Twenty-Eighth Annual Meeting of the Cognitive Science Society* (pp. 261–266). Mahwah, NJ: Erlbaum.

Gentner, D., & Toupin, C. (1986). Systematicity and surface similarity in the development of analogy. *Cognitive Science, 10*, 277–300.

Gick, M. L., & Holyoak, K. J. (1980). Analogical problem solving. *Cognitive Psychology, 12*, 306–355.

Gick, M. L., & Holyoak, K. J. (1983). Schema induction and analogical transfer, *Cognitive Psychology, 15*, 1–38.

Goldstone, R. L., & Medin, D. L. (1994). Similarity, interactive activation, and mapping. *Journal of Experimental Psychology: Learning Memory and Cognition, 20*(1), 3–28.

Goldstone, R. L., Medin, D. L., & Gentner, D. (1991). Relational similarity and the nonindependence of features in similarity judgments. *Cognitive Psychology, 23*(2), 222–262.

Green, A. E., Fugelsang, J. A., Kraemer, D. J., Shamosh, N. A., & Dunbar, K. N. (2006). Frontopolar cortex mediates abstract integration in analogy. *Brain Research, 1096*, 125–137.

Green, A. E., Kraemer, D. J., Fugelsang, J. A., Gray, J. R., & Dunbar, K. N. (2010). Connecting long distance: Semantic distance in analogical reasoning modulates frontopolar cortex activity. *Cerebral Cortex, 21*(1), 70–76.

Gust, H., Kühnberger, K-U., &Schmid, U. (2006). Metaphors and heuristic-driven theory projection (HDTP). *Theoretical Computer Science, 354*(1), 98–117.

Halford, G. S. (1993). *Children's understanding: The development of mental models.* Hillsdale, NJ: Erlbaum.

Haun, D. B, M., &Call, J. (2009). Great apes' capacities to recognize relational similarity. *Cognition, 110*, 147–159

Hofstadter, D. (1995). *Fluid concepts and creative analogies.* New York: Basic Books.

Hofstadter, D. R. (2001). Analogy as the core of cognition. In D. Gentner, K. J. Holyoak, & B. N. Kokinov (Eds.), *The analogical mind: Perspectives from cognitive science* (pp. 499–538). Cambridge, MA: MIT Press.

Holyoak, K. J. (1985). The pragmatics of analogical transfer. In G. H. Bower (Ed.), *The psychology of learning and motivation* (Vol. 19, pp. 59–87). New York: Academic Press.

Holyoak, K. J., & Koh, K. (1987). Surface and structural similarity in analogical transfer. *Memory and Cognition, 15*, 332–340.

Holyoak, K. J., & Thagard, P. (1989). Analogical mapping by constraint satisfaction. *Cognitive Science, 13*, 295–355.

Holyoak, K. J., & Thagard, P. (1997). The analogical mind. *American Psychologist, 52*, 35–44.

Hummel, J. E., & Holyoak, K. J. (1997). Distributed representations of structure: A theory of analogical access and mapping. *Psychological Review, 104*, 427–466.

Kaiser, M., & Proffitt, D. R. (1985). The development of beliefs about falling objects. *Development, 38*(6), 533–539.

Keane, M. T. (1996). On adaptation in analogy: Tests of pragmatic importance and adaptability in analogical problem solving. *Quarterly Journal of Experimental Psychology, 46*, 1062–1085.

Kempton, W. (1986). Two theories used of home heat control. *Cognitive Science, 10*, 75–91.

Kokinov, B., & French, R. M. (2003). Computational models of analogy making. In L. Nadel (Ed.), *Encyclopedia of cognitive science (pp. 113–118).* London: MacMillan.

Kokinov, B. N., & Petrov, A. A. (2001). Integrating memory and reasoning in analogy-making: The AMBR model. In D. Gentner, K. J. Holyoak, & B. N. Kokinov (Eds.), *The analogical mind: Perspectives from cognitive science* (pp. 161–196). Cambridge, MA: MIT Press.

Kotovsky, L., & Gentner, D. (1996). Comparison and categorization in the development of relational similarity. *Child Development, 67*(6), 2797–2822.

Krawczyk, D. C., Holyoak, K. J., & Hummel, J. E. (2005). The one-to-one constraint in analogical mapping and inference. *Cognitive Science, 29*, 797–806.

Krawzyck, D. C., McClelland, M. M., Donovan, C. M., Tillman, G. D., & Maguire, M. J. (2010). An fMRI investigation of cognitive stages in reasoning by analogy. *Brain Research, 1342*, 63–73.

Krawczyk, D. C., Morrison, R. G., Viskontas, I., Holyoak, K. J., Chow, T. W., Mendez, M. F., ... Knowlton, B. J. (2008). Distraction during relational reasoning: The role of prefrontal cortex in interference control. *Neuropsychologia, 46*, 2020–2032.

Kurtz, K. J., Gentner, D., & Gunn, V. (1999). Reasoning. In B. M. Bly & D. E. Rumelhart (Eds.), *Cognitive science: Handbook of perception and cognition* (2nd ed., pp. 145–200). San Diego, CA: Academic Press.

Lakoff, G., & Johnson, M. (1980). *Metaphors we live by.* Chicago: University of Chicago Press.

Larkey, L. B., & Love, B. C. (2003). CAB: Connectionist analogy builder. *Cognitive Science, 27*, 781–794.

Lee, H. S., & Holyoak, K. J. (2008). The role of causal models in analogical inference. *Journal Experimental Psychology: Learning, Memory, and Cognition, 34*(5), 1111–1122.

Loewenstein, J., & Gentner, D. (2001). Spatial mapping in preschoolers: Close comparisons facilitate far mappings. *Journal of Cognition and Development, 2*(2), 189–219.

Loewenstein, J., & Heath, C. (2009). The repetition-break plot structure: A cognitive influence on selection in the marketplace of ideas. *Cognitive Science, 33*(1), 1–19.

Loewenstein, J., Thompson, L., & Gentner, D. (1999). Analogical encoding facilitates knowledge transfer in negotiation. *Psychonomic Bulletin and Review, 6*(4), 586–597.

Markman, A. B. (1997). Constraints on analogical inference. *Cognitive Science, 21*, 373–418.

Markman, A. B., & Gentner, D. (1993a). Splitting the differences: A structural alignment view of similarity. *Journal of Memory and Language, 32*, 517–535.

Markman, A. B., & Gentner, D. (1993b). Structural alignment during similarity comparisons. *Cognitive Psychology, 25*, 431–467.

Marzolf, D. P., & DeLoache, J. S. (1994). Tranfer in young children's understandin of spatial representations. *Child Development, 64*, 1–15.

McCloskey, M. (1983). Intuitive physics. *Scientific American, 248*(4), 122–30.

Medin, D. L., Goldstone, R. L., & Gentner, D. (1993). Respects for similarity. *Psychological Review, 100*(2), 254–278.

Mix, K. S. (2008). Children's equivalence judgments: Crossmapping effects. *Cognitive Development, 23*, 191–203.

Morrison, R. G., Krawczyk, D. C., Holyoak, K. J., Hummel, J. E., Chow, T. W., ... Knowlton, B. J. (2004). A neurocomputational model of analogical reasoning and its breakdown in frontotemporal lobar degeneration. *Journal of Cognitive Neuroscience, 16*, 260–271.

Mussweiler, T., & Epstude, K. (2009). Relatively fast! Efficiency advantages of comparative thinking. *Journal of Experimental Psychology: General, 138*(1), 1.

Mussweiler, T., & Rüter, K. (2003). What friends are for! The use of routine standards in social comparison. *Journal of Personality and Social Psychology, 85*(3), 467–481.

Namy, L. L., & Gentner, D. (2002). Making a silk purse out of two sow's ears: Young children's use of comparison in category learning. *Journal of Experimental Psychology: General, 131*(1), 5–15.

Nersessian, N. J. (1984). *Faraday to Einstein: Constructing meaning in scientific theories.* Dordrecht, The Netherlands: Nijhoff.

Novick, L. R. (1988). Analogical transfer, problem similarity, and expertise. *Journal of Experimental Psychology: Learning, Memory, and Cognition, 14*, 510–520.

Novick, L. R., & Holyoak, K. J. (1991). Mathematical problem solving by analogy. *Journal of Experimental Psychology: Learning, Memory, and Cognition, 17*, 398–415.

Paik, J. H., & Mix, K. S. (2006) Preschoolers' similarity judgments: Taking context into account. *Journal of Experimental Child Psychology, 95*, 194–214.

Penn, D. C., Holyoak, K. J., & Povinelli, D. J. (2008). Darwin's mistake: Explaining the discontinuity between human and nonhuman minds. *Behavioral and Brain Sciences, 31*(02), 109–130.

Reed, S. K. (1987). A structure-mapping model for word problems. *Journal of Experimental Psychology: Learning, Memory, and Cognition, 13*(1), 124–139.

Richland, L. E., Morrison, R. G., & Holyoak, K. J. (2006) Children's development of analogical reasoning: Insights from scene analogy problems. *Journal of Experimental Child Psychology, 94*, 249–273.

Ross, B. H. (1984). Remindings and their effects in learning a cognitive skill. *Cognitive Psychology, 16*, 371–416.

Ross, B. H. (1987). This is like that: The use of earlier problems and the separation of similarity effects. *Journal of Experimental Psychology: Learning, Memory, and Cognition, 13*, 629–639.

Sagi, E., Gentner, D., & Lovett, A. (2012). What difference reveals about similarity. *Cognitive Science, 36*(6), 1019–1050.

Smith, L., & Gentner, D. (2010). Structural constraints and real-world plausibility in analogical inference. In S. Ohlsson & R. Catrambone (Eds.), *Proceedings of the 32nd Annual Meeting of the Cognitive Science Society* (pp. 712–717). Austin, TX: Cognitive Science Society.

Spellman, B. A., & Holyoak, K. J. (1992). If Saddam is Hitler then who is George Bush? Analogical mapping between systems of social roles. *Journal of Personality and Social Psychology, 62*(6), 913–933.

Spellman, B. A., & Holyoak, K. J. (1996). Pragmatics in analogical mapping. *Cognitive Psychology, 31*, 307–346.

Thagard, P. (1992). *Conceptual revolutions.* Princeton, NJ: Princeton University Press.

Thibaut, J.-P., French, R. M., & Vezneva, M. (2010a). The development of analogy making in children: Cognitive load and executive functions. Journal of Experimental Child Psychology, 106(1), 1–19.

Tolley, S. G., & Richmond, S. D. (2003). Use of the LAVA® Lamp as an analogy in the geoscience classroom. *Journal of Geoscience Education, 51*, 217–220.

Tweney, R. D. (1991). Faraday's notebooks: the active organization of creative science. *Physics Education, 26*, 301–306.

Waltz, J. A., Knowlton, B. J., Holyoak, K. J., Boone, K. B., Miskin, F. S., Santos, M. M., ... Miller, B. L. (1999). A system for relational reasoning in human prefrontal cortex. *Psychological Science, 10*, 119–125.

Wharton, C. M., Grafman, J., Flitman, S. S., Hansen, E. K., Brauner, J., Marks, A., & Honda, M. (2000). Toward neuroanatomical models of analogy: A positron emission tomography study of analogical mapping. *Cognitive Psychology, 40*, 173–197.

Whitehead, A. N. (1929): *The aims of education and other essays.* New York: Free Press.

Yan, J., Forbus, K., & Gentner, D. (2003). A theory of rerepresentation in analogical matching. In *Proceedings of the 25th Annual Conference of the Cognitive Science Society.*

# Decision Making

Maarten Speekenbrink *and* David R. Shanks

**Abstract**

This chapter reviews normative and descriptive aspects of decision making. Expected Utility Theory (EUT), the dominant normative theory of decision making, is often thought to provide a relatively poor description of how people actually make decisions. Prospect Theory has been proposed as a more descriptively valid alternative. The failure of EUT seems at least partly due to the fact that people's preferences are often unstable and subject to various influences from the method of elicitation, decision context, and goals. In novel situations, people need to infer their preferences from various cues such as the context and their memories and emotions. Through repeated experience with particular decisions and their outcomes, these inferences can become more stable, resulting in behavior that is more consistent with EUT.

**Key Words:** decision making, preference, expected utility theory, prospect theory, multiattribute decisions, decisions from experience

Should you take the car, bus, or train to work? What should you eat for lunch? Should you join a pension fund or make your own arrangements for retirement? A day is filled with decisions, from mundane to profound. The scientific study of decision making concerns both how people ought to, and how they actually do, make such decisions. It is an interdisciplinary field, with contributions from (in alphabetical order) economics, mathematics, philosophy, psychology, and statistics.

In this chapter, we will provide an introduction to decision-making research. Given the breadth of the field, this overview will necessarily be sketchy at times. Our aim is to provide the reader with key principles and results and to show where (we think) the field is heading. Keeping with tradition, we start with an overview of (subjective) Expected Utility Theory (EUT), the dominant normative theory of decision making. We then discuss problems with this theory as a descriptive account of decision making and present a proposed solution, Prospect Theory.

In the remainder of the chapter, we discuss evidence that preferences are often unstable and subject to influence from the immediate context and currently active goals. Unstable preferences are mainly found in situations in which decision makers have little experience, where they have to infer their preferences from the available information, such as the immediate context or their own memories and emotions. We finish with an overview of recent research that shows that, when people are allowed to repeatedly make decisions and experience their outcomes, preferences can become stable and people can learn to behave in accordance with the principles of EUT.

## How to Make Decisions: Expected Utility Theory

Normative theories of decision making are concerned with how rational people *ought* to make decisions. The most widely accepted normative principle of decision making is the maximization of expected utility. In Expected Utility Theory (EUT), decision problems are analyzed in terms of acts, states, and consequences. Acts are the courses of action a decision maker can follow; they are basic units between which the decision maker can choose and are thus under the control of the decision maker. Each act can have a number of potential consequences and every consequence has some value to the decision maker. Which consequence will actually follow an act depends upon factors outside the control of the decision maker, collectively referred to as "states of nature." While the true state of nature is usually unknown, the decision maker is assumed to have some idea about the probability that states will occur. These probabilities can either be objective ("decisions under risk") or subjective ("decisions under uncertainty"). In either case, the main idea is that the decision maker should choose that act which is expected to provide the most value, or "utility." The expected utility of an act is a weighted sum of the utilities of its potential consequences, where each weight is the probability that the consequence will occur as a result of the act.

As an example, consider a doctor who is visited by a patient complaining of stomach cramps. Based on this symptom, the doctor thinks the patient either has contracted a virus or suffers from a rather serious case of indigestion. Two strains of the virus are going round: Strain A is very serious and, if left untreated, will result in severe disability; strain B is relatively mild and, if untreated, the patient will likely feel ill for a week but get better thereafter. The two strains need different treatments; both involve administration of a medicine with side effects, but the side effects for the treatment of strain A are much more serious than those for the treatment of B. If the patient has indigestion, no treatment is necessary, and the doctor can send him home without serious consequences.

In this example, there are three acts (treatment for virus A, treatment for virus B, and no treatment), three states (virus A, virus B, and indigestion), and nine possible outcomes. The acts ($a$), states ($s$), and outcomes ($o$) can be entered into a decision matrix as in the table below:

The decision problem can be viewed as a game in which Nature chooses a state and the doctor an act. What is the doctor's best strategy? This will depend on the doctor's belief regarding the likelihood that Nature chooses each state and the value of each of the outcomes. To determine the probability of the states, the doctor consulted a recently conducted study, which stated the following probabilities for patients with stomach cramps: $P(\text{"virus A"}) = .05$, $P(\text{"virus B"}) = .1$, and $P(\text{"indigestion"}) = .85$. Although neither virus is very likely, it might be unwise for the doctor to send the patient home, as this could result in severe disability if the patient did happen to have contracted virus A. According to EUT, the doctor should, for each course of action, weight the potential outcomes by their likelihood of occurrence and determine an expectation regarding the outcome of the act. To do so, each outcome has to be assigned a numerical value referred to as its *utility*. Example values are given in the decision matrix. The expected utility of an act is then computed as

$$EU(a_i) = \sum_{j=1}^{n} P(o_{ij}) \times u(o_{ij}) \qquad (1)$$

where $P(o_{ij})$ is the probability that outcome $o_{ij}$ occurs and $u(o_{ij})$ refers to its utility. In decisions under risk, the conditional probabilities of the outcome are given, while they are subjectively determined in decisions under uncertainty. The best decision is then the act with the highest expected utility (for these example values, the expected utilities are $-21$, $-14.5$, and $-5.25$ for the three acts, respectively, so the doctor should decide to send the patient home).

The principle of maximum expected utility was first proposed by Daniel Bernoulli (1738/1954) as a solution to the St Petersburg paradox. Previously, decision making was defined in terms of maximizing expected (monetary) value, but the St Petersburg paradox showed that people are only willing to pay relatively small amounts to play a

| | $s_1$ (strain A) | $s_2$ (strain B) | $s_3$ (indigestion) |
|---|---|---|---|
| $a_1$ (medicine A) | $o_{11}$ (major side effects; $u = -20$) | $o_{12}$ (ill and major side effects; $u = -30$) | $o_{13}$ (major side effects; $u = -20$) |
| $a_2$ (medicine B) | $o_{21}$ (disability and minor side effects; $u = -100$) | $o_{22}$ (minor side effects; $u = -10$) | $o_{23}$ (minor side effects; $u = -10$) |
| $a_3$ (send home) | $o_{31}$ (disability; $u = -95$) | $o_{32}$ (ill; $u = -5$) | $o_{33}$ (fine; $u = 0$) |

game of chance in which the expected winnings are infinite.[1] Bernouilli's solution was based on the idea that the value of a monetary gain is not the same for everyone: 10 dollars means more to a pauper than to a millionaire. In other words, the subjective value (utility) of money has decreasing marginal returns. By proposing that the utility function for money is concave, Bernouilli was able to give a first account for "risk aversion," the finding that a sure win is usually preferred to a gamble with the same expected value.

### The Axioms of Expected Utility Theory

The principle of maximizing expected utility can be justified on the grounds that its consistent application will guarantee that the decision maker obtains the maximum utility "in the long run" (after an infinite number of independent repetitions), but this justification is not to everyone's liking (e.g., Lopes, 1981; Samuelson, 1963). Indeed, it was not until Von Neumann and Morgenstern (1947), in the second edition of their famous book, *Theory of Games and Economic Behavior*, proved that maximizing expected utility uniquely satisfies a set of reasonable a priori axioms that EUT became the cornerstone of rational decision making. The Von Neumann and Morgenstern framework considers decisions between gambles or lotteries. A lottery consists of a set of mutually exclusive outcomes, each with an objective and known probability, such that the probabilities sum to 1 for all outcomes (i.e., the outcomes are exhaustive). Later, Savage (1954) extended their framework from such decisions under risk to decisions under uncertainty, showing that decisions which satisfy a set of axioms are made as if they maximize *subjective* expected utility, taking the expectation with respect to a subjective probability distribution.

Since the seminal work of Von Neumann and Morgenstern, simplified and alternative axiomatizations of EUT have been proposed (see, e.g., Krantz, Luce, Suppes, & Tversky, 1971; Wakker, 1989). The differences between these are not important for our purposes. The four important axioms are as follows:

1. *Completeness*. This axiom concerns the existence of a preference relation for all options. More formally, given two options (lotteries) A and B, either A is preferred to B, B is preferred to A, or the decision maker is indifferent between A and B.

2. *Transitivity*. This axiom concerns the relation between pairwise preferences. More formally, if an option A is considered at least as good as option B, and option B is considered at least as good as option C, then option A must be considered at least as good as option C. The axiom of transitivity guards one against a *money-pump*. Suppose you prefer option A to B, B to C, and C to A. Then you should be willing to pay money to trade option C for B, pay money to subsequently trade option B for A, and then to subsequently trade option A for C, ad infinitum. You would end up without any money, and quite likely with the option you started out with.

3. *Independence*. The axiom of independence states that if option A is preferred to option B, then the lottery $(p:A,(1-p):C)$ should be preferred to the lottery $(p:B,(1-p):C)$, where $(p:A,(1-p):C)$ should be read as saying that outcome A occurs with probability $p$ and outcome C with probability $(1-p)$. As the probability of option C is common to both gambles, this should have no effect on their preference. A similar axiom was proposed by Savage (1954) as the *sure-thing principle*: If someone prefers option A when state S obtains but also when state S does not obtain, then (s)he should prefer option A even when (s)he is uncertain whether state S obtains.

4. *Continuity*. The axiom of continuity states that if A is preferred to B, and B is preferred to C, then it must be possible to construct a lottery $(p:A,(1-p):C)$ such that the decision maker is indifferent between this lottery and option B for sure.

As already mentioned, this is not the only set of axioms that implies the expected utility principle. An important consequence of all of these axiomatizations is that if someone's decisions respect the axioms, the options can be assigned numerical utilities such that the decisions maximize expected utility. In other words, the decisions can be represented *as if* they were made in accordance to maximum expected utility. In this sense, the tenet of rationality lies within the axioms, not in an explicit process of utility maximization. There is no need to assume that the utilities have any reality (that they are somewhere "inside" the people making the decisions); the utilities are merely a representation of the choices made. This representational view contrasts with previous notions of utility, which equated it with experienced pleasure and pain (e.g., Bentham, 1789/1948).

While the axiomatization of rational decision making seems appealing in its simplicity, requiring only consistency in a set of decisions, it is questionable that such internal consistency always implies rationality. Consider the following example by Sen (1993): Suppose a person at a dinner party is offered the last remaining chocolate on a plate. Out of politeness, she chooses to decline. But if the plate contained two chocolates, she might have decided to take one. Based purely on choices, she seems to prefer nothing to a chocolate in the first situation, but a chocolate to nothing in the second situation. Thus, the choices are intransitive over these two situations, while there is nothing irrational in her decisions in light of her social preferences. One may object that the decision alternatives are not the same in the two situations: In the first, she chooses between the last chocolate or nothing, and in the second situation between the second-last chocolate or nothing. While this objection is sensible, it only strengthens the point that the representation of the decision situation must be in accordance to the decision maker's goals: whether decisions are truly transitive may not be immediately obvious.

## Descriptive Failures of Expected Utility Theory

While generally (though not universally) accepted as the normative theory of decision making, EUT offers a relatively poor description of how people actually make decisions. Over the years, many empirical results have questioned the descriptive validity of EUT and the axioms underlying it. We will only mention a few key results here (for a more extensive overview, see e.g., Kahneman & Tversky, 2000; Schoemaker, 1982).

### Allais Paradox

In 1953, Allais presented a major challenge to EUT. He showed that when people are presented with the choice between lotteries

A: Receive $1 million for sure
B: A 10% chance of receiving $5 million and an 89% chance of receiving $1 million (and an implicit 1% chance of receiving nothing)

the large majority prefer A to B. However, when presented with a choice between the lotteries

C: An 11% chance of receiving $1 million
D: A 10% chance of receiving $5 million

the majority prefer D to C. As the two gambles are structurally equivalent between the two situations, this pattern violates the independence axiom.[2] This paradox is characteristic of a general finding referred to as the *common ratio* effect, in which the more risky of two lotteries becomes relatively more attractive when the probability of winning in both lotteries is multiplied by a common ratio.

### Ellsberg Paradox

In 1961, Ellsberg presented a major problem for subjective EUT (Savage, 1954) in decisions under uncertainty, where the probability of the outcomes can only be subjectively determined. Suppose an urn is filled with 90 balls. Thirty balls are colored red and the remainder is a mix of black and yellow balls, in an unknown proportion. One ball is randomly drawn from the urn. When people are presented with the choice between lotteries

A: Receive $100 if the ball is red
B: Receive $100 if the ball is black

most people choose A. But when people are presented with lotteries

C: Receive $100 if the ball is red or yellow
D: Receive $100 if the ball is black or yellow

most people choose D. The first result suggests that the subjective probability of drawing a black ball is less than 1/3, yet the second implies it is larger than 1/3.[3] Like the Allais (1953) paradox, the Ellsberg paradox violates the independence axiom as the probability of obtaining a yellow ball is identical in lotteries C and D. According to Ellsberg, people have an aversion to ambiguity and will avoid it when possible. As the probability of winning is known in gambles A and D, these are preferred.

### Framing

While not explicit in the axioms of EUT, it is generally assumed that decisions should respect the principle of invariance (Slovic, 1995; Tversky & Kahneman, 1986), according to which preferences should be invariant to the way in which the options are formulated. This, however, does not seem to hold. For instance, consider the "Asian disease" problem (Tversky & Kahneman, 1981), which concerns an upcoming outbreak of a rare disease expected to kill 600 people. Participants are asked to choose between two proposed programs to combat the disease. Those who are given the options

Program A: 200 people will be saved
Program B: a 1/3 probability that 600 people will be saved, and a 2/3 probability that no people will be saved

generally choose program A, while participants presented with the options

**Program A'**: 400 people will die

**Program B'**: a 1/3 probability that nobody will die, and a 2/3 probability that 600 people will die

generally choose program B'. It should be clear that, in terms of lives saved, programs A' and B' are identical to programs A and B, respectively. This finding shows that whether a description focuses on gains (people saved) or losses (people died) has a substantial impact on the decisions made. This asymmetry between gains and losses forms an important part of Prospect Theory, to which we turn next.

### Prospect Theory

Prospect Theory (PT; Kahneman & Tversky, 1979; Tversky & Kahneman, 1992) was an attempt to make minimal changes to EUT in order to make it descriptively valid (Kahneman & Tversky, 2000). According to PT, decisions involve two distinct stages: an "editing phase" and an "evaluation phase." In the editing phase, people apply various simplifications to the decision problem. For instance, they will remove from consideration dominated options that are worse than others in every respect, as well as outcomes with extremely small probabilities. In the subsequent evaluation stage, the edited options are evaluated in a similar fashion to EUT, as a weighted sum of the subjective value of the outcomes.

A key principle in the evaluation stage is that the utility of an outcome is determined with respect to a neutral reference point, usually the status quo. Traditionally, the utility of monetary values was defined with reference to a person's overall wealth. According to PT, outcomes are evaluated as changes from the reference point and depending on where the reference point is placed, outcomes are conceived as either gains or losses. The difference between gains and losses has a much greater impact on the resulting decisions than a person's overall final wealth state. This is clearly shown by Kahneman and Tversky (1979), who had one group of participants imagine that they were given $1000. When they were then given the choice between

**A**: A 50% chance of winning $1000

**B**: A sure win of $500

most participants (84%) preferred option B. A second group were told to imagine they had been given $2000. When they were subsequently given the choice between

**A'**: A 50% chance of losing $1000

**B'**: A sure loss of $500

most people (69%) preferred option A'. As options A and A' are equivalent in terms of final wealth (as are B and B'), people who base their decisions on final wealth should make the same decision in both situations. This is not what participants did. Apparently, they did not take the initial bonus of $1000 or $2000 into account, because this aspect was common to the two alternatives. Instead, the choice seemed solely based on the discriminating features, something Kahneman and Tversky refer to as the *isolation effect*. In addition, the results indicate that people react differently to losses and gains. People are risk seeking for losses, preferring a risky option to a certain option with the same expected value, but risk averse for gains. To account for this asymmetry, PT proposes a utility function—now referred to as the value function—for gains and losses as depicted in Figure 43.1. The value function is discontinuous (has a "break") at the reference point; it is concave for gains and convex for losses.

As shown in Figure 43.1, the value function also has a steeper slope for losses than wins, which accounts for a second finding, namely that "losses loom larger than gains." This is illustrated in the *endowment effect* (Thaler, 1980). In a classic study showing this effect (Kahneman, Knetsch, & Thaler, 1990), some university students were given a mug and, in a roundabout way, asked for the minimum price they would accept to sell the mug. Another

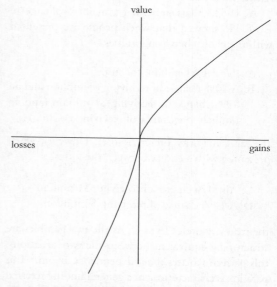

**Figure 43.1** The value function in Prospect Theory.

group was not given a mug and asked for the price they would pay to buy the mug. Kahneman et al. found that the median selling price was over twice as large as the median buying price. This difference between willingness to accept and willingness to pay indicates that the (dis)utility of losing a mug is greater than the utility gained from obtaining it. Another effect illustrating loss aversion is the "status quo bias" (Samuelson & Zeckhauser, 1988), which refers to the tendency to remain in the same state when change involves exchanging a relatively small loss for a larger gain. For instance, Knetsch (1989) randomly gave students either a mug or a chocolate bar. While given the opportunity to trade one for the other, approximately 90% of the students did not do so, showing a preference for whatever they were randomly allocated.

A second key principle in Prospect Theory is the transformation of probabilities by a weighting function. The weighting function reflects the subjective impact of probabilities on decisions. Numerous findings suggest that this impact is not linear (e.g., Camerer & Ho, 1994; Wu & Gonzales, 1996), as it should be according to EUT. Zeckhauser's Russian roulette example gives an intuitive illustration that the effect of changes in probability is not the same over the whole scale:

> Suppose you are compelled to play Russian roulette but are given the opportunity to purchase the removal of one bullet from the loaded gun. Would you pay as much to reduce the number of bullets from four to three as you would to reduce the number of bullets from one to zero? (in Kahneman & Tversky, 1979, p. 283)

Most people would pay substantially more to reduce the number of bullets from 1 to 0 than to reduce it from 4 to 3, while the increase in expected utility should be identical in both cases. This result has been called the *certainty effect* (Kahneman & Tversky, 1979): People seem to overweight certain outcomes (in the example, when the number of bullets is zero, it is certain that you will survive) relative to outcomes that are merely probable. PT accounts for this effect, as well as others, by assuming that the probabilities are distorted by a weighting function. Originally, this weighting function was assumed to be identical for gains and losses and applied directly to the probabilities. This, however, led to some counterintuitive predictions. In a later refinement, called Cumulative Prospect Theory (CPT; Tversky & Kahneman, 1992), the weighting function is applied to cumulative probabilities, as in rank-

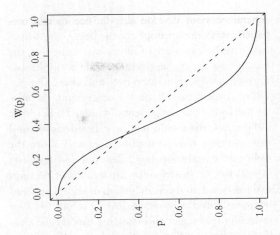

**Figure 43.2** The weighting function ($w$) for cumulative probabilities ($p$) in Cumulative Prospect Theory.

dependent utility theory (Quiggin, 1982). In CPT, the cumulative probabilities are computed separately for each prospect (decision alternative) and separately for gains and losses within each prospect. For gains, the outcomes are ordered in increasing value, and each outcome is associated with a cumulative probability of receiving that outcome or anything better. A weighting function (see Fig. 43.2) is applied to these cumulative probabilities, and for each option, the decision weight is defined as the difference between the transformed cumulative probability for that gain and next highest outcome. The procedure for losses is similar, but the cumulative probabilities are probabilities of obtaining a loss or anything worse, and the decision weights are computed as the difference between the transformed cumulative probability of an outcome and the immediately preceding loss.

This cumulative weighting procedure is intricate and perhaps not immediately plausible from a psychological viewpoint. Regardless, Prospect Theory has proven a successful descriptive account of decision making (see e.g., Edwards, 1996, for a review). On the other hand, it does not provide deep psychological insight into many of the processes it proposed (Newell, Lagnado, & Shanks, 2007), and a complete account of decision making will likely take more factors into account. We will discuss a number of such factors later on, but a prominent one we will briefly mention now is regret (Loomes & Sugden, 1982). When making a decision under uncertainty, the outcome informs us about the actual state of the world. Suppose that, after deciding not to treat the patient, the doctor in the earlier example finds out that the patient had actually contracted virus B. Had she decided to treat the patient with the appropriate medicine, she would have saved him a week of illness. Knowing this, the doctor now regrets her decision, and the displeasure of this regret is something over and above the disutility of the illness. If, on the other hand, the doctor had found out the patient did indeed suffer from indigestion, she would rejoice at her decision, and this rejoicing adds something over and above the utility of a healthy patient. Loomes and Sugden's (1982) Regret Theory offers an account of decision making based on the anticipation of such regret and rejoicing. Effectively, regret theory extends EUT by assuming that regret and rejoicing modify the classic "choiceless" utility function, thus making utility context dependent.

## Multiattribute Decisions

Most real-life decisions are not posed as choices between monetary gambles. For instance, when deciding between two job offers, there are many relevant factors besides monetary outcome (salary), such as the convenience of the location, the sociability of your colleagues, and so on. The decision alternatives have values on many different attributes, and each attribute might be relevant to a different goal (e.g., maximizing earnings, minimizing daily commute, extending social network, etc.). Usually, there is a necessary trade-off between such attributes. For instance, a more highly paid job might require a longer commute. The question then arises how these attributes are integrated when making a decision. Traditionally, Multiattribute Utility Theory has taken the view that people first evaluate each option on every attribute, after which these "single-attribute utilities" are weighted according to the relative importance of the attributes and then summed to give the option's overall utility (e.g., Keeny & Riaffa, 1976). In this view, utility serves as a "common currency" such that a relative lack in one attribute (e.g., salary) can be compensated for by a relative abundance on another attribute (e.g., location). But this compensatory nature of multiattribute decision making has been questioned. For options with many attributes, the computation of overall utility seems too complex, and researchers have proposed that people use a variety of heuristics to deal with this complexity.

One of the first people to propose that a theory of rational decision making should take people's cognitive limitations into account was Simon (1955, 1956), who coined the term "bounded rationality." According to Simon, people *satisfice* rather

than optimize; they look for options that are good enough, rather than the best. In multiattribute decisions, satisficing consists of setting a minimal value for each of the attributes. As soon as an option is found that surpasses all these lower bounds, a decision is made. Satisficing seems like an economical strategy: Options can be searched attribute-wise, and any failing options can be eliminated from the choice set, thus sequentially reducing the complexity of the procedure. There is even research that suggests that while optimizers achieve better outcomes, satisficers are more content with the outcomes they achieve[4] (Iyengar, Wells, & Schwarz, 2006). By considering more options, maximizers may be more prone to anticipate and experience regret (Schwartz et al., 2002).

Tversky's (1972) Elimination-by-Aspects model effectively combines satisficing with optimization. While options that do not meet set criteria are eliminated from the consideration set, this elimination continues until one alternative remains. Elimination-by-Aspects proposes that the search through attribute values is stochastic, with the probability of choosing an attribute dimension depending on its overall importance to the decision maker. As Tversky shows, this model can account for certain violations of the independence axiom. Elimination-by-Aspects is an example of lexicographic decision making, in which attributes are considered sequentially and there is no inter-attribute compensation. A more recently proposed lexicographic decision strategy is Take-the-Best (TTB; Gigerenzer & Goldstein, 1996). This decision-making heuristic was originally proposed for inferential decisions in which there is an objectively correct alternative. TTB is similar to Elimination-by-Aspects, but it does away with random sampling of attribute dimensions in favor of a fixed search order according to attribute validity and eliminates all alternatives that do not have the maximum value on a considered attribute. This last aspect makes TTB a very frugal strategy, as a decision is made as soon as an attribute is found on which a single alternative is best. As lexicographic strategies, Elimination-by-Aspects and Take-the-Best are non-compensatory. They can conflict with compensatory strategies such as Multiattribute Utility Theory, because an alternative that is poor on one attribute, and therefore eliminated by a lexicographic strategy, might be good on all other attributes.

Claims that compensatory strategies are too complex in all but the simplest decision problems have resulted in significant effort to delineate the factors determining decision strategy use. An interesting suggestion is that people adapt their strategies to the decision environment in an attempt to minimize cognitive effort while achieving a satisfactory level of decision accuracy (Gigerenzer, Todd, & the ABC Research Group, 1999; Payne, Bettman, & Johnson, 1993; Rieskamp & Otto, 2006). Simulation studies have shown that in inferential tasks strategies like TTB result in surprisingly accurate decisions, sometimes outperforming compensatory strategies such as linear regression (e.g., Gigerenzer & Goldstein, 1996), although the generality of this conclusion has been questioned (Chater, Oaksford, Nakisa, & Redington, 2003). In any case, potential success provides no direct evidence that people actually employ TTB when making decisions. Studies that have investigated this empirical claim directly have found some evidence for TTB usage (e.g., Bergert & Nosofsky, 2007; Bröder, 2000; Newell & Shanks, 2003; Newell, Weston, & Shanks, 2003; Rieskamp & Hoffrage, 1999). While people usually search information in order of cue validity, they often do not stop their search after the first discriminating cue has been found (e.g., Newell, Weston, & Shanks, 2003). Although simple rules like TTB are employed some of the time, studies show large variability, both within and between people. The growing consensus seems to be that people can use both compensatory and noncompensatory strategies, and adapt their strategies to the requirements of the task (Bröder & Newell, 2008; Gigerenzer & Gaissmaier, 2011; Rieskamp & Otto, 2006).

## The Instability of Preferences

The traditional economic view is that decisions reveal someone's stable preferences. You either prefer the Rolling Stones to the Beatles, or you don't. According to a rather naïve view, people make decisions by reading the utility of the various outcomes from a lookup table. Access to such a stable preference relation implies the principle of invariance (Slovic, 1995; Tversky & Kahneman, 1986), according to which preferences should not depend on the description of the outcomes (description invariance) or on the method of elicitation (procedure invariance). But there is considerable evidence that neither of these holds universally.

### Procedure Variance

Evidence against description invariance has already been mentioned (e.g., the Asian disease problem). A classic study that showed procedure variance was conducted by Lichtenstein and Slovic

(1971). They presented participants with the following lotteries:

**P**: A 95% chance of winning $2.50 and a 5% chance of losing $0.75

**D**: A 40% chance of winning $8.50 and a 60% chance of losing $1.50

In the P ("probability") lottery, there is a relatively large probability of winning a modest amount, while in the D ("dollar") lottery, there is a modest probability of winning a relatively large amount. When asked which gamble they would prefer to play, the majority of the participants chose the P lottery. However, when participants were subsequently asked to give their minimum selling price for a ticket in the lottery, lottery D was usually (in 88% of the cases) given a higher price than lottery P, implying a preference for D.

Preference reversals have subsequently been found when comparing other preference elicitation procedures, such as choice and matching (Slovic, 1975; Tversky, Sattath, & Slovic, 1988), and separate and simultaneous evaluation of options (Hsee, 1996; List, 2002). The study by List (2002) is particularly relevant, as it shows that preference reversals also occur outside the laboratory. List studied people buying baseball cards at a specialist convention. In one condition, people placed bids on two sets of baseball cards viewed simultaneously. One set contained 10 cards, all in excellent condition, while the second set contained three additional cards in very poor condition. As expected, people generally placed somewhat higher bids on the 13-card bundle. However, when people in a second condition evaluated the sets separately (either bidding for the 10-card or the 13-card bundle), the bids for the set of 10 cards were higher than those for the 13-card set. According to Hsee (1996), such effects depend on the "evaluability" of the attributes. Some attributes, like the number of baseball cards in a set, may be difficult to evaluate in isolation; their worth depends on what's offered in other options. Because of this indeterminacy, these attributes will have little influence on separate evaluations. But due to its inherently comparative nature, they will inform joint evaluation.

### Context Effects

The aforementioned finding suggests that the decision alternatives can provide a meaningful context to ground preferences. There are other key findings supporting the general context dependence of

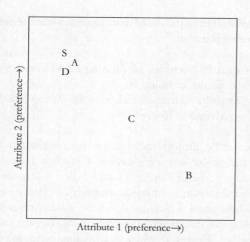

**Figure 43.3** Schematic representation of the decision alternatives in research on context effects. The direction of preference is upward and to the right.

preferences. Three main effects are the similarity, compromise, and attraction effects. These effects all consider how the choice probabilities between two options are affected by the addition of a third alternative and all involve a violation of the axiom of independence.

A schematic representation of the contexts in which these effects are found is given in Figure 43.3. The two-option comparison always concerns options A and B. To describe the effects, suppose that in a binary choice between these two options, (a group of) people show indifference between the options, so that the proportion choosing A equals the proportion choosing B, that is, $P(A|\{A,B\})$ = $P(B|\{A,B\})$.

The *similarity effect* (Tversky, 1972) refers to the finding that the addition of option S (which is similar to option A, but slightly worse on attribute 1 and slightly better on attribute 2) to choice set $\{A,B\}$ mainly takes away from the probability of choosing A, that is, $P(A|\{A,B,S\}) < P(A|\{A,B\})$, while leaving the probability of choosing B relatively intact. As a result, people can prefer A over B in the $\{A,B\}$ context, but B over A in the $\{A,B,S\}$ context, which violates the independence axiom. As argued by Tversky (1972), due to the similarity between options A and S, these may be taken as roughly equivalent, and a choice may be conducted in two stages: In the first stage, people choose between option B or the set A and S. If the set is chosen, then the second stage involves the choice between A and S. Indeed, Tversky's (1972) Elimination-by-Aspects model was explicitly formulated to account for the similarity effect.

The *attraction effect* (Huber, Payne, & Puto, 1982; Simonson, 1989) refers to the finding that the addition of option D (which is similar to A, but worse on both attributes) to the choice set $\{A,B\}$ increases the number of people choosing A, that is, $P(A|\{A,B,D\}) > P(A|\{A,B\})$. A marketing example of the effect is when a manufacturer introduces a new product (D) onto the market that is clearly inferior to one they already produce (A), in the hope of taking market share away from a competitor brand (B). The key difference between the situation leading to the similarity effect and the attraction effect is that option D is asymmetrically dominated (it is worse than A on both attributes, but worse than B on only one attribute), while option S is not dominated (i.e., it is better than A on one attribute). The attraction effect violates the *regularity principle* (Tversky, 1972), according to which the addition of an option to the choice set can never increase the probability of choosing an option relative to the original set (i.e., the principle implies that $P(A|\{A,B\}) \geq P(A|\{A,B,D\})$). The regularity principle is a weaker form of the independence axiom and is implied by many decision-making models, including Elimination-by-Aspects and a large class of random utility models. Therefore, the attraction effect poses a major problem for many accounts of decision making.

Another violation of the regularity principle is found in the *compromise effect* (Simonson, 1989; Tversky & Simonson, 1993). Suppose that people are indifferent between the options in a series of binary choices between pairs $\{A,B\}$, $\{A,C\}$, and $\{B,C\}$, that is, $P(A|\{A,B\}) = P(B|\{B,C\}) = P(C|\{A,C\}) = .5$. The compromise effect refers to the finding that in a choice from the set $\{A,B,C\}$, people often show a clear preference for the compromise option C, that is, $P(C|\{A,B,C\}) > P(C|\{A,C\}) = P(C|\{B,C\})$.

Simonson (1989) proposed that the attraction and compromise effects arise because people find it easier to justify their choices in the enlarged choice sets. For instance, the dominated option D provides a clear justification for choosing A. The importance of such justifications is highlighted in the reason-based choice account of Shafir, Simonson, and Tversky (1993), which shows how various choice anomalies can be more readily understood when considering how the decision context can affect the generation of reasons for and against choosing the alternatives. A more tractable value-, rather than reason-, based account of the attraction and compromise effects was given by Tversky and Simonson (1993) in their context-dependent advantage model. However, this model cannot account for the similarity effect (Roe, Busemeyer, & Townsend, 2001). A theory that can account for all three context effects is Decision Field Theory (Busemeyer & Townsend, 1993; Roe et al., 2001), to which we will return later on.

## Goals

Outcomes with multiple attributes are usually relevant to a number of goals. As people generally have multiple goals at a single time, multiattribute decisions will usually involve a trade-off between the attainment of different goals (Payne, Bettman, & Johnson, 1992). When multiple goals conflict, selective attention to different subsets of these goals can influence both how a decision is made and the outcome of this process (Krantz & Kunreuther, 2007; Markman & Medin, 2002). If there is a shift in the relevance of different goals between one decision and the next, decision makers can seemingly make inconsistent choices, even though these decisions are individually all instrumentally rational.

Brendl, Markman, and Messner (2003) conducted a study that shows how goal activation can affect decisions. They offered habitual smokers the opportunity to buy tickets for a lottery involving either a cash or cigarette prize. Each lottery would be conducted after 2 weeks, so neither prize could be used to satisfy current needs. The crucial manipulation was in the timing of the offer: Half the smokers were asked before and half after having the opportunity for a post-class cigarette. The results showed that those who had not smoked yet bought significantly fewer tickets to win money than those in the other group. The authors also found such devaluation for options irrelevant to currently active goals when hungry participants rated the attractiveness of non-food items (see also Markman, Brendl, & Kim, 2007).

Maintaining a set of conflicting goals may be subserved by a process called mental accounting (Markman & Medin, 2002; Thaler, 1985). Mental accounting is often considered a hindrance to rational decision making, but it may actually help people to obtain long-term goals in the face of currently active short-term goals (Shefrin & Thaler, 1992). An example of mental accounting comes from Kahneman and Tversky (1984), who found that people were less likely to buy a theatre ticket they previously lost compared to people who had not previously bought a ticket but lost an amount of money equal to the ticket price. In contrast to the view that money is "fungible" (substitutable), this finding suggests that people segregate theater costs from other costs. Those who prepurchased a ticket were less willing to spend additional money from the theater account, while the money lost by people in the other condition could have come from any other account. Although this behavior may seem unreasonable (money lost is money lost), associating different goals with separate accounts (e.g., entertainment, education, etc.) may help people protect particular goals from other, more immediately pressing ones.

## The Inference of Preferences

In cases where decision makers have little prior experience with the options, their preferences may not be immediately obvious and they will need to infer the subjective value of the outcomes. Indeed, this may even be true of some decisions made repeatedly. In the literature, this process is often called *preference construction* (e.g., Payne et al., 1992; Slovic, 1995; Tversky & Thaler, 1990), but we prefer the term *preference inference*, as we believe this reflects the aims and constraints of the decision makers better. While preference construction implies the absence of inherent preferences, preference inference implies that underlying preferences may exist, but that these need to be discovered (cf. Plott, 1996; Simonson, 2008). In attempting to infer their preferences, people may rely on a variety of cues, such as those in the immediate decision context, memory of previous experiences, and affective reactions.

## Context Effects (Again)

One notable finding is that the range of attribute values can have a large effect on how they are perceived. For instance, Mellers and Cooke (1994) had students rate the attractiveness of various apartments, which differed in rent and distance to campus. Mellers and Cooke found that the same change on an attribute (e.g., a rent change from $200 to $400) had a greater effect on perceived attractiveness when the range of rents considered was narrow (e.g., all apartments had rents varying between $200 and $400) than when the range was wide (e.g., rent varied from $100 to $1000). Indeed, this effect was so pronounced that it resulted in preference reversals. For instance, a $200 apartment 26 minutes from campus was preferred to a $400 apartment 10 minutes from campus when the range of rents was small but the range of distances was wide, while the opposite was found when the range of rents was wide and the range of distances was narrow. Mellers and Cooke also showed that this effect was not due to a change in relative attribute weight; rather, the perceived value on the attribute differed as a function of the range of values on that attribute. Although the students were presumably quite familiar with the decision context, they seemed to rely on relative rather than absolute attribute values in their preferences. This makes sense if you consider that assessments such as whether an apartment is expensive are inherently relative, as are many other qualities, such as sport achievements and what constitutes a well-paid job. Especially in relatively unknown environments, the distribution of attribute values can provide useful information, if only about what others conceive as important. In support of this, Beattie and Baron (1991) have found that range effects on relative attribute weights depend on participants' experience with a scale.

### Memory

It seems plausible to assume that, in order to estimate the value of various decision outcomes, people will attempt to retrieve from memory prior experiences with similar outcomes. While it is hard to deny such a role of memory in evaluation, there is relatively little work that directly assesses the effect of memory on decision making (Weber & Johnson, 2006).

Stewart, Chater, and Brown (2006) have formulated a theory in which memory plays a central role. According to their Decision by Sampling (DbS) theory, people value decision alternatives by evaluating their attributes against a sample of other attribute values. This decision sample consists of attribute values in the immediate decision context and values from memory of previously encountered attributes. People are assumed to make only ordinal comparisons, and the value of a decision alternative is determined by its relative ranking in the sample. They show that Prospect Theory's value function closely matches relative rankings of credit and debit amounts in actual bank transfers. Assuming that memory provides a veridical representation of the environment, DbS thus provides an explanation for the shape of the value function. In a similar way, it provides an account of the probability weighting function, and hyperbolic time discounting.

DbS assumes, at least as a first approximation, that attributes are sampled randomly from memory. This assumption is unlikely to hold, given what is known about memory. For instance, memory is associative, and retrieved items are likely to be similar to previously retrieved items. In addition, there are interference effects in memory, such that retrieved items can inhibit the retrieval of other items (e.g., Anderson & Spellman, 1995). Johnson, Häubl, and Keinan (2007) argue that such memory interference may play a key role in the endowment effect. According to their Query Theory, people first consider reasons for maintaining the status quo, and then consider reasons for changing it. Reasons are considered to be constructed by queries of memory, and due to memory interference, query order can have strong effects on the outcome of this process. Because sellers first consider reasons for keeping the mug, which enhance its value, retrieval of value-decreasing reasons for selling the mug is inhibited, resulting in a more positive evaluation of the mug compared to buyers who first consider reasons for keeping their money (value decreasing) before reasons for buying the mug (value enhancing). In an experiment, Johnson et al. found some support for this account. In particular, when the assumed natural order of queries was reversed (sellers were guided to give value-decreasing aspects before value-increasing aspects, and vice versa for buyers), the endowment effect was eliminated.

Being able to retrieve any memories for an alternative may in itself be value enhancing. Preferences for products and other objects tend to be related to their familiarity (e.g., Hoyer & Brown, 1990). In this way, recognition can serve as a cue to value. According to Goldstein and Gigerenzer (2002), recognition is a powerful heuristic in decision making. As recognition is often related to quantities of interest, such as the quality of higher education institutes, or a team's success in sports, basing decisions on recognition can give good outcomes. A telling example is in stockmarket investment, where it has been shown that portfolios comprised of the most-recognized options, on average, outperformed investment experts and managed funds such as the Fidelity Growth Fund (Ortmann, Gigerenzer, Borges, & Goldstein, 2008). According to the recognition heuristic, if only one decision alternative is recognized, that alternative is chosen and no further information is used. While most agree that recognition is a useful and often informative cue, this last claim has led to some debate (e.g., Oeusoonthornwattana & Shanks, 2010; Pachur, Bröder, & Marewski, 2008). For instance, Oeusoonthornwattana and Shanks (2010) showed that when, in addition to recognition, other information about options is available, people will not ignore this. As such, recognition may be a cue to value, but it is not used exclusively.

While people may explicitly attempt to retrieve experiences in order to assess the value of decision alternatives, memory effects may be more subtle. As shown in a study by North, Hargreaves, and McKendrick (1997), people can be primed to make certain decisions. North et al. investigated wine-buying behavior in a supermarket where four French and four German wines were displayed. When French background music was played, French wines outsold the German wines, while the reverse was true when German music was played. Questionnaires indicated that the music made people think of its originating country, thereby retrieving more memories relating to a particular wine region. However, most people denied that the music influenced their wine choice. Additional support for priming effects in decision making comes from Berger, Meredith, and Wheeler (2008), who report evidence that the location where people vote can influence their decision. When people were assigned a school as a polling station, they were more likely to support a school-funding initiative than when they voted in other locations. According to the authors, the context may have primed people to retrieve favorable arguments for the school-funding initiative.

By retrieving previous experiences with outcomes, people should be able to make an informed evaluation of the decision alternatives. However, evidence suggests that "remembered utility" is not a veridical representation of directly experienced (dis)pleasure (Kahneman, Wakker, & Sarin, 1997). In a classic study, Redelmeier and Kahneman (1996) asked patients undergoing a painful colonoscopy to rate their level of discomfort every 60 seconds. After the procedure, they were asked to rate their overall discomfort. These final ratings did not reflect an integration of the minute-by-minute experienced discomfort. Rather, total ratings seemed to be formed by a "peak-end" rule, averaging the maximum discomfort and the discomfort experienced just before finishing the procedure. For instance, a patient whose procedure ended with a period of relatively mild discomfort rated the overall discomfort as less than another patient whose procedure ended abruptly at a point of relatively large discomfort, even though the first patient's procedure lasted considerably longer and he thus accumulated more overall discomfort. Similar results were obtained in a study in which participants watched pleasant and unpleasant movies (Fredrickson & Kahneman, 1993).

As shown in the studies by Kahneman and colleagues, we do not always remember events in a way that accurately reflects how they were experienced. Our recollections can distort past events and how enjoyable or unpleasant they were. Therefore, experienced utility is not always a good predictor of future decisions. This is especially clear in a study by Wirtz, Kruger, Scollon, and Diener (2003), who showed that students' desire to repeat a type of vacation was better predicted by their recollected than their actually experienced enjoyment. Although recollections were related to experienced enjoyment, there was also an independent effect of predicted enjoyment before the vacation. Expectations thus seem to have a long-lasting effect which is not overwritten by actual experience. As recollected enjoyment mediates the effect of actual experience, when determining whether someone will repeat an experience such as revisiting a restaurant, asking her during the experience will be less useful than seeking her subsequent remembered experience.

## Emotion

While the traditional revealed preference view on decision making eschewed direct consideration of the hedonic value of decision outcomes, recent work has begun to explore the role of emotion in decision making. Perhaps the most extensive thesis on the role of emotion in decision making is Damasio's (1994, 1996) Somatic Marker Hypothesis. According to Damasio, in complex and conflicting decision problems, people rely on emotion-based biasing signals generated from the body that simplify the problem by marking risky and potentially costly alternatives. Evidence for this Somatic Marker Hypothesis comes from patients with damage to the ventromedial prefrontal cortex (VMPFC), such as the famous Phineas Gage (see Damasio, Grabowski, Frank, Galaburda, & Damasio, 1994), who survived an accident in which an iron rod went through his head and destroyed much of his frontal cortex. While Gage seemed to have no intellectual impairment, he became impulsive and unpredictable and started showing strange social and decision-making behavior, consistent with the loss of his somatic marker system.

Experimental evidence for the Somatic Marker Hypothesis has mainly relied on the Iowa Gambling Task (IGT; Bechara, Damasio, Damasio, & Anderson, 1994), which was designed to simulate real-life decision making in the way it factors uncertainty, reward, and punishment. The IGT is a multiarmed bandit task in which participants repeatedly choose to draw a card from four decks. Each card will provide a (monetary) reward, but some cards also provide an additional punishment. Two decks are disadvantageous: While providing higher rewards, they are also associated with higher punishments, and consistently choosing these decks will result in an overall net loss. The other two decks are advantageous: While providing lower rewards than the disadvantageous decks, the punishments are also lower and consistently choosing these decks will result in an overall net gain. Bechara et al. (1994) found that people with damage to the VMPFC were relatively impaired in this task (choosing more from the disadvantageous decks than healthy controls and patients with other brain lesions) and concluded that the VMPFC plays a key role in the emotional evaluation of decision outcomes. In further support of the Somatic Marker Hypothesis, later studies found that healthy participants, but not those with damage to the VMPFC, developed anticipatory skin conductance responses to choices from the disadvantageous decks (Bechara, Damasio, Tranel, & Damasio, 1997; Bechara, Tranel, Damasio, & Damasio, 1996). These anticipatory reactions correlated with improved performance and apparently developed before participants acquired explicit knowledge about the structure of the task (Bechara et al., 1997). While this suggests that nonconscious emotional signals, or somatic markers, guide normal decision making before conscious knowledge does, this conclusion was later placed in doubt by Maia and McClelland (2004). Using more sensitive questions, they showed that participants developed awareness of the good and bad decks much earlier than previously thought. While the many studies using the IGT have failed to provide compelling support for the Somatic Marker Hypothesis (for a review, see Dunn, Dalgleish, & Lawrence, 2006), there seems little doubt that emotions play a significant role in decision making.

The role of emotional reactions to outcomes as a guide to decision making has been formulated as the *affect heuristic* (e.g., Finucane, Peters, & Slovic, 2003). Decision problems can conjure vivid images with attached affective reactions, which influence the overall evaluation of alternatives. Some evidence for this idea was gathered by Finucane, Alhakami, Slovic, and Johnson (2000), who showed that they could manipulate the perceived benefit of nuclear power by telling participants that the associated risk was either high or low. The authors argued that high risk induces an overall negative affective evaluation, which, via an affect heuristic, results in an inference of low benefit. In a similar way, perceived risk could be manipulated by informing participants that the

benefits were either high or low. According to the "risk as feelings" hypothesis (Loewenstein, Weber, Hsee, & Welch, 2001), such affective reactions can also explain the overweighting of small probabilities discussed previously. According to this account, when moving from impossibility (i.e., $p = 0$) to possibility (e.g., $p = .01$), a threshold is crossed in which a consequence of no concern becomes a source of worry or hope. As possible consequences are imagined, associated emotional reactions arise, but this process is assumed to be little affected by further increases in probability. In the words of Loewenstein et al. (2001, p. 276), "One's mental image of what it would be like to win the state lottery [...] is likely to be about the same, whether there is a 1 in 10,000,000 chance of winning or a 1 in 10,000 chance of winning." The idea that departures from certainty are especially marked for affect-rich compared to affect-poor consequences was supported by Rottenstreich and Hsee (2001), who found a preference reversal between certain and possible outcomes. In their study, participants chose between a lottery with a 1% chance to win a kiss from their favorite movie star (affect-rich) or a lottery with a 1% chance to win $5. The large majority preferred the kiss lottery, even though when participants were given the choice between the outcomes for certain, the large majority preferred the $5 prize. Rottenstreich and Hsee explain this reversal by assuming that the nonlinearity of the probability weighting (the "S-shapedness" in Fig. 43.2) increases for affect-rich outcomes.

The role of emotion in decision making is receiving more and more attention (Weber & Johnson, 2009). It is increasingly common to find dual-process accounts of decision making, which contrast intuitive and analytical decision-making processes (e.g., Kahneman & Frederick, 2002; Sloman, 1996). Intuitive, "System 1" processes are automatic, effortless, and associative, and work on affective reactions and specific memory exemplars. Analytical, "System 2" processes are deliberate, effortful, and deductive and work on abstract, affectively neutral inputs. System 1 processes are assumed to propose intuitive solutions to decision problems. These proposals are monitored by System 2 processes, which may endorse, correct, or override the inputs from System 1 processes (Kahneman & Frederick, 2002). Although the claim of qualitatively separable processing systems is controversial (e.g., Keren & Schul, 2008), it seems plausible that various cognitive and affective processes provide cues to solve a decision problem. This cue generation may appear more or less automatic. Integrating these cues into a final decision may be more akin to what is understood by "System 2" processes. As discussed earlier, there are different strategies for multiattribute decisions, and whether cues are integrated in a compensatory manner may depend on the time available and the effort one is willing to put in.

## Predicting Future Preferences

As noted by March (1978), rational decision making involves two types of inference: "guesses about future consequences of current actions and guesses about future preferences for those consequences" (p. 40). While subjective EUT assumes a completely specified set of potential consequences and their subjective likelihood of occurrence, as well as a complete preference order over them, it seems more realistic to assume that these are only vaguely specified. As current preferences for outcomes may be only weak indicators of future preferences for those outcomes, preference prediction is an inherently uncertain endeavor. For example, when deciding to buy a house, you need not only consider what it would be like to live there immediately but also how you will feel in a few years' time. The difficulty with such prediction is that your needs and preferences are likely to change over time. For instance, an apartment in the heart of the entertainment district may be very satisfactory for a young couple, but it may not be suitable after they have their first child. But even in the absence of such major life changes, people seem to have problems in predicting their future preferences.

Studies on affective forecasting have shown that people are generally poor at predicting their affective reactions to events in the future (Gilbert, Gill, & Wilson, 1998). Perhaps this is not too surprising, as accurate foresight is a desirable but illusive cognitive faculty. While evidence suggests that people are reasonably accurate when predicting their immediate reactions to outcomes, they have little insight into how their preferences will adapt over time (Loewenstein, O'Donoghue, & Rabin, 2003). A common finding is that predictions of future utility are anchored on current utility. For instance, hungry shoppers tend to buy more than intended (e.g., Gilbert et al., 1998), apparently expecting to be as hungry in the future. This unwarranted projection of a current state into the future has been called the *projection bias* (Loewenstein et al., 2003). While current liking of options can be indicative of future liking—people are quite adept at predicting whether future events will be pleasant or unpleasant—people

seem relatively poor at predicting the future intensity of their feelings (Wilson & Gilbert, 2005). For instance, people often overestimate the impact of life-changing events, such as acquiring a medical condition, or a relationship breakup. While people readily adapt to new circumstances, their predictions seem mostly based on the initial impact of the event (Wilson & Gilbert, 2005).

An early study by Kahneman and Snell (1992) illustrates how people fail to predict their changing preferences in a more mundane situation: tasting yogurt. Their participants were unable to predict that repeated exposure to plain yogurt, rather than decreasing, would actually increase their liking. Overall, there was little correlation between participants' predictions and actual liking. In a study by Simonson (1990), participants who chose three snacks in advance for consumption on later occasions made more varied choices than those who chose their snacks on those occasions for immediate consumption. This indicates that participants may have wrongly assumed their tastes would vary. Interestingly, when participants were asked, after an initial choice, to predict their choices on consecutive occasions, the difference between simultaneous and separate choice disappeared. While Simonson found that people's preferences are more stable than they expected, the results of Kahneman and Snell's study suggest that people should expect preference change, but that they have difficulty predicting its direction. That people seem to have little insight into how their preferences will change, even for the very near future, was also shown by Loewenstein and Adler (1995). In their experiment, people were unable to predict how endowment would change their preferences.

## The Process of Preference Inference

If preferences are not simply accessed but inferred, this process should be of interest to decision-making researchers. A common view is that this process involves a form of sequential sampling. Sequential sampling models of decision making have a long history in psychology (e.g., Audley, 1960; Ratcliff, 1978). A common theme is that, during the course of deliberation, evidence in favor of decision alternatives is accumulated until the decision maker is satisfied (s)he has a good-enough basis for making a final choice. Evidence is assumed to be randomly sampled on a moment-by-moment basis (hence the name sequential sampling), resulting in a stochastic process of evidence accumulation. In "race" models, evidence for each alternative is accumulated separately. In "diffusion" models, accumulation involves the relative evidence in favor of one option over others. In both cases, a decision is made when the accumulated evidence (whether absolute or relative) exceeds a threshold. The setting of the threshold is important for speed-accuracy trade-off: Setting a lenient criterion will result in quick but unreliable decisions, while setting a stricter criterion will result in a more reliable but lengthy decision-making process.

An extensive overview of the various sequential sampling models exceeds the scope of this chapter (the interested reader may consult, e.g., Smith, 2000). We will only describe one of them in more detail here, namely Decision Field Theory (DFT; Busemeyer & Townsend, 1993; Roe et al., 2001). DFT assumes a person deliberates over the decision alternatives by thinking about the consequences of each action. During deliberation, attention shifts between the possible consequences, giving rise to affective reactions that are accumulated in an overall preference state for each action. Affective reactions to consequences can be positive or negative. In DFT, these affective reactions result in a valence for each option, which reflects the relative advantage of an option over the other options. Valences are accumulated into an integrated preference state for each option. Crucially, this integration process is competitive and incorporates an inhibitory mechanism that increases the advantage of a preferred option over less preferred, similar options. An example of the dynamic trajectories resulting from this integrative process is given in Figure 43.4. As in other sequential sampling models, a decision is made as soon as a trajectory surpasses a decision threshold.

As already mentioned, Decision Field Theory can account for the similarity, attraction, and compromise effects. The similarity effect results from

the attention-switching process. When considering options S, A, and B (Fig. 43.3), if attention is focused on dimension 1, option B receives a large advantage over S and A. But if attention is focused on dimension 2, both S and A have a positive valence, while option B has a negative valence. Therefore, addition of option S to the choice set takes away from option A, but not option B. The attraction affect results primarily from the competitive integration process. Because option D is similar to option A, they compete more than options D and B, and this results in a relative advantage of option A over D. The compromise effect depends on both attention and inhibition, but the precise explanation for this effect is more intricate (see Roe et al., 2001, for more details). Another sequential sampling model that can account for all three effects is the Leaky Competing Accumulator model (LCA; Usher & McClelland, 2001, 2004). While the relative merits of DFT and the LCA, and other models like them, need further research, sequential sampling models can offer a precise theoretical framework to synthesize a wide variety of empirical results on decision making.

## Learning to Make Decisions

Much of decision research has concerned how people make one-shot decisions between fully specified gambles, or otherwise abstracted choice situations. But how relevant are the results for everyday decision making outside the laboratory? How often does one face a never-to-be-repeated situation in which the options are completely and accurately described? Given relatively little experience with such "decisions from description," it seems hardly surprising that people fail to always decide optimally (Binmore, 1999; Plott, 1996).

A central idea in the preceding discussion was that preferences, rather than being immediately accessed, often need to be inferred. Various sources of information can support this inferential process, such as the decision context, emotions, and memory. These cues vary in their reliability and validity, and they can sometimes conflict. To make a rational decision, the decision maker will need to integrate them appropriately. Although cue integration can be difficult, it can be learned. Thus, if someone learns that current affective reactions are relatively poor predictors of future affective reactions, they may learn to give relatively more weight to other considerations (Beer, Knight, & D'Esposito, 2006).

As people gain more experience with types of decision problems, they should learn to make more

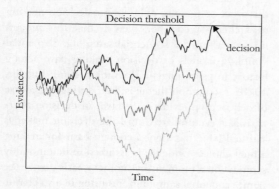

**Figure 43.4** Hypothetical evidence accumulation process for three options.

optimal decisions. Even the expectation that a gamble will be played repeatedly can increase the tendency to choose reward-maximizing alternatives (Lopes, 1981; Wedell & Böckenholt, 1990). According to Friedman (1998, p. 941), 'every choice "anomaly" can be greatly diminished or entirely eliminated in appropriately structured learning environments' and evidence discussed in this section suggests that this may indeed be the case.

## Probability Matching and Maximizing

A phenomenon that has puzzled researchers for a long time and that is closely related to learning in decision making is probability matching. Consider a simple game in which you repeatedly choose to look behind one of two doors. There will be a reward behind one of the doors, but you do not know which one. Unbeknownst to you, the reward is placed behind door A 60% of the time, and behind door B for the remaining 40% of trials. To maximize your overall reward, you should always look behind door A. However, a consistent finding in these probability learning tasks is that people usually fail to display this maximizing behavior. Instead, they often probability-match, looking behind door A roughly 60% of the time and behind door B roughly 40% of the time. Although results also indicate "overshooting" (choosing A somewhat more frequently than its probability of being correct, e.g., Friedman & Massaro, 1998), the proportion of maximizing responses is usually much less than 100%. Various explanations have been offered for this finding. For instance, the reward sequences used in many studies are not exactly random, in which case it is optimal to not always choose the same option (Fiorina, 1971). Also, the reward magnitudes are usually quite small, so that the difference between maximizing and matching may not be notable (e.g., Vulkan, 2000), and people may expect the reward schedules to change over time (Peterson & Ulehla, 1965; Wolford, Newman, Miller, & Wig, 2004), in which case it is good to sometimes check the previously inferior options (this is known as the exploration-exploitation trade-off). Finally, most studies only report group averages, which can mask large individual differences in strategies (Shanks, Tunney, & McCarthy, 2002). All these explanations seem reasonable and Shanks, Tunney, and McCarthy (2002) showed that a large majority of participants can learn to maximize when they are provided with large financial incentives, meaningful and regular feedback (informing participants how much they could have earned), and make many repeated decisions.

## Experience Versus Description

In recent years, researchers have directly compared decisions from experience to decisions from description. Keeping within the monetary gamble framework, Barron and Erev (2003) replicated a number of classic experiments, with the crucial difference that rather than describing the probabilities and rewards associated with each alternative, participants could experience the gambles in a two-armed bandit task, repeatedly choosing which machine to play and observing a randomly drawn reward from the appropriate distribution. Interestingly, Barron and Erev found a number of results that directly oppose the findings of description-based studies. For instance, they found a reversed common ratio effect, in which the riskier of two options became less attractive after multiplying the probability by a common ratio. They also found more risk seeking in the gain than loss domain, and underweighting rather than overweighting of small probabilities. Thus, a number of key results underlying Prospect Theory have not been replicated in experience-based decision making.

Why do experience-based decisions show opposite patterns to description-based decisions? With respect to the underweighting of small probabilities, it might be the result of limited sampling (Fox & Hadar, 2006; Hertwig, Barron, Weber, & Erev, 2004; Rakow, Demes, & Newell, 2008). Because the sampling distribution for the binomial distribution is highly skewed for small samples and low probabilities, rare events are often underrepresented and may not occur at all.[5] However, even when description-based decision scenarios exactly match experienced probabilities, differences between experience- and description-based decisions can be found (Hau, Pleskac, & Herwig, 2010; Ungemach, Chater, & Stewart, 2009; but see Rakow et al., 2008). Underweighting of small probabilities may also result from memory limitations and recency effects, resulting in biased samples from memory, or an exploration-exploitation trade-off in situations where only feedback from chosen options is received. However, neither of these seems sufficient to fully explain the experience-description gap (Camilleri & Newell, 2011; Hertwig & Erev, 2009). Camilleri and Newell (2011) showed that repeated, consequential decisions may play a crucial factor in underweighting. While reliable underweighting was found when participants repeatedly chose which gamble to play and received feedback on the outcome (whether only of the gamble played, or also that of the foregone gamble), this was not the case for a sampling paradigm in which participants first chose a number of gambles to observe before making a final decision. While it is likely that multiple factors play a role in the "experience-description gap," the findings clearly show that results from description-based studies cannot always be generalized to experience-based decision making.

### Discovering Preferences

When people are given the opportunity to learn, they can not only learn about the probabilities of outcomes but also about what those outcomes are like. Plott (1996) argues that preferences are usually not immediately obvious and need to be discovered. According to his "discovered preference hypothesis," decisions may initially be subject to a variety of biases, but after repeatedly making a decision and experiencing its outcome, people will converge to rational decisions consistent with EUT. In contrast to strong claims of preference construction, he argues for stable underlying preferences that can be accessed after sufficient learning. Some evidence for this has been found. For instance, Hoeffler and Ariely (1999) show how experience in a decision environment results in more stable preferences, especially after repeated decisions. A study by Amir and Levav (2008) shows that whether preferences stabilize may depend on the types of decisions encountered. Some decision situations, such as those with an asymmetrically dominated alternative, may lead people to use choice rules with little consideration of attribute trade-offs. Such shallow processing seems to prohibit the formation of stable preferences. When situations require an explicit consideration of attribute trade-offs, and with that a more thorough preference inference process, preferences do tend to stabilize.

Research has shown that experience can reduce or even eliminate preference reversals and other violations of EUT. In the study by List (2002) described earlier, professional card dealers did not show a reliable preference reversal between separate and joint evaluation, although nonprofessional card dealers did. According to Berg, Dickhhaut, and Rietz (2010), preference reversals between choice and pricing can be greatly reduced when participants are given an explicit incentive to reveal their true preference. In a meta-analysis of studies in the Lichtenstein and Slovic (1971) paradigm, they show that with such incentives, behavior is consistent with stable underlying preferences, although expressions of these in different tasks are subject to independent sources of noise. Other work has found that the general willingness to pay/willingness to accept gap (Coursey, Hovis, & Schulze, 1987; Shogren, Shin, Hayes, & Kliebenstein, 1994), the related endowment effect (List, 2004; Plott & Zeiler, 2005), and loss aversion (Myagkov & Plott, 1997) are eliminated or at least substantially diminished in repeated market settings with meaningful feedback and incentives. Similar results were found for preference reversals between choice and pricing (Braga & Starmer, 2003; Cox & Grether, 1996). Christensen, Heckerling, Mackesyamiti, Bernstein, and Elstein (1995) found much smaller framing effects for medical experts compared to novices. In addition, repeated play of gambles with outcome feedback reduces violations of EUT in Allais-type problems (van de Kuilen and Wakker, 2006) and leads people to approach maximizing expected value (Barron & Erev, 2003; Keren & Wagenaar, 1987). More recently, van de Kuilen (2009) conducted a study in which he found that the best-fitting probability weighting of Prospect Theory approached linearity after increased experience.

Taken together, these results indicate that while deviations from EUT are often observed when people make decisions in novel and usually hypothetical situations, after sufficient learning with meaningful feedback and incentives, they can learn to respond in close accordance to EUT. Although there may be limits to this—for instance, due to the consistently found difficulty in predicting future preferences—there seems to be some scope for EUT as both a normative and descriptive theory of decision making.

## Conclusion

During its long history, the scientific study of decision making has progressed from a mainly normative theory to a mainly descriptive account. Common violations of the axioms of Expected Utility Theory (EUT) have led many to question its descriptive validity. However, recent results show that a complete abandonment of normative principles may be premature. Violations are often found when people are presented with decisions between monetary gambles, or other abstract descriptions of decision problems. Research on how people learn to make decisions from experience has shown that, given sufficient practice, people can and often do learn to make decisions in accordance with the principles of EUT. In novel situations, people may need to infer their preferences from various sources, such as the immediate decision context, and their memory and emotions. This inferential process may initially give rise to highly variable preferences and decisions. But repeated exposure to decisions and their consequences may provide people with enough evidence to make informed decisions, pushing them in the direction of rationality.

## Future Directions

• Can repeated experience allow all violations of EUT to be eliminated?

• To what extent (if any) can decisions be guided by unconscious influences?

• How should differences across individuals in decision making (e.g., some people are more risk averse than others) be understood?

• What can decision-making research contribute to the remediation of pathological decision behavior such as addictions?

• How might sequential sampling models of one-shot decisions be extended to repeated decisions that involve learning?

• How does the experience/description contrast apply in more realistic decision problems? In particular, what about contexts where decision makers integrate both forms of information?

## Acknowledgments

Preparation of this chapter was supported by the Economic and Social Research Council (ESRC) grant RES-062-23–1511. We are grateful to David Lagnado and Daniel Reisberg for providing invaluable comments on earlier drafts of this chapter.

## Notes

1. The St Petersburg game involves tossing a fair coin until heads comes up, after which the game ends and the player receives a payout of $2^n$, where $n$ denotes the total number of throws. The expected payout is

$$\left(\frac{1}{2}\right) \times 2 + \left(\frac{1}{4}\right) \times 4 + \left(\frac{1}{8}\right) \times 8$$
$$+ \ldots = \sum_{n=1}^{\infty} \left(\frac{1}{2}\right)^n 2^n = \infty$$

but people generally are typically willing to pay only about $10 to play the game.

2. The first result implies that $u(\$1m) > .1 \times u(\$5m) + .89 \times u(\$1m)$, which can be rearranged to give $.11 \times u(\$1m) > .1 \times u(\$5m)$. Yet the second result implies the opposite, namely that $.11 \times u(\$1m) < .1 \times u(\$5m)$.

3. The first result implies that $1/3 \times u(\$100) > P(\text{black}) \times u(\$100)$, so that $1/3 > P(\text{black})$. However, the second result implies that $(1/3 + (2/3 - P(\text{black}))) \times u(\$100) < 2/3 \times u(\$100)$, which is equivalent to $1 - P(\text{black}) < 2/3$, so that $P(\text{black}) > 1/3$.

4. One could argue that, insofar as decision satisfaction is the ultimate goal, this finding calls into question the normative status of maximizing utility. But this is not necessarily the case. While the results indicate that the utility of outcomes may be affected by the decision context, as also proposed in regret theory (Loomes & Sugden, 1982), one can still argue that maximizing context-specific utility is the normative strategy. Moreover, the results from these studies are correlational, and maximizers and satisficers may differ on a number of personality characteristics which affect their satisfaction.

5. For instance, with 10 draws from a binomial distribution with $p = .1$, the probability of observing no win is roughly $P(X = 0) = .35$; hence, a large proportion of people will experience less than the expected number of wins.

## References

Allais, M. (1953). Le comportement de l'homme rationnel devant le risque: Critique des postulats et axiomes de l'ecole americaine. *Econometrica, 21*, 503–546.

Amir, O., & Levav, J. (2008). Choice construction versus preference construction: The instability of preferences learned in context. *Journal of Marketing Research, 45*, 145–158.

Anderson, M. C., & Spellman, B. A. (1995). On the status of inhibitory mechanisms in cognition: Memory retrieval as a model case. *Psychological Review, 102*, 68–100.

Audley, R. J. (1960). A stochastic model for individual choice behavior. *Psychological Review, 67*, 1–15.

Barron, G., & Erev, I. (2003). Small feedback-based decisions and their limited correspondence to description-based decisions. *Journal of Behavioral Decision Making, 16*, 215–233.

Beattie, J., & Baron, J. (1991). Investigating the effect of stimulus range on attribute weight. *Journal of Experimental Psychology: Human Perception and Performance, 17*, 571–585.

Bechara, A., Damasio, A. R., Damasio, H., & Anderson, S. W. (1994). Insensitivity to future consequences following damage to human prefrontal cortex. *Cognition, 50*, 7–15.

Bechara, A., Damasio, H., Tranel, D., & Damasio, A. H. (1997). Deciding advantageously before knowing the advantageous strategy. *Science, 275*, 1293–1295.

Bechara, A., Tranel, D., Damasio, H., & Damasio, A. H. (1996). Failure to respond autonomically to anticipated future outcomes following damage to prefrontal cortex. *Cerebral Cortex, 6*, 215–225.

Beer, J. S., Knight, R. T., & D'Esposito, M. (2006). Controlling the integration of emotion and cognition: The role of the frontal cortex in distinguishing helpful from hurtful emotional information. *Psychological Science, 17*, 448–453.

Bentham, J. (1948). *An introduction to the principle of morals and legislation*. Oxford, England: Blackwell. (Original work published in 1789)

Berg, J. E., Dickhaut, J. W., & Rietz, T. A. (2010). Preference reversals: The impact of truth-revealing monetary incentives. *Games and Economic Behavior, 68*, 443–468.

Berger, J., Meredith, M., & Wheeler, S. C. (2008). Contextual priming: Where people vote affects how they vote. *Proceedings of the National Academy of Sciences USA, 105*, 8846–8849.

Bergert, F. B., & Nosofsky, R. M. (2007). A response-time approach to comparing generalized rational and take-the-best models of decision making. *Journal of Experimental Psychology: Learning, Memory, and Cognition, 33*, 999–1019.

Bernouilli, D. (1954). Exposition of a new theory on the measurement of risk. *Econometrica, 22*, 23–36. (Original work published in 1738)

Binmore, K. (1999). Why experiment in economics? *Economic Journal, 109*, F16–F24.

Braga, J., & Starmer, C. (2005). Preference anomalies, preference elicitation, and the discovered preference hypothesis. *Environmental and Resource Economics, 32*, 55–89.

Brendl, C. M., Markman, A. B., & Messner, C. (2003). Devaluation of goal-unrelated choice options. *Journal of Consumer Research, 29*, 463–473.

Bröder, A. (2000). Assessing the empirical validity of the "take-the-best" heuristic as a model of human probabilistic inference. *Journal of Experimental Psychology: Learning, Memory, and Cognition, 26*, 1332–1346.

Bröder, A., & Newell, B. R. (2008). Challenging some common beliefs: Empirical work within the adaptive toolbox metaphor. *Judgment and Decision Making, 3*, 205–214.

Busemeyer, J. R., & Townsend, J. T. (1993). Decision field theory: A dynamic-cognitive approach to decision making in an uncertain environment. *Psychological Review, 100*, 432–459.

Camerer, C. F., & Ho, T. H. (1994). Violations of the betweenness axiom and nonlinearity in probability. *Journal of Risk and Uncertainty, 8*, 167–196.

Camilleri, A.R., & Newell, B.R. (2011). When and why rare events are underweighted: A direct comparison of the sampling, partial feedback, full feedback and description choice paradigms. *Psychonomic Bulletin and Review, 18*, 377–384.

Chater, N., Oaksford, M., Nakisa, R., & Redington, M. (2003). Fast, frugal and rational: How rational norms explain behavior. *Organizational Behavior and Human Decision Processes, 90*, 63–86.

Christensen, C., Heckerling, P., Mackesyamiti, M. E., Bernstein, L. M., & Elstein, A. S. (1995). Pervasiveness of framing effects among physicians and medical students. *Journal of Behavioral Decision Making, 8*, 169–180.

Coursey, D. L., Hovis, J. L., & Schulze, W. D. (1987). The disparity between willingness to accept and willingness to pay measures of value. *Quarterly Journal of Economics, 102*, 679–690.

Cox, J. C., & Grether, D. M. (1996). The preference reversal phenomenon: Response mode, markets and incentives. *Economic Theory, 7*, 381–405.

Damasio, A. R. (1994). *Descartes' error: Emotion, reason, and the human brain.* New York: Avon.

Damasio, A. R. (1996). The somatic marker hypothesis and the possible functions of the prefrontal cortex. *Philosophical Transactions of the Royal Society of London: Series B, 351*, 1413–1420.

Damasio, H., Grabowski, T., Frank, R., Galaburda, A. M., & Damasio, A. R. (1994). The return of Phineas Gage: Clues about the brain from the skull of a famous patient. *Science, 264*, 1102–1105.

Dunn, B. D., Dalgleish, T., & Lawrence, A. D. (2006). The somatic marker hypothesis: A critical evaluation. *Neuroscience and Biobehavioral Reviews, 30*, 239–271.

Edwards, K. D. (1996). Prospect theory: A literature review. *International Review of Financial Analysis, 5*, 19–38.

Ellsberg, D. (1961). Risk, ambiguity and the Savage axioms. *Quarterly Journal of Economics, 75*, 643–669.

Finucane, M. L., Alhakami, A., Slovic, P., & Johnson, S. M. (2000). The affect heuristic in judgments of risks and benefits. *Journal of Behavioral Decision Making, 13*, 1–17.

Finucane, M. L., Peters, E., & Slovic, P. (2003). Judgment and decision making: The dance of affect and reason. In S. L. Schneider & J. Shanteau (Eds.), *Emerging perspectives on judgment and decision research* (pp. 327–364). Cambridge, England: Cambridge University Press.

Fiorina, M. P. (1971). A note on probability matching and rational choice. *Behavioral Science, 16*, 158–166.

Fox, C. R., & Hadar, L. (2006). "Decisions from experience" = sampling theory + prospect theory: Reconsidering Hertwig, Barron, Weber & Erev (2004). *Judgment and Decision Making, 1*, 159–161.

Fredrickson, B. L., & Kahneman, D. (1993). Duration neglect in retrospective evaluations of affective responses. *Journal of Personality and Social Psychology, 65*, 45–55.

Friedman, D. (1998). Monty Hall's three doors: Construction and deconstruction of a choice anomaly. *American Economic Review, 88*, 933–946.

Friedman, D., & Massaro, D. W. (1998). Understanding variability in binary and continuous choice. *Psychonomic Bulletin and Review, 5*, 370–389.

Gigerenzer, G., & Gaissmaier, W. (2011). Heuristic decision making. *Annual Review of Psychology, 62*, 451–482.

Gigerenzer, G., & Goldstein, D. G. (1996). Reasoning the fast and frugal way: Models of bounded rationality. *Psychological Review, 103*, 650–669.

Gigerenzer, G., Todd, P. M., & the ABC Research Group (1999). *Simple heuristics that make us smart.* New York: Oxford University Press.

Gilbert, D. T., Gill, M., & Wilson, T. D. (1998). The future is now: Temporal correction for affective forecasting. *Organizational Behavior and Human Decision Processes, 88*, 430–444.

Goldstein, D. G., & Gigerenzer, G. (2002). Models of ecological rationality: The recognition heuristic. *Psychological Review, 109*, 75–90.

Hau, R., Pleskac, T. J., & Hertwig, R. (2010). Decisions from experience and statistical probabilities: Why they trigger different choices than a priori probabilities. *Journal of Behavioral Decision Making, 68*, 48–68.

Hertwig, R., Barron, G., Weber, E. U., & Erev, I. (2004). Decisions from experience and the effect of rare events in risky choice. *Psychological Science, 15*, 534–539.

Hertwig, R., & Erev, I. (2009). The description-experience gap in risky choice. *Trends in Cognitive Science, 13*, 517–523.

Hoeffler, S., & Ariely, D. (1999). Constructing stable preferences: A look into dimensions of experience and their impact on preference stability. *Journal of Consumer Psychology, 8*, 113–139.

Hoyer, W. D., & Brown, S. P. (1990) Effects of brand awareness on choice for a common, repeat-purchase product. *Journal of Consumer Research, 17*, 141–148.

Hsee, C. K. (1996). The evaluability hypothesis: An explanation for preference reversals between joint and separate evaluations of alternatives. *Organizational Behavior and Human Decision Processes, 67*, 247–257.

Huber, J., Payne, J. W., & Puto, C. (1982). Adding asymmetrically dominated alternatives: Violations of regularity and the similarity hypothesis. *Journal of Consumer Research, 9*, 90–98.

Iyengar, S. S., Wells, R. E., & Schwarz, B. (2006). Doing better but feeling worse: Looking for the "best" job undermines satisfaction. *Psychological Science, 17*, 143–150.

Johnson, E. J., Häubl, G., & Keinan, A. (2007). Aspects of endowment: A query theory of value construction. *Journal of Experimental Psychology: Learning, Memory, and Cognition, 33*, 461–474.

Kahneman, D., & Frederick, S. (2002). Representativeness revisited: Attribute substitution in intuitive judgment. In

T. Gilovich, D. Griffin, & D. Kahneman (Eds.). *Heuristics and biases: The psychology of intuitive judgment* (pp. 49–81). Cambridge, England: Cambridge University Press.

Kahneman, D., Knetsch, J. L., & Thaler, R. H. (1990). Experimental tests of the endowment effect and the Coase theorem. *Journal of Political Economy, 98,* 1325–1348.

Kahneman, D., & Snell, J. (1992). Predicting a changing taste: Do people know what they will like? *Journal of Behavioral Decision Making, 5,* 187–200.

Kahneman, D., & Tversky, A. (1979). Prospect theory: An analysis of decision under risk. *Econometrica, 47,* 263–292.

Kahneman, D., & Tversky, A. (1984). Choices, values, and frames. *American Psychologist, 39,* 341–350.

Kahneman, D., & Tversky, A. (2000). *Choices, values, and frames.* New York: Cambridge University Press.

Kahneman, D., Wakker, P. P., & Sarin, R. (1997). Back to Bentham? Explorations of experienced utility. *Quarterly Journal of Economics, 112,* 375–405.

Keeny, R. L., & Raiffa, H. (1976). *Decisions with multiple objectives: Preferences and value tradeoffs.* New York: Wiley.

Keren, G., & Schul, Y. (2008). Two is not always better than one: A critical evaluation of two-system theories. *Perspectives on Psychological Science, 4,* 533–550.

Keren, G., & Wagenaar, W. A. (1987). Violation of utility theory in unique and repeated gambles. *Journal of Experimental Psychology: Learning, Memory, and Cognition, 13,* 387–391.

Knetsch, J. L. (1989). The endowment effect and evidence of nonreversible indifference curves. *American Economic Review, 79,* 1277–1284.

Krantz, D. H., & Kunreuther, H. C. (2007). Goals and plans in decision making. *Judgment and Decision Making, 2,* 137–168.

Krantz, D. H., Luce, R. D., Suppes, P., & Tversky, A. (1971). *Foundations of measurement, Vol. 1. Additive and polynomial representations.* New York: Academic Press.

Lichtenstein, S., & Slovic, P. (1971). Reversals of preference between bids and choices in gambling decisions. *Journal of Experimental Psychology, 89,* 46–55.

List, J. A. (2002). Preference reversals of a different kind: The "more is less" phenomenon. *American Economic Review, 92,* 1636–1643.

List, J. A. (2004). Neoclassical theory versus prospect theory: Evidence from the marketplace. *Econometrica, 72,* 615–625.

Loewenstein, G., & Adler, D. (1995). A bias in the prediction of tastes. *Economic Journal, 105,* 929–937.

Loewenstein, G., O'Donoghue, T., & Rabin, M. (2003). Projection bias in predicting future utility. *Quarterly Journal of Economics, 118,* 1209–1248.

Loewenstein, G., Weber, E. U., Hsee, C. K., & Welch, E. S. (2001). Risk as feelings. *Psychological Bulletin, 127,* 267–286.

Loomes, G., & Sugden, R. (1982). Regret theory: An alternative theory of rational choice under uncertainty. *Economic Journal, 92,* 805–824.

Lopes, L. L. (1981). Decision making in the short run. *Journal of Experimental Psychology: Human Learning and Memory, 7,* 377–385.

Maia, T. V., & McClelland, J. L. (2004). A re-examination of the evidence for the somatic marker hypothesis: What participants know in the Iowa gambling task. *Proceedings of the National Academy of Sciences USA, 101,* 16075–16080.

March, J. G. (1978). Bounded rationality, ambiguity, and the engineering of choice. *Bell Journal of Economics, 9,* 587–608.

Markman, A. B., Brendl, C. M., & Kim, K. (2007). Preference and the specificity of goals. *Emotion, 7,* 680–684.

Markman, A. B., & Medin, D. L. (2002). Decision making. In D.L. Medin & H. Pashler (Eds.), *Stevens' handbook of experimental psychology* (Vol. 2, 3rd ed., pp. 413–466).

Mellers, B. A., & Cooke, A. D. J. (1994). Trade-offs depend on attribute range. *Journal of Experimental Psychology: Human Perception and Performance, 20,* 1055–1067.

Myagkov, M., & Plott, C. R. (1997). Exchange economies and loss exposure: Experiments exploring prospect theory and competitive equilibria in market environments. *American Economic Review, 87,* 801–828

Newell, B. R., Lagnado, D. A., & Shanks, D. R. (2007). *Straight choices: The psychology of decision making.* Hove, England: Psychology Press.

Newell, B. R., & Shanks, D. R. (2003). Take the best or look at the rest? Factors influencing "one-reason" decision making. *Journal of Experimental Psychology: Learning, Memory, and Cognition, 29,* 53–65.

Newell, B. R., Weston, N. J., & Shanks, D. R. (2003). Empirical tests of a fast-and-frugal heuristic: Not everyone "takes-the-best." *Organizational Behavior and Human Decision Processes, 91,* 82–96.

North, A. C., Hargreaves, D. J., & McKendrick, J. (1997). In-store music affects product choice. *Nature, 390,* 132.

Oeusoonthornwattana, O., & Shanks, D. R. (2010). I like what I know: Is recognition a non-compensatory determiner of consumer choice? *Judgment and Decision Making, 5,* 310–325.

Ortmann, A., Gigerenzer, G., Borges, B., & Goldstein, D. G. (2008). The recognition heuristic: A fast and frugal way to investment choice? In C. R. Plott & V. L. Smith (Eds.), *Handbook of experimental economics results* (Vol. 1, pp. 993–1003). Amsterdam, The Netherlands: North-Holland.

Pachur, T., Bröder, A., & Marewski, J. N. (2008). The recognition heuristic in memory-based inference: Is recognition a non-compensatory cue? *Journal of Behavioral Decision Making, 21,* 183–210.

Payne, J. W., Bettman, J. R., & Johnson, E. J. (1992). Behavioral decision research: A constructive processing perspective. *Annual Review of Psychology, 43,* 87–131.

Payne, J. W., Bettman, J. R., & Johnson, E. J. (1993). *The adaptive decision maker.* Cambridge, England: Cambridge University Press.

Peterson, C. R., & Ulehla, Z. J. (1965). Sequential patterns and maximizing. *Journal of Experimental Psychology, 69,* 1–4.

Plott, C. R. (1996). Rational individual behavior in markets and social choice processes: The discovered preference hypothesis. In K. Arrow, E. Colombatto, M. Perleman, & C. Schmidt (Eds.), *Rational foundations of economic behavior* (pp. 225–250). London: Macmillan and St. Martins.

Plott, C. R., & Zeiler, K. (2005). The willingness to pay-willingness to accept gap, the endowment effect, subject misconceptions, and experimental procedures for eliciting valuations. *American Economic Review, 95,* 530–545.

Quiggin, J. (1982). A theory of anticipated utility. *Journal of Economic Behavior and Organization, 3,* 323–343.

Rakow, T., Demes, K. A., & Newell, B. R. (2008). Biased samples not mode of presentation: Re-examining the apparent underweighting of rare events in experience-based choice. *Organizational Behavior and Human Decision Processes, 106,* 168–179.

Ratcliff, R. (1978). A theory of memory retrieval. *Psychological Review, 85*, 59–108.

Redelmeier, D. A., & Kahneman, D. (1996). Patients' memories of painful medical treatments: Real-time and retrospective evaluations of two minimally invasive procedures. *Pain, 66*, 3–8.

Rieskamp, J., & Hoffrage, U. (1999). When do people use simple heuristics and how can we tell? In G. Gigerenzer, P. Todd, & ABC Research Group (Eds.), *Simple heuristics that make us smart* (pp. 141–168). Oxford, England: Oxford University Press.

Rieskamp, J., & Otto, P. E. (2006). SSL: A theory of how people learn to select strategies. *Journal of Experimental Psychology: General, 135*, 207–236.

Roe, R. M., Busemeyer, J. R., & Townsend, J. T. (2001). Multialternative decision field theory: A dynamic connectionist model of decision making. *Psychological Review, 108*, 370–392.

Rottenstreich, Y., & Hsee, C. K. (2001). Money, kisses and electric shocks: On the affective psychology of probability weighting. *Psychological Science, 12*, 185–190.

Samuelson, P. A. (1963). Risk and uncertainty: A fallacy of large numbers. *Scientia, 98*, 108–113.

Samuelson, W., & Zeckhauser, R. (1988). Status quo bias in decision making, *Journal of Risk and Uncertainty, 1*, 7–59.

Savage, L. J. (1954). *The foundations of statistics.* New York: Dover.

Schoemaker, P. (1982). The expected utility model: Its variants, purposes, evidence and limitations. *Journal of Economic Literature, 20*, 529–563.

Schwartz, B., Ward, A., Monterosso, J., Lyubomirsky, S., White, K., & Lehman, D. R. (2002). Maximizing versus satisficing: Happiness is a matter of choice. *Journal of Personality and Social Psychology, 83*, 1178–1197.

Sen, A. (1993). Internal consistency of choice. *Econometrica, 61*, 495–521.

Shafir, E., Simonson, I., & Tversky, A. (1993). Reason-based choice. *Cognition, 49*, 11–36.

Shanks, D. R., Tunney, R. J., & McCarthy, J. D. (2002). A re-examination of probability matching and rational choice. *Journal of Behavioral Decision Making, 15*, 233–250.

Shefrin, H. M., & Thaler, R. H. (1992). Mental accounting, saving, and self- control. In G. Loewenstein & J. Elster (Eds.), *Choice over time* (pp. 287–330). New York: Russell Sage Foundation.

Shogren, J. F., Shin, S. Y., Hayes, D. J., & Kliebenstein, J., (1994) Resolving differences in willingness to pay and willingness to accept. *American Economic Review, 84*, 255–270.

Simon, H. A. (1955). A behavioral model of rational choice. *Quarterly Journal of Economics, 69*, 99–118.

Simon, H. A. (1956). Rational choice and the structure of the environment. *Psychological Review, 63*, 129–138.

Simonson, I. (1989). Choice based on reasons: The case of attraction of compromise effects. *Journal of Consumer Research, 16*, 158–174.

Simonson, I. (1990). The effect of purchase quantity and timing on variety seeking behavior. *Journal of Marketing Research, 27*, 150–162.

Simonson, I. (2008). Will I like a "medium" pillow? Another look at constructed and inherent preferences. *Journal of Consumer Psychology, 18*, 155–169.

Sloman, S. A. (1996). The empirical case for two systems of reasoning. *Psychological Bulletin, 119*, 3–22.

Slovic, P. (1975). Choice between equally valuable alternatives. *Journal of Experimental Psychology: Human Perception and Performance, 1*, 280–287.

Slovic, P. (1995). The construction of preference. *American Psychologist, 50*, 364–371.

Smith, P. L. (2000). Stochastic dynamic models of response time and accuracy: A foundational primer. *Journal of Mathematical Psychology, 44*, 408–463.

Stewart, N., Chater, N., & Brown, G. D. A. (2006). Decision by sampling. *Cognitive Psychology, 53*, 1–26.

Thaler, R. (1980). Towards a positive theory of consumer choice. *Journal of Economic Behavior and Organization, 1*, 39–60.

Thaler, R. (1985). Mental accounting and consumer choice. *Marketing Science, 4*, 199–214.

Tversky, A. (1972). Elimination by aspects: A theory of choice. *Psychological Review, 79*, 281–299.

Tversky, A., & Kahneman, D. (1981). The framing of decisions and the psychology of choice. *Science, 211*, 453–458.

Tversky, A., & Kahneman, D. (1986). Rational choice and the framing of decisions. *Journal of Business, 59*, 251–278.

Tversky, A., & Kahneman, D. (1992). Advances in prospect theory: Cumulative representation of uncertainty. *Journal of Risk and Uncertainty, 323*, 297–323.

Tversky, A., & Simonson, I. (1993). Context-dependent preferences. *Management Science, 39*, 1179–1189.

Tversky, A., Sattath, S., & Slovic, P. (1988). Contingent weighting in judgment and choice. *Psychological Review, 95*, 371–384.

Tversky, A., & Thaler, R. H. (1990). Anomalies: Preference reversals. *Journal of Economic Perspectives, 4*, 201–211.

Ungemach, C., Chater, N., & Stewart, N. (2009). Are probabilities overweighted or underweighted when rare outcomes are experienced (rarely)? *Psychological Science, 20*, 473–479.

Usher, M., & McClelland, J. L. (2001). The time course of perceptual choice: The leaky, competing accumulator model. *Psychological Review, 108*, 550–592.

Usher, M., & McClelland, J. L. (2004). Loss aversion and inhibition in dynamical models of multialternative choice. *Psychological Review, 111*, 757–769.

van de Kuilen, G. (2009). Subjective probability weighting and the discovered preference hypothesis. *Theory and Decision, 67*, 1–22.

van de Kuilen, G., & Wakker, P. P. (2006). Learning in the Allais paradox. *Journal of Risk and Uncertainty, 33*, 155–164.

Von Neumann, J., & Morgenstern, O. (1947). *Theory of games and economic behavior* (2nd ed.). Princeton, NJ. Princeton University Press.

Vulkan, N. (2000). An economist's perspective on probability matching. *Journal of Economic Surveys, 14*, 101–118.

Wakker, P. P. (1989). *Additive representations of preferences: A new foundation of decision analysis.* Dordrecht, The Netherlands: Kluwer Academic.

Weber, E. U., & Johnson, E. J. (2006). Constructing preferences from memories. In S. Lichtenstein & P. Slovic (Eds.), *The construction of preference* (pp. 397–410). New York: Cambridge University Press.

Weber, E. U., & Johnson, E. J. (2009). Mindful judgment and decision making. *Annual Review of Psychology, 60,* 53–85.

Wedell, D. H., & Böckenholt, U. (1990). Moderation of preference reversals in the long run. *Journal of Experimental Psychology: Human Perception and Performance, 16,* 429–438.

Wilson, T. D., & Gilbert, D. T. (2005). Affective forecasting: Knowing what to want. *Current Directions in Psychological Science, 14,* 131–134.

Wirtz, D., Kruger, J., Scollon, C. N., & Diener, E. (2003). What to do on spring break? The role of predicted, on-line, and remembered experience in future choice. *Psychological Science, 14,* 520–524.

Wolford, G., Newman, S. E., Miller, M. B., & Wig, G. S. (2004). Searching for patterns in random sequences. *Canadian Journal of Experimental Psychology, 58,* 221–228.

Wu, G., & Gonzalez, R. (1996). Curvature of the probability weighting function. *Management Science, 42,* 1676–1690

# Affective Forecasting and Well-Being

Barry Schwartz *and* Roseanna Sommers

**Abstract**

Every decision requires a prediction, both about what will happen and about how the decider will *feel* about what happens. Thus, decisions require what is known as *affective forecasting*. This chapter reviews evidence that people systematically mispredict the way experiences will feel. First, predictions about the future are often based on memories of the past, but memories of the past are often inaccurate. Second, people predict that the affective quality of experiences will last, thereby neglecting the widespread phenomenon of adaptation. Third, in anticipating an experience, people focus on aspects of their lives that will be changed by the experience and ignore aspects of their lives that will be unaffected. Fourth, decisions are profoundly affected by the choice context, even though the choice context will no longer be relevant when the chosen object is actually experienced. Each of these affective forecasting "errors" can lead people to mispredict satisfaction with decisions.

**Key Words:** affective forecasting, decision making, subjective experience, misprediction, rational choice

Every decision requires a prediction. The world is an uncertain place, and what may happen is rarely guaranteed to happen. Should you expand your business? Invest in stocks or in bonds? Refinance your home? Carry a new line of products?

As challenging as decisions like these are, there is one respect in which they are simple: Your aim in each of these cases is to maximize return on investment. Return on investment is the consequence that matters. It is an objective outcome that is being pursued, one that can be measured unambiguously. Contrast that with decisions like these: Should you switch jobs? Move to a new neighborhood? Go on vacation to Europe or Mexico? Eat at the Italian restaurant or the Japanese one? These decisions also involve predictions, and no doubt, they, too, have objective, unambiguously measureable characteristics. But now, what you are mainly trying to predict is your subjective experience. How much satisfaction will you get from the new job? How much will

you like living in the new neighborhood (and how big a pain will it be to move)?

There are certainly subjective aspects of your business decisions that matter. How will it feel, for example, to achieve a targeted rate of return, only to discover that a competitor achieved a slightly higher one? And there are certainly objective aspects of decisions about jobs, restaurants, and vacations that matter. So virtually all decisions, in all domains, have both objective and subjective dimensions. But the questions at the heart of most business or other financial decisions concern predicting a future state of the world, whereas the questions at the heart of most of personal decisions concern future states of you. Personal decisions like these ask not "What will happen if I do X?" but rather "How will I feel if I do X?" So, in addition to predicting objective events, you must also predict your subjective response to those events.

This chapter is about people's ability to predict subjective experience, what is sometimes referred to as "affective forecasting" (e.g., Gilbert, 2006; Gilbert & Wilson, 2000, 2007). More precisely, it is about the ways in which people make frequent and systematic errors when endeavoring to predict how they will feel. These errors in prediction can lead to frequent and systematic mistakes in decision making—mistakes in the sense that the decisions people make often do not provide them with the subjective experiences they expect.

The potential significance of these errors cannot be overstated. The aim of rational decision making, economists tell us, is to maximize utility—not wealth, but utility. Though it is hard to pin down exactly what "utility" means, it certainly has a subjective element that cannot be eliminated. Part of deciding what job to take, where to live, where to go on vacation, or pretty much anything else, is predicting how your choice will make you feel. Even if you could predict the objective future perfectly, failure to predict the subjective future would consistently leave you feeling that you made a mistake. So how well do people predict their subjective futures?

## Forecasting Based on Inaccurate Memory

Imagine yourself a college student about to go off to South Florida for spring break. Some psychologists have outfitted you with a personal digital assistant (PDA) that will beep periodically while you are away. When it beeps, your job is to respond to a series of questions designed to assess how you are feeling at that moment. This technique is known as "ecological momentary assessment" (EMA; Kahneman, 1999) or "experience sampling." We might regard the integral, or algebraic sum, of these moment-by-moment affective responses as an objective measure of how happy the students were to be on vacation (Kahneman, 1999, 2000; Kahneman & Thaler, 2006). It is a measure of "experienced utility," or how life is going as it is being lived. Experienced utility is quite different from "remembered utility," which is what you rely on to answer your coworker's query about how your vacation was. To answer her, you survey your memory and form a summary judgment of the entire vacation.

Wirtz, Kruger, Scollon, and Diener (2003) gave PDAs to college students and measured their moment-by-moment affective experience while they were on vacation for spring break. They found that the students misremembered how much fun they had had. Whereas they remembered their vacations as having both intensely positive and intensely negative points, their moment-by-moment reports recorded on their PDAs revealed that they had

had a much more mild time. This disparity raised a key question: If students' in-the-moment ratings of spring break differed from their after-the-fact, memory-based ratings of spring break, which opinion would form the basis of their future decisions? What Wirtz et al. found was that it was the memory of the experience, not the experience itself, that most influenced people's willingness to have the experience again (i.e., to go back to South Florida next year during spring break). Thus, it appears that when experienced utility and remembered utility disagree, it is remembered utility that most influences affective forecasting.

Perhaps this is not so surprising. When making decisions, we draw on our experience with past events to decide how much we will enjoy similar future events (e.g., "How much did I enjoy being in Mexico last spring?"). But we cannot truly relive our old experiences to know how much we enjoyed them; all we have access to is our memories of those experiences. Thus, every prediction requires relying upon memory, and memory is not a veridical representation of moment-by-moment experience.

If our memories were perfectly veridical, then when trying to answer a question such as "How was your break?" people would create a summary judgment by giving each moment of the experience equal weight. But Kahneman (1999, 2000) discovered that memory is *systematically* nonveridical. What Kahneman found is that two moments of an experience have an outsized effect on our memory-based summary judgments: the "peak" and the "end." That is, what seems to be stored in memory is what the experience was like at its most intense point (the peak) and how it ended. Kahneman found that the global, summary evaluation of an experience (i.e., what people rely on to answer "How was your break?") is not very close to people's time-integrated moment-by-moment experiences. Rather, summary evaluations seem to match up with the mathematical average of the peak moment and the end moment.

One of the most important implications of the "peak-end rule" is that the duration of the experience seems not to matter, a phenomenon that has come to be known as "duration neglect." Two weeks on the beach in Florida, *as lived*, will certainly be different from 1 week on the beach. But if the two experiences have similar peaks and similar endings, they will be remembered as affectively equivalent. Indeed, Redelmeier, Katz, and Kahneman (2003) studied patients who underwent painful colonoscopy procedures that ranged in duration from 4 minutes to 69 minutes and found that, surprisingly, duration did not affect patients' retrospective evaluations of the experience. Only the pain felt at the peak and at the end affected patients' memories of the procedure and their likelihood of returning for a repeat procedure years later. Duration mattered so little that some patients even preferred the longer, more painful colonoscopy procedures—as long as those elongated procedures ended on a less painful note.

There is now substantial evidence in support of this peak-end rule for encoding and recalling affect. For example, Kahneman, Fredrickson, Schreiber, and Redelmeier (1993) asked participants to immerse their hands in freezing cold water twice: once in 14°C water for 60 seconds and once in 14°C water for 60 seconds with an additional 30 seconds tacked on at the end, during which the water temperature was gradually raised to 15°C (still painful, but less so). Even though the 90-second trial exposed participants to all the pain of the 60-second trial and more, participants tended to remember the 90-second trial as less painful. When given the choice of which trial they would prefer to repeat for a third dunking, most participants chose the longer trial. Similar results have been found with other unpleasant experiences (e.g., exposing people to loud noises followed by less loud noises) as well as pleasant experiences.

The fact that there are discrepancies between experienced affect and remembered affect raises an important question: Which is more important? If a longer colonoscopy causes you more pain, but you remember it as causing you less, is it worth the extra few minutes of pain to secure a better memory? It might be, especially considering that a better memory might make you more willing to return for future colonoscopies to screen for colorectal cancer. Furthermore, if you remember spring break in South Florida as a fantastic vacation, but your PDA reports reveal that it was rather mundane, are you better off staying home next year? It seems that if you decide to go back for your next spring break, and you have a mediocre time again, but you remember it as a wonderful trip, perhaps the forecasting "error" is not much of an error after all.

The experience of spring break, or ice water dunking, or anything else is just a moment in time. The memory of that experience may last forever. And people do not simply file away the memories of experiences; they "consume" those memories in the future. So there is a sense in which "spring break" is actually "spring break plus all the times I think

about it and talk about it later on." Thus, remembered affect is important beyond its function as the basis for future decisions; it is important because you will consume those memories over and over for the rest of your life.

There are a number of issues regarding the peak-end rule and its role in the encoding and recall of affective experience that remain to be resolved. First, what counts as an "episode" over which affective experience is integrated and summarized? Is spring break one episode or many? Does it have one peak and one end, or several? It remains to be seen whether global judgments are better predicted by the peak/end of each episode or the peak/end of the whole unified experience. Second, how are the positive and negative moments that characterize most real-life experiences combined and integrated? Are there separate positive and negative peaks? Does one get subtracted from the other? Does whichever peak is greater determine whether the experience is summarized as positive or negative? All of these questions require more investigation.

Beyond our tendency to remember peaks and ends, there are other instances of nonveridical memory. There is considerable evidence that people's memories often align with their expectations, even if their actual experiences (as measured by ecological momentary assessments) tell another story. In the 2000 presidential contest between Al Gore and George W. Bush, devoted Republicans and Democrats each made predictions about how they would feel the day after the outcome of the election was decided. Republicans thought they would be elated if Bush won and Democrats thought they would be devastated. But when researchers followed up with them shortly after Bush was certified as the winner, it became evident that both groups had overestimated their affective responses: Bush supporters were happy but not ecstatic, whereas Gore supporters were disappointed but not distraught. Interestingly, when researchers contacted participants 6 months later and asked them to recall how they had felt the day after the election's outcome had been decided, Republicans remembered feeling elated and Democrats remembered feeling devastated. Their recollections matched their expectations, not their actual feelings (Gilbert, Pinel, Wilson, Blumberg, & Wheatley, 1998). Wirtz et al. (2003) found a similar result with the college students on vacation: They remembered spring break being about as much fun as they had expected it to be.

In addition, when asked to recall how they felt after events of a sort they have experienced many times in the past, people tend to recall not a typical instance, but an extreme one. Furthermore, they treat the extreme instance as if it were typical. For example, when students are asked to recall a time when their school's team won a football game, they come up with the most extreme example (e.g., "We had a miraculous last-second comeback and it was unbelievably exciting"; Morewedge, Gilbert, & Wilson, 2005). The fact that the most unusual, affectively intense examples are the ones that come most easily to mind means that forecasts are often based on the most extreme past experiences, causing people to overpredict their emotional reactions (e.g., "I will be ecstatic if my team wins this time"). Morewedge et al. found that people who explicitly corrected for this bias in memory retrieval, either by recounting multiple past experiences to achieve a more representative sample on which to base forecasts or by recognizing that the salient example was actually an outlier, were able to forecast more accurately how exciting they would find the game they were about to watch. But in the absence of retrieval aids like these, the bias in memory retrieval toward affectively intense experiences is another cause of inaccurate forecasts.

## Overestimating Affective Responses to Events: Durability Bias and Focalism

Drawing upon nonveridical memories is one reason people mispredict what will make them happy, but memory is hardly the only source of affective forecasting errors. Another important source of misprediction is a failure to appreciate that by and large, people adapt to new circumstances. They get over bad things and stop enjoying good things (e.g., Brickman, Coates, & Janoff-Bulman, 1978; Fredrick & Loewenstein, 1999; Gilbert, 2006; Lyubomirsky, 2007). Sensory adaptation and neural adaptation are long-known, pervasive features of the organism's response to its environment. Stimuli of constant intensity produce ever-diminishing responses over time, a process known as habituation. The same seems to be true of affective experience. The classic demonstration of what is often called "hedonic adaptation" was provided by Brickman, Coates, and Janoff-Bulman (1978), who compared the subjective states of people who had recently become paralyzed and people who had won significant sums of money in state lotteries. They found that whereas the self-reported life satisfaction ratings of paraplegics and lottery winners were vastly different shortly after the momentous events, as time passed, people's subjective states tended to gravitate back to their

original happiness levels. Furthermore, looking at their projections of how happy they expected to be in the future, it was impossible to tell who had had a tragic accident and who had hit the jackpot. Thus, seemingly life-altering experiences can have merely transient effects on subjective well-being.

People do not adapt to all hedonic experience (see Frederick & Loewenstein, 1999). It may take years to adapt to major life events like divorce, death of a spouse, or job loss, and adaptation may never be complete (Lucas, 2005, 2007; Lucas & Clark, 2006; Lucas, Clark, Geirgellis, & Diener, E., 2004; see Diener & Biswas-Diener, 2008, for a review). Nonetheless, as a general rule, hedonic adaptation reduces the affective impact of experiences over time. This fact has been codified into some theories of well-being. For example, Lyubomirsky (2007) suggests that people have a "set point" for happiness, which may account for as much as 50% reported well-being. This happiness set point acts as a kind of gravitational pull. Good experiences deflect people up from their set points and bad experiences push them down, but over time, gravity does its work and they return, at least partially, to where they started.

If hedonic adaptation is a fact of people's affective lives, the question is, do people expect it and thus predict it? People might not spend months deciding what make and model of new car to buy if they know that they will only get a hedonic "kick" out of the car for a few weeks, after which it will become just their mode of transportation. Gilbert and Wilson (e.g., 2000, 2007; see Gilbert, 2006; Gilbert et al., 1998) provide extensive empirical evidence that people fail to anticipate adaptation. People display what Gilbert and Wilson call "durability bias" in expecting the affective quality of experiences to last. Gilbert and Wilson demonstrate this bias by asking people to predict how it will feel, days, months, and even years after the fact, to get tenure or be denied tenure, to have their favored gubernatorial candidate win or lose an election, or to have their favored team win or lose the big game. They find that people's predictions are largely unaffected by the time interval between the event and the moment of evaluation. This is in marked contrast to queries of other people, days, months, or years after they have actually gotten or been denied tenure, seen their candidates win or lose election, or their favored team win or lose the game. For the "experiencers" of these events, time seems to heal all wounds (or blunt all triumphs). The mismatch between prediction of the future and the actual experience of that future is a powerful example of an error in affective forecasting (Gilbert et al., 1998).

In a detailed, careful investigation of adaptation, Riis, Loewenstein, Baron, Jepson, Fagerlin, and Ubel (2005) combined the "predictor/experiencer" techniques of Gilbert et al. (1998) with the experience sampling techniques of Wirtz et al. (2003) and Kahneman (1999, 2000) in a study of patients with end-stage renal disease, a chronic medical condition. To an outsider, life as an end-stage renal patient looks pretty miserable, as multiple times per week, patients are required to spend several hours hooked up to a machine in a hospital or clinic that performs the blood-cleaning and filtering, a process known as "hemodialysis."

Riis et al. found healthy people to act as a control group, matching each hemodialysis patient with a healthy person who had similar demographic characteristics. The researchers sought to examine how healthy and sick people would imagine being in one another's shoes. Hemodialysis patients were asked to imagine they had never been sick, and healthy people were asked to imagine they had been on hemodialysis for as long as their matched partner had been. The participants estimated what their mood levels would be like if they were in their matched partner's shoes. Riis et al. found that healthy people vastly underestimated the mood levels of hemodialysis patients; they thought chronic kidney disease would cause overall negative mood, whereas in actuality, hemodialysis patients' mood levels were positive overall. Furthermore, the PDA data revealed no differences in mood between the hemodialysis patients and the healthy controls. In other words, the dialysis patients adapted, and the healthy controls did not anticipate this adaptation.

Did the dialysis patients appreciate that they had adapted? Riis et al. reasoned that if a patient were aware of adaptation, then when asked how happy she would be if she had never had kidney problems, her estimate would be about the same as the happiness she currently reported (which the PDA data revealed was about the same as the happiness that healthy controls reported): "Dialysis is bad, but I've adapted, so there's no reason to think that if I weren't on dialysis, I'd be any happier." What the researchers found, however, was that dialysis patients substantially overestimated how happy they would be if they had never been sick. These data suggest that hedonic adaptation is a process of which people are largely unaware.

People not only overestimate the duration of their affective responses to events; they also overestimate how intense those feelings will be. This may be due to what Gilbert and Wilson call "focalism," or the "focusing illusion." When imagining an alternate state of reality, such as what it would be like to become paralyzed, people focus on the aspects of their lives that will be affected by that event, and ignore aspects of their lives that will be unaffected. Mobility expands to fill the entire screen, and people forget that that while becoming paraplegic will affect a person's ability to get around, it might not change the quality of that person's social relationships, or the satisfaction that can be derived from work. Many facets of life will be the same, wheelchair or not, but when imagining the momentous event, all a person can think about is how his or her life will change. In addition, people learn to adjust to the momentous event in ways that they could not have anticipated. They may even be able to find benefits—silver linings—in unfortunate events (e.g., "The accident may have paralyzed me, but it made me appreciate how precious every moment of being alive is").

To summarize this section, people experience hedonic adaptation, yet they fail to predict it. They also exhibit a focusing illusion, whereby they neglect to take into account all the ways their lives will be unaffected by the change in question. Thus, predictions of affect tend to be more intense and longer lasting than reality warrants due to both focalism and the underestimation of adaptation.

But people do not adapt to everything, and even when they do adapt, the pace of adaptation can vary dramatically from one affectively relevant experience to another. We do not yet fully know why people adapt easily to some experiences and not to others. Indeed, there may be no especially perspicuous classification. Possibly, the more important to one's life an experience is, the less one will adapt. Possibly, the more aspects of a person's life an experience affects, the less the person will adapt. Possibly, the adaptation process is dynamic, such that with repeated experiences of a certain type, adaptation occurs more and more rapidly. Though it is important that people be cognizant of hedonic adaptation so that they can predict future affect more accurately and thus be able to make better decisions, it is also apparent that affective adaptation is a mixed bag that we still do not fully understand.

## Preferences Shift Depending on the Context
Another reason it is difficult to make decisions that make us happy is that our preferences are not stable. They are affected by seemingly irrelevant

aspects of the decision context, such as what other options are presented and how those options are described. Our preferences are also affected by our state of arousal. If we fail to understand that our preferences change, we can exhibit a "presentism bias" (Gilbert, 2006): We choose what we want now instead of thinking about what we will want later.

Much of the time, perhaps most of the time, the decisions people make involve not just predicting how some object or event will make them feel, but how that object or event will make them feel in comparison with other objects and events. That is, most of the time, decisions require choices among alternatives. The choice one makes reflects a prediction that the chosen option will make for more satisfaction than the alternatives. Though there is probably seldom an explicit prediction of affect (i.e., people rarely ask themselves, "How will I feel if I have the chicken, as opposed to the beef?"), in effect, making a choice among options amounts to a prediction of affect.

In theory, choice among alternatives should be fairly simple. The rational choice model of economists assumes that people have well-ordered preferences, so that choosing is just a matter of "looking up" those preferences, or of determining which of those preferences each option will allow you to satisfy, and then going with the highest ranked one. Economists further assume that the relation between preferences and behavior is straightforward, so that even when people have not stated their preferences, or "looked them up," we can tell what people like by observing what they choose.

Forty years of research on decision making makes it abundantly clear that this rational choice model provides an extremely inaccurate description of how people actually choose. It is not so much that people go against their preferences when choosing (though this is sometimes the case). It is that people may not even *have* preferences until a choice presents itself. Even more problematic, people may have partial and somewhat incoherent preferences, which then get filled out by the set of options they confront. As both Fischoff (1991) and Slovic (1991) put it, often, preferences are *constructed* rather than consulted, and that construction is heavily influenced by the context in which choices are made.

For example, Brenner, Rottenstreich, and Sood (1999) asked San Francisco Bay Area students to make choices about various travel options. One group was asked, "You are thinking of taking a long weekend out of town. You are considering Seattle, Las Vegas, and Los Angeles. How much would you pay for a roundtrip plane ticket to Seattle?" These respondents were willing to pay an average of $135. The researchers then asked a second group of students, "You are thinking of taking a long weekend out of town. You are considering Seattle. How much would you pay for a roundtrip plane ticket to Seattle?" Students responding to this question were willing to pay $206 for a roundtrip ticket to Seattle, a 50% increase over the other group.

So which is it? Which number reflects the "true" value of a trip to Seattle? This is a question with broad implications, since the mode of inquiry used in this study, known as "contingent valuation," has come to be viewed as the gold standard for assessing the welfare consequences of various public policies. Why does Seattle seem so much less attractive when it is considered alongside Las Vegas and Los Angeles? Brenner et al. suggest that when there are multiple options, people are forced to compare the benefits and drawbacks of each locale. In making such tradeoffs, losses loom larger than gains (see, e.g., Kahneman & Tversky, 1984; Kahneman, 2003 for a discussion of "Prospect Theory," which systematizes this sensitivity to losses). Thus, people are bothered more by what they will lose in passing up Los Angeles and Las Vegas than they are pleased by what they will gain in choosing Seattle. As Brenner et al. argue, everything suffers from comparison.

Interestingly, the presence of Las Vegas and Los Angeles as alternatives only serves to make tradeoffs more easily noticeable; the tradeoffs exist regardless of whether people realize that a choice for Seattle is a choice against going anywhere else. The people who were asked only about Seattle were making tradeoffs as well (i.e., by going to Seattle they were precluding themselves from going to Las Vegas, Los Angeles, and everywhere else they might go), but for these respondents, the foregone alternatives were not as noticeable. It appears that people do not spontaneously generate alternatives. Comparison is not automatic.

Thus, it can be said that how much one likes Seattle depends on how many options are presented. Preferences are shaped by the choice context. Christopher Hsee has done pioneering research on other misleading cues that people use to construct their preferences (e.g., Hsee, 1996; Hsee & Hastie, 2006; Hsee, Hastie, & Chen, 2008; Hsee & Zhang, 2004).

Consider going to choose a new set of speakers for your home theater. In the consumer electronics store, you listen to dozens of possibilities. Some candidates are clearly different, but many seem agonizingly close in sound quality. Nonetheless, when you listen to them side by side, you can detect subtle differences.

You narrow the finalists down to two. One set of speakers sounds better than the other, but it is unattractive and will clash with your décor. The other, slightly less pleasing sounding speakers will fit into your living room perfectly. Faced with this tradeoff, which speakers will you choose? There is no right answer to this question, but as Hsee shows, there may be a substantial difference between what matters in the store and what matters at home. In choosing the speakers, you are performing what Hsee calls a "joint evaluation." That is, you are making a direct, side-by-side comparison between alternatives. Under these conditions, small differences in sound quality will be detectable, and probably quite salient (sound is what speakers are for, after all). Given the detectable difference, you might be tempted to choose the speakers that sound better.

But then, you bring them home, and set them up. Whereas you used joint evaluation in the store, at home you have separate consumption. The differences in sound that seemed significant in the store vanish, because you did not realize—could not realize—that it was only the direct comparison that made them noticeable. Meanwhile, the unattractiveness of your chosen speakers needs no direct comparison. It is obvious, a direct reproach to you for neglecting the difference the choice context makes.

For Hsee, this problem is endemic to the processes of rational choice. Wise choosers are supposed to comparison shop, which means using joint evaluations. But consumption is always separate from the foregone options. As a result, people will consistently overestimate the subjective magnitude and importance of some differences. People will consistently mispredict the satisfaction they will derive from their choice as a result of failing to appreciate that what is best in a side-by-side comparison may not be what is best alone.

A related finding was reported by Dunn, Wilson, and Gilbert (2003) in a study of first-year students at the University of Virginia who participated in the annual housing lottery that determined dorm room assignments for the next 3 years. Students entered the lottery in groups of their own choosing, meaning that no matter where they ended up, they would be with their closest friends. Thus, housing options differed from one another not in terms of social environment but in terms of location, and therefore convenience. Prior to the lottery, students believed

that the outcome of the lottery would have a big impact on the happiness they experienced in the coming years. They were wrong: Housing had virtually no impact on self-reported happiness (determined by follow-up inquiries 12 and 24 months later). The only factor that significantly influenced happiness levels was the social climate at the various houses, and because the houses differed little from one another in this regard, happiness levels were relatively constant. The students had focused, incorrectly, on location.

Why did they make this mistake? It was not because they were unaware that it would be social environment that would actually matter most for happiness. When asked to rate the significance of various aspects of residential life, students showed that they understood that the social dimensions of where they lived were key. Yet they abandoned this understanding when it came to predicting their satisfaction with the various housing options. These students faced a situation not unlike the customer shopping for speakers. In the important respects, the housing options are essentially equivalent—no matter where they end up, their friends will be with them, so that social environment and sense of community were constant across alternatives. So students looked for a way to differentiate the housing options. They focused on the dimension—location—on which options differ, even though it was relatively unimportant. They then elevated the significance of this difference, forgetting that when it came to their overall happiness, any differences in location would be overwhelmed by the impact of their social environments.

In these examples we see that aspects of context at the moment of decision affect the evaluation of options, and thus affect the decision. Dunn et al.'s (2003) housing study provides another example of how affective forecasts may be inaccurate if people focus too much on what is the best among the options, and not enough on what will be best when it is experienced by itself. Thus, people who are influenced by joint evaluation to choose an option on the basis of features that will not matter when they are actually consuming it are making an affective forecasting error, even if it is only implicit.

## Hot-Cold Empathy Gaps: Mispredicting the Effect of Arousal on Decisions

Preferences are unstable in another way: They often fluctuate due to changes in arousal. For example, when you ask people whether they would have sex without a condom, almost everyone says no. Yet lots of people do. When you ask people whether they would drive when impaired by alcohol, almost everyone says no. Yet lots of people do. This mismatch between what people say they will do when in a given state (e.g., when they are sexually aroused) and what they actually do is an error in affective forecasting. But it is different from the ones we have considered thus far. Now, the forecasting error is not about how people will *feel* in the future; it is about how the way they feel will affect what they *do*. It is what Loewenstein (1996) calls the "hot-cold empathy gap."

Loewenstein argues that people in cold states have little empathy for themselves in hot states and, conversely, in hot states people do not anticipate feeling cold. People in cold states find their hot state behavior perplexing (e.g., "How could I have been so tired that I fell asleep in class?"). It is easy to imagine resisting temptation when one is not tempted (e.g., "I don't need coffee before my afternoon class because there is no way I'll be tired enough to doze off"). As a result, people fail to take the kinds of precautions that will prevent them from succumbing to temptation in the future. They rely too heavily on willpower, because when unaroused, they do not appreciate how powerfully arousal will alter their preferences. When unaroused, precautions seem unnecessary.

Perhaps the first demonstration of this hot-cold effect was reported by Nisbett and Kanouse (1968), who showed that people who did their supermarket shopping when hungry bought more food than they needed or wanted later, when they were no longer hungry. They predicted their future feelings inaccurately. Another example of the hot-cold empathy gap is the failure of pregnant women—even women who have given birth before—to anticipate that they will want pain medication during childbirth (Loewenstein, 1996).

More recently, Ariely and Loewenstein (2006) showed that men who answered questions about the desirability of various sexual partners and practices while sexually aroused were considerably more willing to engage in risky sex and unorthodox sex than they were when unaroused. This finding demonstrates that preferences differ when people are in a hot state versus cold state. The forecasting error comes from the fact that people do not appreciate these hot/cold differences.

Loewenstein's (1996) account of this phenomenon suggests that when people are in a hot state, their attentional focus narrows, the value of objects or events relevant to that state is enhanced, and

people's willingness to delay gratification (what is often referred to as their "temporal discount function") plummets. He further suggests that people underestimate the effects of being in hot states and do not remember how powerful past hot states were. As a result, the mistakes people make when aroused are likely to be repeated.

In discussing this phenomenon, Gilbert (2006) suggests that one reason why people fail to allow for the effects of hot states is that no matter how much they try to avoid it, people's predictions regarding future affective states will be anchored, in part, by their current affective (and neural) states. People anchored in how they feel at the moment can try to correct for this starting point, but correction is often insufficient, and thus people exhibit a "presentism bias." As a result, current affective states will always exert an influence on predictions about future states.

Presentism has been demonstrated in another study that is perhaps less dramatic than those involving sexual arousal or intoxication, but no less compelling. Read and Loewenstein (1995) asked undergraduates what snacks they would like to eat during a weekly seminar. Some students selected their snacks every week for 3 weeks, whereas other students were asked on the first week to choose the snacks they would eat over the next 3 weeks. Those who chose every week tended to pick the same snack (their favorite) every time. But those who were asked to choose for 3 weeks at once tended to select more variety: tortilla chips this week, Oreos the next week, and Snickers bars the week after that. They seemed to assume that they would grow bored with the same snack week after week. When it came time to consume their choices, however, those who had chosen ahead of time often wished they could have their favorite snack again. They wanted less variety than they had committed themselves to, a tendency that has come to be called "diversification bias" (Read & Loewenstein, 1995; Simonson, 1990). It is as though at the moment of choice, people imagine eating a bag of tortilla chips, then another, and then another, and surmise that they will get tired of eating tortilla chips. What they cannot do is imagine what it will be like to be offered a bag of tortilla chips a week after having consumed the last one. This is a presentism bias because they are anchored on how they feel now (i.e., three bags of tortilla chips is too much) and do not realize that with a week in between each bag, their appetite for tortilla chips is quite different.

In a somewhat related phenomenon, when people are asked to choose several films to rent, all at the same time, they select something lowbrow and entertaining for now (e.g., *Animal House*) and something respectably edifying for later (e.g., *The Sorrow and the Pity*). But when "later" comes, what people turn out to want is another film in the lowbrow category (Milkman, Rogers, & Bazerman, 2009). Similarly, people ordering groceries online are more likely to order junk food (e.g., ice cream) for now and healthy food (e.g., vegetables) for a few days later (Milkman, Rogers, & Bazerman, 2010; see also Milkman, Rogers, & Bazerman, 2008). As Milkman, Rogers, and Bazerman (2008) put it, people often face a choice between "wants" and "shoulds." They tend to want their "wants" satisfied now and their "shoulds" deferred for later. But when later becomes now, the "shoulds" that seemed attractive enough in the temporal distance lose their attractiveness. Read and Loewenstein (1995) surmised that something similar may have been going on in the snacks study: People who were planning out their snacks for the next 3 weeks had the goal of diversifying their food choices, but when it came time to eat the food, the goal of variety was no longer operative. All they wanted was what would taste the best—their favorite snack.

What all of these studies show is that people have time-inconsistent preferences. To the extent that people know what they want when their passions are cooled and the objects or events are at some temporal distance, it often makes sense for them to bind themselves to these preferences, because they may not still have them at the actual moment of choice. It is not always the case that the cool self knows best (e.g., in the throes of intensely painful labor, it may make sense to abandon your cold-state preferences for a "natural childbirth" and do something to relieve the pain). But regardless of whether your judgment is better in hot or cold states, failing to recognize the extent to which arousal can alter preferences can produce sizable forecasting errors. Though these phenomena are less about predicting how one will feel about a choice in the future, and more about predicting how the way one feels will affect what one chooses in the future, they are nonetheless evidence for the importance of affective forecasting and for people's failure to do that forecasting accurately.

## How "Deep" Are Affective Forecasting Errors?

We have reviewed a variety of respects in which people's predictions of future affect are inaccurate.

We can ask, with regard to each, exactly what the nature of the inaccuracy is. One possibility is that people are aware of such factors as memory distortion, context effects, and adaptation, but that they are badly calibrated. That is, they allow for these inaccuracies, but they do not allow sufficiently for them. If so, correcting mispredictions would involve recalibrating a system that is already attuned to relevant factors. By analogy, one could imagine someone who appreciates that the perceived size of familiar objects is a reliable cue to how far away they are, and thus uses perceived size as a cue to distance, but who nonetheless systematically underestimates distance. If this were the source of inaccuracy, adjustment would probably be fairly simple. In contrast, it is possible that people are simply unaware of any of these sources of misprediction. They cannot adjust, because they do not know what needs to be adjusted. This second possible source of misprediction would be much deeper, and much harder to correct, than a mere problem of calibration. Though there has been little systematic attention devoted to this issue, what evidence there is suggests that miscalibration is not the problem—that people mispredict affect because they simply do not appreciate context effects, adaptation, and memory distortion and other sources of misprediction at all (see Nisbett & Wilson, 1977; Wilson, 2002; and Wilson, Centerbar, & Brekke, 2002, for discussion).

## How Leaky Rationality May Make Forecasts Accurate

The foregoing discussion creates a picture of decision making that makes one wonder how people ever make good decisions. If decisions are aimed at maximizing utility, and utility includes affect, and people mispredict affect, how can they ever get it right? Though there is little doubt that people often do not get it right, there is another perspective on affective forecasting that suggests a mechanism by which forecasting "errors" get "corrected." Keys and Schwartz (2007) wrote a paper in which they introduced a concept they called "leaky rationality." What they meant by the term is that factors that influence a decision may continue to exert their effects after the decision is made. That is, considerations at the moment of decision "leak" into the experience of the decision.

For instance, if people choose burgers that are "75% lean" over burgers that are "25% fat" (obviously the same burgers), they will think the "lean" burgers taste better than the fat ones. It seems irrational for decisions to be influenced by the way in which options are described ("fat" vs. "lean"). But as long as these factors that influence a decision also influence one's experience with the results of that decision, there is nothing irrational about it—at least as long as the aim of decisions is maximizing utility, a subjective entity, rather than some objective outcome.

Consider the following study by Lee, Frederick, and Ariely (2006). Patrons at a bar in Cambridge, Massachusetts, were subjected to a taste test between a popular commercial beer and "M.I.T. Brew," another commercial beer that had been adulterated with a few drops of balsamic vinegar. When participants were unaware of the composition of the M.I.T. Brew, they preferred it to the commercial beer. When they were told in advance that the M.I.T. Brew contained balsamic vinegar, they preferred the commercial beer. But when they were told about the adulteration of M.I.T. brew only *after* they had tasted it, they preferred it to the standard beer. In their account of this finding, Lee, Frederick, and Ariely argue that people's understanding before the experience (the taste) continues to exert its influence during the experience. So when people do not find out until after the fact that M.I.T. Brew has vinegar, they think something like, "What a surprise. Who would have thought that vinegar enhances the taste of beer?" When they find out before the fact, they think something like "Ugh. Beer with vinegar. This will be awful." In other words, conditions of understanding under which people have an experience shape the subjective quality of the experience. The knowledge of M.I.T. Brew's special ingredient actually alters the sensory experience of tasting the beer.

What this means is that, at least some of the time, the context of choice, with all of the misprediction of affect it may contain, will exert enough of an influence on the experience that the "misprediction" turns out not to be so wrong after all. In the study described earlier in which students assigned a price to a trip to Seattle, it seems apparent that it is a mistake to value the trip to Seattle less when it is bracketed with trips to Las Vegas and to Los Angeles. But we suggest that if you spend your time in Seattle thinking about all you have passed up by not going to Las Vegas or Los Angeles, you will not enjoy Seattle nearly as much (see Schwartz, 2004). The context of the decision may leak, affecting the consumption of the experience. The so-called faulty forecast exerts an effect on the experience such that it is not an error.

What the concept of "leaky rationality" means is that at least some of the time, apparent errors of affective forecasting will not be errors. The currently unanswered question is: When do decisions leak? For the students in Dunn's study, for example, the expectation that housing location would affect happiness did not appear to leak into the experience of living in the dorms. Students who got desirable dorm rooms were not more satisfied than those who got undesirable ones. In the example of buying speakers, it is likely that when people bring home the ugly speakers that sounded a little better than the attractive ones in the store, the context of choice will not "leak" into the experience of the choice enough to convince people that they made the right decision. But if the consumer can sit at home feeling satisfied knowing that he most certainly chose the best sounding of speakers in the store, he may be comforted enough to conclude that he had chosen well.

Consider another example: choosing between political candidate A, who has 5 years of experience and is extremely handsome, and political candidate B, who has 15 years of experience and is quite homely. Normally, it is very difficult to judge how many years of experience constitutes a lot of experience—is 5 years a lot or a little? In contrast, it is very easy to judge how attractive someone is, even without a basis of comparison. Thus, you might expect that if you ask people to rate one of the candidates (without knowing about the other candidate—a separate evaluation), candidate A would get higher ratings because his experience level is difficult to evaluate but his attractiveness is easily perceived. But when the two candidates are running against one another, voters can compare them and can determine that 15 years of experience is quite a lot. People given the choice between the two candidates (a joint evaluation) will likely choose candidate B. But the research on evaluability suggests that when candidate B takes office, voters are in separate consumption mode—experience level is no longer perceptible and all they know is that the candidate who won is quite homely. Or will they remember that 15 years of experience is a lot? We submit that, in this example, features of the decision (e.g., the ability to compare years of experience) can be expected to leak into consumption. That is, people will remember that they chose candidate B for a reason and they will be satisfied with their choice, even though experience level is not normally evaluable in the absence of an alternative.

The scope of the effects of leaky rationality is unknown at present. What we are suggesting is that to the extent that leaky rationality operates, it may serve to mitigate affective forecasting errors. Thus, if we are interested in assessing the consequences of these forecasting errors for people's judgments about the quality of their decisions, we must be able to specify when leaky rationality operates and when it does not. This will help to tell us when affective forecasting errors matter, and when they do not.

## Conclusion: What Is Rational?

Even so, the literature on affective forecasting is actually quite agnostic about whether people's mispredictions of the future should properly be considered "errors." Gilbert, Wilson, and their various collaborators are interested in pointing out the systematic ways in which people mispredict future subjective experience, but they rarely discuss whether these mispredictions lead people astray in any way that really matters. Said another way, the research on inaccuracies in affective forecasting is concerned more with predicting what people will choose and why they choose it than it is with judging the rationality of people's choices (see Gilbert, 2006, for an extended discussion of the difficulty in judging the rationality of decisions based on anticipated subjective experience).

In contrast, we think the literature on affective forecasting, along with the concept of leaky rationality, raises deep questions about what it means for a decision to be rational. The problem with the subjectivity that is inherent in the concept of utility is that the only grounds for challenging the rationality of decisions are formal ones (e.g., violations of consistency or transitivity). But sometimes, people will feel good about their decisions for bad reasons. When the aim of an experience is entirely subjective (e.g., good-tasting burgers and beer), there is, perhaps, no harm in people fooling themselves. But even here, there are objective aspects to the subjective experience. If people consistently pay more for "75% lean" meat than for "25% fat" meat, they can waste a lot of money. Thus, we challenge the notion that decisions that are objectively bad can be deemed rational as long as people feel good about (i.e., derive utility from) them. Happiness matters, but it is not the only thing that matters.

Keys and Schwartz (2007) suggest that what is needed is a richer conception of rationality that is not tied exclusively to utility—one that embeds individual decisions in lives lived as a whole. It is not enough to examine one decision to pay extra for 75% lean instead of 25% fat; we must examine the consequences (e.g., wasted money) of making that type of decision every day for an entire lifetime. And these long-range consequences can easily extend beyond the specific domain of the decision (e.g., wasting money on what you eat can limit the resources you have available for other sorts of things). But developing this richer conception of rationality is no easy task, especially at a time and in a culture in which people are reluctant to use any standard for assessing the quality of a life aside from the one adopted by the individual. The attractiveness of "utility" as a concept is that it avoids having to make judgments about what are better and worse decisions—better and worse lived lives. One can fault people for having preferences that are inconsistent, or intransitive. One can, perhaps, fault people for discounting the future so much that they are continually paying big long-term prices for small, short-term satisfactions. These sorts of phenomena can be labeled as mistakes and criticized. But not much else can be. Of course, as Lewis Carroll observed, people can use words in any way they like. But the honorific attached to the word "rational" is unjustified if all it means is "consistent." For the word to deserve the honorific it has, it needs to refer to substantive aspects of decisions, and not just formal ones.

## Future Directions

The research we have reviewed on affective forecasting tells us a lot about how people predict their future subjective states. At the same time, it raises questions for future research. Among the more significant are these:

1. When people evaluate an experience, what counts as an "episode," over which affective experience (whether moment by moment or peak-end) is integrated and summarized? Is "spring break" one episode, or many? Does it have one peak and one end, or several?

2. How are the positive and negative moments that characterize most real-life experiences combined and integrated? Are there separate positive and negative peaks? Does one get subtracted from the other? Does whichever peak is greater determine whether the experience is summarized as positive or negative?

3. In the determination of life satisfaction, how important are the actual experiences people have, and how important are people's memories of the experiences?

4. Can we develop a systematic account of hedonic adaptation that explains differences across domains of experience in the time course of adaptation and its magnitude?

5. Does experience in a particular domain affect the likelihood and magnitude of affective forecasting errors? That is, can people learn to prevent or counteract these errors? If so, what teaches them?

6. What role, in what domains, does "leaky rationality" play in mitigating the effects of affective forecasting errors? One can imagine that there will be cases in which "leakage" is substantial ("Boy, this 90% lean beef sure does taste great!"), and cases in which "leakage" is minimal or nonexistent. Can we find anything systematic to distinguish these two types of cases? Are there individual differences such that some people are much more susceptible to "leakage" than others? At present, nothing much is known about the leakage process except that it sometimes occurs.

## References

Ariely, D., &Loewenstein, G. (2006). The heat of the moment: The effect of sexual arousal on sexual decision making. *Journal of Behavioral Decision Making, 19*, 87–98.

Brenner, L., Rottenstreich, Y., & Sood, S. (1999). Comparison, grouping, and preference. *Psychological Science, 10*, 225–229.

Brickman, P., Coates, D., & Janoff-Bulman, R. (1978). Lottery winners and accident victims: Is happiness relative? *Journal of Personality and Social Psychology, 36*, 917–927.

Diener, E., & Biswas-Diener, R. (2008). *Happiness.* New York: Blackwell.

Dunn, E. W., Wilson, T. D., & Gilbert, D. T. (2003). Location, location, location: The misprediction of satisfaction with housing lotteries. *Personality and Social Psychology Bulletin, 29*, 1421–1432.

Fischoff, B. (1991). Value elicitation: Is there anything in there? *American Psychologist, 46*, 835–847.

Frederick, S., & Loewenstein, G. (1999). Hedonic adaptation. In D. Kahneman, E. Diener, & N. Schwarz (Eds.), *Well-being: The foundations of hedonic psychology* (pp. 302–328). New York: Russell Sage.

Gilbert, D. (2006). *Stumbling on happiness.* New York: Knopf.

Gilbert, D. T., Pinel, E. C., Wilson, T. D., Blumberg, S. T., & Wheatley, T. P. (1998). Durability bias in affective forecasting. *Journal of Personality and Social Psychology, 75*, 617–638.

Gilbert, D. T., & Wilson, T. D. (2000). Miswanting. In J. P. Forgas (Ed.), *Feeling and thinking: The role of affect in social cognition* (pp. 178–197). New York: Cambridge University Press.

Gilbert, D. T., & Wilson, T. D. (2007) Prospection: Experiencing the future. *Science, 317*, 1351–1354.

Hsee, C. K. (1996). Attribute evaluability: Its implications for joint-separate evaluation reversals and beyond. *Organizational Behavior and Human Decision Processes, 67*, 247–257.

Hsee, C. K., & Hastie, R. (2006). Decision and experience: Why don't we choose what makes us happy? *Trends in Cognitive Sciences, 10*, 31–37.

Hsee, C. K., Hastie, R., & Chen, J. (2008). Hedonomics. *Perspectives on Psychological Science, 3*, 224–243.

Hsee, C. K., & Zhang, J. (2004). Distinction bias: Misprediction and mischoice due to joint evaluation. *Journal of Personality and Social Psychology, 86*, 680–695.

Kahneman, D. (1999). Objective happiness. In D. Kahneman, E. Diener, & N. Schwarz (Eds.), *Well-being: The foundations of hedonic psychology* (pp. 3–25). New York: Russell Sage Foundation.

Kahneman, D. (2000). New challenges to the rationality assumption. In D. Kahneman & A. Tversky (Eds.), *Choices, values, and frames* (pp. 758–774). New York: Russell Sage Foundation.

Kahneman, D. (2003). A perspective on judgment and choice. *American Psychologist, 58*, 697–720.

Kahneman, D., Fredrickson, B. L., Schreiber, C. A., & Redelmeier, D. A. (1993). When more pain is preferred to less: Adding a better end. *Psychological Science, 4*, 401–405.

Kahneman, D., &Thaler, R. H. (2006). Utility maximization and experienced utility. *Journal of Economic Perspectives, 20*, 221–234.

Kahneman, D., &Tversky, A. (1984). Choices, values, and frames. *American Psychologist, 39*, 341–350.

Keys, D. J., & Schwartz, B. (2007). "Leaky" rationality: How research on behavioral decision making challenges normative standards of rationality. *Perspectives on Psychological Science, 2*, 162–180.

Lee, L., Frederick, S., & Ariely, D. (2006). Try it, you'll like it: The influence of expectation, consumption, and revelation on preferences for beer. *Psychological Science, 17*, 1054–1058.

Loewenstein, G. (1996). Out of control: Visceral influences on behavior. *Organizational Behavior and Human Decision Processes, 65*, 272–292.

Lucas, R. E. (2005). Time does not heal all wounds: A longitudinal study of reaction and adaptation to divorce. *Psychological Science, 16*, 945–950.

Lucas, R. E. (2007). Adaptation and the set-point model of subjective well-being: Does happiness change after major life events. *Current Directions in Psychological Science, 16*, 1675–1679.

Lucas, R. E., & Clark, A. E. (2006). Do people really adapt to marriage. *Journal of Happiness Studies, 7*, 405–426.

Lucas, R. E., Clark, A. E., Geirgellis, Y., & Diener, E. (2004). Unemployment alters the set point for life satisfaction. *Psychological Science, 15*, 8–13.

Lyubomirsky, S. (2007). *The how of happiness.* New York: Penguin.

Milkman, K. L., Rogers, T., & Bazerman, M. H. (2008). Harnessing our inner angels and demons: What we have learned about want/should conflicts and how that knowledge can help us reduce short-sighted decision making. *Perspectives on Psychological Science, 3*, 324–338.

Milkman, K. L., Rogers, T., & Bazerman, M. H. (2009). Highbrow films gather dust: Time-inconsistent preferences and online DVD rentals. *Management Science, 55*, 1047–1059.

Milkman, K. L., Rogers, T., &Bazerman, M. H. (2010). I'll have the ice cream soon and the vegetables later: A study of online grocery purchases and order lead time. *Marketing Letters, 21*, 17–36.

Morewedge, C. K., Gilbert, D. T., & Wilson, T. D. (2005). The least likely of times: How remembering the past biases forecasts of the future. *Psychological Science, 16*, 626–630.

Nisbett, R. E., & Kanouse, D. E. (1968). *Obesity, hunger, and supermarket shopping behavior. Proceedings of the Annual*

*Convention of the American Psychological Association, 3,* 683–684.

Nisbett, R. E., & Wilson, T. D. (1977). Telling more than we can know: Verbal reports on mental processes. *Psychological Review, 84,* 231–259.

Read, D., & Loewenstein, G. (1995). Diversification bias: Explaining the discrepancy in variety seeking between combined and separated choices. *Journal of Experimental Psychology: Applied, 1,* 34–49.

Redelmeier, D. A., Katz, J., & Kahneman, D. (2003). Memories of colonoscopy: A randomized trial. *Pain, 104,* 187–194.

Riis, J., Loewenstein, G., Baron, J., Jepson, C., Fagerlin, A., & Ubel, P. A. (2005). Ignorance of hedonic adaptation to hemodialysis: A study using ecological momentary assessment. *Journal of Experimental Psychology: General, 134,* 3–9.

Schwartz, B. (2004). *The paradox of choice.* New York: Ecco.

Simonson, I. (1990). The effect of purchase quantity and timing on variety-seeking behavior. *Journal of Marketing Research, 27,* 150–162.

Slovic, P. (1991). The construction of preference. *American Psychologist, 46,* 364–371.

Wilson, T. D. (2002). *Strangers to ourselves.* Cambridge, MA: Harvard University Press.

Wilson, T. D., Centerbar, D. B., & Brekke, N. (2002). Mental contamination and the debiasing problem. In T. Gilovich, D. Griffin, & D. Kahneman (Eds.), *Heuristics and biases: The psychology of intuitive judgment* (pp. 185–200). New York: Cambridge University Press.

Wirtz, D., Kruger, J., Scollon, C. N., & Diener, E. (2003). What to do on spring break? The role of predicted, on-line, and remembered experience on future choice. *Psychological Science, 14,* 520–524.

# PART 8

# Thinking in Specialized Domains

# Spatial Reasoning

Holger Schultheis *and* Laura A. Carlson

## Abstract

Spatial reasoning is the mental transformation of spatial knowledge. Such transformation is an integral component of everyday cognition, occurring within a variety of domains, such as attention, memory, and language, and across a variety of tasks, spatial and nonspatial alike. The structure of this chapter is as follows. In the section entitled "Core Components of Spatial Reasoning," we discuss spatial representations, spatial processes, and spatial memory. In the section entitled "Basic Spatial Tasks," we discuss basic spatial tasks, including navigation, giving directions, imaginal perspective taking, spatial inference, and visualization. In the section entitled "The Broad Influence of Space," we discuss the broader influence of space beyond such basic spatial tasks, as reflected in spatial compatibility effects, the use of space to understand abstract concepts, and reasoning by spatial analogy. In the section entitled "Neural Systems, Variation, and Learning," we discuss neural systems that underlie our spatial abilities, individual differences, and learning. Finally, in the section entitled "Future Directions," we discuss open questions for future research.

**Key Words:** spatial representations, spatial processes, spatial memory systems, spatial abilities and tasks, spatial compatibility effects, spatial grounding of abstract concepts, spatial analogies, spatial functional neuroanatomy, individual differences and spatial education

## Core Components of Spatial Reasoning

The transformation of spatial information requires three components: (1) the representation of this information; (2) a set of processes that operate on these representations; and (3) a memory system that encodes and maintains the spatial information and its transformations.

### Spatial Representations

Spatial reasoning often relies on existing knowledge about the spatial environment. For example, imagine that you are home but need to go to the airport to catch a flight to begin your vacation. Your reasoning about how to accomplish this goal requires knowledge about a number of spatial relations. For example, you need to find your way out of your house; you need to plan a driving route to the

airport; and once there, you need to park your car, noting its location for when you arrive back at the airport after your trip. The way in which the spatial information is represented for each of these pieces of information may influence the way in which that information is used and accessed. For example, if in planning your route to the airport, you rely on your memory of other trips to the airport, you may have difficulty if you encounter a detour that forces you to construct a novel (unexperienced) route. Two important components of spatial representations are their format and the spatial reference frames that are used to organize the information.

#### FORMAT

Spatial representations of well-learned environments that represent information in a survey or birds-eye perspective are commonly referred to as cognitive maps (Tolman, 1948). It was initially assumed that these cognitive maps were similar to two-dimensional maps of the environment, such as a floorplan of your home or a city map showing your house, traffic routes, and the airport. An important feature of this type of representation is that it is spatio-analogical. This means that the spatial relations between entities within the environment are represented by portraying the parts representing these entities in the same spatial relations (Sloman, 1975). For example, the intersection of two streets in an environment is represented on a map by showing that the two lines that represent the streets intersect. Similarly, two buildings that are next to each other are represented on a map in a corresponding adjacency. Support for this spatio-analogical property of cognitive maps is found in research on spatial processes (see section on "Spatial Processes") and spatial inference (see section on "Spatial Inference").

However, the label "cognitive map" may not always fit perfectly for these types of representations. First, mental representations exhibit a number of inaccuracies and distortions not commonly found in external two-dimensional maps. Distances may be represented asymmetrically, with the distance from your house to the airport not necessarily considered the same as the distance from the airport to your house. For example, Sadalla, Burroughs, and Staplin (1980) asked students from Arizona State University to indicate the distance between pairs of locations on the campus (e.g., the distance between the student union and the architecture building). Students were given a sheet of paper with one of the locations at the center of a distance grid. The task was to mark the second location on the grid such that the distance between the two locations was adequately represented. Students received the same pair of locations twice such that each of the locations was indicated at the center of the grid once. Sadalla et al. (1980) found that for several pairs of locations the indicated distances differed significantly depending on which of the two locations was presented at the center. In addition to such asymmetries, distances between objects within a given region tend to be underestimated, whereas distances between objects in different regions tend to be overestimated (McNamara, 1986). Finally, directions are often distorted toward right angles, leading to a bias to represent angles as closer to 90 degrees than they actually are (Moar & Bower, 1983) and a bias to remember regions as aligned (Tversky, 1981).

Second, a spatial representation of a given external environment may actually correspond to a set of multiple representations, each corresponding to a different part of the environment, rather than there being a single all-inclusive representation (Brockmole & Wang, 2002; Lynch, 1960; Tversky, 1993). For example, there may be one spatial representation that corresponds to your office, and another representation that corresponds to the building in which the office is located. Evidence for multiple spatial representations is provided, for instance, by the study of Brockmole and Wang (2002). In this study participants had to judge shown directions to objects in two familiar environments. One environment was their office and the other environment was the corresponding building. On each trial participants had to judge the correctness of a displayed direction to a target object. The target object could either be an object from the office (e.g., file cabinet, computer) or an object from the building (e.g., patio, stairs). Whether the target object was from the office or from the building was manipulated from trial to trial such that participants had to switch between parts of the environment across trials. On average, judging directions after a switch took participants significantly longer than judging directions when no switch was necessary. This switch cost suggests that different representations have to be retrieved for spatial reasoning about different parts of the environment. Multiple spatial representations may be partially interrelated and overlapping, such that their combination yields a (distorted) representation of the overall environment. Given this fractionated nature, *cognitive collage* (Tversky, 1993) and *cognitive atlas* (Hirtle, 1998) are metaphors for human spatial representations that may be more accurate labels for this type of spatial representation.

Third, spatial representations are hierarchical in the sense that knowledge is organized in nested levels of detail (McNamara, 1986; Stevens & Coupe, 1978). The overall space that is represented is divided into several parts that can be further divided into subparts. Each of the (sub)parts is represented by one representational unit, and each division leads to a new (lower) level in the hierarchy. For instance, you may have a representation of your city that is divided into neighborhoods. Your neighborhood may be further divided into the locations of houses; your house may be further divided into its floors and rooms. It is assumed that spatial relations are usually only explicitly represented between entities within the same level of the hierarchy that are subparts of the same part. Thus, the spatial relation between your living room and kitchen may be explicitly represented, but not the relation between the kitchen and other structures in the city. A nice illustration of this aspect of spatial representations is provided by the results of Stevens and Coupe (1978). They asked participants to estimate the cardinal directions between pairs of locations in North and Central America. For example, participants had to estimate the direction between San Diego (California) and Reno (Nevada). While the actual direction from San Diego to Reno is northnorthwest, the direction from California to Nevada is east. Supporting the assumption of hierarchical coding of spatial information, most participants exhibited a distortion of direction estimates toward the direction between California and Nevada. Such a distortion is to be expected given that spatial relations between (sub)parts (San Diego, Reno) of different (super)parts (California, Nevada) are not explicitly represented but are inferred from the relation between the (super)parts.

## REFERENCE FRAMES

The organization of and access to a given spatial representation relies on a reference frame that provides a means for distinguishing parts of that space. As such, spatial reference frames are pervasive in any form of reasoning that involves spatial information. For example, we use reference frames when reasoning about how to get to the airport as quickly as possible, because we need to distinguish the locations of start, end, and intermediate points along the route. It is common to conceptualize a reference frame as a coordinate system that consists of a set of axes (vertical and horizontal) that parse space into distinct regions (Levinson, 2003; Logan & Sadler, 1996). For example, a compass rose on a map distinguishes the main cardinal directions of that space.

There are different types of reference frames, based on the type of information that is used as the basis for distinguishing the different regions of space. For cognitive maps that adopt a survey perspective of an environment, the distinction is based on environmental information, such as cardinal directions or key features of the environment. This type of reference frame is variably known as allocentric or absolute. A key feature is that information is represented independently of a person's orientation or location within the environment. An example would be spatially locating your kitchen as being to the west of your living room. In contrast, a reference frame may distinguish regions of space based on one's current location and perspective. This type of reference frame is variably known as egocentric or relative. An example would be spatially locating your kitchen as behind the living room, from the perspective of someone standing in the front doorway. Both kinds of reference frames are involved in human spatial reasoning (Mou, McNamara, Valiquette, & Rump, 2004; Sholl, 2000; Wang & Spelke, 2002). Egocentric frame seems to be more important for transient representations of immediately surrounding space, and allocentric frames seem to be more important for more enduring representations of larger scale spaces. In addition, egocentric and allocentric reference frames can be coordinated. For example, one may transform egocentric representations into allocentric representations for long-term storage, and one may transform a portion of an allocentric representation back into an egocentric representation as needed. Ontogenetically, the ability to use an egocentric frame precedes the ability to use an allocentric frame (Acredolo, 1988; Piaget & Inhelder, 1960).

### Spatial Processes

Spatial representations are accessed and manipulated by spatial processes. For example, at the airport, imagine that you purchase a map of your destination so that you can plan your visit. To make optimal use of the information represented in the map, you may want to move it in different ways, so that the current area of interest is right before you; to direct your gaze and attention to different locations on the map such as tracing the street route from the airport to your hotel; and to rotate the map. Rotating a map can become necessary due to conflicting coding of spatial information in the egocentric reference frame (see earlier). For instance, depending on how you currently hold the map, the check-in counters indicated on the map may be to your right, whereas the actual counters are to your left. To avoid such confusion and, for example, take the correct turns for leaving the airport, it is helpful to rotate the map such that the conflict is overcome. Although all the spatial information is contained in the map, you can only make suitable use of this information by employing a set of spatial processes. As such, in combination with representations, processes are paramount for making the relevant information available for spatial reasoning. Three prominent spatial processes are mental rotation, mental translation, and mental scanning.

## MENTAL ROTATION

Mental rotation is a process that changes the orientation of a spatial representation. A common example is when you try to imagine whether a piece of luggage may fit at a different orientation into your partially filled car trunk. This process of mentally changing a representation's orientation is called rotation because the performance characteristics of this manipulation are similar to characteristics for a comparable physical rotation. For example, the time needed for conducting a mental rotation increases monotonically and often linearly with the degree of rotation. Just as physically rotating an object 120 degrees would take longer than rotating an object 10 degrees, imagining it rotating 120 degrees takes longer than imagining rotating it 10 degrees. This monotonic relation between the magnitude of rotation and the time to rotate is quite robust and, starting with the study by Shepard and Metzler (1971), has been replicated many times (Cooper, 1976; Cooper & Shepard, 1973, Shepard & Cooper, 1982). This correspondence between physical and mental rotation offers compelling evidence for the spatio-analogical property of spatial representations (Shepard, 1984; see also section on "Format").

Mental rotation can be applied to a wide range of representations. Empirical studies suggest that representations of single objects (Shepard & Cooper, 1982), representations of object arrays (Presson, 1982), representations of oneself (Farrell & Robertson, 1998; but see section on "Imaginal Perspective Taking"), and abstract representations (i.e., reference frames, Hinton & Parsons, 1981) can all be manipulated by mental rotation.

## MENTAL TRANSLATION

Spatial reasoning sometimes requires manipulating spatial location. For example, after mentally rotating a piece of luggage, it may be helpful to mentally imagine moving it to the open space in the partially filled trunk to check whether it will fit. The process by which such a change of location is achieved has been termed "mental translation." Generally, the time required for a mental translation increases monotonically with distance, such that moving larger distances takes more time. This correspondence thus also supports the spatio-analogical nature of representations employed in spatial reasoning. As in the case of mental rotation, mental translation has been argued to be applicable to single objects (Larsen & Bundesen, 1998), representations of one's self (Easton & Sholl, 1995), and abstract representations (Graf, 2006).

## MENTAL SCANNING

Mental scanning is a process that operates on spatial representations to enable inspection and exploration of particular parts of the representation. During this process, a circumscribed field of attention is shifted across the representation to make different parts of the representation more accessible. For example, after mentally rotating and translating a piece of luggage, you may want to more closely inspect the handles of the luggage to make sure that they will be accessible for removing the bag from the trunk when you arrive at the airport.

Research by Kosslyn and colleagues (Borst & Kosslyn, 2008; Denis & Kosslyn, 1999; Kosslyn, 1973) indicates that the time necessary to access a part of the spatial representation increases monotonically with increasing distance between that part and one's current focus. In other words, the time necessary to mentally scan across the representation is proportional to the distance that has to be scanned. Further studies have shown that valid and invalid cues to direct attention to imagined parts of a representation have a similar impact on performance as cues to direct attention in visual perception (Finke & Pinker, 1982; Griffin & Nobre, 2003).

### Spatial Memory Systems

The third core component involved in spatial reasoning is memory for spatial information. However represented, spatial knowledge from previous experience can only be brought to bear during spatial reasoning if this knowledge is stored in one or more memory systems. Following a distinction common in cognitive psychology, spatial memory systems can be roughly divided into a more transient spatial working memory and a more enduring spatial long-term memory.

#### SPATIAL WORKING MEMORY

Several studies (see Baddeley & Logie, 1999, for an overview) support the idea that human working memory is composed of a number of functionally specialized components. One of these components, called the visuospatial sketchpad, is thought to be responsible for the transient storage of visuospatial information. More precisely, the visuospatial sketchpad is assumed to consist of two distinct subcomponents that are responsible for different kinds of information. One component constitutes memory for visual detail such as color and shape or, more generally, the visual appearance of a scene. The other component constitutes memory for locations and sequences of locations that may result from movements through space. These two components have been shown to have functionally different characteristics. For example, Klauer and Zhao (2004) observed that the maintenance of location information in the spatial component was interfered with more strongly by a concurrent spatial (movement discrimination) task than by a concurrent visual (color discrimination) task. On the contrary, the maintenance of shape information was interfered with more by the visual task than by the spatial task. Furthermore, in contrast to the visual component, the spatial component is amodal in the sense that the stored spatial information need not arise from vision but can originate from various perceptual sources such as hearing (Vecchi, Monticellai, & Cornoldi, 1995).

## SPATIAL LONG-TERM MEMORY

Research on the enduring storage of spatial information has revealed two important characteristics of spatial long-term memory. First, the location of an object may be represented by noting its distance and direction relative to surrounding objects (Sholl, 2000). Consider, for example, your memory of the objects in your living room. You may encode the location of your couch as being a certain distance from the coffee table and the TV, and at a certain angular direction from these objects. Second, there are preferences for which objects you encode relative to each other. For example, you may encode the couch relative to the TV but not relative to the sideboard, based on the configuration formed by the objects and their relative locations. A task used to assess this characteristic is the judgment of relative direction task (Mou & McNamara, 2002). In this task, participants memorize a configuration of objects. They then are told to imagine that they are standing at one of the objects and facing a second object, and they are then asked to point to a third object. Pointing responses are typically faster and more accurate for objects that are encoded relative to each other (face TV and point to couch) than objects that are not encoded relative to each other (face TV and point to sideboard).

## Basic Spatial Tasks

Spatial reasoning is a central component of our ability to successfully solve a number of problems that involve spatial information. This section highlights five basic spatial tasks—navigation, giving directions, perspective taking, spatial inference, and employing external visualizations—that rely on spatial reasoning and are frequently encountered in everyday life. The described tasks are considered basic in the sense that performance in other, more complex spatial tasks such as architectural design involves employing several of these basic tasks in combination.

### Navigation

The goal to get from your living room to the airport is an example of a navigational task. Navigation consists of two main subtasks: *wayfinding* and *locomotion* (Montello, 2005). Wayfinding consists of the more cognitive components of the task, including planning, identifying one's current location, and updating that location as one moves. Locomotion consists of the more physical components of the task that enable you to move through the environment in a collision-free manner. We will focus on updating. There are two types of updating (Wang, 2003). The first type employs an egocentric reference frame (see section on "Reference Frames") for representing one's location and involves updating the direction and distance of objects relative to one's position with each movement through the environment. One example of such egocentric updating is dead-reckoning, in which the direction, speed, and time of one's own movement are tracked to maintain one's position relative to a starting point. For example, if you have walked 1 m straight ahead, you know that the starting point is 1 m directly behind you. If you then turn 90 degrees to the right and walk another meter, the starting point is now 1.41 m to your back-right. Although it may seem difficult to do the computations required for dead-reckoning deliberately, a wide range of species, including humans (May & Klatzky, 2000), have been shown to employ dead-reckoning during navigation.

The second type of updating employs an allocentric reference frame (see section on "Reference Frames") for representing one's location in which one's position is updated relative to surrounding features rather than updated relative to the distance and direction of the navigational path. For example, if you walk toward a building in front of you by moving 1 m straight ahead and then 1 m to the right, you may note that you are now west of the building.

While both types of updating can be assumed to be involved in navigation, their relative importance and interplay still need to be clarified. Wang et al (2006), for example, provide evidence for the use of an egocentric frame during updating.

Participants saw a variable number of objects (one, two, or three objects) for several seconds. After a short retention interval, participants had to place the previously seen objects in their respective locations. On half of the trials participants had to move to a new location in the environment before recalling object locations. The movement required spatial updating to be able to correctly reproduce the original object locations. Placing the objects became more error prone with increasing number of objects. In particular, this increase was steeper after movements. These results suggest that participants employed an egocentric reference frame for representation and updating. Such a frame requires storing and changing the direction and distance of oneself to each of the objects. Thus, the more objects had to be placed, the more information had to be updated, leading to a steeper increase in errors after movements. A similar study by Hodgson and Waller (2006) investigating updating with sets of four, six, eight, and ten objects, however, did show no such effect of movement (i.e., need for updating). Against this background, it seems that humans can and do use both egocentric and allocentric updating. At the same time, it is currently unclear what determines the use of the different updating modes and how they may interact to subserve naviagtion.

### Giving Directions

The task of giving directions provides information that allows a person who is unfamiliar with a particular environment to successfully navigate this environment (e.g., to get from an airport to a hotel). Formulating directions consists of three main steps (Lovelace, Hegarty, & Montello, 1999). First, the direction giver has to activate and access her spatial knowledge about the relevant environment. Second, based on this knowledge, a route has to be chosen. Third, the chosen route needs to be translated into a set of verbal instructions. Ideally, these three steps result in directions that are both accurate and easy to follow. Research on direction giving suggests coordination between direction giver and receiver that develops across exchanges, both with respect to the perspective that is adopted (Schober, 1993) and with respect to the labels used for landmarks (Brennan & Clark, 1996). There is also some suggestion that the landmarks that are selected and the way in which they are referenced depend upon a direction giver's assessment of the familiarity of the receiver with the environment (Isaacs & Clark, 1987).

### Imaginal Perspective Taking

The ability to judge spatial relations from perspectives that are different from one's current bodily perspective is important for everyday behavior. Suppose you are attending a talk by a colleague in an auditorium. Choosing a good seat will involve reasoning about how well you would be able to see the speaker if you imagine sitting at different open seats around the room. Such perspective taking has been termed "imaginal perspective taking" and has been investigated in numerous experiments. A typical perspective-taking experiment asks participants to learn the location of a number of objects in the environment from a fixed position. Once object locations have been sufficiently memorized, participants are deprived of vision and hearing except of experimenter instructions. Participants are then instructed to, for example, "point to object x as if you were facing object y" or "point to object x as if you were standing at object y." These two examples ask the participant to imagine a perspective that differs in orientation or location, respectively, from the actual perspective. Such perspective-taking experiments have revealed that imaginal perspective taking is more error prone and slower than judging spatial relations from the actual bodily perspective (e.g., Kelly, Avraamides, & Loomis, 2007; Waller & Hodgson, 2006; Wraga, 2003). This is particularly so in cases where the imaginal and the actual perspective differ in orientation. The larger the angular difference between the actual and the imaginal orientation, the longer and more inaccurate are relation judgments (Creem et al., 2001; Farrell & Robertson, 1998). A similar but weaker and less reliable decrement on performance is found for imaginal perspectives that differ in location from the bodily perspective. However, depending on the setup of the spatial layout involved in imaginal perspective taking, some experiments (Easton & Sholl, 1995; Rieser, 1989) have yielded no such performance decrement.

One explanation for the difficulties observable in imaginal perspective taking has been in terms of the spatial processes of mental rotation (see section on "Mental Rotation") and mental translation (see section on "Mental Translation"). According to this account, taking the imaginal perspective requires mentally rotating (in case of orientation change) and/or mentally translating (in case of a location change) oneself to the imaginal perspective in one's representation of the spatial layout (Sholl, 2000). Due to the analogical nature of these processes, imaginal orientation and location changes require time proportional to the angular difference and distance, respectively, between the imaginal and bodily perspective. However, it has also been suggested that such performance decrements in imaginal perspective taking arise from interference and not from mental transformations (May, 2004; Mou et al., 2004).

## Spatial Inference

New spatial knowledge can be obtained from already existing knowledge by drawing spatial inferences. If, for instance, you know that *Paris* is north of *Algiers* and that *London* is north of *Paris*, you can readily infer that *London* is north of *Algiers*. Spatial inferences of this type are thought to rely on spatial mental models that are integrated and spatio-analogical (see section on "Format") representations of the spatial relations between different objects (Johnson-Laird & Byrne, 1991), although they are normally not assumed to preserve all metric information (Tversky, 1993). Spatial mental models are integrated in the sense that objects and their relations that belong to the same state of affairs are represented in a single mental model. For example, the relation between Paris and Algiers and the relation between London and Paris would be represented together in the same spatial mental model. Furthermore, each spatial mental model represents only one possible situation (Johnson-Laird, 1999). If the known information is consistent with several different spatial situations, representing these different situations would require different spatial mental models.

Evidence in support of using mental models to draw spatial inferences is observed in preferences for certain models when available spatial information does not allow an unambiguous inference. If, for instance, you know that *London* is north of *Paris* and that *Paris* is west of *Prague*, in principle, depending on the distances between *London*, *Paris*, and *Prague*, the relation between *London* and *Prague* can be anything from west to north. However, when asked to report this relation, participants are quite happy to commit to a relation, even though it cannot be determined from the information in the problem (and hence is ambiguous; see Jahn, Knauff, & Johnson-Laird, 2007; Rauh et al., 2005). Moreover, the chosen relation is quite stable both within an individual and across different individuals. Accordingly, the mental model containing this preferred relation has been termed *preferred mental model*.

## Employing External Visualizations

Performance in the basic spatial tasks described so far can profit from employing external visualizations such as sketches, maps, or diagrams. For instance, navigation in an unfamiliar environment can be assisted by the use of a map. Moreover, external visualizations are also used in nonspatial domains to convey complex relationships and mechanisms (e.g., the workings of a combustion engine). One reason for the advantage provided by external visualizations is that their properties beneficially complement the properties of internal mental representations (Tversky, 2005). Whereas mental representations may suffer from memory capacity restrictions, visualizations are, in principle, free of this flaw. On the other hand, internal representations allow manipulating (e.g., mentally rotating; see section on "Mental Rotation") parts of an overall representation without manipulating the overall representation. This is normally impossible with external visualizations, as, for instance, you can only rotate the whole map and not just a single street. Thus, internal representations and external visualizations together provide a more flexible and powerful means to reason about spatial (and other types of) knowledge than a reliance on either individually. In some sense, employing external visualizations is a spatial task itself, because usually the spatial relations between elements within the external visualizations represent relations among elements in the world. For example, larger distances between boxes in a flow diagram typically indicate more intervening steps between the processes represented by the boxes. Accordingly, elements and the spatial relations between them have to be created/interpreted when producing/comprehending external visualizations.

With respect to production, Tversky (1999) suggests that the creation of a visualization reflects the organization and structure of the mental representation from which the information is drawn. If your representation of the layout of your house is hierarchical (see section on "Format"), it is more likely that you will produce a visualization of one of the floors by (1) drawing the outline of the floor, (2) drawing the outline of the rooms on this floor, and (3) drawing the (position of the) furniture inside the rooms in this order, rather than by drawing the elements in the reverse order. With respect to comprehension, Carpenter and Shah (1998) have proposed that understanding external visualizations consists of three processes. The first process recognizes visual patterns such as slopes of lines. The second process translates these visual patterns into quantitative and qualitative interpretations, such as describing a negative slope as a decreasing function. The third process relates existing interpretations to concepts associated with the visualization (e.g., relating decreasing temperature with increasing altitude).

Finally, external visualizations are often subject to schematization, in which certain details are omitted (Tversky, 2005). During production of an external visualization, schematization can occur either because the represented knowledge is missing some detail or is distorted (see section on "Format") or because the producer of the visualization intentionally omits (irrelevant) detail to reduce the complexity of the visualization. For example, a map designer may only include major roads rather than side streets at certain scales. For comprehension of an external visualization, schematization is often advantageous, because too much detail would obscure the relevant information. For example, when reading a map, seeing each house on each road would make identifying the road and planning a path much more difficult.

## The Broad Influence of Space

Spatial concepts are also thought to underlie our understanding of abstract concepts (Gattis, 2001; Lakoff & Johnson, 1980). In this section we discuss how our spatial facilities impact how we process, understand, represent, and reason about abstract concepts.

### Spatial Compatibility Effects

Imagine viewing a display that consists of single numbers that can occur anywhere on the screen, with your task being simply to indicate with one button (held in your right hand) when a number appears on the right side of the screen and another button (held in your left hand) when a number appears on the left side of the screen. When there is a spatial correspondence between the location of the number and the hand making the responses, responses are facilitated (Fitts & Seeger, 1953). This has been referred to as a spatial compability effect. This may not be particularly surprising because the judgment is a left/right judgment and it is made with left/right hands. However, imagine now that the task is to determine whether the number is odd or even, and the odd button is held in your left hand and the even button is held in your right hand. The number may appear to the left or right side of the screen, but this is irrelevant to your judgment of whether it is odd or even. Nevertheless, when an odd number appears on the right (and the odd button is in your

right hand), you make your response faster than when the odd number appears on the left. Similarly, when an even number appears on the left (and the even button is in your left hand), you make your response faster than when the even number appears on the right. This type of spatial compatibility effect that occurs when the spatial location of the stimulus is irrelevant to the task has been termed the "Simon effect" (Hedge & Marsh, 1975; Memelink & Hommel, 2005; Proctor & Vu, 2002; Simon & Rudell, 1967; Wallace, 1971) and indicates that spatial location is ubiquitously processed even when irrelevant, attesting to its primary importance.

### Spatial Grounding of Abstract Concepts

Lakoff and Johnson (1980) argue that humans establish the meaning of abstract concepts such as love, thought, happiness, time, (social) status, and so on by basing them on directly perceivable physical reality: Abstract concepts are grounded in physical reality. One source of support for the significance of space in grounding concepts comes from language. For example, the concept of happiness is grounded in the spatial dimension of up and down. If you are feeling happy, you may say, "I'm feeling up" or "I'm in high spirits." If you are sad, you may say, "I'm feeling down" or "I'm depressed." Similarly, if you state that you are "in love" or "in the middle of something," you allude to the spatial concept of containment. Such linguistic evidence is complemented by experimental work indicating, among others, that numbers are represented along a mental numberline, and that representation of time is grounded in space, as discussed next.

#### THE MENTAL NUMBERLINE

Our understanding of numbers is grounded in spatial representations. One can represent magnitude through spatial concepts like quantity (two piles of items correspond to the number 2) or length (smaller rods correspond to lower numbers than longer rods) or by ordering numbers along a mental numberline, with low numbers anchored at one end and increasing as one moves to the other end. In support of this idea, Moyer and Landauer (1967) found that the difficulty of judging which of two numerals was larger was proportional to the difference of the magnitude of the two numerals: Numbers that are closer together are more difficult than numbers that are far apart, with a monotonic decrease in difficulty with an increase in distance. Further evidence for the existence of the mental numberline has arisen from research on the SNARC (Spatial-Numerical

Association of Response Codes) effect (Dehaene, Bossini, & Giraux, 1993; see Wood, Willmes, Nuerk, & Fischer, 2008, for a recent review). In a typical SNARC experiment, participants judge the parity of digits that are shown in the center of a screen and make an odd or even response by pressing either a left or a right response button. The SNARC effect consists of the observation that left button responses are faster for lower digits than for higher digits, and that right button responses are faster for higher digits than for lower digits. If lower numbers were consistently presented in the left half of the screen and higher numbers were presented in the right half of the screen, such an effect would be expected due to spatial compatibility and the Simon effect (see section on "Spatial Compatibility Effects"). However, in the basic SNARC setup, the numbers are presented in the center of the screen. That a spatial compatibility effect is nevertheless observed suggests that the conceptualization and representation of digits is inherently spatial, aligned along a mental numberline. Additional evidence for a mental numberline comes from neuropsychological investigations. Hemineglect (see section on "Space in the Brain") patients have been reported not only to neglect a portion of perceived space but also to exhibit difficulties representing numbers that would be located on the corresponding side of the mental numberline (Zorzi, Priftis, & Umilta, 2002).

## TIME

Time can be also grounded in space. For instance, Boroditsky (2000) showed that a previously employed spatial frame of reference (see section on "Reference Frames") primes temporal information processing. Participants first had to verify four sentence/picture pairs, making a judgment about the spatial relation between the depicted objects. The sentences defined the spatial relation with respect to an egocentric frame (e.g., The object is in front of me) or with respect to an object-centered frame (e.g., Object 1 is in front of Object 2). After completing the four spatial verification trials, participants were presented with an ambiguous temporal sentence such as "Next Wednesday's meeting has been moved forward 2 days." Their task was to indicate the new day of the meeting. Interestingly, participants for whom the spatial relation was defined in an egocentric frame assumed the meeting had been shifted to Friday (forward 2 days), whereas participants for whom the spatial relation was defined in an object-centered frame assumed the meeting had

been rescheduled to Monday (back 2 days). These results suggest that the understanding of temporal concepts can be grounded in two different spatial metaphors. In the first metaphor the passing of time is understood by analogy to forward movement of oneself through space. If this metaphor is adopted, a forward shift of a meeting indicates that the meeting will take place on a later day. In the second metaphor the passing of time is understood by analogy to an entity moving past the unmoving self that results in one being behind the moving entity. If this metaphor is adopted, a forward shift of a meeting indicates that the meeting will take place on an earlier day.

### Reasoning by Spatial Analogies

As in the spatial domain (see section on "Spatial Inference"), new knowledge about abstract concepts can be inferred from existing knowledge. For example, knowledge about the average temperature for different altitudes can be used to infer the rate of temperature change with increasing/decreasing altitude. Such inferences over abstract domains may be realized and facilitated by drawing on abilities for spatial reasoning (Gattis, 2001). To infer the rate of temperature change with altitude, one may visualize the known temperatures for the different altitudes using two orthogonal axes by mapping altitude onto one axis and mapping temperature onto the other axis. Such mapping of altitude and temperature onto the axes implicitly also maps the rate of temperature change onto the steepness of the curve that connects all the known altitude-temperature combinations. Accordingly, the rate of change can be inferred by determining the steepness of the curve. As in this example, spatial analogies often help to make explicit some abstract relations that may be difficult to compute otherwise. A crucial prerequisite for reasoning by spatial analogies is to establish an appropriate analogy between the abstract and the spatial domain, such that results obtained by spatial reasoning can be transferred to the abstract domain. An important and powerful mechanism by which the analogy can be established is structure-mapping (Gentner, 1983). Structure-mapping, in general, establishes an analogy between two domains by mapping elements, relations between elements, and relations between relations in the different domains onto each other. In the analogy "The atom is like the solar system," for instance, the electrons are mapped onto the planets and the relations between the atomic core and the electrons are mapped onto the relations between the sun and the planets. Gattis (2004) has shown that structure-mapping is also central when employing spatial analogies to infer new knowledge about abstract concepts. In one of the experiments, participants were presented with pictures of gestures that were accompanied by short sentences. The first picture showed a person touching her right ear with the right hand and the second picture showed a person touching her left ear with the right hand. The sentences accompanying the first and second pictures were, for example, "Mouse bites monkey" and "Mouse bites elephant." After studying these two picture-sentence pairs, a third picture with a person touching her left ear with the left hand was shown to the participants and they were probed for the meaning of this new picture by asking them to select one of two sentences written below the third picture. These two sentences were, for example, "Bear bites monkey" and "Bear bites elephant." In the given example, inferring the meaning of the new picture required mapping objects in the sentences to aspects of the picture. For other sets of sentences used in the experiment, relations in the sentences needed to be mapped to aspects of the picture. As predicted by structure-mapping, there was a clear tendency of mapping sentence objects onto picture objects and sentence relations onto spatial relations in the picture.

## Neural Systems, Variation, and Learning

In this section we discuss how spatial information is represented and processed in the brain, identify possible individual differences, and discuss training and learning in spatial reasoning.

### Space in the Brain

Neuroscientific research is beginning to uncover where and how spatial information is maintained and transformed in the brain. At a low level, spatial information obtained by vision is represented in the primary visual cortex (V1) in the occipital lobe. Viewing objects that are close together excites neurons that are close together in V1, suggesting that the spatial layout in the world is partially mapped to the primary visual cortex. Information present in V1 is further processed in two main pathways in the brain called the ventral and dorsal pathways (Ungerleider & Mishkin, 1982). The ventral pathway extends to regions in the temporal lobe and processes nonspatial object information such as color and shape. The dorsal pathway extends to regions in the parietal lobe and processes spatial information such as the location of objects.

The parietal lobe receives and integrates spatial information across the senses (Byrne, Becker, & Burgess 2007), with structures that are thought to be responsible for mapping together different spatial reference frames (see section on "Reference Frames"). This is necessary because the space around the human body is represented in many different frames. For example, a reference frame that may be employed in vision may be centered on the head, whereas a reference frame employed for grasping may be centered on the hand. As a result, the same location in space (e.g., a cup of coffee on your desk) may be coded in two different frames. A further central function supported by areas in the parietal lobe is directing attention to different regions of space. The importance of this function becomes most clear when it breaks down, for example, due to lesions in the parietal lobe which often results in hemineglect, a reduced awareness for one side of peripersonal space. Finally, the parietal lobe serves as a gateway for sensory information to brain structures in the medial temporal lobe such as the hippocampus and entorhinal cortex that are also involved in processing and representing spatial information.

The hippocampus and the entorhinal cortex contain neurons that represent information about one's own location and direction in the environment (Moser, Kropff, & Moser, 2008). Neurons in the hippocampus, called *place cells*, respond selectively to circumscribed regions in the environment: A given place cell only fires when there is stimulation at the location coded by that cell. Different place cells code different places, such that the response of several place cells together allows a fairly precise localization. Similarly, neurons in the entorhinal cortex, called *grid cells*, respond selectively to particular locations in the environment. Grid cells respond to several places, with these places arranged like a grid across the environment. In contrast to earlier processing stages such as V1, the spatial representation in place cells and grid cells is not topographic. Neighboring place and grid cells may represent places that are not adjacent in the environment. A further type of neurons in the entorhinal cortex, called *head direction cells*, complements the location information given in the place and grid cells. Whereas place and grid cells code the current location largely independently from current orientation, head direction cells code the current orientation largely independently from the current location. Thus, the neurons in the hippocampus and the entorhinal cortex provide enough information to determine one's location and orientation in the environment.

## Individual Differences

Different people can vary in spatial reasoning ability, such as the person who gets easily lost in a new environment and the person who can easily find her way when she encounters a detour. Several tests have been developed to assess these individual differences (Hegarty & Waller, 2005), including assessments of mental rotation ability, of the ability to maintain an adequate sense of direction, of the ability to imagine folding a paper in accordance with instructions, and the ability to decide when to start the movement of one object such that it intersects with another already moving object. These types of tests have revealed consistent individual differences, with some of these differences correlating with gender (Halpern & Collaer, 2005). For example, some studies have shown that men perform better than women on mental rotation (see section on "Mental Rotation"). There are also differences in giving directions (see section on "Giving Directions") and in navigation (see section on "Navigation"), with women relying more on landmarks, and men relying more on directions and distances. Whereas men are normally more likely to employ cardinal directions such as east and south when giving directions, females are more likely to refer to landmarks along a route. Furthermore, women are, on average, slower and more error prone than men in navigating virtual environment mazes, which in part may arise from the fact that such mazes tend to be comparatively sparse in landmarks. This may suggest that strategy differences underlie these observed gender effects (Lawton, 1996). More generally, work by Hegarty, Montello, Richardson, Ishikawa, and Lovelace (2006) has shown, that individual differences in a number of spatial abilities as measured by the aforementioned tests jointly determine navigational performance. For instance, higher scores on both the mental rotation test and a sense of direction instrument predict better navigation performance.

## STEM Education and Spatial Skills

Spatial reasoning is important for a number of professions and proficiencies. For example, chemists and biologists may need to understand the spatial layout of chemical compounds and molecules. Similarly, physicists and engineers work on the spatial layout of electrical circuits and mechanical devices. Geoscientists employ spatial transformations when trying to determine the events that led to the current features of a given outcrop. Indeed, Shea, Lubinski, and Benbow (2001) suggest that spatial ability is a good predictor of success in STEM disciplines. They measured spatial ability in a large sample of 13-year-olds and monitored their educational and occupational careers over the next 20 years. One main result was the correlation between spatial ability and involvement in STEM fields: Participants with higher spatial ability at age 13 were more likely to graduate and work in one of the STEM fields than people with lower spatial ability. This relationship between spatial ability and the STEM fields suggests the possibility that involvement and performance in STEM disciplines may be increased by training spatial ability (Baenninger & Newcombe, 1989).

## Future Directions

In this section, we outline five future directions for further research. First, we encourage research on the nature of spatial representations: How are representations that code different types of spatial knowledge integrated? Second, we encourage research on how spatial knowledge from long-term and working memory combines to support spatial task performance. Third, we encourage research on the differential role of egocentric and allocentric reference frames in navigation: How does the use of these frames depend on existing knowledge, task properties, and previous experience, for example? Fourth, we encourage additional research on how space can underlie nonspatial abilities such as understanding, dealing with, and reasoning about time. Lastly, we encourage research on the feasibility of training spatial abilities. (For further discussion related to spatial reasoning, see chapters 8, 25, 32, 41, 42, and 48.)

## References

Acredolo, L. (1988). Infant mobility and spatial development. In J. Stiles-Davis, M. Kritchevsky, & U. Bellugi (Eds.), *Spatial cognition: Brain bases and development*. (pp. 157–166). Hillsdale, NJ: Erlbaum.

Baddeley, A. D., & Logie, R. H. (1999). Working memory: The multiple-component model. In A. Miyake & P. Shah (Eds.), *Models of working memory* (pp. 28–61). Cambridge, England: Cambridge University Press.

Baenninger, M., & Newcombe, N. (1989). The role of experience in spatial test performance: A meta-analysis. *Sex Roles, 20*, 327–344.

Boroditsky, L. (2000). Metaphoric structuring: Understanding time through spatial metaphors. *Cognition, 75*, 1–28.

Borst, G., & Kosslyn, S. M. (2008). Visual mental imagery and visual perception: Structural equivalence revealed by scanning processes. *Memory and Cognition, 36*, 849–862.

Brennan, S. E., & Clark, H. H. (1996). Conceptual pacts and lexical choice in conversation. *Journal of Experimental Psychology: Learning, Memory, and Cognition, 22*, 1482–1493.

Brockmole, J. R., & Wang, R. F. (2002). Switching between environmental representations in memory. *Cognition, 83*, 295–316.

Byrne, P., Becker, S., & Burgess, N. (2007), Remembering the past and imagining the future: A neural model of spatial memory and imagery. *Psychological Review, 114*, 340–375.

Carpenter, P. A., & Shah, P. (1998). A model of the perceptual and conceptual processes in graph comprehension. *Journal of Experimental Psychology: Applied, 4*, 75–100.

Cooper, L. A. (1976) Demonstration of a mental analog of an external rotation. *Perception and Psychophysics, 19*, 296–302.

Cooper, L. A., & Shepard, R. N. (1973). Chronometric studies of the rotation of mental images. In W. G. Chase (Ed.), *Visual information processing* (pp. 75–176). New York: Academic Press.

Creem, S. H., Downs, T. H., Wraga, M., Harrington, G. S.Proffitt, D. R., & Downs, J. H., III. (2001). An fMRI study of imagined self-rotation. *Cognitive, Affective, and Behavioral Neuroscience, 1*, 239–249.

Dehaene, S., Bossini, S., & Giraux, P. (1993). The mental representation of parity and number magnitude. *Journal of Experimental Psychology: General, 122*, 371–396.

Denis, M., & Kosslyn, S. M. (1999). Scanning visual mental images: A window on the mind. *Cahiers Psychologiques Cognitives, 18*, 409–465.

Easton, R. D., & Sholl, M. J. (1995). Object-array structure, frames of reference, and retrieval of spatial knowledge. *Journal of Experimental Psychology: Learning, Memory, and Cognition, 21*, 483–500.

Farrell, M. J., & Robertson, I. H. (1998). Mental rotation and the automatic updating of body-centered spatial relationships. *Journal of Experimental Psychology: Learning, Memory, and Cognition, 24*, 227–233.

Finke, R. A., & Pinker, S. (1982). Spontaneous imagery scanning in mental extrapolation. *Journal of Experimental Psychology: Learning, Memory, and Cognition, 8*, 142–147.

Fitts, P. M., & Seeger, C. M . (1953). S-R compatibility: Spatial characteristics of stimulus and response codes. *Journal of Experimental Psychology, 46*, 199–210.

Gattis, M. (2001). *Spatial schemas and abstract thought.* Cambridge, MA: MIT Press.

Gattis, M. (2004). Mapping relational structure in spatial reasoning. *Cognitive Science, 28*, 589–610.

Gentner, D. (1983). Structure-mapping: A theoretical framework for analogy. *Cognitive Science, 7*, 155–170.

Graf, M. (2006). Coordinate transformations in object recognition. *Psychological Bulletin, 132*, 920–945.

Griffin, I. C., & Nobre, A. C. (2003). Orienting attention to locations in internal representations. *Journal of Cognitive Neuroscience, 15*, 1176–1194.

Halpern, D. F., & Collaer, M. L. (2005). Sex differences in visuospatial abilities: More than meets the eye. In A. Miyake & P. Shah (Eds.), *The Cambridge handbook of visuospatial thinking* (pp. 170–212). Cambridge, England: Cambridge University Press.

Hedge, A., & Marsh, N. W. A. (1975). The effect of irrelevant spatial correspondence on two-choice response time. *Acta Psychologica, 39*, 427–439.

Hegarty, M., Montello, D. R., Richardson, A. E., Ishikawa, T., & Lovelace, K. (2006). Spatial abilities at different scales: Individual differences in aptitude-test performance and spatial-layout learning. *Intelligence, 34*, 151–176.

Hegarty, M., & Waller, D. A. (2005). Individual differences in spatial abilities. In A. Miyake & P. Shah (Eds.), *The Cambridge handbook of visuospatial thinking* (pp. 121–169). Cambridge, England: Cambridge University Press.

Hinton, G. H., & Parsons, L. M. (1981). Frames of reference and mental imagery. In J Long & A. Badddeley (Eds.), *Attention and performance IX* (pp. 261–277). Hillsdale, NJ: Erlbaum.

Hirtle, S. C. (1998). The cognitive atlas: Using GIS as a metaphor for memory. In M. Egenhofer & R. Golledge (Eds.), *Spatial and temporal reasoning in geographic information systems* (pp. 267–276). New York: Oxford University Press.

Hodgson, E., & Waller, D. (2006). Lack of set size effects in spatial updating: Evidence for offline updating. *Journal of Experimental Psychology: Learning, Memory, and Cognition, 32*, 854–866.

Isaacs, E. A., & Clark, H. H. (1987). References in conversations between experts and novices. *Journal of Experimental Psychology: General, 116*, 26–37.

Jahn, G., Knauff, M., & Johnson-Laird, P. N. (2007). Preferred mental models in reasoning about spatial relations. *Memory & Cognition, 35*, 2075–2087.

Johnson-Laird, P. N. (1999). Deductive reasoning. *Annual Review of Psychology, 50*, 109–135.

Johnson-Laird, P. N., & Byrne, R. M. J. (1991). *Deduction.* Hillsdale, NJ: Erlbaum.

Kelly, J. W., Avraamides, M. N., & Loomis, J. M. (2007). Sensorimotor alignment effects in the learning environment and in novel environments. *Journal of Experimental Psychology: Learning, Memory, and Cognition, 33*, 1092–1107.

Klauer, K. C., & Zhao, Z. (2004). Double dissociations in visual and spatial short-term memory. *Journal of Experimental Psychology: General, 133*, 355–381.

Kosslyn, S. M. (1973). Scanning visual images: Some structural implications. *Perception and Psychophysics, 14*, 90–94.

Lakoff, G., & Johnson, M. (1980). *Metaphors we live by.* Chicago: University of Chicago Press.

Larsen, A., & Bundesen, C. (1998). Effects of spatial separation in visual pattern matching: Evidence on the role of mental translation. *Journal of Experimental Psychology: Human Perception and Performance, 24*, 719–731.

Lawton, C. A. (1996). Strategies for indoor wayfinding: The role of orientation. *Journal of Environmental Psychology, 16*, 137–245.

Levinson, S. C. (2003). *Space in language and cognition.* Cambridge, England: Cambridge University Press.

Logan, G. D., & Sadler, D. D. (1996). A computational analysis of the apprehension of spatial relations. In P. Bloom, M. Peterson, M. Garrett, & L. Nadel (Eds.), *Language and space* (pp. 493–529). Cambridge, MA: MIT Press.

Lovelace, K. L., Hegarty, M., & Montello, D. R. (1999). Elements of good route directions in familiar and unfamiliar environments. In C. Freksa & D. M. Mark (Eds.), *Spatial information theory: Cognitive and computational foundations of geographic information science* (pp. 65–82). Berlin: Springer.

Lynch, K. (1960). *The image of the city.* Cambridge, MA: MIT Press.

May, M. (2004). Imaginal perspective switches in remembered environments: Transformation versus interference accounts. *Cognitive Psychology, 48*, 163–206.

May, M., & Klatzky, R. L. (2000). Path integration while ignoring irrelevant movement. *Journal of Experimental Psychology: Learning, Memory and Cognition, 26*, 169–186.

McNamara, T. P. (1986). Mental representations of spatial relations. *Cognitive Psychology, 18*, 87–121.

Memelink, J., & Hommel, B. (2005). Attention, instruction, and response representation. *European Journal of Cognitive Psychology, 17*, 674–685.

Moar, I., & Bower, G. H. (1983). Inconsistency in spatial knowledge. *Memory and Cognition, 11*, 107–113.

Montello, D. R. (2005). Navigation. In A. Miyake & P. Shah (Eds.), *The Cambridge handbook of visuospatial thinking* (pp. 257–294). Cambridge, England: Cambridge University Press.

Moser, E. I., Kropff, E., & Moser, M-B. (2008). Place cells, grid cells, and the brain's spatial representations system. *Annual Review Neuroscience, 31*, 69–89.

Mou, W., & McNamara, T. P. (2002). Intrinsic frames of reference in spatial memory. *Journal of Experimental Psychology: Learning, Memory, and Cognition, 28*, 162–170.

Mou, W., McNamara, T. P., Valiquette, C. M., & Rump, B. (2004). Allocentric and egocentric updating of spatial memories. *Journal of Experimental Psychology: Learning, Memory, and Cognition, 30*, 142–157.

Moyer, R. S., & Landauer, T. K. (1967). Time required for judgments of numerical inequality. *Nature, 215*, 1519–1520.

Piaget, J., & Inhelder, B. (1960). *The child's conception of geometry*. New York: Routledge & Kegan.

Presson, C. C. (1982). Strategies in spatial reasoning. *Journal of Experimental Psychology: Learning, Memory, and Cognition, 8*, 243–251.

Proctor, R. W., & Vu, K-P. L. (2002). Eliminating, magnifying, and reversing spatial compatibility effects with mixed location-relevant and irrelevant trials. In W. Prinz & B. Hommel (Eds.), *Common mechanisms in perception and action: Attention and performance XIX* (pp. 443–473).Oxford, England: Oxford University Press.

Rauh, R., Knauff, M., Schlieder, C., Hagen, C., Kuß, T., & Strube, G. (2005). Preferred and alternative models in spatial reasoning *Spatial Cognition and Computation, 5*, 239–269.

Rieser, J. J. (1989). Access to knowledge of spatial structure at novel points of observation. *Journal of Experimental Psychology: Learning, Memory, and Cognition, 15*, 1157–1165.

Sadalla, E. K., Burroughs, W. J., & Staplin, L. J. (1980). Reference points in spatial cognition. *Journal of Experimental Psychology: Human Learning and Memory, 6*, 516–528.

Schober, M. F. (1993). Spatial perspective-taking in conversation, *Cognition, 47*, 1–24.

Shea, D. L., Lubinksi, D., & Benbow, C. P. (2001). Importance of assessing spatial ability in intellectually talented young adolescents: A 20-year longitudinal study. *Journal of Educational Psychology, 93*(3), 604–614.

Shepard, R. N. (1984). Ecological restraints on internal representations. *Psychological Review, 91*, 417–447.

Shepard, R. N., & Cooper, L. A. (1982). *Mental images and their transformations*. Cambridge, MA: MIT Press.

Shepard, R. N., & Metzler, J. (1971). Mental rotation of three-dimensional objects. *Science, 171*, 701–703.

Sholl, M. J. (2000). The functional separability of self-reference and object-to-object systems in spatial memory. In S. Ó Nualláin (Ed.), *Spatial cognition* (p. 45–67). Amsterdam, The Netherlands: Benjamins.

Simon, J. R., & Rudell, A. P. (1967). Auditory S-R compatibility: The effect of an irrelevant cue on information processing. *Journal of Applied Psychology, 51*, 300–304.

Sloman, A. (1975). Afterthoughts on analogical representations. In B. L. Nash-Webber & R. Schank (Eds.), *Proc. Theoretical Issues in Natural Language Processing (TINLAP-1)* (pp. 164–168). Cambridge, MA: Association for Computer Linguistics.

Stevens, A., & Coupe. P. (1978). Distortions in judged spatial relations. *Cognitive Psychology, 10*, 422–437.

Tolman, E. C. (1948). Cognitive maps in rats and men. *Psychological Review, 55*, 189–208.

Tversky, B. (1981). Distortions in memory for maps. *Cognitive Psychology, 13*, 407–433.

Tversky, B. (1993). Cognitive maps, cognitive collages, and spatial mental models. In A. Frank & I. Campari (Eds.), *Spatial information theory—A theoretical basis for GIS* (pp. 14–24). Berlin: Springer.

Tversky, B. (1999). What does drawing reveal about thinking? In J. S. Gero & B. Tversky (Eds.), *Visual and spatial reasoning in design* (pp. 93–101). Sidney, Australia: Key Centre of Design Computing and Cognition, University of Sydney.

Tversky, B. (2005). Functional significance of visuospatial representations. In P. Shah & A. Miyake (Eds.), *Handbook of higher-level visuospatial thinking* (pp. 1–34). Cambridge, England: Cambridge University Press.

Ungerleider, L. G., & Mishkin, M. (1982). Two cortical visual systems. In M. A. Ingle, M. I. Gooodale, & R. J. W. Masfield (Eds.), *Analysis of visual behavior* (pp. 549–586). Cambridge, MA: MIT Press.

Vecchi, T., Monticellai, M. L., & Cornoldi, C. (1995). Visuo-spatial working memory: Structures and variables affecting a capacity measure. *Neuropsychologia, 33*, 1549–1564.

Wallace, R. J. (1971). S-R compatibility and the idea of a response code. *Journal of Experimental Psychology, 88*, 354–360.

Waller, D., & Hodgson, E. (2006). Transient and enduring spatial representations under disorientation and self-rotation. *Journal of Experimental Psychology: Learning, Memory, and Cognition, 32*, 867–882.

Wang, R. F. (2003). Spatial representations and spatial updating. In D. E. Irwin & B. H. Ross (Eds.), *The psychology of learning and motivation, Vol. 42. Advances in Research and theory: Cognitive vision* (pp. 109–156). San Diego, CA: Academic Press.

Wang, R. F., Crowell, J. A., Simons, D. J., Irwin, D. E., Kramer, A. F., Ambinder, M. S.,...Hsieh, B. (2006). Spatial updating relies on an egocentric representation of space: effects of the number of objects. *Psychonomic Bulletin and Review, 13*, 281–286.

Wang, R. F., & Spelke, E. S. (2002). Human spatial representation: Insights from animals. *Trends in Cognitive Sciences, 6*, 376–382.

Wood, G., Willmes, K., Nuerk, H-C., & Fischer, M. H. (2008). On the cognitive link between space and number: A meta-analysis of the SNARC effect. *Psychology Science Quarterly, 50*(4), 489–525.

Wraga, M. (2003). Thinking outside the body: An advantage for spatial updating during imagined versus physical self-rotation. *Journal of Experimental Psychology: Learning, Memory, and Cognition, 29*, 993–1005.

Zorzi, M., Priftis, K., & Umilta, C. (2002). Neglect disrupts the mental number line. *Nature, 417*, 138–139.

## Further Readings

Kosslyn, S. M. (1973). Scanning visual images: Some structural implications. *Perception and Psychophysics, 14*, 90–94. (spatial representations, spatial processes)

Shepard, R. N., & Metzler, J. (1971). Mental rotation of three-dimensional objects. *Science, 171*, 701–703. (spatial processes)

Ellard, C. (2009). *You are here: Why we can find our way to the moon, but get lost in the mall.* New York: Doubleday. (spatial memory, navigation, design of public places)

Liben, L. S. (2009). The road to map understanding. *Current Directions in Psychological Science, 18*, 310–315. (external visualizations)

Dehaene, S., Bossini, S., & Giraux, P. (1993). The mental representation of parity and number magnitude. *Journal of Experimental Psychology: General, 122*, 371–396. (grounding of abstract concepts, mental numberline)

Gattis, M. (2001). *Spatial schemas and abstract thought.* Cambridge, MA: MIT Press. (grounding of abstract concepts; grounding of time)

Hegarty, M., & Waller, D. A. (2005). Individual differences in spatial abilities. In A. Miyake & P. Shah (Eds.), *The Cambridge handbook of visuospatial thinking* (pp. 121–169). Cambridge: Cambridge University Press. (individual differences)

# Causal Reasoning

Michael R. Waldmann *and* York Hagmayer

### Abstract

Causal reasoning belongs to our most central cognitive competencies. Causal knowledge is used as the basis of predictions and diagnoses, categorization, action planning, decision making, and problem solving. Whereas philosophers have analyzed causal reasoning for many centuries, psychologists have for a long time preferred to view causal reasoning and learning as special cases of domain-general competencies, such as logical reasoning or associative learning. The present chapter gives an overview of recent research about causal reasoning. It discusses competing theories, and it contrasts domain-general accounts with theories that model causal reasoning and learning as attempts to make inferences about stable hidden causal processes.

**Key Words:** causal reasoning, causal learning, causal Bayes nets, causal power, causal mechanisms, associative theories, probabilistic theories, logical theories, force dynamics

Causal reasoning belongs to one of our most central cognitive competencies, which enable us to adapt to our world. Causal knowledge allows us to predict future events or diagnose the causes for observed facts. We plan actions and solve problems using knowledge about cause-effect relations. Without our ability to discover and empirically test causal theories, we would not have made progress in various empirical sciences, such as physics, medicine, biology, or psychology, and we would not have been able to invent various technologies that changed our lives. Yet causal reasoning has been curiously absent from mainstream cognitive psychology for many decades. The situation has dramatically changed in the past two decades with more and more research devoted to causal reasoning and causal learning.

The goal of the present chapter is to present an overview of various theoretical paradigms studying causal reasoning. Whereas cognitive psychology has for a long time neglected this topic, causality and causal reasoning has remained one of the central themes of philosophy throughout its history. In fact,

psychological theories of causal reasoning have been greatly inspired by philosophical accounts. So far there is no dominant overarching theory of causality or causal reasoning that would serve as an organizational foundation for presenting research on different reasoning tasks (e.g., prediction, diagnosis, inductive reasoning, decision making). We have therefore decided to structure the research according to the postulated concept of causality, which, at this stage of research, seemed more natural than organizing the chapter around different types of reasoning tasks.

## Causal Reasoning Without Causation: Associationist, Logical, and Probabilistic Theories

One of the reasons for the neglect of causality in cognitive psychology may have been the widespread skepticism about the reality of causation in philosophy and science. An outspoken proponent of this critical view, Bertrand Russell, stated: "The law of causation ... is a relic of a bygone age, surviving, like the monarchy, only because it is erroneously supposed to do no harm" (1912/1992, p. 193). This skepticism has in the meantime been questioned because a closer look at how scientists actually reason has revealed that causal constructs are central for scientific discovery (see Cartwright, 1999; Pearl, 2000). Nevertheless, many psychological theories have tried to explain causal reasoning with theories that do not contain references to specifically causal concepts.

The following three sections will present three classes of theories that try to reduce causal reasoning to domain-general noncausal reasoning. Although some of these theories acknowledge the difference between causes and effects, the postulated reasoning and learning mechanisms merely capture covariation information or logical relations without expressing causal notions.

## Associative Theories

Skepticism about the usefulness of the concept of causality in psychology can be traced back to the critical analyses of the philosopher David Hume (e.g., Hume, 1748/1977). Hume reflected about situations in which he observed causes and effects, and he did not detect any empirical features that might correspond to evidence for hidden causal powers, which necessitate effects. What he found instead was spatiotemporally ordered successions of events. So, why do we believe in causation? His answer was that our impression of causation was merely an illusion derived from observed associations between event pairs. Contemporary learning theorists have adopted Hume's empiricist approach to causal learning. Associations derived from spatiotemporally connected events, such as through Pavlovian and instrumental conditioning, serve in these theories as the basis for causal predictions (e.g., Allan, 1993; Shanks & Dickinson, 1987; see López & Shanks, 2008, for a recent overview). Although associative theories claim to model causal reasoning, there is actually no place for causation in these theories, regardless of the variant. All associative theories divide learning events in two classes, cues and outcomes, which are distinguished on the basis of temporal order. Cues represent events that are experienced first in a learning context, and which trigger internal representations of outcomes based on the strength of the associations, which reflect the degree of covariation between the learning events.

Associative theories serve as an interesting contrast to causal reasoning. Many reasoning tasks can be successfully solved on the basis of associations and do not require causal knowledge that goes beyond covariations. Covariation information can often be used to make successful predictions and diagnoses, and it can be employed for action planning and decision making. Moreover, covariation information used in modern associative theories is often quite sophisticated. For example, the popular Rescorla-Wagner (1972) model generates associative weights for multiple cues of a single outcome that are (under specific conditions) formally equivalent to partial regression weights in multiple regression analysis. Thus, associative weights do not simply reflect simple unconditional covariations; they take into account the predictive contribution of competing cues (i.e., cue competition).

An example of cue competition, which has also been adopted in research on causal reasoning, is the blocking paradigm, in which in a first learning phase a particular cause A is paired with an effect (e.g., Beckers, De Houwer, Pineño, & Miller, 2005; De Houwer & Beckers, 2003; Chapman & Robbins, 1990; Shanks, 1985; Sobel, Tenenbaum, & Gopnik, 2004; Waldmann & Holyoak, 1992). In a second phase, A is redundantly paired with a novel cause, B, and the compound of causes A and B are now followed by the effect. The consequences of B are never observed on their own. Although both A and B individually covary with the effect, participants view A as a cause but tend to be uncertain about whether B is a cause. This can be interpreted as evidence for cue competition. Once A is known to be a cause, B does not add anything to the predictability of the effect event. Blocking in causal reasoning is just one example of how associative theories proved useful as models of causal reasoning. Numerous other empirical findings (e.g., acquisition curves, trial order effects, sensitivity to contingency) also seem to support the view that causal reasoning does not need the concept of causation and can be reduced to a sophisticated form of covariation learning and associative reasoning.

Despite the success of associative theories, numerous studies in the past two decades have shown that humans are sensitive to aspects of causation that cannot be reduced to covariation information. The first demonstration in which causal and associative theories were directly pitted against each other comes from Waldmann and Holyoak's work on causal model theory, who have shown that learners distinguish between cues that represent causes of outcomes (i.e., predictive learning) and cues that represent effects of outcomes (i.e., diagnostic learning), which indicates that they are sensitive to the directionality of the causal arrow. For example, Waldmann and Holyoak (1992) showed that blocking only occurs when the cues represent causes but not effects (see also Booth & Buehner, 2007; López, Cobos, & Caño, 2005; Waldmann, 2000, 2001, for more recent converging evidence). Causal directionality is an aspect of causation that cannot be reduced to covariation but is an integral component of causal model theory (see section on "Reasoning With Causal Models," for more details).

Other demonstrations of the irreducibility of causation to covariation include the distinction between causal and noncausal (i.e., spurious) covariations (Cheng, 1997; Waldmann & Hagmayer, 2005), the distinction between covariation and causal power (Cheng, 1997), or the capacity of humans to derive differential predictions for hypothetical observations and interventions from identical covariation information (Gopnik et al., 2004; Sloman & Lagnado, 2005; Waldmann & Hagmayer, 2005). All these findings, which will be discussed later in greater detail, demonstrate how humans go beyond the information given and infer causal properties on the basis of covariational learning input (see also Buehner & Cheng, 2005; Gopnik & Schulz, 2007; Holyoak & Cheng, 2011; Waldmann, Hagmayer, & Blaisdell, 2006, for overviews).

## Logical Theories

A second class of theories that attempt to reduce causal reasoning to a domain-general theory are logical theories, which model causal reasoning as a special case of deductive reasoning. Modeling causal reasoning in terms of propositional logic has proven problematic. From "If Cause A, then Effect B" and "Cause A," we cannot infer Effect B ("modus ponens") in many real-world cases because there may be additional disablers of Effect B, or Cause A may be probabilistic, and therefore neither necessary nor sufficient (Cummins, 1995; Markovits & Potvin, 2001; Neys, Shaeken, & Ydewalle, 2002, 2003; Quinn & Markovits, 1998). For the same reasons we cannot infer from the absence of Effect B to the absence of Cause A ("modus tollens").

Moreover, conditionals do not distinguish between causes and effects, and therefore they can equally express "(1) If Cause A, then Effect," and "(2) If Effect, then Cause B," the latter type of rule being used often in diagnostic expert systems. However, the insensitivity of logical rules to causal directionality creates problems. For example, premises (1) and (2) invite the transitive inference from Cause A to Effect, and then from Effect to Cause B, which is clearly an invalid inference since two alternative causes of the same effect do not necessarily occur together (Pearl,

1988). Although some of these problems may be solved if additional premises are added from background knowledge (Cummins, 1995), it can be doubted that this route fixes the underlying problem of neglecting causality (see Pearl, 1988, 2000).

A prominent example of a logical theory of causal reasoning is Goldvarg and Johnson-Laird's (2001) *mental model theory* of causation. The focus of this theory is reasoning with causal propositions. According to mental model theory, people represent propositions by constructing mental models in which each model represents a possible state of affairs consistent with the premises. To distinguish between causes and effects, a temporal priority assumption is added according to which causes precede effects in time. For example, the full representation of proposition "A causes B" assumes three models in which (1) A precedes and co-occurs with B (i.e., a b), (2) the absence of A co-occurs with the absence of B (i.e., ~a ~b), and (3) the absence of A co-occurs with the presence of B (i.e., ~a b). The third possibility describes possible cases in which the effect is caused by some other factor.

Mental model theory assumes that people represent causality as deterministic. "A causes B" excludes as the only case the co-occurrence of A and non-B, thus assuming that A is sufficient (but not necessary) for its effect. According to the theory, "A causes B" can be distinguished from "A enables B" by modifying the third model (i.e., a ~b). Thus, enablers are necessary but not sufficient. Finally, preventing is modeled as causing the absence of the effect.

People often reason with reduced representations that only contain what is mentioned in the proposition (e.g., "A causes B"), which in the example would be the first model (a b). The other models are either neglected or there is a mental footnote referring to them. This assumption predicts that people often represent causal relations as the co-occurrence of two events and forget about other cases consistent with the causal claim.

Mental model theory is strictly Humean by reducing causality to temporal priority, co-occurrence, and determinism. Notably "A causes B" is represented by mental model theory the same way as "If A, then B." Thus, the theory clearly attempts to reduce causation to noncausal domain-general representations, and therefore it shares many of the problems of other noncausal theories. For example, the theory cannot differentiate between causal and noncausal relations in which temporal priority holds. For example, barometer readings precede and co-occur with states of the weather but are clearly not causally related. Moreover, the theory does not distinguish between causes that are observed and causes that are generated by means of interventions (see Sloman & Lagnado, 2005). A further shortcoming of the theory is that the relationship between deterministic relations and probabilistic data is not worked out.

## Probabilistic Theories

Whereas associative theories update associative strength based on trial-by-trial learning, probabilistic theories pick up covariation information from frequency data, which can be presented in various formats. Probabilistic theories typically assume that there are causes and effects, and that covariations need to be assessed in the cause-effect direction. Thus, they also represent a step in the direction of causal theories. However, they are still limited as a causal theory. The distinction between causes and effects is assumed, not an intrinsic part of a causal theory; the principal goal of research is to investigate which covariation metric people use to assess the strength of cause-effect relations. Thus again, causal relations are largely reduced to statistical covariations between causes and effects.

This research was pioneered by Kelley (1973), who postulated that people compute intuitive ANOVA analyses to make causal inferences. His theory proved very influential in social and cognitive psychology, and it was formalized in various directions. A popular rule for measuring causal strength for a single cause-effect relation was the $\Delta P$ rule, which measures contingency as the difference between the conditional probabilities of the effect in the presence ($P(e|c)$) minus the absence of the cause ($P(e|\sim c)$) (Jenkins & Ward, 1965):

$$\Delta P = P(e|c) - P(e|\sim c) \qquad (1)$$

Thus, according to this rule, causes are *difference makers*, which raise (generative cause) or reduce (preventive cause) the probability of the effect. For example, eating nuts may be viewed as a cause of an allergy in a specific person if the person has a higher probability of having an allergy after having eaten nuts in comparison to not having eaten nuts. Interestingly, it can be shown that under certain conditions, the asymptotic strength computed by the Rescorla-Wagner (1972) model of associative learning is equivalent to $\Delta P$ (Danks, 2003).

The $\Delta P$ rule can be successfully applied to single cause effect relations, but it often fails when multiple causes are present, which may introduce

confoundings. For example, the $\Delta P$ rule does not predict the blocking effect that was mentioned earlier because it does not take into account competing causes. Therefore, Cheng and Novick (1992) have developed and tested a formal theory that computes probabilistic contrasts that take into account main effects and interactions, and therefore can deal with situations in which multiple causes converge on a joint effect.

The $\Delta P$ rule is not the only statistical rule that has been postulated as a measure of causal strength; there are numerous alternatives (see Hattori & Oaksford, 2007; Perales & Shanks, 2007, for overviews). However, the $\Delta P$ rule shares with most of these rules the problem of reducing causation to covariation between causes and effects.

### FROM COVARIATION TO CAUSAL POWER

The fact that covariation does not necessarily reflect causation can be seen in various cases. For example, barometer readings covary (to some extent) with the future weather, although there is no causal relation between the two variables. It is also possible that we observe zero covariations despite underlying causal power. If, for example, only people who do not suffer from headaches take aspirin, then aspirin will not covary with the amount of headaches, although they are causally related. In this population aspirin simply cannot display its potential power (see Fig. 46.1).

### Power PC Theory

In a seminal paper, Cheng (1997) has proposed a formal theory of how causal power can be estimated from covariation data when specific preconditions hold. The view that causality can be reduced to some metric of covariation was abandoned and replaced by the theory that causal power is a theoretical concept, which can be estimated under specific circumstances using covariation information and background knowledge. According to Cheng's (1997) power PC theory, causal power represents

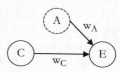

**Figure 46.1** Parameterized causal model of a single causal relation. Nodes indicate the causal variables under consideration (*C* and *E*); the dashed node (*A*) represents additional unobserved causal factors influencing the effect; arrows indicate causal mechanisms having causal powers *w*.

the probability of a cause, acting alone, to generate or prevent a target effect. Given that causes are never observed alone, this is a theoretical entity that needs to be inferred on the basis of observed data. To estimate causal power, several assumptions need to be made. Power PC theory partitions all (observed and unobserved) causes of effect $e$ into the candidate cause in question, $c$, and $a$, a composite of all alternative causes of $e$ (see Fig. 46.1). The variable $a$ represents the compound of all alternative enabling and generative causes. According to power PC theory, people enter the task with the default assumption that $c$ and $a$ independently influence $e$, $a$ produces but does not prevent $e$, that causal powers are independent of the frequencies of $c$ and $a$, and that $e$ does not occur without being caused. These default assumptions may of course be revised on the basis of contradicting evidence.

The unobservable probability with which $c$ produces $e$ is called *generative* power, represented by $w_c$. The generative power of the unobservable set of causes $a$ is analogously termed $w_a$. On the condition that $c$ and $a$ influence $e$ independently, it follows that

$$P(e|c) = w_c + P(a|c) \cdot w_a - w_c \cdot P(a|c) \cdot w_a \quad (2)$$

$$P(e|\sim c) = P(a|\sim c) \cdot w_a \quad (3)$$

Equation 2 implies that effect $e$ is either caused with a specific probability by $c$ or by the unobservable $a$ minus the overlap of the two event classes. The assumption embodied in Equation 2 that $c$ and $a$ are independent causes of $e$ is an instantiation of a *noisy-OR* gate (see Cheng, 1997; Griffiths & Tenenbaum, 2005; Pearl, 1988). According to the noisy-OR integration rule, each cause has an individual chance to produce the effect, and the causes do not interact when they occur simultaneously. The difference between $P(e|c)$ and $P(e|\sim c)$ can be abbreviated as $\Delta P$ (see Equation 1). Thus,

$$\Delta P = w_c + P(a|c) \cdot w_a - w_c \cdot P(a|c) \cdot w_a \\ - P(a|\sim c) \cdot w_a \quad (4)$$

Equation 4 shows why covariations do not directly reflect causality. If we observe the presence of a candidate cause $c$ and its effect $e$, we do not know whether $e$ was actually caused by $c$, by $a$, or by both. If $c$ and $a$ are perfectly correlated, we may observe a perfect covariation between $c$ and $e$, and yet $c$ may not be a cause of $e$ because the confounding variable $a$ may be the actual cause. Ideally reasoners should restrict causal inference to situations

in which $c$ and $a$ occur independently; that is, there is *no confounding*. In this special case, Equation 4 reduces to Equation 5:

$$w_c = \Delta P / (1 - P(e|\sim c)) \quad (5)$$

Of course, since $a$ is unobserved, reasoners cannot be sure whether $a$ and $c$ are indeed independent in a particular case. Cheng (1997) assumes that independence is the *default* assumption people make when there is no evidence to the contrary (but see Hagmayer & Waldmann, 2007; Luhmann & Ahn, 2007). A strategy to ensure independence is to manipulate the presence or absence of $c$ by means of an intervention, as scientists do in experiments. These manipulations make sure that $c$ and $a$ occur independently even when $a$ is unobserved.

This analysis holds for situations in which $\Delta P > 0$ (generative causes). A similar derivation can be made for situations in which $\Delta P < 0$, and one evaluates the *preventive* causal power of $c$.

Confounding may, of course, be due to *observed* alternative causes as well, not only to unobserved ones. Research on confounding by observed causes has shown that people are often aware of the confounding and therefore tend to create independence by holding the alternative cause constant, preferably in its absent value. For example, Waldmann and Hagmayer (2001) have shown that when assessing causal strength between a target cause and a target effect, learners hold a third event constant only when it is an alternative cause but not when it is causally irrelevant or a causal effect (see also Goedert, Harsch, & Spellman, 2005; Spellman, 1996).

Numerous studies have tested power PC theory and related accounts. The typical research strategy in this field is to present participants with various causal scenarios in which the contingencies between a target cause and an effect are varied by manipulating the conditional probabilities of the effect in the presence versus absence of the cause. After the learning phase, causal strength estimates are requested by the participants. To discriminate between the competing theories, contingencies are chosen that entail different causal strength estimates in the competing theories. These studies have generally shown that in many circumstances learners indeed try to estimate causal power and take into account alternative causes when presented with covariation data (Buehner, Cheng, & Clifford, 2003; Cheng, Novick, Liljeholm, & Ford, 2007; Hagmayer & Waldmann, 2007; Novick & Cheng, 2004; Wu & Cheng, 1999), although there are also situations in which learners seem to be trying to estimate covariation or other statistics (see Cheng & Novick, 2005; Hattori & Oaksford, 2007; López & Shanks, 2008; Luhmann & Ahn, 2007; White, 2003).

In sum, Cheng's (1997) theory computes point estimates of $w_c$ causal power. Formally the theory provides an answer to the query for the maximum likelihood estimate of $w_c$. However, power PC theory does not take into account the *uncertainty* of inductive causal inference. In particular, the power PC estimate is insensitive to sample size and other sample statistics that may affect inductive inference.

## Causal Support Theory

Griffiths and Tenenbaum (2005) analyzed causal inference in the context of their *causal support model*, which takes into account the uncertainty of parameter estimates by considering distributions of parameters in contrast to point estimates (see also Griffiths, Kemp, & Tenenbaum, 2008). Like Cheng's (1997) theory, this account is derived from normative considerations about rational inference; both theories postulate that everyday learners strive to reason rationally if possible. Thus, the primary goal of these theories is to provide a computational account of human reasoning, not a theory of cognitive mechanisms.

Whereas Cheng's (1997) focus was judgments of causal strength, which were modeled as parameter estimation tasks, the causal support model focuses on the assessment of the likelihood of the presence of a causal link between a target cause $c$ and an effect $e$. Griffiths and Tenenbaum argued that this is actually the question learners try to answer when estimating causal power. Within a Bayesian account, structure judgments are a case of *model selection* (see Mackay, 2003). The causal support model aims to contrast the evidence in favor of a causal model in which a link exists between $c$ and $e$ (Model 1; see Fig. 46.1) with a causal model in which these two variables are independent, and $e$ is only influenced by the background causes $a$ (Model 0). As in power PC theory, it is assumed that there are additional hidden causes $a$ in the background which affect the base rate of the effect. Also it is assumed that $c$ and $a$ are, in the case of generative causation, combined by the noisy-OR gate.

The center of Bayesian inference is Bayes's rule:

$$P(H \mid D) = \frac{P(D \mid H)P(H)}{P(D)} \quad (6)$$

where $H$ denotes a hypothesis, and $D$ denotes observed data. Bayes's rule provides a formal tool

for modeling the inference concerning the posterior probability of a hypothesis, $P(H \mid D)$, with $P(H)$ representing the prior belief in the hypothesis and $P(D \mid H)$ representing the likelihood of the data given the hypothesis.

In general, there are several competing hypotheses that may explain a given set of data, like Model 1 and Model 0 for a simple causal relation. To compute how likely a model is in comparison to other models, a ratio representation of Bayes's rule is used. In causal support theory the decision for a model is based on the posterior probability ratio of Model 1 and Model 0 by applying Bayes's rule (cf. Equation 6):

$$\log \frac{P(Model1 \mid D)}{P(Model0 \mid D)} = \log \frac{P(D \mid Model1)}{P(D \mid Model0)} \\ + \log \frac{P(Model1)}{P(Model0)} \quad (7)$$

Thus, the log ratio of the posterior probabilities (left side of Eq. 6) equals the sum of the log ratio of the likelihoods of the data given each model (first expression on right side) and the log ratio of the models' prior probabilities (second expression). Assuming equal base rates of Models 1 and 0, causal support is determined by the log likelihood ratio:

$$\text{support} = \log \frac{P(D \mid Model1)}{P(D \mid Model0)} \quad (8)$$

Thus, support represents a measure of the degree of evidence that data $D$ provide in favor of Model 1 over Model 0. The computations of the likelihoods of the data $D$ given the models take into account the uncertainty attached to parameter estimation. The likelihood of $D$ given Model 1 versus Model 0 is computed by averaging over the unknown causal strength parameters $w_a$ and $w_c$, which can vary between 0 and 1.

Griffiths and Tenenbaum (2005) presented experiments providing evidence for their causal support theory, generally using the same research paradigm as power PC theory: Participants are confronted with contingencies that entail different patterns of strength estimates in the competing theories (e.g., causal support theory vs. power PC theory). These experiments showed sensitivity to sample size and demonstrated good fits between power estimates and the Bayesian causal support measure. Thus, these studies suggest that people indeed take into account the uncertainty of statistical inference in causal induction. Their results also raise the possibility that requests to report causal strength estimates may be interpreted as queries about causal structure rather than strength.

Lu, Yuille, Liljeholm, Cheng, and Holyoak (2008) have further developed Bayesian models of power estimation, considering different variants of priors for the causal models and their parameters. Various experiments showed that models incorporating a simplicity bias along with the assumption that causes tend to be strong ("strong and sparse bias") provided the best fit to the data.

### Summary

In sum, the literature on causal power estimation suggests that people often try to go beyond covariation information and are sensitive to causal power. However, there are different ways a learner may interpret a power query. For example, she may provide an estimate of the strength parameter, assess the likelihood of a causal link, or interpret the test question as a request to judge the extent to which the observed cause actually is responsible for the occurrence of the effect in the case at hand (see Cheng & Novick, 2005). The complexity of the task also affects the inference strategies, which sometimes prevents reasoners from reaching their goals to estimate power (see De Houwer & Beckers, 2003; Waldmann & Walker, 2005). Despite the wealth of studies on causal strength estimations, little is known about the interplay between inference goals and task factors in determining how people estimate causal strength.

### Causal Mechanisms, Processes, and Forces

The theories we have discussed so far are all variants of theories that view causes as difference makers. In probabilistic theories, causes change the probability of the effect; counterfactual and logical theories compare the hypothetical or actual absence of the cause with its presence (Dowe, 2000). These accounts can be contrasted with mechanistic *process theories*, which focus on processes and mechanisms initiated by causal events. A popular recent philosophical example of such a theory was developed by Dowe (2000), who characterized causal processes in terms of the transmission of a *conserved quantity*, such as linear momentum or charge. This theory can be applied to physical processes, but it is less clear how such an account would model other domains (e.g., economy). Moreover, it seems unlikely that people who are not scientists know much about conserved quantities. A more general account, which has also

been adopted in psychology, is expressed in theories that focus on the *mechanisms* relating causes and effects (e.g., Machamer, Darden, & Craver, 2000).

### Mechanisms and Covariation

Although Rozenblit and Keil (2002) have shown that people have little knowledge about the mechanisms underlying artifacts from everyday life, it still seems plausible that mechanism information is considered important when it is available. Most of us certainly believe that causes are connected with effects by some mechanism, even when we do not really care to get to know the details.

A number of studies have investigated how covariation and mechanism information interact. Knowledge about potential causal mechanisms typically increases estimates of perceived correlations relative to the objective covariations in the data (Koslowski, 1996)—even when the covariation is zero (Chapman & Chapman, 1967, 1969). Ahn, Kalish, Medin, and Gelman (1995) employed an information search paradigm to pit mechanism against covariation information. In their experiments participants were confronted with various positive and negative fictitious facts, such as the promotion of Mary last year. Participants were requested to ask further questions that would help them to find out which causal factor is responsible for the target event. The general finding of this study was that participants were more interested in potential mechanisms than covariation. For example, participants were more interested in whether Mary did something special that would motivate her raise, rather than information about how many of her colleagues also got raises.

Fugelsang and Thompson (2003) proposed a dual-process theory which claims that causal judgments are influenced by two independent sources: covariation information and mechanism knowledge. The results were not entirely conclusive (see Perales, Shanks, & Lagnado, 2010), but the authors interpret their findings as showing that new data are weighted more heavily in causality judgments when there is a plausible mechanism than when the mechanism is implausible. In contrast, new covariation data are simply combined with information about covariation in the past, regardless of whether the new and old covariation match or mismatch.

All these studies show that people care for mechanism information. However, pitting mechanisms against covariation does not reflect the current state of the field anymore. The previous sections have shown that modern theories of probabilistic causation no longer claim that causation can be reduced to covariation. Covariation is rather an empirical indicator of causal relations, which is especially important in situations in which we do not have prior knowledge and need to induce causal knowledge based on data (see Cheng, 1993). This view is certainly consistent with the findings that knowledge about mechanisms, which might have been induced in previous learning contexts, may influence current judgments. It also makes sense to weigh well-established knowledge more than current data, which is typically noisy and due to its typically small sample size not very reliable.

Moreover, covariation assessment itself is intrinsically linked to mechanism knowledge. If people observe a continuous sequence of events, the number of possible covariations that could be computed clearly surpasses their information processing capacity. Mechanism knowledge can place constraints on the events we consider for covariation assessments. If we suddenly experience nausea, we may hypothesize a drug we ingested 2 hours ago as the cause but not a food item we ate 1 minute ago, or various other irrelevant events. A number of studies have shown that people use their knowledge about typical temporal delays of different mechanisms when making covariation assessments (Buehner & May, 2002, 2003; Buehner, 2005; Greville & Buehner, 2007, 2010; Hagmayer & Waldmann, 2002).

Another reason why mechanism and covariation theories need not be seen as competitors anymore is that the focus on single cause-effect relations has been replaced by a greater interest in other causal models, such as causal chains (see section on "Reasoning With Causal Models"). Within probabilistic theories, mechanisms can be modeled as causal chains in which multiple events form a sequence (see Fig. 46.2c). When knowledge about the potential alternative causal explanations is already available, it seems reasonable to ask for information about the chaining of causal relations, rather than for contrast information that is already known. For example, in

the study of Ahn et al. (1995) participants probably already knew possible causes for salary raises, and therefore needed information that allows them to decide between possible alternative explanations.

### Causal Forces

So far we have discussed theories that postulate causal relations between classes of events, for example, between smoking and lung disease. However, we can also ask about the actual cause in a specific situation (i.e., singular causation), for example, whether the lung disease Peter contracted last year was due to his smoking, exposure to asbestos, or some other cause. According to probabilistic theories, both levels are clearly related; we need generic-level knowledge to answer questions about actual causes, but nevertheless both levels need to be separated. Thus, although in Peter's case we only have observed the presence of smoking and lung disease, which by itself does not ensure a causal relation, smoking is a candidate for his lung disease because we know that in the reference class to which Peter belongs smoking and lung disease are causally related (see Pearl, 2000).

However, there is an alternative view: Some psychologists have argued that the specific level in which no covariation information is available is the primary level, and that we derive generic-level conclusions from collections of specific, singular cases. An example of such an approach is force theories which assume that people represent singular causal events as generated by hidden forces. Whereas philosophical theories of mechanisms and processes try to model causation in terms of normative scientific theories, the forces postulated by the psychological theories bear more similarity to Aristotelian medieval impetus theories (McCloskey, 1983) than to modern Newtonian physics.

White (2006, 2009) uses Michotte-type launching events to demonstrate the difference between intuitive causal representations and physics (see also White, 2005). In Michotte's (1963) famous demonstrations of phenomenal causality, participants observed moving objects. For example, in a launching scenario, Object A moves toward Object B and touches it. This stops Object A and sets Object B into motion at the same or a slightly lesser speed. Observers typically describe this scenario as a case in which the movement of Object B is caused by Object A (i.e., launching). Although according to Newtonian physics the force on body B exerted by body A is equal in magnitude but opposite in direction to that on body A exerted by

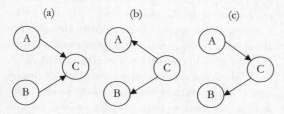

**Figure 46.2** Basic causal models with three causal variables, (*a*) common effect, (*b*) common cause, and (*c*) causal chain model.

**Table 46.1** Force Dynamic Analysis of the Meaning of Causal Concepts

|  | Patient Tendency for End State | Affector-Patient Concordance | End State Approached |
|---|---|---|---|
| Cause | No | No | Yes |
| Allow (enable) | Yes | Yes | Yes |
| Prevent | Yes | No | No |

body B, observers often see Object A as the cause and Object B as the effect (causal asymmetry). Nobody would describe the scenario as a case of Object B stopping Object A, although this would be a legitimate description.

The impression of causal asymmetry is also reflected in judgments about force. White (2009) presented participants with different launching events and asked them to provide estimates of the relevant underlying forces. The results showed that in such events more force is attributed to Object A than Object B, and that Object A is viewed as active and exerting a *force* on Object B, whereas the initially stationary Object B is viewed as inactive, exerting *resistance* to being moved. Thus, causal interactions are perceived as the result of the opposition between forces of agents (e.g., Object A) and resistance of patients (e.g., Object B). Within White's theory, force and resistance are theoretical concepts that need to be estimated based on observable data. White (2009) shows that different observable kinematic features, such as the velocity of objects before and after contact, are the basis for force and resistance attributions.

How can the impression of causal asymmetry be explained? In developmental psychology the hypothesis is popular that force attributions in launching scenarios may be due to an innate module specialized for causal analysis (see Carey, 2009; Leslie & Keeble, 1987). White (2009) disagrees and proposes the theory that our haptically experienced actions are the primary sources of intuitions about force and resistance. When we manipulate objects we experience the required force, and take into account properties of the objects, which are experienced as resistance. These sensorimotoric schemas are used to make sense of analogous causal interactions, which we only passively observe (see also White, 2012).

White's (2009) theory is restricted to launching and similar events. A more general theory that aims at elucidating our understanding of abstract causal concepts, such as *cause*, *prevent*, and *enable*, is Wolff's (2007) theory of *force dynamics* (see also Talmy, 1988; Wolff & Song, 2003). Wolff (2007) also focuses on specific causal events but studies a wide range of scenarios from different domains. As in the theories of White (2009) and Talmy (1988), two entities are distinguished, which Wolff calls affectors and patients (i.e., the entity acted upon by the affector). Force theory states that people evaluate configurations of forces attached to affectors and patients, which may vary in direction and degree, with respect to an end state, that is, the possible result. Forces can be physical, psychological (e.g., intentions), or social (e.g., peer pressure). Causal relations are analyzed in terms of three components, (a) the tendency of a patient for an end state, (b) the presence or absence of concordance between affector and patient, and (c) the degree to which the end state is reached. Table 46.1 summarizes the predictions for how people use the concepts *cause*, *prevent*, and *allow* (*enable*).

For example, force theory would represent the singular causal fact "Winds caused the boat to heel" in terms of a patient (the boat) that had no tendency to heel (Tendency = No), the affector (the wind) acted against the patient (Concordance = No), and the result (heeling) occurred (End state approached = Yes). In contrast, "Vitamin B allowed the body to digest" describes a scenario in which the patient (body) already has a tendency toward the end state (digest), which is reached in accordance with the affector (vitamin B). Preventing, in contrast, refers to cases in which an affector exerts a force that counteracts the tendency of a patient toward an end state (e.g., "Wind prevented the boat from reaching the harbor").

Empirical support for the model was provided in a series of experiments in which participants made judgments about three-dimensional animations of realistically rendered objects (e.g., moving boats on a lake) with trajectories that were wholly determined by the force vectors entered into a physics simulator. For example, participants were asked to judge whether they are viewing a case of *cause*, *enable*, or *prevent* (see Lombrozo, 2010; Wolff, Barbey, & Hausknecht, 2010, for further developments).

Force theories represent an important novel class of theories which highlight aspects of causality that have largely been neglected in previous theories. Causes have mostly been viewed as entities that make a difference with respect to their effects, but little is said about how they make a difference, and why a specific functional form is observed between causes and effects. Force theories also point to the importance of empirical indicators of causation beyond (or instead of) covariation (e.g., velocity). However, research on force theories is still in the beginning stage so that a number of questions remain unanswered. For example, it is unclear how general these theories are. Wolff (2007) thinks that force theories can replace other theories, but at this point it is not clear whether they can successfully model all kinds of causal relation. The model is very convincing in cases of perceptions of cases of singular causation (e.g., moving objects) in which attributions of forces and end states seem natural, but it is less clear whether all causal relations, especially generic ones, are also represented this way. Do we represent causal claims such as "social status influences success" or "interest rates influence spending" in terms of forces and resistance, or forces and end states? Although this may be the case, there is no direct empirical evidence for such a claim. Sloman, Barbey, and Hotaling (2009) have proposed a successful causal model theory of cause, enable, and prevent that does not contain references to forces and tendencies (see also Cheng & Novick, 1991).

Force theories have tried to separate themselves from theories that use covariation as input to causal power assessments. However, it seems implausible to generally dismiss this information. For example, it seems unlikely that people would make force attributions when considering the claim "Vitamin B allowed the body to digest" (Wolff, 2007), when there is no prior covariational knowledge that supports vitamins as potential causal agents. Covariation information allows people to infer causal relations between variables even when no cues relevant for phenomenal causality are present. Schlottmann and Shanks (1992), for example, showed that people can use correlations between color change cues and movements to judge an underlying causal relation, although color changes did not lead to the perception of phenomenal causality.

## Reasoning With Causal Models

Force and mechanism theories have so far primarily been applied to singular causal relations and do not address the question of how notions of forces and mechanisms can be related to covariation information. Causal model representations provide tools to integrate basic intuitions about causal relations with inference and learning methods. A further advantage of causal models is that they can be applied to complex networks of causes and effects, thus overcoming the restrictive focus on individual causal relations.

Networks of cause-effect relations lend themselves to graphical representations, which have been introduced in philosophy (Reichenbach, 1956) and further developed to Bayes net or causal Bayes net theory in both philosophy and Artificial Intelligence (e.g., Pearl, 1988, 2000; Spirtes, Glymour, & Scheines, 1993; see Koller & Friedman, 2009, for a recent textbook). Although Bayes nets have primarily been developed as a practical tool for automated inference and data mining, they have also inspired psychological research (see Gopnik et al., 2004; Sloman, 2005, for overviews). Causal Bayes net theory is not a unified theory but integrates various more specific tools, which are not meant to be plausible as psychological theories. Moreover, a number of formal assumptions are controversial as psychological claims. Therefore, we will use the more neutral term *causal model* in the following discussion except when discussing the specific assumptions underlying causal Bayes nets.

Figure 46.2 shows examples of causal models with three events. In general, causal models include variables that represent causes and effects along with arrows representing direct causal relations. These graphical representations of the structure of the causal models provide useful information about conditional dependence and independence relations. Assuming the *Markov* condition, which states that each variable, conditional upon its direct causes, is independent of all other variables except its direct and indirect effects, the common cause model in Figure 46.2b implies, for example, that effects A and B of the common cause C are correlated but become independent conditional upon their cause. Similarly, in the causal chain model (Fig. 46.2c) the final effect B is correlated with the initial cause A and the intermediate cause C but becomes independent from the initial cause A when the intermediate cause C is kept constant. Finally, the common effect model (Fig. 46.2a) implies that the causes A and B are marginally independent from each other but become dependent once the state of the effect C is known. This feature of common effect models explains the familiar notion of *explaining away* or *discounting*. For example, once we know that we have nausea due to contaminated food, other potential causes, such as an infection, become less probable.

Apart from structure information, causal models also contain parameters that can be estimated based on learning data. These parameters (e.g., $w_c$ in Fig. 46.1) quantify estimates of causal power of generative or preventive causes, and assumptions about the way multiple causes are integrated (e.g., linear additive integration by noisy-OR). Causal models can be learned, and they can support predictive inferences from causes to effects, or diagnostic inferences from effects to causes. The following sections will give an overview of the most important psychological findings motivated by causal model theories.

### Causal Arrows

One of the most fundamental properties setting causal relations apart from mere covariations is the directionality of the causal arrow. Regardless of the order in which causal events are experienced, causal relations are directed from causes to their effects. Causes generate their effects but not vice versa, which can be explained by the unidirectionality of the underlying mechanism.

Waldmann and Holyoak (1992; Waldmann, Holyoak, & Fratianne, 1995) introduced *causal model theory* in cognitive psychology, hypothesizing that learners use abstract causal knowledge about causal networks guiding their processing of the learning input. The general idea of their experimental paradigm was to present participants in different learning conditions with identical covarying events but manipulate subjects' assumptions about which events represent causes and which effects (see also the section on "Associative Theories"). For example, Waldmann (2000, 2001) presented learners first with cues that represented substances in hypothetical patients' blood and then gave feedback about fictitious blood diseases. Two conditions manipulated—through initial instructions—whether learners interpreted the substances as effects of the diseases (common cause model) or as causes (common effect model). Thus, learners represented identical cues either as causes that they used to predict a common effect (i.e., predictive learning) or as effects to diagnose a common cause (i.e., diagnostic learning). In the test phase, learners were asked to estimate the

strength of the relation between substances and disease. The results showed that causal models guided how the learning input was processed. Learners treated the substances as potentially competing explanations of the disease in the common effect condition, whereas the substances were treated as collateral correlated evidence of a common cause in the contrasting condition. Consequently, effects conforming to patterns entailed by cue competition (e.g., blocking) resulted only when the cues represented causes but not effects. These findings demonstrate that people do not simply associate cues with outcomes but represent the learning events within causal model structures.

Further evidence for sensitivity to the direction of the causal arrow comes from a *semantic memory* study by Fenker, Waldmann, and Holyoak (2005). Questions referring to the existence of a causal relation between events described by a pair of words (e.g., spark-fire) were answered faster when the first word of a pair of words referred to a cause and the second word to its effect than vice versa (i.e., fire-spark). No such asymmetry was observed, however, with questions referring to the associative relation between the two words.

Evidence for the asymmetry of causes and effects can also be found in research on *inductive reasoning* about properties. For example, undergraduates are more likely to infer that "lions have enzyme X" from the premise "gazelles have enzyme X" than vice versa because their knowledge about food chains makes it easier for them to imagine the transmission from gazelles to lions than the other way around (Medin, Coley, Storms, & Hayes, 2003).

Finally, Ahn and colleagues, using category membership judgments, have demonstrated that causes often carry more weight than effects in causal *categories* (causal status effect). For example, in Ahn, Kim, Lassaline, and Dennis (2000) participants were instructed about artificial animal categories that were described as possessing three features: eats fruit (X), has sticky feet (Y), and builds nests on trees (Z), which are causally linked within a chain ($X \rightarrow Y \rightarrow Z$). When presented with items in which one feature was missing, subjects showed that they found the item least likely to be a member of the category when X was missing and most likely when only Z was missing (see also Kim & Ahn, 2002, for examples from clinical psychology). The theoretical source and generality of these findings is currently under debate. Rehder and Kim (2006) have questioned the generality of the causal status effect and have shown that a common effect of multiple alternative causes may receive more weight than either of its causes. At any rate, this set of findings does provide additional evidence for the psychological difference between cause and effect representations.

### Causal Structure

One of the main strengths of causal model theories is that they do not only focus on models in which one or more causes converge on a common effect but also on more complex causal models. One key advantage of causal model representation is their parsimony. Only direct causal relations are represented, whereas covariations between indirectly linked events can be computed from the causal model, based on information about the strengths of the direct relations and the structure of the model. A number of studies have investigated whether people are capable of deriving predictions for indirect relations.

For example, Waldmann et al. (1995) have used a *learning* paradigm in which participants were presented with multiple cues that were either described as causes of an effect (common effect model) or as effects of a single cause (common cause model). For example, in one experiment the task was to learn to classify stones as magnetic or nonmagnetic based on the spatial orientation of surrounding iron compounds. In the common effect condition, the iron compounds were described as potential causes of the stones being magnetic, whereas in the common cause condition the magnets were characterized as influencing the spatial orientation of the surrounding iron compounds. Learning difficulty was assessed by measuring the mean number of errors until a criterion was reached. Across different conditions, it was manipulated whether the cues were correlated or independent. The findings showed that participants in the common cause condition learned faster to predict the outcome when the cues were correlated, whereas independent cues yielded faster learning with the common effect model. This finding is consistent with the fact that common cause models entail correlations between their effects, whereas the default assumption of common effect models is that the causes are independent.

Rehder and colleagues have presented a number of studies showing sensitivity to structural implications of causal models in *categorization* tasks. For example, Rehder (2003a, 2003b) presented subjects with fictitious categories of stars (e.g., Myastars) that had five different binary features (e.g., ionized helium, very hot, high density, etc.), which

varied between abnormal and normal values (see also Rehder & Hastie, 2001). Additionally, instructions about the causal model connecting these features were provided (common cause model; chain; common effect model). Then different exemplars with different feature configurations were presented along with the task to rate the degree of category membership (i.e., typicality). One important finding was that subjects rated exemplars as more typical that were consistent with the structural implications of the instructed causal model (coherence effect). For example, subjects expected that in causal chains or common cause models it is very likely that either all features are normal or all abnormal. Thus, subjects expected correlations between indirectly linked events, which is in line with the structural implications of causal models (see also Rehder & Kim, 2006, for more complex causal models).

Sensitivity to the structure of the underlying causal model has also been demonstrated in *inductive inference* tasks (see Rehder, 2009; Rehder & Hastie, 2001). Rehder (2009) used his paradigm in which subjects were informed about fictitious categories with multiple features, for example, Romanian Rogos (a type of automobile). After learning about Rogos, participants in one of the experiments were presented with a series of trials in which they were told about one novel feature, for example, a zinc-laden tank. When subjects were subsequently asked how prevalent the new feature probably was within the category of Rogos, they gave higher ratings when it was causally linked to a common feature than to a rare feature. Thus, subjects used causal knowledge to make inductive inferences about the generality of novel properties.

### Observing Versus Intervening

One of the key differences between causal models and probabilistic or associative models is that they support inferences about the consequences of actions. Probabilistic or associative models tell us how variables are correlated, but they do not distinguish between noncausal (i.e., spurious) and causal correlations. Interventions in a cause lead to its effects, but these effects cannot be generated by an intervention in a spurious correlate. For example, barometers are spuriously correlated with weather and therefore can be used to predict the weather. However, tampering with the barometer does not change the weather because they are not causes of the weather. Thus, causal representations are crucial for correct predictions of the consequences of actions. Another feature of interventions, which is captured by causal Bayes net theories, is the fact that interventions, which deterministically and independently change the states of a target variable, remove all causal influences on the variable that is the target of the intervention. If we tamper with the barometer, then its reading is solely influenced by our manipulation but not by its usual cause, atmospheric pressure (Pearl, 2000; Spirtes et al., 1993; Woodward, 2003). Hence, causal Bayes nets model interventions in variables as a removal of all causal arrows that normally influence this variable ("graph surgery"; see also Waldmann, Cheng, Hagmayer, & Blaisdell, 2008, for an explanation of interventions in terms of discounting and explaining away).

Do people distinguish between observations and interventions as causal Bayes nets predict? Research indicates that they do (see Hagmayer, Sloman, Lagnado, & Waldmann, 2007, for an overview). Sloman and Lagnado (2005) studied reasoning about a number of causal models and interventions that removed individual events. For example, participants were told that "When A happens, it causes B most of the time; when B happens, it causes C most of the time; A is present and C is present." Then they were asked either to imagine that B was observed to be absent or to imagine that B was actively prevented from occurring. In both cases participants were requested to draw inferences about A and C. Subjects generally predicted the absence of C, but they predicted the absence of A only when the absence of B was observed but not when it was removed by an intervention ("undoing"). Thus, subjects had the intuition that the cause of B is unaffected if B is actively removed. Probabilistic theories or theories of propositional logical reasoning including mental model theory do not predict this finding.

Waldmann and Hagmayer (2005) showed that people also distinguish between observations and interventions when subjects receive both instructions about the structure of the underlying causal model and *learning* data about probabilistic relations between causal events (i.e., covariations). The study demonstrates that people use the learning data to infer the parameters of the underlying causal model and are able to use the parameterized causal model to derive estimates about the probabilities resulting from hypothetical interventions and observations. These findings have been confirmed for more complicated models involving confounding causal pathways and a broader variety of learning procedures and species (Blaisdell, Sawa, Leising, & Waldmann, 2006; Blaisdell & Waldmann, 2012; Leising, Wong,

Waldmann, & Blaisdell, 2008; Meder, Hagmayer, & Waldmann, 2008, 2009).

It is particularly important to distinguish between interventional and observational probabilities when we make *choices*. When we decide which action to take, it is the interventional probabilities that matter, and not simply the observed probabilities (Joyce, 1999). Hagmayer and Sloman (2009) examined the question whether subjects use interventional probabilities in decision making. For example, participants were told that men who do the chores are substantially more likely to be in good health than men who do not. In addition, participants were provided with causal explanations for this fact. Participants in one group were informed that the relation is due to a common cause (degree of concern) that causes men to help at home and to care about their health. Another group was told that doing the chores is a form of exercise that positively affects health. Participants were sensitive to the causal structure underlying the probabilistic relation and preferred to start doing the chores when there was a direct causal link. Moreover, participants differentiated between an action that was merely observed versus an action that was actively chosen in their estimates of the probability of the desired outcome. Only choices were treated as hypothetical interventions within a causal Bayes net.

The difference between observations and interventions is not only important in reasoning and decision making, but it can also aid learning. Interventions often allow us to discriminate between alternative causal models. For example, a correlation between bacteria and ulcer does not tell us whether bacteria cause ulcer or whether there is a common cause of both. An intervention (e.g., removing the bacteria) can tell us whether bacteria are the cause. A number of studies have shown that learners can use interventions to aid their learning (Gopnik et al., 2004; Lagnado & Sloman, 2004; Steyvers, Tenenbaum, Wagenmakers, & Blum, 2003).

Most of the research on the difference between hypothetical interventions and observations is motivated by the view that interventions completely remove prior causal influences on the variable that is being manipulated (i.e., graph surgery). More recently, it has been pointed out that other types of interventions are conceivable that do not have this property (Meder, Gerstenberg, Hagmayer, & Waldmann, 2010; Rips, 2010). Interventions may alter the state of the manipulated variable without completely removing prior influences. Moreover, interventions need not necessarily be independent of the variables in the manipulated system.

## Knowledge-Based Causal Induction

Many Bayes net researchers in computer science have focused on the development of statistical tools for scientific research that require minimal prior knowledge. An example of a learning method that uses minimal knowledge is *constraint-based algorithms*, which allow us to induce causal structures on the basis of the patterns of statistical dependency within a set of variables (Pearl, 1988, 2000; Spirtes et al., 1993). A second approach to structure learning is framing the task in terms of Bayesian inference. In this approach the learner must determine the likelihood of a structure hypothesis given data. To achieve generality, all possible structures along with minimal assumptions about the parameters are being considered in these statistical theories. Both approaches make few assumptions about the domain and therefore need vast amounts of reliable data to accomplish their goal.

In psychology there has been a debate whether these algorithms are plausible models of human learning (see Gopnik et al., 2004; Griffiths & Tenenbaum, 2009). The high data demands of the Bayes net algorithms cast doubt on the psychological plausibility of these models given that people often successfully acquire causal knowledge on the basis of very few learning trials. Empirical studies confronting subjects with the task to induce causal models based on covariation data alone have generally shown poor performance with observational data, although these studies typically presented a small number of variables along with information about a limited number of alternative models to be considered (Steyvers et al., 2003). A number of studies have shown that allowing subjects to intervene helps (Gopnik et al., 2004; Steyvers et al., 2003). Kushnir, Gopnik, Lucas, and Schulz (2010) could even show that people can induce hidden causes when people received information about salient (deterministic) covariations. In sum, there is some evidence that people can use covariation information to induce causal structures, but performance is poor unless learning conditions are favorable.

The implausibility of domain-general algorithms of structure induction has led Waldmann (1996) to propose the view that people generally use prior knowledge about the structure of causal models to guide learning in a top-down fashion ("knowledge-based causal induction"; see also Lagnado, Waldmann, Hagmayer, & Sloman,

2007). People use various cues that guide their initial hypotheses about causal structure, including temporal order, interventions, and prior knowledge. Temporal order is a potent cue to causal order (causes typically precede their effects). Prior knowledge may, however, override the temporal cue. For example, a physician may see the symptom of herpes (i.e., effect information) before test results about the cause come in but can nevertheless form the correct causal hypothesis that a herpes virus has caused the observed lesions and not vice versa. Numerous studies have shown that people can disentangle temporal from causal order (see Waldmann et al., 2006). Interventions are a further potent cue that allows us to distinguish causes from effects. Inducing causal structures based on cues simplifies the learning of causal strength parameters because learners may now focus on individual links rather than encoding patterns of dependency (see Fernbach & Sloman, 2009; Waldmann et al., 2008).

Assumptions about integration rules underlying multiple causes (i.e., functional form) also provide knowledge-based constraints on learning. Instead of considering large numbers of possible parameterizations as in Bayesian structure learning, the task may be simplified by considering only plausible default rules (see Griffiths & Tenenbaum, 2009). A typical default assumption underlying common effect models with several generative causes is that the multiple causes independently influence their effect (noisy-OR schema; see Cheng, 1997; Griffiths & Tenenbaum, 2005; Lu et al., 2008).

Although independent causal influences may be the default assumption, multiple causes can also interact (see Novick & Cheng, 2004). Interactions require more complex representations because the causal influence of a configuration of multiple causes cannot be reduced to a function of the individual causes. Empirical work on interactions and integration rules has only just begun. One factor influencing assumptions about integration rules is prior learning. Beckers et al. (2005) and Lucas and Griffiths (2010) have shown that people can transfer nonadditive integration rules from a previous learning context to the present task (see also Shanks & Darby, 1998).

Another factor influencing the choice of integration rules is domain knowledge. Waldmann (1996, 2007) presented subjects with colored liquids that potentially affected the heart rate when consumed. Different conditions showed that subjects tended to add the individual influences when the liquids were introduced as drugs with different *strengths*.

However, subjects averaged the influences when they believed that the heart rate is dependent on the *taste* of the liquids. Here domain knowledge about the different properties of extensive and intensive physical quantities determined the integration rule.

Griffiths and Tenenbaum (2007, 2009) have proposed *hierarchical* Bayesian inference to model knowledge-based (or theory-based) causal induction. The basic idea is that probabilistic inference is carried out at multiple levels of abstraction which influence each other and are updated simultaneously. In causal learning these levels include the data, alternative causal models, and the theory level, which encodes knowledge about the types of events (e.g., causes vs. effects), the plausibility of a causal relationship, and the functional form of these relationships (e.g., noisy-OR). In the hierarchical probabilistic model, the theory level at the top defines a probability distribution over causal model hypotheses, as each hypothesis defines a probability distribution over data. These different levels are then updated based on the data using the basic Bayes's rule (see Equation 5). Hierarchical Bayesian models speed up learning because the range of alternative hypotheses being considered is constrained by both the data and the theory level. Moreover, updating occurs on each level so that it is not necessary to assume fixed innate knowledge. Biases encoded on the theory level can be changed when the data disconfirm them. Finally, hierarchical models have the advantage of being able to generalize to new contexts. In a specific learning context both specific causal model knowledge and abstract theory knowledge are being updated. This abstract knowledge can, in turn, influence learning in novel domains and thereby explain transfer effects (Lucas & Griffiths, 2010).

## Summary

Causal models provide a fruitful framework for modeling reasoning and learning in causal domains. They overcome the traditional restrictive focus on single cause effect relations and have motivated studies on more complex causal scenarios. Moreover, the simultaneous development of causal model theory in both computer sciences and psychology has proven mutually fruitful, although it turned out that not all developments in engineering yield plausible psychological theories. Causal model theories go beyond traditional noncausal theories in that both the postulated representation and the inference and learning mechanisms are causally motivated. Causal models embody information about the structural difference between causes and effects, interventions and observations, and combine causal structure information with parameters reflecting causal power. Moreover, hierarchical knowledge-based theories allow for the integration of abstract theoretical knowledge with the processing of covariation information.

Unlike, for example, force theories, causal models provide an integrated computational mechanism that connects mechanism knowledge with covariation information. However, thus far only very basic information about mechanisms is expressed in causal models. The asymmetry of causal relations is encoded in arrows, which Pearl (2000) has interpreted as "mechanism placeholders." Prior knowledge about causal interactions is being encoded in parameters reflecting functional form and integration rules. Although these are certainly important steps in the direction of encoding mechanism knowledge, mechanism and force theories suggest that we have deeper intuitions about underlying mechanisms which may also need to be expressed in causal model theories. Moreover, singular causation, the main focus of force theories, has been neglected by causal model theories, although there are some attempts to model singular causation (Cheng, 1993; Griffiths & Tenenbaum, 2009; Sloman et al., 2009).

There are also findings that are critical for causal model theories. Empirical evidence for the insufficiency of simple causal models comes from a study by Rehder and Burnett (2005), who have developed a reasoning task that allowed for testing people's intuitions about the Markov condition, which is arguably the most fundamental feature of Bayes nets. In their experiments, subjects had to rate the conditional probability of an effect's presence given the state of its cause C. The crucial manipulation was whether other effects of C were present or absent (i.e., common cause model). According to the Markov condition, participants' ratings should be invariant across these conditions. The probability of each effect should be only dependent on its cause, not the states of the other effects of this cause, which are screened off by this cause. Contrary to this prediction, the ratings were clearly sensitive to the states of other effects of C. The more collateral effects were present, the higher were the ratings of the conditional probability of the target effect given the presence of C. This apparent Markov violation was extremely robust across many cover stories and domains.

One possible explanation of this finding is that people bring to bear additional assumptions about hidden causal events and mechanisms. Possibly the absence of the collateral effects of the target cause led subjects to infer that something was wrong with the underlying mechanism, hence their uncertainty about the target effect. Although such knowledge can be modeled within Bayesian causal models when they are augmented with hidden variables and mechanisms (Rehder & Burnett, 2005), the robustness of the finding indicates that the usually postulated minimal versions of causal models (e.g., Fig. 46.2) do not sufficiently capture our causal intuitions.

## General Summary and Perspectives for Research

Our overview of research on causal reasoning has demonstrated how much progress has been made in this field in the past two decades. Not long ago theories of causal reasoning dominated that tried to get away with subsuming causal reasoning as a special case of more general theories of reasoning, thus ignoring the unique features of causality. In these theories causal reasoning has been viewed as a special case of associative, logical, or probabilistic reasoning with minimal constraints coming from causal notions. Although domain-general reasoning certainly plays a role in causal domains, it has been shown that these theories fail to capture truly causal reasoning. People are sensitive to various aspects of causality, including the directionality of the causal arrow, the structure of causal models, causal power, or forces and mechanisms, and this sensitivity needs to be an integral part of theories of causal reasoning. The present review has discussed a number of recent theories that capture the unique features of causality.

We only could touch upon a subset of studies on causal learning and reasoning. An increasing number of studies are interested in the relationship of causal reasoning with other cognitive tasks, including diagnostic reasoning (Fernbach, Darlow, & Sloman, 2011; Krynski & Tenenbaum, 2007; Meder, Mayrhofer, & Waldmann, 2009), legal reasoning (Lagnado & Harvey, 2008), scientific explanations (Lombrozo, 2007, 2010), decision making (Hagmayer & Sloman, 2009; Hagmayer & Meder, 2012), or analogical problem solving (Holyoak, Lee, & Lu, 2010; Lee & Holyoak, 2008). Moreover, the interaction between category learning and causal induction has been an important recent area of research (Kemp, Goodman, & Tenenbaum, 2010; Lien & Cheng, 2000; Marsh & Ahn, 2009; Waldmann & Hagmayer, 2006; Waldmann, Meder, von Sydow, & Hagmayer, 2010).

We have discussed research in the context of different theoretical paradigms, which have precursors in philosophy and Artificial Intelligence. This leads to the obvious question how the different approaches can be unified. Obviously each theoretical paradigm has its pet empirical paradigm for which it works best, whereas other applications are neglected. Currently promising approaches are the attempts to integrate our knowledge about mechanisms with theories that pick up covariation information to induce causal power and causal structures (e.g., causal model theories). However, the postulated mechanism knowledge is currently far more abstract than what force theories, for example, postulate.

The different levels of abstraction in the competing theories may turn out to be a blessing in disguise. It seems highly implausible that people represent causal relations uniformly at the same level of abstraction (e.g., as forces or as abstract causal arrows). Cartwright (2004) has expressed skepticism about the possibility of reducing causal relations to a few abstract concepts or to a uniform theory. Causal knowledge can be represented on an abstract level, which is sufficiently captured by nodes and arrows in a Bayes net (e.g., "IQ influences motivation") or can make very specific references to various mechanisms, which require more detailed representations (e.g., "the sun attracts the planets"; "pistons compress air in the carburetor chamber"). Often, we may not care about mechanisms. If we intervene in a complex system, such as our economy, we are generally only interested in global outcomes rather than the myriad of arbitrary causal processes that govern complex systems. At other times, we spend huge efforts searching for the underlying mechanisms (e.g., the search for the Higgs boson).

One reason for shifting levels of abstraction is that causal explanations are sometimes more stable on the specific process level, sometimes more on the abstract level. For example, when we send off an e-mail, we are fairly sure that the recipient will receive it, although it is unpredictable what path the message will take in the Internet (see also Cartwright, 2001; Lombrozo, 2010). It seems plausible that various factors, including expertise and goals, influence how we choose to represent and use causal knowledge. This flexibility may in part justify why we have so many theories of causal reasoning.

## Acknowledgments

We would like to thank M. Buehner, D. Lagnado, and K. Holyoak for helpful comments.

# References

Ahn, W.-K., Kalish, C. W., Medin, D. L., & Gelman, S. A. (1995). The role of covariation versus mechanism information in causal attribution. *Cognition, 54,* 299–352.

Ahn, W.-K., Kim, N. S., Lassaline, M. E., & Dennis, M. J. (2000). Causal status as a determinant of feature centrality. *Cognitive Psychology, 41,* 361–416.

Allan, L. G. (1993). Human contingency judgment: Rule based or associative? *Psychological Bulletin, 114,* 435–448.

Beckers, T., De Houwer, J., Pineño, O., & Miller, R. R. (2005). Outcome additivity and outcome maximality influence cue competition in human causal learning. *Journal of Experimental Psychology: Learning, Memory, and Cognition, 31,* 238–249.

Blaisdell, A. P., Sawa, K., Leising, K. J., & Waldmann, M. R. (2006). Causal reasoning in rats. *Science, 311,* 1020–1022.

Blaisdell, A. P., & Waldmann, M. R. (2012). Rational rats: Causal inference and representation. In E. Wasserman & T. Zentall (Eds.), *The Oxford handbook of comparative cognition* (pp. 175–198). Oxford: Oxford University Press.

Booth, S. L., & Buehner, M. J. (2007). Asymmetries in cue competition in forward and backward blocking designs: Further evidence for causal model theory. *Quarterly Journal of Experimental Psychology, 60,* 387–399.

Buehner, M. J. (2005). Contiguity and covariation in human causal inference. *Learning and Behavior, 33,* 230–238.

Buehner, M. J., & Cheng, P. W. (2005). Causal learning. In K. J. Holyoak & R. G. Morrison (Eds.), *Cambridge handbook of thinking and reasoning* (pp. 143–168). Cambridge, England: Cambridge University Press.

Buehner, M. J., & May, J. (2002). Knowledge mediates the time-frame of covariation assessment in human causal induction. *Thinking and Reasoning, 8,* 269–295.

Buehner, M. J., & May, J. (2003). Rethinking temporal contiguity and the judgment of causality: Effects of prior knowledge, experience, and reinforcement procedure. *Quarterly Journal of Experimental Psychology, 56A,* 865–890.

Buehner, M. J., Cheng, P. W., & Clifford, D. (2003). From covariation to causation: A test of the assumption of causal power. *Journal of Experimental Psychology: Learning, Memory, and Cognition, 29,* 1119–1140.

Carey, S. (2009). *The origin of concepts.* Oxford, England: Oxford University Press.

Cartwright, N. (1999). *The dappled world. A study of the boundaries of science.* Cambridge, England: Cambridge University Press.

Cartwright, N. (2001). What is wrong with Bayes nets? *The Monist, 84,* 242–264.

Cartwright, N. (2004). Causation: One word, many things. *Philosophy of Science, 71,* 805–819.

Chapman, L. J., & Chapman, J. P. (1967). Genesis of popular but erroneous psychodiagnostic observations. *Journal of Abnormal Psychology, 72,* 193–204.

Chapman, L. J., & Chapman, J. P. (1969). Illusory correlation as an obstacle to the use of valid diagnostic signs. *Journal of Abnormal Psychology, 74,* 271–280.

Chapman, G. B., & Robbins, S. J. (1990). Cue interaction in human contingency judgment. *Memory and Cognition, 18,* 537–545.

Cheng, P. W. (1993). Separating causal laws from casual facts: Pressing the limits of statistical relevance. In D. L. Medin (Ed.), *The psychology of learning and motivation* (Vol. 30, pp. 215–264). New York: Academic Press.

Cheng, P. W. (1997). From covariation to causation: A causal power theory. *Psychological Review, 104,* 367–405.

Cheng, P. W., & Novick, L. R. (1991). Causes versus enabling conditions. *Cognition, 40,* 83–120.

Cheng, P. W., & Novick, L. R. (1992). Covariation in natural causal induction. *Psychological Review, 99,* 365–382.

Cheng, P. W., & Novick, L. R. (2005). Constraints and non-constraints in causal learning: Reply to White (2005) and to Luhmann and Ahn (2005). *Psychological Review, 112,* 694–706.

Cheng, P. W., Novick, L. R., Liljeholm, M., & Ford, C. (2007). Explaining four psychological asymmetries in causal reasoning: Implications of causal assumptions for coherence. In M. O'Rourke (Ed.), *Topics in contemporary philosophy, Vol. 4. Explanation and causation* (pp. 1–32). Cambridge, MA: MIT Press.

Cummins, D. D. (1995). Naïve theories and causal deduction. *Memory and Cognition, 23,* 646–658.

Danks, D. (2003). Equilibria of the Rescorla-Wagner model. *Journal of Mathematical Psychology, 47,* 109–121.

De Houwer, J., & Beckers, T. (2003). Secondary task difficulty modulates forward blocking in human contingency learning. *Quarterly Journal of Experimental Psychology, 56B,* 345–357.

Dowe, P. (2000). *Physical causation.* Cambridge, England: Cambridge University Press.

Fenker, D. B., Waldmann, M. R., & Holyoak, K. J. (2005). Accessing causal relations in semantic memory. *Memory and Cognition, 33,* 1036–1046.

Fernbach, P. M., & Sloman, S. A. (2009). Causal learning with local computations. *Journal of Experimental Psychology: Learning, Memory, and Cognition, 35,* 678–693.

Fernbach, P. M., Darlow, A., & Sloman, S. A. (2011). Asymmetries in predictive and diagnostic reasoning. *Journal of Experimental Psychology: General, 140,* 168–185.

Fugelsang, J., & Thompson, V. (2003). A dual-process model of belief and evidence interactions in causal reasoning. *Memory and Cognition, 31,* 800–815.

Goedert, K. M., Harsch, J., & Spellman, B. A. (2005). Discounting and conditionalization: Dissociable cognitive processes in human causal inference. *Psychological Science, 16,* 590–595.

Goldvarg, E., & Johnson-Laird, P. N. (2001). Naïve causality: A mental model theory of causal meaning and reasoning. *Cognitive Science, 25,* 565–610.

Gopnik, A., Glymour, C., Sobel, D. M., Schulz, L. E., Kushnir, T., & Danks, D. (2004). A theory of causal learning in children: Causal maps and Bayes nets. *Psychological Review, 111,* 1–30.

Gopnik, A., & Schulz, L. E. (Eds.). (2007). *Causal learning: Psychology, philosophy, and computation.* New York: Oxford University Press.

Greville, W. J., & Buehner, M. J. (2007). The influence of temporal distributions on causal induction from tabular data. *Memory and Cognition, 35,* 444–453.

Greville, W. J., & Buehner, M. J. (2010). Temporal predictability facilitates causal learning. *Journal of Experimental Psychology: General, 139,* 756–771.

Griffiths, T. L., & Tenenbaum, J. B. (2005). Structure and strength in causal induction. *Cognitive Psychology, 51,* 354–384.

Griffiths, T. L., & Tenenbaum, J. B. (2007). Two proposals for causal grammars. In A. Gopnik & L. Schulz (Eds.), *Causal learning: Psychology, philosophy, and computation* (pp. 323–346). New York: Oxford University Press.

Griffiths, T. L., & Tenenbaum, J. B. (2009). Theory-based causal induction. *Psychological Review, 116*, 661–716.

Griffiths, T. L., Kemp, C., & Tenenbaum, J. B. (2008). Bayesian models of cognition. In R. Sun (Ed.), *The Cambridge handbook of computational cognitive modeling* (pp. 59–100). Cambridge, England: Cambridge University Press.

Hagmayer, Y., & Meder, B. (2012). Repeated causal decision making. *Journal of Experimental Psychology: Learning, Memory, and Cognition,* June 1, Online First.

Hagmayer, Y., & Sloman, S. A. (2009). Decision makers conceive of their choices as interventions. *Journal of Experimental Psychology: General, 138*, 22–38.

Hagmayer, Y., Sloman, S. A., Lagnado, D. A., & Waldmann, M. R. (2007). Causal reasoning through intervention. In A. Gopnik & L. E. Schulz (Eds.), *Causal learning: Psychology, philosophy, and computation* (pp. 86–100). New York: Oxford University Press.

Hagmayer, Y., & Waldmann, M. R. (2002). How temporal assumptions influence causal judgments. *Memory and Cognition, 30*, 1128–1137.

Hagmayer, Y., & Waldmann, M. R. (2007). Inferences about unobserved causes in human contingency learning. *Quarterly Journal of Experimental Psychology, 60*, 330–355.

Hattori, M., & Oaksford, M. (2007). Adaptive non-interventional heuristics for covariation detection in causal induction: Model comparison and rational analysis. *Cognitive Science, 31*, 765–814.

Holyoak, K. J., & Cheng, P. W. (2011). Causal learning and inference as a rational process: The new synthesis. Annual Review of Psychology, 62, 135–163.

Holyoak, K. J., Lee, H. S., & Lu, H. (2010). Analogical and category-based inference: A theoretical integration with Bayesian causal models. *Journal of Experimental Psychology: General, 139*, 702–727.

Hume, D. (1748/1977). *An enquiry concerning human understanding.* Indianapolis, IN: Hackett.

Jenkins, H. M., & Ward, W. C. (1965). Judgment of contingency between responses and outcomes. *Psychological Monographs, 79.*

Joyce, J. M. (1999). *The foundations of causal decision theory.* Cambridge, England: Cambridge University Press.

Kelley, H. H. (1973). The process of causal attribution. *American Psychologist, 28*, 107–128.

Kemp, C., Goodman, N., & Tenenbaum, J. B. (2010). Learning to learn causal models. *Cognitive Science, 34*, 1185–1243.

Kim, N. S., & Ahn, W. (2002). Clinical psychologists' theory-based representations of mental disorders predict their diagnostic reasoning and memory. *Journal of Experimental Psychology: General, 131*, 451–476.

Koller, D., & Friedman, N. (2009). *Probabilistic graphical models: Principles and techniques.* Cambridge, MA: MIT Press.

Koslowski, B. (1996). *Theory and evidence: The development of scientific reasoning.* Cambridge, MA: MIT Press.

Krynski, T. R., & Tenenbaum, J. B. (2007). The role of causality in judgment under uncertainty. *Journal of Experimental Psychology: General, 136*, 430–450.

Kushnir, T., Gopnik, A., Lucas, C., & Schulz, L. E. (2010). Inferring hidden causal structure. *Cognitive Science, 34*, 148–160.

Lagnado, D. A., & Harvey, N. (2008). The impact of discredited evidence. *Psychonomic Bulletin and Review, 15(6), 1166–1173.*

Lagnado, D. A., & Sloman, S. A. (2004). The advantage of timely intervention. *Journal of Experimental Psychology: Learning, Memory, and Cognition, 30*, 856–876.

Lagnado, D. A., Waldmann, M. R., Hagmayer, Y., & Sloman, S. A. (2007). Beyond covariation. Cues to causal structure. In A. Gopnik & L. E. Schulz (Eds.), *Causal learning: Psychology, philosophy, and computation* (pp. 154–172). New York: Oxford University Press.

Lee, H. S., & Holyoak, K. J. (2008). The role of causal models in analogical inference. *Journal of Experimental Psychology: Learning, Memory, and Cognition, 34*, 1111–1122.

Leising, K. J., Wong, J., Waldmann, M. R., & Blaisdell, A. P. (2008). The special status of actions in causal reasoning in rats. *Journal of Experimental Psychology: General, 137*, 514–527.

Leslie, A. M., & Keeble, S. (1987). Do six-month-old infants perceive causality? *Cognition, 25*, 265–288.

Lien, Y., & Cheng, P. W. (2000). Distinguishing genuine from spurious causes: A coherence hypothesis. *Cognitive Psychology, 40*, 87–137.

Lombrozo, T. (2007). Simplicity and probability in causal explanation. *Cognitive Psychology, 55*, 232–257.

Lombrozo, T. (2010). Causal-explanatory pluralism: How intentions, functions, and mechanisms influence causal ascriptions. *Cognitive Psychology, 61*, 303–332.

López, F. J., Cobos, P. L., & Caño, A. (2005). Associative and causal reasoning accounts of causal induction: Symmetries and asymmetries in predictive and diagnostic inferences. *Memory and Cognition, 33*, 1388–1398.

López, F. J., & Shanks, D. R. (2008). Models of animal learning and their relations to human learning. In R. Sun (Ed.), *Cambridge handbook of computational psychology* (pp. 589–611). Cambridge, England: Cambridge University Press.

Lu, H., Yuille, A. L., Liljeholm, M., Cheng, P. W., & Holyoak, K. J. (2008). Bayesian generic priors for causal learning. *Psychological Review, 115*, 955–982.

Lucas, C. G., & Griffiths, T. L. (2010). Learning the form of causal relationships using hierarchical Bayesian models. *Cognitive Science, 34*, 113–147.

Luhmann, C. C., & Ahn, W. (2007). BUCKLE: A model of unobserved cause learning. *Psychological Review, 114*, 657–677.

Machamer, P., Darden, L., & Craver, C. F. (2000). Thinking about mechanisms. *Philosophy of Science, 67*, 1–25.

Mackay, D. J. C. (2003). *Information theory, inference, and learning algorithms.* Cambridge, England: Cambridge University Press.

Markovits, H., & Potvin, F. (2001). Suppression of valid inferences and knowledge structures: The curious effect of producing alternative antecedents on reasoning with causal conditionals. *Memory and Cognition, 29*, 736–744.

Marsh, J. K., & Ahn, W. (2009). Spontaneous assimilation of continuous values and temporal information in causal induction. *Journal of Experimental Psychology: Learning, Memory, and Cognition, 35*, 334–352.

McCloskey, M. (1983). Naive theories of motion. In D. Gentner & A. L. Stevens (Eds.), *Mental models* (pp. 299–324). Hillsdale, NJ: Erlbaum.

Meder, B., Gerstenberg, T., Hagmayer, Y., & Waldmann, M. R. (2010). Observing and intervening: Rational and heuristic models of causal decision making. *The Open Psychology Journal, 3*, 119–135.

Meder, B., Hagmayer, Y., & Waldmann, M. R. (2008). Inferring interventional predictions from observational learning data. *Psychonomic Bulletin and Review, 15*, 75–80.

Meder, B., Hagmayer, Y., & Waldmann, M. R. (2009). The role of learning data in causal reasoning about observations and interventions. *Memory and Cognition, 37*, 249–264.

Meder, B., Mayrhofer, R., & Waldmann, M. R. (2009). A rational model of elementary diagnostic inference. In N. Taatgen & H. van Rijn (Eds.), *Proceedings of the Thirty-First Annual Conference of the Cognitive Science Society* (pp. 2176–2181). Austin, TX: Cognitive Science Society.

Medin, D. L., Coley, J. D., Storms, G., & Hayes, B. K. (2003). A relevance theory of induction. *Psychonomic Bulletin and Review, 10*, 517–532.

Michotte, A. E. (1963). *The perception of causality.* New York: Basic Books.

Neys, W., Shaeken, W., & d'Ydewalle, G. (2002). Causal conditional reasoning and semantic memory retrieval: A test of the semantic memory framework. *Memory and Cognition, 30*, 908–920.

Neys, W., Shaeken, W., & d'Ydewalle, G. (2003). Causal conditional reasoning and strength of association: The disabling condition case. *European Journal of Cognitive Psychology, 15*, 161–176.

Novick, L. R., & Cheng, P. W. (2004). Assessing interactive causal power. *Psychological Review, 111*, 455–485.

Pearl, J. (1988). *Probabilistic reasoning in intelligent systems: Networks of plausible inference.* San Mateo, CA: Morgan Kaufmann Publishers.

Pearl, J. (2000). *Causality.* Cambridge, England: Cambridge University Press.

Perales, J. C., & Shanks, D. R. (2007). Models of covariation-based causal judgment: A review and synthesis. *Psychonomic Bulletin and Review, 14*, 577–596.

Perales, J. C., Shanks, D. R., & Lagnado, D. (2010). Causal representation and behavior: The integration of mechanism and covariation. *Open Psychology Journal, 3*, 174–183.

Quinn, W. S., & Markovits, H. (1998). Conditional reasoning, causality, and the structure of semantic memory: Strength of association as a predictive factor for content effects. *Cognition, 68*, B93–B101.

Rehder, B. (2003a). A causal-model theory of conceptual representation and categorization. *Journal of Experimental Psychology: Learning, Memory, and Cognition, 29*, 1141–1159.

Rehder, B. (2003b). Categorization as causal reasoning. *Cognitive Science, 27*, 709–748.

Rehder, B. (2009). Causal-based property generalization. *Cognitive Science, 33*, 301–343.

Rehder, B., & Burnett, R. (2005). Feature inference and the causal structure of categories. *Cognitive Psychology, 50*, 264–314.

Rehder, B., & Hastie, R. (2001). Causal knowledge and categories: The effects of causal beliefs on categorization, induction, and similarity. *Journal of Experimental Psychology: General, 130*, 323–360.

Rehder, B., & Kim, S. (2006). How causal knowledge affects classification: A generative theory of categorization. *Journal of Experimental Psychology: Learning, Memory, and Cognition, 32*, 659–683.

Reichenbach, H. (1956). *The direction of time.* Berkeley and Los Angeles: University of California Press.

Rescorla, R. A., & Wagner, A. R. (1972). A theory of Pavlovian conditioning: Variations in the effectiveness of reinforcement and nonreinforcement. In A. H. Black & W. F. Prokasy (Eds.), *Classical conditioning II: Current theory and research* (pp. 64–99). New York: Appleton-Century-Crofts.

Rips, L. J. (2010). Two causal theories of counterfactual conditionals. *Cognitive Science, 34*, 175–221.

Rozenblit, L., & Keil, F. C. (2002). The misunderstood limits of folk science: An illusion of explanatory depth. *Cognitive Science, 26*, 521–562.

Russell, B. (1912/1992). On the notion of cause. In J. Slater (Ed.), *The collected papers of Bertrand Russell, Vol. 6. Logical and philosophical papers* 1909–1913 (pp. 193–210). London: Routledge Press.

Schlottmann, A., & Shanks, D. R. (1992). Evidence for a distinction between judged and perceived causality. *Quarterly Journal of Experimental Psychology: Human Experimental Psychology, 44(A)*, 321–342.

Shanks, D. R. (1985). Forward and backward blocking in human contingency judgment. *Quarterly Journal of Experimental Psychology, 37B*, 1–21.

Shanks, D. R., & Darby, R. J. (1998). Feature- and rule-based generalization in human associative learning. *Journal of Experimental Psychology: Animal Behavior Processes, 24*, 405–415.

Shanks, D. R., & Dickinson, A. (1987). Associative accounts of causality judgment. In G. H. Bower (Ed.), *The psychology of learning and motivation* (Vol. 21, pp. 229–261). San Diego, CA: Academic Press.

Sloman, S. A. (2005). *Causal models: How people think about the world and its alternatives.* New York: Oxford University Press.

Sloman, S. A., Barbey, A. K., & Hotaling, J. (2009). A causal model theory of the meaning of "cause," "enable," and "prevent." *Cognitive Science, 33*, 21–50.

Sloman, S. A., & Lagnado, D. A. (2005). Do we "do"? *Cognitive Science, 29*, 5–39.

Sobel, D. M., Tenenbaum, J. B., & Gopnik, A. (2004). Children's causal inferences from indirect evidence: Backwards blocking and Bayesian reasoning in preschoolers. *Cognitive Science, 28*, 303–333.

Spellman, B. A. (1996). Acting as intuitive scientists: Contingency judgments are made while controlling for alternative potential causes. *Psychological Science, 7*, 337–342.

Spirtes, P., Glymour, C., & Scheines, P. (1993). *Causation, prediction, and search.* New York: Springer-Verlag.

Steyvers, M., Tenenbaum, J. B., Wagenmakers, E-J., & Blum, B. (2003). Inferring causal networks from observations and interventions. *Cognitive Science, 27*, 453–489.

Talmy, L. (1988). Force dynamics in language and cognition. *Cognitive Science, 12*, 49–100.

Waldmann, M. R. (1996). Knowledge-based causal induction. In D. R. Shanks, K. J. Holyoak & D. L. Medin (Eds.), *The psychology of learning and motivation, Vol. 34. Causal learning* (pp. 47–88). San Diego, CA: Academic Press.

Waldmann, M. R. (2000). Competition among causes but not effects in predictive and diagnostic learning. *Journal of Experimental Psychology: Learning, Memory, and Cognition, 26*, 53–76.

Waldmann, M. R. (2001). Predictive versus diagnostic causal learning: Evidence from an overshadowing paradigm. *Psychological Bulletin and Review, 8*, 600–608.

Waldmann, M. R. (2007). Combining versus analyzing multiple causes: How domain assumptions and task context affect integration rules. *Cognitive Science, 31*, 233–256.

Waldmann, M. R., Cheng, P. W., Hagmayer, Y., & Blaisdell, A. P. (2008). Causal learning in rats and humans: A minimal rational model. In N. Chater & M. Oaksford (Eds.), *The probabilistic mind. Prospects for Bayesian cognitive science* (pp. 453–484). Oxford, England: Oxford University Press.

Waldmann, M. R., & Hagmayer, Y. (2001). Estimating causal strength: The role of structural knowledge and processing effort. *Cognition, 82*, 27–58.

Waldmann, M. R., & Hagmayer, Y. (2005). Seeing vs. doing: Two modes of accessing causal knowledge. *Journal of Experimental Psychology: Learning memory and Cognition, 31*, 216–227.

Waldmann, M. R., & Hagmayer, Y. (2006). Categories and causality: The neglected direction. *Cognitive Psychology, 53,* 27–58.

Waldmann, M. R., Hagmayer, Y., & Blaisdell, A. P. (2006). Beyond the information given: Causal models in learning and reasoning. *Current Directions in Psychological Science, 15,* 307–311.

Waldmann, M. R., & Holyoak, K. J. (1992). Predictive and diagnostic learning within causal models: Asymmetries in cue competition. *Journal of Experimental Psychology: General, 121,* 222–236.

Waldmann, M. R., Holyoak, K. J., & Fratianne, A. (1995). Causal models and the acquisition of category structure. *Journal of Experimental Psychology: General, 124,* 181–206.

Waldmann, M. R., Meder, B., von Sydow, M., & Hagmayer, Y. (2010). The tight coupling between category and causal learning. *Cognitive Processing, 11(2), 143–158.*

Waldmann, M. R., & Walker, J. M. (2005). Competence and performance in causal learning. *Learning and Behavior, 33,* 211–229.

White, P. A. (2003). Making causal judgments from contingency information: The pCI rule. *Journal of Experimental Psychology: Learning, Memory, and Cognition, 29,* 710–727.

White, P. A. (2005). Postscript: Differences between the causal powers theory and the power PC theory. *Psychological Review, 112,* 683–684.

White, P. A. (2006). The causal asymmetry. *Psychological Review, 113,* 132–147.

White, P. A. (2009). Perception of forces exerted by objects in collision events. *Psychological Review, 116,* 580–601.

White, P. A. (2012). The experience of force: The role of haptic experience of forces in visual perception of object motion and interactions, mental simulation, and motion-related judgements. *Psychological Bulletin, 138,* 589–615.

Wolff, P. (2007). Representing causation. *Journal of Experimental Psychology: General, 136,* 82–111.

Wolff, P., Barbey, A. K., & Hausknecht, M. (2010). For want of a nail: How absences cause events. *Journal of Experimental Psychology: General, 139,* 191–221

Wolff, P., & Song, G. (2003). Models of causation and the semantics of causal verbs. *Cognitive Psychology, 47,* 276–332.

Woodward, J. (2003). *Making things happen. A theory of causal explanation.* Oxford, England: Oxford University Press.

Wu, M., & Cheng, P. W. (1999). Why causation need not follow from statistical association: Boundary conditions for the evaluation of generative and preventive causal powers. *Psychological Science, 10,* 92–97.

# Moral Thinking

Liane Young

## Abstract

This chapter presents several current models of moral thinking, with a focus on the cognitive processes that support people's moral judgments and justifications. These models are not mutually exclusive; rather, based on recent evidence from psychology and neuroscience, they posit different cognitive processes as the primary source of moral thinking. This chapter therefore does not quantify the evidence for one model versus another but instead reviews evidence for each model separately. These models, discussed in turn, emphasize the role of conscious principled reasoning, emotional processing, theory of mind, and a domain-specific "moral faculty" that integrates information from other cognitive systems to compute specifically moral judgments.

**Key Words:** moral judgment, justification, reason, emotion, theory of mind, moral faculty

The topic of morality has been of interest to philosophers and indeed ordinary people long before cognitive psychologists and neuroscientists took up their tools to investigate the moral mind and brain. Moral thinking as a topic for empirical science is both rewarding and challenging precisely because people—scientists or not—think about moral thinking. What sorts of behaviors are morally right or wrong? How do we make these judgments? Are there right or wrong ways to go about this? Many people find these questions easy to answer simply by introspecting on their own experience, rather than relying on experiments, either scientific experiments, or, in the case of philosophy, thought experiments. In contrast to vision, language, or motor control, morality appears accessible to everyone—not only do we engage in moral thinking, but we also have a few thoughts on how we do so. For some people, moral thinking feels a lot like thinking: It involves thoughtfully considering pros and cons and rationally reflecting on moral principles. For others, moral thinking reduces to moral feeling: Some things feel right, other things feel wrong, and

our emotions help us track important moral distinctions. Some people recognize culture and education as the primary sources of moral thinking; others appeal to an innate sense of right and wrong, an unconscious moral code. Scientists are people too, and so, not surprisingly, the last decade has seen a frenzy of empirical activity as we begin to put many of these intuitions to the test.

In this chapter, I will present several current models of moral thinking, with a particular focus on how we think about and make moral judgments and justify them, rather than how we actually behave because of or in spite of these judgments. I will discuss evidence from cognitive psychology and neuroscience for each of these models, named here for their primary focus: (1) Reason, (2) Emotion, (3) Theory of Mind (i.e., the processing of mental states such as beliefs and intentions), and (4) Moral Faculty. Importantly, these models are not mutually incompatible. For instance, not all Emotion models will deny roles for Reason or Theory of Mind; Emotion models simply emphasize Emotion as the dominant process in moral judgment. Or, in the case of Theory of Mind, both domain-specific (e.g., specific to Theory of Mind) and domain-general processes (e.g., Reason) may contribute to the influence of mental state factors on moral judgment; however, here, we will focus on evidence for the domain-specific contributions. In the following four sections, I will therefore present evidence for the roles of reason, emotion, theory of mind, and a moral faculty in moral thinking.

## Reason: Moral Thinking Is "Thinking"

On a reason model, moral thinking is dominated by "thinking"—of the conscious, controlled sort. In other words, most of the time, for most of moral thinking, people consult explicit moral principles or theories, engage in conscious reasoning, and in general behave as rational agents. People therefore make moral decisions that they would endorse upon reflection, given the important role of reflection in the first place. Developmental psychologists such as Piaget and Kohlberg supported such reason-based models of moral judgment and, as a consequence, identified participants' ability to articulate justifications for their moral judgments as the primary indication of moral maturity (Kohlberg, 1981; Piaget, 1932/1965). The ability to engage in conscious, principled moral reasoning was supposed to track with stages of moral development, since moral judgment was supposed to reflect directly the reasoning that led to it, and not any funny business operating under our conscious radar.

Contemporary moral psychology arose largely in resistance to rationalist or reason-based models of moral judgment (Cushman, Young, & Hauser, 2006; Greene, Sommerville, Nystrom, Darley, & Cohen, 2001; Haidt, Koller, & Dias, 1993). As a result, much of the evidence that follows for moral thinking as "thinking" is indirect and, in fact, falls out of results primarily seen as supporting a different conclusion, that is, moral thinking is moral feeling. That most of the evidence for moral "thinking" is indirect is also notable. At first, it might appear easy to generate evidence for moral "thinking"—after all, if moral thinking is conscious and controlled, then participants should be able to detect and report engaging in moral thinking. However, the question at hand is not whether people ever consult explicit moral principles or theories, but rather whether conscious moral reasoning is the causal source of moral judgment. This question turns out to be more difficult to address—people may report having made particular moral judgments for particular moral reasons; however, based on this report alone,

the experimenter cannot know whether participants generated those reasons post hoc, after the fact, to rationalize or justify their judgments, or whether those reasons did causally determine those judgments. Most of contemporary moral psychology has emphasized the surprising absence of "thinking" in moral thinking, as we will see in the next section. This section, however, serves to show that thinking may play a greater role in moral judgment than has been recently thought—and in surprising contexts—contexts used to show that feeling, not thinking, dominates moral psychology.

The reason model makes two basic predictions. The first is that moral judgments, moral justifications, and, critically, their correspondence are subject to the influence of demographic variables such as education and culture, which partly determine access to, as well as reliance on, reason. In the first of an important line of studies, Jonathan Haidt and his colleagues investigated moral judgment and justification in participants of low and high socio-economic status (SES) from Brazil and Philadelphia (Haidt et al., 1993). Participants were asked to judge not only harmful actions but also harmless actions that nevertheless violated norms of moral purity, such as consensual incest, eating the family dog upon its demise, and other disgusting but victimless transgressions. Contrary to the reason model, the upshot of this and related work is that many participants are unwilling to endorse taboo violations that elicit strong emotional responses even when they are unable to articulate reasons for their judgments—for instance, why incest is morally wrong even in the absence of any physical or psychological harm (Haidt, 2001).

This particular study, however, allows for a closer look, as its title suggests, at affect, culture, and morality (Haidt et al., 1993). Indeed, high SES participants from Philadelphia (described in the study as college students at elite universities), as compared to low SES participants from Brazil, were more likely to endorse harmless actions they found disgusting. By contrast, low SES participants from Brazil continued to judge these taboo violations as morally forbidden even when they were unable to justify their judgments, thereby revealing poor correspondence between their judgments and justifications. These demographic differences in judgments and justifications were also observed to be more pronounced in adults than children. Over time, then, differences in education and culture may lead to differences in the reliance on conscious principled reasoning for moral judgment and perhaps the resistance to moral judgments that appear not to be based on reason. This study therefore suggests that reasoning abilities, as modulated by culture and education, impact moral judgment even in the presence of strong emotions such as disgust.

A related body of research reveals a dissociation between implicit and explicit attitudes toward race and sexual orientation (Banaji, 2001; Inbar, Pizarro, Knobe, & Bloom, 2009). Very liberal college students from Berkeley, for example, appear capable of overriding their negative emotionally mediated implicit attitudes toward gay and interracial sex in order to explicitly endorse gay and interracial sex across a number of behavioral measures (Inbar, Pizarro, Knobe, et al., 2009). Of course, implicit attitudes may constitute moral judgment in some sense, too. However, to the extent that people's explicit moral attitudes, determined in part by culture and education, drive moral judgment and behavior, these findings are consistent with the rational correction of implicit emotionally mediated attitudes.

The second prediction is related to the first: People make moral judgments based on factors that they endorse as morally relevant (e.g., the distinction between harming via action versus omission), and, correspondingly, people are willing to reject moral judgments made on the basis of factors they regard as morally irrelevant (e.g., the distinction between harming via personal contact versus no contact). Research from Fiery Cushman and his colleagues has provided evidence of conscious reasoning from moral principles to moral judgments (Cushman et al., 2006). One such principle, *it is morally worse to harm by action than omission*, was articulated by participants when required to justify their judgments of particular scenarios, in particular, their response that killing a person in one scenario was worse than letting a person die in another scenario. Because participants were able to articulate this general principle, it is at least possible that they consciously reasoned from this principle to their moral judgments; however, the alternative is that they reconstructed this principle post hoc when required to justify their prior judgments. Importantly, against this alternative, participants who were able to articulate this principle in their justifications showed significantly greater use of this principle in their judgments. Meanwhile, when participants in the same study discovered that their moral judgments were governed by a morally dubious principle (e.g., it is morally worse to harm via physical contact than no contact), they disavowed both the principle and their judgments that were based on the principle. Together, these findings indicate an impact of conscious principled reasoning on moral judgments.

Behavioral evidence from Tania Lombrozo also suggests a relationship between general moral commitments and moral judgments of particular scenarios (Lombrozo, 2009). Participants who explicitly endorsed consequentialist moral theories, that is, theories focused on the moral significance of consequences (e.g., the greatest good for the greatest number) were more likely to ignore nonconsequentialist distinctions between scenarios (e.g., physical contact versus no contact) when the scenarios were presented side by side. In fact, as will be discussed in more depth in the next section, an important body of behavioral and neural evidence suggests a direct correspondence between conscious principled reasoning and consequentialist moral judgments (Greene et al., 2001; Koenigs et al., 2007; Valdesolo & DeSteno, 2006). Extensive work by Josh Greene and his colleagues suggests a correlation between consequentialist moral judgments and activity in brain regions for abstract reasoning, such as the dorsolateral prefrontal cortex (DLPFC), as well as slower consequentialist moral judgments under cognitive load (Greene, Morelli, Lowenberg, Nystrom, & Cohen, 2008; Greene, Nystrom, Engell, Darley, & Cohen, 2004).

In all, these results reveal a substantial role for reason in moral judgment—even in the very cases thought to exemplify the emotion model. Reasoning abilities, determined in part by culture and education, may allow us in some instances to override our initial moral attitudes. As rational moral agents, we may be able to make judgments based on principles and theories that we explicitly endorse and invoke when justifying our judgments. As we will see in the next section, though, not all moral judgments arise from conscious, principled reasoning. Much of moral thinking may be emotionally mediated and immune to conscious correction.

### Emotion: Moral Thinking Is Moral Feeling

The emergence of the Emotion Model accompanied the birth of contemporary moral psychology (Haidt et al., 1993). On this model, most of moral thinking is moral feeling—judgments are made not via conscious, principled reasoning primarily but via emotional responses. These emotions include those, like disgust, that drive Haidt's participants to condemn disgusting but harmless actions (e.g., eating the family dog), as we will discuss next, as well as prosocial emotions, like empathy, disrupted in certain patient populations (e.g., psychopathy, frontotemporal dementia, ventromedial prefrontal damage), as we will discuss later in this section.

Emotion models do not necessarily deny a role for other cognitive processes, as discussed in the prior section ("Reason) and subsequent section ("Theory of Mind"). Haidt, for example, recognizes a limited role for conscious reasoning—in social contexts and motivated moral reasoning. Nevertheless, on Haidt's model, emotions such as disgust dominate, as evident in the title of his seminal paper: "The Emotional Dog and Its Rational Tail" (Haidt, 2001). Conscious reasoning plays a more prominent role in Greene's dual-process model, as discussed later in this section (Greene et al., 2004). Greene's model highlights the competitive interaction between consciously reasoned responses (e.g., consequentialist responses) and emotional responses, including empathy. This section discusses the behavioral, neuroimaging, and neuropsychological evidence for the contribution of emotional processes to moral judgments.

Disgust, in particular, appears to be a key candidate emotion for certain moral judgments. On the one hand, certain actions may be perceived as immoral but not disgusting (e.g., tax fraud) and other actions as purely disgusting but not immoral (e.g., drinking urine). On the other hand, abundant research indicates a complex and often causal relationship between disgust and morality. Recent research suggests, for example, that individual differences in disgust responses may drive moral judgments: Political conservatives are more "disgust sensitive" (Inbar, Pizarro, & Bloom, 2009), a trait that can play a causal role in moral attitudes toward homosexuality (Inbar, Pizarro, Knobe, et al., 2009). In a more direct test of the causal link between disgust and moral judgment, participants were hypnotized to experience disgust at an arbitrary word (e.g., "often") and consequently delivered harsh moral judgments even when this word described benign behaviors (e.g., the student often chose popular topics for discussion) (Wheatley & Haidt, 2005). A related study investigated the impact of disgust induction on moral judgment (i.e., via a disgusting smell, a disgusting testing room, a memory of a physically disgusting experience, and a disgusting video) (Schnall, Haidt, Clore, & Jordan, 2008). After the disgust induction, subjects made harsher moral judgments, particularly if they were sensitive to their own bodily state. Finally, in a surprising study of moral behavior, participants were found to be more likely to engage in physical cleansing after

behaving immorally and, conversely, to engage in immoral behaviors after physical cleansing (Zhong & Liljenquist, 2006). These behavioral findings converge on the notion that our emotional responses, and especially disgust, can dramatically shape our moral thinking.

Studies using functional magnetic resonance imaging (fMRI) have also revealed an important association between activity in brain regions implicated in disgust, including the insula, and moral judgments of purity violations (e.g., incest) (Schaich Borg, Lieberman, & Kiehl, 2008) and even unfair and harmful actions (Hsu, Anen, & Quartz, 2008; Moll et al., 2005). More generally, since its inception, contemporary moral psychology has seen a continuous stream of neuroimaging and neuropsychological research focused on the role of emotion in moral judgment (Young & Koenigs, 2007).

Much of this research has focused on the role of brain regions involved in empathy and emotional responsiveness, in particular, the ventral and medial portions of prefrontal cortex, referred to as ventromedial prefrontal cortex (VMPC). The VMPC includes the medial portions of orbitofrontal cortex (Brodmann areas 11 and 12) and the medial prefrontal cortex from the ventral surface to around the level of the genu of the corpus callosum (Brodmann area 25 and portions of Brodmann areas 10 and 32). The VMPC projects to limbic, hypothalamic, and brainstem regions that execute visceral and autonomic components of emotional responses (Ongur & Price, 2000); neurons within the VMPC encode the emotional value of sensory stimuli (Rolls, 2000). Damage to VMPC results in striking impairments in emotional function, including generally blunted affect, diminished empathy, emotional lability, and poorly regulated anger and frustration (Anderson, Barrash, Bechara, & Tranel, 2006; Barrash, Tranel, & Anderson, 2000). Activation in the VMPC is therefore taken as evidence of emotional processing, as in many of the fMRI studies described next.

Early fMRI studies of moral thinking were designed to isolate whatever cognitive processes or neural substrates might be specific to morality. With domain specificity in mind, these studies relied on paradigms contrasting neural responses to moral stimuli versus nonmoral stimuli. In an early study, subjects viewed emotionally salient scenes with moral content (e.g., physical assaults, war scenes) versus nonmoral content (e.g., body lesions, dangerous animals; Moll, de Oliveira-Souza, Bramati, & Grafman, 2002). Regions of VMPC, in this case the right medial orbitofrontal cortex and medial frontal gyrus (Brodmann areas 10 and 11), were selectively recruited when participants passively viewed the moral scenes. Broadly similar activation patterns in the VMPC (lower medial Brodmann area 10) were observed when moral and nonmoral stimuli were matched for social content (e.g., number of people depicted in the scenes) and when subjects down-regulated their own emotional responses to the moral stimuli (Harenski & Hamaan, 2006). Another series of studies targeted the relationship between emotion and explicit moral judgment, replacing moral scenes with "moral statements," simple descriptions of morally salient behavior. VMPC activation (left medial orbitofrontal cortex) was selectively enhanced during the processing of emotionally salient moral statements (e.g., "He shot the victim to death") versus socially and emotionally salient nonmoral statements (e.g., "He licked the dirty toilet") (Moll, de Oliveira-Souza, Eslinger, et al., 2002). Even in the absence of explicit emotional content, moral statements describing morally inappropriate or appropriate actions (e.g., "A steals a car"/"A admires a car") elicited enhanced VMPC activation (medial Brodmann area 10) compared to nonmoral statements that were either semantically appropriate or inappropriate (e.g., "A takes a walk"/"A waits a walk") (Heekeren, Wartenburger, Schmidt, Schwintowski, & Villringer, 2003). Finally, in a similar vein, VMPC activation was observed for silent "right" or "wrong" judgments of simple statements with moral content (e.g., "We break the law when necessary") versus nonmoral content (e.g., "Stones are made of water") (Moll, Eslinger, & de Oliveira-Souza, 2001). Across these fMRI studies, emotional brain regions, in the VMPC, were recruited for moral thinking, in particular, the processing of moral scenes and statements versus nonmoral scenes and statements controlled for social and emotional content. These early studies set the stage for addressing additional questions about emotion and moral judgment in more detail. Do emotions support the processing of complex moral stimuli such as moral dilemmas? Do emotions systematically drive specific moral judgments?

Greene and his colleagues were the first to investigate whether emotion-related areas, such as the VMPC, support moral judgment in the context of moral dilemmas and, importantly, whether neural activity tracks with different moral content, within the moral domain. An early topic of investigation was the difference between moral scenarios that were "personal" or more emotionally salient and moral scenarios that were "impersonal" or less emotionally salient (Greene et al., 2001). For example, a trolley is headed for five people, and participants can save them by sacrificing the life of one person instead. In the "impersonal" scenario, participants can choose to turn the trolley away from the five people onto a side track where one person where will be hit instead. In the "personal" scenario, participants can choose to push a large stranger off a footbridge onto the tracks below, where his body will stop the trolley from hitting the five, though he, of course, will be hit. Personal moral scenarios selectively recruited VMPC (medial Brodmann area 10).

Greene and colleagues took this finding further when they investigated whether the observed activation patterns track not only emotionally salient scenarios but also emotionally mediated moral judgments. In particular, does emotional engagement track nonconsequentialist moral judgments—judgments based on factors other than consequences (e.g., intention, physical contact)? In Greene's experiments, nonconsequentialist judgments consisted of rejecting harmful actions that maximized good consequences (e.g., killing one to save five), while consequentialist judgments consisted of endorsing such harmful actions (Greene et al., 2004). Participants therefore made judgments for a series of scenarios. For example: Enemy soldiers have taken over your village. They have orders to kill all remaining civilians. You and some of your townspeople have sought refuge in the cellar of a large house. Outside, you hear the voices of soldiers who have come to search the house for valuables. Your baby begins to cry loudly. You cover his mouth to block the sound. If you remove your hand from his mouth, his crying will summon the attention of the soldiers who will kill you, your child, and the others hiding out in the cellar. To save yourself and the others, you must smother your child to death. Is it appropriate for you to smother your child in order to save yourself and the other townspeople? For this scenario, the nonconsequentialist judgment (e.g., "Don't smother the baby") is to reject the harmful action, even though it would maximize the greater good. On Greene's model, this judgment is rooted in an automatic emotional aversion to the harmful act. In other words, participants' prepotent response is an emotional response to the harm, leading participants to reject it. By contrast, consequentialist reasoning requires participants to stifle their emotional response (e.g., "The baby will die no matter what, so smother the baby to save everyone else"), leading to the consciously reasoned and emotionally incongruent judgment. Consistent with Greene's dual-process model, brain regions associated with cognitive conflict and abstract reasoning, such as anterior cingulate and dorsolateral prefrontal cortex, were selectively recruited for consequentialist judgments. Subjects appeared able to override their emotional aversion to the harm and engage in consequentialist reasoning.

The growing body of neuroimaging work suggests emotional engagement during moral judgment and, in particular, nonconsequentialist moral judgments. Neuroimaging methods, however, are currently limited in that they reveal only correlations between neural activity and cognitive processes rather than causally necessary connections. One way to determine whether emotional processing plays a causally necessary role in moral judgment is to test individuals with selective deficits in emotional processing. As we will see, neuropsychological studies suggest a causal connection between prosocial emotions and social cognition. Emotional dysfunction often does lead to deficits in moral judgment, reasoning, and behavior.

An early study investigated moral reasoning in two adult individuals with early-onset VMPC lesions (Anderson, Bechara, Damasio, Tranel, & Damasio, 1999). According to a traditional characterization of moral development (Kohlberg, 1981), both individuals exhibited a "preconventional" stage of moral reasoning. More specifically, both early-onset VMPC lesion patients provided immature moral justifications, engaging in moral reasoning from an egocentric perspective of punishment-avoidance (e.g., reasoning that stealing medicine for a loved one is morally wrong because one might get caught). This finding was especially striking given prior research revealing normal moral reasoning in patients with adult-onset VMPC damage (Saver & Damasio, 1991). The moral reasoning deficit documented in the early-onset cases suggests that areas of prefrontal cortex support the original acquisition of normal moral reasoning abilities (Anderson et al., 1999). A caveat, however, is that these studies target participants' justifications rather than judgments, licensing only limited conclusions about the role of the VMPC in moral thinking.

Investigations of adult and developmental psychopaths have associated emotional impairment with defects in moral behavior and judgment. Psychopathy is typically associated with pronounced emotional impairment, for instance, considerably reduced empathy and guilt, and pronounced behavioral disturbance, for instance, criminal and frequently violent behavior (Hare, 1991). Reports of deficits in prosocial emotions (e.g., empathy) and behavior motivated a pair of studies on moral judgment in psychopathy (Blair, 1995, 1997). James Blair found that both adult and developmental psychopaths were unable to distinguish between unambiguous moral transgressions (e.g., hitting someone) and unambiguous conventional transgressions (e.g., talking out of turn) along the dimensions of permissibility, seriousness, and authority contingence—a distinction that even young children are able to make (Turiel, 1983). Recent work suggests that individuals with psychopathic tendencies may show normal moral judgments in limited contexts but simply lack motivation to behave prosocially in accordance with their judgments (Cima, Tonnaer, & Hauser, 2010).

The first direct investigation of moral judgment (as opposed to behavior or justification) in brain-damaged populations was a study of patients with frontotemporal dementia (FTD; Mendez, Chen, Shapira, & Miller, 2005). FTD involves deterioration of prefrontal and anterior temporal brain areas. FTD patients therefore exhibit blunted emotion and diminished regard for others early in the course of the disease. Similar to psychopathy, FTD is marked by behavioral changes, including transgressive behavior, that is, stealing, physical assault, and inappropriate sexual advances (Mendez, Chen, et al., 2005). In light of the deficits in prosocial emotions and behavior associated with FTD, Mendez and colleagues (Mendez, Anderson, & Shapira, 2005) investigated FTD patients' moral judgments of personal and impersonal moral scenarios (Greene et al., 2001). Again, most healthy participants advocate turning a trolley away from five people and onto one person, in the impersonal scenario, but not pushing a stranger off a footbridge so that his body will stop a trolley from hitting five people, in the personal scenario (Cushman et al., 2006; Hauser, Cushman, Young, Jin, & Mikhail, 2007; Mikhail, 2002) However, most FTD patients endorsed the harmful action for both the impersonal and personal scenarios. Social psychologists have observed similar patterns of judgment after reducing negative affect by exposing subjects to Chris Farley's comedic *Saturday Night Live* skits (Valdesolo & DeSteno, 2006). These results suggest that due to the deterioration of emotional processing mediated by the VMPC, the FTD patients did not fully experience the emotional salience of the personal harm (e.g., pushing the stranger). However, since neurodegeneration in FTD affects multiple prefrontal and temporal areas, precise conclusions about the impact of emotional processing subserved by the VMPC versus other cognitive functions cannot yet be drawn.

Investigating moral judgment in individuals with focal VMPC lesions represents the most direct approach to the relationship between emotional processing in the VMPC and moral judgment. Like FTD patients, VMPC lesion patients exhibit diminished empathy and blunted affect, but, importantly, unlike FTD patients, VMPC lesion patients retain broader intellectual function. VMPC patients can therefore be studied to characterize the specific role of emotion in moral judgment. One study tested a group of six patients with focal, adult-onset, bilateral lesions of VMPC to determine whether emotional processing subserved by VMPC is, in fact, causally necessary for normal moral judgment (Koenigs et al., 2007). In this study, patients evaluated the same impersonal and personal moral scenarios described earlier. As in previous fMRI studies (Greene et al., 2001, 2004), many of the personal scenarios pit an emotionally aversive harm against the "greater good" (e.g., killing one to save many). Like the FTD patients, VMPC patients responded normally to the impersonal moral scenarios, but for the personal scenarios the VMPC patients were significantly more likely to endorse committing an emotionally aversive harm if a greater number of people would benefit—the consequentialist judgment. A second lesion study confirmed this finding (Ciaramelli, Muccioli, Ladavas, & di Pellegrino, 2007). Together, these studies suggest that emotional processing mediated by VMPC is crucial for moral judgment and in particular consequentialist moral judgment (Greene et al., 2004).

All of these studies, however, rely on moral scenarios describing intentional harms: Agents act with the belief and intent, stated or implied, that they will cause the harmful outcome that they, in fact, cause. It is thus unresolved whether the brain regions implicated in emotional processing, such as the VMPC, are involved in processing harmful outcomes or harmful intentions or both. Recent functional neuroimaging and neuropsychological evidence suggests that the VMPC supports the processing of harmful intentions (Young & Saxe, 2009b). In healthy adult participants, moral judgments of failed attempts to harm (harmful intention, neutral outcome) were significantly correlated with the average neural response in the VMPC. Individuals with a high VMPC response, and a stronger emotional response to the harmful intention, assigned more blame for failed attempts to harm, while individuals with a low VMPC response, and a weaker emotional response to the harmful intention, assigned less blame.

A follow-up study investigated moral judgments made by patients with adult-onset VMPC lesions, as in the study described earlier (Young, Bechara, et al., 2010). Consistent with the fMRI evidence, VMPC patients judged attempted harms as significantly more morally permissible, compared to control participants—and even compared to their own judgments of accidental harms. In fact, this pattern reflects a striking reversal of the normal pattern of moral judgments; in judging failed attempts to harm as more permissible than accidental harms, VMPC patients revealed an extreme "no harm, no foul" mentality. VMPC patients showed a selective deficit in moral judgment of attempted harms, including attempted murder, suggesting that although VMPC patients may be able to reason about the content of a belief or an intention, they are unable to trigger normal emotional responses to mental state content for moral judgment—in line with prior work showing deficits in their emotional processing of abstract versus concrete information (Bechara & Damasio, 2005). The finding that the VMPC is associated with processing intentions with high emotional content, that is, harmful intent, for moral judgment, is also consistent with the role of the VMPC in "affective" theory of mind or emotional empathy (Jenkins & Mitchell, 2009; Mitchell, Macrae, & Banaji, 2006; Shamay-Tsoory & Aharon-Peretz, 2007; Vollm et al., 2006). Prior evidence has suggested a specific role for the VMPC in processing affective aspects of another person's mental states (Jenkins & Mitchell, 2009; Mitchell et al., 2006; Shamay-Tsoory & Aharon-Peretz, 2007; Vollm et al., 2006). Therefore, damage to these processes for emotional empathy may lead to deficits in both moral judgment and prosocial behavior.

Research using behavioral methods, fMRI, and neuropsychology has illuminated the specific role of emotion in moral judgment. Manipulating emotions, by either enhancing or suppressing them, can systematically bias people's moral judgments; brain regions associated with emotional processing are recruited for moral judgment, and more for some kinds of moral judgments over others; patients with deficits in emotional processing show systematically abnormal moral cognition in judgment, justification, and behavior.

## Theory of Mind: Moral Thinking Is Thinking About Thinking

A third cognitive model posits that, in addition to conscious reasoning and emotional processing, theory of mind is a key cognitive process for moral judgment, that is, how we reason about the mental states of moral agents, including their innocent and guilty intentions (Hart, 1968; Kamm, 2001; Mikhail, 2007). My colleagues and I have focused on the dominant role of mental states versus outcomes for moral judgment (Young, Cushman, Hauser, & Saxe, 2007). In our studies, participants typically read stories in which agents produced either a negative outcome (harm to another person) or a neutral outcome (no harm), based on the belief that they would cause the negative outcome ("negative" belief or intention) or the neutral outcome ("neutral" belief or intention). Participants then judge whether the action was morally permissible or forbidden, or how much moral blame the agent deserves.

For example, in one scenario, Grace and her coworker are taking a tour of a chemical factory. Grace stops to pour herself and her coworker some coffee. Nearby is a container of sugar. The container, however, has been mislabeled "toxic," so Grace thinks that the powder inside is toxic. She spoons some into her coworker's coffee and takes none for herself. Her coworker drinks the coffee, and nothing bad happens. In an alternative scenario, a container of poison sits near the coffee. The container, however, has been mislabeled "sugar," so Grace thinks the powder inside is sugar. She spoons some into her coworker's coffee. Her coworker drinks her coffee and ends up dead. Across all of our studies using scenarios like these, participants weighed the agent's belief and intent more heavily than the action's outcomes in their moral judgments (Young et al., 2007; Young, Nichols, & Saxe, 2010). A simple metric of this effect is that our participants almost universally judge an attempted harm (negative belief, neutral outcome) as more morally blameworthy and more morally forbidden than an accidental harm (neutral belief, negative outcome).

Cushman (2008) has pushed this line of work even further, directly comparing the roles of outcome, causation, beliefs, and desires for different kinds of moral judgments (e.g., person, permissibility, blame, and punishment) (Cushman, 2008; Cushman, Dreber, Wang, & Costa, 2009). The agent's belief about whether his or her action would cause harm was the most important factor across the board, followed by the agent's desire to cause harm. Notably, though, judgments about how much

to punish the agent relied relatively more on outcomes, as compared to judgments about the moral character of the agent or the moral permissibility of the action, which relied more on beliefs.

What's surprising is that mental state factors dominate even where external outcomes appear to drive moral judgments. For instance, agents who cause harmful outcomes by accident are still judged to be somewhat morally blameworthy in spite of their mental states. Consider again the scenario where Grace accidentally poisons her coworker because she mistakes poison for sugar. Though we mostly let Grace off the hook for her false belief and innocent intention, we still assign some moral blame. Recent research suggests that this negative moral judgment is based not simply on the harmful outcome of Grace's action but largely on participants' assessment of Grace's mental state (Young, Nichols, & Saxe, 2010). In particular, participants judge Grace's false belief as unjustified or unreasonable and therefore Grace as morally blameworthy. So, even when we assign blame for accidents, we may do so on the basis of mental state factors (e.g., negligence) and not simply on the basis of the harmful outcome.

For most healthy adults, mental states, including beliefs, intentions, and desires, carry more moral weight than external outcomes. In some cases, mental states overwhelm other morally relevant external factors, including external constraints, like whether the person could have acted otherwise (Woolfolk, Doris, & Darley, 2006). Woolfolk, Doris, and Darley (2006) presented subjects with variations of one basic story: Bill discovers that his wife Susan and his best friend Frank have been involved in a love affair. All three are flying home from a group vacation on the same airplane. In one variation of the story, their plane is hijacked by a gang of ruthless kidnappers, who surround the passengers with machine guns and order Bill to shoot Frank in the head; otherwise, they will shoot Bill, Frank, and the other passengers. Bill recognizes the opportunity to kill his wife's lover and get away with it. He wants to kill Frank and does so. In another variation: Bill forgives Frank and Susan and is horrified when the situation arises but complies with the kidnappers' demand to kill Frank. On average, observers rate Bill as more responsible for Frank's death, and the killing as more wrong, when Bill wanted to kill Frank, even though this desire played no role in causing the death, in either case.

While assigning moral blame for harmful desires and intentions appears easy and automatic (except in case of VMPC damage), forgiving accidental harms appears to present more of a challenge. Among healthy adults, we have found evidence of substantial individual variability in moral blame assigned to protagonists for accidental harms (Young & Saxe, 2009b). In development, full forgiveness or exculpation for accidents does not emerge until approximately 7 years of age, surprisingly late in childhood. Meanwhile, 5-year-old children are capable of reasoning about false beliefs: In the paradigmatic "false-belief task," children predict that observers will look for a hidden object where they last saw the object, not in its true current location (Flavell, 1999; Wellman, Cross, & Watson, 2001). These same children, however, judge that if a false belief led an observer to unknowingly and accidentally cause harm to another person (e.g., mistake poison for sugar), the agent is just as bad as if he or she had caused the harm on purpose (Piaget, 1932/1965). The ability to integrate beliefs and intentions into moral judgments appears then to be a distinct developmental achievement (Young & Saxe, 2008). Consistent with this idea, high-functioning adults diagnosed with Asperger's syndrome, who also pass standard false-belief tasks, assign abnormally high levels of moral blame for accidental harms as well (Moran et al., 2011).

My colleagues and I have recently investigated the neural mechanisms that support moral judgments based on mental states such as beliefs and intentions. Our results suggest that specific brain regions support multiple distinct cognitive components of mental state reasoning for moral judgment: the initial encoding of the agent's belief, the use and integration of the belief (with outcome information) for moral judgment, as discussed earlier, spontaneous mental state inference when mental state information is not explicitly provided in the moral scenario, and even post hoc reasoning about beliefs and intentions to rationalize or justify moral judgments (Kliemann, Young, Scholz, & Saxe, 2008; Young et al., 2007; Young & Saxe, 2008, 2009a).

Building on prior research on neural substrates for theory of mind in nonmoral contexts (Perner, Aichhorn, Kronbichler, Staffen, & Ladurner, 2006; Saxe & Kanwisher, 2003), our research suggests that the most selective brain region appears to be the right temporo-parietal junction (RTPJ). In one study, individual differences in moral judgments were correlated with individual differences in the RTPJ response (Young & Saxe, 2009b). Participants with a high RTPJ response, and a more robust mental state representation (e.g., false belief, innocent

intention), assigned less blame to agents causing accidental harm. Participants with a low RTPJ response, and a weaker mental state representation, assigned more blame, like young children and our participants with Asperger's Syndrome. One source of developmental change in moral judgments may therefore be the maturation of specific brain regions for representing mental states such as beliefs—consistent with recent research suggesting the RTPJ may be late maturing (Saxe, Whitfield-Gabrieli, Scholz, & Pelphrey, 2009).

The correlation observed here between the use of mental states for moral judgment and the neural response in a brain region dedicated to mental state reasoning suggests that individual differences in moral judgment are not due exclusively to individual differences in domain-general capacities for abstract reasoning or cognitive control, as discussed in the preceding sections. What determines blame or forgiveness is not just the ability to override a prepotent response to a salient harmful outcome (Greene et al., 2004). The conflict between mental state and outcome factors may account for part of the challenge of forgiveness. The neural data suggest that the strength of the mental state representation matters for how the conflict is resolved—and whether forgiveness or blame is offered.

Disrupting RTPJ activity also disrupts the use of mental state information for moral judgment. In a recent study, we produced a temporary "virtual lesion" in the RTPJ, using a neurophysiological technique known as transcranial magnetic stimulation (TMS) (Young, Camprodon, Hauser, Pascual-Leone, & Saxe, 2010). TMS allows the induction of a current in the brain, using a magnetic field to pass the scalp and skull. After using fMRI to identify the RTPJ in each of our participants, and a nearby control region not implicated in mental state reasoning, we used offline and online TMS to modulate neural activity in two experiments. In both experiments, TMS to the RTPJ versus the control region made a significant and selective difference, reducing the impact of intentions and, as a direct result, increasing the impact of outcomes on moral judgments. For example, disrupting RTPJ activity led to more lenient judgments of failed attempts to harm, based on the neutral outcome, and not the harmful intent. Indeed, moral judgment depends critically on specific neural substrates for processing mental states like beliefs and intentions.

Together, these studies provide behavioral and neural evidence for theory of mind as a key cognitive process for moral judgment. Evaluating moral agents and their actions requires an assessment of the agents' mental states. Specific neural substrates support such mental state assessments. Compromised mental state reasoning in the case of neurodevelopmental disorders (e.g., autism) or via TMS therefore leads to abnormal moral thinking.

## Moral Faculty: Moral Thinking Is Uniquely Moral

In contrast to the models presented so far, moral faculty models focus on what, if anything, might be specific to the domain of morality—rather than the contribution of cognitive processes already known to operate in other domains (e.g., reasoning, emotion, theory of mind). Moral faculty models posit a uniquely moral faculty that takes multiple cognitive inputs and computes a uniquely moral judgment (Hauser, 2006; Mikhail, 2002, 2007). Interestingly, at the outset of contemporary moral psychology, the key questions for many focused directly on what was specific to the moral domain. Are moral judgments governed by specific moral rules and computations, or specific moral emotions? Are moral judgments supported by a specific neural substrate or network? An illustration of this domain-specific approach can be found in early fMRI studies of morality, described earlier in the section on "Emotion." Many of these studies were designed around comparing moral stimuli to nonmoral stimuli, while controlling for differences along other dimensions (e.g., emotional salience, social content). Before too long, though, moral psychology saw a subtle shift from these questions of domain specificity toward questions concerning other better studied cognitive processes—how they might interact and contribute to moral judgment.

In some sense, all models of moral judgment depend on some sort of "faculty" that functions to integrate the outputs of others cognitive processes (e.g., theory of mind) in order to compute a distinctly moral judgment. Then, any debate about the future of moral psychology might simply concern where to direct our empirical efforts—the moral faculty or the processes that feed into the faculty. This might turn on the complexity of the computations performed by the moral faculty: How much or how little work is done before the moral faculty runs its moral computations? Current models posit relatively simple moral rules, for example, "ME HURT YOU" (Greene et al., 2004) and "it is wrong to intentionally cause harm" (Cushman, Young, & Hauser, 2011; Mikhail, 2007). The simplicity of these moral computations recommends the worthy

challenge of characterizing the messier processes that provide the inputs to the moral faculty.

It may be also worth noting, however, that while the moral rules themselves may be relatively simple, "hurt" and "harm" may require some deconstruction into further component parts (S. Carey, personal communication). What constitutes "hurt" and "harm"? Causing distress to another person (Leslie, Knobe, & Cohen, 2006)? Violating moral norms that extend beyond physical harms, to norms concerning fairness, community, authority, and purity (Haidt, 2007)? Hindering others—something that even 6-month-old infants recognize as "bad" (Hamlin, Wynn, & Bloom, 2007; Kuhlmeier, Wynn, & Bloom, 2003)? How "hurt" and "harm" are filled out may turn out to be learned or innate (or some combination), learned explicitly or associatively (Blair, 1995), culturally bound or universal. In the meantime, any innate content of "hurt" and "harm" may be one candidate for what is uniquely moral.

Another candidate, though, is the moral faculty itself, in other words, not merely the content of "hurt" and "harm" within the moral computation, but that which performs the computation. Indeed, some mechanism must take nonmoral inputs and deliver a uniquely "moral" judgment. And, yet, it is also possible that whatever integrative mechanism that takes, for example, mental states and outcomes as inputs to compute moral permissibility is no different from that which takes height and radius to compute volume (Anderson & Cuneo, 1978). What would be needed then is positive evidence for a specifically "moral" faculty. This evidence might take the form of a specific neural process dedicated to integrating information for moral judgment (Hsu et al., 2008), or the systematic transformation of the nonmoral inputs, post moral computation. For example, are there unique behavioral or neural signatures of theory of mind for moral judgment, compared to theory of mind deployed in nonmoral contexts, for predicting and explaining behavior (Knobe, 2005; F. Cushman, personal communication)? If so, then searching for a moral faculty may indeed be worth the effort.

## Conclusion

In the past decade, cognitive psychology and neuroscience has started to reveal moral thinking in the mind and brain. Moral judgment includes a complex set of cognitive processes, including reason, emotion, and theory of mind, each with distinct behavioral and neural signatures. Conscious reasoning from explicit principles or theories may lead directly to some moral judgments and allow us to correct others. Emotional processes, including disgust and empathy, may drive us to judge some actions as harmful, unfair, or impure, and also motivate us to behave prosocially. Theory of mind enables us to evaluate moral agents based not only on their actions and effects on the external world but on the internal contents of agents' minds—their beliefs and intentions. Finally, a moral faculty may serve to integrate the information from these cognitive processes and generate a uniquely moral judgment of right or wrong. The science of morality therefore requires at once investigating the multitude of cognitive and neural processes known to function in other domains, as well as exploring the possibility of processes dedicated specifically to morality.

## Future Directions

1. How do different cognitive processes for moral judgment interact?

2. What is the relationship between moral judgment and moral behavior?

3. What are the differences and similarities between moral judgment of self versus other?

4. What are the differences and similarities between moral judgment of ingroup versus outgroup members?

5. Do distinct moral domains (e.g., harm versus purity) follow distinct cognitive rules?

## References

Anderson, N., & Cuneo, D. (1978). The height + width rule in children's judgments of quantity. *Journal of Experimental Psychology: General, 107*(4), 335–378.

Anderson, S., Barrash, J., Bechara, A., & Tranel, D. (2006). Impairments of emotion and real-world complex behavior following childhood—or adult-onset damage to ventromedial prefrontal cortex. *Journal of the International Neuropsychology Society, 12*, 224–235.

Anderson, S. W., Bechara, A., Damasio, H., Tranel, D., & Damasio, A. R. (1999). Impairment of social and moral behavior related to early damage in human prefrontal cortex. *Nature Neuroscience, 2*, 1032–1037.

Banaji, M. R. (2001). Implicit attitudes can be measured. In H. L. Roediger, J. S. Nairne, I. Neath, & A. Surprenant (Eds.), *The nature of remembering: Essays in honor of Robert G. Crowder*. Washington, DC: American Psychological Association.

Barrash, J., Tranel, D., & Anderson, S. (2000). Acquired personality disturbances associated with bilateral damage to the ventromedial prefrontal region. *Developmental Neuropsychology, 18*, 355–381.

Bechara, A., & Damasio, A. R. (2005). The somatic marker hypothesis: A neural theory of economic decision. *Games and Economic Behavior, 52*(2), 336–372.

Blair, R. J. R. (1995). A cognitive developmental approach to morality: Investigating the psychopath. *Cognition, 57*, 1–29.

Blair, R. J. R. (1997). Moral reasoning and the child with psychopathic tendencies. *Personality and Individual Differences, 22*, 731–739.

Ciaramelli, E., Muccioli, M., Ladavas, E., & di Pellegrino, G. (2007). Selective deficit in personal moral judgment following damage to ventromedial prefrontal cortex. *Social Cognitive and Affective Neuroscience, 2*(2), 84–92.

Cima, M., Tonnaer, F., & Hauser, M. D. (2010). Psychopaths know right from wrong but don't care. *Social Cognitive and Affective Neuroscience, 5*(1), 59–67.

Cushman, F. (2008). Crime and punishment: Distinguishing the roles of causal and intentional analysis in moral judgment. *Cognition, 108*(2), 353–380.

Cushman, F., Dreber, A., Wang, Y., & Costa, J. (2009). Accidental outcomes guide punishment in a "trembling hand" game. *PLoS One, 4*(8), e6699.

Cushman, F., Young, L., & Hauser, M. (2011). Patterns of moral judgment derive from non-moral psychological representations. *Cognitive Science, 35*(6), 1052–1075.

Cushman, F., Young, L., & Hauser, M. D. (2006). The role of conscious reasoning and intuitions in moral judgment: Testing three principles of harm. *Psychological Science, 17*(12), 1082–1089.

Flavell, J. H. (1999). Cognitive development: Children's knowledge about the mind. *Annual Review of Psychology, 50*, 21–45.

Greene, J. D., Morelli, S. A., Lowenberg, K., Nystrom, L. E., & Cohen, J. D. (2008). Cognitive load selectively interferes with utilitarian moral judgment. *Cognition, 107*(3), 1144–1154.

Greene, J. D., Nystrom, L. E., Engell, A. D., Darley, J. M., & Cohen, J. D. (2004). The neural bases of cognitive conflict and control in moral judgment. *Neuron, 44*, 389–400.

Greene, J. D., Sommerville, R. B., Nystrom, L. E., Darley, J. M., & Cohen, J. D. (2001). An fMRI investigation of emotional engagement in moral judgment. *Science, 293*, 2105–2108.

Haidt, J. (2001). The emotional dog and its rational tail: A social intuitionist approach to moral judgment. *Psychological Review, 108*, 814–834.

Haidt, J. (2007). The new synthesis in moral psychology. *Science, 316*, 998–1002.

Haidt, J., Koller, S. H., & Dias, M. G. (1993). Affect, culture, and morality, or is it wrong to eat your dog? *Journal of Personal and Social Psychology, 65*(4), 613–628.

Hamlin, J. K., Wynn, K., & Bloom, P. (2007). Social evaluation by preverbal infants. *Nature, 450*(7169), 557–559.

Hare, R. D. (1991). *The hare psychopathy checklist-revised*. Toronto, ON: Multi-Health Systems.

Harenski, C. L., & Hamaan, S. (2006). Neural correlates of regulating negative emotions related to moral violations. *Neuroimage, 30*(1), 313–324.

Hart, H. L. A. (1968). *Punishment and responsibility*. Oxford, England: Oxford University Press.

Hauser, M. D. (2006). *Moral minds: How nature designed a universal sense right and wrong*. New York: Harper Collins.

Hauser, M. D., Cushman, F. A., Young, L., Jin, R., & Mikhail, J. M. (2007). A dissociation between moral judgment and justification. *Mind and Language, 22*, 1–21.

Heekeren, H. R., Wartenburger, I., Schmidt, H., Schwintowski, H. P., & Villringer, A. (2003). An fMRI study of simple ethical decision-making. *Neuroreport, 14*, 1215–1219.

Hsu, M., Anen, C., & Quartz, S. R. (2008). The right and the good: Distributive justice and neural encoding of equity and efficiency. *Science, 320*(5879), 1092–1095.

Inbar, Y., Pizarro, D., & Bloom, P. (2009). Conservatives are more easily disgusted than liberals. *Cognition and Emotion, 23,* 714–725.

Inbar, Y., Pizarro, D. A., Knobe, J., & Bloom, P. (2009). Disgust sensitivity predicts intuitive disapproval of gays. *Emotion, 9*(3), 435–439.

Jenkins, A. C., & Mitchell, J. P. (2009). Mentalizing under uncertainty: Dissociated neural responses to ambiguous and unambiguous mental state inferences. *Cerebral Cortex, 20*(2), 404–410.

Kamm, F. M. (2001). *Morality, mortality: Rights, duties, and status.* New York: Oxford University Press.

Kliemann, D., Young, L., Scholz, J., & Saxe, R. (2008). The influence of prior record on moral judgment. *Neuropsychologia, 46*(12), 2949–2957.

Knobe, J. (2005). Theory of mind and moral cognition: Exploring the connections. *Trends in Cognitive Sciences, 9,* 357–359.

Koenigs, M., Young, L., Adolphs, R., Tranel, D., Cushman, F., Hauser, M., & Damasio, A. (2007). Damage to the prefrontal cortex increases utilitarian moral judgments. *Nature, 446,* 908–911.

Kohlberg, L. (1981). *Essays on moral development, Vol. 1. The philosophy of moral development.* New York: Harper Row.

Kuhlmeier, V., Wynn, K., & Bloom, P. (2003). Attribution of dispositional states by 12-month-olds. *Psychological Science, 14*(5), 402–408.

Leslie, A. M., Knobe, J., & Cohen, A. (2006). Acting intentionally and the side-effect effect: "Theory of mind" and moral judgment. *Psychological Science, 6,* 421–427.

Lombrozo, T. (2009). The role of moral commitments in moral judgment. *Cognitive Science, 33,* 273–286.

Mendez, M., Anderson, E., & Shapira, J. (2005). An investigation of moral judgment in frontotemporal dementia. *Cognitive and Behavioral Neurology, 18*(4), 193–197.

Mendez, M., Chen, A., Shapira, J., & Miller, B. (2005). Acquired sociopathy and frontotemporal dementia. *Dementia and Geriatric Cognitive Disorders, 20*(2–3), 99–104.

Mikhail, J. M. (2002). *Aspects of a theory of moral cognition. Unpublished Public Law and Legal Theory Research Paper Series,* Georgetown University Law Center, Washington, DC.

Mikhail, J. M. (2007). Universal moral grammar: Theory, evidence and the future. *Trends in Cognitive Sciences, 11*(4), 143–152.

Mitchell, J. P., Macrae, C. N., & Banaji, M. R. (2006). Dissociable medial prefrontal contributions to judgments of similar and dissimilar others. *Neuron, 50*(4), 655–663.

Moll, J., de Oliveira-Souza, R., Bramati, I. E., & Grafman, J. (2002). Functional networks in emotional moral and nonmoral social judgments. *Neuroimage, 16,* 696–703.

Moll, J., de Oliveira-Souza, R., Eslinger, P. J., Bramati, I. E., Mourao-Miranda, J., Andreiulo, P. A., & Pessoa, L. (2002). The neural correlates of moral sensitivity: A functional magnetic resonance imaging investigation of basic and moral emotions. *Journal of Neuroscience, 22,* 2730–2736.

Moll, J., de Oliveira-Souza, R., Moll, F. T., Ignacio, F. A., Bramati, I. E., Caparelli-Daquer, E. M., & Eslinger, P. J. (2005). The moral affiliations of disgust. *Journal of Cognitive Behavioral Neurology, 18*(1), 68–78.

Moll, J., Eslinger, P. J., & de Oliveira-Souza, R. (2001). Frontopolar and anterior temporal cortex activation in a moral judgment task: Preliminary functional MRI results in normal subjects. *Arq Neuropsiquiatr, 59*(3-B), 657–664.

Moran, J., Young, L., Saxe, R., Lee, S., O'Young, D., Mavros, P., & Gabrieli, J. (2011). Impaired theory of mind for moral judgment in high functioning autism. *Proceedings of the National Academy of Sciences, 108,* 2688–2692.

Ongur, D., & Price, J. (2000). The organization of networks within the orbital and medial prefrontal cortex of rats, monkeys, and humans. *Cerebral Cortex, 10,* 206–219.

Perner, J., Aichhorn, M., Kronbichler, M., Staffen, W., & Ladurner, G. (2006). Thinking of mental and other representations: The roles of left and right temporo-parietal junction. *Social Neuroscience, 1*(3–4), 245–258.

Piaget, J. (1932/1965). *The moral judgment of the child.* New York: Free Press.

Rolls, E. (2000). The orbitofrontal cortex and reward. *Cerebral Cortex, 3,* 284–294.

Saver, J. L., & Damasio, A. (1991). Preserved access and processing of social knowlede in a patient with acquired sociopathy due to ventromedial frontal damage. *Neuropsychologia, 29,* 1241–1249.

Saxe, R., & Kanwisher, N. (2003). People thinking about thinking people. The role of the temporo-parietal junction in "theory of mind." *Neuroimage, 19*(4), 1835–1842.

Saxe, R. R., Whitfield-Gabrieli, S., Scholz, J., & Pelphrey, K. A. (2009). Brain regions for perceiving and reasoning about other people in school-aged children. *Child Development, 80*(4), 1197–1209.

Schaich Borg, J., Lieberman, D., & Kiehl, K. A. (2008). Infection, incest, and iniquity: Investigating the neural correlates of disgust and morality. *Journal of Cognitive Neuroscience, 20*(9), 1529–1546.

Schnall, S., Haidt, J., Clore, G. L., & Jordan, A. H. (2008). Disgust as embodied moral judgment. *Personal and Social Psychology Bulletin, 34*(8), 1096–1109.

Shamay-Tsoory, S. G., & Aharon-Peretz, J. (2007). Dissociable prefrontal networks for cognitive and affective theory of mind: A lesion study. *Neuropsychologia, 45*(13), 3054–3067.

Turiel, E. (1983). *The development of social knowledge: Morality and convention.* Cambridge, England: Cambridge University Press.

Valdesolo, P., & DeSteno, D. (2006). Manipulations of emotional context shape moral judgment. *Psychological Science, 17*(6), 476.

Vollm, B. A., Taylor, A. N., Richardson, P., Corcoran, R., Stirling, J., McKie, S., ... Elliott, R . (2006). Neuronal correlates of theory of mind and empathy: a functional magnetic resonance imaging study in a nonverbal task. *Neuroimage, 29*(1), 90–98.

Wellman, H. M., Cross, D., & Watson, J. (2001). Meta-analysis of theory-of-mind development: The truth about false belief. *Children Development, 72*(3), 655–684.

Wheatley, T., & Haidt, J. (2005). Hypnotic disgust makes moral judgments more severe. *Psychological Science, 16*(10), 780–784.

Woolfolk, R. L., Doris, J. M., & Darley, J. M. (2006). Identification, situational constraint, and social cognition: Studies in the attribution of moral responsibility. *Cognition, 100*(2), 283–301.

Young, L., Bechara, A., Tranel, D., Damasio, H., Hauser, M., & Damasio, A. (2010). Damage to ventromedial prefrontal cortex impairs judgment of harmful intent. *Neuron, 65*(6), 845–851.

Young, L., Camprodon, J. A., Hauser, M., Pascual-Leone, A., & Saxe, R. (2010). Disruption of the right temporoparietal junction with transcranial magnetic stimulation reduces the role of beliefs in moral judgments. *Proceedings of the National Academy of Sciences USA, 107*(15), 6753–6758.

Young, L., Cushman, F., Hauser, M., & Saxe, R. (2007). The neural basis of the interaction between theory of mind and moral judgment. *Proceedings of the National Academy of Sciences USA, 104*(20), 8235–8240.

Young, L., & Koenigs, M. (2007). Investigating emotion in moral cognition: A review of evidence from functional neuroimaging and neuropsychology. *British Medical Bulletin, 84,* 69–79.

Young, L., Nichols, S., & Saxe, R. (2010). Investigating the neural and cognitive basis of moral luck: It's not what you do but what you know. *Review of Philosophy and Psychology, 1(3),* 333–349.

Young, L., & Saxe, R. (2008). The neural basis of belief encoding and integration in moral judgment. *NeuroImage, 40,* 1912–1920.

Young, L., & Saxe, R. (2009a). An FMRI investigation of spontaneous mental state inference for moral judgment. *Journal of Cognitive Neuroscience, 21*(7), 1396–1405.

Young, L., & Saxe, R. (2009b). Innocent intentions: A correlation between forgiveness for accidental harm and neural activity. *Neuropsychologia, 47*(10), 2065–2072.

Zhong, C. B., & Liljenquist, K. (2006). Washing away your sins: Threatened morality and physical cleansing. *Science, 313*(5792), 1451–1452.

# Problem Solving and Creativity

# Problem Solving

Richard E. Mayer

**Abstract**

Problem solving refers to cognitive processing directed at achieving a goal when the problem solver does not initially know a solution method. A problem exists when someone has a goal but does not know how to achieve it. Problems can be classified as routine or nonroutine, and as well defined or ill defined. The major cognitive processes in problem solving are representing, planning, executing, and monitoring. The major kinds of knowledge required for problem solving are facts, concepts, procedures, strategies, and beliefs. Classic theoretical approaches to the study of problem solving are associationism, Gestalt, and information processing. Current issues and suggested future issues include decision making, intelligence and creativity, teaching of thinking skills, expert problem solving, analogical reasoning, mathematical and scientific thinking, everyday thinking, and the cognitive neuroscience of problem solving. Common themes concern the domain specificity of problem solving and a focus on problem solving in authentic contexts.

**Key Words:** problem solving, problem, cognitive process, transfer, insight, heuristics, decision making, intelligence, creativity, thinking

The study of problem solving begins with defining problem solving, problem, and problem types. This introduction to problem solving is rounded out with an examination of cognitive processes in problem solving, the role of knowledge in problem solving, and historical approaches to the study of problem solving.

## Definition of Problem Solving

Problem solving refers to cognitive processing directed at achieving a goal for which the problem solver does not initially know a solution method. This definition consists of four major elements (Mayer, 1992; Mayer & Wittrock, 2006):

*Cognitive*—Problem solving occurs within the problem solver's cognitive system and can only be inferred indirectly from the problem solver's behavior (including biological changes, introspections, and actions during problem solving).

*Process*—Problem solving involves mental computations in which some operation is applied to a mental representation, sometimes resulting in the creation of a new mental representation.

*Directed*—Problem solving is aimed at achieving a goal.

*Personal*—Problem solving depends on the existing knowledge of the problem solver so that what is a problem for one problem solver may not be a problem for someone who already knows a solution method.

The definition is broad enough to include a wide array of cognitive activities such as deciding which apartment to rent, figuring out how to use a cell phone interface, playing a game of chess, making a medical diagnosis, finding the answer to an arithmetic word problem, or writing a chapter for a handbook. Problem solving is pervasive in human life and is crucial for human survival. Although this chapter focuses on problem solving in humans, problem solving also occurs in nonhuman animals and in intelligent machines.

How is problem solving related to other forms of high-level cognition processing, such as thinking and reasoning? Thinking refers to cognitive processing in individuals but includes both *directed thinking* (which corresponds to the definition of problem solving) and *undirected thinking* such as daydreaming (which does not correspond to the definition of problem solving). Thus, problem solving is a type of thinking (i.e., directed thinking).

Reasoning refers to problem solving within specific classes of problems, such as deductive reasoning or inductive reasoning. In deductive reasoning, the reasoner is given premises and must derive a conclusion by applying the rules of logic. For example, given that "A is greater than B" and "B is greater than C," a reasoner can conclude that "A is greater than C." In inductive reasoning, the reasoner is given (or has experienced) a collection of examples or instances and must infer a rule. For example, given that X, C, and V are in the "yes" group and x, c, and v are in the "no" group, the reasoning may conclude that B is in "yes" group because it is in uppercase format. Thus, reasoning is a type of problem solving.

## Definition of Problem

A problem occurs when someone has a goal but does not know to achieve it. This definition is consistent with how the Gestalt psychologist Karl Duncker (1945, p. 1) defined a problem in his classic monograph, *On Problem Solving*: "A problem arises when a living creature has a goal but does not know how this goal is to be reached." However, today researchers recognize that the definition should be extended to include problem solving by intelligent machines. This definition can be clarified using an information processing approach by noting that a problem occurs when a situation is in the given state, the problem solver wants the situation to be in the goal state, and there is no obvious way to move from the given state to the goal state (Newell & Simon, 1972). Accordingly, the three main elements in describing a problem are the given state (i.e., the current state of the situation), the goal state (i.e., the desired state of the situation), and the set of allowable operators (i.e., the actions the problem solver is allowed to take). The definition of "problem" is broad enough to include the situation confronting a physician who wishes to make a diagnosis on the basis of preliminary tests and a patient examination, as well as a beginning physics student trying to solve a complex physics problem.

## Types of Problems

It is customary in the problem-solving literature to make a distinction between routine and nonroutine problems. Routine problems are problems that are so familiar to the problem solver that the problem solver knows a solution method. For example, for most adults, "What is 365 divided by 12?" is a routine problem because they already know the procedure for long division. Nonroutine problems are so unfamiliar to the problem solver that the problem solver does not know a solution method. For example, figuring out the best way to set up a funding campaign for a nonprofit charity is a nonroutine problem for most volunteers. Technically, routine problems do not meet the definition of problem because the problem solver has a goal but knows how to achieve it. Much research on problem solving has focused on routine problems, although most interesting problems in life are nonroutine.

Another customary distinction is between well-defined and ill-defined problems. Well-defined problems have a clearly specified given state, goal state, and legal operators. Examples include arithmetic computation problems or games such as checkers or tic-tac-toe. Ill-defined problems have a poorly specified given state, goal state, or legal operators, or a combination of poorly defined features. Examples include solving the problem of global warming or finding a life partner. Although, ill-defined problems are more challenging, much research in problem solving has focused on well-defined problems.

## Cognitive Processes in Problem Solving

The process of problem solving can be broken down into two main phases: *problem representation*, in which the problem solver builds a mental representation of the problem situation, and *problem solution*, in which the problem solver works to produce a solution. The major subprocess in problem representation is *representing*, which involves building a *situation model*—that is, a mental representation of the situation described in the problem. The major subprocesses in problem solution are *planning*, which involves devising a plan for how to solve the problem; *executing*, which involves carrying out the plan; and *monitoring*, which involves evaluating and adjusting one's problem solving.

For example, given an arithmetic word problem such as "Alice has three marbles. Sarah has two more marbles than Alice. How many marbles does Sarah have?" the process of representing involves building a situation model in which Alice has a set of marbles, there is set of marbles for the difference between the two girls, and Sarah has a set of marbles that consists of Alice's marbles and the difference set. In the planning process, the problem solver sets a goal of adding 3 and 2. In the executing process, the problem solver carries out the computation, yielding an answer of 5. In the monitoring process, the problem solver looks over what was done and concludes that 5 is a reasonable answer. In most complex problem-solving episodes, the four cognitive processes may not occur in linear order, but rather may interact with one another. Although some research focuses mainly on the execution process, problem solvers may tend to have more difficulty with the processes of representing, planning, and monitoring.

### Knowledge for Problem Solving

An important theme in problem-solving research is that problem-solving proficiency on any task depends on the learner's knowledge (Anderson et al., 2001; Mayer, 1992). Five kinds of knowledge are as follows:

> Facts—factual knowledge about the characteristics of elements in the world, such as "Sacramento is the capital of California"
> Concepts—conceptual knowledge, including categories, schemas, or models, such as knowing the difference between plants and animals or knowing how a battery works
> Procedures—procedural knowledge of step-by-step processes, such as how to carry out long-division computations
> Strategies—strategic knowledge of general methods such as breaking a problem into parts or thinking of a related problem
> Beliefs—attitudinal knowledge about how one's cognitive processing works such as thinking, "I'm good at this"

Although some research focuses mainly on the role of facts and procedures in problem solving, complex problem solving also depends on the problem solver's concepts, strategies, and beliefs (Mayer, 1992).

## Historical Approaches to Problem Solving

Psychological research on problem solving began in the early 1900s, as an outgrowth of mental philosophy (Humphrey, 1963; Mandler & Mandler, 1964). Throughout the 20th century four theoretical approaches developed: early conceptions, associationism, Gestalt psychology, and information processing.

### Early Conceptions

The start of psychology as a science can be set at 1879—the year Wilhelm Wundt opened the first world's psychology laboratory in Leipzig, Germany, and sought to train the world's first cohort of experimental psychologists. Instead of relying solely on philosophical speculations about how the human mind works, Wundt sought to apply the methods of experimental science to issues addressed in mental philosophy. His theoretical approach became *structuralism*—the analysis of consciousness into its basic elements.

Wundt's main contribution to the study of problem solving, however, was to call for its banishment. According to Wundt, complex cognitive processing was too complicated to be studied by experimental methods, so "nothing can be discovered in such experiments" (Wundt, 1911/1973). Despite his admonishments, however, a group of his former students began studying thinking mainly in Wurzburg, Germany. Using the method of introspection, subjects were asked to describe their thought process as they solved word association problems, such as finding the superordinate of "newspaper" (e.g., an answer is "publication"). Although the Wurzburg group—as they came to be called—did not produce a new theoretical approach, they found empirical evidence that challenged some of the key assumptions of mental philosophy. For example, Aristotle had proclaimed that all thinking involves mental imagery, but the Wurzburg group was able to find empirical evidence for *imageless thought*.

### Associationism

The first major theoretical approach to take hold in the scientific study of problem solving was *associationism*—the idea that the cognitive representations in the mind consist of ideas and links between them and that cognitive processing in the mind involves following a chain of associations from one idea to the next (Mandler & Mandler, 1964; Mayer, 1992). For example, in a classic study, E. L. Thorndike (1911) placed a hungry cat in what he called a puzzle box—a wooden crate in which pulling a loop of string that hung from overhead would open a trap door to allow the cat to escape to a bowl of food outside the crate. Thorndike placed the cat in the puzzle box once a day for several weeks. On the first day, the cat engaged in many extraneous behaviors such as pouncing against the wall, pushing its paws through the slats, and meowing, but on successive days the number of extraneous behaviors tended to decrease. Overall, the time required to get out of the puzzle box decreased over the course of the experiment, indicating the cat was learning how to escape.

Thorndike's explanation for how the cat learned to solve the puzzle box problem is based on an associationist view: The cat begins with a *habit family hierarchy*—a set of potential responses (e.g., pouncing, thrusting, meowing, etc.) all associated with the same stimulus (i.e., being hungry and confined) and ordered in terms of strength of association. When placed in the puzzle box, the cat executes its strongest response (e.g., perhaps pouncing against the wall), but when it fails, the strength of the association is weakened, and so on for each unsuccessful action. Eventually, the cat gets down to what was initially a weak response—waving its paw in the air—but when that response leads to accidentally pulling the string and getting out, it is strengthened. Over the course of many trials, the ineffective responses become weak and the successful response becomes strong. Thorndike refers to this process as the *law of effect*: Responses that lead to dissatisfaction become less associated with the situation and responses that lead to satisfaction become more associated with the situation. According to Thorndike's associationist view, solving a problem is simply a matter of trial and error and accidental success. A major challenge to associationist theory concerns the nature of transfer—that is, where does a problem solver find a creative solution that has never been performed before? Associationist conceptions of cognition can be seen in current research, including neural networks, connectionist models, and parallel distributed processing models (Rogers & McClelland, 2004).

### Gestalt Psychology

The Gestalt approach to problem solving developed in the 1930s and 1940s as a counterbalance to the associationist approach. According to the Gestalt approach, cognitive representations consist of coherent structures (rather than individual associations) and the cognitive process of problem solving involves building a coherent structure (rather than strengthening and weakening of associations). For example, in a classic study, Kohler (1925) placed a hungry ape in a play yard that contained several empty shipping crates and a banana attached overhead but out of reach. Based on observing the ape in this situation, Kohler noted that the ape did not randomly try responses until one worked—as suggested by Thorndike's associationist view. Instead, the ape stood under the banana, looked up at it, looked at the crates, and then in a flash of insight stacked the crates under the bananas as a ladder, and walked up the steps in order to reach the banana.

According to Kohler, the ape experienced a sudden visual reorganization in which the elements in the situation fit together in a way to solve the problem; that is, the crates could become a ladder that reduces the distance to the banana. Kohler referred to the underlying mechanism as *insight*—literally seeing into the structure of the situation. A major challenge of Gestalt theory is its lack of precision; for example, naming a process (i.e., insight) is not the same as explaining how it works. Gestalt conceptions can be seen in modern research on mental models and schemas (Gentner & Stevens, 1983).

### Information Processing

The information processing approach to problem solving developed in the 1960s and 1970s and was based on the influence of the computer metaphor—the idea that humans are processors of information (Mayer, 2009). According to the information processing approach, problem solving involves a series of mental computations—each of which consists of applying a process to a mental representation (such as comparing two elements to determine whether they differ).

In their classic book, *Human Problem Solving*, Newell and Simon (1972) proposed that problem solving involved a *problem space* and *search heuristics*. A problem space is a mental representation of the initial state of the problem, the goal state of the problem, and all possible intervening states (based on applying allowable operators). Search heuristics are strategies for moving through the problem space from the given to the goal state. Newell and Simon focused on *means-ends analysis*, in which the problem solver continually sets goals and finds moves to accomplish goals.

Newell and Simon used computer simulation as a research method to test their conception of human problem solving. First, they asked human problem solvers to think aloud as they solved various problems such as logic problems, chess, and cryptarithmetic problems. Then, based on an information processing analysis, Newell and Simon created computer programs that solved these problems. In comparing the solution behavior of humans and computers, they found high similarity, suggesting that the computer programs were solving problems using the same thought processes as humans.

An important advantage of the information processing approach is that problem solving can be described with great clarity—as a computer program. An important limitation of the information processing approach is that it is most useful for describing problem solving for well-defined problems rather than ill-defined problems. The information processing conception of cognition lives on as a keystone of today's cognitive science (Mayer, 2009).

## Classic Issues in Problem Solving

Three classic issues in research on problem solving concern the nature of transfer (suggested by the associationist approach), the nature of insight (suggested by the Gestalt approach), and the role of problem-solving heuristics (suggested by the information processing approach).

### Transfer

*Transfer* refers to the effects of prior learning on new learning (or new problem solving). *Positive transfer* occurs when learning A helps someone learn B. *Negative transfer* occurs when learning A hinders someone from learning B. *Neutral transfer* occurs when learning A has no effect on learning B. Positive transfer is a central goal of education, but research shows that people often do not transfer what they learned to solving problems in new contexts (Mayer, 1992; Singley & Anderson, 1989).

Three conceptions of the mechanisms underlying transfer are *specific transfer*, *general transfer*, and *specific transfer of general principles*. Specific transfer refers to the idea that learning A will help someone learn B only if A and B have specific elements in common. For example, learning Spanish may help someone learn Latin because some of the vocabulary words are similar and the verb conjugation rules are similar. General transfer refers to the idea that learning A can help someone learn B even they have nothing specifically in common but A helps improve the learner's mind in general. For example, learning Latin may help people learn "proper habits of mind" so they are better able to learn completely unrelated subjects as well. Specific transfer of general principles is the idea that learning A will help someone learn B if the same general principle or solution method is required for both even if the specific elements are different.

In a classic study, Thorndike and Woodworth (1901) found that students who learned Latin did not subsequently learn bookkeeping any better than students who had not learned Latin. They interpreted this finding as evidence for specific transfer—learning A did not transfer to learning B because A and B did not have specific elements in common. Modern research on problem-solving transfer continues to show that people often do not demonstrate general transfer (Mayer, 1992). However, it is possible to teach people a general strategy for solving a problem, so that when they see a new problem in a different context they are able to apply the strategy to the new problem (Judd, 1908; Mayer, 2008)—so there is also research support for the idea of specific transfer of general principles.

### Insight

*Insight* refers to a change in a problem solver's mind from not knowing how to solve a problem to knowing how to solve it (Mayer, 1995; Metcalfe & Wiebe, 1987). In short, where does the idea for a creative solution come from? A central goal of problem-solving research is to determine the mechanisms underlying insight.

The search for insight has led to five major (but not mutually exclusive) explanatory mechanisms— insight as completing a schema, insight as suddenly reorganizing visual information, insight as reformulation of a problem, insight as removing mental blocks, and insight as finding a problem analog (Mayer, 1995). Completing a schema is exemplified in a study by Selz (Fridja & de Groot, 1982), in which people were asked to think aloud as they solved word association problems such as "What is the superordinate for newspaper?" To solve the problem, people sometimes thought of a coordinate, such as "magazine," and then searched for a superordinate category that subsumed both terms, such as "publication." According to Selz, finding a solution involved building a schema that consisted of a superordinate and two subordinate categories.

Reorganizing visual information is reflected in Kohler's (1925) study described in a previous section in which a hungry ape figured out how to stack boxes as a ladder to reach a banana hanging above. According to Kohler, the ape looked around the yard and found the solution in a flash of insight by mentally seeing how the parts could be rearranged to accomplish the goal.

Reformulating a problem is reflected in a classic study by Duncker (1945) in which people are asked to think aloud as they solve the tumor problem— how can you destroy a tumor in a patient without destroying surrounding healthy tissue by using rays that at sufficient intensity will destroy any tissue in their path? In analyzing the thinking-aloud protocols—that is, transcripts of what the problem solvers said—Duncker concluded that people reformulated the goal in various ways (e.g., avoid contact with healthy tissue, immunize healthy tissue, have ray be weak in healthy tissue) until they hit upon a productive formulation that led to the solution (i.e., concentrating many weak rays on the tumor).

Removing mental blocks is reflected in classic studies by Duncker (1945) in which solving a problem involved thinking of a novel use for an object, and by Luchins (1942) in which solving a problem involved not using a procedure that had worked well on previous problems. Finding a problem analog is reflected in classic research by Wertheimer (1959) in which learning to find the area of a parallelogram is supported by the insight that one could cut off the triangle on one side and place it on the other side to form a rectangle—so a parallelogram is really a rectangle in disguise. The search for insight along each of these five lines continues in current problem-solving research.

### Heuristics

Heuristics are problem-solving strategies, that is, general approaches to how to solve problems. Newell and Simon (1972) suggested three general problem-solving heuristics for moving from a given state to a goal state: *random trial and error*, *hill climbing*, and *means-ends analysis*. Random trial and error involves randomly selecting a legal move and applying it to create a new problem state, and repeating that process until the goal state is reached. Random trial and error may work for simple problems but is not efficient for complex ones. Hill climbing involves selecting the legal move that moves the problem solver closer to the goal state. Hill climbing will not work for problems in which the problem solver must take a move that temporarily moves away from the goal as is required in many problems.

Means-ends analysis involves creating goals and seeking moves that can accomplish the goal. If a goal cannot be directly accomplished, a subgoal is created to remove one or more obstacles. Newell and Simon (1972) successfully used means-ends analysis as the search heuristic in a computer program aimed at general problem solving, that is, solving a diverse collection of problems. However, people may also use specific heuristics that are designed to work for specific problem-solving situations (Gigerenzer, Todd, & ABC Research Group, 1999; Kahneman & Tversky, 1984).

### Current and Future Issues in Problem Solving

Eight current issues in problem solving involve decision making, intelligence and creativity, teaching of thinking skills, expert problem solving, analogical reasoning, mathematical and scientific problem solving, everyday thinking, and the cognitive neuroscience of problem solving.

### Decision Making

Decision making refers to the cognitive processing involved in choosing between two or more alternatives (Baron, 2000; Markman & Medin, 2002). For example, a decision-making task may involve choosing between getting $240 for sure or having a 25% change of getting $1000. According to economic theories such as expected value theory, people should chose the second option, which is worth $250 (i.e., .25 x $1000) rather than the first option, which is worth $240 (1.00 x $240), but psychological research shows that most people prefer the first option (Kahneman & Tversky, 1984).

Research on decision making has generated three classes of theories (Markman & Medin, 2002): descriptive theories, such as prospect theory (Kahneman & Tversky), which are based on the ideas that people prefer to overweight the cost of a loss and tend to overestimate small probabilities; heuristic theories, which are based on the idea that people use a collection of short-cut strategies such as the availability heuristic (Gigerenzer et al., 1999; Kahneman & Tversky, 2000); and constructive theories, such as mental accounting (Kahneman & Tversky, 2000), in which people build a narrative to justify their choices to themselves. Future research is needed to examine decision making in more realistic settings.

### Intelligence and Creativity

Although researchers do not have complete consensus on the definition of intelligence (Sternberg, 1990), it is reasonable to view intelligence as the ability to learn or adapt to new situations. *Fluid intelligence* refers to the potential to solve problems without any relevant knowledge, whereas *crystallized intelligence* refers to the potential to solve problems based on relevant prior knowledge (Sternberg & Gregorenko, 2003). As people gain more experience in a field, their problem-solving performance depends more on crystallized intelligence (i.e., domain knowledge) than on fluid intelligence (i.e., general ability) (Sternberg & Gregorenko, 2003). The ability to monitor and manage one's cognitive processing during problem solving—which can be called *metacognition*—is an important aspect of intelligence (Sternberg, 1990). Research is needed to pinpoint the knowledge that is needed to support intelligent performance on problem-solving tasks.

Creativity refers to the ability to generate ideas that are original (i.e., other people do not think of the same idea) and functional (i.e., the idea works; Sternberg, 1999). Creativity is often measured using tests of *divergent thinking*—that is, generating as many solutions as possible for a problem (Guilford, 1967). For example, the uses test asks people to list as many uses as they can think of for a brick. Creativity is different from intelligence, and it is at the heart of creative problem solving—generating a novel solution to a problem that the problem solver has never seen before. An important research question concerns whether creative problem solving depends on specific knowledge or creativity ability in general.

### Teaching of Thinking Skills

How can people learn to be better problem solvers? Mayer (2008) proposes four questions concerning teaching of thinking skills:

*What to teach*—Successful programs attempt to teach small component skills (such as how to generate and evaluate hypotheses) rather than improve the mind as a single monolithic skill (Covington, Crutchfield, Davies, & Olton, 1974).
*How to teach*—Successful programs focus on modeling the process of problem solving rather than solely reinforcing the product of problem solving (Bloom & Broder, 1950).
*Where to teach*—Successful programs teach problem-solving skills within the specific context they will be used rather than within a general course on how to solve problems (Nickerson, 1999).
*When to teach*—Successful programs teaching higher order skills early rather than waiting until lower order skills are completely mastered (Tharp & Gallimore, 1988).

Overall, research on teaching of thinking skills points to the domain specificity of problem solving; that is, successful problem solving depends on the problem solver having domain knowledge that is relevant to the problem-solving task.

### Expert Problem Solving

Research on expertise is concerned with differences between how experts and novices solve problems (Ericsson, Feltovich, & Hoffman, 2006).

Expertise can be defined in terms of time (e.g., 10 years of concentrated experience in a field), performance (e.g., earning a perfect score on an assessment), or recognition (e.g., receiving a Nobel Prize or becoming Grand Master in chess). For example, in classic research conducted in the 1940s, de Groot (1965) found that chess experts did not have better general memory than chess novices, but they did have better domain-specific memory for the arrangement of chess pieces on the board. Chase and Simon (1973) replicated this result in a better controlled experiment. An explanation is that experts have developed schemas that allow them to chunk collections of pieces into a single configuration.

In another landmark study, Larkin et al. (1980) compared how experts (e.g., physics professors) and novices (e.g., first-year physics students) solved textbook physics problems about motion. Experts tended to work forward from the given information to the goal, whereas novices tended to work backward from the goal to the givens using a means-ends analysis strategy. Experts tended to store their knowledge in an integrated way, whereas novices tended to store their knowledge in isolated fragments. In another study, Chi, Feltovich, and Glaser (1981) found that experts tended to focus on the underlying physics concepts (such as conservation of energy), whereas novices tended to focus on the surface features of the problem (such as inclined planes or springs). Overall, research on expertise is useful in pinpointing what experts know that is different from what novices know. An important theme is that experts rely on domain-specific knowledge rather than solely general cognitive ability.

### Analogical Reasoning

Analogical reasoning occurs when people solve one problem by using their knowledge about another problem (Holyoak, 2005). For example, suppose a problem solver learns how to solve a problem in one context using one solution method and then is given a problem in another context that requires the same solution method. In this case, the problem solver must recognize that the new problem has structural similarity to the old problem (i.e., it may be solved by the same method), even though they do not have surface similarity (i.e., the cover stories are different). Three steps in analogical reasoning are *recognizing*—seeing that a new problem is similar to a previously solved problem; *abstracting*—finding the general method used to solve the old problem; and *mapping*—using that general method to solve the new problem.

Research on analogical reasoning shows that people often do not recognize that a new problem can be solved by the same method as a previously solved problem (Holyoak, 2005). However, research also shows that successful analogical transfer to a new problem is more likely when the problem solver has experience with two old problems that have the same underlying structural features (i.e., they are solved by the same principle) but different surface features (i.e., they have different cover stories) (Holyoak, 2005). This finding is consistent with the idea of specific transfer of general principles as described in the section on "Transfer."

## Mathematical and Scientific Problem Solving

Research on mathematical problem solving suggests that five kinds of knowledge are needed to solve arithmetic word problems (Mayer, 2008):

*Factual knowledge*—knowledge about the characteristics of problem elements, such as knowing that there are 100 cents in a dollar
*Schematic knowledge*—knowledge of problem types, such as being able to recognize time-rate-distance problems
*Strategic knowledge*—knowledge of general methods, such as how to break a problem into parts
*Procedural knowledge*—knowledge of processes, such as how to carry our arithmetic operations
*Attitudinal knowledge*—beliefs about one's mathematical problem-solving ability, such as thinking, "I am good at this"

People generally possess adequate procedural knowledge but may have difficulty in solving mathematics problems because they lack factual, schematic, strategic, or attitudinal knowledge (Mayer, 2008). Research is needed to pinpoint the role of domain knowledge in mathematical problem solving.

Research on scientific problem solving shows that people harbor misconceptions, such as believing that a force is needed to keep an object in motion (McCloskey, 1983). Learning to solve science problems involves conceptual change, in which the problem solver comes to recognize that previous conceptions are wrong (Mayer, 2008). Students can be taught to engage in scientific reasoning such as hypothesis testing through direct instruction in how to control for variables (Chen & Klahr, 1999). A central theme of research on scientific problem solving concerns the role of domain knowledge.

## Everyday Thinking

Everyday thinking refers to problem solving in the context of one's life outside of school. For example, children who are street vendors tend to use different procedures for solving arithmetic problems when they are working on the streets than when they are in school (Nunes, Schlieman, & Carraher, 1993). This line of research highlights the role of *situated cognition*—the idea that thinking always is shaped by the physical and social context in which it occurs (Robbins & Aydede, 2009). Research is needed to determine how people solve problems in authentic contexts.

## Cognitive Neuroscience of Problem Solving

The cognitive neuroscience of problem solving is concerned with the brain activity that occurs during problem solving. For example, using fMRI brain imaging methodology, Goel (2005) found that people used the language areas of the brain to solve logical reasoning problems presented in sentences (e.g., "All dogs are pets...") and used the spatial areas of the brain to solve logical reasoning problems presented in abstract letters (e.g., "All D are P..."). Cognitive neuroscience holds the potential to make unique contributions to the study of problem solving.

## Conclusion

Problem solving has always been a topic at the fringe of cognitive psychology—too complicated to study intensively but too important to completely ignore. Problem solving—especially in realistic environments—is messy in comparison to studying elementary processes in cognition. The field remains fragmented in the sense that topics such as decision making, reasoning, intelligence, expertise, mathematical problem solving, everyday thinking, and the like are considered to be separate topics, each with its own separate literature. Yet some recurring themes are the role of domain-specific knowledge in problem solving and the advantages of studying problem solving in authentic contexts.

## Future Directions

Some important issues for future research include the three classic issues examined in this chapter—the nature of problem-solving transfer (i.e., How are people able to use what they know about previous problem solving to help them in new problem solving?), the nature of insight (e.g., What is the mechanism by which a creative solution is constructed?), and heuristics (e.g., What are some teachable strategies for problem solving?). In addition, future research in problem solving should continue to pinpoint the role of domain-specific knowledge in problem solving, the nature of cognitive ability in problem solving, how to help people develop proficiency in solving problems, and how to provide aids for problem solving.

# References

Anderson, L. W., Krathwohl, D. R., Airasian, P. W., Cruikshank, K. A., Mayer, R. E., Pintrich, P. R., Raths, J., & Wittrock, M. C. (2001). *A taxonomy for learning, teaching, and assessing: A revision of Bloom's taxonomy of educational objectives.* New York: Longman.

Baron, J. (2000). *Thinking and deciding* (3rd ed.). New York: Cambridge University Press.

Bloom, B. S., & Broder, B. J. (1950). *Problem-solving processes of college students: An exploratory investigation.* Chicago: University of Chicago Press.

Chase, W. G., & Simon, H. A. (1973). Perception in chess. *Cognitive Psychology, 4,* 55–81.

Chen, Z., & Klahr, D. (1999). All other things being equal: Acquisition and transfer of the control of variable strategy. *Child Development, 70,* 1098–1120.

Chi, M. T. H., Feltovich, P. J., & Glaser, R. (1981). Categorization and representation of physics problems by experts and novices. *Cognitive Science, 5,* 121–152.

Covington, M. V., Crutchfield, R. S., Davies, L. B., & Olton, R. M. (1974). *The productive thinking program.* Columbus, OH: Merrill.

de Groot, A. D. (1965). *Thought and choice in chess.* The Hague, The Netherlands: Mouton.

Duncker, K. (1945). On problem solving. *Psychological Monographs, 58*(3) (Whole No. 270).

Ericsson, K. A., Feltovich, P. J., & Hoffman, R. R. (Eds.). (2006). *The Cambridge handbook of expertise and expert performance.* New York: Cambridge University Press.

Fridja, N. H., & de Groot, A. D. (1982). *Otto Selz: His contribution to psychology.* The Hague, The Netherlands: Mouton.

Gentner, D., & Stevens, A. L. (Eds.). (1983). *Mental models.* Hillsdale, NJ: Erlbaum.

Gigerenzer, G., Todd, P. M., & ABC Research Group (Eds.). (1999). *Simple heuristics that make us smart.* Oxford, England: Oxford University Press.

Goel, V. (2005). Cognitive neuroscience of deductive reasoning. In K. J. Holyoak & R. G. Morrison (Eds.), *The Cambridge handbook of thinking and reasoning* (pp. 475–492). New York: Cambridge University Press.

Guilford, J. P. (1967). *The nature of human intelligence.* New York: McGraw-Hill.

Holyoak, K. J. (2005). Analogy. In K. J. Holyoak & R. G. Morrison (Eds.), *The Cambridge handbook of thinking and reasoning* (pp. 117–142). New York: Cambridge University Press.

Humphrey, G. (1963). *Thinking: An introduction to experimental psychology.* New York: Wiley.

Judd, C. H. (1908). The relation of special training and general intelligence. *Educational Review, 36,* 28–42.

Kahneman, D., & Tversky, A. (1984). Choices, values, and frames. *American Psychologist, 39,* 341–350.

Kahneman, D., & Tversky, A. (Eds.). (2000). *Choices, values, and frames.* New York: Cambridge University Press.

Kohler, W. (1925). *The mentality of apes.* New York: Liveright.

Larkin, J. H., McDermott, J., Simon, D. P., & Simon, H. A. (1980). Expert and novice performance in solving physics problems. *Science, 208,* 1335–1342.

Luchins, A. (1942). Mechanization in problem solving. *Psychological Monographs, 54*(6) (Whole No. 248).

Mandler, J. M., & Mandler, G. (1964). *Thinking from associationism to Gestalt.* New York: Wiley.

Markman, A. B., & Medin, D. L. (2002). Decision making. In D. Medin (Ed.), *Stevens' handbook of experimental psychology, Vol. 2. Memory and cognitive processes* (2nd ed., pp. 413–466). New York: Wiley.

Mayer, R. E. (1992). *Thinking, problem solving, cognition* (2nd ed). New York: Freeman.

Mayer, R. E. (1995). The search for insight: Grappling with Gestalt psychology's unanswered questions. In R. J. Sternberg & J. E. Davidson (Eds.), *The nature of insight* (pp. 3–32). Cambridge, MA: MIT Press.

Mayer, R. E. (2008). *Learning and instruction.* Upper Saddle River, NJ: Merrill Prentice Hall.

Mayer, R. E. (2009). Information processing. In T. L. Good (Ed.), *21st century education: A reference handbook* (pp. 168–174). Thousand Oaks, CA: Sage.

Mayer, R. E., & Wittrock, M. C. (2006). Problem solving. In P. A. Alexander & P. H. Winne (Eds.), *Handbook of educational psychology* (2nd ed., pp. 287–304). Mahwah, NJ: Erlbaum.

McCloskey, M. (1983). Intuitive physics. *Scientific American, 248*(4), 122–130.

Metcalfe, J., & Wiebe, D. (1987). Intuition in insight and non-insight problem solving. *Memory and Cognition, 15,* 238–246.

Newell, A., & Simon, H. A. (1972). *Human problem solving.* Englewood Cliffs, NJ: Prentice-Hall.

Nickerson, R. S. (1999). Enhancing creativity. In R. J. Sternberg (Ed.), *Handbook of creativity* (pp. 392–430). New York: Cambridge University Press.

Nunes, T., Schliemann, A. D., & Carraher, D. W. (1993). *Street mathematics and school mathematics.* Cambridge, England: Cambridge University Press.

Robbins, P., & Aydede, M. (Eds.). (2009). *The Cambridge handbook of situated cognition.* New York: Cambridge University Press.

Rogers, T. T., & McClelland, J. L. (2004). *Semantic cognition: A parallel distributed processing approach.* Cambridge, MA: MIT Press.

Singley, M. K., & Anderson, J. R. (1989). *The transfer of cognitive skill.* Cambridge, MA: Harvard University Press.

Sternberg, R. J. (1990). *Metaphors of mind: Conceptions of the nature of intelligence.* New York: Cambridge University Press.

Sternberg, R. J. (1999). *Handbook of creativity.* New York: Cambridge University Press.

Sternberg, R. J., & Gregorenko, E. L. (Eds.). (2003). *The psychology of abilities, competencies, and expertise.* New York: Cambridge University Press.

Tharp, R. G., & Gallimore, R. (1988). *Rousing minds to life: Teaching, learning, and schooling in social context.* New York: Cambridge University Press.

Thorndike, E. L. (1911). *Animal intelligence.* New York: Hafner.

Thorndike, E. L., & Woodworth, R. S. (1901). The influence of improvement in one mental function upon the efficiency of other functions. *Psychological Review, 8,* 247–261.

Wertheimer, M. (1959). *Productive thinking.* New York: Harper and Collins.

Wundt, W. (1973). *An introduction to experimental psychology.* New York: Arno Press. (Original work published in 1911).

## Further Reading

Baron, J. (2008). *Thinking and deciding* (4th ed). New York: Cambridge University Press.

Duncker, K. (1945). On problem solving. *Psychological Monographs, 58*(3) (Whole No. 270).

Holyoak, K. J., & Morrison, R. G. (2005). *The Cambridge handbook of thinking and reasoning.* New York: Cambridge University Press.

Mayer, R. E., & Wittrock, M. C. (2006). Problem solving. In P. A. Alexander & P. H. Winne (Eds.), *Handbook of educational psychology* (2nd ed., pp. 287–304). Mahwah, NJ: Erlbaum.

Sternberg, R. J., & Ben-Zeev, T. (2001). *Complex cognition: The psychology of human thought.* New York: Oxford University Press.

Weisberg, R. W. (2006). *Creativity.* New York: Wiley.

# Insight

Jessica I. Fleck, Mark Beeman, *and* John Kounios

**Abstract**

In the early 1900s, the Gestalt psychologists introduced insight as a component process in perception and problem solving. Since the inception of the scientific study of insight, researchers have examined the phenomenological, behavioral, and neural components of insight, and how insight and other forms of cognition (e.g., analysis) differ in the aforementioned areas. This chapter reviews the historical contributions to the insight field, as well as the most recent and influential research that has shaped our understanding of insight. Of significance is research examining the faciliatory and inhibitory influences of prior knowledge, the antecedents of representational change, the neural components associated with insight, and the recent interest in enhancing rates of insight experiences. We conclude with an integration of research conducted to date, and we posit potential directions for the field as we continue to advance our knowledge of insight and its role in the creative process.

**Key Words:** knowledge, fixation, impasse, restructuring, Gestalt, special process, hemispheric differences, anterior cingulate cortex, superior temporal gyrus

When research on insight was first proposed by the Gestalt psychologists almost a century ago (e.g., Duncker, 1945; Koffka, 1935; Köhler, 1925), the distinction between insight and analysis as separate forms of thought was largely intuitive. The Gestalt psychologists' two-process theory was supported by historical anecdotes detailing experiences that yielded highly creative products (e.g., Archimedes, Poincaré, and Newton) and the ordinary individual's encounters with the phenomenology that accompanies a sudden solution to a previously unanswerable problem (i.e., the Aha! experience). Since that time insight has waxed and waned as a research area in cognitive psychology and related disciplines, and it has changed in scope and method of study. The modern importance of understanding the insight effect, as well as its contribution to the creative process (i.e., illumination; Wallas, 1926), has revitalized theory and research in this fascinating area.

Generally, insight has been described as attaining understanding in a situation that, beforehand, had been misunderstood (Mayer, 1995). In problem solving, the individual initially misrepresents a problem's components in such a way that a solution is not possible, either by focusing on irrelevant information retrieved from long-term memory (Knoblich, Ohlsson, Haider, & Rhenius, 1999; Ohlsson, 1992; Seifert, Meyer, Davidson, Patalano, & Yaniv, 1995) or attempting to craft a solution from incomplete information (Kaplan & Simon, 1990). A discontinuity or restructuring of thought, therefore, is needed to alter the solver's representation (Ohlsson, 1992; Weisberg, 1995) to create the potential for solution. Unique to the insight experience is that many of the components of this process are believed to operate outside the conscious awareness of the problem solver (Bowers, Regehr, Balthazard, & Parker, 1990; Metcalfe & Wiebe, 1987), so much so that the solver may be surprised by the ease and suddenness at which the entire solution is achieved (Smith & Kounios, 1996). Combined, these components describe a process that is distinct from that of analysis (Newell & Simon, 1972) or trial and error (Thorndike, 1898), in which a deliberate, incremental approach is applied.

Historically, *insight* was a term used to describe the sudden and often spontaneous reorganization of thought in a problem solver who was initially misled (see Ohlsson, 1984). Initially, the empirical study of insight involved assessing participants' abilities to solve *classic* insight problems (problems believed to be solved solely with insight; see Fig. 49.1) and the factors that facilitated or impeded participants' success. More recent research in the field has shifted from research centered on the occurrence of solutions to classic insight problems (e.g., Metcalfe &

(A) Problem: Without lifting your pencil, connect the nine dots using four straight lines.

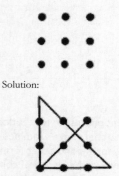

Solution:

(B) Problem: Using the items provided, attach the candle to a door so it can burn properly.

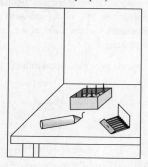

Solution: Empty the tacks from the box and use the box as a ledge to support the candle.

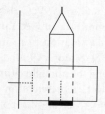

(C) Problem: Given a human being with an inoperable stomach tumor, and lasers which destroy organic tissue at sufficient intensity, how can one cure the person with these lasers and, at the same time, avoid harming the healthy tissue that surrounds the tumor?

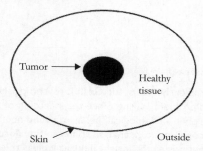

Solution: Use multiple low-intensity lasers applied from different locations outside the body with all lasers converging at the location of the tumor. This will generate sufficient intensity at the tumor site to destroy the tumor but, at the same time, will not destroy the healthy tissue surrounding it.

(D) Problem: Your task is to tie the two stings together. Keep in mind that when you hold one string in your hand, it is not possible for you to reach out and grab the other string.

Solution: Tie the pliers to one of the strings and get the string to swing back and forth like a pendulum. You would then be able to pull the second string over as far as possible and wait for the first string to swing within your reach.

**Figure 49.1** Classic insight problems and their solutions. (A) The nine-dot Problem (Maier, 1930). (B) The Candle Problem (Duncker, 1945); Problem: Reprinted with permission from Cognitive Psychology, Vol 4, Robert W. Weisberg and Jerry M. Suls, An information-processing model of Duncker's Candle Problem, pp. 255–276, Copyright 1973, with permission from Elsevier Inc. Solution: Reprinted with permission from Memory & Cognition, Vol 32, Jessica I. Fleck and Robert W. Weisberg, The use of verbal protocols as data: An analysis of insight in the candle problem, pp. 990–1006, Copyright 2004, by The Psychonomic Society. (C) The Radiation Problem (Duncker, 1945, p. 1); problem: Reprinted from Psychological Science, Vol 14, Elizabeth R. Grant and Michael J. Spivey, Eye movements and problem solving: Guiding attention guides thought, p. 462–466, Copyright 2003, with permission from John Wiley & Sons, Ltd. (D) The Two-string Problem (Maier, 1930); Problem: Reprinted from *Cognitive Psychology and its Implications*, J. R. Anderson, p. 283, Copyright (1980), with permission from W. H. Freeman and Company.

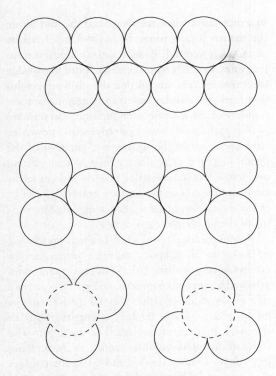

**Figure 49.2** Eight-coin problems and their solution.

Wiebe, 1987; Schooler, Ohlsson, & Brooks, 1993), to research focused on elucidating the cognitive and affective processes that are associated with the insight experience (e.g., Knoblich et al., 1999; MacGregor, Ormerod, & Chronicle, 2001). This shift to process has expanded the stimuli appropriate for study in insight research, to include problems that are primarily, though not exclusively, solved via insight (see the eight-coin problem in Fig. 49.2), or problems that could be solved with or without insight (e.g., anagrams and remote associate problems discussed later).

To isolate insight solutions from those arising from analysis, researchers rely on factors such as self-report (e.g., Jung-Beeman et al., 2004) and eye-movement data (e.g., Thomas & Lleras, 2009a) to determine that insight has occurred. For example, problems such as anagrams are used as stimuli in insight research by examining only the trials reported to have been solved by insight (see Kounios et al., 2008). In contrast, the Gestalt psychologists would have explored all solutions to the nine-dot problem (see Fig. 49.1) as data in the study of insight. The aforementioned changes in stimuli, the shift in research focus from problem solution to the solving process, and the modifications to the very definition of insight, illustrate how broad a construct insight

has become. Existing research elucidating the cognitive, behavioral, and neural components of insight has only begun to address many of the questions surrounding this unique cognitive process (e.g., Sternberg & Davidson, 1995; Weisberg, 2006). In this chapter we address some of the most fundamental and universally held questions concerning the experience of insight and review existing research that attempts to answer them: In what ways can knowledge inhibit or facilitate the occurrence of insight? What factors precipitate restructuring and what is the nature of the representational change itself (e.g., conscious versus unconscious)? Is insight truly unique from other forms of thought? Is it possible to induce a mental state that fosters insight? Finally, what are the future directions for research in this growing field?

## The Role of Knowledge in Insight: From Fixation to Productive Thought

A collection of seminal works published in the early 1900s expressed the core principles held by the Gestalt psychologists (e.g., Duncker, 1945; Koffka, 1935; Köhler, 1925; Wertheimer, 1945/1959). Pivotal to their theory was the proposal of a distinct form of knowledge (i.e., different from that used in trial and error) essential to insight and how the incorrect application of prior knowledge delayed or impeded the insight experience. Though many have criticized the Gestalt psychologists for a lack of methodological rigor in their work (e.g., Mayer, 1995; Ohlsson, 1992), their theories have served as the foundation for modern insight research. An excellent review and integration of the Gestalt principles as they pertain to problem solving is available in Ohlsson (1984).

The Gestalt psychologists proposed that insight required the acquisition of knowledge structures beyond those of ordinary thought, such as trial and error (Duncker, 1945; Köhler, 1925). Ordinary thought could be fueled by reproductive thinking (i.e., reiterating previous ideas or approaches), whereas insight required productive thinking (Wertheimer, 1945/1959; see also Mandler & Mandler, 1964), in which a deeper conceptual understanding directed how/which knowledge components could be combined in novel ways or which stimuli from the environment were relevant to a particular situation. Furthermore, Wertheimer suggested that insight was not the result of the problem solver blindly recombining problem elements in search of a solution but gaining the necessary structure on which to build a solution. Thus, a lack of success in problem solving could stem from the retrieval of irrelevant information from long-term memory, or the retrieval of relevant components but an absence of the necessary structure with which to link these components.

Problem solvers have experienced limited success in solving classic insight problems, such as the nine-dot problem (Maier, 1930; see Fig. 49.1), in the absence of productive thought. One attempt at explaining participants' failure with this problem (solution rates are consistently less than 10% without hints) has been to propose that problem solvers fail to possess solution-relevant knowledge concerning how lines can be extended outside the initial nine-dot square or the memory capacity to mentally construct the solution configuration (e.g., Chronicle, Ormerod, & MacGregor, 2001; Kershaw & Ohlsson, 2004). However, attempts to provide participants with strategies and hints regarding principles for solution (e.g., Lung & Dominowski, 1985; Weisberg & Alba, 1981), as well as perceptual hints signifying the overall solution configuration (Chronicle et al., 2001; MacGregor et al., 2001), have achieved only modest gains in solution rates. For example, in research with the nine-dot problem, Chronicle et al. (2001) provided participants with the problem over the top of a shaded figure whose perimeter mirrored the solution configuration (see Fig. 49.3). This shaded figure was presented with or without the hint that the shaded region would be of value when generating the solution. Despite these hints, only 16% of participants solved the problem when the shaded figure was present; this increased

**Figure 49.3** Nine-dot solution hint.

to a mere 30% when the figure and the hint to use the shaded region where both provided. Kershaw and Olsson were able to substantially facilitate solution rates, but only when extensive prior knowledge was provided (i.e., knowledge about pivoting solution lines on non-dot points, a conceptual understanding of the solution configuration, and training to shift participants away from irrelevant knowledge structures such as the square configuration of the dots). Together, these finding suggest that gaining problem-relevant knowledge may do little to facilitate solution success unless that knowledge results in the acquisition of a deep conceptual understanding of the problem's components.

Recent electrophysiological research conducted by Lang et al. (2006) examined differences in event-related potentials (ERPs) in participants who achieved a conceptual understanding of a patterned rule in the number reduction task (NRT; insight group) and those who did not (no insight group). In the NRT, participants are asked to make pair-wise comparisons of six-number sequences by applying two rules—identity (both numbers in the pair are the same) and difference (both numbers in the pair differ). Of importance is determining the final judgment in the sequence as quickly as possible. For all trials, the pattern of responses was ABCCB, such that the solution response for the final comparison, B, was always the same as the second response in the sequence. Forming an explicit understanding of the sequencing rule was viewed as achieving insight. Lang et al. observed several differences in the ERP waveforms between participants who did and did not achieve insight into the sequencing rule, to include greater slow-positive-waveform (SPW) amplitude across the length of the trial over parietal electrode sites, and enhanced P3a amplitude over frontocentral sites. These effects have been tied to increased working-memory involvement (SPW; Vos, Gunter, Kohk, & Mulder, 2001) and the distinctiveness of encoding each stimulus (P3a; Gaeta, Friedman, & Hunt, 2003) in prior research. Combined, these results suggest that thought processes applied in earlier trials differentiated participants who would/ would not achieve a deep conceptual understanding of the task.

Though the Gestalt psychologists believed that a deep conceptual understanding was necessary to achieve insight, they also proposed that the recurring application of faulty knowledge from long-term memory (i.e., fixation) could thwart an individual's ability to achieve insight (Duncker, 1945; Luchins, 1942; Maier, 1930; Scheerer, 1963). Some of the earliest work on fixation was conducted by Duncker in his research with the candle problem (see Fig. 49.1). In the candle problem, participants are presented with a candle, a book of matches, and a box of tacks, and asked to devise a way to attach the candle to a door so it can burn properly. The insightful solution to this problem is to empty the tack box and use that box as a ledge to support the candle. However, the standard function of the box as a container is activated when solvers initially approach the problem (i.e., functional fixedness), limiting their ability to consider the tack box in other roles that may result in solution. Perseveration on an object's dominant function may be so extensive that an impasse results, in which the solver becomes increasingly fixated on a solution idea following repeated attempts at the same approach (Smith, 1995).

Modern theorists have suggested that when a problem solver's initial problem space contains irrelevant or incorrectly constructed prior knowledge an impasse will result in which no further work on the problem is possible (Knoblich et al., 1999; Ohlsson, 1992). Knoblich et al. proposed that a problem solver's prior knowledge leads him or her to incorrectly apply constraints to the problem-solving situation, limiting solution possibilities. In their research on matchstick arithmetic problems (see Fig. 49.4), participants' prior knowledge of algebra (relevant in most equation solving but not here) was believed to restrict ideas considered during problem solving. For example, participants may have assumed that the operands could be subdivided to correct the equation, whereas the operators could not. Continued progress was only possible if these mental constraints were relaxed and additional ideas could be considered for solution.

Despite the theoretical importance placed on fixation in insight, empirical research on fixation and impasse has been limited. This deficit likely stems from difficulty in operationally defining fixation (a time period of limited progress, the number of applications of the same solution approach) or determining if fixation is sufficient for the problem solver to reach impasse. Although insight problems are created with misleading components designed to generate fixation on irrelevant problem components (Weisberg, 1995), it is not necessarily the case that solvers are misled. Two approaches that have achieved some success in establishing the occurrence of fixation and impasse in problem solving have been the collection of verbal protocols (Fleck & Weisberg, 2004; Kaplan & Simon, 1990) and the use of eye-tracking data (Grant & Spivey, 2003; Jones, 2003; Knoblich, Ohlsson, & Raney, 2001; Thomas & Lleras, 2009a). Fleck and Weisberg examined verbal protocols for the presence of impasse characteristics (e.g., statements of confusion/being unable to generate new ideas and evidence of emotional frustration) and were able to demonstrate that impasse-like characteristics were present in the thought processes of approximately 45% of participants attempting to solve Duncker's (1945) candle problem. Most of these statements reflected confusion with specific problem components or a lack of additional ideas for consideration. In rare instances, the impasse was such that work on the problem ceased. Few participants who experienced impasse went on to generate the insightful solution of this problem within the 10 min solving period (perhaps participants would have achieved insight with a longer solving window). Protocol analysis has been challenged as a technique, however, due to its reliance on what participants actually verbalize and whether those verbalizations genuinely reflect participants' thought processes. Prior research of Schooler et al. (1993) has also raised concerns with the technique due to the detrimental effect of verbalization they observed on solving success. However, subsequent research has failed to replicate this deleterious effect of verbalization on insight (Fleck, 2008; Fleck & Weisberg, 2004; Gilhooly, Fioratou, & Henretty, 2010).

A second approach that has shown promise for empirically assessing fixation in insight has been tracking eye movements and measuring gaze fixation durations during the solving process (e.g., Grant & Spivey, 2003; Jones, 2003). For example, Knoblich et al. (2001) used an increase in gaze fixation duration (i.e., less eye movement) as the solving period progressed to indicate that the solver had reached a state of impasse and gaze fixation on specific problem elements to demonstrate

Problem:  IV = III + III

Solution:  VI = III + III

Problem:  III = III + III

Solution:  III = III = III

**Figure 49.4** Matchstick arithmetic problems.

fixation on incorrect problem components. Mean gaze fixation duration increased across the solving period as participants attempted to solve matchstick arithmetic problems (see Fig. 49.4), indicating that solvers reached an impasse as work on the problem progressed. Furthermore, the duration of fixation during the initial solving period was greatest for problem elements that were irrelevant to the problem's solution and for solvers who shifted to relevant problem elements as the solving period progressed. In a more directed approach, Jones quantified the point at which impasse occurred in the solving process (i.e., gaze fixation was at least two standard deviations above mean gaze fixation for the participant) and, furthermore, indicated that impasse was experienced by all solvers prior to the representational change that led to solution. Thus, eye movement and verbal protocol research have revealed that fixation and impasse play an important role in the insight process, and they may be fundamental in establishing the necessary environment for representational change (to be discussed later).

## Restructuring in Insight—The Mechanisms of Representational Change

No component of the insight process has received more attention than restructuring, frequently used as the characteristic to distinguish insight from the smooth, incremental processing of analysis. The Gestalt psychologists discussed restructuring as a change in mental representation that frees the problem solver from fixation (or impasse) and results in the productive thinking necessary for insight (e.g., Duncker, 1945; Koffka, 1935; Köhler, 1925). Modern researchers have attempted to determine the environment in which restructuring occurs, as well as the cognitive changes that comprise restructuring (e.g., Chronicle, MacGregor, & Ormerod, 2004; Durso, Rea, & Dayton, 1994; Knoblich et al., 1999).

In their *representational change* theory, Knoblich et al. (1999; Knoblich et al., 2001) proposed that restructuring can occur if the problem solver exhausts the initial problem-solving space without achieving solution, thus resulting in impasse. After achieving impasse, an incorrect constraint imposed on the problem-solving situation by the participant's prior knowledge can be relaxed, generating a new problem space for exploration. For example, after reaching impasse in matchstick arithmetic problems (see Fig. 49.4), the participant may decide that problem's operators (e.g., addition and equal signs) may also be modified to change the

arithmetic statement rather than relying only on the conversion of the operands. In contrast, Chronicle, Ormerod, and MacGregor's *progress monitoring* theory (2001; MacGregor et al., 2001; Ormerod, MacGregor, & Chronicle, 2002) suggests that the need for restructuring may arise when the problem solver, monitoring his or her progress through the application of problem-solving heuristics, realizes that successfully solving the problem is not possible under the current parameters. For example, in the nine-dot problem (see Fig. 49.1), potential moves may be more or less likely at different points in the solving process depending on the number of dots a line captures in relation to the number of dots that remain to be captured. The progress monitoring theory indicates that relaxation of mental constraints does not require fixation or impasse but, rather, the understanding that sufficient progress is not being made. Fleck and Weisberg (2004) have found support for this possibility in their research on Duncker's candle problem in which restructuring often occurred when participants generated an incorrect solution or envisioned a solution idea that they deemed implausible prior to implementation.

In addition to discrepancies over the ideal environment for restructuring, theorists have also questioned whether restructuring is consciously directed or occurs outside the awareness of the problem solver. For example, Knoblich et al. (1999, see also Ohlsson, 1992) have suggested that restructuring results from the unconscious reorganization of knowledge structures. In this instance, impasse provides the tension/need for mental reorganization, but the restructuring itself is spontaneous. In fact, several behavioral studies of insight have suggested that insight arises quite suddenly following a spontaneous restructuring of ideas (Metcalfe & Wiebe, 1987), in an all-or-none fashion (Smith & Kounios, 1996). Spontaneous restructuring stemming from exposure to relevant external hints has also been empirically supported in research demonstrating that exposure to problem-relevant information during problem solving, or during incubation periods, can facilitate the insight experience (Maier, 1930; Seifert et al., 1995).

Others are not as sure (e.g., Fleck & Weisberg, 2004; MacGregor et al., 2001), citing instead the possibility that restructuring may occur as the result of an internal or external search for new information following impasse or failure. In an early study on failure and insight, Weisberg and Suls (1973) proposed that failed solutions during the solving process allowed participants to acquire additional knowledge regarding problem components that altered future solution attempts with the candle problem (see Fig. 49.1; e.g., the tacks are too short to go directly through the candle). Furthermore, Durso et al. (1994) reported the gradual accumulation of solution-related knowledge when participants solved anagrams, rather than sudden, all-or-nothing, solutions. Durso et al. had participants make similarity ratings for word pairs to indicate their location within the semantic network and to demonstrate the change in network structure that accompanies restructuring. Similarity ratings for word pairs tied to the critical restructuring shifted gradually in relatedness in ratings made before problem presentation, during the solving process, and after solution, supporting the gradual acquisition of solution-related information.

In a direct comparison of controlled search versus spontaneous forms of restructuring, Ash and Wiley (2006) examined the role of working memory (i.e., the maintenance of problem-solving information during online cognition) in the solution of insight problems with large versus small initial search spaces. For example, participants were presented with an eight-coin problem and were asked to rearrange the initial coin configuration so that each coin touched exactly three others by moving only two coins (see Fig. 49.2). To generate the solution, a three-dimensional configuration is necessary. In the large search-space problem, many possible moves can be made in two dimensions in which a coin can be moved and will touch three others. However, in the small search-space problem, no viable two-dimensional moves exist. Problems with small search spaces were designed to directly assess the restructuring component of insight, whereas problems with large initial search spaces required the exhaustion of solution possibilities from the initial problem-solving space prior to restructuring. Ash and Wiley observed that working memory capacity predicted performance for insight problems with large initial search spaces but not success for problems with smaller initial search spaces. Similar results were obtained by Fleck (2008) and Gilhooly and Murphy (2005). Thus, when restructuring is isolated, the capacity for controlled search and the conscious application of strategies is not related to solving success.

Mai, Luo, Wu, and Luo (2004; Luo, Niki, & Phillips, 2004a; Qiu et al., 2008) have explored the neural components associated with restructuring. In this research, participants were presented with a riddle or an ambiguous sentence designed to initiate an incorrect representation on the part of problem solvers (e.g., riddle: The thing that can move heavy logs but cannot move a small nail; solution: a river; Luo & Knoblich, 2007, p. 79). After a 10 s solving period, the solution to the riddle or sentence was presented and participants indicated via button press if the solution matched the one they had generated during the solving period (noninsight), or if the solution was more likely than the one they had generated during the solving window/no solution was generated initially but the answer made sense (insight). Thus, insight was characterized as achieving a conceptual understanding after the solution's presentation that was absent during the initial problem-solving period. It should be noted that the researchers' classification of experiences as insight may not genuinely reflect insight experiences. First, the paradigm does not actually verify whether an insight occurred during the solving period. Second, the response to the solution's presentation (recognition) may not elicit the same neural processing associated with Aha! experiences in conjunction with self-generated solutions.

Mai, Luo, and colleagues (Mai et al., 2004) proposed that switching from the initial, prepotent response to a representation that coincides with the riddle's solution should initiate cognitive conflict, reflected by increased activation in the anterior cingulate cortex (ACC) during insight solutions. Using ERPs time-locked to the solution word's presentation, Mai et al. observed greater negativity for insight trials 250–500 ms post solution, localized via dipole modeling to the ACC. Associated functional magnetic resonance imaging (fMRI) research conducted by Luo et al. (2004a), using ambiguous sentences rather than riddles, revealed greater ACC and left prefrontal cortex activation for insight trials than noninsight trials. Furthermore, the level of ACC activation present in insight trials decreased across blocks, suggesting that the ACC is more involved when the task is novel and participants have yet to develop strategies that would facilitate the comprehension of sentences of this type. In similar research, Luo and colleagues (Luo, Niki, & Phillips, 2004b, as cited in Luo & Knoblich, 2007) observed greater ACC activation when participants attempted to solve riddles with heterogeneous solution types than when participants were presented with riddles of a single solution type. Therefore, the presence and strength of ACC activation may be related to the need for the problem solver to abandon an incorrect representation formed early in the solving process, in conjunction with the novelty of the problem to the problem solver.

## The Unique Processes of Insight

The dispute over whether insight is genuinely unique from analysis (special-process view) or comprised exclusively of thought processes present in other types of cognition (business as usual) has given rise to research examining potential cognitive, behavioral, and neural differences between insight and analysis (e.g., Bowden & Beeman, 1998; Jung-Beeman et al., 2004; Metcalfe & Wiebe, 1987). Proponents of insight as an ordinary process, most notably Perkins (1981) and Weisberg (1986; Weisberg & Alba, 1981), have suggested that ordinary cognitive processes, such as recognition and long-term memory search, can sufficiently explain the insight experience and that extraordinary mental leaps are not needed to account for the outcomes. In research examining verbal protocols, Perkins reported that participants experienced insight characteristics, such as the Aha! reaction, in conjunction with search solutions (i.e., incremental progress toward solution), suggesting that insight and analysis may not be mutually exclusive processes. More recently, researchers have noted that heuristics traditionally applied during the solution of search problems (e.g., hill climbing and means ends) can be used to explain the processing displayed by participants when solving with insight in problems such as the eight-coin problem (see Fig. 49.2; Chronicle et al., 2004; MacGregor et al., 2001). It is less clear how these heuristics might be adapted when solving classic insight problems, such as the candle problem.

Theorists supporting insight as a special process have been more numerous (e.g., Knoblich et al., 1999; Schooler et al., 1993; Seifert et al., 1995). Some of the first research directly contrasting insight and analysis focused on participants' metacognitions of their solving potential and solution progress for problems of each type. Metcalfe (1986a; Metcalfe & Wiebe, 1987) proposed that insight consists of processes outside conscious awareness of the problem solver, reducing metacognitive access to progress during problem solving or the advance knowledge of the likelihood of achieving solution. When Metcalfe and Wiebe asked participants to report their perceived closeness to solution at 15 s intervals during the solving period, an incremental increase in proximity to the solution was observed for noninsight problems, whereas insight solutions were accompanied by a sudden spike in perceived closeness immediately before the solution itself. In fact, prior research revealed that high warmth ratings during the solving process were actually associated with a decreased likelihood of solution, perhaps indicating a strong conviction by participants in the accuracy of a solution idea that was faulty (Metcalfe, 1986b). Similarly, when participants were asked to predict their likelihood of solution success for insight and trivia problems prior to the solving period, participants were highly accurate in predicting their subsequent ability to answer trivia questions, but their predictions of success for insight problems were at chance levels.

Conscious access to solution information was also found to differ between insight and analytic problem solving in research exploring the effect of concurrent verbalization on problem-solving success (Schooler & Melcher, 1995; Schooler et al., 1993). Schooler et al. reported a significant drop in solution rates when participants solved insight problems while providing verbal protocols as compared to a silent condition, an effect not present for analytic problems. This led Schooler et al. to propose that insight processes occur outside awareness, making them inaccessible to verbalization and, thus, verbalization interferes with solving processes in insight (i.e., verbal overshadowing of insight). In a recent analysis of verbalization effects in insight and noninsight problems, Gilhooly et al. (2010) observed a clear presence of verbal overshadowing for spatial problems that were both insight and noninsight in nature, but no difference in the degree of verbal overshadowing present when insight and noninsight problems (verbal and visual combined) were compared. Therefore, the verbal overshadowing effect observed by Schooler et al. may stem from the visual nature of most problems used as insight stimuli in their research rather than the problems being insight in nature.

Some of the most convincing support for a distinction between insight and analysis has stemmed from research revealing hemispheric differences in achieving solutions with versus without insight (e.g., Aziz-Zadeh, Kaplan, & Iacoboni, 2009; Bowden & Beeman, 1998). Initial research in this area explored differences between the hemispheres in processing benefits following the presentation solution-related hints (e.g., Beeman & Bowden, 2000; Fiore & Schooler, 1998). Fiore and Schooler asked participants to solve a series of classic insight problems during which hints were presented to the right visual field (processed initially by the left hemisphere) or the left visual field (processed initially by the right hemisphere). Participants were most effective in generating solutions to these problems when the hints were presented in the left visual field, supporting a theory of right-hemisphere specialization in insight and related processes (see Bowden, Jung-Beeman, Fleck, & Kounios, 2005, for a review). Furthermore, the beneficial effects stemming from right-hemisphere hint presentation were greatest if the hints were presented after participants had worked unsuccessfully on the problem for a few minutes rather than when hints were presented at the start of the solving window.

Similarly, Bowden and Beeman (1998; Beeman & Bowden, 2000; Bowden & Jung-Beeman, 2003) examined differences between the hemispheres when participants attempted to solve compound remote associate problems (CRAs). CRAs, adapted from Mednick's (1962) remote associates task, are brief problems in which participants are presented with three problem words (e.g., LETTER/PUPPY/TRUE) and need to generate a solution word (e.g., LOVE) that can be combined with each of the problem words to generate a compound word form (e.g., LOVE LETTER, PUPPY LOVE, and TRUE LOVE). Participants were allotted brief solving windows after the presentation of the problem words, too brief to allow most participants to generate a solution (e.g., 7 s; see Bowden & Jung-Beeman, 2003). After this initial solving window, a word was briefly presented in either the right or the left visual field and participants were asked to judge whether this word was the solution to the problem and to provide a self-report rating as to whether insight was experienced in response to the hint's presentation. Bowden and Jung-Beeman reported that participants exhibited the greatest priming for solution hints when the decision words were presented in the left visual field (right hemisphere) and that these judgments were also associated with the highest ratings of insight experiences in response to hint words.

Recent neuroimaging and electrophysiological research has revealed differences in neural activity when insight or search strategies are applied during the solving process. Jung-Beeman, Kounios, and colleagues (Jung-Beeman et al., 2004; Kounios et al., 2006) asked participants to solve a series of CRAs. Neural activity was recorded during the task in one experiment using fMRI and another using electroencephalography (EEG). For solved CRAs, participants indicated if their solution was generated with or without insight. Insight solutions were those in which the solution was achieved suddenly, at times without a clear understanding of the underlying processes, and produced a high level of confidence that the solution was correct. The trial-by-trial

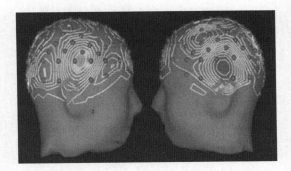

**Figure 49.5** Differences in neural activity immediately preceding insight and noninsight solutions. (*See* color insert.)

classification of experiences as insight or analysis when solving problems of a single type addresses many of the confounds noted in prior research (e.g., Metcalfe & Wiebe, 1987; Schooler et al., 1993) in which unique problem sets are presented as stimuli for insight and noninsight problems.

Unique patterns of activity were present in insightful solutions. First, fMRI analyses revealed greater right-hemisphere activation in the superior temporal gyrus (STG) for insight solutions than was present for noninsight solutions (see Fig. 49.5). Because the bilateral STG is known to be involved in semantic integration, and the right hemisphere has been found to play a significant role in processing distant semantic associations and figurative language (Jung-Beeman, 2005), this activation may be linked to the sudden integration of semantic information resulting in the solution. It should be noted that it is unlikely that the right STG activation observed in insight solutions is linked to an emotional response stemming from solution. Similar activity was observed in the right hemisphere in participants when they first were presented with problems.

High-density EEG data collected as part of a second experiment revealed high-frequency gamma-band activity over the right anterior temporal region 0.3 seconds prior to a bimanual button-press indicating solution (thus, approximately coinciding with solution), which was localized via Lapacian mapping to a region similar to that identified in the fMRI experiment. In addition, a burst of low alpha activity over the right posterior parietal region preceding the right hemisphere gamma burst suggests the possibility of visual gating prior to the insight effect (see Ray & Cole, 1985). This posterior alpha activity was also observed in research exploring chunk decomposition, a form of restructuring, supporting the need to attenuate visual input as a component of restructuring (Wu, Knoblich, Wei, & Luo, 2009). Combined, these data support the sudden integration of distantly related problem components leading to the insight effect, and the need to block the input of sensory information to permit the conscious awareness of information previously at the unconscious level.

The behavioral and imaging research mentioned earlier identifies the right hemisphere as a source of unique/supplementary processing in insight. Additional research further supports this classification for insight experiences. For example, Aziz-Zadeh et al. (2009) observed greater solution-related activity over the right prefrontal cortex when participants solved anagrams with insight. In addition, researchers have identified the right prefrontal cortex as important in generating novel ideas in insight and creativity (Dietrich, 2004; Howard-Jones, Blakemore, Samuel, Summers, & Claxton, 2005). Likewise, patient groups shown to rely more heavily on right-hemisphere processing (e.g., schizotypes—those high in schizophrenia-like traits) have demonstrated higher rates of insightful solutions compared to those exhibited by normal adults (Karimi, Windmann, Güntürkün, & Abraham, 2007). Although these results allude to a unique role of the right hemisphere in insight, they should be interpreted with caution. Greater right-hemisphere processing in insight does not imply a dichotomy, with search solutions involving the left hemisphere and insight solutions involving the right hemisphere. For instance, although Jung-Beeman et al. (2004) observed greater right STG activation for CRAs solved with insight, the activation present in the left STG prior to solution did not differ between insight and noninsight solutions. Therefore, it seems more prudent to support a theory of additional processing components as part of the insight experience rather than insight and noninsight as arising from completely distinct processes.

## Methods of Facilitating Insight

There are situations in which insight/creativity may be optimal for success over analytic strategies (e.g., invention, imagination). This realization has generated a significant increase in research aimed at identifying factors related to situational and overall differences in insight potential. As in other forms of problem solving, individual differences in cognitive function (e.g., working memory, fluid intelligence) are related to success in solving problems with insight (Ash & Wiley, 2006; Davidson, 1995; Fleck, 2008;

Gilhooly & Murphy, 2005; Schooler & Melcher, 1995; Sternberg & Davidson, 1982). Schooler and Melcher revealed that insight problem-solving success was correlated with core cognitive abilities, such as vocabulary level and general problem-solving ability. Similarly, DeYoung, Flanders, and Peterson (2008) observed that insight problem-solving ability was correlated with measures of fluid and crystallized intelligence, as was the ability to solve other problem types, but was uniquely associated with divergent-thinking ability. Divergent thinking, explored extensively in creativity research, assesses one's ability to generate multiple solution ideas for a particular problem (Guilford, 1950). DeYoung et al.'s research extends the findings of prior researchers who also observed relationships between insight and divergent-thinking ability (e.g., Ansburg, 2000; Davidson, 1995).

In addition to cognitive predictors, activity in the brain at rest, when the individual is not engaged in task-directed cognition, may be a reliable indicator of an individual's potential to solve problems with or without insight (Kounios et al., 2008). Kounios et al. grouped participants into high-insight and high-analytic conditions based on the proportion of anagrams they solved using insight. When patterns of resting brain activity were compared between conditions, greater high alpha and low beta activity were observed over visual cortex in the high analytic group, and greater high beta activity was observed over the right temporal region in the high-insight group. The activity patterns at rest observed in high-insight participants complement cognitive components of insight identified in prior research (e.g., Fiore & Schooler, 1998; Jung-Beeman, 2005; Martindale, 1995), to include diffuse attention, the reliance on remote semantic connections, and greater right-hemisphere activation.

Beyond individual differences in insight potential, insight rates have been influenced by situational factors such as behavioral interventions and state affect. A number of researchers have explored the efficacy of brief training intervals in enhancing insight problem solving (e.g., Ansburg & Dominowski, 2000; Cunningham & MacGregor, 2008; Dow & Mayer, 2004; Lung & Dominowski, 1985; Maier, 1933; Schwert, 2007). Training intervals typically involved instruction on principles to alleviate common obstacles to achieving insight (e.g., initial ideas during problem solving are often misleading or problem solving may be difficult because you are applying unnecessary constraints to the problem; see Ansburg & Dominowski, 2000;

and Cunningham & MacGregor, 2008) followed by example problems where the solution and associated logic are demonstrated. Results of such trainings have revealed domain-specific training effects, similar to those present with other problem types (see Gick & Holyoak, 1980), in which training on one type of insight problem (e.g., verbal or spatial) was beneficial in facilitating insight for that type of problem but had limited efficacy or transfer to insight problems of other types (Ansburg & Dominowski, 2000; Dow & Mayer, 2004). Furthermore, training was most beneficial in enhancing solving ability for traditional insight problems, such as riddles and puzzles, and less influential when the insight problems contained real-life contextual information (Cunningham & MacGregor, 2008).

Insight rates have also been enhanced through the introduction of manipulations during the solving process (e.g., Grant & Spivey, 2003; Sio & Ormerod, 2009; Thomas & Lleras, 2007). Taking a break from the problem after impasse (i.e., incubation) can promote the solution of insight problems (Christensen & Schunn, 2005; Segal, 2004). As noted earlier, a critical aspect in the insight process is the ability to overcome an initial misleading solution idea in favor of novel solution ideas (e.g., Martindale, 1995; Metcalfe & Wiebe, 1987; Ohlsson, 1992). Though the exact mechanisms of restructuring are unknown, it has been suggested that an incubation period can increase the potential for representational change (for a review, see Sio & Ormerod, 2009). In research conducted by Segal, solution rates for insight problems improved when participants took either a short or long break after impasse. Furthermore, this break was more successful when the break interval was filled with a cognitively demanding task, supporting the theory that a shift in attention is the basis for success following incubation. In addition, Christensen and Schunn observed an increase in insightful problem solving when external hints related to the solutions were incidentally provided during incubation periods that occurred at regular intervals throughout the problem-solving task. It should be noted, however, that some researchers have questioned the efficacy of incubation intervals (e.g., Olton, 1979; Vul & Pashler, 2007). For example, Vul and Pashler failed to find incubation effects in participants attempting to solve brief verbal problems unless the problem words were presented in conjunction with misleading hints at the outset, perhaps supporting the value of the incubation interval as a means to forget misleading information.

Hints diverting attention from one problem component to another can facilitate the occurrence of insight (e.g., Grant & Spivey, 2003; Kaplan & Simon, 1990; Thomas & Lleras, 2009a). Grant and Spivey were able to enhance solution rates for Duncker's (1945) radiation problem (see Fig. 49.1) by presenting the problem with the outside surface of the body flashing, drawing attention to this component. Thomas and Lleras (2007) also directed participants' attention to the problem's solution by having participants track a series of letters and digits that appeared on the computer screen in a sequence such that the eye-movement pattern mirrored the layout of the problem's solution (i.e., across the surface of the skin and moving in toward the tumor). Similar effects occurred when participants directed their attention to the letter and number locations resembling the solution pattern without physically moving their eyes to track the stimuli (Thomas & Lleras, 2009a). Furthermore, having participants engage in physical movements that coincided with the solution to Maier's (1931) two-string problem (see Fig. 49.1; i.e., participants swung their arms back and forth in a pendulum-like motion) facilitated problem-solving rates (Thomas & Lleras, 2009b). This research collectively supports the role of shifting attention from misleading to relevant problem components in facilitating insight.

Numerous studies have linked positive affect to enhanced creativity (e.g., Amabile, Barsade, Muller, & Staw, 2005). Several of these studies have been aimed directly at examining the role of affect in insight (e.g., Isen, Daubman, & Nowicki, 1987; Subramaniam, Kounios, Parrish, & Jung-Beeman, 2009). Some of the first research in this area was conducted by Isen et al., who observed increased solution rates for Duncker's (1945) candle problem following the inducement of positive affect when participants viewed a brief comedic film. More recently, the work of Subramaniam et al. examined rates of insight and analytic solutions to CRA problems in relation to self-reported affect. Participants were asked to indicate their solution strategy (either insight or analysis) on a trial-by-trial basis for solved CRAs during fMRI recording and to complete self-report measures of affect and anxiety. The researchers observed higher rates of insight solutions in participants who were high in positive affect and low in anxiety. Interestingly, analytic solution rates did not differ based on situational affect. The faciliatory effect of positive affect on insight specifically and creativity generally may stem from a shift from a focused to a global attention spotlight allowing participants to consider ideas for solution that would typically fall outside the scope of attention (Rowe, Hirsch, & Anderson, 2007). In support of this theory, researchers examining differences in the allocation of attentional resources in individuals high versus low in creativity, as measured via scores on Mednick's (1962) RAT, observed that participants high in creativity exhibited an enhanced ability to process hints presented outside the scope of focal attention (Ansburg & Hill, 2003). This coincides with neuroimaging results reported by Subramaniam et al., in which increased activation in the ACC, a region of the brain known for its role in cognitive control and attention, both before and during problem solving, was associated with an increase in insight solutions.

Finally, neural activity prior to the problem-solving interval can reliably differentiate whether solutions will arise with or without insight (Kounios et al., 2006). Kounios et al. asked participants to solve a series of CRAs in a procedure similar to that used by Jung-Beeman et al. (2004) discussed earlier. Of interest was the pretrial interval after participants provided a response to the previous problem but before the current trial's problem words were presented. Activation patterns in the preparatory interval were compared between trials that were solved with versus without insight. The analysis of low alpha activity (8–10 Hz) in the EEG experiment revealed greater preparatory activation for trials subsequently solved with insight over midfrontal, left and right temporal, and bilateral somatosensory regions. In contrast, the interval preceding trials solved without insight was associated with greater activity over posterior brain regions. A second experiment conducted using fMRI replicated the results of the EEG experiment and further clarified the neural components underlying the strategy differences, identifying increased signal strength for insight trials in the ACC, posterior cingulate cortex, and bilateral middle and superior temporal gyri. Combined, these experiments suggest that specific preparatory states prior to problem presentation are associated with the solution of problems with versus without insight.

## Future Directions in Insight

Recent developments in methodology and theory have transformed the concept of insight. A field that began primarily as a collection of anecdotes supporting the probable existence of a unique cognitive process has evolved into one detailing behavioral and neural components that comprise the insight experience. Despite this progress, many unanswered questions remain. Though the nature and variety of stimuli in insight research have developed beyond the classic insight problems presented in Figure 49.1 to include other problem types (e.g., CRAs, anagrams), the majority of stimuli in use are verbal in nature (cf. Gilhooly et al., 2010). Therefore, we must question whether insights to verbal and visual problems would differ and, if so, in what way. Jung-Beeman et al. (2004) observed right STG activity that coincided approximately with solutions for CRAs solved with insight. Because the STG activation in this research was likely tied to the sudden semantic integration of distantly related concepts, it is unlikely that visual insight problems would produce such activation. Therefore, what activation patterns would be observed? Should we expect that visual insight problems will be solved with a sudden burst of gamma frequency activation as were verbal insight problems, or even that visual insights would be associated with unique activation localized to the right hemisphere?

To date, much research on insight has pursued independent insight characteristics, such as restructuring or the Aha! experience (e.g., Ash & Wiley, 2006; Durso et al., 1994; Metcalfe & Wiebe, 1987). The separate study of individual characteristics gives us little information concerning insight as a process, or the influence of early-process components on the subsequent occurrence of late-process components (e.g., the influence of fixation or impasse on the subsequent occurrence of restructuring; cf. Fleck & Weisberg, 2004). If insight is best conceptualized as a process, then the study of the neural underpinnings of insight may need to rely more heavily on imaging techniques that are not limited to the identification of structures that differentiate the insight experience from those of other processing types (e.g., analysis) but instead permit the exploration of brain regions acting in synchrony or succession to produce the experience of insight (i.e., coherence analysis).

In addition to elucidating the insight process, the need for clarification of specific insight components remains (e.g., restructuring). We believe advances in neuroscience may hold the key to further clarifying mechanisms of insight and evaluating contrasting theories. For example, metacognitive research supports the sudden conscious awareness of an insightful solution at the point of solution (Metcalfe & Wiebe, 1987), whereas behavioral research supports the accumulation of partial information prior to solution (Durso et al., 1994). If both veins of research are valid, and the reorganization of thought occurs outside awareness and enters consciousness in a sudden leap, then we should be able to determine the point at which enough solution-relevant information has been acquired on the unconscious level to enter into conscious awareness. This might be possible if existing techniques in metacognitive research were integrated with imaging techniques, thus permitting researchers to synch the conscious experiences of the individual with activity in the brain.

As we continue to learn more about the insight experience, it may be time to consider the possibility for different forms/degrees of insight. For example, is it reasonable to assume that the insight in a scientific discovery mirrors the insight in solving an anagram? Should we expect that the restructuring that occurs after impasse is analogous to the restructuring that arises without impasse? Furthermore, does the degree or duration of impasse or fixation influence the type of restructuring (external search versus sudden internal reorganization) that follows, or the likelihood of experiencing an Aha! reaction? The probable answer is that all of these factors are relevant in some capacity, though the extent and nature of the variation have not been examined empirically.

Beyond expanding our knowledge of the insight experience is the need to clarify how insight is related to other areas of cognition, most notably creativity. Much of the recent interest in insight stems from its likely role as a component of the creative process (Wallas, 1926), but the relationship between insight experiences and creative ability has rarely been examined empirically. In one such study, Ansburg (2000) observed that the ability to solve classic insight problems was more strongly correlated with the ability to solve RAT problems, administered as a standard measure of creativity, than analytic problems. There is also little research directly assessing whether the constructs known to be associated with the enhanced potential for creativity are also associated with the enhanced potential for insight itself. For example, although diffuse semantic networks and a broader attention spotlight have been suggested as sources of enhanced creativity (e.g., Ansburg & Hill, 2003; Carson, Peterson, & Higgins, 2003; Martindale, 1995), there is limited research demonstrating that these factors are associated with enhanced potential for insight. In addition, while research has identified specific groups as likely to be high in creative experiences, such as the first-degree relatives of schizophrenics

and normal adults who are high in schizotypal traits (e.g., Keefe & Magaro, 1980; Weinstein & Graves, 2002), only recently have we begun to see the influence of this research in the field of insight (Karimi et al., 2007).

We concluded this chapter with a review of the existing research demonstrating that insight as a solving approach can be facilitated if the correct environment is created (e.g., Cunningham & MacGregor, 2008; Subramaniam et al., 2009). However, we believe this is just the beginning of research in this area. Research in the field of creativity enhancement has achieved success that we believe could be relevant in insight. For example, Markman, Lindberg, Kray, and Galinsky (2007) have evaluated the use of counterfactual mindsets as a means of enhancing either creative or analytic thought. In their research, additive counterfactuals (i.e., achieved through statements modifying reality by adding elements to a situation) generated a mindset that enhanced the potential for creativity, whereas subtractive counterfactuals (i.e., achieved though statements modifying reality by removing elements from a situation) instead enhanced the potential for analysis. In a similar manner, Friedman and Förster (2005) have successfully enhanced either creative or analytic problem-solving success via approach (i.e., seeking a reward or positive outcome) or avoidance (attempting to avoid a negative outcome) motivational states. If the relationship between insight and creativity is substantiated, then creativity enhancement techniques in addition to counterfactual mindsets and motivational states could be assessed for their efficacy with insight.

## References

Amabile, T. M., Barsade, S. G., Mueller, J. S., & Staw B. M. (2005). Affect and creativity at work. *Administrative Science*, 50, 367–403.

Anderson, J. R. (1980). *Cognitive psychology and its implications*. New York: W. H. Freeman.

Ansburg, P. I. (2000). Individual differences in problem solving via insight. *Current Psychology*, 19, 143–146.

Ansburg, P. I., & Dominowski, R. L. (2000). Promoting insightful problem solving. *Journal of Creative Behavior*, 34, 30–60.

Ansburg, P. I., & Hill, K. (2003). Creative and analytic thinkers differ in their use of attentional resources. *Personality and Individual Differences*, 34, 1141–1152.

Ash, I. K., & Wiley, J. (2006). The nature of restructuring in insight: An individual-differences approach. *Psychonomic Bulletin and Review*, 13, 66–73.

Aziz-Zadeh, L., Kaplan, J. T., & Iacoboni, I. (2009). "Aha!": The neural correlates of verbal insight solutions. *Human Brain Mapping*, 30, 908–916.

Beeman, M. J., & Bowden, E. M. (2000). The hemisphere maintains solution-related activation for yet-to-be-solved problems. *Memory and Cognition, 28,* 1231–1241.

Bowden, E. M., & Beeman, M. J. (1998). Getting the right idea: Semantic activation in the right hemisphere may help solve insight problems. *Psychological Science, 9,* 435–440

Bowden, E. M., & Jung-Beeman, M. (2003). Aha! Insight experience correlates with solution activation in the right hemisphere. *Psychonomic Bulletin and Review, 10,* 730–737.

Bowden, E. M., Jung-Beeman, M., Fleck, J. I., & Kounios, J. (2005). New approaches to demystifying insight. *Trends in Cogntiive Science, 9,* 322–328.

Bowers, K. S., Regehr, G., Balthazard, C., & Parker, K. (1990). Intuition in the context of discovery. *Cognitive Psychology, 22,* 72–110.

Carson, S. H., Peterson, J. B., & Higgins, D. M. (2003). Decreased latent inhibition is associated with increased creative achievement in high-functioning individuals. *Personality Processes and Individual Differences, 85,* 499–506.

Christensen, B. T., & Schunn, C. D. (2005). Spontaneous access and analogical incubation effects. *Creativity Research Journal, 17,* 207–220.

Chronicle, E. P., MacGregor, J. N., & Ormerod, T. C. (2004). What makes an insight problem? The roles of heuristics, goal conception, and solution recoding in knowledge-lean problems. *Journal of Experimental Psychology: Learning, Memory, and Cognition, 30,* 14–27.

Chronicle, E. P., Ormerod, T. C., & MacGregor, J. N. (2001). When insight just won't come: The failure of visual cues in the nine-dot problem. *Quarterly Journal of Experimental Psychology, 54A,* 903–919.

Cunningham, J. B., & MacGregor, J. N. (2008). Training insightful problem solving: Effects of realistic and puzzle-like contexts. *Creativity Research Journal, 20,* 291–296.

Davidson, J. E. (1995) The suddenness of insight. In R. J. Sternberg & J. E. Davidson (Eds.), *The nature of insight* (pp. 125–155). Cambridge, MA: MIT Press.

DeYoung, C. G., Flanders, J. L., & Peterson, J. B. (2008). Cognitiive abilities involved in insight problem solving: An individual differences model. *Creativity Research Journal, 20,* 278–290.

Dietrich, A. (2004). The cognitive neuroscience of creativity. *Psychonomic Bulletin and Review, 11,* 1011–1026.

Dow, G. T., & Mayer, R. E. (2004). Teaching students to solve insight problems: Evidence for domain specificity in creativity training. *Creativity Research Journal, 16,* 389–402.

Duncker, K. (1945). On problem-solving. *Psychological Monographs, 58*(5). Whole No. 270.

Durso, F. T., Rea, C. B., & Dayton, T. (1994). Graph-theoretic confirmation of restructuring during insight. *Psychological Science, 5,* 94–98.

Fiore, S. M., & Schooler, J. W. (1998). Right hemisphere contributions to creative problem solving: Converging evidence for divergent thinking. In M. Beeman & C. Chiarello (Eds.), *Right hemisphere language comprehension: Perspectives from cognitive neuroscience* (pp. 349–371). Mahwah, NJ: Earlbaum.

Fleck, J. I. (2008). Working memory demands in insight versus analytic problem solving. *European Journal of Cognitive Psychology, 20,* 139–176.

Fleck, J. I., & Weisberg, R. W. (2004). The use of verbal protocols as data: An analysis of insight in the candle problem. *Memory and Cognition, 32,* 990–1006.

Friedman, R. S., & Förster, J. (2005). Effects of motivational cues on perceptual asymmetry: Implications for creativity and analytical problem solving. *Journal of Personality and Social Psychology, 88,* 263–275.

Gaeta, H., Friedman, D., & Hunt, G. (2003). Stimulus characteristics and task category dissociate the anterior and posterior aspects of novelty P3. *Psychophysiology, 40,* 198–208.

Gick, M. L., & Holyoak, K. J. (1980). Analogical problem solving. *Cognitive Psychology, 12,* 306–355.

Gilhooly, K. J., Fioratou, E., & Henretty, N. (2010). Verbalization and problem solving: Insight and spatial factors. *British Journal of Psychology, 101,* 81–93.

Gilhooly, K. J., & Murphy, P. (2005). Differentiating insight from noninsight problems. *Thinking and Reasoning, 11,* 279–302.

Grant, E. R., & Spivey, M. J. (2003). Eye movements and problem solving: Guiding attention guides thought. *Psychological Science, 14,* 462–466.

Guilford, J. P. (1950). Creativity. *American Psychologist, 5,* 444–454.

Howard-Jones, P. A., Blakemore, S. J., Samuel, E. A., Summers, I. R., & Claxton, G. (2005). Semantic divergence and creative story generation: An fMRI investigation. *Cognitive Brain Research, 25,* 240–250.

Isen, A. M., Daubman, K. A., & Nowicki, G. P. (1987). PA facilitates creative problem solving. *Journal of Personality and Social Psychology, 32,* 1112–1131.

Jones, G. (2003). Testing two cognitive theories of insight. *Journal of Experimental Psychology: Learning, Memory, and Cognition, 29,* 1017–1027.

Jung-Beeman, M. (2005). Bilateral brain processes for comprehending natural language. *Trends in Cognitive Sciences, 9,* 512–518.

Jung-Beeman, M., Bowden, E. M., Haberman, J., Frymiare, J. L., Arambel-Liu, S., Greenblatt, R.,... Kounios, J. (2004). Neural activity when people solving verbal problems with insight. *PLoS Biology, 2*(4), 0001–0011.

Kaplan, C. A., & Simon, H. A. (1990). In search of insight. *Cognitive Psychology, 22,* 374–419.

Karimi, Z., Windmann, S., Güntürkün, O., & Abraham, A. (2007). Insight problem solving In individuals with high versus low schizotypy. *Journal of Research in Personality, 41,* 473–480.

Keefe, J. A., & Magaro, P., A. (1980). Creativity and schizophrenia: An equivalence of cognitive processing. *Journal of Abnormal Psychology, 89,* 390–398.

Kershaw, T. C., Ohlsson, S. (2004). Multiple causes of difficulty in insight: The case of the nine-dot problem. *Journal of Experimental Psychology: Learning, Memory, and Cognition, 30,* 3–13.

Knoblich, G., Ohlsson, S., Haider, H., & Rhenius, D. (1999). Constraint relaxation and chunk decomposition in insight problem solving. *Journal of Experimental Psychology: Learning, Memory, and Cognition, 25,* 1534–1555.

Knoblich, G., Ohlsson, S., & Raney, G. E. (2001). An eye movement study of insight problem solving. *Memory and Cognition, 29,* 1000–1009.

Koffka, K. (1935). *Principles of Gestalt psychology.* New York: Harcourt, Brace.

Köhler, W. (1925). *The mentality of apes.* London: Routledge and Kegan Paul.

Kounios, J., Fleck, J. I., Green, D. L., Payne, L., Stevenson, J. L., Bowden, E., & Jung-Beeman, M. (2008). The origins of insight in resting-state brain activity. *Neuropsychologia*, *46*, 281–291.

Kounios, J., Frymiare, J. L., Bowden, E. M., Fleck, J. I., Subramaniam, K., Parrish, T. B., & Jung-Beeman, M. (2006). The prepared mind: Neural activity prior to problem presentation predicts subsequent solution by sudden insight. *Psychological Science*, *17*, 882–890.

Lang, S., Kanngieser, N., Jaśkowski, P., Haider, H., Rose, M., & Verleger, R. (2006). Precursors of insight in event-related brain potentials. *Journal of Cognitive Neuroscience*, *18*, 2152–2166.

Luchins, A. S. (1942). Mechanization in problem solving—The effect of Einstellung. *Psychological Monographs*, *54*, 1–95.

Lung, C. T., & Dominowski, R. L. (1985). Effects of strategy instructions and practice on nine-dot problem solving. *Journal of Experimental Psychology: Learning, Memory, and Cognition*, *11*, 804–811.

Luo, J., & Knoblich, G. (2007). Studying insight problem solving with neuroscientific methods. *Methods*, *42*, 77–86.

Luo, J., Niki, K., & Phillips, S. (2004a). Neural correlates of the "Aha! Reaction." *NeuroReport*, *15*, 2013–2017.

Luo, J., Niki, K., & Phillips, S. (2004b). The function of the anterior cingulate cortex (ACC) in insightful problem solving: ACC activated less when the structure of the puzzle is known. *Journal of Chinese Societies*, *5*, 195–213.

MacGregor, J. N., Ormerod, T. C., & Chronicle, E. P. (2001). Information-processing and insight: A process model of performance on the nine-dot problem. *Journal of Experimental Psychology: Learning, Memory, and Cognition*, *27*, 176–201.

Mai, X., Luo, J., Wu, J., & Luo, Y. (2004). "Aha!" effects in a guessing riddle task: An event-related potential study. *Human Brain Mapping*, *22*, 261–270.

Maier, N. R. F. (1930). Reasoning in humans I: On direction. *Journal of Comparative Psychology*, *10*, 115–143.

Maier, N. R. F. (1931). Reasoning in humans II: The solution of a problem and its appearance in consciousness. *Journal of Comparative Psychology*, *12*, 181–194.

Maier, N. R. F. (1933). An aspect of human reasoning. *British Journal of Psychology*, *24*, 144–155.

Mandler, J. M., & Mandler, G. (1964). *Thinking: From association to Gestalt*. New York: Wiley.

Markman, K. D., Lindberg, M. J., Kray, L. J., & Galinsky, A. D. (2007). Implications of counterfactual structure for creative generation and analytic problem solving. *Personality and Social Psychology Bulletin*, *33*, 312–324.

Martindale, C. (1995). Creativity and connectionism. In S. M. Smith, T. B. Ward, & R. A. Finke (Eds.), *The creative cognition approach* (pp. 249–268). Cambridge, MA: MIT Press.

Mayer, R. E. (1995). The search for insight: Grappling with Gestalt psychology's unanswered questions. In R. J. Sternberg & J. E. Davidson (Eds.), *The nature of insight* (pp. 3–32). Cambridge, MA: MIT Press.

Mednick, S. A. (1962). The associative basis of the creative process. *Psychological Review*, *69*, 220–232.

Metcalfe, J. (1986a). Feeling of knowing in memory and problem solving. *Journal of Experimental Psychology: Learning, Memory, and Cognition*, *12*, 288–294.

Metcalfe, J. (1986b). Premonitions of insight predict impending error. *Journal of Experimental Psychology: Learning, Memory, and Cognition*, *12*, 623–634.

Metcalfe, J., & Wiebe, D. (1987). Intuition in insight and noninsight problem solving. *Memory and Cognition*, *15*, 238–246.

Newell, A., & Simon, H. A. (1972). *Human problem solving*. Englewood Cliffs, NJ: Prentice-Hall.

Ohlsson, S. (1984). Restructuring revisited I: Summary and critique of the Gestalt theory of problem solving. *Scandinavian Journal of Psychology*, *25*, 67–78.

Ohlsson, S. (1992). Information-processing explanations of isnight and related phenomena. In M. T. Keane & K. J. Gilhooly (Eds.), *Advances in the psychology of thinking* (Vol. 1, pp. 1–44). London: Harvester-Wheatsheaf.

Olton, R. M. (1979). Experimental studies of incubation: Searching for the elusive. *Journal of Creative Behavior*, *13*, 9–22.

Ormerod, T. C., MacGregor, J. N., & Chronicle, E. P. (2002). Dynamics and constraints in insight problem solving. *Journal of Experimental Psychology: Learning, Memory, and Cognition*, *28*, 791–799.

Perkins, D. N. (1981). *The mind's best work*. Cambridge, MA: Harvard University Press.

Qiu, J., Li, H., Yang, D., Luo, Y., Li, Y., Wu, Z., & Zhang, Q. (2008). The neural basis of insight problem solving: An event-related potential study. *Brain and Cognition*, *68*, 100–106.

Ray, W. J., & Cole, H. W. (1985). EEG alpha activity reflects attentional demands, and beta activity reflects emotional and cognitive processes. *Science*, *228*, 750–752.

Rowe, G., Hirsch, J. B., & Anderson, A. K. (2007). Positive affect increases the breadth of selective attention. *Proceedings of the National Academy of Sciences USA*, *104*, 383–388.

Scheerer, M. (1963). Problem solving. *Scientific American*, *208*, 118–128.

Schooler, J. W., & Melcher, J. (1995). The ineffability of insight. In S. M. Smith, T. B. Ward, & R. A. Finke (Eds.), *The creative cognition approach* (pp. 97–143). Cambridge, MA: MIT Press.

Schooler, J. W., Ohlsson, S., & Brooks, K. (1993). Thoughts beyond words: When language overshadows insight. *Journal of Experimental Psychology: General*, *122*, 166–183.

Schwert, P. M. (2007). Using sentence and picture clues to solve verbal insight problems. *Creativity Research Journal*, *19*, 293–306.

Segal, E. (2004). Incubation in insight problem solving. *Creativity Research Journal*, *16*, 141–148.

Seifert, C. M., Meyer, D. E., Davidson, N., Patalano, A. L., & Yaniv, I. (1995). Demystification of cognitive insight: Opportunistic assimilation and the prepared-mind perspective. In R. J. Sternberg & J. E. Davidson (Eds.), *The nature of insight* (pp. 157–196). Cambridge, MA: MIT Press.

Sio, U. N., & Ormerod, T. C. (2009). Does incubation enhance problem solving? A meta-analytic review. *Psychological Review*, *135*, 94–120.

Smith, S. M. (1995). Getting into and out of mental ruts: A theory of fixation, incubation, and insight. In R. J. Sternberg & J. E. Davidson (Eds.), *The nature of insight* (pp. 229–251). Cambridge, MA: MIT Press.

Smith, R. W., & Kounios, J. (1996). Sudden insight: All-or-none processing revealed by speed-accuracy decomposition. *Journal of Experimental Psychology: Learning, Memory, and Cognition*, *22*, 1443–1462.

Sternberg, R. J., & Davidson, J. E. (1982). The mind of the puzzler. *Psychology Today*, *16*, 37–44.

Sternberg, R. J., & Davidson, J. E. (1995). *The nature of insight*. Cambridge, MA: MIT Press.

Subramaniam, K., Kounios, J., Parrish, T. B., & Jung-Beeman, M. (2009). A brain mechanism for facilitation of insight by positive affect. *Journal of Cognitive Neuroscience, 21*, 415–432.

Thomas, L. E., & Lleras, A. (2007). Moving eyes and moving thought: On the spatial compatibility between eye movements and cognition. *Psychonomic Bulletin and Review, 14*, 663–668.

Thomas, L. E., & Lleras, A. (2009a). Covert shifts of attention function as an implicit aid to insight. *Cognition, 111*, 168–174.

Thomas, L. E., & Lleras, A. (2009b). Swinging into thought: Directed movement guides insight in problem solving. *Psychonomic Bulletin and Review, 16*, 719–723.

Thorndike, E. L. (1898). Animal intelligence: An experimental study of the associative processes in animals. *Psychological Review: Series of Monograph Supplements, 2*(4), Whole No. 8.

Vos, S. H., Gunter, T. C., Kohk, H. H. J., & Mulder, G. (2001). Working memory constraints on syntactic processing: An electrophysiological investigation. *Psychophysiology, 38*, 41–63.

Vul, E., & Pashler, H. (2007). Incubation benefits only after people have been misdirected. *Memory & Cognition, 35*, 701–710.

Wallas, G. (1926). *The art of thought*. London: Cape.

Weinstein, S., & Graves, R. E. (2002). Are creativity and schizotypy products of a right hemisphere bias? *Brain and Cognition, 49*, 138–151.

Weisberg, R. W. (1986). *Creativity: Genius and other myths*. New York: Freeman.

Weisberg, R. W. (1995). Prolegomena to theories of insight in problem solving: A taxonomy of problems. In R. J. Sternberg & J. E. Davidson (Eds.), *The nature of insight* (pp. 157–196). Cambridge, MA: MIT Press.

Weisberg, R. W. (2006). *Creativity: Understanding innovation in problem solving, science, invention, and the arts*. Hoboken, NJ: Wiley.

Weisberg, R. W., & Alba, J. W. (1981). An examination of the alleged role of "fixation" in the solution of several "insight" problems. *Journal of Experimental Psychology: General, 110*, 169–192.

Weisberg, R. W., & Suls, J. M. (1973). An information-processing model of Duncker's candle problem. *Cognitive Psychology, 4*, 255–276.

Wertheimer, M. (1945/1959). *Productive thinking* (Enlarged ed.). London: Tavistock Publications.

Wu, L., Knoblich, G., Wei, G., & Luo, J. (2009). How perceptual processes help to generate new meaning: An EEG study of chunk decomposition in Chinese characters. *Brain Research, 1296*, 104–112.

# Creativity

Dean Keith Simonton *and* Rodica Ioana Damian

**Abstract**

An idea's creativity is most often defined as the joint function of its originality or novelty and its adaptiveness or utility. Creativity is a quantitative property that can range from "little-c" to "Big-C" creativity. Given this definition, creativity can be studied from three different perspectives: the product, the person, and the process. Research adopting the product perspective may examine either the final product or the notebooks or sketchbooks that led to that product. Inquiries into the creative person have tended to pursue two alternative viewpoints, one concentrating on domain-specific expertise and the other on a generic cognitive style. Naturally, cognitive psychologists tend to favor the third perspective, namely that concentrating on the creative process. After discussing the three main theoretical views of this process, the discussion turns to the three principal empirical approaches. The chapter closes with four sets of questions that should guide future research on creativity.

**Key Words:** creativity, products, persons, processes, domain, expertise, cognitive style, creative cognition, neuroscience, social cognition

An idea is most often defined as creative if it fulfills two independent conditions (Simonton, 2000b; cf. Boden, 2004). First, the idea must be original, novel, or surprising. Otherwise, the idea would represent the hackneyed or routine. Second, the idea must be adaptive, functional, or useful—it must satisfy some standard that determines whether the idea actually works. It is this second utility condition that permits the exclusion of ideas produced by schizophrenics or paranoid psychotics. Both of these conditions are quantitative rather than qualitative. In particular, both can be conceived as attributes that vary along some ratio scale. Such a scale has a true zero point. Hence, it becomes possible to say that an idea has zero originality. An example would be the reinvention of the wheel. Similarly, it is reasonable to speak of an idea that has zero adaptiveness or utility, such as an airplane made completely out of cinderblocks. The amount of creativity can then be defined as the product of these two quantitative characteristics. If $C$ = creativity, $O$ = originality, and $A$ = adaptiveness, then $C = O \times A$. Accordingly, if an idea is either unoriginal (a reinvented wheel) or useless (cinderblock airplane), then creativity remains zero even if the other attribute is indefinitely large.

At once, this multiplicative definition forces us to ask: How do we assess variation in an idea's originality or adaptiveness? This twofold issue is far more difficult to address. In fact, different researchers will adopt rather divergent measurement strategies. This methodological diversity partly reflects differences in creative domain. What counts as original or adaptive in the sciences is not equivalent to that in the arts. For example, where scientific ideas must be constrained by fact and logic, artistic ideas can indulge in "poetic license" that requires appreciators to engage in a "willing suspension of disbelief."

Just as important, diversity in assessment reflects the tremendous variation in the magnitude of creativity (cf. Kaufman & Beghetto, 2009). At one extreme is "little-c creativity," where both originality and adaptiveness are noticeable but small. This level represents everyday creativity—the creativity of home and the workplace. These ideas will be creative with respect to the individual but not with respect to the world at large. At the other extreme is "Big-C Creativity," where both originality and adaptiveness are maximized to the point that the idea achieves a high degree of recognition, even universal acclaim. Extreme examples might include Einstein's theories of relativity or Michelangelo's Sistine Chapel frescoes. These creative ideas are both novel and original not only with respect to the individual but also with respect to the larger world. Unlike little-c creativity, Big-C Creativity invariably requires the confirmatory assessment of other individuals, most often judgments made by colleagues working in the same domain (Csikszentmihályi, 1999; Simonton, 2010).

At this point, we must note an enigma. On the one hand, it is patent that creativity is an extremely important cognitive phenomenon. Like language, creativity is one of those cognitive processes that distinguish *Homo sapiens* from other animals, including most primates. Big-C Creativity is highly desired in any creative domain, cognitive psychology not excluded. On the other hand, creativity is a somewhat neglected topic within cognitive psychology in particular and psychology in general (Sternberg & Lubart, 1996). This neglect was apparent in a casual survey of best-selling cognitive psychology textbooks. Only a minority included a specific section on the topic.

To be sure, most cognitive psychology texts will feature major sections devoted to the related topics of insight and problem solving. Even so, a great deal of research on the cognitive psychology of creativity does not overlap either of these phenomena. In the first place, creativity does not have to require insight, and not all insights yield ideas that are highly creative. Indeed, many insight experiments in cognitive psychology entail finding answers to questions whose answers are already known. Secondly, although it is often useful to view creativity as a form of problem solving, not all solutions to problems are creative—nor are all problems creative. This is why creativity researchers sometimes place emphasis on problem *finding* as a core aspect of the phenomenon, with problem solving placed in a secondary role (e.g., Getzels & Csikszentmihalyi, 1976; Rostan, 1994). What is remarkable about Einstein's special theory of relativity is not so much

the solution he offered as the problem he raised. His theory used minimal mathematics and knowledge of physics to respond to a question that only Einstein thought was important, namely certain esoteric inconsistencies between Newtonian mechanics and Maxwellian electromagnetic equations. Some of the problems Einstein raised are still driving research in physics.

Whatever the limitations in the cognitive research, in the following we offer a concise overview of the literature. This survey divides naturally into three parts: product, person, and process. Presumably, creative products are conceived by creative persons using creative processes.

## Creative Products

Frequently a creative idea will result in a creative product—a poem, painting, patent, publication, plan, policy statement, or some other concrete contribution that can be listed on the creator's resumé. In any case, such products have been used to obtain insights into creativity. This usage can be roughly grouped into the following two areas of research.

First, some researchers have concentrated on the final creative product. An example is Sternberg's (1999) propulsion model that identifies seven types of creative contributions, four that attempt to extend current paradigms and three that try to replace those paradigms. Such distinctions are important insofar as the cognitive processes underlying paradigm-accepting contributions probably differ from those responsible for paradigm-rejecting contributions (Simonton, 2009b, 2009c). For example, creativity in the former case is more likely to entail domain-specific methods (e.g., algorithms), whereas creativity in the latter case is more likely to involve domain-general methods (e.g., heuristics). Other investigators have scrutinized individual publication lists to help discern how creativity unfolds during the course of the career (e.g., Feist, 1997; Simonton, 1992, 2000a). As an example, content analyses of publication titles have shown that scientific creativity is hindered by switching around among totally disparate research topics (Feist, 1997; Simonton, 1992). Finally, we should mention empirical efforts to determine why some creative products have a much higher impact than others do, where the products may be either scientific (e.g., Shadish, 1989) or artistic (e.g., Kozbelt & Burger-Pianko, 2007). In the latter case, the question has been a major empirical issue since the advent of experimental aesthetics under Gustav Fechner, the founder of psychophysics. Perhaps for that reason it has proven easier to predict the impact of an artwork than the impact of a scientific publication!

Second, rather than focus on the final products, psychologists might concentrate on the ideational development of those products prior to their attaining finished form. For instance, many creators have left behind introspective reports of the thought processes that led to certain key discoveries (Ghiselin, 1952). Using such reports, Wallas (1926) argued that creativity consisted of the four stages of preparation, incubation, illumination, and verification. Of course, introspective reports are not necessarily reliable sources of data, especially insofar as they are often retrospective and thereby subject to memory distortions. To avoid this problem, researchers can concentrate on notebooks or sketchbooks that provide a contemporary record of the ideational development. Examples of such use include the notebooks of Charles Darwin (Gruber, 1974) and Michael Faraday (Tweney, 1989) as well as Pablo Picasso's sketches for his *Guernica* (Simonton, 2007; Weisberg, 2004). A related alternative is for the investigator to record the ongoing transactions in active research laboratories. The best example is Dunbar's (1995) in-depth study of biomedical research using videotapes, audiotapes, notes from grants, and paper drafts. From these in vivo data, Dunbar was able to discern the specific role that analogies play in the emergence of major discoveries.

It should be apparent that the bulk of the aforementioned research largely concerns Big-C Creativity. An exception is the work using the Consensual Assessment Technique (Amabile, 1982). In this method, participants are instructed to create objects (e.g., collages or poems) under specified laboratory conditions. However, because the actual product produced is less important than the processes underlying its creation, the results of this work are more properly discussed later in this chapter (Amabile, 1996).

## Creative Persons

People vary greatly in the number of creative products they offer the world (Simonton, 1997). In fact, the cross-sectional distribution of lifetime output is so skewed that about half of the contributions come from the top 10% of the contributors. Moreover, the modal level of output is a single contribution, and the bottom half of the distribution contributes only about 15% or so. Significantly, this huge variation applies to quality as well as quantity. On the average, those who contribute the most

products also create the most high-impact products—works that are high in both originality and adaptiveness. Indeed, at the top of the distribution are usually found highly prolific Big-C Creators like Albert Einstein, Igor Stravinsky, or Pablo Picasso. This is not to say that there are not exceptions; any domain of creative achievement includes mass producers who generate numerous low-quality contributions and perfectionists who create a handful of high-quality contributions. Even so, the mass producers and perfectionists are outliers with respect to the overall bivariate distribution linking quantity and quality of lifetime output.

In recognition of this enormous cross-sectional variation, some researchers have chosen to concentrate their inquiries on the creative person. Does the creative individual think differently from the noncreative individual? Do the more prolific creators differ from their less productive colleagues in some special cognitive ability or skill? Investigators addressing this question have tended to adopt one of two contrasting orientations. On the one hand are those psychologists who view creativity as a manifestation of domain-specific expertise. On the other hand are those psychologists who believe that creativity requires a generic cognitive style regardless of the domain in which it is applied. As will be seen shortly, these two perspectives may be contrasting, but they are not necessarily mutually exclusive.

### Domain-Specific Expertise

Starting with the classic research on chess conducted by Chase and Simon (1973), a number of cognitive psychologists have studied how achievement in a diversity of domains depends on the acquisition of the relevant domain-specific expertise (Ericsson, Charness, Feltovich, & Hoffman, 2006). This expertise consists of a large inventory of knowledge and skills that can only be acquired through considerable study and deliberate practice (Ericsson, Krampe, & Tesch-Römer, 1993). One particular manifestation of this requirement is the so-called 10-year rule (Ericsson, 1996). According to this empirical generalization, most domains are sufficiently complex that they require at least a decade of intense preparation and apprenticeship before an aspirant can attain worldclass expertise. Without that level of expertise, that person cannot expect to generate substantial domain-specific achievements. Although this rule was originally established for competitive games and musical performance, the principle applies to creativity as well (Hayes, 1989). On the average, even Big-C Creators must endure a decade-long apprenticeship before beginning to produce unquestioned masterworks rather than mere juvenilia. Hence, creativity may not require any special cognitive capacities. Provided individuals have enough general intelligence and motivation to engage in the necessary practice, then they should eventually emerge as high-impact contributors to their chosen domain of achievement.

Unfortunately, the expertise-acquisition explanation is incomplete. Research findings by creativity researchers have identified three empirical complications (Simonton, 2000a).

First, the 10-year rule is not a really a "rule" but rather a statistical average. Individuals vary greatly in the time necessary to attain domain mastery. Furthermore, these individual differences have a paradoxical consequence: Those persons who take less time to acquire domain-specific expertise tend to be more productive and to attain higher levels of lifetime achievement (e.g., Simonton, 1991, 1992). So, less is more.

Second, the expertise perspective cannot easily explain how some individuals display unusual versatility by making major contributions to two or more distinct domains (Cassandro & Simonton, 2010; White, 1931). Yet such creative versatility has been shown to correlate positively with lifetime achievement (Simonton, 1976; Sulloway, 1996; Ting, 1992). It is difficult to see how this would be possible if creativity in each domain were contingent on the 10-year rule, particularly when the domains overlap very little in requisite expertise.

Third, although a minimum level of domain-specific expertise is clearly required for creative accomplishments, that acquisition alone is by no means sufficient (Simonton, 2000a). Experts need not be creators. Somehow, the person must convert that knowledge and skill into creative ideas, and that conversion seems to require some special way of thinking that is most suitable for genuine creativity (Ansburg & Hill, 2003; Rostan, 1994). Einstein did not know more theoretical physics than did his contemporaries—and, if anything, he knew somewhat less. But what Einstein did know he thought about differently, and that difference gave him an advantage over those who knew much more.

### Generic Cognitive Style

Creativity requires the ability to combine seemingly unrelated ideas in original ways. Hence, researchers have tried to identify the cognitive capacities and inclinations that allow this to happen. These attributes may be loosely collected together as

defining a creative cognitive style that transcends any particular domain (see Chapter 63). More specifically, the accumulated research indicates the following five sets of interconnected results:

1. Creativity correlates positively with divergent thinking, or the ability to come up with many alternative responses to a given stimulus or probe (as contrasted to convergent thinking, or the ability to arrive at the single best response; Guilford, 1967). For example, one frequently used measure requires that the participant come up with many uses for common objects (e.g., a brick). Most often these responses are then scored for (a) fluency (the number of responses), (b) originality (statistical rarity), and (c) flexibility (range of conceptual categories). Fluency, originality, and flexibility not only correlate with each other but also with objective measures of creative behavior (Carson, Peterson, & Higgins, 2005). The latter measures include publishing or exhibiting creative products, receiving critical or professional recognition, and winning local and national awards.

2. Creativity is positively associated with the capacity to generate numerous and unusual associations (Gough, 1976; Rothenberg, 1983). Of special interest is the extensive work using the Remote Association Test (RAT) devised by Mednick (1962). In the RAT the respondent must come up with a fourth word that is the common associate of three stimulus words whose associative connection is not immediately obvious. For example, given "rat," "blue," and "cottage," the respondent should associate the word "cheese." This task requires that the respondent have a flat rather than steep associative hierarchy. That is, high scores depend on having many associations with roughly equal probabilities rather than just a few high-probability associations to any given stimulus. Because the RAT assesses a person's ability to quickly identify relationships among separate ideas, it is important to observe that the latter capacity correlates positively with divergent thinking (Vartanian, Martindale, & Matthews, 2009).

3. Creativity tends to increase with the tendency to lapse into defocused attention (Mendelsohn, 1976), such as gauged by reduced latent inhibition or negative priming (Carson, Peterson, & Higgins, 2003; Eysenck, 1995). In other words, creative individuals are less likely to filter out supposedly "irrelevant" information, thereby enabling them to take advantage of

serendipitous input (Seifert, Meyer, Davidson, Patalano, & Yaniv, 1995). Insofar as creative insight often requires viewing old things in new ways (e.g., to avoid "functional fixedness"), this potential cognitive liability can become a tremendous asset. Notably, persons who are more prone to attend to peripheral cues in the environment tend to score higher on the RAT as well (Ansburg & Hill, 2003).

4. Creativity is positively linked with openness to experience, a personal disposition to have wide interests and to be responsive to a diversity of intellectual or emotional input (Carson et al., 2005; Feist, 1998; Harris, 2004; McCrae, 1987). Openness to experience is also positively correlated with divergent thinking (Carson et al., 2005) and reduced latent inhibition (Peterson & Carson, 2000; Peterson, Smith, & Carson, 2002). A related concept is conceptual or cognitive complexity, which is also correlated with creativity (Charlton & Bakan, 1988–1989; Feist, 1994). Such complexity presupposes openness so that thinking will accommodate multiple and even contradictory perspectives on a given phenomenon.

5. Creativity at the highest levels is likely to be associated with elevated scores on psychoticism or schizotypy, two closely related indicators of a psychological proximity to mental illness (Batey & Furnham, 2008; Brod, 1997; Eysenck, 1995). Although creativity and psychopathology are by no means equivalent, the two mental states share certain characteristics, such as a disposition toward allusive or overinclusive thinking. Thus, reduced negative priming and latent inhibition is positively associated with psychoticism (Eysenck, 1993; Stavridou & Furnham, 1996). However, this cognitive style is less likely to have pathological consequences for highly intelligent individuals (Carson et al., 2003). Certain personality characteristics can also modulate the potential negative effects of this pattern of thinking, such as high ego strength (Eysenck, 1995).

Taken altogether, these correlates of creativity would increase the probability of generating the original ideational combinations required for creative thought. It should be pointed out that the capacity for creativity is neither equivalent to nor even highly correlated with general intelligence (Runco, 2004). The magnitude of the correlation depends on the variation in intellectual ability (e.g., the association can be near zero in highly intelligent college populations) and the type of creativity test

(e.g., more convergent measures like RAT correlate more highly than more divergent measures like Unusual Uses Test). Another factor that lowers the correspondence is that creativity tends to be more domain specific than general intelligence (e.g., Baer, 1994; Diakidoy & Spanoudis, 2002; Han, 2003; Plucker, 2004). This domain specificity is probably especially conspicuous in areas that demand highly technical expertise, as in the sciences (Simonton, 2009c). To illustrate, high-impact scientists tend to display considerable conceptual complexity when they talk about research, but not when they talk about teaching (Feist, 1994). Indeed, the latter is actually negatively associated with creativity in science.

Finally, we should note that to some degree the foregoing cognitive inclinations have a genetic foundation (e.g., Simonton, 2008b). Indeed, part of the reason why creativity and psychopathology have some correspondence is that both may share some genes (while diverging on other genes). At the same time, environmental experiences also play a role. For example, creativity tends to be positively associated with bilingualism (Simonton, 2008b) and with multicultural experiences, such as living abroad (Leung, Maddux, Galinsky, & Chiu, 2008). Those individuals who have both nature and nurture working in their favor are then most likely to exhibit the highest levels of creativity—assuming that they have acquired the threshold level of domain-specific expertise. Expertise provides the necessary condition, and a creative cognitive style provides the sufficient condition.

## Creative Processes

It may come as no surprise that most cognitive psychologists aim their primary research efforts at the creative process rather than the product or person. After all, the creative process must supply the ultimate causal basis for both the creative person and the creative product. Most (if not all) creative products resulted from creative persons who engaged in the appropriate creative process. In any event, cognitive research in this area falls into two broad categories: theoretical and empirical.

### Theoretical Perspectives

Given the importance of the phenomenon, creativity has attracted a large amount of theorizing. Rather than attempt to cover them all, we would like to restrict ourselves to mentioning the three main theoretical approaches:

1. *Gestalt restructuring*—Gestalt psychologists extended their fascination with insight (e.g., Köhler, 1925) to what Max Wertheimer (1945/1982) called "productive thinking," or high-level problem solving. To study the latter, Wertheimer took advantage of the introspections offered by Albert Einstein, his friend and colleague. In line with their basic theoretical orientation, which stressed holistic configurations, Gestalt psychologists viewed creativity as a perceptual or conceptual restructuring process in which the given problem is viewed in an entirely different way (see Chapter 49). Even though Gestalt psychology can no longer be taken as an active research tradition within mainstream cognitive psychology, Gestalt psychologists generated many fundamental issues that are still important today (e.g., the role of incubation in the creative process).

2. *Newell-Simon problem solving*—In 1972 Newell and Simon published their classic work on *Human Problem Solving*. Although originally focused on everyday problems (see Chapter 48), the approach was eventually extended to cover higher forms of creativity, particularly scientific discovery (Klahr & Simon, 1999). This application included not just supportive laboratory experiments (e.g., Qin & Simon, 1990) but also computer simulations that purport to make scientific discoveries (e.g., Langley, Simon, Bradshaw, & Zythow, 1987; Shrager & Langley, 1990). In a nutshell, this tradition views problem solving in terms of both "strong" algorithmic methods that tend to be domain specific and "weak" heuristic methods that are far more general in application (e.g., hill climbing or steepest ascent, means-end analysis, working backward, analogy, and trial and error), where the latter methods play a far larger role in creativity and discovery (Klahr & Simon, 1999; Newell, Shaw, & Simon, 1962). The Newell-Simon approach probably still represents the mainstream perspective on the creative process within cognitive psychology.

3. *Blind variation and selective retention*—Starting with Alexander Bain (1855/1977) and William James (1880) and continuing with Campbell (1960), several psychologists have argued that creativity represents a blind-variation, selective-retention (BVSR) process roughly comparable to the process underlying biological evolution (see also Cziko, 1998; Simonton, 1999, 2009a). BVSR theories can explicate a wide range of data as well as provide the basis for explanatory and predictive mathematical models (e.g., Schilling, 2005). Like the Newell-Simon approach, the BVSR conception has inspired the development of computer programs that exhibit creative problem solving, such as genetic algorithms and genetic programming (Holland, 1992; Koza, Bennett, Andre, & Keane, 1999). The central feature of most BVSR applications is the theoretical assumption that creativity entails some combinatorial mechanism (Simonton, 2003, 2010). Even so, the specific cognitive basis for that mechanism is left as an empirical question. It is also possible to integrate BVSR with the Newell-Simon tradition, particularly insofar as creativity depends on the trial-and-error heuristic (Simonton, 2012).

The foregoing perspectives constitute more or less comprehensive theories of the creative process. However, empirical research is not often guided by any of these theoretical perspectives—and often not by any theories at all.

### Empirical Perspectives

Psychologists who conduct research on the creative process hail from many different psychological subdisciplines, such as personality, developmental, and social psychology. Later we concentrate on the three empirical research domains that are most closely connected to cognitive psychology: the creative cognition approach, cognitive neuroscience, and social cognition.

#### CREATIVE COGNITION APPROACH

Too often creativity is viewed as some mysterious, almost magical process, a perception that may have inhibited cognitive psychologists from studying the phenomenon to the same degree that they have investigated the related phenomena of problem solving and insight. Nonetheless, many researchers hold that creativity does not require any special cognitive processes but rather just the application or coordination of processes available to every intelligent human being (Weisberg, 2006). Perhaps the most conspicuous proponents of this perspective are the advocates of the "creative cognition approach" (Finke, Ward, & Smith, 1992; Smith, Ward, & Finke, 1995; see also Ward, Smith, & Vaid, 1997). This paradigm has been developed in a series of laboratory experiments. One distinctive feature of these experiments is the frequent use of open-ended measures of creativity, in contrast to traditional insight and problem-solving experiments in which a correct answer is already established.

A good illustration of this approach is the experimental research conducted on the Geneplore model of creativity (Finke et al., 1992). According to this model, creativity involves two steps: (a) the generation of ideational combinations and (b) the exploration of their possibilities or implications. To evaluate this model, participants are given forms or shapes—lines, letters, triangles, hooks, rings, circles, spheres, cubes, and so on—from which they are asked to create objects with identifiable functions (e.g., tools and utensils, appliances, furniture, toys, or weapons). Independent judges then score the creativity of the resulting products emerging from this inventive task. Among the ingenious inventions were a shoestring unlacer, a hip exerciser, and a hamburger maker (see Finke et al., 1992, Figure 4.23, for some illustrations). The researchers would then manipulate various experimental conditions to determine how they affected the creativity of the products. For example, whereas in some conditions the participants themselves were allowed to select the shapes, in other conditions the participants were merely given a random selection of forms. In another experimental manipulation, participants could either chose the type of object they were to invent or this would be determined randomly by the experimenter. Curiously, the experiments indicated participants exhibit the most creativity when *both* the forms that they had to work with *and* the type of object they had to create were randomly sampled from the larger set of possibilities. Creativity appears to be enhanced when participants are exposed to serendipitous or incongruous stimulation (see also Proctor, 1993; Rothenberg, 1986; Wan & Chiu, 2002). Such stimulation may permit persons to "think outside the box" or "break set" by priming associative pathways that would otherwise not be pursued. In a sense, the upshot is experimentally induced openness to experience and defocused attention.

## COGNITIVE NEUROSCIENCE

From time to time researchers in the neurosciences have attempted to identify the brain regions and neurological processes that produce creative thought (for review, see Andreasen, 2005). Some of the earliest work in the neurosciences took advantage of electroencephalography (EEG). For example, creativity has been shown to be associated with lower arousal states, as gauged by alpha wave activity (Fink & Neubauer, 2008; Martindale & Armstrong, 1974). This association provides some experimental endorsement for introspective reports

that many Big-C creative ideas emerge when the creative individual is engaged in some mundane, low-arousal activity, such as going for a walk or waking up in the morning (Boden, 2004). Perhaps the most famous illustration is the Eureka experience reported by Archimedes, who solved a particularly difficult problem upon getting into a bath tub.

Other investigators have examined the connection between creativity and the EEG coherence function (e.g., Bechtereva & Nagornova, 2007). The EEG technique has also been applied to the identification of those cortical regions most involved in creative thought (e.g., Grabner, Fink, & Neubauer, 2007). This quest for cortical localization of brain function has been enhanced with the advent of functional magnetic resonance imaging (fMRI). For instance, such research has indicated that the right prefrontal cortex may play an important role in verbal creativity (e.g., Howard-Jones, Blakemore, Samuel, Summers, & Claxton, 2005; Mashal, Faust, Hendler, & Jung-Beeman, 2007). Of course, EEG and fMRI need not be mutually exclusive techniques. As a case in point, the two methods have been fruitfully combined to discern the brain processes underlying the insight or "Aha! moment" (Kounios & Beeman, 2009).

Other research findings have been contingent on surgical interventions that radically altered brain structure and function. The most dramatic of these investigations concerned the consequences of cutting the corpus callosum and thereby separating the right and left cortical hemispheres. Such "split-brain" participants provided evidence that the two hemispheres in the adult human being were often responsible for vastly different functions (Springer & Deutsch, 1989). These findings unfortunately entered popular psychology as people were urged to become more creative by "using their right brain." Empirical research suggests, however, that people are more creative when they can use both hemispheres in an integrative fashion (Hines, 1991). Split-brain patients are at a distinct disadvantage, for example, in comprehending metaphors (Hoppe & Kyle, 1990). That said, it remains apparent from the brain imaging research mentioned earlier that the right prefrontal regions may make a special contribution to creative thought.

Finally, it is clear that chemical features of the brain might also have an effect on the processes supporting creativity. The earliest research on this topic looked at the impact of various psychoactive drugs, especially psychadelics, on the creative process (e.g., Berlin, Guthrie, Weider, Goodell, & Wolff, 1955;

Janiger & de Rios, 1989). Later researchers have concentrated on the more natural biochemistry of creativity in the brain, such as specific hormones and neurotransmitters. For example, lower levels of such catecholamines as norepinephrine and dopamine, by lowering cortical arousal level, can increase the likelihood of creativity (Eysenck, 1995; Heilman, Nadeau, & Beversdorf, 2003). Because the brain chemistry associated with creativity also features connections with that related to psychopathology, this line of inquiry may eventually help resolve the creativity-psychopathology connection discussed earlier.

At present, we think it fair to say that the cognitive neuroscience of creativity has a long way to go before it can provide a complete basis for the phenomenon. One reason for this statement is that such techniques as fMRI are still relatively new, and so the details of their proper application still need refinement (see, e.g., Vul, Harris, Winkielman, & Pashler, 2009). Yet another reason has to do with the state of our understanding of creativity. Because creativity researchers have not yet reached a consensus about the basic processes involved, it would be premature to expect neuroscientists to isolate the neurological underpinnings of those processes. In fact, creativity may assume more than one form, each with its distinct set of brain mechanisms. If so, the problem of finding the neuroscientific basis becomes even more recalcitrant (for further discussion, see Dietrich & Kanso, 2010, and Sawyer, 2011).

### SOCIAL COGNITION

Social psychologists have recently taken an interest in creativity. From their perspective, the most intriguing question concerns the relationship between social context and creative processing. The social context can influence creativity through affective states, motivation, and social power.

Creative processing has long been linked with positive affect. A classic study by Isen, Daubman, and Nowicki (1987) showed that watching funny films or receiving a bag of candy made participants perform better on creative insight tasks. However, more recent studies (e.g., Akinola & Mendes, 2008) suggest the opposite, namely that negative affect increases creative performance.

To integrate these contradictory findings, DeDreu, Baas, and Nijstad (2008) proposed a new model of affect-creativity, emphasizing a dual pathway to creativity. For this purpose, the authors categorized moods based on two independent dimensions: valence (positive vs. negative; e.g., happy vs.

fearful) and activation level (activating vs. deactivating; e.g., angry vs. sad). Using these distinctions, the authors found that activating moods in general (regardless of valence) led to more creative processing than deactivating moods. A potential theoretical explanation would be that activating moods help the release of dopamine and noradrenalin, which enhance working memory and prefrontal cortex control, thus allowing for increased attention focus and creativity. Additionally, the authors found that affective valence also mattered. Positive activating moods increased creativity via cognitive flexibility (i.e., ability to come up with distinct solution categories), while negative activating moods increased creativity via cognitive persistence (i.e., ability to come up with many items per category). Moreover, in a follow-up study, Baas, DeDreu, and Nijstad (2011) found that negative activating moods, such as anger, led to a peak in creative production only at the beginning of the task and showed a decline in creative idea generation as time continued (16 minutes later), suggesting that negative activating moods deplete people's creative resources relatively fast. In these studies, creativity was defined as originality on a variation of Guilford's Unusual Uses Test (1967). The theoretical interpretation for these findings is that moods are used as information (see the cognitive tuning theory; Schwarz & Bless, 1991) in the following way: Positive moods signal a benign environment and encourage eagerness and a broad focus of attention (which lead to cognitive flexibility), while negative moods signal a threatening environment and encourage vigilance and a narrow focus of attention (which lead to persistence). In other words, the hypothesized mechanism behind the affect-creativity link is in part a motivational one, where affect is seen as merely a trigger for approach/avoidance motivation. While DeDreu et al. (2008) seem to suggest that an avoidance motivation marked by vigilant persistence can also lead to creativity, most of the current research on motivation supports more strongly the authors' first claim, namely that an approach motivation leads to creativity.

In exploring the relation between approach/avoidance motivation and creativity more directly, Regulatory Focus Theory (RFT; Higgins, 1997) has become one of the most popular theoretical frameworks. According to the RFT, *promotion focus* is associated with an approach motivation, eagerness, broad thinking, and risk taking, whereas *prevention focus* is associated with an avoidance motivation, vigilance, narrow thinking, and risk avoidance. Considering the different cognitive styles engendered by the two motivational states, Friedman and Förster (2001) showed that promotion focus (rather than prevention focus) led to more creative processing. For a potential cognitive mechanism, the authors propose that promotion focus leads to broader attention deployment. Such defocused attention allows for automatic screening of a larger pool of information, which then leads to an increased probability of remote associations and creativity.

Apart from the type of motivation and its impact on creativity, researchers have also investigated the source of motivation (intrinsic versus extrinsic) and its role in creative processing. Intrinsic motivation is defined as a desire to perform an activity for its own sake (inherent enjoyment), while extrinsic motivation is defined as performing a task in order to receive an external reward (or to avoid punishment). Amabile (1996) showed that participants who wrote essays priming them with an intrinsic motivation scored higher on complex creativity tasks (collages and poems) than participants primed with an extrinsic motivation. Once again, the suggested cognitive mechanism behind these effects is an attentional one. According to Csikszentmihalyi (1978), intrinsic motivation leads to highly concentrated attention and task involvement, which is beneficial for creativity, whereas extrinsic motivation is harmful to creativity because it causes people to divide their attention between their extrinsic goals and the task at hand (Amabile, 1983).

In addition to the type of motivation and the source of motivation, Deci and Ryan (1985) propose research should also focus on how individuals perceive certain kinds of motivation: externally controlling or providing useful and desired information (i.e., allowing for autonomy). Their hypothesis is that not all types of extrinsic motivation are equally harmful for creativity, depending on how they are perceived. In a study testing the effects of controlled versus autonomous motivation on creativity, Koestner, Ryan, Bernieri, and Holt (1984) told their participants that they must be neat while making a painting either because it was a rule (in the controlled motivation condition), or because they should keep the materials in order for other participants (in the autonomous motivation condition). Although both conditions imposed extrinsic constraints, they differed in controlled versus autonomous motivation. As predicted, participants in the autonomous motivation condition produced more creative paintings.

The beneficial effects of autonomous motivation on creativity are also supported by research on social power. According to Galinsky, Gruenfeld, Magee, Whitson, and Liljenquist (2008), individuals high in social power have both control over and independence from others in reaching their goals. The latter characteristic of power, namely the capacity to be uninfluenced by others, should lead to an autonomous motivation and is therefore important in the context of creative thinking. More precisely, Galinsky and colleagues (2008). propose that high-power individuals (as opposed to low-power individuals) are less influenced and constrained by salient information in the environment, and as a result, internal processes and predilections matter more than the situation in determining creative outcomes of the powerful. Supporting this hypothesis, the authors showed that individuals who were primed with high versus low social power were less influenced by salient cues in the environment and produced more creative drawings of imaginary alien life forms. Relating these findings back to Koestner et al.'s (1984) research on autonomous/controlled motivation, one could say that high-power individuals are immune to controlled motivation and therefore their creativity cannot suffer from situational constraints.

In sum, research in social cognition points to very similar prerequisites for creative cognitive processing, namely the following: an approach motivation, a broad attention mindset, and a deep task involvement characterized by intrinsic motivation and immunity from external control.

Dijksterhuis and Nordgren (2006) suggest that unconscious thought (i.e., being distracted while still holding a task-relevant goal) meets all of these requirements. According to their theory, unconscious thought is better at broad associative searches and leads to more remote associations, while conscious thought is better at analytic processing that primarily isolates and discriminates. Additionally, conscious thought is more susceptible to situational constraints and limited working memory capacity. Supporting this theory, Dijksterhuis and Meurs (2006) found that unconscious thought increased creativity more than an equal duration of continuous attention (i.e., conscious thought), suggesting that temporarily distracting attention away from the task of generating creative ideas allowed participants to conduct broader searches that were less constrained by conventional associations. So where does this leave us? Many researchers are still skeptical about the unconscious thought theory (e.g.

Gonzalez-Vallejo, Lassiter, Bellezza, & Lindberg, 2008) and the issue of what cognitive processes lead to creativity remains unresolved.

## Conclusion

Although creativity is not always counted as a core subject in cognitive psychology, the literature review herein suggests that it deserves much more theoretical and empirical attention. Creativity as a psychological phenomenon is far from subsumed by mainstream research on insight and problem solving. To be sure, creativity is not an easy phenomenon to study. One problem is that it can be investigated from a number of distinct perspectives—product, person, and process—that do not always entail the same methods and theories. Furthermore, creativity research often demands techniques that depart from those favored in representative research in cognitive psychology. Examples include such methods as introspective reports, naturalistic observations, content analyses, and open-ended measures. In contrast, reaction times, which have been a mainstay of cognitive research ever since the founding of experimental psychology, play a minimal role in the study of creativity (but see, e.g., Dorfman, Martindale, Gassimova, & Vartanian, 2008). Nevertheless, given that (a) creativity is an intrinsically significant phenomenon and (b) it is a phenomenon that has inherent cognitive features, we hope that the topic will attract more attention in mainstream cognitive psychology.

## Future Directions

Once we recognize that creativity represents a distinct phenomenon from either problem solving or insight, the potential research questions expand tremendously. These questions can be grouped into the following four areas:

1. What is the complete inventory of cognitive processes that participate in creativity? All too often researchers have focused on single-process conceptions. One will put forward their favorite process while another argues for an alternative process. Yet it is very likely that creativity constitutes a very complex phenomenon with multiple processes that interact in intricate ways both simultaneously and over time. These have all to be teased out.

2. What is the neurological substrate of these various processes and their interactions? Cognitive neuroscience has the techniques to address this question, but a satisfactory treatment requires that neuroscientists know where to look. The brain, too, is an extremely complicated phenomenon.

3. How do these processes and interactions relate to individual differences on cognitive and dispositional variables? It is conceivable that different cognitive styles or personality traits might impinge on distinct processes or phases of those processes.

4. What is the developmental basis for the foregoing? How do early experiences in childhood and adolescence influence the acquisition of creative potential? What is the precise contribution of domain-specific expertise?

5. How does the social context affect the operation of creative processes and their interactions? The social milieu can clearly influence creative development as well as the manifestation of creative potential in adulthood. To what extent can we actively intervene in the social environment to increase the amount of creativity?

It is probably clear that the answers to these five questions are intimately connected. That means that progress on one front cannot be achieved without sufficient progress on another. Probably we can only obtain a coherent and comprehensive theory of creativity by answering all questions simultaneously and in a mutually reinforcing manner. That is the hope for the future.

## References

Akinola, M., & Mendes, W. (2008). The dark side of creativity: Biological vulnerability and negative emotions lead to greater artistic creativity. *Personality and Social Psychology Bulletin, 34,* 1677–1686.

Amabile, T. M. (1982). Social psychology of creativity: A consensual assessment technique. *Journal of Personality and Social Psychology, 43,* 997–1013.

Amabile, T. M. (1983). *The social psychology of creativity.* New York: Springer-Verlag.

Amabile, T. M. (1996). *Creativity in context: Update to the social psychology of creativity.* Boulder, CO: Westview.

Andreasen, N. C. (2005). *The creating brain: The neuroscience of genius.* New York: Danna Press.

Ansburg, P. I., & Hill, K. (2003). Creative and analytic thinkers differ in their use of attentional resources. *Personality and Individual Differences, 34,* 1141–1152.

Baas, M., De Dreu, C.K.W., & Nijstad, B.A. (2011). Creative production by angry people peaks early on, decreases over time, and is relatively unstructured. *Journal of Experimental Social Psychology, 47, 1107–1115.*

Baer, J. (1994). Divergent thinking is not a general trait: A multidomain training experiment. *Creativity Research Journal, 7,* 35–46.

Bain, A. (1977). *The senses and the intellect* (D. N. Robinson, Ed.). Washington, DC: University Publications of America. (Original work published 1855).

Batey, M., & Furnham, A. (2008). The relationship between measures of creativity and schizotypy. *Personality and Individual Differences, 45,* 816–821.

Bechtereva, N. P., & Nagornova, Z. V. (2007). Changes in EEG coherence during tests for nonverbal (figurative) creativity. *Human Physiology, 33,* 515–523.

Berlin, L., Guthrie, T., Weider, A., Goodell, H., & Wolff, H. G. (1955). The effects of mescaline and lysergic acid on cerebral processes pertinent to creative activity. *Journal of Nervous and Mental Disease, 122,* 487–491.

Boden, M. A. (2004). *The creative mind: Myths & mechanisms* (2nd ed.). New York: Routledge.

Brod, J. H. (1997). Creativity and schizotypy. In G. Claridge (Ed.), *Schizotypy: Implications for illness and health* (pp. 274–298). Oxford, England: Oxford University Press.

Carson, S., Peterson, J. B., & Higgins, D. M. (2003). Decreased latent inhibition is associated with increased creative achievement in high-functioning individuals. *Journal of Personality and Social Psychology, 85,* 499–506.

Carson, S., Peterson, J. B., & Higgins, D. M. (2005). Reliability, validity, and factor structure of the Creative Achievement Questionnaire. *Creativity Research Journal, 17,* 37–50.

Cassandro, V. J., & Simonton, D. K. (2010). Versatility, openness to experience, and topical diversity in creative products: An exploratory historiometric analysis of scientists, philosophers, and writers. *Journal of Creative Behavior, 44,* 1–18.

Charlton, S., & Bakan, P. (1988–89). Cognitive complexity and creativity. *Imagination, Cognition and Personality, 8,* 315–322.

Chase, W. G., & Simon, H. A. (1973). Perception in chess. *Cognitive Psychology, 4,* 55–81.

Csikszentmihalyi, M. (1978). Attention and the holistic approach to behavior. In K. S. Pope & J. L. Singer (Eds.), *The stream of consciousness* (pp. 335–358). New York: Plenum Press.

Csikszentmihályi, M. (1999). Implications of a systems perspective for the study of creativity. In R. J. Sternberg (Ed.), *Handbook of creativity* (pp. 313–338).Cambridge, England: Cambridge University Press.

Cziko, G. A. (1998). From blind to creative: In defense of Donald Campbell's selectionist theory of human creativity. *Journal of Creative Behavior, 32,* 192–208.

Deci, E. L., & Ryan, R. M. (1985). *Intrinsic motivation and self-determination in human behavior.* New York: Plenum Press.

De Dreu, C., Baas, M., & Nijstad, B. (2008). Hedonic tone and activation level in the mood-creativity link: Toward a dual pathway to creativity model. *Journal of Personality and Social Psychology, 94,* 739–756.

Diakidoy, I-A. N., & Spanoudis, G. (2002). Domain specificity in creativity testing: A comparison of performance on a general divergent-thinking test and a parallel, content-specific test. *Journal of Creative Behavior, 36,* 41–61.

Dietrich, A., & Kanso, R. (2010). A review of EEG, ERP, and neuroimaging studies of creativity and insight. *Psychological Bulletin, 136,* 822–848.

Dijksterhuis, A., & Meurs, T. (2006). Where creativity resides: The generative power of unconscious thought. *Consciousness and Cognition, 15,* 135–146.

Dijksterhuis, A. & Nordgren, L. F. (2006). A theory of unconscious thought. *Perspectives on Psychological Science, 1,* 95–109.

Dorfman, L., Martindale, C., Gassimova, V., & Vartanian, O. (2008). Creativity and speed of information processing: A double dissociation involving elementary versus inhibitory cognitive tasks. *Personality and Individual Differences, 44,* 1382–1390.

Dunbar, K. (1995). How scientists really reason: Scientific reasoning in real-world laboratories. In R. J. Sternberg & J. E. Davidson (Eds.), *The nature of insight* (pp. 365–396). Cambridge, MA: MIT Press.

Ericsson, K. A. (1996). The acquisition of expert performance: An introduction to some of the issues. In K. A. Ericsson (Ed.), *The road to expert performance: Empirical evidence from the arts and sciences, sports, and games* (pp. 1–50). Mahwah, NJ: Erlbaum.

Ericsson, K. A., Charness, N., Feltovich, P. J., & Hoffman, R. R. (Eds.). (2006). *The Cambridge handbook of expertise and expert performance.* New York: Cambridge University Press.

Ericsson, K. A., Krampe, R. T., & Tesch-Römer, C. (1993). The role of deliberate practice in the acquisition of expert performance. *Psychological Review, 100,* 363–406.

Eysenck, H. J. (1993). Creativity and personality: Suggestions for a theory. *Psychological Inquiry, 4,* 147–178.

Eysenck, H. J. (1995). *Genius: The natural history of creativity.* Cambridge, England: Cambridge University Press.

Feist, G. J. (1994). Personality and working style predictors of integrative complexity: A study of scientists' thinking about research and teaching. *Journal of Personality and Social Psychology, 67,* 474–484.

Feist, G. J. (1997). Quantity, quality, and depth of research as influences on scientific eminence: Is quantity most important? *Creativity Research Journal, 10,* 325–335.

Feist, G. J. (1998). A meta-analysis of personality in scientific and artistic creativity. *Personality and Social Psychology Review, 2,* 290–309.

Fink, A., & Neubauer, A. C. (2008). Eysenck meets Martindale: The relationship between extraversion and originality from the neuroscientific perspective. *Personality and Individual Differences, 44,* 299–310.

Finke, R. A., Ward, T. B., & Smith, S. M. (1992). *Creative cognition: Theory, research, applications.* Cambridge, MA: MIT Press.

Friedman, R., & Förster, J. (2001). The effects of promotion and prevention cues on creativity. *Journal of Personality and Social Psychology, 81,* 1001–1013.

Galinsky, A., Gruenfeld, D., Magee, J., Whitson, J., & Liljenquist, K. (2008). Power reduces the press of the situation: Implications for creativity, conformity and dissonance. *Journal of Personality and Social Psychology, 95,* 1450–1466.

Getzels, J., & Csikszentmihalyi, M. (1976). *The creative vision: A longitudinal study of problem finding in art.* New York: Wiley.

Ghiselin, B. (Ed.). (1952). *The creative process: A symposium.* Berkeley: University of California Press.

Gonzalez-Vallejo, C., Lassiter, G. D., Bellezza, F. S., & Lindberg, M. J. (2008). "Save angels perhaps": A critical examination of unconscious thought theory and the deliberation-without-attention effect. *Review of General Psychology, 12,* 282–296.

Gough, H. G. (1976). Studying creativity by means of word association tests. *Journal of Applied Psychology, 61,* 348–353.

Grabner, R. H., Fink, A., & Neubauer, A. C. (2007). Brain correlates of self-rated originality of ideas: Evidence from event-related power and phase-locking changes in the EEG. *Behavioral Neuroscience, 121,* 224–230.

Gruber, H. E. (1974). *Darwin on man: A psychological study of scientific creativity.* New York: Dutton.

Guilford, J. P. (1967). *The nature of human intelligence*. New York: McGraw-Hill.

Han, K. S. (2003). Domain-specificity of creativity in young children: How quantitative and qualitative data support it. *Journal of Creative Behavior, 37*, 117–142.

Harris, J. A. (2004). Measured intelligence, achievement, openness to experience, and creativity. *Personality and Individual Differences, 36*, 913–929.

Higgins, E. T. (1997). Beyond pleasure and pain. *American Psychologist, 52*, 1280–1300.

Hines, T. (1991). The myth of right hemisphere creativity. *Journal of Creative Behavior, 25*, 223–227.

Hoppe, K. D., & Kyle, N. L. (1990). Dual brain, creativity, and health. *Creativity Research Journal, 3*, 150–157.

Hayes, J. R. (1989). *The complete problem solver* (2nd ed.). Hillsdale, NJ: Erlbaum.

Heilman, K. M., Nadeau, S. E., & Beversdorf, D. O. (2003). Creative innovation: Possible brain mechanisms. *Neurocase, 9*, 369–379.

Holland, J. H. (1992). Genetic algorithms. *Scientific American, 267*(1), 66–72.

Howard-Jones, P. A., Blakemore, S-J., Samuel, E. A., Summers, I. R., & Claxton, G. (2005). Semantic divergence and creative story generation: An fMRI investigation. *Cognitive Brain Research, 25*, 240–250.

Isen, A. M., Daubman, K. A., & Nowicki, G. P. (1987). Positive affect facilitates creative problem solving. *Journal of Personality and Social Psychology, 52*, 1122–1131.

James, W. (1880, October). Great men, great thoughts, and the environment. *Atlantic Monthly, 46*, 441–459.

Janiger, O., & de Rios, M. D. (1989). LSD and creativity. *Journal of Psychoactive Drugs, 21*, 129–134.

Kaufman, J. C., & Beghetto, R. A. (2009). Beyond big and little: The four c model of creativity. *Review of General Psychology, 13*, 1–13.

Klahr, D., & Simon, H. A. (1999). Studies of scientific creativity: Complementary approaches and convergent findings. *Psychological Bulletin, 125*, 524–543.

Koestner, R., Ryan, R. M., Bernieri, F., & Holt, K. (1984). Setting limits on children's behavior: The differential effects of controlling versus informational styles on intrinsic motivation and creativity. *Journal of Personality, 52*, 233–248.

Köhler, W. (1925). *The mentality of apes* (E. Winter, Trans.). New York: Harcourt, Brace.

Kounios, J., & Beeman, M. (2009). The Aha! moment: The cognitive neuroscience of insight. *Current Directions in Psychological Science, 18*, 210–216.

Koza, J. R., Bennett, F. H., III, Andre, D., & Keane, M. A. (1999). *Genetic programming III: Darwinian invention and problem solving*. San Francisco: Morgan Kaufmann.

Kozbelt, A., & Burger-Pianko, Z. (2007). Words, music, and other measures: Predicting the repertoire popularity of 597 Schubert lieder. *Psychology of Aesthetics, Creativity, and the Arts, 1*, 191–203.

Langley, P., Simon, H. A., Bradshaw, G. L., & Zythow, J. M. (1987). *Scientific discovery*. Cambridge, MA: MIT Press.

Leung, A. K., Maddux, W. W., Galinsky, A. D., & Chiu, C. (2008). Multicultural experience enhances creativity: The when and how. *American Psychologist, 63*, 169–181.

Martindale, C. & Armstrong, J. (1974). The relationship of creativity to cortical activation and its operant control. *Journal of Genetic Psychology, 124*, 311–320.

Mashal, N., Faust, M., Hendler, T., & Jung-Beeman, M. (2007). An fMRI investigation of the neural correlates underlying the processing of novel metaphoric expressions. *Brain and Language, 100*, 115–126.

McCrae, R. R. (1987). Creativity, divergent thinking, and openness to experience. *Journal of Personality and Social Psychology, 52*, 1258–1265.

Mednick, S. A. (1962). The associative basis of the creative process. *Psychological Review, 69*, 220–232.

Mendelsohn, G. A. (1976). Associative and attentional processes in creative performance. *Journal of Personality, 44*, 341–369.

Newell, A., Shaw, J. C., & Simon, H. A. (1962). The processes of creative thinking. In H. E. Gruber, G. Terrell, & M. Wertheimer (Eds.), *Contemporary approaches to creative thinking* (pp. 63–119). New York: Atherton Press.

Newell, A., & Simon, H. A. (1972). *Human problem solving*. Englewood Cliffs, NJ: Prentice-Hall.

Peterson, J. B., & Carson, S. (2000). Latent inhibition and openness to experience in a high-achieving student population. *Personality and Individual Differences, 28*, 323–332.

Peterson, J. B., Smith, K. W., & Carson, S. (2002). Openness and extraversion are associated with reduced latent inhibition: Replication and commentary. *Personality and Individual Differences, 33*, 1137–1147.

Plucker, J. A. (2004). Generalization of creativity across domains: Examination of the method effect hypothesis. *Journal of Creative Behavior, 38*, 1–12.

Proctor, R. A. (1993). Computer stimulated associations. *Creativity Research Journal, 6*, 391–400.

Qin, Y., & Simon, H. A. (1990). Laboratory replication of scientific discovery processes. *Cognitive Science, 14*, 281–312.

Rostan, S. M. (1994). Problem finding, problem solving, and cognitive controls: An empirical investigation of critically acclaimed productivity. *Creativity Research Journal, 7*, 97–110.

Rothenberg, A. (1983). Psychopathology and creative cognition: A comparison of hospitalized patients, Nobel laureates, and controls. *Archives of General Psychiatry, 40*, 937–942.

Rothenberg, A. (1986). Artistic creation as stimulated by superimposed versus combined-composite visual images. *Journal of Personality and Social Psychology, 50*, 370–381.

Runco, M. (2004). Creativity. *Annual Review of Psychology, 55*, 657–687.

Schilling, M. A. (2005). A "small-world" network model of cognitive insight. *Creativity Research Journal, 17*, 131–154.

Sawyer, R. K. (2011). The cognitive neuroscience of creativity: A critical review. *Creativity Research Journal, 23*, 137–154.

Schwarz, N., & Bless, H. (1991). Happy and mindless, but sad and smart? The impact of affective states on analytic reasoning. In J. P. Forgas (Ed.), *Emotion and social judgments* (pp. 55–71). Elmsford, NY: Pergamon Press.

Seifert, C. M., Meyer, D. E., Davidson, N., Patalano, A. L., & Yaniv, I. (1995). Demystification of cognitive insight: Opportunistic assimilation and the prepared-mind perspective. In R. J. Sternberg & J. E. Davidson (Eds.), *The nature of insight* (pp. 65–124). Cambridge, MA: MIT Press.

Shadish, W. R., Jr. (1989). The perception and evaluation of quality in science. In B. Gholson, W. R. Shadish, Jr., R. A. Neimeyer, & A. C. Houts (Eds.), *The psychology of science: Contributions to metascience* (pp. 383–426). Cambridge, England: Cambridge University Press.

Shrager, J., & Langley, P. (Eds.). (1990). *Computational models of scientific discovery and theory formation*. San Mateo, CA: Kaufmann.

Simonton, D. K. (1976). Biographical determinants of achieved eminence: A multivariate approach to the Cox data. *Journal of Personality and Social Psychology, 33*, 218–226.

Simonton, D. K. (1991). Emergence and realization of genius: The lives and works of 120 classical composers. *Journal of Personality and Social Psychology, 61*, 829–840.

Simonton, D. K. (1992). Leaders of American psychology, 1879–1967: Career development, creative output, and professional achievement. *Journal of Personality and Social Psychology, 62*, 5–17.

Simonton, D. K. (1997). Creative productivity: A predictive and explanatory model of career trajectories and landmarks. *Psychological Review, 104*, 66–89.

Simonton, D. K. (1999). *Origins of genius: Darwinian perspectives on creativity*. New York: Oxford University Press.

Simonton, D. K. (2000a). Creative development as acquired expertise: Theoretical issues and an empirical test. *Developmental Review, 20*, 283–318.

Simonton, D. K. (2000b). Creativity: Cognitive, developmental, personal, and social aspects. *American Psychologist, 55*, 151–158.

Simonton, D. K. (2003). Scientific creativity as constrained stochastic behavior: The integration of product, process, and person perspectives. *Psychological Bulletin, 129*, 475–494.

Simonton, D. K. (2007). The creative imagination in Picasso's Guernica sketches: Monotonic improvements or nonmonotonic variants? *Creativity Research Journal, 19*, 329–344.

Simonton, D. K. (2008a). Bilingualism and creativity. In J. Altarriba & R. R. Heredia (Eds.), *An introduction to bilingualism: Principles and processes* (pp. 147–166). Mahwah, NJ: Erlbaum.

Simonton, D. K. (2008b). Scientific talent, training, and performance: Intellect, personality, and genetic endowment. *Review of General Psychology, 12*, 28–46.

Simonton, D. K. (2009a). Creativity as a Darwinian phenomenon: The blind-variation and selective-retention model. In M. Krausz, D. Dutton, & K. Bardsley (Eds.), *The idea of creativity* (2nd ed., pp. 63–81). Leiden, The Netherlands: Brill.

Simonton, D. K. (2009b). Varieties of perspectives on creativity. *Perspectives on Psychological Science, 4*, 466–467.

Simonton, D. K. (2009c).Varieties of (scientific) creativity: A hierarchical model of disposition, development, and achievement. *Perspectives on Psychological Science, 4*, 441–452.

Simonton, D. K. (2010). Creativity as blind-variation and selective-retention: Combinatorial models of exceptional creativity. *Physics of Life Reviews, 7*, 156–179.

Simonton, D. K. (2012). Scientific creativity as blind variation: Explicit and implicit procedures, mechanisms, and processes. In R. Proctor & E. J. Capaldi (Eds.), *Psychology of science: Implicit and explicit reasoning* (pp. 363–388). New York: Oxford University Press.

Smith, S. M., Ward, T. B., & Finke, R. A. (Eds.). (1995). *The creative cognition approach*. Cambridge, MA: MIT Press.

Springer, S. P., & Deutsch, G. (1989). *Left brain, right brain* (3rd. ed.). San Francisco: Freeman.

Sternberg, R. J. (1999). A propulsion model of types of creative contributions. *Review of General Psychology, 3*, 83–100.

Sternberg, R. J., & Lubart, T. I. (1996). Investing in creativity. *American Psychologist, 51*, 677–688.

Stavridou, A., & Furnham, A. (1996). The relationship between psychoticism, trait-creativity and the attentional mechanism of cognitive inhibition. *Personality and Individual Differences, 21*, 143–153.

Sulloway, F. J. (1996). *Born to rebel: Birth order, family dynamics, and creative lives*. New York: Pantheon.

Ting, S -S. (1992). Chinese literary eminence and personal factors: A recursive structural equation model [Mandarin]. *Chinese Journal of Applied Psychology, 1*, 21–37.

Tweney, R. D. (1989). A framework for the cognitive psychology of science. In B. Gholson, W. R. Shadish, Jr., R. A. Neimeyer, & A. C. Houts (Eds.), *The psychology of science: Contributions to metascience* (pp. 342–366). Cambridge, England: Cambridge University Press.

Vartanian, O., Martindale, C., & Matthews, J. (2009). Divergent thinking ability is related to faster relatedness judgments. *Psychology of Aesthetics, Creativity, and the Arts, 3*, 99–103.

Vul, E., Harris, C., Winkielman, P., & Pashler, H. (2009). Puzzlingly high correlations in fMRI studies of emotion, personality, and social cognition. *Perspectives on Psychological Science, 4*, 274–290.

Wallas, G. (1926). *The art of thought*. New York: Harcourt, Brace.

Wan, W. W. N., & Chiu, C -Y. (2002). Effects of novel conceptual combination on creativity. *Journal of Creative Behavior, 36*, 227–240.

Ward, T. B., Smith, S. M., & Vaid, J. (Eds.). (1997). *Creative thought: An investigation of conceptual structures and processes*. Washington, DC: American Psychological Association.

Weisberg, R. W. (2004). On structure in the creative process: A quantitative case-study of the creation of Picasso's *Guernica*. *Empirical Studies of the Arts, 22*, 23–54.

Weisberg, R. W. (2006). *Creativity: Understanding innovation in problem solving, science, invention, and the arts*. Hoboken, NJ: Wiley.

Wertheimer, M. (1982). *Productive thinking* (M. Wertheimer, Ed.). Chicago: University of Chicago Press. (Original work published 1945).

White, R. K. (1931). The versatility of genius. *Journal of Social Psychology, 2*, 460–489.

## Further Reading

Boden, M. A. (2004). *The creative mind: Myths and mechanisms* (2nd ed.). New York: Routledge.

Kaufman, J. C., & Sternberg, R. J. (2009). (Eds.). *Cambridge handbook of creativity*. New York: Cambridge University Press.

Simonton, D. K. (2003). Scientific creativity as constrained stochastic behavior: The integration of product, process, and person perspectives. *Psychological Bulletin, 129*, 475–494.

Ward, T. B., Smith, S. M., & Vaid, J. (Eds.). (1997). *Creative thought: An investigation of conceptual structures and processes*. Washington, DC: American Psychological Association.

# PART 10

# How Do We Differ?

# Contemporary Theories of Intelligence

James C. Kaufman, Scott Barry Kaufman, *and* Jonathan A. Plucker

**Abstract**

The nature of human intelligence has been discussed and debated for literally thousands of years. The purpose of this chapter is to identify and critique several contemporary theories of human intelligence. In general, we attempted to identify those theories that are currently having a significant impact within the social sciences, including psychology, cognitive science, and education, or those that have potential for having such an impact. We highlight some theories, such as the CHC theory and the PASS model, that are closely tied to the measurement of intelligence. We then discuss theories (such as Multiple Intelligences and Successful Intelligence) that have been created, in part, to respond to what is missing in traditional intelligence tests. Finally, we highlight theories that are grounded in the latest research on cognition and neuroscience. This last group includes the Multiple Mechanisms Approach, the Parieto-frontal Integration, Minimal Cognitive Architecture, and Dual-Process theories.

**Key Words:** intelligence, IQ, cognition, memory, planning, knowledge, attention, nonverbal, verbal, achievement

The nature of human intelligence has been discussed and debated for literally thousands of years, from at least the time of Plato and Aristotle. One reason for its enduring character is that the development of theories and approaches to the study of intelligence has paralleled the history of psychology: a philosophical foundation, a transition to empirical methods in the late 1800s (many of which were developed to facilitate the study of intelligence), more sophisticated systems theories and measures during the 20th century, and the development of interdisciplinary approaches and techniques over the past couple of decades.

The topic is also inherently interesting to most people. An understanding of intelligence often provides insight into people's capabilities, provides insight into why various psychological and educational interventions work for some people and not for others, and helps us grasp how affect develops differently based on individual differences in cognitive ability.

Theories of intelligence also form the basis of attempts to measure and quantify human ability and intellectual potential, with far-reaching implications for learning, program design, and team building, among countless other areas. Although IQ testing certainly has a history of abuse and misuse (see Mackintosh, 1998), cognitive ability testing can be useful when the tests are properly administered and when the scores are properly interpreted (see A. S. Kaufman, 2009). Indeed, global IQ scores remain relatively stable during the course of an individual's life span, and IQ substantially predicts important life outcomes, such as academic achievement and occupational performance (Deary, Strand, Smith, & Fernandes, 2007; Gottfredson, 1997; Mackintosh, 1998; Naglieri & Bornstein, 2003; Rohde & Thompson, 2007; S. B. Kaufman, Reynolds, Liu, A.S. Kaufman, & McGrew, 2012; Watkins, Lei, & Canivez, 2007). Of course, IQ does not predict everything equally well, and no prediction is perfect, but that does not negate the scientific and practical utility of understanding individual differences in cognitive ability. Indeed, as we discuss later, current models of intelligence emphasize specific cognitive abilities over global IQ scores.

The purpose of this chapter is to identify and critique several contemporary theories of human intelligence. In general, we attempted to identify those theories that are currently having a significant impact within the social sciences, including psychology, cognitive science, and education, or those that have the potential for having such an impact. With this goal in mind, we do not review classic theories of intelligence, for example, the voluminous literature on Spearman's g or intellectual assessment. The reader is referred to several excellent overviews of these topics, including Mackintosh (1998) and A. S. Kaufman (2009).

## Contemporary Theories of Intelligence

We acknowledge that there are numerous ways to organize the following information (cf. Davidson & Kemp, 2011; Esping & Plucker, 2008; Gardner, Kornhaber, & Wake, 1996; Sternberg, 1990). The discussion of the following theories is roughly chronological, although somewhat arbitrary, and the reader should not infer a priority based on the order in which the material is presented.

### CHC Theory (Cattell-Horn-Carroll)

The theory of intelligence that is most used in IQ tests is the CHC (Cattell-Horn-Carroll) theory, a combination of the Cattell-Horn theory of fluid and crystallized intelligence (Horn & Cattell, 1966; Horn & Hofer, 1992; Horn & Noll, 1997) and Carroll's (1993) Three-Stratum Theory. Both the Cattell-Horn and Carroll models essentially started from the same point—Spearman's (1904) g-factor theory; though they took different paths, they ended up with remarkably consistent conclusions about the spectrum of broad cognitive abilities. Cattell built upon Spearman's g to posit *two* kinds of g: fluid intelligence (Gf), the ability to solve novel problems by using reasoning—believed by Cattell to be largely a function of biological and neurological factors—and crystallized intelligence (Gc), a knowledge-based ability that is highly dependent on education and acculturation (later articulated in Horn & Cattell, 1966, 1967).

Almost from the beginning of his collaboration with Cattell, Horn believed that the psychometric data, as well as neurocognitive and developmental data, were suggesting more than just these two

general abilities. Horn (1968) quickly identified four additional abilities; by the mid-1990s his model included 9 to 10 Broad Abilities (Horn, 1989; Horn & Hofer, 1992; Horn & Noll, 1997). The initial dichotomy had grown, but not in a hierarchy. Horn retained the name Gf-Gc theory, but the diverse Broad Abilities were treated as equals, not as part of any hierarchy. These included visualization (Gv), short-term memory (Gsm), long-term retrieval (Glr), and processing speed (Gs).

Carroll (1993) developed a hierarchical theory based on his in-depth survey of factor-analytic studies composed of three levels or Strata of abilities: (a) Stratum III (General), a Spearman-like g, which Carroll considered to be a valid construct based on overwhelming evidence from factor analysis; (b) Stratum II (Broad), composed of eight broad factors, that correspond reasonably closely to Horn's Broad Abilities; and (c) Stratum I (Narrow), composed of about 70 fairly specific abilities, organized by the broad factor with which each is most closely associated (many relate to level of mastery, response speed, or rate of learning).

In recent years, Carroll's hierarchical theory and the Horn-Cattell Gf-Gc theory have been merged into the Cattell-Horn-Carroll or CHC theory (Flanagan, McGrew, & Ortiz, 2000; Flanagan, Ortiz, & Alfonso, 2007). The CHC theory has been particularly influential in the development of recent IQ tests, most notably the fifth edition of the Stanford-Binet (Roid, 2003); the Kaufman Assessment Battery for Children, second edition (KABC-II; A. S. Kaufman & N. L. Kaufman, 2004); and the Woodcock-Johnson, third edition (WJ-III; Woodcock, McGrew, & Mather, 2001).

The CHC model incorporates both the concept of a general intelligence (all of the different aspects of intelligence are considered to be related to a common "g," although this aspect is not often emphasized; see Flanagan et al., 2007) and the concept of many different aspects of intelligence. Largely because of the influence of CHC theory, nearly all current IQ tests have shifted the historical focus from a small number of part scores to a contemporary emphasis on anywhere from four to seven cognitive abilities. The debate about which is "better," one intelligence versus many aspects of intelligence, still goes on (for a review, see Sternberg & Grigorenko, 2002).

The CHC model proposes 10 different broad factors of intelligence: Gf (fluid intelligence; the ability to solve novel problems, ones that do not benefit from past learning or experience), Gq (quantitative knowledge, typically math related), Gc (crystallized intelligence; the breadth and depth of a person's accumulated knowledge of a culture and the ability to use that knowledge to solve problems), Grw (reading and writing), Gsm (short-term memory), Gv (visual processing), Ga (auditory processing), Glr (long-term storage and retrieval), Gs (processing speed), and Gt (decision speed/reaction time). Of these 10, only 7 are measured by today's IQ tests; Gq and Grw are in the domain of academic achievement,and, therefore, are measured by individually administered achievement tests, and Gt is not measured by any standardized test of anything.

The CHC theory has only two Strata: Stratum II (Broad), which consists of the 10 abilities identified earlier, and Stratum I (Narrow), which includes more specific abilities similar to Carroll's original theory. A Stratum reserved for a *g*-like general factor is no longer explicitly present in the model (Flanagan et al., 2007).

### PASS Model

Luria's (1966, 1970, 1973) neuropsychological model, which features three Blocks or functional units, has also been applied extensively to IQ tests. According to this model, the first functional unit is responsible for focused and sustained attention. The second functional unit receives and stores information with both simultaneous and successive (or sequential) processing. Simultaneous processing is integrating information together; pieces are synthesized together much as one might appreciate a painting all at once. Successive processing is interpreting each piece of individual separately, in sequential fashion.

Luria's model was the theoretical basis of the Kaufman Assessment Battery for Children (K-ABC; A.S. Kaufman & N.L. Kaufman, 1983), specifically Luria's Block 2 distinction between Sequential and Simultaneous Processing. The key contributions of the K-ABC were, first, to finally produce an IQ test built on theory, and, second, to switch the emphasis from the *content* of the items (verbal vs. nonverbal) to the *process* that children use to solve problems (sequential vs. simultaneous). The PASS (Planning, Attention, Simultaneous, and Successive) theory is a cognitive processing theory based on the works of Luria that represents an important expansion of Luria's model to emphasize all three of the blocks and functional units, not just Block 2 (see Das, Naglieri, & Kirby, 1994, for an overview). The PASS theory is also the basis for the Cognitive Assessment System (Naglieri & Das, 1997).

### Theory of Multiple Intelligences

Howard Gardner's Theory of Multiple Intelligences (MI Theory) was first published in the seminal volume, *Frames of Mind*, in 1983. This and subsequent editions of his book and theory (e.g., Gardner, 2006) stress the need for educators and psychologists to broaden their definitions of human intelligence. Gardner has defined intelligence as "an ability or set of abilities that permit an individual to solve problems or fashion products that are of consequence in a particular cultural setting" (Ramos-Ford & Gardner, 1997). MI Theory proposes eight intelligences: linguistic, logical-mathematical, spatial, bodily-kinesthetic, musical, interpersonal, intrapersonal, and naturalistic. Gardner (1999a, 1999b) has also explored the possibility of additional intelligences, including spiritual and existential intelligences.

Instead of relying primarily on traditional factor analytic analyses, Gardner based his theory on an analysis of the research literature using eight criteria, namely, (a) potential isolation by brain damage; (b) the existence of idiot savants, prodigies, and other exceptional individuals; (c) an identifiable core operation or set of operations; (d) a distinctive development history (i.e., it should be possible to differentiate experts from novices in the domain); (e) an evolutionary history and evolutionary plausibility (i.e., its precursors should be evident in less evolved species); (f) support from experimental psychological tasks, (g) support from psychometric findings, and (h) susceptibility to encoding in a symbol system (e.g., Gardner, 1997).

Gardner asserts that logical-mathematical and linguistic intelligences are overemphasized in traditional models of human intelligence, with that overemphasis carrying over to the design of teaching and curriculum in most schools (Gardner, 1993). The recent emphasis on educational accountability systems focusing on math and language achievement test scores suggests that, if anything, the bias Gardner observed remains firmly rooted in US education today.

Gardner's theory has been highly influential, especially among educators, and given both the popularity and unique approach to the study of intelligence, the frequent criticisms of the theory are not surprising. These criticisms have ranged from the philosophical (White, 2008) to the empirical (Visser, Ashton, & Vernon, 2006), from the conceptual (Jensen, 2002) to the cognitive (Lohman, 1991), with numerous, additional wide-ranging critiques (Klein, 1997).

For example, Lohman (2001) argues that $g$ is largely synonymous with fluid intelligence ($gF$), which in turn represents inductive reasoning ability. Lohman also reviews evidence that a central working memory system underlies inductive reasoning ability; he therefore argues that MI Theory ignores the role of a central working memory system and thus a general inductive reasoning ability that cuts across all of the intelligences.

Another criticism of the theory relates to its validity. Even though assessments exist to test Gardner's various intelligences (e.g., Gardner, Feldman, & Krechevsky, 1998), these assessments have not been associated with high levels of psychometric validity evidence, and the evidence regarding reliability of these and similar measures is mixed (e.g., Plucker, 2000; Plucker, Callahan, & Tomchin, 1996; Visser et al., 2006).

It should be noted that Gardner has been an especially vigorous defender of MI Theory, regardless of the nature of the criticisms (e.g., Gardner, 1998). For example, in the face of consistent criticism of how MI Theory has been applied (or misapplied, as the case may be) to classroom contexts, Gardner (1995, 1998) has noted that such applications are often based on misinterpretations of the theory, and that misapplication of a theory is not necessarily conclusive evidence of the weakness of a theory.

## Theory of Successful Intelligence

The theory of successful intelligence comprises four key elements (Sternberg, 1997). The first key element is that "success is attained through a balance of analytical, creative, and practical abilities" (pp. 297–298). According to Sternberg, these three abilities, in combination, are important for success in life. *Analytical intelligence* is required to solve problems and to judge the quality of ideas. Sternberg believes that most tests of general intelligence are assessing analytical intelligence. *Creative intelligence* is required to formulate good problems and solutions, and *practical intelligence* is needed to use the ideas and analysis in an effective way in one's everyday life.

A second key element is that "intelligence is defined in terms of the ability to achieve success in life in terms of one's personal standards, within one's sociocultural context" (pp. 296–297). Sternberg argues that intelligence testing has primarily focused on the prediction of success in an academic setting. The theory of successful intelligence emphasizes the importance of going beyond just the academic sphere to account for success in whatever goals individuals (or societies) set for themselves. The third element is that "one's ability to achieve success depends on one's capitalizing on one's strengths and correcting or compensating for one's weaknesses (pp. 297–298)." The fourth key element is that "balancing of abilities is achieved to adapt to, shape, and select environments" (p. 298). Intelligence does not involve simply modifying oneself to suit the milieu (adaptation); it also involves the ability to modify the environment to suit oneself (shaping) and, sometimes, to find a new setting that is a better match to one's skills, values, or desires (selection).

Sternberg and his colleagues have achieved success in interventions designed to increase school success by improving analytical, creative, and practical skills (Stemler, Grigorenko, Jarvin, & Sternberg, 2006; Sternberg, Grigorenko, Ferrari, & Clinkenbeard, 1999; Sternberg, J.C. Kaufman, & Grigorenko, 2008). Additionally, they have shown a separation between measures of practical intelligence and analytical intelligence, although the two intelligences overlap to a certain extent (Cianciolo et al., 2006). Furthermore, their measures of creative and practical intelligence predict real-world outcomes and measures of high-order cognition such as the SAT and GPA above and beyond analytical intelligence (Sternberg, 2006). However, much as with MI Theory, it is still an open question about the extent to which analytical, creative, and practical forms of intelligence are correlated, load on $g$, or represent midstratum "group factors" (Brody, 2004; Gottfredson, 2003).

## Emotional Intelligence

Theories of emotional intelligence (EI) are based on the observation that individual differences exist in the extent to which individuals can reason about and use emotions to enhance thought (Salovey & Mayer, 1990). Since its inception, EI has been employed to cover a variety of traits and concepts, mixing personality traits with socioemotional abilities (Bar-On, 1997; Goleman, 1998; Petrides & Furnham, 2003), producing what Mayer et al. (2000) refer to as "mixed models" of EI. This state of affairs has spurred various critiques of EI, arguing that EI is too all encompassing to have scientific utility (Eysenck, 2000; Locke, 2005).

Agreeing with these criticisms, Mayer, Salovey, and Caruso (2008) argue for a four-branch model of EI that offers a more precise, ability-based formulation of the construct. According to their model, EI involves the ability to (ordered from lower level to higher level emotional abilities): "(a) perceive emotions in oneself and others accurately, (b) use emotions to facilitate thinking, (c) understand emotions, emotional language, and the signals conveyed by emotions, and (d) manage emotions so as to attain specific goals (p. 506)." To measure these abilities, the Mayer-Salovey-Caruso Emotional Intelligence Test (MSCEIT) was developed (Mayer, Salovey, & Caruso, 2002). The MSCEIT consists of eight tasks, including two tasks for each branch of the EI model. Correct answers are identified by pooling experts (i.e., emotion researchers), which show strong agreement with each other (Mayer, Salovey, Caruso, & Sitarenios, 2003). Research suggests that the MSCEIT correlates moderately with verbal intelligence as well as the Big Five personality dimensions of Openness and Agreeableness (Brackett & Mayer, 2003; Mayer & Salovey, 1993; Petrides & Furnham, 2001; van der Zee, Thijs, & Schakel, 2002) and predicts various important outcomes such as social competence, quality of relationships, interpersonal sensitivity, work relationships, drug use, deviancy, aggressiveness, and psychiatric symptoms (see Mayer et al., 2008, and Mayer, Roberts, & Barsade, 2008). Many of these relations hold after controlling for measures of general intelligence and personality.

The EI model of Mayer, Salovey, and Caruso (2000) has received various criticisms (Brody, 2004; Oatley, 2004; Zeidner, Matthews, & Roberts, 2001; Zeidner, Roberts, & Matthews, 2004). Brody (2004) argues that the MSCEIT tests knowledge of emotions but not necessarily the ability to put the knowledge to use. Brody also questions the predictive validity of the MSCEIT, arguing that the MSCEIT does not fit the characteristics required to demonstrate adequate evidence of validity.

Speaking to this point, Schulte, Ree, and Carretta (2004) administered the MSCEIT, the Big Five personality dimensions, and a measure of general intelligence. Multiple regression analyses with all of the personality variables and $g$ entered into the equation showed that a model consisting of $g$, agreeableness, and sex of the participant explained 38% of the variance in EI. Correcting for the reliability of both the EI and Agreeableness measures increased the variance accounted for to .81. Other studies, however, have found very weak relations between particular components of EI measures and measures of both fluid and crystallized intelligence in college samples (Barchard & Hakstian, 2004; Davies, Stankov, & Roberts, 1998; Mayer, Caruso, & Salovey, 2000; Roberts, Zeidner, & Matthews, 2001). Therefore,

just like Gardner and Sternberg's theories, the extent to which EI (both a common factor and each of the specific abilities that are hypothesized to comprise EI) can provide incremental validity above and beyond general intelligence and the Big Five personality dimensions remains to be established.

## Multiple Cognitive Mechanisms Approach

Recent evidence suggests that the general cognitive ability factor ($g$) may not be comprised of a single cognitive mechanism but instead is supported by multiple, interacting mechanisms that become associated with each other throughout the course of development (see Conway et al., 2011; S.B. Kaufman et al., 2009; van der Maas et al., 2006). Three cognitive mechanisms that have received the most attention are working memory, processing speed, and explicit associative learning.

Working memory involves the ability to maintain, update, and manipulate information in the face of distraction and competing representations. Participants who score higher on working memory tasks demonstrate an increased ability to control their attention while maintaining their task goals in the presence of interference, and this ability is strongly correlated with $g$ (Conway, Cowan, & Bunting, 2001; Conway, Cowan, Bunting, Therriault, & Minkoff, 2002; Conway, Jarrold, Kane, Miyake, & Towse, 2007; Engle & Kane, 2004; Engle, Tuholski, Laughlin, & Conway, 1999; Heitz, Unsworth, & Engle, 2004; Kane, Bleckley, Conway, & Engle, 2001; Unsworth, Schrock, & Engle, 2004). There is also neurological evidence for substantial overlap between the processes evoked by measures of $g$ and the processes evoked by measure of working memory: Both tasks tend to activate the lateral prefrontal cortex (PFC) as well as left and right parietal regions (Duncan & Owen, 2000; Gray, Chabris, & Braver, 2003; Gray & Thompson, 2004).

Another cognitive mechanism associated with $g$ is processing speed, which involves the speed at which rather simple cognitive operations can be performed. Participants with higher $g$ scores tend to respond faster in simple and choice reaction time paradigms (Deary, Der, & Ford, 2001) and are faster at perceiving whether two similar line segments are the same or different, a task referred to as the inspection time task (Deary, 2000; Grudnik & Kranzler, 2001). In the Horn-Cattell theory of intelligence (Horn & Cattell, 1966), processing speed was referred to as "perceptual speed" (Gs) and in Caroll's three-stratum theory of intelligence (Carroll, 1993), processing speed was referred to as "general speediness." Analysis of the factor structure of the WAIS (a widely administered IQ test) reveals that processing speed is one of four second-level factors consumed by *g* (Deary, 2001).

A third cognitive mechanism that has recently been associated with *g* is explicit associative learning, which involves the ability to remember and voluntarily recall specific associations between stimuli (S.B. Kaufman, DeYoung, Gray, Brown, & Mackintosh, 2009). Early studies found very weak associations between associative learning and *g* (Malmi, Underwood, & Carroll, 1979; Underwood, Boruch, & Malmi, 1978; Woodrow, 1938, 1946). These earlier findings were most likely due to the difficulty level of the associative learning tasks that were administered. Further research, using more difficult associative learning tasks involving multiple response-outcome contingencies, has shown substantial correlations with *g*, sometimes statistically independent of working memory and processing speed (Alexander & Smales, 1997; S.B. Kaufman et al., 2009; Tamez, Myerson, & Hale, 2008; Williams, Myerson, & Hale, 2008; Williams & Pearlberg, 2006).

## Parieto-Frontal Integration Theory

According to the parieto-frontal integration theory (P-FIT), the neural basis of intelligence is distributed throughout the brain. Jung and Haier (2007) reviewed 37 neuroimaging studies of intelligence involving both functional and structural magnetic resonance imaging (MRI) techniques and various measures of psychometric intelligence. They identified some consistency in the brain regions that relate to intelligence. Although Jung and Haier found evidence that related regions were distributed throughout the brain, they also found that brain activations relating to intelligence were mostly in the parietal and frontal regions.

The researchers identified brain region activations based on stages of information processing. In the first stage, temporal and occipital areas aid the individual in acquiring visual and auditory sensory information. These regions facilitate recognition, imagery, and elaboration of visual inputs as well as analysis and elaboration of the syntax of auditory information. In the second stage, sensory results from the first stage are sent to regions in the parietal cortex for integration and abstraction. In the third stage, which consists of problem solving, evaluation, and hypothesis testing, the frontal lobes interact with the parietal areas implicated in the second stage. Once the best solution in this stage is

obtained, the anterior cingulate becomes involved in the final stage to inhibit alternative responses. Jung and Haier argue that white matter, particularly the arcuate fasciculus, plays an important role in the reliable transmission of information among the various processing units, especially in moving information from the posterior to frontal regions of the brain. A major tenet of the P-FIT theory is the notion that different combinations of brain area activations can lead to the same levels of cognitive performance. Jung & Haier (2007) suggest that individual difference in cognitive strengths and weaknesses might be accounted for by an individual's unique pattern of P-FIT activations and the white matter tracts that connect them.

The theory has had some criticism. In the review paper by Haier and Jung, 19 other researchers commented on the theory. While mostly supporting the notion of a distributed network supporting intelligence, the commentators also suggested various tests of the theory and called for more research on larger samples using more varied measures of intelligence than what has typically been studied. Some commentators also discussed linkages between the P-FIT and already existing work on cognitive development, finding both similarities and differences. Jung and Haier (2007) call for more empirical work to address the various criticisms. Indeed, since their 2007 paper, over 40 studies relating to the P-FIT theory have been published (e.g., Colom et al., 2009; Schmithorst, 2009; see Haier, 2011, for a review). These have included developmental studies linking intelligence to brain development as well as work on network efficiency. This research has served both to support and extend the P-FIT. Eleven of these newer studies are included in a special issue of the journal *Intelligence* (see Haier, 2009, for an overview).

## Minimal Cognitive Architecture

Based on Fodor's (1983) distinction between central processes of thought and dedicated processing input modules, M. Anderson's (1992, 2005) theory of minimal cognitive architecture integrates general and specific abilities in a developmental theory of human intelligence. According to Anderson, knowledge is acquired through two different processing routes. Route 1 involves "thoughtful problem solving," displays large individual differences, and is constrained by processing speed. Anderson (2005) argues that "it is this constraint that is the basis of general intelligence and the reason why manifest specific abilities are correlated (p. 280)."

The basic processing mechanism of the first route comprises two processors: verbal and spatial. These two processess should be normally distributed, uncorrelated with each other, and have their own unique explanatory powers.

In contrast, the second route for acquiring knowledge in Anderson's model is related to dedicated information processing modules. Such modules consist of the perception of three-dimensional space, syntactic parsing, phonological encoding, and theory of mind. It is this route that is linked to cognitive development as these modules undergo developmental changes in cognitive competence across the life span. Anderson (2005) argues that modular processes can be acquired through extensive practice, but that the common features of both acquired and innate modules are that they operate automatically and independently of the first route and thus are not constrained by central processing mechanisms.

The modular component of Anderson's cognitive theory is intended to allow a reconciliation between Gardner's MI Theory and notions of a general intelligence by acknowledging the importance of domain-specific abilities as well as a central basic processing mechanism. Furthermore, Anderson believes his theory explains how low-IQ individuals can nonetheless be capable of remarkable feats and how various developmental and learning differences such as dyslexia and autism can occur in the presence of an average or even high IQ (Anderson, 2008).

S. B. Kaufman (2011) has questioned Anderson's notion that there are few meaningful individual differences in route 2. Furthermore, S. B. Kaufman notes that Anderson does not propose more than just processing speed as a central mechanism and does not propose any domain-general learning mechanisms (e.g., implicit learning, latent inhibition) underlying route 2, focusing instead on the Fodorian definition of modules. S. B. Kaufman argues that by focusing on individual differences in processing speed as underlying one information processing route, and species-typical cognitive modules with minimal individual differences underlying the other processing route, Anderson's model unnecessarily restricts the number of cognitive mechanisms that can be investigated within each information processing route.

## Dual-Process Theory

The Dual-Process (DP) theory of human intelligence (Davidson & Kemp, 2011; S. B. Kaufman, 2009, 2011, 2013) incorporates modern dual-process theories of cognition (see Epstein, 1994; Evans, 2008, 2010; Evans & Frankish, 2009; Kahneman, 2011; Kahneman & Frederick, 2002, 2005; Stanovich, 2004, 2011—but also see Keren & Schul, 2009; Kruglanski & Grigerezner, 2011; Osman, 2004) into a theory of human intelligence. By doing so, the Dual-Process theory organizes many constructs relating to both explicit and implicit cognition that are at least partially separable and are meaningfully related to a wide range of socially valued intelligent behaviors. In particular, performance across a wide range of intelligent behaviors—across the arts and sciences—are predicted by a hierarchical structure of goal-directed and spontaneous cognitive processes. Goal-directed processes consume limited attentional resources, whereas spontaneous processes are not dependent on input from higher-level control processes (see Stanovich & Toplak, 2012).

The theory has a few key tenets. The first tenet is that there are meaningful and adaptive individual differences in both goal-directed and spontaneous cognitive processes. The second tenet is that both goal-directed and spontaneous cognitive processes jointly determine all intelligent behaviors, although in varying degrees depending on the behavior. A third tenet is that neither mode of thought is more "intelligent" than any other across the board, but what is important is the ability to flexibly switch mode of thought depending on the situation (for applications of this idea to creativity, see Gabora, 2003, 2010; Gabora & S. B. Kaufman, 2010; Howard-Jones & Murray, 2003; Martindale, 1995, Vartanian, 2009). A fourth tenet is that there are many different paths to the same intelligent behavior, with different people drawing on a different mix of cognitive traits to reach the same outcome. Finally, abilities are not conceptualized as static entities, but are seen as constantly changing through the life span as the individual continually engages with the world. This is where passion and inspiration comes into play (see Thrash & Elliot, 2003; Vallerand et al., 2003). The more one engages in a mode of thought, the more that individual will develop skills in that modality, which in turn increases the desire for engaging with that skill.

Goal-directed *cognition* is at the top of the hierarchy (alongside *spontaneous cognition*). Goal-directed cognition consists of a class of cognitive processes that involve the ability and tendency across situations to think about thinking (i.e., metacognition—see Dennett, 1992; Hertzog

& Robinson, 2005), reflect on prior behavior, and use that information to modify behavior and plan for the future.[1] Constructs that are part of the controlled cognition hierarchy include reflective engagement, self-regulation, self-control, perseverance, long-term planning, dissociable components of executive functioning—working memory, cognitive and affective inhibition, and mental flexibility—explicit cognitive ability (the skill set that lies at the heart of highly *g*-loaded tasks), intellectual engagement, and elementary cognitive tasks that support explicit cognitive ability. What links all of the processes together is that they all draw on a limited pool of attentional resources.

The second main component (alongside controlled cognition) of the DP theory is *spontaneous cognition*. At the broadest level, individual differences in spontaneous cognition reflect the ability to acquire information automatically and the tendency to engage in spontaneous forms of cognition. For instance, whereas most people have the ability to spontaneously experience gut feelings and daydreams, there may be individual differences in the extent to which people are willing to engage with them.[2] Constructs that are part of the spontaneous cognition hierarchy include the following: mind-wandering, daydreaming, implicit learning, latent inhibition, intuition, acquired forms of expertise and long-term memory, and implicit domains of mind that are universal human domains pertaining to knowledge of spatial relations, number, probability, logic, language, people, language, music, aesthetics, living things, the inanimate physical world, or the beliefs and desires of other minds (Gelman, 2009; Hirschfeld & Gelman, 1994; Feist, 2008; Pinker, 1997).

Other technical details about the theory, including the hierarchical nature of the model, can be found in S. B. Kaufman (2009). Thus far, there is support for the theory, from different branches of psychology and neuropsychology. For instance, a recent study found that individual differences in implicit learning predict intelligent behaviors such as language learning and verbal analogical reasoning above and beyond *g* and the cognitive mechanisms underlying *g* (S.B. Kaufman et al., 2010). Since the theory is so new, however, it has not had enough time to garner much criticism or support. The extent to which the various components of the DP theory increase prediction of intelligent behaviors across a wide range of situations remains an open question.

## Theories of Intelligence

Broadly speaking, we can divide the theories we have discussed into three categories. There are theories that are closely tied to the measurement of intelligence. CHC theory and the PASS model (along with Spearman's *g*) form the theoretical foundation for nearly all commercial tests of intelligence. These contemporary theories demonstrate the potential to bring psychometric, experimental, and neuroscientific research more in line with each other. For instance, the PASS model and the development of related testing instruments are explicitly tied to cutting-edge neuroscience findings. Additionally, tests based on the CHC model are also incorporating the latest research on the cognitive mechanisms related to *g*, such as working memory. Still, there is more work to be done to bring these various perspectives together. Clearly, this work is important, since both the PASS model and the CHC model have the most impact in terms of people's lives affected. Decisions about which students have a learning disability or which students are labeled "gifted" are nearly always made based on these theories (S.B. Kaufman & Sternberg, 2008).

The second class of theories comprises those that have been created, in part, to respond to what is missing in traditional intelligence tests. The theories of Multiple Intelligence and Successful Intelligence argue for additional abilities (from creativity to bodily/kinesthetic ability) to be treated with the same importance as the standard analytic abilities measured by most tests. The theory of Emotional Intelligence offers an entirely new "intelligence" that some argue is as important as traditionally conceived intelligence.

The third class of theories (The Multiple Mechanisms Approach and the Parieto-frontal Integration, Minimal Cognitive Architecture, and Dual-Process theories) are grounded in the latest research on cognition and neuroscience. These theories, although advancing the scientific understanding of human intellectual differences, are less clearly tied to practical applications in terms of intelligence testing. This may change, however, as these theories evolve and more tests of the specific predictions of the theories are conducted in applied settings.

## Looking Inside the Crystal Ball

Speculating on the future of intelligence theories is a difficult—yet intriguing—task. Throughout the history of the study of intelligence, related theories have largely reflected the emphases in psychology and even the broader society at the time. For example, it is tempting to criticize Galton's seminal work in the late 1800s as being obsessively focused on an assumption of heredity (and more than a little social Darwinism), but such a criticism takes Galton's work completely out of its historical and cultural context. At that time in Western society, Galton's conclusions were hardly considered revolutionary (his methods, however, were truly innovative). Viewed from this context lens, then, the current move to interdisciplinary theories that incorporate findings from psychology, cognitive science, neurology, and so on is not surprising, and we expect this trend to continue. However, we also note that truly interdisciplinary systems theories, which combine the cognitive and neurological perspectives with those from sociology, education, and related areas are not in wide circulation, and that this area appears to be a likely future direction for theories of intelligence.

## Notes

1. Note that other definitions of "controlled cognition" have been put forward (see Schneider & Shiffrin, 1977).

2. The distinction between goal-directed and spontaneous cognition, according to the DP theory, is not always the same as that between conscious and unconscious cognition. Spontaneous cognitions can be either conscious, such as when an individual is aware of his or her vivid fantasies, or nonconscious such as when an individual feels an intuition without knowing what brought about that intuition or when an individual implicitly learns the underlying rule structure of the environment. Likewise, some goal-directed processes can operate without meta-awareness while still consuming limited attentional resources.

## References

Alexander, J. R., & Smales, S. (1997). Intelligence, learning and long-term memory. *Personality and Individual Differences, 23,* 815–825.

Anderson, M. (1992). *Intelligence and development: A cognitive theory.* Malden, MA: Blackwell.

Anderson, M. (2005). Marrying intelligence and cognition: A developmental review. In R. J. Sternberg & J. E. Pretz (Eds.), *Cognition and intelligence: Identifying the mechanisms of the mind* (pp. 268–288). Cambridge, England: Cambridge University Press.

Anderson, M. (2008). What can autism and dyslexia tell us about intelligence? *Quarterly Journal of Experimental Psychology, 61,* 116–128.

Bar-On, R. (1997). *BarOn Emotional Quotient Inventory: Technical manual.* Toronto, ON: Multi-Health Systems.

Barchard, K. A., & Hakstian, A. R. (2004). The nature and measurement of emotional intelligence abilities: Basic dimensions and their relationships with other cognitive abilities and personality variables. *Educational and Psychological Measurement, 64,* 437–462.

Brackett, M. A., & Mayer, J. D. (2003). Convergent, discriminant, and incremental validity of competing measures of emotional intelligence. *Personality and Social Psychology Bulletin, 29,* 1147–1158.

Brody, N. (2004). What cognitive intelligence is and what emotional intelligence is not. *Psychological Inquiry, 15,* 234–238.

Carroll, J. B. (1993). *Human cognitive abilities: A survey of factor analytic studies.* New York: Cambridge University Press.

Cianciolo, A. T., Grigorenko, E. L., Jarvin, L., Guillermo, G., Drebot, M. E., & Sternberg, R. J. (2006). Practical intelligence and tacit knowledge: Advancements in the measurement of developing expertise. *Learning and Individual Differences, 16,* 235–253.

Colom, R., Haier, R. J., Head, K., Alvarez-Linera, J., Quiroga, M. A., Shih, P. C., & Jung, R. E. (2009). Gray matter correlates of fluid, crystallized, and spatial intelligence: Testing the P-FIT model. *Intelligence, 37,* 124–135.

Conway, A. R. A., Cowan, N., & Bunting, M. F. (2001). The cocktail party phenomenon revisited: The importance of working memory capacity. *Psychonomic Bulletin and Review, 8,* 331–335.

Conway, A. R. A., Cowan, N., Bunting, M. F., Therriault, D. J., & Minkoff, S. R. B. (2002). A latent variable analysis of working memory capacity, short-term memory capacity, processing speed, and general fluid intelligence. *Intelligence, 30,* 163–183.

Conway, A. R. A., Jarrold, C., Kane, M. J., Miyake, A., & Towse, J. N. (2007). *Variation in working memory.* New York: Oxford University Press.

Conway, A. R. A., Getz, S. J., Macnamara, B., & Engel de Abreu, P. M. J. (2011). Working memory and intelligence. In R. J. Sternberg & S. B. Kaufman (Eds.), *The Cambridge handbook of intelligence* (pp. 394–418). New York: Cambridge University Press.

Das, J. P., Naglieri, J. A, & Kirby, J. R. (1994). *Assessment of cognitive process: The PASS theory of intelligence.* Boston: Allyn & Bacon.

Davidson, J. E., & Kemp, I. A. (2011). Contemporary models of intelligence. In R. J. Sternberg & S. B. Kaufman (Eds.), *The Cambridge handbook of intelligence* (pp. 58–84). New York: Cambridge University Press.

Davies, M., Stankov, L., & Roberts, R. D. (1998). Emotional intelligence: In search of an elusive construct. *Journal of Personality and Social Psychology, 75,* 989–1015.

Deary, I. (2000). *Looking down on human intelligence: From psychometrics to the brain.* Oxford, England: Oxford University Press.

Deary, I. (2001). Human intelligence differences: A recent history. *Trends in Cognitive Sciences, 5,* 127–130.

Deary, I., Der, G., & Ford, G. (2001). Reaction times and intelligence differences: A population-based cohort study. *Intelligence, 29,* 389–399.

Deary, I., Strand, S., Smith, P., & Fernandes, C. (2007). Intelligence and educational achievement. *Intelligence, 35,* 13–21.

Dennett, D. C. (1992). *Consciousness explained.* New York: Back Bay Books.

Duncan, J., & Owen, A.M. (2000). Common regions of the human frontal lobe recruited by diverse cognitive demands. *Trends in Neurosciences, 23,* 475–483.

Engle, R. W., & Kane, M. J. (2004). Executive attention, working memory capacity, and a two-factor theory of cognitive control. In B. Ross (Ed.), *The psychology of learning and motivation: Advances in research and theory* (Vol. 44, pp. 145–199). New York: Elsevier.

Engle, R. W., Tuholski, S. W., Laughlin, J. E., & Conway, A. R. A. (1999). Working memory, short-term memory, and general fluid intelligence: A latent-variable approach. *Journal of Experimental Psycholology: General, 128,* 309–331.

Epstein, S. (1994). Integration of the cognitive and the psychodynamic unconscious. *American Psychologist, 49,* 709–724.

Esping, A., & Plucker, J. A. (2008). Theories of intelligence. In F. A. Karnes & K. R. Stephens (Eds.), *Achieving excellence: Educating the gifted and talented* (pp. 36–48). Upper Saddle River, NJ: Pearson Education.

Evans, J. St. B. T. (2008). Dual-processing accounts of reasoning, judgment, and social cognition. *Annual Review of Psychology, 59,* 255–278.

Evans, J. St. B. T. (2010). *Thinking twice: Two minds in one brain.* Oxford, UK: Oxford University Press.

Evans, J. S. B. T., & Frankish, K. (2009). *In two minds: Dual processes and beyond.* New York: Oxford University Press.

Eysenck, H. J. (2000). *Intelligence: A new look.* Edison, NJ: Transaction.

Feist, G. J. (2006). *The psychology of science and the origins of the scientific mind.* New Haven: Yale University Press.

Flanagan, D. P., McGrew, K. S., & Ortiz, S. (2000). *The Wechsler Intelligence Scales and Gf-Gc Theory: A contemporary approach to interpretation.* Boston: Allyn & Bacon.

Flanagan, D. P., Ortiz, S. O., & Alfonso, V. C. (2007). *Essentials of cross-battery assessment (2nd ed.).* New York: Wiley.

Fodor, J. (1983). *The modularity of mind.* Boston: MIT Press.

Gabora, L. (2003). Contextual focus: A tentative cognitive explanation for the cultural transition of the middle/upper Paleolithic. In R. Alterman & D. Hirsch (Eds.), *Proceedings of the 25th Annual Meeting of the Cognitive Science Society.* Mahwah, NJ: Erlbaum.

Gabora, L. (2010). Revenge of the "neurds": Characterizing creative thought in terms of the structure and dynamics of human memory. *Creativity Research Journal, 22,* 1–13

Gabora, L., & Kaufman, S. B. (2010). Evolutionary approaches to creativity. In J. C. Kaufman & R. J. Sternberg (Eds.), *The Cambridge handbook of creativity* (pp. 279–300). Cambridge, England: Cambridge University Press.

Gardner, H. (1983). *Frames of mind: The theory of multiple intelligences.* New York: Basic Books.

Gardner, H. (1993). *Frames of mind: The theory of multiple intelligences (2nd ed.).* New York: Basic Books.

Gardner, H. (1995). Reflections on multiple intelligences: Myths and messages. *Phi Delta Kappan, 77,* 200–209.

Gardner, H. (1997). Extraordinary cognitive achievements: A symbol systems approach. In W. Damon (Editor-in-Chief) & R. Lerner (Ed.), *Handbook of child psychology (5th ed., Vol. 1,* pp. 415–466). New York: Wiley.

Gardner, H. (1998). A reply to Perry D. Klein's "Multiplying the problems of intelligence by eight." *Canadian Journal of Education/Revue canadienne de l'éducation, 23,* 96–102.

Gardner, H. (1999a). Are there additional intelligences? In J. Kane (Ed.), *Education, information and transformation* (pp. 111–131). Upper Saddle River, NJ: Prentice Hall.

Gardner, H. (1999b). *Intelligence reframed: Multiple intelligences for the 21st century.* New York: Basic Books.

Gardner, H. (2006). *Multiple intelligences: New horizons in theory and practice.* New York: Basic Books.

Gardner, H., Feldman, D. H., & Krechevsky, M. (1998). *Project spectrum: Early learning activities.* New York, NY: Teachers College Press.

Gardner, H., Kornhaber, M. L., & Wake, W. K. (1996). *Intelligence: Multiple perspectives.* Fort Worth, TX: Harcourt Brace.

Gelman, R. (2009). Innate learning and beyond. In Piatelli-Palmirini, M., Uriagereka, J. & Salaburu, P. (Eds.), *Of minds and language: A dialogue with Noam Chomsky in the Basque country* (pp. 223–238). New York: Oxford University Press.

Goleman, D. (1998). *Working with emotional intelligence.* New York: Bantam.

Gottfredson, L. S. (1997). Why g matters: The complexity of everyday life. *Intelligence, 24,* 79–132.

Gottfredson, L. S. (2003). Dissecting practical intelligence theory: Its claims and evidence. *Intelligence, 31,* 343–397.

Gray, J. R., Chabris, C. F., & Braver, T. S. (2003). Neural mechanisms of general fluid intelligence. *Nature Neuroscience, 6,* 316–322.

Gray, J. R., & Thompson, P. M. (2004). Neurobiology of intelligence: Science and ethics. *Nature Reviews Neuroscience, 5,* 471–482.

Grudnik, J. L., & Kranzler, J. H. (2001). Meta-analysis of the relationship between intelligence and inspection time. *Intelligence, 29,* 523–535.

Haier, R. J. (2009). Neuro-intelligence, neuro-metrics and the next phase of brain imaging studies. *Intelligence, 37,* 121–123.

Haier, R. J. (2011). Biological basis of intelligence. In R. J. Sternberg & S. B. Kaufman (Eds.), *The Cambridge handbook of intelligence (pp. 351–370).* New York: Cambridge University Press.

Heitz, R. P., Unsworth, N., & Engle, R. W. (2004). Working memory capacity, attention control, and fluid intelligence. In I. O. Wilhelm & R. Engle (Eds.), *Handbook of understanding and measuring intelligence* (pp. 61–77). New York: Sage.

Hertzog, C., & Robinson, A. E. (2005). Metacognition and Intelligence. In O. Wilhelm & R. W. Engle (Eds.), *Handbook of understanding and measuring intelligence* (pp. 101–123). Thousand Oaks, CA: Sage.

Horn, J. L. (1968). Organization of abilities and the development of intelligence. *Psychological Review, 75,* 242–259.

Horn, J. L. (1989). Cognitive diversity: A framework of learning. In P. L. Ackerman, R. J. Sternberg, & R. Glaser (Eds.), *Learning and individual differences* (pp. 61–116). New York: Freeman.

Horn, J. L., & Cattell, R. B. (1966). Refinement and test of the theory of fluid and crystallized intelligence. *Journal of Educational Psychology, 57,* 253–270.

Horn, J. L., & Cattell, R. B. (1967). Age differences in fluid and crystallized intelligence. *Acta Psychologica, 26,* 107–129.

Horn, J. L., & Hofer, S. M. (1992). Major abilities and development in the adult period. In R. J. Sternberg & C. A. Berg (Eds.), *Intellectual development* (pp. 44–99). New York: Cambridge University Press.

Horn, J. L., & Noll, J. (1997). Human cognitive capabilities: Gf-Gc theory. In D. P. Flanagan, J. L. Genshaft, & P. L. Harrison (Eds.), *Beyond traditional intellectual assessment: Contemporary and emerging theories, tests, and issues* (pp. 53–91). New York: Guilford Press.

Howard-Jones, P. A., & Murray, S. (2003). Ideational productivity, focus of attention, and context. *Creativity Research Journal, 15,* 153–166.

Jensen, A. R. (2002). Psychometric g: Definition and substantiation. In R. J. Sternberg & E. L. Grigorenko (Eds.), *The general factor of intelligence: How general is it?* (pp. 39–53). Mahwah, NJ, US: Lawrence Erlbaum.

Jung, R. E., & Haier, R. J. (2007). The parieto-frontal integration theory (P-FIT) of intelligence: Converging neuroimaging evidence. *Behavioral and Brain Sciences, 30*, 135–187.

Kahneman, D. (2011). *Thinking, fast and slow*. New York, NY: Farrar, Straus, and Giroux.

Kahneman, D., & Frederick, S. (2002). Representativeness revisited: Attribute substitution in intuitive judgment. In T. Gilovich, D. Griffin, & D. Kahneman (Eds.), *Heuristics and biases: The psychology of intuitive judgment* (pp. 49–81). New York, NY: Cambridge University Press.

Kahneman, D., & Frederick, S. (2005). A model of heuristic judgment. In K. J. Holyoak & R. G. Morrison (Eds.), *The Cambridge handbook of thinking and reasoning* (pp. 267–293). New York, NY: Cambridge University Press.

Kane, M. J., Bleckley, M. K., Conway, A. R. A., & Engle, R. W. (2001). A controlled-attention view of working-memory capacity. *Journal of Experimental Psychology: General, 130*, 169–183.

Kaufman, A. S. (2009). *IQ testing 101*. New York: Springer.

Kaufman, A. S., & Kaufman, N. L. (1983). *K-ABC interpretive manual*. Circle Pines, MN: American Guidance Service.

Kaufman, A. S., & Kaufman, N. L. (2004). *Manual for Kaufman Assessment Battery for Children—Second Edition (KABC-II)—Comprehensive Form*. Circle Pines, MN: American Guidance Service.

Kaufman, S. B. (2009). *Beyond general intelligence: The dual-process theory of human intelligence (Unpublished Ph.D. dissertation)*. Yale University, New Haven, CT.

Kaufman, S. B. (2011). Intelligence and the cognitive unconscious. In R. J. Sternberg & S. B. Kaufman (Eds.), *The Cambridge handbook of intelligence* (pp. 442–467). New York: Cambridge University Press.

Kaufman, S. B. (2013). *Ungifted: Redefining intelligence*. New York: Basic Books.

Kaufman, S. B., DeYoung, C. G., Gray, J. R., Brown, J., & Mackintosh, N. (2009). Associative learning predicts intelligence above and beyond working memory and processing speed. *Intelligence, 37*, 374–382.

Kaufman, S. B., DeYoung, C. G., Gray, J. R., Jimenéz, L., Brown, J. B., & Mackintosh, N. (2010). Implicit learning as an ability. *Cognition, 116*, 321–340.

Kaufman, S. B., Reynolds, M. R., Liu, X., Kaufman, A. S., & McGrew, K. S. (2012). Are cognitive g and academic achievement g one and the same g? An exploration on the Woodcock-Johnson and Kaufman tests. *Intelligence, 40*, 123–138.

Kaufman, S. B., & Sternberg, R. J. (2008). Conceptions of giftedness. In S. Pfeiffer (Ed.), *Handbook of giftedness in children: Psycho-educational theory, research, and best practices (pp. 71–91)*. New York: Plenum.

Keren, G., & Schul, Y. (2009). Two is not always better than one: A critical evaluation of two-system theories. *Perspective on Psychological Science, 4*, 533–550.

Klein, P. D. (1997). Multiplying the problems of intelligence by eight: A critique of Gardner's theory. *Canadian Journal of Education/Revue canadienne de l'éducation, 22*, 377–394.

Kruglanski, A., & Gigerenzer, G. (2011). Intuitive and deliberate judgments are based on common principles. *Psychological Review, 118*, 97–109.

Locke, E. A. (2005). Why emotional intelligence is an invalid concept. *Journal of Organizational Behavior, 26*, 425–431.

Lohman, D. F. (2001). Fluid intelligence, inductive reasoning, and working memory: Where the theory of multiple intelligences falls short. In N. Colangelo & S. G. Assouline (Eds.), *Talent development IV: Proceedings from the 1998 Henry B. and Jocelyn Wallace National Research Symposium on Talent Development* (pp. 219–227). Scottsdale, AZ: Gifted Psychology Press.

Luria, A. R. (1966) *Human brain and psychological processes*. New York: Harper & Row.

Luria, A. R. (1970). The functional organization of the brain. *Scientific American, 222*, 66–78.

Luria, A. R. (1973). *The working brain: An introduction to neuropsychology*. London: Penguin.

Mackintosh, N. J. (1998). *IQ and human intelligence*. New York: Oxford University Press.

Malmi, R. A., Underwood, B. J., & Carroll, J. B. (1979). The interrelationships among some associative learning tasks. *Bulletin of the Psychonomic Society, 13*, 121–123.

Martindale, C. (1995). Creativity and connectionism. In S. M. Smith, T. B. Ward, & R. A. Finke (Eds.), *The creative cognition approach* (pp. 249–268). Cambridge, MA: MIT Press.

Mayer, J. D., Caruso, D. R., & Salovey, P. (2000). Emotional intelligence meets traditional standards for an intelligence. *Intelligence, 27*, 267–298.

Mayer, J. D., Roberts, R. D., & Barsade, S. G. (2008). Human abilities: Emotional intelligence. *Annual Review of Psychology, 59*, 507–536.

Mayer, J. D., & Salovey, P. (1993). The intelligence of emotional intelligence. *Intelligence, 17*, 433–442.

Mayer, J. D., Salovey, P., & Caruso, D. R. (2000). Models of emotional intelligence. In R. J. Sternberg (Ed.), *Handbook of intelligence* (pp. 396–420). Cambridge, England: Cambridge University Press.

Mayer, J. D., Salovey, P., & Caruso, D. R. (2002). *Mayer-Salovey-Caruso Emotional Intelligence Test (MSCEIT) user's manual*. Toronto, ON: Multi-Health Systems.

Mayer, J. D., Salovey, P., & Caruso, D. R. (2008). Emotional intelligence: New ability or eclectic traits? *American Psychologist, 63*, 503–517.

Mayer, J. D., Salovey, P., Caruso, D. R., & Sitarenios, G. (2003). Measuring emotional intelligence with the MSCEIT V2. 0. *Emotion, 3*, 97–105.

Naglieri, J. A., & Bornstein, B. T. (2003). Intelligence and achievement: Just how correlated are they? *Journal of Psychoeducational Assessment, 21*, 244–260.

Naglieri, J. A., & Das, J. P. (1997). *Cognitive Assessment System (CAS)*. Chicago: Riverside.

Oatley, K. (2004). Emotional intelligence and the intelligence of emotions. *Psychological Inquiry, 15*, 216–221.

Osman, M. (2004). An evaluation of dual-process theories of reasoning. *Psychonomic Bulletin & Review, 11*, 988–1010.

Petrides, K. V., & Furnham, A. (2001). Trait emotional intelligence: Psychometric investigation with reference to established trait taxonomies. *European Journal of Personality, 15*, 425–448.

Petrides, K. V., & Furnham, A. (2003). Trait emotional intelligence: Behavioural validation in two studies of emotion recognition and reactivity to mood induction. *European Journal of Personality, 17*, 39–57.

Pinker, S. (1999). *How the mind works*. New York: W.W. Norton & Company.

Plucker, J. A. (2000). Flip sides of the same coin or marching to the beat of different drummers? A response to Pyryt. *Gifted Child Quarterly, 44*, 193–195.

Plucker, J. A., Callahan, C. M., & Tomchin, E. M. (1996). Wherefore art thou, multiple intelligences? Alternative asessments for identifying talent in ethnically diverse and low income families. *Gifted Child Quarterly, 40*, 81–92.

Ramos-Ford, V., & Gardner, H. (1997). Giftedness from a multiple intelligences perspective. In N. Colangelo & G. A. David (Eds.), *Handbook of gifted education* (2 ed., pp. 439–459). Boston: Allyn & Bacon.

Roberts, R. D., Zeidner, M., & Matthews, G. (2001). Does emotional intelligence meet traditional standards for an intelligence? Some new data and conclusions. *Emotion, 1*, 196–231.

Roid, G. (2003). *Stanford-Binet Fifth Edition.* Itasca, IL: Riverside.

Rohde, T. E., & Thompson, L. A. (2007). Predicting academic achievement with cognitive ability. *Intelligence, 35*, 83–92.

Salovey, P., & Mayer, J. D. (1990). Emotional intelligence. *Imagination, Cognition and Personality, 9*, 185–211.

Schmithorst, V. J. (2009). Developmental sex differences in relation of neuroanatomical connectivity to intelligence. *Intelligence, 37*, 164–173.

Schulte, M. J., Ree, M. J., & Carretta, T. R. (2004). Emotional intelligence: Not much more than g and personality. *Personality and Individual Differences, 37*, 1059–1068.

Spearman, C. (1904). "General intelligence," objectively determined and measured. *American Journal of Psychology, 15*, 201–293.

Stemler, S., Grigorenko, E., Jarvin, L., & Sternberg, R. (2006). Using the theory of successful intelligence as a basis for augmenting AP exams in psychology and statistics. *Contemporary Educational Psychology, 31*, 344–376.

Stanovich, K. E. (2004). *The robot's rebellion: Finding meaning in the age of Darwin.* Chicago, IL: University of Chicago Press.

Stanovich, K. E. (2011). *Rationality and the reflective mind.* New York, NY: Oxford University Press.

Stanovich, K. E., & Toplak, M. E. (2012). Defining features versus incidental correlates of Type 1 and Type 2 processing. *Mind and Society, 11*, 3–13.

Sternberg, R. J. (1990). *Metaphors of mind: Conceptions of the nature of intelligence.* New York: Cambridge University Press.

Sternberg, R. J. (1997). *Successful intelligence: How practical and creative intelligence determine success in life* New York: Plume.

Sternberg, R. J. (2006). The Rainbow Project: Enhancing the SAT through assessments of analytical, practical and creative skills. *Intelligence, 34*, 321–350.

Sternberg, R. J., & Grigorenko, E. L. (2002). *The general factor of intelligence.* Hillsdale, NJ: Erlbaum.

Sternberg, R. J., Grigorenko, E. L., Ferrari, M., & Clinkenbeard, P. (1999). A triarchic analysis of an aptitude-treatment interaction. *European Journal of Psychological Assessment, 15*, 3–13.

Sternberg, R. J., Kaufman, J. C., & Grigorenko, E. L. (2008). *Applied intelligence.* New York: Cambridge University Press.

Tamez, E., Myerson, J., & Hale, S. (2008). Learning, working memory, and intelligence revisited. *Behavioural Processes, 78*, 240–245.

Thrash, T. M., & Elliot, A. J. (2003). Inspiration as a psychological construct. Journal of Personality and Social Psychology, 84, 871–889.

Underwood, B. J., Boruch, R. F., & Malmi, R. A. (1978). Composition of episodic memory. *Journal of Experimental Psychology: General, 107*, 393–419.

Unsworth, N., Schrock, J. C., & Engle, R.W. (2004).Working memory capacity and the antisaccade task: Individual differences in voluntary saccade control. *Journal of Experimental Psychology: Learning, Memory, and Cognition, 30*, 1302–1321.

van der Maas, H. L. J., Dolan, C. V., Grasman, R. P. P. P., Wicherts, J. M., Huizenga, H. M., & Raijmakers, M. E. J. (2006). A dynamical model of general intelligence: The positive manifold of intelligence by mutualism. *Psychological Review, 113*, 842–861.

van der Zee, K., Thijs, M., & Schakel, L. (2002). The relationship of emotional intelligence with academic intelligence and the Big Five. *European Journal of Personality, 16*, 103–125.

Vallerand, R. J., Blanchard, C., Mageau, G. A., Koestner, R., Ratelle, C., Leonard, M.…. Marsolais, J. (2003). Les Passions de l'Ame: On Obsessive and Harmonious Passion. *Journal of Personality and Social Psychology, 85*, 756–767.

Vartanian, O. (2009). Variable attention facilitates creative problem solving. *Psychology of Aesthetics, Creativity, and the Arts, 3*, 57–59.

Visser, B. A., Ashton, M. C., & Vernon, P. A. (2006). Beyond g: Putting multiple intelligences theory to the test. *Intelligence, 34*, 487–502.

Watkins, M. W., Lei, P-W., & Canivez, G. L. (2007). Psychometric intelligence and achievement: A cross-lagged panel analysis. *Intelligence, 35*, 59–68.

White, J. (2008). Illusory intelligences? *Journal of Philosophy of Education, 42*, 611–630.

Williams, B. A., Myerson, J., & Hale, S. (2008). Individual differences, intelligence, and behavior analysis. *Journal of the Experimental Analysis of Behavior, 90*, 219–231

Williams, B. A., & Pearlberg, S. L. (2006). Learning of three-term contingencies correlates with Raven scores, but not with measures of cognitive processing. *Intelligence, 34*, 177–191.

Woodcock, R. W., McGrew, K. S., & Mather, N. (2001). *Woodcock-Johnson Battery—Third Edition (WJ III).* Itasca, IL: Riverside.

Woodrow, H. (1938). The relation between abilities and improvement with practice. *Journal of Educational Psychology, 29*, 215–230.

Woodrow, H. (1946). The ability to learn. *Psychological Review, 53*, 147–158.

Zeidner, M., Matthews, G., & Roberts, R. D. (2001). Slow down, you move too fast: Emotional intelligence remains an "elusive" intelligence. *Emotion, 1*, 265–275.

Zeidner, M., Roberts, R. D., & Matthews, G. (2004). The emotional intelligence bandwagon: Too fast to live, too young to die? *Psychological Inquiry, 15*, 239–248.

# Genes and Intelligence

Thais S. Rizzi *and* Danielle Posthuma

**Abstract**

Intelligence is a highly heritable complex trait. The proportion of variance in intelligence that is attributable to genetic factors ranges from 40% in young childhood to 80% in late adulthood. In the past decade, considerable progress has been made in molecular genetics technologies, which facilitates the detection of the actual genetic factors that underlie the high heritability of intelligence. In this chapter we provide an overview of the progress that has been made to date in identifying genetic variants for intelligence using various methods from genetic linkage to genome-wide association studies. In addition, we discuss a number of challenges to identify genetic variants associated with intelligence and provide suggestions for future directions.

**Key Words:** intelligence, IQ, cognition, heritability, linkage, association, gene, genome, pathway, SNP

This chapter provides an overview of the current state of knowledge on the genetic (and environmental) contribution to individual differences in intelligence. Besides some general explanations on genetics, it will include a brief summary of the literature on the heritability of intelligence, followed by an extensive discussion of the findings of molecular genetic studies on intelligence.

Intelligence is one of the most studied complex behavioral traits and has been a research focus for more than a century. The most accepted view among scientists in the field of intelligence is that intelligence is a very general mental capability that, among other things, involves the ability to reason, plan, solve problems, think abstractly, comprehend complex ideas, learn quickly, and learn from experience (Gottfredson, 1997). Two general views on the nature of intelligence have been formulated. The first encompasses the idea of a single general cognitive factor referred to as "g" or "general cognitive ability" (Spearman, 1904). The second view distinguishes several different, unrelated cognitive abilities (e.g., Thurstone, 1948). The typical statistical model of intelligence takes into account the presence of "g," several different abilities, as well test-specific factors.

Psychometric intelligence tests usually consist of a number of component subtests that taken together are used to infer a general intelligence quotient (IQ) score. Intelligence tests such as the Wechsler Adult Intelligence Scale (WAIS; Wechsler, 1997) and Wechsler Intelligence Scale for children (WISC; Wechsler, 1991) are theoretically based on Thurstone's factor analytic theory of intelligence (Thurstone, 1947) and provide an index of both general IQ and primary abilities such as verbal comprehension, working memory, perceptual speed, and perceptual organization. In a population, large interindividual differences in IQ test scores can be observed. The distribution of IQ scores in the general population follows a Gaussian normal distribution. Ninety-five percent of the population have an IQ score between 75 and 130, and 68% of the general population have an IQ score between 85 and 115 (Gottfredson, 1997; Herrnstein & Murray, 1994; C. R. Reynolds, Chastain, Kaufman,

& McLean, 1987). In the general population, 2.5% have an IQ under 75, and this is generally considered as the threshold for "mental retardation," a condition of limited mental ability, which is characterized by difficulties in adapting to the demands of life (Croen, Grether, & Selvin, 2001; Curry et al., 1997; Roeleveld, Zielhuis, & Gabreels, 1997). In the other extreme (above 140) are the high intellectual quotient/giftedness representing approximately 0.25% of the population (1 in 400) (Gottfredson, 1997; Herrnstein & Murray, 1994; C. R. Reynolds et al., 1987).

Individuals from the same family tend to resemble each other more with respect to their IQ test scores than unrelated people. These differences between unrelated persons and the resemblance between relatives can be due to genetic factors, shared environmental factors, cultural transmission from one generation to the next, social interactions between family members, or a combination of these mechanisms (see Box 52.1).

Heritability is the proportion of phenotypic variation in a population that is due to genetic variation between individuals. Phenotypic variation among individuals may be due to genetic or environmental factors. Heritability estimates are typically based on twin and family studies, in which known genetic relatedness (e.g., parental-child genetic relatedness is 0.5, because each child receives 50% of his or her genetic material from each parent) is used to predict phenotypic resemblance. Due to the rapid advances in genome technology, it has become possible to estimate a lower bound of the heritability of a trait based on actual, *measured* genetic variation. This method does not require genetically related individuals but simply uses an overall measure of the average number of alleles that are physically the same between two unrelated individuals. If a trait is heritable, than the more alleles two individuals have in common, the more they will resemble each other on the trait.

The first scientific study of the heritability of intelligence was published in 1869 by Sir Francis Galton, when he published his *Hereditary Genius*, in which he described his observation that family members tend to be more alike for intellectual capabilities than unrelated persons (Galton, 1869). Multiple twin and family studies were conducted in the second half of the 20th century, which were summarized in a landmark study by Bouchard and McGue, who reviewed all 111 twin and family correlations for IQ published before 1980. The mean correlation of IQ scores between monozygotic

twins was 0.86; between siblings, 0.47; between half-siblings, 0.31; and between cousins, 0.15 (Bouchard & McGue, 1981, 2003; Deary, Spinath, & Bates, 2006; Vinkhuyzen, van der Sluis, & Posthuma, 2011). Twenty-five years later heritability estimates for adult IQ based on twin studies are generally accepted to range from 60% to 80% (e.g., Deary et al., 2006). Using measured genotypes in a sample of 3,500 unrelated adults, Davies et al. (2011) recently confirmed that at least 40% to 50% of individual differences in intelligence could be traced to additive genetic variation.

The estimated heritability of IQ tends to change across the life span: Specifically, it increases from 25% in preschool children to 80% in early adolescence and adulthood (Ando, Ono, & Wright, 2001; Bartels, Rietveld, Van Baal, & Boomsma, 2002; Plomin, 1999; Posthuma, Neale, Boomsma, & de Geus, 2001; Thurstone, 1947). In parallel, shared environmental influences, that is, environmental influences that are shared by members from the same family and render them more alike, explain about half of the variation in intelligence in young children (Bartels et al., 2002), while this effect is decreased drastically once adolescence is reached (Posthuma, de Geus, & Boomsma, 2001).

These longitudinal studies suggest that genetic factors contribute differently to variation in intelligence across the life span, especially during the transition from early to middle childhood and from middle childhood to late adolescence. One possible explanation for this phenomenon is that the same genes might have different (larger) effects in middle/late childhood as compared to early childhood (Plomin, 1986) due to differential gene expression regulation across developmental stages (L. W. Harris et al., 2009). The human biological clock switches genes on or off in a preprogrammed way, affecting physical development. Many critical maturational processes take place in the human brain during postnatal development, in particular during adolescence when white matter expansion takes place (Bartzokis et al., 2001; Rice & Barone, 2000). A recent study showed that the expression pattern of approximately 2,000 genes in the prefrontal cortex was significantly correlated with age (L. W. Harris et al., 2009). For many of these genes, the most dramatic changes in expression occur in early postnatal development (0–2 years), reaching a peak around adolescence (15–25 years) and showing only subtle changes in expression thereafter (35–50 years) (L. W. Harris et al., 2009). RNA expression profiling has revealed peak expression in late adolescence for

**Box 52.1** Genetic Terminology

**Allele** = Allele is an alternative form of a gene or genetic region.

**Biological pathway** = Series of molecule actions in a cell that leads to a certain product.

**Copy number variation (CNV)** = Structural variation that results in abnormal number of copies, deletions or insertions of one or more genetic regions of the DNA.

**Cosegregation** = The transmission of two or more genes (regions) on a chromosome to the same daughter cell leading to the inheritance by the offspring of these genes together.

**Crossing over** = Exchange of genetic material between homologous chromosomes.

**Cultural transmission** = Cultural transmission is the process of passing on culturally relevant knowledge, skills, attitudes, and values from one generation to the next.

**Deoxyribonucleic acid (DNA)** = Nucleic acid that contains the genetic information used in the development and functioning of most of the organisms.

**DNA methylation** = Biochemical process that leads to inhibition of transcription initiation

**Gene** = Genomic region corresponding to a unit of inheritance, which is associated with regulatory regions, transcribed regions (that code for a type of protein or for an RNA chain that has a function in the organism), and or other functional sequence regions.

**Genetic association** = Statistical association between a genetic variant and a trait.

**Genetic dominance** = Non-additive relationship between two variant forms of a single gene, in which one copy of an allele is sufficient to cause a disease.

**Genetic marker** = A DNA sequence with a known location on a chromosome that can be used to identify individuals.

**Genome** = The complete hereditary information of an organism.

**Genome-wide association** = Approach that involves rapidly scanning markers across the genomes of many people to find genetic variants associated with a particular disease or complex trait.

**Haplotype** = Combination of alleles at different loci on the same ancestral chromosome.

**Heritability** = Proportion of variation of a trait within a population that is due to genetic variation.

**Homologous chromosomes** = Chromosome pairs with same length, centromere position and genes for the same characteristics.

**Linkage Analysis** = Statistical method that tests for co-segregation of a chromosomal region and a trait of interest.

**Locus** (Plural: loci) = Specific location of a gene or DNA sequence on a chromosome.

**LOD score** = The Log of the odds (LOD) of obtaining the observed data when two loci (or a trait and a marker) are indeed linked, versus the likelihood of observing the same data purely by chance.

**Mendel's second Law of Independent Assortment** = Two different genes located on different chromosomes or located relatively far from each other will assort independently and thus randomly.

**Monogenic disease** = Disorders caused by the inheritance of a single defective gene.

**Penetrance** = The rate of occurrence of a disease expressed in individuals with the detrimental allele.

**Recombination** = Exchanged of portions of DNA between homologous chromosomes.

**Restriction Fragment Length Polymorphisms** = Genetic variations at the site where a restriction enzyme cuts a piece of DNA resulting in variation in the size of the resulting fragments.

**Ribonucleic acid (RNA)** = RNA is transcribed from DNA and it is central to protein synthesis.

**Shared environmental factors** = Factors in the environment that are shared between siblings and make siblings resemble each other more on a trait.

**Single-nucleotide polymorphism (SNP)** = Genetic variation occurring when a single nucleotide (A, T, C, or G) differs between individuals or paired chromosomes in the same individual.

---

genes involved in energy metabolism, protein and lipid synthesis, together with a decrease of expression of genes associated with signaling and neuronal development such as axon guidance, morphogenesis, and synaptogenesis (L. W. Harris et al., 2009).

Such differential gene expression across developmental stages may explain differences in heritability estimates across the life span.

Alternative explanations for the increased heritability later in life may be (1) active gene–environment correlation, where the environment becomes a function of a person's genetic makeup and is estimated as part of the heritability in the classic twin design, or (2) a decrease in environmental influences with age while genetic influences remain the same—as the heritability estimate is the *proportion* of genetic variance of the total variation, this will also lead to an increase in the heritability estimate with age.

In sum, in adulthood the main factor explaining interindividual variation in intelligence is of a genetic nature (McGuffin, Riley, & Plomin, 2001; Plomin, 1990; Plomin, Owen, & McGuffin, 1994). A logical next question is, Can we identify the genes, or genetic mechanisms, that cause this variation in intelligence? In the past decade, considerable progress has been made in genotyping technologies, which facilitates the detection of the actual genetic variants that underlie the high heritability of intelligence. In the remainder of this chapter, we review the progress that has been made to date in identifying genetic variation for intelligence. Progress in gene finding for intelligence is highly dependent on genotyping technologies; below we will therefore follow the revolution from genetic linkage studies to genome-wide association studies and their impact on finding genes for intelligence. For the genetically less informed reader, Box 52.2 provides a very brief tutorial on gene finding.

## Linkage Studies (Widely Used in the 1980s and 1990s)

Genetic linkage analysis is a statistical method that is used to identify loci that are inherited together with the trait. Genetic linkage was first discovered by the British geneticists William Bateson and Reginald Punnett (Bateson, 1906; Punnett, 1908) shortly after Mendel's laws were rediscovered in 1900.

Linkage can be explained by reference to Mendel's second law—the law of independent assortment. This law states that separate genes for separate traits are passed independently from one another from parents to offspring; in other words, they are segregated independently. During gamete formation, chromosomes assort randomly, such that the segregation of alleles of one locus is independent of the segregation of alleles of another locus. The law of independent assortment always holds for regions that are located on different chromosomes, but not necessarily for loci that are on the same chromosome. When two loci are located on the same chromosome, the chance of a crossover (recombination of genetic material between the paired chromosomes

inherited from each of one's parents) between them is a function of the distance between the two regions. If two loci are located further apart, the chance of crossovers between them increases, whereas if the loci are very close, the chance of crossover is very small, causing the two loci to be inherited together (cosegregate), and assortment of these loci is no longer independent. The basic idea of linkage analysis is to compare resemblance between subjects at a genetic marker with resemblance at a measured trait (e.g., intelligence). Relatives who resemble each other more phenotypically will also resemble each other more genetically if the trait under study is heritable. In 1980 Botstein et al. described a new basis for the construction of a genetic linkage map of the human genome, based on so-called restriction fragment length polymorphisms (RFLPs) (Botstein, White, Skolnick, & Davis, 1980). Pedigrees in which inherited traits are known to be segregating can be tested for cosegregation of an RFLP marker (and unmeasured genes that are physically close to the marker and are coinherited) with the trait. The causal variant might be the genetic marker in study or in a region around this marker that is linked to it. Evidence for linkage is usually expressed in terms of LOD scores, that is, a log of the odds for linkage.

Figure 52.1 explains crossing-over, cosegregation, and how linkage is conducted in more detail.

Linkage studies were widely used in the 1990s and progressed together with other molecular techniques (Barrett et al., 2007; Mathew, 1999; Williamson, 1988). Linkage studies have led to the detection of genetic loci for monogenic diseases using classical penetrance-based linkage analysis methods (Mathew, 1999; Williamson, 1988). This penetrance-based linkage method attempts to characterize the mode of inheritance of a trait, by statistically examining the segregation pattern of the trait through genetic samples of related individuals (as explained previously in Fig. 52.1). Penetrance is a measurement of the proportion of individuals in a population who carry a disease-causing allele and can express the disease phenotype; in other words, if a mutation in the gene responsible for a particular autosomal dominant disorder has 80% penetrance, then 80% of those with the mutation will develop the disease, while 20% will not, even though they carry the mutation. An example of a disease with different levels of penetrance is Huntington's disease (HD). HD is a neurodegenerative genetic disorder that affects muscle coordination and leads to cognitive decline and dementia. HD is one of several trinucleotide repeat disorders, which are caused by the

**Box 52.2** A brief tutorial on gene finding

The human genome is stored on 23 chromosome pairs (total of 46) plus the small mitochondrial DNA as shown in the figure below.

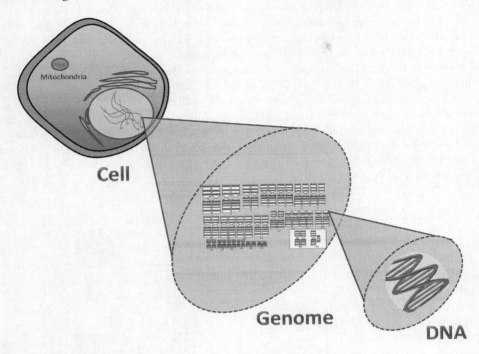

A chromosome is an organized structure of DNA and protein found in each cell. Each individual has two strands of the DNA and the information within a particular gene or DNA region (locus/loci) is not always the same between individuals: Different individuals may carry different copies of a locus. Since, different copies of a gene give different instructions to the cell, genetic variation may lead to phenotypic variation or diseases when a copy of an allele leads to misinstructions of the cell. Each unique form of a single gene is called an allele. For example, two sequenced DNA fragments from two different individuals, TTCG**G**ATAA to TTCG**A**ATAA, contain a difference in a single nucleotide (sequence letter). In this case we say that there are two alleles of this DNA fragment: G and A.

Three nucleotides form a *codon,* which codes for an amino acid. Multiple amino acids form proteins. Genetic mutations can create new alleles and sometimes can lead to diseases such as *Microcephaly*, where mutations in a single gene *ASPM (*abnormal spindle-like microcephaly) cause a brain developmental disorder, altering neuronal migration and cortical layering process (for review see Bond et al., 2002).

The combination of these variants is called a haplotype. Haplotypes that occur more often in a disease group are high-risk haplotypes. For example, in a schizophrenia family based study it was found that a certain combination of 8 allele calls in the *DTNBP1* (dystrobrevin binding protein 1) gene were unique for the disease group (Van den Oord et al., 2003).

Human individuals differ from one another by about one base pair per thousand. If these differences occur within coding or regulatory regions, phenotypic variation in a trait may result. It is estimated that humans have more than 5.9 million sites where genetic variation exists (Durbin et al., 2010). Not all of these variants lead to disease or phenotypic differences, but some will. The molecular biology field is advancing at an exponential rate since the late 1970s, specifically the automated genotyping of thousands of single nucleotide polymorphisms (SNPs) and, more recently, copy number variations (CNVs), have revolutionized our ability to describe variation at all levels of genetic organization: genes, individuals, populations, species, and genera. The past decade is characterized by several milestones in genetics, including the International HapMap project (http://hapmap.ncbi.nlm.nih.gov) aiming to determine common patterns of DNA sequence variation in the human genome, the publication of the first draft sequence of the human genome (Venter et al., 2001), and the recent start of the 1000 genome project (http://www.1000genomes.org/), which aims to find most genetic variants present in the genome. Major efforts in genome-wide association studies (GWAS) have been undertaken since ±2005, where millions of SNPs have been tested for association with diseases and quantitative traits. This has led to the discovery of several genes for Type-II diabetes, Crohn's disease, prostate cancer, inflammatory bowel disease, body mass index and age related macular degeneration (Saxena et al., 2007; Rioux, 2007; Gudmundsson et al., 2007; Dewan et al., 2006; Duerr et al., 2006; Frayling et al., 2007). For complex traits, which are influenced by multiple genetic variants of small effect, GWAS studies have been less successful (Altshuler & Daly, 2007; Maher, 2008). Large study samples (> 40,000 subjects) are needed to detect the multiple variants involved in complex traits (Visscher, 2008). Lately new tools have been developed to test for the combined effect of multiple genetic variants in the same gene or indifferent genes from the same biological pathway, to increase statistical power and allow more biologically driven hypothesis testing (e.g. Ruano et al., 2010; Torkamani, A., Topol, E. J., & Schork, N. J., 2008).

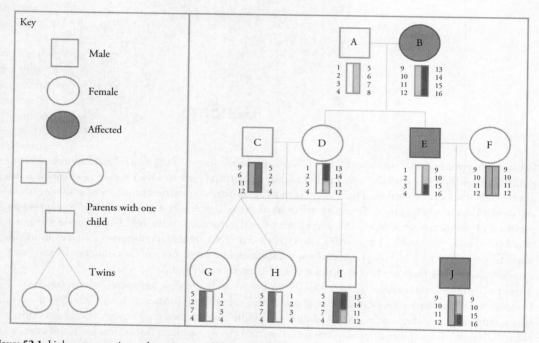

**Figure 52.1** Linkage, segregation and crossing over. (*See* color insert.)

**Note:** This figure shows a pedigree with 10 individuals, identified with letters from A to J. Three individuals (B, E, and J) are affected with a certain disease. Each bar represents one chromosome, and each individual has 1 pair of a chromosome. The two founder individuals (A and B) have colored bars indicating that the white bar was inherited from the father of A, the blue bar from the mother of A, the yellow bar was inherited from the father of B and the red bar from the mother of B. On each chromosome, 4 markers are genotyped. Each pair of chromosomes contains the same markers in the same order, but the sequences are not identical. Numbers 1–16 represent the different alleles from each of the four markers. Each marker has 4 possible alleles. For example, the first marker has possible alleles coded 1, 5, 9, and 13, the second marker has alleles 2, 6, 10, and 14 etcetera. Individual C and F are not genetically related to the two founders and have grey chromosomes that have the same order of markers with the same possible alleles, but not necessarily with the same combination of alleles. Individuals D and E (children from parents A and B) have one chromosome (represented in white) that was inherited from the father. These individuals also have a chromosome inherited from the mother, however a genetic recombination took place and the children inherited a mixture of the two maternal grandparental chromosomes (combination of yellow and red), this phenomenon is known as crossover. If we follow the disease in the pedigree we notice that affected individuals always carry alleles 15 and 16 of the third and fourth marker. These alleles are flanking a region that segregates with the trait. We can conclude from the fictitious family pedigree that the red region (between 15 and 16) shared by all the affected individuals likely contains the gene or casual variant for the disease. We then say that this region is linked to the trait.

length of a repeated DNA section of a gene exceeding a normal range (Walker, 2007).

Linkage studies have also provided evidence of genetic contribution to intelligence. The first whole genome linkage scan for intelligence was published in 2005 (Posthuma et al., 2005). The sample used in this study consisted of a Dutch sample (159 sibling pairs) and an Australian sample (475 sibling pairs). Results indicated two significant areas of linkage to general intelligence on the long arm of chromosome 2 (2q) and the short arm of chromosome 6 (6p), and several areas of suggestive linkage (4p, 7q, 20p, 21p). These first genome-wide linkages show convergence with linkage in clinical disorders that are characterized by cognitive disabilities. For instance, the chromosome 2 area has been implicated in linkage scans for autism, dyslexia, and schizophrenia (Addington et al., 2005; Buxbaum et al., 2001; Fagerheim et al., 1999; IMGSAC, 2001; Kaminen et al., 2003; Ylisaukko-Oja et al., 2005), while the chromosome 6 region is the main linkage area for reading ability and dyslexia (Cardon et al., 1994; Fisher, Stein, & Monaco, 1999; Grigorenko et al., 1997).

Four linkage studies for IQ have been published since (Buyske et al., 2006; Dick et al., 2006; Luciano et al., 2006; Wainwright et al., 2006). Two studies with a partly overlapping sample confirmed the importance of the areas on chromosomes 2 and 6 for specific aspects of intelligence (Luciano et al., 2006), as well as for academic achievement, which is highly correlated with IQ scores (Wainwright et al., 2006). The study by Luciano and colleagues (2006) additionally showed that both word recognition and IQ were linked to chromosome 2, corroborating the notion that the same genes influence different aspects of cognitive ability (Plomin & Kovas, 2005).

Dick and colleagues (2006) also confirmed linkage of intelligence to the chromosome 6 area, and a second scan on the same dataset (Buyske et al., 2006) showed strong evidence for linkage of specific cognitive abilities on chromosome 14, which had shown suggestive linkage in the two previous linkage studies (Dick et al., 2006; Luciano et al., 2006). Converging evidence from these whole genome linkage studies provides support for the involvement of three different chromosomal regions in human intelligence: 2q24.1–31.1, 6p25–21.2, and 14q11.2–12.

The significant genomic regions that result from a linkage study tend to be relatively large (10–20 Mb), harboring many potential candidate genes.

The obvious next step after linkage is therefore to fine map these linkage regions using more DNA markers and/or select genes from these regions for further investigation, using a candidate gene approach.

## Candidate Gene Approach (Widely Used in 1990s–2000s)

The candidate gene approach is a commonly used technique to identify genetic risk factors for complex traits, such as intelligence. In this approach, one gene (or several) is selectively tested for association with a disease or trait. The statistical test for association involves a simple comparison of allele frequencies across cases and controls (dichotomous traits) or a linear regression of genotype on trait level (quantitative traits). The candidate gene approach allows researchers to investigate the validity of a "biological guess" about the genetic basis of a specific phenotype.

A candidate gene study can be performed in unrelated individuals and does not necessarily rely on family data, which are often more difficult to collect. The selection of suitable and promising candidate genes, however, requires prior knowledge, for example, from previous linkage findings or from putative underlying biological mechanisms (or pathways) that might be relevant to intelligence, such as neurotransmission and neurodevelopment. Candidate genes can be selected based on linkage study, known biological processes, adaptive evolution, animal studies, or severe cognitive impairment. Next we present some examples of candidate gene–based studies for intelligence.

### Candidate Gene–Based Studies for Intelligence

GENES SELECTED BASED ON LINKAGE STUDY

The five previous whole-genome linkage scans discussed earlier have pointed to three genomic regions (2q24.1–31.1, 6p25–21.2, and 14q11.2–12) important to human intelligence (Buyske et al., 2006; Dick et al., 2006; Luciano et al., 2006; Posthuma et al., 2005; Wainwright et al., 2006), but they did not identify the responsible genes or variants.

Recently, Rizzi et al. (2011) conducted an in silico fine mapping study of six different chromosomal regions, including these three previously reported linkage regions and three regions that showed suggestive evidence for linkage. For their analysis, the publicly available data of 947 families participating in the International Multi-Centre ADHD (attention deficit/hyperactivity disorder) Genetics (IMAGE) study were used. SNPs that proved significant in the IMAGE samples were subsequently tested in four independent samples (4,357 subjects), one ascertained for ADHD, and three population-based samples. Associations between intelligence and SNPs in the *ATXN1* and *TRIM31* genes (6p25–21.2) and in three intergenic regions (14q11.2–12) showed replicated association, but only in the samples ascertained for ADHD (Rizzi et al., 2011). This finding suggests that genetic variants important for intelligence in a psychiatric (ADHD) population may not necessarily overlap with genetic variants important for intelligence in a nonpsychiatric population.

## CANDIDATE GENES BASED ON KNOWN BIOLOGICAL PROCESSES

Candidate genes may also be selected based on their known role in biological processes that are thought to be important for intelligence. For example, neurotransmission is thought to play a crucial role in cognitive functioning. Genetic variants in genes involved in neurotransmission may have immediate consequences in multiple events in the signaling cascade (release and reuptake process), altering neurotransmitter receptors located in the cell membrane. Examples of candidates for neurotransmission are the catechol-O-methyltransferase (*COMT*), the Cholinergic Muscarinic Receptor 2 (*CHRM2*), and the synaptosomal-associated protein, 25 kDa (*SNAP25*) genes.

COMT is one of the major mammalian enzymes involved in the metabolic degradation of catecholamines (Chen et al., 2004; Gogos et al., 1998) and has been consistently associated with specific cognitive abilities, such as memory and executive functioning (e.g., Gosso et al., 2008a; Savitz, Solms, & Ramesar, 2006; Small, Rosnick, Fratiglioni, & Backman, 2004). Savitz et al. (2006) found that 20 out of 26 studies reported significant association between COMT polymorphisms (Val108/158Met) and cognitive function. Given its broad range of activity, several research groups also reported association of genetic variants in *COMT* with phenotypes other than cognition, such as obsessive-compulsive disorder, schizophrenia, and anorexia nervosa (Frisch et al., 2001; Karayiorgou et al., 1997, 1999; S. G. Lee et al., 2005; Shifman et al., 2002). One specific variant (rs4680) has been associated with various traits such as cognitive ability, schizophrenia, Alzheimer's disease, and pain sensitivity (Gosso et al., 2008a; Nackley et al., 2007; Shifman et al., 2002; Sweet et al., 2005). These findings suggest that this gene is probably not the only one involved

in these traits, and interaction between *COMT* and other genes might influence variation in cognitive function. For instance, Gosso et al. (2008a) found a significant interaction effect between *COMT* and *DRD2* polymorphisms for working memory performance in two independent family-based Dutch samples. Similarly, Qian et al. (2009) reported that the IQ of Chinese boys with ADHD can be predicted by an interaction between *COMT* and *MAOA* (monoamine oxidase A), an isozyme that preferentially deanimates dopamine. These findings suggest that a single polymorphism effect may not be detected easily if the interaction with other genes in the dopaminergic pathway is not taken into account and if the trait is not well defined.

A further example of a neurotransmission-related candidate is the *CHRM2* (cholinergic muscarinic receptor 2) gene. Variants of the *CHRM2* gene were reported to explain 1% to 2% of the variance in intelligence in three independent studies (Comings et al., 2003; Dick et al., 2007; Gosso et al., 2006). The *CHRM2* gene is the most widely replicated gene for IQ, although a recent study could not confirm this association (Lind, et al., 2009).

The SNAP25 (synaptosomal-associated protein, 25kDa) protein is a component of the SNARE (soluble N-ethylmaleimide-sensitive factor attachment protein receptors) complex and has also been associated with intelligence. Variance in a single-nucleotide polymorphism of the *SNAP25* gene was suggested to account for 3.4% of the phenotypic variance in intelligence in two independent Dutch cohorts (Gosso et al., 2008b; Gosso, de Geus, et al., 2006).

Selection of candidate genes for cognitive ability is not limited to neurotransmission. For example, developmental trajectories—cognitive maturation in early childhood and cognitive decline in aging—show considerable variation across individuals as well, with a significant portion of this variation again being due to genetic factors. The insulin-like growth factor 2 receptor (*IGF2R*) and cathepsin D (*CTSD*) genes were both found to be associated with intelligence and are suggested to play a role in the optimal development of the human brain (Chorney et al., 1998; Payton et al., 2003).

Variants in the *PRNP* (prion protein [p27–30]) and *KL* (klotho) genes were found to be associated with general intelligence and play a role in the trajectory of normal cognitive aging (Deary et al., 2005; Kachiwala et al., 2005).

Similarly, neurotrophins, that is, regulatory factors that mediate the differentiation, proliferation, and survival of cholinergic, dopaminergic, and serotonergic neurons, could be related to variation in cognitive ability as well. For instance, one of these neurotrophins, brain-derived neurotrophic factor (BDNF), has been previously associated with intelligence (Tsai, Hong, Yu, & Chen, 2004) and reasoning skills (S. E. Harris et al., 2006).

There are several lines of evidence that suggest that the biosynthetic fatty acid pathway may be imported for IQ. The amount of fatty acid in the blood has been shown to influence cognitive development (for a review, see Innis, 2007), and recently higher fatty acid (DHA) blood level was related to better performance on tests of nonverbal reasoning and mental flexibility, working memory, and vocabulary ($p < .05$) in individuals between 35 and 54 years of age (Muldoon et al., 2010). The *FADS3* gene was associated with IQ in the genome-wide scan of Butcher, Davis, Craig, and Plomin (2008). Caspi et al. (2007) showed a dominant effect of the C allele of the *FADS2* (Fatty Acid Desaturase 2) gene in response to breast feeding: Breastfed children carrying the C allele showed more than a 6 IQ points advantage relative to children not fed with breast milk ($p < .001$), but this effect was later refuted by Martin et al. (2011; Caspi et al., 2007). Genetic variants in the biosynthetic fatty acid pathway might influence the amount of fatty acids in blood and consequently cognitive functioning in early and later age, but the field currently awaits systematic testing of the involvement of candidate genes from the biosynthetic fatty acid pathway in IQ.

### CANDIDATE GENES BASED ON ANIMAL STUDIES

Candidate genes can also be selected based on results from animal studies, as has been shown for memory performance, one of the aspects of cognition. Molecular genetic studies of memory in animals began more than 25 years ago with Seymour Benzer and coworkers (Dudai, Jan, Byers, Quinn, & Benzer, 1976), who identified "dunce," an X-linked mutant fly with defective associative learning. Later it was confirmed that this mutation was in a cAMP-specific phosphodiesterase gene. In the past few years, a series of molecular-genetic, biochemical, cellular, and behavioral studies in fruit flies and mice have confirmed that long-term memory formation is dependent on CREB (cAMP response element binding protein), a constitutively expressed regulatory transcription factor (Bourtchouladze et al., 2003; Guzowski & McGaugh, 1997; Tully, 1997). The importance of CREB in memory likely also extends to humans, where the mutation

of CBP (CREB-binding protein) results in the Rubinstein-Taybi syndrome (Petrij et al., 1995), a condition characterized by mental retardation.

It has also been shown that transgenic mice that overexpress the NMDA receptor 2B (NR2B) gene, a synaptic coincidence detector, exhibit superior ability in learning and memory in various behavioral tasks (Tang et al., 1999). In humans, NR2B is down-regulated in Alzheimer's patients (Hynd, Scott, & Dodd, 2004), and genetic variants in the NR2B subunit gene (GRIN2B) promoter region were associated with sporadic Alzheimer's disease in the North Chinese population (Jiang & Jia, 2009). However, until now no direct association has been found between memory or IQ and *NR2B* in humans.

### CANDIDATE GENES BASED ON SEVERE COGNITIVE IMPAIRMENT

Selection of candidate genes for variation in cognitive ability in the normal population may also be based on genes that have already been associated with severe cognitive impairment such as mental retardation (Inlow & Restifo, 2004; Ramakers, 2002) and Down syndrome. Down syndrome is a medical condition caused by an extra copy of chromosome 21, and it is characterized by an overexpression of cystathionine beta synthase (CBS) and a low level of homocysteine in the blood (Al-Gazali et al., 2001). Barbauz and others have linked variants in the *CBS* genes to individual differences in intelligence in the normal range (Barbaux, Plomin, & Whitehead, 2000).

The *DTNBP1* (dystrobrevin binding protein 1) gene is associated with the clinical expression of schizophrenia (Straub et al., 2002), as well as with Hermansky-Pudlak syndrome type 7 (Li et al., 2003). Variants in the *DTNBP1* gene have also been associated with general cognitive ability ("g") in a clinical and a normal population, including 213 patients with schizophrenia or schizoaffective disorder, and 126 healthy volunteers. In this study, individuals carrying the risk haplotype had lower g-scores compared to noncarriers (Burdick et al., 2006). More recently, an independent study showed that schizophrenic patients carrying the Dysbindin risk haplotype showed significantly lower spatial working memory performance compared to patients who were nonrisk carriers, with genotype explaining 12% of variance in performance (Donohoe et al., 2007).

The *APOE* (apolipoprotein E) variant is the largest known genetic risk factor for late-onset Alzheimer's disease (AD). Carriers of two APOE isoform E4 alleles have between 10 and 30 times increased risk of developing AD by 75 years of age, as compared to those not carrying any E4 alleles (e.g., Jiang et al., 2008; Strittmatter & Roses, 1996). The *APOE* gene has also been consistently associated with specific cognitive abilities, such as memory and executive functioning (e.g., Deary et al., 2002; Savitz et al., 2006; Small et al., 2004).

## CANDIDATE GENES BASED ON ADAPTIVE EVOLUTION

Allelic variants that show continuous adaptive evolution in modern humans have been hypothesized to pose good candidate genes for intelligence. Genetic variants that were positively selected for during human evolution and have swept to high frequency under strong positive selection have been suggested to be related to increased intellectual abilities (Evans et al., 2005; Gilbert, Dobyns, & Lahn, 2005; Posthuma et al., 2002; Thompson et al., 2001; Zhang, 2003). Several studies have shown that genes controlling brain development are favored targets of natural selection during human evolution (Gilbert et al., 2005; Zhang, 2003), and it has been suggested that genes that regulate brain size during development are chief contributors in driving the evolutionary enlargement of the human brain (Gilbert et al., 2005). Humans have an exceptionally large brain relative to their body size. Compared to chimpanzees, the human brain weight is 250% greater, while the body is only 20% heavier (McHenry, 1994). During *Homo sapiens* evolution the brain size tripled over a period of approximately 2 million years, ending around 0.4 million years ago (McHenry, 1994; Wood & Collard, 1999). This brain expansion is believed to be important to the emergence of human language and other higher order cognitive functions that was archived along the human evolution (Deacon, 1992).

Several studies, using a variety of methods, provide lists of genes positively selected during *Homo sapiens* evolution (Dorus et al., 2004; Pollard et al., 2006; Sabeti et al., 2006; Voight, Kudaravalli, Wen, & Pritchard, 2006; Zhang, 2003). However, until now, none of these selected genes could be associated with variation in intelligence. Poor replication of an initially promising association result is a common concern in the molecular genetic study of complex brain functioning. This problem is illustrated by studies with two allelic variants that have been reported to show continuous adaptive evolution in modern humans, *ASPM* (Mekel-Bobrov et al., 2005)

and the microcephalin (*MCPH1*) genes (Evans et al., 2005). These genes are known to be under positive selection and to be involved in human brain volume, and they are therefore expected to pose suitable candidate genes for IQ (see, e.g., Posthuma et al., 2002; Thompson et al., 2001).

To confirm *ASPM* and *MCPH1* findings, Mekel-Bobrov and colleagues tested association of these genes with IQ in a sample of 2,393 subjects from three family-based samples (one Australian and two Dutch), as well as from the population-based Scottish Aberdeen (ABC1936) and Lothian (LBC1921) birth cohorts. If selective pressure is linked to higher IQ, we would expect to see an association between the allele that is positively selected for during evolution (i.e., the derived allele) with higher IQ. A significant association was found for *ASPM* in four of the five samples, with the nonsignificant result in the youngest (12-year-olds) sample (Mekel-Bobrov et al., 2007). However, although in two samples (Dutch adults and LBC1921) the beneficial allele was the allelic variant under selective pressure (the derived allele), in the other two samples it was the ancestral allele that was associated with higher IQ scores. For *MCPH1*, a significant positive association was seen for the derived allele in the Dutch 12-year-olds, but this effect was not replicated in any of the other samples (Mekel-Bobrov et al., 2007). These results thus remain inconclusive, and selective pressure of both *ASPM* and *MCPH1* cannot be explained by selective pressure on brain size or IQ of modern human (Woods et al., 2006).

Candidate gene studies can be performed relatively quickly and inexpensively and may allow identification of genes with relatively small effects. However, the candidate gene approach is limited by how much is already known about the biology or genomic location of the trait being investigated. Without previous knowledge, exploratory, hypothesis-free methods like genome-wide association analysis might be more suitable.

## Genome-Wide Association Analysis (Widely Used from the 2000s to the Present)

Genome-wide association (GWA) analysis allows testing for association between the trait of interest and "all" genetic variants genotyped across the entire genome.

A GWA study is hypothesis-free in the sense that it involves scanning the entire genome for genetic loci that might be associated with intelligence, rather than focusing on small, predetermined, candidate areas or genes. Plomin and coworkers

(Butcher et al., 2005, 2008; Plomin, 1999; Plomin et al., 2004) conducted several whole genome association studies (although smaller scaled, i.e., using 10,000 markers) and showed significant association of a functional polymorphism in *ALDH5A1* (aldehyde dehydrogenase 5 family) on chromosome 6p with intelligence. Recently, the same group identified three novel genes through a whole genome scan using a DNA-pooling approach for low- and high-IQ groups involved in intelligence; *DNAJC13* (DnaJ [Hsp40] homolog, subfamily C, member 13), *FADS3* (fatty acid desaturase 3), and *TBC1D7* (TBC1 domain family, member 7) (Butcher et al., 2008). The chromosome 6 linkage lies close to, but a bit further downstream of, the association that was reported in the genome-wide allelic association study by the same group in 2005 (Butcher et al., 2005). Recently, Ruano et al. (2010) used the traditional GWA strategy in a study with 627 individuals ascertained for ADHD and almost 0.5 million genetic markers, but they did not find any region significantly associated with intelligence.

GWA studies have identified a number of genetic polymorphisms that are involved in common diseases (Hindorff et al., 2009). However, by only associating genotypes with the analyzed phenotype, little can be inferred about the actual biological mechanisms underlying variation in the trait. Moreover, the effect size of genetic associations with trait variance is often small. Therefore, large samples (N > 50,000) are needed to obtain sufficient statistical power for the identification of new causal genetic variants. Several new approaches have emerged as an alternative strategy for detecting genetic variants with small effect size, such as analysis of copy number variation, pathway analysis, and functional gene group analysis.

### Copy Number Variations (Widely Used from 2005 to the Present)

Apart from searching for changes in the genetic code, recent studies have also tested the effects of structural variation such as copy number variants (CNVs) in the DNA on complex traits. American geneticist Calvin Bridges discovered CNVs in 1936, when he noticed that flies that inherit a duplicate copy of a gene called *Bar* develop very small eyes (Bridges, 1936). More than two decades later, Jérôme Lejeune identified CNV as the cause of Down syndrome (extra copy of chromosome 21) (Lejeune, Turpin, & Gautier, 1959).

CNVs are alterations in the genome that result in the cell having an abnormal number of copies of one or more sections of the DNA. CNVs correspond to relatively large regions of the genome that have been deleted or amplified on certain regions of the chromosomes (Conrad et al., 2009; Estivill & Armengol, 2007; Redon et al., 2006; Saus et al., 2010). The mechanisms by which interindividual changes in CNVs can cause variation in complex traits include an altered gene dosage (deletion or duplication) affecting the gene expression levels (Buckland, 2003; McCarroll et al., 2006; Nguyen, Webber, & Ponting, 2006; Repping et al., 2006), or effects on gene structure or regulation (Stranger et al., 2007). These genomic rearrangements can affect normal development or maintenance of the central nervous system (J. A. Lee & Lupski, 2006) and are highly heritable ($h^2$ close to 1.0) (Locke et al., 2006).

CNVs contribute substantially to disease pathogenesis (Conrad et al., 2009; Estivill & Armengol, 2007) and particularly to neurocognitive disorders like intellectual disability (ID) (Mefford et al., 2009). Mefford and colleagues (2009) screened 69 susceptible rearrangement regions in a cohort of 1,105 individuals with unexplained ID. From all tested individuals, 5.4% had pathogenic or potentially pathogenic variants, including deletions at 15q11.2 and 16p11.2, and a duplication at 16p13.11. Compared to reported CNVs in control cohorts, these deleted and duplicated regions are significantly ($p \leq .003$) enriched in children with ID, supporting the hypotheses that they are risk factors for neurocognitive illness (Mefford et al., 2009).

Recently, Moreno-De-Luca et al. described a pathogenic CNV deletion on 17q12 that confers a very high risk for autism and schizophrenia and showed that one or more of the 15 genes in the deleted interval are dosage sensitive and essential for normal brain development and function (Moreno-De-Luca et al., 2010).

These results suggest that normal cognitive function might depend on structural variation in the DNA, and variance in intelligence might be associated with genomic rearrangements. Future functional analyses need to be conducted to confirm these findings.

### Pathway and Functional Gene Group Analysis for Intelligence (2010–Present)

GWA is a successful method for identifying common genes of relatively large effect (Frayling et al., 2007; Saxena et al., 2007) but have been less effective when rare variants of large effect or genes of small effect are of importance (Maher, 2008).

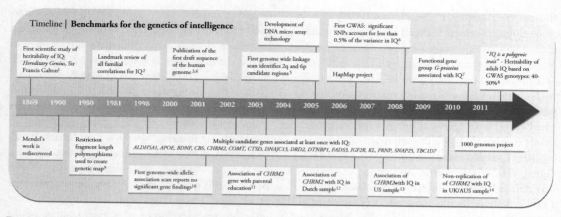

**Figure 52.2** Timeline of benchmark events for research into the genetics of human intelligence.

Most complex traits, such as IQ, are now thought to be influenced by a (large) number of rare and/or low-penetrance variations that possibly interact with environmental factors (Davies et al., 2011; Vinkhuyzen et al., 2011). It is most likely that combined effects of many loci, each making a small contribution to overall disease susceptibility, reveal insights into the genetic basis of common traits (Torkamani, Topol, & Schork, 2008). Such small effects are difficult to detect and collective testing of genes involved in biological pathways has been suggested as an alternative strategy for testing the collective effect of many genetic variants with small effect size (Holmans, 2010; Lips et al., 2011; Ruano et al., 2010; Torkamani et al., 2008). Pathways are defined as a set of proteins that participate in cascades of intracellular reactions, whereas functional gene groups are defined as a set of proteins that share a similar cellular function. Functional mutations presented in the genetic pathways or functional gene groups might lead to changes in cellular responses, gene expression, or cell morphology. Collective testing of the combined effect of these genetic variants involved in the same pathway has been shown to be more powerful than testing single gene effects (Torkamani et al., 2008).

Recently, Ruano and colleagues (Ruano et al., 2010) reported that the combined effect of the heterotrimeric guanine nucleotide–binding proteins (G proteins) genetic variants could explain 3.3% of the variance in cognitive ability. In their novel approach, 900 genes known to be expressed in the synapse were selected and organized in 23 different functional groups, and from all tested groups only the G proteins group showed association with IQ ($p$ = .00019). G proteins are signal transducers that communicate signals from many hormones,

neurotransmitters, chemokines, and autocrine and paracrine factors. Alterations in the G protein pathway might affect the properties of neuronal networks in the brain in such a manner that impaired cognition and lower intelligence result (Hurowitz et al., 2000; Neves, Ram, & Iyengar, 2002).

## Conclusion

The past decade has seen major efforts to elucidate the genetic variants underlying the high heritability of intelligence. Figure 52.2 provides a timeline of crucial events in gene finding for intelligence. The main conclusion that can be drawn is that nearly 150 years after Sir Francis Galton's observation that family members tend to be alike on intellectual capabilities, we can merely confirm that IQ is indeed heritable and that at least 40%–50% can be traced to additive genetic variation. The past century has yielded a handful of putative genes, of which perhaps the most promising (i.e., *CHRM2*) was recently refuted. It has become clear that human intelligence is influenced by multiple genes of small effect, and most likely these genes aggregate in biological pathways or functional gene groups, of which the group of genes encoding G proteins is the first to have been detected (see Fig. 52.2).

The discrepancy between the relative high trait heritability and so little success in gene finding has been observed for many other traits as well and has been called the "missing heritability" (Maher, 2008).

## Explaining the Missing Heritability of Intelligence

One possible explanation of the "missing heritability" concerns the limitations of the applied research approaches (Maher, 2008). The approaches generally employed are limited to the detection of common genetic variants with small effect, or rare variants with high penetrance (Mendelian disease). However, variation in quantitative traits like intelligence is probably due to low-frequency variants with intermediate penetrance effects (Maher, 2008; Manolio et al., 2009; McCarthy et al., 2008). Most study designs that are currently used are unfortunately not well suited to expose these.

GWAs, for example, use just a small fraction of known variants in the genome and do not take into account rare variants that might be present in the region. One possible solution would be to use deep sequencing approaches, which allow exploration of the genetic variation in the genome in a very dense way. At present, deep sequencing studies are still very costly, but this technique will certainly gain in popularity when the costs go down, which is expected to happen within the next couple of years.

GWA techniques do not necessarily include information on structural variants, such as CNVs. These stretches of DNA of tens or hundreds of base pairs long, which are deleted or duplicated between individuals, might, however, account for a considerable part of the genetic variability from person to person and could account for some of those rare mutations with moderate penetrance that GWAs cannot detect.

Another explanation of the missing heritability might be that the heritability estimates of traits like intelligence are actually overestimated. The recent study by Davies et al. (2001) provides a heritability estimate based on measured genotypes and sets the lower bound of the heritability of adult intelligence at 40%–50%. The reported higher heritability of IQ in adults (60%–80%) is derived from classical twin studies in which the phenotypic resemblance of monozygotic twins is compared to the phenotypic resemblance of dizygotic twins. Stronger resemblance between monozygotic twins is taken as evidence for the involvement of genetic factors. These classical twin studies, however, rely on a number of assumptions that may not always be correct. For example, genetic effects are assumed to be stable across different environmental conditions. However, multiple studies have shown that this is not always the case. In the context of intelligence, for instance, Vinkhuizen and colleagues (Vinkhuyzen et al., 2011) studied the heritability of intelligence across samples of subjects who were exposed to different life events. The study showed that the heritability of intelligence ranged from only 9% to above 90% across levels of positive, negative,

and neutral life events, suggesting that genetic and environmental factors influence cognitive variation differently depending on the type of life events that subjects were exposed to. These so-called gene–environment interaction (GxE) studies show that population-based estimates of heritability, that is, averaged across subgroups and various environmental conditions, can be misleading as the heritability may be higher in some subgroups and lower in others. In addition, these studies suggest that the success of genetic association studies might increase when such subgroups and the effects of environmental conditions are taken into account.

Two other assumptions underlying the classical twin design concern random mating (i.e., the phenotypes of the parents of the twins are assumed to be uncorrelated) and the absence of cultural transmission (i.e., environmental factors related to the trait of interest are not transmitted from the parental generation to the offspring). If these assumptions are violated (i.e., assortative mating and cultural transmission do in actuality affect the trait of interest) but the effects are not accommodated explicitly in heritability studies of intelligence, the result may be that effects of genetic dominance (i.e., nonadditive genetic factors) are underestimated (Fulker, 1982; Keller et al., 2009). Since gene-finding methods like GWAs generally assume the absence of genetic dominance, heritability may go missing when nonadditive genetic effects that are actually present are not sufficiently considered. Previous studies indeed suggest that these assumptions may not always hold for intelligence. Various studies have, for example, shown that mates do select each other on the basis of similar cognitive levels (Loehlin, 1978; Mascie-Taylor, 1989; C. A. Reynolds, Baker, & Pedersen, 2000). In a study using an extended family design (twins, and the siblings, children, and parents of these twins, N = 1,314), Vinkhuyzen, van der Sluis, Maes, and Posthuma (2012) showed that the pattern of phenotypic resemblance between family members other than twins did not comply with high heritability due to additive genetic effects. They reported the presence of genetic dominance effects on intelligence besides effects of assortative mating and cultural transmission, and they suggest that heritability estimates based solely on twin samples may not always provide a complete picture of the dynamics between genes and environment.

Another genetic mechanism that is not accounted for in current gene-finding studies is epigenetic inheritance, in which changes in phenotype and RNA expression are passed through from generation to generation without being accompanied by changes in the underlying DNA sequence of the organism. That is, specific changes in the environment or food intake of the first generations can affect the phenotypes of following generations without altering the DNA sequence. As a result, study designs that focus on variation in DNA sequence only will not be able to link the trait to the implicated genetic loci. Generally, animal models, in which external factors can be controlled and manipulated, are necessary to reveal epigenetic effects. A nice example is the coat-color methylation study by Cooney, Dave, and Wolff (2002), who reported that maternal dietary methyl supplements increased DNA methylation of the *agouti* gene and methylation-dependent epigenetic phenotypes in the offspring, resulting in coat colors ranging from yellow to heavily mottled, depending of the combination of the nutrients (Cooney et al., 2002; Waterland, 2003; Waterland & Jirtle, 2003).

In addition to environmental factors like food intake, gene–gene interactions (epistasis) can also influence RNA expression. That is, the expression of a certain gene can be enhanced or reduced by (several) other gene variants and, as in the previous case, the phenotype can be passed through generations even if the genetic variants that caused the effect are not (Lam, Youngren, & Nadeau, 2004). Complex genetic mechanisms like epigenetics and epistasis are practically impossible to track using relatively simple techniques such as GWAs and candidate gene studies, which usually focus on the effects of single genes (rather than studying their concerted effects) and generally make use of information collected in a single generation only. Although studies in which these complex genetic processes are implicated in intelligence are as yet lacking, it is deemed very likely that such complex genetic processes underlie variation in complex traits such as intelligence. The fact that these complex genetic processes are not well accommodated in current behavioral genetic studies could therefore well be one of the reasons that a large part of the heritability of intelligence remains as yet unexplained Future Directions

One of the primary findings of the wide range of GWA studies conducted to date is that single gene effects are usually (very) small, suggesting that most of the genes interact epistatically or work concertedly within pathways. It is, therefore, possible that the effect of one gene on the trait of interest can only be observed when the effects of other genes are taken into account. Functional pathway approaches based on cellular function might promote the identification of genes with small effect that together explain more variance in the phenotype than alone. Future efforts in gene finding for intelligence will benefit from the availability of sequence data and may also benefit from looking at the combined effect of multiple genes as opposed to testing for single SNP effects on intelligence. In addition, unraveling gene environment interaction processes seems of utmost importance. Ideally, future studies aimed at revealing the genetic basis of intelligence should combine these two lines of research by studying groups or networks of genes, including rare variants, that share the same cellular function while controlling for, or accommodating, the effects of environmental factors that induce variation in cognitive functioning.

## References

Addington, A. M., Gornick, M., Duckworth, J., Sporn, A., Gogtay, N., Bobb, A.,... Straub, R. E. (2005). GAD1 (2q31.1), which encodes glutamic acid decarboxylase (GAD67), is associated with childhood-onset schizophrenia and cortical gray matter volume loss. *Molecular Psychiatry*, *10*(6), 581–588.

Al-Gazali, L. I., Padmanabhan, R., Melnyk, S., Yi, P., Pogribny, I. P., Pogribna, M.,... James, S. J. (2001). Abnormal folate metabolism and genetic polymorphism of the folate pathway in a child with Down syndrome and neural tube defect. *American Journal of Medical Genetics*, *103*(2), 128–132.

Ando, J., Ono, Y., & Wright, M. J. (2001). Genetic structure of spatial and verbal working memory. *Behavior Genetics*, *31*(6), 615–624.

Barbaux, S., Plomin, R., & Whitehead, A. S. (2000). Polymorphisms of genes controlling homocysteine/folate metabolism and cognitive function. *Neuroreport*, *11*(5), 1133–1136.

Barrett, J. H., Sheehan, N. A., Cox, A., Worthington, J., Cannings, C., & Teare, M. D. (2007). Family based studies and genetic epidemiology: Theory and practice. *Human Heredity*, *64*(2), 146–148.

Bartels, M., Rietveld, M. J., Van Baal, G. C., & Boomsma, D. I. (2002). Genetic and environmental influences on the development of intelligence. *Behavior Genetics*, *32*(4), 237–249.

Bartzokis, G., Beckson, M., Lu, P. H., Nuechterlein, K. H., Edwards, N., & Mintz, J. (2001). Age-related changes in frontal and temporal lobe volumes in men: A magnetic resonance imaging study. *Archives of General Psychiatry*, *58*(5), 461–465.

Bateson, W. (1906). An Address on mendelian heretity and its application to man. *British Medical Journal*, *2*(2376), 61–67.

Botstein, D., White, R. L., Skolnick, M., & Davis, R. W. (1980). Construction of a genetic linkage map in man using restriction fragment length polymorphisms. *American Journal of Human Genetics*, *32*, 314–331.

Bouchard, T. J., Jr., & McGue, M. (1981). Familial studies of intelligence: A review. *Science*, *212*(4498), 1055–1059.

Bouchard, T. J., Jr., & McGue, M. (2003). Genetic and environmental influences on human psychological differences. *Journal of Neurobiology*, *54*(1), 4–45.

Bourtchouladze, R., Lidge, R., Catapano, R., Stanley, J., Gossweiler, S., Romashko, D., Tully, T . (2003). A mouse model of Rubinstein-Taybi syndrome: Defective long-term memory is ameliorated by inhibitors of phosphodiesterase 4. *Proceedings of the National Academy of Sciences USA, 100*(18), 10518–10522.

Bridges, C. (1936). The bar "gene" a duplication. *Science, 83*(2148), 210–211.

Buckland, P. R. (2003). Polymorphically duplicated genes: Their relevance to phenotypic variation in humans. *Annals of Medicine, 35*(5), 308–315.

Burdick, K. E., Lencz, T., Funke, B., Finn, C. T., Szeszko, P. R., Kane, J. M.,... Malhotra, A. K. (2006). Genetic variation in DTNBP1 influences general cognitive ability. *Human Molecular Genetics, 15*(10), 1563–1568.

Butcher, L. M., Davis, O. S., Craig, I. W., & Plomin, R. (2008). Genome-wide quantitative trait locus association scan of general cognitive ability using pooled DNA and 500K single nucleotide polymorphism microarrays. *Genes, Brain and Behavior, 7*(4), 435–446.

Butcher, L. M., Meaburn, E., Knight, J., Sham, P. C., Schalkwyk, L. C., Craig, I. W., & Plomin, R. (2005). SNPs, microarrays and pooled DNA: identification of four loci associated with mild mental impairment in a sample of 6000 children. *Human Molecular Genetics, 14*(10), 1315–1325.

Buxbaum, J. D., Silverman, J. M., Smith, C. J., Kilifarski, M., Reichert, J., Hollander, E.,... Davis, K. L . (2001). Evidence for a susceptibility gene for autism on chromosome 2 and for genetic heterogeneity. *American Journal of Human Genetics, 68*(6), 1514–1520.

Buyske, S., Bates, M. E., Gharani, N., Matise, T. C., Tischfield, J. A., & Manowitz, P. (2006). Cognitive traits link to human chromosomal regions. *Behavior Genetics, 36*(1), 65–76.

Cardon, L. R., Smith, S. D., Fulker, D. W., Kimberling, W. J., Pennington, B. F., & DeFries, J. C. (1994). Quantitative trait locus for reading disability on chromosome 6. *Science, 266*(5183), 276–279.

Caspi, A., Williams, B., Kim-Cohen, J., Craig, I. W., Milne, B. J., Poulton, R.,... Moffitt, T. E. (2007). Moderation of breastfeeding effects on the IQ by genetic variation in fatty acid metabolism. *Proceedings of the National Academy of Sciences USA, 104*(47), 18860–18865.

Chen, J., Lipska, B. K., Halim, N., Ma, Q. D., Matsumoto, M., Melhem, S.,... Weinberger, D. R. (2004). Functional analysis of genetic variation in catechol-O-methyltransferase (COMT): Effects on mRNA, protein, and enzyme activity in postmortem human brain. *American Journal of Human Genetics, 75*(5), 807–821.

Chorney, M. J., Chorney, K., Seese, N., Owen, M. J., Daniels, J., McGuffin, P.,... Plomin, R. (1998). A quantitative trait locus associated with cognitive ability in children. *Psychological Science, 9*(3), 159–166.

Comings, D. E., Wu, S., Rostamkhani, M., McGue, M., Lacono, W. G., Cheng, L. S., & MacMurray, J. P . (2003). Role of the cholinergic muscarinic 2 receptor (CHRM2) gene in cognition. *Molecular Psychiatry, 8*(1), 10–11.

Conrad, D. F., Pinto, D., Redon, R., Feuk, L., Gokcumen, O., Zhang, Y., et al. (2009). Origins and functional impact of copy number variation in the human genome. *Nature, 464*(7289), 704–712.

Cooney, C. A., Dave, A. A., & Wolff, G. L. (2002). Maternal methyl supplements in mice affect epigenetic variation and DNA methylation of offspring. *Journal of Nutrition, 132*(8 Suppl), 2393S–2400S.

Croen, L. A., Grether, J. K., & Selvin, S. (2001). The epidemiology of mental retardation of unknown cause. *Pediatrics, 107*(6), E86.

Curry, C. J., Stevenson, R. E., Aughton, D., Byrne, J., Carey, J. C., Cassidy, S.,... Opitz, J. (1997). Evaluation of mental retardation: Recommendations of a Consensus Conference: American College of Medical Genetics. *American Journal of Medical Genetics, 72*(4), 468–477.

Davies, G., Tenesa, A., Payton, A., Yang, J., Harris, S. E., Liewald, D.,... Deary, I. J. (2011). Genome-wide association studies establish that human intelligence is highly heritable and polygenic. *Molecular Psychiatry, 16*(10), 996–1005.

Deacon, T. W. (1992). *Biological aspects of language*. In J. Jones, R. Martin, & D. Pilbeam (Eds.), *The Cambridge encyclopedia of human evolution* (pp. 115–123). Cambridge: Cambridge University Press.

Deary, I. J., Harris, S. E., Fox, H. C., Hayward, C., Wright, A. F., Starr, J. M., & Whalley, L. J. (2005). KLOTHO genotype and cognitive ability in childhood and old age in the same individuals. *Neuroscience Letters, 378*(1), 22–27.

Deary, I. J., Spinath, F. M., & Bates, T. C. (2006). Genetics of intelligence. *European Journal of Human Genetics, 14*(6), 690–700.

Deary, I. J., Whiteman, M. C., Pattie, A., Starr, J. M., Hayward, C., Wright, A. F.,... Whalley, L. J. (2002). Cognitive change and the APOE epsilon 4 allele. *Nature, 418*(6901), 932.

Dick, D. M., Aliev, F., Bierut, L., Goate, A., Rice, J., Hinrichs, A.,... Hesselbrock, V. (2006). Linkage analyses of IQ in the collaborative study on the genetics of alcoholism (COGA) sample. *Behavior Genetics, 36*(1), 77–86.

Dick, D. M., Aliev, F., Kramer, J., Wang, J. C., Hinrichs, A., Bertelsen, S.,... Bierut, L. (2007). Association of CHRM2 with IQ: Converging evidence for a gene influencing intelligence. *Behavior Genetics, 37*(2), 265–272.

Donohoe, G., Morris, D. W., Clarke, S., McGhee, K. A., Schwaiger, S., Nangle, J. M., ... Corvin, A. (2007). Variance in neurocognitive performance is associated with dysbindin-1 in schizophrenia: A preliminary study. *Neuropsychologia, 45*(2), 454–458.

Dorus, S., Vallender, E. J., Evans, P. D., Anderson, J. R., Gilbert, S. L., Mahowald, M.,... Lahn, B. T. (2004). Accelerated evolution of nervous system genes in the origin of Homo sapiens. *Cell, 119*(7), 1027–1040.

Dudai, Y., Jan, Y. N., Byers, D., Quinn, W. G., & Benzer, S. (1976). Dunce, a mutant of Drosophila deficient in learning. *Proceedings of the National Academy of Sciences USA, 73*(5), 1684–1688.

1000 Genomes Project Consortium. (2010). A map of human genome variation from population-scale sequencing. *Nature, 467*(7319), 1061–1073.

Estivill, X., & Armengol, L. (2007). Copy number variants and common disorders: Filling the gaps and exploring complexity in genome-wide association studies. *PLoS Genetics, 3*(10), 1787–1799.

Evans, P. D., Gilbert, S. L., Mekel-Bobrov, N., Vallender, E. J., Anderson, J. R., Vaez-Azizi, L. M.,... Lahn, B. T. (2005). Microcephalin, a gene regulating brain size, continues to evolve adaptively in humans. *Science, 309*(5741), 1717–1720.

Fagerheim, T., Raeymaekers, P., Tonnessen, F. E., Pedersen, M., Tranebjaerg, L., & Lubs, H. A. (1999). A new gene (DYX3) for dyslexia is located on chromosome 2. *Journal of Medical Genetics, 36*(9), 664–669.

Fisher, S. E., Stein, J. F., & Monaco, A. P. (1999). A genome-wide search strategy for identifying quantitative trait loci involved in reading and spelling disability (developmental dyslexia). *European Child and Adolescent Psychiatry, 8*(Suppl. 3), 47–51.

Frayling, T. M., Timpson, N. J., Weedon, M. N., Zeggini, E., Freathy, R. M., Lindgren, C. M., McCarthy, M. I. (2007). A common variant in the FTO gene is associated with body mass index and predisposes to childhood and adult obesity. *Science, 316*(5826), 889–894.

Frisch, A., Laufer, N., Danziger, Y., Michaelovsky, E., Leor, S., Carel, C.,... Weizman, A. (2001). Association of anorexia nervosa with the high activity allele of the COMT gene: A family-based study in Israeli patients. *Molecular Psychiatry, 6*(2), 243–245.

Fulker, D. W. (1982). Extensions of the classical twin method. *Progress in Clinical and Biological Research, 103*(Pt. A), 395–406.

Galton, F. (1869). *Hereditary genius: An inquiry into its laws and consequences* (Vol. 27). London: Macmillan.

Gilbert, S. L., Dobyns, W. B., & Lahn, B. T. (2005). Genetic links between brain development and brain evolution. *Nature Reviews Genetics, 6*(7), 581–590.

Gogos, J. A., Morgan, M., Luine, V., Santha, M., Ogawa, S., Pfaff, D., & Karayiorgou, M. (1998). Catechol-O-methyltransferase-deficient mice exhibit sexually dimorphic changes in catecholamine levels and behavior. *Proceedings of the National Academy of Sciences USA, 95*(17), 9991–9996.

Gosso, M. F., van Belzen, M., de Geus, E. J., Polderman, J. C., Heutink, P.,... Posthuma, D. (2006). Association between the CHRM2 gene and intelligence in a sample of 304 Dutch families. *Genes, Brain and Behavior, 5*(8), 577–584.

Gosso, M. F., de Geus, E. J., Polderman, T. J., Boomsma, D. I., Heutink, P., & Posthuma, D. (2008a). Catechol O-methyl transferase and dopamine D2 receptor gene polymorphisms: Evidence of positive heterosis and gene-gene interaction on working memory functioning. *European Journal of Human Genetics, 16*(9), 1075–1082.

Gosso, M. F., de Geus, E. J., Polderman, T. J., Boomsma, D. I., Heutink, P., & Posthuma, D. (2008b). Common variants underlying cognitive ability: Further evidence for association between the SNAP-25 gene and cognition using a family-based study in two independent Dutch cohorts. *Genes, Brain and Behavior, 7*(3), 355–364.

Gosso, M. F., de Geus, E. J., van Belzen, M. J., Polderman, T. J., Heutink, P., Boomsma, D. I., & Posthuma, D. (2006). The SNAP-25 gene is associated with cognitive ability: Evidence from a family-based study in two independent Dutch cohorts. *Molecular Psychiatry, 11*(9), 878–886.

Gottfredson, L. S. (1997). Mainstream science on intelligence: An editorial with 52 signatories, history, and bibliography (Reprinted from The Wall Street Journal, 1994). *Intelligence, 24*(1), 13–23.

Grigorenko, E. L., Wood, F. B., Meyer, M. S., Hart, L. A., Speed, W. C., Shuster, A., & Pauls, D. L. (1997). Susceptibility loci for distinct components of developmental dyslexia on chromosomes 6 and 15. *American Journal of Human Genetics, 60*(1), 27–39.

Guzowski, J. F., & McGaugh, J. L. (1997). Antisense oligodeoxynucleotide-mediated disruption of hippocampal cAMP response element binding protein levels impairs

consolidation of memory for water maze training. *Proceedings of the National Academy of Sciences USA, 94*(6), 2693–2698.

Harris, L. W., Lockstone, H. E., Khaitovich, P., Weickert, C. S., Webster, M. J., & Bahn, S. (2009). Gene expression in the prefrontal cortex during adolescence: Implications for the onset of schizophrenia. *BMC Med Genomics, 2*, 28.

Harris, S. E., Fox, H., Wright, A. F., Hayward, C., Starr, J. M., Whalley, L. J., & Deary, I. J. (2006). The brain-derived neurotrophic factor Val66Met polymorphism is associated with age-related change in reasoning skills. *Molecular Psychiatry, 11*(5), 505–513.

Herrnstein, J., & Murray, C. (1994). *Bell curve: Intelligence and class structure in American life.* New York: Free Press.

Hindorff, L. A., Sethupathy, P., Junkins, H. A., Ramos, E. M., Mehta, J. P., Collins, F. S., & Manolio, T. A. (2009). Potential etiologic and functional implications of genome-wide association loci for human diseases and traits. *Proceedings of the National Academy of Sciences USA, 106*(23), 9362–9367.

Holmans, P. (2010). Statistical methods for pathway analysis of genome-wide data for association with complex genetic traits. *Advances in Genetics, 72*, 141–179.

Hurowitz, E. H., Melnyk, J. M., Chen, Y. J., Kouros-Mehr, H., Simon, M. I., & Shizuya, H. (2000). Genomic characterization of the human heterotrimeric G protein alpha, beta, and gamma subunit genes. *DNA Research, 7*(2), 111–120.

Hynd, M. R., Scott, H. L., & Dodd, P. R. (2004). Differential expression of N-methyl-D-aspartate receptor NR2 isoforms in Alzheimer's disease. *J Neurochem, 90*(4), 913–919.

IMGSAC. (2001). A genomewide screen for autism: strong evidence for linkage to chromosomes 2q, 7q, and 16p. *American Journal of Human Genetics, 69*(3), 570–581.

Inlow, J. K., & Restifo, L. L. (2004). Molecular and comparative genetics of mental retardation. *Genetics, 166*(2), 835–881.

Innis, S. M. (2007). Dietary (n-3) fatty acids and brain development. *Journal of Nutrition, 137*(4), 855–859.

International Human Genome Sequencing Consortium. (2001). Initial sequencing and analysis of the human genome, *409*(6822), 860–921.

Jiang, H., & Jia, J. (2009). Association between NR2B subunit gene (GRIN2B) promoter polymorphisms and sporadic Alzheimer's disease in the North Chinese population. *Neuroscience Letters, 450*(3), 356–360.

Jiang, Q., Lee, C. Y., Mandrekar, S., Wilkinson, B., Cramer, P., Zelcer, N.,... Landreth, G. E. (2008). ApoE promotes the proteolytic degradation of Abeta. *Neuron, 58*(5), 681–693.

Kachiwala, S. J., Harris, S. E., Wright, A. F., Hayward, C., Starr, J. M., Whalley, L. J., & Deary, I. J. (2005). Genetic influences on oxidative stress and their association with normal cognitive ageing. *Neuroscience Letters, 386*(2), 116–120.

Kaminen, N., Hannula-Jouppi, K., Kestila, M., Lahermo, P., Muller, K., Kaaranen, M.,... Kere, J. (2003). A genome scan for developmental dyslexia confirms linkage to chromosome 2p11 and suggests a new locus on 7q32. *Journal of Medical Genetics, 40*(5), 340–345.

Karayiorgou, M., Altemus, M., Galke, B. L., Goldman, D., Murphy, D. L., Ott, J., & Gogos, J. A. (1997). Genotype determining low catechol-O-methyltransferase activity as a risk factor for obsessive-compulsive disorder. *Proceedings of the National Academy of Sciences USA, 94*(9), 4572–4575.

Karayiorgou, M., Sobin, C., Blundell, M. L., Galke, B. L., Malinova, L., Goldberg, P.,... Gogos, J. A. (1999). Family-based association studies support a sexually dimorphic effect of COMT and MAOA on genetic susceptibility to obsessive-compulsive disorder. *Biological Psychiatry, 45*(9), 1178–1189.

Keller, M. C., Medland, S. E., Duncan, L. E., Hatemi, P. K., Neale, M. C., Maes, H. H., & Eaves, L. J. (2009). Modeling extended twin family data I: Description of the Cascade model. *Twin Research and Human Genetics, 12*(1), 8–18.

Lam, M. Y., Youngren, K. K., & Nadeau, J. H. (2004). Enhancers and suppressors of testicular cancer susceptibility in single- and double-mutant mice. *Genetics, 166*(2), 925–933.

Lee, J. A., & Lupski, J. R. (2006). Genomic rearrangements and gene copy-number alterations as a cause of nervous system disorders. *Neuron, 52*(1), 103–121.

Lee, S. G., Joo, Y., Kim, B., Chung, S., Kim, H. L., Lee, I., . . . Song, K. (2005). Association of Ala72Ser polymorphism with COMT enzyme activity and the risk of schizophrenia in Koreans. *Hum Genet, 116*(4), 319–328.

Lejeune, J., Turpin, R., & Gautier, M. (1959). Le mongolisme premier exemple daberration autosomique humaine. Annales de Genetique, 1, 41–49.

Li, W., Zhang, Q., Oiso, N., Novak, E. K., Gautam, R., O'Brien, E. P., . . . Swank, R. T. (2003). Hermansky-Pudlak syndrome type 7 (HPS-7) results from mutant dysbindin, a member of the biogenesis of lysosome-related organelles complex 1 (BLOC-1). *Nature Genetics, 35*(1), 84–89.

Lind, P. A., Luciano, M., Horan, M. A., Marioni, R. E., Wright, M. J., Bates, T. C., . . . Martin, N. G. (2009). No association between Cholinergic Muscarinic Receptor 2 (CHRM2) genetic variation and cognitive abilities in three independent samples. Behavior Genetics, 39, 513–523.

Lips, E. S., Cornelisse, L. N., Toonen, R. F., Min, J. L., Hultman, C. M., Holmans, P. A., . . . Posthuma, D. (2011). Functional gene group analysis identifies synaptic gene groups as risk factor for schizophrenia. *Molecular Psychiatry.* doi: 10.1038/mp.2011.117.

Locke, D. P., Sharp, A. J., McCarroll, S. A., McGrath, S. D., Newman, T. L., Cheng, Z., . . . Eichler, E. (2006). Linkage disequilibrium and heritability of copy-number polymorphisms within duplicated regions of the human genome. *American Journal of Human Genetics, 79*(2), 275–290.

Loehlin, J. C. (1978). Heredity-environment analyses of Jencks's IQ correlations. *Behavior Genetics, 8*(5), 415–436.

Luciano, M., Wright, M. J., Duffy, D. L., Wainwright, M. A., Zhu, G., Evans, D. M., . . . Martin, N. G. (2006). Genome-wide scan of IQ finds significant linkage to a quantitative trait locus on 2q. *Behavior Genetics, 36*(1), 45–55.

Maher, B. (2008). Personal genomes: The case of the missing heritability. *Nature, 456*(7218), 18–21.

Manolio, T. A., Collins, F. S., Cox, N. J., Goldstein, D. B., Hindorff, L. A., Hunter, D. J., . . . Visscher, P. M. (2009). Finding the missing heritability of complex diseases. *Nature, 461*(7265), 747–753.

Martin, N. W., Benyamin, B., Hansell, N. K., Montgomery, G. W., Martin, N. G., Wright, M. J., & Bates, T. C. (2011). Cognitive function in adolescence: Testing for interactions between breast-feeding and FADS2 polymorphisms. *Journal of the American Academy of Child and Adolescent Psychiatry, 50*(1), 55–62 e54.

Mascie-Taylor, C. G. (1989). Spouse similarity for IQ and personality and convergence. *Behavior Genetics, 19*(2), 223–227.

Mathew, C. G. (1999). DNA diagnostics: Goals and challenges. *British Medical Bulletin, 55*(2), 325–339.

McCarroll, S. A., Hadnott, T. N., Perry, G. H., Sabeti, P. C., Zody, M. C., Barrett, J. C., . . . International HapMap Consortium. (2006). Common deletion polymorphisms in the human genome. *Nature Genetics, 38*(1), 86–92.

McCarthy, M. I., Abecasis, G. R., Cardon, L. R., Goldstein, D. B., Little, J., Ioannidis, J. P., & Hirschorn, J. N. (2008). Genome-wide association studies for complex traits: Consensus, uncertainty and challenges. *Nature Reviews Genetics, 9*(5), 356–369.

McGuffin, P., Riley, B., & Plomin, R. (2001). Genomics and behavior. Toward behavioral genomics. *Science, 291*(5507), 1232–1249.

McHenry, H. M. (1994). Tempo and mode in human evolution. *Proceedings of the National Academy of Sciences USA, 91*(15), 6780–6786.

Mefford, H. C., Cooper, G. M., Zerr, T., Smith, J. D., Baker, C., Shafer, N., . . . Eichler, E. E. (2009). A method for rapid, targeted CNV genotyping identifies rare variants associated with neurocognitive disease. *Genome Research, 19*(9), 1579–1585.

Mekel-Bobrov, N., Gilbert, S. L., Evans, P. D., Vallender, E. J., Anderson, J. R., Hudson, R. R., . . . Lahn, B. T. (2005). Ongoing adaptive evolution of ASPM, a brain size determinant in Homo sapiens. *Science, 309*(5741), 1720–1722.

Mekel-Bobrov, N., Posthuma, D., Gilbert, S. L., Lind, P., Gosso, M. F., Luciano, M., . . . Lahn, B. T. (2007). The ongoing adaptive evolution of ASPM and microcephalin is not explained by increased intelligence. *Human Molecular Genetics, 16*(6), 600–608.

Moreno-De-Luca, D., Mulle, J. G., Kaminsky, E. B., Sanders, S. J., Myers, S. M., Adam, M. P., . . . Ledbetter, D. H. (2010). Deletion 17q12 is a recurrent copy number variant that confers high risk of autism and schizophrenia. *American Journal of Human Genetics, 87*(5), 618–630.

Muldoon, M. F., Ryan, C. M., Sheu, L., Yao, J. K., Conklin, S. M., & Manuck, S. B. (2010). Serum phospholipid docosahexaenonic acid is associated with cognitive functioning during middle adulthood. *Journal of Nutrition, 140*(4), 848–853.

Nackley, A. G., Tan, K. S., Fecho, K., Flood, P., Diatchenko, L., & Maixner, W. (2007). Catechol-O-methyltransferase inhibition increases pain sensitivity through activation of both beta2- and beta3-adrenergic receptors. *Pain, 128*(3), 199–208.

Neves, S. R., Ram, P. T., & Iyengar, R. (2002). G protein pathways. *Science, 296*(5573), 1636–1639.

Nguyen, D. Q., Webber, C., & Ponting, C. P. (2006). Bias of selection on human copy-number variants. *PLoS Genet, 2*(2), e20.

Payton, A., Holland, F., Diggle, P., Rabbitt, P., Horan, M., Davidson, Y., . . . Pendelton, N. (2003). Cathepsin D exon 2 polymorphism associated with general intelligence in a healthy older population. *Molecular Psychiatry, 8*(1), 14–18.

Petrij, F., Giles, R. H., Dauwerse, H. G., Saris, J. J., Hennekam, R. C., Masuno, M., . . . Peters, D. J. (1995). Rubinstein-Taybi syndrome caused by mutations in the transcriptional co-activator CBP. *Nature, 376*(6538), 348–351.

Plomin, R. (1986). *Development, genetics, and psychology.* Hillsdale, NJ: Erlbaum.

Plomin, R. (1990). The role of inheritance in behavior. *Science, 248*(4952), 183–188.

Plomin, R. (1999). Genetics and general cognitive ability. *Nature, 402*(6761 Suppl.), C25–C29.

Plomin, R., Hill, L., Craig, I. W., McGuffin, P., Purcell, S., Sham, P.,... Owen, M. J. (2001) A genome-wide scan of 1842 DNA markers for allelic associations with general cognitive ability: a five-stage design using DNA pooling and extreme selected groups. *Behavior Genetics, 31*, 497–509.

Plomin, R., & Kovas, Y. (2005). Generalist genes and learning disabilities. *Psychological Bulletin, 131*(4), 592–617.

Plomin, R., Owen, M. J., & McGuffin, P. (1994). The genetic basis of complex human behaviors. *Science, 264*(5166), 1733–1739.

Plomin, R., Turic, D. M., Hill, L., Turic, D. E., Stephens, M., Williams, J.,... O'Donovan, M. C. (2004). A functional polymorphism in the succinate-semialdehyde dehydrogenase (aldehyde dehydrogenase 5 family, member A1) gene is associated with cognitive ability. *Molecular Psychiatry, 9*(6), 582–586.

Pollard, K. S., Salama, S. R., Lambert, N., Lambot, M. A., Coppens, S., Pedersen, J. S.,... Haussler, D. (2006). An RNA gene expressed during cortical development evolved rapidly in humans. *Nature, 443*(7108), 167–172.

Posthuma, D., De Geus, E. J., Baare, W. F., Hulshoff Pol, H. E., Kahn, R. S., & Boomsma, D. I. (2002). The association between brain volume and intelligence is of genetic origin. *Nature Neuroscience, 5*(2), 83–84.

Posthuma, D., de Geus, E. J., & Boomsma, D. I. (2001). Perceptual speed and IQ are associated through common genetic factors. *Behavior Genetics, 31*(6), 593–602.

Posthuma, D., Luciano, M., Geus, E. J., Wright, M. J., Slagboom, P. E., Montgomery, G. W.,... Martin, N. G. (2005). A genomewide scan for intelligence identifies quantitative trait loci on 2q and 6p. *American Journal of Human Genetics, 77*(2), 318–326.

Posthuma, D., Neale, M. C., Boomsma, D. I., & de Geus, E. J. (2001). Are smarter brains running faster? Heritability of alpha peak frequency, IQ, and their interrelation. *Behavior Genetics, 31*(6), 567–579.

Punnett, R. C. (1908). Mendelism in relation to disease. *Proceedings of the Royal Society of Medicine, 1*(Sect Epidemiol State Med), 135–168.

Qian, Q.-J., Yang, L., Wang, Y.-F., Zhang, H.-B., Guan, L.-L., Chen, Y.,... Faraone, S. (2009) Gene–Gene Interaction Between COMT and MAOA Potentially Predicts the Intelligence of Attention-Deficit Hyperactivity Disorder Boys in China. *Behavior Genetics, 40*, 357–365.

Ramakers, G. J. (2002). Rho proteins, mental retardation and the cellular basis of cognition. *Trends in Neuroscience, 25*(4), 191–199.

Redon, R., Ishikawa, S., Fitch, K. R., Feuk, L., Perry, G. H., Andrews, T. D., ... Hurles, M. E. (2006). Global variation in copy number in the human genome. *Nature, 444*(7118), 444–454.

Repping, S., van Daalen, S. K., Brown, L. G., Korver, C. M., Lange, J., Marszalek, J. D., Rozen, S. (2006). High mutation rates have driven extensive structural polymorphism among human Y chromosomes. *Nature Genetics, 38*(4), 463–467.

Reynolds, C. A., Baker, L. A., & Pedersen, N. L. (2000). Multivariate models of mixed assortment: Phenotypic assortment and social homogamy for education and fluid ability. *Behavior Genetics, 30*(6), 455–476.

Reynolds, C. R., Chastain, R. L., Kaufman, A. S., & McLean, J. E. (1987). Demographic characteristics and IQ among adults: Analysis of the WAIS-R standardization sample as a function of the stratification variables. *Journal of School Psychology, 25*(4), 323–342.

Rice, D., & Barone, S., Jr. (2000). Critical periods of vulnerability for the developing nervous system: Evidence from humans and animal models. *Environmental Health Perspectives, 108*(Suppl 3), 511–533.

Rizzi, T. S., Arias-Vasquez, A., Rommelse, N., Kuntsi, J., Anney, R., Asherson, P.,... Posthuma, D. (2011). The ATXN1 and TRIM31 genes are related to intelligence in an ADHD background: Evidence from a large collaborative study totaling 4,963 subjects. *American Journal of Medical Genetics B: Neuropsychiatric Genetics, 156*(2), 145–157.

Roeleveld, N., Zielhuis, G. A., & Gabreels, F. (1997). The prevalence of mental retardation: A critical review of recent literature. *Developmental and Medical Child Neurology, 39*(2), 125–132.

Ruano, D., Abecasis, G. R., Glaser, B., Lips, E. S., Cornelisse, L. N., de Jong, A. P.,... Posthuma, D. (2010). Functional gene group analysis reveals a role of synaptic heterotrimeric G proteins in cognitive ability. *American Journal of Human Genetics, 86*(2), 113–125.

Sabeti, P. C., Schaffner, S. F., Fry, B., Lohmueller, J., Varilly, P., Shamovsky, O.,... Lander, E. S. (2006). Positive natural selection in the human lineage. *Science, 312*(5780), 1614–1620.

Saus, E., Brunet, A., Armengol, L., Alonso, P., Crespo, J. M., Fernandez-Aranda, F.,... Estevill, X. (2010). Comprehensive copy number variant (CNV) analysis of neuronal pathways genes in psychiatric disorders identifies rare variants within patients. *Journal of Psychiatric Research, 44*(14), 971–978.

Savitz, J., Solms, M., & Ramesar, R. (2006). The molecular genetics of cognition: Dopamine, COMT and BDNF. *Genes, Brain and Behavior, 5*(4), 311–328.

Saxena, R., Voight, B. F., Lyssenko, V., Burtt, N. P., de Bakker, P. I., Chen, H.,... Purcell, S. (2007). Genome-wide association analysis identifies loci for type 2 diabetes and triglyceride levels. *Science, 316*(5829), 1331–1336.

Shifman, S., Bronstein, M., Sternfeld, M., Pisante-Shalom, A., Lev-Lehman, E., Weizman, A.,... Darvasi, A. (2002). A highly significant association between a COMT haplotype and schizophrenia. *American Journal of Human Genetics, 71*(6), 1296–1302.

Small, B. J., Rosnick, C. B., Fratiglioni, L., & Backman, L. (2004). Apolipoprotein E and cognitive performance: A meta-analysis. *Psychology of Aging, 19*(4), 592–600.

Spearman, C. (1904). "General intelligence" objectively determined and measured. *American Journal of Psychology, 15*, 201–293.

Stranger, B. E., Forrest, M. S., Dunning, M., Ingle, C. E., Beazley, C., Thorne, N.,... Dermitzakis, E. T. (2007). Relative impact of nucleotide and copy number variation on gene expression phenotypes. *Science, 315*(5813), 848–853.

Straub, R. E., Jiang, Y., MacLean, C. J., Ma, Y., Webb, B. T., Myakishev, M. V., ... Kendler, K. S. (2002). Genetic variation in the 6p22.3 gene DTNBP1, the human ortholog of the mouse dysbindin gene, is associated with schizophrenia. *American Journal of Human Genetics, 71*(2), 337–348.

Strittmatter, W. J., & Roses, A. D. (1996). Apolipoprotein E and Alzheimer's disease. *Annual Review of Neuroscience, 19*, 53–77.

Sweet, R. A., Devlin, B., Pollock, B. G., Sukonick, D. L., Kastango, K. B., Bacanu, S. A., ... Ferrell, R. E. (2005). Catechol-O-methyltransferase haplotypes are associated with psychosis in Alzheimer disease. *Molecular Psychiatry, 10*(11), 1026–1036.

Tang, Y. P., Shimizu, E., Dube, G. R., Rampon, C., Kerchner, G. A., Zhuo, M.,... Tsien, J. Z. (1999). Genetic enhancement of learning and memory in mice. *Nature, 401*(6748), 63–69.

Thompson, P. M., Cannon, T. D., Narr, K. L., van Erp, T., Poutanen, V. P., Huttunen, M.,... Toga, A. W. (2001). Genetic influences on brain structure. *Nature Neuroscience, 4*(12), 1253–1258.

Thurstone, L. L. (1948). Primary mental abilities. Science, 108, 585.

Thurstone, L. L. (1947). The calibration of test items. *American Psychologist, 2*(3), 103.

Torkamani, A., Topol, E. J., & Schork, N. J. (2008). Pathway analysis of seven common diseases assessed by genome-wide association. *Genomics, 92*(5), 265–272.

Tsai, S. J., Hong, C. J., Yu, Y. W., & Chen, T. J. (2004). Association study of a brain-derived neurotrophic factor (BDNF) Val66Met polymorphism and personality trait and intelligence in healthy young females. *Neuropsychobiology, 49*(1), 13–16.

Tully, T. (1997). Regulation of gene expression and its role in long-term memory and synaptic plasticity. *Proceedings of the National Academy of Sciences USA, 94*(9), 4239–4241.

van den Oord, E. J., Sullivan, P. F., Jiang, Y., Walsh, D., O'Neill, F. A., Kendler, K. S., & Riley, B. P. (2003). Identification of a high-risk haplotype for the dystrobrevin binding protein 1 (DTNBP1) gene in the Irish study of high-density schizophrenia families. *Molecular Psychiatry, 8*(5), 499–510.

Venter, J. C., Adams, M. D., Myers, E. W., Li, P. W., Mural, R. J., Sutton, G. G.,... Zhu, X. (2001). The sequence of the human genome. *Science, 291*(5507), 1304–1351.

Vinkhuyzen, A. A., van der Sluis, S., Maes, H. H. M., & Posthuma, D. (2012). Reconsidering the heritability of intelligence in adulthood: Taking assortative mating and cultural transmission into account. *Behavior Genetics, 42*(2), 187–198.

Vinkhuyzen, A. A., van der Sluis, S., & Posthuma, D. (2011). Life events moderate variation in cognitive ability (g) in adults. *Molecular Psychiatry, 16*(1), 4–6.

Visscher, P. M. (2008). Sizing up human height variation. *Nature Genetics, 40*(5), 489–490.

Voight, B. F., Kudaravalli, S., Wen, X., & Pritchard, J. K. (2006). A map of recent positive selection in the human genome. *PLoS Biol, 4*(3), e72.

Wainwright, M. A., Wright, M. J., Luciano, M., Montgomery, G. W., Geffen, G. M., & Martin, N. G. (2006). A linkage study of academic skills defined by the Queensland core skills test. *Behavior Genetics, 36*(1), 56–64.

Walker, F. O. (2007). Huntington's disease. *Lancet, 369*(9557), 218–228.

Waterland, R. A. (2003). Do maternal methyl supplements in mice affect DNA methylation of offspring? *Journal of Nutrition, 133*(1), 238; author reply 239.

Waterland, R. A., & Jirtle, R. L. (2003). Transposable elements: Targets for early nutritional effects on epigenetic gene regulation. *Molecular Cell Biology, 23*(15), 5293–5300.

Wechsler, D. (1991). *Examiner's manual, Wechsler intelligence scale for children.* New York: Psychological Corporation.

Wechsler, D. (1997). *WAIS-III Wechsler Adult Intelligence Scale.* San Antonio, TX: Psychological Corporation.

Williamson, R. (1988). The molecular genetics of complex inherited diseases. *British Journal Cancer Suppl., 9,* 14–16.

Wood, B., & Collard, M. (1999). The human genus. *Science, 284*(5411), 65–71.

Woods, R. P., Freimer, N. B., De Young, J. A., Fears, S. C., Sicotte, N. L., Service, S. K.,... Mazziotta, J. C. (2006). Normal variants of Microcephalin and ASPM do not account for brain size variability. *Human Molecular Genetics, 15*(12), 2025–2029.

Ylisaukko-Oja, T., Peyrard-Janvid, M., Lindgren, C. M., Rehnstrom, K., Vanhala, R., Peltonen, L.,... Kere, J. (2005). Family-based association study of DYX1C1 variants in autism. *European Journal of Human Genetics, 13*(1), 127–130.

Zhang, J. (2003). Evolution of the human ASPM gene, a major determinant of brain size. *Genetics, 165*(4), 2063–2070.

# Cognitive Style

Maria Kozhevnikov

**Abstract**

This chapter will review research on cognitive style from different traditions in order to revaluate previous and existing theoretical conceptions of cognitive style and to redefine cognitive style in accordance with current cognitive science and neuroscience theories. First, this chapter will review conventional and applied research on cognitive style that introduces the concept of cognitive style as patterns of adaptation to the external world and demonstrate that, although cognitive style develops on the basis of innate abilities, it is modified further as a result of changing environmental demands. Next, we will review the latest trends in cognitive style research that integrate different style dimensions into unifying models as well as recent findings in transcultural neuroscience that have documented the existence of culturally sensitive individual differences in cognition and suggested a close relationship between sociocultural environment and specific neural and cognitive patterns of information processing. Finally, based on our review, we will redefine cognitive style as ontogenetically flexible individual differences representing an individual's adaptation of innate predisposition to external physical and sociocultural environments and expressing themselves as environmentally and culturally sensitive neural and/or cognitive patterns of information processing.

**Key Words:** cognitive style, individual differences, information processing, neural mechanisms, sociocultural environment, innate predispositions

Historically, the term "cognitive style" refers to consistencies in an individual's manner of cognitive functioning, particularly in acquiring and processing information (Ausburn & Ausburn, 1978). Messick (1976) defines cognitive styles as stable attitudes, preferences, or habitual strategies that determine individuals' modes of perception, memory, thought, and problem solving. Witkin, Moore, Goodenough, and Cox (1977) characterize cognitive style as individual differences in the way people perceive, think, solve problems, learn, and relate to others.

While it seems obvious that there are differences among individuals' preferred ways of processing information, what these differences mean and how they might be captured is less apparent. Despite

being extremely popular throughout the 1950s–1970s, research on cognitive style has lost much of its appeal and has been seriously questioned in recent decades, and currently, many cognitive scientists are on the verge of accepting that cognitive style research has reached a standstill. The main reasons for this decline of interest in cognitive style seem to be the lack of a coherent organizing framework, and the lack of understanding of how cognitive style maps onto other psychological concepts and theories (see Kozhevnikov, 2007, for a review). According to its definition, cognitive style should refer to the way individuals process information; however, since the vast majority of cognitive style studies were conducted before the rise of cognitive science, the concept of cognitive style has not been integrated with contemporary cognitive science theories, and the relationship between cognitive style's and cognitive psychology's approaches to individual differences in cognition has not been established (Kozhevnikov, 2007, for a review).

Cognitive psychologists and neuroscientists researching individual differences in cognitive functioning have often focused on such basic dimensions of individual differences as speed of processing, working memory capacity (WMC), and general fluid intelligence (*Gf*). Overall, these reflect *stationary* individual differences in cognition, in the sense that these individual differences are largely genetically predetermined (Ando, Ono, & Wright, 2001; Deary, Penke, & Johnson, 2010; Friedman et al., 2008) and exhibit only limited ontogenetic sensitivity and training-induced plasticity (e.g., Sayala, Sala, & Courtney, 2005). Cognitive style researchers, in contrast, originally introduced the concept of cognitive style as specific modes of adjustment to the external world (Klein, 1951; Witkin, Dyk, Faterson, Goodenough, & Karp, 1962) modifiable by sociocultural and life experiences, and they have been primarily interested in more *flexible*, ontogenetically malleable individual differences that are shaped as a result of physical and sociocultural influences.

The goal of the current chapter is to incorporate the concept of cognitive style into current cognitive science theories of individual differences by integrating research findings on individual differences in cognition and cognitive styles from three different research perspectives: (1) cognitive style, (2) cognitive psychology and neuroscience, and (3) transcultural psychology and neuroscience. First, this chapter will review conventional research on cognitive style that introduces the concept of cognitive style *as patterns of adaptation* or specific modes of adjustment to the external world. Next, the chapter will review cognitive style research in applied fields (education, management) demonstrating that, although cognitive style develops on the basis of innate abilities, it is modified further as a result of changing environmental demands and life experiences, and it must thus be thought of not only in terms of innate predispositions but as a *flexible* construct, in terms of sociocultural interactions regulating an individual's behavior. Third, we will summarize the latest trends in cognitive style research that have attempted to integrate the variety of cognitive style dimensions into unifying hierarchical models, and we relate these models to information processing theories. Fourth, we will review recent findings in transcultural psychology and neuroscience that have documented the existence of culturally sensitive individual differences in cognition and suggested a close relationship between sociocultural environment and specific neural and cognitive patterns of information processing.

Finally, based on our review, we will suggest a dissociation between (1) *stationary individual differences* that are determined primarily by genetic factors and exhibit only limited sensitivity to ontogenetic (environmental and sociocultural) factors; and (2) *flexible individual differences* or *cognitive styles*, whose formation, although affected by genetic factors, is largely influenced by environmental and sociocultural factors during ontogenetic development. According to the aforementioned approach, we will redefine the concept of cognitive style as *ontogenetically flexible individual differences representing an individual's adaptation of innate predisposition to external physical and sociocultural environments and expressing themselves as environmentally and culturally sensitive neural and/or cognitive patterns of information processing.*

## "Conventional" Cognitive Style

"Conventional" cognitive style research began in the late 1940s, with experimental research (e.g., Hanfmann, 1941; Klein, 1951; Klein & Schlesinger, 1951; Witkin & Ash, 1948) that focused on identifying the existence of consistent individual differences in performance on lower order cognitive tasks (e.g., perception, simple categorization). For example, Hanfmann (1941) identified two groups of individuals: those who preferred a perceptual approach when grouping blocks, and others who preferred a more conceptual approach. Klein (1951) identified "sharpeners," who tended to notice differences between visual stimuli, and "levelers," who tended to notice similarities.

These individual differences were first conceptualized as cognitive styles in the early 1950s, with Klein (1951) terming them as "perceptual attitudes." These perceptual attitudes were defined as *patterns of adaptation to the external world* that regulate an individual's cognitive functioning. According to Klein, adaptation requires balancing one's inner needs with the requirements of the external environment. Klein also reported a relationship between cognitive style and personality; levelers exhibited a "self-inwardness" pattern characterized by "a retreat from objects, avoidance of competition," while sharpeners were more manipulative and active (Klein, 1951, p. 339). Klein considered both poles of the leveling/sharpening dimension as equally valid ways for individuals to achieve a satisfactory equilibrium between their inner needs and outer requirements, but different in their repertoire of psychological functions. Several years later, based on Klein's findings, Holzman and Klein (1954, p. 105) defined cognitive styles as "generic regulatory principles" or "preferred forms of cognitive regulation" in the sense that cognitive styles are an "*organism's typical means of resolving adaptive requirements posed by certain types of cognitive problems,*" emphasizing the adaptive and flexible nature of cognitive style.

Around the same time, Witkin et al. (1954) carried out his large-scale experimental study on field dependence/independence, which was central to the further development of cognitive style research. The goal of this study was to investigate individual differences in perception and to associate these differences with particular trends in personality. Subjects were presented with a number of orientation tests aimed at examining their perceptual skills (e.g., Rod-and-Frame Test, in which the subjects determined the upright position of a rod, or Embedded Figure Test [EFT], in which the subjects were asked to find a simple figure inside a complex one) along with various personality measures. Two main groups of subjects were distinguished: field dependent (FD), those who exhibited high dependency on the surrounding field; and field independent (FI), those who displayed low dependency on the field. There was also a significant relationship between subjects' performance on perceptual tests and their personality characteristics: FD individuals were more attentive to social cues than FI individuals. In contrast, the FI group had a more impersonal orientation than the FD group, exhibiting psychological and physical distancing from others. Witkin concluded that that the "core" of cognitive style is rooted in an individual's innate predispositions, such as abilities or personality. Furthermore, Witkin explained individual differences in perception as outcomes of different modes of adjustment to the world, concluding that both FD and FI groups have specific components that are adaptive to particular situations. According to Witkin, Dyk, Paterson, Goodenough, and Karp (1962), field dependence reflects an earlier and less differentiated mode of adjustment to the world, and field independence reflects a later and more differentiated mode. However, although a highly differentiated FI individual could be highly efficient in perceptual and cognitive tasks, he or she may exhibit inappropriate

responses to certain situational requirements and be in disharmony with his or her surroundings. Thus, both Klein and Witkin introduced the notion of cognitive style as patterns or modes of adjustment to the world, which appeared to be equal in their adaptive value but different in their level and repertoire of psychological and/or perceptual functions.

In the late 1950s, Klein's and Witkin's idea of bipolarity (value-equal poles of cognitive style dimensions in terms of adaptive nature) spawned a great deal of interest. As a result, a tremendous number of studies on "style types" appeared in the literature. The most commonly studied cognitive styles of this period are impulsivity/reflectivity (Kagan, 1966), tolerance for instability (Klein & Schlesinger, 1951), breadth of categorization (Pettigrew, 1958), field articulation (Messick & Fritzky, 1963), conceptual articulation (Messick, 1976), conceptual complexity (Harvey, Hunt, & Schroder, 1961), range of scanning, constricted/flexible controls (Gardner, Holzman, Klein, Linton, & Spence, 1959), holist/serialist (Pask, 1972), verbalizer/visualizer (Paivio, 1971), and locus of control (Rotter, 1966). Attempting to organize these numerous dimensions, Messick (1976) proposed a list of 19 cognitive styles; Keefe (1988) synthesized a list of 40 separate styles.

One of the serious limitations of conventional cognitive style research was its narrow focus on lower order cognitive tasks, often assessed by performance ability measures (error rate and response time) with simple "right" and "wrong" answers, which is hypothetically more relevant in testing *abilities*, not styles. Most of the perceptual tasks used as measures of cognitive style were tapping relatively *stationary* individual differences related to personality or intelligence. Ironically, this fact appears especially clear in the most commonly used instruments to measure cognitive styles, such as Witkin's EFT (Witkin et al., 1954) and Kagan's Matching Familiar Figures Test (MFFT; Kagan, Rosman, Day, Albert, & Phillips, 1964). While these instruments were supposed to measure bipolar dimensions representing two equally efficient ways of solving a task, in reality, one strategy was usually more effective than the other (e.g., FI subjects usually perform better than FD on many spatial tasks). It is not surprising then that many researchers who have investigated the correlation between intelligence tests and conventional measures of field dependence such as the Rod-and-Frame or EFT (e.g., Cooperman, 1980; Goodenough & Karp, 1961; McKenna, 1984) consistently report higher intelligence among individuals with an FI style than among those with an FD style.

Thus, despite that literature of that period has suggested the adaptive nature of cognitive style, and proposed that cognitive style refers to specific modes of adjustment to the external world (Klein, 1951; Witkin et al., 1962), early research on cognitive styles often used measures of individual differences sensitive mostly to genetic factors, and it did not clearly distinguish those from adaptive, ontogenetically malleable traits. This caused a situation in which the cognitive styles under study closely resembled genetically predetermined cognitive abilities, sparking later debates as to whether cognitive style and ability were indeed the same. Furthermore, since the majority of the aforementioned studies were conducted before the advent of cognitive science, their main problem was the lack of a unifying theoretical approach to information processing, which could lay the foundation for systematizing numerous overlapping cognitive style dimensions (see Kozhevnikov, 2007 for a review). Consequently, the promising benefits of studying cognitive styles were lost amidst the chaos, and the amount of work devoted to the cognitive style construct declined dramatically by the end of the 1970s, ironically, only a few years before information processing and cognitive science stepped into the forefront of contemporary psychology. Thus, although cognitive style refers to ways of processing information, since the majority of interest in cognitive style was abandoned before the rise of the information processing approach, a close relationship between cognitive style and other psychological concepts from contemporary information processing theories was never properly established.

## Research in Applied Fields: Sociocultural Components of Cognitive Styles

Despite declining theoretical interest in conventional cognitive styles toward the end of the 1970s, the number of publications on cognitive styles in applied fields has continued to increase, reflecting an assumption of a practical necessity of understanding cognitive styles and their important role in real-life activities. Applied research on cognitive style focused on the existence of styles related to higher order cognitive functioning, such as problem solving, decision making, learning, and explanation of causality, as reviewed next.

Kirton (1976, 1989) was the first to consider "decision-making styles" within the cognitive style framework by introducing the adaptor/innovator dimension of managerial style. Kirton defined adaptors as preferring to accept generally recognized policies while proposing ways of "doing things better," and innovators as those who question the problem itself and propose ways "for doing things differently"; Kirton proposed that these differences were evident in personality as well as creativity and problem-solving strategies. Kirton (1989) investigated the adaptation/innovation dimension in organizational settings, widening the concept of cognitive style to characterize not only individuals but also the prevailing style in a group situation (called "organizational cognitive climate"). Kirton argued that overall cognitive climate stems from members of a workgroup sharing similar cognitive styles, that is, with all members within one-half standard deviation around the mean for the workgroup. Other studies on managerial decision-making styles were conducted by Agor (1984), who introduced three broad types of management styles in decision making: intuitive, analytical, and integrated problem-solving styles. Agor (1984) surveyed 2,000 managers of various occupations and managerial levels, and cultural backgrounds, and although it is not clear whether the differences cited are indeed statistically significant, Agor states that the data showed variation in executives' dominant styles of management practice by organizational level, service level, and gender and ethnic background (e.g., women are more intuitive than men, managers of Asian background are more intuitive than the average manager). As did Kirton, Agor pointed out that one's decision-making style not only includes stable individual characteristics but also applies to interpersonal communications and group behavior.

Rowe and Mason (1987) proposed a model of decision-making styles based on cognitive complexity (i.e., an individual's tolerance for ambiguity) and environmental complexity (people-oriented vs. task-oriented work environment). The four styles derived from this model are directive (practical, power-oriented), analytical (logical, task-oriented), conceptual (creative, intuitive), and behavioral (people-oriented, supportive). Rowe and Mason stressed the importance of cognitive style in career success. More recent studies on styles in managerial fields have supported similar ideas. First, that cognitive style is a key "determinant of individual and organizational behavior, which manifests itself in both individual workplace actions and in organizational systems, processes, and routines" (Sadler-Smith & Badger, 1998, p. 247). Second, although tending to be relatively stable, cognitive styles interact with the external environment and can be modified in response to changing situational demands, as well as influenced by life experiences (Allison & Hayes, 1996; Hayes & Allinson, 1998; Leonard & Straus, 1997).

At the same time, by the end of 1970s, a large number of "personal cognitive styles" have arisen in psychotherapy, such as optimistic/pessimistic, explanatory, anxiety-prone, and others (Haeffel et al., 2003; Peterson et al., 1982; Seligman, Abramson, Semmel, & von Baeyer, 1979). One of the first and most elaborated personality-related styles to be used widely in psychotherapy was the explanatory (attributional) style that reflects differences in the manner in which people habitually explain the causes of uncontrollable events (attributing the cause to internal vs. external circumstances). The cognitive component, according to this theory, refers to the ways in which people perceive, explain, and extrapolate events in their lives. Furthermore, the attribution theory suggests that styles are not always inherent to one's personality and intelligence and, although relatively stable, can be acquired as a result of an individual's interaction with the external environment (Peterson, Maier, & Seligman, 1993). It requires some amount of repetition of life events or observing other people's behavior to reinforce or inhibit a certain style.

The Myers-Briggs Type Indicator (MBTI) remains the major tool for describing personal styles (Myers, 1976; Myers & McCaulley, 1985). The MBTI is a self-report instrument, which was developed based on four of Jung's (1923) personality dimensions, extraversion/introversion (EI), sensing/intuition (SI), thinking/feeling (TF), and judging/perceiving (JP). Permutations of the four dimensions form 16 psychological types identified by the MBTI. Although evidence supporting the MBTI as a valid measurement of style is inconclusive (see Coffield, Moseley, Hall, & Ecclestone, 2004, for a review), and there has been considerable controversy regarding its measurement characteristics (Carlson, 1989; Healy, 1989; McCaulley, 1991) and construct validity (e.g., Bess & Harvey, 2002; Girelli & Stake, 1993), similar to other "applied" approaches, the MBTI assumes close connections between one's style and professional specialization and that certain professional settings are suited to individuals with different personality profiles.

The applied field that generated the greatest number of studies on styles was education. In education, research on style was aimed at understanding individual differences (preferences) in learning processes, and thus they were called "learning styles." One of the first models of learning styles was proposed by Kolb (1974, 1984), who suggested that the "cycle of learning" involves four adaptive learning modes—two opposing modes of grasping experience: concrete experience (CE) and abstract conceptualization (AC); and two opposing modes of transforming experience: reflective observation (RO) and active experimentation (AE). Kolb suggested the relationship between learning styles and educational or professional specialization, showing that different job requirements might cause changes in learning styles. Other research on learning styles has focused on the development of psychological instruments to assess individual differences in complex classroom situations (e.g., Dunn, Dunn, & Price, 1989; Entwistle, 1981; Schmeck, 1988). These studies all showed a close connection between educational environment and cognitive style. Overall, learning style research establishes the importance of how education might affect cognitive style and also how cognitive style may affect an individual's preference for certain educational environments.

The main problem with applied research on cognitive style is similar to the problem with conventional cognitive style research: If in the conventional cognitive style research the number of styles was defined by the number of cognitive tasks used as assessors, here the number of styles was defined by the number of applied fields in which styles were studied. As a consequence, the cognitive style construct multiplied, and in addition to conventional cognitive styles, the new terminologies of decision-making styles, learning styles, and personal styles were introduced in the mid-1970s, without clear definitions of what they were or how they differed from conventional cognitive styles. Despite their problems, one of the most significant contributions of the applied studies to cognitive style research is the examination of how external, social-environmental factors affect the formation of cognitive style. Most of the applied studies on cognitive style converged on the conclusion that cognitive styles, although relatively stable, adapt to changing environmental and situational demands and can be modified by life experiences. Furthermore, evidence has accumulated regarding the connection between an individual's cognitive style and the requirements of different social groups—including parent–child relationships, educational and professional societies, and sociocultural environment. Thus, the early definition of cognitive styles as patterns of adjustment to the world was further specified to include descriptions of particular requirements of social and professional groups on an individual's cognitive functioning. Cognitive styles became related not only to personality, ability, or cognition but also to social interactions regulating beliefs and value systems.

Another significant contribution by this line of research is that it expanded the concept of cognitive style to include constructs that might operate not only at perceptual or simple cognitive levels but also on complex, higher order cognitive levels (decision making, learning preferences). Overall, the applied studies on cognitive style seem to more apparently reflect the *flexible* nature of cognitive styles (e.g., interaction and development within professional and educational settings; relevance for sociocultural interactions and overall sociocultural context).

## Recent Developments in Cognitive Style Research

Since the 1970s, conventional cognitive style and applied cognitive style studies have been joined by new trends in cognitive style research, which can be divided into three rough categories. The first includes studies that suggest the existence of cognitive styles (e.g., mobility-fixity), or "metastyles," that operate on the metacognitive level. The second category contains studies that attempt to unite existing models of cognitive style into a unifying theory with a limited number of central dimensions, culminating in a few theoretical studies that aim to build multilevel hierarchical models of cognitive styles.

## The Mobility/Fixity Dimension: "Metastyle"

Studies of the mobility/fixity (also called flexibility/rigidity) dimension attempted to address contradictory results from previous research on conventional cognitive styles, namely, the mobility of cognitive style. Witkin was the first to point out that there might be "mobile" individuals who possess both FD and FI characteristics, and can employ one style or the other depending on the situation (Witkin, 1965; Witkin et al., 1962). According to Witkin, while FI individuals as a group tend to be creative, FI individuals who also possess FD characteristics may be even more creative, since such mobility signifies greater diversity in functioning and is more adaptive than fixed use of a single style.

Furthermore, Niaz (1987) administered the ETF and Raven's Standard Progressive Matrices Test to a group of college freshmen to assess their field dependence/independence and intelligence level. In addition, participants received the Figural Intersection Test to measure mobility/fixity. According to their results on the EFT and Figural Intersection Test, four groups of participants were identified: mobile FI, mobile FD, fixed FI, and fixed FD. Niaz reported that the fixed FI group of students received the highest intelligence scores among all the groups on the Raven's Matrices Test, while mobile individuals (both FD and FI) performed significantly better than all other groups in college chemistry, mathematics, and biology classes. Niaz (1987, p. 755) concluded that "mobile subjects are those who have available to them both a developmentally advanced mode of functioning (field-independence) and a developmentally earlier mode (field-dependence)." Furthermore, she also concluded that in mature individuals, fixed functioning implies a certain degree of inflexibility and inability to regress to earlier perceptual modes.

Furthermore, Russian psychologist Kholodnaya (2002) suggested a quadripolar model of several conventional cognitive styles: field dependence/independence, wide/narrow categorization, constricted/flexible cognitive control, and impulsivity/reflectivity. Participants were administered a number of different cognitive style and intelligence tests (EFT, the MFFT, Raven's Matrices, Stroop task) and a word sorting task. Using cluster analysis, four clusters in the field-dependency/independency dimension were identified. One seemed to represent *fixed FI* individuals, who demonstrated high scores on EFT; however, they showed high interference and longer response times in the Stroop task, as well as low concept formation ability (as measured by the word sorting task). In contrast, another cluster, representing *mobile field independence*, included individuals who, along with high EFT scores, showed relatively high performance on the word sorting task, lower conflict on the Stroop task, and higher ability to integrate sensory information with context. The other two clusters, *fixed FD* and *mobile FD*, were similar in their relatively poor response on the EFT. However, in contrast to fixed FD, mobile FD individuals exhibited low cognitive conflict in the Stroop task and better ability to coordinate their verbal responses with presented sensory information. Kholodnaya found similar patterns for each of the following dimensions: constricted/flexible cognitive control, impulsivity/reflexivity, and narrow/wide range of equivalence. She concluded that mobile individuals can spontaneously regulate their intellectual activities and effectively resolve cognitive conflicts. In contrast, fixed individuals are unable to adapt their strategies to the situation and exhibit difficulties in monitoring their intellectual activity. Thus, according to Kholodnaya, cognitive style represents the extent to which the metacognitive self-monitoring mechanisms are formed in a particular individual, and in the case of a fixed individual, it is more appropriate to talk about a cognitive deficit rather than a cognitive style.

The important contribution of this research is that it introduces the notion of metacognition to the field of cognitive style. However, there is little support for the conclusions that fixed individuals exhibit cognitive deficits, or that cognitive style can be reduced to metacognition, or that the majority of the cognitive styles are quadripolar dimensions. Rather, the results seem to suggest that individuals are different in the extent to which they exhibit flexibility and their degrees of self-monitoring in their choices of different cognitive styles. Mobility/fixity may be better viewed as a metastyle representing the level of flexibility with which an individual applies a particular style in a particular situation. More recently, Kozhevnikov (2007) suggested that the mobility/fixity dimension represents a superordinate *metastyle* dimension, which serves as a control structure for other subordinate cognitive styles. That is, metastyle represents the developmental level of an individual's metacognitive mechanisms—the ability to consciously control and situationally adapt one's own active problem-solving strategies to the degree that he or she has a number of available potential solutions and strategies (which may involve opposing cognitive styles) and can select the most appropriate one for any given task.

## Toward Hierarchical Models of Cognitive Style

The unifying trend emerged in the 1990s as a general response to vagueness in the cognitive style field, and it aimed to unite and systematize multiple cognitive style dimensions. For example, Hayes and Allinson (1994) proposed that the different dimensions of cognitive style can be considered as variations of an overarching analytical-intuitive dimension. Others characterize cognitive style as consisting of two orthogonal dimensions, such as holistic-analytical versus visualizer-verbalizer (Hodgkinson & Sadler-Smith, 2003; Riding & Cheema, 1991). However, these models of cognitive style were too simplistic; they tried to reduce cognitive style to a limited number of dimensions, rather than build a theory that systematizes known

styles into a multidimensional structure. Generally, models of cognitive style do not consider cognitive style in the context of information processing theories; they neither attempt to relate cognitive styles to other psychological theories, nor do they fully account for the complexity of the cognitive style construct. Miller (1987) was the first to consider cognitive style in the context of information processing and proposed that cognitive style consisted of a horizontal analytical-holistic dimension and a vertical dimension representing different stages and levels of information processing, such as perception, memory (representation, organization, and retrieval), and thought. However, Miller's model has been criticized for its lack of empirical support, and that the placement of cognitive style dimensions into the model was based more on convenience than research evidence or theoretical framework (Messick, 1994; Zhang & Sternberg, 2006).

There have been few empirical attempts to systematize cognitive style dimensions (e.g., Leonard, Scholl, & Kowalski, 1999; Bokoros, Goldstein, & Sweeney, 1992). For example, Bokoros et al. (1992) conducted an empirical study based on the factor analysis of correlations between the various subscales of widely used cognitive style instruments. They identified three factors, to which a variety of cognitive style dimensions could be reduced, which were dubbed as the "information-processing domain," the "thinking-feeling dimension," and the "attentional focus dimension." It is interesting to note that the first and second factors identified empirically by Bokoros et al. closely resemble "conventional" and "applied" styles, respectively. While the first factor comprised cognitive style dimensions that operate at perceptual and low-order cognitive levels, the second factor comprised styles related to individual differences in more complex, higher order cognitive activities. As for the third factor, which is described by Bokoros et al. as "internal and external application of the executive cognitive function," it closely resembles the mobility/fixity dimension, or metastyle, described in the mobility/fixity lines of research.

Finally, Nosal (1990) proposed a multidimensional hierarchical model of cognitive style that systematized cognitive style dimensions based on cognitive science theories. Specifically, the model proposes that the variety of cognitive styles can be arranged into a matrix (see Fig. 53.1). The horizontal axis of the matrix represents four hierarchical levels of information processing: *perception* (processing of primary/early perceptual information),

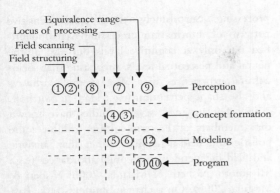

**Figure 53.1** Cognitive styles in relation to levels of information processing and cross-dimensions, according to Nosal's theory. 1 = field dependence-independence; 2 = field articulation; 3 = breadth of categorization; 4 = range of equivalence; 5 = articulation of conceptual structure; 6 = tolerance for unrealistic experience; 7 = leveling-sharpening; 8 = range of scanning; 9 = reflectivity-impulsivity; 10 = rigidity-flexibility; 11 = locus of control; 12 = time orientation.

*concept formation* (formation of conceptual representations in the form of symbolic, semantic, and abstract structures), *modeling* (organizing personal experiences into "schemas," "models," or "theories"), and *program* (goal-directed activity and metacognitive approaches used for complex decision-making tasks).

After positioning different conventional styles into these four levels of information processing, Nosal identified a number of vertical cross-dimensions, which he described as "modules of information processing" that encompass all the variety of cognitive styles. These stylistic cross-dimensions, according to Nosal, reflect regulatory mechanisms responsible for generating four qualitatively different bipolar cognitive style dimensions: (1) *field structuring* (*context dependent vs. context independent*), which describes a tendency to shift attention to perceiving events as separate versus inseparable from their context; (2) *field scanning* (*rule-driven vs. intuitive*), which describes a tendency for directed, driven by rules, versus aleatoric, driven by salient stimuli, information scanning; (3) *control allocation* (*internal vs. external locus of processing*), which describes ways of locating criteria for processing at the internal versus external center; and (4) *equivalence range* (*compartmentalization vs. integration*), which represents a tendency to process and output information globally versus sequentially. The model allows detecting some gaps in the area of cognitive style and identifying yet unknown cognitive styles dimensions in the cells of the matrix. For instance, field-structuring

cross-dimension has been studied so far on the basis of Witkin's field dependence/independence cognitive style, which operates mostly on the perceptual level, so context-dependent/independent styles operating at higher levels of cognitive processing have yet to be identified.

It is interesting to note that the cross-dimensions that Nosal derived from his model resemble the metacomponents suggested by Sternberg's componential theory of intelligence (selection of low-order components, selection of representation or organization of information, and selection of a strategy for combining lower order components), which are defined as the "specific realization of control processes…sometimes collectively (and loosely) referred to as the executive" (Sternberg, 1985, p. 99). Thus, the four major cross-dimensions identified by Nosal seem to reflect four different types of executive functions or cognitive control processes that regulate an individual's perception, thoughts, and actions, and generate four qualitatively different bipolar cognitive style dimensions (i.e., context dependent vs. context independent; rule-driven vs. stimulus-driven information scanning; internal vs. external locus of control; and holistic vs. sequential processing). In this view, any given cognitive style can be viewed as an expression of a particular executive function from these four cross-dimensions, operating at a particular level of information processing. Thus, according to Nosal's categorization, the number of cognitive styles is finite and unknown styles could be predicted and placed into the cells of the matrix.

In summary, the recent studies on cognitive style endeavored to systematize the variety of cognitive styles and establish a possible structural relationship among them. These studies cast serious doubt on the unitary nature of cognitive style and provided evidence for the hierarchical organization of cognitive style dimensions operating at different levels of information processing (from perceptual to metacognitive). Furthermore, Nosal's model allows for mapping existing models of cognitive style onto information processing theories, taking into account the complex structure and multidimensionality of the cognitive style construct. Furthermore, many of the aforementioned studies pointed out the regulatory function of cognitive styles. Nosal's model, in particular, suggested that all the variety of cognitive style dimensions might be clustered around a limited number of stylistic cross-dimensions, related to specific executive functions.

## Perspectives From Cognitive Sciences and Neuroscience

Recent cognitive science and neuroscience studies provided new evidence that shed light on the nature of cognitive style and its relation to other basic psychological constructs and processes. In this section, we will review two categories of recent cognitive science and neuroscience studies.

The first line of research contains a few recent cognitive neuroscience studies that attempted to demonstrate that cognitive style may be more accurately represented by specific patterns of neural activity, and not only by differences in performance on behavioral measures. Gevins and Smith (2000) examined differences between subjects with verbal versus nonverbal cognitive styles by recoding their electroencephalograms (EEGs) while the subjects performed a spatial working memory task. The results showed that although the subjects did not significantly differ in task performance, subjects with a verbal cognitive style tended to make greater use of the left parietal region, whereas subjects with a nonverbal style tended to make greater use of the right parietal region. Furthermore, functional magnetic resonance imaging (fMRI) experiments have revealed that, while performing the EFT (which can be solved with either visual-object or visual-spatial strategies), in the absence of significant behavioral differences in task performance, spatial visualizers (i.e., individuals who prefer to process information spatially in terms of spatial relations and locations) showed greater activation in left occipito-temporal areas, while the object visualizers (i.e., individuals who prefer to process information visually in terms of color, shape, and detail) showed greater activation in the bilateral occipito-parietal junction (Motes, Malach, & Kozhevnikov, 2008), supporting the relationship between individual differences in visual cognitive style and differential use of regions in the dorsal and ventral visual processing streams. The importance of these studies is that they indicate that individuals with different cognitive styles may exhibit different patterns of neural activity, even though their behavioral performance may not significantly differ. That is, the findings imply that the differences underlying individuals' cognitive styles can be associated with different patterns of neural activity in the brain, in addition to the ability to perform a particular task.

The second line of studies is related to the most recent cognitive and cultural neuroscience studies that demonstrated that culture-specific experiences may afford distinct patterns of information processing. Surprisingly, these culture-sensitive patterns of information processing were indentified not only at cognitive levels but also at the neural and perceptual levels, suggesting that sociocultural experiences may affect neural pathways and also shape perception (e.g., Han & Northoff, 2008). For instance, several studies have shown that members of Eastern cultures exhibit more holistic and field-dependent rather than analytic and field-independent perceptual affordances (e.g., Miyamoto, Nisbett, & Masuda, 2006; Nisbett & Masuda, 2003). On a change blindness task, East Asians detected more changes in background context, whereas North Americans detected more changes in foreground objects (Nisbett & Masuda, 2003). Kitayama, Duffy, Kawamura, and Larsen (2003) also found that while North Americans were more accurate in an "absolute task" (drawing a line that was identical to the first line in absolute length), Japanese people were more accurate in a "relative task" (drawing a line that was identical to the first in relation to the surrounding frame), suggesting that the Japanese participants paid more attention to the frame (context) than did the North Americans and were more field dependent. Other studies reported that North Americans recognized previously seen objects in changed contexts better than Asians did, due to their increased focus on objects' features independent of context (Chua, Boland, & Nisbett, 2005). Gutchess, Welsh, Boduroglu, and Park (2006) evaluated neural bases for these cultural differences in fMRI, concluding that cultural experiences subtly direct neural activity, particularly for focal objects in early visual processing.

Differences between members of different cultures were also reported on lower order and higher order cognitive tasks, as well as on tasks that require metacognitive processing. For instance, Chinese participants organized objects more relationally (e.g., grouping "monkey" and "banana" together because monkeys eat bananas) and less categorically (e.g., grouping "panda" and "monkey" together because both are animals) than Westerners (Nisbett, 2003), reflecting differences in field scanning. Significant differences between Easterners and Westerners have also been found in decision making. Kume (1985) discovered that, when making decisions, Easterners adopt an indirect, agreement-centered approach, based on intuition, while Westerners favor a direct, confrontational strategy using rational criteria. There are also cross-cultural differences at the neural level in language processing; English speakers reading English words activate superior temporal gyrus, but Chinese speakers reading Chinese characters activate inferior parietal lobe (Tan, Laird, Li, & Fox, 2005), which might indicate differences in global versus sequential processing.

Furthermore, research also identified self-construal differences: Westerners characterize the self as independent and have self-focused attention, while East Asians emphasize interdependence and social context (Nisbett, Choi, Peng, & Norenzayan, 2001). Also, Americans believe that they have control over events to the extent that they often fail to distinguish between objectively controllable events and uncontrolled ones. In contrast, East Asians are not susceptible to this illusion (Glass & Singer, 1973), reflecting differences in the locus of control dimension.

Overall, the reported cultural differences were identified at all levels of information processing (from perceptual to higher order cognitive reasoning) and can be generally described as tendencies of East Asian people (1) to engage in context-dependent cognitive processes, while Westerners, who tend to think about the environment analytically, engage in context-independent cognitive processes (Goh et al., 2007; Miyamoto et al., 2006); (2) to seek intuitive instantaneous understanding through direct perception, while Westerners favor more logic and abstract principles (Nakamura, 1985); (3) to exhibit more external locus of control in contrast to Westerners, who have stronger internal locus (Glass & Singer, 1973; Nisbett et al., 2001); and (4) to have tendencies to perceive and think about the environment more holistically and globally, in contrast to Westerners, who engage in more sequential processing (Goh et al., 2007).

Interestingly, all the reported culture-sensitive individual difference can be described by Nosal's four style cross-dimensions (executive functions), field scanning, organization, locus of control, and equivalence range, and can therefore be positioned into the cells of Nosal's matrix of cognitive style dimensions, according to the specific executive function they perform and the dominant level of information processing involved in a given task. Thus, culture-sensitive individual differences reported in transcultural psychology and neuroscience seem to represent different dimensions of cognitive style described in the cognitive style literature, and yet unidentified, culture-sensitive individual differences in cognition might be predicted from the Nosal's matrix.

While cognitive psychology research provides evidence that some components of executive functions

(e.g., updating working memory representations, shifting between task sets) are entirely genetic in origin (Friedman et al., 2008), social-constructivist research argues for the sociocultural origin of executive functioning, suggesting its flexible nature (e.g., Ardila, 2008; Vygotsky, 1984). In light of the proposed framework distinguishing between stationary and flexible individual differences, as well as on the basis of the review of culture-sensitive individual differences, we suggest that the four executive functions derived from Nosal's theory represent "flexible" components of executive functioning, which are shaped and mediated by sociocultural environment. On the basis of this approach, cognitive style research can contribute to transcultural psychology and neuroscience research by helping to organize and predict different dimensions of culture-sensitive individual differences.

## Conclusions and Future Directions

The current review attempts to bridge the gap between the large body of traditional cognitive style concepts, cognitive neuroscience, and transcultural psychology and neuroscience research, using an organizing framework that distinguishes between relatively stationary (i.e., abilities, personality traits) and ontogenetically flexible (cognitive styles) individual differences in cognition. As demonstrated throughout the review, the lack of discrimination between stationary and flexible individual differences, as well as the absence of a common theoretical framework for mapping the cognitive style concept onto existing cognitive science and neuroscience research, has led to misinterpretation and underestimation of the cognitive style concept.

The reviewed literature on the state of affairs in the aforementioned three research traditions suggests that the concept of cognitive style has a place in, and should be integrated into, mainstream current cognitive science and neuroscience theories. One of the possible approaches to integrate cognitive style into contemporary cognitive science theories can be based on Nosal's (1990) model, which proposes that the variety of cognitive styles could be structuralized as the elements of a matrix, with the horizontal axis representing different levels of information processing (from perception to metacognition) and the vertical axis representing four major types of stylistic cross-dimensions that reflect specific executive functions responsible for generating four qualitatively different bipolar cognitive style dimensions (i.e., context dependent vs. context independent; rule-driven vs. stimulus-driven information scanning; internal vs. external locus of control; holistic vs. sequential processing). Nosal's model takes into account the complex structure and multidimensionality of the cognitive style construct, and it allows for predicting the existence of other, yet unidentified, styles.

Based on our review, we suggest redefining cognitive style as ontogenetically flexible individual differences representing an individual's adaptation of innate predisposition to external physical and sociocultural environments and expressing themselves as environmentally and culturally sensitive neural and/or cognitive patterns of information processing. To an extent far greater than that seen in other animals, who are born in a given environment and bound for generations to specific environmental conditions and thus might exhibit numerous fixed inborn patterns of behavior that result from long-term evolutionary processes, humans are much less restricted by fixed innate mechanisms suited for specific environmental conditions. This places more importance on the role of postnatal development, which is largely based on social interactions, concepts, and cultural means of learning, and takes place in ever-expanding and changing environments throughout the life span. Thus, the inborn capacities of humans allow for a wide range of possibilities for their future expression and development. Recent evidence from neuroscience indicates that neurogenesis and neural plasticity are affected by social environments (Lu et al., 2003). Research in evolutionary genetics consistently shows evidence of the neural plasticity of human behavior in relation to sociocultural environment, and the coevolution of genes, cognition, and culture (see Li, 2003 for review).

The proposed view on individual differences in cognition is reflected in the model presented in Figure 53.2. The core is formed by the individual's innate predispositions and personality traits, which reflect stationary individual differences. This core is surrounded by cognitive style, reflecting flexible individual differences. The development of cognitive style occurs on the basis of these innate core traits and is shaped through interaction with the surrounding environment. The first environmental layer represents the individual's immediate familial and physical environment, which influences early cognitive development and reinforces certain innate characteristics, while suppressing others. At the next level lies the educational layer, in which the individual progresses through school systems and develops certain problem-solving strategies. The next layer is the professional layer, in which individuals' ways of thinking are sharpened and become more distinct. In the professional layer, an individual's cognitive style is affected by both mediated information contained in the professional media, as well as personal interactions with peers. Surrounding all of these is the final, cultural layer, reflecting mental, behavioral and cognitive processing patterns common to a specific cultural group. All these sociocultural layers affect each other and together shape the different layers of information processing and behavioral patterns of an individual. Metacognitive processes can possibly affect all the subordinate layers of information processing; a person with highly developed metacognitive processes would be aware of his or her preferred style, and, when presented with tasks or situations that require use of a different style, would flexibly adapt his or her strategies. The development of flexible metatstyles would allow an individual to switch between preferred styles. Possible reasons for the formation of flexible metastyles could be experiencing different situational contexts (such as different professional, educational, and cultural settings), changing professional field, or changing cultural context (native language, traditions). Indeed, Bagley and Mallick (1998) indicated malleability of cognitive styles in migrant children and suggested that concept of cognitive style can be deployed as an indicator of process and change in migration and multicultural education, rather than as a description of basic cognitive processes.

The current organizing framework that distinguishes between stationary and ontogenetically flexible individual differences in cognition helps to bridge the gap between the large body of traditional cognitive style concepts, cognitive neuroscience, and transcultural psychology and neuroscience research. We argue for the importance of such a framework for cognitive psychology and neuroscience, which still lacks a coherent framework of individual differences. Moreover, such an organizing framework will

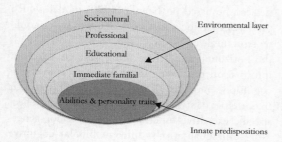

**Figure 53.2** Layers constituting individual differences in cognition. (*See* color insert.)

be crucial for helping transcultural psychology and neuroscience identify the causes of found cross-cultural individual differences (e.g., whether the identified differences are due to long-term evolutionary processes or ontogenetic development) and assign relative weight to such causes (e.g. whether within-culture differences, such as in educational and/or professional contexts, might overshadow the global cultural effect). Finally, such a framework will aid in understanding the relation between cognitive style and other cognitive science concepts, suggesting that cognitive style can be a valuable concept beyond the largely abandoned filed of cognitive style research, and can bring new insights in understanding the individual differences in humans' cognitive functioning.

## References

Ardila, A. (2008). On the evolutionary origins of executive functions. *Brain and Cognition, 68*, 92–99.

Agor, W. H. (1984). *Intuitive management*. Englewood Cliffs, NJ: Prentice Hall.

Allison, J., &Hayes, C. (1996). The Cognitive Style Index, a measure of intuition-analysis for organizational research, *Journal of Management Studies, 33*, 119–135.

Ando J., Ono Y., & Wright M. J. (2001). Genetic structure of spatial and verbal working memory. *Behavior Genetics, 31*, 615–624.

Ausburn, L. J., & Ausburn, F. B. (1978). Cognitive styles: Some information and implications for instructional design. *Educational Communication and Technology, 26*, 337–354.

Bagley, C., & Mallick, K. (1998). Field dependence, cultural context and academic achievement. *British Journal of Educational Psychology, 68*, 581–587.

Bess, T. L., & Harvey, R. J. (2002). Bimodal score distribution and the Myers–Briggs Type Indicator: Fact or artifact? *Journal of Personality Assessment, 78*, 176–186.

Bokoros, M. A., Goldstein, M. B., & Sweeney, M. M. (1992). Common factors in five measures of cognitive style. *Current Psychology: Research and Reviews, 11*, 99–109.

Carlson, G. J. (1989). Affirmative: In support of researching the Myers-Briggs Type Indicator. *Journal of Counseling and Development, 67*, 484–486.

Chua, H. F., Boland, J. E., & Nisbett, R. E. (2005). Cultural variation in eye movements during scene perception. *Proceedings of the National Academy of Sciences USA, 102*, 12629–12633.

Coffield, F., Moseley, D., Hall, E., & Ecclestone, K. (2004). *Learning styles and pedagogy in post-16 learning: A systematic and critical review*. London: Learning & Skills Research Centre.

Cooperman, E. W. (1980). Field differentiation and intelligence. *Journal of Psychology, 105*, 29–33.

Deary, I. J., Penke, L., & Johnson, W. (2010). The neuroscience of human intelligence differences. *Nature Reviews Neuroscience, 11*, 201–211

Dunn, R., Dunn, K., & Price, G. E. (1989). *Learning Styles Inventory*. Lawrence, KS: Price Systems.

Entwistle, N. J. (1981). *Styles of teaching and learning: An integrated outline of educational psychology for students, teachers, and lecturers*. Chichester, England: Wiley.

Friedman, N., Mikaye, A., Young, S. E., De Fries, J. C., Corley, R. P., & Hewitt, J. K. (2008). Individual differences in executive functions are almost entirely genetic in origin. *Journal of Experimental Psychology: General, 137*(2), 201–225.

Gardner, R.W., Holzman, P. S., Klein, G. S., Linton, H. B., & Spence, D. P. (1959). *Cognitive control. A study of individual consistencies in cognitive behavior*. Psychological Issues, Part 4. New York: International Universities Press.

Gevins, A., & Smith, M. (2000). Neurophysiological measures of working memory and individual differences in cognitive ability and cognitive style. *Cerebral Cortex, 10*, 829–839.

Girelli, S. A., & Stake, J. (1993). Bipolarity in Jungian type theory and the Myers–Briggs Type Indicator. *Journal of Personality Assessment, 60*, 290–301.

Glass, D. C., &Singer, J. E. (1973). Experimental studies of uncontrollable and unpredictable noise. *Representative Research in Social Psychology, 4*, 165–183.

Goh, J. O., Chee, M. W., Tan, J. C., Venkatraman, V., Hebrank, A., Leshikar, E. D.,... Park, D. C. (2007). Age and culture modulate object processing and object-scene binding in the ventral visual area. *Cognitive, Affective, and Behavioral Neuroscience, 7*, 44–52.

Goodenough, D. R., &Karp, S. A. (1961). Field dependence and intellectual functioning. *Journal of abnormal and social Psychology, 63*, 243–246.

Gutchess, A. H., Welsh, R. C., Boduroglu, A., Park, D. C. (2006). Cultural differences in neural function associated with object processing. *Cognitive Affective Behavioral Neuroscience, 6*, 102–109.

Haeffel, G. J., Abramson, L. Y., Voelz, Z. R., Metalsky, G. I., Halberstadt, L., Dykman, B. M., & Hogan, M. E. (2003). Cognitive vulnerability to depression and lifetime history of Axis I psychopathology: A comparison of negative cognitive styles (CSQ) and dysfunctional attitudes (DAS). *Journal of Cognitive Psychotherapy, 17*, 3–22.

Han, S., & Northoff, G. (2008). Culture-sensitive neural substrates of human cognition: A transcultural neuroimaging approach. *Nature Reviews Neuroscience, 9*, 646–654.

Hanfmann, E. (1941). A study of personal patterns in an intellectual performance. *Character and Personality, 9*, 315–325.

Harvey, O. J., Hunt, D. E., & Schroder, H. M. (1961). *Conceptual systems and personality organization*. New York: Wiley.

Hayes, J., &Allinson, C. W. (1994). Cognitive style and its relevance for management practice. *British Journal of Management, 5*, 53–71.

Hayes, J., & Allinson, C. W. (1998). Cognitive style and the theory and practice of individual and collective learning in organizations. *Human Relations, 51*, 847–871.

Healy, C. C. (1989). Negative: The MBTI: Not ready for routine use in counseling. *Journal of Counseling and Development, 67*, 487–488.

Hodgkinson, G. P., & Sadler-Smith, E. (2003). Complex or unitary? A critique and empirical re-assessment of the Allinson–Hayes Cognitive Style Index. *Journal of Occupational and Organizational Psychology, 76*, 243–268.

Holzman, P. S., & Klein, G. S. (1954). Cognitive system-principles of leveling and sharpening: Individual differences in assimilation effects in visual time-error. *Journal of Psychology, 37*, 105–122.

Jung, K. (1923). *Psychological types*. New York: Harcourt Brace.

Kagan, J. (1966). Reflection-impulsivity: The generality and dynamics of conceptual tempo. *Journal of Abnormal Psychology, 71*, 17–24.

Kagan, J., Rosman, B. L., Day, D., Albert, J., & Phillips, W. (1964). Information processing in the child: Significance of analytic and reflective attitudes. *Psychological Monographs*, *78*, 1–37.

Keefe, J. W. (1988). Development of the NASSP learning style profile. In J. W. Keefe (Ed.), *Profiling and utilizing learning style* (pp. 1–28). Reston, VA: National Association of Secondary School Principals.

Kholodnaya, M. A. (2002). *Kognitiivnii stili: O prirode individual'nogouma* [Cognitive styles: On the nature of individual mind]. Moscow, Russia: PER SE.

Kirton, M. J. (1976). Adaptors and innovators, a description and measure. *Journal of Applied Psychology*, *61*, 622–629.

Kirton, M. J. (Ed.). (1989). *Adaptors and innovators*. London: Routledge.

Kitayama, S., Duffy, S., Kawamura, T., & Larsen, J. T. (2003). A cultural look at New Look: Perceiving an object and its context in two cultures. *Psychological Science*, *14*, 201–206.

Klein, G. S. (1951). A personal world through perception. In R. R. Blake & G. V. Ramsey (Eds.), *Perception: An approach to personality* (pp. 328–355). New York: Ronald Press.

Klein, G. S., &Schlesinger, H.J. (1951). Perceptual attitudes toward instability: I. Prediction of apparent movement experiences from Rorschach responses. *Journal of Personality*, *19*, 289–302.

Kolb, D. A. (1974). On management and the learning process. In D. A. Kolb, I. M. Rubin, & J. M. McInture (Eds.), *Organizational psychology* (pp.239–252). Englewood Cliffs, NJ: Prentice Hall.

Kolb, D. A. (1984). *Experiential learning: Experience as a source of learning and development*. Englewood Cliffs, NJ: Prentice Hall.

Kozhevnikov, M. (2007). Cognitive styles in the context of modern psychology: Toward an integrated framework of cognitive style. *Psychological Bulletin*, *133*(3), 464–481.

Kume, T. (1985). Managerial attitudes toward decision-making. In W. B. Gudykunst, L. P. Stewart, & S. Ting-Toomey, (Eds.) *Communication, culture, and organizational processes* (pp. 231–251). Beverly Hills, CA: Sage.

Leonard, N. H., Scholl, R. W., & Kowalski, K. B. (1999). Information processing style and decision making. *Journal of Organizational Behaviour*, *20*, 407–420.

Leonard, N. H., & Straus, S. (1997). Putting your company's whole brain to work. *Harvard Business Review*, *75*, 111–121.

Li, S. (2003). Biocultural orchestration of developmental plasticity across levels: The interplay of biology and culture in shaping the mind and behavior across the life span. *Psychological Bulletin*, *129*(2), 171–194.

Lu, L., Bao, G., Chen, H., Xia, P., Fan, X., Zhang, J., Pei, G., & Ma, L. (2003). Modification of hippocampal neurogenesis and neuroplasticity by social environments. *Experimental Neurology*, *183*, 600–609.

McCaulley, M. H. (1991). Additional comments regarding Myers–Briggs Type Indicator: A response to comments. *Measurement and Evaluation in Counseling and Development*, *23*, 182–185.

McKenna, F. P. (1984). Measures of field dependence: Cognitive style or cognitive ability? *Journal of Personality and Social Psychology*, *47*, 593–603.

Messick, S. (1976). Personality consistencies in cognition and creativity. In S. Messick (Eds.), *Individuality in learning* (pp.4–23). San Francisco: Jossey-Bass.

Messick, S., &Fritzky, F.J. (1963). Dimension of analytic attitude in cognition and personality. *Journal of Personality*, *31*, 346–370.

Miller, A. (1987). Cognitive styles: An integrated model. *Educational Psychology*, *7*, 251–268.

Miyamoto, Y., Nisbett, R. E., & Masuda, T. (2006). Culture and physical environment: Holistic versus analytic perceptual affordances. *Psychological Science*, *17*, 113–119.

Motes, M. A., Malach, R., & Kozhevnikov, M. (2008). Object-processing neural efficiency differentiates object from spatial visualizers. *NeuroReport*, *19*(17), 1727–1731

Myers, I. B. (1976). *Introduction to type*. Palo Alto, CA: Consulting Psychologist Press.

Myers, I. B., &McCaulley, M. N. (1985). *Manual: A guide to the development and use of the Myers-Brigs Type Indicator*. Palo Alto, CA: Consulting Psychologist Press.

Nakamura, H. (1985). *Ways of thinking of eastern people*. Honolulu: Unversity of Hawaii Press.

Niaz, M. (1987). Mobility-fixity dimension in Witkin's theory of field-dependence-independence and its implication for problems solving in science. *Perceptual and Motor Skills*, *65*, 755–764.

Nisbett, R. E. (2003). *The geography of thought: How Asians and Westerners think differently... and why*. New York: The Free Press.

Nisbett, R. E., Choi, I., Peng, K., & Norenzayan, A. (2001). Culture and system of thoughts: Holistic versus analytic cognition. *Psychological Review*, *108*, 291–310.

Nisbett, R. E., & Masuda, T. (2003). Culture and point of view. *Proceedings of the National Academy of Sciences USA*, *100*, 11163–11170.

Nosal, C. S. (1990). *Psychologiczne modele umyslu [Psychological models of mind]*. Warsaw, Poland: PWN.

Paivio, A. (1971). *Imagery and verbal processes*. Oxford, England: Holt, Rinehart & Winston.

Pask, G. (1972). A fresh look at cognition and the individual. *International Journal of Man-Machine Studies*, *4*, 211–216.

Peterson, C., Maier, S. F., & Seligman, M. E. P. (1993). *Learned helplessness*. New York: Oxford University Press.

Peterson, C., Semmel, A., Baeyer, C.von Abramson, L. Y., Metalsky, G. L., & Seligman, M. I. P. (1982). The Attribution Style Questionnaire. *Cognitive Therapy and Research*, *6*, 287–299.

Pettigrew, T. F. (1958). The measurement of category width as cognitive variable. *Journal of Personality*, *26*, 532–544.

Riding, R., & Cheema, I. (1991). Cognitive styles—an overview and integration. *Educational Psychology*, *11*, 193–216.

Rotter, J. B. (1966). Generalized expectancies for internal versus external control of reinforcement. *Psychological Monograph*, *80*, 1–28.

Rowe, A. J., & Mason, R. O. (1987). *Managing with style*. San Francisco: Jossey-Bass.

Sadler-Smith, E., &Badger, B. (1998). Cognitive style, learning and innovation. *Technology Analysis and Strategic Management*, *10*(2), 247–266.

Sayala, S., Sala, J. B., & Courtney, S. M. (2005). Increased neural efficiency with repeated performance of a working memory task is information-type dependent. *Cerebral Cortex*, *16*, 609–617.

Schmeck, R. R. (Ed.). (1988). *Strategies and styles of learning*. New York: Plenum Press.

Seligman, M. E. P., Abramson, L. Y., Semmel, A., & von Baeyer, C. (1979). Depressive attributional style. *Journal of Abnormal Psychology*, *88*, 242–247.

Sternberg, R. J. (1985). *Beyond IQ: A triarchic theory of intelligence*. Cambridge, England: Cambridge University Press.

Tan, L. H., Laird, A. R., Li, K., &Fox, P. T. (2005). Neuroanatomical correlates of phonological processing of Chinese characters and alphabetic words: A meta-analysis. *Human Brain Mapping, 25*(1), 83–91.

Vygotsky, L. S. (1984). *Mind in society: The development of higher psychological processes*. (M. Cole, V. John-Steiner, S. Scribner, & E. Souberman, Eds.). Cambridge, MA: Harvard University Press.

Witkin, H. A. (1965). Psychological differentiation and forms of pathology. *Journal of Abnormal Psychology, 70*, 317–336.

Witkin, H. A., &Ash, S. E. (1948). Studies in space orientation: IV. Further experiments on perception of the upright with displaced visual field. *Journal of Experimental Psychology, 43*, 58–67.

Witkin, H. A., Dyk, R. B., Faterson, H. F., Goodenough, D. R., & Karp, S. A. (1962). *Psychological differentiation*. New York: Wiley.

Witkin, H.A., Lewis, H.B., Hertzman, M., Machover, K., Bretnall P. M., & Wapner, S. (1954). *Personality through perception*. New York: Harper & Brothers.

Witkin, H. A., Moore, C. A., Goodenough, D. R., &Cox, P. W. (1977). Field dependent and field independent cognitive styles and their educational implications. *Review of Educational Research, 47*, 1–64.

Zhang, L. F., & Sternberg, R. J. (2006). *The nature of intellectual styles*. Mahwah, NJ: Erlbaum.

# PART 11

# Practice and Skilled Performance

# CHAPTER
# 54

# Planning and Performing Physical Actions

David A. Rosenbaum

**Abstract**

The capacity for planning and performing physical actions enables people and animals to gather information, manipulate objects, express decisions, and communicate with others. Physical actions are not only important for enabling cognition, however. They also manifest what we know, often in subtle ways or in ways that reflect knowledge of domains that have not been traditionally susceptible to analysis by cognitive psychologists (e.g., biomechanics). This chapter reviews cognitive psychological research on planning and performing physical actions, first by focusing on the knowledge revealed through such actions (via practice effects and anticipation effects), and second by focusing on the realization of action, both in verbal and nonverbal domains. The last sections describe a cognitive psychological model of action production and offer reflections on the place of this somewhat neglected area of study in cognitive psychology.

**Key Words:** action, motor control, performance, plans

Cognitive psychology, the study of mental function, focuses on questions of knowing. Such questions were taken up by philosophers who, for centuries, pondered the nature of knowledge. Luminaries such as Plato, Socrates, Aristotle, Descartes, Locke, Berkeley, and Kant developed concepts that inspire and challenge cognitive psychologists today. Concepts they developed, such as nativism, rationalism, and empiricism, lie at the heart of modern cognitive psychology, continuing to define many of the core problems of the field.

There is a side to knowing that, oddly, the classical philosophers did not pick up on. This is a side of knowing that only came to be appreciated in the 20th century and, as it happens, in three countries: in the United States, via John Dewey (1929); in France, via Maurice Merleau-Ponty (1945); and in England, via Michael Polanyi (1958) and Gilbert Ryle (1949). In the United States, Dewey argued that knowing without acting is useless; in France,

Merleau-Ponty argued that much of what we know is embodied; and in England, Polanyi and Ryle argued that much of what we know is reflected in how we act. The second view just mentioned, the one espoused by Merleau-Ponty, finds expression in the modern view that cognition and perception are expressed in terms of what the body can do (Wilson, 2006). The first and third views, the ones espoused by Dewey and by Polanyi and Ryle, respectively, underlie much of the work reviewed here.

Inspired by thinkers like Dewey, Polanyi, and Ryle, as well as my own interest in perceptual-motor skill learning, which was borne largely of my long-standing interest in playing the violin, I have devoted my research to the planning and performance of physical actions. In this chapter I review work on this topic by focusing on two core questions: (1) What knowledge do we reveal through our physical actions? and (2) How does that knowledge come to be physically realized?

## Knowledge Revealed Through Action

When someone answers questions correctly, it is reasonable to conclude that he or she knows the answers to the questions. No matter how the answers are physically realized—whether through speaking, typing, writing, or other means—the person's motor system is brought to bear to express the explicit, declarative knowledge the individual possesses.

The motor system also enables the expression of *implicit* knowledge. When someone completes a word fragment in a way that reflects a bias toward what he or she was exposed to before, but the individual shows no sign of having remembered the material through other tests such as recall or recognition (Schacter, 1987), the motor system helps make such implicit knowledge explicit. It does so by allowing for overt expression of the individual's responses. Similarly, when one responds to signals in ways that betray learning of the signals' sequential structure despite lack of conscious awareness of that structure (Nissen & Bullemer, 1987; Reber, 1992), the motor system helps bring such implicit knowledge to the fore.

Saying that the motor system helps express knowledge is trivial in the sense that without the motor system, we would be unable to communicate with the outside world, except through technical tricks made possible by brain scanning or other means (Owen et., 2006). Of greater interest for the present chapter, more subtle expressions of knowledge are possible through everyday physical behaviors. Those are the ones to which I will turn in the remainder of this section. The phenomena to be covered will fall within two broad categories: practice effects and anticipation effects. After those topics are discussed, I will turn to the realization of action, by which I mean the process through which thoughts are physically expressed.

### Practice Effects

If someone improves on a task, the individual can be said to have acquired knowledge permitting the improvement. This conclusion is justified so long as the improvement is not simply due to nonneural bodily changes such as strengthening of muscles or fortuitous deformation of bones (see Rosenbaum, 2010) or to changes in the external environment that make the task easier (e.g., the wind subsiding during a tennis match).

Consider practice effects that lead to stellar performance. This is a good place to start because many people who first learn about psychomotor research,

as my field of study is sometimes called, immediately turn to superstars. "What makes Tiger Woods so great?" they ask (referring to his golf), and likewise for heroes of other skill domains—athletic, musical, or otherwise. The related, implied, question is what makes the rest of us so ordinary?

Superstars are, by definition, much better than virtually everyone else at the tasks on which they excel. What makes them special is not just that they are reliable; it is also that they are exceptionally creative. The "oohs" and "aahs" bestowed on great athletes like Tiger Woods or Michael Jordan (the great basketball player) are attributable to those performers' extraordinary "generative" capabilities as much as they are to the athletes' reliability. Michael Jordan was able to navigate through thickets of moving players and get the basketball into the basket when, for most of us, doing so would have been inconceivable. Tiger Woods, likewise, made shots that seemed to defy what anyone could reasonably expect.

An important lesson learned about such extraordinary performance is that it does not come easily. Contrary to the view that talent alone accounts for exceptional performance (Galton, 1869/1979), it is now appreciated that sustained, deliberate practice is the key to becoming an Olympian, literally or figuratively. This appreciation is due largely to the work of Ericsson, Krampe, and Tesch-Romer (1993), who analyzed the determinants of exceptional skill. These cognitive psychologists showed that focused practice for long periods of time (typically 10,000 hours) is a prerequisite for expertise. For a popular-audience account of this work, see Malcolm Gladwell's (2008) best-selling book *Outliers*. For an expanded and updated compendium of research on this line of research, see Ericsson et al. (2006).

It turns out that the time course for the development of skills that are traditionally called "perceptual-motor" is remarkably similar to the time course of the development of skills that are traditionally called "intellectual." Chess masters and master computer programmers need about as much time to excel in their disciplines—about 10,000 hours, as mentioned earlier—as do exceptional soccer players and golfers. This might not be expected if one thought that the learning of perceptual-motor skills and the learning of intellectual skills were fundamentally different. The fact that similar amounts of time are needed to achieve expertise in the two domains suggests that the cognitive substrates of perceptual-motor skills and the cognitive substrates of intellectual skills may be more similar than one might expect.

Suggesting that perceptual-motor skills and intellectual skills have common substrates makes the study of the planning and performance of physical actions more interesting for cognitive psychologists than might be the case otherwise. The suggestion that the two kinds of skills share important features was noted by Schmidt and Bjork (1992), whose insights were echoed and elaborated by Rosenbaum, Carlson, and Gilmore (2001). These two groups of authors pointed to several features common to learning of perceptual-motor skills and intellectual skills, some of which are reviewed next.

Both in intellectual skills and in perceptual-motor skills, people need less time to perform a task as they gain more experience with it. The rate of improvement diminishes with practice such that it is possible to express task completion time, $T$, as a function of number of practice trials, $P$, according to the relation $T = aP^b$, where $a$ and $b$ are non-negative empirical constants (i.e., real numbers equal to or above 0 that permit minimization of the difference between theoretical data and actual data). Because the foregoing mathematical relation is obtained on a regular basis and over a wide range of tasks, the relation has come to be called the Power Law of Learning (Crossman, 1959; Newell & Rosenbloom, 1981). The word "power" refers to the fact that task-completion time, $T$, is expressed as a function of the number of practice trials, $P$, raised to a power. The value to which $P$ is raised is negative, so $P$ is also equal to $a$ divided by $P$ raised to the rectified value (the absolute value) of $b$. The Power Law of Learning is one of the few laws in psychology. (Heathcote, Brown, and Mewhort [2000] suggested that an exponential function might provide a better account of the data than does a power function.)

Theories concerning the source of the Power Law of Learning say that the law results from trial-and-error learning (Crossman, 1959) or from chunking (Newell & Rosenbloom, 1981). In the former case, possible methods are tried at random and those that happen to lead to better performance are retained. In the latter case, routines for performing temporally contiguous actions congeal into "chunks" that can be called by other routines. The idea that skills are learned through the formation of hierarchically organized procedures was first suggested by Bryan and Harter (1897). The term "chunk" comes from Miller (1956), who observed that the number of meaningful units in memory, not the number of objectively measured "bits" of information (Shannon & Weaver, 1949), predicts the span of working memory. Chunking is the time- or practice-dependent formation of such meaningful elements. In the case of skill learning, chunking is the formation of groups of elements that tend to co-occur with such regularity that they crystallize as a coherent group that can be retrieved as a unit.

The trial-and-error method and chunking methods are not mutually exclusive, though deciding between them is an empirical enterprise which few cognitive psychologists have pursued (but see Logan, 1988). One reason may be that the trial-and-error account and the chunking account actually focus on different aspects of learning. The trial-and-error account focuses on the process by which learning occurs. The chunking account focuses on the structural changes within memory that tend to promote learning. An important property of both approaches is that neither one says anything that precludes its application to perceptual-motor skills. Both accounts apply to perceptual-motor skills and intellectual skills.

Might it be, however, that chunking theory or trial-and-error theory better accounts for one kind of learning than to the other? A way to pursue this possibility is to consider the measure of learning. The dependent measure for the Power Law of Learning is task completion time, which diminishes with practice at a negatively accelerated rate. This is true for a broad range of tasks: cigar rolling (Crossman, 1959); moving the hand back and forth between targets (Elliott, Helsen, & Chua, 2001); generating responses in response to signals (Seibel, 1963); justifying mathematical proofs (Neves & Anderson, 1981); and writing books (Ohlsson, 1992). Insofar as chunking or trial-and-error learning can give rise to the Power Law of Learning, the success of the Law in both domains makes it difficult to decide which theory applies better to one domain than the other.

There are, however, other measures of performance for which it is less clear that chunking theory or trial-and-error theory applies equally well. Here it helps to focus on features of perceptual-motor tasks that improve with practice in ways that are not simply captured by task-completion time. The most obvious measures concern *quality* of performance, which can be orthogonal to task-completion time. Playing a lament on the violin is not about playing the piece as quickly as possible, nor is painting a portrait of a grieving widow with as much poignancy as possible. The quality of the work—however that is judged—is the relevant index of performance in such cases.

There is relatively little scientific research on judged quality of performance, either with respect to its determinants or with respect to how it changes with practice (but see Ericsson et al., 2006). This is surprising considering how important the quality of performance is in so many domains, not least in trades such as plumbing, carpentry, and glassblowing. On the other hand, within laboratory-based studies of perceptual-motor performance, there has been some documentation of practice-related changes in features of performance other than speed. For example, when people try to bring one hand from a start position to a target as quickly as possible, their movements become smoother with practice (Elliott et al., 2001). This smoothing affords greater metabolic efficiency (Sparrow & Newell, 1998) as well as greater aiming efficiency.

The aiming task just referred to was first studied by Woodworth (1899). Later, Fitts (1954) showed that the time to capture a target increases both with the distance of the target's center from the start point and with the narrowness of the target. More specifically, Fitts showed that target-completion time increases linearly with an index of difficulty (ID), the logarithm of the ratio of target distance to target diameter. This is true for a wide range of tasks, making this relation, along with the Power Law of Learning, discussed above, one of the other laws of psychology. The relation is called Fitts's law (see Elliott et al., 2001). The slope of the function relating movement time to Fitts's ID decreases as practice continues. As the slope decreases, the time to complete the aiming task decreases in a manner consistent with the Power Law of Learning.

Another task where quality of perceptual-motor performance has been analyzed is adaptation to altered stimulus-response mappings. In one of the first versions of this task, George Stratton, in the late 1800s, wore prisms that optically displaced the visual inputs he received (Rosenbaum, 2010). At first, Stratton showed large errors in reaching as he extended his hand to targets that appeared to the left when they were to the right, and vice versa. Over time, he reduced these errors and reached for optically displaced targets as readily as he had reached for targets before, when they were not optically shifted. Later, when he took off the prism, he readapted to normal conditions. In other people, whose prism adaptation abilities have been studied in more detail and with greater quantitative precision, it has been shown that the magnitude of aiming errors decreases at a decreasing rate as practice

continues, again consistent with the Power Law of Learning (Redding & Wallace, 1997).

More recent research concerning adaptation has gone high-tech, using computers instead of glass prisms. An exciting extension of the traditional method has been to use robots to study people's adaptations to altered force fields (Shadmehr & Wise, 2005). Such adaptation occurs in everyday life, though we are rarely aware of it. For example, we can walk with and without backpacks immediately after donning or dropping those extra loads, we can walk without stopping to recalibrate while ambling on a sandy beach, in the surf, and so on.

Robot-based studies of adaptation have examined a wide range of force fields. In such studies, people aim for targets while "holding hands" with a robot. The robot is programmed to resist or assist the participant's movements. Learning to compensate for or capitalize on the robot's mechanical perturbations is nontrivial, but people can do so, usually at rates that depend on the complexity of the perturbations imposed by the robot: The greater the complexity, the longer it takes to reach asymptotic performance. How well people adapt to the force-field perturbations reflects not just the difficulty of the functions to be learned; it also reflects the integrity of the participant's nervous system. This being the case, learning to adapt to robotic force fields may serve useful diagnostic functions, not to mention potentially rehabilitative ones if the robot can assist movements in patients who have difficulty moving and then are weaned from the assistive device (Hogan, 2008).

The fact that people can adapt to altered force fields and then readapt to normal force fields (lest you worry they cannot!) suggests that chunking alone may not be the basis for skill learning. Participants in force-field adaptation studies cannot know in advance which underlying function drives the robot with which they interact, so trial-and-error learning must play some role in this context. What seems more critical than chunking is learning the *mappings* between stimuli and responses. Strengthening those mappings, whether through tightening piecewise associations between stimuli and responses or through assigning more weight to some induced functions than to others is what seems to account for the improved performance observed in such situations.

Another kind of practice effect in perceptual-motor skills that does not seem most easily explained in terms of chunking is shifting frames of reference. This sort of shift was first and most famously demonstrated by Tolman (1948), who placed rats in a maze and recorded the time for the rats to find their way to the (constant) reward site. Rats who had little practice with the maze experienced disruptions in reaching the goal if they were placed in the maze in different places from where they first began their journeys. By contrast, rats who had a great deal of practice with the maze experienced few disruptions in reaching the goal if they were placed in different start places than they experienced before. Because the rats in both groups took less time to reach the goal as practice continued, it was clear they learned something about the environment or the movements within it. The contrasting effects of starting the rats at different places in their practice histories showed that what was learned shifted over the course of learning. Early in practice, the rats learned relatively low-level features of the task—the particular route to be followed or, conceivably, the particular movements to be made. But later, the rats learned relatively high-level features of the task—the layout of the maze or what Tolman called the "cognitive map."

Tolman's choice of the term "cognitive map" was far from accidental. By using this term, he challenged the prevailing view of his time—the behaviorists' insistence that all that was ever learned were associations between stimuli and responses. Showing that rats have information about where they are in a spatial layout challenged the hypothesis that rats' behavior, or for that matter, any animals' behavior, is simply controlled by learning what movement to make in response to what stimulus.

Subsequent work by others confirmed that the information governing behavioral sequences is coded in different ways as practice continues. Support for this idea came from work on spatial navigation in humans and from work on tasks involving eye-hand coordination. For example, studies of the control of golf putting suggested that there is a shift, with practice, in the frame of reference used to control the position of the golfer's head relative to the position of the golfer's club (Lee, Ishikura, Kegel, Gonzalez, & Passmore, 2008). Studies of stimulus-response compatibility effects in manual reaction-time tasks likewise showed that, after practice, the main factor determining stimulus-response compatibility is not the relation between the stimulus and which *hand* is used to make a response but rather the relation between the stimulus and where *in space* the response is made (Brebner, Shephard, & Cairney, 1972; Wallace, 1971). Studies of serial reaction time, where participants typically press keys in response to lights associated with the keys, showed that, over

the course of practice, participants learn the mappings of lights to key *locations*, not the mappings of lights to particular *fingers* (Willingham, Wells, Farrell, & Stemwedel, 2000).

In all these demonstrations, there is no reason, a priori, to expect participants to alter the frame of reference or the manner of coding they use to control sequences of movements. Yet those coding changes occur. Why they do is something that neither chunking theory alone nor (unadorned) trial-and-error learning theory seems to explain. Explaining these sorts of change is an exciting challenge for future research.

### Anticipation Effects

One of the main changes that accompanies improvements in perceptual-motor performance over the course of practice is better anticipation of the consequences of the actions to be performed. Such anticipation is so rich, in terms of the range and quality of events that can be forecast, that it makes a mockery of the notion that planning and performing physical actions are cognitively trivial, if anyone entertains such a view. Even if no one admits to this perspective, the absence of motor control from most cognitive psychology textbooks suggests that this may be a widely held belief; see Rosenbaum (2005).

To convey some of the evidence for perceptual-motor anticipation, I begin with one of my favorite experiments—the demonstration of expectancy in the housefly. Two German scientists, von Holst and Mittelstaedt (1950), wondered why, if a housefly stands on a surface, it may turn to the right or to the left and continue to turn for several steps, provided the visual surroundings are stationary. On the other hand, if the same housefly stands still in visual surroundings that move, the fly turns, apparently trying to keep itself visually situated with respect to its surroundings. The latter response can be understood from the perspective of trying to stay in the same place in the environment. The former response can be understood from the perspective of allowing the fly to move around freely. The question von Holst and Mittelstaedt (1950) wanted to answer is, Why does sight of the surroundings in motion not cause the housefly to take corrective steps when it triggers those visual motions on its own?

von Holst and Mittelstaedt (1950) set out to test the hypothesis that when visual changes are induced by one's actions, the actor (insect or otherwise) anticipates the perceptual consequences of those actions. Such anticipation makes sense from the standpoint of monitoring one's own performance, because expecting some perceptual consequences but not others lets one decide whether one's actions have been successful. If you were a housefly about to turn to the right, you might, conceivably, anticipate a shift of the visual world to the left, in which case seeing the visual world shift that way would indicate that things worked out as planned. By contrast, if you were a housefly about to stand still, you might anticipate *no* shift of the visual world, in which case seeing the visual world shift would indicate that all had *not* gone as planned.

The foregoing account provides a way of explaining the behavior of the housefly when the fly either turns on its own in stationary visual surroundings or turns in response to moving visual surroundings. The account relies on the idea that, in some limited sense, the fly has expectations. How, then, can one tell whether this is really the case?

von Holst and Mittelstaedt (1950) had a brilliant experimental insight into how to solve this problem. They inverted a housefly's head and glued the fly's head to the fly's thorax. Next they observed the fly's behavior as it stood inside a tall tube with vertical black and white stripes. Inverting the fly's head caused the fly (who survived the procedure and could locomote perfectly well) to confront a visual world that was left-right reversed. In effect, the fly underwent the same visual transformation as the human subjects in the prism adaptation experiments pioneered by George Stratton. Unlike the human subjects, however, the fly never adapted. Instead, it spent the rest of its life in a weird limbo. When the fly attempted to move on its own, it took steps one way or the other and kept doing this indefinitely. von Holst and Mittelstaedt referred to the fly's situation as a "catastrophe." The only way to relieve the fly of its catastrophic life while letting it continue to live was to turn the lights out, at which time the fly finally rested.

Seeing the fly act as if it was confused is just what one would expect if one thought the fly expected visual changes related to its locomotion. One need not conclude that the fly consciously anticipated visual changes, of course. Instead, it could be that some neural signal accompanying signals for walking had the effect of canceling visual shifts that arose from that behavior. A number of other authors, including the great German scientist Hermann von Helmholtz (1866/1962) and the Nobel Laureate Roger Sperry (1950), have said exactly this.

In humans, as for flies, it is important to distinguish between perceptual change produced by one's own actions and perceptual change produced by the environment. von Holst and Mittelstaedt called the former type of perceptual change *reafference*, whereas they called the latter type of perceptual change *exafference*. An example of the need to distinguish reafference from exafference arises when we make saccadic eye movements. The retinal shifts that occur when the world is stationary and we move our eyes can be the same as the retinal shifts that occur when the world moves and we keep our eyes still. To distinguish between these two cases, it is important to have information about the source of the retinal shift.

Hermann von Helmholtz, a giant of late 19th- and early 20th-century science, thought carefully about this problem and argued that neural signals accompanying oculomotor commands enable visual centers to discount saccadically induced visual changes. To reach this conclusion, he relied on a variety of ingenious experiments. In one, he gently pressed on his eyelid with his finger and noted that the visual world seemed to jump. By contrast, when he moved his eye in the normal way, Helmholtz reported that he did not see the visual world jump. The difference between these two cases, Helmholtz argued, was that when he moved his eye in the normal way (i.e., through the normal oculomotor channels), neural signals apprised visual centers of the forthcoming visual shift. Conversely, in the abnormal method of moving the eye (the finger-press condition), the visual centers were not similarly apprised.

In another experiment, a heroic participant agreed to have his eyes bunged with putty, thereby preventing him from moving his eyes when he tried to do so. When the participant tried to move his eyes but failed, he saw the visual world jump. If he tried to move his eyes to the right, the visual world seemed to jump to the right. If he tried to move his eyes to the left, the visual world seemed to jump to the left. Such apparent visual shifts are just what one would expect if one thought signals related to saccadic commands are used to discount ensuing visual changes. When those signals are sent to the visual centers and no visual changes are detected, the reasonable inference is that the visual world jumped in the same direction and over the same magnitude as the intended eye movement.

Several additional points are worth making in connection with this classic work. Notice, first, that in both of the demonstrations just reviewed, feedback from the eye muscles was disrupted. When the eye was prevented from moving, the eye muscles contracted but to no avail, and when the eye was pressed with the finger, the eye muscles presumably failed to contract. The fact that strange visual shifts were experienced in these two cases suggests, or were taken to suggest by Helmholtz, that neural inflow from receptors in the eye muscles does not provide input to the visual centers that helps them discount visual changes brought on by eye movements. Rather, Helmholtz argued, neural *outflow* to the eye muscles provided this critical information.

A second point about Helmholtz's argument is that his account includes a claim that is remarkable, though it is easy to gloss over on first reading. The claim is that unconscious inference impacts perception. Saying that the visual world appears to move because the retinal image shifts but no shift is expected relies on the idea that what is seen depends on implicit calculations of the probabilities of relevant sources of perceptual information: "If the retinal image slides across my retina," one might say (for pedagogic purposes), "but my eye didn't move, then the world must have moved." Helmholtz proposed that perception involves such internal reasoning. In making this proposal, he effectively forecast modern cognitive science, with its emphasis on internal computation. Helmholtz also beat Sigmund Freud to the punch when it came to postulating the unconscious. Helmholtz hypothesized unconscious processes before Freud did, although Freud's postulation of those processes was more famous.

A third point about Helmholtz's argument is that it has not gone unchallenged. Although many investigators have embraced the idea that perception involves unconscious inference (Rock, 1983) or implicit computation (Marr, 1982), others have not. Chief among those who have been resistant to this idea was James Gibson (1979), who argued that optical arrays may be sufficiently structured that they do not need to be "figured out." Gibson argued that the layout of the external environment is directly specified by the light it reflects.

It is not critical that we try to decide between these two perspectives here—the computational perspective of Hemholtz, Rock, and Marr, or the ecological perspective of Gibson and his disciples—especially because this chapter is about the planning and performance of physical actions. My rationale for letting the text move toward this debate about perception has been to show that the investigation of the planning and performance of physical actions helps raise questions about other domains of cognitive psychology. Action research has not been removed from other branches of cognitive psychology, nor will it be in the future.

A fourth point about Helmholtz's argument is related to the last one. It turns out that optical information alone is, in fact, sufficient to distinguish between self-induced perceptual changes and externally induced perceptual changes in some cases (Bridgeman, 2007). It also turns out that sensory feedback from the muscles that rotate the eye can tell the brain how the eye has moved, contrary to Helmholtz's original supposition that such feedback is of little help. Recent evidence (Wang, Zhang, Cohen, & Goldberg, 2007) indicates, in fact, that cells in the brain fire in response to sensory feedback from the stretch receptors of the extraocular muscles (the muscles that move the eye). Even if the eye is passively displaced, these cells code the eye's orbital position (how it is oriented in the socket). This outcome helps resolve a puzzle that has long beset Helmholtz's analysis. The puzzle centers on the fact that extraocular muscles are more richly endowed with muscle stretch receptors than are any other muscles of the body. That being the case, researchers have long wondered why those stretch receptors provided no useful input, as Helmholtz supposed. It is now appreciated that they can.

Even if Helmholtz's experiments were not airtight—he was, after all, working in the 19th and early 20th centuries—it does not follow that his main conclusion was wrong. In fact, a great deal of evidence indicates that Helmholtz was basically correct in thinking that the consequences of forthcoming voluntary movements are anticipated. To take one example from research on the neurophysiology of saccadic eye movements, it turns out that some cells in the parietal cortex change their visual receptive field properties before saccades begin (Duhamel, Colby, & Goldberg, 1992). When electrical recordings are made from these cells, it has been found that when the eye points straight ahead, the cells respond to spots of light presented, say, at 11 o'clock. However, just before the animal spontaneously initiates a saccade, the receptive field of the cells changes to the new position on the retina to which the same spot of light will project once the saccade is completed. Thus, the forthcoming target site on the retina is known even before the eye begins to move, and this knowledge, however rudimentary, is registered in the parietal cortex.

The latter finding helps "seal the deal" for sensorimotor anticipation, or at least it does so for sensorimotor anticipation in connection with saccadic eye movements and visual input. Many other studies support the hypothesis that anticipation plays a key role in action control (Wolpert & Flanagan, 2001).

Because much of this research has helped shed light on the processes by which physical actions are realized, I turn next to that topic.

## Realization of Actions

Every performed voluntary act is the culmination of internal events. Discovering what those events are is one of the primary goals of research on motor control. In addition, discovering what the events are in terms of information processing and, specifically, in terms of mental representations and their physical realizations, is the primary goal of cognitive psychological research on motor control.

To make inroads into this problem, it helps to have a roadmap for the sort of model being pursued and to have a clear idea of the methods for drawing inferences about that model.

Virtually all researchers concerned with the cognitive psychology of motor control appreciate that the generation of voluntary actions entails some sort of transformation from one sort of cognitive code to another. At the highest level are intentions. At the lowest level are efferent commands, the neural signals that cause muscles to contract. Between these levels may be intermediate representations. What they are and how they are activated and deactivated over time comprise core questions for this area of study.

### Language Production

Cognitive psychological models that rely on the idea that there are levels of representation for motor output have been explored the most in research on language production. Here it makes intuitive sense that, at the highest level, there are thoughts to be expressed and, at the lowest level, there are commands for the articulators to be moved. The articulators may be of different sorts. They may be tongues, lips, and larynxes for speaking, or there may be fingers for typing, hands for signing, and so on. The face may be involved as well. For that matter, any part of the body may participate, as long as it contributes to nonverbal communication. Whether all the body parts that move in relation to what is being communicated are represented in the intention to be expressed is a fascinating question. If the crook of one's smile, if the tilt of one's head, if the widening of one's eyes are represented in the plan for a forthcoming utterance, it will be interesting to see whether and if so how a conventional representation of language, such as a syntactic tree structure, can accommodate such a plan.

Within conventional models of language production that focus only on the words that are spoken and the way the words are pronounced, the levels residing between intention and physical action represent different aspects of language: semantics, syntax, morphology, prosody, and phonology. That these levels exist in the minds of both speakers and listeners is more than a convenient assumption. There is empirical evidence that such levels have psychological reality for people engaged in producing and perceiving language.

Consider one of the methods used to learn about the generation of overt behavior: the analysis of errors and, in this case, the analysis of speech errors. The logic of speech-error analysis is familiar to anyone who knows something about psychoanalysis. When someone says something by accident, that mistake may be taken to indicate his or her "real thoughts." For cognitive psychologists interested in language production, the speaker's underlying motives—the topic of interest to Freud and his disciples—are generally of less concern than the format of the mental representations they reveal.

Based on analyses of speech errors, Karl Lashley (1951), a psychologist at Harvard, reached the view, which was revolutionary for his time, that forthcoming speech is mentally represented in plans. Subsequent, more detailed analyses of speech errors led to the important discovery that unintended exchanges of speech elements tend to involve like elements. Thus, nouns exchange with other nouns, verbs exchange with other verbs, and so on (Garrett, 1975). This outcome provides evidence for the psychological reality of nouns, verbs, and other grammatical categories.

So do other malapropisms, including some that may be more subtle than exchanging entire words. An example is saying "two out and one runs" while describing a baseball game. If you just now read this sentence in a way that echoes the way it was actually uttered, you pluralized "run" with a "z" sound rather than with a hard "s" sound. The fact that you (and the error-prone sports announcer) used the "z" ending for the semantically unintended "run" suggests that pluralizing is a distinct mental operation with its own rules. In this example, the speaker picked the wrong word to pluralize—"run" rather than "out"—whereupon the rule for pluralizing was deployed.

A picture that has emerged from the analysis of speech errors is one that favors computation over storage. By this I mean speakers appear to *construct* words on the fly rather than retrieve words as wholes, even when one might plausibly imagine that whole words are used. A speech error that bears out this inference concerns syllable exchanges, such as "slicely thinned bread." This is a morphological error, so-called because it exemplifies a mistake in the way the ultimately produced words are formed. Saying "slicely thinned bread" suggests that, while preparing to say "thinly sliced," the speaker added the "-ly" ending to "slice" and the "-ed" ending to "thin." Had those suffixes not existed as free-standing elements applied to the base morphemes, the observed (or heard) mistake would not have happened. Likewise for phonological errors such as "Flow snurries" instead of "snow flurries." This amusing *faux pas* suggests that individual words may be assembled before being spoken. Saying this another way, it is not the case that the words "snow" and "flurries" are unknown; they are. It *is* the case, however, when these words are *spoken*, they are put together element by element but in a way that sometimes goes awry. The problem is reminiscent of illusory conjunctions in vision (Treisman & Gelade, 1980), where different visual features are misapplied to the relevant object files, so one misremembers a briefly seen person's hat as being red and her pocketbook as being black, whereas the hat and pocketbook actually had the opposite colors.

The analysis of speech errors has been a fruitful line of investigation for the dissection of language production. Early models of language production that relied on speech-error analysis assumed that language production proceeds in distinct stages, with each stage awaiting just one input from the stage before it or, saying this another way, with each stage passing its output to the next stage only after its processing has been completed (Levelt, 1989). Some of these early models included an editor that weeded out mistakes (Baars, Motley, & MacKay, 1975). Later models avoided appeal to an editor and relied instead on parallel distributed processing, with excitation and inhibition passing between nodes within and between putative levels (Dell, 1986). Such models may be seen as being preferable to strict stage models insofar as they resemble neural networks, which, of course, underlie perception and performance. Avoiding an editor is preferable a priori to having an editor because positing an editor begs the question of who the little person is in the head who does the editing—the well known *homunculus* problem that runs through all of cognitive science.

Besides relying on speech errors to analyze language production, students of this subject have turned to other measures to shed light on the means by which language is produced. The time required to generate speech in various conditions is one such measure. Here, two findings are especially interesting. One is that the time to start saying a phrase generally increases with the complexity of the phrase. This is true both when the phrase must be assembled, as in describing a picture or recalling which phrase goes with which abstract symbol (Johnson, 1966), and it is also true when the phrase to be said is known in advance and must be spoken as quickly as possible when a "go" signal is presented (Sternberg, Monsell, Knoll, & Wright, 1978). Second, the time to initiate a sentence is shorter if it has the same syntactic structure as the sentence before (Bock, 1982). Such syntactic priming indicates that the abstract procedural frame for sentences persists in working memory and can be used to generate forthcoming sentences.

Within our list of language output that helps students of language production draw inferences about the history of generated language, the final feature is *coarticulation*. This is a change in the way actions are produced depending on what actions will follow. If you are about to say "tulip," for example, your lips round dramatically when you say "t." You can see such early lip rounding if you look at your mouth in a mirror while saying this word. Such lip rounding is nowhere to be seen if you say "tipping" (i.e., in another word that starts with "t" but continues with a different vowel). The presence of anticipatory lip rounding for "tulip" but not for "tipping" shows that information about articulation is available in advance. Such anticipatory effects are abundant in speech.

Recent work using technology that permits visualization of the moving tongue and other articulators has made it possible to observe coarticulation effects unfold within the interior of the mouth. Such work has shown that when people say the same words over and again, to the point that the phrase becomes a tongue twister, it is possible to see blends of the competitor words (Fowler, 2007). This finding reveals a surprising feature of motor behavior, namely, that it is possible to do more than one thing at once. Such simultaneity of performance has been shown in a form of language production that does not involve the vocal tract, namely, typing. It turns out that when skilled typists produce sequences of keystrokes, their hands and fingers move toward forthcoming targets as soon as possible. Only the requirement to use the *same* hand and finger prevents that effector from proceeding to its present key to its target key at the same time (Gentner, Grudin, & Conway, 1980). This conclusion was reached by filming typists' hands (see Rosenbaum, 2010).

A model of typing control that incorporates the simultaneous motion of the hands and fingers in typing (Rumelhart & Norman, 1982) relies on parallel distributed processing within a neural network, similar to the one used to account for speech generation (Dell, 1986). It is hard to see how a strict stage model could account for such results, at least if the stage model had the order of key depressions as the critical determinant of the ordering of the stages. What confounds such a model is that it is necessary to press the keys in the order that properly specifies the order of letters to be typed, but the order in which the fingers start moving toward the keys may be quite different depending on what biomechanical opportunities or obstacles stand in the way (e.g., whether the finger that needs to get to a key must be involved with reaching some other key first).

## Nonverbal Action

The phenomena reviewed in the last section comprise a subset of the phenomena in language production that have been used to analyze the means by which language is generated. Additional phenomena concern the structure of language itself, as in phonological regularities that linguists and psycholinguists have studied to explore how forthcoming phrases are put together, deficits in language production in patients afflicted with damage to various parts of the brain, and activity of different parts of the brain during language production. Similar phenomena and methods have been used to decipher the generation of nonverbal action, which is the subject of this section.

The generation of movements that play little or no role in language is, of course, extremely important in everyday life. Moving through the environment, eating, and manipulating objects are just a few of the activities that must be carried out with a reasonable degree of skill if one is to function effectively. It turns out that the methods of analysis applied to language production have been profitably applied to the analysis of nonverbal actions. Many of the phenomena discovered for language production have been found for nonverbal action as well.

Suppose you are going to reach out and grab an object to be moved to another site. How would you grab the object? With which hand, with which hand orientation, and where on the object? It turns out that the choices made in this situation are decidedly nonrandom, at least for typically developing children and neurologically normal adults. In studies in my lab, for example, we found that the way people grasp a rod depends on what they plan to do with it; for a review, see Rosenbaum et al. (2006). If the rod lies flat on a pair of cradles allowing grasp of the handle along its midsection, the rod tends to be grasped by the right hand with an overhand grasp if the rod will be turned clockwise with that hand. Alternatively, the rod tends to be grasped by the left hand with an overhand grasp if the rod will be turned counterclockwise with that same lefthand. Conversely, the rod tends to be grasped by the right hand with an underhand grasp if the rod will be turned counterclockwise with the right hand, or the rod tends to be grasped by the left hand with an underhand grasp if the rod will be turned clockwise with that same left hand. This set of behavioral preferences was something I first noticed while having a meal in a restaurant. I noticed a waiter filling glasses with water. The glasses were all inverted to start with, and each time the waiter picked up a glass, he did so with an awkward thumb-down posture. The waiter adopted an initially uncomfortable posture for the sake of a comfortable, or easy-to-control final posture. Participants in the lab study did the same thing.

A related phenomenon is grasping a standing rod high up if it is going to be moved to a low position or grasping the same standing rod low down if it is going to be moved to a high position. Always grabbing the rod at the same height would cause the actor to end in an awkward, hard-to-control final posture. The arm would end up at an extreme angle during the critical phase of the task (placement of the end of the rod onto a target). When the precision demands of placing the rod on the target were reduced, this *grasp-height* effect was attenuated (Rosenbaum, Cohen, Meulenbroek, & Vaughan, 2006).

These grasping results are analogous to the verbal coarticulation results summarized in the last section. There you saw that the lips round in anticipation of later lip-rounding requirements (e.g., rounding the lips for the "u" in "tulip"), demonstrating advance knowledge of such lip rounding. The data concerning object grasps demonstrate the same planning ability for manual control. How one performs at a given time reflects knowledge of what will happen later, and this is no less true of object manipulation than it is of speech.

It turns out that anticipatory effects of this sort run rampant in motor control and are demonstrated not just through overt manifestations of behavior, as in the examples just described, but also through more subtle physiological changes, some of which reveal amazingly subtle knowledge of forthcoming physical changes. I refer here, at least to begin with, to research pioneered by three Russian physiologists (Belen'kii, Gurfinkel, & Pal'tsev, 1967) and by two French physiologists (Bouisset & Zattara, 1987). Using electromyographic (EMG) recording techniques, the researchers in these labs attached electrodes to the muscles of the lower back and legs. The investigators were interested in these muscles because they are involved in maintaining postural support. The question the investigators sought to answer was whether activity in the muscles presaged demands of postural support and, if so, by what amount of time and to what level of detail.

The answers the researchers were led to would warm the hearts of cognitive psychologists, or at least those cognitive psychologists who find it appealing to learn that the knowledge possessed by human beings as reflected in their physical actions is rich and well adapted to future needs. What the researchers found, and what many other researchers subsequently found as well (e.g., Lacquaniti & Maioli, 1989), is that prior to the initiation of overt voluntary behavior, postural muscles are activated to offset whatever imbalances are likely to follow. Thus, if a participant is about to lift his or her left hand rather than right, different muscles in the lower back become active. The nature of the EMG signals depends not just on which arm will be raised; it also depends on the speed of the forthcoming movement, how much weight will be lifted, the direction of the lift, and so on. Such findings indicate that people are attuned to the biomechanical demands of their forthcoming physical actions. They are not consciously aware of these demands and cannot articulate the relevant physical principles in terms of physics equations. Yet their knowledge of biomechanics is exquisitely detailed and fully usable. Were it otherwise, we would be unable to move as well as we do.

### Toward a Cognitive Model of Action Realization

We are far from fully articulating all the physical interactions that are implicitly known and unconsciously anticipated in the generation of voluntary physical actions. Nevertheless, it is possible to venture a cognitive psychological model of movement initiation.

My colleagues and I have developed a cognitive model that draws on the findings reviewed earlier as well as numerous other results, including many from the motor-neuroscience literature. These have received short shrift here because of space limitations. The motor neuroscience literature is an enormous and venerable body of research spurred, on the one hand, by interest in ameliorating motorically expressed neurological disorders, and spurred, on the other hand, by the happy convenience that stimulation of the nervous system leads to observable motor output, a fact that makes motor neuroscience an especially workable scientific pursuit.

Our model of movement generation (Rosenbaum et al., 1995; Rosenbaum, Meulenbroek, Vaughan, & Jansen, 2001) says that voluntary movements are generated not by immediately determining what movement should be made but instead by first establishing representations of goal postures. Saying this another way, goal postures comprise a higher functional level of representation than do movements, much as the semantic level is a higher level than the phonological level for speech.

A few more details can give a feeling for how this posture-based motion planning model works. First, goal postures are specified by relying on constraint hierarchies (i.e., prioritized task requirements). The priorities given to different constraints define the task to be performed. Switching tasks, a topic that has received much attention lately in cognitive psychology (Monsell, 2003), entails changing the priorities of task requirements, including assigning extremely low priorities to task requirements that are only implicit and so are irrelevant.

Second, goal postures are chosen through a two-stage process. Initially, remembered goal postures are evaluated for their suitability for the task at hand (i.e., how well they fulfill the current constraint hierarchy). Next, the most suitable remembered goal posture is altered randomly to change its properties in order to make the goal posture potentially more suitable for the current task. This extra step ensures, or increases the likelihood, that the goal posture to be aimed for actually meets the task demand. This is critical because that task demand may be somewhat different from any task encountered before. The capacity for generativity is as important for body motion as it is for language.

Third, once a goal posture is determined, the movement to it is internally specified before being performed. This process entails internal simulation. Insofar as it does, this helps provide a basis for mental imagery, as anticipated by Shepard and Cooper (1982.) The properties of the specified movement are determined according to the constraint hierarchy as well. Canonically, the movement that is specified has no repercussions for the goal posture specified in the preceding step. However, there can be bottom-up as well as top-down control. If the movement that is chosen based on the assumed goal posture is unacceptable, feedback can inform higher centers that a different goal posture is needed. Plainly, some goal postures that were originally thought to be fine may not be reachable—for example, if an obstacle would be encountered on the way to that particular goal posture. In that case, a different goal posture may be needed.

Fourth, the model makes no distinction between initial movements toward targets and subsequent error correction. Both types of movement reduce discrepancies between current positions and goal positions, and the planning processes required to specify a goal posture and the associated movement are the same in both cases. In both circumstances, the motor planning problem is to determine which of the infinite number of possible goal postures and movements that could potentially reduce the distance between the current position and the goal is most suitable (Bernstein, 1967).

Fifth, the model permits a smooth series of movements. Thus, contrary to what one might think given the model's assumption that goal postures are represented at a different level from movements to those goal postures, the model allows for planning of future goal postures and their attendant movements while ongoing moves are occurring.

A sixth and final point about the posture-based motion planning model is that it is just one of several motor planning models that have been developed. Other models have been advanced as well (for a review, see Rosenbaum, 2010), though most of them have been couched in neural network terms or abstract computational terms, removed from the algorithmic level of explanation that is the usual focus of cognitive psychological research (Marr, 1982). The posture-based motion planning model takes as its starting point the need to identify the memory representations relevant to motor control as well as the information processing operations that act on those memory representations. This is the main reason why the model has been covered here. Arguably, it is the most fully developed cognitive psychological model of the planning and performance of bodily movements available today.

What are the model's capabilities? Some of these have been rendered as computer simulations of an artificial creature presented with various reaching tasks. The main question has been whether the artificial creature can move as people do and whether, by the same token, limitations in the abilities of people are reflected in the model.

Many features of the model's performance are encouraging. The model, or its avatar, can move with any part of its body or with extensions of the body (i.e., with tools) to external targets, it can move at different speeds if needed, and it can rely on different effectors, as occurs in natural movement. The model's simulacrum can also compensate for changes in the mobility of different joints, as occurs in biological motion, and it can reach around obstacles, as also occurs in everyday life. Detailed features of the model's movements compare favorably with detailed features of movements made by people carrying out analogous tasks (Rosenbaum, Meulenbroek, Vaughan , & Jansen, 2001; Vaughan, Rosenbaum, & Meulenbroek, 2001). This outcome indicates that the model is adequate in the particular contexts where it has been tested.

No model is perfect, of course, and the posture-based model is far from it, signaling the need for more research. To name one of the limitations of the model, it has so far been implemented in a cartoon world, not in the real world where mechanical forces must be dealt with. Three-dimensional robots that perform in the real world exist, of course, but the range of tasks they can perform is, arguably, smaller than the range of tasks that the posture-based model can perform. It will be important to bring the range of capabilities of the psychologically informed model to life in three-dimensional environments.

The model also learns goal postures rather than movements per se. In the model, movements are generated on the fly, reflecting the conviction, well known in cognitive psychology, that it is sometimes better to rely on problem solving than to rely on retrieval of previously stored solutions. There is a difficulty with this solution, however. Actors (people and animals performing physical actions) learn to generate particular sorts of movements in particular contexts. A violinist learns how quickly or slowly to move his or her bow in various musical passages, for example, or a painter learns how rapidly or lazily to move his or her brush to achieve certain effects. Research has shown that there is considerable carryover in the way successive movements are performed. So, for example, aiming movements with high curvature induced by obstacle avoidance tend to be followed by aiming movements that have higher-than-normal curvatures even when no obstacle is present (Jax,& Rosenbaum, 2007; van der Wel, Fleckenstein, Jax, & Rosenbaum, 2007).

There is a need to account for such effects within the posture-based motion planning model or in some other model of comparable scope. One way to do so may be to build on the idea that constraint hierarchies apply to the specification of movements as well as to the specification of goal postures. It may also be important to allow that constraint hierarchies for recently performed physical actions tend to be preserved. An efficient way to program forthcoming physical actions may be to change just those features of the constraint hierarchy that distinguish the task to be performed coming next from the task that has been performed last (Rosenbaum, Cohen, Jax, van der Wel, & Weiss, 2007). This hypothesis joins recent work on task switching with research on motor control and perceptual-motor learning.

## Conclusions

This chapter has been concerned with the cognitive psychology of the planning and performance of physical actions. The chapter began with the observation that the study of knowing, which arguably occupies the heart of cognitive psychology, needs to include the study of physical action planning and performance, not just because physical action is required to gather information from the external environment but also because the manner in which physical actions are carried out reflects knowledge of an important kind, a kind that classical epistemologists hardly noticed, the kind that permits skillful physical action itself. The fact that people and animals can move as well as they can, even for mundane, everyday tasks like getting out of chairs or picking up and carrying objects, reveals that implicitly actors know physics. How marvelous it would be if there were some way to make this implicit knowledge explicit! Conventional methods of programming robots from scratch might be replaced by drawing on the knowledge that actors already have that enables them to move as well as they do.

Where will this field of study go next? One avenue for future investigation will be delineating those kinds of information relevant to physical action control that actually are knowledge based. I refer to the fact that an exciting development in this area of research has been the identification of *preflexes*. These are mechanically based responses that typically occur with latencies of virtually 0 ms and are attributable to physical features, rather than neural/computational features, of the body. Far from being cognitively trivial, these structural features obviate

the need for computation or neural mediation. An exciting advance in robotics has been to build robots that have appropriate preflexes (Dickinson et al., 2000). So insect-like robots with rotating flipper legs can traverse paths riddled with rocks, logs, mud, and ruts. The physical properties of these robots contribute to their agility.

The human body, too, has similar capabilities. Elastic properties of muscles and tendons are used in everyday activities like bending down to jump up or in cocking one's arm back to throw a ball forward. People learn to exploit such features of their bodies, but it takes time for them to do so. Curiously, it takes children longer to learn not to spill their milk than to generate syntactically complex sentences. Understanding how we control our physical actions will help explain why physical actions take so long to learn and why. Computers can beat the best chess players in the world, but no robot can do what virtually any 3-year-old can: climb a tree, put on a shirt, or catch a butterfly. The great challenge for this field of research is to understand how the endless generativity of physical action is possible. Cognitive psychology will not be complete if it leaves the organism equipped for perceiving, attending, and storing away information, but ill equipped for acting in the world.

## References

Baars, B. J., Motley, M. T., & MacKay, D. G. (1975). Output editing for lexical status in artifically elicited slips of the tongue. *Journal of Verbal Learning and Verbal Behavior, 14,* 382–391.

Belen'kii, V., Gurfinkel, V. S., & Pal'tsev, Y. I. (1967). Elements of control of voluntary movements. *Biofizika, 10,* 135–141.

Bernstein, N. (1967). *The coordination and regulation of movements.* London: Pergamon.

Bock, J. K. (1982). Toward a cognitive psychology of syntax: Information processing contributions to sentence formulation. *Psychological Review, 89,* 1–47.

Bouisset, S., & Zattara, M. (1987) Biomechanical study of the programming of anticipatory postural adjustments associated with voluntary movement. *Journal of Biomechanics, 20,* 735–742.

Brebner, J., Shephard, M., & Cairney, P. (1972). Spatial relationships and S-R compatibility. *Acta Psychologica, 36,* 1–15.

Bridgeman, B. (2007). Efference copy and its limitations. *Computers in Biology and Medicine, 37,* 924–929.

Bryan, W. L., & Harter, N. (1897). Studies in the physiology and psychology of the telegraphic language. *Psychological Review, 4,* 27–53.

Crossman, E. R. F. W. (1959). A theory of the acquisition of speed skill. *Ergonomics, 2,* 153–166.

Dell, G. S. (1986). A spreading activation theory of retrieval in sentence production. *Psychological Review, 93,* 283–321.

Dewey, J. (1929). *The quest for certainty.* New York: Minton, Balch.

Dickinson, M. H., Farley, C. T., Full, R. J., Keohl, M. A., Kram, R., & Lehman, S., (2000). How animals move: An integrative view. *Science, 288*, 100–106.

Duhamel, J-R., Colby, C. L., & Goldberg, M. E. (1992). The updating of the representation of visual space in parietal cortex by intended eye movements. *Science, 255*, 90–92.

Elliott, D., Helsen, W. F., & Chua, R. (2001). A century later: Woodworth's (1899) two-component model of goal-directed aiming. *Psychological Bulletin, 127*, 342–357.

Ericsson, A., Charness, N., Hoffman, P., & Feltovich, R. (Eds.). (2006). *The Cambridge handbook of expertise and expert performance*. Cambridge, England: Cambridge University Press.

Ericsson, K. A., Krampe, R. T., & Tesch-Romer, C. (1993). The role of deliberate practice in the acquisition of expert performance. *Psychological Review, 100*, 363–406.

Fitts, P. M. (1954). The information capacity of the human motor system in controlling the amplitude of movement. *Journal of Experimental Psychology, 47*, 381–391.

Fowler, C. A. (2007). Speech production. In M. G. Gaskell (Ed.), *The Oxford handbook of psycholinguistics* (pp. 489–502). New York: Oxford University Press.

Galton, F. (1979). *Hereditary genius: An inquiry into its laws and consequences*. London: Julian Friedman Publishers. (Original work published in 1869).

Garrett, M. F. (1975). The analysis of sentence production. In G. H. Bower (Ed.), *Psychology of learning and motivation* (Vol. 9, pp. 133–177). New York: Academic Press.

Gentner, D. R., Grudin, J., & Conway, E. (1980). *Finger movements in transcription typing*. (Technical Report 8001). La Jolla, CA: University of California, San Diego, Center for Human Information Processing.

Gibson, J. J. (1979). *The ecological approach to visual perception*. Boston: Houghton-Mifflin.

Gladwell, M. (2008). *Outliers: The story of success*. New York: Little Brown and Company.

Heathcote, A., Brown, S., & Mewhort, D. J. K. (2000). The power law repealed: The case for an exponential law of practice. *Psychonomic Bulletin and Review, 7*, 185–207.

Helmholtz, H. (1866/1962). *Handbook of physiological optics*. New York: Dover. (Translation of Handbuch der physiologischen Optik. Hamburg: Voss.)

Hogan, N. (2008). Intensive sensorimotor arm training mediated by therapist or robot improves hemiparesis in patients with chronic stroke. *Neurorehabilitation and Neural Repair, 22*, 305–310.

Holst, E. von, & Mittelstaedt, H. (1950). Das Reafferenzprinzip. Wechselwirkungen zwischen Zentralnervensystem und Peripherie. *Naturwissenschaften, 37*, 464–476. (English translation in The behavioral physiology of animals and man. London: Methuen, 1973, pp. 139–173).

Jax, S. A., & Rosenbaum, D. A. (2007). Hand path priming in manual obstacle avoidance: Evidence that the dorsal stream does not only control visually guided actions in real time. *Journal of Experimental Psychology: Human Perception and Performance, 33*, 425–441.

Johnson, N. F. (1966). On the relationship between sentence structure and the latency in generating the sentence. *Journal of Verbal Learning and Verbal Behavior, 5*, 375–480.

Lacquaniti, F., & Maioli, C. (1989). The role of preparation in tuning anticipatory and reflex responses during catching. *Journal of Neuroscience, 9*, 134–148.

Lashley, K. S. (1951). The problem of serial order in behavior. In L. A. Jeffress (Ed.), *Cerebral mechanisms in behavior* (pp. 112–131). New York: Wiley.

Lee, T. D., Ishikura, T., Kegel, S., Gonzalez, D., & Passmore, S. (2008). Head–putter coordination patterns in expert and less skilled golfers. *Journal of Motor Behavior, 40*, 267–272.

Levelt, W. (1989). *Speaking*. Cambridge, MA: MIT Press.

Logan, G. D. (1988). Toward an instance theory of automatization. *Psychological Review, 95*, 492–527.

Marr, D. (1982). *Vision*. San Francisco: W. H. Freeman.

Merleau-Ponty, M. (1962). *Phenomenology of perception* (C. Smith, Trans.). New York: Humanities Press. (Original work published in 1945).

Miller, G. A. (1956). The magical number seven plus or minus two: Some limits on our capacity for processing information. *Psychological Review, 63*, 81–97.

Monsell, S. (2003). Task switching. *Trends in Cognitive Sciences, 7*, 134–140.

Neves, D. M., & Anderson, J. R. (1981). Knowledge compilation: Mechanisms for the automatization of cognitive skills. In J. R. Anderson (Ed.), *Cognitive skills and their acquisition* (pp. 57–84). Hillsdale, NJ: Elbaum.

Newell, A. M., & Rosenbloom, P. S. (1981). Mechanisms of skill acquisition and the law of practice. In J. R. Anderson (Ed.), *Cognitive skills and their acquisition* (pp. 1–55). Hillsdale, NJ: Erlbaum.

Nissen, M. J., & Bullemer, P. (1987). Attentional requirements of learning: Evidence from performance measures. *Cognitive Psychology, 19*, 1–32.

Ohlsson, S. (1992). The learning curve for writing books: Evidence from Professor Asimov. *Psychological Science, 3*, 380–383.

Owen, A. M., Coleman, M. R., Boly, M., Davis, M. H., Laureys, S., & Pickard, J. D. (2006). Detecting awareness in the vegetative state. *Science, 313*, 1402.

Polanyi, M. (1958). *Personal knowledge: Towards a post-critical philosophy*. Chicago: University of Chicago Press.

Reber, A. S. (1992). *Implicit learning and tacit knowledge—An essay on the cognitive unconscious*. New York: Oxford University Press.

Redding, G. M., & Wallace, B. (1997). *Adaptive spatial alignment*. Mahwah, NJ: Erlbaum.

Rock, I. (1983). *The logic of perception*. Cambridge, MA: MIT Press.

Rosenbaum, D. A. (2005). The Cinderella of psychology: The neglect of motor control in the science of mental life and behavior. *American Psychologist, 60*, 308–317.

Rosenbaum, D. A. (2010). *Human motor control (2nd ed)*. San Diego, CA: Academic Press/Elsevier.

Rosenbaum, D. A., Carlson, R. A., & Gilmore, R. O. (2001) Acquisition of intellectual and perceptual-motor skills. *Annual Review of Psychology, 52*, 453–470. Rosenbaum, D. A., Cohen, R. G., Jax, S. A., van der Wel, R., & Weiss, D. J. (2007). The problem of serial order in behavior: Lashley's legacy. *Human Movement Science, 26*, 525–554.

Rosenbaum, D. A., Cohen, R. G., Meulenbroek, R. G., & Vaughan, J. (2006). Plans for grasping objects. In M. Latash & F. Lestienne (Ed.), *Motor control and learning over the lifespan* (pp. 9–25). New York: Springer.

Rosenbaum, D. A., Loukopoulos, L. D., Meulenbroek, R. G. M., Vaughan, J., & Engelbrecht, S. E. (1995). Planning reaches by evaluating stored postures. *Psychological Review, 102*, 28–67.

Rosenbaum, D. A., Meulenbroek, R. G., Vaughan, J., & Jansen, C. (2001). Posture-based motion planning: Applications to grasping. *Psychological Review, 108*, 709–734.

Rumelhart, D. E., &Norman, D. A. (1982). Simulating a skilled typist: A study of skilled cognitive-motor performance. *Cognitive Science, 6,* 1–36.

Ryle, G. (1949). *The concept of mind.* Chicago: University of Chicago Press.

Schacter, D. L. (1987). Implicit memory: History and current status. *Journal of Experimental Psychology: Learning, Memory, and Cognition, 13,* 501–518.

Schmidt, R. A., &Bjork, R. A. (1992). New conceptualizations of practice: Common principles in three paradigms suggest new concepts for training. *Psychological Science, 3,* 207–214.

Seibel, R. (1963). Discrimination time for a 1,023-alternative task. *Journal of Experimental Psychology, 66,* 215–255.

Shadmehr, R., &Wise, S. P. (2005). *The computational neurobiology of reaching and pointing.* Cambridge, MA: MIT Press.

Shannon, C., &Weaver, W. (1949). *The mathematical theory of communication.* Urbana: Univeristy of Illinois Press.

Shepard, R. N., &Cooper, L. (1982). *Mental images and their transformations.* Cambridge, MA: MIT Press/Bradford Books.

Sparrow, W. A., &Newell, K. M. (1998). Metabolic energy expenditure and the regulation of movement economy. *Psychonomic Bulletin and Review, 5,* 173–196.

Sperry, R. W. (1950). Neural basis of the spontaneous optokinetic response produced by visual inversion. *Journal of Comparative and Physiological Psychology, 43,* 482–489.

Sternberg, S., Monsell, S.Knoll, R. L., &Wright, C. E. (1978). The latency and duration of rapid movement sequences: Comparisons of speech and typewriting. In G. E. Stelmach

(Ed.), *Information processing in motor control and learning* (pp. 117–152). New York: Academic Press.

Tolman, E. C. (1948). Cognitive maps in rats and men. *Psychological Review, 55,* 189–208.

Treisman, A., &Gelade, G. (1980). A feature integration theory of attention. *Cognitive Psychology, 12,* 97–136.

van der Wel, R. P., Fleckenstein, R., Jax, S., & Rosenbaum, D. A. (2007). Hand path priming in manual obstacle avoidance: Evidence for abstract spatio-temporal forms in human motor control. *Journal of Experimental Psychology: Human Perception and Performance, 33,* 1117–1126.

Vaughan, J., Rosenbaum, D. A., & Meulenbroek, R. G. J. (2001). Planning reaching and grasping movements: The problem of obstacle avoidance. *Motor Control, 5,* 116–135.

Wallace, R. J. (1971). Stimulus-response compatibility and the idea of a response code. *Journal of Experimental Psychology, 88,* 354–360.

Wang, X., Zhang, M., Cohen, I. S., & Goldberg, M. E. (2007). The proprioceptive representation of eye position in monkey primary somatosensory cortex. *Nature Neuroscience, 10,* 640–646.

Willingham, D. B., Wells, L. A., Farrell, J. M., & Stemwedel, M. E. (2000). Implicit motor sequence learning is represented in response locations. *Memory and Cognition, 28,* 366–375.

Wilson, M. (2002). Six views of embodied cognition. *Psychonomic Bulletin & Review, 9,* 625–636.

Wolpert, D. M., &Flanagan, J. R. (2001). Motor prediction. *Current Biology, 11,* 729–732.

Woodworth, R. S. (1899). The accuracy of voluntary movement. *Psychological Review Monograph Supplements, 3,* No. 3.

# The Psychology of Practice: Lessons From Spatial Cognition

David H. Uttal *and* Nathaniel G. Meadow

**Abstract**

Having high levels of spatial skills strongly predicts attainment in science, technology, engineering, and mathematics fields (Shea, Lubinski, & Benbow, 2001; Wai, Lubinski, & Benbow, 2009). The focus of this chapter is on two issues: (a) the effect of training and practice on spatial skills and (b) the cognitive mechanisms that support training-related improvement. We discuss a recently conducted meta-analysis that measures the beneficial effects of practice on spatial ability. On average, training led to an improvement of almost one-half standard deviation. Moreover, in some cases the training-related improvements were durable and transferred to other spatial tasks. Research on the effects of training on one well-known spatial task, mental rotation, has led to specific accounts of the influence of practice and training. Finally, we review the effects of video games on spatial skills and their potential impact on spatial cognition. The ability to improve people's spatial ability provides an avenue to increase participation in mathematics, science, and engineering.

**Key Words**: spatial skills, practice, STEM, transfer, sex differences

The ability to think about and communicate spatial information is critically important to human learning. Spatial cognition is important not only in everyday tasks such as navigation but also in thinking about scientific and mathematical information. Several studies (e.g., Humphreys, Lubinski, & Yao, 1993; Wai et al., 2009) have documented that skill in spatial tasks strongly predicts academic attainment in science, technology, engineering, and mathematics (*STEM*) fields. There is great interest in increasing the number of Americans capable of studying and ultimately obtaining jobs in STEM fields, and spatial practice and training may be one way (of many) (see Sorby, 2009; Spence & Feng, 2010; Terlecki, Newcombe, & Little, 2008; Uttal & Cohen, 2012) to increase STEM attainment.

For all of these reasons, it is critically important to determine how spatial thinking can be improved. Until now, researchers have disagreed substantially on basic questions such as whether, and to what extent, spatial cognition responds to practice and training. Although some researchers have claimed that spatial cognition is highly malleable, others have suggested either that training has no effect or is limited to specific tasks that are similar to the trained tasks (see Uttal et al., 2012). Our goal here is to address these issues by reviewing and systematizing what is known about the influences of practice and training on spatial thinking. We also point out reasons why previous researchers have reached different conclusions regarding the influences of practices, and we attempt to resolve some of these disagreements.

In addition to its importance for improving spatial cognition, investigating the effects of practice on spatial thinking can also shed light on more general issues in cognition. The study of practice is one of the oldest topics in psychology. Even before 1900, researchers were conducting detailed and specific studies of the effect of practice on learning specific skills, such as Morse code (Bryan & Harter, 1897, 1899). More recently, research on the effects of practice has figured prominently in studies of expertise, with many findings indicating it can take years of intensive practice to acquire a high level of competency in domains ranging from musical performance to chess (e.g., Ericcsson, Krampe, & Tesch-Römer, 1993). However, despite the large amount of research that has been conducted on this topic, it is still not easy to answer some fundamental questions regarding the effects of practice. What happens, at a perceptual and cognitive level, when people practice? How do underlying mental representations and processes change with practice? The research discussed next reveals that studying the effects of practice on spatial cognition can shed light on these issues. In several cases (e.g., mental rotation) the cognitive mechanisms that are involved have been well specified, and this work can provide a foundation for understanding the influences of practice. Reviewing this literature can provide insights into whether, and why, spatial thinking is malleable and how it responds to practice and training.

## Organization and Definitions

This chapter is organized as follows: We begin by defining spatial cognition and practice. We then provide reviews of work on spatial training and practice, including both a systematic meta-analysis and a more detailed, focused narrative review of the mechanisms of improvement in two well-known tasks and training paradigms (mental rotation and video game playing). Finally we consider the implications of our findings and highlight important research questions that need to be addressed.

### Defining Spatial Cognition

We define spatial cognition as the representation and transformation of a set of objects in space, or the relations among a set of objects (Uttal & Cohen, 2012). One complication is that there are many different kinds of spatial tasks, and different tasks may respond differently to practice. Defining the individual components of spatial cognition and the underlying cognitive skills or abilities that support these operations has proved to be a challenging task. There is very little agreement (and relatively little psychometric coherence) to the different measures of spatial cognition (Carroll, 1993; Eliot, 1987; Hegarty & Waller, 2005; Lohman, 1988).

The most successful approach to defining the divisions of spatial skills involves a combination of factor-analytic methods and analysis of the cognitive skills and processes that correlate with these factors (see Hegerty & Waller, 2005; Linn & Petersen, 1985; Miyake & Shah, 1999; Uttal et al., 2012). The largest and most consistent factor is *spatial visualization* (Linn & Petersen, 1985), which is the ability to transfer and mentally manipulate representations of objects. A second factor that has shown up in several psychometric studies is sometimes called *spatial memory* (Ekstrom, French, & Harman, 1979), which may include both recognizing and recalling spatial figures and relations.

We also note that specific tasks may involve many steps that tap into different skills. For example, mental rotation not only requires the transformation of spatial information but also the encoding, activation, and recall of the relevant figures. In addition, practice in one kind of skill may transfer to tasks in another skill. For example, the gains from practicing mental rotation may not be limited to the specific dynamics of turning the object over in one's mind. People may also improve at recognizing and representing particular shapes, and hence decisions regarding whether a stimulus is a mirror image of the target may become faster and more accurate.

### Defining Practice

What is practice? What distinguishes practice from other, related activities, such as learning, repetition, and performance? We suggest that practice has two distinguishing characteristics. First, it is intensive; it involves a substantial amount of attention and time. In contrast, performance is not practice, as it typically is not intensive enough to provide the desired outcomes. For example, Ericsson, Krampe, and Tesch-Römer (1993) point out that the average baseball player will see only about 15 pitches in a typical performance—a professional game—but the same baseball player may see hundreds of pitches daily in batting practice.

Note that practice does not need to occur in a single session or single location. Indeed, many studies have now established that practice works best when it is *distributed* across time (e.g., Mumford, Constanza, Baughman, Threlfall, & Fleishman, 1994). Yet, even in the shorter, distributed practice sessions, the participant typically works at the task repeatedly. One-trial learning is not practice; skills or abilities that are acquired without repetition do not require practice.

Second, practice usually involves the same or similar tasks, or at least tasks within the same general domain. The range of skills demanded in that domain determine how much practice is required to obtain a level of expertise or mastery. Well-defined or constrained tasks may improve dramatically with relatively little practice, whereas 10,000 or more hours of practice is typically required to obtain a degree of mastery in highly complex domains, such as chess or music (e.g., Gladwell, 2008; Ericsson & Smith, 1991).

It is also important to point out that the gains from practice are not always available to conscious awareness; the effects of practice can often be implicit in nature. A good example is what may happen as one plays a spatially challenging video game. People practice the video game and are aware that they are improving; however, they may not be aware of the *cause* of this improvement (e.g., Gee, 2003). Playing action video games may in fact facilitate more general abilities, such as the capacity of video-spatial attention, and these improvements facilitate not only playing of the specific video game but also performance on a host of cognitive and psychometric spatial ability tasks. Likewise, people who practice classic implicit motor learning tasks, such as mirror-tracing, may improve dramatically without knowing precisely why or what they have learned. Our review includes literature both on explicit and implicit practice.

## Quantitative and Qualitative Reviews of Research on the Effects of Practice on Spatial Thinking

In this chapter we review literature investigating the effects of spatial practice and training at two complementary levels. The first is broad, course, and quantitative; we present the results of a meta-analysis of the effects of spatial training and practice on a wide variety of outcome measures. The meta-analysis provides a measure of the overall effectiveness of spatial training and practice. It also identifies several factors that may contribute to the large differences in prior findings and claims. Our second approach is more fine and qualitative; we present a narrative review and analysis of the causes of practice-related improvement in mental rotation and video game playing.

Each approach has both advantages and disadvantages. The meta-analysis provides a very accurate measure of the overall effectiveness of spatial training and practice, but it does not provide much information about the mechanisms through which these effects occur. The narrative review provides a much more focused account of the influences of practice and training, but it is limited to only to two

domains that are well established or of great current interest. When taken together, the two approaches provide a reasonably comprehensive account of both whether, and how, spatial practice and training improve spatial thinking.

### Meta-Analysis of Spatial Practice and Training Studies

We recently completed a meta-analysis of the large literature on spatial training and practice (Uttal et al., 2012). We were interested in whether practicing spatial tasks led to improvements in performance and, if so, whether these effects endured over time and whether they transferred to different, untrained tasks. The issue of transfer is particularly important because direct training in spatial tasks will not lead to improvements in STEM unless the knowledge that is gained transfers to other, untrained tasks.

#### METHOD

*Selecting and Finding Articles*

A critical issue in any meta-analysis is the literature search. We sought to provide a comprehensive yet focused review of the literature. We therefore chose to focus on a 25-year period of research, from 1984 through 2009. We searched for relevant literature in digital databases (PsycInfo, ERIC, and ProQuest Dissertations and Theses). We also contacted researchers in the field. We took pains to obtain as much unpublished work as possible. In this regard, the database ProQuest Dissertations and Theses proved to be particularly important as it focuses on dissertations, many of which remain unpublished.

We read the abstracts of all articles that met our criteria. If the study could not be immediately eliminated, we read the full paper. Reliability of these judgments was high, and disagreements were resolved through consensus. In the end, we included over 200 papers, and most studies reported multiple experiments or manipulations. The range of practice and training varied widely from intensive, laboratory-based studies to examination of the effects of more real-world practice opportunities, such as the influences of taking a spatially demanding geology course (e.g., Pibrum, Reynolds, McAuliffe, Leedy, & Birk, 2005).

*Conversion to Effect Sizes*

After deciding that a given article should be included, we then converted the findings to a standard effect size. By expressing observed differences in terms of standard deviation units, effect sizes provide a means of comparing studies despite differences in dependent measures. In this case, the effect size usually involved comparisons of treatment and control groups, as well as comparisons of both groups before and after training.

## RESULTS
### Overall Results
The results indicate that spatial skills respond strongly to practice or training. The overall effect size was 0.47 ($SE = 0.04$).[1] Spatial training and practice improved performance by almost one-half of a standard deviation.

### Duration of Effects
The effects of training and practice are only useful if they last. People will not be able to engage in intense practice forever, so its effects need to endure for it to be of practical use. One of the continuing concerns about attempts to improve spatial reasoning is that the effects are often fleeting (e.g., National Research Council, 2006). However, our comprehensive meta-analysis does provide evidence that the effects of spatial training can endure. In those studies that did include delays, the effects of training were as strong after the delay as immediately after practice or training. One challenge in interpreting this finding is that many studies did not include measures of the effects of practice after delay. In the typical laboratory study, for example, measures are typically taken only during one sitting, and the entire process often lasts less than an hour. Nevertheless, those that did include delays found, on average, that the effects of practice or training can last.

### Transfer
For practice and training to be effective, they also need to transfer to other tasks that are not included in the practice or the training. Moreover, as discussed earlier, the issue of transfer has very important implications for understanding the cognitive changes that occur as a result of practice. Therefore, we paid particular attention to whether practice on one task transferred to other tasks that were not explicitly included in the training or practice. As in the analysis of the duration of effects, our analyses are somewhat limited by researchers' self-selection regarding whether to study transfer. Most researchers did not include a transfer task. However, those studies that did look for transfer usually found it. In fact, the overall effect size for those studies that tested for transfer was also about one-half of a standard deviation improvement.

## MODERATORS
We examined several factors that have been shown, or thought, to influence the magnitude of training effects on spatial thinking, including study design, as well as participants' sex and age.

### Study Design and Control Group Performance
Different researchers used different experimental designs, and these differences substantially affected the findings. There were three main kinds of experimental design. In a *between-subjects* only design, the researcher randomly assigns participants to an experimental or control group. The experimental group receives training or practices specific tasks that are designed to enhance some kind of spatial performance. Performance is measured only after the training or practice is implemented. Thus, between-subjects only designs do not include a pretest. Conversely, in a *within-subjects* only design, performance is measured both before (pretest) and after (posttest) training or practice. However, there is no control group, only one group is assessed. Finally, the most common design, *mixed designs*, combines elements of both; participants are assigned to an experimental or control group, and their performance is measured both before and after training or practice. Approximately two-thirds of the studies in our meta-analysis used the mixed design.

Experimental design affected the magnitude of the reported effects. Studies using the within-only design found significantly higher effects of training than studies that used the between-only or mixed design. This result is not surprising because within-subjects designs do not include a control group; thus, all of the improvement may be attributed to the effects of practice. However, this assumption is methodologically unsound because we know that simply taking a test more than once often leads to improved performance on that test. The magnitude of the test-retest effects can be substantial, and at least part of the larger improvement in studies that used the within-only design can be attributed to the confounding of improvement due to practice or training on the relevant spatial test or ability and the general improvement that would be expected simply from tasking a test. This issue is discussed further later.

### Control Group Performance
To further examine the influences of control groups on overall findings, we separated the control and treatment groups for independent analysis. Note that this analysis was only possible for the

mixed design studies, as only this design includes both a control and treatment group, and measures taken both before and after training or practice.

Two aspects of this analysis were noteworthy. First, the treatment groups ($g = 0.62$, $SE = 0.04$)[2] improved significantly more than the control groups did ($g = 0.45$, $SE = 0.04$), $p < .01$. Second, the magnitude of the control group improvement was surprisingly high. Studies of test-retest effects in other domains have found effect sizes of approximately half the value of the mean-weighted effect size in our control groups (Hauschknecht, Halpert, Di Paolo, & Gerrard, 2007). The high levels of improvement in the control groups have important implications for understanding why different researchers have reached such different conclusions regarding the effectiveness of training and practice.

We suggest that differences in the reported effect sizes and statistical significance of a given study may depend not only on whether there was a control group but also on what the control group did. As shown earlier, the absence of a control group produced significantly larger findings in studies measuring improvement due to practice or training. In the same vein, a highly performing control group could *suppress* the overall finding of a study by rivaling the gains demonstrated by the experimental group.

A very good example of the importance of considering the improvement in control groups comes from the research of Sims and Mayer (2002). They investigated the influences of playing the video game Tetris on participants' performance on a battery of nine spatial ability tests. Experiment 1 was correlational, focusing on differences between people who already played or did not play Tetris frequently. Experiment 2 used an experimental design to investigate the influences of practicing Tetris on the performance on the spatial battery of tests. We focus only on the second experiment here.

The participants in Experiment 2 were 16 women who had no experience playing Tetris. Half of them were assigned to receive 14 sessions of approximately 1-hour practice in playing Tetris, and the other half were assigned to a control question. Both the experimental and control groups took the same tests, completing various measures of spatial ability at sessions 1, 2, 5, 9, and 15. Thus, the only difference between the control and experimental groups was the Tetris training; both groups took the same tests at the same time throughout the practice period.

The training group improved substantially, with a mean effect size of 1.19. However, despite this very large effect, the comparison to the control group did not reach statistical significance. Why? The answer is that the control group also improved greatly, with a mean effect size of 1.11. Based on these results, Sims and Mayer (2002) concluded that training effects are not large or even statistically significant, if comparisons are made with the appropriate control group. They wrote that

> … participants in both groups showed large pretest-to-posttest improvements for all the measures… However, there were no significant main effects for group, nor were there any significant interactions between group and time of test. Thus, there is no evidence that up to 12 hours of Tetris playing had any effect on students' spatial ability skills beyond merely retaking the tests.

We reinterpret these results in a different light. Although it is true that there were no significant differences between the training and control group, the fact that both groups improved so much is remarkable. Whereas Sims and Mayer interpreted the results as indicating that spatial skills do not respond well to training or practice, our analysis leads to the opposite conclusion: Spatial skills respond very well to training or practice, and importantly, this training may take the form of either direct or implicit practice (or both). We suggest that the experience of taking multiple tests throughout the experiment was in itself a form of implicit practice.

More specifically, we are arguing for an expanded view of the interpretation of the improvement that can result from taking tests multiple times. Traditionally, this "retesting effect" is often seen as uninteresting, involving low-level effects such as learning which key to press for a particular response. However, we suggest that in this case something more interesting was taking place; we think that taking multiple, distinct tests at different times distributed throughout the experiment may have led the participants to think more about relevant spatial information and to do better than they would if they simply took a single test twice. Comparing and contrasting across different kinds of tests may help participants think about the similarities and differences among the tests and therefore focus on improving spatial thinking more than they otherwise would (see Bransford & Schwartz, 1999; Gentner & Markman, 1997).

Further support for the claim that multiple testing can be an important source of spatially relevant practice comes from an analysis of the *kinds* of tasks that control groups performed. Across the literature, there was substantial variation in the "filler" tasks that control groups completed while the experimental groups were practicing the relevant spatial skills. In many cases, researchers deliberately used nonspatial filler tasks, such as playing Solitaire or taking vocabulary tests. In other cases, however, the researchers had the control group perform spatial filler tasks that differed from the experimental task in some specific way. For example, Feng, Spence, and Pratt (2007) were specifically interested in the effects of practicing *action* video games on the mental transformation of three-dimensional (3D) shapes. Their control group therefore practiced a nonactive but 3D puzzle video game called *Ballance*.

We coded each control group's filler activity and compared the impact of spatial versus nonspatial fillers on a study's overall effect size. Studies in which the control group performed a spatial filler task had significantly lower effects sizes than studies in which the control group performed a nonspatial filler. This result suggests that control groups learned something from material that was not directly tested—from the filler tasks. Having a spatial filler task led to more improvement in the control group, which had the ironic effect of lowering the overall effect size. The difference between the experimental and control groups was lower because the control group improved so much. Thus, the filler tasks were a form of implicit practice; the participants were not aware they were learning something relevant to the outcome tests that they took, but nevertheless, experiencing the spatial filler tasks facilitated spatial learning.

A second reason to assume that something more interesting than simply practicing the response is going on is that the improvement in the control groups *transferred* to different tasks. That is, being in the *control* group led to better performance on the transfer items. Caution is needed in interpreting this finding because only a relatively small number of studies tested for transfer in the control group. Nonetheless, this result again provides evidence that some of the control-group activities provided real, although implicit, spatial practice. This implicit practice was sufficient both to promote the acquisition of skills and knowledge and the transfer of these skills to new tasks.

*Sex*

Males traditionally perform better than females on tasks involving the mental transformation of spatial information, particularly three-dimensional information (Halpern, 2012; Maccoby & Jacklin, 1974; Voyer, Voyer, & Bryden, 1995). Some researchers (e.g., Feng et al., 2007) have suggested that the sex difference can be reduced or even eliminated with training or practice. We found, however, that both sexes improved equally with practice. On average, males began at higher levels and maintained their advantage over the practice period. Of course, it is certainly possible that sex differences are declining with age, and that future meta-analyses may find smaller, or no, sex differences in spatial cognition (see Hyde & Linn, 2006).

*Age*

Generally speaking, the malleability of thinking declines with age, with children typically benefiting more from training, practice, or experience than adults do (although large effects can still be observed in adults). We did find that children improved more than adults did, but this result did not reach statistical significance. We believe a likely reason for the lack of a significant difference is that very few studies have included participants of substantially different ages. For example, a developmental psychologist might compare the performance of 5-year-olds and 7-year-olds, but he or she is unlikely to also include adolescents in the same study (although see Kail, 1986 for a notable exception). Likewise, it is very unusual to include young adolescents and adults in the same study. Thus, when assessing the effects of age on the magnitude of practice-related improvement, we must rely almost completely on comparisons across studies. Because different studies often vary in many ways, the variability of these cross-study age comparisons tends to be large, and hence it can be difficult to show that the differences between ages are greater than the variability within ages (see Hedges, Tipton, & Johnson, 2010a, 2010b; Uttal et al., 2012).

## Understanding Mechanisms of Improvement

In this section we provide a more detailed, narrative review of two lines of research (practice on mental rotation and the effects of video game playing) to shed light on the *mechanisms* through which practice and training promote improvement in spatial tasks. This review is deliberately *not* comprehensive. Instead, we have chosen to focus on research that highlights the perceptual or cognitive mechanisms that improve with training or practice.

### Mental Rotation

There has been a great deal of research on the cognitive mechanisms that support mental rotation, and a smaller but growing body of work on the effects of practice on mental rotation. In combination, these lines of work have allowed researchers to be very specific about how, when, and why practice leads to improvement in mental rotation.

In classic (e.g., Cooper, 1975; Shepard & Metzler, 1971) mental rotation tasks, participants are asked to judge whether a presented stimulus is a rotated or reflected (mirror) image of a target stimulus. If the stimulus is a rotated transformation of the target, then it can be reoriented (mentally or physically) to match the target. For example, if the stimulus has been rotated 90 degrees relative to the target, then it can be rotated −90 degrees to bring it into alignment with the target. In contrast, no amount of rotation can bring a reflected image into alignment with the target. Researchers typically measure both the accuracy of judgment and the time needed to make the judgments.

There is a strong, linear relation between the degree of angular disparity and reaction time; the more the stimulus is rotated relative to the target, the longer the judgment takes. The very strong, linear relation is often taken as evidence that participants mentally rotate the stimulus (Kosslyn, 1986; Shepard & Metzler, 1971), a claim that has been further supported by neuropsychological evidence (e.g., Kosslyn, 1996; Kosslyn et al., 1993).

Our focus is on whether, and how, practice affects the process of mental rotation. Practice can deliberately improve reaction time and can also improve the accuracy of responses. Addressing when, why, and how this happens turns out to shed light not only on the effects of practice but also on the fundamental mechanisms that support mental rotation.

## EFFECTS OF PRACTICE ON MENTAL ROTATION

Practice leads to substantial improvements in mental rotation response times (e.g., Kail, 1986; Tarr & Pinker, 1989; Widenbauer, Schmid, & Jasnson-Osmann, 2007). Why? Consider first one simple possibility: Maybe practice leads people to simply get faster at rotating the stimulus. However, this ostensibly simple explanation turns out not to be so simple. The process of making a judgment in a mental rotation task, in fact, consists of at least four distinct, serial processes: (1) encoding the stimuli, (2) attempting to transform the stimulus into alignment with the target, (3) comparing stimuli and target to decide whether they are the same, and (4) responding (Cooper & Shepard, 1973; Shepard and Metzler,

1971; Wright, Thompson, Ganis, Newcombe, & Kosslyn, 2008). Each of these components could respond to training or practice, and improvement in any one of them could lead to decreases in reaction time. For example, it is possible that training might facilitate the encoding of the stimuli and thus allow people to make the decision about rotation and reflection more quickly. Likewise, practice could support faster motor responses and thus overall decreases in reaction time. With multiple processes involved, overall response times might decrease, even if the rate of the actual mental reorientation did not change.

How can we determine which processes are influenced by practice? Decomposition of the function that relates the degree of misalignment and reaction time can provide important insights. Generally speaking, the slope of the line represents the speed of the transformation process (Shepard & Metzler, 1971; Wright et al., 2008). Steeper slopes indicate slower responses. Thus, if practice leads to increases in the speed of the transformation process, then slopes will become flatter with practice. In contrast, the level of the Y-intercept reflects overall processing speed and is not affected by the magnitude of the rotation of the stimulus. Changes in the Y-intercept of performance are thus thought to reflect processes other than the actual spatial transformation of the stimulus object or figure.

Several studies have used this decomposition method to assess when and how practice affects performance on mental rotation. For example, Wright et al. (2008) investigated the effect of intensive practice on two spatial tasks, mental rotation and mental paper folding, and a control task, making judgments about similarities in the meanings of pairs of words. Thirty-eight subjects were recruited from a Harvard psychology department Web site with a mean age of 24 years old. Participants first took all three tests to provide baseline measures. They were then assigned to practice either the mental rotation task or the mental paper-folding task. Participants completed 21 daily practice sessions, during which they received 114 trials of the assigned task. In each practice session, approximately half of the items were present in the initial testing, and approximately half were completely new. Each training session lasted about 15 to 20 minutes. After the training sessions, both groups then retook the same tests that they had taken initially.

Practice led to substantial improvements, particularly in reaction time. Participants improved on both the mental rotation and mental paper-folding tasks, regardless of which task they practiced, indicating transfer between the spatial tasks. As expected, there was no transfer to the nonspatial verbal task.

Decomposition of the functions relating reaction time to degree of rotation revealed that much of the effect of practice was on the Y-intercept, not the slope. This result suggests that the effect of practice on mental rotation is *not* on the actual spatial transformation (i.e., mental rotation per se) but rather on other elements of the task. This possibility is discussed in more detail later, as it also relates to a discussion of the influences of video game practice on spatial cognition.

These results should not be interpreted as indicating that practice can never affect the slope of the mental rotation function. There are some cases in which practice may lead to a novel approach to the task, and this difference may be reflected in a changing slope. A classic example comes form the work of Tarr and Pinker (1989). They asked participants to make spatial judgments about a set of letter-like figures that were presented in different orientations. At first, participants seemed to use the standard strategy of rotating each stimulus into alignment with the target; reaction time increased linearly with increases in the angle of rotation, and the slope of this function was similar to that of earlier studies (e.g., Shepard & Metzler, 1971). However, with practice, the slope of the function approached zero, indicating that participants' reaction time was not affected by the degree of rotation. Tarr and Pinker suggested that with practice, participants fundamentally altered how they performed the task. They recognized the figure shapes of the previously displayed orientations and hence could respond with prior knowledge instead of the time-consuming task of rotating the stimulus into orientation with the target. Importantly, this effect did not transfer to different orientations. When the stimuli were presented in orientations that differed from the practice stimuli, the reaction time was again highly correlated with the degree of rotation of the stimulus.

In summary, Tarr and Pinker's (1989) results show that practice can help people to recognize particular figures, but the facilitative effect of doing so is limited to those figures and orientations specifically practiced. The time required to make the judgments was not reduced because people rotated the stimuli more quickly but because practice made it possible to make the judgments without rotating the stimuli at all.

## The Effects of Video Game Practice on Spatial Cognition

Playing video games is another activity that has been show to improve performance on a variety of spatially relevant tasks. Studies of this type have garnered a great deal of attention, in part because of the general interest in video games as contexts for learning. As Gee (2003) has noted, playing video games is fun and does not "feel" like learning, often motivating people to play for countless hours simply to master the challenges offered. Much of the focus on the cognitive benefits of video game playing has been in the area of spatial perception, attention, and cognition (e.g., Spence & Feng, 2010; Subrahmanyam & Greenfield, 1994, 2008). Reviewing this literature sheds substantial light not only on the influence of video game thinking on spatial reasoning but also on the basic mechanisms of spatial cognition.

In several cases, researchers have been very specific about how practice has its effects. For example, a series of studies by Green and Bavelier (2003, 2006a, 2006b, 2007) has shown that playing action video games can enhance both the capacity and resolution of visual-spatial attention. Green and Bevalier first compared experienced gamers' performance on a variety of classic tasks that assess the capacity of visual-spatial attention. One is the flanker compatibility task, which is illustrated in Figure 55.1. The participant's task is to decide whether a circle or a square appeared within the shapes that form the ring, while ignoring the large "flanker" stimulus that appears outside of the ring of circles. As the figure illustrates, sometimes the flanker was the same as the target (compatible trials) and sometimes it was the opposite of the target (incompatible trials). Typically, a compatible flanker improves

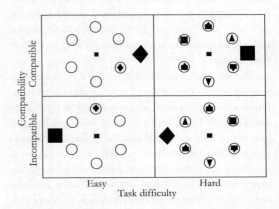

**Figure 55.1** Example of the Flanker Compatibility Task (from Green & Bavelier, 2004).

performance in the easy version of the task, in which the participant needs to search in only one member of the ring to find the target. For most participants, the shape of the flanker has little effect on performance in the difficult version of the task because they cannot simultaneously attend to the flanker and search for the target among the many foils. However, Green and Bavalier found that video game players continue to benefit from a compatible flanker even on the difficult trials. This result suggests that playing video games expands the amount of information to which people can attend. Similar results were found for other tasks that measure the span or capacity of visual attention.

These results were very interesting, but the design of this first study did not allow for the assessment of cause and effect. Perhaps those individuals with exceptional visual-spatial attention are more likely to start playing video games in the first place, or at least more likely to "get hooked" and hence become serious gamers. To address this potential confound, Green and Bevalier conducted an additional experimental study with participants who said they seldom or never played video games. One-half of the participants were randomly assigned to practice video game playing. The remaining participants were assigned to a control group that performed a vocabulary task. Participants practiced for approximately 10 hours.

This experimental design allowed Green and Bevalier to assess whether video game playing *caused* the improvement in visual-spatial capacity. The answer was yes; participants assigned to the video game playing group improved significantly more on the tests of visual-spatial attentional capacity than the control group did. The effect of the 2-week intervention was not as strong as the effect of a lifetime of being a serious gamer, but nevertheless it was strong and statistically significant. This result suggests that practicing video games can cause an increase in visual-spatial attention capacity.

The research presented thus far establishes that playing video games can increase the capacity of visual-spatial attention. In subsequent work, Green and Bavelier (2007) also showed the playing video games can increase the *resolution* of the information in visual-spatial attention as well. This work tested the effect of video game playing on the *crowding* phenomenon. Individual objects become progressively more difficult to identify when they are presented in the same area as other objects than when presented apart from other objects. Each target has

a *crowding region*; the perception of an individual object also sets up a zone of inhibition that makes it more difficult to see surrounding objects. Green and Bavalier showed the crowding region is significantly *smaller* in video game players than in people who do not play video games. Thus, gamers experience *less* crowding and have greater attentional resolution, allowing them to see, identify, and keep track of the locations of more objects.

It is interesting to note that the effects of practice in this case are again largely or even completely implicit. Participants did not try to increase their visual-spatial capacity or resolution while playing video games. They probably were not aware it was happening. Nevertheless, it did happen, again showing that practice need not be deliberate to promote gains in performance that can also transfer to other tasks.

## EXTENSION OF VIDEO GAME PRACTICE TO OTHER SPATIAL TASKS

The studies reviewed thus far demonstrate that playing video games can increase the capacity and resolution of visual-spatial attention capacity. Feng, Spence, and Pratt (2007) extended these results to include other spatial tasks, such as mental rotation. They found that practicing video games leads to substantial improvement in mental rotation, and moreover, that the advantage gets *larger* after a delay; participants performed *better* after a 2-week delay than they did immediately after the experiment. This result is very important because it suggests that the effect was not a fleeting boost that is directly tied to playing the game. Therefore, playing video games may lead to long-term improvement in visual-spatial tasks.

## EXPLAINING THE INFLUENCES OF VIDEO GAME PLAYING

Based on these results, Spence and Feng (2010) offered a general explanation for the effects of playing video games on performance for both video games and spatial cognition tasks. As already mentioned, the effects entail increases in both the capacity and acuity of visual attention. For example, greater visual-spatial attention capacity will allow a player to pick up on approaching "enemies" (and respond appropriately) sooner than someone with less visual-spatial attention capacity. Likewise, the ability to attend to what is happening on a wider portion of the screen will again give the experienced player more time to respond both to threats and opportunities to attack or otherwise score points.

Skilled video game players can attend to a particular event on the screen (e.g., avoiding hitting an asteroid), while simultaneously monitoring what is happening in the periphery.

These skills transfer to other judgments that require actively attending to and making decisions regarding objects. The explanation for the improvement in tasks such as the flanker compatibility effect seem straightforward: If playing video games increases the capacity and resolution of spatial attention, then it will support performance in other tasks that also draw upon these cognitive resources. The far transfer to seemingly less related tasks, such as mental rotation, is particularly intriguing but can also be explained in terms of increases in attention, capacity, and acuity of visual-spatial attention. Mental rotation requires representing objects or figures and holding them in working memory as the transformation is made (e.g., Hyun & Luck, 2007; Miyake & Shah, 1999). Being able to attend to more information, and to hold it in working memory, could benefit the representation of individual figures substantially. For example, individuals with higher levels of spatial attention or working memory may be able to quickly form schematic representations of to-be-rotated figures and keep track of the elements of the figures during the transformation process (e.g., Just & Carpenter, 1985). They may have more time to abstract schematic representations of the to-be-rotated figures and use these schematic representations to facilitate the transformation (see Cooper, 1975). In summary, having greater attentional resources and resolution provides many potential benefits in the representation and recall of spatial figures and relations. This advantage may be domain general and thus may benefit performance in a wide variety of tasks (Spence & Feng, 2010).

Researchers (e.g., Green & Bavelier, 2008; Spence & Feng, 2010) have proposed a neurally motivated explanation for the improvements that practicing video games engenders. Central to the theory is the interaction between lower and higher level visual recognition processes. The visual (occipital) cortex first processes information about components of figures and passes this information on to higher (e.g., parietal and frontal) cortex, which then contribute to the analysis, recognition, and storing of spatial figures and relations. If the information is not sufficient to support the detection and discrimination of features, additional information must be retrieved from the visual cortex (see Ahissar & Hochstein, 2004). Spence and Feng suggested that playing action video games allows people to more often make judgments and discriminations about information in the higher cortical areas without having to refer back to the lower level information. This change decreases the average amount of time that it takes to make decisions but does not affect the time required to transform this information. This explanation thus is consistent with the observation (e.g., Wright et al., 2008) that training affects the Y-intercept of the reaction time and degree of rotation function but does not typically affect the slope of this function. Note also that this capacity increase is not tied to particular stimuli and thus could support transfer to unpracticed tasks.

In summary, research on the effects of video game training has shed light on the mechanisms that are likely implicated when spatial training or practice leads to faster responses. If the right conditions are met, the training can provide precisely the large, durable, and transferable improvements that we reported in our meta-analysis of the research on the effects of spatial training and practice.

## Summary and Conclusions

Our review has revealed that spatial cognition is quite malleable and that some kinds of experiences can have lasting and important benefits. Prior studies that reached other conclusions may have been affected by the unexpected improvement in control groups or by the use of stimuli that could be easily memorized and thus did not support more domain-general improvements. Our discussion of the mental processes that are affected by mental rotation practice or playing video games both supports our conclusions and provides information about how and why these benefits are obtained.

Finding that spatial cognition can be improved may have important implications for other topics, such as research on methods to promote STEM achievement and attainment. For example, we have argued (e.g., Uttal & Cohen, 2012) that spatial training programs, in which people actively practice STEM-relevant spatial tasks, could help to prevent some of the substantial dropout that occurs in STEM majors. Even relatively small amounts of practice could help people cope with the spatial demands of tasks such as representing the structures of molecules or the forces that are acting on a bridge or other structure.

We end by asking whether the experiences of everyday life are sufficient to provide sufficient practice in spatial thinking. When we mention the possibility of including spatial training and practice as part of the STEM curriculum, we are sometimes asked why this is needed, since people use spatial cognition frequently in everyday tasks such as navigation. This question reveals a common assumption—reading and mathematics may take substantial amounts of practice, but spatial thinking does not. We strongly disagree with this assumption; everyday spatial experiences are almost certainly not sufficient to provide the kinds of practice that are needed to support STEM-related spatial thinking. Although everyone navigates, the cognitive skills that support navigation are only modestly related to those that support the processing of spatial figures and diagrams that is required in STEM (e.g., Allen, Kirasic, Dobson, Long, & Beck, 1996; Hegarty, Montello, Richardson, Ishikawa, & Lovelace, 2006). Many kinds of spatial experiences do transfer to other tasks, but navigation does not appear to be one of them. In addition, the very high levels of improvement that are observed after only modest amounts of training suggest that people may enter these tasks with relatively low levels of spatial reasoning. Standard psychometric tests of spatial ability are normed to the population, but it is possible that these norms could be raised substantially with only moderate amounts of training.

In summary, our review of research indicates that spatial cognition is highly malleable, and that these effects both endure and transfer. Given the relatively little amount of time and money required to include spatial practice and training in school curricula, it is time to test whether interventions such as playing video games can improve STEM learning.

## Acknowledgments

The research reported here, and the preparation of the chapter, were supported by the Spatial Intelligence and Learning Center (NSF grant SBE0541957) and by the Institute for Education Sciences (Department of Education grant R305H020088). We thank Kate Bailey, Kate O'Doherty, Linda Liu Hand, Alison Lewis, Nora Newcombe, Kseniya Povod, Elizabeth Tiption, and Chris Warren for their help. Send correspondence to David Uttal (duttal@northwestern.edu), Department of Psychology, Northwestern University, 2029 Sheridan Rd, Evanston, IL 60208–2710.

## Notes

1. Several extreme outliers were removed from this, and all subsequent analyses.

2. $g$ represents Hedges's $g$, the mean-weighted effect size and common metric for our meta-analyses. This statistic is a slightly more conservative version of Cohen's $d$.

## References

Ahissar, M., & Hochstein, S. (2004). The reverse hierarchy theory of visual perceptual learning. *Trends in Cognitive Sciences*, 8, 457–464.

Allen, G. L., Kirasic, K. C., Dobson, S. H., Long, R. G., & Beck, S. (1996). Predicting environmental learning from spatial abilities: An indirect route. *Intelligence*, 22, 325–355.

Bransford, J. D., & Schwartz, D. L. (1999). Rethinking transfer: A simple proposal with multiple implications. *Review of Research in Education*, 24, 61–100.

Bryan, W. L., & Harter, N. (1897). Studies in the physiology and psychology of the telegraphic language. *Psychological Review*, 4, 27–53.

Bryan, W. L., & Harter, N. (1899). Studies on the telegraphic language: The acquisition of a hierarchy of habits. *Psychological Review*, 6, 345–375.

Carroll, J. B. (1993). *Human cognitive abilities: A survey of factor-analytic studies*. New York: Cambridge University Press.

Cooper, L. A. (1975). Mental rotation of random two-dimensional figures. *Cognitive Psychology*, 7, 20–43.

Cooper, L. A., & Shepard, R. N. (1973). Chronometric studies of the rotation of mental images. In W. G. Chase (Ed.), *Visual information processing* (pp. 75–176). New York: Academic Press.

Ekstrom, R. B., French, J. W., & Harman, H. H. (1979). Cognitive factors: Their identification and replication. *Multivariate Behavioral Research Monographs*, 79(2), 3–84.

Eliot, J. (1987). *Models of psychological space: Psychometric, developmental and experimental approaches*. New York: Springer-Verlag.

Ericsson, K. A., Krampe, R. T., & Tesch-Römer, C. (1993). The role of deliberate practice in the acquisition of expert performance. *Psychological Review*, 100(3), 363–406.

Ericsson, K. A., & Smith, J. (1991). Prospects and limits in the empirical study of expertise: An introduction. In K. A. Ericsson & J. Smith (Eds.), *Toward a general theory of expertise: Prospects and limits* (pp. 1–38). Cambridge, England: Cambridge University Press.

Feng, J., Spence, I., & Pratt, J. (2007). Playing and action video game reduces gender differences in spatial cognition. *Psychological Science*, 18(10), 850–855.

Gee, J. P. (2003). *What video games have to teach us about learning and literacy*. New York: Palgrave/Macmillan.

Gentner, D., & Markman, A. B. (1997). Structure mapping in analogy and similarity. *American Psychologist*, 52(1), 45–56.

Gladwell, M. (2008). *Outliers: The story of success*. New York: Little, Brown.

Green, C. S., & Bavelier, D. (2003). Action video game modifies visual selective attention. *Nature*, 423, 534–538.

Green, C. S., & Bavelier, D. (2006a). Effect of action video games on the spatial distribution of visuospatial attention. *Journal of Experimental Psychology: Human Perception and Performance*, 32(6), 1465–1478.

Green, C. S., & Bavelier, D. (2006b). Enumeration versus multiple object tracking the case of action video game players. *Cognition*, 101(1), 217–245.

Green, C. S., & Bavelier, D. (2007). Action video game experience alters the spatial resolution of attention. *Psychological Science*, 18(1), 88–94.

Green, C. S., & Bavelier, D. (2008). Exercising your brain: A review of human brain plasticity and training-induced learning. *Psychology and Aging*, 23, 692–701.

Halpern, D. F. (2012). *Sex differences in cognitive abilities* (4th ed.). New York: Psychology Press.

Hauschknecht, J. P., Halpert, J. A., Di Paolo, N. T., & Gerrard, M. O. M. (2007). Retesting in selection: A meta-analysis of practice effects for tests of cognitive ability. *Journal of Applied Psychology, 92*(2), 373–385.

Hedges, L. V., Tipton, E., & Johnson, M. C. (2010a). Robust variance estimation in meta-regression with dependent effect size estimates. *Research Synthesis Methods, 1*(1), 39–65.

Hedges, L. V., Tipton, E., & Johnson, M. C. (2010b). Erratum: Robust variance estimation in meta-regression with dependent effect size estimates. *Research Synthesis Methods, 1*(2), 164–165.

Hegarty, M., Montello, D. R., Richardson, A. E., Ishikawa, T., & Lovelace, K. (2006). Spatial abilities at different scales: Individual differences in aptitude-test performance and spatial-layout learning. *Intelligence, 34*(2), 151–176.

Hegarty, M., & Waller, D. (2005). Individual differences in spatial abilities. In P. Shah & A. Miyake (Eds.), *The Cambridge handbook of visuospatial thinking* (pp. 121–169). New York: Cambridge University Press.

Humphreys, L. G., Lubinski, D., & Yao, G. (1993). Utility of predicting group membership and the role of spatial visualization in becoming an engineer, physical scientist, or artist. *Journal of Applied Psychology, 78*(2), 250–261. doi:10.1037/0021–9010.78.2.250

Hyde, J. S., & Linn, M. C. (2006). Gender similarities in mathematics and science. *Science, 314*, 599–600.

Hyun, S-K., & Luck, S. L. (2007). Visual working memory as the substrate for mental rotation. *Psychomic Bulletin and Review, 14*(1), 154–158.

Just, M., & Carpenter, P. (1985). Cognitive coordinate systems: Accounts of mental rotation and individual differences in spatial ability. *Psychological Review, 92*, 137–172.

Kail, R. P. (1986). The impact of extended practice on mental rotation. *Journal of Experimental Child Psychology, 42*, 378–391.

Kosslyn, S. M. (1986). *Image and mind*. Cambridge, MA: Harvard University Press.

Kosslyn, S. M. (1996). *Image and brain: The resolution of the mental imagery debate*. Cambridge, MA: MIT Press.

Kosslyn, S. M., Alpert, N. M., Thompson, W. L., Maljkovic, V., Weise, S.B. Z., Chabirs, C. F., … Buonanno, F. S. (1993). Visual mental imagery activates topographically organized visual cortext: PET investigations. *Journal of Cognitive Neuroscience, 5*(3), 263–287.

Linn, M. C., & Petersen, A. C. (1985). Emergence and characterization of sex differences in spatial ability: A meta-analysis. *Child Development, 56*(6), 1479–1498.

Lohman, D. F. (1988). Spatial abilities as traits, processes and knowledge. In R. J. Stermberg ( Ed.), *Advances in the psychology of human intelligence* (Vol. 4, pp. 181–248). Hillsdale, NJ: Erlbaum.

Maccoby, E. E., & Jacklin, C. N. (1974). *The psychology of sex differences*. Stanford, CA: Stanford University Press.

Miyake, A., & Shah, P. (1999). *Models of working memory: Mechanisms of active maintenance and executive control*. New York: Cambridge University Press.

Mumford, M. D., Constanza, D. P.Bughman, W. A., Threlfall, K. V., & Fleishman, E. A. (1994). Influenc of abilities on

performance during practice: Effects of massed and distributed practice. *Journal of Educational Psychology, 86*(1), 134–144.

National Research Council. (2006). *Learning to think spatially*. Washington, DC: National Academies Press.

Pibrum, M. D., Reynolds, S. J., McAuliffe, C., Leedy, D. E., & Birk, J. P. (2005). The role of visualization in learning from computer-based images. *International Journal of Science Education, 27*(5), 513–527.

Shea, D. L., Lubinski, D., & Benbow, C. P. (2001). Importance of assessing spatial ability in intellectually talented young adolescents: A 20-year longitudinal study. *Journal of Educational Psychology, 93*(3), 604–614.

Shepard, R. N., & Metzler, J. (1971). Mental rotation of three-dimensional objects. *Science, 1971*, 701–703

Sims, V. K., & Mayer, R. (2002). Domain specificity of spatial expertise: The case of video game players. *Applied Cognitive Psychology, 16*(1), 97–115.

Sorby, S. A. (2009). Educational research in developing 3-D spatial skills for engineering students. *International Journal of Science Education, 31*(3), 459–480.

Spence, I., & Feng, J. (2010). Video games and spatial cognition. *Review of General Psychology, 14*(2), 92–104.

Subrahmanyam, K., & Greenfield, P. M. (1994). Effect of video game practice on spatial skills in girls and boys. *Journal of Applied Developmental Psychology, 15*(1), 13–32.

Subrahmanyam, K., & Greenfield, P. (2008). Media symbol systems and cognitive processes. In S. Calvert & B. J. Wilson (Eds.), *The Blackwell handbook of children, media, and development* (pp. 166–187). London: Blackwell Publishing

Tarr, M. J., & Pinker, S. (1989). Mental rotation and orientation-dependence in shape recognition. *Cognitive Psychology, 21*, 233–282.

Terlecki, M., Newcombe, N., & Little, M. (2008). Durable and generalized effects of spatial experience on mental rotation: Gender differences in growth patterns. *Applied Cognitive Psychology, 22*, 996–1013.

Uttal, D. H., & Cohen, C. A. (2012). Spatial cognition and STEM education: When, why, and how? In B. Ross (Ed.), *Psychology of Learning and Motivation, 57, 147–181.*

Uttal, D. H., Meadow, N. G., Tipton, E., Hand, L L., Alden, A. R., Warren. C., Newcombe, N. S. (2012). The malleability of spatial skills: A meta-analysis of training studies. *Psychological Bulletin.* ePub ahead of print.

Voyer, D., Voyer, S., & Bryden, M. P. (1995). Magnitude of sex differences in spatial abilities: A meta-analysis and consideration of critical variables. *Psychological Bulletin, 117*(2), 250–270.

Wai, J., Lubinski, D., & Benbow, C. P . (2009). Spatial ability for STEM domains: Aligning over 50 years of cumulative psychological knowledge solidifies its importance. *Journal of Educational Psychology, 101*, 817–835.

Widenbauer, G., Schmid, J., & Jansen-Osmann, P. (2007). Mantual training of mental rotation. *European Journal of Cognitive Psychology, 19*(1), 17–36.

Wright, R., Thompson, W. L., Ganis, G., Newcombe, N. S., & Kosslyn, S. M. (2008). Training generalized spatial skills. *Psychonomic Bulletin and Review, 14*(4), 763–771.

# Experts and Their Superior Performance

K. Anders Ericsson *and* Tyler J. Towne

### Abstract

This chapter reviews recent developments in the study of experts. Particularly, it seeks to contrast two approaches. The first traditional approach defined individual experts by peer nomination or the amount of time they have worked as professionals. The second approach—which is the focus of this review—seeks to identify experts based on objective measurement of their reproducibly superior performance on designed standardized representative tasks. The expert-performance approach seeks to identify cognitive and physiological factors mediating the observed superior performance. The chapter outlines how particular training activities (deliberate practice) have been shown to be related to the acquisition of complex cognitive and biological mechanisms that mediate superior performance in a variety of domains of expertise. The concluding section discusses future directions such as the continued specification of causal biological mechanisms mediating the acquisition of expert performance. Key issues such as motivation to engage in practice are also discussed.

**Key Words:** expertise, experts, expert performance, long-term working memory, skill

The *Merriam-Webster Dictionary* (2009) defines an expert as "having, involving, or displaying special skill or knowledge derived from training or experience." Contemporary psychological research on experts has been motivated by the hypothesis proposed by Simon and Chase (1973) that there are general characteristics of experts that differentiate them from novices and less experienced people in a wide range of domains of expertise. The superior achievement of experts has been found to be related to cumulative effects of their extensive experience in their respective domains (see Ericsson & Lehmann, 1996).

The concept of expertise development can be traced back to the Middle Ages when craftsmen formed guilds. The craftsmen passed on their special knowledge of how to produce products such as lace, barrels, and shoes to their students (apprentices). Apprentices would typically start at around 14 years and commit to serve and study with their master for

about 7 years. The length of time would vary based on the complexity of the craft and the age and prior experience of the apprentice (Epstein, 1991).

Once apprentices had fulfilled their contracts, they would work with other masters for pay, which often involved traveling to other cities and towns; therefore, they were referred to as journeymen. When a journeyman had accumulated enough additional skill and money, he would purchase a shop with tools and apply to become a master of the guild. In most guilds the journeyman's best work (i.e., master pieces) were examined and sometimes special tests were also administered to objectively assess the level of his performance (Epstein, 1991).

When people were accepted as masters, they were held responsible for the quality of the products from their shop and were thereby allowed to take on the training of their own apprentices (see Amirault & Branson, 2006 and Chi, 2006, on the progression toward expertise and mastery of a domain).

In most contemporary professional domains such as medicine, science, and law, individuals have to acquire extensive knowledge and skills—typically in a college or university setting—before becoming a participant in the domain. After graduation the individuals often work as apprentices and are supervised by experienced professionals until they are capable of performing independently. During this learning period they get many opportunities to learn how to apply the knowledge and rules efficiently in professional contexts until the appropriate actions in a context have been repeated so often that the actions are elicited immediately and guided by intuition (Dreyfus & Dreyfus, 1986).

In the 1970s and 1980s there was a rapid increase in the interest in research on experts in which researchers emphasized the relation between domain-related experience and increases in level of perceived expertise. Many researchers began to define level of expertise in terms of the amount of accumulated experience in the domain, where 10 or more years of professional experience started to become synonymous with reaching the status of expert (see Chi, 2006 and Feltovich, Prietula, & Ericsson, 2006 for discussions). However, this experience-based definition of expertise without a concurrent validation by observed superior performance was found to be problematic in the early 1990s (Ericsson & Smith, 1991; Holyoak, 1991).

## Defining Characteristics of Experts: Experience Versus Superior Reproducible Performance

Experience is clearly necessary to become an expert and even to acquire skill for unfamiliar everyday activities. The most influential contemporary model for acquisition of everyday skills such as type writing, diving, and other skills was proposed by Fitts and Posner (1967). This model outlined three discrete stages illustrated in the lower arm of Figure 56.1. When introduced to an unfamiliar domain, people first need to understand the governing rule and acquire other basic knowledge. For example, in the case of touch-typing, beginners must learn the location of all the keys so that they are able to retrieve the location of each letter from memory in order to move their fingers to the key and strike it without looking.

During this first "cognitive" stage of skill acquisition, generation of behavior is typically slow and sometimes associated with errors of execution. These errors lead to clear observable consequences such as a missed ball in tennis or incorrectly typed

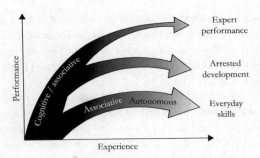

**Figure 56.1** An illustration of the qualitative difference between the course of improvement of expert performance and of everyday activities. The goal for everyday activities is to reach as rapidly as possible a satisfactory level that is stable and "autonomous" (see the gray/white plateau at the bottom of the graph). In contrast, expert performers counteract automaticity by developing increasingly complex mental representations to attain higher levels of control of their performance and will therefore remain within the "cognitive" and "associative" phases. Some experts will at some point in their career stop engaging in deliberate practice and prematurely automate their performance. (Adapted from "The scientific study of expert levels of performance: General implications for optimal learning and creativity" by K. A. Ericsson in *High Ability Studies, 9*, p. 90. Copyright 1998 by European Council for High Ability.)

words and thus can be corrected and gradually improved by repeated practice opportunities. With sufficient experience and with mental concentration on producing the correct actions, individuals are able to increase their speed, especially for frequently encountered patterns.

During the second "associative" stage, individuals are able to learn and execute sequences of associated actions. They become increasingly able to access and execute complex actions rapidly with acceptable outcomes; this is consistent with other theories of skill acquisition (Anderson, 1982). For most recreational activities such as skiing, tennis, and driving a car as well as professional activities such as telegraphy and typing (see Ericsson, 2006a, for a review), 50 hours of experience is sufficient for individuals to successfully adapt to the typical situational demands of the domain. Execution becomes increasingly automated and the performers cease monitoring many aspects of their behavior and are not able to adjust or modify these discrete aspects of their skill (Fitts & Posner, 1967).

According to this framework, the representation of the task is established primarily during the first stage of skill acquisition and improvements during the second two stages are mainly concerned with the speed of execution and reduction of effort. When performance has reached the level of automaticity and execution is "effortless," additional experience will no longer change the accuracy of behavior. Consequently, increases in accumulated experience will not lead to higher levels of performance (Ericsson, 1996, 2006a, 2006b), as illustrated in the lower arm of Figure 56.1.

Most people know from firsthand experience that the number of times or amount of time a person has engaged in an everyday activity like driving, playing tennis, and typing is not closely related to one's level of objective performance. Several reviews (Ericsson & Smith, 1991; Holyoak, 1991) criticized the assumption of a predictable relation between increased experience and performance. These reviews showed that increased domain-related experience is not always associated with improved professional performance in many domains.

Highly experienced individuals frequently do not exhibit superior performance in several domains, including psychotherapy (Dawes, 1994) or financial forecasting (Camerer & Johnson, 1991; Shanteau & Stewart, 1992). Reviews (Ericsson & Lehmann, 1996; Ericsson, Whyte, & Ward, 2007) have shown that the length of domain experience is often unrelated to improvements in professional performance and in some cases the time since graduation is even associated with decrements in performance, most likely due to forgetting (Choudhry, Fletcher, & Soumerai, 2005; Ericsson, 2004, 2007a). Based on observation and interviews with socially recognized experts, such as fire commanders and paramedics, Klein (1990, 1993) inferred characteristics of the described decision-making by the experts, but there were no laboratory studies that validated the link between these characteristics and superior decision accuracy. In fact, Benner (1984) interviewed experienced nurses about their decision making, but laboratory studies of actual decision-making performance by experienced nurses failed to show superior decision performance compared to less experienced nurses (Ericsson, Whyte et al., 2007).

## Contrasting Approaches to the Study of Superior Performance

There are two main approaches to the study of expertise and superior human performance. The traditional expertise approach (Simon & Chase, 1973) focused on the changes in characteristics of individuals' cognitive structure and performance as a function of increased amount of experience and training, namely from beginners to novices to intermediates to experts. This approach has also historically relied on methods for selecting experts by social criteria such as peer nomination (Chi, 2006; Feltovich et al., 2006).

The second approach—referred to as the expert-performance approach—is only concerned with the study of the structure and development of reproducibly superior (expert) performance that captures the essence of expertise in a domain (Ericsson, 2006a, 2006b). These two approaches overlap for domains like chess, where levels of socially defined expertise are defined in terms of objective success at tournaments. They diverge for domains such as medicine, where peer-nominated clinical experts frequently do not display superior accuracy in diagnosing actors trained to portray particular diseases (Ericsson, 2007a). We will review the evidence on the structure and acquisition of superior performance for representative tasks that capture expertise.

## Measurement of Reproducibly Superior (Expert) Performance

In many individual sports, such as running and swimming, performance can be measured objectively, and some individuals consistently perform at a superior level. In other domains of activity, such as ballet, music, diving, and figure skating, measurement of performance is conducted at public competitions by experienced judges, where many of the tasks such as particular dives and routines have been objectively assigned a level of technical difficulty.

Measurement of performance in most professional domains is more difficult because different surgeons operate on patients with different severity of their health condition, different sales people promote the same product to different customers, and programmers are rarely paid to develop independent computer programs for identical tasks. In domains such as chess, fencing, and tennis, each match in a tournament will develop very differently with unique situations facing the two opponents. Although skill levels of various players are accurately estimated by analyzing the final outcomes for approximately 20–30 tournament games, it is nearly impossible to identify those particular behaviors and associated mechanisms that caused the winning players' superior overall performance.

To address this measurement problem, Ericsson and Smith (1991) proposed the expert-performance approach based on methods developed by de Groot (1978) in his pioneering research on chess experts. This approach is based on the identification of challenging representative situations in the domain of expertise where there is a demand for immediate action or behavior as illustrated in Figure 56.2. For

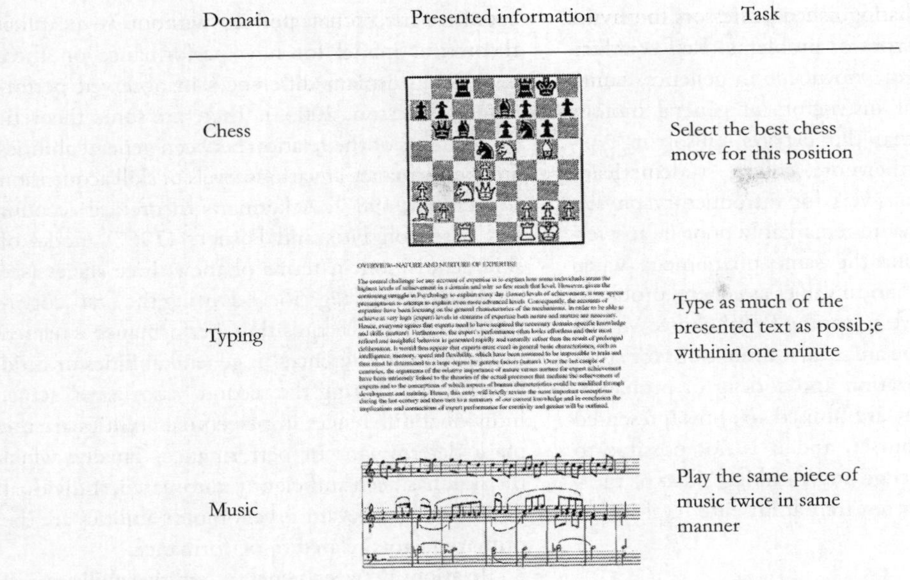

| Domain | Presented information | Task |
|--------|----------------------|------|
| Chess | | Select the best chess move for this position |
| Typing | | Type as much of the presented text as possib;e withinin one minute |
| Music | | Play the same piece of music twice in same manner |

**Figure 56.2** Three examples of laboratory tasks that capture the consistently superior performance of domain experts in chess, typing, and music. (From "Expertise," by K. A. Ericsson and Andreas C. Lehmann, 1999, *Encyclopedia of creativity*. Copyright by Academic Press.)

example, the top panel of Figure 56.2 illustrates a chess position that de Groot identified from a real chess game that required a challenging discovery of the best next move. By presenting the same set of game positions identified from games and requiring players to select the best move, the accuracy of selecting the best move can be measured and compared between players at different skill levels. Performance on these relatively short representative tasks is highly related to past chess tournament success.

Subsequent research has confirmed de Groot's methodology as the best available laboratory measure of expertise in chess (Ericsson, Patel, & Kintsch, 2000; van der Maas & Wagenmakers, 2005) and several other domains (Ericsson, 2006a, 2006b; Ericsson & Williams, 2007) such as medicine (Ericsson, 2004, 2007a), sport (Ward, Hodges, Williams, & Starkes, 2004), SCRABBLE (Tuffiash, Roring, & Ericsson, 2007), and music (Lehmann & Grüber, 2006). The second panel in Figure 56.2 illustrates how the speed of typists can be measured by asking individuals to type as much as possible from a series of provided texts, where the amount of correctly typed text during a 3-minute test period is measured. It is also possible to measure the performance of musicians by having them perform a relatively simple piece several times while playing the piece in as similar a manner as possible. Expert pianists are found to be able to reproduce their original rendition of the piece better than less-skilled

pianists (Ericsson, Krampe, & Tesch-Römer, 1993; Krampe & Ericsson, 1996).

It is informative to compare tasks that capture expert performance with some of the tasks used in the pioneering studies of expertise (Chase & Simon, 1973; Chi, Feltovich, & Glaser, 1981; Simon & Simon, 1978). The most popular task traditionally used to study expertise is Chase and Simon's (1973) memory task, where skilled and less skilled participants are presented representative stimuli from the domains, such as positions from chess games, and randomly rearranged stimuli for a brief time (around 5 seconds). Although memory performance on this task correlates with other measures of expertise, it does not capture the essence of expertise, because with 50 hours of practice a person who does not play chess was able to match the accuracy of chess masters' recall for game positions (Ericsson & Harris, 1990; see Ericsson et al., 2000, and Ericsson and Kintsch, 2000, for an extended discussion and Gobet and Jackson, 2002, for a replication). The pioneering research on expertise in physics focused on solving problems in college introductory physics courses (Simon & Simon, 1978) and categorization of such problems in a sorting task (Chi et al., 1981). These tasks do not capture the essence of true expertise in physics, because these problems do not capture the thinking of individuals who can conduct research and make innovations in physics. For example, it is possible to find college freshmen that outperform distinguished professors in physics on solving these types of problems (Reif & Allen, 1992). In studies of knowledge in genetics, Smith (1992) found that instructors of general biology performed better than the "experts" on solving typical problems. Furthermore, college students learn how to calculate answers for introductory physics problems, but they are remarkably poor in answering problems about the same phenomena when posed without numerical values as general problems requiring qualitative reasoning (VanLehn & Van de Sande, 2009). There are similar limitations for studies of the categorization and sorting of problems, when the problems are limited to those presented in introductory courses, and it is not possible to capture the knowledge and thinking skills of individuals conducting research at an elite level in the domain.

## Mechanisms That Mediate Expert Levels of Performance

One important question regarding the expert performance approach is the extent to which expertise can be discussed in general terms. For example, can we identify mechanisms mediating superior performance that are shared by experts in all domains? Or is it necessary to describe reproducibly superior performance at a domain-specific level? The expert performance view holds that the acquired mechanisms have been developed to increase the domain-specific performance, and thus it is necessary to engage in domain-specific training activities to develop these particular mechanisms. As a consequence, there is essentially no transfer between attaining elite performance in soccer and elite performance in high jump, for example. However, there are general characteristics of how expert performers engage in training to develop physical and cognitive mechanisms that mediate performance during several years or even decades (depending on the competitiveness of the domain) of deliberate practice. Furthermore, one should be able to predict the trajectory of different individuals' development within the same domain based on the type and amount of various practice activities that they engage in. We will also discuss general characteristics of those training activities that are associated with effective improvement.

The second step in the expert-performance approach is to identify the specific physiological and cognitive mechanisms that mediate the experts' performance advantage. Early research on experts administered psychometric tests to measure their general abilities such as intelligence and

cognitive/perceptual abilities without any explicit theoretical model for how performance on these tests could explain differences in observed performance (Ericsson, 2003a). There are some theoretical accounts of the relation between general abilities and performance at various levels of skill acquisition (Ackerman, 1987). Ackerman's theoretical account was based on Fitts and Posner's (1967) model of skill acquisition in terms of their three stages (see the lower arm of Fig. 56.1). During the first "cognitive" stage of skill acquisition, performance is related to individual differences in general abilities or fluid intelligence. During the second "associative" stage, individual differences in perceptual abilities are the main determinant of performance. Finally, when the skill has been sufficiently automated, individual differences in relevant psychomotor abilities are the primary factors related to performance.

Relations between general cognitive abilities and initial performance have been well documented in psychological research, especially for laboratory tasks. In these types of tasks, virtually error-free performance is attained relatively easily and further improvements in performance concern increases in speed of execution. Some relations between general cognitive abilities and initial performance on more complex tasks such as sports or performance in the workplace have been found. With increased experience in a given domain, however, the correlation between performance and general abilities decreases or even vanishes (Ackerman, 1987; Hulin, Henry, & Noon, 1990).

In many domains of expertise the correlation between skilled performance and individual differences in general and specific abilities has not been demonstrated. Research has found no relation between individual differences in general abilities and the associated performance of skilled performers in domains, such as chess, music, and sports (cf. Ericsson, Roring, & Nandagopal, 2007a, 2007b). For example, expert typists do not have superior psychomotor ability measured by simple RT (Salthouse, 1984), nor do soccer goalies possess superior simple RTs.

The expert-performance approach uses a different paradigm and collects data on the concurrent processes that mediate individual differences in superior performance on representative tasks. There are several process-tracing techniques from cognitive psychology that can monitor cognitive and perceptual processes that mediate expert performance such as the analysis of latency components, eye tracking, and concurrent and retrospective verbal reports (for a description, see Ericsson & Oliver, 1988). For example, research has found that superior soccer players make better predictions and decisions for action in presented game situations (Ward et al., 2004), and expert golfers are better at reproducing the same putt many times (Ericsson, 2001; Hill, 1999).

Other studies have uncovered superior ability of experts to monitor and control overall aspects of their performance execution. For instance, elite long-distance runners with increased running economy have been shown to verbally report monitoring their internal states; they also plan their races in more detail than sub-elite runners (Baker, Côté, & Deakin, 2005; Masters & Ogles, 1998).

Compelling scientific evidence for cognitive representations and mechanisms as mediators for the experts' performance advantage (Ericsson & Smith, 1991) has been found in domains of expertise, such as chess, music, and sports. For example, de Groot (1978) analyzed chess players' thought processes by collecting think-aloud protocols while they selected the best move for chess positions. The chess players first verbalized aspects of the structure of the chess position followed by the generation of promising moves and lines of attack. These promising lines of attack were systematically evaluated by planning out their consequences for future moves. During planning, the players generated a new set of possible moves, which were evaluated until their "best" move was selected.

Subsequent investigations have confirmed these results by experimental studies of the mediating cognitive processes. They have demonstrated similar findings in domains such as medicine, computer programming, and games (Ericsson, 2006a; Ericsson & Kintsch, 1995; Ericsson et al. 2000; Ericsson & Lehmann, 1996; Ericsson & Williams, 2007). In a recent review, Hodges, Huys, and Starkes (2007) examined athletes' superior performance in the laboratory and the field. Of particular interest are studies that present the real-world perceptual context with video recordings and then require the participants to generate representative motor actions within natural time constraints. These studies with representative tasks and constraints differ from the typical practice of asking participants to generate ratings for verbally described situations and where time pressure is lacking. Taken together, the results of these investigations suggest that experts maintain a highly complex and sophisticated representation of domain-specific situations in comparison to novices.

Superior performance in sports and other motor activities has traditionally been explained by higher acuity of the perceptual system or faster basic speed of the motor system. However, reviews have shown that the superiority of perception and motor performance is restricted to domain-related stimuli and situations and thus is more likely acquired as the result of training (see Abernethy, 1991; Starkes & Deakin, 1984; and Ward & Williams, 2003). In a series of pioneering studies, Salthouse (1984) demonstrated that superior typing ability required looking ahead in the text. Experimentally restricting how far skilled typists were able to look ahead in the text markedly reduced their typing speed—approaching the speed of novices. More elaborate advance preparation of appropriate actions has been documented for expert performers in several domains such as baseball (Nevett & French, 1997), tennis (McPherson & Kernodle, 2003), and music (Drake & Palmer, 2000). The experts' anticipation leads to rapid execution of actions without the need for faster basic neural speed.

In addition to superior anticipation skills and more refined cognitive representations, experts also acquire an ability to control their motor actions in order to perform very complex motor behaviors consistently. Higher consistency of motor performance has not only been shown in sports but also other domains such as medicine (Ericsson, 2004) and music (Krampe & Ericsson, 1996; Watson, 2006). The experts' complex mental representations can also permit sophisticated and precise access and execution of appropriate actions (Ward & Williams, 2003). These cognitive mechanisms that allow experts to reason and plan, anticipate, and control and monitor their actions require that a vast amount of information is kept accessible in working memory capacity to support these cognitive activities.

## Expertise and Long-Term Working Memory

Early research on the specific mental activities that mediate performance by experts on complex tasks in their domain focused on the role of individual differences in memory between experts and novices, as mentioned in our discussion of using memory tasks instead of representative tasks capturing the essence of expertise in the domain. Specifically, when asked to remember a chessboard presented for 5 seconds, novices would typically show very poor memory performance because they encoded individual pieces or patterns of very small groups of pieces in the chess positions (Chase &

Simon, 1973). The masters were "chunking" much larger groups of meaningful patterns of chess pieces. When stimuli with no meaningful patterns of chess pieces are presented, like in randomly rearranged pieces on a chessboard, the experts' memory performance drops almost to the level of beginners. From this evidence Simon and Chase (1973) concluded that the ability to identify familiar patterns by chunking domain-specific information was crucial for retrieval of past knowledge about chess moves. This view of expert memory has been extended in Gobet and Simon's (1996) work on templates. An alternative view of how chess memory is acquired as a by-product of supporting planning and evaluation for finding the best move in chess positions has been advance by Ericsson and Kintsch (1995; Ericsson et al., 2000) and will be discussed in this section.

Superior memory performance can be explained as an acquired skill based on complex encoding mechanisms and mental representations (Wilding & Valentine, 2006). One of the first theoretical accounts for superior memory was Ericsson and Chase's (1982) skilled memory theory. They showed how—after considerable practice—individuals could increase their performance on digit span tasks from 7 to over 80 digits. Ericsson and Kintsch (1995) expanded this theory to explain superior memory and working memory capacity in a broader range of domains of expertise such as chess, medicine, and mental calculation. They proposed that expert performers acquire encoding methods that allow them to store information and later retrieve it from long-term memory (LTM). Given that many expert performers have been shown to be able to retrieve information from LTM virtually as rapidly as if it has been stored in short-term memory, Ericsson and Kintsch (1995) named this acquired memory capacity long-term working memory (LTWM).

The concept of LTWM has successfully explained the superior memory of mental calculators, waiters, and other individuals with exceptional memory in domains where memory is the focus of the exceptional performance. Studies have examined the superior memory abilities of individuals who have memorized over 30,000 digits (Thompson, Cowan, & Frieman, 1993) and over 60,000 digits (Hu, Ericsson, Yang, & Lu, 2009) of the mathematical constant pi. There is no evidence that these memorists were endowed with an innate advantage in general memory abilities (Ericsson, Delaney, Weaver, & Mahadevan, 2004; Hu et al., 2009).

The superior working memory of experts in their domain has been accounted for by LTWM. Ericsson

et al. (2000) demonstrated that expert performers engaged in deliberate practice to improve their performance; they also acquired skills to expand their functional working memory capacity in order to engage in planning or evaluation of their performance. When selecting a move for chess positions, skilled chess players explore the consequences of long sequences of moves by planning. This requires the storage of manipulated chess positions and the depth of their planning is correlated with chess skill (Charness, 1981). Expert doctors encode information about patients in a higher level representation that permits them to reason about similar diagnostic alternatives (Patel, Kaufman, & Magder, 1996). Elite athletes acquire skills to represent the current game situation in more refined and complex ways when they play tennis (McPherson & Kernodle, 2007) and baseball (McPherson & MacMahon, 2008). Although there is general agreement that experts often display superior memory for stimuli from their domain, there have been considerable disagreements about the theoretical mechanisms accounting for this superiority as shown by a couple of heated exchanges (Ericsson et al., 2000; Gobet & Simon, 2000; Vicente, 2000; Vicente & Wang, 1998; and Ericsson & Kintsch, 2000; Ericsson & Lehmann, 1996; Gobet, 1998, 2000a, 2000b).

## Development of the Structure of Expert Performance

If complex mechanisms and physiological adaptations differentiate experts from less accomplished performers, this raises the questions of whether—and how—these mechanisms have been acquired. The expert performance approach focuses on describing how elite performers develop the complex cognitive mechanisms and physiological adaptations that are responsible for their superior performance. When an individual's performance in a domain is measured objectively as a function of age (aee Fig. 56.3), the data show that no experts began their training as superior performers nor did they spontaneously obtain high levels of objective performance (Bloom, 1985). Only after years of gradual improvement do they reach an international level of performance. Even those individuals considered to be the most "gifted" do not win competitions at international levels with less than 10 years of focused training in the majority of highly competitive domains (Ericsson et al., 1993; Simon & Chase, 1973).

Studies of swimmers and musicians show that the developmental histories of superior performers differ dramatically from their peers. Future elite

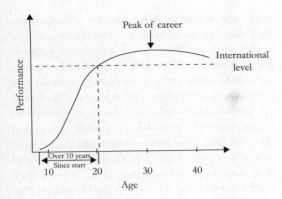

**Figure 56.3** An illustration of the gradual increases in expert performance as a function of age, in domains such as chess. The international level, which is attained after more than around 10 years of involvement in the domain, is indicated by the horizontal dashed line. (From "Expertise," by K. A. Ericsson and Andreas C. Lehmann, 1999, *Encyclopedia of creativity.* Copyright by Academic Press.)

performers often start training in their domain at a very young age and have access to superior training resources from the start of training. Supportive environments also encourage individuals to engage in large amounts of specific and appropriate practice activities.

All children are not equally likely to reach elite levels in sport. In sports such as soccer and hockey, children are grouped by age. A review by Musch and Grondin (2001) described the extensive evidence that those children who were oldest in their age cohort were more likely to be successful. The oldest individuals would be up to almost a year older than the youngest. This difference is crucial at young ages such as 4, 5, or 6 years of age. Even more remarkably the oldest children eventually were more likely to become professional players. This is most likely because they had been given superior training opportunities and more encouragement. Côté, Macdonald, Baker, and Abernethy (2006) showed that children living in medium-sized cities were more likely to become successful in sports than children growing up in large cities. The most likely explanation for these differences is that smaller cities offer optimal levels of resource availability such as competitive leagues, space for practice, and other resources that may be limited in large cities, where space and safety are often concerns.

In an extensive review, Ericsson (2003b) found that improvement and maintenance of superior performance were uniformly observed when individuals were given tasks with well-defined goals, immediate feedback, and appropriate opportunities for repetition and gradual refinement.

It is not simply spending more time in domain-specific activities that predicts superior performance. Only when individuals engage with full concentration on improving specific aspects of performance during practice activities would those activities be considered "deliberate practice." This type of practice requires intense concentration on improving particular aspects of performance and thus leads to modification of mechanisms responsible for improvement. Spending more time simply doing more of the same, which is typical of those engaging in activities with the explicit purpose of recreation or minimal acceptable performance, leads to development of automaticity (lower arm of Fig. 56.1). Some higher performers such as athletes competing regionally also automatize acquired skills by stopping deliberate efforts to keep improving, which leads to prematurely arrested development (middle arm of Fig. 56.1). Still some exceptional individuals are able to avoid automaticity in favor of continually modifying appropriate aspects of their performance (upper arm of Fig. 56.1).

Ericsson et al. (1993) found that expert violinists worked on assignments and exercises designed by their music teachers as the primary activities during their solitary practice. Individual differences in the amount of this type of solitary practice were found to be closely related to the levels of attained music performance. By the time the best expert musicians had reached age 20, they estimated that they had accumulated more than 10,000 hours of deliberate practice. This was several thousand hours more than their less accomplished peers at the same music academy.

Higher chess performance has been found to be correlated with the amount of solitary study in chess (Charness, Tuffiash, Krampe, Reingold, & Vasyukova, 2005). Once the amount of deliberate practice has been statistically controlled, the number of games played in tournaments has not been found to have a unique contribution to predicting chess skill. In sports, higher level of competitive events (amateur, local, district, national, and international) is reliably related to higher amounts of different types of practice activities (Helsen, Starkes, & Hodges, 1998; Starkes, Deakin, Allard, Hodges, & Hayes, 1996; Ward et al., 2004). In sports there are some controversies about which practice activities constitute deliberate practice as opposed to more playful activities (Côté, Ericsson, & Law, 2005). Côté (1999) has proposed that practice activities that combine deliberate practice and play (deliberate play) also contribute to the acquisition of highly skilled performance (Côté, Baker, & Abernethy, 2003).

The role of feedback has been found to be critical for deliberate practice. During deliberate practice in chess, players read books and try to predict the moves made by masters in published games. Players can generate the move for each chess position in the game one at a time and compare their moves to the recorded move of the masters. In this way they can receive immediate feedback on the quality of their moves and then try to identify the source of their mistake and make appropriate improvements in future analyses (Ericsson et al., 1993). The design of situations in which individuals can receive immediate feedback is one of the essential prerequisites for deliberate practice activities that generalize across widely disparate domains. In the earlier example, the chess player would likely read published games and compare his or her chosen moves to the choice of a master, thus obtaining feedback. In a similar way athletes can identify aspects of their current performance and find a practice activity that allows them to stretch those aspects to a higher level of performance with immediate feedback and opportunity to repeat and refine the relevant processes. Once attained, the improved skill will be incorporated in their regular performance.

Another important facet of deliberate practice is the direction or coaching to practice appropriately challenging tasks such as the technical mastery of difficult shots in darts (Duffy, Baluch, & Ericsson, 2004), difficult jumps in figure skating (Deakin & Cobley, 2003; Starkes et al., 1996), and difficult routines in rhythmic gymnastics (Law, Côté, & Ericsson, 2007). In all these cases the performers get almost immediate feedback by the observable outcome itself and, often, additional feedback from coaches.

Immediate informative feedback and the opportunity for subsequent correction of suboptimal actions as well as repetition of the correct actions in the same and similar situations is a key component of deliberate practice. One critical issue concerns significant delay of feedback. In many activities feedback regarding failures is almost instantaneous such as in sports (i.e., missed shots and passes in basketball) and surgery (i.e., incisions with aversive side effects, such as ruptured arteries or nerves). In contrast, the accuracy of many of the decisions made by managers may never be known because the results of any alternative decisions are unknown. Even

when the decisions have negative consequences, they may not be revealed until weeks, months, or even years later. There have been several proposals for how one would be able to provide the opportunities for immediate feedback and, by extension, deliberate practice. One such suggestion is to present professionals with descriptions or simulations of past situations in which the correct actions and outcome have been eventually determined. As soon as the aspiring expert performers have generated their actions, it is possible to provide immediate feedback following their decision (Ericsson, 1996, 2004, 2006a).

The relation between accumulated amounts of deliberate practice and attained skill level could be an artifact of bias introduced by "dropouts." Sternberg (1996) suggested that more talented individuals gain larger improvements from the same amount of deliberate practice. Those benefiting less from practice would eventually be more likely to become discouraged, thus reducing their practice and eventually discontinuing their engagement in the domain. This process would lead to more talented individuals persisting with high levels of practice in a domain and thus creating a false impression that increased practice was the primary cause of superior performance.

De Bruin, Rikers, and Schmidt (2008) directly evaluated this hypothesis by collecting information on the amount of deliberate practice in a group of young elite chess players. This study showed that the amount of deliberate practice was related to the development of performance for all players. They found that a reduction in weekly deliberate practice led to a decrease in performance and eventually to dropping out. Hence, reduced practice leads to reduced performance rather than inferior performance, leading individuals to become discouraged and practice less. Sloboda, Davidson, Howe, and Moore (1996) reported similar findings in the field of music, where music students estimated their level of past practice. They found that contrary to accounts proposed by proponents of innate abilities, none of the highest scoring students reached objectively defined levels of music performance with significantly less solitary practice than their lower performing counterparts.

A recent study by Roring and Charness (2007) suggests that mental performance in chess shows only very slight decline with age and that the declines are smallest for the most skilled individuals who more frequently engage in deliberate practice activities. Studies of aging musicians (Krampe & Ericsson,

1996) have shown that even domains requiring rapid movements may show little age decline with regular engagement in deliberate practice. A study of master athletes in track by Young, Weir, Starkes, and Medic (2008) compared the performance of a longitudinal sample to a cross-sectional sample in three track events. Their analysis indicated that runners who maintained higher levels of practice saw a much slower decline of performance as they aged. These studies suggest that healthy individuals in their sixties and seventies are not subject to inevitable loss of performance and that their decision to continue engagement in deliberate practice drives the maintenance of performance (Ericsson, 2000).

## Deliberate Practice and Changes in Anatomical and Physiological Characteristics

To account for improvements in performance, it is necessary to identify the associated specific cognitive and physiological changes that mediate those improvements. An ultimate theory needs to specify the causal biological factors that can explain how deliberate practice activities lead to sustained elite performance.

In physical activities such as sports, experts continually strive beyond their current performance levels and deliberately push themselves during practice (Ericsson, 2001, 2007b, 2007c). They engage in sustained strenuous physical activity that consumes oxygen and energy at a high level and thus challenges homeostasis of cells' metabolism in some physiological systems. The depleted resources of energy and oxygen force the cells to change their metabolism to produce alternative biochemical compounds, leading to the activation of "dormant" genes within the affected cells' DNA. The activated genes in turn will activate other genes to initiate bodily reorganization and adaptive change.

Research has analyzed the chemical contents of cells such as activated genes and proteins and studied changes in response to vigorous physical activity. Researchers found that over 100 different genes are activated and expressed in mammalian muscle when they are exposed to intense physical exercise (Carson, Nettleton, & Reecy, 2001).

There are many abnormal physiological and anatomical characteristics of expert athletes that can be explained as acquired adaptations to increased demands induced by their intense and extended engagement in practice activities (see Ericsson et al., 1993 and Ericsson 2007a for reviews). Some physiological adaptations result from intense extended practice. In long-distance running the hearts of athletes increase in size as a response to continued physical challenges (increased intensity and duration of physical training). When training is reduced or ceased after their active athletic careers are completed, their enlarged hearts eventually shrink and approach an average size (Pelliccia et al., 2002). Furthermore, certain practice activities that are carried out during critical developmental periods result in dramatic and permanent physical adaptations. Examples are ballet dancers' ability to turn their feet and baseball pitchers' ability to stretch back with their throwing arm. These abilities are related to stretching while practicing the associated movements before the children's bones and cartilage in joints are calcified in late childhood (see Ericsson & Lehmann, 1996).

A relatively new area of expertise research has attempted to determine the neurological correlates of superior performance. Modern neuroimaging techniques have revealed that there may be complex neurological differences in the structure, the composition, and the activation patterns among skilled individuals. For example, Maguire, Valentine, Wilding, and Kapur (2003) conducted an experimental test of the nature and structure of superior memory in 10 of the world's foremost memory performers. When the structural magnetic resonance images for the brains of memory experts and control subjects were compared, Maguire et al. (2003) were unable to find any significant anatomical differences. Most interestingly, the differences in brain activation during memorization between the two groups could be fully explained by the differences in their reports of using sophisticated memory strategies (Ericsson, 2003c).

Another study by Draganski et al. (2004) examined the compositional (white and gray matter) changes after months of juggling training. Their results revealed significant changes in gray matter after a 3-month practice interval. Three months after the second testing participants showed gray matter reductions toward baseline levels. Bengtsson, Nagy, Skare, Forsman, Forsberg, and Ullén (2005) examined white matter (myelin) distribution differences as a function of prior piano practice. They concluded that extended practice could have effects on white matter distribution during periods before maturation. These studies outline emerging research investigating the neurological correlates and changes that occur as a result of practice and demonstrate that complex biological adaptations are mediated by practice; this contrasts with previous beliefs that propensity for a given domain was mediated by fixed biological structures and composition.

## Deliberate Practice Activities Changing Particular Aspects of Performance

Many types of changes in performance concern changes in the cognitive structure of mechanisms mediating higher speed, better selection of actions, and higher consistency of executed motor actions. The development of each of these types of mechanisms requires different types of deliberate practice. Some of the best evidence for how speed of performance can be increased through deliberate practice involves the refinement of the representations of future actions.

Research on increased speed of typists illustrates this type of deliberate practice. Expert typists have modified their mental representations to allow them to look further ahead in the text while typing. Thus they are able to prepare future keystrokes by moving their fingers to the keys in advance (as shown by high-speed filming of anticipatory movements of the fingers of typists). Although most people's typing speed remains pretty constant over decades by regular typing, typists are able to improve by deliberately increasing their speed of typing well beyond their normal speed for short periods. During this type of practice they can reach increases in speed of 10%–20% as long as they are able to maintain full concentration, which is typically between 15–30 minutes per day in the beginning of training (Dvorak, Merrick, Dealey, & Ford, 1936).

The faster speeds help them to identify keystroke combinations that are comparatively slow. They can then improve these weaker components of their skill that will allow them to gradually increase performance during sessions of deliberate practice. A similar type of deliberate practice can explain the superior speed of expert performers in domains such as tennis, soccer, and ice hockey, in which cognitive representations can be acquired in order to anticipate future outcomes and events (for reviews, see Abernethy, 1991; Starkes & Deakin, 1984).

Improvement in the selection of actions in representative situations requires different types of deliberate practice tasks where the trainees' selected actions can be evaluated by comparisons against a gold standard such as the best possible action determined by a computer analysis or world-class individuals. By using archival data from masters, it is possible to allow aspiring expert performers to take on the same task as the masters. They can try to generate the best action and then compare their products or actions with those of the masters. The central argument is that students are able to use their mental representations that aided their generation of moves to identify why they generated an inferior action or did not consider the better action. They can then assess how they need to modify their representations so that they would be able to reproduce the correct action (that of the master) if they were to encounter that or a similar situation in the future.

Chess students can replay old games by masters under self-paced conditions and then make corrections when they select moves inconsistent with the masters.' As chess students' skill increases from deliberate practice, their mental representations are refined in a way that allows them to access domain-specific information more efficiently, increasing the speed at which they can generate superior chess moves (Charness, Krampe, & Mayr, 1996; Charness et al., 2005; Ericsson, 1996; Ericsson et al., 1993).

A study of soccer players by Ward and Williams (2003) demonstrated that more skilled players had developed more sophisticated representations of game situations in videos of soccer matches. By watching soccer games on television or video they would be able to get feedback on their anticipations of players' behaviors and thus constantly improve mental representations of game situations in order to select better actions under actual game situations. Studies of sports such as baseball and tennis have indicated that superior performances are linked to refined representations of game situations (see McPherson & Kernodle, 2003, 2007).

## Conclusions and Future Directions

The scientific study of experts requires that phenomena of superior performance be reproducible, and ideally they should be captured with performance on standardized tasks under controlled conditions. The expert-performance approach has shown that experts' superior performance is primarily mediated by acquired mental and physiological representations.

In several domains, engagement in deliberate practice has been shown to be closely associated with the acquisition of mental representations, which in turn permit monitoring, refinement, and improvement of performance during deliberate practice. The demands for full concentration and effort restrict the time that performers can engage in deliberate practice without a break. These limits also constrain the daily practice amounts, where even experts need sleep and rest in order to recuperate prior to the next training sessions (Ericsson, 2006a; Ericsson et al., 1993). These findings have been further supported by evidence that athletes in multisport events such as triathlons devote similar durations of weekly practice as their single-sport counterparts (Hodges, Kerr, Starkes, Weir, & Naninidou, 2004). Similar daily durations of practice are reported by experts across domains such as sport, chess, and music, suggesting that deliberate practice at elite levels of performance is very demanding and its daily duration is limited to no more than 4 or 5 hours every day to permit sufficient rest and recuperation in order to avoid exhaustion, injury, and burnout (Ericsson et al., 1993).

The most exciting future direction in research on expert performance involves the identification and specification of causal biological mechanisms that mediate the development of expert performance. Identifying the critical training activities (cf. deliberate practice) that induce adaptations of the neural and physiological systems contributing to superior performance could help us better understand the improvement of skill in a variety of domains.

The degree of myelination of specific brain systems has been found to be linked to the level of music practice during specific age intervals (Bengtsson et al., 2005). Ericsson (2007b) discusses the issue of identifying biological markers of increased performance in sports, particularly the activation of genes in DNA that healthy people possess and are thus capable to evoke in response to extended appropriate deliberate practice.

All healthy children appear to possess the critical genes and thus should be able to activate them with a sufficient amount of prerequisite practice. Ericsson et al. (2007b, 2007c) argue that the expert performance approach can be applied equally well to genetic and training-based accounts of superior performance. Once the crucial genes have been identified it will be possible to assess whether the genes are prevalent in healthy children or whether only a small proportion of talented individuals have them as part of their DNA. It is essential that all research regarding exceptional individuals is based on testable hypotheses that can adequately explain the full development of expert performance.

Despite some significant advances in our understanding of the factors that influence development of reproducibly superior performance, it is only a modest beginning. Perhaps the great challenge is to develop methods to measure and capture the full range of performance in many professions and creative domains such as writing, acting, and painting.

Until we are able to capture essential aspects of these types of performance with representative tasks, it seems unlikely that we will make progress in assessing its structure and development. Another major challenge is the identification and measurement of more general skills that will be beneficial for the development of superior expert performance.

The greatest challenge concerns understanding individual differences that are related to engagement in the demanding deliberate practice activities for months, years, and decades. Only future research will tell us about potential factors related to early development and support by parents, coaches, peers, and teachers. This research will inform us about differential development trajectories, stumbling blocks, and sustainable practice levels.

At the basis for research on experts and their performance is the desire to learn how exceptional individuals have been able to attain their superior performance. Emphasis has been placed on identifying specific mediating factors for superior performance. Once identified, factors with a history of development through training can be coached to novices so that motivated individuals can begin and continue on their path to superior performance.

### Glossary

*Associative stage of skill acquisition*: Second stage of skill acquisition proposed by Fitts and Posner (1967) in which skill execution becomes fluid and salient performance errors are rare.

*Automatic stage of skill acquisition*: Last stage of skill acquisition proposed by Fitts and Posner (1967) in which the steps of skill execution have been integrated and are elicited effortlessly and automatically. Intentional changes to aspects of performance are very difficult once this stage has been reached.

*Cognitive stage of skill acquisition*: First stage of skill acquisition posited by Fitts and Posner (1967) in which execution is slow, deliberate, effortful, and prone to errors.

*Expert-performance approach*: Approach to studying experts that focuses on identifying representative tasks in a domain that can measure the superior performance of experts in a standard and reproducible way. The expert-performance approach was originally proposed by Ericsson and Smith (1991) as an alternative to studies of experts based on peer nomination and length of professional experience.

*Long-term working memory (LTWM)*: Theoretical structure of working memory of experts based on Chase and Ericsson's (1982) skilled memory theory and later expanded and generalized by Ericsson and Kintsch (1995). It explains how experts can acquire memory skills to encode and store and later retrieve domain-related information in long-term memory. LTWM theory proposes that experts acquire complex representations to encode information in a manner that allows it to be reliably accessed in relevant future contexts of processing with speeds typically associated with short-term memory.

# References

Abernethy, B. (1991). Visual search strategies and decision-making in sport. *International Journal of Sport Psychology, 22*, 189–210.

Ackerman, P. L. (1987). Individual differences in skill learning: An integration of psychometric and information processing perspectives. *Psychological Bulletin, 102*, 3–27.

Amirault, R. J., & Branson, R. K. (2006). Educators and expertise: A brief history of theories and models. In K. A. Ericsson, N. Charness, P. Feltovich, & R. R. Hoffman (Eds.), *The Cambridge handbook of expertise and expert performance* (pp. 69–86). Cambridge, UK: Cambridge University Press.

Anderson, J. R. (1982). Acquisition of cognitive skill. *Psychological Review, 89*, 369–406.

Baker, J., Côté, J., & Deakin, J. (2005). Cognitive characteristics of expert, middle of the pack, and back of the pack ultra-endurance triathletes. *Psychology of Sport and Exercise, 6*, 551–558.

Bengtsson, S. L., Nagy, Z., Skare, S., Forsman, L., Forssberg, H., & Ullén, F. (2005). Extensive piano practicing has regionally specific effects on white matter development. *Nature Neuroscience, 8*, 1148–1150.

Benner, P. (1984). *From novice to expert: Excellence and power in clinical nursing practice.* Upper Saddle River, NJ: Prentice Hall.

Bloom, B. S. (1985). Generalizations about talent development. In B. S. Bloom (Ed.), *Developing talent in young people* (pp. 507–549). New York: Ballantine Books.

Camerer, C. F., & Johnson, E. J. (1991). The process-performance paradox in expert judgment: How can the experts know so much and predict so badly? In K. A. Ericsson & J. Smith (Eds.), *Toward a general theory of expertise: Prospects and limits* (pp. 195–217). Cambridge, UK: Cambridge University Press.

Carson, J. A., Nettleton, D., & Reecy, J. M. (2001). Differential gene expression in the rat soleus muscle during early work overload-induced hypertrophy. *FASEB Journal, 15*, 261–281.

Charness, N. (1981). Search in chess: Age and skill differences. *Journal of Experimental Psychology: Human Perception and Performance, 7*, 467–476.

Charness, N., Tuffiash, M., Krampe, R., Reingold, E., & Vasyukova, E. (2005). The role of deliberate practice in chess expertise. *Applied Cognitive Psychology, 19*, 151–165.

Charness, N., Krampe, R. T., & Mayr, U. (1996). The role of practice and coaching in entrepreneurial skill domains: An international comparison of life-span chess skill acquisition. In K. A. Ericsson (Ed.), *The road to excellence: The acquisition of expert performance in the arts and sciences, sports, and games* (pp. 51–80). Mahwah, NJ: Erlbaum.

Chase, W., & Simon, H. (1973). The mind's eye in chess. In W. Chase (Ed.), *Visual information processing* (pp. 215–281). Mahwah, NJ: Erlbaum.

Chi, M. T. H. (2006). Two approaches to the study of experts' characteristics. In K. A. Ericsson, N. Charness, P. Feltovich, & R. R. Hoffman (Eds.), *The Cambridge handbook of expertise and expert performance* (pp. 21–38). Cambridge, England: Cambridge University Press.

Chi, M. T. H., Feltovich, P. J., & Glaser, R. (1981). Categorization and representation of physics problems by experts and novices. *Cognitive Science, 5*, 121–152.

Choudhry, N. K., Fletcher, R. H., & Soumerai, S. B. (2005). Systematic review: The relationship between clinical experience and health care. *Annals of Internal Medicine, 142*, 260–273.

Côté, J. (1999). The influence of the family in the development of talent in sports. *The Sport Psychologist, 13*, 395–417.

Côté, J., Baker, J., & Abernethy, B. (2003). From play to practice: A developmental framework for the acquisition of expertise in team sports. In K. A. Ericsson & J. L. Starkes (Eds.), *Expert performance in sports: Advances in research on sport expertise* (pp. 89–113). Champaign, IL: Human Kinetics.

Côté, J., Ericsson, K. A., & Law, M. (2005). Tracing the development of athletes using retrospective interview methods: A proposed interview and validation procedure for reported information. *Journal of Applied Sport Psychology, 17*, 1–19.

Côté, J., Macdonald, D. J., Baker, J., & Abernethy, B. (2006). When "where" is more important than "when": Birthplace and birthdate effects on the achievement of sporting expertise. *Journal of Sports Sciences, 24*, 1065–1073.

Dawes, R. M. (1994). *House of cards: Psychology and psychotherapy built on myth.* New York: Free Press.

de Bruin, A. B. H., Smits, N., Rikers, R. M. J. P., & Schmidt, H. G. (2008). Deliberate practice predicts performance over time in adolescent chess players and drop-outs: A linear mixed models analysis. *British Journal of Psychology, 99*, 473–497.

de Groot, A. (1978). *Thought and choice in chess.* The Hague, The Netherlands: Mouton.

Deakin, J. M., & Cobley, S. (2003). An examination of the practice environments in figure skating and volleyball: A search for deliberate practice. In J. Starkes & K. A. Ericsson (Eds.), *Expert performance in sports: Advances in research on sport expertise* (pp. 90–113). Champaign, IL: Human Kinetics.

Draganski, B., Gaser, C., Busch, V., Schuierer, G., Bogdahn, U., & May, A. (2004). Changes in grey matter induced by training. *Nature, 427*, 311–312.

Drake, C., & Palmer, C. (2000). Skill acquisition in music performance: Relations between planning and temporal control. *Cognition, 74*, 1–32.

Dreyfus, H. L., & Dreyfus, S. E. (1986). *Mind over machine: The power of human intuition and expertise in the era of the computer.* New York: Free Press.

Duffy, L. J., Baluch, B., & Ericsson, K. A. (2004). Dart performance as a function of facets of practice amongst professional and amateur men and women players. *International Journal of Sports Psychology, 35*, 232–245.

Dvorak, A., Merrick, N. L., Dealey, W. L., & Ford, G. C. (1936). *Typewriting behavior.* New York: American Book Company.

Epstein, S. A. (1991). *Wage, labor, and guilds in medieval Europe.* Chapel Hill: North Carolina University Press.

Ericsson, K. A. (1996). The acquisition of expert performance: An introduction to some of the issues. In K. A. Ericsson

(Ed.), *The road to excellence: The acquisition of expert performance in the arts and sciences, sports, and games* (pp. 1–50). Mahwah, NJ: Erlbaum.

Ericsson, K. A. (2000). How experts attain and maintain superior performance: Implications for the enhancement of skilled performance in older individuals. *Journal of Aging and Physical Activity, 8*, 346–352.

Ericsson, K. A. (2001). Expertise in interpreting: An expert-performance perspective. *International Journal of Research and Practice in Interpreting, 5*, 187–220.

Ericsson, K. A. (2003a). The search for general abilities and basic capacities: Theoretical implications from the modifiability and complexity of mechanisms mediating expert performance. In R. J. Sternberg & E. L. Grigorenko (Eds.), *Perspectives on the psychology of abilities, competencies, and expertise* (pp. 93–125). Cambridge: Cambridge University Press.

Ericsson, K. A. (2003b). The acquisition of expert performance as problem solving: Construction and modification of mediating mechanisms through deliberate practice. In J. E. Davidson & R. J. Sternberg (Eds.), *Problem solving* (pp. 31–83). New York: Cambridge University Press.

Ericsson, K. A. (2003c). Exceptional memorizers: Made, not born. *Trends in Cognitive Sciences, 7*, 233–235.

Ericsson, K. A. (2004). Deliberate practice and the acquisition and maintenance of expert performance in medicine and related domains. *Academic Medicine, 79*, S70–S81.

Ericsson, K. A. (2006a). The influence of experience and deliberate practice on the development of superior expert performance. In K. A. Ericsson, N. Charness, P. Feltovich, & R. R. Hoffman (Eds.), *The Cambridge handbook of expertise and expert performance* (pp. 685–706). Cambridge, England: Cambridge University Press.

Ericsson, K. A. (2006b). Protocol analysis and expert thought: Concurrent verbalizations of thinking during experts' performance on representative task. In K. A. Ericsson, N. Charness, P. Feltovich, & R. R. Hoffman (Eds.), *The Cambridge handbook of expertise and expert performance* (pp. 223–242). Cambridge, UK: Cambridge University Press.

Ericsson, K. A. (2007a). An expert-performance perspective of research on medical expertise: The study of clinical performance. *Medical Education, 41*, 1124–1130.

Ericsson, K. A. (2007b). Deliberate practice and the modifiability of body and mind: Toward a science of the structure and acquisition of expert and elite performance. *International Journal of Sport Psychology, 38*, 4–34.

Ericsson, K. A. (2007c). Deliberate practice and the modifiability of body and mind: A reply to the commentaries. *International Journal of Sport Psychology, 38*, 109–123.

Ericsson, K. A., & Chase, W. G. (1982). Exceptional memory. *American Scientist, 70*, 607–615.

Ericsson, K. A., Delaney, P. F., Weaver, G., & Mahadevan, R. (2004). Uncovering the structure of a memorist's superior "basic" memory capacity. *Cognitive Psychology, 49*, 191–237.

Ericsson, K. A., & Harris, M. S. (1990, November 17). *Expert chess memory without chess knowledge: A training study*. Poster presented at the 31st Annual Meeting of the Psychonomic Society, New Orleans, LA.

Ericsson, K. A., & Kintsch, W. (1995). Long-term working memory. *Psychological Review, 102*, 211–245.

Ericsson, K. A., & Kintsch, W. (2000). Shortcomings of generic retrieval structures with slots of the type that Gobet (1993) proposed and modeled. *British Journal of Psychology, 91*, 571–590.

Ericsson, K. A., Krampe, R. T., & Tesch-Römer, C. (1993). The role of deliberate practice in the acquisition of expert performance. *Psychological Review, 100*, 363–406.

Ericsson, K. A., & Lehmann, A. C. (1996). Expert and exceptional performance: Evidence on maximal adaptations on task constraints. *Annual Review of Psychology, 47*, 273–305.

Ericsson, K. A., & Oliver W. L. (1988). Methodology for laboratory research on thinking: Task selection, collection of observations, and data analysis. In R. J. Sternberg & E. E. Smith (Eds.), *The psychology of human thought* (pp. 392–428). Cambridge, UK: Cambridge University Press.

Ericsson, K. A., Patel, V., & Kintsch, W. (2000). How experts' adaptations to representative task demands account for the expertise effect in memory recall: Comment on Vicente and Wang (1998). *Psychological Review, 107*, 578–592.

Ericsson, K. A., Roring, R. W., & Nandagopal, K. (2007a). Giftedness and evidence for reproducibly superior performance: An account based on the expert performance framework. *High Ability Studies, 18*, 3–56.

Ericsson, K. A., Roring, R. W., & Nandagopal, K. (2007b). Misunderstandings, agreements and disagreements: Toward a cumulative science of reproducibly superior aspects of giftedness. *High Ability Studies, 18*, 97–115.

Ericsson, K. A., & Smith, J. (1991). Prospects and limits in the empirical study of expertise: An introduction. In K. A. Ericsson & J. Smith (Eds.), *Toward a general theory of expertise: Prospects and limits* (pp. 1–38). Cambridge, England: Cambridge University Press.

Ericsson, K. A., & Williams, M. A. (2007). Capturing naturally occurring superior performance in the laboratory: Translational research on expert performance. *Journal of Experimental Psychology: Applied, 13*, 115–123.

Ericsson, K. A., Whyte, J., & Ward, P. (2007). Expert performance in nursing: Reviewing research on expertise in nursing within the framework of the expert performance approach. *Advances in Nursing Science, 30*, E58–E71.

Expert . (2009). *Merriam-Webster Online Dictionary*. Retrieved February 8, 2009, from http://www.merriam-webster.com/dictionary/expert.

Feltovich, P., Prietula, M. J., & Ericsson, K. A. (2006). Studies of expertise from psychological perspectives. In K. A. Ericsson, N. Charness, P. Feltovich, & R. R. Hoffman (Eds.), *The Cambridge handbook of expertise and expert performance* (pp. 41–67). Cambridge, UK: Cambridge University Press.

Fitts, P., & Posner, M. I. (1967). *Human performance*. Belmont, CA: Brooks/Cole.

Gobet, F. (1998). Expert memory: A comparison of four theories. *Cognition, 2*, 115–152.

Gobet, F. (2000a). Some shortcomings of long-term working memory. *British Journal of Psychology, 91*, 551–570.

Gobet, F. (2000b). Retrieval structures and schemata: A brief reply to Ericsson and Kintsch. *British Journal of Psychology, 91*, 591–594.

Gobet, F., & Jackson, S. (2002). In search of templates. *Cognitive Systems Research, 3*, 35–44.

Gobet, F., & Simon, H. A. (2000). Expertise effects in memory recall: Comments on Vicente and Wang (1998). *Psychological Review, 107*, 593–600.

Helsen, W. F., Starkes J. L., & Hodges, N. J. (1998). Team sports and the theory of deliberate practice. *Journal of Sport and Exercise Psychology, 20*, 12–34.

Hill, L. A. (1999). *Mental representations in skilled golf putting.* Unpublished Master's thesis, Florida State University, Tallahassee.

Hulin, C. L., Henry, R. A., & Noon, S. L. (1990). Adding a dimension: Time as a factor in the generalizability of predictive relationships. *Psychological Bulletin, 107,* 328–340.

Hodges, N. J., Kerr, T., Starkes, J. L., Weir, P., & Nananidou, A. (2004). Predicting performance from deliberate practice hours for triathletes and swimmers: What, when and where is practice important? *Journal of Experimental Psychology: Applied, 10,* 219–237.

Hodges, N. J., Huys, R., & Starkes, J. L. (2007). A methodological review and evaluation of research of expert performance in sport. In G. Tenenbaum & R. Eklund (Eds.), *Handbook of sport psychology* (3rd ed., pp. 161–183). New York: Wiley.

Holyoak, K. J. (1991). Symbolic connectionism: Toward third-generation theories. In K. A. Ericsson & J. Smith (Eds.), *Toward a general theory of expertise: Prospects and limits* (pp. 301–336). Cambridge, UK: Cambridge University Press.

Hu, Y., Ericsson, K. A., Yang, D., & Lu, C. (2009). Superior self-paced memorization of digits in spite of a normal digit span: The structure of a memorist's skill. *Journal of Experimental Psychology: Learning, Memory, & Cognition, 35,* 1426–42.

Klein, G. A. (1990). *Sources of power: How people make decisions.* Cambridge, MA: MIT Press.

Klein, G. A. (1993). A recognition-primed decision (RPD) model of rapid decision making. In G. A. Klein, J. Orasanu, R. Calderwood, & C. E. Zsambok (Eds.), *Decision making in action: Models and methods* (pp. 138–147). Norwood, NJ: Ablex.

Krampe, R. T., & Ericsson, K. A. (1996). Maintaining excellence: Deliberate practice and elite performance in young and older pianists. *Journal of Experimental Psychology: General, 125,* 331–359.

Law, M., Côté, J., & Ericsson, K. A. (2007). Characteristics of expert development in rhythmic gymnastics: A retrospective study. *International Journal of Exercise and Sport Psychology, 5,* 82–103.

Lehmann, A. C., & Gruber, H. (2006). Music. In K. A. Ericsson, N. Charness, P. Feltovich, & R. R. Hoffman (Eds.), *The Cambridge handbook of expertise and expert performance* (pp. 457–470). Cambridge, UK: Cambridge University Press.

Maguire, E. A., Valentine, E. R., Wilding, J. M., & Kapur, N. (2003). Routes to remembering: The brains behind superior memory. *Nature Neuroscience, 6,* 90–95.

Masters, K. S., & Ogles, B. M. (1998). Associative and dissociative cognitive strategies in exercise and running: 20 years later, what do we know? *The Sport Psychologist, 12,* 253–270.

McPherson, S., & Kernodle, M. W. (2003). Tactics, the neglected attribute of expertise: Problem representations and performance skills in tennis. In J. Starkes & K. A. Ericsson (Eds.), *Expert performance in sport: Recent advances in research on sport expertise* (pp. 137–164). Champaign, IL: Human Kinetics.

McPherson, S., & Kernodle, M. W. (2007). Mapping two new points on the tennis expertise continuum: Tactical skills of adult advanced beginners and entry-level professional during competition. *Journal of Sports Sciences, 25,* 945–959.

McPherson, S. L., & MacMahon, C. (2008). How baseball players prepare to bat: Tactical knowledge as a mediator of expert performance in baseball. *Journal of Sport and Exercise Psychology, 30,* 755–778.

Musch, J., & Grondin, S. (2001). Unequal competition as an impediment to personal development: A review of the relative age effect in sport. *Developmental Review, 21,* 147–167.

Nevett, M. E., & French, K. E. (1997). The development of sport-specific planning, rehearsal, and updating of plans during defensive youth baseball game performance. *Research Quarterly for Exercise and Sport, 68,* 203–214.

Patel, V. L., Kaufman, D. R., & Magder, S. A. (1996). The acquisition of medical expertise in complex dynamic environments. In K. A. Ericsson (Ed.), *The road to excellence: The acquisition of expert performance in the arts and sciences, sports, and games* (pp. 127–165). Hillsdale, NJ: Erlbaum.

Pelliccia, A., Maron, B. J., De Luca, R., Di Paolo, F., Spartaro, A., & Culasso, F. (2002). Remodeling of left ventricular hypertrophy in elite athletes after long-term deconditioning. *Circulation, 105,* 944–949.

Reif, F., & Allen, S. (1992). Cognition for interpreting scientific concepts: A study of acceleration. *Cognition and Instruction, 9,* 1–44.

Roring, R. W., & Charness, N. (2007). A multilevel model analysis of expertise in chess across the life span. *Psychology and Aging, 22,* 291–299.

Salthouse, T. A. (1984). The skill of typing. *Scientific American, 250,* 128–135.

Shanteau, J., & Stewart, T. R. (1992). Why study expert decision making? Some historical perspectives and comments. *Organizational Behavior and Human Decision Processes, 53,* 95–106.

Simon, D. P., & Simon, H. A. (1978). Individual differences in solving physic problems. In R. S. Siegler (Ed.), *Children's thinking; What develops?* (pp. 325–348). Hillsdale, NJ: Erlbaum.

Simon, H. A., & Chase, W. G. (1973). Skill in chess. *American Scientist, 61,* 394–403.

Sloboda, J. A., Davidson, J. W., Howe, M. J. A., & Moore, D. C. (1996). The role of practice in the development of performing musicians. *British Journal of Psychology, 87,* 287–309.

Smith, M. U. (1992). Expertise and the organization of knowledge: Unexpected differences among genetic counselors, faculty, and students on problem categorization tasks. *Journal of Research in Science Teaching, 29,* 179–205.

Starkes, J. L., & Deakin, J. (1984). Perception in sport: A cognitive approach to skilled performance. In W. F. Straub & J. M. Williams (Eds.), *Cognitive sport psychology* (pp. 115–128). Lansing, NY: Sport Science Associates.

Starkes, J. L., Deakin, J. M., Allard, F., Hodges, N. J., & Hayes, A. (1996). Deliberate practice in sports: What is it anyway? In K. A. Ericsson (Ed.), *The road to excellence: The acquisition of expert performance in the arts and sciences, sports and games* (pp. 81–106). Hillsdale, NJ: Erlbaum.

Sternberg, R. J. (1996). Costs of expertise. In K. A. Ericsson (Ed.), *The road to excellence: The acquisition of expert performance in the arts and sciences, sports and games* (pp. 347–354). Mahwah, NJ: Erlbaum.

Thompson, C. P., Cowan, T. M., & Frieman, J. (1993). *Memory search by a memorist.* Hillsdale, NJ: Erlbaum.

Tuffiash, M., Roring, R. W., & Ericsson, K. A. (2007). Expert performance in SCRABBLE: Implications for the study of the structure and acquisition of complex skills. *Journal of Experimental Psychology: Applied, 13,* 124–134.

van der Maas, H. L. J., & Wagenmakers, E. J. (2005). A psychometric analysis of chess expertise. *American Journal of Psychology, 118,* 29–60.

VanLehn, K., & Van de Sande, B. (2009). Acquiring conceptual expertise form modeling: The case of elementary physics. In K. A. Ericsson (Ed.), *The development of professional expertise: Toward measurement of expert performance and design of optimal learning environments* (pp. 356–378). New York: Cambridge University Press.

Vicente, K. J. (2000). Revisiting the constraint attunement hypothesis: Reply to Ericsson, Patel, & Kintsch (2000) and Simon & Gobet (2000). *Psychological Review, 107*, 601–608.

Vicente, K. J., & Wang, J. H. (1998). An ecological theory of expertise effects in memory recall. *Psychological Review, 105*, 33–57.

Ward, P., Hodges, N. J., Williams, A. M., & Starkes, J. L. (2004). Deliberate practice and expert performance. In A. M. Williams & N. J. Hodges (Eds.), *Skill acquisition in sport* (pp. 231–258). London, UK: Routhledge.

Ward, P., & Williams, A. M. (2003). Perceptual and cognitive skill development in soccer: The multidimensional nature of expert performance. *Journal of Sport and Exercise Psychology, 25*, 93–111.

Watson, A. H. D. (2006). What can studying musicians tell us about motor control of the hand? *Journal of Anatomy, 208*, 527–542.

Wilding, J. M., & Valentine, E. M. (2006). Exceptional memory. In K. A. Ericsson, N. Charness, P. Feltovich, & R. R. Hoffman (Eds.), *The Cambridge handbook of expertise and expert performance* (pp. 457–470). Cambridge, UK: Cambridge University Press.

Young, B. W., Weir, P. L., Starkes, J. L., & Medic, N. (2008). Does lifelong training temper age related decline in sport performance? Interpreting differences between cross-sectional and longitudinal data. *Experimental Aging Research, 34*, 27–48.

# PART 12

# The Social and Cultural Context

# Self-Knowledge

Isabelle M. Bauer *and* Roy F. Baumeister

**Abstract**

This chapter broadly addresses the following question: How do people gain knowledge about the self, and is this knowledge accurate and unbiased? To answer this question, we discuss pathways to self-knowledge that involve intrapsychic processes related to introspection and self-perception and interpersonal processes that involve the self in its interaction with the social world. We further expose some of the biases and underlying motives that shape people's search for self-knowledge via these pathways. Specifically, we consider how the biased processing of self-relevant information as well as the varied ways in which people engineer their social world can influence how people perceive and present themselves, and how they are perceived by others. Over time, the reciprocal forces inherent in the search for self-knowledge conspire to give rise to a subjective sense of self that may be experienced as true and unadulterated, notwithstanding possible evidence to the contrary.

**Key Words:** self-knowledge, self-assessment, self-verification, self-enhancement, introspection, self-perception, biased information processing, interpersonal relationships

Self-esteem, self-presentation, self-enhancement, self-regulation, and self-reflection: these are only some of the psychological phenomena that have been studied over the years to unravel the mystery of the self. The sheer number of phenomena related to the self that have intrigued and occupied the minds of researchers and laypeople alike is a testament to people's fascination with understanding the self. At the individual level, people are engaged in a perpetual quest for self-knowledge that can be equally daunting. Notwithstanding these challenges, the importance of "knowing thyself" has been advocated since ancient Greek times and the goal to know oneself—the true and unadulterated self—remains central to the lives of many people. Given that self-knowledge resides within each person, should not everyone therefore be able to turn inward and describe what is in plain view for him or her to see? To the contrary, to access self-knowledge, people must sift through layers and search behind the self's protective walls in order to expose its true nature. In this chapter, we will address two broad questions related to self-knowledge. First, we will explore different pathways toward self-knowledge and discuss the strengths and limitations associated with each. Second, we will examine how self-knowledge is shaped and modified by means of intrapsychic and interpersonal processes that rely on personally and socially based sources of information.[1]

To answer these questions, we will begin by addressing the nature of self-knowledge. Next, we will explore psychological processes that open the window into the self and pave the way toward self-knowledge, as well as the limits inherent in these processes. We will argue that knowledge of the self is derived from the self's capacity to turn attention inward, to observe, think about, and evaluate itself. We will show that self-knowledge does not emerge from the dispassionate operation of cognitive processes, but that it is instead creatively constructed and manufactured in a way that reflects underlying motivations. Next, we will explore how interpersonal processes can represent an important source of complementary self-knowledge. In this respect, we hasten to note that self-knowledge is a highly personal *and* social construct: It resides within each person, yet it takes shape in the social world. People acquire self-knowledge by relying on socially based sources of information, by receiving, eliciting, and internalizing social feedback, and by engineering their social world in a way that will reinforce specific self-views. Through these processes, people's self-concept develops, evolves, and changes over time. Ultimately, this information crystallizes into a self-structure that organizes and makes sense of the wealth of information in the world. For better or for worse, the self serves as a lens through which people experience and interpret their inner and social worlds.

## The Nature of Self-Knowledge

Self-knowledge refers to the beliefs that people hold about themselves, whether these are true or false. It has been proposed that self-knowledge is organized according to self-guides (Higgins, 1987). Based on this conceptualization, people have mental representations of an actual self, an ideal self (which refers to the type of person they would like to be), and an ought self (which embodies the morals and standards that a person should strive to actualize). According to Higgins's theory, these self-guides organize people's knowledge about themselves, direct the processing of self-relevant information, and steer future behaviors.

These different components of the self suggest that self-knowledge can be multifaceted. For example, a person may have self-relevant information to suggest he or she is both introverted and extraverted, and each of these features can be brought into awareness at different times and in different contexts (Fazio, Effrein, & Falender, 1981). Nevertheless, a person can generally maintain a subjective sense of coherence and consistency in his or her sense of self. This is due to the fact that only a circumscribed aspect of the self, referred to as the "phenomenal self" (Jones & Gerard, 1967), is revealed or featured in conscious awareness at any given time.

In addition, self-knowledge is dynamic rather than fixed (e.g., Markus & Wurf, 1987), as evidenced by the fact that it can change, develop, and evolve over time. This may result in a discrepancy between how the self is experienced in the present and memories of the self in the past. To

maintain or restore coherence in spite of these shifts in self-views, Conway and colleagues have theorized and demonstrated that distortions of memory in the Self-Memory System (SMS) serve to increase the accessibility of memories and autobiographical knowledge consistent with how the self is conceived of in the present. By the same token, other biases in the processing of autobiographical memories serve to inhibit and make inaccessible past self-related knowledge that could contradict, threaten, or undermine the integrity and coherence of the self in the present (e.g., Conway & Pleydell-Pearce, 2000; Conway, Singer, & Tagini, 2004).

In addition to the changes that occur as a result of the natural evolution of the self over time, people can accentuate some features and subdue others depending on situational demands, build up self-aspects that are underdeveloped yet valued, and avoid experiences that will expose aspects of themselves that they strive to shed. In this process, people shape, and are shaped by, their inner and outer worlds, including their social relationships. In turn, self-knowledge changes in response to the intrapsychic and interpersonal processes that are brought to bear on it. Viewed in this way, the self is not merely a passive repository of knowledge and information waiting to be discovered. Rather, people mobilize cognitive resources and engineer their social world in the service of bringing to life specific self-conceptions in their mind or in the minds of others.

## Pathways to Self-Knowledge

In this section, we explore how people can gain self-knowledge by looking inward and observing the self, by inferring internal states from behaviors, and by looking to others for feedback. Despite the multiplicity of pathways for accessing knowledge of the self, we will also review findings exposing the limits of intrapsychic and interpersonal processes for accessing self-knowledge and that call into question people's capacity for gaining unobtrusive access to the contents and workings of their mind. Given these considerations, a true understanding of the self may only be possible by learning both about its content and the structure of the processes that organize, filter, and modify it.

### Self-Awareness and Introspection

The search for self-knowledge begins with self-awareness, which is the experience of focusing attention inward. Based on the theory of self-awareness (Duval & Wicklund, 1972), awareness of self invokes a comparison between features of the self against specific standards. Given the relevance of this comparison process for the regulation of behavior, self-awareness became integrated into a theory of self-regulation. According to this theory, self-awareness permits people to compare their actual state against internal standards, to detect the presence or absence of discrepancies between these states, and to regulate behaviors in a way to eliminate them (Carver & Scheier, 1981).

From this perspective, self-awareness is an important source of self-knowledge, as it makes salient features of the self such as personal standards, values, and goals as well as how much people are adhering to or deviating from these self-aspects. This is supported by research showing that people who are made more self-aware are more likely to be conscious of, and to act in accordance with, their attitudes, to be more accurate in their causal attributions for events (e.g., Gibbons, 1983, 1990), to be more self-consistent (Wicklund & Duval, 1971), to act in ways that uphold moral standards (e.g., reduced the tendency to cheat; Diener & Wallbom, 1976), and to display behaviors consistent with inner restraints (e.g., Heatherton, Polivy, Herman, & Baumeister, 1993).

Given that self-awareness permits access to the contents of one's mind, the capacity for introspection should also be facilitated by states of high self-awareness. According to the "perceptual accuracy hypothesis," self-focused attention should increase the accuracy of self-perceptions. Support for this hypothesis was obtained from research showing that self-focused attention allows people to access accurate knowledge about their attitudes, somatic states, emotions, and causal attributions (e.g., Gibbons, 1983, 1990). In addition, research has shown that self-focused attention contributes to greater attitude-behavior consistency (Pryor, Gibbons, Wicklund, Fazio, & Hood, 1977) among participants who were induced into a state of heightened self-awareness by sitting in front of a mirror. The self-awareness appears to have increased the accuracy of people's responses to the attitude questionnaire, which improved the capacity of those responses to predict subsequent behavior.

The assumption that self-focused attention is associated with accurate self-knowledge has been challenged, however, by empirical reports of biases in self-perceptions (e.g., Epley & Dunning, 2006; Pronin & Kugler, 2007; Wilson & Gilbert, 2003), further fueling the debate about the merits of introspection and self-perception for gaining accurate self-knowledge (for a review of empirical evidence

challenging the perceptual accuracy hypothesis, see Silvia & Gendolla, 2001). Presumably, an accurate knowledge of one's values and dispositions should help people predict with some degree of accuracy how they would behave or feel in a situation or to explain why they behaved the way they did. Yet research on behavioral and affective forecasting suggests that people are often incorrect in predicting their future behaviors (Epley & Dunning, 2000), and that they over- and underestimate the amount and intensity of pleasure or displeasure they will experience in reaction to positive and negative events (Wilson & Gilbert, 2005). In addition, people's explanations for their behaviors are often inaccurate (Nisbett & Wilson, 1977) and they are often not aware of (or willing to admit to) their biases in self-perceptions (Epley & Dunning, 2006; Pronin & Kugler, 2007).

The debate surrounding the relationship between introspection and self-insight exposes the complexity of this issue and provides fertile ground for investigating moderators of this relationship. Indeed, this approach proved fruitful in the past, when research revealed that the capacity to derive self-knowledge via introspection was contingent upon the nature of self-knowledge, as well as the type and amount of self-reflection. Specifically, self-reflection was more likely to yield useful insights when it involved salient and unambiguous aspects of self-knowledge, and when people engaged in a moderate amount of self-reflection. Beyond a certain point, people became susceptible to contemplating extraneous and irrelevant information, which yielded misleading insights (Hixon & Swann, 1993).

Recent work suggests that it is when people begin to reflect on the *reasons* for why they are the way they are and why they feel the way they feel that introspection leads them astray (e.g., Wilson & Dunn, 2004). This is evidenced by findings showing that analyzing reasons was associated with lower correlations between self-reported feelings and behaviors (Wilson & Dunn, 1986) and a reduced ability to predict personal future behaviors (Wilson & LaFleur, 1995). Thus, people may be better able to report accurately on their thoughts and emotions than on the reasons underlying these thoughts and emotions.

### Self-Perception

Given the limits of introspection, people would benefit from having an alternative pathway toward gaining self-knowledge that minimizes one's reliance on introspective processes. According to self-perception theory (Bem, 1972), one of the simplest ways of acquiring self-knowledge is by making inferences about conscious or nonconscious opinions, motivations, and beliefs based on observed behaviors. This process is itself replete with ambiguities, however, as it involves a creative and reconstructive process by which people infer states by amalgamating different pieces of self-knowledge and filling in the gaps. For example, one study found that people misattributed the physiological arousal induced by the anxiety experienced while crossing a rickety bridge (or perhaps the relief felt after arriving on solid ground) to the physical attraction felt toward a stranger they encountered after crossing the bridge (Dutton & Aron, 1974). In addition, people tend to place greater weight on internal states and introspective information than on behavioral evidence when making inferences about themselves, and this could further limit their potential to derive self-knowledge through this pathway (Pronin & Kugler, 2007). Thus, despite the allure of being able to infer internal states from overt behaviors, self-perception theory does not appear to capture the complexity of the relationship between people's behaviors and inferences about personal attitudes (e.g., Kelly & Rodriguez, 2006).

## The Social Basis of Self-Knowledge

Thus far, we have reviewed findings to suggest that the quality and accuracy of self-relevant information derived from self-perception and introspection can at times be limited, imprecise, and potentially misleading. Therefore, people may be able to sidestep some of the limits of these processes and improve self-knowledge via an alternative pathway that involves interpersonal processes. Put simply, people can look to others for feedback about the self.

There is a growing body of literature to suggest that ratings made by the self and others diverge and that these can differentially predict a person's behavior. In fact, an individual's self-view is at times a less accurate predictor of behavior than peers' views of the target (e.g., Spain, Eaton, & Funder, 2000). For example, discrepancies have been reported between informant and patient reports of depressive symptoms (e.g., McAvay, Raue, Brown, & Bruce, 2005). Furthermore, a spouse's confidence in a patient's ability to manage his or her illness predicted patient survival following heart failure, after the patient's self-reported self-efficacy was taken into account (Rohrbaugh et al., 2004). A recent study further debunked the notion that a person is the best expert

when it comes to predicting daily behaviors with accuracy. Instead, both self- and other-perspectives contributed independently to the prediction of a person's behavior. More surprisingly perhaps, in some domains, others were more accurate in predicting a person's daily behaviors (Vazire & Mehl, 2008).

These findings suggest that others are privy to unique and complementary insights and viewpoints regarding a person's traits and behavioral patterns, and they can offer a perspective that affords incremental value in the prediction of a person's behavior. Of course, this route toward self-knowledge is plagued with its own set of challenges, as it is often difficult to decode others' perceptions of ourselves. In addition, others are not always candid in the feedback they disclose (Jones & Wortman, 1973). The difficulties associated with using feedback from others to gain self-knowledge are further compounded by self-deceptive processes that are activated to manipulate social feedback in a way to align it with previously held or preferred self-views.

To summarize, people use various pathways to derive self-knowledge. They acquire self-knowledge through introspection and by inferring internal states from behaviors. When internal processes fail to produce a complete or accurate self-portrayal, others can provide a unique and complementary source of valid information about the self. The limitations associated with each pathway expose the limits of self-knowledge, leaving open the possibility that cognitive and motivational factors may play an important role in restricting access to self-knowledge that is impartial and objective. Against this backdrop, in the next section, we consider how self-knowledge can be shaped via intrapsychic processes that rely on personally based sources of information.

## Shaping Self-Knowledge via Intrapsychic Processes
### Self-Motives as Guides to Self-Knowledge

Are people motivated to gain self-knowledge that is accurate, that fits preexisting self-views, or that paints them in a favorable light? Research suggests that the self has multiple motives that can conflict at times (e.g., Sedikides & Strube, 1995). First, people can be motivated by *self-assessment*, suggesting that they process information in ways that are conducive to an accurate assessment of their skills and competencies, whether favorable or unfavorable. Second, people can be motivated by *self-enhancement*, thereby seeking self-knowledge in biased ways designed to boost the ego. Third, people can be motivated by *self-verification*, which can lead them to strategically process feedback in a way that will confirm and reinforce preexisting self-views, regardless of whether favorable.

Research suggests that each of these motives can serve as important guides for cognitive and behavioral processes that shape self-knowledge over time. Several theories, including social comparison theory (Festinger, 1954) and self-assessment theory (Trope, 1979), have suggested that people seek and gain accurate self-knowledge. Specifically, self-assessment has been shown to trump self-enhancement on tasks that are high in diagnosticity (e.g., Trope, 1980) and when attributes are unambiguous, modifiable, and important (e.g., Brown & Gallagher, 1992; Dunning, 1995). The view that people search for accurate self-knowledge has been challenged, however, by findings documenting a lack of correspondence between self-views and objective criteria (e.g., self-reported intelligence and IQ scores; Borkenau & Liebler, 1993). Notwithstanding these claims, the self-assessment motive should not be underestimated given that an accurate assessment of one's strengths and weaknesses is necessary so that people may capitalize on their domains of ability to compensate for their areas of relative deficiency and thereby maintain adaptive levels of functioning.

According to "self-immunization theory," people can maintain a balance between their needs for self-enhancement and accurate self-assessment by adjusting perceptions of the diagnosticity of their skills with respect to traits that are centrally tied to their self-concept. For example, people can rate skills at which they excel as being highly diagnostic of their self-defining traits while minimizing the diagnosticity of skills on which they underperform. Processing personal weaknesses in this way can allow people to maintain some degree of accuracy in their self-perceptions as well as effective levels of functioning that can otherwise be undermined by denying one's shortcomings (Greve & Wentura, 2003).

From a different perspective, self-verification theory (e.g., Swann, 1983) posits that people search for a particular type of self-knowledge that allows them to maintain stability and coherence in their self-views. Toward this end, people selectively attend to, encode, and remember information in the world that confirms their self-views while turning a blind eye to inconsistent feedback. In addition, people interpret information strategically, for example, by discrediting a source that reflects inconsistent feedback (Swann & Read, 1981). Even when people espouse negative self-views, they prefer feedback that confirms rather than discredits these views (e.g., Swann & Pelham, 2002). Together, these processes represent the self's most powerful allies in the quest to ward off threats to the integrity of the self-concept.

Notwithstanding people's preference for feedback that matches their self-perceptions, people also want to see themselves in a positive light and to feel good about themselves, and they are remarkably successful in this respect. In fact, most people espouse self-views that are more than favorable: They are at times self-enhancing to the point of misrepresenting the reality of self-views. This is supported by research showing that people think they are better than the average person on a broad assortment of dimensions (better-than-average effect; Alicke & Govorun, 2005) and exaggerate appraisals of how much control they have over events (positive illusions; e.g., Taylor & Brown, 1988).

Other tactics reflecting flagrant and subtle attempts at boosting the positivity of the self-image abound. For example, people evaluate positively various things associated with the self, including groups to which they belong (Gramzow & Gaertner, 2005) and the letters of the alphabet that correspond to their initials (e.g., Hodson & Olson, 2005). In addition, people eagerly accept positive self-relevant information, but they scrutinize negative information (e.g., Kunda, 1990). Moreover, people judge skills that are within the realm of their competencies as more diagnostic of traits that are central to their self-concept than skills at which they are less proficient (Wentura & Greve, 2005).

Research suggests that the choices people make in their daily lives can represent another method for bolstering self-views that are temporarily shaken. A recent study found that experimentally undermining confidence in one's intelligence increased people's tendency to choose consumer products related to intelligence (Gao, Wheeler, & Shiv, 2009). This suggests that people are motivated to maintain confidence in important self-views and that they make choices strategically as a way to affirm and reassert desired self-views when these are undermined.

The self-serving attribution bias (Brown & Rogers, 1991) is yet another example of a self-protective process that can aid in maintaining favorable self-views. Indeed, people display a well-documented tendency to attribute successes to factors internal to the self (e.g., effort and ability) and failures to external factors (e.g., difficulty and luck). While the self-serving bias has been observed consistently when making success attributions, the evidence on failure attributions has been mixed. Research found that when self-focus was high, performance success was invariably attributed internally, regardless of whether a person could subsequently improve performance. In contrast, high self-focus was associated with internal attributions for failure in the presence of future opportunities to improve and external attributions for failure in the absence of opportunities to improve subsequently (Duval & Silvia, 2002). This suggests that people are only willing to accept blame, albeit temporarily, for a failure that they can undo, but not when the failure risks leaving an indelible mark on the self-concept.

In addition, the self-serving bias appears to become magnified under conditions of self-threat (Campbell & Sedikides, 1999), suggesting that when favorable self-views are threatened by information that is unbecoming to the self, individuals bring out their arsenal of psychological tools to defuse that threat. While these are only some examples of the ways in which self-motives can shape and influence beliefs about the self, it becomes apparent that people process and interpret information about the self strategically, thereby bolstering the view that the process of acquiring self-knowledge is both dynamic and creative.

## Self-Esteem as a Source of, and Guide to, Self-Knowledge

While self-motives guide information processing in the service of acquiring self-knowledge, the self then makes an evaluation of self-worth based on the accumulated self-knowledge, and this gives rise to the subjective experience of self-esteem, which includes both affective (e.g., shame/pride) and cognitive (e.g., "I am competent/incompetent") components. Self-esteem can further bias and shape personal and interpersonal processes in a way that can maintain and reinforce the positive or negative cognitive and affective aspects associated with self-knowledge.

A number of differences have been reported between people with high and low self-esteem on dimensions of self-knowledge. For example, in contrast to people with low self-esteem, those with high self-esteem are more likely to report beliefs about the self that are clear, confidently held, stable, and consistent (e.g., Campbell, 1990). Research also shows that self-esteem is important in further shaping self-knowledge as it influences how people work on and modify self-relevant information in a way

that strengthens and reinforces their self-knowledge over time. In this respect, being confident in one's sense of self has been shown to buffer against threats to self-esteem among high self-esteem people as they are better able to rely on self-serving biases than people with low self-esteem (e.g., Dodgson & Wood, 1998; Suls, Lemos, & Lockett Stewart, 2002).

People with high as opposed to low self-esteem have also been shown to be more oriented toward self-enhancement as opposed to self-protection (Baumeister, Tice, & Hutton, 1989). As a result, they responded to ego threats in a way that would boost and reaffirm positive self-views (e.g., Vohs & Heatherton, 2001, 2004). Together, these findings suggest that the cognitive and affective correlates of high and low self-esteem can become perpetuated by biasing attention to information that confirms the valence of people's self-views and ensuring that people seek self-knowledge in a self-verifying manner.

The importance of social relationships for self-esteem has led researchers to propose the sociometer theory. Specifically, it states that rather than reflecting a personal evaluation based on self-worth, self-esteem signals one's value as a relational partner and represents an internal gauge of interpersonal acceptance and rejection (Leary, 2005; Leary & Baumeister, 2000). Various studies have shown that self-esteem is maintained at a normal to high level to the extent that people appraise their relationships with others as valuable, but it drops when one's value as a relational partner is in doubt or threatened by rejection or exclusion in laboratory and real-world settings (e.g., Leary, Springer, Negel, Ansell, & Evans, 1998; Leary, Tambor, Terdal, & Downs, 1995; Sommer, Williams, Ciarocco, & Baumeister, 2001). A recent meta-analysis confirmed that social acceptance causes self-esteem to rise, but interpersonal rejection did not reliably produce drops in self-esteem, possibly because people have defensive processes that shield their self-appraisals against any sort of threat or loss (Blackhart, Knowles, Nelson, & Baumeister, 2009). From this perspective, self-esteem provides people with information about their value as a relational partner and thus serves as an internal indicator of how well a person is satisfying his or her fundamental need to belong (Baumeister & Leary, 1995).

Confirming the significance of relational information for self-esteem, research has documented differential patterns of information processing in the context of relationships among people with high and low self-esteem. For example, it was found that on traits that were relevant in the context of relationships, high self-esteem people self-enhanced by thinking that their partners viewed them more positively than they viewed themselves. In contrast, people with low self-esteem reported that their partners evaluated them more negatively than they appraised themselves (Sciangula & Morry, 2009). In comparison to people with high self-esteem, those with low self-esteem have also been shown to be less confident in their partner's love and feelings of positive regard for them (Murray, Holmes, & Griffin, 2000), and they anticipated less acceptance from new interaction partners (Anthony, Wood, & Holmes, 2007).

As a result of these differences in the processing of social information, people with high self-esteem have been shown to adopt a relationship-promoting interpersonal style, while people with low self-esteem adopt a self-protective style aimed at minimizing the possibility for rejection. These differential patterns of information processing and interpersonal interaction of people with high and low self-esteem can result in a self-fulfilling prophecy, and thereby perpetuate preexisting beliefs and feelings of self-worth via self-verification (Swann, Chang-Schneider, & McClarty, 2007). This ensures that the cognitive (i.e., self-knowledge) and affective (i.e., evaluation of self-worth based on self-knowledge) aspects of self-esteem endure.

## Shaping Self-Knowledge via Interpersonal Processes

To sidestep some of the limits of intrapsychic processes for gaining self-knowledge, we suggested that people can look to others for feedback about the self. Indeed, the self is embedded in a social context, it is a social construction, and can therefore reveal itself through social and interpersonal processes. In this respect, others can directly offer feedback that may increase self-knowledge. Alternatively, people may solicit feedback from others that may be accurate, self-enhancing, or self-verifying. In less direct ways, people can utilize socially based sources of information to strategically shape self-knowledge. The ambiguity inherent in social information and processes affords the flexibility necessary to artfully shape self-knowledge in line with underlying motivations and goals.

### Reflected Appraisals

Others figure prominently in people's inner and private worlds. For example, people develop meta-perceptions in the form of reflected appraisals that represent theories about how they are perceived by others. These reflected appraisals represent an important source of self-knowledge as well as a means of shaping self-knowledge over time.

For example, research has found that others' perceptions of people can shape self-knowledge via their influence on people's reflected appraisals and their actual behavior. For example, parent and teacher perceptions of students' competence in the academic domain predicted students' self-perceived competence and actual performance (e.g., Eccles, 1993). More recently, research found that students' reflected appraisals of adults' beliefs about their academic competence predicted self-perceptions of students' own competence, and this in turn predicted actual academic performance (Bouchey & Harter, 2005). Consistent with these findings, a longitudinal investigation also found that parents' appraisals of children's physical competence (in sports) at time 1 predicted the children's reflected appraisals of parents' beliefs about their competence at time 2, and children's beliefs concerning how they were perceived by their parents at time 2 influenced their self-appraisals at time 3. Crucially, reflected appraisals mediated the relationship between parents' appraisals of their children's physical competence and the children's self-perceptions of their own competence over time (Bois, Sarrazin, Brustad, Chanal, & Trouilloud, 2005).

This work suggests that a person's self-knowledge is assembled from others' perceptions of him or her as well as his or her own reflected appraisals. People form reflected appraisals by seeing themselves through the eyes of others and they further internalize these perceptions in a way that can shape personally held beliefs and influence their self-concept. This can in turn influence behaviors in a way that can actualize or confirm self-views.

### Self-Presentation

The imaginary or actual presence of others can have an important influence on the type of self-knowledge that people expose and portray in front of others. Concerns over self-presentation are pervasive (Baumeister, 1982), as evidenced by the fact that people strategically accentuate, subdue, or dissimulate desirable and undesirable self-aspects in various contexts and with various goals or intentions (e.g., Tyler & Feldman, 2005). Regardless of the specific motive underlying self-presentation, it has been suggested that people engage in self-presentation with the goal of constructing a self-identity that can be validated in the context of social relationships. Crucially, by influencing others' perceptions of us as well as our own beliefs about how we are viewed by others, self-presentations can influence self-knowledge in a way that can produce a lasting change in the self-concept.

The notion that self-presentations can shape self-knowledge and influence the structure of the self-concept over time has received empirical support. For example, Tice (1992) demonstrated that participants who were induced to present themselves in a specific way were more likely to endorse self-beliefs and engage in behaviors that were consistent with those self-presentations, particularly when these self-presentations were made publicly but not anonymously. Consistent with these results, another study showed that participants who portrayed themselves as extraverted/introverted during a videotaped presentation that was later to be viewed by an audience (but not if it was private) rated themselves as more/less sociable. In addition, their subsequent behaviors matched the self-concept that was featured in their self-presentations (Kelly & Rodriguez, 2006). These findings suggest that people internalize self-aspects that they feature in their self-presentations in a way that can alter their self-concept.

While people can shape self-knowledge through self-presentation, the presence of others can also set important constraints on people's attempts to present themselves in contrived or disingenuous ways. For example, research has shown that people manipulate their self-presentations in a way to enhance the positivity of their public self-views, so long as this embellishment is not likely to be discerned and disputed by others. Specifically, participants represented their level of ability to others in a way that matched their level of performance if their actual level of performance was disclosed to the audience. In contrast, participants presented themselves more favorably regardless of their actual performance if their true performance remained confidential (Baumeister & Jones, 1978). Paralleling these findings, a recent study found that participants who were induced to feel transparent presented themselves as having higher social intelligence in a group context when they were expected to perform well in front of others on a test of social intelligence, but they presented themselves as having lower social intelligence in a group context when they were expected to perform poorly. In contrast, participants induced to feel impenetrable presented themselves as having higher social intelligence regardless of how they were expected to perform on the test (Schlenker & Wowra, 2003).

Thus, it appears that people rely on strategic self-presentations to enhance the self or to communicate specific self-aspects that are valued in different social contexts. In doing so, the self-aspects featured in people's self-presentations can be socially validated, strengthened through feedback and reinforcement received from others (e.g., Schlenker, 1980, 1986), and ultimately incorporated within the self-concept purposefully or inadvertently. Self-presentation may also influence self-knowledge by way of shaping reflected appraisals such that people will think others view them in a way that is consistent with their self-presentation. From yet another perspective related to cognitive dissonance theory, self-presentation may affect change in self-concept as people attempt to increase consistency between self-views and the behaviors featured in their self-presentations.

In these varied ways, the self-concept can be strongly influenced by people's self-presentations in a social context, further buttressing the view that self-knowledge is a social construction in need of social validation. In the process of validating their self-views, people are nevertheless careful to assess the personal and interpersonal tradeoffs between presenting a self-enhancing image and appearing disingenuous, and adjust their self-presentations accordingly. Thus, the presence of others also appears to place constraints on the degree to which people can misrepresent aspects of their self-knowledge.

### Social Comparisons

Social comparisons represent another psychological process that relies on socially based sources of information and that is fundamental in the quest for self-knowledge. The ubiquitous nature of social comparisons is important in this respect, as the mere exposure to others invites voluntary or involuntary comparisons on a vast range of dimensions. In addition to their information value, social comparisons are made for the purpose of, and are an important basis for, self-evaluations based on accumulated self-knowledge. In this respect, the standards on which such self-evaluations rest are derived in relation to how others fare on similar dimensions. Finally, people can manufacture and strategically manipulate social comparison processes in a way to shape self-knowledge. In brief, social comparisons serve the dual function of supporting the acquisition of self-knowledge while also allowing people to actively shape knowledge of the self.

According to social comparison theory (Festinger, 1954), people engage in a quest to discover the truth about themselves through comparisons with others, in domains of both ability and opinions (Suls, Martin, & Wheeler, 2002). For example, people compare themselves with similar others to predict the likelihood of succeeding at a task (Martin, Suls, & Wheeler, 2002). Such comparisons can be made objectively through an unbiased assessment of where one stands in relation to others. For example, people can learn that they are skilled or competent through exposure to others who are perceptibly worse on the corresponding dimension (downward social comparison). Alternatively, the presence of others who are highly skilled in a given domain can expose a person's personal weaknesses (upward social comparison).

Inevitably, however, self-motives are woven into the fabric of social comparison processes in a way that allows people to strategically manipulate the comparison direction and target in order to achieve desired self-perceptions and self-evaluations and to influence the emotional outcome of the comparison process. For example, people facing different kinds of threat that can undermine positive self-perceptions, such as victimized and stigmatized populations and people suffering from various medical conditions, have been shown to display preferences for interacting with others who are worse off and making downward social comparisons (e.g., Buunk & Ybema, 1995; Tennen, McKee, & Affleck, 2000). Making downward social comparisons has further been shown to be associated with an improvement in well-being, which supports their self-enhancing function (Wills, 1981). When such comparison targets cannot be brought to mind or found in one's social network, people can go so far as to actively fabricate or imagine a worse-off target (Taylor, Wood, & Lichtman, 1983).

Despite the self-enhancing nature of downward social comparisons, research suggests that people also intentionally compare themselves with superior others. Because people generally hold positive self-views, they perceive similarities with upward targets and can therefore reinforce the positivity of their self-views by considering themselves among the "elite." In cases when such upward social comparisons are experienced as threatening, however, people can strategically reappraise this information in a way that can ward off the threat of such comparisons. For example, people can label someone who outperformed them as a "genius," a strategy that could explain their lower performance while

maintaining favorable perceptions of their ability (Alicke, LoSchiavo, Zerbst, & Zhang, 1997).

The previous discussion intimates that whether upward and downward social comparisons are experienced as threatening, inspiring, self-enhancing, or self-deflating may depend on a host of moderating variables, one being whether a person engages in assimilation or contrast with the comparison target. Downward social comparisons can be self-enhancing if a person does not foresee the risk of deteriorating to the level of the downward target (contrast) or self-deflating if a person feels vulnerable to experiencing a similar fate (assimilation) (Wheeler & Miyake, 1992). By the same logic, upward social comparisons can be inspiring if a person is confident in his or her capacity to fulfill a high potential (e.g., Lockwood & Kunda, 1997) or threatening if he or she perceives the attainment of higher standards to be out of his or her reach. Given these considerations, a person may strategically increase contrast by emphasizing differences between himself or herself and a downward target, or he or she can increase assimilation by highlighting similarities with an upward target. In this light, social comparison processes can shape self-knowledge to reflect each individual's unique goals and motivations.

Yet another way that people can voluntarily manipulate self-knowledge through social comparison processes is by reappraising the importance of the comparison domains and the closeness with the comparison target. According to the self-evaluation maintenance model (Tesser, 1988), people will experience a greater threat if they are outperformed (upward social comparison) in a domain that is highly central as opposed to peripheral to their self-concept, and when the comparison target involves a close rather than a distant other. To avoid such threats, it was found that people who confronted unfavorable comparisons in domains of high self-relevance subsequently decreased the perceived self-relevance of the task (Tesser & Paulhus, 1983).

In addition, when participants faced an unfavorable comparison in a domain of high self-relevance, they created distance with the comparison target (Pleban & Tesser, 1981). In a similar vein, in order to avoid being outperformed by close others in domains of high ego involvement, people have been shown to select as friends people who are less skilled in domains of high personal importance and more skilled in domains lower in importance (Tesser, Campbell, & Smith, 1984). These findings suggest that people can engineer their social environment by keeping close those who permit self-enhancing comparisons while keeping at a distance those who pose a threat to a person's self-evaluations. In this way, people shape self-knowledge to reinforce desired self-views.

## Self-Motives and the Social World

While comparisons with others can be manufactured in ways that enhance the positivity of self-views, the self-enhancement motive can permeate relationship dynamics in other ways. For example, people can strategically select interaction partners who directly reinforce desired self-views. This was supported in a study in which participants expressed a preference for interacting with a person who described them as extraverted if they thought that extraversion was associated with success in life and with a person who described them as introverted when introversion had been paired with later success. These findings therefore suggest that people can shape their social world to receive personal feedback that is consistent with, and that can reinforce, desired self-views (Sanitioso & Wlodarski, 2004).

There is an extensive line of empirical research showing that people also seek self-verification in their social relationships, by behaving in ways to elicit self-verifying social feedback and by engineering their social world to reinforce preexisting self-views. For example, people selectively choose to interact with partners who confirm their self-views. In addition, people have been shown to step up efforts to display behaviors that are highly diagnostic of self-views so as to elicit self-confirmatory social feedback. Research has also shown that people prefer interaction partners who see them as they see themselves: Participants with positive self-views preferred to interact with a partner who espoused a favorable view of them, whereas participants with negative self-views preferred partners who held unfavorable impressions of them (see Swann, Rentfrow, & Guinn, 2003, for a review of these studies).

In addition to seeking social partners that provide self-verifying feedback, the quality of people's social relationships can be affected by the type of feedback they receive from partners. It was found that marriages in which a spouse's self-view did not match with how the partner perceived him or her were characterized by less intimacy (e.g., Burke & Stets, 1999). Another study found that people who thought their own self-evaluations matched their partner's evaluations of them were more intimate and committed in the relationship (Katz & Joiner, 2002), regardless of whether these self-views were positive or negative. This supports the idea that the self-verification motive pervades relationship dynamics and directly impacts the quality of the interpersonal bond. Relationships that are more satisfying are more likely to endure, further ensuring that people will continue to receive feedback that corresponds to their self-views.

Research suggests that people may be particularly inclined to verify self-views in intimate relationships. Indeed, significant others may be an especially valued source of self-knowledge as they witness people's behaviors across contexts and are privy to the contents of people's mind as a result of frequent and intimate self-disclosures. Thus, people may be particularly inclined to perceive the feedback received from intimate partners as valid. Given these considerations, people may therefore be especially selective when choosing intimate partners so that they can surround themselves with people who confirm rather than undermine their self-views on a daily basis.

The importance of self-verifying feedback in close relationships is supported by research showing people are more likely to seek self-verifying feedback in relationships with significant others and spouses, as well as in long-term relationships (e.g., Campbell, Lackenbauer, & Muise, 2006). In addition, a recent study found that participants who were primed with significant-other representations were more likely to seek feedback that would verify rather than enhance relational self-views that were rated high in importance. In contrast, participants primed with acquaintance representations preferred self-enhancing feedback (Kraus & Chen, 2009). Together, these findings suggest that conscious and automatic processes can jointly conspire toward promoting and reinforcing preexisting self-views in relationship contexts. This pattern of findings attests to the pervasive influence of the social context on self-verification goals.

In this section, we showed that others represent a rich repository of knowledge about the self. Others can provide direct feedback, serve as standards for social comparisons, embody expectations for people's behaviors, and supply the basis of reflected appraisals. In addition, self-knowledge can be shaped via self-presentation in the context of interpersonal interactions. In these varied ways, others may serve as a metaphorical mirror in which self-knowledge is reflected back to the individual.

## Conclusion

In this chapter, we discussed several pathways toward self-knowledge, none of which are foolproof, and each of which had its own set of limitations. While people can acquire self-knowledge by looking inward, inferring internal states from behaviors, and turning to others for feedback, the insights afforded by each of these pathways separately may be incomplete and misleading. This is compounded by the fact that self-knowledge is strategically assembled, accumulated, and shaped by means of intrapsychic and interpersonal processes that reflect the full range of self-motives. This underscores the importance of seeking self-knowledge via different routes, as each may offer different pieces of the puzzle that can be assembled into an accurate self-portrait.

In the quest to know themselves, people take liberties to shape self-knowledge in desired ways. The ego's defenses can hardly be removed to access a pure and unadulterated knowledge base for knowing the self's true nature. This leaves open the possibility that people are not the most sophisticated experts when it comes to telling about themselves. People do, however, conspire in the construction of self-views that suit them, fulfill their needs, and satisfy their underlying motivations. In this light, it remains unclear whether each person can ever unravel the mystery of his or her own self, nor whether this would be entirely beneficial.

## Note

1. We acknowledge that while these pathways and processes may be influenced by, or may differ across, cultural contexts, space limitations preclude a comprehensive discussion of such differences. We therefore reserve our discussion to general processes that operate in the service of acquiring and shaping self-knowledge.

## References

Alicke, M. D., & Govorun, O. (2005). The better-than-average effect. In M. D. Alicke, D. A. Dunning, & J. I. Krueger (Eds.), *Studies in self and identity* (pp. 85–106). New York: Psychology Press.

Alicke, M. D., LoSchiavo, F. M., Zerbst, J., & Zhang, S. (1997). The person who outperforms me is a genius: Maintaining perceived competence in upward social comparison. *Journal of Personality and Social Psychology, 73*, 781–789.

Anthony, D. B., Wood, J. V., & Holmes, J. G. (2007). Testing sociometer theory: Self-esteem and the importance of acceptance for social decision-making. *Journal of Experimental Social Psychology, 43*, 425–432.

Baumeister, R. F. (1982). A self-presentational view of social phenomena. *Psychological Bulletin, 91*, 3–26.

Baumeister, R. F., & Jones, E. E. (1978). When self-presentation is constrained by the target's knowledge: Consistency and compensation. *Journal of Personality and Social Psychology, 36*, 608–618.

Baumeister, R. F., & Leary, M. R. (1995). The need to belong: Desire for interpersonal attachments as a fundamental human motivation. *Psychological Bulletin, 117*, 497–529.

Baumeister, R. F., Tice, D. M., & Hutton, D. G. (1989). Self-presentational motivations and personality differences in self-esteem. *Journal of Personality, 57*, 547–579.

Bem, D. J. (1972). Self-perception theory. In L. Berkowitz (Ed.), *Advances in experimental social psychology* (Vol. 6, pp. 1–62). New York: Academic Press.

Blackhart, G. C., Knowles, M. L., Nelson, B. C., & Baumeister, R. F. (2009). Rejection elicits emotional reactions but neither causes immediate distress nor lowers self-esteem: A meta-analytic review of 192 studies on social exclusion. *Personality and Social Psychology Review, 13(4)*, 269–309.

Bois, J. E., Sarrazin, P. G., Brustad, R. J., Chanal, J. P., & Trouilloud, D. O. (2005). Parents' appraisals, reflected appraisals, and children's self-appraisals of sport competence: A yearlong study. *Journal of Applied Sport psychology, 17*, 273–289.

Borkenau, P., & Liebler, A. (1993). Convergence of stranger ratings of personality and intelligence with self-ratings, partner ratings, and measured intelligence. *Journal of Personality and Social Psychology, 65*, 546–553.

Bouchey, H. A., & Harter, S. (2005). Reflected appraisals, academic self-perceptions, and math/science performance during early adolescence. *Journal of Educational Psychology, 97*, 673–686.

Brown, J. D., & Gallagher, F. M. (1992). Coming to terms with failure: Private self-enhancement and public self-effacement. *Journal of Experimental Social Psychology, 28*, 3–22.

Brown, J. D., & Rogers, R. J. (1991). Self-serving attributions: The role of physiological arousal. *Personality and Social Psychology Bulletin, 17*, 501–506.

Burke, P. J., & Stets, J. E. (1999). Trust and commitment through self-verification. *Social Psychology Quarterly, 62*, 347–366.

Buunk, B. P., & Ybema, J. F. (1995). Selective evaluation and coping with stress: Making one's situation cognitively more livable. *Journal of Applied Social Psychology, 25*, 1499–1517.

Campbell, J. D. (1990). Self-esteem and clarity of the self-concept. *Journal of Personality and Social Psychology, 59*, 538–549.

Campbell, L., Lackenbauer, S. D., & Muise, A. (2006). When is being known or adored by romantic partners most beneficial? Self-perceptions, relationship length, and responses to partner's verifying and enhancing appraisals. *Personality and Social Psychology Bulletin, 32*, 1283–1294.

Campbell, W. K., & Sedikides, C. (1999). Self-threat magnifies the self-serving bias: A meta-analytic integration. *Review of General Psychology, 3*, 23–43.

Carver, C. S., & Scheier, M. F. (1981). *Attention and self-regulation: A control theory approach to human behavior.* New York: Springer-Verlag.

Conway, M. A., & Pleydell-Pearce, C. W. (2000). The construction of autobiographical memories in the self-memory system. *Psychological Review, 107*, 261–288.

Conway, M. A., Singer, J. A., & Tagini, A. (2004). The self and autobiographical memory: Correspondence and coherence. *Social Cognition, 22*, 491–529.

Diener, E., & Wallbom, M. (1976). Effects of self-awareness on anti-normative behavior. *Journal of Research in Personality, 10*, 107–111.

Dodgson, P. G., & Wood, J. V. (1998). Self-esteem and the cognitive accessibility of strengths and weaknesses after failure. *Journal of Personality and Social Psychology, 75*, 178–197.

Dunning, D. (1995). Trait importance and modifiability as factors influencing self-assessment and self-enhancement motives. *Personality and Social Psychology Bulletin, 21,* 1297–1306.

Dutton, D. G., & Aron, A. P. (1974). Some evidence for heightened sexual attraction under conditions of high anxiety. *Journal of Personality and Social Psychology, 30,* 510–517.

Duval, T. S., & Silvia, P. J. (2002). Self-awareness, probability of improvement, and the self-serving bias. *Journal of Personality and Social Psychology, 82,* 49–61.

Duval, S., & Wicklund, R. A. (1972). *A theory of objective self-awareness.* New York: Academic Press.

Eccles, J. S. (1993). School and family effects on the ontogeny of children's interests, self-perceptions, and activity choice. In J. Jacobs (Ed.), *Nebraska Symposium on Motivation, Vol. 40. Developmental perspectives on motivation* (pp. 145–208). Lincoln: University of Nebraska Press.

Epley, N., & Dunning, D. (2000). Feeling "Holier than Thou": Are self-serving assessments produced by errors in self- or social- prediction? *Journal of Personality and Social Psychology, 79,* 861–875.

Epley, N., & Dunning, D. (2006). The mixed blessings of self-knowledge in behavioral prediction: Enhanced discrimination but exacerbated bias. *Personality and Social Psychology Bulletin, 32,* 641–655.

Fazio, R. H., Effrein, E. A., & Falender, V. J. (1981). Self-perceptions following social interactions. *Journal of Personality and Social Psychology, 41,* 232–242.

Festinger, L. (1954). A theory of social comparison processes. *Human Relations, 7,* 117–140.

Gao, L., Wheeler, S. C., & Shiv, B. (2009). The "shaken self": Product choices as a means of restoring self-view confidence. *Journal of Consumer Research, 36,* 29–38.

Gibbons, F. X. (1983). Self-attention and self-report: The "veridicality" hypothesis. *Journal of Personality, 51,* 517–542.

Gibbons, F. X. (1990). Self-attention and behavior: A review and theoretical update. *Advances in Experimental Social Psychology, 23,* 249–303.

Gramzow, R. H., & Gaertner, L. (2005). Self-esteem and favoritism toward novel in-groups: The self as an evaluative base. *Journal of Personality and Social Psychology, 88,* 801–815.

Greve, W., & Wentura, D. (2003). Immunizing the self: Self-concept stabilization through reality-adaptive self-definitions. *Personality and Social Psychology Bulletin, 29,* 39–50.

Heatherton, T. F., Polivy, J., Herman, C. P., & Baumeister, R. F. (1993). Self-awareness, task failure, and disinhibition: How attentional focus affects eating. *Journal of Personality, 61,* 49–61.

Higgins, E. T. (1987). Self-discrepancy: A theory relating self and affect. *Psychological Review, 94,* 319–340.

Hixon, J. G., & Swann, W. B. (1993). When does introspection bear fruit? Self-reflection, self-insight, and interpersonal choices. *Journal of Personality and Social Psychology, 64,* 35–43.

Hodson, G., & Olson, J. M. (2005). Testing the generality of the name letter effect: Name initials and everyday attitudes. *Personality and Social Psychology Bulletin, 31,* 1099–1111.

Jones, E. E., & Gerard, H. B. (1967). *Foundations of social psychology.* New York: Wiley.

Jones, E. E., & Wortman, C. (1973). *Ingratiation: An attributional approach.* Morristown, NJ: General Learning Press.

Katz, J., & Joiner, T. E. (2002). Being known, intimate, and valued: Global self-verification and dyadic adjustment in couples and roommates. *Journal of Personality, 70,* 33–54.

Kelly, A. E., & Rodriguez, R. R. (2006). Publicly committing oneself to an identity. *Basic and Applied Social Psychology, 28,* 185–191.

Kunda, Z. (1990). The case for motivated reasoning. *Psychological Bulletin, 108,* 480–498.

Kraus, M. W., & Chen, S. (2009). Striving to be known by significant others: Automatic activation of self-verification goals in relationship contexts. *Journal of Personality and Social Psychology, 97,* 58–73.

Leary, M. R. (2005). Sociometer theory and the pursuit of relational value: Getting to the root of self-esteem. *European Review of Social Psychology, 16,* 75–111.

Leary, M. R., & Baumeister, R. F. (2000). The nature and function of self-esteem: Sociometer theory. In M. Zanna (Ed.), *Advances in experimental social psychology* (Vol. 32, pp. 1–62). San Diego, CA: Academic Press.

Leary, M. R., Springer, C., Negel, L., Ansell, E., & Evans, K. (1998). The causes, phenomenology, and consequences of hurt feelings. *Journal of Personality and Social Psychology, 74,* 1225–1237.

Leary, M. R., Tambor, E. S., Terdal, S. K., & Downs, D. L. (1995). Self-esteem as an interpersonal monitor: The sociometer hypothesis. *Journal of Personality and Social Psychology, 68,* 518–530.

Lockwood, P., & Kunda, Z. (1997). Superstars and me: Predicting the impact of role models on the self. *Journal of Personality and Social Psychology, 73,* 91–103.

Markus, H., & Wurf, E. (1987). The dynamic self-concept: A social psychological perspective. *Annual Review of Psychology, 38,* 299–337.

Martin, R., Suls, J., & Wheeler, L. (2002). Ability evaluation by proxy: Role of maximum performance and related attributes in social comparison. *Journal of Personality and Social Psychology, 82,* 781–791.

McAvay, G. J., Raue, P. J., & Brown, E. L., & Bruce, M. L. (2005). Symptoms of depression in older home-care patients: Patient and informant reports. *Psychology and Aging, 20,* 507–518.

Murray, S. L., Holmes, J. G., & Griffin, D. W. (2000). Self-esteem and the quest for felt security: How perceived regard regulates attachment processes. *Journal of Personality and Social Psychology, 78,* 478–498.

Nisbett, R. E., & Wilson, T. D. (1977). Telling more than we can know: Verbal reports on mental processes. *Psychological Review, 84,* 231–259.

Pleban, R., & Tesser, A. (1981). The effects of relevance and quality of another's performance on interpersonal closeness. *Social Psychology Quarterly, 44,* 278–285.

Pronin, E., & Kugler, M. B. (2007). Valuing thoughts, ignoring behavior: The introspection illusion as a source of the bias blind spot. *Journal of Experimental Social Psychology, 43,* 565–578.

Pryor, J. B., Gibbons, F. X., Wicklund, R. A., Fazio, R. H., & Hood, R. (1977). Self-focused attention and self-report validity. *Journal of Personality, 45,* 514–527.

Rohrbaugh, M. J., Shoham, V., Coyne, J. C., Cranford, J. A., Sonnega, J. S., & Nicklas, J. M. (2004). Beyond the "self" in self-efficacy: Spouse confidence predicts patient survival following heart failure. *Journal of Family Psychology, 18,* 184–193.

Sanitioso, R. B., & Wlodarski, R. (2004). In search of information that confirms a desired self-perception: Motivated processing of social feedback and choice of social interactions. *Personality and Social Psychology Bulletin, 30,* 412–422.

Schlenker, B. R. (1980). *Impression management: The self-concept, social identity, and interpersonal relations*. Monterey, CA: Brooks/Cole.

Schlenker, B. R. (1986). Self-identification: Toward an integration of the private and public self. In R. Baumeister (Ed.), *Public self and private self* (pp. 21–62). New York: Springer-Verlag.

Schlenker, B. R., & Wowra, S. C. (2003). Carryover effects of feeling socially transparent or impenetrable on strategic self-presentation. *Journal of Personality and Social Psychology, 85*, 871–880.

Sciangula, A., & Morry, M. M. (2009). Self-esteem and perceived regard: How I see myself affects my relationship satisfaction. *Journal of Social Psychology, 149*, 143–158.

Sedikides, C., & Strube, M. J. (1995). The multiply motivated self. *Personality and Social Psychology Bulletin, 21*, 1330–1335.

Silvia, P. J., & Gendolla, G. H. E. (2001). On introspection and self-perception: Does self-focused attention enable accurate self-knowledge? *Review of General Psychology, 5*, 241–269.

Sommer, K. L., Williams, K. D., Ciarocco, N. J., & Baumeister, R. F. (2001). Explorations into the intrapsychic and interpersonal consequences of social ostracism. *Basic and Applied Social Psychology, 23*, 227–245.

Spain, J. S., Eaton, L. G., & Funder, D. C. (2000). Perspectives on personality: The relative accuracy of self versus others for the prediction of emotion and behavior. *Journal of Personality, 68*, 837–867.

Suls, J., Lemos, K., & Lockett Stewart, H. (2002). Self-esteem, construal, and comparisons with the self, friends, and peers. *Journal of Personality and Social Psychology, 82*, 252–261.

Suls, J., Martin, R., & Wheeler, L. (2002). Social comparison: Why, with whom, and with what effect? *Current Directions in Psychological Science, 11*, 159–163.

Swann, W. B., Jr. (1983). Self-verification: Bringing social reality into harmony with the self. In J. Suls & A. G. Greenwald (Eds.), *Psychological perspectives on the self* (Vol. 2, pp. 33–66). Hillsdale, NJ: Erlbaum.

Swann, W. B., Jr., Chang-Schneider, C., & McClarty, K. L. (2007). Do people's self-views matter? Self-concept and self-esteem in everyday life. *American Psychologist, 62*, 84–94.

Swann, W. B., & Pelham, B. (2002). Who wants out when the going gets good? Psychological investment and preference for self-verifying college roommates. *Self and Identity, 1*, 219–233.

Swann, W. B., & Read, S. J. (1981). Acquiring self-knowledge: The search for feedback that fits. *Journal of Personality and Social Psychology, 41*, 1119–1128.

Swann, W. B., Rentfrow, P. J., & Guinn, J. S. (2003). Self-verification: The search for coherence. In M. R. Leary & J. P. Tangney (Eds.), *Handbook of self and identity* (pp. 367–383). New York: Guilford Press.

Taylor, S. E., & Brown, J. D. (1988). Illusion and well-being: A social psychological perspective on mental health. *Psychological Bulletin, 103*, 193–210.

Taylor, S. E., Wood, J. V., & Lichtman, R. R. (1983). It could be worse: Selective evaluation as a response to victimization. *Journal of Social Issues, 39*, 19–40.

Tennen, H., McKee, T. E., & Affleck, G. (2000). Social comparison processes in health and illness. In J. Suls & L. Wheeler (Eds.), *Handbook of social comparison: Theory and research* (pp. 443–483). Dordrecht, The Netherlands: Kluwer Academic.

Tesser, A. (1988). Toward a self-evaluation maintenance model of social behavior. In L. Berkowitz (Ed.), *Advances in experimental social psychology, Vol. 21. Social psychological studies of the self: Perspectives and programs* (pp. 181–227). San Diego, CA: Academic Press.

Tesser, A., Campbell, J., & Smith, M. (1984). Friendship choice and performance: Self-evaluation maintenance in children. *Journal of Personality and Social Psychology, 46*, 561–574.

Tesser, A., & Paulhus, D. (1983). The definition of self: Private and public self-evaluation management strategies. *Journal of Personality and Social Psychology, 44*, 672–682.

Tice, D. M. (1992). Self-concept change and self-presentation: The looking glass self is also a magnifying glass. *Journal of Personality and Social Psychology, 63*, 435–451.

Trope, Y. (1979). Uncertainty-reducing properties of achievement tasks. *Journal of Personality and Social Psychology, 37*, 1505–1518.

Trope, Y. (1980). Self-assessment, self-enhancement, and task preference. *Journal of Experimental Social Psychology, 16*, 116–129.

Tyler, J. M., & Feldman, R. S. (2005). Deflecting threat to one's image: Dissembling personal information as a self-presentation strategy. *Basic and Applied Social Psychology, 27*, 371–378.

Vazire, S., & Mehl, M. R. (2008). Knowing me, knowing you: The accuracy and unique predictive validity of self-ratings and other-ratings of daily behavior. *Journal of Personality and Social Psychology, 95*, 1202–1216.

Vohs, K. D., & Heatherton, T. F. (2001). Self-esteem and threats to self: Implications for self-construals and interpersonal perceptions. *Journal of Personality and Social Psychology, 81*, 1103–1118.

Vohs, K. D., & Heatherton, T. F. (2004). Ego threat elicits different social comparison processes among high and low self-esteem people: Implications for interpersonal perceptions. *Social Cognition, 22*, 168–191.

Wentura, D., & Greve, W. (2005). Assessing the structure of self-concept: Evidence for self-defensive processes by using a sentence priming task. *Self and Identity, 4*, 193–211.

Wheeler, L., & Miyake, K. (1992). Social comparison in everyday life. *Journal of Personality and Social Psychology, 62*, 760–773.

Wicklund, R. A., & Duval, S. (1971). Opinion change and performance facilitation as a result of objective self-awareness. *Journal of Experimental Social Psychology, 7*, 319–342.

Wills, T. A. (1981). Downward comparison principles in social psychology. *Psychological Bulletin, 90*, 245–271.

Wilson, T. D., & Dunn, D. S. (1986). Effects of introspection on attitude-behavior consistency: Analyzing reasons versus focusing on feelings. *Journal of Experimental Social Psychology, 22*, 249–263.

Wilson, T. D., & Dunn, E. W. (2004). Self-knowledge: Its limits, value, and potential for improvement. *Annual Review of Psychology, 55*, 17.1–17.26.

Wilson, T. D., & Gilbert, D. T. (2003). Affective forecasting. In M. P. Zanna (Ed.), *Advances in experimental social psychology* (Vol. 35, pp. 345–411). San Diego, CA: Academic Press.

Wilson, T. D., & Gilbert, D. T. (2005). Affective forecasting. *Current Directions in Psychological Science, 14*, 131–134.

Wilson, T. D., & LaFleur, S. J. (1995). Knowing what you'll do: Effects of analyzing reasons on self-prediction. *Journal of Personality and Social Psychology, 68*, 21–35.

Gordon B. Moskowitz *and* Michael J. Gill

**Abstract**

*Person perception* is the study of the cognitive processes involved in categorizing people and their behavior, forming inferences about their qualities and the causes for their action, arriving at attributions that explain behavior, and making predictions about what people are like and likely to do. It incorporates phenomena that operate outside of conscious awareness and automatically (allocation of attention, feature detection, categorization, trait inference, stereotyping, assimilation, and contrast) as well as cognitive processes that require cognitive effort, attentional resources, and extended mental reasoning. It examines the influences of these processes on social judgment and emotion, as well as on interpersonal behavior and intergroup dynamics. Because all social exchanges begin with inferring the intentions and qualities of others, as well as what they are likely to do, and anticipating their expectations of us, person perception is ubiquitous and essential to social exchanges and structures all interactions.

**Key Words:** attribution, inference, causality, automaticity, correspondence bias, motivated reasoning, stereotyping, priming, social explanations

*Person perception* is the study of how we come to "know" and understand people (self and others). It incorporates phenomena ranging from how perceivers explain single instances of behavior, to how they develop an enduring sense of a person's personality, to how their perceptions and emotions influence relationship regulation. It includes both snap judgments that the individual does not consciously intend or even detect and explanations that require extended mental reasoning. It is premised on the assumption that having such knowledge about people is required to formulate an action strategy—to know how one is to behave and to anticipate how a social interaction will unfold (what a person is likely to do). James (1890/1950, p. 333) asserted that "my thinking is first and last and always for the sake of my doing." This belief was echoed by Allport (1954, p. 167): "By thinking we try to foresee consequences and plan actions."

Because we need to plan behavior and anticipate what others are like and likely to do, all social exchanges begin with person perception. To understand human behavior in its social context thus requires an understanding of person perception. The questions investigated by psychologists interested in this basic aspect of human experience include the following: What categories are used to label humans and identify behavior? Why and when do activation and inhibition of associated categories ensue? Do categories trigger schemas, exemplars, scripts, stereotypes, and other category-based knowledge? How do we assign explanations for the occurrence of behavior? What behavior do we anticipate (predict) will follow based on the cognitive processes just described? To what degree are these inferences based on effortful and rational processes versus biased processing (motivated reasoning) and less effortful heuristics? What goals other than arriving at an accurate inference guide person perception? Are there biases that infiltrate the process more than others, and do some dimensions of explanation (e.g., internal versus external cause; forming a coherent and unified impression; focusing on warmth and competence as dimensions of evaluation; affective reactions) cut across judgment domains? How much of the cognitive work dedicated to these tasks occurs outside of conscious awareness?

The empirical examination of these questions is usually traced to Heider's (1958) book *Interpersonal Relations*, with this term defined therein as "relations between a few, usually between two, people. How one person thinks and feels about another person, how he perceives him and what he does to him, what he expects him to do or think, how he reacts to the actions of the other" (p. 1). Heider saw person perception as ubiquitous, and over the course of his book he systematically analyzed informal observations of social behavior to develop a conceptual analysis of the everyday concepts people use to make sense of each other (what he called *common-sense psychology*). Beyond borrowing much of the conceptual framework developed by Heider, social psychologists also took from him the notion that the fundamental motive of the lay perceiver is *accurate understanding*. As noted earlier, perceivers have the aim of gaining powers of prediction and control in social interaction. Thus, Heider conceptualized the lay perceiver as a *naïve scientist*.

Two streams of research emerged in the decades following Heider's book. One investigates the rapid, implicit cognitive processes that occur in the first moments of thinking about a person. The snap judgments resulting from such processes may serve as anchors to which conscious evaluation is tethered. At times not much further evaluation occurs. A second stream focuses on the perceiver's search for causal understanding of behavior: *Why* did he act that way? *Why* did she experience that outcome? Although Heider focused on conscious cognitive processes underlying this search, it is now seen as involving a mixture of implicit and explicit processes. Before we discuss these two streams of research we will first touch on issues that distinguish person perception from object perception.

## Perceiving People Versus Perceiving Objects

The term *person perception* is a bit of a misnomer since the concern in this field of inquiry is largely not with perception in the manner a cognitive psychologist would define it. The focus is on processes at or after categorization. This is because the goal guiding most research is to study how and when we *make inferences about the causes of others' behavior* (such as whether behavior is intended, what trait it manifests), and how such inferences impact thought, emotion, and behavior. This, of course, is impacted by low-level questions such as who we attend to, what features are detected, and so on, but these feed into higher order cognition. This is not to say that there is no research on how people perceive other people in a manner more consistent with how "perception" is used in neuroscience or cognitive psychology; it is simply less prominent.

### Intentionality and Theory of Mind

A perceived object first becomes present in our life space, occupies our focus of attention, and is categorized (often unconsciously). The raw material on which categorization is based consists primarily of the shape, color, and other physical properties of the object. A perceived person also has properties like shape and color that allow the person to be categorized (e.g., a man, a judge, a Hispanic, etc.). In both object and person perception these raw features become percepts when they are met by the perceptual apparatus and transcribed into sensations to which the mind assigns meaning.

A first difference between person and object perception is that person perception's raw materials include behavior. The movement of objects is due to random forces and external agents (wind, gravity, pressure, collision).While human behavior can be random, often it reflects the willed activity of a sentient creature—a desire, generated in the mind of the perceived person, to act. Humans develop theory of mind (Wellman, 1990) to explain behavior: a belief that the psychological state of others is separate from one's own and serves as the cause for others' action (Tomasello, Carpenter, Call, Behne, & Moll, 2005). Even stationary humans are perceived to have intentions we never infer exist in objects.

This theory creates the drive to understand behavior. We do not have access to the internal states of others, only to their overt responses from which the causes for their responses are deduced. This process of forming inferences about causality requires a perceiver to discern whether the response was intended or was caused by reasons unrelated to the person's momentary or enduring intentions. This process is described as the primary task of humans in social contexts (Jones & Davis, 1965). We must decipher not only who other people are and what they are doing, but *why*. Thus, the research agenda is marked by investigations of processes of categorization, identification, cue detection, and inference, as well as issues of inferring meaning from observed acts, and anticipating behavior that is soon to be observed.

## Intentionality and Interaction

People are likely to be in flux and expected to change from moment to moment, especially as their interaction partner changes (Kenny, 1994). This not only makes person perception more complicated than object perception but raises the issue of why behavior is so variable. One answer is that people act in ways meant to affect their partners, who vary from situation to situation and who are relevant to the person's goals in unique ways that require the person to adjust behavior appropriately. As a perceiver, I need not anticipate an object's reaction to and perceptions of me. While objects can harm or help us, they do not try to. People do, and we adjust accordingly to what we perceive is their current intent. A second answer is that the people we perceive are themselves aware of the fact they are being evaluated and need to accommodate the expectations of the interaction partner who is perceiving them. Thus, when we infer intent from behavior we observe, we must realize the behavior may not only reflect that person's intent but their assumptions about what we expect or want—it is a dynamic process that must account for not only what a person does but the fact that he or she is displaying behavior in anticipation of the reaction of others.

## Intentionality and Traits (The Fundamental Attribution Error)

Because others change from moment to moment, we seek features to perceive in them that will lend some level of control and coherence to the perceptual experience. In this sense, object and person perception each are indebted to the Gestalt tradition. Gestalt principles inform that a stimulus should cohere together in a meaningful way and should have emergent properties that are not revealed by an analysis of the constituent parts. Heider (1994) imported these principles to person perception.[1]

Heider (1994) stated "one of the features of the organization of the social field is the attribution of a change to a perceptual unit" (p. 358). Each time we encounter a person a change to our environment has been produced by that person's actions. This change is unexplained and triggers doubt, or what in a Gestalt perspective would be called a state of disequilibrium. Equilibrium can only be attained by reducing the uncertainty and doubt.

The organization of the perceptual field in a meaningful and coherent fashion is achieved when an underlying cause for the behavior (attribution) is established. The search for meaning that is initiated is seen, from this view, as a perceptual necessity—"a causal drive" (Heider, p. 359).

However, Heider (1994) did not believe all attributions are equal. A fundamental perceptual bias was posited to exist that arises because persons as objects of perception are willful agents who cause change. Heider stated that "changes in the environment are almost always caused by acts of persons in combination with other factors. The tendency exists to ascribe the changes entirely to persons... to be intropunitive... to see the cause of their successes and failures in their personal characteristics" (p. 361). He described a bias for humans to *overperceive a causal role for disposition*. They pay less attention to pressures in the situation that impel people to act, focusing more on the internal qualities of the person from which the behavior must have sprung. Ross (1977) dubbed this tendency a *fundamental attribution error* (FAE).

This belief was grounded in Gestalt principles. First, the person and the person's behavior form a perceptual unit such that the behavior is seen as belonging to, part and parcel of, the person. This creates a sense of causal dependence whereby the person is seen as responsible for the behavior he or she enacts, regardless of the press of the situation. Second, perceivers need to see behavior as coherent and need to impose meaning on the dynamic behavior observed. This is best achieved by assuming a *stable* cause that accounts for fluctuations in behavior. Inferences about a person's *traits* provide this stability that is useful for establishing feelings of predictability and control.

The remainder of this chapter focuses, first, on the diverse implicit cognitive processes that happen within milliseconds of perceiving another person. These processes govern, for example, which stimuli capture our attention, which particular features of those stimuli are processed, and which conceptual categories are activated by a person's appearance or action. Next, we turn to the perceiver's search for causal understanding of the other's action, which involves a mixture of implicit and explicit processes. We then describe how motivational and cognitive biases suffuse the entire person perception process. Finally, we will discuss some of the downstream consequences of social cognitive processing: emotional and evaluative responses to others and the relationship regulation that is governed by these responses.

The manner in which goals guide person perception is a concern throughout.

## Person Perception During the First Ksana: Dominated by Implicit Cognitive Processes

Much of everyday thinking about people occurs (1) despite the fact we *lack conscious intention* to initiate it, (2) beyond our *control*, in that it occurs even if we wish it was not initiated or want it to stop once started, (3) *efficiently* (i.e., with minimal use of cognitive resources), or (4) when we *lack awareness* of it. These four features specify if an aspect of person perception is *automatic*. Consider stereotyping. Devine (1989) stated that upon seeing or thinking about a social group (e.g., Black men), a stereotype is automatically retrieved from memory—without intending it, being aware of it, being able to stop it if made aware of it, and despite other activity consuming one's mind. However, more recent research has revealed that even though stereotypes can be efficiently pulled from memory without one's awareness or conscious intent, this does not mean the process cannot be controlled (e.g., Moskowitz & Li, 2011). This highlights the fact that just because one feature of automaticity (lack of control) is not present, it does not mean stereotyping is conscious or is deliberately willed. The four features do not comprise a discrete class that make a thought categorically automatic. Rather, automaticity is a continuous variable conceptualized as a matter of degree rather than kind, with the combination of features present specifying varieties of automaticity (Bargh, 1994).

The study of automaticity in person perception falls into three general classes. The first is when attention is allocated, judgments are drawn, or beliefs formulated without one's awareness of any such processes. The second is when influences on how one reasons, feels, or acts are exerted, yet one remains unable to detect these influences. The third is when both occur: One engages specific types of processing without realizing it, with processing shaped by undetected forces. We investigate the first class of issues next.

### Processes in Person Perception We Do Not Know We Engage

Bruner (1957) described a series of mental events that happen prior to consciousness: (1) attending to one stimulus versus another, (2) detecting the features that characterize that stimulus, (3) matching those features against stored representations in memory, (4) identifying/classifying the stimulus, and (5) making inferences about other features (not yet seen) that are likely to appear as well. These preconscious steps also occur in the perception of people.

### SELECTIVE ATTENTION

Who do we notice? What behaviors from among all that are enacted in the environment enter consciousness and are further scrutinized? Decisions regarding to what stimuli one will attend are made prior to consciousness. For example, such selectivity is seen in research focused on self-relevant stimuli. Without consciously trying, one detects one's name leaping from what previously was an undecipherable din of noise (the cocktail party effect). Furthermore, Postman, Bruner, and McGinnies (1948) found that self-relevant words rise above the threshold of conscious attention faster than other words. In one study, words specifying values were presented subliminally. Presentation speeds were gradually slowed on successive presentations until the words were consciously identifiable. Words that described values of importance to a person were perceived at faster speeds, rising above the subliminal level more easily.

The automatic nature of attention to self-relevant stimuli has been illustrated in a variety of ways. Bargh (1982) used a dichotic listening task. Headphones delivered separate information to each ear, and participants were instructed to ignore the information in one ear while performing a task focused on the information in the other. Attention was selectively drawn to the unattended ear when it contained self-relevant information. Moskowitz (2002) used a task in which two stimuli were presented on a screen, one moving vertically, the other horizontally, at speeds too fast for conscious recognition. Participants were asked to attend to what moved vertically and ignore what moved horizontally. When the horizontal items were self-relevant, performance on the focal task declined. Roskos-Ewoldsen and Fazio (1992) used a task where an array of items was flashed quickly to participants. Memory for items in the array was later tested. They found memory was biased toward objects one had strong attitudes toward. Attention was selectively allocated despite there being no conscious attempt to do so.

Self-relevance is not only determined by long-standing values but by items relevant to one's temporary goals. Thus, opportunities for goal pursuit grab attention. Moskowitz, Li, Ignarri, and Stone (2011) found that when shown four images of people, and given a goal of focusing on one of them, attention was nonetheless distracted by the images of the people who were to be ignored. This occurred only if participants had another accessible goal that the to-be-ignored images could help them address (despite not knowing the goal existed, these images were relevant to it, or attention was being deflected). In sum, automatic processes of selective attention are impacted by perceiver-based factors. This short review's focus on self-relevance does not mean that self-relevance is the only factor that automatically directs attention. For example, threatening and negative stimuli receive preferential attention (e.g., Pratto & John, 1991). Fiske (1980) described stimulus information that is unusual—such as extreme or negative behavior—as especially able to grab attention. These brief examples focused on self-relevance are a small selection chosen merely for illustrative purposes (a note that applies to all experiments reviewed in all sections of this chapter).

## FEATURE DETECTION

Just as perceiver-based factors lead to selective attention, features of the stimuli being perceived shape how one's limited attentional capacity is rationed. Among the earliest research on implicit processes in person perception is that on features of a social stimulus that are likely to grab attention outside of conscious awareness (e.g., Taylor & Fiske, 1978). Such features not only include negativity and extremity but, as with object perception, include those that are "intense, changing, complex, novel, and unit-forming" (McArthur, 1981, p. 202).

Analyzing the features of a social stimulus occurs quickly not only because it helps to ration our limited attentional capacity but also because it is a precursor to, and necessary for, categorization. The most basic of those categories is whether a person's features put that person in the category of being either harmful or beneficial to one's survival. Facial expressions are a form of nonverbal communication that Darwin (1872/1965) believed transmitted such information about the person's value to the perceiver's survival, and, as such, the processing of facial expressions should become habitual, routine, and happen automatically. Hansen and Hansen (1988) supported this notion that people discern whether another person is to be categorized as a threat through implicit evaluation of the person's facial features (such as frowns). Their experiments revealed asymmetry in how easily people detected positive versus negative faces. Indeed, a rich history of research on the perception of nonverbal

cues, emotional displays, and thin slices of behavior reveals the power of the processing of features automatically.

Many nonverbal behaviors are initiated with the conscious intent of communicating information or a particular feeling. However, information and emotions also leak out through nonverbal behavior without the intent to have them communicated. As one example, Ekman (1992) described a nonverbal sign, a smile of true joy, which involves moving muscles around the eye that are difficult to control and that could not be duplicated regardless of what one consciously wishes to communicate (if trying to fake a smile). A host of automatic features in one's nonverbal display reveal underlying emotions and beliefs, at times having the undesired effect of undermining what is being verbally communicated, such as when facial microexpressions reveal that one is lying (Ekman & Friesen, 1969; Ekman & Rosenberg, 2005; Mehrabian & Wiener, 1967).

Just as with producing nonverbal cues, detecting them is often automatic. Though we can consciously scan for facial features and body language that betray a person's underlying intent, more often perceivers use rules of inference that they do not report knowing, let alone using. For example, Chawla and Krauss (1994) had participants try to determine whether a speech they watched was spontaneous or rehearsed. Without realizing, their attention was focused on features unrelated to the content of what was being said and related instead to how it was being said—how fluent the speech was, hand gestures used, the timing between the gestures and words, and the relationship gestures had with problems of lexical access.

Recent research on feature detection has focused on the question of how people perceive faces (e.g., Zebrowitz & Montepare, 2008), such as what facial features imply traits (e.g., Blair, Judd, & Fallman, 2004; Livingston & Brewer, 2002), how alterations in those features change the perceptual experience (such as the degradation of a facial stimulus and its impact on the perception of the category to which the person belongs, e.g., Martin & Macrae, 2007), and which brain regions are used uniquely to process facial stimuli (e.g., Haxby, Hoffman, & Gobini, 2000; Kanwisher, 2000; Mitchell, Macrae, & Gilchrest, 2002) and allow faces to be processed more easily than other types of visual information (Yin, 1969).

For example, Todorov et al. illustrated that the facial cues perceivers rely on form the perceptual basis of judgment. They identified two broad trait dimensions people use to characterize faces: dominance (power) and valence (trustworthiness). As we review later, this corresponds well with other research suggesting that the dimensions of status/competence and warmth/valence dominate interpersonal judgments (Asch, 1946; Fiske, Cuddy, Glick, & Xu, 2002; Osgood, Suci, & Tannenbaum, 1957). Using computer models, they next generated digitized images of faces that varied according to these two dimensions and systematically examined how the evaluation of a person changes with these slight alterations in the person's facial features. This reveals precisely how cues detected in the face are perceived and signal information to the perceiver about the qualities of the person, allowing for the person to be categorized and inferences drawn.

## CATEGORIZATION

Nonconscious processing of features impacts how a person is categorized. The categories implicitly used to identify features range from group memberships such as sexual orientation (Rule & Ambady, 2008) and race (e.g., Livingston & Brewer, 2002) and their associated stereotypes, to personality characteristics. These include both personality categories that are harmful to a perceiver, such as aggression (Bar, Neta, & Linz, 2006) and threat, and those beneficial to the perceiver, such as trustworthiness (Todorov, Pakrashi, & Oosterhof, 2009) and competence. For example, features detected in faces flashed at extremely fast speeds (100 ms) lead those faces to be categorized as *competent* (even influencing voting behavior and predicting political outcomes; Todorov, Mandisodza, Goren, & Hall, 2005) and *threatening* (Todorov, Said, Engell, & Oosterhof, 2008).

Exactly which from among the many potential categories becomes the one selected and serves as a superordinate category that organizes later processing[2] depends on features of the context, the perceiver, and the target. Fiske and Neuberg (1990, p. 10) state that qualities that "possess temporal primacy, have physical manifestations, are contextually novel, are chronically or acutely accessible in memory, or are related in particular ways to the perceiver's mood will tend to serve the role of category label." Brewer (1988) asserted there are a limited number of social categories that are used consistently enough—for example, age, ethnicity, race, and sex—to be the dominant categories for identifying a person.

Trope (1986) similarly argued that how a person is categorized is shaped by more than the stimulus features detected. The process is shaped by three types of influences. The first is the features detected in the stimulus, such as the behavior enacted. The second is the situation or context in which the observed features are detected. For example, funerals and parties lead the same facial features/expressions (crying) to be categorized differently (sadness versus joy). Casper, Rothermund, and Wentura (2010) showed that in one context a stereotype was, unconsciously, used to categorize a person, yet in a different context it was not. The third is prior information about the stimulus target (e.g., stereotypes about groups the person belongs to and expectancies built up through past experience). For example, past knowledge of a person will affect categorization of her action in that knowing she often cries, or having a stereotype that "women" are prone to crying, will shape whether her current behavior is identified as "crying" (e.g., Hastorf & Cantril, 1954; Trope & Liberman, 1993).

Once having categorized a person, the perceiver is now armed with information, delivered without implicating consciousness, which serves several further functions. First, the person is prepared to make a preconscious decision as to whether further processing is necessary by assessing the relevance of this identified person to current goals (Brewer, 1988). If no relevance is determined, no conscious thought needs to be engaged. Second, the person is able to access associated information in memory that is linked to the category in question and provides inferences for the individual about what, beyond that which has been seen, is likely to be encountered. Third, impressions of other people are not fully formed at the moment they have been categorized. Conscious reasoning about causality ensues, but it typically starts with the implicit inputs categorization provides serving as judgmental anchors (e.g., Gilbert, 1989; Jones, 1979; Trope, 1986).

## INFERENCE

Categories are nested in a mental network of associated concepts, goals, and emotions, all of which can be triggered in memory, thus providing perceivers with knowledge about the category that is useful for making predictions about the social world (Bruner, 1957). For example, McArthur and Apatow (1983–1984) found that a facial appearance with features characteristic of infants (big head and eyes) leads to being perceived as having a "baby face." This category then triggers in perceivers these specific inferred personality traits: nonthreatening, kind, loveable, flexible, weak, and naive.

The entire literature on implicit stereotyping is predicated on the idea that associated with social categories are socially learned/shared beliefs about what it means to be a member of a given category—the stereotype. Stereotypes have been shown to be pulled from memory for most perceivers, even those who denounce the stereotype, each time they encounter the category (e.g., Devine, 1989; Dovidio, Evans, & Tyler, 1986; Macrae & Bodenhausen, 2000). This occurs even if the category is not recognized as being encountered (such as when subliminal presentation is made). This association between the category and the stereotype imbues the perception of the person with inferences that the associated knowledge affords, allowing one to go beyond the information given, to make predictions about what is likely to occur and how to act.

To illustrate that a stereotypic inference has been made outside of consciousness, researchers have drawn from methods developed in cognition. For example, with a lexical decision task (Neely, 1977) stimuli representing the category are presented, and these are followed immediately by words representing a stereotype associated with the category (and control words). Reaction times to the words are assessed. Typically, response times to stereotypic words, not control words, are faster after the category is seen, indicating that the category triggered a stereotype (e.g., Banaji, Hardin, & Rothman, 1993; Dovidio et al., 1986; Macrae, Bodenhausen, Milne, & Jetten, 1994; Moskowitz, Gollwitzer, Wasel, & Schaal, 1999; Spencer, Fein, Wolf, Fong, & Dunn, 1998).

Not all unconscious inferences are about stereotypes. Asch (1946, p. 258) asserted, "we look at a person and immediately a certain impression of his character forms... with remarkable rapidity and great ease." This suggests that part and parcel of categorizing behavior is an inference about what caused it, with one implicit answer being that it resulted from a type of person. A *spontaneous trait inference* is said to occur. Perceivers spontaneously explain another person's behavior with traits. This inference happens without being aware an inference had been formed and with the inference occurring in the absence of an explicit intention to form an impression (e.g., Uleman & Moskowitz, 1994). In illustrating the unconscious nature of inferences about traits, research has again used methods that draw from cognitive psychology (for a review, see Uleman, Newman, & Moskowitz, 1996), such as implicit learning tests (e.g., Nelson, 1985), cued recall tests (Tulving & Thomson, 1973), misattribution of

recognition (e.g., Jacoby & Whitehouse, 1989), and recognition probe reaction time tasks (McKoon & Ratcliff, 1986).

Inferences about the qualities of others occur with even very brief observations of behavior (under 30 seconds; what Ambady, Hallahan, & Conner, 1999 called *thin slices of behavior*), and even in the absence of any information about a person more than a still image (what Kenny, 1994, called *zero acquaintance*). Ambady and Rosenthal (1993) found that judgments formed from "thin slices" are correlated with judgments of perceivers who know the target well, implying a degree of accuracy.

Perhaps the most pervasive inferences perceivers make outside of awareness are about two broad traits: warmth and competence. Several converging lines of research in person perception independently point to the importance of these two traits. In a series of studies where people were asked to form impressions of others from a list of traits, Asch (1946) found the power of the dimension "warmth" to dramatically alter the emerging impression. Twenty years later, using a very different approach, Rosenberg, Nelson, and Vivekananthan (1968) gave participants a list of 64 traits to sort and examined the themes emerging in the sorts. A sociability and intellectual dimension emerged that mirrors what others have called, respectively, warmth and competence. Most recently, Fiske and colleagues (Fiske, Cuddy, & Glick, 2007; Fiske et al., 2002) found that ethnic and gender stereotypes often fit into the four categories resulting from crossing these dimensions: the elderly are stereotyped as warm but incompetent, the rich as disliked but competent, Americans are stereotyped (at least by Americans) as liked and competent, poor Blacks as disliked and incompetent. They further find these four quadrants from crossing these two dimensions result in distinct emotions associated with each quadrant—pity (warmth and incompetence), envy (low warmth and high competence), admiration (warmth and competence), and contempt (low warmth and incompetence).

### The First Ksana and Beyond: A Search for Causal Understanding, Undertaken via a Mixture of Implicit and Explicit Processes

Following the implicit processes just described—which often result in the perceiver achieving a conceptualization of the target's act (e.g., *mean, nice, nervous, bold*)—the perceiver then wonders: *Why* did this person act this way? There is strong reason to believe causal searches happen spontaneously (e.g., Gopnik, 2000; Heider, 1958; Weiner,

1985) and a great deal of theoretical and empirical effort has gone into understanding how lay perceivers select an explanation (see Gilbert, 1998; Malle, 2004; for reviews). Current understanding is that behavior explanation is sometimes an implicit, thoughtless cognitive task (i.e., a spontaneous trait inference can constitute the sum of the perceiver's "causal thinking"). Other times, however, perceivers devote effort and utilize logic as they strive to arrive at a "proper" explanation.

It was Heider who first conceived of social perception as a type of causal analysis and who elucidated the basic conceptual framework underlying the layperson's answers to questions of behavior causality. Specifically, he described the common-sense view that other people "are *affected* by their personal and impersonal environment, [and that] they *cause* changes in the environment, [which] they are able to (*can*) and *try* to cause" (p. 17; italics in original). This distinction between being "affected by" versus "causing" is seen in the attribution theory distinction between *external* (*situational*) *causes*, which involve personal and impersonal forces that surround an actor and shape her acts or outcomes, and *internal* (*dispositional*) *causes*, which involve personal abilities (*can*) and motives (*try*) that are internal to the actor, and which sometimes are related to broader tendencies, such as personality traits and attitudes. Heider's emphasis on *try*—which points to mental phenomena such as intentions and desires—is emphasized in Malle's work on how perceivers deduce others' reasons, desires, and other mental states (for a review, see Malle, 2004).

## Rational-Effortful Models of Behavior Explanation

Two early, important theoretical contributions inspired by Heider come from Jones and Davis (1965) and Kelley (1973). They offered descriptions of inferential rules that perceivers effortfully employ—or *should* employ (more on this later)—when reasoning about causality. Jones and Davis suggested that perceivers first diagnose the *intention* of an actor. At times, if prompted by evidence, they go further to make a *correspondent inference* that the actor's intention corresponds to an underlying, distinguishing character trait. To illustrate, imagine a colleague who combatively argues a policy position at a meeting, creating disharmony and irritation. The question of intention is: *What was he trying to accomplish?* The question of correspondent inference is: *Does this intention suggest a character trait?*

Jones and Davis (1965) proposed that both these inferences depend on the perceiver's analysis of the effects of both the chosen act (combativeness) and alternative acts (e.g., remaining quiet). The perceiver first considers *noncommon effects*, or effects produced by the chosen act that would not have been produced by the unchosen act. Only noncommon effects are informative, because effects common to both acts cannot logically explain why one act was chosen. In our example, combativeness (compared to remaining quiet) might be seen as having two noncommon effects: keeping alive a policy position that one's colleagues had dismissed and also irritating others. If a perceiver thought only of a single noncommon effect, then that noncommon effect would be used to infer the actor's intention (i.e., it *must be* what the actor was aiming for). But surely the existence of a single noncommon effect is rare.

Our example has two noncommon effects and hence ambiguity about intent. How do perceivers resolve the ambiguity? Jones and Davis (1965) suggested that sometimes they do so by considering the *desirability* of the various effects. Perceivers assume the intention was to produce the effect that would be sought by most people. If a perceiver believes keeping alive a personally valued policy position is what most people would desire (whereas irritating others is not), then he or she will infer that this was the intention. If a perceiver believes that getting on others' nerves is something most people find perversely pleasant, he or she will infer the colleague's intention was to have a little fun by "throwing a wrench in the works."

For Jones and Davis (1965), perceivers are interested in more than momentary intentions. Perceivers are also motivated—by their desire for prediction and control—to consider whether an inferred intention points to a potent, distinguishing character trait. How do people reason about such matters? A key variable for Jones and Davis is this: Is the effect that the actor ostensibly intended to bring about one that most people would try to bring about? If not, then the actor has a distinguishing trait. For example, the perceiver who inferred the intention of "keeping the policy proposal alive" might reason that most people value "fighting for what they believe in" and conclude that the actor's behavior is uninformative vis-à-vis distinguishing traits (i.e., he has only an *ordinary disposition*; Gilbert, 1998). In contrast, a different perceiver might think most actors would *not* consider it desirable to fight for a position in a manner that creates irritation in others. Such a perceiver would conclude the actor has a distinguishing trait of being difficult (i.e., he has an *extraordinary disposition*; Gilbert, 1998). Connecting this back to prediction and control, the first perceiver would likely support the efforts of her colleague to join an important committee (e.g., "He'll share his opinion, like any good citizen would"). In contrast, the second perceiver would likely have reservations about the colleague occupying positions of power (e.g., "He'll make everyone's life difficult").

Kelley (1973) developed another theoretical approach to describe how perceivers reason about causality. Kelley's *covariation model* addresses the situation in which one has made multiple observations of the actor across time and contexts. To illustrate, let's stick with the combative colleague. Kelley's model suggests that, to identify the "true" cause, the perceiver considers three questions regarding covariation of the act with time, contexts, and other actors. First, *is he typically disagreeable in faculty meetings* (consistency test)? Second, *is he disagreeable only in faculty meetings* and not elsewhere (distinctiveness test)? And, third, *are others disagreeable in faculty meetings* (consensus test)? If the answers are yes (disagreeable in prior meetings), no (disagreeable many contexts), and no (others are not disagreeable in faculty meetings), then a perceiver makes an internal attribution: The act reflects a trait of the actor (i.e., "He's generally a difficult person"). In contrast, if the answers are yes (disagreeable in past meetings), yes (disagreeable only at such meetings), and yes (others are also disagreeable in these meetings), then a perceiver makes an external attribution: Faculty meetings turn people into ogres. Finally, if the answers are no (not disagreeable in past meetings), yes (disagreeable only at faculty meetings), and no (others are not disagreeable in faculty meetings), then a perceiver makes the inference that this is a unique occurrence: The cause is some temporary factor (e.g., perhaps his manuscript was just rejected). Other combinations of answers are possible, but they are more ambiguous in terms of the inferences that should be drawn.

Kelley (1973) also addressed the situation in which the perceiver makes only a single observation of behavior and lacks prior knowledge for assessing covariation. Imagine, for example, a visiting scholar witnessed the combative colleague. How would she assign causality? Although she has no prior knowledge, it would occur to her that he might be a difficult person. On the other hand, she also knows "tensions arise in group decision making." Two potential causes, one internal (a trait) and one external (group decision-making context), occur to her.

If she construes these as *multiple sufficient causes* (i.e., *either* cause *alone* is sufficient to produce the effect; Kelley, 1972), she will experience uncertainty about the "true" cause. That is, if there is just one plausible cause, the inference is clear. But, as additional plausible causes are considered, it becomes less clear what one's causal inference should be, a phenomenon that Kelley called the *discounting principle*. In contrast, if her operative causal schema were one of *multiple necessary causes* (i.e., *both* causes must be present to produce the effect; Kelley, 1972), then she would not discount but would attribute the act to the combination of the two causes (i.e., group decision making is tense, but only certain personalities respond by becoming combative). Finally, Kelley (1973) also describes the augmentation principle, in which a causal inference is strengthened by the fact that other causes are present that should *prevent* an act from occurring. For example, the visiting scholar might think, "These people will want to make a good impression on their visitor and thus will strive to be pleasant." Because the act of the combative colleague occurred *in spite of this*, the visiting scholar will augment her inference and conclude that the combative colleague is an *extremely* disagreeable person.

These descriptions present the lay perceiver as using *systematic and effortful thought processes*, as naïve scientists. Beyond this, other aspects of these models are worth noting. First, they construe the perceiver as *open minded* in the sense of being without bias for or against internal or external explanations. Second, they construe the process of explanation as driven by *case-specific* information, such as whether *this actor* engaged in a particular behavior before, or whether *this behavior* has produced desirable effects that would not be produced by alternative behaviors.

### Departures From the Rational Baseline: The Fundamental Attribution Error

A major discovery that has energized research for several decades is that lay perceivers are often not so systematic, logical, and open minded. Heider (1944) and Ichheiser (1949) foreshadowed this discovery. Ichheiser spoke of how perceivers fail to see the (external) "invisible jail" surrounding others, preferring to interpret others in terms of (internal) "specific personality characteristics" (p. 47), just as Heider described perceivers as intropunitive. Jones and Harris (1967) were the first to experimentally demonstrate this bias, later dubbed the fundamental attribution error (FAE). In their study, a person delivered a pro-Castro or anti-Castro speech. Participants' task was to infer the true attitude of this person. A crucial manipulation was whether the person had a *choice* regarding the speech topic. According to both Jones and Davis (1965) and Kelley (1972), observers should not attribute an act (giving a speech) to an internal quality of the actor (his true attitude) when there is a plausible external cause of the act (he was forced to do it). Jones and Davis found that perceivers were somewhat sensitive to the choice manipulation, rating the person's true attitude as more in line with the content of his speech when the person had choice, as opposed to no choice, in selecting the topic. Yet perceivers were not quite sensitive enough: They rated the person significantly more pro-Castro when he gave a pro-Castro speech, *even when he had no choice about the content of his speech*! Subsequent research ruled out a variety of alternative explanations for the effect, and all pointed to a bias to overemphasize the person's disposition.

Such research has also provided novel demonstrations of the phenomenon in completely different experimental paradigms. For example, Ross, Amabile, and Steinmetz (1977) assigned participants to the role of Quizmaster or Contestant. The Quizmaster was told—clearly within earshot of the Contestant—to generate trivia questions that relied on esoteric knowledge (e.g., *Who was the drummer on Miles Davis's "Kind of Blue"?*). Next, the Quizmaster asked 10 such self-generated questions of the Contestant and, naturally, the Contestant got very few correct. The Contestant *should* know that the Quizmaster was given a substantial role-conferred advantage (i.e., the ability to draw on an idiosyncratic store of knowledge) and thus Contestants should not infer that the Quizmaster is exceptionally knowledgeable. Yet they inferred precisely that: They rated the Quizmaster as exceedingly knowledgeable!

What these studies—and many more—suggest is that perceivers tend to interpret acts and outcomes as reflecting inner properties of a person and are relatively insensitive to the influence of external factors. Decades of research have been devoted to understanding why this FAE (also termed the *Correspondence Bias*; Jones, 1979) happens. Gilbert and Malone (1995) distill from the literature several distinct causes of the FAE aside from those discussed by Heider. First, perceivers can fail to notice external forces because such forces are invisible from the vantage point of the perceiver (*the invisibility problem*). For example, when a child is defiant in

school, the fact that the child has oppressive parents is invisible to those at the school. Second, perceivers might notice the external force but misconstrue its power (*the construal problem*). For example, they might know that "his commanding officer said he *must* do it" but fail to realize the full power of such a command to a soldier who knows the punishments for insubordination and who needs promotions to support his family. Third, knowledge about the person's situation can lead to an exaggerated view of the extremity of her behavior (*inflated categorization*; e.g., Snyder & Frankel, 1976; Trope, 1986). For example, knowing that a person is in a job interview might lead one to expect anxiety, and this expectation can make mildly anxious behavior appear *very* anxious. Fourth, attributions to internal traits are made easily (e.g., Moskowitz, 1993), whereas making attributions to external forces is more difficult (e.g., Gilbert, Pelham, & Krull, 1988). Thus, under conditions where perceivers lack the ability or motivation to think deeply about the target, internal attributions will persist, but external causes will not be considered, yielding a bias toward internal explanations. For example, Gilbert et al. had participants watch a video of an anxious-behaving woman who was discussing either mundane or anxiety-provoking topics. Results indicated that participants under cognitive load failed to consider the conversation topics—despite being fully aware of them—and thus rated the woman as dispositionally anxious regardless of what she was discussing. Those not under load considered the situation appropriately and rated the woman as less dispositionally anxious if she was discussing anxiety-provoking topics. This last finding has now been qualified. One's initial, automatic inference need not be dispositional. The nature of the spontaneous inference depends on one's goals (e.g., Krull, 1993; Uleman & Moskowitz, 1994) and one's lay theory of behavior causation (e.g., Gill & Andreychik, 2012; Molden, Plaks, & Dweck, 2006). Now we turn attention to such lay theories.

### The Role of Lay Theories in the Attribution Process

A more recent perspective on the process of explanation focuses on the guiding role of *lay theories*—general assumptions held by lay persons about the nature and causes of human characteristics. Some of this work focuses on lay theories of stability versus malleability (see Plaks, Levy, & Dweck, 2009, for a review), some focuses on theories of behavior causality or *social explanatory styles* (see Gill & Andreychik, 2009, for a review), and other work focuses on culture (see Choi, Nisbett, & Norenzayan, 1999, for a review). All three streams of work suggest that broad, preexisting knowledge structures shape explanation, and thus they oppose the notions of open-mindedness and dependence on case-specific information emphasized by earlier models.

The most well-established approach to lay theories comes from Dweck and colleagues (see Plaks et al., 2009, for a review). Their work suggests that lay perceivers can be classified either as *entity theorists*, who believe that the characteristics of human beings are static ("Everyone is a certain kind of person and there is not much that can be done to change that"), or *incremental theorists*, who believe that humans are malleable and dynamic ("All people can change even their most basic qualities"). Research suggests that these theories have effects that reverberate throughout the processes of self- and other-directed cognition. One of the clearest demonstrations of their effects comes from Chiu, Hong, and Dweck (1997). They found that entity theorists were more likely than incremental theorists to believe that an actor's behavior in one context would predict that actor's behavior in a different context (suggesting an internal explanation) and that even a single instance of behavior is relatively indicative of a general disposition (think: FAE). Other work (Hong, 1994) has suggested, in contrast, that incremental theorists tend to explain behavior in terms of dynamic processes within the actor (e.g., temporary feeling, need, or goal states). Interestingly, the divergence between entity and incremental theorists does not map on to the internal-external distinction described earlier but maps more closely on to Weiner's (1985) *internal-stable* (fixed trait) versus *internal-unstable* (temporary state) distinction.

Other work on implicit theories has taken a process-oriented view, considering the automatic and controlled aspects of the attribution process. Molden et al. (2006; Study 1) used Gilbert et al.'s (1988) "anxious woman paradigm." Results indicated that entity theorists *only* considered conversation topics while *not* under cognitive load (like Gilbert et al.'s participants). Incremental theorists considered the conversation topics even when under load. In Study 2, participants watched the same video while under load or not but, rather than learning the discussion topics, they learned the woman was either anxious or calm by disposition (as in Krull, 1993). Participants were asked to infer how anxiety provoking her *conversation topics* were.

Participants should either discount (i.e., "She looks anxious, but that's her nature... the topics are mundane") or augment (i.e., "She looks anxious, but her nature is calm... the topics must be *really* anxiety provoking"). Incremental theorists *only* considered the dispositional information about the target while *not* under cognitive load (like Krull's participants), whereas entity theorists considered the dispositional information even when under load. Taken together, the results suggest incremental theorists are well practiced at thinking about temporary states that are created via situational influence, and entity theorists are well practiced at thinking about stable dispositions. Each type of theorist can automatically, effortlessly factor into his or her judgments the types of information he or she is well practiced at thinking about.

Recently, Gill and Andreychik (2009) offered an alternative conceptual approach to lay theories and behavior explanation. They offered the concept of *social explanatory style*, which refers to a perceiver's consistent pattern of assigning causality across diverse targets. This approach is most clearly distinguished from that of Dweck and colleagues by its emphasis on *externality*, or the extent to which a perceiver chronically views acts and outcomes as caused by external factors. In a number of studies, Gill and his colleagues have either measured social explanatory style or manipulated it using bogus scientific articles that purported to identify the crucial causes of human action (e.g., "external forces are very important" or "external forces are not very important"). This research has linked external social explanatory style to phenomena as diverse as an increased tendency to cite external forces when explaining why a student is struggling with his work and a decreased tendency to conclude the perpetrators of a terrorist atrocity are inherently evil (Andreychik, 2009). Also, Gill and Andreychik (unpublished data) replicated the Jones and Harris (1967) study and found that those with an external explanatory style nearly avoided the FAE altogether.

In addition to exploring individual-level theories, scholars have examined the role of culture in shaping behavior explanations (see Choi et al., 1999, for a review). Much of this work suggests that cultures differ in terms of the lay theories described earlier. Miller (1984) was a pioneer in the cross-cultural study of social explanation. She had 8-year-olds, 11-year-olds, 15-year-olds, and adults in India and the United States explain prosocial and antisocial behaviors. Participants then offered explanations of the acts. Explanations were coded in terms of reference to internal and external causes. With regard to internal explanations, the data revealed no cultural difference among the 8- and 11-year-olds. Among 15-year-olds and adults, however, Americans offered a greater proportion of internal explanations (especially personality traits) than did Indians. This was more evident for the antisocial acts. With regard to external explanations, cultural differences were found only among adults. Indian adults made more reference to situational causes than American adults and this difference was, in contrast to the case with internal explanations, somewhat more evident for prosocial behaviors than for transgressions.

Relatedly, Morris and Peng (1994) explored the tendency for perceivers to explain behavior dispositionally. They argued that members of individualistic cultures (such as the United States) are saturated with messages about, for example, acting in line with personal desire, which tends to encourage a dispositional theory. In contrast, members of collectivistic cultures are saturated with messages about, for example, molding one's actions to fulfill the expectations of others, which will tend to encourage a less dispositional theory. Morris and Peng presented three studies of relevance to this possibility. In Study 1, participants watched cartoon displays of fish engaged in social behaviors (e.g., one fish enters, then a group of fish exits). Cultural differences in explanations were found among high school students: Those from the United States were more likely to view individual fish as the cause of what had happened, whereas high school students from China were more likely to view the group as the cause. Morris and Peng interpreted this as suggesting less dispositionism among Easterners (similar to Miller, 1984). In Studies 2 and 3, they examined explanations for homicide. Study 2 coded explanations given in the newspapers, whereas in Study 3 graduate students rated the importance of various dispositional and external causes. In both studies, greater dispositionism was evident in the US sample. Notably, subsequent work has highlighted a possible alternative explanation for these patterns. Specifically, instead of reflecting less dispositionism among Easterners, Morris and Peng's data might instead reflect an Eastern emphasis on groups being more agentic than individuals (i.e., dispositions reside in groups; see Menon, Morris, Chui, & Hong, 1999). For example, because the "external explanations" preferred by the Chinese in Morris and Peng's Study 3 referenced group-level cultural patterns (e.g., "America's individualistic, selfish values"; "chaotic times of the Cultural Revolution"), the explanations might reflect an Eastern tendency to attribute causality to group dispositions rather than to external causes per se.

Additional work further refines our understanding of cultural differences. Choi and Nisbett (1998) replicated the Jones and Harris (1967) experiment with both American and Korean participants. Surprisingly, in their Study 1, individuals from both cultures were equally likely to show the FAE. Norenzayan, Choi, and Nisbett (2002) add further complexity. In their Study 1, they found that Koreans who were given information about a behavior or trait of an individual used that information to predict the individual's future behavior to the same extent as did Americans. Both these findings suggest that dispositionism with respect to an individual actor can be just as strong in the East as in the West.

How can we reconcile this with the idea that Easterners are less dispositional in their thinking about individuals? One important point involves the salience of the external causal information (see Choi et al., 1999). To illustrate, Choi and Nisbett replicated their Study 1 and added conditions in which, prior to reading the target's essay, participants wrote an essay with no choice about the position to be argued (exposure condition) or experienced this lack of choice plus were also given the specific arguments to be presented in the essay (exposure + arguments condition). Among Koreans the FAE was somewhat reduced in the exposure condition and nearly eliminated in the exposure plus arguments condition. Among Americans, these manipulations had no effect on the extent of the FAE. Similarly, Norenzayan et al. (2002) replicated their behavior prediction task but added a manipulation in which some participants were reminded of situational base rates (e.g., "most people are helpful when the giving is not costly") prior to predicting how the individual target would behave. They found that Koreans were affected by this manipulation—expecting less cross-situational consistency when situational base-rate information had been made salient—whereas Americans were not.

## Biases Capable of Infusing All Stages of the Person Perception Process

Earlier, we reviewed the variety of responses people make that they do not realize they make (e.g., attention allocation, stereotype activation, trait inference). Next we turn to responses people are aware of having made but that are influenced in ways they do not detect. These biases can occur at any stage of the person perception process, and they leave people feeling they see the world in a "true" or "real" way, free from bias, when they do not (a state called *naïve realism*).

## The Role of Motives and Goals in Subjective Perception

One dominant source of influence is one's goals, motives, and needs. Among the earlier illustrations of this point was research by Bruner and Postman (1948) where participants viewed a series of circular discs with symbols on them, with the task being to simply draw the size of the disc. The perceived size of the disc was reliably impacted by the type of symbol inscribed on the disc. Discs with symbols that had value to the perceiver were seen as larger than discs with neutral symbols.

### COHERENCE

Many believe the first formal experiments on person perception to be those by Asch (1946), where people are asked to form impressions of a person from a list of personal qualities. The predictions carried a distinctly Gestalt perspective in that Asch believed the emerging impressions would be more than just a sum of the items on the list but would form in a coherent way, with an overall meaning or unified narrative that the person was motivated to impose on the story so that the pieces fit together as a unit. When the lists varied by one item only, for example, "warm" is replaced by "cold," impressions do not change slightly to reflect one item in the list has been altered; they change dramatically. Though conscious of the fact they formed judgments, participants did not dream those judgments were influenced so heavily, if at all, by a goal to have coherence. In yet another experiment, Asch split a single list into two lists. These lists not only yield impressions that look nothing like each other, but the participants argue they could never incorporate the items from the opposing lists into an impression. Yet participants have no trouble doing so if the items had been encountered initially in one list. In another experiment, participants in two groups were given the exact same qualities on which to base an impression, with the items merely presented to one group in the reverse order of the other. Here Asch introduced the notion of a *primacy effect*, where information encountered first has unusual weight in guiding the emerging narrative. In each of Asch's experiments, altering a focal quality leads one to see the remaining information in a totally different way—the meaning of each item in the set

of information changes, and a new coherent narrative emerges.

Perhaps an even more powerful illustration of Asch's (1946) point is made in experiments where the exact same qualities are presented in the exact same order, yet different memories of the items emerge and different impressions are formed. Why? Because one's goals when encountering the information differ, thus changing the way the items are made to cohere. For example, Hamilton, Katz, and Leirer (1980) asked participants to read the same sentences about a person, but half the participants were asked to do so with the goal of forming an impression of the person and the other half did so with a goal of memorizing the information. Memory of people forming an impression was superior to that of people trying to remember the information, with a more complex and interconnected (coherent) mental representation of the information. This suggests that the two groups structured and organized the information differently as it was being received (encoded).

Attempts to make information cohere when forming an impression also impact how people process information inconsistent with the rest of the information provided. Hastie and Kumar (1979) found that the goal of producing coherence leads inconsistent items to be processed more deeply because these items need to make sense in the overall picture. This requires effort spent on rationalizing why these items can be omitted from the otherwise consistent impression, effort not spent by people who are not pursuing this goal (Bargh & Thein, 1985; Sherman, Lee, Bessenoff, & Frost, 1998). People without the goal can more easily dismiss these items, or at the least they feel no need to give them extra attention. These processing differences are manifested in people with coherence goals having better memory for these inconsistent items, even though these items are omitted from their impressions. This occurs even if the goal of forming an impression is unconscious (Chartrand & Bargh, 1996).

### SELF-ESTEEM PROMOTION

The need to see the self positively and promote self-esteem is one of three needs typically listed as central to social life (another, epistemic needs—to impose meaning on stimuli—has already been reviewed, and the third is the need to affiliate with others). Taylor and Brown (1988) argue that *positive illusions*, or unrealistic positive views of the self, are an important ingredient to maintaining a positive sense of self. They classify these illusions into three general types of undetected influences over person perception: unrealistically positive views of self (and others with whom one shares an important identity), unrealistic optimism about the future, and exaggerated perceptions of personal control.

For example, unrealistic positive views of the self are maintained by selectively weighting and preferentially evaluating information with favorable implications for the self and avoiding information with negative implications. This results, at times, in *self-serving attributions*, where people attribute their own negative outcomes and actions to the situation while positive behaviors are seen as arising from dispositional and stable causes (e.g., Miller, 1976; Sicoly & Ross, 1977; Stevens & Jones, 1976). It also manifests itself in how people handle negative feedback. Ambiguous feedback is interpreted in the most positive light, and when feedback is clearly negative, it tends to be ignored. And if not ignored, the feedback is either seen as illegitimate, or one can denigrate the source of the negative feedback.

Kunda (1987) referred to these strategies for how people handle negative feedback as *motivated reasoning*—a tendency to be skeptical and critically examine information one does not want to receive yet readily accept information that boosts self views. Kunda asked participants to read a supposed *New York Times* article about the negative effects of caffeine consumption and its (fictitious) link in women to fibrocystic disease. When asked to evaluate the evidence in the article, a pattern of defensive processing emerged. People to whom the article was most relevant, yet to whom its conclusions posed a threat (women who were caffeine drinkers), saw the article as providing unconvincing evidence as compared to people who were not personally impacted by the article (men, and women who do not consume caffeine). A similar critical eye turned toward health-relevant negative feedback was shown by participants in an experiment by Ditto and Lopez (1992). Participants were skeptical of and rejected information that suggested they lacked an enzyme that made them at risk for pancreatic disorders later in life (yet easily accepted feedback when it suggested they possessed the enzyme).

## COMPARISON GOALS

Comparison occurs when a perceiver is forming an impression of a person (consciously or not) by making a relative assessment of the degree to which that person exhibits a given trait or behavior relative to a standard of comparison (Herr, Sherman,

& Fazio, 1983). One way this can lead to bias in person perception is when different standards are used to evaluate two different people who perform the same behavior. If one is surprised at the high quality of an essay when written by one person, but not surprised when that same essay is said to have been written by another person, it is clear that the essays were judged against different standards. The goal of comparing the essay against a standard reveals a bias if the standard being used shifts (e.g., Biernat, Manis, & Nelson, 1991). For example, if the exact same essay is seen as "better" and assigned a higher grade when a teacher believes it was written by a woman as opposed to a man, one of two things has just transpired. Either the teacher likes women better and is biased by this preference, or, somewhat counterintuitively, the teacher is biased *against* women, with standards (expectations) for women set lower than for men so that the teacher is pleasantly surprised to find a modicum of intelligence in the essay written by the woman.

Comparison goals can lead to a different form of bias in person perception, one where using an extreme standard produces a *contrast effect*. A contrast effect is when a stimulus is perceived to be less like a standard against which it is compared. For example, a friendly person is actually not seen to be friendly if the standard against which his or her behavior is judged is the kindest, friendliest person in the world. Next to such a standard the person actually seems less friendly than the behavior would have implied if comparison goals had not been in place (e.g., Moskowitz & Skurnik, 1999; Herr, 1986; Herr et al., 1983). Stapel and Koomen (2001) reviewed the existing experimental research in support of this hypothesis. For example, when a comparison goal is implicitly triggered and participants then engage in an impression formation task, the people with comparison goals show contrast effects in that judgments are in the opposite direction of the traits implied by a standard/primed person. When Gandhi had been recently mentioned to a participant with a comparison goal, this "Gandhi prime" became the standard against which a subsequent person was judged, and the new person was seen to have less of the qualities exemplified by Gandhi, such as kindness, than if a different standard (or no standard) had been mentioned—the person is seen in the opposite manner to Gandhi.

## UNCONSCIOUS GOALS

The multitude of goals that bias person perception could occupy an entire volume. These include goals relating to being accurate, accountable, avoidant, consistent, creative, cynical, egalitarian, positive, vengeful, and so on. Many of the effects are unexpected or counterintuitive. For example, the goal of getting along with others has been shown to lead people to mimic the behavior of people they interact with (and occurs without realizing one has the goal or is imitating the person; Chartrand & Bargh, 1999; Tiedens & Fragale, 2003). It also leads people to comply with normative pressures (e.g., Asch, 1952; Packer, 2009). The goal of taking another person's perspective leads people to see increased overlap between the self and others, creates increased empathy for others, makes people more open to seeing how the situation influences others (reducing the FAE), and lowers the degree to which people stereotype others (e.g., Batson, Sympson, Hindman, & Decruz, 1996; Davis, Conklin, Smith, & Luce, 1996; Galinsky & Moskowitz, 2000). Rather than review the vast list of goals that influence person perception, we end by focusing on the fact that the goals, and their influence, are often implicit.

Even when people realize they are engaging in behavior, they may fail to see the role their goals play in shaping that behavior. This can occur when one does not realize a goal is triggered or being pursued, thus precluding them from detecting its influence (e.g., Moskowitz, Li, & Kirk, 2004). One example, with implicit coherence goals, was reviewed earlier (Chartrand & Bargh, 1996). In another, Aarts, Gollwitzer, and Hassin (2004) unconsciously triggered a goal of earning money in participants. The participants then consciously performed a series of tasks on a computer and were told that if time permitted they could do a final task for pay. People with the unconscious goal of earning money as well as the conscious goal of working on the computerized tasks quickly to have a chance to earn money on the last task worked faster on the computer tasks than people with just this conscious goal. Participants did not know the unconscious goal existed, let alone that it impacted how diligently they pursued the task.

Wegner and Wheatley (1999) argue that obliviousness to the impact of unconscious goals on behavior is even more likely in instances where one acts in a way one did not want to act or has thoughts one did not wish to have. Such unwanted responses seem somehow magical, mystical when they occur because they oppose what one set out to do. Many examples exist. Ansfield and Wegner (1996) described the "mystical" movement on Ouija boards

as one's hand being under the direction of goals that remain invisible to the person. Similarly, pendulum divining, where the swing of a pendulum seemingly moves in an uncontrolled way, is described as guided by unconscious goals. Leander, Moore, and Chartrand (2009) describe people's experiences of moods as mysterious, arising from seemingly nowhere. Once again, it is the disconnect between a nonconscious goal and this conscious experience that causes the resulting moods to seem to have emerged from nowhere. Finally, Wegner (1994) described an ironic effect from trying to suppress a thought. The very thoughts one wants not to think become even more pervasive in consciousness than if one had not tried to will them away. However, this feeling of mysteriously doing the opposite of what one wants exists only because one fails to see the unconscious goals that are doing precisely what one wants. To suppress a thought requires scanning or monitoring one's mind for the unwanted thought so it can be inhibited when detected, and searching for information to replace the unwanted thought in consciousness. These mental steps required for not thinking something are rattled off as the goal dictates. The person just does not know it and only has the conscious experience of the unwanted side effects of these steps (the unwanted thought later being more prevalent).

### Nonmotivated Sources of Bias: The Role of Construct Accessibility in Subjective Perception

Not all influences on person perception are motivated. Often it is the case that in perceiving people we use whatever information is most readily available in the mind. For example, Murphy and Zajonc (1993) subliminally showed faces to their participants, manipulating whether the facial expressions depicted positive or negative emotions. Participants did not consciously see the faces, so they could not intend to detect the expression nor intend to have a mood triggered in them by virtue of being exposed to these faces. Furthermore, they could not intend to be influenced in their judgments of some new and unrelated picture by having seen these faces. Nonetheless, having these positive and negative states available in memory was shown to influence the judgment of an ambiguous (neutral) stimulus (a Chinese ideograph). The stimulus was liked more when it was preceded by the subliminal presentation of a positive face.

As a second example, cognitive psychologists have long noted that instead of seeking optimal solutions to problems people use a strategy of satisficing—seeking adequate solutions by relying on shortcuts in processing. These *heuristics* (e.g., Tversky & Kahneman, 1974) provide a way to generate a judgment that may be suboptimal, but one that is largely effective. The availability heuristic, for example, is a rule of thumb we employ in decision making whereby the speed with which information comes to mind (ease of retrieval, or fluency) signifies that the target to which the information refers is encountered frequently, happens often, and is likely to be true. The sensation of information being readily available is used as a proxy for something meaningful about the target with which it is associated. This heuristic is also used in making judgments of people, such as inferring a person (even the self) has specific qualities not because one has thought deeply about the person but because those qualities and its representative behavior come to mind easily (e.g., Schwarz et al., 1991).

Related to the availability heuristic is the impact on how people are judged by information that is primed. The concern here is also with fluency, but not with a theory about what fluency means, such as it meaning that something happens often, or when feeling something is fluent and familiar means that it is true (e.g., Begg, Anas, & Farinacci, 1992), or that when a name feels familiar it must be because the person is famous (e.g., Jacoby & Whitehouse, 1989). Rather, the concern is with how people explain the fact something feels fluent in the first place. Thus, if the quality "generous" suddenly come to mind, there is a need to assign a reason as to why. Such a reason is usually provided by scanning the environment for a way to attribute that fluency. If a person is detected, and that person's behavior can in even the most modest way be labeled as "generous," then there is a tendency to misattribute the fluency to that person's behavior rather than to the actual cause (which may not even be conscious to the perceiver).

## PRIMING AND THE MISATTRIBUTION OF FLUENCY

When one wants to start a lawnmower, or paint a room, there is an initial step of preparedness one takes, a "readiness" for action called *priming*. The human mind also gets primed prior to action. There is a mental preparedness, a perceptual readiness, which precedes responding. This occurs when a category and its associated knowledge is pulled from long-term memory and momentarily resides in working memory, even though the perceiver is unaware of this chain of events. Now prepared to respond, the perceiver can be unknowingly influenced by what has attained this state of fluency. This information is said to be *accessible*, or *primed*, and the stimulus that initiated the retrieval from memory of this information is called a *prime*. Importantly, it does not matter what caused the priming. Once a concept attains this state, it has the power to influence the way people who are next encountered are perceived, often leading a perceiver to misattribute the fluency to the person so that the person's behavior is seen as consistent with the prime (e.g., Higgins, 1996). Bruner (1957, pp. 129–130) identified several aspects of priming that have served as a guide for person perception research:

> The greater the accessibility of a category, (a) the less the input necessary for a categorization to occur in terms of this category, (b) the wider the range of characteristics that will be "accepted" as fitting the category in question, (c) the more likely that categories that provide a better or equally good fit for the input will be masked. To put it in more ordinary language: apples will be more easily and swiftly recognized, a wider range of things will be identified or misidentified as apples, and in consequence the correct or best fitting identity of these other inputs will be masked.

In the language of person perception, this leads us to expect that the greater the accessibility of a concept: (a) the less information needed to identify the type of person and behavior that is present—even ambiguous acts are given meaning, (b) the broader the range of behavior that will be seen as consistent with (or evidence of) the concept—even remotely associated behaviors will now be seen in the light of the concept, and (c) concepts that compete with an accessible one as a potential explanation will not be used but inhibited. More concretely, a behavior that is ambiguous as to whether it is hostile will be seen as hostile, a behavior that is at best remotely hostile will be labeled hostile, and a competing explanation such as "a playful shove" will be inhibited if the concept or quality *hostile* had been made accessible.

## ASSIMILATION

Higgins, Rholes, and Jones (1977) were the first to show that priming impacts person perception. In doing so, Higgins et al. introduced what is now a standard procedure for illustrating a prime's biasing influence: two ostensibly separate experiments in which the first one primes a concept, and the second one measures the primes' impact on judgment.

One type of impact has already been reviewed—a contrast effect. Another type of impact, the more well-researched type, is assimilation. *Assimilation* is when an impression of a person, and the interpretation of his or her behavior, is seen as consistent with the prime. The interpretation is drawn toward, or assimilated into, the meanings offered by an accessible concept. Hundreds of experiments have by now highlighted issues that determine when assimilation occurs, how long a prime's influence lasts, and what features of the prime are important to consider for understanding whether assimilation or contrast will occur.

Accessibility can exist in various degrees of strength, with assimilation getting stronger with accessibility strength. This raises the issue of what determines strength. Accessibility strength is dependent on how *recently* the prime has been encountered, how *frequently* the prime has been encountered, and how strongly the prime is associated with the concept in question. To illustrate the relationship between how recently a concept has been made accessible, accessibility strength, and impact on judgment, experiments have manipulated the amount of time (delay) between when the prime is encountered and when the judgment of the person is made (Bargh, Lombardi, & Higgins, 1988; Higgins, Bargh, & Lombardi, 1985; Srull & Wyer, 1979, 1980). The finding is that assimilation is weaker the longer the delay. To illustrate the relationship between frequency of accessibility, accessibility strength, and impact on judgment, experiments have manipulated the number of times participants are exposed to a prime (e.g., Bargh & Pietromonaco, 1982; Devine, 1989; Srull & Wyer, 1979, 1980). Such experiments reveal that more frequent exposure to a prime leads to a stronger impact on judgment.

Concepts frequently and consistently encountered repeatedly over time represent another manner with which accessibility arises. Rather than these concepts awaiting a priming stimulus from the environment to provide them with a momentary charge, they have a state of permanent charge or *chronic accessibility*, making them relatively more accessible than other concepts and, therefore, pervasive tools in guiding how one sees the world (e.g., Bargh & Pratto, 1986; Markus, 1977; Moskowitz, Salomon, & Taylor, 2000).

Primes exert effects on judgment by altering the meaning of an observed act. It is not that accessibility of positive thoughts makes us judge people positively. It is that a *specific primed quality* alters perception of the behavior and the manner with which it is interpreted (e.g., Higgins et al., 1977; Moskowitz & Roman, 1992). Furthermore, we do not attempt to foist whatever concept is accessible upon every person we see. The impact depends on there being perceived *relevance* between the behavior being observed and the accessible concept. Behavior related to the qualities reckless and adventurous will not be interpreted as intelligent because "intelligence" is primed (e.g., Higgins et al., 1977, 1982).

Not all relevant behavior is seen in the light of what is primed; behavior must be *ambiguous*. Behavior highly diagnostic (clearly indicative) of one quality is not assimilated to a prime. For example, having an accessible stereotype that a member of a group will be passive and timid does not lead one to see behavior that is obviously assertive as timidity (e.g., Locksley, Borgida, Brekke, & Hepburn, 1980). However, it is rare that behavior is so diagnostic and clear that it cannot be open to interpretation. Darley and Gross (1983) suggest that when a construct is well defined and highly accessible (such as a stereotype), only the slimmest of behavioral evidence is required for assimilation to occur (consistent with Bruner's, 1957, points "a" and "b," earlier). In their experiment, participants were primed with either the stereotype for poor or rich people. They then saw a video of a child answering questions in a classroom, with the behavior being ambiguous regarding her intelligence (right and wrong answers were observed). They next rated her intelligence and aptitude at school. The type of prime determined how she was ultimately rated. Importantly, seeing the ambiguous behavior was required for assimilation to appear. A separate group of participants who did not see the video of the girl at school did not have aptitude ratings assimilated to the prime.

## CORRECTION

What happens when one becomes aware of a prime's influence on judgment? Awareness of this process, in most people, leads them to develop theories about the nature of how they were biased, and then apply those theories in attempting to correct that bias—they try to counteract or remove the bias, thus altering how they perceive the person (Martin, 1986; Moskowitz & Skurnik, 1999; Strack & Hannover, 1996; Wegener & Petty, 1995; Wilson & Brekke, 1994). This attempt to not be biased often results in a contrast effect—trying not to see someone as consistent with a primed quality can lead one to go too far in the attempt to not see that quality and thus see the person in the opposite manner. It is important to note that this is a different method of a contrast effect being produced than that reviewed earlier arising from comparison goals. Here the person is not paling in comparison to some standard. Rather, the perceiver is trying to correct a bias and does it inaccurately, producing an opposite bias (seeing the person as unlike, rather than like the prime).

One factor promoting contrast is the prime's extremity (for example, evil is more extreme than mean). However, extremity does not always increase contrast. What must also be considered is whether the prime is an exemplar or a trait (Moskowitz & Skurnik, 1999). Exemplars are specific examples of a concept, such as Gandhi, Hitler, and Bill Murray. Traits are abstract qualities representing general types, such as hero, evil, and funny. These differ in that exemplars are narrower, more exclusive, and more distinct. Exemplars tend to promote comparison goals, and as such they lead to people using standards of comparison in judgment. An extreme exemplar will, therefore, increase contrast because it serves as a distant standard of comparison, sharing few features with the person being judged and making one perceive the person as dissimilar (Herr, 1986). A moderate exemplar leads to assimilation because the person is seen as similar to the standard. Traits, however, being more abstract, are less likely to call to mind comparison standards, and thus contrast will come from correction processes. Extreme traits (evil) serving as primes are less likely to trigger correction relative to moderate traits because extreme traits are less likely to be seen as an influence. We rarely use such extreme characterization, and thus are less likely to think they can bias our impressions. Moderate traits, however, are often used to describe people, so we are more likely to become suspicious of their ability to bias impressions and initiate correction attempts, and contrast (Moskowitz & Skurnik, 1999).

### STEREOTYPING

Person perception is influenced not only by the heightened accessibility of traits and exemplars but also by goals, attitudes, mindsets, behavioral tendencies, emotions, and stereotypes. A stereotype associated with a category can be primed outside of awareness. A perceiver can then be influenced by its accessibility on how he or she judges, and acts toward, others despite not detecting and denying any bias, and despite a conscious goal to not be biased (e.g., Bargh, Chen, & Burrows, 1996; Correll, Park, Judd, Wittenbrink, & 2002; Devine,

1989; Dovidio & Gaertner, 2000; Rudman & Glick, 2001; Sherman et al., 1998; Word, Zanna, & Cooper, 1974). One way research illustrates the automatic, unconscious influence of stereotypes is when the primes that make a stereotype accessible are presented subliminally (e.g., Devine, 1989). Here the influencing agent, the stereotype, is never consciously seen, yet judgments are assimilated toward the stereotype.

Another way primed stereotypes influence person perception is by biasing memory. Sherman and Bessenoff (1999) had participants read lists of friendly and unfriendly behaviors performed by either a skinhead or a priest. Crucially, these lists contained exactly the same number of friendly and unfriendly behaviors being performed by the skinhead and the priest. Subsequently, participants were shown each of the behaviors from the lists, but this time without specifying who performed which behavior. Their task was to remember who performed each behavior. The results indicated they tended to misremember unfriendly, but not friendly, behaviors as having been performed by a skinhead, and to misremember friendly, but not unfriendly, behaviors as performed by the priest.

### INHIBITION

Kunda and Thagard (1996) assert that encountering a person who can be categorized, or observing a behavior that represents a particular category, does not trigger everything in the lexicon associated with the category. Their *parallel-constraint-satisfaction model* states that the activation of a category after encountering information will simultaneously (in parallel) constrain the activation of some information associated with the category, inhibiting that information. They stated, "*aggressive* may activate both *punch* and *argue*. The context in which *aggressive* is activated may serve to narrow its meaning. Thus, *courtroom* may activate *argue* while deactivating *punch* ... a given trait may have a rich and diverse network of associates; only a subset of these is activated on any occasion" (Kunda, Sinclair, & Griffin, 1997, p. 721). For instance, priming a stereotype has been found to not only trigger associated stereotype-consistent traits but to inhibit stereotype-inconsistent traits (Dijksterhuis & van Knippenberg, 1996). Similarly, priming a category has been found to increase the ability to retrieve typical category members, while simultaneously limiting access to atypical ones (Rothbart, Sriram, & Davis-Stitt, 1996). Inhibition in the domain of stereotyping can also happen in the opposite manner of that just described, with typical associates to the category, stereotypic content, inhibited. This occurs when a perceiver has goals antagonistic with stereotyping. Priming the goal leads to the inhibition of the competing content—the stereotype. Moskowitz et al. (1999) illustrated perceivers with goals antithetical to stereotyping inhibited stereotypic associations to the category *woman*, making those qualities less (not more) accessible (as did Moskowitz & Li, 2011, with the category *African Americans*).

## Downstream Consequences of Cognition: Behavior Explanations as a Foundation of Social Emotions and Relationship Regulation

As implied by the title of Heider's (1958) book, *The Psychology of Interpersonal Relations*, person perception is not an end in itself. Rather, it is the stuff out of which social relations are constructed. Indeed, the nature of our relationships depends on emotions and motives that are revealed by questions such as: How do I feel about him? Shall I seek proximity or keep my distance? Shall I punish or forgive? And our explanations regarding others powerfully affect our answers to these questions (e.g., Alicke, 2000; Fincham, 2000; Gill & Andreychik, 2009; Weiner, 2006). These socioemotional and relational implications of explanations sometimes fade to the background in the attribution literature, with its focus on the cognitive operations underlying the selection of an explanation (see earlier). Humans are concerned not merely with gaining a sense of understanding by selecting a subjectively accurate explanation; they are also concerned with assessing goodness, badness, social worth, and with constructing and regulating relationships.

Weiner and colleagues were pioneers in highlighting the socioemotional and relational implications of social explanations (see Weiner, 2006, for a review). For example, Weiner and Kukla (1970) studied how explanations shape punitive responses to academic performance. Participants, playing the role of teachers, received information about the academic performances of hypothetical students, as well as the causes of those performances. The causes involved effort and ability. A key finding was that they were punitive toward students who failed to exert effort, but not toward students who lacked ability (intelligence). Reflecting on this study and his several decades of subsequent work, Weiner (2006; see also Fincham & Jaspars, 1980) has concluded that *perceived controllability* is one of the most important factors governing socioemotional

reactions to negative acts or outcomes. When an actor produces a negative act/outcome, yet *he could and should have done otherwise*, strong levels of anger and punitiveness are created. Not surprisingly, controllability perceptions have continued to be a major focus of research (e.g., Skitka, 1999), and they are clearly distinguishable from the classic internal versus external distinction (e.g., Gill, Andreychik, & Getty, in press; Weiner, 2006).

Alicke (2000) agrees that perceived controllability is an important contributor to socioemotional responses to failures or transgressions. He goes further, however, to make the case that perceivers are biased toward seeing others as exerting control (cf. the work on "Just World" thinking; e.g., Hafer, 2000; Lerner & Miller, 1978). A crucial contribution of Alicke's *culpable control model* is the notion that negative emotional reactions to an act (e.g., moral outrage over an act of violence) are *antecedents* to heightened perceptions of control and blameworthiness, rather than merely being *consequences* of perceived controllability and blame (cf. Lerner & Miller, 1978; Weiner, 2006). Specifically, Alicke states that negative emotions elicited by an act can trigger *blame-validation processing*, in which the perceiver alters evidential standards (Alicke & Davis, 1989) and alters perceptions of evidence (Alicke, Davis, & Pezzo, 1994) to support a view of the target as exerting control and, thus, being blameworthy. A related perspective comes from Tetlock et al. (2007), who show that the perception of widespread norm violation in the community triggers a heightened motivation to blame and punish individual perpetrators. Notably, this work fits well with recent evolutionary accounts of how humans maintain large-scale cooperation and conformity to social norms (e.g., Fehr & Fischbacher, 2004).

Coming from a close relationships perspective, Fincham (2000) points out that, although humans may have biases toward blame and punishment, they are also social beings who need close relationships and social bonds for emotional fulfillment and the attainment of individual goals (see Baumeister & Leary, 1995; de Waal, 1996). If the social-cognitive repertoire included only mechanisms fostering blame and anger, how could relational harmony be maintained (see de Waal, 1996; McCullough, 2008)?

Accordingly, Fincham and his colleagues have spent decades examining how certain types of explanations for injury inflicted by an intimate partner—ranging from insult to infidelity—can mitigate anger and blame reactions, increase pro-relationship responses, and promote forgiveness (see Bradbury & Fincham, 1990; Fincham, 2000). Bradbury and Fincham's (1990) review suggested that marital contentment is most strongly facilitated by a tendency to explain a partner's negative behavior in terms of a highly specific, context-dependent cause (e.g., *She gets cranky only when she thinks about her parents*) and to explain a partner's positive behavior in terms of highly general causes (e.g., *She's a great person*). Furthermore, Fincham and Bradbury (1992) developed the Relationship Attribution Measure (RAM), a standardized measure of how one characteristically explains *negative* partner behavior. Research with the RAM suggests that marital disharmony is increased when partners explain each other's negative behavior as being done intentionally and as being motivated by selfishness. This relates to Weiner's (2006) emphasis on controllability but adds the notion of *egoistic motivation* to the mix. The relation between explanations and marital harmony, although typically assessed with correlational data, does not appear to be explicable based on any trivial third variable explanation and, indeed, seems to be a causal relation (see Fincham, 2001, for a review). Thus, behavior explanation is integral to the successful regulation of our most enduring and important relationships.

Finally, Gill and Andreychik (2009) link externality of social explanatory style (discussed earlier) to heightened levels of dispositional compassion. In one study, they manipulated externality using bogus scientific articles and then had participants learn about a college student struggling with his coursework (Andreychik, 2009). Those primed with an external explanatory style responded to the student's struggles with more compassionate emotions (e.g., concern, sympathy) than did those primed to downplay external causes. In another study, participants learned about Chechen terrorists who took hostages and committed murder at an elementary school in Beslan. Those who spontaneously interpreted the terrorist act as indicating inherent evil expressed a lack of sympathy for suffering that had occurred on the Chechen's side *unless* they also had an external explanatory style, in which case compassion was not denied to those who suffered on the Chechen side (Andreychik, 2009). This work suggests that behavior explanations are also relevant to how we regulate our relationships with peers and perhaps even to international relations.

## Conclusion

Person perception involves automatic processing to which the perceiver is naïve, the use of heuristics learned through a lifetime of experience with people and situations, and systematic evaluation, or rational processes. Though this is true of object perception as well, person perception has an extra layer of complexity—knowing the target of perception is impelled by intentions, intentions that (a) one needs to infer and (b) are impacted by one's own presence as a perceiver (he or she forms inferences about the perceiver, anticipating the perceiver's qualities and behavior). It is guided by attempts at finding meaning in the form of causal explanation, attempts that involve processing ranging from the implicit and immediate to explicit and extended. It involves attending to behavior and features such as nonverbal cues, categorizing, predicting the qualities others will reveal, and anticipating their goals and behavior. Each of these forms of cognitive processing can be described as essentially rational in that perceivers are doing the best they can with the information they have. Even apparent violations to a normative model (such normative models include Kelley's 1967 model, and Jones & Davis's 1965 theory of correspondent inference) do not necessarily indicate bias.

Of course, the collection of processes that contribute to our perceptions of others is fraught with bias as well. One can decide a person is aggressive/hostile not because that person's behavior is objectively threatening, but because notions of hostility and aggressiveness were already in working memory before seeing the person's behavior, even for reasons that have nothing to do with the person. People use faulty heuristics when they should use systematic analyses. They give unusual weight to spontaneous inferences, accessible knowledge, and lay theories. They are often biased without knowing by goals, standards of comparison, stereotypes, and traits. Perceivers also exert effort to seek out information that supports their biases and to dispel that which would undermine it. This unseen bias pervading social cognition leaves us unable to accurately specify why and how we think the thoughts we think. We generate what we believe to be reasons for our beliefs and judgments, the rules and logic that guide our inferences and predictions, but we lack introspective awareness of their true root cause (e.g., Nisbett & Wilson, 1977; Wilson & Brekke, 1994). The naïve scientist can, however, become a little less naïve by turning to the science of person perception as it unearths the diverse and fascinating machinations that underlie social knowledge.

## Notes

1. A result of Heider having been a student of Wolfgang Köhler and Max Wertheimer in Berlin during the heyday of the Gestalt movement in perception (and furthered by having been colleagues with Kurt Koffka at Smith College starting in 1930, after fleeing Germany during Hitler's rise to power).

2. Macrae, Bodenhausen, and Milne (1995) found that once a person is categorized according to one group, inhibition of competing categories ensues. Thus, reacting to a person in terms of race inhibits categories such as gender (and vice versa).

## References

Aarts, H., Gollwitzer, P. M., & Hassin, R. R. (2004). Goal contagion: Perceiving is for pursuing. *Journal of Personality and Social Psychology*, *87*, 23–37.

Alicke, M. D. (2000). Culpable control and the psychology of blame. *Psychological Bulletin*, *126*, 556–574.

Alicke, M. D., & Davis, T. I. (1989). The role of a posteriori victim information in judgments of blame and sanction. *Journal of Experimental Social Psychology*, *25*, 362–377.

Alicke, M. D., Davis, T. L., & Pezzo, M. V. (1994). A posteriori adjustment of a priori decision criteria. *Social Cognition*, *12*(4), 281–308.

Allport, G. W. (1954). *The nature of prejudice*. Reading, MA: Addison-Wesley

Ambady, N., & Rosenthal, R. (1993). Half a minute: Predicting teacher evaluations from thin slices of nonverbal behavior and physical attractiveness. *Journal of Personality and Social Psychology*, *64*(3), 431–441.

Ambady, N., Hallahan, M., & Conner, B. (1999). Accuracy of judgments of sexual orientation from thin slices of behavior. *Journal of Personality and Social Psychology*, *77*, 538–547.

Andreychik, M. R. (2009). *Social explanatory style as a foundation of social orientation*. Unpublished Master's thesis, Lehigh University, Bethlehem, PA.

Andreychik, M. R., & Gill, M. J. (2009). Ingroup identity moderates the impact of social explanations on intergroup attitudes: External explanations are not inherently prosocial. *Personality and Social Psychology Bulletin*, *35*(12), 1632–1645.

Ansfield, M. E., & Wegner, D. M., (1996). The feeling of doing. In P. M. Gollwitzer, & E. J. A. Bargh (Ed.), *The psychology of action: Linking cognition and motivation to behavior (pp. 482–506)*. New York: Guilford Press.

Asch, S. E. (1946). Forming impressions of personality. *Journal of Abnormal and Social Psychology*, *41*, 258–290.

Asch, S. E. (1952a). Effects of group pressure on the modification and distortion of judgments. In G. E. Swanson, T. M. Newcomb, & E. L. Hartley (Eds.), *Reading in social psychology* (2nd ed., pp. 2–11). New York: Holt.

Banaji, M. R., Hardin, C., & Rothman, A. J. (1993). Implicit stereotyping in person judgment. *Journal of Personality and Social Psychology*, *65*, 272–281.

Bar, M., Neta, M., & Linz, H. (2006). Very first impressions. *Emotion*, *6*(2), 269–278.

Bargh, J. A. (1982). Attention and automaticity in the processing of self-relevant information. *Journal of Personality and Social Psychology*, *43*, 425–436.

Bargh, J. A. (1994) The four horsemen of automaticity: Awareness, efficiency, intention, and control in social cognition. In R. S. Wyer, Jr. & T. K. Srull (Eds.), *Handbook of social cognition* (2nd ed., pp.1–40). Hillsdale, NJ: Erlbaum.

Bargh, J. A., Chen, M., & Burrows, L. (1996). Automaticity of social behavior: Direct effects of trait construct and stereotype activation on action. *Journal of Personality and Social Psychology*, *71*, 230–244.

Bargh, J. A., Lombardi, W. J., & Higgins, E. T. (1988). Automaticity of chronically accessible constructs in person x situation effects on person perception: It's just a matter of time. *Journal of Personality and Social Psychology*, *55*, 599–605.

Bargh, J. A., & Pietromonaco, P. (1982). Automatic information processing and social perceptions: The influence of trait information presented outside of conscious awareness on impression formation. *Journal of Personality and Social Psychology*, *43*, 437–44

Bargh, J. A., & Pratto, F. (1986). Individual construct accessibility and perceptual selection. *Journal of Experimental Social Psychology*, *22*, 293–311.

Bargh, J. A., & Thein, R. D. (1985). Individual construct accessibility, person memory, and the recall-judgment link: The case of information overload. *Journal of Personality and Social Psychology*, *49*, 1129–1146.

Batson, C. D., Sympson, S. C., Hindman J. L., &Decruz, P. (1996). "I've been there, too": Effect on empathy of prior experience with a need. *Personality and Social Psychology Bulletin*, *22*(5), 474–482.

Baumeister, R. F., & Leary, M. R. (1995). The need to belong: Desire for interpersonal attachments as a fundamental human motivation. *Psychological Bulletin*, *117*(3), 497–529.

Begg, I. M., Anas, A., & Farinacci, S. (1992). Dissociation of processes in belief: Source recollection, statement familiarity, and the illusion of truth. *Journal of Experimental Psychology: General*, *121*, 446 458.

Biernat, M., Manis, M., & Nelson, T. E. (1991). Stereotypes and standards of judgment. *Journal of Personality and Social Psychology*, *60*, 485–499.

Blair, I. V., Judd, C. M, & Fallman, J. L. (2004). The automaticity of race and afrocentric facial features in social judgments. *Journal of Personality and Social Psychology*, *87*(6), 763–778.

Bradbury, T. N., &Fincham, F. D. (1990). Attributions in marriage: Review and critique. *Psychological Bulletin*, *107*(1), 3–33.

Brewer, M. B. (1988). A dual process model of impression formation. In T. K. Srull & R. S. Wyer (Eds.), *Advances in social cognition* (Vol. 1, pp. 1–36). Hillsdale, NJ: Erlbaum.

Bruner, J. S. (1957). Going beyond the information given. In H. E. Gruber, K. R. Hammond, & R. Jessor (Eds.), *Contemporary approaches to cognition* (pp. 41–69). Cambridge, MA: Harvard University Press.

Bruner, J. S., &Postman, L. (1948). Symbolic value as an organizing factor in perception. *Journal of Social Psychology*, *27*, 203–208.

Casper, C., Rothermund, K., & Wentura, D. (2010). Automatic stereotype activation is context dependent. *Social Psychology*, *41*, 131–136.

Chartrand, T. L., & Bargh, J. A. (1996). Automatic activation of impression formation goals: Nonconscious goal priming reproduces effects of explicit task instructions. *Journal of Personality and Social Psychology*, *71*, 464–478.

Chartrand, T. L., & Bargh, J. A. (1999). The chameleon effect: The perception-behavior link and social interaction. *Journal of Personality and Social Psychology*, *76*, 893–910.

Chawla, P., & Krauss, R. M. (1994). Gesture and speech in spontaneous and rehearsed narratives. *Journal of Experimental Social Psychology, 30*(6), 580–601.

Chiu, C., Hong, Y., & Dweck, C. S. (1997). Lay dispositionism and implicit theories of personality. *Journal of Personality and Social Psychology, 73*, 19–30.

Choi, I., & Nisbet, R. E. (1998). Situational salience and cultural differences in the correspondence bias and actor-observer bias. *Personality and Social Psychology Bulletin, 24*, 949–960.

Choi, I., Nisbett, R. E., & Norenzayan, A. (1999). Causal attribution across cultures: Variation and universality. *Psychological Bulletin, 125*, 47–63.

Correll, J., Park, B., Judd, C. M., &Wittenbrink, B. (2002). The police officer's dilemma: Using ethnicity to disambiguate potentially threatening individuals, *Journal of Personality and Social Psychology, 83*(6), 1314–1329.

Darley, J. M., & Gross, P. H. (1983). A hypothesis-confirming bias in labelling effects. *Journal of Personality and Social Psychology, 44*, 20–33.

Darwin, C. (1965). *The expression of the emotions in man and animals*. Chicago: University of Chicago Press. (Original work published 1872).

Davis, M. H., Conklin, L., Smith, A., & Luce, C. (1996). Effect of perspective taking on the cognitive representation of persons: A merging of self and other. *Journal of Personality and Social Psychology, 70*, 713–726.

de Waal, F. B. M. (1996). *Good natured: The origins of right and wrong in humans and other animals*. Cambridge, MA: Harvard University Press.

Devine, P. G. (1989). Stereotypes and prejudice: Their automatic and controlled components. *Journal of Personality and Social Psychology, 56*, 5–18.

Dijksterhuis, A., & van Knippenberg, A. (1996). The knife that cuts both ways: Facilitated and inhibited access to traits as a result of stereotype activation. *Journal of Experimental Social Psychology, 32*, 271–288.

Ditto, P. H., & Lopez, D. F. (1992). Motivated skepticism: Use of differential decision criteria for preferred and nonpreferred conclusions. *Journal of Personality and Social Psychology, 63*, 568–584.

Dovidio, J. F., & Gaertner, S. L. (2000). Aversive racism and selection decisions: 1989 and 1999. *Psychological Science, 11*, 319–323.

Dovidio, J. F., Evans, N., & Tyler, R. B. (1986). Racial stereotypes: The contents of their cognitive representations. *Journal of Experimental Social Psychology, 22*, 22–37.

Ekman, P. (1992). *Telling lies: Clues to deceit in the marketplace, marriage, and politics*. New York: W.W. Norton.

Ekman, P., & Friesen, W. V. (1969). Nonverbal leakage and clues to deception. *Psychiatry, 32*, 88–106.

Ekman, P., & Rosenberg, E. L. (Eds.). (2005). *What the face reveals: Basic and applied studies of spontaneous expression using the Facial Action Coding System (FACS)* (2nd ed.). New York: Oxford University Press.

Fehr, E., & Fischbacher, U. (2004). Social norms and human cooperation. *Trends in Cognitive Sciences, 8*(4), 187–190.

Fincham, F. D. (2000). The kiss of the porcupines: From attributing responsibility to forgiving. *Personal Relationships, 7*, 1–23.

Fincham, F. D. (2001). Attributions and close relationships: From balkanization to integration. In G. J. Fletcher & M. Clark (Eds.), *Blackwell handbook of social psychology* (pp. 3–31). Oxford, England: Blackwell.

Fincham, F. D., & Bradbury, T. N. (1992). Assessing attributions in marriage: The relationship attribution measure. *Journal of Personality and Social Psychology, 62*(3), 457–468.

Fincham, F. D., & Jaspars, J. M. (1980). Attribution of responsibility: From man the scientist to man as lawyer. In L. Berkowitz (Ed.), *Advances in experimental social psychology* (Vol. 13, pp.81–138). New York: Academic Press.

Fiske, S. T. (1980). Attention and weight in person perception: The impact of negative and extreme behavior. *Journal of Personality and Social Psychology, 38*, 889–906.

Fiske, S. T., Cuddy, A. J. C., & Glick, P. (2007). First judge warmth, then competence: Fundamental social dimensions. *Trends in Cognitive Sciences, 11*, 77–83.

Fiske, S. T., Cuddy, A. J. C., Glick, P., & Xu, J. (2002). A model of (often mixed) stereotype content: Competence and warmth respectively follow from perceived status and competition. *Journal of Personality and Social Psychology, 82*, 878–902.

Fiske, S. T., & Neuberg, S. L. (1990). A continuum model of impression formation, from category based to individuating processes: Influences of information and motivation on attention and interpretation. In M. P. Zanna (Ed.), *Advances in experimental social psychology* (Vol. 23, pp. 1–74). New York: Academic Press.

Galinsky, A. D., & Moskowitz, G. B. (2000). Perspective taking: Decreasing stereotype expression, stereotype accessibility and in-group favoritism. *Journal of Personality and Social Psychology, 78*, 708–724.

Gilbert, D. T. (1989). Thinking lightly about others: Automatic components of the social inference process. In J. S. Uleman, & J. A. Bargh (Eds.), *Unintended thought* (pp. 189–211). New York: Guilford Press.

Gilbert, D. T. (1998). Ordinary personology. In D. T. Gilbert, S. T. Fiske, & G. Lindzey (Eds.), *The handbook of social psychology* (4th ed., Vol. 2, pp. 89–150). New York: McGraw-Hill.

Gilbert, D. T., & Malone, P. S. (1995). The correspondence bias. *Psychological Bulletin, 117*, 21–38.

Gilbert, D. T., Pelham, B. W., & Krull, D. S. (1988). On cognitive busyness: When person perceivers meet persons perceived. *Journal of Personality and Social Psychology, 54*, 733–740.

Gill, M. J., & Andreychik, M. R. (2009). Getting emotional about explanations: Social explanations and social explanatory styles as bases of prosocial emotions and intergroup attitudes. *Social and Personality Psychology Compass, 3*(6), 1038–1054.

Gill, M. J., Andreychik, M. R., & Getty, P. D. (in press). More than a lack of control: External explanations can evoke compassion for outgroups by increasing perceptions of suffering (independent of perceived control). *Personality and Social Psychology Bulletin*.

Gopnik, A. (2000). Explanation as orgasm and the drive for causal knowledge: The function, evolution, and phenomenology of the theory formation system. In F. C. Keil & R. A. Wilson (Eds.), *Explanation and cognition* (pp. 299–323). Cambridge, MA: MIT Press.

Hafer, C. L . (2000). Do innocent victims threaten the belief in a just world? Evidence from a modified stroop task. *Journal of Personality and Social Psychology, 79*, 165–173.

Hamilton, D. L., Katz, L. B., & Leirer, V. O. (1980). Cognitive representation of personality impressions: Organizational processes in first impression formation. *Journal of Personality and Social Psychology, 39*, 1050–1063.

Hansen, C. H., & Hansen, R. D. (1988). Finding the face in the crowd: An anger superiority effect. *Journal of Personality and Social Psychology*, *54*(6), 917–924.

Hastie, R., & Kumar, P. A. (1979). Person memory: Personality traits as organizing principles in memory for behavior. *Journal of Personality and Social Psychology*, *37*, 25–38.

Hastorf, A., & Cantril, H. (1954) They saw a game: A case study. *Journal of Abnormal and Social Psychology*, *49*, 129–134.

Haxby, J., Hoffman, E., & Gobbini, M. (2000). The distributed human neural system for face perception. *Trends in Cognitive Sciences*, *4*, 223–233.

Heider, F. (1958). *The psychology of interpersonal relations*. New York: Wiley.

Heider, F. (1994). Social perception and phenomena causality. *Psychological Review*, *51*, 358–374.

Herr, P. M. (1986). Consequences of priming: Judgment and behavior. *Journal of Personality and Social Psychology*, *51*, 1106–1115.

Herr, P. M., Sherman, S. J., & Fazio, R. H. (1983). On the consequences of priming: Assimilation and contrast effects. *Journal of Experimental Social Psychology*, *19*, 323–340.

Higgins, E. T. (1996). Knowledge activation: Accessibility, applicability, and salience. In E. T. Higgins & A.W. Kruglanski (Eds.), *Social psychology: Handbook of basic principles* (pp. 133–168). New York: Guilford Press.

Higgins, E. T., Bargh, J. A., & Lombardi, W. (1985). Nature of priming effects on categorization. *Journal of Experimental Psychology: Learning, Memory, and Cognition*, *11*, 59–69.

Higgins, E. T., Rholes, W. S., & Jones, C. R. (1977). Category accessibility and impression formation. *Journal of Experimental Social Psychology*, *13*, 141–154.

Hong, Y. (1994). Predicting trait versus process inferences: The role of implicit theories. *Dissertation Abstracts International: Section B: The Sciences and Engineering*, *55*(6), 2436.

Ichhesier, G. (1949). *Misunderstandings in human relations: A study of false social perception*. Chicago: University of Chicago Press.

Jacoby, L. L., & Whitehouse, K. (1989). An illusion of memory: False recognition influenced by unconscious perception. *Journal of Experimental Psychology: Learning, Memory, and Cognition*, *20*, 304 317.

Jacoby, L. L., & Whitehouse, K. (1989). An illusion of memory: False recognition influenced by unconscious perception. *Journal of Experimental Psychology: Learning, Memory, and Cognition*, *20*, 304 317.

James, W. (1890/1950). *The principles of psychology* (Vols. 1 & 2). New York: Dover.

Jones, E. E. (1979). The rocky road from acts to dispositions. *American Psychologist*, *34*, 107–117.

Jones, E. E., & Davis, K. E. (1965). From acts to dispositions: The attribution process in person perception. In L. Berkowitz (Ed.), *Advances in experimental social psychology* (Vol. 2, pp. 219–266). New York: Academic Press.

Jones, E. E., & Harris, V. A. (1967). The attribution of attitudes. *Journal of Experimental Social Psychology*, *3*, 1–24.

Kanwisher, N. (2000) Domain specificity in face perception. *Nature Neuroscience*, *3*(8) 759–763

Kelley, H. H. (1972). Attribution in social interaction. In E. E. Jones, D. E. Kanouse, H. H. Kelley, R. E. Nisbett, S. Valens, & B. Weiner (Eds.), *Attribution: Perceiving the causes of behavior* (pp. 1–26). Morristown, NJ: General Learning Press.

Kelley, H. H. (1973). Processes of causal attribution. *American Psychologist*, *28*, 107–128.

Kenny, D. A. (1994). *Interpersonal perception: A social relations analysis*. New York: Guilford Press.

Krull, D. S. (1993). Does the grist change the mill?: The effect of the perceiver's inferential goal on the process of social inference. *Personality and Social Psychology Bulletin*, *19*(3), 340–348.

Kunda, Z. (1987). Motivated inference: Self-serving generation and evaluations of causal theories. *Journal of Personality and Social Psychology*, *53*, 636–647.

Kunda, Z., Sinclair, L., & Griffin, D. (1997). Equal ratings but separate meanings: Stereotypes and the construal of traits. *Journal of Personality and Social Psychology*, *72*(4), 720–734.

Kunda, Z., & Thagard, P. (1996). Forming impressions from stereotypes, trait, and behaviors: A parallel constraint satisfaction theory. *Psychological Review*, *103*, 284–308.

Leander, N. P., Moore, S. M., & Chartrand, T. L. (2009). Mystery moods: Their origins and consequences. In G. Moskowitz & H. Grant (Eds.), *The psychology of goals* (pp. 480–504). New York: Guilford Press.

Lerner, M. J., & Miller, D. T. (1978). Just world research and the attribution process: Looking back and ahead. *Psychological Bulletin*, *85*(5), 1030–1051.

Livingston, R. W., & Brewer, M. B. (2002). What are we really priming? Cue-based versus category-based processing of facial stimuli. *Journal of Personality and Social Psychology*, *82*(1), 5–18.

Locksley, A., Borgida, E., Brekke, N., & Hepburn, C. (1980). Sex stereotypes and social judgment. *Journal of Personality and Social Psychology*, *39*, 821–831.

Macrae, C. N., & Bodenhausen, G. V. (2000). Social cognition: Thinking categorically about others. *Annual Review of Psychology*, *51*, 93–120.

Macrae, C. N., Bodenhausen, G. V., & Milne, A. B. (1995). The dissection of selection in person perception: Inhibitory processes in social stereotyping. *Journal of Personality and Social Psychology*, *69*, 397–407.

Macrae, C. N., Bodenhausen, G. V., Milne, A. B., & Jetten, J. (1994). Out of mind but back in sight: Stereotypes on the rebound. *Journal of Personality and Social Psychology*, *67*(5), 808–817.

Malle, B. F. (2004). *How the mind explains behavior: Folk explanations, meaning, and social interaction*. Cambridge, MA: MIT Press.

Markus, H. (1977). Self-schemata and processing information about the self. *Journal of Personality and Social Psychology*, *35*, 63–78.

Martin, L. L. (1986). Set/reset: Use and disuse of concepts in impression formation. *Journal of Personality and Social Psychology*, *51*, 493–504.

Martin, D., & Macrae, C. N. (2007). A face with a cue: Exploring the inevitability of person categorization. *European Journal of Social Psychology*, *37*(5), 806–816.

McArthur, L. (1981). What grabs you? The role of attention in impression formation and causal attribution. In E. T. Higgins, C. P. Herman, & M. P. Zanna (Eds.), *Social cognition: The Ontario symposium* (Vol. 1, 201–246). Hillsdale, NJ: Erlbaum.

McArthur, L. Z., & Apatow, K. (1983–1984). Impressions of baby-faced adults. *Social Cognition*, *2*, 315–342.

McCullough, M. (2008). *Beyond revenge: The evolution of the forgiveness instinct*. San Francisco: Jossey-Bass.

McKoon, G., & Ratcliff, R. (1986). The automatic activation of episodic information in a semantic memory task. *Journal of Experimental Psychology: Learning, Memory, and Cognition, 12*, 108–115.

Mehrabian, A., & Wiener, M. (1967). Decoding of inconsistent communications. *Journal of Personality and Social Psychology, 6*(1), 109–114.

Menon, T., Morris, M., Chui, C. Y., & Hong, Y. Y. (1999). Culture and the construal of agency: Attribution to individual versus group dispositions. *Journal of Personality and Social Psychology, 76*, 701–717.

Miller, C. T. (1984). Self-schemas, gender, and social comparison: A clarification of the related attributes hypothesis. *Journal of Personality and Social Psychology, 46*, 1222–1228.

Miller, D. T. (1976). Ego involvement and attributions for success and failure. *Journal of Personality and Social Psychology, 34*, 901–906.

Mitchell, J. P., Macrae, C. N., & Gilchrest, I. D. (2002). Working memory and the suppression of reflexive saccades. *Journal of Cognitive Neuroscience, 14*, 95–103.

Molden, D. C., Plaks, J. E., & Dweck, C. S. (2006). "Meaningful" social inferences: Lay theories and inferential processes. *Journal of Experimental Social Psychology, 42*, 738–752.

Morris, M. W., & Peng, K. (1994). Culture and cause: American and Chinese attributions for social and physical events. *Journal of Personality and Social Psychology, 67*, 949–971.

Moskowitz, G. B. (1993). Individual differences in social categorization: The effects of personal need for structure on spontaneous trait inferences. *Journal of Personality and Social Psychology, 65*, 132–142.

Moskowitz, G. B. (2002). Preconscious effects of temporary goals on attention. *Journal of Experimental Social Psychology, 38*, 397–404.

Moskowitz, G. B., Gollwitzer, P. M., Wasel, W., & Schaal, B. (1999). Preconscious control of stereotype activation through chronic egalitarian goals. *Journal of Personality and Social Psychology, 77*, 167–184.

Moskowitz, G. B., & Li, P. (2011). Egalitarian goals trigger stereotype inhibition: A proactive form of stereotype control. *Journal of Experimental Social Psychology, 47*, 103–116.

Moskowitz, G. B., Li, P., Ignarri, C., & Stone, J. (2011). Compensatory cognition associated with egalitarian goals. *Journal of Experimental Social Psychology, 47*, 344–349.

Moskowitz, G. B., Li, P., & Kirk, E. (2004). The implicit volition model: On the preconscious regulation of temporarily adopted goals. In M. Zanna (Ed.), *Advances in experimental social psychology* (Vol. 36, pp. 317–413). San Diego, CA: Academic Press.

Moskowitz, G. B., & Roman, R. J. (1992). Spontaneous trait inferences as self generated primes: Implications for conscious social judgment. *Journal of Personality and Social Psychology, 62*, 728–738.

Moskowitz, G. B., Salomon, A. R., & Taylor, C. M. (2000). Implicit control of stereotype activation through the preconscious operation of egalitarian goals. *Social Cognition, 18*, 151–177.

Moskowitz, G. B., & Skurnik, I. W. (1999). Contrast effects as determined by the type of prime: Trait versus exemplar primes initiate processing strategies that differ in how accessible constructs are used. *Journal of Personality and Social Psychology, 76*, 911–927.

Murphy, S. T., & Zajonc, R. B. (1993). Affect, cognition, and awareness: Affective priming with optimal and suboptimal stimulus exposures. *Journal of Personality and Social Psychology, 64*, 723–739.

Neely, J. H. (1977). Semantic priming and retrieval from lexical memory: Roles of inhibitionless spreading activation and limited-capacity attention. *Journal of Experimental Psychology: General, 106*, 226–254.

Nelson, O. T. (1985). Ebbinghaus's contribution to the measurement of retention: Savings during relearning. *Journal of Experimental Psychology: Learning, Memory and Cognition, 11*(3), 471–479.

Nisbett, R. E., & Wilson, T. D. (1977). Telling more than we can know: Verbal reports on mental processes. *Psychological Review, 84*, 231–259.

Norenzayan, A., Choi, I., & Nisbett, R.E. (2002). Cultural similarities and differences in social inference: Evidence from behavioral predictions and lay theories of behavior. *Personality and Social Psychology Bulletin, 28*, 109–120.

Osgood, C. E., Suci, G. J., & Tannenbaum, P. H. (1957). *The measurement of meaning*. Chicago: University of Illinois Press.

Packer, D. J. (2009). Avoiding groupthink: Whereas weakly identified members remain silent, strongly identified members dissent about collective problems. *Psychological Science, 20*, 546–548.

Plaks, J., Levy, S. R., & Dweck, C. (2009). Lay theories of personality: Cornerstones of meaning in social cognition. *Social and Personality Psychology Compass, 3*, 1069–1081.

Postman, L., Bruner, J. S., & McGinnies, E. (1948). Personal values as selective factors in perception. *Journal of Abnormal and Social Psychology, 43*, 142–154.

Pratto, F., & John, O. (1991). Automatic vigilance: The attention grabbing power of negative social information. *Journal of Personality and Social Psychology, 61*, 380–391.

Rosenberg, S., Nelson, C., & Vivekanathan, P. S. (1968). A multidimensional approach to the structure of personality impressions. *Journal of Personality and Social Psychology, 9*, 283–294.

Roskos-Ewoldsen, D. R., & Fazio, R. H. (1992). On the orienting value of attitudes: Attitude accessibility as a determinant of an object's attraction of visual attention. *Journal of Personality and Social Psychology, 63*, 198–211.

Ross, L. (1977). The intuitive psychologist and his shortcomings: Distortions in the attribution process. In L. Berkowitz (Ed.), *Advances in experimental social psychology* (Vol. 10, pp. 174–221). New York: Academic Press.

Ross, L., Amabile, T. M., & Steinmetz, J. L. (1977). Social roles, social control, and biases in social-perception processes. *Journal of Personality and Social Psychology, 35*, 484–494.

Rothbart, M., Sriram, N., & Davis Stitt, C. (1996). The retrieval of typical and atypical category members. *Journal of Experimental Social Psychology, 32*, 1–29.

Rudman, L. A., & Glick, P. (2001). Prescriptive gender stereotypes and backlash toward agentic women. *Journal of Social Issues, 57*, 743–762.

Rule, N. O., & Ambady, N. (2008). Brief exposures: Male sexual orientation is accurately perceived at 50 ms. *Journal of Experimental Social Psychology, 44*, 1100–1105.

Schwarz, N., Bless, H., Strack, F., Klumpp, G., Rittenauer Schatka, H., & Simons, A. (1991). Ease of retrieval as information: Another look at the availability heuristic. *Journal of Personality and Social Psychology, 61*, 195 202.

Sherman, J. W., & Bessenoff, G. R. (1999). Stereotypes as source monitoring cues: On the interaction bewteen episodic and semantic memory. *Psychological Science, 10*, 100–110.

Sherman, J. W., Lee, A. Y., Bessenoff, G. R., & Frost, L. A. (1998). Stereotype efficiency reconsidered: Encoding flexibility under cognitive load. *Journal of Personality and Social Psychology, 75,* 589–606.

Sicoly, F., & Ross, M. (1977). Facilitation of ego-biased attributions by means of self-serving observer feedback. *Journal of Personality and Social Psychology, 35*(10), 734–741.

Skitka, L. J. (1999). Ideological and attributional boundaries on public compassion: Reactions to individuals and communities affected by a natural disaster. *Personality and Social Psychology Bulletin, 25*(7), 793–808.

Snyder, M. L., & Frankel, A. (1976). Observer bias: A stringent test of behavior engulfing the field. *Journal of Personality and Social Psychology, 34,* 857–864.

Spencer, S. J., Fein, S., Wolfe, C. T., Fong, C., & Dunn, M. A. (1998). Automatic activation of stereotypes: The role of self-image threat. *Personality and Social Psychology Bulletin, 24,* 1139–1152.

Srull, T. K., & Wyer, R. S., Jr. (1979). The role of category accessibility in the interpretation of information about persons: Some determinants and implications. *Journal of Personality and Social Psychology, 37,* 1660–1672.

Srull, T. K., & Wyer, R. S., Jr. (1980). Category accessibility and social perception: Some implications for the study of person memory and interpersonal judgment. *Journal of Personality and Social Psychology, 38,* 841–856.

Stapel, D. A., & Koomen, W. (2001). Let's not forget the past when we go to the future: On our knowledge of knowledge accessibility. In G. B. Moskowitz (Ed.), *Cognitive social psychology: The Princeton symposium on the legacy and future of social cognition* (pp.229–246). Hillsdale, NJ: Erlbaum.

Stevens, L., & Jones, E. E. (1976). Defensive attribution and the Kelley cube. *Journal of Personality and Social Psychology, 34,* 809–820.

Strack, F., & Hannover, B. (1996). Awareness of influence as a precondition for implementing correctional goals. In P. M. Gollwitzer & J. A. Bargh (Eds.), *The psychology of action: Linking cognition and motivation to behavior.* New York: Guilford Press.

Taylor, S. E., &Brown J. D. (1988). Illusion and well being: A social psychological perspective n mental health. *Psychological Bulletin, 103,* 193–210.

Taylor, S. E., & Fiske, S. T. (1978). Salience, attention, and attribution: Top of the head phenomena. In L. Berkowitz (Ed.), *Advances in experimental social psychology* (Vol. 11, pp. 249–288). San Diego, CA: Academic Press.

Tetlock, P. E., Visser, P. S., Singh, R., Polifroni, M., Scott, A., Elson, S. B.,... Rescober, P. (2007). People as intuitive prosecutors: The impact of social-control goals on attributions of responsibility. *Journal of Experimental Social Psychology, 43,* 195–209.

Tiedens, L. Z., &Fragale, A. R. (2003). Power moves: Complementarity in submissive and dominant nonverbal behavior. *Journal of Personality and Social Psychology, 84,* 558–568.

Todorov, A., Mandisodza, A. N., Goren, A., & Hall, C. C. (2005). Inferences of competence from faces predict election outcomes. *Science, 308,* 1623–1626.

Todorov, A., Pakrashi, M., & Oosterhof, N. N. (2009). Evaluating faces on trustworthiness after minimal time exposure. *Social Cognition, 27,* 813–833.

Todorov, A., Said, C. P., Engell, A. D., & Oosterhof, N. N. (2008). Understanding evaluation of faces on social dimensions. *Trends in Cognitive Sciences, 12,* 455–460.

Tomasello, M., Carpenter, M., Call, J., Behne, T., & Moll, H. (2005). Understanding and sharing intentions: The origins of cultural cognition. *Behavioral and Brain Sciences, 28,* 675–735.

Trope, Y. (1986). Identification and inferential processes in dispositional attribution. *Psychological Review, 93,* 239–257.

Trope, Y., & Liberman, A. (1993). The use of trait conceptions to identify other people's behavior and to draw inferences about their personalities. *Personality and Social Psychology Bulletin, 19,* 553–562.

Tulving, E., & Thomson, D. M. (1973). Encoding specificity and retrieval processes in episodic memory. *Psychological Review, 80,* 352–373.

Tversky, A., & Kahneman, D. (1974). Judgment under uncertainty: Heuristics and biases. *Science, 185,* 1124–1131.

Uleman, J. S., & Moskowitz, G. B. (1994). Unintended effects of goals on unintended inferences. *Journal of Personality and Social Psychology, 66,* 490–501.

Uleman, J. S., Newman, L. S., & Moskowitz, G. B. (1996). People as flexible interpreters: Evidence and issues from spontaneous trait inference. In M. Zanna (Ed.), *Advances in experimental social psychology* (Vol. 28, pp. 211–280). San Diego, CA: Academic Press.

Wegener, D. T., & Petty, R. E. (1995). Flexible correction processes in social judgment: The role of naive theories in corrections for perceived bias. *Journal of Personality and Social Psychology, 68,* 36 51.

Wegner, D. M. (1994). Ironic processes of mental control. *Psychological Review, 101,* 34–52.

Wegner, D. M., & Wheatley, T. (1999). Apparent mental causation: Sources of the experience of will. *American Psychologist, 54,* 480–492.

Weiner, B. (1985). "Spontaneous" causal thinking. *Psychological Bulletin, 97,* 74–84.

Weiner, B. (2006). *Social motivation, justice, and the moral emotions: An attributional approach.* Mahwah, NJ: Erlbaum.

Weiner, B., & Kukla, A. (1970). An attributional analysis of achievement motivation. *Journal of Personality and Social Psychology, 15,* 1–20.

Wellman, H. M. (1990). *The child's theory of mind.* Cambridge, MA: Bradford Books/MIT Press.

Wilson, T. D., & Brekke, N. (1994). Mental contamination and mental correction: Unwanted influences on judgments and evaluations. *Psychological Bulletin, 116,* 117–142.

Word, C. O., Zanna, M. P., & Cooper, J. (1974). The nonverbal mediation of self-fulfilling prophecies in interracial interaction. *Journal of Experimental Social Psychology, 10,* 109–120.

Yin, R. K. (1969). Looking at upside-down faces. *Journal of Experimental Psychology, 81,* 141–145

Zebrowitz, L. A., &Montepare, J. M. (2008). Social psychological face perception: Why appearance matters. *Social and Personality Psychology Compass, 2,* 1497–1517.

# Theory of Mind

Dana Samson

**Abstract**

To navigate successfully in the social environment, we need to be able to understand and predict other people's behavior so that we can respond appropriately. One way by which we make sense of other people's behavior is by inferring their mental states (such as what they see, want, know, or think), an ability usually referred to as having and using a Theory of Mind. This chapter will first summarize the classic findings and debates that have shaped our views of Theory of Mind over the past three decades. The chapter will then present a series of recent controversial findings that provide new avenues for understanding how we read other people's minds.

**Key Words:** Theory of Mind, perspective taking, mind reading, mentalizing, mental states, false belief

Imagine yourself sitting at the terrace of a café and looking around while you are waiting for someone. You see passersby and although they may be strangers to you, what they do will probably not appear meaningless. You may see, for example, a man running in the street and there will be certainly several possible stories crossing your mind: He is running late and he wants to catch his train; he just realized that he left an important belonging behind and he runs to get it back before someone takes it away, and so on. We can easily come up with various explanations for people's behavior and these will include what may be going on in the other person's mind such as percepts, feelings, desires, intentions, knowledge, or beliefs. In fact, even when we watch simple geometric shapes moving, we often use words that denote mental states to describe what we see (Heider & Simmel, 1944).

The ability to ascribe mental states to others (and also to oneself) in order to explain and predict behavior is often referred to as Theory of Mind (ToM), a concept that was first popularized with the seminal paper by Premack and Woodruff (1978), in which they discussed whether chimpanzees are capable of

inferring mental states. In this chapter, I will first describe the key findings and theoretical frameworks that have dominated the field of research on ToM for the past three decades. I will then describe some recent findings that invite us to consider mind reading under a different light. Finally, I will sketch some future research directions.

## The Standard View
### Typical Theory of Mind Development

There are already signs very early in life that infants are interested and tuned to animate objects. For example, within the first few months of life, infants show great interest in biological stimuli such as faces (e.g., Johnson, Dziurawiec, Ellis, & Morton, 1991) and biological movement (e.g., Fox & McDaniel, 1982), and they start following other people's gaze direction (e.g., Hood, Willen, & Driver, 1998). At the age of 1 year, infants also already understand some characteristics of animate agents such as the fact that their movements are self-propelled and goal directed (Gergely & Csibra, 2003). For example, if 1-year-old infants are habituated to see an agent jumping over an obstacle to reach an object, they are surprised to see the same agent continuing to jump to reach the object once the obstacle has been removed (Gergely, Nádasdy, Csibra, & Bíró, 1995). However, they are not surprised at all to see the agent moving straight ahead after the obstacle has been removed. These results indicate that by the age of 1, infants interpret actions as goal directed and expect agents to achieve their goal in the most efficient way given the environmental constraints at hand. From the age of 2, children start to show signs of mental state attributions per se. They show signs that they can ascribe to other people mental states that have a direct connection with the external world such as percepts, emotions, and desires (Bartsch & Wellman, 1995; Flavell, Everett, Croft, & Flavell, 1981). For example, Wellman and Woolley (1990) told 2 year-old children a story of a child who is looking for a specific object that could be in one of two locations. In one condition, the story ends with the child going to the location where the object is, successfully finding the object ("Watch, she's looking for her mittens in her backpack. Look. She finds her mittens," experiment 1). In another condition, the story ends with the child going to the location where the object is not ("Watch, she's looking for her horse in the green barn. Look. She doesn't find her horse"). When the 2 year-old children were asked whether the child in the story would be happy or sad, they correctly said that the child would be happy in the former condition where the desire was fulfilled but sad in the latter condition where the desire was not fulfilled. However, something more remarkable happens from the age of 4, when children now start to accurately ascribe "representational" mental states such as beliefs. These are mental states that are meant to represent the external world but do not necessarily match the external world (such as in the case of false beliefs). These mental states allow children to understand, for example, that people may be mistaken or may intentionally deceive. The ability to understand and process representational mental states has been seen as a significant milestone after which the child's ToM becomes more adult-like (Wellman, Cross, & Watson, 2001). Of course, children after the age of 5 still continue to develop their ToM. For example, from the age of 6, children start to correctly ascribe second-order mental states such as second-order beliefs (e.g., *Mary thinks that Peter thinks that*...; Perner & Wimmer, 1985). Children from the age of 6 also start to understand the hidden intention in some forms of social communication such as in the case of irony and double bluff (e.g., Capelli,

Nakagawa, & Madden, 1990). However, the first signs of success in solving first-order belief problems, which appear around the age of 4, are usually seen as the most significant achievement in a child's ToM development.

### The False-Belief Task

Given the importance of the understanding of representational mental states in ToM, it was essential to find a reliable paradigm that would test whether an individual can understand that mental states do not necessarily match the real state of the world. This was achieved with the now classical false-belief paradigm first designed by Wimmer and Perner (1983). In the original version, children were presented with a story along the following lines: Maxi puts his chocolate in the blue cupboard and goes outside to play in the playground. While he is out of the house, his mum takes the chocolate out of the blue cupboard and puts it in the green cupboard. Mum then goes out of the house and Maxi comes back to get his chocolate. The child is then asked which cupboard Maxi will open *first*[1] to get his chocolate: the blue or the green cupboard? Correct belief reasoning consists in inferring that Maxi will open first the blue cupboard,—even though that's not where the chocolate really is-because this is where Maxi last saw the chocolate. It is only from the age of 4 that children reliably give the correct response (Wellman et al., 2001). Three-year-old children do not respond randomly but systematically respond that Maxi will open the green cupboard, a response suggesting that they do not realize that Maxi's belief does not match the real state of the world.

There are several variations of the false-belief paradigm. In some cases, the change of the state of the world consists in the change of the location of an object like in the Maxi story (change of location paradigm), whereas in other variations the content of a box is changed (change of content paradigm) or is unexpected (deceptive box paradigm). In that latter case, children are presented, for example, with a familiar box such as a Smarties box and they are asked what they think is inside the box. Children usually correctly respond that there are chocolates inside. Children are then shown that the box does not contain chocolates but pencils instead. The experimenter then asks what they first thought was inside the box (probing the child to reason about his or her own belief) or what someone else would think is inside the box (Gopnik & Astington, 1988). Across all variations of the false-belief paradigm, the classic finding is that children start to correctly ascribe a false belief to the protagonist or themselves from the age of 4 (Wellman et al., 2001).

Despite its widespread use, the false-belief task has not been without criticism. For example, it has been argued that the task is too complex and that failing on a false-belief task does not necessarily mean that one does not understand beliefs (Bloom & German, 2000). False-belief tasks require keeping track of the different events in the scenario (who did what and who saw what), and simply forgetting one of these events can lead to an incorrect response. Several improvements to the false-belief paradigm have been made over time to deal with this criticism, with researchers reducing unnecessary incidental task demands and controlling for the remaining incidental demands by including control questions that allow researchers to objectively measure whether the individual remembers the crucial elements of the story (e.g., Baron-Cohen, Leslie, & Frith, 1985). Independently of the high incidental demands of false-belief tasks, reasoning about *false* rather than true beliefs also places particular high demands on inhibition, as participants need to resist interference from their own knowledge of the real state of the world. Thus, children may understand the representational nature of belief (they may understand that where people think an object is located is not necessarily where the object really is), but while performing the false-belief task they may not be able to inhibit their knowledge of where the object is located because of insufficient inhibitory abilities (Russell, Saltmarsh, & Hill, 1999).

A second type of criticism that has been put forward is that failing on the false-belief task does not mean that the individual has no ToM at all (Bloom & German, 2000). As described in the previous section, children already show signs that they understand some aspects of other people's mind before they pass the false-belief task. Thus, performance on the false-belief task is not representative of *all* the individual's ToM abilities. Over the years, the false-belief paradigm has lost some of its status of *litmus* test for ToM, but it is still widely used to specifically test the understanding and ability to reason about beliefs.

In addition to the false-belief tasks, researchers have developed other ToM tasks that test for the ability to process complex mental states, and that are particularly suitable for older children and adults. The most popular ones are the Mind in the Eyes test (Baron-Cohen, Wheelwright, Hill, Raste, & Plumb, 2001), where participants have to decode various cognitive and affective mental states from the expression of someone's eyes (e.g., bored, amused); the Strange Stories (Happé, 1994), where participants have to detect the nonliteral meaning of what someone says (e.g., detecting jokes, lies, double bluffs); and the Faux Pas task (Baron-Cohen, O'Riordan, Stone, Jones, & Plaisted, 1999), where participants have to detect that a person's mistake may unintentionally upset another person.

### Atypical Theory of Mind Development

One of the first reports of atypical ToM development came from research that tested children with autism. From the outset, autism has been associated with problems in social interactions, but it was in 1985 that the disorder became linked to a ToM impairment (Baron-Cohen et al., 1985). In their seminal study, Baron-Cohen and collaborators compared performance on a false-belief task between subgroups of high-functioning autistic children, typically developing children, and mentally retarded Down syndrome children. More than 85% of the typically developing children and children with Down syndrome passed the task compared to only 20% of the autistic children. However, as shown by these initial results, it appears that a subset of children with autism (20% in the study above) is able to pass false-belief tasks. It was even shown that some individuals with autism pass second-order false-belief tasks (Bowler, 1992). This observation led to the question of how universal ToM impairments are across children diagnosed with autism and led to the suggestion that children with autism simply show a delay in ToM development (Baron-Cohen, 1989) or that their problem lies more in dealing with the incidental or cognitive control demands of the false-belief task (e.g., Russel et al., 1999). The controversy regarding the universality of ToM impairment in autism remains up to this date. It is also currently debated whether individuals with autism are impaired for less complex mental states than beliefs such as desires and intentions (see, for example, Hamilton, 2009). Perhaps most consistent findings of ToM impairment in autism come from the more complex ToM tasks such as the Mind in the Eyes test, the Strange Stories test, and the Faux Pas test (Baron-Cohen et al., 2001). However, even in those cases it has been shown that the impairment may not be universal (Back, Ropar, & Mitchell, 2007).

Several studies have also raised the possibility that atypical ToM development could be associated with other developmental disorders such as

Williams syndrome (Santos & Deruelle, 2009) or schizophrenia (Sprong, Shothorst, Vos, Hox, & Van Engeland, 2007). In all those cases, there are signs of impaired performance on some ToM tasks, but similar to the literature on ToM and autism, how universal the impairments are across subjects and tasks is still a very debated issue.

## Classic Debates
### HOW DO WE READ OTHER PEOPLE'S MINDS?

It is quite remarkable that we are able to read *other* people's minds, even though we have no direct access to other people's mental states. How do we achieve this? Originally, the dominant view was that we have a folk psychology or theory about how the mind works. The theory would be made of mental state concepts and general principles or rules about the ways in which mental states are related to the external world, the ways in which they are causally linked to one another, and the ways in which they are causally linked to behavior. To explain and predict other people's behavior, we would use our theory to make inferences. To take the example of the false-belief task described earlier (Wimmer & Perner, 1983), we would predict the behavior of Maxi by referring to principles such as "people look for objects where they think the objects are and not where the objects really are; people's belief about the location of an object depends on where they have last seen the object; etc." In fact, the idea that we use a theory to impute mental states to others is what led to the use of the term "*Theory* of Mind" in the first place (Premack & Woodruff, 1978), but this was later more specifically referred to as the "Theory Theory" position (see, for example, Gopnik & Meltzoff, 1997; Gopnik & Wellman, 1992). Nowadays, the term "ToM" is more neutral as to whether imputing mental states requires a theory.

The Theory Theory position was strongly criticized by philosophers and developmental psychologists (e.g., Gordon, 1986; Harris, 1992). The crucial point of disagreement was whether a child or an adult really needs in all cases to invoke a sophisticated theory to impute mental states to other people. The alternative proposal is that we can instead simply put ourselves in the other person's shoes and find out what kind of mental states we would have or what decision we would make if we were in the other person's situation. For example, in the case of Maxi's story, we would pretend that we are Maxi and simulate in our mind (without enacting it) which cupboard we would open if,

like Maxi, we would have put the chocolate in the blue cupboard, then walked outside the room, and finally came back to the room to get the chocolate. This alternative position has been referred to as the Simulation Theory (Goldman, 1992; Gordon, 1986).

Whether it is the Theory-Theory or the Simulation Theory that provides the best account for how we explain and predict other people's behaviors has been and remains a fiercely debated issue (see, for example, the debate in Mind and Language, 1992, volume 7, issues 1 and 2). It has led to the proposal of several variants, including hybrid versions (e.g., Goldman, 2006; Mitchell, Currie, & Ziegler, 2009), or even the claim that the debate may be fruitless as the two positions, in their current versions, cannot be properly put to empirical test by cognitive scientists (Apperly, 2008).

A different approach to explain how we read other people's minds has been to describe the processes involved in terms of an information processing model. An example and probably the most detailed model proposed to date is the one developed by Leslie and collaborators to account for how we reason about people's beliefs and desires (Leslie, Friedman, & German, 2004; Leslie, German, & Polizzi, 2005). The model is based on the principles of selective attention. It incorporates a first component, the Theory of Mind Mechanism, which plays two important roles. First, and particularly important for ToM development, the Theory of Mind Mechanism directs the child's attention to people's mental states so that the child can learn about mental states. Secondly, it plays an important role during online processing of mental states (even in adults) by ascribing by default some specific mental states based on information salience. People's beliefs' are usually true and people most often have a desire to approach objects; thus, these will be the states and actions that the Theory of Mind Mechanism will ascribe by default. In the cases where the mental states ascribed and actions predicted by default are not appropriate, such as in the cases where the other person has a false belief or when a person wants to avoid a certain object, a second component, the Selection Process, will need to intervene to override the default information and select more appropriate alternative options. This Selection Process is thought to be a cognitively effortful process, whereas the Theory of Mind Mechanism is thought to operate in a more automatic fashion.

## HOW DO WE ACCOUNT FOR THE SHIFT IN THEORY OF MIND DEVELOPMENT BETWEEN THE AGES OF 3 AND 5?

The sudden improvement observed between the ages of 3 and 5 when typically developing children start to successfully pass the false-belief task has been seen as a universal milestone in ToM development (Wellman et al., 2001). However, scientists are divided as to what explains the sudden improvement in the child's performance. On the one hand, it has been argued that the transition reflects a radical change in how the child understands how the mind works, a view referred to as the conceptual change position. For example, Wellman (1990) proposed that the change reflects the transition between the use of a theory about desires to the use of a more sophisticated theory that incorporates both beliefs and desires. In a slight variation, Perner (1991) proposed that the transition reflects the acquisition of knowledge about the nature of representations in general (not only mental states but also other forms of representations like photographs, pictures, etc.); in other words, the transition reflects the fact that children start to understand that representations do not necessarily match reality.

Opponents to the conceptual change position argue that children have an understanding of beliefs all along, but what improves between the ages of 3 and 5 is their ability to use that knowledge to make accurate predictions about other people's behavior (Fodor, 1992; Leslie et al., 2005). Children between the ages of 3 and 5 undergo major changes in their language abilities and their abilities to control their thoughts and actions (an ability often denoted by the construct of executive function), which makes them better equipped to deal with complex tasks such as false-belief tasks.

The debate as to whether 3-year-olds' failure in belief reasoning tasks is due to a *competence* or simply a *performance* problem is still open and has been revived recently by the unexpected finding that infants well below the age of 3 can pass some false-belief tasks (see the section on "Signs of Early Theory of Mind Competence in Infants").

## IS THEORY OF MIND UNIQUELY HUMAN?

ToM is seen as a fundamental ability for successful navigation in the social world. However, it is not only humans who live in groups and who show social behaviors such as cooperation, competition, or reciprocity; some nonhuman animals do as well. The critical question is thus whether nonhuman animals also impute mental states during their social interactions and whether they do so in the same way as humans do. In their seminal paper, Premack and Woodruff (1978) showed that chimpanzees took into account the goals and intentions of a human actor and concluded that chimpanzees have a ToM. Subsequent studies not only tested whether chimpanzees can infer goals and intentions (Buttelmann, Carpenter, Call, & Tomasello, 2007) but also whether they can infer percepts, knowledge, and beliefs (Hare, Call, Agnetta, & Tomasello, 2000; Hare, Call, & Tomasello, 2001, 2006). This was tested with ever more elegant experimental paradigms which incorporated situations that are relevant for chimpanzees (e.g., situations where chimpanzees compete for food). The picture that emerged was that chimpanzees can solve ToM problems that require taking into account someone else's goal, intention, percept, and knowledge, though to date there has been no evidence that they can pass a false-belief task (Call & Tomasello, 2008).

Of course, solving a ToM problem is no direct proof that the problem was solved by imputing mental states. This is the core issue of debate. Some researchers have argued that chimpanzees do not impute mental states, and instead use behavioral abstractions to solve ToM problems (Penn & Povinelli, 2007; Povinelli & Vonk, 2003). For example, if chimpanzees prefer to beg for food to a human who is looking at them than to a human who is not looking at them, on the face of it, this could be taken as evidence that chimpanzees can reason about whether the person can or cannot *see* their gesture (imputing a percept to the other person). However, it is possible that the preference for one over the other human simply results from their past experience that a human looking at them more often responded to their food request gestures than a human not looking at them. This would not mean that they construe the humans as *seeing* or *not seeing* their gesture (for a discussion, see Povinelli & Vonk, 2004). On the other hand, other researchers have argued that chimpanzees successfully solve ToM problems in a variety of novel situations, which makes it less likely that they rely on previously learned behavioral abstractions and suggests instead that they know something about mental states (Call & Tomasello, 2008). However, even for those who argue today that chimpanzees have a ToM, the idea is that it would be a different ToM to the one humans have. In particular, chimpanzees would only have knowledge about perceptions and goals but perhaps not about beliefs and desires (Call & Tomasello, 2008; Tomasello, Call, & Hare, 2003).

Researchers have also started to investigate whether the social behaviors observed in other species than chimpanzees reflect the presence of a ToM. For example, researchers have looked at the sophisticated food-caching behavior of some birds (especially birds from the corvids family like crows, magpies, jays). Field observations show that corvids use quite sophisticated strategies to avoid food theft, such as caching only when no other bird is around, caching when the other bird is distracted or its line of sight is obstructed, or even sometimes recaching the food once the observer has left the area. Such behaviors have been confirmed in experimental settings (Clayton, Dally, & Emery, 2007) and suggest that corvids may have at least a rudimentary ToM. But again, it is hard to demonstrate that the birds behave the way they do because they are able to impute mental states to others.

## IS THEORY OF MIND DOMAIN SPECIFIC?

Another question that has interested researchers is whether ToM processes are encapsulated within a cognitive module. This led to a substantial program of research aiming at establishing the degree to which ToM is independent from or dependent on general cognitive processes, in particular language and executive function abilities.

There are several ways in which language and executive function can be related to ToM. First, at the most basic level, language and executive function abilities are necessary to deal with the incidental demands of ToM tasks as they allow remembering and understanding the critical features of a ToM problem without which there would be no input to the mental state inference process. This is not the link of most interest, but it needs to be taken into account so that it can be discounted as a sole explanation for any relation observed between ToM tasks and performance on language and executive function tasks (Apperly, Samson, & Humphreys, 2005).

Secondly, it has been argued that language and executive function play a precursor role for the development of ToM. For example, language has been seen as an important medium for children to learn about mental states from their interactions with adults (Sabbagh & Callanan, 1998). Consistent with this view, it has been shown that language abilities in young typically developing children predict their performance on ToM tasks at on older age (Astington & Jenkins, 1999; de Villiers, &

Pyers, 2002; Ruffman, Slade, Rowlandson, Rumsey, & Garnham, 2003). It has also been shown that deaf children who are raised by nondeaf parents and who, consequently, do not have sign language readily available as an alternative means of communication show a delay in their ToM development (Peterson & Siegal, 1995; Russell et al., 1998).

Executive function, in particular inhibitory control, has also been hypothesized to play a precursor role in ToM development. Being able to disengage from salient information has been seen as critical to learn that other people may have different mental states to oneself, and particularly in the case of representational mental states, to learn that they do not necessarily match the outside world (Carlson & Moses, 2001; Russell, 1996). In line with this claim, it has been shown that children's inhibitory abilities predict how they perform on ToM tasks later in their development (Carlson, Mandell, & Williams, 2004).

Finally, it has been proposed that language and executive function play a more enduring role in the actual process of mental state inference per se, in addition or beyond any scaffolding role in ToM development. In the case of language, it is grammar, and in particular the mastering of embedded clauses, that has received most attention. The verbal expression of someone's representational mental states requires the use of embedded complement clauses such as *Maxi thinks the chocolate is in the blue cupboard*. Being able to process such sentences would not only be critical to learn about representational mental states but also to hold these mental states in mind. In line with this view, it has been shown that children's ability to deal with complement clauses predicts their performance in false-belief tasks (de Villiers & Pyers, 2002). However, recent findings from adults who lost their ability to process complex grammatical structures following brain damage showed that these patients were still able to infer false beliefs (Apperly, Samson, Carroll, Hussain, & Humphreys, 2006; Varley & Siegal, 2000; Varley, Siegal, & Want, 2001), suggesting that the role of grammar may be more crucial in the development of ToM than for mental state processing per se.

In the case of executive function, working memory has been claimed to be essential for holding in mind multiple perspectives, and inhibitory control for disengaging from one's own salient perspective or, in the case of false-belief reasoning, for disengaging from one's knowledge of the real state of the world. There is evidence that children's performance on working memory tasks and their performance on inhibitory tasks correlate with their ability to solve ToM tasks (in particular, false-belief tasks; Carlson, Moses, & Breton, 2002; Sabbagh, Moses, & Shiverick, 2006). Furthermore, there is also evidence that working memory and inhibitory control play a fundamental role in ToM during adulthood. For example, it has been shown that performing a concurrent task which taxes working memory disrupts healthy adults' performance in second-order, false-belief tasks that require dealing with multiple representations (Mckinnon & Moscovitch, 2007). Likewise, it was found that traumatic brain injury patients' performance on working memory tasks predicted the patients' performance on a second-order, false-belief task but not a first-order, false-belief task (Bibby & McDonald, 2005). Furthermore, it has been shown that impaired inhibitory control following brain damage acquired in adulthood was associated with a specific deficit in resisting interference from one's own perspective (Samson, Apperly, Kathirgamanathan, & Humphreys, 2005). So far, these results suggest that even in adults, reasoning about mental states requires executive function abilities, in line with the idea that beyond any scaffolding role during development, working memory and inhibitor control also play an enduring role in ToM reasoning (Apperly, Samson, & Humphreys, 2009).

## New Outlook on Mind Reading
### Signs of Early Theory of Mind Competence in Infants

For more than 25 years, there was a general consensus that children only start to be able to reason about beliefs from around the age of 4 (at best around the age of 3, if the task was sufficiently simplified, e.g., Clements & Perner, 1994). It came thus as a completely unexpected finding that 15-month-old infants are able to detect someone else's false belief (Onishi & Baillargeon, 2005). In the study by Onishi and Baillargeon (2005), infants watched an adult actor placing an object in one of two boxes. A barrier then appeared occluding the view of the adult, and the object was displaced to the other box in full view of the infant (but unbeknown to the actor). The barrier was then removed and the actor reached either to the box where the object really was or to the box where the object was originally (in line with the actor's false belief). Onishi and Baillargeon were interested in the looking patterns of infants. Would infants be more surprised and hence look longer when the adult reaches for the box where the object is not? This would indicate that infants did

not understand that the adult has a false belief and they were thus expecting the adult to reach for the box where the object really is. Or conversely, would infants be more surprised when the adult reaches for where the object really is? This would suggest that infants were expecting the adult to reach for the empty box, in line with the actor's false belief. Strikingly, the results conformed to that latter pattern. Since Onishi and Baillargeon's initial findings, many other studies have elegantly modified complex ToM problems to make them suitable for young infants and showed signs of surprisingly early ToM competence in infants (e.g., Kovacs, Teglas, & Endress, 2010; Sodian, Thoermer, & Metz, 2007; Song & Baillargeon, 2008; Southgate, Senju, & Csibra, 2007; Surian, Caldi, & Sperber, 2007).

On the one hand, the results could be seen as evidence that infants already understand quite complex mental state concepts such as beliefs or at least ignorance (e.g., Csibra & Southgate, 2006; Leslie, 2005; Onishi & Baillargeon, 2005; Southgate et al., 2007; Surian et al., 2007). On the other hand, it is possible that infants did not solve the tasks by imputing mental states. For example, infants may simply have encoded associations between an agent, an object, and a location without any reasoning about mental states. When the actor reaches for the box that contains the object (i.e., the condition that surprised infants in the false-belief condition of Onishi and Baillargeon's study [2005]), the actor's behavior would violate a previously encoded association between the agent, the object, and its location. Increased looking time would simply result from the detection of this new association and from the encoding of the new three-way association in memory (Perner & Ruffman, 2005). Alternatively, infants may be using behavioral rules or behavioral abstractions, such as "agents return to objects where they looked at them." Increased looking time would then simply reflect the infants' surprise at the nonfulfillment of the rule (Ruffman & Perner, 2005; see also Penn & Povinelli, 2007). This debate is very far from being resolved and highlights the same difficulty in interpreting the results as in animal research (see the section on "Is Theory of Mind Uniquely Human?"): Does solving a ToM problem really mean that the problem was solved by imputing mental states?

### Easy and Hard Theory of Mind Problems for Adults

When presented with the classic false-belief paradigm, adults usually give the correct response, and thus for many years, investigating ToM in adults did not seem to be a fruitful avenue to pursue. In parallel streams of research, however, social psychologists had already described biases in adults' reasoning which gave clear signs that adults are not always accurate in daily life situations when they read other people's minds. For example, it has been well documented that adults tend to overestimate the extent to which other people share their own beliefs, attitudes, or feelings (i.e., *the false-consensus effect*, Ross, Greene, & House, 1977). Adults also tend to overestimate the ease with which their own mental states (such as the fact that they lie) are detectable by others (*the illusion of transparency effect*, Gilovich, Savitsky, & Medvec, 1998). However, it is only recently that researchers started to develop new methods to investigate the limits of adults' performance in *ToM tasks*. For example, instead of simply recording a pass or fail to a ToM problem, researchers started to use parametric measures (reaction time, error rate, probability estimates) over a series of trials. Furthermore, adults started to be tested under time pressure in situations that better match the demands of online mental state processing in daily life situations.

Equipped with better tasks, researchers started to show that although adults have presumably reached the end point of ToM development, their performance on ToM tasks is not flawless. In false-belief tasks, for example, adults show difficulties in resisting interference from their knowledge of the real state of the world (Birch & Bloom, 2007). Even simply holding in mind a false belief has been shown to be cognitively costly for adults (Apperly, Back, Samson, & France, 2008). In fact, inferring someone else's belief does not seem to be an activity that adults engage in automatically (Apperly, Riggs, Simpson, Chiavarino, & Samson, 2006), consistent with the idea that using one's ToM recruits effortful processes.

It is not only false-belief reasoning that is hard; even taking into account someone else's visual perspective during conversations is not so easy for adults. In one study (Keysar, Barr, Balin, & Brauner, 2000), adults were asked to follow the instructions of another person (referred to as the Director). The Director would ask the participant to move objects around a grid that was placed between them. The critical feature of the grid was that although all the objects in it were visible to the participant, some of these objects were not visible to the Director (some cells were closed on the side of the Director so that he could not see the content of those cells). Participants

were made fully aware of this feature, and the question was whether they would take this into account in their online processing of what the Director says. On a critical trial, for example, the grid would contain, among other items, three similar objects of different sizes (a small candle, a medium size candle, and a large candle). All the objects would be visible to the participant, but the smallest object would not be visible to the Director. The director would then ask to move the "small candle," an utterance referring in fact to the medium size candle from the participant's perspective. The recording of the eye movements while participants were listening to the Director showed that participants first looked at the object that the Director could not see (the small object from the participant's perspective rather than the small object from the Director's perspective). Furthermore, in 20% of the cases, participants even reached out toward that object without realizing that this was not the object meant by the Director. Thus, these results show that even for adults who have a fully developed ToM, it is not that easy to use one's ToM in online processing.

Another line of research highlighted circumstances in which it was very easy for adults to take into account someone else's perspective (Samson, Apperly, Braithwaite, Andrews, & Bodley Scott, 2010). Adults were presented with the picture of a room with red discs pinned on the wall and a person in the middle of the room facing either the left or the right wall. On half of the trials, the person in the picture could see the same discs as the participants (consistent perspective condition), but on the other half of the trials, the person in the picture could not see some of the discs that were visible to the participants (inconsistent perspective condition). When participants were asked to judge how many discs they could see in the room (a question that should be trivial), participants were affected by what the person in the picture could see: They were slower and more error prone in the inconsistent perspective condition. It seems that adults automatically computed what the person in the picture could see even when it was not necessary to do so, and even when it had detrimental effects on the task performance. In the same study, when comparing the ease with which participants judged the person's perspective compared to their own perspective, it appeared that (in some conditions at least), participants found it even easier to judge the person's perspective then their own perspective.

Thus, in line with the paradoxical findings in children where some false-belief tasks are only reliably passed by children from the age of 4 whereas other false-belief tasks seem to be solved successfully by young infants, findings from studies with adults point to two classes of ToM problems, some that are effortful to solve and some that are solved more automatically (Samson & Apperly, 2010).

## The Neural Basis of Mind Reading

While paradoxical findings emerged from behavioral studies investigating ToM abilities in infants and adults, neuroscientists started to unravel the neural substrate of mind reading. Two main lines of research were undertaken in parallel.

The first line of research highlighted brain regions that are activated when we simply watch biologically meaningful stimuli without necessarily engaging in mental state reasoning. Some of these brain areas, in particular the superior temporal sulcus, have been shown to play a critical role in recognizing biological cues that signal where someone is attending, such as gaze or head direction (for a review, see Allison, Puce, & McCarthy, 2000). Other areas are activated both during the execution and the observation of actions and seem to provide a means by which we can process in a fine-grained manner the other person's action as if we were performing the action ourselves. This is the so-called mirror neuron system, first discovered in monkeys (Di Pellegrino, Fadiga, Fogassi, Gallese, & Rizzolatti, 1992) and which in humans includes the inferior frontal gyrus and the inferior parietal lobule (Rizzolatti & Craighero, 2004). These areas may be the neural basis for low-level mechanisms that, in simple situations, may provide very quickly and efficiently useful information about what the other person is seeing and what he or she wants to do.

The second line of research investigated more directly the brain areas recruited when we impute mental states to other people. Over the years, researchers have used a variety of tasks to investigate with various neuroimaging techniques which areas of the brain are activated when healthy adults reason about mental states. The tasks used include, for example, classic false-belief tasks (Saxe & Kanwisher, 2003), more complex stories such as the Strange Stories (Fletcher et al., 1995; Gallagher et al., 2000), watching moving geometrical shapes (Castelli, Happé, Frith, & Frith, 2000), or playing a competitive game against someone else (Gallagher, Jack, Roepstorff, & Frith, 2002). These different studies have highlighted a similar network of brain areas associated with ToM (sometimes referred to as the "ToM network"), including the medial prefrontal cortex, the temporo-parietal junction, and the temporal poles (for a review, see Carrington & Bailey, 2009; Frith & Frith, 2003). There are several hypotheses regarding the role of the medial prefrontal cortex. Some authors have suggested that this region plays a role in processing more enduring social information than transient mental states such as personality traits (Van Overwalle, 2009). Other authors proposed that this region may process the behavioral or emotional consequences of the protagonists' mental states (e.g., Aichhorn, Perner, Kronbichler, Staffen, & Ladurner, 2006). More recently, it has been proposed that the medial prefrontal cortex is involved in generating possible hypotheses about what is going on in the other person's mind when the situation is ambiguous (perhaps by referring to one's own experiences, e.g., Jenkins & Mitchell, 2010). There is also some debate about the role of the left and the right temporo-parietal junction. Both regions have been found to be more activated when adults reason about mental states than when they reason about other social or human aspects (Saxe & Powell, 2006). It has been proposed that the role of the right temporo-parietal junction is specific to mental states, whereas the left temporo-parietal junction would process both social and nonsocial representations of the world (Aichhorn et al., 2009; but see Decety & Lamm, 2007, for an alternative hypothesis). Finally, as regards the temporal poles, it has been proposed that these regions are involved in the retrieval of social conceptual knowledge (Frith & Frith, 2003; Ross & Olson, 2010).

Neuropsychological studies have looked at the impact of various brain lesions on ToM and showed that lesions to the prefrontal cortex (e.g., Lough et al., 2006; Rowe, Bullock, Polkey, & Morris, 2001; Stone, Baron-Cohen, & Knight, 1998; but for evidence against the necessary role of the prefrontal cortex, see Bird, Castelli, Malik, Frith, & Husain, 2004) and to the temporo-parietal junction (Samson, Apperly, Chiavarino, & Humphreys, 2004) affected patients' ability to reason about mental states. There are signs, however, that, depending on the location of the brain lesion, different aspects of ToM may be affected (Samson, 2009). For example, it has been shown that a lesion to the right lateral prefrontal cortex impacts on the patient's ability to resist interference from his own perspective (Samson et al., 2005; Samson, Apperly, & Humphreys, 2007). In contrast, a lesion to the temporo-parietal junction affects the patient's ability to pay attention to the objects and events in the environment that are relevant for inferring someone's mental state (Samson et al., 2007). In both cases, it was shown that the patients still had ToM concepts, but that they were unable to use these efficiently in some situations, either because they lacked the cognitive resources to inhibit their own perspective or because they lacked the resources to monitor the external world for relevant cues (Samson, 2009).

Thus, collectively, the evidence from neuroscience points to some brain areas which underpin low-level mechanisms that can provide useful information when we read other people's minds (e.g., the mirror neuron system) and other areas which sustain mental state reasoning per se (the ToM network). Researchers have only just begun to investigate the specific roles played by the different areas within the ToM network.

## The New Picture Arising

There seem to be various routes available to humans to read other people's minds. One type of route seems to make mind reading effortless and efficient, and it appears to be available even to young infants. However, efficiency usually comes at the cost of flexibility, and it is therefore likely that this route can only operate efficiently in specific contexts—for example, when there is a limited amount of information to process or when the relevant information is very salient (Apperly & Butterfill, 2009). It is worthwhile noting that the studies showing early competence in infancy (e.g., Onishi & Baillargeon, 2005) or automatic perspective-taking processes in adults (Samson et al., 2010) used purified tasks with little irrelevant information. These may be precisely the type of situations where a low-level mind-reading route can be used. However, it is hard to determine whether this type of processing route truly processes *mental states*.

In addition to low-level mind-reading routes, humans are able to use a more sophisticated route that allows them to navigate more flexibly in the social world and to infer much richer content to other people's mental states. This is the route that has been more traditionally associated with ToM and that truly processes *mental states*. The price to pay for the flexibility of this mind-reading route is that its use (and possibly its development) relies on more cognitively effortful processes which are only available to older children and perhaps only humans.

## Conclusion

Our ability to explain and predict other people's behavior plays a fundamental role in our social interactions and has been receiving increasing attention from developmental psychologists, comparative psychologists, philosophers, linguists, and cognitive (neuro)scientists. Much of the research in the past three decades has concentrated on one way in which we explain and predict behavior, namely by inferring the other person's mental states, an ability referred to as using a *Theory of Mind*. This has led to a fruitful program of research in which researchers investigated, among other issues, when and how children acquire a ToM and whether nonhuman species have a ToM. Central to the cognitive sciences is also the question of how we should describe the collection of processes recruited when we reason about mental states and how these processes are related to language and executive function. The first answers to these questions have consisted of a broad description of the type of computation that would be required to infer someone else's mental state, with the opposing views between those who have argued that we use a theory (e.g., the Theory Theory position) and those who have argued that we simply put ourselves in the other person's shoes (the Simulation Theory position). In parallel to this mainly theoretical debate, evidence from children, healthy adults, and adults with brain damage have highlighted that there is more to ToM than having ToM concepts (Apperly et al., 2009; Samson, 2009; Samson & Apperly, 2010), and that there are probably a collection of diverse and quite effortful processes that are necessary to implement ToM concepts in online reasoning about mental states. Unraveling these processes and describing them in terms of an information processing model is a task that has only just begun.

Ascribing mental states is one way in which we can explain and predict other people's behavior, but this is perhaps not the only way. While looking into how ToM could be tested in nonhuman animals and infants, researchers started to move away from complex and verbal tasks, and found that mind reading may be surprisingly easy for very young infants and nonhuman species. It is still unclear whether the newly developed ToM tasks really require inferring mental states to be solved, but at the very least they have shown that mind reading does not always rely on effortful mental state reasoning, and that instead there may be more low-level, mind-reading routes available to us, even as adults (Apperly & Butterfill, 2009; Samson et al., in press).

## Future Directions

There are many exciting years ahead of cognitive scientists as there is a need for a much more fine-grained cognitive approach to the study of ToM and mind reading. Here, I will sketch some of the broad and most pressing questions that will need to be addressed.

(1) Reasoning about mental states or ToM is not seen as a unitary function anymore. What are the dimensions that are relevant to separate out the building blocks of this ability? What are the common and unique processes recruited across the different types of mental states (e.g., percepts, intentions, desires, knowledge, beliefs)?

(2) It appears that mind reading can be achieved without engaging in complex mental state reasoning. What are the alternative routes that we use? What is the scope of ToM problems that can be solved with these routes? What cues in the environment do these mind-reading routes respond to? How rich is the information extracted? Are the underlying processes the same in infants and adults as well as across animal species or are these low-level processes shaped by the cognitive apparatus of the mind reader?

(3) Older children and adults seem to have available to them both the more effortful mind-reading route (traditionally referred to as ToM) and the alternative low-level, mind-reading routes. How separate are these two types of routes? If they interact with one another, what are the points of contact?

## Note

1. In the original study, the question did not include the word "first." This made the question pragmatically ambiguous and subsequent studies showed that the inclusion of the word "first" allowed for a more reliable assessment of a child's understanding of beliefs (e.g., Siegal & Beattie, 1991).

## References

Aichhorn, M., Perner, J., Kronbichler, M., Staffen, W., & Ladurner, G. (2006). Do visual perspective tasks need theory of mind? *NeuroImage, 30*, 1059–1068.

Aichhorn, M., Perner, J., Weiss, B., Kronbichler, M., Staffen, W., & Ladurner, G. (2009). Temporo-parietal junction activity in theory-of-mind tasks: Falseness, beliefs, or attention. *Journal of Cognitive Neuroscience, 21*, 1179–1192.

Allison, T., Puce, A., & McCarthy, G. (2000). Social perception from visual cues: Role of the STS region. *Trends in Cognitive Sciences, 4*, 267–278.

Apperly, I. A. (2008). Beyond simulation–theory and theory–theory: Why social cognitive neuroscience should use its own concepts to study "theory of mind." *Cognition, 107*, 266–283.

Apperly, I. A., Back, E., Samson, D., & France, L. (2008). The cost of thinking about false beliefs: Evidence from adults' performance on a non-inferential theory of mind task. *Cognition, 106*, 1093–1108.

Apperly, I. A., & Butterfill, S. A. (2009). Do humans have two systems to track beliefs and belief-like states? *Psychological Review, 116(4)*, 953–970.

Apperly, I. A., Riggs, K. J., Simpson, A., Chiavarino, C., & Samson, D. (2006). Is belief reasoning automatic? *Psychological Science, 17*, 841–844.

Apperly, I. A., Samson, D., Carroll, N., Hussain, S., & Humphreys, G. (2006). Intact first- and second-order false belief reasoning in a patient with severely impaired grammar. *Social Neuroscience, 1*, 334–348.

Apperly, I. A., Samson, D., & Humphreys, G. W. (2005). Domain-specificity and theory of mind: Evaluating neuropsychological evidence. *Trends in Cognitive Sciences, 9*, 572–577.

Apperly, I. A., Samson, D., & Humphreys, G. W. (2009). Studies of adults can inform accounts of theory of mind development. *Developmental Psychology, 45*, 190–201.

Astington, J. W., & Jenkins, J. M. (1999). A longitudinal study of the relation between language and theory-of-mind development. *Developmental Psychology, 35*, 1311–1320.

Back, E., Ropar, D., & Mitchell, P. (2007). Do the eyes have it? Inferring mental states from animated faces in autism. *Child Development, 78(2)*, 397–411.

Baron-Cohen, S. (1989). The autistic child's theory of mind—a case of specific developmental delay. *Journal of Child Psychology and Psychiatry and Allied Disciplines, 30*, 285–297.

Baron-Cohen, S., Leslie, A. M., & Frith, U. T. (1985). Does the autistic child have a "theory of mind"? *Cognition, 21*, 37–46.

Baron-Cohen, S., O'Riordan, M., Stone, V., Jones, R., & Plaisted, K. (1999). Recognition of faux pas by normally developing children and children with Asperger syndrome or high-functioning autism. *Journal of Autism and Developmental Disorders, 29(5)*, 407–418.

Baron-Cohen, S., Wheelwright, S., Hill, J., Raste, Y., & Plumb, I. (2001). The "reading the mind in the eyes" test revised version: A study with normal adults, and adults with Asperger syndrome or high-functioning autism. *Journal of Child Psychology and Psychiatry, 42(2)*, 241–251.

Bartsch, K., & Wellman, H. M. (1995). *Children talk about the mind.* New York: Oxford University Press.

Bibby, H., & McDonald, S. (2005). Theory of mind after traumatic brain injury. *Neuropsychologia, 43(1)*, 99–114.

Birch, S. A. J., & Bloom, P. (2007). The curse of knowledge in reasoning about false beliefs. *Psychological Science, 18*, 382–386.

Bird, C. M., Castelli, F., Malik, O., Frith, U., & Husain, M. (2004). The impact of extensive medial frontal lobe damage on "theory of mind" and cognition. *Brain, 127*, 914–928.

Bloom, P., & German, T. P. (2000). Two reasons to abandon the false belief task as a test of theory of mind. *Cognition, 77*, 25–31.

Bowler, D. M. (1992). Theory of mind in aspergers syndrome. *Journal of Child Psychology and Psychiatry and Allied Disciplines, 33(5)*, 877–893.

Buttelmann, D., Carpenter, M., Call, J., & Tomasello, M. (2007). Enculturated chimpanzees imitate rationally. *Developmental Science, 10*, F31–F38.

Call, J., & Tomasello, M. (2008). Does the chimpanzee have a theory of mind? 30 years later. *Trends in Cognitive Sciences, 12(5)*, 187–192.

Capelli, C. A., Nakagawa, N., & Madden, C. M. (1990). How children understand sarcasm—the role of context and intonation. *Child Development, 61*, 1824–1841.

Carlson, S. M., Mandell, D. J., & Williams, L. (2004). Executive function and theory of mind: Stability and prediction from ages 2 to 3. *Developmental Psychology, 40,* 1105–1122.

Carlson, S. M., & Moses, L. J. (2001). Individual differences in inhibitory control and children's theory of mind. *Child Development, 72,* 1032–1053.

Carlson, S. M., Moses, L. J., & Breton, C. (2002). How specific is the relation between executive function and theory of mind? Contributions of inhibitory control and working memory. *Infant and Child Development, 11,* 73–92.

Carrington, S. J., & Bailey, A. J. (2009). Are there theory of mind regions in the brain? A review of the neuroimaging literature. *Human Brain Mapping, 30,* 2313–2335.

Castelli, F., Happé, F., Frith, U., & Frith, C. (2000). Movement and mind: A functional imaging study of perception and interpretation of complex intentional movement patterns. *NeuroImage, 12,* 314–325.

Clayton, N. S., Dally, J. M., & Emery, N. J. (2007). Social cognition by food-caching corvids. The western scrub-jay as a natural psychologist. *Philosophcal Transactions of the Royal Society, Series B: Biological Sciences, 362,* 507–522.

Clements, W. A., & Perner, J. (1994). Implicit understanding of belief. *Cognitive Development, 9,* 377–395.

Csibra, G., & Southgate, V. (2006). Evidence for infants' understanding of false beliefs should not be dismissed. *Trends in Cognitive Sciences, 10,* 4–5.

Decety, J., & Lamm, C. (2007). The role of the right temporoparietal junction in social interaction: How low-level computational processes contribute to meta-cognition. *Neuroscientist, 13*(6), 580–593.

de Villiers, J. G., & Pyers, J. E. (2002). Complements to cognition: A longitudinal study of the relationship between complex syntax and false-belief-understanding. *Cognitive Development, 17,* 1037–1060.

Di Pellegrino, G., Fadiga, L., Fogassi, L., Gallese, V., & Rizzolatti, G. (1992). Understanding motor events: A neurophysiological study. *Experimental Brain Research, 91,* 176–80.

Flavell, J. H., Everett, B. A., Croft, K., & Flavell, E. R. (1981). Young children's knowledge about visual perception: Further evidence for the level 1-level 2 distinction. *Developmental Psychology, 17*(1), 99–103.

Fletcher, P. C., Happé, F., Frith, U., Baker, S. C., Dolan, R. J., Frackowiak, R. S., & Frith, C. D . (1995). Other minds in the brain: A functional imaging study of "theory of mind" in story comprehension. *Cognition, 57,* 109–128.

Fodor, J. A. (1992). A theory of the child's theory of mind. *Cognition, 44,* 283–296.

Fox, R., & McDaniel, C. (1982). Perception of biological motion by human infants. *Science, 218,* 486–487.

Frith, U., & Frith, C. D. (2003). Development and neurophysiology of mentalizing. *Philosophical Transactions of the Royal Society of London, Series B: Biological Sciences, 358,* 459–473.

Gallagher, H. L., Happé, F., Brunswick, N., Fletcher, P. C., Frith, U., & Frith, C. D. (2000). Reading the mind in cartoons and stories: An fMRI study of `theory of mind' in verbal and nonverbal tasks. *Neuropsychologia, 38,* 11–21.

Gallagher, H. L., Jack, A. I., Roepstorff, A., & Frith, C. D. (2002). Imaging the intentional stance in a competitive game. *NeuroImage, 16,* 814–821.

Gergely, G., & Csibra, G. (2003). Teleological reasoning in infancy: The naïve theory of rational action. *Trends in Cognitive Sciences, 7,* 287–292.

Gergely, G., Nádasdy, Z., Csibra, G., & Bíró, S. (1995). Taking the intentional stance at 12 months of age. *Cognition, 56,* 165–193.

Gilovich, T., Savitsky, K., & Medvec, V. H. (1998). The illusion of transparency: Biased assessments of others ability to read our emotional states. *Journal of Personality and Social Psychology, 75,* 332–346.

Goldman, A. (1992). In defense of the simulation theory. *Mind and Language, 7,* 104–119.

Goldman, A., (2006). *Simulating minds: The philosophy, psychology, and neuroscience of mind reading.* Oxford, England: Oxford University Press.

Gopnik, A., & Astington, J.W. (1988). Children's understanding of representational change and its relation to the understanding of false beliefs and the appearance-reality distinction. *Child Development, 59,* 26–37.

Gopnik, A., & Meltzoff, A. (1997). *Words, thoughts and theories.* Cambridge, MA: MIT Press.

Gopnik, A., & Wellman, H. (1992). Why the child's theory of mind really is a theory. *Mind and Language, 7,* 145–171.

Gordon, R. (1986). Folk psychology as simulation. *Mind and Language, 1,* 158–170.

Hamilton, A. F. de C. (2009). Research review: Goals, intentions and mental states: Challenges for theories of autism. *Journal of Child Psychology and Psychiatry, 8,* 881–892.

Happé, F. (1994). An advanced test of theory of mind: Understanding of story characters' thoughts and feelings by able autistic, mentally handicapped, and normal children and adults. *Journal of Autism and Developmental Disorders, 24*(2), 129–154.

Hare, B., Call, J., Agnetta, B., & Tomasello, M. (2000). Chimpanzees know what conspecifics do and do not see. *Animal Behaviour, 59,* 771–785.

Hare, B., Call, J., & Tomasello, M. (2001). Do chimpanzees know what conspecifics know? *Animal Behaviour, 61,* 139–151.

Hare, B., Call, J., & Tomasello, M. (2006). Chimpanzees deceive a human competitor by hiding. *Cognition, 101,* 495–514.

Harris, P. (1992). From simulation to folk psychology: The case for development. *Mind and Language, 7,* 120–144.

Heider, F., & Simmel, M. (1944). An experimental study of apparent behavior. *American Journal of Psychology, 57,* 243–259.

Hood, B. M., Willen, J. D., & Driver, J. (1998). Adult's eyes trigger shifts of visual attention in human infants. *Psychological Science, 9*(2), 131–134.

Jenkins, A. C., & Mitchell, J. P. (2010). Mentalizing under uncertainty: Dissociated neural responses to ambiguous and unambiguous mental state inferences. *Cerebral Cortex, 20,* 404–410.

Johnson, M. H., Dziurawiec, S., Ellis, H., & Morton, J. (1991). Newborns' preferential tracking of face-like stimuli and its subsequent decline. *Cognition, 40,* 1–19.

Keysar, B., Barr, D. J., Balin, J. A., & Brauner, J. S. (2000). Taking perspective in conversation: The role of mutual knowledge in comprehension. *Psychological Science, 11,* 32–38.

Kovacs, A. M., Teglas, E., & Endress, A. D. (2010). The social sense: Susceptibility to others' beliefs in human infants and adults. *Science, 330*(6012), 1830–1834.

Leslie, A. M. (2005). Developmental parallels in understanding minds and bodies. *Trends in Cognitive Sciences, 9,* 459–462.

Leslie, A. M., Friedman, O., & German, T. P. (2004). Core mechanisms in "theory of mind." *Trends in Cognitive Sciences*, 8(12), 528–533.

Leslie, A. M., German, T. P., & Polizzi, P. (2005). Belief-desire reasoning as a process of selection. *Cognitive Psychology*, 50, 45–85.

Lough, S., Kipps, C. M., Treise, C., Watson, P., Blair, J. R., & Hodges, J. R. (2006). Social reasoning, emotion and empathy in frontotemporal dementia. *Neuropsychologia*, 44, 950–958.

Mckinnon, M. C., & Moscovitch, M. (2007). Domain-general contributions to social reasoning: Theory of mind and deontic reasoning re-explored. *Cognition*, 102, 179–218.

Mitchell, P., Currie, G., & Ziegler, F. (2009). Two routes to perspective: Simulation and rule-use as approaches to mentalizing. *British Journal of Developmental Psychology*, 27, 513–543.

Onishi, K. H., & Baillargeon, R. (2005). Do 15-month-old infants understand false beliefs? *Science*, 308, 255–258.

Penn, D. C., & Povinelli, D. J. (2007). On the lack of evidence that non-human animals possess anything remotely resembling a "theory of mind." *Philosophical Transactions of the Royal Society, Series B: Biological Sciences*, 362, 731–744.

Perner, J. (1991). *Understanding the representational mind*. Cambridge, MA: MIT Press.

Perner, J., & Ruffman, T. (2005). Infants' insight into the mind: How deep? *Science*, 308, 214–216.

Perner, J., & Wimmer, H. (1985). "John thinks that Mary thinks that . . ." Attribution of second-order beliefs by 5- to 10-year-old children. *Journal of Experimental Child Psychology*, 39, 437–471.

Peterson, C. C., & Siegal M. (1995). Deafness, conversation and theory of mind. *Journal of Child Psychology and Psychiatry*, 36, 459–474.

Povinelli, D. J., & Vonk, J. (2003). Chimpanzee minds: Suspiciously human? *Trends in Cognitive Sciences*, 7, 157–160.

Povinelli, D. J., & Vonk, J. (2004). We don't need a microscope to explore the chimpanzee's mind. *Mind and Language*, 19, 1–28.

Premack, D., & Woodruff, G. (1978). Does the chimpanzee have a theory of mind. *Behavioral and Brain Sciences*, 4, 515–526.

Rizzolatti, G., & Craighero, L. (2004). The mirror-neuron system. *Annual Review of Neuroscience*, 27, 169–192.

Ross, L., Greene, D., & House, P. (1977). The false consensus effect: An egocentric bias in social perception and attribution processes. *Journal of Experimental Social Psychology*, 13, 279–301.

Ross, L. A., & Olson, I. R. (2010). Social cognition and the anterior temporal lobes. *NeuroImage*, 49, 3452–3462.

Rowe, A. D., Bullock, P. R., Polkey, C. E., & Morris, R. G. (2001). "Theory of mind" impairments and their relationship to executive functioning following frontal lobe excisions. *Brain*, 124, 600–616.

Ruffman, T., & Perner, J. (2005). Do infants really understand false belief? *Trends in Cognitive Sciences*, 9, 462–463.

Ruffman, T., Slade, L., Rowlandson, K., Rumsey, C., & Garnham, A. (2003). How language relates to belief, desire, and emotion understanding. *Cognitive Development*, 18, 139–158.

Russell, J. (1996). *Agency: Its role in mental development*. Hove, England: Erlbaum.

Russell, P. A., Hosie, J. A., Gray, C. D., Scott, C., Hunter, N., Banks, J. S., & Macaulay, M. C. (1998). The development of theory of mind in deaf children. *Journal of Child Psychology and Psychiatry*, 39, 903–910.

Russell, J., Saltmarsh, R., & Hill, E. (1999). What do executive factors contribute to the failure on false belief tasks by children with autism? *Psychiatry: Interpersonal and Biological Processes*, 40, 859–868.

Sabbagh, M. A., & Callanan, M. A. (1998). Metarepresentation in action: 3-, 4-, and 5-year-olds' developing theories of mind in parent-child conversations. *Developmental Psychology*, 34, 491–502.

Sabbagh, M. A., Moses, L. J., & Shiverick, S. (2006). Executive functioning and preschoolers' understanding of false beliefs, false photographs, and false signs. *Child Development*, 77, 1034–1049.

Samson, D. (2009). Reading other people's mind: Insights from neuropsychology. *Journal of Neuropsychology*, 3, 3–16.

Samson, D. & Apperly, I.A. (2010). There is more to mind reading than having theory of mind concepts: New directions in theory of mind research. *Infant and Child Development*, 19, 443–454.

Samson, D., Apperly, I. A., Braithwaite, J. J., Andrews, B. J., & Bodley Scott, S. E. (2010). Seeing it their way: Evidence for rapid and involuntary computation of what other people see. *Journal of Experimental Psychology: Human Perception and Performance*. doi: 10.1037/a0018729

Samson, D., Apperly, I. A., Chiavarino, C., & Humphreys, G. W. (2004). Left temporoparietal junction is necessary for representing someone else's belief. *Nature Neuroscience*, 7, 499–500.

Samson, D., Apperly, I. A., & Humphreys, G. W. (2007). Error analyses reveal contrasting deficits in "theory of mind": Neuropsychological evidence from a 3-option false belief task. *Neuropsychologia*, 45(11), 2561–2569.

Samson, D., Apperly, I. A., Kathirgamanathan, U., & Humphreys, G. W. (2005). Seeing it my way: A case of a selective deficit in inhibiting self-perspective. *Brain*, 128, 1102–1111.

Santos, A., & Deruelle, C. (2009). Verbal peaks and visual valleys in theory of mind ability in Williams syndrome. *Journal of Autism and Developmental Disorders*, 39, 651–659.

Saxe, R., & Kanwisher, N. (2003). People thinking about thinking people: The role of the temporo-parietal junction in "theory of mind." *NeuroImage*, 19, 1835–1842.

Saxe, R., & Powell, L. J. (2006). It's the thought that counts. Specific brain regions for one component of theory of mind. *Psychological Science*, 17, 692–699.

Siegal, M., & Beattie, K. (1991). Where to look first for children's knowledge of false beliefs. *Cognition*, 38, 1–12.

Sodian, B., Thoermer, C., & Metz, U. (2007). Now I see it but you don't: 14-month-olds can represent another person's visual perspective. *Developmental Science*, 10, 199–204.

Song, H., & Baillargeon, R. (2008). Infants' reasoning about others' false perceptions. *Developmental Psychology*, 44, 1789–1795.

Southgate, V., Senju, A., & Csibra, G. (2007). Action anticipation through attribution of false belief by 2-year-olds. *Psychological Science*, 18, 587–592.

Sprong, M., Schothorst, P., Vos, E., Hox, J., & Van Engeland, H. (2007). Theory of mind in schizophrenia—meta-analysis. *British Journal of Psychiatry*, 191, 5–13.

Stone, V. E., Baron-Cohen, S., & Knight, R. T. (1998). Frontal lobe contributions to theory of mind. *Journal of Cognitive Neuroscience*, 10, 640–656.

Surian, L., Caldi, S., & Sperber, D. (2007). Attribution of beliefs by 13-month-old infants. *Psychological Science*, *18*, 580–586.

Tomasello, M., Call, J., & Hare, B. (2003). Chimpanzees understand psychological states—the question is which ones and to what extent. *Trends in Cognitive Sciences*, *7*(4), 153–156.

Van Overwalle, F. (2009). Social cognition and the brain: A meta-analysis. *Human Brain Mapping*, *30*, 829–858.

Varley, R., & Siegal, M. (2000). Evidence for cognition without grammar from causal reasoning and "theory of mind" in an agrammatic aphasic patient. *Current Biology*, *10*, 723–726.

Varley, R., Siegal, M., & Want, S. C. (2001). Severe impairment in grammar does not preclude theory of mind. *Neurocase*, *7*, 489–493.

Wellman, H. M. (1990). *The child's theory of mind*. Cambridge, MA: MIT Press/ Bradford Books.

Wellman, H. M., Cross, D., & Watson, J. (2001). Meta-analysis of theory-of-mind development: The truth about false belief. *Child Development*, *72*(3), 655–684.

Wellman, H. M., & Woolley, J. D. (1990). From simple desires to ordinary beliefs: The early development of everyday psychology. *Cognition*, *35*, 245–275.

Wimmer, H., & Perner, J. (1983). Beliefs about beliefs: Representation and constraircing function of wrong beliefs in young children's understanding of deception. *Cognition*, *13*, 103–128.

## Further Reading

Apperly, I. A., & Butterfill, S. A. (2009). Do humans have two systems to track beliefs and belief-like states? *Psychological Review, 116(4), 953–970.*

Call, J., & Tomasello, M. (2008). Does the chimpanzee have a theory of mind? 30 years later. *Trends in Cognitive Sciences*, *12*(5), 187–192.

Caron, A. J. (2009). Comprehension of the representation mind in infancy. *Developmental Review*, *29*, 69–95.

Frith, C. D., & Frith, U. (2012). Mechanisms of social cognition. Annual Review of Psychology, 63, 287–313.

Samson, D. & Apperly, I.A. (2010). There is more to mind reading than having theory of mind concepts: New directions in theory of mind research. *Infant and Child Development, 19, 443–454.*

Wellman, H. M., Cross, D., & Watson, J. (2001). Meta-analysis of theory-of-mind development: The truth about false belief. *Child Development*, *72*(3), 655–684.

# Attitude Change

Galen V. Bodenhausen *and* Bertram Gawronski

**Abstract**

The ability to produce meaningful evaluations of the external world (i.e., attitudes) is critical for adaptive functioning. However, to be fully adaptive, such evaluations must be flexible enough to change when circumstances warrant. The psychological processes involved in attitude change have been the subject of intensive investigation for over 50 years. We review the major themes of this literature, paying particular attention to the distinction between explicitly endorsed propositional evaluations and more automatic forms of evaluative response, often referred to as implicit attitudes. In particular, we begin by discussing the precursors of attitudinal stability versus malleability. Next, we review the role of learning in producing attitude change, with a focus on both propositional learning and affective conditioning. We then consider how external constraints on behavior and changes in evaluative context can lead to the modification of attitudes. Finally, we consider the determinants and mechanisms of resistance to attitude change.

**Key Words:** attitudes, evaluation, implicit attitudes, attitude change, persuasion, evaluative conditioning, cognitive dissonance

Arguably, two of the most fundamental and adaptive capacities any agent could possess would be the ability to construct meaningful evaluations of external stimuli (determining which entities are helpful, useful, gratifying, or valuable versus dangerous, confounding, unpleasant, or useless) and the ability to later retrieve or reconstruct these evaluations in the presence of the same or related stimuli. Once activated, such evaluations provide a basis for deciding whether to approach and engage with an entity or to avoid it all costs. These capacities are at the heart of the psychology of attitudes. Of course, environments are dynamic and a given entity's evaluative significance could easily change over time. A person who is helpful at one point in time might prove to be untrustworthy in a subsequent situation. As a result, an adaptive attitude system must be amenable to modification in light of new experiences; attitudes that are characterized by rigid stability run the risk of providing obsolete or overly general behavioral guidance. The processes governing attitude change are the focus of this chapter.

## Automatic Versus Deliberate Evaluation

Historically, the primary focus of attitude research was on deliberate evaluative judgments of the sort that could be verbally reported in interviews and questionnaires. Many hundreds of studies have been conducted on the factors that result in modification of these deliberated expressions of attitudes. Such evaluations consist of assertions about the evaluative properties of a stimulus (e.g., "X is good" or "I like X"), and we refer to them as *propositional evaluations* in light of their explicit, declarative nature. However, in recent years there has been a growing appreciation that evaluative reactions also occur in a more immediate, less deliberate manner (e.g., Petty, Fazio, & Briñol, 2009). Even preverbal infants who are not yet able to make propositional assertions are nevertheless quite capable of learning and expressing evaluations (Hamlin, Wynn, & Bloom, 2007). Whereas propositional evaluations consist of articulated beliefs, these latter, more immediate evaluative responses are more akin to automatic affective reactions toward the attitude object. Drawing on the assumption that these reactions result from the activation of automatic associations, we refer to them as *associative evaluations*. Instead of relying on self-report questionnaires and surveys, the assessment of associative evaluations focuses on performance on a variety of behavioral tasks that are assumed to be influenced by automatic associations (see Gawronski & Payne, 2010). This distinction between associative and propositional evaluations is analogous to the distinction between "alief" and belief in recent philosophy of epistemology (e.g., Gendler, 2008).

The term "automatic" carries multiple implications, including rapidity, spontaneity, efficiency, and uncontrollability (see Moors & De Houwer, 2006). It is also often taken to imply that a process is implicit or introspectively unavailable. The causes and consequences of associative evaluations may indeed often remain introspectively unidentified or misidentified, but assertions that associative evaluations per se are commonly unconscious remain controversial (e.g., Gawronski, Hofmann, & Wilbur, 2006). Although associative and propositional evaluations differ in several respects, Gawronski and Bodenhausen (2006, 2011) argue that the key qualitative difference between them lies in the fact that propositional evaluations are subject to assessments of their truth value; propositional claims are regarded as true or false to some degree, depending on their consistency with other salient propositions (see Festinger, 1957). In contrast, truth and falsity have no relevance when it comes to one's automatic affective reactions; such associative evaluations simply are what they are. The Associative-Propositional Evaluation (APE) Model proposed by Gawronski and Bodenhausen (2006; 2011) provides an extensive consideration of how the processes underlying the two kinds of evaluation can interact in different circumstances, but by default, it is assumed that people will commonly propositionalize their automatic affect, turning an immediate feeling state (e.g., the unpleasant taste of brussels sprouts) into an assertion about the world that is held to be true (e.g., "brussels sprouts are horrible"). However, if contradictory propositions happen to be salient (e.g., "brussels sprouts are extremely nutritious"), then it

becomes possible for propositional evaluations to dissociate from associative ones. Research has found such dissociations to be more pronounced in certain domains, such as racial and other intergroup attitudes (e.g., Greenwald, Poehlman, Uhlmann, & Banaji, 2009). Thus, in examining the nature of attitude change it is necessary to consider processes that influence both associative and propositional forms of evaluation.

## Malleability Versus Stability of Attitudes

In addition to serving the fundamental object appraisal function described earlier, attitudes can serve a multitude of other psychological functions (e.g., Shavitt, 1989). For example, they can provide a means for connecting with others, for self-expression, and for the maintenance of self-esteem, among others. Thus, the stability versus malleability of attitudes has important implications for their functionality. The stability of propositional evaluations has been investigated extensively. In the domain of political attitudes (e.g., Converse, 1964), early research suggested a great deal of stability in many of these attitudes (e.g., attitudes toward political parties), and such attitudes were characterized as being "crystallized." A crystallized attitude is conceptualized as being stored in memory in an encapsulated manner and subsequently retrieved, whenever the attitude object is considered, presumably producing very similar evaluations across time. A more contemporary version of this approach can be found in the work of Fazio (1995), who defines attitudes as stored object-evaluation associations. From this perspective, a given evaluative association exists as a stable structure in memory, and given that it is activated, it can produce a consistent pattern of evaluative responses over time. In essence, attitudes are viewed as evaluative dispositions in this approach.

The view of attitudes as stable memory structures that are retrieved and applied across various episodes was challenged by an alternative viewpoint asserting that attitudes are constructed on the fly, based on a variety of informational inputs—implying that attitudes should in fact commonly be malleable (e.g., Schwarz, 2007; Smith & Conrey, 2007). This perspective views attitudes as being transitory states triggered by the interaction of stored memories and environmental inputs, rather than as enduring traits; it makes no assumption of an enduring, encapsulated attitude representation that operates independently of context. To the extent that stability of attitude expression is observed, it is assumed to result largely from the stability of relevant environmental cues.

These two perspectives represent fundamentally distinct approaches to understanding what attitudes are and how stable they are likely to be. Empirically speaking, there is certainly ample evidence for both the stability and the malleability of attitudes. Thus, the identification of relevant moderator variables becomes important. General characteristics of the attitude holder and specific characteristics of the attitude have been shown to be influential moderators of stability.

## Characteristics of the Attitude

Many approaches to understanding variations in attitude malleability have focused on the possibility that there are different types of attitude that vary in their potency and stability. For example, political attitudes were held to vary on a continuum from being highly symbolic to nonsymbolic (e.g., Sears, 1975). Symbolic attitudes are assumed to be acquired quite early in life and to be based mostly on affect rather than well-articulated knowledge. Nonsymbolic attitudes, in contrast, involve thoughtful integration of information (and can only form at later developmental stages, after a capacity for reasoning develops). The latter type of attitude was assumed to be more susceptible to modification, via persuasive arguments or changing political realities, whereas the former was thought to be more deeply ingrained and impervious to change. Although research initially supported this contention, it was ultimately shown to rest on a methodological artifact, and the claim that symbolic attitudes are inherently less susceptible to change was thrown into doubt (Krosnick, 1991). This symbolic-nonsymbolic distinction bears a good deal of similarity to our distinction between associative and propositional evaluations, and analogous arguments have been put forth suggesting that implicit or associative evaluations should have developmental priority and be more difficult to change, compared to explicit or propositional evaluations (e.g., Rudman, 2004; Wilson, Lindsay, & Schooler, 2000); however, a considerable body of research has shown that automatic evaluations are in fact readily malleable (e.g., Blair, 2002).

Taking a different approach, some researchers have conceptualized attitudes as varying on a strength continuum, with stability being one of the properties of strong attitudes. Within this tradition, it has been demonstrated that the presence of other indicators of attitude strength, such as high importance,

certainty, extremity, or accessibility of the attitude, imply an attitude's stability (e.g., Krosnick, 1988). Several variables have been documented as precursors of attitude strength. For example, attitudes vary in the degree to which they are genetically heritable (presumably because of the effects of genes on relevant psychological factors such as temperament, sensory processes, intelligence, etc.) and those with a higher heritability are generally stronger and more stable (e.g., Olson, Vernon, Harris, & Jang, 2001). In terms of the social environment, Visser and Mirabile (2004) showed that individuals who are situated within relatively more attitudinally homogeneous social networks tend to have stronger, more stable attitudes.

Another characteristic of an attitude that relates to its stability is valence. Negative attitudes are often harder to change than positive ones. One reason this may be the case is the fact that negative information is perceived as less ambiguous and more diagnostic than positive information (for a review, see Skowronski & Carlston, 1989), implying that attitudes formed on the basis of positive information are more amenable to subsequent reevaluation. Another important valence-related moderator has been documented by Fazio, Eiser, and Shook (2004); because people with negative attitudes often avoid the disliked entity, they are less likely to have new experiences with it that might cause them to update their views. In contrast, people holding a positive attitude are likely to interact with the attitude object and thus are much more likely to have new, potentially counterattitudinal experiences. In sum, negative attitudes in general, and any attitudes that are regularly socially reinforced or undergirded by genetically influenced processes, tend to be stronger and therefore are less easily modified.

## Characteristics of the Attitude Holder

Certain dispositional characteristics are known to be associated with greater or lesser degrees of attitude stability. Of the "Big Five" fundamental personality dimensions, it is openness to experience that has the most consistent bearing on social attitudes (McCrae, 1996). Dogmatism, for example, represents a form of closedness that is fundamentally characterized by a rigidity of attitudes (Miller, 1965). Individuals who are high in the dispositional need for closure are more resistant to persuasion (Webster & Kruglanski, 1994). A certainty orientation is also associated with a tendency to forget information that is incongruent with one's expectations (Driscoll, Hamilton, & Sorrentino, 1991), creating a substantial disadvantage for counterattitudinal information.

Another personality variable that has often been shown to have great significance for attitudinal phenomena is self-monitoring, which refers to the degree to which people are habitually concerned with the impression they are making on others (Snyder & Tanke, 1976). Because high self-monitors are oriented toward social acceptance, they are often readily willing to modify their evaluations to fit in with their current social milieu. Low self-monitors, in contrast, are more likely to express cross-situationally stable evaluations. The bulk of the research on dispositional variations in attitude stability has focused on explicit, propositional evaluations. A useful direction for future research would be to determine whether these same dispositional factors, or different ones, predict the relative stability of automatic evaluations.

## Mechanisms of Attitude Change
### Learning-Based Attitude Change

What psychological processes bring about attitude change? The most common and long-standing assumption is that learning drives attitude change (e.g., Hovland, Janis, & Kelley, 1953). We first consider the case of *propositional learning*, which can be conceptualized as the acquisition of new propositional information about an attitude object. We then we turn to *associative learning*, which can be described as the formation of new associative links in memory on the basis of mere co-occurrences between objects and events. In each case, the underlying assumption is that learning new information (whether acquired vicariously or via new experiences with an attitude object) is the critical determinant of any observed change in evaluation.

In one of the first comprehensive theoretical models of attitude change, Hovland et al. (1953) proposed that the essence of persuasion lies in the (propositional) learning of persuasive messages. Message learning was viewed as depending on (a) attention to the message, (b) comprehension of the message, (c) yielding to the arguments contained in the message, and (d) retention of these arguments. Other variables (e.g., communicator characteristics, message format, type of audience, etc.) were thought to be important only to the extent that they influenced one (or more) of these four key processes mediating persuasion. Although the program of research stimulated by this theoretical model was hugely influential in shaping attitude change research for decades, its core assumption

came into question in a seminal analysis conducted by Greenwald (1968). Greenwald noted that the central implication of this message-learning model of persuasion was that the degree of attitude change should be robustly correlated with recall of the message contents. In fact, this was typically not the case (but see Chattopadhyay & Alba, 1988, for evidence that more sensitive measures of message learning can indeed evince stronger correlations with attitude change). Instead, what Greenwald showed was that the nature of message recipients' own self-generated thoughts (termed "cognitive responses" to the persuasive appeal) predicted whether attitude change ultimately occurred. When counterattitudinal information resulted in positive thoughts, persuasion was likely, but when it produced counterarguing, persuasion was typically not evident. It quickly became evident that message recipients are not merely passive receptacles who can be spoon-fed new information; rather, they actively generate their own propositional assertions in response to a persuasive appeal. In this sense, the relevant mediating process is focused less on the learning of new, externally provided propositions per se and more on working out the propositional implications of provided information when considered in relation to the recipients' other knowledge and beliefs (see also Festinger, 1957). In cases where persuasion does occur, this kind of cognitive elaboration can still be construed as a case of propositional learning, but the process is much more active and dynamic than Hovland and colleagues realized.

As the message-learning approach yielded to the cognitive-responses approach (Petty, Ostrom, & Brock, 1981), the underlying process model shifted to a focus on message reception (attention and comprehension), elaboration (active cognitive responses), and retention (not necessarily of the message per se, but of the evaluative implications of the elaborative thinking that has occurred). Persuasion-related variables were viewed as having their impact in large part via their influence on the content and extent of elaborative processes rather than on message learning. Prominent models that emerged from this perspective (e.g., Petty & Cacioppo, 1981) emphasized the importance of two critical factors in shaping the outcome of propositional reasoning in response to persuasive messages. First, the quality of the message content (e.g., the strength of the propositional logic and the supporting evidence provided in favor of the advocated position) was viewed as determining whether message recipients' cognitive responses were likely to be positive or negative. Second, a variety of elaboration moderators were assumed to determine the extent to which recipients will engage in propositional analysis. Two principal classes of elaboration moderators were identified (see Petty & Briñol, 2012): variables that bear on the ability to reason about a message (e.g., distraction, time pressure, or topical knowledge) and variables that bear on the motivation to do so (e.g., personal relevance of the issue, accuracy concerns, or dispositional enjoyment of cognitive analysis). Attitude change based on propositional reasoning was thus predicted to emerge only to the extent that (a) message recipients are both motivated and able to engage in cognitive elaboration, and (b) informational cues provided in the persuasive message are strong and compelling. This prediction has been frequently confirmed in empirical research (see Petty & Briñol, 2012).

At the same time that Hovland and colleagues were laying out their message-learning model of persuasion, other attitude researchers were emphasizing a quite different approach, linked to prevailing behaviorist models of conditioning. Here, the focus was much more on the formation of evaluative associations rather than propositional reasoning. For example, Staats and Staats (1957, 1958) conducted research using a classical conditioning procedure and argued that when an attitude object is consistently paired with other stimuli that have clear positive or negative connotations, those same connotations come to be associated with the attitude object, without any conscious awareness of the conditioning process. Although research on such forms of evaluative conditioning (EC) languished for years, increasing attention to unconscious processes and automatic evaluation in recent years has prompted a resurgence of interest in this topic (see De Houwer, Thomas, & Baeyens, 2001; Hofmann, De Houwer, Perugini, Baeyens, & Crombez, 2010).

An interesting question in the context of attitude change is what kinds of associations are formed during EC. One possibility that has been explored is that the formerly neutral conditioned stimulus (CS) acquires its valence *indirectly* through a mental link to the positive or negative unconditioned stimulus (US) it has been paired with (i.e., stimulus-stimulus learning). An alternative is that the CS becomes *directly* associated with a positive or negative response independent of the particular US (i.e., stimulus-response learning). An important difference between the two accounts is that subsequent changes in the valence of the US should lead to corresponding changes in the evaluation of the CS in cases of stimulus-stimulus learning, but not in cases

of stimulus-response learning (Walther, Gawronski, Blank, & Langer, 2009). Importantly, the effects of US-revaluation predicted by the stimulus-stimulus learning account may occur in the absence of any new experiences with the CS. For instance, when an initially likeable celebrity falls out of favor due to socially undesirable behavior (as in the cases of Tiger Woods or Kobe Bryant), the new evaluation of the celebrity may associatively spread to products that have been associated with the celebrity in previous advertisements. Providing deeper insights into the boundary conditions of such US revaluation effects, a recent study by Sweldens, Van Osselaer, and Janiszewski (2010) showed that pairings of a CS with the same US produced EC effects via stimulus-stimulus learning regardless of whether the CS and the US were presented simultaneously or sequentially. In contrast, pairings of a CS with multiple different US of the same valence produced EC effects via stimulus-response learning for simultaneous presentations. Sequential pairings of a CS with multiple US of the same valence failed to produce any significant EC effects.

Given the research showing that attitudes can be shaped by processes that are relatively devoid of propositional thinking, attitude theorists developed dual-process models of persuasion that viewed attitude change as taking relative thoughtless as well as more thoughtful forms (Chaiken, Liberman, & Eagly, 1989; Petty & Cacioppo, 1981). These models held that even when there were constraints on propositional analysis (i.e., factors that limit the recipients' ability or motivation to think about a persuasive appeal), attitude change could still occur by less thoughtful means. In such circumstances, individuals can still rely on "peripheral cues" or simple persuasive heuristics to quickly determine the valence of the attitude object. Such cues could include affective associations (e.g., a highly attractive spokesperson leads to positive feelings about the associated attitude object) or simple cognitive rules of thumb (e.g., a spokesperson who appears to be an expert invokes the belief that "experts are usually right"). From the standpoint of these theories, the aforementioned elaboration moderators play the critical role in determining which of two qualitatively different persuasion routes will be engaged: systematic thinking or heuristic processing. This assumption came under close scrutiny by Kruglanski and Thompson (1999), who argued that the case for qualitatively distinct processes was actually quite weak. In the view of their "unimodel," so-called heuristic processes can simply be viewed as less effortful and less extensive forms of propositional thinking. Determining whether persuasion heuristics constitute a distinct form of persuasion is complicated by the diversity of meanings that have been attached to the term "heuristic" (see Shah & Oppenheimer, 2008). In reviewing the heuristics literature, Shah and Oppenheimer emphasized effort reduction as the sine qua non of heuristic processing, and this perspective accords nicely with Kruglanski and Thompson's claim that heuristics should be regarded as representing a simplified or scaled-down form of propositional thinking, rather than a qualitatively different phenomenon.

Though the heuristic-systematic distinction per se seems insufficient to characterize qualitatively different evaluative processes, alternative dual-process models may provide a more promising basis for doing so. As previously noted, Gawronski and Bodenhausen's (2006, 2011) APE model draws upon the distinction between associative and propositional processes and views the critical qualitative difference between the two processes as being the extent to which an evaluative reaction is subjected to validation or truth testing. Associative evaluations are hypothesized to involve the mere activation of an affective reaction that cannot meaningfully be said to be "true" or "false"—it simply *is*. Propositional evaluations, in contrast, must necessarily be regarded as either true or false, to some degree, and this implies their eligibility for syllogistic reasoning processes and concerns about their consistency with other relevant propositions. From this perspective, some of the persuasion heuristics identified in previous research are considered associative in nature (those that involve the formation of associative links on the basis of mere co-occurrences, such as in the case of the attractive spokesperson), while others are propositional (e.g., "experts are usually right").

The APE model's analysis points to two qualitatively different learning mechanisms in attitude change: the automatic formation of new associations on the basis of mere co-occurrences between objects and events (*associative learning*) versus mechanisms involving logical reasoning and a systematic assessment of the validity of available information (*propositional learning*). At the same time, it heavily emphasizes the intricate interactions between associative and propositional processes. In many circumstances, these processes are likely to work in concert to produce well-aligned automatic and deliberated evaluations regardless of whether new information has been acquired through associative or propositional learning (e.g., Whitfield & Jordan, 2009).

Yet associative and propositional evaluations have also been shown to be dissociated under a variety of circumstances, and the APE model attempts to provide a comprehensive account of the conditions under which the two learning mechanisms produce either congruent or incongruent evaluations. For instance, in line with the predictions of the APE model, EC-related pairings of an attitude object with positive or negative stimuli have been shown to produce corresponding changes in associative and propositional evaluations when participants used their affective responses as a basis for evaluative judgments, but not when they introspected on reasons for their preferences (e.g., Gawronski & LeBel, 2008). Conversely, associative and propositional evaluations have been shown to be equally affected by newly acquired propositional information when this information was regarded as valid (e.g., Whitfield & Jordan, 2009). Yet a rejection of newly acquired information as false influenced only propositional, but not associative, evaluations (e.g., Gregg, Seibt, & Banaji, 2006).

### Behavior-Induced Attitude Change

In the majority of research on attitude change, the focus has been on the influence of environmental cues and persuasive messages on the contents of evaluative representations, which are thought in turn to play an important role in guiding behavioral responses to attitude objects (e.g., Fishbein & Ajzen, 2010). For example, a TV advertisement might provide a consumer with good reasons to form a positive attitude toward a new fast food restaurant, so she decides to try it. However, some research has turned this sequence on its head, asking instead, How does one's behavior toward an attitude object influence one's evaluation of it (Olson & Stone, 2005)? There might be many reasons why a consumer would try a new restaurant that have nothing to do with her attitude—going along with friends, convenience of the location, and so on. In such a case, does the act of going to the restaurant have any influence on the consumer's attitude toward it? If positive attitudes engender approach behavior, does approach behavior engender positive attitudes?

Undoubtedly the most famous explanatory account for behavior-induced attitude change is the one provided by cognitive dissonance theory (Festinger, 1957). Of primary interest are cases in which thoughts of one's behavior are inconsistent with one's attitude. Festinger proposed that these inconsistencies between cognitive elements are aversive, and they motivate efforts to restore consonance. If they cannot be sufficiently justified by external factors, then attitudes will likely be modified to bring them in line with the behavior that has been performed. This phenomenon has been frequently documented in the "induced compliance" paradigm, in which individuals are led to engage in a counterattitudinal behavior through the application of social influence (although the individuals feel that they have freely chosen to engage in the behavior). In such cases, as long as there is strong external justification for the behavior, such as a sizable cash reward, attitudes remain unchanged; however, if external justifications are insufficient, then attitudes are observed to shift in the direction of the counterattitudinal behavior, in order to provide an internal justification for it (Festinger & Carlsmith, 1959). Another frequently studied dissonance paradigm involves choice-induced preference shifts (e.g., Brehm, 1956). When individuals must choose between similarly valued options, making a choice can evoke dissonance (e.g., "I chose *A*, but *B* has so many positive features"). In order to eradicate this inconsistency and justify the choice that has been made, choosers must convince themselves that the chosen option is actually clearly preferable. This dissonance reduction process results in a "spreading of alternatives," in which the chosen option comes to be evaluated more favorably and the nonchosen option evaluated less favorably, compared to prechoice attitudes.

An alternate account of these sorts of findings is provided by Bem's (1967) self-perception theory. Unlike Festinger's theory, Bem makes no assumptions about aversive motivational states that drive individuals to construct logically consistent accounts of their own behavior. Instead, he simply assumes that people make inferences about the reasons for their own behavior based on available evidence (much as an independent observer would do). If I engaged in a given behavior without external justification, then I must possess an internal, attitudinal reason for doing so. Bem's theory has proven fruitful in attitude research (e.g., Fazio, 1987). Although Bem cast his theory specifically as an alternative to dissonance theory, most scholars have come to the conclusion that the two theories each have merits and are ultimately compatible with one another (e.g., Fazio, Zanna, & Cooper, 1977). However, it is important to note that both dissonance theory and self-perception theory are rooted in propositional reasoning processes. Dissonance, by its very nature, is concerned with the logical consistency of cognitive elements, and self-perception involves inferential processes that are similarly concerned with determining what is true and what is not true. Thus, although these processes have been well documented in the domain of propositional evaluations, they might be expected to have little influence on associative evaluations. Indeed, Gawronski and Strack (2004) used a classic induced compliance manipulation to show that counterattitudinal behavior (when not externally justified) produced the expected shifts in self-reported attitudes, but the same manipulation had no effect on automatic evaluations (for related findings, see Wilson et al., 2000).

One might expect the same dissociation to be evident in the case of choice-induced preference shifts, but the situation in that paradigm is more complicated. For one thing, there have been several demonstrations showing that similar preference shifts can occur in situations where an individual receives an object through no choice of her own (e.g., Egan, Bloom, & Santos, 2010). Research on the mere ownership effect (Beggan, 1992) and the endowment effect (Kahneman, Knetsch, & Thaler, 1990) similarly show that even when an object is received as a gift, its evaluation shifts (compared to how the same object is evaluated when it is not owned). Clearly, choice behavior is not an essential ingredient in these effects, and indeed, there is no behavior that needs to be justified or explained (whether by dissonance-reduction or self-perception mechanisms). Instead, a quite different mechanism may be a common denominator across these scenarios. Gawronski, Bodenhausen, and Becker (2007) argued that a simple associative process is involved whenever an object comes to be possessed, whether by choice, as a gift, or by random happenstance. Specifically, the things we own become associated with the self. Consequently, self-evaluations become associated with the objects we possess (Zhang & Chan, 2009). For the majority of individuals, automatic self-evaluations are decidedly positive (e.g., Yamaguchi et al., 2007). In their experiments, Gawronski et al. documented the formation of self-object associations following the choice of a given object, and they further showed that automatic evaluations of the chosen object were more positive to the extent that the individual had a positive automatic self-evaluation. Among those individuals who did not have a positive automatic self-evaluation, choosing an object did not result in subsequently enhanced automatic evaluations of it (see also Prestwich, Perugini, Hurling, & Richetin, 2010). Although these findings do not imply that propositional reasoning processes are irrelevant in producing choice-induced preference shifts, they do document a role for associative mechanisms in these phenomena. Given the existence of both propositional and associative mechanisms that can lead to postchoice evaluative shifts, it is perhaps not surprising that these effects are evident both in self-reported and automatic evaluations.

## Context-Induced Variations in Attitudes

The term "attitude change" usually connotes some sort of relatively enduring change. Whether speaking of automatic or more deliberate evaluative processes, one would typically expect such a change to be more than fleeting. However, it is clearly also the case that attitudes can vary over much shorter timescales. Such variations are typically not random or capricious, but rather reflect changes in the context in which a given attitude object is encountered.

It has long been recognized that self-reported evaluations can vary, sometimes markedly, as a function of the context in which questions about the attitude object are posed (for a review, see Tourangeau & Rasinski, 1988). The context in which an entity is evaluated can trigger a variety of psychological processes that are likely to sway deliberations and judgments about it. Knowledge about many attitude objects is both extensive and diverse. As such, it is unlikely that individuals will retrieve all of this knowledge and use it in deriving their evaluative judgments of a given object. When stored knowledge is characterized by evaluative heterogeneity, then sampling of different subsets of knowledge might result in notably distinct evaluations. For example, when thinking about ice cream, if one thinks mostly about the delicious flavor and creamy texture, the evaluation will likely be much more positive than if one thinks mostly about its artery-clogging fat and waistline-expanding calories. Contextual cues can play an important role in directly activating different subsets of stored knowledge. For example, attitudes reported in political surveys often are strongly influenced by the order in which particular topics are raised. Tourangeau, Rasinski, Bradburn, and D'Andrade (1989) showed that these effects can be attributed to the role prior questions play in activating beliefs that have relevance to subsequently evaluated issues. Thus, earlier topics can bias the subset of available knowledge that is considered in reaching an evaluative judgment of a focal attitude object.

A different sort of bias emerges from the role of context cues in the resolution of stimulus ambiguity. Whichever features of an attitude object happen to be salient, it is often the case that their evaluative meaning is at least somewhat open to interpretation, and contextual stimuli can provide a standard that is used to fine-tune such interpretations. Two effects have been noted in the literature. Assimilation effects occur when the evaluation of a stimulus shifts in the direction of the evaluative tone of a salient contextual cue, while contrast effects occur when the evaluation shifts in the opposite direction (e.g., evaluating a vacation in California less favorably after thinking about a vacation in Hawaii). These effects are usually considered to be perceptual in nature (Sheriff & Hovland, 1961), although it is surely the case that contrast and assimilation effects can also emerge from the activation of different subsets of knowledge following exposure to a particular context stimulus. For example, evaluations of the group "African Americans" are more sympathetic after people have been thinking about specific, positively evaluated group members (Bodenhausen, Schwarz, Bless, & Wänke, 1995), and this effect is presumably driven by the activation of a different subset of knowledge about the group after exposure to the positive exemplars. Schwarz and Bless (1992) developed a comprehensive model of the determinants of assimilation versus contrast effects in evaluative judgment. In their approach, the key moderating process lies in the categorization of the relevant stimuli. When a target stimulus is seen as belonging to the same category as the context stimulus, assimilation effects are observed such that the target is evaluated more in line with attitudes toward the context stimulus. However, when the target and context stimuli seem to belong in different categories, contrast effects emerge. The great majority of research on attitudinal context effects has focused on propositional evaluations. When individuals become aware that their propositional inferences may have been inappropriately influenced by a contextual stimulus, they often take steps to "correct" or debias their judgments, subtracting out the contextual influence (Strack & Hannover, 1996). However, such efforts are often poorly calibrated and result in either under- or overcorrection—most often the latter (see Wegener & Petty, 1997).

The extensive evidence of context effects in evaluative judgments raises questions concerning the situational variability of automatic affective reactions. As we previously noted, some theorists have assumed that automatic evaluations are likely to be much more stable than their deliberate counterparts (e.g., Wilson et al., 2000). However, given that prior research has implicated spreading activation within memory networks as playing a role in the generation of context effects based on question order (Judd, Drake, Downing, & Krosnick, 1991), the possibility that associative evaluations shift across different contexts would seem to be highly likely. Indeed, they do (Gawronski & Sritharan, 2010). For example, automatic racial biases are stronger when individuals have just read a newspaper story about a Black criminal (Correll, Park, Judd, & Wittenbrink, 2007), and they are weaker when African Americans are depicted in relatively unthreatening environments, such as in a church (Wittenbrink, Judd, & Park, 2001). When memory representations of an attitude object are evaluatively heterogeneous, the different subsets of associations that are triggered in different contexts can produce substantially different automatic evaluative reactions. These different automatic evaluations will then be likely to result in corresponding differences in propositional evaluations, provided that there are no salient propositions that invalidate the propositional implications of the affect (Gawronski & Bodenhausen, 2006). For example, if a given context activates a more negative set of associations about African Americans, this could result in more negative propositional judgments as well, unless the individual considers conflicting propositions (e.g., "I should not think negative thoughts about minority groups") and modifies explicit evaluative judgments accordingly. Thus, this analysis indicates that context-driven biases in association activation can often mediate corresponding context effects in evaluative judgments. Although it is certainly not the case that all context effects rely on this mechanism, it does provide one common process through which context-induced variations occur at both associative and propositional levels.

It is thus apparent that, although attitudes have often been considered to have a stable, dispositional quality (e.g., see Eagly & Chaiken, 2007), they can also be highly sensitive to situational variations. This seeming paradox raises fundamental questions about what is stable and general versus what is context specific in our evaluative representations of the external world. Some new leverage on this issue was provided in recent research by Gawronski, Rydell, Vervliet, and De Houwer (2010). Their research focused on the role of attention to context cues during the acquisition of evaluative knowledge. When initial attitudes are formed in settings where context cues are not particularly salient, their relevance would not be expected to be context delimited;

under these circumstances, the acquired knowledge may later be triggered in a variety of different circumstances involving the attitude object. However, if a subsequent encounter with the attitude object produces unexpected affective experiences, then attention will be drawn to the context (to explain the unexpected state of affairs) and the newly acquired knowledge will be linked to the salient context cues. Thus, whenever these context cues are present during subsequent encounters with the attitude object, the newly acquired knowledge should be activated ("occasion setting"), but in any other context, the initial, domain-general knowledge would be triggered ("renewal"). Working out the full range of factors underlying relative stability versus malleability of automatic associations remains an intriguing and important topic for further investigation.

## Resistance to Attitude Change

With respect to long-term changes in attitudes, researchers have traditionally focused their attention on the identification of factors that facilitate change (e.g., the variables in a communication setting that maximize persuasive impact). However, attention has also been directed to the countervailing forces that mitigate change (Knowles & Linn, 2004), recognizing that they are not likely to simply be the mirror image of the facilitating factors. In this final section, we examine some of the most noteworthy resistance processes.

### Selective Exposure

Because counterattitudinal information is likely to create cognitive dissonance, given its logical incompatibility with one's current attitude, Festinger (1964) argued that people will routinely avoid such information when they can. A variety of evidence has confirmed that people do in fact attempt to selectively expose themselves to attitudinally congenial information (e.g., Frey, 1986). However, if people invariably engaged in such selective exposure, they would run the risk of having very poorly tuned evaluations of the world. Thus, there is a tension between the need to have an accurate understanding of the world and the desire for feelings of relative security and personal validity that can only exist when one's views of the world are not challenged. In a recent meta-analysis, Hart, Albarracín, Eagly, Brechan, Lindberg, and Merrill (2009) provided evidence that selective exposure to attitudinally relevant information is indeed modulated by the relative priority of accuracy versus defensive motives. They provided evidence of a moderate overall tendency for individuals to prefer attitudinally congenial information, but this tendency was significantly moderated by numerous variables. The tendency grew stronger under circumstances where defensive concerns are stronger (e.g., when the attitude in question is strongly linked to personal values, is held with strong conviction, or when the individual is dispositionally closed minded). The tendency reversed (i.e., an "uncongeniality bias") when accuracy motives were activated (e.g., when the accuracy of an attitude has a direct bearing on the accomplishment of a salient goal). Thus, selective exposure is indeed a common but by no means universal mechanism that can produce attitudinal stability.

### Defensive Elaboration

When people choose, or are situationally forced, to pay attention to counterattitudinal information, a variety of defensive processes can be unleashed in the service of protecting their attitudes from modification (Jacks & Cameron, 2003). In various ways, these processes involve the recruitment of propositional knowledge that is intended to undermine the persuasive force of an appeal. *Attitude bolstering* refers to the retrieval and rehearsal of arguments supporting one's current attitude. *Social validation* involves calling to mind other individuals who share one's attitude, thereby providing a reassuring sense of its appropriateness. *Counterarguing* involves scrutinizing presented counterattitudinal information in an effort to detect weaknesses in the logic or evidence provided that would permit the information to be discredited and dismissed. *Source derogation* focuses on constructing ad hominem arguments for mistrusting or disregarding the claims of the communicator. The research of Jacks and Cameron showed that, of these strategies, people expect to commonly use—and actually do commonly use—bolstering and counterarguing strategies. However, whereas respondents generally indicated that they would be unlikely to rely on source derogation, in an actual persuasion situation, derogation was in fact a relatively commonly deployed defensive strategy. In their analysis of resistance to persuasion in the domain of death-penalty attitudes, they found that counterarguing was generally the most effective resistance strategy, as the cognitive-responses approach would anticipate (Greenwald, 1968). Counterarguing can be encouraged by forewarning individuals that they will be targeted for persuasion (Petty & Cacioppo, 1977) or by giving them specious, easily refuted counterattitudinal information

prior to a strong persuasive attack (i.e., the "inoculation" strategy; McGuire & Papageorgis, 1961). Overall, defensive elaboration is most likely to be triggered whenever individuals feel that a persuasive appeal involves an unwarranted manipulative intent on the part of the source and they feel relatively vulnerable to such manipulation (Sagarin, Cialdini, Rice, & Serna, 2002).

### Overcoming Resistance

Marketers, politicians, and others who are in the business of influencing people's attitudes have sought to identify strategies for overcoming the forces of resistance that tend to hold attitudes in place. One approach has been to camouflage the persuasion, so that targets are not made to feel vulnerable to manipulation. Narrative persuasion (Green, Strange, & Brock, 2002) involves using stories (rather than persuasive essays or speeches) to imply the validity of particular attitudes. This approach is founded on the notion that when people enter narrative worlds, they routinely suspend their disbelief and engage in a relatively uncritical way with the premises of the story. Research has indeed confirmed that, to the extent that audiences have been psychologically "transported" into a narrative world (Gerrig, 1993), they are unlikely to counterargue or resist the attitudinal implications of the story and their attitudes are thus more likely to change (Green & Brock, 2000).

Taking the camouflage idea one step further, some agents of social influence have pursued the possibility of subliminal persuasion, in which cues that might influence attitudes are presented below the threshold of conscious awareness. Obviously, if persuasive information is not detected, it cannot be strategically resisted. Although psychologists have often been highly skeptical of claims of subliminal influence (e.g., Pratkanis, 1992), there is no doubt that many replicable experiments have documented the potential for subliminal stimuli to influence evaluations. For example, Monahan, Murphy, and Zajonc (2000) produced a subliminal mere exposure effect, such that multiple subliminal presentations of a novel stimulus resulted in subsequently more favorable evaluative judgments of it. Krosnick, Betz, Jussim, and Lynn (1992) produced evaluative conditioning effects using affectively potent but subliminally presented photos as the unconditioned stimuli that were paired with supraliminal photographs of a target person; the valence of the subliminal photos influenced propositional evaluations of the target. Despite findings of this sort, evidence for effective behavioral social influence via subliminal stimulation has been scant. One exception is a study by Karremans, Stroebe, and Claus (2006), who found that subliminal presentation of the name of a particular brand of beverage ("Lipton Ice") resulted in a greater likelihood of immediately subsequent choice of the brand, particularly among individuals who were thirsty at the time. Thus, motivational relevance may moderate susceptibility to subliminal influence (see also Strahan, Spencer, & Zanna, 2002). Much remains to be learned about the viability of subliminal methods for influencing attitudes, but if and when they occur, such influences are likely to be only very short lived.

## Conclusion

We began by arguing that the ability to produce meaningful evaluations of the external world is a critical cognitive capacity for adaptive functioning. Many decades of focused empirical attention have produced an extensive database documenting the processes governing the construction and modification of attitudes. We have provided a necessarily selective overview of this work, which has shed a great deal of light on the psychology of attitude change. Despite the extensive progress that has been made, many questions remain open, and new discoveries continue to emerge. Evaluating the state of research on attitude change will, no doubt, require its own updating in years to come.

## References

Blair, I. V. (2002). The malleability of automatic stereotypes and prejudice. *Personality and Social Psychology Review, 6*, 242–261.

Beggan, J. K. (1992). On the social nature of nonsocial perception: The mere ownership effect. *Journal of Personality and Social Psychology, 62*, 229–237.

Bem, D. J. (1967). Self-perception: An alternative interpretation of cognitive dissonance phenomena. *Psychological Review, 74*, 183–200.

Bodenhausen, G. V., Schwarz, N., Bless, H., & Wänke, M. (1995). Effects of atypical exemplars on racial beliefs: Enlightened racism or generalized appraisals? *Journal of Experimental Social Psychology, 31*, 48–63.

Brehm, J. W. (1956). Post-decision changes in desirability of alternatives. *Journal of Abnormal and Social Psychology, 52*, 384–389.

Chaiken, S., Liberman, A., & Eagly, A. H. (1989). Heuristic and systematic processing within and beyond the persuasion context. In J. S. Uleman & J. A. Bargh (Eds.), *Unintended thought* (pp. 212–252). New York: Guilford Press.

Chattopadhyay, A. , & Alba, J. W. (1988). The situational importance of recall and inference in consumer decision making. *Journal of Consumer Research, 15*, 1–12.

Converse, P. E. (1964). The nature of belief systems in the mass public. In D. E. Apter (Ed.), *Ideology and discontent* (pp. 206–261). New York: Free Press.

Correll, J., Park, B., Judd, C. M., & Wittenbrink, B. (2007). The influence of stereotypes on decisions to shoot. *European Journal of Social Psychology, 37*, 1102–1117.

De Houwer, J., Thomas, S., & Baeyens, F. (2001) Associative learning of likes and dislikes: A review of 25 years of research on human evaluative conditioning. *Psychological Bulletin, 127*, 853–869.

Driscoll, D., Hamilton, D. L., & Sorrentino, R. (1991). Uncertainty orientation and recall of person-descriptive information. *Personality and Social Psychology Bulletin, 17*, 494–500.

Eagly, A. H., & Chaiken, S. (2007). The advantages of an inclusive definition of attitude. *Social Cognition, 25*, 582–602.

Egan, L. C., Bloom, P., & Santos, L. R. (2010). Choice-induced preferences in the absence of choice: Evidence from a blind two-choice paradigm with young children and capuchin monkeys. *Journal of Experimental Social Psychology, 46*, 204–207.

Fazio, R. H. (1987). Self-perception theory: A current perspective. In M. P. Zanna, J. M. Olson, & C. P. Herman (Eds.), *Social influence: The Ontario symposium* (Vol. 5, pp. 129–150). Hillsdale, NJ: Erlbaum.

Fazio, R. H. (1995). Attitudes as object-evaluation associations: Determinants, consequences, and correlates of attitude accessibility. In R. E. Petty & J. A. Krosnick (Eds.), *Attitude strength* (pp. 247–282). Mahwah, NJ: Erlbaum.

Fazio, R. H., Eiser, J. R., & Shook, N. J. (2004). Attitude formation through exploration: Valence asymmetries. *Journal of Personality and Social Psychology, 87*, 293–311.

Fazio, R. H., Zanna, M. P., & Cooper, J. (1977). Dissonance and self-perception: An integrative view of each theory's proper domain of application. *Journal of Experimental Social Psychology, 13*, 464–479.

Festinger, L. (1957). *A theory of cognitive dissonance.* Stanford, CA: Stanford University Press.

Festinger, L. (1964). *Conflict, decision, and dissonance.* Stanford, CA: Stanford University Press.

Festinger, L., & Carlsmith, J. M. (1959). Cognitive consequences of forced compliance. *Journal of Abnormal and Social Psychology, 58*, 203–210.

Fishbein, M., & Ajzen, I. (2010). *Predicting and changing behavior: The reasoned action approach.* New York: Psychology Press.

Frey, D. (1986). Recent research on selective exposure to information. In L. Berkowitz (Ed.), *Advances in experimental social psychology* (Vol. 19, pp. 41–80). New York: Academic Press.

Gawronski, B., & Bodenhausen, G. V. (2006). Associative and propositional processes in evaluation: An integrative review of implicit and explicit attitude change. *Psychological Bulletin, 132*, 692–731.

Gawronski, B., & Bodenhausen, G. V. (2011). The associative-propositional evaluation model: Theory, evidence, and open questions. *Advances in Experimental Social Psychology, 44*, 59–127.

Gawronski, B., Bodenhausen, G. V., & Becker, A. P. (2007). I like it because I like myself: Associative self-anchoring and post-decisional change of implicit evaluations. *Journal of Experimental Social Psychology, 43*, 221–232.

Gawronski, B., Hofmann, W., & Wilbur, C. J. (2006). Are "implicit" attitudes unconscious? *Consciousness and Cognition, 15*, 485–499.

Gawronski, B., & LeBel, E. P. (2008). Understanding patterns of attitude change: When implicit measures show change, but explicit measures do not. *Journal of Experimental Social Psychology, 44*, 1355–1361.

Gawronski, B., & Payne, B. K. (Eds.). (2010). *Handbook of implicit social cognition: Measurement, theory, and practice.* New York: Guilford Press.

Gawronski, B., Rydell, R. J., Vervliet, B., & De Houwer, J. (2010). Generalization versus contextualization in automatic evaluation. *Journal of Experimental Psychology: General, 139*, 683–701.

Gawronski, B., & Sritharan, R. (2010). Formation, change, and contextualization of mental associations: Determinants and principles of variations in implicit measures. In B. Gawronski & B. K Payne (Eds.), *Handbook of implicit social cognition: Measurement, theory, and practice* (pp. 216–240). New York: Guilford Press.

Gawronski, B., & Strack, F. (2004). On the propositional nature of cognitive consistency: Dissonance changes explicit, but not implicit attitudes. *Journal of Experimental Social Psychology, 40*, 535–542.

Gendler, T. S. (2008). Alief in action (and reaction). *Mind and Language, 23*, 552–585.

Gerrig, R. J. (1993). *Experiencing narrative worlds.* New Haven, CT: Yale University Press.

Green, M. C., & Brock, T. C. (2000). The role of transportation in the persuasiveness of public narratives. *Journal of Personality and Social Psychology, 79*, 701–721.

Green, M. C., Strange, J. J., & Brock, T. C. (Eds.) (2002). *Narrative impact: Social and cognitive foundations.* Mahwah, NJ: Erlbaum.

Greenwald, A. G. (1968). Cognitive learning, cognitive response to persuasion, and attitude change. In A. G. Greenwald, T. C. Brock, & T. M. Ostrom (Eds.), *Psychological foundations of attitudes* (pp. 147–170). New York: Academic Press.

Greenwald, A. G., Poehlman, T. A., Uhlmann, E. L., & Banaji, M. R. (2009). Understanding and using the implicit association test: III. Meta-analysis of predictive validity. *Journal of Personality and Social Psychology, 97*, 17–41.

Gregg, A. P., Seibt, B., & Banaji, M. R. (2006). Easier done than undone: Asymmetry in the malleability of implicit preferences. *Journal of Personality and Social Psychology, 90*, 1–20.

Hamlin, J. K., Wynn, K., & Bloom, P. (2007). Social evaluation by preverbal infants. *Nature, 450*, 557–559.

Hart, W., Albarracín, D., Eagly, A. H., Brechan, I., Lindberg, M. J., & Merrill, L. (2009). Feeling validated versus being correct: A meta-analysis of selective exposure to information. *Psychological Bulletin, 135*, 555–588.

Hofmann, W., De Houwer, J., Perugini, M., Baeyens, F., & Crombez, G. (2010). Evaluative conditioning in humans: A meta-analysis. *Psychological Bulletin, 136*, 390–421.

Hovland, C. I., Janis, I. L., & Kelley, J. J. (1953). *Communication and persuasion.* New Haven, CT: Yale University Press.

Jacks, J. Z., & Cameron, K. A. (2003). Strategies for resisting persuasion. *Basic and Applied Social Psychology, 25*, 145–161.

Judd, C. M., Drake, R. A., Downing, J. W., & Krosnick, J. A. (1991). Some dynamic properties of attitude structures: Context-induced response facilitation and polarization. *Journal of Personality and Social Psychology, 60*, 193–202.

Kahneman, D., Knetsch, J. L., & Thaler, R. H. (1990). Experimental tests of the endowment effect and the Coase theorem. *Journal of Political Economy, 98*, 1325–1347.

Karremans, J. C., Stroebe, W., & Claus, J. (2006). Beyond Vicary's fantasies: The impact of subliminal priming and brand choice. *Journal of Experimental Social Psychology, 42*, 792–798.

Knowles, E. S., & Linn, J. A. (Eds.). (2004). *Resistance and persuasion.* Mahwah, NJ: Erlbaum.

Krosnick, J. A. (1988). Attitude importance and attitude change. *Journal of Experimental Social Psychology, 24*, 240–255.

Krosnick, J. A. (1991). The stability of political preferences: Comparisons of symbolic and nonsymbolic attitudes. *American Journal of Political Science, 35*, 547–576.

Krosnick, J. A., Betz, A. L., Jussim, L. J., & Lynn, A. R. (1992). Subliminal conditioning of attitudes. *Personality and Social Psychology Bulletin, 18*, 152–162.

Kruglanski, A. W., & Thompson, E. P. (1999). Persuasion by a single route: A view from the unimodel. *Psychological Inquiry, 10*, 83–109.

McCrae, R. R. (1996). Social consequences of experiential openness. *Psychological Bulletin, 120*, 323–337.

McGuire, W. J., & Papageorgis, D. (1961). The relative efficacy of various types of prior belief-defense in producing immunity against persuasion. *Journal of Abnormal and Social Psychology, 62*, 327–337.

Miller, N. (1965). Involvement and dogmatism as inhibitors of attitude change. *Journal of Experimental Social Psychology, 1*, 121–132.

Monahan, J. L., Murphy, S. T., & Zajonc, R. B. (2000). Subliminal mere exposure: Specific, general, and diffuse effects. *Psychological Science, 11*, 462–466.

Moors, A., & De Houwer, J. (2006). Automaticity: A theoretical and conceptual analysis. *Psychological Bulletin, 132*, 297–326.

Olson, J. M., & Stone, J. (2005). The influence of behavior on attitudes. In D. Albarracín, B. T. Johnson, & M. P. Zanna (Eds.), *Handbook of attitudes and attitude change* (pp. 223–271). Mahwah, NJ: Erlbaum.

Olson, J. M., Vernon, P. A., Harris, J. A., & Jang, K. L. (2001). The heritability of attitudes: A study of twins. *Journal of Personality and Social Psychology, 80*, 845–860.

Petty, R. E., & Briñol, P. (2012). The elaboration likelihood model. In P. A. M. Van Lange, A. W. Kruglanski, & E. T. Higgins (Eds.), *Handbook of theories in social psychology (Vol. 1, pp. 224–245).* London: Sage.

Petty, R. E., & Cacioppo, J. T. (1977). Forewarning, cognitive responding, and resistance to persuasion. *Journal of Personality and Social Psychology, 35*, 645–655.

Petty, R. E., & Cacioppo, J. T. (1981). *Attitudes and persuasion: Classic and contemporary approaches.* Dubuque, IA: Wm. C. Brown.

Petty, R. E., Fazio, R. H., & Briñol, P. (Eds.). (2009). *Attitudes: Insights from the new implicit measures.* New York: Psychology Press.

Petty, R. E., Ostrom, T. M., & Brock, T. (Eds.). (1981). *Cognitive responses in persuasion.* Hillsdale, NJ: Erlbaum.

Pratkanis, A. R. (1992). The cargo-cult science of subliminal persuasion. *Skeptical Inquirer, 16*(3), 273–281.

Prestwich, A., Perugini, M., Hurling, R., & Richetin, J. (2010). Using the self to change implicit attitudes. *European Journal of Social Psychology, 40*, 61–71.

Rudman, L. A. (2004). Sources of implicit attitudes. *Current Directions in Psychological Science, 13*, 79–82.

Sagarin, B. J., Cialdini, R. B., Rice, W. E., & Serna, S. B. (2002). Dispelling the illusion of invulnerability: The motivations and mechanisms of resistance to persuasion. *Journal of Personality and Social Psychology, 83,* 526–541.

Schwarz, N. (2007). Attitude construction: Evaluation in context. *Social Cognition, 25,* 638–656.

Schwarz, N., & Bless, H. (1992). Constructing reality and its alternatives: An inclusion/exclusion model of assimilation and contrast effects in social judgment. In L. L. Martin & A. Tesser (Eds.), *The construction of social judgments* (pp. 217–245). Hillsdale, NJ: Erlbaum.

Sears, D. O. (1975). Political socialization. In F. I. Greenstein & N. W. Polsby (Eds.), *Handbook of political science* (pp. 93–153). Reading, MA: Addison-Wesley.

Shah, A. K., & Oppenheimer, D. M. (2008). Heuristics made easy: An effort-reduction framework. *Psychological Bulletin, 134,* 207–222.

Shavitt, S. (1989). Operationalizing functional theories of attitude. In A. R. Pratkanis, S. J. Breckler, & A. G. Greenwald (Eds.), *Attitude structure and function* (pp. 311–337). Hillsdale, NJ: Erlbaum.

Sheriff, M., & Hovland, C. I. (1961). *Social judgment: Assimilation and contrast effects in communication and attitude change.* New Haven, CT: Yale University Press.

Skowronski, J. J., & Carlston, D. E. (1989). Negativity and extremity biases in impression formation: A review of explanations. *Psychological Bulletin, 105,* 131–142.

Smith, E. R., & Conrey, F. R. (2007). Mental representations are states, not things: Implications for implicit and explicit measurement. In B. Wittenbrink & N. Schwarz (Eds.), *Implicit measures of attitudes* (pp. 247–264). New York: Guilford Press.

Snyder, M., & Tanke, E. D. (1976). Behavior and attitude: Some people are more consistent than others. *Journal of Personality, 44,* 501–517.

Staats, A. W., & Staats, C. K. (1957). Meaning established by classical conditioning. *Journal of Experimental Psychology, 54,* 74–80

Staats, A. W., & Staats, C. K. (1958). Attitudes established by classical conditioning. *Journal of Abnormal and Social Psychology, 57,* 37–40.

Strack, F., & Hannover, B. (1996). Awareness of influence as a precondition for implementing correctional goals. In P. M. Gollwitzer & J. A. Bargh (Eds.), *The psychology of action: Linking cognition and motivation to behavior* (pp. 579–596). New York: Guilford Press.

Strahan, E. J., Spencer, S. J., & Zanna, M. P. (2002). Subliminal priming and persuasion: Striking while the iron is hot. *Journal of Experimental Social Psychology, 38,* 556–568.

Sweldens, S., Van Osselaer, S., & Janiszewski, C. (2010). Evaluative conditioning procedures and the resilience of conditioned brand attitudes. *Journal of Consumer Research, 37,* 473–489.

Tourangeau, R., & Rasinski, K. A. (1988). Cognitive processes underlying context effects in attitude measurement. *Psychological Bulletin, 103,* 299–314.

Tourangeau, R., Rasinski, K. A., Bradburn, N., & D'Andrade, R. (1989). Belief accessibility and context effects in attitude measurement. *Journal of Experimental Social Psychology, 25,* 401–421.

Visser, P. S., & Mirabile, R. R. (2004). Attitudes in the social context: The impact of social network composition on individual-level attitude strength. *Journal of Personality and Social Psychology, 87,* 779–795.

Walther, E., Gawronski, B., Blank, H., & Langer, T. (2009). Changing likes and dislikes through the backdoor: The US-revaluation effect. *Cognition and Emotion, 23,* 889–917.

Webster, D. M., & Kruglanski, A. W. (1994). Individual differences in need for cognitive closure. *Journal of Personality and Social Psychology, 67,* 1049–1062.

Wegener, D. T., & Petty, R. E. (1997). The flexible correction model: The role of naïve theories of bias in bias correction. In M. P. Zanna (Ed.), *Advances in experimental social psychology* (Vol. 29, pp. 141–208). New York: Academic Press.

Whitfield, M., & Jordan, C. H. (2009). Mutual influences of explicit and implicit attitudes. *Journal of Experimental Social Psychology, 45,* 748–759.

Wilson, T. D., Lindsay, S., & Schooler, T. Y. (2000). A model of dual attitudes. *Psychological Review, 107,* 101–126.

Wittenbrink, B., Judd, C. M., & Park, B. (2001). Spontaneous prejudice in context: Variability in automatically activated attitudes. *Journal of Personality and Social Psychology, 81,* 815–827.

Yamaguchi, S., Greenwald, A. G., Banaji, M. R., Murakami, F., Chen, D., Shiomura, K.,…Krendl, A. (2007). Apparent universality of positive implicit self-esteem. *Psychological Science, 18,* 498–500.

Zhang, H., & Chan, D. K-S. (2009). Self-esteem as a source of evaluative conditioning. *European Journal of Social Psychology, 39,* 1065–1074.

# Cultural Differences and Their Mechanisms

Yuri Miyamoto *and* Brooke Wilken

## Abstract

Growing evidence has demonstrated cultural differences in cognitive processes. Whereas individuals living in interdependent social worlds, as illustrated by East Asian cultures, have been shown to have a more holistic cognitive style, those living in independent social environments, as exemplified by Western cultures, have been shown to have a more analytic cognitive style. Recent evidence has also begun to show the mechanisms underlying cultural differences, both by examining within-cultural differences and by showing effects of sociocultural contexts on cognitive processes. This chapter aims to highlight dynamic relationships between sociocultural contexts and cognitive processes by providing an overview of research on cultural differences and their mechanisms. First, we briefly summarize different approaches to studying cultural differences in cognition. Then, we review studies showing cultural differences in various cognitive processes, by focusing on holistic versus analytic cognition. Finally, we outline recent evidence showing the causes and mechanisms of cultural differences, as well as suggest future directions.

**Key Words:** culture, cognition, holistic and analytic cognition, mechanisms

Studies on cross-cultural differences in cognitive processes have been rapidly accumulating over the past decade across various fields in psychology. These studies have not only shown cultural differences in a wide range of cognitive processes but have also begun to reveal mechanisms underlying these cultural differences. In this chapter, our goal is to highlight dynamic relationships between sociocultural contexts and cognitive processes. First, we briefly introduce different approaches to understanding cultural differences in cognition. Next, we review studies showing cultural differences in various cognitive processes, including attention, categorization, attribution, and dialecticism. Then, we outline recent evidence showing causes and mechanisms of cultural differences and propose directions for future research.

## Different Approaches to Cultural Differences in Cognition

Anthropologists and psychologists have been examining the cultural groundings of our cognition for more than a century, prior to the recent reemergence of interest in cultural differences. There have been at least five approaches to cultural differences in cognition (Berry, Poortinga, Segall, & Dasen, 2002): (1) early studies on visual illusion, (2) studies on linguistic relativity, (3) studies on cognitive ability, (4) studies from the cultural-historical approach, and (5) studies on the sociocultural system.

Probably the earliest researcher who showed cultural differences in basic perception was Rivers (1901, 1905). Through examining the Torres Straits Islanders and the Todas in Southern India, Rivers found that, compared to a Western sample, the non-Western samples were more susceptible to a horizontal-vertical illusion and less susceptible to the Müller-Lyer illusion. Segall, Campbell, and Herskovits (1966) further reasoned that these differences in visual illusions could reflect differences in ecological and cultural environments. By conducting extensive experiments across 15 societies, Segall et al. found that Western samples which lived in highly carpentered environments were more susceptible to the Müller-Lyer illusion than non-Western samples which lived in less carpentered environments. On the other hand, they also showed a trend that individuals who lived in open, flat terrain were more susceptible to the horizontal-vertical illusion than those who lived in environments without open vistas. These studies demonstrated that even a process as basic as visual perception can be influenced by cultural and ecological environments.

Research on linguistic relativity is also relevant when discussing cultural influences on cognition. The linguistic relativity (Whorfian) hypothesis, at least its weaker version which states that the language we speak influences how we think, has received some empirical support (for a review, see Lucy, 1997; Hunt & Agnoli, 1991). However, early studies on color terms also presented evidence against the Whorfian hypothesis. Berlin and Kay (1969) showed that there are universal laws underlying basic color terms. Moreover, Rosch Heider demonstrated that Dani speakers recognize focal colors better than nonfocal colors, even though their language has only two color terms (i.e., dark and light; Heider, 1972; Heider & Olivier, 1972), suggesting that lack of color terms does not prevent them from perceiving the colors. More recent studies, however, have shown that color terms influence perception by increasing perceived distances at category boundaries (Kay & Kempton, 1984; Robertson, Davidoff, & Davies, 2005; Roberson, Davies, & Davidoff, 2000). Effects of language on cognition have also been demonstrated in a number of other domains, such as spatial orientation (Levinson, 1997), understanding of time (Boroditsky, 2001), category learning (Lupyan, Rakison, & McClelland, 2007), and numerical cognition (Gordon, 2004; Pica, Lemer, Izard, & Dahaene, 2004).

While the previous two approaches focus on specific domains of cognition, some cross-cultural psychologists have focused on cultural differences in general cognitive ability. An overwhelming amount of studies have shown that Westerners tend to perform better than non-Westerners on intelligence tests developed in Western cultures, even with supposedly "culture fair" tests (e.g., Vernon, 1969).

Additionally, exposure to Western-style schooling has been linked to increased performance on these intelligence tests (Ceci, 1991). At the same time, researchers have recognized the difficulty of transferring intelligence tests to other cultures, not only because of issues associated with translating materials and settings but also because of cultural differences in the meaning and function of intelligence (Greenfield, 1997; Sternberg & Kaufman, 1998).

From the cultural-historical perspective, Cole and his colleagues (Cole, 1996; Cole & Scribner, 1974) have criticized the view that there are cultural differences in a general cognitive capacity which can be measured by general cognitive tasks. Instead, they have suggested the importance of examining specific cognitive performances in proper cultural-historical context and pragmatic activity, where cognitive operations are usually carried out. For example, Kpelle rice farmers in Liberia, who often sell rice in a market setting, were found to be more accurate than American adults in estimating quantities of rice (Gay & Cole, 1967), even though Kpelle adults had difficulty sorting patterned cards according to a simple rule.

With the same emphasis on situating cognitive processes within the demands of cultural and ecological contexts, other researchers have proposed that different social and cultural worlds can foster qualitatively different types of cognitive processes (Nisbett, 2003; Nisbett & Miyamoto, 2005; Nisbett, Peng, Choi, & Norenzayan, 2001; Witkin, Dyk, Faterson, Goodenough, & Karp, 1974). Interdependent, collective social organizations have been theorized to foster attention to relationships and to the context. On the other hand, independent, individualistic social worlds have been theorized to encourage individuals to focus on a single object and one's goal with respect to it without being overly constrained by the surrounding context or others' demands. Researchers have called the style of thinking found in the former sociocultural system a holistic or field-dependent cognition, and the style of thinking found in the latter an analytic or field-independent cognition (Nisbett, 2003; Witkin et al., 1974).

In this chapter, we mainly focus on the last approach because it is the area where growing evidence has been accumulating in the past decade, by employing a wide range of methodologies. In the following section, we first summarize studies documenting cultural differences in various cognitive tasks, by focusing on holistic versus analytic cognition. In the latter half of the chapter, we review evidence showing how differences in sociocultural environments underlie differences in cognitive processes. Although this chapter focuses on cultural differences in relatively general cognitive processes that are assumed to operate across various domains, it is important to note that there are also studies demonstrating cultural influences on domain-specific knowledge (see Chapter 22).

## Cognitive Differences
### Attention

Recent studies have shown cultural differences in the visual perception of focal and contextual information. In an illustrative study, Masuda and Nisbett (2001) presented Japanese and American participants with animated video clips of underwater scenes that contained focal fish within a background. When asked to describe what they saw in the scenes, Japanese were more likely than Americans to refer to the background and to relationships between focal objects and the background. Moreover, in a subsequent recognition task, participants were presented with both previously seen and novel objects, with either the original or a novel background. Whereas Japanese recognition was facilitated when objects were presented with their original background, American recognition was not influenced by the changes in background, indicating that objects are more bound to their contexts for Japanese.

Cultural differences are not confined to the perception of complex natural scenes. Researchers have also used stimuli stripped of any sociocultural context. Ji, Peng, and Nisbett (2000) found that Americans were more accurate than Chinese on the Rod-and-Frame Test (Witkin et al., 1954), which measures the ability to focus on a focal object (i.e., rod) while ignoring contextual information (i.e., square frame). Kitayama, Duffy, Kawamura, and Larsen (2003) further developed the Framed-Line Task (FLT) to examine the ability to incorporate or ignore contextual information. Participants were first shown a square frame with a vertical line in it and then presented with another square frame of either the same or a different size. In the second square, participants were asked to draw a line that was identical to the first line in either absolute or relative length. As expected, Americans were more accurate than Japanese on the absolute task where they had to ignore the frame, whereas Japanese were more accurate than Americans on the relative task where they had to incorporate the frame.

Further evidence supporting culturally divergent attentional styles has been provided by a wider range of behavioral measures and stimuli, such as context sensitivity in the Ebbinghaus illusion (Doherty, Tsuji, & Phillips, 2008), susceptibility to a mnemonic context effect (Duffy & Kitayama, 2007), allocation of attention to both contextual information (Masuda & Nisbett, 2006) and to a wider region (Boduroglu, Shah, & Nisbett, 2009) using a change blindness paradigm, attention to contextual information (i.e., vocal tone) using an auditory stroop task (Ishii, Reyes, & Kitayama, 2003; Kitayama & Ishii, 2002), and eye movements (Chua, Boland, & Nisbett, 2005; Masuda et al., 2008; Rayner, Li, Williams, Cave, & Well, 2007). For example, Chua and her colleagues measured the eye movements of American and Chinese participants while they viewed natural scenes that contained a focal object and its background (e.g., a tiger in a jungle). Although Americans looked at the focal objects sooner and fixated on them longer than Chinese did, Chinese made more saccades to the background than Americans did. These findings suggest that Easterners and Westerners are not only reporting and memorizing different things but are also actually looking at different things.

Recent neurophysiological studies have started to accumulate evidence for neural correlates of cultural differences in attention. A functional magnetic resonance imaging (fMRI) study found that, when viewing focal objects, Americans showed greater activation than did East Asians in the areas associated with object processing, such as the middle temporal cortex (Gutchess, Welsh, Boduroglu, & Park, 2006), suggesting that Americans have greater processing of focal objects. Consistent evidence was provided by Lewis, Goto, and Kong (2008), who examined P3 event-related potentials (ERPs) during a three-stimulus oddball task. Whereas European Americans showed larger target P3 amplitudes, indicating their greater attention to target objects, East Asian Americans showed larger novelty P3 amplitudes, indicating their greater attention to events that deviate from the stimulus context. These studies provide neural evidence for Americans' greater attention to focal objects and East Asians' greater attention to contextual information. Furthermore, Hedden, Ketay, Aron, Markus, and Gabrieli (2008) found that when people need to engage in a perceptual task incompatible with their cultural background, it requires greater attentional control. They assessed fMRI responses while American and East Asian participants performed the FLT (Kitayama et al., 2003) and found that, in both cultural groups, engaging in culturally incompatible tasks (i.e., the relative task for Americans and the absolute task for East Asians) increased activation in the frontal and parietal regions commonly associated with attentional control, more than did engaging in culturally compatible tasks.

Studies reviewed thus far have focused on attention to focal objects versus contextual information. East Asian holistic perceptual styles, however, seem to extend to attention to discrete features versus configural relationships when perceiving a single stimulus. In an early study, Abel and Hsu (1949) presented Rorschach cards to China-born Chinese and American-born Chinese participants in the United States. Their results indicated that whereas China-born participants were more likely than American-born participants to attend to the configuration and perceive the blots as a whole pattern, American-born participants were more likely than China-born participants to attend to discrete parts of the blots. More recently, research demonstrated that, when perceiving faces, Japanese were more sensitive to changes in configural information (i.e., distance between eyes) than Americans (Miyamoto, Yoshikawa, & Kitayama, 2011). The existence of cultural differences in face perception also suggests that cultural variation exists even in a domain that is typically viewed as configural and holistic in nature. Such a finding points out the possibility that there is cultural variation in other perceptual processing in which even Westerners are known to show a holistic pattern, such as boundary extension (Intraub, Gottesman, Willey, & Zuk, 1996).

## Categorization and Reasoning

If Easterners attend to contextual and relational information more than Westerners do, Easterners may also rely more on contextual cues when categorizing objects. When presented with three objects (e.g., a monkey, a panda, and a banana) and asked to choose the two that should be grouped together, Chinese children and adults tended to group on the basis of thematic relations (e.g., grouping a monkey and a banana, because monkeys eat bananas), whereas American children and adults tended to group on the basis of categorical relations (e.g., grouping a monkey and a panda, because monkeys and pandas are both animals; Chiu, 1972; Ji, Zhang, & Nisbett, 2004).

These cultural differences in categorization were also observed for more perceptual stimuli. Norenzayan, Smith, Kim, and Nisbett (2002) presented a target

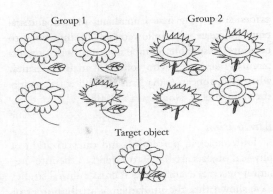

**Figure 61.1** An example of a categorization task (Norenzayan et al., 2002). Participants were asked to judge to which group the target object was most similar. In this example, whereas all the members in group 2 shared a single feature with the target object (the unidimensional rule group), members in group 1 shared a larger number of features with the target object, though no single feature was shared by all members (the family resemblance group). (Reprinted from Norenzayan, Smith, et al., 2002, with permission of Cognitive Science Society, Inc.)

object and two groups of four objects to participants, and then asked them to judge to which group the target object was most similar (Fig. 61.1). All members of one group shared a single feature with the target object (i.e., the unidimensional rule group), whereas all members of the other group were holistically similar to the target, because they shared a larger number of features with the target object, though no single feature was shared by all members (i.e., the family resemblance group). The results showed that European Americans were more likely than East Asians to choose the unidimensional rule group, whereas East Asians were more likely than European Americans to choose the family resemblance group. Asian Americans showed intermediate responses.

Researchers have extended these differences in categorization to examine differences in other types of reasoning, such as deductive reasoning. East Asians' reliance on overall similarity, rather than a unidimensional rule, indicates their use of an intuitive strategy to categorize objects. This suggests the possibility that East Asians may also rely more on intuitive plausibility than on formal rules when making deductive inferences. Supporting this possibility, when there was a conflict between logical structure of a deductive argument and the empirical plausibility of the argument's conclusion, Koreans were more likely than European Americans to rely on plausibility and mistakenly judge valid arguments with implausible conclusions as invalid (Norenzayan, Smith, et al., 2002). In addition, different reasoning styles are *perceived* differently across cultures. Asian Canadians judged a company manager who followed holistic intuitions to be more reasonable, competent, and wiser than a company manager who followed analytical rules, whereas European Canadians showed equal preference (Buchtel & Norenzayan, 2008).

## Attribution

Differences in perception and categorization of physical objects are likely to extend to the interpretation of social events. In fact, cross-cultural studies have shown that the fundamental attribution error (Ross, 1977)—a tendency to overestimate the internal cause (e.g., personal disposition) and underestimate the external cause (e.g., situational forces) of behavior—is especially strong among Westerners, who tend to focus on focal objects. Early evidence for cultural differences in attribution was provided by Miller (1984). She asked American and Indian adults to describe a behavior of a person they knew and to explain why the behavior was undertaken. American adults were more likely to attribute the behavior to general dispositions of the person than to contextual factors, thus demonstrating the fundamental attribution error, whereas Indian adults were more likely to attribute the behavior to contextual factors than to general dispositions. Morris and Peng (1994) replicated similar cultural differences between Americans and Chinese by using controlled stimuli (i.e., animated displays of fish's behavior).

At the same time, research has suggested that cultural differences in attribution depend on the relative salience of contextual information and the diagnosticity of the behavior. Asians are as likely as Americans to infer that behavior is caused by internal dispositions (thus showing correspondence bias) when a behavior is diagnostic of the actor's attitude, or when situational information either is not salient or is absent (Choi & Nisbett, 1998; Krull et al., 1999; Masuda & Kitayama, 2004; Miyamoto & Kitayama, 2002; Norenzayan, Choi, & Nisbett, 2002). However, when behavior is less diagnostic of the actor's attitude (Miyamoto & Kitayama, 2002) or when situational information is made salient (Choi & Nisbett, 1998; Masuda & Kitayama, 2004; Norenzayan, Choi, et al., 2002), Americans have still been found to attribute behavior to internal dispositions, whereas Asians have been found to take situational information into greater consideration.

These cultural differences have also been shown with implicit measures of attribution. The type of lexicon one chooses to describe a behavior reflects one's implicit causal judgment (Semin & Fiedler, 1988). If Easterners are more likely than Westerners to spontaneously make situational inferences, they may also prefer to use more verbs, which provide information about the situation (e.g., *Tom helped his mother*), than adjectives, which provide information about the disposition of an actor that transcends situations (e.g., *Tom is helpful*). Supporting this possibility, Maass, Karasawa, Politi, and Suga (2006) showed that Japanese used more verbs and fewer adjectives than Italians when describing others. Moreover, in a memory task, Japanese were more likely to unintentionally transform adjectives into verbs, whereas Italians showed the opposite pattern. These findings suggest that situational inferences can occur spontaneously and automatically for Asians, whereas dispositional inferences can occur automatically for Westerners (for relevant findings with Latinos, see Zárate, Uleman, & Voils, 2001; see also Knowles, Morrs, Chiu, & Hong, 2001; but also see Lieberman, Jarcho, & Obayashi, 2005).

These differences in causal attribution are likewise reflected in the amount of information considered to explain a behavior. Because a holistic explanation style involves attribution to a larger number of factors (e.g., situational factors, the interaction between personal and situational factors) than does an analytic explanation style, East Asians consider a greater amount of information than Americans do to explain an event (Choi, Dalal, Kim-Prieto, & Park, 2003). For example, when judging the causal relevance of various items in order to solve a case involving a graduate student who murdered a professor, Korean participants considered a larger number of items (e.g., the graduate student's zodiac sign) as relevant than Americans did. These differences are also found to extend to the temporal dimension. Although Chinese and Canadians have been found to be equally likely to attend to present information, Chinese were found to be more likely than Canadians to attend to past information (Ji, Guo, Zhang, & Messervey, 2009). In addition, Japanese participants were shown to be more aware of indirect and distal consequences of a given event than Americans were (Maddux & Yuki, 2006), pointing out the possibility that Asians are also more likely than Americans to attend to future information. Supporting this possibility, a recent study which examined achievement behavior showed that whereas East Asians are more motivated than Americans when a task has utility to fulfill long-term goals, Americans were more motivated than East Asians when a task has utility to fulfill short-term goals (Shechter, Durik, Miyamoto, & Harackiewicz, 2011).

## Dialecticism

If East Asians take a broader range of factors into consideration, they may also tend to tolerate contradictions that are inherent in the factors. Peng and Nisbett (1999) conducted a series of studies to demonstrate how Chinese and Americans approach contradictions. Compared to Americans, Chinese preferred more proverbs involving a contradiction (e.g., "beware of your friends, not your enemies"), indicating a Chinese preference for contradictions. In addition, when approaching contradictory arguments, Chinese tended to seek a middle way by moderately endorsing both views, whereas Americans tended toward polarizing attitudes. This tendency to seek a middle way was also reflected in the way they approached social conflicts, such as conflicts between mothers and daughters. Chinese were more likely than Americans to attribute the causes to both sides and recommend resolving the conflicts by compromising.

Because of their dialectical thinking, East Asians may take information that contradicts their expectations for granted. Choi and Nisbett (2000) presented participants with a scenario about a good Samaritan (Darley & Batson, 1973), where a religious student who was in a hurry ended up not helping a victim. Some participants received the scenario with the outcome (i.e., the student did not help the victim), while others did not. When no outcome was provided, Koreans and Americans were equally likely to predict that the person would help the victim, suggesting that neither Koreans nor Americans could predict the actual outcome. However, after being told the outcome, Koreans were less likely to be surprised and more likely to report that they could have predicted the outcome than were Americans, thereby demonstrating a stronger hindsight bias.

The dialectical approach toward contradictions can be closely related to beliefs about change, because if opposite sides of a contradiction coexist, it also means that one side can easily transform into the other side. To explore cultural differences in beliefs about change, Ji, Nisbett, and Su (2001) presented participants with graphs depicting certain trends (e.g., gross domestic product) over three time points. Americans were more likely than Chinese to predict that current trends would continue, whereas Chinese were more likely than Americans to predict that current trends would slow or reverse direction. These cultural differences in beliefs about change

are also manifested in stock market decisions (Ji, Zhang, & Guo, 2008). Canadians were more willing than Chinese to buy a rising stock, whereas Chinese were more willing than Canadians to buy a falling stock.

## Summary

In this section, we reviewed evidence showing cultural differences in various cognitive processes, ranging from attention and categorization to attribution and dialectical thinking. Miyamoto, Talhelm, and Kitayama (unpublished manuscript) conducted a meta-analysis of these cultural differences in cognitive processes and found the overall effect size (Cohen's d) to be 0.56, which is a moderate to large effect (Cohen, 1977). Level of cognitive processing was not a significant moderator, suggesting that these cultural differences in cognitive processes can be as strong in the lower level processes (e.g., eye-tracking measure) as in the higher level processes (e.g., causal attribution task).

## Causes and Mechanisms

In the previous section, we summarized cultural differences in a wide range of cognitive processes. Although evidence showing between-cultural differences in cognition is crucial for understanding the nature and scope of cultural influences, such evidence does not specify why there are cultural differences in cognition to begin with. Researchers have proposed that differences in ecological environments and social structures, at a distal level, and everyday practices, at a proximal level, underlie differences in holistic vs. analytic cognitive processes.

## Differences in Ecological Environments

Nisbett and his colleagues proposed that cultural differences in cognitive processes can be traced back to the different ecological and social environments of ancient Greek and Chinese societies (Nisbett, 2003; Nisbett et al., 2001). Chinese civilization was based on large-scale agriculture, which required cooperation and coordination with a substantial number of individuals, in order to effectively perform economic activity. In Chinese society, the social structure was thus complex and hierarchical, and social relations were characterized by mutual dependence. Individuals living in such an interdependent, collectivistic social environment may have needed to attend to relationships and to the context. On the other hand, the ecological environments of the Greeks were suited to herding, fishing, and small-scale agriculture—economic activities that did not require cooperation among many individuals. A sense of personal agency and freedom thus became characteristics of Greek society. From living in such an independent, individualistic social structure, individuals within this type of society may have gradually developed the ability to focus on an object and their individual goal with respect to it without being overly constrained by surrounding contexts or others' demands.

In line with this contention, different ecology and social structures have been linked to different cognitive styles (Witkin & Berry, 1975). Berry (1966) compared Temne communities in West Africa with Canadian Eskimo communities. The Temne engage in rice farming and their social relations emphasize conformity and strict social order, whereas the Eskimo engage in hunting and their social structure is more flexible. As expected, Berry found that individuals in Eskimo communities showed more field-independent performance compared to those in Temne communities on the Embedded Figure Test (Witkin, 1950). Summarizing similar studies conducted across 20 communities around the world, Berry (1976) further showed that economic activity of the community correlated with the tightness of social structure, and that the combined index of economy and social structure highly correlated with field-independent cognitive performance.

Although these findings are informative, the communities that were examined differed not only in economic activities but also in various other aspects, such as languages and ethnicities, which could have been potential confounds. More recently, Uskul, Kitayama, and Nisbett (2008) compared three communities within Turkey that engage in different types of economic activities—farming, fishing, and herding—but share the same language and ethnicity. Farmers and fishers, whose economic activities require close cooperation among the family members, were more likely to show a holistic perceptual style on the FLT (Kitayama et al., 2003) and to categorize objects based on thematic relations and overall family resemblance than were herders, whose community emphasizes autonomy.

## Differences in Social Structures: Regions, Religions, and Socioeconomic Contexts

To examine the contention that differences in social structures underlie East-West differences in cognitive processes, recent studies have begun to explore whether individuals who belong to groups or communities that differ in their social structures due to regional, religious, or socioeconomic backgrounds (Cohen, 2009) show different cognitive styles even within the same culture.

### REGIONAL DIFFERENCES

Some investigators have contrasted different regions within Europe. Social relations have historically been hierarchical and close-knit in southern Italy and in Central and Eastern Europe, whereas voluntary association between independent individuals was more characteristic of social relations in northern Italy and in Western Europe. If social practices underlie cognitive processes, southern Italians and Central and Eastern Europeans may show more context-dependent cognitive style compared to northern Italians and Western Europeans. In support of this hypothesis, southern Italian high school students were more likely than their northern counterparts to categorize objects based on thematic relations (Knight & Nisbett, 2007). Furthermore, Central and Eastern European college students were more likely than Western European and American students to categorize objects based on thematic relations (Varnum, Grossmann, Katunar, Nisbett, & Kitayama, 2008).

Kitayama, Ishii, Imada, Takemura, and Ramaswamy (2006) focused on another type of regional difference—societies and regions rooted in a history of voluntary settlement. Voluntary settlement in a frontier, which is motivated by pursuit of personal wealth and freedom, has been theorized to foster social structures that place few restraints on individuals and promote independent agency (Turner, 1920). To examine the effects of voluntary settlement, Kitayama and his colleagues compared a voluntary settlement society in Japan (i.e., Hokkaido) with a nonvoluntary settlement society in Japan (i.e., mainland). Those who were born in Hokkaido were more likely than those in mainland Japan to show an independent social orientation and to attribute the cause of behavior to internal rather than external causes, thereby exhibiting an analytic pattern of cognition. Furthermore, voluntary settlement led North American societies to be even more independent than Western European societies. On the FLT, North Americans showed a more analytic perceptual style compared to Western Europeans, who in turn showed a more analytic perceptual style than did Japanese (Kitayama, Park, Sevincer, Karasawa, & Uskul, 2009).

### RELIGIOUS DIFFERENCES

The religious beliefs and practices one is exposed to may also influence characteristics of social structures. Dershowitz (1971) contrasted Orthodox Jewish boys, whose families stress strict adherence to specified religious structures, with secular Jewish and Protestant boys, whose social settings involve looser social constraints. As expected, Orthodox Jewish boys showed more field-dependent cognitive performance than did Protestant boys, and secular Jewish boys fell between the two groups. More recently, Colzato, van den Wildenberg, and Hommel (2008) contrasted Calvinists and atheists in the Netherlands, who were matched with respect to race, age, sex, and intelligence. In Dutch neo-Calvinism, there is a principle of *sphere sovereignty*, which emphasizes independence and autonomy of each sphere of society. Emphasis on the segregated, independent sections in social structures was hypothesized to lead Calvinists to focus on parts within a field without attending much to the larger field. Supporting this hypothesis, compared to Dutch atheists, Dutch Calvinists were relatively faster at identifying small letters embedded within larger letters, which is assumed to reflect their analytic, focused perceptual style.

## SOCIOECONOMIC DIFFERENCES

Socioeconomic backgrounds provide social contexts in which one is embedded as well. By examining a community sample of adults with different educational backgrounds, Na and colleagues (2010) showed that compared to people with lower educational attainment, those with higher educational attainment are more likely to show an analytic cognitive style. In addition to objective socioeconomic status, subjective perception of one's social class has also been shown to predict holistic patterns of cognition. Those who perceive themselves to be lower on the social class ladder tend to prefer contextual explanations for various social events compared to those who perceive themselves to be higher on the social class ladder (Kraus, Piff, & Keltner, 2009). Moreover, various sociocultural factors have been shown to explain socioeconomic status differences in cognition, such as a sense of control and perceived influence (Kraus et al., 2009; Miyamoto & Ji, 2011) or inflated self-views (Grossmann & Varnum, 2011).

## Differences in Everyday Practices

Cultures differ not only in the social structures at a distal, abstract level but also in the nature of daily practices at a proximal level. Ecological and social environments influence and shape what kind of daily practices people in the community are likely to be exposed to and to engage in. Through participating in these practices, people's cognitive processes may become attuned to cultural ideas and beliefs that are embodied in these practices.

## CULTURAL PRODUCTS

Cultural ideas and beliefs are embodied in cultural products and environments to which individuals are exposed in daily life (for a meta-analysis, see Morling & Lamoreaux, 2008). For example, by randomly sampling hotels, public elementary schools, and post offices in small, medium, and large cities in both Japan and the United States, and taking photographs at each selected location, Miyamoto, Nisbett, and Masuda (2006) showed that Japanese perceptual environments are more complex and ambiguous than American perceptual environments (Fig. 61.2). Moreover, exposure to complex and ambiguous Japanese perceptual environments encouraged attention to the overall context for individuals from both cultures, whereas exposure to simple American perceptual environments fostered attention to a few salient objects. Another example of cultural products is mass media coverage. When covering Olympic athletes, American mass media focuses more on personal characteristics of athletes, whereas Japanese mass media focuses more on the background and others surrounding athletes (Markus, Uchida, Omoregie, Townsend, & Kitayama, 2006; see also Lee, Hallahan, & Herzog, 1996; Morris & Peng, 1994). Being exposed to such cultural products may lead people to make attributions characteristics of each culture. The relations between cultural products and cognitive styles may be bidirectional. Those who have a holistic cognitive style might be more likely than those with an analytic cognitive style to create products and environments that include more contextual information. Supporting this contention, when asked to take photographs or to draw landscape pictures, East Asians include a larger amount of context or background than Americans do (Masuda, Gonzalez, Kwan, & Nisbett, 2008). These findings suggest that cognitive styles and cultural environments can mutually sustain and reinforce each other. Not only do cultures influence individuals, but individuals also actively create and sustain cultures.

## SOCIALIZATION PRACTICES

Pedagogical and parental practices have been known to differ across cultures. Whereas Chinese

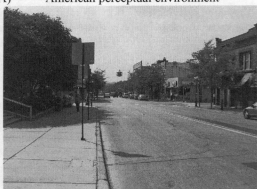

(A) American perceptual environment    (B) Japanese perceptual environment

**Figure 61.2** Examples of an American perceptual environment and a Japanese perceptual environment (Miyamoto et al., 2006). Hotels, public elementary schools, and post offices in small, medium, and large cities in both Japan and the United States were randomly sampled, and photographs were taken at each sampled location. (*See* color insert.)

and Japanese preschool teachers tend to support a larger class size and engage children in various group activities, American preschool teachers tend to value a smaller class size and encourage personal choice and verbalization of thinking processes (Tobin, Wu, & Davidson, 1989). The educational practices of Asian preschools appear to lead children to attend to complex relationships among group members, whereas the educational practices of American preschools seem to guide children's attention to the target of one's goal. In addition to pedagogical practices at school, there are cultural differences in parental practices that take place at home. When playing with toys, Japanese mothers were more likely than American mothers to engage infants in social routines, such as greeting and exchange, whereas American mothers were more likely than Japanese mothers to label toys for infants (Fernald & Morikawa, 1993; Tamis-LeMonda, Bornstein, Cyphers & Toda, 1992). American mothers' emphasis on labeling objects could be said to lead infants to focus on objects, whereas Japanese mothers' emphasis on social practices could direct infants' attention to relationships or to the context in which an object is located. Reflecting this emphasis on labeling objects, American mothers tend to produce more nouns than verbs when talking with their toddlers, whereas Mandarin-speaking mothers tend to produce more verbs than nouns when talking with their toddlers (Tardif, Gelman, & Xu, 1999). Such cultural differences in communication practices can guide children's attention to either the object (i.e., noun) or to the relationship between the object and the field (i.e., verb).

## Proving Causality by Manipulating General Cultural Mindsets

Although the previous studies based on between-group comparisons suggest that different cognitive styles are associated with different social structures or practices, between-group comparisons do not provide direct causal evidence. Some researchers have tried to test causal mechanisms underlying cultural differences by experimentally manipulating culture. There are mainly two approaches to the experimental manipulation of culture: biculturalism and cultural mindset priming.

### BICULTURALISM

The bicultural approach capitalizes on the fact that some individuals are bicultural (e.g., Asian Americans) and thus might have internalized two cultural knowledge systems (e.g., Asian and American cultural meaning systems). If this is the case, priming one cultural knowledge system (e.g., Asian cultural meaning system) should increase the accessibility of declarative and procedural knowledge (e.g., situational attribution) that belongs to the primed knowledge system. Various studies have provided support to this contention. Hong Kong Chinese have been found to make more situational attributions (thus showing more holistic cognitive patterns) after being exposed to Chinese cultural icons, such as a Chinese dragon, than after being exposed to American cultural icons, such as the American flag (Hong, Morris, Chiu, & Benet-Martínez, 2000). Recalling experiences that highlight either one of biculturals' identities has also been shown to influence patterns of attribution (Peng & Knowles, 2003). For example, Chinese

Americans produced more situational attributions after recalling an experience that made their Asian identity salient than after recalling an experience that made their American identity salient.

At the same time, there are individual differences among bicultural individuals in whether cultural priming increases the accessibility of the primed cultural knowledge system. The ways bicultural individuals integrate their two identities have been shown to influence the direction of cultural priming (Benet-Martínez, Leu, Lee, & Morris, 2002). Cultural priming leads Chinese American biculturals who perceive their two identities as compatible (e.g., "I am both") to show culturally congruent patterns of attribution, replicating Hong et al.'s (2000) findings. However, those Chinese Americans who perceive their two identities as mutually exclusive (e.g., "I am simply a Chinese who lives in America") show a reverse pattern: They produce more contextual explanations after being primed with American icons than after being primed with Chinese icons.

### CULTURAL MINDSET PRIMING

Whereas the bicultural approach manipulates culture only among bicultural individuals, the cultural mindset priming approach manipulates culture even among *monocultural* individuals. It starts from identifying critical mindsets that are supposed to underlie cultural differences. Mindset priming manipulations typically ask participants to first work on a task that employs a certain mindset, and they subsequently examine whether this mindset carries over to a new context. The cultural mindsets that have been most frequently examined are individualism and collectivism (for a meta-analysis, see Oyserman & Lee, 2008). Multiple procedures have been proposed to prime individualism and collectivism. For example, Gardner and her colleagues primed individualism by making participants focus on first-person singular pronouns (I, my, me, mine) and primed collectivism by making them focus on first-person plural pronouns (we, our, us, ours; Gardner, Gabriel, & Lee, 1999).

These cultural priming tasks have been shown to influence patterns of cognition. Compared to participants who were primed with individualism, those who were primed with collectivism showed facilitated identification of global features (i.e., identifying a large letter composed of smaller letters) and increased recall of objects' location (Kühnen & Oyserman, 2002). There is also neural evidence to suggest that global versus local perceptual processing is influenced by cultural priming. Lin, Lin, and

Han (2008) found that the P1 amplitude at lateral occipital electrodes was larger for local than global targets after being primed with individualism, whereas the pattern was reversed after being primed with collectivism. These findings suggest that individualism priming facilitated local perceptual processing by increasing the extrastriate activity.

### Proving Causality by Examining Affordances of Proximal Cultural Practices

Although the manipulation of general cultural mindsets provides strong evidence for a causal factor underlying cultural differences in cognition, such studies locate the source of cultural differences exclusively inside individuals' minds. As we have reviewed in the previous section, cultural differences are also embodied in proximal daily experiences, such as cultural products and socialization processes. Repeated exposure to such different cultural practices may afford and shape people's cognitive styles in a way that reinforces the cultural pattern. For example, Koo and Choi (2005) examined the effect of Oriental medicine training practices. Oriental medicine embodies core aspects of East Asian holistic thinking, such as attention to relations between parts and the whole, and an emphasis on maintaining balance. Koo and Choi reasoned that being exposed to the practices of Oriental medicine may foster holistic ways of thinking. Supporting their hypothesis, students in Oriental medicine considered a larger number of items as relevant to solving a murder case than did students in psychology. Furthermore, the longer the students gained training in Oriental medicine, the larger the number of items they considered.

Another example is the aforementioned study on cultural differences in the physical environment. Miyamoto et al. (2006) hypothesized that holistic and analytic cognitive styles are partly shaped by being exposed to culturally specific physical environments that afford such cognitive styles. To test this hypothesis, participants were first exposed to either complex and ambiguous Japanese perceptual environments or simple and organized American perceptual environments (Fig. 61.2). Subsequently, they worked on a change blindness task, which measured their patterns of attention. The results demonstrated that both Americans and Japanese participants were able to identify a larger number of contextual changes, thus showing a more holistic attentional pattern, after being exposed to the Japanese perceptual environments than after being exposed to the American perceptual environments.

## Culturally Contingent Causality

Most studies that examine causes of culturally divergent cognitive styles propose that the same mechanism underlies cognitive processes across cultures. For example, as reviewed earlier, priming people with collectivism or with complex and ambiguous Japanese environments has been shown to lead to context-dependent, holistic patterns of cognition in both Western and Eastern cultures. However, there might also be culturally contingent sources of cognitive styles. That is, some factors might be linked to holistic cognition in a certain cultural context but not in other cultural contexts.

For example, in Western cultures, a higher sense of control has been linked to more analytic patterns of cognition (Kraus et al., 2009; Miyamoto & Ji, 2011), possibly because those who have control over their surroundings can focus on their goals and the target of their goals without a need to pay much attention to the context. On the other hand, those who are in a position to exert control over others (i.e., leaders) are more likely to attend to relational cues in order to effectively govern the group in Japan than in the United States (Misumi & Peterson, 1985). In such a cultural context, influencing others may require attention to contextual cues, leading to a more holistic attentional style. Supporting this possibility, our recent studies have shown that although having control and influence over others leads to analytic patterns of attention among Americans, this effect was nonexistent or even reversed among Japanese (Miyamoto & Wilken, 2010). These findings highlight the importance of situating causes of perceptual styles in a larger cultural context. Perceptual styles can be shaped by the nature of interpersonal contexts, but how they are shaped depends on the larger cultural contexts in which they are embedded.

## Developmental Trajectories

Studies that experimentally manipulate cultural constructs have identified the short-term effects of culture on cognitive processes. Such short-term effects of exposure to cultural contexts might have long-term consequences on cognitive styles. That is, repeated exposure to cultural practices in everyday life may change a habitual cognitive style for individuals as they develop and accumulate experiences in cultural contexts. To examine long-term consequences of exposure to cultural contexts, researchers have examined both the early development of cognitive styles and cognitive changes that happen in the later stages of development.

As summarized earlier, there are cultural differences in pedagogical and parenting practices. If extended exposure to such socialization practices shapes children's cognitive styles, cultural differences in cognitive styles should become larger as children grow older and gain more experiences in each culture. Developmental studies have provided supporting evidence. In the aforementioned study focusing on causal attribution in India and the United States, Miller (1984) examined both adults and children (ages 8, 11, and 15 years). Although American adults made more dispositional and less contextual attributions than did Indian adults, the cultural differences were smaller among 15- and 11-year-olds, and no cultural differences were observed among 8-year-olds (Miller, 1984). Interestingly, younger children in both cultures made more contextual than dispositional attributions, suggesting that children in both cultures have a relatively context-dependent, holistic cognitive style. Similar developmental patterns were observed for predictions of changes (Ji, 2008) as well as for perceptual processing (Duffy, Toriyama, Itakura, & Kitayama, 2009). Using the FLT (Kitayama et al., 2003), Duffy and his colleagues found that both American and Japanese 4- to 5-year-olds were more accurate on the relative task than on the absolute task, thus showing a more holistic attentional style. In contrast, older American children were more accurate on the absolute task than on the relative task, whereas older Japanese children showed the reverse pattern. These findings indicate that children start out from having a relatively holistic cognitive style across cultures and that children increasingly acquire patterns of cognition consistent with their cultural background as they grow older, though the exact age at which cultural differences start to emerge seems to differ across tasks.

Studies have also shown that prolonged experiences in a cultural context foster culturally specific patterns of cognition and perception across the life span as adults age. Blanchard-Fields, Chen, Horhota, and Wang (2007) examined the degree of correspondence bias among college students and older adults (aged 58–80) in the United States and China. Consistent with the previous studies on attitude attribution that did not find cultural differences when situational information was not salient, there were no cultural differences in the degree of correspondence bias among younger adults. However, among older adults, Americans showed a stronger correspondence bias than Chinese, suggesting that longer exposure to cultural contexts reinforced cognitive styles dominant in each culture. A similar pattern was found for categorical clustering in the United States and China (Gutchess et al., 2006). Cultural differences in categorical clustering were larger for older adults (ages 60–78) than for younger adults (ages 18–22). Such age differences have also been observed in an fMRI study (Goh et al., 2007). When viewing a set of pictures where a focal object or the background varied, although there were no cultural differences in adaptation response among younger adults, older American adults showed a larger adaptation response in areas associated with object processing (i.e., lateral occipital regions) than did older Chinese adults, suggesting that older American adults engaged their object-processing areas to a greater extent than older Chinese adults did.

## Summary

This section reviewed studies that examined the causes and mechanisms of cultural differences in cognitive processes. Both distal and proximal causes have been proposed. Some studies have attributed the cultural differences in cognition to distal causes, such as different ecologies and social structures. At the same time, differences in daily social practices and cultural products have also been linked to cultural differences in cognition. Recent studies have begun to test causal mechanisms using various experimental manipulations. Both activation of general cultural constructs and exposure to specific cultural contexts have been shown to induce patterns of cognition specific to each culture. Furthermore, developmental studies provide evidence that prolonged exposure to cultural contexts fosters culturally specific cognitive patterns.

## Conclusion and Future Directions

Emerging evidence suggests that sociocultural contexts influence cognitive processes. Individuals living in interdependent or collectivistic social worlds, as illustrated by East Asian cultures, have been shown to have a more holistic cognitive style, whereas those living in independent or individualistic social environments, as exemplified by Western cultures, have been shown to have a more analytic cognitive style. Furthermore, recent evidence has begun to show the mechanisms underlying cultural differences in cognitive processes. These studies suggest that participating in certain social and ecological environments fosters divergent cognitive processes both in the short term (e.g., as shown in priming studies) and in the long term (as illustrated by developmental studies).

If repeated exposure to one's own cultural practices through developmental processes shapes one's cognitive style, being exposed to and living in different cultural environments might also change cognitive style. Although some studies have found that East Asians living in the United States show more analytic patterns of cognition compared to East Asians living in East Asia (Kitayama et al., 2003; Norenzayan et al., 2002), it is not clear whether the differences are due either to exposure to American cultural practices or to self-selection; East Asians who came to the United States might have had more analytic cognitive styles before immigrating than might have East Asians who did not come to the United States. Studies examining acculturation processes in longitudinal designs would be useful for disentangling acculturation and self-selection effects, as well as for identifying factors that may facilitate (or hinder) dynamic changes in cognitive styles. For example, what distinguishes individuals whose cognitive styles become attuned to the new culture from those whose cognitive styles remain the same? Is there a critical period for acquiring a new cognitive style?

Another direction for future research is to examine consequences of engaging in certain cognitive processes. Although cross-cultural studies in cognition have mainly examined cognitive styles as an end state, cognitive styles may have consequences on the nature of interpersonal relationships. For example, van Baaren, Horgan, Chartrand, and Dijkmans (2004) have shown that participants who are induced to engage in holistic cognitive processing evidence a greater tendency to mimic each other's behavior. Since mimicry works as the "social glue" that fosters empathy and smooth interaction (Chartrand & Bargh, 1999), holistic cognitive styles may have the function of increasing interpersonal closeness, thus leading to more interdependent social relationships. Cognitive styles may also influence other aspects of interpersonal relationships, such as attention to others and sensitivity to others' needs. Research on these interpersonal consequences of cognitive processes could shed light on the bidirectional relationship between cognitive processes and social contexts.

Lastly, although recent studies have sought mechanisms underlying cognitive styles, most studies have been conducted in Western cultural contexts. Although these findings are informative in identifying factors underlying cognitive styles in

Western cultures, future research needs to examine whether these factors have the same effects across cultures or whether the factors are grounded in particular cultural contexts. For example, as reviewed earlier, having control over others leads to analytic patterns of cognition among Americans but not among Japanese, possibly because exerting control requires different cognitive styles across cultures (Miyamoto & Wilken, 2010). These findings point out the importance of studying mechanisms not only within Western cultural contexts but also within other cultural contexts. For example, it is an open question as to whether high socioeconomic status is associated with analytic patterns of cognition across cultures or whether socioeconomic contexts have different cognitive consequences in Eastern cultural contexts.

Human cognition has long been assumed to be a fixed and universal information-processing system, where only the input to the system differs across cultures. However, growing evidence accumulated over the past decade suggests that cognitive processes are shaped through participation in social and cultural environments. It is our hope that advances in studies on the cultural grounding of cognitive processes will contribute to a better understanding of not only cultural diversity but also the nature of the human mind in general.

## References

Abel, T. M., & Hsu, F. L. K. (1949). Chinese personality revealed by the Rorschach. *Rorschach Research Exchange, 13*, 285–301.

Benet-Martínez, V., Leu, J., Lee, F., & Morris, M. W. (2002). Negotiating biculturalism. *Journal of Cross-Cultural Psychology, 33*, 492–516.

Berlin, B., & Kay, P. (1969). *Basic color terms: Their universality and evolution.* Berkeley: University of California Press.

Berry, J. W. (1966). Temne and Eskimo perceptual skills. *International Journal of Psychology, 1*, 207–229.

Berry, J. W. (1976). *Human ecology and cognitive style: Comparative studies in cultural and psychological adaptation.* New York: Sage.

Berry, J. W., Poortinga, Y. H., Segall, M. H., & Dasen, P. R. (2002). *Cross-cultural psychology: Research and applications.* Cambridge University Press.

Blanchard-Fields, F., Chen, Y., Horhota, M., & Wang, M. (2007). Cultural differences in the relationship between aging and the correspondence bias. *Journal of Gerontology, Series B: Psychological Sciences and Social Sciences, 62*, 362–365.

Boduroglu, A., Shah, P., & Nisbett, R. E. (2009). Cultural differences in allocation of attention in visual information processing. *Journal of Cross-Cultural Psychology, 40*, 349–360.

Boroditsky, L. (2001). Does language shape thought? Mandarin and English speakers' conceptions of time. *Cognitive Psychology, 43*, 1–22.

Buchtel, E. E., & Norenzayan, A. (2008). Which should you use, intuition or logic? Cultural differences in injunctive norms about reasoning. *Asian Journal of Social Psychology, 11*, 264–273.

Ceci, S. J. (1991). How much does schooling influence general intelligence and its cognitive components? A reassessment of the evidence. *Developmental Psychology, 27*, 703–722.

Chartrand, T. L., & Bargh, J. A. (1999). The chameleon effect: The perception-behavior link and social interaction. *Journal of Personality and Social Psychology, 76*, 893–910.

Chiu, L. H. (1972). A cross-cultural comparison of cognitive styles in Chinese and American children. *International Journal of Psychology, 7*, 235–242.

Choi, I., Dalal, R., Kim-Prieto, C., & Park, H. (2003). Culture and judgement of causal relevance. *Journal of Personality and Social Psychology, 84*, 46–59.

Choi, I., & Nisbett, R. E. (1998). Situational salience and cultural differences in the correspondence bias and actor-observer bias. *Personality and Social Psychology Bulletin, 24*, 949–960.

Choi, I., & Nisbett, R. E. (2000). Cultural psychology of surprise: Holistic theories and recognition of contradiction. *Journal of Personality and Social Psychology, 79*, 890–905.

Chua, H. F., Boland, J. E., & Nisbett, R. E. (2005). Cultural variation in eye movements during scene perception. *Proceedings of the National Academy of Sciences USA, 102*, 12929–12633.

Cohen, A. B. (2009). Many forms of culture. *American Psychologist, 64*, 194–204.

Cohen, J. (1977). *Statistical power analysis for the behavioral sciences (Rev. ed).* Hillsdale, NJ: Erlbaum.

Cole, M. (1996). *Cultural psychology.* Cambridge, MA: Harvard University Press.

Cole, M., & Scribner, S. (1974). *Culture and thought: A psychological introduction.* Oxford, England: John Wiley & Sons.

Colzato, L. S., van den Wildenberg, W. P. M., & Hommel, B. (2008). Losing the big picture: How religion may control visual attention. *PLoS ONE, 3*, 3679–3681.

Darley, J. M., & Batson, C. D. (1973). "From Jerusalem to Jericho": A study of situational and dispositional variables in helping behavior. *Journal of Personality and Social Psychology, 27*, 100–108.

Dershowitz, Z. (1971). Jewish subcultural patterns and psychological differentiation. *International Journal of Psychology, 6*, 223–231.

Doherty, M. J., Tsuji, H., & Phillips, W. A. (2008). The context sensitivity of visual size perception varies across cultures. *Perception, 37*, 1426–1433.

Duffy, S., & Kitayama, S. (2007). Mnemonic context effect in two cultures: Attention to memory representations? *Cognitive Science, 31*, 1009–1020.

Duffy, S., Toriyama, R., Itakura, S., & Kitayama, S. (2009). Development of cultural strategies of attention in North American and Japanese children. *Journal of Experimental Child Psychology, 102*, 351–359.

Fernald, A., & Morikawa, H. (1993). Common themes and cultural variations in Japanese and American mothers' speech to infants. *Child Development, 64*, 637–656.

Gardner, W. L., Gabriel, S., & Lee, A. L. (1999). "I" value freedom, but "we" value relationships: Self-construal priming mirrors cultural differences in judgment. *Psychological Science, 10*, 321–326.

Gay, J., & Cole, M. (1967). *The new mathematics and an old culture: A study of learning among the Kpelle of Liberia.* New York: Holt, Rhinehart & Winston.

Goh, J. O., Chee, M. W., Tan, J. C., Venkatraman, V., Hebrank, A., Leshikar, E. D., ... Park, D. C . (2007). Age and culture modulate object processing and object-scene binding in the ventral visual area. *Cognitive, Affective, and Behavioral Neuroscience, 7,* 44–52.

Gordon, P. (2004). Numerical cognition without words: Evidence from Amazonia. *Science, 306,* 496–499.

Greenfield, P. M. (1997). You can't take it with you: Why ability assessments don't cross cultures. *American Psychologist, 52,* 1115–1124.

Grossmann, I., & Varnum, M. E. W. (2011). Social class, culture, and cognition. *Social Psychological and Personality Science, 2,* 81–89.

Gutchess, A. H., Welsh, R. C., Boduroglu, A., & Park, D. C. (2006). Cultural differences in neural function associated with object processing. *Cognitive, Affective and Behavioral Neuroscience, 6,* 102–109.

Gutchess, A. H., Yoon, C., Luo, T., Feinberg, F., Hedden, T., Jing, Q., ... Park, D. C. (2006). Categorical organization in free recall across culture and age. *Gerontology, 52,* 314–323.

Hedden, T., Ketay, S., Aron, A., Markus, H. R., & Gabrieli, J. D. E. (2008). Cultural influences on neural substrates of attentional control. *Psychological Science, 19,* 12–17.

Heider, E. R. (1972). Universals in color naming and memory. *Journal of Experimental Psychology, 93,* 10–20.

Heider, E. R., & Olivier, D. C. (1972). The structure of the color space in naming and memory for two languages. *Cognitive Psychology, 3,* 337–354.

Hong, Y. Y., Morris, M. W., Chiu, C. Y., & Benet-Martínez, V. (2000). Multicultural minds: A dynamic constructivist approach to culture and cognition. *American Psychologist, 55,* 709–720.

Hunt, E., & Agnoli, F. (1991). The Whorfian hypothesis: A cognitive psychology perspective. *Psychological Review, 98,* 377–389.

Intraub, H., Gottesman, C., Willey, E., & Zuk, I. (1996). Boundary extension for briefly glimpsed photographs: Do common perceptual processes result in unexpected memory distortions? *Journal of Memory and Language, 35,* 118–134.

Ishii, K., Reyes, J. A., & Kitayama, S. (2003). Spontaneous attention to word content versus emotional tone: Differences among three cultures. *Psychological Science, 14,* 39–46.

Ji, L. J. (2008). The leopard cannot change his spots, or can he? Culture and the development of lay theories of change. *Personality and Social Psychology Bulletin, 34,* 613–622.

Ji, L. J., Guo, T., Zhang, Z., & Messervey, D. (2009). Looking into the past: Cultural differences in perception and representation of past information. *Journal of Personality and Social Psychology, 96,* 761–769.

Ji, L., Nisbett, R., & Su, Y. (2001). Culture, change, and prediction. *Psychological Science, 12,* 450–456.

Ji, L. J., Peng, K., & Nisbett, R. E. (2000). Culture, control, and perception of relationships in the environment. *Journal of Personality and Social Psychology, 78,* 943–955.

Ji, L. J., Zhang, Z., & Guo, T. (2008). To buy or to sell: Cultural differences in stock market decisions based on price trends. *Journal of Behavioral Decision Making, 21,* 399–413.

Ji, L. J., Zhang, Z., & Nisbett, R. E. (2004). Is it culture or is it language? Examination of language effects in cross-cultural research on categorization. *Journal of Personality and Social Psychology, 87,* 57–65.

Kay, P., & Kempton, W. (1984). What is the Sapir-Whorf hypothesis? *American Anthropologist, 86,* 65–79.

Kitayama, S., Duffy, S., Kawamura, T., & Larsen, J. T. (2003). Perceiving an object and its context in different cultures: A cultural look at New Look. *Psychological Science, 14,* 201–206.

Kitayama, S., & Ishii, K. (2002). Word and voice: Spontaneous attention to emotional utterances in two languages. *Cognition and Emotion, 16,* 29–59

Kitayama, S., Ishii, K., Imada, T., Takemura, K., & Ramaswamy, J. (2006). Voluntary settlement and the spirit of independence: Evidence from Japan's "northern frontier." *Journal of Personality and Social Psychology, 91,* 369–384.

Kitayama, S., Park, H., Sevincer, A. T., Karasawa, M., & Uskul, A. K. (2009). A cultural task analysis of implicit independence: Comparing North America, Western Europe, and East Asia. *Journal of Personality and Social Psychology, 97,* 236–255.

Knight, N., & Nisbett, R. E. (2007). Culture, class and cognition: Evidence from Italy. *Journal of Cognition and Culture, 7,* 283–291.

Knowles, E. D., Morris, M. W., Chiu, C. Y., & Hong, Y. Y. (2001). Culture and the process of person perception: Evidence for automaticity among East Asians in correcting for situational influences on behavior. *Personality and Social Psychology Bulletin, 27,* 1344–1356.

Koo, M., & Choi, I. (2005). Becoming a holistic thinker: Training effect of Oriental medicine on reasoning. *Personality and Social Psychology Bulletin, 31,* 1264–1272.

Kraus, M. W., Piff, P. K., & Keltner, D. (2009). Social class, the sense of control, and social explanation. *Journal of Personality and Social Psychology, 97,* 992–1004.

Krull, D. S., Loy, M. H-M., Lin, J., Wang, C-F., Chen, S., & Zhao, X. (1999). The fundamental fundamental attribution error: Correspondence bias in individualist and collectivist cultures. *Personality and Social Psychology Bulletin, 25,* 1208–1219.

Kühnen, U., & Oyserman, D. (2002). Thinking about the self influences thinking in general: Cognitive consequences of salient self-concept. *Journal of Experimental Social Psychology, 38,* 492–499.

Lee, F., Hallahan, M., & Herzog, T. (1996). Explaining real-life events: How culture and domain shape attributions. *Personality and Social Psychology Bulletin, 22,* 732–741.

Levinson, S. C. (1997). Language and cognition: The cognitive consequences of spatial description in Guugu Yimithirr. *Journal of Linguistic Anthropology, 7,* 98–131.

Lewis, R. S., Goto, S. G., & Kong, L. L. (2008). Culture and context: East Asian American and European American differences in P3 event-related potentials and self-construal. *Personality and Social Psychology Bulletin, 34,* 623–634.

Lieberman, M. D., Jarcho, J. M., & Obayashi, J. (2005). Attributional inference across cultures: Similar automatic attributions and different controlled corrections. *Personality and Social Psychology Bulletin, 31,* 889–901.

Lin, Z., Lin, Y., & Han, S. (2008). Self-construal priming modulates visual activity underlying global/local perception. *Biological Psychology, 77,* 93–97.

Lucy, J. A. (1997). Linguistic relativity. *Annual Review of Anthropology, 26,* 291–312.

Lupyan, G., Rakison, D., & Mc Clelland, J. (2007). Language is not just for talking: Redundant labels facilitate learning of novel categories. *Psychological Science, 18,* 1077–1083.

Maass, A., Karasawa, M., Politi, F., & Suga, S. (2006). Do verbs and adjectives play different roles in different cultures? A cross-linguistic analysis of person representation. *Journal of Personality and Social Psychology, 90*, 734–750.

Maddux, W. W., & Yuki, M. (2006). The "ripple effect": Cultural differences in perceptions of the consequences of events. *Personality and Social Psychology Bulletin, 32*, 669–683.

Markus, H. R., Uchida, Y., Omoregie, H., Townsend, S. S. M., & Kitayama, S. (2006). Going for the gold: Models of agency in Japanese and American contexts. *Psychological Science, 17*, 103–112.

Masuda, T., Ellsworth, P. C., Mesquita, B., Leu, J., Tanida, S., & Van de Veerdonk, E. (2008). Placing the face in context: Cultural differences in the perception of facial emotion. *Journal of Personality and Social Psychology, 94*, 365–381.

Masuda, T., Gonzalez, R., Kwan, L., & Nisbett, R. E. (2008). Culture and aesthetic preference: Comparing the attention to context of East Asians and Americans. *Personality and Social Psychology Bulletin, 34*, 1260–1275.

Masuda, T., & Kitayama, S. (2004). Perceiver-induced constraint and attitude attribution in Japan and the US: A case for the cultural dependence of the correspondence bias. *Journal of Experimental Social Psychology, 40*, 409–416.

Masuda, T., & Nisbett, R. E. (2001). Attending holistically versus analytically: Comparing the context sensitivity of Japanese and Americans. *Journal of Personality and Social Psychology, 81*, 922–934.

Masuda, T., & Nisbett, R. E. (2006). Culture and change blindness. *Cognitive Science, 30*, 381–399.

Miller, J. G. (1984). Culture and the development of everyday social explanation. *Journal of Personality and Social Psychology, 46*, 961–978.

Misumi, J., & Peterson, M. (1985). *The behavioral science of leadership: An interdisciplinary Japanese research program.* Ann Arbor: University of Michigan Press.

Miyamoto, Y., & Ji, L. J. (2011). Power fosters context-independent, analytic cognition. *Personality and Social Psychology Bulletin, 37*, 1449–1458.

Miyamoto, Y., & Kitayama, S. (2002). Cultural variation in correspondence bias: The critical role of attitude diagnosticity of socially constrained behavior. *Journal of Personality and Social Psychology, 83*, 1239–1248.

Miyamoto, Y., Nisbett, R. E., & Masuda, T. (2006). Culture and the physical environment: Holistic versus analytic perceptual affordances. *Psychological Science, 17*, 113–119.

Miyamoto, Y., Yoshikawa, S. & Kitayama, S. (2011). Feature and configuration in face processing: Japanese are more configural than Americans. *Cognitive Science, 35*, 563–574.

Miyamoto, Y. & Wilken, B. (2010). Culturally contingent situated cognition: Influencing others fosters analytic perception in the U.S. but not in Japan. *Psychological Science, 21*, 1616–1622.

Morling, B., & Lamoreaux, M. (2008). Measuring culture outside the head: A meta-analysis of individualism-collectivism in cultural products. *Personality and Social Psychology Review, 12*, 199–221.

Morris, M. W., & Peng, K. (1994). Culture and cause: American and Chinese attributions for social and physical events. *Journal of Personality and Social Psychology, 67*, 949–971.

Na, J., Grossman, I., Varnum, M. E. W., Kitayama, S., Gonzalez, R., & Nisbett, R. E. (2010). Cultural differences are not always reducible to individual differences. *Proceedings of the National Academy of Sciences USA, 107*, 6192–6197.

Nisbett, R. E. (2003). *The geography of thought: How Asians and Westerners think differently… and why.* New York: Free Press.

Nisbett, R. E., & Miyamoto, Y. (2005). The influence of culture: Holistic versus analytic perception. *Trends in Cognitive Sciences, 9*, 467–473.

Nisbett, R. E., Peng, K., Choi, I., & Norenzayan, A. (2001). Culture and systems of thought: Holistic versus analytic cognition. *Psychological Review, 108*, 291–310.

Norenzayan, A., Choi, I., & Nisbett, R. E. (2002). Cultural similarities and differences in social inference: Evidence from behavioral predictions and lay theories of behavior. *Personality and Social Psychology Bulletin, 28*, 109–120.

Norenzayan, A., Smith, E. E., Kim, B. J., & Nisbett, R. E. (2002). Cultural preferences for formal versus intuitive reasoning. *Cognitive Science, 26*, 653–684.

Oyserman, D., & Lee, S. W. S. (2008). Does culture influence what and how we think? Effects of priming individualism and collectivism. *Psychological Bulletin, 134*, 311–342.

Peng, K., & Knowles, E. D. (2003). Culture, education, and the attribution of physical causality. *Personality and Social Psychology Bulletin, 29*, 1272–1284.

Peng, K., & Nisbett, R. E. (1999). Culture, dialectics, and reasoning about contradiction. *American Psychologist, 54*, 741–754.

Pica, P., Lemer, C., Izard, V., & Dahaene, S. (2004). Exact and approximate arithmetic in an Amazonian indigene group. *Science, 306*, 499–503.

Rayner, K., Li, X., Williams, C. C., Cave, K. R., & Well, A. D. (2007). Eye movements during information processing tasks: Individual differences and cultural effects. *Vision Research, 47*, 2714–2726.

Rivers, W. H. R. (1901). Introduction and Vision. In A. C. Haddon (Ed.), *Reports of the Cambridge Anthropological Expedition to the Torres Straits* (Vol. 2, Part 1). Cambridge University Press.

Rivers, W. H. R. (1905). Observations on the senses of the Todas. *British Journal of Psychology, 1*, 321–396.

Robertson, D., Davidoff, J., & Davies, I. (2005). Color categories: Evidence for the cultural relativity hypothesis. *Cognitive Psychology, 50*, 378–411.

Roberson, D., Davies, I., & Davidoff, J. (2000). Color categories are not universal: Replications and new evidence from a stone-age culture. *Journal of Experimental Psychology: General, 129*, 369–398.

Ross, L. (1977). The intuitive psychologist and his shortcomings. In L. Berkowitz (Ed.), *Advances in experimental social psychology* (Vol. 10, pp. 173–220). San Diego, CA: Academic Press.

Segall, M. H., Campbell, D. T., & Herskovit, M. J. (1966). *The influence of culture on visual perception.* Indianapolis, IN: Bobbs-Merrill.

Semin, G., & Fiedler, K. (1988). The cognitive functions of linguistic categories in describing persons: Social cognition and language. *Journal of Personality and Social Psychology, 54*, 558–568.

Shechter, O. G., Durik, A. M., Miyamoto, Y., & Harackiewicz, J. M. (2011). The role of utility value in achievement behavior: The importance of culture. *Personality and Social Psychology Bulletin, 37*, 303–317.

Sternberg, R. J., & Kaufman, J. C. (1998). Human abilities. *Annual Review of Psychology, 49*, 479–502.

Tamis-LeMonda, C. S., Bornstein, M. H., Cyphers, L., Toda, S., & Ogino, M. (1992). Language and play at one year: A comparison of toddlers and mothers in the United States and Japan. *International Journal of Behavioral Development, 15,* 19–42.

Tardif, T., Gelman, S. A., & Xu, F. (1999). Putting the "noun bias" in context: A comparison of English and Mandarin. *Child Development, 70,* 620–635.

Tobin, J. J., Wu, D. Y. H., & Davidson, D. H. (1989). *Preschool in three cultures.* New Haven, CT: Yale University Press.

Turner, F. J. (1920). *The frontier in American history.* New York: Henry Holt.

Uskul, A. K., Kitayama, S., & Nisbett, R. E. (2008). Ecocultural basis of cognition: Farmers and fishermen are more holistic than herders. *Proceedings of the National Academy of Sciences USA, 105,* 8552–8556.

Van Baaren, E. R., Horgan, T. G., Chartrand, T. L., & Dijkmans, M. (2004). The forest, the trees, and the chameleon: Context dependence and mimicry. *Journal of Personality and Social Psychology, 86,* 453–459.

Varnum, M. E. W., Grossmann, I., Katunar, D., Nisbett, R. E., & Kitayama, S. (2008). Holism in a European cultural context: Differences in cognitive style between Central and East Europeans and Westerners. *Journal of Cognition and Culture, 8,* 321–333.

Vernon, P. E. (1969). *Intelligence and cultural environment.* London: Methuen.

Witkin, H. A. (1950). Individual differences in ease of perception of embedded figures. *Journal of Personality, 19,* 1–15.

Witkin, H., & Berry, J. (1975). Psychological differentiation in cross-cultural perspective. *Journal of Cross-Cultural Psychology, 6,* 4–87.

Witkin, H. A., Dyk, R. B., Faterson, H. F., Goodenough, D. R., & Karp, S. A. (1974). *Psychological differentiation.* Potomac, MD: Erlbaum.

Witkin, H. A., Lewis, H. B., Hertzman, M., Machover, K., Meissner, P. B., & Wapner, S. (1954). *Personality through perception.* New York: Harper.

Zárate, M. A., Uleman, J. S., & Voils, C. I. (2001). Effects of culture and processing goals on the activation and binding of trait concepts. *Social Cognition, 19,* 295–323.

PART 13

# A Developmental Perspective

# The Development of Cognitive Control From Infancy Through Childhood

Katherine C. Morasch, Vinaya Raj, *and* Martha Ann Bell

**Abstract**

Cognitive control is a strategic, regulatory ability guiding and organizing thoughts and actions that lead to goal-directed behavior. As such, it is a critical aspect of cognitive development and fundamental to higher order processing. In this review, we focus on the developmental periods of infancy through childhood to examine the early foundations of cognitive control. We adopt a dual-process theory of executive function, highlighting working memory and inhibitory control, as we discuss individual differences in behavioral and physiological mechanisms contributing to the development of cognitive control. We conclude with a discussion of the educational implications related to differences in this ability as well as suggestions for future research.

**Key Words:** cognitive control, early development, working memory, inhibitory control, frontal lobe

One of the most critical issues in contemporary cognitive development focuses on early executive functions and the neurological systems that support the foundations of these abilities. In this chapter, we approach executive functions from the perspective of cognitive control, an organizing process guiding goal-related actions. We first describe the defining characteristics of cognitive control, including an emphasis on working memory and inhibitory control mechanisms. Next, we detail typical tasks used in the study of early behavioral development of cognitive control. Then, we selectively review empirical studies examining the developmental psychophysiology of cognitive control in infancy and childhood. Finally, we discuss the implications of individual differences in cognitive control as well as potential research questions on higher order cognitive abilities in early development.

## Characteristics of Cognitive Control

Executive functions refer to a collection of higher order cognitive processes responsible for organizing and coordinating behavior in order to perform complex goal-related actions (Miyake, Friedman, Emerson, Witzki, & Howerter, 2000). These include planning, set shifting, error detection and correction, working memory, and inhibitory control (Blair, Zelazo, & Greenberg, 2005; Roberts, Robbins, & Weiskrantz, 1998). One of the main questions in the study of higher order processes is whether executive function operates as a unitary construct or whether its subcomponents should be examined in isolation (Eslinger, 1996; Garon, Bryson, & Smith, 2008; Miyake et al., 2000; Roberts & Pennington, 1996). Our conceptualization of executive function aligns with Roberts and Pennington's interactive framework.

In describing their framework of executive function, based on prefrontal cognitive processes, Roberts and Pennington (1996) suggest that the umbrella term of "executive functions" could effectively be reduced to a smaller set of core processes. They propose that the two main executive functions that best represent the role of the prefrontal cortex are working memory (the ability to sustain and manipulate short-term information needed for performing future action; Baddeley, 1986; Reznick, 2007) and inhibitory control (the ability to inhibit inappropriate or inaccurate action, such as a prepotent response; Diamond, 1990; Goldman-Rakic, 1987).

Working memory (WM) is assumed to involve maintaining transient information in short-term storage while actively manipulating or "working" with that information in order to achieve a goal (Baddeley, 1986; Pennington, 1994). This goal may be externally defined, or it may be as basic as the intrinsic desire to not make an error. WM is thought to have a limited capacity that is constrained by the amount of information that can be held and manipulated simultaneously and by the length of time that information can be kept online (Baddeley, 1992; Kane & Engle, 2002).

Baddeley (1986) provides a well-established, comprehensive theory of WM. In his updated model, Baddeley describes WM as being parsed into three slave systems, a visuospatial sketchpad, a phonological loop, and an episodic buffer, which are organized by a central executive regulatory component (Baddeley, 2000). The central executive is viewed as having a coordinative function (Baddeley, 1992), directing attention, and balancing the storage and active requirements inherent in WM processing.

Inhibitory control (IC) is a central component of executive function and generally focuses on the ability to actively inhibit or delay a dominant response to achieve a goal (Roberts & Pennington, 1996). As in real-world situations demanding inhibitory abilities, what is being inhibited varies as a function of experimental task. Thus, inhibited responses may include reflexive reactions in response to external stimuli (e.g., antisaccade tasks), as well as learned automatic responses to more cognitively demanding tasks (i.e., go/no-go and Stroop tasks). In these tasks, individuals may be required to suppress reactions to recently established rules or perhaps to focus on local characteristics (color of printed words) in the face of more salient, automatic responses (reading a printed word). Although these tasks elicit inhibitory abilities in different ways, they all require top-down control of behavior (Kok, 1999).

In summary, WM processes are required for producing and performing correct responses, whereas IC is necessary for suppressing interfering dominant responses (Roberts & Pennington, 1996). Whereas WM and IC can each be considered independently to characterize specific aspects of cognitive regulation (Demetriou, Christou, Spanoudis, & Platsidou,

2002; Luna, Garver, Urban, Lazar, & Sweeney, 2004), there is evidence that WM and IC work in concert to support goal-driven behavior (Miller & Cohen, 2001; Roberts & Pennington, 1996; Wolfe & Bell, 2004, 2007). Roberts and Pennington (1996) argue that an interactive, dual-component process, comprised of WM and IC, functions distinctly from either process in isolation. We consider this interactive skill, WMIC, to underlie the executive process known as cognitive control.

The term *cognitive control* was first described by Posner and Snyder (1975) in a chapter contrasting automatic activation processes against more strategic or conscious controls of behavior and/or cognition. More recently, cognitive control has been defined as the strategic, regulatory ability guiding and organizing thoughts and actions that lead to goal-directed behavior (Davidson, Amaso, Anderson, & Diamond, 2006; Luna, Padmanabhan, & O'Hearn, 2010). We conceptualize cognitive control as frontally mediated executive abilities binding WM and IC into the interactive component WMIC (Davidson et al., 2006; Luna et al., 2010; Roberts & Pennington, 1996).

In our program of research, we examine cognitive control based on the model of executive processes set forth by Engle and colleagues (Barrett, Tugade, & Engle, 2004; Engle, Kane, & Tuholski, 1999; Unsworth, Schrock, & Engle, 2004). Engle characterizes WM as a system of highly salient long-term memory traces that are held active above a threshold via short-term memory representational abilities. Included in this description are the skills and processes necessary to achieve and maintain this activation, as well as a limited-capacity, domain-general attentional control component responsible for the regulation of higher level cognitive demands. The function of this executive attention component is perhaps the most intriguing part of Engle's model and effectively captures our conceptualization of cognitive control (Bell & Morasch, 2007).

Similar to Engle and colleagues' description of a controlled attentional capacity, cognitive control is the maintenance of short-term memory representations in the presence of interference or response competition. In the absence of interference, various components of information, goals, and planned actions are accessed from long-term memory stores with few errors. However, when faced with interfering conditions, it is likely that inaccurate information and incorrect responses are produced (Kane & Engle, 2002). Thus, cognitive control is not needed for all mental processing, but it is elicited in circumstances that require response inhibition under cognitively challenging conditions (Engle et al., 1999; Unsworth et al., 2004).

Additionally, this domain-general executive attention ability of cognitive control has been shown to predict performance on higher order cognitive tasks (Kane & Engle, 2002). Individual differences in executive attention (Engle et al., 1999; Kane & Engle, 2002, 2003; Unsworth et al., 2004) have been associated with a wide variety of cognitive abilities, including general fluid intelligence (Engle et al., 1999). According to Engle's model, these individual differences in cognitive control reflect the ability to apply activation to short-term memory representations, to bring these representations into focus and actively maintain them, and to do so in the face of interference or distraction (Engle et al., 1999; Kane & Engle, 2003). Therefore, individuals who score high on tasks assessing cognitive control are more effective at ignoring task-irrelevant information and maintaining a focus on pertinent information than individuals low in cognitive control. Indeed, individuals who are low in cognitive control have been described as more likely to break focus and orient to distracting, attention-capturing external cues (Unsworth et al., 2004). In addition to emphasizing the central role of the attentional control component, Engle and colleagues assert that this model can be appropriately applied to research with children and that individual differences in this ability are likely supported by prefrontal mechanisms (Engle et al., 1999).

## Early Behavioral Development of Cognitive Control

Individual differences in executive function have been associated with developmental improvements in socialization (Hughes, Dunn, & White, 1998), conscience (Kochanska, Murray, & Coy, 1997), and school readiness (Blair, 2002; Diamond, Barnett, Thomas, & Munroe, 2007). Age-related changes in cognitive control, operationally defined as WMIC performance, have been examined behaviorally (Davidson et al., 2006; Diamond, Prevor, Callender, & Druin, 1997; Gerstadt, Hong, & Diamond, 1994; Welsh, Pennington, & Groisser, 1991), electrophysiologically (Bell, 2001, 2002; Bell & Fox, 1992, 1997), and neuroanatomically (Casey et al., 1997; Diamond, 1990, 1991; Diamond & Goldman-Rakic, 1989; Diamond, Zola-Morgan, & Squire, 1989). The converging evidence from these studies suggests that the biological substrates of successful performance on WMIC tasks are developing throughout infancy, toddlerhood, and the early childhood period.

Investigations of WMIC abilities often highlight cognitive tasks that require the participant to hold some information in memory and to simultaneously inhibit a prepotent response. Significant changes in WMIC processes are clearly identifiable from infancy through early childhood. As is the case with executive functions in general, there is currently no universal agreement on a single unifying measure of WMIC, and there are multiple approaches to the study of this ability (Blair, Granger, & Razza, 2005; Carlson, 2005; Diamond et al., 1997; Espy, 2004). We will discuss relevant tasks and age-related trends in cognitive control measured across early development. As we discuss these studies, it will be evident that most are correlational in nature, although the assumption is that brain maturation is driving these trends in developmental processes (Diamond, 2002).

In infancy, one age-appropriate WMIC task is Piaget's (1954) classic A-not-B task, which is comparable to Jacobsen's (1935) delayed response paradigm (Bell & Fox, 1992, 1997; Bell & Morasch, 2007; Diamond, 1990; Diamond et al., 1997; Pelphrey et al., 2004; Reznick, 2007). Although one recent framework of executive functions in childhood describes the A-not-B task as a measure of set shifting (Garon et al., 2008), the work of Diamond and others focuses on the executive functions of WM and IC as critical for success on this task (Braver & Barch, 2002; Diamond et al., 1997, Roberts & Pennington, 1996).

In the A-not-B task, a toy is hidden in one of two locations (i.e., A or B) in full view of the infant and then the infant is encouraged to "find the toy." After two correct searches to location A, the infant observes as the toy is hidden in the opposite location, and the infant is again encouraged to find the toy. Infants younger than 8 months have the tendency to search for the toy at location A, not location B, even though they observed the toy being hidden at B. Research and theory about this phenomenon maintain that successful performance on this task (i.e., searching at location B) requires simultaneous cognitive skills of WM and IC. Indeed, infants are required to constantly update and maintain knowledge of where the toy is hidden as subsequent trials occur, and to simultaneously inhibit the prepotent response to search at the location where they were previously rewarded. With age, infants become more successful in correctly searching at location B, even after a brief delay (Diamond, 1990; Diamond et al., 1997).

During the toddler period, individual differences in language ability are markedly high. Therefore, similar to the testing demands in place during infancy, toddler WMIC has often been examined using nonverbal assessments of visuospatial conflict (Diamond et al., 1997). Similar to the classic infant A-not-B task, success on the A-not-B task with invisible displacement requires the toddler to be able to remember where a reward is hidden across a 5-second standard delay and to inhibit responding based on the location of previous rewards (i.e., conflicting conditions; Diamond et al., 1997). In this task, a toy is hidden at a central location and the hiding apparatus is shifted to a lateral location in full view of the child. A barrier is placed between the child and the hiding location, and during a brief delay period, a second potential hiding location is added behind the barrier. Following the delay, the barrier is lifted and the child is allowed to search. Just as with the infant A-not-B task, the child accrues two consecutive correct responses on the same side and then the hiding location is switched to the opposite side. As consecutive correct responses accrue to same-side trials, so does the prepotency of the dominant response to return to the location of previous reward. Thus, the reversal trials, ones where the hiding location is switched to the opposite side, are the source of WMIC-related conflict-based behavior. As during infancy, with age, toddlers' accuracy increases on reversal trials (Diamond et al., 1997).

WMIC tasks that have been used with children from 3½ to 7 years of age include Stroop-like tasks such as Day/Night (Carlson, 2005; Diamond et al., 1997). In the Day/Night task, children are instructed to say "day" when they are shown a drawing of a yellow crescent moon and stars on a black card and are instructed to say "night" when shown a yellow sun on a white card. Children, therefore, are required to remember two rules (i.e., the instructed responses for each picture stimulus) and to also inhibit a dominant response (i.e., the tendency to label the picture with the congruent label). Because successful performance on the Day/Night task involves WMIC skills, it is hypothesized to involve prefrontal functioning as well. The percentage of correct response on this Stroop-like task increases with age (Carlson, 2005; Diamond et al., 1997; Wolfe & Bell, 2007).

In a recent examination of the development of cognitive control from 4–13 years of age, Davidson et al. (2006) found that WM tasks which included IC demands accounted for more variability in performance in younger children than in older children and adults. Indeed, using spatial tasks presenting either congruent or incongruent stimuli and response expectations, Davidson et al. (2006) showed that the incongruent trials were more difficult overall, and these interfering effects were most pronounced for younger children. Additionally, even the 13-year-olds were affected by the more challenging conditions of tasks assessing both WM and IC, rather than just one or the other.

One interesting finding from Davidson and colleagues' (2006) work was that as age-related IC abilities improved, WM capacity demands became more challenging relative to inhibitory demands. Indeed, due to immaturity of inhibitory skills, younger children's performance was more susceptible to interference from distracters, which acted to mask WM success in tasks presenting conflicting conditions (Bjorklund & Harnishfeger, 1990; Luna et al., 2010). Before age 10, introducing distracting or conflicting task demands resulted in more dramatic losses in performance accuracy than did taxing the capacity of working memory. The opposite trend was true for older children. Additionally, across age, performance on tasks specifically designed to separately assess either WM or IC control were highly correlated with one another (ranging from 0.7 to 0.8; Davidson et al., 2006). Thus, it may be that the interactive components of WMIC are codeveloping throughout this childhood period.

## Neural Correlates of Cognitive Control Development

In our examination of the role of prefrontal function, we highlight our own research on the development of individual differences in cognitive control, as well as selectively review the work of others. Our research takes a decidedly psychobiological approach to examine cognitive control performance, focusing on behavior as well as patterns of brain electrical activity associated with WMIC task performance. The focus of our research program is one of individual differences in frontal lobe development, with an emphasis on WMIC components of cognitive control.

Evidence from atypical and healthy populations has consistently highlighted the integrity and function of the frontal lobe as the neurological substrate for the development and function of executive processes (Diamond, 2001; Diamond et al., 1997; Nelson & Luciana, 2008; Welsh & Pennington, 1988). Additionally, within both the human and nonhuman primate literatures, it has been hypothesized that individual differences in cognitive control are associated with individual differences in the functioning of the prefrontal cortex (Astle & Scerif, 2008; Davidson et al., 2006; Goghari & MacDonald, 2009; Kane & Engle, 2002; Luna et al., 2010). Indeed, Miller and Cohen (2001) strongly argue that the capacity for cognitive control is the primary function of the prefrontal cortex. Anatomical, neuropsychological, and biobehavioral work with developmental populations have all implicated the unique development and function of the frontal cortex in supporting individual and age-related differences in WMIC mechanisms (Bell & Morasch, 2007; Bell & Wolfe, 2007a; Diamond, 2001, 2002; Diamond et al., 1997; Luria, 1973; Morasch & Bell, 2011; Passler, Isaac, & Hynde, 1985). For example, behavioral neuroscience investigations reveal that tasks tapping the integration of WM and IC are dependent on the prefrontal cortex and lesions to this area, specifically the dorsolateral prefrontal cortex, impair WMIC performance (Diamond, 1988, 1990; Diamond & Goldman-Rakic, 1989). Despite direct calls for work focusing on neural correlates of executive function development, including WMIC and other processes (Diamond, 2002; Diamond et al., 1997; Reznick, 2007), there remain few empirical investigations directly exploring the biobehavioral expression of WMIC in early development.

The development of the neural circuitry that subserves cognitive control, particularly the prefrontal cortex, is delayed compared to other cortical regions (Goldman-Rakic, 1987; Goldman-Rakic & Leung, 2002). The presence of this delayed maturation is evident in resting metabolism (Chugani, 1994, 1998; Chugani & Phelps, 1986), cortical gray matter reduction (Giedd et al., 1999), increases in cerebral white matter (Jernigan et al., 1991), and changes in synaptogenesis (Huttenlocher, 1979; for reviews, see Casey, Geidd, & Thomas, 2000; Diamond, 2002). Indeed, the frontal lobes are typically not functionally mature until the second half of the first year of life, as indicated by associations with WMIC task performance (Bell & Fox, 1994). Additionally, the development of frontal architecture is also protracted, as it continues to structurally develop from infancy through early adulthood (Luna et al., 2004). Evidence that age-related improvements in WMIC skills develop gradually throughout childhood lends support to the hypothesis that the immaturity of the prefrontal cortex is a limiting factor in the development of cognitive control.

A useful strategy in exploring the neural processes associated with these early executive function skills is to employ psychophysiological recording techniques that allow for the examination of age-related changes in brain functioning during cognitive processing. More specifically, the electroencephalogram (EEG) is advantageous as an electrophysiological technique because it provides a method for relating brain development to resting and activity-related differences in cognitive processing. The EEG records brain electrical activity emitted from the scalp, with the assumption that these electrical signals originate from the brain itself (Berger, 1929, 1932; Stern, Ray, & Quigley, 2001). EEG is advantageous in developmental research settings because it is relatively inexpensive, noninvasive, easily used with infants and children, and offers greater temporal resolution of brain–behavior processes (Bell & Wolfe, 2007b; Bell, Wolfe, & Adkins, 2007; Casey & de Haan, 2002) than more metabolic-based measurements. Taking these advantages into account, our research program has relied heavily on incorporating EEG technology to the study of early cognitive functions and changes in brain development. While relatively few developmental investigations have explored the direct link between changes in prefrontal functioning and improvements in cognitive control, we attempt to offer a selective review of the psychophysiological literature exploring these associations from infancy, toddlerhood, and early childhood.

As previously noted, successful performance on the infant A-not-B task has been anatomically linked to the integrity and development of the dorsolateral prefrontal cortex (Diamond & Goldman-Rakic, 1989; Diamond, Zola-Morgan, & Squire, 1989; Nelson, 1995). EEG studies measuring changes in brain electrical activity have provided a great deal of insight to understanding the relations between frontal lobe development and WMIC processes associated with the A-not-B task. In a longitudinal assessment, Bell and Fox (1992) reported that baseline frontal EEG power from 7 to 12 months was associated with performance on a reaching A-not-B task. EEG power reflects the excitability of groups of neurons, and increases in power values during infancy are considered to be a marker of brain maturation (see Bell, 1998; Bell & Fox, 1994 for reviews). In this study, infants who by 12 months of age were able to tolerate long delays between hiding of the object and subsequent manual search on the A-not-B task exhibited greater increases in baseline frontal and occipital EEG power across age from 7 to 12 months, whereas infants who were unable to tolerate such delays by 12 months did not display these changes in power values. The association between EEG power values and A-not-B task performance was replicated in an age-held-constant study with a sample of 8-month-olds. Specifically, higher levels of task performance were associated with greater baseline EEG power values at frontal and occipital scalp locations (Bell & Fox, 1997).

In subsequent research investigations utilizing task-related EEG, we demonstrated that infants with higher levels of performance on a looking version of the A-not-B task exhibited baseline-to-task increases in EEG power values at frontal and posterior scalp locations. This was observed specifically during the delay phase of the toy-hiding procedure when WMIC demands are highest. However, infants with low levels of performance had task-related EEG power values that did not differ from their baseline values (Bell, 2001). Importantly, task-related EEG was able to not only distinguish between high and low levels of overall performance but also between correct and incorrect individual responses during the looking A-not-B task (Bell, 2002). Taken together, these data demonstrate links between emerging WMIC skills and frontal and some posterior involvement during infancy.

Much less is known about the psychophysiological changes associated with executive functioning skills during the toddler period. As noted by Diamond (2002), relatively little is known about frontal lobe maturation between the ages of 1 and 3 years, and the developmental psychophysiological literature is limited with respect to EEG data during the toddler period (Bell & Wolfe, 2007b). To our knowledge, Morasch and Bell (2011) provide the first known investigation describing patterns of brain electrical activity during WMIC function in toddlers. This study gave special focus to the cognitive control component of inhibitory functioning, which can be regarded as a particularly salient skill necessary for both higher order cognitive processing and self-regulation during the toddler years. Baseline-to-task changes in EEG power were examined during a looking version of the A-not-B task with invisible displacement, which taps the executive skill of WMIC (Diamond et al., 1997) and allows for the recording of continuous EEG during task performance. Results demonstrated that changes in brain electrical activity at medial frontal, parietal, and occipital scalp locations uniquely predicted maternal ratings of toddler inhibitory control, even after controlling for concurrent WMIC

task performance on A-not-B task (Morasch & Bell, 2011). These findings coincide with previous investigations implicating the role of frontal lobe activity in cognitive control function, and they are particularly exciting because they provide the first known simultaneous exploration of WMIC and continuous EEG during the toddler period.

Relatively few research investigations have explored EEG studies of cognitive control in early childhood. In our research lab, we have extended our infant and toddler investigations of the beginnings of WMIC skills and their associated patterns of electrophysiology to the preschool years. Wolfe and Bell (2004) investigated the neural correlates of WMIC in a sample of preschool children, aged 4.5 years. Patterns of baseline-to-task changes in EEG power values were compared using age-appropriate WMIC tasks, such as the Day-Night Stroop (Diamond et al., 1997). Results from this study provided further confirming evidence linking physiological changes in cognitive control to frontal lobe involvement in early childhood. Specifically, baseline-to-task increases in EEG power at the medial frontal region (assumed to reflect prefrontal cortex activation) were evident in children who demonstrated higher levels of WMIC performance, in contrast to the low-performance group, which showed no task-related changes in EEG power (Wolfe & Bell, 2004). This pattern of frontally mediated differences related to WMIC performance echoes our findings in infancy and toddlerhood.

In a longitudinal study, Bell and Wolfe (2007a) examined both the developmental progression of executive function skills from infancy to early childhood and the corresponding changes in brain maturation that take place during this time span. A comparison of patterns of brain electrical activity during WMIC processing between infancy and early childhood revealed a pattern of widespread brain electrical activity during infancy, as reported earlier. More specifically, increases in EEG power from baseline to task were evident at frontal scalp locations as well as across the entire scalp (Bell & Wolfe, 2007a). In contrast, when these same infants reached 4.5 years of age, a more specified pattern of frontal activation emerged, signifying that WMIC processing may have become more localized to frontal brain areas.

Exploring age-related changes in WMIC functioning during early childhood, Wolfe and Bell (2007) examined three groups of children (3½-, 4-, and 4½-year-olds) to further pinpoint when during this developmental period brain functioning becomes more specified. Wolfe and Bell (2007) showed that with increasing age-related specificity, WMIC processing depended on frontal lobe activation. Additionally, increases in EEG power at left medial frontal scalp locations were able to explain variability in WMIC performance above and beyond the variable of age (Wolfe & Bell, 2007).

Although baseline to task increases in EEG power values have been associated with the development of WMIC in infants, toddlers, and children, functional magnetic resonance imaging (fMRI) data have been collected with 7- and 8-year-olds using a go/no-go IC reaction-time task that induced conflict between responding and withholding a response (Casey et al., 1997; Durston et al., 2002). This work has shown cortical activation along the frontal midline, rather than from diffuse cortical sites. This is a notably different pattern of activation than was found in the infant, toddler, and preschool EEG research, where most scalp locations were indicated, and may reflect increasing specificity with development. EEG replication of this fMRI WMIC activation pattern in young children is needed and would validate EEG as a psychophysiological measure of cognitive control in young children.

## Implications and Future Directions

The development of cognitive control has implications for adjustment in many areas of functioning. Cognitive control is a critical component for higher order cognitive functioning, and the early development of cognitive control processes has implications for school readiness and later academic success (Blair et al., 2005; Diamond et al., 2007; Gathercole & Alloway, 2006). Recent conceptual and empirical work suggests that regulatory control over behavior, including cognitive and emotion control, is a better predictor of successfully transitioning into the school setting than actual scholastic knowledge (Bierman, Nix, Greenberg, Blair, & Domitrovich, 2008; Blair, 2002; Denham, 2006).

From a purely cognitive point of view, however, knowledge about early developing WMIC skills is critical for understanding early academic performance. For example, WM predicts emerging mathematic skills in preschool children (Espy et al., 2004) and poor WM performance at age 5 is associated with poor reading assessments at age 8 (Gathercole, Tiffany, Briscoe, & Thorn, 2005). Thus, there is an important need for accurate diagnosis and remediation of poor WM skills.

Gathercole and colleagues have proposed a method for diagnosing WM impairments and have recently reported on a training technique to enhance poor WM in older children (Gathercole & Alloway, 2006; Holmes, Gathercole, & Dunning, 2009). WM is considered to be impaired if a child falls one standard deviation below the mean on typical forward and backward digit span tasks or on a standardized battery, such as the Working Memory Test Battery for Children (Gathercole & Alloway, 2006; Pickering & Gathercole, 2001). The training task used with a group of 10-year-olds by Gathercole and colleagues consisted of a variety of computerized WM games with which the children engaged for 35 minutes a day for at least 20 days across a 6-week period of time. The tasks were adapted to each child's current WM skills so that participating in the computerized games taxed the limits of WM for the individual child. Participation in this behavioral intervention increased the WM skills of the children to age-appropriate levels and the increase in WM was sustained with respect to a 6-month follow-up assessment (Holmes et al, 2009). These enhancements in WM were relative to children who participated in computerized WM games that did not tax WM skills. Furthermore, the children's mathematical skills also improved following the taxing WM training, demonstrating that scholastic achievement was enhanced with the training of WM skills in middle childhood.

Arguing that executive function skills, particularly those associated with WM and IC, need to be improved prior to school entry, Diamond and colleagues assessed the Tools of the Mind curriculum for efficacy in improving cognitive control in low-income children attending preschool (Diamond et al., 2007). The Tools curriculum consists of a series of games and activities designed to promote cognitive control skills throughout the preschool day. Relative to children in a preschool curriculum that did not focus on cognitive control games, children in the Tools curriculum performed higher on WMIC tasks. It is important to note that the tasks used at assessment were different from the tasks/games on which the children were trained. Furthermore, performance on the cognitive control outcome tasks was correlated with reading readiness scores (Diamond et al., 2007).

Our goal in this chapter has been to demonstrate that the development of cognitive control is multi-faceted in infancy and childhood. We have focused on behavioral and cortical indicators of WMIC development, as well as academic correlates of early WMIC skills. We briefly highlighted two training programs, one designed to enhance WM skills in school-aged children who are deficient in this cognitive control skill and another designed to enhance WMIC skills in preschool children who are at risk for academic difficulties. Although we did not focus our review on situational influences on the development of cognitive control, we conclude by briefly noting the potential for environmental factors to impact early WMIC development.

In the developmental psychology literature, much attention has been given to the role of maternal interactive style on child emotion control (e.g., Calkins & Bell, 2010); however, little attention has been given to the potential role of parenting behaviors in the development of executive functions. Colombo and Saxon (2002) argue that perhaps individual differences in early memory and attention abilities interact with characteristics of parental caregiving behaviors to influence child cognitive development. Studies designed to determine how parents influence child cognitive control would fill a major void in the cognitive development literature.

Finally, the functional architecture of the prefrontal cortex continues to develop through adolescence and into early adulthood (Luna et al., 2004) and exhibits age-related changes toward the end of the life span. Evidence from the adult cognitive neuroscience and cognitive aging literatures indicates that performance on executive function tasks is dependent on the integrity of the prefrontal cortex across adulthood (Miller & Cohen, 2001; Luna et al., 2010). Further cross-sectional and longitudinal studies examining factors contributing to the expression of higher order abilities in early, middle, and late adulthood will contribute to the complete picture of the development of cognitive control.

## Acknowledgments

This writing of this chapter was supported by grant HD049878 from the *Eunice Kennedy Shriver* National Institute of Child Health and Human Development (NICHD). The content of this manuscript is solely the responsibility of the authors and does not necessarily represent the official views of the NICHD or the National Institutes of Health. We thank Dr. Kimberly Cuevas for her feedback on a previous version of this chapter.

## References

Astle, D. E., & Scerif, G. (2008). Using developmental cognitive neuroscience to study behavioral and attentional control. *Developmental Psychobiology, 51,* 107–118.

Baddeley, A. (1986). *Working memory.* Oxford, England: Oxford University Press.

Baddeley, A. (1992). Working memory. *Science, 255,* 556–559.

Baddeley, A. (2000). The episodic buffer: A new component of working memory? *Trends in Cognitive Sciences, 4,* 417–423.

Barrett, L. F., Tugade, M. M., & Engle, R. W. (2004). Individual differences in working memory capacity and dual-process theories of the mind. *Psychological Bulletin, 130,* 553–573.

Bell, M. A. (1998). The ontogeny of the EEG during infancy and childhood: Implications for cognitive development. In B. Garreau (Ed.), *Neuroimaging in child neuropsychiatric disorders* (pp. 97–111) Berlin: Springer-Verlag.

Bell, M. A. (2001). Brain electrical activity associated with cognitive processing during a looking version of the A-not-B task. *Infancy, 2,* 311–330.

Bell, M. A. (2002). Power changes in infant EEG frequency bands during a spatial working memory task. *Psychophysiology, 39,* 450–458.

Bell, M. A., & Fox, N. A. (1992). The relations between frontal brain electrical activity and cognitive development during infancy. *Child Development, 63,* 1142–1163.

Bell, M. A., & Fox, N. A. (1994). Brain development over the first year of life: Relations between electroencephalographic frequency and coherence and cognitive and affective behaviors. In G. Dawson & K. Fischer (Eds.), *Human behavior and the developing brain* (pp. 314–345). New York: Guilford Press.

Bell, M. A., & Fox, N. A. (1997). Individual differences in object permanence performance at 8 months: Locomotor experience and brain electrical activity. *Developmental Psychobiology, 31,* 287–297.

Bell, M. A., & Morasch, K. C. (2007). Individual differences in the development of working memory during infancy and early childhood. In L. M. Oakes & P. J. Bauer (Eds.), *Short- and long-term memory in early childhood: Taking the first steps toward remembering* (pp. 27–50). New York: Oxford University Press.

Bell, M. A., & Wolfe, C. D. (2007a). Changes in brain function from infancy to early childhood: Evidence from EEG power and coherence during working memory tasks. *Developmental Neuropsychology, 31,* 21–38.

Bell, M. A., & Wolfe, C. D. (2007b). The use of electroencephalogram in research on cognitive development. In L. A. Schmidt & S. J. Segalowitz (Eds.), *Developmental psychophysiology: Theory, systems, and methods* (pp. 150–170). New York: Cambridge University Press.

Bell, M. A., Wolfe, C. D., & Adkins, D. R. (2007). Frontal lobe development during infancy and childhood. In D. Coch, G. Dawson, & K.W. Fischer (Eds.), *Human behavior, learning, and the developing brain: Typical development* (pp. 247–276). New York: Guilford Press.

Berger, H. (1929). On the human electroencephalogram. *Archiv für Psychiatrie und Nervenkrankheiten, 87,* 527–70.

Berger, H. (1932). The human electroencephalogram and its significance for psychophysiology. *Zeitschrift für Psychologie, 126,* 1–13.

Bierman, K. L., Nix, R. L., Greenberg, M. T., Blair, C., & Domitrovich, C. E. (2008). Executive functions and school readiness intervention: Impact, moderation, and mediation in the Head Start REDI program. *Development and Psychopathology, 20,* 821–843.

Bjorklund, D. F., & Harnishfeger, K. K. (1990). The resource construct in cognitive development: Diverse sources of evidence and a theory of inefficient inhibition. *Developmental Review, 10,* 48–71.

Blair, C. (2002). School readiness: Integrating cognition and emotion in a neurobiological conceptualization of children's functioning at school entry. *American Psychologist, 57,* 111–127.

Blair, C., Granger, D., & Razza, R. P. (2005). Cortisol reactivity is positively related to executive function in preschool children attending head start. *Child Development, 76,* 554–567.

Blair, C., Zelazo, P. D., & Greenberg, M. T. (2005). The measurement of executive function in early childhood. *Developmental Neuropsychology, 28,* 561–571.

Braver, T. S., & Barch, D. M. (2002). A theory of cognitive control, aging cognition, and neuromodulation. *Neuroscience and Biobehavioral Reviews, 26,* 571–593.

Calkins, S. D., & Bell, M. A. (2010). *Child development at the intersection of emotion and cognition.* Washington, DC: American Psychological Association.

Carlson, S. M. (2005). Developmentally sensitive measures of executive function in preschool children. *Developmental Neuropsychology, 28,* 595–616.

Casey, B. J., & de Haan, M. (2002). Introduction: New methods in developmental science. *Developmental Science, 5,* 265–267.

Casey, B. J., Giedd, J. N., & Thomas, K. M. (2000). Structural and functional brain development and its relation to cognitive development. *Biological Psychology, 54,* 241–257.

Casey, B. J., Trainor, R. J., Orendi, J. L., Schubert, A. B., Nystrom, L. E., Giedd, J. N.,...Rapoport, J. L. (1997). A developmental functional MRI study of prefrontal activation during performance of a go-no-go task. *Journal of Cognitive Neuroscience, 9,* 835–847.

Chugani, H. T. (1994). Development of regional brain glucose metabolism in relation to behavior and plasticity. In G. Dawson & K. Fischer (Eds.), *Human behavior and the developing brain* (pp. 153–175). New York: Guilford Press.

Chugani, H. T. (1998). A critical period of brain development: Studies of cerebral glucose utilization with PET. *Preventive Medicine, 27,* 184–188.

Chugani, H. T. & Phelps, M. E. (1986). Maturational changes in cerebral function in infants determined by 18FDG positron emission tomography. *Science, 231,* 840–843.

Colombo, J., & Saxon, T. F. (2002). Infant attention and the development of cognition: Does the environment moderate continuity? In H. E. Fitzgerald, K. H. Karraker, & T. Luster (Eds.), *Infant development: Ecological perspectives* (pp. 35–60). Washington, DC: Garland Press.

Davidson, M. C., Amso, D., Anderson, L. C., & Diamond, A. (2006). Development of cognitive control and executive functions from 4 to 13 years: Evidence from manipulations of memory, inhibition, and task switching. *Neuropsychologia, 44,* 2037–2078.

Demetriou, A., Christou, C., Spanoudis, G., & Platsidou, M. (2002). The development of mental processing: Efficiency, working memory, and thinking. *Monographs of the Society for Research in Child Development, 67*(1, Serial No. 268).

Denham, S. A. (2006). Social-emotional competence as support for school readiness: What it is and how do we assess it? *Early Education and Development, 17,* 57–89.

Diamond, A. (1988). Abilities and neural mechanisms underlying AB performance. *Child Development, 59,* 523–527.

Diamond, A. (1990). The development and neural bases of memory functions as indexed by the AB and delayed response tasks in human infants and infant monkeys. *Annals of the New York Academy of Sciences, 608,* 267–317.

Diamond, A. (1991). Frontal lobe involvement in cognitive changes during the first year of life. In K. R. Gibson & A. C. Petersen (Eds.) *Brain maturation and cognitive development: Comparative and cross-cultural perspectives (pp. 127–180).* New York: Aldine de Grutyer.

Diamond, A. (2001). A model system for studying the role of dopamine in the prefrontal cortex during early development in humans: Early and continuously treated phenylketonuria. In C. A. Nelson & M. Luciana (Eds.) *Handbook of developmental cognitive neuroscience* (pp. 433–472). Cambridge, MA: MIT Press.

Diamond, A. (2002). Normal development of prefrontal cortex from birth to young adulthood: Cognitive functions, anatomy, and biochemistry. In D. T. Stuss & R. T. Knight (Eds.), *Principles of frontal lobe function* (pp. 466–503). London: Oxford University Press.

Diamond, A., Barnett, W. S., Thomas, J., & Munro, S. (2007). Preschool program improves cognitive control. *Science, 381,* 1387–1388.

Diamond, A., & Goldman-Rakic, P. S. (1989). Comparison of human infants and rhesus monkeys on Piaget's A-not-B task: Evidence for dependence on dorsolateral prefrontal cortex. *Experimental Brain Research, 74,* 24–40.

Diamond, A., Prevor, M. B., Callendar, G., & Druin, D. P. (1997). Prefrontal cortex cognitive deficits in children treated early and continuously for PKU. *Monographs of the Society for Research in Child Development, 62* (4, Serial No. 252).

Diamond, A., Zola-Morgan, S., & Squire, L. (1989). Successful performance by monkeys with lesions of the hippocampal formation on AB and object retrieval, two tasks that mark developmental changes in humans. *Behavioral Neuroscience, 103,* 526–537.

Durston, S., Thomas, K. M., Yang, Y., Ulug, A., Zimmerman, R. D., & Casey, B. J. (2002). A neural basis for the development of inhibitory control. *Developmental Science, 5,* 9–16.

Engle, R. W., Kane, M. J., & Tulholski, S. J. (1999). Individual differences in working memory capacity and what they tell us about controlled attention, general fluid intelligence, and functions of the prefrontal cortex. In A. Miyake & P. Shah (Eds.), *Models of working memory: Mechanisms of active maintenance and executive control* (pp. 102–134). New York: Cambridge University Press.

Eslinger, P. J. (1996). Conceptualizing, describing, and measuring components of executive function: A summary. In G. R. Lyon & N. A. Krasnegor (Eds.), *Attention, memory, and executive function* (pp. 367–395). Baltimore: Paul H Brookes.

Espy, K. A. (2004). Using developmental, cognitive, and neuroscience approaches to understand executive control in young children. *Developmental Neuropsychology, 26,* 379–384.

Espy, K. A., McDiarmid, M. M., Cwik, M. F., Stalets, M. M., Hamby, A., & Senn, T. E. (2004). The contribution of executive functions to emergent mathematic skills in preschool children. *Developmental Neuropsychology, 26,* 465–486.

Garon, N., Bryson, S. E., & Smtih, I. M. (2008). Executive function in preschoolers: A review using an integrative framework. *Psychological Bulletin, 134,* 31–60.

Gathercole, S. E., & Alloway, T. P. (2006). Practitioner review: Short-term and working memory impairments of neurodevelopmental disorders: Diagnosis and remedial support. *Journal of Child Psychology and Psychiatry, 47,* 4–15.

Gathercole, S. E., Tiffany, C., Briscoe, J., & Thorn, A. (2005). Developmental consequences of poor phonological short-term memory function in childhood: A longitudinal study. *Journal of Child Psychology and Psychiatry, 46*, 598–611.

Gerstadt, C., Hong, Y., & Diamond, A. (1994). The relationship between cognition and action: Performance of 3½–7-year old children on a Stroop-like day-night test. *Cognition, 53*, 129–153.

Giedd, J. N., Blumenthal, J., Jeffries, N. O., Castellanos, F. X., Liu, H., Zijdenbos, A.,…Rapoport, J. L. (1999). Brain development during childhood and adolescence: A longitudinal MRI study. *Nature Neuroscience, 2*, 861–863.

Goghari, V. M., & MacDonald, A. W., III. (2009). The neural basis of cognitive control: Response selection and inhibition. *Brain and Cognition, 71*, 72–83.

Goldman-Rakic, P. S. (1987). Circuitry of primate prefrontal cortex and regulation of behavior by representational memory. In F. Plum (Ed.), *Handbook of physiology: The nervous system* (Vol. 5, pp. 373–417). Bethesda, MD: American Physiological Society.

Goldman-Rakic, P. S., & Leung, H. C. (2002). Functional architecture of the dorsolateral prefrontal cortex in monkeys and humans. In D. Stuss & R. Knight (Eds.), *Principles of frontal lobe function* (pp. 85–95). New York: Oxford University Press.

Holmes, J., Gathercole, S. E., & Dunning, D. L. (2009). Adaptive training leads to sustained enhancement of poor working memory in children. *Developmental Science, 12*, F9–F15.

Hughes, C., Dunn, J., & White, A. (1998). Trick or treat? Uneven understanding of mind and emotion and executive dysfunction in "hard-to-manage" preschoolers. *Journal of Child Psychology and Psychiatry, 39*, 981–994.

Huttenlocher, P. R. (1979). Synaptic density in human frontal cortex—developmental changes and effects of aging. *Brain Research, 163*, 195–205.

Jacobsen, C. F. (1935). Functions of the frontal association areas in primates. *Archives of Neurology and Psychiatry, 33*, 558–560.

Jernigan, T. L., Archibald, S. L., Berhow, M. T., Sowell, E. R., Foster, D. S., & Hesselink, J. R. (1991). Cerebral structure on MRI, part I: Localization of age-related changes. *Biological Psychiatry, 29*, 55–67.

Kane, M. J., & Engle, R. W. (2002). The role of the prefrontal cortex in working memory capacity, executive attention, and general fluid intelligence: An individual-differences perspective. *Psychonomic Bulletin and Review, 9*, 637–671.

Kane, M. J., & Engle, R. W. (2003). Working-memory capacity and the control of attention: The contributions of goal neglect, response competition, and task set to Stroop interference. *Journal of Experimental Psychology: General, 132*, 47–70.

Kochanska, G., Murray, K., & Coy, K. C. (1997). Inhibitory control as a contributor to conscience in childhood: From toddler to early school age. *Child Development, 68*, 263–277.

Kok, A. (1999). Varieties of inhibition: Manifestations in cognition, event-related potentials and aging. *Acta Psychologica, 10*, 129–158.

Luna, B., Garver, K. E., Urban, T. A., Lazar, N. A., & Sweeney, J. A. (2004). Maturation of cognitive processes from late childhood to adulthood. *Child Development, 75*, 1357–1372.

Luna, B., Padmanabhan, A., & O'Hearn, K. (2010). What has fMRI told us about the development of cognitive control through adolescence? *Brain and Cognition, 72*, 101–113.

Luria, A. R. (1973). The frontal lobes and the regulation of behavior. In K. H. Pribram & A. R. Luria (Eds.), *Psychophysiology of the frontal lobes* (pp. 3–28). Oxford, England: Academic Press.

Miller, E., & Cohen, J. (2001). An integrative theory of prefrontal cortex function. *Annual Review of Neuroscience, 24*, 167–202.

Miyake, A., Friedman, N. P., Emerson, M. J., Witzki, A. J., Howerter, A., & Wager, T. D. (2000). The unity and diversity of executive functions and their contributions to complex "frontal lobe" tasks: A latent variable analysis. *Cognitive Psychology, 41*, 49–100.

Morasch, K. C., & Bell, M. A. (2011). The role of inhibitory control in behavioral and physiological expressions of toddler executive function. *Journal of Child Psychology, 108*(3), 593–606.

Nelson, C. A. (1995). The ontogeny of human memory: A cognitive neuroscience perspective. *Developmental Psychology, 31*, 723–738.

Nelson, C. A., & Luciana, M. (2008). *Handbook of developmental cognitive neuroscience.* Cambridge, MA: MIT Press.

Passler, M. A., Isaac, W., & Hynde, G. W. (1985). Neuropsychological development of behavior attributed to frontal lobe functioning in children. *Developmental Neuropsychology, 1*, 349–370.

Pelphrey, K. A., Reznick, J. S., Goldman, B. D., Sasson, N., Morrow, J., Donahoe, A., & Hodgson, K. (2004). Development of visuospatial short-term memory in the second half of the first year. *Developmental Psychology, 40*, 836–851.

Pennington, B. F. (1994). The working memory function of the prefrontal cortices: Implications for developmental and individual differences in cognition. In M. M. Haith, J. Benson, R. J. Roberts, Jr., & B. F. Pennington (Eds.), *The development of future oriented processes* (pp. 243–289). Chicago: University of Chicago Press.

Piaget, J. (1954). *The construction of reality in the child.* New York: Basic Books.

Pickering, S. J., & Gathercole, S. E. (2001) *Working Memory Test Battery for Children.* Hove, England: Psychological Corporation.

Posner, M. I., & Snyder, C. R. (1975). Attention and cognitive control. In R. L. Solso (Ed.), *Information processing and cognition: The Loyola symposium* (pp. 55–85). Hillsdale, NJ: Erlbaum.

Reznick, J. S. (2007). Working memory in infants and toddlers. In L. M. Oakes & P. J. Bauer (Eds.), *Short and long-term memory in infancy and early childhood* (pp. 3–26). New York: Oxford University Press.

Roberts, A. C., Robbins, T. W., & Weiskrantz, L. (1998). *The prefrontal cortex: Executive and cognitive functions.* New York: Oxford University Press.

Roberts, R. J., & Pennington, B. F. (1996). An interactive framework for examining prefrontal cognitive processes. *Developmental Neuropsychology, 12*, 105–126.

Stern, R. M., Ray, W. J., & Quigley, K. S. (2001). *Psychophysiological recording (2nd ed.).* New York: Oxford University Press.

Unsworth, N., Schrock, J. C., & Engle, R. W. (2004). Working memory capacity and the antisaccade task: Individual differences in voluntary saccade control. *Journal of Experimental Psychology: Learning, Memory, and Cognition, 30*, 1302–1321.

Welsh, M. C., & Pennington, B. F. (1988). Assessing frontal lobe functioning in children: Views from developmental psychology. *Developmental Neuropsychology, 4*, 199–230.

Welsh, M. C., Pennington, B. F., & Groisser, D. B. (1991). A normative-developmental study of executive function: A window on prefrontal function in children. *Developmental Neuropsychology, 72*, 131–149.

Wolfe, C. D., & Bell, M. A. (2004). Working memory and inhibitory control in early childhood: Contributions from electrophysiology, temperament, and language. *Developmental Psychobiology, 44*, 68–83.

Wolfe, C. D., & Bell, M. A. (2007). Sources of variability in working memory in early childhood: A consideration of age, temperament, language, and brain electrical activity. *Cognitive Development, 22*, 431–455.

# The Development of Attention

Greg D. Reynolds, Mary L. Courage, *and* John E. Richards

**Abstract**

This chapter reviews past research and theory related to the early development of attention beginning with the most commonly used behavioral measures of infant visual attention. The developmental course of visual attention in infancy and early childhood is then described with a focus on the relevant behavioral and psychophysiological findings and recent work relating these findings to developmental change occurring in the brain in early development. Several theoretical models of the development of visual attention are discussed, including Richards' (2001, 2008, 2010) model of a general arousal/attention system. We conclude with a discussion of individual differences in infant attention and present a series of suggestions for future directions in research on attention in infancy and early childhood.

**Key Words:** infancy, visual attention, event-related potentials, cognitive development, source analysis

Attention is a core component of adaptive responsiveness to the environment, and it is integral to all explicit cognitive processing. However, a clear and concise definition of attention as a global construct remains somewhat elusive (Colombo, 2001; Moray, 1969, 1993). It is generally agreed that there are multiple forms of attention and several component processes involved in attention. In one way or another nearly all of these forms of attention relate to focusing perceptual processing toward a particular aspect of the environment. Much developmental research has focused on the ability of infants and children of different ages to engage in selective attention, including orienting toward a specific stimulus and subsequently maintaining attention toward that central stimulus over distracters in the periphery. Rapid early developments in these aspects of attention are evident in a wide range of behaviors and also in the underlying brain structures that mediate them. Ultimately, they will have a significant impact on whether and

how infants and young children will attend to people and events in their environment.

In this chapter we review past research and theory related to the early development of attention. We begin with a brief description of the most commonly used behavioral measures of infant visual attention. We then describe the developmental course of visual attention in infancy and early childhood. We review the relevant behavioral and psychophysiological findings and subsequently cover recent work relating these findings to developmental change occurring in the brain in early development. Additionally, we present Richards' (2001, 2008, 2010) model of a general arousal/attention system that provides a coherent and biologically plausible framework for understanding developmental changes that have been observed in attention across the first 2 years of postnatal life. We describe the impact of developmental change in Richards' general arousal/attention system on development of specific attention systems related to eye-movement control. We conclude with a discussion of the significance of individual differences in infant attention and present a series of suggestions for future directions in research on attention in infancy and early childhood.

## Historical Background and Behavioral Measures

Developmental research on attention in infancy has a relatively recent history. In the early years, the study of attention was of secondary interest in research where processes such as perception, discrimination, learning, strategy acquisition, planning, or working memory were of primary concern. Measuring any of these processes in early development is not a straightforward process because the human infant is incapable of making verbal responses or engaging in complex behavioral responses. Historically, researchers have thus utilized infant looking behavior as a window into attention and cognitive processing in infancy. Fantz (1964) was among the first to document a systematic decline in looking toward a stimulus with repeated presentations (i.e., habituation). In the habituation procedure, infants are exposed to repeated presentations of a single stimulus; once looking drops to a set criteria from the initial (or peak) looks (i.e., habituates), the stimulus is changed and subsequent looking to the new stimulus is examined. If the infant looks longer after the change has occurred, then the assumption is made that the infant recognized the difference between the new stimulus and the stimulus he or she was habituated to. This increase in looking following a stimulus change is often referred to as dishabituation or recovery of looking.

The paired comparison task is another procedure commonly used to examine infant looking behavior. In this procedure infants are shown a single stimulus during a brief familiarization phase. Following a delay interval, there is a recognition memory test in which the familiar stimulus is paired with a novel stimulus that has not been seen previously. Recognition memory for the familiar stimulus is inferred if the infants show greater attention (i.e., longer looking) to the novel stimulus than to the familiar stimulus during the paired comparison test. This procedure can also be applied without a familiarization phase to test the relative salience of stimuli based on previous experience outside of the laboratory. These looking time methods have provided a wealth of data on the conditions under which infants encode, store, and retrieve information. These include the facts that (1) encoding, storage, and retrieval processes in preverbal children could be examined objectively and scientifically; (2) even very young infants were able to recognize stimuli that they had seen before and in certain conditions could retain that information over several weeks; and (3) many of the processes and variables that were known to affect encoding, storage, and retrieval in older children and adults were integral to infant memory processes as well (for reviews, see Haith & Benson, 1998; Kellman & Banks, 1998; Mandler, 1992; Rose, Feldman, & Jankowski, 2004).

More recently, the study of attention has become important in its own right, as cognitive developmental research has become increasingly integrated with research in cognitive neuroscience. A number of practical issues have also contributed to the growing interest in the development of attention. For example, individual differences in attention observed during infancy are predictive of achievements in language, cognition, and play later in childhood. In addition, a number of deficits in attention processes contribute to or are symptomatic of the learning and behavior difficulties experienced by children with conditions such as attention-deficit/hyperactivity disorder (ADHD), fetal alcohol spectrum disorder (FASD), autism, and early exposure to teratogenic agents and environmental contaminants.

One focus that has emerged from the abundant data available from habituation and preferential looking experiments is the development of look duration in infancy. Changes in look duration occurring across infancy and early childhood are believed to reflect further development of areas of the brain involved in the control of eye movements and visual attention. Thus, the timing of change in visual behavior provides insight into the emergence of functional attention systems in the brain. Several models have been proposed to explain the development of visual attention from this perspective (e.g., Bronson, 1974, 1997; Hood, 1995; Johnson, 1990; Maurer & Lewis, 1979, 1998; Posner & Peterson, 1998; Richards, 2008, 2010; Richards, Reynolds, & Courage, 2010; Ruff & Rothbart, 1996). Many of these models were influenced by Schiller's (1985) work on primate eye-movement systems. In the next section we discuss the development of three specific attention systems: the reflexive system, the posterior orienting system, and the anterior attention system (or executive attention system). These systems involve networks of brain areas dedicated to particular aspects or forms of attention. We also discuss a general arousal/attention system that influences all of these specific attention systems and also plays a key role in the developmental of attention.

## Developments in Visual Attention
### The Reflexive System

In the newborn period, it is generally agreed that visual attention is primarily under the control of a reflexive system involving the lateral geniculate nucleus, primary visual cortex, and superior colliculus. Yet, in spite of the immaturity in both structure (e.g., retino-geniculo-cortical pathway) and function (e.g., spatial vision, color vision) of the human visual system (e.g., Atkinson, 2000; Banks & Salapatek, 1983; Hickey & Peduzzi, 1987), newborn infants do attend selectively to stimuli during their brief periods of alert inactivity. In his seminal research, Fantz (1963, 1964) showed that between birth and 2 months of age infants looked longer at patterned than at unpatterned stimuli and that depending on factors such as familiarity, size, and the amount of contrast, they preferred to look (i.e., looked longer) at some stimuli over others. Although visual reflexes (e.g., saccadic and pursuit movements) are present at birth, more general visuomotor immaturity restricts infants' ability to scan stimuli extensively or to detect stimuli beyond about 30 degrees in the peripheral visual field (e.g., Aslin, 1987; Lewis & Maurer, 1992). Moreover, when infants visually fixate on an element in the environment, they may have trouble disengaging from it, a phenomenon referred to as obligatory looking or "sticky fixation" (e.g., Hood, 1995). This is most evident between 1 and 2 months of age, a brief period when certain inhibitory mechanisms that limit eye movements come online. These early immaturities in the visual system do not last long. The rapid neurological development that occurs in the retina and in the visual pathways to the cortex between 2 and 3 postnatal months of age coincides with significant improvement in all aspects of visual functioning, an expansion of the effective visual field, moderation of inhibitory mechanisms that restricted eye movements, and the onset of more mature perceptual abilities whereby infants come to recognize objects and to determine their spatial layout. Coincident with this shift toward greater cortical control of vision, infants begin to spend more time awake and in an alert state. They look about the environment in a way that is less reflexive and more "voluntary" in nature (see Colombo, 2001; Haith, 1980).

### Posterior Orienting System

From 3 to 6 months of age, a posterior orienting network becomes functional (Posner & Peterson, 1990). Ruff and Rothbart (1996) described infants' visual behavior during much of the first postnatal year of life as dominated by an *orienting/investigative system* of attention. There are two interrelated components in this system. First, a spatial *orienting* network (including the posterior parietal cortex with several subcortical systems such as the superior colliculus, pulvinar, and the locus coeruleus in the brainstem), is alerted by peripheral stimuli and directs attention to potentially important locations in the environment (i.e, "where"an object is). This component mediates attention functions such as engagement, disengagement, shifting, and inhibition of return. Areas within the parietal cortex along with the frontal eye fields are integral for disengaging and shifting attention. As these areas develop, infants will be less prone to "sticky fixation" and develop greater ability to voluntarily shift attention. Second, an *object recognition* network (including the dorsal and ventral pathways from the primary visual cortex to the parietal cortex and the inferior temporal cortex) mediates attention to object features and gathers detailed information (e.g., form, color, pattern) that enables object identification (i.e., "what" an object is).

There is a marked developmental transition in the structure and function of this system between 3 and 9 months of age. Rapid maturation at all levels of the visual system along with increased periods of arousal and alertness enables infants to deploy their attention more flexibly and quickly and to respond to stimuli in terms of experiential factors such as the novelty or complexity of objects and events rather than by their intensity alone. As this attention system develops across this age range, infants will focus on the relevant features of objects and demonstrate clear visual preferences based on previous experience. The increased ability to shift attention combined with more efficient information processing leads to a linear decrease in looking from 3 to 6 months.

### Anterior Attention System

After 6 months of age, the rudiments of another major attention system, one in which the infant begins to acquire a system of higher level, endogenous, or voluntary control over the allocation and deployment of cognitive resources, begins to emerge. This capacity is evident in a wide range of behaviors. For example, infants' look duration to static stimuli and simple objects continues to decline, whereas their look duration to complex objects increases (Courage, Reynolds, & Richards, 2006; Ruff & Saltarelli, 1993). Infants also look more to their caregivers in situations that call for social referencing (Bertenthal & Campos, 1990) and joint attention (Bakeman & Adamson, 1984). At the same time, infants show the beginnings of behavioral inhibition on the A-not-B task (Diamond, 1985). Further evidence of emerging intentionality is evident in improvements in deferred imitation (Barr, Dowden, & Hayne, 1996; Barr & Hayne, 2000), means-end problem solving (Willatts & Rosie, 1989), and recall memory (Bauer, Wiebe, Waters, & Nelson, 2003) that occur late in the first year of life. By about 18 months of age, the endogenous control of attention acquires an increasingly executive function as toddlers also evaluate behavior progress and direct activity with goals and plans. The system involved in all of these developmental changes is called the anterior attention system because developments in executive attention and functioning are closely related to frontal brain activity, in particular the orbitofrontal cortex, dorsolateral prefrontal cortex, and anterior cingulate cortex (e.g., Bell & Fox, 1994; Chugani, 1994; Diamond & Goldman-Rakic, 1989; Posner, 1995). These changes in visual attention and their neural substrates enable (and may be enabled by) coincident changes in language (e.g., comprehension), cognition (e.g., representation), and self-regulation (e.g., behavioral inhibition) that begin in this time frame and continue to advance across the preschool years.

Colombo (2001) has proposed a triphasic theory of look duration that describes the overall trajectory of early developments in looking. This model fits well with the developing attention systems described earlier. The triphasic theory proposes that look duration increases from birth to 2 months of age, followed by a consistent decrease in looking from 3 to 6 months. After 6 months of age, there is a plateau in look duration. Courage, Reynolds, and Richards (2006) tested the triphasic theory in a developmental study of look duration in infants from 3 to 12 months of age. Infants were exposed to several different types of stimuli, including achromatic computer-generated patterns, a female face, and scenes from Sesame Street. Additionally, each stimulus type was presented in both static and dynamic conditions. Figure 63.1 shows the results of our analysis. The triphasic theory was supported overall with a clear drop in looking from 3 to 6 months of age (i.e., 14 to 26 weeks). However, after 6 months, the stimulus type began to have a significant impact

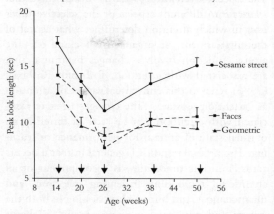

Developmental course of look duration in infancy

**Figure 63.1** The developmental course of look duration to patterns, faces, and Sesame Street across infancy. The Y-axis represents infants' peak look lengths, and age (in weeks) is shown on the X-axis. Fourteen weeks corresponds to 3 months of age, 26 weeks corresponds to 6 months of age, and 52 weeks corresponds to 1 year of age. Arrows show exact test age. (Adapted with permission from Courage, M.L., Reynolds, G.D., & Richards, J.E. [2006]. Infants' visual attention to patterned stimuli: Developmental change from 3- to 12-months of age. *Child Development*, 77[3], 680–695.)

on look duration. Infants began to look longer to complex, interesting stimuli (faces, Sesame Street), whereas looking remained very low to basic, achromatic visual patterns. There was also a strong main effect for dynamic stimuli, with infants looking longer to dynamic as opposed to static stimuli regardless of the specific type of stimulus (pattens, faces, Sesame Street). These data provide a clear picture of the development of visual attention systems and their impact on infant looking. The drop from 3 to 6 months in looking represents the onset of functioning of the posterior orienting system. The infant becomes able to shift fixation voluntarily from one stimulus to another, and this shifting becomes more rapid with increasing age. However, after 6 months, the anterior attention system begins to influence looking. Thus, looking remains brief to stimuli that require no further processing. But in situations where sustained attention is called for (dynamic patterns, faces, Sesame Street), the infant demonstrates increased looking and resistance to distracters. In addition to these three specific attention systems, there is a more general system that impacts attention throughout development.

## General Arousal/Attention System

Attention can be seen as having two major functions: a selective function and an arousal function.

The specific attention systems discussed earlier all relate to different aspects of the selective function in which attention determines what aspect of the environment the organism is focused on. The arousal function involves changes in arousal that are associated with attention. Ruff and Rothbart (1996) refer to this conceptualization of attention as "attention as state." The changes in state associated with attention can be seen as fostering an optimal state of arousal for performance or learning. This arousal response is general in that it occurs across multiple modalities, is a component of all attentional responding (orienting, selection, and maintenance), and impacts functioning in both the central and peripheral nervous systems. Richards (2001, 2008, 2010) proposes that there is a general arousal/attention system in the brain composed of neuroanatomical connections between the mesencephalic reticular activation system and the cortex (Heilman, Watson, Valenstein, & Goldberg, 1987; Mesulam, 1983). Additionally, the noradrenergic and cholinergic neurotransmitter systems are highly involved in this system (Robbins & Everitt, 1995). This system shows substantial growth across early development with infants and children showing greater magnitude arousal responses associated with attention and children spending longer periods within this arousal state across age (e.g., Richards & Cronise, 2000).

Research over the past quarter of a century has been characterized by a steady increase in the sophistication of the tools available for measuring the arousal response associated with attention. Earlier work was aimed at establishing psychophysiological measures of infant attention and integrating these measures with existing behavioral measures of infant attention. Heart rate is the most notable of these psychophysiological measures and provides highly informative data regarding the process of attention in infancy. More recent work has established a link between behavioral and heart rate measures of attention and neural correlates of infant attention. Richards refers to times when the infant is attentive and the general arousal/attention system is engaged as "sustained attention."

## Sustained Attention

Sustained attention to stimulus features, also called focused attention, is the extended selective engagement of a behavior system that primarily enhances information processing in that system (e.g., see Richards, 2003). Many of the infant's cognitive and social activities occur during episodes of sustained attention, and it is during this time that active information processing occurs (see Oakes & Tellinghuisen, 1994; Reynolds & Richards, 2008; Ruff & Rothbart, 1996). Novel objects and events typically first elicit stimulus orienting followed by sustained attention. Maintenance of sustained attention facilitates the infant's learning and memory for aspects of the stimulus as it becomes familiar (Colombo, Richman, Shaddy, Greenhoot, & Maikranz, 2001; Frick & Richards, 2001; Richards, 1997a, 2003a). Infants are also less distractible by a peripheral stimulus and slower to orient to it when they are in sustained attention (Hicks & Richards, 1998; Hunter & Richards, 2003; Richards, 1997b; Ruff & Capozzoli, 2003). Infants as young as 3 months of age will engage in 5- to 10-second periods of sustained attention, and the duration that sustained attention can be maintained increases markedly to several minutes or more over the first 2 years of life (Reynolds & Richards, 2008; Ruff & Capozzolli, 2003). The development of sustained attention during the period of infancy is closely related to the development of brain systems controlling arousal and state (see Richards, 2001, 2008, 2010). These include the neuroanatomical connections between the mesencephalic reticular activating system in the brainstem, the thalamus, and the cortex. The mesencephalic reticular activating system also stimulates extrinsic neurotransmitters that in turn influence the limbic system areas. Sustained attention is a manifestation of this global arousal system of the brain that controls responsiveness to events in the environment. Sustained attention has been operationalized using both behavioral (i.e., looking) measures and heart rate, and we discuss details associated with each approach in the following sections.

## Sustained Attention: Looking

The duration and direction of looking have been central measures of infants' attention to a variety of stimuli and over the years have provided important information about infants' sensory, perceptual, and cognitive processes and how they change with age. However, it is now evident that attention and looking are not isomorphic—there are varieties of attention and varieties of looking (see Colombo, 2001). Ruff and colleagues (Ruff, 1986; Ruff & Capozzoli, 2003; Ruff, Capozzoli, & Saltarelli, 1996; Ruff, Capozzoli, & Weissberg, 1998) identified and investigated two different patterns of looking that infants and young children display when given a novel toy to play with. An infant or child in "focused" attention showed a characteristic pattern of examination of the toy in which he or she looked at it with an intense facial expression and knit brows, in conjunction with reduced body movement, and manual rotation and finger examination of the toy. In contrast, during periods of "casual" attention, the infant continued to look at the toy but without the intensity of expression and the manual exploration of the toy. During casual attention the infant often waved or shook the toy, appearing to enjoy its sensory qualities (see also Oakes & Tellinghausen, 1994). Information processing occurs during focused attention but not in casual attention (see Oakes & Tellinghuisen, 1994; Ruff et al., 1996; Tellinghuisen & Oakes, 1997).

### Sustained Attention: Heart Rate

Sustained attention is also indicated when infants are presented with a novel stimulus and an extended deceleration in heart rate accompanies looking at the stimulus. Richards and colleagues (Richards & Casey, 1992) proposed a model in which the phasic changes in infants' heart rates that occur as they look at a stimulus correspond to different levels of attentional engagement. There are four key phases in this model illustrated in Figure 63.2. First, when the stimulus is initially presented, there is a brief automatic interrupt phase that reflects the detection of a change in environmental stimulation. A very brief, reflexive, biphasic deceleration-acceleration in heart rate occurs. The second phase is stimulus orienting. Stimulus orienting indicates the beginning of attentional engagement and initiates preliminary processing of the information in the stimulus. A large, rapid deceleration in heart rate from its pre-stimulus level occurs during this phase. The third phase is sustained attention. Sustained attention reflects the activation of the alertness/arousal system of the brain and involves voluntary, subject-controlled cognitive processing of the stimulus information. The heart rate deceleration that was reached during stimulus orienting is maintained during this phase. Heart rate also shows decreased variability, and certain other somatic changes that facilitate attentiveness such as reduced body movement and slower respiration may also occur. Infants require less time to process and subsequently recognize a stimulus if exposure occurs during sustained attention than if exposure occurs during other heart rate phases (Richards, 1997a). The fourth phase is attention termination. During this last phase the infant continues to look at the stimulus but is no longer processing its information (i.e., is inattentive) and heart rate begins to return to prestimulus levels. Infants fail to demonstrate evidence of recognition memory for a previously viewed stimulus if exposure occurs during attention termination (Richards, 1997a).

The behavioral (looking) and psychophysiological (heart rate) indices of sustained attention are highly correlated (Lansink & Richards, 1997). The implications for information processing of focused and casual attention are similar to those of sustained attention and attention termination. Focused attention and casual attention are behaviorally defined periods of attention and inattention. Sustained attention and attention termination are heart rate–defined periods of attention and inattention. For example, infants take longer to disengage from a central stimulus and shift attention to a distracter stimulus during focused attention than during casual attention (Oakes & Tellinghuisen, 1994; Ruff et al., 1996; Tellinghuisen & Oakes, 1997). Similarly, infants demonstrate longer distraction latency to a peripheral stimulus presented during sustained attention than during attention termination (Casey & Richards, 1988; Hunter & Richards, 2003; Richards, 1987, 1997b). Sustained attention and focused attention are operationally defined phases of attention that represent periods when the infant is actively engaged in information processing. Distraction latencies are longer when infants are engaged in these phases of attention because infants are most likely processing information provided by a central stimulus. During casual attention or attention termination, infants respond more rapidly

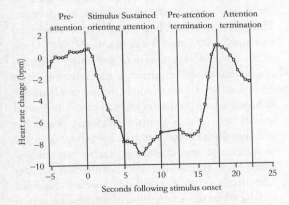

**Figure 63.2** Richards' heart rate phases of attention. The average heart rate change as a function of seconds following stimulus onset during the heart rate–defined attention phases is shown (data from Richards & Casey, 1992). Change in heart rate from prestimulus levels is indicated on the X-axis, and time following stimulus onset is shown on the Y-axis.

to peripheral stimuli because they are no longer engaged in attention to the central stimulus.

Heart rate and behavioral measures of infant attention also correlate with measures of brain activity associated with attention and recognition memory. Event-related potentials (ERPs) have been used to investigate the neural correlates of infant visual attention and recognition memory (e.g., Nelson & Collins, 1991, 1992; Reynolds, Courage, & Richards, 2010; Reynolds & Richards, 2005; Richards, 2003a,b). ERPs refer to voltage oscillations in the electroencephalogram (EEG) that are time-locked with an event of interest (Fabiani, Gratton, & Coles, 2000; Picton et al., 2000). Stimuli are presented briefly and repeatedly to each participant, and then trials are averaged together by experimental condition to identify the ERP. This averaging technique increases the signal-to-noise ratio in the EEG so that waveform components associated with a particular stage of processing can be identified. Of particular interest is the Negative central (Nc) component. The Nc is a component of negative polarity located over frontal and central electrodes with a peak latency of between 400 and 800 ms following stimulus onset. This component is ubiquitous in research on infant attention and memory and has been proposed to reflect novelty detection, general orienting, or amount of attentional engagement (e.g., Carver, Bauer, & Nelson, 2000; Courchesne, 1977; Courchesne, Ganz, & Norcia, 1981; de Haan & Nelson, 1997, 1999; Karrer & Ackles, 1987; 1988; Karrer & Monti, 1995; Nikkel & Karrer, 1994; Reynolds & Richards, 2005, 2009; Richards, 2003a; Webb, Long, & Nelson, 2005).

Richards (2003a) explored the relationship between the Nc component and attention processes in a modified-oddball procedure that exposes infants to frequent familiar, infrequent familiar, and infrequent novel stimuli (Nelson & Collins, 1991, 1992). Infants of 4.5, 6, or 7.5 months of age were presented with a video of a Sesame Street movie as a background stimulus. Heart rate changes elicited by the video were used to distinguish periods of time during sustained attentiveness (during heart rate deceleration) and during inattentiveness (when heart rate was at prestimulus levels) (e.g., Casey & Richards, 1988; Reynolds & Richards, 2008; Richards, 1997, 2001; Richards & Casey, 1992). Nc amplitude was greater during periods of attention than inattention and also increased in magnitude across age, but only during periods of attentiveness. Reynolds and Richards (2005) used a high-density 128-channel EEG recording system

that enabled the application of cortical source analysis of the ERP data for identification of locations in the cortex that could be potential generators of Nc (Reynolds & Richards, 2009; Richards, 2003b, 2004, 2005). Nc was found to be greater in amplitude to novel stimuli than familiar stimuli (see Fig. 63.3). Figure 63.4 shows the results of the source analysis displayed on a series of magnetic resonance imaging (MRI) images. The results of the cortical source analyses identified areas of prefrontal cortex, including the anterior cingulate, as likely sources of the Nc component.

To determine the relationship between ERP and behavioral correlates of infant attention and memory, Reynolds, Courage, and Richards (2010) designed a procedure with alternating blocks of ERP trials followed by paired-comparison choice trials. This design allowed for the analysis of the distribution of infant visual preferences throughout ERP testing. There were several findings of interest. First, there was a main effect for age with Nc increasing in amplitude from 4.5 to 7.5 months of age. This may reflect the increasing involvement of prefrontal cortical areas in visual attention across infancy. Second, there was a main effect for attention replicating Richards (2003) with Nc being greater in amplitude during sustained attention. Third, there was an interaction of preference with stimulus type. Infants that demonstrated novelty preferences demonstrated greater amplitude Nc in response to novel versus familiar stimuli. The opposite pattern was found for those that demonstrated familiarity preferences.

These findings indicate that Nc is impacted by stimulus salience. Thus, Nc reflects activation of the general arousal system involved in attention. Through the use of heart rate, ERPs, behavioral measures, and source localization, different levels of this general arousal system governing attention can be examined. Activation of this system leads to decreased heart rate through the parasympathetic influence of the brainstem on the heart. The general arousal system also involves enhanced processing throughout the cortex through the influence of the noradrenergic and cholinergic neurochemical systems. Thus, areas of the brain involved in the specific attention systems will demonstrate enhanced activity when the general arousal/attention system is engaged. Our results support this proposal showing that areas of the cortex that demonstrate enhanced activation when this attention system was engaged include inferior and superior prefrontal cortex, and the anterior cingulate cortex (all structures involved

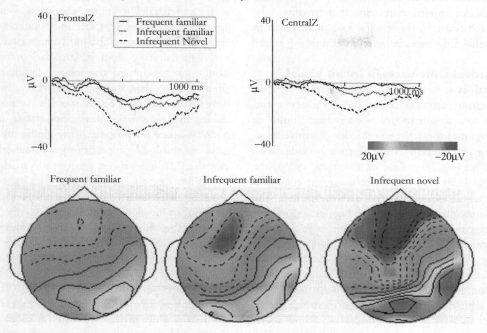

Nc following familiar and novel stimulus presentations

Frequent familiar    Infrequent familiar    Infrequent novel

**Figure 63.3** The Nc component following frequent familiar, infrequent familiar, and infrequent novel stimulus presentations. The event-related potential waveforms are shown by stimulus type in the top panel at FrontalZ and CentralZ electrode locations (see Reynolds & Richards, 2005). The bottom panel shows the topographical scalp potential maps of the distribution of this component for the three stimulus types at the peak of Nc (approximately 500 ms following stimulus onset). (*See* color insert.)

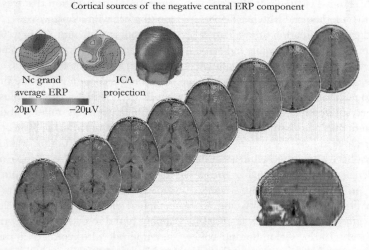

Cortical sources of the negative central ERP component

Nc grand average ERP    ICA projection

**Figure 63.4** The sequence of magnetic resonance imaging (MRI) slides shows the dipole locations (yellow circles) for an event-related potential (ERP) component known as the Negative central (Nc) (topographical scalp potential maps on upper left figures). The dipoles represent the best-fitting cortical sources of the Nc for individual participants obtained through cortical source analysis of high-density ERP data. (*See* color insert.)

in the anterior attention system). Neuroimaging work with adult participants has shown that these areas are active in a wide range of tasks involving attention (see review, Duncan & Owen, 2000).

Thus, with advances in technology and increased sophistication of tools available to developmental scientists, a clearer picture has emerged of the normal course of early development of attention and the role that brain development plays in this process. An important question that remains to be answered concerns the specific role of the brain in individual differences in infant attention.

## Individual Differences in Infant Visual Attention

Because performance on the habituation and paired-comparison procedures has been found to have significant predictive value for cognitive functioning in childhood (e.g., Bornstein & Sigman, 1986; Fagan, 1984; Rose & Feldman, 1995), the study of individual differences in infant cognition has emerged as an important area of research. The best known approach to studying individual differences in infant visual attention is to examine differences across infants in their look durations during habituation to or during familiarization with a novel stimulus. Using this approach, look duration has been found to be negatively correlated with measures of cognitive performance in infancy as well as certain measures of intellectual performance obtained in later childhood years (Bornstein & Sigman, 1986; Colombo, 1993; Colombo & Mitchell, 1990; Colombo, Mitchell, Coldren, & Freeseman, 1991; Colombo, Mitchell, & Horowitz, 1988; McCall & Carriger, 1993; Rose, Slater, & Perry, 1986; Sigman, Cohen, Beckwith, & Parmalee, 1986; Tamis-LeMonda & Bornstein, 1989). According to Colombo and Mitchell (1990), peak look-length during habituation or familiarization provides the most reliable and stable indicator of individual differences in attention and cognitive processing. Infants that demonstrate brief visual fixations (i.e., short-lookers) are more likely to demonstrate evidence of recognition memory for a familiar stimulus than infants that demonstrate long visual fixations (i.e., long-lookers).

Mechanisms that have been proposed to account for individual differences in infant visual attention include speed of processing, processing strategy, and the ability to disengage attention (Colombo, 1993; Colombo, Freeseman, Coldren, & Frick, 1995; Colombo et al., 2001). Colombo and colleagues (2001) tested speed of processing and processing strategy with 4-month-old infants using the paired-comparison procedure, which consisted of the simultaneous presentation of two novel stimuli that differed from the familiar on either global or local stimulus properties. Familiarization time was also manipulated. Results indicate that with brief familiarization time (20 s), short-lookers only demonstrated preferences (i.e., looked longer) based on

global differences; long-lookers failed to demonstrate a preference for either condition. With longer familiarization times (30s), short-lookers shifted from demonstrating global-differences preferences to demonstrating local-differences preferences. Long-lookers required the longest familiarization time (50s) to demonstrate a preference, and this only occurred to local differences. The authors concluded that (1) short-lookers demonstrate a dominant tendency for processing the global properties prior to the local properties of a visual stimulus and that (2) long-lookers process information at a slower rate than short-lookers and use a less efficient visual intake strategy by processing the local properties prior to the global ones.

Colombo, Richman, Shaddy, Greenhoot, and Maikranz (2001) found that long-lookers spend proportionately more time in attention termination than short-lookers. This indicates that long-lookers may have problems disengaging fixation. Long-lookers are more likely to continue looking at a stimulus while inattentive, whereas short-lookers are more likely to shift fixation away from a stimulus once attention has waned. Thus, the addition of heart rate measures to the video analysis of looking behavior provided a much more accurate measure of infant attention and provided a level of insight into possible mechanisms behind individual differences in infant attention that was not possible with looking behavior alone.

Reynolds, Guy, and Zhang (2011) conducted an investigation of individual differences in infant visual attention and ERPs. Infants of 6 and 7.5 months of age were tested in a procedure in which they were familiarized with a single stimulus, and then shown the familiar stimulus on 50% of the ERP trials, and novel stimuli on the other 50% of trials. Look duration during familiarization was used to determine looker type. There were a couple of interesting findings. There was a significant interaction of looker type and stimulus type on the late slow wave at right temporal electrodes. The late slow wave is commonly found to occur on novel trials and decreases in amplitude with repeated exposure (e.g., de Haan & Nelson, 1997; Quinn, Westerlund, & Nelson, 2006; Snyder, 2010). Short-lookers demonstrated a late slow wave to novel stimuli and a return to baseline to the familiar stimulus. The return to baseline following familiar presentations indicates the short-lookers fully processed and recognized the familiar stimulus. Long-lookers demonstrated no differences in late slow waves to both novel and familiar stimuli, indicating incomplete processing and lack of recognition of the familiar stimulus. These findings demonstrate that individual differences in visual attention are related to differences in cortical activity across infants.

## Conclusion

There is a rich history of research on the early development of visual attention. Early work in the area capitalized on the natural tendency of human infants to look longer at novel compared to familiar stimuli. Habituation and preferential looking measures have provided a wealth of information regarding the developmental course of looking and visual attention in infancy and early childhood (for reviews, see Colombo, 2001; Haith & Benson, 1998; Keller & Banks, 1998; Mandler, 1992; Rose, 2007). Models of the development of visual attention and the underlying changes in the brain responsible for this development have been traditionally based on behavioral data obtained through looking measures with human infants, integrated with neuroanatomical data obtained through comparative animal research (e.g., Bachevalier, 2008; Schiller, 1985). This application of comparative data to explain developmental change in human infants has been useful but has certain limitations (see Richards, 2010 for a detailed discussion). More recent work has utilized noninvasive measures of infant brain activity (e.g., EEG, ERP, structural MRI, source analysis) to test these models directly in human participants (e.g., Reynolds & Richards, 2005; Richards, 2001, 2005, 2007).

The extant findings provide support for the proposal that there are several attention systems that show substantial development in infancy. Most notable are the posterior orienting system, anterior attention system, and a general arousal/attention system (see Ruff & Rothbart, 1996; Posner & Peterson, 1990; Richards, 2001, 2008, 2010). As these systems become functional, visual attention and looking show clear developmental change. Early attention is primarily under the control of a reflexive system that is characterized by obligatory attention to salient stimuli and motion in the periphery and also is highly susceptible to sticky fixation. As the posterior attention system develops, areas of posterior parietal cortex (PG), and the frontal eye fields become involved in voluntary shifts of attention. This system shows substantial development across 3 to 6 months of age, a time when visual attention is characterized by increasingly shorter looking. From 6 months on, the anterior attention system becomes functional, and frontal areas (inferior and superior

prefrontal cortex, anterior cingulate) begin to play a role in sustained attention toward stimuli when attention and information processing is required. Attention to distracters is inhibited in these cases. Thus, visual attention and looking become increasingly voluntary and functional after 6 months of age, representing early examples of "executive attention."

The general arousal/attention system influences all three of these more specific attention systems. As the child develops, the ability to maintain an aroused/attentive state increases. During activation of the general arousal/attention system, activity of the specific attention systems in the brain is enhanced through a generalized spread of arousal (decreased heart rate, activation of the noradrenergic and cholinergic neurochemical systems). Alternatively, as the anterior attention system becomes functional, the child develops the ability to voluntarily maintain attention toward a central stimulus while inhibiting attention to distracters. This voluntary control of attention allows the child to actively maintain sustained attention—the primary component of the general arousal/attention response. This rudimentary form of executive attention will be critical for the development of more complex behaviors and cognitive processes (e.g., language, self-regulation, mental representation).

## Future Directions

1. Further refinement is needed for applying cortical source analysis to infant EEG/ERP data. The existing models for estimating the cortical sources of EEG activity are based on adult parameters (skull/scalp thickness, etc.). Richards (see Reynolds & Richards, 2009) is currently developing a technique that uses structural MRIs from individual infant participants to model the brain activity that produces their EEG data based on the anatomical features of their own brain as opposed to the typical anatomy of the adult brain. Ultimately, the ability to apply a direct measure of brain activity (e.g., fMRI) with infant participants is needed; however, practical and ethical concerns currently preclude the use of fMRI with normal infant participants. Structural MRIs are typically obtained from infants while sleeping.

2. The research described in this chapter is based largely on studies of attention processes in normally developing infants and children. Little is known about the development of attention in atypical and clinical populations. Once progress

had been made with this, subsequent work could enable the identification of infants who are at risk for developmental disorders. Ultimately, identifying early markers for children at risk for developing attention-related disorders or learning disabilities will facilitate early intervention and potentially better outcomes.

# References

Aslin, R. N. (1987). Visual and auditory development in infancy. In J. D. Osoksky (Ed.), *Handbook of infant development* (pp. 5–97). New York: Wiley.

Atkinson, J. (2000). *The developing visual brain*. Oxford, England: Oxford University Press.

Bachevalier, J. (2008). Non-human models of primate memory development. In C. A. Nelson & M. Luciana (Eds.), *Handbook of developmental cognitive neuroscience* (pp. 499–508). Cambridge, MA: MIT Press.

Bakeman, R., & Adamson, L. B. (1984). Coordinat-ing attention to people and objects in mother-infant and peer-infant interaction. *Child Development, 55,* 1278–1289.

Banks, M., & Salapatek, P. (1983). Infant visual perception. In P. H. Mussen (Series Ed.), M. M. Haith & J. J. Campos (Vol. Eds.), & P. H. Mussen (Ed.), *Handbook of child psychology, Vol. 2. Infancy and developmental psychobiology* (4th ed., pp. 435–572). New York: Wiley.

Barr, R., Dowden, A., & Hayne, H. (1996).Developmental changes in deferred imitation by 6-to 24-month-old infants. *Infant Behavior and Development, 19,* 159–170.

Barr, R., & Hayne, H. (2000). Age-related changes in imitation: Implications for memory development. In C. Rovee-Collier, L. Lipsitt, & H. Haynee (Eds.), *Progress in infancy research* (Vol. 1, pp. 21–67). Mahwah, NJ: Erlbaum.

Bauer, P. J., Wiebe, S. A., Carver, L. J., Waters, J. M., & Nelson, C. A. (2003). Developments in long-term explicit memory late in the first year of life: Behavioral and electrophysiological indices. *Psychological Science, 14,* 629–635.

Bell, M. A., & Fox, N. A. (1994). Brain development over the first year of life: Relations between EEG frequency and coherence and cognitive and affective behaviors. In G. Dawson & K. Fischer (Eds.), *Human behavior and the developing brain* (pp. 314–345). New York: Guilford Press.

Bertenthal, B. I., & Campos, J. J. (1990). A systems approach to the organizing effects of self-produced locomotion during infancy. In C. Rovee-Collier & L. P. Lipsitt (Eds.), *Advances in infancy research* (Vol. 6, pp. 1–60). Norwood, NJ: Ablex.

Bornstein, M. H., & Sigman, M. D. (1986). Continuity in mental development from infancy. *Child Development, 57,* 81–99.

Bronson, G. W. (1974). The postnatal growth of visual capacity. *Child Development, 45,* 873–890.

Bronson, G. W. (1997). The growth of visual capacity: Evidence from infant scanning patterns. In C. Rovee-Collier & L.P. Lipsitt (Eds.), *Advances in infancy research* (Vol. 11, pp. 109–141). Greenwich, CT: Ablex.

Carver, L. J., Bauer, P. J., & Nelson, C. A. (2000). Associations between infant brain activity and recall memory. *Developmental Science, 3,* 234–246.

Casey, B. J., & Richards, J. E. (1988). Sustained visual attention in young infants measured with an adapted version of the visual preference paradigm. *Child Development, 59,* 1514–1521.

Chugani, H. T. (1994). Development of regional brain glucose metabolism in relation to behavior and plasticity. In G. Dawson & K. W. Fischer (Eds.), *Human behavior and the developing brain* (pp. 153–175). New York: Guilford Press.

Colombo, J. (1993). *Infant cognition: Predicting later intellectual functioning*. Newbury Park, CA: Sage.

Colombo, J. (2001). The development of visual attention in infancy. *Annual Review of Psychology, 52,* 337–367.

Colombo, J., Freeseman, L. J., Coldren, J. T., & Frick, J. E. (1995). Individual differences in infant fixation duration: Dominance of global versus local stimulus properties. *Cognitive Development, 10,* 271–285.

Colombo, J., & Mitchell, D. W. (1990). Individual and developmental differences in infant visual attention: Fixation time and information processing. In J. Colombo & J. W. Fagen (Eds.), *Individual differences in infancy* (pp. 193–227). Hillsdale, NJ: Erlbaum.

Colombo, J., Mitchell, D. W., Coldren, J. T., & Freeseman, L. J. (1991). Individual differences in infant attention: Are short lookers faster processors or feature processors? *Child Development, 62,* 1247–1257.

Colombo, J., Mitchell, D. W., & Horowitz, F. D. (1988). Infant visual attention in the paired-comparison paradigm: Test-retest and attention-performance relations. *Child Development, 59,* 1198–1210.

Colombo, J., Richman, W. A., Shaddy, D. J., Greenhoot, A. F., & Maikranz, J. M. (2001). HR-defined phases of attention, look duration, and infant performance in the paired comparison paradigm. *Child Development, 72,* 1605–1616.

Courage, M. L., Reynolds, G. D., & Richards, J. E. (2006). Infants' visual attention to patterned stimuli: Developmental change from 3- to 12-months of age. *Child Development, 77*(3), 680–695.

Courchesne, E. (1977). Event-related brain potentials: Comparison between children and adults. *Science, 197,* 589–592.

Courchesne, E., Ganz, L., & Norcia, A. M. (1981). Event-related brain potentials to human faces in infants. *Child Development, 52,* 804–811.

de Haan, M., & Nelson, C. A. (1997). Recognition of the mother's face by six-month-old infants: A neurobehavioral study. *Child Development, 68,* 187–210.

de Haan, M., & Nelson, C. A. (1999). Brain activity differentiates face and object processing in 6-month-old infants. *Developmental Psychology, 35,* 1113–1121. by infants' performance on AB. *Child Development, 56,* 868–883.

Diamond, A, & Goldman-Rakic, P. S. (1989). Comparison of human infants and rhesus monkeys on Piaget's A-not-B task: Evidence for dependence on dorsolateral

Diamond, A. (1985). Development of the ability to use recall to guide action, as indicated prefrontal cortex. *Experimental Brain Research, 74,* 24–40.

Duncan, J., & Owen, A. M. (2000). Common regions of the human frontal lobe recruited by diverse cognitive demands. *Trends in Neuroscience, 23,* 475–483.

Fabiani, M., Gratton, G., & Coles, M. G. H. (2000). Event-related brain potentials: Methods, theory, and applications. In J. T. Cacioppo, L. G. Tassinary, & G. G. Berntson (Eds.), *Handbook of psychophysiology* (pp. 53–84). New York: Cambridge University Press.

Fagan, J. F. (1984). The relationship of novelty preference during infancy to later intelligence and later recognition memory. *Intelligence, 8,* 339–346.

Fantz, R. L. (1963). Pattern vision in newborn infants. *Science, 140,* 296–297.

Fantz, J. F. (1964). Visual experience in infants: Decreased attention to familiar patterns relative to novel ones. *Science, 146,* 668–670.

Frick, J. E., & Richards, J. E. (2001). Individual differences in infants' recognition of briefly presented visual stimuli. *Infancy, 2,* 331–352.

Goldman-Rakic, P. S. (1987). Circuitry of primate prefrontal cortex and regulation of behaviour by representational memory. In *Handbook of physiology: The nervous system (Vol. 5,* pp. 373–417). Bethesda, MD: American Physiological Society.

Haith, M. M. (1980). *Rules that babies look by.* Hillsdale, NJ: Erlbaum.

Haith, M. M., & Benson, J. B. (1998). Infant cognition. In D. Kuhn & R. S. Siegler (Eds.), *Handbook of child psychology, Vol. 2. Cognition, perception, and language* (5th ed., pp. 199–254). New York: Wiley.

Heilman, K. M., Watson, R. T., Valenstein, E., & Goldberg, M. E. (1987). Attention: Behavior and neural mechanisms. In V. B. Mountcastle, F. Plum, & S. R. Geiger (Eds.), *Handbook of physiology: The nervous system* (Vol 5, pp. 461–481). Bethesda, MD: American Physiological Society.

Hickey, T. L., & Peduzzi, J. D . (1987). Structure and development of the visual system. In L. Cohen & P. Salapatek (Eds.), *Handbook of infant perception* (pp. 1–42). New York: Academic Press.

Hicks, J. M., & Richards, J. E. (1998). The effects of stimulus movement and attention on peripheral stimulus localization by 8- to 26-week-old infants. *Infant Behavior and Development, 21,* 571–589.

Hood, B. M. (1995). Shifts of visual attention in the human infant: A neuroscientific approach. *Advances in Infancy Research, 10,* 163–216.

Hunter, S. K., & Richards, J. E. (2003). Peripheral stimulus localization by 5- to 14-week-old infants during phases of attention. *Infancy, 4,* 1–25.

Johnson, M. H. (1990). Cortical maturation and the development of visual attention in early infancy. *Journal of Cognitive Neuroscience, 2,* 81–95.

Karrer, R., & Ackles, P. K. (1987). Visual event-related potentials of infants during a modified oddball procedure. In R. Johnson, J. W. Rohrbaugh, & R. Parasuraman (Eds.), *Current trends in event-related potential research* (pp. 603–608). Amsterdam, The Netherlands: Elsevier Science.

Karrer, R., & Ackles, P. K. (1988). Brain organization and perceptual/cognitive development in normal and Down syndrome infants: A research program. In P. Vietze & H. G. Vaughan, Jr. (Eds.), *The early identification of infants with developmental disabilities* (pp. 210–234). Philadelphia: Grune & Stratton.

Karrer, R., & Monti, L. A. (1995). Event-related potentials of 4–7 week-old infants in a visual recognition memory task. *Electroencephalography and Clinical Neurophysiology, 94,* 414–424.

Kellman, P. J., & Banks, M. S. (1998). Infant visual perception. In D. Kuhn & R. S. Siegler (Eds.), *Handbook of child psychology, Vol. 2. Cognition, perception, and language* (5th ed., pp. 103–146). New York: Wiley.

Lansink, J. M., & Richards, J. E. (1997). Heart rate and behavioral measures of attention in 6-, 9-, & 12-month-old infants during object exploration. *Child Development, 68,* 610–620.

Lewis, T. L., & Maurer, D. (1992). The development of the temporal and nasal visual field during infancy. *Vision Research, 32,* 903–911.

Mandler, J. M. (1992). How to build a baby: II. Conceptual primitives. *Psychological Review, 99,* 587–604.

Maurer, D., & Lewis, T. L. (1979). A physiological explanation of infants' early visual development. *Canadian Journal of Psychology, 33,* 232–252.

Maurer, D., & Lewis, T. L. (1998). Overt orienting toward peripheral stimuli: Normal development and underlying mechanisms. In J. E. Richards (Ed.), *Cognitive neuroscience of attention: A developmental perspective* (pp. 51–102). Hillsdale, NJ: Erlbaum.

Mesulam, M. M. (1983). The functional anatomy and hemispheric specialization for directed attention. *Trends in Neuroscience, 6,* 384–387.

McCall, R. B., & Carriger, M. (1993). A meta-analysis of infant habituation and recognition memory performance as predictors of later IQ. *Child Development, 64,* 57–79.

Moray, N. (1969). *Attention: Selective processes in vision and hearing.* London: Hutchinson Educational.

Moray, N. (1993). Designing for attention. In A. D. Baddeley & L. Weiskrantz (Eds.), *Attention: Selection, awareness, and control* (pp. 111–34). New York: Oxford University Press.

Nelson, C. A., & Collins, P. F. (1991). Event-related potential and looking-time analysis of infants' responses to familiar and novel events: Implications for visual recognition memory. *Developmental Psychology, 27,* 50–58.

Nelson, C. A., & Collins, P. F. (1992). Neural and behavioral correlates of visual recognition memory in 4- and 8-month-old infants. *Brain and Cognition, 19,* 105–121.

Nikkel, L., & Karrer, R. (1994). Differential effects of experience on the ERP and behavior of 6-month-old infants: Trends during repeated stimulus presentation. *Developmental Neuropsychology, 10,* 1–11.

Oakes, L. M., & Tellinghuisen, D. J. (1994). Examining in infancy: Does it reflect active processing? *Developmental Psychology, 30,* 748–756.

Picton, T. W., Bentin, S., Berg, P., Donchin, E., Hillyard, S. A., Johnson, R., ... Taylor, M. J. (2000). Guidelines for using human event-related potentials to study cognition: Recording standards and publication criteria. *Psychophysiology, 37,* 127–152.

Posner, M. I. (1995). Attention in cognitive neuroscience: An overview. In M. Gazzaniga (Ed.), *The cognitive neurosciences* (pp. 615–624). Cambridge, MA: MIT Press.

Posner, M. I., & Peterson, S. (1990). The attention system of the human brain. *Annual. Review of Neuroscience, 13,* 25–42.

Reynolds, G. D., Courage, M. L., & Richards, J. E. (2010). Infant attention and visual preferences: Converging evidence from behavior, event-related potentials, and cortical source localization. *Developmental Psychology, 46,* 886–904.

Reynolds, G. D, Guy, M. W., & Zhang, D. (2011). Neural correlates of individual differences in infant visual attention and recognition memory. *Infancy, 16(4),* 368–391.

Reynolds, G. D., & Richards, J. E. (2005). Familiarization, attention, and recognition memory in infancy: An ERP and cortical source localization study. *Developmental Psychology,* *41,* 598–615.

Reynolds, G. D., & Richards, J. E. (2008). Infant heart rate: A developmental psychophysiological perspective. In L. A. Schmidt & S. J. Segalowitz (Eds.), *Developmental psychophysiology: Theory, systems, and applications.* New York, NY: Cambridge University Press.

Reynolds, G. D., & Richards, J. E. (2009). Cortical source localization of infant cognition. *Developmental Neuropsychology,* *34*(3), 312–329.

Reynolds, G. D., Riggs, M. W., Davidson, S. A., Silander, A. E., & Cannon, R., (2009, April). *Individual differences in infant visual attention and event-related potentials.* Poster presented at the Biennial Meeting of the Society for Research in Child Development, Denver, CO.

Richards, J. E. (1987). Infant visual sustained attention and respiratory sinus arrhythmia. *Child Development,* *58,* 488–498.

Richards, J. E. (1997a). Effects of attention on infants' preferences for briefly exposed visual stimuli in the paired-comparison recognition-memory paradigm. *Developmental Psychology,* *33,* 22–31.

Richards, J. E. (1997b). Peripheral stimulus localization by infants: Attention, age, and individual differences in heart rate variability. *Journal of Experimental Psychology: Human Perception and Performance,* *23,* 667–680.

Richards, J. E. (2001). Cortical indices of saccade planning following covert orienting in 20-week-old infants. *Infancy,* *2,* 135–157.

Richards, J. E. (2002). Development of attentional systems. In M. De Haan & M. H. Johnson (Eds.), *The cognitive neuroscience of development.* East Sussex, England: Psychology Press.

Richards, J. E. (2003a). Attention affects the recognition of briefly presented visual stimuli in infants: An ERP study. *Developmental Science,* *6,* 312–328.

Richards, J. E. (2003b). Cortical sources of event-related-potentials in the prosaccade and antisaccade task. *Psychophysiology,* *40,* 878–894.

Richards, J. E. (2004). Recovering cortical dipole sources from scalp-recorded event-related-potentials using component analysis: Principal component analysis and independent component analysis. *International Journal of Psychophysiology,* *54,* 201–220.

Richards, J. E. (2005). Localizing cortical sources of event-related potentials in infants' covert orienting. *Developmental Science,* *8,* 255–278

Richards, J. E. (2008). Attention in young infants: A developmental psychophysiological perspective. In C. A. Nelson & M. Luciana (Eds.), *Handbook of developmental cognitive neuroscience* (pp. 479–497). Cambridge, MA: MIT Press.

Richards, J. E. (2010). Attention in the brain and early infancy. In S. P. Johnson (Ed.), *Neoconstructivism: The new science of cognitive development* (pp. 3–31). New York: Oxford University Press.

Richards, J. E., & Casey, B. J. (1991). Heart rate variability during attention phases in young infants. *Psychophysiology,* *28,* 43–53.

Richards, J. E., & Casey, B. J. (1992). Development of sustained visual attention in the human infant. In B. A. Campbell & H. Hayne (Eds.), *Attention and information processing in infants and adults: Perspectives from human and animal research* (pp. 30–60). Hillsdale, NJ: Erlbaum.

Richards, J. E., & Cronise, K. (2000). Extended visual fixation in the early preschool years: Look duration, heart rate changes, and attentional inertia. *Child Development,* *71,* 602–620.

Richards, J. E., Reynolds, G. D., & Courage, M. L. (2010). The neural bases of infant attention. *Current Directions in Psychological Science,* *19*(1), 41–46.

Robbins, T. W., & Everitt, B. J. (1995). Arousal systems and attention. In M. S. Gazzaniga (Ed.), *Cognitive neurosciences* (pp. 703–720). Cambridge, MA: MIT Press.

Rose, S. A., & Feldman, J. F. (1995). Predicting IQ and specific cognitive abilities at 11 years from infancy measures. *Developmental Psychology,* *31,* 685–696.

Rose, S. A., Feldman, J. F., & Jankowski, J. J. (2004). Infant visual recognition memory. *Developmental Review,* *24,* 74–100.

Rose, D. H., Slater, A., & Perry, H. (1986). Prediction of childhood intelligence from habituation in early infancy. *Intelligence,* *10,* 251–263.

Ruff, H. A. (1986). Components of attention during infants' manipulative exploration. *Developmental Psychology,* *20,* 9–20.

Ruff, H. A., & Capozzoli, M. C. (2003). Development of attention and distractibility in the first 4 years of life. *Developmental Psychology,* *39,* 877–890.

Ruff, H. A., Capozzoli, M., & Saltarelli, L. M. (1996). Focused visual attention and distractibility in 10-month-old infants. *Infant Behavior and Development,* *19,* 281–293.

Ruff, H. A., Capozzoli, M., & Weissberg, R. (1998). Age, individuality, and context as factors in sustained visual attention during the preschool years. *Developmental Psychology,* *34,* 454–464.

Ruff, H. A., & Rothbart, M. K. (1996). *Attention in early development.* New York: Oxford University Press.

Ruff, H. A., & Saltarelli, L. M. (1993). Exploratory play with objects: Basic cognitive processes and individual differences. In M. Bornstein & A. O'Reilly (Eds.), *New directions for child development, Vol. 59. The role of play in the development of thought* (pp. 5–15). San Francisco, CA: Josey-Bass.

Schiller, P. H. (1985). A model for the generation of visually guided saccadic eye movements. In D. Rose & V. G. Dobson (Eds.), *Models of the visual cortex* (pp. 62–70). New York: John Wiley.

Sigman, M., Cohen, S. E., Beckwith, L., & Parmelee, A. H. (1986). Infant attention in relation to intellectual abilities in childhood. *Developmental Psychology,* *23,* 788–792.

Tamis-LeMonda, C. S., & Bornstein, M. H. (1989). Habituation and maternal encouragement of attention in infancy as predictors of toddler language, play, and representational competence. *Child Development,* *60,* 738–751.

Tellinghuisen, D. J., & Oakes, L. M. (1997). Distractibility in infancy: The effects of distractor characteristics and type of attention. *Journal of Experimental Child Psychology,* *64,* 232–254.

Webb, S. J., Long, J. D., & Nelson, C. A. (2005). A longitudinal investigation of visual event-related potentials in the first year of life. *Developmental Science,* *8,* 605–616.

Willatts, P., & Rosie, K. (1989, April). *Planning by 12-month-old infants.* Paper presented at the Biennial Meeting of the Society for Research in Child Development, Kansas City, MO.

## Further Reading

Colombo, J. (2001). The development of visual attention in infancy. *Annual Review of Psychology, 52,* 337–367.

Hood, B. M. (1995). Shifts of visual attention in the human infant: A neuroscientific approach. *Advances in Infancy Research, 10,* 163–216.

Johnson, M. H. (1995). The development of visual attention: A cognitive neuroscience perspective. In M. S. Gazzaniga (Ed.), *The cognitive neurosciences* (pp. 735–747). Cambridge, MA: MIT Press.

Richards, J. E. (2008). Attention in young infants: A developmental psychophysiological perspective. In C. A. Nelson & M. Luciana (Eds.), *Handbook of developmental cognitive neuroscience* (pps 479–497). Cambridge, MA: MIT Press.

Richards, J. E., Reynolds, G. D., & Courage, M. L. (2010). The neural bases of infant attention. *Current Directions in Psychological Science, 19(1), 41–46.*

# Cognitive Aging

Paul Verhaeghen

**Abstract**

This chapter provides an overview of cognitive changes associated with normal, nonpathological aging. Many aspects of fluid cognition show declines (speed of processing, working memory, divided attention, the size of the attentional field, episodic and prospective memory, fluid intelligence), while some aspects of cognition remain largely intact (lexical processing, familiarity-driven processing, selective attention, semantic memory, and crystallized intelligence). Explanatory frameworks include cognitive explanations (declines in a common factor or the cascading effects of cognitive slowing and working memory deficits), predicated on changes in brain morphology and functioning, as well as in cardiovascular health. Issues of culture are briefly discussed, as well as the disuse hypothesis (an enriched lifestyle is associated with higher levels of cognitive functioning). The chapter ends with an overview of changes in assembled cognition (expertise, creativity, and wisdom) and openings for healthy cognitive aging—the promises of physical fitness, cognitive training, and selective optimization with compensation.

**Key Words:** aging, disuse, wisdom, plasticity, cognitive slowing

It is a truism that as people grow older, performance on a large number of cognitive tasks declines. Figure 64.1 (compiled by Salthouse, 2010) shows life-span trends obtained from the norming samples of three intelligence tests (KBIT, WASI, Woodcock-Johnson III). I will return to these later in the chapter, but for now it is important to note the bifurcation: Performance tests peak at around age 20 and then show a steady and accelerated decline, all going down at about the same rate; verbal tests remain relatively stable throughout middle adulthood, but at around age 60, a steady and accelerated decline sets in as well. Given that we are all interested parties, these results are quite frightening. Older adults are frightened, too. For instance, a 2006 survey by the MetLife Foundation found that while Americans fear getting cancer more than they fear getting any other disease, for those 55 years or older, Alzheimer's (the ultimate insult to cognitive

functioning) is the disease most dreaded. Older adults routinely complain about memory loss (e.g., Blazer, Hays, Fillenbaum, & Gold, 1997; Cutler & Grams, 1988). The association between aging and cognitive decline is even encoded in our language. The term *senior moment*, for instance, does not refer to a revelatory flash of increased maturity but to brief memory lapses, experiences of cognitive impairment, and even to functional incompetence (Bonnesen & Burgess, 2004).

In this chapter, I will discuss three aspects of older adults' cognition. First, I will give an all-too-brief overview of research findings that document age-related changes in speed of information processing, attention, memory, and intelligence. Second, I will give a brief overview of explanatory mechanisms. Third, I will discuss forms of cognition and of intelligent behavior that expand or transcend the traditional definition of cognition—complex

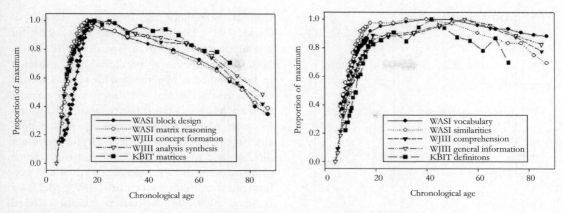

**Figure 64.1** Life-span trends in cognition as derived from the test manuals for the KBIT, WASI, and Woodcock-Johnson III. (From Salthouse, 2010.)

assemblages of different psychological aspects of performance: expertise, creativity, and wisdom. The final part discusses mechanisms used to cope with cognitive decline. I restrict myself here to the "normal" aging process at the exclusion of age-related pathologies (e.g., different forms of dementia).

## Age Differences in Cognitive Performance
### Speed of Information Processing

It has long been known that the increase in response time (RT) with adult age is monotonic. In a large meta-analysis on studies using continuous age samples, Verhaeghen and Salthouse (1997) reported an age-speed correlation of –.52, and Welford (1977) estimated that each additional year of adult age increases choice reaction time by 1.5 ms. In fact, the increase is more than linear, and it accelerates notably with advancing age (Cerella & Hale, 1994; Verhaeghen & Salthouse, 1997). Cerella and Hale (1994) estimated that the average 70-year-old functions at the speed of the average 8-year-old—a large effect.

One way to zoom in on this age-related slowing is to consider the average response time of older adults as a function of the average response time of younger adults. The resulting graph is called a Brinley plot, after Brinley (1965). Figure 64.2 depicts such a plot, with data culled from a total of 190 studies representing a wide range of tasks and subjects (Verhaeghen, in press; similar result shave been obtained in other studies, e.g. Cerella, Poon, & Williams, 1980; Lima, Hale, & Myerson, 1991). A first finding is that older adults are indeed consistently slower than younger adults: The graph contains 1,354 data points, and only 19 of those are situated on or below the diagonal. A second conclusion is that age-related slowing is not random but predictable. All points on the graph fall within a relatively narrow range (I address the scatter below); $R^2$ (weighted for sample size) is .87. This is a powerful result: We can explain 87% of the differences between mean performance of older adult groups simply from knowing what the speed of the corresponding group of younger adults is, regardless of the nature of the task. A third conclusion is that age-related slowing is proportional: The regression line through the data points has a slope larger than one and an intercept close to zero. Thus, to predict the average speed of a group of older adults from the average speed of a group of younger adults performing the same task, one simply needs to multiply the average speed of younger adults by a certain factor. The regression line shows that this factor is close to 1.4—that is, the average 70-year-old is about 1.4 times slower than the average 20-year-old. One of the consequences of proportional slowing is that, measured in absolute time, older adults will be much slower on tasks that generally take longer than on tasks that are generally fast. This has consequences for the interpretation of interactions in ANOVA: Tasks with added components (e.g., an executive control requirement) will by necessity result in larger age differences. As a consequence, some correction (such as a log-transform; Faust, Balota, Spieler, & Ferraro, 1999) is necessary to take this "general" slowing effect into account. A fourth conclusion is that not all studies or tasks show the same slowing factor. Even though the band is relatively narrow and predictability is good, there is still a fan, indicating variability in slowing factors. Further analysis shows the presence of at least three slowing factors in the data: (a) tasks that require simple lexical/verbal identifications show a slowing factor (which is, in fact, a speedup) of about 0.8; (b) sensorimotor

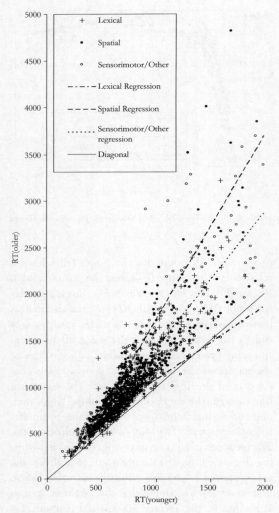

**Figure 64.2** Mean response time of groups of older adults as a function of mean response times of groups of younger adults performing the same task, as a function of task type; the graph contains 1,354 data points culled from 190 studies (Verhaeghen, in press).

tasks with simple decision components (e.g., choice reaction time tasks) show a slowing factor of about 1.5; and (c) tasks that involve spatial processing (e.g., visual search or mental rotation) show a slowing factor of about 2.0.

### Attention and Executive Control

At least three types of attentional control processes have been extensively researched in the field of cognitive aging (see Miyake, Friedman, Emerson, Witzki, & Howerter, 2000, for a factor-analytic categorization of control processes). First, *resistance to interference*, also known as inhibitory control, has been a central explanatory construct in aging

theories throughout the 1990s (e.g., Hasher & Zacks, 1988; Hasher, Zacks, & May, 1999; for a computational approach, see Braver & Barch, 2002). An age-related breakdown in resistance to interference is hypothesized to lead to mental clutter in older adults' working memory, thereby limiting its functional capacity, and perhaps also its speed of operation. Second, age-related deficits have been posited in the ability to *coordinate* distinct tasks or distinct processing streams. Some of the relevant literature pertains to dual-task performance (e.g., Hartley & Little, 1999; McDowd & Shaw, 2000), but the concept has also received some attention in the working memory literature (e.g., Mayr & Kliegl, 1993). Third, the late 1990s and early 2000s have seen a surge in the number of publications devoted to aging and *task switching* (e.g., Mayr, Spieler, & Kliegl, 2001). A fourth factor, working memory *updating*, has been investigated relatively rarely in an aging context (e.g., Van der Linden, Brédart, & Beerten, 1994; Verhaeghen, 2012).

Recently, Verhaeghen and Cerella (2002) pooled the available aging literature on resistance to interference (viz. the Stroop effect and negative priming), dual-task performance, and task switching, using different meta-analytic techniques to control for the effects of general slowing. (Controlling for general slowing is necessary to avoid Type-I error, that is, false positives, but it is often neglected or impossible to do in primary studies.) They found that age effects were absent in tasks measuring resistance to interference and in tasks measuring local task-switching costs (i.e., the comparison, within a block of task-switching trials, between trials in which task switching is actually required with trials in which the task did not switch). In contrast, age effects were seen in dual-task performance and global task switching (i.e., the comparison between reaction times in single-task blocks with reaction times in blocks when the participant has to switch between tasks). One possible interpretation is that age differences only emerge in tasks that involve the maintenance of two (or more) distinct mental task sets, and not in tasks that involve active selection of relevant information. Multiple task-set maintenance could challenge the control system in several ways. The deficit could arise from the need for coordination inherent in dual-task and global switching paradigms. A second possibility is that an age-related deficit in the capacity of working memory may be responsible for the difficulty in maintaining multiple sets. In that case, the underlying problem would arise from a structural limit rather than from a specific control process (Verhaeghen, Cerella, Bopp, & Basak, 2005, expand on this point). One thing is clear from this meta-analysis: There is no general age-related deficit in executive control processes. Some are spared by age, and others are disproportionately damaged.

I note here that dual-task costs also operate in more ecologically valid circumstances, and that younger and older adults deal with the dual-task requirements in different ways. Li, Lindenberger, Freund, and Baltes (2001) had participants walk around a room, tracking a particular route indicated on the floor while learning a list of words for later retrieval; the words were presented over wireless headphones. Both age groups showed dual-task costs, but older adults tended to show larger costs on the cognitive task than the motor task; the opposite was true for the younger adults. Similar results were obtained in a study where younger and older adults were studying words while standing on a platform that simply recorded the variation in their center of gravity (Rapp, Krampe, & Baltes, 2005): Younger adults showed larger costs in balance performance than in memory; older adults showed larger costs in memory than in balance. Clearly, in old age the cost of falling is potentially much higher than the cost of forgetting the occasional word, and in both studies older adults shifted their priorities accordingly.

One aspect of attention that is particularly vulnerable to age is the size of the attentional field, especially as measured by the useful field of view (UFOV) task (e.g., Owsley et al., 1998). The difference between this task and traditional visual search tasks is that UFOV tasks are dynamic: The participant has to quickly and accurately detect changes in the field of view. Participants fixate the center of a computer monitor; targets and/or distractors are flashed at smaller or larger distances from the point of fixation. The distance at which targets can be located with high accuracy indicates the boundary of the useful field of view. The shrinkage of the UFOV in old age has real-world consequences: UFOV was the single best predictor for past at-fault accidents in one study of 294 older adult drivers (Ball, Owlsey, Sloan, Roenker, & Bruni, 1993; the other predictors were visual acuity, contrast sensitivity, stereopsis, color discrimination, and a static visual search task); it also predicted future accidents over a 3-year period with a correlation of about .50 (Owsley et al., 1998).

## Memory

### AGE DIFFERENCES IN WORKING MEMORY

Working memory can be defined as the ability to simultaneously store and actively transform information (e.g., Baddeley, 1986; Engle, 2002). Small but reliable age differences are already found in tasks that require simple storage, such as simple digit tasks. In a meta-analysis of 123 studies of diverse working memory measures, Bopp and Verhaeghen (2005) concluded that older adults have a span of about 7.1 digits, compared to a span of 7.6 digits for younger adults. The difference is larger for tasks that tap into simultaneous storage and processing, such as reading span, listening span, or operation span: The same meta-analysis found that younger adults can hold about four items in working memory, whereas older adults can retain only three. Age differences in working memory are likely to have consequences for the rest of the cognitive system. Research has consistently found that especially the active version of working memory correlates well with tests of intelligence (e.g., Engle, Kane, & Tuholksi, 1999) as well as with general language abilities (e.g., Kemper, Herman, & Lian, 2003).

### AGE DIFFERENCES IN LONG-TERM MEMORY
#### Recollection and Familiarity

Many varieties of memory are supported by two distinct processes, recollection and familiarity (e.g., Yonelinas, 2002), which tend to be map onto different brain substrates (Kahn, Davachi, & Wagner, 2004; Parkin & Walter, 1992; Yonelinas, Otten, Shaw, & Rugg, 2005). Recollection refers to a detailed memory of an event, typically including contextual detail (such as time or place), and it is typically considered a slow, controlled, all-or-none process; familiarity refers to an automatic, gradated feeling of knowing that the event has been encountered before, but without retrieval of specific information. One method to assess the contributions of recollection and familiarity to memory is Jacoby's (1991) process-dissociation procedure. Subjects typically study two lists (A and B) and are then given two types of instructions for a memory test (both recall and recognition tests have been used, as well as more implicit tests of memory, such as word stem completion). Under the inclusion instruction, the subject selects or recalls words from either list—this should tap both recollection and familiarity. Under the exclusion instruction, the subject selects or recalls only words from list A (or B), not B (or A)—in this scenario, only recollection will presumably lead to correct exclusions. The standard finding with this procedure is an age constancy in familiarity in the presence of a sizeable age-related decrease in measures of recollection (for a meta-analysis, see Light, Prull, LaVoie, & Healy, 2000; the average recollection estimates were .49 and .29 for younger and older adults, respectively, and the average familiarity estimates were .41 and .48). Another procedure for distinguishing between recollection and familiarity is the remember/know paradigm. In this paradigm, participants are simply asked to indicate, for each item recognized, whether they remember it (i.e., whether any contextual detail is available), or whether the item just provokes a sense of familiarity. Light et al.'s (2000) meta-analysis again shows age differences in recollection. Conclusions for familiarity, however, depend on the assumptions made about the relationship between recollection and familiarity: When the processes are assumed to be mutually exclusive, the data support age constancy in familiarity; if one assumes the two processes are independent, then familiarity appears to be age sensitive as well, but less so than recollection. The third approach is to use receiver-operating-curves (ROC curves; e.g., Yonelinas, 1997). Here, participants perform a recognition task and provide confidence ratings for each item. Hit and false alarm rates are calculated for each level of confidence, and then an ROC curve is constructed in hit-false alarm space. Results here are sparse. Age differences in recollection are ubiquitous, but the picture on age differences in familiarity is mixed (e.g., Healy, Light, & Chung, 2005, found age differences in familiarity in three studies under the independence assumption; Howard, Bessette-Symons, Zhang, & Hoyer, 2006, did not).

## Episodic and Semantic Memory

Probably the best-documented finding in cognitive aging is the large decline in episodic memory functioning coupled with an absence of age differences in semantic memory. Figure 64.3 (Salthouse, 2010) illustrates this: Performance on a paired-associates test, which taps episodic memory, declines steadily over the adult age range, whereas performance on a synonym vocabulary test, which taps semantic memory, increases until age 60 and then starts showing a modest decline. (Note that there are indications that semantic memory does show marked decline in extreme old age, that is, after age 90 or so; Singer, Verhaeghen, Ghisletta, Lindenberger, & Baltes, 2003). Meta-analyses confirm the bifurcation: Verhaeghen, Marcoen, and Goossens (1993) concluded that the difference between 20-year-olds

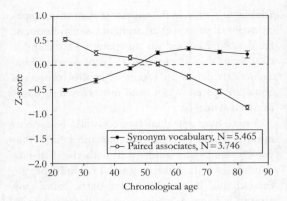

**Figure 64.3** Large-sample age trajectories for synonym vocabulary and paired-associate memory (Salthouse, 2010).

and 70-year-olds on memory for word lists, prose, and word pairs was about 1 standard deviation, and Verhaeghen (2003) found that 70-year-olds outperform 20-year-olds on vocabulary tests by about 0.8 standard deviation. (Both meta-analyses included primarily experimental studies on cognition, which tend to use highly educated and highly accomplished healthy older adults, thus likely underestimating the episodic memory decline and overestimating the semantic memory advantage.) The vocabulary advantage exhibited by older adults is larger for verification or recognition measures than for measures that require the production of synonyms or definitions. Part of this difference can be attributed to possible differences in the retrieval demands of the tasks; or it could be the case that production measures underestimate the extent to which our knowledge about word meanings and language accumulates over the adult life span. One potential reason for the difference in age trajectories between the two types of memory is that semantic information is widely distributed across the cortex (Eichenbaum, 2003). For that reason alone it is less vulnerable to changes in brain volume and connectivity than episodic memory, which relies heavily on the intactness of the hippocampus, at least for the encoding of new memories. In addition to the negative effects of attentional demands at retrieval as reported in studies of the recollection process in recognition and recall, age-related deficits in episodic memory are also associated with associative deficits or binding deficits at encoding (e.g., Naveh-Benjamin, 2001) and with increased attentional demands at encoding (e.g., Castel & Craik, 2003).

One very important aspect of aging in episodic memory is that the pattern of age-related loss is quantitative rather than qualitative in nature. In the

Verhaeghen et al. (1993) meta-analysis, for instance, the most striking pattern was an across-the-board decrease in performance, with few areas of either sparing or of exacerbated problems. This suggests that the same principles that govern memory performance of younger adults also govern memory performance of older adults, and to the same degree. For instance, the meta-analysis showed that younger and older adults benefit equally (in effect-size measures) from the reinstatement of the study context at recall (thus, the encoding specificity principle is not differentially affected by age); that older adults benefit as much as younger adults from semantic orienting questions (i.e., the levels-of-processing mechanism is not differentially affected by age); or that age differences are identical across different hierarchical levels of a text (i.e., the principle of organization is not specifically affected by age). What does influence age differences is the type of retrieval task. The findings mentioned previously all concern recall. Age differences are much smaller (about 0.5 standard deviations; LaVoie & Light, 1994) when memory is tested using recognition, that is, when participants have to point out the correct answer from a number of alternatives.

Two complaints often voiced by older adults concern retrieval of semantic or quasi-semantic information, namely forgetting names (or, put more accurately, problems with retrieval of the name associated with a familiar person about whom everything else is remembered) and word-finding problems. Studies show that older adults indeed experience an increase in tip-of-the-tongue states, but not dramatically so. In a laboratory study, Heine, Ober, and Shenaut (1999) found that older adults experience about 20% more tip-of-the-tongue states than younger adults. This difference is about 0.5 standard deviations, considerably smaller than what is typically found in episodic memory recall. Heine et al. also asked their participants to keep a diary for 28 days. Younger adults reported on average 5.2 tip-of-the-tongue experiences; older adults, 6.6. For both age groups, most tip-of-the-tongue states resolved spontaneously. Older adults then do show more word-finding problems than younger adults, but these problems are less severe than those experienced in episodic recall; such (quasi-) semantic problems are, however, perhaps more likely to lead to complaints because they are more salient or disruptive. For one, failure to retrieve a name of a word is immediately noticeable to the individual (unlike, say, forgetting to put an item on a grocery list); additionally, failure to retrieve someone's name in a social context is often considered embarrassing, and so is failure to come up with the right word during conversation.

Episodic and semantic memory are most often probed by looking at memories for facts and events. In real life, however, facts and events are always embedded in a context—a specific temporal sequence, a location, a source, or another co-occurring item or event. In a recent meta-analysis, Old and Naveh-Benjamin (2008) directly compared age-related differences in episodic memory for items with memory for their associated context. They found that age differences were generally smaller for memory for items (0.7 standard deviations) than for their associated context (0.9 standard deviations). Memory for source and nonfocal context (e.g., the font in which a word was presented) is generally less age-sensitive (0.6 standard deviations) than memory for location, temporal order, modality, or an item paired with the target item at study. Importantly, there was no specific age-related deficit in associative memory when learning of associations and items was incidental; age-related differences only emerged when subjects were told to study and remember the associated context together with item. This suggests that younger adults deploy efficient strategies to bind items to contexts, but older adults do not. This is at least partially a production deficit (i.e., older adults simply do not produce efficient strategies): Providing subjects with associative strategies under intentional encoding reduces age differences in associative binding (Naveh-Benjamin, Keshet-Brav, & Levy, 2007).

*Prospective Memory*

Episodic and semantic memory are retrospective forms of memory—they record the past. Prospective memory looks toward the future: It is the memory for intentions that need to be carried out sometime later—appointments to keep, errands to run, the mental to-do list. Older adults outperform younger adults in naturalistic studies, where the participant is asked to perform some task in the days or weeks following an initial contact with the research team—call a particular phone number at a particular time, or mail back postcards at specific times. A recent meta-analysis (Henry, MacLeod, Philips, & Crawford, 2004) shows that such studies yield an age difference favoring the old of about 1 standard deviation. The reason for this age-related increase in prospective memory performance may be the effective use of strategies, for instance, a better use of a calendar, honed through decades of compensating for declining memory ability. Prospective memory can also be measured in the lab. Typically, the participant is engaged in a background task (e.g., a series of faces is projected on a computer screen, and the participant has to decide whether each face is famous); at the same time, she is also performing a prospective task (e.g., press a key when the face shown has facial hair, or turn a dial every 2 minutes). On these tasks, older adults do worse than younger adults, but the age difference, about 0.75 standard deviations, is smaller than the deficit usually observed in retrospective episodic memory. The age difference does not covary with the nature of the task: Time-based prospective memory (i.e., remembering to do something at a particular time) yields the same effects as event-based prospective memory (i.e., remembering to do something when a particular event occurs). Age differences do, however, covary with task difficulty, at least in event-based tasks: Age differences tend to be larger when the demands on prospective memory are higher (e.g., when cues are not particularly salient, when the association between cue and action is weak, or when the embedded task is highly engaging).

*Very Long-Term Memory*

Some gerontologists make a distinction within long-term memory between secondary and tertiary memory. The latter denotes memory for facts or events that occurred in the distant past. This distinction resonates with many older adults. They complain that it is impossible to retain new information but that they have flawless memory for events from the distant past (e.g., "Don't ask me what I had for breakfast, but ask me anything you want about my daughter's wedding.") Research on this topic has used memory for high-school classmates or for materials learned in school or college and unlikely to have been revisited since (e.g., Bahrick, 1984; Bahrick, Bahrick, & Wittlinger, 1975; Conway, Cohen, & Stanhope, 1991). A period of relatively rapid forgetting, lasting 1 to 6 years, is followed by a long period of stable retention, lasting 30 years or longer, possibly followed by a second period of decline (Bahrick et al., 1975). Active knowledge (e.g., production of the correct translation of a Spanish word, or production of the name of a classmate from a photograph) declines faster than passive knowledge does (e.g., Spanish reading comprehension or recognition of a classmate's name). Another important determinant of long-term retention is the original level of proficiency: The better

the material was mastered, the higher the ultimate level of retention.

It is sometimes assumed that older adults live in the past. Research into autobiographical memory does not confirm this claim. Using the memory probe method, in which a subject is given words as a prompt for autobiographical memories, Rubin, Wetzler, and Nebes (1986) obtained a nonmonotonic temporal distribution of autobiographical memories. Most of the memories generated were not from the distant past but from recent events: Spontaneous memories are fresh, not decades old. Second, they found evidence for childhood amnesia: Participants responded with relatively few early childhood memories (age 1–10). Third, the curve showed a bump (the reminiscence bump) between the age of 15 and 30.

Early explanations for the bump stressed that the period covered by the bump is typically marked by novel and salient life events. Later work, however, suggests that reminiscence bumps tend to occur around positive, not negative events (Rubin & Berntsen, 2003), and that bump memories do not include very many novel events at all (Fitzgerald, 1988), thus suggesting that the bump is not generated by novelty but by the presence of culturally prescribed or expected life scripts (starting a family is expected for people in their 20s; losing a parent is not). More recently, Rathbone, Moulin, and Conway (2008) suggested that the bump occurs for periods when a new sense of self emerges; this can happen for both normatively timed, scripted events, and for unscripted events. This hypothesis is strengthened by data showing that Hispanic immigrants in the United States show a reminiscence bump that corresponds to their age at immigration, when a new, "American" self is being formed (Schrauf & Rubin, 2001).

## Intelligence
### AGE DIFFERENCES IN SCORES ON INTELLIGENCE TESTS

The study of adult age differences in intelligence is almost as old as intelligence testing itself—the earliest large-scale studies appeared in the 1930s. These studies often showed peak performance around age 20 and a steady decline after that—not that different from the picture shown in Figure 64.1. One problem inherent in these studies (and with all the work on speed, attention, and memory cited earlier) is that they are all cross-sectional in nature, that is, a single group of participants varying in age is tested at a single point in time. It is entirely possible that all or some of the differences noted between younger and older adults are due not to age but to generational differences—differences in access to education, differences in life experiences, differences in childhood nutrition, and so on. If later-born cohorts are advantaged in terms of opportunities, cross-sectional studies will overestimate age effects because they are contaminated with cohort effects favoring the young.

One way to deal with cohort effects is to conduct longitudinal research, where one group of subjects, by preference of different ages, is followed over a period of time (popular intervals are 3 and 7 years). The first large-scale longitudinal study was Warner Schaie's Seattle Longitudinal Study, started in the 1950s (see Schaie, 2005, for an overview). Figure 64.4 illustrates the longitudinal trajectory of six subsets of intelligence in the Seattle Longitudinal Study. It is immediately clear that although all abilities show accelerated decline after about age 60, peak performance for most abilities occurs much later than indicated by cross-sectional research (as expressed, e.g., in Figure 64.1). Only one ability—numeric ability—peaks in early adulthood. Perceptual speed peaks around age 40. Two abilities peak around age 50—verbal ability and verbal memory. (The latter result differs from most other longitudinal studies, which show an earlier peak

for memory. This is probably due to retest effects: The Seattle Longitudinal Study used the exact same list of 20 words at each measurement occasion.) There also appears to be a correlation between the time when decline becomes apparent and the size of the age effect: The abilities with the largest drop over the adult life span are perceptual speed and numeric ability, variables declining first. All other abilities show less drastic declines. Some even show an increase from young adulthood to early old age. A few other results from this study are noteworthy. Schaie discovered that there are no universal patterns of change and that decline is not universal. Around age 50, for instance, about half of the participants experienced a decrease on at least two abilities. At age 88, almost all participants experienced decline on at least two abilities. But the identity of these two (or more) abilities differs across participants— there is no preordained pattern. Moreover, even at age 88, hardly any participant showed decline on all six measures. The group curves simply do not generalize to the level of the individual. Schaie also stresses that decline is no universal given. He calculated the number of participants whose scores declined, remained stable, or improved over the 7-year interval between testing occasions. Over the course of adulthood, the number of participants whose scores increase declines (from 12% to 0%),

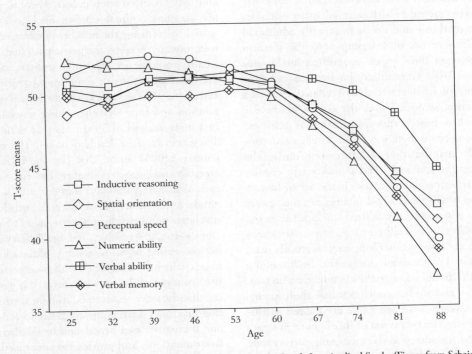

**Figure 64.4** Longitudinal age trajectories of six subsets of intelligence in the Seattle Longitudinal Study. (Figure from Schaie, 2005.)

and the number of participants who scores decline increases (from 20% to 50%). What is most striking, however, is that the majority of subjects (50% to 60%) show no significant difference in tests scores at all, and that this percentage does not covary with age. In other words, most 80-year-olds experience stability in their test scores, not decline. As expected, cohort effects turned out to be quite important in the Seattle Longitudinal Study. For almost all abilities, participants born earlier score lower, independent of age. Exceptions are verbal ability and numeric ability—those abilities peak for people born between roughly 1930 and 1950 and show a steady decline over successive cohorts. This suggests that a large part of the age-related decline observed in cross-sectional studies is not due to age at all, but to cohort differences—an indicator of a worse starting point rather than of a steep decline. Schaie's conclusions, then, are ultimately optimistic: At the group level, decline happens much later than typically assumed, and, at the individual level, stability, not decline, is the norm.

Not everyone, however, agrees with these conclusions. Salthouse (1991), for instance, observes that in the Seattle study, cohort effects are taken into account, but historic effects (related to time of measurement) are not. Salthouse reanalyzed the data and found that when time of measurement is taken into account, longitudinal results do not differ much from cross-sectional results: Only verbal ability increases with age; all other variables decline markedly and do so from early adulthood on. Salthouse fits these results into the classical framework of fluid versus crystallized intelligence (Horn, 1970). Crystallized intelligence concerns that part of intelligence that is related to stored information, acquired over the course of the life span; when tested, this information is retrieved from long-term memory. Fluid intelligence concerns the manipulation of information during the course of the test itself. Verbal ability taps crystallized intelligence; all other tests in the Schaie battery tap fluid intelligence. Fluid intelligence then peaks in early adulthood; crystallized intelligence in old age. The results of Salthouse's reanalysis have been confirmed in many other longitudinal studies (e.g., the Duke Longitudinal Study, the Berlin Aging Study, the Bonner Laengschnittstudie des Alterns). Each of those studies concludes that fluid intelligence decreases with age while crystallized intelligence soars. The two types of intelligence intersect at around age 40. (It is thus tempting to conclude that younger adults are equipped with a lot of fluid

resources to make up for a severe lack of experience.) Part of Schaie's optimistic conclusions may also be tied to selection effects. Singer et al. (2003) analyzed data from the Berlin Aging Study and obtained the typical result that cross-sectional age effects were larger than longitudinal age effects. When, however, only the profiles for those participants who returned for a second and third round of testing were considered, cross-sectional and longitudinal results overlapped quite nicely. This suggests that selection is a major problem in longitudinal research—we only keep testing the fittest, and that leads to an underestimation of age effects.

### EVERYDAY INTELLIGENCE

At least on the face of it, standard intelligence tests have little ecological validity—the materials and tasks have little to do with most adults' daily life. (This bias is intentional; otherwise the tests run the risk of being very vulnerable to ethnic, educational, gender, generational, or other cultural biases.) Everyday intelligence tests, in contrast, have subjects work on tasks that have high relevance for daily living, such as financial problems or medication-related issues. Often, these tests are presented under the form of brief vignettes (e.g., "An older women with no other source of income learns that because of an administrative error, her pension check will be a month late. What should she do?"), and they are often open ended: There is, just as in life, no single optimal solution. Such tests are often scored by counting the number of effective and safe solutions advanced by the participant (e.g., robbing a bank would be an effective but unsafe solution to the financial problem); sometimes participants are asked after the fact how satisfied they are with their solution and how well they think it would work. In a meta-analysis of 33 studies that examined age differences in these kinds of tasks, Thornton and Dumke (2005) found that the age difference in everyday intelligence is smaller than the age difference observed in standard tests for reasoning—0.5 standard deviations versus 0.9 standard deviations (the latter number is from Verhaeghen & Salthouse, 1997)—but still reliable. The age difference favoring the young notwithstanding, older adults tend to generally be more pleased with their performance than younger adults are with theirs. It is worth noting that the same seems to be true for medical decision making: Older adults are faster to zoom in on one alternative (and hence tend to ask their doctor fewer questions) and provide fewer detailed reasons for their decisions (Park & Hall Gutchess, 2000).

One possible reason for this finding is that older adults are more easily satisfied with their initial solutions and do not explore other options, even if (at least as rated by the experimenters) older adults do not actually provide better solutions. This might be due to working memory limitations in old age, which might preclude searching through a very large problem space until an ultimate solution is found. It is also possible to interpret the results from an expertise perspective: Older adults know from experience that everyday problems do not have ideal solutions and that it is simply best to focus one's attention on a single workable solution and implement it as well as one can. One additional result from this meta-analysis was that age differences were identical whether the problem was designed to be of concern primarily for older adults (such as the right choice of retirement plan) or for younger adults (such as decisions about an unwanted pregnancy). Age differences were, however, smaller for problems that had an interpersonal component (e.g., what to do when someone misbehaves at a party; 0.2 standard deviations) versus problems that had not (e.g., what to do when your freezer breaks down in the middle of the night; 0.5 standard deviations).

## Explanations for Age Differences in Cognitive Performance

Description is obviously not the only goal of gerontological research. We need explanations for cognitive changes as well. I briefly describe two approaches that are currently en vogue: cognitive-psychological explanations and biological explanations. These are not mutually exclusive: Cognition is built on biology.

### *Cognitive-Psychological Explanations*

Researchers in the field have taken primarily two approaches to explain age-related differences. Experimental psychologists (this approach is well represented by Kausler's 1991 monograph *Experimental psychology, cognition, and human aging*) tend toward high precision and high detail: They investigate age by condition interactions in experiments in which the manipulations are purposefully designed to measure (or at least differentially emphasize) different types of processes. (I noted a few examples in the section on memory earlier). The conclusion of most of these studies is not just that many cognitive processes show age-related decline, but that the age-related effects in most of these processes can be reliably dissociated from the age-related effects in almost any other process. One

current in this process-oriented camp is computational—starting with mathematical models from cognitive psychology, the goal is to isolate those parameters whose modification reproduces the observed pattern of age effects (see, e.g., the strong positions taken by Byrne, 1998; Kahana, Howard, Zaromb, & Wingfield, 2002; Meyer, Glass, Mueller, Seymour, & Kieras, 2001; and Ratcliff, Spieler, & McKoon, 2000).

Psychometrically inclined researchers, on the other hand (see, e.g., Salthouse's 1991 *Theoretical perspectives on cognitive aging*), tend to focus on between-task correlations in large data sets. (In these studies, the level at which tasks or constructs are typically considered would be considered coarse by most cognitive psychologists—psychometricians tend to look at the level of ability factors rather than at the level of processes. Thus, "episodic memory" is often measured by recall or recognition of a list of items; no attempt is made at disentangling the effects of, for instance, spontaneous versus deliberate encoding, or to separate out effects on encoding from those of retrieval.) Psychometricians in the field of cognitive aging have typically noticed large commonalities among different tasks, pointing to a few (perhaps a single) underlying factors. The variables considered tend to be basic aspects of cognition: The idea is that deficits in very general mechanisms will lead to deficits in higher order aspects of cognition as well. The hypothesis that only a few basic mechanisms are responsible for the plethora of findings in the literature gains credibility when we consider that adult age differences in cognitive functioning tend to be quantitative rather than qualitative in nature. The current aspiration among these researchers is of cross-level unification, building explanations for cognitive aging from the bottom up, starting with gross changes in brain structure or neuronal functioning (see, e.g., the strong claims in Li, Lindenberger, & Frensch, 2000, and Park, Polk, Mikels, Taylor, & Marshuetz, 2001). The psychometric approach comes in two flavors: common-cause or common-factor models, and meditational models.

Common-cause or *common-factor models* originate in the finding that sensory and cognitive measures correlate very highly in old age (Lindenberger & Baltes, 1994, 1997). This finding has given rise to the hypothesis that the declines in both domains must be due to a common cause, identified with a general, unspecified decline in the functional integrity of the brain (see also Anstey, Hofer, & Luszcz, 2003; Salthouse, Hancock, Meinz, & Hambrick,

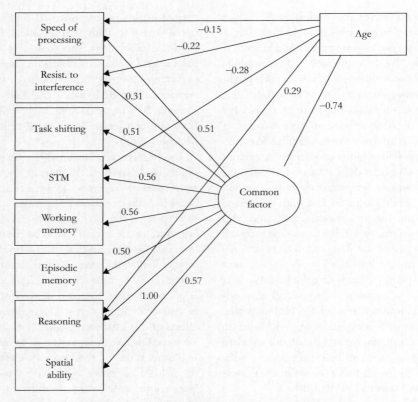

**Figure 64.5** A common-factor model to explain age-related differences in eight aspects of cognition; correlations are derived from a meta-analysis on 119 studies (Verhaeghen, in press).

1996). Recent versions of this hypothesis emphasize a common factor among cognitive variables rather than a common cause connecting many diverse aspects of physiological functioning (Allen et al., 2001; Schmiedek & Li, 2004). Figure 64.5 shows the fit of a common-factor model to correlation matrix derived from a meta-analysis of 119 studies (all studies used a continuous age range rather than extreme age groups; Verhaeghen, in press). In this model, direct paths from age to a variable suggest misspecifications of the model—there are quite a few.

*Mediational models* often assume a cascade of effects, starting with decline in one or more basic aspects of cognition that reverberates through the system. One such proposed basic aspect is speed of information processing (Salthouse, 1996). As mentioned earlier, age-related slowing is a rather general phenomenon, which already appears in very simple tasks. The hypothesis is that this slowing will have two consequences: (a) Performance will break down when information is streaming too fast; and (b) information will be lost when tasks require multiple steps with storage of intermediate results.

This mechanism can explain age-related differences in multitasking or task switching: While one task is being performed, the other one needs to be kept more or less active in working memory. If the foreground task takes longer, it is likely that the background task may have faded from active memory. A second proposed mediator is working memory capacity. Given that working memory capacity correlates with many other cognitive tasks (Engle et al., 1999), it is plausible that the age-related decline in working memory capacity plays a role in age differences in fluid cognition. A third proposed mediator concerns deficient executive control processes, likely related to age-specific changes in the prefrontal cortex (Braver & West, 2007; Raz, 2000; West, 1996). Probably the best-known version of this hypothesis is the inhibition-deficit hypothesis (e.g., Hasher & Zacks, 1988): A purported breakdown in resistance to inference from irrelevant stimuli or tasks leads to mental clutter in working memory, thereby limiting its functional capacity and perhaps also its speed of operation. (Note that the meta-analyses reported earlier do not give much credence to the existence a specific age-related breakdown in inhibition.).

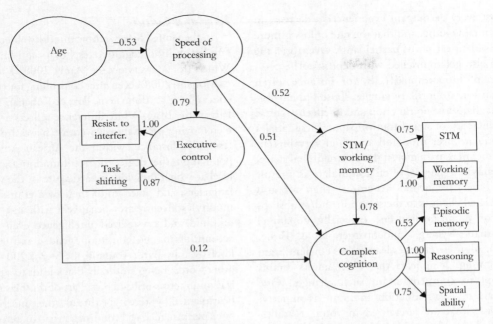

**Figure 64.6** A cascade model to explain age-related differences in eight aspects of cognition; correlations are derived from a meta-analysis on 119 studies (Verhaeghen, in press).

Figure 64.6 shows fit of one cascade model to the same dataset as used for Figure 64.5. The model suggests that both speed and working memory capacity are important mediators of more complex aspects of cognition; executive control measures do not carry any influence down the line.

### *Biological Explanations*

#### BRAIN AGING

There is no doubt that with advancing age the brain undergoes drastic changes. The brain of an average 20-year-old weighs 1,500 grams, that of the average 70-year-old 1,250 grams. Part of the weight loss is due to neuronal death, another part to shrinking of the mass of surviving neurons, and a third to white matter loss. Not all brain structures are affected to the same degree. The frontal lobes show the largest volume loss, the temporal and parietal lobes are a little less affected, and the motor and sensory cortex are relatively spared (Raz, 2000). Figure 64.7 illustrates longitudinal changes in two specific areas of the frontal cortex—the part of the brain that is, among other things, responsible for mental coordination and cognitive control. Each of the lines in the plot describes the trajectory for a single participant. It is clear that

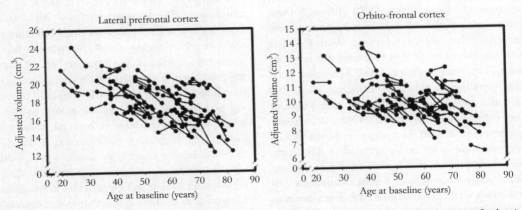

**Figure 64.7** Age trajectories for brain volume in two cortical regions. Each dot represents a person; connected dots signify a longitudinal measurement. (Figure from Raz et al., 2005.)

almost every participant experienced a decrease in prefrontal volume, and that the rate of loss is more or less identical across participants. Over time, the brain also gets burdened with deposits. The cytoplasm of hippocampal cells, for instance, often contains neurofibrillary tangles, loose protein segments that serve no function and in effect decrease the efficiency of signal transmission. These tangles accumulate over time and are often very present in Alzheimer's patients. In the interneuronal space, beta-amyloid plaques often accumulate as a result of degenerative neural structures. There are also age-related changes in the secretion and/or absorption of neurotransmitters, especially dopamine (Bäckman, Nyberg, Lindenberger, Li, & Farde, 2006). All these changes lead to less efficient brain functioning. It appears that older adults' brains attempt to compensate for such changes. One mechanism is a reduction in brain asymmetry: For tasks that are lateralized in younger adults, older adults often additionally activate areas in the opposite hemisphere (Cabeza, 2002). Another such mechanism is the so-called posterior-anterior shift: an age-related reduction in occipital activity coupled with increased frontal activity, possibly reflecting enhanced strategic processing (Davis, Dennis, Daselaar, Fleck, & Cabeza, 2008). It is important to note here that these changes in brain structure and functioning are not pathological but part of the normal aging process.

## HEALTH

Physical health plays an important role in cognitive functioning. Brain damage, hypertension and other cardiovascular disorders, thyroid disorders, stroke, hypoxemia, medication or alcohol abuse, untreated diabetes, epilepsy, and Alzheimer's disease all have a negative impact on cognitive functioning (e.g., Anstey & Christensen, 2000). Although these ailments are not part of the normal aging process, they tend to become more prevalent with age. The effects on cognition of these illnesses are far from modest: One study estimates it at 0.5 standard deviations (Verhaeghen, Borchelt, & Smith, 2003). This study also found that the effects of cardiovascular abnormalities and diabetes decreased with advancing age—after age 90, the presence or absence of these four syndromes no longer made a difference. One possible reason is that with advancing age the normal progression of brain deterioration is no longer distinguishable from the effects of cardiovascular problems and diabetes, which then have little to add to the picture.

### Race and Culture

In the United States, ethnic minority older adults fare less well on cognitive tests than non-Hispanic Whites (for an overview, see Manly, 2008; Whitfield & Morgan, 2008), even after controlling for years of education (e.g., Bohnstedt, Fox, & Kohatsu, 1994). Part of the Black-White difference reflects a failure of removing pro-Caucasian ethnic biases from the tests. For instance, within the African American population the degree of acculturation (i.e., the level at which individuals participate in the values, languages, and practices of their own ethnic community) still correlates negatively with test scores on fluid and crystallized intelligence even when accounting for age, education, gender, and reading level (Manly, Byrd, Touradji, & Stern, 2004)—in other words: Being culturally Black leads to a penalization in terms of IQ scores. Part of this bias might be explained by stereotype threat—the concern that one's performance will confirm a negative stereotype about one's group drains attention away from the test (Steele & Aronson, 1995). Another part of the picture is health—the prevalence of several risk factors for cardiovascular disease are higher in African Americans than in Whites, leading to higher incidences of stroke and white-matter abnormalities (Manly, 2008). A third might be differential racial/ethic access to high-level educational opportunities, certainly in the first half of the 20th century.

### Disuse (or Use It or Lose It)

The hypothesis (or the belief) that an engaged lifestyle can counter some of the age-related decline in basic cognitive abilities is an appealing one, but the scientific verdict is still out. To wit, two recent and comprehensive reviews of the literature (Hertzog, Kramer, Wilson, & Lindenberger, 2009, and Salthouse, 2006) appear to arrive at opposite conclusions. The former asserts that "the available evidence favors the hypothesis that maintaining an intellectually engaging and physically active lifestyle promotes successful cognitive aging" (p. 1), the latter that "there is currently little scientific evidence that differential engagement in mentally stimulating activities alters the rate of mental aging" (p. 84). Both, however, seem to be right. One crucial problem in evaluating the evidence is the causal direction of the effect: Do people who are more able engage in more demanding activities, or does engagement in demanding activities keep one able? Longitudinal studies suggest that the relationship is reciprocal, that is, both mechanisms are at play— cognition pushes activity, which in turn pushes cognition, and so on (e.g., Bosma et al., 2002; Schooler & Mulatu, 2001). What Salthouse notes is one very important caveat: Although cognitive activities tend to increase one's level of performance, they do not change the rate of age-related decline. This is still good news, of course: At the very least, an engaged lifestyle postpones reaching a critical threshold in cognitive functioning. A second caveat (with the possible exception of true expertise in a specific domain, see the next paragraph) is that the effects of cognitive activities are often restricted to knowledge rather than influencing all of cognition (Salthouse, Berish, & Miles, 2002). In other words, an avid crossword puzzle solver will be excellent at solving crossword puzzles but might still fare poorly in the grocery store.

## Assembled Cognition

The previous paragraphs centered on cognition as it is typically defined in psychology textbooks: a set of abilities as measured by tests. There are, however, forms of cognitive and intelligent behavior that transcend the traditional definition of cognition, among other things because they are complex assemblages of different psychological aspects of performance. Here, I briefly discuss three of such assembled types of cognition: expertise, creativity, and wisdom.

### *Expertise*

A very specific form of crystallized intelligence is the knowledge base an individual has acquired over a lifetime of experience in the life domains in which she has invested most. Such accumulated knowledge can compensate for age-related changes in basic abilities.[1] One example is chess playing (e.g., Charness & Bosman, 1995). Age-sensitive cognitive abilities such as speed of processing, working memory, long-term memory, and reasoning ability all contribute to high performance in the game. If only these were at play, chess players' performance should peak when these constituent abilities peak: in their 20s. Top performers in chess, however, tend to be around 40 years of age. The reason is that peak performance in chess relies on the acquisition and use of a gigantic knowledge base of possible board positions and the best moves associated with each position (Elo, 1965). Research shows that chess grandmasters have no less than 50,000 of these positions stored in memory (compare this to the about 20,000 words of native-language vocabulary typically acquired by a college graduate; Nation & Waring, 1997) (Chase & Simon, 1973). Building

up this knowledge takes many decades, during which performance continues to rise; after this peak the decline in fluid intelligence starts taking its toll.

The study of expertise has focused on the comparison of novices and experts in different domains such as musicianship, flying, graphic design, typing, baseball, crossword puzzles, chess, bridge, and the game Go (a review can be found in Hess, 2005). In each of these domains, expertise has a positive impact on performance. Expertise does not, however, appear to influence age differences: The differences between younger and older experts tend to be identical to those between younger and older novices. Expertise then serves to lift performance, not to stop decline. In the rare studies that do find smaller age differences for experts (graphic design in one study, flying an airplane in another) expertise does not make age differences disappear. (And in these instances, it can be questioned whether expertise was properly matched—expertise was simply defined as being a graphic designer or a pilot, respectively.) An interesting finding from a number of studies is that growing expertise, although domain-specific, can have positive consequences for those aspects of the cognitive system that the expertise relies on. For instance, Clarkson-Smith and Hartley (1990) found that bridge experts had a larger working memory, although they did not differ from novices on measures of speed and verbal abilities. Shimamura, Berry, Rustig, and Jurica (1995) studied university professors of different ages and found the usual age-related differences in memory performance, with one exception: memory for text, which remained stable over age. Older typists (Salthouse, 1984) store more words in working memory while typing than younger typists. The conclusion is that the repeated and intensive practice of a specific ability can lead to preservation of that ability with age.

One terrain in which expertise is relevant is on-the-job performance. Even within samples of unskilled laborers there is a positive correlation between intelligence and job ratings by supervisors (e.g., Schmidt, Hunter, & Outerbridge, 1986). A corollary could be that with advancing age, when abilities decline, on-the-job performance would decline as well. This is clearly not the case: Meta-analyses find no relationship between age and job performance (Ng & Feldman, 2008; Rhodes, 1983; Waldman & Avolio, 1986). The most comprehensive of those analyses (Ng & Feldman) included 380 studies, and it found no age effects on core job performance, creativity, or trainability, regardless of whether these were objectively measured, rated by supervisors, or rated by the subjects themselves, and regardless of job complexity. Park (1994) offers a few reasons why this may be the case. First, the positive effects of increasing expertise might compensate for the decline in basic abilities, as explained earlier. Second, this effect might be enhanced because most older workers work in a stable environment, which allows them to keep using the skills they have acquired over the years. When the job requires a new skill set, for instance, when a new piece of information technology is introduced in the workplace, older adults tend to learn slower than younger adults. Research shows that lower processing speed and smaller working memory capacity is to blame for this age difference in learning rate (e.g., Echt, Morrell, & Park, 1998). The same research also shows, however, that given enough time older workers can reach the same level as younger workers. Third, older workers often have more detailed knowledge about the job than younger adults. This is especially true for tacit knowledge—the kind of (often essential) knowledge that is hard to put into words and that is therefore hard to teach or train. In a study of 200 managers in a bank, Colonia-Willner (1998) found that tacit knowledge about interpersonal problems was a much better predictor of a manager's performance than any cognitive ability; this tacit knowledge also declined much less rapidly than any of the cognitive abilities tested. Fourth, older adults seek advice from other colleagues more often, they are better team players, and they often choose positions that emphasize fluid abilities less but depend much more on judgment and social skills. In this way, older workers capitalize on their strong points while avoiding their potential weaknesses.

## Creativity

Creativity can be considered a special form of expertise. Although the ability to produce original ideas—one core aspect of creativity—appears to be rather hardwired, time and experience are needed to elaborate on these original ideas and make them work, and those are at least partially a function of experience (Simonton, 1994). It is clear that old age does not preclude creative peak performance. Bach composed the *Art of the Fugue* at age 65; Verdi wrote *Falstaff* when he was 80; Rembrandt's later self-portraits are among his best work; Picasso kept working until he died, at age 92; Stravinsky mastered serialism when he was 70 and delivered a few of the masterpieces in the genre (*Agon, Threni*); Goethe

finished his *Faust* when he was 80. All of these artists, writers, and composers were also very active when young; there are only a handful of examples of artists who become creative in advanced age (the writer Annie Proulx is an interesting exception; she published her first book, *Postcards*, when she was 57). The artists who stay active longest tend to be the ones who started earliest and produced their first masterpiece at an early age—creativity is a lifelong habit. Such lifelong habits can lead to increasingly more interesting work. Painters who elaborate on a single theme for a lifetime, such as Cezanne or Degas, make their literally most valuable work late in life (Galenson, 1999).

Research on the age trajectory of creativity in science and the arts often finds a curvilinear association: There is an initial rise in productivity and quality, a short plateau, and then a decline (e.g., Lehman, 1953; Simonton, 1994). The placement of the peak differs across disciplines. Scientists often peak around age 35–40. Poets and mathematicians peak earlier. But philosophers and historians peak rather late: around age 60 or 70. The decline in productivity is usually steeper for artists than for scientists. There are also differences within disciplines. Within the group of classical composers, for instance, the peak for symphonic music is around age 30–35; for operas, around age 40–45. Poets peak earlier than novelists. The differences might be due to the time needed to acquire the skills and experiences necessary to make a top work: Operas are more complex than purely instrumental music, novels might be invested with more life experience than poems, and philosophers and historians need a lifetime to work their way through a gigantic library. Sometimes knowledge can also hamper creativity. The pioneers of relativity theory and quantum physics in the early 20th century were all younger than 30, unimpeded by preconceived notions about how physics should work. This curvilinear association has also been found in samples that are more representative of the total population: Participants in the Baltimore Longitudinal Study of Aging (McCrae, Arenberg, & Costa, 1987) showed a peak around age 40 in a standard test for creativity.

## Wisdom

One of the few positive clichés about aging is that older adults are wiser than younger adults. Most of the research on wisdom in old age has been done by the group around Paul Baltes (a review can be found in Baltes & Staudinger, 2000). Baltes defines wisdom as a system of knowledge about the meaning of life and how to be a good person—a constellation of personal characteristics that reflects a high level of cognitive, affective, and behavioral maturity and reveals an unusual degree of sensitivity, openness of mind, and care for humanity. (No easy feat.) Wisdom is measured by confronting participants with life problems of fictitious individuals ("Someone receives a phone call from a good friend who tells her that she cannot keep on living like this and has decided to commit suicide. What kinds of things could someone in this situation consider and do?"; or "In reflecting about life, people often realize they have not attained their dreams. What could one then do and consider?") Participants think out loud and trained observers judge their utterings on five criteria: (a) factual knowledge about the problems presented; (b) pragmatic procedural knowledge (e.g., knowing how to listen and to give advice); (c) the degree to which the problem is embedded in the life context of the fictitious person; (d) the degree to which the fictitious person's life choices and values are being accepted; and (e) the degree to which the participant understands and deals with uncertainty. The most important finding from this line of research is that wisdom is not related to age. A second important finding is that certain life patterns lead more easily to wisdom. Clinical psychologists, for instance, tend to score above the mean. They do not, however, score in the top range of the samples, indicating that there is more to wisdom than life experience. The third finding is that wisdom is clearly separate from cognition as traditionally defined: The correlations between wisdom and intelligence, creativity, and even personality are small. A final conclusion is that wisdom scores tend to be lower when people think about a situation alone than when they do so with a partner. Wisdom only truly blossoms in an interpersonal context.

## Coping With Cognitive Limitations

The previous paragraphs have made it clear that aging comes with serious limitations on the functioning of the cognitive system, especially in the domains of speed, divided attention, episodic memory, and fluid intelligence. What is to be done?

### Fitness Training

Colcombe and Kramer (2003) conducted a meta-analysis of 18 studies published between 1966 and 2001 in which the effects of cardiovascular fitness training on cognition were examined. The training interventions ranged from dancing to aerobic training combined with muscle training.

The control groups in these interventions (mostly training programs aimed at flexibility or power) obtained a 0.2 standard deviation increase in their cognitive functioning, whereas the cardiovascular fitness groups saw an increase in cognitive functioning of 0.5 standard deviations. The net effect of aerobic training on cognition is therefore 0.3 standard deviations. Given that the difference in fluid aspects of cognitive functioning between a 20-year-old and a 70-year-old is about 1 standard deviation, this is a sizable effect. Several variables moderated the effect: (a) The effect was larger in females than in males; (b) the effect was only significant for programs with sessions that lasted 30 minutes or longer; (c) short interventions (1 to 3 months) were effective, but the largest gain was observed with programs that lasted at least 6 months; (d) the effect was larger for individuals older than 65 than for younger older adults; (e) demented older adults gained as much as normal older adults; and (f) the effect was largest on control processes in working memory, but there were also measurable effects on spatial ability and speed of processing. It is plausible to assume that aerobic training impacts brain functioning directly. Colcombe and colleagues (2004) scanned the brains of 15 individuals who took part in a 45-minute/day walking program and compared the scans with those of age-matched individuals who were part of an equally intensive program aimed at increasing flexibility and musculature. The aerobic group performed better on tests of attention, and this change correlated with imaging results: They showed heightened activation in the frontal and parietal cortex (areas associated with the attention network) and a stronger suppression of activity in the posterior cortex. Aerobic fitness then did not result in a general effect, but rather it allowed individuals to steer activation to the areas relevant for the cognitive task at hand.

The exact neuronal mechanism that underlies these changes is still unclear. It is possible that cardiovascular fitness increases the oxygen supply in the brain and thereby leads to more precise recruitment of the necessary brain areas; it is also possible that cardiovascular fitness enhances the release of particular hormones (such as neurotropin) that have a direct impact on the number of neurons and their connections. In any case, relatively short and simple aerobic interventions appear to lead to increased cerebral fitness. These effects can be demonstrated both on standard cognitive tests and on brain activity. It is plausible that these changes will also influence everyday functioning.

## Cognitive Training

Cognitive performance is not merely a function of cognitive ability. Strategy use can be important as well, especially in memory functioning. A large number of studies have investigated what happens when older adults are instructed in new, more optimal memory strategies. These memory-training programs appear to work. Verhaeghen, Marcoen, and Goossens (1992) conducted a meta-analysis on 33 training studies. In these studies, researchers concentrate typically on a single memory strategy, such as the use of imagery, the combined use of labels and imagery to connect names to faces, or more specialized techniques, such as the method of loci. Memory training increased scores on a memory test by about 0.7 standard deviations, compared with a 0.4 increase in control groups. The net gain is then about 0.3 standard deviations, comparable to the gain obtained after aerobic training. The bad news is that the effects of strategy training, contrary to those of aerobic training, result in a Matthew effect ("the rich get richer, the poor get poorer"). Younger adults show larger gain than older adults; younger older adult show larger gain than older older adults (Singer, Lindenberger, & Baltes, 2003), and Alzheimer's patients show no gain at all (Baltes, Kühl, & Sowarka, 1992). Within the group of older adults, gain correlates positively with working memory capacity, speed of processing, reasoning ability, or episodic memory (e.g., Verhaeghen & Marcoen, 1996). Thus, training gains are larger for the initially more able. The effects are also very limited: Participants who have been taught a technique to associate names and faces will do well on a face-name test, but not on a test for, say, grocery lists (Verhaeghen et al., 1992). Similar results were obtained in the largest cognitive training study ever conducted, the ACTIVE trial (Ball et al., 2002; the study involved 2,832 older adults). Different training regimes were implemented—one for reasoning, one for memory, one for speed—and the effects were impressive (a net effect of about 0.5 standard deviations for reasoning, 0.2 for memory, and 1.5 for speed), but very specific: Untrained abilities typically showed zero net gain.

## The Competent Older Adult: Selective Optimization With Compensation

Older adults somehow need to learn to cope with their growing cognitive limitations. One framework that is often used to examine such coping behavior is the model of selective optimization with compensation (SOC; Baltes & Baltes, 1990). SOC is not a theory (it cannot be falsified by research), but it is a good guiding principle to organize the everyday reality of aging. The starting point of the SOC model is that individuals guide their own development using three principles: selection, optimization, and compensation. Selection stands for making choices between the several alternatives life throws one's way. Selection can happen as a consequence of temporary limitations or as a shift in priorities (e.g., putting one's hobbies on hold to concentrate on one's career), or it can reflect a more permanent change (e.g., marrying one's boyfriend [usually] puts a halt on dating). Optimization means to try to find and apply new means to reaching one's goals or to refine existing means (e.g., downshifting to part-time work to accommodate a new baby). Compensation operates when the means at the individual's disposal are no longer sufficient; she then needs to find alternative ways to reach her goals (e.g., hiring a nanny when there is a crunch at work). SOC is a contextual model: The concrete content of the concepts depends on the individual's context and on the specific behavioral domain—SOC is ultimately about expertise in one's own life span. Baltes (1997) offers an example that might clarify these rather abstract statements. In a television interview, the then 80-year-old pianist Arthur Rubinstein explained how he maintained such a high level of performance at such an advanced age. First, he focused on a smaller number of pieces (selection). Second, he practiced more often than he used to (optimization). Third, he used a psychological technique to compensate for the loss of physical finger speed: Right before a fast passage, he would slow down so that the contrast made the (not-so-) fast passage sound faster than it was actually played (compensation). Earlier in this chapter we encountered other examples of SOC in action. During dual tasking, older adults tend to protect motor tasks (balancing, walking) more than younger adults do, almost certainly because the consequences of a fall are more severe in old age. Another example is that older adults more than younger adults use external support to compensate for memory problems (e.g., Bouazzaoui et al., 2010). Viewed from an SOC perspective, these changes are clever ways to cope with likely permanent changes in cognitive functioning. Research into SOC is difficult, precisely because SOC operates at the level of the individual—it is a function of an individual's highly idiosyncratic goals and means, which are hard to capture. In a recent study, Freund and Baltes (2002) therefore tried to operationalize SOC processes in a broader sense. They asked their subjects rather general questions (e.g., selection: "When I think about what is important in life, I restrict myself to one or two goals"; optimization: "When I consider something to be truly important, I will dedicate myself to it fully"; compensation: "When things don't go very well, I look for help or advice"). They found shifts in what type of SOC strategies were favored along what portion of the life span. Older adults used selection strategies more often than younger adults; younger adults relied more often on compensation strategies. Competent aging then seems to be a matter of adapting one's goals, not one's means. A second finding was that SOC strategy use did not covary with crystallized intelligence: Expertise in one's life course is not related to general intelligence. Third, each of the SOC processes turned out to be important for well-being: Subjects who indicated using SOC processes more often experienced more positive emotions and scored higher on tests for general well-being. Well-being then is not only caused by living in objectively happy circumstances; it is also born out of the ability to creatively cope with one's limitations, and in mastery over one's own life course.

## Conclusion

As stated often throughout this chapter, the news for older adults does not appear to be good. Fluid intelligence and memory abilities decline, and this decline appears to be hardwired, linked to changes in brain functioning and in basic cognitive abilities. Basically, only verbal and other knowledge-based, crystallized abilities are generally spared. Looking at the picture more carefully, however, we found that older adults are not powerless vis-à-vis this decline. Living healthily and avoiding risk factors for diabetes and cardiovascular disease can counteract part of the deficit; so might an active, engaged lifestyle. Part of the decline can be compensated for by aerobic training. Expertise is another buffer against the negative effects of aging. One unique type of expertise is expertise in one's own personal life course. This form of expertise, built on increasing selection as well as optimization and compensation, can help older adults to live competently and happily until a very advanced age.

## Note

1. Or the other way round: Perhaps younger adults are gifted with such a high level of cognitive ability to compensate for their lack of experience.

## References

Allen, P. A., Hall, R. J., Druley, J. A., Smith, A. F., Sanders, R. E, & Murphy, M. D. (2001). How shared are age-related influences on cognitive and noncognitive variables? *Psychology and Aging, 16*, 532–549.

Anstey, K. J., & Christensen, H. (2000). Education, activity, health, blood pressure and Apolipoprotein E as predictors of cognitive change in old age: A review. *Gerontology, 46*, 163–177.

Anstey, K. J., Hofer, S. M., & Luszcz, (2003). Cross-sectional and longitudinal patterns of dedifferentiation in late-life cognitive and sensory function: The effects of age, ability, attrition, and occasion of measurement. *Journal of Experimental Psychology: General, 132*, 470–487.

Bäckman, L., Nyberg, L., Lindenberger, U., Li, S-C., & Farde, L. (2006). The correlative triad among aging, dopamine, and cognition: Current status and future prospects. *Neuroscience and Biobehavioral Reviews, 30*, 791–807.

Baddeley, A. D. (1986). *Working memory*. New York: Oxford University Press.

Bahrick, H. P. (1984). Semantic memory content in the permastore: 50 years of memory for Spanish learned in school. *Journal of Experimental Psychology: General, 113*, 1–29.

Bahrick, H. P, Bahrick, P. O., & Wittlinger, R. P. (1975). Fifty years of memory for names and faces: A crosssectional approach. *Journal of Experimental Psychology: General, 104*, 54–75.

Ball, K., Berch, D. B., Helmers, K. F., Jobe, J. B., Leveck, M. D., Marsiske, M., …; Advanced Cognitive Training for Independent and Vital Elderly Study Group. (2002). Effects of cognitive training interventions with older adults: A randomized controlled trial. *Journal of the American Medical Association, 288*, 2271–2281.

Ball, K., Owsley, C., Sloane, M. E., Roenker, D. L., & Bruni, J. R. (1993). Visual attention problems as a predictor of vehicle crashes among older drivers. *Investigative Ophthalmology and Visual Science, 34*, 3110–3123.

Baltes, M. M., & Baltes, P. B. (1990). *Successful aging: Perspectives from the behavioral sciences*. New York: Cambridge University Press.

Baltes, M. M., Kühl, K-R, & Sowarka, D. (1992). Testing for limits of cognitive reserve capacity: A promising strategy for early diagnosis of dementia? *Journal of Gerontology: Psychological Sciences, 47*, 165–167.

Baltes, P. B. (1997). On the incomplete architecture of human ontogeny: Selection, optimization, and compensation as foundation of developmental theory. *American Psychologist, 52*, 366–380.

Baltes, P. B., & Staudinger, U. M. (2000). Wisdom: A metaheuristic (pragmatic) to orchestrate mind and virtue toward excellence. *American Psychologist, 55*, 122–136.

Blazer, D. G., Hays, J. C., Fillenbaum, G. G., & Gold, D. T. (1997). Memory complaint as a predictor of cognitive decline. *Journal of Aging and Health, 9*, 171–184.

Bohnstedt, M., Fox, P. J., & Kohatsu, N. D. (1994). Correlates of mini-mental status examination scores among elderly demented patients: The influence of race-ethnicity. *Journal of Clinical Epidemiology, 47*, 1381–1387.

Bonnesen, J. L., & Burgess, E. O. (2004). Senior moments: The acceptability of an ageist phrase. *Journal of Aging Studies, 18*, 123–142.

Bopp, K. L., & Verhaeghen, P. (2005). Aging and verbal memory span: A meta-analysis. *Journal of Gerontology: Psychological Sciences, 60B*, 223–233.

Bosma, H., van Boxtel, M. P., Ponds, R. W., Jelicic, M., Houx, P., Metsemakers, J., & Jolles, J. (2002). Engaged lifestyle and cognitive function in middle and old-aged, non-demented persons: A reciprocal association? *Zeitschrift fuer Gerontologie und Geriatrie, 35*, 575–581.

Bouazzaoui, B., Isingrini, M., Fay, S., Angel, L., Vanneste, S., Clarys, D., & Taconnat, L. (2010). Aging, executive functioning and self-reported memory strategy use. *Acta Psychologica, 135*, 59–66.

Braver, T. S., & Barch, D. M. (2002). A theory of cognitive control, aging cognition, and neuromodulation. *Neuroscience and Biobehavioral Reviews, 26*, 809–817.

Braver, T. S., & West, R. (2007). Working memory, executive control, and aging. In F. I. Craik & T. Salthouse (Eds.), *The handbook of aging and cognition* (3rd ed., pp. 311–372). New York: Psychology Press.

Brinley, J. F. (1965). Cognitive sets, speed and accuracy of performance in the elderly. In A. T. Welford & J. E. Birren (Eds.), *Behavior, aging and the nervous system* (pp. 114–149). Springfield, IL: Thomas.

Byrne, M. D. (1998). Taking a computational approach to aging: The SPAN theory of working memory. *Psychology and Aging, 13*, 309–322.

Cabeza, R. (2002). Hemispheric asymmetry reduction in old adults: The HAROLD Model. *Psychology and Aging, 17*, 85–100.

Castel, A. D., & Craik, F. I. M. (2003). The effects of aging and divided attention on memory for item and associative information. *Psychology and Aging, 18*, 873–885.

Cerella, J., & Hale, S. (1994). The rise and fall in information-processing rates over the life span. *Acta Psychologica, 86*, 109–197.

Cerella, J., Poon, L. W., & Williams, D. H. (1980). Age and the complexity hypothesis. In L. W. Poon (Ed.), *Aging in the 1980's* (pp. 332–340). Washington, DC: American Psychological Association.

Charness, N., & Bosman, E. A. (1995). Expertise and age. In G. Maddox (Ed.), *Encyclopedia of aging* (2nd ed., pp. 352–354). New York: Springer.

Chase, W. G., & Simon, H. A. (1973). Perception in chess. *Cognitive Psychology, 4*, 55–81.

Clarkson-Smith, L., & Hartley, A. A. (1990). The game of bridge as an exercise in working memory and reasoning. *Journal of Gerontology, 45*, 233–238.

Colcombe, S. J., & Kramer, A. F. (2003), Fitness effects on the cognitive function of older adults: A meta-analytic study. *Psychological Science, 14*, 25–130.

Colcombe, S. J., Kramer, A. F., Erickson, K. I., Scalf, P., McAuley, E., Cohen, N.J., … Elavsky, S. (2004). Cardiovascular fitness, cortical plasticity, and aging. *Proceedings of the National Academy of Sciences USA, 11*, 3316–3321.

Colonia-Willner, R. (1998). Practical intelligence at work: Relationship between aging and cognitive efficiency among managers in a bank environment. *Psychology and Aging, 13*, 45–57.

Conway, M. A., Cohen, G., & Stanhope, N. (1991). Very long-term memory of knowledge acquired at school and university. *Applied Cognitive Psychology, 6*, 467–482.

Cutler, S. J., & Grams, A. E. (1988). Correlates of self-reported everyday memory problems. *Journal of Gerontology: Social Sciences, 43*, 82–90.

Davis, S. W., Dennis, N. A., Daselaar, S. M., Fleck, M. S., & Cabeza, R. (2008). Que PASA? The posterior-anterior shift in aging. *Cerebral Cortex, 18*, 1201–1209.

Echt, K. V., Morrell, R. W., & Park, D. C. (1998). Effects of age and training formats on basic computer skill acquisition in older adults. *Educational Gerontology, 24*, 3–25.

Eichenbaum, H. (2003). How does the hippocampus contribute to memory? *Trends in Cognitive Science, 7*, 427–429.

Elo, A. E. (1965). Age changes in master chess performances. *Journal of Gerontology, 20*, 289–299.

Engle, R. W. (2002). Working memory capacity as executive attention. *Current Directions in Psychological Science, 11*, 19–23.

Engle, R. W., Kane, M. J., & Tuholski, S. W. (1999). Individual differences in working memory capacity and what they tell us about controlled attention, general fluid intelligence, and functions of the prefrontal cortex. In A. Miyake & P. Shah (Eds.), *Models of working memory: Mechanisms of active maintenance and executive control* (pp. 102–134). New York: Cambridge University Press.

Faust, M. E., Balota, D. A., Spieler, D. H., & Ferraro, F. R. (1999). Individual differences in information-processing rate and amount: Implications for group differences in response latency. *Psychological Bulletin, 125*, 777–799.

Fitzgerald, J. M. (1988). Vivid memories and the reminiscence phenomenon: The role of a self narrative. *Human Development, 31*, 261–273.

Freund, A. M., & Baltes, P. B. (2002). Life-management strategies of selection, optimization, and compensation: Measurement by self-report and construct validity. *Journal of Personality and Social Psychology, 82*, 642–662.

Galenson, D. W. (1999). *Quantifying artistic success: Ranking French painters—and paintings—from Impressionism to Cubism.* NBER Working Papers 7407. National Bureau of Economic Research, Inc.

Hartley, A. A., & Little, D. M. (1999). Age-related differences and similarities in dual task interference. *Journal of Experimental Psychology: General, 128*, 416–449.

Hasher, L., & Zacks, R. T. (1988). Working memory, comprehension, and aging: A review and a new view. In G. H. Bower (Ed.), *The psychology of learning and motivation* (Vol. 22, pp. 193–225). San Diego, CA: Academic Press.

Hasher, L., Zacks, R. T., & May, C. P. (1999). *Inhibitory control, circadian arousal, and age.* In D. Gopher & A. Koriat (Eds.), *Attention and performance, XVII, Cognitive regulation of performance: Interaction of theory and application* (pp. 653–675). Cambridge, MA: MIT Press.

Healy, M. R., Light, L. L., & Chung, C. (2005). Dual-process models of associative recognition in young and older adults: Evidence from receiver operating characteristics. *Journal of Experimental Psychology: Learning, Memory, and Cognition, 31*, 768–788.

Heine, M. K., Ober, B. A., & Shenaut, G. K. (1999). Naturally occurring and experimentally induced tip-of-the-tongue experiences in three adult age groups. *Psychology and Aging, 14*, 445–457.

Henry, J. D., MacLeod, M. S., Phillips, L. H., & Crawford, J. R. (2004). A meta-analytic review of prospective memory and aging. *Psychology and Aging, 19*, 27–39.

Hertzog, C., Kramer, A. F., Wilson, R. S., & Lindenberger, U. (2009). Enrichment effects on adult cognitive development: Can the functional capacity of older adults be preserved and enhanced? *Psychological Science in the Public Interest, 9*, 1–65.

Hess, T. M. (2005). Memory and aging in context. *Psychological Bulletin, 131*, 383–406.

Horn, J. (1970). Organization of data on life-span development of human abilities. In R. Goulet & P. B. Baltes (Eds.), *Life-span developmental psychology: Research and theory (pp. xx–xx)*. New York: Academic Press.

Howard, M. W., Bessette-Symons, B., Zhang, Y., & Hoyer, W. J. (2006). Aging selectively impairs recollection in recognition memory for pictures: Evidence from modeling and receiver-operating characteristic curves. *Psychology and Aging, 21*, 96–106.

Jacoby, L. L. (1991). A process dissociation framework: Separating automatic from intentional uses of memory. *Journal of Memory and Language, 30*, 513–541.

Kahana, M. J., Howard, M. W., Zaromb, F., & Wingfield, A. (2002). Age dissociates recency and lag recency effects in free recall. *Journal of Experimental Research: Learning, Memory, and Cognition, 28*, 530–540.

Kahn, I., Davachi, L., & Wagner, A. D. (2004). Functional neuroanatomic correlates of recollection: Implications for models of recognition memory. *Journal of Neuroscience, 24*, 4172–4180.

Kausler, D. H. (1991). *Experimental psychology, cognition, and human aging (2nd ed.)*. New York: Springer-Verlag.

Kemper, S., Herman, R. E., & Lian, C. H. T. (2003). The costs of doing two things at once for young and older adults: Talking while walking, finger tapping, and ignoring speech noise. *Psychology and Aging, 18*, 181–192.

La Voie, D. J., & Light, L. L. (1994). Adult age differences in repetition priming: A meta-analysis. *Psychology and Aging, 9*, 539–553.

Lehman, H. C. (1953). *Age and achievement*. Princeton, NJ: Princeton University Press.

Li, S-C., Lindenberger, U., & Frensch, P. (2000). Unifying cognitive aging: From neuromodulation to representation to cognition. *Neurocomputing, 32–33*, 879–890.

Li, K. Z. H., Lindenberger, U., Freund, A. M., & Baltes, P. B. (2001). Walking while memorizing: Age-related differences in compensatory behavior. *Psychological Science, 12*, 230–237.

Light, L. L., Prull, M. W., La Voie, D. J., & Healy, M. R. (2000). Dual-process theories of memory in old age. In T. J. Perfect & E. A. Maylor (Eds.), *Models of cognitive aging* (pp. 238–300). Oxford, England: Oxford University Press.

Lima, S. D, Hale, S., & Myerson, J. (1991). How general is general slowing? Evidence from the lexical domain. *Psychology and Aging, 6*, 416–425.

Lindenberger, U., & Baltes, P. B. (1994). Sensory functioning and intelligence in old age: A strong connection. *Psychology and Aging, 9*, 339–355.

Lindenberger, U., & Baltes, P. B. (1997). Intellectual functioning in old and very old age: Cross-sectional results from the Berlin Aging Study. *Psychology and Aging, 12*, 410–432.

Miyake, A., Friedman, N. P., Emerson, M. J., Witzki, A. H., & Howerter, A. (2000). The unity and diversity of executive functions and their contributions to complex "frontal lobe" tasks: A latent variable analysis. *Cognitive Psychology, 41*, 49–100.

Manly, J. J. (2008). Race, culture, education, and cognitive test performance among older adults. In S. M. Hofer & D. F. Alwin (Eds.) *Handbook of cognitive aging: Interdisciplinary perspectives* (pp. 398–417). Thousand Okas, CA: Sage.

Manly, J. J., Byrd, D. A., Touradji, P., & Stern, Y. (2004). Acculturation, reading level, and neuropsychological test performance among African American elders. *Applied Neuropsychology, 11*, 37–46.

Mayr, U., & Kliegl, R. (1993). Sequential and coordinative complexity: Age-based processing limitations in figural transformations. *Journal of Experimental Psychology: Learning, Memory, and Cognition, 19*, 1297–1320.

Mayr, U., Spieler, D. H., & Kliegl, R. (2001). *Aging and executive control*. New York: Routledge.

McCrae, R. R., Arenberg, D., & Costa, P. T. (1987). Declines in divergent thinking with age: Cross-sectional, longitudinal, and cross-sequential analyses. *Psychology and Aging, 2*, 130–137.

McDowd, J. M., & Shaw, R. J. (2000). Attention and aging: A functional perspective. In F. I. M. Craik & T. A. Salthouse (Eds.), *The handbook of aging and cognition* (2nd ed., pp.221–292). Mahwah, NJ: Erlbaum.

Meyer, D. E., Glass, J. M., Mueller, S. T., Seymour, T. L., & Kieras, D. E. (2001). Executive-process interactive control: A unified computational theory for answering 20 questions (and more) about cognitive aging. *European Journal of Cognitive Psychology, 13*, 123–164.

Nation, P., & Waring, R. (1997). Vocabulary size, text coverage, and word lists. In N. Schmitt & M. McCarthy (Eds.), *Vocabulary: Description, acquisition, pedagogy* (pp. 6–19). New York: Cambridge University Press.

Naveh-Benjamin, M. (2001). The effects of divided attention on encoding processes: Underlying mechanisms. In M. Naveh-Benjamin, M. Moscovitch, & H. L. Roediger, III (Eds.), *Perspectives on human memory and cognitive aging: Essays in honour of Fergus Craik* (pp. 193–207). Philadelphia: Psychology Press.

Naveh-Benjamin, M., Keshet Brav, T., & Levy, O. (2007). The associative memory deficit of older adults: The role of strategy utilization. *Psychology and Aging, 22*, 202–208.

Ng, T. W. H., & Feldman, D. C. (2008). The relationship of age to ten dimensions of job performance. *Journal of Applied Psychology, 93*, 392–423.

Old, S. R., & Naveh-Benjamin, M. (2008). Differential effects of age on item and associative measures of memory: A meta-analysis. *Psychology and Aging, 23*, 104–118.

Owsley, C., Ball, K., McGwin, G., Sloane, M. E., Roenker, D. L., White, M. F., & Overley, E. T. (1998). Visual processing impairment and risk of motor vehicle crash among older adults. *Journal of the American Medical Association, 279*, 1083–1088.

Park, D. C. (1994). Aging, cognition, and work. *Human Performance, 7*, 181–205.

Park, D. C., & Hall Gutchess, A. (2000). Cognitive aging and every day life. In D. C. & N. Schwarz (Eds.), *Cognitive aging: A primer (pp. xx–xx)*. Philadelphia: Psychology Press.

Park, D. C., Polk, T., Mikels, J., Taylor, S. F., & Marshuetz, C. (2001). Cerebral aging: Integration of brain and behavioral Models of cognitive function, *Dialogues in Clinical Neuroscience, 3*, 151–165.

Parkin, A. J., & Walter, B. M. (1992). Recollective experience, normal aging, and frontal dysfunction. *Psychology and Aging, 7*, 290–298.

Rapp, M., Krampe, R. T., & Baltes, P. B. (2005). Adaptive task prioritization in aging: Selective resource allocation to postural control is preserved in Alzheimer disease. *American Journal of Geriatric Psychiatry, 14*, 52–61.

Ratcliff, R., Spieler, D., & McKoon, G. (2000). Explicitly modeling the effects of aging on response time. *Psychonomic Bulletin and Review, 7*, 1–25.

Rathbone, C. J., Moulin, C. J. A., & Conway, M. A. (2008). Self-centred memories: The reminiscence bump and the self. *Memory and Cognition, 36*, 1403–1414.

Raz, N. (2000). Aging of the brain and its impact on cognitive performance: Integration of structural and functional findings. In: F. I. M. Craik & T. A. Salthouse (Eds.), *Handbook of aging and cognition* (2nd ed., pp. 1–90). Mahwah, NJ: Erlbaum.

Raz, N., Lindenberger, U., Rodrigue, K. M., Kennedy, K. M., Head, D., Williamson, A., Dahle, C., ... Acker, J. D. (2005). Regional brain changes in aging healthy adults: General trends, individual differences, and modifiers. *Cerebral Cortex, 15*, 1676–1689.

Rhodes, S. R. (1983). Age-related differences in work attitudes and behavior: A review and conceptual analysis. *Psychological Bulletin, 93*, 328–367.

Rubin, D. C., & Berntsen, D. (2003). Life scripts help to maintain autobiographical memories of highly positive, but not highly negative, events. *Memory and Cognition, 31*, 1–14.

Rubin, D. C., Wetzler, S. E., & Nebes, R. D. (1986). Autobiographical memory across the adult lifespan. In D. C. Rubin (Ed.), *Autobiographical memory* (pp. 202–221). Cambridge: Cambridge University Press.

Salthouse, T.A. (1984). Effects of age and skill in typing. *Journal of Experimental Pyschology: General, 113*, 345–371.

Salthouse, T. A. (1991). *Theoretical perspectives on cognitive aging*. Hillsdale, NJ: Erlbaum.

Salthouse, T. A. (1996). The processing-speed theory of adult age differences in cognition. *Psychological Review, 103*, 403–428.

Salthouse, T. A. (2006). Mental Exercise and mental aging: Evaluating the validity of the use it or lose it hypothesis. *Perspectives on Psychological Science, 1*, 68–87.

Salthouse, T. A. (2010). *Major issues in cognitive aging*. New York: Oxford University Press.

Salthouse, T. A., Berish, D. E., & Miles, J. D., (2002). The role of cognitive stimulation on the relations between age and cognitive functioning. *Psychology and Aging, 17*, 548–557.

Salthouse, T. A., Hancock, H. E., Meinz, E. J., & Hambrick, D. Z. (1996). Interrelations of age, visual acuity, and cognitive functioning. *Journal of Gerontology, Series B: Psychological Sciences and Social Sciences, 51B*, P317–P330.

Schaie, K. W. (2005). What can we learn from longitudinal studies of adult intellectual development. *Research in Human Development, 2*, 133–158.

Schmidt, F. L., Hunter, J. E. & Outerbridge, A. N. (1986). The impact of job experience and ability on job knowledge, work sample performance, and supervisory ratings of job performance. *Journal of Applied Psychology, 71*, 432–439.

Schmiedek, F., & Li, S-C. (2004). Towards an alternative representation for disentangling age-associated differences in general and specific cognitive abilities. *Psychology and Aging, 19*, 40–56.

Schooler, C., & Mulatu, M. S. (2001). The reciprocal effects of leisure time activities and intellectual functioning in older people: A longitudinal analysis. *Psychology and Aging, 16*, 466–482.

Schrauf, R. W., & Rubin, D. C. (2001). Effects of voluntary immigration on the distribution of autobiographical memory over the lifespan. *Applied Cognitive Psychology, 15*, 75–88.

Shimamura, A. P., Berry, J. A., Mangels, J. A., Rusting, S., & Jurica, P. J. (1995). Memory and cognitive abilities in academic professors: Evidence for successful aging. *Psychological Science, 6(5)*, 271–277.

Simonton, D. K. (1994). *Greatness: Who makes history and why*. New York: Guilford Press.

Singer, T., Lindenberger, U., & Baltes, P. B. (2003). Plasticity of memory for new learning in very old age: A story of major loss? *Psychology and Aging, 18*, 306–317.

Singer, T., Verhaeghen, P., Ghisletta, P., Lindenberger, U., & Baltes, P. B. (2003). The fate of cognition in very old age: Six-year longitudinal findings in the Berlin Aging Study (BASE). *Psychology and Aging, 18*, 318–331.

Steele, C. M., & Aronson, J. (1995). Stereotype threat and the intellectual test performance of African-Americans. *Journal of Personality and Social Psychology, 69*, 797–811.

Thornton, W. J. L., & Dumke, H. A. (2005). Age differences in everyday problem-solving and decision-making effectiveness: A meta-analytic review. *Psychology and Aging, 20*, 85–99.

Van der Linden, M., Brédart, S., & Beerten, A. (1994). Age-related differences in updating working memory. *British Journal of Psychology, 85*, 145–152.

Verhaeghen, P. (2003). Aging and vocabulary scores: A meta-analysis. *Psychology and Aging, 18*, 332–339.

Verhaeghen, P. (2012). Working memory still working: Age-related differences in working memory and executive control. In N. Ohta & M. Naveh-Benjamin (Eds.), *Memory and aging* (pp. 3–30). Psychology Press.

Verhaeghen, P. (in press). *The elements of cognitive aging: Meta-analyses of cognitive speed and its consequences*. New York, NY: Oxford University Press.

Verhaeghen, P., Borchelt, M., & Smith, J. (2003). The relation between cardiovascular and metabolic disease and cognition in very old age: Cross-sectional and longitudinal findings from the Berlin Aging Study. *Health Psychology, 22*, 559–569.

Verhaeghen, P., & Cerella, J. (2002). Aging, executive control, and attention: A review of meta-analyses. *Neuroscience and Biobehavioral Reviews, 26*, 849–857.

Verhaeghen, P., Cerella, J., Bopp, K. L., & Basak, C. (2005). Aging and varieties of cognitive control: A review of meta-analyses on resistance to interference, coordination and task switching, and an experimental exploration of age-sensitivity in the newly identified process of focus switching. In R. W. Engle, G. Sedek, U. von Hecker, & D. N. McIntosh (Eds.), *Cognitive limitations in aging and psychopathology: Attention, working memory, and executive functions* (pp. 160–189). Cambridge, MA: Cambridge University Press.

Verhaeghen, P., & Marcoen, A. (1996). On the mechanisms of plasticity in young and older adults after instruction in the method of loci: Evidence for an amplification model. *Psychology and Aging, 11*, 164–178.

Verhaeghen, P., Marcoen, A., & Goossens, L. (1992). Improving memory performance in the aged through mnemonic training: A meta-analytic study. *Psychology and Aging, 7*, 242–251.

Verhaeghen, P., Marcoen, A., & Goossens, L. (1993). Facts and fiction about memory aging: A quantitative integration of research findings. *Journals of Gerontology: Psychological Sciences, 48*, P157–P171.

Verhaeghen, P., & Salthouse, T. A. (1997). Meta-analyses of age-cognition relations in adulthood: Estimates of linear and non-linear age effects and structural models. *Psychological Bulletin, 122*, 231–249.

Waldman, D. A., & Avolio, B. J. (1986). A meta-analysis of age differences in job performance. *Journal of Applied Psychology, 71*, 33–38.

West, R. L. (1996). An application of prefrontal cortex function theory to cognitive aging. *Psychological Bulletin, 120,* 272–292.

Whitfield, K., & Morgan, A. A. (2008). Minority populations and cognitive aging. In S. M. Hofer & D. F. Alwin (Eds.), *Handbook of cognitive aging: Interdisciplinary perspectives* (pp. 384–396). Thousand Okas, CA: Sage.

Yonelinas, A. P. (1997). Recognition memory ROCs for item and associative information: Evidence for a single-process signal-detection model. *Memory and Cognition, 25,* 747–763.

Yonelinas, A. P. (2002). The nature of recollection and familiarity: A review of 30 years of research. *Journal of Memory and Language, 46,* 441–517.

Yonelinas, A. P., Otten, L. J., Shaw, K. N., & Rugg, M. D. (2005). Separating the brain regions involved in recollection and familiarity in recognition memory. *Journal of Neuroscience, 25,* 3002–3008.

# Epilogue

## Looking Forward

Daniel Reisberg

**Abstract**

In this final chapter, I offer speculations about future changes in the field of cognitive psychology. Topics covered include phenomenology, the study of individual differences, the prospect for partnerships with other specialties within psychology, and the future of applied work in cognition.

**Key Words:** future research, cognitive psychology, phenomenology, individual differences

The chapters in this volume provide an enormous quantity of information, and I hope readers find the information as interesting and as useful as I do. In this Epilogue, however, I want to look at the chapters collectively, because, as a package, the contributions provide a remarkable portrait of both the range and power of the 2013 field of Cognitive Psychology.

It should be obvious that the chapters in this handbook cover a broad set of topics and rely on an impressive variety of methods and dependent measures. The chapters also differ enormously in their language of explanation. In some chapters, data are explained in terms of complex (and perhaps conscious) strategies; in other chapters, the explanation depends on constraints or biases that derive from unconscious algorithms. Some observations are attributed to large brain structures (e.g., the fusiform area or the amygdala); other observations are attributed to the traits of individual neurons; still other observations are explained in terms of the genome. For some explanations, the relevant time scale involves the milliseconds in which a process unfolds; for others, the time scale spans months of practice; for others, the relevant frame is ontogenetic or even phylogenetic.

Let's be clear, though, that this mention of methods, or measures, or modes of explanation, reflects only the variety of research tools in use in our field. More important—and more impressive—is what we have achieved with these tools. Cognitive psychologists know a lot, and what we know is well rooted in good evidence, theoretically rich, and, in many cases, of considerable practical importance.

However, this celebration of what we have accomplished so far invites a question about what is still to come, and this final chapter seems a plausible place to explore that issue. What unsolved puzzles or untouched mysteries remain for us? What form will our theories take as we progress? I will offer my speculations about these points in a moment, but let's be clear that these are speculations, and readers are likely to have their own views about these points. (Indeed, I would be delighted if readers are provoked to think through why they disagree with my conjectures and what their own proposals might be.) So, with that base, here are some thoughts on how this handbook might be different when some subsequent edition is published in, say, a dozen years.

## Phenomenology

When psychology emerged as a separate research endeavor, more than a century ago, the study of conscious experience was a central concern. However, in its determination to be scientific and objective, the field largely set this topic to the side. In American laboratories under the influence of behaviorism, discussion of conscious experience was essentially forbidden.

In the last decades, psychology has reversed this trend, and, indeed, discussion of consciousness is threaded throughout this book. Thus, research on perception is routinely concerned with how the world looks to (i.e., is experienced by) the perceiver. Research on attention illuminates the processes governing the selectivity of experience. Research on memory has tackled both the conscious experience of familiarity and also the intriguing ways we are influenced by memories of which we are not aware. Cutting across these areas, there is rich discussion of the power of, and limits on, the cognitive unconscious. And, alongside of these endeavors, our colleagues in cognitive neuroscience are charting the neural correlates of consciousness.

To a large extent, though, this research focuses on the "information content" of consciousness. We ask what information people have, what cues they are aware of, and what inferences they draw from this information. But we less often ask how this content *is actually experienced* by the individual, that is, how the information "feels" from the point of view of the person aware of the information. Likewise, we rarely ask *whether it matters* that there is a "subjective side" to cognition. As John Kihlstrom put it (personal communication), we rarely ask, "Why are there subjective states at all? Why doesn't cognition all just go on in the dark?"

The issues in play here are mysteries associated with *qualia*—and, specifically, mysteries about what qualia are, how they are produced by neural tissue, and what function they might have. These issues are difficult, of course, for many reasons, including the simple fact that no one other than the experiencers themselves has access to qualia. There is thus no way to measure qualia or to provide a direct comparison between your qualia and mine.

Even so, there may be paths that can carry research forward, and, in truth, intriguing hints about qualia have been in the literature for years. For example, consider the fact that people seem to experience their own mental processes as sometimes more "fluent" and sometimes less so, and often seem to have expectations for how fluent these processes should be. In some settings, people seem influenced by the fluency itself; in other settings, they seem influenced by discrepancies between the experience

and expectations. One way or another, notice that this may be a domain in which people are relying on the actual "feel" of their mental lives, and so this may be one domain in which we can gather data on the use of subjective states.

In what arenas does this sense of fluency matter? Research on judgment indicates that the conclusions people draw about the *plausibility of a suggestion*, or the *likelihood of a future event*, can be influenced by how readily examples of the target idea can be brought to mind. Choices of *judgment strategy* may also be shaped by a sense of fluency, with people apparently switching strategy when their initial path feels less fluent than they had wished. In addition, the degree of *confidence* one places in a memory is likely shaped by how fluently the memory comes to mind. The feeling of *familiarity* may also be rooted in a feeling of greater-than-expected fluency. With this, studies of implicit memory imply that a range of attributions (e.g., "Is this a famous name?" "Is this sentence credible?" "Is this polygon attractive?") may also be guided by a sense of fluency. (For some of the relevant research, see Alter & Oppenheimer, 2009; Carroll, 1978; Jacoby, Woloshyn & Kelley, 1989; Oppenheimer, 2008; Tversky & Kahneman, 1974; Whittlesea & Leboe, 2000, and others.)

Let's be clear that the subjective experience in play here is rather different from the more-often-mentioned examples of qualia (e.g., the exact experience of tasting chocolate or the exact experience of seeing a particular hue). Nonetheless, the experience of one's own fluency does seem a subjective experience, not shared (or sharable) with anyone else, and seemingly impossible to describe in words or gesture. Hence, this does seem an example of a quale—and so the behavioral consequences of this quale may open a research avenue for exploring the functional role of conscious experience.

## Many-Way Interactions

In reading through these chapters, one is reminded of the futility of dichotomies—pitting *this* theory against *that* one—since, almost invariably, the data force us toward some hybrid that incorporates both sides of the dichotomy. And surely, we would find a similar pattern—with dichotomies posed and then rejected—in a handbook of developmental or social psychology (e.g., nature vs. nurture, person vs. situation).

Psychologists have been alert to this pattern for many years. Neisser (1963) noted with some chagrin that "the psychology of thinking seems to breed dichotomies." Newell (1973) famously admonished us all that "you can't play 20 questions with nature and win." McGuire (1983), in his contextualist framework, argued that all theories are true, and the task of the scientist is to discover the circumstances under which they are true. Over and over, then, theorists have warned us against an arguably simplistic "either/or" perspective, and yet we all seem to return to this perspective in our framing of the issues.

In the same vein, many chapters in this handbook offer yes/no questions (e.g., "Does variable $X$ matter for this behavior?") and then retreat from the question, acknowledging that the answer is likely to be, "Sometimes yes, sometimes no." (More precisely, the answer is likely to be, "Well, it depends on other factors, such as . . . ") In case after case, then, it seems that our behaviors are best described by multifactor interactions, rather than main effects.

What lessons can we draw from these points? As a start, perhaps we should regard the futility of dichotomies, and the dominance of interactions over main effects, as sources of insight, not frustrations. Said differently, we might set aside the notion that our explanations can be conveyed in streamlined, narrative form, and we might seek instead to explore the complex interplay among multiple factors.

In a similar way, psychologists often celebrate a variable as important even though that variable accounts for only a thin slice of the data. We showcase, for example, correlations of .3 and .4, knowing that these leave more than four-fifths of the variance unaccounted for. We discuss effect sizes in a meta-analysis that, by our own standards, we regard as "small." We dismiss large parts of the data pattern as mere "scree." Why is this? The answer in

many cases is obviously a "small-increment problem": To handle even a bit more of the variance, we would need to add many variables to our explanatory account. Thus, we choose explanatory elegance over empirical power, and prefer straightforward accounts over complete accounts.

There is much to be said for this pattern of preferences—but our field's current inclination is not inevitable, nor is it self-evident that more complete accounts will be hopelessly complex. As one illustration, consider a pattern familiar to most psychologists: the Yerkes-Dodson function. This inverted-U curve allegedly describes the relationship between arousal and performance in many domains, with performance best at some moderate level of arousal. In truth, this is a remarkably bold claim—resting on the ambitious idea that we can isolate just one factor (arousal) and use it to make substantial predictions, essentially ignoring in our predictions the myriad other factors on the scene. To bring the boldness into plain view, contrast this idea with a proposal, illustrated in Figure 65.1, offered years ago by Fazey and Hardy (1988). To be sure, the empirical basis for this figure is thinner than one might like, but even so it is interesting to contemplate the suggestions inherent in this proposed data pattern.

The figure obviously introduces a third dimension and proposes that the relationship between arousal and performance is modulated by a factor of cognitive anxiety. Having taken this step, though, why stop with a *third* dimension? We can, after all, find indications in the research literature that other factors are also important here. The list includes task complexity, task familiarity, audience effects, and a fractionation of the term "physiological arousal." A

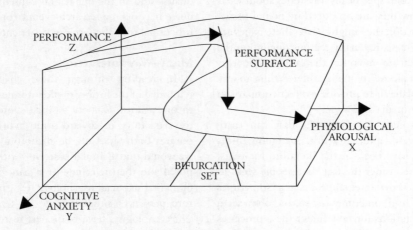

**Figure 65.1** Hardy and Fazey's Catastrophe Model illustrating the proposed (and complex) interplay among arousal, anxiety and performance.

further set of complications includes variations in a person's *goal* when aroused—escape versus enjoyment versus confrontation. With all of these ideas in view, the often-mentioned inverted-U is likely to be an oversimplification, and it may have misled us in important ways.

In addition, how should we think about the infolding depicted in the figure? One idea is that mental states are "asynchronic"—not existing just at a single point in time but instead having a history. Thus, the consequences of someone's arousal status may depend on whether the person has recently been *more* aroused or *less*.

Indeed, the role of "asynchronic" states in psychology is itself worth highlighting. Students of perception have known for years that an organism's adaptation state is crucial for determining the impact of a new stimulus. Likewise, one of the many insights offered by Daniel Kahneman and Amos Tversky is that *decision making* is guided, not by "wealth states" but by *changes* in wealth state, and so (for example) a gain moving you from $100 to $200 is psychologically very different from a loss that moves you from $300 to $200 (e.g., Kahneman, 2011).

What would our theorizing look like if we seek to accommodate all of these complications—an inclusion of other factors, a celebration of interaction effects, and a consideration of *changes* rather than *states*? After all, Figure 65.1, taken at face value, tells us only that our data contain higher order interactions, and we obviously want to ask *why* the fifth-order interactions (say) are as they are, and are as *powerful* as they are. It seems unlikely that a plausible account will take the form of a simple narrative, well captured in a journal article's General Discussion section, but that invites speculation about what the alternative might be.

One suggestion is already in view: Many forms of computer modeling (e.g., PDP theorizing, or neural net modeling, or modeling rooted in dynamic systems theory) rely on some version of *simultaneous multiple constraint satisfaction*. The idea, roughly, is that, for most mental processes, many factors are in play at the same time, all shaping (and thus constraining) the mental or behavioral outcome. Rather than seeking to work through these factors one by one, the mind may allow all these factors to operate in parallel, with each factor in essence "tugging" a mental representation toward the requirements and goals pertinent to just that factor. As a result, with all the factors operative at the same time, the mental representation that emerges from this process will reflect the best compromise among all of these "tugs"—often satisfying none of the constraints fully, but shaped nonetheless by all of the constraints.

Various colleagues have urged us all to rely more on this type of multiple-constraint satisfaction, but even so most theorizing in cognition (and throughout psychology) continues to have a simpler, narrative form. Time will tell whether this pattern shifts in coming years.

## Individual Differences

Cognitive psychology has made huge progress in cataloguing lawful principles that apply to nearly all people, but it has had less to say about principles describing how people differ. Variations from one person to the next have, in most research, been consigned to the category of "error variance" and left unexplored. The obvious exception is research on intelligence, but, even here, many cognitive psychologists seem to regard this topic as a problem in psychometrics, not cognition, and so (for example) many textbooks in cognition do not cover this research, and many introductory texts place this research alongside of their coverage of personality and clinical assessment, and not their coverage of memory, attention, or judgment.

Plainly, though, this tradition is shifting, and psychologists have made considerable headway in describing the cognitive capacities that underlie differences in intelligence, and also in cataloging other ways in which individuals, genders, and even cultures differ in their cognition. Thus, researchers are offering important claims about individual differences in creativity, expertise in a given domain, cognitive style, decision-making style, executive control, visualization prowess, and more. Discussions of cultural differences have likewise extended into more and more domains, including a set of surprising implications for perception and attention. One of the issues we should watch with interest, therefore, is how discussion in these domains will broaden, as we learn more about the ways in which people vary, and deepen, as we gain insights into what these variations entail.

It is also worth emphasizing that there is a double "payoff" from the individual-differences and cross-cultural research. First, for many purposes, the individual differences are themselves of interest. Thus, at a theoretical level, we are learning about the extent to which diverse variations (e.g., differences in problem-solving skill or differences in reading comprehension) can be traced to a common root (e.g., differences in working-memory capacity). For applied purposes, progress in this domain helps us in optimizing educational programs, in personnel decisions, and more.

Second, the individual differences can illuminate broader questions. For example, how are people influenced by their own visual imagery? How does visual imagery contribute, say, to decision making? We can get some leverage on these questions by comparing the performance of people with clear, vivid imagery and those without. Or, as a very different case, research on *judgment* has invited debate about the nature of rationality, and Stanovich (e.g., 2012) has argued powerfully that a consideration of individual differences provides new insights into (and may resolve) this issue. It simply remains to be seen what other domains will also be clarified by a consideration of the differences from one person to the next.

## Special Talents

The study of individual differences is typically understood as describing the range of the ordinary—how "normal" people differ from each other. A related question asks: Where are the limits? What can people manage to do, either because of some inborn advantage or because of extensive practice? And when we do find people with special talents of one sort or another, should we think of them merely as the extremes of an ordinary distribution? Or is it possible we will need new theorizing to describe these exceptional cases?

Consider a few examples. Individuals with autism sometimes have extraordinary talents, and so some have remarkable musical skill or skill in learning languages; others can form exquisitely detailed visual memories of complex scenes after a single, brief view. Likewise, a number of (apparently normal) individuals have been located who seem to have nearly perfect autobiographical recall—able to remember specific and mundane details of even ordinary events, such as what they ate and what they wore at an inconsequential lunch gathering decades ago (e.g., Parker, Cahill, & McGaugh, 2006). Similarly, studies suggest that some London taxi drivers may have an extraordinary memory for, and an ability to navigate through, the 25,000 streets of their city (e.g., Woolett, Spiers, & Maguire, 2008). Or, from a very different tradition, Buddhist monks tell us that they can create magnificently detailed visual images, with a degree of detail and resolution far beyond what we would expect, based on laboratory studies of imagery (e.g., Kosslyn, Reisberg, &

Behrman, 2006). Perhaps related, we have known for decades that some people have *eidetic* imagery—again, a level of visualization skill that goes far beyond what we observe in the lab (e.g., Stromeyer & Psotka, 1970).

What should we make of these cases? We do know that extension of human abilities is possible through well-practiced use of conventional strategies. This is plainly the case, for example, with many stage mnemonists; it is also the likely explanation of the individual studied by Chase and Ericsson (Chase & Ericsson, 1982; Ericsson, 2003), who had an apparent digit span of more than 75 digits. We must not trivialize these cases, but let us also note that these cases do not demand new theory; they seem instead instances in which truly extraordinary performance derives from ordinary mechanisms.

Some of the cases listed earlier, however, do not seem open to this sort of explanation. Instead, people with eidetic imagery or perfect autographical recall seem to be relying on processes truly different from those used for "normal" visualization or memory. What are these processes? And no matter what the nature of these processes, how does one gain these remarkable skills? Little research has tackled these issues (although there are some wonderful exceptions—e.g., Ericsson, 2003; Simonton, 2012; Spelke, Hirst, & Neisser, 1976), and this seems a fertile area for upcoming work.

## Links to Social Psychology

The various boundaries that subdivide psychology have long been permeable, and it is interesting to ask what will happen in upcoming years to the boundary between cognitive psychology and social psychology, or that between cognitive and developmental psychology. Likewise, there is ongoing discussion about the relationship between cognitive psychology and cognitive neuroscience, and that relationship is sure to evolve.

I have not done a systematic assessment, but it seems to me that discussion of the social context is becoming more and more visible in cognitive psychology. There are, for example, studies of "collaborative" problem solving, remembering, and decision making. The literature on "false memories" contains a strong emphasis on social influence; this theme is especially visible in discussions of *false confessions,* in which an interrogator's encouragement can lead someone to "remember" his or her own misdeeds (e.g., Kassin et al., 2010). Discussion of stereotype threat is prominent in the literature on intelligence, drawing our attention to the fact that performance of "intellectual tasks" (including, but not limited to, those on the intelligence tests) is shaped by a person's expectations for his or her own performance—expectations shaped by the social milieu—and also by how the person believes his or her performance will be perceived and interpreted by others (e.g., Steele, 2010). There can be no question, therefore, that issues central to cognition are shaped by social forces (e.g., Michael, Garry, & Kirsch, 2012), and it seems clear that the interplay between cognitive and social psychology will increase in the coming years.

## Links to Developmental Psychology

There is of course a substantial history of studying the *development* of cognition—and so we know a lot about how children gain skill in remembering or in paying attention. There is a rich literature on children's concepts (e.g., Carey, 2011), and their ability to reason (e.g., Gelman & Frazier, 2012), and on executive function in children (e.g., Zelazo & Müller, 2011).

To my eye, though, there is less "cross-talk" than one might hope for between research in these developmental areas and research in adult cognition. As informal evidence for this point, we might again use coverage in textbooks as our index, and, in fact, there's rarely any mention of developmental research in undergraduate cognition texts. Perhaps more compelling, there is also a clean separation between the professional journals in cognition and those in developmental psychology (with the conspicuous exception, of course, being the journal *Cognition*). This separation of the journals virtually guarantees that colleagues in each specialty will not be keeping up with findings in the other, a point that plainly limits the prospects for cross-fertilization.

What cross-talk should we seek? I leave it to the developmentalists to think through what more they might learn from studies of adult cognition, but, in the other direction, it is easy to find research under way in developmental psychology that could inform discussions in cognitive psychology. For example, it seems plausible that we might gain insights into how adults develop specialized expertise by asking how children gain an understanding of everyday domains. Likewise, we can gain important clues about the functioning of various cognitive resources by asking how children progress once these resources come "online." Studies of development may also provide guidance for us in domains in which we seek remediation for cognitive shortcomings in adults (in attention, perhaps, or in reasoning, or in memory). For these and other questions, therefore, I will

express a hope, rather than a forecast, for an increase across the next decade in the interactions between cognitive psychologists and developmentalists.

## Links to Neuroscience

One last partnership for cognitive psychology has been contentious: the partnership with cognitive neuroscience. Some of our colleagues seem to suggest that this is no partnership at all; instead, neuroscience is better understood as the eventual "replacement" for cognitive psychology, so that biologically rooted theorizing will soon supplant the psychological claims. Other colleagues apparently take a very different view, arguing that neuroscience is, in essence, wholly dependent on cognitive psychology, so that we first need to figure out—with a full and rich functional account—how the mind works; only then can we tackle questions about how the brain supports these functions.

My own view is that (like most either/or choices in psychology) neither of these extreme positions is correct. To be sure, many in the general public (and some of our colleagues) are overimpressed by the beautifully colored functional magnetic resonance images (fMRI) and seem sometimes confused about the difference between a neuroimage and an explanation. And, likewise, some of the early neuroscience work simply corroborated claims that had already been well established through functional data. As I indicated in Chapter 1, however, there can now be no question that information is flowing back and forth between cognitive psychology and cognitive neuroscience in ways that are instructive and intriguing.

Here's just one example of a case in which I, as a cognitive psychologist, have had my thinking changed by neuroscience data. We know from various localization studies that the amygdala plays an important role in supporting emotion-based processing. Having learned this, it was then instructive to learn that the amygdala also has a role in supporting the feeling of *familiarity* that accompanies some memories; this taught me something about familiarity, and it has made me curious to learn more about affect's role within familiarity. Likewise, I have been interested to see how widespread the amygdala's role seems to be in decision making; this too was instructive for me.

I realize I risk embarrassing myself here; and perhaps others, more insightful than I, learned these points about familiarity or decision making without the neuroscience data. (I might also mention, in my own defense, that neither of these lessons came as a complete surprise for me.) Even so, there is no question that my thinking was guided and broadened by the relevant biology, and I suspect that colleagues can find their own analogous examples.

What, then, will the future hold? I think it is clear that there will be some phenomena for which neuroscience explanations will be more straightforward, more compelling than psychological explanations, and also phenomena for which the reverse will be true. In that regard, there will sometimes be a "competition" of sorts between the different levels of explanation. There will also be arenas in which the two disciplines ask separate questions, and so there is no issue of competition. But there will also be topics for which we will trade insights back and forth. I see no way to forecast which domains are which (competing, separate, or interacting), and so I am driven to the cheerful and perhaps banal notion that the two areas simply need to keep listening to each other, and to glean insights from each other where they can.

## Methodology

Another issue is linked to several points already discussed: Will the *methods* in use in cognitive psychology be the same in a decade as they are now? This is a question about lab procedures, statistical methods, means of recruiting research participants, and more. What does the future hold?

One hint of possible changes arises from the recent flurry of calls for caution in interpreting our data, a possible reconsideration of our statistical procedures, and also a broad push toward more replication studies. Consider, for example, the widespread discussion of Bem's research on precognition (Bem, 2011, but then see, for example, Alcock, 2011). Whatever one makes of this research, Psychology has surely benefited from the ensuing discussion—a discussion that forced many of us to rethink our assumptions about methodology and statistics. Likewise, note the 2012 news article in *Science*, entitled "Psychology's Bold Initiative." The main focus of this article was on the group calling itself the Open Science Collaboration—a collection of our colleagues coordinating a systematic effort to replicate studies in our field's leading journals (Carpenter, 2012; also see Yong, 2012, for a parallel report in *Nature*, and also Ritchie, Wiseman & French, 2012, for a similar effort in the United Kingdom).

There is surely no debate about the value of replication, nor is there any question about the need for care here: This renewed worry about Type 1 errors may trigger research that encourages Type 2 errors, especially if the replication attempts are underpowered. But various cross-lab collaborations have been proposed as a way of dealing with these concerns, and it seems likely that some form of widespread, systematic double-checking on our data will emerge as a new research priority and will likely (from the laboratory side) join meta-analysis (from the statistical side) in ensuring our results are solid.

Overall, then, it seems plausible that some future edition of this handbook might add a chapter roughly entitled "New Developments in Cognition Research Methods," and I expect that at least part of this chapter would discuss where things stand in this broad effort toward promoting replication. In addition, a methodological chapter might also tackle a different topic—the new options for online data collection. These steps are encouraged by several developments: the increasing sophistication of the online survey sites, the improved options for client-side response timing (so that transmission times do not compromise response-time measures), and also the prospect of recruiting participants through other agencies, such as Amazon's MTurk service (see, for example, Buhrmester, Kwang, & Gosling, 2011; Paolacci, Chandler, & Ipeirotis, 2010).

These online options are, in important ways, risky. Investigators have no direct contact with the research participants, creating a danger of miscommunication (e.g., in the task instructions or in what a participant intends by a particular response). There is also no explicit way to make certain participants are taking the procedure seriously or running the study in a suitably nondistracting environment. Investigators also lose the option of viewing the study under way, in order to gain a firsthand impression of what the task involves, or how the participants are dealing with the experiments' challenges.

At the same time, these online procedures can offer important benefits. As a start, online research allows a much larger N, and this point would help us address the chronic problem of underpowered studies. The ease with which data can be gathered in these studies also makes it possible to run studies that would be hopelessly inefficient in the laboratory—for example, procedures that collect one observation per participant. With this, the online procedures broaden the set of potential *researchers*, by making a key resource (research participants) available to colleagues at small or specialized institutions. Online studies also allow the recruitment of a more *diverse* sample, and this diversity would, as an immediate gain, strengthen the claim that our results are generalizable. In addition, this diversity, together with the large N, would make individual-difference studies more plausible, encouraging work in this direction. Finally, the worldwide participant recruiting available via the Internet opens the door to more cross-cultural comparisons, allowing us to explore this underresearched domain.

Will these benefits outweigh the concerns about online data gathering? This seems another point in which the question must be settled on a case-by-case basis. Even so, I will forecast that the prospect of online data gathering will enlarge and enrich cognition research, and I look forward to reading the Research Methods chapter in the 2023 edition of this handbook.

## New Applications

Finally, I note that it has been more than 40 years since George Miller, in his 1969 APA Presidential address, urged us to "give psychology away"—that is, to make sure our knowledge was available to and useful for *non*psychologists. This message has been taken seriously throughout our discipline, and has surely shaped research in cognition. Indeed, the journal *Applied Cognitive Psychology* published its first volume in 1987 and has published more than two dozen volumes since then; a second applied journal, the *Journal of Applied Research in Memory and Cognition*, has recently been launched.

In fact, the applications of cognitive psychology are numerous and diverse, and how could they not be? In a wide range of real-world settings, people need to perceive and understand the world around them, to remember and draw conclusions from what they have seen, to make judgments and solve problems, and so on. It cannot be surprising, therefore, that research on *learning and memory* has often been used to inform educational practices. There are studies of *implicit memory's* influence on consumer choice, and *decision making* in physicians. Cognitive psychology has also had a substantial impact on the legal system—with suggestions for how witnesses should be questioned, how identification procedures should be conducted, how we might evaluate witness memory in the courtroom, how jury instructions should be framed, and so on.

There are many advantages associated with this applied work. One obvious point is that we can, rather directly, use our science to improve our world. Other benefits, though, feed back to the field: A focus on applied issues can highlight new phenomena for us to explore, or new questions for us to address, or possible boundary conditions on

claims made so far. Applied work also forces us to examine the external validity of our research—and whether we are illuminating the processes that ultimately we wish to understand. Establishing external validity is sometimes difficult, but studies aimed at applied concerns can obviously help with this important issue.

I should pause to acknowledge the tensions that sometimes flare up between applied research and "pure" work in the laboratory. (The "classic" flare-up, of course, was Neisser, 1988; then Banaji & Crowder, 1989; Roediger, 1991; etc.) Surely, though, this tension is misplaced, for the simple reason that we need research in both arenas. I have just noted the advantages of applied work, but there are, of course, powerful methodological advantages gained by doing research in the controlled world of the laboratory. (Indeed, I am broadly skeptical about applied work not rooted in the good science often possible only in the laboratory.) Likewise, the problem of external validity is itself sometimes misunderstood, and this form of validity does *not* uniformly require procedures that resemble real-world settings. What matters instead, of course, is whether the mental processes in play in a procedure resemble those used outside of the lab, and this point can sometimes be established even with seemingly peculiar, seemingly "unnatural" tasks.

However, having now celebrated the value of applied work, my point is not to chastise colleagues toward doing more of this work or to urge psychologists to seek out new applications. I believe we are doing well on those fronts, and I am impressed by the flow of applied studies. I do look forward, though, to enlargement of the applied work so far—and so I would not be surprised if some future edition of this handbook needed a chapter on "Cognitive Psychology and Law," or, for that matter, chapters on "Cognition and Clinical Diagnosis," or "Decision Making in Business." (I note that one of Oxford's other, more specialized, handbooks has already stepped in this direction: see Spellman & Schauer, 2012; Patel, Arocha, & Zhang, 2012; or Loewenstein, 2012.) Indeed, I can imagine that future editions will include applied work in domains so far untouched by our research.

The pace of this applied work is often slowed, however, not by the psychology researchers, but by those working in the applied arenas. Indeed, it has been an uphill climb to get psychology research integrated into the justice system (e.g., Wells et al., 2000) and, for other potential applications, it is easy to find considerable gaps between research and practice—including some outright contradictions between research data and real-world policies. Consider, for example, the case of cell-phone use while driving. The research has accumulated that this phone use is dangerous and does increase the danger of various mishaps, ranging from minor (missed exits) to horrific (serious accidents). Crucially, the data also make it clear that the problem is the telephone conversation itself, independent of whether the conversation is conducted on a hand-held or hands-free phone (e.g., Strayer & Drews, 2007). In many jurisdictions, however, legislation now prohibits hand-held cell-phone use, but—contrary to the data—allows the equally hazardous use of hands-free phones.

This is one issue, therefore, in which public policies seem out of step with the available data. Indeed, it seems likely that the policies limiting cell-phone use by drivers were not formulated in the first place with an eye on the data but were instead shaped by anecdotal, common-sense observations. I therefore flag—as a topic for discussion, and exploration, and perhaps research—the problem of how we persuade nonpsychologists to take our data seriously. George Miller enjoined us to give psychology away, and plainly we are ready to do that. The field might benefit from some discussion, however, about how we convince others to accept our gift and to value our contribution.

## Conclusion

I am sure others will have their own forecasts for what topics will likely be included in subsequent editions of this handbook, and, with that, which topics may drop from view. Indeed, if I may echo a comment I made at the start, I would count this epilogue as successful if it provokes readers into thinking through what their own forecasts might be. I would suggest, though, that this *uncertainty* about the forecast is itself an important point. It is remarkably easy to think of new avenues, new topics, for cognitive psychology research—and that is an exciting prospect. We have, I have said repeatedly, learned a great deal in the last few decades and, as I have highlighted, our knowledge is firmly established, theoretically rich, and pragmatically useful. But this record of achievement does not, of course, change the cheerful fact that there is much still to be done.

## Acknowledgments

This chapter was fun—but challenging—to write, and I am deeply grateful to John Kihlstrom and Friderike Heuer for their help.

## References

Alcock, J. (2011). Back from the future: Parapsychology and the Bem affair. *Skeptical Inquirer, 35,* 31–39.

Alter, A., & Oppenheimer, D. (2009). Uniting the tribes of fluency to form a metacognitive nation. *Personality and Social Psychology Review, 13,* 219–235.

Banaji, M. R., & Crowder, R. G. (1989). The bankruptcy of everyday memory. *American Psychologist, 44,* 1185–1193.

Bem, D. J. (2011). Feeling the future: Experimental evidence for anomalous retroactive influences on cognition and affect. *Journal of Personality and Social Psychology, 100,* 407–427.

Buhrmester, M., Kwang, T., & Gosling, S.D. (2011). Amazon's Mechanical Turk: A new source of inexpensive, yet high-quality, data? *Perspectives on Psychological Science, 6,* 3–5.

Carey, S. (2011). The origin of concepts: A précis. *Behavioral and Brain Sciences, 34,* 113–167.

Carpenter, S. (2012). Psychology's bold initiative. *Science, 335,* 1558–1561.

Carroll, J. (1978). The effect of imagining an event on expectations for the event: An interpretation in terms of the availability heuristic. *Journal of Experimental Social Psychology, 14,* 88–96.

Chase, W., & Ericsson, K. A. (1982). Skill and working memory. In G. H. Bower (Ed.), *The psychology of learning and motivation* (pp. 1–58). New York: Academic Press.

Ericsson, K. A. (2003). Exceptional memorizers: Made, not born. *Trends in Cognitive Sciences, 7,* 233–235.

Fazey, J., & Hardy, L. (1988). *The inverted-U hypothesis: A castrophe for sport psychology.* British Association of Sports Sciences Monograph No. 1. Leeds, England: The National Coaching Foundation.

Gelman, S. A., & Frzier, B. N. (2012). Development of thinking in children. In K. J. Holyoak & R. G. Morrison (Eds.), *The Oxford handbook of thinking and reasoning* (pp. 513–455). New York: Oxford University Press.

Jacoby, L. L., Woloshyn, V., & Kelley, C. (1989). Becoming famous without being recognized: Unconscious influences on memory produced by dividing attention. *Journal of Experimental Psychology: General, 118,* 115–125.

Kahneman, D. (2011). *Thinking, fast and slow.* New York: Farrar, Straus and Giroux.

Kassin, S. M., Drizin, S. A., Grisso, T., Gudjonsson, G. H., Leo, R. A., & Redlich, A. D. (2010). Police-induced confessions: Risk factors and recommendations. *Law and Human Behavior, 34,* 3–38.

Kosslyn, S., Reisberg, D., & Behrman, M. (2006). Introspection and mechanism in mental imagery. In A. Harrington & A. Zajonc (Eds.), *The Dalai Lama at MIT* (pp. 79–114). Cambridge, MA: Harvard University Press

Loewenstein, J. (2012). Thinking in business. In K. J. Holyoak & R. G. Morrison (Eds.), *The Oxford handbook of thinking and reasoning* (pp. 755–773). New York: Oxford University Press.

McGuire, W. (1983). A contextualist theory of knowledge: Its implications for innovation and reform in psychological research. In L. Berkowitz (Ed.), *Advances in experimental social psychology* (pp. 1–47). New York: Academic Press.

Michael, R. B., Garry, M., & Kirsch, I. (2012). Suggestion, cognition, and behavior. *Current Directions in Psychological Science, 21,* 151–156.

Neisser, U. (1963). The multiplicity of thought. *British Journal of Psychology, 54,* 1–14.

Neisser, U. (1988). New vistas in the study of memory. In U. Neisser & E. Winograd (Eds.), *Remembering reconsidered: Ecological and traditional approaches to the study of memory* (pp. 1–10). New York: Cambridge University Press.

Newell, A. (1973). You can't play 20 questions with nature and win. In W. G. Chase (Ed.), *Visual information processing (pp. 283–308).* New York: Academic Press.

Oppenheimer, D. M. (2008). The secret life of fluency. *Trends in Cognitive Sciences, 12,* 237–241.

Paolacci, G., Chandler, J., & Ipeirotis, P. G. (2010). Running experiments on Amazon Mechanical Turk. *Judgment and Decision Making, 5,* 411–419.

Parker, E. S., Cahill, L., & McGaugh, J. L. (2006). A case of unusual autobiographical remembering. *Neurocase, 12,* 35–49.

Patel, V. L., Arocha, J. F., & Zhang, J. (2012). Medical reasoning and thinking. In K. J. Holyoak & R. G. Morrison (Eds.), *The Oxford handbook of thinking and reasoning* (pp. 736–754). New York: Oxford University Press.

Ritchie, S., Wiseman, R., & French, C. (2012). Replication, replication, replication. *The Psychologist, 25,* 346–348.

Roediger, H. L. (1991). They read an article? A comment on the everday memory controversy. *American Psychologist, 46,* 37–40.

Simonton, D. K. (2012). Genius. In K. J. Holyoak & R. G. Morrison (Eds.), *The Oxford handbook of thinking and reasoning* (pp. 492–509). New York: Oxford University Press.

Spelke, E., Hirst, W., & Neisser, U. (1976). Skills of divided attention. *Cognition, 4,* 215–230.

Spellman, B. A., & Schauer, F. (2012). Legal reasoning. In K. J. Holyoak & R. G. Morrison (Eds.), *The Oxford handbook of thinking and reasoning* (pp. 719–735). New York: Oxford University Press.

Stanovich, K. E. (2012). On the distinction between rationality and intelligence: Implications for understanding individual differences in reasoning. In K. J. Holyoak & R. G. Morrison (Eds.), *The Oxford handbook of thinking and reasoning* (pp. 433–455). New York: Oxford University Press.

Steele, C. M. (2010). *Whistling Vivaldi and other clues to how stereotypes affect us.* New York: W.W. Norton.

Strayer, D. L., & Drews, F. A. (2007). Cell-phone induced driver distraction. *Current Directions in Psychological Science, 16,* 128–131.

Stromeyer, C. F., & Psotka, J. (1970). The detailed texture of eidetic images. *Nature, 225,* 346–349

Tversky, A., & Kahneman, D. (1974). Judgment under uncertainty: Heuristics and biases. *Science, 185,* 1124–1131.

Wells, G., Malpass, R. S., Lindsay, R. C. L., Fisher, R. P., Turtle, J. W., & Fulero, S. M. (2000). From the lab to the police station: A successful application of eyewitness research. *American Psychologist, 55,* 581–598.

Whittlesea, B. W., & Leboe, J. P. (2000). The heuristic basis of remembering and classification: Fluency, generation, and resemblance. *Journal of Experimental Psychology: General, 129,* 84–106.

Woolett, K., Spiers, H., & Maguire, E. A. (2008). Talent in the taxi: A model system for exploring expertise. *Philosophical Transactions of the Royal Society, 1522,* 1407–1416.

Yong, E. (2012). Replication studies: Bad copy. *Nature, 485,* 298–300.

Zelazo, P. D., & Müller, U. (2011). Executive function in typical and atypical development. In U. Goswami (Ed.), *The Blackwell handbook of childhood cognitive development (2nd ed.,* pp. 574–603). Malden, MA: Blackwell.

# INDEX

*Note: Page numbers followed by "f" and "t" denote figures and tables, respectively.*

activation of, 691
attention influenced by, 170–72
Bloom's taxonomy and, 311
of cognitive psychology, 299
comparison, 931
defined, 174n1
EUT and, 691
in everyday life, 279–80
expertise and, 338
neglect, 143–44
person perception and, 930–32
postures and, 869–70
of reader, 481
relevance of, 672
during retrieval, 236
unconscious, 931–32
good continuation, principle of, 16, 17f, 19
good judgment, 603–4
gradient, attentional, 120–21
grammatical class, 415
grasp-height effect, 868
grid cells, 728
grooming/gossip theory, 529
ground, 9. See also figure-ground perception
grounded cognition, 207, 359, 368, 370
grouped array hypothesis, 128
grouping
assessment methods, 21, 23–27, 24f–28f
cue integration, 18–19, 20f
as early or late process, 19–21, 21f
edge-region principle, 21
image-based factors in, 16–17, 17f
overview of, 9, 16
segregation related to, 21
subjective factors in, 17–18, 17f–18f
guided search, 104
GWA analysis. See genome-wide association analysis

## H

habit family hierarchy, 772
habituation procedure, 1001
HAL. See hyperspace analogue to language model
hand gestures, 541
haplotypes, 825, 827
happiness set point, 707
Hart, Joseph, 284–85
H-A theory of reasoning. See heuristic-analytic theory of reasoning
HD. See Huntington's disease
head direction cells, 728
health, cognitive aging and, 1026
heart rate, sustained attention and, 1005–8, 1005f, 1007f
hedonic adaptation, 707–8, 714
Helmholtz, Hermann von, 864–65
hemineglect, 102, 727
hemispheric differences, in insight, 786–88, 787f, 790

hemodialysis, 708
Hension effect, 255
heritability, 824–26, 834–36
heuristic-analytic (H-A) theory of reasoning, 639
heuristics. See also judgment heuristics and biases
adjustment, 608
affect, 577–78, 608, 694
availability, 578, 607–8, 933
biases in, 640t
brand, 578
change, 260
cognitive processing style and, 577–78
ease-of-retrieval, 578
fast and frugal
adaptive toolbox metaphor and, 610
critiqued, 611–12
empirical evidence for, 610–11
in judgment under uncertainty, 609–12
fluency, 260, 611
generation, 260
in H-A theory of reasoning, 639
persuasion, 961–62
problem solving and, 774
recognition, 692
representativeness and, 607
resemblance, 260
search, 772
TTB, 610–11
hierarchical models
Bayesian, 747
of cognitive style, 848–49, 849f
higher order cognition, 4
highlighting, as learning strategy, 303–4
hill climbing, 774
hippocampus
memory and, 197, 559–66
plasticity, 562
space in brain and, 728
stress and, 559–66
holding. See attentional holding
holistic coding, in face recognition, 47–50, 48f, 56, 60–61
holistic cognition, 970–71, 973–81
holistic representations of shape, 34
holophrastic protolanguage, 530–31
horizontal explanation, 164
hot-cold empathy gaps, 710–12
housefly, expectancy in, 863–64
HSR. See human speech recognition
HTT. See hypothetical thinking theory
hue perception, 507–8
human speech recognition (HSR), 406–7
Hume, David, 734
Huntington's disease (HD), 826–27
hybrid model, of object recognition, 35, 41–42
hyperspace analogue to language model (HAL), 214–15
hypothetical thinking theory (HTT), 643

## I

IAT. See Implicit Association Test
IB. See inattentional blindness
IB judgments. See information-based judgments
IC. See inhibitory control
iconicity, 651–52, 664
ideals, expertise and, 338
identity aftereffect, 51, 60–61
IGT. See Iowa Gambling Task
illusory conjunctions, 104, 148f, 150, 155
illusory sentential inferences, 658–60
image. See also mental images
gist of, 102–3
schema theory, 211–12
image-based discovery, 378–80, 379f
image-based factors
Gestalt, 10–11, 10f, 12f–13f, 16, 17f
in grouping, 16–17, 17f
new, 11, 13f, 16–17, 17f
in segregation, 10–15, 10f, 12f–14f
imageless thought, 771
imaginal perspective taking, 724–25
immediate priming, 246–53
implementation intentions, PM and, 269–71
Implicit Association Test (IAT), 183
implicit attitudes, 578, 957–59
implicit emotion, 182–83
implicit-explicit attitude correspondence, 578
implicit knowledge, 860
implicit learning, 180–81, 183, 260
implicit memory
Alzheimer's disease and, 178
amnesia and, 221–22, 225–29
breadth of, 226–27
categories and, 322
in cognitive unconscious, 178–79, 181, 183–84, 190
dissociations with explicit memory
functional dissociations, 224–25
neuroimaging dissociations, 225–26
pharmacological dissociations, 225
population dissociations, 222–24
emerging research issues, 229
episodic memory and, 181, 190, 194
explicit contamination and, 226
history of, 220–21
in modern era, 221–22
repetition priming and, 222
theoretical frameworks, 227–29
implicit motivation, 182
implicit perception, 99, 108, 179–80, 183–84
implicit processing, in neglect, 137–39, 138f
implicit stereotyping, 921, 923–24
implicit thought, 181–84
inattentional blindness (IB)
attentional filtering and, 101
implicit perception and, 179
incomplete records and, 234
visual resources and, 148f, 150, 155–56, 156f

perception (*Cont.*)
  concepts reunited with, 341–42
  distributional models and, 215–16
  of events
    action-object couplets in, 90–92
      using brain and body, 91–92
    early research on, 83–85
    EST and, 89–90
    kinds of events in, 85
    parts of events in, 86–90
  explicit, 179, 184
  face, 50–53, 51*f*–52*f*, 60–61, 74, 77
  figure-ground
    attentional binding and, 105
    conditions of, 23
    early and late, 16
  hue, 507–8
  imagery and, 381
  implicit, 99, 108, 179–80, 183–84
  inferences influencing, 865, 923–24
  scene, 74, 79
  self-perception, 907–8, 963
  of spatial relations, 148*f*, 150–51, 158
  subjective
    construct accessibility in, 932–36
    motives and goals in, 930–32
  subliminal, 103, 179
percepts, 332, 378
perceptual accuracy hypothesis, 907
perceptual attitudes, 843
perceptual effects, attentional filtering and cuing effects, 100
  inattentional blindness, 101
  interference effects, 101
  interocular suppression, 101–2
  search asymmetry, 100–101
perceptual expertise, 55, 338–40
perceptual learning, 332, 339, 404–6
perceptual-motor skills, 860–62
perceptual neglect, 132–34, 137, 139
perceptual organization, in vision
  grouping
    assessment methods, 21, 23–27, 24*f*–28*f*
    cue integration, 18–19, 20*f*
    as early or late process, 19–21, 21*f*
    edge-region principle, 21
    image-based factors in, 16–17, 17*f*
    overview of, 9, 16
    segregation related to, 21
    subjective factors in, 17–18, 17*f*–18*f*
  overview of, 9–10, 27–28
  segregation
    grouping related to, 21
    image-based factors in, 10–15, 10*f*, 12*f*–14*f*
    methods of assessing, 21–23, 22*f*–24*f*
    overview of, 9–10
    subjective factors in, 12–16, 14*f*
  structuralism and, 9
perceptual reference frame, 378

perceptual representation, of categories
  in brain, 362–66, 363*f*–366*f*
  domain-specific deficits in, 363–66, 363*f*–366*f*
  evidence for, 359–62
  future directions, 370
  language in, 366–68
  sensory-motor processing in, 359–63, 367–70
  theories, 358–59
perceptual set, as subjective factor, 14–15
perceptual simulation
  in brain, 362–66, 363*f*–366*f*
  evidence for, 359–62
  need for, 368–69
perceptual span, in reading, 444–45, 444*f*
Perceptual Symbols theory, 358–59
performance
  deliberate practice changing, 896
  by experts, 888–90, 889*f*, 892–95, 893*f*, 897
  job, 1027–28
  mechanisms mediating, 890–91
  of physical actions, 859–71
  structure, development of, 892–95, 893*f*
  superior reproducible, 886–90, 887*f*, 889*f*
peripheral cuing. *See* exogenous cuing
perseveration, 783
personality, reasoning and, 665
personal neglect, 132
person perception
  automaticity in
    categorization, 923
    feature detection, 922–23
    inference, 923–24
    selective attention, 921–22
  behavior explanations and, 936–37
  biases in, 929
    assimilation and, 933–34
    coherence in, 930
    correction and, 934–35
    inhibition and, 935–36
    motives and goals in, 930–32
    nonmotivated sources of, 932–36
    priming and, 933–35
    stereotyping and, 935
  causality, 924
    FAE and, 926–27
    lay theories in, 927–29
    rational-effortful models, 925–26
  defined, 918
  object perception *vs.*
    intentionality and, 919–21
    interaction and, 920
    theory of mind and, 919–20
    traits and, 920–21
  overview of, 918–19, 937
perspective shifts, 640*t*, 641
perspective taking
  imaginal, 724–25
  Theory of Mind and, 952

persuasion
  affect–cognition interactions and, 578
  attitude change and, 959–62, 965–67
  camouflaged, 966
  heuristics, 961–62
  message-learning model of, 960–61
  subliminal, 966–67
PET. *See* positron emission tomography
PFC. *See* prefrontal cortex
P-FIT. *See* parieto-frontal integration theory
pharmacological dissociations, between implicit and explicit memory, 225
phenomenal causality, 740
phenomenal-consciousness (P-consciousness), 103, 171
phenomenal self, 906
phenomenology, 1036–37
phonemes
  defined, 391
  in speech perception, 391–403, 398*f*, 401*f*, 403*f*, 405, 407
phonetic context, 396
phonetic learning, 499–501
phonological coding, 453–55
phonological form, 414–15
phonology, 454
physical actions
  future directions, 871
  knowledge revealed through, 860–66
  motor control and, 863, 866, 868, 870–71
  overview of, 859
  planning and performing, 859–71
  realization of
    cognitive model of, 869–71
    language production, 866–68
    nonverbal action, 868–69
physiological characteristics, deliberate practice changing, 895–96
pictures
  mental images differing from
    image-based discovery and, 378–80, 379*f*
    neutral and organized depictions, 377–78, 378*f*
  mental images resembling
    brain and, 376–77
    chronometric studies of, 375–76
    sensory effects in, 377
    viewing position in, 375
  in word-to-picture matching, 421*t*
pile sorting behavior, 334–35
place cells, 728
planning
  intelligence and, 813
  in PASS model, 813, 818
  physical actions, 859–71
Planning, Attention, Simultaneous, and Successive model. *See* PASS model
plasticity, 562, 1014

Printed and bound by CPI Group (UK) Ltd, Croydon, CR0 4YY